图书在版编目（CIP）数据

"一带一路"沿线国家法律环境国别报告. 第三卷/中华全国律师协会编. — 北京：北京大学出版社，2018.12

ISBN 978-7-301-29998-2

Ⅰ.①一… Ⅱ.①中… Ⅲ.①国际投资法学—指南 Ⅳ.①D996.4-62

中国版本图书馆CIP数据核字（2018）第240659号

书　　　名	"一带一路"沿线国家法律环境国别报告（第三卷） "YI DAI YI LU" YANXIAN GUOJIA FALÜ HUANJING GUOBIE BAOGAO（DI-SAN JUAN）
著作责任者	中华全国律师协会　编
责 任 编 辑	王建君　陈　康
标 准 书 号	ISBN 978-7-301-29998-2
出 版 发 行	北京大学出版社
地　　　址	北京市海淀区成府路205号　100871
网　　　址	http://www.pup.cn　http://www.yandayuanzhao.com
电 子 信 箱	yandayuanzhao@163.com
新 浪 微 博	@北京大学出版社　@北大出版社燕大元照法律图书
电　　　话	邮购部 010-62752015　发行部 010-62750672　编辑部 010-62117788
印 刷 者	南京爱德印刷有限公司
经 销 者	新华书店
	720毫米×1020毫米　16开本　68.25印张　2210千字 2018年12月第1版　2018年12月第1次印刷
定　　　价	398.00元

未经许可，不得以任何方式复制或抄袭本书之部分或全部内容。
版权所有，侵权必究
举报电话：010-62752024　电子信箱：fd@pup.pku.edu.cn
图书如有印装质量问题，请与出版部联系，电话：010-62756370

出版说明

共同建设"丝绸之路经济带"和"21世纪海上丝绸之路"（以下简称"一带一路"）是中国主动适应全球经济形势深刻变化提出的重大合作倡议。为推进律师行业投身"一带一路"建设，中华全国律师协会于2016年启动中国律师服务"一带一路"建设项目，着手编写了《"一带一路"沿线国家法律环境国别报告》（以下简称《报告》）第一卷、第二卷。2017年12月，中华全国律师协会又启动了《报告》第三卷、第四卷的编写工作。

《报告》旨在介绍"一带一路"沿线国家的基本法律制度和法律环境。本次出版的是《报告》的第三卷、第四卷，含"一带一路"沿线38个国家的投资法律环境报告。报告内容涉及投资、贸易、劳动、环境保护、知识产权、争议解决等领域。具体包括相关国家的法律制度及基本法律环境概述，相关国家的市场准入、外汇管理、融资、土地政策、公司设立与解散、并购、竞争管制、税收政策、证券交易、投资优惠、贸易法律规定及管理、工会与劳动组织、劳动争议解决、知识产权保护、环境保护、争议解决方式及机构等具体法律制度。

本书编写特点及特别声明：

一、《报告》由中华全国律师协会国际业务专业委员会委员和中华全国律师协会涉外律师领军人才联手"一带一路"沿线国家律师事务所的律师共同撰写。"一带一路"沿线国家参与撰稿的律师事务所的选择，是按照国际著名法律评级机构评定前五名的律师事务所。中国律师两人一组作为一个国家的国别协调人，负责联络该国家的律师事务所，请他们指定本所律师根据中华全国律师协会拟定的写作提纲及要求，撰写本国英文版法律环境报告。报告在规定的时间完成后，中国律师将英文稿翻译成中文稿，交中华全国律师协会编审汇总后，交付出版机构。

二、《报告》真实反映了"一带一路"沿线国家实际法律环境状况，具有很强的实用性、权威性和可操作性，可以为社会各界与"一带一路"沿线国家开展官方与民间交流提供科学准确的法律环境参考，同时《报告》在附录部分收录了参与写作的境内外律师事务所、律师介绍，可以为参与"一带一路"建设的中国企业聘请中外律师提供相关参考信息。

三、《报告》编写所依据的法律及实践截至2018年1月31日，包含了"一带一路"沿线国家所适用、已颁布并且现行有效的当地投资法律及参与撰写《报告》的"一带一路"沿线国家律师事务所的实践。中华全国律师协会并未调查、未明示或暗示地运用上述日期以后的"一带一路"沿线国家投资法律和实践或除"一带一路"沿线国家以外其他任何国家的法律和实践。

四、《报告》中对于"一带一路"沿线国家投资法律概念的解释均以中文直译。有关的法律概念也许不会与在其他司法管辖区内对应的英语术语表达的法律概念完全等同。因此,《报告》只可能在其明确表达下对基于"一带一路"沿线国家投资法律管辖下产生的解释或法律责任问题负责。中华全国律师协会不对外国司法体系下法官、仲裁员等如何解释"一带一路"沿线国家投资法律概念及法律表述提供任何意见。

五、《报告》中引用及使用的术语或概念的中文翻译,在"一带一路"沿线国家投资法律中可能不具有完全等同的术语或概念。《报告》仅为社会各界了解"一带一路"沿线国家的相关投资法律和实践时参考使用,不代表中华全国律师协会、相关律师事务所和律师对其中所述任何事项的法律意见。受限于客观条件,中华全国律师协会并未核查《报告》中相关内容的真实性、合法性和有效性,参与撰写《报告》的"一带一路"沿线国家的律师事务所对其所撰写的内容独自承担责任。

六、《报告》的相关知识产权归中华全国律师协会所有,包括但不限于著作权、邻接权与标识,非经中华全国律师协会事先书面同意和批准,《报告》不得用于营利或据以向中华全国律师协会追究任何责任。对《报告》解释和修改的权利归中华全国律师协会所有。

由于各个国家的社会制度不同,法律环境各异,作者来自不同国家,在撰稿、编译及编辑过程中难免出现各种不同理解及错误遗漏,希望各位读者及时反馈,以便我们在后续的项目中日臻完善。

七、本说明中文文本与英文文本不一致的,以中文文本为准。

中华全国律师协会

2018 年 12 月

NOTIFICATION OF PUBLICATION

Joint construction of the "Silk Road Economic Belt" and the "21st Century Maritime Silk Road" (hereinafter referred to as the "Belt and Road Initiative") is a milestone cooperative initiative proposed by China to actively adapt to profound changes in the ever-changing global economic environment. To more effectively integrate the legal profession/industry into the establishment of the "Belt and Road Initiative", All China Lawyers Association (ACLA) launched the "Belt and Road Initiative" developmental project for Chinese attorneys in 2016, and initiated the composition of the First and Second Volume of the "National Legal Environment Report along the 'Belt and Road Initiative'"(hereinafter referred to as the "Report"). In December 2017, the All China Lawyers Association initiated preparation of the Third and Fourth Volume of the Report.

The tenet of the "Report" aims at introducing the fundamentals of legal system and legal environment of countries along the "Belt and Road Initiative". The most recent publication of both the Third and Fourth Volume of the "Report" contains detailed descriptions of investment legal environment of the 38 countries along the "Belt and Road Initiative". Scope of the report covers issues such as investment, trade, labor, environmental protection, intellectual property right, as well as dispute resolution. The "Report" includes overviews of the legal system and basic legal environment of pertinent countries along the "Belt and Road Initiative". More specifically, it includes these countries' legal organization on issues such as requirement/standard of market access, foreign exchange regulations, finance, land policy, company establishment and dissolution, mergers and acquisitions, competition control, taxation policies, securities transactions, investment preferences, legal regulation and management of trade, trade unions and labor organizations, labor dispute resolution, intellectual property protection, environmental protection, as well as methods and institutions of dispute resolution.

Unique features and special announcements of the "Report":

1. The "Report" is co-authored by Members of the International Business Professional Committee of the All China Lawyers Association and Leading Lawyers for Foreign Related Issues from the All China Lawyers Association, in cooperation with lawyers of law firms from countries along the "Belt and Road Initiative". Law firms that participated in drafting of the "Report" are selected from top five law firms of corresponding countries pursuant to ratings from internationally renowned legal rating agencies. Two attorneys from China are assigned to a team, with each team designated as a particular country's

national coordinator; each team is responsible for liaising with that country's law firms and inquire from them English version of legal environment reports in accordance with the written outlines and requirements of the All China Lawyers Association. After the report is completed within the prescribed time, the attorneys from China then translate the English text into a Chinese manuscript. The manuscript is then submitted to ACLA for review, and is eventually delivered to the publishing agency.

2. The "Report" truthfully reflects actual legal environment of countries along the "Belt and Road Initiative", it is highly practical, authoritative, and operable. The "Report" serves the purpose of promoting communications between various sectors of the society (world) and countries along the "Belt and Road Initiative" as an accurate scientific standard of reference, on both governmental and private-sector levels. Meanwhile, provided in the appendix are the introductions of domestic and foreign law firms and lawyers that participated in the composition of the "Report". For Chinese companies that participate in the construction of the "Belt and Road Initiative", the "Report" can provide relevant referential information for those companies that are interested in hiring domestic and foreign attorneys.

3. As of January 31st, 2018, laws and legal practices on which the Report is based on include local investment laws that have been adopted, promulgated, and are currently in force along the "Belt and Road Initiative" countries, as well as actual practice experiences of law firms that participated in the composition of the "Report" from countries along the "Belt and Road Initiative" countries. The All China Lawyers Association has not investigated, nor explicitly or implicitly incorporated, laws and practices of countries along the "Belt and Road Initiative", or laws and practices of countries not included in the "Belt and Road Initiative", subsequent to the above date.

4. Within the "Report", interpretations of legal investment concepts (and or definitions) of all countries along the "Belt and Road Initiative" are translated directly (verbatim) into Chinese. There is a possibility that such legal concepts or definitions of one particular jurisdiction do not exactly/precisely correspond to a suitable legal concept or definition within the realm of legal English in a different jurisdiction. Thus, unless a statement is made clearly in the "Report", the "Report" shall not be legally responsible or liable for issues arising out of such interpretations. Among the countries along the "Belt and Road Initiative", the All China Lawyers Association did not and will not provide suggestions or recommendations to professionals such as judges or arbitrators from a foreign judicial system on interpretations of legal investment concepts and relevant laws.

5. There is the possibility that the Chinese translation of professional terms or concepts cited and used in the "Report" do not correspond precisely/exactly to a suitable and equivalent professional term or concept in a country along the "Belt and Road Initiative". The "Report" is composed only for purpose of reference to aid various sectors of the society/world to better understand relevant investment laws and legal practices of countries along the "Belt and Road Initiative". Any issues within the "Report" shall not be considered in any way as legal opinions presented by the All China Lawyers Association, nor any law firms or lawyers participated in the composition of the Report. Subject to practical limitations, the All China Lawyers Association did not verify the authenticity, legitimacy, and validity of the relevant contents of the "Report". Law firms from various countries along the "Belt and Road Initiative" shall be solely responsible for the contents to which it participated in drafting.

6. Relevant intellectual property rights of the "Report" are retained by the All China Lawyers Association, including but is not limited to copyright, its neighboring rights, and logos. Without prior written consent/approval from the All China Lawyers Association, the "Report" shall not be used for purposes of generating profits, or as evidence of any liability perused against the All China Lawyers Association. The All China Lawyers Association retains the right to interpret and amend this "Report".

Taking into consideration of the differences among socio-political system, legal environment, and diverse background of the authors (of the "Report"), it is reasonably foreseeable that there might exist various (subjective) interpretations and/or mistakes within the "Report". It is our sincerest hope that the readers conveniently provide us with timely feedbacks, so that we can follow up and make appropriate adjustments in our subsequent projects.

7. Should there be any inconsistencies in between the Chinese text of this notification and its English translation, the Chinese text shall prevail.

All China Lawyers Association
December 2018

总目录
SUMMARY OF CONTENTS

（以国家名称英文字母排序）　　　　　　　　　　第三卷
LISTED BY ALPHABETICAL ORDER　　　　　　　VOLUME Ⅲ

A	阿富汗	1
	Afghanistan	26
	阿尔巴尼亚	54
	Albania	77
	阿根廷	102
	Argentina	126
	亚美尼亚	153
	Armenia	178
	澳大利亚	207
	Australia	244
	阿塞拜疆	283
	Azerbaijan	315
B	巴林	351
	Bahrain	370
	波斯尼亚和黑塞哥维那	390
	Bosnia and Herzegovina	411
	巴西	435
	Brazil	465
	文莱	499
	Brunei	516

C	智利 ……………………………………………………	534
	Chile ……………………………………………………	564
D	吉布提 …………………………………………………	597
	Djibouti …………………………………………………	615
E	埃塞俄比亚 ……………………………………………	635
	Ethiopia …………………………………………………	657
I	伊拉克 …………………………………………………	682
	Iraq ………………………………………………………	706
	意大利 …………………………………………………	732
	Italy ………………………………………………………	762
J	日本 ……………………………………………………	796
	Japan ……………………………………………………	820
K	肯尼亚 …………………………………………………	848
	Kenya ……………………………………………………	876
	韩国 ……………………………………………………	906
	Republic of Korea ………………………………………	931
	科威特 …………………………………………………	960
	Kuwait ……………………………………………………	985
	附录 ……………………………………………………	1013
	APPENDIX ………………………………………………	1013

目录 CONTENTS

A

阿富汉 / Afghanistan

- 一、概述 1
- 二、投资 3
- 三、贸易 13
- 四、劳动 15
- 五、知识产权 18
- 六、环境保护 21
- 七、争议解决 23
- 八、其他 24

- I. Overview 26
- II. Investment 28
- III. Trade 39
- IV. Labour 42
- V. Intellectual Property 45
- VI. Environmental Protection 49
- VII. Dispute Resolution 51
- VIII. Others 52

阿尔巴尼亚 / Albania

- 一、概述 54
- 二、投资 55
- 三、贸易 67
- 四、劳动 68
- 五、知识产权 71
- 六、环境保护 72
- 七、争议解决 73
- 八、其他 74

- I. Overview 77
- II. Investment 79
- III. Trade 92
- IV. Labour 93
- V. Intellectual Property 96
- VI. Environmental Protection 97
- VII. Dispute Resolution 98
- VIII. Others 99

阿根廷 / Argentina

- 一、概述 102
- 二、投资 104
- 三、贸易 114
- 四、劳动 116
- 五、知识产权 119

- I. Overview 126
- II. Investment 128
- III. Trade 140
- IV. Labour 142
- V. Intellectual Property 146

六、环境保护 …………………… 121	VI. Environmental Protection …………… 147
七、争议解决 …………………… 122	VII. Dispute Resolution …………………… 148
八、其他 ………………………… 124	VIII. Others ………………………………… 150

亚美尼亚 / Armenia

一、概述 ………………………… 153	I. Overview ………………………………… 178
二、投资 ………………………… 154	II. Investment …………………………… 180
三、贸易 ………………………… 164	III. Trade ………………………………… 191
四、劳动 ………………………… 166	IV. Labour ………………………………… 193
五、知识产权 …………………… 168	V. Intellectual Property ………………… 195
六、环境保护 …………………… 170	VI. Environmental Protection …………… 197
七、争议解决 …………………… 171	VII. Dispute Resolution …………………… 199
八、其他 ………………………… 176	VIII. Others ………………………………… 205

澳大利亚 / Australia

一、概述 ………………………… 207	I. Overview ………………………………… 244
二、投资 ………………………… 211	II. Investment …………………………… 248
三、贸易 ………………………… 229	III. Trade ………………………………… 267
四、劳动 ………………………… 231	IV. Labour ………………………………… 269
五、知识产权 …………………… 236	V. Intellectual Property ………………… 274
六、环境保护 …………………… 238	VI. Environmental Protection …………… 276
七、争议解决 …………………… 239	VII. Dispute Resolution …………………… 278
八、其他 ………………………… 241	VIII. Others ………………………………… 280

阿塞拜疆 / Azerbaijan

一、概述 ………………………… 283	I. Overview ………………………………… 315
二、投资 ………………………… 284	II. Investment …………………………… 316
三、贸易 ………………………… 298	III. Trade ………………………………… 332
四、劳动 ………………………… 300	IV. Labour ………………………………… 335
五、知识产权 …………………… 305	V. Intellectual Property ………………… 340
六、环境保护 …………………… 308	VI. Environmental Protection …………… 343
七、争议解决 …………………… 309	VII. Dispute Resolution …………………… 345
八、其他 ………………………… 311	VIII. Others ………………………………… 347

B

巴林 / Bahrain

- 一、概述 ·········· 351
- 二、投资 ·········· 352
- 三、贸易 ·········· 360
- 四、劳动 ·········· 361
- 五、知识产权 ·········· 363
- 六、环境保护 ·········· 365
- 七、争议解决 ·········· 365
- 八、其他 ·········· 366

- I. Overview ·········· 370
- II. Investment ·········· 371
- III. Trade ·········· 379
- IV. Labour ·········· 381
- V. Intellectual Property ·········· 383
- VI. Environmental Protection ·········· 385
- VII. Dispute Resolution ·········· 386
- VIII. Others ·········· 387

波斯尼亚和黑塞哥维那 / Bosnia and Herzegovina

- 一、概述 ·········· 390
- 二、投资 ·········· 391
- 三、贸易 ·········· 401
- 四、劳动 ·········· 402
- 五、知识产权 ·········· 405
- 六、环境保护 ·········· 407
- 七、争议解决 ·········· 408
- 八、其他 ·········· 409

- I. Overview ·········· 411
- II. Investment ·········· 412
- III. Trade ·········· 423
- IV. Labour ·········· 424
- V. Intellectual Property ·········· 427
- VI. Environmental Protection ·········· 430
- VII. Dispute Resolution ·········· 432
- VIII. Others ·········· 433

巴西 / Brazil

- 一、概述 ·········· 435
- 二、投资 ·········· 437
- 三、贸易 ·········· 454
- 四、劳动 ·········· 455
- 五、知识产权 ·········· 457
- 六、环境保护 ·········· 458
- 七、争议解决 ·········· 460
- 八、其他 ·········· 462

- I. Overview ·········· 465
- II. Investment ·········· 468
- III. Trade ·········· 487
- IV. Labour ·········· 488
- V. Intellectual Property ·········· 490
- VI. Environmental Protection ·········· 491
- VII. Dispute Resolution ·········· 493
- VIII. Others ·········· 495

文莱

一、概述	499
二、投资	500
三、贸易	506
四、劳动	507
五、知识产权	509
六、环境保护	512
七、争议解决	513
八、其他	513

Brunei

I. Overview	516
II. Investment	517
III. Trade	523
IV. Labour	524
V. Intellectual Property	526
VI. Environmental Protection	530
VII. Dispute Resolution	531
VIII. Others	531

C

智利

一、概述	534
二、投资	535
三、贸易	550
四、劳动	552
五、知识产权	558
六、环境保护	559
七、争议解决	561
八、其他	561

Chile

I. Overview	564
II. Investment	565
III. Trade	582
IV. Labour	584
V. Intellectual Property	590
VI. Environmental Protection	591
VII. Dispute Resolution	594
VIII. Others	594

D

吉布提

一、概述	597
二、投资	597
三、贸易	607
四、劳动	609
五、知识产权	611
六、环境保护	612
七、争议解决	613
八、其他	614

Djibouti

I. Overview	615
II. Investment	615
III. Trade	627
IV. Labour	629
V. Intellectual Property	630
VI. Environmental Protection	632
VII. Dispute Resolution	633
VIII. Others	634

E

埃塞俄比亚

一、概述 ………………………………… 635
二、投资 ………………………………… 636
三、贸易 ………………………………… 646
四、劳动 ………………………………… 648
五、知识产权 …………………………… 651
六、环境保护 …………………………… 652
七、争议解决 …………………………… 653
八、其他 ………………………………… 654

Ethiopia

I. Overview ……………………………… 657
II. Investment …………………………… 659
III. Trade ………………………………… 669
IV. Labour ……………………………… 671
V. Intellectual Property ………………… 674
VI. Environmental Protection ………… 676
VII. Dispute Resolution ………………… 677
VIII. Others ……………………………… 679

I

伊拉克

一、概述 ………………………………… 682
二、投资 ………………………………… 685
三、贸易 ………………………………… 694
四、劳动 ………………………………… 696
五、知识产权 …………………………… 699
六、环境保护 …………………………… 700
七、争议解决 …………………………… 700
八、其他 ………………………………… 702

Iraq

I. Overview ……………………………… 706
II. Investment …………………………… 709
III. Trade ………………………………… 718
IV. Labour ……………………………… 720
V. Intellectual Property ………………… 723
VI. Environmental Protection ………… 725
VII. Dispute Resolution ………………… 726
VIII. Others ……………………………… 727

意大利

一、概述 ………………………………… 732
二、投资 ………………………………… 733
三、贸易 ………………………………… 751
四、劳动 ………………………………… 752
五、知识产权 …………………………… 757
六、环境保护 …………………………… 758
七、争议解决 …………………………… 758
八、其他 ………………………………… 759

Italy

I. Overview ……………………………… 762
II. Investment …………………………… 763
III. Trade ………………………………… 783
IV. Labour ……………………………… 784
V. Intellectual Property ………………… 790
VI. Environmental Protection ………… 791
VII. Dispute Resolution ………………… 792
VIII. Others ……………………………… 792

J

日本

一、概述……………………………796
二、投资……………………………797
三、贸易……………………………810
四、劳动……………………………812
五、知识产权………………………813
六、环境保护………………………816
七、争议解决………………………817
八、其他……………………………818

Japan

I. Overview …………………………820
II. Investment ………………………822
III. Trade ……………………………837
IV. Labour …………………………839
V. Intellectual Property ……………840
VI. Environmental Protection ……844
VII. Dispute Resolution ……………845
VIII. Others …………………………846

K

肯尼亚

一、概述……………………………848
二、投资……………………………848
三、贸易……………………………864
四、劳动……………………………865
五、知识产权………………………868
六、环境保护………………………870
七、争议解决………………………870
八、其他……………………………873

Kenya

I. Overview …………………………876
II. Investment ………………………877
III. Trade ……………………………892
IV. Labour …………………………894
V. Intellectual Property ……………897
VI. Environmental Protection ……899
VII. Dispute Resolution ……………900
VIII. Others …………………………903

韩国

一、概述……………………………906
二、投资……………………………907
三、贸易……………………………920
四、劳动……………………………922
五、知识产权………………………924
六、环境保护………………………926
七、争议解决………………………928
八、其他……………………………929

Republic of Korea

I. Overview …………………………931
II. Investment ………………………932
III. Trade ……………………………948
IV. Labour …………………………949
V. Intellectual Property ……………951
VI. Environmental Protection ……954
VII. Dispute Resolution ……………956
VIII. Others …………………………957

科威特	Kuwait
一、概述……………………960	I. Overview ……………………985
二、投资……………………961	II. Investment ……………………986
三、贸易……………………972	III. Trade ……………………998
四、劳动……………………973	IV. Labour ……………………999
五、知识产权………………975	V. Intellectual Property ……………1001
六、环境保护………………978	VI. Environmental Protection ………1004
七、争议解决………………979	VII. Dispute Resolution ……………1006
八、其他……………………981	VIII. Others ……………………1007

附录……………………………………………………………………1013

APPENDIX ……………………………………………………………1013

阿富汗

作者：刘晓炜、江知芸
译者：刘晓炜、江知芸

一、概述

（一）政治、经济、社会和法律环境概述

阿富汗伊斯兰共和国（以下简称"阿富汗"）是一个亚洲内陆国家，位于南亚，与中国、伊朗、巴基斯坦、塔吉克斯坦、土库曼斯坦和乌兹别克斯坦接壤。阿富汗有着长期动荡的历史，已经历了持续近20年的战火。

普什图语和达里语（阿富汗波斯语）是阿富汗的官方语言和使用最广泛的语言。

1. 政治环境

2003年支尔格大会（阿富汗大国民会议）批准了阿富汗《宪法》，重构了阿富汗政府，阿富汗成为伊斯兰共和国，行政、立法、司法三权分立。

2004年，阿富汗新《宪法》生效，选举了总统，次年普选议员。

国民议会是阿富汗国家立法机关，实行两院制，包括人民院和长老院。首届国民议会在2005年选举产生。最高法院由总统任命组成司法机关。

阿富汗与伊朗关系密切，两国有着共同的语言和文化，是大波斯的一部分。近些年，阿富汗与巴基斯坦经常发生纠纷并且关系持续恶化。

阿富汗与其北部盟友保持着良好的关系，包括乌兹别克斯坦、塔吉克斯坦和土库曼斯坦，它们有相似的文化。阿富汗与俄罗斯和印度的关系很好，而且印度在阿富汗的投资比较多。阿富汗与其他阿拉伯国家和穆斯林国家关系很好。

目前，反政府与政治暴力经常发生，公众对安全的关注制约了经济活动。安全是投资者首要关注的问题。外国公司不得不将大量收益用于安全方面的基础设施建设和运营费用。

阿富汗是南亚区域合作联盟成员。

2. 经济环境

阿富汗是世界上贫穷和欠发达国家之一，主要为农业经济，制造业基础差，很少有附加值的工业。阿富汗有着计划经济体系，中央政府指挥经济生产和物资分配。阿富汗有富裕的自然资源，尤其是天然气、煤和铜矿。

自从塔利班政权垮台后，得益于数十亿美元的援助和国际社会的投资，阿富汗经济稳步增长。

正常的经济活动仍然极少，频繁的战争和地方军阀对道路的阻隔抑制了正常的经济活动。北部地区时有盗抢事件发生。商业贸易在一些非塔利班地区被妨碍，因为地方军阀继续通过征收过路费和偶尔关闭道路来表示他们对道路的控制。

国际部队的撤离显著阻碍了经济的增长，因为撤离导致对交通、建设、通信和其他服务的需求下滑。

农业是阿富汗经济中最重要的部门，占GDP的35%，大部分人口依赖于农作物。公共部门的复兴导致公共事业机构的增多，现在已占到GDP的40%左右。由于对大量的矿产资源的开采，如锂、宝石，采矿业增长迅速。[①]

农业，包括高水平的罂粟种植，是经济的支柱，并且是最重要的工作来源：60%～80%的人口在

---

① 参见 https://tradingeconomics.com/afghanistan/gdp-growth-annual。

农业部门工作,虽然农业只占 GDP 的第三位,原因在于缺乏灌溉、降水不均衡、市场准入的限制以及其他结构性障碍。

阿富汗有着世界上第二高的鸦片产量,贸易主要是水果、矿石、宝石,还有其他走私到巴基斯坦的货物。

阿富汗需要更高的经济增长率来支撑 3% 的人口增长率和接纳每年新增 40 万名左右的就业者进入劳动力市场。但是,安全威胁、基础设施缺乏和特有的腐败已经在阻碍着经济活动。

为了改善商业环境,阿富汗政府在各种场合公开强调其培养以私营部门为主导的发展和增加国内外投资的决心。政府和民间社会正在努力建构一个有利于私营经济的环境,并且通过开发自然资源和进行基础建设来扩大私营经济的投资。之前,因为来已久的能力问题、依赖于自上而下作决定和寻租严重阻碍了这些领域的发展。2016 年进行了经营许可方面的改革,包括经营和投资许可统一在一个部门,经营许可由 1 年延长到 3 年。另外,政府采用了开放准入的政策,号召电信业自由化,现正在等待实施。①

2016 年,经议会批准阿富汗成为 WTO 第 164 个成员,这对商业和贸易来说是一个积极的信号。阿富汗同时还是南亚自由贸易区成员,与印度和巴基斯坦签订了贸易协定。阿富汗政府一直期望外国投资来提升和稳定其经济。

3. 社会环境

阿富汗的安全问题,特别是对商业安全的挑战仍然是头条新闻。然而,大多数在阿富汗的国内外商业人士认为,比安全问题更严重的是腐败和政府索要赞助。

阿富汗生产世界上超过 90% 的非药品鸦片,毒品收益是不安全的持续的根源,从军阀到毒枭,再到塔利班,都从毒品中获利。阿富汗现在还时刻面临着武器的威胁——这是数十年几乎持续不断的战争留下来的。根据人权研究和倡导联盟的报告《把枪拿开》,在 2004 年的调查中,2/3 的阿富汗被调查者认为,裁军是阿富汗改善安全问题最重要的事情。

4. 法律环境

阿富汗的法律、法规框架和执行机制仍然是不规则地实施。在阿富汗有三种重叠的法律制度——伊斯兰法、舒拉(习惯法)和正规法(大陆法系)。

2004 年生效的《宪法》确立了强有力的总统制。阿富汗总统由阿富汗人民直接选举,任期 5 年,连任不得超过两届。总统同时是武装部队的总司令。

总统的责任包括:经国民议会批准决定政策;任命经主要立法机关人民议院批准的国家各部部长、总检察官、中央银行总裁、最高法院法官;任命国家第一副总统和第二副总统。

根据阿富汗《宪法》第 81 条的规定,阿富汗国民议会作为最高立法机构,显示了人民的意志和代表整个国家。每个国会议员在投票表决时应考虑公共福利和阿富汗所有人民的最高利益。

国民议会由两院,即人民院 249 席,长老院 102 席,组成立法机关。

根据阿富汗《宪法》第 116 条的规定,司法机关是阿富汗独立的机关。司法权包括最高法院、高等法院和上诉法院、初级法院,这些法院的职权由法律规定。巡回法庭根据需要由最高法院院长建议,总统批准设立。

9 名最高法院法官经人民院批准后由总统任命。

腐败阻碍了法律的公平适用,商业监督机构人员缺乏,且能力不够。金融数据系统有限。重要部门如矿业、水电缺乏规则的环境和政策制定者对投资有益的支持。

不过,阿富汗于 2016 年加入了世界贸易组织(WTO),这对商业和贸易是一个积极的信号。

(二)"一带一路"倡议下与中国企业合作的现状与方向

中国和阿富汗的关系可以追溯到古代。古丝绸之路紧紧连接了中国和阿富汗。古老的"丝绸之路"是汉武帝时的特使张骞开辟的,从中国一直延伸到罗马。从那以后,许多阿富汗的智者和商人来到中

---

① 参见 https://www.state.gov/e/eb/rls/othr/ics/investmentclimatestatements/index.htm#wrapper。

国，为中国的经济与文化发展作出了贡献。

两国现代外交关系始于20世纪后期，已实现了两国政府领导首次互访。[①]

中国现在已是阿富汗最大的投资来源。2007年一家中国公司以30亿美元的价格租了阿富汗艾娜克铜矿，签署了为期30年的租赁协议。

2016年阿富汗与中国签订了关于"一带一路"的备忘录，2017年加入了亚洲基础建设投资银行。

两国在2016年9月连通了铁路，货物可以从中国运到阿富汗海拉顿铁路口岸，该铁路也是连接中国和阿富汗、乌兹别克斯坦、哈萨克斯坦和伊朗等国家的中国"一带一路"商贸走廊的一部分。中阿铁路使同样距离的陆路货运从原来的6个月缩短到两个星期。中阿铁路必将促进阿富汗尼输入中国，从中国吸引更多的投资。[②]

在2015年7月的出访中，阿富汗总统阿什拉夫·加尼·艾哈近德扎伊说，阿富汗希望参与到与中国"一带一路"倡议相关的在阿富汗的任何项目，欢迎中国投资阿富汗基础设施建设。

很多商人希望融入中国的两个区域性项目，一个是"一带一路"，另一个是中—巴能源走廊。

阿富汗的基础设施建设项目，比如，阿富汗铁路网、开发未利用的矿产资源、环阿公路，都与中国的"一带一路"倡议有联系。

阿富汗的政治家已表示对中—巴能源走廊的支持，并表示有兴趣加入。

中国、巴基斯坦和阿富汗已同意合作在喀布尔河流域的库纳尔河上建造一座水力发电的大坝。根据阿富汗跨部级能源委员会的估计，喀布尔河流域每年能产出超过2 800兆瓦的电能。[③]

今天，中国和阿富汗共同响应"一带一路"倡议，这必将重现丝绸之路，并且会使它更美丽，为两国的未来作出贡献。

二、投资

（一）市场准入

1. 投资监管部门

高级投资委员会（HCI）负责阿富汗投资政策的制定。高级投资委员会成员包括农业部长、畜牧业和食品部长、商业部长、财政部长、外交部长、矿产和工业部长、央行行长、阿富汗投资支持局首席执行官，商业部长为高级投资委员会主席。

高级经济委员会（HEC）根据阿富汗总统令于2016年4月14日成立，阿富汗总统是该委员会的主席，成员包括高级投资委员会成员、总统高级顾问、中央统计办公室主任、学术与私人部门的代表和其他需要参与的人员。

高级经济委员会的主要职责是：

（1）根据国家预算结构决定基本的财政和经济目标、政策，短期、中期、长期政府优先发展事项；

（2）评估和决定国家经济发展规划和改革方案；

（3）协调发展和经济部门的政策、项目；

（4）创造合适的环境吸引商人投资；

（5）就响应和协调国家优先项目、区域性合作项目和国家及国际经济会议发布必要的指令。[④]

投资支持局（AISA）是投资促进机构，已于2016年10月并入工商部（MOCI）。目前仍处于过渡期，因此投资支持局继续扮演一个半独立的角色。工商部已承担起促进商业增长、投资和贸易的职责。

高级经济委员会、高级投资委员会、工商部、阿富汗工商总会和投资支持局都有保持对话和解决与政府的商业纠纷的责任。

---

① 参见https://www.c3sindia.org/geopolitics-strategy/chinas-interests-in-afghanistan-by-adithya-krishna/。
② 参见https://www.forbes.com/sites/ralphjennings/2018/02/27/china-needs-a-win-in-afghanistan-to-keep-its-edge-in-asian-trade/#c35c3101d5c7。
③ 参见https://thediplomat.com/2017/04/linking-afghanistan-to-chinas-belt-and-road/。
④ 参见https://president.gov.af/en/about-high-economic-council/?q=council。

2. 投资行业的法律、法规

阿富汗《宪法》规定了在阿富汗投资的主要原则。

2005年《私人投资法》（PIL）取代了《国内和外国私人投资法》。

《私人投资法》第2条规定："本法宗旨为促进国内和外国对阿富汗的经济投资，创造一个鼓励、支持和保护外国和国内私人投资者，为了促进经济发展、扩大劳动力市场、增加产品和出口创汇、促进技术转让、增加国家繁荣和提高生活水准的法律制度和行政结构。"

目前，阿富汗新的投资法已由工商部起草，正在等待部长委员会的审议。

阿富汗其他与投资相关的法律有《合伙企业法》《股份及有限公司法》《竞争法》和《公共采购法》。

《合伙企业法》和《股份及有限公司法》是外国律师起草的，他们没有花太多的时间在阿富汗，没有从阿富汗国内的人们和企业那里获得多少信息。这两部法律被一个外国政府机构批评制定得太匆忙而没有充足的国内信息的国内投入。另外，一些条款过于复杂，很多条款反映了鼓励投资的国际上最好的实践，但却不适用于阿富汗特殊的环境。

阿富汗《合同法》包含在1955年阿富汗《商法典》和1977年阿富汗《民法典》中。1955年阿富汗《商法典》和1977年阿富汗《民法典》基于埃及法制定，而埃及法又是源自法国民法。

根据这些法典，当事方总体而言可以自由地：订立和执行任何商业主题的合同，只要该商业主题或合同的履行不违反法律、公共政策、伊斯兰法；同意由外国法管辖他们的合同。

《公共采购法》于2015年10月7日生效，它坚持国家资源和国内产品优先的原则。

2016年7月29日，阿富汗正式加入WTO，意味着在阿富汗投资要遵守WTO规则。

3. 投资方式

根据《私人投资法》的规定，经批准的企业所有权应当是以下两种形式之一：

（1）100%的私人所有；

（2）私人投资者与阿富汗政府的合资。

4. 准入条件及审查

在阿富汗开设企业，应当符合以下条件：

（1）根据阿富汗法律规定开设企业；

（2）根据外国法开设企业，但须按照阿富汗法律、法规的规定经批准和注册在阿富汗从事贸易和投资。

根据2005年《私人投资法》的规定，外国和国内私人实体有同等的地位，可以创设和拥有商事企业，从事所有形式的获取利益的活动，自由地获得和处理商事企业的利润。

根据《私人投资法》的规定，投资须以现金、实物（包括机器、设备和工业和知识产权）投入注册的企业来获得股份或其他所有者权益。

《私人投资法》允许投资除核能、博彩业、毒品和麻醉剂产品外的几乎所有行业。另外，在关于动画、道路交通（客运和货运）业的交易和资产总价值上以及证券公司雇用的总人数上有所限制。

虽然高级经济委员会有权限制外国投资在一些行业、特殊的经济部门和特定公司占有的股份，但实际上这个权力从来没有行使过。实践中，外国投资者可拥有100%股份。

投资于特定的部门，比如武器与爆炸物的生产和销售，非银行金融活动、保险、自然资源和基础设施建设（界定为污水、废物处理、空港、通信和健康、教育设施），需要遵从高级经济委员会在与相关政府部门协商后的具体决定。高级经济委员会可选择适用投资限制部门的具体要求。直接投资超过300万美元需要经过高级经济委员会批准。

外国或国内公司在阿富汗投资必须从阿富汗商业注册中心（ACBR）获得公司注册和税务部发放的税务识别码。

从事证券、通信、农业和健康等行业需要从相关部门取得另外的许可。

提供咨询、法律或审计服务的公司其高级管理人员须符合对教育或相关经验的要求才能获得许可。

外国公司初始许可证的发放、更新、许可事项的变更，首先要取得阿富汗外交部的介绍信，呈交工商部。要取得外交部的介绍信，须向驻外国公司所在国的阿富汗大使馆申请或从该外国驻喀布尔的大使馆或商务参赞处取得介绍信。取得介绍信后，阿富汗外交部就会介绍该外国公司给工商部或者投资支持局，从而进入领取营业执照的程序。

2016年的商业简便化改革，导致投资支持局为了吸引投资开始颁发3年期的执照，之前只颁发1年期的执照。取得营业执照相对简单，但是，申请更新要具备财政部的所有税收义务均已履行的证书。尽管财政部保证税务审计不妨碍投资支持局执照的换发，一些公司发现，在财政部进行税务审计的同时，执照被投资支持局延迟换发。

（二）外汇管理

1. 外汇主管部门

官方货币是阿富汗尼（AFN）。虽然立法规定日常交易必须使用阿富汗尼，但美元仍被广泛使用。

阿富汗银行（DAB）是阿富汗的中央银行。阿富汗《银行法》规定的阿富汗银行的一些目标和基本任务包括：

阿富汗银行享有自主的管理权力和权威，包括通过法规为阿富汗银行、其他银行及其客户之间的电子交易提供便利。

阿富汗银行由总督管理。最高委员会是阿富汗银行的最高政策和决策机构，由总督（最高委员会主席）、第一副总督（最高委员会副主席）和其他5名成员组成。最高委员会的所有成员应由阿富汗总统在征得阿富汗议会的意见和同意后任命。

2. 外汇法律、法规概况

阿富汗《银行法》第72条规定，阿富汗银行对外汇有专有的职责。

《银行法》第8条规定，阿富汗银行最高委员会有权制定和批准外汇政策和外汇安排，有权决定阿富汗银行外汇储备和其他金融资源适合于投资的资产类别。

在阿富汗，对于任何与投资有关的资金在法定市场清算率下转换或转移为国际货币没有任何限制。若相关税收已缴纳，对利润汇款、偿债、资本、资本收益、知识产权收益或进口原材料的资金流入和流出也没有任何限制。为反洗钱的目的，对资金外流的唯一要求是遵守程序性规定。任何相当于或超过100万阿富汗尼（20 000美元）的国外转账必须通过银行或有执照的外汇交易商进行，并向中央银行报告。在主要城市和省份有可兑换主要货币的大型非正式外汇市场。

携带100万及以上阿富汗尼或同等金额的其他货币现金出境到另外一个国家，必须事先向阿富汗央行金融调查局报告。

进行投资的外汇不受任何法律或法规的限制。在主要城市和省份，有大量的、非正式的外汇市场，美元、英镑和欧元都有。希望在阿富汗买卖外汇的实体必须向阿富汗银行登记，但大量的哈瓦拉交易系统没有按规定登记却继续从事他们的交易。非官方货币服务提供商常常以货币兑换部门缺乏执行力以及由此导致的对持牌货币兑换商的竞争劣势为由，不想成为持牌货币兑换商。

2014年中期，由于阿富汗未能及时通过金融行动特别工作组（FATF）的反洗钱/打击资助恐怖主义（AML/CFT）的法律的合规性审查，一些国际代理银行开始关闭阿富汗银行在海外持有的美元账户，这增加了出入境资金调拨的费用和时间成本。目前，阿富汗只有一家银行与一家在美国设有分行的银行有代理关系。自那时以来，阿富汗已采取措施改进反洗钱/打击资助恐怖主义的制度。

3. 外资企业外汇管理要求

私人投资者有权将资本和利润从阿富汗转移出去，包括离岸贷款还本付息。没有限制将与投资有关的资金，如股息、资本回报率、利息和私人外债本金、租赁付款或特许权使用费和管理费，以合法的市场清算率转换、汇出或转移为可自由使用的货币。

在阿富汗，主要交易如出售汽车或财产，经常以美元或邻国的货币进行。阿富汗没有实行双重汇率政策、货币管制、资本管制或对资金自由流动的任何其他限制。阿富汗采用管理的浮动汇率制度，汇率由市场决定。通过陆路或空运将超过100万阿富汗尼（约17 200美元）或等值的外币运出阿富汗是非法的；数额超过50万阿富汗尼（约8 600美元）但低于100万阿富汗尼的，必须申报。实际执行可能与上述规定不一致。

《私人投资法》规定，投资者可以自由地将投资红利或出售已批准企业的收益转移到国外。财政部在某些情况下，比如有税收争议，才会冻结公司国内银行账户，有效地禁止了资本的转移。

（三）金融融资

1. 主要金融机构

阿富汗的银行系统有着悠久的历史，但直到最近几年才根据现代标准发展起来。阿富汗中央银行是对银行和非银行金融机构进行许可和监管的唯一实体。阿富汗银行还负责维持货币供应、货币流通并间接负责通货膨胀和汇率。阿富汗中央银行现已在全国 34 个省设立分支机构，并通过环球同业银行金融电讯协会结算系统（SWIFT）进行资金转移。

原则上阿富汗欢迎外国证券投资，但金融机构和市场正处于早期发展阶段。外国投资者获得信贷没有任何限制，银行一般只提供短期贷款。

在 2010 年喀布尔银行危机之后，中央银行在监测和监督银行部门方面有了改进。加尼总统还采取措施追究责任人的责任。阿富汗政府计划从实施大规模银行欺诈的人手中追回资产，尽管进展仍然缓慢。

大多数阿富汗人被排除在正规银行外。阿富汗人继续依靠非正式的基于信任的程序——哈瓦拉交易系统获得资金和转移资金，部分原因是宗教信仰、对正规银行系统的不熟悉以及农村地区银行的准入限制。四大移动网络运营商中的三家——Etisalat、AWCC 和 Roshan 提供有限的移动支付服务。此外，阿富汗政府计划在劳工部推出移动支付方式支付工资，如果成功，政府计划将移动支付推广至教育和内政部。

尽管如此，金融仍然是阿富汗仅次于电信的第二大服务业，也是私人投资和经济增长的重要推动力。阿富汗有 15 家商业银行，总资产约 44.8 亿美元。有三家国有银行：阿富汗 E-Millie 银行（阿富汗国家银行）、普什塔尼银行和新喀布尔银行（原为私人拥有的喀布尔银行），还有外国银行的分支机构，其中包括巴基斯坦阿尔法拉银行、巴基斯坦哈比卜银行和巴基斯坦国家银行。

银行业务高度集中，大部分贷款是由喀布尔银行提供的。由于法律和监管制度的影响，阻碍了产权的执行和抵押品的发展，银行贷款受到影响。2015 年通过的一项银行业改革法可能会改善现状。银行业的总存贷比率约为 11%，大多数银行集中于收费服务和对知名客户的短期信贷。通过银行和其他正规金融机构获得信贷的困难使现有公司更依赖家庭资金和留存收益，限制了创业机会，并加剧了对非正规金融部门的依赖。

阿富汗的保险业仍处于初级阶段。保险委员会成立于 2006 年中期，并且对国内外投资者在该领域的投资规定了许可程序。截至 2014 年 6 月，已有四家公司取得营业执照。

2. 外资企业融资条件

私营企业的正规信贷不到国内生产总值的 10%，大大低于该地区其他国家。在世界银行 2017 年贸易报告中，阿富汗在 189 个经济体中排名第 101 位，容易获得授信。阿富汗企业家抱怨当地银行的商业贷款利率高，平均约为 15.5%。在这种情况下，投资基金、租赁、小额融资和中小企业融资公司纷纷进入市场。美国国际开发署正在与阿富汗政府和银行部门合作，以促进更好地获得资金和扩大金融包容性。

那些希望在阿富汗开设银行账户的外国人必须持有有效护照和签证或工作许可证。非居民要接受更严格的打击洗钱和恐怖主义融资调查。

（四）土地政策

1. 土地法律、法规概况

阿富汗《宪法》规定，财产不受侵犯，除非法律有禁止规定，任何人都可以拥有和取得财产，私人财产只能由法律命令没收。

法律禁止在未经政府批准的情况下非法取得土地（《民法典》第 1991 条），取得任何类型的土地都必须得到政府许可。

即使没有所有者的贫瘠土地，也只能经政府许可才能取得。经政府许可取得和开发贫瘠土地的人，应当拥有该土地（《民法典》第1992条）。任何财产在指定用于公共用途的期限届满后，即不再属于公共财产。公用期限的届满由继承法或在公有制的目的不再存在时确定（《民法典》第483条）。

根据《民法典》第481条的规定，个人拥有的不动产被视为私人财产。《民法典》没有规定由集体或公司拥有的私有财产。但是，根据伊斯兰法，私人财产可以单独或集体所有。阿富汗《民法典》第1900条赋予所有者使用和开发其财产的排他性权利，这一权利被解释为所有者可以在法律规定的范围内自由使用和处置其财产。

私人可以通过购买、市政当局土地划拨、所有权让渡的方式取得土地所有权。另外，在理论上，土地可以通过运用"不毛之地"或"无主土地"原则取得。

总统令（第83号法令）规定，公民对由国家所有已超过37年的土地主张所有权的，将被阻止。国家被视为土地的所有者（第2条）。此外，该法令还规定，凡未合法确立个人所有权的土地，均应视为国家财产（第3条）。①

关于喀布尔市住宅、商业和多层建筑国有土地的分配和出售的总统令（第794号）规定了喀布尔市国有土地的分配。根据该法令，没有住房、公寓或地块的个人有资格从市政府购买土地。此外，法律规定申请购买土地的人的未成年子女与配偶不得拥有任何住房、公寓或土地，以便有资格从国家获得土地分配（第3条第1款）。

根据《地方行政管理法》和随后颁布的实施条例（第753号）的规定，省长被授权出售国有土地以及代表国家购买土地。

然而，全国各地普遍存在攫取土地、非法占有和其他非法占用土地的现象。大部分房地产交易是通过非正式的市场机制进行的。另外，正式的产权制度不利于土地的有效利用或促进房地产市场的运作。鉴于其目前的腐败和低效率，正式的土地所有权取得程序没有提供一个适当的机制来满足对房地产交易的潜在需求。

土地政策改革正在进行，但进展缓慢，城市的土地管理能力仍然薄弱并且有待改善。阿富汗政府正在努力通过修订和更新土地法，为土地占有权创建一个连贯的法律框架。继承规定在《民法典》中，体现了伊斯兰法（伊斯兰教法）的精神。

2007年的土地政策允许非正式住宅区土地权利的正规化，并解决了土地权利管理方面的瓶颈，以及不同机构在土地问题上的管理重叠问题。

新《土地法》于2008年出台，定义了各种土地类型和分类、土地契约的要求，以及关于国家土地分配、土地出租、土地征用、土地权利安置和土地储存的原则。然而，目前的法律框架仍有过去土地所有权改革的残余。此外，虽然习惯法很重要且具有社会合法性，但它并未与正式法律和政策融合。

2. 外资企业获得土地的规定

阿富汗《宪法》和《私人投资法》禁止外国人拥有土地所有权。实践中，大多数外国公司认为和阿富汗伙伴一起合作是必要的。

阿富汗《宪法》第41条规定，外国个人无权在阿富汗拥有不动产。依照法律规定，以资本投资为目的的不动产租赁应予以准许。根据法律规定允许向外国外交使团以及阿富汗加入的国际组织出售财产。《宪法》第41条中的"外国个人"，是指自然人和法人实体。因此，在没有关于这一问题的其他立法的情况下，无论外国所有权的比例如何，对外国人拥有土地所有权的限制是绝对的。

阿富汗《宪法》第21条对土地租赁作了规定，该条允许经批准的企业有权租赁土地用于经营目的，根据法律规定，租期最长可达50年。因此，租赁似乎是外国人开展需要长期拥有土地的项目的唯一可行办法。

（五）企业设立与解散

1. 企业形式

阿富汗有五种形式的商业组织：个人独资企业、普通合伙、特殊（有限）合伙、股份公司、有限

---

① 参见 Dr. Yohannes Gebremedhin, Legal Issues in Afghanistan Land Titling and Registration. 2005, www.terrainstitute.org/pdf/Legal_Analysis_of_Land_Laws.pdf。

公司。

根据《合伙企业法》的规定，合伙是两个或两个以上的人通过提交和注册他们的合伙协议创设。合伙企业一经设立即具有法律人格，就能够进行交易、签订合同和拥有财产。《合伙企业法》规定了两种合伙，普通合伙和特殊合伙。

《股份及有限责任公司法》（CLLCL）第4条规定，股份公司是指一种商业公司，其公司的资本是确定的并且分成等额份额，每个股东的股份和责任以其持有股份的比例为限。有限责任公司是一种商业公司，其资本不分成等额份额，股东的责任限于其同意出资的金额。

《股份及有限责任公司法》明确了股份公司的注册要求，包括营业执照、公司章程和年度报告在内的相关文件可以在注册中心登记。

股份公司有两重董事会，包括监事会，负责监督董事会，检查公司登记簿和记录。该法还规定了董事会的职责和要求，包括披露关于影响公司交易的利益冲突的义务。

股份公司必须召开年度会议，在会上选举董事，决定重大事务。在召开年度董事会之前，股份公司必须向股东递交财务报告，财务报告包括资产负债表，必须遵守国际会计准则。《股份及有限公司法》还规定了更多的股东知情权和其他对股东权益的保护，比如检查公司登记簿和记录，以及股东对董事或公司高级管理人员在管理公司过程中失职、违反职责追诉的权利。同时，该法对股份公司可以支付多少红利、保留多少必须的资金设置了规则。

《股份及有限责任公司法》限定有限责任公司股东为2～50名，股份不能公开上市交易。

2. 设立程序

根据1955年《商法典》的规定，不想将企业作为法人实体注册的独资企业和家族企业不再被强制要求登记。外国独资企业必须在阿富汗投资支持局登记。对阿富汗独资企业和家族企业的唯一法律要求是，他们必须取得税务识别号码或TIN并且向地区和市政当局登记。有些人选择向商业登记中心（ACBR）、投资支持局登记或申请工商部商业（或贸易商）许可证。有建议要求阿富汗独资企业向行政当局登记。这些建议的现况可在工商部查阅。

2007年《股份及有限责任公司法》通过后，所有在阿富汗设立法人企业的国内外投资者都需要在商务部商业登记中心登记。《股份及有限公司法》规定阿富汗商业登记中心设立于工商部之下。

根据企业从事的具体部门，它们可能被要求获得相关部门的许可，特别是在下列任何一个部门开展活动的企业（独资企业、合伙企业或公司实体）都必须获得部门许可证。

外国投资者第一次向投资支持局登记其公司/投资时，需要提供其投资支持局许可证的副本，作为为其雇员申请工作许可证程序的一部分。

有签证的外国雇员应申请外国人工作许可。

为了在阿富汗设立企业，必须对申请人进行犯罪记录调查。外国申请人必须提供他/她的大使馆或政府提供的证明或此种类型的文件，明确表明他/她没有参与过任何类型的犯罪、非法活动，目前没有受到起诉。

阿富汗申请人将通过警察局长办公室的刑事部门进行犯罪记录调查。这是商业登记中心和投资支持局进行的登记的一部分。

3. 解散方式及要求

根据《公司及有限责任公司法》的规定，阿富汗有两种解散公司的方式，决议解散和判决解散。

（1）决议解散

《公司及有限责任公司法》第103条规定："董事会过半数票通过即可批准解散公司，并将提案（无论是有条件的还是无条件的）提交股东会通过和批准。"

公司可向登记中心提交解散决议，公司在登记解散之日解散。公司股东大会可以自登记公告之日起5日内撤销解散。当解散的撤销生效时，公司恢复经营业务。解散的撤销具有追溯效力。

（2）判决解散

具有管辖权的商事法院可以根据工商部、一名或多名股东或债权人的起诉判决公司解散。

如果在公司设立时有以下情况，工商部可以启动解散程序：

① 公司通过欺诈取得公司设立许可证书；
② 公司超过或者滥用了法律赋予的权限。
当公司出现以下情形时，一名或多名股东可以启动解散程序：
① 董事在公司事务的管理上陷入僵局，股东无法打破僵局，公司及其资产受到不可弥补的损害；
② 公司的董事或控制者已有或正在进行非法或欺诈的行为；
③ 股东在投票权方面陷入僵局，在至少连续两次定期/年度会议上，未能选举董事。
具有以下情形时，债权人也可以启动解散程序：
① 债权人的债权：已有生效判决；对判决的执行不满意；且企业已无力偿债；
② 企业书面承认该债权人的债权已到期且公司已无力偿债。
当债权人已向公司提出索赔时，公司的主动解散应当在法院监督下进行。
根据《股份及有限责任公司法》的规定，在公司解散程序中，法院可委任一名或一名以上接管人清盘及清算，或委任一名或一名以上托管人管理企业在解散期间的业务及事务。托管人可以在必要的范围内通过或者代替公司董事会行使管理公司的权力来管理公司事务，但须符合股东和债权人最佳利益。
如果法院认定存在判决解散的一个或多个理由，可以根据《股份及有限责任公司法》第107条的规定作出解散公司的法令，并规定解散的公告日期。
法院应当向中央登记机关提交解散令的副本。在颁布解散令后，法院应当主导公司业务和事务的清盘和清算。
对于合伙企业，可以因合伙人死亡、破产、退伙、合伙目标的实现或法院的命令等多种原因解散。合伙企业解散时，必须遵循清算程序，以保护债权人和合伙企业的资产。

（六）合并收购

《公司及有限责任公司法》第41条规定，受公司章程限制，董事会有权执行并签署任何法律文件，并在合法交易中代表公司。该法第51条和第52条规定了董事会批准与股东对交易的批准。因此，公司并购活动要遵从公司章程的规定，并且要经董事会和股东的批准。

同时，根据该法第51条的规定，只要不存在董事利益冲突，不被法院在股东诉讼中禁止，或者董事利益冲突所衍生的程序，并且不被判处支付损害赔偿或其他限制，并购交易就应当由公司（或者公司的子公司或者其他控制实体）实施或建议实施。

（七）竞争管制

1. 竞争管制主管机构

《竞争法》第14条规定，设立国家竞争理事会，其主要职责是"促进公平竞争和防止垄断"。

工商部内设的竞争促进与消费者保护专门委员会（CPCPD）作为国家竞争理事会的秘书处，其职责是监督市场活动。

2. 竞争法概况

现行阿富汗《竞争法》于2010年1月25日颁布。该法对"竞争"的定义是：竞争是一种状态，在这种状态下，存在大量独立的生产者、买者和卖者，在市场上生产、买卖相似商品或服务，没有人能独立地决定产品数量与价格。

该法规定了政府五个方面的责任：
（1）保护市场上合理的竞争；
（2）防止有害竞争、不公正的协议、决定和履行不公平的限制性的、扰乱或阻止竞争的货物、服务和产品的合同；
（3）在商事活动中防止垄断；
（4）预防市场受垄断企业家的影响；
（5）促进形成公平竞争和宽松的总体经济环境。

但当前的《竞争法》有些不合时宜。在与巴基斯坦竞争委员会（CCP）和巴基斯坦消费者权益委员会（CRCP）的紧密合作之下，美国商事法律发展课程组织（CLDP）在巴基斯坦伊斯兰堡为阿富汗竞争促进与消费者保护专门委员会组织了一个竞争与消费者保护法项目。这个项目是商事法律发展课程组织持续努力构建阿富汗竞争促进与消费者保护专门委员会的内在能力，发展一个可持续的竞争与消费者保护制度，以帮助在阿富汗建立一个透明和平稳的商业竞技场。①

阿富汗工商部竞争促进与消费者保护专门委员会委托一家印度的律师事务所 ELP 起草了一部《竞争法》草案。②

这是一部更为现代的《竞争法》，但是国会并未通过。新法涵盖垄断行为、非法串通和反竞争行为——倾销、固定价格、排他性交易、拒绝交易、限定区域、捆绑、转售价格维持等。

3. 竞争管制措施

《竞争法》第 7 条规定，禁止任何类型的企业家、商人、组织和公司之间的旨在阻止、限制或干扰竞争，或有损于消费者的谅解、协议和合同（书面、电子或口头的）。

《竞争法》第 8 条规定，禁止不公平的商业行为。

《竞争法》第 11 条规定了收购公司和组织的限制情形。公司或组织不能独自、双方或多方在以下情况下收购：

（1）收购的结果或在收购过程中出现反竞争的行为；

（2）导致货物或服务价格急剧增长；

（3）导致市场中强烈的集中（由竞争理事会决定什么是强烈的集中）；

（4）收购导致产生了一个市场控制的公司或组织。

（八）税收

1. 税收体系与规则

近年来，阿富汗的国家税收体系已经改变，简化了一系列的小额税收，税务机关和投资者都接受了培养和教育，对于税务机关来说可以有效且高效地管理税收，对于投资者来说，纳税是一项义务。

纳税人需获得纳税人识别号（每一个纳税人有唯一的编码），所有的投资者应上报他们的利润，即使利润不属于应纳税收入。除非法律授权，纳税人提供的信息在财政部是保密的。纳税人应使用权责发生制方式记账及保存。纳税年度开始于 12 月 21 日终于下一年的 12 月 20 日。③

2. 主要税赋与税率

在阿富汗，税种包括个人所得税、企业所得税、工资预扣税、独资企业税、小企业固定税、展览固定税、进口固定税、承包商固定税、商业运输固定税等。

所得税是在每一个应纳税年度，对个人、股份公司、有限责任公司或者其他实体所征收的税种，纳税年度以一年为基准，除非法律有特别规定。应纳税收入是从个人、股份公司、有限责任公司及其他组织的所有收入中除去法律、法规所规定的扣减之后的余额。

法人、公司、有限责任公司及普通合伙的企业所得税占财政年度应纳税收入的 20%。

外国货币收入应转为阿富汗尼纳税。外国货币转换比率是阿富汗银行每月月底购买这些外国货币的汇率。

根据《所得税法》第 3 条的规定，所有的国家及市政的合伙、组织、代理处、部门及公司，所有的企业及有限责任公司在一年中的任意 1 个月内雇用 2 名或 2 名以上雇员的，必须从薪金、工资收入中代扣代缴税款至政府账户。

累进的个人所得税税率如下：

收入 0～5 000 阿富汗尼，税率为 0，在此范围内的工资收入不需纳税；

收入 5 001～12 500 阿富汗尼，税率为 2%，5 000 阿富汗尼免征，剩余的 7 500 阿富汗尼按 2% 的

---

① 参见 http://cldp.doc.gov/programs/cldp-in-action/details/1183。
② 参见 http://moci.gov.af/en/page/5976。
③ 参见 http://investinafghanistan.af/taxation-in-afghanistan/。

税率征收 150 阿富汗尼；

收入 12 501～100 000 阿富汗尼，税率为 10%，150 阿富汗尼+剩余数额的 10%（约为 8 750 阿富汗尼）；

收入 100 001 阿富汗尼以上的，税率为 20%，8 900 阿富汗尼+剩余数额的 20%。

另外，出租建筑物给法人和自然人用于商业目的或办公的，租金超过 15 000 阿富汗尼的，应缴纳 20% 的所得税。

商业收入所得税是对有限责任公司、公司、普通合伙及组织收取的税种：

（1）本财政年度的佣金、费用、利息、股息、租金、版税及相似收入等总收入（抵扣前）的 5%，但是不适用于自然人的租金收入。

（2）本财政年度的材料、设备、服务、运输及基于合同条款的建筑总收入（抵扣前）的 2%。

（3）本财政年度保险额外收入（抵扣前）的 2%。

（4）本财政年度的公共娱乐门票收入，包括电影、戏剧、音乐会、展出、体育及其他表演总收入（抵扣前）的 2%。

（5）本财政年度的产品、货物、资产和其他服务的销售总收入（抵扣前）的 2%。

（6）根据财政部的规定，法人或者自然人每月来源于提供服务的收入超过 50 000 阿富汗尼的，征收收入的 10%。①

3. 纳税申报与优惠

根据《所得税法》的规定，拥有营业执照（包括投资支持局投资许可及工商部商业贸易许可）能有一系列的优惠。这些优惠主要是减少政府合同税及进口固定税，特别是：

（1）减少进口固定税：进口产品及有商业许可证的贸易征进口商品总额（包括关税）2% 的固定税。根据《所得税法》的规定，纳税可以计入个人年度收入税收评估的信用评分。没有许可证的公司应征收进口商品总额（包括关税）3% 的固定税。

（2）政府合同减税：

① 没有贸易许可证的个人为政府部门、市政、国有企业、私人实体及其他人提供物资、材料、施工及服务，应缴纳 7% 的固定税代替所得税。税收将从付给承包商的总金额中代扣代缴。

② 有贸易许可证的人为前述提到的实体提供服务或者其他活动的，应缴纳 2% 的承包税。此处的税款可以抵减随后的纳税义务。

③ 前述提到的税收应由付款人代扣代缴并且应在 10 天之内交到相关的账户。承包商应在签订合同之后发送副本至相关的税收部门。根据《所得税法》第 17 条第 1 款的规定，自然人获得的应税收入应按本条款的规定。

（九）证券交易

阿富汗没有证券交易市场，因此没有相关证券法律、法规。

（十）投资优惠及保护

1. 优惠政策框架

促进和为国内外投资提供便利是阿富汗工商部的职责之一。

《阿富汗国家发展战略（ANDS）(2008—2013 年)》，是在联合国开发计划署的协助下完成的。该战略旨在通过优先级项目来指导特定领域的投资，这些优先级项目要选择能为创造就业机会作贡献、具有广泛的地理影响和可能吸引额外投资的项目。

阿富汗政府在 2013 年 7 月批准了"投资激励政策"，给将要投资的投资者以及在过渡转型的 10 年中继续投资的投资者以特别的优惠。

2016 年 3 月，阿富汗投资支持局建议政府考虑制定新政策，主要集中于工业、发电、税收改革、工业支持、海关、科技和农业部门。但该政策至今没有出台。

---

① 参见 http://ard.gov.af/?page_id=2686。

2. 行业与地区支持

2013 年 7 月的"投资激励政策"特别重视发展五个部门,即工业、建筑业、出口、农业和采矿业。该政策旨在为发展这些部门提供基本的基础,为了吸引外国投资者对这些潜在的商业机会的注意力。

对外国投资者的优惠待遇有:

(1) 工业部门:
① 为投资 100 万美元以上的实业家免费提供政府所有的土地;
② 可以 10 年分期付款购买工业园区的土地;
③ 政府所有的未开发的土地 30 年租期,第一个 5 年租期免费;
④ 免除 10 年的各类税费(除市政当局征收的除外);
⑤ 免除机器设备的进口关税,原材料的进口关税仅为 1%。

(2) 建筑业:
① 简化签证发放程序(市政当局已规定签证发放最多只要 6 个部门的签名,时间为 21 天以内);
② 在喀布尔投资 500 万美元以上或在省级投资 200 万美元的,可购买政府拥有的土地 2 000 平方米;
③ 对在喀布尔投资 200 万美元以上、省级投资 100 万美元以上的,简化住宅区变更成商业用途的行政程序,并且不收取费用。

(3) 出口产业:
① 为出口商,特别是食品、干湿加工、毛毯和动物产品加工出口,免费提供土地(取代之前的每 100 万美元买 4 000 平方米);
② 免除 10 年的各类税费(除市政当局征收的除外);
③ 免除进口机器设备关税。

(4) 农业:
① 可租赁政府所有的未开发的土地 30 年,第一个 5 年租期免费,尤其是投资冷藏、温室和食品加工的,取代之前的每 50 万美元买 4 000 平方米;
② 投资 1 000 万美元的可以租赁政府所有的未开发的土地 30 年,第一个 10 年租期免费;
③ 中小企业可以租赁政府所有的未开发的土地 15 年,第一个两年租期免费。

(5) 采矿产:
① 免除进口机器设备关税;
② 只要经营和商业意向事先经矿产和石油部批准,能开采 10 年,投资在 200 万美元的中小矿可以不招标。

但是,这些政策需要政府各部门采取必要的措施来执行。比如,外交部必须采取签证便利化的措施,给外国投资者一年期多次往返签证;高级委员会、农业灌溉和牲畜部与阿富汗投资支持局要加快土地流转进程。

值得一提的是,这些政策的落地需要修订几部法律和规章。

3. 特殊经济区域

阿富汗目前没有特殊经济区。阿富汗政府正通过阿富汗机场经济发展委员会(AAEDC)考虑建立特殊经济区(SEZs)来开发最终要转为民用的某些军事基地和机场。如果这个计划被批准,阿富汗需要在建设这些经济区之前制定相应的法律、法规。

4. 投资保护

保护外国和国内私人在阿富汗的投资是《私人投资法》的主要目标之一。《私人投资法》第 16 条规定,根据阿富汗法律,经批准的国内外具有相似目标的公司均享有相同的权利,对歧视性的政府行为享有相同的保护。

然而,由于缺乏土地清册或者完善的土地所有权制度,加之存在争议的土地权证和无能为力的商事法院以及普遍的腐败,阿富汗对财产权的保护非常赢弱。阿富汗的土地法前后矛盾、交叉、不完整,在有效土地的管理细节上缺乏规定。法官和律师没有处理土地争议相关的经验。而且,抵押和留置权处于发展的早期阶段。外国投资者寻求与阿富汗公民合作购买财产的，应当做好尽职调查，以确定可靠的合作伙伴。

三、贸易①

阿富汗和中国是传统友好邻邦，两国友好关系历史悠久。阿富汗于1955年1月20日与中国建交。2006年6月卡尔扎伊总统对中国进行国事访问，两国元首共同签署了《中阿睦邻友好合作条约》，2010年3月，卡尔扎伊总统再次来华进行国事访问，双方签署了以下协议：《中华人民共和国政府和阿富汗伊斯兰共和国政府经济技术合作协定》《中华人民共和国政府和阿富汗伊斯兰共和国政府关于培训项目的换文》和《中华人民共和国政府关于给予原产于阿富汗的部分输华产品特别优惠关税待遇的换文》。

中国是阿富汗重要贸易伙伴，占阿富汗外贸总额约11.69%。巴基斯坦、乌兹别克斯坦分别是阿富汗第一、第二大贸易伙伴。主要出口对象为巴基斯坦、印度、伊朗、俄罗斯和美国。

（一）贸易主管部门

阿富汗主管贸易的政府部门是商业和工业部（简称"商工部"），其下属的对外贸易司主管贸易政策制定和外贸的协调管理，外交部内设经济事务司，负责政府层面的对外经济贸易关系的协调。此外专设由商工部主管的出口促进局，负责政策贯彻、贸易推动、组织会展、出口手续、出具单证如货物原产地证等事务性业务，进口货物由海关监管。

（二）贸易法律、法规概况

与贸易相关的法律有《海关法》《合同法》《保险法》《仲裁法》《调解法》《大阿富汗银行法》《货币和商业银行法》等。2015年12月17日，在肯尼亚首都内罗毕举行的WTO第十届部长级会议上，WTO成员国同意阿富汗加入WTO。

据阿富汗《每日瞭望报》报道，2016年6月21日，阿富汗议会批准阿加入世界贸易组织（WTO）。②阿富汗上议院第二副主席哈西布拉·卡里姆扎指出，加入WTO能让阿富汗经济增长提高2.5%。7月29日，阿富汗正式成为WTO第164个成员。

阿富汗还是南亚区域合作联盟（SAARC）、中亚区域经济合作组织（CAREC）和经济合作组织（ECO）的成员国。

（三）贸易管理

阿富汗货币为阿富汗尼。③战后阿富汗进行货币改革，发行新的阿富汗尼，实行相对固定的汇率，基本稳定在1美元兑换50阿富汗尼左右。阿富汗纸币有七种面值，分别为1 000、500、100、50、20、10、5阿富汗尼，硬币面值为5、2、1阿富汗尼三种。受国际金融危机影响，2008年11月阿富汗尼出现首次贬值，比价为1∶54。

阿富汗对投资换汇和汇款没有限制，只要按规定缴税，对利润、债务服务、资本、资本所得、知识产权收入等的汇款不设限制。但为了防止洗钱，规定国际汇款100万阿富汗尼（2万美元）以上的必须通过银行或有资质的外汇交易机构，并向阿富汗央行备案。

阿富汗对大宗商品进口没有限制。禁止进口的商品有：酒、生猪、猪肉、猪油脂、棉籽、毒品、枪支炸药。阿富汗政府鼓励本国商品出口。禁止出口的商品有：毒品、古董、稀有矿产资源和其他政府规定禁止出口的物品。

（四）进出口商品检验检疫

进口货物由阿富汗海关进行检验，但是检验检疫设备和技术相对落后。中国出口阿富汗的货物应

---

① 参见http://af.mofcom.gov.cn/article/ddfg/201109/20110907755599.shtml。
② 参见http://af.mofcom.gov.cn/article/afjj/201609/20160901394480.shtml。
③ 根据2018年7月的汇率，100万阿富汗尼约等于90 420元人民币。

按规定出具中国商检报告。

（五）海关管理

1. 概况

阿富汗《海关法》[①]（2005年3月20日）规定，财政部负责收取国家的海关收入，执行本法和其他有关海关立法的规定。

海关监管是指当局为确保出入境的货物遵守海关立法和其他适用于受海关监管货物的规定而进行的检查，包括必要时可能实施海关监管的措施。

进出口商有义务将进出口货物交由财政部许可的报关经纪人办理清关手续。根据《海关法》第42条、第45条的规定，前述规定不适用于邮政物品和入境旅行者携带的物品。[②]

2. 关税

（1）海关总署按照世界海关组织统一制度，对货物的说明和编码进行关税分类，并对相应的关税进行评估。

货物价值以阿富汗货币计算。当货物的价值以外币表示，需要确定关税价值时，货物的价值应按照大阿富汗银行（Da Afghanistan Bank）[③]的汇率确定。

该汇率应是大阿富汗银行在每月最后一个工作日宣布的汇率，有效期从每月6日起至次月6日止。

（2）对下列进口货物免征关税：

① 国家官员在公务旅行期间进口的货物，其价值不超过海关关税所规定的10万阿富汗尼。

② 政治代表和国际机构的办公材料和设备，拟在主管当局批准后用于外国驻阿富汗代表的住所和办事处。

③ 根据合同条款和条件，在阿富汗工作的外国人个人使用的物品。

④ 被允许的书籍、公报、杂志和报纸。

⑤ 为政府资助的项目提供的货物，由政府批准的公营和私营外国和国际救济和发展机构向该国提供贷款或进口的货物。

⑥ 阿富汗代表团或阿富汗国际工作人员及其家属在国外使用的个人物品。

⑦ 按照海关关税的规定属于旅客个人的物品。

⑧ 商业样品和广告礼品。

⑨ 价值5 000阿富汗尼或以下的邮包。

⑩ 荣誉勋章或奖章。

⑪ 寄给保护著作权或者专利权的工商组织的样品。

⑫ 属于自然人使用的动产，按照海关征收关税的规定，将其经常居住地从另一个国家转移到本国的。

⑬ 托运的货物价值低于1 000阿富汗尼。

⑭ 纯种繁殖动物、昆虫和实验动物；科学研究所需的生物或化学物质。

⑮ 用于人体治疗的血型和组织分型试剂等物质。

⑯ 控制药品质量的器材。

⑰ 按照有关程序办理的运输车辆携带的必要的燃料、润滑油和设备。

⑱ 经财政部长理事会推荐和批准的其他可以免税的货物。

3. 报关

非阿富汗货物出入必须报关，报关员有义务在报关单提交之日起5日内完成所需的报关单。特殊情况下，海关可以缩短或者批准延长期限。

[①] 参见 http://www.wipo.int/wipolex/en/details.jsp?id=10722，阿富汗《海关法》，此译文为非官方的英文翻译，仅作学术研究参考之用。

[②] 参见阿富汗《海关法》第42条邮品报关单和第45条旅行者行李的海关管制。

[③] Da Afghanistan Bank 为阿富汗的中央银行。

过关货物的临时仓储期为 30 天，任何情况下，如果没有对该货物负责的海关当局向海关总理事会提交一份完整的报告，证明延期是合理的，该期限不得延长。

4. 走私货物及其处罚

（1）从事下列活动，可能被认为是走私，按照该法及其他与海关相关的法律规定，行为人将被处以相关处罚：

①违反本法和其他海关法规的规定，将货物带入本国的海关关境内或者出境的，其目的是避免海关管制或者监督。

②未经有关主管部门许可，擅自携带禁止进口、出口、储存的货物。

③在不缴纳关税的情况下，在运输过程中出售或购买货物。

④重复进行下列活动或者有下列活动意图的视为走私：

- 违反第 66 条最终使用部分或者全部免除关税债务的货物的放行条件；
- 持有违反第 61 条第 2 款规定的货物；
- 删除或伪造运输工具的识别号码；
- 假定明知在仓库储存的是走私货物的情况下，仍购买、销售、储存和持有这些进口货物；
- 破坏密封或替换在运输工具或货物上的安全验证标识；
- 未经海关许可，擅自将货物、旅客及其行李从一种运输工具运往另一种运输工具的，在未经批准的地方装卸、搬运的。

⑤飞机机长在下列情况下被认为是走私：

- 在没有有关舱单的情况下运输货物，或在舱单上填写货物虚假信息；
- 在舱单上已被带入国家海关领域内，未向海关申报的货物，在离开关境时，也不在飞机上；
- 不在海关机场着陆，并且在最短的时间内未告知海关或其他有关部门。

（2）处罚：

- 没收走私货物；
- 罚款金额为走私货物适用的关税债务的 2～5 倍；
- 按照第 179 条的规定处罚。

（3）一人以上违反的，依照其参与的比例处以罚款。

如果一方支付全部金额，另一方则不承担任何有关罚款的义务。

（4）同一违反者同时犯有多项违法行为的，对每一项违法行为分别给予处罚。

5. 对海关处罚裁决有异议的处理机构

海关对违反《海关法》行为的处罚必须进行听证，并确定听证的日期、时间和地点，收集文件和证据，并记录证人的申报。举行听证的期限自通知之日起不得超过 72 个小时。

在听证中，海关可以允许被检举或者检举人出示、记载其陈述，因而听证时无须在场。被控违反法律的人或者证人，不会讲达里语、普什图语的，听证会将在一名翻译人员在场的情况下进行，翻译程序由翻译人员负责。

对海关的裁决有异议的，可提交海关仲裁管理机构裁决。该机构设立在财政部内部，行政仲裁员为 3 人，行政仲裁员由财政部长提议，由国家元首任命。

四、劳动

（一）劳动法律、法规概况

阿富汗《劳动法》[①]于 1999 年 11 月 1 日颁布。2006 年对该法进行了进一步修改，对劳工组织和雇员的权利及义务作出了如下规定：

（1）规定阿富汗人有劳动和获得报酬的权利。

---

① 参见 http://www.asianlii.org/af/legis/laws/lloaogn790p1999110114200722a443/。

（2）规定了解除劳动合同的前提条件和在解除合同后对员工的补偿，如解除合约，对工作 1～5 年的员工应补偿 2 个月的工资，工作 5～10 年的员工补偿 4 个月的工资，工作 10 年以上的员工补偿 6 个月的工资。

（3）对工作时间、加班和假期的规定。员工一天正常工作时间不能超过 8 个小时，周四的工作时间不能超过 5 个小时。晚上 7 点以后的加班不能超过 1 个小时。管理人员晚上加班工资最低为原工资的 115%，生产工人晚上加班工资最低为原工资的 125%，不允许工人连续工作两个班次。周末和节日加班工资按 150% 计算。雇员享受 5～45 个工作日的带薪休假。

（4）工资。不能低于政府规定的最低工资。

（5）工作不能损害工人健康。

（6）工人有权利参加工会。男性退休年龄为 65 岁，最高不能超过 70 岁；女性退休年龄为 55 岁，最高不能超过 60 岁。退休养老金由工人每月工资的 3% 和政府与企业支付的每月工资的 8% 组成。

（7）性别和文化。女性医务工作人员晚上不允许加班，公司一般要为女性员工上下班提供交通工具，男女用餐一般分开，要给工人留有祈祷时间，并分别男女不同祈祷场所等。

尽管已经有健康补偿法，规定了加班工资，健康保险，退休权利，孕妇、哺乳母亲和未成年人的标准工作周减少等劳工权利，但这些规定没有得到很好的施行，工人们也没有意识到可以拥有这些权利。

（二）外国人在当地工作规定

1. 工作许可和申请程序

根据《关于在阿富汗组织中雇用外国公民的法规》[①]第 2 条的规定，驻扎在阿富汗的政府、合资企业、私营和非政府组织，雇用没有阿富汗国籍的外国人，必须签订协议，该协议是与驻阿富汗政府、合资企业、私营和非政府组织以及外国和国际组织签署的与就业有关的文件。还需要取得工作许可证，该证是由劳工部根据本法的规定向合格的外国公民颁发的书面认可文件。外国人还需与雇用机构签署书面劳动合同，内容包含双方约定的工作条件和义务、有效期、薪酬支付标准和其他福利标准。

外国人的雇用程序应由外交部和劳工部规定和批准。受雇用的外国人要遵守法律和执行法规的强制性规定，并尊重阿富汗人民的信仰和传统。

《关于在阿富汗组织中雇用外国公民的法规》第 7 条规定了工作许可证的授予内容：

（1）阿富汗劳工部负责发放工作许可证，要取得该证需要支付固定的费用；

（2）本条款第（1）项所述许可费用的标准限期应由劳动和社会事务部、财政部确定。

（3）工作许可证应规定员工身份，如工作地点、工作规范、工作开始日期和有效期等都应在工作许可证中明确列明。工作许可证有效期为 1 年。如果需要延长工作许可证，则需另行申请一个许可期限。

《关于在阿富汗组织中雇用外国公民的法规》第 5 条规定，外国人在阿富汗就业必须符合以下标准：

（1）已满 18 周岁且未达到劳动法规定的退休年龄的外国人，持有原籍国和阿富汗卫生部的健康证明，可在阿富汗的组织或机构中以下列形式就业：

- 基于政府组织和国家之间达成的协议的要求，并由外交和社会事务部批准。
- 基于在阿富汗获得居留许可签证的外国公民个人请求，并且这些组织也需要外国公民为其工作。

（2）不允许在外国公民专业领域以外雇用他 / 她。

（3）用人单位必须对雇员的行为进行实时监督。

《关于在阿富汗组织中雇用外国公民的法规》第 6 条对就业的限制性规定：如果是国内和国外的工人都可以做的工作，则优先考虑国内员工。

2. 社会保障

阿富汗《劳动法》第 123 条规定：

（1）社会保障应通过阿富汗伊斯兰酋长国的企业和工人的缴费提供。

---

① 参见 http://www.worldlii.org/af/legis/laws/soteffcbao716/。

（2）职工社会保障规模应随国民经济的增长而增加。

第124条进一步规定：

（1）第124条对家属的经济援助（丧葬费）另有规定：按已故工人的级别和职位计算，给已故工人的遗属发放相当于6个月的酬金和津贴。

（2）按照卫生部和劳动和社会事务部规定的规则，对患病期间的国内工作人员提供医疗救助。

（3）按照阿富汗伊斯兰酋长国的规则和规定，分配土地、住宅区和公寓的待遇平等。

（4）退休时给予工人的经济援助，相当于其上一年级别和职位的10个月的报酬和津贴。

（5）企业有义务向工人提供食品和消费品或者相应的补助。

（6）接受强制性国民服务的工作人员的家属有权享受本条第（5）款规定的特权以及医疗设施。

（7）企业有义务为工人提供交通服务。如果没有提供这种服务，企业应按照现行的费率向工人提供交通费用。

（三）出入境[①]

1. 签证类型

（1）旅游签证。旅游签证是为有兴趣单独或集体前往阿富汗旅游或探亲的外国人签发的，由阿富汗驻外使团签发。这类签证的有效期为1个月，经阿富汗旅游组织同意，内政部只能延期一次。

（2）工作许可的入境签证。工作许可的入境签证是为商务、经济、商业、文化、工业目的，以及为政府或非政府组织工作而签发的，这类签证可以从阿富汗外交部的领事馆处获得。雇主或担保人应直接与外交部有关部门联系。该类签证可以通过内政部延期。

（3）居留签证。居留签证是由内政部发给持有普通护照的外国公民的，该护照的持有人已经持合法的签证进入阿富汗。该类签证的有效期是1个月到6个月，可以延期。

（4）过境签证。过境签证是由阿富汗驻外使团发给经由阿富汗前往第三国的外国公民的。对航空旅客签证的有效期为72个小时，对陆路旅客签证的有效期为6天。

（5）双入境签证。双入境签证是发给持有签证的外国人，签证有效期可以延长。

（6）外交签证。外交签证发给打算前往阿富汗的外交护照持有者。外交护照持有者可以从阿富汗使团那里获得该类签证。但他们必须通过在喀布尔的使团直接与阿富汗外交部的"外交护照和外交签证"部门取得联系。

（7）服务签证。服务签证由阿富汗驻外使团发给持有服务或特殊护照的外国公民。

（8）学生签证。学生签证由阿富汗驻外使团签发给有意在阿富汗学习的外国学生。有关院校或研究机构必须直接与"阿富汗外交部文化关系部"联系。

（9）出境签证。出境签证发给持入境工作许可签证入境的外国人，该类签证的有效期为1～6天，特殊情况下可以延期。

所有拥有双重国籍的阿富汗人都需要从阿富汗驻外使领馆获得例外签证函。

2. 签证的申请

鉴于不同类型的签证办理的规定可能会有所不同。办理签证之前，先向当地的阿富汗大使馆或领事馆咨询。同时，也可登录阿富汗海外使团网站了解更多有关签证部门的开放时间、所需文件、等待时间等信息。

3. 出入境限制

（1）重要信息和规定。如果希望逗留的时间超过许可期限，则应在签证到期前申请延期。如果签证在到期日没有延期，对护照持有者在延期的第一个月按2美元/天罚款，在延期的第二个月按5美元/天罚款，罚款可在港口支付。逾期超过两个月的，除罚款外，还将被驱逐出境。

外国游客在抵达阿富汗后应到驻喀布尔大使馆、当地阿富汗警察局和阿富汗旅游组织（如果是旅游目的）登记。

---

① 以下有关签证的信息参见 http://mfa.gov.af/en/page/consular-affairs/visa-information。

（2）特殊要求、禁止携带和必须申报的物品。在获得位于信息文化大楼一楼的旅游局新闻部的书面许可后，才可以拍摄照片和电影胶片。

运送一些稀有鸟类出境是非法的。因此，游客必须与阿富汗旅游局联系，获取更多信息和相关出口证明。

游客可以免税带出境的物品有：30平方米地毯，10张皮（不包括卡拉库尔地毯），切割和抛光的宝石，包括天青石、手工艺品和各种古董。

到达后，如果游客所携带的所有外币，金额超过100万阿富汗尼或与其等值的货币，必须在机场索取"安萨里申请表"①进行申报。

（3）特殊的文化和宗教信仰要求。应尊重阿富汗当地的宗教习俗、文化。阿富汗是伊斯兰国家，衣着比较保守，男士不要穿短裤上街，女士不要穿窄小和暴露的服装，最好能戴头巾。

（四）工会与劳工组织

阿富汗设有全国总工会，创建于1965年，总部设在首都喀布尔，各省有省级工会。工会组织属于非政治团体、非政府组织。目前，阿富汗全国总工会约有20万名会员。工人有权利参加工会。

（五）劳动争议

企业对员工的处罚，如果员工认为不合理，可以向劳动争议解决委员会提出申诉。

未经有关单位解决的与工作有关的争议，应当通过下列方式解决：

（1）由劳动争议解决委员会处理；

（2）由劳动和社会事务部行政委员会处理；

（3）由有管辖权的法院处理。

除依法应当由法院裁决的纠纷外，劳动争议解决委员会是对劳动争议进行初步调查的主管机关。劳动争议解决委员会的决定应取得当事人的同意，并具有约束力。

劳动和社会事务部行政委员会应在下列情况下对劳动争议进行调查：

（1）争议解决不能使当事人满意时，应将问题提交劳动和社会事务部管理委员会处理；

（2）当事人之一就决定存在的缺陷提出书面投诉。

如果当事各方反对劳动和社会事务部行政委员会的决定，则应通过提交书面申请将问题提交有管辖权的法院。

企业有义务在10日内履行劳动争议解决委员会的决定。

五、知识产权

（一）知识产权法律、法规概况

由阿富汗立法机关制定的主要知识产权法律有②：

（1）《专利权保护法》，1967年6月10日颁行；

（2）阿富汗《商标注册法律》，2009年9月1日颁行；

（3）《支持作者、作曲家、艺术家和研究者权利的法律（版权法）》，2008年7月21日颁行。

（二）版权保护③

《支持作者、作曲家、艺术家和研究者权利的法律（版权法）》2008年7月21日由总统签署生效。

1. 根据该法，下列作品应受到保护

（1）书、小册子、论文、散文、戏剧和其他学院的专业和艺术作品；

---

① "安萨里申请表"为海关申报表的名称。——译者注

② 法规信息参见 http://www.wipo.int/wipolex/en/profile.jsp?code=AF。

③ 版权保护的法规参见 http://www.wipo.int/wipolex/en/details.jsp?id=10197。

（2）使用任何手段编写、录制或出版的诗歌、旋律、歌曲和作曲；
（3）视听作品，用于在电影场景上表演，或使用任何手段书写、录制或出版的广播或电视广播；
（4）已经写好、录制或已发表的音乐作品；
（5）绘画、图画、设计、绘图、创新地理制图、线形绘画、装饰线条和其他装饰和虚构作品，是使用任何简单或组合的方式或模式创作的；
（6）雕像（雕塑）；
（7）使用创新模式创作的摄影作品；
（8）手工艺或工艺艺术的创新作品（地毯设计、地毯、毡毯及其附件等）；
（9）根据公共文化（民间文学艺术）或国家文化遗产和艺术创作的创新作品；
（10）具有创新性的技术工作；
（11）电脑程序；
（12）衍生作品。
该法的规定适用于根据阿富汗签署和批准的国际条约、协定和公约规定的所有符合条件的其他作品。

2. 作品的保护期限

（1）作者生前出版或播出作品的保护期限为作者有生之年至其去世后 50 年，除非作者作出不同的决定。
（2）作者生前出版或播出的合作作品的保护期为最后一个受保护的作者死后 50 年。
（3）用化名出版或播出的作品的保护期为第一年之后保护 50 年。如果提交人被确定，则适用本条第 1 款的规定。
（4）在作者有生之年未发表的作品以及在最后作者去世前没有发表的合作作品的保护期为从出版和播出的第一年起保护 50 年。
（5）视听作品自出版或播出第一年起保护 50 年。
（6）摄影和绘画作品自出版和展示第一年起保护 50 年。
该法第 15 条规定，在视听内容固定之日起生效的未经宣传、播放的视听作品，应当保护 50 年。

3. 作品保护期限的开始日期

如果保护的起算期从发布和播出之日起，那么发布的第一个日期应是起算日，除非作者在复制作品时使作品发生根本性变化，从而导致原作品成为新作品。如果作品由多个部分组成或在不同阶段出版，每一部分作品的保护期限应分开单独计算。

4. 处罚

（1）在该法第 19 条规定的时间范围内，未经作品作者核证的书面授权，任何人发布其不享有著作权的作品的，应根据情况处以 1 年以下的监禁或金额为 50 000 阿富汗尼至 100 000 阿富汗尼的罚款。
（2）任何人在该法第 22 条所述的保护期内，未经作品的表演者书面同意重复播放和展示作品或作品的一部分，视具体情节处以最高 1 年的监禁或金额为 50 000 阿富汗尼至 100 000 阿富汗尼的罚款，或者给予其他处罚。
（3）在未经作者书面同意的情况下，任何人出版、广播作品，或以其自己的名义或别人的名字翻译作品，视具体情形，应处以 1 年以下的监禁及／或金额为 50 000 阿富汗尼至 100 000 阿富汗尼的罚款或给予其他处罚。
（4）由最高法院建议、经部长理事会同意和阿富汗伊斯兰共和国总统背书，可以修改该条第 1、2、3 款提及的罚款金额。

（三）注册商标

1. 商标注册申请

阿富汗《商标注册法》[①]于 2009 年 9 月 1 日颁行，该法规定，个人或者单位可以亲自或者通过各自

---

① 该法的信息参见 http://www.wipo.int/wipolex/en/text.jsp?file_id=235961。

的法定代表人申请商标注册。

由中央注册办公室商标注册处负责办理商标注册。对外国人申请商标注册的优先权，优先权日为其在外国提出申请的日期。

接受申请后，中央注册办公室商标注册处从形式、性质以及与现行法律规定的兼容性的角度审查申请。从收到申请之日起，在30天内作出接受或拒绝申请的决定。如果拒绝申请，中央注册办公室商标注册处有义务说明拒绝的理由。在这种情况下，申请人可以在15天内寻求救济，重新向中央注册办公室商标注册处提出申请，或者向当地商业法院提出上诉。如申请人未在规定的期限内对拒绝理由进行反驳或者未向法院提起诉讼的，视为已经放弃申请。

该法第6条规定，下列符号不得作为商标使用或注册：

（1）国旗、国徽和其他与国内外组织或机构、国际组织或机构或任何外国郡县有关的标志，除非有书面形式授权使用。

（2）内殿和讲坛或任何与纯粹宗教性质的符号相同或类似的标记。

（3）国家领导人和政府高级官员的照片。

（4）可能与阿富汗政府部门混淆的词和短语。

（5）官方组织的标志，如红新月、红十字或任何其他类似的标志，以及任何模仿该标志的标志。

（6）任何与贞操、道德和公共秩序相抵触的标志。

（7）在本质或特性上不具有特色的标记，或该标记是传统上通常赋予货物、产品或服务的名称，或由熟悉的图纸和标志组成。如商品和产品的普通图片，该标志可以通用使用，但不得作为商标使用或注册，也不得给予任何保护。

（8）地理名称，如使用该名称可能导致对货物、产品或服务的产地或来源产生混淆。

（9）第三者的姓名、姓氏、照片或徽章，除非他／她或他／她的继承人事先同意使用。

（10）可能误导公众或含有虚假或欺骗性信息的标志，如货物、产品或服务的原产地、来源或任何其他特征，以及含有虚构、模仿或伪造商号的标志。

（11）包含虚构、模仿或伪造名称的标记。

（12）禁止使用与法律或法律实体有关的标志。

（13）使用在阿富汗的公司出版和传播的标志，除非有其所有者授权。

（14）与相同的商品或服务或类似的注册商标或符号有关的标志。

（15）用于特定目的的标记。相同或类似的标志，用于与注册商标相同或类似的商品或服务，而使用该商标可能导致混淆。

2. 商标注册的有效期限

商标自向中央注册办公室商标处提交申请之日起受保护。商标所有权属于第一次使用商标的人，除非法庭另有证明。注册商标的有效期通常为10年，期限届满前6个月内，商标所有人可向中央注册办公室商标注册处提交续期申请，可续期10年。

3. 商标所有权终止的情形

（1）与特定的商标的所有权有关的贸易、工业、农业和服务业停止经营；

（2）依照法律规定出售或以其他形式将所有权的权利转移给第三方；

（3）商标注册权期满后6个月内未申请续展的；

（4）如果证明商标连续3年未被使用，相关商业法院可以发布关于终止该商标的命令，除非在指定的期限内商标所有人（第一人）提供了不使用的理由。在这种情况下，商标的注册申请人应当按照《商标注册法》第2条第2项规定的条件进行注册。

4. 商标争议的诉讼时效期间

与商标注册相关诉讼的时效期限为1年，自商标注册之日起一年内未提出异议，之后再提起的请求无效。

5. 罚则

（1）由于实施下列违法行为，视情况需要，相关人员应根据造成的损害按比例赔偿：

以误导公众的方式，故意使用虚假或伪造的已经按照本法规定向中央注册局商标注册处注册的商标；故意使用伪造或仿造的商标；未经商标所有者同意，将属于第三方的商标用于他/她自己的商业产品；故意销售、供应销售、分销或拥有伪造、模仿或非法商标的商品、产品或服务；使用该法第6条规定的商标；在产品的宣传中，提及可能与之无关的商品、产品或服务，或者这些商业机构或实体实际上可能尚未获得的奖章证书、奖励或荣誉等级；在商品、在展览中展示的产品或服务上使用特殊的区别标志，并明确指出其来源和性质，除非这些标志已经在这些载体上自然体现；在商品、在展览中展示的产品或服务上使用地区的著名地理标志，以表明在该地区内制造此类货物、产品和提供了相关的服务，并产生误导公众的结果。

（2）屡次实施违反前述规定的违法行为，违法者应当承担双倍损害赔偿责任或者判处6个月以上1年以下有期徒刑。

（3）主管法院除对违法者进行定罪处罚外，还应责令扣押货物和构成违法标的物的产品、违法所得的款项、违法行为所使用工具，并关闭工作场所6个月，如果反复违规，可责令违法者永久停工。

（四）申请专利[①]

阿富汗专利管理机构为商工部商标注册办公室。根据阿富汗《外国专利注册法》的规定，阿富汗可为过去在其他国家获得过的专利提供当地注册，申请时间必须在原批准国批准该项专利的2年之内。申请专利时需提交如下文件：

（1）申请人和发明人资料，包括名字、地址、联系方式、身份证明等；
（2）如外国人申请专利，需出示原批准国的相关资料；
（3）相关技术资料；
（4）图片或照片等。

此外，需要在商标注册办公室填写申请表格，一般可委托当地律师代为办理。

六、环境保护

水和森林是阿富汗短缺的资源。研究发现，将环境保护计划纳入对阿富汗的人道主义行动中，实现计划的可能性非常小。2007年，阿富汗制定了严格的保护环境法规——阿富汗《环境法》。[②]

（一）环境保护主管部门

国家环境保护局作为一个独立的机构，负责协调和监督环境的保护和恢复，并执行该法案。
国家环境保护局履行下列职责：
（1）保持环境完整性，促进自然资源的可持续利用；
（2）促进环境的保护和恢复；
（3）协调地方、国家和国际环境事务；
（4）制定和实施国家环境政策和战略，以便将环境问题和可持续发展方法纳入法律和监管框架；
（5）在环境影响评估、空气和水质管理、废物管理、污染控制和相关活动许可等方面提供环境管理服务；
（6）为环境信息建立沟通和外联，以确保提高对环境问题的认识；
（7）执行阿富汗加入的双边或多边环境协定；
（8）执行《濒危野生动植物种国际贸易公约》（CITES）；
（9）代表政府签订关于保护和修复环境的协议；
（10）促进和管理阿富汗加入和批准的双边和多边环境协定；
（11）协调国家环境监测计划的制订和实施，并有效利用该计划提供的数据；
（12）每两年针对城市、每五年针对农村准备一份阿富汗的环境状况报告，提交总统办公室；

[①] 参见 http://af.mofcom.gov.cn/article/ddfg/201109/20110907755599.shtml。
[②] 参见 https://www.afghan-web.com/environment/environmental_law/。

（13）至少每两年编写一份关于阿富汗环境新出现的问题的临时环境状况报告；

（14）在本法颁布3年期间制定国家环境行动计划，评估短期、中期和长期应采取的行动的紧迫性和重要性，以预防、消除和减少最新环境状况报告中所述的不利影响，并与有关部委和机构协商，确定执行这些行动的协调战略和时间表；

（15）定期编制和发布重要环境指标报告；

（16）每年编制并出版一份报告，详细说明国家环境保护局的授权和开展的活动；

（17）评估《环境法》和任何依据《环境法》而制定的提升自然资源利用与管理的可持续性以及环境保护与修复的法规的实施的有效性；

（18）与相关部委和公共机构合作制定和实施环境培训、环境教育和环境意识的计划；

（19）就可持续利用自然资源和保护、恢复环境的所有问题，与各部委、省议会、区和村委员会、公共机构和私营部门积极协调和合作；

（20）监督《环境法》目标和规定的执行情况；

（21）履行部长理事会分配的其他职能。

（二）环境保护法律、法规概况

阿富汗《环境法》[①]依据阿富汗《宪法》第15条规定了与恢复环境、保护和可持续利用自然资源、活生物体和非生物有关的问题。

（1）在环境影响方面，该法确立了公众参与原则。

在项目、方案、政策或活动获得批准之前，受影响人可以就拟议的项目、计划、政策或活动、初步评估、环境影响报告、最终意见记录和综合缓解计划发表意见，并且提议者必须向国家环境保护局证明，受影响的人通过独立协商和参加公开听证会有机会及时就这些事项发表意见。

对于可能对环境造成重大不利影响的拟议项目、计划、政策或活动，国家环境保护局和相关机构必须允许受影响的人有机会参与国家环境保护局和有关机构在前述每一个阶段的活动。

在申请人关于申请项目的论证获得国家环境保护局认可，且已将该申请文件的副本分发给受影响人员之前，国家环境保护局不得就任何许可申请作出决定。该申请文件须通过公告告知公众并提供文件副本供公众查阅，并且要召开公证听证会并记录听证过程。

在审查了前述规定的条件后，国家环境保护局应作出决定并告知公众，并提供相关文件或信息供公众审查。

（2）与废物管理有关的一般禁止和注意义务。

任何人不得以导致重大不利影响的方式收集、运输、分类、回收、储存、处置或以其他方式管理废物。凡进口、生产、收集、回收、运输、保存、处理或处置废弃物的人员均应采取一切合理措施，防止对环境产生重大不利影响。

生产危险废物的场所的所有者或占用者应确保所有危险废物与其他废物分开，并按照国家环境保护局公布的指导方针或许可条件的要求将危险废物储存在待处理的单独容器中。任何人不得以废物或变为垃圾的方式处置废物。

（3）制定专项清单，保护水资源，控制和防治沙漠化，并优先考虑当地树种的造林和植被恢复措施。

（三）环保评估

根据该法案，每个人，特别是国家环境保护局的职责包括：在阿富汗《环境法》颁布3年内制定国家环境行动计划，评估短期、中期和长期应采取的行动的紧迫性和重要性，以预防、消除和减少最新环境状况报告中所述的不利影响；与有关部委和机构协商，确定执行这些行动的协调战略和时间表。

设立环境协调委员会，以促进环境问题的整合和协调以及本法规定的基本原则。委员会由相关部委、国家机构、省议会、区和村委员会以及民间社会组织的代表组成，提出协调环境活动的建议，包

[①] 参见 https://www.afghan-web.com/environment/environmental_law/。

括合作开展环境影响评估程序。

七、争议解决

(一) 争端解决方式及机构①

在阿富汗,争端解决的方式有两种:法院判决和仲裁裁决。

1. 法院系统

阿富汗司法系统分为三级。最基层为地方法院,全国共有 350 个左右;中级为上诉法院,分设于阿富汗各省;高级为最高法院,设在首都喀布尔。

《法院组织和管辖法》(2013 年 6 月 30 日) 和《特别法院组织和管辖法》(2010 年 7 月 12 日)② 规定:

最高法院设立专门法庭来处理特殊案件。

这些法院的名称为:

① 初级和上诉麻醉品法庭;

② 关于危害内部和外部安全的罪行初审法院和上诉法院;

③ 财产纠纷初审法院和终审法院;

④ 专门家庭法院;

⑤ 专门少年法院;

⑥ 商业文书和商标的登记,由商业法院管辖。

2. 仲裁机构

2015 年 9 月,由阿富汗商工会和一家名为 Harakat 的工业和金融机构联合经营的阿富汗商业纠纷仲裁中心 (ACDR)③在喀布尔举行揭幕仪式。成立后,该中心将处理来自阿富汗全国各地的商业纠纷。

商业纠纷专业调解机构不足是贸易商们面临的一大问题,过去在阿富汗国内解决商业纠纷需要经过 47 个阶段,耗时 1 600 余天,并且要耗费大量的金钱。

阿富汗的替代性争端解决 (ADR) 由《商业调解法》和《商业仲裁法》④调整,废除了 1995 年的《商业调解法》。阿富汗商工会通过提供调解和仲裁服务在解决商业纠纷方面发挥着至关重要的作用。

(1)《商业仲裁法》的适用范围

除《商业仲裁法》第 11 条和第 7 条外,本法的规定仅适用于仲裁地在阿富汗的情况。本法不适用于某些不适用于仲裁或其他立法规定了解决方式的争议。仲裁可以通过国内或国际仲裁两种方式完成。在下列情况下仲裁是国际性的,如果在合同中约定为这样;如果交易发生在两个或两个以上的国家之间,尽管协议中没有提及这一点。如果协议中未提及的,则适用当事人开展业务国家的法律;在本条第 1 款没有规定的情况下,称为国内仲裁。

(2) 仲裁庭的管辖权

仲裁庭具有以下权力:解决其管辖范围内的任何问题,解决有关仲裁协议存在或有效性的异议。构成仲裁合同一部分的条款应视为独立协议,仲裁庭认为合同无效的决定不应使该条款或仲裁合同条款无效。

(3) 仲裁机构的选择

如果双方当事人没有通过仲裁机构进行仲裁的协议,如果当事人没有明确规定并且不能就仲裁机构达成一致,则仲裁机构应由法院决定,对该裁决不得再提出上诉。

---

① 参见 http://www.wipo.int/wipolex/en/details.jsp?id=13856, Law on Organization and Jurisdiction of Courts (《法院组织和管辖的法》)。
② 参见 http://www.wipo.int/wipolex/en/details.jsp?id=13855, Law on Organization and Jurisdiction of Special Courts (《特别法院组织和管辖的法》)。
③ 参见 http://af.mofcom.gov.cn/article/ddfg/201509/20150901103735.shtml。
④ 参见 http://www.wipo.int/edocs/lexdocs/laws/en/af/af027en.pdf。

（4）仲裁程序中使用的语言

争议双方可以自由地就在仲裁程序中使用的语言达成一致意见。如果没有这样的协议，仲裁庭应确定程序中使用的语言。任何关于语言的协议或决定，除非当事人另有约定，应适用于任何一方的书面陈述、仲裁庭的任何听证和任何裁决、决定或其他通讯信息。仲裁庭可以下令将所有文件证据翻译成双方商定的或仲裁庭裁定的语言文本。

（二）适用法律

阿富汗商工会通过提供调解和仲裁服务，在解决商业纠纷方面发挥着重要作用。依据《商业仲裁法》（2007年）的规定，仲裁庭应根据当事人选择的法律来裁决争议，如果当事人未指定或法律有冲突，仲裁庭应适用其认为可以适用的法律。

八、其他

（一）招投标

1. 招标投标

阿富汗各部委的工程项目和外国援助阿富汗的项目多采用国际招标方式，项目招标公告将公布在报纸、媒体和网络上，并列明对参与项目投标者的企业资质、资金、技术要求。有些项目，业主也可能采取议标的方式，指定企业执行项目。

2. 许可程序

企业如参加投标，会被要求提供资质证明、过去业绩（完成项目）的相关资料和标书、保函等，这些资料和证明需得到业主或承包商的确认。

（二）其他注意事项

在阿富汗开展投资、贸易、承包工程和劳务合作过程中，要特别注意事前调查、分析、评估相关风险，事中做好风险规避和管理工作，切实保障自身利益。包括对项目或贸易客户及相关方的资信调查和评估，对投资或承包工程国家的政治风险和商业风险分析和规避，对实施项目的可行性分析等。建议相关企业积极利用保险、担保、银行等保险金融机构和其他专业风险管理机构的相关业务保障自身利益，包括贸易、投资、承包工程和劳务类信用保险、财产保险、人身安全保险等，银行保理业务和福费廷业务，各类担保业务（政府担保、商业担保、保函）等。

开展投资合作最应注意的是安全问题，避免到安全无保障地点投资或承包工程。已在危险区域实施项目的，应加强安全意识，高度重视安全防范，确保安全。此外，应该遵守当地法律、法规，尊重当地的风俗习惯。

（三）主要官方机构的联系方式[①]

1. 阿富汗商工部（Ministry of Commerce and Industries）

地址：Darluman Road Kabul, Afghanistan
传真：0093-798013276
网址：www.commerce.gov.af

2. 阿富汗外交部（Ministry of Foreign Affairs）

地址：Ministry of Foreign Affairs of Afghanistan Malek Asghar St. Kabul, Afghanistan
网址：www.mfa.gov.af

---

① 参见 http://af.mofcom.gov.cn/article/ddfg/201109/20110907755599.shtml。

3. 阿富汗司法部（Ministry of Justice）

网址：www.moj.gov.af
电话：0093-202100322

4. 阿富汗投资促进局（Afghanistan Investment Support Agency）

地址：Opposite to Ministry of Foreign Affairs, Kabul-Afghanistan

Afghanistan

Authors: Liu Xiaowei, Dennia Jiang
Translators: Liu Xiaowei, Dennia Jiang

I. Overview

A. General Introduction to the Political, Economic, Social and Legal Environment of the Country Receiving Investment

Afghanistan is a landlocked, impoverished Asian country located in Southern Asia that borders China, Iran, Pakistan, Tajikistan, Turkmenistan, and Uzbekistan, with a long history of turbulence, which has experienced almost two decades of constant warfare.

Pushtu (also known as Pashto or Pushto) and Dari (Dari is the official name of the Persian language in Afghanistan) are both official and most widely spoken.

a. Political Environment

The constitution of Afghanistan ratified by the 2003 Loya Jirga restructured the Afghan government into an Islamic republic consisting of three branches-executive, legislative, and judicial.

In 2004, the nation's new constitution was adopted and a president was elected. The following year a general election to choose parliamentarians took place.

The National Assembly is Afghanistan's national legislature. It is a bicameral body, composed of the House of the People and the House of Elders. The first legislature was elected in 2005. Members of the Supreme Court were appointed by the president to form the judiciary.

Relations between Afghanistan and Iran are strong. The two nations share the same language and culture, and both countries are part of Greater Persia. Afghanistan's relationship with Pakistan is not as stalwart. The two nations are often in dispute and relations have deteriorated significantly in recent years.

Afghanistan maintains excellent relations with its northern allies, including Uzbekistan, Tajikistan, and Turkmenistan as all four countries share a similar culture. Afghanistan also has good relations with Russia and India. India is a leading investor in Afghanistan. Afghanistan has excellent relations with the rest of the Arab and Muslim world.

Currently, anti-government and political violence are common and public concerns regarding security constrain economic activity. Security is a primary concern for investors. Foreign firms have to spend a significant percentage of revenues on security infrastructure and operating expenses.

Afghanistan is a member of the South Asian Association for Regional Cooperation (SAARC).

b. Economic Environment

Afghanistan is one of the poorest and least developed countries in the world, has a poor, agrarian economy with a small manufacturing base, few value-added industries, has a controlled economic system in which the central government directs the economy regarding the production and distribution of goods. Afghanistan has a rich endowment of natural resources, notably natural gas, coal and copper.

Since the collapse of the Taliban government , the economy has been steadily growing due to multi-billion dollar aid infusions and investments from the international society.

Formal economic activity remains minimal and is inhibited by recurrent fighting and roads blocked by local commanders. The northern areas all suffer from brigandage. Commercial trade is impeded in certain non-Taleban areas, as local commanders continue to demonstrate their control over the roads by demanding road tolls and sometimes closing roads.

The drawdown of international forces significantly slowed economic growth as demand for transport, construction, telecommunications and other services fell.

Agriculture (35 percent of GDP) is the most important sector of the economy, as the majority of the population is dependent on crops. The resurgence of the public sector has led to growth in services, which now account for around 40 percent of GDP. Mining has also been growing rapidly due to exploration of the country's vast mineral resources, such as lithium, and precious stones.①

Agriculture, including high levels of opium poppy cultivation, is the mainstay of the economy, remains Afghanistan's most important source of employment: 60-80 percent of Afghanistan's population works in this sector, although it accounts for just a third of GDP due to insufficient irrigation, uneven rainfall, lack of market access, and other structural impediments.

Afghanistan remains the second largest opium producer in the world. Trade is mainly in fruits, minerals, and gems, as well as goods smuggled to Pakistan.

Much higher growth rates are required to support a three percent population growth and roughly 400,000 new entrants into the labor market each year. However, security threats, the lack of infrastructure and endemic corruption have been hampering economic activity.

On the enabling environment for business, the Afghan government at all levels has publicly emphasized its commitment to fostering private sector-led development and increasing domestic and foreign investment. Important government and civil society efforts to build an enabling environment for the private sector and to expand investment by developing natural resources and infrastructure have been hindered by institutional capacity, reliance on top-down decision making and rent-seeking. Some improvements are underway in business licensing in 2016, including the consolidation of business and investment licenses within one ministry and the extension of business license validity from one to three years. Additionally, the government adopted an open access policy calling for liberalization of the telecoms sector, which now awaits implementation.②

In 2016, Afghanistan became the 164th WTO member after parliamentary ratification, which is a positive sign for business and trade. It is also a member of the South Asian Free Trade Area (SAFTA) and signed trade agreements with India and Pakistan. The Afghan government has long been pleading for foreign investment in order to grow and stabilise its economy.

c. Social Environment

Afghanistan's security challenges remain headline news, particularly for businesses. Nevertheless, domestic and foreign business leaders in most of Afghanistan report corruption and patronage in government are tougher challenges than security.

Afghanistan produces over 90% of the world's non-pharmaceutical opium. Drug profits create a sustainable base for insecurity, funding everyone from warlords to drug barons to the Taliban. Afghanistan is also awash in weapons-the legacy of decades of near-constant warfare. According to Take the Guns Away, a report produced by the Human Rights Research and Advocacy Consortium, almost two-thirds of Afghans surveyed in 2004 believe that disarmament is the single most important factor to improve security in Afghanistan.

d. Legal Enverionment

Afghanistan's legal and regulatory frameworks and enforcement mechanisms remain irregularly implemented. The existence of three overlapping legal systems—Sharia (Islamic Law), Shura (customary rules and practice), and the formal system (the Continental Law System).

The Constitution which came into force in 2004 involves a strong presidential system. The President of Afghanistan is elected directly by the Afghan people to a five-year term, and can be elected no more than twice. The president is the commander-in-chief of the armed forces.

Presidential responsibilities include:

Determining policies with the approval of the National Assembly; Appointing the nation's ministers, the attorney general, the director of the central bank, and the justices of the Supreme Court with the approval of the main legislative body, the Wolesi Jirga; Appointing the nation's first and second vice presidents.

Article Eighty-One of Constitution of the Islamic Republic of Afghanistan stupulates that The National Assembly of the Islamic Republic of Afghanistan as the highest legislative organ is the manifestation of the will of its people and represents the whole nation. Every member of the National Assembly takes into judgment the general welfare and supreme interests of all people of Afghanistan at the time of casting their vote.

A National Assembly consisting of two Houses, the House of People (Wolesi Jirga) with 249 seats, and the House of Elders (Meshrano Jirga) with 102 seats, forms the Legislative Branch.

In accordance with article 116 of the Constitution of Islamic Republic of Afghanistan the judiciary is an independent body of the Islamic Republic of Afghanistan. The judicial power is comprised of the Supreme Court, (Stera Mahkama), High Courts and Appeal Courts, Primary Courts the authorities of which are regulated by law. Travelling courts may be established when needed, on recommendation by the Supreme Court and approval of

---

① https://tradingeconomics.com/afghanistan/gdp-growth-annual.
② https://www.state.gov/e/eb/rls/othr/ics/investmentclimatestatements/index.htm#wrapper.

the President.

The President appoints the nine members of the Supreme Court with the approval of the Wolesi Jirga.

Corruption hampers fair application of the laws. Commercial regulatory bodies are often understaffed and under capacity. Financial data systems are limited. Crucial sectors such as mining and hydropower stations lack a regulatory environment and policymaker support conducive to investment.

However, Afghanistan accessed to the World Trade Organization(WTO) in 2016, a positive sign for business and trade.

B. The Status and Direction of the Cooperation with Chinese Enterprises Under the B&R

Sino-Afghan relations can be traced back to the ancient age. The ancient Silk Road connected China and Afghanistan closely. The old 'Silk road' stretching from China to Rome was opened by Chang Chien, a special envoy of Emperor Wu of the Han dynasty. Since then, many wise men and businessmen from Afghanistan traveled to China, made contribution to China's economic and cultural development.

Modern diplomatic relations between the two countries was first established in the later part of the 20th century and exchanging bilateral visits by the head of governments for the first time. [1]

China is already Afghanistan's biggest investor. In 2007 a Chinese firm took a $3 billion, 30-year lease for the Aynak copper mine in Afghanistan.

Afghanistan and China signed an MoU on OBOR in 2016, and then in 2017, Afghanistan joined the the Asian Infrastructure Investment Bank(AIIB).

The two countries established a railway link in September 2016, allowing freight to travel from far eastern China to the Afghani rail port of Hairatan, which is one part of China's "Belt and Road" trade corridor that connects China to Afghanistan, Uzbekistan, Kazakhstan and Iran, among others. Shipments over that distance now take two weeks, down from six months by road. The railway link should boost Afghani exports into China, while allowing more investment from China. [2]

In his trip to China in July 2015, Afghan President Ashraf Ghani said Afghanistan was looking forward to participating in any relevant projects under China's Belt and Road Initiative to his country, welcoming Chinese investment in the country's infrastructure.

Many businessmen wish to be a part of two Chinese regional projects—the Belt and Road (OBOR) initiative and the China-Pakistan Energy Corridor (CPEC).

Afghan infrastructure projects-such as the Afghan Railway Network, developing untapped mineral resources, and the National Afghan ring road-correlate with China's OBOR.

Politician of Afghanistan have already extended supported for the China—Pakistan Energy Corridor (CPEC) and showed interest of joining it.

China, Pakistan and Afghanistan have already agreed to cooperate in making a hydroelectric dam on the Kunar river in the Kabul river basin. According to the estimates of the Afghan inter-ministerial energy commission, the Kabul river basin can produce more than 2,800 MWs of electricity annually. [3]

Today, China and Afghanistan are jointly building the Belt and Road Initiative, which will revive the Silk Road, make it more beautiful, and contribute a shared future of the two counties.

II. Investment

A. Market Access

a. Department Supervising Investment

The High Commission on Investment (HCI) is responsible for investment policy making in Afghanistan. The HCI includes the Ministers of Agriculture, Animal Husbandry and Food, Commerce, Finance, Foreign Affairs, Mines and Industries, the Governor of the Central Bank (Da Afghanistan Bank), and the Chief Executive Officer of Afghanistan Investment Support Agency (AISA). The Minister of Commerce chairs the HCI.

The High Economic Council (HEC) was constituted on 14 April 2016 in accordance with Decree issued by President of the Islamic Republic of Afghanistan, which is chaired by the President and includes both the HCI

---

[1] https://www.c3sindia.org/geopolitics-strategy/chinas-interests-in-afghanistan-by-adithya-krishna/.
[2] https://www.forbes.com/sites/ralphjennings/2018/02/27/china-needs-a-win-in-afghanistan-to-keep-its-edge-in-asian-trade/#c35c3101d5c7.
[3] https://thediplomat.com/2017/04/linking-afghanistan-to-chinas-belt-and-road/.

members, Senior Advisor to the President, Director of Central Statistics Office, and representatives from academia, the private sector, other members may participate if necessaryalso plays a role in investment policy development.

Main duties of High Economic Council:

(i) To determine essential financial and economic objectives and policies, short-term, medium-term and long-term development priorities of the government in accordance with national budget structure;

(ii) To evaluate and make decisions on national economic plans and reforms;

(iii) To initiate coordination on policies and programs of development and economic sectors;

(iv) To create a suitable environment for coaxing business people to invest;

(v) To issues necessary instructions on following and coordinating nationally prioritized programs, regional economic cooperation programs and national and international economic meetings.[1]

Afghanistan Investment Support Agency (AISA) is an investment promotion agency that was merged into the Ministry of Commerce and Industries (MOCI) in October 2016. The transition period is ongoing so the AISA continues to play a semi-independent role. MOCI has taken on the role of promoting business growth, investment, and trade.

The HEC, HCI, MOCI, Afghan Chamber of Commerce and Industries, and AISA are tasked with maintaining a dialogue and resolving business disputes with the government.

b. Laws and Regulations of Investment Industry

Afghan Constitution stipulates the main principles upon investment in Afghanistan.

The Private Investment Law 2005 (PIL) replaced the Law on Domestic and Foreign Private Investment in Afghanistan in 2005.

Article 2 of PIL provides that "The purposes of this Law are to promote the role of private investment, both domestic and foreign, in the economy of the country, and to create a legal regime together with an administrative structure that will encourage, support and protect foreign and domestic private investors in order to promote economic development, expand the labor market, increase production and export earnings, promote technology transfer, improve national prosperity and advance the standard of living. "

Currently a new investment law has been drafted by MoCI and is awaiting review by the Council of Ministers.

Other laws relevant to investment in Afghanistan are Partnership Law, Corporation & LLC Law, Competition Law and The Public Procurement Law.

The Partnership Law and the Corporations and Limited Liability Companies Law were written by foreign lawyers who did not spend much time in Afghanistan and who received little input from people and businesses inside Afghanistan. The laws have been criticized by at least one foreign government agency as developed in haste without adequate domestic input. In addition, some provisions are unnecessarily complex. Many provisions reflect international best practices which encourage foreign investment, but may not respond to Afghanistan's unique circumstances.

Contract law in Afghanistan is set out in the Afghanistan Commercial Code 1955 and the Afghanistan Civil Code 1977. Both the 1977 Civil Code and the 1955 Commercial Code are based on the laws of Egypt, which in turn are based on French civil law.

Under these codes, parties are generally free to: (i) enter into and perform a contract on any commercial subject matter provided that subject matter or performance is not contrary to law, public policy, or sharia; and (ii) agree to have the law of a foreign state govern their contract.

The Public Procurement Law of 2015 went into effect October 7, 2015. The law retains a preference for national sources and domestic products.

On July 29, 2016, Afghanistan was formally admitted to the WTO which means that the regulations of WTO shall be complied with inviting in Afghanistan.

c. Forms of Investment

Pursuant to the Private Investment Law, the ownership of approved enterprises shall be one of the following forms:

(i) 100% private ownership;

(ii) Joint ownership by the Afghan Government and private investors.

d. Standards of Market Access and Examination

Approved enterprises shall be one of the following types:

(i) Enterprises organized according to Afghan law;

(ii) Enterprises organized under foreign law, but the approval and registration to trade and invest in

---

[1] https://president.gov.af/en/about-high-economic-council/?q=council.

Afghanistan has taken place as per Afghan law and regulations.

Under the Private Investment Law of 2005 (PIL), foreign and domestic private entities have equal standing and may establish and own business enterprises, engage in all forms of remunerative activity, and freely acquire and dispose of interests in business enterprises.

Under the PIL, investment is defined as currency and contributions in kind, including machinery, equipment, and industrial and intellectual-property rights provided for the purpose of acquiring shares of stock or other ownership interests in a registered enterprise.

The PIL permits investments in nearly all sectors except nuclear power, gambling, and production of narcotics and intoxicants. There are also limitations on the total value of service transactions or assets with respect to motion pictures, road transport (passenger and freight), and on the total number of people that can be employed in security companies.

Although the HCI has authority to limit the share of foreign investment in some industries, specific economic sectors, and specific companies, that authority has never been exercised. In practice, investments may be 100 percent foreign owned.

Investment in certain sectors, such as production and sales of weapons and explosives, non-banking financial activities, insurance, natural resources, and infrastructure (defined as sewage, waste-treatment, airports, telecommunications, and health and education facilities) is subject to special consideration by the HCI, in consultation with relevant government ministries. The HCI may choose to apply specific requirements for investments in restricted sectors. Direct investment exceeding USD 3 million requires HCI approval of the investment application.

Foreign or domestic companies investing in Afghanistan must obtain a corporate registration from the Afghanistan Central Business Registry (ACBR) and a Tax Identification Number issued by the Department of Revenue.

Companies operating in the security, telecommunications, agriculture, and health sectors require additional licenses from the relevant ministries.

Companies seeking licenses to provide consultancy, legal, or audit services must meet requirements for education or related experience for top officers.

To begin the process for initial issuance of licenses, renewals, and material changes to the license, foreign firms must first obtain an introduction letter from the Ministry of Foreign Affairs (MOFA) addressed to the Ministry of Commerce and Industries. Obtaining this letter typically requires an application to the Afghan embassy located in the country where the company is incorporated or a letter of introduction from the embassy or commercial attaché in Kabul representing the country where the company is incorporated. Once this process is complete, the company will be introduced by MOFA to MOCI / AISA and may proceed to obtain a license.

Ease of doing business reforms in 2016 led AISA to begin issuing licenses for three years, as opposed to one year, to attract investment. Obtaining a business license is relatively simple, however, applications for renewal are contingent upon certification from the Ministry of Finance (MOF) that all tax obligations have been met. Some companies have seen AISA license renewals delayed while MOF audits their tax status, despite MOF assurances that an ongoing tax audit should not impede AISA license renewal.

B. Foreign Exchange Regulation

a. Department Supervising Foreign Exchange

The official currency is the Afghani (AFN). There is legislation requiring the use of AFN for day to day transactions but US dollars are still widely accepted.

Da Afghanistan Bank (DAB) is the central bank of Afghanistan. Some of the objectives and basic tasks of DAB as set out in the Da Afghanistan Bank Law include:

DAB enjoys autonomous regulatory powers and authority, including those to pass regulations to facilitate orderly electronic transactions between DAB and banks and their respective customers.

DAB is managed by its Governor. The Supreme Council is DAB's highest policy and decision making body and is made up of the Governor (Chairman of the Supreme Council); First Deputy Governor (Vice Chairman of the Supreme Council); and five other members. All members of the Supreme Council shall be appointed by the President of Afghanistan with the advice and consent of the Parliament of Afghanistan.

b. Brief Introduction of Laws and Regulations of Foreign Exchange

Article 72 of Da Afghanistan Bank Law provides that Da Afghanistan Bank shall have exclusive responsibility for foreign exchange.

Article 8 of Da Afghanistan Bank Law provides that the Supreme Council of DAB shall have powers to formulate and adopt the foreign exchange policy and the exchange arrangements of Afghanistan and to determine the categories of assets that shall be suitable for investment of the foreign exchange reserves and other financial resources of Da Afghanistan Bank.

There are no restrictions on converting or transferring funds associated with any investment into international currencies at the legal market clearing rate. There is no limitation on the inflow and outflow of funds for remittances of profits, debt service, capital, capital gains, returns on intellectual property or imported inputs, provided that applicable taxes have been paid. The only requirements placed on the outflow of funds are procedural, for the purposes of anti-money laundering. Any transfer abroad that equals or exceeds AFN 1 million ($20,000) must be carried out via a bank or licensed foreign exchange dealer and is reported to the Central Bank. There are large, informal foreign exchange markets in major cities and provinces where major currencies can be exchanged.

The transport of more than AFN 1 million or equivalent in cash across the border of Afghanistan into another country must be reported in advance to the Financial Intelligence Unit of the Da Afghanistan (Central) Bank.

Access to foreign exchange for investment is not restricted by any law or regulation. There are large, yet informal, foreign exchange markets in major cities and provinces where U.S. dollars, British pounds, and euros are readily available. Entities wishing to buy and sell foreign exchange in Afghanistan must register with the central bank, Da Afghanistan Bank, but thousands of Hawalas continue to practice their trade. Non-official money service providers often cite the lack of enforcement in the currency exchange sector, and the resulting competitive disadvantage to licensed exchangers, as a disincentive to becoming licensed.

In mid-2014, due in part to Afghanistan's failure to pass Financial Action Task Force (FATF)-compliant Anti-Money Laundering / Combating the Financing of Terrorism (AML / CFT) laws in a timely manner, some international correspondent banks began closing USD accounts held for Afghan banks abroad, which increased costs and processing times for inbound and outbound international funds transfers. Currently there is only one bank in Afghanistan with a correspondent relationship with a bank that has a U.S. branch. Since then, Afghanistan has taken steps towards improving its AML / CFT regime.

c. Requirements of Foreign Exchange Management for Foreign Enterprises

Private investors have the right to transfer capital and profits out of Afghanistan, including for off-shore loan debt service. There are no restrictions on converting, remitting, or transferring funds associated with investment, such as dividends, return on capital, interest and principal on private foreign debt, lease payments, or royalties and management fees, into a freely usable currency at a legal market clearing rate.

Major transactions in Afghanistan, such as sale of autos or property, are frequently conducted in dollars or in the currency of neighboring countries. Afghanistan does not maintain a dual-exchange-rate policy, currency controls, capital controls, or any other restrictions on the free flow of funds abroad. Afghanistan uses a managed floating exchange rate regime under which the exchange rate is determined by market forces. It is illegal to transport more than AFN 1,000,000 (approximately USD 17,200) or the foreign currency equivalent out of Afghanistan via land or air; amounts over AFN 500,000 (approximately USD 8,600), but beneath AFN 1,000,000, must be declared. Enforcement is reported to be inconsistent.

The PIL states that an investor may freely transfer investment dividends or proceeds from the sale of an approved enterprise abroad. MOF has in some instances frozen the domestic bank accounts of companies over tax disputes, which has effectively served to prohibit transfers of capital.

C. Financing

a. Main Financial Institutions

The banking system of Afghanistan has a long history of operations but has been developed on modern standards only in the recent years. The central bank of Afghanistan (Da Afghanistan Bank) is the sole entity of licensing and regulating the banks and non-banking financial institutions. Da Afghanistan Bank (DAB) is also responsible for the maintaining the money supply, currency circulation and indirectly the inflation and exchange rates. DAB has now established branches in all 34 provinces of the country and introduced the transfer of funds through SWIFT.

Afghanistan is in principle welcoming toward foreign portfolio investment, but financial institutions and markets are at an early stage of development. There are no limitations of foreign investors obtaining credit. The banking sector generally only provides short-term loans.

DAB has made improvements in monitoring and supervising the banking sector, following the 2010 Kabul Bank crisis. President Ghani also took steps to hold those responsible accountable. The Afghan Government has a plan to recover assets from perpetrators of the large-scale bank fraud, though progress on its implementation remains slow.

Most Afghans remain outside the formal banking sector. Afghans continue to rely on an informal trust-based process referred to as Hawala to access finance and transfer money, due in part to religious acceptance, unfamiliarity with a formal banking system and limited access to banks in rural areas. Three of the four major mobile network operators-Etisalat, AWCC, and Roshan-offer limited mobile money services. Further, the Afghan government plans to launch mobile money salary payments in the Ministry of Labor. If successful, the government plans to expand mobile money payments to the ministries of Education and Interior Affairs.

Still, finance is Afghanistan's second-largest service industry behind telecommunications and is potentially an important driver of private investment and economic growth. There are 15 commercial banks were operating in Afghanistan, with total assets of approximately USD 4.48 billion. There are three state banks: Bank-E-Millie Afghan (Afghan National Bank), Pashtany Bank, and New Kabul Bank (formerly the privately owned Kabul Bank), and there are also branch offices of foreign banks, including Alfalah Bank (Pakistan), Habib Bank of Pakistan, and National Bank of Pakistan.

Banking remains highly centralized, with a considerable majority of total loans made in Kabul. Bank lending is undermined by the legal and regulatory infrastructure that impedes the enforcement of property rights and development of collateral, though a banking reform law passed in 2015 could improve conditions. The aggregate loan-to-deposit ratio for the banking sector is approximately 11 percent, and most banks concentrate on fee-based services and short-term credit to well-known customers. The difficulty of accessing credit through banks and other formal financial institutions makes existing firms dependent on family funds and retained earnings, limits opportunities for entrepreneurialism, and reinforces dependence on the informal financial sector.

The insurance sector is still in its infancy in Afghanistan. An Insurance Commission was established in mid-2006 and has a licensing procedure for foreign and domestic investors in the sector. As of June 2014, four companies had been licensed.

b. Financing Conditions for Foreign Enterprises

Formal credit to the private sector stands at less than 10 percent of GDP, significantly lower than other countries in the region. Afghanistan ranks 101 out of 189 economies for ease of obtaining credit in the World Bank's Doing Business 2017. Afghan entrepreneurs complain interest rates for commercial loans from local banks are high, averaging around 15.5 percent. In response to this situation, investment funds, leasing, micro-financing and SME-financing companies have entered the market. USAID is working with the Afghan government and the banking sector to promote improved access to finance and the expansion of financial inclusion.

Foreigners who would like to establish a bank account in Afghanistan are required to hold a valid passport and visa or work permit. Non-resident customers are subject to enhanced due diligence in an effort to combat money laundering and terrorism finance.

D. Land Policy

a. Brief Introduction of Land-related Laws and Regulations

The Constitution of Afghanistan provides that property shall be safe from violation, no one shall be forbidden from owning and acquiring property except by law, and private property can only be confiscated by legal order.

The law prohibits acquisition of such land without the permission of the government in violation of the law (Article 1991 Civil Code.) Government permission is necessary for acquiring any type of land.

Even barren land (zameen-e-bayer) that does not have an owner may only be acquired with the permission of the government. The person who acquires and develops barren land with the permission of the government shall own the land (Article 1992 Civil Code.) Any property shall cease to be public property upon the expiry of its designation for public use. Such expiry of the period of public utility is determined either by a successive law or when the purpose for staying under public ownership ceases to exist (Article 483 Civil Code).

According to Article 481of the Civil Code, immovable property that is owned by individuals is considered as private property. The Civil Code does not envisage private property owned by a group of individuals or body corporate. However, according to Islamic Law, private property can be held either individually or collectively. Article 1900 of the Afghan Civil Code confers an entitlement on the owner to use and exploit his property to the exclusion of all others. This right is construed to mean that the owner may, within the limits of law, use and dispose of his property freely.

Private ownership may be acquired through purchase, land allocation from the Municipality, and through transfer of ownership. Moreover, in theory, land may be acquired through the application of the principle of "dead land" or "zameen-e-bayer".

Presidential Decree (Issue 83 dated 18/8/1382) states that all individual claims to land that has been held by the state for a period exceeding 37 years shall be barred and the state shall be considered the owner of the property (Article 2). Moreover, the decree provides that all land in which the ownership of individuals is not established legally shall be considered the property of the state (Article 3.).[1]

The distribution of state land in Kabul is governed by a Presidential Decree on Distribution and Sale of State Owned Land for Residential, Commercial, and Multi-Storied Buildings in Kabul City (OG, , No, 794, 25/6/1421, 2000). According to this decree, individuals who do not own a residential house, apartment or plot of land are eligible to purchase land from the Municipality. Further the law provides that the spouse and minor children of a person who applies to purchase land must not own any house, apartment, or land in order to be eligible for land allocation from the state (Article 3 (1)).

According to the Law on Local Administration and subsequent order on its enforcement (OG, no753, October, 7, 1991), the provincial governor is authorized to sell state owned land as well as purchase land on behalf of the state.

However, land grabbing, squatting and other forms of irregular occupation of land are widespread throughout the country. A large percentage of real estate transactions take place through informal market mechanisms. On the other hand, the formal property titling system does not facilitate the efficient use of land or promote the operation of a real estate market. Given its current corrupt and inefficient nature, the formal land titling process does not provide a suitable mechanism to accommodate the potential demand for real estate transactions.

Reform of land policy is ongoing but slow and land administration capacity remains weak and mostly improved in urban areas. The government of Afghanistan is working towards creating a cohesive legal framework for land tenure, by revising and updating land law. Inheritance is covered by the Civil Code, which reflects Islamic law (Sharia).

The 2007 Land Policy Allows for the formalization of land rights in informal settlements, and addresses bottlenecks in land rights administration as well as the overlap in different institutions' authority over questions of land rights.

The new land laws in 2008, which sets out definitions for various land types and classifications, requirements for land deeds, and principles governing allocations of state land, land leasing, land expropriation, settlement of land rights, and restoration of lands. However, the current legal framework still has remnants of past land rights reforms. Moreover, although customary law is important and has social legitimacy, it remains poorly integrated with formal law and policy.

b. Rules of Land Acquisition for Foreign Enterprises

The Afghan Constitution and the PIL prohibit foreign ownership of land. In practice most foreign firms find it necessary to work with an Afghan partner.

Article 41 of Constitution states that Foreign individuals shall not have the right to own immovable property in Afghanistan. Lease of immovable property for the purpose of capital investment shall be permitted in accordance with the provisions of the law. The sale of estates to diplomatic missions of foreign countries as well as international organization's to which Afghanistan is a member, shall be allowed in accordance with the provisions of the law. "Foreign individuals" in Section 41 of Constitution refers to natural and legal entities, and therefore the restriction on foreign ownership of land appears, in the absence of other legislation on the subject, absolute and applies regardless of the foreign ownership percentage.

Land leasing is addressed in Article 21 of Constitution which allows approved enterprises to have the right lease land, for business purposes, as provided by law, for up to 50 years. Leasing therefore appears to be the only viable alternative for foreigners to carry out projects requiring long term land possession.

E. The Establishment and Dissolution of Companies

a. The Forms of Enterprises

There are five kinds of forms of business organization: sole proprietorship, general partnership, special (or limited) partnership, corporation, limited liability company (LLC).

Under the Partnership Law (PL), a partnership is created by two or more persons who file and register their partnership agreement. When a partnership is created, it has a legal personality and can execute transactions, sign contracts and own property. The Law defines two types of partnerships; General Partnership and Special Partnership.

Article 4 of the Corporations and Limited Liability Companies Law (CLLCL) provides: "Corporation": a business company whose capital is definite and divided into shares, with the share and responsibility of each shareholder

---

[1] Dr. Yohannes Gebremedhin,Legal Issues in Afghanistan Land Titling and Registration.2005. www.terrainstitute.org/pdf/Legal_Analysis_of_Land_Laws.pdf.

limited to the proportion of his share; and "Limited Liability company"; "Limited" is a business company whose capital is not divided into shares with the responsibility of each shareholder limited to the amount of capital agreed to [by such shareholder] in the company.

The Law sets the registration requirements for corporations by indicating the documents that may be registered in a Central Registry, which include a Business License, the Articles of Incorporation and Annual Reports.

The Corporation under this law has a two-tier Board of Directors including a Board of Supervisors that oversees the Board of Directors and can inspect the Corporation"s books and records. The Law provides for duties and standards of the Board of Directors including the duty to disclose a conflict of interest regarding transaction effected by the corporation.

Corporations must hold Annual Meetings where Directors are elected and other business is transacted. Before such meetings, the Corporation must deliver the financial statement to all Shareholders and the financial statement, including the balance sheets, must comply with international accounting standards. The law also provides more transparent rights and protections of shareholders such as the ability to inspect the books and records of the corporation and lawsuits by a shareholder in the right of a corporation against a Director or Officer for failure to perform, or other violation of his duties in management of the Corporation. The law sets the rules for when a corporation may pay dividends and how much of a reserve fund is necessary.

The law also defines a limited liability company that has between 2 to 50 shareholders and whose shares are not to be sold on a public stock exchange.

b. The Procedure of Establishment

The sections of the Commercial Code of 1955, under which sole proprietors and family businesses who do not want to establish a business as a legal entity are required to register with the Commercial Court, are no longer enforced. Sole proprietors who are foreign must register with AISA. The only legal requirements for Afghan sole proprietors and family businesses are that they obtain a tax identification number or TIN and register with the district and municipal authorities. Some choose to register with Afghanistan Central Business Registry (ACBR), AISA or apply for MOCIs Business (or Traders) License. There are proposals to require Afghan sole proprietors to register with the ACBR. The status of these proposals can be checked on MOCIs.

Following the passage of the 2007 Corporations and Limited Liability Companies Law, all investors, both domestic and foreign, wishing to establish a business as a legal entity in Afghanistan need to be registered with the Afghanistan Central Business Registry in the Ministry of Commerce. The Law establishes the Afghanistan Central Business Registry within MOCIs.

Depending on the specific sector in which businesses engage, they may be required to obtain sector licenses. In particular, all businesses (sole proprietors, partnerships or incorporated entities) with activities in any of the following sectors must obtain sector licenses.

The first time foreign investor should then proceed to register his / her company / investment with AISA as a copy of his/her AISA License needs to be provided as part of the process for applying for a work permit for his / her employee.

Once a foreign employee has a visa, he / she must then apply for a work-permit for foreigners.

In order to establish a business in Afghanistan a criminal background check must be conducted on an applicant. A foreign applicant must provide a certificate or some type of documentation from His / her embassy or government, which clearly states that he / she has not been involved in any kind of crime, illegal activity and is not currently under prosecution.

Afghan applicants will have a criminal background check done through the Criminal Department of the Police Head-office. This is done as part of the registration process with ACBR and AISA.

c. Routes and Requirements of Dissolution

Pursuant to Corporations and Limited Liability Companies Law (CLLCL), there are two kinds of method of company dissolutions in Afganistan: determined dissolution and judicial dissolution.

a) Determined Dissolution

Article 103 of Corporations and Limited Liability Companies Law (CLLCL) stipulates that the Board of Directors may approve the dissolution of the Corporation by majority of votes and present the proposal (whether conditional or unconditional) to Shareholders meeting for adoption and approval.

The Corporation may deliver to the Central Registry for filing Articles of dissolution and the Corporation shall be dissolved upon the date of registering the Articles of dissolution. The general meeting of Shareholders of a Corporation may revoke its dissolution within five days of its Registration and advertisement date. When the revocation of dissolution is effective, the Corporation resumes carrying on its business as if dissolution had never occurred. Revocation of dissolution is retroactive.

b) Judicial Dissolution

The Commercial Court of proper jurisdiction may dissolve a Corporation in a proceeding, which is initiated by the Ministry of Commerce and Industry, by one or more Shareholders, or by a creditor.

The Ministry of Commerce can initiate this proceeding if a Corporation is established that:

(i) The Corporation obtained its Certificate of Incorporation through fraud;

(ii) The Corporation has exceeded, or abused, the authority conferred upon it by Law.

If there are situations in a Corporation as below, one or more Shareholders can initiate this proceeding:

(i) The Directors are deadlocked in the management of the Corporation's affairs, the Shareholder s are unable to break the deadlock, and irreparable injury to the Corporation and its assets is being suffered;

(ii) The Directors, or those in control, of the Corporation have acted, or are acting, in a manner that is illegal or fraudulent;

(iii) The Shareholders are deadlocked in voting power and have failed, for a period that includes at least two consecutive Regular / Annual Meetings, to elect Directors.

A creditor can initiate this proceeding when:

(i) The creditor's claim: has been reduced to judgment; and the execution on the judgment is unsatisfied; and the Corporation is insolvent; or

(ii) The Corporation has admitted in writing that the creditor's claim is due and owing and the Corporation is insolvent.

When a claim is filed against the Corporation, the Corporation's voluntary dissolution shall be executed under Court supervision.

According to Corporations and Limited Liability Companies Law (CLLCL), in a Court Proceeding brought to dissolve the Corporation, a Court may appoint one or more receivers to wind up and liquidate, or one or more custodians to manage the business and affairs of the Corporation during such dissolution. The custodian may exercise all of the powers of the Corporation through or in place of the Board of Directors to the extent necessary to manage the affairs of the Corporation in the best interests of its Shareholders and creditors.

If the Court determines that one or more grounds for judicial dissolution exist, it may enter a decree dissolving the Corporation in accordance with Article 107 of CLLCL and specify the announcement date of the dissolution.

The Court shall deliver a certified copy of the decree of dissolution to the Central Registry. After entering the decree of dissolution, the Court shall direct the winding up and liquidation of the Corporation's business and affairs.

As for a partnership, it may dissolve for many reasons such as death, bankruptcy, or withdrawal of a partner, the realization of the objective of the partnership or upon the order of the court. Upon dissolution, the partnership must follow liquidation procedures to protect creditors and partnership assets.

F. Merger and Acquisition

Article 41 of Corporations and Limited Liability Companies Law provides that subject to the limitations within the Articles of Incorporation, the Board of Directors is entitled to execute and sign any legal document and to represent the Corporation in legal transactions. Article 51 and 52 of this law provide the approval of directors and shareholders regarding a transaction. Therefore, merger and acquisition activities shall comply with the Articles of Incorporation of a Corporation and be approved by the directors as well as the shareholders of the Corporations.

Meanwhile, in accordance with Article 51 of this law, a transaction shall be effected, or proposed to be effected, by a Corporation (or by a subsidiary of the Corporation or by any other controlled Entity) when it is not a Director's conflicting interest transaction, is not prohibited or enjoined by the court in an action by a Shareholder, or a Derivative Proceeding based on such Director's interest in the transaction, and is not sentenced to payment of damages or to other limitations.

G. Competition Regulation

a. Department Supervising Competition Regulation

The National Competition Board is to be constituted as provided in Article 14 of the Competition Law. The prime responsibility of the Board is "To Promote Fair Competition and prevent Monopoly."

The Competition Promotion and Consumer Protection Directorate(CPCPD) in MOCI acts as the secretariat of the Board, who undertakes the function of market surveillance activities.

b. Brief Introduction of Competition Law

The Competition Law was enacted on January 25, 2010. The Law defines the word "Competition" as: "a situation wherein a number of independent producers, buyers and sellers for producing, buying or selling of similar commodities or services operate in such a manner that none of them has the power of determining quantity and price in the market independently".

The law aims to meet five obligations as below:

(i) Protect sound competition in the market.

(ii) Prevent unsound competition, unfair agreements, decisions as well as implementation of unfair contracts restricting, disrupting or preventing competition in the markets of goods, services and products.

(iii) To prevent monopoly in commercial activities.

(iv) Prevent influence of monopolist entrepreneurs in the market.

(v) To facilitate the environment for a fair competition and for relief of general economy.

But the current Competition Law is inappropriate and obsolete. In close coordination with the Competition Commission of Pakistan (CCP) and the Consumer Rights Commission of Pakistan (CRCP), the Commercial Law Development Program (CLDP) of US conducted a competition and consumer protection law program for the Afghan Competition Promotion and Consumer Protection Directorate (CPCPD) in Islamabad, Pakistan. This program was a continuation of CLDP efforts to build the CPCPD's internal capacity to develop a sustainable competition and consumer protection regime that will help create a transparent and level playing field for businesses in Afghanistan.[1]

A now draft of the Competition Law for Afghanistan is developed by the Competition Promotion and Consumer Protection Directorate (CPCPD) of the Ministry of Commerce and Industries (MoCI), through the legal services of Economic Legal Practice (ELP), an Indian law firm.[2]

It is a more modern Competition Law but has yet to be passed by Parliament. The new law covers monopolistic practices, outlaws collusion and anti-competitive practices dumping, price-fixing, exclusive dealing, refusal to deal, dividing territories, tying, resale price maintenance, etc.

c. Measures Regulating Competition

Article 7 of the Competition Law states that any kind of understanding, agreement and contract (written, electronic or oral), among the entrepreneurs, merchants, organizations and those corporations whose objectives are to prevent, limit or disrupt competition or harm the consumers are prohibited.

Article 8 of the Competition Law provides that unfair commercial practices shall be prohibited.

Article 11 regulates the limitation on merging of companies and organizations. A company or an organization cannot merge unilaterally, bilaterally or multilaterally in the following circumstances:

(i) If as a result of merger or during the merger anticompetitive practices emerge in the market.

(ii) If as a result of merger prices of goods or services increase dramatically.

(iii) If merger causes intense concentration in the market (Determination of intense concentration is undertaken by Competition Board).

(iv) Where merger causes the creation of a controlling organization or company in the market.

H. Tax

a. Tax Regime and Rules

The national taxation system of Afghanistan has been altered in recent years; new changes were brought in to simplify a wide range of nuisance taxes. Both tax authorities and investors were trained and educated; for authorities to effectively and efficiently administer tax payments while for investors on their tax obligations.

The taxpayer must acquire a tax identification number (a unique number for every taxpayer). All investors need to file their returns even if the returns are not taxable. Information provided by the taxpayers is kept confidential in the Ministry of Finance (MoF) unless authorized by law. The taxpayers are also required to maintain books and records using an accrual method of accounting. The taxation year starts from 1st of Jaddi (21st of December) to last day of Qaws (20th of December).[3]

b. Main Categories and Rates of Tax

In Afghanistan, there are personal tax, corporate tax, wage withholding tax, sole proprietors tax, fixed tax on small businesses, fixed tax on exhibitions, fixed tax on imports, fixed tax on contractors, fixed tax on transport of goods & people for business purpose, etc.

The income tax is imposed for each taxable year on the taxable income of each person, corporation, limited

---

[1] http://cldp.doc.gov/programs/cldp-in-action/details/1183.
[2] http://moci.gov.af/en/page/5976.
[3] http://investinafghanistan.af/taxation-in-afghanistan/.

liability company, or other entity. The taxable year is the solar year except as otherwise provided in this Law. The taxable income is the sum remaining after all the deductions and exclusions authorized in this Law and its regulations are deducted from the total of all receipts of the person, corporation, Limited Liability Company or organization.

The income tax of legal persons, corporations, limited liability companies, and general partnerships is 20 percent of its taxable income in the fiscal year.

Income in foreign money shall be converted to Afghanis for purposes of taxation. The rate of conversion shall be the average of free rates used by Da Afghanistan Bank to purchase such foreign money at the end of each month.

All partnerships, organizations, agencies, departments, and enterprises of the State and municipalities; all corporations and limited liability companies employing two or more persons in any month of a year are required to withhold taxes as provided in Article 3 of Income Tax Law from all salary and wage payments, and pay the amount withheld to the Government account.

The graduated personal tax of rates are as follows:

(i) AFS 0-5000, no tax, No tax is imposed on salaries / wages up to mentioned amount.

(ii) AFS 5001-12500, 2%, AFS 5000 Tax free, AFS 7500 taxed at 2% which equals AFS 150.

(iii) AFS12501-100000, 10%, AFS 150 + 10% Tax remaining amount which equals AFS 8750.

(iv) AFS100001-above, 20%, AFS 8900 + 20% Tax on remaining amount.

In addition, payments of rent for buildings and constructions which are rented to legal or natural persons and are used for business purposes or offices where the monthly rent is more than AFS 15,000, are subject to a 20 percent income tax.

The business receipts tax is collected from limited liability companies, corporations, general partnerships and organizations as follows:

(i) Five percent of the gross receipts (before any deductions) during the fiscal year of commissions, fees, interest, dividends, rent, royalties, and similar income. However, the business receipt tax does not apply to the rental income of a natural person;

(ii) Two percent of all the gross receipts (before any deductions) during the fiscal year for materials, equipment, services, transportation, and construction provided under terms of a contract;

(iii) Two percent of the gross receipts (before any deductions) during the fiscal year from premium income for insurance;

(iv) Two percent of the gross receipts (before any deductions) during the fiscal year from sale of admissions to public entertainment including cinema shows, plays, concerts, exhibitions, sports and other shows;

(v) Two percent of the gross receipts (before any deductions) during the fiscal year from sales of products, good s, assets, and other services;

(vi) Ten percent of the income derived from the services provided by a legal or natural person which is AFS 50,000 or more per month in accordance with the rulings issued by Ministry of Finance.[①]

c. Tax Declaration and Preference

Under the Income Tax Law, having a business license (including an AISA Investment License or MOCIs Business or Traders License) gives rise to a number of benefits. These benefits relate to reduced fixed taxes on imports and on government contracts. In particular:

a) Reduced fixed tax on imports: Businesses which import goods and have a business license are subject to two percent fixed tax on the total value (including custom duties) of the goods imported. The tax paid is allowed as a credit in the calculation of the person"s annual income tax assessment in accordance with the provisions of the Income Tax Law. Companies which import goods without having a business license are subject to three percent fixed tax on the total value (including customs duties) of the goods imported.

b) Reduced tax on government contracts:

(i) "Persons who, without a business license who provide supplies, materials, construction and services under contract to government agencies, municipalities, state entities, private entities and other persons shall be subject to 7 percent fixed tax in lieu of income tax. This tax is withheld from the gross amount payable to the contractor.

(ii) Persons who have a business license and provide the services and other activities mentioned in paragraph (1) of this Article to the specified entities shall be subject to 2 percent contractor tax. The tax levied by this paragraph is creditable against subsequent tax liabilities.

(iii) The tax mentioned in paragraph (i) and (ii) of this Article shall be withheld by the payer from payment and shall be transferred to the relevant account within ten days. Contractors subject to this Article shall be required to,

---

① http://ard.gov.af/?page_id=2686.

upon signing the contract, send a copy thereof to the relevant tax administration. Natural persons who, according to provision of paragraph (1) of Article 17 of this Law, earn taxable salaries shall be excluded from this provision.

I. Securities

Afghanistan does not have a stock market, so there are no laws or regulations upon securities.

J. Preference and Protection of Investment

a. The Structure of Preference Policies

It is one of responsibilities of Ministry of Commerce and Industry of Afghanistan to promote and facilitate domestic and foreign investment.

The United Nations Development Program (UNDP) assisted the Afghanistan government to develop the Afghanistan National Development Strategy (ANDS) from 2008 to 2013, which attempted to guide development investments in specific focus areas, through high-priority programs chosen for contributions to job creation, broad geographic impact, and likelihood of attracting additional investment.

Afghan government approved the Investment Incentive Policy in July 2013 to provide special privileges for investors who either will invest or extend their businesses during the transition and transformation decade. While it has been approved, as yet it has not been implemented.

As of March 2016 the Afghanistan Investment Support Agency (AISA) is urging the government to consider an updated strategy, potentially focusing on support to industry, electricity generation, taxation reform, industry supports, customs, technology, and the agricultural sector. However, so far the strategy hasn't appeared on the horizon.

b. Support for Specific Industries and Regions

The Investment Incentive Policy in July 2013 has particularly been designed to develop five strategic sectors such as industry, construction, export, agriculture and mining. The policy aims to pave essential grounds for developing these sectors, to draw up attention of foreign investors to the existing potential investments opportunities.

The productive and favorable privileges for investors are as follow:

a) Industry Sector:

(i) Allocate the government possessed lands as free of charge for industrialists who will invest at least in value USD 1 million;

(ii) Sell lands of industrial parks by 10-year settlements;

(iii) Rent unused lands of government possessed by 30 years in term exemption rent of first five years;

(iv) Exempt all kind of taxes by 10 years except municipality's duty;

(v) Exempt custom duty free for machinery and 1 percent on raw materials only.

b) Construction Sector:

(i) Facilitate visa issuance processing (municipalities have to set a form that in maximum 6 signatures would be required for visa issuance and be processed by 21 days);

(ii) Sell the lands possessed by municipalities (who will invest in value USD 5 million in Kabul or USD 2 million in provinces at least, will get 2000 m2);

(iii) Facilitate administrative processing of modification of residence areas' identification to commercial use free of charge for who will invest in value USD 2 million in Kabul or 1 million in the provinces at least.

c) Export Sector:

(i) Allocate land free of charge for exporters especially who have occupied in foodstuff, dried and fresh processing, carpeting, and animal products manufacturing (instead of each USD 1 million, 4000 m2);

(ii) Exempt all kinds of taxes by 10 years except municipality's duty;

(iii) Exempt custom duty free for machinery.

d) Agriculture Sector:

(i) Rent unused government possessed lands by 30 years, in term exemption rent of first five years especially for who will invest in cool storages, greenhouses and foodstuff manufacturing (instead of USD half million, 4000 m2);

(ii) Rent unused government possessed lands by 30 years, in term exemption rent of first ten years for who will invest in value USD 10 million;

(iii) Rent unused government possessed lands by 15 years, in term exemption rent of first two years for small and medium enterprises.

e) Mining Sector:

(i) Exempt custom duty free for machinery;

(ii) Not bidding is required for small and medium mines where can be exploited by 10 years and needed USD 2 million investments, in terms that operation and commercial proposals have to be approved by the Ministry of Mines and Petroleum first.

However, the policy persuades government respective entities to take necessary measurements toward implementation of the policy. For example; Ministry of Foreign Affairs have to facilitate visa issuance processing and offer one-year valued and multiple entry visas for foreign investors. High Investment Council, Ministry of Agriculture, Irrigation and Livestock and AISA have to accelerate land distribution processing.

It's mentionable; implantation of the policy is required to modify several laws and regulations.

c. Special Economic Areas

There are no special economic zone currently. The Afghan government, through the Afghan Airfield Economic Development Commission (AAEDC), is considering Special Economic Zones (SEZs) to develop certain military bases and airfields that will eventually be transferred to Afghan civilian control. If the plan is approved the Afghan government will need to enact laws and regulations before such zones can be established.

d. Investment Protection

To protect foreign and domestic private investment in Afghanistan is one of the main targets of the Private Investment Law(PIL). Article 16 of the PIL states that approved domestic and foreign companies with similar objectives are subject to the same rights under Afghan law and the same protections against discriminatory governmental actions.

However, property rights protection is weak due to a lack of cadasters or a comprehensive land titling system, disputed land titles, incapacity of commercial courts, and widespread corruption. Land laws in Afghanistan are inconsistent, overlapping, incomplete, or silent with regard to details of effective land management. Judges and attorneys are often without expertise in land matters. Moreover, mortgages and liens are at an early stage of development. Therefore, foreign investors seeking to work with Afghan citizens to purchase property should conduct thorough due diligence to identify reliable partners.

III. Trade[①]

Afghanistan and China are traditional good-neighborly and friendly neighbors with a long history of friendly relations. Afghanistan established diplomatic relations with China on January 20, 1955. In June 2006, President Hamid Karzai paid a state visit to China. The two heads of state jointly signed the treaty of good-neighborliness, friendship and cooperation between China and Afghanistan. In March 2010, the state visit to China again, the two sides signed the following agreement: the government of the People's Republic of China and the Islamic republic of Afghanistan government economic and technological cooperation agreement, the law of the People's Republic of China government and government of the Islamic republic of Afghanistan on training project on, the government of the People's Republic of China's part of the product imports originating in Afghanistan on special preferential tariff treatment.

China is an important trading partner of Afghanistan, accounting for about 11.69 percent of its total foreign trade. Pakistan and Uzbekistan are Afghanistan's first and second largest trading partners. Exports are mainly to Pakistan, India, Iran, Russia and the United States.

A. The Competent Trade Department

Afghanistan government, who is in charge of trade department is business and industry (hereinafter referred to as the ministry of commerce), its foreign trade department in charge of trade policy and foreign trade coordination and administration, the ministry of foreign affairs with economic affairs department, responsible for foreign economic and trade relations and coordination of the government level. In addition, the export promotion bureau, headed by the ministry of commerce and industry, is responsible for policy implementation, trade promotion, organization of exhibitions, export procedures, issuance of documents (such as certificate of origin of goods) and other affairs. Imports are also subject to customs supervision.

B. Overview of Trade Laws and Regulations

Trade-related laws are customs law, contract law, insurance law, arbitration act, the act of settlement the banking act of Afghanistan, the currency and the commercial banking law, etc. On December 17, 2015, WTO

---

① This information comes from the URL: http://af.mofcom.gov.cn/article/ddfg/201109/20110907755599.shtml.

member states agreed to accede to the WTO at the 10th ministerial conference of the WTO held in Nairobi, Kenya.[①]

Afghanistan's parliament approved Afghanistan's entry into the world trade organization (WTO) on June 21, 2016, according to the Afghanistan daily outlook. The second deputy chairman of the upper house of the Afghan parliament Haseebullah Kalimzai said joining the WTO could boost Afghanistan's economic growth by 2.5 percent. Afghanistan officially became the 164th member of the WTO on July 29.

It is also a member of the south Asian association for regional cooperation (SAARC), the central Asian regional economic cooperation organization (CAREC) and the economic cooperation organization (ECO).

C. Trade Management

The name of the Afghan currency is Afghani.[②] After the war, Afghanistan carried out currency reform, issued new Afghanis, and implemented a relatively fixed exchange rate, which basically stabilized at around 50 Afghanis per dollar. There are seven denominations of Afghan banknotes: 1000, 500, 100, 50, 20, 10 and 5 ANI, and 5, 2 and 1 ANI. Affected by the international financial crisis, ANI depreciated for the first time in November 2008, with a ratio of 1:54.

Afghanistan has no restrictions on the exchange of investment and remittances, as long as they are taxed without restrictions on remittances such as profits, debt services, capital, capital gains and intellectual property income. But to prevent money laundering, international remittances of more than 1 million ANI ($20,000) must go through Banks or qualified foreign exchange trading institutions and be filed with the central bank.

Afghanistan has no restrictions on commodity imports. Prohibited imports include: alcohol, live pigs, pork, pig fat, cottonseed, drugs, firearms and explosives. The Afghan government is encouraging exports of its goods. Goods prohibited from export: drugs, antiques, rare mineral resources, and other goods regulated by the government.

D. Inspection and Quarantine of Import and Export Commodities

The Afghan customs has inspected the imported goods, but the inspection and quarantine equipment and technology are backward. China's exports to Afghanistan shall be subject to the issuance of a Chinese inspection report.

E. Customs Administration

a. The General Situation

Provisions of The Customs Law of Afghanistan (20 March 2005)[③], The Ministry of Finance is responsible for the collection of customs revenues of the state, and for enforcing the provisions of this law and any other relevant customs legislation.

Customs supervision means the inspection done by those authorities with a view to ensuring that customs legislation and, other provisions applicable to goods subject to customs supervision are observed, and may include measures for exercising customs control, when necessary.

Importers and exporters of goods shall execute the customs clearance of the relevant import and export of goods by a customs broker licensed by the Ministry of Finance. The provisions of paragraph 1 do not apply to Postal goods and goods imported by travelers pursuant to Articles 42 and 45 of this law.[④]

b. Tariffs

a) The General Directorate of Customs is responsible for carrying out the tariff classification of goods concerning description and coding in accordance with the Harmonized System of the World Customs Organization and for assessing any corresponding duty under the Customs Tariff.

The value of goods shall be computed in Afghan currency. When the value of goods is expressed in foreign currency and there is need to determine customs value, the value of goods shall be determined in accordance with the Da Afghanistan Bank[⑤] exchange rate.

The exchange rate shall be the rate announced by The Afghanistan Bank on the last working day of the month

---

① This information comes from the URL: http://af.mofcom.gov.cn/article/afjj/201609/20160901394480.shtml.
② According to the exchange rate in July 2018, 1 million Afghanis is equal to 90, 420 yuan.
③ The content of law comes from: http://www.wipo.int/wipolex/en/details.jsp?id=10722, please note that this translation is an unofficial English translation. For academic research purposes only.
④ For details, see Article 42 of the Afghan Customs Act and the customs control of Article 45 passenger baggage.
⑤ Da Afghanistan Bank is the central bank of Afghanistan.

and shall be valid for a period starting from the 6th day of every month and ending on the 6th day of the following month.

b) Exemption from customs duties on the following imported goods:

(i) Goods imported by officials of the State during official travels not in excess of Afghani 100,000 as provided by the Customs Tariff.

(ii) Office materials and equipment of political representatives and international agencies, intended to be used in residences and offices of representatives of foreign countries in Afghanistan, after confirmation of permission to do so by competent authorities.

(iii) Items intended for personal use by foreigners working in Afghanistan according to the terms and conditions of their contract.

(iv) Permitted books, gazettes, magazines and newspapers.

(v) Goods provided for government projects funded by Loans or imported into the country by or for public and private foreign and International relief and development agencies approved by the government.

(vi) Personal effects used by Afghan delegations or Afghan international workers and their family members while abroad.

(vii) Travelers' personal goods in accordance with the Customs Tariff.

(viii) Commercial samples and advertising gifts.

(ix) Post parcels valued at Afghani 5000 or less.

(x) Honorary decorations or awards.

(xi) Samples sent to organizations protecting copyrights or industrial or commercial patent rights.

(xii) Used movable property belonging to natural persons, who transfers their normal place of residence from another country to the State, as provided in the Customs Tariff.

(xiii) a consignment of less than Afghani 1000 value.

(xiv) Pure-bred breeding animals and insects and laboratory animals; biological or chemical substances needed for Scientific researches.

(xv) Therapeutic substances of human origin and blood grouping and tissue typing reagents.

(xvi) Substances for the quality control of medicinal products.

(xvii) Fuels, lubricants and equipment's carried with and necessary for the normal functioning of transport vehicles in accordance with the relevant procedure.

(xviii) Other goods may be included as exempted goods upon recommendation of Minister of Finance and approval of Council of Ministers as required.

c. Customs Declaration

Non-afghan goods must be declared at customs, The declarant is obliged to complete required customs declarations within 5 days from the date on which the summary declarations were submitted. Where circumstances so warrant, Customs may set a shorter period or authorize an extension to the periods referred to in paragraph 1.

The temporary storage period shall be 30 days and it will terminate at any time that duties, storage and other obligations accrued under this law equal the value of the goods. In no event shall the period be extended in the absence of a complete report by the responsible customs authority to the General Directorate of Customs justifying the delay.

d. Smuggling of Goods and its Penalties

a) Carrying out the following activities is deemed to be smuggling and the offender shall be punished in accordance with this law and any other customs legislation:

(i) Introduction of goods into the customs territory of the State, or the exit of goods, in violation of the provisions of this Law and other customs legislation, with the intent of avoiding (ejtinab) customs control or supervision.

(ii) to carry prohibited goods for the purpose of import, export, or storing without permission of the relevant authorities.

(iii) Selling or purchasing of goods in a transit process without paying customs duties.

(iv) carrying out the following activities repeatedly, or showing intent to carry out the following activities shall be considered smuggling:

• Violate the conditions for use of goods that occasioned a partial or total relief from customs debt by reason of their end-use pursuant to Article 66;

• Possess goods against the provisions of article 61, paragraph 2 ;

• Remove or falsify the identification number of the means of transport;

• Purchase, sell, store, and possess imported goods with knowledge that they are smuggled goods; such

knowledge will be presumed in the case of a warehouse;
 • Break the seal or substitute or change other security verifications placed on the means of transport or goods;
 • Load, unload, or move goods, travelers or their luggage, from one means of transport to the other without permission from the customs, in an unauthorized place.
  (v) Smuggling is considered to have been committed by the Captain of an aircraft who:
 • Transports goods without the relevant manifest, or with a manifest that misrepresents the goods on board;
 • Has not presented goods to customs which were brought into the customs territory of the State according to the manifest but are not on board at the time of departure;
 • Lands out of a customs airport, and does not notify its landing to the customs or other relevant authorities within the shortest time.
  b) The violators shall be punished with:
 • Confiscation of the smuggled goods;
 • A fine from two to five times the amount equal to the applicable customs debt of the smuggled goods; and
 • Punishment in accordance with Article 179.
  c) In case of committing a violation by more than one person, each one shall be fined proportionate to that person's participation in the violation. If one of the parties pays the full amount, the others are free of any obligation to Customs for the fine in question.
  d) When the same violator commits at the same time several violations referred to in chapter 14, the violator shall be punished for each of the violations separately.

e. A Handling Agency that has Objections to a Customs Penalty Award

Customs must conduct a hearing for violations of the Customs Law, collect documents and proofs, and record the declaration of witnesses. Customs will set a date and time and place for that purpose. The time limit for holding the hearing may not exceed 72 hours from the date of notification.

The persons charged or witnessing the violation may be allowed by Customs to present and record their statement to the charges instead of being present at the hearing.

When any persons charged with the violation, or a witness, does not speak Dari or Pashtu, the hearing will be carried out in the presence of an interpreter who shall be responsible for the translation of the proceedings.

If there is any objection to the customs award, it may be submitted to the customs arbitration administration for adjudication. The Customs Arbitration Administration will be established within the framework of the Ministry of Finance for the purpose of taking care of objections to the decisions of Customs. The Arbitration Administration shall be composed of three members to be appointed upon proposal of the Minister of Finance by the Head of State.

IV. Labour

A. Overview of Labour Laws and Regulations

The Labour Law of the Islamic Emirate of Afghanistan[1] was promulgated on 1 November 1999. The law was further developed and improved in 2006, with the following new provisions on the rights and obligations of Labour organization and its employees:
  (i) Provide for the right of Afghans to work and to be remunerated;
  (ii) The prerequisite to terminate the labour contract and after the cancellation of the contract for the employee compensation, such as remove contract, 1-5 years of working staff should compensate for 2 months salary, 5-10 years 4 months salary employee compensation, work more than 10 years of employee compensation 6 monthly wages;
  (iii) The working hours, overtime and holiday regulation, normal work time can't more than eight hours a day, work time can't more than five hours on Thursday. No more than an hour's overtime after 7:00 p.m. The minimum wage for managers to work overtime at night is 115%, and the minimum wage for production workers to work overtime at night is 125%. Workers are not allowed to work two consecutive shifts. Weekend and holiday overtime pay at 150%. Employees are entitled to 5–45 working days of paid leave;
  (iv) Wages shall not be lower than the minimum wage stipulated by the government;
  (v) Work shall not impair the health of workers;

---

[1] This legal information comes from the URL, please note that this translation is an unofficial English translation. http://www.asianlii.org/af/legis/laws/lloaogn790p1999110114200722a443/.

(vi) Workers have the right to join trade unions. The retirement age for men is 65, up to 70. Women are 55, up to 60. Retirement pensions, in which workers pay 3% of their monthly wages, are paid 8% by the government and enterprises;

(vii) Gender and culture, the female medical personnel, are not allowed to work overtime at night, the company in general to provide transportation for women to work, dinner usually separate men and women, to give workers left a prayer time, men and women in different places and so on.

Despite the health compensation law, overtime wages, health insurance, pension rights, pregnant women and nursing mothers and the standard working week of minors to reduce workers' rights, such as but these standards are not maintenance, workers also didn't realize that you can have these rights.

B. Regulations on the Work of Foreigners in Local Areas

a. Work Permit and Application Procedures

According to article 2 of Statutes on the Employment of Foreign Citizens by Afghan Organizations[①]: A person who does not have the Afghan citizenship shall has An "Agreement" is signed between governmental, joint ventures, private, and Non-Governmental Organizations stationed in Afghanistan on one hand and foreign countries and International Organizations on the other hand. Get a "Work Permit" is a printed endorsed document, issued by the Ministry of Labor and Social Affairs to the qualified foreign citizens according to the provisions of these Statutes. A "Work Contract" is a written document signed by a foreign citizen and the organization, containing work conditions, obligations of the two parties, terms of validity, norms and criteria for payment of salaries ad other benefits.

Procedures for the employment of Foreign Citizens in the organizations shall be designed, prepared and approved by the Ministries of Foreign Affairs and Labor and Foreign citizens employed in organizations are obliged to observe the provisions of the enforced laws and these Statutes and respect the beliefs and traditions of the people of Afghanistan.

Article 7 of this regulation provides the Issuance of Work Permit:

(i) The Ministry of Labor and Social Affairs issues the Work Permit against a fixed cost.

(ii) The cost of the permit mentioned under item (1) of this article considering criteria For time limit shall be fixed by the ministries of Labor and Social Affairs and Finance.

(iii) Identification of employee such as location of work, work specification, date of beginning of duty and time validity, shall be specified in the Work Permit. Validity of Work Permit is one year. If the Work Permit is extended, it may be for another term.

According to the article 5 of the act, foreigners must meet the following Criteria for Employment in Afghanistan:

(i) Foreign citizens who have completed 18 years of age, have not reached the final age for retirement, which is enacted in Labor Law, holds the health certificate from the country of citizenship and the Ministry of Public Health of Afghanistan, may be employed in the following forms in the organizations in Afghanistan.

• On the basis of agreement based on the request of governmental organizations and the countries and processed through the ministries of Foreign Affairs and Social Affairs.

• On the basis of individual request of the foreign citizens who have obtained the stay permit (visa) in Afghanistan and the organizations need them.

(ii) Employment of foreign citizens outside their field of specializations is not allowed.

(iii) The employing organization shall supervise the activities of the employee from time to time.

As the meanwhile, restrictions on the employment Article 6: If both domestic and foreign workers are available; priority is given to domestic workers.

b. Social Security

Article 123 of the Islamic emirate of Afghanistan Labor law provides that:

(i) Social security shall be provided through financial contribution of the establishment and workers of the Islamic Emirate of Afghanistan.

(ii) The scale of workers' social security shall increase in proportion to the growth of national economy.

Article 124 further provisions:

(i) Financial assistance (funeral expenses) to the family of the Article 124 further provisions: deceased worker for the purposes of his obsequies equivalent to six month remuneration and allowances on the basis of his last grade and position.

(ii) Assistance for medical treatment of the worker inside the country during his sickness shall be granted in

---

① This legal information comes from the URL http://www.worldlii.org/af/legis/laws/soteffcbao716/.

accordance with the rule laid down by the Ministry of Public Health and the General Department of Labor & Social Affairs.

(iii) Equality of treatment in the allotment of land, residential quarters and apartments in accordance with the rules and regulations of the Islamic Emirate of Afghanistan.

(iv) Financial assistance to the worker at the time of his retirement equivalent to his 10-month remunerations and allowances on the basis of his last grade and position.

(v) The establishment shall be obligated to provide foodstuff and consumable items, or the pecuniary difference thereof to the worker.

(vi) The family members of the worker undergoing his compulsory national service shall be entitled to the privilege prescribed in paragraph (5) of this article, as well as to medical facilities.

(vii) The establishment shall be obligated to provide transportation services to the workers. In case such services are not provided, the establishment may provide transportation costs to the workers in accordance with the prevailing rates.

C. Immigration[①]

a. Types of Visa

(i) Tourist Visa. Tourist visa is issued for foreign nationals who are interested to travel to Afghanistan individually or with a group for the purpose of visiting Afghanistan or their relatives. This type of visa is issued by the Afghan Missions aboard. The validity of this type of visa is for one month, which can be extend only once by the Ministry of Interior with the agreement of the Afghan Tourism Organization.

(ii) Entry Visa for Work Permit. Entry visa for work permit is issued for business, economic, commercial, cultural, industrial purposes and working for the governmental or non governmental organizations, This type pf visa can be obtained from the Consulate Section of the Afghan Ministry of Foreign Affairs. Your employer or sponsor should contact the concerned department of Ministry of Foreign Affairs directly. However, this type of visa can be extended through the Ministry of Interior.

(iii) Resident Visa. This type of visa is issued by the Ministry of Interior to the foreign nationals holding ordinary passport, which has already entered Afghanistan with a proper visa. The validity of this type of visa is from one month to six months and can be extended.

(iv) Transit Visa. This type of visa is issued by the Afghan Missions aboard to those foreign nationals who pass through Afghanistan to a third country. The validity of this type of visa is for 72 hours for air passengers' and six days for those who travel by land.

(v) Double Entry Visa. This type of visa is issued to the foreign nationals who has stay visa and the validity of the visa can be extended.

(vi) Diplomatic. This visa is issued for holders of diplomatic passports who intend to travel to Afghanistan. Diplomatic passport holder can obtain this type of visa from the Afghan Missions aboard. However, they must contact the 'Section of Diplomatic passport and Diplomatic Visa' of the Afghan Ministry of Foreign Affairs directly through their mission in Kabul.

(vii) Service Visa. This type of visa is issued by the Afghan Missions abroad to the foreign nationals who hold service or special passports.

(viii) Student Visa. This type of visa is issued by the Afghan Missions aboard to the foreign students who intend to study in Afghanistan. The relevant university / academic institution must contact the 'Cultural Relations Department of the Afghan Ministry of Foreign Affairs' directly.

(ix) Exit Visa. This type of visa is issued to the foreign nationals who have entered the country with entry work permit visa. The validity of this type of visa is one to six days; in some circumstances this can be extended.

All Afghans with Duel Citizenship required to obtain a Visa Exception letter from the Afghan Embassies or Consulates abroad.

b. Visa Application

Considering that different types of visa processing requirements may vary Check with the local Afghan embassy or consulate before applying for a visa. At the same time, you can also learn more about the opening time of the visa department, required documents, waiting time and other information from the website of the overseas mission of Afghanistan.

---

① This information comes from the URL http://mfa.gov.af/en/page/consular-affairs/visa-information.

c. Entry and Exit Restrictions

(i) Important Information and Regulations. Must to extend your visa prior to expiry, if you wish to stay longer than the permitted duration. If the visa is not extended on the due date, the holder of the passport will be fined US$2 for each day during the first month of the delay, US$5 for each day during the second month of the delay (fined can be paid at ports). If the delay is more than two months, in addition to the fine, the holder will be deported.

Foreign visitors shall to register with their embassy in Kabul, the local Afghan Police Department and the Afghan Tourist Organization (if the visit is for tourism purposes only) on arrival.

(ii) Special Requirements, Prohibited Items And Items That Must Be Declared. Photos and Cinematographic films can be taken after obtaining previous permission in writing from the Tourist Bureau, Press Department, located on the first floor of the Ministry of Information and Culture Building.

Transportation of some rare birds out of the country is illegal. Therefore, visitors must contact the Afghan Tourist Bureau to obtain more information and relevant export certificate.

Tourists may export duty free 30 sqm carpets, 10 skins excluding Karakul, cut and polished precious stones including Lapis Lazuli, handicrafts and a limited variety of antiques.

Upon arrival, visitors are required to declare all foreign currency (If the amount exceeds 1million AFS or its equivalent value) that they carry. Please ask for 'Ansari Application Form' at the airport.

(iii) Special Cultural And Religious Requirements. Afghanistan's local religious customs and culture should be respected and its sensitivities should be noted. Afghanistan is an Islamic country with conservative clothes. Men should not wear shorts on the street. Women should not wear narrow and exposed clothing; it is best to wear a headscarf.

D. Trade Unions and Labor Organizations

Afghanistan has a national federation of trade unions, founded in 1965, with headquarters in the capital Kabul, and provincial provinces with provincial unions. A trade union organization is a non-political group and a non-governmental organization. At present, the National Federation of Trade Unions has about 200,000 members. Workers have the right to join a trade union.

E. Work-related Disputes

The penalties imposed on the employees by the enterprise may be appealed to the labor dispute resolution committee if the employee believes that it is unreasonable.

Where disputes in relation to work, which are not settled by the relevant establishment shall be settled by the following sources:

(i) By the labor disputes settlement commission;

(ii) By the Administrative Council of the General Department of Labor & Social Affairs;

(iii) By a competent court.

In addition to disputes that should be decided by the court according to law, the labor dispute handling committee is the competent authority for preliminary investigation of labor disputes. The decision of the Labor Dispute Resolution Committee shall be agreed with the parties and binding.

The Administrative Council of the General Department of Labor & Social Affairs shall investigate work-related disputes under the following circumstances:

(i) where settlement of dispute does not satisfy the parties, the issue shall be referred to the Administrative Council of the General Department of Labor & Social Affairs for settlement.

(ii) one of the parties has lodged a written complaint concerning unsoundness of the decision.

In case the decision of the Administrative Council of the General Department of Labor & Social Affairs is objected to by the parties, the issue shall be referred to a competent court through submission of a written request.

The establishment shall be obligated to carry out the decision of the dispute settlement commission within 10 days.

V. Intellectual Property

A. Overview of Intellectual Property Laws and Regulations

The main intellectual property laws enacted by the Afghan legislature[1]:

---

[1] Regulatory information from the URL http://www.wipo.int/wipolex/en/profile.jsp?code=AF.

(i) Protection of Patent Rights Act June 10, 1967.
(ii) Afghanistan Trademark Registration Law (2009).
(iii) The Law on the support the right of authors, composers, artists and researchers (Copyright Law) (21 July, 2008).

B. Copyright Protection[①]

Decree of President of Government of Islamic Republic of Afghanistan regarding signing The Law on the support the right of authors, composers, artists and researchers (Copyright Law) on July 21, 2008.

a. According to the Act, the Following Works Should be Protected

(i) Book, pamphlet, brochure, essay, play and other academic technical and artistic writings;

(ii) Poem, melody, song and compose that has been written, recorded or published using any mean;

(iii) Audiovisual work for the purpose of performance on a movies scene or broadcast from radio or television that has been written, recorded or published using any mean;

(iv) Musical work, which has been written, recorded or published by any mean;

(v) Painting, picture, design, drawing, innovate geographical cartography, linear writings, decorative lines and other decorative and imaginary works which have been created using any simple or combinatory mean or mode;

(vi) Statuary (sculpture);

(vii) Photography work that has been created using an innovative mode;

(viii) Innovative work of handicraft or industrial art(carpet designs, rugs, felt carpet and its attachments etc.);

(ix) Innovative work which has been created based on the public culture (folklore) or national cultural heritage and art;

(x) Technical works with an innovative aspect;

(xi) Computer programs;

(xii) Derivative works.

The provisions of this Law shall apply to all other works eligible in accordance with all international treaties, agreements and conventions that Afghanistan is a party to.

b. Timeline to Protect the Works

(i) Works published or broadcast during the life cycle of the author shall be protected fifty calendar years after his / her death unless the author has decided differently.

(ii) Joint works published or broadcast during the life cycle of the authors shall be protected for fifty years after the death of the last author.

(iii) Works published or broadcast with metaphorical (pseudonym) names shall be protected for fifty years after the first year of the publication. If the author is identified, the provisions of the clause 1 of this article shall apply.

(iv) Works not published during the life cycle of the author and in the case of the joint work, which have not been published during the life cycle of the last author, shall be protected for fifty years effective from the first year of publication and broadcast.

(v) Audiovisual works shall be protected for fifty years effective from the first year of the publication or broadcast.

(vi) Photography and painting works shall be protected fifty years effective from the first year of publication and broadcast.

Provisions of the article 15 of this Law for the publication of the audiovisual work in the case of not being publicized and broadcast, effective from the date of phonogram's fixation shall be protected for fifty years.

c. Start Date of the Timeline for the Protection of the Work

If the timeline of the protection starts from the date of the publication and broadcast, therefore the first date of the publication shall be the date for the protection timeline unless the author when reproducing the work brings fundamental changes in the work in way that results into a new work. If the work is consisted of several components or is published in different phases, the timeline for the protection shall be accounted for each component as a separate work.

d. Penalties

(i) Any Person who publishes a Work he or she does not own, in the time frame mentioned in Article (19) of this law, without a certified written authorization from the Author of the Work, with a consideration of the

---

① Regulatory information from the URL http://www.wipo.int/wipolex/en/details.jsp?id=10197.

circumstances shall be punished by imprisonment for a period up to one year or with a fine of not less than (50,000.00 Afs) and not more than (100,000.00 Afs), or by either punishment.

(ii) Any Person who repeats broadcast and show of a Work or a part of a Work without a certified written agreement from the Performer of the Work, in the time frame mentioned in Article (22) of this law, with a consideration of circumstances shall be punished by imprisonment for a period up to one year or with a fine of not less than (50,000.00 Afs) and not more than (100,000.00 Afs), or by either punishment.

(iii) Any Person who Publishes broadcasts, airs the translation of the Work under his own name or somebody else name, without a written agreement from the Author of the Work, with a consideration of circumstances shall be punished by imprisonment for a period up to one year and or with a fine of not less than (50,000.00 Afs) and not more than (100,000.00 Afs), or by either punishment.

(iv) The amounts mentioned in paragraphs (1,2,3) of this article may be amended by a suggestion of the Supreme Court and approval of Council of Minister and endorsement of the President [of the Islamic Republic of Afghanistan].

C. Registered Trademarks

a. Trademark Registration Application

Afghanistan Trademark Registration Law[①] was enacted on September 1, 2009. The law provides:

Persons or entities may apply for registration of a trademark either personally or through their respective legal representatives.

The Central Registration Office (the Trademarks Section) shall be obligated to enter the contents of trademarks into the registration book and give or send it to the applicant. The priority for a foreigner to apply for trademark registration shall be counted from the date of filing an application in a foreign country.

The Central Registration Office (the Trademarks Registration Section) shall be obligated to review the applications from the point of view of their form, nature and their compatibility with the provisions of the present law and shall either accept or reject the application within 30 days from the day of the receipt of the application. In case of rejection, the Central Registration Office shall be obligated to clearly mention the reasons for rejection. In such a case, the applicant may, within 15 days seek the remedy and resubmit his application to the Central Registration Office (the Trademarks Registration Section) or appeal the rejection to the local commercial court. If the applicant has not, within the prescribed time limit, refuted the reasons for refusal or brought a lawsuit to the court, it shall be deemed to have abandoned the application.

Article 6 of the act provides that:

The following symbols may not be used or registered as trademarks:

(i) National flag, State emblems and other symbols pertaining to domestic or foreign organizations or institutions, international organizations or institutions, or any foreign county unless their use is authorized in writing.

(ii) Adytum and pulpit or any marks which are identical or similar to symbols of a purely religious nature.

(iii) The pictures of national leaders and high-ranking authorities o f the State.

(iv) Words and 'phrases that could be confused with the government departments of Afghanistan.

(v) Marks of official organizations such as: the Red Crescent, the Red Cross, or any other similar symbols as well as any mark which is an imitation thereof.

(vi) Any marks repugnant to chastity, morality and public order.

(vii) A mark which is not distinctive in character or property or where the mark consists of names commonly given by tradition to goods, products or services, or familiar drawings and Ordinary pictures of goods and products. Such marks may be used generally, but may not be used or registered, and shall not be given any protection, as a trademark.

(viii) Geographical names where the use thereof may cause confusion as to the origin or source of the goods, products or services.

(ix) The name, surname, photograph or emblem of a third party, unless he / she or his / her heirs' prior consent to use has been obtained.

(x) Marks which may mislead the public or which contain false or deceptive information as to the origin, source, or any other characteristics of the goods, products or services, as well as marks containing an imaginary, imitated or forged trade name.

(xi) Marks containing imaginary, imitative or forged names.

(xii) Marks related to juristic or legal entities and the use of which is prohibited.

---

① Regulatory information from the URL sitehttp://www.wipo.int/wipolex/en/text.jsp?file_id=235961.

(xiii) Use of company marks published and disseminated in Afghanistan unless authorized by their owners.

(xiv) Marks related to identical goods or services or similar registered trademarks or symbols.

(xv) Marks, which are used for specific purposes. Identical or similar signs for goods or services which are identical or similar to those in respect of which the trademark is registered where such use would result in a likelihood of confusion.

b. Validity Period of Trademarks Registration

The trademarks shall be protected from the date of the submission of the application to the Central Registration Office (Trademarks Registration section). The ownership of a trademark belongs to the person that used it for the first time, unless proven otherwise by a court. A registered trademark shall be valid for a period often (10) years, which may, upon request by the owner, be extended for successive 10-year periods, the owner of the trademark shall, within six months prior to expiry o f the period set forth.

c. The Right to Ownership of the Trademark Shall Terminate in the Following Cases

(i) Cessation of trade, industry, agriculture and services, which may relate to ownership of specific trademarks;

(ii) Sale or other transfers of the right of ownership to a third party in accordance with Provisions of law;

(iii) Failure to apply for renewal o f the trademark registration right within six months o f expiration of the registration;

(iv) where it is proved that the trademark has not been used for three consecutive years, the relevant commercial court may issue an order concerning termination thereof, unless the owner of the trademark (the first person) provides justification for the non-use thereof within the specified period of time. Under such circumstances, the trademark shall, upon application by the person in whose name the trademark has been registered, be registered taking into account the provision set forth in sub-Article (2) of Article (9) of the present law.

d. Period of Limitations of the Lawsuit

The period of limitations for hearing the lawsuit related to registration trademark shall be one year, and the claim of those who fail to object thereto within the said period following the registration date of the trademark shall not be valid.

e. Punishments

(i) A person shall, on account of the following violations, be convicted, as the circumstances may warrant, to make compensation in proportion to the damages being incurred.

Use of a false or forged trademark, which has already been registered with the Central Registration Office (Trademarks Registration Section) in accordance with the provisions of the present law in such a way as to mislead the public. Deliberate use of a forged or imitated trademark. Use of a trademark belonging to a third party for his / her own commercial products without the consent o f the owner thereof. Deliberate sale, supply for sale, distribution or possession of goods, products or services bearing a forged, imitative or unlawful mark.Use of a mark set forth under Article 6 of the present law. Mention of medals diplomas, rewards or grades of distinction in respect of goods, products or services which may not relate thereto, or in respect of commercial institution or entity, which it may not have acquired in fact. Use of distinctions being granted to the goods, products to be displayed in exhibition, or common services unless the source and nature of the said distinctions are clearly indicated. Use of geographical indications of a famous area in manufacturing goods, products or fixed services on the goods, products or services in such a manner as to indicate as if such goods, products or services have been manufactured and created in the said area, and resulting in misleading the public.

(ii) In case of repeated violations as provided for in sub-Article (1) of the present Article, the violator shall be incur double damages or a term of imprisonment not less than 6 months and not exceeding one year.

(iii) The competent court shall, in addition to convicting the violator of punishments provided for in the present chapter, order sequestration of goods and the products constituting subject matter of the violation, sums acquired as the result of the violation, means being employed in perpetration of violation, as well as closing down of the work site for a period of six months, and in case of repeated violation, stoppage of work permanently.

D. Apply for Patent[①]

The Afghan Patent Management Agency is the Trademark Registration Office of the Ministry of Commerce and Industry. According to the Afghan Foreign Patent Registration Act, Afghanistan can provide local registration for patents that have been obtained in other countries in the past, and the application must be within 2 years of the approval of the patent by the original ratifying country. The documents to be submitted when applying for a patent

---

① Regulatory information from the URL http://af.mofcom.gov.cn/article/ddfg/201109/20110907755599.shtml.

are as follows:
  (i) Information of the applicant and the inventor, including name, address, contact information, identification, etc.;
  (ii) If a foreigner applies for a patent, he / she must present relevant information of the original ratifying country;
  (iii) Relevant technical information;
  (iv) Pictures or photos, etc.
  In addition, you need to fill in the application form at the trademark registration office, and you can usually entrust a local lawyer to handle it.

VI. Environmental Protection

Water and forests are among the scarcest resources in Afghanistan. The study found that humanitarian action to integrate the environment into Afghanistan is very limited. In 2007, Afghanistan enacted strict environmental protection regulations—Islamic Republic of Afghanistan Environment Law.[1]

A. The Competent Department of Environmental Protection

The National Environmental Protection Agency, as an independent institutional entity, is responsible for coordinating and monitoring conservation and rehabilitation of the environment, and for implementing this Act.
  The National Environmental Protection Agency shall carry out the following functions and powers:
  (i) Maintain environmental integrity and promote the sustainable use of natural resources;
  (ii) Promote conservation and rehabilitation of the environment;
  (iii) Coordinate environmental affairs at the local, national and international levels;
  (iv) Develop and implement national environmental policies and strategies in order to integrate environmental issues and sustainable development approaches into the legal and regulatory frameworks;
  (v) Provide environmental management services in the areas of environmental impact assessment, air and water quality management, waste management, pollution control, and permitting of related activities;
  (vi) Establish communication and outreach for environmental information to ensure improved awareness of environmental issues;
  (vii) Implement bilateral or multilateral environmental agreements to which Afghanistan is a Party;
  (viii) Implement the Convention on the International Trade in Endangered Species of Fauna and Flora (CITES);
  (ix) Sign on behalf of the government agreements regarding the protection and rehabilitation of the environment;
  (x) Promote and manage the Islamic Republic of Afghanistan's accession to and ratification of bilateral and multilateral environmental agreements;
  (xi) Coordinate the preparation and implementation of a national programme for environmental monitoring and effectively utilize the data provided by that programmed;
  (xii) prepare every two years in relation to urban areas and every five years in relation to rural areas a State of the Environment report for the Islamic Republic of Afghanistan for submission to the President's Office;
  (xiii) Prepare an interim State of the Environment report on emerging issues relevant to the environment in Afghanistan not less than every two years;
  (xiv) Within a period of three years of promulgation of this Act, develop a national environmental action plan, which assesses the urgency and importance of actions that should be taken in the short, medium and long-term in order to prevent, eliminate and reduce adverse effects as described in the most recent State of the Environment report, and, in consultation with relevant ministries and institutions, determines a coordinated strategy and schedule for the implementation of those actions;
  (xv) Periodically compile and publish reports on significant environmental indicators;
  (xvi) On an annual basis, compile and publish a report that details the authorizations granted and activities undertaken by the National Environmental Protection Agency;
  (xvii) Assess the effectiveness of the implementation of the Act and any regulations made under it in improving the sustainability of the use and management of natural resources and conservation and rehabilitation of the environment;
  (xviii) Develop and implement plans for environmental training, environmental education and environmental awareness-raising in cooperation with relevant ministries and public bodies;
  (xix) Actively coordinate and cooperate with ministries, Provincial Councils and District and Village Councils,

---

[1] Regulatory information from the URL https://www.afghan-web.com/environment/environmental_law/.

public bodies and the private sector on all issues related to sustainable use of natural resources and conservation and rehabilitation of the environment;

(xx) Monitor the implementation of the objectives and provisions of this law;

(xxi) Fulfill any other functions that may be assigned by the Council of Ministers.

B. Overview of Environmental Laws and Regulations

Islamic Republic of Afghanistan Environment Law (25 January 2007)[①]. This Act has been promulgated to give effect to Article 15 of the Constitution of Afghanistan and provide for the management of issues relating to rehabilitation of the environment and the conservation and sustainable use of natural resources, living organisms and non-living organisms.

(i) This Law Establishes The Principle Of Public Participation In The Environmental Impact.

Affected persons may express their opinion on the proposed project, plan, policy or activity, the preliminary assessment, the environmental impact statement, the final record of opinion and the comprehensive mitigation plan, before the approval of the project, plan, policy or activity, and the proponent must demonstrate to the National Environmental Protection Agency that affected persons have had meaningful opportunities, through independent consultation and participation in public hearings, to express their opinions on these matters on a timely basis.

In regard to a proposed project, plan, policy or activity that is likely to have highly significant adverse effects on the environment, affected persons must be allowed the opportunity to participate at each of the phases referred to in sub-article 1 by the National Environmental Protection Agency and relevant institutions.

The National Environmental Protection Agency shall not reach a decision on any application for a permit until such time that the proponent has demonstrated to the satisfaction of the National Environmental Protection Agency that the proponent has distributed copies of the document to affected persons, informed the public that the document is being made available for public review by advertising the document and displaying a copy of it for inspection, and convened and recorded the proceedings of a public hearing.

After the National Environmental Protection Agency has reviewed the conditions set forth in sub-article 3, the National Environmental Protection Agency shall reach a decision and inform the public of that decision and make available any relevant documentation or information for public review.

(ii) General Prohibition And Duty Of Care In Relation To Waste Management.

No person may collect, transport, sort, recover, store, dispose of or otherwise manage waste in a manner that results in a significant adverse effect. Every person who imports, produces, collects, recovers, transports, keeps, treats or disposes of waste shall take all reasonable measures to prevent a significant adverse effect on the environment from occurring.

The owner or occupier of every premises upon which hazardous waste is produced shall ensure that all hazardous waste is separated from other waste, and is stored in separate containers pending disposal, in accordance with the requirements of the National Environmental Protection Agency as set out in regulations, published guidelines or license conditions. A person shall not dispose of waste in such a manner that it becomes litter or is likely to become litter.

(iii) Make a special list to protect water resources, control and prevent desertification, and give priority to, afforestation and vegetation restoration measures of local species.

C. Environmental Assessment

Every person, pursuant to this Act, Specifically, the responsibilities of the national environmental protection agency are included: Within a period of three years of promulgation of this Act, develop a national environmental action plan, which assesses the urgency and importance of actions that should be taken in the short, medium and long-term in order to prevent, eliminate and reduce adverse effects as described in the most recent State of the Environment report, and, in consultation with relevant ministries and institutions, determines a coordinated strategy and schedule for the implementation of those actions.

The Committee for Environmental Coordination is hereby established in order to promote the integration and coordination of environmental issues and the fundamental principles set out in this Act. The Committee will be composed of representatives of all relevant ministries, national institutions, Provincial Councils and District and Village Councils, and civil society organizations. Making recommendations to coordinate environmental activities including cooperation on environmental impact assessment procedures.

---

① Regulatory information from the URL https://www.afghan-web.com/environment/environmental_law/.

VII. Dispute Resolution

A. Dispute Resolution Methods and Institutions[①]

In Afghanistan, disputes can be settled in two ways: by court decision and by arbitration.

a. Court System

Afghanistan's judicial system is divided into three levels. At the most basic level, there are about 350 local courts. The middle level is the appeals court, which is located in Afghan provinces; the highest level is the Supreme Court in the capital Kabul.

Law on Organization and Jurisdiction of Courts (June 30, 2013) and Law on Organization and Jurisdiction of Special Courts[②](July 12, 2010) provide that:

The Supreme Court has established Special Courts within the structure of the Supreme Court to resolve special cases.

These courts are named the following:
(i) The Primary and Appellate Narcotics Courts;
(ii) The Primary and Appellate Courts of Crimes against Internal and External Security;
(iii) The Primary and Final Courts of Property Disputes;
(iv) The Specialized Family Court;
(v) The Specialized Juvenile Court;
(vi) The registration of commercial documents and trademarks shall be governed by the jurisdiction of the commercial court.

b. Arbitration Institution

In September 2015, the Afghan commercial dispute arbitration center (ACDR)[③], jointly run by the Afghan chamber of commerce and industry and a financial institution called Harakat, opened in Kabul. Once established, the center will handle commercial disputes from all over the country.

Commercial disputes the shortage of professional mediation organization is traders face a big problem, in the past, in the domestic need to solve business disputes through the stage of 47, spent more than 1600 days, and consume a large amount of money.

The Alternative dispute resolution (ADR) in Afghanistan is governed by the Commercial Mediation Law and Commercial Arbitration Law[④], which repeal the Commercial Mediation Law of 1995. The Afghanistan Chamber of Commerce and Industries (ACCI) plays a vital role in resolving business disputes by offering mediation and arbitration services.

a) The Scope of Application of Commercial Arbitration Law (2007)

The provisions of this Law, except ARTICLEs 11 and CHAPTER 7, apply only if the place of Arbitration is in Afghanistan. This Law shall not apply to certain disputes, which are not subject to Arbitration or the resolution of which is regulated under other legislation. Arbitration can be done in two ways, domestic or international. Arbitration is international: If in the contract it is described as such; If the transaction occurs between two or more countries although this has not been mentioned in the agreement. If it has not been mentioned in the agreement, the law of the country where the parties are transacting business shall be applicable; In situations not stipulated by paragraph a) of this article it is called domestic arbitration.

b) Jurisdiction of the Arbitral Tribunal

The Arbitral Tribunal has the following powers: To resolve any matter within its jurisdiction. To resolve objections with respect to the existence or validity of the Arbitration Agreement. A provision or clause that forms part of an Arbitration contract shall be treated as an independent Agreement and a decision by the Arbitral Tribunal that the contract is null and void shall not invalidate that provision or clause of the Arbitration contract.

c) Selection of Arbitral Institution

Absent an Agreement by the parties to conduct an Arbitration without using an Arbitral institution, if the parties do not specify and cannot agree upon an Arbitral institution under which the Arbitration will be conducted, the

---

① Regulatory information from the URL http://www.wipo.int/wipolex/en/details.jsp?id=13856, Law on Organization and Jurisdiction of Courts..
② Regulatory information from the URL http://www.wipo.int/wipolex/en/details.jsp?id=13855, Law on Organization and Jurisdiction of Special Courts http://www.wipo.int/wipolex/en/details.jsp?id=13857, Commercial Arbitration Law.
③ Regulatory information from the URL http://af.mofcom.gov.cn/article/ddfg/201509/20150901103735.shtml.
④ Regulatory information from the URL http://www.wipo.int/edocs/lexdocs/laws/en/af/af027en.pdf.

Arbitral institution shall be determined by a Court, which decision shall not be subject to further appeal.

d) Usage of Language in Arbitration Proceeding

The parties are free to agree on the language or languages to be used in the Arbitral proceedings. Failing such Agreement, the Arbitral Tribunal shall determine the language or languages to be used in the proceedings. Any Agreement or determination as to language, unless otherwise agreed upon by the parties, shall apply to any written statement by a party, any hearing and any Award, decision or other communication by the Arbitral Tribunal. The Arbitral Tribunal may order that any documentary evidence be accompanied by a translation into the language or languages agreed upon by the parties or determined by the Arbitral Tribunal.

B. Applicable Law

The Afghan chamber of commerce and industry plays an important role in resolving commercial disputes by providing mediation and arbitration services. Under Commercial Arbitration Law (2007), the Arbitral Tribunal shall decide the dispute in accordance with the rules of Law chosen by the parties. Failing any designation by the parties or when there is a conflict of laws, the Arbitral Tribunal shall apply the Law it considers applicable.

VIII. Others

A. Invitation of Tender and Tender

a. Invitation of Tender and Tender

Afghan ministries and commissions and foreign aid projects in Afghanistan use international bidding methods. The project tender notice will be published on newspapers, media and networks, and list the qualifications, funds and technical requirements for bidders. In some projects, the owner may also adopt a negotiation method to designate the enterprise to execute the project.

b. Licensing Procedures

If the enterprise participates in the bidding, it will be required to provide the qualification certificate, the relevant information of the past performance (completion of the project) and the bidding documents, guarantee letters, etc., and these materials and certificates need to be confirmed by the owner or contractor.

B. Other Matters Needing Attention

In the process of investment, trade, contracting engineering and labor cooperation in Afghanistan, special attention should be paid to the investigation, analysis and assessment of relevant risks beforehand, and risk avoidance and management should be done in a timely manner to effectively protect their own interests. This includes credit investigations and assessments of project or trade customers and related parties, analysis and avoidance of political and commercial risks in investment or contracted engineering countries, and feasibility analysis of implementation projects. It is recommended that relevant enterprises actively use insurance, guarantees, banks and other insurance financial institutions and other professional risk management agencies to protect their own interests. Including trade, investment, contracting and labor credit insurance, property insurance, personal safety insurance, bank factoring business and Forfeiting business, various types of guarantee business (government guarantee, commercial guarantee, guarantee).

The most important thing to pay attention to when investing in cooperation is to avoid safety and avoid investing in safe and unsafe locations or contracting projects. Projects have been implemented in hazardous areas, safety awareness should be strengthened, safety precautions should be taken seriously, and safety should be ensured. In addition, local laws and regulations should be observed and local customs and practices should be respected.

C. Contact Information of Major Official Institutions[①]

a. Ministry of Commerce and Industries

Address: Darluman Road Kabul, Afghanistan
fax: 0093-798013276
URL: www.commerce.gov.af

---

① This information comes from the following url: http://af.mofcom.gov.cn/article/ddfg/201109/20110907755599.shtml.

b. Ministry of Foreign Affairs

Address: Ministry of Foreign Affairs of Afghanistan Malek Asghar St. Kabul, Afghanistan
URL: www.mfa.gov.af

c. Ministry of Justice

URL: www.moj.gov.af
Tel: 0093 -202100322

d. Afghanistan Investment Support Agency

Address: Opposite to Ministry of Foreign Affairs, Kabul-Afghanistan

阿尔巴尼亚

作者：Genc Boga、Jonida Skendaj、Elion Shkodrani、Dorant Ekmekçiu
译者：胡静、陈赞

一、概述

（一）政治、经济、社会和法律环境概述

阿尔巴尼亚地处东欧和西欧主要走廊的天然十字路口，据有重要的战略、经济和地理位置。阿尔巴尼亚是一个改革中国家。改革重点是提供商业便利、市场自由、低税率和强有力的激励机制以及提供积极主动、受过良好教育并且具有成本竞争力的劳动力。近年来，随着国内经济增长和出口不断扩大，阿尔巴尼亚经济一直朝着更加开放和自由的模式快速发展，对内投资在整体经济转型中发挥着关键作用。

阿尔巴尼亚语是该国官方语言，隶属印欧语系。意大利语和英语是该国最常用的外语。

阿尔巴尼亚是欧洲人口最年轻的国家之一。根据阿尔巴尼亚统计局的数据，截至2017年1月1日，阿尔巴尼亚的人口数量为2 874 800人。

1. 政治体系

阿尔巴尼亚是一个议会制共和国，立法、行政和司法部门分权制衡。根据1998年《宪法》的规定，议会共140席，从地区党派的名单中选出。阿尔巴尼亚议会是阿尔巴尼亚人民根据自己的意愿行使选举权选举出的代表合法组成的机构。

根据《宪法》规定，总统由议会选举产生，任期5年。阿尔巴尼亚总统是国家元首。部长理事会是国家最高执行机构，总理为部长理事会主席，由总统任命。部长人选由总理建议，通过总统令提名，最后由议会批准本届政府的组成。

全国分为12个行政区域。部长理事会选举地方行政长官为该地区的代表。每四年举行一次地方选举，选举地区议会。市长直接通过公开投票选出。司法系统由宪法法院、最高法院、上诉法院和地区法院组成。2014年7月31日，阿尔巴尼亚议会通过第115/2014号法律《阿尔巴尼亚共和国地方政府单位的行政和领土划分法》，将此前的384个城市整改为61个地方政府单位。通过2015年6月选举后，该61个地方政府单位正式设立。

2. 经济发展

为了加快经济增长步伐，阿尔巴尼亚正在实施结构化改革，进一步提高经济竞争力和生产力，创造更多的就业机会，改善治理手段并提高公共服务。

从世界银行2017年10月统计的阿尔巴尼亚最新概况可以看出，该国经济在2016年因国内需求支撑增长了3.4%。其中，两项大型外商直接投融资能源项目的私人投资和个人消费的复苏分别贡献了1.8%和2.1%的经济增长率。信贷增长和就业改善也刺激了2017年的个人消费。GDP的0.7%基本盈余第一次帮助降低了自全球经济危机以来的债务与GDP的比率，该比率在2016年达到了72.4%。平均年通货膨胀率从2015年的1.9%降至2016年的1.3%，低于阿尔巴尼亚银行目标3±1%（或2%～4%）。但阿尔巴尼亚汇款额保持稳定。由于与能源项目相关的资金流入，外商直接投资净值从2015年GDP的8%增长至8.9%。受到工业和服务业的推动，2016年就业率增长了2.5个百分点，达到48.7%，从而进一步推动了就业机会的增长。预计阿尔巴尼亚的经济前景将有所改善。在私人投资和个人消费的推动下，2017—2019年的经济增长率预计达3.5%。

3. 法律制度

阿尔巴尼亚为大陆法系国家。外国投资仍然处于优先地位，阿尔巴尼亚政府已经通过改革来促进

外国投资。法律规定对下列行业的投资为战略投资：

① 能源和采矿；
② 运输；
③ 电信；
④ 基础设施和城市废物处理；
⑤ 旅游；
⑥ 农业和渔业。

《外国投资法》意在创造一个友善的投资环境。该法旨在为所有拟在阿尔巴尼亚投资的外国人（包括自然人及法人）提供保障。以下将简要介绍阿尔巴尼亚法律框架下对外国投资的保护和特别规定：

① 无须事先获得政府授权，也没有任何行业禁止外国人投资；
② 外国资本在公司中的参股比例没有限制——允许100%全外资公司；
③ 外国投资者有权将所有资金和出资汇回国外；
④ 阿尔巴尼亚税收制度不区分对待外国和本国投资者；
⑤ 不限制购买私人住宅；
⑥ 除法律规定的为公共目的外，外国投资不得被直接或间接地征收或国有化，也不会受到任何类似措施或行动的约束；
⑦ 外国投资享有非歧视待遇，并按照法律公平有效，即时兑现；
⑧ 在任何情况下和任何时候，投资均享有平等和无差别待遇，并得到完全保护；
⑨ 该自由投资制度中适用于购买大部分不动产存在有限的例外情形：
- 外国人和外国实体不能购买农业用地，但可以租用，租期可长达99年；
- 仅当拟投资额是土地价格的3倍时，可购买建设用地；

（10）阿尔巴尼亚的投资者的与其投资相关的合法权利有权获得司法保护。阿尔巴尼亚《民事诉讼法》中有关于国际仲裁的相关规定。

（11）阿尔巴尼亚法律承认多种企业形式。

（二）"一带一路"倡议下与中国企业合作的现状和方向

"一带一路"被视为中国长期发展经济战略的重要推动力，预期将在很多方面对地区企业产生重大影响。中国提出了"一带一路"倡议，并对其具有很高的期待。

阿尔巴尼亚政府支持任何形式的在阿尔巴尼亚的投资计划。"一带一路"计划为改善涉及区域的基础设施创造了必要条件，从而为创建连接亚洲和欧洲的"新丝绸之路"想法提供助力，阿尔巴尼亚期望引进项目并成功实施。从历史的角度来看，由于国外对中国丝绸需求的不断增长，丝绸之路在两千多年前就已出现。

阿尔巴尼亚鼓励在互利原则基础上加强在基础设施、道路、铁路、港口和机场发展方面的合作。阿尔巴尼亚政府的目标是促进经济贸易和投资合作的发展，为经济和贸易的可持续增长创造更好的条件。

阿尔巴尼亚政府在很多场合强调，愿意增加阿尔巴尼亚产品向中国市场的出口。阿尔巴尼亚政府称，中国海关当局签订减少对阿尔巴尼亚食品检疫条款的协议将有助于其出口或有关当局之间的持续沟通，以实现进出口增长。

二、投资

（一）市场准入

1. 投资监管部门

阿尔巴尼亚没有投资监管部门。阿尔巴尼亚的外国投资不受初步授权的限制。外国投资与本国类似投资享受相同的条件和待遇。在任何情况下和任何时候，外国投资都享有平等和无差别待遇，享有充分的保护和保障。

阿尔巴尼亚仅设立少数预算机构以最大限度地利用国内外投资并促进政府与投资者之间的对话。

阿尔巴尼亚投资发展局（AIDA）是根据2010年7月15日颁布的第10303号法律《阿尔巴尼亚投资发展机构的设立、组织和运作》而设立的主管行政单位，其职能主要为：促进并支持对阿尔巴尼亚的直接投资；增强中小企业竞争力；促进货物和服务出口。

成立国家经济商业议会和投资议会，主要职能为：帮助商业团体代表、捐助者（私营部门）和阿尔巴尼亚政府之间进行调解对话，以创造有利的、非歧视性和透明的商业待遇和投资环境等。

2. 投资行业法律、法规

外国投资应遵守1993年11月2日颁布的第7764号《外国投资法》、投资双边条约、避免收入和资本双重征税的双重税收协定，并根据其性质亦应遵守2010年9月16日颁布的第10316号法律和第55/2015号法律《阿尔巴尼亚共和国战略投资法》（以下简称《战略投资法》）、第125/2013号法律《特许经营权和公私合营法》，以及其他规范市场和领域（如银行、能源、电信、视听传媒）的专门法律。

3. 投资形式

外国投资根据其性质可以采用不同的形式。外国投资可以由外国投资者直接或间接拥有，并包含在下列形式中：

① 公司（权利源自该公司的所有权益）；
② 具有经济价值并与投资有关活动中的贷款、货币负债或负债；
③ 知识产权和工业产权；
④ 动产或不动产，有形或无形或任何其他类型的所有权（应遵守"土地政策"部分规定的购买土地的某些限制）；
⑤ 法律或合同承认的任何其他权利，以及依法授予的任何许可。

4. 市场准入和审查标准

阿尔巴尼亚和中国于1993年2月13日签署了双边投资协定，规定了两国公司在彼此国家都将受到公平公正待遇和投资保护。

此外，阿尔巴尼亚和欧盟已经签署了《稳定与联合协议》，阿尔巴尼亚必须遵守欧盟委员会法规并与欧盟共同体协调立法，包括适用于一般市场和受特定监管市场的标准。

（二）外汇管理

1. 外汇监管部门

阿尔巴尼亚银行是管理持有外汇牌照从事外汇活动的实体的主要监管机构。此外，阿尔巴尼亚银行负责起草、批准和实施阿尔巴尼亚共和国的外汇制度和汇率政策。

2. 外汇法律、法规简要介绍

外汇活动应遵守阿尔巴尼亚银行监督管理委员会（BoA）于2009年9月30日由第70号决议通过的修订版《关于外汇活动的规定》。

3. 外国企业的外汇管理要求

阿尔巴尼亚不存在外汇管制。非居民可以自由地将资金和交易转让给阿尔巴尼亚居民。

从阿尔巴尼亚向国外转出资金由阿尔巴尼亚银行许可的实体代表其客户进行，客户应在此前提交法规中规定需要提交的文件以及该实体可能要求其提交的额外文件：

① 企业家和法人实体应提交：申报资金转出的目的以及转出资金的来源、资金数额和转出地址；提交决策机构关于转出执行情况的决议和国家商业中心发布的资金状态摘要；
② 个人应提交申报资金转出的目的和转出资金来源、资金数额和转出地址。

此外，在以下情况，还存在如下附加要求：

① 如果最初通过非居民银行转入到阿尔巴尼亚进行投资的资金未被使用，则向国外转出的资金需向银行提交该实体决策机构的决议，决议内容需确认投资中断且不再使用最初转入阿尔巴尼亚的资本。
② 转出公司利润（与在阿尔巴尼亚注册资本有关的收入和投资所产生的收入）需提交决策机构关

于分配和使用利润的决议。
③ 阿尔巴尼亚共和国境内往来账户或存款账户中进行的存款交易应提交相关证明文件。
④ 与国际贸易和服务条款直接相关的期限不超过一期的商业贷款需提交贷款合同。
⑤ 源自非居民个人存款和/或由此产生收入的货币转移需提交银行对账单，以确认从所述存款转移的金额。
⑥ 出售股份以及清算部分或全部投资所产生的股本和收入的转让，需提交由决策机构出具的出售或清算决议。

与商业贸易（货物）有关的转让，需提供下述文件：
① 转让请求，包含转让性质和目的的文件以及此前未提交过转让相同货物文件的说明；
② 指明付款方式的形式发票和/或合同。

提供服务相关的转让，除上述转让请求外，还应提交证明转让目的和/或各自合同的发票或文件。非商业转让，除上述转让请求外，还应申报与转让相关的收入来源。证券和类似金融工具的交易以及行使相关权利，只能根据双方签订的合同通过银行机构或其他许可机构进行。阿尔巴尼亚居民或非居民拟向阿尔巴尼亚境外实际转移金额超过100万列克的或对应金额的外币，应向海关当局申报转移的来源和目的。

临时访问阿尔巴尼亚的非居民可将境外货币兑换为阿尔巴尼亚的现金和/或旅行支票，兑换的金额以入境阿尔巴尼亚共和国时向海关当局申报的金额为准。根据入关时填写的申报表和申报金额差异的支持文件，该等金额应被认定具有合理性。

（三）金融

1. 主要金融机构

（1）银行系统

2006年12月通过的银行法规定了双重银行体系。私人银行注册资本不得低于10亿阿尔巴尼亚列克，并且必须注册为股份制公司。商业银行和其他金融机构可在阿尔巴尼亚银行监督管理委员会的监管下提供一系列服务。

（2）中央银行

阿尔巴尼亚银行负责制作和提供金融部门和对外部门的数据，在国家统计系统中发挥着重要作用。对外部门的数据包含收支平衡、国际储备和外汇流动性、商品进出口、国际投资头寸、外汇汇率和外债的指标。

阿尔巴尼亚银行监督管理委员会是直接对阿尔巴尼亚议会负责的独立法律实体，其主要目标为实现和维持币值稳定。阿尔巴尼亚银行监督管理委员会同时也是负责制定和执行阿尔巴尼亚货币政策的机构。

具体而言，阿尔巴尼亚银行监督管理委员会享有下列专有权力和职责：
① 制定和执行货币政策和外汇政策。
② 阿尔巴尼亚共和国国内货币的唯一发行主体。
③ 许可、监管、规范银行和其他金融机构的活动。
④ 为银行提供信贷。
⑤ 对阿尔巴尼亚共和国的支付系统进行监管，同时促进形成高效的银行间支付和清算。
⑥ 控制和管理阿尔巴尼亚共和国国家外汇储备。
⑦ 发行国家债券和阿尔巴尼亚银行债券。

所有在阿尔巴尼亚运营的二级银行有义务：
① 按月向阿尔巴尼亚银行监督管理委员会进行报告，该报告应包括资产负债表和月度损益表、外汇账户余额、银行董事会管理的变更（如有）、银行的网络结构数据、利率、信贷敞口、各经济部门的信贷情况、高风险控制、资本充足率（包括所有风险）、风险加权资产、表外项目和监管资本金。
② 维持阿尔巴尼亚银行监督管理委员会监管法案要求的强制准备金。
③ 按月报告呆账。

④ 维持《巴塞尔协议》规定的至少 12% 的资本充足率。
⑤ 向位于财政部附近的预防洗钱总理事会报告：
- 在 24 小时内以一笔交易或者几笔关联交易的形式实施的所有金额大于或等于 100 万阿尔巴尼亚列克或者等价的其他货币的现金交易；
- 所有其他可疑交易。
⑥ 在阿尔巴尼亚银行监督管理委员会限定的范围内维持开放的货币地位。
⑦ 遵守阿尔巴尼亚银行监督管理委员会批准的规范外汇活动的规定。

2. 外国企业融资条件

阿尔巴尼亚对外国企业不存在特别的或差异性的融资条件。根据外国企业在阿尔巴尼亚拟从事的投资项目，融资可能包括特许经营权/PPP 立法下的项目融资或额外抵押融资。

（四）土地政策

根据 1995 年 7 月 27 日颁布的第 7980 号法律《关于土地买卖》第 5 条的规定，外国个人或公司可以在已经进行土地投资的情况下取得本国土地，但投资不得少于土地价值的 3 倍。根据施工许可，他们可以直接租用当地土地。该限制不适用于被外国人拥有或控制的或存在外国董事的或主要项目由外商投资的当地企业。

在阿尔巴尼亚拥有建筑物或者农业用地不动产的外国个人或法人应缴纳建筑物和农业用地税。地拉那建筑工程不动产的税率是投资价值的 2%～4%，其他地区为 1%～3%。财产税也适用于农业用地，税率从每公顷 700～5 600 阿尔巴尼亚列克不等，视使用情况而定。商业用途建筑物的财产税率为每平方米 200～400 阿尔巴尼亚列克不等，取决于建筑物所在的位置。自 2018 年 4 月 1 日起，财产税将从每平方米固定金额变更为超出建筑物市值的 a%。自 2016 年 1 月 1 日起，城市土地也开始以每公顷 1 400～5 600 阿尔巴尼亚列克征税。

（五）公司的成立和解散

阿尔巴尼亚现行有效的规制商业组织的商法（第 9901 号《关于股东和商业公司法》）于 2008 年 5 月 21 日生效。该法效仿德国、意大利和英国的商业立法。商法是商业组织立法的主要法律，旨在使阿尔巴尼亚的法律和其他欧洲国家以及欧盟的法律协调一致。

1. 企业形式

阿尔巴尼亚的外国投资者对于业务运营的组织形式有多种选择，可以设立本地公司、分支机构或者代表处。国家注册中心（NRC）根据 2007 年 5 月 3 日的第 9723 号法律《关于国家注册中心》于 2007 年 9 月 1 日开始承担阿尔巴尼亚新实体的注册登记业务，旨在实施一站式服务制度。但是，2015 年 11 月 26 日第 131 号法律《关于国家商业中心》颁布，该法旨在通过国家商业中心（NBC）一站式完成注册和许可手续，进一步促进阿尔巴尼亚的商业发展便利化。因此，国家商业中心将取代国家注册中心和国家许可中心。

根据阿尔巴尼亚的法律框架，以下商业实体需要在国家商业中心注册：
- 个人独资企业——Tregtari；
- 无限合伙企业——Shoqeri Kolektive；
- 有限合伙企业——Shoqeri Komandite；
- 有限责任公司——Shoqeri me Pergjegjesi te Kufizuar；
- 股份有限公司——Shoqeri Aksionare；
- 合资企业—Shoqeria e Thjeshte。

（1）个人独资企业

个人独资企业以该个人的名义进行交易。成立个人独资企业的个人需向开展业务地区的国家商业中心提交申请表和身份证明。申请表包括个人的详细信息、地址、经营类型和本人的签名样本。

（2）无限合伙企业

全体合伙人对合伙企业债务承担连带责任。无限合伙企业中，除非章程另有约定，全体合伙人均被认为是合伙企业的管理人。每一合伙人在面对第三方时均代表合伙企业。无限合伙企业应发布年度财务报告。合伙人的权利、义务和责任应以书面形式规定在章程中，并在国家商业中心备案。

（3）有限合伙企业

有限合伙企业在实践中很少存在，通常包括一个或多个承担无限责任的合伙人和一个或多个以其在初始资本中的出资额为限承担责任的合伙人。有限合伙人即使被授予代理权，也不参与合伙企业的管理。如果其参与管理，则将承担无限责任。有限合伙企业不会因一个或多个有限合伙人的死亡或退出而解散。

（4）有限责任公司

有限责任公司为阿尔巴尼亚最常见的商业组织形式。有限责任公司可以由一个或多个个人或法人设立。通常情况下，股东以出资额为限对公司的损失承担责任。

有限责任公司的最低出资额为 100 阿尔巴尼亚列克。出资形式可以为现金或实物（有形资产或无形资产）。

董事由股东大会提名，任期不超过 5 年，可连任。股东大会的普通决议，必须经持有公司 30% 以上股份的股东到场并通过方为有效。

股东大会作出修改公司章程、增加或者减少注册资本、公司合并和分立或者利润分配的特别决议，必须经出席会议的股东 3/4 以上多数通过，且到会参与表决的股东必须超过拥有表决权的股东的半数。

股东大会的决议应当制作会议记录，会议记录由董事会保存。

（5）股份有限公司

股份有限公司的股本由股份组成，一般情况下，股东以其认购的股本为限对公司的损失承担责任。非公开募集的私人公司的初始资本最低为 3 500 000 阿尔巴尼亚列克，上市公司最低为 10 000 000 阿尔巴尼亚列克。

当股东已承诺将资产以现金或等价实物的形式转移至公司时，资本即已足额认缴。在认缴股本时，就现金出资的股份，至少 1/4 的股本票面价值必须以现金形式支付。剩余股本经公司管理层同意可以分期缴纳。实物出资的股东在认缴时须完成全部交付。商法不允许以服务形式出资。

在国家商业中心完成登记之前，股份上附加的权利不得转让。每股票面价值相同。

股份有限公司可以发行"普通股"或"优先股"。优先股不享有投票权且在任何情况下不得超过注册股本的 49%。

商法规定股份公司可以采用灵活的管理制度。股份公司可以选择采用"单层"制（董事会兼具管理和监督职能）或者"双层"制（设立董事会和独立履行监督职能的监事会）。

（6）合资企业

阿尔巴尼亚法律承认"简单公司"条款下的合资企业，其基于合伙人之间的协议而产生。

根据《民法典》(第 1074—1112 条）的规定，合资企业可由两个或两个以上同意从事经济活动并分享由此产生利润的主体设立，包括自然人或法人，外国人或本国人。合伙企业没有最低资本要求。合伙人有义务按照协议出资。除非另有约定，每一合伙人都可参加合资企业的管理，并拥有完全的权利在合伙范围内开展活动。

除另有约定外，每一合伙人均有权在账目被批准后获得其利润份额。除非其能够证明不存在过错，否则合伙人应共同承担法律和合伙协议所规定的义务。

2. 设立程序

在国家商业中心注册新公司，需要提供下列文件：

① 公司法定代表人或授权委托书中授权人员填写并提交的申请表（标准表格）；

② 公司章程和/或章程；

③ 公司董事提名决议；

④ 根据商业实体的法律形式，可能需要在公司章程/章程中陈述或向国家商业中心提交的额外和特殊信息。

向国家商业中心申请注册分支机构或代表处，需要提交下列文件：

① 分公司／代表处或母公司的代表或上述任何人签发的授权委托书中授权人员填写并提交的申请表（标准表格）。

② 母公司的公司章程和章程以及所有修正案。

③ 近期从母公司所在国家商业协会获取并在申请日前 90 天内出具的文件，以确认下列内容：

• 母公司原所在国商业登记处的注册登记证；

• 公司不存在解散或破产的情况；

• 公司管理层的组成。

④ 母公司董事会或根据其章程授权的公司任何其他机构的决议，内容包括在阿尔巴尼亚设立分支机构或代表处并任命该阿尔巴尼亚分支机构或代表处的法定代表人（经理）。

⑤ 母公司上一财政年度的财务报表和审计报告。

3. 公司解散的程序和要求

发生下述情形时，商业公司将予以解散：

① 营业期限到期；

② 破产程序完成或资产不足以支付破产费用；

③ 由于公司法人团体持续不运作或其他情况，使得商业活动无法继续，从而导致商业目的无法实现；

④ 公司章程无效；

⑤ 由于亏损或公司决定减少股本（并且不存在通过后续增资以弥补该减少的有效条件）导致公司净资产低于最低注册资本价值；

⑥ 公司章程规定的其他情形；

⑦ 法律规定的其他情形；

⑧ 股东大会决定的其他原因。

（六）清算程序

根据 2008 年 4 月 14 日颁布的第 9901 号法律《股东和商业公司法》及其修正案，以及 2007 年 5 月 3 日生效的第 9723 号法律《关于国家商业中心》，公司的解散包括清算和从阿尔巴尼亚商业注册处注销两个阶段的程序。

1. 第一阶段

第一阶段，独资股东必须向国家商业中心提交以下文件：

① 独资股东决议：结束公司活动及开始清算程序；任命清算人。

② 独资公司所注册的商业注册处出具的最新摘录（出具日不早于向国家商业中心申请日期前 90 天），该摘录反映了股东在原所在国的商业注册处的注册及其管理机构的组成（合法认证）。

③ 签署上述决议的独资股东代表的护照复印件。

上述所有文件必须翻译成阿尔巴尼亚语并且由公证处进行公证（认证）。

上述文件向国家商业中心提交后，公司的管理者将不再享有公司的管理权，且视为自动解职。清算人应向第三方（包括银行）代表公司。此外，在这一阶段，清算人应履行以下职责：

① 编制清算开始阶段的财务报表；如清算时间持续超过 1 年，清算人应同时编制公司的年度财务报表。

② 准备并向国家商业中心提交两份通知，间隔 30 天向公司的债权人通知清算程序启动。根据第 9901/2008 号法律《股东和商业公司法》第 199 条的规定，清算人不得在早于第二份通知发出后 1 个月内结束清算程序。

③ 编制清算结束财务报表。为确认公司的税务状况，税务机关通常在纳税人清算过程中进行税务审计。实践中，公司／清算人应向当地税务机关提交一份说明经营活动已结束并要求税务审计或其他注销相关行为的请求。上述与税务机关相关程序可能持续 6～8 个月。

2. 第二阶段

第二阶段，清算人应进行不同的必要交易，以偿还未清偿的债务、出售公司资产（如有）、终止雇用合同和／或其他合同（基于公司的需要）、向公司的债权人付款（如有）、将余额转交给股东等。此外，清算人应在清算过程中编制最终财务报表和公司管理最终报告。

上述行为完成后，清算人应邀请独资股东就以下事项达成决议：

① 批准最终财务报表和清算人对公司的管理行为合规（两者均由清算人准备）；
② 撤销对清算人的授权；
③ 批准结束清算。

在国外签署的该决议应为原件，以独资股东的抬头纸打印（无须公证或合法认证）。该决议应在30日内向国家商业中心备案，以便公司在商业公司注册处注销。

（七）并购

阿尔巴尼亚共和国境内的并购主要由以下法律、法规进行调整：

① 2008年4月14日颁布的第9901号法律《股东和商业公司法》及其修正案；
② 2003年7月28日颁布的第9121号法律《保护竞争法》及其修正案；
③ 阿尔巴尼亚竞争管理局发布的指令和规定。

其他适用于特定行业并购的法规包括：

① 视听传媒业：任何实体或个人均不允许持有国有视听传媒公司超过40%的股份。持有一家国有视听传媒公司股份的实体或个人不允许在另一家国有视听传媒公司持有超过20%的股份。持有一家当地或区域性的视听传媒公司股份的实体或个人不允许在另一家当地或区域性的视听传媒公司持有超过40%的股份。任何所有权或相关事项的变更应获得视听传媒管理局的事先书面批准。

② 银行业：BoA有权批准或拒绝10%以上的银行股份转让或足够使股东对银行管理或政策产生重大影响的股份转让。

③ 保险业：金融监管局作为监管机构有权批准或拒绝从事保险和／或再保险的公司中大于或等于10%的有投票权的股份转让，以及虽然小于10%但能够授予对保险公司管理控制权的股份转让。此外，公司如需进一步持有保险公司投票权或股本达到或超过20%、30%、50%或75%，另需获得金融监管局的批准。

④ 电信业：电信牌照持有人的任何变更应通知电子与邮政通信管理局或获得其批准。

（八）竞争监管

1. 竞争监管部门

阿尔巴尼亚竞争管理局负责2003年7月28日颁布的第9121号法律《保护竞争法》有关规定的监管和执行。

2. 竞争法简介

根据阿尔巴尼亚和欧盟签署的《稳定与联合协议》，阿尔巴尼亚法律框架中的竞争法接近欧盟既有法规。

该法管辖以限制或阻碍竞争为目标或效果的协议（禁止协议），例如瓜分市场、固定定价或其他交易条件、同一交易适用不同条件、一家或多家公司滥用其支配地位（如通过固定滥用的交易条件和价格、拒绝供应等）以及满足特定要求的集中，其评估标准为是否在阿尔巴尼亚市场造成竞争隐患问题（如建立或加强支配地位）。

此外，竞争管理局还需对具有竞争法律维度的法律及相关法律文件提出意见。

3. 调控竞争的措施

竞争管理局发布了适用于阿尔巴尼亚公司和外国公司的法规和指令，只要其活动在阿尔巴尼亚市场具有影响力，即应适用。

（九）税收

1. 税收制度和规定

税收制度包括企业所得税、增值税、消费税、个人所得税、小企业简易利得税和地方税。企业所得税的征税期为日历年，而增值税、消费税、个人所得税的征税期为日历月。

税收制度的现代化开始于 1997 年 10 月，增值税自此取代了营业税。初始增值税税率为 12.5%，随后上调至 20%。1999 年 1 月，为符合 WTO 的要求而制定的《海关法》生效，该法适用更加简便，留给个人解释的空间更少。1998 年颁布的所得税法废除了此前的大部分免税政策。

阿尔巴尼亚政府于 2006 年实施了鼓励投资的低税率政策。2008 年，政府对所有收入（无论是个人收入或商业收入）均按 10% 的统一税率进行征税，有专门法律规定的行业部门除外（如烃类）。

此外，2008 年 5 月通过了一部关于税收程序的新法律，该法规定了纳税人权利细则、强制纳税的程序、为会计目的适当记录交易的要求等。

自 2014 年 1 月 1 日起，政府将企业所得税从 10% 上调至 15%，对就业所得实行累进税率（取代 10% 的统一税率），并提高了医疗保险缴费的计算基准。

2014 年 7 月通过的新增值税法，广泛反映了欧盟《增值税指令》。该法于 2015 年 1 月 1 日生效。

新《海关法》于 2014 年 7 月获得通过，该法完全符合《欧盟海关法典》的规定。新《海关法》部分条款于 2015 年 1 月生效，其他条款在 2018 年财政一揽子方案制定之前逐步生效。

2. 主要税种和税率

（1）企业所得税

年营业额超过 800 万阿尔巴尼亚列克的公司应按 15% 的税率缴纳企业所得税。年营业额在 500 万阿尔巴尼亚列克与 800 万阿尔巴尼亚列克之间的实体适用 5% 的简易企业所得税率。年营业额低于 500 万阿尔巴尼亚列克的实体免征简易企业所得税。

应税基数按照损益表中反映的利润确定。利润应按照现行的会计法规和财政部相关指令进行计算。

（2）个人所得税

按照阿尔巴尼亚法律，所有个人均须缴纳个人所得税。居民应对其在全球范围内的收入纳税，非居民仅对其源自阿尔巴尼亚境内的收入所得纳税。

（3）居民

经常居住地位于阿尔巴尼亚或在任何日历年内在阿尔巴尼亚累计居住超过 183 天的个人应视为阿尔巴尼亚税收居民。

（4）个人所得税税率

雇员的工资、薪水和其他收入按如下税率征税：

月度应税收入（阿尔巴尼亚列克）	税率
0～30 000	无
30 000～130 000	超过 30 000 列克的部分按 13% 征税
130 000 及以上	13 000 列克 + 超过 130 000 列克的部分按 23% 征税

其他应税收入，适用 15% 的统一税率。

（5）纳税申报及优惠

应税人应在每一纳税期间结束后下一日历月的 14 之前提交纳税申报并汇付相关款项。增值税分类账应于每一纳税期间结束后下一日历月的 10 日之前提交。

（6）个人所得税申报

年度总收入达到或超过 2 000 000 阿尔巴尼亚列克的所有居民及非居民应当填写并提交年度所得税申报表。个体经营者在商业活动中产生的收入（适用小企业简易利得税或利得税）不纳入上述阈值的计算。该申报必须在纳税期间后下一年的 4 月 30 日之前向居住地的税务理事会提交。

任何到期个人所得税（以最终税额和当期任何预缴税额和／或预扣税额的差额进行计算）当日即

应缴付。个人在当期多缴税费的,差额将予返还或用作预缴下一年度个人所得税。

(十) 证券

1. 证券相关法律、法规简介

阿尔巴尼亚证券管理法律框架主要包括 2008 年 2 月 21 日颁布的第 9879 号法律《证券法》、2009 年 10 月 15 日颁布的第 10158 号法律《公司和本地政府债券法》、2010 年 2 月 18 日颁布的第 10236 号法律《公开收购法》,以及金融监管局颁布的若干规定。

第 9879 号法律确立了证券的类型,规定了证券发行的方式和条件,证券交易和登记、证券交易的识别和履行,经授权可以从事证券交易的个人,进行公开交易证券的机构条件,投资者和证券权利人保护,无纸化证券的条件,证券登记机构的组织和运作,证券市场的交易和监管。

第 9879 号法律适用于监管投资服务、启动和停止金融工具交易程序、未来的金融交易、金融分析和上市公司股东持有的有投票权股份的变动。该法关于价格操纵和金融工具分析的条款同样适用于金融监管局授权的实体在阿尔巴尼亚境外从事的对阿尔巴尼亚证券市场的证券交易造成影响的作为和不作为。

证券是通过对持有其所衍生的权利进行管理以达到获利目的而发行或交易的金融工具。"证券"应当包括但不限于股份、企业和当地政府债券、短期国库券和阿尔巴尼亚政府债券、阿尔巴尼亚银行发行的证券、商业票据、投资基金份额或股份,或其他由金融监管局(以下简称"监管局")认可与股份、债券相当的金融工具。

证券可以是股票、债务证券、投资或养老基金份额或股份。

股票应当是证明与股份公司最低股本或注册资本份额相关权利义务的有价证券。债券应当是证明与发行人和证券持有人之间债权债务关系相关权利义务的工具。

投资基金份额或股份应当是承载与投资基金资本金份额相关权利义务的证券。养老金份额应当是承载与养老金基金资本份额相关权利义务的证券。证券应由财政经济部、阿尔巴尼亚银行、地方政府、公司或其他法人实体(以下统称"发行人")代表部长理事会发行。证券应以阿尔巴尼亚列克或其他外币发行。

证券应当在专门从事证券登记的中心进行登记,中心应当根据有关法律组建,并经监管局许可开展证券登记业务。

证券应当由证券登记机构按照有关法律规定的方式及监管局施行的规定进行发行、转让并作为电子记录留存。

2. 证券市场的监管

证券市场由金融监管局实施监管。

3. 外国企业从事证券交易的要求

可转让证券包括:
① 股票、债券和与股票、债券相当的其他证券;
② 合同或签署合同的权利,购买或收购前述第 ① 项下的证券;
③ 期货、期权和前述第 ① 项下与证券相关的金融合同,允许在证券市场上交易并由监管局监管;

代表客户从事证券交易的外国机构必须得到金融监管局的许可。

下列活动应为与证券交易相关的活动:
① 根据客户指令买进或卖出证券;
② 自行买进或卖出自有账户的证券;
③ 为投资组合所有人客户代管证券投资组合;
④ 发行代理人开展业务,包括组织、准备和实施证券认购和付款,与证券发行、公开市场上市交易准备工作相关的包括代表发行人提交上市申请在内的其他为发行人开展的工作;
⑤ 为发行筹措资金,包括为进一步向潜在投资人销售而为发行人组织、准备和实施证券发行,全

部证券或未认购证券的相关认购和付款;

⑥ 证券投资建议;

⑦ 与证券结算、交割、保管和登记相关的活动;

⑧ 证券的捐赠、交易和出借;

⑨ 为回购之目的出售证券和／或反之亦然;

⑩ 一般而言,任何被监管局认定为与证券交易相关的证券操作或合法交易。

除证券保管外,证券交易作为商业活动,只有经监管局许可且在经营内容条款中包含此类交易的经纪公司或银行方可从事此类业务。

经纪公司应为阿尔巴尼亚境内的股份公司,其业务应当是根据《证券法》的规定和监管局颁发的牌照而从事的证券交易。

对于拟从事经纪活动或证券交易等商业活动的外国实体,还应遵守以下规则:

(1) 公开发行和交易

任何拟进行公开发行的人都应依照阿尔巴尼亚金融监管局发布的规定向金融监管局提交批准招股说明书的请求。

未经金融监管局批准公开招股说明书,不可公开发售。根据《证券法》的规定,在发行人为下列特定目的发行股票的情形下,公开招股说明书不作为强制性的程序要求,例如:将利润、储备金或留存收益转增为初始股本;因公司合并增加初始股本;持有发行人75%以上表决权的股东认购并付款而增加初始股本;仅有机构投资者参与而增加初始股本;将可转换债转换为股票,且发行人在向投资人发行可转换债时已向投资者公开或交付了招股说明书;将其他形式的公司变更为股份公司。

如证券拟在受监管的市场中交易,则证券交易所应批准验收规则和规定。

拟公开发行的外国实体只能通过金融监管局正式许可的中介机构(即经纪公司或银行)进行公开发行。

外国发行人应为阿尔巴尼亚境外的证券发行人。

外国发行人只能通过该外国公司聘用为发行代理人的授权公司在阿尔巴尼亚进行证券公开发行。

授权公司可以是监管局许可从事证券交易的股票经纪公司或银行。

阿尔巴尼亚受管制市场进行的证券交易受到《证券法》有关市场滥用规定的限制。另外,拥有内幕信息的人禁止从事证券交易。

此外,禁止市场操纵行为,包括交易不会导致证券持有人变更或交易使用虚假手段,例如为了营造"真实交易正在进行"的假象进行证券买卖的虚拟订单从而抬高价格。

(2) 收购法规

《公开收购法》规定了两种要约收购行为:自愿要约收购和强制要约收购。

作为一般性规则,任何拟进行公开要约(自愿要约收购)的人须将其要约收购的决定告知金融监管局和公司管理人员。此人必须自发出该通知之日起10日内,向金融监管局提交要约收购的文件以请求批准。

任何直接或间接(即与一致行动人一同)持有足以使其控制公司的投票权份额的人,必须发起要约收购(强制要约收购)。

金融监管局应当在要约文件提交登记之日起10个工作日内作出决定。金融监管局未能在上述期限内作出决定将视为同意批准,要约人有权公布要约文件。

要约文件应当在取得金融监管局批准后立即公布。对要约的接受应当在要约文件发布之日起3～10周之内进行。

法律规定了要约收购中与要约价格相关的特殊条件。

证券交易应当在证券交易所以有组织的方式进行,以提供符合证券供求的条件。

阿尔巴尼亚的证券交易所运营应当得到金融监管局的许可。2017年7月,金融监管局向一家证券交易所颁发了牌照,名称为阿尔巴尼亚证券交易所。

(十一）优惠政策和投资保护

1. 优惠政策的框架

法律和其他法规根据不同的投资领域制定了不同的优惠政策，作为对投资者（不论是外国人或阿尔巴尼亚人）的激励。

（1）对特定行业和地区的支持

阿尔巴尼亚议会于 2015 年 5 月颁布了第 55/2015 号法律《战略投资法》，作为促进和提升国内外战略投资举措的一部分。

《战略投资法》旨在激励和吸引国内外在该法确定的战略性投资领域的战略投资，通过设立特别优惠政策，促进或加快行政程序以为投资者提供支持和服务。该法确立了国家机构审查、通过和支持国内外战略投资以及通过"特别窗口"（负责向战略投资者提供服务的部门）向战略投资者提供服务的程序和规则。

此外，《战略投资法》确定了以下领域为战略领域：能源和矿业；运输、电子通信基础设施以及城市垃圾；旅游（旅游结构）；农业（大型农场）和渔业；经济地区；优先发展地区。

确定战略投资的标准是投资价值，《战略投资法》对不同领域的标准均作出了规定。例如，在对运输、电子通信基础设施以及城市垃圾行业的投资中，获得"战略投资者，辅助程序"地位并获益的投资人或项目，投资额必须等于或大于 3 000 万欧元；获得"战略投资者，特别程序"地位并获益的投资者或项目，投资额必须等于或大于 5 000 万欧元（获得战略投资者地位的程序类型见下文）。

其他标准包括投资的实施时间表、投资产能和增值；创造新的就业岗位；行业的经济次序；区域和地方经济发展；发展或提高产品生产或服务提供的条件或标准；提供新技术以有效地增加竞争和投资；提高总体安全水平以及城市居民的生活质量；保护环境和消费者。

《战略投资法》规定了两种申请程序："辅助程序"，公共行政机构在实施的整个阶段跟进、协调、帮助、监管，以及根据具体情况代表战略投资；"特别程序"，对在经济、就业、工业、技术和/或地区发展等领域有影响的战略投资提供支持或特别规定，以促进和加强投资。

《战略投资法》还规定设立战略投资委员会（以下简称"委员会"），该委员会是设立在部长理事会内的合议行政机构，由总理担任主席，成员为副总理和相关战略部门的部长。该委员会获得了阿尔巴尼亚投资发展署（AIDA）的支持。AIDA 是通过"特别窗口"给投资者提供服务的行政主管单位，面向申请并获得"战略投资辅助/特别程序"地位的投资者或投资项目。

此外，AIDA 保有"战略投资登记册"，包含阿尔巴尼亚境内所有战略投资的数据。根据《战略投资法》的规定，在该法范围内与战略投资相关的、战略投资项目的准备、执行、发展和实现以及依照该法颁布许可证/同意/授权方面的行政程序均享有优先权，所有涉及的机构/实体/公共机构均采用快速程序。

（2）战略投资地位

有兴趣获得战略投资地位的投资者，无论是以辅助程序或特别程序的方式，均需向 AIDA 申请并提交以下材料：

① 商业计划、金融投资计划和为了实现项目/战略投资的工作计划；
② 社会影响评估报告；
③ 实现该投资项目的财务能力证明材料；
④ 关于数据准确性的声明；
⑤ 投资者书面授权，授权 AIDA 采取必要手段验证其提交的数据，以及同意 AIDA 公布投资的有关细节，除非投资者认为这些数据具有保密性质；
⑥ 支付申请费用的凭证。

在辅助程序下，可为投资者提供下述措施：
① 实施初步行动并准备行政文件；
② 确认土地状况，支持项目；
③ 通过辅助基础设施提供支持；

④通过销售或租赁协议，提供可获得的国家不动产，用以开发和完成战略投资项目。

在特别程序下，可为投资者提供下述措施和保证：

①征用私人拥有的不动产以完成战略投资项目；

②议会批准相关战略投资合同，以提高与阿尔巴尼亚政府合同关系的安全性。

《战略投资法》规定了批准"战略投资"地位的程序，以及 AIDA 为投资者提供的获得相关项目实施启动许可和授权的协助。

申请获得战略投资地位的文件提交截止日期为 2018 年年末。

（3）旅游业

《旅游法》规定，向旅游教育、推广和研究提供财政支持，以帮助旅游业发展。投资者可取得位于具有发展旅游优势地区的国有不动产长达 99 年。使用权可以以 1 欧元的象征性价格转让。

若投资者获得战略特别投资者地位，部长理事会可以视个案情况，将国有不动产的所有权转让给私人投资者，条件是全面实现投资。若部长理事会认为必要，则实现战略投资协议将提交给议会根据特定法律批准。

（4）农业

2007 年 10 月 22 日第 9817 号《农业和农村发展法》规定了支持农业发展的项目。

农业补贴方案用于增加产品竞争力的投资，以确保市场供应的稳定；提高种植技术；保护区内蔬菜种植；水产养殖和畜牧业；市场的供应稳定及农村地区家庭收入增长；增加农业市场部门的投资；提高农民使用机械工具的可能性；加强农业合作公司的形式、合作和组织。

（5）可再生能源

阿尔巴尼亚政府通过 2016 年 1 月 20 日第 27 号决定批准了《2015—2020 年可再生能源国家行动计划》，政府承诺，到 2020 年可再生能源占国家能源生产目标的 38%。"激励计划"是政府为实现目标直接参与的一项计划。这些计划与该地区其他国家相类似，指通过减少可再生能源的成本，提高出售的价格或通过可再生能源的购买义务增加购买量，或以其他方式来鼓励可再生能源的利用的任何工具、计划或机制，包括但不限于支持投资、运营、免税或降低税收、退税等。

差价合约（CFD）是合同的一种，其模式已由部长理事会批准，是可再生能源运营商和可再生资源能源生产商之间签订的合同，该生产商在拍卖中成为受益于激励方案的中标人。差价合约的激励由不断变化的补偿构成，根据可再生能源生产商作为中标人获得的奖励（确定价格）和电力能源的市场价（参考价格）之间的差额计算得出的。部长理事会在相关部长的提议下，批准组织拍卖程序以向优先能源生产商提供激励措施奖励。"优先生产商"的定义是任何可再生能源的发电商，以及发电机组装机容量达 15 兆瓦的水力生产商，这些生产商从激励计划中获益；已与可再生能源运营商签订差价合约，并在监管市场上出售能源。

参考价格是产品在监管市场中的交易价格，或直至其作为相同产品的市场可比价格出现。

根据会计准则和此前给予的其他投资支持，对可再生能源生产商的该等支持必须在其工厂投资全部支付完成时给予。差价合约的合同最长期限为 15 年。

当参考价格高于确定价格时，可再生能源生产商有义务向可再生能源运营商支付参考价和确定价格之间的差额。

（6）特殊经济领域

技术和经济开发区的发展应遵守 2007 年 7 月 19 日颁布的第 9789 号法律《技术和经济开发区的设立与运行法》。任何拟开发此类开发区的人必须获得许可。技术和经济开发区主要有以下激励措施：

①从开发区进出口货物必须遵守《海关法》的规定；

②开发者和使用者在前五年的活动中有资格享有 50% 的所得税减免；

③开发区开发者和使用者在投资前三年可享有其每年资本支出 20% 的税收减免（适用于正常折旧以外的支出），期限为 2 年；

④开发区开发者免征新建筑对基础设施的影响税；

⑤开发区内的新建筑可免征 5 年的建筑税；

⑥开发区开发者和使用者免征不动产转让税；

⑦ 雇主在开发区内第一年运营所支付的相当于工资、社会和健康支出金额的150%可予抵扣税款；此后年度中，任何额外的工资、社会和健康支出（与前一年相比）可在150%的水平上扣除；

⑧ 培训成本和研发支出按实际发生费用的200%可用于税收目的，此项优惠适用于商业活动开始后的10年期间；

⑨ 向开发区供应阿尔巴尼亚货物可视为出口，增值税率为0%。

位于科普利克（斯库台）的技术与经济开发区向外国投资者开放。① 该开发区开放制造业、工业、农产品加工业以及贸易和货物存储，为给外国投资者提供更多投资选择，将被分成三个较小区域。

另一技术与经济开发区位于阿尔巴尼亚北部，由15个地级单位和约61公顷的农田和牧场组成。

阿尔巴尼亚首都地拉那预计还将"托管"一个位于卡塞尔的技术和经济开发区。②

2. 投资保护

《外国投资法》对投资额超过10 000 000欧元，且依据《战略投资法》被认为是战略性的投资/项目提供"特别国家保护"。如外国投资者和私人之间就项目所在地和/或即将建设和/或开发的土地权属发生争议，那么其将受到此等保护。

该保护包括，在法庭纠纷调解中心，国家替代外国投资者，在法院规则对索赔人有利时承担赔偿责任。

其他法律激励措施包括：

（1）平等对待外国和本国投资者；

（2）税后全部利润和股息汇回国外；

（3）公司清算后的资金汇回国外。

三、贸易

（一）贸易监管部门

阿尔巴尼亚贸易监管部门是中央国家监察局，该机构是阿尔巴尼亚经济和财政部的下属机构。

根据政府的改革监察职能，中央国家监察局集中了监察机构的组织和职能，这些监察机构以前曾根据"部门监察机构"的原则运作。

中央国家监察局的主要职责之一是确保对企业和个人的日常运营的强制性规则的实施。贸易监管是通过部门监督机构进行的，例如国家市场监督检查机构。

进口由阿尔巴尼亚海关当局管理，该局是经济和财政部下属的一个中央机构。

（二）贸易法律、法规简介

阿尔巴尼亚的贸易立法（贸易法律、法规）由若干部门议会法案以及政府和有关部委发布的二级立法法案组成。

除了《海关法》③和为执行《海关法》颁布的二级立法④以外，阿尔巴尼亚没有针对贸易制定统一的法案。

阿尔巴尼亚还根据世界贸易组织的规定制定了标准化制度体系⑤，并设立标准化总局，以负责执行欧洲、国际和国家标准。除法律另有规定，该标准的适用是自愿的。

对贸易有重要意义的另一法案是《货物综合税则目录》⑥，通常每年更新一次。

---

① 来源：财政部。
② 来源：ATA。
③ 《海关法》第102/2014号经修正的法律批准。
④ 2017年10月11日，部长理事会《关于批准第102/2014号法律〈海关法〉实施规则》的第651号决定。
⑤ 2008年2月4日发布的第9870号经修正的《标准化规则》。
⑥ 1999年14日，第8474号法律《关于批准税则和关税——货物综合税则目录》。

(三)贸易管理

阿尔巴尼亚的贸易体制相对开放,对进出口限制有限。采取了一些反倾销、反补贴和保障措施。[①]对被认为对公共健康有危害的产品(如废物、臭氧消耗物质或放射性物质等)禁止进口。

进口许可证管制主要用于卫生和植物检疫目的,以确保安全和环保。进口管制也适用于遵守国际公约规定的义务。

阿尔巴尼亚于 2000 年 9 月 8 日成为世界贸易组织成员,并为其所有的贸易伙伴提供了"最惠国待遇"。此外,阿尔巴尼亚还签署了一系列区域贸易协定,例如中欧自由贸易协定、与欧洲自由贸易联盟的协定[②],以及与欧盟及其成员国[③]签订的自由贸易协定等。

阿尔巴尼亚对来自与其签订自由贸易协定[④]的国家(欧盟成员国、中欧自由贸易区、欧洲自由贸易联盟成员国以及土耳其)的产品实施一系列优惠关税和配额。

(四)进出口商品的检验检疫

阿尔巴尼亚根据国家法律实施严格的检验检疫规定,以求达到欧盟标准以及世界贸易组织卫生和植物检疫措施(SPS)的要求。

因此,对有关活体动物进出口、动物源性产品、未加工材料、生物材料、生物产品等的检查配备有整套的程序(并在必要时进行检疫)。

进口/出口检查由海关和兽医检查员根据 2011 年 9 月 29 日颁布的第 10465 号法律《兽医服务和其他行业法律(经修订)》(例如 2012 年 5 月 31 日第 64/2012 号法律《渔业法》等)实施。兽医检查员组成海关队伍的一部分,有权检查进口货物的兽医卫生状况,并取样分析,没收托运货物或采取其他预防措施等。

营养食品的进出口将依据经修订的 2008 年 1 月 28 日第 9863 号法律《食品法》以及在其基础上批准的相关二级法规进行检验。

阿尔巴尼亚批准了《野生动植物濒危物种国际贸易公约》(2008 年 1 月 31 日颁布的第 9867 号法律),因此受保护动植物物种的进出口将严格根据该有关条款执行。

此外,阿尔巴尼亚还建立了一个海关实验室,协助海关当局拥有分析商品进出口分析参数的专属权限,这是确定和核查货物税则分类所必需的,并最大限度地对有关货物征收间接税(消费税、特许权使用费、增值税等)。

(五)海关管理

海关当局作为财政和经济部下属的中央机构,是实施和监督实施海关法律、法规以及其他与进出阿尔巴尼亚的货物相关的部门法规/规章的行政机构。

除了主要征收货物进出口的主要税之外,海关还与其他国家机构合作,目的是:
① 确保阿尔巴尼亚的财政和环境利益不受不公平和非法贸易侵害;
② 确保阿尔巴尼亚及其居民以及环境的安全;
③ 通过确保阿尔巴尼亚的财政和环境利益不受不公平和非法贸易侵害,为阿尔巴尼亚的公平贸易做出贡献;
④ 通过对反倾销和进口假冒商品采取行动,确保阿尔巴尼亚的公平贸易。

四、劳动

阿尔巴尼亚人的劳动问题主要受第 7961/1995 号法律批准的经修正的阿尔巴尼亚《劳动法》(ALC)的管辖。

---

① 参见 https://www.wto.org/english/thewto_e/countries_e/albania_e.htm。
② 包括冰岛、列支敦士登、挪威、瑞士。
③ 参见阿尔巴尼亚共和国与欧盟及其成员国签订的《稳定与联合协议》。
④ 参见 http://www.dogana.gov.al/english/d/182/249/0/266/preferential-tariff-and-quotas。

《劳动法》调整劳动合同的各个方面以及雇员的权利，它还调整诸如但不限于就业协议的形式和内容、最低工资、休假、工期、轮班、节假日、裁员、劳工组织、罢工权等。

《劳动法》适用于所有在阿尔巴尼亚境内履行职责的雇员的劳动关系，即使该雇员暂时在其他国家执行工作任务。《劳动法》也适用于临时在阿尔巴尼亚工作的外国人。

如果员工在阿尔巴尼亚和海外平等地履行职责，则适用的就业法应为其就业所在地国家的法律，就业所在地不能确定的，适用雇主总部所在地国家的法律。

当事人可以为他们的劳动关系选择不同的管辖法律，只要该等选择不会剥夺法律在不存在该等选择的情况下所赋予雇员的强制性保护。

（一）劳动法律、法规简介

除《劳动法》以外，该领域的其他重要法律还包括2011年6月16日颁布的经修订的第10433号法律《监察法》（以下简称"第10433号法律"），以及1993年5月11日颁布的第7703号法律《社会保障法》（以下简称"第7703号法律"）和1994年10月13日第7870号经修正的法律《医疗保险法》（以下简称"第7870号法律"）等。

第10433号法律规定设立劳动监察局，并将其作为负责监督和检查技术、卫生和法律雇用条件等在劳动法下的适用和遵守情况的主要机构。

阿尔巴尼亚还另外批准并遵守一些国际劳工组织公约[①]，例如1930年《禁止强迫或强制劳动公约》（第29号），1948年《结社自由和组织权利保护公约》（第87号），1958年《消除（就业和职业）歧视公约》（第111号）等。

（二）雇用外籍员工的要求

外国公民必须获得以下许可才能在阿尔巴尼亚合法入境、居住和工作：工作许可证[②]、入境签证（D类）[③]、居留许可证。

1. 工作许可

打算在阿尔巴尼亚工作的外国人需要获得工作许可证。

工作许可证由阿尔巴尼亚劳工当局签发，为期1年，根据就业的目的和期限，可以延期1年或2年。

在阿尔巴尼亚连续工作5年后，可申请永久工作许可证。

现有工作许可的类型如下：

A类工作许可证：根据雇员的经济活动，包括以下子类别："A/P"适用于员工，"A/PS"适用于季节性就业；"A/TN"适用于受让人；"A/S"适用于学生；"A/NK"适用于跨境就业；"A/FP"适用于专业培训；"A/SHV"适用于志愿服务；"A/AF"适用于家庭成员以家庭团聚为目的进入阿尔巴尼亚；"A/KL"适用于高素质员工；"A/SP"适用于运动员；"A/PSH"适用于家庭雇员。

B类工作许可证：根据独立的经济活动，包括以下子类别："B/VP"适用于个体经营者；"B/I"适用于投资者。

C类工作许可证：特殊情况下，承包服务有以下子类别："C/SHK"；

D类工作许可证：永久工作许可证——在阿尔巴尼亚连续居住5年，并且在第一次工作许可证颁发后续签2次每次2年才可签发。

如果员工在阿尔巴尼亚短期工作（长达90天），将发放"工作登记证"，而不是工作许可证。

欧盟和美国公民可免于获得阿尔巴尼亚工作许可。这些国民享有与阿尔巴尼亚国民相似的就业权利，并获得阿尔巴尼亚劳工当局颁发的就业证明。

---

① 参见 http://www.ilo.org/dyn/normlex/en/f?p=1000:11200:0::NO:11200:P11200_COUNTRY_ID:102532。
② 某些国家的公民获得免于满足工作许可的要求，如欧盟公民、美国公民。
③ 某些国家的公民可以在180天内累计90天免签证进入阿尔巴尼亚。国家签证要求的完整名单可通过以下链接查询：http://www.punetejashtme.gov.al/en/services/consular-services/visa-regime-for-foreign-citizens/。

2. 申请程序

在申请工作许可的过程中，外籍员工必须由阿尔巴尼亚雇主代表并办理工作许可证。雇主必须提供基本的申请文件，例如劳动合同、支持信、健康保险、在阿尔巴尼亚的住宿等。

阿尔巴尼亚劳工当局将根据当地就业市场的报价/需求状况以及失业的阿尔巴尼亚公民的可用情况来评估申请情况，以填补这一职位。

工作许可申请通常在提交所有必要文件后30天内处理，应支付6 000列克（约45欧元或56美元）的申请费用。

在获得工作许可后的90天内，外籍员工需要获得阿尔巴尼亚签证（D类签证），入境阿尔巴尼亚并开始工作。如果这个条件不符合，工作许可证将被认为是无效的。如果外籍员工是阿尔巴尼亚实行免签证制度的国家[①]的国籍，则此要求不适用。

3. 社会保险

除非有基于阿尔巴尼亚签订的国际协议的例外情况，外国雇员需要支付类似于阿尔巴尼亚员工所支付的社会保险。

（三）出入境

1. 签证类型

进入阿尔巴尼亚的可用签证类型如下：

A类签证：用于过境；

C类签证：180天内入境和停留长达90天；

D类签证：在180天内进入和停留超过90天。

某些国家的公民可以免签进入阿尔巴尼亚并在180天内累计停留不超过90天。

2. 出入境限制

阿尔巴尼亚通常不会适用基于国籍的入境歧视。外国人违反了允许逗留期限（无论是基于签证还是免签证机制），但自愿离开该国，应在支付50 000阿尔巴尼亚列克罚金（约380欧元或465美元）后才可离开。如果在逗留期满后有效停留时间超过1个月，则罚款加倍。

（四）工会和劳工组织

阿尔巴尼亚《宪法》授予雇员组织工会和罢工的自由的权利依法得到保障。

尽管阿尔巴尼亚有许多工会，但它们在私营企业中并不十分活跃，以前在国家机构或国有公司中经营的私有化的企业除外（如采矿部门、采油部门、某些工业工厂等）。

根据《劳动法》的规定，禁止基于工会成员资格而进行就业歧视和/或终止就业。《劳动法》进一步对罢工被视为合法的条款和条件作出了规定。

根据《劳动法》的规定，集体劳动协议可以在私人企业或经济部门签署，签署该等协议可以在一方为一个或几个雇主或一方雇主协会与另一方为一个或多个工会之间进行。

集体劳动协议一经签订，对所有遵守该协议的雇员都具有约束力，并且适用于所有雇员，不论其是否为各工会成员。

根据《劳动法》的规定，工会在裁员程序和公司限制期间也充当谈判的角色。

（五）劳动纠纷

阿尔巴尼亚的劳动纠纷属于普通法院的管辖范围。作为规则的例外情况，公共机构和公务员之间的劳资纠纷属于行政法院系统的管辖范围。

对于集体纠纷（如劳工组织或更多雇员与雇主或工会之间的纠纷），《劳动法》提供了通过调解、

---

① 国家签证要求的完整名单可通过以下链接查询：http://www.punetejashtme.gov.al/en/services/consular-services/visa-regime-for-foreign-citizens。

和解到最终仲裁的程序。但是，这一程序从未应用过。

实践中，由雇佣关系引起的最常见的争议为雇主单方面终止雇佣协议。其他不太常见的争议涉及违反强制性健康和安全规则而导致的侵犯员工权利和工伤。

《劳动法》十分注重对员工权利的保护。通常雇主需要证明单方面终止雇佣协议的合理性。此外，雇主仍需要遵守严格的合同终止程序，若雇主没有遵循该程序，其将面临相当于雇员两个月工资的处罚。

对于终止无限期合同，除有合理理由和满足终止程序的要求外，雇主还必须根据劳动关系存续时间给予员工2周至3个月的期限通知。

此外，如果法院认为单方面终止雇佣协议不合理或出于歧视性理由，雇主可能会被处以相当于雇员12个月工资的罚款。

如果员工在同一雇主处工作了3年，那么在终止雇用时，雇员有权获得每年工作年度最后一次工资的50%的工龄奖金。如果终止是因员工的过错造成的，则员工丧失获得该奖金的权利。

ALC规定劳动相关索赔的期限为3年，在该期限届满后索赔无法进行。如果雇员声称雇主没有正当理由单方面终止合同，则适用180天的期限。

五、知识产权

（一）知识产权法律、法规概述

阿尔巴尼亚立法认可的主要知识产权是：
《工业产权法》——第9947号法律：
① 专利；
② 商标（贸易或服务商标）；
③ 设计；
④ 实用新型；
⑤ 地理标志。
《版权与邻接权法》——第35/2016号法律：
① 作者的权利；
② 表演者的权利；
③ 其他邻接权；
④ 数据库；
⑤ 软件。
此外，阿尔巴尼亚根据第8488号法律保护集成电路拓扑图。

阿尔巴尼亚是世界知识产权组织的成员国，并且已经批准了许多与知识产权有关的条约和公约，如《巴黎公约》《伯尔尼公约》《与贸易有关的知识产权协定》，等等。

（二）专利申请

专利申请可以由任何人或与法人相当的其他实体提出。专利申请可以由多个申请人共同提出。

专利权适用于发明人或其继承人。如果发明是以工作或其他协议为基础作出的，专利权归属于委托研究的一方。如果专利的价值远远高于合同报酬，除了合同中约定的补偿外，员工还有权获得特别补偿。

专利申请可在阿尔巴尼亚要求优先权日，如果该优先权要求是同一专利申请基于以下情形定期提交之后的12个月内提出：
①《巴黎公约》一个成员国的国家立法；
② 世界贸易组织的一个成员国的国家立法。
如果提出优先权要求，阿尔巴尼亚专利申请日与上述国家之一申请日期相同。

成功申请专利的主要条件是：

① 新颖性（本发明不构成现有技术的一部分）；
② 创新步骤（根据现有技术，本发明对于本领域技术人员来说不是显而易见的）；
③ 工业应用（本发明必须在任何工业或农业中有实际应用）。

阿尔巴尼亚工业产权总局对这些条件进行正式评估，而无须进行实际测试。

注册专利授予专利所有人对专利所涵盖的发明的专有权，自申请日起期限为 20 年，但前提是在专利申请日起 10 年内，所有者能够提交欧洲专利局对该专利的可专利性出具的书面证明，或由阿尔巴尼亚工业产权总局认可的该专利基于条约（即 PCT）或双边协议所具有的足够的检测能力。

有效的专利还需要及时支付相关年费。

（三）商标注册

商标或服务标志（共同称为"商标"）被定义为能够将企业的商品或服务与其他企业的商品或服务相区别的图形代表标志。

商标可以由符号、文字、形状、颜色或它们的任何组合构成，包括图形表示的声音或光信号。

商标申请可以由开展业务的任何人向阿尔巴尼亚工业产权总局提出。

商标注册在以下情形中可被驳回：绝对理由；相对理由。例如，没有明显特征（例如通用产品名称）、使用保留的名称/标志（例如州和国际组织的名称和符号等），以及与先前注册的商标冲突。

除本国申请的外，商标权也可基于马德里国际商标体系在阿尔巴尼亚得以保障。

商标申请可在阿尔巴尼亚要求优先权日，如果该优先权要求是同一商标申请基于以下情形定期提交之后的 6 个月内提出：
① 《巴黎公约》一个成员国的国家立法；
② 世界贸易组织的一个成员国的国家立法。

如果提出优先权要求，阿尔巴尼亚商标申请日与上述国家之一申请日期相同。

如果申请人在阿尔巴尼亚国际展览会或其他成员国的其他国家举办的国际展会上已经展示了该商品/服务标志，那么在商标申请前 6 个月内还可以申请优先权日。

自申请之日起 10 年内，注册商标赋予商标所有者在商业过程中对其申请的相同类别商品/服务的专有权利。

（四）知识产权保护措施

基于知识产权派生的权利通过法院系统执行。知识产权权利人被侵权时，可以向法院主张采取如下措施：
① 确定发生了侵权行为；
② 根据侵权行为要求支付赔偿金；
③ 查获或销毁侵权产品和/或用于生产侵权产品的工具；
④ 签发针对侵权方的禁令；
⑤ 在媒体上公布法院的判决，由侵权方支付费用。

如果侵犯知识产权的产品是故意制造的，则可能构成行政违法，可被处以罚款，甚至构成刑事犯罪，可被处以罚金和/或监禁。

六、环境保护

（一）环境保护监督局

阿尔巴尼亚旅游和环境部（MTE）是负责起草和实施旨在保护环境的政策的国家机构，具体职能包括可持续利用自然资源、保护自然和生物多样性、森林和牧场的可持续发展和管理、空气和水质监测、废物管理、噪音、工业污染、化学品、气候变化影响、保护区和环境影响评估等。

关于起草具体法律框架问题，MTE 定期编制和更新国家环境保护计划和战略，并由政府决定批准。

环境保护的具体行动和措施由国家环境局（NEA）和区域环境机构（REA）执行。国家环境局是由环境部长负责的中央政府机构，负责管理、组织和协调地方一级的若干区域环境机构。

阿尔巴尼亚旅游和环境部、国家环境局、区域环境机构也负责评估过程并批准所需的环境许可证。国家环境、林业和水域督察局负责控制和检查对环境法律、规则和要求的实施。

此外，地方政府一级市政当局负责按照国家战略批准环境的地方计划和战略，采取适当措施以保护空气、土壤和水质免受污染，包括防止和减少噪音的污染等。

（二）环境保护法律、法规简介

阿尔巴尼亚共和国通过了一项广泛的环境立法，大部分与欧盟法律协调一致。迄今为止，基于欧盟与阿尔巴尼亚共和国于2009年签署生效的《稳定与联合协议》所承担的义务，欧盟法与国内法的转换正在所有环境专题领域取得进展。

此外，阿尔巴尼亚议会还批准了若干与环境保护有关的国际协定和条约，包括《卡塔赫纳生物安全议定书》《气候变化框架公约》《气候变化框架公约京都议定书》《生物多样性公约》《保护臭氧层维也纳公约》《关于消耗臭氧层物质的蒙特利尔议定书》《关于持久性有机污染物的斯德哥尔摩公约》《海洋法公约》和《防治荒漠化公约》等。

国内关于环境的立法主要有2011年6月9日颁布的第10431号法律《环境保护法》、2011年7月7日第10440号法律《环境影响评估法》、2011年7月14日第10448号法律《环境许可法》、2005年5月4日第9385号法律《森林和森林服务法》、2010年4月15日第10266号法律《防止空气污染法》、2011年9月22日第10463号法律《综合废物管理法》、2006年7月20日第9587号法律《保护生物多样性法》、2002年6月6日第8906号法律《保护区法》和第111/2012号法律《水资源综合管理法》。

（三）环境保护评估

环境保护对阿尔巴尼亚仍然是一个挑战，并且与城市快速发展和经济活动的增长相对立。一个非常积极的方面是，国家环境立法和政策的起草几乎是依据欧盟立法和政策所规定的要求而进行的。

此外，阿尔巴尼亚与周边国家和地区就环境问题进行了良好的合作，并积极参与国际倡议。一方面，公民、社会和非政府组织的作用越来越大，人们对环境保护重要性的教育和认知程度也越来越高。另一方面，尽管阿尔巴尼亚当局做出了努力，但在达到环境保护的良好标准方面仍面临一些困难。

尽管环境立法规定了环境监测和检查，但阿尔巴尼亚的主要问题与立法和规则的正确实施、控制和监督有关。检查和地区控制仍然存在问题，部分做法与国际做法保持一致，但部分经营者仍然在没有环境许可的情况下运作，或者没有按照要求开展活动。

执法水平较低主要是由于缺乏行政能力、财政资源减少、地区差异控制，以及中央和地方政府机构之间协调不当等。

七、争议解决

根据阿尔巴尼亚《宪法》的规定，地方法院、上诉法院和高等法院行使司法权。

高等法院被视为仅处理有关法律适用不当和/或违反程序事项的案件的法院。然而，高等法院在对共和国总统、总理、部长理事会成员、高等法院法官、宪法法院法官等进行刑事指控的审理时具有初始管辖权。高等法院也有权制定判例法。

目前在阿尔巴尼亚设立了下列法院：

① 民事上诉法院和地方法院，处理民事/私法事务，如就业、劳工、合同、家庭等；
② 行政上诉法院和地区法院，处理行政/公法方面的事务，例如对行政行为的索赔；
③ 处理刑法事务的刑事上诉法院和地区法院；
④ 上诉和地区重罪法院，处理某些严重的重罪，如有组织的犯罪集团犯下的罪行等。

《宪法》还设定了一个宪法法院，该法院只对有关个人投诉违反其宪法权利的事项进行最终裁决，以便在所有用于保护这些权利的法律手段都已用尽之后得到公正审判。

当事人向各有管辖权的地方法院提起诉讼和随附证据后案件即进入诉讼程序。法庭书记员应将这些文件送达被告方，被告方应提交答辩状和/或反诉状以及支持其立场的证据。当事双方提交诉讼请求和证据后，法院将要求当事人在开庭时以口头方式提供解释。

法院通常会在一些法庭听证会中审结案件。

高等法院的诉讼只限于违反程序事项、违反高等法院基于裁量权认为对于判例法非常重要的实体法的事项，以及下级法院的判决违反了高等法院统一判决形成的判例法的事项。

关于国内和国际仲裁程序的国内法规定载于阿尔巴尼亚《民事诉讼法》（ACPC）。

2001年5月17日第8812号法令废除了有关国际仲裁的条款。现在，《民事诉讼法》要求有关国际仲裁的条款应包含在单独的法律中。《民事诉讼法》第399条（现仍生效）进一步规定：承认及执行外国法院裁决的程序也应适用于承认及执行国际仲裁裁决。迄今为止，议会尚未批准适用于国际仲裁的法律。

但是，阿尔巴尼亚已批准1958年《承认及执行外国仲裁裁决公约》（以下简称《纽约公约》），因此《纽约公约》的自行执行条款已成为阿尔巴尼亚国内立法的一部分。此外，如果发生冲突，《纽约公约》的规定应优先于国内法的规定。

（一）争议解决的方法和机构

新近调整的非诉讼纠纷解决机制并未在阿尔巴尼亚广泛运用。2011年阿尔巴尼亚通过了一个新的调解和非诉讼纠纷解决法律框架，目的是为非诉讼纠纷解决机制提供更好的支持。国际仲裁仅限于在少数具有重大价值/要求损害赔偿的民事案件中由当事人选择，但国内仲裁的优先性较低。

（二）法律的适用

第10428号法律《国际私法》规定了阿尔巴尼亚的法律适用问题。它规定了有关阿尔巴尼亚人和涉外因素的私人民事事务，例如对法律人格、家庭继承、财产、合同等事宜的法律适用。

第10428号法律基本上与欧盟第593/2008号《合同义务法律适用条例》和欧盟第864/2007号《非合同义务法律适用条例》相一致。

八、其他

（一）反商业贿赂

1. 反商业贿赂法律、法规简介

私人和公共部门的腐败和贿赂行为属于刑事犯罪，因此根据阿尔巴尼亚《刑法》（APC）的规定，应处以高额罚款和/或监禁。应受惩罚的罪行涵盖了主动犯罪和被动犯罪。

此外，阿尔巴尼亚还批准了若干与腐败有关的国际条约和公约，并且是处理腐败和/或有组织犯罪[①]的主要国际组织和项目的成员。

尽管现行法律及已批准的条约和公约将腐败和贿赂行为认定为犯罪，但腐败仍然是阿尔巴尼亚面临的一大问题，因为其一直处在腐败指数高的国家之中。

为了解决这个问题，阿尔巴尼亚最近在司法领域通过了一个宪法改革，目的是解决公共行政最高层的腐败和贿赂问题。

改革还将设立独立检察官和专门调查组，对腐败和有组织犯罪进行调查和起诉。改革一旦全面实施，新成立的机构将重点打击腐败并促进国内外投资。

2. 反商业贿赂监督部门

到目前为止，负责监督反商业贿赂行为的部门是检察官办公室。

根据最近的改革，反商业贿赂工作将由一个特别检察官办公室进行调查和起诉，该办公室将专注

---

① 如《民法反腐败公约》（欧洲委员会）、《刑法反腐败公约》（欧洲委员会）、《刑法反腐败公约附加议定书》（欧洲委员会）以及《联合国反腐败公约》（简称UNCAC）等。

于腐败和贿赂事宜以及与有组织犯罪的联系。

除了检察官办公室之外，公共部门的反商业贿赂也在行政层面上由资产申报审计和利益冲突审计高级监察局、阿尔巴尼亚部长理事会以及反腐败部门进行调查。

这些机构在特别检察官办公室成立之后也将继续在行政层面上运作。

3. 惩罚性行为

以下是对阿尔巴尼亚腐败行为的惩罚：

（1）私营部门
- 主动犯罪，监禁长达 3 年。
- 被动犯罪，监禁长达 5 年。

（2）公职人员
- 主动犯罪，监禁长达 3 年。
- 被动犯罪，监禁长达 8 年。

（3）外国公职人员
- 主动犯罪，监禁长达 3 年。
- 被动犯罪，监禁长达 8 年。

（4）高级国家官员/地方选举官员
- 主动犯罪，监禁长达 5 年。
- 被动犯罪，监禁长达 12 年。

（5）中介机构——对公职人员产生不当影响
- 主动犯罪，监禁长达 3 年。
- 被动犯罪，监禁长达 4 年。

（6）选举官员
- 主动犯罪，监禁长达 5 年。
- 被动犯罪，监禁长达 5 年。

（7）法庭证人、专家或翻译
- 主动犯罪，监禁长达 4 年。

（8）法官、检察官或其他司法官员
- 主动犯罪，监禁长达 4 年。
- 被动犯罪，监禁长达 10 年。

（9）外国法院法官或其他司法官员
- 主动犯罪，监禁长达 4 年。
- 被动犯罪，监禁长达 10 年。

（10）本地或外国仲裁员
- 主动犯罪，监禁长达 4 年。
- 被动犯罪，监禁长达 8 年。

（11）外籍陪审员
- 主动犯罪，监禁长达 4 年。
- 被动犯罪，监禁长达 8 年。

除了监禁刑之外，次级处罚还可能包括没收通过刑事犯罪获得的财产或不当得利，以及在特定时期内停止执行公职、从事商业、贸易、专业执业等。

（二）项目外包

公共机构在阿尔巴尼亚的项目外包是根据 2006 年 11 月 20 日颁布的经修订后第 9643 号法律《公共采购法》以及在其基础上批准的二级立法（统称为"公共采购规则"）进行规制。

1. 许可制度

阿尔巴尼亚的项目发展许可制度是依据第107/2014号法令《领土规划与发展法》以及经修订的二级立法（统称"规划与发展规则"）建立。

规划和发展规则旨在：

① 确保领土的可持续发展；

② 评估国家和地方一级目前和潜在的领土发展潜力；

③ 促进保护、恢复和提高自然和文化遗产质量的适当行动；

④ 实现使用和开发财产的权利；

⑤ 为所有社会类别的住房、经济和社会活动、经济和社会凝聚力以及享有财产权创造适当的条件和平等机会；

⑥ 确保国家和地方规划机构起草和定期更新规划文件，确保规划部门协调其规划活动，促进和谐和统一的地区规划。

阿尔巴尼亚已经建立了国家地区规划登记处（电子规划），作为综合电子地区规划平台，服务于中央和地方一级的阿尔巴尼亚所有规划机构。

通过电子规划，让利益相关者、社会团体和广大公众更广泛地参与，是所有地区规划中最为重要和切实的程序。

电子规划平台的两个组成部分包括：

① 注册，或起草或正在起草的计划文件库；

② 网络GIS门户，整合规划文件的绘图资料。

有关规模的项目由国家领土委员会批准，由少数政府部长组成，总理主持。

2. 招标邀请和招标

公共采购规则概述了招标邀请和招标过程的各个阶段。

公共采购规则根据项目的类型和价值提供不同类型的程序和投标阶段。

投标过程可能是开放的（即任何有关方可参与并提交投标）或受限制的（即只允许邀请方参与）。

在公开程序中，投标人的经验和资格与其资金计划书一起评估，而在限制程序中，投标人的经验和资格在财务报价提交前进行评估。

实践中，对于期望投标人达到一定水平的专业知识和资质的高价值项目，项目外包当局经常采用限制性流程。该限制性流程首先要注意：对相关方进行资格预审；邀请符合资格要求的利害关系方参加投标程序。

随着公共采购规则进一步授权项目外包当局，由其细化招标程序的条款和条件，并为该项目选择最合适的招标结构，项目外包当局将根据个案的具体情况设计所适用的程序。

Albania

Authors: Genc Boga, Jonida Skendaj, Elion Shkodrani, Dorant Ekmekçiu
Translators: Dora Hu, Chen Zan

I. Overview

A. Introduction to the Political, Economic, Social and Legal Environment

Albania is situated at a natural crossroad of Europe's major transit corridors between Eastern Europe and the West. It boasts a strong strategic, economic and geographic position. Described as a reforming country with a focus on the ease of doing business, free markets, low taxation and powerful incentives, as well as a motivated, well-educated and cost-competitive work force, Albania is considered a vital and interesting country to invest in by international businesses. During recent years, with the domestic economy and exports expanding, the Albanian economy has been moving quickly towards a more open and liberal model with inward investment playing a key role in the overall economic transformation.

Albanian is the official language.It belongs to the Indo-European family of languages. Italian and English are the most commonly spoken foreign languages in the country.

The population of Albania, one of the youngest populations in Europe, is 2,874,800 inhabitants as of 1 January 2017, according to the Albanian Institute of Statistics.

a. Political System

Albania is a parliamentary republic based on the separation and balancing of powers in legislative, executive and judicial branches.Governed by a constitution of 1998, one hundred and forty members, elected through regional party lists, sit in its parliament. The Parliament of Albania is an institution legitimated by the will of Albanian people through their right to vote and elect their representatives.

According to the Constitution, the Parliament elects the country's President for a five-year term. The President of Albania is the head of the state and represents the unity of the country. The President in turn appoints a Prime Minister, who is the head of the Council of Ministers, the highest executive body in Albania. Ministers are nominated by presidential decree based on the Prime Minister's recommendation and it is then for the Parliament to give its final approval to the composition of the Government.

The country is divided into 12 administrative counties.The Council of Ministers elects prefects to be its representatives in the regions. Local elections are held every four years to elect district councils. City mayors are directly elected by public ballot. The judicial system is made up of a Constitutional Court, a Supreme Court, an Appeal Court and a District Court. On 31 July 2014 the Albanian Parliament passed law no.115/2014 "On the Administrative and Territorial Division of Local Government Units in the Republic of Albania", which reorganizes the previous 384 municipalities to 61 local government units. The 61 local government units were constituted after the June 2015 elections.

b. Economic Development

With the aim of accelerating the pace of economic growth, Albania is implementing structural reforms that will have an impact on competitiveness and productivity in the economy, create more jobs, and improve governance and public service delivery.

According to the most recent overview of the World Bank in Albania, in October 2017, the country's economy expanded by 3.4% in 2016 supported by domestic demand.Private investment in two large FDI-financed energy projects and a recovery in private consumption drove growth, contributing by 1.8% and 2.1% points respectively. Improvement in credit growth and employment also encouraged private consumption in 2017. The primary surplus of 0.7% of GDP helped lower the debt to GDP ratio for the first time since the global crisis, reaching 72.4% of GDP in 2016. Average annual inflation fell from 1.9% in 2015 to 1.3% in 2016, below the Bank of Albania's target of 3±1 percent. Remittances are stable in spite of weak growth in source EU countries.Net FDI's increased to 8.9% of GDP from 8% in 2015, helped by inflows associated with energy projects. Stronger growth further stimulated job creation in 2016 where the employment grew by 2.5% points reaching 48.7%, driven by industry and services. Albania's economic outlook is expected to improve over the medium term. Growth is projected at 3.5% during

2017-2019 driven by private investments and private consumption.

c. Legal System

Albania has a civil law system. Foreign investments remain a priority and the Albanian government has set up reforms to boost foreign investment.The law foresees as strategic, the investments in these sectors:

(i) Energy and mining.
(ii) Transport.
(iii) Telecommunications.
(iv) Infrastructure and urban waste.
(v) Tourism.
(vi) Agriculture and fisheries.

The Law on Foreign Investments intends to create a hospitable investment climate.The law provides guarantees to all foreigners (either physical or judicial persons) willing to invest in Albania.Below we present a brief information on the foreign investment protection or particularities of Albanian legal framework:

(i) no prior government authorization is needed, and no sector is closed to foreign investment.

(ii) there is no limitation on the percentage share of foreign participation in companies—100% foreign ownership is possible;

(iii) foreign investors have the right to expatriate all funds and contributions in kind of their investment.

(iv) Albania's tax system does not distinguish between foreign and domestic investors.

(v) there are no restrictions on the purchase of private residential property.

(vi) foreign investments may not be expropriated or nationalized directly or indirectly and will not be subject to any measure or similar action, except for public purposes determined by law.

(vii) foreign investments will be treated in a non-discriminatory manner and paid immediately, in a fair and effective manner, in accordance with the law.

(viii) in all cases and at all times investments will have an equal and unbiased treatment, and will have complete protection.

(ix) there are limited exceptions to this liberal investment regime, most of which apply to the purchase of real estate:

• Agricultural land cannot be purchased by foreigners and foreign entities, but may be rented for up to 99 years; and

• Constructible land may be purchased, but only if the proposed investment is worth three times the price of the land.

(x) investors in Albania are entitled to judicial protection of legal rights related to their investments.The Albanian Civil Procedure Code outlines provisions regarding international arbitration.

(xi) Albanian law recognizes a variety of legal forms for businesses entities.

B. The Status and Direction of the Cooperation with Chinese Enterprises Under the B&R

B&R regarded as a very important driver of China's long-term development economic strategy, is expected to have a major impact on regional businesses in many ways.The development of the corridors was formerly being envisioned by China itself and expectations for the initiative are high.

The Albanian Government supports any kind of initiative for strategic investments in Albania.It is acknowledged that the B&R initiative creates the compulsory conditions for improving the infrastructure of the region, thus serving the idea of creating a "New Silk Road" linking Asia with Europe, and that Albania wants to see the actualization of the incoming projects.From an historical perspective, silk routes emerged more than 2,000 years ago, due to increasing foreign demand for Chinese silk.

Albania is open in strengthening cooperation for the development of infrastructure, road, rail, port and airport under the principle of mutual benefit. The Albanian government aims at boosting economic, trade and investment cooperation and creating better conditions for a sustainable growth of the economy and trade.

In many occasions, the Albanian government statements highlighted the willing to increase the exports of Albanian products towards the Chinese market.According to them "the signing of an agreement to reduce the quarantine terms by the Chinese customs authorities for Albanian foodstuffs would facilitate their export or continuous communication between the relevant authorities realizing the growth of import-exports".

II. Investment

A. Market Access

a. Department Supervising Investment

In Albania there is no supervising authority on investments.Foreign investments in Albania are not conditioned by a preliminary authorization.They are treated and allowed based on the same conditions as those offered to similar local investments.In any case and at any time foreign investments have an equal and unbiased treatment and enjoy full protection and security.

There are few budgetary bodies established to inter alia maximize foreign and domestic investments and facilitate the dialogue between government and investors:

Albanian Agency of Investment Development ("AIDA") established by Law no.10303, dated 15.7.2010 On the Establishment, Organization and Functioning of the Albanian Agency of Investment Development is the competent administrative unit serving as a facilitator and supporter of direct investments in the Republic of Albania; enhancer of SME's competition capabilities; promoter of export of goods and services.

National Economic Business Council and Council of Investments are established to serve as mediators of the dialogue between representatives of business community, donors (private sector) and the Albanian government for the creation of a favorable, non-discriminatory and transparent business and investments' environment etc.

b. Laws and Regulations of Investment Industry

Foreign investments are subject to Law no.7764, dated 02.11.1993 "On Foreign Investments", bilateral treaties on investments, double tax treaties on avoidance of double taxation of income and capital, and depending on their nature can be governed also by Law no.10316, dated 16.9.2010, Law no.55/2015 "On the Strategic Investments in the Republic of Albania", Law no.125/2013 "On Concessions and Public Private Partnership", and other specific laws applicable to regulated markets and sectors (such as banking, energy, telecommunications, audiovisual media).

c. Forms of Investment

Foreign investments can adopt different forms, depending on their nature.Foreign investments can be directly or indirectly owned by a foreign investor, and may consists in:

(i) A company, rights deriving from all kind of interest in a company;

(ii) Loans, monetary liabilities or liabilities in an activity which has an economic value and related to an investment;

(iii) Intellectual and industrial property;

(iv) Movable or immovable property, tangible or intangible or any other kind of ownership right (subject to some restrictions on the purchase of land as set forth in Section D of this section);

(v) Any other right acknowledged by laws or contracts, and any license or permit granted pursuant to law.

d. Standards of Market Access and Examination

Albania and China have signed a bilateral investments treaty on 13.02.1993.The treaty provides for the fair and equitable treatment of companies of both countries in either country and protection of the investments.

Also, Albania and EU have signed the Stabilization and Association Agreement, under which Albania is abide to follow and harmonize its legislation with the EU acquis communautaire including standards applicable to the market in general and to specific regulated markets.

B. Foreign Exchange Regulation

a. Department Supervising Foreign Exchange

The Bank of Albania is the authority having supervisory powers of entities licensed to perform foreign exchange activities.Also, the Bank of Albania is responsible to draft, approve and implement the regime of foreign exchange and the policies of foreign exchange rate in the Republic of Albania.

b. Brief Introduction of Laws and Regulations of Foreign Exchange

Foreign exchange activities are governed by regulation "On Foreign Exchange Activities" approved by decision No.70, dated 30 September 2009 of the Supervisory Council of the Bank of Albania (BoA) as amended.

c. Requirements of Foreign Exchange Management for Foreign Enterprises

No foreign exchange controls apply in Albania.Transfer of money and transactions are freely carried out from non-residents to residents of Albania.

Capital transfers from Albania to a foreign country are made by entities licensed by the Bank of Albania on behalf of their clients after the clients submit them the documentation mentioned in the Regulation and additional documentation as may be required by these entities:

(i) entrepreneurs and legal entities should (i) declare the purpose of transfer of capital and the source of creation of the capital to be transferred, the amount of capital and the address of transfer, (ii) submit the resolution of the decision-making body on the performance of the transfer and the extract on the status issued by the National Business Center;

(ii) individuals should declare the purpose of transfer of capital and the source of creation of the capital to be transferred, the amount of capital and the address of transfer.

Further, in the following cases, additional requirements apply:

(i) if the capital initially transferred in Albania through a non-resident bank for purposes of investment, is not used, the transfer to the foreign country is made upon submission to the bank of the resolution of the decision-making body of the entity confirming the interruption of the investment and the non-use of the capital initially transferred in Albania.

(ii) for the transfer of a company's profit (income related to the registered share capital in Albania and income generated from the investment of that amount), it must be submitted also the resolution of the decision-making body of the entity determining the distribution and use of profit.

(iii) for transactions of deposits that include actions in a current account or deposit account from the territory of the Republic of Albania, relevant supporting documents are to be submitted.

(iv) for commercial loans with a maturity term up to one term, which relate directly with international trade and provision of services, it is necessary to submit the loan contract.

(v) for transfer of currencies that derives from the deposits of a non-resident person and/or the so generated income, it is necessary to submit the bank statement that confirms the amount that will be transferred from the said deposits.

(vi) For the transfer of the share capital and income that result from sale of shares, as well as of partial or entire liquidation of an investment, it must be submitted the act of sale or the liquidation act issued by the decision-making body.

For transfers related to commercial trade (goods), the institution requires the following documents:

(i) request for the transfer containing the nature and purpose of the transfer as well as a statement that the documentation is not submitted before to justify transfers for the same goods; and

(ii) the pro-forma invoice and/or the contract which shall indicate the form of payment.

For transfers related to provision of services, besides the abovementioned request for transfer, the invoice or document that certifies the purpose of the transfer and/or respective contract must be submitted as well. For non-commercial transfers, besides the abovementioned request for transfer, it must be declared the source of income related to the transfer. Transactions with securities and similar instruments as well as the exercise of rights that derive therefrom, are performed only through banking institutions or other licensed institutions pursuant to a contract entered by the parties. Resident and non-residents seeking to transfer physically outside Albania amounts exceeding ALL 1 million or the counterparty in foreign exchange currencies, are required to declare to customs authorities the source and purpose of transfer.

Non-residents that visit temporarily the Republic of Albania may transfer outside Albania currencies in "cash" and/or travellers cheque up to the amount declared to the entrance customs authorities at the moment of entrance in the territory of the Republic of Albania. This amount is justified upon submission of the declaration filled-in at the moment of entrance and documents that support any differences to the amounts declared.

C. Financing

a. Main Financial Institutions

a) Banking System

The banking law, approved in December 2006, formalized a two-tiered banking system.Private banks are required to have a minimum capital of ALL 1 billion and should be incorporated as joint-stock companies. Commercial banks and other financial institutions can provide a range of services under the supervision of the BoA.

b) The Central Bank

The Bank of Albania plays an important role in the national statistical system, as the institution responsible for producing and providing data on the financial sector and the external sector. The external sector of statistics encompass indicators on the balance of payments, statements of international reserves and foreign currency liquidity, merchandise imports and exports, international investments position, exchange rates and external debt.

BoA operates as an independent legal entity accountable directly to the Albanian Parliament and its principal objective is to achieve and maintain the price stability.BoA is responsible for the formulation and implementation of monetary policy in Albania.

Specifically, BoA has the exclusive power and the duty to:

(i) formulate and implement monetary policy and foreign exchange policies.
(ii) act as a sole issuer of domestic currency in the Republic of Albania.
(iii) license, supervise and regulate the activities of banks and other financial institutions.
(iv) provide credit for banks.
(v) oversee the payment system in the Republic of Albania and facilitate efficient inter-bank payments and settlements.
(vi) hold and manage the official foreign reserves of the Republic of Albania.
(vii) distribute securities for the state account and issue securities for its own account.

All second-tier banks operating in Albania are obliged to:

(i) report monthly to the BoA.These reports should include the balance sheet and profit and loss account for the month, foreign currency balances, changes, if any, to the management of the Board of Directors of the bank, data on the bank's network structure, interest rates, credit exposures, credit per economic sector, high risk control, adequacy ratio (including total risk), weighted assets and off-balance sheet items and regulatory capital.
(ii) maintain the compulsory reserve required by the BoA's regulatory acts.
(iii) report on a monthly basis the provision of doubtful debt.
(iv) maintain a capital adequacy ratio as defined by the Basel Accord of at least 12%.
(v) report to the General Directorate for the Prevention of Money Laundering, located near the Ministry of Finance.
• all transactions in cash with a value equal to or higher than ALL 1,000,000, or its equivalent in other currencies, executed as a single transaction or as a several related transactions within 24 hours;
• all other suspected transactions.
(vi) maintain an open currency position with certain limits established by the BoA.
(vii) comply with the provisions of the regulation on foreign exchange activities as approved by the BoA.

b. Financing Conditions for Foreign Enterprises

There is no particular or discriminatory financing conditions for foreign enterprises. Depending on the investments that a foreign enterprise seek to make in Albania, financing may consist of a project financing under the concessions/PPP legislation or financing with additional collateral.

D. Land Policy

According to the article 5 of the law no.7980, dated 27.07.1995 "On Buying and Selling of land", foreign individuals and companies are permitted to own local land on the condition of carrying out investments on the land, not less than three times the value of the land, in accordance with the construction permit, whilst they can lease local land directly. This prohibition is not applicable in case of local corporations owned or controlled by foreigners or having foreign directors or for foreign investments consisting of major projects.

All foreign individuals and legal entities, which own real estate property consisting of buildings or agricultural land, are subject to tax on buildings and agricultural land.A real estate tax on construction projects is levied on the value of a new investment at a rate from 2% to 4% in Tirana, and 1% to 3% in other municipalities. Property tax is also applicable to agricultural land, at rates ranging from ALL 700 to ALL 5,600 per hectare, depending on the use. Property tax rates on buildings used for commercial purposes range from ALL 200 per square meter to ALL 400 per square meter, depending on the cadastral area in which the building is situated. From 01 April 2018, property tax will change from a fixed amount per m2 to a % over the market value of the building. As from 1 January 2016, urban land also is subject to property tax, with the amount ranging from ALL 1,400 per hectare to ALL 5,600 per hectare.

E. The Establishment and Dissolution of Companies

The current Commercial Law governing business organizations in Albania (Law no.9901 "On Entrepreneurs and Commercial Companies") has entered into force on 21 May 2008.It is modeled after the commercial legislation of Germany, Italy and Great Britain.The Commercial Law constitutes the main body of legislation for business organizations and aims to harmonize Albanian law with the laws of other European countries and the acquis communautaire.

a. The Forms of Enterprises

The foreign investors have numerous options available to organize its business operations in Albania.This may be achieved either by establishing a locally incorporated company, a branch or a representative office.The registration of new entities in Albania, since 1 September 2007, is carried out by the National Registration Center ("NRC") established under law no.9723, dated 3 May 2007 "On the National Registration Center", which aimed to implement a "one stop shop" system.As of 26 November 2015, a new law no.131/2015 has been enacted "On National Business Centre".The said law aims to further facilitate doing business in Albania by offering the registration and licensing procedures through only one institution, which is the National Business Centre ("NBC"). Therefore, the National Business Centre will replace both the National Registration Centre and the National Licensing Centre.

According to the Albanian legal framework, the following business entities need to be registered with the NBC:
- Sole Entrepreneur—Tregtari;
- Unlimited Partnership—Shoqeri Kolektive;
- Limited Partnership—Shoqeri Komandite;
- Limited Liability Company—Shoqeri me Pergjegjesi te Kufizuar;
- Joint Stock Company—Shoqeri Aksionare;
- Joint Ventures—Shoqeria e Thjeshte.

a) Sole Entrepreneur

The Sole Entrepreneur trades under his/her own name.Individuals interested in establishing this type of business should file an application and an identification document with the NBC of the district where the business will be conducted.The application form includes the individual's personal details, address, type of business and a specimen of his signature.

b) Unlimited Partnership

All partners are jointly liable for the debts of the partnership.In unlimited partnerships, the partners are all considered administrators of the partnership, unless the contrary is stipulated in the bylaws.Each partner represents the partnership in relation to third parties.An unlimited partnership should issue annual financial reports. The rights, duties and obligations of partners are governed by written bylaws, which should be filed with the NBC.

c) Limited Partnership

A limited partnership, which is seldom used in practice, consists of one or more partners with unlimited liability and one or more partners whose liability is limited to the amount of their contributions in the initial capital.A limited liability partner may not take part in the management of the partnership, even if he/she is given a proxy, and if he/she does so, he/she will incur unlimited liability.The limited partnership is not dissolved on the death or dissolution of one or more limited partners.

d) Limited Liability Company (SHPK)

This is the most common used legal form for conducting business in Albania.It can be established by one or more individuals or legal entities.Under normal circumstances, shareholders are held responsible for losses only to the extent of their contribution to the capital.

The minimum required capital for the limited liability company is ALL 100. Contributions to the capital can be in cash or in kind by any asset, tangible or intangible.

Directors are nominated by the General Assembly of the shareholders for a period of no more than five years, though this term can be renewed.Ordinary decisions may be validly taken by the General Assembly of shareholders provided that a quorum representing more than 30% of the company's shares is present in the meeting.

Extraordinary decisions, such as changes to the bylaws, increase or decrease of share capital, mergers and acquisitions or distribution of profits, may be validly taken by the General Assembly of the shareholders upon a majority vote of ¾ of the shareholders present in the meeting, provided that shareholders holding more than half of the total number of votes are present at the meeting.

Decisions of the General Assembly of shareholders are recorded in the minutes of the meeting, which are kept by the directors of the company.

e) Joint Stock Company (SHA)

The capital of a joint stock company is divided into shares, and, under normal circumstances, its shareholders are held responsible for losses only to the extent of their contribution to the capital.The minimum initial capital required is ALL 3.5 million for privately held companies with no public offering, and ALL 10 million for companies which are publicly listed.

The capital is fully subscribed when the shareholders have promised to transfer assets to the company in cash or in kind to an amount equaling the capital.At the point of subscription, for shares being paid for in cash, at least one quarter of the nominal value of the shares must be paid in cash.Payment of the remaining value can be made in installments with the agreement of the management bodies of the company.Contributions in kind must be fully paid in at the time of subscription.The Commercial Law does not allow contributions by way of services.

The rights attached to shares may not be transferred before registration of the company with the NBC.All shares bear the same nominal value.

The joint stock company may have "ordinary shares" or "privileged shares".The latter may also have no voting rights and in any case may not represent more than 49% of the registered share capital.

The Commercial Law provides for the adoption by joint stock companies of a flexible administration system. Joint stock companies may choose to adopt either a "one-tier" system (with a board of directors conducting both management and supervisory functions) or a "two-tier" system (with a board of directors and a separate supervisory board carrying out supervisory functions).

f) Joint Ventures

Albanian legislation recognizes joint ventures under the term "simple company", since it is based on an agreement between partners.

Joint ventures are foreseen by the provisions of the Civil Code (articles 1074-1112) and may be concluded by two or more persons, whether individuals or legal entities, foreign or national, agreeing to engage in an economic activity in order to share profits deriving there from.There is no minimum capital requirement.Partners are liable to make the contributions provided in the agreement.Unless otherwise agreed, each partner may take part in the management of the partnership and has full power to carry out any acts which are within the scope of the partnership.

Each partner is entitled to receive its share of profits after the accounts have been approved, unless otherwise agreed.Partners are jointly responsible for fulfilling the obligations imposed upon them by law and by the partnership agreement, unless they prove they were not at fault.

b. The Procedure of Establishment

To register a new company with the National Business Center (NBC) the following documents are required:

(i) application form (standard form) filled in and filed by the legal representatives of the company or by a person authorized by a power of attorney;

(ii) articles of Incorporation and/or Bylaws;

(iii) resolution nominating the director of the company;

(iv) depending on the legal form of the business entity, additional and specific information may be required to be stated in the Articles of Incorporation/Bylaws or filed with the NBC.

To register a branch or representative office with the NBC the following documents are required:

(i) application form (standard form) filled in and filed by the representative of the branch/representative office or of the parent company or by a person authorized by a power of attorney issued by either of the above-mentioned persons.

(ii) articles of Incorporation and Bylaws of parent company and any amendments.

(iii) recent extract from the Chamber of Commerce of the country where the parent company is located, issued no more than 90 days before the date of application, and confirming:

• the registration of the parent company in the Commercial Register of the country of origin;

• that the company is not subject to dissolution or bankruptcy;

• the composition of the managing bodies of the company.

(iv) Resolution of the parent company's board of directors or of any other body of the company authorized under its bylaws, to establish the branch or representative office in Albania and appoint a legal representative (manager) of the branch or representative office in Albania.

(v) financial statements for the last financial year of the parent company and the auditor's report.

c. Routes and Requirements of Dissolution

A commercial company is dissolved in the following cases:

(i) expiry of the duration;

(ii) completion of bankruptcy proceedings or insufficiency of assets to cover the expenses of the bankruptcy proceedings;

(iii) the object becomes non-realizable due to a continuous non-functioning of the corporate bodies of the company or for other cases that make impossible the continuation of the commercial activity;

(iv) invalidity of the constitution of the company;

(v) the net assets become less than the minimum registered share capital value as a result of losses or when the company decides to decrease the share capital below this value and the effectiveness of this decrease is not

conditioned with a subsequent increase that would remedy the situation;
(vi) in other cases, determined in the bylaws;
(vii) in other cases, determined in the law;
(viii) for any reason decided by the shareholders meeting.

F. Liquidation Procedures

Based on law no.9901, dated 14 April 2008 (Commercial Companies Law) as amended and law no.9723, dated 03 May 2007 "On National Business Centre", the dissolution of the company involves the liquidation and deregistration from the Albanian Commercial Register, which is subject to a two-phase procedure.

a. First Phase

In this phase, the sole shareholder must submit the following documents to the National Business Center (NBC):

(i) resolution of the sole shareholder (i) the closing of the activity of the company and opening of the liquidation procedure and (ii) the appointment of the liquidator.

(ii) recently issued extract of the Commercial Register where the sole shareholder company is registered (issued not earlier than 90 days before the date of application with the NBC), which reflects the registration of the shareholder with the Commercial Register of the country of origin and the composition of its managing body [legalized with apostille].

(iii) copy of the passport of the representative(s) of the sole shareholder who will sign the resolution mentioned above.

All documents listed above must be translated into Albanian language and notarized (certified) by a notary public.

Upon filing of the above documents with the NBC, the administrator of the company will no longer have any powers in connection with the company administration and is considered automatically dismissed.The liquidator shall represent the company before third parties, including banks.Further, during this phase, the liquidator shall perform the following:

(i) prepare the financial statements of the opening phase of the liquidation; in case the liquidation will last more than one year the liquidator should also prepare the annual financial statements of the company.

(ii) prepare and deliver to NBC two notices, with an interval of 30 days informing the possible creditors of the company about the initiation of the liquidation procedure.Pursuant to article 199 of the law 9901/2008 "On Entrepreneurs and Commercial Companies", the liquidator may not close the liquidation procedure earlier than one month from the second notice.

(iii) prepare the financial statements of closing of liquidation. In order to confirm the tax status of the company, the tax authorities usually conduct a tax audit near the taxpayer under liquidation process.In practice, the company/liquidator should submit to the local tax office a request indicating the closing of the activity and seeking the performance of the tax audit or any other relevant actions for the deregistration.The above procedure with the tax authorities may last from 6 to 8 months.

b. Second Phase

In the second phase, the liquidator shall perform different transactions necessary to collect the outstanding claims, sell the assets of the company (if any), terminate employment contracts and/or other contracts (depending on the needs of the company), pay the creditors of the company (if any), transfer the remaining amount to the shareholder etc.In addition, the liquidator should prepare the final financial statements and the report on the administration of the company during the liquidation process.

Upon completion of the above activities, the liquidator shall invite the sole shareholder to resolve on the following:

(i) approval of the final financial statements and act of compliance of the administration of the company from the liquidator; both acts are prepared by the liquidator;

(ii) withdrawal of the liquidator's mandate;

(iii) approval of closing of the liquidation.

Same as above, this resolution executed abroad should be in original, printed in letterhead of the sole shareholder (but not notarized and legalized). Such resolution shall be filed with the NBC, within 30 days in order for the company to be de-registered from the Commercial Company Register.

G. Merger and Acquisition

Mergers in the Republic of Albania are mainly governed by:

(i) Law no.9901, dated 14 April 2008, "On Entrepreneurs and Commercial Companies", as amended;
(ii) Law no.9121, dated 28 July 2003, "On Protection of Competition" ("Competition Law"), as amended; and
(iii) instructions and regulations issued by the Albanian Competition Authority.

Other legislation applies to mergers in particular sectors such as:

(i) the audiovisual broadcasting sector: where an entity or person may not hold more than 40% of the share capital in a national audiovisual company.An entity or person holding shares in a national audiovisual company may not hold more than 20% of the share capital in another national audiovisual company.An entity or person that holds shares in local or regional audiovisual companies may not hold more than 40% of the share capital in another local or regional audiovisual company.Any change in the ownership, or matters related to it, is subject to prior written approval by the Audiovisual Media Authority.

(ii) the banking sector: where BoA has the power to approve or decline any transfer of at least 10% of a bank's share capital or such a percentage that enables a shareholder to influence considerably in the management or policies of a bank.

(iii) the insurance sector: where the Authority of Financial Supervision is the regulatory body having the power to approve or decline any transfer of 10% or more of the shares with voting rights held in a company engaged in insurance and/or reinsurance activity as well as any transfer which affects less than 10% of the said shares but confers a control over the management of the insurance company.In addition, companies shall be subject to approval from the Authority of Financial Supervision for any further participation that reaches or exceeds 20%, 30%, 50% or 75% of the voting rights or the share capital of the insurance company; and

(iv) the telecommunications sector: where changes related to the licensee may be subject to notification to, or approval by, the Authority of Electronic and Postal Communication.

H. Competition Regulation

a. Department Supervising Competition Regulation

Albanian Competition Authority is the authority in charge with the supervision and implementation of requirements of law no.9121, dated 28 July 2003 "On Competition Protection".

b. Brief Introduction of Competition Law

The Competition Law approximates the competition law acquis communautaire in the Albanian legal framework pursuant to the Stablization and Association Agreement entered between Albania and the EU.

The said law governs those agreements that by object or effect restrict or hinder the competition (prohibited agreements) such as sharing the market, or fixing prices or other trade conditions, applying dissimilar conditions to same transactions, and the abuse of one or more companies with its/their dominant position (eg.by fixing abusive trade conditions and prices, refusing to supply, etc) as well as concentrations that meet certain requirements, which are assessed whether create competition concerns in the Albanian market (such as creation or strengthening of the dominant position).

The Competition Authority is also required to provide its opinion to legal and sublegal acts that have a competition law dimension.

c. Measures Regulating Competition

The Competition Authority issues regulations and instructions applicable to the companies located in Albania and foreign companies insofar as their activity presents effects in the Albanian market.

I. Tax

a. Tax Regime and Rules

The tax system includes corporate income tax, value added tax (VAT), excise tax, personal income tax, and simplified profit tax on small businesses and local taxes.The tax period for corporate income tax is the calendar year, while for VAT, excise tax, and personal income tax, the tax period is the calendar month.

The modernization of the tax regime started in October 1997 with the introduction of VAT, replacing the turnover tax.The initial VAT rate of 12.5% was later increased to 20%.In January 1999, the Customs Code came into force, which was simpler to apply, left less space for individual interpretation and was designed to comply with WTO requirements.The law on income tax introduced in 1998 abolished most tax exemptions granted previously.

The Albanian Government in 2006 implemented a policy of low tax rates to encourage investment.In 2008, the Government introduced a flat tax rate of 10% for all income, whether personal or business, except for that from industry sectors covered by specific laws, such as hydrocarbons.

Furthermore, in May 2008, a new law on tax procedures was adopted, providing detailed rules about taxpayers' rights, procedures for enforcing tax payment, requirements for transactions to be documented appropriately for fiscal purposes etc.

Effective from 1 January 2014, the Government introduced inter alia an increase of the corporate income tax rate from 10% to 15%, progressive tax rates on income deriving from employment (instead of the flat rate of 10%) and an increase of the basis of calculation of the health insurance contributions.

The new law on VAT, approved on July 2014, broadly reflects the EU Directive "On Value Added Tax".The law entered into force in 1 January 2015.

A new Customs Code was also adopted on July 2014, which is in full compliance with the Regulation "Union Customs Code".Certain provisions of the new Customs Code entered into force in January 2015, the other provisions gradually became effective until 2018 fiscal package.

b. Main Categories and Rates of Tax

a) Corporate Income Tax

Companies with an annual turnover exceeding ALL 8 million are subject to a 15% tax rate of corporate income tax.If the annual turnover is between ALL 5 million and ALL 8 million, the entity is subject to the simplified corporate income tax rate of 5%.Entities with a total annual turnover below ALL 5 million are exempt from the simplified corporate income tax.

The determination of taxable base starts with the profit shown in the profit and loss account.The profit calculation should be made according to the current accounting legislation and relevant instructions issued by the Ministry of Finance.

b) Taxation of Individuals

Under Albanian law, all individuals are liable to income tax.While residents pay tax on their worldwide income, non-residents pay tax only on income generated within the territory of Albania.

c) Residence

Individuals having their habitual residence in Albania or who reside in Albania for an aggregate period of more than 183 days in any calendar year are considered Albanian tax residents.

d) Personal Income Tax Rates

Wages, salaries and other compensation for employees are taxed as follows:

Monthly taxable income		Rate
Over (ALL)	Until (ALL)	
0	30,000	Nil
30,000	130,000	13 percent of the amount over ALL 30,000
130,000	and above	ALL 13,000 + 23 percent of the amount over ALL 130,000

For other taxable income, a flat rate of 15% is applied.

e) Tax Declaration and Preference

A taxable person shall submit a tax declaration and remit the related payment not later than the 14th of the calendar month following the end of each tax period.The VAT ledgers have to be filed within the 10th of the calendar month following the end of each tax period.

f) Personal Income Tax Declaration

All resident and non-resident persons, whose gross annual income reaches or exceeds ALL 2 million, must complete and submit an annual income tax declaration.Income generated from business activities carried out by self-employed individuals (subject to simplified profit tax on small businesses or profit tax) is not considered for purposes of calculating the said threshold.The declaration must be filed with the Tax Directorate, of the region in which the individual resides by 30 April of the year following the tax period for which the declaration is made.

If any personal income tax is due (calculated as the difference between the final tax amount and any tax prepaid and/or withheld during the tax period) it is payable by the same date.If the individual has overpaid tax during the tax period, the difference will be either reimbursed to the taxpayer or used as a prepayment for the following year's personal income tax.

J. Securities

a. Brief Introduction of Securities-Related Laws and Regulations

The legal framework governing securities in Albania is the Albanian Law no.9879, dated 21 February 2008

"On Securities", Law no.10158, dated 15 October 2009 "On corporate and local government bonds", and Law no.10236, dated 18 February 2010 "On Public Takeover", as well as several regulations issued by the Financial Supervisory Authority.

Law no.9879 determines the types of securities, regulates the manner of and conditions for issuance of securities, trading and registration, identification and performance of transactions with securities and persons and individuals authorized to perform transactions withsecurities, the conditions for the organization of the public trading of securities, the protection of investors and the securities right holders, and the conditionsfor dematerialized securities, the organization and functioning of securities registries, exchanging and regulation of the securities market.

Law no.9879 shall apply to regulating services in investment, opening and closing the financial instrument trading process, future financial transactions, financial analyses and changes to voting rights shares owned by listed company shareholders.The provisions of this law on price manipulation and financial instrument analysis shall also apply to the actions and omissions that entities licensed by the Financial Supervision Authority conduct outside the Republic of Albania to the extent that they affect the trading of securities in a securities market in the Republic of Albania.

Securities are financial instruments that are issued and traded with the goal of making a profit through the management of the rights deriving from owning them.The term "Securities" shall include, but shall not be limited to, shares, corporate and local government bonds, treasury bills and Albanian government bonds, securities issued by the Bank of Albania, commercial papers, investment fund shares or stakes, and other financial instruments that are comparable to shares and bonds and are regarded as such by the Financial Supervision Authority (hereinafter called "the Authority").

Securities can be equity securities, debt securities, and investment or pension fund shares or stakes.

Equity securities shall be securities that prove rights and obligations related to a share of a joint-stock company minimum or registered capital.Debt securities shall be instruments that prove rights and obligations related to the debtor-creditor relationship between the issuer and the security owner.

Investment fund shares or stakes shall be securities that confer rights and obligations related to a share of the investment fund capital.Pension fund shares shall be securities that confer rights and obligations related to a share of the pension fund capital.

Securities shall be issued by the Council of Ministers, as represented by the Ministry of Finance and Economy, the Bank of Albania, local governments, corporations and other legal entities (hereinafter called "issuers"). Securities shall be issued in Albanian Lekë or other foreign currency.

Securities shall be registered in centers specialized in maintaining security registers, which shall be organized in accordance with relevant Law and licensed by the Authority to operate as securities registries.

Securities shall be issued, transferred and kept as electronic records with securities registries, in the way prescribed in relevant Law and as per the rules adopted by the Authority.

b. Supervision and Regulation of Securities Market

The securities market is supervised by the Financial Supervisory Authority.

c. Requirements for Engagement in Securities Trading for Foreign Enterprises

Transferable securities shall be:

(i) shares, debt securities and other securities that are comparable to shares and debt securities;

(ii) contracts or the rights to signing them, purchase or acquisition of securities referred to in item (i) of this paragraph;

(iii) futures and options and financial contracts that are related to securities referred to item (i) above, where these are allowed to be traded in a securities market, which is regulated and supervised by the Authority.

A foreign entity seeking to perform transactions with securities on behalf of clients must be licensed from the Financial Supervisory Authority.

The following shall be activities related to transactions with securities:

(i) purchase and sale of securities by a customer's order;

(ii) purchase and sale of securities on one's own behalf and for one's own account;

(iii) management of a security portfolio on behalf of a customer that is the owner of the portfolio;

(iv) performance of the business of an issuing agent, including the organization, preparation and implementation of subscription and payment of securities, and performance of other activities for the issuer related to issuance of securities, preparation for the listing of securities on an exchange and regulated public market including the filing of the listing on behalf of the issuer;

(v) financing an issue, including the organization, preparation and implementation of issuance of securities for the issuer and related subscription and payment of all securities or only unsubscribed titles, for their further sale to potential investors;

(vi) advice on investment in securities;

(vii) activities related to clearing, settlement, custody and registration of securities;

(viii) donation, exchange and lending of securities;

(ix) selling securities for repurchasing them and/or vice-versa;

(x) generally, any operations or legal transactions with securities that are considered as such by the Authority.

Transactions with securities as a business activity, with the exception of security custody, may be performed exclusively by brokerage companies or banks that have been licensed by the Authority to conduct such transactions and have included such transactions in their objects clause.

A brokerage company shall be a joint-stock company seated in the Republic of Albania, the business of which shall be the transactions with securities in accordance with the provisions of the Securities Law and the license issued by the Authority.

Additional rules are applicable to foreign entities seeking to conduct brokerage activities or perform transactions with securities as a business activity.

a) Public Offerings and Trading

Any person intending to make a public sale offer shall submit to the Albanian Financial Supervisory Authority (FSA) a request for the approval of the prospectus, according to the regulations issued by the FSA.

A public sale offering cannot be made without the publication of a prospectus approved by the FSA. By way of derogation, the Law on Securities provides that publication of a prospectus is not mandatory in certain cases when the issuer issues shares for certain purposes, such as: increase of the initial share capital, by using for this purpose the profit, reserves or the retained earnings; increase of the initial share capital, as a result of a merger of companies; increase of the initial share capital, by which the subscription and the payment of securities are carried out by the shareholder of the issuer, which owns more than 75 per cent of the voting rights; increase of the initial share capital, in which only the institutional investors participate; conversion of convertible bonds into shares, if at the time of issuing the convertible bonds the issuer has published or delivered the prospectus to the investors; and converting the company of another form to a joint-stock company.

In its decision, the FSA confirms that the prospectus contains all the information required by the Securities Law and that it can be published.

If the securities are intended to be admitted for trading on a regulated market, the stock exchange is required to approve the acceptance rules and regulations.

Foreign entities willing to make a public sale offer can only do so through an intermediary (i.e.brokerage companies or banks) that is duly licensed by the FSA.

A foreign issuer shall be a securities issuer whose seat is registered outside the Republic of Albania.

A foreign issuer may issue securities in the Republic of Albania by a public offering only through an authorized company that the foreign issuer has engaged to act as an issuing agent.

The authorized company may be a stockbroker company or a bank that has received from the Authority the license to perform securities transactions.

Trading of securities admitted on the Albanian regulated market is limited by the Securities Law provisions concerning market abuse.

Furthermore, a person who possesses inside information shall be prohibited from engaging in trading securities. Additionally, market manipulation, such as transactions which do not lead to a change in the holder of a security or transactions which employ fictitious devices, for example, placing a fictitious order for the purchase or sale of securities in order to create the idea that a real trade is going on and therefore inflate the price is also prohibited.

b) Takeover Rules

The Public Takeover Law provides two types of takeover bids: voluntary takeover bids and mandatory takeover bids.

As a general rule, any person intending to make a public offer (voluntary takeover offer) must notify their decision on the takeover bid to the Financial Supervisory Authority and the administrators of the company. Within 10 days from the notice, the person must submit for approval to the FSA the takeover offer document.

A person holding, directly or indirectly, (i.e.together with persons acting in concert) a percentage of the voting rights that enables them to control the company must initiate a takeover bid (mandatory takeover bid).

The FSA shall decide within ten (10) business days from the registration of the offer document. If the FSA does not provide a decision in this time period, the approval will be considered granted and the offeror shall have the right to publish the offer document.

The offer document shall be published immediately after approval from the FSA has been granted.Acceptance of a bid may not occur less than 3 weeks before and more than 10 weeks after the date of publication of the offer document.

The legislation provides for certain special conditions relating to the offering price in a takeover bid.

Trading in securities shall be performed in an organized manner on stock exchanges established to provide conditions to match the supply and demand of securities.

Stock exchanges operating in the Republic of Albania shall be licensed by the Authority.In July 2017, the Authority licensed one stock exchange, called Albanian Stock Exchange.

K. Preference and Protection of Investment

a. The Structure of Preference Policies

Incentives to investors, either foreigners or Albanian, are set forth in laws and sub-legal acts depending on the sector to be incentivized and invested.

a) Support for Specific Industries and Regions

The Albanian Parliament has enacted in May 2015 the law no.55/2015 "On Strategic Investments in the Republic of Albania" (the "Law") as part of the initiative for facilitating and improving foreign and domestic strategic investments.

The Law aims to incentivize and attract strategic foreign and domestic investments, in sectors identified by the Law as strategic ones, by establishing special benefits, facilitating or accelerating administrative procedures to support and serve investors.It determines procedures and rules to be applied by state bodies for the review, approval and support of strategic investments, foreign or domestic ones, as well as services rendered to strategic investors via the "unique window" (the agency responsible for the services towards strategic investors).

Furthermore, it identifies as strategic the following sectors: energy and mining; transport, electronic communication infrastructure, and urban waste; tourism (tourism structures); agriculture (large agricultural farms) and fishing; "economic areas"; and priority development areas.

The criteria for determining strategic investments will be based on the value of the investment, which are specified in this Law for different sectors.For instance, for the sector of transport, electronic communication infrastructure, and urban waste the investment must be equal to or larger than EUR 30,000,000 for investors or projects benefiting from the status "strategic investor, assisted procedure", and equal to or larger than EUR 50,000,000 for investors or projects benefiting from the status "strategic investor, special procedure" (see below on the types of procedure to obtain the strategic investor status).

Other criteria include the timeline of investment implementation; investment productivity and added value; creation of new jobs; sectors' economic priorities; regional and local economic development; development or improvements of conditions or standards for the production of goods or provision of services; offering new technologies to effectively increase competition and investments; increase of the general level of security and citizens' quality of life; and protection of the environment and consumers.

The Law defines two types of application procedures: "assisted procedure", in which the public administration follows, coordinates, assists, supervises, and depending on the circumstances, represents the strategic investment during all phases of implementation"; and "special procedure", in which is given support and special regulations for strategic investments with impact in the economy, employment, industry, technology and/or regional development, with the goal of facilitating and accelerating investments.

Moreover, it provides for the creation of a Strategic Investment Committee (the "Committee"), a collegial administrative body, established within the Council of Ministers, and chaired by the Prime Minister, which members are the Deputy Prime Minister and the relevant ministers covering the strategic sectors.The Committee is supported by the Albanian Agency of Investment Development.AIDA is the competent administrative unit for delivering services to investors via a "unique window", towards investors/projects which apply and obtain the status of "Strategic Investment Assisted/Special Procedure".

In addition, AIDA keeps the "Register of Strategic Investment", which contains all the data for each strategic investment that will be performed in the Republic of Albania.According to the Law, the administrative procedures related to strategic investments within the scope of this Law, regarding preparation, implementation, development and realization of a strategic investment project, as well as issuing licenses/permits/authorizations pursuant to this Law, have priority and all institutions/entities/public authorities involved shall apply an accelerated procedure.

b) The Status of Strategic Investment

The interested investor, which seeks to obtain the status of "Strategic Investment", either in the form of assisted procedure or special procedure, has to file a request with AIDA by attaching these documents:

(i) business plan, financial investment plan and the working program for the realization of the project/strategic investment;

(ii) social impact evaluation;

(iii) documentation that proves the financial capacities for realizing this investment project;

(iv) the subject declaration over the accuracy of the data;

(v) written authorization by the investor, authorizing AIDA to perform all necessary verifications to the data submitted with the file along with the consent to publish details related with the investment, except for the data considered by the investor as confidential;

(vi) proof of payment for the applicable fee.

Some of the facilities offered to an investor in case of assisted procedure are:

(i) performance of preliminary actions and preparing of administrative documents;

(ii) land status confirmation, supporting programs;

(iii) supporting through auxiliary infrastructure;

(iv) making available state immovable property, through sale or lease agreements, for the development and completion of strategic investment projects.

In case of special procedure, some of facilities and guarantees to the investor are:

(i) expropriation of immovable properties owned by private owners, in order to realize strategic investment projects;

(ii) approval from the Parliament of relevant strategic investments contracts, in order to enhance the security of the contractual relationship entered into with the Albanian state.

The Law establishes the procedures to be followed for the approval of "strategic investment" status, and the assistance to be granted by AIDA to the investor for obtaining the relevant permits and authorizations to start the project implementation.

Applications for obtaining the strategic investment status may be filed until the end of year 2018.

c) Tourism

The Law "On Tourism" provides for a financial support to touristic educational, promotional, studies helping the development of the tourism.State-owned immovable properties that are located in areas having as priority the development of the tourism can be made available to investors for a duration of up to 99 years.The transfer of rights of use over these properties can also be made against the symbolic price of 1 Euro.

In case of investors having the status of Strategic Special Investor, the Council of Ministers may decide, case by case, to transfer the ownership right over the state-owned immovable properties to the private investor by conditioning it with a full realization of the investment.In case the Council of Ministers considers so, the agreement for realization of the strategic investment is proposed to the Parliament for approval upon a specific law.

d) Agriculture

Law no.9817, dated 22 October 2007 "On Agriculture and Rural Development" provides for programs of support of the development of agriculture.

Subsidies schemes in agriculture are applied for investments in the increase of competition of products for guaranteeing the stable supply of market; improvement of the cultivation technology; production of vegetables in protected areas; aquaculture and livestock breeding; stable supply of market and increase of income for rural zones families; increase of investments in the sector of marketing of the agriculture; increase of the possibility of farmers to use mechanic means; increase of formalities, cooperation and organization of companies of agriculture cooperation.

e) Renewable Energy

The Albanian government has approved, through decision no.27, dated 20 January 2016, the National Action Plan on Renewable Energy Sources 2015–2020, where the government undertakes to achieve the national objective of energy production from renewable resources in the amount of 38% until 2020.Incentive Schemes" as a direct engagement of the government in order to reach the target.These schemes, similar to countries in the region, mean any instrument, scheme or mechanism for encouraging utilization of energy from renewable resources by reducing the costs of such energy, raising the price it could be sold, or by increasing the volume of purchased energy through obligations for renewable energy or other means.This includes, but is not limited to, support for the investment, operation, tax exemptions or lower taxes, tax reimbursement, etc.

The Contract for Difference (CFD) is a contract, the model of which is approved by the Council of Ministers, entered into with the Operator of Renewable Energy and the producer of energy from renewable resources, which has been selected as the successful bidder in the auction to benefit from the incentive scheme.The incentive through this CFD consists of a changing compensation, calculated as a difference between the price, with which the renewable energy producer has been awarded the incentive as the successful bidder (determined price), and the market price of electric energy (reference price).The Council of Ministers, with the proposal of the relevant minister, approves the procedure for the organization of the auction for awarding the incentive to the priority producers of energy."Priority producers" are defined as any producer of electricity from renewable energy resources, and for hydro energy with an installed capacity of up to 15 MW for generating unit, which: benefits from the incentive scheme; has entered into a CFD with the Operator of Renewable Energy and sells the energy in the regulated market.

The reference price is the price of the product as traded in the regulated energy market, or otherwise until its creation will serve a market comparable price for the same product.

Such support for producers of renewable energy shall be given until the full payment of the plant investment, according to the accounting rules and other investment support given before.The CFD shall have a maximum duration of 15 years.

The producers of renewable energy shall be obliged to pay the difference between the reference price and the determined price to the Operator of Renewable Energy when the reference price exceeds the determined price.

f) Special Economic Areas

Areas of technology and economic development are governed by law no.9789, dated 19 July 2007 "On Creation and Functioning of Areas of Technology and Economic Development". Any person seeking to develop these areas must obtain a license to do so.

The areas of technology and economic development are subject to the following incentives:

(i) entrance and exit of goods in and from the areas is subject to the provisions of the Customs Code;

(ii) the developer and users are eligible to a reduced income tax rate of 50% for the first 5 years of activity;

(iii) area developers and area users benefit from a tax deduction of 20% of their annual capital expenditure (this applies in addition to the normal depreciation), for a period of 2 years, during the first three years of investment;

(iv) area developers are exempted from the tax on impact of new construction on infrastructure;

(v) new constructions on the area are exempted from the tax on building for a period of 5 years;

(vi) area developers and area users are exempted from the tax on transfer of immovable property;

(vii) an amount equal to 150% of wages and social & health contributions paid by employers in the zone is recognized as tax deductible during the first year of operation.In the subsequent years, any additional expense for wages and social & health contributions (compared to the previous year) shall be deductible at the level of 150 percent;

(viii) training costs and research & development expenditure are recognized for tax purposes at a level of 200% of the amount actually incurred.This benefit applies for a period of 10 years from the commencement of the business activity:

(ix) supply of Albanian goods destined to be located in the area is considered as export with VAT at 0% rate.

The area of technology and economic development located in the city of Koplik (Shkoder) is open to foreign investors.[1] The zone, opened for manufacturing, industrial and agro-processing activities as well as trading and storing goods, will be divided into three smaller districts in order to provide more investing options to foreign investors.Another area of technology and economic development is situated in Northern Albania, which consists of 15 cadastral units and about 61 hectares of agricultural fields and pastures.

The capital of Albania, Tirana, is also expected to "host" an area of technology and economic development, located in Kashar.[2]

b. Investment Protection

The Law on Foreign Investments provides "special state protection" for investments/projects exceeding EUR 10 million and those investments considered as strategic pursuant to the Strategic Investments Law.Such protection is granted where a dispute arises between the foreign investor and a private party claiming title over the land where the project is or will be built and/or developed.

This protection involves the state replacing the foreign investor in a court dispute and undertaking to compensate the claimant if the court rules in its favor.

Other legal incentives include:

(i) Equal treatment of foreign and domestic investors;

(ii) Full profit and dividend repatriation, after taxation;

(iii) Repatriation of funds from liquidated companies.

---

[1] Source: Ministry of Finance.
[2] Source: ATA.

III. Trade

A. Department Supervising Trade

The department supervising trade in Albania is the Central State Inspectorate (CSI), an agency of the Albanian Ministry of Economy and Finance.

Based on the reform inspection functions of the government, CSI has centralized the organization and function of inspection bodies, which were previously operated based on the principle "an inspectorate for a ministry".

One of the main duties of the CSI is to guarantee the implementation of mandatory rules on daily operations of businesses and individuals.The trade supervision is performed through sector inspectorate bodies, such as the state inspectorate for market surveillance (SIMS).

Imports are managed by the Albanian Customs Authority, which is a central agency under the Ministry of Economy and Finance.

B. Brief Introduction of Trade Laws and Regulations

Albania's legislation on trade (trade laws and regulations) is composed of a number of sectorial parliamentary acts, as well as secondary legislation acts issued by the Government and by the relevant line ministries.

With the exception of the Customs Code[1] and the secondary legislation issued for its implementation[2] there is no unified legal acts on trade.

Albania has additionally developed a regime on standardization[3], in compliance with WTO regulations, and has established the General Directorate of Standardization as agency responsible to implement European, international and national standards.The application of standards is voluntary unless otherwise specified by law.

Another act with relevant importance for trade is the Combined Nomenclature of Goods[4], which is usually updated on an annual basis.

C. Trade Management

Albania has a relatively open trade regime, with limited restrictions on imports and exports.It applies a number of anti-dumping, countervailing, and safeguard measures.[5]

Import prohibitions are imposed on products that are considered to be dangerous for public health (e.g.waste, ozone depleting substances or radioactive materials etc.).

Import licensing controls are mainly applied for sanitary and phytosanitary purposes, for security and protection of the environment.Import controls are also applied for compliance with obligations under international conventions.

Albania became a Member of the WTO on 8 September 2000, and grants a "most favoured nation" treatment to all its trading partners.Albania has additionally signed a number of regional trade agreements, such as the Central European Free Trade Agreement, agreement with the EFTA States[6] a free Trade Agreement with the EU and its Member States[7] etc.

Albania applies a number of preferential tariffs and quotas on products with origin from the countries with which it has entered into free trade agreements[8] (EU member states, CEFTA, EFTA countries as well as Turkey).

D. The Inspection and Quarantine of Import and Export Commodities

Albania applies strict rules on inspection and quarantine based on national laws, aiming to meet EU standards as well as WTO sanitary and phytosanitary measures (SPS).

As such, procedures are in place for the inspection (and quarantine, when necessary) of import/export of live

---

[1] Approved with law no.102/2014 "The Customs Code of the Republic of Albania", as amended.
[2] Decision of the Council of Ministers no.651, dated 10 November 2017 On the approval of the implementation provisions to the Law no.102/2014 "The Customs Code of the Republic of Albania".
[3] Law no.9870, dated 04 February 2008 "On standardization", as amended.
[4] Introduced with Law 8474, dated 14, 1999: "On the approval of the nomenclature and customs tariffs, for goods Combined Nomenclature of Goods."
[5] https://www.wto.org/english/thewto_e/countries_e/albania_e.htm.
[6] Iceland, the Principality of Liechtenstein, the Kingdom of Norway, the Swiss Confederation.
[7] Stabilisation and Association Agreement between the European Communities and their Member States, of the one part, and the Republic of Albania, of the other part.
[8] http://www.dogana.gov.al/english/d/182/249/0/266/preferential-tariff-and-quotas.

animals, products of animal origin, unprocessed materials, biologic materials, bio-products, etc.

Inspection of imports/exports are performed by custom authorities and the veterinary inspectors, based on law on 10465, dated 29 September 2011 On veterinary service in the republic of Albania, as amended, and other sector laws (e.g.Law No.64/2012 of 31 May 2012 "On Fishery", etc.).Veterinary inspectors form part of the customs team, and have the authority to inspect the sanitary-veterinary conditions of import shipments as well as to take samples for analysis, and confiscate the consignment or take other preventative measures.

Inspection of imports/exports for alimentary goods are performed pursuant to Law no.no.9863, dated 28 January 2008 "On Food", as amended, and the relevant secondary legislation approved on its basis.

Albania has ratified the Convention on International Trade in Endangered Species (CITES) of Wild Fauna and Flora (Law no.9867, dated 31 January 2008), and therefore the imports/exports of protected fauna and flora species are restricted pursuant to the relevant provisions.

Additionally, Albania has established a customs laboratory to assist the customs authorities, having the exclusive competence to analyse the analytical parameters imports/exports of commodities, necessary for the determination and verification of the tariff classification of goods and to maximize collection of indirect taxes (excise, royalties, VAT etc.) for relevant products.

E. Customs Management

The Customs Authorities, as central agency under the Ministry of Finance and Economy, is the administrative body that implements and supervises the implantation of customs laws and regulations, as well as of other sector laws that are relevant for the import/export of goods to/from the Republic of Albania.

In addition to the main role as revenue generating agency from the import/export of goods, the customs authorities also collaborate with other state institutions for the purpose of:

(i) ensuring financial and environmental interests of the Republic of Albania from unfair and illegal trade;

(ii) ensuring security and safety of the Republic of Albania, its inhabitants, as well as of environment;

(iii) contributing to a fair trade the Republic of Albania, by ensuring financial and environmental interests of the Republic of Albania from unfair and illegal trade;

(iv) contributing to a fair trade the Republic of Albania, by taking actions against the antidumping practices and the importation of counterfeited goods.

IV. Labour

Labour matters in Albanian are mainly governed by the Albanian Labour Code ("ALC") approved with the Law 7961/1995, as amended.

The ALC regulates all aspects of the employment contract, as well as rights of the employees.It also deals with matters such as, without limitation, the forma and content of the employment agreement, minimum wage, vacations, duration, shifts, holidays, layoffs, labour organizations, right to strike etc.

The ALC applies to all employment relations where the employee usually performs his/her duties in the territory of the Republic of Albania, even if the employee is temporarily on a working mission in another country. The ALC also applies to the temporary employment of foreigners working in Albania.

If the employee performs his/her duties equally in Albania as well as abroad, the applicable law of the employment shall be the law of the country where his/her employment centre is located, or if this may not be determined, the employment is regulated by the law of the country where the head office of the employer is located.

The parties may chose a different governing law for their employment relations, provided however that such choice does not deprive the employee from the mandatory protection granted by the law that would have been applicable in the absence of such choice/.

A. Brief Introduction of Labour Laws and Regulations

In addition to the ALC, other important laws in this area include, the Law No.10433, dated 16 June 2011 "On inspection in the Republic of Albania" as amended ("Law 10433"), the Law no.7703, dated 11 May 1993 "On Social Security in the Republic of Albania", as amended ("Law 7703") and Law no.7870, dated 13 October 1994 "On healthcare insurance in the Republic of Albania", as amended ("Law 7870"), etc.

The Law 10433, has established the Labour Inspectorate as the main agency to supervise and inspect the application and compliance of the technical, health, legal employment conditions, with the ALC.

Albania has additionally ratified, and complies with a number of conventions of the International Labour

Organization[1], such as C029 - Forced Labour Convention, 1930 (No.29), C087–Freedom of Association and Protection of the Right to Organise Convention, 1948 (No.87), C111 - Discrimination (Employment and Occupation) Convention, 1958 (No.111) etc.

B. Requirements of Employing Foreign Employees

Foreign nationals are required to obtain the following permits to be able to legally enter, reside and work in Albania: "Work Permit[2]", "Entry Visa (Type - D)[3]", "Residence Permit"

a. Work Permit

Foreign nationals intending to work in Albania are required to obtain a "Work Permit".

The work permit is issued by the Albanian labour authorities for a 1 year period and is renewable for the same term or for 2 year terms based on the purpose and duration of the employment.

A permanent work permit may be requested following 5 years of continuous work in Albania.

The types of available work permits are as follows:

Type "A" Work Permit—economic activities as employees, with the following subcategories: "A/P" for employees; "A/PS", for seasonal employment; "A/TN", for transferees; "A/S", for students; "A/NK", for cross-border employment; "A/FP", for professional training; "A/SHV", for voluntary services; "A/AF", for family members entering Albania on basis of the family reunion; "A/KL", for highly qualified employees; "A/SP", for athletes; and "A/PSH", for household employees;

Type "B" Work Permit—independent economic activities, with the following subcategories: "B/VP", for self - employed; and "B/I", for investors;

Type "C" Work Permit—special cases, with the following subcategory: "C/SHK", for contracting services;

Type "D" Work permit—permanent work permit-issued after 5 year of continuous residency in Albania and after 2 renewals of 2 years from the first work permit.

In case the employee will work in Albania for a short term (up to 90 days), a "Work Registration Certificate" is issued instead of the work permit.

EU and USA nationals are exempt from the obligation to obtain an Albanian work permit.These nationals enjoy similar employment rights with Albanian nationals, and are granted with an Attestation of Employment, issued by the Albanian labour authorities.

b. Application Procedure

During the application procedure for a work permit, the foreign employee must be represented and supported by the Albanian employer.The employer, is required to provide the basic application documentation, such as: the work contract, support letter, health insurance, accommodation in Albania, etc.

The Albanian labour authorities will assess the application on the basis of the offer/demand status of the local employment market and availability of unemployed Albanian citizens to fill in the position.

The work permit application is usually processed within 30 days following submission of all required documentation.An application fee of ALL 6,000 (approximately Euro 45, or 56 USD) is required.

Within a 90 day period from the obtainment of the work permit, the foreign employees are required to obtain the Albanian visa (Type –D Entry Visa), as well as enter and commence their work in Albania.If such term is not met, the work permit is considered invalid.This requirement does not apply if the foreign employee is national of a country for which Albania applies a visa free regime.[4]

c. Social Insurance

Unless there is an exception based on an international agreement entered into by Albania, foreign employees are required to pay social security similarly to Albanian employees.

---

[1] http://www.ilo.org/dyn/normlex/en/f?p=1000:11200:0::NO:11200:P11200_COUNTRY_ID:102532.
[2] Nations of certain countries, such as EU and US nationals, are exempted from the Work Permit requirement.
[3] Nations of certain countries may enter Albania, and stay visa free, for up to 90 days within a 180 day period.The full list of country based visa requirements may be found here http://www.punetejashtme.gov.al/en/services/consular-services/visa-regime-for-foreign-citizens.
[4] The full list of country based visa requirements may be found here http://www.punetejashtme.gov.al/en/services/consular-services/visa-regime-for-foreign-citizens.

C. Exit and Entry

a. Visa Types

The available visa types to enter Albania are as follows:
Type—A visa—for transit;
Type—C visa—for entry and stay of up to 90 days within 180 days;
Type—D visa—for entry and stay of more than 90 days within 180 days.
Nations of certain countries may enter Albania, and stay visa free, for up to 90 days within a 180 day period.

b. Restrictions for Exit and Entry

Albania does not generally apply entry discrimination based on nationality.The foreign national having breached the terms of allowed stay (either based on a visa or a visa free regime), but willing to voluntarily leave the country, are restricted from leaving the country without paying a fine of 50,000 lekë (approx.EUR 380 or USD 465). If the effective stay was longer than 1 month after the expiry of the allowed stay period, than the fine is doubled.

D. Trade Union and Labour Organizations

The freedom of employees to organize in trade unions and to strike, pursuant to the law, is guaranteed under the Albanian Constitution.

Even though there are a number of Trade Unions in Albania, they are not very active the private sector, except for privatized enterprises (e.g.mining sector, oil extraction sector, certain industrial plants etc.) formerly operating under state agencies or state owned companies).

Under the ALC prohibits employment discrimination and/or termination of employment on the basis of membership in trade unions.The ALC further sets certain terms and conditions for the strike to be deemed legitimate.

Based on the ALC, collective labour agreements may be entered at individual enterprise or at economic sector level, between one or several employers or employers' associations from one side and one or more trade unions from the other.

Upon its execution, the collective labour agreement becomes binding for all employees having adhered to it, and applicable to all or their employees, irrespective of the employee membership in the respective trade union.

Under the ALC Trade Unions have also a negotiating role during lay-off procedures and company restricting.

E. Labour Disputes

Labour disputes in Albania fall under the jurisdiction of the ordinary court system.As an exception to the rule, labour disputes between public agencies and civil servants fall under the jurisdiction of the Administrative court system.

In case of collective disputes (e.g.disputes between labour organizations or more employees and employer or trade unions), the ALC provides for a different procedure, through mediation, reconciliation and finally Arbitration Tribunal.However, due to the limited activity of trade unions, this procedure is almost never applied.

In practice, the most common disputes arising from the employment relationship relate to the unilateral termination of the employment agreement from the employer.Other, less common disputes, are related to breach of employee's rights and work-related injuries from the breach of the compulsory health and safety rules.

The ALC, is quite defensive to the employee's rights.The employer is always required to justify the unilateral termination of the employment agreement.Moreover, the employer is always required to follow a strict termination procedure, and failure to do so exposes the employer to a penalty equal to salary of the employee for two months.

In case of termination of an unlimited term contras, in addition to the justification and to the requirement to follow the termination procedure, the employer must also give to the employee a term notice, between 2 weeks and up to 3 months, depending on the duration of the employment relation.

Additionally, if the unilateral termination of the employee is deemed by the court to be unjustified, or based on discriminatory grounds, the employer may be fined with penalty equal to up to salary of the employee for twelve months.

In case the employee has worked for the same employer for a 3 year period, then upon termination of the employment, the employee is entitled to a seniority bonus of 50% of the last salary, for each year of work.The employee loses the right for the seniority bonus in case the termination is due to the fault of the employee.

The ALC provides for time limit of 3 years for labour related claims, and upon the expiry of said period the claim is time barred.A time limit of 180 days applies in case the employee claims that the unilateral termination of the contract was made without justified grounds by the employer.

V. Intellectual Property

A. Brief Introduction of IP Laws and Regulations

The main IP rights recognised by the Albanian legislation are:
Industrial Property Law-Law No.9947
(i) Patents;
(ii) Marks (trade or service marks);
(iii) Designs;
(iv) Utility Models;
(v) Geographical indications.
Copyright and Neighbouring Rights-Law No.35/2016
(i) Rights of authors;
(ii) Rights of performers;
(iii) other neighbouring rights;
(iv) Databases;
(v) Software.
Further, Albania protects the topographies of integrated circuits based on law no.8488.

Albania is a WIPO member and has ratified a number of relevant IP related treaties and conventions such as Paris Union Convention (CUP), Berne Union Convention (CUB), WTO's TRIPS Agreement, just to name a few.

B. Patent Application

A patent application may be filed by any person or any other entity that is equivalent to a legal person.A patent application may be filed jointly by more than one applicant.

The right for the patent applies to the inventor or to his/her successor.If the invention has been made on that basis of an employment or other agreement, the ruler is that the right for the patent is for the party having commissioned the research.If the value of the patent is significantly higher than the contractual remuneration, the employee has the right for a special compensation, in addition to the compensation agreed in the contract.

A patent application may claim a priority date in Albania, if a priority claim is filed no later than 12 months after the same patent application has been regularly made on:
(i) The basis of the national legislation of one of the CUP member states; or
(ii) The basis of the national legislation of one of the WOT member states.

If a priority claim is made, the Albanian patent with have the same application date as the date of the previous application in one of the above countries.

The main conditions for a successful patent application are:
(i) Novelty (the invention does not form part of the state of the art);
(ii) Inventive step (the invention is not obvious to the skilled person in the light of the state of the art);
(iii) Industrial application (the invention must have a practical application in any industry or in the agriculture).

The Albanian General Directorate of Industrial Property makes a formal assessment of these conditions, without performing actual testing.

A registered patent gives to the owner exclusivity on the invention covered by the patent, for a period of 20 years from the date of application, provided that within a period of 10 years from the patent application date, the owner is able to submit documentary evidence on the patentability of the same invention, issued by the European Patent Office, or by any other national patent office that is recognized by Albanian General Directorate of Industrial Property as having adequate testing capabilities based on treaties (i.e.PCT) or based on bilateral agreements.

A patent validly will be also subject to the timely payment of the relevant annuities.

C. Trademark Registration

A trademark or service mark (jointly "trademarks") is defined as a graphically represented sign that is able to distinguish the goods or services of an undertaking from those of other undertakings.

Trademarks may be composed of signs, words, shapes, colours, or any combination of them, including graphically represented sounds or light signals.

A trademark application may be filed at Albanian General Directorate of Industrial Property by anyone performing a business.

The registration of a trademark can be rejected on the basis of (i) absolute grounds; or (ii) relative grounds, such a such as the absence of a distinctive character (e.g.generic product names), use of reserved names/signs (e.g.names and symbols of states, international organisations, etc.), and conflicts with earlier registered marks.

In additional to a national application, rights on a trademark may be also extended in Albania based on the Madrid International Trademark System.

A trademark application may claim a priority date in Albania, if a priority claim is filed no later than 6 months after the same trademark application has been regularly made on:

(i) The basis of the national legislation of one of the CUP member states; or

(ii) The basis of the national legislation of one of the WOT member states.

If a priority claim is made, the Albanian trademark with have the same application date as the date of the previous application in one of the above countries.

A priority date may be also claimed in within a period of 6 months prior to the trademark application, the applicant has exposed the sign on goods/services during international exhibitions in Albania or in another the CUP member states.

A registered mark gives to the owner an exclusive right to use it in the course of business, for the same classes of goods/services it has been applied for, for a period of 10 years from the date of application.

D. Measures for IP Protection

Rights deriving from an IP are enforced through the court system.The main measures available to an IP owner in case of an infringement include the right to claim for the courts to:

(i) Establish that an infringement has occurred.

(ii) Order the payment of compensation caused by the infringement.

(iii) Order the seizure or destruction of infringing goods and/or of tools used to produce the goods.

(iv) Issue injunctions against the infringing party.

(v) Order publication of the court's decision in the media at the expense of the infringing party.

In case the IP infringement is made intentionally, it may amount to an administrative offence punishable by fines as well as criminal offence, punishable by fines and/or imprisonment.

VI. Environmental Protection

A. Department Supervising Environmental Protection

The Albanian Ministry of Tourism and Environment ("MTE") is the responsible state body for drafting and implementation of policies aimed at environmental protection.The specific sectors of responsibility includes also sustainable use of natural resources, nature and biodiversity protection, sustainable development and management of forests and pastures, monitoring of air and water quality, waste management, noises, industrial pollution, chemicals, climate change effects, protected areas and environmental impact assessment.

For what concerns the drafting of the specific legal framework, the MTE prepares and updates periodically the national plans and strategies for environment protection, which are approved by government decisions.

The concrete actions and measures for environment protection are enforced by the National Environmental Agency ("NEA") and the Regional Environmental Agencies ("REA").NEA is a central governmental agency under the responsibility of the minister responsible for environment, which control, organize and coordinate several regional environment agencies at the local level.

MTE, NEA and REA's are also responsible for the evaluation process and approval of the required environment permits.The control and inspection for the implementation of the environment law, rules and requirements is executed by the State Inspectorate of Environment, Forestry and Waters.

Furthermore, at the local government level, municipalities are responsible for the approval of environment local plans and strategies, in accordance with the national strategies and for granting adequate measures to protect air, soil and water quality from pollution, including measure to prevent and reduce acoustic pollution.

B. Brief Introduction of Laws and Regulations of Environmental Protection

The Republic of Albania has adopted a vast environment legislation, which very often, is harmonized with the European Union acquis communautaire.To date the transposition of EU acquis is advancing in all the environmental thematic areas, as a result of obligations raising from the Stabilization and Association Agreement signed between EU and Republic of Albania, which entered into force in 2009.

Furthermore Albanian Parliament has ratified several international agreements and treaties related to environment protection, including Cartagena Protocol on Biosafety, Framework Convention on Climate Change,

Kyoto Protocol to the Framework Convention on Climate Change, Convention on Biological Diversity, Vienna Convention for the Protection of the Ozone Layer, Montreal Protocol on Substances that deplete the Ozone Layer, Stockholm Convention on Persistent Organic Pollutants, Convention of the Law of the Sea and Convention to Combat Desertification.

The main domestic laws on environment to be mentioned are Law 10431, dated 09 June 2011, "On environment protection", Law 10440, dated 07 July 2011, "On the Environmental Impact Assessment", Law 10448, dated 14 July 2011, "On environment permits", law 9385, dated 04 May 2005, "On forests and forest services", Law 10266, dated 15 April 2010 "On air protection from pollution", Law 10463, dated 22 September 2011, "On the integrated waste management", Law 9587, dated 20 July 2006, "On biodiversity protection", Law 8906, dated 6 June 2002, On Protected Areas" and Law 111/2012, "On the integrated water resources management".

C. Evaluation of Environment Protection

The environment protection remains a challenge in Albania and is in opposition with the rapid urban development and growth of the economic activities.A very positive aspect is the fact that the process of drafting national environmental legislation and policies is based on requirements defined by the approximation to the EU legislation and policies.

Moreover, Albanian has a good cooperation on environment issues with neighbouring countries and regional ones and is actively involved in the international initiatives.The role of the civil society and NGO's is growing together with a higher level of education and awareness of the population on environment protection importance. To the other hand, despite the efforts, Albania face several difficulties to reach good standards on environment protection.

Although environmental monitoring and inspection are stipulated in the environmental legislation, Albania main problems are related to the correct implementation, control and monitoring of the legislation and rules.Inspection and territory control is still problematic, partly aligned with international good practices and several operators still operate without environmental permits or do not exercise their activity in compliance with the requirements.

The low enforcement levels are mainly due to lack of administrative capacity, reduced financial resources, control of territory gaps and inappropriate coordination between central and local state bodies.

VII. Dispute Resolution

The Constitution of the Republic of Albania provides that the judicial power is exercised by the District Courts the Courts of Appeal and the High Court.

The High Court is considered as a court of law dealing only on matters regarding the misapplication of the law and/or procedural breaches.However, the High Court has original jurisdiction when adjudicating criminal charges against the President of the Republic, the Prime Minister, members of the Council of Ministers, deputies, judges of the High Court, and judges of the Constitutional Court.The High Court has also the right to set case laws.

Currently in Albania are established the following courts:

(i) Civil Courts of Appeal and District Courts, which deal for matters of the civil/private law, such as employment, labour, contractual, familiar, etc.;

(ii) Administrative Courts of Appeal and District Courts, which deal for matters of the administrative/public law, such as claims against administrative acts;

(iii) Criminal Courts of Appeal and District Courts, which deal for matters of the criminal law;

(iv) The Appeal and the District Court of Serious Crimes, which deals for certain felonies considered as serious, such as crimes made by structural criminal groups, etc.

The Constitution establishes also a Constitutional Court, which deals only for matters that regard the final adjudication of the individual complaints for the violation of their constitutional rights for a fair trial after all legal means for the protection of those rights have been exhausted.

The cases are commenced upon filing of a lawsuit and the accompanying evidence, at the competent district court.The court clerks shall serve these documents to the respondent party, who on the other hand should submit the declaration of defence and/or counterclaim and evidence supporting their position.After the parties have submitted their claims and evidence, the court shall request the parties to provide their explanations in an oral hearing.

The court usually will settle the case in a few hearings.

The access at the High Court is limited only for matters concerning procedural breaches and in breaches of the material law which are considered, upon discretion of the High Court, as highly important for the case laws and in cases when the decisions of the lower instances are in violation with the case laws of settled by the unifying decisions of the High Court.

The domestic law provisions governing both domestic and international arbitration procedures were contained in the Albanian Civil Procedure Code (the "ACPC").

Law no.8812, dated 17 May 2001 has repealed provisions governing international arbitration.Now the ACPC requires that provisions governing international arbitration shall be contained in a separate law.Article 399 of the ACPC (which is still in force) further provides that the procedure for the recognition and enforcement of decisions of courts of foreign jurisdictions shall apply also for the recognition and enforcement of international arbitration awards.To date the Parliament has not approved a law governing international arbitration.

However, the Republic of Albania has ratified the 1958 New York Convention on the Recognition and Enforcement of Foreign Arbitral Awards, therefore self-executing provisions of the New York Convention have become part of the domestic legislation in Albania.Moreover, in case of conflict, provisions of the New York Convention shall prevail with respect to provisions of the domestic law.

A. Methods and Bodies of Dispute Resolution

Alternative dispute resolution has been recently regulated and is not widely spread in Albania.A new legal framework on mediation and alternative dispute resolution has been adopted in 2011, aiming to offer a better support on the matter.International arbitration has been chosen by the parties in several civil cases having significant values/claimed damages, while domestic arbitration has a lower preference.

B. Application of Laws

The matter of applicable of laws is governed in Albania pursuant to law no.10428 "On international private law". It sets rules on the law governing private civil matters, in case the matter has an Albanian as well as a foreign element, such as matters of applicable law to legal personality, family inheritance, property, contracts etc.

Law no.10428 law is substantial approximated to EU Regulation no.593/2008 on the law applicable to contractual obligations (Rome I) as well as to the EU Regulation no.864/2007 on the law applicable to non-contractual obligations (Rome II).

VIII. Others

A. Anti-commercial Bribery

a. Brief Introduction of Anti-commercial Bribery Laws and Regulations

Corruptive and bribery practices, both in the private and public sector, are a criminal offence and as such punishable under the Albanian Penal Code (APC) with significant fines and/or imprisonment.The punishable offences cover both active and passive parts of the practice.

Albania has moreover ratified several corruption-related international treaties and conventions and is member of major international organizations and programs dealing with corruption and/or organized crime[1].

Despite the existing legal provisions criminalizing corruption and bribery practices, as well as the ratified treaties and conventions, corruption remains big problem for Albania, as it is constantly ranked between countries with a high corruption index.

To tackle the issue, Albania has recently passed a constitutional reform in the judicial sector, with the aim to tackle corruption and bribery at the highest level of the public administration.

The reform will also establish an independent prosecutor and specialized investigation unit to investigate and prosecute corruption and organized crime.Once fully implemented, the newly established institutions aim to discourage corruption and promote foreign and domestic investment.

b. Department Supervising Anti-commercial Bribery

Up to now, the department supervising anti-commercial bribery practices has been the Public Prosecutor's Office.

Based on the recent reform, anti-commercial bribery practices will be investigated and prosecuted by an ad

---

[1] Such as, just to name a few, the Civil Law Convention on Corruption (Council of Europe), the Criminal Law Convention on Corruption (Council of Europe), the Additional Protocol to Criminal Law Convention on Corruption (Council of Europe), and the United Nations Convention against Corruption (UNCAC) etc.

hoc Special Prosecutor's Office, which will focus on the corruption and bribery matters, as well as links with the organized crime.

In addition to the Public Prosecutor's Public Prosecutor's Office, anti-commercial bribery in the public sector are also investigated on an administrative level by the High Inspectorate of Declaration and Audit of Assets and Conflict of Interests as well as the Anticorruption Department near the Council of Ministers of the Republic of Albania.

These bodies will continue to operate at an administrative level also after the Special Prosecutor's Office.

c. Punitive Actions

The following are the punishment for corruption practices in Albania:
a) Private sector:
• Active   Imprisonment for up to 3 years.
• Passive   Imprisonment for up to 5 years.
b) Public officers:
• Active   Imprisonment for up to 3 years.
• Passive   Imprisonment for up to 8 years.
c) Foreign public officers:
• Active   Imprisonment for up to 3 years.
• Passive   Imprisonment for up to 8 years.
d) High state officials / local elected officials:
• Active   Imprisonment for up to 5 years.
• Passive   Imprisonment for up to 12 years.
e) Intermediaries—undue influence in public officers:
• Active   Imprisonment for up to 3 years.
• Passive   Imprisonment for up to 4 years.
f) Elections officer:
• Active   Imprisonment for up to 5 years.
• Passive   Imprisonment for up to 5 years.
g) Court witness, expert or translator:
• Active   Imprisonment for up to 4 years.
h) Judge, prosecutor or other justice official:
• Active   Imprisonment for up to 4 years.
• Passive   Imprisonment for up to 10 years.
i) Judge or other justice official of foreign courts:
• Active   Imprisonment for up to 4 years.
• Passive   Imprisonment for up to 10 years.
j) Local or foreign arbiter:
• Active   Imprisonment for up to 4 years.
• Passive   Imprisonment for up to 8 years.
k) Member of foreign juries:
• Active   Imprisonment for up to 4 years.
• Passive   Imprisonment for up to 8 years.

In addition to the imprisonment, secondary punishment may include the seizure of the property/benefit realized through the criminal offence, and banishment for holding public office/performing business/trade/profession for a specific period of time.

B. Project Contracting

Project contracting in Albania by public institutions is based on the rules set forth by Law no.9643, dated 20 November 2006 "On public procurement", as amended, and by the secondary legislation approved on its basis (jointly the "Public Procurement Rules").

a. Permission System

The permission system in Albania for project developments is based on Law no.107/2014 "On territory planning and development", as amended, and by the secondary legislation approved on its basis (jointly the "Planning and Development Rules").

Planning and Development Rules aim to:
(i) ensure the sustainable development of the territory;

(ii) assess the current and prospective potential for territorial development at the national and local level;

(iii) promote appropriate actions for the protection, restoration and enhancement of the quality of natural and cultural heritage;

(iv) enable the right to use and develop property;

(v) create appropriate conditions and equal opportunities and equal opportunities for housing, economic and social activities for all social categories, economic and social cohesion and enjoyment of property rights;

(vi) ensure that national and local planning authorities draft and regularly update planning documents; ensure that planning authorities co-ordinate their planning activities to promote harmonized and integrated territorial planning.

Albania has established the National Territorial Planning Register (e-Planning), as the integrated electronic territorial planning platform, serving all planning authorities in Albania, both at the central and local level.

Through e-Planning, the broader involvement of stakeholders, civil society and the general public is envisaged in the process, so important and tangible by all, territorial planning.

The two components of the e-Planning platform consist of:

(i) Register, or library of planning documents, drafted or under drafting process;

(ii) The web-GIS portal, integrating the mapping material of planning documents.

Relevant size projects are approved by the National Territory Council, composed of several ministers of the government, and chaired by the Prime Minister.

b. Invitation to Bid and Bidding

The invitation to bid as well as the phases of the bidding process are outlined in the Public Procurement Rules.

The Public Procurement Rules provide for different types of procedures and bidding phases, depending on the type and value of the project.

A bidding process may be open (i.e.any interested party may participate and submit a bid) or restricted (i.e.only invited parties are allowed to participate).

In an open procedure, the experience and qualifications of the bidders are assessed jointly with their financial proposal, while in the restricted procedure, the bidder experience and qualifications are assessed before a financial price is submitted.

In practice, in cases of high value project where it was expected that bidders meet a certain level of expertise and qualification, the Contracting Authorities have often applied the restricted process, with a first stare, pre-qualification of interested parties, followed by second stage; invitation of the interested parties meeting the qualification requirements, to participate in the bidding process.

As the Public Procurement Rules further delegate to the Contracting Authority the right to detail the terms and conditions of the bidding procedure, and to choose the most appropriate bidding structure for the project, the applicable procedure shall be a case by case design of the Contracting Authority.

阿根廷

作者：Valeriano Guevara Lynch、Raúl Fratantoni、Roberto A.Fortunati、Nicolás Rukavina Mikusic
译者：林翠珠、郭芳

一、概述

（一）经济、政治、法律体系和社会概述

1. 政治

阿根廷共和国（以下简称"阿根廷"）是联邦国家，划分为23个省和1个自治城市（布宜诺斯艾利斯）。作为联邦国家，除了阿根廷宪法授权联邦政府的事务外，所有省份均实行自治。

联邦政府的主要权力有三项：行政权（总统）、立法权（参、众两院组成的议会）和司法权（最高法院及各地方法院）。总统和议员由直选选举产生，最高法院的5名大法官则由总统提名后参议院批准任命。各地方法院的法官由行政官委员会提名后经相应的国家或省级立法机构批准任命。

最近一次总统选举是2015年，毛里西奥·马克里当选总统，任期至2019年12月。

马克里是共和国方案党（PRO）的创始人之一，并于2015年与激进公民联盟（UCR）和公民联盟（CC）组成"我们一起改变"（Cambiemos）政治联盟，该政治联盟服务于国家、省和地方政府选举任命总统、省长和地方市长。"我们一起改变"联盟还参与了2017年国家、省和地方政府选举，并在大部分行政辖区胜过庇隆党，成为全国得票最高的政治力量。此外，该联盟在布宜诺斯艾利斯、科尔多瓦、恩特雷里奥斯、门多萨、萨尔塔和圣菲等重要辖区都占有优势。

2. 经济

阿根廷的经济结构包括三大支柱：收入多样化；自然资源可得性；高质量的人力资源。为提高国家生产力，政府着重提高国家基础建设，鼓励国家去官僚化。

阿根廷是拉丁美洲第三经济强国，2017年其国内生产总值（GDP）超过6 000亿美元。其人口总数约为4 400万，人均GDP为22 500美元。阿根廷GDP在2016年缩减了2.2%，但2017年相比2016年增长了2.7%。此外，GDP基本赤字从2016年的4.3%降低至2017年的1.9%。

阿根廷作为全球国土面积第八大国家（面积约280万平方公里），在能源和农业方面坐拥数量多、品种繁的自然资源，有着发展农业和畜牧业、油气、矿业和再生能源的好机遇。

关于阿根廷2017年进出口相关数据统计见图1、图2。

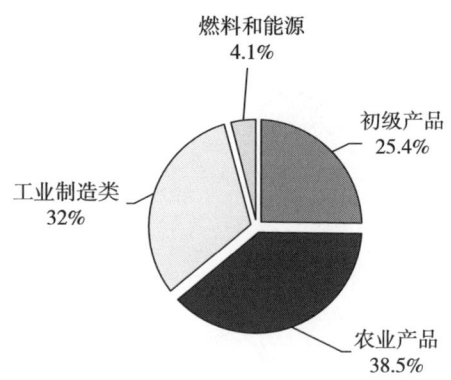

图1　阿根廷2017年出口数据

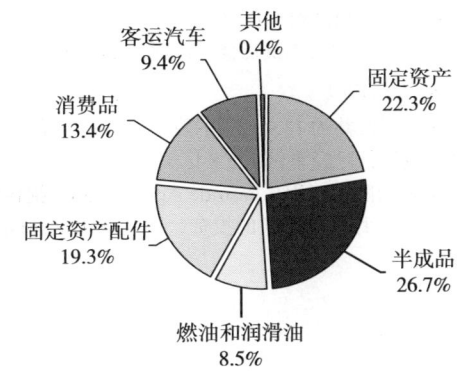

图 2　阿根廷 2017 年进口数据

3. 法律体系

阿根廷的最高司法机构是最高法院，由 5 名大法官组成。

阿根廷法律系统不采用遵循先例原则，因此各地方法院没有遵循其高级法院判决的法律义务。然而，在实践中，律师却会引用判例，且地方法院的法官在判决案件时也会根据这些判例，以免判决被高级法院推翻。

此外，阿根廷在行政、民事和商事诉讼方面，既没有口头程序，也没有陪审团审案制度。司法程序多数由书面陈述和仅一名法官介入完成。如果该法官的最终判决被上诉，该案件将被移交给高级法院或由 3 名法官组成的上诉法庭，而数量极为有限的案件能够进行再次上诉，由（省级或国家）最高法院进行最终调停。

4. 社会

阿根廷有约 4 300 万人口，2016 年人口增长率为 0.99%。

阿根廷人口受以前移民潮的影响有所增长。1850 年代到 1950 年代，阿根廷接收的欧洲移民，主要来自意大利和西班牙。近十年，移民群体主要为中国和韩国移民。近来来自邻近国家的移民数量有所上升。

2010 年阿根廷人口年龄构成如下：15 岁以下人口占 25.5%；15～65 岁人口占 64.3%；65 岁以上人口占 10.2%。

关于教育水平，10 岁以上的阿根廷人识字率为 98%，20 岁以上的居民有 7% 完成了大学教育。

2015 年，联合国发布的人类发展指数中衡量人类发展的关键标准方面——即预期寿命、教育水平和生活质量，阿根廷在拉丁美洲排名第二位，在全球排名第四十五位。

（二）"一带一路"倡议下与中国企业的合作

中国驻阿根廷大使杨万明指出，"一带一路"倡议在推进国际和区域发展计划及目前美洲区域基础设施一体化。他还指出，在阿根廷发展"一带一路"建设的核心内容为"五通"：政策沟通，进一步密切高层双边对话机制；设施联通，特别着重于水电、核电、铁路、光伏发电等重大合作项目，加强发展公路、港口、海上和内河运输、航空、能源管道、海底电缆、光纤、电信、信息通信技术等领域的合作；贸易畅通；资金融通；民心相通。[①]

虽然目前并无任何关于中国企业参与阿根廷"一带一路"建设的官方消息，但据很多杂志报道，在中国政府的支持下，中国企业将要或可能参与阿根廷数个建设项目，比如：

1. 贝尔格拉诺货运（Belgrano Cargas）

根据阿根廷政府第 868/2016 号行政法令批准的合约条款，恢复火车"贝尔格拉诺货运"线项目由

---

① 参见 https://www.lanacion.com.ar/2037609-nuevas-oportunidades-de-desarrollo。

一个中国公司（中国机械设备工程股份有限公司）负责。

该工程投资 2 470 万美元，由中国开发银行提供资金。特别是该项目包括安装恢复 3 800 公里的铁轨。

2. 黑水隧道（Agua Negra Tunnel）

黑水隧道是一个基建工程，包括两段共约 13.9 公里的隧道，穿过安第斯山脉，连接阿根廷和智利。该工程总造价 150 亿美元，美洲开发银行已经垫付了 2.8 亿美元。

智利和阿根廷同意为黑水安第斯山隧道工程（Paso de Agua Negra）提供优惠预算。该隧道位于阿根廷和智利的战略位置，同时该工程号称当务之急的投资，旨在解决交通问题，无须和邻近交通道路竞争。①

二、投资

（一）市场准入

1. 投资主管部门

阿根廷没有专门负责监督外国投资的部门。但是阿根廷投资和国际贸易机构负责与政府部门吸引投资者促进工程快速进行，在投资生命期帮助投资者解决冲突，就投资相关问题提供最新统计数据，并就各个方面提供具体信息，为潜在投资者提供专门分析和信息包。

2. 投资行业规定

根据《外商直接投资法》（FDI 法案）的规定，外国直接投资在执行前无须经过任何官方机构批准。根据宪法训令，FDI 法案规定国内外投资者不论投资商务类型都可享受同等权利。这些权利包括汇出利润、调回投资、按照阿根廷法律许可的任何公司类型构建企业、享受与国内公司同等条件的国内信贷便利。

3. 投资方式

根据《外商直接投资法》的规定，海外投资者在下述领域可以无限制投资：自由兑换外币、资本货物及其零配件、合法汇回海外投资者拥有的外币利润或资本、可自由兑换的外币的国外贷款资本化以及无形财产。

需要注意的是，在阿根廷以永久方式进行投资活动必须在国内注册分公司或当地子公司。从这个意义上讲，投资者在阿根廷进行投资项目时有三个选择：一是在阿根廷设立外国分公司；二是获取已存续公司的股权；三是组建新公司。后两个选择需要外国投资者向当地商业公共登记处登记备案为股东。

4. 准入条件及审查

阿根廷宪法规定国内外投资者享有同等权利，但也有一些具体法规条款对在阿根廷的国外投资者进行了明确约束，其中最主要的约束有：

①《农村土地法案》明确了国外投资个人或公司获取农地的限制，详情参见"土地政策"部分。

②《文化遗产法案》规定对于任何国家广播公司，国外公司最多只能拥有 30% 的股票或投票权。

③ 内政部发布的第 15385/1944 号法令和第 166/2009 号决议规定国外投资个人或公司在获取国际边界附近的土地时应得到政府的特别授权。

④《航空法》规定服务于国内客运、货运或邮政的国家航空公司的大多数股票或投票权必须由阿根廷公司或定居于阿根廷的个人拥有或控制。

（二）外汇管理

1. 外汇管理部门

阿根廷的外汇市场由独立于联邦政府的自主公司——阿根廷中央银行（CBA）监管。阿根廷中央银行章程规定：所有个人或法人实体，无论是否为本地居民，都可在外汇市场进行自由操作；所有操

---

① 参见 https://www.ebitan.org/en/proyecto.php。

作依当事方合意的汇率结算；金融和外汇实体操作无时间限制；汇票或誓章无强制签名要求，除非实体有核实客户身份和登记操作的义务。

2. 外汇法律、法规概况

2015年12月，阿根廷政府启动外汇市场的撤销管制规定程序和"去科层化"，这一结果结束了严格的外汇管制时代。

在现行规则下，如果作为跨境或本地交易的一个环节，阿根廷居民（包括有国外股东的当地实体）可无限制地购买外汇并汇至国外。一般来说，跨境交易包括阿根廷和非阿根廷居民之间的交易（比如进口货物或服务、支付股东股息等）。此外，阿根廷居民可购买外汇并存放于国内外作如下用途：本地存款；国外房地产投资；贷款给非本地居民；国外直接投资；国外间接投资。

另外，非阿根廷居民可购买外汇用于收回投资。

外汇市场的汇率是由外汇货币的供求决定的，但阿根廷中央银行也通过自身账户买卖外币进行市场干预。

3. 外资企业外汇管理要求

自2015年12月起，政府启动撤销管制规定和简化外汇市场的程序，此后在外汇管理方面对外国企业不作特殊限制。

（三）金融融资

1. 主要金融机构

根据阿根廷中央银行2017年9月发布的排名，阿根廷前十大民营银行（基于自有总资产）为：加利西亚银行（Banco de Galicia y Buenos Aires S.A.）、中国工商银行（Industrial and Commercial Bank of China）、美国花旗银行（Citibank N.A）、阿根廷法国银行（BBVA Banco Frances S.A）、金融银行（Banco Supervielle S.A）、巴塔哥尼亚银行（Banco Patagonia S.A）、桑坦德瑞欧银行（Banco Santander Rio S.A）、阿根廷汇丰银行（HSBC Bank Argentina S.A）、阿根廷信贷合作银行（Banco CredicoopCooperativoLimitado）和宏观银行（Banco Macro S.A）。

此外，还有其他几家阿根廷大众银行，例如阿根廷国家银行、布宜诺斯艾利斯省银行、科尔多瓦省银行和布宜诺斯艾利斯市银行及其他银行。

2. 外资企业融资条件

很多（公共或私人的）金融机构向本地和国外投资者提供信用额度，举例如下：

① 阿根廷国家银行向公司提供信用额度，包括运营资本和投资的贷款，用于产品和销售成本、出口前融资和筹资、参加国际展会等。同时也提供资本租赁和代收服务。

② 投资外贸银行（BICE）向其客户提供美元或比索的信用额度。该银行主要产品之一，允许投资者在发展区域生产的再生能源相关项目中筹资高达总额的70%，通过该信用额度最多可借贷约1 000万美元。

③ 联邦投资委员会（CFI）本着促进阿根廷区域和各省发展目的为中小型企业提供财政资助。这些信用额度旨在筹备运营资本、固定资产和投资前融资。此外还提供出口前融资和支持出口产品的特殊资助。

④ 发展中小型和微型企业国家基金会向中小型企业提供低成本信贷，用于投资项目、促进劳动、资本和提高节能。

（四）土地政策

1. 土地法律、法规概况

与土地相关的最重要的法规是《农村土地法案》及其监管法令（合称"农村土地法规"）。这些法规规范限制外国人（法人或个人）因生产性或非生产性原因收购农村土地（例如市区外的小地块，无论其土地用途是什么）。

此外，内政部发布的第 15385/1944 号法令和第 166/2009 号决议规定了当地居民或外国人通过任何途径（租赁或其他）拥有或使用国际边界附近的财产的特殊要求。基于国家安全原因，外国人在拥有或使用边界附近财产时必须取得政府的额外授权。

2. 外资企业获得土地规定

农村土地法规中，"外资拥有权"表示以下述各方为受益人的农村土地所有权（包括少数股东权益）的获得、过户和转让：

① 外国个人，法律规定豁免的除外（符合最低居住要求者）；
② 对法人实体直接控股超过 51% 的，或对该法人实体决策有决定权的外国个人或实体；
③ 外国实体或个人通过投票在当地决策过程胜出而进行控制的法人实体。

农村土地规章中与外资企业获得土地最密切相关的约束如下：

① 外资对农村土地的拥有权或占有不得超过阿根廷领土农村土地总面积的 15%，该比例在计算时包括相关土地所在的省份和自治市领土在内。
② 同一国籍的外国人持有阿根廷国家级、省级和市级农村土地面积不得超过上述①"阿根廷领土农村土地总面积的 15%"中的 30%。
③ 对于同一外国所有者的土地拥有权或占有：阿根廷"核心地区"[①]不得超过 1 000 公顷；国内其他地区不得超过一定公顷数（关于具体公顷数值，1 000 公顷为"核心地区"的临界数值）。
④ 外国实体或个人不得成为"永久的标志性水源"部分或其临近农村土地的所有人或占有人。

根据农村土地法规，位于工业区、工业产区或工业园区的土地不视为农村土地。

（五）企业设立与解散

1. 企业形式

在阿根廷，外国企业需通过其全资或部分拥有的子公司或分公司运营。该类子公司可在几种集团类型下运营，其中最常见的是：股份有限责任公司；有限责任公司。此外，近来出现了两种新的股份有限责任公司，单一股东股份有限责任公司和简化股份有限责任公司。

无论是外国股东的子公司、外国总部的分公司或是作为本地公司股东的外国公司，作为企业，其登记都受到阿根廷商业公共登记处的管辖控制。

（1）子公司

外国公司可选择设立本地子公司。这种情况要求外国公司先在阿根廷注册为外国股东，根据阿根廷相关法律要求该公司必须符合企业设立要求。

一旦建立子公司，就是不同于外国股东的法人实体。这些实体适用通常责任限制，外国股东需承担的本地责任将限制为该股东所持的股权（法庭裁定否定法人人格或认定股东有责等特殊情况除外，但该类情况鲜有发生）。

以下是关于阿根廷最常见公司实体类型的特征和组建要求：

① 股份有限责任公司

A. 基本要求

组建股份有限责任公司时有几个要求必须特别重视。其中最显著的要求是股份有限责任公司必须至少有两个持重要股权的股东（至少持有公司股份的 5%）；公司名称必须真实、原创无误；章程中需准确描述公司的目的。

B. 资本

股份有限责任公司的资本以股票形式表现，以阿根廷比索为基准，并有平等稳定的票面值。资本金额必须在附中写明。根据现行规章，股份有限责任公司的最低资本金额为 100 000 比索（约 5 000 美元）。附则订立完成时，资本总金额应是被认购完毕的，且每位申购股东都必须缴款，至少 25% 的资本需以现金实缴，其余 75% 的资本在后续两年需完成缴款。如无法以现金实缴，则需在认购时全额付讫。

---

① 由布宜诺斯艾利斯、科尔多瓦和圣达菲省的一些部门组成。

C. 管理

股份有限责任公司由 1 名或多名董事组成的董事会管理，受政府"永久监管"的公司除外。这类公司的董事会需由不少于 3 名董事组成。董事可以是阿根廷人或外国人，无须是股东。然而，大多数股东必须是阿根廷居民或其真实住所在阿根廷。董事经股东大会任免。董事最多可被选任 3 个财政年度，且可以连任。附则必须明确每位董事的任期。

董事至少每季度要开一次会，并按每人一票进行投票。在董事会大部分成员都出席会议的情况下可授权 1 名董事代表投票。

D. 政府永久监管

被政府永久监管的公司，申报要求更为严格。受永久监管的公司实体（股份有限责任公司、有限责任公司、单一股份有限责任公司、简化股份有限责任公司）有以下几个特征：公开发行股票或证券；资本超过 10 000 000 比索（约 500 000 美元）；以收益或未来收益为承诺向公众进行资本化、储蓄业务或以各种方式筹集金钱或证券；进行特许公共服务；控制或曾控制其他受政府永久监管的公司。

受永久监管的公司需遵守下述要求：公司需指定一个正式审计师和一个候补审计师（需为本地会计师或律师），不受该政府监管的公司也可任命审计师，但非强制；每次股东大会需提前至少 15 个工作日通知商业公共登记处，商业公共登记处可决定是否派督察员参会，核实公司是否遵守所有适用的公司规章；董事会准备详细的年度财政报告，向股东们汇报公司财务状况；资本认购，即便是现金认购，需在认购时全额付讫。

② 有限责任公司

有限责任公司和股份有限责任公司有很多共同特征，也遵守很多相同要求。这两种公司实体的主要不同是：有限责任公司的合伙人数不得超过 50 人（而股份有限责任公司对股东人数并无限制）；有时选择有限责任公司是因为其在某些辖区的有利税率（例如作为美国纳税中间实体）；有限责任公司的资本均分为等价配额，且每份配额有相同投票权；配额转让需向商业公共登记处登记备案；有限责任公司对资本没有最低要求，但公司资本需用于满足实现公司的目的；有限责任公司管理人任命期限可以是定期或无限期；如任命 1 名以上管理人，附则必须阐明各管理人行使权力的方法，如单独行使、交替行使、模糊行使或作为一个整体行使。

③ 单一股东股份有限责任公司

单一股东股份有限责任公司和股份有限责任公司有很多共同特征，遵守很多相同要求。这两种公司实体的主要不同是：单一股东股份有限责任公司仅有一名股东，而股份有限责任公司需至少两名股东；尽管公司性质如此，单一股东股份有限责任公司资本在认购当时需完全整合（无论是以现金或其他方式）；单一股东股份有限责任公司的股东不能是另一单一股东股份有限责任公司的股东，但股份有限责任公司可以；单一股东股份有限责任公司永远受限于政府监管，不论该公司资本是否超过 1 000 万比索（约 50 万美元）。

④ 简化股份有限责任公司

简化股份有限责任公司是近年才出现的公司形式，以便企业家快速简易地注册法人组建公司。而对本地或大中型外资公司来说，组建此类法人并无障碍。简化股份有限责任公司与其他公司形式的不同之处在于：24 小时就可成立（前提是使用了法律规定的附则格式），且其组织文件可通过数码形式执行并提交商业公共登记处；公司账簿记录需以数码格式保存；公司资本最少为最低工资的两倍，新近定额为 10 000 比索（约 500 美元）；股东可决定简化股份有限责任公司运行的具体重要事项，比如组织文件的大部分内容、公司法人团体的构成和机能。

（2）分公司

如以分公司形式运营，总公司需承担责任。因此，涉及授信业务时，大部分外资公司倾向于通过子公司而不是分公司来经营。

税收对分公司和子公司是一视同仁的。一般来说，分公司的维护费用比子公司要低。因为分公司无须在阿根廷任命本地董事及法定审计师，也不用在当地开股东大会，不会产生其他额外开销。然而，选择以分公司形式在当地运营时，低维护成本并非关键因素。因为通常来说，维护费用并不高于总公司承担的责任风险。

通常来说，一方面，并不强制要求总公司分配资本到分公司，但这基本上由分公司实际经营的业务而定。另一方面，分公司需强制在阿根廷开设独立账户，准备和提交财务报表和纳税表。

分公司由总公司任命的1名或多名法人代表管理。总公司以授权委托书形式准确说明法人代表的权限。被任命的管理人承担与股份有限责任公司董事相同的义务和责任。

2. 设立程序

阿根廷《公司法》规定了外国人（个人或法人）建立法人实体或在阿根廷注册分公司时必须遵守的具体规定。

（1）子公司

如果有意在当地设立子公司的外国投资者系法人实体而非个人，必须在商业公共登记处注册为外国股东。为此，外国实体须提交以下文件：

① 外国实体董事会的决议。表明同意公司注册为外国股东，并授权法定代表人在地方公司行使投票权。

② 信誉凭证。由外国实体注册地所在司法辖区的相关机关签发。

③ 公司组织文件的副本（公司章程和附则）及其任何修正案。

④ 最近期审计的财务报表的副本，如无法提供，则附上类似的会计书面凭证。

⑤ 外国实体股东的身份凭证。

⑥ 书面陈述。表明是否存在个人直接或间接持有20%或以上的外国实体股份或投票权的情况，或者是否存在个人直接或间接以其他方式控制外国实体的情况。如有，则提供任何此类个人的特定信息。

上述文件必须：由外国实体董事会正式授权的高级职员核实签署；由公证人公证，该公证须根据1961年《关于取消要求外国公文书认证的公约》认证文件的合法性（海牙认证）。如果相关辖区无法提供海牙认证，则须取得领事馆认证。

如果外国股东按上述要求在商业公共登记处完成注册（如果要求如上所述），在当地成立子公司需要完成以下步骤：

① 提交公司名称变更预留申请书，确保公司名称的可用性。

② 视公司形式而定，将新实体的附则纳入公契或经公证的私人文书（简化股份有限责任公司除外，该公司类型可使用数码形式的文件，详见前述）。

③ 向商业公共登记处提交新实体的附则，登记处将根据义务公示和资本支付的有关要求之合规性批准登记。

（2）分公司

有意在阿根廷注册分公司的外国实体必须向商业公共登记处提交以下文件：

① 外国实体的公司章程和附则的副本。

② 证明该外国实体信誉良好的公司凭证副本。

③ 董事会决议副本。表示同意成立和注册阿根廷分公司并确定其当地资本（如有）。

④ 董事会决议副本。任命阿根廷分公司总经理，向其授予授权委托书以执行分公司的所有事务。

⑤ 特别授权书。内容为：在阿根廷当局注册分公司；执行法律手续所需的一切步骤；代表分公司与行政机关和司法机关交涉。

⑥ 相关证据，显示外国公司在其所属司法管辖区开展主要业务和经营活动的行为能力不受任何限制或禁令的影响。

⑦ 书面证据，披露外国公司股东或成员身份。

⑧ 书面证据，证明在阿根廷境外至少符合以下条件之一：

• 存在一个或多个代理、分公司或常驻代表处，必须出示各机构的信誉凭证以证明该机构的存在。该等凭证由与该代理、分公司或常驻代表处相关的权威机构出具。

• 拥有其他公司股权的所有权。根据公认会计准则，该所有权将被视为非流动资产。根据公司账簿中的会计记录，提供外国公司的年度财务报表和/或外国公司的授权签字人签署的证书作证明。

• 在注册所在地拥有固定资产的所有权，其存在和价值被证明属于前述所述的股权。

• 上述文件必须：由外国实体董事会正式授权的高级职员核实签署；由公证人公证，该公证须根据 1961 年《关于取消要求外国公文书认证的公约》认证文件的合法性（海牙认证）。如果相关辖区无法提供海牙认证，则须取得领使馆认证。

注册登记阿根廷分公司或子公司须在官方公报中发布为期一天的通知。

3. 解散方式及要求

（1）解散子公司

启动解散和清算程序，必须采取以下步骤：

① 公司董事会必须召开定期和临时股东大会，批准关闭和清算公司，及委任个人担任该公司的清算人。在此阶段，公司必须在公司名称中添加"停业清算"一词。

② 股东大会的决议和清算人的委任必须在商业公共登记处登记备案。清算人只能处理紧急事宜和采取一切必要措施进行公司清盘。

③ 所有资产处置完毕并清偿债务后，公司必须出具清盘余额明细表，并将注销书报批商业公共登记处。

④ 公司必须向税务机关（联邦和地方）和与其经营活动相关的任何其他公共办事处提交注销申请书。

（2）解散分公司

向地方当局注销分公司，必须采取以下步骤：

① 分公司总部必须决定解散、清算和注销阿根廷分公司并指定清算人。在此阶段，分公司必须在公司名称中添加"停业清算"一词。

② 清算人必须清算资产并偿清阿根廷分公司的债务。

③ 清算结清后，必须发布清算余额明细表。

④ 分公司必须向商业公共登记处、税务机关和任何其他主管办公室注销其注册。

如果分公司尚有未尽义务，在尽义务前不得予以注销（例如，未偿清对税务机关的税款、未遵守提交财务报表的规则等）。

（六）合并收购

1. 规则

《反托拉斯法》要求当事各方就部分经济集中交易（以下简称"集中交易"）报批阿根廷反垄断局（以下简称"反垄断局"）。受《反托拉斯法》影响的交易会对一个或多个企业产生直接或间接的控制力或实质影响。必须上报反垄断局的集中交易包括合并、持续进行的转移、股票收购、股东协议、合资协议和其他就企业管理决策授予基于法律或基于事实的控制权或者实质控制权的协议。

《反托拉斯法》要求在集中交易结束后一周内补交报告和申请。如果交易未能获得反垄断许可，反垄断局有权命令各方解除交易或让买方放弃收购。然而，由于通常在各方已经结束集中交易并合并相关业务之后，反垄断局才提出反对。因此，实际上反垄断局通常要求原买方为其获得的资产或业务寻找合适的新买家以恢复竞争状态。

2. 涵盖的交易

如果出现以下情况，相关协议的签署方应向反垄断局报告集中交易：

① 收购集团和被收购集团在阿根廷的年销售净额总和超过 2 亿阿根廷比索（约合 1 000 万美元）；

② 交易中阿根廷部分的金额或待转移的阿根廷资产的价值超过 2 000 万阿根廷比索（约合 100 万美元）。

如果集中交易不符合上述金额条件，但在过去 12 个月内收购集团从事的一项阿根廷集中交易价值 2 000 万阿根廷比索（约合 100 万美元），或过去 36 个月内收购集团从事的一项阿根廷集中交易价值 6 000 万阿根廷比索（约合 300 万美元），则须上报并获得批准。上述通知和批准申请均无须支付费用。

3. 豁免的交易

下列集中交易免除通知要求：

① 收购公司时买方已拥有该公司 50% 以上的股份和投票权。

② 收购政府债券、公司债券、票据及无投票权的股份。

③ 未拥有阿根廷资产或未拥有其他阿根廷公司股份的外国公司收购一家阿根廷公司。需注意的是，反垄断局已将不同的协议类型（例如分销协议和授权协议）视为阿根廷资产。

④ 收购清算停业的公司，该公司在上一年未在阿根廷进行交易。

4. 程序

根据《反托拉斯法》的规定，反垄断局最迟在公司提交集中交易报告日期后的 45 个工作日内出示决定。如果在这段时间内未出示决定，则被视为批准该集中交易。

但是，反垄断局可能会暂缓 45 天的期限，以便更详细地审查其他信息。

5. 实质性测试

根据《反托拉斯法》的规定，禁止以违背整体经济利益的方式进行以限制或破坏竞争为目的或产生类似影响的经济集中交易。法案中整体经济利益的概念和经济效率相差无几，但整体经济利益更侧重于消费者剩余而非总剩余。

（七）竞争管制

1. 竞争管制主管机构

反垄断局系负责监管竞争规范的部门。反垄断局主要规范三类行为活动：经济集中、反竞争行为和竞争促进。

2. 竞争法概况

《反托拉斯法》是阿根廷反垄断监管最重要的法律文书。该法不包括任何本身违法的行为或反竞争行为。因此，为了确定一项商业行为是否违法，《反托拉斯法》要求反垄断局进行详细的市场分析，旨在证明（在个案基础上且调查遵循特定的程序）该商业行为具有反竞争性，可能会损害整体经济利益。

为了确定一项行为是否违法，反垄断局必须遵循以下所有要点：

① 证明存在以减少竞争或滥用支配地位为手段的反竞争行为。

② 证明当事方参与上述行为。

③ 明确相关的地理和产品市场。

④ 证明被调查方有能力（例如市场支配力）对相关市场的整体经济利益构成潜在损害。

⑤ 证明对整体经济利益存在潜在损害。如果被指控的参与方没有足够的市场势力对整体经济利益造成潜在损害，该反竞争行为不应被视为《反托拉斯法》规定的非法行为。

基于审查的案件的具体事实，上述部分要点由行政和司法部门据其不同的解读而确定。

3. 竞争管制措施

《反托拉斯法》的宗旨是防止可能限制或扭曲竞争、损害整体经济利益的部分行为和经济交易。《反托拉斯法》旨在保护整体经济利益。

《反托拉斯法》可能对涉及受禁行为的公司实施如下制裁措施：

① 停止该活动或行为，并解除其导致的相关影响。

② 对于《反托拉斯法》禁止的任何反竞争行为，罚款 1 万至 150 万阿根廷比索（约合 500 万至 750 万美元），并应按以下基准进行调整：受该被禁止的活动影响而对个人造成的损失；个人因参与该被禁止的活动而获得的利益；在违规行为发生时，上述个人的相关资产的价值。对于付款违约者，罚款金额加倍。

（八）税收

1. 税收体系与制度

因为阿根廷是联邦共和制国家，阿根廷的征税权分为国家、省和市三个层面。宪法赋予联邦和省政府征收间接税的权力（关税除外，只能由联邦政府征收）。

阿根廷宪法规定，所得税等直接税由各省政府征收。然而，联邦政府有权在有限时间段内征收直接税，但需在领土内等比例征收，且需以国防、国家安全和公共福利要求为前提。

2. 主要税赋与税率

（1）联邦税

① 增值税

增值税是国家最重要的间接税之一。间接税定义为纳税义务人不是税收的实际负担人的税务。

该税收自 1975 年 1 月 1 日起生效，并由《增值税法》规范约束。一般税率为 21%，但在特殊情况下适用较高或较低的税率。增值税的课税对象是商品或服务在经济链各阶段产生的增值额。

增值税按月进行申报和支付，但农业公司可选择月度税务评估和年度支付。

根据《增值税法》第 1 条的规定，增值税适用于：

- 位于或置于阿根廷的动产的销售额；
- 在阿根廷进行的工程、租赁和服务；
- 第 3 条中列出的动产和服务的最终进口。该等服务的执行地点为国外，有效使用地点为国内（但是服务的进口商是注册纳税人，且因其他应税事件而需缴纳增值税）。

② 联邦所得税

联邦所得税的课税对象为个人收入、公司收入、一般阿根廷业务收入和其他法人实体的阿根廷业务收入（包括分支机构）。

对于阿根廷居民，根据相关规定确定的应税活动系指在阿根廷境内外获得收入的活动。

法律根据分类方法将收入分为不同的收入类别。四个传统类别为房地产收益、投资收入、业务收入和个人工作收入。例如，第四类征税采用累进税率，税率为 5%～35% 不等，但始终遵循现行的减税立法。属于第三类别的企业实体在 2018 财年和 2019 财年采用 30% 的统一税率，从 2020 财年开始下降到 25%。

最新立法还规定，2018 财年和 2019 财年的股息和利润分配率为 7%，2020 财年起为 13%。

居民实体必须在纳税年度结束时提交年度所得税申报表（内容包括税收、税损、免税收入）以及一份资产和负债声明。居民个人也须提交年度所得税申报表。

③ 最低预期收入税

在各财年末，对当地企业实体在境内外持有的资产价值征收该特殊税费，税率为 1%。该税种也对部分个人和未分配产业征税。

课税起征点为 20 万比索，低于此值不须征税。同年的所得税可抵扣此税，因此它在实践中起到最低收入税的作用。

根据最新立法的规定，该税种被废除，对 2019 年 1 月开始及以后的财年无法律约束力。

④ 个人资产税

个人资产税适用于在阿根廷境内居住的个人（居民）持有的资产和境内未分配产业，直至该产业分配给继承人，无论该资产位于国内或国外。

非居民个人和境外的未分配产业仅对其阿根廷境内资产有纳税义务。根据《个人资产税法》的规定，作为非居民纳税人资产的共同所有人、持有人、使用人、存管人、管理人或托管人，个人和企业实体均应以替代义务人身份支付适用的税额。此外，非居民外国人在阿根廷公司或企业的股权投资按 0.5% 的年税率征税。

目前，《个人资产税法》规定该税种起征点为 105 万比索（约合 5.25 万美元），低于此值不须纳税。当地个人和未分配产业的税率如下：

征税时间	资产价值	税率
2017 年	低于或等于 950 000 比索（约 47 500 美元）	无须征税
	高于 950 000 比索（约 47 500 美元）	超出 950 000 比索（约 47 500 美元）部分按 0.5% 的税率
2018 年	低于或等于 1 050 000 比索（约 52 500 美元）	无须征税
	高于 1 050 000 比索（约 52 500 美元）	超出 1 050 000 比索（约 52 500 美元）部分按 0.25% 的税率

⑤ 银行账户支出及收入税

该税种是阿根廷银行（和其他储蓄机构）扣缴的国家税，它适用于从支票或储蓄账户中提款或转账的任何存款。应税基数为提取或转移的金额。一般税率为 0.6%，但存在少数免税情况。如因避免使用银行账户而使用定期托收业务，税率是普通税率的两倍。

⑥ 关税

关税的课税对象为阿根廷境内的货物进出口活动。过去几年，出口税是联邦政府最重要的收入来源。阿根廷是世界贸易组织成员国，1994 年《关税与贸易总协定》也于同年纳入了该国的法律。

阿根廷于 1994 年与巴西、乌拉圭、巴拉圭和委内瑞拉成立了共同市场，阿根廷是共同市场中最活跃的成员国之一。成员国需要就南方共同市场内部和外部的进出口设定不同的关税。

（2）省税

① 营业税

营业税是一项省级税，以给定辖区内的商业、专业或业务等惯常的有偿行为所获得的总收益为征税对象。适用的税率视行为和行为的辖区而定。一般而言，适用的税率为 3%。

为了避免对在多个辖区开展业务的纳税人征收双重或多重税务，税额按各省签订的多边公约中规定的条款进行计算和支付。

② 印花税

印花税是一种以有偿合同为征税对象的地方税。尽管印花税的税率视管辖区而定，大部分省份的普遍税率为 1%（房地产转移除外，税率较高，在部分管辖区高达 4%）。

联邦最高法院的几项裁决决定，以部分不成文的方式接受合同的，不适用印花税（例如，一方发出书面要约，确定另一方的某些行为将使协议生效）。

③ 房地产税

房地产税定义为向给定省份内房地产的所有权征收的直接税。

各辖区自行制定税率，通常税基是由主管税务机关确定的财政估值。

（3）市政税

市政府可就其辖区内的公共服务设定一定的税费，包括公共用地占用费、房地产税费、公墓税费、工程建设税费、卫生保护服务税费、广告税费和公共工程融资税费。

具体市政税通常由《市政税法典》或《市政税法令》规定。

（九）证券交易

1. 证券法律、法规概况

阿根廷主要的证券法规是国家证券委员会（CNV）颁布的《资本市场法案》和《一般决议》。

实践中，阿根廷的主要证券交易所是布宜诺斯艾利斯证券交易所。约有 200 名授权经纪人在布宜诺斯艾利斯证券交易所进行股票交易，其中部分经纪人与国内或国际银行有关联。布宜诺斯艾利斯证券交易所也进行流通票据和可转让期权交易。该系统由国家证券委员会监管，国家证券委员会所起的作用与美国证券交易委员会（SEC）相似。上市公司必须每季度向国家证券委员会提交财务报表和董事会报告，且提交经审核的年度财务报表。

国家证券委员会也负责监管场外交易市场。该市场的股票日交易量与布宜诺斯艾利斯证券交易所几乎无异，且在此进行的政府证券的交易量要大得多。在该市场上流通的股票是在布宜诺斯艾利斯证券交易所上市的公司的股票。

2. 证券市场监管

如果要在证券交易所上市股票，公司必须在国家证券委员会注册进行公开募股，并且必须提交包含以下信息和文件的申请：

① 实体信息（例如，实体类型、总部所在地、注册信息）。

② 发行人股本的组成（例如，股权和优先股、股东描述、发行人的经济集团结构）。

③ 发行人背景和活动说明。

④ 发行人的会计和财务信息（例如，最近三个财年的资产负债表）。
⑤ 表决进行上市的临时股东大会会议记录副本。
⑥ 公司章程附则的副本。
⑦ 董事、法定审计师和管理人员名单（正式和候补），具体说明其住址和职位。
⑧ 申请前 12 个月内在股东和董事会会议上讨论的项目议程清单。
⑨ 证明公司持续经营，拥有适当的技术或行政组织，其市场和财务状况前景良好，有利于为股东权益创造利润的证据。

虽然目前由现行的《资本市场法》对阿根廷资本市场进行规范，但预计数月后联邦国会将颁布一项规制资本市场的新法律，该法律由联邦政府起草并促进通过（以下简称"法案"）。众议院已经批准了该法案，待参议院批准之后即可生效。该法案对外公开，其中几项更新的法规为：

① 撤销国家证券委员会的以下行为能力：指派对发行人管理机构采用的决议拥有否决权的审计师；以中止董事权力 180 天的方式干预公司管理。
② 当认为法令违反国家证券委员会颁布或批准的规章、制度或裁决时，国家证券委员会有义务在宣布法令无效之前出示充分的决定和总结。
③ 修改公开募股优先权。在资本增加或公开发行强制性可转换票据的情况下，应根据由各自公开募股前景决定的配股流程行使优先权。申请此类流程的条件是：章程附则明确授权该程序；决定发行股票或强制性可转换票据的各股东大会批准该程序。
④ 本法案允许海外注册的法人实体参与公司股东大会，在无附加前提的情况下，该公司的股票被国家证券委员会授权在市场上报价。
⑤ 因修改国家证券委员会的制裁而产生的任何争议，应由联邦商业法院而非行政法院管辖。

此外，该法案规定所得税豁免条款适用于在国家证券委员会授权的市场上公开发售股票所得的资本收益。另外，如果这些股票不在公募范畴内，但资本收益是公开发行股票的结果，则同样适用豁免条款。该豁免也适用于对阿根廷投资的信托和共同基金，并就其参与证书和/或可转让价值进行公开募股。当指定的可转让价值不在国家证券委员会授权的市场上公开发行时，豁免条款不适用。

3. 外资企业参与证券交易要求

虽然外国人不需事先授权便可在阿根廷从事证券交易，但境内外公司和个人应符合一定要求。

托管账户的开设是强制性的，像明讯或欧洲清算这样的银行或国际公司等代理商被授权开户。个人开户时，应提供以下信息：姓名、出生地点和日期、国籍、性别、婚姻状况、身份证号码、财务标识号（CDI）、地址、电话和职业。提供最新的工资支票存根以核实资金来源。公司开户时，应提供以下信息：法定代表人的身份证复印件、章程附则、公司股票所有权、职位安排记录、向税务局提交的注册凭证（AFIP），并应提交最新的财务报表供核实资金来源。

当投资者是外国实体时，如果其唯一活动是从事阿根廷证券交易，则有理由认为该实体没有必要在商业公共登记处注册。根据阿根廷《公司法》的规定，当公司在该国的活动正常时，须强制进行注册登记。考虑到该账户只能开设一次，如果公司并无常规运作，则该公司不需要注册。

（十）投资优惠及保护

1. 优惠政策框架

阿根廷没有制定具体的优惠政策。根据《外商直接投资法》的规定，外国投资者与阿根廷投资者享有同等权利并履行同等义务。

2. 行业与地区鼓励

阿根廷政府目前正在开展和/或推广最重要的基础设施项目，目标对象为阿根廷北部和南部地区。贝尔格拉诺计划是旨在发展阿根廷北部地区（该国欠发达地区）的社会、生产和基础设施建设项目。预计拨给该项目的总金额为 163 亿美元。关于基础设施方面，贝尔格拉诺计划的目标是改善南北/东西连通性；改善主要城市地区与偏远小镇之间的连通性；开发适应所有汽车类型和气候条件的国道和省道；减少瓶颈路段，缓解关键节点的拥堵；改建铁路，长度为 3 800 公里；完善铁路，长度为 850

公里；建造和完善四个机场，连接阿根廷北部与世界各地。

此外，在南方开展与贝尔格拉诺计划相似的巴塔哥尼亚计划。巴塔哥尼亚计划重点关注基础设施、连通性、城市发展、水文工程、海洋和可再生能源等问题。在第一阶段，该计划拨款 800 万美元用于改建沿贝尔科机场，约 1.9 亿美元保养道路和扩建乌斯怀亚港口。

对于政府支持的特定行业，联邦国会制定了第 27424 号法案，支持发展可再生能源的分布式发电，为此类市场的参与者提供了几项优惠，例如免税或专项授信额度。第 23877 号法案为技术行业提供了若干优惠，体现了国家对特定行业的支持。

3. 特殊经济区域

阿根廷在全国设有 11 个自由贸易区（FTZ）。在自由贸易区，货物不受常规海关管制，货物进口、提取或出口不须征税（惩罚性关税除外），且不受经济禁令管制。在自由贸易区内可以开展的活动有：储存、商业化和工业化。但是，自由贸易区用户在享受自由贸易区优惠时不得加入其他产业振兴的特殊体制。

火地岛省作为阿根廷南部的自由贸易区，《火地岛法案》的财政和海关制度规定，如果火地岛省内设立的产业向该省的部分地区进口货物，应免收国家税。

4. 投资保护

阿根廷与若干国家签署了双边投资协定，是多边投资担保机构（MIGA）、海外私人投资公司和国际投资争端解决中心（ICSID）的成员。这些举措进一步为外国投资者提供了保护。

三、贸易

（一）贸易主管部门

1. 对外贸易

生产部旨在推动和促进阿根廷融入全球经济，维护竞争和制度的有效执行，并将生产纳入联邦政府管辖。

2. 国际贸易秘书室

国际贸易秘书室的主要目的是使阿根廷融入全球商业价值链，促进投资，以及扩大阿根廷产品的销售市场。此外，其目标是使贸易透明化，提高价值链的效率，简化商业程序，及进一步维护消费者权益。

在其职能范围内，竞争保护委员会作为一个分权机构进行运作，旨在力促防止竞争遭受任何形式的市场扭曲。国际贸易秘书室详细阐述、提出并参与实施国际商业政策的战略指导方针，使阿根廷能够融入全球经济。

3. 海关

该国负责进出口业务的主管部门是海关总署，其隶属于联邦公共收入管理局（AFIP），主要目的之一是维护国家在税收方面的利益以及发现与外贸业务有关的具体违规行为。

阿根廷的海关立法基本上是由《海关法典》（第 22415 号法律）、《亚松森条约》（第 01001/82 号监管法令）组成的。需注意的是，向阿根廷进口货物时，相关商品的关税分类。

阿根廷采用了以世界海关组织制定的《商品名称及编码协调制度》为南方共同市场通用命名法（MCN）。根据南方共同市场通用命名法，使用一个八位数的海关编码来表示进口到阿根廷的货物。构成海关编码的第七位和第八位数字是南方共同市场所独有的。对于国内货物，阿根廷增加了三个数字。确定了具体要求及/或限制的适用性，并在某些情况下确定了共同对外关税的例外情况。

4. 南方共同市场

南方共同市场是一个关税联盟，来自南方共同市场国家的货物贸易不受进口关税的限制（某些特定情况除外），并且免除统计费。

为了取得南方共同市场货物的资格，产品必须符合《南方共同市场服务原产地规则》中载明的原产地条例，生产商或出口商必须向进口商提供规定的南方共同市场原产地证书。

上述规则规定，符合下列条件的货物将被视为来自南方共同市场成员国：

① 产品完全在南方共同市场成员国制造，且仅使用来自南方共同市场成员国的材料。

② 产品原料来自第三国家，在南方共同市场加工"转换"为南方共同市场产品。经过这种"转换"的产品不使用原料的税号，而使用南方共同市场通用命名法编码的（四位数）税号。

③ 产品符合60%的增值规定。也就是说，如果由于转换过程不需要为了获得南方共同市场原产地产品的资格而改变海关编号，导致未能符合前述第②项中载明的要求，那么第三国的组件在目的港的到岸价格（CIF）或在海港的到岸价格必须等于或低于产品"离岸价格"的40%。

④ 采用仅在南方共同市场成员国开展的组装流程、使用非南方共同市场成员国的材料制造的产品，前提是第三国组件在目的港的到岸价格或在海港的到岸价格等于或低于产品"离岸价格"的40%。

⑤ 资本资产符合60%的增值规定。

⑥ 产品受到特定原产地要求的限制。此类要求优先于前述①~⑤项中提到的一般要求，对于完全在南方共同市场成员国生产的产品，则无须遵守此类要求。

（二）贸易法律、法规概况

1. 进口许可证

生产部重新修订了自动及非自动进口许可证制度。属于南方共同市场通用命名法关税类别中界定的进口消费品的所有货物都需要申报许可证。对于所有进口货物，其必须申报自动许可证，但需申报非自动许可证的货物除外。

为了申报非自动许可证，进口商必须在生产部的唯一注册处进行登记。

自批准之日起，进口许可证的有效期为180个日历日。

2. 补贴

关于出口补贴，阿根廷向消费品出口商提供全部或部分增值税退税。此外，对于有地理或原产地标志的产品、经认证的有机产品以及符合质量和创新标准、有资格贴上"阿根廷食品，天然之选"标签的产品，第1341/16号法令还为出口商提供了0.5%的额外退税。

此外，对于火地岛省生产的货物也给予补贴。火地岛省是一个免税贸易区，称为特殊关税区域（AAE）。

3. 二手货物

国家立法要求进口二手资本货物须严格遵守有关条件，具体如下：

① 二手固定资产只能由最终用户直接进口。

② 仅在由原始制造商进行翻新的情况下，才允许在国外对货物进行翻新。不允许进行第三方技术评估。

③ 在当地对货物进行翻新时，需要由工业技术研究院对货物进行技术评估，但飞机除外。

④ 无论在哪里进行翻新，阿根廷海关当局都要求在进口时提交"二手货物证明"。

4. 在海关办理进出口商登记

在阿根廷进出口货物的个人或公司，通常必须在海关的进出口商登记处进行登记。

5. 临时进口

临时进口系指将货物运入阿根廷领土，在有限的时间内停留于该国，并用于特定目的。只要满足某些条件，可以延展最初批准的期限。

临时进口程序基本上有两种类型：

① 按照进口条件出口的货物，此类货物必须根据其性质在一定时间内再出口；

② 将经过转换、制造或修理等流程和再出口的货物。一般来说，此类货物必须在两年内再出口。

进口关税不适用于按照该制度进口的货物，但某些服务费除外。为了按照该制度进口货物，必须向海关提供担保，以确保缴纳适用的关税及／或罚款。

6. "厂房海关"

第 688/02 号法令描述了在阿根廷境内建立工业厂房的"厂房海关"制度。该制度对进口生产过程中直接使用的原材料、零部件及组件和／或为货物后续出口或最终进口所需进行的转换作出了规定。

考虑到在所有情况下，海关已经对货物进行了核查，所以上述货物应按《海关法典》载明的规定办理海关仓储手续。因此，不适用进口关税和统计费。

进口商必须遵守税收、海关和社会保障义务，并提供担保，以确保缴纳适用的关税及／或罚款。

（三）贸易管理

请参见上文的第（一）和第（二）部分。

（四）进出口商品检验检疫

进口及／或出口商品的检验检疫制度不适用于大多数情况。但是，作为第三方机构，国家农产食品卫生和质量服务局有权在进出口蔬菜和动物时对此类商品进行检验检疫。

（五）海关管理

请参见上文的第（一）和第（二）部分。

四、劳动

（一）劳动法律、法规概况

劳工关系主要受《雇佣合同法》（ECL）、国家宪法、国际条约、集体谈判协议和个人雇佣合同的制约。下文对与此有关的法规进行简要阐述。

1. 试用期

聘用员工时应签订固定期限合同、临时合同或无限期合同。在最后一种情况中，聘用的前 3 个月为试用期。在此期间，雇主经提前 15 天发送通知后可以终止合同。

2. 工作天数

《劳工法》规定了工作时间限制，包括每天 9 小时或每周 48 小时。如果超过最高时间限制，则需支付加班费。工作日加班的，需多付 50% 的工资；星期六下午 1 点以后、星期日和节假日加班的，需多付 100% 的工资。公司董事不受工作时间限制。

3. 支付薪酬

可每月、每天或每两周支付一次薪酬，并可采取薪水、销售佣金、参与利润等形式。按月结算的，必须在相关工作月份结束后的 4 个工作日内支付薪酬；按两周结算的，必须在两个星期结束后的 4 个工作日内支付薪酬；按周支付薪酬的，必须在 3 个工作日内予以支付。

4. 强制性奖金（第 13 个月的工资）

该笔奖金于每年 6 月 30 日和 12 月 18 日支付，分别为当年上半年和下半年向员工支付的最高工资的 50%。在终止雇佣关系时，员工有权根据相应半年内的工作时间按比例获得第 13 个月的工资。

5. 假期

员工按其服务年限有权享有 14～35 天不等的年假。假期工资的计算方法是将员工的工资除以 25，并将该结果乘以假期天数。在雇佣关系终止时，员工有权根据上一年的工作时间按比例获得假期工资。

6. 特殊休假

在某些情况下，员工可以获得短暂的特殊休假，例如，孩子出生、结婚、近亲死亡以及高中和大学考试。特殊休假的工资与假期工资的计算基准相同。集体谈判协议规定可以延长期限及／或安排其他休假。

女性员工有权在产前 45 天和产后 45 天休产假。在此期间，由家庭津贴基金支付工资。

如果员工患有疾病或残疾（与工作无关），合同将持续完全有效，并且员工有权根据其服务年限和家庭义务（抚养／赡养近亲属）获得 3～12 个月的正常工资。

7. 终止雇佣合同

员工提前 15 天给出通知后，可以辞职为由终止雇佣合同。

雇主可以无故终止无限期合同。在此情况下，雇主应提前通知。通知期限取决于员工的服务年限（从 15 天到两个月不等）；未能作出通知的，雇主需向员工支付与员工在此期间应得薪酬相等的赔偿金。

此外，雇主应根据上一年最高月薪支付工龄补偿金，按服务每满 1 年支付 1 个月的工资，或服务不满 1 年但超过 3 个月的，按比例支付。考虑到适用的集体谈判协议和判例法，可以设定上限。

员工在怀孕、作为工会代表和结婚等特定情况下，有权在该时期获得特殊保护。在此情况下，遣散费金额将大幅提高。

雇主也可以因员工严重违纪而解聘员工。在此情况下，雇主无须支付遣散费，但雇主对员工的严重违纪负有举证责任，劳工法官有权判定此类决定是否合理。

经双方一致同意，以及员工退休、死亡或发生伤残时，也可以终止雇佣合同。

8. 一致同意

双方一致同意后可以随时终止合同。《雇佣合同法》特别规定，在此情况下，终止合同需提供公证文件。《雇佣合同法》还允许当事人在劳工法庭或劳工部门解除合同。

9. 伤残

如果因员工永久和完全残疾而终止雇佣关系，则员工有权获得与其资历补偿金相等的赔偿。

10. 退休

员工在达到依法可获得正常退休福利的年龄时，可以终止雇佣合同。在此情况下，雇主必须通知员工其有义务开始办理退休手续。在一年后或者一旦员工开始获得养老金福利（以较早发生者为准），雇主有权终止雇佣合同，而无须支付遣散费。

11. 死亡

员工死亡时雇佣合同终止。在此情况下，其家属有权获得特殊补偿金，金额相当于在无故解聘员工时所支付的资历补偿金的 50%。

12. 员工登记

员工的每一次入职和每一次终止雇佣合同都必须通过互联网通知税务机构。

另外，雇主必须保存一份特殊劳工手册，登记雇主和员工的信息、薪水等。

13. 社会保险缴费和税费

根据第 24.241 号法律的规定，在阿根廷向员工支付的任何款额都需要由员工和雇主缴纳（不同比例的）社会保险费用。

员工必须支付工资总额的 17%，而从事服务业的雇主须支付工资总额的 20.7%，从事其他营业活动的雇主需支付工资总额的 17.5%。

社会保险的缴款用于支持退休和抚恤金系统、退休人员医疗保险、家庭补贴基金、失业基金和强制医疗保险。

雇主还必须支付额外的费用（金额不尽相同），为员工购买强制性人寿保险和职业风险保险。

当年度所得超过税务机构规定的最低限额时，雇主有义务从员工的薪酬中扣缴所得税。

（二）外国人在当地工作规定

1. 工作许可

根据当地的移民法规，在阿根廷居住并从事任何形式的有偿活动的外国人，必须获得阿根廷移民局颁发的居留许可。居留权可以是短期的（即授予 1 年期并可以按照相同年限进行续展）或永久的

(授权外国人无限期在该国工作和居住)。

2. 申请程序

外国人可以按照下列方式申请居留许可:阿根廷境外的申请人可以向原籍国的阿根廷领事馆申请居留许可(在提出申请之前,必须获得阿根廷移民局颁发的入境许可证);游客可以在入境阿根廷后向阿根廷移民局申请短期居留许可。若为短期居留许可,那么外国公民不得从事任何有报酬或获利的活动。

申请居留许可的文件和要求各不相同,不论申请人是南方共同市场成员国公民(玻利维亚、巴西、哥伦比亚、智利、厄瓜多尔、巴拉圭、秘鲁、乌拉圭、委内瑞拉、圭亚那和苏里南)还是非南方共同市场成员国公民,取决于所申请的居留许可的类型(见签证类型)。

3. 社会保险

地方立法授予移民及其家属在特定情况下享有与国民相同的社会保障福利(退休、失业、伤残等)。

此外,阿根廷与其他国家签署了若干双边条约,确立如下规定:

① 在一段有限的时间内,外籍务工人员可以继续为其原籍国的国家安全体系效力;

② 外籍务工人员缴纳阿根廷社会保险的数额和期限将由其原籍国的社会保障体系根据相关条约进行审议。

(三)出入境

1. 签证类型

(1)永久居留许可

下列人士可获得永久居留许可:

① 南方共同市场成员国的公民连续两年或以上持有短期居留许可后,可以获得永久居留许可;

② 连续3年或以上持有短期居留许可的非南方共同市场成员国的公民;

③ 阿根廷公民的配偶、子女和父母;

④ 永久居民的配偶、未满18周岁的子女及父母;

⑤ 曾履行过外交或领事职务或者在国际组织工作过的人士。

阿根廷移民局在颁发永久居留许可前会要求申请人提供一些个人文件,例如出生/结婚证明、无犯罪记录证明等。

持永久居留许可的人士获准无限期在阿根廷工作和居住。

(2)短期居留许可

短期居留许可分为几类(如外籍务工人员、科学家、公司高级管理人员等)。

为申请短暂居留许可,申请人需要向阿根廷移民局或阿根廷领事馆提交一些个人文件,如出生/结婚证明、无犯罪记录证明等。

非南方共同市场成员国的公民需要由当地公司/作为其雇主的个人提供担保。担保人应在国家移民局的申请人国籍登记处(RENURE)进行登记。需要提供与阿根廷公司签订的雇佣合同、申请人国籍登记处颁发的雇主注册证明以及雇主向联邦公共收入管理局登记的证明等文件。

南方共同市场成员国的公民不需要当地实体提供担保。

短期居留许可为期1年,并可以按照相同年限续展。持短期居留许可的人士在授权期限内可以从事各种有报酬的活动。

(3)临时居留许可

在授予短期及/或永久居留许可之前,国家移民局可以提供有效期为3个月的临时居留许可(并且可以续展,直至获得短期/永久居留许可时为止)。在这段时间内,持临时居留许可的人士可以从事各种有报酬的活动。

2. 出入境限制

只要居民向移民当局提交了能证明其身份和居留状态的文件,就可以在授权逗留期间自由出入阿根廷。

(四)工会与劳工组织

1. 工会

工会可以代表某些特定群体或行业的工人,例如在特定机构提供服务的工人、其雇主的营业活动相同的工人及/或开展特定工作及/或工种类似的工人。

工人拥有加入(或退出)任何工会及/或创建新工会的不可撤销的权利,雇主不得干涉。

此外,工会有权要求进行选举,以便委任受法律特别保护的工会代表;未经劳工法官的事先授权,不得终止或暂时取消此类代表,亦不得对此类代表采取惩戒措施。

2. 集体谈判协议

一般情况下,某些集体谈判协议的适用取决于雇主的活动及/或员工的类别。

通常情况下,集体谈判协议适用于去分级化员工。

集体谈判协议由工会和雇主代表一致同意,其提出的条件必须优于《雇佣合同法》规定的条件。

所有集体谈判协议都制定了最低工资标准,通过工会与雇主代表之间的直接谈判定期更新。

确定是否适用集体谈判协议,必须具体情况具体分析。

(五)劳动争议

1. 个人纠纷

当员工称雇主违反劳工法规(《雇佣合同法》、集体谈判协议和个人雇佣合同)而向雇主提出索赔时,即为个人纠纷。

此类索赔的审理程序根据司法管辖区而定。

在布宜诺斯艾利斯市,员工需要向劳工部提起行政索赔,然后再提起诉讼。

与劳工有关的审判可以持续4~5年。当事人可在法院作出最终裁决之前随时达成和解协议。

2. 集体纠纷

当与由工会代表的一组员工发生纠纷及/或与工会发生冲突时,即为集体纠纷。

此类纠纷通常在劳工部进行审理,劳工部应作为调解人并鼓励当事人达成友好和解协议。

在特定情况下,集体纠纷也可以在劳工法庭进行审理。

五、知识产权

(一)知识产权法律、法规概况

知识产权保护的首要依据是《宪法》。《宪法》第17条规定,所有作者或发明人可以就其作品、发明或发现在法律规定的期限内获得保护。

执行机构于2018年颁布了第27号紧急法令,旨在简化和加速专利及商标的注册程序。由于这一紧急法令仍有待国会批准,在此未提及任何修正案。

(二)申请专利

专利受第24481号法律(经修订)和第260/96号监管法令的特别管辖。

关于国际条约,阿根廷是《巴黎公约》和《与贸易有关的知识产权协定》的缔约国。阿根廷不是《专利合作条约》的缔约国。为了保护植物,阿根廷加入了《国际植物新品种保护公约》。

法律规定,新的产品发明或者具有独创性和产生工业结果的流程应受专利保护。

因此,专利申请的基本要求如下:

① 新颖;
② 工业应用;
③ 独创性。

专利权人自申请之日起获得使用该项发明20年(不可续展)的专有权。获得专利后,必须缴纳年费,以维持专利的有效性。

法律规定,以下事项不得被视为发明:

① 发现、科学理论和数学方法;

② 文学艺术作品或任何其他美学创作和科学著作;

③ 用于开展智力活动、游戏或经济商业活动的计划、规则和方法以及计算机程序;

④ 可以呈现信息的其他方式;

⑤ 用于人类以及与动物有关的手术、治疗或诊断治疗的方法;

⑥ 已知发明或已知产品组合的并置,其形式、尺寸或组成材料发生的变化,但所述组合或合并使得其组成部分无法单独运作,或者修改了固有特性或功能但所取得的工业效果被该领域专家认为不明显;

⑦ 自然界已经存在的任何种类的生命和物质。

药品特别归类为可获得专利的发明,目前受到阿根廷法律的保护。但是,其规定严重限制了制药和化学领域多个发明种类的可专利性。

可以许可和转让专利,但是此类转让必须在专利局进行注册后才能对第三方有效。

(三)注册商标

第 22362 号法律及其条例、第 558/81 号法令规制与阿根廷商标有关的所有事宜。关于国际条约,阿根廷是《巴黎公约》和《与贸易有关的知识产权协定》的缔约国。

法律提供了一个弱化权限系统,规定商标权及其专有使用权自登记(而非使用)时产生,但明确了与商标续展有关的使用要求。

此外,阿根廷采用国际商品和服务分类,与发达国家统一商标分类标准。

法规对于哪些标志可以用作商标没有作出严格限制:特殊名称、徽章、组合图案、广告标语、印章、小插图、浮雕标志、带图画的字母和数字、容器或标签或者用于区分所有者的产品和服务的其他标志。至今,一些非传统商标[如声音、嗅觉、动作和三维(3D)商标]也已获准进行注册登记。

商标的保护期为自注册之日起 10 年,每 10 年可延展一次,并且可以无限次延展,前提是在续展日期前连续使用商标 5 年。

商标可以转让,但只有在国家工业产权局进行登记注册后才对第三方有效。

(四)保护知识产权措施

关于专利,为避免第三方向专利局申请制造和销售专利产品或使用专利方法的强制许可,以下事项至关重要:在授予专利后的 3 年内或在提交申请后的 4 年内使用发明;在所述期限内为使用发明做好有效和严格的准备;发明的使用不得中断 1 年以上。

另外,为了向专利所有人提供救济措施来对抗无权使用专利、但违反法律要求获得专利的任何人,法律提出了无效诉讼。

专利侵权属于违法犯罪行为,将被判处罚金或予以监禁。受侵害方可以请求法院发布命令,以防止继续侵权和获得损害赔偿。

关于商标,如果某人注册了商标,并且知道或本应知道该商标属于他人,或者如果授予的商标与法令的任何规定相冲突,那么商标权人可以向法院提起诉讼请求宣告该商标无效。

此外,如果在取消诉讼之日前的 5 年内未于国内使用该商标,可根据一方当事人的请求取消商标。

商标侵权属于违法犯罪行为,将被判处罚金或予以监禁。可以请求法院发布命令,以防止继续侵权和获得损害赔偿。

版权侵权也属于违法犯罪行为,将被判处罚金或予以监禁。可以请求法院发布命令,以防止继续侵权和获得损害赔偿。

六、环境保护

(一) 环境保护主管机构

在所有监管环境保护及具有环境管辖权的机构中,阿根廷环境与可持续发展部(MAyDS)是国家级的环保机构。环境与可持续发展部设有秘书处、次级秘书处和办公室,负责处理环境管理和保护方面的问题,包括但不限于林业、荒漠化、生物多样性、受保护物种、气候变化、可持续发展、可持续消费、水资源、环境影响评估、环境教育、预防污染、危险废物和废物越境转移。

2016年,阿根廷组建了气候变化内阁,旨在制定气候变化政策。气候变化内阁由内阁幕僚长统辖,由环境与可持续发展部、能源和矿业部、经济发展部、农业部、交通部、社会发展部、教育部、科学部、内政部、文化部和外交部等共同参与管理。

监管环境问题的其他国家机构包括:监管燃料储存条件的碳氢化合物秘书处(隶属能源和矿业部)以及监管化学物质的反贩毒秘书室(隶属安全部)。

在省级层面,阿根廷的23个省均设有环境保护机构,主要是环境保护部门或环境保护秘书处。布宜诺斯艾利斯市于2008年1月成立了市环境保护机构。在布宜诺斯艾利斯省(全国绝大多数工业活动所在地),省级可持续发展署和水务局在环境监管和审批方面发挥着至关重要的作用。

2006年12月,阿根廷国会创建了马坦萨河—里亚丘埃洛河流域管理局(ACUMAR)。当时,最高法院审理了一宗影响极为广泛和严重的大型环境污染案件(即"里亚丘埃洛河"案),由此阿根廷设立了跨区的监管机构马坦萨河—里亚丘埃洛河流域管理局,对布宜诺斯艾利斯市和布宜诺斯艾利斯省的流域具有优先管辖权。自设立以来,马坦萨河—里亚丘埃洛河流域管理局积极规范管理标准,在流域开展生态恢复活动以及落实环境法规。

(二) 环境保护法律、法规概况

阿根廷是一个联邦共和国,由布宜诺斯艾利斯自治市(联邦政府的办事处所在地)和多个省组成。根据阿根廷《宪法》的规定,各省可保留未授权予联邦政府的所有权力。

阿根廷《宪法》1994年修订后承认公民享有健康、协调的环境的权利和知情权,制定了可持续发展原则和"污染者付费"原则(即破坏环境的人有义务"恢复"环境),以及颁布了禁止危险废弃物入境的禁令。

根据《宪法》规定的联邦制结构,保护环境的权力基本属于警察权限的范畴。因此,这种权力属于各省和联邦政府,但是联邦政府只能以授权的形式获得这种权力。尽管如此,联邦政府有权出台全国各地均需达标的最低标准。因此,自2002年7月以来,国会制定了11项法律,对以下问题规定了最低环境保护标准:生物多样性的保全和保护以及可持续发展的实施,即《环境框架法》(EFL);工业废物和服务活动管理产生的废物;多氯联苯的监管;水资源的保存、开发和合理利用;免费和公开获取环境信息的权利;家庭废物管理;原始森林的扩展、恢复、保护、可持续利用和管理;燃烧活动的监控;冰川和冰缘地带保全;用火管理;闲置植物检疫集装箱的管理。

因此,各省颁布了地方法律,此类法律适用于其所在辖区,并与全国适用的联邦法律共存。

(三) 环境保护评估

在国家层面,针对环境有效可持续管理的一般环境保护标准颁布的第25675号法律规定,如果阿根廷境内的任何工作或活动可能会破坏环境或任何环境组成,或者对居民的生活质量造成严重损害,应在开展之前进行环境影响评估(EIA)。《环境框架法》进一步规定,该等评估程序应首先提交一份宣誓书,说明相关工作或活动是否会对环境造成影响。然后,项目倡议人必须提交环境影响研究报告。此后,环境保护机构将进行评估,并发布环境影响声明,表示接受或拒绝提交的研究报告。

几项联邦条例载明了对具体活动进行强制性环境影响评估的规定(即勘探、开采和碳氢化合物运输、危险废物处理和处置设施、公共投资项目和采矿项目),省级法规则载明了与环境影响评估流程有关的规定。

已颁布环境影响评估法律和法规的省份包括布宜诺斯艾利斯省、卡塔马卡省、丘布特省、科尔多瓦省、科连特斯省、恩特雷里奥斯省、胡胡伊省、拉潘帕省、拉里奥哈省、门多萨省、米西奥斯内斯省、内乌肯省、里奥内格罗省、萨尔塔省、圣胡安省、圣路易斯省、圣克鲁斯省、圣菲省、圣地亚哥—德尔埃斯特罗省、图库曼省和布宜诺斯艾利斯市。在部分司法管辖区，申请项目的实体只能任用特别授权的环境顾问进行环境影响评估。

七、争议解决

（一）纠纷解决方式及机构

在阿根廷，在法庭上进行对抗制诉讼是处理大规模商业纠纷的主要纠纷解决方式，同时也会考虑采用仲裁和调解等替代性纠纷解决方式。

1. 法院诉讼

（1）法院结构

阿根廷国家宪法确立了双重司法体系，由联邦司法管辖权和一般司法管辖权构成。据此，各辖区都设有专项法庭，涵盖不同的法律领域。各辖区均设有一审法院（由一名法官审理案件）和上诉法院（由多名法官审理案件）。

（2）法院管辖权

在布宜诺斯艾利斯市，联邦民事和商业法庭对海事和航空纠纷、知识产权和司法辖区内的运输纠纷等行使管辖权。普通商业法庭对一般商事纠纷、工程协议纠纷、租赁纠纷、企业纠纷以及其他一般商业事务行使管辖权。

2. 替代性争议解决方法（ADR）

根据程序法规则，主要的替代性争议解决方法是调解和仲裁。提供替代性争议解决服务的主要机构是：布宜诺斯艾利斯证券交易所的普通仲裁法庭；商业调解和仲裁中心；阿根廷商会调解和仲裁中心；布宜诺斯艾利斯谷物交易所仲裁庭。

（1）调解

在多个司法管辖区（例如布宜诺斯艾利斯市）经常使用调解，因此，申诉人必须在提起司法诉讼之前启动调解程序。

（2）仲裁

仲裁具有契约性质，因此需要达成协议，以便将争议提请仲裁。根据《国家民事和商事诉讼法典》载明的程序，无论诉讼状态如何，当事人都可以在法院审理任何诉讼之前或期间将争议提请仲裁。

阿根廷被视为适用仲裁的国家。通常对大型国际商业交易进行仲裁，特别是在涉及外国投资者的情况下，各方同意将潜在争议提请仲裁。仲裁尤其适用于解决石油和天然气行业、能源、建筑和汽车行业的纠纷、并购交易、企业纠纷等。

对法庭诉讼进行仲裁的主要优点是：

① 仲裁员的专业知识：当事人可以根据仲裁员在纠纷领域的技术知识和专业知识选择仲裁员。

② 保密性：《国家民商法》第1658条允许当事人就仲裁的保密性达成一致。

③ 更快捷并具有灵活性：仲裁程序往往比法庭程序更快捷。当事人可以选择适用的规则，根据其需要以及当事人和仲裁员的法律文化来定制程序。

④ 便于进行成本管理：当事人可以就如何分摊仲裁程序的费用达成一致。

（3）对仲裁提出上诉和执行仲裁裁决

① 上诉权。当事人可以放弃上诉权。此种情况下，当事人只能申请撤销追索权（基于诉讼中的根本错误）或请求进行澄清。

② 执行国内裁决。国内裁决可以作为国内法院的最终裁决（例如，即审即决程序中的裁决）予以执行。

③ 执行国外裁决。承认和执行外国裁决主要受阿根廷签署的下列条约的制约：

- 《纽约公约》;
- 1975 年《美洲国家国际商事仲裁公约》(即《巴拿马公约》);
- 1984 年美洲国家组织《关于在国际范围内实现外国判决域外效力的管辖权公约》。

此外,条约范围以外的仲裁裁决如果符合《国家民事和商事诉讼法典》第 517 条的要求(例如,裁决必须是最终裁决,并且必须由具有管辖权的仲裁庭发布;仲裁裁决的被执行人必须被亲自传唤,并且其为合法权益进行辩护的权利必须得到保证等),则可以强制执行,并且所依据的法律将予接受。

3. 跨境诉讼

(1)适用法的选择

法院尊重合同中适用法律的选择,但须遵守《国家民商法》第 2599 条和第 2600 条的某些限制。阿根廷法律的国际强制性规则优先于当事人就管辖法律达成的协议,并排除适用外国法律,尽管当事人可能就此类法律达成一致。此外,当外国法律导致产生与阿根廷公共秩序原则不相容的解决方案时,不适用外国法律。

(2)司法管辖权的选择

根据《国家民商法》第 2605 条的规定,当事人可以同意外国法官或仲裁员对财产/家庭事务和国际事务具有管辖权。

(二)适用法律

1. 诉讼

(1)国家规定

《国家民商法》包含与程序性事宜有关的若干规则,例如:
- 诉讼时效(第 2560 条及后续条款);
- 国际未决诉讼案件原则(第 2604 条);
- 预防行动(第 1711 条及后续条款)。

(2)程序性规定

由于阿根廷是联邦制国家,每个省都可以规范制定的程序性规则,包括与诉讼、仲裁和调解有关的程序性规定。《国家民事和商事诉讼法典》适用于布宜诺斯艾利斯市的诉讼程序以及向省内的联邦法院提起的诉讼。

2. 仲裁

(1)国内规定

《国家民商法》对联邦层面的仲裁作出了规定,其中包含涉及以下方面的条款:
- 仲裁协议的形式和类型;
- 向仲裁庭提交的事项的可仲裁性;
- 任命和罢免仲裁员;
- 针对仲裁裁决的初步措施和上诉。

(2)程序性规定

当事人可在仲裁庭执行仲裁程序的过程中达成一致意见[《国家民商法》第 1658(3)项],未能达成一致的,应适用普通司法程序规则(《国家民事和商事诉讼法典》第 751 条)。

《国家民事和商事诉讼法典》包含与以下内容有关的程序性规定:
- 仲裁程序;
- 法院与仲裁庭之间的关系。

(3)国际公约

阿根廷签署了以下国际公约:
- 1958 年《承认及执行外国仲裁裁决公约》(即《纽约公约》);
- 1975 年《美洲国家国际商事仲裁公约》(即《巴拿马公约》);
- 南方共同市场 1998 年《国际商事仲裁协议》。

3. 调解

在布宜诺斯艾利斯市，根据《国家民事和商事诉讼法典》和《调解与和解法》（第 26589 号法律）的规定进行调解。《调解与和解法》规定，（和许多其他司法管辖区一样）在提交司法诉讼之前必须开展事先调解程序。

八、其他

（一）反商业贿赂

1. 反商业贿赂法律、法规概况

阿根廷《刑法典》属于联邦法律，其第 256 条至第 259 条与惩罚贿赂和腐败有关。此外，2017 年颁布的第 27401 号法律载明了涉腐犯罪活动的公司刑事责任制度。但是，贿赂罪并不适用于私人之间的贿赂，而仅适用于涉事公职人员和雇员的贿赂。该制度存在一个例外，即该制度对金融实体雇员贿赂罪作出了最新解释（阿根廷《刑法典》第 312 条）。该条规定，在证券交易所运作的金融实体的雇员，如亲自或通过中间人收受金钱或任何其他好处以作为提供贷款、融资或股票交易的条件，将被处以 1~6 年的监禁，并被吊销资格 6 年。

此外，在某些情况下，根据阿根廷《刑法典》第 173 条第 7 款的规定，商业贿赂可被视为欺诈行为。就此，任何人根据法律、授权或合同而管理、支配或照管属于另一个人的货物或金钱利益，却为了自身或第三方谋取非法利益违反其义务滥用职权，或者过度开支、损害其所代表的人士的利益的，将被处以 1~6 年的监禁。

值得一提的是，与阿根廷《刑法典》有关的改革项目目前正在审议中，以解决私人贿赂问题。

2. 主管部门

阿根廷没有专职负责监督反商业贿赂的部门。联邦刑事和惩教事务法院是处理公职人员贿赂和腐败问题的主管法院，国家《宪法》规定了撤销和起诉官员和法官的弹劾机制，指派联邦法官进行贿赂和腐败调查。此外，以下机构也很重要：

- 反贪局；
- 行政调查：总检察长办公室的特设检察官办公室，负责调查以及力促调查腐败和行政违规行为；
- 经济犯罪和洗钱活动检察官办公室：该机构隶属于总检察长办公室，其旨在打击洗钱和其他经济犯罪活动。

3. 惩处措施

个人和公司欺诈也可能构成民事责任，此类行为对某人造成损害，并且只有该当事人（或其代理人或继任人）才能提出索赔。这方面的责任可以基于侵权产生，以防止损害他人。这一原则载于阿根廷《宪法》第 19 条，并已在《国家民法典》第 1716 条中进行了明确规定。

对于构成民事责任的公司或商业欺诈，必须具备以下条件：违反法定或合同义务，构成违法行为；造成实际损害；违法行为与损害之间具有充分的因果关联；由损害方的疏忽或故意不当行为造成。

（二）工程承包

1. 许可制度

所有商业和工业活动的开发都需要获得许可和授权，其中一些活动受到阿根廷不同层级政府的专属管辖（例如，联邦政府有权颁发电力运输和分配许可证，市政当局有权确定市内公共空间的使用或授予商业许可），其他活动需要不止一个层级的政府给予许可和授权后才能开展。例如，虽然《国家环保政策》（第 25675 号法律）规定了环境保护的最低要求，但省级法规可以进一步扩展此类要求。

2. 禁止领域

不适用。

3. 招投标

所有层级政府的公共采购活动都受到具体原则的制约，此类原则要求对公共资源的使用保持公开透明并确保高效。

从这个意义上说，在选择国家项目的承包商时，通常采用的机制是投标（第 1023/01 号法令第 24 条）。通过该机制，不定数量的要约人根据招标文件的具体条款提供报价。在提供的报价中，发出招标的公共实体将根据所涉公共利益选择最合适的要约人。

如上所述，第 1023/01 号法令和第 1030/16 号法令确定了国家公共采购制度。对于其他承包活动，还纳入了一些协议，包括交易和供应合同、租赁协议、咨询服务和行政特许权合同。此外，其他规定还考虑到了具体的特许权，例如公共工程特许权合同（第 13064 号法律）或电力分配和运输特许权合同（第 24065 号法律）。

（三）个人数据保护

如果在阿根廷处理个人数据（系指涉及个人或法律实体的信息，无论通过关联程序已被识别还是可以识别），则适用有关个人数据保护的第 25326 号法令、第 1558/2001 号法令和相关法律规定处置。

一般情况下，必须获得数据所有者的同意，以便收集和处理个人数据。

对于将个人数据传输到国外（即使仅用于存储目的），阿根廷法规禁止将个人数据传输至未能提供充分保护的国家。但是，禁止规定不适用于下列情况：

① 数据所有者已明确同意了此类传输；

② 出于外包目的，通过转让人与受让人签署国际数据传输协议的方式传输数据，根据该协议，后者承诺遵守阿根廷的数据保护条例和其他义务。

阿根廷数据保护局列出了符合其标准的、提供充分保护水平的国家。截至目前，中国未被列入该名单。

Argentina

Authors: Valeriano Guevara Lynch, Raúl Fratantoni, Roberto A.Fortunati, Nicolás Rukavina Mikusic
Translators: Lin Cuizhu, Guo Fang

I. Overview

A. Economic, Political and Legal System-an Overview of the Society

a. Political System

The Republic of Argentina is a federal country divided in 23 provinces and the Autonomous City of Buenos Aires.

As a federal country, the provinces are autonomous except for the matters that pursuant to the Argentine Constitution are delegated in favor of the Federal Government.

The Federal Government is divided into three main powers: the Executive Power (Presidency), the Legislative Power (the National Congress composed with a Senate and a House of Representatives), and the Judiciary Power (Supreme Court and lower courts). The President and the congressmen are elected by popular vote, while the five members of the Supreme Court are nominated by the President and approved by the Senate. Judges of lower courts are nominated by the Council of Magistracy and subject to the approval of the corresponding national or provincial legislative authority.

Last presidential election took place in 2015 and Mr. Mauricio Macri was elected President. Mr. Macri will stay in office until December 2019, and may be re-elected if he seeks another 4 year term.

Mr. Macri is a founding member of the Republican Proposal political party (PRO), which in 2015 formed the coalition Let's Change (Cambiemos, in Spanish) together with the Radical Civic Party (UCR) and the Civic Coalition (CC) for the national, provincial and municipal elections of that year for the appointment of the President and several governors and municipal mayors. The Let's Change coalition also participated in the 2017 mid-term elections at the national, provincial and municipal levels and prevailed over the Peronist party in most jurisdictions, resulting the most voted political force in the country. Additionally, Let's Change prevailed in important jurisdictions such as the Province of Buenos Aires, Córdoba, Entre Ríos, Mendoza, Salta and Santa Fe.

b. Economic Structure

Argentina's economic structure could be summarized into 3 pillars: the diversification of its revenues; the availability of natural resources; and the high quality of human capital. To improve the Country's productivity, this Government put emphasis in improving the national infrastructure and encouraging the de-bureaucratization of the State.

Argentina is the 3rd largest economy in Latin America and its Gross Domestic Product ("GDP") in 2017 was above US$ 600 billion. With a population of around 44 million inhabitants, its GDP per capita is US$ 22,500. Argentina's GDP concentrated 2. 2% in 2016, but grew 2. 7% in 2017, as compared to 2016. In addition, the primary deficit was reduced from 4. 3% of the GDP in 2016 to 1. 9% in 2017.

Being the 8th largest country in the world (with almost 2. 8 million square meters), Argentina offers a vast and diverse variety of natural resources in energy and agriculture, which represents an opportunity for the development of the agribusiness and the livestock industry, as well as in terms of oil and gas, mining and renewable energy activities.

Regarding Argentina's performance on international commerce, the following graphs show some relevant statistics, referred to Argentina's exports and imports in 2017:

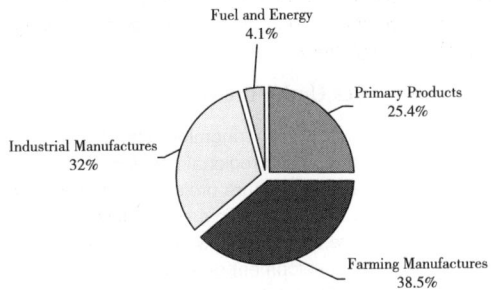

Argentine Exports- 2017

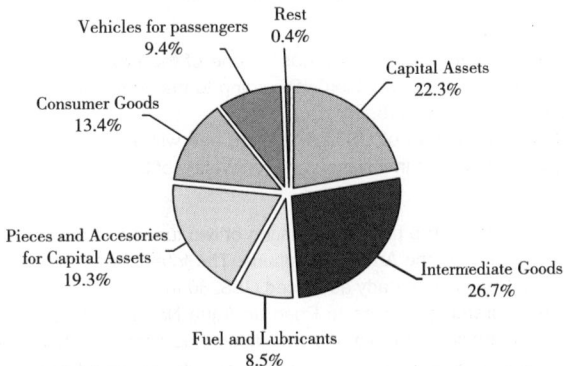

Argentine Imports- 2017

c. Legal System

The highest authority of the National Judicial Power is the Supreme Court, which is composed of five members.

Argentina's legal system does not follow the stare decisis doctrine, and therefore lower courts do not have a legal obligation to follow the decisions made by their higher courts. However, in practice attorneys do quote precedents, and judges of lower courts actually decide many of their cases following such precedents, in the understanding that their decisions may be otherwise revised by the higher courts.

In addition, Argentina has not developed oral procedures in administrative, civil and commercial litigation; neither has introduced jury trials in those kinds of procedures. Judicial procedures are mostly completed by written presentations, and with the mere intervention of a judge. When the final decision of such judge is appealed, the case can be taken to a higher court or court of appeals generally formed by three members, and in a restricted number of cases this last decision can be appealed again with the final intervention of a supreme court (provincial or national).

d. Social

Argentina has approximately 44 million inhabitants, and its annual population growth rate in 2016 was 0. 99%.

The influence of the past immigration wave boosted such population. From the 1850s to the 1950s, Argentina received European immigrants, mostly from Italy and Spain. In the last decades, the migratory flow consisted of Chinese and Korean immigrants. Lately, the inflow of migrants from neighbor countries has risen.

The age rate composition of the Argentine population in 2010 was structured as follows: 25. 5% of the population was under 15; 64. 3% was between 15 and 65; and 10. 2% was over 65.

Regarding the education level of such groups, the literacy rate of the Argentines over 10 years old is 98% and 7% of the inhabitants over 20 have a completed university level.

In 2015, the Human Development Index published by the United Nations that measures key dimensions of human development, such as life expectancy, knowledge and standards of living, placed Argentina in the 2nd place in Latin America, and in the 45th place globally.

B. Cooperation With Chinese Enterprises Under the B&R

The Chinese ambassador in Argentina, Mr. Yang Wangming, stated that the One Bel- One Road initiative (the "B&R") seeks to promote plans of international and regional development and integration currently in place in Latin America, in conjunction with the regional infrastructure projects. In addition, he stated that the 5 main pillars of the OBOR integration project in Argentina are: the political connectivity, through the application of high level bilateral dialogue mechanisms; the infrastructure connectivity, with an special emphasis in hydro-electricity, nuclear energy, railroads and photovoltaic energy, the development of highways, ports, aquatic transport, aviation, energy piping and tubing, underwater cables, optical fiber, telecommunications and information technology applied to communication; the commercial connectivity; the capital investment connectivity; and the social connectivity[1].

Although there are not official sources informing about enterprises under the B&R, many journals have informed about some projects with Chinese companies and with the support of the Chinese Government that are or may be carried out in Argentina. The following are some examples:

a. Belgrano Cargas

The reconversion of the train line "Belgrano Cargas" is one of the projects being conducted by a Chinese company (China Machinery Engineering Corporation), according to the contractual terms ratification made by the Argentine Government in Decree No. 868/2016.

This project represents an investment of US$2,47 billion, and will be financed by the China Development Bank. In particular, this project includes the installation and renovation of 3,800 kilometers of railroad tracks.

b. Agua Negra Tunnel

Agua Negra Tunnel is an infrastructure project consisting of two tunnels of around 13. 9 kilometers long each connecting Argentina and Chile through the Andes Mountains. The total cost of this project is US$15 billion, and the Interamerican Development Bank has already advanced US$280 million.

Chile and Argentina have agreed to provide to Paso de Agua Negra preferential budgetary attention. It is strategically located between Argentina and Chile and was labeled as a top priority in terms of investment as it is expected to solve traffic problems without competing with other possible traffic adjacent paths.[2]

II. Investment

A. Market Access

a. Department Supervising Investments

Argentina does not count with a public office specifically dedicated to the supervision of foreign investments. However, the Argentine Agency of Investment and International Trade (Agencia Argentina de Inversiones y Comercio Internacional, in Spanish) is in charge of engaging investors with government entities to facilitate and fast-track processes; assisting investors in alternate conflict resolution proceedings throughout the investment life-cycle; providing updated statistics on investment-related issues and specific information in every sector; and developing ad-hoc analysis and information packages for potential investors.

b. Laws and Regulations of Investment Industry

According to the Foreign Direct Invest Act (the "FDI Act"), foreign direct investments do not need to be approved by any authority prior to their execution. Following the constitutional mandate, the FDI Act establishes that domestic and foreign investors enjoy the same rights, irrespective of the type of business they invest in. This includes their right to remit profits and to repatriate their investments, the right to structure their business in accordance with any of the types of entities available under Argentine law and the right to access domestic credit facilities and loans under the same conditions applicable to domestic companies, among others.

---

[1] Source:https : //www.lanacion.com.ar/2037609-nuevas-oportunidades-de-desarrollo.
[2] Source:http : //www.ebitan.org/en/proyecto.php.

c. Forms of Investment

In accordance with the FDI Act, foreign investors can invest, without limitation, in the following operations: foreign currencies of free convertibility; capital goods, its spare parts and accessories; profits or capital in foreign currency owned by foreign investors, provided that the legal conditions to repatriation are met; capitalization of foreign loans in foreign currencies of free convertibility; and immaterial goods.

Note that investors seeking to conduct activities on a permanent basis in Argentina must register a branch or a local subsidiary in the country. In this sense, investors have three possible paths to follow when starting an investment project in Argentina. First, they can establish a foreign branch office; second, they can acquire ownership interests in an existing company; and, finally, they can incorporate a new company. The last two options require the foreign investor to register as a foreign shareholder with the local Public Registry of Commerce (the "Public Registry of Commerce" or Registro Público de Comercio, in Spanish).

d. Standards of Market Access and Examination

As stated above, the Argentine Constitution provides that foreign and local investors enjoy the same rights. However, there are certain regulatory provisions that establish certain restrictions to investment by foreign enterprises in Argentina, the most relevant of these restrictions being the following:

(i) The Rural Lands Act provides limits for the acquisition of rural lands by foreign individuals or entities, according to the details further developed in section "D" under the title "Land Policy".

(ii) The Cultural Heritage Act provides that foreign companies can own up to 30% of the stocks or voting rights of any national broadcasting company.

(iii) The Decree-Law No. 15385/1944 and the Resolution 166/2009 issued by the Ministry of Domestic Affairs provide that foreign individuals or entities shall require an exceptional governmental authorization in order to acquire lands located near international borders with.

(iv) The Aeronautic Code provides that the majority of the stocks or voting rights of national aviation companies dedicated to the internal transportation of passengers, cargo or mail must be owned or controlled by Argentine companies or individuals domiciled in Argentina.

B. Foreign Exchange Regulation

a. Department Supervising Foreign Exchange

The Argentine foreign exchange market is regulated and supervised by the Central Bank of Argentina (the "CBA" or Banco Central de la República Argentina, in Spanish), an autonomous and independent entity from the federal government. The CBA charter provides that: every individual or legal entity can freely operate in the foreign exchange market, whether it is the case of local residents or not; the operations will be settled at the exchange rate freely agreed between the parties; the financial and exchange entities can operate with no time limits; and the signature of bills of exchange or affidavits are not mandatory, in spite of the obligation for the entities of identifying their clients and registering their operations.

b. Brief Introduction of Laws and Regulations of Foreign Exchange

In December 2015, the Argentine Government started a process of deregulation and de-bureaucratization of the Foreign Exchange Market, putting an end to a period of very strict exchange control regulations.

Under the rules currently in force, Argentine residents (including local entities with foreign shareholders) are allowed with no restrictions to buy foreign currency and transfer it abroad if they are part of a cross-border or local transaction. In general, cross-border transactions include transactions performed between Argentine and non-Argentine residents (e.g. , import of goods or services, payment of dividends to foreign shareholders, etc.). Moreover, Argentine residents are allowed to buy foreign currency to keep it outside of Argentina or within the country for local savings, real estate investments abroad, loans to non-residents, direct investments abroad, and portfolio investments abroad.

Also, non-Argentine residents are allowed to buy foreign currency in order to repatriate their investments.

The exchange rate in the foreign exchange market is determined by the supply and the demand of foreign exchange currency, although the CBA does also intervene in the market by selling and purchasing foreign currency on its own account.

c. Requirements of Foreign Exchange Management for Foreign Enterprises

Since December 2015, the Government initiated a process of deregulation and simplification of the foreign exchange market and, as a consequence of such process, there are no special restrictions for foreign enterprises regarding the foreign exchange management.

C. Financing

a. Main Financial Institutions

The top 10 Argentine private banks (based on the total owned assets) according to the raking issued by the CBA as of September 2017, are the following: Banco de Galicia y Buenos Aires S. A. , Industrial and Commercial Bank of China, Citibank N. A. , BBVA Banco Frances S. A. , Banco Supervielle S. A. , Banco Patagonia S. A. , Banco Santander Rio S. A. , HSBC Bank Argentina S. A. , Banco Credicoop Cooperativo Limitado, and Banco Macro S. A.

In addition, there are several public banks in Argentina, such as the Argentine Nation Bank, the Bank of the Province of Buenos Aires, the Bank of the Province of Córdoba, and the Bank of the City of Buenos Aires, among others.

b. Financing Conditions for Foreign Enterprises

Many financial entities (public or private) offer credit lines to local and foreign investors. Some of them are the following:

(i) The Argentine National Bank (Banco de la Nación Argentina, in Spanish) offers credit lines to companies, which includes loans for working capital and investments to cover production and sales costs, pre-financing and financing of exports and for the participation in international fairs or exhibitions. It also offers capital leases and factoring services.

(ii) The Investment and Foreign Trade Bank ("BICE" or Banco de Inversión y Comercio Exterior, in Spanish) provides its clients with several credit lines in dollars o pesos. One of its principal products allows investors to finance up to 70% of the total amounts of projects related to the generation of renewable energy, which contributes to the development of regional productive sectors. The maximum amount to be borrowed through this credit line is approximately US$ 10,000,000.

(iii) The Federal Investment Council ("CFI" or Consejo Federal de Inversiones, in Spanish) offers financial assistance to small and medium-sized enterprises with the aim of promoting the development of Argentine regions and provinces. These credit lines are meant to finance working capital, fixed assets and pre-investment. In addition, special financing is offered as export pre-financing and support to exportable production.

(iv) The National Fund for the Development of Micro, Small and Medium-sized Enterprises (Fondo Nacional para el Desarrollo de la Micro, Pequeña y Mediana Empresa, in Spanish) offers low cost credits to small and medium-sized enterprises for investment projects, promoting labor, capital, and energy efficiency improvements.

D. Land Policy

a. Brief Introduction of Land-Related Laws and Regulations

The most important land-related regulation is the Rural Lands Act, and its Regulatory Decree (together, the "Rural Lands Regulation"). These statutes regulate and limit the acquisition of rural lands (i. e. , plots located outside an urban area, independently of their destination) by foreigners (legal entities or individuals), whether for productive or non-productive ends.

Additionally, Decree-Law No. 15385/1944 and Resolution 166/2009 issued by the Ministry of Domestic Affairs govern the specific requirements in order for local residents or foreigners to own or use by any means (either under a lease or otherwise) properties located near international borders, based on national security purposes, requiring foreigner to request an exceptional authorization in order to own or use such near-the-border properties.

b. Rules of Land Acquisition for Foreign Enterprises

For purposes of the Rural Lands Regulation, "foreign ownership" means any acquisition, transfer or assignment of rights over rural land (including minority equity interests) performed in favor of any of the following, among others:

(i) Foreign individuals other than those exempted by the law (for complying with certain minimum residency requirements).

(ii) Legal entities with more than 51% of their stock directly owned by foreign individuals or entities or in which the latter control the entity's decision-making process.

(iii) Legal entities controlled by foreign entities or individuals through a number of votes sufficient to prevail in the local entity's decision-making process.

The most relevant restrictions under the Rural Lands Regulation are the following:

(i) Foreign ownership or possession of rural land shall not exceed 15% of the total amount of rural land in the Argentine territory. This percentage is to be calculated also in relation to the territory of the province or municipality where the relevant land is located.

(ii) Foreign owners from the same nationality cannot hold rural land exceeding 30% of the 15% mentioned in (i) above at the national, provincial and municipality levels.

(iii) Ownership or possession by the same foreign owner shall not exceed 1,000 hectares in the "core area"[1] of Argentina, or certain number of hectares in other regions of the country (which number of hectares have been set vis-à-vis the 1,000-hectare threshold applicable in the "core area").

(iv) Foreign entities or individuals are prevented from becoming owners or possessors of rural lands that comprise or are adjacent to "permanent and significant bodies of water".

Note that lands located in "Industrial Zones", "Industrial Areas", or "Industrial Parks" are not considered as rural lands for purposes of the Rural Lands Regulation.

E. The Establishment and Dissolution of Companies

a. The Forms of Enterprises

Foreign companies may operate in Argentina either through a wholly or partially owned subsidiary or through a branch. Any such subsidiary may operate under any of the several types of corporate entities available. The most common are the stock corporation ("S. A. " or Sociedad Anónima, in Spanish); and the limited liability company ("S. R. L" or . Sociedad de Responsabilidad Limitada, in Spanish). In addition, two new kinds of stock corporations were recently created, the sole-shareholder stock corporation ("S. A. U" or Sociedad Anónima Unipersonal, in Spanish) and the simplified stock corporation ("S. A. S" or Sociedad Anónima Simplificada, in Spanish).

Enterprises, whether subsidiaries of foreign shareholders or branches of a foreign main office, as well as foreign entities acting as shareholders of a local entity, are governed and controlled, from a corporate perspective, by the Public Registry of Commerce of the Argentine jurisdiction of their registration.

a) Subsidiaries

A foreign company may elect to establish a local subsidiary, in which case the foreign company must first register itself as a foreign shareholder in Argentina, pursuant to certain legal requirements it must fulfill for corporate purposes.

Once a subsidiary is established, it will be a different legal entity than the foreign shareholder. Usual limitations of liability apply to these entities and, therefore, the exposure of the foreign shareholder to local liabilities will be limited to the equity held by said foreign shareholder (except for certain specific situations in which courts may decide to pierce the corporate veil or otherwise hold the shareholder liable, although this very rarely occurs).

Below is a brief description of the characteristics and requirements of the most common types of corporate entities in Argentina:

(i) Sociedad Anónima or S. A.

• General Requirements

There are several requirements that must be particularly taken into account when incorporating an S. A. The most notorious requirements are that S. A. s must have at least two shareholders with "substantial participation" (which has been interpreted as at least 5% of the shares of the company); that the corporate name shall be truthful, novel and unmistakable; and that the corporate purpose must be precisely described in the by-laws.

• Capital

The capital of an S. A. is represented by shares, which must be denominated in Argentine pesos and have an equal, fixed par value. The amount of the capital must be stated in the by-laws, and under current regulations, the minimum capital of an S. A. is AR$ 100,000 (approximately US$ 5,000). Upon execution of the by-laws, the total amount of capital must be subscribed and each shareholder shall pay-in, at least, 25% of the capital to be contributed in cash, while the other 75% should be paid-in within the following 2 years. If the capital is not contributed in cash, it must be fully paid-in at the time of its subscription.

• Management

An S. A. is managed by a Board of Directors composed of one or more directors, except for companies under "permanent surveillance" by the Government, as explained further below, in which case the Board of Directors must be composed of at least three directors. Directors may be Argentines or foreigners and need not be shareholders. However, the majority of the directors must be Argentine residents or have their real domicile in Argentina. directors are appointed and removed by the shareholders' meeting. Directors may be elected for up to three fiscal years and may be reelected. The by-laws must establish the period for which Directors are elected.

Directors must meet at least quarterly. They must cast their votes personally, although they may authorize another director to vote on their behalf if the absolute majority of the Board of Directors is present at the meeting.

---

[1] Formed by certain departments of the provinces of Buenos Aires, Cordoba and Santa Fé.

• Permanent Governmental Surveillance

More stringent reporting requirements are imposed on those companies that are subject to what is known as "permanent surveillance" by the Government. The companies that are subject to permanent surveillance are those entities (whether S. A. s, S. R. L. s, S. A. S. s or S. A. U. s) that: make public offering of their shares or securities; have a capital in excess of AR$ 10,000,000 (approximately US$ 500,000); make capitalization or saving operations or in any way request money or securities to the public with promise of benefits or future benefits; exploit public concessions of services; are controlling or controlled companies of another company that is under permanent surveillance of the government.

Companies under "permanent surveillance" are subject to the following requirements: companies must appoint a regular and an alternate auditor (who shall be local accountants or attorneys at law), which can be done but is not mandatory for companies that are not under such government's surveillance regime; companies must inform to the Public Registry of Commerce that a shareholders' meeting will be held at least 15 business days in advance to each meeting, and the Public Registry of Commerce may decide to send an inspector to the meeting to verify that all applicable corporate regulations are complied with; the Board of Directors has to prepare a more detailed annual report introducing the financial statements to the shareholders; and capital contributions, even when made in cash, must be fully paid-in at the time of the contribution.

(ii) Sociedad de Responsabilidad Limitada or S. R. L.

S. R. L. s share many of the characteristics and are subject to many of the requirements applicable to S. A. s. The main differences between the two types of corporate entities are the following: the number of partners of S. R. L. s cannot exceed 50 (whereas there is no limitation in the number of shareholders of an S. A.); S. R. L. s are sometimes chosen due to their tax advantages in certain jurisdictions (for instance, this may be considered a pass-through entity for U. S. tax purposes); the capital of an S. R. L. is divided into quotas of equal value and must grant equal voting rights; all transfers of quotas must be registered with the Public Registry of Commerce; there is no minimum required capital for the S. R. L. , although the capital must be sufficient to carry out the corporate purpose of the S. R. L. ; managers of an S. R. L. may be appointed for a fixed or indefinite term; and if more than one manager is appointed, the by-laws must state the manner in which they shall exercise their powers, i. e. , individually, alternatively, indistinctly or as a body.

(iii) Sociedad Anónima Unipersonal or S. A. U.

S. A. U. s also share many of the characteristics and are subject to many of the requirements applicable to S. A. s. The main differences between the two types of corporate entities are the following: S. A. U. s are companies with only one shareholder, whereas S. A. s require at least two shareholders, as explained above; the capital of S. A. U. s must be fully integrated at the time of subscription notwithstanding its nature (i. e. , whether the capital is contributed in cash or in kind); S. A. U. s cannot be shareholders of another S. A. U. , whereas S. A. s can; and S. A. U. s are always subject to permanent governmental surveillance, whether or not their capital exceeds AR$ 10,000,000 (approximately US$ 500,000).

(iv) Sociedad Anónima Simplificada or S. A. S.

S. A. S. s were recently created with the main purpose of allowing entrepreneurs to register legal entities so as to start their businesses quickly and easily, although there is no obstacle for local or foreign medium-sized and large companies to incorporate such types of entities. The main characteristics of S. A. S. s that distinguish such corporate form from all others are the following: they can be incorporated in 24 hours (provided the standard by-laws form provided by law is used), and their organizational documentation can be digitally executed and submitted with the Public Registry of Commerce; corporate books and records are kept in digital form; their capital must be at least two times the minimum wage, which is currently fixed at AR$ 10,000 (approximately US$ 500); and the shareholders can decide on certain important matters of the functioning of the S. A. S. s, such as most of the content of the organizational documents, and the structure and functioning of the corporate bodies of the company.

b) Branches

Operating through a branch entails the liability of the main office. Because of this, when engaged in active business, most foreign companies prefer to conduct their business through subsidiaries rather than through branches.

Taxwise, both a branch and a subsidiary are treated the same. In general, maintenance costs of a branch are lower than those of a subsidiary, as a branch is not required to have local directors and statutory auditors, hold shareholders' meetings in Argentina and incur in other ancillary expenses. However, the lower maintenance costs are not a decisive factor, insofar as they generally do not outweigh the liability exposure of the main office.

In general, it is not mandatory for the main office to assign capital to the branch, although this will ultimately depend on the actual business to be conducted by the branch. On the other hand, it is mandatory for the branch to maintain separate accounts in Argentina and to prepare and submit financial statements and tax returns.

Branches are managed by one or more legal representatives appointed by the main office under a power of attorney that must precisely describe the extent of their authority. The managers so appointed are subject to the same duties and liabilities than the directors of S. A. s.

b. The Procedure of Establishment

There are certain requirements set forth in the Argentine Companies Law that foreigners (either individuals or legal entities) must follow in order to establish a legal entity or to register a branch of a foreign company in Argentina.

a) Subsidiaries

If the foreign investors seeking to establish a local subsidiary are legal entities rather than individuals, they must register themselves as foreign shareholders with the Public Registry of Commerce. To that end, the foreign entity must file the following documents:

(i) Resolution of the Board of Directors of the foreign entity approving the registration of the company as a foreign shareholder and appointing legal representatives with power to vote its shares in local companies.

(ii) Certificate of good standing issued by the appropriate authorities of the jurisdiction where the foreign entity is incorporated.

(iii) Copy of the organizational documents (articles of incorporation and by-laws), and any amendments thereto.

(iv) Copy of the latest audited financial statements or, if unavailable, a similar accounting affidavit.

(v) Identification of the foreign entity's shareholders.

(vi) Indication of whether there are individuals directly or indirectly holding 20% or more of the foreign entity's shares or voting rights, or otherwise with the direct or indirect control of the foreign entity, and if applicable, certain personal information of any such individual.

The documents listed above must be executed by an officer duly authorized by the Board of Directors of the foreign entity, and certified by notary public and legalized pursuant to the 1961 Hague Convention (Apostille), or have consular legalization if the Apostille is not available in the relevant jurisdiction.

Once the foreign shareholder is registered as such with the Public Registry of Commerce (if required as stated above), the incorporation of the local subsidiary will require the completion of the following steps:

(i) To file a name reservation application form to ensure the availability of the corporate name.

(ii) To pass the by-laws of the new entity into a public deed or into a private instrument certified by a notary public, depending on the corporate form (except for S. A. S. s, which can be instrumented in digital form, as explained above).

(iii) To submit the by-laws of the new entity with the Public Registry of Commerce, which will approve registration upon compliance with certain requirements related to mandatory publications and payment of capital.

b) Branches

Foreign entities seeking to register a branch in Argentina must submit to the Public Registry of Commerce the following documentation:

(i) Copy of the articles of incorporation and by-laws of the foreign entity.

(ii) Copy of the certificate of incorporation evidencing that the foreign entity is in good standing.

(iii) Copy of the Board of Directors' resolution approving the establishment and registration of an Argentine branch and determining its local capital, if any.

(iv) Copy of the Board of Directors' resolution appointing the general manager of the Argentine branch and granting him/her a general power of attorney for conducting all the affairs of the Argentine branch.

(v) A special power of attorney to register the branch with the Argentine authorities, carry out all steps needed to comply with all legal formalities, and act on behalf of the branch to deal with the administrative and judicial authorities.

(vi) Evidence that there are no restrictions or prohibitions affecting the ability of the foreign company to carry out its principal activity or activities in the jurisdiction where the foreign company is incorporated.

(vii) Written evidence of the disclosure of the shareholders or members of the foreign company.

(viii) Written evidence of compliance with at least one of the following conditions outside of Argentina:

• The existence of one or more agencies, branches or permanent representations, any of which evidence must be in the form of a certificate of good standing issued by the applicable authorities corresponding to such agency, branch or permanent representation.

• The ownership of equity interests in other companies, which under Generally Accepted Accounting Principles would be considered non-current assets, evidenced by the annual financial statements of the foreign company and/or a certificate signed by an authorized signatory of the foreign company, based on the accounting records contained in the company books.

• The ownership of fixed assets at its place of incorporation, the existence and value of which shall be proved as the equity interests mentioned in above.

• The documents listed above must be executed by an officer duly authorized by the Board of Directors of the foreign entity, and certified by notary public and legalized pursuant to the 1961 Hague Convention (Apostille), or have consular legalization if the Apostille is not available in the relevant jurisdiction.

The registration of the Argentine branch or a subsidiary must be announced by means of a notice published for one day in the Official Gazette.

c. Routes and Requirements of Dissolution

a) Dissolution of Subsidiaries

To initiate the dissolution and liquidation process, the following steps must be taken:

(i) the Board of Directors of the company must call for a regular and special shareholders' meeting which shall approve the dissolution and liquidation of the company; and appoint an individual to act as liquidator of the company. At this stage the company must add the term "in liquidation" to its corporate name.

(ii) The resolution of the shareholders' meeting and the appointment of the liquidator must be filed and registered with the Public Registry of Commerce. The liquidator can only deal with urgent matters and shall adopt all necessary measures to proceed with the liquidation of the company.

(iii) Once all the assets are disposed of and the liabilities are settled, the company must issue a winding-up balance statement and submit the cancellation before the Public Registry of Commerce for approval.

(iv) The company must file the request for cancellation with the tax authorities (federal and local) as well as any other public office that may correspond according to its activity.

b) Dissolution of Branches

In order to cancel the registration of a branch before local authorities, the following steps must be taken:

(i) The head office of the branch must decide to dissolve, liquidate and cancel the branch in Argentina and appoint a liquidator. At this stage the branch must add the term "in liquidation" to its corporate name.

(ii) The liquidator must then liquidate the assets and settle the liabilities of the branch in Argentina.

(iii) Once settled and liquidated, a winding-up balance statement must be issued.

(iv) The branch must cancel its registration with the Public Registry of Commerce, the tax authorities and any other competent Public Office.

If the branch has any outstanding obligation, the cancellation of the registration will be delayed until this issue is resolved (e. g. , pending payments with the tax authorities, failure to comply with the filing of financial statements, among others).

F. Merger and Acquisitions

a. The Regulations

The Argentine Antitrust Act (the "Antitrust Act") requires the parties to notify and obtain the approval of the Argentine Antitrust Authority (the "Antitrust Authority", or Comisión Nacional de Defensa de la Competencia, in Spanish) for certain economic concentration transactions (the "Concentration Transactions"). Transactions affected by the Antitrust Act are those resulting in the control or substantial influence, directly or indirectly, of one or more companies. Concentration Transactions that must be notified to the Antitrust Authority include mergers, transfers of ongoing concerns, stock acquisitions, shareholders' agreements, joint venture agreements and other agreements granting de iure or de facto control or substantial influence over management decisions of a business.

Note that the Antitrust Act requires the notification and request for approval to be made up to one week after the closing of the Concentration Transactions. If the transaction does not obtain anti-trust clearance, the Antitrust Authority has the power to order the parties to unwind the deal or to make the purchaser divest the acquisition. However, since most rejections are issued well after the parties have already closed the Concentration Transaction and combined the relevant businesses, in practice the Antitrust Authority generally requests the original purchaser to find a suitable new purchaser for the acquired assets or business in order to restore competition.

b. Transactions Covered

A Concentration Transaction should be notified to the Antitrust Authority by the signing parties of the relevant agreement if:

(i) the combined Argentine annual net sales of the acquiring group and the acquired group exceed AR$ 200 million (approximately US$ 10 million); and

(ii) either the amount of the Argentine portion of the transaction or the value of the assets in Argentina to be transferred, exceeds AR$ 20 million (approximately US$ 1 million).

Concentration Transactions that do not meet these monetary thresholds are nonetheless subject to notification and approval where the acquiring group was involved in a Concentration Transaction in Argentina valued in AR$ 20 million (approximately US$ 1 million) during the preceding 12-month period, or AR$ 60 million (approximately US$ 3 million), during the preceding 36-month period. Neither of these notifications and requests for approval require the payment of a filing price.

c. Exempt Transactions

The following Concentration Transactions are exempted from the notification requirement:

(i) Acquisitions of companies in which the buyer already owns more than 50% of the shares and of the voting rights.

(ii) Acquisitions of bonds, debentures, notes and non-voting shares.

(iii) Acquisitions of a single Argentine company by a foreign company which owns no assets in Argentina or shares in other Argentine companies. Note, however, that different types of agreements (e. g. , distribution and license agreements) have been considered as being assets in Argentina by the Antitrust Authority.

(iv) Acquisitions of companies in liquidation that did not transact business in Argentina in the preceding year.

d. Procedure

The Antitrust Act provides that the Antitrust Authority has a maximum of 45 business days after the filing date to issue a decision. If no decision is issued within this period, the Concentration Transaction is to be considered approved.

However, the 45-day period may be suspended by the Antitrust Authority for a more detailed examination for additional information and.

e. Substantive Test

The Antitrust Act provides that economic concentrations with the purpose or effect of restricting or distorting competition in a manner which may be contrary to the general economic interest are prohibited. The general economic interest has been interpreted as comparable to the concept of economic efficiency, although more inclined to consumer surplus rather than to total surplus.

G. Competition Regulation

a. Department Supervising Competition Regulation

The Department supervising antitrust regulation is the Antitrust Authority. The three main activities that are regulated by the Antitrust Authority are: economic concentrations, anticompetitive conducts, and promotion of competition.

b. Brief Introduction of Competition Law

The Antitrust Act is the most important legal instrument regarding antitrust regulation in Argentina. It does not contemplate any per se illegal or anticompetitive conducts. Thus, in order to determine if a business practice is unlawful, the Antitrust Act requires the Antitrust Authority to perform a detailed market analysis aimed at proving (on a case-by-case basis and through an investigation that must follow a specific procedure) that the alleged conduct is anticompetitive and can potentially damage the general economic interest.

In order for the Antitrust Authority to be able to determine if a conduct is unlawful, it must comply with all of the following points:

(i) Proving the existence of an anticompetitive behavior, by either diminishing competition or constituting an abuse of a dominant position.

(ii) Proving the participation of the parties in said conduct.

(iii) Defining a relevant geographic and product market.

(iv) Proving the capacity (i. e. , market power) of the investigated parties to be able to potentially damage the general economic interest in the relevant market.

(v) Proving the potential damage to the general economic interest. An anticompetitive conduct shall not be considered unlawful under the Antitrust Act if those accused of having engaged in such practice do not have enough market power to potentially damage the general economic interest.

Some of these points were defined by administrative and judiciary authorities based on the specific facts of the cases under review, according to their variable interpretation.

c. Measures Regulating Competition

The purpose of the Antitrust Act is to prevent certain behaviors and economic transactions that may limit, restrict or distort competition to the detriment of the general economic interest, which is the goal protected by the

Antitrust Act.

Pursuant to the Antitrust Law the sanctions which may be imposed to companies involved in prohibited conducts are the following:

(i) The cessation of the acts or conducts and, if relevant, the removal of its effects.

(ii) In case of performance of any of the anticompetitive acts forbidden by the Antitrust Act, fines from AR$ 10,000 to AR$ 150,000,000 (approximately from US$ 500 to US$ 7.5 million), which shall be adjusted on the following basis: the loss suffered by the persons affected by the forbidden activity; the benefit obtained by the persons involved in the forbidden activity; and the value of the assets involved belonging to the persons indicated in item above at the moment when the violation was performed. In case of default in the payment, the amounts of the fine shall be doubled.

H. Tax

a. Tax Regime and Rules

Due to its organization as a federal republic, Argentine taxing powers are distributed on three levels: national, provincial and municipal. The Constitution grants both the federal and provincial governments the authority to levy indirect taxes (except for custom duties, which shall only be collected by the federal government).

According to the Argentine Constitution, provinces shall levy direct taxes such as income tax. However, the federal government is authorized to impose direct taxes for a limited time, provided they are proportionately equal within the territory, and that defense, national security, and common welfare so require it.

b. Main Categories, Rates of Tax and Tax Declaration

a) Federal Taxes

(i) Value Added Tax (Impuesto al Valor Agregado, in Spanish)

Value Added Tax ("VAT") is one of the most important indirect taxes of the country. Indirect taxes can be defined as those burdened on someone other than the person responsible for paying the taxes.

This tax is in force as of January 1, 1975, and is regulated by the VAT Act. The general tax rate is 21%, but there are special situations where higher or lower tax rates are applied. It is levied in each stage of the economic chain of a product or a service where a value is added.

The reporting and payment of VAT are made on a monthly basis, though agricultural companies may choose to assess the tax monthly and pay it annually.

According to Section 1 of the VAT Act, this tax applies to:

• Sale of movable assets located or placed in Argentina;

• Performance of works, leases and services within the country; and

• Final imports of movable assets and the import of services, included in Section 3. These are services carried out outside the country, which are effectively used or exploited within the country (provided that the importer of the services is subject to VAT on account of other taxable events and is a registered taxpayer).

(ii) Federal Income Tax (Impuesto a las Ganancias, in Spanish)

Income tax is levied on the income of individuals, companies and Argentine businesses in general (branches included) and other legal entities.

The taxable event established in the corresponding regulation is obtaining income within the territory of Argentina or outside the country, in the case of Argentine residents.

The law follows a category method, whereby earnings are grouped into different classes of income. The four traditional categories are: real estate income; investment income, business income; and personal work earnings. For example, the fourth category is subject to progressive tax rates ranging from 5% to 35% but pursuant to recent legislation reducing taxes, the different business entities which belong to the third category are subject to a flat 30% tax rate for fiscal years 2018 and 2019, which will be decreased to a rate of 25% starting on fiscal year 2020.

Recent legislation also provides that dividends and profits distributions are subject to a 7% rate for fiscal years 2018 and 2019, and a 13% rate starting on fiscal year 2020.

Resident entities must file an annual income tax return reporting income subject to tax, tax losses, exempt income and a declaration of assets and liabilities existing at the closing of the taxable year. Resident individuals must also file an annual income tax return.

(iii) Tax on Deemed Minimum Income (Impuesto a la Ganancia Mínima Presunta, in Spanish)

This particular tax levies at a 1% rate on the value of the assets held locally or abroad, by local business entities, at the end of each fiscal year. It also taxes certain individuals and undistributed estates.

There is a minimum threshold of AR$ 200,000 below which the tax shall not apply. The income tax of the same year is creditable against this tax, so it works -in practice- as a minimum income tax burden.

Pursuant to recent legislation, this tax is repealed for fiscal years commencing from January 1, 2019 onwards.

(iv) Personal Assets Tax (Impuesto a los Bienes Personales, in Spanish)

This tax applies on assets held by individuals domiciled in Argentina (residents) and undivided estates located within the country until distribution to the heirs. These assets could be either located in the country or abroad.

Non-resident individuals and undistributed estates located abroad are exclusively taxed on their holdings of property located within the country. According to the Personal Assets Tax Act, individuals and business entities that are co-owners, possessors, users, depositories, administrators or custodians of assets belonging to non-resident taxpayers are liable as substitute obligors for payment of the tax applicable thereon. In addition, equity investments of non-resident aliens in Argentine companies or businesses are taxed at a 0. 5% annual levy.

The Personal Assets Tax Act currently includes a minimum threshold of AR$ 1,050,000 (approximately US$ 52,500), below which the tax is not applicable. The tax rates for local individuals and undivided estates are:

Tax Period	Value of the assets	Tax Rate
2017	Less or equal to ARS 950,000 (approximately US$ 47,500)	Non-taxable
	Higher than ARS 950,000 (approximately US$ 47,500)	0,5% rate in excess of ARS$ 950,000 (approximately US$ 47,500)
2018	Less or equal to ARS 1.050.000	Non-taxable
	Higher than ARS$ 1,050,00 000 (approximately US$ 52,500)	0,25% rate in excess of ARS$ 1,050,00 000 (approximately US$ 52,500)

(v) Debits and Credits in Bank Accounts Tax (Impuesto sobre créditos y débitos en cuentas bancarias y otras operatorias, in Spanish)

This tax is a national level tax withheld by Argentine banks (and other savings institutions). It applies on any deposited funds that are either withdrawn or transferred from checking or savings account. The taxable base is the amount withdrawn or transferred. The general tax rate is 0. 6 %, but there are very limited exemptions. Regular collection mechanisms made to avoid the use of bank accounts are burdened with a tax rate that doubles the general rate.

(vi) Custom Duties (Impuestos aduaneros, in Spanish)

Custom duties are taxed on import and export activities of goods to or from Argentine territory. During the last years, export duties represented the most important source of revenue of the federal government.

Argentina is a member of the World Trade Organization and that the 1994 General Agreement on Tariffs and Trade was incorporated in the country's legislation in the same year.

Argentina is one of the most relevant members of a common market between this country, Brazil, Uruguay, Paraguay and Venezuela, created in 1994. A reasonable consequence of this membership is that differential duties and tariffs are set forth with respect to intra- Mercosur and extra- Mercosur imports and exports.

b) Provincial Taxes

(i) Gross Turnover Tax (Impuesto a los Ingresos Brutos, in Spanish)

The gross turnover is a provincial tax assessed on the gross revenues obtained from the habitual onerous exercise of activities, such as commerce, profession or business, within a given jurisdiction. The applicable tax rates may vary according to the activity and the jurisdiction where they are conducted. Generally, the applicable tax rate is 3%.

In order to achieve the avoidance of double or multiple taxation in case of taxpayers conducting business in more than one jurisdiction, the tax is calculated and paid pursuant to the provisions set forth in a Multilateral Convention entered into among the provinces.

(ii) Stamp Tax (Impuesto de Sellos, in Spanish)

The Stamp Tax is a local tax levying the instrumentation of onerous contracts. Although Stamp Tax rates may vary from jurisdiction to jurisdiction, the general rate in most provinces is 1% (except for real estate property transfer which is higher and goes, in some jurisdiction, up to 4%).

Several Federal Supreme Court rulings have determined the inapplicability of the tax whenever acceptance of the contract takes place through partially unwritten means (e. g. the written offers sent out by one party, which determine that an agreement will be sealed provided that the other party performs a certain activity).

(iii) Tax on Real Estate Property (Impuesto inmobiliario, in Spanish)

Tax on real estate property can be defined as a direct tax levied on the ownership of real estate property located within the territory of a given province.

Each jurisdiction establishes its own tax rates and normally the tax base is the fiscal valuation determined by the competent tax authority.

c) Municipal Taxes

Municipalities may establish certain contributions and levies for public services rendered in their jurisdictions, including contributions on the occupation and use of public spaces; contributions on real estate property; contributions on cemeteries; contributions on work construction; contributions on services of sanitary protection; contributions of advertising and taxes for financing public works.

These particular municipal taxes are generally regulated in Municipal Tax Codes or the Municipal Tax Ordinances.

I. Securities

a. Brief Introduction to the Argentine Securities-Related Laws and Regulations

The main Argentine securities-related laws and regulations are the Capital Markets Act and the General Resolutions periodically issued by the National Securities Commission (the "CNV" or the Comisión Nacional de Valores, in Spanish).

In practice, the main stock exchange in Argentina is the Buenos Aires Stock Exchange. Shares are purchased and sold on the Buenos Aires Stock Exchange through one of approximately 200 authorized brokers, some of whom are related to national or international banks. Negotiable instruments and options are also traded on the Buenos Aires Stock Exchange. The system is supervised by the CNV, which has functions similar to those of the Securities and Exchange Commission (SEC) in the United States. Listed companies must file their financial statements and board of directors' reports with the CNV on a quarterly basis, and must file their annual audited financial statements.

The CNV also regulates the over-the-counter market. The daily volume of shares traded is similar to that of the Buenos Aires Stock Exchange, and the volume of government securities traded is considerably higher. The shares traded in this market are those of the companies listed on the Buenos Aires Stock Exchange.

b. Supervision and Regulation of Securities Market

To list shares on the stock exchange, a company must be registered for public offering with the CNV and must submit an application including the following information and documentation:

(i) Entity information (e. g. , type of entity, location of its head office, incorporation data).

(ii) Composition of issuer's capital stock (e. g. , stock's rights and preferences, description of its shareholders, structure of issuer's economic group).

(iii) Description of issuer's background and activities.

(iv) Accounting and financial information of the issuer (e. g. , balance sheet for the last three financial years).

(v) Copy of the minutes of the extraordinary meeting of shareholders resolving to list the shares.

(vi) Copy of the company's bylaws.

(vii) List of its directors, statutory auditors and managers (regular and alternate), specifying their domicile and positions held in other companies.

(viii) List of the agenda of items dealt with in shareholders and board of directors' meetings held in the 12 months prior to application.

(ix) Evidence that the company is a going concern, with an appropriate technical or administrative organization, and a market and financial position that show good prospects for generating profits on shareholders' equity.

Although the Capital Markets Act is the current statute regulating the Argentine capital markets, it is expected that in the following months the Federal Congress will enact a new law regulating capital markets that was drafted and is being promoted by the Federal Government (the "Bill"). The House of Representative has already approved that Bill, so it is only pending the approval of the Senate. The Bill is publicly known, and some of the regulatory updates that it brings are:

(i) The elimination of the CNV's capacity to designate auditors with veto power on the resolutions adopted by the management bodies of the issuers, and intervene the management of the company by suspending the power of the directors for a period of 180 days.

(ii) The obligation to the CNV to issue funded decisions and summaries prior to the declaration of irregularities o nullities of acts, when considered illegal or against the regulations and statues or dispositions issued or approved by the CNV.

(iii) The modification of the right of preference in public offerings. In the cases of capital increase or mandatory convertible notes offered by public offerings, the right of preference shall be exercised through the placement procedure determined in the respective public offering prospect. The conditions for the application of such procedure are: the existence of an expressed inclusion in the bylaws that authorize it and that it is approved by every shareholder meeting that passes every issuance of shares or mandatory convertible notes.

(iv) The Bill enables legal entities incorporated abroad to take part in the shareholders' meetings of the companies whose stocks are being quoted in the markets authorized by the CNV, without any further requisite.

(v) In case of any controversy derived from the revision of sanctions imposed by the CNV, the federal commercial courts shall have jurisdiction, instead of the administrative ones.

In addition, the Bill includes an exemption to the income tax applicable to the capital gain triggered by the sale of the stock from companies with public offerings in markets authorized by the CNV. Also, when such stocks are not in public offering regimes, but the capital gain is a result of a public offering of such stocks, the exemption shall also apply. The exemption shall also apply for trusts and mutual funds that invest in Argentina and make public offerings of their participation certificates and/or negotiable values. When the indicated negotiable values are not in the public offering in markets authorized by the CNV, these exemptions shall not apply.

c. Requirements for Engagement in Securities Trading for Foreign Entities

Although no prior authorization is needed in order for foreigners to engage in securities trading in Argentina, foreign and local companies and individuals shall fulfill certain requirements to do so.

Particularly, the opening of a custody account is mandatory and agents such as banks or international companies as Clearstream or Euroclear are authorized to that end. When an individual is to open an account, the following information shall be provided: name, place and date of birth, nationality, gender, marital status, ID number, Fiscal Identification Key ("CDI" or Clave de Indentificación Tributaria, in Spanish), address, telephone and profession. The verification of the funds' origin is proved by the provision of the last paycheck stub. In the case of a company seeking to open an account, the required information includes: ID copy of the legal representatives, by-laws, ownership of the company's stock, minutes regarding distribution of positions, certification of inscription before the Tax Authority (the "AFIP" or Administración Federal de Ingresos Públicos, in Spanish). In order to verify the origin of the funds, the last financial statement shall be presented.

When the investor is a foreign entity, it would be reasonable to conclude that there is no need for such entity to be registered with the Public Registry of Commerce if its sole activity is to engage in the trading of securities in Argentina. According to the Argentine Companies Act, such registration is obligatory when the activities of the company in the country are usual. Considering that the opening of such account is an activity to be performed only one time, such regularity is not met and the registration of the company would not be needed.

J. Preference and Protection of Investment

a. The Structure of Preference Policies

There are no particular preference policies in Argentina. The FDI Act provides that the foreign investors shall enjoy the same rights and have the same obligations as Argentine investors.

b. Support for Specific Industries and Regions

The northern and the southern regions of Argentina are the targets of the latest and most important infrastructure projects conducted and/or promoted by the National Government.

The Plan Belgrano is a social, productive and infrastructural project to develop the Northern region of the Argentina (the less advanced region of the country). The total amount that will be destined to this project is US$ 16,300 million. Regarding its infrastructure aspect, the Plan Belgrano has the objectives of improving the North-South / East-West connectivity; boost the connectivity between main urban areas and small isolated towns; develop the national and provincial roads with improvements for all type of vehicle and climate condition; reduce the bottlenecks and congestions in key nodes; start a process of renovation of 3,800 km and the improvement of 850 km of railway; and the building and conditioning of four airports to connect the North of Argentina with the rest of the world.

On other hand, the Plan Patagonia is the southern version of the Plan Belgrano and is focused on matters as infrastructure, connectivity, urban development, hydric works, the ocean and renewable energies. In its first phase, it includes improvements of the Chapelco Airport for US$ 8 million and the conditioning of routes and the expansion of Usuahia's port for almost US$ 190 million.

Regarding specific industries supported by the Government, the Federal Congress has recently enacted the Act No. 27424, for the support of distributed generation of renewable energy, providing the actors of such market with several benefits, such as tax exemptions or special credit lines. Other example of the National support for an industry is Act No. 23877, which establishes several benefits to the technological industry.

c. Special Economic Areas

Argentina has 11 Free Trade Zones (the "FTZ") over the country, where the goods are not subject to the usual custom controls and their import, extract or export are not taxed with tributes (with the exception of retributive taxes), neither subject to economic prohibitions. The activities which can be developed in the FTZ are: storing, commercialization and industrialization. However, the users of the FTZ cannot enter other special regime of industry promotion, while being users of the FTZ.

Particularly, Tierra del Fuego is a FTZ in the south of Argentina. The Fiscal and Custom Regime for Tierra del Fuego Act provide that the industries set in Tierra del Fuego shall enjoy exemptions of national tax, when goods are imported or located into the determined zone of the province.

d. Investment Protection

Argentina has executed a number of Bilateral Investment Treaties with third countries and is a member of the Multilateral Investment Guarantee Agency (MIGA), the Overseas Private Investment Corporation, and the International Centre for the Settlement of Investment Disputes (ICSID), which further strengthen the protections for foreign investors.

III. Trade

A. Department Supervising Trade

a. Foreign Trade

The Ministry of Production aims to promote and foster the international insertion of the Argentine economy, secure competition and institutional quality as well as to federalize production.

b. Subsecretariat of International Trade

The Subsecretariat of International Trades main purposes are the commercial insertion of Argentina in the global value chains, the promotion of investment, and the expansion of the markets for the sale of Argentine products. In addition, its aim is to make trade transparent, improve the efficiency of the chains, simplify commercial procedures and strengthen consumer rights.

Within its scope, the Commission for the Defense of Competition operates as a decentralized institution that promotes the defense of competition against any form of market distortion. The Subsecretariat of International Trade elaborates, proposes and participates in the implementation of strategic guidelines of the international commercial policy that allows the integration of Argentina in the world.

c. Customs

The competent authority on import and export operations in the country is the General Direction of Customs. As a dependency of the Federal Administration of Public Income ("AFIP", for its acronym in Spanish), one of its main purposes is to safeguard the State's interests regarding tax collection and specific infractions associated with foreign trade operations.

The Argentine customs legislation is composed, basically by the Customs Code-Law No. 22415 ("Customs Code"), its regulatory Decree No. 1001/82, the Treaty of Asuncion. The key issue when importing goods into Argentina is the tariff classification of the underlying goods.

Argentina has adopted the MERCOSUR Common Nomenclature ("MCN"), which is based on the Harmonized Commodity Description and Coding System developed by the World Customs Organization. Under MCN, an eight-digit tariff number identifies goods imported into Argentina. Digits seven and eight, which make up the tariff item, are unique to MERCOSUR. Argentina has three additional digits for domestic purposes. They determine the applicability of certain requirements and/or restrictions and, in some cases, exceptions to the common external tariff.

d. MERCOSUR

As a customs union, the trade of goods originating and proceeding from MERCOSUR countries are not subject to import duties -except in some specific cases- and are exempt from statistic fees.

In order to qualify as MERCOSUR goods, the products must meet the rules of origin set forth in the MERCOSUR Origin Regime, and the producer or exporter will have to provide to the importer the prescribed MERCOSUR certificate of origin.

The aforementioned regime establishes that goods will be considered originated from a MERCOSUR country when:

(i) The products are totally manufactured in a MERCOSUR country: exclusively manufactured with materials originated from MERCOSUR countries.

(ii) The products are manufactured with materials of a third country and are "transformed" in a MERCOSUR country product, and the "transformation" allows the product to be classified under a Tariff Number of the MCN (4 digits) different from the Tariff Number of the manufacture materials.

(iii) The products comply with the 60% added value rule. In other words, if the requirement indicated above in b) is not satisfied because the transformation process does not entail a change in the Tariff Number to qualify as a MERCOSUR origin product, the CIF port of destiny value or the CIF maritime port value of the third country components must be equal to or less than 40% of the "Free On Board" value of the product.

(iv) Products resulting from a process consisting only in the assembly made in a MERCOSUR country, using non-MERCOSUR materials, when the CIF port of destiny value or the CIF maritime port value of the third country components be equal to or less than 40% of the "Free On Board" value of the product.

(v) Capital assets comply with the 60% added value rule.

(vi) Products are subject to specific origin requirements. These requirements will prevail over the general requirements mentioned above in (i) to (v), and shall not be required for products totally manufactured in a MERCOSUR country.

B. Brief Introduction of Trade Laws and Regulations

a. Import Licenses

The Ministry of Production reinstated the regime of Automatic and Non-Automatic Licenses of Importation. All the tariff positions of the MCN destined for definitive importation for consumption are subject to the processing of licenses. For all of them they must process automatic licenses, except those that are subject to Non-Automatic Licenses.

To process these Non-Automatic Licenses, it is necessary that the importer is registered in the Unique Registry of the Ministry of Production.

Import licenses have a validity period of 180 calendar days counted from the date of their approval.

b. Subsidies

Regarding export subsidies, Argentina provides total or partial VAT refunds to exporters of consumer goods. Also, Decree No. 1341/16 provides an additional 0.5 percent refund to exporters of certified products with geographical or originating indications, certified organic products and products that comply with the standards of quality and innovation that qualify the goods so that they are labeled as "Argentine Foods a Natural Option".

In addition, there are subsidies for goods produced in the Province of Tierra del Fuego, which is a tax-exempt trade zone called the Special Customs Area (AAE).

c. Used-Goods

The national legislation requires compliance with strict conditions on the importation of used capital goods that can be imported. In order to import these kind of goods it is required:

(i) The capital assets of use can only be imported directly by the final user.

(ii) The reconditioning of the goods abroad is only allowed if it is made by the original manufacturer. Third-party technical evaluations are not allowed.

(iii) The local reconditioning of the goods is subject to the technical evaluation carried out by the Industrial Technology Institute, with the exception of aircraft.

(iv) Regardless of the place where the reconditioning is carried out, the Argentine Customs Authority requires, at the time of importation, the presentation of a "Used-Goods Certificate".

d. Importers and Exporters' Registration Before the Customs Service

Individuals or corporations wishing to import or export goods into or from Argentina must generally be registered in the Importers and Exporters' Registry before the Customs Service.

e. Temporary Imports

A temporary importation involves the entry of goods into the Argentine territory to remain in the country for a limited period of time and for a specific purpose. Extensions of the terms originally granted may be authorized, as long as certain conditions are met.

There are basically two types of temporary importation procedures:

(i) Goods which are to be exported in the same condition as they entered the country. Such goods must be re-exported in certain periods of time, depending on their nature; and

(ii) Goods which will undergo a process of transformation, manufacturing or repairing and be re-exported. In general, such goods must be re-exported within a 2-year term.

No import duties are applicable to the importation of goods under these regimes, except certain service fees. In order to import goods under these regimes, a guarantee must be provided to the Customs Service to ensure the payment of duties and/or penalties that may apply.

f. "Aduana en Factoría"

Decree No. 688/02 sets out the "Aduana en Factoría" regime for industrial factories established within the Argentine territory. Such regime provides for the importation of raw materials, parts, components, which are directly used in the productive process and/or transformation of goods for their subsequent exportation or definitive importation.

The above mentioned goods should be placed under customs warehousing procedure in the terms set forth in the Customs Code, considering that in all cases, the verification of the goods by the Customs Service has taken place. Therefore, import duties and statistics fees are not applicable.

The importers will have to comply with their tax, customs and social security obligations and provide a guarantee to secure the payment of duties and/or penalties that may apply.

C. Trade Management

Please see items A and B above.

D. The Inspection and Quarantine of Import and Export Commodities

The regime of inspection and quarantine of import and/or export commodities does not apply to most cases. However, as a third-party organism, the National Agrifood Health and Quality Service Agency is empowered to require the quarantine and inspection of commodities, in cases of import and/or export operations of vegetables and animals.

E. Custom's Management

Please see items A and B above.

IV. Labour

A. Brief Introduction of Labour Laws and Regulations

Labour relationships are mainly regulated by the Employment Contract Law ("ECL"), the National Constitution, International Treaties, the Collective Bargaining Agreements and individual employment contracts. The following is a brief summary of the most outstanding regulations on this matter.

a. Probationary Period

Employees shall be hired with a fixed term contract, a temporary contract or for an indefinite term. In this last case, the three first months of employment is the probationary period. During such period the employer may terminate the contract with the only obligation of giving a 15 day prior notice.

b. Work Day

Labour law establishes limits to working hours, consisting of 9 daily hours or 48 hours per week. If maximum limits are exceeded, overtime shall be paid, with 50% of surcharge when extra hours are made during week days and 100% surcharge when they are made on Saturdays after 1 pm, Sundays and national holidays. Directors in such Company are exempt from workday limitations.

c. Payment of Remunerations

Remunerations may be paid monthly, daily, or on a fortnight basis and can take the form of salary, commissions on sales, participation in profits, and so forth. Remunerations must be paid within four working days following the end of the relevant month or fortnight, or three working days when paid weekly.

d. Mandatory Bonus: (13th Salary)

This bonus is paid on June 30 and December 18 every year, and amounts to 50% of the best salary paid to the worker during the first and second halves of the year, respectively. When an employment relationship is terminated, the employee is entitled to the payment of the proportional 13th salary, considering the time worked during the corresponding semester.

e. Vacation

Employees are entitled to annual vacation periods which vary from 14 to 35 calendar days depending on their seniority. Vacation payment is calculated by dividing the employee's salary by 25 and multiplying this result by the number of vacation days. Upon termination of the employment relationship, employees are entitled to the payment of the proportional vacations, considering the time worked during the last year.

f. Special Leaves

Employees are granted with a short special leave of absence in certain events such as: birth of a child, marriage, death of close relatives and high school and university tests. The payment of special leaves is calculated on the same basis as vacation payments. Collective Bargaining Agreements can extend the periods and/or establish additional leaves.

Female employees are also entitled with maternity leave of 45 days before and 45 days after birth. During this period salary is paid by the Family Allowance Fund.

In case of employees' illnesses or disability (not related to work), the contract will continue in full force and effect and the employee will be entitled to receive the usual salary payments for a period of 3 to 12 months depending on the employees' seniority and family obligations (supports of close relatives).

g. Termination of an Employment Contract

The employment contract may be terminated by the employee's resignation, by giving 15 days prior notice.

Indefinite term contracts can be terminated by the employer without cause. In such case prior notice shall be given. Its duration depends on the employee's seniority (from 15 days to two months) and failure to give notice will result in the payment of an indemnity equal to the salaries the employee would have collected during those periods.

Additionally, the employer shall pay the seniority indemnity, which is equivalent to one monthly salary per each year of service or fraction over three months, on the basis of the best ordinary usual monthly remuneration accrued during the last year. A cap may be applied considering the applicable Collective Bargaining Agreement and case law.

Employees are entitled to special protection for a certain period of time in specific situations such as pregnancy, union representation and marriage. In these cases, the amounts due as severance payments are substantially increased.

The employer may also dismiss the employee for gross misconduct. In such case no severance compensations are owed, but the employer has the burden of proof of the gross misconduct and the labor judge is who has the capacity to decide whether such decision was or not justified.

Other ways in which the employment contract can be terminated are mutual consent of the parties, and the employee's retirement, death or disability.

h. Mutual Agreement

Both parties may terminate the contract at any time by mutual consent. The ECL specifically provides that in this case the termination requires a notarized document. It also allows the parties to terminate the contract before a labor court or the Ministry of Labor.

i. Disability

In the event the employment relationship ends due to the employee's permanent and total disability, he/she is entitled to obtain an indemnity equal to the seniority indemnity.

j. Retirement

The employment contract may be terminated when the employee has reached the age required by law to obtain the benefit of ordinary retirement. In this sense, the employer will have to notify the employee that he/she is under the obligation to commence the retirement procedure. After a year or once the employee has obtained the pension benefit, whichever occurs first, the employer is entitled to terminate the employment agreement without severance payments.

k. Death

The employment contract may also terminate in case of death of the employee. In such event, certain family dependents are entitled to a special indemnity of an amount equivalent to 50% of the seniority indemnity provided for dismissal without cause.

l. Employees' Registration

Every new hiring and every termination of an employment contract must be communicated to the Tax Authority. This communication is made through the internet.

Additionally, the employer must keep a Special Labor Book in which the employer and employee's information, salaries, etc. shall be registered.

m. Social Security Contributions and Taxes

Any amount paid to employees in Argentina is subject to social security contributions to be paid by employee and employer (in different proportions), according to Law No. 24241.

Employees have to pay 17% of their gross salary, while employers have to pay 20. 7% of the gross salaries when their activity is the provision of services and 17. 5% of the gross salaries when their activity is a different one.

Social security contributions are destined to fund the Pension and Retirement System, the Medical Protection to the Retired, the Family Allowance Funds, the Unemployment Fund and the Mandatory Medical Care Insurance.

In addition, employers have to make additional payments (which amounts may vary) to grant employees with a mandatory life insurance and an occupational risk insurance.

Finally, employers are obliged to withhold income tax from their employees' remuneration when the annual amount exceeds a certain minimum set by the Tax Authority.

B. Requirements of Employing Foreign Employees

a. Work Permit

According to local regulations on immigration, in order to reside and perform any kind of remunerated activities in Argentina, foreigners must obtain a residence permit issued by the Argentine Immigration Agency. Residencies can be temporary (which are granted for a year and renewable for an identical period), or permanent (which grant the foreigner the right to work and reside in the country for an undetermined period of time).

b. Application Procedure

Foreigners may request residence permits abroad, at the Argentine consulate in the applicant's home country (this application must be preceded by the issuance of an entry permit emitted by the Argentine Immigration Office); or at the Argentine Immigrations Office after entering the country as tourists, with a transitory residence permits. While being a transitory resident, the foreign citizen cannot perform any kind of remunerated or lucrative activities.

The documents and requirements to apply for a residence permit differ whether the applicant is a citizen of a MERCOSUR country (Bolivia, Brazil, Colombia, Chile, Ecuador, Paraguay, Peru, Uruguay, Venezuela, Guyana and Suriname) or a non-MERCOSUR citizen; and also depending on the type of residence permit that will be requested (See Visa types).

c. Social Insurance

Local legislation grants immigrants and their families with access to the same social security benefits that are granted to nationals under specific circumstances (retirement, unemployment, disablement, etc.).

In addition, Argentina has executed several bilateral treaties with other countries which establish that:

(i) for a limited period of time foreign workers can keep on contributing to their home country national security system; and

(ii) the amounts and periods during which the foreign worker contributed to the Argentine social security system will be considered by their home country social security system pursuant to such treaties.

C. Exit and Entry

a. Visa Types

a) Permanent Residency Permit

Permanent residency permits may be granted to:

(i) MERCOSUR country members citizens after holding a temporary residency permit for two or more consecutive years;

(ii) non-MERCOSUR citizens after holding a temporary residency permit for three or more consecutive years;

(iii) spouses, children and parents of Argentine citizens;

(iv) spouses, children under 18 and parents of a permanent resident; and

(v) those who have performed diplomatic or consular duties or worked in international organizations.

In order to grant this permit, the Argentine Immigrations Office will require several personal documents of the applicant such as birth/marriage certificate, affidavit of criminal records, etc.

This permit allows its holder to work and reside in the country for an undefined period of time.

b) Temporary Residency Permit

There are several categories of temporary residency permits (i. e. migratory worker, scientist, company executive, etc).

To apply for this visa, the applicant will need to submit before the Argentine Immigrations Office or the Argentine Consulate, several personal documents such as birth/marriage certificate, affidavit of criminal records, etc.

Non-MERCOSUR citizens need to be sponsored by the local company/individual that will act as employer. Sponsors shall be registered before the National Registry of Applicants of the National Immigration Office ("RENURE", for its acronym in Spanish). Documents such as the employment contract signed with the Argentine company, a certificate of registration of the employer in the RENURE, and a certificate of the employer's inscription before the AFIP will be required.

MERCOSUR citizens do not need to be sponsored by any local entity.

This permit is granted for a year and renewable for an identical period and will allow its holder to perform all kinds of remunerated activities during the authorized period.

c) Provisional Residency Permit

Until the temporary and/or permanent residency permit is granted, the National Immigrations Office may provide with a provisional residency permit valid for three months (and renewable until the temporary/permanent residency permit has been granted). During this period of time, provisional residents may perform all kinds of remunerated activities.

b. Restrictions for Exit and Entry

Residents may depart and enter the country freely during the period of their authorized stay, as long as they present before the immigration authorities the documents that proof their identity and residency status.

D. Trade Union and Labor Organizations

a. Trade Unions

Trade Unions can represent certain defined groups or sectors of workers such as workers that render services in a specific establishment, workers whose employers' activity is the same, and/or workers that render a specific task, and/or share a similar category.

Workers have an irrevocable right to join any Trade Union (or leave them), and/or to create new ones and employers cannot interfere in those decisions.

In addition, Trade Unions have the right to call for elections to appoint Union Representatives that are specially protected by law, they cannot be terminated or suspended and no disciplinary measures can be taken against them without a prior authorization is granted by the labor judge.

b. Collective Bargaining Agreements

The application of certain Collective Bargaining Agreement ("CBA") in general terms depends on the employer's activity and/or on the employees' category.

Commonly, CBAs apply to non-hierarchical employees.

CBAs are agreed between Trade Unions and Employer representatives and they can only create better conditions than the ones established by the ECL.

All CBAs establish a minimum wage scale, which is updated periodically through direct negotiations between the Trade Unions and the Employer representatives.

In order to determine whether there is an applicable CBA, a case by case analysis has to be made.

E. Labour Disputes

a. Individual Disputes

Individual disputes occur when an employee files a claim against the employer arguing the existence of breaches to labour regulations (ECL, CBA and the individual employment contract).

The procedure through which these claims shall be substantiated will depend on the jurisdiction.

In the City of Buenos Aires, the employees need to file an administrative claim before the Labour Ministry before filing their lawsuit.

A labour trial can last between 4 and 5 years. Parties may reach a settlement agreement at any time before the final court ruling is notified.

b. Collective Disputes

These types of conflicts arise when there is a dispute with a group of employees that are represented by a Trade Union, and/or there is a conflict with the Trade Union.

These disputes are generally substantiated before the Labor Ministry, entity which will act as a mediator and encourage the parties to reach an amicable agreement.

In specific cases, collective disputes can also be substantiated before Labor Courts.

V. Intellectual Property

A. Brief Introduction of IP Laws and Regulations

The first source of protection of Intellectual Property rights is our National Constitution. Section 17 grants protection to all authors or inventors regarding their works, inventions or discoveries, for a period of time granted by the law.

It is worth mentioning that the Executive Branch has recently issued an Urgency Decree No. 27/2018 which aims at simplifying and accelerating the patents and trademarks registration proceedings. Since this Urgency Decree is still to be approved by the Congress, we have not mentioned herein any of its amendments.

B. Patent Application

Patents are specifically governed by Law No. 24481 (as amended) and its Regulatory Decree No. 260/96.

Regarding international treaties, Argentina is a party to the Paris Convention and the TRIPS Agreement (Trade-Related Aspects of Intellectual Property Agreement). Argentina is not a party to the PCT (Patent Cooperation Treaty). For the protection of plants, Argentina has acceded to the UPOV Convention (International Convention for the Protection of New Varieties of Plants).

The law grants that new inventions of products or proceedings involving an inventive step and leading to an industrial result shall be patentable.

Consequently, the basic requirements for a patent application are the following:

(i) Novelty;
(ii) Industrial application;
(iii) Inventive step.

A patent grants the owner the exclusive right of exploiting the invention for a non-renewable 20 years counted as from the application date. Annual fees are mandatory to keep the patent in force once the patent has been granted.

The law determines that the following are not considered inventions:

(i) discoveries, scientific theories and mathematic methods;
(ii) literary or artistic works or any other aesthetic creation, as well as scientific works;
(iii) plans, rules and methods for carrying out intellectual activities, for games or for economic-commercial activities, as well as computer programs;
(iv) other manners in which information can be presented;
(v) methods of surgical, therapeutical or diagnostic treatment for use on human beings and those related to animals;
(vi) juxtaposition of known inventions or combinations of known products, changes in their form, size or component materials, except when said combination or merger is such that the components thereof cannot operate separately or when the characteristic properties or functions thereof are modified to obtain an industrial result being not obvious to an expert in the art; and
(vii) any kind of life matter and substance pre-existing in nature.

Pharmaceutical products are specifically included as patentable inventions and are currently protected by Argentine law. However, its regulation severely restricts the patentability of many categories of inventions in the pharmaceutical and chemical fields.

Patents may be licensed and transferred, but such transfer must be registered with the Patent Office in order to be enforceable against third parties.

C. Trademark Registration

Law No. 22362 and its regulation, Decree No. 558/81, govern all matters relating to trademarks in Argentina. Regarding international treaties, Argentina is a party to the Paris Convention and the TRIPS Agreement.

The law provides for an attenuated attributive system by which trademark rights and their exclusive use arise from registration -as opposed to use-, but establishes the requirement of use for renewal purposes.

Also, Argentina has adopted the international classification of goods and services unifying classification trademarks criteria with developed countries.

The statute is permissive in relation to which signs may be used as trademarks: special names, emblems, monograms, advertising slogans, stamps, vignettes, embossed marks, letters and numbers with drawings, containers or labels, or other signs to distinguish the owner's products and services. To this day, a few non-traditional trademarks such as sound, olfactory, motion and three dimensional (3D) trademarks have also been accepted for registration.

The term of protection of trademarks is ten years as from the registration date, and may be indefinitely renewed for periods of ten years, so long as the trademark has been used within the last five years prior to the renewal date.

Trademarks may be transferred, but such transfer will only be valid with respect to third parties once registered with the National Institute of Industrial Property.

D. Measures for IP Protection

Regarding patents, in order to avoid that a third party requests before the Patent Office a compulsory license for the manufacture and sale of the patented product or the use of the patented process, it is important that: the invention is exploited within three years after the granting of the patent, or four as from the filing of the application or that effective and serious preparations have been made for the exploitation of the invention within said period, and that the exploitation is not interrupted for more than a year.

Also, in order to give the patent owners a remedy against anyone, without any right, that has obtained a patent that violates any of the requirements established by the law, a nullity action is set forth by the law.

Patent infringement is considered a crime sanctioned with fines or imprisonment. A court order may be obtained to prevent the continuation of the infringement and the collection of damages.

Considering trademarks, if someone registered a trademark and was aware or should have been aware that the trademark belonged to someone else, or if the granted trademark collides with any provision of the statute, the trademark owner can request the declaration of the nullity through a court action.

Trademarks can be declared invalid through a court action against those who were aware, or should have been aware, that the trademark belonged to someone else, or if the granted trademark collides with any provision of the statute.

In addition, trademarks can also be cancelled at the request of a party, if said trademark has not been used in the country within five years before the date on which the cancellation action is brought.

Trademark infringement is considered a crime sanctioned with fines or imprisonment. A court order may be obtained to prevent the continuation of the infringement and the collection of damages.

Finally, also copyright infringement is considered a crime sanctioned with fines or imprisonment. A court order may be obtained to prevent the continuation of the infringement and the collection of damages.

VI. Environmental Protection

A. Department Supervising Environmental Protection

Regarding agencies with environmental jurisdiction and supervising environmental protection, the national environmental agency is the Ministry of Environment and Sustainable Development (Ministerio de Ambiente y Desarrollo Sustentable, "MAyDS", for its acronym in Spanish). The MAyDS has Secretariats, Subsecretariats and Offices that address various aspects of environmental management and protection, including but not limited to, forestry, desertification, biodiversity, protected species, climate change, sustainable development, sustainable consumption, water resources, environmental impact assessment, environmental education, pollution prevention, hazardous waste and transboundary movements of wastes.

In 2016, the Argentine Cabinet on Climate Change was created to design climate change policies. It is presided by the Chief of Staff and runs with the participation of the MAyDS, the Ministries of Energy and Mining, Economic Development, Agriculture, Transport, Social Development, Education, Science, Interior, Culture and the Foreign Ministry.

Other national agencies that regulate environmental issues are the Secretariat of Hydrocarbons (Ministry of Energy and Mining) regarding fuel storage conditions; and the Subsecretariat of Fight against Drug Trafficking (Ministry of Security) concerning chemical substances.

At the provincial level, the twenty three Argentine provinces have environmental agencies, mainly at the ministerial or secretariat level. And the City of Buenos Aires created its own environmental protection agency in January 2008. In the Province of Buenos Aires-where the vast majority of the industrial activity is conducted in the country- the Provincial Sustainable Development Agency and the Water Authority play a very important role in environmental regulation and permitting.

In December 2006, the Argentine Congress created the Matanza-Riachuelo Basin Authority (Autoridad de Cuenca Matanza-Riachuelo, "ACUMAR", for its acronym in Spanish). ACUMAR was created in the context of a particularly large and extensive environmental contamination case heard by the Supreme Court of Justice (known as the Riachuelo case), as an interjurisdictional agency with preemptive jurisdiction over the river basin area of the City of Buenos Aires and the Province of Buenos Aires. Since its creation, ACUMAR has been very active in regulating standards, implementing reconversion activities in the basin, and enforcing environmental regulations.

B. Brief introduction of Laws and Regulations of Environmental Protection

Argentina is organized as a federal republic. As such is composed by provinces and one autonomous city, the City of Buenos Aires, where the federal government has its offices. Provinces retain all powers that have not been delegated to the federal government in conformity with the Argentine National Constitution.

The Argentine National Constitution, as amended in 1994, recognizes the right to a healthy, balanced environment; the principle of sustainable development; the "polluter pays" principle, whereby environmental damage generates the obligation to "restore"; the right to information; and a ban on the entry into the country of hazardous waste.

Because the power to protect the environment basically falls within the police power, according to the federal structure of the constitution, such power is vested in the provinces, and only by delegation, in the federal government. Nevertheless, the federal government is vested with the power to legislate the minimum standards to be met throughout the country. Consequently, eleven laws were enacted by the National Congress as from July 2002 regulating minimum environmental protection standards on the following issues: preservation and protection of biological diversity and the implementation of sustainable development, known as the Environmental Framework Law ("EFL"); industrial waste and waste generated by service activities management; polychlorinated biphenyls ("PCBs") management; preservation, development and rational utilization of water; free and public access right to environmental information; household waste management; enrichment, restoration, conservation, sustainable use and management of native forests; control of burning activities; preservation of glacial and periglacial zones; fire management; and empty phytosanitary containers management.

As a result, local laws enacted by the provinces and applicable in their own jurisdiction coexist with federal laws that apply to the whole country.

C. Evaluation of Environmental Protection

At a national level, Law No. 25675 on general environmental protection standards for the adequate and sustainable management of the environment, known as the "LGA", provides that any work or activity that, within the Argentine territory, may degrade the environment or any of its components, or significantly impair the quality of life of the population, shall be subject to an environmental impact assessment ("EIA") procedure before any operations commence. The EFL further establishes that the procedure shall begin with the submission of an affidavit stating whether the work or activities will affect the environment. Subsequently, an environmental impact study must be submitted by the project proponent. Thereafter, the authorities will make an assessment, and issue an environmental impact statement either accepting or rejecting the studies filed.

There are federal rules that provide for mandatory EIAs for specific activities (namely exploration, exploitation, and transport of hydrocarbons, hazardous waste treatment and disposal facilities, public investment projects, and mining projects), and provincial regulations on EIAs procedures.

The Provinces that have passed EIA laws and regulations include the Province of Buenos Aires, Catamarca, Chubut, Córdoba, Corrientes, Entre Ríos, Jujuy, La Pampa, La Rioja, Mendoza, Misiones, Neuquén, Río Negro, Salta, San Juan, San Luis, Santa Cruz, Santa Fe, Santiago del Estero, Tucumán, and the City of Buenos Aires. In some jurisdictions, the entity filing the project is required to hire only specially licensed environmental consultants to conduct the EIA.

VII. Dispute Resolution

A. Methods and Bodies of Dispute Resolution

The main dispute resolution method used in Argentina to settle large commercial disputes is adversarial litigation through the courts. Alternative dispute resolution ("ADR") methods, such as arbitration and mediation, are being also considered.

a. Court Litigation

a) Court Structure

The Argentine National Constitution establishes a dual judicial system consisting of the federal and the ordinary jurisdictions. In turn, each jurisdiction has specific courts that cover different areas of law. Within each jurisdiction, there are courts of first instance (headed by a judge) and appellate courts (with several judges).

b) Court jurisdiction

In the City of Buenos Aires, federal civil and commercial courts exercise jurisdiction over maritime and aviation disputes, intellectual property and inter-jurisdictional transport disputes, among other things. Ordinary commercial courts exercise jurisdiction over ordinary commercial law disputes, construction agreement disputes, leasing disputes, corporate disputes and the remaining general commercial matters.

b. ADR Methods

The main ADR methods under the procedural rules are mediation and arbitration. The main bodies that offer ADR services are: The General Arbitration Tribunal of the Buenos Aires Stock Exchange; Business Mediation and Arbitration Centre; Centre for Mediation and Arbitration of the Argentine Chamber of Commerce; Arbitral Chamber of the Grain Exchange of Buenos Aires.

a) Mediation

Mediation is frequently used in several jurisdictions (such as the City of Buenos Aires) it is mandatory for the claimant to initiate a mediation proceeding before bringing a judicial claim.

b) Arbitration

Arbitration has a contractual nature and therefore an agreement is required to submit a dispute to arbitration. Under the CCPC procedure, the parties can submit their disputes to arbitration before or during any court proceeding, regardless of the status of the proceedings.

Argentina is considered an arbitration-friendly country. It is generally used in large international commercial transactions, particularly when foreign investors are involved, for parties to agree to submit potential disputes to arbitration. Arbitration is particularly used to solve disputes in the oil and gas industry, energy, construction and automotive industries, M&A transactions, corporate disputes, and so on.

The main advantages of arbitration over court litigation are:

(i) Expertise of the arbitrators: Parties can select the arbitrators according to their technical knowledge and expertise in the field in question.

(ii) Confidentiality: Section 1658 of the CCC allows parties to agree on the confidentiality of the arbitration.

(iii) Speed and flexibility of proceedings: Arbitration proceedings tend to be faster than court proceedings. Parties can choose the applicable rules, customising the procedure according to both their needs and the legal culture of the parties and the arbitrators.

(iv) Management of costs: Parties can agree on how the costs of the arbitration proceedings are apportioned.

c) Appeal and Enforcement of Arbitral Awards

(i) Right to appeal. Parties can waive the right to appeal. In such case, they can only file an annulment recourse (grounded on a fundamental fault in the procedure) or a request for clarification.

(ii) Enforcement of domestic awards. A domestic award may be enforced as any domestic court's final decision (i. e. in summary enforcement proceedings).

(iii) Enforcement of foreign awards. The recognition and enforcement of foreign awards is primarily governed by the following treaties signed by Argentina:

• New York Convention.

• OAS Inter-American Convention on International Commercial Arbitration 1975 (Panama Convention).

• OAS Inter-American Convention on Jurisdiction in the International Sphere for the Extraterritorial Validity of Foreign Judgments 1984.

In addition, arbitral awards outside the scope of the treaties are enforceable if the requirements governed by Section 517 of the CCPC are met (i. e. the award must be final and must be issued by a competent tribunal; the party against whom the award is being enforced must have been personally summoned and the defense of its legal rights must be guaranteed; etc.) and the choice of law is admissible.

c. Cross-Border Litigation

• Choice of governing law. Courts respect the choice of governing law in a contract, subject to certain restrictions under Sections 2599 and 2600 of the National Civil and Commercial Code ("CCC"). International mandatory rules of Argentine law prevail over the agreement between the parties with regard to the governing law, and exclude the application of foreign law despite whatever the parties may have agreed upon. In addition, foreign law will not be applied when it leads to solutions that are incompatible with Argentine public order principles.

• Choice of Jurisdiction. Under section 2605 of the CCC, parties can agree the jurisdiction of foreign judges or arbitrators acting abroad regarding property/patrimonial and international matters.

B. Application of Laws

a. Litigation

a) National Provisions

The CCC contains several rules on procedural matters, such as:
- Statute of limitations (Section 2560 et seq.);
- International lis pendens (Section 2604);
- Preventive action (Section 1711 et seq.).

b) Procedural Provisions

Since Argentina is a federal country, each province can regulate its own rules of procedure, including the procedural provisions on litigation, arbitration and mediation. The Civil and Commercial Procedural Code ("CCPC") applies to proceedings seated in the City of Buenos Aires as well as to the claims brought before the federal courts within the provinces.

b. Arbitration

a) National Provisions

The CCC regulates arbitration at a federal level, containing provisions on the:
- Form and type of arbitration agreements.
- Arbitrability of the matters before the arbitration tribunal.
- Appointment and removal of arbitrators.
- Preliminary measures and appeals against arbitral awards.

b) Procedural Provisions

The parties can agree upon the procedure to be followed by the arbitral tribunal during the proceedings (Section 1658 (3) of the CCC). In absence of agreement, rules governing ordinary judicial proceedings shall apply (Section 751, CCPC).

The CCPC contains procedural provisions related to:
- Arbitration proceedings.
- The relationship between the courts and the arbitration tribunal.

c) International Conventions

Argentina is signatory to international conventions such as the following:
- Convention on the Recognition and Enforcement of Foreign Arbitral Awards 1958 (New York Convention).
- Inter-American Convention on International Commercial Arbitration (Panama Convention 1975).
- MERCOSUR's (Southern Common Market) Agreement on International Commercial Arbitration 1998.

c. Mediation

In the City of Buenos Aires mediation is governed by the CCPC and the Law on Mediation and Conciliation No. 26589, which establishes (as in many other jurisdictions) that a prior mediation procedure is mandatory before filing a judicial claim.

VIII. Others

A. Anti–commercial Bribery

a. Brief Introduction of Anti-commercial Bribery Laws and Regulations

The Argentine Criminal Code ("ACC") is the Federal Law that punishes bribery and corruption through Sections 256 to 259. Furthermore, recently enacted Law No. 27401 sets forth the corporate criminal liability regime for certain crimes related to corruption cases. However, the offence of bribery does not apply to bribery between private individuals, but only where public officials and employees are involved. The exception to this regime is the recent introduction of the offence of bribery for employees of financial entities (Section 312, ACC). This provides that employees of financial entities operating on the stock exchange shall be punished with imprisonment from one to six years and special disqualification of up to six years if they personally, or through an intermediary, receive money or any other benefit as a condition of providing loans, finance or stock exchange transactions.

Additionally, in certain cases, commercial bribery could be construed as a fraud under the terms of Section 173, subsection 7 of the ACC. In this regard, any person who, under the law, by authority or contract, is vested with the management, administration or care of goods or pecuniary interests belonging to another person and, with the purpose of obtaining an unlawful gain for himself or herself or a third party or violating his or her duties, damages such interests conferred upon him or her or makes excessive expenses to the detriment of the person he or she represents, shall be punished with prison from one to six years.

It is worth mentioning that a reform project of the ACC is being considered, which will address bribery between private individuals.

b. Department Supervising Anti-commercial Bribery

There is no department supervising anti-commercial bribery. The Federal Court on Criminal and Correctional Matters is the competent court for bribery and corruption matters concerning public officers, and the National Constitution provides an impeachment mechanism for removal and prosecution of officials and judges. Federal judges are assigned to conduct bribery and corruption investigations and the following institutions are important:

• Anti-corruption Bureau.

• Administrative Investigations: A special prosecutor's office within the Attorney General's Office ("AGO"), this investigates and promotes the investigation of crimes concerning corruption and administrative irregularities.

• Office of the Prosecutor for Economic Crime and Money Laundering: This unit within the AGO is designed to combat money laundering and other economic crimes.

c. Punitive Actions

On the other hand, individual and corporate fraud can also give rise to civil liability, which requires damage to a certain person to occur, and only that person (or an agent or successor) can bring a claim. Liability in this area can arise under tort, which precludes individuals from harming others. This principle is set out in Section 19 of the Argentine National Constitution and has been expressly regulated in Section 1716 of the CCC, among others.

For corporate or business fraud to give rise to civil liability, the following elements must be present: a breach of either a legal or contractual obligation, constituting an illicit act; the existence of actual damage; a sufficient causal relationship between the illicit act and the damage; and negligence or willful misconduct from the damaging party.

B. Project Contracting

a. Permission System

Permits and authorizations are required for the development of all commercial and industrial activities. Some of these activities are subject to the exclusive jurisdiction of the different governmental dimensions of the country (i. e. federal government is entitled to grant licenses for transportation and distribution of electricity; municipalities are entitled to determine the use of public spaces or grant commercial permits within their territory) and other activities are reached by more than one of said stages of government, with regards to the requirement of permits and authorizations. For instance, Law No. 25675 of National Environmental Policies states the minimum requirements for environmental protection, which might be then extended by provincial regulations.

b. Prohibited Areas

Not applicable.

c. Invitation to bid and Bidding

In all of said stages, public procurements are governed by specific principles which tend to grant transparency and efficiency in the use of public resources.

In this sense, the mechanism generally chosen for selection of the state's contracting party are bids (Decree No. 1023/01 Section 24), by means of which an undetermined amount of offerors are invited to file their offers according to the specific terms of the bidding documents. Among the presented offers, the requiring public entity will chose the most convenient according to the public interest involved.

As said, Decree No. 1023/01 and 1030/16 determine the national public procurement regime. Among other contracts, some of the agreements included are trading and supply contracts, lease agreements, consultancy services and administrative concessions. Also, other previsions contemplate specific concessions, such as public work concession contracts (Law No. 13064) or electricity distribution and transportation concession contracts (Law 24 065).

C. Personal Data Protection

In case personal data (understood as the information of any kind referred to individuals or legal entities, whether identified or identifiable by an associative process) is processed in Argentina, Law No. 25326 on Personal Data Protection, Decree No. 1558/2001 and related dispositions shall be applicable.

As a general rule, data owner's consent is necessary in order to collect and process the personal data.

Regarding the transfer of personal data abroad (even if only for storage purposes), Argentine regulations prohibit the transfer of personal data to countries that do not provide an adequate level of protection. However, the prohibition is not applicable when either:

(i) the data owner has expressly consented to such transfer; or

(ii) when data is exported for outsourcing purposes, by means of an International Data Transfer Agreement between the transferor and the transferee, under which the latter undertakes to comply with the Argentine data protection regulations, among other obligations.

The Argentine Data Protection Authority has listed the countries that in accordance to its criterion have an adequate level of protection. Up to date, China was not included in such list.

亚美尼亚

作者：Sedrak Asatryan、Roustam Badasyan、Hakob Tadevosyan、Tatevik Harutyunyan
译者：李玛林、李结华

一、概述

（一）政治、经济、社会和法律环境概述

亚美尼亚共和国（以下简称亚美尼亚）是一个具有悠久文化历史的独立主权、统一、民主和社会化国家。第一次提到亚美尼亚人及其祖先的历史作品可以追溯到公元前 3000 年的铭文。亚美尼亚是世界上第一个将基督教作为官方宗教的国家（公元 301 年）。现代亚美尼亚认可世界上最古老的国家教会——亚美尼亚使徒教会是该国的主要宗教机构。亚美尼亚人拥有独特的文字语言亚美尼亚语，该语言于公元 405 年由梅斯罗普·马什托茨创造。

亚美尼亚国土面积 29 800 平方公里。它位于南高加索地区，北与格鲁吉亚接壤，东邻阿塞拜疆，西与土耳其接壤，南与伊朗接壤。

亚美尼亚是一个多山的内陆国家，平均海拔 1 800 米。亚美尼亚的气候属于强烈的大陆性气候（夏天很热，冬天很冷），湿度很低。

亚美尼亚人口约为 300 万，其中 95% 以上的人口是亚美尼亚族，其余主要是俄罗斯族、库尔德族、亚述族、希腊族和乌克兰族。其中，城市人口约占总人口的 64%。

亚美尼亚货币是亚美尼亚德拉姆。① 亚美尼亚中央银行公布亚美尼亚货币对外币的市场平均汇率。

亚美尼亚首都是埃里温（约有 100 万人口），另外两个较大的城市是久姆里和瓦纳佐。

1991 年 9 月 21 日，亚美尼亚于加入苏联 70 年后宣布独立。亚美尼亚国旗由三个宽度相等的长方形组成，顶部为红色，中部为蓝色，底部为橙。

亚美尼亚的国徽为盾牌造型，盾牌上刻有阿拉腊山与诺亚方舟，盾牌周围是亚美尼亚四个王国的徽章。盾牌由一头狮子和一只鹰护持，盾牌下面则刻有剑、麦穗、箭头、树枝和绶带。

亚美尼亚目前与全球 180 多个国家建立了外交关系。亚美尼亚是联合国组织（UNO）、国际货币基金组织（IMF）、世界银行（WB）、欧洲复兴开发银行（EBRD）、欧洲理事会、欧洲安全与合作组织和世界贸易组织的成员。亚美尼亚也是独立国家联合体（独联体）的成员。1994 年 10 月，亚美尼亚与北大西洋公约组织（北约）签署了有限的军事合作协议，并于 2017 年 11 月与欧盟签署了全面和加强伙伴关系协定。

1. 政治

根据 2015 年 12 月的《宪法修正案》，目前亚美尼亚正从半总统制向议会制过渡。根据上述《宪法修正案》，新国民议会选举已于 2017 年 4 月 2 日举行，从国家和地区的政党选举名单提名的候选人中，选举出 102 人组成议会。

亚美尼亚上一任总统是谢尔日·萨尔基相，他通过 2013 年 2 月举行的普通、平等和直接的选举当选，任期 5 年。任期于 2018 年 4 月结束，亚美尼亚驻美大使阿曼·萨尔基相接任总统，任期 7 年。

亚美尼亚新总统一旦上任，包括总理和部长在内的行使亚美尼亚行政权力的政府应当提出解散，新总统应立即接受。

新政府由总理、副总理和部长组成，副总理不得超过 3 人，部长不得超过 18 人。新总理由国会通过多数选举产生。新总理一旦选出，总统应立即任命其就职，政府应在总理任命后的 15 天内由总理提名的候选人组成。现任亚美尼亚总理为卡伦·卡拉佩强。

---

① 2017 年的平均汇率：1 美元 =482.63 德拉姆；1 欧元 =546.15 德拉姆；1 元 =71.52 德拉姆。

2. 经济

1991年获得独立后,亚美尼亚采取了自由市场经济政策并启动了私有化计划。尽管2008—2009年发生了经济衰退,但目前亚美尼亚经济正逐渐向好。此外,根据2018年经济自由度指数(排名第44位)和2018年营商环境报告的"营商易"(排名第47位),亚美尼亚的投资自由度高于世界平均水平。2016年,亚美尼亚的国内生产总值达到5 079.9亿德拉姆。

快速增长的经济部门主要包括采矿、能源、可再生能源、建筑、信息技术、食品加工和饮料、珠宝和钻石加工以及旅游和金融服务等。亚美尼亚在廉价但高技能的劳动力(人类发展指数排名第84位)、发展中的和相当宽松的银行业监管、有利的投资法规、设立自由经济区等很多方面具有优势。

3. 社会

总的来说,外国人在亚美尼亚合法居住期间,能够享受这个国家的诸多社会政策(例如国家福利制度、国家养老金计划、累积养老金计划等)。

根据亚美尼亚国家统计局的数据,该国2016年的失业率约为18%。同年国家平均每月养老金金额为40 397德拉姆。

4. 法律

亚美尼亚最重要的国家法律是1995年通过、并于2005年11月和2015年12月通过公民投票进行修订的《宪法》,其中规定了基本权利和自由,并针对侵犯基本权利和自由的行为制定了保障措施。《宪法》还规定了三权分立的政治体制(立法、行政和司法权力的分离与平衡原则)。

其他的国家性法律都应与《宪法》和宪法性法律相一致(2015年12月《宪法修正案》引入了宪法性法律的概念,旨在区分某些与一般法律相比规定得更加严格的法律,宪法性法律的清单由《宪法修正案》规定)。国际条约只有在符合《宪法》的情况下才能得到认可。亚美尼亚在与国际法的关系上采用一元论,因此,被认可的国际法将立即转化为国内法,这意味着国际法可由国内法官直接适用,并且可以由公民直接援引,如同本国法律一般。

司法权由三审级的法院系统和宪法法院行使(仅限于宪法司法问题)。

亚美尼亚的法院体系由初审法院〔普通法院和行政法院(预计还将设立破产法院作为专门法院)〕、上诉法院和最高法院组成。普通法院对所有民事和刑事案件有管辖权,行政法院仅针对行政案件有管辖权(破产法庭对破产案件有管辖权)。对初审法院的判决可向上诉法院提出上诉,再从上诉法院进入最高法院审理。如果所有司法救济措施都已用尽并且符合相应的条件,当事人可以向宪法法院提出申请,要求审查法院审理适用的法律规定的合宪性。

此外,在用尽所有国内救济办法(根据公认的国际法规则)后,当事人可以在最后判决作出之日起6个月内向欧洲人权法院提出申请,主张根据1950年在罗马签署的《保护人权与基本自由公约》的规定,国家侵犯了其权利(上述提出申请的期限在该公约第15号修正案生效后变更为4个月)。

(二)"一带一路"倡议下与中国企业合作的现状和方向

2017年11月,"一带一路"协同创新中心资助的亚美尼亚合作办事处设立仪式在青岛举行。该办事处旨在促进建中—亚商业关系。亚美尼亚工商会、亚美尼亚制造商和商人(雇主)联盟、亚美尼亚驻华大使馆和"一带一路"倡议协作创新中心分别签订了有关协议。

据亚美尼亚国家统计局称,亚美尼亚2017年前11个月与中国的贸易额为5.483亿美元,与去年同期相比,增长态势强劲。

二、投资

(一)市场准入

1. 部门监督投资

亚美尼亚政府积极鼓励外国投资,遵循"开放门户"政策的原则,并持续放宽外国直接投资进入亚美尼亚的自由度。

亚美尼亚促进外国投资的主要部门是经济发展和投资部以及亚美尼亚发展基金会。

2. 投资部门的法律、法规

外国投资领域主要受 1994 年 7 月 31 日通过的《外国投资法》调整，该法规定了外国投资的类型和形式，确保对外国投资的保护和对外资实体的额外权利（适用于设立时外国资金不低于 30% 的投资），以及解决与外国投资有关的纠纷的程序。

下列所有民事领域的对象都能够由"外国投资者"投资，即任何外国国家、法律实体、国民、无国籍人、永久居住在亚美尼亚境外的亚美尼亚公民，以及任何有资格根据适用的个人法进行投资的国际组织：

① 货币，包括外币、亚美尼亚德拉姆；
② 动产或不动产或任何产权，包括楼宇、建筑物、设备、其他有形资产等；
③ 股票、债券和其他类型的证券；
④ 货币性债权或针对具有合同价值的债务的债权的诉求；
⑤ 知识产权；
⑥ 根据亚美尼亚法律或合同进行某些经济活动的权利，包括探索自然资源、采矿权等的权利；
⑦ 服务业；
⑧ 不为法律所禁止的其他事务。

3. 投资方式

外国人在亚美尼亚投资，有以下几种方式：

① 设立拥有 100% 外资的商业法人实体、分支机构或收购现有亚美尼亚公司的全部股份；
② 与亚美尼亚实体创建合资企业，或部分收购现有亚美尼亚公司的股份；
③ 收购债券和其他证券；
④ 获得其他财产权利；
⑤ 基于与亚美尼亚实体达成的协议，进行亚美尼亚法律不禁止的其他形式的投资。

4. 市场准入和检验标准

投资不需要任何事前批准，一般来说，对外国投资者没有特别的限制。外国投资者仅在土地所有权方面受到部分限制，具体内容将在"土地政策"部分阐述。

实践中，外国公司在亚美尼亚通过当地分支机构开展符合许可要求的活动时会面临一些问题，特别是，政府部门拒绝向外国公司的当地分支机构颁发许可证，并建议设立当地公司，以便获得相应许可证并按照许可证的要求进行相关活动。

（二）外汇管理

1. 外汇管理部门

对未经亚美尼亚中央银行或财政部发放许可的实体 / 人员遵守外汇管理条例的监督控制权，主要由亚美尼亚税务机关行使。

2. 外汇法律、法规简介

2004 年 11 月 24 日通过的《货币管理和控制法》对外汇交易、执行条件、使用和处置货币进行了规定。违反外汇管理规定的制裁由该法律（针对亚美尼亚中央银行或财政部许可的实体 / 人员）以及《行政违法条例》（针对其他实体 / 人员）规定。

根据该法规定的一般原则，亚美尼亚境内的货物（库存）销售、提供服务和劳动报酬应以亚美尼亚货币计价，但本法规定例外的除外。

亚美尼亚和外国货币之间不存在转换限制，亚美尼亚银行可以保留外币账户。上述法律定义的居民和非居民均有权不受即时或推迟支付条款的限制购买 / 出售外汇，并有权利和义务在一定时期以特定价格回购、转换为其他货币或者其他条件的权利或义务。外币买卖交易通过专业实体进行。专业实体应根据亚美尼亚中央银行正式确定的亚美尼亚货币平均汇率确定其进行的外币买卖交易的汇率和交易量。

3. 外国企业的外汇管理要求

《货币管理和控制法》规定，外国组织及其分支机构和代表处，包括在亚美尼亚设立的分支机构和代表处、外国领事馆和亚美尼亚使馆，以及在1年内（从1月1日至12月31日）或任意12个月期间没有居住在亚美尼亚达到183天或更长时间，其重要利益中心不在亚美尼亚的自然人，被视为非居民。

作为上述法律一般规则的例外规定，如果居民法人或个体工商户与非居民法人或个体工商户之间以电汇作为付款方式的交易应以书面形式进行，价格面额可以以外币计价。此外，在这些情况下，交易双方之间的付款也可能以外币进行。

（三）金融融资

1. 主要金融机构

亚美尼亚的银行体系最近调整为《巴塞尔协议Ⅲ》标准。目前，亚美尼亚银行业市场包括17家商业银行，其中包括数家由外国知名银行设立的银行，以及在亚美尼亚和纳戈尔诺－卡拉巴赫共和国设立的531家分支机构。

亚美尼亚中央银行对包括银行在内的金融机构进行控制。亚美尼亚中央银行的主要任务是保持价格稳定，自2006年以来，它实施着通过影响国内利率以控制通货膨胀的策略并作为其操作目标。此外，它还将通货膨胀的可预测水平作为附带目标。亚美尼亚中央银行还监测金融市场趋势，评估风险并衡量金融体系发展的影响。

2005年，中央银行设立了银行存款担保基金，该基金目前担保的金额为1 000万德拉姆的银行存款以及500万德拉姆的外币存款。

2. 外资企业的融资条件

外国实体（包括在亚美尼亚没有常设机构的外国实体）在亚美尼亚银行开立和运营银行账户或从中获得融资没有任何限制，只要相关银行内部规定所要求的所有文件，包括根据反洗钱法规和披露外国实体的实际受益人的文件予以提交，并提供必要的抵押品以确保相关的安排。

（四）土地政策

1. 土地法律、法规简介

土地问题主要受《土地法》《民法典》和《宪法》规范。除了另有规定，《宪法》规定了外国人和无国籍人无权享有土地所有权的主要原则/限制。特别是《土地法》规定，这种限制不适用于在亚美尼亚获得特殊居住身份的人，以及土地上的私人住房、公共建筑和生产建筑、多户住宅等建筑物。土地所有权在合法的基础上转移给外国人或无国籍人的，该外国人或无国籍人应在1年内转让。如果在上述期限内土地所有权未被转让的，根据《民法典》的规定，该土地所有权可经法院判决并被强制执行转让。

《土地法》还规定了永远不会成为自然人或法人实体所有权客体的土地种类（例如国家森林、公园、矿区等），无论其是当地法律实体还是外国法律实体。

2. 外国企业取得土地的规则

没有针对外国实体取得土地的具体规定。相关规则对于所有类型的实体都是相同的。根据《土地法》的规定，在不违反法律规定的情形下，国家和社区的土地可被转让。一般而言，国有土地转让是通过公开拍卖的方式进行的，个别情况下通过直接出售、无偿分配或实物交易的方式被转让。

（五）公司的设立和解散

1. 企业的形式

商业法人可以以股份有限公司、有限责任公司、补充责任公司、普通合伙企业或有限合伙企业、商业合作社的形式成立。最常用的企业类型是有限责任公司和股份有限公司。

法律实体的设立（管理）文件是章程。章程确定了实体资本的规模、治理结构的组成和权力以及决策规则、参与者/股东/合伙人的权利和义务、参与者/股东/合伙人的退出和股份转让规则。

注册分支机构（分公司或代表处）而非单独的法律实体也是被广泛适用的，这种形式经常被外国人选择。应该指出的是，分支机构不具有独立的法律行为能力，并且只能根据其发起人的授权行事。代表处和分公司之间的唯一区别在于，代表处只是有权代表并维护其发起人的利益，分公司则可以执行发起人可以执行的所有职能，最重要的是，其可以执行代表处的所有职能。

2016年的立法变化中引入了迁册程序，目前希望将住所转移至亚美尼亚的外国法律实体能够在不清算的情况下启动这一程序，希望在国外迁册的当地法律实体也有同样的机会。

（1）有限责任公司

有限责任公司是一个经济实体，其资本划分为股份，数量由其章程确定。公司股东对公司的义务不承担责任，仅以其出资对公司活动造成的损失承担责任。有限责任公司的参与者人数不得超过49人。

有限责任公司可以由自然人或法律实体建立。应当指出的是，有限责任公司不得作为另一个商业实体的唯一发起人或股东。

对于有限责任公司，没有强制性的最低注册资本要求，除非法律对某些特定事项的最低资本另有规定。出资的形式可以是货币、证券、其他财产或以金钱估价的权利。如果出资包含非货币性资产，并且相对应的股份面值不超过500 000德拉姆，则应由创立大会或股东会议评估。否则，非货币资产形式的出资应由独立评估师评估。

出资应在有限责任公司创立协议中约定的期限内完成（不超过公司注册后1年）。

有限责任公司的股份登记簿由国家法人登记机构管理，并可供公众查阅。

有限责任公司至少应有以下管理机构：

① 股东大会（最高管理机构）由有限责任公司的股东组成，每个股东均按其在公司资本中的权益按比例投票；

② 负责管理有限责任公司日常活动的执行机构负责人，对外代表公司。

有限责任公司股东超过20人的，应当设立监事会或者提名监事。有限责任公司的章程可设立一个额外的管理机构（如董事会）。

有限责任公司的有关要点如下：

① 在其他股东没有以高于出售给第三方的价格行使优先购买权的前提下，有限责任公司的股东可以将其持有的股份转让给第三方（非参与者）。

② 股东可以随时退出有限责任公司。退出后，有限责任公司需要在6个月内清偿股东股份的金额。

③ 如果股东的作为或不作为使得有限责任公司的日常活动变得困难或无法经营，根据另一个持有至少10%股份股东的请求，有限责任公司的股东身份可以通过司法程序被解除。有限责任公司应在6个月内清偿被解除股东股份的金额。

④ 如果股东的其他财产不足以满足债权人的债权请求，股东个人的债权人可以扣押股东在有限责任公司中的股份以实现债务人履行法院裁决的义务。

（2）股份有限公司

股份有限公司是一个法人实体，由其资本确定一定数量的股份。股份有限公司股东的责任仅限于其出资额。股份有限公司有两种：开放式股份有限公司和封闭式股份有限公司。开放式股份有限公司可以不受限制地公开发行股票。每个股东都有权在未经其他股东同意的情况下出售股份。在封闭式股份有限公司中，股票仅分配给其股东（包括发起人）或预先确定的人员，股东人数也受到限制（法律规定最多49名股东）。此外，封闭式股份有限公司的现有股东对其他股东出售的股份拥有优先购买权。

股份有限公司的法律结构大部分与适用于有限责任公司的法律框架类似。与有限责任公司一样，股份有限公司不存在强制性的最低注册资本要求。这些股份可以通过多种形式，包括货币、证券和财产权以及知识产权缴纳。股份有限公司成立时以非货币性资产支付股份的，应当由发起人约定其估算的价值。如果非货币性资产是为额外股份出资的，则应由独立评估师按照董事会决议规定的方式进行估算（如果股份有限公司的章程中未设立董事会，则解决此问题属于股东大会的权限范围）。

与有限责任公司不同，股份有限公司的股份登记由专门的登记机构管理。此外，股份有限公司可以发行和设置不同的股权。特别是可以发行优先股，其总面值不得超过股份公司载明资本的25%。一般而言，优先股股东在股东大会上没有投票权。但当同时提出主张时，优先股股东的主张优先于普通股东。

股份有限公司的管理机构：

① 股东大会（最高管理机构）由股份有限公司的股东组成，除优先股股东外，每个股东均拥有与其在公司资本中的权益等比例的票数；

② 执行机构，为首席执行官（董事、总监）或者首席执行官和联合执行机构（执行委员会、管理委员会）负责管理股份有限公司的日常活动；

③ 负责对股份有限公司的金融活动实施监管的监事或监事会。

如果股份有限公司的股东人数超过49人，应该设立至少由3名成员组成的董事会。除股份有限公司的章程另有规定外，股份有限公司股东或其代表人以外的人也可被选举为董事会成员。

与有限责任公司的法律框架不同，股份有限公司的法律框架详细规定了有投票权的股东可以行使看跌期权的权利，而有表决权的股东有义务购买其股份以确保看跌期权被行使。特别是，这种情况多发生在股东对公司通过的影响其股东权利的决议投出反对票或未参与投票的情况下。

2. 设立程序

包括分支机构在内的商业实体在统一的国家法人注册备案机构进行注册。一经注册，该实体自动被记录在税务机构中，并被授予纳税人身份号。

在提交正确的文件后，商业实体通常在2个工作日内成立。

设立一个商业实体包含两个阶段：

① 收集和制作法律所要求的文件；

② 提交国家登记所需的国家法人登记机构文件。

应注意的是，法人实体的注册是免费的。没有任何国家义务。对于法人实体的注册，应向注册机构提交以下文件：

① 发起人／执行机构负责人或法人实体发起人授权人的申请；

② 关于创立法人的决定或法人组成大会的会议记录[如果该法人是由一个以上的人创立的（如果法人的发起人之一是另一个法人实体，其授权机构的决议也应提交）]；

③ 由发起人或创立大会批准的法人实体章程的副本（至少两份副本，每增加一份副本，需支付2000德拉姆）；

④ 执行机构负责人的护照详情和社会服务号码（如果没有可提交有效证明号码）（护照复印件，如果是外国人还需提交经翻译和核证的护照复本）及电子邮件地址；

⑤ 关于实际受益人的声明。

如果发起人或发起人之一是外国法律实体，还应将以下文件翻译为亚美尼亚语并公证：

① 发起人的原籍国商业登记处的登记副本；

② 外国法人的创设文件，例如章程或其他同等文件。

这些文件应包含以下信息：

① 发起人的法律性质和组织形式；

② 在居住国的注册日期；

③ 发起人的法人名称；

④ 发起人的居住地；

⑤ 发起人管理机构的权力，包括有权决定发起另一法律实体的能力。

如果发起人或发起人之一是外国自然人，则应将其公证的护照翻译件连同一般要求的文件一起提交。

注册程序可以通过电子方式进行。与法人实体注册不同的是，商业法人分支机构的注册需要12 000德拉姆的税金。分支机构登记，应向登记机关提交以下文件：

① 发起人的执行机构负责人或发起人的授权人或包含发起人姓名和国家注册号的分支机构负责人的申请、分支机构负责人的详细信息[护照详情和社会服务号码（如果没有可提交连署证明号码）、住

址、具体联系方式]及其电子邮件地址；
②关于设立分支机构和批准章程的决定以及分支机构部门负责人的提名决定；
③分支机构章程的副本；
④支付税金的证明文件。

如果发起人是外国法律实体，应将上述文件翻译成亚美尼亚文并公证（包括商业登记册副本及其创设文件）。

以迁册目的，外国法人实体应进行以下注册程序：
①迁册初步注册；
②迁册最后登记。

对于第一个过程，特定的外国法人应提交：

• 初步注册申请，包含有关其当前名称和特定外国法人实体未来希望运营的新名称的信息，以及其活动的主要类型，特定法人实体登记的国家以及与该国内有效的法律形式相对应的法律形式的信息；特定外国法人实体主管机构的决议或相应会议记录或摘录，其中包含关于特定法人实体迁册至亚美尼亚的条款，关于按照当地法律选择的法律形式和名称，以及对其新章程的批准；

• 商业登记处对特定外国法律实体的登记副本及其创设文件；

• 外国法律实体执行机构负责人的信息（护照、联系方式及电子邮件地址）；

• 证明已支付相当于 10 000 德拉姆的税金的文件；

• 根据当地法规批准的章程副本；

• 特定外国法人股东的信息，如果股东是当地法人，要求提供姓名和国家登记号；如果股东是自然人或外国法人实体（要求股东登记由登记机关保管），需要护照复印件或商业登记簿中有关外国股东的信息摘要以及法人实体的创设文件；

• 在迁册前有效的该外国法律实体的章程副本。

如果上述任何文件仅以外文编写，则应将公证过的亚美尼亚文的翻译件附在其中。该要求同样适用于提交最终注册的文件。

如果上述文件已经充分提交并且没有被驳回的理由，需要迁册的外国法人实体便完成了初步注册记录。此类记录应在国外商业法人申请的 3 天内作出。

外国法人在最终注册时应提交：

• 申请；

• 证明外国法定实体在相应外国管辖区内迁册或终止活动的信息文件；

• 指定的外国法律实体的主管机构未参与任何交易的声明，未交易期间自收到迁册初步注册文件起至最终注册日期止（该声明提交时，初步注册的日期应视为最终注册日期）。

3. 解散的流程和要求

法人可在以下情况解散：
① 根据其发起人/股东的决定或主管机构根据其章程通过的决定，包括法定实体的指定经营期限届满或其创立经营计划已经实现；
② 因注册期间发生的违规事件而导致法律实体的注册无效，可以由法院判决解散；
③ 法院判决其多次或严重违反法律规定以及《民法》特别规定的情况下。

例如，如果根据每下一财政年度的结果，有限责任公司或股份有限公司的净资产值为负值或低于法律规定的最低额，则法人实体应进行清算。

如果法人实体的财产不足以偿还所有债务，法人实体只能通过破产程序进行清算。除了银行、信贷机构、保险公司、投资公司、投资基金管理人以外，法律实体的破产受 2006 年 12 月 25 日通过的《破产法》规制。

（六）兼并和收购

在亚美尼亚，公司的兼并和收购是公司重组的形式（其他形式还有分立、让产易股、转型）。在法人实体并购中，各方的权利和义务应当依据转让协议转移至新设立的法人实体。在股份公司并购中，并购方签署一份并购协议。并购重组的决定将由并购各方的股东大会商定。各方股东大会还负责审议通过并购协议、转让方案、并购的程序和条款,以及将并购各方的股票和其他证券转换为新设公司的股票和其他证券的程序。并购各方股东的联合股东大会将被视为新设立公司的创立大会,由机构依据在合并协议中规定的时间框架召集,并对与创立相关的主要事项作出决定。

在法人实体收购另外一个法人实体的情形下,被收购方的权利和义务将依据转让协议转移给收购方。在股份公司收购中,收购参与方签署一份收购协议。收购重组决定应由各方股东大会商定。各方股东大会还负责审议通过收购协议、转让方案、收购的程序和条款,以及将收购各方的股票和其他证券转换为新设公司的股票和其他证券的程序。参与并购或收购的股东组成联合股东大会,应对修改和完善收购方公司章程、通过收购协议和转让方案以及其他必要事项决定进行审议。

在法人以并购形式重组的情形下,应当自新产生的法人完成登记备案时视为重组。

在法人以收购形式重组的情形下,前一个法人实体在关联法人实体在一国完成解除登记时被视为重组。

公司并购或者收购时,应当载明转让文件,其中包括对其债权人和债务人全部责任的法律继承的规定,包括有争议的义务。转让文件应由法人的参与者/股东或由其公司已批准重组的章程授权的机构批准,该章程必须与该即将产生的新法人实体的章程一起提交用于国家登记,或对原法律实体的章程进行修改。未能提供相应的转让文件及公司章程,并且其中缺少关于重组法人的法定继承的规定或者缺少资产和责任分配比例条款的,将被拒绝进行国家登记。

公司债权人有权知悉关于公司的重组(法律采用股份公司的通知条款:自作出重新决定的 30 日内),并在之后有权主张对关于全额履约的额外保证条款,或者终止,或者当重组法律实体是债务人时,债权人有权要求提前履约并对造成的损害要求补偿。在股份公司并购或者收购的情形下,债权人有权在收到通知后 30 日内主张上述权利。

(七)竞争管制

1. 竞争管制的主管部门

竞争管理机构是国家经济竞争保护委员会,该委员会网站(www.competition.am)提供了关于竞争法规则的指导,包括:

① 必须申报的时效;
② 由形成主导或垄断地位的实体提交的报告的表格。

2. 竞争法简介

《经济竞争保护法》禁止限制性协议和行为。法律将限制性协议和行为定义为间接或可能导致限制、妨碍或禁止竞争的协议和行为,包括:

① 经济实体之间的合同和协议;
② 直接或间接的联合行动或行为;
③ 一致行动;
④ 经济实体联盟作出的决定。

其他限制性协议和行为包括以下内容:

① 市场或供应来源的分配或划分;
② 设置不公平价格;
③ 限制其他经济实体进入市场。

《保护经济竞争法》禁止滥用支配地位、垄断地位、不正当竞争、非法国家支持,并规定了应向委员会申报的集中情形:

① 经济实体在采取联合行动前必须作出声明;
② 在任何市场中,至少有一家公司处于支配地位。

同业联合,是指联合之前,基于前一个财政年度业绩基础,有以下两种情形之一:

① 联合各方的总资产达到 15 亿德拉姆或更多,并且其中一方的总资产达到 10 亿德拉姆或更多;

② 联合各方的利润达到 3 亿德拉姆或更多，并且其中一方的利润达到 20 亿德拉姆或更多。

上述规定同样适用于垂直或者混合联合。

3. 竞争管制的措施

在竞争法中有多种制裁措施，针对违反法律的具体规定，包括罚款、制裁、裁决限制不正当竞争，或者解除违反法律和其他措施的交易（包括提起刑事诉讼）。例如，滥用市场支配地位可被处以 500 万德拉姆到 2 亿德拉姆的罚款。

（八）税收

1. 税收体系与制度

通过统一的《税法》于 2016 年 10 月由国民议会，用以规范亚美尼亚的财政关系。

国家税收包括利润税、所得税、消费税、增值税、自然保护税、道路税、营业税和专利税。

地方税包括物业税和土地税，但从 2019 年 1 月起，这些将被房地产税和车辆税取代。

税务局监管国家税收计算和支付程序，在法律规定的某些情况下，则由海关监管。同时，地方税计算和征收的权力属于地方自治当局。

《税法》规定了一般税制和三种特殊税制（营业税制度、专利税制度和家族企业制度）。一般来说，一般税收制度下的实体、企业家和公证人缴纳增值税和利润税。在适用营业税制度、专利税制度的情况下，相关的纳税人分别缴纳营业税或专利税，分别代替增值税和 / 或利得税。在适用家族企业制度的情况下，对纳税人免征增值税和 / 或利润税、营业税，以及某些特定的专利税。

2. 主要税种与税率、报税单与优惠

（1）利润税

亚美尼亚居民，即在亚美尼亚注册的组织、企业家、公证人和契约型基金需要缴纳利润税，但养老金和非居民（即国际组织、在国外设立的其他组织、在亚美尼亚活动的非居民自然人或通过常设机构在亚美尼亚获得的收入）不需缴纳利润税。

亚美尼亚居民需对在亚美尼亚境内或境外获得的利润缴纳利润税，而非居民仅针对从亚美尼亚获得的利润缴纳利润税。

亚美尼亚居民以及通过常设机构在亚美尼亚实施活动的非居民纳税人，适用 20% 的年度利润税率。利润税根据应纳税利润计算，相当于总收入扣除法律规定的数额（由相应的文件证明生产活动所需的费用，折旧免税额等）。

在亚美尼亚没有设立常设机构的非居民纳税人，其利润所得应当按照下列税率缴纳税款，并由税务机关上缴国家财政：

① 保险赔偿、再保险费和运费收入——5%；

② 被动收入，包括股息，在 Panarmenian 银行储蓄所得的收益、利息、特许权使用费、财产租赁所得、财产增值（资本增值）、证券增值——10%；

③ 从亚美尼亚 Panarmenian 银行收取的股息——0%；

④ 因有价证券转让而产生的资本增值——0%；

⑤ 其他收入——20%。

纳税人必须在不迟于次年 4 月 20 日前向税务机关报送纳税年度的利润税纳税额，并在次年 4 月 25 日前缴纳税款。

一般情况下，居民和通过常设机构在亚美尼亚境内实施活动的非居民，应当按季度预先支付税款（不迟于本季度最后一个月的第二十日），除非纳税人申请替代方案，否则一律按前一年利润税实际金额的 20% 计算。需要注意的是，纳税人可以在本年度 3 月 20 日前向税务机关提交替代方案申请。如果纳税人选择替代方案，那么其应于每季（不迟于本季度最后一个月的第二十日）预付税款，税款支付标准为上一季度货物供应、准备金 / 服务 / 工作收入总额的 2%。

（2）所得税

在亚美尼亚，包括亚美尼亚公民和外国公民在内的居民和非居民自然人都应缴纳所得税。若企业家和公证人取得的收入根据税法的规定是属于私人的，应当缴纳所得税。如果在各纳税年度（从1月1日到12月31日），其在亚美尼亚居住的时间多于183天或其利益中心在亚美尼亚，则应将其视为居民。

对居民而言，从亚美尼亚境内或境外收到的应纳税所得都应被视为征税对象。对非居民而言，仅对来源为亚美尼亚的应纳税所得视为征税对象，但通过驻亚美尼亚常设机构获得的收入以及由于从事外国经济活动而获得的收入除外。

一般而言，当收入由税务代理人支付给自然人时，税务代理人有义务计算和扣缴所得额。

根据纳税人获得收入的类型、性质以及公民身份的不同，法律规定适用不同的所得税税率。

除非某些收入类型另有规定，根据适用月度或年度税率来决定最终税额：

每月应纳税所得额	税　额
不高于150 000德拉姆	应纳税额的23%
150 000～2 000 000德拉姆	34 500德拉姆加上超过150 000德拉姆部分的28%
超过2 000 000德拉姆	552 500德拉姆加上超过2 000 000德拉姆部分的36%

年度应纳税所得额	税　额
不高于1 800 000德拉姆	应纳税额的23%
1 800 000～24 000 000德拉姆	414 000德拉姆加上超过1 800 000德拉姆部分的28%
超过24 000 000德拉姆	6 630 000德拉姆加上超过24 000 000德拉姆部分的36%

作为一般规则的例外，特许权使用费、利息收入所得以及购置财产所得应按10%的税率计算所得税。

需要指出的是，在《税法》通过前，股息可以在应纳税所得额中扣除。但是，根据新《税法》的规定，外国人获得的股息应按10%的税率纳税，亚美尼亚公民获得的股息按5%的税率缴纳所得税。

对税务代理机构而言，一个所得税的报告期是一个自然月。每月20日之前，税务代理机构应向税务机关提交上个月所得税的相关计算数据。计算出来的所得税额由税务代理机构在同一期间内支付。

同时，每年应纳税所得额应于次年4月20日前由纳税人以电子表格的形式提交，单独载明本年度纳税所得额。按照该表格计算出来的应纳税所得额应当在同一期限内纳入国家预算。

（3）增值税

增值税是一种间接税，针对特定交易和活动征收，例如供应商品、提供服务（包括财产租赁、提供贷款、转让无形资产）按照"国内消费通关"的海关程序进口商品以及从欧亚经济联盟成员国进口商品。

一般情况下，如果组织、企业家和公证人不符合选择营业税制度的资格或他们未能提交其被视为营业税纳税人或适合家族企业制度的证明，则应被视为增值税纳税人。

非商业性组织和农产品生产者应被视为增值税纳税人，如上一年度增值税纳税营业额超过5 835万德拉姆，或者在一个报告年度内营业额超过以上数字，或者向税务机关提交书面声明达到该数额。

需要注意的是，在亚美尼亚境内没有常设机构的非居民在亚美尼亚境内进行增值税应税交易时，且他们的交易对方为居民并为增值税纳税人的，应当代表该机构承担缴纳增值税的责任。

增值税的税率为商品和服务的应税营业额的20%。在货物和服务的总补偿金额（包括20%税率）范围内的增值税金额，课以16.67%的增值税。出口的货物和服务的增值税为0%。

亚美尼亚的财政法律规定了投入一产出模型。增值税纳税人在扣除为货物或者服务所缴纳的增值税（投入增值税）后，缴纳增值税。

申报期是一个自然月。增值税纳税人在每个申报期间，必须提交统一核算增值税和消费税的计算结果。统一核算结果必须用书面形式提交，并在申报期满后 20 日内支付增值税。

（4）消费税

消费税应由个体企业主和特定法律实体缴纳，这些特定法律实体的营业范围涵盖进口商品（须按照"国内消费通关"的海关程序进口或从欧亚经济联盟成员国进口），或生产（以瓶装或其他方式包装）并转让在亚美尼亚缴纳消费税的商品，或者在天然气车辆加气站提供压缩天然气。

以下货物应缴纳消费税：啤酒、葡萄酒和其他酒类、烈酒（白兰地除外），酒精类饮料，烟草（包括烟草工业替代商品、雪茄、小雪茄），润滑剂，汽油，柴油，原料油，油类物质，石油气，压缩天然气和其他碳氢化合物（除了非压缩天然气）。

消费税的税基是上述产品的价格/海关完税价格（如从欧亚经济联盟成员国进口的货物应减去货物购买价格），或实物每一单位的重量/体积或包装上标明的最高零售价格。

应注意的是，有些消费税应税产品是根据其标签课税，这些产品的名单特别列载于《税法》。

消费税的数额按月计算，并于下个月 20 日前支付。下个月 20 日前，应向税务机关申报每季度计算后的金额。

出口关税程序下的应税出口货物，以及出口到欧亚经济联盟其他成员国的出口货物，免征消费税。

（5）财产税

财产税是对被视为应税对象的财产的直接征税，不依赖于纳税人的经济活动。

财产税应由在亚美尼亚或其他国家设立的组织、国际组织及其在亚美尼亚境外设立的组织、亚美尼亚公民、外国公民以及无国籍人在亚美尼亚拥有财产所有权的人支付。必须注意的是，建设中的建筑物或者未授权的建筑物/建筑物的所有权未正式登记的，不能成为免缴财产税的理由。

公共或生产用途的建筑物、工程（公寓、别墅等），包括未完工的建筑物和在建建筑物、车库、机动车，包括汽车、水运工具、雪地摩托、四轮机车和摩托车，都被视为应征税对象。

建筑物和工程的税基是他们的不动产清册载明的价值，机动车辆的税基则是发动机马力大小。财产税以年为单位按一定税率计算。

自然人支付的财产税的申报期为自然年。法律明确了自然人提交财产纳税申报表的自愿原则（截止日期为报告期公历年的 10 月 1 日）。同时，需注意的是，地方政府有义务向自然人发送通知，告知他们的纳税义务。年度财产税额由自然人于报告年度的 12 月 1 日前支付。

由组织缴纳财产税的纳税申报周期为半年。相关税务申报表应在半年期后的下一个月的 20 日前提交。财产税的数额由组织在相同的时限内支付。

（6）土地税

土地所有者、国有土地的永久使用者（自然人、组织）为土地税的纳税人。土地租赁的，由出租人支付土地税。土地税的数额不取决于纳税人的经济活动，而是取决于每单位土地年度征收的固定费用。

农业用地的税基是土地的地籍评估计算确定的净收益。非农业土地的税基是土地的地籍价值。

自然人的土地税纳税申报周期为自然年。地方政府有义务通知自然人他们的税负数额。自然人支付的土地税年度数额将被均分为两期：第一期于申报期的 11 月 15 日之前支付，第二期于第二年的 4 月 15 日之前支付。

由组织缴纳土地税的纳税申报周期为半年。相关税务申报表应在半年期后的下一个月的 20 日前提交。组织应在相同期限内缴纳土地税。

（九）证券交易

1. 相关法律、法规简述

目前，这一领域由 2007 年 10 月 11 日通过的《证券市场法》规范。该法律的主要目的是保护投资者的合法权益，确保证券市场的透明度、可持续性和有效地发展，证券价格体系的可靠性，并缓解证券市场的系统性风险。上述法律主要规范证券公开发行和公开买卖证券、证券市场上的投资服务、证券交易和托管等，并对衍生品进行了规定，主要是对被允许在市场交易的衍生品。

该部法律未涉及的问题主要由亚美尼亚中央银行通过的法案来规范。

2. 证券市场的监督和规范

亚美尼亚纳斯达克 OMX 集团是亚美尼亚唯一受监管的市场运营商，亚美尼亚中央托管银行是唯一的证券清算结算系统运营商。由亚美尼亚中央银行对证券市场进行全面控制。

3. 外国企业参与证券交易的要求

对于外国实体发行和交易的准入，亚美尼亚纳斯达克 OMX 集团的规则不包含任何具体要求。当证券发行商不具备发行资格时，可以适用交易准入程序。在这种情况下，该发行商可申请其股票或债券在 C 和 Cbond 自由市场交易。

发行商不需要达到特定要求就可以让其股票在 C 自由市场交易。然而，要获准在 Cbond 自由市场交易，股票发行量至少要达到 1 亿德拉姆。

（十）投资优惠及保护

1. 优惠政策框架

给予投资者优惠的基本原则是，在亚美尼亚境内适用的关于外国投资者的法律体系的优惠不低于给予本国投资者的优惠。这一原则体现在 1994 年的亚美尼亚《外国投资法》中。另一方面，这项法律又为外国投资者提供了额外的激励措施，比如在投资后的 5 年里，不受法律、法规改变的影响、投资不被征用、没收等。

2. 行业与地区鼓励

亚美尼亚立法规定了对某些行业和地区的投资者的特殊优惠。

在税收和/或关税支付方面获得鼓励的部门是 IT 初创企业、建筑和装配、农副产品、医疗服务、手工地毯产品和被政府列为优先的部门。在亚美尼亚边境地区工作的投资者可以获得特殊的税收和关税优惠。

其中一些鼓励机制自动生效，并且投资者可以减少纳税，但某些鼓励措施需要经过由政府法令规定的申请程序。

3. 特殊经济区

亚美尼亚法律为两种不同体制的经济特区的创建提供了可能性：自由经济区和工业园区。工业园区的特殊性在于，工业园区适用的鼓励措施单独适用于每个区域。政府颁布的创建工业园区的法令也提供了一些激励措施，这些激励措施只适用于这个区域。目前，亚美尼亚没有工业园区。

目前在亚美尼亚有三个自由经济区（FEZ）：联盟自由经济区、子午线自由经济区和梅戈里自由经济区。梅戈里自由经济区是在 2017 年年底建立的，目前基础设施建设已接近尾声。

4. 投资保护

关于保护外国投资的法案主要是 1994 年的亚美尼亚《外国投资法》。亚美尼亚还是多个双边投资保护条约的签署国，也是 1965 年签署的《关于解决各国和其他国家国民之间的投资争端公约》的成员国。因此，国际投资争端解决中心（ICSID）可以解决其涉及外国投资的争议。这些协议确保了对外国投资者公平和公正的待遇，并为纠纷解决提供了有效的机制。

三、贸易

（一）贸易主管部门

当地社区以及若干国家机构负责监管该行业是否符合要求，每个国家机构都在其被授权的范围内行使其职权，包括亚美尼亚税务局、海关、国家食品安全局等。

(二)贸易法律、法规概况

贸易、公共饮食和消费服务受2004年11月24日通过的《贸易和服务法》和亚美尼亚政府通过的若干决定约束。对外贸易受当地法规和亚美尼亚加入的欧亚经济联盟的法律以及亚美尼亚加入的其他国际协定的制约。亚美尼亚与格鲁吉亚、摩尔多瓦、塔吉克斯坦、土库曼斯坦和乌克兰签订了双边自由贸易协定。

(三)贸易管理

自2003年2月5日以来,亚美尼亚一直是世界贸易组织的成员。亚美尼亚在各方面履行了入世承诺,并继续采取一切必要措施,确保进一步履行《世界贸易组织协定》及其在各方面的承诺。

世界贸易组织于2010年4月6日和8日第一次对亚美尼亚贸易政策进行了审查。审查得出两个结论:一是亚美尼亚面临的主要挑战是摆脱对以矿产出口和国外汇款流入为基础的狭隘经济的依赖;二是由于亚美尼亚对贸易和投资抱有的开放态度,大量的侨民,丰富的矿产资源,悠久的历史和旅游潜力,使其具有很大潜力。从那时起,亚美尼亚实施了重大改革,以确保亚美尼亚经济进一步发展。

(四)进出口商品检验检疫

申报的货物将会按照有关海关程序就卫生防疫、兽医、检疫、植物检疫和辐射要求的遵守情况进行检验。具体地讲,通常的海关报关规则是报关员还应提供相应的文件以证明该货物符合要求。这些要求由亚美尼亚认可的国际协定、欧亚经济联盟委员会的各个决定和亚美尼亚颁布的地方法规规定。

(五)海关管理

亚美尼亚于2015年1月2日成为欧亚经济联盟(目前包括白俄罗斯、哈萨克斯坦、俄罗斯和吉尔吉斯共和国)的一员,因此,亚美尼亚海关事务同时受亚美尼亚当地法律和该联盟法案的约束。根据这些文件,所有的欧亚经济联盟成员国境内构成一个单独关税区。经上述任何国家海关放行的货物,以及在该国境内生产的货物,可以在欧亚经济联盟的关税区内自由流通,不需经过任何其他会员国的任何海关手续。在某些情况下,如果仅以报税为目的,可以要求提交某些文件。

当货物和运输工具跨越欧亚经济联盟海关边境时,须征收以下特定费用/税款:

(1)进出口关税

· 当携带货物跨越关税边境时,按照货物各自报关价值的一定百分比或者以相关货物计量单位的固定税率征收;

· 货物从亚美尼亚出口,除非亚美尼亚法律另有规定,出口关税税率为0%;

· 货物进口到亚美尼亚,税率按照欧亚经济联盟的统一关税政策,根据FEACN的相关规定,各成员国的国际协定另有规定的除外;

· 必须在海关程序根据具体货物所规定的时间内支付。

(2)报关费

是就跨境运输货物履行海关手续的强制性费用,按照各成员国地方法律所规定的数额征收。

(3)税费

具体是:

· "国内消费放行"海关程序下进口的货物将被征收增值税,须在按照上述海关程序放行货物之前付款;

· "国内消费放行"海关程序项下进口的某些货物将被征收消费税,须在按照上述海关程序放行货物之前付款;

· 自然保护税在进口的货物对环境有害(如原油、油料、轮胎等)时征收,须在办理海关手续时或在完成海关手续之前付款;外国登记的运输工具在进入亚美尼亚时征收,因其将有害物质排放到大气,须在入境时付款;

· 在外国登记的车辆进入亚美尼亚使用国家公共道路时将被征收道路税,按照每旅行15天一个周期征收;在进入亚美尼亚时须支付第一个15天周期的道路税费。

货物和运输工具跨越欧亚经济联盟海关边境时，按照以下相关程序报关：
- 国内消费放行；
- 出口；
- 海关过境；
- 海关仓库；
- 关税边境内加工；
- 关税边境外加工；
- 为内需加工；
- 临时进口；
- 临时出口；
- 再进口；
- 再出口；
- 免税商店；
- 销毁；
- 为国家利益而抛弃；
- 自由关税区；
- 自由仓库；
- 特殊海关程序（适用于某些类别的货物）。

四、劳动

（一）劳动法律、法规简述

劳动法的相关法规主要来自亚美尼亚共和国《劳动法》，亚美尼亚《民法典》中《劳动法》未能涵盖的部分法规、《公务员法》、亚美尼亚共和国《公共服务法》、其他调整劳动关系的法律、部门集体劳动协议以及涉及劳动安全标准的政府法令。此外，亚美尼亚也是一些规制雇佣法律问题的国际劳工组织会议的成员国。

劳动关系和其他与其直接相关的关系，可以按照《劳动法》的规定，由职工和用人单位订立的集体劳动合同和劳动合同执行。

劳动关系建立在劳动者和用人单位共同约定的基础上。在此基础上，劳动者在遵守内部劳动纪律的前提下，以个人名义履行其职责，以换取报酬，同时用人单位应当保证《劳动法》规定的必要劳动条件。额外改善条件的问题可以通过集体协议来规定，不是强制性的，但是可以通过亚美尼亚共和国的劳动立法来达成。

（二）雇用外籍员工的要求

外国工人可以在亚美尼亚工作并且与亚美尼亚公民享有相同的权利和义务，没有任何限制。唯一的要求是他们应按下列方式进行注册：

1. 工作许可

尽管亚美尼亚法律规定外国人需要获得工作许可证才能在该国工作，但相关程序的适用将截止至2019年1月。这意味着外国人只要拥有有效的居留许可，在2019年1月1日之前，便可以在没有任何工作许可证的情况下在亚美尼亚工作。针对外国人有三种不同类型的居留许可：

① 为期1年的临时许可证，需要大约220美元的费用——主管机关自提交之日起30天内作出接受或拒绝申请的决定；

② 为期5年的长期许可证，需要大约290美元的费用——主管机关自提交之日起30天内作出接受或拒绝申请的决定；

③ 为亚美尼亚人后裔以及在亚美尼亚从事经济或文化活动的外国人提供的10年特别居留许可，费

用约为 310 美元——该许可证可在约 6 个月内获得，取决于许多不同的因素。

2. 申请程序

截至 2019 年 1 月 1 日，除了获得前述提到的居留许可外，无须其他程序。

3. 社会保险

亚美尼亚共和国私营部门的雇主依据法律没有任何需要承担的社会保险，除非在雇员暂时伤残情况下支付临时伤残津贴。然而，实际上大多数外国公司都向其员工提供不同的社会福利，例如员工及其家属的健康保险，为员工参加体育俱乐部以保持员工的健康生活方式支付相关费用等。

（三）出入境

1. 签证类型

入境亚美尼亚有四种类型的签证。签证的一般类型是访问入境签证，这是对游客和医学治疗为目的的入境，对亚美尼亚机构的研究，参加体育、科学、文化活动和不同活动的访问，以及许多其他常见的短期访问。有效期为 1 年的一次入境签证或多次入境签证。

官方入境签证发给持有官方（公务）护照的人员。外交签证签发给持有外交护照或外交身份的人员。过境签证发放给在亚美尼亚中转的旅游者，此种签证准予在亚美尼亚居留 3 天，最长可延长 4 天。

亚美尼亚政府有权为某些州或某些类别的人制定无签证制度。不受入境签证限制的国家公民，在 1 年内可以在亚美尼亚境内停留最长达 180 天，除非国际公约另有约定。

外籍人士签证到期，或者特定国籍公民虽无须办理签证但其法定停留期限到期，仍希望合法居住在亚美尼亚境内的，应当申请居留许可。允许外籍人士申请的居留许可，有以下三种不同类型：

- 1 年期的短期许可，需要 220 美元的费用，在申请提交后 30 日内作出是否批准的决定。
- 5 年期的永久许可，需要 290 美元的费用，在申请提交后 30 日内作出是否批准的决定。
- 10 年期的居留许可，给予亚美尼亚血统和参与亚美尼亚经济或者文化活动的人，需要大约 310 美元的费用。根据不同因素，取得该居留许可大概需要 6 个月的时间。

2. 出入境限制

下列情况下，外籍人士的签证申请会被拒绝，或者其持有的签证将失效：

- 此等人员已被驱逐出亚美尼亚，或其居留许可在 3 年以前被撤销；
- 此等人员在一年内违反了亚美尼亚关于外国人的法律规定并被要求承担相应的责任，但未予履行；
- 有证据证明此等人员参与了危险的活动，例如恐怖主义、走私毒品或军火等；
- 此等人员感染了传染性疾病，对公众健康构成威胁；
- 在申请入境签证时，此等人员提供虚假资料，或未能提供必要的资料；
- 它们对亚美尼亚的国家安全或公共秩序构成严重威胁；
- 此等人员在一年内违反了亚美尼亚交通法规并被要求承担行政责任，但未予履行。

按照亚美尼亚的立法规定，下列情况下，外籍人士不得离开亚美尼亚：

- 此等人员已经被判刑，并且只能在亚美尼亚执行这一判决；
- 此等人员在刑事调查的范围内被采取了限制措施。

（四）工会与劳工组织

在亚美尼亚，工会受亚美尼亚共和国加入的国际条约、《劳动法》《工会法》和其他法律、法规的共同约束。

工会具有以下权力：起草章程和规定；自由选举代表；安排行政人员及其活动；制订计划；按照《劳动法》规定的方式从雇主处获得信息；向雇主提交有关工作组织的建议；在组织内进行集体谈判；缔结集体协议并对其执行情况进行监督；在组织内执行《劳动法》和其他包含劳动法律规范的法律、法规中规定的非国家监督；通过司法程序申诉雇主及其授权人员违反亚美尼亚共和国法律、集体协议和雇佣合同的决定和活动，或侵犯组织内雇员代表的权利的行为；确保劳动关系中雇员和雇主在不同社会合作关系层面的利益协调一致;向国家和地方自治机构提出建议;组织和领导罢工;参与制订并实施组织内提高生产的计划;向雇主提交改善雇员工作和休闲条件的建议,引进新的技术设备,减少体力劳动,修改生产规范及工作报酬的数量和程序;其他不违反法律规定的权力。

工会有权组织、举行和领导罢工和公开活动,并有权与国家机构、地方自治机构、其他组织及其官员进行谈判。在下列情况下,工会有权组织罢工:

① 因调解程序原因,涉及缔结集体劳动合同的有关纠纷未得到解决;

② 雇主回避调解程序;

③ 雇主未能履行雇员认可的调解委员会的决定,或者未能履行事先订立的集体雇佣协议中所应承担的义务。

然而,工会组织在亚美尼亚并不活跃,迄今为止,亚美尼亚工会并没能开展太多实际工作。

(五)劳动争议

雇员与雇主之间关于行使权利、履行《劳动法》或其他规范性法律文件、劳动合同或集体协议中规定的职责所产生的劳资纠纷和分歧,可以通过双方谈判解决。此外,各方还可以将劳资纠纷提交给调解员。

如果当事人不能通过上述方式解决纠纷的,可以通过司法途径解决。

在亚美尼亚,如果雇主是一个行政机构,则涉及的劳资纠纷需同时按民事诉讼程序由有管辖权的法院或行政法院解决。

五、知识产权

(一)知识产权法律、法规简介

在亚美尼亚,知识产权问题由《民法》和针对具体种类知识产权的法律予以规范。亚美尼亚自1993以来一直是世界知识产权组织(WIPO)的成员,并且是世界知识产权组织管理条约以及许多与知识产权有关的多边、区域和双边条约的签署国。

(二)专利申请

专利保护发明和实用新型,并从注册时起提供保护。专利受《民法》第65章的规定以及2008年6月10日通过的《发明、实用新型和工业设计法律》规范。

专利权人享有使用受保护发明或者实用新型的专有权,有权为发明或者实用新型命名,并基于各自专利的权责发生制,获得一项发明或者实用新型的署名权和其他道德权利。

侵犯专利权,是指未经专利权人许可,制造、使用、销售或者进口专利产品或者工艺。下列情况下,未经专利权人许可使用该发明或者实用新型,将不被视为侵权:

- 为个人需要,而不是为了获得利润;
- 作为科学实验或科学研究的对象;
- 按医生处方在药房一次性配药;
- 专利用在属于任何其他国家的运输工具(车辆)上,意外通过或暂时停留在亚美尼亚,在这种情况下,对该专利的应用应当以其于交通工具中的既定用途为限(考虑到国家关系);
- 用于医学产品(包括植物检疫)的测试、研究和临床——在专利有效期的最后2年。

发明专利有效期为自申请时起20年,实用新型专利有效期为自申请时起10年。

专利申请应当包括:

- 专利授予的请求;
- 对发明或实用新型的描述;
- 对发明或实用新型的权利要求的定义,包括至少一个独立的物品;
- 图纸和其他文件,有必要用于了解发明或实用新型的内容;
- 发明或实用新型的摘要。

专利权的申请应用亚美尼亚文书写。对于外国申请者，若能在申请之日起 3 个月内向国家主管机关提交亚美尼亚文译本，可以其本国语言填写申请文件。专利申请应附有授权书，证明申请人代表（如有）的权限，以及本国缴税凭证。

国家主管机关应于申请之日起 3 个月内核实申请书和文件是否符合法律规定。若符合规定，国家主管机关应当审查要求保护的发明或实用新型是否符合上述法律规定的专利申请条件的要求。如条件达到，主管机关应于公报和专利发行刊物上公示决定。应在申请日起 18 个月内填写申请书。一般来说，公示不会提前。

（三）注册商标

《民法》第 69 章和 2010 年 4 月 29 日通过的《商标法》对商标作了规定。

商标（或服务标记）是一种能将自己的商品或服务与他人的同种商品和服务区分开的注册标志（包括文字、图形、特点或其他设计）。注册是商标获得法律保护的保障和依据。商标权经证书确认。

商标注册由知识产权代理机构或根据国际条约由受亚美尼亚法律保护的国际组织办理。商标持有者具有专有的使用和处置权。

以下行为构成对商标的侵权：

• 在商品或包装上粘贴标志，同样，在三维商标情况下，将其附于物品或包装上，或将其作为包装使用。

• 以侵犯商标权为目的提供、出售或储存商品，或者提供带有该标志的服务。

• 使用标志进口或出口物品。

• 将标志用于文件资料和广告。

• 在网络或其他全球通信网络上，尤其是通过寻址模式，例如域名使用该商标标识的。

• 基于以上用途对标志进行复制、存储或销售。

商标注册自申请之日起，有效期为 10 年。

商标注册申请应当以书面或电子邮件方式提交且只能申请一个商标，并应以亚美尼亚文字书写。同时，外国人如果能在申请日后 2 个月内提供亚美尼亚文译本，也可以提交外国语言书写的申请资料。

申请必须包括以下信息：

• 申请者或代理人的身份信息（如有）；

• 独特图案（复印件，如果是声音商标须注明五角星图案）和对其的描述；

• 依照尼斯分类法，将标记注册的商品和/或服务分组清单按升序排列；

• 声明申请的标记应是三维的（如有需要）；

• 声明申请的标记应是全息的（如有需要）；

• 声明申请的标记应包含声音标志（如有需要）

• 声明颜色组合是商标的显著特征（如有需要）；

• 声明商标组成的要素，以及哪些部分不受保护（如有需要）；

• 商标或其要素的音译和亚美尼亚文翻译（如有需要）；

• 声明是集体商标（如有需要）；

• 声明商标是被认证的（如有需要）；

• 声明优先申请的日期和原因。

申请必须有以下材料作为补充：

• 对商标的申请和审查的缴税付款收据；

• 若由代理人提出申请，则需要提交确认其权责的证明材料；

• 要求优先权的申请（如需要）；

• 若商标包括国家标志、旗帜、符号、国家官方名称、象征特殊公共利益的标志，需要主管机关颁发的许可证（如需要）；

• 如果商标复制了或包含了其他更优先的知识产权对象，须获得知识产权所有人的同意（如需要）；

- 集体商标的使用管理规制（如需要）；
- 认证商标的使用管理规制（如需要）。

商标注册流程如下：
- 提交商标注册申请书和缴税的付款收据；
- 国家主管机关应于提交后的 10 个工作日内将申请材料作登记并初步专业评估申请材料，若材料符合相关要求，主管机关应予以公示并作出全面专业评估；
- 作出如上决定的 15 个工作日内，申请应予以公示，其被公示后的 2 个月内，商标的任何利害关系人均可向国家主管机关提出异议；
- 国家主管机关应于公示后的 3 个月内对商标进行全面专业审查，若鉴定结果无疑义，则决定予以登记。一旦作出登记决定，主管机关应通知申请人并收取注册税费；
- 提供支付税金凭证之后 10 个工作日内，主管机关应完成商标注册。

（四）知识产权保护措施

除了对公民权利的一般保护，知识产权人的专有权保护也可通过如下方式实现：
- 侵犯专有权以及因侵权所得实物一律予以没收；
- 由知识产权人选择，强制公开侵权行为，包含被侵权人信息以及法院判决全文或者在媒体上公开部分信息，产生的费用由侵权人支付；
- 与具体种类知识产权相关的法律所规定的其他方法。

六、环境保护

（一）环境保护主管部门

在亚美尼亚，被授权监督环境保护的国家机构是亚美尼亚共和国自然保护部。自然保护部是亚美尼亚共和国的执行机关，执行亚美尼亚共和国保护环境和合理利用自然资源的国家政策。分配给该部门的职能由体制内的及独立的人员团体以及部门内设立的国家非营利组织和公司实施。亚美尼亚自然保护和地下资源部是一个独立的分部，负责监控环境保护规范的遵守情况，发现违规行为并采取相应的措施。区域政府机构和地方自治团体也会捍卫环境保护法，并采取措施预防违法行为。他们有义务在 3 天内向国家环境监察局汇报并及时披露违法行为。所有这些机构都会采取相应的行动，致力于解决其管辖范围内的环境问题。

（二）环境保护法律、法规概况

亚美尼亚《宪法》确定了环境保护的基本原则和国家发挥的作用。这一领域的事务主要由四个法案规制。

亚美尼亚《森林法案》规定了亚美尼亚林区和林地的保护、修复、造林和有效利用，还规定了林区的登记、监测、管理以及其他与林地有关的事务。

亚美尼亚《地下资源法案》设立了亚美尼亚领土地下资源的使用原则和程序。此法案规定的事务还包括如何在地下资源的使用过程中保护自然环境、消除有害影响、开发工程活动中有关安全保障的规定，以及在地下资源使用过程中有关保护国家和个人的合法权益的事务。本法案还规定了授予开采矿物许可证的程序、许可条款和续期程序、地下资源使用者的权利和义务等。

为了利用和维护为人们生命活动提供了条件的亚美尼亚共和国土地，亚美尼亚《土地法》为国家土地法规的完善、各种土地管理的组织上和法律形式上的发展、土地肥力和利用效率的提高、人们的生命健康的维护和环境改善，以及基于环境、经济和社会意义的土地权益保护奠定了法律基础。这一法案确定了土地的现实意义和用途。

亚美尼亚《水资源法》为水资源相关管理机制的设立、水资源的保护、确保污染的减少、保护水质和国家水资源总量、对水资源污染的预防、水资源登记的规定、制定与人口和经济相关的用水量和用水质量的条款及订立收费标准提供了法律依据。

许多部门法也规定了与环境相关的事务，包括：亚美尼亚《动物法》、亚美尼亚《植物法》、亚美尼亚《废品法》、亚美尼亚《环境监管法》、亚美尼亚《环境处罚法》、亚美尼亚《特别保护区法》、亚美尼亚《环境评估和专业评审法》等。

许多有关环境保护的国际公约已经得到了亚美尼亚的签署生效，以下条约也被视为亚美尼亚法律制度的一部分：《联合国防治荒漠化公约》《控制危险废物越境转移及其处置巴塞尔公约》《消耗臭氧层物质的蒙特利尔议定书》。

（三）环境保护的评估

近年来，亚美尼亚在环境政策、立法和体制改革方面采取了许多切实的举措。部门环境立法已更新并适应现代要求，并根据宪法的要求，通过了《环境影响评估法》。该法律规范了拟开展活动和设想对环境影响之评估机制的法律、经济和组织基础。该法的主要目的是对可能对环境产生影响的拟议活动进行管制。该法首次提及有关社区和公众听证程序，以鼓励公众参与环境问题的决策。公开听证会确保公众认识并参与评估和专业评审过程。发起人和被授权机构应当考虑公众的合理意见和建议。对于不理解的，应当给予合理的解释。与此相适应的是，行政诉讼法中的一个重要变化是公共组织代表着环境保护领域受益者的利益。公共组织如果根据亚美尼亚《环境评估和专业评审法》参加了基本文件或拟开展活动的公开听证会，或没有机会参加公开讨论，均可以向法院提出诉讼。

七、争议解决

（一）争议解决方式和机构

1. 程序的效力

亚美尼亚法院系统是一个三审级的司法系统，除涉及宪法制度的单独交由宪法法院以外，所有案件都由该司法系统审理。

法院系统主要有以下特点：

法院系统在《宪法》和《司法法典》中有详细说明。不同的程序法（刑事、民事、行政）和破产法规定了不同的司法程序。

亚美尼亚普通法院审理所有刑事和民事案件，包括商业和破产案件。

亚美尼亚行政法院是负责审理公共法律关系案件的专门法院，对行政权力（执行）的监督起到关键作用。

亚美尼亚民事上诉法院和刑事上诉法院审理对普通法院判决的上诉，行政上诉法院审理对行政法院行为的上诉。

最高法院是有权受理除宪政诉讼以外所有诉讼的最高司法机构。

一般来说，如果起诉符合适当程序规范的要求（包括所需资料、随附列出的文件、行为已签署等），法院会受理听审。相同情况时上诉亦会被允许听审。

撤销申诉的受理是一个复杂的问题，因为最高法院的宗旨已载入《宪法》（旨在确保统一适用法律，并消除对人权和自由的根本侵犯）。一般来说，最高法院接受符合形式要求和法院宗旨的申诉。近期有关接受原告的撤销申诉，需要经过宪法法院的审查。预计这种做法将有相应改变，如果明确规定受理撤销申诉的形式要求，审理的次数将会增加。

在初审法院（除了刑事诉讼程序和破产分别适用刑事诉讼法和破产法），案件在受理后主要经历以下三个阶段：初步听审；一审；判决和公开判决。

上诉法院在上诉和证据范围内审查案件，不接受未在一审中提交的任何证据或主张。在法庭审理公开的情况下，上诉法院将进行开庭审理（一次或两次），随后进行判决并公布裁判。

上诉法院的判决可能会受到申诉要求撤销，如果该申诉被受理，则会进行一次法庭听审，并最终作出不可上诉判决。

亚美尼亚通过立法确定了时效期间。尽管如此，适用时效期间的申请应由法院在对案件进行全面审查的同时进行审查,即申请适用时效并不会立即停止诉讼程序。

亚美尼亚立法承认替代性争端解决方案。下面介绍相关章程中的调解和替代性争端解决机制详细信息。

(1) 替代性争端解决机制机制的适用

亚美尼亚法律承认调解和仲裁。尽管多年来仲裁已经出现在法律中,但正式的调解(于 2015 年推出)还是相当新颖的。

仲裁在特定领域得到了广泛认可(大多数是银行和信贷机构使用,用以作为处理不良贷款的快捷方式)。但总的来说,仲裁实践依然有所欠缺。另外,部分仲裁机构的名录中有着经验丰富的仲裁员,立法却没有规定担任仲裁员应当具备特殊许可或背景的要求。

仲裁程序由单独的仲裁法、仲裁中心的内部规定(及特设仲裁条例)和争议双方的协议进行规定。通常它的程序类似于法院的诉讼程序;但它不那么正式,速度更快。如果双方当事人没有另行约定,仲裁裁决将不可上诉,并且是终局的、有约束力的:在有限情况下法院可以进行审查(例如,没有仲裁协议或其他严重违反程序的情况)。

调解方面,如果当事人希望他们的调解得到法院的批准,调解人必须持有调解员执照。最近许多法律和非法律专家申请并获得许可作为调解人。然而,由于调解是一种新颖的争端解决方式,目前尚没有足够的数据来阐述非法律专家担任调解员的有效性。

当事人也可以进行庭外调解,在某些情况下,庭外调解也将由法院进行调查。

如果调解不成功,当事人仍可通过仲裁或法院继续解决争议。

(2) 电子司法工具提高司法效率和实现诉权的适用

目前,没有通过在线系统向法院提起诉讼申请的方式。该在线系统由司法部门和司法部在 Concern Dialog 律师事务所及欧盟代表团的财务和技术支持下开发并测试。一些立法和监管问题阻碍了该系统的应用。由于法律要求是基于纸质的诉讼申请,在线申请流程可能需要经一些细微的法律改革调整后方能实施。相比之下,仲裁在操作上更容易通过电子邮件或专门开发的平台接受在线申请。

与此同时,法院所有案件的数据都在亚美尼亚网络司法系统 Datalex 上公布(需要进行非公开听审的案件数据除外),并可在 http://datalex.am 查阅。它仅可在亚美尼亚境内使用,并且一方可以在线查询其申请和有关程序(例如接受程序、开庭日期、一些诉讼过程中的司法行为、最终判决文本、上诉和撤销索赔信息等),也可以跟踪并审查有关案件。

其他公布法院裁决的资源包含复杂的检索和索引机制,如:免费的官方资源 http://arlis.am 和 http://www.court.am;私人付费资源 http://www.armlaw.am 和 Irtekhttp://www.irtek.am,两者都包含最高法院和宪法法院的裁决。

2. 程序的完整性

亚美尼亚的法律制度体现了自然正义的原则。亚美尼亚《宪法》保障每个人有权就其案件进行公开听审,以恢复其被侵犯的权利,并在合理期间内,接受独立、公正的法院基于公平、平等原则就对其的指控进行审理。

根据国际公认的、作为自然正义基本规则的司法保护权(诉权),亚美尼亚《司法法典》规定,人人有权对其权利和自由寻求司法保护,不得剥夺其在合理的时间内,在平等的条件下,充分尊重公平的所有要求的,由合格、独立和公正的法院公开审查案件的权利。

亚美尼亚的法律中包含一些机制来保护避免偏见原则(任何人不能作为自己的案件的法官)。如果仲裁当事人认为法官存在偏见,他们可以提出一个包含理由的、必须由法官决定的自我拒绝申请。如果法官存在偏见,或者存在可能被认为有偏见的情况,其应主动放弃或通过该申请将案件转移给另一名法官。如果当事人对法院驳回自行回避申请的决定不满意,其可以将它作为对最终裁决提出上诉的理由。

至于获得听审的机会,法院在听取案件其他参与者的意见后,就案件参与人的申请和请求进行判决。

在亚美尼亚,人人有权通过代表人、辩护人或自行行使其获得司法保护的权利(获得法律代表权)。

亚美尼亚司法部门是独立和自治的。法院的独立性由《宪法》《司法法典》和程序法确定。《司法词典》规定，除法律另有规定，法官是独立的，不对任何人负责，不需要作出任何解释。此外，法官不能加入任何党派或参与政治活动。在任何情况下，法官都必须表现出政治克制和中立态度。

法官不得容忍任何对司法的干涉，无论该干涉是来自立法权力、行政权力的代表，或是其他公职人员或普通市民。

对法官独立性的保证在于，如果其根据司法权或其他法律授予的权力受到干涉，且该种干涉并非法律所规定的，法官必须立即通知道德委员会。如果道德委员会发现法官的活动受到非法干扰，就必须请求主管当局追究违法者的责任。任何此类行为都会受到刑事起诉；对公务员来说，它也会引起纪律责任，甚至包括解职。

此外，在其任职期间和终止后，法官不得作为他所审判案件的证人被讯问。

《宪法》规定了法院公正性原则的基础，规定人人有权由独立和公正的法院进行公正和公开的听审，法官应是独立的、公正的，只依据宪法和法律行事。根据《司法法典》的规定，法官在行使权力时，必须避免表现出言论或行为上的歧视或给人留下这样的印象。

刑事诉讼法和民事诉讼法中体现了对法官在具体案件中保持公正的要求。

亚美尼亚的法律体系整合并具体规定了《司法法典》所设定的一系列保障公正性的机制和机构。其中包括：
- 法官不可被解除职务；
- 薪水；
- 养老金/社会保障特权；
- 对法官进行刑事起诉的司法特别程序；
- 政治中立；
- 不能兼职（法官仍可从事志愿活动或从事有偿教育或科学工作）；
- 复杂的任用程序。

3. 权利及披露

（1）权利

任何人都有权拒绝提供对其本人、配偶及直系亲属不利的证言。

律师（辩护人）、人权捍卫者、法官、仲裁员、调解员及承认指控者在民事（包括破产）、行政和刑事诉讼中不能作证。此外，媒体代表人对于可能披露信息来源的问题，有权不予回答。

亚美尼亚《辩护人及辩护人行为法》针对保密信息的保护作出了多项规定，例如：
①除当事人同意外，禁止披露任何信息；
②禁止从与法律服务相关的律师资料中查抄（调取）保密信息，并禁止将其作为证据；
③禁止调查辩护人的住所、车辆、办公场所以及律师事务所的办公场所，禁止在律师履行职责期间对其进行审查。

（2）披露

亚美尼亚法律保护保密信息和个人信息。因此，保密信息（涵盖商业、银行、国家、公务、公证、家庭及个人生活等）包括个人信息（即可直接或间接确定自然人身份的信息）可以在诉前或诉中在当事人同意或法院裁定的范围内予以披露。

与其他法院不同，亚美尼亚行政法院可依其职权要求提供包含保密信息的证据。其他法院则不得启动此类程序，但对诉讼参与人向法院提出的提供保密数据的请求，有权进行审查，并作出相应决定。获准提出该请求的诉讼参与人必须证明或表明，若未经法院批准，其将无法获得此类数据，并且该证据或信息与案件相关。

无论保密信息所有权人在案件中是否享有诉讼地位，经法院裁定，均可请求并获得保密数据。

一般说来，案件应公开审理，但一方当事人为保护收养的保密性、家庭成员隐私以及商业或其他秘密而申请不公开审理的，经法院批准后，可不公开审理。

不公开审理的，无法从公开途径获得案件的相关信息，即从 www.datales.am 中仅可获得案号及诉讼各方的相关信息。

4. 费用

诉讼请求须缴纳国家费用（非金钱案件或无法以金钱估值的案件须缴纳象征性数量的费用，金钱案件则缴纳诉讼标的的 2%～3%，具体标准取决于受理法院的审级）。某些案件可免于缴纳国家费用（例如，劳务案件中雇员的诉讼请求）。当事人无法及时缴纳国家费用的，亚美尼亚法律对迟延缴纳作出了相关规定，但当事人须提交申请，并说明其无法缴纳该项费用的理由。此外，近年来的司法实践表明，法院在批准此类申请时愈加严格。

通常由败诉方偿付已支付的各项费用，诉讼费用包括律师费。但是，仅当有证据证明其他费用的计算依赖于当事人已实际支付的金额时，律师费应视为满足"合理数额"。对于律师费的计算办法或已实际支付的金额，当事人需提供证据（例如付款凭证）。法院在综合考虑各种因素后，裁定费用的合理数额，由败诉方向胜诉方偿付。

目前尚无针对诉讼费用的担保规定，但临时措施机制可以有限地满足此类目的。

目前尚无限定诉讼费用或限制诉讼费用可偿付性的其他规定（唯一适用的费用为律师费）。

目前，当事人尚无其他途径寻求资助诉讼费用，但当事人可寻找第三方资助人。一些国际基金项目曾经资助过策略性的诉讼案件，但近年来，大多数此类项目已经终止。

5. 诉讼资助

根据亚美尼亚法律，任何有关诉讼的费用均可要求偿付。该费用合理的偿付主张可予以支持，但国家费用除外（国家费用按照得到支持的请求金额予以支持）。目前尚无任何标准确定费用是否合理或合法，但法官可以自由裁量。司法实践中，费用（律师费、翻译费、专家费等）的偿付金额根据市场均价、花费时间以及案件性质等确定。

已经支付或将要支付的律师费可得到偿付。因此，胜诉酬金应在合理金额范围内，并由法院批准。实践中，收回债款服务大多采用此种模式，通常法院会批准偿付协议规定的全部金额。

诉讼费用既可以在原案件审理中一并主张，也可以另案主张。后者包括若干法律问题，例如请求的法律性质和实体法中的法律依据等，其法律地位各不相同。在主要听审范围内，诉讼费用可向与提起诉讼相关的法院寻求支持，例如，上诉费用可直接向上诉法院提起偿付。

当事人能够证明无法支付国家费用的，可以迟延缴付。

法律服务费用由当事人或第三方支付。为策略性诉讼案件提供资金支持的机构正逐渐减少，目前数量几乎为零。

同时，为发展公益法律服务，各方面展开了广泛的商议。目前，公益法律服务主要由公共辩护人办公室提供，服务范围包括对社会弱势群体的刑事、民事、行政以及宪法诉讼的法律援助。

6. 临时救济

对于民事诉讼，亚美尼亚《民事诉讼法》第98条规定了禁令救济的范围。以下为救济方式：

- 对被告人财产或金融资产按照案件标的金额予以扣押；
- 禁止被告人的某些特定行为；
- 禁止与争议标的相关的其他人员的某些特定行为；
- 不得出售撤销扣押的财产；
- 对由原告所有但由被告占有的财产予以扣押。

行政诉讼中的救济方式与《民事诉讼法》中规定的救济方式不同。根据亚美尼亚《行政诉讼法》的规定，法院可临时批准救济行为。

申请救济行为，原告需证明采取担保措施的必要性。实践中，采取合理担保措施的申请需要得到批准。必要时，法院有权采用多种担保方式。

相应的，经案件参与人申请，法院有权变更临时救济措施，并经案件参与方申请，终止临时救济措施。终止担保措施经庭审决定。作为一种保护措施，被告人可以要求原告支付与其所主张的损失相当的钱款作为法院实施保全措施的担保金，并向同一法院请求支付因临时措施导致的损害赔偿金。

亚美尼亚是独联体《关于民事、家庭和刑事案件中的法律协助和法律关系公约》的缔约国。该公约对全球冻结令的执行进行了规范。通常，若亚美尼亚法院发出冻结令，其效力涉及被告人在亚美尼亚以及全球的资金。但是，亚美尼亚法院的裁定必须得到资金所在国法院的承认，该资金方能冻结。

7. 判决的执行

亚美尼亚是独联体《关于民事、家庭和刑事案件中的法律援助和法律关系公约》的缔约国，并与很多国家签订了互惠协定，如希腊、伊朗、保加利亚、罗马尼亚、格鲁吉亚、阿拉伯联合酋长国、立陶宛。对于未与亚美尼亚签订任何协定的国家，判决和裁决的执行以互惠为基础。

根据《强制执行法》的规定，若亚美尼亚参加的国际条约有规定的，由亚美尼亚法院对有关外国法院判决和裁定在亚美尼亚境内的效力予以认定，并签发执行该判决和裁定的执行令状。

通常，诉讼各方应履行各自的义务，无须强制执行。然而，在终局性司法行为或临时措施裁定生效后，当事人可向法院申请司法执行令（执行令状），并递交给国家强制执行服务部门。

执行时限为执行案件启动后2个月，用于执行强制措施，法律另行规定在个别情况下可以延长的除外。

通常，执行程序耗时不长，尤其是在涉及申请采取临时措施的情况下：一旦原告财产确认，即可扣押，或者如若涉及禁止令的，由国家强制执行服务局直接签发并执行。

强制执行的，另行缴付执行费用（约5%），在将判决金额交付胜诉方之前，从缴付金额中予以扣除。债权人撤销执行令状的，应承担执行费用（额度根据撤销时间节点在1%～5%之间）。

撤销强制执行的事由由亚美尼亚司法行为《强制执行法》第42条规定。例如，这些情况包括：

- 权利人放弃强制执行的；
- 权利人和债务人达成和解协议，并经法院同意；
- 作为权利人或债务人的自然人死亡，并且该司法行为确立的权利或义务无法由继承人继承；
- 作为签发执行令状基础的司法行为被推翻；
- 作为债务人的法人经法院判决宣告破产；
- 作为债务人的法律实体解散。

诉讼各方可就争议达成和解，并签订和解协议。该和解协议经法院确认后发布，成为司法行为。各方也可对协议的执行作互惠安排。另一种选择（仅涉及司法行为的履行顺序）是各方就司法命令的执行顺序达成协议。这一选择要求案件存在终局性司法行为，并且诉讼各方根据自己的意愿和协议，希望规范各自履行法律行为义务的顺序。如若违反该协议，可向国家强制执行服务局申请执行法院判决。

国家强制执行服务局发现原告无力偿债的，将停止执行，并告知债权人提起破产之诉。

已经履行义务并有证据证明的，执行服务仅收取执行费用。对于不履行司法行为的，亚美尼亚《刑法》规定对强制执行机构和拒不执行的个人可以提出刑事指控。

对于执行仲裁裁决问题，《强制执行法》规定强制执行仲裁裁决书的执行令状由适格的亚美尼亚法院签发。该法院有权根据亚美尼亚《商事仲裁法》的规定，拒绝签发执行令状。

虽然亚美尼亚法律没有规定特别案外债务人程序，但有类似的机制。若强制执行者意欲扣押债务人的货币性资金，可在终局性判决生效后，函告银行以及债务人雇主请求冻结债务人的资金和未付薪金。

8. 跨国诉讼

为完成某些诉讼，亚美尼亚法院可向管辖地以外发送裁决令，但这仅限于亚美尼亚领土范围内。对于涉外案件，亚美尼亚法院可就协助事项寻求他国协助，例如了解他国法律的内容。如前所述，其他类型的合作仅以国际条约或外交合作关系为基础，但要求民事诉讼以抗辩为基础并且当事人向法院提交了证据（在个别情况下，当事人提出书面申请说明为何无法收集证据后，法院方可代为收集证据）。

裁决令的境外执行也依赖于国际条约或外交手段。亚美尼亚裁决令的境外执行在实践中鲜有发生，可能需要耗时数月。

通常，由诉讼当事人在境外司法管辖领域内实施所要求的司法行为。

9. 国际仲裁

亚美尼亚是《承认及执行外国仲裁裁决公约》（以下简称《纽约公约》）的缔约国，因此，亚美尼亚承认并执行外国仲裁裁决，亚美尼亚的仲裁裁决亦可在其他《纽约公约》缔约国得到承认并执行。相关程序包含在诉讼法典和规范仲裁的法律中。根据国际指引性文件以及亚美尼亚的诉讼法律、法规，尽管外国仲裁裁决在亚美尼亚的承认和执行鲜有发生，但承认与执行并无重大困难。

10. 调解和非诉讼纠纷解决程序

在亚美尼亚，调解是一种很新的机制。诉讼各方可随时申请调解。协议中规定调解的，法院须在调解结束后方可作出判决。调解的时限完全取决于各方的意愿。

负责调解的专业人士（不一定需要有法律背景）需要获得司法部的调解员证书。

调解需要支付费用，但为强化这一新制度，亚美尼亚法律规定，前4个小时为免费调解时间。

经数次修订，很多专业人士申请并获得了调解员证书，但实践中，调解并未被广泛采用。

11. 监管调查

政府当局负责监管适当区域的经济行为，包括消费者权利保护。根据行政法律，监管调查属于行政程序。

政府或市政当局作出的决定可由行政法院审查。

行政法院可审查政府或市政当局（包括中央银行、国家保护经济竞争委员会以及公共服务监管委员会）的规范性法律行为是否与更高位阶的法律行为相一致（宪法除外）。

行政法院有权审查公证人员以及负责监管并保护个人信息机构的行为。

（二）法律适用

在程序法上，诉讼分别以《民事诉讼法》《刑事诉讼法》和《行政诉讼法》为基础。设立在亚美尼亚的仲裁庭受到基于《联合国示范法》的亚美尼亚《商事仲裁法》规制，但当事人可以自由就程序事项达成一致，包括纳入其仲裁协议的希望适用的仲裁规则。

至于实体法，如果争端提交至亚美尼亚法院，则适用于涉外关系的法律将根据亚美尼亚《冲突法规则》确定。作为一般规则，当事人可以自由选择适用于其合同的法律，法律选择对法院具有约束力。对法院无法根据具体的《冲突法规则》决定适用法律的案件，将适用与该案件关系最密切的法律。

设立在亚美尼亚的仲裁庭，仲裁员在仲裁中必须适用当事人选择的法律。当事人没有选择适用于案件的法律的，仲裁员根据《冲突法规则》决定其认为适用的法律。如果争端的一方是亚美尼亚公民或在亚美尼亚注册的法人实体，并且当事方未能选择适用于其案件的法律时，仲裁员应适用亚美尼亚法律。

八、其他

（一）反商业贿赂

1. 反商业贿赂法律、法规概况

商业贿赂，包括与商业贿赂行为有关的钓鱼执法，受亚美尼亚《刑法》的管制，即根据亚美尼亚法律，商业贿赂被认为是一种刑事犯罪。

亚美尼亚《刑法》第200条第1款规定：向商业或其他机构雇员、仲裁员（包括依据外国仲裁法律进行仲裁的仲裁员）、审计员、律师（以下简称为"特定人员"）行贿的，构成商业贿赂。行贿人或中间人实施下列行为，从而使特定人员为行贿人或行贿者代表的他人利益作为或不作为的，构成行贿：

① 非法向特定人员或其他人员许诺、提供或汇寄现金；
② 非法向特定人员或其他人员许诺、提供或转让财产；
③ 非法向特定人员或其他人员许诺、提供或转让财产权利；
④ 非法向特定人员或其他人员许诺、提供或转让有价证券；
⑤ 非法向特定人员或其他人员许诺、提供或转让其他利益。

亚美尼亚《刑法》第200条第3款规定：商业或其他机构雇员、仲裁员（包括依据外国仲裁法律进行仲裁的仲裁员）、审计员、律师（以下简称为"特定人员"）接受贿赂的，构成商业受贿。特定人

员为行贿人或行贿人代表的他人利益作为或不作为,从而直接或通过中间人实施下列行为的,构成受贿:

① 接收、要求、许诺接收或接受向特定人员或其他人员提供的现金;
② 接收、要求、许诺接收或接受向特定人员或其他人员提供的财产;
③ 接收、要求、许诺接收或接受向特定人员或其他人员提供的财产权利;
④ 接收、要求、许诺接收或接受向特定人员或其他人员提供的有价证券;
⑤ 接收、要求、许诺接收或接受向特定人员或其他人员提供的其他利益。

除亚美尼亚《刑法》外,于2017年9月6日通过并于2018年1月1日起正式实施的亚美尼亚《刑法》外,关于讯号行为的法律还规定了社会组织(即提供公共服务如电信、供水、供电以及供气的组织)、政府和市政机构、国家机关和组织的讯号行为。讯号行为指以下事项的书面或口头通知:腐败事件;利益冲突;违反道德规范;违反合规条例或其他限制;违反申报规定;损害公共利益;威胁公共利益。讯号行为可分为内部和外部两种。作出讯号行为的人员应谨慎。

2. 反商业贿赂行为的主管部门

商业贿赂行为是相关执法机构调查的重点。

内部讯号行为由机构(组织)负责人或主管部门监管。外部讯号行为交由防止腐败委员会监管。讯号行为也可以由检察机关通过提交特殊平台监管。

存在犯罪事实或犯罪嫌疑的,案件将移交给有管辖权的执法机构。

3. 惩处措施

实施亚美尼亚《刑法》第200条第1款或第3款规定的(商业贿赂)犯罪行为的,处罚金200 000～400 000德拉姆(1美元可兑换480德拉姆),或最长3年内不得担任某些职位或从事某些职业,或最高3年的有期徒刑。

事先定有协议的犯罪集团或有组织的犯罪集团实施相同行为的,处罚金300 000～500 000德拉姆,或最高4年的有期徒刑。

实施亚美尼亚《刑法》第200条第3款规定的(商业贿赂)犯罪行为,并有敲诈情节的,处罚金300 000～500 000德拉姆,或最长5年内不得担任某些职位或从事某些职业,或最高5年的有期徒刑。

(二) 项目承包

亚美尼亚《采购法》和相关法案规定了采购规则,亚美尼亚共和国的州政府机构或社区机构有义务遵守亚美尼亚关于采购的法律和相关的监管法律,通过采购的方式购买货物、工程和服务。这些机构包括亚美尼亚中央银行、国家或社区非商业组织、国家或社区参股超过50%的组织,由国家或社区或者非商业性国家组织或社区组织或者国家或社区参股超过50%的组织建立的(包括重组)基金会或单位、公共组织(电力生产、电力和天然气的流通和分配、电力和天然气部门的运营商、水的供应、电子通信公共网络的开发等)。

采购的方式包括电子交易、招标(包括公开招标和定向招标)、费用报价请求和单一来源购买。在例外情况下,允许从单一来源购买商品、劳务和服务,例如合同价格不高于购买的基础价格,即100万德拉姆。

法律规定了招投标若干事项的程序,包括投标邀请、投标人及中标人资格的形式和确认、报名、评标、合同订立和违反程序的责任。此外,还规定了提交标书的程序以及就采购进行合规审查的程序。

Armenia

Authors: Sedrak Asatryan, Roustam Badasyan, Hakob Tadevosyan, Tatevik Harutyunyan
Translators: Li Malin, Li Jiehua

I. Overview

A. General Introduction to the Political, Economic, Social and Legal Environment of the Country Receiving Investment

Armenia, officially the Republic of Armenia, is a sovereign, unitary, democratic and social state with ancient cultural heritage. The first mention of Armenians and their ancestors in historical writings is found in inscriptions which date back to the third millennium B.C.Armenians are the first nation to adopt Christianity as the official religion of their state (301 A.D.). The modern Armenia recognizes the Armenian Apostolic Church, the world's oldest national church, as the country's primary religious establishment. Armenians have their own unique alphabet invented by Mesrop Mashtots in 405 A.D.

Armenia occupies 29,800 km². It is located in the Southern Caucasus and borders with Georgia in the north, Azerbaijan to the east, Turkey in the west, and Iran to the south.

Armenia is a mountainous land-locked country, the average altitude of which is 1800 m above the mean sea level. Its climate is sharp continental (very hot in summer and very cold in winter), humidity is low.

The population of Armenia is about 3 million. More than 95% of the population of Armenia are Armenians. The rest are mostly Russians, Kurds, Assyrians, Greeks and Ukrainians. Of the general population, the urban population comprises around 64%.

The monetary unit of Armenia is the Armenian dram (AMD). The market based average exchange rates of Armenian dram vis-à-vis foreign currency are published by the Central Bank of Armenia_a.

The capital of Armenia is Yerevan (with approximately 1 million of population), Gyumri and Vanadzor are the other two largest cities.

Armenia proclaimed its independence on September 21, 1991, after 70 years within the Soviet Union. The national flag of Armenia consists of three horizontal bands of equal width, red on the top, blue in the middle, and the color of apricot on the bottom.

The national coat of arms of Armenia depicts Mount Ararat with Noah's Ark in the centre on a shield, and the coats of arms of the four kingdoms of historical Armenia. The shield is supported by a lion and an eagle while a sword, a branch, a sheaf, a chain and a ribbon are portrayed under the shield.

Armenia currently has diplomatic relations with more than 180 countries worldwide. Armenia is a member of the United Nations Organization (UNO), International Monetary Fund (IMF), The World Bank (WB), European Bank for Reconstruction and Development (EBRD), Council of Europe, Organization for Security and Co-operation in Europe (OSCE) and the World Trade Organization (WTO). Armenia is also a member of the Commonwealth of Independent States (CIS). In October 1994 Armenia signed a limited military cooperation agreement with the North Atlantic Treaty Organization (NATO) and in November 2017–Comprehensive and Enhanced Partnership Agreement with the European Union.

a. Political

Currently Armenia is set to transition from semi-presidential to parliamentary system of governance in accordance with the amendments made to the Constitution in December 2015. The election of the new National Assembly in line with the said constitutional amendment was held on April 02, 2017 and is comprised of 102 members of parliament (deputies) elected through proportional electoral system from among candidates nominated in the national and district electoral lists of political parties.

The incumbent President of Armenia is SerzhSargsyan who was elected for a 5 year term through general, equal and direct elections which took place in February 2013. His mandates will expire in April 2018 and the new President of Armenia will be elected by the National Assembly for a 7 year term.

As soon as the new President of Armenia assumes office the Government comprised of the Prime Minister

---

① Average exchange rate in 2017: 1 USD = 482.63 AMD; 1 EUR = 546.15 AMD, 1 CNY = 71.52 AMD.

and the Ministers and exercising the executive power in Armenia shall submit its resignation and the new President shall immediately accept it.

The new Government shall be composed of the Prime Minister, Deputy Prime Ministers and Ministers provided that the number of Deputy Prime Ministers may not exceed 3, whereas that of the Ministers may not exceed 18. The new Prime Minister shall be elected by the National Assembly at the majority of votes of the total number of deputies. As soon as the new Prime Minister is elected, the President shall immediately appoint the former to the said position and the Government shall be formed within a period of 15 days following appointment of the Prime Minister from among the candidates proposed by the latter. The incumbent Prime Minister of Armenia is Karen Karapetyan.

b. Economic

After gaining independence in 1991, Armenia adopted a policy of liberal market economies and initiated a privatization program. Despite the recession suffered in 2008-2009, currently the Armenian economy is moving towards improvement. Furthermore Armenia rates higher than the world and regional averages in terms of Investment Freedom according to 2018 Index of Economic Freedom (the 44th freest) and Ease of Doing Business according to Doing Business 2018 (overall rank: 47). In 2016 Armenia recorded GDP in the amount of AMD 5,079.9 billion.

The main sectors of the economy undergoing rapid growth include mining, energy, including renewable energy, construction, IT, food processing and beverages, jewellery and diamond processing, as well as tourism and financial services. Armenia stands out for a number of advantages such as: inexpensive but highly skilled labour force (Human Development Index Rank 84), developing and rather liberal banking regulations, favourable investment legislation, existence of free economic zones, etc.

c. Social

In general, state social systems are fully accessible to foreigners having a residence status in Armenia for the whole period of validity of such status (e.g.state benefits system, state pension scheme, cumulative pension scheme, etc.).

According to the National Statistical Service of Armenia, the country's unemployment rate was equal to 18% in 2016. The average state monthly pension constituted AMD 40,397 for the same year.

d. Legal

The main national law of Armenia is the Constitution, adopted in 1995 and amended by the referendums in November 2005 and December 2015, which sets out basic rights and freedoms, as well as establishes guaranties and safeguards against their violation. The Constitution also specifies the tripartite system of government (the principle of separation and balance of the legislative, executive and judicial powers).

The other national legal acts should all be in consistency with the Constitution and constitutional laws (the concept of constitutional laws was introduced by the amendments to the Constitution made in December 2015 aimed at distinguishing certain laws which might be adopted at a higher threshold of votes as compared to laws, the list of the constitutional laws is specified by the given amendments to the Constitution). Even international treaties may be ratified only in case they are in compliance with the Constitution. Armenia is monist in its relationship with international law, thus the act of ratifying the international law immediately incorporates it into national law, which means that international law can be directly applied by a national judge, and can be directly invoked by citizens, just as if it were national law.

The judicial power is exercised by the three-level court system and by the Constitutional Court (only for matters of constitutional justice).

The court system in Armenia consists of the Courts of First Instance (Courts of General Instance and Administrative Court (it is anticipated to establish also a Bankruptcy court as a specialized court)), Courts of Appeal and the Court of Cassation. Courts of General Instance have jurisdiction over all civil and criminal cases and the Administrative Court - only over administrative cases (the Bankruptcy court will have jurisdiction over bankruptcy cases). Decisions from First Instance Courts may be appealed to the Courts of Appeal, and from there to the Court of Cassation. In case all judicial remedies are exhausted and a final court act is available, it is possible to file an application to the Constitutional Court challenging the constitutionality of a legal provision applied upon the court act.

Moreover, upon exhaustion of all domestic remedies (according to the generally recognized rules of international law), an application may be filed to the European Court of Human Rights within a period of 6 months from the date on which the final decision was taken, asserting that the state violates their rights under the Convention for the Protection of Human Rights and Fundamental Freedoms signed in Rome in 1950 (the abovementioned period for filing an application would be changed to 4 months, upon the entry into force of Protocol 15 amending the Convention).

B. The Status and Direction of the Cooperation with Chinese Enterprises Under the B&R

In November 2017 the opening ceremony of the office of cooperation of Armenia took place in Qingdao being financed by the Collaborative Innovation Centre of the B&R Initiative. The activities of the said office are aimed at promoting establishment of Armenian-Chinese business ties. In this connection respective agreements were entered into between the Chamber of Commerce and Industry of Armenia, the Union of Manufacturers and Businessmen (Employers) of Armenia, the Embassy of Armenia in China and the Collaborative Innovation Centre of the B&R Initiative.

According to the National Statistical Service of Armenia, the country's trade turnover with China in the first 11 months of 2017 was worth USD 548.3 million and continues recording intense growth year-over-year.

II. Investment

A. Market Access

a. Department Supervising Investment

In Armenia making foreign investments is actively encouraged by the Government. The latter follows the principle of "Open Doors" policy and is continuously liberalizing the entry of foreign direct investments into the Armenian economy.

Promotion of foreign investments to Armenia is mainly carried out by the Ministry of Economic Development and Investments and by the Development Foundation of Armenia.

b. Laws and Regulations of Investment Industry

The field of foreign investments is regulated mainly by the Law "On Foreign Investments" adopted as of July 31, 1994, which provides the types and forms of foreign investments, guarantees securing protection of foreign investments and additional privileges to foreign owned entities (applicable in case if foreign investment in the capital fund is no less than 30% at the moment of establishment), as well as procedure for settlement of any dispute arisen in connection with foreign investments.

Any of the following objects of civil circulation might be invested in Armenia by "foreign investors", i.e.by any foreign state, entity, national, person having no citizenship, Armenian citizen permanently residing outside of Armenia, as well as any international organisation eligible to make investments according to the applicable personal law:

(i) currency values, including foreign currencies, Armenian dram;

(ii) movable or immovable property or any property right, including buildings, constructions, equipment, other tangible assets, etc.;

(iii) shares, bonds, other types of securities;

(iv) rights to monetary claims or claims for performance of liabilities having contractual value;

(v) intellectual property rights;

(vi) right to conduct certain economic activity on the basis of the Armenian legislation or a contract, including the right to explore natural resources, mining rights, etc.;

(vii) services;

(viii) any other object not prohibited by the Armenian legislation.

c. Forms of Investment

Foreigners are suggested various methods of investments to be made in the Armenia, including:

(i) foundation of commercial legal entities with 100% foreign capital, or of subdivisions, or acquisition of all shares of an existing Armenian company;

(ii) creation of joint ventures with participation of Armenian entities, or partial acquisition of shares of an existing Armenian company;

(iii) acquisition of bonds and other securities;

(iv) acquisition of other property rights;

(v) other forms of investment not prohibited by the Armenian legislation, based on agreements with Armenian entities.

d. Standards of Market Access and Examination

Making investment does not require any preliminary authorization. In general, no specific restrictions are applicable to foreign investors. Certain restrictions are only envisaged in terms of land ownership by foreigners which will be disclosed under the section D. "Land Policy" below.

Meanwhile, in practice foreign companies encounter certain problems when carrying out activities subject to licensing requirements in Armenia through a local branch. Particularly, state authorities refuse granting licenses to local branches of foreign companies and suggest establishing a local company for the purposes of performance of relevant activities subject to licensing requirements and obtainment of respective license.

B. Foreign Exchange Regulation

a. Department Supervising Foreign Exchange

Control over compliance with the foreign exchange regulations by entities / persons not being licensed by the Central Bank of Armenia or the Ministry of Finances is mainly being exercised by the Armenian tax authorities.

b. Brief Introduction of Laws and Regulations of Foreign Exchange

Transactions in foreign currency, conditions of their execution, order for use and disposal of currency values are regulated by the Law "On Currency Regulations and Currency Control" adopted as of November 24, 2004. Sanctions for breach of foreign exchange regulations are foreseen by the said law (for entities / persons being licensed by the Central Bank of Armenia or the Ministry of Finances), as well as by the Code on Administrative Offences (for other entities / persons).

According to the general principle envisaged under the said law, sale of goods (inventory), rendering services and labour remuneration in the territory of Armenia shall be denominated in the Armenian currency, save for certain exceptions specified by the same law.

There are no conversion restrictions between Armenian and foreign currencies, and foreign currency accounts may be maintained in Armenian banks. Both residents and non-residents as defined by the abovementioned law have a right to purchase / sell foreign currency without limitations on immediate or inferred payment terms, assuming a right or an obligation to repurchase or convert to other currencies at a certain price in a certain period or on any other terms. Foreign currency purchase / sale transactions are performed through specialised entities. Specialised entities shall determine the exchange rate and volumes of foreign currency purchase / sale transactions performed by them with account of the Armenian dram / foreign currency average exchange rate being officially set by the Central Bank of Armenia.

c. Requirements of Foreign Exchange Management for Foreign Enterprises

In the meaning of the Law "On Currency Regulations and Currency Control" foreign organizations, their branches and representation offices, including those established in Armenia, foreign consulates and embassies in Armenia, as well as physical persons who has not been residing in Armenia for a total duration of 183 days or more during any 12 month period starting or ending in a year (from January 1 to December 31 inclusive) or whose centre of vital interests is not in Armenia are considered as non-residents.

As an exception to the general rule specified by the said law it is established that should a transaction envisaging wire transfer as a payment mode be executed in writing between a resident legal entity or individual entrepreneur and a non-resident legal entity or individual entrepreneur, the denomination of prices might be made in foreign currency. In addition, in those cases payments between the parties to such transaction might be also made in foreign currency.

C. Financing

a. Main Financial Institutions

Armenia's banking system has recently shifted to Basel III standards. Currently, the Armenian banking market includes 17 commercial banks, including several banks established by foreign esteemed banks, with 531 branch offices in Armenia and Nagorno-Karabakh Republic.

Control over financial institutions, including banks, is exercised by the Central Bank of Armenia. The principal mission of the Central Bank of Armenia is to maintain price stability, and since 2006 it has exercised an inflation targeting strategy that influences domestic interest rates as an operational goal. Additionally, it addresses the forecasted level of inflation as an intermediate goal. The Central Bank of Armenia also monitors trends in the financial markets, evaluates risk and measures the impact of developments in the financial system.

In the summer of 2005, a bank deposit guarantee fund was created, which currently guarantees bank deposits for an amount of AMD 10 million for deposits made in drams and AMD 5 million for deposits made in foreign currency.

b. Financing Conditions for Foreign Enterprises

There are no certain restrictions impeding foreign entities, including those having no permanent presence in

Armenia, to open and operate bank accounts with an Armenian bank or obtain financing there from provided that all documents required by the internal regulations of the respective bank, including those required under the money laundering regulations and those disclosing the actual beneficiaries of the given foreign entity are duly submitted, as well as necessary collaterals are provided for securing relevant facility arrangements.

D. Land Policy

a. Brief Introduction of Land-Related Laws and Regulations

Land issues are mainly regulated by the Land Code and Civil Code, as well as by the Constitution. The latter establishes the main principle / restriction according to which foreigners and stateless persons (apatrides) are not entitled to ownership right towards land, save for the case specified by the law. Particularly, the Land Code specifies that this restriction does not apply to those individuals having been granted special residence status in Armenia, as well as over lands for private housing, construction of public and production objects, multi-apartment buildings, etc. In case an ownership right to land passes to a foreigner or stateless person on a lawful basis, the latter shall alienate it within 1-year period. In case the respective land plot is not alienated within the said period, it shall be alienated in an enforcement procedure on the basis of a court decision in accordance with the Civil Code.

The Land Code also establishes the categories of lands which might not ever become the ownership of a physical person or a legal entity irrespective of the fact whether it is a local or foreign legal entity (e.g.state forests, parks, mine sites, etc.).

b. Rules of Land Acquisition for Foreign Enterprises

There are no specific rules regulating acquisition of land by foreign entities. The rules are same for all type of entities. Under the Land Code state and community lands might be alienated for use with the purposes not prohibited by law. In general, state lands are being alienated either at public auction or in limited cases through direct sale, gratuitous assignment or under barter arrangements.

E. The Establishment and Dissolution of Companies

a. The Forms of Enterprises

Commercial legal entities may be established in the form of joint stock companies, limited liability companies, supplementary liability companies, general partnerships or limited partnerships, commercial cooperatives. Most frequently used types of legal entities are: a limited liability company and a joint stock company.

The founding (governing) document of a legal entity is its charter. The charter determines the size of the entity's statutory capital, the composition and competencies of the governing bodies and the rules for decision-making, the rights and obligations of the participants / shareholders / partners, the rules for exit and the transfer of shares of a participant / shareholder / partner to another person.

It is also widely applicable to register a subdivision (either a branch, or a representation office) rather than a separate legal entity. Particularly, this form is frequently chosen by foreigners. It should be noted that a subdivision is deprived of any separate legal capacity and acts only in accordance with the powers delegated by its founder. The sole difference between a representation office and a branch is that the former is only entitled to represent and defend the interests of its founder, while a branch can implement all those functions, which the founder can perform, on top of that, it can perform all functions of a representation office.

According to the legislative changes made in 2016 the process of re-domiciliation was introduced and currently foreign legal entities wishing to transfer their domicile to Armenia are able to do so without winding-up their legal entity. The same opportunity is also introduced for local legal entities wishing to be "re-domiciliated" abroad.

a) Limited Liability Companies

A limited liability company is an economic entity, the charter capital of which is divided into shares the number of which is determined by its charter. The participants of the company are not liable for the obligations of the company and within the values of their contributions shall bear responsibility for the risks of losses related to the activity of the company. The number of the participants of a limited liability company may not exceed 49.

A limited liability company may be founded by a physical or a legal entity. It should be noted that a limited liability company may not act as a sole founder / shareholder of another business entity.

There is no mandatory minimum charter capital requirement for a limited liability company, except for cases when the law envisages minimum capital requirements for certain types of activity. Contributions to the charter capital may be in the form of money, securities, other property or rights estimable in money. In case contributions consist of non-monetary assets and the nominal value of the shares for which the contributions are made does not exceed AMD 500,000, they should be estimated by the meeting of the founders / participants. Otherwise, the contributions in the form of non-monetary assets should be estimated by an independent appraiser.

The contributions should be totally made within the term (no longer than 1 year upon the registration of the company) agreed by the founding agreement of the limited liability company.

The shares register of a limited liability company is kept by the State Register Agency of Legal Entities and is available for public.

A limited liability company should have at least the following governing bodies:

(i) the General Meeting of the participants (supreme governing body) consisted of the participants of the limited liability company, each of which has votes proportionally to its interest in the company charter capital;

(ii) the Head of executive body responsible for managing the day-to-day activities of the limited liability company and representing the latter against third persons.

In case the number of participants of a limited liability company exceeds 20, a Supervisory Board should also be established or a Supervisor shall be nominated. Establishment of an additional governing body (e.g. Board) may be envisaged by the charter of the limited liability company.

The key points pertaining to a limited liability company are as follows:

(i) participants of a limited liability company may transfer their shares in the company's capital to third parties (non-participants) only if the other participants do not exercise their priority right to purchase at the price at which the shares will be sold to third parties.

(ii) a participant may withdraw from a limited liability company at any time. Upon withdrawal, the limited liability company is required within 6 months to repay the value of the participant's share.

(iii) a participant in a limited liability company may be removed by judicial procedure upon the request of another participant/s holding at least 10% of the shares, if the participant's activity or inactivity makes the usual activities of the limited liability company difficult or impossible. The limited liability company would be required within 6 months to repay the value of the excluded participant's share.

(iv) a participant's personal creditors may seize the participant's share in a limited liability company to settle obligations upon a court decision, if the participant's other property is insufficient to satisfy the creditors' claims.

b) Joint Stock Companies

A joint stock company is a legal entity, the charter capital of which is distributed into a certain number of shares. The liability of shareholders in a joint stock company is limited to the value of their capital contribution. There are two types of joint stock companies: joint stock companies of open type and joint stock companies of closed type. An open joint stock company may, without restrictions, issue shares and sell them to public. Every shareholder has the right to sell shares without consent of the other shareholders. In closed joint stock companies, shares are distributed only among its shareholders (including founders) or pre-decided persons, and the number of shareholders is restrained (maximum envisaged by the law: 49 shareholders). Moreover, existing shareholders in a closed joint stock company also have pre-emptive purchase rights for shares offered for sale by the other shareholders.

The legal framework for joint stock companies is mostly similar to that applied for limited liability companies. As is the case with a limited liability company, there is no mandatory minimum charter capital requirement for a joint stock company. The shares may be paid for by means of property, including money, securities and property rights, and intellectual property. In case the shares are paid for by means of non-monetary assets upon the establishment of a joint stock company, the order for their estimation should be agreed between the founders. In case non-monetary assets are contributed for additional shares, they should be estimated by an independent appraiser in the manner specified by the Board's decision (in case no Board has been created by the charter of the joint stock company, settlement of this issue shall fall within the competence of the General Meeting of the shareholders) of the joint stock company.

Unlike the limited liability companies, the shares register of a joint stock company is kept by a specialized register keeping organization. Moreover, a joint stock company may issue and allocate shares granting different rights to their owners. Particularly, privileged shares may be issued, the total nominal value of which may not exceed 25% of the charter capital of the joint stock company. In general, the holders of privileged shares do not have voting rights at the General Meeting of the shareholders. But at the same time claims of privileged shareholders are satisfied in priority to those of ordinary shareholders.

The governing bodies of a joint stock company are:

(i) the General Meeting of the shareholders (supreme governing body) consisted of the shareholders of the joint stock company, each of whom has votes proportionally to its interest in the company capital, except privileged shareholders;

(ii) the executive body, either a CEO (director, general director), or a CEO and a collegial executive body (Executive Board, Management Board), responsible for managing the day-to-day activities of the joint stock company;

(iii) the Supervisor or the Supervisory Board responsible for exercising control over the financial activities of the joint stock company.

In case the number of shareholders of a joint stock company exceeds 49, a Board consisting of at least 3 members should also be established. Persons who are neither shareholders of the joint stock company nor their representatives may also be elected as members of the Board, unless otherwise specified by the charter of the joint stock company.

Unlike the legal framework of limited liability companies, the legal framework of joint stock companies defines in details the cases when the owner of a voting share may exercise its right for a put option and the joint stock company is obliged to buy the shares for which a put option is exercised. Particularly, this refers to cases when an important decision affecting shareholder's rights was adopted and if the latter voted against such decision or did not participate in the vote.

b. The Procedure of Establishment

Business entities, including subdivisions, are registered with a unified register kept by the State Register Agency of Legal Entities. Upon the registration the given entity is deemed automatically recorded with the tax body and is awarded a Taxpayer Identification Number.

The incorporation of a business entity takes in general 2 working days once the correct documents are filed.

The creation of a business entity consists of two stages:

(i) elaboration and collection of documents envisaged by the law;

(ii) submission of documents to the State Register Agency of Legal Entities required for state registration.

It should be noted that the registration of a legal entity is free of charge. No state duty is imposed. For registration of a legal entity, the following documents should be submitted to the registration authority:

(i) the application of the founder/s or the head of the executive body or the authorized person of the founder/s of the legal entity;

(ii) the decision on the creation of the legal entity or the minutes of the constituent assembly of the legal entity (if the latter is founded by more than one person (in case one of the founders of the legal entity is another legal entity, the decision of the authorized body of the latter should be also submitted));

(iii) the copies of the charter of the legal entity (at least two copies, for each additional copy a duty shall be paid in the amount of AMD 2,000) approved by the founder or constituent assembly;

(iv) the passport details and the social services number (or the number of attestation on absence thereof) of the head of the executive body (a copy of his/her passport, and in the case of a foreigner-a translated and certified copy of the passport), as well as the e-mail address of the latter;

(v) statement about actual beneficiaries.

If the founder or one of the founders is a foreign legal entity, then notarized translations into Armenian of the following documents should be also submitted:

(i) extract from the commercial registry of the country of origin of the founder;

(ii) founding documents of the foreign legal entity, for instance, the charter of the latter or other equivalent documents.

These documents should contain the following information on:

(i) the legal status and organizational form of the founder;

(ii) the registration date in the country of residence;

(iii) the juridical name of the founder;

(iv) the place of residence of the founder;

(v) the competences of the managing bodies of the founder, including of the body competent to make decisions on the foundation of another legal entity.

In case the founder or one of the founders is a foreign physical entity, the notarized translation of his/her passport shall be submitted together with the generally required documents.

The registration procedure can be carried out electronically. Unlike the registration of a legal entity, for the registration of a subdivision of a commercial legal entity there is a state duty in the amount of AMD 12,000. For registration of a subdivision, the following documents should be submitted to the registration authority:

(i) the application of the head of the executive body of the founder or the authorized person of the founder or the head of the subdivision containing the name of the founder and its state registration number, details of the head of the subdivision (passport details and the social services number (or the number of attestation on absence thereof), residence address, contact details), as well as the e-mail address of the latter;

(ii) the decision on the establishment of the subdivision and approval of its charter, as well as on the nomination of the head of the subdivision;
(iii) the copies of the charter of the subdivision;
(iv) the document proving the payment of the state duty.

If the founder is a foreign legal entity, then the notarized translations into Armenian of the abovementioned documents (including the extract from the commercial registry and its founding documents) should also be submitted.

For re-domiciliation purposes the foreign legal entity shall undergo the following registration processes:
(i) preliminary registration of re-domiciliation;
(ii) final registration of re-domiciliation.

In connection with the first process the given foreign legal entity shall submit:
• the application on preliminary registration containing information on its current name and the new name under which the given foreign legal entity wishes to operate in future, as well as on the main types of its activity, jurisdiction where the given legal entity is registered and on the legal form corresponding to the legal form valid in such jurisdiction; the decision of the competent body of the given foreign legal entity or respective minutes or excerpt thereof containing provisions on the re-domiciliation of the given legal entity to Armenia, on the legal form and name chosen in accordance with the local legislation, as well as on approval of its new charter;
• the extract from the commercial registry on the given foreign legal entity and its founding documents;
• the data on the head of the executive body of the given foreign legal entity (passport, contact details, as well as the e-mail address of the former);
• the document proving the payment of the state duty which is equal to AMD 10,000;
• the copies of the charter approved in conformity with the local legislation;
• the data on shareholders of the given foreign legal entity: in case of a shareholder being a local legal entity the name and state registration number are requested; in case of a shareholder being a physical person or a foreign legal entity (requested if the shares register is to be kept by the registration authority)– either the copy of his / her passport or the extract from the commercial registry on such foreign shareholder and its founding documents;
• the copy of the charter of the given foreign legal entity valid before re-domiciliation.

In case any of the documents mentioned above are drawn up solely in a foreign language, they should be accompanied with their notarized translations into Armenian. The same rule applies also to the documents to be submitted for final registration.

In case the abovementioned documents are duly submitted and there is no legal basis for rejection of the application, a record on preliminary registration of the foreign legal entity subject to re-domiciliation is made. Such record shall be made within 3 days in case of foreign business legal entities.

For the final registration the given foreign legal entity shall submit:
• the application;
• the document proving the registration of the data on re-domiciliation or termination of activities of the given foreign legal entity in the respective foreign jurisdiction;
• the declaration of the competent body of the given foreign legal entity on non-performance of any transaction during the period starting from the date of receipt of the document proving the preliminary registration of re-domiciliation up to final registration date (in case such declaration is submitted, the date of preliminary registration shall be deemed as the final registration date).

c. Routes and Requirements of Dissolution

A legal entity may be dissolved:
(i) upon the decision of its founders / participants or upon the decision of the competent body entrusted with the authority to adopt such decisions in accordance with its charter, including in cases when the term of activities of the given legal entity has expires or the goal of its establishment has been achieved;
(ii) by the court in case of invalidating the registration of the given legal entity due to the breaches committed during the registration;
(iii) upon the court decision for multiple or serious breaches of the legislative requirements, as well as in cases specified by the Civil Code.

For example, if upon the results of the second or each next financial year the value of net assets of a limited liability company or a joint stock company is a negative or is lower than the minimum charter amount specified by the law, the given legal entity is subject to liquidation.

In case the property of a legal entity is insufficient for covering all the claims of creditors, the legal entity might be liquidated only through bankruptcy procedure. The bankruptcy of legal entities, save for banks, credit organizations, insurance companies, investment companies, managers of investment funds, is regulated by the Law "On Bankruptcy" adopted as of December 25, 2006.

F. Merger and Acquisition

Merger and acquisition (accession) of a company are the forms of reorganization of a companion in Armenia (the other forms are division, spin-off and transformation). In case of the merger of legal entities, the rights and duties of each of them shall pass to the newly arising legal entity in accordance with the transfer documents.In case of merger of a JSC, merging companies sign an agreement on merger. A decision on reorganization in the form of merger shall be adopted by the General meetings (GM) of each of the merging companies, which will also approve the merger agreement, the transfer act, the procedure and terms of merger, as well as the procedure of converting the shares and other securities of each of the merging companies into shares and / or other securities of the newly created company. The joint GM of Shareholders of the merging companies shall be deemed the Founding Meeting of newly created company, which will be assembled by the body and in the timeframe mentioned in the merger agreement, and will adopt decisions on the matters which are subject to founding decision.

In case of acquisition (accession) of a legal entity by another legal entity, the rights and duties of the acceding legal entity shall move to the latter in accordance with the transfer document. In case of acquisition of a JSC, the companies participating in the acquisition sign an acquisition agreement. A decision on reorganization in the form of acquisition shall be adopted by the GMs of each of the merging company, which will also approve the acquisition agreement, the transfer act, the procedure and terms of acquisition, as well as the procedure of converting the shares and other securities of each of the acquired companies into shares and / or other securities of the acquiring company. The joint General Meeting of Shareholders of the companies involved in the merger or acquisition shall adopt decisions on making necessary amendments and modifications to the Charter of the acquiring company, approving the acquisition agreement and transfer act, and if necessary, on other issues, as well.

In case of reorganization of a legal entity in the form of merger, a legal entity shall be considered reorganized, from the time of state registration of the newly arising legal entities.

In case of reorganization of a legal entity in the form of accession of another legal entity to it, the first of them shall be considered reorganized from the time of making in the single state register of legal entities of an entry on the termination of activity of the joining legal entity.

While merger or accession a company shall set forth the transfer document which shall contain provisions on legal succession for all obligations of the reorganized legal entity with respect to all its creditors and debtors, including also obligations contested by the parties. The transfer document shall be approved by participants / shareholders of the legal entity or by the body of the legal entity empowered thereto by the Articles of Association that has taken the decision to reorganize the legal entity and must be presented together with the Article of association for state registration of the newly arising legal entities or for entering changes in the charters of existing legal entities. Failure to present the corresponding transfer document together with the Articles of Association, and also the absence in them of provisions on legal succession to the obligations of the reorganized legal entity or provision on distribution of assets and obligation proportionally shall entail a refusal of state registrations concerning reorganization.

The creditors of a company shall be notified about its reorganization of the company (the law is enshrined the term of notification for JSC: within 30 days since making decision on reorganizations) and afterwards will be entitled to demand on provision of additional warranties on fulfilment of obligations of a legal entity or termination or early performance of legal obligations for which the reorganized legal entity is a debtor and compensation for damages. In case of merger or accession of the JSC, the creditors to be entitled to the mentioned demands within 30 days after receipt of the notification.

G. Competition Regulation

a. Department Supervising Competition Regulation

The competition authority is the State Commission for the Protection of Economic Competition. Its website (www.competition.am) gives guidance on the competition law rules, including:

(i) When a concentration must be declared.

(ii) Forms for the reports to be submitted by entities who hold dominant or monopoly positions.

b.Brief Introduction of Competition Law

The Law on the Protection of Economic Competition prohibits restrictive agreements and practices. The law defines restrictive agreements and practices as those that indirectly result or might result in the restriction,

prevention or prohibition of competition, including:
(i) Contracts and agreements between economic entities.
(ii) Direct or indirect joint actions or behaviour.
(iii) Concerted practices.
(iv) Decisions made by unions of economic entities.
Restrictive agreements and practices relate to the following, among other things:
(i) Distribution or division of markets or supply sources.
(ii) Setting unfair prices.
(iii) Restricting other economic entities from entering the market .

The Law on the Protection of Economic Competition prohibits the abuse of dominant or monopoly position, unfair competition, illegal State support, sets the cases of concentration which shall be declared to the Commission.

(i) Economic entities must declare the concentration before putting it into action if:
(ii) At least one of the parties of concentration holds dominant position in any market.

There is a horizontal concentration where, based on the results of previous financial year preceding the concentration, either:

(i) the total assets of the parties to the concentration equal AMD1 billion and 500 million or more [and] the total assets of one of the parties equal AMD1 billion or more;

(ii) the total gross income of the parties of the concentration equals AMD3 billion or more [and] the gross income of one of the parties equals AMD 2 billion or more;

Thresholds are also set for vertical and mixed concentrations.

c. Measures Regulating Competition

There are various sanctions provided for in the Competition Law, dealing with non-compliance of specific regulations of the Law, including fines, sanctions, rulings to restrict unfair competition or dissolving transactions concluded in breach of Law and other measures (including initiation of criminal proceedings). For example, the abuse of dominant position can be fined by the amount from AMD 5 million to AMD 200 million.

H. Tax

a. Tax Regime and Rules

Fiscal relations in Armenia are currently regulated by a unified Tax Code adopted by the National Assembly in October 2016.

Presently, state taxes include profit tax, income tax, excise tax, value added tax (VAT), nature protection tax, road tax, turnover tax and patent tax.

As regards local taxes, they include property tax and land tax which will be replaced by real estate tax and vehicle tax starting from January 01, 2019.

Control over the procedure for calculation and payment of state taxes is carried out by tax authorities and, in certain cases as specified by the law, by customs authorities. Concurrently, the authority to exercise control over the calculation of local taxes and their collection is vested with local self-governing authorities.

The Tax Code specifies a general taxation regime and 3 special taxation regimes (turnover tax regime, patent tax regime and family entrepreneurship regime). As a general rule, under the general taxation regime entities, individual entrepreneurs and notaries are subject to VAT and / or profit tax. In case of application of turnover tax or patent tax regime respective taxpayers are subject to turnover tax or patent tax respectively which substitute VAT and / or profit tax. In case of application of family entrepreneurship regime respective taxpayers are exempt from VAT and / or profit tax, as well as from turnover tax, save for patent tax for certain activities.

b. Main Categories and Rates of Tax, Tax Declaration and Preference

a) Profit Tax

Profit tax is to be paid both by residents, i.e. organisations, individual entrepreneurs registered in Armenia, notaries and contractual funds, except for the pension funds, and non-residents, i.e. international organisations, other organizations established abroad, non-resident physical persons implementing activities in Armenia or generating incomes from Armenian sources through a permanent establishment.

Residents are taxed on the profit gained in the territory of Armenia and outside; while non-residents are taxed solely on profit gained from Armenian sources.

The annual profit tax rate applicable to residents, as well as to non-residents implementing activities in Armenia through a permanent establishment, is 20%. The profit tax is calculated on the basis of the taxable profit, which corresponds to gross income, deducting the amounts specified by the law (expenses required for conducting activities and justified by corresponding documents, depreciation allowances, etc.).

For the incomes payable to non-residents not having a permanent establishment in Armenia the amount of the profit tax shall be withheld at the source at the following rates and paid to the state budget by a tax agent:

(i) insurance compensation, reinsurance payments and income received from the freight-5%;

(ii) passive incomes, including dividends, save for dividends received from the Panarmenian Bank, interests, royalties, income from the lease of property, increase in the value (capital gain) of property, save for securities-10%;

(iii) dividends received from the Panarmenian Bank-0%;

(iv) capital gain arisen as a result of alienation of securities-0%;

(v) other incomes-20%.

A taxpayer must submit to the tax authorities its profit tax calculations for the respective tax year no later than April 20 of the following year, and the tax must be paid before April 25 of the following year.

As a general rule, the residents and non-residents implementing activities in Armenia through a permanent establishment shall make advance payments quarterly (no later than on the 20th of the last month of the respective quarter), at 20% of the actual amount of the profit tax for the previous year, unless the respective taxpayer has applied for an alternative option. Particularly, a taxpayer may chose this option provided that respective application is submitted to the tax authorities till March 20 of the current year. In case the alternative option is chosen, the taxpayer shall quarterly (no later than on the 20th of the last month of the respective quarter) make advance payments at 2% of the total amount of incomes received from supply of goods, provision/ performance of services / works during the previous quarter.

b) Income Tax

In Armenia both resident and non-resident physical persons, including citizens of Armenia and foreign citizens, are entitled to pay income tax. Individual entrepreneurs and notaries shall pay income tax only in respect of those incomes which are considered as personal in the light of the Tax Code. An individual shall be considered a resident if during respective tax year (from January 1 to December 31 inclusive) he / she has been residing in Armenia for a total duration of 183 days or more, or whose centre of vital interests is in Armenia.

For a resident the taxable income received within or outside the territory of Armenia is considered to be the object of taxation. For a non-resident the taxable income received only from Armenian sources is considered to be the object of taxation, save for incomes received through a permanent establishment in Armenia and incomes received as a result of external economic activities.

As a general rule, when incomes are payable to physical persons by a tax agent, the latter shall be obliged to calculate and withhold the amount of the income.

Different income tax rates are imposed by the law depending on the type of income payable, status of the taxpayer within the framework of the activities aimed at gaining respective income, as well as his / her citizenship.

Unless otherwise specified below in terms of certain income type, the following rates shall be applied depending on the fact whether monthly or annual tax rates are applicable:

MonthlyTaxable Income Amount	Tax Amount
Up to AMD 150,000	23% of taxable income
AMD 150,000 – 2,000,000	AMD 34,500 plus 28% of the amount exceeding AMD 150,000
Over AMD 2,000,000	AMD 552,500 plus 36% of the amount exceeding AMD 2,000,000

Amount of Annual Taxable Income	Tax Amount
Up to AMD 1,800,000	23% of taxable income
AMD 1,800,000 – 24,000,000	AMD 414,000 plus 28% of the amount exceeding AMD 1,800,000
Over AMD 24,000,000	AMD 6,630,000 plus 36% of the amount exceeding AMD 24,000,000

As an exception to the general rule, income tax on royalties and interest income, as well as on income gained from acquisition of property shall be calculated at the rate of 10%.

It should be noted that before the adoption of the Tax Code dividends were considered as incomes subject to deduction from the taxable object. However, in accordance with the provisions of the Tax Code the dividends received by foreigners are taxable at the rate of 10% and the dividends received by Armenian nationals - at the rate of 5%.

For tax agents the reporting period in terms of income tax is a calendar month. Till the 20th of each month the tax agent should present to the tax authority relevant calculation of income tax for the previous month. The amount of income tax included in the relevant calculation should be paid by the tax agent within the same period.

Concurrently, the incomes taxable on annual basis shall be declared by the taxpayer till April 20 of the following year by submitting an annual calculation exclusively in electronic format. The amount of the income tax payable in accordance with the presented calculation shall be paid to the state budget within the same period.

c) Value Added Tax (VAT)

VAT is a type of indirect tax, which is imposed on certain transactions and operations, i.e. supply of goods, provision of services (including lease of property, provision of loan, transfer of intangibles) and import of goods under "release for domestic consumption" customs procedure, as well as import of goods from member states of the Eurasian Economic Union.

As a general rule, organizations, individual entrepreneurs and notaries are considered as VAT payers in case they are not eligible for opting turnover tax regime or in case they have failed to submit respective declaration for being considered as turnover taxpayer or for application of family entrepreneurship regime.

As regards non-commercial organizations and producers of agriculture products they shall be considered as VAT payers in case the turnover of transactions taxable with VAT exceeded the threshold of AMD 58.35 million during the previous year or upon exceeding the given threshold during the reporting year or upon submitting a written declaration to the tax authorities for obtaining such status.

It should be noted that in case non-residents not having permanent establishment in Armenia carry out transactions taxable with VAT on the territory of Armenia their resident counterparties being VAT payers shall bear VAT liability on their behalf.

The rate of VAT is determined at 20% of taxable turnover of goods and services. The amount of VAT within the amount of the total indemnity for the goods and services (including 20% rate) shall be determined at the rate of 16.67 %. The exported goods and services are subject to VAT at the rate of 0%.

The Armenian fiscal legislation specifies the input-output model. A VAT payer accounts for output VAT after deducting VAT paid for the goods or services received (input VAT).

The reporting period is a calendar month. VAT payers are required to submit a unified calculation of VAT and excise tax for each reporting period. Those unified calculations must be filed and VAT amounts shall be paid within 20 days after the expiry of the reporting period.

d) Excise Tax

Excise tax shall be paid by individual entrepreneurs and legal entities importing (under "release for domestic consumption" customs procedure or from member states of the Eurasian Economic Union) or producing (bottling or otherwise packaging) and alienating goods subject to excise tax in Armenia or supplying compressed natural gas at NGV-refuelling compressor station.

The following goods shall be subject to excise tax: beer, grape wines and other wines, spirits (except cognac spirit), alcoholic drinks, cigarettes (including tobacco industrial substitutes, cigars, cigarillos), lubricants, gasoline and diesel fuel, raw oil and oil materials, oil gas, pressurized natural gas and other hydro-carbons (except natural gas not being considered as pressurized).

The taxable base of the excise tax is either the price / customs value (in case of goods imported from member states of the Eurasian Economic Union–goods purchase price) of the abovementioned products or their quantity / volume expressed in physical units or the maximum retail price labelled on the package.

It should be noted that some products taxable with excise tax are subject to labelling, the list of which is specified by the Tax Code.

The amounts of the excise tax shall be calculated per each month and paid till the 20th of the following month. The calculated amount shall be reported to the tax authorities per each quarter till the 20th of the following month.

Export of goods taxable by excise tax under "export" customs procedure, as well as their export to other member states of the Eurasian Economic Union are exempt from excise tax.

e) Property Tax

Property tax is a direct tax on the property considered as a taxable object and does not depend on the outcomes of the taxpayers' economic activity.

The property tax shall be paid by the organizations set up in Armenia or in other countries, international organizations and those created by them outside Armenia, citizens of Armenia, foreign citizens, as well as those without citizenship who have ownership right to a property in Armenia. It should be noted that absence of formal registration of ownership right to buildings under construction or to unauthorized buildings / constructions may not serve as a basis for exemption from property tax.

Buildings, constructions of residential use (apartments, villas, etc.), of public or production use, including unfinished buildings and buildings under construction, garages, motor vehicles, including motor cars, watercrafts, snowmobiles, four-wheelers and motorcycles are considered as taxable objects.

The taxable base for buildings and constructions is their cadastral value and for motor vehicles—engine power. Property tax is calculated on annual basis at certain rates.

The reporting period in terms of property tax payable by physical persons is the calendar year. The law specifies the principle of voluntariness for submission of property tax returns by physical persons (deadline— October 01 of the reporting year). Concurrently, it is worth noting that the local authorities are obliged to send notifications to physical persons on the amount of their tax liabilities. The annual amount of the property tax shall be paid by physical persons till December 01 of the reporting year.

The reporting period in terms of property tax payable by organizations is the half-year period. The relevant returns shall be submitted till 20th of the month following the respective half-year period. The amount of the property tax shall be paid by organizations in the same timeline.

f) Land Tax

Landowners, permanent users of the state-owned land (physical persons, organizations) are considered payers of land tax. In case of land lease the amount of the land tax shall be paid by the lessor. The amount of the land tax shall not depend on the results of the taxpayer's economic activity and is defined as an annually paid fixed payment per unit of the land lot area.

The calculated net income determined by the cadastral evaluation of the land shall be the taxable base for agricultural lands. The cadastral value of the land shall be the taxable base for non-agricultural lands.

The reporting period in terms of land tax payable by physical persons is the calendar year. The local authorities are obliged to send notifications to physical persons on the amount of their tax liabilities. The annual amount of the land tax shall be paid by physical persons in two equal instalments: the 1st instalment should be paid till November 15 of the reporting period, and the 2nd instalment—till April 15 of the following year.

The reporting period in terms of land tax payable by organizations is the half-year period. The relevant returns shall be submitted till 20th of the month following the respective half-year period. The amount of the land tax shall be paid by organizations in the same timeline.

I. Securities

a. Brief Introduction of Securities-Related Laws and Regulations

Currently, this sector is regulated by the Law "On Securities Market" adopted as of October 11, 2007. The main objectives of the said law is the protection of the rights and lawful interests of investors, ensuring the transparency and sustainable and efficient development of the securities market and reliability of securities price formation system, as well as mitigation of system risks in the securities market. The abovementioned law mainly regulates public offering and public sale of securities, provision of investment services in the securities market, public trade and custody of securities, etc. The given law also establishes rules on derivatives, mainly in respect of derivatives permitted to trade in the regulated market.

Issues not being regulated by the said law are mainly established by the acts adopted by the Central Bank of Armenia.

b. Supervision and Regulation of Securities Market

NASDAQ OMX Armenia is the sole regulated market operator in Armenia and the Central Depositary of Armenia is the sole operator of the clearing and settlement system of securities. The overall control over the securities market is exercised by the Central Bank of Armenia.

c. Requirements for Engagement in Securities Trading for Foreign Enterprises

The rules of NASDAQ OMX Armenia both for listing of securities and admission to trading do not contain any specific requirements in case when the issuer of respective securities is a foreign entity. The procedure of admission to trading is generally applicable in case when the respective issuer of securities is not yet eligible for listing. In such case the respective issuer might apply for its shares or bonds to be admitted to trading in C and Cbond free markets.

There are no specific requirements to be met by the issuer for its shares to be admitted to trading in C free market. Meanwhile, for being admitted to trading in Cbond free market the volume of the issue shall be at least AMD 100 million.

J. Preference and Protection of Investment

a. The Structure of Preference Policies

The principle underlying the preferences granted to investors is that the legal regime applicable to foreign investments in Armenia cannot be less preferential than the one applicable to the local investments. This principle is enshrined in the RA Law on Foreign Investments of 1994. The Law, on the other hand, proscribes additional incentives for foreign investors, such as protection from legislative changes during 5 years after the investment, protection from expropriation of their investment, etc.

b. Support for Specific Industries and Regions

Armenian legislation prescribes special preferences for investors working in certain industries and regions.

The sectors that are covered by incentives concerning taxation and/or payment of custom duties are IT startups, construction and installation, agricultural production, medical services, production of handmade carpets and sectors declared as prioritized by the Government. Special tax and customs incentives are granted to the investors working in the frontier regions of Armenia.

Some of the incentives apply automatically and the investor pays taxes with deductions. However, certain incentives require an application procedure which are regulated by government decrees.

c. Special Economic Areas

Armenian legislation provides a possibility of creation of two types of special economic zones with different regimes: free economic zones and industrial zones. The specificity of the second one is that the incentives applicable in the industrial zone are regulated for each zone separately. The governmental decree on creation of the industrial zone also provides with incentives which will be applicable in that specific zone. Currently, there are no industrial zones in Armenia.

There are currently three Free Economic Zones (FEZ) in Armenia: Alliance FEZ, Meridian FEZ and Meghri FEZ. The latter has been established at the end of 2017 and is in the process of infrastructural finalization.

d. Investment Protection

The major national legal act on protection of foreign investments is the RA Law on Foreign Investments of 1994. However, Armenia is also signatory to multiple bilateral investment protection treaties and is party to 1965 Convention on the Settlement of Investment Disputes between States and Nationals of Other States. Therefore, disputes concerning foreign investments can be resolved by the International Centre for Settlement of Investment Disputes (ICSID). These agreements insure fair and equitable treatment of foreign investors and provide effective mechanism for dispute resolution.

III. Trade

A. Department Supervising Trade

Control over the requirements applicable in this sector is exercised by local communities, as well as by several state bodies–each to the extent of the authorities entrusted to it, including Armenian tax authorities, customs authorities, state service for food safety, etc.

B. Brief Introduction of Trade Laws and Regulations

The sector of trade, public catering and consumer services is regulated by the Law "On Trade and Services" adopted as of November 24, 2004 and several decisions adopted by the Armenian Government. External trade is regulated both by the local rules and the legal acts of the Eurasian Economic Union to which Armenia has acceded, as well as by other international agreements being ratified by Armenia. Armenia has bilateral free trade agreements with Georgia, Moldova, Tajikistan, Turkmenistan, and Ukraine.

C. Trade Management

Armenia has been a member of the World Trade Organization (WTO) since February 5, 2003. By accession Armenia has undertaken extensive WTO commitments in all the areas and continues taking all the necessary measures to ensure further implementation of the WTO Agreement and its commitments in all the areas.

The first Trade Policy Review of Armenia by WTO was held on 6 and 8 April 2010. As a result of the said Review it was concluded that the main challenge for Armenia was to escape dependence on a narrow economic base of exports of minerals and inflows of remittances from abroad and that Armenia had a lot of potential from its open attitude to trade and investment, a huge diaspora, its mineral wealth, its long history and related tourist potential, and so on. Since then significant reforms have been implemented to ensure further growth of the Armenian economy.

D. The Inspection and Quarantine of Import and Export Commodities

The compliance with the sanitary-epidemiological, veterinary, quarantine, phytosanitary and radiation requirements are being checked upon the declaration of respective goods under relevant customs procedure. Particularly, as a general rule along with the customs declaration the declarant shall also provide respective documents substantiating the compliance of the given goods with the applicable requirements. Those requirements are set forth by the international agreements ratified by Armenia, respective decisions of the Commission of the Eurasian Economic Union and local rules enacted in Armenia.

E. Customs Management

Since January 02, 2015 Armenia became one of the member states of the Eurasian Economic Union (which currently comprises also Belarus, Kazakhstan, Russia and the Kyrgyz Republic), therefore, customs affairs in Armenia are currently regulated not only by the local Armenian legislation, but also by the legal acts of the said Economic Union. According to these documents the territories of all the member states of the Eurasian Economic Union constitute one unique customs territory and goods imported into any of the abovementioned states being cleared through customs, as well as goods produced within such state may freely circulate within the customs territory of the Eurasian Economic Union without any customs clearance procedure in any other member state. In such case, certain documents may be required to be submitted only for tax purposes.

Goods and vehicles carried across the customs border of the Eurasian Economic Union shall be subject to imposition of certain charges / taxes, including.

a) import / export customs duties

• are levied for carrying goods across the customs border either at percentage applied to the customs value of the respective goods or at fixed rates applied per measurement unit of the relevant goods;

• in case of goods being exported from Armenia, export duties are levied at 0%, unless otherwise specified by the laws of Armenia;

• in case of goods being imported into Armenia, the rates specified by the unified tariff policy of the Eurasian Economic Union depending on the relevant code under the FEACN shall be applied, unless otherwise specified by the international agreements of the member states;

• are to be paid within specific period of time depending on the customs procedure being applied to the respective goods.

b) customs fees

which are mandatory charges for performing customs formalities in respect of the goods carried across the customs border and are levied in the amounts specified by the local legislation of the respective member state.

c) taxes

particularly:

• value added tax (VAT) imposed on import of goods under "release for domestic consumption" customs procedure and payable before the release of the respective goods under the said customs procedure;

• excise tax imposed on import of certain type of goods under "release for domestic consumption" customs procedure and payable before the release of the respective goods under the said customs procedure;

• nature protection tax imposed in case of import of goods being hazardous for the environment (e.g.raw oil and oil materials, tyres, etc.) and subject to payment before completing customs formalities or during their completion, or levied for ejection of harmful substances into the air basin in case of entering Armenia by vehicles registered in foreign countries which are payable upon their entry;

• road tax levied for the use of state public roadways in case of entering Armenia by vehicles registered in foreign countries and payable per each 15-day period of travelling time in Armenia; payment of road tax for the 1st 15-day period shall be made upon the entry of the relevant vehicles into Armenia.

Goods and vehicles carried across the customs border of the Eurasian Economic Union shall be declared under the relevant customs procedure specified below:

• release for domestic consumption;

• export;

- customs transit;
- customs warehouse;
- processing within the customs territory;
- processing beyond the customs territory;
- processing for domestic consumption;
- temporary import;
- temporary export;
- re-import;
- re-export;
- duty free shop;
- destruction;
- abandonment to the benefit of the state;
- free customs zone;
- free warehouse;
- special customs procedure (applicable for certain categories of goods).

IV. Labour

A. Brief Introduction of Labour Laws and Regulations

The major sources of labour law are the Labour Code of the Republic of Armenia (RA), the Civil Code of the RA, to the extent not covered by the Labour Code, the Law on Civil Service, the Law on Public Service of the Republic of Armenia, and other RA laws regulating labour relations, sectoral collective labour agreements, and Decrees of Government regulating different technical issues, including work security standards. In addition, Armenia is party to several ILO Conventions regulating employment law issue.

The regulation of labour and other relationships directly related to it, may be exercised by collective and labour contracts concluded by and between employees and employers in accordance with labour legislation.

Labour relations are based on the mutual agreement of employee and employer, under which the employee shall personally perform their functions in exchange for remuneration all while abiding by the internal disciplinary rules, while the employer shall insure necessary working conditions prescribed by labour legislation. Issues that improve some additional conditions may be regulated by a collective agreement, which is not mandatory, but can be concluded by labour legislation of the Republic of Armenia.

B. Requirements of Employing Foreign Employee

Foreign workers can work and have the same rights and duties as Armenian citizens without any limitations. The only requirement is that they shall be correctly registered in below mentioned way.

a. Work Permit

Even though it is established by Armenian law that foreigners need to obtain a work permit to work in the country, the application of respective procedure is suspended until January 2019. This means that foreigners can work in Armenia without any work permit until 1 January 2019 if they have a valid residency permit. There are three different types of residency permits for foreigners:

(i) a temporary permit is given for the duration of one year, and entails a fee of approximately USD 220–the decision to accept or reject an application is made within 30 days from the date of submission;

(ii) a permanent permit is given for five years, and entails a fee of approximately USD 290 USD–the decision to accept or reject an application is made within 30 days from the date of submission;

(iii) a special residence permit is provided for ten years to people of Armenian descent, as well as to foreigners who are engaged in economic or cultural activities in Armenia, and entails a fee of approximately USD 310–the permit can be obtained in approximately six months, depending on a number of different factors.

b. Application Procedure

Until 1 January 2019 there are not any additional applicant procedure for foreigners except of getting the residence permit mentioned in point a of this paragraph.

c. Social Insurance

Employers in the private sector in the Republic of Armenia do not have any social insurance commitments as defined by legislation, except for paying to employees temporary disability benefits in cases of temporary disability.

However in practice most of foreign companies provide to their employees different social benefits like as health insurance for employees and their families, payments to visit sport clubs to keep employees in health life style, etc.

C. Exit and Entry

a. Visa Types

There are four types of visa for the entry into the territory of Armenia. The general type of visa is the visit entry visa, which is previewed for touristic and treatment visits, studies in Armenian institutions, participation in different events such as sports, scientific, cultural events, and many other usual short term visitors. It is issued as one time entry visa or multiple entry visa with the expiration period of one year.

Official entry visa is issued to persons who possess official (service) passport and the diplomatic entry visa is issued to persons who possess a diplomatic passport or diplomatic status. Finally, the transit visa is issued to the persons who travel through the territory of Armenia and grants a permission to be in Armenia for 3 days, which can be extended for maximum another 4 days.

The RA Government has the power to stipulate no visa regime for some States or some category of persons. The citizens of States which are exempt from the obligation to obtain entry visa, can stay in the territory of Armenia for maximum 180 days during one year, unless it is otherwise previewed by the international convention of the RA.

In case where the visa issued to the foreigner or the period for visit provided by law, where the citizens of a particular State are exempt from obligation to obtain visa, expires, the foreigner who wishes to lawfully reside in the territory of Armenia, shall apply for residency permit. There are three different types of residency permits for foreigners:

• a temporary permit is given for the duration of one year, and entails a fee of approximately USD 220-the decision to satisfy or reject an application is made within 30 days from the date of submission;

• a permanent permit is given for five years, and entails a fee of approximately USD 290–the decision to satisfy or reject an application is made within 30 days from the date of submission;

• a special residence permit is provided for ten years to persons of Armenian descent, as well as to foreigners who are engaged in economic or cultural activities in Armenia, and entails a fee of approximately USD 310–the permit can be obtained in approximately six months, depending on a number of different factors.

b. Restrictions for Exit and Entry

The application of the foreigner for a visa is rejected and the visa issued to them is invalidated, if:

• They have been deported from Armenia or their residency permit has been revoked not later than 3 years ago;

• They have been subjected to administrative responsibility for violation of Armenian legislation on foreigners not later than 1 year ago and have not performed obligations imposed on them;

• Reliable information is available pointing to their involvement in dangerous activities, such as terrorism, trafficking of drugs or ammunitions, etc.;

• They are infected with contagious illness that can be a threat to the public health;

• They have presented fraudulent information when applying for entry visa or have failed to present necessary information;

• They represent a serious threat to the national security or public order of Armenia;

• They have been subjected to administrative responsibility for violation of Armenian legislation on transport circulation not later than 1 year ago and have not performed obligations imposed on them.

The foreigner is restricted from leaving Armenia, if, in accordance with the RA legislation:

• They have been sentenced and the execution of that sentence in possible only in Armenia;

• They have been subjected to preventive measures in the scope of criminal investigation.

D. Trade Union and Labour Organizations

In the RA, trade unions are regulated by the international treaties of the Republic of Armenia, the Labour Code, the Trade Unions Law and other legal acts.

Trade unions are entitled to: draft their statutes and regulations; freely elect their representatives; arrange their administrative staff and their activities; draw up their programmes; acquire information from the employer in the manner prescribed by the Labour Code; submit proposals to the employer on work organisation; conduct collective bargaining within the organisation; conclude collective agreements and exercise supervision over their execution; exercise non-state supervision within an organisation over implementation of labour legislation and other regulatory legal acts containing rules of labour law; appeal through judicial procedure the decisions and activities of an employer and the authorised persons thereof contradicting the legislation of the Republic of Armenia, as well as collective agreements and employment contracts or violating rights of the representatives of employees within the organisation; ensure the coordination of employees' and employers' interests in collective employment relations at different levels of social partnership; submit proposals to state and local self-government bodies; organise and lead strikes; participate in the development of production plans and their implementation within the organisation; submit proposals to the employer on improvement of working and leisure conditions of employees, introduction of new technical equipment, reduction of the amount of manual labour, revision of the production norms, as well as the amount of and procedure for the remuneration of work; and other additional powers not contradicting the legislation.

Trade unions are entitled to organise, hold and lead strikes and public events and conduct bargaining on the issue with State bodies, local self-government bodies, other organisations and their officials. Trade unions are entitled to organise a strike if:

(i) because of conciliation processes, the dispute related to the conclusion of a collective employment agreement has not been settled;

(ii) the employer avoids carrying out a conciliation process; and

(iii) the employer fails to execute a decision of the Conciliation Commission that satisfies the employees, or fails to perform his or her obligations assumed by the collective employment agreement having been concluded beforehand.

However, the trade unions are not very active in Armenia, and so far there has not been formed much practice regarding their work in the country.

E. Labour Disputes

Labour disputes and disagreements between the employee and the employer regarding the exercise of rights and the fulfilment of the duties established in the Labour Code or other normative legal acts, an employment contract or a collective agreement can be resolved between the parties by negotiation. Also the parties can also resolve labour disputes to mediators.

If parties cannot resolve disputes by above mentioned way disputes can be solve at court.

In the RA, labour disputes are considered in the courts of general jurisdiction within the framework of civil proceedings as well as in the Administrative Court if the employer is an administrative body.

V. Intellectual Property

A. Brief Introduction of IP Laws and Regulations

In Armenia, intellectual property rights issues are regulated by the Civil Code and laws regulating specific objects of intellectual property rights. Armenia has been a member of the World Intellectual Property Organisation (WIPO) since 1993 and is signatory to WIPO-Administered Treaties, as well as numerous IP-related multilateral, regional and bilateral treaties.

B. Patent Application

Patents protect inventions and utility models. Protection is provided from the moment of registration. Patents are regulated by the provisions of chapter 65 of the Civil Code and the Law "On Inventions, Utility Models and Industrial Designs" adopted as of June 10, 2008.

The patent holder has the exclusive right to use the protected invention or utility model at his discretion and the right to give a name to the invention or utility model. The right of authorship and other moral rights to an invention or utility model arise upon the accrual of rights based on the respective patent.

Infringing a patent means manufacturing, using, selling or importing patented products or processes without the patent holder's permission. Using the invention or utility model without the patent holder's permission is not considered an infringement, when it is used:

- for personal needs, without the purpose of getting profit;
- as an object of scientific experience or scientific study;
- for one-time preparation of medicine in pharmacies by the doctors' prescription;
- on the transport means (vehicles), which belong to any other state and accidentally pass through or temporarily stay in Armenia, in case the use of the relevant patent object is conditioned with the needs of the given transport means (with account of the principle of mutuality);
- for tests, studies and trials of medical (including phytosanitary) products—during the last 2 years of the validity

of the patent.

Patents for inventions are valid for 20 years from the filing date. Patents for utility models are valid for 10 years from the filing date.

A patent application shall include:
• request for granting a patent;
• description of the respective of invention / utility model;
• definition of the claim for the invention or utility model, which includes at least one independent item;
• drawings and other documentation, if they are necessary for understanding the substance of invention or utility model;
• summary (abstract) of invention or utility model.

The request for granting a patent shall be filed in Armenian. In case of a foreign applicant, the rest of documents might be filed in a foreign language provided that their duly translations are submitted to the competent state authority within 3-month period from the filing date. The patent application shall be accompanied with respective power of attorney substantiating the authorities of the representative (if any) of the applicant, as well as with respective receipt on state duty payment.

Within 3-month period from the filing date the state competent body shall verify the compliance of the application and documents attached thereto with the legislative requirements in terms of their filing. In case all the requirements are met the state competent body shall proceed with the expertise of the compliance of claimed invention / utility model with the requirements of patentability conditions specified by the said Law. If the requirements are met, the state competent body shall adopt decision on publication of the application into the official bulletin and on patent issuance. The application shall be filed after the expiry of 18-month period from the filing date. In limited cases it can be published at an earlier date.

C. Trademark Registration

Trademarks are regulated by the provisions of chapter 69 of the Civil Code and the Law "On Trademarks" adopted as of April 29, 2010.

A trademark (or service mark) is a registered verbal, pictorial, special, or other designation serving to distinguish the goods or services of one person from the same kind of goods and services of another person. Legal protection of a trademark is ensured on the basis of and provided upon its registration. The right to a trademark is confirmed by a certificate.

A trademark registered by the Intellectual Property Agency or by an international organisation by virtue of an international treaty grants legal protection in Armenia. A trademark holder has the exclusive right to use and dispose the trademark.

The following can be considered as infringements of a trademark:
• affixing the sign on the goods or on the packaging thereof, as well as, in case of a three-dimensional trademark, its use as packaging of such goods;
• offering the goods, their sale or storage for these purposes, or supplying or offering services under that sign;
• importing or exporting goods under that sign;
• using the sign on documents and in advertising;
• using the sign on the Internet or on other global computer telecommunication networks, in particular by any modes of addressing, including internet domains;
• reproducing, storing or selling the sign for the above mentioned purposes.

The validity of the trademark registration is 10 years from the filing date with the right to extension.

The application for trademark registration shall be submitted either in writing or electronically and shall be related to one trademark. The application shall be filed in Armenian. Concurrently, documents attached thereto might be submitted in foreign language by foreign applicants provided that their Armenian translation are provided within 2-month period from the filing date.

The application must contain the following:
• information identifying the applicant and its representative (if any);
• distinct image (reproduction, in case of sound trademark the pentagram) and description of the claimed sign;
• list of goods and / or services for which the registration of the mark is claimed, grouped in accordance with the Nice classification, in ascending order of numbers of classification;
• statement that the claimed mark is three-dimensional (in appropriate case);
• statement that the claimed mark is holographic (in appropriate case);
• statement that the claimed mark is a sound mark (in appropriate case);
• statement that colour combination is the distinctive feature of the mark (in appropriate case);

- statement on the elements of the claimed mark, which are considered as unprotected (in appropriate case);
- transliteration of the mark or its verbal elements, also their Armenian translation (in appropriate case);
- statement that the claimed mark is a collective mark (in appropriate case);
- statement that the claimed mark is a certification mark (in appropriate case);
- statement on the date of priority of filing and the grounds thereof.

The application must be supplemented by the following:
- payment receipt of the state duty for the filing of the application and its examination;
- document certifying the power of the representative, if the application is filed through a representative;
- request for claiming a priority (if necessary);
- permission issued by the competent body, in case the trademark includes state emblems, flags, symbols, official state names, marks or emblems re[resenting particular public interest (if necessary);
- consent of the proprietor, in case the trademark reproduces or includes other objects of intellectual property rights with an earlier date of priority (if necessary);
- regulations for the use of a collective mark (if necessary);
- regulations for the use of a certification mark (if necessary).

The procedure of trademark registration is as follows:
- submission of application for the registration of the trademark and payment of state duty;
- during 10 working days upon submission of the application the state competent body shall register the application and perform a preliminary expertise to check the compliance of the submitted application and documents; should the documents be in compliance with the respective requirements, the state competent body shall adopt decision on publishing the submitted application and on commissioning a full expertise;
- during 15 working days upon adoption of the abovementioned decision the submitted application shall be published and during 2-month period upon its publication any interested party may address objections to the state competent body in connection with the registration of the given trademark;
- during 3-month period upon the publication of the application the state competent body shall perform the full expertise of the trademark. In case upon the results of the expertise no basis for rejection of the registration is identified, the state competent body shall adopt decision on the registration of the given trademark. Upon adoption of such decision the state competent body shall notify thereon and request paying state duty for registration of the trademark;
- during 10 working days upon submission of the document proving the payment of the state duty the state competent body shall finally register the trademark.

D. Measures for IP Protection

In addition to general means specified for protection of civil rights the protection of the exclusive rights of intellectual property right holders might be also conducted by way of:
- seizure of material objects violating the exclusive rights, as well as of material objects created as the result of such violation;
- compulsory publication about the breach committed, with an inclusion therein of information about to whom the violated rights belong along with the publication of the whole text of the court decision or a part thereof in mass media chosen by the respective intellectual property right holder at the account of the person having committed the given breach;
- other means provided by laws regulating issues in connection with each type of intellectual property right objects.

VI. Environmental Protection

A. Department Supervising Environmental Protection

In Republic of Armenia the state body, which is authorized to supervise the environmental protection is The Ministry of Nature Protection of the Republic of Armenia ("The Ministry"). The Ministry is a republican body of executive power that implements the state policy in the field of environmental protection and rational use of natural resources of the Republic of Armenia ("RA"). The functions assigned to the Ministry are implemented by the structural and detached units of the ministry personnel and state non-profit organizations and companies established within the ministry system. Nature Protection and subsoil the Ministry of Armenia is a separate subdivision which controls compliance with environment protection norms, discovers violations and undertakes appropriate measures. Territorial governance bodies and local self-governing bodies also carry out control on the protection of environmental legislation and undertake measures to prevent the offense. Within three days, they are obliged to inform the State Environmental Inspectorate about duly disclosed violations. Accordingly, all these bodies are engaged in carrying out certain action aimed at tackling environmental issues within their jurisdiction.

B. Brief Introduction of Laws and Regulations of Environmental Protection

The Constitution of the RA which determines the basic principles of environmental protection and state's role in it. There are four Codes which are regulate the main relations in this area.

The Forest Code of the RA regulates the relations in area RA forests and forest lands management, protection, restoration, forestation and effective use of its. It also regulates relations in area forests registration, monitoring, control and other relations connected with forest lands.

The Subsoil Code of the RA establishes the principles and procedures of subsoils use in the territory of the RA. This Code also regulates relations of nature and environment protection from harmful impacts during the use of subsoil, provision of security of work execution, as well as relations related to the protection of the rights and legitimate interests of the state and persons during the use of the subsoil. This Code also regulates procedure of granting permission for extraction of useful minerals, terms of permission and its extension procedure, rights and responsibilities of subsoil users and other relations.

The Land Code of the RA establishes the legal basis for the improvement of the state regulation of land relations, the development of various organizational and legal forms of land management, improvement of land fertility and efficiency of land use, conservation and improvement of favourable environment for human life and health and protection of rights over lands based on important environmental, economic and social significance, thanks to which the land in the Republic of Armenia is used and maintained as the condition of the vital activity of people. This Code defines operational significance and purpose of lands.

The Water Code of the RA establishes legal basis for creation of relevant management mechanisms of water resources, preservation and protection of water resources, ensuring the reduction of pollution, preservation of the standards of water and the level of national water resources, prevention of harmful impact of waters, provision of registration of water resources, provision of the population and the economy with the required quantity and quality of water with regulated tariffs.

There are also many sectoral laws which are regulate environmental relations. They are the following: the RA law on Animal World, the RA law on Plant World, the RA law on Wastes, the RA law on Environmental Control, the RA law on Provisions of Environmental Payments, the RA law on Special Protective Territories, the RA law on Environmental Assessment and Expertise on Environment and other laws.

In these field are many international conventions which have been ratified by RA; United Nations Convention to Combat Desertification, Basel Convention on the Control of Transboundary Movement and disposal of Hazardous Wastes, Montreal Protocol On ozone depleting substances. This treaties also considered part of RA legal system.

C. Evaluation of Environmental Protection

During the recent years, tangible steps have been taken in the RA towards environmental policy, legislation and institutional reforms. The sectoral environmental legislation has been updated and adapted to modern requirements. In accordance with the constitutional requirements, the Law on Environmental Impact Assessment was adopted. The said law regulates legal, economic and organizational bases of assessment of the environmental impact of the proposed activities and concepts. The main goal of the Law is to regulate proposed activities which are likely to have impact on the environment. This document for the first time contains a reference to concerned communities as well as public hearing processes, which motivate the involvement of public in decision making on environmental issues. Public hearings ensure public awareness and participation in assessments and expertise processes. Public reasonable comments and suggestions should be taken into account by the initiator and the authorized body. In case of non-taking account its, reasonable explanations should be given. Connected with this an important change has been in Administrative Procedure Code of the RA according to which public organization represents the interests of its beneficiaries in the field of environmental protection. Organization can submit a lawsuit to the court if within the framework of the RA law on Environmental Impact Assessment and Expertise, it has participated in the public hearings on fundamental documents or envisaged activity or it has not given opportunity to participate in public discussions.

VII. Dispute Resolution

A. Methods and Bodies of Dispute Resolution

a. Efficiency of Process

The Court System of the Republic of Armenia (Armenia) is a three-stage judicial system, and all cases except matters of constitutional justice, which are subject to the separate Constitutional Court, are handled by the said judicial system.

The system is as follows:

The system is described in detail in the Constitution and the Judicial Code. Separate codes for procedures (criminal, civil, administrative) and the law on bankruptcy regulate the particularities of different processes in the courts.

The Court of General Competence of Armenia hears all criminal and civil cases, including commercial and bankruptcy cases.

The Administrative Court of Armenia is a specialized court with jurisdiction to examine cases arising from public legal relationships, with the key role of overseeing the activities of administration (executive power).

The Civil Court of Appeal and the Criminal Court of Appeal of Armenia review appeals to acts of the Courts of General Competence, and the Administrative Court of Appeal reviews appeals to acts of the Administrative Court.

The Court of Cassation is the highest juridical instance that is eligible to examine all claims except those concerning constitutional jurisdiction.

As a general rule, if the claim meets the formal requirement of proper procedural code (includes required data, the listed documents are enclosed, the action is signed, etc.) it is accepted to the hearings. Appeal complaints are accepted to hearings under the same grounds.

Acceptance of a cassation complaint is a sophisticated issue as this court's purposes are enshrined in the Constitution (to ensure uniform application of legislation and eliminate fundamental violation of human rights and freedoms). In general, the Cassation court accepts complaints which comply with formal requirements as well as the court's purposes. Regulations related to acceptance of cassation complaints were recently subject to review of the Constitutional court and it is anticipated that the practice will be changed accordingly, i.e.the number of acceptances to hearings will increase if the formal requirements are provided.

In the first instance courts (except for the criminal procedure and bankruptcy peculiarity, which are enshrined in the Criminal procedural code and Law on bankruptcy respectively), the case passes the following main stages after acceptance of the claim: preliminary hearing; trial; judgment and publication of the decision.

The Appeal court examines the case within the scope of the complaint and evidences, not accepting any evidences or positions which were not presented in the first instance court. As far as court hearings shall be public, the Appeal court assigns hearing (one or two) of the case, has a stage of judgment and publishes its decision as well.

The decision of the Appeal court may be subject to cassation complaint and, if accepted for review, one court hearing, and publication of the final and non-appealable decision, take place.

The prescription period is recognized by Armenian legislation. Nonetheless, the motion to apply the prescription period shall be reviewed by the court simultaneously with the review of the case in total, i.e.the declaration of application of the prescription period does not cease the procedure in court immediately.

Alternative dispute resolution is recognized by Armenian legislation. Details on Mediation and ADR in the proper charters are presented below.

a) Availability of ADR Mechanisms

Armenian law recognizes mediation and arbitration. While arbitration has been present in legislation for many years, formal mediation is quite new (and was introduced in 2015).

Arbitration is widely accepted in specific areas (mostly used by banks and credit organizations as faster ways to deal with non-performing loans), however in general there is still a lack of practice in arbitration. On the other hand, there are several arbitration institutions with their lists of rather experienced arbitrators. The legislation does not stipulate requirements for arbitrators to have special permission or background.

The arbitration process is regulated by a separate Law on arbitration as well as internal regulations of arbitration centers (and regulations for ad hoc arbitration) and agreement of the parties. Normally it comprises stages similar to court stages; however, it is less formal and faster. If not agreed otherwise by the parties, the arbitral award will not be appealable, and will be final and binding: it can be reviewed on very limited grounds by a court (e.g. absence of arbitration agreement or other grave breach of procedure).

For mediation, if the parties want to have their conciliation approved by court, the mediator must be the one with an acting mediator license. Many legal and non-legal specialists have recently applied and become licensed as mediators; however, since mediation is new, there is not sufficient data to elaborate the effectiveness of the latter.

Parties may also use out-of-court mediation, and in some limited cases this decision will also be verified by court.

In any case, if the mediation is not successful, the parties shall continue their dispute resolution via arbitration or court.

b) E-Justice availability as a tool to increase the efficiency of justice and access to justice

Currently, there is no online filing of lawsuit applications in courts available. The system was developed by the Judicial Department and the Ministry of Justice with the financial and technical assistance of Concern Dialog law firm as well as the EU Delegation, and has been tested. Some legislative and regulatory concerns are still hindering the application of the system. Provided that legal requirements are based on paper lawsuit applications, the online application process will probably require a minor legal reform. In contrast, arbitrations are easier and, in practice, accept online filing via email or specially developed platforms.

Meantime, data on all cases in the courts are published (except for data on cases subject to close hearings) in the Online Armenian Judicial System known as Datalex and available at http://datalex.am.It is available only in Armenian, and a party can nearly always follow its application and procedure (e.g.acceptance, hearing dates, some intermediate judicial acts, final decision text, information on appeal and cassation claims, etc.) online, as well as trace and examine relevant cases.

Other resources publishing court decisions and containing sophisticated search and indexing mechanisms are also available, i.e.there are: non-paid official resources http://arlis.am and http://www.court.am; and private and paid resources http://www.armlaw.am and Irtek http://www.irtek.am, both of which contain decisions of the Court of Cassation and of the Constitutional court.

b. Integrity of Process

The principles of natural justice are implemented in Armenia's legal system. The Constitution of Armenia safeguards everyone's right to a public hearing of his case in order to have his violated rights restored and to have charges against him determined by an independent and impartial court, within a reasonable period, under equal conditions, with due respect for all the requirements of fairness.

In accordance with the internationally recognized right of judicial protection (access to justice), which is the fundamental rule of natural justice, the Judicial Code of Armenia states that everyone has the right to judicial protection of his rights and freedoms and no-one may be deprived of the right to have his case publicly examined by a competent, independent, and impartial court within a reasonable time, under equal conditions, with due respect for all requirements of fairness.

The legislation of Armenia contains some mechanisms to protect the principle of nemo judex in causa sua. If a party to arbitration believes that the judge is partial, they can bring a self-recusal motion, which must be decided by the judge, with the consideration of arguments brought in the motion. If the judge is biased, or the situation can be perceived as biased, he / she is expected to abandon the case and pass it to another judge on their own initiative or by the motion of the party. If the party is not satisfied with the decision of the court rejecting the self-recusal, he / she can recall it as grounds for appeal of the final decision.

As for opportunity to be heard, the court resolves the applications and motions on all issues relevant to the consideration of the case filed by the participants of the case after having heard the opinions of other participants of the case.

In Armenia, everyone has the right to exercise his right to judicial protection either through a representative or advocate, or personally (right to legal representation).

The judiciary of Armenia is autonomous and self-governed. The independence of the court is declared by the Constitution, Judicial Code and procedural codes. The Judicial Code states that the judge is independent and not accountable to anyone and, among other things, is not required to give any explanation, save for cases provided by law. Additionally, a judge may not be a member of any party or otherwise engage in political activities. In all circumstances, a judge must demonstrate political restraint and neutrality.

A judge must not tolerate any interference with the administration of justice, regardless of whether it is performed by representatives of the legislative or executive powers, other public officials, or ordinary citizens.

The guarantee of judges' independence is the rule that a judge must immediately inform the Ethics Committee about any interference with his activities related to the administration of justice and the performance of other powers stipulated by law, if such interference is not provided by law. If the Ethics Committee finds that the judge's activities have been interfered with in a way that is not provided by law, it must petition the competent authorities to hold the guilty ones liable. Any such act is subject to criminal prosecution. For public servants, it gives rise also to disciplinary liability, up to and including dismissal from office or service.

In addition, during his term of office and after the termination thereof, a judge may not be interrogated as a witness about a case tried by him.

The basis of the principle of the impartiality of the court is stated in the Constitution, which declares that everyone shall have the right to a fair and public hearing [...] by an independent and impartial court, and that a judge shall be independent, impartial and act only in accordance with the Constitution and laws. According to the Judicial Code, when exercising his powers, a judge must refrain from displaying discrimination with speech or conduct, as well as making such an impression.

The requirement for judges to be impartial in specific cases is reflected in the criminal and civil procedure codes.

The Armenia's legal system integrates a number of impartiality guarantee mechanisms and institutions, foreseen by the Judicial Code. Among them are, inter alia:
- non-dismissibility of judges;
- salary;
- pension / social security prerogatives;
- special procedures of judicial control in criminal prosecution against a judge;
- political impartiality;
- impossibility of parallel jobs (judges still can engage in volunteer activities or undertake paid educational or scientific work); and
- complex appointment procedures.

c. Privilege and Disclosure

a) Privileges

No-one is obliged to give testimony against himself / herself, his / her spouse and immediate relatives.

The Attorneys at law (advocates), the Defender of human rights, judges, arbitrators, mediators and confessors cannot testify in the scope of civil (including bankruptcy), administrative and criminal procedures. In addition, representatives of mass media are entitled not to answer if it may disclose the source of their information.

The Armenian law on Advocates and Advocates' Activities enshrines a number of guarantees of confidentiality as well, e.g.it is banned:

(i) to disclose any information unless the client agrees;

(ii) to confiscate (take) from the advocate materials concerning legal support provided and to use them us evidence; or

(iii) to investigate advocates' apartments, vehicles, offices and offices of law firms, as well as to examine the advocate while he / she performs his / her professional duties.

b) Disclosure

Armenian legislation protects confidential information as well as personal data. Thus, confidential information (commercial, bank, state, official, notary, family and private life, etc.), including personal data (data allowing a natural person to be identified directly or indirectly) may be disclosed in the scope of pre-court or court procedures either by the consent of its owner or by the court decision thereon.

The Administrative court, unlike the others, is entitled by its own ex officio authority to initiate a request to provide evidences containing confidential information. The other courts may not initiate this kind of procedure, but they are entitled to review the petitions of participants on providing confidential data to the court, and may decide accordingly. A participant of this procedure who is allowed to bring such a petition must prove / show that he / she is not able to receive data without the court's approval, as well as the relevance of the evidence or data to the case.

The confidential data may be requested and received under the court's decision by its owner regardless of whether the latter has status or not in the scope of case.

In general, cases are considered in open hearings, but closed-door hearings are allowed if the court accepts the relevant petition of a party, which latter can present for protection of confidentiality of adoption, privacy of citizens of their families, as well as protection of commercial or other secrets.

Closed-door hearing allows public access to information about the case to be banned as well, i.e.one can find merely information about the number of case and parties at www.datales.am.

d. Costs

Applications require state fees (symbolic amounts for cases related to non-monetary, or not subject to monetary evaluation, and percentages of 2–3% for cases of a monetary nature, depending on the instance of the court it is presented to). Some cases are exempt from state fee (e.g.lawsuit applications of employees in labor matters); the law also provides a possibility to postpone the state fee if the party is unable to pay at that moment; however, he / she needs to submit a motion and ground his / her inability to pay the state fee. Moreover, the recent practice indicates that the courts are stricter in approving such motions.

Normally, the losing party is obliged to recover the fees paid. In the structure of costs, attorney fees are also included; however, while amounts of other costs are based on the factual amounts paid by the parties, attorney fees are considered to be satisfied in "reasonable amounts" and only if proved. Parties need to present proofs about the mechanism of attorney cost calculations or the factually paid sums (e.g.payment receipts are provided). Considering different factors, at its discretion, the court will, however, decide a reasonable sum, which the losing party will have to compensate to the winning party.

There are no securities for costs available; however, the institution of interim measures, though very limited, may serve such purpose.

Similarly, there are no other mechanisms available for capping costs or limiting recoverability of costs (the only one applicable is the attorney fee).

There are no other options available to litigants in funding the litigation; however, they are free to find third party founders. Some internationally funded projects have financed strategic litigation cases; however, recently most such projects have closed.

e. Litigation Funding

Any costs related to the procedure may be subject to recovery under Armenian legislation. Nonetheless, the claim may be approved if the costs, except for the state fee (the state fee is approved in compliance with the amount of satisfied demand), are reasonable. There are not any criteria to define whether costs are reasonable or not under the law, but a judge decides at his / her discretion. In practice, recovery amount of costs (attorney's fee, translator's fee, expertise, etc.) are derived from average market prices, the time consumed for fulfilment of tasks and the character of the case, etc.

The attorney's fee may be recovered if payment thereof has already been made or shall be made in future. Thus, contingency fee arrangements are subject to approval by the court but, again, in the scope of reasonable amount thereof. Practically, this model is mostly applied for debt collection services and usually the courts approve refund of the whole sum enshrined in the agreement.

Recovery of litigation costs may be either subject to the hearing in the scope of the main hearing, or be the subject of a separate claim. The latter has a few legal issues such as the legal character of the demand, legal grounds in material law, etc.; the positions are not yet similar. In the scope of main hearings, legal costs may be sought in the court for representation in relation to which they have arisen, e.g.costs for an appeal complaint may be presented directly to the appeal court.

Postponement of payment of the state fee may be applicable as well if the claimant is able to prove inability to pay it.

Legal services can be paid either by the Client or by the third party. The number of organizations that provide financing for strategic cases is decreasing, and now it is almost zero.

Meanwhile, pro bono legal services are discussed by different structures with the aim of development of this sector as well. Today, pro bono legal services are mostly provided by the Office of the Public Defender and include support in criminal, civil, administrative and constitutional procedures of socially vulnerable classes.

f. Interim Relief

In the civil procedure of Armenia, the range of injunctive relief is provided by Article 98 of the Civil Procedure Code. The following are the means of relief:
- imposing an arrest on the defendant's property or financial assets in the amount of lawsuit;
- prohibiting the committal of certain actions by the defendant;
- prohibiting the committal of certain actions by other persons in relation to the object of the dispute;
- preventing the sale of property, in case of bringing a case concerning the lifting of the arrest on the property; and
- imposing an arrest on the plaintiff's property which is in the defendant's possession.

In administrative procedure there is means of relief, which is not similar to the means provided by the Civil Procedure Code. According to the Administrative Procedure Code of Armenia, the court can temporarily satisfy the action.

To apply one, the plaintiff needs to ground the necessity of the security measure. In practice, motions for reasonable security measures are satisfied. When necessary, the court is entitled to apply several means of securing the action.

In the countermeasure, by motion of a person participating in the case, the court is entitled to replace one provisional remedy with another, and by motion of a participating party, can terminate the provisional remedy. The issue of termination of a security is resolved at court session. As a protective measure, the defendant can demand the plaintiff pay an amount equal to its damages as a security to the court deposit, as well as apply to the same court demanding the damages caused by the interim measure.

The Republic of Armenia is a party to the CIS Convention on legal assistance and legal relations in civil, family and criminal cases and has reciprocal agreements with a number of countries. The mentioned treaties regulate the enforcement of worldwide freezing orders. Also, normally, when Armenian courts give freezing orders, it relates not only to a defendant's funds in Armenia, but also worldwide funds. Nevertheless, the decision of the Armenian court must be recognized by the courts of the countries in which these funds are kept in order to have the corresponding funds frozen.

g. Enforcement of Judgments

The Republic of Armenia is a party to the CIS Convention on legal assistance and legal relations in civil, family and criminal cases and has reciprocal agreements with a number of countries, for instance with Greece, Iran, Bulgaria, Romania, Georgia, UAE and Lithuania. With the countries with which Armenia doesn't have any agreements, the enforcement of judgments / awards is performed on a reciprocal basis.

According to the Law on Compulsory Enforcement, in cases provided for by international treaties of the Republic of Armenia, the writ of execution on enforcement of judgments and decisions of courts of foreign states shall be issued by the court of the Republic of Armenia which has taken a decision on the recognition in the Republic of Armenia of the judgment, and decision of the court of the foreign State concerned.

Normally, parties are expected to fulfil their obligations without waiting for compulsory enforcement. However, after the entry into force of the final judicial act, or the decision on an interim measure, the party may apply to the court for a judicial enforcement order (enforcement writ), which he / she can present to the State Service of Compulsory Enforcement.

The time limit for enforcement is two months after the opening of the enforcement case, and is established for carrying out enforcement actions, except for cases provided by law, which can be prolonged in limited cases.

Normally, enforcement procedures do not take long, especially when they concern the application of interim measures: once the property of the plaintiff is identified, it is attached, or if it concerns injunction, the State Service of Compulsory Enforcement simply orders the injunction and follows up its performance.

If enforced, the fees (some 5%) are collected additionally and held from the collected amount before transferring the adjudged amount to the winning party. If the creditor takes back the enforcement writ, he bears the enforcement fee (from 1–5%, depending at which stage it is done).

The grounds for avoiding enforcement are stated in Article 42 of Law of The Republic of Armenia on compulsory enforcement of judicial acts. For instance, among them are cases where:

- the claimant has renounced the levy of execution;
- the claimant and the debtor have entered into a settlement agreement, and it has been approved by the court;
- the claimant or debtor-citizen has died, and claims or obligations established by the judicial act may not pass to his or her successor;
- the judicial act, based on which the writ of execution has been issued, has been reversed;
- the debtor-legal person has been declared bankrupt by a court judgment; or
- the debtor-legal entity has been dissolved.

The parties are free to come to a peaceful settlement of their dispute and conclude a conciliation agreement, which is later confirmed by the court and published as a judicial act. There, the parties can also regulate reciprocal arrangements for enforcement of the agreement. Another option is (and it only concerns the order of fulfilment of the judicial act), the possibility of the parties to agree on the order of realization of the judicial orders. This concerns cases where the final judicial act is present, and parties, of their own will and agreement, want to regulate the order of fulfilment of the obligations under the respective judicial act. If the agreement is violated, the State Service of Compulsory Enforcement will be called to apply the decision of the court.

If the plaintiff is insolvent, and the State Service of Compulsory Enforcement finds out, it will stop the enforcement and invite the creditor to initiate a bankruptcy case.

If the obligation is already performed and proof is provided, the enforcement service will only enforce the service fee confiscation. For the non-performance of a judicial act, the Armenian Criminal Code provides criminal charges both for Compulsory Enforcers and persons intentionally avoiding enforcement.

As for enforcement of awards, the Law on Compulsory Enforcement states that writs of execution for compulsory enforcement of awards of arbitral tribunals shall be issued by the competent court of the Republic of Armenia. The court shall have the right to refuse issuance of the writ of execution based on the grounds provided for by the Law of the Republic of Armenia on commercial arbitration.

Armenia's legislation does not provide special garnishee proceedings but it has mechanisms which are similar to garnishee proceedings. When a Compulsory Enforcer imposes attachment on a debtor's monetary funds, he or she send messages to the banks and employer of the debtor and asks for freezing of funds and future payments to the debtor until the final judgment comes into force.

h. Cross-Border Litigation

An Armenian court can send judicial orders outside its territorial jurisdiction, in order to accomplish several actions. This is limited to the territory of the Republic of Armenia. For foreign matters, Armenian courts may seek the help of a foreign country on assistance matters, such as finding the contents of the foreign law. Other kinds of cooperation are based solely on international treaties, as explained in the previous section, or on diplomatic cooperation, provided that civil procedure is based on competition and parties provide the court with proofs (the obtaining of the proofs by the court is only possible in limited cases, where the party so requests by written motion, and grounds why he / she cannot acquire them himself / herself).

Enforcement of judicial orders abroad is possible, again based on international treaty or diplomatic means. There is little practice in relation to the application of Armenian judicial orders abroad; it can take a couple of months.

Generally, it is up to the parties to pursue the acquired judicial acts in foreign jurisdictions for their application.

i. International Arbitration

Armenia is party to the New York Convention on Recognition and Enforcement of Foreign Arbitral Awards, which makes it possible to recognize and enforce foreign arbitral awards in Armenia, as well as local arbitral awards in other NY Convention member-countries. Relevant procedures are incorporated in procedural codes and in the law on regulating arbitration. Based on the international instruments, as well as local procedural legislation, recognition and enforcement of foreign arbitral awards is done without major difficulties, although there is not much practice on this side either.

j. Mediation and ADR

Mediation is a very new institution in Armenia. Parties can apply for mediation at any moment. If the agreement provides for mediation, the court cannot decide the case until mediation is over. The mediation length completely depends on the will of parties.

To mediate, a specialist (not necessarily with a legal background) needs to acquire a mediator certificate from the Ministry of Justice.

Mediation is a paid service, but to strengthen the new institution, the Armenian legislator has provided free mediation hours by law. These are the first four hours.

After the amendments, many specialists have applied and received mediator certificates; however, there is still no widespread practice of mediation

k. Regulatory Investigations

Governmental authority regulates the economic activities of proper areas, including protection of consumers' rights; the regulatory investigations thereof are implemented as administrative procedure under administrative law.

Decision is made by governmental or municipal authority and may be reviewed by the Administrative court.

Normative legal acts of governmental and municipal authorities (including the Central Bank, State Commission for the Protection of Economic Competition and the Public Services Regulatory Commission) may be reviewed by the Administrative court subject to its compliance with legal acts which hold higher position in the hierarchy thereof (except for the Constitution).

The Administrative court is entitled to review notaries' activities, as well as activity of the body responsible for overview and providing protection of personal data.

B. Application of Laws

With regards to procedural law, the litigation is conducted based on Civil Procedure Code, Criminal Procedure Code and Administrative Procedure Code respectively. The arbitration having its seat in Armenia is subjected to the RA Law on Commercial Arbitration which is based on UNCITRAL Model Law, however the parties are free to agree on procedural matters, including incorporate in their arbitration agreement arbitration rules that they wish to be applicable.

As to substantial law, if the dispute is submitted to the Armenian court, the law applicable to the relations with foreign element will be decided based in the conflict of laws rules of Armenia. As a general rule, the parties are free to choose the law applicable to their contract and that choice of law will be binding for the court. In the cases, where it is impossible for the court to decide on the issue of applicable law based on the specific conflict of laws rules, the law with the closest connection to the relations is applied.

During arbitration, with its seat in Armenia, the arbitrators are bound by choice of law of the parties. Whenever the parties fail to choose law applicable to the merits of the case, the arbitrator decides on the applicable law based on the conflict of laws rules that the arbitrator finds applicable. If one of the parties to the dispute is Armenian citizen or legal entity incorporated in Armenia, and the parties have failed to choose the law applicable to their relations, the arbitrator shall apply Armenian law.

VIII. Others

A. Anti–commercial Bribery

a. Brief Introduction of Anti-commercial Bribery Laws and Regulations

Commercial bribe, including entrapment for it, is subject to regulation of Criminal Code of Armenia, i.e.pursuant to Armenian legislation commercial bribe is a crime.

Article 200 (1) of Criminal Code: Bribe to an employee of commercial or other organization, an arbitrator, including an arbitrator who acts in accordance with the law on arbitration of foreign state, auditor or attorney (hereinafter named persons), shall be classified as a commercial bribe. The following shall be considered as bribe if it is performed by the briber or intermediator with the aim the named persons perform action or non-action in favor of the briber or person represented by the latter:

(i) Illegal promise, offer or transfer of the cash for the named persons or to the other persons

(ii) Illegal promise, offer or transfer of the property for the named persons or to the other persons

(iii) Illegal promise, offer or transfer of the rights towards the property for the named persons or to the other persons

(iv) Illegal promise, offer or transfer of securities for the named persons or to the other persons,

(v) Illegal promise, offer or transfer of the other advantage for the named persons or to the other persons

Article 200 (3) of Criminal Code: Acceptance of the bribe by an employee of commercial or other organization, an arbitrator, including an arbitrator who acts in accordance with the law on arbitration of foreign state, auditor or attorney (hereinafter named persons) shall be classified as commercial bribe as well. The following shall be considered as bribe if it is performed by named persons directly or via intermediator in exchange of acting or non-acting in favor of the briber or person represented by the latter:

(i) To receive, demand, promise to receive or accept offer of the cash for the named person or to the other persons,

(ii) To receive, demand, promise to receive or accept offer of the property for the named persons or to the other persons,

(iii) To receive, demand, promise to receive or accept offer of the rights towards the property for the named persons or to the other persons,

(iv) To receive, demand, promise to receive or accept offer of securities for the named persons or to the other persons,

(v) To receive, demand, promise to receive or accept offer of of the other advantage for the named persons or to the other persons.

In addition to the Criminal Code of Armenia, the Law on signaling, adopted on 09.06.2017 and entered into force since 01.01.2018, regulates signaling in public-purpose organization (organizations provided publicly regulated services such as telecommunication, water, electricity and gas supply) in addition to the regulation of signaling in the governmental and municipal bodies, state institution and organizations. Signaling stands for informing in written or oral about corruption incident, conflict of interest, violation of the rules of ethic violation of rules of non-compliance or other restrictions, violation concerning declaration or damages to the public interest or threats to the public interests. The signaling may be internal or external. The person who is signaling shall act diligently.

b. Department Supervising Anti-commercial Bribery

Commercial bribe is the subject to investigation to the relevant law enforcement agency.

Internal signaling is supervised by a head of a body (organization) or by a supervisor of a body (organization). External signaling is presented to the Corruption prevention commission. There will be an opportunity to submit signaling to the special platform to which Prosecutor office shall have access.

In case there is corpus delicti or suspicion to the crime committed the case shall be transferred to the appropriate law enforcement agency

c. Punitive Actions

The one, who committed the crime (commercial bribe) under the Article 200 (1) or the Article (3) of Criminal code is punished with fine AMD 200 000 – 400 000 (1 USD is around 480 AMD) or with deprivation of the right to hold certain posts or practice certain activities for up to 3 years or with imprisonment for the term of maximum 3 years.

The same action committed by a group with prior agreement or by an organized group is punished with fine AMD 300 000 – 500 000 or with imprisonment for the term of maximum 4 years.

The crime under the Article 200 (3) committed with extortion is punished with fine AMD 300 000- 500 000 or with deprivation of the right to hold certain posts or practice certain activities for up to 5 years or with imprisonment for the term of maximum 5 years.

B. Project Contracting

The state governmental bodies or community bodies of the Republic of Armenia, institutions thereof, the Central Bank of Armenia, state or community non-commercial organizations, organizations with the participation of state or community by more than 50%, foundation or units established (including reorganizations) by the state or community or non-commercial state or community organization or organization with state or community participation (more than 50%), public organizations (production of electricity, transfer and distribution of electricity and natural gases, operators of electricity and natural gas sectors, supply of water, exploitation of public net of electronic communication etc.) is obliged to purchase goods, works and services via procurement by providing rules stipulated in the Law on procurement of Armenia and connected regulatory legal acts.

The procurement can be provided via electronic trades, tender (open and close), fee quote request and purchase from the one source. Goods, works or services is allowed to purchase from one source in exceptional cases, e.g.the price of contract is no more than basic amount of purchase, i.e.1 million AMD.

The Law established procedures for invitation to bid, formation and confirmation of requirement to the participants and winner, submission for participation, choosing of the winner and signing the contract, liability for breaching the procedure, as well as procedure on submission and hearing of compliance as regards to the procurement procedures provided.

澳大利亚

作者：Will Heath、Charles Coorey、Michael Williams
译者：莫海波、陶海英

一、概述

（一）政治、经济、社会和法律环境概况

澳大利亚联邦（以下简称"澳大利亚"）是一个稳定、高度自由民主的国家，人口约 2450 万。
澳大利亚设有三级行政区划：
- 联邦政府（澳大利亚政府），法律由位于澳大利亚首都堪培拉的联邦议会制定。
- 州/领地政府，法律由位于各州和各领地首府城市的 6 个州议会和 2 个领地议会制定。①
- 地方政府，"地方政府法规"由澳大利亚约 546 个地方议会制定。②

1. 行政制度

澳大利亚联邦议会由以下部分组成：
- 英女皇，由总督代表。
- 参议院，由来自每个州的各 12 名参议员以及来自 2 个主要领地的各 2 名参议员组成（共 76 人）。
- 众议院，由 150 个地区（或"选区"）的议员组成，每个选区的人口大致相同。

众议院和参议院是联邦议会的两个议事机构。法案必须在众议院和参议院均获得过半数票数并取得总督的批准方可通过。澳大利亚现任总理是斯科特·莫里森。

2. 权力分立

澳大利亚宪法将澳大利亚政府的权力分成三个部分：
- 立法机构（联邦议会），负责就法案进行辩论及表决。
- 行政机构（澳大利亚政府），负责颁布并维护立法机构制定的法律。行政机构由在众议院中获得多数席位的政党或政党联盟组成。澳大利亚当前的政府及行政机构由联邦总理斯科特·莫里森领导的自由党组成。
- 司法机构（法院），法院是澳大利亚政府的司法机构。法院独立于立法机构以及行政机构，并确保立法机构以及行政机构在其各自的权力范围内规范运作。

上述制度称为"权力分立"。

3. 澳大利亚的司法体制

澳大利亚拥有稳定且备受尊重的司法体制，其核心原则如下：
- 法治；
- 听证原则；
- 法律面前人人平等；
- 公正；
- 公平；
- 透明。

澳大利亚是"普通法"司法地区。普通法是以遵循先例的原则作为基础，即在法院作出决定（判决）前，必须首先参考其他法院，尤其是上级法院曾经作出的相关判例，这可以逐步丰富法院判例以

---

① 澳大利亚各州均有自己的宪法，并遵循权力分立原则。
② 各州/领地的地方议会的角色及责任均有所不同。

及确保法院判例的体系化。议会可以制定成文法以推翻现有的普通法，但普通法不得推翻成文法。

尽管大部分法律是由澳大利亚议会制定的成文法，但普通法仍然是澳大利亚法律制度不可缺少的一部分。

4. 社会经济环境

澳大利亚的经济已实现连续27年增长，目前是世界第13大经济体。[1]澳大利亚拥有以服务业为基础的多元化经济，并且政府负债率低。[2]

澳大利亚拥有受过高等教育、技能熟练、通晓多国语言的劳动力。[3]澳大利亚也是众多国际组织以及国际金融机构的成员，包括G20、世界银行集团以及经济合作与发展组织。在透明国际组织"最清廉国家"评选中，澳大利亚排在第13位。[4]

5. 投资者利益保护

澳大利亚可为外国投资者提供可观的投资收益和优越的投资环境。澳大利亚的经济充满活力、结构多元、通胀率低，并且拥有透明宽松的外商投资审批程序、低贸易壁垒、以商业利益为导向的公司监管以及极具吸引力的公司税率。

正如澳大利亚政府所称："澳大利亚一直依靠外国投资来弥补国内储蓄以及投资的差额。外国投资推动了澳大利亚的经济增长、创造了技术类就业岗位、改善了进入海外市场的渠道并提高了生产力，是澳大利亚经济重要且有益的组成部分。"[5]

澳大利亚的经济由多个优势产业组成，包括：
- 金融市场；
- 食品及综合农业；
- 能源及矿产资源；
- 医疗保健；
- 基础设施。

得益于其开放、透明的经济环境，澳大利亚在其他产业领域也产生了一批成功企业，包括工业产品、消费品、技术、传媒、旅游业以及专业服务等产业。

6. 金融市场

澳大利亚成熟、创新且备受认可的金融市场在汇集储蓄与投资、高效配置资本、管理投资者、企业以及政府现金流量以及资产负债表的风险等方面均扮演着重要角色。澳大利亚的金融市场拥有各类本国以及外国投资者。

澳大利亚金融市场上许多产业领域的交易活跃程度均高于澳大利亚经济规模所能反映的情况。例如，在2016年至2017年：
- 投资级债券（在债务证券市场）的总发行量为1 300亿澳元；
- 外汇交易总计37万亿澳元；
- 柜台交易衍生品的日均成交量为49万亿澳元。[6]

澳元是世界上交易最活跃的10种货币之一。虽然澳大利亚的债券市场规模从全球范围来看相对较小，但以澳元计价的债券已被纳入机构投资者们常用的国际主流债券指数。

目前，澳大利亚的强制退休金（退休储蓄金）规模合计已达约2.5万亿澳元。[7]澳大利亚的基金以及退休金产业是区域内最大、最成熟的产业之一，其拥有与中国及国际投资者共同投资的经验，且重

---

[1] 参见澳大利亚贸易投资委员会，Why Australia: Benchmark Report 2018 (2018)，第3、4页。
[2] 同上注，第11页。
[3] 截至2017年12月，澳大利亚的失业率为5.4%。
[4] 参见 https://www.transparency.org/country/AUS。
[5] 外国投资审查委员会，Annual Report 2015-16，第9页，载 https://cdn.tspace.gov.au/uploads/sites/79/2017/04/1516-FIRB-Annual-Report.pdf。
[6] 参见澳大利亚金融市场协会，2017 Australian Financial Markets Report，第1、6、7页，载 https://afma.com.au/data/afmr/2017%20AUSTRALIAN%20FINANCIAL%20MARKETS%20REPORT.pdf。
[7] 参见澳大利亚统计局，5655.0 - Managed Funds, Australia, Sep 2017，载 http://www.abs.gov.au/ausstats/abs@.nsf/mf/5655.0。

要的是其具备长远投资眼光。

7. 证券交易市场

澳大利亚最大的证券交易市场是澳大利亚证券交易所（ASX），约占澳大利亚全部股票市场交易总量的 79%。

ASX——截至 2017 年 6 月 30 日财政年度[①]				
IPO——首次募集	二次募集	总市值	上市公司数量	外国公司
152（146 亿澳元）	371 亿澳元	1.7 万亿澳元	2 239	266

自 2015 年以来，澳大利亚的另类股票交易平台 Chi-X 以其针对独家交易产品的定价模式与 ASX 形成竞争。Chi-X 约占澳大利亚全部股票市场交易总量的 21%。

8. 食品、综合农业

相较于其他国家，澳大利亚的可用土地较多，因此在大规模的大田农业方面具有相对优势。

投资澳大利亚综合农业能为投资者带来潜在的战略利益及机遇。食品以及其他农产品的需求预计会有大幅增长，澳大利亚将会是一个理想的投资目的地，具体优势包括：

- 毗邻亚洲的成长型市场；
- 稳健的生物安全制度；
- 生产高品质、安全产品的创新性以及声誉记录；
- 技术熟练的劳动力。

澳大利亚生产多种多样的食品以及纤维制品。前四大农产品分别为食用牛养殖、奶牛养殖、谷物种植以及绵羊养殖，其次是蔬菜、水果、坚果、羊肉和棉花。该产业已引起了国外养老基金以及一些当地退休金基金的浓厚兴趣，预计未来将会受到进一步的关注，原因包括：

- 更多的资本需求（至 2025 年估计有 1 090 亿澳元的资本需求）；
- 该产业可提供年均 10%～12% 的长期回报；
- 该产业是一个绝佳的投资组合多样化工具（该产业可对冲通胀、与传统资产关联性较小并且较少受到经济衰退的影响）；
- 由于农业用地较为分散，该产业可发展集约经营。

2015 年至 2016 年，澳大利亚农产品出口额达 446 亿澳元。相比之下，澳大利亚在同时期的农产品进口额为 172 亿澳元。

截至 2017 年 6 月 30 日，澳大利亚含有外资权属成分的农业用地总计为 5 050 万公顷，占澳大利亚全部农用地的 13.6%。[②] 中国公司以及个人拥有澳大利亚全部农用地的约 0.4%。[③]

澳大利亚也是一些亚洲食品以及营养品的主要供应商，包括婴儿食品、维生素和益生菌。

9. 能源及矿产资源

澳大利亚是自然资源的主要生产国。正如澳大利亚政府所称："澳大利亚拥有丰富多样的矿产以及自然能源资源。该产业在过去以及将来都将继续为国家的繁荣作出贡献。澳大利亚拥有世界上最为丰富的铁矿石、黄金和铅资源，以及第二大的铝土矿储备。"[④]

化石燃料在澳大利亚的能源构成中同样占有主要地位，尤其是液化天然气以及煤炭。尽管冶金煤的合同价格一度达到 2011 年以来的最高点，但由于供给量高于钢铁市场的预期需求，且随着传统市场参与者开始退出煤炭市场，煤炭产业正在经历重大的结构性变化，同时也意味着煤炭行业将有越来越

---

① 参见澳大利亚证券交易所有限公司，Annual Report 2017，第 33、34、77 页，载 https://www.asx.com.au/documents/investor-relations/AnnualReport2017.pdf。
② 参见澳大利亚税务局，Register of Foreign Ownership of Agricultural Land，第 5 页，载 https://cdn.tspace.gov.au/uploads/sites/79/2017/09/Register_of_Foreign_ownership_of_Agricultural_Land_2017.pdf。
③ 参见外国投资审查委员会，Annual Report 2015-16，第 7 页，载 https://cdn.tspace.gov.au/uploads/sites/79/2017/04/1516-FIRB-Annual-Report.pdf。
④ 参见澳大利亚贸易投资委员会，Why Australia: Benchmark Report 2018 (2018)，第 15 页。

多的投资机会。在天然气方面,将会有更多的机会促进并开发更多的天然气资源以服务澳大利亚的国内市场。

尽管煤炭仍是澳大利亚主要的能源,以风能和太阳能为主的可再生能源也在稳步发展。得益于技术的进步以及在澳大利亚拟实现2020年可再生能源目标的大趋势下,澳大利亚的可再生产业将会有越来越多的投资机会。2016年,澳大利亚17.3%的电力由可再生能源提供,并且大规模的可再生能源投资较2015年增长了5倍,相应的投资额超过40亿澳元。

考虑到在澳大利亚各州以及各领地均发现了自然资源,因此仍有机会在全国范围内投资未充分开发利用的资源。矿业在经历了澳大利亚以及全球市场的不确定性后已经复苏,预计投资者对澳大利亚资源产业的信心也将恢复。进一步而言,市场参与者可能会利用股价低迷的机会适时出价,澳大利亚的资源产业仍将维持其收益丰厚的特点。

10. 医疗保健

澳大利亚的医疗保健系统由各级政府组织、管理并出资,同时由私人健康保险系统提供支持。

- 澳大利亚政府:负责调控医疗政策、提供资金并进行监管。其管理医疗保险制度以及澳大利亚公众健康保险计划,包括为公立医院的患者提供免费的药物或相应补贴以及免费住院治疗。
- 州及领地政府:负责提供包括公立医院在内的公众医疗服务,并监管私人医疗服务以及设施。

互联网以及智能手机用户的迅速增长,使进入国际健康科技市场的澳大利亚新兴企业数量剧增。通过与活跃的医疗投资基金的合作,该等企业已开发了包括穿戴式设备、医疗应用程序、在线医疗信息服务以及病患护理工具在内的一系列创新技术。

澳大利亚有多元化的医疗设备产业,涵盖了世界知名技术制造商、供应商以及小型新兴企业。医疗设备产业受到严格的监管,但同时得到澳大利亚政府强有力的政策支持,例如MTPConnect以及R&D税收激励措施。

11. 基础设施

在澳大利亚的联邦、州以及领地投资不同产业的基础设施,均有明确的重点关注领域。

- 交通:2017—2018年澳大利亚预算加大了对交通基础设施项目的总投资以及融资承诺,年度预算自2013—2014年起至2020—2021年将超过700亿澳元,其中包括就墨尔本至布里斯班内陆铁路项目向澳大利亚铁路轨道公司进行84亿澳元的股权投资。
- 住房:一些州及领地已意识到澳大利亚不断增长的人口对于规划良好的新型或替代型社会福利住房以及平价的公共住房的需求。
- 健康及老年护理:随着澳大利亚人口的老龄化以及生活成本的增加,对于健康护理,尤其是针对老年人的护理将产生更大的需求。该等不断增长的需求需要建设更多的公共以及私营的健康护理设施,以及提供更多的政府服务来满足。
- 公私合作模式:迄今为止,澳大利亚已有相当数量采用公私合作模式(PPP)的成功案例,在相关案例中,该等模式确保了公共以及私营主体共同合作,根据预算及时交付重要基础设施项目。在澳大利亚,以PPP模式开发基础设施项目,是具有明朗前景的开发方式。

澳大利亚公司在亚洲以及其他地区对于大规模项目的设计、建设以及管理均有良好的业绩记录。除此之外,澳大利亚还能够提供世界一流的建筑、设计、工程以及环境服务。

(二)在"一带一路"倡议下与中国企业合作的现状及趋势

"一带一路"将给予中国以及澳大利亚企业在区域基础设施发展中共同扮演重要角色的机会,以及建立新型资产区域基础设施框架的机遇。"一带一路"不仅为对接中国的资本提供了渠道,也为澳大利亚基础设施承包商、资产管理人、融资人、顾问以及投资者与中国相对应的主体进行合作提供了可能性,同时也为利用各自的经验以成功交付在澳大利亚以及新丝绸之路沿线以及其他区域的基础设施项目提供了可能性。

澳大利亚是亚洲太平洋经济合作组织(APEC)成员,该组织是促进亚太地区经济发展、合作、贸易以及投资的重要平台。

澳大利亚与许多国家建立了自由贸易协定关系，包括马来西亚、泰国、新加坡、韩国、日本、美国、智利、新西兰、中国以及东盟。

2016 年 1 月 1 日生效的《中澳自由贸易协定》（ChAFTA）是中澳之间重要的自由贸易协定。《中澳自由贸易协定》为澳大利亚以及中国企业进行广泛的商业合作提供了一个平台。

在《中澳自由贸易协定》下，澳大利亚向中国出口的 96% 的货物将享受免税优惠，为澳大利亚以及中国企业都带来了一系列好处，包括：

- 移除、减少关税壁垒（农业以及资源产业和特定的工业产品获益最大）；
- 放宽跨境投资的监管壁垒；
- 促进中澳之间的跨境投资；
- 放宽移民的法定要求以促进中澳之间劳动力的流动；
- 改善澳大利亚企业进入中国开展经营活动的渠道；
- 通过投资者国家争端解决机制提供投资者保护。

澳大利亚是亚洲基础设施投资银行的创始成员国之一。作为亚洲基础设施投资银行的成员，澳大利亚在未来 5 年将出资超过 9.3 亿澳元，成为该区域性商业银行的第六大股东，为澳大利亚的私人产业参与银行可担保项目提供了机会。

悉尼是全世界范围内仅有的 20 个官方离岸人民币交易中心之一，是亚洲知名的人民币现金以及证券结算中心。凭借悉尼的 G20 全球基础设施中心、活跃的金融科技产业以及人民币在贸易、金融以及投资领域更广泛的使用，悉尼已拥有必要的金融基础设施，足以成为资本进出中国的主要枢纽。

二、投资

（一）市场准入

1. 投资监管部门

澳大利亚联邦财政部（以下简称"财政部"）负责监管澳大利亚的外商投资事宜。财政部由澳大利亚外商投资审核委员会（FIRB）提供建议以及协助。

外国人士在进行特定投资前需要取得财政部以"无异议通知"的形式作出的事先批准（澳大利亚外商投资审核委员会的批准）。澳大利亚外商投资审核委员会的批准需要由申请人向澳大利亚外商投资审核委员会提出申请并由财政部处理。财政部将根据澳大利亚外商投资审核委员会的分析以及建议作出决定。澳大利亚外商投资审核委员会鼓励外国投资者在投资项目前期与其联系并讨论投资者可能采取的投资方案。

2. 投资产业法律、法规

财政部须根据 1975 年《外资收购及接管法》（FATA）判断是否发放澳大利亚外商投资审核委员会的批准。该法对在澳大利亚进行外商投资作出了原则性的规定。根据《外资收购及接管法》的规定，"外国人士"具有广泛的含义，包括：

- 非经常居住在澳大利亚的个人；
- 外国个人、外国公司或外国政府持有实质权益（单独或与其他联合体持有 20% 或以上）的公司；
- 外国政府或外国政府投资者（包括但不限于外国政府或独立政府实体持有至少 20% 权益的公司或受托人）。

澳大利亚外商投资审核委员会批准制度旨在授权财政部对认定外国投资方案是否违反澳大利亚的国家利益作出最终决定。"国家利益"在《外资收购及接管法》下并无定义，何等情况会被财政部（根据澳大利亚外商投资审核委员会的建议）认为违反国家利益将视个案情况而定。在对投资方案进行国家利益评估时，特别是针对涉及敏感产业（例如农业或国家基础设施）的大规模投资方案时，可能会纳入考虑的因素包括但不限于：

- 国家安全；
- 投资方案对经济、整个澳大利亚以及当地社区可能带来的影响（包括市场竞争问题以及税收合规）；
- 投资方案是否主要受商业利益驱动（也就是说，并非受外国政府的非商业利益驱动）；
- 社区对外资持有澳大利亚特定资产的顾虑；
- 投资方案对澳大利亚外商投资制度的公众支持度的影响。

如果财政部认为其有必要保护国家利益，则会在澳大利亚外商投资审核委员会批准上附加条件。如果投资者不遵守该等条件，将会被视为违反国家利益，并且财政部将再次行使其监管权力。未能遵守财政部附加的任何条件的投资者将会面临高额处罚。

3. 投资形式

只有特定的投资以及收购行为需要取得澳大利亚外商投资审核委员会的批准。以下是判断一名受《外资收购及接管法》规范的外国人士是否需要取得澳大利亚外商投资审核委员会的批准的考量因素：
- 投资者是否为私人，是否为外国政府实体，或是否来自与澳大利亚有自由贸易协定的国家（协约国投资者）；
- 收购的类型；
- 收购是否达到了相关的金额或权益申报门槛；
- 是否可获得豁免。

视投资是否属于涉及综合农业或特定土地的敏感行业收购，申报门槛将有所不同。敏感行业的收购将适用低金额批准门槛，并且澳大利亚外商投资审核委员会会进行更审慎的审查，该等敏感行业包括：
- 传媒；
- 电信；
- 交通；
- 军事以及国防相关的活动；
- 加密以及安全技术；
- 核设施的运营（或提取铀或钚的业务）。

作为协约国投资者，中国个人或企业直接投资澳大利亚时适用更高的申报门槛，这相应地降低了需要澳大利亚外商投资审核委员会批准的收购行为的数量。

中国个人和企业投资者目前在以下类型的收购中适用更高的比例以及金额批准门槛：
- 业务收购（敏感）：权益达到20%并且投资标的的全部资产价值达到2.62亿澳元；
- 业务收购（非敏感）：权益达到20%并且投资标的的全部资产价值达到11.34亿澳元。

金额批准门槛每年1月1日会根据相关指数进行调整。值得注意的是，外国政府投资者（包括来自中国的外国政府投资者）并不适用更高的申报门槛。在一些情况下，外国政府投资者仍将适用低申报门槛。

此外，协约国投资者在该协约国以外的地区设立的子公司（包括在澳大利亚设立的子公司）将不能适用更高的申报门槛。这意味着在澳大利亚设立子公司的中国个人以及企业投资者将不能适用更高的申报门槛。

4. 市场准入及审查标准

外国政府投资者就潜在交易申请澳大利亚外商投资审核委员会批准时，财政部往往会考虑以下因素：
- 拟议投资对澳大利亚国家安全的影响；
- 拟议投资是否会阻碍相关产业或行业的竞争；
- 投资者对澳大利亚政府的财政收入以及政策的影响；
- 拟议投资对澳大利亚商业的运营以及发展方向的影响及其对澳大利亚经济以及整个社区的贡献；
- 投资者的性质（尤其是投资者的经营是否独立于相关外国政府，并且投资者是否受限于并坚持贯彻法律，以及是否遵守商业行为的通用标准）。

下表概括了 2015 年至 2016 年间向澳大利亚外商投资审核委员会提出的申请:

FIRB 申请（2015—2016）[①]	数量	比例	拟议投资的价值
批准（无条件）	26 954	62.66%	970 亿澳元
批准（有条件）	14 491	33.69%	1 508 亿澳元
合计批准	41 445	96.35%	2 478 亿澳元
否决	5	0.01%	—
撤回	1 319	3.07%	—
豁免	244	0.57%	—
合计	43 013	100%	2 478 亿澳元

（二）外汇管理

1. 外汇监管部门

澳大利亚未设有专门监管外汇或货币流动的部门。

尽管澳大利亚未设有相当于中国"国家外汇管理局"的机构，但部分监管部门对外汇制度会产生特定的影响，例如澳大利亚交易报告分析中心（AUSTRAC）以及澳大利亚证券投资委员会（ASIC）。

2. 外汇法律、法规简介

澳大利亚一般不会限制货币进出，并且澳元可自由兑换。政府一向采取浮动汇率的政策，汇率由国际市场的供求来决定。因此澳大利亚储备银行（RBA）不会给汇率水平设定特定的目标，但在外汇领域仍存在部分报告义务以及零散的监管规定。

（1）报告义务

外汇方面最主要的报告义务来自 1988 年《金融交易报告法》的规定，即要求 1 万澳元或以上的国际汇款向澳大利亚交易报告分析中心报告。此外，2006 年《反洗钱及打击恐怖主义融资法》下的报告主体（例如银行、金融服务提供者）同样有类似的报告义务。该等报告义务的目的在于防止逃税、洗钱以及恐怖主义融资。因此，澳大利亚交易报告分析中心并不会阻止任何与国际贸易相关的常规汇款。

如果与澳大利亚有足够的地缘上的联系，那么提供支付服务（例如，接受零售支付指示、兑换货币或提供资金）可能会受到反洗钱及打击恐怖主义融资的相关立法的规制。相关立法所约束的支付服务提供者应当在澳大利亚交易报告分析中心进行登记、遵守交易报告要求以及实施"了解你的客户"活动，并履行其他义务。

（2）零散的监管

澳大利亚现行的零散的监管以及限制规定如下：

- 从向非澳大利亚居民支付利息、非免税投资收益或使用费中预提税款；
- 受澳大利亚对外经贸部管理的各种制裁制度规制。

（3）外国企业的外汇管理要求

任何希望在澳大利亚从事外汇兑换活动的商家（例如向消费者提供货币兑换服务的商家）都可能需要取得澳大利亚证券投资委员会颁发的澳大利亚金融服务牌照（AFSL）。

提供立即（即"现场"兑换）或在 3 天内结算的外汇兑换的外汇经营商一般不需要取得澳大利亚金融服务牌照。除此之外的所有外汇经营商（即提供超过 3 天的远期外汇/期货）均需要取得澳大利亚金融服务牌照并需遵守 2001 年《公司法》有关报告以及经营的规定。

（4）电子支付监管（澳大利亚境内）

澳大利亚的支付系统能够使消费者以及商家通过现金、支票以及电子资金转账的方式进行价值

[①] 参见外商投资审核委员会, Annual Report 2015—2016, 第 19 页, 载 https://cdn.tspace.gov.au/uploads/sites/79/2017/04/1516-FIRB-Annual-Report.pdf。

交换。

澳大利亚储备银行以及澳大利亚支付清算协会（APCA）负责监督管理澳大利亚不同的支付系统。如需直接与其他金融机构进行交易结算，一方需要在澳大利亚储备银行有一个结汇账户并成为澳大利亚支付清算协会或其他系统管理机构所管理的相关支付系统的会员。

如果支付服务提供者有意或可能诱导消费者购买"金融产品"（包括无现金支付工具、外汇兑换或对外汇产品以及其他衍生品进行做市），则该支付服务提供者需要取得澳大利亚金融服务牌照。取得澳大利亚金融服务牌照需要非常多的前期投入以及持续的合规成本支出，但在特定情况下可能会获得相关豁免。

（三）融资

1. 主要金融机构

澳大利亚金融监管体系由五个主要机构组成，各自承担特定的职能：

- 澳大利亚审慎监管局（APRA），负责储蓄机构（即银行、建房互助协会以及信用合作社）、寿险机构、普通保险机构、再保险机构以及退休金机构的审慎监管以及监督。
- 澳大利亚证券投资委员会，负责监管澳大利亚金融系统的市场行为以及对投资者的保护。澳大利亚证券投资委员会监管金融市场、金融服务提供者、市场交易、金融产业中介以及金融产品，包括投资、保险、退休金以及储蓄业务（不包括放贷业务）。
- 澳大利亚储备银行，负责货币政策、支付系统以及澳大利亚金融系统的整体稳定性。
- 财政部，负责发展以及引导澳大利亚经济政策的部门。
- 金融监管委员会，负责协调澳大利亚审慎监管局、澳大利亚证券投资委员会、澳大利亚储备银行以及财政部。

2. 外国企业的融资条件

在《公司法》下，未在澳大利亚登记的外国公司不得在澳大利亚经营业务。

"外国公司"包括法人实体和一些非法人实体。对于一个在澳大利亚以外的地区成立且在澳大利亚未设总部或主要营业场所的非法人实体，如果其可以自己的名义起诉或被起诉，或可以其秘书或高级管理人员（高级管理人员系为持有财产之目的适当任命）的名义持有财产，则该主体属于"外国公司"。

拟在澳大利亚经营业务的外国公司必须在澳大利亚证券投资委员会登记。在《公司法》下，如果法人团体有以下行为，则属于经营业务：

- 在澳大利亚有经营场所（例如常驻办事机构）；
- 在澳大利亚建立或使用股份转让办事处或股份登记办事处；
- 作为代理、合法遗产代理人或受托人在澳大利亚掌管、管理或买卖位于澳大利亚的财产（无论通过雇员、代理或者其他人士）。

《公司法》未对在澳大利亚经营业务给予详尽的定义，因此，需根据普通法进行考虑。在普通法下，是否"经营业务"属于一个事实问题。

在普通法下，一个公司是否在澳大利亚经营业务取决于"机制""重复"以及"连续性"三个概念。一个公司即使在澳大利亚没有固定的经营场所也可能被认为经营业务。进一步而言，经营业务一般需要进行一些人身活动，该等活动本身就已构成了一部分经营业务。

其他可能会导致外国主体被视为在澳大利亚经营业务的活动包括：

- 在澳大利亚拥有有权约束外国主体的代表；
- 在澳大利亚任命代表（例如代理人），且该等代表的行为可能会被认为是外国主体的行为而不仅仅是该等代表自身的行为，或该等代表的行为已不仅仅属于"行政上"的范畴；
- 对在澳大利亚的任何代理或其他代表的行为实施明显的控制；
- 在澳大利亚发展重要的客户群；
- 在澳大利亚从事一系列日常或连续的交易；

- 支付其在澳大利亚的场所的运营或其代理或代表的场所的运营的成本，或为上述场所的运营提供资助；
- 在澳大利亚聘请人员，或支付代理或代表聘请的人员的薪酬或向其提供资助；
- 在澳大利亚安置或使用业务设施（例如IT服务器）。

在澳大利亚，经营金融服务业务需要满足以下条件：
- 持有澳大利亚金融服务牌照；
- 被任命为授权代表；
- 根据《公司法》的规定，获得豁免而不需持有澳大利亚金融服务牌照。

在澳大利亚法律下，即使金融服务提供者在澳大利亚并无实体存在，其仍有可能被认为在澳大利亚经营金融业务。

澳大利亚证券投资委员会将向符合标准的牌照申请人颁发澳大利亚金融服务牌照。申请牌照可能需要繁杂的证明文件。取得牌照后，持牌人将承担许多义务。在澳大利亚，零售客户和批发客户适用不同的金融服务制度。如向零售客户提供金融服务，则须遵循大量额外的披露及操守规定。违反澳大利亚金融服务牌照制度者可被追究刑事责任，而交易对手可能会撤销交易。

在澳大利亚，通常不要求公司实体取得提供贷款的牌照后方可提供贷款。但是，如果贷款过程中包含出借人对外提供金融产品（例如衍生品）的情况，则出借人需要持有澳大利亚金融服务牌照。

根据澳大利亚法律，向公司实体提供贷款的主体可能会被要求进行登记。例如，2001年《金融产业（数据收集）法》要求特定的公司（包括在澳大利亚唯一或主要业务是借款或提供融资的公司）在澳大利亚审慎监管局进行登记。

向2009年《国家消费者信贷保护法》（包括《国家信贷守则》）规定的人士提供信贷需要依法取得澳大利亚信贷许可证。《国家消费者信贷保护法》适用于为以下目的向个人提供信贷的情形：
- 为个人、家庭或日常之目的；
- 为投资之目的购买、更新或改善住宅物业；
- 对为投资之目的购买、更新或改善住宅物业所提供的再融资贷款。

《公司法》要求出借人需持有澳大利亚金融服务牌照方可向个人提供边际贷款（或者提供与贷款有关的任何其他金融产品）。根据澳大利亚法律，向个人提供贷款的主体也可能被要求进行登记。

（四）土地政策

1. 土地相关法律、法规简介

澳大利亚各州及各领地一般采用托伦斯登记制进行土地登记。在该制度下，州以及领地的产权登记处存有每个地块目前的所有权人的登记信息。澳大利亚的大多数土地都按照托伦斯登记制进行登记。

土地一般由买卖双方通过合同进行转让，相关合同将规定各方的权利、义务以及责任，并规定拟出售土地的相关条款。土地出售合同可由买卖双方自行约定，但含有外资成分的土地所有权则需要根据《外资收购及接管法》在联邦层面进行规范。

2. 外国企业收购土地的规定

外国政府投资者收购澳大利亚土地适用"0元申报门槛"且需取得澳大利亚外商投资审核委员会的批准。外国政府投资者收购采矿、矿产或矿权相关的权益同样如此。

（1）商业用地

外国投资者在收购澳大利亚商业用地的权益前可能需要取得澳大利亚外商投资审核委员会的批准。根据以下不同情况将适用不同的规定：
- 土地是否空置；
- 拟进行的收购是否满足"低门槛土地"的条件；
- 拟进行的收购的金额。

低门槛土地将受到更审慎的审查（以及更低的申报门槛），包括：
- 矿山、石油或天然气井，矿场或类似的业务；

- 是否存在因该土地上部分通信网络部件缺失而导致在其他土地上无法提供电话或互联网服务的情况；
- 该土地上是否设置有公共基础设施（包括机场、港口，或者有关电力、天然气、水的传输、分配或供给，或者有关污水处理的基础设施）。

（2）农业用地

如外国人士拟持有的农业用地的累计价值超过 1 500 万澳元，则该等农业用地的投资一般需要取得批准，但来自协约国（例如中国）的投资者除外。

农业用地是指用于或可以合理地用于初级生产业务的土地，包括培养及繁殖植物、饲养直接用于出售或加工后出售的动物、鱼类养殖及树木种植。需要注意的是，超过一定金额标准的综合农业（例如进行肉类、家禽、谷物、乳制品、牛奶、水果或蔬菜加工的企业）的收购通常需要取得澳大利亚外商投资审核委员会的批准。

一般而言，除非土地已被广泛营销，否则外国投资者将无法取得澳大利亚外商投资审核委员会的批准以购买该农业用地。作为澳大利亚外商投资审核委员会的批准的考量因素的一部分，外国投资者需要告知澳大利亚外商投资审核委员会该农业用地销售的过程。澳大利亚外商投资审核委员会所指的公开透明的销售过程是指：

- 房地产"广泛营销"，意味着其必须在广泛使用的房地产网站或在区域性/全国性媒体上进行广告宣传；
- 房地产应当进行至少 30 天的广告宣传；
- 有平等的机会可以就未出售的农业用地提出报价。

为遵守该新规定，外国投资者需要向澳大利亚外商投资审核委员会说明其如何注意到该农业用地已在市场上出售的信息，以及后续的收购如何以公开透明的过程进行，但以下情况除外：

- 外国投资者收购在过去 6 个月已进行公开广告宣传（但并未出售）的房地产；
- 外国投资者的权益实质上由澳大利亚人士所拥有（即至少 50% 的权益由澳大利亚人士所拥有，但该比例会根据外国投资者的情况上调）；
- 外国投资者为符合澳大利亚法律的要求进行收购（例如，采矿缓冲区域）。

（3）居住用地

外国人士在澳大利亚收购住宅房地产的权益前一般需要取得澳大利亚外商投资审核委员会的批准。"收购权益"包括但不限于：

- 签署无条件的合同约定购买一处住所；
- 收购不动产抵押项下的担保权益，即使持有房地产的是澳大利亚公民或永久居民；
- 拥有在将来以约定价格购买房地产的选择权（例如，出售选择权或购买选择权）。

澳大利亚外商投资审核委员会通常无条件通过对于购买新住所以及空置的居住用地的申请。相反，非居民外国人士以及外国控制的公司一般禁止在澳大利亚购买已建成的住所，但在澳大利亚有实质业务的外国公司除外。

（五）公司设立及解散

1. 企业的组织形式

澳大利亚实行多种企业组织形式及商业结构。

在澳大利亚，投资、经营业务的形式及组织结构的选择是获得市场成功的关键，且会受到业务性质、税务及投资者需求等一系列因素的影响。商业组织形式包括公司、信托或管理投资计划（MIS）、合资企业及合伙。

企业/商业组织结构	主要特点	监管规则
私营公司	• 必须至少有1名股东，但非员工股东不得超过50名。 • 必须至少有1名通常居住在澳大利亚的董事。 • 可以（但不强制要求）聘任公司秘书。 • 因税务目的必须有1名公共事务人员。 • 必须在澳大利亚有注册办公室。 • 主要决策机构是董事会。 • 与公司相关的股东权利由章程或法定的可更换规则进行规范，股东协议可规范股东之间的关系。 • 不得从事需要提交证券发行说明书的活动（即向不特定公众发行证券），但可以向员工给付证券。 • 不需要召开年度股东大会（AGMs）。	• 由澳大利亚证券投资委员会根据《公司法》监管。
公众公司	• 必须至少有1名股东。 • 必须至少有3名董事（其中两名应通常居住在澳大利亚）。 • 必须至少有1名通常居住在澳大利亚的公司秘书。 • 因税务目的必须有1名公共事务人员。 • 必须在澳大利亚有注册办公室。 • 主要决策机构是董事会。 • 由公司章程对与公司相关的股东权利进行规范，股东协议对公众公司而言并不常见。 • 可以是上市公司或非上市公司，上市公司指在澳大利亚证券交易所等交易所挂牌交易的公司。 • 可根据证券法及其他适用的法律公告关于发行股票、债券或其他证券的发行说明书。 • 必须召开年度股东大会。	• 由澳大利亚证券投资委员会根据《公司法》监管。 • 由澳大利亚证券交易所（如在澳大利亚证券交易所上市）或其他市场交易所监管。
信托/管理型投资信托（以下简称"MIS"）	• 受托人拥有企业的资产，并代表信托受益人开展交易活动。 • 受托人可以是个人或企业。 • MIS是一种常用的信托结构，可让人们为共同目的集中资金并从中获利。 • MIS由受托人/责任实体（RE）及/或投资经理管理。	• 注册为MIS的信托产品有较重的监管及合规负担（此外，如有散户投资者，还存在信息披露的合规责任）。 • 部分情况下，因融资需要会要求对投资者进行信息披露。
	• 信托受益人为大额投资者。 • 构成MIS的信托至少需要两个权益持有人。 • 如果信托的所有投资者均为大额投资者，则该信托不必注册为MIS。	• 运营时须持有澳大利亚金融服务牌照。 • 澳大利亚金融服务牌照通常由受托人、投资经理或由外部主体通过代表人及/或中介机构持有。 • 根据一般信托法规及《公司法》进行监管。
	• 信托受益人为散户投资者。 • 如果MIS有超过20名"成员"参与，则其必须在澳大利亚证券投资委员会注册。如其中有散户投资者，该信托可能需要登记为MIS，这样可以从更广大的潜在投资者群体中融资。 • 可在澳大利亚证券交易所上市。	• 注册为MIS的信托产品有较重的监管及合规负担（此外，如其中有散户投资者，还可能存在信息披露的合规责任）。 • 注册后，责任实体必须为公众公司并持有澳大利亚金融服务牌照。 • 根据一般信托法规及《公司法》进行监管。
合资企业	• 合资企业指由具有共同目标或项目的各方共同组建、经营且共同所有的企业。 • 合资企业可以为法人性质或非法人性质。 • 投资者权利由合资协议、单位证券信托持有人协议（合资企业的形式为信托时）或股东协议（合资企业的形式为公司时）进行规范。 • 可通过所有上述企业组织结构进行合资经营，或以非法人企业的形式（契约式）合资经营。 • 实现与其他市场参与者的共同合作（如获取合资经营方的资源）。	• 所适用的监管规定取决于合资企业的具体形式（如信托或公司）。

(续表)

企业/商业 组织结构	主要特点	监管规则
合伙企业	• 并非单独的法律实体——合伙人对企业债务承担连带责任。 • 除若干例外情形外，合伙企业不得拥有超过20名合伙人。 • 合伙人共享企业的管理和经营权。 • 合伙人之间的合伙关系受合伙协议规范、管理。	• 各州及领地的《合伙法》。 • 合伙协议。 • 普通法。

在澳大利亚经营业务，公司是最常见的企业组织形式。公司可用私营形式或公众形式。根据《公司法》的规定，公众公司负有更为繁重的披露及报告义务。私营公司在澳大利亚所有注册公司中占比约99%。

（1）董事的职责

公司董事会有管理公司事务的主要权力。公司的董事必须遵守《公司法》及一般法规所规范的多种不同义务（包括衡平法的信义义务、侵权法的注意义务及普通法的合同义务），违反董事义务会受到民事及刑事处罚。《公司法》规定的董事义务适用于"影子董事""实际董事"以及公司高级管理人员。而董事及高级管理人员对违反《公司法》所规定的义务的抗辩理由较为有限。

澳大利亚公司的董事必须遵守下列原则及规定：

• 谨慎勤勉：董事及高级管理人员行使职权履行义务时，必须达到一个理性人在同样的环境下作为公司董事及高级管理人员、承担同样公司职责时所能达到的谨慎、勤勉程度。

• 诚实及为正当目的行事：公司董事及其他高级管理人员必须诚实（为公司最佳利益）且出于正当目的行事。

• 利益冲突：董事必须避免个人或第三方与公司之间的利益冲突，该义务包括披露重要的个人利害关系，并避免不恰当地利用个人职位或公司信息。

• 破产交易：董事在合理相信公司处于资不抵债的状况或很可能因承担债务而破产时必须防止公司产生债务。

（2）董事及高级管理人员的责任保险

责任保险可用于补偿被保险董事及高级管理人员因履行管理职责被指控行为不当时所承受的损失或应诉成本。特定的行为或损失不在保险政策的承保范围内，例如，故意诈骗或欺瞒。保险索赔请求必须针对发生在承保期间的行为，且保险政策通常会明确赔偿金额限制。

2. 公司设立程序

在澳大利亚设立或"组建"公司的程序相对简单且直接。

（1）注册设立

向澳大利亚证券投资委员会登记时须提交申请，申请中应包含下列信息（如适用于具体公司类型）：

• 公司类型；

• 拟用公司名称或澳大利亚公司注册号（ACN）；

• 各发起股东、拟任董事、公司秘书的书面同意及详细信息；

• 公司注册地址及经营时间；

• 主要经营地；

• 最终控股公司的证照信息；

• 股权结构。

澳大利亚证券投资委员会将在必要的登记费用缴纳完成后出具公司商业登记证明。

（2）章程

制定公司章程时可以采纳《公司法》的可替换规则，亦可自行起草章程内容，或结合上述方法制定。公众公司还需要在公司章程获得通过后的14天内，向澳大利亚证券投资委员会提交一份正式通过章程的特别决议副本和章程副本。

（3）常住要求

澳大利亚的常住要求适用于在根据《公司法》成立的公司中担任董事的个人。根据《公司法》注册的私营公司必须至少有一位"通常居住"在澳大利亚的董事。公众公司（包括在澳大利亚证券交易所上市）必须至少有两名通常居住在澳大利亚的董事。

《公司法》没有对通常居住进行定义。一般来说，如果个人与澳大利亚有持续的联系并把它视为居住地，则会被认定为在澳大利亚通常居住。个人可以是多个国家的居民，这实际上是一个事实认定问题。

举个例子，《外资收购及接管法》将"常住居民"定义为在过去 12 个月内在澳大利亚至少居住 200 天，且其在澳大利亚的居住并不受任何澳大利亚法律限制的个人（例如，临时签证的持有者不是澳大利亚的常住居民）。

（4）经审计的财务报告

除了保留财务记录外，某些公司还必须准备向澳大利亚证券投资委员会提交经审计的财务报告。该类公司见下表：

公司类型	标　准	向澳大利亚证券投资委员会提交的时间安排
公众公司	适用于所有公众公司。	公司的财政年度结束后 4 个月内。
披露实体	适用于所有披露实体。 披露实体有几种不同的类型，其中最常见的一种是在交易所（例如澳大利亚证券交易所）挂牌交易的公众公司。	披露实体的财政年度结束后 3 个月内。
大型私营公司	若该公司（或其控制的任何实体）符合下列因素中至少两项： • 在该财政年度，公司的合并收入达到或超过 2 500 万澳元。 • 在财政年度结束时，其合并总资产的价值达到或超过 1 250 万澳元。 • 在财政年度结束时，其雇有 50 个或更多的雇员。	公司财政年度结束后 4 个月内。
外资控股的小型私营公司	如下列所有因素均符合： • 全年或部分时间由一家外国公司控制； • 当年向澳大利亚证券投资委员会提交的财务报表中，未被已注册的外国公司或公司、注册计划或者披露实体合并计算的； • 该公司（或其所控制的任何实体）符合大型私营公司标准中的至少两项（见上）。	公司的财政年度结束后 4 个月内。

一些外国控股的小型私营公司可能会因澳大利亚证券投资委员会减少这类报告要求而从中受益。如果澳大利亚证券投资委员会或持有 5% 以上表决权的股东提出要求，小型私营公司必须准备并提交经审计的财务报告。

3. 公司解散的途径和要求

解散公司至少有四种方法。

（1）自愿注销登记

公司在满足以下要求时可以通过通知澳大利亚证券投资委员会的方式自愿注销登记：
• 所有股东都同意注销登记；
• 该公司停止运营；
• 该公司的资产价值低于 1 000 澳元；
• 公司没有负债；
• 公司不涉及任何法律诉讼；
• 该公司已向澳大利亚证券投资委员会支付了所有费用和罚金。

（2）清算

有偿付能力和资不抵债的公司都可以进入清算程序：
• 有偿付能力：公司经营目的已经实现，股东想对公司资产进行分配。
• 资不抵债：公司不能正常运作，债权人希望得到偿还。

清算意味着公司解散。公司的资产被清算（即转化为现金），并按照法定优先规则分配给债权人和股东。公司随后会被注销。

清算人的主要目标是将可分配给无担保债权人的现金池最大化。因此，清算人除了出售资产，收回公司在一般经营过程中积累的所有账款外，还将积极实施追索诉讼。

清算程序与接管程序（非管理程序）可同时分别进行。

（3）管理程序

独立的管理人从董事手中接管破产或濒临破产的公司，随后有一个法定的短期中止程序以评估公司是否能够并应当继续经营，或者是否应当被清算。

对公司全部财产或者实质上的全部财产有担保权的债权人可以在"决定期间"（任命管理人之日起13个工作日内）指定一个接管人（或者执行担保物权）。

管理程序与接管程序（非清算程序）可同时分别进行。

（4）接管程序

接管人从董事手中接管、控制有担保权的资产，并用担保资产来偿还相关的有担保债权人。根据担保合同的具体条款，指定接管人时可针对具体资产（如一座建筑物），也可针对公司的全部业务。

接管人可以决定出售资产，或者管理资产以提高其价值，或者将其出租以收取租金和利润。如果公司的有担保债务得到清偿使公司避免被强制清算，则公司在接管程序后仍可存续。

接管程序与管理程序或清算程序（但不会两者兼有）可同时分别进行。

（六）兼并和收购

收购和投资澳大利亚的公众公司主要受到以下机构的监管：

兼并和收购的监管	
澳大利亚证券投资委员会（ASIC）	澳大利亚证券投资委员会是澳大利亚关于公众公司收购、企业和证券法的主要监管机构。澳大利亚证券投资委员会有权修改《公司法》多项规定的实践操作，并有权豁免各公司遵守《公司法》的义务。澳大利亚证券投资委员会发布对立法条款的解释，并对其作出《公司法》修改和义务豁免的情况发布详细指导。
澳大利亚证券交易所（ASX）	如果澳大利亚证券交易所认为收购各方没有遵守交易所规则，那么其可能会参与收购程序。澳大利亚证券交易所的主要关注点是确保目标公司（以及收购方，如已上市）的证券信息在市场上披露畅通。
收购委员会	收购委员会是一个非司法机构，由银行家、律师和公司董事在内的一系列并购行业专家组成。在澳大利亚，收购委员会是收购结束前负责解决收购争议的主要机构。 收购委员会拥有广泛的法定权力： • 在对公司重大利益的接管或收购中作出"不可接受情况"的声明； • 作出临时或者最终的决定以纠正"不可接受情况"，保护遭受该等不利影响的人员和团体的权利，如目标公司的股东； • 审查澳大利亚证券投资委员会关于是否豁免某人遵守收购条款义务或者修改收购条款的决定。 当事人必须将拟议事项向委员会提出申请。投标人、目标公司、澳大利亚证券投资委员会或任何利益受该收购影响的人士，都可以申请收购委员会的声明或决定。
澳大利亚竞争及消费者委员会（ACCC）	澳大利亚竞争及消费者委员会将会介入具有或可能具有显著减少澳大利亚任何市场竞争之效果的收购交易（详见下文）。

交易管制的概要	
20%规则	如果收购人及其关联方因该次收购将控制目标公司超过20%的证券（或从持股比例高于20%、低于90%的收购线开始增持），则《公司法》将禁止收购人的该次收购（不管是通过购买现有的证券或发行新证券）("20%规则")。 如果个人（包括实体）有以下情况，则通常被认为对证券有相关权益： • 是证券的持有者； • 有权行使或者控制行使该等证券所代表的表决权； • 有权出售或控制对证券的出售。

(续表)

20%规则的例外	个人或实体可以通过多种方法突破20%规则，主要的两种方法是接管收购和协议安排。 其他例外情况将在下文介绍。
接管收购	接管收购可以通过场外要约收购或场内要约收购的方式进行。场外要约收购是最常见的收购方式。两种情形都将在下文介绍。
协议安排	根据协议安排，目标公司请求法院和股东批准将目标公司股份转让给收购方。 为获得审议通过，协议安排需经代表75%以上出资额出席会议的股东同意及超过50%的出席股东的同意（不包括收购人或其关联方作出的任何表决）。协议安排必须得到法庭的批准。

20%规则限制下允许的收购途径	
股东批准	经与收购无关联的独立目标公司股东批准的收购。
渐进式收购	由至少已经持有19%投票权的股东在6个月内收购公司不超过3%的股票投票权。
配股	向所有股东按比例公平配股所产生的收购。
承销	承销人根据招股说明书或者其他披露文件收购发行的证券。
下游收购	收购在澳大利亚证券交易所（或其他经批准的外国市场）上市的"上游"公司证券时，因其对某家在澳大利亚证券交易所上市的"下游"公司持有相关权益，因而产生的间接收购。

1. 场外要约收购

在场外要约收购中，收购人对目标公司的所有证券持有人分别进行相同报价以取得证券持有人的证券。当证券持有人接受要约时，即可达成对相关证券的收购协议。

收购人必须准备包含相关背景信息和收购条款的收购人声明。该声明会提交给澳大利亚证券投资委员会、澳大利亚证券交易所和目标公司。声明副本必须同时发送给目标公司的股东。

在宣布要约收购之日起2个月内，收购人向目标公司的股东发出书面要约，且必须保持开放至少1个月，但最长不得超过12个月。无异议的场外要约收购通常需要至少3个月的时间才能完成。如果被提出异议，收购的持续时间可能会显著增加。

场外收购要约可以是有条件的或无条件的、全面的或部分的，且对价可以是现金、证券或两者的结合。场外收购要约通常是在满足或豁免多项条件的基础上作出的有条件的要约，例如，收购人至少达到最低持股比例（通常是50%或90%），或者取得如澳大利亚外商投资审核委员会或竞争及消费者委员会批准等特定的监管批准。

如果收购人及其关联方拥有至少90%的某类证券的相关权益，收购人可强制性收购剩余的该类证券。

场外收购可能是善意收购（即根据目标公司董事会的建议作出），也可能是敌意收购。

2. 场内要约收购

场内要约收购由收购人通过经纪人在澳大利亚证券交易所提出特定价格的要约。在澳大利亚，场内要约收购比较罕见，因为场内要约收购必须是无条件、以现金为对价的，并且须收购目标公司相关类别的所有证券。

可以更为快捷地实施收购是场内要约收购的战略优势。场内要约收购的时间比场外要约收购的时间短，因为场内要约收购必须在公告发布后的15天内向股东发出收购要约。对目标公司100%股权进行收购时，场内收购的批准门槛和场外收购相同。

3. 协议安排

鉴于目标公司和收购方需要就协议安排达成约定，协议安排一般仅用于实施善意要约收购。该计划的结果是"要么全有，要么全无"，因此该计划在100%权益的收购中被频繁使用。

协议安排的进程由目标公司推进。目标公司和收购方达成一项正式的收购实施协议，该协议的条款构成向目标公司股东和董事提出的协议安排。

协议安排比要约收购更灵活，允许收购方以现金或代币的任何组合作为支付对价，并可以特定事件的发生（或不发生）作为支付条件，例如，以是否取得监管批准为条件。协议安排可以使收购包含更为多样化的交易结构，例如，减少目标公司的资本。协议安排也可达到全有或全无的效果，并经常被用于全面收购。

4. 关联交易（涉及公众公司）

澳大利亚对关联交易有严格的规定，尤其是对公众公司。当公众公司或 MIS 的责任实体与关联方进行与提供财务利益相关的交易时，就会发生关联交易。关联方包括：
- 公众公司或相关实体的控股公司；
- 公众公司或相关实体的任何董事，或是公众公司或相关实体之控股公司的任何董事；
- 董事的配偶、父母和子女；
- 任何由上述实体或个人所控制的实体。

一般来说，交易必须经股东批准，除非交易按照独立交易原则进行。这种情况在任何一方都不受自身利益的影响行事也不承担任何特殊责任或义务时发生。股东在考虑是否批准一项关联交易时可以借助于独立专家的报告。

如果交易需要股东批准，则应召开股东大会通过普通决议（即获得超过 50% 的投票）批准关联交易。

在交易所（例如澳大利亚证券交易所）上市的公司必须遵守关于关联交易的额外规则。

5. 私营公司

在澳大利亚收购私营公司很大程度上由合同法进行规范。《公司法》《外资收购及接管法》和 2010 年《竞争和消费者法》（CCA）的某些规定通常也适用于私营公司的合并和收购。

出售过程中涉及双方就起草出售协议所进行的谈判，协议中的条款是对交易内容以及双方的风险分配的书面表述。

收购私营公司主要有两种方法：
- 收购私营公司的股权（"股权出售"）；
- 收购私营公司所有（或部分）的资产和商誉（"资产出售"）。

	股权出售	资产出售
结构	买方购买经营业务的目标公司的股份。因此，买方将获得对目标公司及其业务和资产的控制权。	将目标公司部分或全部资产卖给买方，但目标公司的股权所有权保持不变。 转让资产通常包括雇员、知识产权和设备。
债务	买方将承担目标公司的所有债务。 但是，买方通常会在销售协议中加入保证和赔偿条款来减轻需承担的负债。	买方不承担目标公司过去或现在的负债。 但是根据双方之间存在的商业交易，买方可以选择承担过去的负债。
优点	与资产出售相比，交易程序的复杂程度较低，因为标的类别通常只有一种（即目标公司的股份）。 商业运作的公司结构和劳动合同仍将保留，对于拟将目标公司作为子公司经营的买方而言可能是有利的。	具有确定性和灵活性，因为买方可以选择从目标公司获得的确切资产。 买方还可以限制转让给其的债务，并将剩余债务留给目标公司。
潜在问题	• 如果某些目标公司的资产由另一个实体持有，则出售前需要进行内部重组，情况可能较为复杂。 • 双方关于债务承担的协商。	• 可能因转让引起重大的重组问题（对双方而言均存在该等问题）。 • 根据澳大利亚法律，买方必须与目标公司的现有雇员签订劳动合同，没有雇员的同意，劳动合同的权利和义务不能转让。因此，存在关键雇员不接受雇员转让条款的风险。 • 重要合同可能存在要求第三方同意的转让条款。如果待变更的合同和第三方的数量较多，情况可能会很复杂。 • 税务影响。

（续表）

	股权出售	资产出售
保证	·转让方保证的重点是股权所有权的有效性，以及目标公司的历史经营和负债问题。 ·收购方在承担目标公司过往负债的情况下，通常会要求转让方作出覆盖范围更为广泛的保证。	转让方保证的重点是所收购资产的属性（例如，机器应满足工作条件，公寓应取得土地所有权）。

（七）竞争法

在澳大利亚市场开展业务之前，熟悉澳大利亚的竞争法是很重要的，竞争法限制了澳大利亚企业从事某些活动。

澳大利亚的反垄断法和消费者保护法包含在《竞争和消费者法》中。《竞争和消费者法》的目的是通过促进竞争、公平贸易以及为消费者提供保护来提高澳大利亚人的福利。

1. 竞争监管部门

澳大利亚竞争及消费者委员会是澳大利亚一个独立的法定机构，负责实施澳大利亚的竞争法规。该机构对可能违反《竞争和消费者法》的行为展开调查，并有权通过行政手段处理问题、发布侵权通知，或向澳大利亚法庭起诉（以自身名义或代表他人）。

企业不确定所从事行为是否违反澳大利亚竞争法时，可寻求澳大利亚竞争及消费者委员会批准以消除澳大利亚竞争及消费者委员会对它们提起诉讼的风险。

2. 竞争法简要介绍

在澳大利亚，以下领域属于竞争法的范畴：
· 兼并及投资控制；
· 卡特尔法；
· 其他形式的反竞争行为；
· 消费者保护。

澳大利亚联邦法院可能对违反《竞争和消费者法》竞争条款的行为进行实质性处罚。在民事和刑事禁令中，公司面临的最高的罚款和罚金为以下金额较高者：
· 1 000 万澳元；
· 违法所得的 3 倍；
· 当违法所得数额难以确定时，集团企业年营业额中来源于澳大利亚收入的 10%。

针对各项卡特尔刑事指控，个人将面临最高 10 年的监禁或最高 42 万澳元的罚款或二者相结合的处罚；而针对违反任何其他竞争禁令的行为，个人面临的最高民事罚金为 50 万澳元。高级管理人员因应对卡特尔刑事指控而承担的法律费用和受到的任何经济损失，企业不得进行补偿，否则亦构成违法行为。

3. 规范竞争的措施

（1）兼并及投资管控

澳大利亚的兼并管控制度不包含强制性通知程序。然而在澳大利亚的收购实践中，有一套被广泛使用的自愿通知程序。股权或者资产的收购人可以：
· 就拟进行的收购交易礼节性地通知澳大利亚竞争及消费者委员会（包括保密的情况）
· 基于拟议收购并不会显著减少竞争向澳大利亚竞争及消费者委员会申请非正式许可；
· 基于该次收购将产生或者可能产生公共利益向澳大利亚竞争及消费者委员会申请正式许可。

在实践中，收购人通常会在完成交易之前向澳大利亚竞争及消费者委员会请求许可，如果该交易将会：
· 导致收购方占有 20% 或以上的市场份额；
· 排除一个有力的实际竞争对手；
· 产生明显的垂直集中问题；
· 可能被其他的监管机构［例如，澳大利亚外商投资审核委员会、澳大利亚税务局（ATO）、澳大利亚证券投资委员会或澳大利亚审慎监管局］转交给澳大利亚竞争及消费者委员会；

- 受到公众关注或竞争对手、供应商或客户的投诉。

(2) 卡特尔法

在澳大利亚，竞争者之间制定或达成包含卡特尔条款的合同、安排或谅解都将可能构成民事和刑事违法行为。卡特尔条款指：

- 具有固定、控制、维持商品或者服务价格的目的或者效果；
- 具有下列目的：
  —— 阻碍、限制或制约商品或服务的产量、产能、供应或获取途径；
  —— 划分客户或地理区域；
  —— 串通投标。

若该卡特尔条款有助于实现合资企业的设立目的，而且是经营合资企业的合理且必要的条件，则参与合资协议或谅解的竞争者可以不受上述规则的约束。

澳大利亚竞争及消费者委员会还拥有豁免和宽免的权限。只有第一个向澳大利亚竞争及消费者委员会披露卡特尔行为并同意全面配合澳大利亚竞争及消费者委员会调查的当事人才符合民事豁免的条件。

(3) 其他反竞争行为

澳大利亚的竞争法同样禁止下列行为：

- 任何具有显著减少竞争目的或效果的合同、安排或谅解。
- 个人或多人参与有显著减少竞争目的或效果的联合行为。"联合行为"没有正式定义，但是立法指导思想认为联合行为是违反竞争规则的沟通，或虽不存在合同、协议或谅解，但已超出独立应对多变的市场行情的业务范围的合作行为。
- 在市场上拥有支配地位的公司从事具有显著减少竞争目的或效果的行为。
- 供应或收购条件中包含以显著减少竞争为目的或效果的非价格垂直限制条件。
- 公司对其产品或服务的最低转售价格进行规定。

(4) 消费者保护

在澳大利亚经营业务的公司必须遵守澳大利亚的消费者保护法。这些条款可能会对企业—企业、企业—消费者的交易产生很大影响。这些规定包括：

- 禁止误导性或欺骗性的行为，包括使用误导性或虚假广告、误导性的名称或市场行为（包括外观相似的产品）和在谈判过程中作出误导性陈述；
- 禁止在贸易或商业中作出不合理的行为；
- 提供法定担保（例如，保证货物质量可以接受），适用于价值小于 40 000 澳元的商品和服务供应，或者通常为个人、家庭或日常使用（但不包括用于再补给或用于制造或维修的商品）而供应的商品和服务。
- 法院有权宣布与消费者或小企业签订的格式合同因存在不公平条款而无效。

(八) 税务

1. 税务制度及规则

澳大利亚有一个较为全面的税收制度，在联邦和州/领地上都有征税。澳大利亚税务局负责管理联邦级别的税法。每个州和领地都有不同的机构负责管理在该特定管辖范围内实施的税法。

澳大利亚税收规则的适用取决于经营实体管理事务所采用的组织形式（即作为个人、公司、合伙或信托运营）。澳大利亚居民实体和非居民实体的税收规定也有所不同。

2. 主要税项及税率

(1) 所得税

澳大利亚的所得税根据一个实体的应纳税所得额征收，这相当于一个实体的应税收入减去准予扣减数。澳大利亚的财政年度自 7 月 1 日至次年 6 月 30 日。

一个实体的应税收入是基于其纳税居民的性质决定的。概括而言：

- 澳大利亚居民的应税收入中必须包括所有来源（即全球收入）的普通收入（例如，收入利得）

和法定收入（例如，净资本收益）；

- 非居民实体的可评估收入中必须包括源于澳大利亚的普通收入和根据税法规定的其他收入（例如，在处理澳大利亚不动产权益时产生的资本收益）。

准予扣减数包括在获得或产生应税收入或经营业务时所产生的一般业务支出。税法也提供了一些具体的扣减数。

在某一特定财政年度，如纳税义务人的准予扣减数超过其可纳税所得额，则可能导致当年的税收损失，在一定情况下，该年度的税款可在以后的财政年度内从纳税义务人的应税收入中进行征缴。

澳大利亚与其他国家订立了一系列关于所得税的综合性双重税收条约。这些都与在澳大利亚开展活动的非居民实体有关，也与在澳大利亚以外从事活动的澳大利亚居民有关。

非居民实体的某些收入，如股息、利息和从澳大利亚实体获得的特许权使用费，也可能通过征收最终预扣税的方式被澳大利亚征收所得税。

澳大利亚有严格的转移定价规则，目的是防止纳税人通过从事跨境交易增加扣减额或减少收入额，从而规避其对澳大利亚的纳税责任。澳大利亚的税法也包含了各种各样的反规避规则。

（2）其他税项

除了所得税外，澳大利亚还征收其他一系列的税。

澳大利亚征收10%的商品和服务税（GST）。商品和服务税的概念与许多经合组织国家的增值税类似。商品和服务税是由消费者承担的消费税，通常已包含在澳大利亚商品的购买价格中。纳税人一般可以在经营企业的过程中为他们所承担的任何商品和服务税申报税收抵免。

澳大利亚的雇主也要缴纳一定的雇佣税，包括预扣税款，向雇员或与雇员相关的人员提供的非现金福利的雇员附加福利税，雇主向雇员或有关承包商支付高于一定工资标准时所缴工资税，以及退休金、员工赔偿转让保险等。

此外，每个州和领地对一系列不同的交易征收印花税。值得一提的是：

- 所有州和领地对其管辖范围内的土地权属转让或者土地上的任何利益的转让征税；
- 所有州和领地针对使收购方获得土地所有者一定权益的间接收购征税；
- 一些州和领地（但并非全部）对涉及某些商业资产（例如，商誉、知识产权）的一系列交易征收转让税。

澳大利亚某些进口商品（包括豪华车）要承担比常规关税更多的纳税义务。某些情形下也适用其他税项（例如，葡萄酒平衡税、消费税）。

（3）税率

澳大利亚现行所得税税率如下[①]：

澳大利亚居民个人税率	
应纳税所得额	应缴税款
0～18 200 澳元	无
18 201～37 000 澳元	超过 18 201 澳元部分每澳元征税 19 澳分
37 001～87 000 澳元	在 3 572 澳元基础上对超过 37 000 澳元部分每澳元征税 32.5 澳分
87 001～180 000 澳元	在 19 822 澳元基础上对超过 87 000 澳元部分每澳元征税 37 澳分
180 001 澳元及以上	在 54 232 澳元基础上对超过 180 000 澳元部分每澳元征税 45 澳分

---

① 2018年6月21日，澳大利亚通过了一项总规模高达1440亿澳元（合1060亿美元）的减税计划。根据这一为期7年的税收计划，到2025年财年，94%的纳税人的所得税税率将下调至32.5%，甚至更低。

澳大利亚非居民个人税率	
应纳税所得额	应缴税款
0～87 000 澳元	每澳元征税 32.5 澳分
87 001～180 000 澳元	在 28 275 澳元基础上对超过 87 000 澳元部分每澳元征税 37 澳分
180 001 澳元及以上	在 62 685 澳元基础上对超过 180 000 澳元部分每澳元征税 45 澳分

澳大利亚居民及非居民企业税率（2017—2018 财年）	
营业额	适用税率
低于 2 500 万澳元	27.5% 固定税率
高于 2 500 万澳元	30% 固定税率
说明：公司税率在逐年下降。预计在 2026—2027 财年，营业额少于 5 000 万澳元的公司适用税率将为 25%。	

其他税务相关问题：

• 每个州和领地都有自己的印花税制度，不同交易将适用不同税率（最高可达 5.75%）。在某些州，还会就外国投资者直接或间接购得土地权益的事项征收印花税附加费。附加费范围在 3% 到 7% 之间。

• 目前的员工附加福利税税率为 47%，但联邦议会正在考虑将税率提高到 47.5%（从 2019 年 7 月 1 日起）。

• 目前的养老金最低缴款率是雇员薪酬或工资的 9.5%（有最高缴款限额）。

• 不同的州和领地在各自的辖区内征收工资税。目前的工资税税率在不同的辖区有所不同，但一般在 5% 左右。

3. 纳税申报和优先权

（1）税务表格及纳税申报

澳大利亚的所得税缴纳责任基于自行评估制度，它需要每年提交纳税申报表。澳大利亚税务局可以对纳税人进行审计，以确保他们遵守税收法规。

在澳大利亚注册的企业必须按月、按季度或按年度缴纳间接的税务负担，并且必须向澳大利亚税务局提交一份商业活动声明。必须定期申报与其他税务事项（如工资税、员工附加福利税）有关的申报文件。

为了在澳大利亚开展业务，各实体应获得一个税务号（TFN）和澳大利亚商业编号（ABN）。此外，其还必须在开展业务或在澳大利亚获得收入之日起 3 个月内委任一名公共事务人员。公共事务人员必须是年满 18 岁的自然人，通常居住在澳大利亚。

（2）优先权、纳税减免及优惠

澳大利亚没有规定任何免税期或减税政策。

在某些情况下可以适用一系列的纳税减免和豁免。例如，澳大利亚的某些商品和服务免除了类似商品和服务税的间接税收（例如，某些食品的供应、某些卫生服务的供应）。此外，诸如研发、天使投资、风险投资等活动可以享受与行业激励相关的纳税补偿。

澳大利亚有一种股息归属抵免制度，意味着公司的某些股息分配可能会存在税收抵免（红利抵免），澳大利亚的居民股东可针对公司以股息收益分红所应向澳大利亚缴纳的税款申报纳税抵免。它还使非居民股东获得该类股息时免缴任何股息预扣税。

此外，澳大利亚的税法允许独资企业集团成立一个"税务合并集团"。这意味着，该集团的所有成员都被视为为特定的所得税目的成立的单一实体。在澳大利亚的企业集团中，税务合并非常普遍。类似的集团可以为其他税务目的而成立（例如商品和服务税）。

（九）证券

1. 证券相关法律、法规概述

澳大利亚的公司可进行首次公开发行证券（IPO），并在交易所中进行交易。在交易所上市增加了公司股票的流动性。

然而，在上市之前，公司必须首先满足某些要求。对于澳大利亚证券交易所来说，关键要求是：

通过标准	一般要求
股东数量（股东分布要求）	至少有 300 个非关联投资者，每人持有价值 2 000 澳元或以上的证券
公众持股量	20% 或以上。 公众持股量指以下证券占公司证券的比例： • 不受托管安排的限制； • 由非关联投资者持有。
公司规模	利润标准： 过去 3 年持续运营的利润合计达到 100 万澳元，且过去 12 个月持续运营的合并利润达到 50 万澳元。 或 资产标准： • 有形资产净值达到 400 万澳元； • 市值达到 1 500 万澳元。
股价	该公司寻求的所有证券的发行价格或售价必须至少为 0.20 澳元
良好品质	公司各董事必须符合澳大利亚证券交易所关于董事良好声誉和品质的要求

外国公司如要取得澳大利亚证券交易所的上市交易批准，必须根据《公司法》注册为一家在澳大利亚从事商业活动的外国公司。

（1）持续要求

当公众公司成为在澳大利亚证券交易所上市的公司（上市公司）后，它必须遵守澳大利亚证券交易所上市规则（上市规则）以及《公司法》。上市规则对上市公司进行了一系列要求，例如：

• 定期向股东和公众进行报告和公告（持续披露）；
• 提交年度和半年度的财务报告；
• 拟进行部分交易前应事先披露并取得股东批准；
• 确保管理事务（例如，出具证券的持有声明）和交易（例如，市场上的股票回购）符合一定的要求和标准；
• 遵守澳大利亚证券交易所的公司治理原则和建议（澳大利亚证券交易所原则）。

（2）澳大利亚证券交易所原则

澳大利亚证券交易所原则要求上市公司每年在"不遵守，应解释"的基础上报告合规情况。

在澳大利亚，上市公司的董事会常由非执行董事、独立董事组成，非执行的独立董事通常多于负责执行的独立董事。在澳大利亚，上市公司的董事长很少在公司内部担任高级管理人员职务。上市公司还应明确董事会和管理层各自的角色、职责和资质要求并进行披露。大型上市公司通常成立董事会下属委员会，以解决审计、风险控制、合规、提名和薪酬问题。

澳大利亚证券交易所原则规定，澳大利亚上市公司的审计委员会应仅由非执行董事组成，其中应多数为独立董事。根据上市规则，这项要求对应标普/澳大利亚证券交易所指数排名前 300 位的上市公司具有强制性。

2. 证券市场的监管及法规

澳大利亚的证券市场主要由澳大利亚证券投资委员会监管。澳大利亚证券投资委员会负责监督公司是否遵守《公司法》的规定，并对上市公司的信息披露和公司活动享有广泛的调查权力。澳大利亚证券投资委员会还负责对澳大利亚的交易所（例如澳大利亚证券交易所）进行监管。

(1) 内幕交易

证券和其他金融、投资产品的内幕交易行为是被严格禁止的。

上市公司的交易政策必须包含特定内容,包括明确关键管理人员不得在禁止期内(包括年度股东大会召开前和年度、半年度财务报表公告前)买卖公司证券或公司发行或创设的金融产品。《公司法》禁止对激励报酬进行套期保值。上市公司的董事必须披露其证券交易的全部细节。

(2) 市场不正当行为

操纵证券和金融市场的行为是被禁止的。证券和金融市场的运营者有义务积极监控市场交易,并向澳大利亚证券投资委员会报告任何可疑交易。此外,澳大利亚法律最重要的规定,即禁止任何人在金融交易中从事误导性或欺骗性的行为。

3. 外国企业参与证券交易的要求

除了澳大利亚外商投资审核委员会的批准要求,外国企业可以以自己的名义、为自身目的在澳大利亚买卖证券,且不受一般限制。

(十) 投资优惠和投资保护

1. 优惠政策概述

澳大利亚没有官方的优惠政策,但可能有非官方的投资优惠,澳大利亚政府与州政府和领地政府共同合作:

- 积极鼓励外商对澳大利亚的直接投资;
- 旨在帮助外国投资者在澳大利亚建立或扩大业务。①

2. 对特定行业和地区的支持

和世界上大多数国家一样,澳大利亚为一些行业、业务部门和地区提供补贴。补贴往往因政府和政治局势而有所不同。

例如,澳大利亚政府最近在澳大利亚北部设立了总额高达 50 亿澳元的基础设施发展贷款计划(NAIF)。根据该贷款计划,澳大利亚政府在 2021 年 6 月 30 日前可通过贷款、优惠或替代融资机制为澳大利亚北部的经济基础设施建设项目提供资助,包括为符合基础设施发展贷款计划资格标准的机场、铁路、水、港口和住房项目提供资金。

3. 经济特区

澳大利亚没有经济特区。

4. 投资保护

得益于澳大利亚的先进经济和法治,澳大利亚的投资和所有权得到了很好的保护。

(1) 知识产权及品牌保护

澳大利亚拥有大量知识产权法律,可以保护与大多数企业业务相关的品牌和构思。该知识产权法律体系由澳大利亚政府机构"澳大利亚知识产权局"管理。在澳大利亚受保护的知识产权形式包括:

- 商标;
- 著作权;
- 专利;
- 设计。

更详细的信息可参见"知识产权"部分。

(2) 资产的担保权益

2009 年《动产担保法》(PPSA)允许公司和个人注册并保护在澳大利亚的某些担保利益。该法案不适用于土地权益。

根据《动产担保法》的规定,有担保权的债权人(有效的担保利益)拥有优先于其他权益/债权

---

① 参见澳大利亚贸易投资委员会,在澳大利亚投资:投资指引,载 https://www.austrade.gov.au/International/Invest/Guide-to-investing/Australian-Government-support-programs。

人的担保利益。这种担保权益在公司破产的情况下可以执行且可以向第三方主张。

根据《动产担保法》的规定，可通过以下任一方式使动产的担保权益生效：
- 在动产保护注册表上注册——这是最常见的生效方法；
- 动产和其他抵押物由被担保的一方占有；
- 金融资产（包括股票、债券和由澳大利亚授权的存款机构的某些账户）由被担保人控制。

在行使执行权之前，通常不必获得法院判决。执行权可以在担保协议中约定。此外，《动产担保法》还提供了除担保协议中约定的选项之外的一系列法定执行选项。

（3）土地抵押

在不涉及个人财产时（以最常见的不动产为例），担保事项涉及不同担保文件。对于土地而言，通常是抵押贷款文件。

州和领地法律对不动产抵押进行监管。抵押权意味着有权出售被抵押的土地权益。在大多数州，行使抵押权之前必须按规定进行违约通知；但行使抵押权时不需要向法院提出申请。排序在有担保债权人出售权之后的其他权益不会影响买方对土地的权益。然而，某些受成文法保护的有限权益可能会制约买方权益。

（4）澳大利亚法院保护和双边投资条约

除了上述投资保护制度，根据澳大利亚法律规定，澳大利亚法院也是裁决商业法律纠纷的独立机构。澳大利亚法院也会作出有利于外国企业、不利于澳大利亚公司和澳大利亚政府的裁定和判决。

此外，澳大利亚还参与了多项双边投资条约。① 这些条约为投资澳大利亚提供了额外的保护，进一步兑现了澳大利亚鼓励外商投资的承诺。

三、贸易

（一）贸易行政管理部门

澳大利亚的贸易法律并非由单一的政府部门全权负责管理，而是由多个政府部门各自分工、共同负责贸易政策的制定与执行：
- 外交和贸易部：负责所有外交事务，包括双边、区域性和多边贸易政策，条约管理，国际贸易和投资促进；
- 财政部：负责研订竞争法、消费者保护法、证券和投资法、外商投资审查政策；
- 内务部：负责边境管制和海关；
- 农业和水资源部：负责生物安全和检疫；
- 工业、创新与科学部：负责工业和市场的开发、知识产权、反倾销法；
- 就业与小企业部：负责就业；
- 基础设施、区域发展与城市部：负责民用航空、海运和航运政策。

由于澳大利亚是一个联邦制国家，每个州和领地政府都负责制定各自与贸易相关的法律，因此，澳大利亚各州和领地之间的法律可能会有所不同。

（二）贸易法律、法规概述

由于大量政府部门实施各自的贸易政策，澳大利亚没有统一管理国际贸易的一般性立法或监管制度，目前，澳大利亚管理国际贸易的法律、法规包括：
- 1901年《海关法》：管理澳大利亚的海关监管程序；规定了安全和控制程序；制定货物进出口管理办法；并监管堆场、仓库、货运站和航空的各类活动。
- 1995年《海关关税法》：对进口至澳大利亚的货物规定了进口关税。
- 1975年《外国收购法》：管理澳大利亚境内大型土地或公司收购的评估机制，以确保其符合国家利益。

---

① 条约清单可在以下网页获取：http://dfat.gov.au/trade/topics/investment/Pages/australias-bilateral-investment-treaties.aspx。

- 1985年《澳大利亚贸易和投资委员会法案》：设立澳大利亚贸易和投资委员会（以下简称"澳贸委"），系全国贸易、投资和教育促进机构。
- 1956年《海关（禁止进口）条例》、1992年《进口食品管理法》：明确了允许进口和禁止进口至澳大利亚的产品。
- 1901年《消费税法》：规定了澳大利亚进出口消费税管理制度。
- 1995年《刑法典》：规定了与进出口货物有关的刑事犯罪。
- 1999年《新税法（商品和服务税法）》：规定了进出口所征收的增值税（在澳大利亚称为商品和服务税——GST）。
- 2010年《竞争和消费者法》：建立限制性贸易惯例、反垄断及其他竞争法相关的制度；制定了澳大利亚消费者保护制度。适用于所有在澳大利亚进行贸易或商业行为的主体。

澳大利亚是WTO的创始成员，与诸多国家或地区签订了影响其贸易和关税制度的双边、区域性和多边贸易协定，包括文莱、加拿大、柬埔寨、智利、印度尼西亚、日本、韩国、老挝、马来西亚、缅甸、新西兰、巴布亚新几内亚、菲律宾、新加坡、泰国、美国和越南。在诸多区域性协定中，例如东南亚国家联盟、亚太经合组织，澳大利亚作出了更多承诺。澳大利亚正在继续与印度和印度尼西亚就若干其他双边协议进行谈判，并且还参与跨太平洋伙伴关系协定（TPP）、澳大利亚—海湾合作委员会（GCC）区域贸易协定、太平洋更紧密经济关系协定（PACER Plus）、区域全面经济伙伴关系协定（RCEP）等相关的谈判。

（三）贸易管理

澳大利亚一直保持着其作为世界上最开放的经济体之一的地位，尽管"资源热潮"于2011年达到顶峰后，其地位已处于不稳定状态。随着国际贸易领域越来越广泛，澳大利亚的经济进入了一个新的过渡时期，国际贸易目前约占全国GDP的40%。

澳大利亚政府的贸易远景是根据所谓的"亚洲世纪"而改变的，国际贸易的新趋势反映了澳大利亚进出口市场的变化，澳大利亚五大双向贸易伙伴中有三个（中国、日本和韩国）均位于亚洲。澳大利亚正继续积极推行双边、区域性和多边贸易协定及一系列其他政府政策，旨在加强贸易开放和经济增长。

澳大利亚获取贸易收入的主要手段是关税。约96%适用于最惠国的关税低于5%。此外，99.5%以上的关税是从价关税，这提高了澳大利亚贸易环境的可预测性和透明度。在某些受政府支持的领域，澳大利亚的关税明显较高，即纺织品、服装、鞋类和机动车辆。

澳大利亚对外国直接投资（FDI）持开放态度，仅对大型投资项目进行审查以确保其符合国家利益。尽管附带一定的条件，但是外国直接投资项目很少被直接拒绝。出于对澳大利亚公民的保障，对住宅房地产和农用地的投资进行限制。此外，对民用航空、海运和电信基础设施也有股权限制。

（四）进出口商品的检验检疫

澳大利亚以其独特而多样的动植物而闻名。由于其具有隔离型的地理位置，澳大利亚有严格的检疫法律。鉴于联邦分权制度和生物多样性的明显差异，不同的检疫措施不仅适用于进入澳大利亚的情形，而且适用于澳大利亚境内的交易。

- 检疫法律涵盖所有进口和出口事项，包括但不限于植物、动物、食品。联邦农业和水资源部（DAWR）主要负责实施和管理澳大利亚的检疫系统，这些职能包括颁发进出口许可证和实施检查。卫生部还提供有关进口许可的意见和建议，并对与公共卫生有关的生物材料进行评估。
- 食品进口由1992年《进口食品管理法》以及1993年《进口食品管理法规》规制。联邦农业和水资源部根据《进口食品检验计划》制定了管理流程。澳大利亚新西兰食品标准部门作为提供有关食品安全的建议和制定标准的独立法定机构，负责协助联邦农业和水资源部进行风险管理工作。所有进口食品必须按照食品标准法规的规定对食品添加标签。

对于纺织品、服装、太阳镜和化妆品的卫生和产品护理同样有着强制性的产品标签信息标准。电子设备如洗衣机、洗碗机、冰箱、空调以及机动车辆必须通过产品标签标注其能耗。在烟草方面，澳大利亚拥有特别完善的法律，包括禁止所有广告营销并要求烟草平装。

虽然澳大利亚对于申请进口许可证没有必然要求，但基于包括公共卫生、环境保护和国际义务等诸多原因，对某些产品有许可要求。这些许可要求对150多种产品实行禁令或一系列严格的检验和检疫程序，包括：
- 农产品；
- 动物皮毛制品，濒危动植物物种；
- 抗生素，其他治疗药物和物质；
- 烟草制品；
- 氢氟烃（HFCs），臭氧消耗物质/合成温室气体，农药和其他危险化学品。

除非有特定的许可证要求，否则所有价值超过2 000澳元的出口货物必须在海关注册。澳大利亚多数出口报关都使用澳大利亚政府营运的电子报告工具—一体化货物通关系统（ICS），也可以在海关柜台填写出口报关单（B957表格）。根据出口货物的具体情况，海关可以代表授权出口许可的机构或政府部门进行合规审查。澳大利亚在农产品出口方面拥有较大的市场。为了缓解国际贸易摩擦，海关可以对某些产品实施出口管制，以符合目的地国家的进口要求。

（五）海关管理

澳大利亚拥有现代化的海关管理基础设施，最大限度地减少了纸质文件的要求，几乎所有进出口活动都可通过电脑化流程完成。内务部的主要业务部门是澳大利亚边境执法署（ABF）。为推进政府鼓励国际贸易的目标，澳大利亚边境执法署通过以下方式进行海关管理：
- 实现现代化和提高数字化能力，包括自助身份/实体验证。
- 实现低风险、大批量交易的自动化，以便将资源分配给风险较高的区域（例如，通过澳大利亚可信赖贸易商进行快速处理）。
- 通过积极协商与行业合作。
- 加大力度提高透明度和一致性。

近年来，为避免与贸易商仅在海关处、仅就单笔交易进行单一交流，澳大利亚海关的管理流程转向更全面渠道的交流。现在，澳大利亚边境执法署通过积极的行业参与和建议（包括合规培训、估值、关税建议）来提高海关管理的确定性。

根据澳大利亚法律，澳大利亚边境执法署可以使用一系列合规工具。在确定适当的监管补救措施时，澳大利亚边境执法署将考虑诸多因素，包括历史背景、具体意图、减轻处罚的情况、纠正措施、对经济或社区的影响、对澳大利亚边境执法署运营资源的影响、合作和披露。

四、劳动

（一）劳动立法概述

1. 概要

澳大利亚的雇佣法源自普通法，其义务来自法律和适用的法规以及行业规定，例如现代奖励制度和企业协议。

2. 普通法

普通法主要源自雇佣合同，是澳大利亚雇员和雇主的义务的主要来源。普通法中也有一些通常适用的原则。

雇佣合同的条款和条件有各种来源。首先，部分条款是由各方口头或书面明确同意的；其次，根据周围环境、习惯和实践，法律也隐含着部分适用于雇佣合同的条款。书面的雇佣合同通常会列明雇佣的主要条款，包括雇员的职位、工作地点、雇用状况、薪酬、奖励津贴、有关使用和披露保密信息的义务、知识产权、交易限制（如适用）、终止和附则。

3. 法令框架

（1）最低雇用条件

适用于澳大利亚企业的主要雇用立法是 2009 年《公平工作法》。

《公平工作法》规定了最低限度的法定雇用条件，即"全国就业标准"（NES）。全国就业标准适用于所有国家系统雇员，不论雇员的收入或职位如何，包括每周最长工作时间、要求灵活安排工作的权利、育儿假、年假、个人/看护人休假、社区服务假、长期服务休假、公众假期、终止通知和裁员费。这些条件不能通过合同、奖励或企业协议修改从而减损雇员的利益。

（2）最低工资

最低工资标准通过现代奖励、企业协议和国家最低工资标准列明。目前的全国最低工资是每小时 18.29 澳元或每周 38 小时 694.90 澳元（税前）。《公平工作法》规定了临时雇员的默认补助金比率为 25%，但现代奖励和企业协议可能会规定不同的临时雇员的补助金比率。

（3）终止雇用

所有雇主必须根据《公平工作法》的规定提供终止通知（如适用，支付裁员费）。

（4）不当解雇

《公平工作法》允许一些雇员就雇主苛刻、不公正、不合理地解除劳动合同提起诉讼。

一旦雇员完成了最低雇用期限（对于拥有超过 15 个雇员的雇主，其最低雇用期限为 6 个月），所有雇主，无论其规模大小，将可能因不公平解雇雇员的行为而被诉至公平工作委员会（FWC）并遭受索赔。

针对不公平解雇的主要补救措施是恢复该雇员被解雇前的职位或该雇主选择另一合适的职位重新雇用该雇员，同时，雇员可能因此收到相应补偿或所欠薪酬。

（5）一般保护

《公平工作法》包含"一般保护"条款，旨在保护雇员免受雇主因法律所禁止的事由而采取的不利行动。实质上，不利行动是指雇主采取的导致雇员在其工作中受到不利影响或歧视的行为的情况。例如，因法律所禁止的事由（例如，雇员的年龄、性别、婚姻状况、性取向、种族或宗教），雇主所采取的导致雇员被解雇、工伤、受到歧视、岗位下调的不利行为。

雇员可向公平工作委员会主张雇主违反一般保护的规定，《公平工作法》也明确规定了相应的补救措施（包括损害赔偿和复职）。

（6）退休金

联邦退休金保障立法目前要求雇主按照雇员平时收入的一定比例（目前为 9.5%）支付给独立管理且通常与雇主无关的核准养老基金。养老金存在最高缴纳基数的限制，即雇主无须为超过最低收入标准的收入缴纳养老金，目前最低收入标准为每季度 50 810 澳元。

（7）反歧视与欺凌

就业歧视被一系列州和联邦的法律明确禁止。以如下理由歧视雇员的行为是违法的，包括种族、性别、性取向、怀孕、婚姻状况、残疾、跨性别身份、年龄、父亲或母亲的身份或看护人身份。

除非雇主制定了适当的政策并就歧视问题对其雇员进行了培训，否则雇主可能会对其雇员作出的歧视性行为承担连带责任。

在工作中被欺凌的劳动者（包括雇员和承包商）可向公平工作委员会申请停止欺凌行为的命令。欺凌是指个人或群体反复对劳动者进行不合理的行为，且这种行为给该劳动者的健康和安全造成威胁。如果公平工作委员会确信劳动者受到欺凌且有可能继续受到欺凌，则可作出其认为合适的任何命令以停止欺凌行为（除了要求支付金钱的命令外）。

欺凌也属于工作健康和安全（WHS）法律制度的管制范围，即雇主有义务通过一定的行为，例如防止和应对工作场所中的欺凌，以确保其劳动者的健康和安全。

4. 行业规定

（1）现代奖励制度

一些雇员适用的最低条款和条件受"现代奖励制度"的规制。现代奖励制度是由公平工作委员会批准的文件与全国就业标准共同规定了最低雇佣条款和条件。现代奖励制度适用于某些行业和职业的雇员。

雇主和"高收入雇员"可书面同意在约定期限内不适用现代奖励制度。高收入雇员是指固定年收入超过 142 000 澳元的雇员，该金额会根据通货膨胀指数每年调整一次。

（2）企业协议

企业协议是指雇主与雇员团体以及最常见的——行业工会之间签订的协议，其中约定了适用于协议所涵盖的雇员的最低雇用条件。为了使企业协议获得行业的认可，每个雇员或潜在雇员在该协议项下享受的待遇必须优于所适用的现代奖励制度。

5. 工作健康与安全

澳大利亚境内的每个州和领地对工作健康与安全问题都有大量立法。除维多利亚州和西澳州之外，其他各州和领地的立法都是一致的（尽管西澳州预计在适当的时候也将采用示范法的立法标准）。

《工作健康与安全示范法》对从商人员、高级职员、工人和其他访问工作场所的人员都规定了各种义务，如违反这些义务将受到包括监禁在内的重大处罚。

雇主还必须为其雇员缴纳工伤补偿保险，每个州和领地的费率和制度都有所不同。

（二）雇用外国雇员的条件

1958 年《移民法》（及其相关法规和政策）与《公平工作法》项下的雇用条款共同对在澳大利亚雇用外国雇员作出规定。

所有没有澳大利亚护照进入澳大利亚的人员，都必须持有相关签证才能在澳大利亚从事其预期的活动，雇主雇用不符合签证要求的外国雇员，将遭受严格的处罚。签证持有者若违反相关条件可能会被取消签证并会被遣返。

负责管理澳大利亚签证的主管部门为内务部（DOHA）。

1. 工作许可

对于以在澳大利亚工作为主要目的的短暂停留，主要有两种类型的工作许可（即工作签证），包括：

（1）临时工作（短暂停留专家）签证（第 400 类）

临时工作（短暂停留专家）签证（第 400 类）（以下简称"400 签证"）允许持证人通过"高度专业化工作"渠道进入澳大利亚从事最长为期 6 个月的短期高度专业化工作，既可通过澳大利亚企业邀请，也可通过海外企业委派特定雇员在澳大利亚履行相关合同的方式进行，但需确保该工作本身是"非持续"的。若被认定为具有持续性，则需要申请长期工作签证。

签证持有人持 400 签证在澳大利亚进行的活动不得对澳大利亚人的就业或培训机会带来不利后果。

另外，特别 400 签证渠道允许将澳大利亚利益纳入对申请人的评估范围。该渠道仅当存在影响澳大利亚利益，迫切需要申请人入境并停留在澳大利亚的情况下适用。例如，国家紧急情况或澳大利亚的贸易机会将受到不利影响的情况。

（2）临时技能短缺签证

临时技能短缺签证（以下简称"TSS 签证"）从 2018 年 3 月初引入澳大利亚移民计划，替代之前的临时工作（技术）签证（第 457 类）（以下简称"457 签证"）。

根据所申请的技术性职业列表中的职业，TSS 签证允许 2 年或 4 年的临时工作签证。申请短期技术职业清单（STSOL）中的职业，将有资格获得 2 年签证，并可续签 2 年；申请中长期技能短缺名单中的职业，将有资格获得 4 年签证，并可续签。若申请创业公司中的职位（即公司成立时间少于 12 个月），签证期限最多只有 18 个月。

每项申请都必须严格符合薪酬、技能和英语的要求，且大多数申请都要求提供澳大利亚劳动力市场测试数据。

2. 申请手续

（1）临时工作（短暂停留专家）签证（第 400 类）

为获得 400 签证，申请人必须：

- 具有与其申请参加的活动或工作相符且相关的个人技能或/和就业背景;
- 具有短暂停留澳大利亚的真实意向;
- 具有足够支持自己在澳大利亚生活的能力——通常通过澳大利亚公司或其所在国家的雇主支付的薪水体现;
- 通过与其在澳大利亚停留期间相关的各项健康检查和品行考核。

400 签证申请对英文没有要求,对申请人的薪资也没有具体规定,但不得用于规避澳大利亚市场工资标准的要求,且根据现有政策的规定,高技能职业的最低工资应符合"临时技术移民收入标准"(TSMIT)(目前定为 53 900 澳元),其他所有职业的最低工资应当符合澳大利亚最低工资标准。

(2) 临时技能短缺签证

对于需要为雇员申请 TSS 签证的雇主,需要通过以下三个步骤:

①雇主必须符合相关要求,包括积极合法经营,以获得批准成为担保雇主。

②雇主从技能型职业列表中申请的职位是澳大利亚公民无法从事的,然而:

- 若适用《中澳自由贸易协定》或其他免除劳动力市场测试的国际贸易协定时,所申请的职位不受劳动力市场测试的限制;
- 所申请的职位必须提供至少与临时技术移民收入标准相当的薪水,并与澳大利亚市场工资标准保持一致。

③申请人需证明其具有从事所申请职位的相关技能。若所申请职位是从申请短期技术职业清单中选取的,则"临时入境者"的真实性审核要求也适用于该等签证申请。申请人还必须符合健康、品行和英语的要求。

对于 400 签证和 TSS 签证,申请人和/或企业应根据每项标准提供相应的文件以证明其满足这些要求。申请的准备、提交和管理将在线上直接与内务部对接。

申请的处理时间因人而异,但大多数 400 签证申请会在 1 个月内完成,457/TSS 签证会在 5 个月内完成,对于持有"认证担保雇主"身份的企业可加速处理。

3. 社会保险

400 签证持有者不需要在澳大利亚缴纳社会保险(通常指健康保险)。

然而,对于 457/TSS 签证,所有签证持有者在签证有效期间持有适当的澳大利亚或同类健康保险是申请签证的一项条件,包括任何家属签证持有人。

(三) 出入境

1. 签证种类

澳大利亚拥有适用于各类活动的签证类型,这些活动既贡献于澳大利亚的劳动力市场与经济,也通过家庭团聚或澳大利亚人道主义计划惠及澳大利亚公民。

(1) 工作或学习签证

以临时工作为目的的,根据预期停留时间的长短,申请 400 签证和 457/TSS 签证是最为合适的。一般技术和永久雇主担保签证允许 45 岁以下的高技能工人办理永久性移民,部分雇主担保签证类别还可有限地豁免年龄限制。

工作假期(第 462 类)签证适用于年龄在 18~30 岁之间具有大专学历及基本英语应用水平的中国护照持有者。

澳大利亚学生签证适合获批在澳大利亚进行学习的各国学生。

(2) 商务访问

前往澳大利亚进行商务访问活动的人士,应当申请访问签证(第 600 类)。

申请的准备、提交和管理将在线上直接与内务部对接,处理时间通常少于 1 个月,且中国护照持有者可享受 48 小时"快速通道"服务。2016 年 12 月,新的 10 年多次往返旅行签证开始试行,可在澳大利亚停留最多 3 个月并允许多次入境。

（3）其他签证种类

有经验的企业主、企业家或投资者亦可选择商业创新和投资签证。特别是重要投资者签证类别提供了有关英语语言要求的特殊豁免，对被动投资历史的要求更灵活，对在澳大利亚的居住条件要求更宽松，这一类别中来自中国的申请人人数最多。

2. 出入境限制

所有以非澳大利亚护照进入澳大利亚的人都必须在入境前持有澳大利亚签证。对于中国护照持有人，必须在旅行前申请并取得签证。

此外，所有入境者必须持有效护照才能进入澳大利亚。虽然澳大利亚政府对外国入境者护照的有效期限没有限制，但一些国际航空公司可能要求至少有 6 个月的有效期。

（四）工会和劳工组织

工会或劳工组织是指由个人组成的（雇员或承包商）联合，代表特定行业或职业内工人的诸如最低工资标准、工作时间以及日益增多的工作条件弹性化等诉求的共同利益体。

工会的主要职责通常包括：担任工人代言人、调查涉嫌违反雇用或工作健康与安全立法的行为、确保雇主遵守最低就业条件、在工作中出现问题时协助解决。工会可以根据 2009 年《公平工作（注册组织）法》在公平工作委员会注册，但这不是强制性要求。

（五）劳动争议

雇员和/或工会与雇主之间可能会产生纠纷，通常被称为"行业争议"，包括例如雇员罢工和实行工作禁令。

1. 劳工行动

根据《公平工作法》的规定，劳工行动发生在雇员以不同于普通工作方式的方式进行工作的情况下；雇员的工作行为受到禁止、限制或束缚；雇员无法或拒绝上班或工作；和/或雇员被雇主"拒之门外"。在某些特定情况下，劳工行动可以"受保护"，这基本上意味着工业行为的参与者大部分将被免除民事诉案。劳工行动只有在涉及企业协议谈判时才会被视为"受保护"。《公平工作法》中明确规定了何时以及如何采取受保护的劳工行动。

如果雇员参加劳工行动，雇主在雇员实施该行为期间没有义务向该雇员支付工资。

2. 谈判

受保护的劳工行动可由一位谈判代表通过向公平工作委员会申请"受保护行动表决令"的方式发起。

公平工作委员会批准该等申请需满足一定的要求。如果获得批准，公平工作委员会将发布受保护行动表决令，实质上使企业协议所涉及的雇员能够通过投票决定是否参与受保护的劳工行动。如果受保护的劳工行动是由雇员发起的，当取得投票名册中过半数雇员的投票、过半数有效投票同意该行动且该劳工行动将在表决结果宣布后 30 日内举行（除非公平工作委员会批准额外的期限），则该劳工行动可获得授权实施。

3. 争议解决程序

公平工作委员会有权根据《公平工作法》以调解或仲裁的方式处理与国家系统雇员相关的特定类型的争议，包括但不限于协商企业协议时的谈判争议、一般性保护争议、入职与离职的权利。对于非国家系统雇员（例如，公共部门雇员、地方政府雇员和位于西澳州私营部门的非适用联邦宪法公司的雇员），雇员可适用其所在的州或领地的劳动法。通常而言，大多数州和领地的裁决和/或协议包含涉及争议解决程序的条款，并且通常要求当事方在进行诉讼之前通过商业途径尝试解决争议。

五、知识产权

(一) 知识产权法律概述

只有澳大利亚联邦政府有权制定关于版权、专利、外观设计和商标方面的法律。

澳大利亚知识产权局是负责管理澳大利亚知识产权体系的联邦政府机构,具体包含商标权、专利权、外观设计权和植物育种权。

澳大利亚是主要知识产权国际多边公约和条约的缔约国,包括《伯尔尼公约》《与贸易有关的知识产权协定》(1994年)和《专利合作条约》(1970年),且与各国签订了一系列有关的双边条约(主要为自由贸易协定)。澳大利亚在条约项下的义务并非自动生效,在生效前需经国内立法转化。

1. 版权

版权法律仅由澳大利亚1968年《版权法》进行规定,澳大利亚没有关于版权的普通法。《版权法》将版权分为两类:第一类,"作品",包括原创文学、戏剧、音乐和艺术作品;第二类,特定的"除作品以外的客体",包括录音、电影、广播电视节目和出版的作品。通常而言,如果一方未经许可使用或授权他人使用版权所有人对版权材料享有的专有权利,则侵犯了版权。

根据《版权法》制定的条例中同样可找到关于版权的规定。1969年《版权(国际保护)条例》对"作品"和"除作品以外客体"互惠版权的保护,不仅限于本国国民,还扩大到其他国家的公民和居民,只要该等国家加入了主要版权公约(《伯尔尼公约》《世界版权公约》《世界知识产权组织版权条约》《世界知识产权组织表演和录音制品条约》和《罗马公约》)或是世界贸易组织成员,并且作品在这些国家制作或首次出版。

2. 商标

澳大利亚关于商标的法律由1995年《商标法》规定。除了《商标法》外,联邦政府还根据《商标法》颁布了法规,即1995年《商标法规》。《商标法》对"标志"未进行穷尽列举,包括但不限于任何字母、单词、名称、签名、数字、图形、品牌、标题、标签、票证、包装方面、形状、颜色、声音、气味或其任何组合。澳大利亚对商标的有效期限没有限制,只要商标得到持续更新便可取得永久的商标专有权。为得到《商标法》的保护,商标所有者必须向澳大利亚知识产权局提交商标申请。

澳大利亚《消费者法》(载于2010年《竞争和消费者法》附表2)也与商标有关。澳大利亚《消费者法》明确了涉及商标的行为符合商业行为的适当标准,包括不合情理行为、不公平行为、产品安全和产品信息有关的各项原则。普通法中关于仿冒行为的规定同样是商标法的法律渊源。

3. 专利

澳大利亚关于专利的法律由1990年《专利法》规定。专利赋予发明人在特定时间内独家使用该发明的法定权利。《专利法》规定了两种类型的专利:标准专利和创新专利。创新专利的注册门槛较低,但保护期较短。

澳大利亚也是《专利合作条约》的缔约国,根据该制度,在澳大利亚或其他缔约国申请专利,可在每个缔约国获得专利保护。

4. 设计

澳大利亚关于注册外观设计的法律由2003年《外观设计法》规定。外观设计注册保护产品的视觉外观设计,而不像专利保护产品功能。但如果产品的外观或视觉特征与产品功能相关,亦不影响其申请外观设计注册。

为得到《外观设计法》的保护,所有权人必须向澳大利亚知识产权局提交申请。注册外观设计的保护期限为10年,并保护设计的视觉特征,如形状、构造、图案和装饰。在澳大利亚,对注册外观设计的评估标准包括两个方面,即原创性和独特性。

5. 知识产权法院系统

知识产权诉讼案件的实务操作和程序一般由1976年澳大利亚《联邦法院法》及根据该法制定的2011年《联邦法院规则》规定。其中《联邦法院规则》第34.3条是处理知识产权诉讼所适用的一般规则。如果在澳大利亚联邦巡回法院（以前称为联邦裁判法院）进行诉讼，案件的实务操作和程序将适用 1999 年澳大利亚《联邦巡回法院法》和 2001 年《联邦巡回法院规则》。联邦巡回法院于 2003 年被授予司法管辖权以处理简易的版权问题。澳大利亚联邦法院和澳大利亚联邦巡回法院也不时发布执业指引，为从业人员提供指导。1995 年《证据法》则规定了澳大利亚的证据适用规则。

（二）专利申请

专利权申请人必须向澳大利亚知识产权局申请专利，其可根据需要获得保护的国家选择申请澳大利亚专利或《专利合作条约》专利。

为了注册为标准专利，专利申请必须体现"创造性步骤"，即为所在行业中新颖的、非显而易见的且具实用性的发明。对于创新型专利，则必须体现"革新性步骤"，即对现有知识进行逐步改进。

在起草申请材料时，申请人可以选择对形式要求较少的临时申请，也可以选择标准较高、要求在专利申请书中披露申请人所知的执行该发明的"最佳方法"的完整申请。临时申请可以在申请日起 12 个月内转换为完整申请，在这种情况下，原申请日将被视为该发明的优先权日。

所有专利申请必须采用指定表格（且用英语填写）并符合形式要求，以足够清楚和完整地对发明进行披露，使该发明相关领域的技术人员可以执行该发明。任何含糊或相对性的术语都必须进行量化，并且任何外部参考资料必须为业界常识。完整申请通常（但并不强制要求）包括该发明的附图和工作示例。

申请人在提交申请之后、取得专利之前必须采取多项措施，申请由澳大利亚知识产权局负责管理专利申请的专利审查专员（以下简称"专员"）进行专利审查，该专员将评估该专利是否符合《专利法》的各项要求。

经审查，专员可以选择授予、拒绝授予专利或出具否定意见报告。出具否定意见报告的，申请人则有时间纠正专员指出的任何错误，任何纠正必须在原始报告发布后 12 个月内作出。

创新专利的审查程序与标准专利不同，专员只会进行形式审查，如形式要件符合要求，该项申请将被授予专利并在专利局官方公报中发布。

在提交专利申请满 18 个月后，专利将通过官方公报发布，任何第三方有权提出异议。如果在所有流程中都未被提出异议，申请人将被授予专利。创新专利的保护期限为 8 年，而标准专利的保护期限为 20 年，并允许专利权人对该发明享有专有权。为维持专利权属，专利权人必须定期支付专利维持费。

（三）商标注册

商标在商标局进行注册，由商标注册处登记生效。商标是以申请人的名义对申请文件中指定的商品和/或服务进行注册。

申请商标注册的申请人应当正在使用或有意使用该商标，或已授权或有意授权他人使用该商标，或有意将该商标转让给即将设立的法人团体以期由该法人团体使用该商标。

商标按商品和服务的类别进行注册，单项申请可以涵盖一个、几个或全部类别。在提出申请时，必须对商品和/或服务范围进行明确的描述，并以此确定商标所有者的专属权利范围。

澳大利亚是建立国际商标注册体系的《马德里议定书》的 98 个成员国之一。根据《马德里议定书》的规定，商标申请人可指定澳大利亚为商标保护国家，该商标通过当地审查后即可在澳大利亚注册。

外国公司申请在澳大利亚注册之前，应核实该项商标是否已经通过《马德里议定书》在澳大利亚完成注册。如果申请人在其他缔约国初次提交申请后 6 个月内在澳大利亚提交申请，根据《巴黎公约》的规定，申请人可以适用与初次申请相同的优先权日。外国公司在澳大利亚展开任何交易前，应先考虑在澳大利亚完成其商标注册。

申请提交后，审查员将对商标进行审查，并决定该商标是否已经根据商标法提出了申请，以及是否存在驳回申请的事由。审查过程中，将对已注册的商标进行检索，以确定是否存在任何阻却该申请的已注册商标。审查员报告发布后，申请人可以通过书面形式作出答复。申请人有 15 个月的时间对审查员提出的异议进行抗辩。

注册处必须以书面形式将同意或否决申请的决定告知申请人,且必须将审查决定在商标期刊上进行公布。如果注册处同意该申请,仍可能收到第三方的异议。任何第三方在同意申请的决定公布后的 2 个月内可提出异议。申请人和异议方均可提交证据,由注册处听取(当面或书面)相关事宜。当事方也可(在注册处作出决定后的 21 天内)就注册处的决定诉至联邦法院或联邦巡回法院。

商标申请获得通过后,注册处将向商标注册所有人颁发证书,并在商标期刊上进行公布。初始注册有效期为自申请之日起 10 年,每满 10 年需进行续期。

六、环境保护

(一)环境保护监督部门

联邦环境与能源部(DoEE)是监管澳大利亚联邦环境保护的主要联邦机构。联邦环境与能源部设计并实施澳大利亚政府的政策和计划,以保护环境、水和自然遗产。

澳大利亚的每个州和领地政府都有各自的部门负责监管相应管辖地区的环境保护。通过指导,在新南威尔士州,主要的环境监管机构是新南威尔士州环境保护局,负责颁发环境保护许可证、调查和管理污染事故(空气、水、土地和噪音)以及清理污染。在新南威尔士州负责环境保护的其他重要部门包括:
- 新南威尔士州规划和环境部——负责土地使用规划和战略规划政策;
- 新南威尔士州环境与遗产办公室——负责国家公园和保护区、原住民遗产和非原住民遗产;
- 新南威尔士州水务局——负责保护地表水和地下水资源。

虽然每个州和领地的政府都采用自己的环境保护法,但监督环境保护法律实施的部门结构通常与新南威尔士州相似。

地方政府理事会在澳大利亚的每个州和领地也拥有广泛的权力,有权在规划审批中增加保护环境的要求,根据规划要求和环境保护法律调查及执法。

(二)环境保护立法概述

环境保护法律以州和领地的法律为主,以联邦层面的环境保护立法及监管为辅。

在联邦层面,环境保护的主要立法是 1999 年《环境保护和生物多样性保护法》。

该法的主要目标是对可能影响国家环境的重要事项提案进行规范,其中包括世界遗产、国家遗产名录、国际重要湿地、濒危物种和生态群落、迁徙物种、联邦海域、核活动(包括铀矿开采)以及受煤层气与大型煤矿开发影响的水资源。

如果拟议行动涉及原住民遗产、核安全、危险废物进口或出口和海上石油活动,则可能违反其他联邦环境保护法。

澳大利亚每个州和领地的政府都制定了一套环境保护法律,总的来说,可能影响环境的开发通常需要规划审批和环境保护许可证。

此类项目的审批通常需要编写详细的环境评估报告并进行公开,任何人可提交意见反对或支持该项目。

相关授权机构拥有广泛的自由裁量权,决定同意或拒绝环境许可批准。如果获得批准,监管机构通常会规定一系列要求来缓解和管理该提案的潜在环境影响,通过严格的条件限制输出和排放,并要求提供财务保证。

实施某些行动前,比如可能影响原住民遗产和非原住民遗产、受保护物种的行动,或需要供应或储存水资源、废物、危险化学品和危险物品的行动,可能需要取得其他特定环境许可的授权。

州和领地层面的环境保护法对各种环境违法行为作出了规定,包括不得造成环境损害的概括环境责任及一系列特定污染类型的违法行为。

所有州和领地政府都制定了法律,规定董事和参与公司管理的人员对公司作出的违法行为承担法律责任。监管机构是否起诉董事或经理,通常取决于他们对事件的控制和影响程度,作为为法人团体行为承担个人责任的被告,也享有特定的抗辩事由。

大多数州和领地政府也制定了具体的法律以规范土地污染问题——包括向监管机构通报污染的法定义务。

通常而言,根据州和领地污染法律的规定,制造污染的责任人(污染者)对治理污染负主要责任。

若无法要求污染者采取补救措施(例如,污染者无法确定或资不抵债),监管机构通常有权要求土地所有权人(在某些辖区内,可要求土地占用人)治理污染问题,无论是否是该土地所有权人或占用人造成的污染。

对收购或处置污染土地的主体、或在澳大利亚拥有处置污染土地的公司、或基于租赁产生的合同义务主体,潜在的污染责任将导致重大风险。

(三)环境保护评价

澳大利亚正处于环境监管的时代。在过去的20年,环境保护法发生了重大变化——联邦、州和地方政府层面愈发倾向于引入和执行环境保护法。

毫不夸张地说,环境保护立法、战略政策、指导方针、判例法和/或监管指引每周都会发生变化,为澳大利亚企业带来了风险和机遇。

虽然导致变化的原因多种多样,但可以确定的是,社会和政治层面对某些行业潜在环境影响的敏感度和意识都有所提高,且环境保护对澳大利亚未来繁荣非常重要。

国家对环境遗留问题的潜在责任是澳大利亚环境保护法的重点,并形成了一套新的制度,包括更高的财务保证义务,以确保公司无法规避停运和重建的重大成本。在昆士兰州,该制度包括新的"责任链"权力,即如果公司规避环境保护义务且牵涉了相关人员(即因公司从事相关活动可获得重大经济利益的人员,或能够影响公司行为的人员),相关人员将面临收到环境保护令的风险。

澳大利亚环境保护的其他重点关注领域与危险废物和污染土地的管理相关。许多州建立了具体的工作小组,调查和执行有关危险废物来源、运输和处置的监管制度,以及对受污染土地的补救和管理。

七、争议解决

(一)争议解决方式与主体

1. 法律渊源

由英国发展而来的普通法制度构成了澳大利亚法理学的基础,体现为法官造法、法院制定法律规则与先例。在适用类似事实或法律原则时,法官必须遵循上级法院对法律的解释。

立法是当今法律的主体,即使在仍旧主要依据普通法的地区,也通过立法作出了重大修改。法院在诸如公司法(具有全面的法规)等领域的作用则是对法律规则的法定解释和执行。

2. 澳大利亚法院系统

澳大利亚法院系统由联邦、州和领地法院组成。澳大利亚高等法院是最高上诉法院。高等法院判决联邦具有特殊意义的案件,包括对法律的合宪有效提出质疑的案件以及来自联邦、州和领地法院的上诉案件(经特别许可)。

澳大利亚联邦法院通常处理公司、竞争、宪法和行政法相关的案件,以及联邦立法项下产生的其他问题,如税收和移民问题。公司和证券诉讼案件由联邦和州法院共同管辖。

澳大利亚联邦巡回法院负责家庭法、破产、非法歧视、消费者保护、竞争、隐私、移民、版权和工业法的相关案件,对几乎所有案件与家庭法院或澳大利亚联邦法院共享管辖权。

州和领地法院系统独立运作,这些法院对除联邦立法之外的所有争议具有固有的管辖权。每个州和领地都有一个称为最高法院的高级法院。除了某些专业领域(如家庭法和竞争法),联邦通过立法赋予各最高法院对所有事项的联邦管辖权。州法院通常处理合同、侵权和刑事事宜以及在州法项下引起的案件。

较低级别的法院,包括地区和地方法院在内,有权对一定数额内的大多数严重刑事犯罪和民事诉讼进行裁决。每个州都有一系列专门的法院和法庭，其中包括收购委员会、澳大利亚竞争法庭、各种行政决定审查法庭、移民审查法庭、土地和环境法庭、工业法庭、家庭法院和各种消费者索赔法庭。

（二）适用法律

1. 启动程序

启动诉讼程序时选择正确的法院尤为重要，因为法院必须对所要审理的事项拥有必要的管辖权。诉讼时效根据不同的诉讼类型和不同的法院而有所不同，例如，合同和侵权行为必须在导致行为发生的事由首次发生之日起 6 年内提起诉讼。

2. 法院程序

每个联邦、州和领地法院和法庭都有其自有的程序规则，这些程序规则体现在法案、实践指引和具体规则中，为每个法庭审议事项提供了程序框架。

所有上级法院有权在紧急情况下单方面作出临时命令，包括在等待最后听证和确定诉讼程序时的中间禁令、资产保全令和搜查令。每个法庭都有一名值勤法官，在普通体系之外（工作时间以外）可及时听取按照一般程序难以妥善处置的紧急申请。在特别紧急情况下，可通过电话接收申请及发出指令。

除为公正利益而另有要求外，推定民事诉讼程序将在没有陪审团的情况下进行。民事诉讼通常在没有陪审团的情况下由法官或裁判官裁决，但诽谤、人身伤害民事诉讼除外。民事诉讼中的举证责任则适用"盖然性权衡"原则。

3. 费用

在澳大利亚所有管辖区内，法院都有酌情决定收取诉讼费用的裁量权。大多数情况下，败诉方将被要求向胜诉方支付费用，通常有两种类型的费用：

- 律师与客户之间的费用是指因聘用律师参与诉讼工作而产生的律师费用；
- 双方当事人之间的费用是指根据法院出具的指令，一方当事人可要求另一方补偿的费用。

双方当事人之间的费用是根据法院规模以相当严格的原则确定的（实际上意味着胜诉方只能收回已发生的律师与客户之间的费用总额的 50%～70%）。某些情况下，律师与客户之间的费用或者基于"补偿"形成的费用，除了不合理的费用以外，都可能被追回。赔偿费用基于充分的理由可酌情确定并根据申请给付，例如，支付费用的一方不合理地拒绝了一项比最终的判决更好的和解方案，或者在审判期间有不恰当的行为导致延误或产生额外费用。

4. 文书制作

"证据开示"是法院下令普遍执行的一个过程，即一方当事人被要求向另一方当事人出示其拥有、保管或支配范围内的所有文件，以阐明诉讼中的任何问题。在某些情况下，一方当事人可能还需要提供代理人或雇员占有、保管或在其支配范围内的文件、一方当事人有权从第三方获得的文件，以及一方当事人向文件所有者提出请求后可能会获得的文件。

机密的非特许文件仍应遵循"证据开示"原则（但可能另一方当事人需作出保密承诺）。因每个法院的规则不同，与"证据开示"有关的规则也存在重大差异。

5. 特权

证据规则允许对特定类型的文件提出特权，法律因司法辖区而异，特权文件通常包含以下类别：

- 法律专业特权——使客户有权不提供律师（一名或多名）为其提供法律意见时所出具的文件。客户可提出或放弃该权利，但法律专业特权不适用于犯罪或欺诈案件。
- 反对自证的特权——若证人作出回答将导致其倾向于自认澳大利亚或外国法律项下的犯罪或导致其可能遭受民事处罚，则证人有权反对回答该问题。该特权不适用于公司。
- 公共利益豁免——若对国家事务相关的文件或信息保密所带来的公共利益，超出了将这些文件或信息作为证据或在诉讼中公平处理所带来的公共利益，则法院可主动或经一方当事人申请指定该文件具有特权。

6. 替代性争议解决

替代传统法院程序的争议解决程序，通常被称为"替代性争议解决"（ADR），调解和仲裁是较为常见的形式。替代性争议解决程序通常涉及第三方，由该第三方协助争议或冲突各方达成协议，或作出对双方具有或不具有约束力的决定。

澳大利亚各州和领地根据《联合国国际贸易法委员会示范仲裁规则》颁布了商业仲裁法以进行国内仲裁，联邦层面则颁布了1974年《国际仲裁法》。根据上述法案，法院均有权如同执行法院判决一样执行仲裁裁决。

调解在澳大利亚极为普遍，建立法院的大多数法规、诸多法院规则和一些法院实践指引都包含了参与调解的程序规则与要求。其他形式的替代性争议解决还包括专家决定、裁判与裁决。专家决定由具有专业知识的人员积极收集与争议有关的信息后出具，而并非听取当事人的意见。在不存在欺诈或串通等因素的情况下，经授权的专家作出的决定在澳大利亚具有法律约束力。所有最高法院和大多数法庭都有权将这些问题交由仲裁员处理。涉及复杂技术问题的案例，如建筑类案例，通常都包含来自技术专家的决定。

7. 外国判决

1991年《外国判决法》制定了一项法定清单，根据该清单，澳大利亚对特定外国法院的判决予以承认并执行，包括双方当事人之间最终的、确定的可执行的货币类判决。值得注意的是，该清单不包括美国的任何法院。为执行判决，判决债权人必须在判决作出之日起6年内向适当的澳大利亚法院申请执行登记；为实现判决的执行，已注册的外国判决与其注册法院的判决具有相同的效力，包括累积计算判决金额的利息。判决的债务人可以基于一些特定的理由申请驳回判决。根据《外国判决法》的规定，对于可注册但未进行注册的判决应当适用禁止反言原则。

澳大利亚颁布了《跨境破产示范法》，允许外国代表人（如外国清盘人）向澳大利亚法院申请承认在澳大利亚的任命。承认任命后，应外国代表人的请求，澳大利亚法院可以给予救济，以帮助其在澳大利亚对具有资产、权利、义务或责任的公司或个人进行重组或清算。

八、其他

（一）反商业贿赂

1. 反商业贿赂立法概述

商业贿赂在澳大利亚国家与各州的立法制度层面都被定为犯罪行为。

根据各州和领地的刑事立法，贿赂公职人员和私人代理人是犯罪行为，即1990年《刑法》（新南威尔士州）、1958年《犯罪法》（维多利亚州）、1899年《刑法》（昆士兰州）、1935年《刑法整合法》（南澳大利亚州）、1913年《刑法典汇编法》（西澳大利亚州）、1924年《刑法法案》（塔斯马尼亚州）、2002年《刑法》（澳大利亚首都地区）和刑法法典（北部地区）。虽然各州认定的贿赂的特征有相似之处，但具体细节各有不同。通常而言，国家法律项下认定的贿赂包含向公职人员或私人代理人提供利益以实现影响其作为或不作为的目的。

根据1995年《刑法典》的规定，贿赂联邦公职人员和外国公职人员系犯罪行为。对"外国公职人员"的定义较为广泛，既包括外国政府的雇员，也包括行使贿赂的介绍人员。《刑法典》规定的贿赂包括向政府官员提供任何利益，影响其行使职权以取得或保留业务或业务优势。

2. 反商业贿赂监管部门

澳大利亚没有单独负责调查贿赂犯罪的政府部门。根据所适用的州或联邦制度，澳大利亚联邦警察局、州警察部门或澳大利亚证券和投资委员会将与相关州或联邦检察官共同进行调查。每个州还设有一个法定机构负责调查有关公共机构的贿赂和腐败犯罪，这些机构具有极为广泛的调查权力，但不能向个人或公司提出指控。

3. 惩罚措施

（1）概览

虽然联邦及各州的具体制度不同，但对贿赂行为所采用的认定方式大体相同。通常而言，贿赂包括提供或承诺给予货币或非货币的利益，可以采用现金、现金等价物（例如礼品券或贷款）、其他利益（如物质礼品、招待或娱乐、赞助旅行、捐赠或奖学金）或提供优惠（例如折扣或"免费"使用公司服务、设施或财产）或对接收方而言具有重大价值的任何其他物品或利益。

即使并非以获得利益回报而作出的行为，也可被认定为贿赂。只要为了使接收方在未来某个时间可取得某种优势而给予接收方好处，即可被认定为贿赂，且并不要求贿赂行为人明确表达对公职人员或私人代理人施加影响的意图。

作为一般规则，企业可以出于合法目的给予或接收适当的礼物或招待，例如为了建立商业关系、维护声誉或销售产品和服务。但是，所有提供或接收的礼品、招待和赞助旅行都必须在日常业务过程中提供，且不得期望任何利益回报。

习俗和惯例不得用于为贿赂辩护。但是，就涉嫌贿赂的外国公职人员而言，如果该行为在其所在的国家是合法的，或者为了加快或确保执行相对不重要的日常政府行为而作出的小额付款行为，则可以作为辩护事由。

需注意的是，反洗钱和反恐怖主义融资同样被视为刑事犯罪，由不同的法律进行规制。

（2）公司对其代表所承担的责任

在某些州，公司可能因其雇员或代理人的贿赂行为而被追究刑事责任。而在另一些州，只有当董事或高级管理人员参与贿赂行为时，公司才会被追究刑事责任。在联邦制度项下，2017年《犯罪立法修正案（打击企业犯罪）法案》中的拟议修正案规定，公司将对"合伙人"（其定义较为广泛，包括雇员、承包商或其他服务提供者）贿赂外国公职人员的行为负责，除非公司能够证明其为了防止犯罪行为的发生已经制定了适当的程序规则。

（3）惩罚性行为和处罚

适用于贿赂犯罪的处罚因体制而异，但可能包括罚款和监禁。

贿赂州政府或地区系统下的公职人员或私人代理人可能导致的最高监禁刑期从7年（新南威尔士州、西澳大利亚州、北部地区）至21年（塔斯马尼亚州）不等，同时也可能受到没收贿赂和罚款的处罚。收受贿赂的雇员也可能违反2001年《公司法》的规定，并可能因此被要求支付高达20万澳元的罚款。

根据《刑法典》的规定，个人贿赂公共官员和外国公职人员的，可导致最高达10年的徒刑和最高210万澳元的罚金。对于公司而言，最高罚款是2 100万澳元或通过贿赂所获利益的3倍，或公司年营业额的10%。

需要注意的是，2017年《犯罪立法修正案（打击企业犯罪）法案》的修正案将延期起诉协议计划引入刑法。根据该计划，被控贿赂犯罪的公司可以同意某些要求（例如，承担责任和/或支付经济处罚），以换取联邦检察官停止起诉。

（二）工程承包

1. 许可制度

在澳大利亚，政府部门和私营部门的采购明显不同。

（1）政府部门

澳大利亚（各级）政府通常制定政策明确规定如何采购商品和服务，通常要求具有较大价值或风险的项目通过公开招标等更加公开的采购流程进行，而较小的项目可以使用更有限的流程进行，例如，使用现有的供应商小组或从有限数量的供应商处获取报价。

举例来说，2018年《联邦采购规则》（CTRs）是联邦政府采购政策框架的基础，所有作为澳大利亚政府潜在供应商的主体都适用《联邦采购规则》的各项规则。《联邦采购规则》的核心准则是物有所值。根据《联邦采购规则》的规定，联邦政府主体必须向满足条件和评估标准、完全具备履行合同能力并最物有所值的投标人授予合同。

根据采购项目的价值和采购机构的不同，适用不同的程序规则。价值等于或高于某个门槛的项目对透明度的要求更为严格。

联邦政府招标采用以下三种方式进行：公开招标、资格预审或有限招标。超过相关门槛的采购必须采用公开招标程序。公开招标将公开面向市场并征求建议书。资格预审仅接受在已有的供应商清单中进行采购。如果公开招标或资格预审均不适用，则可采用有限招标，直接要求潜在供应商提交资料。有限招标一般只在采购项目风险相对较低且低于相关门槛的情况下采用。

虽然每个州和地区以及地方政府的政策与联邦的政策大致相似，但具体细节各不相同。

（2）私营部门

与政府部门不同，对私营部门的采购程序没有任何规定。尽管有时私营部门可能会选择采用类似于政府部门采用的采购流程，但在私营部门采购中，客户可以完全选择性地确定采购流程、具体安排和潜在供应商。例如，私营部门客户可能更倾向于只允许受邀供应商参与，或者（如果对现有的供应安排满意）在不面向市场的情况下直接与其现有供应商合作。

2. 限制领域

只有在政府采购流程中才存在限制领域的概念。某些地区的政府部门建立自有的采购流程，或在某些情况下未采取通常所需的采购流程，这些情况并不罕见。

以联邦政府为例，为维护或恢复国际和平与安全，或保护人类健康、基本安全利益或国家艺术、历史或考古宝藏，某些类型的采购不适用《联邦采购规则》第二部分的规定。这赋予招标流程更大的灵活性以适应其需求和目的。

澳大利亚政府主体有权认定签订某项合同不符合公共利益。公共利益事由可能包括严重影响采购项目基本目标或原因的意外事件或其他信息。另外，联邦政府可能依据贸易协议条款允许限制投标人或选择性采购。

此外，联邦政府同时采用联合国安理会的制裁措施及其自己实施的制裁，这可能会影响与外国承包商相关的采购。一般而言，政府不采用较大范围的贸易抵制或禁运。相反，该种制裁通常针对某些商品或服务而实施于特定行业部门的指定人员或实体。通常针对武器和相关原料供应、或使受制裁的司法管辖区受益的服务采取这些措施。

据此，《联邦采购规则》遵循非歧视原则，并规定采购和关于价值的评估必须是非歧视性的。这体现了澳大利亚政府在自由贸易协定下的义务。

同样，虽然每个州和地区以及地方政府的政策与联邦的政策大致相似，但具体细节各不相同。

Australia

Authors: Will Heath, Charles Coorey, Michael Williams
Translators: Mo haibo, Tao Haiying

I. Overview

A. General Introduction to the Political, Economic, Social and Legal Environment of the Country Receiving Investment

The Commonwealth of Australia (Australia) is a stable and advanced liberal democratic nation of approximately 24.5 million people.

It has three levels of government:

- Federal government (Australian Government): Laws are passed by the Commonwealth Parliament (Federal Parliament), located in Australia's capital city, Canberra.
- State / territory government: Laws are passed by the 6 state parliaments and 2 territory parliaments, located in the capital city of each state and territory.①
- Local government: "By-laws" are passed by approximately 546 local councils in Australia.②

a. Political System

Australia's Federal Parliament is comprised of:
- The Queen: Represented by the Governor-General.
- The Senate: Comprised of 12 senators from each state and 2 senators from each of Australia's two mainland territories (76 in total).
- The House of Representatives (House): Comprised of 150 members who each represent a different geographical region (or electorate). Each electorate has roughly the same number of people.

The House and the Senate are the two deliberative chambers in Federal Parliament. Proposed laws must receive a majority of votes in both the House and the Senate, and then receive approval from the Governor-General. The current Prime Minister of Australia is the Honourable Scott Morrison MP.

b. Separation of Powers

Australia's Constitution divides power between three arms of the Australian Government:
- The legislature (Federal Parliament): Responsible for debating and voting on proposed laws.
- The executive (Australian Government): Responsible for enacting and upholding the laws established by the legislature. The executive is formed by the political party, or group of political parties, who have a majority of members in the House. The current Australian Government and executive are formed by the Liberal-National Party Coalition, led by Prime Minister Scott Morrison.
- The judiciary (courts): The legal arm of the Australian Government. It is independent from the legislature and executive, and it must ensure that they do not act inappropriately beyond their powers.

This division is known as the "separation of powers".

c. Australia's Legal (court) System

Australia has a stable and well-respected legal system, which is based on the following core principles:
- The rule of law;
- The right to be heard;
- Equality before the law;
- Freedom from bias;
- Fairness;
- Transparency.

---

① Each state in Australia has its own constitution and also applies the "separation of powers" principle.
② The roles and responsibilities of local councils differ in each state / territory.

Australia is a 'common law' jurisdiction. Common law is based on the concept of precedent. This means that, before a court can make a decision (or 'judgment'), it must first consider previous and relevant court decisions, especially those made by higher courts. This ensures incremental and principled decision-making. Whereas common law cannot override statute law, parliaments can create statute law to override existing common law.

While most laws are created by parliaments in Australia, via "statute law", common law is still an integral part of Australia's legal system.

d. Economic and Social Conditions

Australia has had 27 consecutive years of economic growth and is currently the world's 13th largest economy.[1] It has a diverse, services-based economy with low government debt.[2]

Australia has a highly educated, skilled and multi-lingual labour force.[3] It is also a member of numerous international organisations and financial institutions including the G20, the World Bank and the OECD. Transparency International ranks Australia as the 13th least corrupt nation in the world.[4]

e. Benefits for Investors

Australia offers significant benefits for foreign investors and has an open and favourable investment environment. It has a resilient and diverse economy with low inflation, a transparent and liberal process for approving foreign investment, low barriers to trade, business-oriented corporate regulation, and a competitive company tax rate.

As the Australian Government has acknowledged: "Australia has traditionally relied on inward foreign investment to meet the shortfall between domestic saving and domestic investment. Foreign investment plays an important and beneficial role in the Australian economy because it helps drive economic growth, creates skilled jobs, improves access to overseas markets and enhances productivity."[5]

Australia's economy is comprised of a diverse mix of well-performing sectors, including:
- Financial markets;
- Food and Agribusiness;
- Energy and Resources;
- Healthcare;
- Infrastructure.

Australia's open and transparent economy has also generated successful enterprises in other sectors, including industrial products, consumer products, technology, media, tourism and professional services.

f. Financial Markets

Australia's sophisticated, innovative and highly-regarded financial markets play an essential role in bringing together saving and investment, allocating capital to its most efficient uses, and managing cash flow and balance sheet risks for investors, business and government. Australia's financial markets have a diverse mix of Australian and foreign investors.

Trading activity in many Australian financial market sectors is higher than the size of Australia's economy might indicate. For example, during 2016-17:
- the total issuance of investment grade bonds (on the debt securities market) was A$133 billion;
- foreign exchange transactions totalled A$37 trillion; and
- average daily turnover of over-the-counter derivatives was A$49 trillion.[6]

The Australian dollar is one of the 10 most actively traded currencies in the world. While the Australian debt market is relatively small, on a global scale, Australian dollar denominated debt is included in several key global indices used by institutional investors.

Australia has a compulsory superannuation (retirement savings) sector, which currently totals approximately A$2.5 trillion.[7] Australia's funds and superannuation sector is one of the largest and most sophisticated in the region, with experience in co-investing with Chinese and international investors, importantly with an increasingly

---

[1] Australian Trade and Investment Commission, Why Australia: Benchmark Report 2018 (2018), pg. 3 and 4.
[2] Ibid, pg. 11.
[3] As at December 2017, Australia's unemployment rate was 5.4%.
[4] See https://www.transparency.org/country/AUS.
[5] Foreign Investment Review Board, Annual Report 2015-2016, pg. 9, https://cdn.tspace.gov.au/uploads/sites/79/2017/04/1516-FIRB-Annual-Report.pdf.
[6] Australian Financial Markets Association, 2017 Australian Financial Markets Report, pg. 1, 6 and 7, https://afma.com.au/data/afmr/2017%20AUSTRALIAN%20FINANCIAL%20MARKETS%20REPORT.pdf.
[7] Australian Bureau of Statistics, 5655.0-Managed Funds, Australia, Sep 2017, http://www.abs.gov.au/ausstats/abs@.nsf/mf/5655.0.

longer-term investment horizon.

g. Market Exchanges

The largest market exchange in Australia is the Australian Securities Exchange (ASX) which accounts for approximately 79% of all equity market turnover in Australia.

ASX–as at financial year end 30 June 2017[1]				
IPOs-new raisings	Secondary raisings	Total market capitalisation	Number of listed companies	Foreign companies
152 (A$14.6 billion)	A$37.1 billion	A$1.7 trillion	2,239	266

Since 2015, Chi-X Australia ("Chi-X") has offered an investment products platform that enables it to compete with ASX in the quotation of investment products that are exclusively traded on the Chi-X market. Chi-X accounts for approximately 21% of equity market turnover in Australia.

h. Food and Agribusiness

Australia has a comparative advantage in extensive broadacre agriculture due to the relatively large amount of land available compared to other countries.

Investing in Australian agribusiness can potentially provide strategic benefits and opportunities for investors. With demand for food and other agricultural products expected to grow substantially, Australia is ideally placed to capitalise on these trends due to its:
- close proximity to growth markets in Asia;
- robust biosecurity system;
- record of innovation and reputation for producing high quality and safe products; and
- skilled workforce.

A diverse range of food and fibre products are produced in Australia. The top four commodities are beef and dairy cattle farming, grain growing and sheep farming. This is followed by vegetables, fruits and nuts, lamb meat and wool. The sector has already seen active interest from foreign pension funds and some local superannuation funds. Further interest is expected given:
- the need for additional capital (estimated at A$109 billion by 2025);
- it has provided long-term returns of 10-12% per annum;
- it presents a great option as a portfolio diversification tool (as investments in the sector provide a hedge against inflation, offer low correlation to traditional asset classes and are less impacted by economic slowdowns); and
- it provides an opportunity to pursue aggregation due to the fragmented nature of agricultural land holdings.

Australia's farm exports were worth A$44.6 billion in 2015-2016. By contrast, Australia imported only A$17.2 billion in agricultural products over the same period.

As at 30 June 2017, agricultural land in Australia with a level of foreign ownership totalled 50.5 million hectares. This figure represents 13.6% of all agricultural land in Australia.[2] Chinese companies and nationals own approximately 0.4% of Australia's total agricultural land.[3]

Australia is also home to some of Asia's leading food and nutritional products, including infant formula, vitamins and probiotics.

i. Energy and Resources

Australia is a major producer of natural resources. As the Australian Government explains: "Australia is endowed with a rich variety of mineral and natural energy resources. The sector has been and continues to be an important contributor to the nation's wealth. Australia has the world's largest resources of iron ore, gold and lead,

---

[1] Australian Securities Exchange Limited, Annual Report 2017, pg. 33, 34 and 77, https://www.asx.com.au/documents/investor-relations/AnnualReport2017.pdf.

[2] Australian Taxation Office, Register of Foreign Ownership of Agricultural Land, pg. 5, https://cdn.tspace.gov.au/uploads/sites/79/2017/09/Register_of_Foreign_ownership_of_Agricultural_Land_2017.pdf.

[3] Foreign Investment Review Board, Annual Report 2015-16, pg. 7, https://cdn.tspace.gov.au/uploads/sites/79/2017/04/1516-FIRB-Annual-Report.pdf.

as well as the second largest bauxite reserves."[1]

Fossil fuels also continue to dominate Australia's energy mix, particularly significant liquefied natural gas and coal. While contract prices for metallurgical coal have surged to their highest levels since 2011, due to higher than expected demand from steelmakers, the coal industry is undergoing significant structural changes as traditional players begin to exit some coal markets. This means that there will be increasing opportunities to acquire coal assets. In relation to gas, there will be increased opportunities to assist and develop additional gas resources to serve Australia's domestic market.

Despite coal's dominance as Australia's primary energy source, there has also been a steady uptake in renewable sources of energy, primarily in wind and solar. With technological improvements and increasing momentum to meet Australia's renewable energy target by 2020, there are growing opportunities for investment in Australia's renewables sector. In 2016, 17.3% of Australia's electricity was generated from renewable energy sources, and large-scale renewable investment was five times greater than 2015, representing an investment of over A$4 billion.

Given Australia's resources are found across the states and territories, there will continue to be opportunities to invest in under-explored and untapped resources throughout the country. As the mining sector recovers from uncertainty in both Australian and global markets, it is expected that confidence in Australia's resources sector will return. It is further expected that market players will seek to take advantage of share price weakness and submit opportunistically timed offers, and that resources will continue to be extremely profitable in Australia.

j. Healthcare

Australia's healthcare system is organised, administered and funded by multiple levels of government and supported by a private health insurance system.

• Australian Government: Responsible for directing and coordinating healthcare policy, funding and regulation. It administers Medicare, Australia's public health insurance scheme, which encompasses the provision of free or subsidised medicines and free hospital treatment to patients in public hospitals.

• State and territory governments: Responsible for providing public health services, including public hospitals, and regulating private healthcare services and facilities.

The rapid increase in internet and smartphone users has seen a boost in the number of Australian start-ups entering the international HealthTech market. In collaboration with active healthcare investment funds, they have developed a range of innovative technologies including wearable devices, healthcare applications, online healthcare information services and direct patient care tools.

Australia has a diverse medical device industry, spanning manufacturers and suppliers of world-renowned technologies through to smaller, start-up ventures. The medical device industry is closely regulated but enjoys a strong level of support from the Australian Government through measures such as MTPConnect and the R&D tax incentive scheme.

k. Infrastructure

There are clear areas of focus for infrastructure investment in Australia at the federal, state and territory levels across different sectors.

• Transport: The 2017-2018 Australian Budget contained an increase to total funding and financing commitments for transport infrastructure projects to over A$70 billion from 2013-14 to 2020-21, including an A$8.4 billion equity investment in the Australian Rail Track Corporation for the Melbourne to Brisbane Inland Rail project.

• Housing: Some states and territories have identified the need for well-planned new or replacement social, affordable and public housing to respond to the needs of Australia's growing population.

• Health and aged care: With Australia's ageing population and the increased cost of living, there will be greater demand for health care, particularly for the elderly. Increased health care infrastructure and the delivery of government services, involving both the public and private sectors, will be required to meet this growing demand.

• Public Private Partnership model: To date, Australia has had considerable success employing the Public Private Partnership (PPP) model to ensure that the public and private sectors work together to deliver priority infrastructure projects in a timely manner and to budget. There is a clear commitment in Australia to develop infrastructure projects using the PPP model.

Australian companies have proven records in the design, construction and management of large scale projects across Asia and in other regions. Alongside them, Australia has world-class architectural, design, engineering and environmental services.

---

[1] Australian Trade and Investment Commission, Why Australia: Benchmark Report 2018 (2018), pg. 15.

B. The Status and Direction of the Cooperation with Chinese Enterprises Under the B&R

The B&R will give Chinese and Australian enterprises a chance to work together to take a leading role in the growth of regional infrastructure, and build the framework for regional infrastructure as a new asset class. The B&R offers not just access to Chinese capital, but the potential for Australian infrastructure contractors, asset managers, financiers, advisors and investors to partner with Chinese counterparts, to build relationships, as well as to leverage each other's experience to successfully deliver infrastructure projects in Australia, along the New Silk Road, and beyond.

Australia is a member of the Asia-Pacific Economic Cooperation (APEC) which is the premier forum for facilitating economic growth, cooperation, trade and investment in the Asia-Pacific region.

Australia is party to a number of significant free trade agreements with various countries including Malaysia, Thailand, Singapore, South Korea, Japan, the United States of America, Chile, New Zealand, China and ASEAN.

A key free trade agreement is the China-Australia Free Trade Agreement (ChAFTA) which came into effect on 1 January 2016. ChAFTA creates a platform for Australian and Chinese businesses to engage in wide-ranging business relationships.

Under ChAFTA, 96% of Australia's goods that are exported to China will enter duty free. It will deliver a range of benefits to Australian and Chinese businesses, including:

- removal and reduction of tariff barriers (with the agriculture and resources sectors, in particular, being the big winners along with certain manufactured products);
- relaxation of regulatory barriers to cross-border investments;
- facilitation of cross-border investments between China and Australia;
- relaxation of immigration law requirements to facilitate the movement of labour between China and Australia;
- improved access for Australian businesses to establish operations in China; and
- investor protections through Investor-State Dispute Settlement mechanisms.

Australia is a founding member of the Asian Infrastructure Investment Bank (AIIB). As part of AIIB, Australia will contribute A$930 million over the next five years as paid in capital. That makes Australia the 6thlargest shareholder in the commercially focussed regional bank. It also opens opportunities for the private sector in Australia to participate in bankable projects.

Sydney is one of only 20 official offshore Renminbi (RMB) hubs around the world and is developing a reputation as the go-to hub for RMB cash and securities settlement in Asia. With the G20 Global Infrastructure Hub located in Sydney, a dynamic fintech industry, and the rapidly growing use of RMB as a trade, finance and investment currency, Sydney has the "financial infrastructure" necessary to become a major gateway for capital flows in and out of China.

II. Investment

A. Market Access

a. Department Supervising Investment

Australia's Federal Treasurer (Treasurer) oversees all decisions regarding foreign investment in Australia. The Treasurer is advised and assisted by an Australian governmental body, the Foreign Investment Review Board (FIRB).

Before they can proceed, certain investments by foreign persons require the prior approval of the Treasurer in the form of a "no objections notification" (FIRB Approval). Applications for FIRB Approval are made through FIRB and processed by the Federal Department of Treasury (Treasury). All decisions by the Treasurer relating to foreign investment will be underpinned by the analysis and recommendation of FIRB. FIRB encourages early contact by foreign investors to discuss potential proposals.

b. Laws and Regulations of Investment Industry

When considering whether to grant FIRB Approval, the Treasurer must have regard to the Foreign Acquisitions and Takeovers Act 1975 (FATA). This legislation principally regulates foreign investment in Australia. "Foreign persons" is defined broadly under FATA, and includes:

- individuals who are not ordinarily resident in Australia;
- corporations in which a foreign individual, a foreign corporation or a foreign government holds a substantial interest (20% or more held solely or together with associates); or
- a foreign government or a foreign government investor (which includes, but is not limited to, corporations or

trustees where a foreign government or separate government entity holds an interest of at least 20%).

The purpose of the FIRB regime is to empower the Treasurer to make orders in respect of foreign investment proposals that are ultimately considered by the Treasurer to be contrary to Australia's national interest. While "national interest" is not defined under FATA, what is considered to be against the national interest by the Treasurer (as advised by FIRB) is determined on a case-by-case basis. Factors that may be considered as part of the national interest assessment, particularly for large scale proposals in sensitive sectors (such as agriculture and national infrastructure), include, but are not limited to:
- national security concerns;
- the impact the proposal would have on the economy and the broader Australian and local community (including market competition issues and taxation compliance);
- whether the proposal is primarily commercially motivated (i.e. rather than motivated by the non-commercial interests of a foreign government);
- community concerns about foreign ownership of certain Australian assets; and
- the impact the proposal would have on public support for Australia's foreign investment regime.

The Treasurer may impose conditions on a FIRB Approval if the Treasurer considers them necessary to protect the national interest. If a condition is not complied with, this would be contrary to the national interest and would reactivate the Treasurer's powers. Substantial penalties apply for failure to comply with any conditions imposed by the Treasurer.

c. Forms of Investment

Only certain investments and acquisitions require FIRB Approval. A foreign person, to whom FATA applies, will be required to obtain FIRB Approval subject to the following factors:
- whether the investor is privately owned, a foreign government entity, or from a country with whom Australia has a free trade agreement (an "agreement country investor");
- the type of acquisition;
- whether the acquisition meets relevant monetary or interest thresholds (notification thresholds); and
- whether an exemption is available.

The notification thresholds vary depending on whether the investment is a sensitive business acquisition or involves the acquisition of an agribusiness or certain classes of land. Sensitive business acquisitions are subject to lower monetary thresholds and increased FIRB scrutiny, and include acquisitions in the following industry sectors:
- media;
- telecommunications;
- transport;
- military and defence related activities;
- encryption and security technologies; and
- the operation of nuclear facilities (or businesses that extract uranium or plutonium).

As an agreement country investor, Chinese individuals or enterprises that directly invest in Australia are subject to higher notification thresholds which reduce the number of acquisitions requiring FIRB Approval.

Chinese individuals and enterprise investors are currently subject to the following increased percentage and monetary thresholds for the following types of acquisitions:
- business acquisitions (sensitive): a percentage interest of 20% and total asset value of the target of A$262 million; and
- business acquisitions (non-sensitive): a percentage interest of 20% and a total asset value of the target of A$1,134 million.

These monetary thresholds are indexed annually on 1 January. It is important to note that foreign government investors (including Chinese foreign government investors) do not qualify for the increased notification thresholds. In some circumstances, foreign government investors will be subject to lower notification thresholds.

Additionally, an agreement country investor's subsidiary that is incorporated outside of the agreement country (including one incorporated in Australia) would not benefit from the higher thresholds. This means that Chinese individuals and enterprise investors, who establish subsidiaries in Australia, would not benefit from the higher thresholds.

d. Standards of Market Access and Examination

Where a foreign government investor seeks FIRB Approval for a potential transaction, the Treasurer will typically have regard to the following factors:
- the proposed investment's impact on Australia's national security;
- whether the proposed investment may hinder competition in the industry or sector concerned;

• the investor's impact on Australia's revenue or policies of the Australian Government;
• the proposed investment's impact on the operations and directions of an Australian business, as well as its contribution to the Australian economy and broader community; and
• the character of the investor, particularly whether the investor's operations are independent from the relevant foreign government and whether the investor is subject to, and adheres to, the law and observes common standards of business behaviour.

The following table summarises the applications made to FIRB during 2015-16:

FIRB applications (2015-16) [1]	Number	Percentage	Value of proposed investment
Approved (without conditions)	26,954	62.66%	A$97 billion
Approved (with conditions)	14,491	33.69%	A$150.8 billion
Total approved	41,445	96.35%	A$247.8 billion
Rejected	5	0.01%	—
Withdrawn	1,319	3.07%	—
Exempt	244	0.57%	—
Total considered	43,013	100%	A$247.8 billion

B. Foreign Exchange Regulation

a. Department Supervising Foreign Exchange

In Australia, there is no department dedicated to supervising foreign exchange or the flow of currency.

Despite there being no equivalent to China's "State Administration of Foreign Exchange" in Australia, some regulators such as the Australian Transaction Reports and Analysis Centre (AUSTRAC) and the Australian Securities and Investments Commission (ASIC) have certain functions that impact the foreign currency exchange system.

b. Brief Introduction of Laws and Regulations of Foreign Exchange

Australia generally does not restrict the flow of currency into or out of the country and the Australian dollar is freely convertible. It has been longstanding government policy to have a floating exchange rate that is determined by international supply and demand. As such, the Reserve Bank of Australia (RBA) does not target any particular exchange rate level. Nevertheless, there are a number of foreign exchange reporting obligations and discrete controls.

a) Reporting Obligations

The principal reporting obligations arise under the Financial Transaction Reports Act 1988 and require international currency transfers of A$10,000 or more to be reported to AUSTRAC. Additionally, similar reporting obligations are placed on reporting entities (e.g. banks, financial service providers) under the Anti-Money Laundering and Counter-Terrorism Financing Act 2006. The purpose of these reporting obligations is to prohibit tax evasion, money laundering and terrorism-financing. As such, AUSTRAC does not prevent any normal currency transfers associated with international trade.

Providing a payment service (such as accepting retail payment instructions, exchanging currencies or making funds available) may be caught by anti-money laundering and counter-terrorism financing legislation if there is a sufficient geographical link to Australia. Payment service providers that are subject to the legislation are required to register with AUSTRAC, comply with transaction reporting requirements and apply "know your customer" procedures, among other obligations.

b) Discrete Controls

The key discrete controls and restrictions applicable in Australia are:
• the requirement to withhold tax from interest payments, unfranked dividends or royalties paid to persons who are not Australian residents; and
• various sanctions regimes administered by the Department of Foreign Affairs and Trade.

---

[1] Foreign Investment Review Board, Annual Report 2015-16, pg. 19, https://cdn.tspace.gov.au/uploads/sites/79/2017/04/1516-FIRB-Annual-Report.pdf.

c) Requirements of Foreign Exchange Management For Foreign Enterprises

Any business that wishes to act as a foreign exchange provider in Australia (i.e. a business that offers currency conversion services to consumers) may require an Australian Financial Services Licence (AFSL) from ASIC.

Foreign exchange dealers that provide foreign exchange contracts that settle immediately (i.e. "spot" conversions) or within 3 days do not generally require an AFSL. All other foreign exchange dealers (i.e. those providing foreign currency forwards / futures that extend beyond 3 days) require an AFSL and are subject to the reporting and conduct rules in the Corporations Act 2001 (Corporations Act).

d) Regulation of Electronic Payments (Within Australia)

The payments systems in Australia enable consumers and businesses to exchange value using cash, cheques and electronic funds transfers.

The RBA and Australian Payments Clearing Association (APCA) oversee and administer the different payments systems in Australia. To settle transactions directly with other financial institutions, a party needs to have an Exchange Settlement Account at the RBA and be a member of the relevant payments systems administered by APCA or other scheme administrator.

An AFSL may also be required if a payments service is intended or likely to induce a consumer to buy a "financial product" (including non-cash payment facilities, foreign exchange contracts or making a market in foreign exchange products and other derivatives). There are significant upfront and ongoing compliance costs to holding an AFSL, but exemptions may be available in certain circumstances.

C. Financing

a. Main Financial Institutions

Australia's financial regulatory framework consists of 5 key agencies, each with specific functional responsibilities:

- Australian Prudential Regulation Authority (APRA): APRA is responsible for the prudential regulation and supervision of deposit-taking institutions (i.e. banks, building societies and credit unions), life insurers, general insurance providers, reinsurers and superannuation entities.
- ASIC: ASIC is responsible for market conduct and investor protection in Australia's financial system. It regulates financial markets, financial services providers, market exchanges, financial sector intermediaries and financial products, including investments, insurance, and superannuation and deposit-taking activities (but not lending).
- RBA: RBA is responsible for monetary policy, the payments system and the overall stability of Australia's financial system.
- Treasury: Treasury is the Australian government department (run by the Treasurer) which develops and leads Australia's economic policy.
- Council of Financial Regulators: This is the coordinating body for APRA, ASIC, RBA and Treasury.

b. Financing Conditions for Foreign Enterprises

Under the Corporations Act, a foreign company cannot carry on business in Australia unless it is registered.

"Foreign companies" include bodies corporate and some unincorporated bodies. An unincorporated body formed outside Australia, that does not have a head or principal place of business in Australia, is a "foreign company" if it may sue or be sued, or may hold property in the name of its secretary or an officer of the body duly appointed for that purpose.

A foreign company wishing to carry on business in Australia must be registered with ASIC. Under the Corporations Act, a body corporate carries on business in Australia if it:

- has a place of business in Australia (e.g. a permanent office);
- establishes or uses a share transfer office or share registration office in Australia; or
- administers, manages or otherwise deals with property situated in Australia as an agent, legal personal representative or trustee, whether by employees or agents or otherwise.

The Corporations Act does not give an exhaustive definition of carrying on business in Australia. As such, the common law must also be considered. Under the common law, whether a person is "carrying on business" is a question of fact.

Under common law, whether a company is carrying on business in Australia depends on notions of "system", "repetition" and "continuity". A company may be carrying on business in Australia even if it does not have a fixed place of business in Australia. Further, traditionally there is a need for some physical activity in Australia that itself forms part of the course of conducting business.

Other activities which may result in a foreign entity carrying on business in Australia include:
- having a representative in Australia who has authority to bind the foreign entity;
- appointing a representative (such as an agent) in Australia whose activities would be regarded as forming part of the activities of the foreign entity rather than merely of the representative, or whose activities go beyond merely 'ministerial' matters;
   - exercising a significant degree of control over the activities of any agent or other representative in Australia;
   - developing a significant client base in Australia;
   - conducting a series of regular or continuous dealings in Australia;
   - paying or contributing to the costs of running an office in Australia or the office of an agent or representative;
- employing staff in Australia, or paying or contributing to the salaries of staff employed by an agent or representative; or
   - locating or using business infrastructure in Australia (e.g. IT servers).

In Australia, if you carry on a financial services business, you need:
- to hold an AFSL;
- to be appointed as an authorised representative; or
- to be exempt from the requirement to hold an AFSL (under the Corporations Act).

Under Australian law, a financial services provider may be deemed to carry on a financial services business in Australia even though it has no physical presence in Australia.

AFSLs are issued by ASIC on satisfaction of the relevant licensing application criteria. Licence applications can require extensive evidence. AFSL holders have a large range of obligations imposed on them. The Australian financial services regime differentiates between retail and wholesale clients. There are significant additional disclosure and conduct requirements where financial services are provided to retail clients. Breaches of the AFSL regime can lead to criminal sanctions and the possibility that counterparties may rescind transactions.

In Australia, there is no general restriction or requirement for a person to have a licence to provide a loan to a corporate entity. However, if the loan also involves the provision of a financial product by the lender (such as a derivative) they may need to hold an AFSL.

Entities that provide loans to corporate entities may also be required to register under some Australian legislation. For example, the Financial Sector (Collection of Data) Act 2001 requires certain corporations to register with APRA, including where the sole or principal business activities in Australia of the corporation are the borrowing of money and the provision of finance.

There is a statutory requirement for a person to hold an Australian Credit Licence where credit is provided to a person who falls within the scope of the National Consumer Credit Protection Act 2009 (including the National Credit Code) (Credit Act). The Credit Act will apply where credit is provided to an individual:
- for personal, domestic or household purposes;
- to purchase, renovate or improve residential property for investment purposes; or
- to refinance credit that has been provided to purchase, renovate or improve residential property for investment purposes.

The Corporations Act also requires a lender to hold an AFSL in order to issue a margin lending facility to an individual (or to provide any other financial product in connection with the loan). Entities that provide loans to individuals may also be required to register under Australian law.

D. Land Policy

a. Brief Introduction of Land-related Laws and Regulations

Australian states and territories generally operate a Torrens system of land registration, under which the Registrar of Titles in the relevant state or territory keeps a register to record the current owner of each parcel of land. Most land in Australia is held under the Torrens system.

Land is ordinarily transferred through a contract of sale between the vendor and the purchaser which defines the rights, obligations and duties of the parties, and sets out the terms upon which the land will be sold. Contracts for the sale of land are privately determined, but foreign ownership of land is federally regulated under FATA.

b. Rules of Land Acquisition for Foreign Enterprises

All acquisitions of Australian land by foreign government investors will require FIRB Approval, regardless of value. This is also the case for all acquisitions by foreign government investors of any interest in a mining, production or exploration tenement.

a) Commercial

Foreign persons may require FIRB Approval before acquiring an interest in commercial land in Australia.

Different rules apply depending on whether:
- the land is vacant;
- the proposed acquisition meets the conditions for "low threshold land"; and
- the value of the proposed acquisition.

Low threshold land is subject to greater scrutiny (and lower notification thresholds) and includes:
- mines, oil or gas wells, quarries or similar operations;
- land where the failure of a part of a telecommunications network unit on the land would result in telephone or internet services not being provided on other land; and
- land where public infrastructure will be located (including airports, ports, or infrastructure related to the transmission, distribution or supply of electricity, gas, water or the treatment of sewage).

b) Agricultural

Proposed investments in agricultural land by foreign persons generally require approval where the cumulative value of a foreign person's agricultural land holdings exceeds A$15 million, with exceptions applying to investors from agreement countries (e.g. China).

Agricultural land is land that is used, or that could reasonably be used, for a primary production business. This includes cultivating or propagating plants, maintaining animals for the purpose of selling them or their bodily products, fish farming or tree plantations. It is also important to note that acquisitions over a certain monetary threshold in agribusinesses, such as businesses which conduct meat, poultry, grain, dairy, milk, fruit or vegetable processing, will usually require FIRB Approval.

In general, foreign investors will not be able to obtain FIRB Approval to purchase agricultural land unless the land has been marketed widely. Foreign investors have been requested to inform FIRB of the sale process as part of the consideration of their FIRB applications. FIRB has indicated that an open and transparent sale process means:
- the property is "marketed widely," meaning that it must be advertised on widely used real estate listing websites or in regional / national media;
- the property was advertised for a minimum of 30 days; and
- there was equal opportunity for offers to be made for the agricultural land while it was still available for purchase.

To comply with this new requirement, the foreign investor will need to demonstrate (to FIRB) how it became aware that the agricultural land was marketed for sale and how the acquisition followed an open and transparent sale process. Certain exceptions to this restriction include acquisitions where the foreign investor:
- is acquiring a property that had been publically advertised in the preceding six months (but had not sold);
- has a substantial Australian ownership (at least 50% but could vary upwards depending on the foreign owners); or
- is required to make the acquisition in order to comply with Australian law (e.g. mining buffer zones).

c) Residential

Foreign persons generally need to obtain FIRB Approval before acquiring an interest in residential real estate in Australia. "Acquiring an interest" includes, but is not limited to:
- signing an unconditional contract agreeing to purchase a dwelling;
- acquiring a security interest under a real property mortgage, even if the person that possesses the property is an Australia citizen or permanent resident; or
- holding an option that provides the right to purchase a property at an agreed price at some time in the future (such as a put or call option).

Applications for FIRB Approval for the purchase of new dwellings and vacant residential land will usually be approved unconditionally. In contrast, non-resident foreign persons and foreign controlled companies are generally prohibited from purchasing established dwellings in Australia, although there are some exceptions for foreign companies which have a substantial Australian business.

E. The Establishment and Dissolution of Companies

a. The Forms of Enterprises

There are many different forms of enterprise and business structures available in Australia.

The choice of form and structure used to invest and to conduct business in Australia is central to success in the market, and will be influenced by a number of factors including the nature of the business, tax issues and the needs of investors. Business structures include companies, trusts or managed investment schemes ("MISs"), joint ventures and partnerships.

Enterprise / Business structure	Key Features	Regulation
Proprietary companies	• Must have at least 1 shareholder but no more than 50 nonemployee shareholders. • Must have at least 1 director who is ordinarily resident in Australia. • Can, but not required to, have a company secretary. • Must have a public officer for tax purposes. • Must have a registered office in Australia. • The board of directors is the primary decision-making body. • Shareholders' rights in relation to the company are governed by the constitution or statutory replaceable rules. A shareholders' agreement can govern the relationship between the shareholders. • Cannot engage in any activity that would require the lodgement of a prospectus (i.e. issuing securities to the general public). However, they can offer securities to employees. • Not required to hold annual general meetings (AGMs).	• Regulated by ASIC under the Corporations Act.
Public companies	• Must have at least 1 shareholder. • Must have at least 3 directors (2 of whom are ordinarily resident in Australia). • Must have at least 1 company secretary who is ordinarily resident in Australia. • Must have a public officer for tax purposes. • Must have a registered office in Australia. • The board of directors is the primary decision-making body. • Shareholders' rights in relation to the company are governed by the constitution. Shareholders' agreements are unusual for public companies. • Can be listed or unlisted. Listed companies are those which are listed on a market exchange such as ASX. • Subject to securities and other applicable laws, may issue a prospectus for the offer of shares, debentures or other securities. • Must hold AGMs.	• Regulated by ASIC under the Corporations Act. • Regulated by ASX (if listed on ASX) or by another market exchange.
Trusts/MISs	• A trustee owns the assets of the business and carries on the business for the benefit of the beneficiaries of the trust. • The trustee may be an individual or a corporation. • An MIS is a common trust structure which allows people to pool funds for a common purpose and make a profit. • The MIS is managed by a trustee / responsible entity (RE) and / or investment manager.	• If the trust is registered as an MIS, there is a heavier regulatory and compliance burden (additionally, there are likely to be disclosure compliance obligations if there are retail investors). • In some cases, disclosure to investors may be required for capital raising purposes.
	• Wholesale investors as beneficiaries • A trust needs to have at least 2 holders of interests to be an MIS. • If investors are all wholesale, the trust will not need to be registered as an MIS.	• Need to operate under an AFSL. • The AFSL is usually held by the trustee, by the investment manager, or by an external party through representative and / or intermediary arrangements. • Regulated by the general law of trusts and the Corporations Act.

(continued)

Enterprise / Business structure	Key Features	Regulation
	• Retail investors as beneficiaries • If the MIS has more than 20 "members", it must be registered with ASIC. If there are retail investors, the trust may need to be registered as a MIS. This also allows the MIS to raise capital from a larger pool of potential investors. • May be listed on ASX.	• If the trust is registered as an MIS, there is a heavier regulatory and compliance burden (additionally, there are likely to be disclosure compliance obligations if there are retail investors). • If registered, the RE must be a public company and hold an AFSL. • Regulated by the general law of trusts and the Corporations Act.
Joint ventures	• A joint venture creates a common enterprise for parties to assist each other with a common goal or project. • Joint ventures can be incorporated or unincorporated. • Investors' rights are governed by a joint venture agreement, a unitholders' agreement (where the joint venture vehicle is a trust) or a shareholders' agreement (where the joint venture vehicle is a company). • Can be used in conjunction with all the above structures or in an unincorporated (contractual only) form. • Enables co-operation with other market participants (e.g. ability to access another joint venture party's resources).	• Regulation can depend on the type of joint venture vehicle (e.g. a trust or company).
Partnerships	• Not a separate legal entity - the partners are jointly and severally liable for the debts of the business. • Subject to certain exceptions, there cannot be more than 20 partners. • Shared control and management of the business by the partners. • A partnership deed would govern and regulate the relationship between partners.	• Partnership laws of the states and territories. • Partnership deed. • Common law.

The most common form of enterprise for conducting business in Australia is the company. A company can be either proprietary or public. Public companies have more onerous disclosure and reporting obligations under the Corporations Act. Proprietary companies represent approximately 99% of all registered companies in Australia.

a) Directors' Duties

Each company's board of directors has primary oversight and power to direct the company's affairs. Each Australian company director is subject to a wide range of duties under the Corporations Act and general law (including fiduciary duties in equity, duty of care in negligence and contractual duties in common law). Consequences of breaching a directors' duty include both civil and criminal penalties. The duties under the Corporations Act apply to "shadow" and "de-facto" directors as well as officers of the company. There are some limited defences available to directors and officers for a breach of duties under the Corporations Act.

Directors in Australia must adhere to the following principles and rules:

• Care and diligence: Directors and officers must exercise their powers and discharge their duties with the degree of care and diligence that a reasonable person would exercise if they were a director or officer of a company in the company's circumstances and occupied the office held by, and had the same responsibilities within the company as, a director or officer.

• Good faith and proper purpose: Directors and other officers of the company must exercise their powers and discharge their duties in good faith (in the best interests of the company) and for a proper purpose.

• Conflicts of interest: A director must avoid being put in a position of conflict between the interest of the company and their personal, or a third party's interests. This includes disclosing material personal interests and not improperly using their position or company information.

• Insolvent trading: Directors must prevent the company from incurring debts in circumstances where there are reasonable grounds for believing that the company is insolvent or would likely become insolvent by incurring the debt.

b) Directors' and Officers' Indemnity Insurance

Liability insurance can be paid to directors and officers of a company as indemnification for losses or costs in the event legal action is brought against the insured party for wrongful acts in their capacity as directors and / or officers. Certain acts or losses, such as deliberate fraud or dishonesty, will not be covered by the policy. Claims must also be for acts that occurred within the policy period and there will be a monetary limit for the indemnity specified in the policy.

b. The Procedure of Establishment

Establishing or 'incorporating' a company in Australia is relatively straightforward.

a) Incorporation

An application must be lodged with ASIC that includes the following information (if applicable to the company type):
- type of company;
- proposed company name or Australian Company Number ("ACN");
- written consent and details of each proposed shareholder, director and secretary;
- registered office address and opening hours;
- principal place of business;
- identification of ultimate holding company; and
- share structure.

Once the requisite lodgement fee is paid, ASIC will issue a certificate of registration.

b) Constitutions

A constitution can be created by either adopting the replaceable rules in the Corporations Act, drafting a constitution or a combination of these methods. Public companies also need to lodge a copy of the special resolution that adopts the constitution, along with a copy of the constitution, with ASIC within 14 days after it is passed.

c) Residency Requirements

Australian residency requirements apply to individuals who form part of the board of a company incorporated under the Corporations Act. A proprietary company incorporated under the Corporations Act must have at least one director who "ordinary resides" in Australia. Public companies, which includes those listed on ASX, must have at least two directors who ordinary reside in Australia.

The term ordinarily resides is not defined in the Corporations Act. In general, a person will be held to ordinarily reside in Australia if they have a continuous association with Australia and treat it as their home. A person can be a resident in more than one country. It is ultimately a question of fact.

As an example, FATA defines "ordinarily resident" as a person being resident in Australia for 200 days or more in the last 12 months and whose presence is not subject to any limitation imposed by Australian law (e.g. a holder of a temporary visa would not be ordinarily resident in Australia).

d) Audited Financial Reports

Along with keeping financial records, certain companies must also prepare and lodge their audited financial reports with ASIC. Some of these companies are:

Type of company	Test	Timing (for ASIC lodgement)
Public companies	This applies to all public companies.	Within 4 months after the company's financial year.
Disclosing entities	This applies to all disclosing entities. There are several different types of disclosing entities, one of the most common being a public company that is also listed on a market exchange (e.g. ASX).	Within 3 months after the disclosing entity's financial year.
Large proprietary companies	If the company (or any entities it controls) satisfies at least two of the following elements: • During the financial year, its consolidated revenue is A$25 million or more. • At the end of the financial year, the value of its consolidated gross assets is A$12.5 million or more. • At the end of the financial year, it has 50 or more employees.	Within 4 months after the company's financial year.

(continued)

Type of company	Test	Timing (for ASIC lodgement)
Small proprietary companies that are foreign controlled	If all of the following elements are satisfied: • It is controlled by a foreign company for all or part of the year; • it is not consolidated for that period in financial statements for that year lodged with ASIC by a registered foreign company or a company, registered scheme or disclosing entity; and • it (or any entities it controls) satisfies at least two of the elements of the test for large proprietary companies (above).	Within 4 months after the company's financial year.

Certain small proprietary companies that are foreign controlled may benefit from ASIC relief from these reporting requirements. A small proprietary company must also prepare and lodge audited financial reports if it is directed to do so by ASIC or by shareholders with at least 5% of the vote.

c. Routes and Requirements of Dissolution

There are four main methods by which companies can dissolve.

a) Voluntary Deregistration

A company can voluntarily deregister by notifying ASIC and fulfilling the following requirements:
- all shareholders agree to deregister;
- the company is no longer operating;
- the company's assets are worth less than A$1,000;
- the company has no liabilities;
- the company is not party to any legal proceedings; and
- the company has paid all fees and penalties payable to ASIC.

b) Liquidation

Both solvent and insolvent companies can enter liquidation:
- Solvent: The company's purpose has come to an end and its shareholders want to distribute the company's assets.
- Insolvent: The company can no longer function properly and its creditors want to be repaid.

Liquidation means a company is dissolved. The company's assets are liquidated (i.e. turned into cash) and distributed among creditors and shareholders according to statutory priority rules. The company is then deregistered.

The liquidator's primary objective is to maximise the pool of cash available for distribution to unsecured creditors. Thus, in addition to selling off assets and getting in all debts accrued to the company in the ordinary course of its business, the liquidator will actively consider recovery actions.

The liquidation process can be run separately to, but in parallel with, the receivership process, but not the administration process.

c) Administration

An independent administrator takes control of an insolvent or near insolvent company from the directors, and then has a short statutory moratorium to assess whether the company can and should be salvaged, or whether it should be put into liquidation.

A secured creditor who has a security interest over the whole, or substantially the whole, of the property of a company can appoint a receiver (and otherwise enforce the security) during the "decision period", being the 13 business days after the administrator is appointed.

The administration process can be run separately to, but in parallel with, the receivership process, but not the liquidation process.

d) Receivership

A receiver takes possession and control of secured asset(s) from the directors and uses the assets to repay the relevant secured creditor. A receiver may be appointed over specific assets (e.g. a building) or over the whole business of the company, depending on the terms of the security.

The receiver can decide to sell the assets, or manage the assets for the purpose of enhancing their value, or just take the rents and profits. A company can survive a receivership if the secured debt can be discharged without the company being forced into liquidation.

The receivership process can be run separately to, but in parallel with, either the administration and liquidation process (but not both).

F. Mergers and Acquisitions

Acquisitions of, and investments in, public companies in Australia are predominantly regulated by the following bodies:

Regulation of mergers and acquisitions	
ASIC	ASIC is the main regulator and supervisor of takeovers of public companies, corporate and securities law in Australia. ASIC has powers to modify the operation of, and grant parties exemption from compliance with, various provisions of the Corporations Act. ASIC publishes detailed guidance on its interpretation of legislative provisions and when it may consider granting such modifications and exemptions.
ASX	ASX may become involved in a takeover if it is concerned that its rules are not being complied with by the parties involved in the takeover. The principal concern of ASX is to ensure there is an informed market in the securities of the target company (and the acquirer, if listed).
The Takeovers Panel	The Panel is a non-judicial body comprising of specialists in mergers and acquisitions across a range of professions, including bankers, lawyers and company directors. It is the principal forum in Australia for resolving disputes about a takeover bid until the end of the bid period. The Panel also has broad statutory powers to: • make declarations of "unacceptable circumstances" in relation to a takeover or acquisition of a substantial interest in the company; • make interim or final orders to remedy those circumstances and protect the rights of persons and groups affected by the circumstances, such as target company shareholders; and • review decisions of ASIC which relate to modifying the operation of, or granting exemptions from, takeover provisions. A party must apply to the Panel for a matter to be considered. An application for a declaration or an order can be made by the bidder, the target company, ASIC, or any person whose interests are affected by the takeover.
Australian Competition and Consumer Commission (ACCC)	The ACCC will intervene in a transaction where the acquisition would have the effect, or be likely to have the effect, of substantially lessening competition in any market in Australia (see more, below).

Control transactions at a glance	
The 20% Rule	The Corporations Act broadly prohibits a person from acquiring (whether by way of a purchase of existing securities or an issue of new securities) securities in a company that is subject to the takeover rules if, because of the acquisition, the number of securities controlled by that person and their associates would exceed 20% (or increase from a starting point that is above 20% and below 90%) (20% Rule). A person (including an entity) will generally have a relevant interest in securities if the person: • is the holder of the securities; • has power to exercise or control the exercise of the voting power attached to the securities; or • has power to dispose of, or control the disposal of, the securities.
Exceptions to the 20% Rule	There are a number of methods that enable a person or entity to overcome the 20% Rule. The two main methods are via takeover bids and schemes of arrangement. Some other exceptions are explained below.
Takeover bids	A takeover bid may be take the form of an off-market or market bid. Off-market bids are the most common form of takeover bids. Both are explained below.
Schemes of arrangement (scheme)	Under a scheme, a target company seeks court and shareholder approval for the transfer of target company shares to the bidder. In order to be successful, a scheme needs the approval of 75% by value and more than 50% by number of each class of shareholders present and voting at a scheme meeting (excluding any votes cast by the bidder or any of its associates). It must also be approved by the court.

Some key gateways through the 20% Rule	
Shareholder approval	Acquisitions made with the approval of independent target company shareholders not affiliated with the acquisition.
Creeping acquisition	Acquisitions of not more than 3% of the voting power in a company in a 6 month period by a shareholder already holding at least 19%.
Rights issue	Acquisitions resulting from pro-rata rights issues offered equally to all shareholders.
Underwriting	Acquisitions by an underwriter of an issue of securities made pursuant to a prospectus or other disclosure document.
Downstream acquisition	Indirect acquisitions resulting from an acquisition of securities in an "upstream" company listed on the ASX (or other approved foreign market) which itself has a relevant interest in a "downstream" ASX listed company.

a. Off-market Bids

Under an off-market bid, a bidder makes separate but identical offers to all holders of securities in a target company to acquire their securities. When a holder accepts the offer, an agreement for the acquisition of their securities results.

The bidder is required to prepare a bidder's statement containing relevant background information and terms of the bid. This is lodged with ASIC, ASX and the target company. Copies must also be sent to the target company's shareholders.

Off-market bids are made by written offers to a target company's shareholders within two months of the announcement of a bid, and must stay open for at least one month, but no longer than 12 months. An uncontested off-market bid usually takes a minimum of 3 months from announcement to completion. If a bid is contested, the duration of the bid may be increased significantly.

Off-market bids may be conditional or unconditional, full or partial, and the consideration offered may be cash, securities or a combination of both. However, off-market takeover bids are often made conditional upon the satisfaction or waiver of a number of conditions, such as that the bidder reaches a minimum level of acceptances (usually 50% or 90%) or obtains specified regulatory approvals such as FIRB or ACCC approval.

A bidder may compulsorily acquire the remaining securities in the bid class if the bidder and their associates have relevant interests in at least 90% of the securities in the bid class.

Off-market takeover bids may be friendly (i.e. made with the recommendation of the target company's board) or hostile.

b. On-market Bids

On-market bids are made on ASX by the bidder at a specified offer price through a broker. On-market bids are rare in Australia due to the requirement that the offer must be cash-only, unconditional and relate to all securities in the target company of the relevant class.

The strategic merit of an on-market takeover bid is the potential for a faster implementation. The timing of an on-market takeover bid is shorter than off-market, as offers to shareholders must be made within 15 days of the announcement. The approval threshold to acquire 100% of the target company is the same as an off-market takeover bid.

c. Schemes

As schemes require agreement between the target company and the acquirer, they are generally only used for friendly acquisitions. The binary (all or nothing) outcome means schemes are frequently used to effect 100% acquisitions.

The scheme process is driven by the target company. The target company and acquirer enter into a formal merger implementation agreement that sets out the terms upon which a scheme will be proposed to the target company's shareholders and directors.

Schemes are more flexible than takeover bids, allowing an acquirer to pay any combination of cash or scrip as consideration, and may be conditional on the occurrence (or non-occurrence) of specific events, such as obtaining regulatory approval. It enables an acquisition to incorporate additional complexities, such as the reduction of a target company's capital. Schemes also achieve an all-or-nothing outcome and are frequently used to achieve 100% acquisitions.

d. Related Party Transactions (Involving Public Companies)

Australia has strict rules about related party transactions, particularly for public companies. A related party

transaction occurs when a public company, or RE of an MIS, engages in a transaction to give a financial benefit to a related party. "Related parties" include:
- a company that controls the public company or related entity;
- any director of, the public company or related entity, or the company that controls the public company or related entity;
- the spouses, parents and children of those directors; and
- any entity controlled by any of the entities or persons listed above.

In general, shareholder approval is required unless a transaction is entered into on arm's length terms. This occurs when neither party is influenced nor acting in their own interests, or bears any special duty or obligation. An independent expert report may be obtained to assist shareholders in considering whether to approve a related party transaction.

If shareholder approval is required, a shareholder meeting must be held to pass an ordinary resolution (more than 50% of votes) approving the related party transaction.

Companies listed on a market exchange (e.g. ASX) are subject to additional rules for related party dealings.

e. Proprietary Companies

Acquiring a proprietary company in Australia is largely governed by general principles of contract law. Certain provisions of the Corporations Act, FATA and the Competition and Consumer Act 2010 (CCA) also commonly apply to mergers and acquisitions of proprietary companies.

The sale process involves negotiations between the parties to draft a sale agreement that sets out the agreed terms - it is the written expression of the "deal" and how risk will be allocated between the parties.

There are two principal methods by which proprietary companies can be acquired:
- acquiring the shares of the proprietary company (Share Sale); or
- acquiring all (or some) of the proprietary company's assets and goodwill (Asset Sale).

	Share Sale	Asset Sale
Structure	Where the buyer purchases the shares in the target company which operates the business. As a result, the buyer will acquire control over the target company, its business and its assets.	Where some or all of the assets of the target company are sold to the buyer, but ownership of shares in the target company remains unchanged. Commonly transferred assets include employees, intellectual property and equipment.
Liabilities	The buyer will also acquire all of the target company's liabilities. However, the buyer will generally try to mitigate any liabilities by including warranties and indemnities in the sale agreement.	The starting point is that none of the target company's past or present liabilities are assumed by the buyer. However, a buyer may choose to assume some past liabilities if this is the commercial deal between the parties.
Advantages	Procedurally less complex than an asset sale as generally only one class of asset is acquired (i.e. the shares in the target company). The corporate structure and employment contracts for the operation of the business will remain in place, which may be advantageous if the buyer seeks to operate it as a subsidiary.	Provides certainty and flexibility as the buyer can select the precise assets it wants to acquire from the target company. The buyer can also limit the liabilities transferred to it and leave certain residual liabilities with the target company.
Potential issues	• May be complex if some of the target company's assets are held by another entity, requiring an internal restructure prior to the sale. • Discussions between the parties about liabilities.	• Can raise significant restructure problems with the transfer (for both parties). • Employment offers will need to be made by the buyer to existing employees of the target company- under Australian law, employment contracts cannot be transferred without an employee's consent. There is a risk that key employees will not accept the terms offered. • Key contracts will likely have assignment provisions requiring consent of the counterparty. This can be complicated due to the volume of novation documents and third party consents. • Tax implications.

	Share Sale	Asset Sale
Warranties	• Warranties focus on good title to the shares and the past history and liabilities of the target company. • More extensive warranties are typically given as the buyer will acquire the past liabilities of the target company.	Warranties focus on the type of asset acquired (e.g. machinery in working condition; title to land tenements).

G. Competition Regulation

Before commencing business in the Australian market, it is important to be familiar with Australia's competition laws, which restrict certain activities by businesses in Australia.

Australia's antitrust and consumer protection legislation is contained in the CCA. The object of the CCA is to enhance the welfare of Australians through the promotion of competition and fair trading and provision for consumer protection.

a. Department Supervising Competition Regulation

The ACCC is an independent Australian statutory authority that enforces competition regulation in Australia. The ACCC can investigate possible breaches of the CCA, and can resolve matters administratively, issue infringement notices, or take legal action in an Australian court (in its own name or on behalf of others).

Businesses can seek authorisation from the ACCC to engage in conduct which they are concerned may be in breach of Australian competition law, removing the risk of legal action being taken against them.

b. Brief Introduction of Competition Law

In Australia, the following areas fall under the umbrella of competition law:
- Merger and investment control;
- Cartel laws;
- Other forms of anti-competitive conduct;
- Consumer Protection.

The Federal Court of Australia may impose substantial penalties for breaches of the competition provisions in the CCA. For both civil and criminal prohibitions, corporations face maximum fines and pecuniary penalties of the greater of:
- A$10 million;
- three times the gain from the contravening conduct; or
- where the gain cannot be ascertained, 10% of the corporate group's annual turnover attributable to Australia.

Individuals face up to 10 years in prison or fines of up to A$420,000 or both for each criminal cartel offence, while the maximum civil pecuniary penalty for individuals for a contravention of any other competition prohibition is A$500,000. It is also illegal for a corporation to indemnify its officers against legal costs and any financial penalty.

c. Measures Regulating Competition

a) Merger and Investment Control

Australia's merger control regime does not contain a mandatory notification procedure. However, in practice, Australia has a much-used voluntary notification procedure for mergers and acquisitions. An acquirer of shares or assets may:
- notify the ACCC of their proposed acquisition as a matter of courtesy (including on a confidential basis);
- seek informal clearance from the ACCC on the basis that the proposed acquisition does not substantially lessen competition; or
- seek formal clearance on the basis that the acquisition would, or is likely to, result in a net public benefit.

In practice, acquirers usually seek clearance from the ACCC in advance of completion if their transaction would:
- result in the acquirer having a market share of 20% or more;
- remove a vigorous and effective competitor;
- create significant vertical integration issues;
- be likely to be referred to the ACCC by other regulators (e.g. FIRB, the Australian Tax Office (ATO), ASIC or APRA); or
- attract public attention or complaints from competitors, suppliers or customers.

b) Cartel Laws

In Australia, it is a civil and criminal offence to make or give effect to a contract, arrangement or understanding between competitors that contains a cartel provision. A 'cartel provision' is a provision that has:
- the purpose or effect of fixing, controlling or maintaining the price of goods or services; or
- the purpose of:
  - preventing, restricting or limiting the production, capacity, supply or acquisition of goods or services;
  - allocating customers or geographic areas; or
  - bid rigging.

Competitors involved in joint venture arrangements or understandings may be exempt from the above rules, provided that the cartel provision in question is for the purposes of the joint venture and is reasonably necessary for undertaking the joint venture.

The ACCC also has immunity and leniency policies. Civil immunity is only available to the first eligible party to disclose the cartel conduct to the ACCC who agrees to fully cooperate with the ACCC.

c) Other Anti-competitive Eonduct

Australia's competition laws also prohibit:
- any contract, arrangement or understanding that has the purpose or effect of substantially lessening competition.
- one or more persons from engaging in a concerted practice that has the purpose or effect of substantially lessening competition. "Concerted practice" is not defined, but legislative guidance indicates this is intended to capture anti-competitive communication or cooperative behaviour that may not amount to a "contract, arrangement or understanding", but goes beyond a business independently responding to changing market conditions.
- a corporation which has a substantial degree of power in a market from engaging in conduct which has the purpose or effect of substantially lessening competition.
- non-price vertical restraints imposed as a condition of supply or acquisition, which have the purpose or effect of substantially lessening competition.
- corporations from specifying a minimum price at which its goods or services may be resold.

d) Consumer Protection

Companies doing business in Australia must also comply with Australia's consumer protection laws. A number of these provisions can impact a wide range of both business-to-business, and business-to-consumer transactions. These provisions include:
- a prohibition against misleading or deceptive conduct, which includes the use of misleading or false advertising, misleading names or market practices (including lookalike products), and representations made during negotiations;
- a prohibition against unconscionable conduct in trade or commerce;
- statutory guarantees (e.g. a guarantee that goods are of acceptable quality) which apply to the supply of goods and services that are less than A$40,000, or of a kind ordinarily acquired for personal, domestic or household use (but excludes goods acquired for re-supply or that are used in manufacturing or repairs); and
- a regime for courts to declare terms in standard-form contracts with consumers or small businesses to be "unfair" and therefore void.

H. Tax

a. Tax Regime and Rules

Australia has a comprehensive tax regime with taxes imposed at both the federal and state / territory level. The ATO is responsible for administering the tax laws imposed at the federal level. Each state and territory has a different body which administers the tax laws imposed in that particular jurisdiction.

The application of Australia's tax rules differs depending on the structure that is adopted by entities to regulate and order their affairs (i.e. whether they operate as an individual, company, partnership, or trust). The tax rules also differ between Australian resident entities for tax purposes and those that are non-residents.

b. Main Categories and Rates of Tax

a) Income Tax

Australian income tax is levied annually on the "taxable income" of an entity, which is equal to an entity's "assessable income" less allowable "deductions". The income year in Australia runs from 1 July to 30 June.

The assessable income of an entity is based upon its tax residency. Broadly:
- Australian residents must include, in their assessable income, both ordinary income (e.g. revenue gains) and statutory income (e.g. net capital gains) from all sources (i.e. their worldwide income); and

• non-resident entities must include, in their assessable income, both ordinary income which has an Australian source and other amounts which are specifically required to be included pursuant to the tax law (e.g. capital gains arising on the disposal of Australian real property interests).

Allowable deductions include general business outgoings to the extent they are incurred in gaining or producing assessable income or in carrying on a business. A number of specific deductions are also provided for in the tax law.

If a taxpayer's allowable deductions exceed their assessable income for a particular income year, this may give rise to a tax loss for that year which, in certain circumstances, may be carried forward and applied against their assessable income in a subsequent income year.

Australia also has a comprehensive set of double tax treaties, with other jurisdictions, in relation to income tax matters. These are relevant to non-resident entities that undertake activities in Australia, and also to Australian residents that undertake activities outside of Australia.

Certain types of income received by a non-resident entity, such as dividends, interest and royalty payments received from an Australian entity, may also be subject to Australian income tax by way of a final withholding tax.

Australia has stringent transfer pricing rules designed to prevent taxpayers engaged in cross-border transactions from increasing deductions or decreasing income to reduce their Australian tax liability. The Australian tax laws also contain various anti-avoidance rules.

b) Other Taxes

A range of taxes apply in Australia besides income tax.

Australia imposes a Goods and Services Tax (GST) of 10%. GST is conceptually similar to the Value Added Taxes operating in many OECD countries. GST is a consumption tax borne by consumers and is usually included in the purchase price in Australia. Taxpayers will generally be able to claim input tax credits for any GST they incur in the course of carrying on a business.

Employers in Australia are also subject to certain employment taxes. These include pay-as-you-go withholding, fringe benefits tax on the value of taxable benefits provided to employees or their associates in relation to employment, payroll tax on the value of taxable wages paid or payable by employers to employees or relevant contractors above an applicable threshold, superannuation and workers' compensation insurance liabilities.

Additionally, each state and territory imposes stamp duty on a range of different transactions. In particular:

• all states and territories levy transfer duty on the transfer of land or any interest in land in the jurisdiction in which the land is located;

• all states and territories levy landholder duty on the indirect acquisition of land that entitles the acquirer to an interest in a landholder at or above an applicable acquisition threshold; and

• some (but not all) states and territories impose transfer duty on a range of transactions relating to certain business assets (e.g. goodwill, intellectual property).

Certain imports into Australia, including luxury cars, attract their own tax liability above regular customs duty. A range of other taxes also apply in certain circumstances (e.g. wine equalisation tax, excise duty).

c) Tax Rates

The following income tax rates currently apply in Australia[1]:

Australian resident individual tax rates	
Taxable Income	**Tax Payable**
A$0–A$18,200	Nil
A$18,201–A$37,000	19 cents for each A$1 over A$18,201
A$37,001–A$87,000	A$3,572 plus 32.5 cents for each A$1 over A$37,000
A$87,001–A$180,000	A$19,822 plus 37 cents for each A$1 over A$87,000
A$180,001 and over	A$54,232 plus 45 cents for each A$1 over A$180,000

---

[1] On June 21, 2018, Australia passed a AUD 144 billion ($106 billion) package of income tax cuts. Accroding to this seven-year Personal Income Tax Plan, approximately 94% of all taxpayers will face a marginal tax rate of 32.5% or less in the 2025 income year.

| Australian non-resident individual tax rates ||
Taxable Income	Tax payable
A$0–A$87,000	32.5 cents for each A$1
A$87,001–A$180,000	A$28,275 plus 37 cents for each A$1 over A$87,000
A$180,001 and over	A$62,685 plus 45 cents for each A$1 over A$180,000

| Australian resident and non-resident company tax rates FY 17-18 ||
Turnover	Applicable Tax Rate
<A$25million	27.5% flat rate
>A$25million	30% flat rate
Note: Company tax rates are being reduced annually. It is expected that by FY 26-27 there will be a tax rate of 25% for companies with a turnover of less than A$50million.	

In relation to other tax matters:
• Each state and territory has its own stamp duty regime applicable to transactions at varying rates (of up to 5.75%). In some states, a stamp duty surcharge may also apply where foreign persons acquire direct or indirect interest in land. The surcharges range between 3% and 7%.
• The current rate of fringe benefits tax is 47%, but Federal Parliament is currently considering increasing rate to 47.5% (from 1 July 2019).
• The current minimum contribution rate, for superannuation purposes, is 9.5% of an employee's salary or wages (capped to a maximum contribution).
• The different states and territories impose payroll tax in their respective jurisdictions. The current rates of payroll tax vary between jurisdictions, but are generally around 5%.

c. Tax Declaration and Preference

a) Taxation Forms and Declarations

Income tax liability in Australia functions on a self-assessment regime that requires lodging an annual tax return. The ATO is able to audit a taxpayer to ensure their compliance with tax legislation.

Businesses registered for GST in Australia are required to pay their indirect tax liability on either a monthly, quarterly or yearly basis and must lodge a Business Activity Statement with the ATO. Periodic filings are also required in relation to other tax matters (e.g. payroll tax, fringe benefits tax).

In order to carry on business in Australia, entities are required to obtain a Tax File Number (TFN) and Australian Business Number (ABN). It is also necessary to appoint a public officer within three months of carrying on a business or deriving income in Australia. A public officer must be a natural person of at least 18 years of age who is ordinarily resident in Australia.

b) Preferences, Abatements and Incentives

Australia does not offer any tax holidays or tax abatements.

A range of tax concessions and exemptions apply in relevant circumstances. For example, certain goods and services in Australia are exempt from the indirect taxes like GST (e.g. supplies of certain food, supplies of certain health services). Additionally, some incentive related tax offsets are available for a range of activities (e.g. research and development and angel and venture capital).

Australia has a dividend imputation system, which means that certain distributions made by companies may attach tax credits (franking credits) to allow Australian resident shareholders to claim a credit for Australian tax paid by a company on the profits from which the dividend is paid. It also allows a non-resident shareholder to receive any such dividend free from any dividend withholding taxes.

Further, Australian tax laws permit wholly-owned corporate groups to form a "tax consolidated group". This means that all members of the group are treated as a single entity for certain income tax purposes. Tax consolidation is very common among corporate groups in Australia. Similar groups can be formed for other tax purposes (e.g. GST).

I. Securities

a. Brief Introduction of Securities-related Laws and Regulations

Companies in Australia may conduct an initial public offering (IPO) and have their securities traded on a market exchange. Becoming listed on a market exchange increases the liquidity of a company's shares.

Before being listed, however, companies must first satisfy certain requirements. For ASX, the current key requirements are:

Admission criterion	General requirement
Number of shareholders (spread requirement)	At least 300 non-affiliated investors who each hold a parcel of securities worth A$2,000 or more.
Free float	20% or more. Free float means the percentage of the company's securities that: • are not restricted via an escrow arrangement; and • are held by non-affiliated investors.
Company size	Profits test A$1 million aggregated profit from continuing operations over past 3 years plus A$500,000 consolidated profit from continuing operations over the last 12 months. or Assets test • A$4 million net tangible assets; or • A$15 million market capitalisation.
Share price	The issue price or sale price of all the securities for which the company seeks quotation must be at least A$0.20.
Character	The company must satisfy ASX that each director is of good fame and character.

If the company seeking admission on ASX is a foreign company, it must be registered as a foreign company carrying on business in Australia under the Corporations Act.

a) Ongoing Requirements

Once a public company becomes listed on ASX (Listed Company) it must comply with the ASX Listing Rules (Listing Rules) as well as the Corporations Act. The Listing Rules impose a range of requirements on Listed Companies, such as:
- making regular reports and announcements to their shareholders and the public ('continuous disclosure');
- lodging financial reports on a half-yearly and annual basis;
- making prior disclosure and seeking shareholder approval if they wish to undertake certain transactions;
- ensuring that matters of administration (e.g. issuance of holding statements for securities) and transactions (e.g. on-market share buy-backs) conform to certain requirements and standards; and
- complying with the ASX Corporate Governance Principles and Recommendations (ASX Principles).

b) ASX Principles

The ASX Principles require Listed Companies to report their compliance, annually, on an "if not, why not" basis.

Most Listed Companies in Australia have boards of directors which are comprised of more non-executive, independent directors than executive non-independent directors. In Australia, it is rare for the chairperson of a Listed Company to hold an executive position within the company. Listed Companies should also establish and disclose the respective roles, responsibilities and skills of the board and management. Larger Listed Companies usually establish board committees to address oversight of audit, risk, compliance, nomination and remuneration issues.

The ASX Principles state that Listed Companies in Australia should have audit committees comprised only of non-executive directors, a majority of whom are independent directors. This is mandatory under the Listing Rules for Listed Companies in the top 300 of the S&P / ASX All Ordinaries Index.

b. Supervision and Regulation of Securities Market

The securities market in Australia is predominately regulated by ASIC. ASIC is responsible for monitoring compliance with the Corporations Act and has wide powers to investigate, amongst other things, the conduct of disclosure and corporate activity by Listed Companies. ASIC also has responsibility for the supervision of Australia's market exchanges (e.g. ASX).

a) Insider Trading

Insider trading in securities and other financial and investment products is strictly prohibited.

Listed Companies must have trading policies which comply with minimum content requirements, including specifying that key management personnel cannot trade in the company's securities or in financial products issued, created over or in respect of the company's securities during prohibited periods (including the periods before the AGM and before the release of annual and half-yearly financial statements). The Corporations Act prohibits hedging of incentive remuneration. Directors of Listed Companies must disclose to ASX full details of their trading in securities.

b) Market Misconduct

Manipulation of securities and financial markets is prohibited. The operators of those markets are also required to actively monitor transactions in their markets and report any suspicious trading to ASIC. Further, Australia's laws include an overriding requirement that extends to financial transactions, which prohibits any person from engaging in misleading or deceptive conduct.

c) Requirements for Engagement in Securities Trading for Foreign Enterprises

Aside from any FIRB Approval requirements, there are no general restrictions for foreign enterprises to buy and sell securities, in Australia, on their own behalf and for their own purposes.

J. Preference and Protection of Investment

a. The Structure of Preference Policies

There are no official preference policies in Australia. While unofficial preferences for investment may exist, the Australian Government, working in partnership with Australian state and territory governments:
- actively encourages foreign direct investment into Australia; and
- aims to help foreign investors establish or expand a business in Australia.①

b. Support for Specific Industries and Regions

Like most countries around the world, Australia subsidises some industries, sectors and regions. The subsidies tend to vary depending on the government and political climate.

For example, the Australian Government recently established a A$5 billion Northern Australia Infrastructure Facility (NAIF). Under NAIF, the Australian Government may provide loans, concessions or alternative financing mechanisms to fund economic infrastructure projects in northern Australia until 30 June 2021. This includes financing for airports, rail, water, ports and housing projects that meet NAIF's eligibility criteria.

c. Special Economic Areas

There are no special economic areas or zones in Australia.

d. Investment Protection

Due to Australia's advanced economy and rule of law, investments and ownership rights in Australia are well protected.

a) Intellectual Property and Brand Protection

Australia has extensive intellectual property laws that can protect the branding and ideas associated with most business ventures. The system is administered by IP Australia, an Australian government agency. Forms of intellectual property protected in Australia include:
- trade marks;
- copyright;
- patents; and
- designs.

See Section [iv.], below, for further information.

b) Secured Interests Over Assets

The Personal Property Securities Act 2009 (PPSA) enables companies and persons to register, and protect, certain security interests in Australia. It does not apply to interests in land.

Under the PPSA, a secured creditor (with a perfected security interest) has a security interest which has priority over other interests / creditors. This interest can be enforced on insolvency and can be asserted against third parties.

The PPSA provides for perfection of a security interest in personal property by one of three ways:

---

① Australian Trade and Investment Commission, Invest in Australia: Guide to Investing, https://www.austrade.gov.au/International/Invest/Guide-to-investing/Australian-Government-support-programs.

- registration on the PPS register - this is the most common method of perfection;
- in the case of chattels and other physical collateral, possession by the secured party; or
- in the case of certain financial assets (including shares, bonds and certain accounts with Australian authorised deposit-taking institutions), control by the secured party.

There is usually no requirement to obtain a judgment before exercising enforcement rights. Enforcement rights may be set out in the security agreement. In addition, the PPSA provides a range of statutory enforcement options which are in addition to any options agreed in the security agreement.

c) Mortgages Over Land

If personal property is not involved (real property is the most common example), different security documents will be required. For land, that ordinarily would be a mortgage.

State and territory laws regulate real property mortgages. Mortgages will ordinarily contain an implied power to sell the interest in land that is the subject of the mortgage. In most states, a prescribed default notice must be served before the power of sale can be exercised under the mortgage. Enforcement does not, however, require an application to a court. The purchaser takes an interest in land free from all prior interests that rank below the secured creditor exercising the power of sale. However, this may be subject to certain limited interests that are protected by statute law.

d) Australian Court Protection and Bilateral Investment Treaties

In addition to the systems of investment protection described above, Australian courts operate under the rule of Australian law and act as independent tribunals on commercial law disputes. Australian courts will, and do, make court awards and judgments in favour of foreign enterprises against Australian companies and the Australian Government.

In addition, Australia is party to a number of bilateral investment treaties.[1] These treaties provide additional protection for investments in Australia and underpin Australia's commitment to encouraging foreign investment into Australia.

III. Trade

A. Department Supervising Trade

There is no one single government department in Australia with sole responsibility for governing the laws of trade. Instead, a number of government departments have certain responsibilities in relation to Australian trade policy and enforcement:
- The Department of Foreign Affairs and Trade: responsible for all external affairs issues such as bilateral, regional and multilateral trade policy; treaty administration; international trade and investment promotion;
- Department of the Treasury: Competition law; consumer protection law; Securities and Investment law; foreign investment review;
- Department of Home Affairs: border control and customs;
- Department of Agriculture and Water Resources: biosecurity and quarantine;
- Department of Industry, Innovation and Science: Industry and market development; intellectual property; anti-dumping laws;
- Department of Jobs and Small Business: employment; and
- Department of Infrastructure, Regional Development and Cities: civil aviation, maritime and shipping policy.

As Australia is a federal system, each state and territory government is also responsible for aspects of trade-related laws. As a result, laws can vary between states and territories within Australia.

B. Brief Introduction of Trade Laws and Regulations

As a result of the piece-meal way in which trade policy is administered across a large number of government departments, there is no general legislative or regulatory scheme to govern international trade in Australia. There are a number of laws and regulations that govern international trade in Australia, including:
- Customs Act 1901 (Cth): governs the customs control process in Australia; sets out the security and control processes; establishes rules governing the import and export of goods; the activities of depots, warehouses, cargo terminals and aviation;
- Customs Tariff Act 1995 (Cth): sets out the import duties to be paid on goods imported into Australia;

---

[1] A list of treaties can be found here: http://dfat.gov.au/trade/topics/investment/Pages/australias-bilateral-investment-treaties.aspx.

• Foreign Acquisitions and Takeovers Act 1975 (Cth): Governs the regime for assessing large purchases of land or business in Australia to ensure they are in the national interest;
• Australian Trade and Investment Commission 1985 (Cth): Establishes the Australian Trade and Investment Commission (Austrade), the national trade, investment and education promotion agency;
• Customs (Prohibited Imports) Regulations 1956 (Cth); Imported Food Control Act 1992 (Cth): set out the products that can and cannot be imported into Australia;
• Excise Act 1901 (Cth): sets out the regime governing excises on imports and exports in Australia;
• Criminal Code Act 1995 (Cth): sets out the criminal offences related to the import and export of goods in Australia;
• A New Tax System (Goods and Services Tax) Act 1999 (Cth): sets out the Value Added Tax (referred to in Australia as the Goods and Services Tax - GST) on imports and exports;
• Competition and Consumer Act 2010 (Cth): establishes the regime governing restrictive trade practices, antitrust and other competition law issues; sets out the consumer protection scheme in Australia. Applies to all entities conduct trade or commerce in Australia.

Australia is an original Member of the WTO. Australia has a number of bilateral, regional and multilateral trade agreements which impact its trade and tariff regime. These include agreements with Brunei Darussalam; Canada; Cambodia; Chile; Indonesia; Japan; Republic of Korea; Lao People's Democratic Republic; Malaysia; Myanmar; New Zealand; Papua New Guinea; the Philippines; Singapore; Thailand; the United States; and Vietnam. Australia has additional commitments under regional trade agreements such as ASEAN and APEC. Australia continues to negotiate a number of other bilateral agreements with India and Indonesia, and is also participating in negotiations relating to the Trans-Pacific Partnership (TPP); the Australia-Gulf Cooperation Council (GCC) RTA; the Pacific Trade and Economic Partnership Agreement (PACER Plus); and, the Regional Comprehensive Economic Partnership (RCEP) negotiations.

C. Trade Management

Australia maintains its status as one of the most open economies in the world, albeit one in a state of flux following the end of the resources boom which peaked in 2011. The economy has entered a new transitional period with Australia's international trade portfolio moving towards a broader range of sectors, currently representing around 40% of national GDP.

The Australian Government's trade outlook has pivoted in light of what is commonly referred to as the 'Asian Century'. Emerging trends in international trade reflect the changing shape of the Australian import / export market, with three (China, Japan and South Korea) of the country's five largest two-way trading partners being located within Asia. Australia actively continues to pursue bilateral, regional and multilateral trade agreements and a range of other government policies targeted at enhancing trade openness and economic growth.

Australia's primary means of collecting revenue on trade is the tariff. Approximately 96% of tariffs applied to most favoured nations are below 5%. Further, over 99.5% are ad valorem, increasing predictability and transparency in the Australian trading environment. Australia's tariff regime is noticeably higher in certain sectors supported by government support, namely: textiles, clothing, footwear and motor vehicles.

Australia has an open stance towards foreign direct investment (FDI), though subjects large investment projects to review to ensure they are in the national interest. It is rare for FDI proposals to be rejected outright, though many have conditions attached. Concerns over accessibility for Australian citizens has resulted in restrictions on residential real estate and agricultural land being put in pace. Further, there are equity limits on civil aviation, maritime transport and telecommunications infrastructure.

D. The Inspection and Quarantine of Import and Export Commodities

Australia is well known for its unique and diverse flora and fauna. As a result of its isolated global location, Australia has strict quarantine laws. Given the federal separation of powers and the distinct differences in biodiversity, different quarantine measures apply not only to entering Australia, but when trading within Australia.

• Quarantine laws capture all imports and exports, including but not limited to plants, animals, food products, and people. The Commonwealth Department of Agriculture and Water Resources (DAWR) has the primary responsibility to implement and administer Australia's quarantine systems. These functions include the issuing of import / export permits and conducting inspections. The Department of Health also provides input and advice in relation to import permits, and may also assess biological materials that are of concern to public health.

• The importation of food is subject to the Imported Food Control Act 1992 (Cth), as well as the Imported Food Control Regulations 1993 (Cth). The DAWR administers the process based on the Imported Food Inspection Scheme. The DAWR is assisted in its risk management efforts by Food Standards Australia New Zealand, an independent statutory body that provides advice and develops standards regarding food safety. All imported foods must comply with the food labelling requirements under the Food Standards Code.

There are also mandatory product labelling information standards in relation to health and product care for textiles, clothing, sunglasses and cosmetics. Electronic appliances such as washing machines, dishwashers, fridges, and air-conditioners, as well as motor vehicles, must disclose their energy consumption via product labels. Australia has particularly strong laws in relation to tobacco, including a ban on all marketing and requiring plain packaging.

While Australia has no automatic requirement to seek an import licence, there are licensing requirements in relation to certain products on a number of grounds including public health, environmental protection and international obligations. These licensing requirements impose prohibitions or a range of stringent inspection and quarantine procedures in relation to over 150 products. These include:

- Agricultural produce;
- Animal fur products; endangered animal and plant species;
- Antibiotics; other therapeutic drugs and substances;
- Tobacco products;
- Hydroflurocarbons (HFCs); ozone-depleting substances / synthetic greenhouse gases; pesticides and other hazardous chemicals.

Unless there are specific permit requirements, the general rule is that all goods to be exported with a value greater than AUDA$2,000 must be registered with Customs. The Australian Government operates the Integrated Cargo System (ICS), and is the electronic reporting tool used for most export declarations in Australia. Export declarations can also take the form of an Export Declaration (B957 Form) completed at a Customs counter. Depending on the goods to be exported, Customs may conduct a compliance examination on behalf of the agency or government department authorising the export permit. Australia has a strong export market for its agricultural produce. To ease international trade, Customs may impose export controls on certain products to align with the importing requirements in the destination country.

E. Customs Management

Australia maintains a modern customs management infrastructure, focusing on minimising documentation requirements and using computerised processes for almost all import and export activity. The Home Affairs Department's primary operational arm is the Australian Border Force (ABF). The ABF's approach to customs management is to further the government's aim to encourage international trade through:

- modernising and increasing our digital capabilities, including self-service identity / entity verification;
- automating low-risk, high-volume transactions so that resources can be allocated to areas of higher risk (such as through the Australian Trusted Trader for expedited treatment); and
- collaborating with industry through active consultation; and
- increasing efforts to enhance transparency and consistency.

Australia's Customs management process has in recent years shifted to a more holistic approach aimed at avoiding the only interaction with traders being at the border and relating only to each transaction in isolation. The ABF approach now entails active industry engagement and advice (including compliance training, valuations, tariff advice) to increase certainty.

Under Australian Law, there are a range of compliance tools available to the ABF. In determining the appropriate regulatory remedy, the ABF will consider previous history, level of intent, mitigating circumstances, corrective actions, impact on the economy or community, impact on ABF operational resources, cooperation and disclosure.

IV. Labour

A. Brief Introduction of Labour Laws and Regulations

a. Overview

Employment law in Australia is derived from the common law, obligations arising under statute and applicable regulations, and industrial instruments such as modern awards and enterprise agreements.

b. Common Law

The common law is a primary source of obligations for Australian employees and employers, and primarily arises from the contract of employment. There are also principles that apply generally at common law.

The terms and conditions of an employee's contract come from various sources. First, some terms are expressly agreed by the parties orally or in writing. Second, there are terms implied into the contract by law, from surrounding circumstances, custom and practice. A written employment contract will ordinarily set out the key terms of employment, including the employee's position title, location, employment status, remuneration, incentive entitlements, obligations with respect to the use and disclosure of confidential information, intellectual property rights, restraints of trade (if any), termination and redundancy.

c. Statutory Framework

a) Minimum Employment Conditions

The primary employment legislation that applies to businesses in Australia is the Fair Work Act 2009 (Cth) (FW Act).

The FW Act sets out minimum statutory conditions of employment known as the National Employment Standards (NES). The NES apply to all national system employees irrespective of the employee's income or position and include maximum weekly hours of work, a right to request flexible work arrangements, parental leave, annual leave, personal / carer's leave, community service leave, long service leave, public holidays, notice of termination and redundancy pay. These conditions cannot be modified to an employee's detriment by a contract, award or enterprise agreement.

b) Minimum Pay Rates

Minimum pay rates are set out in modern awards, enterprise agreements and national minimum wage orders. The current national minimum wage is A$18.29 per hour or A$694.90 per 38 hour week (before tax). The FW Act specifies a default casual loading of 25% which applies to casual employees, however, modern awards and enterprise agreements may prescribe a different casual loading rate.

c) Termination of Employment

All employers must provide notice of termination (and if applicable, redundancy pay) in accordance with the FW Act.

d) Unfair Dismissal

The FW Act contains provisions allowing some employees to commence proceedings alleging that the termination of their employment was harsh, unjust or unreasonable.

All employers, regardless of their size, may be subject to a claim in the Fair Work Commission (FWC) for unfair dismissal once an employee has completed a minimum period of employment (6 months for employers with 15 or more employees).

The primary remedy in unfair dismissal applications is reinstatement to the position held prior to termination or re-employment in another suitable position within the employers business. An employee may also receive compensation or back pay.

e) General Protections

The FW Act contains general protections provisions which are intended to protect employees from adverse action taken for a prohibited reason. In essence, adverse action refers to circumstances where an employer engages in a course of conduct which results in an employee being detrimentally affected or prejudiced in his / her employment. For example, adverse action may be taken by an employer if an employee is dismissed, injured in his / her employment, discriminated against or has his / her position altered to their detriment because of a prohibited reason (for example, an employee's age, gender, marriage status, sexuality, ethnicity or religion).

A person may apply to the FWC claiming a breach of the general protections provisions and the FW Act provides remedies (including damages and reinstatement) where the protections have been contravened.

f) Superannuation

The Commonwealth superannuation guarantee legislation currently requires employers to pay a percentage of their employees' ordinary time earnings (currently 9.5%) to an approved superannuation fund which is independently administered and generally unrelated to the employer. A maximum superannuation contribution base exists whereby employers are not required to contribute superannuation with respect to income in excess of minimum earnings. That amount is currently A$50,810 per quarter.

g) Anti-discrimination and Bullying

There is a range of State and Federal legislation prohibiting discrimination in employment. It is unlawful to discriminate against an employee on various grounds including race, gender, sexual preference, pregnancy, marital status, disability, transgender status, age and status as a parent or carer.

Employers may be held vicariously liable for discriminatory conduct engaged in by its employees unless the employer has developed appropriate policies and trained its employees with respect to discrimination matters.

Workers (including employees and contractors) who are bullied at work can apply to the FWC for an order to stop the bullying. Bullying refers to situations where an individual or group repeatedly behaves unreasonably towards a worker and that behaviour creates a risk to health and safety. If the FWC is satisfied that a worker has been bullied and that there is a risk that they will continue to be bullied, it may make any order it considers appropriate to stop the bullying (other than an order requiring payment of a pecuniary amount).

Bullying also falls within the ambit of the work health and safety (WHS) statutory regime, which means that an employer will have an obligation to ensure the health and safety of its workers by, for example, preventing and responding to workplace bullying.

d. Industrial Instruments

a) Modern Awards

The minimum terms and conditions of some employees are governed by modern awards. Modern awards are documents approved by the FWC which, together with the NES, set out minimum terms and conditions of employment. Modern awards apply to employees in certain industries and occupations.

An employer and a high income employee may agree in writing that a modern award will not apply to them for an agreed period. A high income employee is an employee with a guaranteed annual income that exceeds A$142,000. That amount is indexed to inflation and adjusted annually.

b) Enterprise Agreements

An enterprise agreement is an agreement between an employer, a group of employees and, most often, an industrial union which sets out the minimum terms of employment applicable to those employees who are covered by the agreement. In order for an enterprise agreement to be approved, each employee or prospective employee must be better off under the agreement compared with an applicable modern award.

e. Work Health and Safety

Each State and Territory within Australia has extensive legislation dealing with WHS issues. That legislation is consistent across all States except Victoria and Western Australia (although it is expected that Western Australia will adopt the model legislation in due course).

The model WHS laws impose various duties on persons conducting a business or undertaking, officers, workers and other persons who visit the workplace. Significant penalties, including prison sentences, can apply for breach of those duties.

Employers are also required to obtain workers compensation insurance for their employees which covers them for workplace injuries. The rates and regimes differ between each State and Territory.

B. Requirements of Employing Foreign Employees

In conjunction with employment laws under the FW Act, the Migration Act 1958 (together with its associated regulations and policy) (Migration Act) governs the employment of foreign employees in Australia.

All persons that enter Australia without an Australian passport are required to hold a relevant visa to undertake their intended activity in Australia. Strict penalties apply to employers who allow foreign nationals to work in Australia in breach of a visa condition. Visa holders in breach of conditions may be subject to visa cancellation and removal from Australia.

The governing authority for visas to enter Australia is the Department of Home Affairs (DOHA).

a. Work Permit

For a temporary stay in Australia for the main purpose of undertaking work, there are two main types of Australian work permits (known as visas) available. These visas are:

a) Temporary Work (Short Stay Specialist) visa (Subclass 400)

The Temporary Work (Short Stay Specialist) visa (Subclass 400) (400 visa) allows for a person to enter Australia to undertake short-term, highly specialised work for a period of up to six months under the highly specialised work stream. An Australian business should invite a candidate to undertake this work, or alternatively an overseas business may send a specific employee to fulfil a contractual arrangement in Australia. The activity itself needs to be non-ongoing. Where it is considered ongoing, the longer term sponsored work visa should be applied for.

The activities undertaken on this visa by a visa holder should not have adverse consequences for employment or training opportunities for Australians.

Additionally, there is a 400 visa stream that allows for Australias interests to be considered in assessment of a candidate. This stream will only be relevant where there are compelling circumstances affecting Australias interest that require the Applicants entry and stay in Australia. For example, where there is national emergency or where Australias trade opportunities would be adversely affected.

b) Temporary Skills Shortage visa

The Temporary Skills Shortage visa (TSS visa) was introduced to the Australian immigration program from early March 2018, as a replacement for the previous Temporary Work (Skilled) visa (Subclass 457) (457 visa).

The TSS visa allows for either a two year or four year temporary work visa dependent on the nominated occupation from the skilled occupation list. Where nominated from the Short Term Skilled Occupation List (STSOL), a person will be eligible for a two year visa, with the ability to apply for one two year renewal whilst in Australia; those candidates with occupations on the Medium to Long Term Skills Shortage List will have access to a four visa with the ability to renew following this period. Where the candidate is nominated by a start-up business (ie. operating for less than 12 months), the length of the visa will be up to 18 months only.

Each application must meet strict salary, skill and English requirements, and most applications will be required to include evidence of labour market testing in Australia.

b. Application Procedure

a) Temporary Work (Short Stay Specialist) visa (Subclass 400)

To be eligible for a 400 visa, the candidate must:

• hold personal attributes, an employment background, or both, that are relevant to, and consistent with, the nature of the candidates proposed participation in an event, or proposed engagement in an activity or work;

• genuinely intend to stay in Australia temporarily;

• have adequate means to support themselves in Australia usually by way of salary from the inviting Australian company or home employer; and

• meet health and character checks where relevant to the stay period in Australia.

There is no English requirement attached to this application. The salary offered to 400 visa candidates is not specifically prescribed however the 400 visa should not be used to circumvent payment of the Australian market rate requirements and under current policy it is expected that higher skilled occupations would be paid at least the Temporary Skilled Migration Income Threshold (TSMIT) (currently set at AUD 53,900) and that all other occupations would be paid at least Australian minimum wage.

b) Temporary Skills Shortage visa

For employers to support a candidate on a TSS visa, there is three step process:

(i) An employer must be approved as a business sponsor by meeting relevant requirements, including being actively and lawfully operating.

(ii) An employer nominates a position from the skilled occupation list in accordance with the role available that cannot be filled by an Australian. However:

• nominated positions will not be subject to labour market testing where the China-Australia Free Trade Agreement (CHaFTA), or another international trade agreement that exempts labour market testing, applies; and

• the position nominated must offer a salary that is at least equivalent to TSMIT and be consistent with Australian market rates.

(iii) A candidate makes a correlating visa application to the nomination evidencing that they have the relevant skills to fill the role. Where the candidate's position is nominated from the STSOL, a genuine temporary entrant requirement will apply to the visa application. The candidate must also meet health, character and English criteria.

For both the 400 and TSS visas, the candidate and / or business should meet these requirements by providing relevant documents in line with each specific criterion. The application is prepared, lodged and managed online directly with the DOHA.

Processing times for applications will vary. However, most applications are finalised within one month for 400 visas, and within five months for 457 / TSS visas. Faster processing times are available to businesses who hold Accredited Sponsorship status.

c. Social Insurance

It is not required that 400 visa holders hold social insurance (commonly referred to as health insurance) in Australia.

For the 457 / TSS visas however it is a condition of the visa that all visa holders hold appropriate Australian or equivalent health insurance for the duration of their visa. This includes any dependent visa holders.

C. Exit and Entry

a. Visa Types

Australia has various visa types that cover a range of activities that either contribute to the Australian labour force, economy or benefit Australian citizens through family reunion or Australias humanitarian program.

a) Work or Study Visas

For the purposes of temporary work, the 400 visa and 457 / TSS visa are most appropriate depending on the intended length of stay. The General Skilled and permanent employer sponsored visa programs allow for permanent migration of highly skilled workers aged under 45. Some limited age exemptions apply to the employer sponsored visa categories.

The Work and Holiday (subclass 462) visa is available to Chinese passport holders aged between 18 and 30 who have tertiary qualifications and functional English.

Australias student visa program caters for international students who wish to undertake approved study in Australia.

b) Business Visitors

To travel to Australia for business visitor activities, a person should make an application for a Visitor Visa (subclass 600).

This application is prepared, lodged and managed online directly with DOHA. Processing times are usually less than 1 month although a 48 hour fast track service is available for Chinese passport holders. In December 2016, a trial of a new 10 year Frequent Traveller visa commenced allowing stays in Australia for up to three months per visit, with multiple entries permitted.

c) Other Visa Types

Business innovation and investment options may also available for experienced business owners, entrepreneurs or investors. In particular, the Significant Investor visa category provides for particular exemptions regarding English language requirements, and further flexibility regarding passive investment history and lower requirements of residence in Australia. This has resulted in China being the number one source country in this category.

b. Restrictions for Exit and Entry

All persons entering Australia with a non-Australian passport are required to hold an Australian visa prior to entry. For Chinese passport holders, this visa must be applied for and finalised prior to travel.

Further, all entrants must hold a valid passport to enter Australia. Whilst the Australian government does not have a restriction on the length of validity of a foreign entrant's passport some international airlines may for example, require a minimum 6 months validity.

D. Trade Union and Labour Organizations

A trade union or labour organisation refers to a group of individuals (either employees or contractors) who band together to represent the common interests of workers within a particular industry or occupation. This will generally include issues such as minimum pay rates, hours of work and, increasingly, flexible working arrangements.

The key responsibilities of a trade union generally include acting as an advocate for workers, investigating suspected breaches of employment or WHS legislation, ensuring employers are complying with minimum conditions of employment and assisting in the resolution of workplace issues as and when they arise. A trade union may be registered with the FWC under the Fair Work (Registered Organisations) Act 2009 (Cth), although it is not a mandatory requirement.

E. Labour Disputes

There are circumstances in which disputes may arise between employees and / or a trade union and an employer. This is generally referred to as industrial disputation and can include, for example, employees going on strike and the imposition of work bans.

a. Industrial Action

Under the FW Act, industrial action will occur in circumstances where an employee performs work in a way that is different from the way in which work is usually performed; a ban, limitation or restriction is placed on the performance of work by an employee; an employee fails or refuses to attend for work or perform work; and / or employees are locked out by their employer. Industrial action can be classified as protected in certain circumstances, which essentially means that participants in the industrial action will broadly be exempt from civil action. Industrial action will only be considered protected if it relates to the negotiation of a proposed enterprise agreement. There are rules contained in the FW Act which dictate when and how protected industrial action may be taken.

If an employee engages in industrial action, the employer will not be obligated to pay the employee for the duration of that period of industrial action.

b. Bargaining Negotiations

Protected industrial action can be initiated by a bargaining representative by applying to the FWC for a protected action ballot order.

There are certain requirements which must be satisfied in order for the FWC to approve an application. If approved, the FWC will issue a protection action ballot order. This essentially enables employees covered by the enterprise agreement to vote on whether they will engage in protected industrial action. If protected industrial action is initiated by employees, it will be authorised by the protected action ballot if at least 50% of the employees on the roll of voters voted in the ballot, more than 50% of the valid votes approved the action and the industrial action commenced within 30 days of the declaration of the results of the ballot (unless a further period is authorised by the FWC).

c. Dispute Resolution Procedures

There are specific types of disputes relating to national system employees that the FWC is authorised to deal with under the FW Act by way of conciliation or arbitration. This includes, for example, bargaining disputes in connection with the negotiation of an enterprise agreement, general protections disputes, right of entry and stand downs. For non-national system employees (such as public sector employees, local government employees and private sector employees in Western Australia who are not employed by constitutional corporations), industrial laws in the applicable State or Territory in which the employee is based will apply. Generally speaking, awards and / or agreements in most States and Territories will contain a provision which deals with dispute resolution procedures, and will ordinarily require the parties to attempt to resolve the dispute commercially prior to engaging in litigation.

V. Intellectual Property

A. Brief Introduction of IP Laws and Regulations

The power to make laws with respect to copyright, patents, designs and trade marks is conferred exclusively on the Australian Federal Government.

IP Australia is the Federal Government agency responsible for administering Australias intellectual property rights system, specifically trademarks, patents, designs and plant breeder's rights.

Australia is a party to the main international multi-party conventions and treaties on IP law including the Berne Convention, the TRIPS Agreement (1994) and the Patent Cooperation Treaty (1970). Australia has also entered into a range of relevant bilateral treaties (predominantly free trade agreements) with countries. Australias treaty obligations are not self-executing and require local legislation before they are effective under Australian law.

a. Copyright

Copyright law in Australia is exclusively governed by the Copyright Act 1968 (Cth) (Copyright Act) there is no common law copyright in Australia. The Copyright Act recognises copyright in 2 distinct categories of copyright subject matter: first, works which include original literary, dramatic, musical and artistic works, and secondly specific subject matter other than works, including sound recordings, cinematograph films, radio and television broadcasts and published editions of works. As a general rule, copyright is infringed if a person does or authorises another person to exercise without permission one of the copyright owner's exclusive rights in relation to the copyrighted material.

Copyright law is also found in regulations made under the Copyright Act. The Copyright (International Protection) Regulations 1969 (Cth) extends reciprocal copyright protection to the works and subject matters other than works of nationals, citizens and residents of other countries to the extent those countries are party to the relevant core copyright conventions (the Berne Convention, the Universal Copyright Convention, the WIPO Copyright Treaty, the WIPO Performances and Phonograms Treaty and the Rome Convention) or are members of the World Trade Organization, and to works made or first published in those countries.

b. Trade Mark

Trade mark law in Australia is governed by the Trade Marks Act 1995 (Cth) (Trade Marks Act). In addition to the Trade Marks Act, the Federal Government has promulgated regulations pursuant to the Trade Marks Act, known as the Trade Marks Regulations 1995 (Cth). The definition of a sign is not defined exhaustively in the Trade Marks Act, and includes any letter, word, name, signature, numeral, device, brand, heading, label, ticket, aspect of packaging, shape, colour, sound or scent, or any combination thereof. Trade marks are not limited in duration in Australia provided they are renewed, they can create perpetual monopoly. To obtain protection under the Trade Marks Act, the owner must lodge a trade mark application with IP Australia.

The Australian Consumer Law (set out in schedule 2 of the Competition and Consumer Act 2010 (Cth)) is also relevant to trade marks. The Australian Consumer Law ensures that conduct in relation to trade marks meets appropriate standards of business conduct, including principles relating to unconscionable conduct, unfair practices, product safety and product information. The common law of passing off is also a source of law relating to trade marks.

c. Patent

Patent law in Australia is governed by the Patents Act 1990 (Cth) (Patents Act). A patent confers a statutory right to the inventor to exploit that invention exclusively for a specified period of time. The Patents Act provides for two types of patents: standard patents and innovation patents. Innovation patents require a lower threshold of registrability but have a shorter period of protection.

Australia is also part of the Patent Cooperation Treaty, (PCT), and filing a patent under this regime in Australia or another signatory country will grant protection of that patent in each of those countries.

d. Design

Registered design law in Australia is governed by the Designs Act 2003 (Cth) (Designs Act). A registered design protects the visual appearance of products, as opposed to patent protection which protects a product's functionality. However, the fact that the appearance or a visual feature of a product is associated with the products function does not disqualify it from design registration.

To obtain protection under the Designs Act, the owner must lodge a design application with IP Australia. A registered design provides protection for 10 years and protects visual features of a design such as shape, configuration, pattern and ornamentation. Registered designs in Australia are subject to an assessment criteria with two facets; originality and distinctiveness.

e. Intellectual Property Court System

Practice and procedure in intellectual property litigation matters are generally governed by the Federal Court of Australia Act 1976(Cth) and the Federal Court Rules (2011) made pursuant to that Act. In particular, Division 34.3 of the Federal Court Rules deals with intellectual property proceedings generally. If the proceedings are commenced in the Federal Circuit Court of Australia (previously known as the Federal Magistrates Court), practice and procedure in the Court will be governed by the Federal Circuit Court of Australia Act 1999 (Cth) and the Federal Circuit Court Rules (2001). The Federal Circuit Court was invested with jurisdiction to hear less complex and shorter copyright matters in 2003. Both the Federal Court of Australia and the Federal Circuit Court of Australia also issues practice notes from time to time which provide guidance for practitioners. The Evidence Act 1995 (Cth) sets out the rules of evidence applicable in Australia.

B. Patent Application

Prospective patentees must apply for a patent through IP Australia, and can file for either an Australian patent or for a PCT patent, with the applicant selecting which countries they would like to gain protection under.

In order to be registrable as a standard patent, an application must contain an inventive step which entails a new, non-obvious invention with applicability in industry. For an innovation patent there must be an innovative step, which represents an incremental improvement on existing knowledge.

In drafting an application, applicants have the choice of using a provisional application with fewer formality requirements, or a complete application which is held to a higher standard and requires that specifications disclose the best method an applicant knows for performing the invention. A provisional application can be converted into a complete application no longer than 12 months from its filing date, in which case the original filing date will be used as the priority date of the prospective invention.

All patent applications must comply with an approved form (including an English language requirement) and formality requirements, primarily disclosing the invention in a manner which is clear enough and complete enough for the invention to be performed by a person skilled in the relevant art. Any ambiguous or relative terms must be quantified, and any external references must be to common knowledge. A complete application will commonly include drawings and working examples of the invention, though this is not mandatory.

There are a number of steps that must be taken after filing before a patent will be granted. The applicant must request an examination of the patent by the Commissioner of Patents (the Commissioner), which functions as an office within IP Australia responsible for the administration of patent applications. The Commissioner will assess a patents compliance with the requirements of the Patents Act.

Upon examination, the Commissioner can choose to either grant, refuse, or issue an adverse report regarding the application. Issuing an adverse report will give the applicant time to rectify any errors the examiner believes have been made. Any rectifications must be made within 12 months of issue of the original report.

An innovation patent will not go through the same examination process as a standard patent, and the Commissioner will merely check to ensure that formalities have been complied with, if so the patent will be granted and published in Patent Office's Official Journal.

18 months after the filing of a patent application, the patent will be published through the Official Journal, which enables third parties to oppose its grant. If all of these steps have been followed unopposed, the applicant will be granted a patent. In the case of an innovation patent, protection will last 8 years, while protection for a standard patent lasts 20, and allows the patentee exclusive rights to exploit that invention. To maintain the patent, the patentee must pay periodic renewal fees.

C. Trademark Registration

Trade marks are registered with the Trade Marks Office, and registration is effected by the Registrar of Trade Marks. Trade marks are registered in the name of the applicant(s) and in respect of goods and / or services specified in the application.

The applicant(s) should be using or have an intention to use the trade mark, or have authorised or intend to authorise another person to use the trade mark, or intend to assign the trade mark to a body corporate that is about to be constituted with a view to its use by the body corporate.

Trade marks are registered in classes of goods and services. A single application can cover one, some, or all classes. When an application is made, a description of the scope of the goods and / or services must be given, which then defines the monopoly given to the trade mark owner.

Australia is one of the 98 members of the Madrid Protocol which establishes an international system for the registration of trade marks. Under the Madrid Protocol, an applicant for a trade mark may designate Australia as a country for which protection is sought and that trade mark becomes registered in Australia following local examination.

A foreign company should check whether its trade marks have already been registered in Australia by virtue of a Madrid Protocol registration before troubling themselves with a national Australian registration. Under the Paris Convention, it may be possible to claim the same priority date as overseas applications if the application is filed in Australia within 6 months. Foreign companies should always consider acquiring registration for their trade marks in Australia prior to the commencement of any dealings.

Following lodgement of an application, the mark is examined and a decision made on whether the application has been made in accordance with the Trade Marks Act and whether there are any grounds for rejecting the application. During the examination process, a search of the Register of Trade Marks will be made to determine if there are any registered marks that would prevent registration in accordance with the application. An Examiners report is issued and the applicant has an opportunity to make a response in writing. The applicant has 15 months to contest any objections to the application raised by the Examiner.

The Registrar must notify the applicant in writing of the decision to accept or reject the application and must advertise that decision in the Trade Marks Journal. If the Registrar has accepted an application, it may be opposed by any third party. Objections may be made during the 2 month period after acceptance is advertised. The applicant and the opposing party have the opportunity to file evidence and the matter is heard (either in person or on the papers) by the Registrar. The Registrars decision may be appealed to the Federal Court or the Federal Circuit Court (within 21 days of the decision).

Once the trade mark application has been accepted for registration, the Registrar will give the registered owner a certificate and advertise the registration in the Trade Marks Journal. Initial registration is 10 years from the filing date. Renewal of the trade mark is required every 10 years.

VI. Environmental Protection

A. Department Supervising Environmental Protection

The Commonwealth Department of the Environment and Energy (DoEE) is the key Federal department supervising environment protection in Australia. The DoEE designs and implements Australian Government's policy and programs to protect and conserve the environment, water and heritage.

Each State and Territory Government in Australia has its own suite of departments supervising environment protection in those jurisdictions. By way of guidance, in New South Wales (NSW) the primary environmental regulator is the NSW Environment Protection Authority which is responsible for issuing, and enforcing compliance with, environment protection licences, investigation and management of pollution incidents (air, water, land and noise) and the clean-up of contamination. Other Departments which play a key environment protection in NSW include:

• NSW Department of Planning and the Environment responsible for land use planning and strategic planning policies;

• NSW Office of Environment and Heritage responsible for national parks and protected areas, Aboriginal and non-Aboriginal heritage; and

• NSW Office of Water responsible for protecting surface water and groundwater resources.

While each State and Territory Government has adopted their own environment protection laws, the Departments supervising those laws are generally structured along similar lines to the approach outlined above in relation to NSW.

Local Government Councils also have broad powers in each State and Territory of Australia to impose conditions in planning approvals to protect the environment, and to investigate and enforce compliance with planning approvals and environmental laws.

B. Brief Introduction of Laws and Regulations of Environment Protection

Environmental protection laws are primarily State and Territory based, with limited environment protection legislation and involvement of regulators at a Federal level.

At a Federal level, the key piece of environment protection legislation is the Environmental Protection and Biodiversity Conservation Act 1999 (Cth) (EPBC Act).

The primary objective of the EPBC Act is to regulate proposals that have the potential to impact matters of national environmental significance. These include world heritage properties, national heritage places, wetlands of international importance, listed threatened species and ecological communities, migratory species, Commonwealth marine areas, nuclear actions (including mining of uranium), and water resources in respect of impacts from coalseams gas and large coal mining development.

Other Federal environment protection laws may be triggered if the proposed action involves indigenous heritage, nuclear safety, the import and export of hazardous waste or offshore petroleum activities.

Each State and Territory Government in Australia has introduced a suite of environment protection laws. By way of overview, development that has the potential to significantly impact the environment will typically require planning approval and an environment protection license.

The approval pathway for such project typically requires the preparation of detailed environmental assessment, together with public exhibition and opportunities for any person to make submissions objecting or supporting the project.

The relevant consent authority has broad discretionary powers whether to approve or refuse to grant environmental approvals. If approved, the regulator will typically impose a suite of conditions to mitigate and manage the potential environmental impacts of the proposal. Stringent conditions can be imposed in relation to limits on emissions and discharges, and the requirement to provide financial assurances.

Other specific environmental approvals may also be required to authorize actions that may impact on Indigenous and non-Indigenous heritage or protected species, or require the supply or storage of water resources, waste, hazardous chemicals and dangerous goods.

Environment protection laws at a State and Territory level create various environmental offences. There is typically a general environmental duty not to cause environmental harm and a suite of specific pollution type offences.

All State and Territory Governments have introduced laws which make directors and persons involved in the management of a corporation deemed liable for offences by their corporations. Whether a regulator will prosecute a director or manager typically turns on the level of control and influence that they had in respect of the incident. There are also specific defenses available to defendants in respect of personal liability for the offence of a body corporate.

Most State and Territory Governments have also introduced specific legislation to regulate contaminated land including a statutory duty to notify the regulator of contamination.

In general, the person responsible for causing contamination (the polluter) is primarily liable under State and Territory contamination legislation to remediate that contamination.

If it is not practicable for the regulator to pursue the polluter (such as, for example, where the polluter cannot be identified or is insolvent) then the regulator typically has powers to pursue the land owner (and in certain jurisdictions the occupier) to remediate that contamination, regardless of whether the land owner or occupier caused the contamination.

Potential liability for contamination can give rise to material risks in respect of the acquisition or disposal of contaminated land, or for corporations which own or disposed of contaminated land in Australia, or the contractual liabilities under leases.

C. Evaluation of Environmental Protection

Australia is living in the age of environmental regulation. Over the last two decades environment protection laws have undergone significant change and there is increasing appetite at a Federal, State and Local Government level to introduce, and enforce compliance with, environment protection laws.

It is no exaggeration to say that on a weekly basis there are changes to environment protection legislation, strategic policy, guidelines, case law and / or regulatory bodies which presents risks and opportunities for businesses in Australia.

The drivers for change are varied, however, are certainly a product of increased sensitivity and awareness at a social and political level to the potential environmental impacts of certain industry sectors and the critical importance of environment protection to the future prosperity of Australia.

The potential liability of the State for legacy environmental issues is a key focus of environment protection laws in Australia. This has resulted in a suite of new regimes including more robust financial assurance obligations to ensure that companies cannot avoid material decommissioning and rehabilitation costs. In Queensland, that regime includes new chain of responsibility powers whereby related persons (being those who have significantly benefitted financially from the carrying out of a relevant activity by a company, or are in a position to influence the company's conduct) are now at risk of being issued with an environmental protection order where a company has avoided environmental obligations and the related person has participated in this conduct.

Other key focus areas for environment protection in Australia relate to the management of hazardous wastes and contaminated land. Many States have created specific task forces to investigate and enforce compliance with the regulatory regimes in respect of the generation, transport and disposal of hazardous wastes and the remediation and management of contaminated land.

VII. Dispute Resolution

A. Methods and Bodies of Dispute Resolution

a. Sources of Law

The common law system, as developed in the United Kingdom, forms the basis of Australian jurisprudence. It embodies judge-made law, whereby rules of law and precedent have been developed by the court. Judges are bound to follow interpretations of the law made by higher courts in cases with similar facts or legal principles.

Legislation is the primary body of law today. Even in areas which are still primarily based on the common law, important modifications have been made by statute. The role of the courts in areas such as corporations law (where a comprehensive statute has been enacted) is statutory interpretation and enforcement of its rules.

b. Court System in Australia

The Australian court system comprises Commonwealth (or federal), state and territory courts. The High Court of Australia is the highest court of appeal. The High Court decides cases of special federal significance, including challenges to the constitutional validity of laws, and hears appeals (by special leave) from the federal, state and territory courts.

The Federal Court of Australia typically deals with corporations, competition, constitutional and administrative law, along with other matters arising under Commonwealth legislation such as tax and migration matters. The workload in respect of companies and securities litigation is shared between the federal and state courts.

The Federal Circuit Court of Australia oversees family law, bankruptcy, unlawful discrimination, consumer protection, competition, privacy, migration, copyright and industrial law. Nearly all of its jurisdiction is shared with the Family Court or the Federal Court of Australia.

State and territory court systems operate independently. These courts have inherent jurisdiction in respect of all disputes other than those arising under Commonwealth legislation. Each state and territory has a superior court known as a Supreme Court. The Commonwealth has enacted legislation conferring federal jurisdiction on the various Supreme Courts, in all matters except in certain specialist areas such as family law and competition law. State courts typically deal with contract, tort and criminal matters, as well as cases arising under state legislation.

Lower-level courts, including district and local courts, decide the majority of serious criminal offences and civil litigation up to certain monetary limits. There are a range of specialist courts and tribunals in each state. They include the Takeovers Panel, the Australian Competition Tribunal, various administrative decision review tribunals, migration review tribunals, land and environment courts, industrial courts, the Family Court and various consumer claims tribunals.

B. Application of Laws

a. Commencement of Proceedings

Selecting the correct court in which to commence proceedings is important, as the court must have the requisite jurisdiction for the matter to be heard. Limitation periods for commencing proceedings differ according to the type of action and the court in which the action is to be commenced. For example, actions founded in contract and tort must be commenced within six years running from the date the cause of action first accrues.

b. Court Procedure

Each federal, state and territory court and tribunal has its own procedural rules which are embodied in acts, practice notes and rules and which provide the procedural framework within which matters are commenced and conducted in each forum.

The superior courts in all jurisdictions have the power to make interim orders on an urgent and ex parte basis. This includes interlocutory injunctions to operate pending a final hearing and determination of a proceeding, asset preservation orders and search orders. Each court has a duty judge who is available on short notice (outside business hours) to hear urgent applications which cannot be satisfactorily accommodated within the ordinary system. In particularly urgent cases, applications can be heard and orders made by telephone.

The presumption in civil proceedings is that they will be tried without a jury, unless the interests of justice otherwise require. Civil proceedings are usually determined by a judge, or magistrate, without a jury. Exceptions include defamation and personal injury proceedings. The burden of proof in civil proceedings is on the balance of probabilities.

c. Costs

In all Australian jurisdictions, the courts have a discretion to award costs as they see fit. In most cases, an unsuccessful party will be required to pay the successful party's costs. There are generally two types of costs in Australia:
- solicitor / client costs are the costs incurred by the client for the work performed, pursuant to the retainer between the solicitor and the client; and
- party / party costs are costs recoverable by the client from the other party, if a cost order is made in their favour.

Party / party costs are determined under a court scale with fairly rigid principles (which in practice means the successful party will only recover around 50%-70% of the total solicitor / client costs that they have incurred). In some cases, costs will be awarded on a solicitor / client, or indemnity basis, where all but unreasonably incurred costs may be recovered. Indemnity costs are discretionary and awarded upon application, where there are good reasons for doing so for example, where the party paying the costs unreasonably refused a settlement offer that was better than the judgment ultimately awarded or where there has been inappropriate conduct during the trial resulting in delays or additional costs.

d. Production of Documents

"Discovery" is a process often ordered by a court, whereby a party is required to produce to the other party all documents within a party's possession, custody or power that may shed light on any of the issues in the proceedings. In some situations, a party may also be required to discover documents in the possession, custody or power of an agent or employee, documents which a party has a right to obtain from another person and documents which a party would be likely to obtain, if it made a request to the owner of the document.

Confidential non-privileged documents are not exempt from production (but may be the subject of confidentiality undertakings given by the other party). There are substantial differences to rules relating to discovery, depending on the rules for each court.

e. Privilege

The rules of evidence allow privilege to be claimed on certain types of documentation. The law varies between jurisdictions. Privileged documents usually fall within the following categories:
- legal professional privilege: gives a client the right to refrain from producing documents prepared for the dominant purpose of a lawyer, or one or more lawyers, providing legal advice to the client. The claim is for the client to make and may be waived. Legal professional privilege does not extend to cases of crime or fraud;
- privilege against self-incrimination: a witness is entitled to object to answering a question on the grounds

that answering would have a tendency to show that they have committed an offence arising under an Australian or foreign law, or are liable to a civil penalty. This form of privilege does not extend to corporations; and

• public interest immunity: if the public interest in preserving secrecy or confidentiality over a document or information that relates to matters of state outweighs the public interest in admitting it into evidence or disposing fairly of the proceedings, a court may of its own initiative, or on application by a party, direct that document to be privileged.

f. Alternative Dispute Resolution

Dispute resolution processes that are alternative to traditional court proceedings are often referred to as "alternative dispute resolution" (ADR). Mediation and arbitration are common forms. ADR processes often involve a third party who either assists the parties in dispute or conflict to reach an agreement by consent or make a decision which may be binding or non-binding on the parties.

Each of the Australian states and territories has enacted a Commercial Arbitration Act for the conduct of domestic arbitration, based on the UNCITRAL Model Arbitration Rules. The Commonwealth has enacted the International Arbitration Act 1974 (Cth). Under each Act there is provision for the courts to enforce arbitral awards as if they were judgments of the court.

Mediations are extremely common in Australia. Most statutes establishing the courts, many court rules and some court practice notes contain procedural rules and requirements to attend mediation. Other forms of ADR include expert determinations, referees and adjudication. Expert determinations are carried out by persons with specialised knowledge who actively gather information relevant to the dispute, rather than hear arguments from the parties. In the absence of factors such as fraud or collusion, expert determinations are binding in Australia if accompanied by an enabling contact. All Supreme Courts and most tribunals have the power to defer such issues to a referee. Referrals involve complex technical issues such as building cases which involve determination by a technical expert.

g. Foreign Judgments

The Foreign Judgments Act 1991 (Cth) (Foreign Judgments Act) establishes a statutory scheme under which judgments of specified foreign courts are recognised and enforced in Australia. It includes enforceable monetary judgments which are final and conclusive as between the parties. Notably, the Schedule excludes any courts of the United States. To enforce a judgment, the judgment creditor must apply to the appropriate Australian court for registration within six years of the date of the judgment. For the purpose of enforcement, a registered foreign judgment has the same force and effect as a judgment given in the court in which it is registered, including the accumulation of interest on the judgment debt. A judgment debtor can apply to have the judgment set aside on a number of specified grounds. Under the Foreign Judgments Act, judgments which are registrable but not registered may still operate as an estoppel.

Australia has enacted the Model Law on Cross-Border Insolvency, which allows a foreign representative, such as a foreign liquidator, to apply to an Australian court for recognition of the appointment in Australia. Upon recognition, at the request of the foreign representative an Australian court may grant relief to assist with the reorganisation or liquidation of a company or individual with assets, rights, obligations or liabilities in Australia.

VIII. Others

A. Anti-commercial Bribery

a. Brief Introduction of Anti-commercial Bribery Laws and Regulations

Commercial bribery is criminalised in Australia under separate state and national legislative regimes.

Bribery of public officials and private agents is criminalised under the criminal legislation in each individual state and territory, ie, Crimes Act 1900 (NSW), Crimes Act 1958 (Vic), Criminal Code Act 1899 (Qld), Criminal Law Consolidation Act 1935 (SA), Criminal Code Act Compilation Act 1913 (WA), Criminal Code Act 1924 (Tas), Criminal Code 2002 (ACT), and Criminal Code Act (NT). The details of what is considered bribery differs between states although there are similar features. In general, bribery under the state laws involves the provision of a benefit to a public official or private agent with the intention of influencing the person to do or not do something.

Bribery of Commonwealth public officials and foreign public officials is criminalised under the Criminal Code Act 1995 (Cth) (Criminal Code). Foreign public official is defined broadly and includes both employees of foreign governments as well as their intermediaries. Bribery under the Criminal Code includes any benefit provided with the intention of influencing the official in the exercise of their official duties to obtain or retain business or to obtain or retain a business advantage.

b. Department Supervising Anti-commercial Bribery

There is no single government department responsible for investigating bribery offences in Australia. Depending on which state or Commonwealth regime applies, investigations may be conducted by the Australian Federal Police, state police forces, or the Australian Securities and Investments Commission, working together with the relevant state or Commonwealth prosecutor. Each state also has a statutory authority in charge of investigating bribery and corruption offences in relation to public institutions. These authorities have broad investigative powers, although they cannot charge individuals or companies with offences.

c. Punitive Actions

a) Overview

Although the details of the regimes vary, the state and Commonwealth regimes adopt similar approaches to conduct that will be considered bribery. In general, bribery will include the providing, offering or promising of a benefit, which can be either monetary or non-monetary. Bribes can take the form of cash, cash equivalents (eg. gift vouchers or loans), other benefits (eg. material gifts, hospitality or entertainment, sponsored travel, donations or scholarships), or the provision of favours (eg. discounted or free use of company services, facilities or property) or anything else that is of significant value to the recipient.

Conduct can be considered bribery even where there is no specific objective sought in return for the benefit. That is, it is sufficient if the benefit is given in order to encourage the other party to show some favour at some point in the future. There is also no requirement for the intention to influence the public official or private agent to have been explicitly expressed.

As a general rule, businesses may give or accept appropriate gifts or hospitality for legitimate purposes such as building relationships, maintaining reputation, or marketing products and services. However, all gifts, hospitality and sponsored travel offered or received must be given in the ordinary course of business, without an expectation of any benefit in return.

Custom and practice is no defence to bribery. However in respect of the alleged bribery of a foreign public official, it is a defence where the conduct was lawful in the official's country, or where a minor payment was made to expedite or secure the performance of a routine government action of a minor nature.

Note that anti-money laundering and counter terrorism financing is covered under separate legislation and are also considered to be a criminal offence.

b) Liability of Companies for its Representatives

In certain states, a company may be held criminally liable for bribery committed by its employees or agents. In others states, a company will only be held criminally liable where a director or senior manager is involved in the offence. Under the Commonwealth regime, proposed amendments in the Crimes Legislation Amendment (Combatting Corporate Crime) Bill 2017 will hold a company liable where an associate (which is defined broadly to include employees, contractors, or other service providers) bribes a foreign public official unless the company can demonstrate that it had in place adequate procedures designed to prevent the offence.

c) Punitive Actions and Penalties

Penalties applicable to bribery offences vary according to the regime but may include both fines and imprisonment.

Bribery of public officials or private agents under the state or territory regimes can result in maximum prison sentences that range from 7 years (NSW, WA, NT) up to 21 years (Tas). Bribery under the state or territory regimes can also result in the confiscation of the bribe as well as pecuniary penalties. An employee who receives a bribe may also contravene the Corporations Act 2001 (Cth) and may be required to pay pecuniary penalty of up to A$200,000.

Bribery of public Commonwealth officials and foreign public officials under the Criminal Code by individuals can result in a maximum prison sentence of up to 10 years and a fine of up to A$2,100,000. For a corporation, the maximum fine is the greater of A$21 million or 3 times the benefit obtained through the bribery or 10% of the company's annual turnover.

Note that proposed amendments in the Crimes Legislation Amendment (Combatting Corporate Crime) Bill 2017 will introduce to the Criminal Code a deferred prosecution agreement scheme. Under this scheme a defendant company charged with a bribery offence can agree to certain requirements (such as an admission of liability and/or paying a financial penalty) in exchange for the Commonwealth prosecutor discontinuing proceedings.

B. Project Contracting

a. Permission system

In Australia, procurement differs distinctly between the government and private sectors.

a) Government Sector

Governments in Australia (at all levels) typically have policies which describe how they procure goods and services. These normally require that projects of greater value or risk are conducted by more open procurement processes such as open tenders, whereas smaller projects may be capable of being conducted using more limited processes such as using existing supplier panels or obtaining quotes from a limited number of suppliers.

By way of example, the Commonwealth Procurement Rules 2018 (CPRs) underpin the federal government's procurement policy framework. All entities that are potential suppliers to the Australian Government are subject to these CPRs. The core guideline of the CPRs is value for money. Under the CPRs, federal government entities must award contracts to the tenderer that satisfies the conditions and evaluation criteria, is fully capable of undertaking the contract and will provide best value for money.

Different procedural rules apply based on the value of the procurement project and depending on the procurement agency. Projects that are valued at or above a certain threshold are subject to more stringent transparency requirements.

Commonwealth government tenders are operated in one of three ways: open tender, prequalified tender or limited tender. Procurements above the relevant threshold must use an open tender process. Open tenders involve publishing an open approach to market and inviting submissions through a request for proposal. Prequalified tenders accept procurements only from an established list of suppliers that has already been established. Limited tenders involve direct sourcing by approaching potential suppliers to make submissions where the conditions for open or prequalified tenders do not apply. Limited tenders are generally only conducted where the procurement project is relatively low risk and below the relevant threshold.

While the policies of each state and territory, as well as local government, are broadly similar to those of the Commonwealth, they differ in their detail.

b) Private Sector

Unlike the government sector, the procurement process in the private sector is entirely non-prescriptive. While sometimes the private sector may choose to adopt similar procurement processes to those used by the government, in private-sector procurement the customer is able to be completely selective in determining the procurement process, arrangements and potential suppliers. Private sector customers may, for example, be more inclined to only permit invited suppliers to participate, or (if they are happy with existing supply arrangements) to use their existing suppliers without approaching the market.

b. Prohibited Areas

The concept of prohibited areas is really only relevant to government procurement processes. It is not uncommon for certain areas of government to be able to develop their own procurement processes, or to depart from the generally required procurement processes in certain circumstances.

Using the federal government as an example again, certain types of procurements are exempt from Division 2 of the CPRs in the interests of maintaining or restoring international peace and security, or protecting human health, essential security interests or national treasures of artistic, historic or archaeological value. This entitles the entity to greater flexibility in conducting the tender process to suit their needs and purposes.

Further, Australian Government entities may determine that it is not in the public interest to award a contract. Public interest grounds may include unforeseen events or additional information that materially affects the objectives or reasons that are fundamental to the procurement project. Alternatively, the federal government may rely on a trade agreement provision allowing for the limitation of bidders or selective sourcing.

In addition, the federal government adopts the sanctions of the United Nations Security Council and applies its own sanctions, which may affect procurement with foreign contractors. Generally, the government does not adopt jurisdiction-wide trading boycotts or embargoes. Rather, such sanctions are usually with designated persons or entities in a specific industry-sector to target trade in certain goods or services. The main target of such measures is typically the provision of arms and related materials or services to benefit a jurisdiction under sanction.

That said, the CPRs follow a principle of non-discrimination, and specify that procurement and the assessment of value for money must be non-discriminatory. This reflects the Australian Governments obligations under free trade agreements.

Again, while the policies of each state and territory, as well as local government, are broadly similar to those of the Commonwealth, they differ in their detail.

阿塞拜疆

作者：Ilgar Mehti
译者：刘克江、程义贵

一、概述

（一）政治、经济、社会和法律环境概述

阿塞拜疆共和国[①]（以下简称"阿塞拜疆"）于1991年11月18日获得独立，并于同年12月通过全民众投确认独立。独立后的第一年，即笼罩在亚美尼亚与阿塞拜疆的纳戈尔诺-卡拉巴赫冲突（Armenia-Azerbaijan Nagorno-Karabakh conflict）之中，该冲突造成约3万人丧生，近100万人流离失所。

1994年两国停火，阿塞拜疆继续完善其政治体制，并于1995年11月12日通过了新《宪法》。阿塞拜疆采用大陆法系，规定《宪法》在阿塞拜疆境内具有最高的法律效力。《宪法》规定阿塞拜疆是民主、法治、世俗的单一制共和国。其国家政权基于分权原则分配如下：

立法权由一院制国会（"国民议会"）[②]行使。议会由125名议员组成，议员选举采取多数表决制，在全民、平等、直接的基础上，通过自由、独立和匿名的方式进行投票。选举每5年举行一次，由议会发起，年满25岁的阿塞拜疆公民都有权被提名，其资质由宪法、法律和法令规定。目前，新阿塞拜疆党占据大多数席位（72席）。

行政权属于阿塞拜疆总统。总统任期5年，在全民、直接和平等的基础上，按照自由、独立和匿名的方式投票产生，选票过半数当选。阿塞拜疆第一副总统和其他副总统由总统任命和免职。总统有权组建部长内阁，该内阁是对总统和国民议会集体负责的执行机构，由总理、副总理以及各部部长组成。伊尔哈姆·阿利耶夫是阿塞拜疆的现任总统。

司法权由阿塞拜疆法院行使。具体由宪法法院、最高法院以及上诉法院、普通法院和专门法院，通过宪法、民事和刑事法律程序以及法律规定的其他形式实施。法官是独立的，他们只受阿塞拜疆的宪法和法律制约，在任期内不能被更换。

《阿塞拜疆商业报告》显示，2017年，其商业环境在190个国家中排名第65位，其中创业环境排名第5位。2008年，阿塞拜疆政府成立"一站式服务"，减少了创立企业的时间、成本和繁杂的程序。现在，阿塞拜疆已成为国际货币基金组织、世界银行、欧洲复兴开发银行、伊斯兰开发银行和亚洲开发银行的成员。2016年2月1日，作为国际上鼓励外国投资趋势的一部分，阿塞拜疆加入了《联合国国际货物销售合同公约》。

（二）"一带一路"倡议下阿塞拜疆与中国企业合作的现状和方向

2016年第一季度，中国政府在阿塞拜疆的各个领域投资共计4.19亿美元，而阿塞拜疆在中国的投资项目59个，总投资额达780万美元[③]，至2017年，两国贸易额增加至12亿美元。阿塞拜疆和中国之间签署了66个文件，其中22个与贸易和经济相关。例如，华为和中兴通讯是阿塞拜疆电信市场的重要利益相关者；阿塞拜疆国家石油公司（SOCAR）与中国石油天然气集团有限公司（CNPC）合作，向其购买了价值超过5亿美元的石油化工设备；此外，许多阿塞拜疆公司与中国徐州工程机械集团有限公司、中国重型汽车集团有限公司等公司也进行了成功的合作。

[①] 根据2016年的数据统计，阿塞拜疆的人口约为9 755 000人，其中女性占50.2%，男性占49.8%。巴库是首都和最大的城市。
[②] 最高国民议会在纳希切万自治共和国同样行使立法权。
[③] 数据来源于阿塞拜疆共和国国家海关委员会。

二、投资

(一) 市场准入

1. 投资监督部门

(1) 阿塞拜疆出口和投资促进基金会

阿塞拜疆经济部于 2003 年成立了阿塞拜疆出口和投资促进基金会 (AZPROMO),该基金会的性质为公私合作组织,旨在通过吸引外国投资者投资本国非石油领域以及扩大本国非石油产品的输出,从而促进经济发展。该组织作为阿塞拜疆的特殊主体,通过"一站式"服务,为希望在阿塞拜疆了解和寻找投资机会的外国公司提供协助和咨询服务。作为独立主体,基金会在促成外国投资者与当地政府机构和企业家谈判方面起着至关重要的作用。它提升了阿塞拜疆的商业地位,协助国际企业在阿塞拜疆开展业务,帮助阿塞拜疆公司拓展海外市场,并促进阿塞拜疆商业和投资环境的改善。

(2) 阿塞拜疆投资公司

阿塞拜疆投资公司 (AIC) 是一家国有股权基金公司,该基金由阿塞拜疆总统于 2006 年 3 月 30 日颁布的第 1395 号总统令《关于促进投资活动的其他措施》设立,旨在整合全国各行业新技术和专有技术,激励当代企业的现代化和竞争力,促进阿塞拜疆资本市场发展。该公司的首要目的是通过"股权投资"计划,鼓励境内外投资者投资绿地和棕地项目,以支持国内非石油领域的发展;在支持对该领域感兴趣的境内外投资者的同时,阿塞拜疆投资公司严格遵守国际公司治理原则。除股权投资外,它还提供关于国民经济重点领域的市场趋势信息,为境内外投资者寻求投资机会,并为投资者开展市场调查以及商业发展计划提供技术支持。

2. 投资领域的法律、法规

1995 年 1 月 13 日实施的《投资活动法》规定了阿塞拜疆境内投资活动的一般社会、经济和法律环境。其旨在将投资活动常规化,有效利用投资促进对外经济关系和经济一体化,并平等保护各类投资者的权利,无论投资者是何种法律形式的主体。该法还定义了投资与投资活动、利益相关者的权利和责任、国家监管、担保和投资保护等。

1992 年 1 月 15 日实施的《外国投资保护法》旨在确定外商在阿塞拜疆境内投资的经济和法律制度,吸引和有效利用外国资源、金融资金、先进技术、工艺以及管理经验等,保护外国投资者的权益。另外,该法还界定了外国投资及投资形式,并为外国投资制定了国家担保条款。

2010 年 10 月 22 日实施的《投资基金法》界定了投资基金在阿塞拜疆的机构组织、管理和清算的一般原则和规定,为投资基金领域的监管和监督奠定了法律和经济基础。根据该法第 42 条的规定,外国投资基金或其代表有权在阿塞拜疆金融市场监管委员会批准后在阿塞拜疆境内运作。

2000 年 5 月 16 日实施的《国有资产私有化法》规定了国有资产私有化的组织、经济和法律准则。根据该法第 1.0.9 条的规定,外国投资者应为外国公民或非本国公民、外国企业及其代表,或外国股东持有 50% 股份的阿塞拜疆企业。该法还要求为私有化过程中外国投资者的参与制定规则。

2000 年 8 月 10 日实施的《阿塞拜疆第二期国有资产私有化方案》的主要目的之一是吸引外国投资以促进阿塞拜疆经济发展。根据该方案,外国投资者有权依据该方案及阿塞拜疆的其他法律规定参与拍卖。

2016 年 1 月 18 日实施的《关于促进投资附加措施的总统令》规定了用投资证书激励投资的制度。只要实缴投资项目中法定最低投资额的 10% 以上,并提交商业计划和税务登记证副本,就可以授予投资证书,投资者凭此证书可以享受税收优惠和海关特权。

3. 投资形式

根据《外国投资保护法》第 3 条的规定,外国投资可以采取以下任何一种形式:

① 与阿塞拜疆企业或公民共同设立企业;

② 设立外商独资企业;

③ 依照阿塞拜疆法律购买外国投资者依法所有的企业、专有复合物、建筑物、构筑物、企业股

份、债券、证券及其他各类财产;

④ 取得土地或其他自然资源的使用权或其他所有权;

⑤ 与阿塞拜疆的企业或公民自行约定其他形式的外国投资。

4. 市场准入和审查标准

《标准化法》是关于为产品、工作及服务界定标准、规则和特征的主要规范性法律文件。负责制定阿塞拜疆境内产品标准的机构是阿塞拜疆国家标准化、计量和专利机构(AZSTAND)。除制定国家标准外,该机构还负责管理产品认证事宜,也是阿塞拜疆的国家认证机构和主要的合格评定机构。阿塞拜疆国家标准化、计量和专利机构提供在阿塞拜疆生效的技术法规,投资者可以通过该机构网站(阿塞拜疆文、英文和俄文)查寻关于特定产品的标准和技术法规。

农业部国家植物检疫管理处负责审查植物产品的进出口情况,国家兽医管制局负责检查动物产品。新成立的食品安全局将承担与现有机构不同的职责,涉及食品安全和其他安全保护。

(二)外汇管理

1. 外汇监督部门

阿塞拜疆中央银行和阿塞拜疆金融市场监管局负责阿塞拜疆货币政策的总体实施。

(1)阿塞拜疆金融市场监管局

金融市场监管局于2016年2月3日根据第760号总统令成立,是一个公共机构,负责信贷机构、保险部门和证券市场的许可、监管和监督。金融市场监管局的主要目标是通过其直属部门以及其他金融市场监管机构确保金融市场的有效稳定运行,并保护债权人、投资者、投保人以及其他金融市场消费者的权利。金融市场监管局的职责包括管理阿塞拜疆法律中规定的"银行""非银行金融机构""信用合作社""邮政服务""保险活动""强制保险""证券市场""投资基金""奖券""货币管制""储蓄保险""违法犯罪所得的合法化""打击为反恐融资行为",以及其他法律行为。

(2)阿塞拜疆中央银行

阿塞拜疆中央银行是一个公共法律实体,根据《宪法》第19条第2款的规定由国家所有。阿塞拜疆《中央银行法》规定的中央银行的主要职能是:

① 制定并执行国家货币和外汇政策;

② 按照《宪法》第19条第2款及本法管理现金流、货币发放和货币退市;

③ 定期制定并宣布马纳特(阿塞拜疆货币单位)的官方汇率;

④ 按照阿塞拜疆《货币管理法》的规定管理和控制外币;

⑤ 维护和管理国际黄金和外汇储备;

⑥ 制定国际收支报告并参与制定国际收支预算;

⑦ 制定、汇总和发布国家整合的外债和国际投资平衡统计数据及其他数据(公共或非公共);

⑧ 组织、协调、监管和监督中央银行拆借业务和其他无证支付系统的活动;

⑨ 履行阿塞拜疆《中央银行法》或法律规定的其他职能。

2. 外汇法律、法规简介

外汇业务受《货币管理法》规制。根据该法的规定,外币、外币证券、贵金属和宝石被视为货币资金。根据《货币管理条例》的规定,外汇是:

① 在某个或几个国家领土内正式发行并可以流通的纸币、国库券和硬币,以及已经或正在退出流动但可以在上述领土内兑换现币的流通物;

② 以外国货币单位、国际货币单位或其他结算单位结算的资金。

根据《货币管理条例》的规定,以下个人或机构属于"非居民":

① 永久居住在阿塞拜疆境外的个人,包括在阿塞拜疆境内临时居住的个人;

② 在阿塞拜疆境外成立但是依据阿塞拜疆法律不具有法人地位的公司、企业和机构;

③ 设立于阿塞拜疆境内的外国外交部门或其他官方代表处,以及国际组织及其分支机构或代表处;

④ 根据②项中的机构在阿塞拜疆境内设立的分支机构和代表处。

（1）货币经营活动

根据《货币管理法》的规定，以下行为属于货币经营活动：将所有权和其他权利转化为货币权利的相关业务，包括使用外币和以外币作为支付工具的付款文件；将货币资金流入和流出阿塞拜疆；国际汇款。使用外币和外币证券的行为被归类为流通行为以及与资本流动相关的行为。

当前货币经营活动包括：

① 货物、工程和服务的进出口结算以及进出口贸易中 180 天以内的外汇转账入账；

② 获得和发行最长 180 天的金融贷款；

③ 向阿塞拜疆转入或转出的与存款、投资、贷款和其他与资本流动有关的业务产生的利息、股息或其他收入；

④ 因非贸易业务产生的货币流通，包括工资和薪金、养老金、赡养费和遗产以及其他相关业务。

（2）与资本流动相关的货币运营

① 直接投资，即投资企业注册资本以实现盈利并获得参与管理的权利；

② 收购证券；

③ 根据本国法的规定，购买建筑物、构筑物或其他根据本国法属于不动产的财产，包括土地及其内部土地和其他房地产权利；

④ 支付或收取超过 180 天的货物、工程和服务的进出口延期付款；

⑤ 将货币基金存放于指定银行超过 180 天；

⑥ 除当前货币运营外的所有其他货币运营。

3. 外国企业的外汇管理要求

马纳特是阿塞拜疆境内货物和服务买卖合同项下的唯一可支付货币。在阿塞拜疆境内买卖外汇应按照阿塞拜疆中央银行的规定，通过指定银行完成。买卖外汇的交易可以直接在指定的银行之间进行，也可以按照中央银行和金融市场监管局规定的货币兑换方式进行。不通过指定银行进行的外汇交易是被禁止的。为了确保马纳特的稳定，中央银行可以干预外汇市场，并通过外币交易来限制买卖汇率差价。

非阿塞拜疆居民的货币经营活动。非居民有权通过汇款方式将货币带入或转出阿塞拜疆，也可以根据海关条例携带现金入境或出境。他们可以将转入或转出阿塞拜疆的外汇自由汇出。在阿塞拜疆中央银行依据其管理规定发放证明文件后，非居民可以将其先前转入阿塞拜疆的外币提现，但是要符合海关条例规定的数额。

非居民可以依据海关条例的规定将其货币资金以现金形式带入阿塞拜疆。入境货币资金超过 50 000 美元时，海关当局应在 7 日内将有关资金数额、日期、人员和国家以及资金来源的信息提交给中央银行、金融监督机构和相关执行机构。

非居民可以从阿塞拜疆汇出不超过 50 000 美元的货币资金，且不得超过其先前凭海关文件带入的现金数量。当汇出超过 50 000 美元的货币资金时，非居民应提交相关银行或货币资金来源地信贷机构的确认文件。

按照海关条例，非居民个人可以将 50 000 美元以内的货币资金提现，且不得超过其先前以现金形式带入阿塞拜疆的货币资金数量。

非居民个人汇款以及提现的手续应符合海关条例的规定，除非是阿塞拜疆中央银行特殊规定的汇入及携带现金的手续。依照阿塞拜疆中央银行的管理规定，非居民有权以马纳特购买或出售其持有的他国货币。

（三）金融市场管理

1. 主要金融机构

（1）银行

银行可以根据金融市场监管局颁发的特别许可证在阿塞拜疆境内开展银行业务。金融市场监管局具有颁发和撤销银行执照，批准银行增设分支机构、部门和代表处，以及撤销许可证的权力。银行执照和许可证应以无限期的书面形式签发。根据法律规定，银行必须是有至少3个法人和/或个人发起的开放式股份公司。银行应按照金融市场监管局和中央银行的要求，履行忠实和审慎义务。根据法律规定，除金融市场监管局颁发的从业许可证的限制外，银行可以开展以下业务：

① 吸收活期和定期存款（储蓄）及其他可补偿资金；
② 发放贷款（担保和/或无担保），包括消费贷款和抵押贷款、有或没有退货权的保理业务、票据买断、租赁服务以及其他类型的贷款；
③ 开放和维护个人或法人的账户，包括银行的代理账户；
④ 结算服务，现金支付和接收服务，资金、证券和支付工具转账服务；
⑤ 发行支付工具（包括信用卡和借记卡、旅行支票和汇票）；
⑥ 购买和出售金融资产（包括支票、汇票、债务负债和存单）、外汇、贵金属和宝石、货币和利息工具、股票和其他证券，以及自费或由客户付费购买和出售以货币、股票、债券、贵金属或利率为基础的远期合同、货币互换协议、期货、期权和其他衍生产品；
⑦ 吸收和分配作存款用途的贵金属；
⑧ 提供担保，包括保证、自费开设信用证或者客户付费开设信用证；
⑨ 提供财务咨询、代理及其他咨询服务；
⑩ 提供贷款信息和服务以及信用查询服务；
⑪ 提供文件和贵重物品储存服务，包括用于储存的货币资金（存放在专用房间和保险柜中）；
⑫ 收集和运输贵重物品，包括纸币和硬币。

（2）非银行金融机构

同银行一样，非银行金融机构（NBFI）可以根据金融市场监管局颁发的特别许可证在阿塞拜疆境内开展业务。此类机构既可以由阿塞拜疆和/或其他国家的法人和个人设立，也可以由在阿塞拜疆民法典规定的具有法人地位的国际组织设立。非银行金融机构分为两类，即有权接受抵押存款和无权接受抵押存款的非银行金融机构。有权接受抵押存款的非银行金融机构，其获颁发的许可证应包含可以接受抵押存款的特别授权。

根据金融市场监管局颁发的许可证种类，非银行金融机构可以提供有担保贷款或无担保贷款。非银行金融机构发行的贷款可以接受房地产或动产、抵押存款、担保、保证以及法律规定的其他手段进行的担保。只有在金融市场监管局许可证中有特别授权，非银行金融机构才可以提供预付定金托管服务。

获得贷款许可证的非银行金融机构也可以开展以下业务：

① 购买和出售债务负债（保理、票据买断）；
② 租赁；
③ 汇票登记；
④ 提供担保；
⑤ 提供保险代理服务；
⑥ 向借款人和联合借款人提供财务、技术和管理咨询服务。

如果上述业务需要特殊许可证，非银行金融机构应在获得相关许可证后才能开展相关业务。禁止非银行金融机构接受企业或个人的存款。

（3）信用社

信用社是一种非银行金融机构，其成员为固定提供可流通资金的个人和（或）小型企业，自愿为共同利益而设立该机构，成员间能够相互借贷。根据法律规定，贷款来源于信用社中的固定资金，种类包括短期贷款和（或）长期贷款，目的是满足信用社成员的经济和社会需求。

信用社可以：获得银行、国际和国外金融或信贷机构的贷款和赠与；根据章程的规定向其成员发放贷款；向银行存入可流通的现金，或用其购买国家证券。信用社的实收资本由成员股份组成。

2. 外国企业的融资条件

一般来说，外资企业融资条件与本国企业没有区别。对于不同形式的企业，发起的资本要求也不同，例如封闭式股份公司的最低资本为2 000马纳特，开放式股份公司的最低资本为4 000马纳特。在银行业和保险业这些需要特殊许可证的领域，对外国人和外国企业的融资有特殊要求。例如，《银行法》规定，金融市场监督管理局应设定外国银行在阿塞拜疆银行投资的限制，以及外国人和外国企业在当地银行投资的限制。《保险业务法》规定，金融市场监督管理局应设定境外资本在所有阿塞拜疆保险公司注册资本中的比例，外国自然人投资比例不得超过10%，外国企业不得超过30%。

（四）土地政策

1. 与土地有关的法律、法规简介

管理土地相关问题的主要法律、法规如下：
① 《租赁法》，1992年4月30日；
② 《土地肥力法》，1992年12月30日；
③ 《宪法》；
④ 《土地改革法》，1996年7月16日；
⑤ 《土地租赁法》，1998年12月11日；
⑥ 《国家土地清册、土地监察和土地结构法》，1998年12月22日；
⑦ 《土地市场法》，1999年5月7日；
⑧ 《市政区域和土地法》，1999年12月7日；
⑨ 《公证法》，1999年11月26日；
⑩ 《土地法典》；
⑪ 《民法典》；
⑫ 《国有资产私有化法》，2000年5月16日；
⑬ 《城市土地管理法》，2001年6月29日；
⑭ 《国家不动产登记法》，2004年6月29日；
⑮ 《抵押法》，2005年4月15日；
⑯ 《土地征收法》，2010年4月20日；
⑰ 《城市规划和建设规范法》。

2. 法定土地权益种类

根据阿塞拜疆的法律，土地上有三种主要法定权益：
① 完全所有权；
② 使用权；
③ 租赁权。

土地上的私有财产权（完全所有权）只能由阿塞拜疆公民和法人实体取得。①
外国人和外国法人实体只能获得土地的租赁权。②
值得注意的是，"外国企业"是指在阿塞拜疆境外设立的法人实体。③ 该解释也适用于外国企业的分支机构或代表处。
因此，外国法人实体的分支机构或代表处不得在阿塞拜疆的土地上取得私人财产权（即完全所有权）。
如上所述，在阿塞拜疆的公民和法人实体可以根据财产权、使用权和租赁权获得土地。④

（1）财产权

私有财产权（完全所有权）可通过以下方式获得：
① 国家和城市拥有的土地私有化；
② 买卖合同；

---

① 《土地改革法》第4条，1996年7月16日。
② 《土地法典》第48.3条；《土地租赁法》第21条，1998年12月11日。
③ 《国家法人注册法》第2.0.2条，2003年12月12日。
④ 《土地法典》第48.2条。

③ 继承；
④ 赠与；
⑤ 交换合同；
⑥ 其他与土地有关的交易；
⑦ 向法人实体出资。

《国有资产私有化法》（2000 年 5 月 16 日）不适用于土地私有化，但私人机构和设施之下的土地以及自然人或非国有企业拥有的建筑物下的土地除外（《国有资产私有化法》第 1.0.3 条、第 4.0.1 条）。

私有化设施的所有者可以购买或租赁该设施所附着的土地；但如果该设施的所有人是外国人或外国企业，则对该土地只有租赁权而无购买权（《国有资产私有化法》第 29.6 条和《土地法典》第 60 条）。

（2）使用权

土地使用权分为永久使用权和非永久使用权。

非永久土地使用权分为长期土地使用权和短期土地使用权。

短期土地使用权期限最长为 15 年，对私有土地的长期土地使用权期限为 15 年至 99 年，对国有土地和市有土地的长期土地使用权期限为 15 年至 49 年。[①]

为保证以下机构的职能，国有土地和地方政府拥有的土地通常对以下主体设立永久使用权：
① 国家机构和地方自治机构；
② 由国家或市政资助的机构和组织；
③ 工会和教会；
④ 与国计民生相关领域的实体和机构，如矿业、石油化工、能源、运输、通信、国防、自然保护、历史文化、科学研究、教育等；
⑤ 国有或市政拥有的其他机构和组织。[②]

地方行政机关（或国家房地产问题委员会，视情况而定）或市政府有权批准国有或市有土地上的永久使用权或非永久使用权。

私有土地使用权可依据土地所有者与使用者之间签订的合同设立。

《土地法典》第 46.1 条规定了国有土地的广义定义，其中包括：
① 国家机构所在地；
② 国家设施所在地；
③ 冬季和夏季牧场；
④ 林地；
⑤ 阿塞拜疆里海水资源基金会所在地；
⑥ 里海属于阿塞拜疆 20～50 米宽的沿海地带；
⑦ 其他特别保护区的土地，如疗养、旅游娱乐、历史文化地等；
⑧ 国家科研教育机构所在地，包括其实践基地、机械检测站、国家分类检测服务机构、种苗繁育场；
⑨ 批准给国有企事业单位和机构永久使用的土地或者准备建设国有设施的土地；
⑩ 国家储备基金土地。

根据《土地法典》第 46.2 条的规定，上述土地属于国家独有。

《土地法典》第 86.2 条规定："《土地法典》中规定的国有土地……不得进行买卖。"

另外，需注意的是，《土地法典》第 109 条规定，交易（或合同）违反《土地法典》规定的，该交易（或合同）视为无效。

（3）租赁权

如上所述，阿塞拜疆公民和法人、外国人和无国籍人、外国法人、国际机构和组织以及外国政府

---
① 《土地法典》第 50.3 条。
② 《土地法典》第 50.2 条。

都可以取得土地租赁权。

对于国有土地,有关行政机关(比如国家产权委员会、环境和自然资源部、地方行政机关)作为出租人。

租约的条款和条件、租期和租金由双方当事人在双方合意后通过合同约定。

经土地所有人同意,承租人可以转租土地。

3. 土地用途

土地用途十分重要。例如,如果土地用途是住宅或农业用地,则不可能将该土地改为工业用途。只有在特殊情况下,部长内阁可批准改变土地用途。

(五)公司的设立和解散

1. 公司的形式

根据阿塞拜疆的法律,对于公司和投资没有当地成分的要求,对其中的涉外部分也没有份额限制或其他法律限制。除某些特许业务外,设立公司只需要在国家部门注册,没有其他附加审批或批准程序。

《民法典》和《外国投资保护法》的相关规定构成了阿塞拜疆公司法的核心,规定了以下公司结构:

① 股份公司(Joint-stock company, JSC),至少由一个法人或自然人设立,股东责任仅限于其持有的股份价值。股份公司分为"封闭"式和"开放"式两类。封闭式股份公司的股票不能转让,公司的最低股本为 2 000 马纳特;开放式股份公司的股票可以自由转让,但这类公司的最低股本为 4 000 马纳特。

② 有限责任公司(Limited liability company, LLC),由一个或多个自然人和/或法人出资设立。只有一个股东的有限责任公司或其他公司不能成为另一个有限责任公司的唯一股东。股东仅对其出资承担责任。有限责任公司不承担其股东对第三方的债务。法律对有限责任公司的注册资本不设定任何限制。除非公司章程另有规定,股东在有限责任公司的权益可以自由转让给第三方。

③ 普通合伙企业与有限合伙企业(General and limited partnership),至少由两个法人或自然人设立,所有合伙人均承担无限责任。有限合伙企业至少有两个法人或自然人设立,至少有一个合伙人承担无限责任。

④ 补充责任公司(Additional liability company, ALC),由一个或多个自然人和/或法人出资设立。补充责任公司的法律结构与有限责任公司相似,区别在于补充责任公司股东可能会承担超过公司章程规定的出资责任。

⑤ 合作社(Cooperative),由至少 5 个自然人和/或法人为了成员间的相互利益,整合每个成员拥有的资源自愿成立的,旨在通过整合参与者的资源来满足参与者的物质和其他需求。根据经营目的,合作社可以分为不同的形式,比如消费者合作社。

⑥ 分支机构和代表处(Branch and Representative Office),不是独立的法人,而是公司总部的下属公司或延伸部门,由公司总部制定并批准其章程。分公司与代表处的区别在于:代表处的活动范围要窄得多,根据《民法典》的规定,代表处只能代表和保护总部的利益;分公司可以像总部一样开展所有业务,包括通常分配给代表处进行的业务。总部指定分公司/代表处的主管负责进行管理,主管只能在总部的授权范围内行使其管理职能。

注意:根据对《民法典》的修订建议,公司法预计会有很多变化,例如取消额外责任公司类型、取消股份公司开放式和封闭式的分类、对有限责任公司增加最低注册资本限制等。

2. 设立程序

所有在阿塞拜疆经营的合法实体都必须依法注册登记,非经注册登记不得在阿塞拜疆开展经营活动(例如,开设银行账户、通过海关清算货物等)。自 2008 年 1 月 1 日起政府实行"一站式服务",这也是正在进行的商法改革的一部分。原本涉及多个行政部门(司法部、税务部、社会保险基金会和统计署)的注册程序经过简化后,现在企业只需向税务部注册登记。

在提交所有文件后，税务部会在两个工作日内发放经注册的公司章程、国家登记备案的摘要以及该公司独有的税号。

税务部接受 1961 年《关于取消外国公文书认证要求的公约》成员国有权机关的认证文件。在阿塞拜疆接受特定国家发布的公文书，同时，在进行此类认证之前，应先向有关部门核查。

通过注册后，公司需要制作公章、开设银行账户、制作电子签名。

银行、保险公司、分支机构/代表处和其他特定种类公司的国家注册税是 220 马纳特（约 129.40 美元），普通公司仅需 11 马纳特（约 6.47 美元）。

自 2012 年 1 月起，针对本地出资的有限责任公司可以通过"法人在线注册系统"注册。网上注册完全免费。对于电子注册，申请表和由创始人的电子签名签署的章程必须通过税务部的在线系统提交。网上注册只需要一天时间，核准公司注册文件的副本也可以从税务局获得，获得注册号码即可开始营业。

除了电子注册之外，传统纸质申请方式依然可以接受，而且由于网上注册技术尚未完善，纸质申请更受青睐。纸质申请注册有限责任公司所需文件如下：

① 由发起人或其代表签署的标准申请表格；
② 由发起人或其代表批准的在阿塞拜疆设立有限责任公司的章程；
③ 关于成立有限责任公司的决议、批准公司章程的决议、发起人或其代表签署的任命董事的决议；
④ 如果公司发起人是外国投资者，则须提供发起公司时的公司法律文件（公司章程或公司章程条款、注册证书或国家登记备案摘要）；
⑤ 如果发起人是自然人，则需提供身份证复印件；
⑥ 注册资金实缴证明（银行账户报表）；
⑦ 国家注册税缴足证明；
⑧ 有限责任公司董事的身份证明文件复印件；
⑨ 有限责任公司在阿塞拜疆有合法地址的证明文件。

根据《国家法人登记注册法》（2017 年 10 月）最近的修订，网上注册有限责任公司也适用于外国人和无国籍人。不过根据"阿塞拜疆数字贸易中心"的总统令的要求，外国人和无国籍人需要通过阿塞拜疆的使领馆取得电子签名。

3. 公司解散的途径和要求

公司和分支机构/代表处的清算程序受《民法典》和《国家法人登记注册法》规制。清算程序相当漫长，持续 6～12 个月，每个阶段都有法律规定的强制性程序。

启动清算程序前，董事应签署能力声明，说明公司的资产和负债，确认公司有能力解决所有债权人在未来 12 个月内可能申报的债权。之后，发起人需要通过清算决议并指定清算人。公司清算的信息也应登报公告。所有需要的文件以及公司公章都需提交给国家税务部。国家税务部在接受清算申请后，所有债权人应在两个月的法定期限内申报债权。如果公司财产不足以偿还所有债权，该公司只能通过破产解散。在上述期间，公司应当制作新的公司公章，其上标明公司正在"清算过程中"，关闭所有银行账户，解雇员工，提交所有法定文件等。两个月期满后，如果没有债权人申报债权，国家税务部会停止申报并开始最后一步税务审计程序。审计期限取决于公司的规模和运营情况。审计之后，公司进行剩余财产分割，准备清算余额，并将其与公司公章和公司文件一并提交给国家税务部。国家税务部应在 1 周内发布解散通知，声明该公司已从国家登记处注销。如果清算过程持续时间超过 1 年，则需要重新开始。

注意：根据《民法典》修正案的建议，清算程序的期限可以延长 6 个月。

（六）兼并和收购

根据《民法典》的规定，并购是法人的重组方式之一。

在合并中，每个公司的权利和义务根据转让行为将转移给新成立的公司。

在一个公司被另一个公司收购后，根据转让行为将前者的权利和义务转移给后者。

转让行为及资产负债表应包括重组后的法人应当承继原公司对其所有债权人和债务人的义务，包括原公司提出抗辩的义务。

在兼并或收购过程中，还应考虑到《反垄断法》的规定。该法旨在防止、限制和压制垄断行为。依据该法的规定，在出现以下情况时，合并或收购应经过国家经济部下属的国家反垄断政策和消费者权益保护服务处批准：

① 该新设公司占有的市场份额超过 35%；
② 市场上全部相关公司的资产总价值超过 975 万马纳特。

行政机关应在收到申请文件后 15 天内作出决定。如果合并或收购未经过行政机关同意，法院可以直接宣告合并或收购无效。

不属于上述类别的重组行为不在反垄断规制范围之内。

新成立的法人自国家登记注册时起，重组就被视为完成了。在与另一法人实体合并重组中，合并方自被合并方完成国家注销登记后视为重组完成。

（七）市场竞争监管

1. 市场竞争监督部门

国家经济部下属的国家反垄断政策和消费者权益保护服务处（以下简称"服务处"）负责监督阿塞拜疆境内的市场竞争行为，负责执行反垄断、反不正当竞争、公共采购、广告和消费者维权等相关的国家政策和规定。根据服务处制定的相关条例，其职能（共 57 项）可以分为以下几类：

（1）法律职能（制定法律）和机构职能：
① 参与制定相关领域（在其职能范围内）的立法、国家项目和规划；
② 协调国家、市政和非政府组织在相关领域的工作。

（2）执行以下法律规定的国家合规管理（审计）职能：
①《反垄断法》；
②《公平竞争立法和规则》；
③《公共采购法》；
④《食品安全标准和规范》；
⑤《粮食产品安全法》；
⑥《消费者保护法》；
⑦《商标保护法》。

（3）若有违反上述第（2）项法律规定的行为，可以通过以下方式对其进行制裁：
① 承担行政责任和罚款；
② 要求有关部门吊销其执照。

2. 市场竞争法律体系简介

市场竞争法律体系包括以下法律和法律文件：

《反不正当竞争法》（1995 年 6 月 2 日，第 1049 号），为防止和消除不正当竞争行为提供了法律依据，为商事活动确立了诚实原则，并规定了不正当竞争的法律责任。根据该法规定，不正当竞争是指市场参与者通过违反现行法律的不正当手段获得市场优势，损害其他市场参与者（或竞争者）的利益或商业信誉的行为。此外，该法还确定了不公平竞争的种类以及制裁方式。

《反垄断法》（1993 年 3 月 4 日，第 526 号），确定了预防、限制和制止垄断活动的机构和法律依据，以及支配地位、垄断活动、限制性行动手段、市场壁垒、横向和纵向协议的定义，垄断行为形式、反垄断规制手段和垄断行为的法律责任。

《反自然垄断法》（1998 年 12 月 15 日，第 590-IQ 号），规定了与自然垄断有关的国家控制的机构和法律依据。另外，"自然垄断名单"由阿塞拜疆部长内阁以法律文件形式通过。

有关垄断活动和不正当竞争的法律文件还包括其他部门法，如《海港法》《非银行信贷机构法》等，但是，它们都包含上述法律的内容。

《刑法典》(1999年)，该法规定了违反上述法律的刑事责任。

3. 市场竞争的监管措施

由于阿塞拜疆近期才经历了从计划经济向市场经济的转型，其市场竞争监管历史相对较短。如上所述，现代市场竞争规则体系是在20世纪90年代通过《反不正当竞争法》和《反垄断法》的制定而形成的。

市场竞争法律体系的关键是禁止滥用支配地位、限制性协议、不公平竞争措施和合并控制。

（1）滥用支配地位

根据《反垄断法》的规定，支配地位是一个经营实体的特殊地位，使其能够利用经济潜力影响市场竞争，从而限制其他市场参与者进入市场。如果一个经营实体在市场上所占份额超过35%或法律规定的其他份额，将被视为具有市场支配地位。有10项行为被视为滥用支配地位，例如，定价过高、限制生产、拒绝交易，以及通过倾销价格挤压竞争对手等。市场支配地位不能是推定的，这意味着在所有情况下，国家反垄断政策和消费者权益保护服务处应当证明某个经营实体具有市场支配地位。

（2）限制性协议

《反垄断法》规定了两种限制性协议，即横向协议和纵向协议。横向协议是指在生产过程中处于同一阶段或在同一市场从业的经营实体之间为了避免竞争而达成的协议；垂直协议是指在生产过程中处于不同阶段的经营实体之间或经营实体与其客户或供应商之间达成的协议。在非市场竞争主体之间，如果其中一个占据主导地位，而另一个作为其供应商或买方（客户），制定了有可能限制市场竞争的协议，则认为该协议具有限制性。

（3）合并控制

国家反垄断政策和消费者权益保护服务处对以下情况进行监控：

① 经营者合并（如果将导致新成立主体占据的市场份额超过35%）；

② 经营者联合或合并后，其总资产超过975万马纳特；

③ 经营者清算（法院裁决清算的除外）以及国有企业或市政企业分立后，其总资产超过650万马纳特（或者在此情况下设立了新主体的，其市场份额超过35%）。

自然人或经营者对某个经营者经过新设、重组和清算后符合上述条件时，应向服务处申请批准。

（八）税法

1. 税制及规则

阿塞拜疆目前采取三种不同的税收制度：

① 法定税制；

② 产品分成合同（Production Sharing Agreements, PSA）；

③ 东道国政府协议（Host Government Agreements, HGA），仅适用于巴库—第比利斯—杰伊汉管线和南高加索管线。

法定税制适用于所有法人实体（包括本地企业和外国企业），但受产品分成合同或东道国政府协议规制的除外，后两类企业都有自己的税收规则。产品分成合同/东道国政府协议税收制度一般也适用于相关石油公司、作为承包方的外国投资者以及与这些公司合作的外国服务公司。阿塞拜疆迄今已签署并批准了三十多个产品分成合同或东道国政府协议，均用于石油和天然气的生产和运输。其中部分已经终止履行或暂停履行。每个产品分成合同或东道国政府协议都有其特殊的税收和会计制度，为其合同方、承包商和分包商提供更有利的法律和税收制度（例如，更简单的报告制度、费用优惠、固定利润税率、免除某些税收和义务等）。

2. 主要税种和税率

税率	纳税者	税基	例外
1. 企业所得税：一般为20%	所有企业（居民或非居民）；居民企业应对其全部利润征税；通过常设机构在阿塞拜疆经营的非居民企业，须就其在阿塞拜疆的经营利润征税；其他非居民企业仅对其在阿塞拜疆的经营利润征税。	总收入（不含免税收入）减去可抵扣费用；对于非居民常设机构，对其在阿塞拜疆通过常设机构获得的总收入减去与这些收入相关的费用。	慈善机构收入（由企业活动获得的收入除外）；非商业机构获得的无偿汇款、会费和捐款；国际、国家间和政府间组织的收入（由企业活动获得的收入除外）；取得阿塞拜疆投资促进文件的机构，7年内减半征税；进驻工业园区和科技园区内的企业在园区内经营所得；在根据阿塞拜疆总统令决定设立的工业园区或科技园区中，管理机构或建设商直接从建设和维护园区基础设施取得的部分收入，以及其从园区中取得的其他收入，从税收登记年起7年内免税；农产品制造企业（包括其以工业方法生产的产品）2019年1月1日之前的所得利润免税，但仍需缴纳土地税。
2. 非居民企业预扣所得税：根据收入类型分为4%、6%、10%和14%	企业或企业家向非居民支付的费用；非居民企业常设机构支付的费用与居民企业支付的费用同等对待。	非居民来自于阿塞拜疆境内未经费用扣除的全部所得，且前述收入不属于该非居民设立在阿塞拜疆境内的常设机构；非居民从其在阿塞拜疆境内的常设机构汇款到总部的利润，应缴纳10%的利润汇汇出税。	
3. 个人所得税：收入在2 500马纳特（1 480美元）以内的按14%缴纳；收入超过2500马特纳部分按25%缴纳（即应纳税款=350马特纳+超过2500马特纳的全额×25%）	在阿塞拜疆工作的居民和非居民员工；非居民常设机构的员工与居民企业的员工相同；阿塞拜疆居民应对其全球所得纳税，非居民只需对其从阿塞拜疆境内所得纳税。	员工因工作所得到的任何薪金、报酬或利润，无论支付地点在何处。	非阿塞拜疆公民的外交官或领事雇员的收入；非居民企业或以其名义向非居民员工支付的劳动报酬，但通过该非居民企业在阿塞拜疆境内设立的常设机构或以常设机构之名支付的除外；赠与所得、物质援助和继承所得；《税法典》规定的其他减免优待。
4. 增值税：18%	所有已登记或应登记的增值税纳税人（如果营业额超过规定，则必须注册成为增值税纳税人）；进口应税商品的应缴纳增值税；未登记而应当缴纳增值税的在阿塞拜疆经营或者提供服务的非居民纳税人；消费品生产者以及从事住宅建设并且未申报简化税的生产者。	货物、工程和服务的申报价值，应税进口商品的申报价值，在阿塞拜疆境内生产的农产品在零售环节中产生的增值；增值税纳税人可以通过销项税额或其他税来抵扣其采购中包含的增值税（进项税额）。	以私有化形式赎买的国有企业财产的价值，以及出租国有财产获得的应列入预算的部分租金；提供财政服务等。零税率纳税：购买商品或服务；进口商品或服务；接受境外赠与；出口等。获得投资促进文件的企业或企业家7年内，对已固定的进口设备、技术设备和仪器免征增值税。

（续表）

税率	纳税者	税基	例外
5.消费税：多种税率（例如按商品单位体积缴税）	在阿塞拜疆境内生产的以及从国外进口的法定应税商品。	在阿塞拜疆生产的以及从国外进口的法定应税商品；消费品指烈酒、啤酒及所有酒精，烟草制品，石油产品，休闲或体育运动交通工具或游艇，铂金、黄金和珠宝及其制品，皮毛制品。	经过阿塞拜疆的联运过境商品；暂时向阿塞拜疆境内引进，用于再出口的商品；规定再出口及被抵押的商品。
6.财产税：根据资产类型不同征收不同税率 个人房产税：根据房产位置的不同，每平方米征收 0.1～0.4 马纳特 企业固定资产税：资产价值的1% 水上交通工具和航空器也是征税对象	拥有资产（建筑物或建筑物的组成部分、固定资产等）的个人和企业；居民企业以及通过其在阿塞拜疆境内常设机构开展业务的非居民企业。	对于个人纳税者：其在阿塞拜疆境内居民和非居民个人拥有的建筑物，居民个人拥有的水上交通工具和航空器；对于居民企业：其账面固定资产的年平均价值；对于在阿塞拜疆开展业务活动的法人：其常设机构固定资产的年平均价值。	用于环境保护、防火或民防目的的设施；运输货物的管道、铁路和高速公路，通信、输电线路，灌溉系统设施，卫星和其他空间设备，机动车等；对拥有投资促进文件的企业或企业家7年内免征财产税；工业园区和科技园区的进驻企业对其在园区内的财产。
7.土地税：根据土地位置和类型征收不同税率	所有在阿塞拜疆境内拥有或使用土地的人。	土地使用权或所有权。	住宅土地、国家边境地区和用于国防的土地等；持有投资促进证书的所有机构或企业家免征土地税7年；工业园区和科技园区的进驻企业。
8.资源开采税（使用费）：3%～26%	在阿塞拜疆境内（包括阿塞拜疆所属里海部分）的底土和地层从事矿产资源商用开采的企业和个人。	在阿塞拜疆境内（包括阿塞拜疆所属里海部分）的底土和地层开采的矿产资源。	
9.简化税（营业税）：巴库纳税人：4%；其他地区纳税人：2%；营业额超过 200 000 马纳特的贸易行业税率为6%，餐饮行业为8%；体育博彩运营商税率为6%；体育博彩专员为4%	年营业额不超过一定限额的企业和个人（目前为20万马纳特，约118 000美元）；连续12个月内任何月份的应税营业额超过 200 000 马纳特；贸易和餐饮行业从业者；在阿塞拜疆境内从事乘客和货物运输的从业者；建筑施工行业从业者亦可申请成为简化税纳税人；体育博彩运营商和专员等。	纳税人销售货物或提供服务以及从事非销售相关活动中获得的总收益。	
10.员工应缴纳的社会保险金	阿塞拜疆员工和外籍员工。	雇主应在工资之外为员工缴纳22%的社会保险，3%的养老保险。	根据产品分成协议提供劳务的外国员工不享受国家社会保险。

3.税务申报和优惠

为了管理税收，法人纳税主体应当向注册地（依据国家登记簿记载的地址）或者在阿塞拜疆境内的收入来源地税收机关进行税务登记；在收入来源地不是纳税主体的非居民自然人、企业家和居民自然人应向居住地税收机关进行税务登记；私人公证机构向其营业地税务机关登记。

外商投资企业应按照阿塞拜疆的规定记账和准备报告，必要时还需遵循其本国规章制度的规定。

不同行业领域的法人企业（外国投资企业）根据其行业向阿塞拜疆税务部提交不同的税务申报。

更多信息可以在阿塞拜疆税务部网站上找到（http://taxes.gov.az/index.php）。

（九）证券

1. 证券业相关法律、法规简介

阿塞拜疆主要的证券业相关法律是《民法典》和《证券市场法》。《证券市场法》于 2015 年 7 月 15 日通过，以规范证券发行、国家注册登记、投资证券上市、存管和交易、证券和衍生金融工具的分配，确定有牌照的证券交易者和中央存管处的设立、管理和撤销登记等规则，保护在阿塞拜疆投资者的权益，以及建立公平透明的公开证券交易和自由竞争秩序。

《证券市场法》确定了证券市场、本地和外国投资公司等诸多定义，确定了本地和外国投资公司及其分支机构的注册程序，列出金融商品清单。根据《民法典》的规定，衍生金融工具包括期货、期权和掉期交易。拥有公司 10% 以上股份的股东被视为重要股东。

除上述规范性文件之外，同时应当注意金融市场监管局通过的以下其他条例：
①《有关在阿塞拜疆共和国境外发行和招募投资性证券的规定》；
②《有关投资性证券销售合同的规定》；
③《关于防止证券市场腐败的规定》。

2. 证券市场监管

阿塞拜疆金融市场监督管理局监管地方证券市场，其基于国际上通行的金融市场准则和标准成立。该机构的法律地位为公法人，负责监督和维持阿塞拜疆金融市场的稳定，保护债权人、被保险人、投资者以及其他金融市场消费者的权利，可通过制定条例来行使其监管职能。

3. 外国企业从事证券交易的要求

根据《民法典》第 1078-25A 条的规定，外国投资者在购买阿塞拜疆发行人发行的证券时不受限制，但法律另有规定的除外。外国企业可以通过其有资质的分支机构参与证券交易。金融市场监督管理局负责发放外国企业分支机构的相关许可证。《证券市场法》第 71 条规定了许可程序和所需文件。当拒绝向外国企业颁发许可证时，应当使用与当地企业相同的理由，不得区别对待。对于外国企业来说，另外一个条件是要求对企业原籍国投资领域的管理应与阿塞拜疆的要求相同或更严格。

（十）投资保护与投资优惠

1. 对特定行业和地区的支持

（1）信息与通信技术产业

阿塞拜疆总统宣布 2013 年为阿塞拜疆的"信息通信年"。对于信息通信技术的投资者而言，阿塞拜疆提供了便利的基础设施。阿塞拜疆于 2013 年发射了第一颗卫星，这不仅为阿塞拜疆的通信和信息技术领域发展提供了巨大的机遇，也为该地区其他相关领域的发展提供了机遇。2012 年 11 月，阿塞拜疆总统通过了建立高科技工业园区的决议，该决议有利于为信息/通信领域投资者提供简便、有利的商业环境。阿塞拜疆人口的识字率高达 99.6%，且具有出色的信息技术和外语能力。

（2）物流业

阿塞拜疆位于亚洲和欧洲交界处，是该地区经济和政治情况最稳定的国家。由于其还是欧洲和中亚之间的桥梁，连接东北欧和中东，因此阿塞拜疆也是整个里海地区的物流枢纽。

（3）工业

工业是阿塞拜疆的名片。阿塞拜疆在该地区工业领域一直处于前沿地位。石油和天然气的开采和加工、建筑工程、冶金以及电力是该国制造业的支柱。政府将后三个领域放在加工行业优先发展的位置，尤其是化工行业，2011 年 12 月 21 日在该行业成立了苏姆盖特化学工业园有限责任公司。该举措旨在提供便利简化的商业环境，向投资者提供包括税收减免在内的实质性激励措施，以发展创新和尖端技术，培养有竞争力的化工产业。

（4）替代能源和可再生能源

在阿塞拜疆，该领域对投资者来说具有天然吸引力。阿塞拜疆的气候和景观条件对于可再生能源工业的发展特别有利，每年有280多天阳光明媚，能够供应大量太阳能；全年都有"强劲的风力"，能够持续供应涡轮机风力；里海的潮汐周期很长，而且有大量流速极快的山区河流，有利于水力发电的发展；土地肥沃，生物资源丰富。

（5）旅游业

阿塞拜疆的旅游业正在快速发展。政府正在大力建设基础设施，以促进该国旅游业的发展。2012年，阿塞拜疆举办了欧洲歌唱大赛、国际足联U-17女子世界杯。许多全球品牌的五星级豪华酒店近年来进驻巴库，沙赫达格冬夏娱乐中心于2013年1月完成初始建设。阿塞拜疆成功申办了2015年第一届欧洲运动会。计划在不久的将来举办奥运会和欧洲足球锦标赛。

（6）农业

粮食安全和区域发展是阿塞拜疆非石油经济领域的重中之重，对于提高该国的出口收入也具有重大意义。阿塞拜疆在生产传统农产品方面具有优势，优越的土壤气候条件、悠久的农业传统和发达的交通基础设施使得农业部门成为非石油部门的龙头部门之一。政府已经出台了几项国家项目和法律来支持和进一步推动阿塞拜疆的农业发展。自2001年以来，除基本土地税外，农业部门已经取消了所有税种。

2. 特殊经济领域

20世纪90年代的国家立法中首次提到经济特区概念的是《保护外国投资法》和《税法典》。阿塞拜疆经济特区战略的新时代从2007年签署的《关于在阿塞拜疆建立经济特区》的总统令开始，随后在2009年制定了规制经济特区的专门法律。

此类法律颁布后，阿塞拜疆在8年内在苏姆盖特、明盖恰乌尔、加拉达（位于巴库）、马萨雷、涅夫捷恰拉、卡齐穆罕默德以及阿拉特（位于巴库）的免税区建立了工业园区。其中一些工业园区已经开始运作，比如苏姆盖特化学工业园和巴拉肯工业园，并已经有企业进驻登记。

3. 投资保护

（1）投资利益相关者的权利

国家为投资活动顺利进行提供了稳定的条件，保护投资者的合法权益。

投资活动主体之间的合同条款在合同履行期间保持有效；只要合同双方没有同意修改合同条款，即使履约条件恶化或限制了主体的法定权利，该合同依旧有效。

国家机构及其行政人员不得干涉投资活动相关主体的事务，除非法律授权该机构并允许其行政人员行使该权力。

除法律规定的情况外，投资者可以自由选择投资项目。

如果国家机关或其他机构侵害了投资者或其他投资活动主体的权利，应补偿受害者的损失。损害赔偿案件由法院或仲裁庭审理。

（2）保护投资措施

国家为包括外国投资在内的所有投资提供保护。

阿塞拜疆的相应立法以及与其他国家缔结的协议/协定保证投资活动的正常进行，为包括外国投资者在内的所有投资者提供平等的法律环境，排除阻碍管理、使用和清算投资资产的歧视性措施，同时确定了从阿塞拜疆转出投资所得的条件。

如果出现了新的不利于保护投资所得的立法，则在整个投资合同期限内适用投资时的法律。

在没有补偿的情况下，不得将投资资产无偿国有化或者没收投资资产，或采取其他类似行为。只有依据阿塞拜疆法律才能采取这些措施，但须赔偿包括利润损失在内的全部实际价值损失。赔偿顺序由法律规定。

根据阿塞拜疆的立法，投资者购买的银行存款产品、认缴股本以及投资者存储或获得的其他证券，应在依法赔偿投资者的资产或租赁权后，依法返还投资者；但要扣除投资者自身消耗的部分以及因经营不善产生的损失。

投资者可以对其投资购买保险，在某些特定情况下法律规定必须投保。

三、贸易

（一）贸易监督部门

经济部是阿塞拜疆对外经济贸易关系的主要监管机关。经济部与相关机构合作制定经贸关系领域的国家政策，并落实推进，以发展和规范对外经贸关系。经济部是由以促进贸易关系为目的设立的部门、地区分部和机构组成的。贸易政策和世界贸易组织部是主管贸易关系相关事务的机关。经济部有权起草相关贸易决定及规范性法律文件，建立和发展与国际组织在贸易政策上的合作。此外，该部门还负责组织和实施阿塞拜疆加入世界贸易组织的必要行动，包括使其立法最大限度地符合世界贸易组织的要求。

（二）贸易法律、法规简介

1. 现行法律、法规

贸易行为受国际条约和国内立法双重规制。根据《宪法》的规定，阿塞拜疆加入的国际条约优先适用于国内法（《宪法》以及公民投票通过的法律除外）。

国内主要的贸易法律、法规有《投资保护法》《投资活动法》《海关法》和《贸易航运法》等。此外，以下立法亦被采纳用以规范贸易活动：

① 阿塞拜疆《海关关税法》，2013年6月13日；

② 阿塞拜疆《海关法典批准法》，2011年6月24日；

③ 阿塞拜疆内阁《关于对外经济活动中商品命名法以及进出口贸易关税税率的决定》，2017年11月13日；

④ 阿塞拜疆总统令《关于加强阿塞拜疆作为数字贸易枢纽地位和扩大对外贸易业务操作的补充措施的法令》，2017年2月22日；

⑤ 总统令《关于颁布阿塞拜疆共和国海关法典批准决议》，2011年9月15日；

⑥ 阿塞拜疆内阁《关于批准原产国决定规则的法令》，2007年11月29日；

⑦ 阿塞拜疆内阁《关于征收阿塞拜疆共和国进口消费产品消费税的决定》，2001年1月19日；

⑧ 阿塞拜疆总统令《关于阿塞拜疆共和国进一步放宽对外贸易自由化的法令》，1997年6月24日。

2. 近期立法发展

根据阿塞拜疆内阁最新通过的《关于修改阿塞拜疆共和国进口消费产品征收消费税指令的决定》，从2018年起，消费品加征消费税的比例升高。

在近期立法发展中，值得一提的是《阿拉特免税区法》。该法已经议会审核通过，将在总统批准后生效。《阿拉特免税区法》确立了阿拉特免税区（FTZ）的行动开发和管理的法律制度。根据该法的规定，除刑事立法外，免税区不适用阿塞拜疆的其他立法，将会有自己的法律。

在免税区注册的公司及其雇员工享受免税待遇。对于进口到自由贸易区的货物不征收关税，然而就免税区出口到阿塞拜疆的货物而言，将受到阿塞拜疆海关法的约束。

免税区允许阿塞拜疆本币和外币直接交易流通，所获利润可以无限制地转移到境外。就其他方面而言，免税区将拥有自己的争端解决机构，阿塞拜疆的法院除对免税区刑事案件具有管辖权外，对与免税区或其居民有关的案件不具有管辖权。

（三）贸易管理

1. 总体概述

本地和外国法律实体可以在阿塞拜疆进行贸易活动。外国法律实体可以通过开设分支机构、代表处或在当地设立公司参与贸易。法律允许分支机构从事商业活动，代表处只能保护总公司的利益，监督其在国内市场上的产品销售等。此外，外国公司的产品也可以通过分销商分销，并与各分销商分别签订分销协议。任何情形下，在阿塞拜疆注册商标都是避免未来可能发生的侵权案件的有效方法。

阿塞拜疆法律对有标识的食品和农产品实施特别规定。此类产品应妥善包装，以确保其安全存放和使用。应该适当地标识，至少要说明产品的名称、类型、成分、使用范围和条件、生产和到期日期、储存条件、生产商的名称和地址。即使允许在商品外包装上标识外文标签，这些标签、进口产品上的名称及其说明书也必须附有阿塞拜疆语翻译。为了加强这一规定，《消费者权益保护法》规定，消费者应该被告知上述产品的特征。审查标签条例合规事项的主管部门是经济部下属的国家反垄断政策和消费者保护局。

2. 电子商务

阿塞拜疆的电子贸易由2005年通过的《电子商务法》规制。《电子商务法》通过规定当事方的权利和义务以及违反电子商务立法的责任来确立《电子商务法》的立法基础。依据2017年生效的《税法修正案》，税务部门对电子贸易业务加征增值税。依据修订，参与在线竞购和购买服务的居民（机票和酒店服务除外）均需缴纳增值税。

（四）进出口商品的检验检疫

进出口货物由借助现代技术的海关部门进行海关监管。阿塞拜疆法律认可进口到该国的货物所适用的相关海关程序，其中最重要的是过境（跨境与境内）、保税仓（临时保税仓和/或海关保税仓）、免税区、特殊用途（临时进口和/或终端应用）以及加工（在海关辖区内外）的有关程序。

一站式系统也应用于检查越过国界的货物和车辆。海关委员会是中央政府机构，具有实施国家关税政策的法律执行组织的地位，同时还负责主管对货物、运输单证、出口证书以及兽医、植物检疫及卫生控制进行的检查。此外，电子政务门户网站提供多样而广泛的电子服务，阿塞拜疆国家海关委员会还引入了含电子申报在内的多项服务的"电子海关"系统。

"一站式服务"出口支持中心于2017年成立，目的是实现线上文件的起草和签署，包括在阿塞拜疆注册纳税人与其外国商业伙伴之间以电子形式签订合同，同时还提供跨境在线电子服务。

"一站式服务"出口支持中心提供出口所需证书：

① 出口动物、动物产品和原材料的国际兽医证书；
② 出口植物和植物产品的植物检疫（再出口植物检疫）证书；
③ 向欧盟国家出口食品的质量证书；
④ 产品原产地证明证书；
⑤ 出口野生动植物濒危物种许可（证书）；
⑥ 文化资产出口保护证书；
⑦ 出版宗教文献（平装和/或电子格式）、音频和视频材料（产品）及其他具有宗教内容的信息材料的许可证。

2016年，在进行一些自由改革的同时，阿塞拜疆在海关立法中引入了"绿色和其他进入渠道系统"。该系统旨在对货物和车辆进入关税区之前的风险评估，其设计了四种类型的通道（绿色、蓝色、黄色和红色），由自动数字信息系统进行识别确定。绿色通道使有资格的法人实体通过填写电子申报进口货物，而无须额外检查，因此地位突出；蓝色通道入关除了要求对电子申报的评估之外，货物还必须经过海关审核；黄色通道为需要特别进口许可证的货物使用；红色通道则需要强制检查。显而易见，其中最有利的是绿色通道，也是主要进口商们追求的通道。根据海关委员会的资料，目前大约有30家公司获得了绿色通道许可证。

（五）关税管理

1. 海关法

《海关法》规制海关程序。阿塞拜疆于2012年通过并生效一部新的《海关法》，自此旧的法典作废。《海关法》确定了阿塞拜疆海关事务的法律、经济和组织基础，其中包括以出口、中转为目的的进口到阿塞拜疆海关地区的货物和车辆所适用的一般程序和规则，以及海关事务领域人员的权力和义务。

2. 海关关税

2013年6月13日起实施的《关税法》规定了海关关税的有关事宜。该法确定了关税的实施情况以及关于对通过该国境内的货物征收关税的规定。

根据阿塞拜疆总统批准的《关于发放投资促进证书细则》的规定，投资促进证书将颁发给投资项目符合规则中特定标准的商事主体。持有证书的公司有权获得《关税法》和《税法典》所规定的关税及税收豁免。

《关税法》规定了关于部分商品免征关税的17种情况，现已调整为20种。根据新的理由，进口用于投资经济重点行业的机器、器材和设备可免除长达7年的关税。此外，投资证书持有者可免交50%的所得税和土地税。

3. 自由贸易协定

阿塞拜疆与俄罗斯、乌克兰、格鲁吉亚、哈萨克斯坦、吉尔吉斯斯坦、塔吉克斯坦、乌兹别克斯坦、摩尔多瓦和白俄罗斯有自由贸易协定。基于自由贸易协定，阿塞拜疆从这些国家进口的货物免征关税。阿塞拜疆还加入了《联合国国际货物销售合同公约》。

4. 经济发展

阿塞拜疆开始在其他国家注册贸易公司，以增加与这些国家的贸易额，推进出口进程，促进具有竞争力的国内产品出口，支持出口商以"阿塞拜疆制造"品牌实现产品推广，并使各国扩大贸易业务。白俄罗斯和拉脱维亚的两家贸易行已经开业，关于继续推广贸易公司项目的可行性讨论正在进行中。统计数据显示，在白俄罗斯成立的第一家贸易公司使得阿塞拜疆与该国的贸易额增加了约两倍。

2017年10月投入运营的巴库—第比利斯—卡尔斯铁路，其目标在于完成连通中亚和中国通往欧洲的铁路运输走廊，此举从贸易角度来看是非常重要的。巴库—第比利斯—卡尔斯铁路的启动正在改变该地区的物流地图，吸引了来自西方和东方贸易伙伴的关注。

阿塞拜疆政府同时也非常重视机构改革。2017年2月成立并于2018年1月1日开始开展活动的新设机构食品安全局主要服务于实施农产品生产和加工。经济部、农业部和卫生部的部分职能部门已移交食品安全局主管。

此外，政府还出台了出口补助计划，通过支持出口商参与国际展销会、组织出口任务、进行市场调查、促进货物进入国外市场链和免税店、在国外推广"阿塞拜疆制造"品牌及与出口产品相关的研发项目。

5. 统计

中国是阿塞拜疆的主要贸易伙伴之一，在阿塞拜疆对外贸易总额中排名第四。阿塞拜疆与中国的贸易额在2017年增长了43%，达12亿美元。

阿塞拜疆与中国于2005年签署的双边税收协定对各国间贸易额的增长具有重要意义。该协定规定预扣税率为10%的股息（收益）和10%的特许权使用费。

作为阿塞拜疆与中国经济关系发展的一个标志，阿塞拜疆新贸易代表办事处于2018年2月在中国开业。

四、劳动

（一）劳动法律、法规简介

阿塞拜疆的雇佣关系主要受《阿塞拜疆共和国劳动法》（以下简称《劳动法》）和其他规定劳工权利最低标准的法令所规范。除非国际协议另有规定，外国和无国籍员工在阿塞拜疆工作期间享有与阿塞拜疆公民同等的权利和义务。但阿塞拜疆《劳动法》不适用于以下人员：

① 军事人员；
② 法官；
③ 阿塞拜疆议会议员和市政机构的当职人员；
④ 与外国法律实体签署就业协议，并履行该实体在阿塞拜疆设立的分支机构和/或代表处的工作

职能的外国人；

⑤ 基于承包关系、委托关系、知识产权协议和 / 或其他民事合同进行工作的人员。

雇佣关系是在雇主与雇员达成雇佣协议时建立的。雇佣协议只有在阿塞拜疆劳动和社会保障部（以下简称"劳工部"）电子数据库登记后方可生效。雇佣协议的各方可以协商适用协议签订后不超过 3 个月的试用期。雇佣协议可以是固定的或无限期的。所有雇佣协议的登记、修改和终止都必须通过劳工部的电子数据库进行。

最低工资：每位员工有权获得不低于国家最低工资标准的工资，目前最低工资标准为每月 130 马纳特。

工作制度：全职员工的正常工作时间为每周 40 个小时，某些特定群体以及在特定工作场所工作者的工作时间可以协商缩短。每周工作 40 个小时的，日标准工作时间不得超过 8 个小时。雇主和雇员在签署就业协议时可以在标准工作时间以下协商工作时间、工作日和工作周期。

因防止自然灾害、工业事故或其他紧急事件，或因消除其后果以及防止易腐货物的损失等情况，允许加班。加班时间不得超过《劳动法》规定的限度。对于每一加班小时，员工必须按正常每小时费用的至少两倍获得补偿。

假期、休假和休息时间：根据《劳动法》的规定，员工最低带薪年假为 21 天，对于某些员工强制规定更长年限。员工还享有法定社会假（产假）、病假、教育或科学创新假和法律规定情形下的无薪假待遇。

根据每种情况，员工有权享有以下主要类型的休假：

① 年假；

② 产假和社会休假；

③ 教育和研究假；

④ 无薪假期。

年假包括基本假和加休假期。专业和管理人员的基本假期为 30 天，非专业人员的基本假期为 21 天。加休假期限根据工作条件、工龄等确定。根据员工的资历，加休假期如下：

① 5～10 年的工作时限——加休 2 天；

② 10～15 年的工作时限——加休 4 天；

③ 超过 15 年的工作时限——加休 6 天。

在恶劣和有害条件下工作的员工也有权享受最少 6 天的加休假期。

年假可以一次性休或部分多次休（假期分割）。《劳动法》规定，至少有一部分年假必须持续休两周。

产假和社会休假：妇女有权享受产前 70 天和产后 56 天的产假（共 126 天）。如果难产或多胞胎，产后假期将延长至 70 天（共 140 天）；

休完产假后，符合条件的员工可以享受抚养子女的社会假。社会假期可以持续到孩子满 3 岁。

哺乳假：如果员工决定不休社会假并在孩子出生后继续工作的，将有权享受哺乳假，直到孩子满 18 个月。

教育和研究假：教育假是学生在校期间进行实验室研究、考试以及撰写毕业论文所休的假期。在此假期期间，支付给雇员的平均工资按照《劳动法》规定的方式计算。教育假可以持续长达两个月。

研究假针对正在获取学位的员工，最长为 3 个月。

无薪假：员工有权享受无薪休假，以便于去处理紧急个人、家庭事务或其他社会需求；每个工作年度无薪假期的累计总时间不得超过 6 个月。

终止雇佣协议：阿塞拜疆法律对终止雇用协议规定了严格的要求。在严格符合《劳动法》规定的理由和程序的情况下，就业协议可以终止。终止的理由是：

① 一方主动提出；

② 雇佣协议到期；

③ 改变工作条件；

④ 公司所有权变更；

⑤ 超出各方控制的情况；
⑥ 合同方在雇佣协议（包括合同方一致同意）中商定的补充终止理由。

雇员可以提前1个月（日历月）书面通知雇主终止雇佣协议。如果有特定和有效的理由（如员工达到退休年龄、残疾、入学教育机构、搬到新的居住地或与另一雇主签订雇佣协议、性骚扰或法律规定的其他情形），雇佣协议于雇员申请中表明的日期终止。

在以下情况下，雇主可主动终止雇佣协议：
① 公司进入清算；
② 裁员；
③ 员工未能达到能力评估机构的决议规定的能力标准；
④ 严重违反雇佣协议或劳动法确定的工作职责；
⑤ 员工在试用期内未能满足雇主的期望；
⑥ 国有公司员工达到退休年龄。

对解雇某些类别的员工有法定的限制。法律禁止终止与孕妇、有3岁以下子女的妇女和专门列于《劳动法》中的其他类别的雇员间达成的雇佣协议，除非雇主正在进行清算或固定期限劳动合同的期限已届满。

雇主不能根据上述两个或两个以上的理由终止雇佣协议，也不得适用法律未规定的任何其他终止理由。

（二）雇用外籍雇员的规定

《阿塞拜疆共和国移民法》（以下简称《移民法》）是落实国家移民政策的主要成文法案，规范下列法律关系：
① 出境/入境阿塞拜疆的本国公民；
② 出境/入境阿塞拜疆的外国人和无国籍人及其在阿塞拜疆临时居留和登记；
③ 颁发临时和永久居留证以及工作许可证；
④ 移民流程参与者的权利和义务；劳工移民以及国家对移民的控制和对非法移民的打击等。

如上所述，受雇于在阿塞拜疆经营的企业（子公司）、分支机构或代表处的外国雇员受阿塞拜疆劳动法的约束，除非该外国雇员（在阿塞拜疆的分支机构或代表处工作）的雇佣合同是与在他国的外国公司签订的。

1. 工作许可证

前往阿塞拜疆就业的外国人必须获得工作许可证和暂住证。这些许可证由国家移民局（SMS）颁发，最长期限为1年。有效期每次可以延长1年。

法律禁止雇用未获得工作许可证的外国人。雇用未获得工作许可证的外国人的公司会被处以高达20 000马纳特的罚款。非法工作的外籍人士也将被处以300～400马纳特的处罚，并在被有关当局判决后立即遣离阿塞拜疆境内。

某些类别的外国人（永久居民、在阿塞拜疆从事创业活动的人员、外交使团、领事馆和国际组织的工作人员、由国际协议设立的组织的正副级负责人、有关行政当局雇用的人员、在某些法定地区借调的每年不超过90天的人员、阿塞拜疆外国法人实体的分支机构和代表处的正副级负责人、由外国法人实体或外国个人和其他一些类别的外国侨民在阿塞拜疆成立的合法实体的正副级负责人）不需要工作许可证。

如上所述，阿塞拜疆法律规定了在以下八类活动中，雇用外籍人士在1年内累计工作长达90天的，可以不需要工作许可证：
① 采矿业；
② 信息和交流；
③ 运输；
④ 加工业；
⑤ 金融和保险；

⑥ 教育；
⑦ 电力、燃气、蒸汽和经调节温湿度空气；
⑧ 供水、废水和废物处理。
这种派遣需借调命令/信件证明。

2. 申请程序

对于工作许可申请，国家移民局要求雇主公司首先向国家移民局登记注册其代表。该代表必须是该公司的雇员。

申请工作许可不需要外籍人员在该国境内，但公司可以同时申请工作许可证和暂住证。如果是临时居留许可申请，外籍人士应在该国境内。

《移民法》明确规定了申请材料清单。

许可申请可以通过书面和电子方式提交。电子申请中，公司代表只需在国家移民局的数据库中注册，然后上传所需的文件。

国家移民局的许可考量期最长为 20 个工作日。一旦作出决定（不论工作许可被批准还是被拒绝），公司代表会收到一封国家移民局发来的电子邮件。

根据工作许可证的期限，授予工作许可证的审查费最高可征收 1 000 马纳特，并应在收到工作许可证时支付。根据临时居住许可的期限，审查费最高可征收 120 马纳特，未满 18 岁人士申请临时居住许可（TRP）的，可享受 50% 的折扣。

3. 社会保险

阿塞拜疆国民和外国人都应当缴纳社会保险费。雇主有义务按照工资总额的 22% 支付社会保险费，其中 3% 从员工的工资总额中扣除，作为员工自己缴纳的社会保险部分。根据阿塞拜疆签订的相关国际协议，外国公民可免交阿塞拜疆社会保险费。

自 2018 年 1 月 1 日起征收失业保险费用，目的在于为某些类别的失业人员提供更多福利。因此，从员工工资总额中扣除的款项增加到 3.5%（3% 的社会保险费 + 0.5% 的失业保险费）；雇主向国家社会保障基金支付的款项也增加到 22.5%（22% + 0.5%）；雇主提供社会保险、失业保险以及针对职工的职业病和工伤的强制性保险。

（三）出入境

1. 签证类型

所有外国人和无国籍人士必须首先获得签证才能进入阿塞拜疆境内，除非阿塞拜疆与他们的来源地国家所达成的协议中另有规定。他们应当向有关州的阿塞拜疆外交使团或领事馆申请签证。而一些签订双边协议/协定国家的国民，则可以直接在机场获得签证。上述情况也适用于电子申请。

根据入境次数，入境签证分为单次入境签证和多次入境签证，过境签证分为单次过境签证和双程签证。单次入境/出境签证的有效期最长为 90 天，多次入境/出境签证的有效期最长为 2 年。

签证类型因访问目的的不同而不同，列举如下：
① 旅游；
② 科学和教育；医疗；
③ 商务旅行/出差；
④ 文化和体育；
⑤ 个人旅行；
⑥ 劳务/工作；
⑦ 人道主义；
⑧ 正式访问/公务。

商务访问签发的签证可能会限定在该国的停留期最长可达 180 天，而劳务签证则为 90 天。如果签发这类签证，阿塞拜疆驻不同国家的使领馆要求提供一封由阿塞拜疆外交部（MFA）在阿塞拜疆的邀请公司所发出邀请信的基础上批准的特别信（电传）。邀请公司可以在 3～4 个工作日内通过指定的旅行社缴纳特定费用（根据申请人国籍的不同，从 190 美元到 550 美元不等）获得此电传。

2016 年推出 Asan 签证系统，用以简化电子签证系统。电子签证只发给已经获得外交部批准的国家的公民以及永久居住在这些国家的无国籍人士。电子签证通过门户网站（https://evisa.gov.az/en/）进行申请，两种类型的电子签证有所不同：

① 标准签证（3 天内签发）；

② 紧急签证（3 小时内发出）。

电子签证适用于单次入境，有效期为 90 天。在该国停留的时间不得超过 30 天。

在阿塞拜疆临时居留超过 10 天的外国人和无国籍人士（包括在国内变更居住地的情况）应在阿塞拜疆国家移民局在线提交申请，或在抵达该国后的 10 天内直接向当地移民部门提出申请。注册不收取任何费用。注册期间是：

① 持签证的来访人员——签证上标明的停留期限；

② 免签证制度的来访人员——90 天。

未在停留地注册的，最高处罚罚金 400 马纳特。

2. 出入境限制规定

持各自的签证进入该国的外籍人士应该遵守其已声明的访问目的。据此，外籍人士在入境前应获得相应类型的签证。

《移民法》对外国人和无国籍人士进入该国规定了一些限制。下列情况下，外国人和无国籍人可能被禁止入境阿塞拜疆：

① 出于国家安全或维护公共秩序的目的或为了保护阿塞拜疆公民和其他人的权利和合法利益而需要这样做；

② 如果有资料显示某人犯有危害和平与人道主义、恐怖主义、资助恐怖主义罪或其是跨国有组织犯罪集团的成员；

③ 该个人因对阿塞拜疆公民或阿塞拜疆利益进行犯罪而被监禁的，当其监禁尚未终结或取消时；

④ 该个人先前被阿塞拜疆驱逐出境，且对其的入境限制仍然存在；

⑤ 该个人在阿塞拜疆被视为不受欢迎的人；

⑥ 该个人先前违反过其在阿塞拜疆时所宣称之目的；

⑦ 在提交阿塞拜疆的入境申请时，该个人提供虚假的旅行目的信息的；

⑧ 该个人最近三年因两次或两次以上违反移民法律、法规而被指控的；

在上述第⑥至⑧项列明的情况下，外国人和无国籍人士在 5 年内被禁止进入该国。

（四）工会和工人组织

员工可自愿组建工会，并不需要雇主事先许可。和工会一样，雇员也可以建立其他自治机构，雇主有权建立代表机构。

工会独立于政府机关、企业、政党和社会团体，也无须向这些机构报告。他们可以参与劳动、社会和经济立法行为的工作。工会和其他代表有权起草、订立和修改集体合同和协议。《工会法》和《工会条例》界定了工会的权利、职责和权限。

一般来说，工会和/或劳工代表是集体就业协议的一方。协议条款和条件，包括但不限于累积工作制度（工作日和休息日）、优先授予年假、实施补偿制度，健康与安全（HSE）培训和评估程序等也要与工会／代表进行协调配合。

阿塞拜疆的工会隶属于阿塞拜疆工会联盟。虽然其他国家的工会在集体谈判中仍然是雇主的典型合作对象，但在阿塞拜疆，这些工会和／或代表对劳资关系没有显著影响。

因此，在实践中，员工和私人公司都不倾向于建立工会和／或代表或与之协作，仅在少数公司（主要是国有企业）中可以看到工会活动的积极成果。

（五）劳工纠纷

可能会产生两种类型的劳动纠纷：
① 个人纠纷；
② 集体纠纷（或集体诉讼案）。
集体诉讼案的争议主体事项如下：
① 关于签订集体协议和合同的讨论；
② 集体协议和合同的签订；
③ 现有协议和合同的修改和增补；
④ 集体协议和合同的执行；
⑤ 解决其他以维护成员利益为目的的劳工和社会问题。

收到集体要求后，雇主必须在5个工作日内以书面形式回复雇员或工会。有关集体协议的要求应在1个月内进行审查。如果雇主对集体要求完全或部分无视或未能及时回应，则应视为集体劳动争议已经开始。

虽然没有专门的劳工法庭，但有些特定职业的工会会向打算对雇主提起诉讼的雇员提供专门的法律帮助。

作为初步措施，工会的员工代表可以向有关雇主/公司发起对该案件的讨论，以寻求在法庭外解决争议的可能性。

虽然这些案件频繁发生，但这类程序在立法中并没有明确规定。

如果发生个人劳动纠纷，雇员也可以向劳动部下属的劳动监察局提出申请，或直接向阿塞拜疆法院主张索赔。

大部分劳动争议由具有一般管辖权的主管法院解决，涵盖所有事项，部分较小比例的争议则通过诉讼外争议解决机制解决。

一般而言，法院对具有管辖权的事项可以根据法律、阿塞拜疆参加的国际和双边协议的规定进行仲裁。

阿塞拜疆《劳动法》并未规定直接适用仲裁和调解协议。因此，能够推定当事人可以自由选择仲裁，或其他需通过协议且依照如《国际仲裁法和民事诉讼法》等法律文件规定的解决争议的方式解决纠纷。

除上述情况外，各方可以使用下述调解方法来解决集体劳动争议：
- 和解委员会；
- 调解员；
- 劳动仲裁。

尽管在阿塞拜疆这样做并不实际，但各方仍然有权不向法院提交申请而选择通过诉讼外争端解决方法解决劳动纠纷。

五、知识产权

（一）知识产权法律、法规简介

阿塞拜疆《宪法》认可知识产权，并确保保护所有人的知识产权。为了释明《宪法》的规定，并建立保护知识产权的法律基础，阿塞拜疆议会通过了若干法律，并批准了一些国际协议。

以下法律是规范知识产权的主要立法：
① 第504-IQ号《商标和地理标志法》，1998年6月12日；
② 第312-IQ号《专利法》，1997年7月25日；
③ 第115-IQ号《版权及相关权法》，1996年7月5日；
④ 第337-IIQ号《集成电路布图法律保护》，2002年5月31日；
⑤ 第365-IVQ号《保护知识产权和打击盗版法》，2012年5月22日；

⑥第460-IIQ号《阿塞拜疆民俗表达法律保护法》,2003年5月16日;
⑦第755-IIQ号《数据汇编的法律保护法》,2004年9月14日;
⑧第197-IQ号《选育作物成果法》,1996年11月15日。
另外,以下是旨在防止知识产权侵权的主要法律:
①《刑法典》;
②《民事诉讼法典》;
③《行政违法行为法典》;
④《关于批准转让受知识产权保护货物的海关监管条例的决议法令》;
⑤《反垄断活动法》;
⑥《反不正当竞争法》。

《商标和地理标志法》主要规定了阿塞拜疆境内商标和地理标志的注册、法律保护和使用。
- 商标——可以用图形代表并能够区分商标注册人之间的商品和服务的任何标志或标志的组合;
- 地理标志——能够识别出该商品源自某国领土或地区或位于该领土的某个地点,而该商品的特定质量、声誉或其他特征实质上归因于此来源地;
- 集体商标——以团体、协会和任何其他组织的名义注册的任何标志或标志组合;
- 音译——用一种语言的语音表达代替另一种语言的语音表达。

没有在阿塞拜疆注册但在阿塞拜疆加入的国际条约下具有合法效力的商标和地理标志依照该法获得保护。

《专利法》对创造、法律保护、发明、实用新型及工业品外观设计的使用所产生的财产关系和相关的人身非财产关系作了规定。
- 发明——关于任何领域的产品或技术的技术解决方案;
- 实用新型——有关产品构造的技术解决方案;
- 外观设计——工业品的新颖外观、工业品的外观在艺术结构上的解决方案。

在阿塞拜疆没有住所或场所的外国自然人或法律实体与国内自然人和法律实体就其发明具有相同的受保护的权利,这种待遇来自阿塞拜疆签署的国际条约。

《刑法典》关于侵犯知识产权的规定很少。禁止非法使用、进口、生产、出口、投放市场和其他有关知识产权的违法行为。可对侵犯版权或违反专利权施加从罚款到监禁不等的处罚,监禁期可长达2年。

(二)专利申请

向主管机构提交申请表示启动保护发明的程序。该申请可以用阿塞拜疆以外的语言提交,但此种情形必须提交阿塞拜疆语翻译版本。该申请的组成部分为:附图、方案、作者信息、发明的详细描述。

外国法人或自然人(如果没有阿塞拜疆参加的国际协议中载明的其他情况)则由在阿塞拜疆有关行政权力机构注册的专利律师向有关的行政权力机构提出申请。

发明或者实用新型的申请,应只涉及一项发明或者实用新型,或者一组之间关联紧密因而能够形成一个整体的要求的发明和实用新型。申请应包含以下内容:
①授予专利的申请,说明发明人或设计人(们)的姓名和以其名义申请专利的法人或自然人的姓名,及他们的居住地或营业场所的地址;
②一份能够清楚、完整地描述发明或者实用新型技术内容的说明,且以其能够被实现为准;
③权利要求,应明确界定发明或实用新型的技术特征,并以说明书为依据;
④有助于理解所申请的标的物所需的附图和其他材料;
⑤摘要。

(三)商标注册

商标注册程序从提出商标注册申请开始。可以用任何语言向主管当局提出申请,但同时也要附上阿塞拜疆语的翻译件。

申请内容包括：商标注册请求、申请人信息、申请保护的标识、标识简要说明、商品和服务清单（尼斯分类）。从申请到商标权授予的期间从3个月到8个月不等。

外国自然人或法人可以通过专利代理人提出商标注册申请。专利代理人名单可以在由主管当局留存的专利代理人名单中找到。

阿塞拜疆是世界知识产权组织（WIPO）成员国，也可以通过向世界知识产权组织申请注册商标。

（四）知识产权保护措施

标准化、计量、专利委员会和国家版权机构是知识产权保护的主要机关，与有关法院以及其他部委和国家服务机关一起负责知识产权保护。

1. 版权及相关权利的保护

根据阿塞拜疆《刑法典》的规定，侵犯版权和相关权利的行为如下：

非法使用版权和相关权利客体，即非法发表或发行他人的科学、文学、艺术或其他作品，发表或发行此类被盗用的作品，以及强行合著并且违法行为所致损失巨大的——处罚范围可从罚款至两年以下的监禁。

根据《知识产权执行与打击盗版法》的规定，版权及相关权利客体（视听作品、录音制品、录像、计算机程序、数据库、书籍等）的副本，应被标记上有关执行机构为版权问题所颁发的管制标识。蓄意破坏、伪造、非法生产、使用和销售管制标志的皆被禁止。

2. 从市场上扣押和没收侵权或假冒商品

国家反垄断政策和消费者权益保护服务处负责从市场和相关法院扣押和没收侵权商品。

权利人可以向反垄断局发送信函，要求其检查市场上是否存在假冒或侵权商品。如确有这类商品，反垄断服务机构可以采取措施扣押和没收侵权或假冒商品。

3. 专利保护

根据阿塞拜疆《刑法典》的规定，侵犯专利权是指未经专利权人同意非法使用专利保护的技术方案。前述行为造成的损害的处罚范围可从罚款至2年以下的监禁。

4. 商标保护

未经所有人同意而使用商标被视为侵犯受保护的商标权。未经所有人同意而使用商标，包括葡萄酒和烈酒上的地理标志，被视为侵犯了注册商标权。

对侵权行为的制裁：

任何非法使用商标和地理标志的人依据权利人的要求应当全部或部分地停止非法使用行为，并赔偿对商标所有人造成的损害。

非法使用与其相似且达到混淆程度的商标、地理标识或符号的商品属于假冒产品。

在民事法庭庭审中审查争议焦点时，在没有损害第三方合法权利的条件下，法院可以判决将以下商品从商贸流通中移除或进行后续销毁，不再予以赔偿，且此种处理不受违法的危险程度和范围的影响：

① 作为侵犯权利客体的货物；

② 在制造假冒商品中广泛使用的材料和设备（以防止今后可能实现的侵权行为）。

权利人可以以法律形式要求生产假冒产品的人（以及标签或标志）或知道或应该知道他/她使用了这些产品的人支付赔偿，以弥补其所造成的损害。

当非法使用商标和地理标志的商品被带入阿塞拜疆时（转运商品、因权利人自由销售而获得的商品或在其他国家领土上经权利人许可而获得的商品除外），在权利人的要求下，这些货物的自由流通可能会被海关当局推迟10个工作日。

海关当局应当停止意图从海关辖区出口的假冒商品的清关。

权利所有人有权向海关提出具有充分证据的请求，要求扣留在阿塞拜疆过境的非法使用其标志的货物，并披露出口商、进口商、运输商名称和侵权商品数量。

六、环境保护

(一) 环境保护监督部门

环境保护主要由阿塞拜疆生态和自然资源部(以下简称"生态部")负责。生态部依 2001 年 5 月 23 日颁发的阿塞拜疆第 485 号总统令设立。它是国家执行机构,负责在以下领域实施国家政策:环境保护、组织自然管理、有效利用和恢复地下水、矿物原料和陆地自然资源储量、水文气象过程的监测和预报、土壤肥力恢复和改良、土地监测、阿塞拜疆领土内〔包括归阿塞拜疆所有的里海(湖泊)地区〕的土地测量和制图。

在组织架构上,生态部由以下部门组成:环境保护部、里海沿岸水域环境控制和保护中心、规范和技术规范法律行为科学中心、"危险废弃物"有限责任公司等。

根据技术规范相关法律的规定,生态部负责起草法律草案和附则,执行调整环境保护的法律,制定次级法规(例如规则手册、命令或指令)以及检查和监督公司的合规情况。

国家环境保护监测部门主要负责维护环境保护 IT 系统,监测大气质量、地表水、环境放射性以及实施为质量控制而设立的项目,环境保护数据收集处理以及编写关于当前环境状况的报告。国家环境保护监测部门的中央分析实验室(环境污染监测中心)由在巴库的七个分析实验室和其他两个在分区(哈萨克和贝拉干)的实验室组成。上述所有的实验室都通过了官方认证。

生态技术委员会是负责在阿塞拜疆境内通过和实施国际和政府间准则的联合委员会。它是由生态部和国家标准委、计量和专利委员会于 2010 年 6 月 29 日联合创立的。生态技术委员会采用了环境管理、水质、空气质量和土壤质量的标准,有多种如 ISO14031-1999、AZS ISO15799-2013、AZS ISO10381-1-2014 和 ISO6060-1989 等国际标准登记在册。

里海综合监测局在 341 个监测点上对阿塞拜疆长达 955 公里的海岸进行监测,进入里海的径流和海上作业的工业设施(如平台)均受到监测。阿塞拜疆积极参与 2007 年开发的里海跨界诊断分析(TDA)(首次于 2002 年)。TDA 是一项科学技术评估,通过该评估确定和量化了里海地区与水有关的环境问题,分析其成因并评估了其对环境和经济的影响。

(二) 环境法律、法规简介

环境保护是通过大量法律和细则进行调整的,该领域法律相当完善。有关环境保护的基本法律框架由以下法律和附则规定:

①《环境保护法》(1999 年 6 月 8 日,No 678-IQ)是环境保护法律框架的基础法。该法确定了保护环境的法律、经济和社会规则。该法的目的是确保环境的生态平衡,维护领域的生态安全,防止工业和其他类别作业对自然生态系统的有害影响,保护生物多样性和组织有效利用自然资源。

②《环境安全法》(1999 年 6 月 8 日,No 677-IQ)。其立法本意是建立法律基本框架,目的是保护个人和公众的生命和健康,及其物质和道德价值、环境,包括大气、宇宙空间、水体、地下、土壤、自然景观、动植物免受由于自然和人为因素的影响而可能引起的危害。

③《水资源法》(1997 年 12 月 26 日,No 418-IQ)。该法规定了阿塞拜疆与水资源使用和保护有关的法律关系,内陆水域和属于阿塞拜疆的里海(湖泊)部分均涵盖在内。

④《森林法》(1997 年 12 月 30 日,No 424-IQ)。该法为规制森林相关的法律、使用、保护、维护森林和森林培育种植,为阿塞拜疆境内的生态和资源潜力的增长奠定了法律基础。

⑤《工业和生活垃圾法》(1998 年 6 月 30 日,No 514-IQ)。该法在工业和生活垃圾环境保护领域制定了国家政策,确定了生活垃圾是以人类活动形成的物质和物质形式的概念,减少垃圾的危险影响,保持生态平衡,规范废弃物作为二等原材料的使用,并且管理与垃圾有关的事宜(除有害气体、污水和放射性废物)。

⑥《空气保护法》(2001 年 3 月 27 日,No 109-IIQ)。该法确立了保护大气的法律依据,旨在实现人类生活在良好环境中的权利以及获取正确的环境信息的权利。

⑦《供水和污水处理法》(1999 年 10 月 28 日,No 723-IQ)。该法以管理向居民、企业、场所和组

织按需供应质量符合国家标准的优质用水以及规范污水排放事项为目标。

⑧《土地肥力法》（1999年10月30日，No 788-IQ）。该法为恢复、增加和保护国家、城市和私人财产下的土地肥力建立了法律基础。

⑨《污染辐射安全法》（1997年12月30日，No 423-IQ）。该法明确了在电离辐射源、辐射防护和公共保健领域实现零事故的法律依据。

⑩《底土法》（1998年2月13日，No 439-IQ）。本法管理因研究（搜索、调查）、合理使用和保护本国领土的底土，包括在阿塞拜疆的里海（湖泊）安全作业所产生的法律关系，规定主体在使用底土时对国家、底土使用者、公民的利益保护。

⑪《刑法典》（1999年）。该法规定了违反上述生态法律的刑事责任。生态犯罪条目包括工程制造、环境污染、水（水源）污染、大气污染、森林破坏或损毁等违反生态保护规定的行为。

⑫《行政违法行为法典》（2015年）。该法规定了违反上述生态法的行政责任。

（三）环境保护评估

阿塞拜疆在20世纪末至21世纪初就建立了自己的环境保护体系。在过去的5年内，生态和自然资源部采取了大量的措施。《2008—2015年国家减贫与可持续发展方案》《2014—2018年阿塞拜疆共和国地区社会经济发展国家方案》《阿塞拜疆共和国替代能源和可再生能源国家方案》《2014—2016年巴库及其郊区社会经济发展国家计划》等活动以及经政府首脑确认项目内的其他事件。环境保护政策主要集中体现在地表保护，废物管理，动植物保护，大气空气调控，土壤、水资源保护以及提高公众意识等方面。

根据2011年由联合国欧洲经济委员会发布的第二次阿塞拜疆环境绩效评估报告，自2001年成立以来，生态部通过发展环境项目和行动计划，通过推进与其他部委和国家机构合作的可持续发展项目的发展，成功地促进了部门一体化。

2015年，阿塞拜疆开始评估《环境影响评估法草案》，该草案是在联合国欧洲经济委员会的支持下编写的。此外，2009年5月，经济部代表阿塞拜疆政府和世界银行在阿布歇隆康复计划框架内签署了《综合固体废物管理》项目贷款协议。项目旨在改进和支持固体废物管理体系的现代化。2014年缔结了《综合固体废物管理》项目下的扩充资金协议，以进一步改善首都的生态状况。主要的垃圾填埋场得到了修复，独联体和东欧最大的固体废物焚烧计划启动，提议体制改革并根据欧盟在该项目中的相关规定起草了新的法律框架。目前，该项目已进入最后阶段，预计将会进行相应的立法修订。

此外，2014年阿塞拜疆当局转为采用欧IV生态标准，目的是减少汽车污染物排入大气，并改善该国的环境状况。阿塞拜疆作为《京都议定书》附件一的缔约方加入了清洁发展机制（CDM）。

总而言之，阿塞拜疆已经拥有保障环境保护体系的必要法律框架，改善这一框架也是政府实现现代化的首要任务之一，并且符合最佳做法的范畴。

七、争议解决

（一）争议解决的方法和机构

1. 阿塞拜疆的传统争议解决机制——诉讼

（1）阿塞拜疆的法院系统由三个审级组成：

① 一审法院——地区（市）法院、军事法院、行政经济法院和重罪法院。

② 上诉法院——在全国6个地区开展工作，由4个法庭组成——民事、刑事、军事和行政经济法庭。

③ 高级法院——最高法院有4个审判庭——民事、刑事、军事和行政经济法庭。

还有一些例外情况，例如宪法法院和最高法院审理特定案件的审判监督庭。

诉讼程序，特别是诉讼的时间框架在下文详细介绍。

- 一审法院：

案件必须在法院收到起诉状之日起 3 个月内审理并解决。劳动诉讼和因抵押协议而产生的争议的处理期限为 1 个月。

生效：如果未对法院的判决上诉，判决送达 1 个月后即生效。

上诉期限：上诉可在法院判决正式送达后的 1 个月内提交。

- 上诉法院：

上诉法院必须在提交上诉后的 3 个月内审理案件。

生效：如果未对上诉法院的判决上诉，判决送达 2 个月后即生效。

上诉期限：可在法院判决正式送达后的 2 个月内向高级法院提交上诉申请。

- 高级法院：

高级法院必须在提交上诉后的 2 个月内审理案件。

生效：高级法院的判决一经作出即生效。

这是法院体系和诉讼期间的总体概述。在特定情况下，除本文所述之外，可能存在不同的条款。

民事和商业诉讼主要受阿塞拜疆《民事诉讼法》和 1997 年 6 月 10 日颁布的《法院和法官法》规制。

（2）阿塞拜疆法院的专属管辖权

根据《民事诉讼法》第 444 条的规定，以下案件阿塞拜疆法院具有专属管辖权：

① 涉及不动产财产权的案件，包括有关该不动产租赁或抵押的案件，且其标的物位于阿塞拜疆境内；

② 法律实体在阿塞拜疆境内有法定地址（所在地）的情况下，有关确认法律实体是否具有有效性的案件以及法律实体解散的案件，或请求终止该法律实体所作决议的案件；

③ 有关请求确定专利、商标或其他权利有效性的案件，且上述权利是在阿塞拜疆进行注册和申请的；

④ 法院审查强制执行诉讼期间所作出的决定，该决定是在阿塞拜疆提出或执行的；

⑤ 有关运输合同引起的针对承运人索赔的案件；

⑥ 夫妻双方在阿塞拜疆有住所的情况下，有关阿塞拜疆公民与外国人或无国籍人解除结婚的案件。

2. 仲裁

根据 1992 年 1 月 15 日颁布的《保护外国投资法》第 42 条的规定，外国投资者、外国投资实体和阿塞拜疆的国家机构、企业、公共组织和其他法律实体之间的争议可以通过仲裁或根据双方协定的国际仲裁规范予以解决。

仲裁的主要法律文件是 1999 年 11 月 18 日颁布的《国际仲裁法》。

本法适用于：国际商事仲裁；约定阿塞拜疆为仲裁地的。

1992 年 10 月 18 日，阿塞拜疆加入了《解决国家与他国国民之间投资争端公约》（ICSID），该公约于 1965 在华盛顿签订。

阿塞拜疆还是《欧洲国际商事仲裁公约》（1961 年 4 月 21 日，日内瓦）的缔约方。

（1）在阿塞拜疆承认和执行外国仲裁裁决

根据《民事诉讼法》的规定，阿塞拜疆最高法院是审理外国仲裁裁决确认和执行申请的主管法院。依据一般规则，最高法院在申请提交法院之时起的 2 个月内审理。

（2）承认或驳回申请

最高法院既可以承认外国仲裁裁决也可以驳回要求承认和执行的申请。在所有文件均符合《民事诉讼法》规定的要求，且没有理由对申请进行驳回的情况下，最高法院对外国仲裁裁决予以承认。

尽管如此，最高法院在下列情形下，可以驳回要求承认和执行外国仲裁裁决的申请：

① 如果案件涉及阿塞拜疆法院的专属管辖权；

② 由于未及时并适时通知审理的日期和时间而导致一方未能出席审理；

③ 阿塞拜疆法院就同一标的和同一理由已经在相同当事方之间作出生效的判决；

④ 在外国仲裁庭开始审理此案之前，阿塞拜疆法院在同一当事人之间就相同标的及相同理由已经启动程序的；

⑤ 依据作出裁决的国家的法律，裁决尚未生效的；

⑥ 执行裁决与阿塞拜疆立法和主权的主要原则有冲突的;
⑦ 不符合互惠原则的;
⑧ 仲裁协议的当事方缺乏法定资格的;
⑨ 仲裁协议被认定无效的;
⑩ 所作出的仲裁裁决中的争议事项不在仲裁协议的协商范围内;
⑪ 所作出的仲裁裁决中的争议事项与仲裁协议中的条款不相符;
⑫ 仲裁庭的组成或仲裁规则与当事人的协议不符;
⑬ 裁决根据发布国的法律被取消或暂停的。

阿塞拜疆是 1958 年《承认及执行外国仲裁裁决公约》(以下简称《纽约公约》)(2000 年 2 月 29 日加入)的缔约方。除《民事诉讼法》外,《纽约公约》适用于承认和执行外国仲裁裁决。

(3) 执行

一旦法院的决定生效,法院会签发执行令并将其发送给相应的执法部门。

如果被告是自然人,执行令就会在其居住地或其工作场所或其财产所在地执行。如果被告是法人实体,执行令就在该法人实体登记地(法定地址所在地)或其财产所在地执行。

执法官收到执行令后,其会:
① 签发执行程序开始的决定;
② 发送通知要求被告在 10 天内主动履行执行令。

如果被告未能在 10 天内主动履行执行令,执行官有权实行强制执行措施(如扣押工资、银行资产、车辆、不动产等)。根据执法人员的请求,被告离开阿塞拜疆领土的权利也可能受到法院的限制。

需要注意的是,法定执行期限为 2 个月,特殊情况下可以延长 1 个月。然而,在实践中,执法程序为实施执行令,可能会比《执行法》规定的期限更长。

执法速度在很大程度上取决于第三方的合作与否,例如银行和国家机构(国家不动产登记处、税务机关、国家交通警察部门等)。

还应该强调的是,《执行法》有权酌情向被执行人收取被执行金额的 7% 作为强制执行费。

3. 调解

对阿塞拜疆而言,调解是一种新的非诉讼争议解决机制。关于调解没有具体的规定,但是,阿塞拜疆法律并不禁止将调解作为解决争议的一种方法。

八、其他

(一) 反商业贿赂

1. 反商业贿赂法律、法规简介

在阿塞拜疆,《刑法典》和有关反贪污的法律是反贿赂和反贪污的主要立法文件。

自 2000 年代中期以来,阿塞拜疆已经通过并实施了若干关于打击贪污的国家方案、国家行动计划和国家战略文件。阿塞拜疆还是下列国际公约的缔约国:
① 欧洲委员会《反腐败民法公约》(1999 年);
② 欧洲委员会《反腐败刑法公约》(1999 年);
③《联合国反腐败公约》(2004 年)。

2. 反商业贿赂监督部门

总检察长下属的国家反贪污总局,成立于 2004 年。国家反贪污总局领导开展对贪污犯罪及违反反贪污法规的调查,与国际及非政府组织、公共媒体、专业人士进行合作,以便提升在反贪污问题上的意识并且加强国家实施该领域政策的力度。

政府反贪污委员会是打击腐败的专门机构。政府反贪污委员会成立于 2004 年,参与制定反腐政策,为立法作贡献,协调公共机构和国家机构的工作,以便整体打击贪污、收集财务申报等。该委员会由 15 名成员组成,并在此结构下行使职能。委员会中 5 名成员由阿塞拜疆总统任命,5 名由议会任

命，其余 5 名由宪法法院任命。委员会参与国家腐败政策的制定，并协调该领域公共机构的活动。

3. 惩罚性措施

阿塞拜疆《刑法典》对这些行为均有所规定。只有《刑法典》界定的违法行为才会被视为犯罪行为。阿塞拜疆立法确认的在贿赂和腐败领域的犯罪是：

① 恶意履行公务；
② 将国家预算、划定的国家资金和预算外国家资金用于规定以外的目的；
③ 不按采购程序使用国家资金或非法国家采购；
④ 滥用职权；
⑤ 滥用他人职权；
⑥ 索要/接受贿赂（被动贿赂）；
⑦ 提供/给予贿赂（主动贿赂）；
⑧ 对官方决定产生非法影响；
⑨ 服务造假；
⑩ 玩忽职守；
⑪ 批准关于归属于国家的土地的违法决定；
⑫ 指定承包，或准许建设违反法律规定的建筑工程；
⑬ 未能阻止违反立法规定的建筑工程启动。

（1）贿赂

贿赂是指国家和公职人员、法官、私人、法人或国际组织直接或间接索要、接受、提供、赠与物质或非物质价值、豁免权、特权的行为。根据《反贪污法》的规定，禁止公职人员以其名义或为他人索要或接受可能影响公正执行公务的礼品，或暗示他人行贿，或者接收以期行政不作为的礼物或暗示其为前述类型的行为。只要对公正执行公务不产生任何影响，公职人员每年可以收取金额合计为 55 马纳特（约合 32 美元）的小礼品或基本招待费。

在阿塞拜疆，疏通费是被禁止的且被视为贿赂。收受贿赂是犯罪行为。未能防止贿赂不属于犯罪行为。

法律体系涵盖董事和/或商业实体或独资企业的授权职员/经理之间的贿赂。

（2）会计规定

在阿塞拜疆，下列是被定义为有关会计/账簿的犯罪：

① 将通过非法手段获得的金钱/财产合法化；
② 在取得金钱/财产之时知晓其是通过非法途径获得的；
③ 侵占、挪用、盗用金钱、物质商品。

（3）介绍贿赂人

根据法律规定，介绍贿赂人的违法行为也被认定为参与犯罪。

（4）贿赂罪

贿赂罪的定罪在于确定该行为是否由官职人员（公职人员，选举产生的官员，国有企业、公共法人、商业组织、非商业组织的官员）通过使用其职权所犯，以及非官职人员通过赠与、提供贿赂所犯。

这些罪行要求犯罪人具有获取物质或非物质价值，或具有获得豁免、特权的意图和动机。

（5）范围

根据阿塞拜疆的法律，贪污被认定为重罪，诉讼时效为 12 年。

刑事立法适用于阿塞拜疆境内、领海、属于阿塞拜疆的里海部分、领空以及在阿塞拜疆注册的并悬挂阿塞拜疆国旗的船只上。

刑事立法适用于在另一个司法管辖区犯贪污罪但尚未被定罪的人。

犯罪责任人为：

① 政府机构选举或任命的人员；
② 所有担任行政职务的公务员；

③ 任何在政府、市政或准政府实体中具有管理或行政职能的人员；
④ 职位选举的登记候选人；
⑤ 国有企业、公共法人、商业组织、非商业组织的职务人员。

这些人为其行为承担完全刑事责任。但是，立法并未表示要为他人的行为承担任何责任。替代责任不适用于公司层面，立法尚未要求公司对其雇员的行为承担责任。

（6）定罪处罚

一经定罪，对上述罪行的处罚为：
① 财产刑；
② 禁止担任任何公职；
③ 不超过 12 年的监禁刑。

这些处罚的适用取决于：
① 是否为首次犯罪；
② 一人或团伙犯罪；
③ 争议金额；
④ 是否在威胁下犯罪。

（二）工程承包

1. 许可制度

所有权人应向有关地方机构申请，以获得建筑工程许可证，申请材料包括以下文件：
① 关于土地所有权、使用权或租赁权的文件；
② 项目文件。

此外，如果所有权人是法人实体，则需要提供法人实体国家注册摘录。

地方机构在 5 天内对申请的完整性进行审查。如果任何文件缺失或需要更正，地方机构会通知申请人在 10 天内补齐或进行更正。

如果申请是完备的，地方机构会征求国家有关部门的意见，例如，紧急情况部、国家城市建设和建筑委员会等。地方机构还会通知相邻主体并将其意见列入考虑范围。此外，未完成许可程序，地方机构还需向紧急情况部下属（General）国家专家审查部门征求一份专家意见。2014 年第 348 号总统令通过了《建筑工程专家审查规则》，确定了建设工程合规专家审查机制。总体而言，地方机关应在 3 个月内就建设许可申请作出回应。

如果申请通过，地方机构决定颁发许可证，许可证是建设工程开展的基础，以及施工的技术条件。

在许可证签发之日起 3 年内未开始施工，或施工暂停 3 年的，则许可证失去其效力。

使用已竣工建筑必须取得使用许可证。所有权人在向地方机构申请使用许可证时，需提供下列文件：
① 施工许可证；
② 有关组织颁发的关于内外部通信工程系统已经随时可以投入使用的确认文件；
③ 有关施工地址的确认函；
④ 电梯可投放使用的验收文件；
⑤ 地方行政部门关于接收连接通信线路的信函；
⑥ 卫生和流行病学中心关于建筑符合卫生与防疫要求的信函；
⑦ 关于该设施的主要规划和事实特征的信函；
⑧ 关于该设施财务费用开支的信函（如果该项目由国家资金建设）；
⑨ 设施符合消防安全要求的文件；
⑩ 生态和自然资源部发放的有关工业和生产设施生态安全的确认文件；
⑪ 紧急情况部下属的国家安全监督局就所有权人、承包商和设计师代表参与该建筑工程符合《城市和建筑规范法案》以及建设项目要求的确认文件；
⑫ 于该设施最终及全面使用之前发放的部分建筑使用许可。

某些特定类型的设施可能需要额外的文件方能获得使用许可。如所有权人需要向内政部国家交通警察部门提交有关道路使用准备就绪的确认文件，以获得道路使用许可证。地方机构在30天内回复该申请。地方机构可以拒绝申请或授予使用许可证。除了惯常的许可证外，某些地区（如文化和历史保护区）的建筑工程需要国家机构的额外授权。

2. 禁业区域

内阁法令禁止在山体滑坡区进行施工。紧急情况部、生态和国家资源部负责开展研究以确定该区域具有发生山体滑坡的潜在危险，并向内阁报告，禁止在这些地区进行建筑工程（除了山体滑坡防护工程）。此类地区的地图由内阁确认。

3. 招标与投标

所有居民、非居民自然人、法人、法人联盟，无论属于哪个国家，均有权参加在阿塞拜疆举行的作为投标人的公共采购程序。采购代理机构在招标文件批准并经招标委员会公告后，发布招标公告或发送个人邀请函给委托人（承包商）参加投标。在公开招标公告发布的同时，采购代理机构可以向委托人（承包商）发送参加投标的个人邀请。为了吸引其他采购形式的提案、报价和估价，招标委员会制作数量充足（不少于3个）的潜在的委托人（承包商）名单并向其发送个人邀请。

招标公告（邀请）需表明以下信息：
① 有关投标组织者的信息；
② 招标程序开始的时间和地点；
③ 与采购合同有关的税收和关税待遇（如有）；
④ 参加投标所需的文件；
⑤ 协调员的办公室电话和传真号码，以获取更多信息；
⑥ 招标方案的保证条件；货物名称、数量（体积）、货物交付地点、所实施工作的特点和地点以及所提供服务的描述和地点；
⑦ 所需的货物运输条件和完成工程或提供服务的时间表；
⑧ 评估和比选委托人（承包商）资质指标中的优选标准和程序；
⑨ 因涉及国有资产而限制委托人（承包商）参与采购程序的条件；
⑩ 参加费的数额及其支付程序；
⑪ 制定投标文件所用的一种或多种语言；
⑫ 提交投标书的截止日期和地点。

①、②、⑦—⑩和⑫项也被添加到资质合规确定程序的招标文件中。在编制文件时，反映招标程序第一阶段的特点，采购代理有权排除或改变任何有关采购货物（工程和服务）的技术或质量特征的事项，评估标准、投标书的比选和确定以及增加新特点和标准的事项。在发送关于提交最终投标提案的邀请时，发货人（承包商）会被告知有关任何此类信息的所有更改及增加情况。

Azerbaijan

Authors: Ilgar Mehti
Translators: Liu Kejiang, Cheng Yigui

I. Overview

A. General Introduction to the Polictical, Economic, Social and Legal Environment of the Country Receiving Investment

The Republic of Azerbaijan[①] (hereinafter referred to as "Azerbaijan") gained independence on 18 November 1991 which was affirmed by a nationwide referendum in December 1991, when the Soviet Union officially collapsed on 26 December 1991. The first years of the independence were overshadowed by the Armenia-Azerbaijan Nagorno-Karabakh conflict which resulted in killing of an estimated 30,000 people and internal displacement of nearly 1,000,000 people.

Azerbaijan continued to build structural formation of its political system after the conflict was frozen as a result of 1994 ceasefire and completed by adopting a new Constitution on 12 November 1995. Azerbaijani legal system is based on civil law system and the Constitution has the highest legal force in the territory of Azerbaijan. In accordance with the Constitution Azerbaijani state is democratic, legal, secular, unitary republic. State power in Azerbaijan is based on a principle of division of powers:

Legislative power is exercised by unicameral National Assembly ("Milli Majlis")[②]. Milli Majlis consists of 125 members of parliament (MPs) that are elected based on majority voting system and general, direct and equal elections by free, personal and secret ballot. Elections to each call of the Milli Majlis are held every five years. Every citizen of Azerbaijan that is not younger than 25 has right to be nominated as an MP. Milli Majlis adopts Constitutional laws, laws and decrees regarding the questions of its competence. Currently majority of the seats at Milli Majlis are held by New Azerbaijan Party (72).

Executive power belongs to the President of Azerbaijan. The President is elected for a 5-year term by general, direct and equal elections, by free, personal and secret ballot by the majority of more than the half of votes. The first vice-president and vice-presidents of Azerbaijan are appointed and dismissed by the President. The president is authorized to form the Cabinet of Ministers, a collective executive body accountable to both the President and Milli Majlis. The Cabinet of Ministers consists primarily of the Prime Minister, his deputies and Ministers. Ilham Aliyev is the incumbent President of Azerbaijan.

Judicial power is exercised by courts of law of Azerbaijan. It is implemented through the Constitutional Court, Supreme Court, and appeal courts, ordinary and specialized courts of law of Azerbaijan. Judicial power is implemented by constitutional, civil and criminal legal proceedings and other forms of legislation provided for by law. Judges are independent, they are subordinate only to Constitution and laws of Azerbaijan, and they cannot be replaced during the term of their authority.

Azerbaijan's Doing Business overall ranking is 65 among 190 countries for 2017. It ranks no. 5 for starting a business. In 2008 it started operating a one-stop shop that halved the time, cost and number of procedures to start a business. Today Azerbaijan is the member of the International Monetary Fund, the World Bank, the European Bank for Reconstruction and Development, the Islamic Development Bank and the Asian Development Bank. On 1 February 2016 Azerbaijan became a party to United Nations Convention on Contracts for the International Sale of Goods as a part of the trend on stimulating foreign investment.

B. The Status and Direction of the Cooperation with Chinese Enterprises under the B&R

In the first quarter of 2016, the Chinese government invested $419 million in various spheres of Azerbaijan. Azerbaijan invested in 59 projects implemented in China and the total amount of these investments amounted to

---

① According to 2016 estimates, Azerbaijan's population is 9,755,000 people of which 50.2% is women and 49.8% is men. Baku is the capital and the largest city.
② The Supreme National Assembly exercises legislative power in the Autonomous Republic of Nakhchivan.

$7.8 million.[1] The trade turnover between the two countries increased and amounted to $1.2 billion in 2017. More than 66 documents, including 22 in the field of trade and economic relations, were signed between Azerbaijan and China. Companies Huawei and ZTE are important stakeholders in Azerbaijani telecommunication market. State Oil Company of Azerbaijan (SOCAR) has been cooperating with China National Petroleum Corporation (CNPC), from which it bought equipment used in the petrochemical sphere that worth more than $500 million. In addition, many companies have had successfully cooperated with Chinese counterparts such as XCMG, Sinotruk, etc.

II. Investment

A. Market Access

a. Department Supervising Investments

a) Azpromo

Azerbaijan Export and Investment Promotion Foundation (AZPROMO) is a joint public-private-initiative, established by the Ministry of Economy of Azerbaijan in 2003 with the aim to contribute to the economic development through attracting foreign investments in the non-oil sectors of economy and stimulating expansion of country's exports of non-oil goods to the overseas markets. It is a unique body in Azerbaijan that operates as a "one-stop-shop" for assisting and advising foreign-based companies interested in investigating and utilizing investment opportunities in Azerbaijan. AZPROMO plays a role of a single body guiding foreign investors in their negotiations with all relevant Government agencies and local entrepreneurs. It Promotes Azerbaijan as a business location, assists international companies setting up business in Azerbaijan, assists companies based in Azerbaijan with reaching foreign markets and promotes improvement of business and investment climate.

b) Azerbaijan Investment Company

Azerbaijan Investment Company (AIC) is a state owned equity fund that was established by the Decree number 1395 of the President of Azerbaijan "On additional measures to promote investment activity" signed on March 30, 2006. Integration of new technologies and know-how in industries nationwide, stimulation of modernization and competitiveness of local businesses, as well as contribution to the development of capital markets in Azerbaijan are among the priority objectives of AIC. The main purpose of AIC is to support the development of the non-oil sector of the economy via termed equity injection along with local and foreign co-investors into the greenfield and brownfield projects on the territory of Azerbaijan. AIC upholds the concept of supporting local and foreign investors interested in commercially feasible projects in the non-oil sector of the national economy, and adheres to principles of strict compliance to international corporate governance. In addition to equity investment, it also offers expertise in current market trends in the priority sectors of the national economy, identify investment opportunities to foreign and local investors, and provide technical support in carrying out and preparing market research and surveys, as well as in development of business plans.

b. Laws and Regulations of Investment Industry

The Law on Investment Activity dated January 13, 1995. This legislative act defines the general social, economic and legal environment for investment activity in the territory of Azerbaijan. The Law on Investment Activity is aimed at regular involvement of investment to the Azerbaijani economy, as well as efficient use of investment for international economic relations and integration and guarantees equal protection of investor rights regardless of their legal form. It defines investment and investment activity, rights and responsibilities if stakeholders, state regulation, guaranties, and investment protection, etc.

The Law on Protection of Foreign Investment dated January 15, 1992. It defines legal and economic basis for foreign investment in the territory of Azerbaijan. The Law on Protection of Foreign Investment aimed at involvement of foreign material and financial funds, advanced foreign technologies and engineering, their efficient use and guarantees protection for rights of foreign investors. It also defines foreign investment, investment forms and sets the provisions for state guaranties for foreign investment.

The Law on Investment Funds, dated October 22, 2010. The Law on Investment Funds defines the principles and regulations for organization, management and liquidation of investment funds in Azerbaijan. It also sets legal and economic basis for regulation and oversight in the field of investment funds. Pursuant to article 42 of the law, foreign investment funds or their representatives have right to function in Azerbaijan upon approval of Financial Markets Supervision Chamber of Azerbaijan.

---

[1] State Customs Committee of the Republic of Azerbaijan.

The Law on Privatization of State Property dated May 16, 2000. This legislative act sets the organizational, economical and legal principles for privatization of state property. Pursuant to article 1.0.9 of the Law on Privatization of State Property, foreign investors are foreign nationals, non-citizens, foreign legal entities and their representatives, or Azerbaijani legal entities of which 50% of shares belong to foreign shareholders. It also requires state privatization programs to stipulate rules for participation of foreign investors in privatization of the state property.

The Second Program for Privatization of State Property of Azerbaijan dated 10 August, 2000. One of the main purposes of the Program is to strengthen Azerbaijani economy by involving foreign investment. According to the Program foreign investors have right to participate in auctions pursuant to regulations stipulated in the Program and other legislative acts of Azerbaijan.

Presidential Decree on Additional Measures to Promote Investment dated January 18, 2016. The decree defines regulations on stimulating investment in Azerbaijan using investment certificates. An Investment Certificate grants individuals and legal entities tax and customs privileges and can be obtained by confirming payment of at least 10% of the statutory minimum investment under the investment project and submitting a business plan along with a copy of a taxpayer's registration certificate

c. Forms of Investment

In accordance with article 3 of the Law on Protection of Foreign Investment, foreign investment may take any of the following forms:

(i) Participation in entities established jointly with legal entities and citizens of Azerbaijan;

(ii) Establishment of enterprises solely owned by foreign investors;

(iii) Purchase of enterprises, proprietary complexes, buildings, structures, shares in enterprises, bonds, securities, and other kinds of property which may be owned by foreign investors under the laws of Azerbaijan;

(iv) Acquisition of rights to use land and other natural resources, as well as other proprietary rights; and

(v) Conclusion of agreements with legal entities and citizens of Azerbaijan providing for other forms of foreign investment.

d. Standards of Market Access and Examination

The Law on Standardization is the main normative act on activities to define norms, rules, and characteristics for products, works and services. The agency responsible for laying down product standards in Azerbaijan is The State Agency on Standardization, Metrology and Patents of Azerbaijan (AZSTAND). It develops national standards, exercises authority over product certification matters. AZSTAND is also the national accreditation body and the main conformity assessment body in Azerbaijan. It publishes technical regulations being in force in the country. Investors can consult the Agency's website (available in Azerbaijani, English, and Russian) on standards and technical regulations for specific products.

State Phytosanitary Control Service in the Ministry of Agriculture examines the imports and exports of plant products, while State Veterinary Control Service examines animal products. Newly established Food Safety Agency is expected to take upon the relevant competencies of different existing bodies in connection to food safety and security.

B. Foreign Exchange Regulation

a. Department Supervising Foreign Exchange

Central Bank of Azerbaijan and Financial Market Supervisory Authority of Azerbaijan control the overall enforcement of currency regulation in Azerbaijan.

a) Financial Market Supervisory Authority of Azerbaijan

Financial Market Supervisory Authority was established as public legal entity on 03 February 2016 by the Presidential Decree no. 760. It is in charge of licensing, regulation and supervision of the credit institutions, insurance sector and securities market. The main aim of Financial Market Supervisory Authority is to ensure the effective performance and sustainability of the financial markets and protect the rights of creditors, investors, insured parties and other consumers in the financial markets. It exercises powers the control body and financial monitoring body meant in the laws of Azerbaijan on "Banks", "Non-bank financial institutions", "Credit Unions", "Postal service", "Insurance activity", "Compulsory insurance", "Securities Market", "Investment funds", "Lotteries", "Currency Regulation", "Insurance of savings", "Legalization of money funds or other property gained through criminal way and struggle against financing the terrorism" and other legislative acts.

b) Central Bank of Azerbaijan

Central Bank of Azerbaijan is a public legal entity and is owned by the state in accordance with II part of article 19 of the Constitution. Following are the main functions of the Central Bank pursuant to the Law on "Central Bank of the Republic of Azerbaijan":

(i) To establish and implement the state monetary and foreign exchange policy;

(ii) To organize cash flow, issue banknotes to and withdraw from flow according to Part II of Article 19 of the Constitution and the present Law;

(iii) To regularly set and announce an official exchange rate of Manat;

(iv) To regulate and control the foreign currency in accordance with the Law of the Republic of Azerbaijan on Currency Regulation;

(v) To maintain and manage international gold and foreign exchange reserves in its charge;

(vi) To develop a reporting balance of payments and participate in development of the projected balance of payments of the country;

(vii) To develop the state's consolidated (public and non-public) foreign debt statistics and international investment balance, summarize and disseminate data;

(viii) To organize, coordinate, regulate activities of and oversee centralized interbank and other unlicensed payment systems;

(ix) To discharge other functions stipulated by the Law on Central Bank of the Republic of Azerbaijan and other laws.

b. Brief Introduction of Laws and Regulations of Foreign Exchange

Foreign exchange operations are governed by the Law on Currency Regulation. Pursuant to this Law foreign currency, along with securities in foreign currency, precious metal, and precious stones are considered as currency resources. The Law on Currency Regulation states that foreign currency is:

(i) money in the form of banknotes, treasury notes and coins in circulation which are a legal tender in the territory of a relevant country or group of countries, as well as those that have been or are being withdrawn from flow, however can be exchanged for money in flow in the said territories;

(ii) funds in monetary units of foreign countries, international monetary or settlement units.

In compliance with the Law on Currency Regulation:

(i) individuals permanently residing outside Azerbaijan, including those temporarily living in the territory of Azerbaijan;

(ii) legal entities and enterprises and organizations located outside Azerbaijan established according to the legislation of Azerbaijan, however, with no status of a legal entity;

(iii) foreign diplomatic and other official representative offices, as well as international organizations, their branches and representative offices located in Azerbaijan;

(iv) branches and representative offices of non-residents (bureaus and agencies) specified in sub-item (ii) herein which are located in Azerbaijan are considered as non-residents.

a) Currency Operations

Pursuant to this Law operations related to transfer of the proprietary right and other rights onto currency resources, including use of the foreign currency and payment documents in a foreign currency as a payment facility; bringing in and out of and transfer of currency resources to and from Azerbaijan; and international money transfers are considered as currency operations. Operations with a foreign currency and securities in a foreign currency are grouped as current operations and operations related to capital movement.

Current currency operations:

(i) transfers of foreign currency to and from the Republic of Azerbaijan to accomplish settlements connected with export and import of goods, works and services, as well as crediting of export-import operations for a term of maximum 180 days;

(ii) obtaining and issue of financial loans for a term of maximum 180 days;

(iii) transfer of interest rates, dividends and other revenues, connected with deposits, investments, loans and other operations related to capital movement, to and from Azerbaijan;

(iv) non-trade related transfers to and from Azerbaijan, including transfers of wages and salaries, pensions, alimonies and legacies and other similar operations.

b) Currency Operations Related to Capital Movement

(i) direct investments, i.e. investment contributions to the chartered capital of an enterprise to make profits and obtain the right for participation in management;

(ii) acquisition of securities;

(iii) transfers covering payments for proprietary rights on buildings, structures and other property which according to the legislation of the home country is considered real estate, including land and its entrails, and other rights on real estate;

(iv) giving and obtaining deferments in payments for export and import of goods, works and services for a term

exceeding 180 days;
    (v) placement of currency funds on deposits by authorized banks for a term of over 180 days;
    (vi) all other operations with currency other than current operations.

c. Requirements of Foreign Exchange Management for Foreign Enterprises

Manat is the only currency for payment under a contract for the sale and purchase of goods and services in Azerbaijan. Buy and sale of a foreign currency in Azerbaijan shall be accomplished through assigned banks in the order established by the Central Bank of Azerbaijan. Deals on buy-and-sale of a foreign currency may be carried out directly between assigned banks and also through currency exchanges functioning under the terms and conditions and regulations established by the Central Bank upon coordinating with the Financial Market Supervisory Authority. Buy and sale of a foreign currency without participation of assigned banks shall not be permitted. In order to ensure stability of Manat the Central Bank may intervene the foreign exchange market and set a limit on a gap between selling and buying rates through the foreign currency buy-and-sale transactions.

Currency operations of non-residents in Azerbaijan. Non-residents have the right to bring and take their currency resources in and from the Azerbaijan via remittance, as well as bring in and take out in cash in compliance with customs regulations. They may freely remit the foreign currency, previously transferred to and from Azerbaijan. Non-residents may take out their previously transferred foreign currency resources from Azerbaijan, in cash within the limits of customs regulations, on the basis of certificates issued by assigned banks in compliance with the regulations, stipulated by the Central Bank of Azerbaijan.

Non-residents may bring into Azerbaijan their currency resources in cash in compliance with customs regulations. Information on the amount of funds, date, person and country, the source of money that is being brought in, shall be presented by customs authorities to the Central Bank, the financial monitoring service and relevant executive authority within 7 (seven) days, in the event the amount of currency resources that are being brought into Azerbaijan by non-residents exceed the equivalent of USD 50.000 (fifty thousand US dollars).

They may remit from Azerbaijan their currency resources not exceeding the equivalent of USD 50.000 (fifty thousand US dollars) previously brought into Azerbaijan in cash on the basis of custom documents in evidence thereof. When transferring currency resources in the amount exceeding the equivalent of USD 50.000 (fifty thousand US dollars) from Azerbaijan, previously brought into Azerbaijan in cash, non-residents should submit a certificate, confirming issue of such cash money by a relevant bank or other credit institution of the country wherefrom the currency was brought.

Non-resident individuals may take out currency resources not exceeding the equivalent of USD 50.000 (fifty thousand US dollars), previously brought into Azerbaijan in cash in compliance with customs regulations.

The procedures of remittance and taking out of currency resources in cash from Azerbaijan by non-resident individuals in compliance with customs regulations, except for currency resources, remitted or brought into Azerbaijan in the order specified in paragraphs above must be established by the Central Bank of Azerbaijan. They are entitled to purchase and sell their currency resources in Manat in the order established by the Central Bank of Azerbaijan.

C. Financing

a. Main Financial Institutions

a) Banks

Banks may exercise banking activities in the territory of Azerbaijan on the basis of a special permit (license), issued by the Financial Markets Supervisory Authority. It enjoys exclusive rights to issue and revoke banking licenses, as well as issue permits to banks to open branches, departments and representative offices, and revoke issued permits. Banking licenses and permits shall be issued in writing for unlimited period of time. In accordance with the legislation a bank must be established by at least three legal entities and/or individuals as an open joint-stock company. Banks shall implement the management and current operations in a reliable and prudential manner in accordance with the requirements of, inter alia financial markets supervisory authority and the Central Bank. In accordance with the Law, Banks, unless it is restricted by the bank license obtained from the financial markets supervisory authority, may be engaged in the following activities:
    (i) attract demand and term deposits (savings) and other reimbursable funds;
    (ii) issue loans (secured and/or unsecured), including consumer and mortgage lending, factoring with and without the right of regress, forfeiting, lease services and other types of lending;
    (iii) open and maintain accounts of individuals and legal entities, including correspondent accounts of banks;
    (iv) clearing, cash paying and receiving services, transfer of funds, securities and payment instruments;
    (v) issue payment instruments (including credit and debit cards, traveler checks and bills of exchange);
    (vi) purchase and sell financial assets (including checks, bills of exchange, debt liabilities and deposit

certificates), foreign currency, precious metals and precious stones, currency and interest instruments, shares and other securities, as well as forward contracts, swap agreements, futures, options and other derivatives, related to currency, shares, bonds, precious metals or interest rates at its own expense or at the expense of its clients;

(vii) attract and allocate precious metals as deposits;

(viii) issue guarantees, including warranties to implement liabilities or open letters of credit at own expenses or at the expense of clients;

(ix) provide financial consulting, agent and advisory services;

(x) provide information and services on loans and checking creditability;

(xi) accept documents and valuables, including monetary funds for storage (store in dedicated rooms and safes);

(xii) collection and transportation of valuables, including banknotes and coins.

b) Non-bank Financial Institutions

Just like banks, non-bank financial institutions (NBFI) may exercise its activities in the territory of Azerbaijan on the basis of a special permit (license), issued by the Financial Markets Supervisory Authority. NBFIs may be established by legal entities and individuals of Azerbaijan and (or) foreign countries, as well as by international organizations in the organizational-legal form implied for legal entities in the Civil Code of Azerbaijan. NBFIs are divided into two groups—those entitled and not entitled to accept pledged deposits. The license issued to the NBFI shall contain a special permission required for acceptance of pledged deposits.

NBFIs grant secured and unsecured loans based on the license received from the Financial Markets Supervisory Authority. Loans issued by NBFIs may be secured with real estate and movable property, pledged deposit, guarantee, warranty and other means provided for in the legislation. Pledged deposit may be accepted only if it is stipulated in the permit given to the NBCI by the financial markets supervisory authority.

The NBFI that received license for provision of loans may also be involved in the following activities:

(i) purchase and sale of debt liabilities (factoring, forfeiting);

(ii) leasing;

(iii) registration of bills of exchange;

(iv) issuing guarantees;

(v) provision of insurance agency services;

(vi) provision of financial, technical and management consulting services to borrowers and a group of joint borrowers.

In case a license is required for the operations stipulated herein, NBFI may perform this operation only upon obtaining a relevant license. NBFIs are prohibited to accept deposits from legal entities and individuals.

c) Credit Unions

A credit union is defined as a non-bank financial institution established for mutual crediting of its members by fixing free funds of joined individuals and (or) legal entities that are small entrepreneurs, voluntarily united for common interests. Pursuant to the legislation, mutual crediting is short and (or) long-term loan issued to cover economic and social needs of credit union members at the expense of fixed funds.

Credit unions have right to obtain loans and grants from banks, international and foreign financial and credit institutions; issue loans to its own members as established in the charter; deposit free cash with banks, as well as use it for purchase of state securities. The paid-in capital of credit union is formed by shares of its members.

b. Financing Conditions for Foreign Enterprises

In general, there are no specific conditions for financing of foreign enterprises different from local enterprises. For different forms of legal entities there are requirements for starting capital amount, e.g. minimum capital of AZN 2,000 for closed joint-stock companies and AZN 4,000 for open joint-stock companies etc. In specific sectors where there are licensing requirements such as banking and insurance sectors, financing requirements for foreign persons and companies can exist. E.g. according to the Law on Banks, the limit on participation of foreign bank capital in Azerbaijan's banking system is identified by Financial Markets Supervision Authority. The Authority also defines the limit for participation of foreigners and foreign legal entities in the local banks. According to the Law on Insurance Activity, the limit of foreign capital in all insurers' charter capital in Azerbaijan is defined by the Financial Markets Supervision Authority, too. Foreign physical person's share cannot be more than 10% in one insurer's charter capital, while foreign legal person's shares can go up to 30% of all shares.

D. Land Policy

a. Brief Introduction of Land-Related Laws and Regulations

The main regulatory instruments governing the land related issues are the followings:

(i) The Law on "Lease", dated 30 April 1992;
(ii) The Law on "Fertility of Lands", dated 30 December 1992;
(iii) The Constitution of the Republic of Azerbaijan;
(iv) The Law on "Land Reforms", dated 16 July 1996;
(v) The Law on "Land Lease", dated 11 December 1998;
(vi) The Law on "State Land Cadaster, Land Monitoring and Land Structure", dated 22 December 1998;
(vii) The Law on "Land Market" dated 07 May 1999;
(viii) The Law on "Territories and Lands of Municipalities", dated 07 December 1999;
(ix) The Law on "Notary", dated 26 November 1999;
(x) The Land Code;
(xi) The Civil Code;
(xii) The Law on "Privatization of State-Owned Property", dated 16 May 2000;
(xiii) The Law on "Management of Lands of Municipalities", dated 29 June 2001;
(xiv) The Law on "State Registry of Immovable Property", dated 29 June 2004
(xv) The Law on "Mortgage", dated 15 April 2005;
(xvi) The Law on "Acquisition of Lands for State Needs", dated 20 April 2010;
(xvii) The Urban Planning and Construction Code.

b. Types of Legal Interest in Land

Under Azerbaijani law, there are three following main types of legal interest in land:
(i) Full ownership;
(ii) Right to use;
(iii) Right to lease.

Private property right (full ownership) over the land plot may only be acquired by citizens and legal entities of the Republic of Azerbaijan.[1]

Foreigners and foreign legal entities may only acquire land plots on the basis of the right to lease. [2]

It is important to note that "foreign legal entity" means legal entity established outside the territory of the Republic of Azerbaijan.[3] The references to foreign legal entity are construed as the references to its branches or representative offices, as well.

Therefore, branches or representative offices of foreign legal entities may not acquire private property rights (full ownership) over plot of land in the Republic of Azerbaijan.

As stated above, citizens of and legal entities established in Azerbaijan may acquire land plots on the basis of the right to property, use and lease. [4]

a) Right to Property

Private property right (full ownership) may be acquired through:
(i) Privatization of land plots owned by state and municipality;
(ii) Sale and purchase contract;
(iii) Inheritance;
(iv) Gift;
(v) Exchange contract;
(vi) Other transactions with regard to land plots;
(vii) Transfer to charter capital of legal entities.

The Law on Privatization of State-Owned Property (dated 16 May 2000) does not apply to privatization of lands, with exception of land plots under privatized entities and facilities, as well as, land plots under the entities constructed by natural persons or non-state legal entities (Articles 1.0.3 and 4.0.1).

The owners of the privatized facilities may either buy or lease land plots on which the privatized facilities are located. If the owners of the privatized facilities are foreigners or foreign legal entities they can only lease the said land plot without the right to buy it (Article 29.6 of the Law on Privatization of State-Owned Property and Article 60 of the Land Code).

b) Right to Use

Right to use land plot may be permanent and temporary.
Temporary use of land plot may be long-term and short-term.

---

[1] Article 4 of the Law on Land Reforms, dated 16 July 1996.
[2] Article 48.3 of the Land Code and Article 21 of the Law on Land Lease dated 11 December 1998.
[3] Article 2.0.2 of the Law on State Registration and State Registry of Legal Entities, dated 12 December 2003.
[4] Article 48.2 of the Land Code.

Short-term use may be granted up to 15 (fifteen) years, while long-term use may be granted from 15 (fifteen) years up to 99 (ninety nine) years–for privately owned land plots and from 15 (fifteen) years up to 49 (forty nine) years–for land plots owned by state and municipality.[①]

As a rule, land plots owned by state and municipality may be given to permanent use to exercise their respective functions to:

(i) state authorities and local self-governing bodies;

(ii) entities and organisations financed by state or municipality;

(iii) trade unions and ecclesiastical authorities;

(iv) entities and institutions related to specific areas, such as, mining, petrochemical, energy, transport, communications, defense, natural preservation, historical-cultural, scientific-research, education that are of national importance;

(v) other entities and organizations owned by state or municipality.[②]

The right to permanent or temporary use of land plots owned by state or municipalities are granted by local executive authorities (or by State Committee on Property Issues as the case may be) or municipalities.

The right to use of privately owned land plots may be granted on the basis of the contracts entered into between landowners and users.

Article 46.1 of the Land Code sets out the broad definition of the state lands which include:

(i) lands where the state authorities are located;

(ii) lands where state facilities are located;

(iii) lands of winter and summer pastures;

(iv) forest lands;

(v) lands of water fund of the sector of the Caspian Sea belonging to the Republic of Azerbaijan;

(vi) lands along the coastal 20-50 meter wide strip of the sector of the Caspian Sea belonging to the Republic of Azerbaijan;

(vii) lands of other protected areas, such as land related to health improvement, tourism and recreation, historical and cultural lands etc.;

(viii) lands of state scientific-research and educational institutions, their practice bases, machinery testing stations, state sort-testing service, seed-growing and breeding farms;

(ix) lands designated for the permanent use of state-owned enterprises, institutions and organizations or for the construction of state-owned facilities;

(x) lands of state reserve fund.

In accordance with Article 46.2 of the Land Code, the above-mentioned lands are in the exclusive ownership of the state.

Article 86.2 of the Land Code states that "the state lands contemplated in the [Land] Code··· may not be subject to the sale and purchase."

Please also note that Article 109 of the Land Code states that if the transactions (contracts) are made by breaching the rules set out in the Land Code, then such transactions (contracts) may be deemed invalid.

c) Right to Lease

As noted hereinbefore, right to lease of land plot may be granted to the citizens and legal entities of the Republic of Azerbaijan, foreigners and stateless persons, foreign legal entities, international associations and organisations, and foreign states.

In relation to state-owned land plots relevant executive authorities (it can be the State Committee on Property Issues, the Ministry of the Environment and Natural Resources and local executive authorities as the case may be) act in the capacity of lessor.

Terms and conditions of the lease, its duration, and rental fee are set out in the contract entered into between the parties thereof upon their mutual consent.

Upon consent of the landowner, a lessee may sublease land plot.

c. Intended Purpose

Intended purpose of land plot is of importance. For instance, if the intended purpose of the land is residential or agricultural, then it will be impossible to use the land plot for industrial purposes. Changing the intended purpose of land is possible only in exceptional circumstances by the Cabinet of Ministers.

---

① Article 50.3 of the Land Code.
② Article 50.2 of the Land Code.

E. The Establishment and Dissolution of Companies

a. The Forms of Enterprises

In accordance with the legislation of the Republic of Azerbaijan, there is no local content requirement and no specific requirements for the size of share or legal limitations for the foreign component in a company and investment. With the exception of certain licensed activities, there are no additional general approvals or permissions to be given apart from state registration for the start up.

The Civil Code and the Law on Protection of Foreign Investment being the core corporate laws of the Republic of Azerbaijan, provide a number of different business structures as described below:

(i) Joint-stock company (JSC) can be established by at least one legal entity or an individual.Shareholder liabilities of a JSC are limited to the amount of its shares' value. JSCs fall into two categories — "closed" and "open" JSCs. In closed JSCs shares cannot be transferred and the company must have a minimum share capital of AZN 2,000. In open JSCs shares are freely transferable, but this type of companies must have a minimum share capital of AZN 4,000.

(ii) Limited liability Company (LLC) is an entity established by one or more individuals and/or legal entities contributing their shares to the charter capital. An LLC or any other company that has only one participant may not be the sole participant of another LLC. The participants of an LLC are liable only to the extent of their contributions. An LLC is not responsible for the obligations of its participants to third parties. The law sets no finical limit for LLC's charter capital. Participation interest in LLC can be freely transferable to third parties, unless provided otherwise by the Charter.

(iii) General and limited partnership is established by at least two legal entities or individual entrepreneurs with all partners having unlimited liability. A limited partnership is established by at least two legal entities or individual entrepreneurs with at least one partner having unlimited liability.

(iv) Additional liability company (ALC) is an entity established by one or more individuals and/or legal entities contributing their shares to the charter capital. The legal structure of an ALC is similar to LLC. The distinction between an ALC and an LLC is that the participants in the former may assume liability for the company in excess of their contributions as regulated by the charter.

(v) Cooperative is a voluntary union of at least five individuals and legal entities for the purpose of satisfying the material and other needs of the participants through the consolidation of their material contributions. Depending on the purpose of their activity, cooperatives can be in different forms, such as consumer cooperatives and condominiums.

(vi) Branch and Representative Office are not separate legal entities, but subdivisions or extensions of the corporate head office which establishes them and approves their Regulations. To draw a line between the Branch and Representative office, the latter's activities are much narrower. Under the Civil Code, a representative office may only represent and protect the interests of the head office. A Branch office, on the other hand, may engage in all commercial activities as the same with the head office, including those typically assigned to the Representative office. Management of the Branch/Representative Office is usually carried out by director(s) appointed by the head office. Director(s) exercise their duties on the basis of a limited POA issued by the head office.

NOTE: Based on the proposed amendments to the Civil Code, numerous changes are expected in corporate law, such as elimination of an ALC incorporation type, abolishment of division of JSCs into open and closed types, imposing minimal charter capital requirement on LLC, etc.

b. The Procedure of Establishment

All legal entities operating in Azerbaijan are required to be registered. Without formal registration, a company cannot conduct business in Azerbaijan (e.g., maintain a bank account, clear goods through customs, etc.). As a part of the ongoing business law reforms, a "One Stop Shop" principle was introduced as of 1 January, 2008. The registration procedures involving several government authorities (Ministry of Justice, Ministry of Taxes, Social Insurance Fund and Statistics Committee) have been simplified allowing businesses to register only with the Ministry of Taxes.

Upon submission of all the required documents, the Ministry of Taxes issues registered charter, an extract from the state register and a unique tax identification number within 2 business days.

The Ministry of Taxes accepts documents with an apostille issued abroad by member countries of the 1961 Hague Convention Abolishing the Requirement of Legalization for Foreign Public Documents. The acceptability in Azerbaijan of an apostille certification issued in a particular foreign country, and vice versa, should be checked with the relevant authorities before proceeding with such certification.

Following state registration the company needs to obtain an official seal, to open bank accounts and to obtain e-signature.

The state registration duty for banks, insurance companies, branch/representative offices and certain other types of companies is AZN 220 (~USD 129.40); for ordinary companies it is AZN 11 (~USD 6.47).

An "online registration" system of legal entities has been available since January 2012 for limited liability companies with local investment. Online registration has been exempted from state fees and is completely free. For e-registration, application form and the charter signed by e-signature of founder(s) have to be submitted through the online system of the Ministry of Taxes. Online registration takes only a day and hard copies of the approved incorporation documents can also be obtained from the Tax Office. Having a registration number is sufficient to start operation.

Besides the e-registration, the traditional way of incorporation with submission of documents in hard copy exists as well and is preferred due to technical shortcomings of the e-registration. Documents required for a traditional registration of an LLC include the following:

(i) Standard application form on foundation of the LLC signed by or on behalf of the Founder(s);

(ii) LLC's charter in Azerbaijani approved by or on behalf of the Founder(s);

(iii) Resolution on establishment of an LLC, approval of its charter and appointment of its director(s) signed by or on behalf the Founder(s);

(iv) In case of corporate founder depending on the country of origin apostilled or legalized corporate documents (charter or articles of association, certificate of registration or extract from the state register) of the founding company;

(v) In case of individual founder - copy of his/her identity card;

(vi) Confirmation of payment of charter capital (statement from a bank account);

(vii) Confirmation of payment of the state duty;

(viii) Copy of the identification document for director(s) of the LLC.

(ix) Document confirming the LLC's legal address in Azerbaijan.

As per the recent changes in the Law on State Registration of Legal Entities and State Register (October 2017), online registration of an LLC is also applicable for foreigners and stateless persons. In this regard they need to obtain e-signature via embassies and consulates of Azerbaijan in accordance with the Decree of the President on "Digital Trade Hub of Azerbaijan".

c. Routes and Requirements of Dissolution

The liquidation process of legal entities and branch/representative offices is regulated by the Civil Code and the Law on State Registration of Legal Entities and State Register. The procedure being a quite long process lasts from 6 to 12 months and requires mandatory actions prescribed by the legislation at each stage of the process.

In order to start the liquidation process the director should sign a capability statement which states assets and liabilities of the company and confirms that the company is capable to settle all creditor claims that may arise in the next 12 months. Afterwards, the founder(s) needs to adopt the resolution on liquidation and appoint a liquidator(s). The liquidation should be announced in the press release as well. Subsequently, all the required documents alongside with the company's stamp needs to be submitted to the Ministry of Taxes. Acceptance of the application by the Ministry of Taxes is followed by 2 months statutory period for any possible creditor claims. If the value of the company's property is not sufficient to satisfy creditor claims, such company may only be dissolved by bankruptcy. During the mentioned period the company needs to order a new stamp with the note that the company is "under liquidation process", close all bank accounts, dismiss employees, submit all statutory reports, etc. After the expiration of 2 month period, if there is not any claim raised by the creditors, the Ministry of Taxes commences the closure (final) tax audit. Duration of the audit depends on the size and operations of the company. In the aftermath of the audit, the company carries out division of residual property, prepares liquidation balance and presents them alongside with the company's stamp and incorporation documents to the Ministry of Taxes. The Ministry of Taxes issues a notification on dissolution stating that the company is removed from the State Registry within a week from the date of submission. If liquidation process takes more than a year, it needs to be started over.

NOTE: Based on the proposed amendments to the Civil Code, the term of the liquidation process can be extended for additional 6 months.

F. Merger and Acquisition

In accordance with the Civil Code, merger and acquisition are types of the reorganization of a legal entity.

In case of consolidation, the rights and obligations of each legal entity are transferred to the newly emerged legal entity pursuant to an act of transfer.

Upon the acquisition of one legal entity by another legal entity, the rights and obligations of the former are transferred to the latter pursuant to an act of transfer.

An act of transfer and a balance statement of division shall contain provisions on legal succession for all obligations of the reorganized legal entity with respect to all of its creditors and debtors, including obligations which the parties contest.

During merger or acquisitions provisions of the Law on Antimonopoly Activities should be taken into account as well. The Law is aimed to prevent, restrict and suppress monopoly activities and requires the consent of the State Service for Antimonopoly Policy and Consumer Rights Protection under the Ministry of Economy for mergers or acquisitions described below:

(i) in case of an emerging entity holds more than 35% of the market share;

(ii) if the total value of the assets of the relevant legal entities exceeds AZN 9.75 million.

The decision of the government authority can be received in 15 days after submission of the documents. If the companies merge or acquire without receiving the prior consent, the reorganization can be annulled by the court decision.

The remaining reorganizations falling outside of the above-mentioned category are not subject to merger control.

A legal entity is deemed reorganized from the moment of the state registration of newly emerged legal entities. In the reorganization of a legal entity through the merger with another legal entity, the former is deemed reorganized from the moment of its entry in the state register of legal entities of the notation of the termination of activities of the merged legal entity.

G. Competition Regulation

a. Department Supervising Competition Regulation

The State Service for Anti-Monopoly Policy and Consumer Protection under the Ministry of Economy (hereinafter "the Service") is a department supervising competition regulation in the Republic of Azerbaijan. The Service is responsible for exerting the state policy and control over the compliance with anti-monopoly, unfair competition, public procurement, advertisement and consumer rights protection legislation and rules. The regulations of the Service provide a long list of its obligations (57 in total) under each of those directions which can be grouped as following:

a) Legal (Law Making) and Institutional

(i) Partakes in the preparation of the legislation, state programs and concepts in the relevant fields (in its domain);

(ii) Coordinates the efforts of the state, municipal and non-governmental organizations in the relevant fields;

b) Exerts The State Control (audit) over Compliance With

(i) Anti-trust Legislation;

(ii) Fair Competition Legislation and Rules;

(iii) The Law on Public Procurement;

(iv) Food Safety Standards and Norms;

(v) Grain Products Safety

(vi) Consumer Protection Legislation;

(vii) Trademark Protection Legislation.

c) Sanction The Violations of The Above (point B) by

(i) Instigating administrative liability and fines;

(ii) Requesting license cancellations before other state.

b. Brief Introduction of Competition Law

The basic legal framework pertaining to the competition law is set out by the following laws and by-laws:

The Law "on Unfair Competition" (June 2, 1995, № 1049). The Law establishes legal basis for preventing and removing the unfair competition, creates legal ground for carrying out business activity by honest methods and stipulates responsibility of parties for application of methods of unfair competition. According to this Law, unfair competition covers the actions of a market party aimed at achieving an advantage in business by applying unscrupulous methods that are contrary to the current legislation and may damage other market players (competitors) or diminish their business credibility. Also the Law determines the types of the unfair competition and the sanctions for this conduct.

The Law "on Antimonopoly Activity" (March 4, 1993, № 526). The Law determines organizational and legal grounds for prevention, restriction and suppression of the monopoly activity. Definitions of dominating position, monopoly activity, restrictive means of action, market barriers, horizontal and vertical agreements are defined in this Law. Also forms of monopoly activity, means of antimonopoly regulation and liability for monopoly activity are provided thereby.

The Law "on Natural Monopolies" (December 15, 1998, № 590-IQ). The Law regulates organizational and legal grounds of state control related to natural monopolies in the country. Related to this law, "The list of the natural monopolies" was adopted by act of the Cabinet of Ministers of the Republic of Azerbaijan in a form of by-law.

Provisions relating to monopoly activities and unfair competition are provided by sectorial regulations such as the law on seaports, non-bank credit organizations, etc. as well. However, they contain references to the above-mentioned laws.

Criminal Code (1999). The Code provides criminal liability for the breach of the above-mentioned laws.

c. Measures Regulating Competition

The regulation of competition in Azerbaijan has a relatively short history, due to the recent transition from the planned economy to the market economy. As also stated above, modern competition rules system was constructed in Azerbaijan in 90s by adopting the law "on Unfair Competition" and the law "on Antimonopoly Activity".

The key pillars of competition law are the prohibition of abuse of dominance, restrictive agreements, measures of unfair competition and merger control.

a) Abuse of domination

According to the Law "on Antimonopoly Activity", dominating position is an exceptional position of a commercial entity which allows by using its economic potential to influence competition so that to restrict access of other market participants to the market. If the commercial entity has a share in the market exceeding 35 percent or other ultimate figure specified by the legislation, its position will be considered as dominating. The list of 10 actions is considered as abuse of domination. For instance, charging excessive prices, limiting production, refusing supply, and squeezing competitors from the market by dumping prices. Dominance is not presumed, meaning that in all cases the Service should prove that commercial entity is dominant.

b) Restrictive agreements

Two kinds of restrictive agreements are provided by the Law "on Antimonopoly Activity"–horizontal and vertical agreements. Horizontal agreements are the agreements concluded between commercial entities being at one and the same level of production sequence or acting in one and the same market, in order to avoid competition; vertical agreements are the agreements concluded between commercial entities being at different levels of production sequence or between commercial entity and their clients and suppliers of commodities. Agreements between non-competing market subjects are considered as restrictive if one of them occupying dominating position and another being its supplier or buyer (customer), which are or might become the cause of restriction of competition in the market,.

c) Merger control

Service implements state control on the following cases:

(i) merger commercial entities (if it will be resulted in establishment of commercial entities, the share of which exceeds 35% at respective commercial market);

(ii) association and merger of commercial entity, the total value of which assets exceeds AZN 9.75 million;

(iii) liquidation (except for cases of liquidation of enterprises according to judgment of court) and division of the national and municipal enterprises, the total value of assets of which exceeds AZN 6.5 million (if it will be resulted in establishment of commercial entity, the share of which exceeds 35% at respective commercial market).

Individuals or commercial entities, making the decision on establishing, reorganizing and liquidating a commercial entity falling under the above-mentioned criteria should apply to Service for approval.

H. Tax

a. Tax Regime and Rules

Azerbaijan currently has three different tax regimes:

(i) The statutory tax regime;

(ii) Production Sharing Agreements (PSA) and

(iii) Host Government Agreements (HGA), which are exclusively for the BTC and South Caucasus pipelines.

The statutory tax regime applies to all legal entities (both local and foreign) with the exception of those that are governed by a PSA or HGA, each of which has its own tax rules. The PSA/ HGA tax regimes also generally apply to relevant oil operating companies, foreign investors serving as contractor parties and all Foreign Service companies working with such parties. Azerbaijan has to date signed and ratified over 30 PSAs and HGAs for oil and gas production and transportation. Some of them have been terminated or remain dormant. Each PSA and HGA is subject to its own exclusive tax and accounting regime. PSAs and HGAs provide more favourable legal and tax regime (e.g., simpler reporting regime, deductibility of expenses, fixed rate of Profits Tax, exemption from certain taxes and duties, etc.) for its participants, contractor parties and subcontractors.

b. Main Categories and Rates of Tax

Rate	Payers	Taxablebase	Exemptions
1. Corporate Profit Tax Generally–20%	All enterprises (resident and non-resident). Resident enterprises are subject to tax on their total profit. Non-resident enterprises operating in Azerbaijan through permanent establishments ("PE") are subject to tax on profit from such operations. Non-residents are taxable only on profits from activities performed in Azerbaijan.	Difference between total gross income (excluding the income exempted from tax) and deductible expenses. In case of a PE, total gross income generated from Azerbaijani sources through a PE less the amount of expenses incurred with respect to such income.	Profit of charity organizations (except from entrepreneurial activity); Grants, membership fees and donations received by non-commercial organizations; Income of international, interstate and intergovernmental organizations (Except from entrepreneurial activity) etc. 50 percent of the profit of entities that have obtained an Investment Promotion Certificate will be exempt from income tax for seven years. Any income generated from activities in the industrial and technology parks by legal persons that are residents of such parks. Part of income directed to the construction and maintenance of the infrastructure of the parks by the management organisation or the operator of the industrial or technological parks, founded by the decision of the President of the Republic of Azerbaijan, as well as income from the activity of the resident legal entity in this parks for a period of 7 years, starting from their registration reporting year. Legal entities involved in production of agricultural products (including production by industrial method) are exempt from profit tax, except of land tax, up to January 1, 2019.
2. Withholding Tax from the income of non-residents 4%, 6%, 10% and 14% depending on type of income	Enterprises or entrepreneurs making payments to non-residents. Payments made by the PE of non-residents are treated the same as the payments of resident enterprises.	The gross income of a non-resident from an Azerbaijani source not attributable to a PE of a non-resident on the territory of Azerbaijan is subject to taxation at the source of payment, without deduction of expenses. The remittance of profits, derived from a permanent establishment in Azerbaijan, to the head office is subject to a branch remittance tax of 10%.	
3. Income Tax of Employees–14% for up to 2500 AZN (1480 USD); 25% for over 2500 AZN (350 AZN+ 25% of the amount of exceeding 2500 AZN)	Resident and non-resident employees working in Azerbaijan. Payments made by the PE of non-residents are treated the same as the payments of resident enterprises. Residents are taxed on their worldwide income, while non-residents are taxed only on Azerbaijani source income.	Any salaries, payments or benefits received by an employee in respect of employment, regardless the place of payment.	Income of diplomats or consular employees who are not citizens of Azerbaijan; Employment income from the work-place of a person who is not a resident of the Republic of Azerbaijan–if this income is paid by an employer or in the name of an employer who is not a resident of Azerbaijan and is not paid by or on behalf of a PE of a non-resident; gifts, material aid and inheritance up. Other Exemptions and privileges on income tax stipulated in the tax code.

(continued)

Rate	Payers	Taxablebase	Exemptions
4. Value-Added Tax ("VAT")–18%	Any person registered or required to register as a VAT payer (there is a requirement to register for VAT purposes if turnover of a taxpayer exceeds a certain threshold); Persons importing goods to which VAT applies are considered payers of VAT on goods so imported; A non-resident person performing work or providing service, without registration for VAT purposes and being subject to tax on such works or services; Producers of the excise goods and those who are involved in residential housing construction and not using the right to be the simplified tax payer.	Value of goods, works, and services provided, value of taxable import and trade addition during the retail sale of agricultural goods produced on the territory of Azerbaijan; VAT payers are entitled to recover the amount of VAT paid on purchases (input VAT) by offsetting it with its output tax or any other taxes.	The cost of property purchased from state enterprises in the course of privatization; The provision of financial services etc. The following are subject to '0' (zero) rate: The purchase of goods or services, or importation thereof, with the proceeds of foreign grants; Exports, etc. Any entity or individual entrepreneur having obtained an Investment Promotion Certificate will be exempt, for the period of seven years, from VAT upon confirmed import of equipment, technological equipment and devices.
5. Excise Tax–Various rates (perunit, volume, etc.)	All persons engaged in the production of excisable goods in Azerbaijan or importation of such goods into Azerbaijan.	Release of excise goods produced in Azerbaijan and import of excisable goods into Azerbaijan. Excisable goods are spirits, beer and all kinds of alcohol, tobacco products, petroleum products, and vehicles, yachts for sports and leisure, platinum, gold and jewelry products made from them, fur-leather products.	Transit transportation of goods through the territory of Azerbaijan; Temporary imports of goods into Azerbaijan, except for goods intended for re-export; Goods that are intended for re-export and secured under a pledge etc.
6. Property Tax (Different rates depending on type of assets) –Individuals–depending on the region where the property is located between AZN 0.1-0.4 for each square meter of the property; legalentities –1% of the value of fixed assets ; Other rates are applicable for possession of watercrafts and aircrafts	All persons and legal entities having assets (buildings or their parts, fixed assets etc.) in ownership. Resident enterprises, as well as non-resident enterprises carrying our business activity through its permanent establishment in the Republic of Azerbaijan, are subject to property tax.	For individuals, buildings owned by resident and non-residentindividuals in the Republic of Azerbaijan, plus watercraft and aircraft owned by resident individuals; For resident enterprises average annual value of fixed assets on the balance sheet of the enterprise; For legal entities carrying out business activities in Azerbaijan through a permanent establishment annual average valueof only those fixed assets which are related to the PE.	Facilities that are used for environmental preservation, fire protection or civil defense purposes; Pipelines carrying products, rail and motorways, communication, power transmission lines, irrigation system facilities, satellites and other space objects, mechanical vehicles etc; Any entity or individual entrepreneur that has obtained an Investment Promotion Certificate is exempt from property tax for seven years; Residents of industrial and technology parks for the property used in the parks.

Rate	Payers	Taxablebase	Exemptions
7. Land Tax–Different rates depending on location and type of land plots	All persons owning or using land in Azerbaijan.	Land plots granted for use or ownership.	Common use residential land plots, national border zones and land designated for defense purposes etc. Any entity or individual entrepreneur that has obtained an Investment Promotion Certificate is exempt from land tax for seven years. Residents of industrial and technology parks for land used in the parks.
8. Mining Tax (Royalty)–3% - 26%	All individuals and legal entities engaged in extraction of commercial minerals from subsoil strata of the earth within the territory of the Azerbaijan Republic, (including in the Azerbaijani sector of the Caspian Sea).	Commercial minerals extracted from subsoil strata in the territory of Azerbaijan (including in the Azerbaijani sector of the Caspian Sea).	
9. Simplified (System) Tax 4% for taxpayers operating in Baku; and 2% for taxpayers operating in other regions; 6% for trading activities and 8% for catering activities with more than AZN 200,000 turnover; 6% for operators of sports betting; 4% for commissioners of sports betting	Enterprises and individuals with a yearly turnover not exceeding a certain limit (currently 200,000 AZN - around USD 118,000); whose taxable turnover exceeds AZN 200,000 in any month within consecutive twelve months are entitled to a simplified tax; Persons engaged in trading and catering activities; Persons engaged in the passengers and cargo transportation on territory of the Republic of Azerbaijan; Persons engaged in the construction of buildings are also entitled to register as simplified tax payers voluntarily; Operators and commissioners of sports betting etc.	Total proceeds realized by a taxpayer from the sale of goods or services and from non-sales related activity.	
10. Social insurance fund contributions payable by the employee	Azerbaijani and foreign employees.	Employer is responsible for Social Insurance Fund Contribution on behalf of employees at the rate of 22% paid by employer on top of the gross wages, and 3% Contribution to State Pension fund, withheld at from employee's gross salary.	Foreign Employees providing services under PSA regime are exempted from Social Protection Fund Contributions.

c. Tax Declaration and Preference

For the purposes of tax control implementation, taxpayer legal entities shall be registered with tax authorities at place of registration (legal address, indicated in the state registration documents), at the place of received income from the Azerbaijani source, if taxable income contains Azerbaijani source and non-residents, who are not subject at the place of income payment, and individual entrepreneurs and residents - natural persons, which shall submit declaration in accordance with provisions of the Code hereof – at place of residence, and private notaries - at the place of their business.

Enterprise with foreign investments should keep accounts and prepare reports in accordance with regulations of the Azerbaijan Republic and, if necessary, in accordance with regulations existing in the country of origin of foreign investor.

Depending on the field of activity, legal entity (foreign investment enterprise) should provide different tax declaration(s) to the Ministry of Taxes of the Republic of Azerbaijan.

More information can be found on web page of Ministry of Taxes of the Republic of Azerbaijan: http://taxes.gov.az/index.php

I. Securities

a. Brief Introduction of Securities-Related Laws and Regulations

The main securities related laws of the Republic of Azerbaijan are the Civil Code and the Law "on Securities Markets" (hereinafter: Securities Markets Law). The law was adopted on July 15, 2015, to regulate the issuance, state registration, public offer of investment securities, depository and post-trading systems, distribution of securities and derivative financial instruments, to determine the principles of establishment, management, and deregistration of licensed persons and the central depository in the securities market, as well as to protect the rights and interests of investors in Azerbaijan, as well as to establish fair and transparent public trading in securities and free competition.

The Securities Markets Law includes main definitions, such as definitions for securities market, local and foreign investment companies, the procedure of the registration of local and foreign investment companies and their branches; and the list of financial instruments. According to the Civil Code the list of derivative financial instruments consists of futures, options and swaps. Shareholder that owns 10 per cent of the shares of the company is considered as the significant shareholder.

Except for the above normative acts, it is necessary to mention by-laws adopted by Financial Market Supervisory Authority of the Republic of Azerbaijan:

(i) The Rules on procedures for issuance and placement of investment securities outside the Republic of Azerbaijan;

(ii) Rules for concluding a contract for the purchase and sale of investment securities;

(iii) Rules on the prevention of corruption in the securities market.

b. Supervision and Regulation of Securities Market

The local securities market is supervised by the Financial Market Supervisory Authority of the Republic of Azerbaijan (hereinafter FIMSA). This authority was established in a form of public legal entity. The main purpose of FIMSA is to provide effective oversight and stability for the financial markets of the Republic of Azerbaijan, to protect the rights of creditors, insured persons, investors and other consumers of financial markets. FIMSA is based on leading international principles and standards in the field of regulation of financial markets. The FIMSA is entitled to adopt bylaws to regulate the manners in which it applies its supervisory powers.

c. Requirements for Engagement in Securities Trading for Foreign Enterprises

According to the Article 1078-25A of the Civil Code, the purchase of securities of issuers of the Azerbaijan Republic by foreign investors is not limited, except for cases provided for by law. Foreign legal person may participate in securities exchange through its licensed branch office. The license for the branch office of the foreign enterprises is issued by the FIMSA. Procedure of the licensing and the list of the necessary documents that should be applied for the license are listed in the Article 71 of the Securities Markets Law. The grounds for refusal to register coincide with similar grounds relating to local enterprises. An additional condition for foreign enterprises is the requirement that the regulation of the investment sphere in the country of origin of the enterprise should be on equal terms with Azerbaijan requirements or stricter.

J. Preference and Protection of Investment

a. Support for Specific Industries and Regions

a) ICT

2013 has been declared the "Year of ICT" in Azerbaijan by the President of Azerbaijan. For investors in ICT Azerbaijan offers excellent infrastructure. Azerbaijan is launching its first satellite into the space in 2013, which will offer tremendous opportunities in telecommunications and IT not only in the country but in the region at large. As recently as in November 2012 the President of Azerbaijan decreed establishment of a hi-tech industrial park in the country, which will, yet again, offer investors simplified and the most favorable business environment in IT/Telecoms in the country. Azerbaijan prides itself with high literacy levels (99.6%) of its population with excellent IT and foreign language skills.

b) Logistics

Located at the crossroads between Asia and Europe, Azerbaijan is the most stable country in the region in both economic and political terms. Bridging between Europe and Central Asia, as well as connecting the North-Eastern Europe with the Middle East, Azerbaijan is also a logistics hub for the entire Caspian region.

c) Industry

It is the term that defines Azerbaijan in its entirety. The country has always been at the forefront of the regional industrial development. Along with oil and natural gas extraction and processing, engineering, metallurgy and electric power make up the pillars of the manufacturing industry of the country. The government has already prioritized development of the latter three segments of the manufacturing industry with a particular focus on the chemical industry, which saw establishment of Sumgayit Chemical Industrial Park LLC on the 21st of December 2011. The initiative will serve the purpose of developing a competitive chemical industry via innovative and cutting-edge technologies by creating favorable and simplified business environment, and by offering investors substantial incentives including tax breaks.

d) Alternative and Renewable Energy

This sector in Azerbaijan is as attractive to investors as the Mother Nature has prescribed it. Azerbaijan offers the most favorable climate and landscape conditions to foster renewable energy industry. For solar panels Azerbaijan offers over 280 days of bright sunshine a year, for wind turbines there is a "guaranteed continuous supply" of strong winds throughout the year, the Caspian see with high tidal cycles and an abundance of fast flowing mountain rivers are there for hydro-power plants, and last but not the least, the soil of Azerbaijan is renowned for its arable qualities, which is capable of producing a high yield of biomasses.

e) Tourism

It is a fast developing industry in Azerbaijan. The government is investing heavily in infrastructure to facilitate tourism in the country. In 2012 Azerbaijan hosted the Eurovision Song Contest, FIFA U-17 Women's World Cup. A number of five-star luxury hotels of global brands opened their doors in Baku in the recent years. The initial phase of Shahdagh Winter-Summer Recreation Center was completed in January 2013. Just recently Azerbaijan successfully bid to host the First European Games in 2015. Azerbaijan has ambitious plans to host Olympics and the European Football Championship in near future.

f) Agriculture

Food security and regional development are among top priorities for Azerbaijan's non-oil economy, and has significant potential for boosting export revenues for the country. Azerbaijan has comparative advantages in producing traditional agricultural products. Favorable soil-climatic condition, rich traditions, and access to developed transport infrastructure make the agrarian sector one of the major priorities of the non-oil sector. The government has introduced several state programs and other legislative acts to support and further promote development of the agriculture in Azerbaijan. The agricultural sector has been completely relieved from all taxes but the land tax since 2001.

b. Special Economic Areas

The first reference to SEZ in national legislation dates back to 90s–The Law on protection of Foreign Investment, Tax Code. The new age in SEZ strategy of Azerbaijan started from the Presidential Decree signed in 2007 on establishment of SEZ in Azerbaijan. Later followed the law on SEZ dated 2009.

Within 8 years after the Law Azerbaijan has established industrial parks and sites in Sumgayıt, Mingachevir, Garadagh, Masallı, Neftchala, Hacıgabul and a free zone in Alat. Some of them like Sumgayıt Chemical Industrial Park, Balakhanı Industrial Park are already operative and several residents have been registered in them.

c. Investment Protection

a) Rights of Investment Stakeholders

The state provides the stability of realizing conditions of investment activity and protection of rights and legal interests of its subjects.

The terms of the contract made between the subjects of investment activity remain in force during the entire period of this contract and even when the conditions that worsen the situation or limit the rights of the subjects are defined by legislation, if they have not agreed on amending the terms of the contract.

State bodies and their officials cannot interfere with the affairs of subjects of investment activity, unless it is admissible by legislation and included to their authority.

Apart from circumstances specified by the present Law, investors' rights cannot be limited in the choice of projects.

At the adoption of acts that infringe the rights of investors and the other subjects of investment activity by state bodies and other authorities, the said bodies are to fully pay the damage, incurred to the subjects of investment activity. Disputes about damage compensation are to be considered in court or arbitrage.

b) Protection of Investment

The state provides guarantee for the protection of all investments, including foreign investments.

Protection of investments is provided by the corresponding legislation of the Azerbaijan Republic, as well as contracts, concluded with other states. Investors, including foreign ones, are provided with equal legal regime that excludes discrimination based measures that prevent from managing, using and liquidating investments, also determining the terms and conditions of taking the results of deposited wealth and investment out of the republic.

Provided further legislation of the Azerbaijan Republic worsens the conditions of investment depositing, the legislation that was in force at the moment of deposition of investment is applied for the period specified in the contract on investment activity.

Investments are not to be nationalized without compensation, confiscated and no other similar measures are to be applied on the territory of the Azerbaijan Republic. Such measures may be applied by full payment of damage on real value, including lost profits, only on the basis of legislation acts of Azerbaijan Republic. The order of payment of damage is determined by the given legislation.

The purchase of bank deposits, the contribution of shares and other securities deposited or acquired by investors, at the compensation for payments for purchased property or right for lease is received according to the legislation acts of Azerbaijan Republic, excluding amounts used or lost as a result of their own actions or actions conducted with their participation, are to be returned to investors.

Investments may be insured, and in cases specified by the legislation must be insured.

III. Trade

A. Department Supervising Trade

The Ministry of Economy (MOE) is the main governing authorities of foreign economic and trade relations of Azerbaijan. The MOE prepares state policy in the field of economic and trade relations in cooperation with the relevant bodies and carries out its implementation in order to develop and regulate foreign economic and trade relations. Structure of the MOE consists of departments, regional divisions and the institutions founded by the MOE for promoting trade relations. The main department related to trade relations is the Department on Trade policy and World Trade Organization. The Department is empowered to draft actions and normative legal acts on trade policy, establish and develop cooperation with international organizations on trade policy. Further, this Department is charged in organizing and implementing necessary actions for Azerbaijan's accession to WTO, including approximation of the legislation to the requirements of WTO.

B. Brief Introduction of Trade Laws and Regulations

a. Existing Laws and Regulations

Trade is regulated by international treaties and domestic legislation. According to the Constitution, international treaties that Azerbaijan is a party, prevails over domestic laws (except the Constitution and acts adopted by referendum).

The Law on Protection of Investment, the Law on Investment Activity, Customs Code and Trade Shipping Code are among the core domestic trade laws. In addition, the below mentioned legislative acts have been adopted to regulate the trade:

(i) The law of the Republic of Azerbaijan "On customs tariff" dated 13 June 2013;

(ii) The law "on approval of the Customs Code of the Republic of Azerbaijan" dated 24 June 2011;

(iii) The decision of the Cabinet of Ministers of the Republic of Azerbaijan on "Commodity Nomenclature of Foreign Economic Activity, Rates of Import and Export Customs Duties" dated 13 November 2017;

(iv) The decree of the President of the Republic of Azerbaijan on additional measures for strengthening Azerbaijan's position as a Digital Trade Hub and the expansion of foreign trade operations dated 22 February 2017;

(v) The decree of the President of "on enactment of the Law on approval of the Customs Code of the Republic of Azerbaijan" dated 15 September 2011;

(vi) The decree of the Cabinet of Ministers of the Republic of Azerbaijan "On approval of Rules of determination of countries of origin" dated 29 November 2007;

(vii) The decision of the Cabinet of Ministers of the Republic of Azerbaijan "On excise duties of excised products imported to the Republic of Azerbaijan" dated 19 January 2001;

(viii) The decree of the President of the Republic of Azerbaijan "On further liberalization of foreign trade in the Republic of Azerbaijan" dated 24 June 1997;

b. Recent Legislative Developments

Pursuant to the recently adopted Decision of the Cabinet of Ministers that modified the order "On excise duties of excised products imported to the Republic of Azerbaijan", excise duties of excised products have been increased as of 2018.

Among the recent legislative developments it is worth mentioning the Law on Alat Free Zone. The Law has already been approved by the parliament and expected to come into force following presidential approval. The Law on Alat Free Zone determines the legal regime of activities, development and management of the Alat Free Zone (FTZ). According to the Law, except the criminal legislation, laws of the Republic of Azerbaijan will not be applicable in the FTZ, since it will have its own laws.

All the companies incorporated in FTZ and their employees will be exempt from taxes. Customs duties will not be imposed on the goods to be imported to the FTZ and as far as the goods exported from the FTZ to Azerbaijan considered, they will be subject to the customs law of the Republic of Azerbaijan.

Both Azerbaijani national currency and foreign currency can be used for transactions in the FTZ and the gained profits can be transferred abroad without any restriction. Among other things, the FTZ will have its own dispute resolution authority and the courts of the Republic of Azerbaijan, with the exception of the criminal jurisdiction, will not have a jurisdiction over the cases related to the FTZ or its residents.

C. Trade Management

a. General Overview

Local and foreign legal entities can conduct trade activities in Azerbaijan. Foreign legal entities can be part of the trade either with opening branch office, representative office or establishing local presence. Even though branch offices allowed to carry out commercial activities, representative offices can only protect the interest of the main company, supervise the sale of their products in domestic markets etc. In addition, products of foreign companies can also be distributed through distributors with concluding respective distributorship agreement. In all the cases, registration of the trademarks in Azerbaijan is an effective way to avoid possible future infringement cases.

Under Azerbaijani law, special rules are imposed on labeling food and agricultural products. This type of products should be properly packed to ensure its safe storage and usage. They should also be properly labeled at least describing the products name, type, ingredients, usage area and conditions, production and expiration dates, storage conditions, name and address of the producer. Even though the labels in foreign languages are acceptable, those labels and the names on imported products, their description sheets have to be accompanied in Azerbaijani translation as well.To strengthen this rule, the law on Protection of Consumer Rights stipulates that consumers should be informed on the above mentioned features of products. The State Service for Anti-Monopoly Policy and Consumer Protection under the Ministry of Economy is the competent authority for examining the compliance with the labeling rules.

b. E-commerce

Electronic trade in Azerbaijan is regulated by the law on Electronic Commerce adopted in 2005. Determining the legal basis of e-commerce the law sets rights and obligations of its parties and responsibility for violation of e-commerce legislation. In accordance with the amendments to the tax legislation effective as of 2017, Value Added Tax (VAT) was imposed on electronic trade operations. As per the amendments, the residents participating in online competitions and purchasing services, with the exception of flight tickets and hotel services, are subject to VAT.

D. The Inspection and Quarantine of Import and Export Commodities

Imported and exported of goods undergo customs control by the customs authorities with assistance of modern technologies. Azerbaijani law recognizes several customs procedures applicable to goods imported into the country, the most important of which are transit (international and national), warehouse (temporary storage and customs warehouse), free zone, special use (temporary import and end use), and processing (in and outside customs territories).

A one-stop-shop system is applied for the inspection of goods and vehicles crossing the state borders. The Customs Committee is the central governmental institution with a law enforcement organization status implementing state customs policy and the competent authority carrying out inspection of goods, transport documents, export certificates, as well as the veterinary, Phytosanitary, sanitary control. Moreover, wide ranges of e-services are gathered at the e-government portal and the State Customs Committee of Azerbaijan introduced "e-Customs" for a number of services including e-declaration.

Export Support Centre of "One Stop Shop" was set up in 2017 to enable drafting and signing of documents, including contracts between persons registered as tax payers in Azerbaijan and their foreign business partners in an electronic form, as well as providing of cross-border online electronic services.

Export Support Centre of "One Stop Shop" provides certificates required for the export:

(i) International veterinary certificate for animals, animal products and raw materials exported;
(ii) Phytosanitary (re-export Phytosanitary) certificate for export of plant and plant growing products;
(iii) Certificate of quality for export of food products to the countries of the European Union,
(iv) Certificate verifying the country of origin of the product;
(v) Permit (certificate) for export of endangered species of wild fauna and flora;
(vi) Protection certificate of cultural assets for export of cultural assets;
(vii) Permit for export of religious literature (in paperback and electronic formats), audio and video materials (products) and other informational materials with religious content.

In 2016, alongside with a number of liberal reforms in the country, Azerbaijan introduced "Green and other Entry Channel Systems" to the customs legislation. The system is based on risk assessment prior to entry of goods and vehicles into the customs territory. Four types of corridor (green, blue, yellow and red) are designed which is to be determined by the automated digital information system. The green entry channel being the most important entitles entrepreneurs to import goods by filling out electronic declaration without a need for additional checking the goods. Under the blue entry channel, besides assessment of the electronic declaration, goods also have to undergo examination by customs. The yellow corridor is designated for the goods that require special license for import. As for the red corridor, it requires mandatory inspection. As obvious, the green entry channel is the most advantageous corridor and main importers are seeking permit for this channel. According to the Customs Committee, circa 30 companies were granted with the permits so far as a part of the green corridor.

E. Customs Management

a. Customs Law

Customs procedures are regulated by the Customs Code. Azerbaijan adopted a new Customs Code effective as of 2012 which abolished the previous Code. The Customs Code determines legal, economic and organizational basis of customs affairs in Azerbaijan, including the general procedures and rules applied in relation to the goods and vehicles imported on customs area of Azerbaijan, exported from this territory, moved through it with transit, the rights and obligations of persons in the field of customs affairs.

b. Customs Tariff

Customs tariffs are determined by the law "On customs tariff" dated 13 June 2013. The Law determines implementation of customs tariff, as well as rules on levying custom duties from the goods passing through the borders of the country.

In accordance with the Rules "On Issuance Certificate on Investment Promotion" approved by the president of Azerbaijan, investment promotion certificate is issued to entrepreneurs if they present investment projects in line with the certain criteria specified in the Rules. The companies holding the Certificate are entitled for customs and tax exemptions set forth by the Law "On Customs Tariffs" and the Tax Code.

17 grounds provided by the Law "On Customs Tariffs" for exempting certain goods from customs duties have been rounded up to 20. Pursuant to the new grounds, import of machinery, equipment, and devices for investment purposes in priority industries of the economy are exonerated from custom duties for up to 7 years. Additionally, the Investment certificate holders are exempt from paying 50 percent of income tax and land tax.

c. Free Trade Agreements

Azerbaijan has free trade agreements with Russia, Ukraine, Georgia, Kazakhstan, Kyrgyzstan, Tajikistan, Uzbekistan, Moldova and Belarus. Goods imported from these countries are free of customs duties. Azerbaijan has also ratified the United Nations Convention on Contracts for the International Sale of Goods (Vienna, 1980).

d. Economic Developments

Azerbaijan started registering trade houses in other countries in order to increase trade turnover with them, facilitate the export process, promote an export of competitive national production, support promotion of products under the "Made in Azerbaijan" brand and enable the countries to expand trade operations. Two trade houses in Belarus and Latvia have already been opened and further discussions are continuing to raise their number. The statistics reveals that the first trade house set up in Belarus resulted in circa double increase of the trade turnover with the respective country.

Baku-Tbilisi-Gars railway that became operational in October 2017 aimed to complete the transport corridor linking Central Asia and China to Europe by rail is of great importance from the trade perspective. Launch of Baku-Tbilisi-Gars railway is already changing logistics map of the region attracting attention of both Western and Eastern trading partners.

Institutional reforms are among the priorities of the government as well. A new institution–the Food Safety Agency was established in February 2017 and started its activities as of January 1st, 2018. The establishment of the Agency serves the implementation of the roadmap on production and processing of agricultural products. Some authorities of the Ministry of Economy, the Ministry of Agriculture and Ministry of Health were passed to the Food Safety Agency.

Moreover, export grant scheme was introduced to support exporters' participation in international exhibitions, organization of export missions, market researches, entry of goods into the foreign market chains and duty-free shops, promotion of "Made in Azerbaijan" brand in foreign countries and export product related R&D programs.

e. Statistics

Ranking 4th for total turnover, China is one of the major trading partners of Azerbaijan. The trade turnover of Azerbaijan with China increased by 43% in 2017 accounting USD 1.2 bn.

Double tax treaty between Azerbaijan and China signed in 2005 is of importance in growth of the trade turnover between the countries. The Treaty sets out the rates of withholding tax as dividends at 10% and royalties at 10%.

As an indicator of the development of economic relations between Azerbaijan and China a new trade representative office of Azerbaijan was opened in China on February 2018.

IV. Labour

A. Brief Introduction of Labour Laws and Regulations

Employment relations in Azerbaijan are primarily regulated by the Labour Code of the Republic of Azerbaijan and other legislative acts providing minimum standards for provision of labour rights. Foreign and stateless employees have the same labour rights and duties with Azerbaijani citizens during the period they work in Azerbaijan, unless otherwise provided by international agreements. Azerbaijani Labour Code does not apply to the following people:

(i) military personnel;
(ii) judges;
(iii) deputies of the Milli Majlis of the Republic of Azerbaijan and persons elected to municipal bodies;
(iv) foreigners signing employment agreements with a foreign legal entity and fulfilling work functions in their branch and/or representative offices operating in the Republic of Azerbaijan;
(v) persons performing work under contractor, commission, copyright and other civil contracts.

Employment relations are established with the conclusion of an employment agreement between the employer and the employee. Employment agreement becomes effective only after its registration at the electronic database of the Ministry of Labour and Social Protection of the Population of the Republic of Azerbaijan ("Labour Ministry"). Parties to the employment agreement may agree on a probation period not exceeding 3 months upon execution of the agreement. Employment agreements may be entered into for a fixed or indefinite term. Registration of all employment agreements, amendments to them and their termination must be carried out through the electronic database of the Labour Ministry.

Minimum salary: Each employee has a right to get a salary not lower than the minimum salary determined by the state, which is currently 130 AZN per month.

Work regime. Regular work week for full-time employees is 40 hours, reduced for certain groups of people and workplaces. Daily standard working hours for 40 hours working week is 8 hours. Employer and employee may agree on short working hours, short workdays and short workweeks upon execution of an employment agreement.

Overtime work is allowed in order to prevent a natural disaster, an industrial accident, or other emergency events, or to eliminate their consequences, as well as to prevent the loss of perishable goods. The duration of overtime work may not exceed a certain limit established by the Labor Code. For each hour of overtime work, an employee must be compensated at a rate at least double of a normal hourly rate.

Vacation, Leave and Rest Time. In accordance with the Labour Code, minimum paid annual leave is 21 days, and for certain group of employees a longer period is mandated. Employees also have rights to social leave (maternity leave), sick leave, educational or scientific creativity leave and unpaid leave under conditions provided by law.

Employees are entitled to the following main types of leaves depending on the circumstances of each case:

(i) Annual leave;
(ii) Maternity & Social leave;
(iii) Educational & Research leave;
(iv) Unpaid leave.

Annual leave consists of base leave and additional leave. Base leave is 30 days for professional and managerial staff, and 21 days for non-professional staff. Additional leaves are determined on the basis of working conditions, seniority, etc. Depending on employees' seniority, additional leaves are as follows:

(i) seniority of five to ten years–2 additional calendar days;
(ii) seniority of ten to fifteen years–4 additional calendar days;
(iii) seniority of over fifteen years–6 additional calendar days.

Employees working under heavy and harmful conditions are also entitled to minimum of extra 6 days.

Annual leave may be taken wholly or in parts (split vacation).The Labour Code requires that at least one part of annual leave must be 2 weeks in duration.

Maternity & Social leave: Women are entitled to maternity leave of 70 days before and 56 days after the birth (total of 126 days). In case of hard or multiple births, the term of leave after the birth will be extended to 70 days (total of 140 days).

Upon completion of maternity leave, eligible employees may take social leave for raising their child. The term of social leave may last till the child reaches the age of three.

Rest-time for breastfeeding: If employees decide not to take social leave and continue to work after the birth of their child, they will be entitled to a breastfeeding break until the child reaches the age of 18 months.

Educational and Research Leave: Educational leave is granted to the students for laboratory researches and examinations during semesters, as well as for writing a graduation thesis. During such leave average salary paid to the employee is calculated in the manner stipulated by the Labour Code. Educational leave may last up to 2 months.

Research leave is granted to the employees obtaining academic degree. This kind of leave is granted for up to 3 months.

Unpaid Leave: Employees are entitled to unpaid leave to take time-off for urgent family, personal or other social needs. Overall accumulated duration of unpaid leave per one employment year may not exceed 6 (six) months.

Termination of Employment Agreement. Azerbaijani law establishes strict requirements for termination of employment agreements. Employment agreement may be terminated subject to strict compliance with the grounds and procedures stipulated in the Labour Code. The grounds for termination are:

(i) initiative of one of the parties;
(ii) expiration of the employment agreement;
(iii) change of working conditions;
(iv) change in the ownership of the company;
(v) cases falling beyond parties' control;
(vi) additional grounds for termination established by the parties in the employment agreement (including, parties' mutual consent).

Employee may terminate employment agreement by notifying the employer in writing one calendar month in advance. In case there are specific and valid reasons (such as employee's reaching retirement age, disability, admission to an educational institution, moving to a new place of residence or entering into an employment agreement with another employer, sexual harassment, or other cases provided by law), employment agreement is terminated on the date indicated in employee's application.

Employment agreement may be terminated upon employer's initiative in the following cases:

(i) liquidation of the company;
(ii) staff redundancy;
(iii) employee's failure to meet required competency standards as determined by the decision of a competency assessment body;
(iv) gross violation of employment duties as determined by the employment agreement or labour law;
(v) employee's failure to meet expectations of the employer within a probation period;
(vi) with respect to state-owned companies, employee's reaching of retirement age.

There are statutory restrictions relating to dismissal of certain categories of employees. Law prohibits terminating employment agreement with pregnant women, women with children under the age of three and other categories of employees, exclusively listed in the Labour Code, unless employer is in the process of being liquidated or the term of the fixed-term agreement is expired.

Employer cannot terminate the employment agreement on the basis of two or more grounds specified above or may not apply for any other termination ground that is not prescribed by law.

B. Requirements of Employing Foreing Employees

Migration Code of the Republic of Azerbaijan is the main statutory act aiming to implement the state migration policy, and Azerbaijani migration law regulates the relations in the following spheres:

(i) exit from/entry to the country of Azerbaijani citizens;

(ii) foreigners' and stateless persons' entry to/exit from the Republic of Azerbaijan, their temporary stay and registration in the Republic of Azerbaijan;

(iii) issuance of temporary and permanent residence permits, as well as work permits;

(iv) rights and obligations of the migration processes' participants; labour migration, as well as state control over migration and fighting against illegal migration, etc.

As mentioned above, foreign employees who are employed by enterprises (subsidiaries), branches or representative offices operating in Azerbaijan are subject to Azerbaijani labour law, except for those working in branches or representative offices located in Azerbaijan under employment contracts concluded with the foreign state's enterprise in that state.

a. Work Permit

Expatriates travelling to Azerbaijan to take employment here have to obtain work and temporary residence permits. These permits are issued by the State Migration Service ("SMS") for the period of up to one year. The term of validity can be extended every time for another period of up to one year.

Employing expatriates without obtaining work permit is prohibited by law. Companies employing expatriates without work permit are subject to imposition of penalty in amount of up to AZN 20 000. Illegal working expatriates will also be penalised in the amount of AZN 300–400 and be forced to leave the territory of Azerbaijan immediately after the decision of the relevant authority.

Certain categories of foreigners (permanent residents, persons engaged in entrepreneurship activities in Azerbaijan, staff of diplomatic missions, consulates and international organizations, heads and deputy heads of organizations established by international agreements, persons employed by relevant executive authorities, persons on secondment in certain statutorily listed areas for no more than 90 days a year, heads and deputy heads of branches and representative offices of foreign legal entities in Azerbaijan, heads and deputy heads of legal entities founded in Azerbaijan by a foreign legal entity or a foreign individual and some other categories of foreign nationals) do not require work permit.

As stated above, Azerbaijani law provides 8 categories of activity not requiring work permit for engaging expatriates to work for up to 90 cumulative days within one calendar year. These activity spheres are:

(i) mining industry;
(ii) information and communication;
(iii) transport;
(iv) processing industry;
(v) finance and insurance;
(vi) education;
(vii) power, gas, steam and conditioned air supply;
(viii) water supply, waste water and waste treatment.

Such trip is documented by secondment order / letter.

b. Application Procedure

For work permit application, SMS requires that the employing company firstly registers their representative with SMS. This representative must be an employee of that company.

Expatriate's presence in the country is not required for work permit application. However, company may apply for work and temporary residence permits at the same time. But in case if there is temporary residence permit application as well, expatriate should be in the country.

List of documents for application package is clearly reflected in the Migration Code.

Permit application may be submitted both in paper and electronically. For electronic application, company representative just needs to register in the database of SMS and then upload all required documents.

SMS's permit consideration takes up to 20 working days. Once the decision is made (whether the work permit is granted or rejected), company representative receives an email from SMS.

State duty for granted work permit is up to AZN 1000 based on duration of the permit and is paid on receipt. State duty for temporary residence permit depending on its duration is up to AZN 120 and people under 18 years enjoy 50% discount for TRP state duty.

c. Social Insurance

Both Azerbaijani nationals and foreign individuals are subject to social insurance contribution requirement. Employers are liable for paying social insurance contributions at a rate of 22% of the employee's gross salary, and 3% is deducted from employee's gross salary as the employee's portion of the social insurance contribution. Subject to relevant international agreements of Azerbaijan, foreign citizens may be exempted from paying Azerbaijani social insurance contributions.

With effect from 01 January 2018, unemployment insurance fee is applied in order to provide more benefits to certain categories of unemployed people. Therefore, payments deducted from employee's gross salary increased to 3.5% (3% social insurance fee + 0.5% unemployment insurance). Accordingly, payment to the State Social Protection Fund made by Employer is also increased to 22.5% (22% + 0.5%). Consequently, employers provide social insurance, insurance from unemployment and mandatory insurance against occupational illness and workplace injuries of the employees.

C. Exit and Entry

a. Visa Types

All foreigners and stateless persons must firstly obtain a visa in order to enter the territory of Azerbaijan unless Azerbaijan has an agreement with the country they come from providing otherwise. In order to get a visa they have to apply to diplomatic missions or consulates of the Republic of Azerbaijan in relevant states. For some countries it is possible to obtain the visa directly at the airports. Electronic application is also possible.

Depending on the number of entries, entry visas are divided into single entry and multiple entry visas, and transit visas are divided into single transit and double transit visas. Entry visas are valid up to 90 days for single entry/exit, and up to 2 years for multiple entry/exit.

Visa types differ depending on the purpose of visit, such as:
(i) Tourism;
(ii) Science and Education;
(iii) Medical treatment;
(iv) Business trip;
(v) Culture and Sports;
(vi) Personal trip;
(vii) Labour/work;
(viii) Humanitarian;
(ix) Official trip.

Visa issued for business visit may define a period of stay in the country for up to 180 days, while it is 90 days for labour visas. In order to issue those types of visa, the embassies and consulates of the Republic of Azerbaijan in different countries require a special letter (telex) approved by the Ministry of Foreign Affairs of the Republic of Azerbaijan ("MFA") based on the letter of invitation issued by the inviting company in Azerbaijan. The inviting company can get this telex within 3-4 working days via nominated travel agents at certain fees (which vary from USD 190 to USD 550 depending on the nationality of the applicant).

Asan Visa system has been introduced in 2016 in order to simplify the electronic visa system. Electronic visas are issued only to the citizens of the countries, the list of which has been approved by the MFA, and to stateless persons permanently residing in those countries. Electronic visa application is made through https://evisa.gov.az/en/ portal and 2 types of electronic visas differ:
(i) Standard visa (issued within 3 days);
(ii) Urgent visa (issued within 3 hours).

An electronic visa is for single entry and valid for 90 days. Duration of stay in the country may not exceed 30 days.

Foreigners and stateless persons temporarily residing in the Republic of Azerbaijan for more than 10 days (including cases when they change residence within the country) should apply to the State Migration Service of the Republic of Azerbaijan online or by directly applying to regional migration departments within 10 days after arriving in the country. No fee will be charged for the registration. Registration periods are:
(i) Persons arriving upon visa—or the period of stay indicated on visa;
(ii) Persons arriving under visa-free regime—for 90 days.

Penalty for failure to register upon place of stay is up to AZN 400.

b. Restrictions for Exit and Entry

Expatriates entering the country based on respective visas should observe the declared purpose of their visit. Accordingly, expatriate should obtain appropriate type of visa before entering the country.

Migration Code states some restrictions to foreigners and stateless persons for entering the country. Entry of foreigners and stateless persons to the Republic of Azerbaijan may be prohibited in the following cases:

(i) if this is required for the purposes of national security or maintenance of public order, or protection of the rights and legal interests of Azerbaijani citizens and other persons;

(ii) if there is information that a person committed an offence against peace and humanity, terrorism, financing of terrorism, or he/she is a member of a transnational organized criminal group;

(iii) if a person is imprisoned for committing a crime against citizens of the Republic of Azerbaijan or interests of the Republic of Azerbaijan, if his/her imprisonment has not been terminated or annulled;

(iv) if a person deported from the Republic of Azerbaijan previously, and such restriction to his/her entry to the country still exists;

(v) if a person is considered a persona-non-grata in the Republic of Azerbaijan;

(vi) if a person violated the purposes which he/she declared when he/she was in the Republic of Azerbaijan previously;

(vii) if a person gives false information of the purpose of his/her travel, when submitting an application for entry to the Republic of Azerbaijan;

(viii) when a person has been charged with administrative liabilities for violating the migration laws and regulations twice or more in the last 3 years;

In cases set forth in points (vi) to (viii) above, foreigners and stateless persons are prohibited to enter the country for 5 years.

D. Trade Union and Labour Organizations

Employees may establish a trade union on a voluntary basis without any prior permission of employers. Together with trade unions, employees may also establish other self-government agencies and the employers are entitled to establish representations.

Trade unions are not dependent on government agencies, enterprises, political parties and public associations and do not report to those authorities. They can participate in the preparation of labour, social and economic legislative acts. Trade unions and other representations are entitled to draft, enter into and amend collective contracts and agreements. Rights, duties and authorities of trade unions are defined in the Law on Trade Unions and in the regulations of the trade unions.

Generally, unions and /or labour representations are one party of collective employment agreements. Agreement terms and conditions, including, but not limited to cumulative working regime (working days and days-off), as well as priority on granting of annual leave, implementation of compensation system, HSE trainings and assessment procedure, etc. are also coordinated with unions / representations.

Trade unions in Azerbaijan are united in the activity of Azerbaijan Trade Unions Confederation. While trade unions in other countries are still typical partners of employer in collective bargaining, in Azerbaijan such unions and / or representations do not have striking effect on labour relations.

So in practice, neither employees nor private companies tend to establish or coordinate with trade unions and / or representations. Positive results of unions' activity can be observed in a few companies (mostly state-owned).

E. Labour Disputes

Two types of labour disputes may be brought:
(i) Individual disputes;
(ii) Collective disputes (or class action claims).
Subject of collective dispute claims are the followings:
(i) discussions on entering into collective agreements and contracts;
(ii) execution of collective agreements and contracts;
(iii) amendments and addendums to existing agreements and contracts;
(iv) implementation of collective agreements and contracts;
(v) resolution of other labour and social problems to preserve the interests of members.

On receipt of a collective request, employer must respond to the employees or trade union in writing within five working days. Requests regarding collective agreements are reviewed within one month. If the employer completely or partially ignores the collective request or fails to respond in time, a collective labour dispute shall be considered to have begun.

While there are no specialized employment forums, trade unions of certain types of professionals provide specialized legal help to employees, who intend to bring a legal action against their employers.

As a preliminary step employee's representative from the trade union may initiate a discussion of the case with the concerned employer/company to seek for possibility of settling the dispute outside the court.

Although these cases happen quite often, the process is not expressly laid out in the legislation.

In case of individual labour disputes, an employee may also apply to the Labour Inspectorate under the Labour Ministry or file a claim directly to Azerbaijani courts.

Majority of labour disputes are resolved by a competent court of general jurisdiction, covering all the subject-matters, while a smaller percentage is resolved in alternative dispute resolution mechanism.

In general, matters over which courts have jurisdiction can be arbitrated in cases provided by law, international and bilateral agreements of Azerbaijan.

Labour Code of the Republic of Azerbaijan does not provide direct application to arbitration and mediation agreements. Hence, it is assumed that the parties have liberty to choose arbitration or other means of alternative dispute resolution through an agreement and in accordance with legislative acts, such as Law on International Arbitration and Civil Procedure Code.

In addition to above, we would like to inform that parties may use below-mentioned reconciliation methods to resolve collective labour disputes:
• reconciliation commission;
• mediator;
• labour arbitration.

Although it is not practical in Azerbaijan to do so, parties enjoy the right to go through alternative dispute resolution methods for labour disputes instead of applying to the courts.

V. Intellectual Property

A. Brief Introduction of IP Laws and Regulations

The Constitution of Azerbaijan recognizes the right to intellectual property (IP), and ensures the protection of IP rights of all persons. In order to clarify the norm of Constitution, and establish the legal basis of the protection of intellectual property rights, the Parliament of Azerbaijan approved some laws, and ratified international agreements.

The following laws are the primary pieces of legislation regulating the intellectual property rights:

(i) Law No. 504-IQ "Trademarks and Geographical Indications", adopted on 12th June 1998;
(ii) Law No. 312-IQ "On Patents", adopted on 25th July 1997;
(iii) Law No. 115-IQ "On Copyright and Related Rights", adopted on 5th July 1996;
(iv) Law No. 337-IIQ "On Legal Protection of Topographies of Integrated Circuits", adopted on 31st May 2002;
(v) Law No. 365-IVQ "On Protection of Intellectual Property Rights and Combatting Piracy", adopted on 22nd May 2012;
(vi) Law No. 460-IIQ "On Legal Protection of Azerbaijani Folklore Expressions", adopted on 16th May 2003;
(vii) Law No. 755-IIQ "On Legal Protection of Compilations of Data", adopted on 14th September 2004;
(viii) Law No. 197-IQ "On Selection Achievements", adopted on 15th November 1996.

In addition, below are the major laws that are designed to prevent intellectual property infringements:
(i) Criminal Code;
(ii) Civil Procedure Code;
(iii) Administrative Offences Code;
(iv) Law on approval of the Decision of the Rules on Customs Control of Transfer of Goods Protected by Intellectual Property Rights;
(v) Law on Anti-Monopoly Activity;
(vi) Law on Unfair Competition.

Law on Trademarks and Geographical Indications governs the relations arising out the registration, legal protection and use of trademarks and geographical indications in the Republic of Azerbaijan.

• Trademark–any sign or combination of signs which can be represented graphically and is capable of distinguishing the goods and services of one undertaker from those of another undertaker;

• Geographical indication–an indication which identify a good as originating in the territory of a State or region or locality in that territory, where a given quality, reputation or other characteristic of the good is essentially

attributable to its geographic origin;
- Collective mark–any sign, or combination of signs, registered under the name of union, association, and any other union;
- Transliteration–representation of letters of one alphabet with letters of another alphabet.

Trademarks and geographical indications, which are not registered in the Republic of Azerbaijan, but having force under the international treaties to which the Republic of Azerbaijan is a party have protection in accordance to the Law.

Law on Patents regulates property relationships and related personal non-property relationships arising out of creation, legal protection, and use of inventions, utility models and industrial designs.
- Invention–technical solutions relating to a product or technique in any sphere;
- Utility model–technical solutions relating to a facility;
- Industrial Design–the novel outward appearance of an article, art-constructive solution outward appearance of an article.

A foreign natural person or legal entity that do not have their residence or seat in Azerbaijan, have the same rights regarding the protection of their inventions as a domestic natural person and a legal entity, where such treatment derives from international treaties binding Azerbaijan.

The Criminal Code contains few provisions regarding violation of intellectual rights. In proscribes illegal use, import, producing, export, placing in the market and some other actions regarding objects of intellectual property. The penalty for violation of copyright rights or violation of patent rights can range from a fine to imprisonment for a period for up to 2 years.

B. Patent Application

Filing the application with the competent authority represents the initiation of the procedure for the protection of an invention. The application may be filed in a language other than Azerbaijan, but in that case the translation to Azerbaijani must be submitted as well. The elements of the application are: drawings, schemes, information about the author, detailed description of invention.

Foreign legal entities or natural persons, if there are no other cases stipulated by international agreements, which the Republic of Azerbaijan participates in, file application to respective body of executive power by patent attorney registered in the respective body of executive power of the Republic of Azerbaijan.

The application for invention or utility model shall relate to one invention or utility model only or to a group of inventions or utility models so linked as to satisfy the requirement of unity. Application shall contain the following:

(i) a request for the grant of patent, stating the names of the author (authors) and the legal entity or natural persons in whose name the grant of patent is sought, together with addresses of their places of residence or of business;

(ii) a description disclosing the subject matter of the invention or utility model sufficiently clear and complete for it to be carried out;

(iii) the claims shall define the subject matter of invention or utility model and supported by the description;

(iv) drawing and other material where necessary for the understanding of the subject matter of the application;

(v) an abstract.

C. Trademark Registration

Procedure of Trademark registration starts by filling an application for trademark registration. An application can be provided to competent authority in any language, but at the same time it must be submitted in Azeri language as well.

The elements of the application are: the request for trademark registration, information about applicant, the sign the protection is requested for, brief description of a sign, the list of goods and services (Nice Classification). The period from the time of application to certification can vary from 3 to 8 months.

A foreign natural person or legal entity can provide their application for registration of trademark through Patent Attorney. List of Patent Attorneys can be found in the Register of Patent Attorneys, kept by competent authority.

Trademark can also be registered in Azerbaijan through application to International Bureau (WIPO) indicating the Republic of Azerbaijan in the list of designated countries.

D. Measures for IP Protection

Standardization, Metrology and Patent Committee and State Copyright Agency are the main institutions in charge for protection of intellectual property rights, together with relevant courts and some other ministries and state services.

a. Protection of Copyright and Related Rights

According to the Criminal Code of the Republic of Azerbaijan violation of Copyright and related rights:

Illegal use of copyright and related rights objects, meaning illegal publishing or distribution of another's scientific, literary, art or other work, publishing or distribution of such misappropriated work, as well as compulsion to co-authorship and as a result of these acts damage caused was in significant size—Punishment can range from a fine to imprisonment for a period for up to 2 years.

According to the Law on Enforcement of Intellectual Property Rights and Fight against Piracy copies of the objects of copyright and related rights (audiovisual works, phonograms, videograms, computer programs, databases, books etc.) shall be marked with control mark issued by relevant executive agency for copyright issues. Deliberate destruction, falsification, illegal production, utilization and sale of control marks are prohibited.

b. Seizure and Confiscation of Infringing or Counterfeit Goods Rrom the Market

State Service for Antimonopoly Policy and Consumer Rights Protection is in charge for seizure and confiscation of infringing goods from market as well as a relevant court.

Right holder can send a letter to the Antimonopoly Service with a request to the check the market for presence of counterfeit or infringing goods. If such goods are identified the Antimonopoly Service can take measures on seizure and confiscation of infringing or counterfeit goods.

c. Protection of Patents

According to the Criminal Code of the Republic of Azerbaijan violation of invention and patent rights: Infringement of invention and patent rights is illegal use of invention or efficiency proposal, disclosure without well of author of essence of invention and efficiency proposal before official publication of data on them, assignment of authorship, compulsion to co-authorship and as a result of these acts the damage caused was in significant size— Punishment can range from a fine to imprisonment for a period for up to 2 years.

d. Protection of Trademarks

The use of trademark without consent of its owner is deemed to be the infringement of right to the protected trademark. The use of trademark, containing geographical indication on wines and spirits without consent of its owner is considered the infringement of right for the registered trademark.

Sanctions for infringement of rights:

Any person, who unlawfully uses a trademark and geographical indication, on the demand of the right owner, either fully or in part, shall be to discontinue the unlawful use and recompense the damage caused to the owner of the trademark.

The goods illegally provided with trademarks, geographical indications or signs which are similar with them to the extent of confuse are counterfeit.

When reviewing arguments in the civil court examination order, provided not damage legal rights of third parties, the court can make a decision on the removal from the commercial circulation or later destruction of below goods without paying compensation, independent of the danger level and scale of the violation of the law:

(i) of the goods that are object of violation of rights;

(ii) of the materials and equipment widely used in the production of counterfeit goods with the purpose of preventing rights violation that is feasible in the future.

The rights holder may request in the legal form the payment of compensation in return for the damage and expenditures caused by the person that produces counterfeit goods (as well as label or signs) or the person that knows or should know that s/he uses these goods (as well as label or signs).

When goods that are illegally supplied with trademarks and geographical indications are brought into the Republic of Azerbaijan (except transit goods or the goods that are obtained from free sale by the rights holder or with his/her permission in another country's territory), with the request of the right holder, the release of such goods to free circulation may be delayed for 10 business days by customs authorities.

The clearance of counterfeit products from customs territory those are intended for exportation shall be stopped with the decision of the customs authorities.

The rights owner shall have the right to file with customs a substantiated request to detain goods unlawfully bearing his sign while in transit across the border of the Republic of Azerbaijan and to disclose the name of the exporter, importer, transporter and the quantity of infringing goods.

VI. Environmental Protection

A. Department Supervising Environmental Protection

The environment protection primarily falls under the competence of the Ministry of Ecology and Natural Resources of the Republic of Azerbaijan (hereinafter "the Ministry of Ecology"). The Ministry of Ecology was established under the decree № 485 of the president of the Republic of Azerbaijan dated 23 May 2001. It is the executive state body implementing state policy in the field of protection of environment, organization of nature management, effective use and recovery of the underground water, reserves of mineral raw materials and terrestrial natural resources, monitoring and forecasting of hydro meteorological processes, restoration and improvement of soil fertility, land monitoring, geodesy and cartography within the territory of Azerbaijan, including the Caspian Sea (lake) area which is under the ownership of Azerbaijan.

Structurally, the Ministry of Ecology consists of such departments as: Department of Environmental Protection, Center of environmental control and protection of the Caspian coastal waters, scientific center on normative and technical normative legal acts, "Dangerous Wastes" Limited Liability Company and others.

Through Scientific center on normative and technical normative legal acts the Ministry of Ecology executes preparation of drafts laws and by-laws, enforcement of the laws regulating the environment protection, enacting secondary pieces of legislation (e.g. rulebooks, orders or instructions) and inspection and supervision of the companies' compliance with laws.

The National Monitoring Department on Environment Protection is mainly responsible for maintenance of the IT system of environment protection, monitoring quality of atmosphere, surface waters, environmental radioactivity and implementation of enacted programs for the control of quality, collection and processing of data on environment protection and preparation of reports on current situation of the environment. The Central analytical laboratory (Centre for Environmental Pollution Monitoring) of the National Monitoring Department on Environmental Protection consists of seven analytical laboratories in Baku and two in Districts (Gazakh and Beilagan). All of the laboratories have been accredited.

The Technical Committee on Ecology is a joint committee responsible for the adoption and implementation of international and intergovernmental standards in the territory of the Republic of Azerbaijan. It was created by the joint decree of the Ministry of the Ecology and State Committee on Standardization, Metrology and Patent on 29 June 2010. The Technical Committee on Ecology adopts standards in the field of environment management, quality of water, quality of air and quality of soil. Wide variety of such international standards as ISO 14031-99, AZS ISO 15799-2013, AZS ISO 10381-1-2014, and ISO 6060-1989 etc. were registered by the Committee.

The Caspian Complex Monitoring Administration conducts monitoring of 955 km long shore of Azerbaijan at 341 monitoring points, both run-offs entering the Caspian Sea and industrial installations (e.g. platforms) are functioning at the sea. Azerbaijan actively participated in the Transboundary Diagnostic Analysis (TDA) of the Caspian Sea developed in 2007 (the first one happened in 2002). TDA was a scientific and technical assessment, through which the water-related environmental problems of the Caspian Sea region were identified and quantified, their causes analyzed and their impacts, both environmental and economic were assessed.

B. Brief Introduction of Laws and Regulations of Environmental Protection

The environment protection is regulated through a vast number of laws and by-laws; this field of law is quite well developed. The basic legal framework pertaining to the environment protection is set out by the following laws and by-laws:

(i) The Law "on the Protection of Environment" (June 8, 1999, № 678-IQ) is the ground law in the environment protection legal framework. The Law determines legal, economic and social grounds for the protection of the environment. Purpose of the Law is ensuring ecological safety in the field of maintenance of ecological balance of the environment, prevention of harmful impacts of industrial and other categories of operations upon natural ecological systems, protection of biological diversity and organization of efficient use of nature;

(ii) The Law "on Environmental Safety" (June 8, 1999, № 677-IQ). Purpose of the Law is establishment of the legal framework for the purpose of protection of lives and health of individuals, the public, material and moral values thereof, the environment, including atmospheric air, cosmic space, water objects, subsurface, soils, natural landscapes, flora and fauna from hazards which may arise as a result of impact of natural and anthropogenic factors;

(iii) The Water Code (December 26, 1997, № 418-IQ). The Water Code regulates the legal relations connected with the usage and protection of water objects in Azerbaijan, covering both inland waters and the sector of Caspian Sea (lake) belonging to Azerbaijan;

(iv) The Forest Code (December 30, 1997, № 424-IQ). The Code establishes legal bases of regulation of forest relations, use, protection, preservation and reproduction of forests, growth of their ecological and resource potential on the territory of Azerbaijan;

(v) The Law "On Industrial and Domestic Waste" (June 30, 1998, № 514-IQ). The Law establishes the state policy in the area of environment protection from industrial and domestic waste in the form of substances and things formed in the country as a result of human activity, decrease of dangerous influence of the given waste, maintenance of ecological balance in the nature, use of waste as a secondary raw material, regulates the relations connected with the waste, except the harmful gases, polluted waters and radioactive waste;

(vi) The Law "On Protection of Air" (March 27, 2001, № 109-IIQ). The Law establishes legal bases for protection of atmospheric air; and is directed to realization of the right of humans to live in favorable environment and to receive correct information on environment;

(vii) The Law "on Water Supply and Sewage" (October 28, 1999, № 723-IQ). Purpose of the Law consists of regulating relations in the area of supply of the people, enterprises, establishments and organizations with good quality water meeting the requirements of state standards in necessary quantity, discharge sewage;

(viii) The Law "On Land Fertility" (October 30, 1999, № 788-IQ). The Law establishes legal basis of restoration, increase and protection of the land fertility which is under the state, municipal and private property;

(ix) The Law "On radiation safety of the population" (December 30, 1997, № 423-IQ). The Law defines legal basis of accident-free activity in the field of ionizing radiation sources, radiation protection and public health care;

(x) The Law "On Subsoil" (February 13, 1998, № 439-IQ). The Law governs the relations arising out of study (search, investigation), rational use and protection of subsoil of the country's territory, including the Azerbaijani sector of the Caspian Sea (lake) with safe work, provides when using subsoil protection of interests of the state, subsoil users and citizens when using subsoil;

(xi) Criminal Code (1999). The Code provides criminal liability for the breach of the abovementioned ecological laws. The list of the ecological crimes includes among others, infringement of protection rules on environment by manufacture of works, water (water sources) pollution, pollution of the atmospheric air, destruction or damage of woods etc.;

(xii) Code on Administrative Offences (2015). The Code provides administrative liability for the breach of the abovementioned ecological laws.

C. Evaluation of Environmental Protection

The Republic of Azerbaijan created its system of the environmental protection at the end of the 20th and the beginning of 21st Century. However, during the last 5 years a large number of activities have been implemented by the Ministry of Ecology and Natural Resources. "State Program on Poverty Reduction and Sustainable Development in the Republic of Azerbaijan for 2008-2015", "State Program of socio-economic development of regions of the Republic of Azerbaijan for 2014-2018", "State Program on alternative and renewable energy sources in the Republic of Azerbaijan", "State program on the socio-economic development of Baku and its suburban settlements for 2014-2016" and other events were intended in the programs confirmed by the head of the government. The environmental protection policy is mainly focused on earth surface protection, waste management, flora and fauna protection, control of atmosphere air, soil, water resources protection, raise of public awareness and etc.

According to the Second Environmental Performance Review of Azerbaijan by the United Nations Economic Commission for Europe dated 2011, since its establishment in 2001, the Ministry of Ecology has succeeded in promoting sectorial integration by developing environmental programs and action plans, and by contributing to the development of programs on sustainable development in cooperation with other ministries and State agencies.

Azerbaijan started assessing a draft law on Environmental Impact Assessment in 2015, prepared with support of UNECE. Also, on May 2009 the loan agreement on "Integrated Solid Waste Management" Project was signed between the Ministry of Economy on behalf of the Government of Azerbaijan and the World Bank in the framework of the Absheron Rehabilitation Program. Project intends to improve and support the modernization of the solid waste management system. An additional funding agreement within the Integrated Solid Waste Management Project was concluded in 2014 in order to further improve the ecological situation of the capital city. The main waste landfill was rehabilitated, the biggest solid waste incineration plan in CIS and Eastern Europe was opened, institutional reforms were proposed and a new legal framework was drafted in line with the relevant EU acquits within the Project. Currently, the Project is on the final phase and respective legislative amendments are expected to happen.

In addition, Azerbaijan shifted to the Euro-4 ecological standard in 2014, seeking to reduce the emission of vehicle pollutants into the atmosphere and improve the environmental situation in the country. Azerbaijan participates in the Clean Development Mechanism (CDM) as a non-Annex 1 party to the Kyoto Protocol.

To conclude, Azerbaijan has the necessary legal framework for ensuring the environmental protection system and improvement of this framework is among the top priorities of the government in order to modernize it and comply with the best practice.

VII. Dispute Resolution

A. Methods and Bodies of Dispute Resolution

a. The Traditional Dispute Resolution Mechanism in Azerbaijan is the Litigation

a) The court system of Azerbaijan consists of three instances:

(i) Courts of first instance—district (city) courts, military courts, administrative-economical courts and courts on grave crimes.

(ii) Courts of appeal—function in 6 regions of the country and consist of 4 boards—civil, criminal, military and administrative-economical boards.

(iii) Court of cassation—there are 4 boards under the Supreme Court—civil, criminal, military and administrative-economical boards.

There are also exceptional instances such as the Constitutional Court and additional cassation in the Supreme Court which hear specific cases.

The litigation process, especially time frame of litigation has been described below in detail.

• Courts of first instance:

A case must be heard and settled within 3 (three) months from the date of receipt of a statement of claim by the court. In employment litigation and in disputes arising out of the mortgage agreement this period is 1 (one) month.

Entry into legal force: If the court decision has not been appealed, it enters into legal force after 1 (one) month upon its issue.

Period for an appeal: Appeal may be submitted within 1 (one) month upon official submission of the court decision.

• Courts of appeal:

A case must be heard in courts of appeal within 3 (three) months of its submission to the court.

Entry into legal force: If the decision of the court of appeal has not been appealed, it enters into legal force after 2 (two) months upon its issue.

Period for cassation appeal: The appeal may be submitted within 2 (two) months upon official submission of the court decision.

• Court of cassation:

A case must be heard in court of cassation within 2 (two) months of its submission to the court.

Entry into legal force: The decision of the court of cassation enters into legal force from the moment of its issuance.

This is the general overview of the court system and the period of litigation. In specific circumstances, there may be different terms other than stated herein.

Civil and commercial litigation are mainly regulated by the Civil Procedural Code of the Republic of Azerbaijan and the Law on "Courts and Judges" dated 10 June 1997.

b) Exclusive jurisdiction of Azerbaijani courts

Under Article 444 of the Civil Procedural Code of the Republic of Azerbaijan, the followings fall under the exclusive jurisdiction of Azerbaijani courts:

(i) Cases relating to property right over immovable property, including cases with regard to lease or mortgage of such immovable property, if their subject-matter is located in the territory of the Republic of Azerbaijan;

(ii) Cases relating to recognition of validity or invalidity of legal entity and dissolution of legal entity, or cases on claims for termination of its decisions, if the legal entity has legal address (place of location) in the Republic of Azerbaijan;

(iii) Cases relating to claims in respect of recognition of validity of patents, marks or other rights where registration or application for registration of these rights has been carried out in the Republic of Azerbaijan;

(iv) If the decision rendered during court review on mandatory enforcement proceedings, raised or enforced in the Republic of Azerbaijan;

(v) Cases relating to claims against carriers arising out of carriage contracts;

(vi) Cases relating to dissolution of marriage of citizens of the Republic of Azerbaijan with foreigners or stateless persons, if both spouses have place of residence in the Republic of Azerbaijan.

b. Arbitration

Under Article 42 of the Law on "Protection of Foreign Investment" dated 15 January 1992, the disputes between foreign investors, entities with foreign investments and the state authorities of the Republic of Azerbaijan, enterprises, public organizations, and other legal entities may be settled in the arbitration or in an international arbitration upon mutual agreement of the parties.

The main legal instrument on arbitration is the Law on "International Arbitration", dated 18 November 1999.

This Law applies: to international commercial arbitration; and if the place of arbitration is the Republic of Azerbaijan.

On 18 October 1992, Azerbaijan acceded to the "Convention on the settlement of investment disputes between States and nationals of other States", Washington 1965 ("ICSID").

Azerbaijan also is a party to European Convention on International Commercial Arbitration (Geneva, 21 April 1961).

a) Recognition and enforcement of foreign arbitral awards in the Republic of Azerbaijan

Under the Civil Procedural Code, the competent court for hearing the application on recognition and enforcement of foreign arbitral awards is the Supreme Court of the Republic of Azerbaijan. As a general rule, the Supreme Court hears the case within two months from the moment when the application entered into the court.

b) Recognition or Dismissal of Application

The Supreme Court may either recognize the foreign arbitral award or dismiss the application on recognition and enforcement. If all the documents meet the requirements set out in the Civil Procedural Code and if there is no grounds for dismissal of application, then the Supreme Court recognizes the foreign arbitral award.

Nevertheless, the Supreme Court may dismiss the application on recognition and enforcement of foreign arbitral awards in the following circumstances:

(i) If the case refers to the exclusive jurisdiction of the courts of the Republic of Azerbaijan;

(ii) If a party failed to attend the hearing as a result of not being timely and duly notified as to the date and time of the hearing;

(iii) If there is a decision of the courts of the Republic of Azerbaijan which have already entered into force between the same parties, on the same subject-matter and on the same grounds;

(iv) If Azerbaijani courts have commenced, prior to commencement of the case in the arbitration tribunal of foreign countries, proceeding on the case between the same parties, the same subject-matter and based on the same grounds;

(v) If the award has not entered into force in accordance with the legislation of the state where the award was issued;

(vi) If the enforcement of the award contradicts with the main principles of the legislation and sovereignty of the Republic of Azerbaijan;

(vii) If the reciprocity principle has not been met;

(viii) If a party to the arbitration agreement was lacking of legal capacity;

(ix) If the arbitration agreement has been deemed to be invalid;

(x) If an award was issued with respect to a dispute not contemplated in the arbitration agreement;

(xi) If an award was issued with respect to a dispute that does not match to the terms of the arbitration agreement;

(xii) If a composition of arbitration or arbitration rules does not correspond to the agreement of the parties;

(xiii) If an award has been cancelled or suspended under the laws of a state where it was issued.

The Republic of Azerbaijan is a party to Convention on the Recognition and Enforcement of Foreign Arbitral Awards (New York, 1958) (accessed on 29 February 2000). In addition to Civil Procedural Code New York Convention is applied to the recognition and enforcement of foreign arbitral awards.

c) Enforcement

Once the decision of the court comes into force, then the court issues a writ of execution and sends it to the respective law enforcement office.

If a defendant is physical person, then the writ of execution is enforced either in the place of its residence, or in its workplace or in a place where its property located. If a defendant is a legal entity, then the writ of execution is enforced either in the place where such legal entity is registered (where the legal address is) or in the place where its property located.

Once the enforcement officer receives a writ of execution, then it:

(i) Issues a decision on commencement of enforcement proceedings;

(ii) Sends a notification to the defendant to voluntarily perform the writ of execution within 10 (ten) days.

If a defendant fails to voluntarily perform the writ of execution within 10 (ten) days, then the enforcement officer is entitled to perform mandatory enforcement measures (such as attachment of salary, attachment of bank assets, attachment of vehicles, attachment of immovable properties etc.). The defendant's right to leave the territory of the Republic of Azerbaijan may also be restricted by the court based on the request of enforcement officer.

It should be noted that the statutory time limit for enforcement is 2 (two) months and in exceptional cases it may be extended for 1 (one) month. However, in practice enforcement proceedings may last longer than the period stated in the Law on Enforcement to enforce the writ of execution.

The speediness of enforcement also largely depends on cooperation of third parties, such as the banks and state authorities (the State Registry Service of Immovable Property, tax authorities, the State Traffic Police and so on).

It should also be emphasized that the Law on Enforcement contemplates 7% (seven per cent) enforcement fee of the amount to be enforced from the defendant.

c. Mediation

Mediation as a type of alternative dispute resolution is new to Azerbaijan. There is no specific regulation with regard to mediation. However, Azerbaijani law does not prohibit to use the mediation as a method of dispute resolution.

VIII. Others

A. Anti-commercial Bribery

a. Brief Introduction of Anti-commercial Bribery Laws and Regulations

The Criminal Code of the Republic of Azerbaijan and the law on Combating Corruption are the main legislative acts relating to anti-bribery and anti-corruption in Azerbaijan.

Since the mid-2000s Azerbaijan has adopted and implemented state programs, national action plans and national strategy documents on combatting corruption. Azerbaijan is also party to the following international conventions:
 (i) the Council of Europe Civil Law Convention on Corruption (1999);
 (ii) the Council of Europe Criminal Law Convention on Corruption (1999); and
 (iii) the United Nations Convention against Corruption (2004).

b. Department Supervising Anti-commercial Bribery

A state agency Anti-Corruption General Directorate under the Prosecutor General, established in 2004, heads the investigations upon corruption offences and violations against anti-corruption regulations, cooperates with international and non-governmental organizations, public and media institutions, specialized experts in order to spread the awareness in anti-corruption issues and strengthen in-field policy implementing by state.

Governmental Commission on Combating Corruption is the specialized body on fighting against the corruption. Established in 2004, the Commission participates in formation of anti-corruption policy, makes legislative contributions, coordinates the public institutions' and state bodies' work in order to provide general fight against corruption, collects financial declarations and so on. The Commission functions with the structure composed of 15 members. 5 members of the Commission are appointed by the President of Republic of Azerbaijan, 5 by the Parliament and the rest 5 by Constitutional Court. It participates in the formation of the state policy on corruption and coordinates the activity of public institutions in this area;

c. Punitive Actions

The offences are all to be found within the Criminal Code of the Republic of Azerbaijan. Only those offences defined by the Criminal Code will be considered to be an offence. The offences in the area of bribery and corruption that are recognized under the legislation in Azerbaijan are:
 (i) fulfillment of official duties in bad faith;
 (ii) spending state budget, defined state funds and off-budget state funds for purposes other than the defined;
 (iii) spending state funds without procurement processes or illegal state procurement;
 (iv) overuse of official duties;
 (v) embezzlement of another official's duties;
 (vi) requesting/accepting bribe (Passive bribe);
 (vii) offering/giving bribe (Active bribe);
 (viii) illegal influence to official decisions;
 (ix) service forgery;
 (x) negligence;
 (xi) adopting illegal decisions on parcel that solely belong to the state;

(xii) designating parcels, or allowing construction works by breaching legislative regulations; and
(xiii) failure to prevent construction works launched by breaching legislative regulations.

a) Bribery

A bribe is defined as directly or indirectly requesting/accepting/offering/giving material or non-material values/immunity/privilege by state and public officials, judges, private persons, legal entities, or international organisations. In accordance with the Law on Combating Corruption, public officials, either on their own behalf or for others, are prohibited from requesting or receiving gifts that can influence impartial execution of its official duties, or that give the impression of doing so, or gifts that are given against the execution of its official duties or establish an impression that it is a gift of that kind. As long as it does not have any influence on the impartial execution of their official duties, public officials may receive small gifts or basic hospitality in the amount of a total of AZN55 (approximately USD32) during one calendar year.

Facilitation payments are prohibited and are treated as a bribe in Azerbaijan. The receipt of a bribe is an offence. Failure to prevent bribery is not an offence.

Bribery between directors and authorized officials/managers of commercial entities or sole proprietors is covered by the legal framework.

b) Accounting Provisions

The following offences are defined as relating to accounting/book keeping in Azerbaijan:
(i) the legalization of money/property acquired by illegal means;
(ii) the acquisition of money/property whilst being aware that it had previously been illegally obtained; and
(iii) the embezzlement of money/material goods.

c) Intermediaries

In accordance with the legislation, an offence committed by intermediaries renders them participants in the crime as well.

d) Corruption

The relevant tests for corruption offences are to establish whether they have been committed by officials (public officials, elected officials, officials of SOEs/public legal persons/commercial organisations/non-commercial organisations) by the use of their authority and by non-official persons (for giving/offering bribery);

The requirements for these offences are that the offender's intention and motive is to obtain material or non-material values, or immunity, or privilege.

e) Scope

Corruption is considered to be a grave crime, according to Azerbaijani law, and the statute of limitation is 12 years.

Criminal legislation is applicable to the offences committed within the borders of the Republic of Azerbaijan, also in its territorial waters, the part of the Caspian Sea that belongs to Azerbaijan, in aerial territory above Azerbaijan, and on the ships that are registered in Azerbaijan and carry the Azerbaijani flag.

Criminal legislation is applicable to a person who has committed a corruption crime in another jurisdiction but has not been convicted for it.

The persons who are liable for these offences are:
(i) elected or appointed persons in governmental authorities;
(ii) all civil servants holding administrative positions;
(iii) any person with managerial or administrative functions in governmental, municipal or quasi-governmental entities;
(iv) registered candidates for elected positions; and
(v) officials of SOEs/public legal persons/commercial organisations/non-commercial organisations.

These persons hold complete criminal liability for their own actions. However, the legislation does not imply any liability for the acts of others. Vicarious liability does not apply at corporate level; the legislation does not yet hold corporations liable for actions of their employees.

f) Penalties on Conviction

Upon conviction, the penalties for the offences described above are:
(i) monetary penalties;
(ii) A ban on taking any official position;
(iii) imprisonment of up to 12 years.

The application of these penalties depend on:
(i) whether or not they have been committed for the first time;
(ii) whether they have been committed by one person or a group;
(iii) The amount in question; and
(iv) whether or not they have been committed under threat.

B. Project Contracting

a. Permission System

An owner should apply to relevant local authority with an application, which contains following documents, in order to obtain a permit for construction works:

(i) Document on ownership, use or lease rights over the land;
(ii) Project documentation.

Additionally, an extract from the state register of legal entities is needed, if the owner is a legal entity.

The local authority checks the application for completeness within five days. The local authority notifies the applicant if any document is missing or correction is needed and provides ten days to present the missing document or correction.

If the application is completed, the local authority obtains opinions of the relevant state bodies, such as Ministry of Emergencies, State Committee for Urban Construction and Architecture and so on. The local authority also notifies neighbors and takes their views into account. Moreover, the local authority must obtain an expert opinion of General State Department for Expert Examinations under Ministry of Emergencies for the permit proceedings. Rules on Expert Examination of Construction Projects were adopted by Presidential Decree No. 348, 2014, which determines the mechanism for expert examination of the compliance of construction projects. Overall, the local authority responses on the application for a construction permit within three months.

If the application is successful, the local authority decides to issue a permit, which is the basis for commencement of the construction works, and the technical conditions for the construction.

The permit loses its validity, if the construction is not commenced within three years of the date of the permit, or if the construction is suspended for three years.

Finally, one cannot use a completed construction without an exploitation permit. The owner applies to the local authority with following documents for an exploitation permit:

(i) construction permit;
(ii) acts issued by relevant organizations confirming that internal and external engineering-communication systems are ready for exploitation;
(iii) letter regarding the address of construction;
(iv) act of acceptance of the elevators for exploitation;
(v) letter from the local executive authority regarding the acceptance of connected communication lines;
(vi) letter from the Center for Hygiene and Epidemiology regarding the compliance of the construction with sanitary-hygienic and sanitary-epidemiological requirements;
(vii) letter regarding the main project and factual characteristics of the facility;
(viii) letter regarding the financial expenses of the facility (if the object is constructed with state funds);
(ix) act of the facility's compliance with fire safety requirements;
(x) ecological safety act for industrial and production facilities from the Ministry of Ecology and Natural Resources;
(xi) act of State Agency for Supervision of Safety in Construction under Ministry of Emergencies issued along with participation of the representatives of the owner, contractor and the designer regarding the compliance of the construction works with the urban and construction normative acts and the construction project;
(xii) Permits for the parts of the construction which were issued before the final and full use of the facility.

Some specific types of facilities may require additional documents in order to obtain an exploitation permit. For example, the owner needs to submit an act from State Traffic Police of Ministry of Internal Affairs on the readiness of the roads for use for obtaining an exploitation permit for roads. The local authority responds to the application within thirty days. It may either reject the application or grant a permit for exploitation of the construction. Apart from the usual permits, construction works in certain areas (such as cultural and historical reserves) require additional authorization from state authorities.

b. Prohibited Areas

Landslide areas are prohibited to conduct construction works by the Decree of Cabinet of Ministers. Ministry of Emergencies and Ministry of Ecology and National Resources deal with conduction of researches to determine the areas with potential landslide danger and report it to Cabinet of Ministers, which prohibits conducting construction works (except the works conducting against landslide) at those areas. The map of these areas is confirmed by Cabinet of Ministers.

c. Invitation to Bid and Bidding

All resident and non-resident physical or legal persons or union of legal persons irrespective of state belonging may be entitled to take part in public procurement procedures held in Azerbaijan as bidders. Procurement agency publish announcement about tender or send personal invitation to consignors (contractors) for participation in tender after the approval of tender documents and tender announcement by tender committee. Along with issuance of announcement about open tender, procurement agency may send personal invitation to consigners (contractors) for participation in tender. In order to attract proposals, offers and quotations at other procurement methods, Tender Committee produces list of sufficient number (not less than three) of potential consignors (contractors) and send personal invitation to them.

The following are indicated in announcement (invitation) about tender:

(i) information about organizer of tender;

(ii) time and place of commencement of tender procedures;

(iii) tax and duty benefits (if provided) relating to procurement contract;

(iv) documents necessary to take part in tender;

(v) office telephone and fax number of coordinator to get additional information;

(vi) conditions of tender proposal's guarantee; name, quantity (volume), place of delivery of goods, features and place of works performed, description and place of services provided;

(vii) required terms of shipping of goods and completion of works or schedule of provision of services;

(viii) criteria and procedures which are given preference in assessment and comparison of qualification indices of consignors (contractors);

(ix) conditions limiting participation of consignors (contractors) in procurement procedures because of state belonging;

(x) amount of participation fee and its payment procedure;

(xi) language or languages which bidding documents has been prepared in;

(xii) Deadline and place of submission of tender proposals.

(i), (ii), (vii)-(x) and (xii)th are also added to collection of documents on qualification compliance determination procedures. At preparation of documents, reflecting features at first stage of tender procedures, procurement agency isentitled to exclude or change any aspect of technical or qualitative characteristics of procured goods (works and services), any criteria for assessment, comparison of tender proposals and determination of tender proposal as well as add new characteristics and criteria. Information about any such change or addition is provided to consignors (contractors) when invitation about submission of final tender proposal is sent.

巴林

作者：Abdulrahman Zainal、Qays H. Zu'bi、Noor Al Taraif
译者：刘炯、杨晨

一、概述

（一）政治、经济、社会与法律环境概述

巴林王国（以下简称"巴林"）是位于波斯湾的阿拉伯君主立宪制国家。巴林与沙特阿拉伯通过26公里的大桥相连，由30多个岛屿组成，面积约765平方公里。巴林人口约150万[1]，其中一半以上是非本国国民。尽管阿拉伯语是巴林的官方语言，但大多数人都会说英语，并且通常将英语作为商业语言。

随着1602年葡萄牙占领的结束，波斯人对巴林的控制也在1783年阿勒哈利法部落夺取控制权时结束。作为一个受英国保护的前酋长国，巴林于1971年宣布独立，并决定不加入先前的"特鲁西尔酋长国"，也就是后来的阿拉伯联合酋长国。

1. 政治

自现任国王哈马德本·伊萨·阿勒哈利法（Hamad bin Isa bin Salman Al Khalifa）于1999年成为巴林第一任君主以来，巴林政府一直处于稳定状态。哈马德国王确立了议会选举制度，授予女性投票权，并释放了所有政治犯。2002年，随着该国成为君主立宪制国家，他成为巴林的第一位国王。相应地，国王享有广泛的行政权力，其中包括任命总理及其部长、指挥该国的军队、担任最高司法委员会主席、任命议会上议院（Majlis Al-Shura）议员和解散议会民选下议院（Majlis Al-Nuwab）。

根据巴林宪法，立法权归国王和国民议会。国民议会由上议院和下议院组成，讨论和审议共同关心的问题。议员共80人（每个议院各40人），任期4年，上议院的成员由国王任命，下议院的成员则由选举产生。上议院对当选的下议院通过的法案有事实上的否决权，因为法案在被提交给国王并可能通过成为法律之前，必须先得到他们的批准。

2. 经济

尽管受旅游业强劲推动，但巴林的经济仍然严重依赖石油、铝和建筑材料等的出口。不过更重要的是，通信部门和金融/银行部门的繁荣。

虽然由于石油收入下降导致经济总体上增长缓慢，但巴林已实施财政整顿措施。征税、增加政府服务费和补贴改革将有助于经济复苏。此外，海湾阿拉伯国家合作委员会（GCC）发展基金赞助的投资数量不断增加，也使得非石油部门充满活力。

3. 社会

巴林是一个限制很少、生活成本相对较低的国家，它是众多备受认可的跨国公司和主要工业项目的所在地。2017年，巴林被认为是最适合外籍人士居住的国家。[2] 外籍员工主要是来自世界各地的政府雇员、专业人士、技术人员、劳工和商人。鉴于此，巴林没有外汇管制或对货币汇出进行管制。

4. 法律

巴林制定了国家宪法和法律。正如其他海湾阿拉伯国家合作委员会成员国构建了自己的民法体系或罗马日耳曼法律体系一样，巴林也是这样做的。其法律制度有各种来源，如伊斯兰教法、埃及法（民事、刑事和商业）和英国普通法，例如，巴林有自己的《民法》《商业公司法》《商法》《劳动法》等。此外，只有巴林的上诉法院——巴林最高上诉法院作出的判决才是具有约束力的判例。

---

[1] 参见 http://www.worldometers.info/world-population/bahrain-population/。
[2] 参见 https://www.thenational.ae/business/economy/bahrain-tops-best-expat-country-in-the-world-to-live-survey-1.626406。

由于法律现代化的必要性，巴林中央银行（CBB）也推出了资本市场《规则手册》，规定了有关营销、发行和销售各种金融产品的规则和程序。[①] 还有一套关于集体投资事业的先进法规，以确保巴林中央银行的充分监督。因此，许多主要的国际银行和保险集团都已进驻巴林。

（二）"一带一路"倡议下与中国企业合作的现状及趋势

2016年1月，中国外交部发布了中国对阿拉伯国家政策文件。[②] 该文件阐述了中国与阿拉伯国家之间的历史关系，同时着重强调了维护这种关系的倡议，以共同构建"丝绸之路经济带"。

鉴于上述情况，中国与阿拉伯国家之间始终保持着健康的经济关系，特别是因为这些国家是中国主要的原油供应国和第七大贸易伙伴。这种合作预计将会继续下去，以实现政策目标。为实现"1+2+3"合作模式的目标，各方将以能源合作为重点，以贸易与基础设施建设为两翼，以核能、卫星和新能源领域的创新技术进步三项为发展目标，达成业务合作。

如今，基于中国的"一带一路"倡议，巴林已经成为中国企业进入中东地区的枢纽（例如华为技术有限公司和中国银行）。中国不仅是巴林经济发展委员会（EDB）最重要的贸易伙伴之一，而且自1990年成立中国、巴林经济、贸易和技术合作混合委员会以来，中国已经成为巴林最大的非海湾阿拉伯国家合作委员会成员的出口市场和主要进口国之一。

二、投资

（一）市场准入

1. 投资监管部门

致力于促进投资的政府部门包括巴林经济发展委员会（负责评估和制定巴林经济战略并吸引投资的机构）和巴林 Mumtalakat 控股公司（巴林主权财富基金，旨在投资债券、股份和股票）。后者主要投资石油和天然气以外的资产，并持有一系列公司的股份。

2. 投资行业法律、法规

虽然《商业公司法》（CCL）[③] 对商业活动进行监管并规定相关手续和程序，但目前还没有直接管理外国投资的法律。不过，目前也有其他专门管理特定行业的法律，其中包括巴林《海商法》[④]（涉及航运法的各个方面）、《保险法》（涵盖与保险公司有关的事宜，但不得违反巴林中央银行法律）[⑤] 以及巴林中央银行与金融机构法[⑥]。

巴林中央银行《规则手册》为受监管行业的特定主体提供了进一步的规则。例如，《规则手册》第三卷为保险公司和再保险公司提供了规则，并对违规行为设置了处罚。

3. 投资方式

通过一系列投资形式，外国公司可以在巴林设立全资子公司和分支机构，且对其监管要求很少，例如，在某些情况下，不要求在巴林国内具有担保人。此外，尽管巴林的数个自由贸易区为投资提供了更便利的条件（例如，零关税和国内劳动力雇用豁免），但因为没有企业或个人所得税（参见下文的税收部分），该国自由贸易区以外的地区也为投资创造了理想的环境。

4. 准入条件及审查

对外国投资的主要限制是，在巴林成立的公司必须至少有51%的股份由巴林国民所有。但是，这取决于该外国公司的分支机构是否是以运营办公室的形式而存在，以及该公司所从事的业务活动是否允许由100%的外资所有。当外资为海湾阿拉伯国家合作委员会成员国的国民所有，或者公司设立在

---

① 巴林中央银行《规则手册》和法规参见 http://www.cbb.gov.bh/home.php。
② 参见 http://www.china.org.cn/world/2016-01/14/content_37573547.htm。
③ 经2014年第50号法令修正的2001年第21号法令。
④ 经2014年第35号法令修正的1982年第23号法令。
⑤ 1987年第17号法令。
⑥ 经2015年第34号法令修正的2006年第64号法令。

自由贸易区时，情况也可能有所不同。

某些行业和活动可能还会受到如行业许可等进一步的限制，也可能会使公司受到额外的监管。

（二）外汇管理

1. 外汇监管部门

暂无。

2. 外汇法律、法规简介

巴林的自由市场经济提高了透明度，没有对外汇的管制或对资本、利润、股息汇回的限制。因此，这些资本、利润、股息可以实现自由流通。

3. 外资企业外汇管理要求

暂无。

（三）融资

1. 主要金融机构

根据 2006 年第 64 号关于施行《巴林中央银行和金融机构法》的法令，巴林中央银行成立（以前称为巴林货币机构）。巴林中央银行总部设在首都麦纳麦的外交区。巴林中央银行负责各种事宜，包括实施货币政策、监管金融部门、担任政府的财政代理人、管理巴林的外汇现金和黄金储备。

由于巴林中央银行涵盖了银行业、保险业、投资业务和资本市场业务，巴林中央银行负责许可和监管众多实体。除此之外，它还负责确定巴林第纳尔兑换主要外币（目前与美元挂钩）的汇率。

巴林在金融领域享有盛誉，许多外国公司在此处设立商业中心，许多本国和外国银行在此处设址。这里不仅汇集了零售、投资和伊斯兰银行产业，还吸引了多家外国银行在巴林设立代表处。

2. 外资企业融资条件

对于设立于巴林的主体而言，开设银行账户是一个相对简单和直接的过程。受到反洗钱措施的限制，银行通常只允许为巴林国民和居民开立银行账户，这使得营业地不在巴林的商业实体难以使用账户服务。应当注意到，支票簿的开立也仅限于巴林国民和居民，而不包括外国公司或个人。

巴林境内的公司也可以更便捷地享受融资服务。尽管如此，这并不妨碍外国实体获得相同的服务，即使其营业地不在巴林。在享受相关便利服务前，这些实体需要依照惯例接受信用评级核查及其他的必要检查。

（四）土地政策

1. 土地法律、法规简介

调查和土地登记局（SLRB）是负责进行土地登记的政府机构，其登记土地的所有权由国王担保。2017 年第 27 号法令颁布的《房地产行业管理法》取代了 2014 年第 28 号法令颁布的《房地产开发法》。虽然新法与旧法相似，但其目的在于使巴林的房地产现代化，并对新的问题和概念作出回应。还建立了房地产管理局（RERA），作为巴林所有房地产的监管机构，以及必要的许可证的颁发机构。

2. 外资企业获得土地规定

根据 2001 年第 2 号立法令的规定，外国买家（自然人和公司）可以在巴林特定地区购买特定类型的房产。就购买程序而言，与世界各地的做法非常相似。

（五）企业设立与关闭

1. 企业形式

《商业公司法》承认八种类型的企业形式并允许外资在以上所有类型的企业中持有股权（外资完全所有则可能有不同规定）。以其他形式设立公司的，无效，以该企业名义签订合约的个人将向第三方承担连带责任。企业的合法形式如下：

- 普通合伙公司；
- 有限合伙公司；
- 参股合作公司（合资企业）；
- 股份制公司；
- 股份制有限合伙；
- 有限责任公司；
- 一人公司；
- 控股公司。

根据法律规定，外国公司设立的分支机构不构成独立的公司，被认为是外国母公司的一部分，受到该公司的规章或决定的约束，因此将其承担的责任限定在母公司的资产范围内。通过提供担保和任命当地经理人，外国公司即可建立一家分支机构，且没有最低资本要求。外国公司的分支机构可采取以下形式：

- 代表处或区域办事处：不得进行经营活动，仅用于在巴林设立商业存在且只能进行营销和推广活动。
- 运营办公室：可以开展业务，包括银行业务和保险业务（须经巴林中央银行批准），但需要来自巴林交易商的保证。

巴林政府通常不会参与公司的所有权和经营权，除非该行业或活动关乎国家利益（例如石油和天然气工业）。

公司可以从一种法律形式转换为另一种法律形式，但公司须在注册后至少持续两个财政年度才可转换为股份制公司。对于公司形式的转换，除在官方公报上和报纸上通知债权人外，必须在获得主管当局批准转换前偿还贷款和银行融资或确保其债权人同意该转换。公司的转换并不需要收购一个新的公司机构，但需要保留公司在转换之前的所有权利和义务。

（1）普通合伙公司

普通合伙公司是由两个以上主体（自然人或法人）组成的公司，这些主体应当具备交易者的资质且对该公司的债务和义务共同承担无限责任。这意味着，除了拥有对公司资产的追索权外，债权人对合伙人个人财产也享有追索权。其名称必须包含所有合作伙伴的名称或其中一个名称并同时添加"& Co."（或其同义词），并加后缀"巴林合伙公司"。

普通合伙允许持有100%的外资所有权，并且没有最低股本要求。此外，除非另有约定，公司的管理职责由所有合伙人共同承担。在任何情况下，公司须至少有一名管理人。公司应当对管理人在其职权范围内所做的任何行为负责。

未经全体合伙人同意，股份不得兑现、不得转让。除非公司章程另有规定，否则其决议须经一致同意方可通过。每个合伙人的损益和股份，应在公司财务年度末根据资产负债表和损益表确定。

（2）有限合伙公司

有限合伙公司由1名或1名以上以其全部财产承担公司债务的合伙人（连带合伙人）和另外1名或1名以上对公司投资但不承担管理职责的合伙人（隐名合伙人）组成，隐名合伙人在投资份额限度内对公司的债务承担责任。因此，即使凭借授权文件，隐名合伙人也不能干涉公司的管理，否则将作为连带合伙人，就管理公司事务而产生的公司债务与其他连带合伙人承担相同的责任。

有限合伙公司允许持有100%的份额外资持有（即两种类型的合伙人都可以是外国主体），并且没有最低股本要求。普通合伙公司的条款也适用于有限合伙公司的设立、管理、解散和清算。

有限合伙公司的名称只能包含连带合伙人的姓名或一个合伙人的姓名（如果他是唯一一个人所有财产负责的合伙人）及"& Co."，隐名合伙人的姓名不必在公司的公共记录或公司的名称中出现，只需要记录于公司章程。如果他们的姓名在他们知情的情况下包含在公司的名称中，他们将作为连带合伙人向善意第三方承担责任。

（3）合资企业

合资企业不具有法律人格，也不受公示程序的限制。合资企业的章程决定了合伙人的权利和义务以及利润和损失的分配方式。与其他企业不同，合资企业的章程不需要采用阿拉伯语或进行公证。

第三方不会因为企业的经营活动而与其发生任何法律关系，第三方仅与与其来往的企业合伙人（必须是巴林国籍或由巴林人担保）发生法律关系。合伙人可就公司经营活动以及合伙人与公司有关的行为发生的债务向其他合伙人在其份额内相互追索。

（4）股份制公司（公众公司或封闭公司）

① 公众公司。公众公司至少有 7 名股东，且每一位股东基于其出资份额承担责任。这类公司允许进行银行和投资活动，并可以外国资本或专业知识出资。外资以及专业知识参股的具体比例，需遵守部长针对不同行业、活动发布的命令。该公司的名称不必源于自然人的姓名，但后面必须加上"巴林股份公司"一词。

上市公司要求最低股本为 1 000 000 第纳尔，公司章程可以在不超过已发行股本的 10 倍范围内规定授权股本。股票可以转让，但不得以低于票面价值的价格发行。股份可以由两人或多人所有，但是需要选出一名代表向公司作出意思表示。发起人必须认购代表公司至少 10% 的股份，并应在公开招股说明书之前支付相当于公众就认购每股股份所需支付百分比的金额。虽然股份和内部出资证明书可以交易，但未经注册，出售以及转让股份将不会对公司或任何第三方有效。

一家公众公司须至少有 5 名董事，其任期不得超过 3 年，但可续任。他们有权根据公司目标实施公司管理行为。这些权力和行为不受《商业公司法》、公司章程或股东大会决议之外的规定的限制。公司章程规定了董事的薪酬方式，其总额不得超过扣除法定储备金及分配不少于公司已实缴股本的 5% 的利润之后的净利润的 10%。法定储备金是指每年必须扣除的净利润的 10%，直到储备金达到实缴股本的 50% 方可停止（除非公司章程规定了更高的比例）。

② 封闭公司。封闭公司须至少有两名股东，这些股东就其出资份额承担责任，且公司须至少有 3 名董事。封闭股份制公司最低股本要求为 250 000 第纳尔，可从事银行业务和投资活动，并视从事的业务确定外资持股比例（最高可达 100%）。至少 50% 的注册资本必须在公司成立之初支付，剩余部分应在 3 年内支付。因此，非上市公司的股份在实缴出资前不得转让，且如果股份已经出售，公司股东享有优先购买权。

在不违反封闭性公司相关规定的情况下，封闭性公司应当遵守公众公司的有关规定。

（5）股份制有限合伙

股份制有限合伙由两类合伙人组成：以其所有财产对公司承担连带责任的合伙人（连带合伙人）和以其投资份额对公司承担责任的合伙人（隐名合伙人）。这类企业的名称必须由一个或多个连带合伙人的名字组成，并可包含源自公司目标的创新名称。但是，隐名合伙人的名字不得出现。如果在隐名合伙人知情的情况下其名字包含在企业名称中，则将视为对第三方承担连带责任的合伙人。

该类公司的资本可以 100% 是外资，必须划分为可转让的、不可分割的同等价值股份，在不违反《商业公司法》对股份制有限合伙的规定的前提下，隐名合伙人应遵守和股份制公司相同的规定。因此，有关股份制公司发行股权证明的条文适用于股份制有限合伙公司发行的股份权证。

股份制有限合伙须至少有 4 名合伙人，由一名或一名以上连带合伙人进行管理，且其名称须出现在合伙协议中并作为发起人以其财产承担责任。股份合伙人不得干涉公司管理，并且即使经过授权也不得涉足与第三方的经营活动。但他们可以根据合伙备忘录的规定参与内部管理。如果合伙人人数超过 10 人，则需选举成立一个由 3 名成员组成的监事会来监督公司的活动。此外，公司章程必须明确管理者的薪酬方式。

（6）有限责任公司

有限责任公司是拥有至少两名最多 50 名（自然人或公司）股东的公司，股东责任仅限于其股权份额。如果股东人数低于两人，公司将依法成为一人公司，除非该公司在将公司股份集中到一个股东手中之日起 30 天内达到最低股东人数要求。有限责任公司在名称最后带有"有限责任"字样，公司的名称可能包含一个特殊名称或源于其目的的名称，并且可能包含合伙人的名称。这些细节应在公司的所有合同、发票、广告、文件和出版物内均有提及，否则公司的管理人员将因此以其私人财产对第三方承担连带责任。

此类公司不能发行可转让股票或债券，任何合伙人股份的转让都受到优先购买权和公司章程的约束。这类公司不得从事保险或银行业务，但根据业务类型，可能允许外资比例达到100%。如果商业活动需要当地保证人，则外国主体占股一般将被限制在已发行股本的49%以下。同时也有类似股份制公司的维持法定储备金之义务。

公司的股份必须划分为每股价值不低于50第纳尔的若干等份，但并无最低股本要求，不过股本必须足以实现公司的目标。两人或两人以上可以共同持有一股，只要仅一人代表他们向公司行事即可，且双方应共同承担由此产生的义务。直到出资全部实缴且实物出资也已经转让给公司后，公司才能成立。

有限责任公司必须至少任命一名合伙人或非合伙人担任经理，管理并代表公司。经理应对公司、合伙人和第三方承担的任何违规或管理不善的责任承担连带责任。这些管理人员不得参与竞争公司或具有类似目标的公司的管理。经理的职责、义务和责任应与股份制公司董事会成员相同。他们还必须为每个财政年度准备公司的资产负债表、损益表、公司活动和财务状况报告以及利润分配建议。但是，公司的审计师由年度合伙人大会任命。

（7）一人公司

一人公司完全由一人（自然人或公司）所有，但所有人仅以其出资份额承担责任。该类公司应具备一个特殊的商业名称或来自其设立目的的名称，以及出资人的名称，并附后缀"一人公司"。在不违反其性质的前提下，此类公司应当遵守有限责任公司的相关规定。

除非指定一名或多名管理人员，否则，一人公司由资本所有者进行管理，但必须至少有一名经理。只要业务活动允许，个人公司允许100%外资所有。一人公司也没有最低股本要求，但须满足经营所需。

公司应当在资本所有者去世后终止，除非在所有者去世后的6个月内，将所有继承人的股份转让给同一人，或者分配给多人，这些人选择让公司以另一种法律形式存续。此外，如果所有人是法人，则一人公司将在所有人清算时终止。

除上述情况外，如果一人公司的所有者在公司经营期限结束前或者在实现其设立目标之前恶意进行清算或中止公司经营，所有者将以其个人财产承担责任。如果公司所有者故意使自身利益与公司利益相冲突，情况也是如此。

（8）控股公司

控股公司是以持有巴林或外国公司的股份为目的，或以参与其成立为目的的公司。它必须持有关联公司至少50%的股份，必须采用股份制公司、有限责任公司或一人公司的形式，并在所有相关文件中包含其商业名称以及"控股公司"后缀。该公司受其所采用的公司形式的相关法律规定的约束。

关联公司不得持有控股公司的股份，并且除非与关联公司的股东或合伙人另有约定，控股公司必须按其持股比例在关联公司的董事会中委任其代表。

其目标如下：

① 管理其关联公司或参与公司的管理并提供必要的支持。

② 将其资金投资于股票、债券和证券。

③ 在法律允许的范围内，拥有进行商务活动所需的不动产和动产。

④ 向其关联公司提供贷款、担保及融资。

⑤ 享有工业产权，如专利、商业和工业标识和特许权，以及其他无形权利，并将其使用或出租给其关联公司或其他公司。

在每个财政年度结束时，控股公司必须制定综合报表，其中包含其自身以及所有关联公司的资产负债表和损益表，并须附有符合国际会计准则的必要说明和声明。

2. 设立程序

选择了设立公司的类型和相关的业务活动确定后，除合资企业外，通常会采取以下步骤：

① 向工商部（MOIC）提交申请并附上相关文件以进行预先批准。

② 经预先批准后，申请人须提交公司章程文件草案（即公司备忘录和章程）以及租赁合同以证明公司的办公地址。

③ 提交文件后，工商部将根据所选择的业务活动与需要批准的相关部门联系。不同部门有其特定的必须符合的要求。

④ 经上述主体许可后，工商部通知公证人并要求其对公司的章程文件进行公证和准备。
⑤ 申请人须在当地一家银行开设账户，以便将资金存入其中。随后，银行会提供存款证明。
⑥ 向工商部递交公证文件并支付相关费用以获得商业注册号和包含公共记录信息的公司摘录。
⑦ 此后，官方公报正式公布，公司自公布之日起被视为已经依法注册成立。

合资公司的设立没有特别的程序要求，因为此类企业不需要注册。合营协议必须明确各方的权利和义务，并确定利润和损失的分配。

3. 解散的方式及要求

根据《商业公司法》的规定，公司因下列原因解散：
① 超出其存续期限，但公司备忘录或章程续期的除外；
② 公司设立的目标已经实现；
③ 公司所有财产或其相当一部分财产受损使其无法继续存续；
④ 在公司存续到期前，经合伙人一致决定解散公司，除非章程或备忘录规定特别多数即可决定解散；
⑤ 与其他公司合并。

若公司没有正当理由，自成立起 1 年内或暂停其活动 1 年后未进行业务活动的，公司的商业登记将根据工商部部长的指令而撤销。

此外，除公众股份制公司外，经任何合伙人申请，法院可以支持该公司的解散申请，前提是存在解散的重要理由。合伙人不履行其义务的，法院可以根据其他合伙人的申请解散公司。

如果合伙人之一无期限退出企业（在对其他合伙人进行适当通知的前提下），或一方合伙人去世，普通合伙公司、有限合伙企业和合资企业应当解散。如果其中一个合伙人破产，无力偿债或收到扣押令的，法院也可以解散该公司。除非公司章程另有约定，股份制有限合伙公司也适用此规定。如果股份制有限合伙公司的章程没有这方面的特别规定，则特别股东大会可以决定公司的存续。

有限责任公司不会因其中一名或更多合伙人的撤资而解散，也不会因一名合伙人死亡而解散。除非公司章程另有规定，即使法院针对去世的合伙人作出扣押令或者一名合伙人被判定破产或资不抵债，情况依然如此。

（六）合并收购

并购的规定和程序适用巴林《商业公司法》。可通过两种方式实现：被收购公司被清盘并将其资产转移到现有公司（收购），或者现有公司均被清盘并组建新公司（合并）。在任何情况下，合并不得导致对某项活动或产品的垄断，并且合并通知必须在官方公报和一份新闻日报上公布，给予债权人 60 天的时间提出反对意见。

那些被许可或调整的实体，如由巴林中央银行或电信管理局（TRA）等机构所批准或管理的机构的并购，需要事先得到其主管部门的批准，该主管部门可能会在合并前提出进一步的要求。此外，巴林中央银行《规则手册》中的收购兼并模块[①]，对在巴林证券交易所（BHB）上市的巴林公司以及在巴林证券交易所初次上市的普通股权的海外公司的收购、兼并作出了规定。当公司超过 30% 的投票权被收购时，通常适用该模块的规定。

（七）竞争规制

1. 竞争监管机构

现阶段，巴林并没有专门监管竞争的政府部门。

2. 竞争法简介

虽然巴林目前没有正式的竞争法，但一些立法中还是以禁止某些行为的方式规制了竞争行为。例如，1987 年第 7 号法令颁布的《商业法》一般性地禁止对竞争产生不利影响的活动。此外，公司不得实施损害竞争对手或吸引竞争对手客户的行为。

---

① 巴林中央银行《规则手册》第六卷。

消费者保护局以及关于消费者保护的 2012 年第 35 号法令同样对竞争进行了一定的规制，这些规定确保有关确定价格和控制的法律得到充分执行。此外，还有一项法律力图防止水泥贸易的垄断。

此外，《民法典》①对限制性协议的问题进行了规定。对于有强制性条款的协议可能会被法官修改。

3. 竞争规制措施

尽管已经有适用于不合规行为的一般性惩罚，例如《刑法典》（如罚金和徒刑）和《消费者保护法》规定，任何人违反有关竞争的规定，将处以 5 年以下的监禁和不超过 5 000 第纳尔的罚款或择一适用。

（八）税收

1. 税收体系与制度

由于纳税义务很轻，巴林通常被认为是避税天堂。巴林没有像其他海湾阿拉伯国家合作委员会成员国（例如沙特阿拉伯和阿联酋）那样的指定税务机关。除了经营石油和天然气的企业或在巴林以浓缩或提炼化石燃料获得利润的企业以外，巴林目前没有所得、销售额以及资本利得税。不论是本地公司还是外国公司，对上述公司的净利润，都要按照 46% 的税率征税。

巴林对支付股息、特许权使用费或利息没有任何预扣税，但却与许多国家签署了有效的双重征税协定，其中包括阿尔及利亚、奥地利、巴巴多斯、白俄罗斯、比利时、文莱、保加利亚、中国、塞浦路斯、捷克、埃及、爱沙尼亚、法国、格鲁吉亚、匈牙利、伊朗、爱尔兰、约旦、韩国、黎巴嫩、卢森堡、马来西亚、马耳他、墨西哥、摩洛哥、荷兰、巴基斯坦、菲律宾、葡萄牙、塞舌尔、新加坡、斯里兰卡、苏丹、叙利亚、泰国、塔吉克斯坦、土耳其、土库曼斯坦、英国、乌兹别克斯坦和也门等。

2. 主要税种与税率

除了适用于石油和天然气行业的企业所得税外，巴林以 10% 的税率对于向外籍人士出租的商业和住宅物业征收市政税。巴林还对房地产转让和登记征收 2% 的印花税，如果在交易日后的前两个月内支付款项，税率可降至 1.7%。

自 2017 年 12 月 30 日起，巴林一直对烟草（100%征税）、能量饮料（100%征税）和软饮料（税率50%）等有害产品征收消费税。目前，因巴林于 2017 年 2 月 1 日签署了海湾阿拉伯国家合作委员会统一增值税和消费税条约，巴林正在实行增值税。根据海湾阿拉伯国家合作委员会增值税协议，巴林将在 2019 年 1 月 1 日之前实施协议。根据该条约，对大多数商品和服务征收增值税的标准税率为 5%，但存在一些例外。目前还没有关于何时引入增值税的实施法规或确定日期。

3. 纳税申报与优惠

在巴林不适用。

（九）证券交易

1. 证券法律、法规简介

除巴林《商业公司法》规定了哪些企业可以发行可转让的证券外，巴林《证券交易法》②引入并规制了自我管理市场——巴林证券交易所（现称为巴林交易所）③。巴林中央银行《规则手册》提供了有关证券事宜的具体规则。

2. 证券市场监管

巴林中央银行通过遵守最佳国际标准和惯例来调整和监管巴林金融市场并保护投资者，其根据所有披露要求和条件来批准公开发行任何证券或金融工具的申请。

巴林中央银行还采用国际披露标准，旨在提高市场透明度，监控证券交易所、清算交易、存款系统、经纪公司和做市商。

---

① 2001 年第 19 号法令。
② 1975 年第 4 号法令。
③ 2009 年第 57 号法令。

3. 外国企业进行证券贸易的要求

在上市前,证券发行人必须申请并获得巴林中央银行的批准。与此同时,他们还必须遵守巴林《商业公司法》和1996年第6号决议的以下规定:

① 申请公司须是在其设立国的证券交易所合法上市的公众持股公司,或在申请之日前已经设立至少3年的封闭性公司。
② 公司的实收资本不得低于3 770 000第纳尔,或其他任何等值的货币。
③ 公司主营业务须在上市申请前的3年内保持净盈利。
④ 公司章程或公司设立国的法律对投资者之间的股份转让没有限制。
⑤ 公司的财务状况必须良好。
⑥ 公司股东人数应不少于100人。
⑦ 公司应在需要时在巴林派遣代表处负责股权转让、分红、财报和其他相关事宜。
⑧ 公司须遵守同巴林证券交易所签署的上市协议。

外国企业拟收购公众股份制公司股份的,必须经工商部批准。发行人拟在巴林证券交易所发行上市债券或伊斯兰债券的,必须遵守以下规定:

① 2006年《巴林中央银行和金融机构法》;
② 2012年第17号决议关于巴林中央银行批准的交易工具的规则和条例;
③ 外国债券需要按照发行国的相关法律发行;
④ 须从巴林中央银行获得适当的批准;
⑤ 发行人必须至少运营两年;
⑥ 发行人经济状况良好;
⑦ 发行人的实收资本不得少于10 000 000美元;
⑧ 发行人应遵守与巴林证券交易所签署的上市协议;
⑨ 发行人应在巴林指定代表处办理债券/伊斯兰债券登记、股息分配、报告及其他相关事宜;
⑩ 发行人应通过各类媒介发布其资产负债表和财务结果。

(十)投资优惠及保护

1. 优惠政策框架

虽然巴林没有正式的优惠政策,但巴林国民和国内公司通常能享受优惠待遇。然而,巴林同他国保持着良好的外交关系且签订了诸多协定,积极鼓励外国投资并寻求投资者。

2. 特定行业与地区支持

巴林强力推动针对特定行业的投资。尽管该国预算依赖于石油和天然气领域,但巴林的多元化经济刺激了对其他经济领域的投资。因此,能源开发局(EBD)的目标是将外国直接投资纳入对经济有重大贡献的其他主要部门:制造业和物流业、金融服务业、信息和通信技术(ICT)以及旅游业。

3. 特殊经济区域

巴林认可大多数行业中外资占比可以达到100%,资本和利润的无限制汇回政策,以及极低的税收和关税,在某种程度上整个国家都可以被视为一个自由贸易区,巴林自由贸易区提供的减免政策,使其成为寻求区域制造或分销基地的客户的首选。

4. 投资保护

巴林已与不同国家签署了30多个双边投资协定,其中包括与中国签署的双边投资协定。[①]该协议于1999年签署,旨在鼓励、保护和创造两国之间投资的有利条件。

---

① 参见 http://www.dezshira.com/library/treaties/bilateral-investment-treaty-between-bahrain-and-china-4135.html。

三、贸易

（一）贸易监管部门

工商业和旅游业部（MOICT）与其他部委以及与贸易相关的部门和机构共同负责实施巴林的贸易政策及规定，相关机构包括经济发展委（EDB）、财政部和巴林中央银行。其中私营部门是通过巴林工商会（BCCI）参与贸易政策的制定的。

工商业和旅游业部负责组织构成商业环境的一系列经济活动，包括各种商业性质业务的注册登记、商业代理、工业产权、经济计量以及对外贸易。概言之，工商业和旅游业部的目标是确保巴林保持商业环境的开放、透明和市场驱动力，从而提升巴林的经济竞争力，鼓励外来投资，同时促进国内就业。

经济发展委是根据巴林2000年第9号法令建立的，目标是为巴林经济管理提供战略性指导，特别是为私营部门和对外投资的发展提供便利。经济发展委帮助提高巴林的经济竞争力、生产力，特别是为巴林的经济发展提供技术娴熟的劳动力。巴林的王储负责监督经济发展委及其董事会的日常工作，董事会成员包括政府部门部长和产业执行委员，各成员紧密配合加强公共部门和私营部门的紧密合作。

（二）贸易法律、法规简介

巴林的贸易主要通过以下法律进行规制：
①《商法》，由巴林1987年第7号法令颁布实施并修订；
②《商业公司法》，由巴林2001年第21号法令颁布实施并修订；
③《商事登记法》，由巴林2015年第27号法令颁布实施。

巴林为加强与外界的经济联系，增加贸易机会和贸易增长，与美国签订了巴林—美国自由贸易协定，该协定于2006年1月11日生效。自由贸易协定的总目标是取消进出口的贸易关税，以及促进制造服务行业的发展。

（三）贸易管理

数千年来，巴林一直处在商业历史发展的交叉路口。"巴林"的字面含义是阿拉伯的"两片海"，暗示国家所处地理位置的重要性，在历史长河中一直都是连接东西方的贸易中心。巴林作为一个商人主要的停靠站，一个采集珍珠工厂的聚集地，是波斯湾名副其实的著名贸易中心。近些年，巴林的经济发展更加多样化，成为波斯湾众多跨国公司的母国。

作为海湾阿拉伯国家合作委员会的一员，从2003年起，巴林一直施行海湾阿拉伯国家合作委员会的共同对外关税。一般来说，巴林的贸易政策和规定是开放的，实施较为简单的最惠国待遇税则。巴林没有关税配额，没有繁杂捐税，也没有其他关税和进口费用。巴林有本国规定的限制及禁止进出口货物清单。

（四）进出口商品检验检疫

为统一和规制海湾阿拉伯国家合作委员会成员国之间的海关程序，海湾阿拉伯国家合作委员会成员国的海关总署在2002年制定了《统一海关法》。

针对相关机构有进口限制的货物，必须附带相关证书。在巴林，大多数进口限制是出于安全、健康或道德层面的考虑，实行限制的货物包括：特殊种马、武器、杀虫剂、杀真菌剂以及放射性物质。为保护生命健康，对食品、植物、动物产品限制进口，进口产品必须附带出口国卫生与动植物检疫证书。进口食品必须附带证书，该证书用以证明进口产品无辐射、无二噁英。另外，医药产品必须从有科研部门的生产商处直接进口，产品必须在生产国和除巴林以外的两个海湾阿拉伯国家合作委员会的成员国获得生产许可，其中必须包括沙特阿拉伯。

所有进口到巴林（包含保税区）的产品，必须附随：
①4份货运提单（空运货物的空运提单）；

②原产地证明的原件（出于统计目的）；
③三份商业发票；
④所有由出口商或托运人投保的货运保险单；
⑤原产国商会对产品出口原产地和现价的陈述，必须与商业发票印证；
⑥巴林相应的领事馆在产品进口到巴林之前，必须在原产国证照或原产国国内其他阿拉伯国家大使馆的证明上加盖印章，美国贸易商免除签证手续费；
⑦如果文件没有经过认证，商品也可以经过海关检查之后清关，并以存款方式支付关税。如果在进口之日起6个月内不提供认证文件，则为仿冒品。

对于进口成药、食材、活畜、鸟类、鱼类以及全部的肉禽产品，巴林也同样要求附随特定产品证明文件。某些产品必须附随进口准许证，包括特殊种马（阿拉伯马）、武器、杀虫剂以及杀真菌剂。全部进口商和出口商都必须在巴林工商业和旅游业部以及巴林工商会的商业登记处注册登记。

巴林没有要求进口商必须通过代理商进行交易。巴林对于装船前检查没有法律和制度规定。目的地在巴林之外并经陆路运输的货物，获得一张联运提单，就会通过一张货物免税通行证（transit bill）完成清关。海关事务部门要求提供定金或者保证，在有证据证明货物出口之后，定金将会在免税通行证日期30日内返还。如果货物直接由港口发出（船—岸—船或船—船）、通过海运，则货物由转船提单完成清关。

2011年，巴林搭建了一个通过单一窗口管理、促进国际货物便利化的新型网络用户系统，即OFOQ。OFOQ旨在为巴林的关税管理机构和贸易与物流操作人员之间提供综合性、无缝化的电子贸易操作。OFOQ是一个单一窗口平台，可以进行文件提交和问题咨询，尤其侧重于减少交易的费用和时间，同时确保通过智能化任务管理进行合规审查。这一系统能够便利贸易商完成简易发货和清关程序。目前，OFOQ已经在巴林港口以及国际机场投入使用。

（五）海关管理

为了方便关税管理及操作，巴林关税机构将关税系统电子化，创建了eCAS。eCAS使得原来大部分关税机构的人工操作升级为自动化操作，创造了更优质的办公环境，能够实现更准确的数据捕获，以及更高效的报告程序。eCAS还包含了一个校验系统，用以核验如原产地证明等文件，也可用来存档集装箱的检查证书。

四、劳动

（一）劳动法律、法规简介

2012年，巴林第36号法令颁布的《私营部门劳动法》（以下简称《劳动法》）对巴林劳工问题进行了规范，《劳动法》取代了1976年第19号劳动法令。

《劳动法》与几个巴林作为签署国的阿拉伯和国际劳工条约和公约一致，并且这些公约和条约在过去的几十年里已经生效，通过赋予雇员更多权利，振兴了私营部门劳动力市场，其中包括改善工作条件，禁止性别歧视，禁止基于性别、族裔、语言、宗教或信仰等支付工资上等。《劳动法》还对劳工休年假、产假、病假的权利和解决劳动争议进行了改进和细化。

《劳动法》的大多数条款适用于所有私营部门的雇员，除根据第2条豁免的雇员外，即：
①家庭佣人和为其雇主或亲属利益而履行其工作职责的雇员，如园丁、房屋安全警卫、保姆、司机和厨师等；
②实际上由雇主供养的家庭成员，即雇主的丈夫、妻子、血亲和姻亲。

（二）雇用外籍员工的要求

1. 工作许可

如聘请外籍员工，雇主必须为每名外籍员工获取工作许可证和居留许可。外籍员工的工作许可证由劳动市场管理局（LMRA）颁发并可能受到劳动市场管理局的数量限制。此类许可证有效期为2年。

"巴林标准化"要求,对于雇员在10名及以上的公司,需按照一定比例聘用巴林本土雇员。雇主的商业活动由"巴林标准化"表格进行规范,该表格可在劳动市场管理局或其网站上查询并下载。

基本上来说,在巴林工作的外国雇员应满足:身体健康、合法进入巴林以及应持有有效的护照、居住证和工作许可证。

2. 申请程序

申请工作许可证所需的文件如下:
① 一份工作许可证申请表;
② 一份雇员护照的副本;
③ 雇主与雇员之间的聘用信或雇佣合同;
④ 外籍员工的体检报告。

3. 社会保险

根据工商业和旅游业部的规定,所有外籍和当地工作人员都必须在社会保险组织(SIO)注册。

社会保险组织基金构成如下:对于巴林员工,雇主支付基本工资和经常性津贴的10%,雇员支付基本工资和经常性津贴的5%。对于外籍员工,雇主支付基本工资和经常性津贴的3%。

(三) 出入境

1. 签证类型

所有进入巴林的人均需签证,但海湾阿拉伯国家合作委员会成员国的公民除外。

(1) 旅游签证

此类签证给予欧盟、澳大利亚、加拿大、中国香港特别行政区、日本、新西兰和美国公民两周的停留期限。申请人须持有有效的新型护照和回程票。这种签证不允许个人在巴林从事任何工作。

(2) 访客签证

此类签证需要巴林公民的担保,巴林公民必须代表参观者向国籍、护照和居住事务局申请。该类签证有效期为1个月,不允许就业。

(3) 72小时以及7日签证

此类签证可供短期入住巴林的商务旅客使用,在入境时获得。申请人须提供回程票和有效护照。

(4) 商务签证

停留时间超过一周的个人必须通过位于其国家的巴林大使馆获得商务签证。此类签证有效期长达4周。申请人须填写申请表,并出示护照、照片、雇主的信函,说明旅行的目的和无异议函。

(5) 工作签证

此类签证有效期为1年或2年,申请人有权居住在巴林。申请人需要进行体检并支付费用。必要的相关文书通常由申请人的担保人提供。

(6) 家庭签证

在巴林工作的工人,其直系亲属可获得此类签证,在工人就业期间,其直系亲属有权享受居留身份。家庭成员不得工作,除非单独安排并获得适当的工作签证。

2. 出入境限制

劳动市场管理局实施了一项"简易退出计划",针对逾期居留的个人,可以在缴纳最低罚款后离开巴林。具体而言,根据该计划,持工作签证而逾期居留的人,可以在缴纳巴林BHD 15/-的罚款后离开巴林;持旅游签证而逾期居留的人,可以在缴纳巴林BHD 25/-的罚款后离开巴林。

(四) 工会与劳工组织

《劳动法》对巴林劳工组织和工会的建立与监管进行了规范。根据《劳动法》第176条的规定,雇用50名以上工人的企业,应当与工会组织(如有)或工会代表共同为其工人提供必要的社会和文化服务。巴林工会总联合会于2002年根据《工人工会法》成立,该法规定工人有权进行集体组织管理。

(五）劳动争议

1. 纪律规范

根据《劳动法》的规定，任何拥有 10 名以上（包括 10 名）工人的雇主都应制定工作场所规则和明确的纪律规范，该规范须经劳动和社会发展部批准，而且必须进行明确的公示。

如果雇主希望采取惩戒措施或解雇雇员，应首先查阅《劳动法》。对员工可采取的惩戒措施包括罚款、暂停工作、警告和解雇。

如果雇主/雇员打算投诉，应该首先遵循劳资纠纷法定程序，须首先向劳动和社会发展部提出索赔。所有索赔文件都提交至劳工案件管理办公室，劳工案件管理部门的法官将审理案件、编写报告及处理和解程序（如达成和解）。

如果双方未达成和解，劳工案件管理部门法官会将争议事项转交给高等法院，启动诉讼程序，高等法院将在自提起诉讼之日起两个月内处理，并应在第一次听证之日起 30 日内作出判决。高等法院法官的裁决是终局的，当事人只能就实质性法律问题向最高法院提出上诉。

2. 集体谈判（《劳动法》第 137—141 条）

《劳动法》赋予劳动者集体谈判权，但须符合法律的具体规定。

在集体谈判过程中，除紧急情况外，雇主不得采用与谈判议题有关的任何临时性决定或措施。在集体谈判成功的情况下，根据和解协议签订集体劳动合同。如果达不成和解协议，任何一方都可以根据《劳动法》第 158 条的规定，向集体争端解决委员会或仲裁委员会提出请求。

五、知识产权

（一）知识产权法律、法规简介

巴林的知识产权法涵盖了专利、商标、版权和工业品外观设计等多个领域。目前，巴林已经实施了若干法律制度，以确保对知识产权的监管和保护。截至 2006 年，巴林加入了多个国际和区域协定，如《世界知识产权组织版权条约》(WIPO)、《与贸易有关的知识产权协定》(TRIPs)、《保护工业产权巴黎公约》。与此同时，《保护文学和艺术作品伯尔尼公约》和《美国—巴林自由贸易协定》承诺对巴林提供世界一流的知识产权保护措施。

1. 专利权保护

巴林在 2004 年对《专利法》进行了修订，并颁布了 2004 年第 1 号法令，对专利和实用新型的取得和使用进行了进一步规范。作为《专利合作条约》（PCT）的签署国，巴林提交专利申请时，也需遵循《专利合作条约》统一程序，需符合每个《专利合作条约》缔约国的标准。此外，巴林还受海湾阿拉伯国家合作委员会专利局相关规定的约束，特别是颁布于 1996 年的《海湾阿拉伯国家合作委员会专利条例》，该条例于 1999 进行了修改。

2. 版权保护

根据 2004 年第 14 号法令和 1996 年第 30 号法令的规定，巴林正式成为《保护文学和艺术作品伯尔尼公约》和《世界知识产权组织版权条约》的缔约国，从而为作者的人身权利和经济权利提供了广泛保障。

2006 年，巴林对《版权法》进行了修订，颁布了 2006 年第 22 号法令，即新修订的《版权法》，该部法律同时取代了 1993 年第 10 号法令，为著作权亦提供了更广泛的保护。

新修订的《版权法》将保护期延长至作者的终生及其死亡后 70 年（此前为 50 年），并增加了相关初审程序的规定。

3. 商标权保护

2006 年第 11 号法令为商标领域提供了法律规范。同时，根据《商标注册用商品和服务国际分类》（第十版），在巴林进行商标注册时，也需遵循《商品和服务国际分类标准》。

(二)专利申请

巴林根据《专利法》保护专利,为专利发明和实用新型提供保护。

根据《专利法》第 1 条的规定,如果发明具有以下特征,则该发明在巴林能够得到保护:
① 新颖性;
② 创造性;
③ 工业实用性,并且最终不被认为是现有技术的一部分。

《专利法》第 3 条明确规定,不保护与道德或公共秩序、科学理论、数学方法、植物、动物和治疗方法相矛盾的发明。

1. 注册

专利和实用新型应在工商业和旅游业部下属的巴林工业产权局申请注册。

2. 申请类型

在巴林,可通过三种方式申请保护发明:
① 根据《巴黎公约》有权申请优先权,申请人有权通过巴林工业产权局申请国家保护;
② 在提交国际申请后,通过《专利合作条约》进入国家申请保护阶段;
③ 通过海湾阿拉伯国家合作委员会专利局。海湾阿拉伯国家合作委员会《专利法》于 1992 年获得批准,通过 2014 年第 6 号法令在巴林实施,规定海湾阿拉伯国家合作委员会专利局授予的专利适用于巴林。

3. 申请要求

在提交专利申请时,必须满足两项要求:以阿拉伯语提交申请;申请必须提交附有签名的授权书。

申请日后 90 天内,必须提交进一步证明文件,包括:
① 经公证及合法化的授权书副本;
② 申请人的商业登记证副本或商业登记簿摘录,并经巴林大使馆认证;
③ 经过公证及合法化的转让契据;
④ 优先权文件的核证副本(如有声明),翻译成英文和阿拉伯文。

《专利法》规定,专利申请人在被授予专利后 3 年内或在提交申请后 4 年内(以较晚者为准)在巴林有利用或使用该项发明的权利。如果该专利在这段时间内没有被使用,将受到强制许可。

(三)注册商标

巴林遵循《商标注册用商品和服务国际分类》下用于商标和注册商标的国际商品和服务分类,并于 2005 年 7 月 1 日通过了该分类对第 42 类的修订以及新添加的第 43—45 类。

针对每类商品或服务必须提交一份单独的申请。一旦提交贸易 / 服务商标申请,将会审查其商标的可注册性。注册官接受的商标申请将在官方公报上公布,并且利益相关方有 60 天的异议期。对于商标注册的任何异议,均应在公布之日起的规定期限内由授权代理人或所有人本人向注册人提交。这种异议案应由注册官处理。在没有异议的情况下,公布的商标得以注册,并且发放注册证书。商标权通过注册获得。但是,在巴林和世界其他地方提出异议并提供充足的先前商标使用证明之后,商标申请异议成功。

商标注册从提出申请之日起 10 年内有效,并可以续期 10 年。《商标法》为延迟续展商标规定了 6 个月的宽限期。如果不续展商标,根据《商标法》的规定从商标注销之日起 3 年内不允许第三方对该商标进行注册。一旦商标被注册,商标的授权和授权用户可以记录。该记录发表在官方公报上。只有在基于商誉和业务考虑下才允许商标转让。所有其他变更可在商标注册后记录。

(四)保护知识产权措施

巴林根据国际标准实施了保护该国知识产权的条款。如上所述,这些规定因地而异,所有这些都包含了对知识产权进行有效管理的重要性,诸如自由贸易协定等协议中都包含了巴林在这些领域所付出的努力。

巴林拥有悠久而完善的知识产权立法和基础设施。1955年巴林针对专利、设计和商标保护颁布了第一部《工业和知识产权法》。巴林的工业产权局是波斯湾最古老的知识产权局之一，在知识产权执法方面，巴林在阿拉伯国家中也享誉甚高。

巴林是《马德里议定书》缔约国中为数不多的阿拉伯国家之一，其同时还是《伯尔尼公约》《布鲁塞尔公约》《巴黎公约》《专利法条约》《罗马公约》《商标法条约》《世界知识产权组织版权条约》《世界知识产权组织表演和录音制品条约》《专利合作条约》《商标注册用商品和服务国际分类尼斯协定》和海湾阿拉伯国家合作委员会《专利法》的成员国。

六、环境保护

(一) 环境保护监管部门

巴林的环境保护监督部门是最高环境委员会（SCE）。最高环境委员会最终能成立，不仅仅是为协助巴林政府管理环境，而且也为了保护环境、自然和海洋资源、野生动植物及其生物多样性。为实现上述目标，最高环境委员会已经实施了许多项目。

最高环境委员会议程的核心是：所有发展部门，无论是经济、社会还是政治部门，都必须在制定战略计划时着重考虑环境保护，只有这样才能实现上述目标。因此，最高环境委员会的策略不仅是以现在为中心，最重要的是非常关注长期发展。最高环境委员会的努力和坚持得到了国际认可，2005年，总部位于英国的绿色组织授予巴林海洋资源、环境和野生动植物保护公共委员会（委员会）国际"青苹果环境"奖，奖励委员会为建立Hafira工业垃圾填埋场所并最终提供可供安全处置危险废物的区域所做出的努力。

(二) 环境保护法律、法规简介

巴林在环境保护方面已做出巨大努力，一方面确保发展部门各行业取得有效进展，另一方面确保环境保护和可持续发展。在巴林2030年经济远景战略和2030年国家战略计划中都突出反映出对维持两方面平衡的愿景。

此外，与上述战略相结合，巴林为实现可持续发展目标成立了许多机构，制定了许多政策和战略，还增设了许多与可持续发展目标实施相关的法律，这些法律已成为巴林经济、社会和政治向国际社会过渡的前提条件。

为加强环境保护，巴林已实施了多项法令，主要监管来源是1996年关于环境保护的第21号法令，为在岛上开展环境倡议奠定了坚实的基础。此后，针对环境保护特定问题，委员会通过了许多具体方面的立法，其中包括关于维护石棉设备和建筑物许可证的第4号决议、2001年关于环境检查工作人员代表团的第2号决议，2005年关于废油管理的第4号决议和2006年关于危险废物管理的第3号决议。

(三) 环境保护评估

不能否认的是，为实施而且确保其环境保护政策的有效性，巴林已经做出了持续性的努力。

巴林在环境保护方面所取得的进展中，最高环境委员会发挥了重要作用。最高环境委员会具有持续性和创新性的努力不仅使巴林本地的环境得到保护，而且在更广泛的层面上，促成巴林与众多国家和国际组织的密切合作、参与并签订保护环境的协议。

七、争议解决

(一) 争端解决方式及机构

巴林争议解决庭（BCDR）是一个独立的争端解决机构，根据2009年第30号法令设立，负责解决巴林的经济、金融和投资争议，经2009年第30号法令修订，自2010年1月起开始审理案件。

巴林争议解决庭与美国仲裁协会（AAA）合作，为海湾地区及其他地区的商业和政府合作伙伴在经济、金融和投资方面的争端提供快速有效的解决方案。

巴林争议解决庭位于巴林，致力于区域和国际仲裁与调解。案件管理团队由纽约美国仲裁协会总部和其他场所培训的双语律师组成，他们接受持续的培训和专业发展训练。巴林争议解决庭在商业和投资领域拥有优秀的专业人才，为商业纠纷的调解和仲裁提供先进的解决方案。

1. 巴林争议解决庭

巴林争议解决庭位于巴林金融中心麦纳麦的外交区，旨在提供前沿、有效的非诉讼纠纷解决机制，提供商业纠纷的终局且有约束力的裁决。巴林争议解决庭提供的服务包括仲裁和调解，改变了巴林处理某些特定类型争端的方式。

2. 巴林争议解决庭的管辖权

（1）法定仲裁：依法管辖（2009年第30号法令第1条）

对于任何超过500 000第纳尔且涉及商业纠纷中的国际方或涉及巴林中央银行许可的当事方的索赔，巴林争议解决庭拥有自动和强制管辖权（2009年第30号法令第9条）。

如果纠纷内容具有商业性质，如包括提供商品或服务、分销协议、投融资、保险或咨询服务的交易，则为商业纠纷。

（2）约定仲裁：管辖权来源于当事人的协议约定（2009年第30号法令第2条）

如果双方已经以书面方式明确同意根据巴林争议解决庭的规则，以仲裁或调解方式解决争议，巴林争议解决庭也将获得管辖权（2009年第30号法令第19条）。

3. 外国律师的受众权利

根据2009年第30号法令第30条的规定，非巴林籍律师可以在巴林争议解决庭出庭。但是，非巴林籍律师参加任何法定仲裁时都必须由巴林籍律师陪同。

4. 规则和程序

巴林争议解决庭的规则严格遵循国际争议解决中心（ICDR）的规则，即美国仲裁协会的国际部门。其规则经过了检验和测试，通常被认为是国际标准。

（二）适用法律

对于所有巴林争议解决庭仲裁的案件，双方可以协商适用与争议事项相关的法律。在双方没有达成合意的情况下：

① 按照2009年第30号法令第11条的规定，法定仲裁中适用巴林法律；

② 在双方同意的仲裁中，应由仲裁庭确定仲裁适用的法律，根据2009年第30号法令第21条的规定，应根据争议内容选择适用的法律；

③ 根据2009年第30号法令第15条的规定，仲裁庭颁发的法定仲裁裁决是巴林法院的最终裁决。

八、其他

（一）反商业贿赂

1. 反商业贿赂法律、法规简介

1976年巴林《刑法》将公职人员的腐败行为定义为犯罪行为。

2013年第1号法（《刑法修正案》）颁布了关于修改《刑法》的某些规定，对1976年第15号法令颁布的《刑法》进行修订，将《刑法》中的腐败罪的入罪范围扩大至包括私营部门。

《刑法》第186、188、189、190条和《刑法修正案》第418、419、421条对积极腐败（提供贿赂或同意支付贿赂）和被动腐败（受贿或索贿）进行了定义。根据《刑法》第36条的规定，试图实施贿赂行为，同样构成犯罪。

根据《刑法》第186条的规定，国家公务人员或公共机构的官员，利用自己职务便利以作为或不作为的方式，直接或间接索取、非法为自己或他人接受财物、特权或给予利益许诺，处10年以下有

期徒刑。

根据《刑法》第188条的规定，国家公务人员或公共机构的官员，违反职务规定以作为或不作为的方式，以直接或间接方式索取、非法为自己或他人接受财物、特权或给予利益许诺的，将处以10年以下有期徒刑。如果其作为或不作为在其权力范围之内，处以监禁。

根据《刑法》第189条的规定，国家公务人员或公共机构的官员，直接或间接索取、非法为自己或他人接受财物、特权或给予利益许诺作为或不作为，其声称或错认为在其职责范围之内，但实际不在的，处5年以下有期徒刑。

根据《刑法》第190条的规定，为谋求不正当利益，向国家公务人员或公共机构的官员提供财物、特权或给予利益的许诺，让其以作为或不作为的方式违反其工作职责的，处3个月以上有期徒刑。如果国家公务人员或公共机构的官员的作为或不作为行为在其职责范围之内，则应处以1年以下有期徒刑或罚款。

根据《刑法修正案》增加的《刑法》第418条的规定，公司雇员、董事会成员或公司受托人直接或间接为自己或他人的利益接受或索取他人财物、特权或给予利益的许诺，从而为他人执行任务或不履行自身职责，若该任务或职责与其工作、职责或地位相关，并且/或者会对企业或公司的所有者产生负面影响，处10年以下有期徒刑。该条款同样适用于已经接受贿赂并打算作为或不作为的人。

根据《刑法修正案》增加的《刑法》第419条、第420条的规定，公司雇员、董事会成员或公司受托人收受贿赂，为行贿人谋取利益，利用职务上的便利而徇私和舞弊、滥用职权，致使公司或公司股东遭受损失的，处10年以下有期徒刑。

根据《刑法修正案》增加的《刑法》第421条的规定，给予国家公务人员、公司员工、董事会成员或私人公司的受托人以财物或特权的，属于犯罪行为。

贿赂并不必然是金钱利益，任何形式的财物、特权以及许诺给予利益，都属于立法上的贿赂形式。根据《刑法》或《刑法修正案》的规定，没有具体的财产金额门槛，也就是说，任何金钱利益都可构成贿赂。

2. 反商业贿赂监管部门

国家审计署是一个非政府组织，进行独立调查并将其调查结果报告检察机关，由检察机关提起公诉。国家审计署进行财务审计，涉及审计对象的合规性审计、绩效考核和行政审计并发布年度报告。年度报告将会呈交巴林国王。

反腐及经济电子安全总局负责调查和起诉与腐败有关的犯罪，负责初步调查并将其调查结果提交给检察机关。

3. 惩处措施

对公职人员适用的最高刑罚为处3个月（《刑法》第190条）至10年有期徒刑（《刑法》第186条），罚款应与其所接受、索取或许诺的贿赂价值相等，最低处100第纳尔的罚款（《刑法》第191条）。

对私营部门人员适用的最高处罚是处有期徒刑10年（根据《刑法修正案》增加的《刑法》第418条）和处500~10 000第纳尔的罚款（根据《刑法修正案》增加的《刑法》第426条）。

《刑法》第193条规定，如果在案件被提交至法院之前，同案人向司法或行政当局报告或承认犯罪，则应视为减轻处罚的情况。如果其行为在法律上正当合理，法官可以免除对其处罚。根据《刑法修正案》增加的《刑法》第427条的规定，给予私营部门的犯罪分子同样的减免刑罚条件。

（二）工程承包

1. 许可制度

招标委员会是根据2002年第36号法令成立的，对巴林政府的采购活动实行独立监管。其中，商品或建筑购销合同需以公开招标方式签订。

招标委员会流程分为四个主要步骤：

① 准备招标；

② 提交投标；

③ 开始招标;
④ 招标评估与奖励。

2. 禁止领域

根据第 36 号法令第 3 条的规定,本法规定适用于所有有独立或附加预算的部委、组织、公共机构、市政机构和政府机关,以及由政府、咨询委员会和众议院全资拥有的公司。巴林国防部队、公安部队和国民警卫队在购买具有军事、国防安全或保密性质的商品、建筑或服务时,或为公共利益不得公布购买或在出现不适用本法规定的情形时,不适用本法。

3. 招投标

根据第 36 号法令第 19 条的规定,公开招标分为当地招标和国际招标。当地招标范围应限于在巴林注册的公司和组织。国际招标应允许在巴林注册的本地公司和未在巴林注册的国际公司参与,未注册的国际公司应在中标之日起 30 日内依法在巴林完成商业注册。区分当地招标和国际招标的标准应基于购买货物、建筑或服务的性质、数量、复杂程度和所需标准确定。

但是,买方可以根据投标委员会的决定以下列任何一种方式签订合同:

(1)两阶段招标

根据第 36 号法令第 41 条的规定,如果可以确定货物或建筑物的详细规格或服务特性以获得最佳解决方案满足买方的要求,则可通过两阶段招标方式签订合同。合同需满足下列要求:

① 提供技术评估报价的明确标准;
② 有充足的时间进行两阶段招标;
③ 具有订立一次总付合同的意图;
④ 期望收到多个投标。

两阶段招标的第一阶段,是通过挂号信发送邀请函,提交初步投标书,投标书内不包含价格,但包含技术、质量或其他关于货物、建筑物或服务的提案,针对合同条款以及所获取的有关投标人的能力和资格提出建议。

谈判可以在这一阶段进行,与在投标的任何方面都未被拒绝的投标人进行谈判。

两阶段招标的第二阶段,邀请其投标未被拒绝的投标人根据一组产品规格提交包括价格的最终投标。在此阶段,在通知全体投标人的前提下,可以对原始文件任何产品的规格作出修改。

(2)限制投标

依照第 36 号法令第 43 条的规定,可以在下列情形下通过限制投标的方式签订合同:

① 如果货物、建筑物或服务由于其具有高灵敏度的性质而不可用,除了有限的巴林或国外的特定供应商、承包商、顾问、技术人员或专家;
② 如果货物、建筑物或服务的价值较小,而与审查和评估大量投标所需的时间和成本不成比例;
③ 如果特定供应商、承包商、顾问、技术人员或专家采购产品是为了发展国家经济,特别是为了国际收支或外汇储备。

(3)竞争性谈判

根据第 36 号法令第 45 条的规定,在下列情况下,可以通过竞争性谈判的方式达成合同:

① 无法通过精确规格识别的商品;
② 技术工作本身需要技术人员、专家或指定专家执行;
③ 为了获得产品、建筑物或服务而需从其制造地点购买;
④ 物资、建筑物、服务没有投标人提交投标书或投标书中的价格极不合理;
⑤ 如发生灾难和紧急情况,导致迫切需要货物、工程或服务,从而不能进行公开招标程序。

(4)直接采购

根据第 36 号法令第 50 条的规定,合同可以在下列情况下通过直接购买的方式订立:

① 如果除了特定供应商或承包商可以利用货物、建筑物或服务之外,其不能被利用且没有可接受的替代品;
② 不能够遵循各种招标程序或竞争性谈判的紧急情况;

③ 在发生灾难和紧急情况时，迫切需要商品、建筑物或服务，而不可能遵循公开招标程序；

④ 在现有可利用商品、设备、技术或服务所具有的标准化／兼容性情况下，考虑到与原始采购相比拟购买行为的局限性、价格的适合性、替代品的不适用性；

⑤ 用于调研、实验、研究或开发的购买行为；

⑥ 如需要从供应商或承包商处购买以发展国民经济，例如国际收支或外汇储备。

（5）要求提交提案

根据第 36 号法令第 51 条的规定，在下列情况下，可以直接要求供应商或承包商提交提案：

① 除少量供应商或承包商可以利用该服务之外，不能被利用；

② 研究和评估的时间和费用与所需服务的价值（服务价值较低）不成比例；

③ 为保密或维护国家利益。

Bahrain

Authors: Abdulrahman Zainal, Qays H. Zu'bi, Noor Al Taraif
Translators: John Liu, Yang Chen

I. Overview

A. General Introduction to the Political, Economic, Social and Legal Environment of the Country Receiving Investment

The Kingdom of Bahrain is an Arab constitutional monarchy situated in the Persian Gulf. Linked to Saudi Arabia by a 26km causeway, Bahrain is comprised of more than 30 islands and is around 765 km in size. Bahrain has a population of approximately 1.5 million[1], more than half of which are non-nationals. Although Arabic is Bahrain's official language, English is spoken by most and is generally regarded as the business language.

Following the Portuguese occupation which ended in 1602, the Persians' control of Bahrain came to an end in 1783 when the Al Khalifa tribe seized control. As a former Emirate under British protection, Bahrain was declared independent from Britain in 1971 and decided not to join the earlier "Trucial States" in the formation of the subsequent United Arab Emirates.

a. Political

Despite the 2011-2013 protests which were inspired by the regional Arab Spring, Bahrain has had a stable government since the current King, Hamad bin Isa bin Salman Al Khalifa, first became the Emir of Bahrain in 1999 and ended the 1994 uprising. He brought about parliamentary elections, granted women voting rights, and released all political prisoners. In 2002, as a result of the country turning into a constitutional monarchy, he became the first King of Bahrain. Accordingly, the King enjoys a wide range of executive powers. These include: appointing the Prime Minister and his ministers, commanding the country's army, chairing the Supreme Judicial Council, assigning parliament's upper house (Majlis Al-Shura) members and dissolving parliament's lower elected house (Majlis Al-Nuwab).

Pursuant to Bahrain's constitution, the legislative authority is vested in the King and the National Assembly. Majlis Al Shura and Majlis Al Nuwab together form the National Assembly which discusses and scrutinizes matters of mutual interest. Consisting of a total of 80 members (40 per council) who serve a four-year term, the former council's members are appointed by the King whilst the latter council's members are elected. Majlis Al-Shura exercises a de facto veto over the elected Majlis Al-Nuwab since bills must first be approved by them before being referred to the King and potentially passed as laws.

b. Economic

Whilst strongly driven by tourism, Bahrain's economy is also heavily reliant on exports such as petroleum, aluminum, and construction materials. More importantly however, are the booming communications sector and financial/banking sector today.

Although its economy has been generally growing at a moderate pace due to the decline in oil revenues, Bahrain has implemented measures for fiscal consolidation. The introduction of taxes, increase in government services fees, and subsidy reform should help it recover. Moreover, the growing number of investments complimented by the GCC Development Fund has kept the non-oil sector fairly active.

c. Social

Bahrain is a small country with very few restrictions and relatively low living costs. It is home to various esteemed multinational firms and major industrial projects. In 2017, it was considered the best expat country to live in.[2] The majority of expatriate workers include government employees, professionals, technicians, laborers, and businessmen from across the globe. With that said, Bahrain has no foreign exchange controls or restrictions on the repatriation of money.

---

[1] http://www.worldometers.info/world-population/bahrain-population/.
[2] https://www.thenational.ae/business/economy/bahrain-tops-best-expat-country-in-the-world-to-live-survey-1.626406.

d. Legal

Bahrain has a national constitution and laws that are codified. Just like other GCC states adopted their own versions of the Civil Law system or the Romano-Germanic law system, Bahrain did the same. Its legal system derives from various sources such as Islamic Shari'a, Egyptian law (civil, criminal, and commercial), and English common law. For example, Bahrain has its own version of "Civil Law", "Commercial Companies Law", "Commercial Law", "Labour Law", etc. Moreover, the concept of binding precedents in Bahrain is limited to the judgments of the court of cassation - Bahrain's supreme court of appeal.

Due to the necessity of modernizing the law, the Central Bank of Bahrain (CBB) also introduced the Capital Markets Rulebook which sets out the rules and procedures in relation to the marketing, offering and selling of various financial products.[1] It also has a set of advanced regulations with respect to Collective Investment Undertakings to ensure adequate supervision by the CBB. Consequently, many major international banking and insurance groups have been based in Bahrain.

B. The Status and Direction of the Cooperation with Chinese Enterprises Under the B&R

In January 2016, the Ministry of Foreign Affairs of China published China's Arab Policy Paper.[2] The paper sets out the historical relationship between China and the Arab nations whilst highlighting its strategy for maintaining such ties so as to collectively construct the "Silk Road Economic Belt" initiative.

In light of the above, there has always been a healthy economic relationship between China and the Arab states, especially since they are China's main supplier of crude oil and its 7th biggest trading partner. Such cooperation is expected to continue in order to achieve their goals under the policy. By aiming to adopt a the "1+2+3" cooperation pattern, they aim to cultivate practical collaboration by taking energy cooperation as the key point, trade and infrastructure erection as the two wings, and innovative technological advancements with regards to nuclear energy, satellites, and new energy as the three developments.

Today, as per China's Belt and Road policy, Bahrain is used as a hub for Chinese businesses seeking admission to the Middle East region (e. g. Huawei Technologies and the Bank of China). In addition to being one of the Economic Development Board of Bahrain's (EDB) most crucial trading partners, ever since the establishment of the Sino-Bahrain Committee for Economic, Trade and Technological Cooperation in 1990, China has become one of the largest non-GCC markets for Bahraini exports and one of the major importers into Bahrain.

II. Investment

A. Market Access

a. Department Supervising Investment

Governmental departments dedicated to promoting investment include the EDB (an agency responsible for assessing and devising the economic strategy of Bahrain and attracting investment); and Bahrain Mumtalakat Holding Company (a sovereign wealth fund of Bahrain which seeks to invest in bonds, stocks, and equities). It invests mainly in non-oil and gas related assets and has a portfolio of companies in which it is a stakeholder.

b. Laws and Regulations of Investment Industry

While the Commercial Companies Law (CCL)[3] regulates businesses and covers the relevant formalities and procedures, there are currently no laws directly governing foreign investments. However, there exist other laws which cover different industries. These include Bahrain's Maritime Law[4] (addresses aspects of shipping law), Insurance Law (covers matters regarding insurance companies provided they do not contradict the CBB laws)[5], and the CBB & Financial Institutions Law.[6]

The CBB Rulebook provides further regulations for specific entities of regulated industries. For example, Volume 3 of the CBB Rulebook provides rules for insurance and re-insurance companies as well as penalties for non-compliance.

---

[1] Central Bank of Bahrain Rulebook and regulations are available at http://www.cbb.gov.bh/home.php.
[2] http://www.china.org.cn/world/2016-01/14/content_37573547.htm.
[3] Legislative Decree No.21 of 2001 as amended by Law No.50 of 2014.
[4] Decree No.23 of 1982 as amended by Law No.35 of 2014.
[5] Legislative Decree No.17 of 1987.
[6] Law No.64 of 2006 as amended by Legislative Decree No.34 of 2015.

c. Forms of Investment

With a range of investment forms, foreign companies are allowed to establish wholly owned subsidiaries and branches in Bahrain with very few requirements such as, in some instances, a Bahraini national sponsor. Additionally, despite having a few free trade zones in Bahrain which offer even more leniency (e. g. zero custom duties and exemptions on national labor hiring), the country sets an ideal climate for investment due to the fact that there is no corporate or personal income tax (see Tax section below).

d. Standards of Market Access and Examination

The main restriction on foreign investment is that a company established in Bahrain must sometimes be at least 51% owned by Bahraini nationals. However, this depends on whether a foreign company's branch is being formed as an operational office, and whether the business activities a company is undertaking permit 100% foreign ownership. This also differs where the foreign ownership is of GCC nationals, or if the company is established in one of the free trade zones.

There may be further restrictions such as licensing requirements for certain sectors and activities which may also subject the company to additional regulations and approvals.

B. Foreign Exchange Regulation

a. Department Supervising Foreign Exchange

Not applicable to Bahrain.

b. Brief Introduction of Laws and Regulations for Foreign Exchange

Bahrain has a free market economy that promotes transparency. There are no foreign exchange controls or restrictions on the repatriation of capital, profits, and dividends, thus permitting full transferability of such means.

c. Requirements for Foreign Exchange Management for Foreign Enterprises

Not applicable to Bahrain.

C. Financing

a. Main Financial Institutions

Following Decree No.64 of 2006 with respect to promulgating the Central Bank of Bahrain and Financial Institutions Law, the Central Bank of Bahrain (CBB) was established (previously known as the Bahrain Monetary Agency). It is headquartered in the Diplomatic Area in the country's capital - Manama. The CBB is responsible for various matters, including: implementing monetary policies, regulating the financial sector, serving as the government's fiscal agent, and managing Bahrain's foreign currency cash and gold reserves.

The CBB licenses and regulates numerous entities as it covers the full range of banking, insurance, investment business, and capital markets activities. It is also responsible for setting the exchange rate of the Bahraini Dinar against major foreign currencies (currently pegged to the US Dollar).

Having a strong reputation in the financial sector and being the business hub for numerous foreign companies, Bahrain is home to many local and foreign banks. With a mix of retail, investment, and Islamic banks, there are also several foreign banks which have established representative offices in Bahrain.

b. Financial Conditions for Foreign Enterprises

With regards to opening a bank account, it is a relatively easy and straight-forward process for those residing in Bahrain. Subject to money laundering precautionary formalities that banks have to undertake, banks generally only permit the opening of bank accounts to Bahraini nationals and residents, making it difficult for entities without a presence in Bahrain to access current account facilities. It should be duly noted that the issuance of check books is limited to Bahraini nationals and residents, not foreign companies or individuals outside of Bahrain.

In terms of financing, it is easier and quicker for companies within Bahrain to receive such form of services. Nonetheless, this does not prevent foreign entities from obtaining the same services even if they do not have a presence in Bahrain. Such entities will be subject to the customary credit checks and measures necessary before they can be provided with the relevant facilities.

D. Land Policy

a. Brief Introduction of Land-related Laws and Regulations

The Survey and Land Registration Bureau (SLRB) is the governmental body responsible for maintaining a land register, with title to registered land being guaranteed by the King.The Law No.27 of 2017 Concerning the

Promulgation of the Real Estate Sector Regulation Law replaced Law No.28 of 2014 Concerning Real Estate Development. Whilst the new law is similar to the old one, it aims to modernize real estate in Bahrain and address new matters/concepts. It also established the Real Estate Regulation Authority (RERA) to be the regulator of all real estate in Bahrain, and issuer of the necessary licenses.

b. Rules of Land Acquisition for Foreign Enterprises

In accordance with the Legislative Decree No.2 of 2001, foreign buyers (natural and corporate) are permitted to purchase certain types of property in Bahrain in particular areas.In terms of the purchasing process, it is quite similar to that practiced throughout the world.

E. The Establishment and Dissolution of Companies

a. The Forms of Enterprises

The CCL recognizes eight types of companies for formation and permits foreign equity in all of them (complete ownership may vary). Any company that does not take one of the forms shall be null and void, holding any persons contracting in its name personally and jointly liable to third party obligations.The forms of legal structures are as follows:
- General Partnership Company ("General Partnership");
- Limited Partnership Company ("Limited Partnership");
- Association in Participation (Joint Venture);
- Shareholding Company ("BSC");
- Limited Partnership by Shares;
- Limited Liability Company ("WLL");
- Single Person Company ("SPC");
- Holding Company.

A branch established by a foreign entity does not constitute a separate company under the law. It is considered as part of the foreign parent company and so is bound by the laws/decisions of that company, hence limiting its liability to the parent company's assets. By providing a guarantee and appointing a local manager, a branch of a foreign company may be established with no minimum capital requirement. A foreign company's branch may take the form of:
- Representative or Regional Office: these cannot carry out operations.They are used purely to set up a presence in Bahrain and can only undertake marketing and promotional activities.
- Operational Office: can carry out operations, including banking and insurance activities (subject to the CBB's approval).However, a local sponsorship from a Bahraini trader is required.

Bahrain's government does not generally associate itself with ownership and operation/participation in companies, except where the industry or activity is in the interest of the nation (e.g.oil and gas industry).

A company can covert from one legal form to another. However, if conversion is to a BSC, at least two financial years must have lapsed since the company was registered.For all companies to convert, in addition to the notifying creditors of such conversion by way of publication in the Official Gazette and a daily newspaper, they must pay the loans and banking facilities or secure their creditors' approval of such conversion before the approval of the competent authorities of their conversion. The conversion of the company does not entail acquiring a new corporate body, but it does maintain all the rights and obligations of a company before the conversion.

a) General Partnership Company

A General Partnership is a company formed by two or more persons (natural or corporate) who shall assume the nature of a trader and are jointly responsible for the company's debts and obligations on an unlimited liability basis.This means that, in addition to having a right of recourse against the company's assets, creditors have a right of recourse against the private property of the partners.Its name must consist of the names of all partners or the name of one of them while adding "& Co." (or its equivalent) and must be followed by "a Bahraini Partnership Company".

General Partnerships allow up to 100% foreign ownership and do not have a minimum share capital requirement. Further, the company's management is undertaken by all partners unless agreed otherwise. In any case, there must be at least one manager. The company is bound by whatever acts performed by its manager(s) which fall within their functions and powers for the company.

Shares are not negotiable and cannot be assigned without the consent of all partners. Its resolutions are adopted on a unanimous vote basis unless the Memorandum of Association states otherwise. The profits and losses and the shares of each partner in them shall be determined at the end of the company's financial year on the basis of the balance sheet and the profit and loss account.

b) Limited Partnership Company

A Limited Partnership is a company established between one partner or more, who are jointly and severally liable for the company's obligations in all their fortune (joint partners), and another partner or more who have invested capital in the company but are not undertaking management (sleeping partners) who shall not be liable for the company's obligations save to the extent of their shares in the capital. Accordingly, sleeping partners cannot interfere in the management of the company even by virtue of a letter of authority. Doing so shall hold them liable as joint partners with the other joint partners for the obligations of the company arising from their management.

Limited Partnerships allow up to 100% foreign ownership (i.e.both types of partners can be foreign) and do not have a minimum share capital requirement. The provisions of a General Partnership also apply to Limited Partnerships in terms of incorporation, management, winding up, and liquidation.

The name of the Limited Partnership company must only include the names of the joint partners or the name of one partner (if he is the only one liable for all his fortune) followed by "& Co." The sleeping partners' names do not have to be mentioned in the company's public records nor appear in the company's name, only the memorandum of association. If their names are included in the company's name with their knowledge, they become liable as joint partners to third parties acting in good faith.

c) Association in Participation

An Association in Participation is a company that conceals itself from others and does not have a juristic entity, nor is it subject to publication procedures. The partners' rights and obligations, as well as the manner in which profits and losses will be allocated, are determined by the Memorandum of Association. Unlike other companies, the Memorandum of Association does not need to be in Arabic or notarized.

Third parties do not have a legal relationship in respect of the company's activities except with the partner or partners (must be of Bahraini nationality or sponsored by a Bahraini) whom they have dealt with. There after, the partners may have recourse against each other in respect of the company's activities and in respect of their association with it and in the share of each partner.

d) Shareholding Company (Public or Closed)

(i) Public: A public BSC is a company with a minimum of seven shareholders who are liable to the extent of their shares. Such companies permit banking and investment activities and can be established with the participation of foreign capital or expertise. Such condition is subject to the minister's order which shall specify the percentages of participation of foreign capital or expertise in certain sectors/activities. The company's name, which may not derive from a natural person's name, must be followed by the phrase "a Bahraini Shareholding Company".

It requires a minimum share capital of BHD 1,000,000 and the company's Articles of Association may specify an authorized capital exceeding the issued capital by not more than ten times. Shares are negotiable but may not be issued in a lesser value than that of their nominal. They may be owned by two or more persons provided they are represented by one person towards the company. The promoters must subscribe for shares representing at least 10% of the company's capital, and shall pay, before the publication of the subscription prospectus, the amount equivalent to the percentage required to be paid by the public for each share on subscription. Whilst Shares and interim certificates may be traded, disposals/transfers of shares will not be effective against the company or third parties unless registered.

A BSC must have at least five directors and their term must not exceed three years subject to renewal. They have the powers to perform the acts necessary for the administration of the company in accordance with its objectives. These powers and acts shall not be limited except as provided by the CCL, the company's Articles of Association or the resolutions of the general assembly. The company's Articles of Association shall provide for the manner of specifying remuneration of these directors, the total of which cannot exceed 10% of the net profit after deducting statutory reserves and after distributing a profit of not less than five 5% of the company's paid capital. With that said, the statutory reserve refers to a 10% of the net profits which must be deducted every year and set aside (unless the Articles of Association specify a higher percentage) until the reserve amounts to 50% of the paid-up capital.

(ii) Closed: A closed BSC is a company with a minimum of two shareholders who are liable to the extent of their shares, and at least three directors. It requires a minimum share capital of BHD 250,000 and permits banking and investment activities as well as foreign ownership of up to 100% depending on activity. A minimum of 50% of the capital must be paid initially at the time of incorporation; the remaining to be paid within three years. As such, shares of a closed BSC may not become negotiable except after payment of the full value of the shares and, in case the shares are sold, preference of purchase must be given to the company's shareholders.

It is governed by the same provisions relating to a public BSC which do not contravene the provisions of a closed BSC in the CCL.

e) Limited Partnership by Shares

A Limited Partnership by Shares is a company which consists of two categories of partners: partners who are jointly and severally liable for the company's obligations in all their fortune (joint partners), and partners who shall not be liable for the company's obligations save to the extent of their shares in the capital (sleeping partners). The name of such a company must consist of the names of one or more joint partners and can include an innovative name derived from the company's objects. However, the names of the sleeping partners may not be added. If their names are added with their knowledge, they would be considered joint partners towards third parties.

The company's capital, which can be 100% foreign owned, must be divided into negotiable, indivisible shares of equal value and sleeping partners are subject to the same provisions concerning shareholders in a BSC to the extent that they do not contravene the CCL's provisions governing a Limited Partnership by Shares. Accordingly, the provisions relating to share certificates issued by BSCs apply to the share warrants issued by a Limited Partnership by Shares.

Having a minimum of four partners, management is undertaken by one or more joint partners, whose names must be mentioned in the Articles of Association, and they shall be liable in their capacity as promoters of the company. Shareholding partners may not interfere in the administration of the company's activities related to third parties, even with authorization. However, they are able to participate in internal management within the limits set out in the Memorandum of Association. If the number of partners exceeds 10, an elected supervisory board of three members needs to be established to supervise the company's activities. Moreover, the company's Articles of Association must specify the manner of remunerating the managers.

f) Limited Liability Company

A WLL company is a company with a minimum of two shareholders and a maximum of 50 (natural or corporate) whose liability is limited to their shareholding. If the number of partners falls below two, the company will, by force of law, turn into an SPC unless the company completes the number within 30 days from the date of pooling the company's shares into the hands of one partner. Followed by the phrase "With Limited Liability" at the end, the company's name may comprise of a special name or one that derives from its purpose, and can include the name of the partners. Such particulars must be mentioned in all the company's contracts, invoices, advertisements, papers and publications, or else the company's managers shall be jointly liable to the extent of their private property towards third parties.

The company cannot issue negotiable shares or bonds, and any transfer of partners' shares is subject to preemptive rights and the company's constitution. It may not undertake insurance or banking activities but foreign ownership is allowed up to 100% depending on the business activity. If the business activity requires a local sponsor, foreign ownership will generally be limited to 49% of the issued share capital. There is also an obligation to maintain a statutory reserve similar to that of a BSC.

Whilst the company's shares must be divided equally with a value not less than BHD 50, there is no minimum share capital requirement; the capital must simply be sufficient to achieve the company's objectives. Two or more persons may jointly own one share, provided that one person shall represent them towards the company and both shall be jointly liable for the obligations arising from them. The company cannot be incorporated until the shares are fully paid and in-kind shares are delivered to it.

A WLL must have at least one manager appointed from the partners or non-partners to manage the company and represent it. They shall be jointly liable towards the company, partners and third parties for any breaches or mismanagement. Such managers may not engage in the management of a competing company or one with similar objectives. The duties, obligations and responsibilities of the manager(s) shall be the same as those of the members of the board of directors in a BSC. They must also prepare, for each financial year, the company's balance sheet, profit and loss account and a report on the company's activities and financial position together with their recommendations as regards profit distribution. However, the company's auditor(s) are appointed by the ordinary general assembly of partners annually.

g) Single Person Company

An SPC is a company that is wholly-owned by one person (natural or corporate), where the owner is liable only to the extent of the company's capital. It should have a special commercial name or a name derived from the purpose of its establishment accompanied by the name of the capital's proprietor, and followed by "Single Person Company." This form of company is governed by the provisions regulating a WLL to the extent that they do not contravene its nature.

Management of the company is undertaken by the proprietor of its capital, unless one or more managers are appointed. In any case, there must be at least one manager. Under an SPC, 100% foreign ownership is permitted, provided the business activity allows it. There is also no minimum share capital requirement; the capital must simply be adequate for the company to conduct its business.

The company shall terminate upon the death of its capital's owner, unless, within six months from the owner's death, the shares of the heirs are transferred to one person or, if they are distributed amongst them, they choose to continue with it in another legal form. Further, if the owner is a corporate person, the SPC will terminate in the event that the owner is wound up.

In addition to the abovementioned, if the owner of an SPC, in bad faith, liquidates or suspends the company's activities before its expiry period or before it realizes its objects for which it was established, he will be liable for his obligations in his personal funds. The same applies if the owner places himself in a position where his interests conflict with the interests of the company.

h) Holding Company

A Holding Company is a company whose purpose is to own shares in Bahraini or foreign companies, or participate in their establishment. It must hold at least 50% of the affiliated company and must take the form of a BSC, WLL, or SPC and include the phrase "Holding Company" on all the relevant documents, together with its commercial name. The company is governed by the provisions of the company which it has taken its form.

An affiliated company is not permitted to own shares or stakes in the Holding Company, and the Holding Company has to appoint its representatives on the boards of directors of its affiliated companies in proportion to its holdings, unless agreed otherwise with the shareholders or partners in the affiliated company.

Its objects are as follows:

(i) To manage its affiliated companies or to participate in the administration of other companies in which it is participating and to provide the necessary support therefore.

(ii) To invest its funds in stocks, bonds and securities.

(iii) To own property and chattels necessary to undertake its business activities within the limits allowed by the Law.

(iv) To provide loans, guarantees and financing for its affiliated companies.

(v) To own industrial property rights, such as patents, commercial and industrial marks and concessions, and such other intangible rights and utilize and lease them to its affiliated companies or other companies.

At the end of every financial year, the Holding Company must prepare a consolidated statement containing its balance sheet and profit and loss account for itself along with all its affiliated companies. This must also be accompanied by the requisite notes and statements in accordance with the international accounting principles.

b. The Procedure for Establishment

Having chosen the type of company to establish and the relevant business activities it will be undertaking, except for Associations in Participation, the following steps will generally apply:

(i) An application is made to the Ministry of Industry and Commerce (MOIC) along with the relevant documents for pre-approval.

(ii) Upon pre-approval, the applicant must submit the company's draft constitutional documents (i.e.memorandum of association and articles of association) and an address for the company's office supported by a lease agreement.

(iii) After the submissions, MOIC will contact the relevant authorities whose approvals are required depending on the business activities selected. Each authority has its own requirements that must be satisfied.

(iv) Following clearance from the authorities, MOIC informs the Notary Public and requests it to facilitate the notarization and incorporation of the constitutional documents of the company.

(v) A bank account must then be opened for the company in one of the local banks so the capital is deposited in it. Afterwards, a certificate of deposit will be issued by the bank.

(vi) The notarized documents must be submitted to MOIC with the relevant fees to obtain a commercial registration number along with the company's extract which contains information for its public records.

(vii) An official publication is then made in the Official Gazette and the company is considered legally incorporated from the date following the publication.

Associations in Participation do not have specific formalities as they do not need to be registered. The joint venture agreement must specify the parties' rights and obligations as well as determine the division of profits and losses.

c. Routes and Requirements of Dissolution

According to the CCL, a company shall be dissolved for any of the following reasons:

(i) Expiry of its specified period, unless the company's Memorandum or Articles of Association provide for its renewal.

(ii) Fulfillment of the objects for which it was incorporated.

(iii) Destruction of all its property or a sizable portion thereof, making its continuation unfeasible.

(iv) A unanimous resolution by the partners to dissolve the company before the expiry of its term, unless the company's Memorandum or Articles of Association provide for a special majority.

(v) Merger with another company.

In the event that a company, without a justifiable reason, does not undertake its business activities for a period of one year since incorporation or suspends its activities for a period of one year, the commercial registration of the company will be struck off by an order of the Minister of Industry and Commerce.

Furthermore, except for public BSCs, the court may, on an application by any partner, order the dissolution of the company if it finds serious reasons justifying it. The court may dissolve a company upon the application of a partner due to another partner not honoring his obligations.

General Partnerships, Limited Partnerships and Associations in Participation shall be dissolved if one of the partners withdraws from the company (provided adequate notice was given to the other partners) if its term is indefinite, or in the event of the death of one of the partners. The court may also dissolve the company if one of the partners becomes bankrupt/insolvent or obtains a distrait order. The same applies for Limited Partnerships by Shares, unless the company's Articles of Association state otherwise. If the Articles of Association of a Limited Partnership by Shares do not contain any provision in this respect, the extraordinary general assembly may decide upon the continuation of the company.

As for WLLs, they do not dissolve upon the withdrawal of one of the partners or more, nor will it dissolve in the event of a partner's death. Unless the Memorandum of Association states otherwise, the position remains the same, even if a distrait order is issued by the court against a partner is passed by or if a partner is adjudged bankrupt/insolvent.

F. Mergers and Acquisition

The rules and procedures applicable to mergers are governed by Bahrain's CCL. It can be done in two ways: the acquired company is wound up and its assets are transferred to an existing company (acquisition), or the existing companies are wound up and a new company is formed (consolidation). In all cases, a merger must not result in a monopoly of an activity or product and notice of the merger must be published in the Official Gazette and one daily newspaper, thus giving creditors 60 days to object to the merger.

Licensed or regulated entities such as those under the CBB or the Telecommunications Regulatory Authority (TRA) require prior approval from their governing bodies who may place further requirements before the merger. Furthermore, the Takeovers, Mergers and Acquisitions Module[1] of the CBB Rulebook covers takeovers, mergers and acquisitions of Bahrain domiciled companies that are listed on the Bahrain Bourse (BHB) and overseas companies whose primary listing of ordinary voting equity securities is on the BHB. The module is generally triggered when 30% or more of a company's voting rights are being acquired.

G. Competition Regulation

a. Department Supervising Competition Regulation

There is currently no specific competition authority in Bahrain.

b. Brief Introduction of Competition Law

Whilst Bahrain does not currently have a formal competition law, competition is addressed in some legislations to prohibit certain acts. For example, Legislative Decree No.7 of 1987 promulgating the Law of Commerce generally prohibits activities that would have an adverse effect on competition. Moreover, companies are not permitted to undertake practices damaging to their competitors or attracting the customs of their competitors.

Also, the Consumer Protection Directorate and Law No.35 of 2012 with respect to Consumer Protection offer some input on competition. They ensure that the law with respect to determining prices and control is adequately enforced. Furthermore, there is a law in force which seeks to prevent the monopoly of the cement trade.

Moreover, the Civil Code[2] addresses the issue of restrictive agreements. An agreement with arbitrary provisions can be amended by a judge.

c. Measures Regulating Competition

Whilst there are general sanctions applicable for non-compliance of laws as per the Penal Code (e.g.fines and prison sentences), the Consumer Protection Law states that a prison sentence for a period of no more than five years and a fine not exceeding BHD 5,000, or either penalty, shall be inflicted upon anyone who violates the provisions concerning competition.

---

[1] CBB Rulebook, Volume 6.
[2] Legislative Decree No.19 of 2001.

H. Tax

a. Tax Regime and Rules

Bahrain is generally considered a tax haven due to its minimal tax obligations. It has no designated tax authority as opposed to other GCC member states (e.g.Saudi Arabia and UAE). There is currently no income, sales, or capital gains tax in Bahrain except for, in certain circumstances, businesses operating in the oil and gas sector or those which generate profit from extracting or refining fossil fuels in Bahrain. A rate of 46% is levied on the net profits of such companies regardless of whether they are local or foreign.

Bahrain does not have any withholding taxes on the payment of dividends, royalties, or interest. However, it does have effective double tax treaties with numerous countries. These include: Algeria, Austria, Barbados, Belarus, Belgium, Brunei, Bulgaria, China, Cyprus, Czech Republic, Egypt, Estonia, France, Georgia, Hungary, Iran, Ireland, Jordan, Republic of Korea, Lebanon, Luxembourg, Malaysia, Malta, Mexico, Morocco, the Netherlands, Pakistan, Philippines, Portugal, Seychelles, Singapore, Sri Lanka, Sudan, Syria, Thailand, Tajikistan, Turkey, Turkmenistan, the United Kingdom, Uzbekistan, and Yemen.

b. Main Categories and Rates of Tax

In addition to the corporate income tax applicable to the oil and gas sector, municipality tax exists in Bahrain at a 10% rate levied on renting commercial and residential properties to expatriates. Bahrain also imposes stamp duty on the transfer and/or registration of real estate at a 2% rate. The rate can be reduced to 1.7% if payment is made within the first two months following the transaction date.

Since 30 December 2017, Bahrain has been imposing excise tax on harmful products such as tobacco (taxed at 100%), energy drinks (taxed at 100%), and soft drinks (taxed at 50%). In addition, Bahrain is currently working on the implementation of VAT as it signed the GCC unified VAT and Excise Treaties on 1 February 2017. Accordingly, pursuant to the GCC VAT agreement, Bahrain has until 1 January 2019 to implement it. As per the treaty, VAT will be taxed at a standard rate of 5% on most goods and services with some limited exceptions. There are currently no implementation regulations or set date as to when VAT will be introduced.

c. Tax Declaration and Preference

Not applicable to Bahrain.

I. Securities

a. Brief Introduction of Securities-related Laws and Regulations

In addition to the CCL which stipulates which corporate entities may issue negotiable securities, the Bahrain Stock Exchange Law[1] introduced and governed the self-regulated marketplace - the Bahrain Stock Exchange (now known as the Bahrain Bourse).[2] The CBB Rulebook provides for detailed regulations on security-related matters.

b. Supervision and Regulation of Securities Market

The CBB regulates and monitors Bahrain's financial markets through adherence to the best international standards and practices whilst protecting investors. It approves all the applications for the public offering of any securities or financial instruments based on compliance with all the disclosure requirements and conditions.

The CBB also applies the international disclosure standards with the aim of improving market transparency, monitoring the stock exchange, clearance transactions, deposit systems, brokerage companies and the market makers.

c. Requirements for Engagement in Securities Trading for Foreign Enterprises

Security issuers must apply, and obtain the CBB's approval before listing. Further to complying with the requisite conditions, foreign companies wishing to list their shares on the BHB must comply with the CCL, and Resolution No 6 of 1996 stating:

(i) The applicant company shall either be a public shareholding company, duly listed on the stock exchange in the country of incorporation, or a closed company which has been established for at least three years prior to the date of application.

(ii) The paid-up capital of the company must not be less than BHD 3,770,000, or the equivalent in any other currency.

(iii) The company should have maintained net profits from its principal activities for the last 3 years prior the

---

[1] Decree Law No.4 of 1975.
[2] Law No.57 of 2009.

listing application.

(iv) No restrictions on the transfer of the company's share ownership between the investors are imposed by the company's Articles of Association, or by the laws of the country of its incorporation.

(v) The company's financial position must be sound.

(vi) The number of shareholders in the company should not be less than 100.

(vii) The company should assign a representative office in Bahrain to undertake the transfer of share ownership, distribution of dividends, financial reports and other related issues, as and when required.

(viii) The company must comply with the Listing Agreement signed with the Bourse.

With respect to foreign enterprises seeking to buy shares of a public BSC, they will need approval from MOIC. As for issuers who are interested in listing bonds/sukuk on BHB, they must comply with the following:

(i) The Central Bank of Bahrain and Financial Institution Law of 2006.

(ii) Resolution No.17 of 2012 of the rules and regulations of the trading instruments licensed by the Central Bank of Bahrain.

(iii) Foreign bonds are required to be issued in accordance with the relevant laws of the issuing country.

(iv) Appropriate approvals need to be in place from the Central Bank of Bahrain.

(v) The issuer must be operational for at least two years.

(vi) The issuer's financial position must be sound.

(vii) The issuer's paid-up capital should not be less than US$10,000,000.

(viii) The issuer should abide by the Listing Agreement to be signed with Bahrain Bourse.

(ix) The issuer should appoint a representative office in Bahrain for the registration of the bonds/sukuk, distribution of dividends, reports and other related matters.

(x) The issuer should publish its balance sheets and financial results in various media outlets.

J. Preference and Protection of Investment

a. The Structure of Preference Policies

Although Bahrain has no official preference policies, preference is generally given to Bahraini nationals and local companies. Nonetheless, taking into account Bahrain's excellent foreign relations and the numerous treaties in place, it actively encourages foreign investment and seeks investors.

b. Support for Specific Industries and Regions

Industry-specific investment is strongly promoted in Bahrain. Despite the reliance by the country's budget on the oil and gas sector, Bahrain's diverse economy stimulates contribution in other economic sectors. As such, the EDB targets Foreign Direct Investment in other major sectors which heavily contribute to its economy: manufacturing and logistics, financial services, information and communication technology (ICT), and tourism.

c. Special Economic Areas

Whilst the entire country is somewhat of a free zone due to its recognition for 100% foreign ownership in most industries, unrestricted repatriation of capital and profits policy, and its minimal tax obligations and customs duties, Bahrain's Free Trade zones are amongst the most popular and are perfect for those looking to use Bahrain as a regional manufacturing or distribution base due to the exemptions/reductions they offer.

d. Investment Protection

Bahrain has signed over 30 bilateral investment treaties (BITs) with different countries, including one with China.[①] Entered into in 1999, the agreement seeks to encourage, protect, and create favorable conditions for investment between the two nations.

III. Trade

A. Department Supervising Trade

The Ministry of Industry, Commerce and Tourism ("MOICT") implements Bahrain's trade policies and regulations, in coordination with other ministries and trade-related bodies including the Economic Development Board ("EDB"), Ministry of Finance, and Central Bank of Bahrain. The private sector's participation in trade policy formulation is through the Bahrain Chamber of Commerce and Industry ("BCCI").

The MOICT is responsible for a diverse range of activities which make up the commercial environment in

---

① http://www.dezshira.com/library/treaties/bilateral-investment-treaty-between-bahrain-and-china-4135.html.

Bahrain, including the registration of all forms of commercial business, commercial agencies, industrial property, standards and metrology and foreign trade. In general, the MOICT's aim is to ensure the maintenance of an open, transparent and market driven commercial environment so as develop Bahrain's economic competitiveness, and to encourage inward investment, at the same time promoting employment for the local population.

The EDB was established pursuant to Decree No.9 of 2000, with a focus on providing strategic direction on the management of the Bahrain economy, and in particular facilitating private sector and foreign investment. The EDB aims to increase economic competitiveness, raise productivity levels, and focus on creating a skilled workforce that contributes to the development of Bahrain. Bahrain's Crown Prince provides oversight over the EDB alongside its Board of Directors, which includes government ministers as well as industry executives, enabling the public and private sectors to work closely together.

B. Brief Introduction of Trade Laws and Regulations

Trade is regulated through the following key laws:
(i) The Law of Commerce, promulgated by Legislative Decree No.7 of 1987, as amended;
(ii) The Commercial Companies Law, promulgated by Legislative Decree No.21 of 2001, as amended; and
(iii) The Commercial Registration Law, promulgated by Legislative Decree No.27 of 2015.

Bahrain, in an effort to strengthen economic ties and increase trading opportunities and growth, signed the Bahrain-U.S. Free Trade Agreement ("FTA"), which entered into force on 11 January 2006. The overall objectives of the FTA are the elimination of trade tariffs on imports and exports and expansion of manufacturing service sectors.

C. Trade Management

Bahrain has been a commercial crossroad for thousands of years. The word Bahrain means 'two seas' in Arabic, indicating how the country's geographic position has been important throughout its long history as a trading center linking east and west. A major stopping point for merchants and home to the rich pearl diving industry, Bahrain made a name for itself as the Gulf's pre-eminent trade hub. Bahrain has in recent years diversified its economy and has become home to numerous multinational firms in the Gulf.

As a member of the GCC, Bahrain has been applying the GCC Common External Tariff (CET) since 2003. Generally, Bahrain's trade policies and regulations are liberal, applying a relatively simple most-favored-nation (MFN) tariff. There are no tariff quotas, no nuisance rates, and no other duties and charges on imports. Bahrain maintains its own list of restricted and prohibited goods.

D. The Inspection and Quarantine of Import and Export Commodities

In an effort to unify and regulate customs procedures between the Gulf Cooperation Council member states, the customs administrations of the GCC member states established a Unified Customs Law in 2002.

Certificates must accompany goods subject to import restrictions from the relevant authorities. Most of the import restrictions maintained by Bahrain are on safety, health or moral grounds, and apply to, inter alia, special breed horses, armaments, insecticides and fungicides, and radioactive materials. Food, plant, and animal imports that are restricted for health reasons must be accompanied by sanitary and phytosanitary health certificates from the exporting country. A certificate declaring them to be free of radiation and dioxin must accompany imports of food products. In addition, pharmaceutical products must be imported directly from a manufacturer with a research department, and the products must be licensed in the country of manufacture and in at least two GCC countries other than Bahrain, one of which must be the Kingdom of Saudi Arabia.

All imports into Bahrain, including those destined for bonded areas, must be accompanied by:
(i) Four copies of the bill of landing (airway bill for air cargo);
(ii) The original of the certificate of origin (for statistical purposes);
(iii) Three copies of the commercial invoice;
(iv) Insurance certificates for all shipments insured by the exporter or shipper;
(v) A Chamber of Commerce in the country of origin, stating origin and current export price of the product, must certify commercial invoices;
(vi) The relevant Consulate of Bahrain must stamp the certificate of origin or any Arab Embassy in the country of origin before the goods may be exported to Bahrain. Consular fees are waived for U.S. traders;
(vii) In the event that the documents are not authenticated, the goods may still be cleared after inspection by Customs and duties paid in the form of a deposit, which is forfeited if the authenticated documents are not provided within six months of the date of import.

Product-specific documentation is also required for imports of drugs and medicines, food products, live animals, birds and fish, and all meat and poultry products. Import permits must accompany certain products, including special breed horses (Arabian horses), armaments, insecticides, and fungicides. All importers and exporters must be listed in the commercial registry maintained by the MOICT and BCCI.

Importers in Bahrain are not required to use a commercial agent. Bahrain has no laws or regulations on pre-shipment inspection. Goods received on a through-bill-of-lading, for a destination outside Bahrain and dispatched overland, are cleared on a transit bill. A deposit or guarantee is required by Customs Affairs, and is refunded on proof of exit of the goods from Bahrain within 30 days of the date of the transit bill. If the consignment is dispatched by sea, directly from the port (ship-shore-ship or ship-to-ship), the goods are cleared on a transshipment bill.

In 2011, a new eCustoms System for Single Window and International Trade Facilitation known as OFOQ was established. OFOQ aims to provide integrated, seamless, electronic trade operations between Bahrain's customs and regulatory authorities and the trade and logistics operators. It is a single window platform for submissions and enquiries, with particular emphasis on reducing the cost and time of transactions whilst ensuring compliance through intelligent risk management. The system allows traders to expedite the release and clearance process of goods. OFOQ is fully operational at Bahrain ports and its international airport.

E. Customs Management

In an effort to ease customs management and operations, Bahrain Customs Authority computerized their system and created eCAS. The purpose behind eCAS is to automate most of the manual processes, which were being carried out by the Customs Authority. The implementation of the eCAS system has resulted in enhanced working environments, more accurate data capturing and efficient reporting and management. eCAS also incorporates a verification system where documents such as Certificate of Origin are verified and container level inspection notes are stored.

IV. Labour

A. Brief Introduction of Labour Laws and Regulations

Labour matters in the Kingdom of Bahrain are governed by Law No.36 of 2012 promulgating the Labour Law for the Private Sector, as amended (the "Labour Law"), which replaced the previous labour legislation, Legislative Decree No.19 of 1976.

The Labour Law has been aligned with several Arab and international labour treaties and conventions to which Bahrain is a signatory and which have come into effect over the last few decades, and has revitalised the private sector labour market by giving more rights to employees, such as improvement of working conditions, prohibition of discriminating practices such as discrimination in the payment of wages based on gender, ethnic origin, language, religion or beliefs. The Labour Law also introduced improvements in terms of annual leave, maternity leave, sick leave entitlements, and labour dispute resolution.

The majority of the provisions of the Labour Law apply to all private sector employees, except those exempt under Article 2 thereof, namely:

(i) domestic servants and persons regarded as such namely gardeners, house security guards, nannies, drivers and cooks for carrying out their job duties for the benefit of an employer or his relatives; and

(ii) an employer's family members who are actually supported by him namely the husband, wife, blood relatives and in-laws.

B. Requirements of Employing Foreign Employees

a. Work Permit

In order to hire any foreign employee, the employer is required to obtain a work permit and residence permit for each expatriate employee. Work permits for expatriate employees are issued by the Labour Market Regulatory Authority ("LMRA") and may be subject to numerical restrictions by the LMRA. Such permits are valid for 2 years.

"Bahrainisation" requirements, i.e.requirements to hire a certain number of Bahraini employees for every group of foreign employees, apply to companies who hire ten or more expatriates. A Bahrainisation table organised by business activities of employers is available in person at the LMRA, or on its website.

Essentially, to work in the Kingdom, foreign employees should be medically fit, should have entered the country lawfully, and should possess a valid passport and retain a residence and work permit.

b. Application Procedure

The documents that are required in the application procedure for a work permit are as follows:
(i) a work permit application form;
(ii) a copy of the employee's passport;
(iii) offer letter or employment contract between the employer and the employee; and
(iv) medical check up report for foreign employees.

c. Social Insurance

As stipulated by the Ministry of Industry, Commerce and Tourism, all foreign and local staff are required to be registered with the Social Insurance Organisation ("SIO").

SIO contributions are as follows: for Bahraini employees, the employer pays 10% of basic salary and recurring allowances and the employee pays 5% of basic salary and recurring allowances. For expatriate employees, the employer pays 3% of basic salary and recurring allowances.

C. Exit and Entry

a. Visa Types

All persons who wish to enter Bahrain need a visa except citizens of the Gulf Cooperation Council.

a) Tourist Visa

Such visas are issued for stays of 2 weeks to citizens of the EU, Australia, Canada, Hong Kong (China), Japan, New Zealand and the US. Applicants must possess valid, up-to-date passports and a return ticket. Such visas do not allow the individual to engage in any employment.

b) Visitor Visa

Such visas require the sponsorship of a Bahraini, who must apply to the Nationality, Passport and Residence Affairs on the visitor's behalf. They are valid for 1 month and do not allow employment.

c) 72-Hour and 7-Day Visa

Such visas are obtainable at the point of entry for short-stay business visitors. What needs to be presented is a return ticket and a valid passport.

d) Business Visa

Individuals intending to stay for longer than 1 week on business must obtain a business visa through the Bahrain embassy located in their country. Such visas are valid for up to four weeks. An application form must be completed and the passport, photographs, employer's letter indicating the purpose of the trip and a letter of no-objection must be presented.

e) Work Visa

Such visas are valid for one or two years and they entitle the individual to reside in the country. A medical examination is required and fees are applicable. The necessary and relevant paperwork is usually arranged by the individual's sponsor.

f) Family Visa

The immediate family of those working in Bahrain can obtain this visa, which entitled them to residence status for the period of employment. Members of the family aren't allowed to work, unless separate arrangements are made and the appropriate work visas obtained.

b. Restrictions for Exit and Entry

The LMRA has implemented an 'Easy Exit Scheme' for individual overstaying their visa, enabling them to leave the country upon paying minimal fines. Under the scheme, expats who overstay their work visas can leave Bahrain after paying a fine of BHD 15/-, while those who overstay visit visas can leave Bahrain after paying BHD 25/-.

D. Trade Union and Labour Organizations

The Labour Law governs the formation and regulation of labour organizations and trade unions in Bahrain. As stipulated by Article 176 thereof, an establishment that employs fifty workers or more shall provide the necessary social and cultural services to its workers in agreement with the trade union organization, if any, or with the workers' representatives. The General Federation of Bahrain Trade Unions was established in 2002 under the Workers Trade Union Law, which recognizes the right of workers to organize collectively.

E. Labour Disputes

a. Disciplinary Procedures

As stipulated by the Labour Law, any employer with ten or more workers should establish rules in respect of the workplace, and a disciplinary procedure, as approved by the Ministry of Labour and Social Development, which should be clearly displayed.

If an employer wishes to take disciplinary action or dismiss an employee, the Labour Law should first be consulted. The disciplinary measures that can be undertaken against an employee include fines, suspension, warnings and dismissal.

If an employer/employee intends to make a complaint, he should first follow the statutory procedure applicable to all labour disputes. A claim must first be presented to the Ministry of Labour and Social Development.

All claims are now filed with Labour Case Administration Office, wherein the Labour Case Administration Judge will hear the case and prepare a report, aiming to reach an amicable settlement.

However, if the parties do not reach an amicable settlement, the Labour Case Administration Judge passes on the matter to the High Civil Court, who will then hear the labour dispute on an urgent basis within two months from date of filing the case, and the judgment should be rendered within 30 days from the date of its first hearing. The decision of the High Court judge is final and the parties may appeal to the Court of Cassation only on matters of law.

b. Collective Bargaining (Articles 137-141 of the Labour Law)

The Labour Law grants the right to collective bargaining, subject to the specific provisions stipulated in its provisions.

In the course of collective bargaining, an employer shall not adopt any decisions or actions related to the topics subject to bargaining except in the case of exigency and urgency, provided that such measures or resolutions are of a temporary nature. In the event that collective bargaining succeeds, a collective contract of employment shall be concluded on the basis of the agreement. If no agreement is reached, either party may request to refer the matter to the Collective Disputes Settlement Board or the Arbitration Board, as the case may be according to the provisions of Article 158 of the Labour Law.

V. Intellectual Property

A. Brief Introduction of IP Laws and Regulations

Intellectual property laws in Bahrain cover patents, trademarks, copyright and industrial design. Bahrain has implemented several legislations to ensure the regulation and protection of intellectual property rights in Bahrain. Bahrain is also a member of multiple international and regional agreements, namely the world intellectual property organization (WIPO), the Agreement on Trade Related Aspects of Intellectual Property Rights (TRIPS), the Paris Convention for the protection of Industrial Property all of which have been ratified in 2006 , the Berne Convention for the Protection of Literary and Artistic works and the US-Bahrain Free Trade Agreement ("FTA"), which has committed Bahrain to enforcing world-class intellectual property rights.

a. Patent Protection

Law No. (1) for the year 2004 on Patents and Utility Models, as amended ("Patent Law") is the relevant law governing patents in Bahrain. Moreover, since Bahrain is also signatory to the Patent Cooperation Treaty (PCT), filing patent applications in Bahrain is a unified procedure that meets standards of each of the PCT contracting states. Furthermore, Bahrain is also subject to the regulations of the GCC Patent Office, specifically, the Patent Regulation of the Cooperation Council for the Arab States of the Gulf, issued in 1996 and amended in 1999.

b. Copyright Protection

As stipulated by Law No.14 of 2004 and Law No.30 of 1996, Bahrain is a member of the Berne Convention and the WIPO Copyright Treaty. Such membership has provided wide protection for copyright in respect of both moral and financial rights.

The Bahraini Copyright Law No.22 of 2006 as amended ("Copyright Law") replaced Law No.10 of 1993, providing wider protection. Further, copyright protection is not only imposed by the Copyright Law. The Press and Publication Law No.47 of 2002 sets out certain rights in respect of attribution, publishing and distribution.

The Copyright Law extends the protection period to be the authors' life plus 70 years instead of 50 years, and adds specific provisions in relation to customs and preliminary procedures.

c. Trademark Protection

Trademark protection in Bahrain is primarily governed by Law No.11 of 2006 with respect to Trademarks ("Trademark Law"). Bahrain also follows and utilizes the International Classification of Goods and Services for the Purpose of the registration of marks as per the tenth edition of the Nice Agreement.

B. Patent Application

Patents are protected in Bahrain under the Patent Law, which provides protection for patentable inventions and for utility models.

As per Article 1 of the Patent Law, an invention is capable of protection in Bahrain if it is:

(i) novel;

(ii) involves an inventive step; and

(iii) industrially applicable, and ultimately not considered to be part of prior art.

Protection cannot be obtained for inventions which are considered contradictory to morals or public order, scientific theories, mathematical methods, plants, animals, and methods of treatment. This is expressly stipulated in Article 3 of the Patent Law.

a. Registration

Patent and utility model applications are registered at the Bahrain Industrial Property Office, which sits within the Ministry of Industry, Commerce and Tourism.

b. Filing Options

There are three ways in which an invention can be protected in Bahrain:

(i) A national filing at the Bahrain Industrial Property Office, if appropriate claiming priority under the Paris Convention from an earlier application;

(ii) A national phase entry following an international filing via the Patent Cooperation Treaty (PCT); or

(iii) Via the GCC Patent Office. The GCC Patent Law, which was approved in 1992, was implemented in Bahrain by way of Law No.6 of 2014, stipulating that patents granted by the GCC Patent Office are applicable in Bahrain.

c. Filing Requirements

At the time of filing a patent application, two requirements must be fulfilled: the application be filed in Arabic, and the application must be accompanied by a signed Power of Attorney.

Within 90 days after the filing date, further supporting documents must be filed. These include:

(i) the notarised and legalised copy of the Power of Attorney;

(ii) a copy of the applicant's Commercial Registration Certificate or an extract from the commercial register, legalised up to the Bahraini Embassy;

(iii) a notarised and legalised Deed of Assignment; and

(iv) A certified copy of the priority document (if claimed), translated into English and Arabic.

The Patent Law provides an applicant for a patent the right to exploit or use the invention in Bahrain within three years of the grant date, or within four years of filing, whichever is the later. If the patent has not been used within this time, it will be subject to compulsory licensing.

C. Trademark Registration

The International Classification of Goods and Services for the Purposes of the Registration of Marks under the Nice Agreement is followed in Bahrain and the revision of class 42 with the creation of classes 43 to 45 has been adopted as of July 1, 2005.

A separate application must be filed for each class of goods or services. Once a trade/service mark application is filed, the trademark is examined as to its registrability. Trademark applications accepted by the Registrar are published in the Official Gazette and there is a 60-day period open for filing an opposition by any interested party. Any opposition to the registration of a trademark should be filed before the Registrar by an authorized agent or the proprietors themselves within the prescribed period as of the date of publication. Such an opposition case should be settled by the Registrar. In the absence of an opposition, a published trademark is registered, and the certificate of registration will be issued. Trademark rights are acquired by registration. However, a trademark application can be opposed successfully upon producing sufficient proof of the prior use of the mark in Bahrain and elsewhere in the world.

A trademark registration is valid for 10 years as of the date of filing the application, and it can be renewed for subsequent periods of 10 years. The Trademark Law provides for a 6-month grace period for late renewal of a trademark. If a trademark is not renewed, the Trademark Law does not allow third parties to register the trademark, unless after the lapse of 3 years from the date of cancellation. The assignment and the authorized user of a trademark can be recorded once the trademark is registered. Such a recording is published in the Official Gazette. The assignment of a trademark can be accepted only with the goodwill and the business' concern together. All other changes can be recorded after the registration of a trademark.

D. Measures for IP Protection

Bahrain has implemented provisions that protect intellectual property in the country in accordance with international standards. As evidenced above, such provisions vary from local to international, all of which encompass the significance of effective management of intellectual property. Agreements, such as the FTA, encapsulate the serious efforts taken by Bahrain in these areas.

Bahrain has a long and well established intellectual property legislations and infrastructure. The first Industrial and Intellectual Property Law was issued in Bahrain in 1955 for patents, design & trademarks. Bahrain's Industrial Property Office is one of the oldest IP offices in the Arabian Gulf and the country is known to be one of the most reputable Arab countries as far as enforcement of intellectual property rights are concerned.

Bahrain is one of the few Arab countries members of the Madrid Protocol, with memberships in the Berne Convention, Brussels Convention, Paris Convention, Patent Law Treaty, Rome Convention, Trademark Law Treaty, WIPO Copyright Treaty, WIPO Performances & Phonograms Treaty, Patent Cooperation Treaty, Nice Agreement, and GCC Patent Law.

VI. Environmental Protection

A. Department Supervising Environmental Protection

The department supervising environment protection is the Supreme Council for the Environment ("SCE"). The SCE was ultimately set up to assist the Bahraini government in not only the management, but also the preservation of its environment, its natural and marine resources, its wildlife, and its biodiversity. In light of these aims, a myriad of objectives have been implemented in ensuring this is achievable.

At the heart of the SCE's agenda is the strong conception that all sectors of development, whether economic, social or political, must take into strong consideration the preservation of the environment, when strategizing, and only then will goals be achieved. Accordingly, the strategies of the SCE are not only present-centric, but most importantly, very focused on long term progress. As a result of its dedication and perseverance, Bahrain's Public Commission for the Protection of Marine Resources, Environment and Wildlife (the "Commission") received international recognition when it was presented with the international 'Green Apple Environment' award in 2005 from the Green Organization based in the UK. This award was presented to the Commission for setting up the Hafira Industrial Landfill site, and ultimately, for its initiatives in providing areas which allow for safe disposal of dangerous waste.

B. Brief Introduction of Laws and Regulations of Environmental Protection

Great efforts have been made by Bahrain to ensure, on the one hand, efficient progress in various industries of the development sector, and on the other, maintaining the protection and sustainability of the environment. Such a balanced vision has been strongly reflected in the strategy of Bahrain Economic Vision 2030 and the National Strategic Plan 2030.

Moreover, and in conjunction with the aforementioned strategy, Bahrain has established many institutions, policies and strategies to achieve sustainability. It has also enhanced the number of laws related to sustainable development applications that have become a requirement in economic, social and political transitions to the international community.

Numerous decrees have been implemented for greater protection of the environment, the main source of regulation being Law No.21 of 1996 on the Environment, setting a firm foundation for the development of environmental initiatives on the island. Subsequent to this, many more specific legislations have been passed, focusing the efforts of the Commission on particular problem areas. These include Resolution No.4 1999 on Licenses to work on the Maintenance of Equipment and Buildings containing Asbestos, Resolution No.2 of 2001 on Environment Inspection Staff Delegation, Resolution No.4 of 2005 on the Management of Used Oil and Resolution No.3 of 2006 on Hazardous Waste Management.

C. Evaluation of Environmental Protection

It cannot be denied that regular efforts have been made by the Kingdom to not only implement but also ensure the effectiveness of its environmental protection policies.

The SCE has played a major role in the progress Bahrain has been making in this regard and should be commended on its continuous and innovative efforts in ensuring the Kingdom not only works on the protection of the environment on a local level, but also on a broader one, as evidenced by its participation and agreements with various international players and organizations.

VII. Dispute Resolution

A. Methods and Bodies of Dispute Resolution

The Bahrain Chamber for Dispute Resolution ("BCDR") is an independent dispute-settlement institution established by Legislative Decree No.30 of 2009 with respect to the Bahrain Chamber for Economic, Financial and Investment Dispute Resolution, as amended (the "BCDR Law") and has been in operation since January 2010.

In partnership with the American Arbitration Association ("AAA"), the BCDR provides commercial and governmental parties contracting in the Gulf and beyond with solutions for rapid and effective resolution of economic, financial and investment disputes.

Located in Bahrain, the BCDR is dedicated to regional and international arbitration and mediation. The case management team is composed of bilingual lawyers trained at the headquarters of AAA in New York and in other venues. They undergo continuous training and professional development. BCDR provides state-of-the-art facilities for mediation and arbitration of commercial disputes, with particular expertise in the commercial and investment sectors.

a. BCDR

Based in the Diplomatic Area of Manama, the financial hub of Bahrain, the BCDR aims to provide a modern, effective alternative dispute resolution service that results in final and binding resolution of commercial disputes. The BCDR offers and provides both arbitration and mediation services. The introduction of the BCDR has significantly changed the way in which certain types of disputes are dealt with in Bahrain.

b. BCDR Jurisdiction

a) Tatutory Arbitration: Jurisdiction by Law (Section 1 of the BCDR Law)

the BCDR will have automatic and mandatory jurisdiction over any claim exceeding BHD 500,000 which involves either an international party in a commercial dispute or a party licensed by the Central Bank of Bahrain (Article 9 of BCDR Law).

A dispute is commercial if its subject matter is of a commercial nature, including any transaction for the supply of goods or services, distribution agreements, investment and financing, insurance or consultation services.

b) Consensual Arbitration: Jurisdiction by Parties' Agreement (Section 2 of the BCDR Law)

the BCDR will also have jurisdiction if the parties have expressly agreed in writing to refer any dispute for resolution by arbitration or mediation under the BCDR's rules (Article 19 of the BCDR Law).

c. Rights of Audience for Foreign Lawyers

As stipulated by Article 30 of the BCDR Law, non-Bahraini lawyers are permitted to appear before any BCDR tribunal. However, any non-Bahraini lawyer must be accompanied by a Bahraini lawyer in any statutory arbitration.

d. Rules and Procedures

The rules of the BCDR closely follow those of the International Centre for Dispute Resolution (ICDR), the international division of the AAA. Its rules are tried and tested and are generally regarded as the international standard.

B. Application of Laws

For all BCDR arbitrations, the parties may agree upon the applicable law relevant to the subject matter of the dispute. In the absence of such agreement:

(i) In statutory arbitrations, Bahrain law will apply, as per Article 11 of the BCDR Law;

(ii) In consensual arbitration, the tribunal shall determine the applicable law on the basis that it should be the law most applicable to the subject matter of the dispute, as per Article 21 of the BCDR Law;

(iii) An award issued by the tribunal in statutory arbitrations will be a final judgment issued by the courts of

Bahrain, as per Article 15 of the BCDR Law.

VIII. Others

A. Anti-commmercial Bribery

a. Brief Introduction of Anti-commmercial Bribery Laws and Regulation

The Bahrain Penal Code of 1976 makes the corruption of public officials an offence.

Law No.(1) of 2013 With Respect to Amending Certain Provisions of the Penal Code Promulgated by Legislative Decree No.(15) of 1976 (the "Amendment") extends the offence of corruption within the Penal Code to include the private sector.

Articles 186-190 of the Penal Code and Articles 418-421 of the Amendment refer to the concepts of active corruption (the offering of a bribe or accepting to pay for a bribe) and passive corruption (asking for or taking a bribe). An attempt to commit the offence of bribery is an offence under Article 36 of the Penal Code.

Under Article 186 of the Penal Code, imprisonment shall be the punishment for every civil servant or officer entrusted with a public service who asks for or accepts for himself or others, directly or indirectly, a gift or privilege of any kind or a promise to be given any of the above in consideration of doing an act or omitting to do an act involved in the duties of this office. If the doing of an act or omission to do such act actually takes place, the punishment shall be imprisonment for a period of no more than 10 years.

Under Article 188 of the Penal Code, a punishment of imprisonment for a period not exceeding 10 years shall be inflicted upon every civil servant or officer entrusted with a public service who asks for or accepts for himself or others, directly or indirectly, a gift or privilege of any kind whatsoever after having completed doing an act or omitting to do such act in violation of the duties of his office. If the doing of an act or omission to do such act is a right, the punishment shall be a prison sentence.

Under Article 189 of the Penal Code, a punishment of imprisonment for a period not exceeding five years shall be inflicted upon every civil servant or officer entrusted with a public service who asks for or accepts for himself or others, directly or indirectly, a gift or privilege of any kind whatsoever for doing an act or omitting to do such act not constituting a part of his duties, but has alleged or wrongly believed it.

Under Article 190 of the Penal Code, a punishment of imprisonment for a period of no less than 3 months shall be inflicted upon any person who offers to give a civil servant or an officer entrusted with a public service a gift or privilege of any kind whatsoever or a promise to give such a thing for doing an act or omitting to do such act in breach of the duties of his office. Should the doing of an act or omitting to do such act be a right, the punishment shall be imprisonment for a period not exceeding one year or payment of a fine.

Article 418 of the Penal Code, added pursuant to the Amendment, provides that any employee, board member, or corporate trustee who has accepted, or requested for himself or another, whether directly or indirectly, a gift or benefit of any kind - or a promise of the same - in exchange for performing a task/duty or refraining from its performance, where such task/duty is related to the person's work, duties, or position, and/or will negatively affect the owner of a business or company shall be punished with imprisonment for a period not exceeding 10 years. This applies regardless of whether the person accepting the offer already intended to do the act/omission that was being sought.

Articles 419 and 420 of the Penal Code, added pursuant to the Amendment, provide that it is illegal to accept a gift for causing or monitoring the performance or the omission of performance of a task/duty, where such task/duty is not within the scope of the employee, board member, or corporate trustee's employment, and such action results in harm to the owner of a business or company. The punishment in this case is imprisonment for a period not exceeding 10 years.

Under Article 421 of the Penal Code, added pursuant to the Amendment, it is now an offence to offer gifts or privileges to civil servants, company employees, board members, or corporate trustees of a private corporation.

The benefit does not necessarily have to be monetary in order to be considered a bribe. Gifts, privileges of any kind and promises are caught by the legislation. There are no specific monetary thresholds according to the Penal Code or the Amendment. There is no minimum financial value threshold in order for a gift to be considered a bribe.

b. Department Supervising Anti-commmercial Bribery

The National Audit Office is a non-governmental organisation which independently investigates suspicious activities and reports its findings to the Public Prosecution for prosecution. The NAO has practiced financial auditing, involving regularity, performance and administrative audits of entities subject to its audit, and issued annual reports thereon. The annual reports are then presented to the King of Bahrain.

The General Directorate of Anti-Corruption and Economic and Electronic Security is responsible for investigation and prosecution of offences related to corruption. It conducts initial investigations and submits its findings to the Public Prosecution.

c. Punitive Actions

Maximum penalties for a public official ranges from 3 months (Article 190 of the Penal Code) to 10 years imprisonment (Article 186 of the Penal Code) and the fine shall be equal to the value of the bribe that was accepted, offered or promised. There is a minimum fine of 100 Bahraini Dinars (Article 191 of the Penal Code).

Maximum penalties for the private sector are up to 10 years imprisonment (Article 418 of the Penal Code, added pursuant to the Amendment) and a fine of no less than 500 Bahraini Dinars up to a maximum of 10,000 Bahraini Dinars (Article 426 of the Penal Code, added pursuant to the Amendment).

Article 193 of the Penal Code provides that if a partner reports the offence to the judicial or administrative authorities or admits it before reference of the case to the Court, this shall be considered as a mitigating circumstance. A judge may exempt him from punishment, if such course of action is justified. Article 427 of the Penal Code, added pursuant to the Amendment, provides the same mitigating circumstance to private sector offenders.

B. Project Contracting

a. Permission System

The Tender Board was established by Legislative Decree No.36 of 2002 as an independent regulator of government procurement practices in the Kingdom of Bahrain. Contracts for the purchase of goods or constructions shall be concluded by public tender method.

The Tender Board process is split into four (4) main steps:
(i) Tender Preparation;
(ii) Bid Submission;
(iii) Tender Opening;
(iv) Tender Evaluation & Award.

b. Prohibited Fields

In accordance with Article 3 of the Law, the provisions of the Law apply to all ministries, organisations, public institutions, municipalities and government authorities that have an independent or supplementary budget and the companies that are fully owned by the government, Consultative Council and House of Representatives. The Bahrain Defence Force, Public Security Forces and National Guard are exempted from this Law with respect to the purchase of goods, constructions and services of a military, security or confidential nature or when required by public interest not to be announced or not to apply the procedures stipulated under the Law.

c. Tender and Bidding

In accordance with Article 19 of the Law, a public tender shall be local or international. A local tender shall be limited to companies and organisations registered in the Kingdom of Bahrain. An international tender shall allow the participation of local and international companies and firms that are registered or unregistered in the Kingdom of Bahrain, provided that the unregistered international companies and firms shall complete commercial registration according to the applicable regulations within 30 days from the date of awarding the tender thereto. The criteria for distinction between local and international tenders shall be based upon the nature of goods, constructions or services required to be purchased, volume thereof, extent of their complexity and standards required.

However, a buyer may, pursuant to a decision of the Tender Board, enter into a contract in any of the following methods:

a) Tender in Two Phases

In accordance with Article 41 of the Law, a contract may be entered into by a two-phase tender if it is feasible to draft detailed specifications for the goods or constructions or to determine the characteristics of services to obtain the best solutions to meet the buyer's requirements if the following conditions are fulfilled:
(i) Availability of clear criteria for technical evaluation of offers;
(ii) Sufficient time for holding a two-phase tender;
(iii) Intent to conclude a lump-sum contract; and
(iv) Expectation to receive more than one bid.

The first phase of a two-phase tender takes place by an invitation to be sent by registered letters with notes of delivery to submit preliminary bids without quoting a price but containing technical, quality or other proposals for the goods, constructions or services and suggestions with respect to terms of the contract and information about the competence and qualifications of bidders.

Negotiation may take place at this stage with any bidder whose bid has not been rejected concerning any aspect of the bid.

The second phase of a two-phase tender takes place by inviting bidders whose bids have not been rejected to submit final bids inclusive of prices on the basis of one set of the specifications. At this stage it is possible to amend any specifications contained in the original documents, provided that all bidders will be notified of such amendments.

b) Limited Tender

In accordance with Article 43 of the Law, a contract may be entered into by a limited tender the following cases:

(i) If the goods, constructions or services are not available because of their highly sensitive nature except with a limited number of suppliers, contractors, consultants, technical personnel or experts whether in Bahrain or abroad.

(ii) If the goods, constructions or services are of a small value so that such value is not proportionate to the necessary time and cost for review and evaluation a large number of bids.

(iii) If the purchase takes place from a limited number of suppliers, contractors, consultants, technical personnel or experts necessary for strengthening the national economy especially supporting the balance of payments or foreign exchange reserves.

c) Competitive Negotiation

In accordance with Article 45 of the Law, a contract may be entered into by way of competitive negotiation in any of the following cases:

(i) Goods that cannot be identified by precise specifications;

(ii) Technical works which by their very nature require the execution thereof by technical personnel, specialists or appointed experts;

(iii) Goods, constructions or services which by their very nature or purpose of obtaining them are required to be purchased from their points of manufacture;

(iv) Supplies, constructions and services for which no bids have been submitted in the tenders or bids were submitted at unreasonable prices;

(v) In cases of disasters and urgent necessity that cause an urgent need for goods, constructions or services where it is not likely to allow the following of the public tendering procedures.

d) Direct Purchasing

In accordance with Article 50 of the Law, contracts may be entered into by way of direct purchase in any of the following cases:

(i) If the goods, constructions or services are not available except with a certain supplier or contractor and there is no acceptable substitute;

(ii) Emergency cases that do not allow following the tendering procedures of all their kinds or competitive negotiation;

(iii) In cases of disasters and urgent necessity that cause an urgent need for goods, constructions or services where the public tendering procedures are not likely to be followed;

(iv) In cases of standardization or compatibility with the available goods, equipment, technology or services while taking into account the limitation of proposed purchase as compared with the original purchase, suitability of the price and unsuitability of the substitute;

(v) In cases of purchase for research, experimentation, study or development;

(vi) If the purchase from a certain supplier or contractor is necessary to strengthen the national economy such as the balance of payments or foreign currency reserve.

e) Request to Present Proposals

In accordance with Article 51 of the Law, requests for submission of proposals may be made directly to a number of suppliers or contractors in any of the following cases:

(i) If the services are unavailable except with a limited number of suppliers or contractors;

(ii) If the time and costs of the study and evaluation are not proportionate to the value of the required services;

(iii) If confidentiality or national interest so require.

波斯尼亚和黑塞哥维那

作者：Olodar Prebanic、Tijana Blesic
译者：刘尔婵、张玉明

一、概述

（一）政治、经济、社会文化及法律环境概述

波斯尼亚和黑塞哥维那（以下简称"波黑"）位于欧洲东南部，地处巴尔干半岛。该国在南斯拉夫社会主义联邦共和国解体后，于1992年宣告独立。

根据《代顿协定》的规定，波黑具有多层级政治结构。该国划分为两大政治实体：一个为波黑联邦（下设10个州）；另一个为塞族共和国。从面积上看，波黑联邦占波黑国土总面积的51%，塞族共和国占国土总面积的49%。2000年，波黑北部地区成立布尔奇科特区，该特区由波黑联邦及塞族共和国的部分土地共同组成。名义上该特区同时隶属于上述两个政治实体，但实际上其并不受上述任何一个实体的统治，并以权力分散制为治理机制接受当地政府管理。

波黑是有实力的欧盟候选成员国，并自2010年4月起被列入北大西洋公约组织候选成员国名单。此外，波黑自2002年4月起成为欧洲委员会成员，并且是于2008年7月成立的地中海联盟的创始国家之一。

波黑的官方语言为波斯尼亚语、克罗地亚语以及塞尔维亚语。此外，英语作为波黑第二语言被大多数人使用。

1. 政治

根据《代顿协定》的规定，社会秩序的稳定由和平执行委员会选举产生的波黑高级议员代表进行监管。该高级代表被授予包括有权解雇无论是否经选举产生的公职人员等众多政治及立法方面的权利。近年来，在部分司法权由各政治实体向国家转移的过程中，一些核心机构陆续成立（如国防部、国家安全部、法院、间接税收服务部门等）。

波黑主席团由分属波什尼亚克族、塞尔维亚族和克罗地亚族的3人组成，每届任期4年，4年中每人轮流就任8个月主席团主席的职位。主席团3名成员由人民直接选举产生，其中波什尼亚克族、克罗地亚族成员由波黑联邦选举产生，塞尔维亚族成员由塞族共和国选举产生。

主席团提名部长会议主席，并经议会审议通过任命。部长会议主席负责任命外交部长、对外贸易部部长及其他各部部长。

议会为波黑的立法机关，分为两院：人民院和代表院。人民院议员由各政治实体议会选举产生的15名代表组成，其中2/3的议员选举自波黑联邦（克罗地亚族和波什尼亚克族各5人），另1/3的议员选举自塞族共和国（塞尔维亚族5人）。代表院由42名代表组成，采用比例代表制由人民选出，其中2/3的成员由波黑联邦选举产生，1/3的成员由塞族共和国选举产生。

宪法法院为波黑最高司法权力机关，同时是裁决各实体之间及各实体内部机构间纠纷的唯一法律授权机构，其裁定为终审裁定。宪法法院由9名法官组成，其中4人由波黑联邦代表院选举产生，2人由塞族共和国议会选举产生，其余3人是在与主席团磋商后，由欧洲人权法院院长推选出的非波黑公民成员。

然而，波黑最高政治权力为高级代表享有，作为国际民事代表的首席执行官员由欧盟选举产生。自1995年始，该高级代表的权力便凌驾于议会立法权之上，且自1997年始，该高级代表有权辞退经选举产生的行政官员。当波黑被认为在政治和民主上趋于稳定且可以自我维持的时候，国际监督就结束了。

2. 经济

波黑属中高收入国家，当前，在经历缓慢增长和受全球金融危机的影响下，波黑施行了新的经济

增长模式，进入有限的市场改革所带来的经济转型时期。相比于私有领域，当前公共政策及相关激励手段向公共领域倾斜所导致的经济模式的不平衡成为当下波黑经济所面临的最为严峻的挑战。

波黑第纳尔（可兑换马克）作为1998年引入的国家货币，通过货币发行局与欧元挂钩，可兑换马克与欧元间兑换实行固定兑换率，该机制有助于维持货币流通过程中各主体间的信任，同时推动了波黑同欧盟成员国之间可信赖的贸易往来。2016年，波黑开启了为期3年的国际货币基金组织贷款程序，该程序要求波黑经济改革达到可接收未来分期付款的标准。

波黑经济的重中之重在于：加速加入欧盟进程；强化财政系统；推进公共行政改革；争取加入世界贸易组织；通过培育有活力、有竞争力的私有领域确保国家经济增长。

3. 社会文化

波黑作为欧洲小国，其大部分外国劳动者为来自世界各地的工人、专业人士及技术人员。波黑规定了国民待遇原则，保证了外国人在波黑享有国民待遇，为外国劳动者依法在波黑开展工作并享有居留权提供了政策支持。

4. 法律

波黑不同政府体制的结合导致其法律架构十分复杂，除了波黑之外，两大政治实体均有其各自的法律体系，此外布尔奇科特区有其独立的法律架构。因此，只有极少部分法律能够适用于整个国家层面（该部分法律包括：与外交政策、外贸政策、关税政策、货币政策、金融机构及国际义务相关的法律；移民、难民、庇护政策/规定；国际及各政治实体间刑事执法；国际通信设施的建立及运行；各政治实体间运输及航空管控）。依《波黑宪法》第3条第3款之规定，除以上权力外，其他权力都自动归属于各政治实体。

因各政治实体均拥有宽泛的立法权，故其各自施行的法律也大不相同。然而在高级议员代表处的推动之下，各实体开始制定"参照法律"，即涵盖的法律内容相同，但具体条文由各实体议会分别制定。

因政权结构复杂，波黑的法制改革自波黑战争后直至2002年都难以实现。可喜的是，这种局面已逐步改善，并且在高级议员代表处的支持下，有了积极进展。其中，独立的商业经济领域的开创使波黑面临巨大的法律挑战。为了实现高级代表办公室的倡议（该倡议旨在政、商之间建立起工作合作模式），大量法制改革通过在各实体间实施相似的法律得以实现。

（二）"一带一路"倡议下和中国企业合作的现状及未来

中国与波黑间的交往自2013年起趋于紧密，两国至今保持着长期稳定的不同层级政治交流。

中国同波黑之间的商业合作产生了良好结果，2017年5月，位于波黑境内的斯坦纳里发电站由中国企业承包建造。这是两国间首次开展的重要合作项目，同时是中国—中东欧百亿美元专项信贷额度支持下的首次合作。[①]

二、投资

（一）市场准入

1. 投资监管部门

在波黑主管推动投资领域的政府机构中，居于首位的为波黑外商投资促进局。该机构属国家政府部门，设立的目的是最大限度地吸引外资，并鼓励波黑现有的外资企业扩大其经营规模，激励其业务不断开拓发展，从而促进了公共领域及私有领域间交流合作，并对波黑商业投资环境的改善及波黑经济持续稳定发展提供了积极的政策支持。

2. 投资行业法律、法规

波黑投资行业主要受三部法律、法规调整，分别为《波黑外商直接投资法》《波黑联邦外商投资法》和《塞族共和国外商投资法》。

---

① 参见http://www.fmprc.gov.cn/mfa_eng/wjb_663304/zzjg_663340/xos_664404/gjlb_664408/3145_664450/。

《波黑外商直接投资法》对外国投资者参与波黑经济活动的基本原则和基础政策作出了相关规定。该法规定，外国投资者有权向波黑所有经济领域内投资，并有权使用该投资收益进行再次投资。依波黑、波黑联邦、塞族共和国及布尔奇科特区相关法律、法规的规定，外国投资与本国投资形式相同并享受相同政策。

根据波黑关于外商直接投资的相关政策及法律规定，外国投资者在波黑可享受的相关激励政策有：

① 外国投资者享受国民待遇，即外国投资者在波黑与波黑本国公民享有同等权利，同时应承担同等义务。

② 外国投资者有权在波黑境内的任何一家商业银行开立账户，并且/或者在波黑境内进行货币的自由兑换。

③ 外国投资者有权在不违反波黑劳动法及移民法的前提下，自由雇用外籍劳动者。

④ 外国投资者被保护不受国有化、征收、征用及其他可能导致类似后果的措施影响。为公共利益，根据相关法律、法规采取以上措施时，给予适当补偿，该补偿应充分、实际有效且迅速及时。

⑤ 对作为股本的进口设备减免关税（客车、赌博机除外）。

⑥ 法律赋予外国投资者的权益以及法律规定应承担的义务不因新法的出台而被废止或否决，如新法的规定对外国投资者更为有利，则该外国投资者有权选择其投资行为适用新法或旧法。

⑦ 外国投资者在波黑可拥有不动产，对不动产享有与波黑法人同等的权利。

⑧ 外国投资者在波黑境内投资的过程中，有权自由且及时地将其资金以可兑换货币形式转移至境外。

⑨ 自由贸易区属波黑关税区的一部分，具有法人地位。依据《波黑自由贸易区法》的规定，自由贸易区的发起人可以是一个或一个以上的国内外自然人或法人，且须证明其成立具有经济价值（如递交的可行性研究材料或其他相关证据证明自由贸易区出口的货物价值至少超过过去 12 个月从自由贸易区输出的加工后产品总值的 50%，则可视为该自由贸易区的成立具有经济意义）。自由贸易区的用户可免交增值税及进口关税。自由贸易区内的投资、利润及投资的转移均无须缴纳费用。

3. 投资形式

直接投资只能通过经济投资实现（将资本投入现有的或新设立的公司）。

捐赠、借款及补助金不视为投资，但对波黑经济有直接影响。

4. 市场准入和审查标准

根据波黑现行法律的规定，外国投资者享有国民待遇，即外国投资者被赋予包括自由市场准入在内的与波黑本国国民同等的权利及义务。

（二）外汇监管

1. 外汇监管部门

波黑的外汇监管部门为波黑联邦财政部及塞族共和国财政部。

2. 外汇相关法律、法规简介

波黑外汇由《波黑联邦外汇管理法》及《塞族共和国外汇管理法》调整。

3. 外国企业外汇管理要求

外国企业向其所在地的有关部门缴纳相应的税款及其他费用后，有权自由转移其通过直接投资所获得的收益。

外国企业向其所在地的有关部门缴纳相应的税款及其他费用后，有权对企业破产及清算后的剩余资产进行自由转移。

纳税义务的履行由主管税务机关出具证明予以确认。

（三）财政

1. 主要金融机构

波斯尼亚和黑塞哥维那中央银行（以下简称"央行"）根据议会通过的相关法律的规定，于 1997

年6月20日成立。

央行的主要宗旨和任务由相关法律及《代顿协定》予以规定。央行通过货币发行局发行本国货币,并提供以1可兑换马克:0.51129欧元为固定汇率的他国外汇基金的自由兑换,以此来维持货币稳定。同时,央行受托制定波黑货币政策并对该政策的实施进行宏观调控。此外,央行还负责支持及维护适当的支付和结算系统,并对负责银行许可与监督的实体银行机构的相关活动予以协调配合。

2. 外国企业融资条件

外国企业有权与当地企业在同等条件下在其所在地以外币或当地货币自由地开立银行账户。

(四)土地政策

1. 与土地相关的法律、法规简介

波黑与土地有关的法律、法规包括《波黑联邦土地登记法》《塞族共和国土地登记法》《波黑联邦所有权权益保护法》《塞族共和国所有权权益保护法》。

《波黑联邦所有权权益保护法》对所有权的取得、使用、处分、保护、终止及其他财产权和占有进行了规定,依该法规定,任何自然人或法人均有权作为所有权及其他物权的权利人。

在波黑联邦,土地簿由市法院土地登记管理办公室负责保存,并负责行使土地登记法院的全部职权,特别是对土地簿现有内容的监管与审查、接收申请、作出登记决定、执行登记、传达、保管以及如所有权登记、地块及原木登记的附属登记,并在土地登记法院留档。依登记决定对不动产及相关不动产权利进行登记,是土地登记管理办公室工作任务的基本内容。在对财产权利的管理及对法律的应用中的主要挑战是土地簿毁损、灭失或未经监管。因此,一些合同因未建立土地簿或未按法定程序建立所有权登记而无法执行。进行土地簿登记所需时间长短取决于个案具体情况、合同项下包括一个或多个地块,同时取决于该土地簿的现有情况,该土地簿项下是否有其他已登记的地籍地块等,一般来说,注册登记所需时间为10~15天。

在塞族共和国,共和国土地测量和财产事务管理局是独立的管理机关,负责保存财产及相关财产权利记录,不动产地籍保护、地籍分类及土地质量评估。

2. 外国企业征地规则

同波黑法人实体一样,外国企业对不动产财产享有同等权利。

通过签署销售合同并经公证人对各缔约方的签署进行公证之后,标的土地所在地的地政登记处对该土地及该土地的新产权人进行注册登记。

向市级法院所在地的土地登记部门提交土地登记查询申请以及修改登记申请。

外国企业有权在不获得相关部门颁发出租许可的情况下出租其在波黑的地产,但该出租权利可以通过合同约定予以限制。

(五)企业的设立和解散

1. 企业形式

波黑企业的设立、运行、管理和解散由《波黑联邦企业法》《塞族共和国企业法》《布尔奇科特区企业法》进行调整。根据上述法律,波黑企业可区分为以下类型:

(1) 无限责任公司

无限责任公司需至少两名股东对公司承担无限连带责任。该类公司经两个或两个以上的本国/外国的自然人/法人共同签署发起人协议后方可成立。该成立合同中需包括公司名称及地址、公司经营范围、各发起人的基本情况及其各自的权利义务。发起人可通过资金、实物、权利及服务等形式出资,但应当在协议中对非货币形式的出资进行评估作价。所有发起人的出资效力平等并成为公司资产。无限责任公司无须规定公司章程,且不设立公司管理部门,这是因为各发起人包括法定代表人均对公司进行直接管理,对公司负责。此外,相关法律对发起人的出资额度无限额要求。

(2) 有限责任公司

有限责任公司基于成立行为成立或者经一人或一人以上的本国或外国的自然人或法人签署发起人

协议后成立。该类公司的原始资本按发起人出资比例划分，各发起人仅在其出资范围内对公司承担责任。有限责任公司需制定公司章程。公司管理机构设股东会（一人成立的有限责任公司由该发起人行使全部股东权利）、董事会（一人以上的发起人成立的公司设董事会）、监事会对公司事务进行管理。股东达10人以上及注册资本达100万马克以上的有限责任公司须设立监事会。其余未设立监事会的，监事职责由股东承担。波黑联邦规定有限责任公司的注册资本不得低于10万马克（约5万欧元），塞族共和国规定有限责任公司的注册资本不得低于1马克（约0.5欧元）。有限责任公司是波黑最为普遍的公司形式。

（3）股份公司

股份公司将其资本划分为股份，经一人或一人以上本国或外国的自然人或法人签署发起人协议后方可成立，并应签署资金协议。股份公司不对股东义务负责。股份公司的注册资本最低为5万马克（约2.5万欧元），每股票面价值不得低于1马克（约0.5欧元）。股份公司设股东会、监事会管理和修正会。股份公司可划分为开放式股份制和封闭式股份制。开放式股份公司为银行或保险业公司或其他根据波黑联邦规定注册资本不低于400万马克（约200万欧元）、塞族共和国则规定不低于500万马克（约250万欧元）的公司，其股份可通过公开上市方式发行；封闭式股份公司的股份仅在有限的股东之间流转，其注册资本在波黑联邦不得低于5万马克（约2.5万欧元），在塞族共和国不得低于2万马克（约1万欧元）。

（4）有限合伙企业

有限合伙企业需一名或一名以上的普通合伙人以其私人财产在内的全部资产对公司承担无限连带责任，其余有限合伙人以其出资额为限对公司承担有限责任。有限合伙企业由两名或两名以上的本国或外国的自然人或法人基于协议成立。有限合伙企业可转化为股份制有限合伙企业。每位普通合伙人的管理都可以代表公司。

2. 设立程序

根据上述法律规定，波黑的公司作为法人实体，以盈利为目的独立运营。公司可通过如下方式设立：

① 本国自然人、法人设立；

② 外国自然人、法人设立；

③ 本国、外国自然人、法人共同设立。

商业实体的设立需进行登记，即由主管部门对其根据法律规定开展商业活动进行授权。波黑公司注册管理机关包括波黑联邦注册登记法院、塞族共和国信息科技产业中介机构及金融服务机构。

波黑公司注册的程序由《波黑企业注册登记框架法》《波黑联邦企业注册登记法》《塞族共和国企业注册登记法》《布尔奇科特区企业注册登记法》进行规定。

就波黑最为普遍的公司类型（有限责任公司和股份公司）而言，其设立程序可概述如下。

① 有限责任公司可基于发起人协议或发起决定成立。由一名自然人或法人单独成立的，该公司基于发起决定即可成立；由多方自然人或法人共同成立的，发起人签署发起人协议后方可成立公司。波黑各政治实体的公司法均对发起人协议中所必须包括的法定内容进行了规定，此外，发起人间可依意思自治，在法律允许的范围内约定其他条款。波黑各实体对发起人协议的法定内容的规定大致相同，发起人协议需包含以下内容：

• 发起人姓名及联系地址（发起人为自然人的）或发起人名称及所在地（发起人为法人的）；

• 拟设立公司名称、所在地及其经营范围；

• 原始资本总额；

• 发起人权利义务（运营管理、利润分配等）；

• 对发起人未在指定期限内缴足其认缴的出资额或未履行协议中约定的义务等违约行为所应承担的违约责任；

• 公司筹建费用（由发起人支付或以公司财产支付）；

• 公司高级管理人员及法定代表人；

• 对拟设立公司最终因故未能成立的处理方式；

• 对无法定成立期限的公司的特别规定。

② 股本出资。有限责任公司应根据其公司业务类型，按照发起决定或发起人协议约定向波黑联邦注册登记法院或塞族共和国信息科技产业中介机构、金融服务机构递交注册申请，并同时递交发起人出资证明及申请注册所需的其他文件。

③ 公司注册由波黑联邦注册登记法院或塞族共和国信息科技产业中介机构、金融服务机构管辖。基于属地原则，由拟设立公司所在地的注册管理机关对其行使管辖权。有限责任公司注册需提交如下文件：
- 经公证的法定代表人签字；
- 发起决定或发起人协议；
- 以货币形式进行出资的银行证明，或以实物或权利出资的等价评估证明；
- 如发起人决定，发起人协议中未对法定代表人进行约定，则需提交法定代表人委任决定；
- 公司的注册摘录来自发起人登记的注册（发起人为法人的）或经公证的发起人护照复印件（发起人为自然人的）；
- 法定代表人身份证明文件复印件；
- 提供发起人在波黑无任何未付的税务责任且不是波黑另一家企业的发起人的声明。

④ 制作公章（公章应包括拟设立公司的名称及地址）。
⑤ 开立公司账户。
⑥ 在税务局登记。
⑦ 经市政公告开始运营（该公告应交相关审查部门进行审查）。

各政治实体的法律规定均允许外国企业在其各自区域内设立分支机构，分支机构必须依据相关法律进行登记。外国企业分支机构需依法经公司总部所在地的波黑联邦注册登记法院或塞族共和国信息科技产业中介机构、金融服务机构注册登记后方可设立。与公司不同，公司的分支机构不具有法人资格，分支机构可以公司名义并代表公司同第三人进行商业往来。

外国企业想在波黑运营的另一个选择是在波黑境内设立公司的代表机构。代表机构由《波黑外资企业代表机构设立及运行规定决定》进行调整。根据前述规定，外国企业可在波黑境内设代表机构，并以公司名义进行市场调研、信息采集及业务推动，从而积累经验，扩大其在波黑市场的经营规模并增强企业竞争力。公司代表机构不具有法人资格，其性质上仅为其所属公司的延伸机构，该机构仅可进行非营利性活动，并无权代表公司对外签署协议。代表机构的设立需经波黑对外经贸部外商企业代表机构注册管理机关登记批准。

3. 企业解散的程序和要求

波黑现行法律规定公司可经两种途径解散：清算和破产。

清算与破产之间的主要区别在于公司是否有能力偿还其债务。清算指公司在有足够资金偿还债务的情况下暂停其业务，而破产指对债务人的财产进行控制，以实现债权人的主张的程序。

不考虑其产生原因，清算常指有偿还能力的公司之解散，破产代表无偿还能力的公司（其资金无法偿还其债务的公司）之解散。在部分情况下，如公司在清算中被认定为无偿还能力或该公司的资产不足以偿还其全部债权，则破产有可能发生于清算过程中。

4. 公司兼并与收购

在波黑，涉及私人收购的最为普遍的企业类型为有限责任公司，位居第二位的为股份公司。

附条件的股份未获得公司书面批准不得随意转让。在对公司股权进行转让时，《公司法》同时赋予股东以优先购买权。此外，相关法律还对特殊行业的股份转让进行了限制（如银行业、保险业），即该等行业需经波黑相关管理部门批准，方可对公司股份进行转让。股东有权在公司成立文件中对股份转让进行约定。兼并私有企业最普遍的方式是基于买卖合同收购其股份或资产。

外国企业有权在与本国企业同等的条件下收购波黑公司的股份，但是《外商投资法》对外国企业从事生产及销售军用武器、弹药、爆炸物、军用设备的公司及传媒公司的投资份额进行了相应限制，即投资额度不能超过该等公司股本总额的49%。

(六) 竞争法

1. 竞争法的监管部门

波黑的市场竞争由波黑竞争管理委员会进行监管。该委员会作为独立性的公共团体，于2004年成立，旨在确保《波黑竞争法》的贯彻实施。该委员会对确定波黑市场中的禁止性竞争行为具有排他性权力，并针对市场竞争控制的不同方面（实施步骤、最终裁定如何作出、惩罚制度、程序时长等）实施不同的行政和专业职责。

2.《波黑竞争法》简介

波黑的市场竞争规则由《波黑竞争法》规定。该法所确立的竞争政策成为波黑市场创新及强化的重要工具和支柱。《波黑竞争法》与欧盟在市场竞争方面的相关法律规定的一致性确保了法律适用的有效性及公开性，简化了相关程序，缩短了相关进程所耗费的时间，并且降低了国家干预程度。《波黑竞争法》认可对企业实施积极的惩罚政策（宽恕政策），对市场施行有效的监管机制，并支持与竞争领域的国际机构间建立合作关系。该法适用于波黑境内或境外对波黑市场带来重大影响的一切形式的禁止性、限制性以及扭曲的市场竞争行为。该法特别重视关于市场支配地位及滥用市场支配地位的规定，以及对竞争程序的规定。《波黑竞争法》对于部分项目和事项只进行了概括定义，并在附例法令中作出了更加详细的规定。该等项目及事项包括相关市场定义、对非重要条款的定义、对特定款项的豁免、对支配地位的定义等。

《波黑竞争法》针对违反具体条款的行为制定了多种制裁手段，如罚金、转让已取得的股份等。

(七) 税收

1. 税收制度和规则

波黑税收实行分级管理，分为国家层面和实体层面税收。税收制度由下述法律规定：《波黑间接税法》《波黑增值税法》《波黑消费税法》《波黑联邦企业所得税法》《塞族共和国企业所得税法》《布尔奇科特区公司所得税法》《波黑联邦个人所得税法》《塞族共和国个人所得税法》《布尔奇科特区个人所得税法》。

波黑已同下述国家签署了关于避免重复征税的协定：阿尔巴尼亚、阿尔及利亚、奥地利、阿塞拜疆、比利时、黑山、捷克共和国、埃及、芬兰、法国、希腊、德国、克罗地亚、荷兰、伊朗、爱尔兰、意大利、约旦、科威特、卡塔尔、中国、塞浦路斯、匈牙利、马来西亚、马其顿、摩尔多瓦、挪威、巴基斯坦、波兰、罗马尼亚、斯洛伐克、斯洛文尼亚、塞尔维亚、西班牙、瑞典、斯里兰卡、土耳其、阿拉伯联合酋长国、英国。

2. 主要税种和税率

国家层级的税种包括：增值税及消费税。

实体层级的税种包括：企业所得税、个人所得税、不动产税。

（1）增值税

增值税的纳税人为独立进行经济活动（制造商、交易商或服务提供者以获得收入为目的而进行的活动，包括对自然资源的开采、农业、林业及专业性活动）的任何个体。纳税人包括为了其自身收益而以其本人名义提供货物、服务或进口商品，或者为了他人收益而以其本人名义提供货物、服务或进口商品的人。增值税的纳税人应界定为：在波黑境内进行经济活动，提供货物或服务，或向波黑境内进口货物的人。波黑所有的间接税均由间接税务局负责收取。该领域活动的开展以四个区域为中心：萨拉热窝、巴尼亚卢卡、莫斯塔尔、图兹拉，共设34个海关分局和57个海关检查站，其中40个边境关口、4个机场、7个铁路边境关口、3个海外邮政局以及4个免税区。增值税税率为17%。

（2）消费税

消费税是营业税的一种特殊种类，适用于如油品、烟草产品、软饮料（不含酒精饮料）、酒精饮料、啤酒、红酒、咖啡等特种商品的销售。消费税的纳税人包括在波黑境内进出口应纳税商品的法人、企业家（意为任何自然人）。法律规定，对在波黑境内制造的消费产品的交易征税，通常发生在制造商第一次出售和/或向波黑进口商品时。纳税计税基数取决于：应纳税商品的数量，消费税按照每测量单位支付；零售价格，不包括价值、增值税，法律另行规定的除外（如对烟草制品营业税的规定）。消费税作为间接税由间接税务局负责收取，并基于测量单位按照适当税率足额缴纳。

（3）波黑联邦企业所得税

波黑联邦企业所得税的纳税人为在波黑境内设立的以营利为目的，通过向波黑联邦、塞族共和国、布尔奇科特区或国外市场销售货物或提供服务而进行独立且持续的经济活动的公司或其他法人组织。该税种的纳税人包括波黑联邦登记的法人实体为了实现其在波黑联邦境内的利益而在塞族共和国及布尔奇科特区所设立的子公司，同时还包括非居民法人在波黑联邦境内设立的营业机构，以及其收入主要来源于波黑联邦的非居民法人。该税种计税基数由税务结余、支出和收入调整以及财务报表中报告的资本收益或损失来确定。计税基数以财务报表中显示的利润进行计算，因不可抵扣的支出及其他不可抵扣项目而增加，因免税项目而减少。纳税人所获取的任何收入及资本收益都须纳入计税基数，《波黑联邦企业所得税法》未规定者除外。所得税的计算方式为计税基数乘以所得税税率。波黑税务系统具有低税率的特点。收益税的应缴税额为抵扣后纳税基数的10%。

波黑联邦预扣税税率：预扣税的标准税率为10%，且对于支付给非波黑联邦居民的股息须缴纳5%的预扣税，依相关税收协定降低该税率的除外。波黑联邦税务管理局通过其州立分支机构依职责实施税务评估、税费收取及管控。

《波黑联邦企业所得税法》规定外国投资者享有如下权益：

① 纳税人以其自有资金投资生产设备，超过当前税期收益总额50%的，可免收该年应缴税款的30%。

② 纳税人连续5年以其自有资金投资，总金额达1 000万欧元，且首年投资额超过200万欧元的，可免收该年应缴税款的50%。

③ 下述条件下，纳税人可享受数额相当于其向新员工支付工资总额2倍的税费减免：

- 以全职工作时间计算，劳动合同期限超过12个月的；
- 新员工在之前的5年内未受雇于纳税人及其关联人的。

（4）塞族共和国企业所得税

塞族共和国企业所得税的纳税人包括：以从波黑联邦、塞族共和国、布尔奇科特区及国外获取利润为目的的塞族共和国居民法人；在塞族共和国注册的法人以获取来自塞族共和国境内的利润为目的，而在波黑联邦及布尔奇科特区成立的子公司；以其在塞族共和国境内的不动产获取利润的波黑联邦及布尔奇科特区的法人；营业地位于塞族共和国且其利润来源于塞族共和国的非居民法人；利润来源于塞族共和国的非居民法人。《塞族共和国企业所得税法》规定，该税种年度计税基数以该财政年度发生的应纳税收入与可扣减支出的差额进行计算。应纳入计税基数的收入包括：无论其来源，且无论其是否与公司经营有关的以现金或其他任何形式获取的所有应纳税收入。企业所得税的年税率为10%，且对于支付给非塞族共和国居民的股息须缴纳5%的预扣税，依相关税收协定降低该税率的除外。塞族共和国税务局负责执行与税务相关的法律及规定（直接税）。

（5）布尔奇科特区企业所得税

布尔奇科特区企业所得税的纳税人包括：无论其收入来源于波黑国内还是国外的布尔奇科特区法人；其总部位于两大政治实体的，利润来源于布尔奇科特区的法人分支机构；在布尔奇科特区内进行交易并有常设机构，通过该常设机构获取利润的外国法人；通过位于布尔奇科特区内的资产获取利润及通过对非流动资产投资获取收益的外国企业；在布尔奇科特区获得收入的外国自然人。年计税基数为抵税后的应纳税收入。《会计法》规定，应纳税收入通过财务报表中报告的收入及支出确定，法律另有规定者除外。企业所得税税额记为该纳税年应纳税收入的10%。布尔奇科特区金融理事会负责对直接税进行管理。

（6）波黑联邦个人所得税

波黑联邦个人所得税的纳税人包括以下波黑联邦居民以及非波黑联邦居民：在波黑联邦境内、境外获得收入的波黑联邦居民；通过位于波黑联邦境内的常设经营机构进行商业活动并获得收入的非波黑联邦居民；在波黑联邦境内独立进行商业活动的非波黑联邦居民；通过波黑联邦境内的流动资产、非流动资产、版权、专利、执照、资本收益以及其他能获得应纳税收入的商业活动取得收入的非波黑联邦居民。纳税人通过以下途径取得的收入需缴纳个人所得税：独立性商业活动；非独立性商业活动、财产及财产权利、资本收益等。居民个人所得税基数为一个纳税期内取得的应纳税收入总额和可扣减税务收入总额（累计损失、为取得收入的必要支出、个人扣除费用等）之间的差额。个人所得税的计税基数代表了已支出税款。收入和支出按银行制定的规则确定。个人所得税税率为10%。

（7）塞族共和国个人所得税

塞族共和国个人所得税依照《塞族共和国个人所得税法》规定，由取得应纳税收入的自然人缴纳。纳税人为从塞族共和国、波黑联邦、布尔奇科特区或其他国家取得法律规定的应纳税收入的塞族共和国居民。纳税人应该对纳税期间内获取的以下种类的收入缴纳个人所得税：个人收入、自主创业、版权、资本收益及其他收入。塞族共和国个人所得税税率为10%。应纳税收入依如下条件减免：家庭中依赖纳税人扶养的直系亲属，每人每年可减免20%的个人所得税，纳税人年付房屋贷款利息或人寿保险费每年最高不超过12万马克。

（8）布尔奇科特区个人所得税

布尔奇科特区个人所得税的纳税人包括通过以下途径取得收入的布尔奇科特区居民或非特区居民：在特区范围内、特区范围外获得收入的特区居民；通过位于特区内的常设经营机构进行商业活动的非特区居民；在特区内进行独立性商业活动的非特区居民；通过特区内的流动资产、非流动资产、版权、专利、执照、资本收益以及其他能够获得应纳税收入的商业活动取得收入的非特区居民。纳税人通过以下途径取得的收入需缴纳个人所得税：独立性商业活动、非独立性商业活动、财产及财产权利、资本收益及参与抽奖等。《布尔奇科特区个人所得税法》规定了相关激励政策，如税务的减免，包括对受扶养的家庭成员的税费扣减，增加或减少了所得税的计税基数。个人所得税税率为10%。

（9）波黑联邦财产转让税

波黑联邦财产转让税的税率为5%。计税基数为由该转让财产所在地税务管理机关指定的评估机构对该财产的评估价值。财产转让税通常由卖方缴纳（具体取决于该转让财产所处地点），只有在萨拉热窝州和黑塞哥维纳-涅雷特瓦州财产转让税由买方缴纳。

（10）塞族共和国财产税

用于生产活动（原材料的生产及储藏、半成品加工以及成品加工）的不动产的不动产税计为该不动产市场评估价值的0.1%；其他不动产的不动产税计为该不动产市场评估价值的0.2%。

（11）布尔奇科特区财产税

不动产的财产税不得低于该不动产评估价值的0.05%，且不得高于该不动产评估价值的1%。各行政单位在订立销售合同时产生纳税义务。

3. 税收的申报和优惠

在波黑联邦，纳税人在以下情况下享受税收优惠：

① 纳税人以其自有财产投资生产设备总额超过该纳税期间其所获得收入总额的50%以上的，其当年应缴利润税可减免30%；

② 纳税人连续5年投资总额达2 000万马克以上（其中首年投资达400万马克以上）的，其当年应缴利润税可减免50%。

塞族共和国纳税人投资设备、工厂及不动产以进行其注册的经营活动，投资总额超过该纳税期间所获得收入总额50%以上的，其应缴利润税可减免30%。

（八）证券交易

1. 证券相关法律、法规简介

波黑从政治实体层面对资本市场进行管控（波黑联邦和塞族共和国），因此，波黑联邦资本市场有其自身的管理框架及机构，该管理架构同样适用于塞族共和国。总之，两大实体对于资本市场的管控机制表现出极大的一致性。

证券市场监管的法律框架由波黑联邦及塞族共和国《证券市场法》规定。相关法律对证券市场相关的核心问题进行了规定，如术语定义、参与人、机构及其在波黑资本市场中的权力、权利和义务。塞族共和国最近的法律调整使银行丧失了在金融中介市场直接发挥作用的能力，使得塞族共和国至少在金融市场的立法上，与波黑联邦趋于一致。

根据上述法律规定，证券持有人需以其名义对其所持有的证券进行登记后，方可取得证券的所有权。该所有权的设立及转让均通过合法交易实现。

购买权通过证券销售合同取得，银行作为卖方，与买方之间以指定价格、指定日期进行交易，以实现证券所有权的流转。

证券交易在证券交易所及其他受管制的、为满足证券需求给证券发行创造条件而建立的公共市场中进行。

2. 证券市场的监管与调控

波黑两个政治实体的证券管理委员会都建立了证券发行人的登记制度（以下简称"发行人登记"），其内容包括：依相关法律需要提供的相关数据、发行基本信息、发行人以及证券及股本的相关数据。

证券发行方式分为公开发行、私募发行或定向发行。公开发行的过程为公开邀请、认购并支付相应款项。依证券管理委员会的规定，公开发行通过证券交易所进行。发行人须提供包含充分信息的招股说明书，供投资者对该发行人的资产、债务、损益、财务状况和前景进行评估，并向投资者说明发行证券中所包含的各项权利。认购证券的最长期限为90日，自发行之日计算，以现金形式认购并分期付款的，其期限可延长至6个月。

私募发行的认购及支付期限为45日，最长不可超过90日。

《证券市场法》对证券机构的相关职责进行了如下规定：

① 中介机构的职责包括以客户名义买卖证券，并收取费用。

② 证券交易机构包括以本人名义买卖证券，以赚取差价。

③ 市场业务开拓机构的职责包括以本人名义销售股票同时强调证券的持续供应，以满足特定证券的持续性供应和市场需求。

④ 证券投资组合管理机构的职责是指由专业的中介机构以其名义代理客户投资证券以争取最大利润，即持有并管理由客户出资购买的证券。

⑤ 发行代理机构的职责包括帮助发行人组织、准备并实施证券的发行，对于未售出证券无须承担购买义务，而需将该证券引入公开市场中。

⑥ 发行保荐人的职责包括帮助发行人组织、准备并实施证券的发行，并对所有证券或未售出的证券进行支付和承销，将其出售给潜在投资者，从而确保发行成功。

⑦ 证券投资顾问的职责为向客户提供证券操作的建议。

⑧ 证券托管人的职责包括：

- 在登记机关以持股客户名义开设账户（名为托管账户），并对该账户进行管理；
- 在登记机关以其本人名义代表持股客户开设账户，或以非证券持有人的其他客户名义代表证券实际持有人开设账户（联合账户）；
- 根据客户指令转移证券所有权，在证券上注明第三人权利，或转移该证券项下的权利；
- 基于已发行证券向发行人主张收益，如证券持有人应得股息及分红，并保证客户其他权利的行使；
- 提供证券借贷服务；
- 通知持股人参加大会，并在会上代表他们进行发言；
- 告知持有人其证券项下的相关权利，并执行他们在行使权利过程中的相关指令；
- 告知客户对证券托管条件产生直接或间接影响的法律调整；
- 确保持股人已履行纳税义务；
- 客户与托管银行间约定的与证券权利义务相关且不违反法律规定的其他服务。

⑨ 保管人的职责包括在证券交易所及其他有序的公开市场进行的证券发行及与证券交易相关的货币交易。

波黑资本市场的相关规定还包括《证券管理委员会规则》《证券登记规则》，上述规则确定了证券管理委员会及证券登记机关的地点、地位及基本职权，使之作为管理机构保证了波黑资本市场的平稳运行。

证券管理委员会的职权依以下法规确定：《证券法》《证券管理委员会规则》《证券登记规则》《公司资金管理法》《投资基金和公司法》。作为根据以上法律对金融市场进行监管的独立机构，证券管理委员会享有以下职权：

① 对证券发行及交易方式进行监管。

② 对证券商就其交易活动向投资人及公众进行披露的标准、股份公司的管理、投资人利益的保护、与证券发行及交易相关法律法规的实施、股票市场的运行、证券登记、专业中介机构、托管银行以及基金管理公司进行监管。

③ 根据法律、法规的规定，在其职权范围内采取相关措施。

④ 法律或相关法规规定的其他职责。

证券管理委员会被授予广泛的权力，包括：

① 规定证券发行及交易方式；

② 批准企业和银行发行股票及其他证券；

③ 批准基金管理公司、投资基金、共同基金以及其他有证券发行权的机构发行证券；

④ 规定州和市政债券的发行要求和方式；

⑤ 利于电子报价系统，制定证券交易规则，监督证券交易；

⑥ 保护投资者权益；

⑦ 对证券商就其交易活动向投资人及公众进行披露的标准订立规则，并实施监管；

⑧ 对股份公司的管理制定规则并实施监管；

⑨ 对专业中间机构（如中介及经销商）以及其他证券交易参与者作出规定，给予批准和监督，并对其实施监管。

证券登记机关行使以下职权：

① 对证券进行登记和保管，以及保管所有涉及证券所有权转让或变更的交易的相关数据资料；

② 根据合同、法院判决或其他管理部门的决定，保留和撤销与证券有关的第三人权利及对相关权利的限制；

③ 开立证券账户并对之进行管理，出具股东名单，并出具有关这些账户状况和变更情况的发行报告、报表和收据；

④ 基于股票市场或其他受管制的公共市场中进行的与证券相关的交易，对证券进行统计、处置及转移；

⑤ 记录、转移、统计在证券交易所或其他受管制的公开市场中产生的金融衍生品交易，并确保该金融衍生品交易均已履行；

⑥ 相关法律及规则规定的其他职责。

3. 外国企业参与证券交易的要求

外国企业有权在与本国企业同等的条件下参与证券交易。

（九）投资优惠与保护

1. 经济特区

自由贸易区属波黑关税区的一部分，具有法人地位。根据《波黑自由贸易区法》的规定，自由贸易区的发起人须为一个或一个以上的国内外自然人或法人，且自由贸易区的成立需具有经济价值，如递交的可行性研究材料或有其他相关证据证明过去12个月内自由贸易区出口的货物价值至少超过从自由贸易区输出的加工后产品总值的50%，则可视为该自由贸易区的成立具有经济价值。

2. 投资保护

波黑签署了多部双边投资条约，其中，波黑同中国之间（以下简称"中波"）在投资领域签订了以下两部主要双边条约：

①《波中经济贸易协定》（正式批准决议刊登于《波黑公报》）；

②《波中投资促进及保护协定》（正式批准决议发布于《波黑公报》）。
以上两个协定旨在加强两国之间的经济合作以及促进两国间的投资。

三、贸易

（一）贸易监管部门

波黑贸易监管部门是波黑联邦贸易部及塞族共和国贸易和旅游部。

波黑联邦贸易部承担的主要职责涉及国际和国内贸易，单一市场运作，经济制度和经济政策对货物和服务市场的影响；供求比例，货物和服务价格；消费者保护以及法律规定的其他职责。

塞族共和国贸易和旅游部承担组织贸易、分析和跟踪贸易运作、发展贸易、提供干预市场、规范活动的措施等。

（二）贸易法律、法规简介

波黑的贸易在实体层面上进行规定。关于贸易的主要规定是《波黑联邦贸易法》和《塞族共和国贸易法》。

（三）贸易管理

在平等的市场条件下，所有的贸易经营者，包括外国企业，在波黑自由地从事贸易经营活动。交易的货物必须符合法律规定的技术和质量标准。

货物以本地货币计价。价格不受任何国家的影响，法律实体有权根据市场条件决定价格，依据相关法律规定，某些种类产品的价格除外。

如遇自然灾害、战争、市场违规行为或其他灾害，可以对贸易经营进行暂时限制。在该情形下，实体政府将公布措施，包括对某些货物的贸易进行限制或规定条件和明令禁止等。

（四）进出口商品检验检疫

由于需要通过对植物、植物产品、动物、动物产品、监管对象和其他国际贸易中能够传播有害生物的对象的健康检验程序提供对本地生产、市场和消费者的健康保护以及通过质量控制、跟踪和记录产品运输从而保护植物、混合肥料和土壤改良剂、动物和动物产品，必须进行检验管理（控制）。为保证国际运输中植物、植物产品、动物、动物产品的健康，也要进行管理。检验管理在进口、出口和边境管制下的包裹转运时实施。

（五）海关管理

海关事务依据《波黑海关政策法》进行调整。

进口关税税率同欧盟关税分类一致。根据产品种类的不同，有的关税税率降低到之前的 90%、75% 或 50%，同时一些产品的关税税率将被取消。只是对原产于欧盟的货物适用降低关税税率，并非适用于从欧盟进口的所有货物。对农产品仍然提供海关保护，按税率计算的关税大部分和之前一样进行征收。

依据《波黑海关政策法》的规定，下列货物免征关税：作为外国投资组成部分的进口设备，不包括乘用车、赌博机、全部由捐赠者资助用于军队和警察队伍的设备、用于经部长会议批准和完全由捐赠者或国际社会资助的波黑重建项目的设备。

作为外国投资组成部分的设备未经海关事先同意不得用于出借、担保、租赁或让与。如该设备被出借、担保、租赁或让与，应对该设备征收相应关税。

下列项目免征进口关税：固定资产、工业库存和因从国外转移到波黑从事商业活动而进口的设备，用于制造出口货物的中间材料、广告材料，用于慈善和人道主义机构的样品、商品目录、货物等。

波黑部长会议决定给予货物在自由流通状态下的奖励措施和免征关税政策。所有可以免征关税的货物规定在《波黑海关政策法》附件 4 中。

《波黑海关政策法》也对作为国外投资部分的设备作出了限制——该设备生产日期不得超过 10 年。

需要提供权威机构签发的证明，确认设备符合环境保护和工作保护的标准。

四、劳动

（一）劳动法律、法规简介

在波黑国家层面上没有总的劳动法立法框架。波黑通过了政府机构中有关劳动者和公务员的规定，在特别法中对警察和武装力量涉及劳动的事宜作出一些规定。除了调整有关波黑政府机构公务员和非公务员的法律外，布尔奇科特区在波黑有排他的劳动立法权。有关波黑的劳动事宜在实体和布尔奇科特区的层级上主要由劳动法来调整。除了劳动法，劳动事宜还可由总集体协议和在实体层级上采用的分集体协议具体调整，而劳动法提供总的原则和限制。三方当事人——雇主、雇员和特定实体的政府决定采用总集体协议程序，该协议签订后在固定期限内有效。

《波黑联邦劳动法》适用于用人单位和劳动者之间基于雇佣合同而设立的雇佣关系。该法同样适用于基于合同的固定期限和临时工作，劳动法考虑到未设立劳动关系而进行的职业培训，考虑到这类人没有与雇主建立劳动关系因而不享有劳动法意义上的雇员地位；但是他们在健康保险、工资和伤残保险领域确实享有劳动法及其他法律、法规规定的权利。《波黑联邦劳动法》考虑到管理委员会或其他管理机构的主席和成员（执行董事），无论是否建立雇佣关系，但按照劳动规则手册规定履行职责的可能性，因此，没有建立雇佣关系而开展工作的管理委员会主席和成员或执行董事不受劳动法的约束。取而代之的是，这些人的责任和义务由根据涉及雇主的一般法令而签订的合同进行调整。

塞族共和国劳动法调整塞族共和国境内因雇用而发生的劳动关系、权利、义务和责任以及其他关系，特别法另有规定的除外。除了调整雇用权利和义务，也调整雇佣关系以外的短期雇用，该雇用基于签订的固定期限和临时雇佣合同、服务合同、职业和额外培训合同及辅助工作或境外就业合同。这类雇佣关系之外的人员没有劳动法意义上的雇员地位，但是他们在健康保险和社会保障及其他领域同样享有劳动法及其他法律、法规规定的权利。

布尔奇科特区劳动法调整区内因雇用或其他因雇用而发生的劳动关系、权利、义务和责任及其他关系。

（二）雇用外国雇员的要求

要雇用外国雇员，要求该雇员必须取得工作许可和居住许可。

1. 工作许可

在波黑，工作许可由法律授权，允许外国人个人接受国内自然人或法人的有薪雇用，在这方面外国人享有与被雇用的波黑公民相同的与工作相关的权利、义务和责任，国际协议另有规定的除外。工作许可为特定的岗位和/或工种签发。工作许可根据特定的配额签发，配额即每年签发给在波黑一些行业工作的外国人的工作许可数量。年度配额由波黑部长会议根据移民政策和劳动力市场决定。某些情形下可以超出配额签发，这些情形包括：具备波黑高等教育、研究生或博士学位的外国人，基于国际协议在波黑工作的外国人，在企业承担主要任务但基于国际协议未被要求免予取得工作许可的外国人。工作许可的有效期为1年。

外国人在波黑确定居住地前，雇主不得与外国人订立雇佣合同或相应协议，通常需要暂住许可。

波黑法律规定了免除取得工作许可的情形，即：外国人只要持有之前从事下列活动取得的工作证明，每个公历年可以工作90日而无须工作许可；是法律实体的委员会中有较高职位的人或对部门进行管理、监督其他雇员工作的人；具有丰富的知识和对法律实体运营、设备研发、技术或管理而言必不可少的专家，且他们在法律实体中被雇用至少1年，或在来到波黑工作之前作为合伙人履行职责，如果委派不具有雇佣性质，外国人应是在波黑设立的公司发起人，如果该公司平均每雇用一个外国人就至少雇用五个本国人，支付给每个雇员的全部工资总额至少和波黑的平均工资总额相当，按时承担纳税责任及法律规定的其他义务。

雇用外国人的条件和程序由下列法律规定：《波黑外国人法》《波黑联邦外国人雇用法》《塞族共和

国外国公民和无国籍人雇用法》和《布尔奇科特区外国人雇用法》。

根据雇主住所的不同,分别由波黑联邦、塞族共和国和布尔奇科特区雇用外国人就业管理部门负责签发工作许可。在波黑联邦,州就业服务局经联邦就业服务局批准后签发工作许可。在塞族共和国,雇主主要办事机构所在地的就业服务地区办公室负责签发工作许可。在布尔奇科特区,政府职业和管理事务部签发外国人工作许可。

2. 申请程序

根据准备雇用外国人的雇主的请求签发工作许可。雇主代表雇员向雇主住所地有管辖权的就业服务机构提交申请。

申请签发工作许可,雇主有义务提交下列经认证的复印件:

(1)塞族共和国

① 注册决定,由负责雇主主要业务的机构出具;

② 据以签订工作合同或其他所需合同的外国人的信息,特别是姓名、父母姓名、出生日期、性别、出生国住所地和地址、档案编号、有效旅行文件的签发日期和签发地;

③ 工作地点信息或工作种类和工作条件;

④ 雇用外国人的合理解释——外国人被雇用从事的工作的描述、资格种类和专业知识种类及该工作所需的资格;

⑤ 健康证明书(只适用于一次签发工作许可);

⑥ 认证的护照复印件。

(2)波黑联邦

① 来自有关法院相关登记的摘录或有关当局依照关于职业技能和相关活动的法律签发的经营活动注册证明;

② 依据《波黑联邦劳动法》第2条规定的准备雇用的外国人的信息:姓名、父母姓名、出生日期、性别、出生国住所地和地址、档案编号、有效旅行文件的签发日期和签发地;

③ 工作职位、种类和工作条件信息;

④ 雇主开立账户的银行出具的雇主偿付能力证明;

⑤ 证明对现有的雇员已经履行纳税义务和缴纳税款的书面文件,包括申请许可展期的外国人;

⑥ 雇用外国人的理由说明,雇员的教育种类、职业技能和该工作所需的资格;

⑦ 公证的外国人学校毕业证,且需翻译成波黑联邦一种官方语言。

3. 社会保险

在塞族共和国及波黑联邦,社会保险费缴费数额按薪资总额计算。薪资总额包括正式雇用的纯薪资,乘以确定的系数,加上薪资中代扣代缴的缴费数额。在布尔奇科特区,缴纳养老保险由实体的法律进行规范。

在波黑联邦雇员承担的份额分别是:17%的养老保险,12.5%的医疗保险,1.5%的失业保险(总计为薪资总额的31%)。在塞族共和国雇员承担的份额分别是:18.5%的养老保险,12%的医疗保险,1%的失业保险,1.5%的儿童保护保险(总计为薪资总额的33%)。在布尔奇科特区,适用波黑联邦法律,雇主缴纳17%的养老保险,适用塞族共和国的法律,雇主缴纳18%的养老保险、12%的医疗保险、1.5%的失业保险(总计为薪资总额的30.5%或31.5%)。在波黑联邦雇主承担的份额分别是:6%的养老保险,4%的医疗保险,0.5%的失业保险(总计为薪资总额的10.5%)。在塞族共和国,免缴。在布尔奇科特区,适用波黑联邦法律,雇主根据薪资总额缴纳6%的养老保险。

(三)出入境

1. 签证种类

签证只能签发给持有有效护照的外国人,护照有效期至少超过签证有效期3个月。申请签证需要提交准确和全面填写的表格。

机场过境签证(签证A)使外国人可以在不连续或连续国际飞行期间可以通过机场国际中转区而

不实际进入该国家。为外国人签发签证，在中转期间可以一次、两次或者多次通过机场国际中转区，签证有效期 3 个月。

短期居留签证（签证 C）使外国人可以在该国一次或多次居留，前提是在波黑没有连续居留或多次连续居留，总的期限有限制。该签证从第一次入境开始，在 6 个月内有效期为 90 天，短期居留签证为一次或多次进入波黑而签发。短期居留签证有效期不超过 1 年，例外情形是，如果波黑外交部认为有效期超过 1 年的符合本国利益并获得其同意，可以签发短期居留签证。短期居留签证因商务、教育、培训或相似目的，旅游、私人旅行，参加政治、科学、文化、体育、宗教及其他需要短期停留理由的旅行而签发。短期居留签证因不可抗力、人道主义、职业或个人原因可以展期，但是应符合签证签发的规定。

长期居留签证（签证 D）使外国人可以从第一次进入该国起 1 年内居留达 6 个月。长期居留签证为一次或多次进入波黑，特别是为在波黑居留之目的，6 个月内居留期限超过 90 日，需要签发长期居留签证。长期居留签证有效期不超过 1 年，例外情形是，如果波黑外交部认为有效期超过 1 年的符合本国利益并获得其同意，可以签发长期居留签证。

2. 出入境限制

依据《波黑外国人法》的规定，如果不符合一般入境要求，不符合波黑签署的国际条约的要求，或不符合部长会议、法庭或检察官办公室允许入境和在波黑暂时居住许可决定（特殊条件下的入境），外国人将被拒绝入境。

除了前述原因，有以下情形的，外国人可以被拒绝进入波黑：
① 提供假旅行文件试图进入波黑；
② 提供假签证或居住许可试图进入波黑；
③ 任何在 6 个月内已经在波黑停留 90 日的免签证制度国家的公民，该期限指之前每次暂住天数，除非他/她遵守特殊条件下入境的规定；
④ 波黑签署的国际协议允许的暂住期限已经到期，除非基于其他理由许可入境；
⑤ 有理由怀疑他/她进入波黑是为了工作，但无工作许可证，且不符合《波黑外国人法》规定的为工作而暂时居住且不需要工作证的情形；
⑥ 符合入境时波黑签证取消和作废的规定。

如果外国人未持有适当的工作许可但被雇用，或处于无谋生手段的状态，或许可居住的情况发生变化，以致不再符合居住许可的条件，可能终止暂住。如果外国人被判有罪，或拒绝执行波黑管理部门最终或应执行的决定，或滥用其暂住资格给其他进入波黑需要登证的国家的公民寄送邀请函却不履行因邀请/担保发生的相应义务的，其暂住资格将被取消。

（四）工会和劳工组织

在波黑的雇员有权建立和注册工会，并成为会员。两个实体的劳动法都保障该项权利。

波黑独立工会联盟是通过该联盟所属机构——分支工会组织起来的体现工人利益的自发组织，该联盟和其成立的工会是民主的、多种族的、跨国的，独立于政府、雇主、政党和宗教团体。

波黑独立工会联盟包括 24 个分支工会，同时有 7 个该联盟州委员会在波黑联邦 9 个州开展工作。该联盟被认为是联邦政府和波黑联邦雇主联盟的社会合作伙伴，参与联盟境内经济和社会委员会的工作。

（五）劳动争议

个人和集体劳动争议由塞族共和国、波黑联邦、布尔奇科特区和州的各级法院解决，涉及波黑政府机构的雇员除外，该劳动争议由波黑法院管辖。在波黑联邦，《法院法》规定市法院对所有民事争议的管辖，即对所有个人和集体劳动争议进行裁判。在塞族共和国，具有普遍管辖权的法院负责裁判劳动争议。在布尔奇科特区，地方法院对民事争议具有一审管辖权，该争议包括个人和集体劳动争议。劳动争议作为一般的诉讼争议，但应遵守一些特别规定，例如该争议被视为优先解决的争议，雇员免缴诉讼费，缩短诉讼期限以加速争议解决。所有争议的解决只能使用波斯尼亚语。提交的文件必须用波斯尼亚语，因此，所有外文文件必由法院指定的翻译人员翻译成当地语言。在波黑，劳动争议通常审理两年后才能作出终局和有约束力的裁判。

五、知识产权

（一）知识产权法律、法规简介

经过 2010 年的全面改革，波黑立法完全符合欧盟的规定。同时，欧盟也通过新的决定和法令，因此，需要对立法进行修订以符合欧盟立法。波黑在知识产权领域很大程度上遵守了《稳定与结盟协议》。

波黑关于知识产权领域的立法包括：《著作权及相关权利法》《工业设计法》《专利法》《著作权和相关权利集体管理法》《地理标志来源保护法》《集成电路拓扑图保护法》和《商标法》。

依据可适用的法规，知识产权是指思维创意、用于商业用途的发明、文学艺术作品、符号、名称、形象和设计。

知识产权分为两类：工业产权，包括发明（专利）、商标、工业设计、来源地标志、集成电路拓扑图和植物品种。著作权，包括文学艺术作品，如小说、诗歌和戏剧、电影、音乐作品；艺术作品，如图纸、绘画、照片和雕塑及建筑设计。与著作权相关的权利包括表演中表演艺术家、录音中录音制品制作人和广播电视节目中播音员的权利。

取得、维持、登记转让和终止专利和商标的程序向波黑知识产权局申请办理。波黑知识产权局为保护商标之目的负责商标注册申请、商标注册和代理人注册。

专利是保护技术领域发明的权利。为了使发明获得专利，必须符合三个要求：

① 新颖性；
② 创造性；
③ 实用性。

专利权由国家权威机构负责授予并需缴纳费用，在一定的地域和期限内有效。如果在每个可以寻求专利保护的国家申请、审查和授予发明专利权，同一发明可以同时在几个国家受到保护。

专利权被授予一定的期限。专利权期限为 20 年，非实质审查的专利权期限为 10 年，均自提交申请之日起计算。

下列各项不视为发明：发现、科学理论和数学方法、艺术创作、智力活动、游戏，商业经营的方案、规则和方法，计算机程序及限于信息内容本身的信息演示。

商标是能够使一个企业的产品或服务区别于其他企业的同样或相似的产品或服务的标记。申请取得商标专用权的产品或服务的性质不影响商标注册。

标记能区分相同或相似的产品或服务，商标保护用图形表示的标记。标记包括：文字（包括如姓名）、图案、字母、数字、形象、产品形状或其包装、颜色、三维标志或这些要素的组合。

作为身份标记的商标有四个作用：区分产品或服务、来源、质量和市场推广。商标由国家管理部门负责核准注册并需缴纳费用，在特定区域和一定期限内有效。

外国法人和自然人只能通过在波黑知识产权局登记在册的授权代表办理知识产权事务。在波黑知识产权局办理工业产权保护中提供代理服务的法人和自然人必须由波黑知识产权局进行相应的授权代表登记造册。在研究所进行的程序中，专利代理人和商标、工业设计及地理标志来源的代理人可以代理法人和自然人办理知识产权事务。

（二）专利申请

专利申请首先应向波黑知识产权局提出。提出授予专利权的请求，同时提供支付涉及成本的文件和证明。申请以书面形式、当面或邮寄提交，或以数据电文的方式发送至知识产权局官方电子邮箱，按照规定，自知识产权局收到申请之日起 15 日内，向知识产权局提交书面申请。每一个发明填写一份申请。

专利申请文件包括授予专利权请求书、反映实质特点的发明属性、申请人信息和发明人信息。

专利申请包括以下内容：

① 对发明详细和清楚的说明，一项或多项清楚和简要的权利要求，并且有发明和附图说明书完整支持；

② 任何有关发明和专利权利要求的说明；
③ 仅用于提供技术信息的发明实质特点的摘要。
用电脑或打字机填写表格，使用波黑官方语言。提交两份副本以及其他附件。一份由研究院留存，另一份注明日期，注明专利申请号和来函序列号，加盖公章用作记载申请人申请日的证明。

专利申请提交的随附文件：
① 发明者不公布姓名的声明；
② 通过授权代表提出申请时的授权委托书；
③ 有多个申请人时的共同代理人声明。

（三）商标注册

申请商标注册前，需要针对商标相同或相似性进行检索以避免在注册程序或市场中与此前已注册商标或此前已申请注册商标相冲突。及时了解商标注册可能遇到的障碍或避免市场中的冲突，从而及时采取法律行动或进行商业运作。

在申请商标注册审查程序中，波黑知识产权局应审查障碍是否存在。如果申请注册的商标同之前商标持有人的货物或服务的商标相同或相似，可能造成对之前商标持有者的侵权，特别是如果申请人已经在商业活动中使用了该标记。检索服务可以按照各种标准进行（相同、相似、涉及申请人/持有人或特别限定的要求）。

注册商标持有人或申请准予商标注册的申请人可以是本国或外国自然人或法律实体。外国自然人或法律实体在波黑的商标保护与本国自然人或法律实体享有同样的权利，如果该权利来源于波黑加入的国际条约或批准或互惠原则。

申请准予商标注册应首先提出准予商标注册申请。步骤包括：
① 向波黑知识产权局提交申请；
② 波黑知识产权局对申请进行形式审查；
③ 波黑知识产权局在其可以查询官方公报上和网站公布专利申请；
④ 知识产权局作出准予注册决定，发给商标注册证。

申请程序自向知识产权局申请准予商标注册开始，有必要提交完整的准予商标注册的请求、随附文件和支付费用的证明，申请以书面形式当面或邮寄提交，或通过电传发送至知识产权局官方电子邮箱，按照规定，自知识产权局收到申请之日起8日内，向知识产权局提交书面申请。

（四）知识产权保护措施

波黑众多的各级管理机构承担着知识产权权利保护职能。波黑知识产权研究所负责对工业产权保护领域行政和专业事务、著作权和相关权利的保护，包括对著作权集体管理组织的监督。波黑知识产权局负责知识产权保护事宜；波黑国家间接税管理局负责海关监管；各级市场监督管理局负责市场监管；波黑法院负责行政争议诉讼；波黑联邦和布尔奇科特区普通法院及塞族共和国商业法院负责民事法律保护；波黑国家检察院同有管辖权的警察局、各实体检察院和各级法院合作，负责刑事司法保护；实体普通法院负责对轻罪作出裁决。

在国家层面，波黑知识产权局管辖知识产权保护领域专业和合作事务，包括监督著作权集体管理组织，受理知识产权保护事宜。波黑知识产权局的二审机构是复审委员会，当事人可以向波黑法院提起行政诉讼请求对抗波黑知识产权局的决定。

波黑国家间接税管理局负责知识产权权利保护执行的职能部门包括：知识产权保护部；海关办公室和海关邮政；区域中心预防走私和犯罪小组。海关办公室和海关邮政依照海关程序，通过对进口、出口和中转货物的海关监管实施对知识产权的保护措施。

国家调查和保护局（SIPA）的管辖权之一是预防、侦查和调查侵犯知识产权和相关权利的刑事犯罪。国家调查和保护局在其要求范围内可以请求波黑法律执行机构和其他管理部门提供涉及刑事犯罪的信息和调查结果，其中包括侵犯知识产权的刑事犯罪。国家调查和保护局也可以定期向波黑有管辖权的检察院和机构通报，启动预防和侦查有关刑事犯罪的联合行动。国家调查和保护局在收集情报时也向波黑国家检察院和国家法院提供支持,根据这些机构的要求就某些调查结果及必要的事实、证据和资料提供报告。

六、环境保护

(一)环境保护监管部门

根据波黑国家法院和现行法律架构的规定,环境保护活动由波黑、实体、州和自治团体不同的各行政机构执行。

在波黑层面,波黑对外贸易和经济关系部被赋予特别环境保护管辖权。水资源局、旅游和环境保护局是该部的组成部门。

实体、布尔奇科特区、波黑联邦州和自治市及塞族共和国自治市对波黑环境和水资源行使管理职责由宪法授权。

环境保护部门从事下列活动:对政策、基本原则提出建议,协调实体管理部门和机构开展环境保护工作的分工和国际合作,尤其是准备、建议和协调执行波黑的发展政策、国际合作和项目,及波黑层面的法律、法规和其他立法,承担分析监控和收集最新的专家分析、信息和意见。水务管理活动由波黑各主管机构的协调会议定期进行协调。

在波黑层面上制定、贯彻和执行环境立法和政策属于各部的职责,其负责环境保护、预防和消除环境危险、恢复和逐步改善环境;确定环境保护优先任务;介绍环境保护法律、经济和技术措施;开发、维护和运行用作基础保障的系统,对测量、监测、管控和环境评估信息进行收集和处理;提供有关环境潜在影响的资料;采用环境保护金融立法;与塞族共和国进行合作。

此外,塞族共和国社会规划、建设和生态部有权在环境保护领域开展活动,该部门通过采取环境保护措施开展整体的环境保护和促进、研究和管理,保护自然资源、自然与文化遗产、参与国内和国际项目行动的执行和发展,建立和协调同国内外环境保护管理部门、机构和非政府组织之间就环境保护开展专业合作和经验交流,参与国际金融组织为环境保护而赞助的项目的执行,起草有关环境保护的法律和法规。

(二)环境保护法律、法规简介

波黑没有一个普遍的作为其他环境立法基础的环境保护框架性法令。波黑联邦、塞族共和国、布尔奇科特区和一些州通过了关于环境保护的法律及规范环境事宜的其他法律,在此基础上,通过了相关法规,使得法律在该领域得以实施。

在州级行政层级上,共6个州施行《波黑联邦环境保护法》,与此同时,州颁布的环境保护法律在4个州仍然有效。

《波黑环境保护法》调整以下范围:生态质量和环境能力及生活质量的保持、保护、恢复和提高;管理措施和条件、保持和合理使用自然资源;保持、保护和提高环境保护法律措施和机构的框架,对环境保护和志愿措施的资金支持,各级政府行政管理部门的职责和任务。《水资源法》调整水资源保护。

《塞族共和国环境保护法》是总的环境保护框架性法令。本法调整环境保护事宜,从而保护环境、减少人类生存和健康风险,同时保障和提高生活质量、保护环境因素、提供和获取环境保护信息,制定环境保护规划,包括环境影响战略性评价,预防大规模自然灾害,管理生态标识和环境保护,资金支持与环境相关的活动,环境损害的责任,包括依照本法开展活动的自然人和法人的责任。

《布尔奇科特区环境保护法》是相关环境保护立法的基础。本法调整环境保护事宜,从而保护环境、减少人类生存和健康风险,同时保障和提高生活质量、保护环境因素、提供和获取环境保护信息,涉及环境保护规划,环境影响战略性评价,颁发环境保护许可证程序,预防大规模自然灾害,管理生态标识和环境保护,资金支持与环境相关的活动,环境损害的责任,包括依照本法开展活动的自然人和法人的权利和义务。

各实体和布尔奇科特区环境保护法律的主要原则是:

① 可持续发展原则。该原则指通过对自然资源的保护实现环境的可持续性,从而达到再生材料、

水和能源资源的消耗不超过自然界可以补偿的限度，不可再生资源的消耗不超过持续可再生资源可以被替代的限度，排放的污染物的水平不超过空气、水和土壤吸收和处理的能力，以及持续保持生物多样性（biodiversity）、人体健康、空气、水和土地质量，提供人类、植物和动物生存的必要条件。

② 谨慎和预防原则。该原则通过环境影响评估和使用现有的、可用的、最好的工艺、技术和设备加以实现，促进防止环境污染，避免给环境和人类健康带来危害的活动，每一个活动必须作出计划并且带来最小可能的变化，从而降低对环境和人类健康构成的风险；减少对空间的负担和在建设、生产、分配和使用中对原材料和能源的消耗；采用可能的再循环；预防和限制每个污染源对环境的影响。

③ 替代原则。该原则指每一个对环境有损害影响的活动应当由实质上对环境造成较小风险和危害的活动替代。

④ 整体方案原则。该原则指预防整体环境损害的风险或将风险控制在最低范围内。规定对环境的高水平保护和提高环境质量是所有政策和战略的整体组成部分，目标是推进环境保护，确保与可持续发展原则相一致。

⑤ 合作和责任划分原则。该原则指只有通过与有义务进行合作的利益相关者的协调联合行动才能取得可持续发展的目标，从而基于责任划分，实现环境保护为目的，通过与政府管理部门、自然人、法人和其他机构进行合作。为了更好地保护环境，鼓励实体间的合作、签署有关环境保护双边或多边国际协议和其他合作协议，以及提供与环境保护有关的，尤其是与周边国家环境保护有关的信息和支持。

⑥ 公众参与和获取信息原则。在行使健康环境权时，每个人都有权获取环境状况信息，参与可能影响环境的决策程序，同时有关环境状况的数据应对外公开。

⑦ 损害责任原则。该原则指污染者的活动造成或可能造成环境污染的，污染者承担污染环境的费用，即污染者有生产、使用和投入流通的原材料、半成品和产品带有对环境有害物质情形之一的。同时，该原则指污染者承担全部预防和减少污染措施的成本，包括环境风险成本和恢复遭受损害的环境的成本。

以上提及的原则也构成了其他环境法律的基础。

（三）环境保护评估

在国家层面，除涉及健康保护或健康生命和环境权利的情形以外，没有关于环境保护和可持续发展的宪法规定。虽然波黑各部、实体和州负责环境保护事宜，但是国家、实体和州之间的权限划分规定得非常不明确，在国家层面上能力不足（雇员必须具有较高的能力从而对环境情况、可持续发展和气候变化提供更有效和全面的监测）。应在国家层面扩大和增加授权以期同这一地区的情况和管理相一致。目前而言，关于环境保护情况的实施、监测和评估没有完善的结构和机制，此外，环境保护部门的能力也很有限，责任落在国家议会上。

七、争议解决

（一）争议解决的方法和机构

在波黑有四个体现宪法和地方机构的司法体系，即：波黑司法体系、波黑联邦司法体系、塞族共和国司法体系和布尔奇科特区司法体系。

因此，在规定法院结构和作用的立法框架方面，有四部关于法院的法律，规定设立法院和明确其管辖权、组织、内部设置、资金来源和与其作用相关的其他事宜。

在波黑层面，有波黑宪法法院、波黑国家法院和波黑国家检察院。波黑宪法没有关于波黑普通司法体系的规定或司法管理部门总的规定。宪法只有关于波黑宪法法院的规定。波黑国家法院具有刑事、行政和上诉案件管辖权。

《波黑联邦宪法》规定了其境内的司法管辖权，由波黑联邦宪法法院、最高法院、州法院和自治市法院行使。

依据《塞族共和国宪法》的规定，司法权由法院行使，基于宪法和法律规定，法院是自治和独立的。在塞族共和国，司法权由宪法法院、最高法院、高等法院和初级法院行使。除了一般的管辖法院外,《塞族共和国法院法》设立具有专门管辖权的法院——地区商事法院和高级商事法院。

《布尔奇科特区法令》规定特区内的司法是独立和公正的,司法体系包括初级法院和上诉法院。

波黑联邦自治市法院、塞族共和国和布尔奇科特区初级法院对刑事案件一审、民事、轻罪、商事和其他案件有管辖权,例外的是,塞族共和国内商事案件不由初级法院管辖而由地区商事法院管辖。

除了其他权限,布尔奇科特区初级法院不考虑可能判处的刑期,对所有刑事案件具有管辖权,而其他初级和自治市法院审理可能判处10年以下有期徒刑的刑事案例。

塞族共和国地区法院和波黑联邦州法院一审管辖权包括可能判处10年有期徒刑或长期监禁的刑事犯罪案件和行政争议案件。

二审管辖权包括不服自治市法院和初级法院在各自管辖范围内作出的裁判提起上诉而进行的上诉程序,也裁定自治市法院之间的地域管辖冲突和移送管辖,提供刑事事宜国际司法协助。

《塞族共和国法院法》也规定在塞族共和国设立地区商事法院,受理一审商事案件、民事案件和货物合法交易、服务、证券、房地产所有权和其他权利中有关权利义务的非诉争议等,诉讼程序中的双方当事人是企业家或以其他身份进行经济或业务活动的法人或自然人。这些法院也裁决相关争议,涉及船舶、航行、飞机、著作权和相关权利及知识产权、不正当竞争、破产或清算、经营实体注册活动、外国投资、法律援助等。高级商事法院针对地区商事法院的判决作出上诉判决;其裁定法律规定的一审中的其他事宜,裁定地区商业法院之间的管辖冲突和移送管辖,阐明法律立场,从而保证地区商事法院法律适用的连续性。

波黑联邦和塞族共和国最高法院和布尔奇科特区上诉法院对于州和地区法院及布尔奇科特区初级法院判决提供通常的法律救济,对于终审法院的判决提供特别的法律救济。

上诉是通常的法律救济途径。每个人都有权上诉或请求撤销影响其权利或利益的判决。

民事和商事案件中可以缩短或简化的程序包括:基于自认作出的判决、基于放弃作出的判决和缺席审判。

(二)法律适用

程序法规定法院应当在法律规定的审理期限内作出判决,在整个诉讼程序中,法院应当依职权关注其管辖权。

程序法具体规定法院的地域管辖,具有诉讼标的管辖权的法院在其各自的区域内就特定法律争议进行裁判的权利和义务。

八、其他

(一)反商业贿赂

1.反商业贿赂法律、法规简介

波黑部长会议通过了2015—2019年《反腐败战略和行动计划》。目前,为了进一步执行该计划,波黑完善和通过了八项反腐败战略和十项行动计划。

相关反腐败国际组织和机构的建议得到了持续的核查和执行,已经通过了波黑刑事立法修正案,包括对利用影响力受贿的定罪。根据这些修正案,当某人为自己或他人的利益,自己或通过贿赂介绍人向波黑机构官员或负责人,包括外国官员、国际官员、仲裁员或陪审员在内,给予或承诺给予礼物或其他利益,以便在其职权范围内违反规定地作为或不作为,成立商业贿赂罪。

2.反商业贿赂监督部门

波黑设立了下列预防腐败机构:
① 预防腐败和协作反腐败局;
② 波黑联邦政府反腐败组;
③ 塞族共和国执行反腐败战略委员会;

④布尔奇科特区预防腐败和联合行动压制腐败委员会；

⑤在各州设立的反腐败机构。

这些机构监督和协调在相应的管理部门层面战略性反腐败文件的执行过程。预防腐败和协作反腐败局作为波黑国家层面的唯一机构，倡议在波黑其他政府层面上设立反腐败机构。

除了这些具有预防性质的机构，波黑设有具有反腐败管辖权的机构，这些机构有强制权力（警察局、检察官办公室和法院等）。

3. 处罚措施

对于贿赂犯罪，除了判处徒刑外，规定了诸如没收礼物、薪酬、财产或其他获取的利益的处罚。除了强制的特点外，逾期惩罚也有预防性的效果从而预防腐败。

（二）工程承包

1. 许可制度

政府采购须经过招标，符合招标程序。对于私有领域，企业有权自主订立合同。

如果合同涉及法律规定范围内的项目或涉及医院工作、运动设施、娱乐和休闲、学校和大学建筑及用于行政管理的建筑，管理部门作为合同一方且直接出资超过 50% 时，签订的合同须符合政府采购规定。

2. 邀标和投标

编制的投标文件应该包括所有必要的资料，以便法律实体请求参加投标竞争。对于政府采购项目，合同主管部门确定具体或符合条件的采购主体的数量。

合同主管部门确定中标候选人和 / 或要约方的资金、技术和专业能力条件，满足这些条件是评估中标候选人和 / 或要约方是否具有履行合同能力必要的依据。

Bosnia and Herzegovina

Authors: Olodar Prebanic, Tijana Blesic
Translators: Liu Erchan, Zhang Yuming

I. Overview

A. General Introduction to the Political, Economic, Social and Legal Environment of the Country Receiving Investment

Bosnia and Herzegovina (B&H) is a country in Southeastern Europe, located on the Balkan Peninsula.B&H proclaimed independence in 1992, following the dissolution of Socialist Federal Republic of Yugoslavia.

B&H has several levels of political structuring, according to the Dayton Accords. The most important of these levels is the division of the country into two entities: Republic of Srpska (RS) and the Federation of Bosnia and Herzegovina (FB&H). Furthermore, the FB&H is divided into 10 cantons. The B&H covers 51% of B&H's total area while RS covers 49%. Brcko District in the north of the country was created in 2000, out of land from both entities. It officially belongs to both, but is governed by neither and functions under a decentralized system of local government.

B&H is a potential candidate for membership to the European Union and has been a candidate for North Atlantic Treaty Organization membership since April 2010.Additionally, B&H has been a member of the Council of Europe since April 2002 and a founding member of the Mediterranean Union upon its establishment in July 2008.

Official languages of B&H are Bosnian, Croatian and Serbian. English is taught as a second language and is spoken by the majority of the population.

a. Political

As a result of the Dayton Accords, the civilian peace implementation is supervised by the High Representative for B&H selected by the Peace Implementation Council.The High Representative has many governmental and legislative powers, including the dismissal of elected and non-elected officials. More recently, several central institutions have been established (such as defense ministry, security ministry, state court, indirect taxation service) in the process of transferring part of the jurisdiction from the entities to the state.

The Chair of the Presidency of B&H rotates among three members (Bosniak, Serb, Croat), each elected as the Chair for an eight-month term within their four-year term as a member. The three members of the Presidency are elected directly by the people with Federation voters voting for the Bosniak and the Croat, and the Republika Srpska voters for the Serb.

The Chair of the Council of Ministers is nominated by the Presidency and approved by the House of Representatives.He or she is then responsible for appointing a Foreign Minister, Minister of Foreign Trade, and others as appropriate.

The Parliamentary Assembly is the lawmaking body in B&H. It consists of two houses: the House of Peoples and the House of Representatives. The House of Peoples has 15 delegates chosen by parliaments of the entities, two-thirds of which come from the Federation (5 Croat and 5 Bosniaks) and one-third from the Republika Srpska (5 Serbs). The House of Representatives is composed of 42 Members elected by the people under a form of proportional representation (PR), two-thirds elected from the Federation and one-third elected from the Republika Srpska.

The Constitutional Court of B&H is the supreme, final arbiter of legal matters. It is composed of nine members: four members are selected by the House of Representatives of the Federation, two by the Assembly of the Republika Srpska, and three by the President of the European Court of Human Rights after consultation with the Presidency, but cannot be Bosnian citizens.

However, the highest political authority in the country is the High Representative in B&H, the chief executive officer for the international civilian presence in the country and is selected by the European Union. Since 1995, the High Representative has been able to bypass the elected parliamentary assembly, and since 1997 has been able to remove elected officials. International supervision is to end when the country is deemed politically and democratically stable and self-sustaining.

b. Economic

B&H is an upper middle-income country and is currently embarking on a new growth model amid a period of slow growth and the global financial crisis. B&H has a transitional economy with limited market reforms. The key economic challenge for B&H in the imbalance of its economic model is that public policies and incentives are skewed toward the public rather than the private sector.

The konvertibilna marka (convertible mark)–the national currency introduced in 1998–is pegged to the euro through a currency board arrangement, which has maintained confidence in the currency and has facilitated reliable trade links with European partners. In 2016, Bosnia began a three-year IMF loan program that requires Bosnia to meet economic reform benchmarks to receive future funding installments.

B&H's top economic priorities are: acceleration of integration into the EU; strengthening the fiscal system; public administration reform; World Trade Organization membership; and securing economic growth by fostering a dynamic, competitive private sector.

c. Social

B&H is a small country with the majority of foreign employees consisting of laborers, professionals and technicians from all over the world. B&H regulations guarantee the same rights to foreigners, provided they regulate their work and residence in B&H in accordance with applicable regulations.

d. Legal

The legal framework in B&H is quite complex due to the combination of different government systems. In addition to B&H itself, the two entities have their own legal systems. In addition, the Brcko District has a separate legal framework. Only a small number of laws are adopted at B&H level (laws relating to foreign policy, foreign trade policy, customs policy, monetary policy, finances of the institutions and for the international obligations, immigration, refugee and asylum policy/regulation, international and inter-entity criminal law enforcement, establishment and operation of common international communications facilities, regulation of inter-entity transportation and air traffic control). Pursuant to Article 3.3 of the Constitution, any residual powers are automatically assigned to the entities.

As the entities have wide legislative competences, each of them may adopt different laws. However, with the stimulus of the Office of the High Representative (OHR), the entities started enacting the so-called "mirror laws", i.e.laws being identical but enacted separately by the parliaments in each entity.

As a result of the country's political structure, legal reform was very difficult to achieve during the period after the war and up until 2002.However, the situation is improving and a number of substantial positive developments occured under the auspices of the OHR. One of the main legal challenges facing the country is creating a single economic space in which to do business. Pursuant to the "Bulldozer Initiative" (an OHR initiative to build a working partnership between politicians and business people), a number of legal reforms have been enacted to this end through the mechanism of having the entities enacting similar laws.

B. The Status and Direction of the Cooperation with Chinese Enterprises Under the B&R

The People's Republic of China and B&H reached steady growth in 2013.The two countries maintained political exchanges at various levels.

Business cooperation between China and B&H produced great results. In May, construction of the Stanari Power Plant in B&H undertaken by a Chinese company started. This it the first major cooperative project between the two countries and also the first project under the US$10 billion special credit line for China-CEECs cooperation.[①]

II. Investment

A. Market Access

a. Department Supervising Investment

Governmental departments devoted to the promotion of investment include are mainly the Foreign Investment Promotion Agency (FIPA) of B&H. FIPA is a State agency established with the mission to attract and maximize the

---

[①] China and Bosnia and Herzegovina.Available from: http://www.fmprc.gov.cn/mfa_eng/wjb_663304/zzjg_663340/xos_664404/gjlb_664408/3145_664450/.

flow of foreign direct investment into B&H and encourage existing foreign investors to further expand and develop their businesses in B&H, to facilitate the interaction between public and private sectors and have an active role in policy advocacy in order to contribute to continually improving environment for business investment and economic development.

b. Laws and Regulations of Investment Industry

There are three main laws and regulations regulating investment industry. Those are: Law on the Policy of Foreign Direct Investment of B&H, Law on Foreign Investment of the FB&H and Law on Foreign Investment of the RS.

The Law on the Policy of Foreign Direct Investment regulates basic policies and principles of the participation of foreign investors in the economy of B&H. According to this Law, foreign investors are entitled to invest and reinvest profits of such investments into any and all sectors of the economy of B&H, in the same form and under same conditions as defined for the residents of B&H under applicable laws and regulations of B&H, entities and Brcko District.

According to the Law on the Policy of Foreign Direct Investments of B&H, many incentives are offered to foreign investors, such as:

(i) National treatment of foreign investors, i.e., foreign investors have the same rights and obligations as residents of B&H;

(ii) Foreign investors are entitled to open accounts in any commercial bank in domestic and/or any freely convertible currency on the territory of B&H;

(iii) Foreign investors are entitled to freely employ foreign nationals, subject to the labor and immigration laws in B&H;

(iv) Foreign investors are protected against nationalization, expropriation, requisition or measures having similar effects; such measures may take place only in the public interest in accordance with the applicable laws and regulations and against the payment of an appropriate compensation, i.e.compensation that is adequate, effective and prompt;

(v) Equipment being imported as part of share capital is exempt from paying customs duties (with the exception of passenger cars, slot and gambling machines);

(vi) The rights and benefits of foreign investors granted and obligations imposed by the Law (mentioned above) cannot be terminated or overruled by subsequent laws and regulations.Should a subsequent law or regulation be more favorable to foreign investor, the investor will have the right to choose the regime by which the investment will be regulated;

(vii) Foreign investors may own real estate in B&H. Foreign investors enjoy the same property rights in respect to real estate as B&H legal entities;

(viii) Foreign investors are entitled to transfer abroad, freely and without delay, in convertible currency, proceeds resulting from their investment in B&H;

(ix) Free trade zones in B&H are part of the customs territory of B&H and have status of legal entity. According to the Law on Free Trade Zones of B&H, free trade zone founders may be one or more domestic and foreign legal entities or natural persons and establishment must be economically justified (the free zone establishment is considered economically justified if the submitted feasibility study and other evidence can prove that the value of goods exported from a free zone will exceed at least 50% of the total value of manufactured goods leaving the free zone within the period of 12 months). The users of free zone do not pay VAT and import customs.Investment in the free zone, transfer of profit and transfer of investment are free of charge.

c. Forms of Investment

Direct investment exclusively entails investment into economy (into new or existing companies).
Donations, loans or grants are not considered as investments but have indirect influence on B&H economy.

d. Standards of Market Access and Examination

According to applicable B&H regulations, foreign investors have national treatment, i.e.they are granted the same rights and have the same obligations as B&H residents, including free market access.

B. Foreign Exchange Regulation

a. Department Supervising Foreign Exchange

Departments supervising foreign exchange in B&H are the Ministry of Finances of the FB&H and the Ministry of Finances of RS.

b. Brief Introduction of Laws and Regulations of Foreign Exchange

Foreign exchange is regulated by the Law on Foreign Exchange Operations of the FB&H and the Law on

Foreign Exchange Operations of RS.

c. Requirements of Foreign Exchange Management for Foreign Enterprises

Foreign enterprises are entitled to transfer profit made via direct investment freely, under the condition that all respective taxes and contributions towards the entity where the company's seat is located are settled.

Transfer of remaining parts of liquidation or bankruptcy mass is free, under the condition that all respective taxes and contributions towards the entity where the company's seat is located are settled.

Settlement of tax obligations is proven by the competent tax office's credential.

C. Financing

a. Main Financial Institutions

The Central Bank of B&H was established in accordance with the Law adopted at the Parliament of B&H on 20 June 1997.

The main goals and tasks of the Central Bank of B&H are defined by the Law and in accordance with the Dayton Accords.Central Bank of B&H maintains monetary stability by issuing domestic currency according to the Currency Board arrangement with full coverage in freely convertible foreign exchange funds under fixed exchange rate 1 KM: 0,51129 EURO. Central Bank defines and controls the implementation of monetary policy of B&H. It also supports and maintains appropriate payment and settlement systems and coordinates the activities of the entities' banking agencies which are in charge of bank licensing and supervision.

b.Financing Conditions for Foreign Enterprises

Foreign Enterprises are entitled to open a bank account in a local bank freely, under the same conditions as local entities.Bank accounts can be opened in a foreign or local currency.

D. Land Policy

a. Brief Introduction of Land-related Laws and Regulations

Land-related Laws and Regulations in B&H include the Law on Land Registry of the FB&H, Law on Land Registry of the RS, Law on Proprietary Rights of the FB&H and Law on Proprietary Rights of the RS.

Law on Proprietary Rights of the FB&H governs the acquisition, use, disposal of, protection and cease of ownership rights and other proprietary rights and possessions. In accordance with this Law, any natural person or legal entity may be the holder of ownership right and other real rights.

In the FB&H, municipal courts are competent to keep deed books.Within the court organization, the court department in charge of keeping deed books is the land registry office. Keeping of deed books encompasses all actions of the land registry court, in particular the supervision over performing insight into deed books, reception of requests, decisions on entry into deed books, conducting of entry, communicating it and keeping and entries into accessory registries such as the registry of owners, registry of land parcels and logs, as well as archiving at the land registry court itself.The entry of real estate and the entry of the rights to real estate–following the decision on entry–constitute the basic task of the land registry offices.The basic and main challenge in terms of regulation of property rights and application of laws is that the status of deed books is either destroyed or non-regulated. Therefore, some contracts cannot be enforced without either establishment of deed books or enforcement of the procedure to establish ownership.The period needed for registration in the deed books depends on each individual case, and then also on the contents of the contract that pertains to one or more land parcels, the current content of the deed book - in terms of whether a number of requests have been processed that pertain to the same deed book insert in which cadastre particles have been entered, etc. On average, registration takes 10 to 15 days.

In RS, the Republic Administration for Geodetic and Property Affairs is an independent administration responsible for keeping records of properties and property rights, maintenance of real estate cadastre, cadastral classification and land quality evaluation.

b. Rules of Land Acquisition for Foreign Enterprises

Foreign Enterprises have the same property rights in respect to real estate as legal entities of B&H.

Upon signing of a sales contract and certification of signatures of the contracting parties by the public notary, the land and the new owner are registered in the Land Registry of the entity where the land is located.

Requests for land registry extracts, as well as requests for alterations in land register records, are submitted to the land register offices located within municipal courts in the FB&H and each municipality in the RS.

Foreign enterprises are also allowed to rent out their B&H property without any requirement of obtaining a rental license from the authorities, but such rent out can be limited by a signed contract.

E. The Establishment and Dissolution of Companies

a. The Forms of Enterprises

Business establishment, operation, management and termination of business in B&H is regulated by the Law on Companies of the FB&H, Law on Companies of RS and Law on Enterprises of BD. These company laws distinguish the following types of companies in B&H:

a) Unlimited Joint Liability Company (d.n.o./ o.d./ UnLtd)

This is a company of at least two persons who bear unlimited mutual liability of the company. The company is founded by a Founding Contract of two or more domestic/foreign natural and/or legal entities. The contract must contain the name and address of the residence or company and address of company members, company address and activity of the company and the rights and obligations of members. Investments of the members may be in cash, kinds, rights or services. Value of investment must be estimated in the Founding Contract. Members' investments have equal value and become the property of the company. Every member has the right and obligation to manage the company. The company has no statute, no management bodies because members manage the company directly, including the representation of the company. There are no requirements for minimum or maximum contributions.

b) Limited Liability Company (d.o.o./ LLC)

This is a company founded by the establishment act or establishment contract by one or more domestic/ foreign natural and/or legal entities with basic capital divided in parts. A member in a limited company is liable for the value of his investment in that company. Limited Liability Company adopts Articles of Association. Management of the company is made by the Assembly (if it is only one founder it has all the authority of the Assembly), by the administration (which may have more members) and the Supervisory Board, which must be appointed in cases when the company has at least ten founders, and capital of one million BAM. In the Limited Liability Company that has no Supervisory Board its members are held liable. Minimum basic capital for LLCs in the FB&H amounts to 1.000,00 KM (app.500,00 EUR) and 1,00 BAM (app.0,5 EUR) in the RS. LLCs are the most common company form in B&H.

c) Joint-Stock Company (d.d./ a.d./ JSC)

This is founded by the establishment contract of one or more domestic/foreign natural or legal shareholders with basic capital divided into shares. A Joint Stock Company is founded by the Foundation Contract. Joint Stock Company is not liable for the obligations of shareholders, and can be established by one or more founders. The founders are the shareholders in joint-stock company. The minimum basic capital is BAM 50, 000 (25,000 EUR). Nominal value of one share cannot be less than 1,00 KM (approx.0,5 EUR). The bodies of Joint Stock Company are: assembly, supervisory board, administrati on and revision board. Joint Stock Company can be open and close: Open Joint-Stock Company is a legal entity–banks and insurance companies or company with minimum basic capital of BAM 4,000,000,00 (approx.2,000,000 EUR) in the FB&H and BAM 50.000,00 (approx. 25.000,00 EUR) in RS whose shareholders' shares are issued through public offering; Closed Joint-Stock company is a legal entity, whose shares are distributed among a limited number of shareholders. The minimum basic capital is BAM 50,000 (approx.25,000 EUR) in the FB&H and BAM 20.000,00 (approx.10.000,00 EUR) in RS.

d) Limited Partnership (k.d./ LP)

This is a company in which one or more members has unlimited solidarity liability for the liabilities of the company including member's private assets (general partner), and risk of one or more members is limited by the value of their share in that company; Limited Partnership is founded by the contract of two or more domestic/ foreign natural and/or legal entities. Limited Partnership can be transformed into Limited Partnership with share capital. General partners manage the business of the company and company is represented by each general partner.

b. The Procedure of Establishment

According to the above-mentioned laws, a company is a legal entity, which independently performs business activities with the aim of earning profit. A company can be established by:

(i) domestic natural and legal entities;
(ii) foreign natural and legal entities; or
(iii) domestic and foreign natural and legal entities.

Establishment of a business entity requires registration–a procedure within the competent authority providing an authorization to perform certain activities in manner and under conditions prescribed by law. Authorities competent to register companies in B&H are Court Registries in the FB&H and Intermediary Agency for IT and financial services in the RS.

The procedure of registration of business entities in B&H is regulated by the Framework Law on Registration of Business Entities in B&H, Law on Registration of Business Entities of the FB&H, Law on Registration of Business Entities of the RS and Law on Registration of Business Entities of District Brcko.

Taking into account the most common forms of companies in B&H (limited liability company and joint-stock company), procedures for establishment of those will be provided below in more detail.

(i) Adoption of the Founding Decision/Founding Contract–a Ltd (d.o.o.) company can be established either by a founding contract or founding decision. If the company is to be established by one physical or legal entity, this establishment will be made by the founding decision.If there are more founders, the company will be established by the founding contract. Company laws of both entities provide legally minimum elements which are to be incorporated into the founding decision/contracts. Founders are free to include all regulations they consider necessary, as long as they are compliant with the applicable laws. Both entities' Company laws prescribe similar elements to be incorporated:

• name and address of the founder (for physical persons) or name and seat of the founder (for legal entities);
• name, seat and activity of the new company;
• amount of the original capital;
• founders' rights and obligations (management, distribution of profit, etc;
• procedure in case that one of the founders did not deposit their share in the specified period or did not fulfil any of their obligations;
• payment of costs of establishment (by founders or new company;
• management and representation of the company;
• consequences in case of an unsuccessful establishment;
• special regulations if the company is being established for unspecified duration of time.

(ii) Payment of capital–Upon adoption of the founding decision/founding contract, when submitting the application for entry into the court registry/ Intermediary Agency for IT and financial services office, depending on the type of the business entity concerned, along with the other documents required for registration, it is necessary to attach the certificate of payment of the founders' equity.

(iii) Registration within the competent Court/ Intermediary Agency for IT and financial services–Registration shall be done at the competent Court/ Intermediary Agency for IT and financial services office with territorial jurisdiction according to the seat of the newly established company. Registration entails submitting documentation as follows:

• notarized signatures of persons authorized to represent the company;
• founding decision/founding contract;
• bank certificate of payment of capital in cash or evidence of the monetary value of things and rights entered into company;
• decision on the appointment of the person authorized for representation unless this person is appointed by the founding decision/founding contract;
• company's registry excerpt from the register where the founder is registered (if the founder is a legal entity) or certified photocopies of the founder's passport (if the founder is a physical person);
• photocopies of personal identification documents for persons authorized for representation;
• founder's statement that it does not have any unpaid tax liabilities in B&H and that it is not a founder of another company in B&H.

(iv) Manufacturing the Stamp–Stamp must contain the name and address of the company.
(v) Opening a Bank Account.
(vi) Registration at the Tax Administration.
(vii) Starting Activity Through the Municipality Notification–This notification is submitted to a competent inspection department.

Both entities' regulations enable foreign legal entities to establish subsidiaries within the entities' territories. Subsidiaries must be registered in accordance with applicable regulations. A subsidiary of a foreign company shall be entered in the register of the court/Intermediary Agency for IT and financial services of the RS Office where the headquarters of the subsidiary is located. Important difference between a subsidiary and a company is that subsidiaries do not have the capacity of a legal entity. Subsidiaries conduct business with third persons in the name and on behalf of the founder company.

Another option for operating in B&H is representative offices of foreign entities. Opening of representative offices is regulated by the Decision on Establishment and Operation of Representative Offices of Foreign Persons of B&H. In accordance with the aforementioned Decision, foreign entities can establish representative offices in B&H for performing market research, informative and promotional activities and for its own representation. Foreign entities may choose to set up a representative office in order to gain experience and a better perception of the size and potential of the B&H market. Representative offices do not have the status of legal entities–they are extensions of their founders.They may only engage in non-profit activities. Representative offices cannot conclude agreements on behalf of their founder. Representative offices become operational upon entering into the Register of Foreign Representative Offices kept by the Ministry of Foreign Trade and Economic Relations of B&H.

c. Routes and Requirements of Dissolution

B&H applicable regulations provide two routes for dissolution of companies: liquidation and bankruptcy.

The main difference between liquidation and bankruptcy is the fact whether a company is capable to settle their obligations or not. Liquidation represents cessation of work of a company in situations when the company has enough means for settling its obligations.Bankruptcy is a procedure conducted over debtor's property in order to settle creditors' claims.

Without regards to the cause, liquidation always represents dissolution of a solvent company. Bankruptcy represents dissolution of an insolvent company (one that is not able to settle its creditors). Bankruptcy can sometimes occur during liquidation, in cases where it is determined that the company is insolvent and that the company's assets are not sufficient to settle all creditors of the company.

d. Mergers and Acquisition

The main corporate entity commonly involved in private acquisitions in B&H is a limited liability company (LLC) and the second most common corporate entity is the joint-stock company (JSC).

Shares subject to conditions cannot be transferred without first obtaining corporate approval in writing. Company Laws also entitle shareholders to a right of first refusal in cases of share transfers. Additionally, specific laws may provide for other restrictions for companies that are registered to carry out specific activities (for example, banks and insurance companies) by requiring that the transfer must receive the approval of a relevant B&H regulatory body.Shareholders are entitled to incorporate additional restrictions in respect of share transfer in their incorporation documents.The most common ways of acquiring a private company is purchasing its shares or its assets under a contract executed between the seller and the buyer.

Foreign entities can acquire shares in B&H companies under the same conditions as local entities. However, the Law on Foreign Investments provides restriction of foreign investments in the capital of companies engaged in the production and sale of arms, ammunition and explosives for military purposes, companies engaged in the production and sale of military equipment and media companies. These investments cannot exceed 49% of the capital of the company.

F. Competition Regulation

a. Department Supervising Competition Regulation

Competition regulation is supervised by the Council of Competition of B&H. It was established in 2004 as an independent public body mandated to ensure consistent implementation of the Act on Competition. Council of Competition of B&H has exclusive competence to decide on the presence of prohibited competition activities in the market of B&H. It carries out different administrational and professional duties referred to different aspects of market competition control (methods of carrying out proceedings, final decision making, penalty policy, duration of proceedings).

b. Brief Introduction of Competition Law

Competition law in B&H is regulated by the Competition Act of B&H. It establishes the competition policy as one of more important instrument and pillar in creation and strengthening the market of B&H. Compatibility of the Competition Act of B&H with stipulations and regulations of the EU legislation in the field of market competition ensured the effective and transparent application of laws, simplified procedures, reduced durations of proceedings and reduced levels of state intervention in this field.Competition Act of B&H grants the motivated penalty policy for undertakings (leniency policy), effective mechanism of market control and establishes cooperation with international agencies in the competition field. The Competition Act of B&H applies to all forms of prevention, restriction and distortion of market competition on the whole territory of B&H or out of its territory, provided the existence of substantial effect on the market of B&H. Special attention is directed towards agreements on dominant position and abuses of dominant positions and on rules and procedures concerning competition.As some items and matters are defined in general by the Competition Act of B&H, they are more closely defined by by-law acts. These matters include definitions of relevant market, definitions of agreements of minor importance, block exemption granted to certain categories of agreements, definitions of dominant position, etc.

There are various sanctions provided for in the Competition Law, dealing with non-compliance with specific articles of the law, such as fines and transfer of acquired shares.

G. Tax

a. Tax Regime and Rules

Tax regime in B&H is divided between taxes on state level and taxes on entities' levels. Tax regime is regulated by the following laws: Law on Indirect Taxation System in B&H, Law on Value Added Tax in B&H, Law on Excises in B&H, Law on Corporate Income Tax of FB&H, Law on Corporate Income Tax of the RS, Law on Corporate Income Tax of Brcko District, Law on Personal Income Tax of FB&H, Law on Personal Income Tax of the RS, Law on Personal Income Tax of Brcko District.

B&H has signed agreements on avoidance of double taxation with the following countries: Albania, Algeria, Austria, Azerbaijan, Belgium, Montenegro, Czech Republic, Egypt, Finland, France, Greece, Germany, Croatia, Holland, Iran, Ireland, Italy, Jordan, Kuwait, Qatar, China, Cyprus, Hungary, Malaysia, Macedonia, Moldova, Norway, Pakistan, Poland, Romania, Slovakia, Slovenia, Serbia, Spain, Sweden, Sri Lanka, Turkey, United Arab Emirates, United Kingdom and Northern Ireland.

b. Main Categories and Rates of Tax

State level tax categories are: Value Added Tax (VAT) and excises.

Entity level tax categories are: corporate income tax, personal income tax and real estate tax.

a) VAT

A taxpayer is any person who independently carries out any economic activity (activity of a manufacturer, trader or supplier of services performed with a view to generating income, including the activity of exploitation of natural resources, agriculture, forestry and professional activities). The taxpayer shall be the person in whose name and for whose account goods or services are supplied or goods imported. The taxpayer shall also be the person who supplies goods or services or imports goods in his own name, but for the account of another.Subject of taxation of VAT shall be calculated on: –Supplies of goods and services which a taxpayer, within the performance of his economic activities, makes for consideration within the territory of B&H - Importation of goods into B&H.The Indirect Taxation Authority is responsible for the collection of all indirect taxes at on the entire territory of B&H.The field activities are run by four regional centres in: Sarajevo, Banja Luka, Mostar and Tuzla, 34 customs suboffices and 57 customs posts, out of which 40 are border crossings, 4 airports, 7 railway border crossings, 3 overseas mail offices and 4 free zones.VAT rate is flat rate of 17%.

b) Excises

Excises are a special type of sales tax paid on some commodities like oil products, tobacco products, soft drinks, alcohol drinks, beer, wine and coffee.The taxpayer shall be the legal person and entrepreneur (means any physical person) that imports or exports the excise products in the territory of B&H. The Law stipulates that the subject of taxation is the trade of excise products that are manufactured in B&H, when the manufacturer for the first time trade with them and / or import of excise products in B&H. The tax base shall be determined by: quantity of excise products for which excise duty is to be paid per measuring unit, retail price, which does not include the value, added tax (VAT), and until it is introduced (the sales tax on products for tobacco products). The Indirect Taxation Authority is responsible for the collection of excise as a form of indirect taxes.The excise duty shall be paid in the absolute amount per unit of measure or at a proportional rate.

c) Corporate Income Tax - FB&H

A taxpayer shall be company and other legal entities resident of FB&H performing an independent permanent economic activity through the sales of goods and/or provision of services on the market in the FB&H, RS and Brcko District or in foreign market in order to make profit.Taxpayer is a subsidiary of the legal entity from the RS and Brcko District, which is registered in the territory of the FB&H, for the profits realized on the territory of the FB&H. Taxpayer is a business unit of non-resident legal entity that operates through a fixed place of business in the territory of the FB&H and which is a resident of the FB&H. The taxpayer is non-resident, on the basis of revenues derived from the resident of the FB&H. The tax base is determined in the tax balance, alignment of of expenditures and revenues and capital gains/losses reported in the financial statements. The tax base is calculated as the profit shown in the financial statements, increased by nondeductible expenses and other non-deductible items, and reduced by non-taxable items. Any income and capital gains earned by the taxpayer shall be included in the tax base, except for items that are not included in accordance with Law on the Corporate Income Tax. Income tax is calculated by multiplying the tax base with the rate of income tax. Taxation system in B&H is characterized with low tax rates.Profit tax is paid per rate of 10% on the assessed tax base from the Tax Balance.

Withholding tax rates in FB&H: The standard rate of withholding tax is 10%, and dividends paid to a nonresident are subject to a 5% withholding tax unless the rate is reduced under a tax treaty. Tax Administration of the FB&H is responsible for the implementation of tax assessment, tax collection and control through its cantonal branch offices.

The FB&H Law on Corporate Income Tax enables foreign investors to enjoy the following benefits:

(i) The taxpayer who invests, from its own funds, in production equipment more than 50% of the total profit in the current tax period, shall be reduced of the obligation of the calculated tax for 30% of the amount in the year of investment.

(ii) The taxpayer who in a period of 5 consecutive years makes investments from its own funds, in the total amount of 10 million EUR, starting with the first year when taxpayer has to invest at least 2 million EUR, shall be reduced of the obligations of the calculated income tax for 50% of the amount in the year of investment.

(iii) The taxpayer is entitled to a tax-deductible expense in the double amount of the gross wage paid to newly employees if meets the following conditions:
- Duration of the employment contract must be at least for a period of 12 months with full-time working hour;
- New employee was not employed with the taxpayer or a related person in the previous five years.

d) Corporate Income Tax–RS

Taxpayers of corporate income tax in RS are: legal entity, resident of the RS for profits realized from any source in the RS, FB&H, Brcko District or abroad, subsidiary of a legal person from the FB&H or Brcko District, which is registered in the territory of the RS, for the profits obtained from sources in the RS, legal entity from the FB&H or Brcko District for the income earned from real estate located in the territory of the RS, non-resident who operates through a permanent place of business, for the profit earned from sources in the RS, and non-resident for the revenues in terms of profits earned from sources in the RS. The tax base for the tax year is the difference between taxable income and deductible expenditures for this fiscal year, in accordance with the Law on Corporate Income Tax of the RS.Revenues which are included in the calculation of the tax base: taxable income for the purpose of calculating the tax base includes all income from any source, whether in cash or in any other type of income, and whether it is linked to the performance of business.Corporate income tax is payable at the rate of 10% on the tax base for that tax year.Withholding tax rates in RS is the standard rate of 10%, and dividends paid to a nonresident are subject to a 5% withholding tax unless the rate is reduced under a tax treaty. Tax Administration of RS is responsible for implementation of all tax laws (direct taxes).

e) Corporate Income Tax–Brcko District

The taxpayer is: legal entity from Brcko District, the profits obtained from any source in B&H or abroad, branch legal entity headquartered in the entities, the profits obtained in Brcko District, foreign legal entity which deals and has a permanent place of business in Brcko District, profit which contributes to the permanent establishment, foreign business which receives income from property located in Brcko District, the profit which contributes to immovable assets and foreign person which generates revenue in Brcko District. Tax base for the tax year is the taxable profit determined in the tax balance. Taxable income is determined by adjusting income and expenditure of taxpayers reported in the income statement, in accordance with the law governing accounting, except for revenues and expenditures for which the law prescribes a different way of determining. Corporate income tax is payable at the rate of 10% on taxable income for that tax year. Directorate for Finance of BrckoDistrict is the institution responsible for the direct taxes.

f) Personal Income Tax–FB&H

Taxpayer of Personal Income Tax is a resident of the FB&H and non-resident as follows: resident making income in a territory of the FB&H, and outside the territory of the FB&H, non-resident who performs an activity through a permanent place of business in the territory of the FB&H, non-resident who performs independent activity in the territory of the FB&H, non-resident who receives income in the territory of the FB&H from movable and immovable property, copyrights, patents, licenses, investment of capital or any other activity resulting achievement of income that is taxable.Personal income tax on taxable income that taxpayer realizes from: dependent activity, independent activity, property and property rights, investment of capital Personal income tax base of resident represents the difference between the total taxable incomes produced in one tax period and the total deductions that can be recognized in relation with the acquisition of the income (accumulated losses, expenses necessary for the acquisition of income and personal deduction). Income tax basis represents disbursed tax.Income and expenses are determined by the principle of cash desk.Personal income tax is paid at the rate of 10%.

g) Personal Income Tax–Republic of Srpska

Income tax is paid in accordance with the provisions of Law on Personal Income Tax, by natural persons who have an income. The taxpayer is a natural person who under the provisions of this law taxable income.Income tax payer is a resident of the Republic of Srpska for income in the Republic of Srpska, other entity, Brcko District or another state. The subject of taxation is the income derived by an individual in a tax period is calculated and paid to the following types of income: personal income, self-employment, income from capital, copyright, capital gains and other incomes. Personal income tax rate in the Republic of Srpska is 10%. Taxable income is reduced by: 20% non-taxable part of income for each household dependent member of the immediate family, amount of interest paid on housing loans and amount paid for life insurance up to 1.200,00 BAM per year.

h) Personal Income Tax—Brcko District

Personal Income taxpayer is a resident of the District and non-resident that derives income as: an individual/ resident who derives income in the District and outside the District, non-resident who performs an activity through a permanent place of business in the territory of District, non-resident who performs independent activity in the territory of the District, generates revenue in the District of movable and immovable property, copyrights, patents, licenses, capital investment, or any other activity that results in the realization of income that is taxable. Taxable income that a taxpayer realizes from: employment and occupation, self-employment, property and property rights, investment capital and participation in the sweepstakes.Certain incentives are provided with the Law on Personal Income Tax of Brcko District such as tax deductions that include personal exemption and deduction for each dependent family member, which increases and decreases the basis for calculation of income tax. Personal income tax is paid at the rate of 10%. Certain incentives are provided with the Law on Personal Income Tax of Brcko District such as tax deductions that include personal exemption and deduction for each dependent family member, which increases and decreases the basis for calculation of income tax.Personal income tax is paid at the rate of 10%.

i) Property Transfer Tax—FB&H

Property transfer tax rate is 5%.The tax base is the value of the property estimated by the commission appointed by the local tax administration office (according to the seat of the property). Payer of property transfer tax is most often the seller of the property (depending on the location of the property being sold). Only in Canton Sarajevo and Hercegovačko-neretvanski Canton the buyer is the payer of property transfer tax.

j) Property Tax—Republic of Srpska

Real estate tax rate is to 0.10% of the estimated market value of real estate for real estate which is directly responsible for production activities (facilities for the production and storage facilities for raw materials, intermediate products and final products), and the tax rate is to 0.20% of the estimated market value real estate to other real estate.

k) Property Tax—Brcko District

The tax rate on real estate cannot be less than 0.05% of the appraised value of real estate, and shall not exceed 1.0% of the appraised value of real estate. For all administrative units the obligation to pay taxes arises in the moment of concluding the sale contract.

c. Tax Declaration and Preference

In the FB&H, if a taxpayer:

(i) invests into production equipment with their own means in the value of more than 50% of profit made during the current tax period, their calculated profit tax shall be reduced for 30% during the year of investment;

(ii) invests a total of at least 20.000.000,00 BAM into production in five consequent years (at least four million BAM during the first year), their calculated profit tax shall be reduced for 50% for years of investment.

In RS, if a taxpayer invests into equipment, plants and immovable property for performing their registered activity in the value of more than 50% of made profit (tax base) of the current tax period, their profit tax obligation is reduced for 30%.

H. Securities

a.Brief Introduction of Securities-related Laws and Regulations

Capital markets in B&H are regulated at Entity level (FB&H and RS). Thus, regulations pertain to the capital market in FB&H, which has a regulatory framework and institutions of its own, or the RS capital market, to which the same applies.However, there is considerable harmonization of regulations between the two entities.

The legal framework for capital markets is to be found in the FB&H and RS Securities Market Acts (ZOTVP). These Acts regulate core issues related to definitions of terms, participants, institutions, and their authorities, rights, and obligations with regard to the capital markets in B&H. Recent legal changes in the RS did away with the banks' ability to take a direct role in operations on the financial intermediation market there, bringing RS legislation into line with the FB&H, at least as regards financial markets.

These legal frameworks also define the ownership rights over a security, acquired by registering it with the Register in the name of the security holder.

obtained on the basis of a contract of security sale, i.e.the transfer of ownership of a security, between the bank as seller and the buyer, at a specified price on a specified date.

The trade of securities is conducted on the Stock Exchange and other regulated public markets that are established for the purpose of creating the conditions for matching the demand and offer of securities.

b. Supervision and Regulation of Securities Market

The Commissions of both entities keep a register of security issuers (henceforth: the issuer register), which includes, alongside data required under another law, information on the issue, the issuer, and certain basic data on the securities and the equity.

Securities are issued by public offer, private placement, or special issue. A public offer is conducted on the basis of a public invitation to underwrite and pay for securities. This is done through a stock exchange, as and when prescribed by the Commissions. The issuer must prepare a prospectus with sufficient information for investors to assess the issuer's assets, obligations, loss and profit, financial position and prospects, as well as what rights will be contained in the securities being issued. The securities can be underwritten for no longer than 90 days from the day of publication of the offer, except for payments in cash by installments, when it can last up to six months.

Underwriting and paying for securities under private placement should be completed within 45 days, or a maximum of 90 days.

The ZOTVP defines the following securities-related tasks:

(i) Brokering tasks include buying and selling securities in one's own name for a client, for a fee.

(ii) Dealing includes buying and selling securities on one's own behalf to benefit from a price differential.

(iii) Market-making tasks include simultaneously stressing the continuous supply and sale of securities on one's own behalf, in order to establish a continuous supply and demand for specific securities.

(iv) Securities portfolio management involves tasks where a professional intermediary undertakes to invest a client's money in securities with maximum benefit, in his own name, but on the client's behalf, i.e.to hold and manage the client's securities, for which the client pays a fee.

(v) The issuing agent's tasks include organizing, preparing and conducting a securities issue for the issuer, without obligation to buy unsold securities, thus introducing the securities to an organized public market.

(vi) The issue sponsor's tasks include organizing, preparing and conducting the securities issue for the issuer and underwriting and paying for all the securities, or those that remain unsold, to sell them on to potential investors and so ensure the success of the issue.

(vii) The investment advisor's tasks include offering advice to clients on handling securities.

(viii) The Custodian's tasks include:

• Opening and managing an account with the Register on behalf and in the name of a shareholding client (named custodial account);

• Opening and keeping an account with the Register in his own name, on behalf of a shareholding client, or in the name of clients who are not the owners of these securities, on behalf of the actual owner (joint custodial account);

• Executing orders to transfer ownership, inscribe third parties' rights on the security, or transfer the rights under the security;

• Collecting claims against the issuer based on mature securities, e.g.interest and dividends, for the security holder and ensuring the exercise of the clients' other rights;

• Providing services by lending securities;

• Informing shareholders of annual general meetings and representing them at the meetings;

• Informing them of their rights under the securities and carrying out their orders pertaining their exercise;

• Informing their clients of changes in the law that directly or indirectly affect the condition of securities held by the custodian;

• Ensuring that the securities holder's tax obligations are met;

• Other services related to securities, rights, and obligations arising under securities negotiated between the client and the custodian bank, which are not against the law.

(ix) The depositary's tasks include securities issuance and monetary transactions related to trade in securities on the stock exchange or other organized public market.

The regulatory framework of capital markets in BiH also includes the Act on the Securities Commission and the Act on the Securities Register. These acts define the place and role, as well as the basic authorities of the Securities Commission and Securities Register, as institutions that allow the normal functioning of the capital market.

The Commission's authorities derive from the Securities Act, the Securities Commission Act, the Securities Register Act, the Fund Management Companies Act, and the Investment Funds and Companies Act. As an independent institution responsible for the supervision and regulation of financial markets under these laws, the Commission has the following authorities:

(i) Regulating how securities are issued and traded;

(ii) Supervising standards for reporting to investors and the public on securities traders "operations, the management of joint-stock companies, the protection of investors" interests, the implementation of legal and other regulations pertaining to issuing and trading in securities, stock-market operations, the Securities Register, professional intermediaries, depository banks, and fund management companies;

(iii) Taking measures within its authorities, pursuant to legal and other regulations;

(iv) Other jobs and tasks pursuant to legal and other regulations.

The Securities Commission has broad regulatory authorities.These authorities and responsibilities include:

(i) Regulating how securities are issued and traded;

(ii) Approving issues of shares and other securities by enterprises and banks;

(iii) Approving securities issues by fund management companies, investment funds, mutual funds, and other legal entities involved in issuing securities;

(iv) Regulating the requirements for and ways to issue cantonal and municipal bonds;

(v) Prescribing rules and supervising trading in securities on the securities exchange, using the electronic quotation system;

(vi) Protecting investors' interests;

(vii) Prescribing and supervising the application of reporting standards vis-à-vis investors and the public on securities traders' operations;

(viii) Prescribing and supervising management standards for joint-stock companies;

(ix) Prescribing requirements and granting approval for the operations of and supervising professional intermediaries (e.g.brokers and dealers) and other participants in the securities trade.

The Securities Register performs the following tasks:

(i) Registering and safekeeping securities, as well as safekeeping data on securities and all transactions related to transfer of ownership or change in their status;

(ii) Recording and deleting third party rights related to securities and recording and deleting restrictions on rights on the basis of contracts, court decisions, or decisions by the relevant authorities;

(iii) Opening and keeping securities accounts and a shareholder list and issuing reports, statements, and receipts on the status of and changes to those accounts;

(iv) Calculating, settling, and transferring securities based on securities-related transactions on the stock market or other regulated public market;

(v) Recording, transferring, calculating, and ensuring obligations resulting from transactions in financial derivatives on the stock exchange or other regulated public market are met;

(vi) Other tasks under the relevant laws and the Commission's general documents.

c. Requirements for Engagement in Securities Trading for Foreign Enterprise

Foreign enterprises are entitled to engage in securities trading under the same conditions provided to local entities.

I. Preference and Protection of Investment

a. Special Economic Areas

Free trade zones in B&H are part of the customs territory of B&H and have status of legal entity.According to the Law on Free Trade Zones of B&H, free trade zone founders may be one or more domestic and foreign legal entities or natural persons.The free zone establishment is considered economically justified if the submitted feasibility study and other evidence can prove that the value of goods exported from a free zone will exceed at least 50% of the total value of manufactured goods leaving the free zone within the period of 12 months.

b. Investment Protection

B&H is signatory to various bilateral investment treaties. B&H and China have two main bilateral treaties when it comes to investment.Those are:

(i) Treaty between B&H and the People's Republic of China on Trade and Economic Cooperation (Decision on Ratification was published in the "Official Gazette of B&H", no.1/01-1);

(ii) Treaty between B&H and the People's Republic of China on the Promotion and Protection of Investments (Decision on Ratification was published in the "Official Gazette of B&H", no.17/03-511);

Both treaties aim at increased economic cooperation and the promotion of investment by and between the two nations.

III. Trade

A. Department Supervising Trade

Departments supervising trade in B&H are the Ministry of Trade of the FB&H and the Ministry of Trade and Tourism of RS.

Ministry of Trade of the FB&H carries out primarily the tasks related to: foreignand domestic trade, functioning of a single market, impacts of economicsystem and economic policy to goods and services market; supplyand demand ratios, goods and services pricing; consumers' protection, as well asother tasks defined by the law.

Ministry of Trade and Tourism of RS carries out organization of trade, analysis and following the functioning of trade, development of trade, proposing measures in order to intervene on the market, normative activities, etc.

B. Brief Introduction of Trade Laws and Regulations

Trade in B&H is regulated on the entities' levels. The main regulations in regard to trade are the Law on Trade of the FB&H and Law on Trade of RS.

C. Trade Management

Trading in B&H is performed freely, under equal market conditions, for all traders, foreign enterprises included. Traded goods must be conformed to standards, technical and quality norms prescribed by applicable laws.

Price of goods is formed and expressed in the local currency. Price forming is free from any state influence– legal entities are entitled to form prices in accordance with market conditions, except for certain categories of products prescribed by applicable laws.

Trade can be temporarily limited in cases of natural disasters, wars, irregularities on the market or other disasters.In such cases, the entity's government will issue measures including limitations for trade of certain goods or conditions for trade of certain goods, prohibition of trade of certain goods, etc.

D. The Inspection and Quarantine of Import and Export Commodities

Inspection control is conducted due to health protection of local production, market and consumers, via the procedure of health inspection of plants, plant products, animals, animal products, regulated objects and other objects which are able to transmit harmful organisms in international trade as well as through control of quality, tracking and recording traffic of products for protection of plants, compost and soil enhancers, animals and animal products. Controls are also conducted to ensure international traffic with healthy plants, plant products, animals and animal products during export. Inspection controls are conducted during import, export and transit of parcels on border controls.

E. Customs Management

Customs issues are regulated by the Customs Policy Law of B&H.

Import customs rates are harmonized with the EU Nomenclature.Depending on the type of products, customs rates are being reduced to 90%, 75% or 50% of the previous rate, while customs rates will be completely eliminated for some products.The reduction of customs rates is valid only for goods originating from the EU, not all the goods being imported from the EU.Customs protection is still provided for agricultural products for which customs rated will mostly be paid as previously.

Under provisions of the Customs Policy Law, the following goods are exempt from customs duties: equipment being imported as a part of foreign investment, except for passenger cars, slot and gambling machines, equipment for military and police forces of the entities financed entirely by donors, equipment for reconstruction projects in B&H that have been approved by the Council of Ministers and are fully financed by donors or by international community.

The equipment that makes part of a foreign investment cannot be lent, pledged as a guarantee, rented or given up without previous consent of the customs administration.If such equipment is lent, pledged as a guarantee, rented or given up, corresponding customs duty would have to be paid on it.

The following items are also exempt from import duties: fixed assets, industrial inventory and equipment imported on the basis of transfer of business activities from abroad to B&H, intermediate materials to be used for manufacturing of goods for export, advertising material, samples, catalogues, goods for charity and humanitarian agencies, etc.

Incentives and exemptions from payment of custom duties when putting the goods in free circulation are determined and granted by the Council of Ministers of B&H. All goods that may be exempt from payment of customs duties are stated in the Annex 4 to the Customs Policy Law.

The Laws also provide a restriction in regard to equipment that is part of foreign investment—such equipment must not be older than 10 years.A certificate issued by an authorized body needs to be provided, confirming that the equipment meets necessary standards on environmental protection and protection at work.

IV. Labour

A. Brief Introduction of Labor Laws and Regulations

At the level of B&H there is no framework labor legislation. Regulations on labor and civil service in the institutions of B&H were passed and, in special laws, certain provisions regarding labor matters of police officers and armed forces were defined. Apart from laws regulating labor matters of non-civil servants and civil servants in the institutions of B&H, entities and authorities of Brcko District have exclusive competence for labor legislation in B&H.Labor matters in B&H are regulated primarily by labor laws on entities' and Brcko District level.Apart from labor laws, labor matters are regulated by general collective agreements and branch collective agreements adopted on entities' levels which regulate labor issues in more detail whereas labor laws provide general guidelines and limitations. The procedure of adoption of general collective agreements is governed by three parties—employers, employees and the government of specific entity. General collective agreements are concluded for a limited period of time.

Labor Law of the FB&H applies to employment concluded based on an employment contract between an employer and an employee. The same applies to employment based on contracts for fixed-term and temporary jobs. The Labor Law foresees for a possibility of professional training without establishing employment.Considering that such persons are hired beyond the labor relation, they do not enjoy the status of an employed person within the meaning of the Labor Law; however, they do enjoy certain rights under the Labor Law as well as other regulations in the field of health insurance and pension and disability insurance. The Labor Law of the FB&H foresees a possibility for the chair and members of the management board or a management body of another name (managing director) to perform a business function in employment relation or without any, in accordance with labor rulebooks.Therefore, the chair and members of the management board or the managing director who carry out the work without employment are not subject to the Labor Law.Instead, responsibilities and obligations of such persons are regulated by a contract in accordance with the general acts of the employer.

Labor Law of RS regulates labor relations, rights, obligations and responsibilities from employment and other relations arising from employment in RS, unless otherwise provided for by special laws. In addition to regulation of rights and obligations from employment, also regulates engagements beyond the employment relationship, based on concluded contracts on fixed term and temporary employment, service contracts, contracts on professional and additional training and contracts on supplementary work/outside employment. Persons engaged outside the employment relationship have no status in terms of the Labor Law, but do enjoy certain rights established under the Law and other rights in accordance with regulations in the field of occupational health and safety, social security and other.

Labor Law of Brcko District regulates labor relations, rights, obligations and responsibilities from employment and other relations arising from employment in Brcko District.

B. Requirements of Employing Foreign Employees

In order to employ foreign employees, such employees' status must be regulated in such way to firstly obtain a work permit and subsequently a residence permit.

a. Work Permit

Work permits in B&H are legal authorizations, individual acts, which allow foreigners to take paid employment with domestic natural or legal persons, whereby the foreigner has the same work-related rights, obligations and responsibilities as employed citizens of B&H, unless otherwise is specified under an international agreement. Work permits are issued for specific posts and/or for specific types of jobs. Work permits are issued within the specified work permit quota which is the number of work permits that may be issued to foreigners in certain occupations in B&H, during one year. Annual quota is determined by the Council of Ministers of B&H in accordance with the migration policy and the situation in the labor market. There are certain situations where work permits that can be issued outside of the determined quota.Those work permits are issued in situations which, among others, include: a foreigner who has an education that corresponds to higher education, completed post-graduate or doctoral studies in B&H, foreigners whose work in B&H is based on an international agreement, foreigners who perform key tasks in a business entity, who are not exempt from the requirement of obtaining work permits on the basis of international agreements. All work permits are issued for a period of one year.

Employers cannot conclude employment contracts or other appropriate agreements with foreigners prior to foreigner regulating their residence in B&H, usually on basis of a temporary residence permit.

B&H laws provide certain exemptions from the obligation of possessing a work permit. Namely, foreigners can work without a working permit up to 90 days per calendar year, with previously obtained certificate of work if they perform, among others, the following activities: key persons in a legal entity that has a higher position in the board or manages with departments, monitors and supervises the work of other employees, are experts who have excellent knowledge and are essential to the operation of a legal entity, research equipment, techniques or management if they were employed in that legal entity at least one year or has acted as a partner shortly before movement in B&H, if the appointment does not have characteristics of employment, foreigners who are founders of a company based in B&H, if such company employs a minimum of five nationals of B&H on every foreigner, pays a gross salary per employee at least equal to average gross salary in B&H and regularly settles tax liabilities as well as other categories provided by laws.

Conditions and procedures of employment of foreigners are: Law on Foreigners of B&H, Law on Employment of Foreigners of the FB&H, Law on Employment of Foreign Citizens and Stateless Persons of the RS and Law on Employment of Foreigners of Brcko District.

Depending on the location of the employer, a work permit is issued by the authorities responsible for the employment of foreigners in the FB&H, the RS or Brcko District. In the FB&H, work permits are issued by Cantonal Employment Services upon approval of the Federal Employment Service. In RS, work permits for foreign nationals are issued by the RS Employment Service regional offices responsible for the region of employer's head office. In Brcko District, work permits for foreign nationals are issued by the Department for Professional and Administrative Affairs in the Government of the Brcko District.

b. Application Procedure

Work permits are issued to foreigners at the request of the person who intends to employ the foreigner (the employer). Employers submit, on behalf of foreign employees, the application for a work permit to the competent employment service having territorial jurisdiction for the location of the employer's seat.

With the application for issuance of the work permit, the employer is obliged to submit certified photocopies of the following documents:

a) RS

(i) Decision on registration, issued by the body responsible for employer's prevailing activity;

(ii) Data about foreigner with whom they intend to conclude work contract or other adequate contract, in particular: given name and surname, given names and surnames of parents, date of birth, sex, place of residence and address in the country of origin, reference number, date and place of issue of valid travel document;

(iii) Information about workplace or type of tasks, and work conditions;

(iv) Justification of reasons for employment of a foreigner–description of job at which foreigner will be employed and type of qualification and professional knowledge and qualification required for that job;

(v)Medical certificate (only for the first issuance of work permit);

(vi)Certified passport copy.

b) FB&H

(i) excerpt from the relevant register of the competent court or a certificate of registration for the activity issued by the competent authority in accordance with the Law on craft and related activities;

(ii) information about the foreigner that he intends to employ in terms of Article 2 of this law in particular: full name, names and surnames of the parents; date of birth; sex; place of residence and address in the country of origin; number, date and place of issuance of the current travel documents;

(iii) information on the job position, kind and conditions of work;

(iv) evidence on employer's solvency issued by a bank where the employer has their account;

(v) written document that represents a proof that all tax obligations and contributions have been paid for all already existing employees, including the foreigner in case of permit extension application;

(vi) explanation of justified reasons of hiring an foreigner, the type of education and professional skills and qualifications required for this job and

(vii) nostrified diploma of education of the foreigner that must be translated into one of the languages in official use in FB&H.

c. Social Insurance

In RS, as well as in the FB&H, contributions are calculated on the basis of gross salary. Gross salary includes net salary earned by regular employment, multiplied by the determined coefficient, plus contributions from salary.In Brcko Distrct, pension insurance contributions are regulated by entity laws.

Employee's share: the FB&H: 17% for pension insurance, 12.5% for health insurance, 1.5% for unemployment insurance (in total: 31% on gross salary). RS: 18,5% for pension insurance, 12% for health insurance, 1% for unemployment insurance, 1,5% for child protection (in total: 33% on gross wage) Brcko District: 17% for pension insurance for employers who apply FB&H law and 18% for pension insurance for employers who apply RS law, 12% for health insurance and 1.5% for unemployment insurance (in total 30.5 or 31.5% on gross wage). Employer's share: the FB&H: 6% for pension insurance, 4% for health insurance, 0.50% for unemployment insurance (in total: 10.50% on gross wage). RS: no such contributions are paid. Brcko District: 6% on gross salary for pension insurance for employers who apply the FB&H law.

C. Exit and Entry

a. Visa Types

A visa can only be issued to an foreigner who is a holder of a valid passport whose validity exceeds the validity of the visa for at least three months. A visa application shall be submitted on a form, which must be filled in accurately and completely.

The airport transit visa (Visa A) enables the foreigner to pass through an international transit area of an airport without an actual entry into the country, during the discontinuation or continuation of an international flight. It may be issued to an foreigner for one, two or more transits through the international area of the airport during the transit and shall be issued with a term period of up to three months.

A short term stay visa (Visa C) enables an foreigner to have a single or multiple stays in the country, provided that no continuous stay, or the total duration of several consecutive stays in B&H, may last for more than 90 days within a six month period, commencing from the date of first entry. A short term stay visa shall be issued for a single or multiple entries into B&H. A short-term stay visa shall be issued for a validity period not exceeding one year.Exceptionally, a short-term stay visa may also be issued for a validity period of longer than one year if this is in the interest of B&H, which is decided by the Ministry of Foreign Affairs of B&H upon the consent obtained from the Ministry. A short-term stay visa shall be issued for business, education, training and similar purposes, for tourist or other travel for the private purposes, travels to political, scientific, cultural, sports, religious or other events, as well as the travels for other reasons requiring only a short-term stay. A short-term visa (Visa C) may be renewed due to force majeure, for humanitarian, serious professional or personal reasons, but in accordance with the rules applicable to visa issuing.

A long–term stay visa (Visa D) shall enable a foreigner to enter and stay in B&H within the period of up to six months within one year, commencing from the date of the first entry. A long-term visa shall be issued for a single or multiple entries into B&H. A long–term stay visa shall be issued exceptionally in such situations where for the purposes of stay in B&H a period of more than 90 days is required within the period of six (6) months. A long–term stay visa shall be issued for a validity period not exceeding one year. Exceptionally, A long–term stay visa may be issued for a period of longer than one year if this is in the interest of B&H, which shall be decided by the Ministry of Foreign Affairs of B&H.

b. Restrictions for Exit and Entry

Pursuant to the Law on Foreigners of B&H, a foreigner will be refused entry to B&H if they fail to meet general entry requirements, and are not subject to an international treaty to which B&H is a signatory, or to a decision of the Council of Ministers, court or prosecutor's office granting the entry and temporary residence in B&H (entry under special conditions).

Apart from these reasons, a foreigner may be refused entry to B&H if he/she:

(i) presents a falsified travel document while attempting to enter B&H;

(ii) presents a falsified visa or residence permit while attempting to enter B&H;

(iii) is a citizen of visa-free regime country who had already stayed 90 days in the territory of B&H during any period of 180 days, where the 180-day period refers to the period preceding each day of the temporary residence, unless he/she is subject to the provisions on entry under special conditions;

(iv) had already completed the period of temporary residence allowed under an international agreement to which B&H is signatory, unless the entry was granted on other grounds;

(v) there are grounds for suspicion that he/she will perform work which requires work permit, and he/she is not a subject to the provisions of the Law on Foreigners of B&H governing temporary residence for the purpose of employment without a work permit;

(vi) was subject to B&H visa cancellation or annulment upon entry.

Temporary residence may be terminated if the foreigner is employed without holding the appropriate work permit, or if the foreigner is left without means or subsistence, or if circumstances under which the residence permit was issued have changed to such an extent that the alien no longer qualifies for the residence permit. Also, the already granter residence or visa-free stay may be terminated if the foreigner is convicted of a criminal offence, or if they refuse the enforcement of a final or enforceable decision of authorities in B&H or if they abuse the granted temporary residence by sending invitation letters to other persons from the visa regime and failing to fulfill obligations arising from the invitation/guarantee letter.

D. Trade Union and Labor Organizations

Employees in B&H are entitled to form and register trade unions and become members of trade unions.This right is guaranteed by the Labor Laws of both entities.

Confederation of Independent Trade Unions of B&H is a voluntary and interest organization of workers who are organized through branch trade unions–affiliates of the CITU B&H. CITU B&H and trade unions organized within are democratic, multiethnic, multinational and independent of the government, employers, political parties and religious communities.

Confederation of Independent Trade Unions of B&H is comprised of 24 branch unions. At the same time there are 7 Cantonal Boards of CITU B&H, operating in the nine cantons in the FB&H. CITU B&H is recognized as a relevant social partner of the Federal Government and the Association of Employers of the FB&H and participates in the work of the Economic and Social Council for the territory of the FB&H.

E. Labor Disputes

Individual and collective labor disputes are resolved by courts at the levels of the entities of the RS and the FB&H, Brcko District and the cantons, with the exception of labor disputes concerning employees of the institutions of B&H, which are within the jurisdiction of the court at the level of B&H. The Law on Courts in the FB&H provides for jurisdiction of municipal courts in all civil disputes, i.e.municipal courts decide in all individual and collective labor disputes. In RS, courts of general jurisdiction are responsible for deciding labor disputes. In Brcko District, the Basic Court of the Brcko District has first instance jurisdiction for all civil disputes, which includes all individual and collective labor disputes. Labor disputes are conducted as regular litigation disputes but are subject to some special rules, such as that they are considered priority disputes, employees are freed from payment of court fees and certain deadlines within the procedure are shortened in order to speed the disputes up. All disputes are conducted in Bosnian language exclusively.All documents must be submitted in Bosnian language.Therefore, all documents in foreign language must be translated to a local language by a court-appointed interpreter. Labor disputes in B&H are usually conducted for 2 years until a final and binding decision is issued.

V. Intellectual Property

A. Brief Introduction of IP Laws and Regulations

Following its comprehensive reform in 2010, the legislation of B&H was fully complied with EU regulations.In the meantime, the EU adopted some new decisions and directives so that amendments to legislation are required for the purpose of its compliance with the new EU legislation.B&H legislation is in its most part complied with the SAA in IP fields.

Main legislation regulating the IP field in B&H includes: Law on Copyright and Related Rights of B&H, Law on Industrial Designs of B&H, Law on Patents of B&H, Law on the Collective Management of Copyright and Related Rights of B&H, Law on the Protection of Indications of Geographical Origin of B&H, Law on the Protection of Topographies of Integrated Circuits of B&H and Law on Trademarks of B&H.

According to applicable regulations, intellectual property (IP) refers to creations of the mind: inventions, literary and artistic works, and symbols, names, images, and designs used in commerce.

IP is divided into two categories: Industrial property, which includes inventions (patents), trademarks, industrial designs, geographic indications of source, topographies of integrated circuits and plant varieties; and Copyright, which includes literary and artistic works such as novels, poems and plays, films, musical works, artistic works such as drawings, paintings, photographs and sculptures, and architectural designs. Rights related to copyright include those of performing artists in their performances, producers of phonograms in their recordings, and those of broadcasters in their radio and television programs.

The procedure for the acquisition, maintenance, record keeping of the transfer, and termination of patents and trademarks is conducted before the Institute for Intellectual Property of B&H (the Institute). The Institute maintains Register of Trademark Applications, Register of Trademarks, and Register of Representatives for the Protection of Trademarks.

A patent is the right protecting an invention in any field of technology. In order for an invention to be patentable, it must meet three requirements:

(i) being new;
(ii) involving an inventive step;
(iii) being susceptible of industrial application.

Patent right is granted by the responsible state auhority with the payment of the fee, and it lasts for a certain period of time in a certain territory. The same invention may be protected simultaneously in several countries, provided that it has been applied for, examined, and granted at national level in every country where patent protection is sought.

A patent is granted for a fixed number of years.Patents last 20 years, and consensual patents last 10 years from the filing date of the application.

The following shall not be regarded as inventions: discoveries, scientific theories and mathematical methods, aesthetic creations, schemes, rules and methods for performing mental acts, playing games or doing business, computer programs, and presentation of information defined by the content of such information itself.

A trademark is the right protecting a sign capable of distinguishing the products or services of one undertaking from the same or similar products/services of other undertakings. The nature of the products/services to which a trademark is to be applied shall not constitute an obstacle to registration of the trademark.

A sign that is capable of distinguishing identical or similar products/services, and that may be represented graphically may be protected by a trademark.A sign may consist of: words, including personal names, drawings, letters, numerals, images, the shape of a product or its packaging, colours, tri-dimensional forms or the combination of such elements.

A trademark as an identity sign has four main functions: distinguishing products/services, their source, quality, and market promotion. A trademark is granted by a responsible authority of a state with the payment of fees, and it lasts for a certain period of time in a certain territory.

Foreign legal and natural persons exercise their rights in proceedings before the Institute only through a representative authorized to represent and who is enrolled in the appropriate register maintained by the Institute. Legal and natural persons that provide service of representation in the proceedings for protection of industrial property rights before the Institute must be entered in the respective register of representatives kept by the Institute.In proceedings before the Institute, legal and natural persons can be represented by patent agents and agents for trademarks, industrial designs and indications of geographical origin.

B. Patent Application

The procedure for patent application is initiated by filing an application for the grant of a patent with the Institute for Intellectual Property of B&H. It is necessary to furnish a completed request for the grant of a patent, accompanying documents and proof of payment of the costs involved.The application is filed in written form, directly or by mail, by fax or electronically to the official e-mail of the Institute, provided that within 15 days from the date of its receipt by the Institute, it is furnished to the Institute in written form.A separate application is filed for each invention.

A patent application consists of a request for the grant of a patent with an indication that the grant of a patent is requested, the title of the invention reflecting its essence, information concerning the applicant, and information concerning the inventor.

The patent application contains:

(i) a detailed and clear description of the invention, one or more patent claims that need to be clear, concise, and fully supported by the description of the invention and drawings, if any;

(ii) any drawings referred to in the description of the invention and patent claims;

(iii) an abstract of the essence of the invention serving exclusively the purpose of providing technical information.

The form is completed on a computer or a typewriter, in one of the official languages of B&H. It is furnished in two copies, and other accompanying documents in one copy. One copy of the form is retained by the Institute, and the other copy, date stamped, with the number of the patent application entered, incoming correspondence serial number, and official seal is furnished to the applicant as proof of accordal of the filing date to the application.

The following accompanying documents are furnished with the patent application:
(i) declaration of the inventor in the event that he does not wish to be mentioned in the application;
(ii) power of attorney if the application is filed through a representative;
(iii) declaration on a common representative where there are several applicants.

C. Trademark Registration

Prior to filing an application for the registration of a trademark, it is to do a trademark search in respect of identity and similarity, in order to avoid conflicts during the registration procedure or in the marketplace with an earlier registered trademark or a trademark earlier applied for. The timely knowledge of possible obstacles to the registration of a trademark or of the conflict in the marketplace allows for timely taking certain legal actions or business moves.

During the procedure for the examination of an application for the registration of a trademark, the Institute examines the existence of obstacles to the trademark registration. Where a trademark application is filed for an identical and/or similar sign for identical or similar goods and/or services of an earlier trademark holder, it may give rise to the infringement of the rights of earlier trademark holders, in particular if the applicant had used such sign in commerce.Search services may be requested as to various search criteria (identity, similarity, in respect of an applicant/holder or a specifically defined request).

The holder of a registered trademark or the applicant for the grant of a trademark may be a national or foreign natural person or legal entity. Foreign natural persons and legal entities enjoy the same rights as are enjoyed by national natural persons and legal entities in respect of the trademark protection in BIH, provided that it arises from the international treaties or conventions acceded to or ratified by BIH or from the principle of reciprocity.

A procedure for the grant of a trademark is initiated by filing an application for the grant of a trademark.The steps include:
(i) Filing an application with the Institute.
(ii) Formal examination of the application in the Institute.
(iii) Publication of the trademark application in the Official Gazette of the Institute that is available in paper and electronic forms on the Institute website.
(iv) Issuing a trademark certificate along with the decision to register a trademark in the Institute.

The procedure is initiated by filing an application for the grant of a trademark with the Institute.It is necessary to submit a completed request for the grant of a trademark, accompanying documents, and proof that the costs have been paid.The application is filed in written form, directly or through the post, by telefax or at the official e-mail of the Institute, provided that within eight days of its receipt it is furnished to the Institute in writing.

D. Measures for IP Protection

Competence in the field of enforcement of intellectual property rights in B&H share a large number of institutions at different levels of authority (for administrative and expert affairs in the field of protection of industrial property, protection of copyright and related rights, including supervision of collective organizations for copyright management and for the issues of protection of intellectual property: Institute for Intellectual Property of B&H, for customs control: Indirect Taxation Authority of B&H, for inspection: inspectorates competent on market control; for administrative disputes: Court of B&H; for civil law protection: ordinary courts in the FB&H and Brcko District and commercial courts in the RS; for criminal justice protection: Prosecutor's Office of B&H in cooperation with competent police agencies, prosecutor's offices of entities and courts on all levels; for decision making on minor offence liability: ordinary courts in entities).

At state level, the Institute for Intellectual Property of B&H is competent for expert and operative affairs in the field of protection of IP rights, including supervision of organizations for collective management of copyright, and for the issues of protection of IP. Second-instance body is the Institute's Board of Appeal. The parties may initiate administrative dispute before the Court of B&H against final decisions of the Institute.

Institutional structure of Indirect Taxation Authority of B&H competent on the enforcement of intellectual property rights includes the following organizational units: Section for protection of IP, prohibition and restrictions; customs offices and customs post; and smuggling and prevention of offences groups in regional centers. Customs offices and customs post implement IP rights protection measures through customs control of goods being imported, exported or in transfer through B&H customs area, by enforcing customs procedures.

One of competencies of the State Investigation and Protection Agency (SIPA) is prevention, detection, and investigation of criminal offences against copyright and related rights. Within its scope of work, the SIPA may request the law enforcement agencies in B&H and other authorities to provide information and findings related to criminal offences in its competence, including among others criminal offences of infringement of copyright and related rights.Also, the SIPA may report on regular basis to the competent offices and bodies in B&H and initiate joint activities to prevent and detect concerned criminal offences. The SIPA is also providing support to the Prosecutor's Office of B&H and Court of B&H in collecting information and it acts at requests by those bodies and submits reports on results of certain investigations as well as all facts, evidence and materials as necessary.

VI. Environmental Protection

A. Department Supervising Environmental Protection

In accordance with the constitutional competences and existing legal framework, environmental protection activities are performed by various administrative bodies at the levels of B&H, entities, cantons and local self-government units.

At the B&H level, the Ministry of Foreign Trade and Economic Relations of B&H is assigned with specific competences in environmental protection. Part of this Ministry is its Division for Water Resources, Tourism and Environmental Protection.

The environmental and water management in B&H falls within the constitutional competence of the entities and Brcko District, cantons and municipalities in the FB&H and municipalities in RS.

The Section for Environmental Protection performs the following activities: proposals of policies, basic principles, coordination of competence and international alignment of environmental protection plans of the entity authorities and institutions, particularly preparation, proposals and coordination of implementation of development policy, international cooperation and programs of B&H, laws, regulations and other legislation at the B&H level, analytical monitoring and development of expert analyses, information and opinions.Water management activities are coordinated in regular coordination meetings of all the competent institutions from B&H.

Enactment, implementation and enforcement of environmental legislation and policies at the FB&H level are competences of various ministries that are responsible for: environmental protection, prevention and elimination of dangers and damage to the environment, renewal and gradual improvement of the environment; identification of priority tasks for environmental protection; introduction of legal, economic and technical measures for environmental protection; development, maintenance and operation of the system serving as the basis for collection and processing of information on measurements, monitoring, control, assessment of the environment, and provision of information on potential effects on the environment; adoption of financial legislation on environmental protection; and cooperation with RS.

The RS Ministry of Social Planning, Construction and Ecology is, among others, competent for activities within the sector for environment protection. This sector performs activities of overall environment protection and promotion, research, planning and management through environmental protection measures, protection of natural resources, and natural and cultural heritage, participation in development and implementation of domestic and international program acts on environmental protection, establishment and coordination of expert cooperation exchange of experience with international and domestic authorities and organizations and non-governmental organizations for environmental protection, participation in implementation of projects financed by international financial organizations for environmental protection, drafting of laws and regulations on environmental protection, etc.

B. Brief Introduction of Laws and Regulations of Environmental Protection

There is no general environmental protection framework act in B&H, serving as a basis for other environmental legislation.Laws on environmental protection as well as other laws governing the issue of environment have been adopted in the FB&H, Republic of Srpska, Brcko District and some cantons, on the basis of which regulations are adopted enabling law enforcement in this field.

At cantonal administrative level, a total of six cantons implement Law on Environmental Protection of the FB&H, while cantonal laws on environmental protection are also in force in four cantons.

Law on Environmental Protection of the FB&H is in force and it governs the following: preservation, protection, restoration and improvement of the ecological quality and capacity of environment as well as of the quality of life; measures and conditions for managing, preserving, and for rational use of natural resources; the framework for legal measures and institutions for the preservation, protection and improvement of environmental protection, financing of activities related to the environment and voluntary measures, duties and tasks of the administrative authorities at different levels of government. The issue of water protection is covered by the Law on Water.

The Law on Environmental Protection of the Republic of Srpska is the general environmental protection framework act in RS.This Law governs the protection of the environment for the purpose of its preservation, decrease of risks for human life and health, as well as ensuring and improving the quality of life, protection of all environmental elements, informing and access to information in the field of environmental protection, environment planning and protection, strategic environmental impact assessment, procedures for issuing environmental permits and prevention of large-scale disasters, ecosystem labeling and environmental protection management, financing of activities related to the environment, liability for environmental damage, including rights and obligations of natural and legal persons performing activities in accordance with this Law.

The Law on Environmental Protection of Brcko District is in force and it serves as a basis for adoption of related environmental protection legislation. This Law regulates the protection of the environment for the purpose of its preservation, decrease of risks for human life and health, as well as ensuring and improving the quality of life, protection of all environmental elements, informing and access to information in the field of environmental protection, environment planning and protection, strategic environmental impact assessment, procedures for issuing environmental permits and prevention of large-scale disasters, ecosystem labeling and environmental protection management, financing of activities related to the environment, issues related to damage caused to the environment, including rights and obligations of natural and legal persons performing activities under this Law.

The main principles underlying the laws on environmental protection in the entities and in the Brcko District are:

(i) Principle of Sustainable Development. The principle of sustainable development implies that the sustainability of the environment is effected through the preservation of natural resources so that the consumption of renewable materials, water and energy resources does not exceed the boundaries in which natural systems can compensate that and that the consumption of non-renewable resources does not exceed the boundaries in which sustainable renewable resources are substituted, that the level of pollutants being emitted does not exceed the capacity of the air, water and soil to absorb and process them, as well as through continuous preservation of biological diversity (biodiversity), human health, the quality of air, water and land, under the conditions necessary for human life, plants and animals.

(ii) Precautionary and Prevention Principle. The precautionary and prevention principle is realized by assessing the effects on the environment and by using the best available and accessible technologies, techniques and equipment, promotes prevention of the environment from pollution, it promotes avoidance of activities representing a hazard to the environment or to human health and every activity must be planned and implemented in such a way as to: cause the least possible change in the environment; constitutes the minimum risk to the environment and to human health; reduce the burden on the space and consumption of raw materials and energy in construction, production, distribution and use; include a possibility of recycling; prevent or limit the effect on the environment at the very source of pollution.

(iii) Substitution Principle. The substitution principle implies that every activity, which might have harmful effect on the environment should be substituted by another activity, which represents a substantially lesser risk and hazard to the environment.

(iv) Principle of Integral Approach. The principle of integral approach means the prevention from or bringing to the smallest possible measures the risk from damage to the environment in entirety. The requirements for the high level of protection of the environment and the improvement of the quality of the environment are an integral part of all policies and strategies, which aim is to advance the environment, and are secured in accordance with the principle of sustainable development.

(v) Principle of Cooperation and Division of Responsibility. The principle of cooperation and division of responsibility implies that the goal of sustainable development may only be achieved through coordinated joint action of the relevant stakeholders, who are obliged to cooperate, through joint work with the government authorities, natural and legal persons and other institutions, with the aim of protecting the environment based on the division of responsibility. The pursuance of interests related to the environmental protection is encouraged through inter-entity cooperation, bilateral or multilateral international agreements on the environment protection and other agreements on cooperation, as well as by providing information and support in relation to the environmental protection, particularly in relations with the neighboring countries.

(vi) Principle of the Participation of Public and Access to Information. In exercising the right to a healthy environment, everyone is entitled to be informed of the state of the environment and to participate in the procedure of decision-making, which enforcement might affect the environment, while the data on the state of the environment are public.

(vii) Polluter Pays Principle. The polluter pays principle implies that the polluter of the environment pays a fee for polluting the environment in cases where its activities cause or may cause the burden on the environment, i.e.if they produce, use or put into circulation a raw material, a semi-finished product or a product which contains substances harmful to the environment.Also, this principle implies that the polluter covers the total costs of the measures for the prevention and reduction of pollution, which includes the costs of the risk to the environment and the costs of the restoration of the damage inflicted on the environment.

The mentioned principles underlie other environmental laws too.

C. Evaluation of Environmental Protection

On the state level, except in the case of health protection or the right to a healthy life and environment, there is no constitutional provision on the environmental protection and sustainable development. The distribution of competences between the state, entities and cantons is poorly defined although ministries on the level of B&H, entities and cantons are liable for the environmental protection. Capacities are insufficient on the state level (a number of employees must be higher in order to provide a more efficient and comprehensive monitoring and improvement of the environmental situation, sustainable development and climate changes). Authorizations should be expanded and increased on the state level in order to harmonize the situation and regulations in this area. At this moment, there is no wellestablished structure and mechanism for implementation, monitoring and assessment of the situation regarding environmental protection, and there are weak capacities of environmental divisions where the responsibility lies on the National Parliament.

VII. Dispute Resolution

A. Methods and Bodies of Dispute Resolution

There are four judicial systems in B&H reflecting its constitutional and territorial organization. Those are: the judicial system of B&H, the judicial system of the FB&H, the judicial system of RS and the judicial system of Brcko District.

Accordingly, in terms of legislative framework that underpins the structure and functioning of courts, there are four laws on courts, which established courts and specified their jurisdiction, organization, internal structure, funding and other matters of relevance to their functioning.

At B&H level, there are the Constitutional Court of B&H, the Court of B&H and the Prosecutor's Office of B&H. The Constitution of B&H contains no provisions relating ot the regular judicial system in B&H or the judicial authorities in general. It only includes provisions pertaining to the Constitutional Court of B&H. The Court of B&H is established with criminal, administrative and appellate jurisdiction.

The Constitution of the FB&H sets forth that the judicial authority in the FB&H will be performed by the Constitutional Court of the FB&H, the Supreme Court of the FB&H, Cantonal Courts of the FB&H and Municipal Courts of the FB&H.

In accordance with the Constitution of the RS, judicial authority is exercised by courts, which are autonomous and independent and adjudicate on the basis of the Constitution and laws. In RS, judicial power is exercised by the Constitutional Court of RS, the Supreme Court of RS, Higher Courts of the RS and Basic Courts of the RS. In addition to general jurisdiction courts, the RS Law on Courts established the courts with special jurisdiction - district commercial courts and the High Commercial Court.

Statute of Brcko District specifies that the judiciary in the District is independent and impartial and it consists of the Basic Court and the Appellate Court of Brcko District.

Municipal courts in the FB&H and Basic courts in RS and Brcko District have jurisdiction in criminal cases in the first instance, civil, minor offence, commercial and other cases, with the exception of commercial cases in the RS which instead of basic courts are handled by district commercial courts.

In addition to all its other competences, the Basic Court of Brcko District has jurisdiction to process all criminal cases irrespective of the prescribed sentence, while basic and municipal courts handle criminal cases with the prescribed sentence of up to ten years.

The first instance jurisdiction of district courts in the RS and cantonal courts in the FB&H includes criminal offences with the prescribed sentence of 10 years or more or long-term imprisonment, and administrative disputes.

The second instance jurisdiction, inter alia, covers the appeal proceedings upon appeals against decisions of municipal or basic courts within their respective jurisdictions. They also decide on the conflict and transfer of territorial jurisdiction between municipal courts and provide international legal assistance in criminal matters.

In RS, the RS Law on Courts has also established district commercial courts, with the first instance jurisdiction in commercial cases, civil cases and non-contentious disputes relating to the rights and duties involved in the legal transaction in goods, services, securities, ownership and other property rights over the real estate etc., and when both parties in the proceedings are legal or natural persons who perform any economic or other registered activity as an independent entrepreneur or in other capacity. These courts also decide disputes pertaining to ships, navigation, airplanes, copy and related rights and intellectual property rights, unfair competition, bankruptcy or liquidation, activities of registration of business entities, foreign investments, legal assistance, etc. High Commercial Court decides appeals against the decisions of district commercial courts; in the first instance it decides on other matters as specified in the law, it decided on the conflict of jurisdiction and transfer of jurisdiction between district commercial courts, formulates legal positions for the purpose of consistent application of laws relevant to the work of district commercial courts, etc.

Supreme Courts of the FB&H and RS and the Appellate Court of Brcko District decide on the regular legal remedies against the decisions of the cantonal and district courts as well as the Basic Court of Brcko District, and on the extraordinary legal remedies against final court decisions.

Appeal is a regular legal remedy. Everyone has a right to appeal or invoke other legal remedies against decision that affect their rights or lawful interests.

Procedures in civil and commercial cases that may shorten or simplify the proceedings include: judgment based on confession, judgment based on waiver and default judgment.

B. Application of Laws

Procedural codes prescribe that courts should adjudicate within the limits of their subject-matter jurisdiction prescribed by law, and that during the entire course of the proceedings, they should pay attention, ex officio, to their subject-matter jurisdiction.

Procedural codes prescribe in detail the territorial jurisdiction of courts, as well as the right and duty of courts with subject-matter jurisdiction to decide any specific legal matter within their respective territories.

VIII. Others

A. Anti-commercial Bribery

a. Brief Introduction of Anti-commercial Bribery Laws and Regulations

The Council of Ministers of B&H adopted the Anti-corruption Strategy 2015-2019 and the Action Plan for its implementation.Presently, there are eight anti-corruption strategies and ten action plans for their implementation that were developed and adopted in B&H.

Recommendations of the relevant anti-corruption international organizations and institutions are continuously monitored and implemented. Amendments to the criminal legislation in B&H were adopted, including incrimination of the trading in influence.In accordance with these amendments, giving gifts and other forms of benefit (active corruption) exists when someone gives or promises a gift or another benefit to an official or responsible person in the institutions of B&H including also a foreign official person or an international official or arbitrator or lay judge, for himself or another person, in order to perform, within the scope of his official function, an act that ought not to be performed by him, or to refrain from performing an act that ought to be performed by him or mediates in such bribing of an official or responsible person.

b. Department Supervising Anti-commercial Bribery

There are 13 bodies for corruption prevention established in B&H, as follows:

(i) Agency for the Prevention of Corruption and Coordination of the Fight against Corruption;

(ii) Anti-Corruption Team of the FB&H Government;

(iii) Commission for the Implementation of the Anti-corruption Strategy in RS;

(iv) Commission for the Prevention of Corruption and Coordination of Activities on the Suppression of Corruption of Brcko District;

(v) The remaining anti-corruption bodies are established on cantons' levels.

These bodies monitor and coordinate the implementation process of strategic anti-corruption documents at the level of the appropriate authorities. The Agency, as the only institution at the level of B&H, initiated the establishment of bodies at other governmental levels in B&H and created recommendations for their establishment where necessary.

In addition to the bodies whose role is of a preventive nature, there are institutions with anti-corruption jurisdictions in B&H that have repressive powers (police agencies, prosecutors' offices, courts, etc.).

c.Punitive Actions

In addition to the prison sentence, measures such as seizure of gifts, rewards, property or other acquired benefits are provided.The intended sanctions, apart from the repressive character, also have a preventive impact in order to prevent corruption.

B.Project Contracting

a.Permission System

Public procurement is always subject to bidding and bidding procedure.When it comes to private sector, enterprises are entitled to contract projects freely.

Contracts where an authority acts as a contracting party and directly subsidizes with more than 50% will be subject to public procurement if the contracts include works in the context of fields provided by applicable regulations or if the contracts include works in hospitals, facilities intended for sports, recreation and pastime, school and university buildings and buildings used for administrative purposes.

b.Invitation to Bid and Bidding

Bidding documentation is prepared in such way to contain all necessary data which enable a legal entity to prepare a request for participation and/or bidding. Contractual authority in bidding documentation when it comes to public procurement determines the exact or frame quantity of procurement subject.

Contractual authority determines conditions of financial and/or technical and professional capability of a candidate/offering party in cases when meeting those conditions is a necessary base for evaluating a candidate's/offering party's capability for executing a certain contract.

巴西

作者：Celso Costa、Thales Saito
译者：高文杰、冯婧

一、概述

（一）政治、经济、社会和法律环境概述

1. 政治

巴西是由联邦政府、26个州、一个联邦区和多个直辖市组成的联邦共和国。联邦政府对中央政府行使控制权，并划分为三个独立的分支机构：行政机构、立法机构和司法机构。州是自身拥有政府机构的自治实体，与其他联邦行政编制共同组成联邦共和国。每个市有一个由市长和立法机构组成的自治地方政府。

2. 经济

1990年至2002年间，巴西经历了大规模的私有化活动，放宽国内经济管制，移除阻碍国家发展的落后政策，鼓励竞争，刺激国家各经济部门的发展。私有化活动包括出售由联邦政府、州和市政府拥有的国有工业和公共服务公司。特许私有经济提供公共服务和开发自然资源。上述一系列举措使得更多的资源投资于社会，减少了公共部门的债务，竞争更加充分，当地证券市场也得到了振兴，为如今巴西成为拉丁美洲最大的经济体，并且成为当今世界上经济最多元化的经济体之一作出了贡献。

此外，在此期间联邦政府逐渐从经济活动中退出。在这方面的重大举措包括建立了自由的外汇市场，取消了价格管制，减少了外贸和资本流动领域的官僚作风，建立了允许外国投资者进入巴西证券市场的机制，以及减少了对外商投资的限制。

巴西政府持续鼓励私营经济进入曾经一直由政府负责的相关部门，尤其是基础设施部门。巴西的石油工业、电力能源、电信和某些其他公共服务等经济部门目前也已经对私营企业和外资开放。

巴西证券市场也经历了重大变革。2000年12月，巴西证券交易所推出了一个新的板块，称为"新板市场"，是新的挂牌类别，旨在通过设置更严格的公司治理规则、会计和披露规则，同时改善小股东待遇，将更多优质的外资引入巴西。

与阿根廷、巴拉圭、乌拉圭和委内瑞拉一样，巴西也是南方共同市场的成员。玻利维亚于2015年7月17日签署了《南方共同市场议定书》，该议定书必须经成员国批准才能生效。[1] 巴西还是世界贸易组织、20国集团、拉丁美洲一体化协会、拉美及加勒比国家共同体（CELAC）的成员。同时，巴西还是安第斯国家共同体的联系国。

巴西在过去的10年中发展迅速，国力增长显著，但是近期外部环境变得不是十分有利，国内环境也更为复杂。巴西经济在经历了2015年和2016年两年的严重收缩之后，2017年开始恢复增长。最初由农业推动，随后经济复苏的范围日益扩大。零售业正在增长，其中包括耐用品、汽车和建材。据巴西地理和统计研究所（IBGE）统计，2017年第三季度国内生产总值与2016年第三季度相比增长了1.4%。[2] 同时，据巴西地理和统计研究所统计，2017年通过全国普通消费者物价指数计算得出的通货膨胀率为2.95%。[3] 投资的恢复得益于信心的改善和通货膨胀率的下降，这为降低利率和融资成本提供了空间。

---

[1] 南方共同市场（MERCOUSUR, "Países do MERCOSUL"），参见http://www.mercosur.int/innovaportal/v/7824/12/innova.front/paises-do-mercosul。

[2] IBGE. Available on https://agenciadenoticias.ibge.gov.br/agencia-noticias/2013-agencia-de-noticias/releases/18458-pib-varia-0-1-em-relacao-ao-2-tri-e-chega-a-r-1-641-trilhao.html.

[3] 参见https://agenciadenoticias.ibge.gov.br/en/agencia-press-room/2185-news-agency/releases-en/19450-ipca-rises-0-44-in-december-and-closes-2017-at-2-95.html。

根据经济合作与发展组织（OECD）的报告，由于通货膨胀率下降使得实际收入增加，巴西的个人消费趋于改善，预计巴西经济将在 2018 年和 2019 年逐步增长。① 巴西中央银行预测，2018 年国内生产总值将增长 2.70%，2019 年将增长 3.00%。②

3. 社会环境

巴西具有多样的文化背景，这种背景源于殖民时期发生的种族和文化混合，其中包括原住民、葡萄牙和非洲人，以及在 19 世纪末和 20 世纪初期移民来的意大利人、西班牙人、德国人、阿拉伯人和日本人所带来的多元文化。由于葡萄牙帝国的殖民化，巴西文化主要来源于葡萄牙，其主流宗教和殖民时期的建筑风格都来源于葡萄牙，同时巴西文化也受到了原住民传统和非洲传统的深厚影响。

巴西在 2013 年至 2014 年期间经历了令人瞩目的经济和社会进步，使 2 900 多万人摆脱了贫困，并显著地改善了不平等。2003 年至 2014 年间，相较于巴西全部人口收入增长率的 4.4%，巴西 40% 的贫困人口收入增长率约为 7.1%。③

虽然巴西在 2014 年之前一直保持较高的就业率，但由于政治和经济危机，失业率从 2013 年的 6.8% 上升至 2016 年年底的 12.6%。不过，经济合作与发展组织预计 2018 年的就业情况将好转，失业率将下降。④

根据经济合作与发展组织的研究，巴西在福利方面有多个优势领域，包括工作时间、社会支持、选民参与投票率和空气质量。此外，在其他许多方面，巴西也被认为高于伙伴国家的平均水平，包括就业率、基本卫生条件、预期寿命和水质。⑤

4. 法律环境

巴西是一个大陆法国家，这意味着巴西拥有全面并且不断更新的法律和法典，这些法律几乎具体规定了所有能够提交给巴西法院审理的事宜。像巴西这样的大陆法国家，法官的主要作用是确认事实并适用由一整套法律建立的法律框架中的条款。判例不具有约束力，仅用于协助法官解释法律并填补法律空白。法官应当遵守法律，但可以援引法律的次要来源，如法律原则、立法目的，或援引巴西《联邦宪法》本身或类推。

巴西《联邦宪法》是巴西的最高法律，因为它是巴西联邦制度所依据的法律权力的基础和来源。它为巴西政府提供了组织框架，并确立了联邦政府与州、市和巴西人民之间的关系。

在巴西，适用于外国投资的法律监管体系主要是由以下几部法律构成的：2002 年 1 月 10 日修订的巴西《民法典》（第 10406 号法律）、1976 年 12 月 15 日修订的巴西《公司法》（第 6404 号法律）、1962 年 9 月 3 日修订的第 4131 号法律（第 4131 号法）、2010 年 3 月 23 日通过的第 3844 号决议、2015 年 3 月 30 日通过的第 4373 号决议（第 4373 号决议案）、2013 年 12 月 16 日发布的第 3689 号通知以及 2015 年 3 月 27 日发布的巴西证券委员会第 560 号指令（巴西证券委员会第 560 号决议案）。

有关适用于巴西外国投资的监管体系的进一步信息，参见"投资形式"部分。

（二）"一带一路"倡议下巴西与中国企业合作的现状和方向

自 1974 年以来，中巴两国的外交关系日益加深。

1993 年，巴西和中国一同建立了中巴高层协调与合作委员会（COSBAN，以下简称"高委会"）。高委会目前是中巴两国之间最高的永久性对话与双边合作论坛。通过其小组委员会和工作组，高委会负责处理经济、金融与政治关系、农业、能源、采矿、文化与教育交流、技术、创新以及航空方面的合作问题。⑥

2010 年，中国和巴西签署了《中华人民共和国政府和巴西联邦共和国政府 2010 年至 2014 年共同行动计划》（PAC，以下简称《共同行动计划》），明确了两国双边关系的目标和指导方针。2015 年，李

---

① 参见《经合组织成员的发展和选定的非成员经济体——巴西》，载 http://www.oecd.org/eco/outlook/economic-forecast-summary-brazil-oecd-economic-outlook.pdf。
② 参见巴西中央银行：《聚焦——市场报告》，载 https://www.bcb.gov.br/pec/GCI/PORT/readout/R20180202.pdf。
③ 参见世界银行：《在巴西的世界银行》，载 http://www.worldbank.org/en/country/brazil/overview。
④ 参见经合组织：《巴西如何比较？2017 年就业展望》，载 http://www.oecd.org/brazil/Employment-Outlook-Brazil-EN.pdf。
⑤ 参见经合组织：《生活在巴西的感觉如何》，载 http://www.oecd.org/brazil/Better-Life-Initiative-country-note-Brazil.pdf。
⑥ 参见 http://www.itamaraty.gov.br/pt-BR/ficha-pais/4926-republica-popular-da-china。

克强总理和迪尔玛·罗塞夫总统签署了《共同行动计划》的更新版本。2012年，中国和巴西签署了《10年合作规划》，目的是将两国的合作提升到全球战略伙伴关系层面。目前，《共同行动计划》和《10年合作规划》为中巴双边关系提供了主要指导方针，在科学、技术、创新与空间合作、能源、采矿、基础设施与运输、投资、工业及经济合作、经商合作以及两国的文化合作与交流等诸多领域建立了长久的合作关系。①

除了双边协议之外，中国和巴西还共同参与了数个多边论坛，如巴西、俄罗斯、印度和中国的金砖四国（BRIC，以下简称"金砖四国"）、G20以及巴西、南非、印度和中国峰会（BASIC）。2014年7月在福塔莱萨举行的第六届金砖国家峰会期间，新开发银行（NDB）成立，金砖国家之间建立了应急储备基金并签署了协议。这些措施的主要目的在于拓宽项目筹集资金的渠道，并保护金砖国家成员免受支付不平衡的影响。此外，巴西于2015年4月成为亚洲基础设施投资银行（AIIB）的创始成员国。②

基于两国之间的外交和经济关系，2009年以来，中国始终是巴西最大的贸易伙伴。巴西与中国之间的贸易额从2001年的32亿美元大幅增加到2017年的748亿美元。2017年，巴西对中国的出口贸易额为475亿美元、进口贸易额为273亿美元（而这一数据在2016年分别为351亿美元和233亿美元），双边贸易顺差达202亿美元。③

目前，中国也是巴西境外直接投资的主要来源之一，尤其是在能源和采矿、钢铁冶金和农业综合企业领域。近期，中国在巴西其他领域的多样化投资也备受关注，如电信、汽车、机械和银行业务。近年来，在中国对巴西的重大投资中值得一提的包括但不限于以下项目：

① 国家电网收购CPFL Energia 23%的股权；

② 复星收购Rio Bravo Investimentos 50.1%的股权；

③ 中国与Wtorre交通建设公司（CCCC）签署协议，投资15亿雷亚尔在马拉尼昂州圣路易斯市建设港口码头④；

④ 国家电力投资公司投资São Simão HP的特许权。⑤

2018年1月22日在智利首都圣地亚哥召开的中国—拉共体（CELAC）论坛第二届部长级会议期间，中国邀请了包括巴西在内的拉共体成员参与"一带一路"倡议。根据中华人民共和国国务院办公厅提供的资料，习近平主席向中国—拉共体论坛第二届部长级会议发来贺信，借此呼吁拉美国家积极参与"一带一路"倡议。⑥虽然有强烈迹象表明拉共体成员将会在短期内加入"一带一路"倡议⑦，但是除巴拿马已与中国达成了加入"一带一路"倡议的合作协议外，其他国家尚未有实质性进展。⑧

二、投资

（一）市场准入

1. 外资监管部门

巴西的外商投资由巴西中央银行负责监管，中央银行还负责控制和监管巴西外汇往来情况。如下文"外商投资行业的法律、法规"和"投资形式"部分所述，巴西的外商投资需要在巴西中央银行登记。

巴西货币委员会（CMN）是巴西负责全面监督货币、信贷、预算、财政和公共债务政策的最高权力机构。因此，在监管外商投资时，巴西中央银行需要遵守巴西货币委员会的政策规定。

此外，外商投资也受巴西证券委员会（CVM）的监管，该委员会负责依据国家货币委员会制定的证券和交易政策管理、发展、控制和监督巴西证券市场。

---

① 参见 http://www.itamaraty.gov.br/pt-BR/ficha-pais/4926-republica-popular-da-china。
② 参见 http://www.itamaraty.gov.br/pt-BR/ficha-pais/4926-republica-popular-da-china。
③ 参见 http://www.mdic.gov.br/index.php/comercio-exterior/estatisticas-de-comercio-exterior/balanca-comercial-brasileira-mensal-2。
④ 参见 http://www2.planalto.gov.br/acompanhe-planalto/noticias/2016/09/china-e-brasil-assinam-acordos-de-investimento-e-cooperacao。
⑤ 参见 http://eng.spic.com.cn/NewsCenter/CorporateNews/201711/t20171120_282752.htm。
⑥ 参见 http://www.scio.gov.cn/31773/35507/35520/Document/1617809/1617809.htm。
⑦ 参见 http://www.fmprc.gov.cn/mfa_eng/wjbxw/t1527941.shtml。
⑧ 参见 https://www.yidaiyilu.gov.cn/info/iList.jsp?cat_id=10037。

2. 外商投资行业的法律、法规

巴西的外商投资主要受第 4131 号法律、第 3844 号决议、第 4373 号决议、第 3689 号通知和巴西证券委员会第 560 号指令的约束，详见"投资形式"部分。

3. 投资形式

在巴西，"外资"被定义为：在没有任何初始外汇支出的情况下进入巴西的货物、机器和设备，并且将用于货物或服务的生产，以及投资于巴西境内经济活动的资金。通常情况下，任何此类资产可以由居住或定居外国的居民或公司总部位于国外的企业，或注册地在外国的企业持有。

巴西的外商投资按性质分为外商股权投资和外商债权投资。

外资股权投资按控制和注册目的也分为两类，即生产性活动的长期投资（以下简称"4131 投资"）和组合投资。

（1）外商股权投资

① 4131 投资

根据第 4131 号法律、第 3844 号决议和第 3689 号通知的规定，可通过以下方式投资于生产活动：外币汇款（作为对巴西公司的出资或作为购买现有股权的价款）或实物出资（如设备或机器）。在这两种情况下，出资金额或实物价值都符合向巴西中央银行登记的条件。

如外国投资者撤资并将投资款汇回，或者外国投资者将在巴西所得利润以及其他资本收益汇回或进行再投资，必须向巴西中央银行进行外商投资登记。[①]

外国投资应在巴西中央银行进行登记，如果其投资被用于以下生产性活动：该生产性活动可由外国投资者全部或部分控制，且此投资完全符合巴西现行法律规定的外资投资条件。因此，投资于贸易、制造或提供服务等业务的资本符合登记初始投资、撤资和汇回分配股息的条件。

自 2000 年以来，外商投资必须由被投资方及投资者（通过其在巴西的代表）通过向巴西中央银行的外商直接投资（RDE-IED）电子登记系统（SISBACEN）提供相关信息来进行电子登记。此类电子登记必须在投资进入巴西之日起 30 天内完成。

为了运行外商直接投资，被投资方和外国投资者必须通过注册电子登记系统的外商直接投资模块从巴西中央银行取得"CADEMP 代码"。在为巴西公司和外国投资者签发 CADEMP 代码后，必须为相关投资者／被投资者创建一个特定的外商直接投资编号。此类外商直接投资编号必须包含在与相关投资者／被投资方"4131 投资"相关的所有外汇交易协议中。

一般来说，巴西央行在获得外国投资者的 CADEMP 代码后，会自动将申请请求转发给巴西税务局，以便外国投资者在巴西税务机关登记，并取得相应的公司纳税人登记册（即所谓的"CNPJ／MF"）。

外商投资以有效进入巴西的货币进行登记。股息以投资者居住国或总部所在国的货币或作出投资的分支机构所在地的货币汇出。利润的再投资以按照上述规定可以汇出的国家的货币进行登记。

已登记的"4131 投资"没有必须留在巴西的最短期限要求。因此，在投资完成后的任何时间，外国投资者都可以在巴西处置资产或清算投资从而撤回投资。

② 组合投资

根据第 4373 号决议的规定，非居民投资者可以通过固收工具（债券、存款证明、公司债券）、衍生工具（互换、期货、远期、灵活期权）、证券（股票、股票期权、股票指数、权证）、投资基金（信用权基金、私募股权基金、多种市场基金、房地产基金等），以及巴西居民可普遍使用的其他金融工具在巴西的金融和资本市场进行投资。

在巴西进行组合投资需要采取以下步骤：

• 外国投资者必须在巴西指定代理人（金融机构或经巴西中央银行授权经营的其他类型的机构）作为面对第三方（该代理人可以是或不是该投资者当地的税务代表，如下所述）的代表（以下简称"投资组合代理人"）。

• 外国投资者必须指定一名当地代表，负责履行代表相关外国投资者所进行的投资而产生的纳税义

---

① 再投资的定义为，非居民个人或企业的收入（利润和资本收益）再次投入到产生该收入的同一家公司或巴西的其他经济部门。

务（实践中，这种服务通常由上一项中提及的代理人提供）。

- 投资组合代理人必须根据巴西证券委员会第 560 号指令为外国投资者向巴西证券委员会登记；
- 投资组合代理人必须根据第 4373 号决议通过电子登记系统投资组合模块（RDE-Portfolio）向巴西中央银行为外国投资者注册。注册取得的 RDE-Portfolio 代码编号归属于投资者，并且此类代码编号需要被包含在代表投资者执行的与投资组合相关的所有外汇交易协议中；
- 投资者必须通过签订托管服务协议，委任一名或多名由巴西证券委员会正式授权的托管代理人。

外围投资者在巴西证券委员会登记后，巴西证券委员会自动将申请请求转发给巴西税务局，以便巴西税务机关对外国投资者进行登记，以及投资者取得各自的公司纳税人登记册。

所有投资、撤资、赎回、收入收据、股息、利息或资本收益、转移投资以及外国投资者投资组合的其他变化都必须由投资组合代理人在电子登记系统的投资组合模块中注册登记。

此外，应当注意的是，外国投资者根据第 4373 号决议进行的所有资产和证券交易以及其他类别的金融交易，必须在由巴西中央银行或证券委员会根据其法律权限授权提供此类服务的机构或实体注册、登记，并在其监管下经营、存放，或在巴西中央银行或证券委员会认可的清算系统中注册。

按照巴西证券委员会第 560 号指令第 20 条的规定，除吸收合并、新设合并、分立、重组和继承外，不得向海外转让和/或分配投资组合。

同时，根据第 4373 号决议的规定，外国投资者也被禁止使用在巴西的资金在规定之外的交易市场（股票或商品交易所、电子系统、有组织的场外市场）之外购买或出售证券产品。

尽管有上述规定，根据巴西证券委员会第 560 号指令第 19 条的规定，上述限制不适用于通过以下方式进行的证券收购或出售：初始认购；奖金；将债券或其他可转换工具转换为股份；法律规定的赎回和补偿；股票的股息；认购、摊销或赎回由巴西证券委员会监管的投资资金配额；经相关巴西证券委员会条例授权，分配或转让开放式投资基金的配额；向旨在关闭托管账户的外国投资者免费或严格地分配到期和未支付的收益；免费转让认购收据，即外国投资者的转让人或受让人；司法判决、司法决定、仲裁决定、行政决定；出售股票发行人在有组织的市场内的交易权利已被取消或中止的股票；根据已经签署并在巴西证券委员会注册超过 6 个月的股东协议出售股份；公开发售证券；如果此前已经巴西证券委员会批准，在销售过程不属于有组织市场中的拍卖之外的情况下公开要约出售股份；在要约收购中为剩余股东提供期权；以及上述项目中未提及的在交易市场之外进行的其他购买或销售交易的行为，该行为需提前向巴西证券委员会提出合理申请并获得其许可。

最后，需要指出的是，投资组合投资只能通过在巴西金融机构开办的以下类型的账户进行：

- 专有账户：投资者只能以自己的名义投资；
- 参加综合账户或集合账户：账户持有人不仅可以以自己的名义运营，还可以以其他非居民投资者的名义运营。在这种情况下，所有投资者都将使用账户持有人的 RDE-Portfolio。

非居民投资者既可以是账户持有人，也可以是一个或多个账户的参与者。只要申请被登记，综合账户的账户持有人可以将自己的资金投入同一账户。以第三方投资者的名义运营的外国金融机构或经纪商都可以使用综合账户。

（2）外商债权投资

在巴西，跨国融资可以通过以下方式实施：

① 一般融资，由外国个人或法人实体（通常是金融机构）直接向巴西公司提供，或通过巴西公司在国际资本市场发行债券；

② 通过出口预付款进行出口融资交易，包括在货物装船或提供服务前至少 360 天收到与货物和服务出口有关的付款；

③ 付款期限超过 360 天的进口融资交易；

④ 租期超过 360 天的租赁交易（合称"外商债权投资"）。

上述所有外商债权投资都必须通过专门用于债权交易设计的电子登记系统模块在巴西中央银行进行注册（RDE-ROF）。

与我们在上文解释的情况类似，为了运行 RDE-ROF，被投资方和外国投资者必须通过电子登记系统注册相关信息，进而从巴西中央银行获得一个"CADEMP 代码"。在为每个巴西公司和外国投资者发放 CADEMP 代码后，必须为相关交易创建一个特定的 RDE-ROF 编号。此编号必须被包含在与有关外商债权投资相关的所有外汇交易协议中。

注册 RDE-ROF 需要列出所有的关键财务条款和交易条件。如未确定到期日或费用和利息，或未确定与借款人或第三方履行有关的其他费用的，将不允许注册。

作为一般规则，RDE-ROF 注册由巴西中央银行自动同意，除非相关外商债权交易的条件与当前市场条件不一致或其结构不符合现有 RDE-ROF 系统标准。

修改外商债权交易的主要条款和条件（如变更付款期限、利率等）可能需要与一个有权在巴西外汇市场上经营的巴西金融机构同时进行外汇交易（模拟资金从国家流出和流入）。

4. 市场准入和检验标准

一般来说，在巴西的外国投资不需要获得巴西政府的事先批准。

但是需要指出的是，某些战略部门对外国所有权和/或许可证要求有限制，具体如下：

（1）金融机构

按照巴西《联邦宪法》的要求，在巴西金融体系中增加外国投资者的参与份额需要总统令。但是根据 1996 年 12 月 9 日颁布的《总统令》的规定，这种限制不适用于外国投资者收购金融机构发行的无表决权股票，这些股票无须特别授权即可在证券交易所交易。此外，根据 2012 年 8 月 2 日发布的第 4122 号决议的规定，在建立巴西金融机构和变更巴西金融机构控制权的交易中，无论涉及的是外国投资者还是本地投资者，都需事先获得巴西中央银行的批准。

（2）采矿

根据 1967 年 2 月 28 日颁布的第 227 号法令的规定，只有在巴西注册成立的公司，包括受外国公司控制的巴西公司，才有资格在巴西从事采矿活动。此外，想在巴西边境地区（与国境线平行的 150 公里宽的地带）开展采矿活动的公司必须遵守附加要求才能有资格开展此类活动，这些要求包括：

① 外资比例不超过 49%（即必须由巴西的公司或者个人持有公司 51% 的资本）；

② 公司的员工至少有 2/3 是巴西人；

③ 公司的管理权必须由具有主导权的巴西大股东拥有。

只有满足以上要求后，想要在巴西边境地区开展采矿活动的公司才可以向国家安全委员会申请授权许可。

（3）核能

在该领域外商投资仅限于商业化活动，放射性同位素用于医学、农业和工业终端，半衰期等于或低于两小时的放射性同位素的生产和使用。这些活动只能由政府特许经营的私营实体发展。私营企业不能开设核能服务和设施或开采铀等放射性物质。尽管如此，还是有一个议案建议修改巴西宪法，目的是为了打破核反应堆的建设和运行的联盟垄断，从而促进能源生产（PEC 122/2007）。这个议案自 2007 年在众议院提出。

（4）机场

主要的有权接受商业航线的机场均由联邦国有公司巴西机场管理公司（INFRAERO）或经特许的个别私人投资者管理和运营。在 2012 年第二轮和 2013 年第三轮特许中，圣保罗、坎皮纳斯、巴西利亚、里约热内卢和米纳斯吉拉斯的国际机场，其中 49% 的有表决权的股份由巴西机场管理公司强制持有，私人投资者们持有其余 51% 有表决权的股份。自 2016 年起，包括弗洛里亚诺波利斯、阿雷格里港、福塔雷萨和萨尔瓦多国际机场在内的多家机场的特许权都没有巴西机场管理公司的参与，因此，在相应的特许协议下，私人投资者是管理和运营这些机场公司的唯一股东。国内外的私营部门实体可以拥有为公务机和直升机设计的机场，但是这些机场不允许接收民航航班，除非根据某些规定获得特别授权。

（5）航空公司和出租飞机公司

定期提供航空服务需要事先获得巴西当局的特许权，非定期提供航空服务需要获得巴西当局的授权。关于外商投资，根据 1986 年 12 月 19 日颁布的第 7565 号法律第 181 条的规定，只有符合以下要求的实体才能被授予开展航空业务的特许权：总部在巴西；外商投资者只持有不超过 20% 有表决权的股份；并且管理权完全由巴西人掌握。目前有两项待投票法案可能改变对外国投资者持有表决权股份份额的限制：2015 年第 2724 号法案，建议对 1986 年第 7565 号法律第 181 条进行修改，使外商投资者可以拥有 49% 的有表决权的股份；2016 年第 258 号法案提出一部新的巴西《航空法典》，其中规定不限制非巴西人持有表决权股份的数量。

（6）健康服务

最初，除少数情况外，巴西法律禁止外国投资者持有医疗救助机构（如医院、诊所、实验室）的股权。然而，根据 2015 年 1 月 19 日第 13097 号法律修订的 1990 年 9 月 19 日第 8080 号法律的规定，外国投资者现在可以直接或间接持有当地医疗机构的股权。但是，应当指出的是，这种立法的合宪性受到了质疑，联邦最高法院仍然需要就此事作出最终决定。

（7）媒体公司

外国投资者在报社（在线新闻服务除外）、免费电视节目、广播电台、广播公司中所持有的有表决权的股份不能超过有表决权的股份的 30%，且上述公司的管理权和编辑控制权需由巴西国民掌握。[1] 外国投资者可以在巴西拥有付费电视节目公司，不受任何相关限制。此外，在巴西分发当地印刷或者编辑的出版物需要任命一名负责编辑工作的劳动部人员。

（8）邮政服务

根据修订版 1978 年 6 月 22 日第 6538 号法律第 9 条的规定，巴西境内的邮政服务只能由巴西政府直接控制的公司提供（如巴西邮政和电报公司）。

（9）农村房地产

外国企业在巴西购置和租赁农村房地产是有一定限制的。与此相关的更多信息，请参阅"二、（四）2"部分。

（二）外汇管理

1. 外汇监管部门

根据巴西国家货币委员会（CMN）规定的准则，巴西中央银行是负责管理和监督外汇市场的部门。

2. 外汇法律、法规简介

巴西外汇市场目前受 2008 年 5 月 29 日第 3568 号决议、2013 年 12 月 16 日第 3691 号通告（《外汇管理条例》）的约束。

3. 外国企业的外汇管理要求

根据《外汇管理条例》的规定，任何个人或法人都可以不受任何性质和价值限制地买卖外汇或以雷亚尔进行国际转账，只要有相关证明文件能够证明该交易具有经济实质意义并且是合法的。

巴西居民可以通过外汇协议与一个经巴西中央银行许可的巴西银行在外汇市场上进行汇款或者接收国外资金。在这种外汇交易协议下，巴西居民可以从巴西银行处购买外币，这些外币将在境外进行交付；或者巴西居民可以通过授权巴西银行出售外币，在这种情况下，巴西银行将接收外币并将等额的雷亚尔交付给巴西居民。

每一份购买或出售外币的外汇协议都必须按照外汇交易性质进行分类。例如，给巴西居民的国外贷款、进出口贸易的付款、当地或外国公司的直接投资均有一个具体的分类编码。《外汇管理条例》详尽地规定了外汇购买协议中可能存在的外汇交易类别。

（三）金融

1. 主要的金融机构

巴西的金融体系由金融机构、证券交易所、保险公司和养老基金等组成，主要由以下监管机构进行管理和监督：巴西国家货币委员会，巴西中央银行，巴西证券委员会（CVM），全国私营保险理事会，私人保险监督局，全国补充养老理事会，补充养老金国家监管局。

巴西的金融机构大致有以下几类：复合服务银行、商业银行、开发银行、投资银行，信贷、金融

---

[1] 参见巴西《联邦宪法》第 222 条。

和投资机构（消费者信贷），房贷机构，经纪行，证券交易商以及房地产融资机构。

根据巴西中央银行提供的数据，目前共有1 727家金融机构或同类机构获准在巴西金融体系中运营，其中包括132家复合银行、21家商业银行、4家开发银行、13家投资银行。①

巴西联邦政府和州政府仍然控制着重要的商业银行和金融机构，以促进经济发展，尤其是制造业和农业领域的发展。此外，开发银行在巴西作为开发机构运营。

巴西的公共金融机构可以分为：开发银行，在联邦层面（如国家经济和社会发展银行——国家开发银行）以及州和地区层面开展业务；储蓄银行，在联邦层面（如巴西联邦储蓄银行）以及州层面开展业务；巴西政府或其他政府实体直接或间接持有其大多数有投票权股份的商业银行、复合服务银行和其他金融机构。据巴西出版物《检视》杂志统计，2016年巴西三大收入最高的金融机构分别为伊塔乌联合银行、布拉德斯科银行和巴西银行。②

目前巴西有132家金融机构由外国投资者控制③，其中8家由中国投资者控制④。此外，目前有50家外国银行在巴西设有代表处。⑤

2. 外国企业融资条件

巴西金融机构并未被禁止向外国实体贷款。然而，巴西历史上曾出现的高利率使得地方融资成本更高，导致其在国际市场上可提供的借贷交易方面没有竞争力。因此，除了由巴西开发银行向位于海外的某些实体提供融资（提供更具竞争力的利率）或以雷亚尔作为结算货币进行付款，并且自然对冲对其履行有重大影响的交易（在这种情况下，融资通常由巴西子公司而不是外国实体获得），更常见的情况是外国企业在国际市场上获得融资，而不是在巴西。

（四）土地政策

1. 土地相关法律、法规简介

根据巴西的法律体系，房地产的分类及其所衍生的法律关系适用房地产所在国的法律。巴西的房地产法律主要以1988年的《联邦宪法》为依据，以巴西《民法典》为特别规定。除其他概念外，上述法律规定了房地产的所有权可以通过直接购买、逆权侵占、添附或继承取得。巴西《民法典》还规定了不以个人关系为依据的房地产（"对物权"）的其他权利，但是可以对抗第三方，例如地上权、地役权、用益物权、使用权和居住权等。

此外，其他管辖巴西房地产的联邦法律如下：

① 1964年12月16日颁布的《房地产开发法》（第4591号法律），主要涉及两个主要方面：由自治机构组成的房地产企业的发展和建造共管公寓；

② 1964年11月30日颁布的《土地法》（第4504号法律），其中规定了巴西农村土地的使用、占有及关系；该法律规定，国家负有保证在该土地上生活和工作的人有获得该农村土地通行地役权的责任和义务；

③ 2001年7月10日颁布的《城市法》（第10257号法律），其中总体规定了城市土地政策，以及旨在帮助促进城市发展的其他规定；

④ 1979年12月19日颁布的《不动产划分法》（第6766号法律），涉及个人地块的城市化，方法是将土地划分或重新划分为用于行使基本城市功能和修建建筑物的地块；

⑤ 1973年12月31日颁布的《公共登记法》（第6015号法律），该法管理巴西各类公共登记处，包括不动产登记处，其中不动产所有权必须登记。

---

① 参见http://www.bcb.gov.br/htms/deorf/d201801/Quadro%2001%20-%20Quantitativo%20de%20institui%C3%A7%C3%B5es%20por%20segmento.pdf。
② 参见https://exame.abril.com.br/revista-exame/maiores-em-financas/。
③ 参见http://www.bcb.gov.br/htms/deorf/d201801/Quadro%2012%20-%20Participa%C3%A7%C3%A3o%20Estrangeira%20no%20capital%20votante%20e%20IFs%20do%20SFN.pdf。
④ 中国参股巴西的最大金融机构包括：中国工商银行、中国银行、海通、中国建设银行和交通银行。
⑤ 参见http://www.bcb.gov.br/htms/deorf/d201801/Quadro%2015%20-%20Representantes%20de%20Institui%C3%A7%C3%B5es%20Financeiras%20no%20Pa%C3%ADs.pdf。

值得注意的是，某些房地产事宜受到州或市法律的管制，而不是由联邦法律规定，如房地产税、房地产登记程序、城市区划、建筑规则和环境法规。

2. 外国企业购地规则

巴西的城市土地可以被外国企业取得而没有法律限制，仅需要其提供公司纳税人登记册的注册证明。但是，外国企业收购和租赁农村房地产的行为受到一定的限制。2010 年 8 月 23 日联邦政府办公厅总法律顾问（CGU/AGU 01/2008-RVJ），批准并公布了关于 1971 年 10 月 7 日第 5709 号法律的新的合宪性解释（Opinion CGU/AGU），扩大了上述限制范围。

根据合宪性解释的规定，为了限制对农村土地的收购，外国公司的法律概念也包括由外国法人或个人持有股份的巴西公司，只要该巴西公司符合以下条件：外国法人或个人持有的股份可确保外国法人或个人有权执行股东大会决议从而去选举公司大多数管理人员，开展公司经营活动，指导公司运营（股权控制），或持股超过 50%。因此，在上述条件下的巴西公司在购买或租赁巴西的农村房地产上受到限制。

关于目前的立法情况，有一项立法议案正在进行，它附加了 6 项其他法案。该法案旨在允许由外国法人或个人持有多数股份或控制的巴西公司购买和租赁巴西农村房地产。此项立法议案自 2015 年 9 月起即被列入下议院审议事项，但一直被推迟。

此外，2018 年 2 月，另一部明确涉及能源部门法律体系的法案被提交给共和国总统，该法案建议取消对外国企业购买和租赁农村房地产的限制，以促进国家的能源开发。

此外，出于国家安全的考虑，外国人（包括受外国控制的巴西公司）在边境地区（沿国家陆地边界 150 公里宽的地带，该地带被认为是保卫巴西领土所必不可少的）购买土地也受到一定的限制。除其他要求外，购置此类土地须取得国家安全委员会办公室的事先授权。

（五）公司的建立和解散

1. 公司的形式

根据巴西法律的规定，国内外投资者可注册各种类型的公司，包括有限责任公司（Limitadas）、股份有限公司（Corporations）、个人有限责任公司、公私合营企业、非法人合资企业。

在巴西最为常见的公司类型为有限责任公司和股份有限公司，上述两种类型的公司的主要特点和注册条件具体如下：

（1）股份公司

① 管辖法律。股份有限公司主要受巴西《公司法》管辖。

② 投资形式。公司可以是封闭式或开放式公司，前提是股份有限公司是巴西公开招股公司的强制性公司类型。

③ 股东人数。公司必须有 2 名以上的股东，他们可以是自然人或法人实体（在巴西或国外设立）。特殊情况下，公司可能由另一家巴西公司全资拥有。如果股东在国外居住，他们必须签署一份授权居住在巴西的代表的授权书。

④ 股本。公司注册成立时必须交纳至少 10% 的注册资本。

作为一般规则，附加资本要求不适用于股份有限公司，但某些特定情况除外，如成立金融机构和为其外国管理人员申请签证的公司（有关获得签证所需资本要求的信息，参见"雇用外籍员工的要求"部分）。

公司可以以全部认购股本或法定股本设立（在这种情况下，董事会可以在公司章程规定的限额内批准增资，而无须经由股东大会同意）。

公司的股本可分为普通股和优先股。优先股通常（但不一定）是无表决权的股票。无论何时，无表决权股份不得超过公司发行股份的 50%。优先股必须赋予其持有人一定的利益或优先权（与普通股相比），如：获得股息的优先权、资本偿还的优先权（有或无溢价支付），或前述权利的组合。

股份的所有权和转让需要在公司的实体名册上登记，或者交由有权经营此种业务的金融机构登记在簿。

⑤ 股东责任。除非有滥用股东权利、违反法律或公司章程的情形，股东责任仅限于支付认购股票

的价款。

⑥ 投票权及股东大会。持有具有表决权股票的股东在股东大会上每股享有一票表决权（根据公司章程规定，优先股也可能赋予其持有人对某些事项的表决权），除非法律或公司章程就某一事项表决的法定人数有更高要求，通常会议决议经市面流通的有表决权股份的多数同意通过。因此，股东大会决议事项一般由代表超过公司市面流通总股本50%加1票的股东表决同意通过。

股东可以订立股东协议以便约定对公司事务的股权参与关系，包括投票权、否决权、股权转让限制、退出机制及竞业禁止等。在巴西，股东协议对签字人及投资目标公司均有约束力，并可由法院执行（强制履行）。依具体情形，投票有违股东协议的，股东大会主席或董事会主席应认定其无效。

⑦ 经营管理。公司通常由高级管理人员委员会或董事会管理，法律没有要求封闭式公司设立高级管理人员委员会的除外。公司应依法设立常设或非常设的监事会。管理机构的所有成员均应当是个人。

董事会应当由3人以上组成，负责选举和任命高级管理人员，制定或核准公司重大政策。董事会成员由股东大会选举产生。成员可以不是公司股东或巴西居民，但如果其他成员均在巴西境外居住，法定代表人应当是巴西居民。董事会成员对外无权代表公司。

高级管理人员委员会至少由2人组成，有权对外代表公司并直接参与公司活动。高级管理人员不必是股东，由董事会或股东大会（如果公司没有董事会）选任，每届任期不超过3年。高级管理人员必须获得巴西永久居住权，即仅有巴西公民或持有有效签证在巴西合法定居的外国人才有资格担任公司的管理人。

监事会由3～5人组成。监事会的主要职权是监督董事会，还包括其他职权：对公司经营者进行监督、对管理层制作的年报及议案（包括关于修改资本、发行债券及担保等）等须提交股东大会进行审议的事项进行质询、审议公司财务报表。监事会成员通过股东大会选举产生，不必是公司股东。监事会为非常设机构，只有持有10%以上有表决权股份的股东或持有5%以上无表决权股份的股东要求时才可召开监事会。

⑧ 利润。分配股息需要年度一般股东大会的批准，公司章程可以允许董事会批准同意将上一年度、半年度或季度资产负债表上登记的留存收益或利润准备金用于分配中期股息。

公司应至少支付年利润的25%作为股息给股东（除非公司章程有更低要求）。公司也可以依据股东权益给股东分配利息，该利息可以从上述最低股息中扣除。

巴西《公司法》要求公司应当留存净利润的5%作为法定准备金。公司法定准备金累计提取到公司总股本的20%的，可以不再提取。法定准备金仅可用于弥补亏损或增资，不得用于分配利润。

（2）有限责任公司

① 管辖法律。有限责任公司主要受巴西《民法典》管辖。在公司章程另有约定且不与巴西《民法典》相冲突的情况下，还受巴西《公司法》的管辖。

② 投资形式。禁止公开认购股权。有限责任公司不允许交易股权、发行债券（债权证券）或在证券交易所报价。

③ 股东人数。公司可以由2名以上的自然人或者法人出资设立。自然人或者法人股东可以是外国居民或居住在外国。若所有出资人均为外国居民，他们应向居住在巴西的代表出具一份授权委托书。

④ 股本。作为一般规则，最低资本要求不适用于有限责任公司，但某些特定情况除外，如成立金融机构和为其外国管理人申请签证的公司。

对有限责任公司应预先支付的最低股本金不作要求，对全部股本缴足亦无强制性时间限制（缴足时间由出资人在公司章程中商定）。

股份没有证券或证书凭证。股份的所有权登记在公司章程中，股份转让应当相应修改公司章程。持有公司股份25%的股东有权否决向非现有股东转让份额，有限责任公司的公司章程另有规定的除外。

尽管巴西《民法典》对有限责任公司发行不同类型的股份没有规定，但最近修改[①]的《商业登记条例》明确规定，有限责任公司发行的优先股由巴西《公司法》补充管辖。

经股东多数通过，可以将有不法行为或其他影响公司存续行为的股东除名。

---

① 公司注册和一体化部于2017年3月2日发布的第38号规范性指示。

⑤ 股东的责任。股东以其认购的出资额为限对公司的债务承担责任，但全体股东对于未能缴纳的出资额承担共同连带责任。出资人已经足额缴纳出资的，不再承担其他责任，但违反法律、公司章程或滥用权利等情形除外。

⑥ 投票权及股东会。持有具有表决权股份的股东在股东会议上每股享有一票表决权。股东会决议通常由出席会议的股东多数同意通过，但法律或有限责任公司章程对某一事项的表决有更高法定人数要求的除外。例如，根据巴西《民法典》的规定，有限责任公司的合并或解散应当经过代表市面流通股份总数的75%的股东同意通过。

有限责任公司的股东可就其股权参与公司事项的权益订立股东协议，包括投票权和否决权，股权转让限制、退出机制、竞业禁止等。在巴西，股东协议对签字人及投资的有限责任公司均有约束力，并可以得到法院执行。

⑦ 经营管理。有限责任公司应当由公司章程或股东订立的其他文件中指定的一个或多个自然人管理。有限责任公司的事务可以由公司章程授权的股东或第三人执行，执行人应当在巴西居住或定居。这意味着只有巴西公民或者持有有效签证在巴西合法定居的外国人才有资格担任有限责任公司的管理人。

⑧ 利润。有限责任公司的利润分配应当经过股东会同意。

巴西《民法典》未规定有限责任公司应当分配利润的最低数额。

（3）投资基金

法人和自然人通过投资基金在巴西投资已十分常见。

虽然巴西对投资基金的法律性质存在理论上的争议[1]，但大多数巴西学者[2]、巴西适用的法律和条例以及大多数法律先例将它们及所有的形态归类为由巴西《民法典》和巴西证券委员会颁布的条例所管辖的特殊实体。

作为特殊实体，巴西《民法典》第44条并没有赋予巴西投资基金法律人格。尽管如此，值得注意的是，投资基金能够在适用的法律及其设立文件（如规章或制度）允许的范围内享有法定权利和义务。[3]作为一般规则，无论出于什么法律目的，投资基金必须由其管理人员代表。在大多数情况下，管理人员需要取得由巴西证券委员会授予的当地执业资格才能开展资产管理活动。

就权利能力而言，一般具有法人资格的实体可以从事任何类型的交易，除非法律或其设立文件另有规定。[4]另一方面，没有法律能力的实体（如投资基金）只允许进行法律或其设立文件明文授权的交易。因此，考虑到投资基金没有法人资格，他们只能开展其章程及巴西证券委员会颁布的可适用规定明确允许的活动。

必须指出的是，由于投资基金没有法律人格，因此在巴西法律及税收意义上它们不是法律实体，一般来讲，它们不是纳税单位并且并不受特殊税收体系的管辖。因此，投资基金组合所取得的所有收入及资本收益既不用缴纳企业所得税（CIT，下文详述）也不用缴纳营业税（社会一体化税及"社保资助"特别税是法人应当承担的社会税）。因此，只有股权持有者需要对增值收益纳税（依据分配或者权责发生制原则），各自的税收待遇取决于股东所在地。

巴西投资基金的形式有很多，包括：固定收益基金、公众公司基金、外汇基金、多层次市场基金、私募股权基金、不动产基金以及应收信贷基金。

成立投资基金需要有管理人员设立基金的行为，并取得巴西证券委员会授予的运营许可证。此外，投资基金发行和分配股份必须遵守巴西公开发行证券的相关条例，对此将在"证券市场的监督和管理"部分解释说明。

2. 公司设立的程序

股份有限公司和有限责任公司都可以通过私人文书或公共契约设立。无论在何种情形下，公司设立文书、公司规章（股份有限公司）及公司章程（有限责任公司）都应当到对公司总部所在地有管辖

---

[1] 参见卡瓦罗，马里奥·塔沃纳德·马丁斯：《投资基金法律制度》，拉丁区出版社2012年版，第184—185页。
[2] 参见艾兹瑞克，纳尔逊：《资本市场的法律制度》（第三版），里约热内卢出版社2011年版，第82—83页。
[3] 参见科埃略、法比奥·伍尔哈：《商法—公司法教程》（第十版），冰雹出版社2007年版，第9页。
[4] 参见科埃略、法比奥·伍尔哈：《商法—公司法教程》（第十版），冰雹出版社2007年版，第10页。

权的贸易委员会进行登记。

一般地，成立股份有限公司和有限责任公司无须取得巴西任何政府机关的事先批准，但是例如设立金融机构等某些特殊情形除外。有关政府许可和授权的更多信息请参见"市场准入和检验标准"部分。

3. 公司解散途径及要求

出现下列任一情形，股份有限公司应当解散：

① 在以下情形中基于法律效力解散：存续期限届满；公司章程规定解散的情形；一般股东大会决议解散；股东大会年会证实公司仅有一名股东，而次年股东大会年会依然未能达到最少有 2 名股东的要求；对公司经营的授权被依法取消；

② 在以下情形中基于法院命令解散：在任一股东启动的诉讼中，公司设立行为被宣布无效时；在代表公司 5% 或以上股权的股东提起的诉讼中该公司被证明无法达到其公司目的时；如公司破产，按照相关法律规定的方式进行解散时；

③ 根据任何特别法律规定的情形或方式基于主管当局的行政命令解散。

根据法律规定，有限责任公司在以下任一情况下应当解散：公司存续期限届满（如适用）；在公司存续期限届满前全体股东一致同意解散；在无存续期限的有限责任公司中，绝对多数股东同意解散；公司仅有 1 名股东持续超过 180 天；对公司经营的授权依法废止；公司被宣布破产。

2015 年 3 月 16 日颁布的第 13105 号法律规定了基于以下原因而向法院提起部分解散股份有限公司或有限责任公司的法律诉讼：因股东死亡或被除名，或者行使退出权或休会权而脱离公司；对前述股东进行了资产清算；股东分裂或资产清算。

（六）兼并和收购

一般而言，巴西的收购可以通过下列方式实施：

① 直接或者间接地收购目标公司的股权；

② 执行有关表决权或其他权利的协定；

③ 购置资产；

④ 公司重组（吸收合并、剥离、新设合并、分拆等）。

最有效的收购方法取决于诸多因素，其中包括法律、税务影响（包括取得新设企业税务许可证等）、商业考虑、第三方同意及交割时间等。

1. 文书

在巴西进行并购所需的文书与美国、英国法律下跨国并购所需的文书类似。

就文书而言，巴西通常采用的主要交易文件包括：

① 初步文件（术语表、禁止披露协议、谅解备忘录、意向书等）；

② 股权或资产购买协议，以及相关明细表及附表；

③ 代管协议；

④ 投资协议；

⑤ 股东协议。

一般来说，通常谈判双方进行更多的工作和更密集的谈判的都是与陈述、保证和赔偿有关的条款。

购买协议中陈述和保证条款的主要目的是：

① 披露以下重要信息：关于目标公司（包括其经营、业务和紧急情况）的重要信息，待出售的股份或资产，以及当事人订立有关协议的权利；

② 在当事人之间分配风险，并在违约发生时作为索赔的依据；

③ 使当事人在违约行为发生时、交割时间前，提前终止协议。作为一般规则，陈述与保证条款的范围受到"重大""知晓""时间"以及购买协议披露明细中的"证明"等概念的限制。

至于赔偿，购买协议中通常涉及：因违反陈述和保证或陈述保证有误造成的损失，未能履行约定义务造成的损失，以及明确分配给一方当事人承担的责任。

与其他司法辖区不同的是，巴西合同中非常普遍地包括一项兜底条款（也称为"我方注意/你方注意"条款）（除陈述与保证的违反或有误之外），其规定卖方有义务赔偿买方在交割前因发生的行为、事实或事件遭受的所有损失。在此情况下，尽管有陈述与保证条款，交割前由行为、事实或事件产生的一切风险还是被分配给了卖方。赔偿条款通常的限制包括：存续期间，最高限额，门槛、一揽子条款及扣减，迷你一揽子或最低减让标准，以及附属文件（代管、暂停、承诺）。

2. 尽职调查

巴西并购交易通常涉及法律、金融及会计事务。尽职调查的目的是了解卖方和目标公司的情况，并确定与收购有关的问题。

巴西的法律尽职调查报告通常包含下列事项：环境，民事，反垄断，商业和金融协议，不动产，知识产权，监管，保险，公司，劳务，税务，以及反腐败与合规。

和我们在许多其他司法辖区见到的不同，巴西当地目标公司大量卷入司法和行政诉讼是十分常见的事情，并且诉讼多集中在劳务和税收领域。在尽职调查中发现的紧急情况和债务通常是通过调整交易价格或在协议中增加具体的赔偿条款以将风险分配给卖方来解决的。从这个意义上讲，买方通常希望在交易达成前发现卖方存在的重大问题，以便在谈判中调整交易价格或者放弃收购。

3. 并购相关的手续和程序

（1）收购有限责任公司

有限责任公司的股权转让需要修改公司章程。为使转让能够有效对抗第三方，章程修改后要到具备相应资格的商业委员会备案。

（2）收购封闭型股份有限公司

封闭型股份有限公司的股权转让需要在公司的实体名册中登记，或者交给有权经营此种业务的金融机构以簿记的形式登记。封闭公司的股权转让无须再进行额外的备案或披露即具有对世效力。

（3）收购公开招股的股份有限公司

上述收购封闭型股份有限公司的手续同样适用于公开招股的股份有限公司的股权转让。

此外，在一家公开招股的公司中，一旦任何投资导致股东持有的某种类型的股份（或与此类股份相关的可转换债券或衍生工具）达到公司控制权的5%或5%的倍数，股东都必须立即通知该公司，公司须立即向市场、巴西证券委员会及证券交易所提供相关信息。公告必须明确表明并购中买方是否有意变更公司控制权。公司控制权每次增加或减少5%或5%的倍数都需要另行发布公告。

在开放型公司中，当控制权发生变化时，考虑到股东的控制利益，巴西《公司法》要求收购方向剩余的所有普通股股东发起投标要约，每股按照股东已支付的每股价格的80%投标。上述规则适用于巴西股票交易所第二层次（Nivel 2）B3板块下的上市公司。新板市场要求在上述情形下，强制性投标要约中每股（包括在巴西交易所第二层次上市公司的优先股）的价格与收购方对已购股票支付的价格相同，作为收购人取得控制利益的对价。

4. 反垄断审批

如下文"竞争规范举措"部分所述，在巴西，一些并购交易的交割需要事前取得保护经济行政委员会（定义见下文）的批准。

（七）竞争监管

1. 竞争监督部门

保护经济行政委员会（CADE）负责2011年11月30号颁布的《竞争法》（第12529号法）的实施。

保护经济行政委员会由总监管处（SG，负责一级并购审查和不正当竞争行为调查），由1名主席和6名委员组成的行政法庭（CADE Tribunal），及经济研究部组成。

2.《竞争法》简介

巴西的竞争制度目前受《竞争法》的制约，该法律确立了兼并前审查制度，并规定了对不正当竞争行为的惩罚措施。

3. 竞争规范举措

（1）并购

① 司法辖区/门槛

在巴西开展并购时，如果该交易对巴西产生了影响并构成了经济集中以及达到了一定的收入界限时就应当向保护经济行政委员会提交并购申请。这是一项强制性要求。无论是直接形式还是间接形式（例如通过出口外销到巴西）的跨国交易，还是主要在巴西履行的交易，只要交易在巴西产生了实际或潜在的影响，就达到了审查标准。对于启动审查的出口销售数量或价值没有最低要求。

经济集中的概念包括兼并、资产控制权或非控制权权益的收购（如果收购方和目标公司既不是竞争对手，在垂直相关市场也不相关，应收购至少20%的股权；如果收购者和目标公司是竞争对手或在垂直相关市场十分相关，应收购至少5%的股权）以及设立合资企业、合伙企业，签订联合协议。①

当参与交易的经济集团在巴西的年度收入总额/年度总量最低为7.5亿雷亚尔，参与交易的另一经济集团在巴西的上一会计年度收入总额/总量最低7 500万雷亚尔时，就达到了审查的收入门槛。

② 程序

参与交易的各方共同负责并购申请和支付8.5万雷亚尔的备案费。申请可以在交易结束前的任何时候提交，不过，最好是在双方当事人之间签订有约束力的文件之后。

在取得保护经济行政委员会官方许可前，各方应保持独立，不得干涉彼此的经营活动——如有违反静止义务等同于提前偷偷行动，当事人可能会受到6万雷亚尔到6 000万雷亚尔的处罚，以及撤销其违法行为，并/或开展针对并购各方不正当竞争行为的正式调查，调查还可能产生额外的罚款和处罚。

在证券交易所或有组织的场外交易市场上的交易不需经保护经济行政委员会批准即可进行，但是所有与在交易中所获取的利益的所有权相关的政治权利未经保护经济行政委员会的批准是无法行使的。

从保护经济行政委员会宣布并购申请提交之日起，并购审查的过程可能长达330天。然而，大多数的并购案件都是在快速通道下审查的，官方许可可在提交正式申请后30日内作出。

③ 结果

如果总监管处发布的许可没有受到第三方质疑，也没有收到保护经济行政委员会法庭中任何成员对许可提出的修订意见，总监管处将许可在巴西官方报纸上发布15天后，该许可将成为最终的可执行决定。

如果总监管处的结论是交易有可能导致不正当竞争，它会将此交易提交给保护经济行政委员会法庭，由它来决定是否应当无条件地授予许可，或纠正后许可还是不予许可。在此二级审查中，最终许可会在保护经济行政委员会法庭决定后立即作出。

纠正措施可以采用结构性承诺或行动承诺的形式，实践中通过并购各方与保护经济行政委员会之间的合并控制协议（ACC）来协商。

（2）不正当竞争行为

① 可审查的行为

在巴西不正当竞争行为由总监管处在行政层面提起诉讼并由保护经济行政委员会法庭裁决。根据《竞争法》的规定，如果在境外实施的不正当竞争行为实际已经或可能在巴西产生影响，保护经济行政委员会法庭对此具有管辖权。

不正当竞争行为包括寻求或实际产生下列影响的一些行为，不论是否有过错，即使没有产生实际影响：限制、约束或以任何方式损害自由竞争或自主创新；控制相关商品或服务市场；任意提高利润；滥用支配地位。

上述行为涵盖了广泛的实践，包括联合行动（固定价格、分配市场、限制产量、操纵投标、联合抵制等）以及单方行动（排他、歧视、掠夺性定价、维持转售价格、拒绝交易及搭售行为等）。

② 处罚

对公司处以该公司、其集团或企业集团在行政程序启动前一年的年度总收入的0.1%～20%的

---

① 竞争法免除了为参与公开投标设立的合伙、合资企业及签订联合协议报告的义务。

处罚。①②

对公司管理人员及董事处以罚金，金额按照对公司罚款金额的1%～20%收取。对公司职员和如贸易协会等无须登记营业额的组织处以5万雷亚尔到20亿雷亚尔的罚款。

根据1990年12月27日第8137号法律的规定，硬核卡特尔行为（定价、市场分配、产量限制、串通投标）在巴西构成刑事犯罪。另外，在保护经济行政委员会的诉讼中，由检察官办公室对犯有硬核卡特尔行为的公司提起公诉并由法院审判。根据上述法律的规定，只有自然人能够对卡特尔行为承担刑事责任，并将面临2至5年监禁及罚款的处罚。

③ 豁免

《竞争法》规定了宽容制度。据此，与保护经济行政委员会订立了宽容协议的公司和／或个人有权享受行政监管层面的全部或部分豁免。宽容协议也保护个人不受刑事起诉。然而无论是公司还是个人，都不能据此免于遭受卡特尔损害的第三方提起的私人损害赔偿诉讼。

如果一个调查已经开始，被告可与保护经济行政委员会就接受调查的行为进行谈判达成和解协议（TCC）。与保护经济行政委员会协商时，其中一项义务是支付不低于保护经济行政委员会预期最低金额的罚款作为财政缴款。如果保护经济行政委员会接受了这项提议，针对已和解的被告人的行政诉讼中止，对其他被告人的诉讼照常进行。

（八）税务

1. 税收体制及规则

正如上文"政治"部分所述，巴西联邦共和国是由26个州和一个联邦区组成的联邦，联邦区享有政治和经济独立，区和州下设市。

巴西的税收体系规定在《联邦宪法》中，《联邦宪法》规定了联邦、州及地方政府的可征税事项。

通常，联邦政府可以对所得、资本收入、制造业、进口、出口、薪资（社会保障金）和金融交易等征税。州政府可以对商品流通、机动车及赠予征税。最后，市政府可以对服务、不动产及房地产转让征税。

下文中我们仅讨论联邦、州及市层面最为相关的税种。

2. 主要的税种及税率

（1）联邦税

① 企业税

A. 企业所得税（IRPJ）和法人盈利税（CSLL）——针对企业所得的税项

企业所得税（CIT）是对位于巴西或在巴西经营的所有法人的应纳税利润征收的一种税。通常企业所得税的累计税率为34%，包括：公司所得税，利润低于24万雷亚尔的部分税率为15%，另对利润超出24万雷亚尔的部分可能会加课10%③，以及法人营业税，税率为9%。

尽管计算企业所得税的税基有几种，巴西公司一般采用实际利润或推定利润：

- 实际利润：公司应计的会计利润，根据法律规定的增项和减项调整；
- 推定利润：参考预先确定的总收入的百分比来确定应税活动的利润（不考虑费用和成本）。公司上一年的年度总收入未超过7 800万雷亚尔的，可以采用推定利润制度。

B. 社会一体化税（PIS）和"社会资助"特别税（COFINS）——社会性开支

公司应缴纳社会一体化税／"社会资助"特别税，以总收入为计算基础（除了适用于薪金和工资的社保费）。社会一体化税／"社会资助"特别税采用两种税制：

- 非累计税制：9.25%的合并税率，并可能从满足条件的成本和费用（如投入）中扣除一些款额；

---

① "商业活动行业"未必与反垄断意义上的相关市场完全一致。根据2012年5月29日保护经济行政委员会制定的第3号决议的规定，在计算罚款金额时应当参考一个行业列表。
② 此外，公司可能会受到非经济处罚，包括5年以内禁止参与政府采购或从公共金融机构融资等。
③ 值得一提的是，在巴西银行业务产生的利润适用45%的累积税率缴纳企业所得税，包括：①公司所得税，按照税收调整后净利润的15%征收。净利润部分，经过税收加减调整，每年超过24万雷亚尔的要额外缴纳10%的收入税；②法人营业税，截至2018年12月31日税率为20%。自2019年1月1日起，适用税率将调整为15%。

- 累计税制：3.65% 的合并税率并且没有抵消项目。①

作为一般规则，按照实际利润缴纳企业所得税的法人适用非累计税制缴纳社会一体化税/"社会资助"特别税（金融机构等除外）。另一方面，适用推定利润的法律实体强制适用累计税制。

社会一体化税/"社会资助"特别税也适用于进口货物及服务。对于进口货物，一般税率按照商品报关金额的 2.1% 到 9.65% 征收，对于进口服务税率按照汇款金额的 1.65% 到 7.6% 计算。

C. 工业产品税——针对工业制成品的税项

工业产品税是对工业制成品的交易征税，包括进口或国内销售。法律上，工业制成品是指任何符合工业化流程的产品。

进口交易方面，工业产品税征收于产品清关之时，征收基数为产品的报关金额加上进口应纳关税金额。对于国内交易，基本规则是以交易价格为税基。工业产品税的适用税率是根据海关编码中产品税项编码确定的，工业产品税的税率表以海关编码为基础。

D. 关税——针对进口的税项

关税是针对外国产品进口的税项。关税的税基为报关金额，海关估价协定对报关金额有定义。通常而言，报关金额与进口货物的成本、保险加运费价格一致。适用税率是根据海关编码中产品税项编码而变化。

E. 金融操作税——针对金融交易的税项

金融操作税是针对包括但不限于如下多项金融交易征收的税项：

- 信用交易：税基和适用税率根据信用交易特点的不同而不同。通常而言，最高税率为 1.88%，而某些交易免于缴纳金融交易税。
- 外汇交易税：外汇交易的通常税率为 0.38%，但也有例外。

金融交易税的税率可由总统令随时调整，最高税率不超过 25%。

F. 国家社会福利基金——社会保障金

国家社会福利基金是一种社会保障基金。国家社会福利基金由雇主和雇员缴纳，其中雇员应缴纳的份额应由公司代扣并汇缴给联邦政府。

通常而言，社会保障金的缴纳比例如下：

- 雇主应当按照向雇员或独立工人支付薪酬的 20% 缴纳社会保障金。某些特定情况则适用额外比例；
- 工人工伤保险的比例是工资的 1%、2% 或 3%；
- 雇员应按照薪酬的 9%～11% 缴纳社会保障金，但是不得超过某一上限；
- 其他机构缴纳的社会保障金累积比例不得超过 5.8%。

② 个人税

个人所得税——收入税。

居民应就个人在全球范围内的收入缴纳收入税（个人所得税），但可以进行税收抵免。根据收入类型的不同，有时可以进行代扣所得税，代扣的税款视为纳税人缴纳收入税的最终付款或预付款。居民个人的收入可分为两大类：

- 资本收入和财务盈利：根据个人收入的金额实行 15%～22.5% 的累进税率；
- 普通收入，包括工资：实行 7.5%～27.5% 的累进税率。

巴西的公司派发的股息免于征税。

（2）州政府税

流通税——对买卖征收的税项。

流通税类似于一种增值税，是针对与货物有关的进口、买卖以及其他商业交易，提供跨市或跨省交通服务以及通信服务的提供征收的一种税项。流通税是非累进制税项，因此每个交易中支付的流通税可以与后续交易或服务应纳税额进行抵扣。

流通税应于产品交易时缴纳，纳税基数通常为交易的价格，加上有条件的折扣和运费（如果是卖方分别收费并由卖方自行或委托提供运输服务）。进口货物的流通税税基为货物的报关金额加所有进口

---

① 对金融机构而言，社会一体化税/"社会资助"特别税综合税率为 4.65%。

联邦税和清关费用,按总额计算。

进口交易和国内交易的税率均由各州决定,不同产品适用不同的税率,最高可达32%(通常进口/跨州交易税率为17%~20%)。州内纳税人之间进行的交易税率由联邦参议院制定,通常为4%、7%或12%。

(3)市政府税

社会服务税——针对服务的税项。

社会服务税征收对象为所有性质的服务以及服务的进口,根据城市及服务性质的不同,税率从2%到5%不等。社会服务税的税基为服务的价格。

(4)总结——巴西主要税种

巴西的主要税种		
税 种	计税基础	税 率
社会一体化费/"社会资助"特别税(PIS/COFINS)	总收入或报关金额/向外汇款金额	分别为1.65%和7.6%(非累进制) 分别为0.65%和3%(累进制) 分别为2.1%和9.65%(进口货物) 分别为1.65%和7.6%(服务进口)
工业产品税(IPI)	工业产品的价格或报关金额加关税	依产品类型而定
关税(II)	进口货物的报关金额	依产品类型而定
企业所得税(IRPJ)	应纳税所得(利润或损失)	25%(15%加10%)
法人盈利税(CSLL)	应纳税所得	9%
国家社会福利基金(INSS)	员工薪酬总额	通常为26.8%到28.8%
金融操作税(IOF)	金融交易	依交易类型而定
流通税(ICMS)	产品价格或报关金额加联邦税和清关费用(以总额计)	通常为18%
社会服务税(ISS)	针对服务的市政府税项	2%~5%

(5)国际税务

①跨国支付

巴西境内向境外居民支付的薪酬,不论何种性质(例如利息、版税、服务费用以及其他),均应缴纳收入预提税。收款人如果位于低税国家,通常预提税率为15%到25%。[1]

---

[1] 第1037/2010号规范文件列出了巴西法下的低税国家和地区:美属萨摩亚,安道尔,安圭拉,安提瓜和巴布达,阿鲁巴,阿森松岛,巴哈马,巴林,巴巴多斯,伯利兹,百慕大,英属维尔京群岛,文莱,坎皮奥德意大利,开曼群岛,海峡群岛(泽西岛、格恩西岛、奥尔德尼岛和萨克岛),库克群岛,库拉索岛,塞浦路斯,吉布提,多米尼加,法属波利尼西亚,直布罗陀,格林纳达,中国香港、澳门特别行政区,马恩岛,基里巴斯,爱尔兰,黎巴嫩,纳闽,利比里亚,列支敦士登,马尔代夫,马绍尔群岛,毛里求斯,摩纳哥,蒙特塞拉特,瑙鲁,纽埃岛,诺福克岛,巴拿马,皮特凯恩群岛,格什姆岛,圣克里斯托弗和尼维斯,圣赫勒拿,圣卢西亚,圣马丁,圣文森特,萨摩亚,圣马力诺,塞舌尔,所罗门群岛,圣皮埃尔和密克隆群岛,阿曼,斯威士兰,汤加,特里斯坦达库尼亚,特克斯和凯科斯群岛,阿拉伯联合酋长国,美属维尔京群岛以及瓦努阿图。
第1037/2010号规范性文件列举了以下特殊税制:①关于丹麦,该税制适用于不开展实质性经济活动的控股公司,即指控股公司在居住国并不具有开展业务的经营能力,这体现在缺少相应员工和实际办公场地;②关于荷兰,该税制适用于不开展实质性经济活动的控股公司,即指控股公司在居住国并不具有开展业务的经营能力,主要证明是缺少相应员工和实际办公场地;③关于冰岛,适用于国际贸易公司(ITC);④关于美国,适用于非居民控制的、作为州有限责任公司注册成立的公司,无须缴纳联邦税;⑤关于西班牙,适用于作为西班牙控股公司(ETVEs)成立的公司——目前暂停;⑥关于马耳他,适用于国际贸易公司(ITC)和国际控股公司(IHC)的制度;⑦关于瑞士,作为控股公司成立的瑞士法人实体、当地公司、附属公司、混合公司、行政公司或任何其他当地税务机关签发的公司形式,且所得税税率低于20%(联邦、州和市联合税率)的,适用于特殊税制;⑧关于奥地利,适用于不发展实质性经济活动的控股公司;⑨关于哥斯达黎加,适用于自由贸易区制度(Zonas Francas);⑩关于葡萄牙,马德拉国际商业中心(马德拉国际中心);⑪关于新加坡,适用以下特殊税收制度:(a)非居民船东或承租人或航空运输企业的特殊税率;(b)保险和再保险业务的免税和特许税率;(c)金融与资金管理中心特许税率;(d)信托公司的特许税率;(e)债务证券所得收入的特许税率;(f)全球贸易公司和适格公司的特许税率;(g)金融业鼓励公司的特许税率;(h)为金融机构提供流程服务的特许税率;(i)航运投资管理公司的特许税率;(j)信托受益人收入的特许税率;(k)飞机和飞机发动机租赁的特许税率;(l)飞机投资管理公司的特许税率;(m)集装箱投资企业的特许税率;(n)集装箱投资管理公司的特许税率;(o)核框保险经纪人的特许税率;(p)管理合格注册商业信托或所得收入的特许税率;(q)船舶经纪和远期货运协议交易的特许税率;(r)与航运有关的支持服务的特许税率;(s)管理经核准风险投资公司的收入的特许税率;(t)国际成长型公司的特许税率。

- 支付股息。目前巴西的公司向境外支付股息不需向巴西缴纳预提税，只要股息与 1996 年 1 月 1 日后产生的利润相关。
- 所有者权益的支付。公司可以向其股东支付所有者权益利息（一种混合型的资本回报）。所有者权益利息的计算不得超过巴西每日变动的长期利率。[①]向抵税国家的外国投资者支付的所有者权益利息需缴纳 15% 或 25% 的预提税。

如果所有者权益利息的金额达到了法律规定的上限，可以与企业所得税进行抵扣。

② 资本收益

非居民通过资本减持或向居民或非居民购买者转让巴西境内资产的方式获得的资本收益，通常需根据收益总额缴纳 15% 到 22.5% 的累进税。[②]对于低税国家的居民，该税率是 25%。

③ 转移定价

巴西的公司与低税国家的关联方或国家主体进行的跨境交易应受到转移定价的管制。巴西转移定价规则对于利息的支付、进口交易以及出口交易都有详细的规定。

④ 资本弱化

通常而言，巴西公司纳税人向非低税国家的或享受特殊税制的境外关联方支付利息，只有在满足以下条件时方可抵扣企业所得税：

- 公司经营所必需的；
- 达到以下三项要求：第一，巴西主体对关联方的负债率不超过关联方在巴西借方处持有所有者权益的两倍；第二，对于不持有巴西主体所有者权益的关联方，巴西主体对关联方的负债率不超过巴西借方所有者权益的两倍；第三，所有情况下，巴西借方对关联方的总负债率不高于所有关联方在巴西借方处持有所有者权益的两倍（在关联方不持有巴西主体所有者权益的情况下不适用）。

⑤ 避免双重征税协定

巴西目前与 29 个国家和地区签订了《避免双重征税协定》。尽管巴西不是经济发展与合作组织的成员，但巴西签署的《避免双重征税协定》在很大程度上与签订时生效的经济发展与合作组织及联合国《避免双重征税协定》的模板是一致的。

巴西与中国签订的《避免双重征税协议》涵盖了包括如下收入在内的多项内容：

- 利息。利息的支付需在支付国缴纳最高不超过 15% 的预提税。
- 股息。股息的支付需在支付国缴纳最高不超过 15% 的预提税。巴西居民支付的股息不需缴纳预提税。
- 版税。版税须缴纳的预提税不得超过 25%（商标权在工业或商业领域的使用或使用权）或 15%（其他情形）。版税的概念适用于与技术协助或技术服务相关的款项支付。
- 资本收益。资本收益在双方国家均需纳税，且没有最高上限。
- 避免双重征税的方式。巴西与中国签订的《避免双重征税协议》采用了抵补机制来避免双重征税。

3. 税务申报和特别待遇

巴西纳税人必须提交强制的纳税申报表，是对税务机关的辅助义务。联邦政府的纳税申报表包括[③]：

巴西联邦纳税申报表	
纳税申报表	描述
税务账簿	公司必须提交税务账簿以向税务机关提供所有影响公司所得税和法人盈利税计算基础的交易信息。
联邦税务借贷申报表	该表必须包含每个月的缴纳的税金和其他费用信息。

---

① 由巴西中央银行不时公布。
② 适用于巴西金融和资本市场的具体规则。
③ 各州和各市可能提出其他附带义务。

（续表）

巴西联邦纳税申报表	
纳税申报表	描述
税务账簿——缴费部分	该表必须包含公司缴纳社会一体化税/"社会资助"特别税以及社会保障金的信息。
电子税务账簿	该表是法人主体税务审计的记录，替代了原有的纸质审计簿，包括记账分录、总账以及资产负债日报。

（九）证券

1. 证券相关法律、法规简介

巴西规范证券关系的主要成文法是 1976 年 12 月 7 日修改的第 6385 号法（《证券法》）。巴西证券委员会依据《证券法》设立，《证券法》对证券公开发行、证券上市交易、信息披露要求、中介、中介机构以及中间商的行为、可交易证券种类以及可以公开发行股票的公司类型等证券市场的整体运行进行管理。巴西《公司法》也包含巴西证券市场管理的相关规定。

2. 证券市场的监督和管理

根据《证券法》的规定，巴西证券委员会负责巴西证券市场的监督和管理。

通常而言，在巴西进行公开发行要先根据 2003 年 12 月 29 日修改的巴西证券委员会第 400 号令在巴西证券委员会进行登记，但是根据 2009 年 1 月 16 日修改的巴西证券委员会第 476 号令的规定，限制承销方式的特定类型股票的公开发行不需要提前登记（面向不超过 75 位专业投资者发行，条件是仅限 50 个专业投资人认购或购买相应股票）。

根据《证券法》的规定，下列资产被视为证券：

① 股票、债券和认股权证；
② 证券认购券、前述证券的权利、收据和证书；
③ 证券存款凭证；
④ 债券证书；
⑤ 互惠基金或任何投资俱乐部的份额；
⑥ 商业票据；
⑦ 基于证券资产品的衍生品交易合同；
⑧ 基于任何产品的衍生品交易合同；
⑨ 向公众开放，提供参与权、合伙身份或薪酬（包括提供服务所得、管理行为所得或第三方行为所得）的集合投资合同。

上述定义并非采用物权法定原则，巴西证券委员会通常运用类比原则以便对其他具有证券性质的产品进行管理，并对投资者和巴西市场加以总体保护。

巴西目前使用的公开募集概念（包括巴西证券委员会通过法律部制定的多个意见所体现的概念）主要采用的是世界上其他主要国家所采用的定义（即公开发行针对不特定人群，而非特定人群，例如发行人的股东或属于专业人士或合格的投资群体）。

值得一提的是，根据巴西证券委员会第 400 号令及其法律部 2005 年 9 月 30 日作出的第 32 号法令的规定，巴西证券委员会认为互联网属于与电视或报纸相似的大众传媒工具，可用于推广证券发行。巴西证券委员会这一立场与国际证券事务监察委员会组织（IOSCO）的指导意见相一致。后者的指导意见认为证券监管的基本原则不因相关传播工具的改变而改变。因此，利用互联网将证券（包括海外发行的证券）提供给巴西居民，构成证券的公开发行（因此要求向巴西证券委员会进行预先登记），除非网站的主办者利用特殊程序对巴西普通公众认购证券进行限制。

3. 外国企业参与证券交易的要求

参见"投资形式"部分的内容。

(十)优惠待遇及投资保护

1. 优惠政策的结构

通常而言,巴西没有优惠待遇政策。然而如上述"市场准入和检验标准"部分所述,某些行为只能由巴西政府或巴西政府控制的公司来实施,或必须事先取得巴西政府的授权或许可。

此外,如下文所述,巴西政府可能会采取某些税收激励措施。

2. 对特定行业和特定地区的扶持

巴西实行税收激励措施,如降低收入税、进口税、工业产品税、流通税等。通常是为了降低零件、设备、船舶等的进口和生产成本。还有与巴西基础建设(能源和交通等)、港口现代化、石油天然气行业开发、半导体生产以及IT产业发展相关的税收激励措施。

3. 经济特区

(1)亚马逊地区和自由贸易区

亚马逊地区享有更多的巴西联邦税收优惠,因为巴西《联邦宪法》规定了联邦政府有义务促进此地区的发展。已施行的税收优惠包括公司所得税、关税、工业产品税、社会一体化税和"社会资助"特别税的减免政策,而且仅适用于亚马逊地区的特定地域。

亚马逊发展管理局(SUDAM)负责上述税收优惠的管理。税收优惠可适用于亚马逊地区或西亚马逊地区设立的、根据现行法律要求享受税收优惠的适格公司,此类公司可根据开发利润、固定资产加速折旧和免税额计算的企业所得税享受高达75%的减免。

玛瑙斯自由贸易区管理局负责的税收优惠适用于在玛瑙斯自由贸易区设立的公司,税收优惠根据现行法律的要求予以适用,主要包括对进口到该区域用于生产的产品的关税减免、工业产品税和社会一体化税/"社会资助"特别税的免除,前提是享受该优惠政策的公司满足立法要求的最低工业流程。

关于流通税,输入至玛瑙斯自由贸易区用于商业化或生产的国内产品可以根据一份《流通税协定》免除流通税,亚马逊州也可根据此《流通税协定》给予买方一定流通税减免额度。

(2)东北地区

东北地区和米纳斯吉拉斯州和圣埃斯皮里图州的欠发达市的发展也被列入政府的经济计划当中。因此在这些地区设立的公司也享受一些税收优惠,由东北发展管理局(SUDENE)负责上述税收优惠的管理。

可享受的税收优惠包括对根据开发利润、固定资产加速折旧和免税额计算的公司所得税高达75%的减免。

4. 投资保护

根据第4131号法律的规定,外国投资者应与本国投资者享有同等待遇,不允许对外国投资者给予任何歧视待遇。1995年巴西国会还通过了一则巴西《联邦宪法修正案》,目的是消除外国资本和本国资本的差别待遇。

巴西还是多个双边和多边投资计划以及投资协定的成员国。巴西与中国之间的外交关系请参阅"一、(二)"部分的内容。

三、贸易

(一)贸易监管部门

国内和国外贸易的政策由工业及外贸服务部(MDIC)来管理,该部由多个秘书处组成,包括工业发展与竞争处(SDCI)、外贸处(SECEX)以及贸易服务处(SCS)。

(二)贸易法律法规简介

工业及外贸服务部会签发(或建议总统签发)规范性文件,目的是鼓励或抑制在巴西的投资和/或产品贸易,需考虑的因素有贸易平衡(出口交易以及进口交易)以及国内行业的发展策略。

工业及外贸服务部签发的大多数规范性文件对相关的进口交易、出口交易、进出口交易的流程进行了规定，第 23/2011 号外贸处法令对其进行了列举。

（三）贸易管理

巴西贸易管理主要由前述几个秘书处与财政部和总统联合管理。

总体而言，巴西贸易管理的目标是发展和保护国内产业，但有时会采取一些受到世界贸易组织中其他国家挑战的发展保护措施和机制。

（四）进口出口商品的检验检疫

除了工业及外贸服务部制定的贸易政策，其他部门也可能对商品的进口及出口进行审查，主要是农业畜牧及供应部（MAPA）和矿产能源部（MME），通常会确定记录产品／进出口主体的预先登记情况。

（五）海关监管

1. 总体情况

目前所有巴西进出口产品都需要在抵达巴西关税边界或出口装船前向巴西联邦税务局进行清关。清关流程第一步就是向外贸综合管理系统（SISCOMEX）进行相关进口或出口登记。

外贸综合管理系统是用于向监管进口的巴西外贸部、巴西中央银行和巴西联邦税务局汇报相关数据的信息科技系统。

进口商向巴西联邦税务局提交了申请并在确认符合相关法规要求后（即取得进出口许可证），便可进入外贸综合管理系统进行登记。进出口许可证分为以下几种，以授权公司进行不同的进口和出口业务：

① 限制性进出口许可证：仅限于进行小额对外贸易的公司；
② 非限制性进出口许可证：用于进行常规性进出口交易并具有良好经济实力的进出口商；
③ 专用进出口许可证：颁发给特定公司使用。

巴西联邦税务局会根据公司在提交申请前 5 年内的纳税情况来决定公司的进出口资质。

2. 进口许可

根据巴西法律规定，自动许可或特定种类产品适用的非自动许可的必要性。

此外，目前尚允许将二手产品进口到巴西，这通常属于非自动许可证类别，只有非巴西制造的产品或不能由其他类似产品替代时方可进口。临时特许进口的情况下，也是可以进口二手产品的。

3. 海关估价

进口税的税基为报关金额，而报关金额则需依据海关估价协议确定。根据《海关估价协议》，报关金额应当主要依据与正常市场交易价格相当的交易价格，加上进口交易的相关金额（可能由各进口国根据协定进行限定）。

四、劳动

（一）《劳动法》简要介绍

巴西国民的雇佣关系主要由巴西《联邦宪法》制定的规则和原则、1943 年 5 月 1 日的巴西《劳动法》（第 5452 号法律）、巴西劳动部签发的规范性文件、其他劳动及雇用方面的具体法规以及适用于各具体劳动类别的集体劳资协议和巴西判例法规范。

巴西《劳动法》受 2017 年 7 月 13 日第 13467 号法（《劳动与雇佣改革法》）的更新调整。《劳动与雇佣改革法》在 2017 年 11 月 11 日生效，对现行巴西《劳动法》进行了几项重大改变。其中较为值得注意的变化是：将假期拆分为最多三个时间段的权利；同工同酬规则的变化；工作时长及其抵消的新规则；在家办公的新规则；收取工会费的规则变化；终止雇佣关系的新规则；双方解约的新规则；群体解约的新规则。

（二）雇用外籍员工的要求

巴西实体雇用外籍人士主要由 2017 年 5 月 24 日的第 13445 号法律、2017 年 11 月 20 日的第 9199 号法令以及劳工部移民局制定的多个规范性文件以及在特定情况下也受巴西《劳动法》的规范。

根据进行的活动类型不同，在巴西的外籍人士需要申请的签证类型也不同。总之，最常见的是临时签证，该签证允许外籍人士被雇用为管理人员、经理、董事和普通雇员。

（1）管理人员、经理、董事的临时签证

被巴西的公司任命为代表巴西公司、履行管理职责和／或进行公司决策的管理人员、经理或董事的外籍人士可以取得临时签证。

巴西公司必须提供如下证明以便为外籍人士取得临时签证：该巴西实体或海外公司已作出不低于 15 万雷亚尔的投资，而且巴西实体成立后或该外籍管理人员或董事到达巴西后 2 年内该主体至少已创造 10 个新的工作机会；或者该巴西实体或海外公司已经作出不低于 60 万雷亚尔的投资。每个欲取得临时签证的外籍人士均需提供投资证明，而且该外国人必须是在该巴西公司里担任法定管理职务。

（2）外籍普通雇员的临时签证

如果公司想将外籍员工调到巴西生活并工作一段时间，可以为他们申请临时签证。此时需提供外籍员工与巴西公司签署的书面雇佣合同，而且该外籍员工不可担任该巴西公司的法定代表人。作为雇员，外籍人士可以享有巴西劳动法律规定的所有权利。通常此类临时签证的期限最长为 2 年。

签证申请流程根据签证类型的不同有所不同，但都必须是由欲聘用外籍人士的巴西公司来提交申请。

在巴西工作的所有雇员和法定的管理人员（包括外籍人士）都必须受到巴西社会保障局（INSS）的管理。

巴西社会保障局旨在保障与病假（无论是否由工作引起的疾病）、产假、永久残疾、退休和死亡相关的社会福利。

（三）出入境

1. 签证类型

除适用于到巴西工作的外籍人士的签证外，外籍人士也可持有旅游或商务签证进入巴西领土。

根据规定，不时进入巴西领土的外籍人士必须在进入该国家之前取得合适的签证。在巴西，旅游及商务签证亦受 2017 年 5 月 24 日第 13445 号法律及 2017 年 11 月 20 日第 9199 号法律之规范。

对于为旅游或探亲访友之目的（不涉及任何类型的工作或薪酬支付）而进入巴西的人士，巴西将签发旅游签证。

为方便外籍人士前往巴西担任外国公司的代表，开展业务联络，开展工作面试，参加商业相关展览会，代表会及会议，寻找商业机会，签署合同及开展审计或咨询活动，巴西会向外籍人士签发商务签证。除其他业务相关活动外，商务签证的持证人可推广某些外国产品，除了其他与商业有关的活动外，还可开展与巴西市场有关的研究和评估活动。尽管旅游签证的持证人不得进行商业活动，但商务签证的持证人可以进行旅游签证允许的娱乐活动。

除需要提交位于外籍人士母国的当地巴西领事馆对于申请旅游或商务签证所要求的常见文件外，巴西无其他特别要求。

2. 出入境限制

旅游及商务签证允许外籍人士在巴西停留的时间最长达 90 天，总天数可延长到 180 天（在外籍人士首次进入巴西领土后的 12 个月内），这一规定依外籍人士国籍而有所不同。

（四）工会及劳工组织

巴西《联邦宪法》规定雇主及雇员可为捍卫经济及／或专业权益而自由结社。它专门规定了雇主及雇员必须根据其地点及主要活动类型由一个工会作为代表，即工会强制性代表各方，无论其隶属关系如何。

公司及雇员可自愿向其各自的工会支付会费。

(五) 劳动争议

通常情况下,劳动法院有两个审级:初级法院及上诉法院。巴西还设有特别上诉法院:高等劳动法院及最高法院,这些法院均具有审理特定诉求的权利(比如因超出地区劳动法院管辖权的集体劳动协议而产生的诉求、缺乏管辖权的抗辩理由及违反宪法条款的行为)。

因个体劳动关系而产生的劳动诉讼通常在初级法院提起。但是,针对一些特别的诉求(比如因集体劳动协议而产生的诉求)可直接在上诉法院提起诉讼。

提起劳动诉讼的诉讼时效为自劳动关系终止之日起 2 年,劳动者可对诉讼开始前 5 年[①]的薪酬提出请求。

根据规定,仲裁程序对雇员及雇主不具有约束力。这是因为劳动法院有权审理劳动相关争议。但是,自 2017 年 11 月起,《劳动与就业改革法》的规定,在持有高等教育学位且月工资达到或超过 11 291.60[②] 雷亚尔的员工同意仲裁条款的情况下,仲裁条款具有约束力。

五、知识产权

(一) 知识产权法律、法规简介

通常情况下,根据相关法律的规定,巴西法律将知识产权分为著作权(包括软件)、工业产权(包括发明专利及实用新型专利、工业设计、集成电路布图设计及特有标识和商标、地理标志、公司名称及商号、互联网域名及掩膜作品)及新品种。

在巴西,规范知识产权的主要联邦法律有:

① 1996 年 5 月 14 日《工业产权法》(第 9279 号法律),该法律为商标、专利、实用新型、工业设计、地理标志、技术转让及反不正当竞争行为设立的法律框架;

② 1998 年 2 月 19 日《著作权法》(第 9610 号法律),该法律规定了著作权及相关权利应享有的保护;

③ 1998 年 2 月 19 日《软件法》(第 9609 号法律),该法律规定了软件保护的法律框架;

④ 1997 年 4 月 25 日《品种权保护法》(第 9456 号法律),该法律规定了对新品种的保护及相关权利和义务;及

⑤ 2007 年 5 月 31 日《集成电路布图设计保护法》(第 11484 号法律),该法律规定了对集成电路布图设计的保护。

除《与贸易有关的知识产权协定》外,巴西已签署并批准了其他一些关于知识产权的主要国际条约,包括:

① 1883 年《保护工业产权巴黎公约》(并于 1967 年在斯德哥尔摩进行了修订),它旨在保护工业产权;

② 1886 年《保护文学和艺术作品伯尔尼公约》(并于 1971 年进行了修订),它规定了文学及艺术作品受到的著作权保护;

③ 1961 年《保护表演者、音像制品作者和广播组织罗马公约》,它为表演者、其他艺术家、录音制品制作者和广播组织提供了保护;

④《专利合作协定》。

无论是否进行了登记,著作权及软件均会得到保护。但是,工业产权及新品种必须在主管机关进行登记,才能得到保护。在巴西,巴西专利及商标局(INPI)是负责完善、宣传及管理巴西工业知识产权授予及保证体系的联邦政府自治机构,其负责对商标、专利、工业设计、地理标志、软件和集成电路布图设计,以及因商标及专利许可协议、技术转让(即专有技术和技术协助服务)和特许协议而

---

① The statute of limitations for filing a labour lawsuit is of two years as from the termination of the employment, reaching instalments of the last five years prior to the filing of the lawsuit.

② 该金额在 2018 年有效。随着巴西一般社会保障计划所支付福利的增加,该金额可能会逐年增加。

产生的其他权利进行登记,使这些权利能够对抗第三方。对于新品种权,主管登记机关为国家新品种保护署(SNPC),其为巴西农业部下属的机构。

(二)专利申请

专利系指对发明或实用新型暂时享有的权利,由巴西专利及商标局向发明人、作者或对该等创造持有权利的其他个人或法律实体授予。相应地,发明人应详细披露受专利保护的事项的完整技术内容。专利可分为:

①发明,指符合非显而易见性、绝对新颖性及工业实用性的产品或工艺,保护期为20年,从申请之日起算;

②实用新型,指具有工业实用性和实际用途的物品或该等物品的一部分,且具有新的形式或构造,具有创造性,引发使用或生产上的功能改进,实用新型的保护期为15年,自申请之日起算。

(三)商标登记

在巴西,商标分为四类:文字商标(仅由文字构成的符号或文字及/或数字的组合,非虚幻的外观)、图案商标(由图样、图像、一般样式构成的符号)、组合商标(文字及图形)及三维商标(产品的独特外形)。

根据商标的性质可以分为产品商标(对产品与其他相同、类似或相关产品进行区分)、服务商标(对服务与其他相同、类似或相关服务进行区分)、集体商标(识别由某个集团或实体的成员提供的产品或服务)及证明商标(证明产品或服务符合某些规则或技术规格)。

值得注意的是巴西未采纳"一标多类"商标申请制度。相应地,商标注册仅对应一类特定的服务或产品。巴西于2000年采用了《商标注册用商品和服务国际分类》(尼斯分类),对商品和服务的分类依此进行。

巴西专利及商标局签发的商标注册证书有效期为10年,期满可续展。在该注册有效期的最后一年,相应的商标持有人应向巴西专利及商标局支付商标续展注册费,以便将商标保护续展10年。与其他一些国家的规则不同,除缴纳相应费用外,巴西的商标续展无其他特定程序。若注册商标的持有人未能在法定期间内缴纳续展商标注册费,商标保护期将届满,该商标持有人将不再享有独家使用该商标的权利。

(四)知识产权保护措施

上述关于知识产权的巴西联邦法律还规定了知识产权保护措施。为此,《工业产权法》及《软件法》列出了被认定为针对知识产权的犯罪行为,如未经知识产权所有人同意,制造受专利或工业设计保护的产品;未经所有权人同意,复制或模仿注册商标;侵犯软件著作权及其他。

最后,在2004年10月,巴西通过司法部行政秘书处设立了国际打击盗版和侵犯知识产权犯罪委员会(CNCP)。国际打击盗版和侵犯知识产权犯罪委员会是一个集体咨询机构,是司法部基本架构的一部分,旨在为制订和提出打击盗版、盗版导致的逃税及知识产权相关犯罪活动的全国计划提供指引。国际打击盗版和侵犯知识产权犯罪委员会提出的打击盗版的倡议集中在三个优先行动领域:制止、教育及经济处罚。

六、环境保护

(一)监督环境保护的部门

根据巴西《联邦宪法》第24条的规定,联邦及各州政府同时具有就环境问题制定法律法规的权力,这意味着联邦政府有权制定总体原则及指导方针,而各州可对其加以补充并予以实施。各州可制定比联邦政府所制定法律更严格的法律。此外,各州有权就联邦法律尚未涉及的具体环境问题颁布法律。但是,在为应对该问题制定联邦法律时,各州法律中与联邦法律不一致的条款将被撤销。相应地,各市政当局有权在可能的情况下,为联邦及各州法律提供补充,依据巴西《联邦宪法》第30条之规定，制定符合本地利益的法律。

经修订的 1981 年 8 月 31 日第 6938 号法确立了巴西环境政策并建立了全国环境体系，它由有权保护环境的环境机关组成，比如：

① 环境部，它具有就全国政策及指导方针向总统提出建议的责任；
② 全国环境委员会，作为咨询及监管机关；
③ 巴西环境与可再生资源署以及奇科门德斯生物多样性保护研究所，它有权实施及执行国家政策及政府方针；
④ 地区机构，比如各州的环境机关；
⑤ 本地机构，比如本地环境机关。

根据第 140/2011 号补充法的规定，联邦环境机关巴西环境与可再生资源署根据不同地区及企业性质（例如经营核电站、水电站等），负责许可事宜。市级环境机关负责对有地方影响的企业和行为发放许可，而各州环境机关对联邦或市级机关未涉及的企业和活动的环境许可程序具有一般管辖权。

环境机关还有权评估和执行对环境行政违法行为的处罚。根据第 140/2011 号补充法令的规定，授权机关作出的处罚优先于其他机关作出的处罚。此外，联邦及各州检察官办公室负责监督遵守环境法规的情况，并寻求恢复、修复和补偿环境损害。在构成犯罪时，警方有权开展调查并向检察官提供关于最终发生的环境犯罪的证据，因此扮演着重要角色。

（二）环境保护法律、法规简介

巴西《联邦宪法》第 225 条规定了当前及下一代维护环境的责任，根据该法的规定，无论是个人或法律实体，违法犯罪者均将面临刑事及行政处罚，该法还规定了修复环境损害的义务。

《巴西环境政策》旨在维护、改善及恢复环境质量，以确保社会经济的发展、国家安全利益及人权保护。这些规则还确定了上述负责环境保护的机关及其落实环境保护政策的工具（比如环境许可），并界定了环境损害的民事责任。

环境许可程序在联邦层面受第 6938 号法律、1997 年 12 月 19 日第 237 号决议、1986 年 1 月 23 日第 01 号决议之规范，它们均由全国环境委员会起草制定。总的来说，环境许可程序由一个三阶段体系构成，其中的每项许可均以前一项许可的签发为前提，具体如下：基础许可；安装许可；运营许可。此外，2015 年 3 月 24 日第 60 号跨部委命令确立了在巴西环境与可再生资源署执行的环境许可程序中，国家土著基金会（FUNAI）、国家历史及艺术遗产署（IPHAN）及 / 或帕尔马里斯文化基金会（FCP）介入的行政程序。

固体废弃物的管理受 2010 年 8 月 2 日第 12305 号法律及 2010 年 12 月 23 日第 7404 号令所确立的巴西《固体残渣全国政策》规范。此外，在各州及地方层面，还有多项适用于固体废弃物的具体标准。

水资源的使用受 1997 年 1 月 8 日巴西《水资源政策》（第 9433 号法律，该法律建立了巴西水资源体系）及 1934 年 7 月 10 日《水法典》（第 24643 号令）监管。

对于受特别保护的区域，受 2002 年 8 月 22 日第 4340 号令约束的 2000 年 7 月 18 日第 9985 号法律确立了全国保护区体系，为保护区的设立、运行及管理设立了准则及标准。保护区被视为绿色区域，根据保护制度的规定，保护区分为两组：全面保护区；可持续使用区。这些分组涵盖了 12 类保护区，每类均具有自身的特点。

根据 2012 年 5 月 25 日巴西《森林法典》（第 12651 号法律）的规定，某些被称作永久保护区的地区由于其在水资源维护、生态稳定性维持、生物多样性保护及水土流失控制方面的重要性将受到特别的法律保护。根据巴西《森林法典》的规定每个乡村物业均应保留最低比例的本地植被作为法定储备，以确保可持续使用自然资源，维护生物多样性，并保护本土动植物群。

2006 年 12 月 22 日第 11428 号法律及 2008 年 11 月 21 日第 6600 号令规定了对近大西洋的森林植被进行的特别法律保护。受 2008 年 11 月 7 日第 6640 号令规范的 1990 年 10 月 1 日第 99556 号法律规定了对巴西天然洞穴进行的特别保护，这些洞穴可分为如下保护级别：低级、中级、高级以及最大级。

受 2010 年 12 月 9 日第 7390 号令规范的 2009 年 12 月 29 日第 12187 号法律制定了国家气候变化政策，包括辅助实现其目标的指引及机制。

最后，值得注意的是，1998年2月12日《环境犯罪法》（第9605号法律）规定了对有害环境之行为采取的刑事及行政制裁措施，2008年7月22日第6514号法律规定了行政环境违法行为及相应的处罚。

（三）环境保护评估

在巴西，环境机关及检察官均承担着执行环境法律的主要责任。

环境机关有权评估和执行对环境行政违法行为作出的处罚。根据2008年7月22日第6514号令的规定，违反使用、享用、维护、保护及恢复环境有关的法律规则的行为或不作为均应视为违反行政规定的行为或违法行为。违规者可能面临行政处罚，比如罚款、禁运及中止活动。请注意，即便在理论上仅对实施此违法行为的人士处以行政处罚，环境机关通常也会将严格责任的概念沿用到行政领域。

此外，联邦及各州检察官办公室有保护环境的职责，且在环境问题上要求十分严格。因此，在有证据表明环境面临威胁或环境许可的程序或环境法规被违反时，巴西检察官办公室通常会对企业及授权机关提起民事公益诉讼。通常民事公益诉讼会申请禁止令，这就涉及环境许可的中止，中止决定将持到作出最终裁决，因此项目开支及期限可能受到影响。

巴西环境政策规定了环境民事责任，该政策规定的环境民事责任为严格责任（无论是否有过错），这意味着仅证明损害与相关行为之间的因果关系就足以引发弥补环境损害的义务。

对此，提及揭开公司面纱理论十分重要，这意味着股东可能会承担环境损害责任。在公司的存在危害环境损害的恢复或构成原环境条件之适当补偿或补救的阻碍时，该理论可能适用。相应地，除了不当利用法人主体的责任之外，公司的股东可能会被认定应该对公司导致的环境损害承担补偿责任，且其私人财产可能被用于恢复环境损害。

最后，《环境犯罪法》规定了刑事责任，根据该法律的规定，当某些环境违法行为被认定为犯罪时，无论是个人或法律实体都将可能会承担环境刑事责任。刑事责任与过错或故意的认定有关。

七、争议解决

首先，正如上文"政治"部分所阐述的，巴西是由26个州及一个联邦区组成的联邦共和国，所有州及联邦区均为联邦司法体系的一部分。此外，正如上文"法律环境"部分所提及的，在争议解决上，巴西沿袭大陆法系，讲求合法性原则，以成文法为主要法律渊源。

（一）争议解决方法及机构

1. 司法程序

在巴西，司法途径是常规的争议解决方式。巴西司法体系由联邦及州法院构成，分为普通管辖和特别管辖。依据争议对象不同，初级法院分为州法院和联邦法院，具体职责分工如下：

① 州法院有权裁决所有事项，但不影响联邦政府权益的事项及与劳动、选举及军事法院无关的事项除外；
② 联邦法官裁决涉及联邦政府权益的所有事项；
③ 劳动法官裁决因劳动关系而产生的争议；
④ 选举法官裁决因《选举法》而产生的争议；
⑤ 联邦及州军事法官裁决与武装力量（比如陆军及海军）有关的争议。

上诉权受巴西《联邦宪法》保障，且上述初级法院均有对应的上诉法院，分别为：
① 上诉法院；
② 联邦地区法院；
③ 地区劳动法院；
④ 地区选举法院；
⑤ 军事法院。

此外，巴西法院还有特别审程序，适用于巴西全境范围内，相关当事人可在法律规定的有限具体情况下提起上诉：
①高等法院；
②高等劳动法院；
③高等选举法院；
④高等军事法院。

最后，巴西还设有联邦最高法院，该法院对所有宪法相关问题作出最终裁决。

巴西还设有负责设立巴西司法体系指引及架构的行政机关，即全国司法委员会。

巴西法院仅对巴西境内的纠纷进行裁判，或其中一名被告永久居住在巴西；争议的其中一项义务必须在巴西领土内履行；产生争议的事实发生在巴西境内；与位于巴西境内的房地产有关的争议；遗产位于巴西。

2. 行政程序

巴西未设立行政司法权，司法权仅由法官享有。但是，公共机关可设立内部行政程序，当事人可向公共机关提交争议。行政程序仅对公共机关具有约束力，私人可随后向司法机关提出异议。

3. 仲裁

1996年9月23日巴西《仲裁法》（第9307号法律）明确了在巴西领土内与仲裁有关的所有事项。仲裁允许当事人在各州法院之外解决争议，但仅适用于与可自由转让的财产权利有关的争议，比如合同争议。与法庭程序相比，仲裁具有如下优势：更迅速，可在保密状态下进行，且允许当事人指定专业仲裁员解决争议。对于涉及可自由转让财产权利的争议，公共部门也可约定使用仲裁，并参与仲裁程序。

巴西《仲裁法》的规定的主要概念与联合国国际贸易法委员会《国际商事仲裁示范法》类似，并可概括如下：

①仲裁协议约束各方只能向仲裁庭而非各州法院提交争议；
②在仲裁员接受指定时，仲裁程序视为开始；
③仲裁裁决对各方的效力如同由法院作出的决定，并具有法律执行力。仲裁裁决不得上诉，且一旦在巴西作出，无须法院认可；
④外国仲裁裁决（及外国司法判决）的执行由巴西高等法院决定，并适用1958年《承认及执行外国仲裁裁决公约》的相关规定。

此外，在股份公司的章程细则中纳入仲裁条款对所有股东具有约束力，并确保异议股东有权在按股份价值获得补偿后从公司退出。但是，股东若在章程细则中纳入仲裁条款后加入公司，应视为股东同意将争议提交仲裁。

4. 调解及协商

根据2015年6月26日第13140号法律的规定，若争议双方达成一致，调解则具有约束力。在处理多层次争议解决条款时这一点很重要。若各方未就争议问题达成和解，所有披露信息及让步条件均不得在后续诉讼中使用。调解或协商中的和解具有约束力，并可由法官执行。

调解被视作协助各方创造性解决争议问题的工具，正在快速发展。各方可在仲裁前以及法院司法制度中进行调解。巴西设立了专门的调解及协商中心，使各方可聘用专业人士协助其进行调解。

（二）法律适用

巴西《联邦宪法》确立了关于行政、司法及立法机关的总体原则。它规定了巴西联邦共和国由联邦政府、各州和联邦区、市构成。根据这种划分，这些主体的立法被划分为联邦法律、各州及联邦区法律（联邦区包含各州及市级法律）、市级法律，所有这些法律均可在其管辖范围内执行。

《联邦宪法》还确立了每个实体的权力范围。一些事项仅可由联邦进行立法（比如刑法）。一些事项可共享立法权力，比如税法。但是，即便权力共享，法律限制了管辖范围，且法律之间不得彼此冲突。

由于巴西沿用大陆法系传统，法官严格地运用法律。先例不具有约束力，但可用于协助法官解释法律，填补空白。法官应当适用法律，但也可考虑法律的次级来源，比如原则、法律的宗旨、宪法或类推。

高等法院（裁决与联邦法律有关的法律事项）及联邦最高法院（裁决与宪法有关的所有事项）承担着协调法律解释及宪法解释原则的职责，并根据法律及宪法确立的内容，解释和发布相互间不冲突的裁决。

八、其他

（一）反商业贿赂

1. 反商业贿赂法律、法规简介

巴西未专门针对私人商业贿赂制定法规。[①]在另一方面，巴西制定了一系列反公共腐败的法律，根据这些法律的规定，个人及法律实体均可能因公司腐败行为承担责任。

在个人可能因腐败行为承担民事及刑事责任[②]的同时（根据《刑法典》第333条），腐败行为还可能导致法律实体需要承担责任。上述责任可能由个人行为（导致可诉民事后果及法庭职权以外的后果，比如合同终止）引起或基于存在竞合的不同反腐败法律的制裁。这些责任在行政或民事领域由不同的法律规范确立，会导致不同的制裁后果，涉及多个执法机关。

因此，对于涉及公共腐败的非法行为，多种不同的法律可能同时适用。在此领域最重要的法律是2013年8月1日巴西《廉洁公司法》（第12846号法律），该法律自2014年1月29日生效，适用于发生在该日期之后的违法行为。

巴西《廉洁公司法》基于严格责任设立了一个责任体系，据此，无论是否存在过错、故意的不当行为或知悉不当行为的证据，该行为均可能被认定为犯罪。的确，根据巴西《廉洁公司法》设立的体系，原则上，给予被调查公司的一项好处原则上足以引发对公司违法责任的认定，甚至使其对第三方以公司名义实施的行为承担责任。此外，该法律还规定了关联企业、子公司、控股公司或母公司，甚至联合体成员的共同责任。

此外，巴西《廉洁公司法》不仅适用于贿赂公务人员的行为，它还列出了五种潜在的违法行为：
① 向公务人员或与其有关的第三方直接或间接承诺、提议或提供任何不正当利益；
② 资助、赞助或以任何方式补贴针对公共管理的非法行为；
③ 使用中介（个人或法律实体）隐藏或掩盖真实利益或所开展行为之受益人的身份；
④ 对公开招标及合同，进行阻挠、诈骗、阻碍或干扰公开招标程序及影响其竞争性的，操纵或骗取公共机构的经济合同余额的；
⑤ 阻碍公共机关、机构或人员的调查评估活动，干扰其工作，包括监管机关及全国金融体系监督机构相应范围内的活动。

2. 反商业贿赂的监督部门

负责执行个人制裁的公共机构为检察官办公室。

联邦层面负责巴西《廉洁公司法》制定的机关是透明、监管及内部控制部。但是，根据受不法活动影响的公共机构的不同，行政、立法或执法各机构的最高权力机构也可能参与执法程序，取决于受不法活动影响的政府官员服务的机构的不同。

3. 处罚

下表总结了对单独或同时适用于参与公共腐败行为的法律实体或个人的法律处罚的法律规范：

---

① 原则上，商业贿赂行为可能构成1940年12月7日《刑法典》（第2848号法）第171条中的欺诈，个人将因"通过任何类型的欺诈，引起误解或对第三方进行误导，从而为自身或他人获取非法利益，并因此导致第三方遭受损失"而构成犯罪。此外，关于个人根据1986年6月16日第7492号法第4条的规定，仅对金融机构而言，欺诈管理构成犯罪。依据《工业产权法》第195条Ⅲ的规定，若欺诈旨在使客户脱离其他公司，个人也可能受到处罚。

② 在巴西，公司可能仅就某些环境问题承担刑事责任。

法律基础	活动类型	潜在执法者	法律实体可能面临的处罚
巴西《民法典》	针对法律实体及个人的民事损害赔偿诉讼。	受害实体及检察官办公室均可向相应的民事法院申请启动诉讼。	向公共部门支付损害赔偿
1992年6月2日《反不诚信法》（第8429号法）	针对法律实体及个人的民事不诚信诉讼。	受害实体及检察官办公室均可向相应的民事法院申请启动诉讼。	没收非法获得的资产或款项；支付民事罚款，金额最高可达所获取利益或所造成损失的3倍；禁止与公共行政机关缔结新合同或获得税务或信贷优惠或激励措施，即便是通过其为主要合伙人的法律实体，禁止期限最长可达10年。
巴西《廉洁公司法》	巴西《廉洁公司法》中仅针对法律实体的民事程序。	受害实体及检察官办公室均可向相应的民事法院申请启动诉讼。	丧失权利、财产和价值，价值相当于从不法行为中获得的直接或间接优势或利益，但受损害方或第三方的善意权利除外；终止或部分禁止其活动；强制解散法律实体；禁止其从公共实体及公共金融机构或公权力控制的金融机构中获得奖励、补贴、捐赠或贷款，期间为1到5年。
巴西《廉洁公司法》	巴西《廉洁公司法》中仅针对法律实体的行政程序。	受害实体及其他机关，比如相应的内部控制办公室（比如对于涉及联邦行政机关的诉讼），透明、监管及内部控制部可依职权启动调查。	罚款、公开谴责。
《公共招标法》及其他公开采购法律及合同	《公共招标法》及特许权法项下的行政责任诉讼，大多针对法律实体。	受害实体及其他机构可依职权启动调查。	警告、罚款，中止其参与竞标程序并禁止其与公共行政机关缔结合同，期限最长为2年；宣布丧失竞标或与公共行政机关缔结合同的资格。
1992年7月16日《联邦审计法院组织法》（第8443号法律）	《联邦审计法院组织法》项下的行政责任诉讼，大多针对法律实体。	联邦审计法院可依职权启动调查。	取消其参与联邦公共行政机关竞标的资格，期限最长为5年。
1990年12月27日《竞争法》（第8137号法令）	针对法律实体的行政责任（该法律包含了针对个人刑事责任的条款）。	巴西保护经济行政委员会。	罚款、公开处罚、取消其获得官方融资及参与竞标的资格；在国家消费者保护登记处进行登记；通知管理知识产权及税务问题的公共机关；公司剥离、转让控制权、出售资产或部分中止活动；禁止自行或代替他人开展贸易活动；为消除对经济秩序的有害影响而需要采取的其他行动或措施。

（二）项目承包

1. 许可体系

在巴西，政府外包应在1993年6月21日《公共招标法》（第8666号法律）、1995年2月13日《特许权法》（第8987号法律）、2004年12月30日《公私合营企业法》（第11079号法律）、2016年6月30日《国有企业法》（第13303号法）及2011年8月4日《公共外包区分制度法》（第12462号法律）所设立的法律框架下开展。

《公共招标法》在公共行政部门范围内对为建设、服务、购买、出售及租赁行为而开展的拍卖和缔约活动进行监管。所有该等合同均以拍卖程序为前置条件。2002年7月17日第10520号法律（《反向拍卖法》）及各州和市级立法为其规定了补充规则。

《特许权法》监管常见的特许权，即公共行政部门经拍卖程序将公共服务或资产的开发权转移给私营部门，或从私营部门获得公共服务或资产。根据《特许权法》的规定，政府可通过合同将某些公共服务或公共工程交给私营部门来经营，在此过程中，特许权人对项目的实施及融资承担全部责任（若适用），并在特许权协议的期间内对项目运营及维护承担全部责任。私营企业的收入由终端客户缴纳的费用构成。

《公私合营企业法》对特许权进行了规定。通过特许权，公共行政部门或间接行政机构聘请私营机构提供公共服务，或者由其直接或间接向国家提供服务（具有较高投资金额及长期的付款期限）。公私合营企业合同中最低投资为 2 000 万雷亚尔，且相关合同有效期为 5 年至 35 年（包括续展期间，不因费用而可延期）。

《国有企业法》适用于为向公众及混合资本公司提供服务而与第三方缔结的合同，包括工程及广告服务，资产的采购、出售及租赁等。《公共外包区分制度法》对该法律确定的特定事项的项目外包制定了规则。

尽管有既定的框架，在巴西，政府签订合同以平等竞争的理念为基础。因此，在公共采购中，外国公司也应遵守在资格遴选程序中适用于巴西公司的规则，且相关活动有相应要求时提交一份授权其在巴西运营的命令及主管机关批准其在巴西经营的登记册或授权。为此，在进入巴西公共采购程序之前，外国公司必须获得授权。

尽管有上述规定，外国公司若未在巴西运营，也就是说公司若未在巴西领土内开展永久性或持续性的活动且未履行合同而开展活动时，外国公司可免于提交上述授权。在此情况下，外国公司仅需提交与巴西国内办理同类业务需要提交的文件相对应的文件（经相应领事馆认证或海牙认证，并由经认证的译员翻译），且必须任命一名法定代表人（并赋予其接受法定通知，在司法及行政程序中答辩的权利），但在法律所列的某些情况下，这些要求可被豁免。

若外国公司在订立合同后（《公私合营企业法》强制要求）在巴西注册设立特殊目的机构，并具有所有适当的授权或参与了巴西公司领导的企业联合体，外国公司也可参与公共采购而无须获得授权。

在适用有利于国民的平局决胜规则时及在与外包项目有关的行业，政府外包中的平等原则可能受到限制。根据平局决胜规则，优先支持国内公司、供应国产产品或遵守国内可持续发展的。

2. 禁止领域

即便在 1995 年宪法改革后，巴西经济实现了重大突破，但在某些战略领域，外国投资仍受到限制。

关于这些限制的进一步说明，请参见上文"市场准入和检验标准"部分内容。

对于外国人在边境地区购买和租赁农村土地及不动产的限制，请参见上文"外国企业购地规则"部分内容。

3. 邀标及竞标

《公共招标法》规定了多种可用于与公共行政机关缔约的竞标模式，包括但不限于邀标、公开招标及拍卖。《国有企业法》及《公共外包区分制度法》规定了不同的竞标程序。

对于特许企业及公私合营企业，在授权机关公开邀标后，有兴趣的企业应提交其资格文件进行评阅，在随后的竞标阶段提案将被公开，并宣布中标情况。

Brazil

Authors: Celso Costa, Thales Saito
Translators: Gao Wenjie, Feng Jing

I. Overview

A. General Introduction to the Political, Economic, Social and Legal Environment of the Country Receiving Investment

a. Political

Brazil is a federative republic comprised by the federal government, 26 states, the federal district and the municipalities. Federal government exercises control over the central government and is divided into 3 independent branches: executive, legislative and judiciary. States are autonomous entities with their own governments that, together with the other federal units, form the federative republic. Each municipality has an autonomous local government, which is comprised by a mayor and a legislative body.

b. Economic

Between 1990 and 2002, Brazil underwent a massive privatization programme to deregulate the domestic economy, remove anachronisms which had hindered the country's development and allow competition in order to stimulate various sectors of the economy. The programme included the sale of public industries and public service companies owned by federal, state and municipal governments. Concessions were also granted to the private sector for the provision of public services and exploitation of natural resources. As a result of the programme, more resources were assigned to social investment, public sector debt was reduced, competition was encouraged and local securities markets were strengthened, thus contributing to the current status of Brazil's economy as one of the most diversified in the world and the largest in Latin America.

Moreover, during this period, the federal government phased out its presence in economic activities. Important developments in this regard included the establishment of a free foreign exchange market, elimination of price controls, reduction in the bureaucracy surrounding foreign trade and capital flows, and creation of mechanisms to allow foreign investors to access Brazilian securities markets, as well as the reduction in restrictions on foreign investment.

The Brazilian government has been continuously encouraging the private sector to invest in segment of the economy which historically were the government's responsibility, particularly infrastructure. Other segments of the Brazilian economy, such as the oil industry, electrical energy, telecommunications and certain other utility services, have been opened up to private enterprise and foreign capital.

The Brazilian securities market has also undergone major changes. In December 2000, the Brazilian stock exchange (B3 S.A.-Brasil, Bolsa, Balcão-"B3") introduced the so-called New Market (Novo Mercado), a listing category which aims to bring about greater foreign investment in Brazilian companies by applying stricter rules on corporate governance, accounting and disclosure, whilst improving the treatment of minority shareholders.

Brazil, along with Argentina, Paraguay, Uruguay and Venezuela, is a member of the Southern Common Market ("MERCOSUR"). Bolivia signed a Protocol of Accession to MERCOSUR on July 17, 2015, which has to be approved by the member countries in order for its adhesion to become effective.[1] Brazil is also a member of the World Trade Organization (WTO), the G20, the Latin American Integration Association (LAIA) and the Community of Latin American and Caribbean States ("CELAC"). It also has associate membership of the Andean Community.

Brazil experienced remarkable growth in the last decade, but recently, the external context has become less favorable and the domestic environment more complex. After facing a deep contraction in 2015 and 2016, the Brazilian economy resumed growing in 2017. Initially driven by agriculture, the recovery appears increasingly broad-based. Retail sales are rising, including durable goods, automobiles and construction material. Gross domestic product ("GDP") increased by 1.4% in the third quarter of 2017 as compared to the third quarter of 2016

---

[1] MERCOSUR, "Países do MERCOSUL". Available on http://www.mercosur.int/innovaportal/v/7824/12/innova.front/paises-do-mercosul.

according to the Brazilian Institute of Geography and Statistics (Instituto Brasileiro de Geografia e Estatística, or "IBGE").[1] At the same time, inflation as measured by the General National Consumer Price Index ("IPCA") was 2.95% in 2017 according to IBGE.[2] The recovery of investment is supported by improvements in confidence and the fall in the inflation, which provided room for interest rates cuts and reduction in financing costs.

According to the Organization for Economic Co-operation and Development ("OECD"), private consumption in Brazil tend to improve as a result of the back of rising real incomes due to lower inflation, and Brazil's growth is expected to rise gradually in 2018 and 2019.[3] The Central Bank of Brazil forecasts that GDP will increase by 2.70% in 2018 and by 3.00% in 2019.[4]

c. Social

Brazil has a diverse cultural background resulting from ethnic and cultural mixing that took place in the colonial period, involving indigenous, Portuguese and African people, and in the late of the 19th and the early 20th centuries, with the immigration of Italians, Spaniards, Germans, Arabs and Japanese. As a result of the colonization by the Portuguese empire, Brazilian culture is mainly derived from Portugal, including predominant religion and colonial architecture style, added by the strong of indigenous and African traditions.

Brazil experienced a remarkable economic and social progress from 2013 to 2014, lifting more than 29 million people out of poverty and dropping inequality significantly. The income rate of the poorest 40% of the population rose approximately 7.1% between 2003 and 2014, compared to a 4.4% income growth for the population as a whole.[5]

Although Brazil sustained high employment rates until 2014, unemployment increased from 6.8% in 2013 to 12.6% at the end of 2016 as a result of the political and economic crisis. However, OECD projects a better scenario for 2018 with employment rising and unemployment retracting.[6]

According to a research carried out by OECD, Brazil has several areas of strength in relation to well-being, including working hours, social support, voter turnout and air quality. In addition, Brazil is considered to be above average in relation to partner countries in several aspects, including employment rate, basic sanitation, life expectancy and water quality.[7]

d. Legal

Brazil is a civil law country, which means that it has comprehensive and continuously updated laws and legal codes that specify virtually all matters capable of being brought before Brazilian courts. In a civil law system such as Brazil, the judge's main role is to establish the facts and to apply the provisions of a framework established by a comprehensive set of laws. Precedents are not binding and are used to aid judges in interpreting the law and fill in gaps. A judge may not refrain from the law, but can resort to secondary sources of Law, such as principles, following the purpose of a law, or the Brazilian Federal Constitution itself, or analogy.

The Brazilian Federal Constitution is the supreme law of Brazil, in the sense that it is the foundation and source of the legal authority underlying the Brazilian federal system. The Brazilian Federal Constitution provides the framework for organization of the Brazilian government and for the relationship of the federal government with the states, the municipalities and the people.

The main legal regulatory framework applicable to foreign investments in Brazil are Law No. 10406, of January 10, 2002, as amended ("Brazilian Civil Code"), Law No. 6404, of December 15, 1976, as amended ("Brazilian Corporations Law"), Law No. 4131, of September 3, 1962, as amended ("Law No. 4131"), Resolution No. 3844, of March 23, 2010 ("Resolution No. 3844"), Resolution No. 4373, of March 30, 2015 ("Resolution 4373"), Circular No. 3689, of December 16, 2013 ("Circular No. 3689"), and CVM Instruction No. 560, of March 27, 2015 ("CVM Resolution 560").

For further information on the regulatory framework applicable to foreign investments in Brazil, please refer to item II.A.c. below.

---

[1] IBGE. Available on https://agenciadenoticias.ibge.gov.br/agencia-noticias/2013-agencia-de-noticias/releases/18458-pib-varia-0-1-em-relacao-ao-2-tri-e-chega-a-r-1-641-trilhao.html.
[2] IBGE. Available on https://agenciadenoticias.ibge.gov.br/en/agencia-press-room/2185-news-agency/releases-en/19450-ipca-rises-0-44-in-december-and-closes-2017-at-2-95.html.
[3] OECD, "Developments in Individual OECD and Selected Non-Member Economies-BRAZIL". Available on http://www.oecd.org/eco/outlook/economic-forecast-summary-brazil-oecd-economic-outlook.pdf.
[4] Central Bank of Brazil, "Focus-Relatório de Mercado" dated February 2, 2018. Available on https://www.bcb.gov.br/pec/GCI/PORT/readout/R20180202.pdf.
[5] The World Bank, "The World Bank in Brazil". Available on http://www.worldbank.org/en/country/brazil/overview.
[6] OECD, "How does Brazil compare? Employment Outlook 2017". Available on http://www.oecd.org/brazil/Employment-Outlook-Brazil-EN.pdf.
[7] OECD, "How's Life in Brazil". Available on http://www.oecd.org/brazil/Better-Life-Initiative-country-note-Brazil.pdf.

B. The Status and Direction of the Cooperation with Chinese Enterprises Under the B&R

The diplomatic relations between Brazil and China have been deepening increasingly since 1974.

In 1993, Brazil and China created the China-Brazil High-Level Coordination and Cooperation Committee ("COSBAN"). COSCAN currently is the highest permanent dialogue and bilateral cooperation forum between Brazil and China. Through its subcommittees and working groups, COSCAN deals with issues related to economic, financial and political relations, agriculture, energy, mining, cultural and educational exchange, as well as technology, innovation and aerospace cooperation.[1]

In 2010, Brazil and China entered into the 2010-2014 Joint Action Plan ("PAC"), which defined the goals and guidelines of the bilateral relations between both countries. An updated version of the PAC was signed by President Dilma Rousseff and Prime Minister Li Keqiang in 2015. In 2012, Brazil and China entered into the 10-Year Cooperation Plan with the purpose of elevating cooperation to the level of global strategic partnership ("10-Year Cooperation Plan"). Currently, the PAC and the 10-Year Cooperation Plan set forth the main guidelines for the bilateral relationship between Brazil and China, establishing long-term actions in key areas such as science, technology, innovation and spatial cooperation, energy, mining, infrastructure and transport, investments and industrial and economic cooperation, economic-commercial cooperation, as well as cultural cooperation and exchange between both countries.[2]

In addition to bilateral initiatives, Brazil and China have been acting jointly in several multilateral forums, such as the Brazil, Russia, India and China ("BRIC"), the G20 and the Brazil, South Africa, India and China ("BASIC") summits. During the 6th BRICs Summit in Fortaleza in July 2014, the New Development Bank - NDB was created and the Contingency Reserve Fund Agreement was entered by and among the BRIC countries. Those measures had the purpose of broadening the channels to raise funds for projects and protecting BRIC member countries against imbalance of payments. In addition, Brazil became a founding member of the Asian Infrastructure Investment Bank (AIIB) in April 2015.[3]

As a result of the diplomatic and economic relations between both countries, China has been Brazil's largest trading partner since 2009. Trade between Brazil and China strongly increased from the level of USD 3.2 billion in 2001 to USD 74.8 billion in 2017. In 2017, Brazil exported to, and imported from China, USD 47.5 billion and USD 27.3 billion, respectively (versus USD 35.1 billion and USD 23.3 billion in 2016, respectively), having as result a surplus in bilateral trade of USD 20.2 billion.[4]

Currently, China is also one of the main sources of foreign direct investment in Brazil, particularly in the areas of energy and mining, iron and steel metallurgy, and agribusiness. Recently, a diversification of Chinese investments in Brazil in other areas such as telecommunications, automobiles, machinery, and banking services has been noticed. Among material Chinese investments in Brazil in the recent years, it is possible to point out:

(i) the acquisition of a 23% stack in CPFL Energia by State Grid;

(ii) the acquisition of 50.1% of the capital stock of Rio Bravo Investimentos by Fosun;

(iii) the agreement between Wtorre and China Communications and Construction Company (CCCC) to invest R$1.5 billion in the construction of a port terminal in the city of São Luis, State of Maranhão,[5] and;

(iv) the State Power Investment Corp.'s investment in the concession of São Simão HP.[6]

During the Second Ministerial Meeting of the Forum of China and CELAC, which took place on January 22, 2018 in the city of Santiago, Chile, China invited the members of the CELAC, including Brazil, to take part in the B&R initiative. According to the information made available by the State Council Office of the People's Republic of China, President Xi Jinping sent a congratulatory letter to the Second Ministerial Meeting of the Forum of China and CELAC whereby Mr. Xi called on Latin American countries to actively participate in the B&R initiative.[7] Although there is a strong indication that the CELAC's members will join the B&R initiative in a short term[8], no

---

[1] The Ministry of Foreign Affairs, Brazil. Available on http://www.itamaraty.gov.br/pt-BR/ficha-pais/4926-republica-popular-da-china.
[2] The Ministry of Foreign Affairs, Brazil. Available on http://www.itamaraty.gov.br/pt-BR/ficha-pais/4926-republica-popular-da-china.
[3] The Ministry of Foreign Affairs, Brazil. Available on http://www.itamaraty.gov.br/pt-BR/ficha-pais/4926-republica-popular-da-china.
[4] The Ministry of Industry, Foreign Trade and Services, Brazil. Available on http://www.mdic.gov.br/index.php/comercio-exterior/estatisticas-de-comercio-exterior/balanca-comercial-brasileira-mensal-2.
[5] The President of the Republic Office, Brazil. Available on http://www2.planalto.gov.br/acompanhe-planalto/noticias/2016/09/china-e-brasil-assinam-acordos-de-investimento-e-cooperacao.
[6] SPIC, China, corporate news. Available on http://eng.spic.com.cn/NewsCenter/CorporateNews/201711/t20171120_282752.htm.
[7] State Council Office of the People's Republic of China, China. Available on http://www.scio.gov.cn/31773/35507/35520/Document/1617809/1617809.htm.
[8] The Ministry of Foreign Affairs of the People's Republic of China, China. Available on http://www.fmprc.gov.cn/mfa_eng/wjbxw/t1527941.shtml.

steps have been taken to formalize such participation yet, except in case of Panama, which has already entered into B&R collaboration agreements with China.[1]

II. Investment

A. Market Access

a. Department Supervising Foreign Investment

Foreign investments in Brazil are regulated and supervised by the Central Bank of Brazil, which is also responsible for controlling and monitoring the flow of foreign currency to and from Brazil. As explained in items II.A.b and II.A.c below, foreign investments in Brazil need to be registered before the Central Bank of Brazil.

The Brazilian Monetary Council (Conselho Monetário Nacional, "CMN") is the highest authority in Brazil responsible for the overall supervision of Brazilian monetary, credit, budgetary, fiscal and public debt policies. Accordingly, in regulating and supervising foreign investments, the Central Bank of Brazil needs to follow the policies set forth by the CMN.

Foreign investments are also regulated and supervised by the Brazilian Securities Commission (Comissão de Valores Mobiliários-"CVM"), which is responsible for regulating, developing, controlling and supervising the Brazilian securities markets in accordance with the securities and exchange policies established by the CMN.

b. Laws and Regulations of the Foreign Investment Industry

Foreign investments in Brazil are mainly governed by Law No. 4131, Resolution No. 3844, Resolution No. 4373, Circular No. 3689, and CVM Instruction No. 560, as detailed in item II.A.c. below.

c. Forms of Investment

Foreign capital in Brazil is defined as goods, machinery and equipment which have been brought into Brazil without any initial expenditure of foreign currency, and which will be used in the production of goods or services, and financial resources which have been brought into the country to be invested in economic activities. As general rule, any of such assets could be held by individuals or corporate entities resident, domiciled or with their registered offices abroad.

Foreign investments in Brazil are classified by nature in foreign equity investments, and foreign debt investments.

For control and registration purposes, equity foreign investments are also divided into 2 separate categories, namely: long-term investments in productive activities ("4131 Investments") and portfolio investments ("Portfolio Investments").

a) Foreign Equity Investments
(i) 4131 Investments

Pursuant to Law No. 4131, Resolution No. 3844, and Circular No. 3689, investments in productive activities can be made either through the remittance of an amount in foreign currency (as capital contribution to a Brazilian company or as the purchase price of existing equity interests) or the capitalization of companies with goods (i.e., equipment or machinery). In both cases, the amount of the currency or the value of such goods is eligible for registration with the Central Bank of Brazil.

The registration of a foreign investment with the Central Bank of Brazil is mandatory if the investor intends to repatriate the capital invested and to make remittances or reinvestments of profits and other forms of remuneration of the capital brought into Brazil.[2]

A foreign investment is eligible for registration with the Central Bank of Brazil if such investment is made in a productive activity which may, in whole or in part, be conducted by a foreign investor, and the investment fully qualifies as a foreign capital investment under the Brazilian applicable legislation. Therefore, investments made in a business activity like trade, manufacturing or rendering of services are eligible for registration of the initial investment, repatriation of capital and remittance of dividends.

Since 2000, the registration of foreign investments has to be made electronically by the company receiving the investment (investee) and the foreign investor (through its representative in Brazil) by submitting the relevant information through the electronic registry system ("SISBACEN") of direct foreign investments of the Central

---

[1] Belt and Road Portal. Available on https://www.yidaiyilu.gov.cn/info/iList.jsp?cat_id=10037.
[2] Reinvestments are defined as income (profits and capital gains) attributed to non-resident individuals or corporate entities that are reinvested in the same company which generated the income or in another sector of the Brazilian economy.

Bank of Brazil (Registro Declaratório Eletrônico de Investimentos Externos Diretos-"RDE-IED"). Such electronic registration must be done within 30 days from the date of entry of the investment into Brazil.

In order to operate the RDE-IED, the investee and the foreign investor must obtain a "CADEMP code" from the Central Bank of Brazil by means of the enrollment of the relevant investor and investee with the RDE-IED module of the SISBACEN. After the issuance of the CADEMP codes for each of the Brazilian company and for the foreign investor, a specific RDE-IED number must be created for the relevant investor / investee. Such RDE-IED number must be included in all foreign exchange agreements to be executed in connection with the relevant investor / investee 4131 Investment.

As general rule, after obtaining the CADEMP code for the foreign investor, the Central Bank of Brazil automatically forwards an application request to the Brazilian Revenue Service (Receita Federal do Brasil) for the registration of the foreign investor before the Brazilian tax authorities and the obtaining of the respective corporate taxpayers registry (the so-called "CNPJ / MF").

Foreign investments are registered in the currency that has effectively entered Brazil. Dividends are remitted in the currency of the country where the investor is resident or has its head office or where the branch making the investment is located. Reinvestments of profits are registered in the currency of the country to which such profits could have been remitted pursuant to the aforesaid rules.

There is no minimum period during which a registered 4131 Investment must remain in Brazil. Therefore, at any time after the investment is made, the foreign investor may dispose of the assets in Brazil or liquidate the investment and thereafter repatriate the capital invested in the country.

(ii) Portfolio Investments

Pursuant to Resolution No. 4373, non-resident investors are authorized to make investments in the Brazilian financial and capital markets by acquiring fixed income instruments (bonds, certificates of deposit, debentures), derivative instruments (swaps, futures, forwards, flexible options), securities (shares, stock options, stock index, warrants), investment funds (credit rights funds, private equity funds, multimarket funds, real estate funds, etc.) and other financial instruments generally available to Brazilian residents.

The implementation of Portfolio Investments in Brazil requires the adoption of the following measures:

• the foreign investor must appoint an agent (financial institution or other type of institution authorized to operate by the Central Bank of Brazil) in Brazil for the purpose of its representation before third parties (who may or may not be the local representative for tax purposes, as describe below) ("Portfolio Agent");

• the foreign investor must appoint a local representative to be responsible for compliance with tax obligations arising from the investments carried out on behalf of the relevant foreign investor (in practice, such service is usually rendered by the agent mentioned in item (a) above);

• the Portfolio Agent must enroll the foreign investor with the CVM pursuant to CVM Instruction No. 560;

• the Portfolio Agent must enroll the foreign investor with the Central Bank of Brazil through the portfolio module of the SISBACEN ("RDE-Portfolio") pursuant to Resolution No. 4373. As a result of such registration, a RDE-Portfolio code number is attributed to the investor and such code number needs to be included in all foreign exchange agreements to be executed on its behalf and in connection with his portfolio investment; and

• the investor must appoint one or more custody agents duly authorized by CVM, by means of entering into a custody services agreement.

After obtaining the registration of the foreign investor mentioned in item (c) above, CVM automatically forwards an application request to the Brazilian Revenue Service (Receita Federal do Brasil) for the registration of the foreign investor before the Brazilian tax authorities and the obtaining of the respective CNPJ / MF.

All investments, withdrawals, redemptions, receipt of revenues, dividends, interest or capital gains, transfers of investment and other changes in the portfolio of the foreign investor must be registered by the Portfolio Agent in the RDE-Portfolio module of the SISBACEN.

In addition, it should be noted that all assets and securities traded, as well as the other categories of financial transactions entered into by a foreign investors under Resolution No. 4373 must be registered, book-entered, maintained under custody or deposited in institutions or entities authorized to render such services by the Central Bank of Brazil or the CVM, pursuant to their legal competence, or be registered in clearing systems recognized by the Central Bank of Brazil or the CVM.

The transfer and / or assignment of a Portfolio Investment abroad is not allowed, except in case of merger, amalgamation, spin-off, corporate reorganization and succession, as provided for in article 20 of CVM Instruction No. 560.

Foreign investors are also prevented from using funds brought into Brazil under the regime set forth in Resolution No. 4373 in any purchase or sale of securities carried out outside of organized markets (stock or commodities exchanges, electronic systems or organized over-the counter markets).

Notwithstanding the above, article 19 of CVM Instruction No. 560 sets forth that such limitation do not apply to acquisition or sale of securities carried out by means of: initial subscriptions; bonifications; conversions of debentures or other convertible instruments into shares; redemption and reimbursement, when provided by law; payment of dividends in securities; subscription, amortization or redemption of quotas of investment funds regulated by CVM; assignment or transfer of quotas of open-ended investment funds when authorized by the relevant CVM regulation; free or onerous assignment of due and not paid proceeds to foreign investor who aims to close the custody account; free assignment of subscription receipts, being the foreign investor the assignor or the assignee; judicial settlement or judicial, arbitral or administrative decision; sale of securities which issuer's authorization to trade on organized markets has been cancelled or suspended; sale of shares subject to shareholders agreements entered into and registered with CVM for more than 6 months; public offer of securities; if previously approved by CVM, public tender offer of shares when the sale process is any other than the auction in an organized market; put option for remaining shareholders in a tender offer; and other purchase or sale transactions not mentioned in the items above taking place outside an organized market, if approved by CVM upon previous and reasoned request.

Finally, it is important to point out that Portfolio Investments may be carried only through the following types of accounts to be held with Brazilian financial institutions:

• proprietary account: the investor may only invest in his / its own name;

• participant in an omnibus or collective account: the account holder may operate not only in his / its name but also in the name of other non-resident investors. In this case, all passengers (investors) will use the RDE-Portfolio of the account holder.

The non-resident investor can be both the account holder and also a participant in one or more accounts. The accountholder of an omnibus account may invest its own funds in this same account, as long as registration for this purpose has been requested. Omnibus accounts are generally available to foreign financial institutions or broker-dealers which operate in the name of third-party investors.

b) Foreign Debt Investments

In Brazil, cross-border financing may be raised either as:

(i) general financing, extended directly to a Brazilian company by foreign individuals or legal entities (usually financial institutions) or through the issuance by a Brazilian company of debt securities in the international capital markets;

(ii) export financing transactions, through export prepayment transactions, including the receipt of payments in connection with the export of goods and services at least 360 days before the shipment of the goods or the rendering of the services;

(iii) import financing transactions with term for payment exceeding 360 days; or

(iv) leasing transactions with term exceeding 360 days (jointly, "Foreign Debt Investments").

All Foreign Debt Investments mentioned above must be registered with the Central Bank of Brazil through the module of the SISBACEN designed for registration of debt transactions (Módulo Registro de Operação Financeira- "RDE-ROF").

Similarly to what we explained in item above, in order to operate the RDE-ROF, the investee and the foreign investor must obtain a "CADEMP code" from the Central Bank of Brazil by means of the enrollment of the relevant investor and investee with the SISBACEN. After the issuance of the CADEMP codes for each of the Brazilian company and for the foreign investor, a specific RDE-ROF number must be created for the relevant transaction. Such RDE-ROF number must be included in all foreign exchange agreements to be executed in connection with the relevant foreign debt investment.

The RDE-ROF registration shall list all key financial terms and conditions of the transaction. Undetermined maturity dates or fees and interest, fees or other charges linked to the performance of the borrower or third parties on an unlimited basis are not eligible for registration.

As general rule, RDE-ROF registrations are automatically granted by the Central Bank of Brazil, unless the conditions of the relevant foreign debt transaction are not compatible with prevailing market conditions or its structure does not fit within the existing standards of the RDE-ROF system.

Amendments to the main terms and conditions of Foreign Debt Transactions (e.g., change of term for payment, interest rates etc.) may require the execution of simultaneous foreign exchange transactions (simulating the outflow of funds from the country and the inflow of funds) with a Brazilian financial institution authorized to operate in the Brazilian foreign exchange market.

d. Standards of Market Access and Examination

As general rule, foreign investments in Brazil do not require prior authorization from the Brazilian government.

It should be noted, however, that restrictions on foreign ownership and / or licensing requirements apply to certain strategic sectors, as described below:

a) Financial institutions

Brazilian Federal Constitution requires a presidential decree to allow the increase in the participation of foreigners in the Brazilian financial system. Such limitation does not apply to the acquisition by foreign investors of shares issued by financial institutions, without voting rights, which are traded on stock exchanges, which can be implemented without any specific authorization, pursuant to the terms of the Presidential Decree of December 9, 1996. In addition, pursuant to Resolution No. 4122, of August 2, 2012, the incorporation and the change of control of Brazilian financial institutions in transactions involving either foreign or local investors requires prior authorization from the Central Bank of Brazil.

b) Mining: pursuant to Law-Decree No. 227, of February 28, 1967, only companies incorporated in Brazil, which includes Brazilian entities under foreign corporate control, may qualify for mining activities in Brazil. Furthermore, companies interested in performing mining activities at the Brazilian border zone (the 150km-wide strip parallel to the national border) must observe additional requirements in order to qualify for such activities, which include:

(i) limitation of foreign investment to up to 49% of the company corporate capital (i.e., at least 51% of the company's corporate capital must be held by Brazilian individuals or entities);

(ii) at least 2/3 (two thirds) of the company's workforce is formed by Brazilian citizens; and

(iii) the company's management must be carried out by a Brazilian majority which must have predominant powers.

Only after those requirements are met, the interested company may request an authorization for border zone mining before the National Security Council.

c) Nuclear energy

foreign investment is only allowed in activities that involve the commercialization, use of radioisotopes for medical, agricultural and industrial ends and for the production, commercialization and utilization of radioisotopes of half-life equal to or lower than two hours. Such activities can only be developed by private entities as per government concessions. Private entities cannot operate nuclear energy services and facilities or exploit radioactive substances such as uranium. Nevertheless, there is a project to amend the Brazilian Constitution in order to exclude from the Union monopoly the construction and operation of nuclear reactors for the purpose of generating energy (PEC 122/2007). This project has been in the House of Representatives since 2007.

d) Airports

the main airports authorized to receive commercial airlines are managed and operated by INFRAERO, a federal state-owned company, or by concession to private investors. In the second (2012) and third (2013) round of concessions, which comprised the International Airports of São Paulo (Guarulhos), Campinas (Viracopos), Brasília, Rio de Janeiro (Galeão) and Minas Gerais (Confins), 49% of the voting capital of the operating company would mandatorily be held by INFRAERO, while the private investors hold the remaining 51% of the voting shares. Concessions from 2016 onwards, which encompassed the International Airports of Florianópolis, Porto Alegre, Fortaleza and Salvador, did not include the participation of INFRAERO, therefore, the private investors are the sole shareholders of the companies managing and operating such airports, under the corresponding concession agreements. Private sector entities, domestic and foreign, may own airports designed for executive jets and helicopters. Such airports cannot receive air carrier flights, except pursuant to a special authorization under certain regulations.

e) Airlines and air taxis

the rendering of airline services on a regular basis requires the obtaining of a prior concession with the Brazilian authorities, and the rendering of services on a non-regular basis requires the obtaining of an authorization with the Brazilian authorities. With respect to foreign investment, article 181 of Law No. 7565, of December 19, 1986, sets forth that concessions to explore airline services in Brazil can only be granted to entities that comply with the following requirements: head offices are located in Brazil, equity foreign investments are limited to 20% of the company's voting shares, and management is assigned exclusively to Brazilian individuals. There are currently two (2) bills to be voted that may change the limitations of voting shares owned by foreigners: Bill n° 2724/2015, suggesting an amendment to the article 181 of Law 7565/86, whereby 49% of a company's shares with voting rights may be owned by foreigners; and Bill n° 258/2016, suggesting a new Brazilian Aeronautical Code, in which there is no restriction with respect to the amount of voting shares owned by non-Brazilians.

f) Health services

originally Brazilian law prevented foreign investors to hold equity investments in entities engaged in health assistance, such as hospitals, clinics and laboratories, with few exceptions. However, by virtue of Law No. 8080, of September 19, 1990, as amended by Law No. 13097, of January 19, 2015, foreign investors are now allowed to hold direct or indirect equity participation in local healthcare entities. It should be noted, however, that the constitutionality of such legislation has been challenged and the Federal Supreme Court still needs to render a final decision on this matter.

g) Media companies

foreign investment in press (except for online news services) and free to air television and radio and broadcasting companies shall not exceed 30% of their total voting capital and the management and editorial control of the company need to be carried out by Brazilian nationals[①]. Foreign investors may own paid television programming companies in Brazil without any relevant restrictions. Furthermore, distribution in Brazil of publications printed or edited locally require the appointment of a person editorially responsible with the Ministry of Labour.

h) Postal services

pursuant to Article 9 of Law 6538 of June 22, 1978, as amended, postal services within the Brazilian territory can only be rendered by the Brazilian government, either directly or through companies controlled by it (i.e., the Empresa Brasileira de Correios e Telégrafos).

i) Rural real estate properties

there are certain certain restrictions for the acquisition and lease of rural real estate properties in Brazil by foreign enterprises. For further information on this matter, please refer to item II.D.b below.

B. Foreign Exchange Regulation

a. Department Supervising Foreign Exchange

The Central Bank of Brazil is the Brazilian authority responsible for regulating and supervising the foreign exchange market in accordance with the guidelines set forth by the CMN.

b. Brief Introduction of Laws and Regulations of Foreign Exchange

The foreign exchange market in Brazil is currently governed by Resolution No. 3568, of May 29, 2008, Circular No. 3691, of December 16, 2013 ("Foreign Exchange Regulations").

c. Requirements of Foreign Exchange Management for Foreign Enterprises

Pursuant to the Foreign Exchange Regulations, any individual or legal entity may purchase and sell foreign currency, or make international transfers in reais, of any nature and without value limitation, provided that the transaction is legitimate and has economic substance evidenced by the respective supporting documentation.

The remittance or the receipt of funds to or from abroad, respectively, by a Brazilian resident, is made through the execution of a foreign exchange agreement with a Brazilian bank licensed by the Central Bank of Brazil to operate in the foreign exchange market. In such foreign exchange agreement, the Brazilian resident may purchase foreign currency from the Brazilian bank, which will deliver such foreign currency outside Brazil; or the Brazilian resident may sell foreign currency which it is entitled to receive from abroad to the Brazilian bank, in which case the Brazilian bank will receive the foreign currency and pay the equivalent amount in reais to the Brazilian resident.

Every foreign exchange agreement for the purchase or sale of foreign currency has to be classified in accordance with the nature of the transaction underlying the foreign exchange transaction. For instance, foreign loans granted to a Brazilian resident, payments of exports or imports and direct investments made in a local or foreign company have a specific classification code. An extensive list with the possible natures of transactions comprising foreign exchange agreements is provided for in the Foreign Exchange Regulations.

C. Financing

a. Main Financial Institutions

The Brazilian financial system is comprised by financial institutions, stock exchanges, insurance companies and pension funds, among others, and is regulated and supervised mainly by the following regulatory bodies: the CMN; the Central Bank of Brazil; the CVM; the National Council of Private Insurance; the Superintendence of Private Insurance; the National Council of Complementary Pensions; and the National Superintendency of Complementary Pensions.

Financial institutions in Brazil may be incorporated as multiple service banks, commercial banks, development banks, investment banks, credit, financial and investment institutions (consumer credit), housing loan institutions, brokerage houses, securities dealers and real estate financing institutions.

Pursuant to the data made available by the Central Bank of Brazil, currently there are 1,727 financial

---

[①] Article 222 of the Federal Constitution.

institutions, or assimilated entities, authorized to operate in the Brazilian financial system, out of which 132 are multiple banks, 21 are commercial banks, 4 are development banks and 13 are investment banks.[1]

Brazil's federal and state governments still control important commercial banks and financial institutions with the purpose of fostering economic development, especially in the manufacturing and agricultural industries. In addition, development banks operate as development agencies in Brazil.

Public financial institutions in Brazilian may be incorporated either as: development banks that operate at the federal level (e.g., National Bank for Economic and Social Development - BNDES), as well as state and regional levels; savings banks that operate at the federal level (e.g., Caixa Econômica Federal), as well as the state level; and commercial banks, multiple service banks and other financial institutions whose majority of voting stock is held, directly or indirectly, by the Brazilian government or by other governmental entities. According to the Brazilian publication "Exame", the 3 biggest financial institutions in Brazil based on revenue in 2016 were Itaú Unibanco, Bradesco and Banco do Brasil, respectively.[2]

Currently there are 132 financial institutions in Brazil which are controlled by foreign investors[3], out of which 8 are controlled by investors located in China.[4] In addition, there are 50 foreign banks currently have representation offices located in Brazil.[5]

b. Financing Conditions for Foreign Enterprises

Brazilian financial institutions are not prevented from lending money to foreign entities. However, Brazil has historically experienced high rates, what makes the costs of local financing higher and usually not competitive in relation to debt transactions available in the international market. For this reason, except for financing extended by Brazilian development banks to certain entities located abroad (which offer more competitive rates) or transactions which payments are originated in reais and natural hedging is material for its implementation (in which case, financing is usually obtained by the Brazilian subsidiary instead of the foreign entity), it is more common to see foreign enterprises obtaining financing in the international market rather than in Brazil.

D. Land Policy

a. Brief Introduction of Land-related Laws and Regulations

According to the Brazilian legal framework, the law of the country whereupon a real estate property is located is the relevant one to govern its classification and the relations arising thereof. Real estate law in Brazil is primarily guided by the Federal Constitution of 1988 and in special by the Brazilian Civil Code, which provides, among other concepts, that ownership to a real estate property may be acquired either by direct acquisition, adverse possession, accession or succession rights. The Brazilian Civil Code also establishes other rights over real estate properties ("in rem rights"), which are not based on any personal relationship yet enforceable against third parties, such as surface rights, easements, usufruct, use, housing, among others.

Moreover, other federal laws govern real estate in Brazil. They include the following:

(i) Law No. 4591, of December 16, 1964 ("Real Estate Development Law"), which approaches two main subjects: the development of real estate enterprises comprised by autonomous units; and building condominiums;

(ii) Law No. 4504, of November 30, 1964 ("Land Statute"), which regulates the use, occupation and relations of rural land in Brazil. The aforementioned sets forth the country's responsibility and obligation to guarantee the right of access to rural land for those who live and work within it;

(iii) Law No. 10257, of July 10, 2001 ("City Statute"), which provides urban land policies in general, as well as other instruments that aim to help the implementation of urban developments;

(iv) Law No. 6766, of December 19, 1979 ("Parcelling of Real Estate Property Law"), which concerns the urbanisation of individual plots of land by dividing or redeploying them into parcels intended for the exercise of elementary urbanistic functions and building; and

(v) Law No. 6015, of December 31, 1973 ("Public Registry Law"), which regulates every kind of public registry in Brazil, including the Real Estate Registries where ownership to a real estate property must necessarily be

---

[1] The Central Bank of Brazil. Data available on http://www.bcb.gov.br/htms/deorf/d201801/Quadro%2001%20-%20 Quantitativo%20de%20institui%C3%A7%C3%B5es%20por%20segmento.pdf.
[2] Exame. Data available on https://exame.abril.com.br/revista-exame/maiores-em-financas/.
[3] The Central Bank of Brazil. Data available on http://www.bcb.gov.br/htms/deorf/d201801/Quadro%2012%20-%20 Participa%C3%A7%C3%A3o%20Estrangeira%20no%20capital%20votante%20de%20IFs%20do%20SFN.pdf.
[4] The biggest financial institutions with Chinese equity participation in Brazil are the following: Industrial and Commercial Bank of China (ICBC), Bank of China, Haitong, China Construction Bank (CCB), and Bank of Communications (BoCom).
[5] The Central Bank of Brazil. Data available on http://www.bcb.gov.br/htms/deorf/d201801/Quadro%2015%20-%20 Representantes%20de%20Institui%C3%A7%C3%B5es%20Financeiras%20no%20Pa%C3%ADs.pdf.

registered.

It is also worth noting that certain real estate matters are regulated by either state or municipal laws, rather than by federal laws, such as real estate taxes, real estate registry proceedings, urban zoning, construction rules and environmental regulations.

b. Rules of Land Acquisition for Foreign Enterprises

Urban lands in Brazil can be acquired by foreigner enterprises with no legal restriction, being required only the proof of their CNPJ registration. However, certain limitations are imposed for the acquisition and lease of rural real estate properties by foreign enterprises. The range of application of such restrictions was widened on August 23, 2010, due to a new opinion on the interpretation of the constitutionality of Law No. 5709, of October 7, 1971, issued by the General Counsel of the Federal Government Office (CGU / AGU 01/2008-RVJ), which was duly approved and published ("Opinion CGU / AGU").

According to the Opinion CGU / AGU, for purposes of applying restrictions on the acquisition of rural land, the legal concept of foreign companies also comprises Brazilian companies in which foreign individuals or legal entities hold interests, on any account, whenever (i) such interests ensures their holders with the power to conduct the resolutions of the general meeting to elect the majority of managers of the company and to run the corporate activities and instruct the operation of company's bodies (shareholding control) or (ii) such interest represents more than 50% of its shares. Therefore, Brazilian companies under the above conditions are also restricted from acquiring or leasing rural properties in Brazil.

With respect to the current legislative scenario, there is one legislative bill in progress, which has six other bills attached. This legislative bill aims to allow acquisition and rural lease of rural properties in Brazil by Brazilian companies in which foreign individuals or legal entities hold the majority of the capital stock or its control. The legislative bill has been on queue for deliberation by the Chamber of Deputies since September 2015 and has been postponed since then.

Additionally, another legislative bill specifically regarding the legal framework of the energy sector has been sent to the Presidency of the Republic in February 2018, proposing the extinction of the restrictions on the acquisition and lease of rural properties by foreign enterprises for purposes of energy developments in the country.

Besides, for national security reasons, there are certain limitations on the acquisition of real property by foreigners, including Brazilian companies under foreign control, in border areas (the strip of up to 150 kilometres' width along the country's land borders, which is deemed essential to the defence of the Brazilian territory). Acquisition of such land is, among other requirements, conditional on prior authorization from the General Office of the National Security Council.

E. Establishment and Dissolution of Companies

a. Forms of Enterprises

Various types of corporate entities are available to domestic and foreign investors under Brazilian law, including limited liability companies ("Limitadas"), joint-stock corporations ("Corporations"), individual limited liability companies, public-private partnerships, and unincorporated joint venture companies.

As Corporations and Limitadas are the most common types of enterprises adopted by investors in Brazil, please find below a summary of the main features and requirements applicable to those types of companies.

a) Corporations

(i) Governing law. Corporations are governed by the Brazilian Corporations Law.

(ii) Form of investment. Corporations could be closed-end or publicly-held companies, provided that Corporation is the mandatory corporate type for publicly-held companies in Brazil.

(iii) Number of shareholders. Corporations must have at least 2 shareholders, who may be either individuals or legal entities (incorporated either in Brazil or abroad). Exceptionally, Corporations may be wholly owned by another Brazilian company. If shareholders are domiciled abroad, they must grant a power-of-attorney to a representative residing in Brazil.

(iv) Capital stock. At least 10% of the subscribed capital must be paid up at the time of incorporation.

As a general rule, additional capital requirements do not apply to Corporations, except in certain specific cases, such as in the incorporation of financial institutions and companies filing for visas on behalf of their foreign managers (for information on capital requirements necessary for obtaining of visas, please refer to item IV.B. below).

A Corporation may be set up with fully subscribed or with authorized share capital (in which case, the board of directors may approve capital increases within the limits set forth in the Corporation's by-laws without the need of shareholders' meeting).

The capital stock of a Corporation may be divided into common and preferred shares. Preferred shares usually (but not necessarily) are non-voting shares. Whenever adopted, non-voting shares may not exceed 50% of the shares issued by the Corporation. Preferred shares must entitle their holder to certain advantages or preferences (when compared to the common shares), such as the priority right to receive dividends; the priority right to receive reimbursement of capital (with or without a premium payment) or the combination of the preceding rights.

The ownership and transfer of shares need to be registered either in the physical books of the Corporation, or kept in the form of book entries with a financial institution authorized to carry out such services.

(v) Shareholders' liability. shareholder's liability is limited to the payment of the shares subscribed by them, except in case of abuse of powers and of violation of the law or of the Corporation's by-laws.

(vi) Voting rights. shareholders' meetings: Each voting share entitles its holder to one vote at the general shareholders' meeting (preferred shares may also entitle their holders to cast votes in relation to certain matters according to the rules set forth in the by-laws) and resolutions at the meeting are usually passed by a majority of the outstanding voting shares, except if a higher quorum is set forth by law or by the Corporation's by-laws for a specific matter. Therefore, matters subject to the shareholders' meeting are generally approved by shareholders representing 50% plus one share of the total outstanding capital of the Corporation.

Shareholders may enter into a shareholders' agreement in order to govern their relationship in connection with their equity participation in a certain Corporation, including voting and veto rights, restrictions on transfer of shares, withdrawal mechanisms, non-competition etc. Shareholders' agreements in Brazil are binding on their signatories and on the invested Corporation and can be enforced in court (specific performance). Votes cast in breach of shareholders' agreements must be disregarded by the chairman of the shareholders' meeting or by the chairman of the meeting of the board of officers, as the case may be.

(vii) Management. Corporations are usually managed by a board of executive officers (diretoria) and a board of directors (conselho de administração), provided that closed-end Corporations are not legally required to have a board of executive officers. Corporations are also legally required to have a supervisory board (conselho fiscal), which may or may not be permanently in operation. All members of the management must be individuals.

The board of directors shall be composed of at least 3 members. It is responsible for electing and removing officers and for taking or approving major policy decisions. The members of the board of directors, who are elected by the shareholders' meeting, may or may not be shareholders of the company and do not need to be resident in Brazil, provided that a legal representative resident in Brazil is appointed in case of members resident outside Brazil. The members of the board of directors do not have powers to represent the Corporation before third parties.

The board of executive officers is composed by at least 2 officers, who have powers to represent the Corporation before third parties and are directly engaged in the company's activities. Executive officers may or may not be shareholders, and are elected by the board of directors or by the general shareholders' meeting (if the Corporation does not have a board of directors) for a term not exceeding 3 years. Executive officers must be domiciled in Brazil, which means that only Brazilian citizens or foreigners domiciled in Brazil who are holders of the appropriate visa are allowed to act as executive officers of a Corporation.

The supervisory board shall be composed of 3 to 5 members. It is incumbent on the supervise board, among other duties the supervision of the managers of the Corporation; the rendering of an opinion on the annual report prepared by the management and on any proposal by the management bodies that shall be submitted for voting to the shareholders' meeting (regarding the amendment of the share capital, the issuance of debt securities or warrants, among other proposals); reviewing the financial statements of the Corporation. The members of the supervisory board are elected by the shareholders' meeting and may or may not be shareholders of the company. When the supervisory board operates on a non-permanent basis, it will only be activated if requested by the Corporation's shareholders representing at least 10% of the voting shares or 5% of the non-voting shares.

(viii) Profits. Dividend distributions need to be approved at the annual general shareholders' meeting, provided that the Corporation's by-laws may allow the board of directors to approve interim dividends based on retained earnings or profit reserves registered in the previous annual, semi-annual or quarterly balance sheets.

Corporations are required to pay at least 25% of its annual profits as dividends to their shareholders (unless the by-laws provide for a lower threshold). Corporations may also pay interest in return for shareholder's equity, which is deductible from the mandatory minimum dividend.

The Brazilian Corporations Law requires that 5% of the Corporations' net profits are retained as legal reserve, up to an aggregate amount equal to 20% of its share capital. Such legal reserve may only be used to offset losses and for capital increases and may not be paid as dividends.

b) Limitadas

(i) Governing law. Limitadas are governed by the Brazilian Civil Code, provided that they may be subsidiarily governed by the Brazilian Corporations Law if provided so in their articles of association and to the extent there is no conflict with the Brazilian Civil Code.

(ii) Form of investment. no public subscription of quotas is allowed and Limitadas are not allowed to trade quotas, issue debentures (debt securities) or be quoted on the stock exchange.

(iii) Number of shareholders. Limitadas can be incorporated by 2 or more individuals or legal entities. Any of the partners, whether individuals or legal entities, may be resident or domiciled abroad. If the partners are domiciled abroad, they must grant a power-of-attorney to a representative residing in Brazil.

(iv) Corporate Capital. As general rule, no minimum capital requirements apply to Limitadas, except in certain specific cases, such as in the incorporation of financial institutions and companies filing for visas on behalf of their foreign managers.

There is no requirement of minimum amount of capital to be paid up front, nor is there any mandatory time limit for the capital to be fully paid (the time frame is established by the partners themselves in the articles of association).

Quotas are not represented by securities or certificates. Their ownership is registered in the articles of association, and transfers are subject to amendments thereto. Transfer of quotas to non-partners may be rejected by quotaholders representing 25% of the corporate capital, except as otherwise provided in the Limitada's articles of association.

Although the Brazilian Civil Code is silent on the possibility of Limitadas issuing different types of quotas, regulations governing commercial registries have been modified recently[1] to expressly admit the issuance of preferred quotas by Limitadas that are subsidiarily governed by the Brazilian Corporations Law.

A majority of quotas may exclude partners for their unlawful misconduct or commitment of acts that could impair the company's existence.

(v) Quotaholders' liability. quotaholders' liability is limited to the total amount of the quotas subscribed by them, but all quotaholders are jointly and severally liable for the unpaid subscribed capital. Quotaholders shall have no further liability once all quotas have been fully paid, except in cases of violation of law, breach of the articles of association or abuse of power.

(vi) Voting rights. quotaholders' meetings: Each voting quota entitles its holder to one vote at the quotaholders' meeting and resolutions at the meeting are usually passed by a majority of the quotaholders present at the meeting, except if a higher quorum is set forth by law or by the Limitada's articles of association for a specific matter. For instance, the Brazilian Civil Code sets forth a quorum of 75% of the outstanding capital for the approval of merger or dissolution of the Limitada.

Quotaholders may enter into a quotaholders' agreement in order to govern their relationship in connection with their equity participation in a certain Limitada, including voting and veto rights, restrictions on transfer of quotas, withdrawal mechanisms, non-competition etc. Quotaholders' agreements in Brazil are binding on their signatories and on the invested Limitada and can be enforced in court.

(vii) Management. Limitadas shall be managed by 1 or more individuals appointed in the articles of association or in a separate document or act (by the partners). The management of Limitadas is carried out either by the partners or by third parties if the articles of association so authorize, provided that the managers shall be resident and domiciled in Brazil. This means that only Brazilian citizens or foreigners domiciled in Brazil who are holders of the appropriate visa are allowed to act as managers of Limitadas.

(viii) Profits. Dividend distributions by Limitadas need to be approved at the quotaholders' meeting.

Brazilian Civil Code does not require Limitadas to distribute minimum profits.

c) Investment Funds

It is also very common to see legal entities and individuals investing in Brazil through investment funds.

Although there is a doctrinal controversy in Brazil as to the legal nature of investment funds[2], the majority of the Brazilian scholars[3], Brazilian applicable laws and regulations, and the majority of legal precedents classify them, in of all of their modalities, as special condominiums governed by the Brazilian Civil Code and the regulations issued by CVM.

Being special condominiums, Article 44 of the Brazilian Civil Code does not confer legal personality to investment funds in Brazil. Notwithstanding such fact, it is worth noting that investment funds are capable of being entitled to legal rights and obligations to the extent permitted by applicable legislation and their incorporation

---

[1] Normative Instruction No. 38, of March 2, 2017 issued by the Department of Corporate Registration and Integration (DREI).
[2] CARVALHO, Mário Tavernard Martins de. Regime Jurídico dos Fundos de Investimento. Editora Quartier-Latin. São Paulo, 2012 (pp. 184-185).
[3] EIZIRIK, Nelson e OUTROS. Regime Jurídico do Mercado de Capitais. 3º Edição. Editora Renovar. Rio de Janeiro, 2011 (pp.82-83).

documents (e.g., bylaws or regulamento)[1]. As a general rule, investment funds must be represented for all legal purposes by their administrators, which, in most cases, need to be locally licensed by CVM to carry out asset management activities.

With respect to legal capacity, as a general rule, entities granted with legal personality are allowed to enter into any type of transactions, except otherwise prohibited by law or their incorporation documents. Entities conferred with no legal capacity (such as investment funds), on the other hand, are only allowed to enter into transactions expressly authorized by law or their incorporation documents.[2] Therefore, considering that investment funds have no legal personality, they are allowed to carry out only the activities expressly permitted by their bylaws and the applicable regulations issued by CVM.

It is also important to note that, based on the fact that investment funds have no legal personality, they are not considered as legal entities for the purposes of Brazilian laws and, as a general rule, for tax purposes, they are not treated as a taxable unit and are subject to a special taxation regime. In this context, all income and capital gains earned by the portfolio of investment funds are neither subject to the imposition of CIT (as defined below) nor to taxes on gross revenues (PIS and COFINS contributions, which are social contributions due by legal entities). Accordingly, taxation over accrued gains only occurs at the level of their quotaholders (either upon distribution or on an accrual basis (come-quotas)), and the respective tax treatment will depend on the quotaholder's location.

Several modalities of investment funds are available in Brazil, including fixed income funds, publicly-held corporations funds, foreign exchange funds, multi-market funds, private equity funds, real estate properties funds, and credit receivables funds.

The incorporation of investment funds require the execution of an incorporation act by their administrators, and the obtaining of an operation license from the CVM. In addition, the issuance and distribution of quotas issued by investment funds must to comply with the regulations applicable to public offering of securities in Brazil, as explained in item II.I.2 below.

b. Procedure of Establishment of Companies

Corporations and Limitadas may be incorporated either by private instrument or public deed. In any case, the incorporation instrument and the respective by-laws (in case of Corporations) or the articles of association (in case of Limitadas) must be registered with the Board of Trade with jurisdiction over the location of the company's headquarters.

As general rule, the incorporation of Corporations and Limitadas do not require prior approval from any Brazilian governmental authorities, except in certain specific cases, such as the incorporation of financial institutions. For further information on governmental licenses and authorizations, please refer to item II.A.4 above.

c. Routes and Requirements for Dissolution of Companies

Corporations shall be dissolved in any of the following events:

(i) by force of law in the following situations: upon expiration of its term of duration; in the cases provided for in the by-laws; by resolution of a general meeting of shareholders; by the existence of only a single shareholder, verified at an annual general meeting, if the minimum of two shareholders is not observed by the annual general meeting of the following year and by the cancellation, according to law, of its authorization to operate;

(ii) by court order in the following situations: when its incorporation is annulled in proceedings commenced by any shareholder; when it is proved, in proceedings commenced by shareholders representing 5% or more of the capital, that the corporation cannot achieve its corporate purposes; and in the event of bankruptcy, in the manner provided for by the relevant law;

(iii) by the decision of a competent administrative authority, in the cases and in the manner provided for any special law.

Limitadas shall be dissolved, by operation of law, in any of the following events: expiration of the term of duration of the Limitada (if applicable); unanimous decision of the quotaholders to dissolve the Limitada prior to the expiration of its term; in an Limitada for a undefined term, a decision by an absolute majority of the quotaholders to dissolve the Limitada; the existence of only one partner, if not remedied within a period of 180 (one hundred and eighty) days; extinction, in the cases provided for by law, of the Limitada's authorization to operate; and after the Limitada is declared bankrupt.

Law No. 13105, of March 16, 2015, introduced the legal action for partial dissolution of either Corporations or

---

[1] COELHO, Fábio Ulhôa. Curso de Direito Comercial - Direito de Empresa. 10ª Edição, Volume 2. Editora Saraiva. São Paulo, 2007 (p. 9).
[2] COELHO, Fábio Ulhôa. Curso de Direito Comercial - Direito de Empresa. 10ª Edição, Volume 2. Editora Saraiva. São Paulo, 2007 (p. 10).

Limitadas aiming at: the dissociation of Corporations or Limitadas in relation to the deceased or excluded partner, or the partner who exercised the right to withdraw or to opt for a recess; and the liquidation of assets of the deceased or excluded partner, or the partner who exercised the right to withdraw or to opt for a recess; or (c) only the dissociation or the liquidation of assets.

F. Mergers and Acquisitions

Generally, acquisitions in Brazil may be carried out by means of:
(i) direct or indirect acquisition of equity interest in the target entity;
(ii) execution of agreements governing voting and other rights;
(iii) acquisition of assets; or
(iv) corporate reorganization (merger, spin-off, amalgamation, drop down etc.).

The definition of the most effective method of acquisition depends on several factors, including legal and tax implications (including the need to file for new operation licenses), commercial considerations, third-party consents and timing required for closing.

a. Documentation

The documentation usually adopted in local mergers and acquisitions ("M&A") are very similar to the ones used in international deals governed by United States or United Kingdom laws.

In terms of documentation, the main transaction documents usually adopted in Brazil are:
(i) preliminary documents (term-sheets, non-disclosure agreements, memoranda of understanding, letters of intent etc.);
(ii) share, quota or asset purchase agreements, and schedules and exhibits thereto;
(iii) escrow agreements;
(iv) investment agreements; and
(v) shareholders' or quotaholders' agreements.

As general rule, the provisions that usually require more intensive work and negotiations are those related to representations and warranties and indemnification.

The main purposes of the representations and warranties provisions in purchase agreements are to:
(i) disclose material information on the target company (including its operations, business and contingencies), the quotas, shares or assets to be sold; and the parties right to enter into the relevant purchase agreement;
(ii) allocate risk between the parties, serving as basis for indemnification claim in case of their breach; and
(iii) enable the parties to terminate the agreement in case of their breach before closing. As general rule, the scope of the representations and warranties provisions can be limited by concepts of materiality, knowledge, time, and carve out references in the disclosure schedules to the purchase agreement.

With respect to indemnification, the provisions of purchase agreements usually address losses resulting from breach or inaccuracy of representations and warranties, failure to perform covenants, and certain liabilities expressly allocated to one of the parties.

Differently from other jurisdictions, it is very common in Brazil to include a catch-all provision (also known as "my watch / your watch" provision) (in addition to the breach or inaccuracy of representations and warranties) setting forth the seller's obligation to indemnify the buyer for any and all losses arising from acts, facts or events occurred before closing. With the inclusion of such provision, the risk arising from acts, facts or events occurred before closing are allocated to the seller, despite the content of the representation and warranties. Usual limitations on the indemnification provisions include survival period, caps, thresholds, baskets or deductibles, mini-basket or de minimis, and collateral (escrow, hold back, pledge).

b. Due Diligence

M&A transactions in Brazil usually involve legal, financial and accounting matters. The purpose of the due diligence is to find out about the seller and the target company and to determine the issues which are relevant to the acquisition.

Legal due diligence in Brazil usually convers the following matters: environmental, civil, antitrust, commercial and financial agreements, real estate, intellectual property, regulatory, insurance, corporate, labor, tax, and anticorruption and compliance.

Differently from what we see in many other jurisdictions, it is very common to find local target companies being party to a high number of judicial and administrative proceedings, mainly in the labour and tax spheres. Contingencies and liabilities found in the due diligence process are usually addressed by an adjustment to the purchase price, or by including specific indemnification provisions in the relevant purchase agreement allocating the risk to the seller. In this sense, buyers usually prefer to find out about material issues before the closing of the deal so they could be able negotiate an adjustment to the purchase price, or to pull out of the acquisition.

c. Relevant Formalities and Procedures for the Acquisition of Companies

a) Acquisition of Limitadas

The transfer of quotas in a Limitada requires an amendment to its articles of association. In order for the transfer to be effective against third-parties, such amendment needs to be registered before the competent Board of Trade.

b) Acquisition of Closed-end Corporations

The transfer of shares in a closed-end Corporation needs to be registered either in the physical books of the Corporation, or kept in the form of book entries with a financial institution authorized to carry out such services. No additional registration or disclosure is required for the transfer of shares to be effective against third-parties.

c) Acquisition of Publicly-held Corporations

The same comments of item F.3.2 above also apply to the transfer of shares of publicly-held corporations.

In addition, any investment in a publicly-held Corporation leading to ownership of multiples of 5% of a type of its share (or convertible bonds or derivative instruments related to such shares) must be immediately notified by the investor to the Corporation, which shall provide such information to the market, the CVM and the stock exchange on which the relevant shares are traded. The notice must specify if, with the acquisition, the investor intends to change the Corporation's control. Additional notices are required every time such ownership increases or decreases by multiples of 5%.

Whenever a change of control occurs in relation to a publicly-held Corporation, the Brazilian Corporations Law requires the acquiring party to launch a tender offer directed to all of the remaining holders of common shares to buy each of their shares for 80% of the price, per share, paid in consideration for the controlling interest. The rules applicable to companies listed on B3 under its segments 2 (Nível 2) and Novo Mercado require that the price paid per share (including preferred shares in case of companies listed in Nível 2) in a mandatory tender offer involving such companies must be 100% of the price paid, per share, in consideration for the controlling interest.

d. Antitrust Approval

As explained in item G.c. below, closing of certain M&A deals in Brazil shall be conditioned upon the obtaining of CADE's (as defined below) prior approval.

G. Competition Regulation

a. Department Supervising Competition Regulation

The Administrative Council for Economic Defense ("CADE") is responsible for the enforcement of Law No. 12529, of November 30, 2011 ("Competition Law").

CADE is composed of a General Superintendence ("SG", which is responsible for the first-level merger review and for the investigation of anticompetitive practices), an Administrative Tribunal with a chairman and six commissioners ("CADE Tribunal"), and a Department of Economic Studies.

b. Brief Introduction of Competition Law

The Brazilian competition system is currently governed by the Competition Law, which establishes a pre-merger review system, and provides for penalties for anticompetitive practices.

c. Measures Regulating Competition

a) M&A

(i) Jurisdiction / Thresholds

M&A filing with CADE will be mandatory whenever a transaction has effects in Brazil, it constitutes an economic concentration, and it meets the revenue thresholds. A foreign to foreign transaction meets the effects requirement when it has actual or potential effects in Brazil by either direct presence, indirect presence (e.g., through export sales to Brazil) or concrete plans to be active in Brazil. There is no de minimis rule on the volume or value of export sales that meets this test.

The notion of economic concentration encompasses mergers, acquisitions of assets, acquisitions of control or of minority interests (acquisition of an interest of at least 20% if the acquirer and target are neither competitors nor active in vertically related markets; or acquisition of an interest of at least 5% if the acquirer and target are competitors or active in vertically related markets) in addition to the creation of joint ventures, consortia, and associative agreements.①

The revenue thresholds are met when one of the economic groups involved in the transaction had annual gross revenue / volume of business in Brazil of at least R$750 million, and one of the other economic groups involved in the transaction had gross revenue / volume of business in Brazil of at least R$75 million, in the fiscal year immediately prior to the transaction.

(ii) Procedure

The parties involved in the transaction are jointly responsible for the merger filing and for the payment of a filing fee of R$85 thousand. The filing can be submitted at any time before the closing of the transaction, ideally after the execution of a binding document between the parties.

Before obtaining CADE's clearance, the parties shall remain independent, with no intervention to each other's activities - any violation to the standstill obligation amounts to "gun jumping", subjecting the parties to fines from R$60 thousand to R$60 million, in addition to the annulment of the infringing acts and / or a formal investigation for anticompetitive behaviour against the merging parties, which may lead to additional fines and penalties.

Transactions carried out on stock exchanges or on organized over-the-counter markets may take place (e.g., the subscription of shares may occur) before CADE's decision, as long as any political rights relating to the ownership of the interests acquired in such transactions are not exercised before CADE's clearance.

The merger review process may take up to 330 days from the day the filing is declared complete by CADE. However, the majority of merger cases are reviewed under the fast-track procedure, with clearance decision being issued within 30 days from formal filing.

(iii) Outcome

If the SG issues a clearance opinion that is not challenged by a third party or subject to a revision request of any member of CADE Tribunal, the SG's opinion becomes a final and enforceable decision after 15 days from its publication on the national official gazette.

Should the SG conclude that the transaction raises competition concerns, it shall challenge the transaction before CADE Tribunal, which will decide whether the merger should be unconditionally cleared, cleared subject to remedies or blocked. In this second-level review, final clearance occurs right after CADE Tribunal issues its decision.

Remedies can take the form of structural or behavioural commitments, and in practice have been negotiated among the merging parties and CADE through a Merger Control Agreement ("ACC", for its acronym in Portuguese).

b) Anticompetitive Practices

(i) Reviewable Practices

Competition violations are prosecuted at the administrative level in Brazil by the SG and ruled by CADE Tribunal. Pursuant to the Competition Law, CADE has jurisdiction over anticompetitive conducts carried out abroad, provided that such acts produce actual or potential effects in Brazil.

Competition violations comprise acts that aim to, or result in, the following effects, regardless of fault, even if not achieved: to limit, restrain or in any way injure free competition or free initiative; to control the relevant market of goods or services; to arbitrarily increase profits; and to exercise a dominant position abusively.

Such conducts encompass a wide range of practices including collusive practices (price fixing, market allocation, output restriction, bid rigging, boycott, etc.) as well as unilateral practices (exclusivity, discrimination, predatory pricing, resale price maintenance, refusal to deal, tying arrangements, etc.).

(ii) Penalties

Companies are subject to fines ranging from 0.1% to 20% of the annual gross revenue of the company, its group or conglomerate in the sector of business activity affected by the violation, in the year prior to the launch of the Administrative Proceeding②③.

Officers and directors are subject to fines ranging from 1% to 20% of the fine levied against the company, and fines for employees or entities such as trade associations which do not register turnover range from R$50 thousand to R$2 billion.

Hard-core cartels (price fixing, market allocation, output restriction, bid rigging) are also a criminal offense in Brazil under Law No. 8137, of December 27, 1990. In addition to prosecution at CADE's level, hard-core cartels

---

① The Competition Law exempts consortia, joint ventures and associative agreements created for participating in public bids from the duty to file.
② The term "sector of business activity" does not necessarily coincide with a relevant market for antitrust purposes. A list of sectors to be taken into account when calculating a fine is provided in Resolution No. 3, of May 29, 2012, enacted by CADE.
③ Additionally, companies are subject to non-monetary penalties including, inter alia, prohibition from participating in public procurement procedures and obtaining funds from public financial institutions for up to five years.

are prosecuted by the Public Prosecutor's Office and are ruled by a court of law. Only individuals can be held liable for cartel under the referred law, being subject to imprisonment from 2 to 5 years, and fine.

(iii) Immunity

The Competition Law provides for a leniency program, pursuant to which companies and / or individuals who execute a leniency agreement with CADE are entitled to full or partial immunity at administrative level. A leniency agreement also protects individuals from criminal prosecution. However, neither companies nor individuals are sheltered from private actions for damages, which may be filed by third parties harmed by the cartel.

If an investigation is already in place, the defendants can negotiate a settlement agreement ("TCC", for its acronym in Portuguese) with CADE related to the practice under investigation. Amongst the obligations negotiated with CADE is the payment of a financial contribution not lower than the minimum value of the expected fine to be imposed by CADE. If the settlement proposal is accepted by CADE, the administrative proceeding is suspended vis-à-vis the defendant(s) who settled, and the procedure will follow its regular course concerning the other defendants.

H. Tax

a. Tax Regime and Rules

As mentioned in item I.A.1 above, the Federative Republic of Brazil is a federation composed by 26 States and the federal district with political and economic independency, which are, on their turn, composed by municipalities.

The framework of the Brazilian tax system is set forth in the Federal Constitution, which determines the taxable events that can be imposed by each of the Federal, State and Municipal governments.

In general, but not limited to, the federal government can impose taxes on income, capital gains, manufacturing, imports, exports, payroll (social security contributions), and financial transactions. States may levy taxes on sales, motor vehicle property and gifts. Finally, Municipalities can impose taxes on services, real estate property and sale of real estate.

On the comments below, we will only address the most relevant taxes at Federal, State and Municipal levels.

b. Main Categories and Rates of Tax

a) Federal Taxes

(i) Corporate Taxes

- IRPJ and CSLL - Corporate Income Taxes

Corporate Income Taxes ("CIT") are imposed on the taxable profit of all legal entities located in or operating within Brazil. CIT are imposed, in general, at an aggregate rate of 34% and include the following taxes: IRPJ, imposed at the rate of 15% plus a potential surtax of 10% over profits, and CSLL, imposed at the rate of 9%[1].

Despite the existence of some few regimes for calculation of CIT, Brazilian companies typically opt for the Real Profits or the Presumed Profits Regime:

• Real Profits Regime: accounting profit accrued by the company, adjusted by additions and exclusions provided by law.

• Presumed Profit Regime: takes into account a pre-defined percentage of gross revenues do determine the profit of the taxable activity (expenses and costs are not contemplated). Brazilian companies are entitled to adopt the presumed profits regime if the annual gross revenues do not exceed R$78,000,000 in the previous year.

- PIS and COFINS - Social Contributions

Companies are also subject to PIS / COFINS, which apply over gross revenues (in addition to social security charges applied on salaries and wages). PIS / COFINS applies under two regimes:

• Non-Cumulative Regime: 9.25% combined rate and the possibility to deduct credits from qualifying costs and expenses (e.g. inputs); and

• Cumulative Regime: 3.65% combined rate and no credits offset[2].

As a general rule, gross revenues derived by the legal entities under the Real Profit Regime for CIT purposes are subject to PIS / COFINS under the non-cumulative regime (with some exceptions, such as financial institutions). On the other hand, legal entities subject to the Presumed Profits Regime are mandatorily under the

---

[1] It is worth mentioning that profits derived by banking activities in Brazil are taxed by CIT at an aggregate rate of 45% - including (i) IRPJ, which is due at the rate of 15% on net profits after tax adjustments. The portion of net profit, adjusted by tax additions and exclusions, which exceeds BRL 240,000 per year is subject to additional income tax of 10%; and (ii) CSLL, imposed at a 20% rate until December 31, 2018. From January 1, 2019, the applicable rate will be 15%.

[2] For financial institutions, the aggregate rate of PIS/COFINS is 4.65%.

cumulative regime.

PIS / COFINS are also imposed on the import of goods and services. On import of goods the general rates corresponds to 2.1% and 9.65% over the customs value of the good, and on import of services the rates are 1.65% and 7.6% on the value remitted abroad.

- IPI - Tax on Manufactured Goods

IPI is imposed on transactions with manufactured products, including imports or domestic sales. The legislation defines manufactured product as any product subject to industrialization process.

On the import, IPI is imposed on the customs clearance of the products, over the customs value added by the amount of II due on the import. On domestic sales, the taxable basis, as a rule, is the value of the transaction. The applicable IPI rates vary in accordance with the tax classification code of the product under the NCM, used as a basis for the IPI table of rates.

- II - Import Tax

II is imposed on the import of foreign products. The taxable basis is the customs value, for which definition follows the Customs Valuation Agreement. In general, the customs value corresponds to the Cost, Insurance and Freight value of the imported products. The rates vary in accordance with the tax classification code of the imported product in the NCM.

- IOF - Tax on Financial Transactions

IOF is imposed on several financial transactions, including, among others:

• Credit Transactions ("IOF / Credit"): the taxable basis and applicable rates vary according to the characteristics of the credit transaction. In general, the maximum rate is of 1.88% and there are some transactions exempted from IOF / Credit taxation.

• Exchange Transactions ("IOF / Exchange"): the general rate is 0.38% on the amount of the currency exchange transaction, with exceptions.

IOF rates can be altered by Presidential Decree at any time. Maximum rate possible is 25%.

- INSS - Social Security Contribution

INSS is a social security contribution. The financing of INSS is made by means of contributions from both employers and employees. The contribution due by the employee must be withheld by the company and duly remitted to the Federal Government.

In general, social security contributions are imposed at the following rates:

• Employer's contribution is imposed at a rate of 20% on remuneration paid or credited to employees and independent workers. Some specific activities are subject to an additional rate.

• Workers' Compensation Insurance imposed at the rate of 1%, 2% or 3% on the payroll.

• Employees' contribution is imposed at a rate that vary between 9% up to 11% on the remuneration paid or credited to the employees. The employee contribution, however, is subject to a "ceiling" amount.

• Contributions to other official agencies at aggregate rates of up to 5.8%.

(ii) Individual Taxes

Resident individuals are subject to income taxation (IRPF) on worldwide basis. Tax credits may be accepted. Withholding tax may apply in some cases, which, depending on the type of income, may be deemed as a final payment or treated as an advance payment of the income tax due by the taxpayer. Income earned by an individual resident may be divided into two distinct categories:

• Capital Gain and Financial Earnings: taxed at progressive rates ranging from 15% to 22.5%, depending on the amount of gain derived by the individual.

• General Earnings, including salary: Taxed at progressive rates that vary from 7.5% to 27.5%.

Dividend received from Brazilian companies are exempt from taxation.

b) State Taxes

ICMS is similar to a value-added tax (VAT) and is imposed on transactions involving the import, sales and other commercial transactions with goods, the rendering of any type of intermunicipal or interstate transport services and on communication services. ICMS is a non-cumulative tax, which means that the ICMS paid in each transaction may be offset against the tax due on upcoming transactions or services renderings.

The taxable basis of the ICMS due on the sale of products, in general, is the value of the transaction, added by conditional discounts and freight, if charged separately and rendered by the seller or on its behalf. On the import the ICMS taxable basis is the customs value of the good, plus all federal taxes imposed on import and customs expenses, calculated in a gross-up basis.

For import and domestic transactions, the respective tax rates will be determined by each State and may depend on the product, and may reach up to 32% (the general rate on import / intrastate transactions vary from 17% up to 20%). On interstate transactions carried out between taxpayers, the rate is established by the Federal

Senate and may be 4%, 7% or 12%.

c) Municipal Taxes

ISS is imposed on the rendering of services of any nature and on the import of services and its rate may vary from 2% to 5%, depending on the municipality and the nature of the service. The ISS taxable basis is the price of the service.

d) Summary–Brazilian Main Taxes

Brazilian main taxes		
Tax	**Calculation Basis**	**Rate**
PIS and COFINS	Calculated on gross revenue or on the customs value / value remitted abroad	1.65% and 7.6% (respectively, for the noncumulative regime) 0.65% and 3% (respectively, for the cumulative regime) 2.1% and 9.65% (respectively on import of goods) 1.65% and 7.6% (respectively on import of services)
IPI	Price of the industrialized good / customs value added by II	Variable by product
II	Custom value of the imported good	Variable by product
IRPJ	Taxable income (profit or loss)	25% (15% plus 10%)
CSLL	Taxable income	9%
INSS	Total gross compensation	Usually ranging from 26.8% to 28.8%
IOF	Financial transaction	Variable by transaction
ICMS	Price of the product or the customs value added by federal taxes and customs expenses, in a gross-up basis	Usually 18%
ISS	Municipal tax on services	2%–5%

e) International Tax Matters

(i) Cross Border Payments

The payment or credit of remuneration of any nature (including, for instance, interest, royalties, payment of services, among others) from a Brazilian source to a beneficiary resident abroad is subject to the imposition of the withholding income tax (WHT), in general, at the rate of 15% or at a 25% rate if the beneficiary is located in a low tax jurisdiction ("LTJ")[1]

• Remittance of Dividends. Dividends paid by a Brazilian company are currently exempt from the WHT in Brazil, given that such amounts relate to profits generated after January 1st, 1996.

• Remittance of Interest on Equity - JCP . Companies may distribute JCP to their shareholders or quotaholders, which is a hybrid form of capital remuneration. JCP calculation is limited to the daily pro rata variation of the Brazilian long-term interest rate[2]. JCP payments to foreign investors are subject to WHT at the rate of 15% or 25%, if the non-resident is domiciled in a LTJ.

If the limits established by law on the JCP payment are observed, JCP payments are deductible for CIT purposes.

(ii) Capital Gain

In general, capital gains recognized by non-residents as a result of capital reduction or disposition of Brazilian assets to resident or non-resident purchasers are subject to WHT at progressive rates that vary from 15% to 22.5%, depending on the amount of gain[3]. For residents of LTJ, the applicable WHT rate for capital gains is 25%.

(iii) Transfer Pricing

The cross-border transactions carried out by Brazilian companies shall be subject to the transfer pricing controls when they are entered into with related parties or parties located in LTJ. The Brazilian TP Rules provides specific rules for interest payments; import transactions and export transactions.

(iv) Thin Capitalization

In general, interest paid by Brazilian corporate taxpayers to foreign related parties not located in LTJ or benefiting from privileged tax regimes, are only deductible for CIT purposes, provided that:

---

[1] Normative Ruling 1,037/2010 lists the following countries and regions as low tax jurisdictions for purposes of Brazilian law: American Samoa, Andorra, Anguilla, Antigua and Barbuda, Aruba, the Ascension Islands, the Bahamas, Bahrain, Barbados, Belize, the Bermudas, the British Virgin Islands, Brunei, Campione D'Italia, the Cayman Islands, the Channel Islands (Jersey, Guernsey, Alderney and Sark), the Cook Islands, Curaçao, Cyprus, Djibouti, Dominica, French Polynesia, Gibraltar, Grenada, Hong Kong(China), the Isle of Man, Kiribati, Ireland, Lebanon, Labuan, Liberia, Liechtenstein, Macau(China), the Maldives, the Marshall Islands, the Mauritius Island, Monaco, Montserrat, Nauru, Niue Island, Norfolk Island, Panama, the Pitcairn Islands, Qeshm Island, Saint Cristopher e Nevis, Saint Helena, Saint Lucia, Saint Martin, Saint Vincent, Samoa, San Marino, the Seychelles, the Solomon Islands, St. Peter and Miquelon Island, Oman, Swaziland, Tonga, Tristan da Cunha, the Turks and Caicos Islands, the United Arab Emirates, the US Virgin Islands and Vanuatu.

Normative Ruling 1,037/2010 lists the following privileged tax regimes: (i) with respect to the legislation of Denmark, the regime applicable to holding companies which do not develop substantial economic activity, meaning the holding companies that, in the country of residence, do not hold operational capacity to develop its activities, which is evidenced by lack of employees and absence of a physical establishment; (ii) regarding the Netherlands legislation, the regime applicable to holding companies which do not develop substantial economic activity, meaning the holding companies that, in the country of residence, do not hold operational capacity to develop its activities, which is evidenced by lack of employees and absence of a physical establishment; (iii) in relation to the legislation of Iceland, the regime applicable to International Trading Companies (ITC); (iv) in what concerns the legislation of the United States, the regime applicable to companies incorporated as state Limited Liability Companies (LLC), controlled by non-residents, not subject to the federal income tax; (v) regarding the Spanish legislation, the regime applicable to companies incorporated as Entidad de Tenencia de Valores Extranjeros (ETVEs) - currently suspended; (vi) in connection with the legislation of Malta, the regime applicable to International Trading Companies (ITC) and International Holding Companies (IHC); (vii) with reference to Switzerland, Swiss legal entities which are incorporated as holding companies, domiciliary companies, auxiliary companies, mixed companies, administrative companies or in any other corporate form via a ruling issued by the local tax authorities and that are subject to a corporate income tax rate lower than 20% (combined federal, cantonal and municipal rate) are considered to be subject to a privileged tax regime; (viii) regarding the Austrian legislation, the regime applicable to holding companies which do not develop substantial economic activity; (ix) with respect to the legislation of Costa Rica, the Free Zones Regime (Zonas Francas); (x) concerning the Portuguese legislation, the International Business Centers of Madeira (Centro Internacional de Negócios da Madeira - CINM) and (xi) regarding Singapure, the following special tax regimes: a) special rate of tax for non-resident shipowner or charterer or air transport undertaking, b) exemption and concessionary rate of tax for insurance and reinsurance business, c) concessionary rate of tax for Finance and Treasury Centre, d) concessionary rate of tax for trustee company, e) concessionary rate of tax for income derived from debt securities, f) concessionary rate of tax for global trading company and qualifying company, g) concessionary rate of tax for financial sector incentive company, h) concessionary rate of tax for provision of processing services for financial institutions, i) concessionary rate of tax for shipping investment manager, j) concessionary rate of tax for trust income to which beneficiary is entitled, k) concessionary rate of tax for leasing of aircraft and aircraft engines, l) concessionary rate of tax for aircraft investment manager, m) concessionary rate of tax for container investment enterprise, n) concessionary rate of tax for container investment manager, o) concessionary rate of tax for approved insurance brokers, p) concessionary rate of tax for income derived from managing qualifying registered business trust or company, q) concessionary rate of tax for ship broking and forward freight agreement trading, r) concessionary rate of tax for shipping-related support services, s) concessionary rate of tax for income derived from managing approved venture company and t) concessionary rate of tax for international growth company.

[2] Determined by Central Bank of Brazil from time to time.

[3] Specific rules apply to investors in the Brazilian financial and capital markets.

- are necessary for the company's activities; and
- three thresholds are met: the amount of the Brazilian entity's indebtness towards the related party does not exceed twice the value of the interest held by the related party in the equity of the Brazilian borrower; in relation to indebtness towards related parties not holding interest in the Brazilian entity, the Brazilian entity's indebtness towards the related party is not higher than twice the equity value of the Brazilian borrower and in all cases, the total indebtness of the Brazilian borrower towards related parties is not higher than twice the value of interest held by all related parties in the Brazilian borrower's equity (this requirement is not applicable in situations involving indebtness towards non-investing related parties only).

(v) Double Tax Treaties (DTTs)

Brazil currently has DTTs in force with 29 jurisdictions. Notwithstanding the fact that Brazil is not a member of the OECD, Brazilian DTTs follow to a great extent OECD and UN models in force at the time DTTs were signed.

The Brazil-China DDT, among other subjects, regulates the following earnings:
- Interest: Payments of interests may be subject to WHT at the source country at up to 15% rate.
- Dividends: Dividend payments may be subject to WHT at the source country at up to 15% rate. Regarding dividends paid by a Brazilian resident, dividend distributions are exempt of WHT.
- Royalties: WHT imposed on the royalties payments may not exceed: 25% regarding royalties related to the use or right to use trademarks of industry or commerce and 15% to other cases. The concept of royalties is applicable to any payment related to technical assistance or technical services.
- Capital Gain: The capital gain is taxable in both countries and there is no maximum rate applicable.
- Method to avoid double taxation: The Brazil - China DTT provides the crediting mechanism to prevent double taxation.

c. Tax Declaration and Preference

In Brazil, taxpayers must file the following mandatory tax returns, which represent ancillary obligations before the tax authorities. The main tax returns in the federal level are the following[①]:

Brazilian Federal Tax Returns	
Tax Return	**Description**
Tax Accounting Book	ECF is a tax return in which the company must inform all transactions that affect the IRPJ and CSLL calculation basis.
Federal Taxes Debit and Credit Return	DCTF must contain the information regarding the taxes and contributions in relation to each month.
Tax Accounting Book - Contributions	EFD-Contributions must contain the information regarding PIS/COFINS and social security contributions.
Digital Tax Accounting Book	ECD is the record of the legal entity's accounting. It replaces the old physical accounting book. It shall contain the journal entries, the ledger and the daily balance sheets.

I. Securities

a. Brief Introduction of Securities-related Laws and Regulations

The main statute dealing with securities in Brazil is Law No. 6385, of December 07, 1976, as amended ("Securities Law"). The Securities Law set up the CVM and regulates the overall operation of the securities market, the public distribution of securities, the listing of securities on exchanges, disclosure requirements, activities of brokers, broker dealers and intermediaries, types of securities traded and the types of company the shares of which may be traded on the securities market. The Brazilian Corporations Law also contains provisions which are relevant for regulation of the securities market in Brazil.

b. Supervision and Regulation of the Securities Market

Pursuant to the Securities Law, CVM is responsible for supervising and regulating the securities market in Brazil.

As general rule, the public offering of securities in Brazil requires prior registration with CVM pursuant to Instruction CVM No. 400 of December 29, 2003, as amended ("Instruction CVM No. 400"), provided that public

---

[①] Other ancillary obligations might be required at State and Municipal levels.

offerings of certain securities with restricted efforts (those directed to up to 75 professional investors, provided that only 50 professional investor may subscribe or acquire the relevant securities) pursuant to Instruction 476, of January 16, 2009, as amended, are exempt from registration with CVM.

According to the Securities Law, the following assets are considered securities in Brazil:
(i) stocks, debentures, and warrants;
(ii) securities subscription coupons, rights and receipts and certificates of the aforesaid securities;
(iii) securities deposit certificates;
(iv) debentures certificates (cédulas de debêntures);
(v) quotas of mutual funds or any investment clubs;
(vi) commercial papers;
(vii) derivative contracts in which the underlying assets are securities;
(viii) derivative contracts regardless of the underlying assets; and
(ix) collective investment contracts offered to the public, giving rights of participation, partnership or remuneration, including rights resulting from the rendering of services, the income of which arises out of the activities of the entrepreneur or of third parties.

The above definition of securities is not numerus clausus and CVM tends to use analogy principles in order to declare its jurisdiction over other types of products having securities nature and to protect the investors and the Brazilian market in general.

The concept of public offering currently adopted in Brazil (including by CVM, as expressed in several opinions issued by its legal department) follows the definition found in other major jurisdictions (i.e., a public offer takes place whenever it is made to an indeterminate group of people and not to a determined one, such as, for instance, the shareholders of the issuer or a certain group of professional or qualified investors).

It is worth mentioning that, according to Instruction CVM No. 400 and CVM Legal Orientation No. 32, dated September 30, 2005 ("CVM Legal Orientation No. 32"), CVM considers internet a mass communication vehicle such as television or newspapers, which may be used to promote an offering of securities. CVM adopted the position, consistently with the guidelines issued by the International Organization of Securities Commissions ("IOSCO"), that the fundamental principles of securities regulation do not change based on the relevant vehicles. Accordingly, the use of the internet in order to make securities available to Brazilian residents (including securities issued abroad) constitutes a public offering of securities (being subject to prior registration with CVM) unless the website's sponsor adopts special procedures to restrict the access of the Brazilian public in general.

c. Requirements for Engagement in Securities Trading for Foreign Enterprises

Please refer to item II.A.c above for information on the requirements to be complied with by foreign investors in trading securities in Brazil.

J. Preference and Protection of Investment

a. The Structure of Preference Policies

As general rule, Brazil does not have any preference policies. As mentioned in item II.A.d. above, however, certain activities may only be carried out by the Brazilian government, or by companies controlled by it, or may require the obtaining of previous authorization or license from the Brazilian government.

In addition, Brazilian government may offer certain tax incentives, as described in items below.

b. Support for Specific Industries and Regions

Brazil provides for tax incentives, which may grant reductions on the income tax, import tax, IPI, ICMS, etc. Typically, the incentives aim at reducing the import and manufacturing cost of parts, equipment, ships, etc. There are incentives related to the development of the Brazilian infrastructure (energy, transportation, etc.), modernization of ports, development of the Oil and Gas industries, production of semiconductors, development of the IT industry, etc.

c. Special Economic Areas

a) Amazon Area and Free-Trade Zones

The Amazon region is the one with more federal tax benefits in Brazil, being included in the Federal Constitution the obligation of the federal government to promote the development of such area. The benefits granted include IRPJ benefits as well as II, IPI, PIS and COFINS reductions, and may be restricted to certain location with the Amazon region.

The benefits managed by the Superintendence of the Development of Amazon ("SUDAM"), which may apply to eligible companies installed in the Amazon or Western Amazon that request the benefits according to the legislation in force, include a reduction of up to 75% of the IRPJ calculated on the exploration profit, accelerated depreciation of fixed assets and exemptions.

Regarding the benefits managed by the Superintendence of Manaus Free Trade Zone ("SUFRAMA"), applicable to companies installed in Manaus Free-Trade Zone, under the terms determined by the legislation in force, they mainly consist in reduction of the II, exemption of IPI and PIS / COFINS on the import of inputs to be used in the manufacture of products carried out in the region, as long as the minimum industrial process established by the legislation is complied with.

Regarding ICMS, there is an ICMS Agreement exempting the remittance of national products for commercialization or manufacturing in the Manaus free-trade zone, and authorizing the state of Amazonas to grant the acquirer a presumed ICMS credit.

b) Northeast

The development of the northeast region and also of underdeveloped municipalities in the State of Minas Gerais and Espirito Santo is also part of the government's economic policy. Therefore, companies installed therein are also granted some tax benefits, managed by Superintendence of the Northeast Development ("SUDENE").

Among the benefits granted are the reduction of up to 75% of IRPJ calculated on the exploration profit, accelerated depreciation of fixed assets and exemptions.

d. Investment Protection

Law No. 4131 sets forth that foreign investors should be given the same legal treatment as local investors, disallowing any discrimination against foreign investors. In 1995, the Brazilian Congress also approved an amendment to the Brazilian Federal Constitution aimed at eliminating any distinction between foreign and national capital.

Brazil is also a party to several bilateral and multilateral investment initiatives and agreements. For information on diplomatic relations and initiatives between Brazil and China, please refer to item I.B above.

III. Trade

A. Department Supervising Trade

The policy regarding the domestic and foreign trade is defined by Ministry of Industry, Foreign Trade and Services ("MDIC"), which is composed by several Secretariats, specially the Secretariat of Industrial Development and Competitiveness ("SDCI"), the Secretariat of Foreign Trade ("SECEX"); and the Secretariat of Trade and Services ("SCS").

B. Brief Introduction of Trade Laws and Regulations

MDIC may issue normative rulings (or suggest to the President to issue them) in order to encourage or discourage investments and / or the trade of products in Brazil, especially considering the trade balance (export transactions vs import transactions), as well as the strategy for the domestic industry.

Most of the rules issued by MDIC deals with the import and export transactions, establishing the procedures and documents necessary for the carrying out of such operations, as set forth by Ordinance SECEX No. 23/2011.

C. Trade Management

Trade management in Brazil is carried out mainly by the Secretariats mentioned above, in connection with the Ministry of Finance and the President.

As a rule, the trade management in Brazil is oriented to develop and protect the national industry, sometimes through regimes and mechanisms that are challenged by other countries in World Trade Organization.

D. The Inspection and Quarantine of Import and Export Commodities

Apart from the trade policies defined by MDIC, the import and export of commodities may be subject to inspections by other relevant authorities, mainly the Ministry of Agriculture, Livestock and Supply ("MAPA") and the Ministry of Mines and Energy ("MME"), which may determine the previous registration of the products and / or the entities in their records.

E. Customs Management

a. General Comments

Currently, all imports and exports to / from Brazil are subject to customs clearance with the RFB, once they arrive in the Brazilian customs territory or, for export purposes, previously to the shipment of the products. The customs clearance process begins with the enrolment of the relevant import or export statement in the Foreign Integrated System ("SISCOMEX").

SISCOMEX is an information technology system used to inform relevant data to the Brazilian Ministry of Foreign Trade, Central Bank of Brazil and RFB, which supervise the import process.

SISCOMEX will be available to the importer after it submits an application to RFB and complies with the requirements provided in the relevant legislation, being the RADAR granted. There are different kinds of RADAR which authorize companies to carry out imports and exports:

(i) Limited RADAR is granted to companies that carry out foreign trade transactions in a small volume.

(ii) Non-limited RADAR applies to companies that regularly carry on foreign trade transactions and have a good financial capacity.

(iii) Express RADAR is granted to specific companies.

The qualification of the company will be determined by RFB based on the corporate taxes paid in the previous 5 years before presenting the requirement.

b. Import License

The legislation establishes the necessity of an automatic licensing or a non-automatic licensing to certain classes of products.

In addition, as regards the import of used products, currently there is a bureaucracy process to import them into Brazil; the import is in general conditioned to a non-automatic licensing, which is only granted if they are not manufactured in Brazil or may not be replaced by other similar products. There are some cases in which the import of used products may be allowed, such as when they are imported under a temporary admission regime.

c. Customs Valuation

The taxable basis of taxes imposed on import is based on the customs value, whose definition follow the Customs Valuation Agreement. As prescribed by the Customs Valuation Agreement, the customs value must be based primarily on the transaction value, which shall correspond to the market value in an arm's length transactions, added with some amounts related to the import transactions, which may be defined by each importing country under the restrictions imposed by the agreement.

IV. Labour

A. Brief Introduction of Labour Laws and Regulations

Brazilian employment relationships are mainly governed by the rules and principles set forth by the Brazilian Federal Constitution, Decree-Law No. 5452, of May 1, 1943 ("Brazilian Labour Law"), normative rules issued by the Brazilian Ministry of Labour, other specific employment and labour laws, collective bargaining agreements applicable to each labour category and Brazilian case law.

The Brazilian Labour Law has been recently updated by Law No. 13467, of July 13, 2017 (the so called "Labour and Employment Reform"). The Labour and Employment Reform implemented major changes in the current Brazilian Labour Law, effective as of November 11, 2017. Among those changes we can highlight the possibility of splitting vacations in up to 3 periods; changes in equal pay for equal work rules; new rules regarding working hours and offsetting of working hours; new rules regarding home office; changes in the rules regarding the collection of union dues; new rules regarding termination of employment; new rules regarding mutual agreement termination; and new rules regarding mass terminations.

B. Requirements of Employing Foreign Employees

The engagement of foreigners by Brazilian entities is mainly regulated by Law No. 13445, of May 24, 2017, and Decree No. 9199, of November 20, 2017, several Normative Rules issued by the National Immigration Council, of the Ministry of Labour and, as applicable, the Brazilian Labour Law.

Depending on the type of activity to be carried out by the foreigner in Brazil, different types of visa may apply. In any case, temporary visas are the most common as they allow the engagement of officers, managers, directors and executives and of employees.

a) Temporary Visa for Officers, Managers, Directors and Executives

A temporary visa may be obtained by foreigners appointed as officers, managers, directors and executives with powers to represent the company in Brazil, performing, managing activities and / or with decision-making powers in the Brazilian company.

In order to obtain a temporary visa, a Brazilian company must provide evidence that: an investment of at least R$150,000.00 was made by the Brazilian entity or the company abroad, and that at least 10 new jobs will be created during a 2-year period following the incorporation of the Brazilian entity or of the arrival in Brazil of the foreign director or officer; or an investment of at least R$600,000.00 was made by the Brazilian entity or the company abroad. This investment must be evidenced in respect of each foreign individual that will hold a statutory management position in a Brazilian company.

b) Temporary Visa for Foreigners Engaged As Employees

Companies that need to relocate employees to reside and work in Brazil for a certain period of time may apply for a temporary visa. A written employment agreement with the Brazilian company is required and the employee cannot be appointed as legal representative of the Brazilian company. As an employee, the foreign individual is entitled to all the benefits granted by the Brazilian labour laws. As a rule, the term of this type of visa is up to 2 years.

Application procedures may vary depending on the type of visa. In any case, the visa application must be made by the Brazilian company intending to engage the foreigner.

All employees and statutory officers (including foreigners) working in Brazil are mandatorily covered by the Brazilian Social Security Institute (so called "INSS").

The INSS guarantees a social security benefit in case of sick leaves (work-related or not), maternity leave, permanent disabilities, retirement and death.

C. Exit and Entry

a. Visa Types

In addition to the visas applicable for those foreigners coming to Brazil to work, foreigners may also enter the Brazilian territory holding temporary tourist or business visas.

As a rule, foreigners entering the Brazilian territory from time to time must obtain adequate visas before they travel to the country. Tourist and business visas are also regulated in Brazil by Law No. 13445, of May 24, 2017 and Decree No. 9199, of November 20, 2017.

A tourist visa is granted to a person who wishes to enter Brazil for tourism purposes or to visit friends or relatives (not involving any kind of work or payment of remuneration).

A business visa is granted to foreigners in order to enable them to come to Brazil as representatives of foreign companies, to make business contacts, to hold job interviews, to attend business-related fairs, congresses and meetings, prospect business opportunities, sign contracts and carry out audit or consulting activities. The bearer of a business visa is allowed to promote certain foreign products, develop certain research / evaluation activities related to the Brazilian market, among other business-related activities. Although such business-related activities are not allowed to be performed by a bearer of a tourist visa, recreational activities allowed by the tourist visa may be also performed by the bearer of a business visa.

There is no special requirement other than the usual documentation requested by the local Brazilian consulate in the foreigner's home country to obtain a tourist or business visa.

b. Restrictions for Exit and Entry

Both tourist and business visas allow foreigners to stay in Brazil for a period of up to 90 days, extendable to a total of 180 days (within the 12 months following the first entrance in the Brazilian territory by the foreigner), depending on the nationality of the foreigner.

D. Trade Union and Labour Organizations

Brazilian Federal Constitution determines that employers and employees are free to associate in a union in order to defend economic and / or professional interests. It specifically establishes that employers and employees must be represented by a union, in accordance with their location and main activity, being compulsorily represented, regardless of affiliation.

Companies and employees may voluntarily pay union dues to their respective unions.

E. Labour Disputes

Labour Courts are organized in two general instances: lower courts and courts of appeals. There is also extraordinary courts of appeal: the Superior Labour Court and the Supreme Court that have jurisdiction to analyse, respectively, specific claims (such as those arising from collective bargaining agreements that overreach the jurisdiction of the Regional Labour Courts, pleas of lack of jurisdiction action and violations to constitutional provisions).

Labour lawsuits arising from individual employment relationships are usually initiated at the lower courts. However, some specific claims (such as the ones arising from collective bargaining agreements) may initiate directly at the Court of Appeal's level.

The statute of limitations for filing a labour lawsuit is of two years as from the termination of the employment, reaching instalments of the last five years[①] prior to the filing of the lawsuit.

As a rule, arbitration procedures are not binding between employees and employers. This is so because employment-related disputes cannot be prevented to be analysed by labour courts. However, as of November 2017, the Labour and Employment Reform allows employees who hold higher education degree and receive a monthly salary equal or greater than R$11,291.60[②] to agree on arbitration clauses, in which case the arbitration clause will be binding.

V. Intellectual Property

A. Brief Introduction of IP Laws and Regulations

Generally, Brazilian law divides intellectual property into copyright (including software), industrial property rights (including patents, for inventions as well utility models, industrial designs, integrated circuit layout design and distinctive signs and trademarks, geographic indications, corporate and commercial names, Internet domain names and mask works) and cultivars, as regulated by the applicable laws.

The main federal laws governing intellectual property ("IP") in Brazil are:

(i) Law 9279, of May 14, 1996 ("Industrial Property Law"), which regulates the legal framework for trademarks, patents, utility models, industrial designs, geographic indications, technology transfer, and actions against unfair competition;

(ii) Law 9610, of February 19, 1998 ("Copyright Law"), which regulates the protection accorded to copyrights and related rights;

(iii) Law 9609, of February 19, 1998 ("Software Law"), which regulates the legal framework for software protection;

(vi) Law 9456, of April 25, 1997 ("Cultivar Protection Law"), which regulates the protection regarding cultivars and related rights and obligations; and

(v) Law 11484, of May 31, 2007 ("Integrated Circuit Layout Design Protection Law"), which regulates the protection regarding integrated circuit layout designs.

In addition to the Trade Related Aspects of Intellectual Property Rights (TRIPS) agreement, Brazil has signed and ratified the major international treaties dealing with intellectual property rights, including:

(i) the Paris Convention of 1883, revised in Stockholm in 1967, which features industrial property protections;

(ii) the Berne Convention of 1886, revised in 1971, which deals with copyright protection for literary and artistic works;

(iii) the Rome Convention of 1961, which grants protection to singers and other artists, producers of phonograms and broadcasting organizations; and

(iv) the Patent Cooperation Treaty (PCT).

Copyright and software are protected whether or not they are registered. However, industrial property rights and cultivars must be registered with the competent agency in order to ensure protection. In Brazil, the Brazilian patent and trademark office (Instituto Nacional da Propriedade Industrial, "INPI") is the autonomous federal government agency responsible for the perfecting, dissemination and management of the Brazilian system for the granting and guarantee of intellectual property rights for the industry, therefore it is responsible for registering

---

① The statute of limitations for filing a labour lawsuit is of two years as from the termination of the employment, reaching instalments of the last five years prior to the filing of the lawsuit.

② This amount is valid for 2018. This amount may be increased on an annual basis in accordance with the increases of the benefits paid by the Social Security General Regime.

trademarks, patents, industrial designs, geographic indications, software and layout designs of integrated circuits, as well as other rights arising from trademark and patent licensing agreements, technology transfer (i.e., know-how and technical assistance services) and franchise agreements, in order to make them enforceable vis-à-vis third parties. With regard to cultivars, the competent authority for their registration is the Cultivars Protection National Service (Serviço Nacional de Proteção de Cultivares, "SNPC"), an entity of the Brazilian Ministry of Agriculture.

B. Patent Application

Patents refer to titles temporarily held over an invention or utility model, granted by INPI to inventors or authors or other individuals or legal entities holding rights over such creation. In contrast, the inventor is required to disclose in details the entire technical content of the matter protected by the patent. Patents may be classified as:

(i) invention, which are those products or processes meeting the requirements of no obviousness, absolute novelty and industrial application, and it is valid for twenty (20) years as from the filing date of application;

(ii) utility model, which are practical use objects, or portions of such objects, subject to industrial application, having a new form or disposition, involving inventive act, resulting in functional improvements of use or manufacturing, and it is valid for fifteen (15) years as from the filing date of application.

C. Trademark Registration

Trademarks in Brazil are into four categories: word, a symbol constituted only by words, or a combination of words and / or numbers, with no fantasy representation; device, a symbol constituted by a drawing, image, general forms; combination, a symbol constituted of elements combining nominative and figurative presentations; and tri-dimensional, a symbol constituted by the plastic different and necessarily unusual form of the product.

As to the nature of trademarks, they can be product (distinguishes products from other identical, similar or related products), service (distinguishes services from other identical, similar or related services), collective (identifies products from, or services provided by, members of a certain group or entity) and certification (certifies conformity of products or services to certain rules or technical specifications).

It is worth noting that the single deposit in multiple classes is not adopted in Brazil. Accordingly, registration of a trademark is granted to a specific class of services or products, which are organized pursuant to the International Classification of Products and Services (Nice Classification), adopted in Brazil since 2000.

Each registration certificate issued by INPI is valid for 10 years and may be extended every 10 years. During the last year of validity of such registration, the respective holder of such registration shall pay the extension fee to INPI, in order to renew trademark protection for additional 10 years. In contrast to the rules of several other countries, no specific procedure is required in Brazil for trademark renewal other than payment of the respective fee. If the holder of such registered trademark fails to pay the fee within the legal period, trademark protection will expire and the trademark-holder will no longer have the right to use such trademark with exclusivity.

D. Measures for IP Protection

The abovementioned Brazilian federal laws governing IP in Brazil also provide for IP protection measures. In this sense, the Industrial Property Law and Software Law set forth the actions that are considered crimes against IP rights, e.g., the manufacture of a product that is protected by a patent or an industrial design without the consent of its IP owner; the reproduction or imitation of a registered trademark without the consent of its owner; the infringement of software copyrights, among others.

Finally, in October 2004, through the Executive Secretariat of the Ministry of Justice, the National Council for Combating Piracy ("CNCP") was created. CNCP, a collegiate consultative body, which is part of the basic structure of the Ministry of Justice, has the purpose of establishing the guidelines for the formulation and proposal of a national plan to combat piracy, tax evasion resulting from it and IP related crimes. The initiatives designed by CNPC against piracy aimed to contemplate three priority areas of action: repressive, educational and economic.

VI. Environmental Protection

A. Department Supervising Environmental Protection

According to the article 24 of the Brazilian Federal Constitution, the authority to enact laws and regulations regarding environmental matters is concurrent between federal and state governments, which means that the federal government is entitled to enact general rules and guidelines, and states can supplement and enforce them.

States are allowed to create more stringent laws than those established by the federal government. Additionally, states also have the authority to enact laws about specific environmental topics that have not been addressed by a federal law. However, in the case of a federal law being enacted in order to address this topic, the provisions of the state law that are contrary to this federal law will be revoked. Municipalities, in turn, have the authority to supplement federal and state laws, whenever possible, and to enact laws regarding local interests, according to Article 30 of the Brazilian Federal Constitution.

Law No. 6938, of August 31, 1981, as amended ("Law No. 6,938"), established the Brazilian environmental policy ("Brazilian Environmental Policy") and created the National Environment System ("SISNAMA"), comprising the environmental agencies that have the jurisdiction to protect the environment, such as:

(i) the Ministry of the Environment ("MMA"), which has the task of advising the President on the national policy and guidelines;

(ii) the National Environment Council ("CONAMA") as the advisory and regulatory agency;

(iii) Brazilian Institute for Environment and Natural Renewable Resources ("IBAMA") and Chico Mendes Institute for Biodiversity Conservation ("ICMBio") that have authority to implement and enforce the national policy and governmental guidelines;

(iv) regional bodies, such as state-wide environment agencies; and

(v) local bodies, such as local environment agencies.

According to the Complementary Law No. 140/2011, the federal environmental agency, IBAMA, has jurisdiction for licensing depending on the locality and the characteristics of the enterprise (i.e., nuclear power plants, hydroelectric power plants, among others). The municipal environmental agencies have jurisdiction to license enterprises and activities with local impacts, while the state environmental agencies have a general jurisdiction over the environmental licensing proceedings of enterprises and activities that are not covered by federal or municipal agencies.

Environment agencies also have authority to review and enforce penalties for administrative environmental infractions. Pursuant to Complementary Law No. 140/2011, a penalty imposed by the licensing agency prevails over any penalties imposed by other agencies. In addition, the Federal and State Public Prosecutor's Offices (Ministérios Públicos Federal e Estadual) monitor the compliance with the environmental legislation, as well as seek the recovery, repair and compensation of any environmental damage. In the criminal sphere, the police has an important role, since it is has the authority to conduct investigations and provides the Public Prosecutors with evidence on eventual environmental crimes.

B. Brief Introduction of Laws and Regulations of Environmental Protection

Article 225 of the Brazilian Federal Constitution sets forth the duty to preserve the environment for present and future generations and subjects wrongdoers to criminal and administrative sanctions, both for individual and legal entities, as well as the obligation to repair the environmental damage.

The Brazilian Environmental Policy aims at preserving, improving and recovering the environmental quality, in order to ensure the socio-economic development, the interests of national security and the protection of human rights. Such rule also establishes the environmental agencies that are responsible for the environmental protection, as mentioned above, instruments for its implementation (such as the environmental licensing) and define the outlines of civil liability for environmental damage.

The environmental licensing process is governed at the federal level by Law No. 6,938, Resolution No. 237, of December 19, 1997, and Resolution No. 01, of January 23, 1986, both enacted by the National Council for the Environment ("CONAMA"). In summary, it is comprised of a three-phase system, in which each license is conditioned upon the issuance of the preceding one, as follows: Preliminary License, Installation License and Operation License. Moreover, the Interministerial Ordinance No. 60, of March 24, 2015, establishes the administrative procedures for the intervention of the National Foundation for Indigenous ("FUNAI"), the National Historical and Artistic Heritage Institute ("IPHAN") and / or the Palmares Cultural Foundation ("FCP") during the environmental licensing processes conducted by IBAMA.

The management of solid waste is regulated by the Brazilian Solid Residues National Policy, established by Law No. 12305, of August 2, 2010, and Decree No. 7404, of December 23, 2010. In addition, there are several specific standards applicable to solid waste at the state and local levels.

The use of water resources is regulated by Law No. 9433, January 8, 1997 ("Brazilian Water Resources Policy"), creating the Brazilian Water Resources System, and Decree No. 24643, of July 10, 1934 ("Water Code").

In relation to specially protected areas, Law No. 9985, of July 18, 2000, regulated by Decree No. 4340, of August 22, 2002, established the National System for Conservation Units, contemplating criteria and standards for the creation, implementation and management of conservation units. Conservation units are considered as green areas, which are divided, according to their regime of protection, into two distinct groups: full protection conservation units; and sustainable use units. These groups include twelve (12) categories of conservation units, each one with its own specificities.

According to Law No. 12651, of May 25, 2012 ("Brazilian Forest Code"), certain locations referred to as Permanent Preservation Areas ("APPs") shall receive special legal protection because of their importance for preserving water resources, geological stability, biodiversity protection and erosion control. The Brazilian Forest Code also sets forth that every rural property shall preserve a minimum percentage rate of the local vegetation as Legal Reserve, aimed at the sustainable use of the natural resources, conservation of the biodiversity and protection of native fauna and flora.

Law No. 11428, of December 22, 2006, and Decree No. 6600, November 21, 2008, establish special legal protection to Atlantic forest vegetation. Law No. 99556, October 1, 1990, regulated by Decree No. 6640, November 7, 2008, regulates natural caves in Brazil, which are specially protected and may be classified into the following protection levels: low, medium, high and maximum relevance.

Law No. 12187, December 29, 2009, regulated by Decree No. 7390, December 9, 2010, created the National Climate Change Policy, including guidelines and mechanisms to achieve its goals.

Finally, it is worth mentioning Law No. 9605, February 12, 1998 ("Environmental Crimes Act") that provides for criminal and administrative sanctions for conducts and activities harmful to the environment and Decree No. 6514, of July 22, 2008, that regulates administrative environmental infractions and the respective penalties.

C. Evaluation of Environmental Protection

In Brazil, both environmental agencies and Public Prosecutors have the main role in the enforcement of the environmental legislation.

Environment agencies have authority to review and enforce penalties for administrative environmental infractions. Decree No. 6514, of July 22, 2008, establishes that any action or omission that infringes legal rules pertaining to the usage, enjoyment, support, protection and restoration of the environment is deemed to be an administrative violation or infraction. Perpetrators may face administrative penalties, such as fines, embargoes and suspension of activities. Please note that, even though, in theory, only the causer of the infraction should be subject to administrative penalties, the environmental authorities usually extend the concept of the strict liability to the administrative sphere.

Additionally, both Federal and State Public Prosecutor's Offices have jurisdiction for protecting the environment and are very stringent and combative in relation to environmental matters. Therefore, it is usual for the Brazilian Prosecutor's Offices to file a Public Civil Action ("ACP") against the entrepreneur and the licensing authority when there is evidence that there is any threat to the environment; that procedural steps of the environmental licensing or the environmental legislation have been violated. Usually the ACPs are proposed seeking an injunction involving the suspension of the environmental licensing until the final judicial is rendered, what may impact the costs and timeline of the project.

The environmental civil liability is provided by the Brazilian Environmental Policy, which sets forth that environmental civil liability is strict (irrespective of fault), meaning that demonstration of cause-effect relationship between the damage and the agent's conduct suffices to trigger the obligation to redress the environmental damage.

In this sense, it is important to mention the theory of the piercing of the corporate veil, by which shareholders can be liable for environmental damage. Such theory may apply whenever the existence of the company jeopardises the recovery of environmental damages or act as an obstacle to the proper reimbursement or remediation of the former environmental conditions. Accordingly, the shareholders of a corporation may be held liable for indemnification of the damage caused by the corporation to the environment and their patrimony may be affected for the recovery of the environmental damage independently of wrongful use of the legal entity.

Finally, the criminal liability is outlined by the Environmental Crimes Act, which establishes that environmental criminal liability applies to every person, whether individual or legal entity, which concurs with certain offences considered as crimes. The criminal liability depends on the verification of fault or intent.

VII. Dispute Resolution

Firstly, as explained in item I.A.a above, Brazil is a federative republic composed of 26 states and the federal district, all of which are part of the federal judicial system. In addition, as mentioned in item I.A.d above, Brazil adopts a civil law system in governing its disputes, embracing the concept of legality, in which statutes prevail as a source of law.

A. Methods and Bodies of Dispute Resolution

a. Judiciary

The regular form of dispute resolution in Brazil is the judicial dispute resolution. Brazil's judiciary system consists of federal and state courts, divided into common and specialized jurisdictions. The lower jurisdiction is divided by state and federal courts in accordance with the subject of the dispute, as follows:

(i) State Judges have authority to decide all matters except the ones not affecting any interest of the Federal Government and not concerning Labour, Electoral or Military Courts;

(ii) Federal Judges decide all matters of interest of the Federal Government;

(iii) Labour Judges decide on disputes arising from labour relationships;

(iv) Electoral Judges decide on disputes arising from Electoral Law; and

(v) Federal and State Military Judges decide on disputes regarding the Forces (e.g., Army and Navy).

The right to appeal is assured by Brazilian Federal Constitution and each of the abovementioned lower courts have an appealing court, being respectively:

(i) Appellate Courts of Justice ("TJ");

(ii) Federal Regional Courts ("TRF");

(iii) Regional Courts of Labour ("TRT");

(iv) Regional Electoral Courts ("TRE"); and

(v) Military Justice Courts ("TJM").

Moreover, Brazil has Special Instances with jurisdiction over the entire Brazilian territory, to which parties may appeal in very limited and specific cases determined by law:

(i) Superior Court of Justice ("STJ");

(ii) Superior Labour Court ("TST");

(iii) Superior Electoral Court ("TSE"); and

(iv) Superior Military Court ("STM").

Finally, Brazil has a Federal Supreme Court ("STF"), which decides on final basis over all constitutional-related matters.

Brazil has also an administrative body in charge of establishing guidelines and structure of the Brazilian Judiciary, which is the National Justice Board ("CNJ").

All decisions by the Brazilian Judiciary must address disputes within the Brazilian territory, or if: one of the defendants is domiciled in Brazil, an obligation must be complied within the territory, the dispute arises from facts occurred in Brazil, disputes concerning real-estate in the territory, and when probate assets are located in Brazil.

b. Administrative

Brazil does not have an administrative jurisdiction, being the jurisdiction solely held in the judiciary. However, public entities establish internal administrative proceedings in which a party may dispute before the public entity. The administrative proceeding is only binding to the public entity, and can be later questioned by the private party before the Judiciary.

c. Arbitration

Law 9 307, of September 23, 1996 ("Brazilian Arbitration Law"), establishes all matters related to Arbitration within the Brazilian territory. Arbitration allows for resolution of disputes outside of state courts and may only be resorted to for disputes relating to freely transferable property rights, such as contractual disputes. Arbitration offers advantages in comparison to court proceedings: it is more expeditious, can be confidential and allows parties to appoint specialized arbitrators to resolve the dispute. The public administration can also contract the use of arbitration and participate in arbitration proceedings in connection with disputes involving freely transferable property rights.

The main concepts set forth by the Brazilian Arbitration Law are similar to the UNCITRAL Model Law and can be summarized as follows:

(i) An arbitration agreement binds the parties to refer any dispute to an arbitral tribunal instead of state courts;

(ii) Arbitration proceedings are deemed to have commenced when the arbitrators accept their mandate;

(iii) The arbitration award has the same effect on the parties as a decision handed down by the courts and is a judicially enforceable instrument. The arbitration award is not subject to appeal, and, once issued in Brazil, there is no longer any need for it to be recognized by the courts; and

(iv) Enforcement of foreign arbitration awards (as well as foreign judicial awards) depends on the recognition by the Superior Court of Justice (STJ), which applies the 1958 New York Convention on the Recognition and Enforcement of Foreign Arbitration Awards.

In addition, the inclusion of arbitration rules in the bylaws of a joint-stock company binds all shareholders and ensures the dissenting shareholder the right to withdraw from the company upon reimbursement of the value of its shares. However, if a shareholder joins the company after the insertion of an arbitration clause in its by-laws, it is deemed that it has accepted the submission of any disputes to arbitration.

d. Mediation and Negotiation

According to Law 13140, of June 26, 2015, mediation is binding if contractually established. This is important when dealing with multi-tiered dispute resolution clauses. If the parties do not reach a settlement regarding their dispute, any of the disclosed information and concessions cannot be used in subsequent litigation. Any settlement in mediation or negotiation is binding and enforceable before a judge.

Mediation is in full growth, being adopted as a tool to assist parties to find creative solutions to their disputes. Parties are adopting mediation before arbitration and in the Judiciary system. Brazil has specialized centres for mediation and negotiation, which enables parties to hire professionals to assist them in mediation.

B. Application of Laws

The Brazilian Federal Constitution establishes general rules regarding the executive, judicial and legislative branches. It provides the Federal Republic of Brazil to be composed by the Federal Government, the States and the Federal District, and the Municipalities. From this division, all legislation derives from these entities, being: Federal Laws, State and Federal District Laws (the Federal District encompasses the competence of State and Municipal Laws), Municipal Laws, all of which enforceable within their territorial limits.

The Constitution also establishes the limits of the competence of each entity. Some matters are legislated only by federal law (e.g., criminal law). Other matters have shared competence, such as tax law. However, even when competence is shared, the law limits the scope of territorial application and the laws cannot conflict among each other.

Since Brazil has a civil law tradition, Judges vigorously apply the law. Precedents are not binding and are used to aid Judges in interpreting the law and fill in gaps. A Judge may not refrain from the law, but can resort to secondary sources of Law, such as principles, following the purpose of a law, or the Constitution itself, or analogy.

The STJ (which decides about legal matters regarding federal laws) and the STF (which decides about all constitutional-related matters) have the function of harmonizing the interpretation of legal and constitutional rules and interpreting and issuing non-conflicting decisions, following what the laws and the Constitution establish.

VIII. Others

A. Anti-commercial Bribery

a. Brief Introduction of Anti-commercial Bribery Laws and Regulations

Brazil does not have a specific legislation focused on private commercial bribery.[1] On the other hand, it does have a series of public corruption legislation, under which both individuals and legal entities may be liable for acts of corporate corruption.

While individuals may be criminally and civilly liable[2] (according to the Criminal Code, article 333), corruption acts may also cause legal entities to face liability. This liability may be considered either because of the individual's action (that can lead to litigious civil consequences and extrajudicial consequences, such as contracts termination) or because of sanctions based on a variety of anti-corruption laws that sometimes overlap, leading to different sanctions, established by different regulations, involving multiple enforcement agencies, in the administrative and civil spheres.

In this sense, there are a number of different statutes that could be simultaneously applied in case of illegal acts involving public corruption. The most significant law in this regard is Law No. 12846, of August 1, 2013

---

[1] A commercial bribery act could constitute, in principle, fraud pursuant to Article 171 of Law-Decree No. 2848, of December 7, 1940 ("Criminal Code"), which criminalizes the individual for "obtaining, for oneself or a third party, an illegitimate benefit, thereby causing losses to third parties, by inducing mistake or misleading someone through any kind of fraud" . Also regarding individuals, Article 4 of Law no. 7492, of June 16, 1986, provides fraud management as a crime, applicable to financial institutions only. If the fraud aims to deviate clients from another company, the individual may be also punished, according to article 195, III, of the Industrial Property Law.

[2] In Brazil, companies may only have criminal liability concerning certain environmental issues.

("Brazilian Clean Company Act" or "BCCA"), which is in force since January 29, 2014, applicable to occurrences after such date.

The BCCA has created a system of responsibility based on strict liability, under which a conviction can be imposed irrespectively to any proof of fault, wilful misconduct or even knowledge of the wrongdoing. Indeed, according to the system established by the BCCA, a benefit to the investigated company is in principle a sufficient trigger for establishing the company's liability, making it responsible even for acts committed by third parties on its behalf. Additionally, it provides for the joint responsibility of affiliates, subsidiaries, controlling or parent companies, and even members of consortia.

In addition to that, the BCCA is not applied exclusively to cases of bribery of a public official, setting out five main potential offences:

(i) to promise, offer or give, directly or indirectly, any improper advantage to a public official, or third person related to him or her;

(ii) to finance, fund, sponsor or in any way subsidize illicit acts against the public administration;

(iii) to make use of an intermediary (individual or legal entity) to conceal or disguise the real interests or the identity of the beneficiaries of the acts performed;

(iv) regarding public tenders and contracts, to thwart, defraud, impede or disturb any act of public bidding procedure and its competitive nature, to manipulate or defraud the balance of economic and financial contracts with the public administration; and

(v) to hinder the investigation or assessment activity of public agencies, entities or officials, or to interfere with their work, including activities falling within the scope of regulatory agencies and supervisory bodies of the national financial system.

b. Department Supervising Anti-commercial Bribery

The public office responsible for the enforcement of the individuals' sanctions is the Public Prosecutor's Office.

Regarding the BCCA, the responsible for the enforcement at federal level is the Ministry of Transparency, Supervision and Internal Control ("CGU"). There is, however, a multiplicity of possible enforcers, considering that the highest authority within each agency or entity of the Executive, Legislative or Judicial Branches may be involved in the enforcement procedure, depending on the public office victimized by the wrongdoing.

c. Punitive Actions

The table below is an attempt to summarize the complex backdrop of legal penalties that might be discretely or simultaneously applied to legal entities and individuals involved in public corruption acts:

Statutory basis	Kind of action	Potential enforcers	Potential sanctions for legal entities
Brazilian Civil Code	Civil action for damages against legal entities and individuals.	Both the indemnified entity and the Public Prosecutor's Office can start a lawsuit before the appropriate civil court.	Payment of the damages suffered by the public party.
Law No. 8429, of June 2, 1992 ("Improbity Law")	Civil improbity action against legal entities and individuals.	Both the damaged entity and the Public Prosecutor's Office can start a lawsuit before the appropriate civil court.	Loss of assets or amounts unlawfully acquired; payment of a civil fine of up to three times of the benefits gained or damages caused; prohibition from entering into new contracts with the public administration or from receiving tax or credit benefits or incentives, even if through a legal entity of which it is a majority partner, for up to 10 years.

(continued)

Statutory basis	Kind of action	Potential enforcers	Potential sanctions for legal entities
BCCA	Civil proceeding under the BCCA against legal entities only.	Both the damaged entity and the Public Prosecutor's Office can start a lawsuit before the appropriate civil court.	Loss of assets, rights or values that represent a direct or indirect advantage or benefit obtained from the infraction, except for the right of the injured party or third party in good faith; suspension or partial prohibition of its activities; compulsory dissolution of the legal entity; prohibition on receiving incentives, subsidies, donations or loans from public entities and public financial institutions or controlled by the public power, for one to five years.
BCCA	administrative proceeding under the BCCA against legal entities only.	The damaged entity and other agencies, such as the appropriate Internal Control Offices (e.g., the CGU, in case of actions involving the federal administration) can start an investigation ex officio.	Fine; public exposure of the condemnation.
The Public Bidding Law and other public procurement laws and contracts	Administrative liability action under the Public Bidding Law and the Concession Law, mostly against legal entities.	The damaged entity and other agencies can start an investigation ex officio.	Warning; fine; temporary suspension from participation on bidding procedures and prohibition of contracting with the Public Administration, for up to 2 years; declaration of inability to bid or contract with the Public Administration.
Law No. 8443, of July 16, 1992 ("Organic Law of the Federal Court of Accounts")	Administrative liability under the Organic Law of the Federal Court of Accounts, mostly against legal entities.	The Federal Court of Accounts can start an investigation ex officio.	Disbarment to participate, for up to five years, on biddings of the Federal Public Administration.
Law No. 8137, of December 27, 1990 and the Competition Law	Administrative liability against the legal entities (the law includes provisions regarding criminal liability to individuals as well).	CADE.	Fine; publication of the conviction; ineligibility for official financing and for participation in biddings; registration on the National Registry for Consumer Protection; recommendation to the respective public agencies regarding intellectual property and tax matters; company divestiture, transfer of corporate control, sale of assets or partial interruption of activity; prohibition to carry on trade on its own behalf or as representative; any other act or measure required to eliminate harmful effects to the economic order.

B. Project Contracting

a. Permissions System

Government contracting in Brazil can be conducted under the legal framework established by Law No. 8666, of June 21, 1993 ("Public Bidding Law" or "PBL"), Law No. 8987, of February 13, 1995 ("Concession Law" or "CL"), Law No. 11079, of December 30, 2004 ("Public-Private Partnerships Law" or "PPPL"), Law No. 13303, June 30, 2016 ("State Owned Companies Law" or "SOCL") and Law No. 12462, of August 4, 2011 ("Differentiated Regime for Public Contracting Law" or "DRPCL").

The PBL regulates auctions and contracts with the Public Administration for the construction, services, purchase, sale and rental under the scope of the Public Administration. Any such contract shall generally be preceded by an auction process. Additional rules are set forth in Law No. 10,520, of July 17, 2002 ("Reverse Auction Law") and in state and municipal legislation.

The CL regulates common concessions by which the Public Administration transfers the exploitation of a public service or asset to / from the private sector after an auction process. Under the CL, the Government may transfer the performance of certain public services or public works to the private sector by means of a contractual arrangement, in which the concessionaire takes full responsibility for the implementation and financing of the project - if applicable, as well as for its operation and maintenance during the term of the concession agreement. The revenue of the private agent is composed by the tariffs paid by the end users.

The PPPL regulates the concession by which the Public Administration or an indirect administration body engages a private party for the rendering of a public service or the rendering of a service directly or indirectly to the state itself, entailing a high investment and a long-term payment term. The minimum investment under a Public Private Partnership contract is R$20 million and the relevant contract is valid for a term of 5 to 35 years, including any renewal (not sustainable by tariffs).

The SOCL applies to contracts with third parties for the provision of services to public and mixed-capital companies, including engineering and advertising services, acquisition, sale and rental of assets, among others. The DRPCL rules project contracting for specific events as determined by the law.

Regardless of the chosen framework, government contracting in Brazil relies on the idea of isonomic competition. Therefore, in public procurements, foreign companies are also subject to the rules applied to national legal entities in habilitation processes and are required to present a decree authorizing its functioning in Brazil and registry or authorization of the competent authorities to operate in Brazil whenever the activity so requires. In this regard, the foreign company must have obtained its authorization prior to entering the public procurement process in Brazil.

Despite the above, the foreign company shall be exempt of presenting such authorization if the company does not operate in Brazil, in other words, when the company does not have a permanent or continuous activity in Brazilian territory and does not directly act for the execution of the contract. In this case the foreign company will only have to present the equivalent of the applicable Brazilian documents as required by law, duly authenticated by the respective consulate (or apostilled) and translated by a certified translator, and must appoint a legal representative in Brazil with express powers to receive judicial notices and respond in judicial and administrative processes, although those requirements may be waived in certain cases set forth in the law.

The foreign company may also participate in a public procurement without having an authorization in cases where there is the incorporation of a Special Purposes Vehicle, after the awarding of the contract (mandatory under PPPL), which shall be incorporated in Brazil with all the due authorizations, or by participation in a consortium by which a Brazilian entity shall necessarily be the consortium leader.

The isonomy in government contracting may be restrained in the application of tie-break criteria in favour of nationals - according to which national companies, supply of national products or the observance of a sustainable national development may be favoured and in the sector related to the project that is being contracted.

b. Prohibited Areas

Even though after 1995 constitutional reform Brazil achieved significant breakthroughs within the economy, foreign investment is limited or restrict in certain strategic areas.

For further notes on such limitations and restrictions, please refer to item II.A.d above.

For limitations on the acquisition and lease of rural land and real estate property by foreigners in frontier areas, please refer to item II.D.b above.

c. Invitation to Bid and Bidding

PBL establishes several bidding modalities that can be used for contracting with the Public Administration, including but not limited to invitation to bid, public tender and auction. The SOCL and the DRPCL have different bidding procedures.

With respect to Concessions and Public Private Partnerships, after the publication of the Invitation to Bid by the Granting Authority, the companies interested in participating in the respective process present their qualifying documents for analysis and, subsequently, in the bid phase, the proposals are opened and the winning bid is announced.

文莱

作者：Philip Fong、Kennedy Chen、Pengiran Izad、Karen Foong
译者：黄永庆、吴坚

一、概述

(一) 政治、经济和法律环境概述

文莱达鲁萨兰国（以下简称"文莱"）是一个石油储量丰富的伊斯兰教君主国，位于婆罗洲（加里曼丹岛）北岸，于1984年宣布独立，结束了自1888年起作为英国的保护国的局面。

文莱的官方语言是马来语，英语是其第二大语言。文莱人口超过43.2万人[1]，其中近2/3人口被称为马来人，不仅包括马来族，还有一些原住民；约1/10人口为中国人；其余人口包括其他原住民和外籍人士。[2]

文莱的官方宗教是伊斯兰教，其人口主要为穆斯林逊尼派教徒。[3]

1. 政治

文莱苏丹是国家元首和政府首脑。根据1959年《文莱达鲁萨兰国宪法》（以下简称"1959年《宪法》"），苏丹拥有全部行政权力。

文莱分为四个州（daerah）/区，各州/区由被任命的区官员领导；每个州/区又被进一步分为若干个乡镇（mukim），各乡镇由乡镇的各部落（kampungs）或村选举的首领领导。

2. 经济

文莱的经济主要依靠石油和天然气工业，石油和天然气持续占据其国内GDP的一半以上。但近年来，文莱政府加大了发展多样化经济的力度。文莱大部分的石油和天然气产自海上油田，并主要出口到亚洲国家。根据文莱经济规划和发展部的统计，2011年文莱的石油和液化天然气出口收入占出口收入总额的91.5%。[4]

3. 法律

作为政府首脑，文莱苏丹领导五个委员会，即王位继承委员会、部长委员会、枢密委员会、文莱伊斯兰宗教委员会和立法委员会。

王位继承委员会负责决定王位继承人以及因继承事宜发生争议时是否需要摄政者。

部长委员会/内阁是政府部门的首席行政机构，其成员由苏丹任命。苏丹还履行总理、财政部长和国防部长的职能。

枢密委员会负责就宪法问题、马来习俗、授予头衔和奖励以及发布官方赦免等问题向苏丹提出建议，其成员由苏丹任命，包括王室成员和现任及前任高级内阁成员。

文莱伊斯兰宗教委员会负责就伊斯兰教相关问题向苏丹提出建议，其成员由苏丹任命，包括政府部长、国家穆夫提和伊斯兰教教法法官。

立法委员会最初根据1959年《宪法》设立，并于1962年举行第一次选举。1984年文莱宣布独立后，苏丹宣布暂时终止立法委员会。2004年，苏丹恢复了立法委员会并任命了21名成员。2005年，立法委员会成员人数增至29名。据披露，2011年立法委员会新成员将会通过选举产生。

---

[1] 参见世界人口普查之2018年文莱人口（http://worldpopulationreview.com/countries/brunei-population/）。
[2] 参见《大英百科全书》文莱篇（https://www.britannica.com/place/Brunei）。
[3] 参见《大英百科全书》文莱篇（https://www.britannica.com/place/Brunei）。
[4] 参见牛津商业集团：《文莱达鲁萨兰国2013年报告》，第43页。

(二)"一带一路"倡议下与中国企业合作的现状和趋势

近年来,中国在文莱的投资显著增加。2016 年上半年,中国在文莱的投资增长了 9 倍,达 8 600 万美元。① 鉴于中—文关系的进步和发展,文莱与中国企业的合作将更加活跃。

2014 年,中国和文莱签署了建设经济走廊的合作协议,旨在为农业和食品生产领域创造约 5 亿美元的贸易和投资。②

2016 年 7 月,文莱中国企业协会(CEAB)成立,意在促进中文两国企业间的合作,进一步深化两国经贸关系。③

2017 年 2 月,一家中国与文莱合资企业开始接管文莱最大的集装箱码头——穆阿拉港集装箱码头。此外,中国最大的私营化学纤维供应商正在文莱建设一座石化工厂,总投资额近 40 亿美元,预计 2019 年投入使用。④

2017 年 9 月 13 日,中国国家主席习近平与文莱苏丹哈吉·哈桑纳尔·博尔基亚举行会谈。两国领导人就在基础设施、能源、清真食品、农业、渔业和数字化经济等领域推动"一带一路"倡议的合作并努力加强双边关系事宜达成一致。⑤

继 2017 年 9 月 13 日中国对文莱进行国事访问之后,文莱企业已于 2017 年 9 月 15 日与中国企业签署了五项重要的经济和双边合作协议。⑥

二、投资

(一)市场准入

1. 投资监管部门

文莱政府已经成立若干服务机构,以促进外国投资。服务机构包括:

① 文莱经济发展理事会(BEDB):一个法定机构,旨在促进和推动外商对文莱的五个重点商业领域进行投资,即清真产品、技术和创意产业、商业服务、旅游业以及石油和天然气下游产业。⑦

② 外国直接投资行动与支持中心(FAST):该中心为总理办公室下设机构,与文莱经济发展理事会紧密合作,通过协助投资者在文莱开展业务,为未来的投资打下基础。从获得高层审批到推进建立商业运营,外国直接投资行动与支持中心为高价值的投资提供了快速审批流程。⑧

③ 文莱工业发展局(BINA):该局为工业和初级资源部下设机构,负责审批投资项目并监督税收优惠的管理工作。⑨

值得一提的是,文莱政府还于 2016 年宣布将设立外国直接投资和下游产业委员会(FDIDIC),以方便执行全部外国直接投资项目的审批程序,为投资者的项目实施提供一个独立的联络点。⑩

2. 投资行业法律、法规

文莱关于投资的主要立法是 2001 年《投资促进法令》,与《所得税法》共同发挥作用,为投资者提供税收减免的投资激励。

2001 年《投资促进法令》涵盖了一系列符合税收减免条件的先锋行业,主要为非石油经济行业,包括农业、建设业、建筑和重型设备业、化学业、石化和塑料业、消费品业、环境技术业、食品加工

---

① 参见 Singh, D., & Cook, M.,《南洋问题研究》(2017),东南亚研究院—尤索夫伊萨研究所。
② 参见"一带一路"文莱篇(http://beltandroad.hktdc.com/en/country-profiles/brunei)。
③ 参见中华人民共和国驻文莱达鲁萨兰国大使馆网(http://bn.china-embassy.org/eng/sgxws/t1383138.htm)。
④ 参见"一带一路"文莱篇(http://beltandroad.hktdc.com/en/country-profiles/brunei)。
⑤ 参见《中国与文莱联系加强》(http://www.xinhuanet.com/english/2017-09/13/c_136607304.htm)。
⑥ 参见《婆罗洲公报》发表的《文莱企业与中国企业签署了五项重要协议》(https://borneobulletin.com.bn/brunei-companies-ink-five-key-agreements-with-chinese-firms/)。
⑦ 参见文莱经济发展理事会《投资机会》(http://www.bedb.com.bn/invest-bd)。
⑧ 参见文莱商业《重要的服务中介机构》(http://business.gov.bn/SitePages/Your%20Partners.aspx)。
⑨ 参见 http://unctad.org/sections/dite_fdistat/docs/wid_cp_bn_en.pdf。
⑩ 参见文莱达鲁萨兰国能源与工业部《文莱致力于创造利于经商的环境》(http://www.ei.gov.bn/Lists/Industry%20News/NewDispForm.aspx?ID=148)。

业、信息和通信技术业、工业设备业、海洋技术业、金属制造业和一些服务业。[①]

其他对商业有影响的重要法律包括《公司法》(第39号法案)。

3. 投资方式

在文莱注册成立的公司可以由外商100%控股。

外商在文莱直接投资通常采取与本地公司合资的方式。

4. 市场准入和审查标准

如上所述,对于在文莱注册成立的公司的外商持股总额没有限制。有关外商投资的唯一限制是,当公司有2名董事时,至少有1名必须是文莱公民;当公司有2名以上董事时,至少有2名必须是文莱公民。

(二)外汇监管

1. 外汇监管部门

文莱无相关部门。

2. 外汇法律、法规简介

文莱没有外汇管制,非文莱居民可以开设银行账户,在借贷款方面也没有外汇管制。[②]

3. 外国企业外汇管理要求

文莱无相关要求。

(三)金融

1. 主要金融机构

文莱金融管理局根据2010年《文莱金融管理局法令》设立,是文莱的中央银行。其主要职能为制定和执行货币政策、金融机构监管和货币管理。[③]

文莱有许多本国、外国和伊斯兰银行。文莱伊斯兰银行在传统领域和伊斯兰教领域均是文莱规模较大的银行。

2. 外国企业的融资条件

如上所述,非文莱居民可以开设银行账户,在借贷款方面也没有外汇管制。[④]根据洗钱和反恐制度的相关规定,文莱对外国企业的融资没有管制。

(四)土地政策

1. 土地相关法律、法规简介

《土地法》(第40号法案)、《土地分层式所有权法》(第189号法案)[⑤]和《土地获得法》(第41号法案)是文莱与土地相关的三部主要法律。

2. 外国企业获得土地的规定

根据《土地法》的规定,只有文莱公民才被允许拥有土地。然而,根据2009年颁布的《土地分层式所有权法》(第189号法案)的规定,允许外国人申请土地分层式所有权,期限最长为99年。[⑥]

---

① 参见2001年《投资促进法令》第17条。
② 参见国际贸易管理局,美国商务部《文莱——外汇管制》(https://www.export.gov/article?id=Brunei-Foreign-Exchange-Controls)。
③ 参见文莱金融管理局《文莱金融管理局(AMBD)的设立》(http://www.ambd.gov.bn/about-ambd)。
④ 参见国际贸易管理局,美国商务部《文莱——外汇管制》(https://www.export.gov/article?id=Brunei-Foreign-Exchange-Controls)。
⑤ 此处的"土地分层式所有权"可参照我国"建筑物区分所有权"的内容理解,下同。——译者注
⑥ 参见文莱达鲁萨兰国发展部土地局《分层所有权指南》(http://www.tanah.gov.bn/SitePages/Information%20on%20Strata%20Ownership.aspx)。

（五）企业的设立和解散

1. 企业类型及设立程序

在文莱可以设立的企业类型有：
- 独资企业；
- 合伙企业；
- 公司（非上市公司和上市公司）；
- 外国公司的分支机构。①

（1）独资企业

独资企业仅由一人所有和管理。独资企业的所有人对独资企业的债务承担绝对责任。申请设立独资企业获得批准后，相关部门会颁发企业名称证书，费用为 30 文莱元。独资企业的所有人无须缴纳所得税。一般来说，外国人申请设立独资企业不会获得批准。②

（2）合伙企业

《合同法》（第 106 号法案）对合伙企业作了规定。合伙企业可由自然人、文莱本地公司和/或外国公司的分支机构组成，合伙成员数量不得超过 20 个。外国自然人必须事先经移民局批准，方可申请设立合伙企业。申请获得批准后，相关部门会颁发企业名称证书，费用为 30 文莱元。合伙企业无须缴纳企业税或所得税。③

此外，根据《合同法》第 202 条、第 206 条（b）款的规定，合伙人对合伙企业的债务承担连带责任。

（3）公司

根据《公司法》（第 39 号法案）第 4 条的规定，上市公司和非上市公司可以分为以下四种类型：
① 股份有限公司；
② 担保有限公司；
③ 股份和担保有限公司；
④ 无限责任公司。

根据公司类型的不同，股东将承担不同的责任。

非上市公司必须通过其章程限制股东转让股份的权利，其股东数量最少为 2 个，最多为 50 个。股东可以是非文莱公民或居民。子公司可以持有母公司的股份。设立非上市公司无最低股本要求。公司必须有至少 2 名董事。当公司有 2 名董事时，至少有 1 名必须是文莱公民；当公司有 2 名以上董事时，至少有 2 名必须是文莱公民。④

上市公司可以向公众发行可自由流通的股份，其股东数量最少为 7 个。股东可以是非文莱公民或居民。子公司可以持有母公司的股份。设立上市公司原则上无最低股本要求，但可能会受到股份、担保或两者共同的限制。《公司法》对于公司所有者权益没有限制。上述非上市公司董事的相关要求也适用于上市公司。

在文莱设立公司的主要要求如下：

申请人应按表格 A [《公司法》（第 39 号法案）规定的有关待注册公司名称的审批及保留的申请]的规定向公司注册处提交申请，以确定待注册公司名称是否合格。

为使用经批准的名称，申请人应向公司注册处提交以下文件：
① 备忘录和公司章程；
② 法定符合性声明书；
③ 董事名单；
④ 全体董事推选董事长的决议；

---

① 参见文莱达鲁萨兰国外交与贸易部《企业的设立》(http://www.mofat.gov.bn/Pages/Setting-Up-Businesses.aspx)。
② 参见文莱达鲁萨兰国外交与贸易部《企业的设立》(http://www.mofat.gov.bn/Pages/Setting-Up-Businesses.aspx)。
③ 参见文莱达鲁萨兰国外交与贸易部《企业的设立》(http://www.mofat.gov.bn/Pages/Setting-Up-Businesses.aspx)。
④ 参见《公司法》（第 39 号法案）第 138 条。

⑤ 注册办公场所的情况通知；
⑥ 全体股东和董事的身份证或护照的复印件。
注册费根据公司法定股本进行分级收取。公司备忘录及章程中应载明法定股本及分立的股份。注册费用从 300 文莱元（公司法定股本不超过 2.5 万文莱元）至 3.5 万文莱元（公司法定股本超过 1.5 亿文莱元）不等。申请获得批准后，相关部门会颁发公司注册证明书，费用为 25 文莱元。①

（4）外国公司的分支机构

根据《公司法》第九章的规定，如外国公司计划在文莱经营但不在文莱设立公司，则须在文莱注册分支机构。该分支机构须在文莱注册办公场所并雇用文莱本地人作为授权代表。《公司法》还规定了外国公司在文莱注册分支机构的其他要求。分支机构在批准设立前，其注册名称须先由公司注册处批准。②

根据《公司法》第九章的规定，外国公司的分支机构不是独立的法人。因此，外国公司应对其在文莱的分支机构的损失和债务承担全部责任。

外国公司注册分支机构应提交以下文件：
① 表格 A；
② 经认证的外国公司原始注册国家的注册证明复印件；
③ 全体董事的护照或身份证复印件；
④ 规定了公司组织结构的执照、章程及其他文件的复印件，该复印件应经正式认证，并在必要时应进行英文翻译；
⑤ 外国公司董事会关于同意在文莱设立分支机构的决议原件；
⑥ 董事名单及其详细资料、经公司授权代表公司接收通知的一名或多名文莱公民授权代表的姓名、住址。

申请获得批准后，相关部门会颁发注册证明书，费用为 25 文莱元。

注册费根据外国公司法定股本进行分级收取，但以在文莱本地注册公司的注册费为基础减半收取。例如，法定股本不超过 2.5 万文莱元的外国公司将支付 150 文莱元注册费；法定股本超过 1.5 亿文莱元的外国公司最多将支付 1.75 万文莱元注册费。③

2.《公司法》的适用

《公司法》适用于在文莱设立的所有公司以及外国公司的分支机构，但不适用于独资企业或合伙企业。如上所述，《公司法》第 138 条关于对文莱公民的董事人数的规定，对外国投资者尤其重要。

财政部负责监督《公司法》的实施。

3. 解散的方式和要求

在公司清算事项中，股东和成员（视情况而定）将根据公司类型，对公司债务以及清算费用承担相应的责任。④

例如，如果是股份有限公司，公司股东仅需以其股份尚未实缴的部分对公司债务承担责任。如果是担保有限公司，公司成员仅需以其担保的金额对公司承担责任。

在合伙企业解散后，合伙人对合伙企业的债务应承担连带责任。⑤ 在无相反的合同约定的情况下，法院也有权清算合伙企业的业务，用于清偿其债务，并根据合伙成员各自所占份额分配盈余。⑥

（1）解散和清算

根据《合同法》第 207 条的规定，法院可以在特定情况下解散合伙企业。此外，合伙企业也可能因某位合伙人的退伙或死亡而解散。⑦

---

① 参见文莱达鲁萨兰国外交与贸易部《企业的设立》(http://www.mofat.gov.bn/Pages/Setting-Up-Businesses.aspx)。
② 参见文莱达鲁萨兰国外交与贸易部《企业的设立》(http://www.mofat.gov.bn/Pages/Setting-Up-Businesses.aspx)。
③ 参见文莱达鲁萨兰国外交与贸易部《企业的设立》(http://www.mofat.gov.bn/Pages/Setting-Up-Businesses.aspx)。
④ 参见《公司法》(第 39 号法案) 第 155 条第 1 款。
⑤ 参见《合同法》(第 106 号法案) 第 216 条。
⑥ 参见《合同法》(第 106 号法案) 第 218 条。
⑦ 参见《合同法》(第 106 号法案) 第 206 条。

根据《公司法》的规定，经 3/4 以上（含本数）股东同意作出特别决议，文莱的公司可以自愿启动清算程序。此外，法院也可以强制启动清算程序。公司也将被注销。①

（2）破产

2016 年，文莱颁布了《破产法令》，该法令收录了《公司法》中与破产相关的所有条文以及从英国和新加坡借鉴的其他条款。②

值得一提的是，2016 年《破产法令》新增了"公司自愿偿债安排"的章节，内容包括：

① 安排偿还债务的组成部分；
② 就继续偿债事宜，通过重申资产和债务以及与债权人签订合同的方式重组债务；
③ 通过重组公司的股权及管理的方式重组公司，以改善决策的制定和执行；
④ 采取其他必要的恢复或救济公司的行为。

（六）合并和收购

文莱没有关于公司合并和收购的相关立法及法典。

2015 年《竞争法令》禁止已导致或可能导致文莱市场的商品或服务竞争力实质性下降的合并行为。③计划参与合并或已参与合并的一方如认为该合并行为可能违反上述法令的禁止性规定，可向竞争委员会申请由其作出决定。如竞争委员会认为该合并行为违反上述法律的禁止性规定，申请方不服的，可随后就相同事宜向负责管理竞争事宜的部长（目前尚未任命）提出申请。④然而应注意的是，2015 年《竞争法令》中的上述规定尚未生效。

此外，《金融公司法》（第 89 号法案）规定，金融公司与其他金融公司合并或收购其他金融公司的大部分股权，应经财政部长批准。

（七）竞争法规

1. 竞争监管部门

目前文莱没有负责监督竞争管理的部门，但竞争委员会正在组建。⑤

2. 竞争法简介

2015 年《竞争法令》于 2015 年 1 月颁布，但尚未全部生效。该法令旨在禁止三种关键行为：

① 反竞争协议；
② 滥用支配地位；
③ 反竞争合并。⑥

3. 监管竞争的具体举措

2015 年《竞争法令》已生效部分规定了竞争委员会的章程、职能和权力范围。针对反竞争行为应对举措的相关条款尚未生效。

（八）税收

1. 税收制度和规则

《所得税法》（第 35 号法案）和《所得税（石油）法》（第 119 号法案）规定了文莱的税收制度。根据文莱税收制度，仅公司需要纳税。文莱没有个人所得税，也没有营业税或增值税。

---

① 参见《公司法》（第 39 号法案）第 276 条。
② 参见文莱达鲁萨兰国财政部（http://www.mof.gov.bn/divisions/company-insolvency.aspx）。
③ 参见《2015 年竞争法令》第 23 条。
④ 参见《2015 年竞争法令》第 26、27 条。
⑤ 参见 https://asean-competition.org/selectcountry=Brunei。
⑥ 参见文莱达鲁萨兰国经济计划发展部 2015 年《竞争法令》（http://fwww.depd.gov.bn/SitePages/Competition%20Order%202015.aspx）。

2. 主要税收类别和税率

文莱本地和非本地公司的当前税率均为 18.5%，但从事石油和天然气勘探和生产的公司税率为 55%。[①]

3. 税收申报及优惠

如上所述，2001 年《投资促进法令》规定了一系列符合税收减免要求的行业。还有其他类型的公司符合税收减免要求，包括出口具有相关从业资质的服务的公司、生产出口产品的公司以及从事国际贸易的公司。

（九）证券

1. 证券法律、法规简介

尽管文莱自 2013 年就计划建立证券市场，但目前仍未建成。

文莱已颁布 2013 年《证券市场法令》和 2014 年《证券市场规则》，为建设证券市场做准备。

2. 证券市场的监督与管理

根据 2013 年《证券市场法令》的规定，文莱金融管理局将成为文莱证券交易所的监管机构。

3. 外国企业参与证券交易的要求

公司须先向文莱金融管理局提交注册声明和公开招股说明书，并经文莱金融管理局公布生效后，方可进行公开发行的证券交易。

文莱证券交易所对于公司上市的要求尚未发布。

（十）投资优惠与投资保护

1. 优惠政策结构

文莱目前没有官方的优惠政策。

2. 特殊行业和区域支持

国家计划为 2017—2018 财政年度的国家发展预算提供 10 亿美元的支持。以下是预算分配明细[②]：

① 运输和通信部门：37.6%；
② 综合部门（处理已完成但仍负债的项目的融资问题）：24.8%；
③ 工业和贸易部门：19%；
④ 社会服务部门：9.8%；
⑤ 公共设施部门：6.4%；
⑥ 科学与信息技术、研究、开发和创新部门：1.1%；
⑦ 安全部门：1%；
⑧ 公共建筑部门：0.3%。

3. 经济特区

文莱目前没有经济特区，但未来可能将很快建立起来。2017 年 5 月 3 日，华夏幸福基业发展国际（新加坡）投资有限公司（CFLD）、文莱政府和文莱资产公司三方签订了谅解备忘录，建立了公私合作伙伴关系，依照 CFLD 工业城市模型，共同开发经济特区。[③]

4. 投资保护

文莱已与包括中国在内的 8 个国家签署了双边投资协定。文莱与中国的双边投资协定于 2000 年 11

---

① 参见文莱达鲁萨兰国财政部（http://www.mof.gov.bn/divisions/income-tax.aspx）。
② 参见《国家发展预算拨款》，载《文莱时报》（https://www.brudirect.com/news.php?id=24655）。
③ 参见《华夏幸福基金发展国际（新加坡）投资有限公司与文莱政府、文莱资产公司在文莱签署了具有里程碑意义的谅解备忘录，建立战略伙伴关系》，载 https://finance.yahoo.com/news/cfld-international-inks-landmark-mou-093200105.html。

月 17 日签署，但尚未生效。①

三、贸易

（一）贸易监管部门

总理办公室全权负责制定经济和贸易政策。外交与贸易部负责与贸易相关的协议与条约的谈判工作，并主管产地来源证明文件的签发。另外，文莱经济发展理事会和达鲁萨兰公司是文莱法定的发展对外贸易与管理境外投资的机构。其他监管部门包括财政部、卫生部和宗教部。财政部下设皇家海关和税务司，卫生部负责食药和化妆品的监管工作，宗教部负责批准国内的"清真食品"标志。

（二）相关法律、法规简介

管理进出口领域的主要法律是 2006 年《海关法令》和 2006 年《税务法令》。

在进口领域，食品主要受《公共卫生（食品）法》（第 182 号法案）和《公共卫生（食品）规定》规制；药品和化妆用品则主要受 2007 年《药品法令》和 2007 年《药品（化妆品）规定》规制。

鸡肉、牛肉、羊肉和其他清真肉类的进口受《清真肉类法》规制。

根据 2014 年《自贸区法令》的规定，自贸区内可进行免税申报，从而在自贸区内不适用海关法的相关规定。尽管 2014 年《自贸区法令》已经颁布，但迄今为止并没有自贸区。

2015 年《竞争法令》设立了竞争委员会，其目的是为了改善和保证文莱市场的竞争环境。

（三）贸易管理

文莱是东南亚国家联盟（以下简称"东盟"）的成员，该联盟成员国有新加坡、印度尼西亚、文莱、马来西亚、泰国、菲律宾、缅甸、柬埔寨、老挝和越南。

2017 年 4 月 1 日，文莱发布了新的关税价目表和贸易商品分类。新的规则将《东盟关税协议》中确立的规则更加具体化。东盟成员国出于促进东盟内部贸易的考量，制定了统一的商品分类标准。

不仅文莱是《东盟关税协议》的签署方，东盟同澳大利亚和新西兰、中国、印度、日本和韩国之间都有多边自贸协定。

文莱还与日本签订了双边经济伙伴协议（即《文莱—日本经济伙伴协议》），并与智利、新西兰和新加坡签订了《跨太平洋战略经济伙伴关系协议》。

（四）进出口商品的检验、检疫

为了确保食品进口和分销过程中的质量和安全，文莱要求食品贸易商和进口经销商必须遵守 1998 年《公共卫生（食品）法》（以下简称《食品法》）和 2000 年《公共卫生（食品）规定》（以下简称《食品规定》）。

《食品法》第 2 条第 1 款规定，"食品"指的是任何用来制造、加工、出售或供人消化、咀嚼的物质和其中的任何成分。

《食品规定》第 9 条第 1 款规定，未在食品包装上依照本规定标明成分，任何人都不得对该食品进行进口、广告、制造、出售、托运或邮寄。法律要求必须标明的项目包括食品名称、成分列表和原材料来源（包括添加剂的来源）、净重/净含量、生产日期、保质期、原产国名称以及进口食品的本地进口商的名称及地址。

《食品规定》第 9 条第 4 款第 f 项规定，任何食品如含有食品添加剂，必须说明添加剂的类型和来源，即是来自动物、化学物质还是植物。

《食品规定》第 20 条第 1 款规定，在食品中含有本规定不允许添加的添加剂时，任何人都不得以销售为目的进口、制造或零售此类食品。

---

① 参见《中华人民共和国政府和文莱达鲁萨兰国政府关于鼓励、促进和保护投资协定》（2000 年 11 月 17 日），载 http://investmentpolicyhub.unctad.org/Download/TreatyFile/514。

《食品规定》第 20 条第 4 款进一步规定，即使是被许可的食品添加剂，在纯度未达到本规定要求的标准时，任何人不得进口、销售、广告、制造、托运或邮寄。如本规定未对某食品添加剂的纯度进行规定，则应参照世界粮农组织和世界卫生组织食品添加剂专家联合委员会所推荐的食品添加剂纯度标准。

《食品规定》第 19 条规定，需要标明生产日期的食品如未在卫生服务司下设的食品安全与质量控制局注册，任何人不得将其进口至文莱。虽然《食品规定》没有明确要求食品原料/添加剂应分别注册，但其应符合《食品规定》中的相关要求。如《食品规定》未作具体要求，则根据《食品规定》第 20 条第 4 款的规定，该食品原料/添加剂的纯度应参照世界粮农组织和世界卫生组织关于其纯度的要求。

根据《药品法令》的规定，所有药品及化妆品在文莱市场上进行销售前，都应在卫生部的医药服务司进行备案。

根据《清真肉类法》的规定，任何进口至文莱的鸡肉、牛肉、羊肉和其他清真肉类都需要获得批准，包括检查屠宰场以证明进口肉类符合清真标准。

（五）海关管理

对于进口事宜，进口商应首先在皇家海关和税务司进行线上注册。如其拟进口受管制的货物，必须事先获得许可，然后网上申报、支付关税、检验货物和清关。

对于出口事宜，出口商应首先在皇家海关和税务司进行线上注册。如其拟出口受管制的货物，必须事先获得许可，然后进行申报、支付关税和清关。

四、劳动

（一）劳动法律、法规简介

2009 年《劳工法令》仅规定了几种特定类型的劳动合同，不适用于从事管理、行政或保密工作的雇员，此类雇员的劳动合同由一般合同原则进行调整。

2009 年《劳工法令》规定雇员须年满 16 周岁方可签订劳动合同。劳动合同必须包括以下内容：姓名、雇佣性质、工作期限、终止合同的通知期限、工资、遣返条件。

2009 年《劳工法令》还规定了通知期限、立即解雇、准予扣除额、薪酬、休息日、假期、工作时间和加班及病假。

根据《劳工赔偿法》（第 74 号法案）的规定，凡属"劳工"定义范围内的雇员，雇主必须为其购买劳工赔偿保险，以便在劳工发生工伤事故或患疾病时可根据本法的规定取得固定的费用。

2009 年《工作场所安全与卫生法令》（WHSO）的实施，旨在保障工作场所人员的安全、健康和福利，并规定了其他有关事宜。

《工作场所安全与卫生法令》规定：

① 场所使用人有义务确保其使用场所的卫生与安全；
② 雇主有义务采取合理措施确保雇员及所有在工作场所可能受影响的人员的健康和安全；
③ 负责人有义务确保其承包商、分包商及其雇员的健康与安全；
④ 确保工作场所任何机器设备的安全和维护的义务；
⑤ 以安全且不危害健康的方式改造或安装机械或设备的义务。

2009 年《工作场所安全与卫生法令》将维护雇员安全、健康和福利方面的权力授予其任命的权力机构。如果情况严重，机构的委员可发布在指定日期生效的"停工令"，有效地停止一切工作或程序。

2009 年《工作场所安全与卫生法令》第 28 条规定，法令中规定的特定级别或明确规定的工作场所必须配有一名工作场所卫生与安全人员。第 29 条、第 30 条规定，特定级别或明确规定的工作场所必须设立工作场所卫生与安全委员会，并配有一名卫生与安全审核员。

2009 年《工作场所安全与卫生法令》还规定，卫生与安全检查员、官员、审核员和培训人员拥有检查、调查及审批的权力。

（二）雇用外国劳工的要求

1. 工作许可

在文莱雇用外国劳工，雇主必须首先自劳动委员会处取得外国劳工工作许可证。并且，雇主还需证明他们曾尝试从文莱就业中心招聘文莱本地人从事该职位。

2. 申请程序

① 在文莱就业中心登记公司信息。
② 在文莱就业中心发布招聘信息达两周时间。如果本地求职者前来应聘该职位，则必须优先考虑。
③ 如两周内没有招聘到合适的本地人选，则需向文莱就业中心申请许可函件，该程序可能需要 3 日。
④ 向劳工局申请外国劳工工作许可证，劳工局须在 7 日内作出决定。
⑤ 申请必须由已注册的劳动中介公司（B 类）提交。
⑥ 必须填写外国劳工工作许可证申请表。
⑦ 一经批准，必须向劳工局缴纳安全保证金。
⑧ 为外国劳工向移民局申请外国劳工工作签证。所需文件包括：
• 雇主申请函；
• 签证申请表；
• 表格 23 工作准证申请；
• 两张护照复印件；
• 劳工局批准的外国劳工工作许可证；
• 工作中介公司的证件；
• 向卫生部申请体检的材料（可能需要 1～2 周时间）。
⑨ 劳工须至劳工局签订劳动合同。
⑩ 劳动合同签订后，劳工必须到移民局申请工作证和绿卡。该程序可能需要 1 周时间。所需文件包括：
• 身份证申请表；
• 带有照片页和有效工作签证的旅行证件（原件和复印件）。
⑪ 劳工工作准证经批准后 3～6 个月内，将接受强制审查。

3. 社会保险

根据《信托基金劳动法》（第 167 号法案）（TAP）的规定，文莱的雇主和雇员，不论其是文莱永久居民还是公民，均需按其工资的 5% 缴纳员工信托基金。

2010 年又增设了一项计划——补充退休养老基金（SCP）。补充退休养老基金计划与 TAP 类似，公私部门的所有雇员须强制缴纳。根据补充退休养老基金计划的有关规定，雇主和雇员需按工资的 3% 缴纳补充退休养老基金，最高为 98 文莱元。

综上所述，每位员工需缴纳的员工信托基金和补充退休养老基金分别为其工资的 10% 和 6%。员工的扣减额和缴纳额计入员工信托基金和补充退休养老基金，并于员工退休时从中向其支付相应金额。

（三）出入境

1. 签证类型

下列入境签证可供使用：
① 社交访问签证；
② 专业访问签证；
③ 工作签证；
④ 亲属准证。

2. 出入境限制

中国的外交护照和公务护照持有者可以免签进入文莱。对于其他护照持有者，可在落地后办理社交访问签证。前往文莱无工作的护照持有者可办理社交访问签证。专业访问签证需在抵达文莱之前办理；由雇主提出签证申请，签证有效期由移民局工作人员决定，最长为3个月，可续签。

持有专业访问签证或工作签证的人不得携其他人一同在文莱工作。亲属准证可签发给工作签证持有者的亲属。

（四）工会和劳工组织

根据《工会法》（第128号法案）的规定，工会可在文莱进行登记。已登记的工会禁止与文莱境外的工会建立关系。文莱的工会很少，登记在册的不足3个。

（五）劳动争议

《贸易争端法》（第129号法案）对贸易争议作出了规定，将某些行为规定为犯罪，如恐吓行为、基本服务违约行为、可能危及生命或财产的违约行为。该法规定了某些类型的罢工或停工是非法行为，允许已登记的工会采取和平的整改措施，同时规定了任何贸易争端均可采取仲裁措施。

五、知识产权

（一）知识产权法律、法规简介

文莱知识产权局（BruIPO）于2013年设立，旨在重组和管理其国内知识产权的行政工作。知识产权局目前负责监管国内专利、商标、外观设计和植物新品种保护的注册工作。其设立的目的是提供一个简单、实用和被广泛认可的知识产权体系，这个体系不但会保护观念和创新，更会促进"知识产权文化"中的创造力和创新的不断涌现。

文莱自1999年起通过了多部有关商标、外观设计、版权和专利的法律，同时一直以来不断引进新的法律、法规来构建本国的知识产权法律体系。文莱与知识产权的注册和保护相关的法律有：

① 1999年《版权法令》；
② 1999年《外观设计法令》；
③ 《外观设计法则》；
④ 2014年《外观设计（国际注册）法则》；
⑤ 2011年《专利法令》；
⑥ 2012年《专利法则》；
⑦ 2015年《植物新品种保护法令》；
⑧ 2016年《植物新品种保护法则》；
⑨ 《商标法》（第98号法案）；
⑩ 2000年《商标法则》；
⑪ 《（进口侵权货物）商标规定》。

文莱知识产权法律、法规符合国际标准，其严格遵守世界知识产权组织（WIPO）项下的相关国际条约和协议。文莱是多个国际公约的成员国，例如《巴黎公约》《保护文学和艺术作品伯尔尼公约》《专利合作条约》和《工业品外观设计国际注册海牙协定》，同时也是《与贸易有关的知识产权协定》（TRIPS）和《商标国际注册马德里协定》（《马德里协定》）的成员。

尽管文莱已有专利、著作权、商标和外观设计等基本知识产权的法律保护体系，然而尚未对地理标志和商业秘密等知识产权进行立法保护，目前仅通过普通法律对其进行保护。

（二）专利注册

文莱的专利保护依据的是2011年《专利法令》和2012年《专利法则》，其专利申请体系适用"先申请原则"，即第一个提交申请的人相较于在其后提交同样专利申请的人享有优先权。文莱专利体系的主要特点是"自我评定"，即由申请人决定程序如何进行以及何时进行。另外，文莱专利体系还仅实行"形式审查"，实质审查工作则外包给奥地利、丹麦和匈牙利的外国专利局。

文莱的所有专利申请必须以英文提交，使用其他语言的申请文件必须提供英文翻译。

申请步骤

步骤	程序
1	申请人提交申请表（表格 PE1）以及： • 法定费用（160 文莱元）； • 必要的申请文件和/或信息。 包括说明书和摘要。
2	文莱知识产权局会进行初审并发布确认函。
3	一旦一项申请满 18 个月，文莱知识产权局将会在《专利期刊》上公示。
4	自申请之日（即步骤 1）起 21 个月内，申请人可提交如下申请： A. 检索—审查申请（表格 PF11 和 PF16）； B. 检索和审查综合申请（表格 PF12）； C. 根据向规定的专利局或依照《专利合作条约》申请优先权的结果，提交申请； D. 根据相应申请的检索结果提交申请，并提交审查申请（表格 PF16）。
5	申请人自申请之日（即步骤 1）起 42 个月内提出申请，文莱知识产权局视专利发明的复杂程度会在 2~4 年内授予专利权。

来源：文莱知识产权局官网

一项专利如计划在文莱注册，该发明必须同时满足以下条件：
① 必须是新型的（新颖性）；
② 必须具有独创性和工业应用性。

人和/或动物的手术、治疗或诊断的方法发明不予注册专利，因其不能应用于工业。鼓励攻击、不道德或反社会行为的发明，即使满足获得专利的条件，也不予注册。

文莱是《专利合作条约》的成员国。文莱公民和居民有权依据该条约提交国际申请，并可通过 PCT 系统提交国际专利申请，以寻求同时在各成员国获得专利保护。

另外，文莱也是东盟专利审查合作项目（ASPEC）的参与国。该项目是一个区域工作共享计划，由东盟成员国的 9 个知识产权局参与。其设立的目的是减少重复的专利检索和审查工作，使参与国的申请人的专利申请更快、更高效。东盟专利审查合作项目是免费的，英语为其工作语言（缅甸除外）。

已注册的专利自申请日起保护期为 20 年，专利权人需按年续费。

（三）外观设计注册

《外观设计法令》于 2000 年生效，其规定了新型外观设计或产品实用新型可以注册。文莱知识产权局管理与此相关的注册申请，其只进行形式审查，且不做任何的前案检索。

如在文莱注册外观设计，在申请日提交的外观设计必须是新颖的，即在申请日前在文莱没有被注册、公开、使用或出售。一旦被注册，外观设计将会在《外观设计期刊》上公示，同时文莱知识产权局会授予申请人注册证书。注册后初始保护期限为 5 年，其后可续展两次，每次 5 年，最长保护期限共计 15 年，权利人应在每个 5 年期限届满时续费。

外观设计注册须向文莱知识产权局外观设计登记处申请，并提交以下文件：
① 一张填写完整的申请表——设计表格 1；
② 一个非成套物品的外观设计；
③ 一个成套物品的外观设计。
在文莱注册一项外观设计通常需要 8~12 周。

如上所述，文莱是《工业品外观设计国际注册海牙协定》的成员国，该协定为外国企业在文莱注册外观设计提供了便利。

（四）商标注册

依据《商标法》（第 98 号法案）和 2000 年《商标法则》的规定，注册商标受保护。如在文莱注册商标，商标应在视觉上可感知并可用图形表示。另外，拟注册的商标还应在形式与实质上满足《商标法》（第 98 号法案）和 2000 年《商标法则》的要求。如果拟注册的商标是由非英语字母的字符组成，例如中国文字、日本文字或阿拉伯字母，还必须提供其翻译及音译。

从 2017 年起，文莱也接受非传统商标的注册，例如，气味、声音和味道，条件是申请人可以将商标以书面形式可视化地呈现出来。

申请步骤

步骤	程序
1	申请人申请商标注册应提交： • 封面； • 对拟注册商标的描述（规格为 A4 纸）； • 表格 TM1（外国申请人需提交表格 TM22）； • 法定费用，每类商标 150 文莱元。
2	申请人将会收到一份载明商标及申请日期详情的通知。
3	文莱知识产权局将会审查申请是否有缺漏（形式审查），以及是否满足法律对商标注册的要求。
4	一旦申请被批准，文莱知识产权局将签发表格 T27，申请人需支付 125 文莱元的公告费。
5	文莱知识产权局在《商标期刊》上公示 3 个月（异议期）。
6	文莱知识产权局向申请人颁发商标注册证。

来源：文莱知识产权局官网

商标的保护期为自申请注册之日起 10 年，可无限续期，但应缴纳续期费用。

商标的保护具有地域性，任何在文莱知识产权局注册的商标，只能在文莱获得保护。但是，如上所述，文莱是《马德里协定》的成员国，如任何文莱的申请人希望商标在外国获得保护，可通过马德里体系完成，但需缴纳费用。

（五）植物新品种注册

植物新品种在文莱是一项独立的知识产权，该保护体系激励了私人不断从事研究与开发，从而推动新的育种技术出现。所有的植物属种都可依据 2015 年《植物新品种保护法令》受到保护。

对植物新品种给予保护同样会激励研发新的、有益的植物品种，供农民和消费者使用，同时也促进了农业、园艺业和林业的发展。此外，该做法也同样使植物育种者获得排他的生产、销售植物新品种育种材料的权利，以及禁止他人未经允许使用其植物新品种。

申请步骤

步骤	程序
1	提交填写完整的申请表（表格 PVP3），其应包括如下几项： • 用英文表述的技术性问卷（表格 PVP-TQ）； • 法定费用，1 600 文莱元； • 其他必要的相关证明材料和信息。
2	文莱知识产权局将会对其进行初审（形式审查）并向申请人发布确认函。
3	申请信息及拟注册的名称将会在《植物新品种保护期刊》上公示。
4	文莱知识产权局的外国专业审查合作伙伴负责进行技术审查。
5	申请人提出申请，知识产权局会向其颁发权利证书。注册的植物新品种的详细信息将在《植物品种保护期刊》上公示。

来源：文莱知识产权局官网

为了使植物新品种在文莱受到保护，其必须符合 2015 年《植物新品种保护法令》的要求。植物新品种的保护具有属地性，在文莱知识产权局注册的植物新品种只能在文莱获得保护。

（六）知识产权保护措施

依据国际标准，文莱已在本国建立了完善的知识产权法律体系，以实现对知识产权的管理与保护，并且重视对法律的修改与更新，以确保知识产权法适应不断变化发展的实践。

2017年8月，文莱知识产权局在国际商标协会（INTA）的支持下主持了以"商标执法最佳实践"为主题的政策对话会议，并计划在文莱建立综合执法体系。文莱政府代表出席了该会议。

2017年8月，文莱知识产权局与丹麦专利商标局（DKPTO）就专利实质检索和审查的转接安排事宜签署了一份谅解备忘录。自2012年文莱实施专利体系以来，丹麦专利商标局就一直为文莱知识产权局提供审查服务，而该谅解备忘录的达成，标志着两国知识产权局在专利领域的下一个5年合作的开始。

2017年9月，文莱知识产权局和日本专利局签署了《专利审查快速通道意向书》，旨在通过一项新的专利审查合作共享倡议，为在参与合作的知识产权局提交相关专利申请的日本申请人提供更快速的审核流程，以加强知识产权保护。根据《专利审查快速通道意向书》的规定，每个参与合作的专利局都可借助其他专利局已完成的工作成果，从而减轻审查工作负担，提高专利质量。文莱知识产权局还曾于2015年与日本专利局签署了合作备忘录，旨在加强两国在商标、专利、外观设计等工业产权领域的合作。

六、环境保护

（一）监管环境保护的部门

文莱政府十分坚定地将"可持续发展"作为社会经济发展的核心。在国家发展计划（2012—2017年）中，环境战略是已确定的八项战略之一，旨在确保各方面发展都能以有组织、有成效的方式实施。作为国家承诺坚持促进环境可持续发展的一部分，文莱于2016年签署了《巴黎协定》，成为东盟成员国中交存《巴黎协定》批准书的首批国家之一。

负责监督国内环境保护的主要政府机构是发展部下属的环境、公园和娱乐司，该司发布了《环境法案和指南》《工业发展的污染控制指南》和《回收123手册》等指南和手册，亦不时发布有关公共回收的参考资料和建议。此外，环境、公园和娱乐司还负责废物管理、环境养护和管理、景观和休闲区管理以及国内、双边和国际间的环境合作事宜。

（二）环境保护法律、法规简介

2016年《环境保护和管理法令》于2016年9月19日正式生效，是文莱第一部与环境相关的立法。在其颁布之前，有关环境的重要法律曾经或仍然存在于以下立法：

①《石油开采法》（第44号法案）；
②《石油（管道）法》（第45号法案）；
③《采矿法》（第42号法案）；
④《森林法》（第46号法案）；
⑤《供水法》（第121号法案）；
⑥《土地法》（第40号法案）；
⑦《毒品管理法》（第114号法案）；
⑧《港口法》（第144号法案）；
⑨《城乡规划（发展控制）法》（第143号法案）。

根据2016年《环境保护和管理法令》的规定，文莱公民有义务采取切实措施，确保对环境的保护和管理以及防止、减少或控制任何可能导致污染或破坏环境的潜在危害。文莱公民也都应遵守该法令的要求以及后续制定的任何附属规定。

新颁布的法律也规定每个计划开展农业、渔业、林业和工业工程等活动的人员都有义务向当局或任何授权官员提交书面通知，以便其能够在开展前述活动之前考虑有关环境问题的相关事项。如任何人员在未向当局或任何授权官员提交书面通知的情况下开展2016年《环境保护和管理法令》中所列的活动，即属犯罪，一经定罪将被处以100万文莱元以下的罚款、3年以下的监禁或两者并罚。

(三) 环境保护的评估

文莱政府正与企业和非营利组织合作，通过实施回收服务、执行环保意识方案和活动以及建立环保俱乐部等多项措施，来帮助兑现养护和保护该国生态系统的承诺。文莱除了在国内作出努力外，也在国际上作出承诺。文莱是若干联合国公约的缔约国，例如《维也纳公约》《蒙特利尔议定书》和《控制危险废物越境转移及其处置巴塞尔公约》。

从区域上看，文莱是"婆罗洲之心"计划的缔约方，该计划是由世界自然基金会在2005年发起的一项保护协议，旨在保护婆罗洲岛的一个22万平方公里的森林区域。文莱与其他两个共同拥有婆罗洲岛的国家进行可持续地管理。

近年来，文莱为确保其在快速城市化和发展中实现环境可持续发展的目标作出了可信的努力。然而，其环境法律框架仍处于初期阶段，并且需要填补空白，以为全国环境保护提供更明确的指导。

新的法规和指导已经起草以填补这些空白，但尚未全部生效。这些规定如下：
① 2005年《海洋污染防治法令》；
② 2008年《海洋污染防治（授权机构）规定》（尚未生效）；
③ 2008年《海洋污染防治（综合罪行）规定》（尚未生效）；
④ 2008年《海洋污染防治（散装有毒液体物质）规定》（尚未生效）；
⑤ 2008年《海洋污染防治（石油）规定》（尚未生效）；
⑥ 2008年《污染防治（报告事件）规定》（尚未生效）；
⑦ 2008年《污染防治（垃圾）规定》（尚未生效）；
⑧《工业发展的污染控制指南》。

七、争议解决

（一）争议解决的方法和机构

《最高法院法》（第5号法案）在文莱建立了民事法庭体系。一审法院分为三级：地方法院负责审理涉案金额为5万文莱元以下的纠纷或索赔案件；中级法院负责审理涉案金额为5万文莱元至30万文莱元的纠纷或索赔案件；高级法院负责审理涉案金额为30万文莱元以上的纠纷或索赔案件。中级法院设立了专门的商事法庭来处理商事案件，以快速跟进商事案件。高级法院拥有与英国法院类似的海事管辖权。

对地方法院的审理结果不服，可上诉至高级法院。对中级法院和高级法院的审理结果不服，可上诉至上诉法院，上诉法院由3名法官组成。只要双方在上诉法院裁决之前达成一致，就可以进一步上诉至伦敦的最高法院。

在文莱，各方可以选择仲裁的方式解决争议。2009年《仲裁法令》规定了文莱当事人之间的仲裁。文莱是《纽约公约》的签署国，外国仲裁裁决可像文莱法院的判决一样，可以在文莱强制执行。

文莱仲裁中心的设立是为了提供一个实际场地为文莱的仲裁提供支持。

（二）法律适用

文莱法院承认并执行各方的仲裁约定，如果各方同意通过仲裁解决争议，而一方当事人将争议诉至法院寻求救济，文莱法院将中止诉讼程序，以便仲裁继续进行。文莱法院承认各方自行选择适用何种准据法的一般约定，但该约定不得以规避文莱法律的规定为目的。

八、其他

（一）反商业贿赂

1. 反商业贿赂法律、法规简介

《防止腐败法》（第131号法案）分为七个部分，规定了反腐局的管理权、腐败的罪名、搜查和调

查权、证据及起诉。

2. 反商业贿赂监管部门

文莱苏丹可任命一名反腐局局长，局长不受除苏丹以外的其他任何人的控制或指示。

《防止腐败法》第 4A 条规定了反腐局的职责：

① 接受并考虑该法规定的犯罪行为的任何报告；
② 调查涉嫌犯有该法所规定罪行的行为以及企图犯罪和共谋行为；
③ 审查公共机构的实践和操作程序，以利于发现相关犯罪和更正此类实践和操作程序；
④ 建议公共机构在实践和制度上作出调整，以降低腐败的可能性；
⑤ 教育公众以提高其反腐意识；
⑥ 获得公众对反腐机构打击腐败行动的支持和协助。

反腐局拥有逮捕和调查的权力。《防止腐败法》第 20 条规定，所有人必须协助反腐局官员履行职责。

《防止腐败法》第 22 条规定，当反腐局要求提供有关犯罪的任何信息时，所有人均有法定义务提供该信息。本条规定，不提供信息视为犯罪，可被处以 2 万文莱元的罚款及 1 年的监禁。

《防止腐败法》第 23 条规定，当一个人被合理怀疑有犯罪嫌疑时，反腐局官员有权查询此人全部银行账户，银行有义务提供这些信息。

《防止腐败法》第 23 条 A 至 C 款规定，任何反腐局官员可向第三方寻求关于被调查人的资产或办公室情况的说明，有权限制被调查人处置其一切资产并冻结其银行账户，有权扣留其护照长达 6 个月。

《防止腐败法》保留了律师和当事人之间的（保密）特权。

《防止腐败法》第 24 条 A 款规定，在刑事诉讼中，被告人在任何情况下所作的任何陈述，无论是向警察或是向反腐局作出的，无论在作出陈述前是否被警示过，都可作为证据。

3. 惩罚措施

《防止腐败法》第 5 条规定了以下情形构成犯罪：任何人向他人承诺或提供其他任何以促成或避免正在进行中、可能发生或拟发生的特定交易为引诱或报酬，索取、接受或同意接受好处；任何人向负责特定交易项目或将要负责该交易项目的公共机构的成员、官员、雇员提供好处以促成或避免正在进行中、可能发生或拟发生的任何与该公共机构相关的特定交易。

《防止腐败法》第 6 条规定了与代理人的贿赂交易，并规定了以下情况视为犯罪：

① 代理人接受、同意接受或获得好处，以做或不做其委托人安排的事宜；
② 允诺给予、同意给予代理人好处，以使该代理人做或不做与其委托人相关的事宜；
③ 任何人为欺骗代理人的委托人，故意向代理人提供与其委托人相关的错误、虚假、不完整的收款账户或其他文件，以误导其委托人。

《防止腐败法》第 5 条、第 6 条规定，对该罪行可处以 3 万文莱元以下的罚款和 7 年以下的监禁。如果该行为是已与或拟与公共机构签订合同，则可处以 3 万文莱元以下的罚款和 10 年以下的监禁。

《防止腐败法》第 8 条规定，即使没有达到目的，第 6 条规定的收受好处者也可能被认定有罪。

《防止腐败法》第 9 条规定，以贿赂方式获取已撤回的招标视为犯罪；第 10 条规定，贿赂立法机关成员的视为犯罪。

《防止腐败法》第 11 条规定，如因下述事宜向公共机构成员提供好处或奖励，或公共机构成员因下述事宜向任何人索取好处或奖励，即构成犯罪：

① 对公共机构的任何措施决议或问题投票赞成、反对或弃权；
② 执行、不执行或采取行动促进、妨碍或推迟官方行为；
③ 通过表决、放弃表决或同意（签署）合同的方式使他人获利或受益；
④ 以公共机构成员的身份表示或压制他人的支持或反对意见。

《防止腐败法》第 12 条规定，离任或现任公职人员的生活水平或拥有资产与其目前或过去的收入不相符，即构成犯罪，除非其能向法院合理解释维持其生活水平的方法或资产来源。

对《防止腐败法》第 9 条、第 10 条、第 11 条、第 12 条规定的罪行可处以 3 万文莱元以下的罚款及 7 年以下的监禁。

《防止腐败法》第 13 条、第 14 条和第 15 条规定了教唆、预谋和共谋。

《防止腐败法》第 16 条规定，任何公职人员都有义务向反腐局提供和贿赂性礼物、承诺给予或收受贿赂相关的一切信息，否则可被处以 500 文莱元以下的罚款及 6 个月以下的监禁。

《防止腐败法》第 25 条规定，除非相反情况得到证实，否则收受好处都将被认为是受贿行为。根据《防止腐败法》第 27 条的规定，个人资产证明可作为佐证，证明某人接受过、获得过、同意接受或同意获得好处。

《防止腐败法》第 33 条规定，轻率地或毫无根据地报告贪污、贿赂行为也是一种犯罪；第 35 条规定，向任何人透露自己为涉嫌贪污、贿赂的调查对象视为犯罪；第 37 条规定，在文莱，文莱公民应为其在文莱境外的贪污、贿赂行为负刑事责任。

"好处"的定义较广，包括：
① 金钱、礼物、贷款、酬金、证券、资产、动产或不动产的权益；
② 提供办公场所、礼遇、就业机会；
③ 债务的支付、解除、免除或者清偿；
④ 任何形式的有价值的建议；
⑤ 延展资金的债务偿还期；
⑥ 对某事的帮助、投票赞成、同意或施加影响；
⑦ 任何其他服务、帮助、利益，包括延缓行使债权人权利。

（二）工程承包

只有在发展部登记过的承包商才可能被邀请参加文莱政府公共基础设施项目的招标或竞标。不同类型的许可授予不同类型的工程承包，较低等级的工程承包项目对文莱本地公司参与及本地化管理程度要求更高，技术或资本密集型的工程承包项目对文莱本地公司参与及本地化管理程度要求较低。

在石油和天然气领域，主要石油公司在投标文莱的项目和工程时，应遵守总理办公室下属的能源部发布的《本地商业发展指南》的规定。该指南规定："文莱的石油和天然气行业的石油和天然气中游和下游运营商应采用《本地商业发展指南》中的分配方式……进行商品和服务的承包活动的分配。"可分为以下四个方面：

① 基础项目（低技术、低标的额）：仅对文莱本地公司开放，公司的本地就业比例要求为 90%，本地出资比例要求为 70%，管理层本地化比例要求为 100%，并由本地的经理或经营者管理。

② 开发项目（低技术、高标的额）：仅对文莱本地公司开放，公司的本地就业比例要求为 50% 到 90% 之间，本地出资比例要求为 70%，管理层本地化比例要求为 50%，并且他们必须最大限度地利用本地的分包商。

③ 核心项目（高技术、高标的额）：向所有公司开放，公司的本地就业比例要求为 50% 到 90% 之间，本地出资比例要求为 50%，管理层本地化比例要求为 50%，并且他们必须最大限度地利用本地的分包商。

④ 高度专业化项目（高技术、低标的额）：向所有公司开放，并且尽量提供本地就业和本地管理。

Brunei

Authors: Philip Fong, Kennedy Chen, Pengiran Izad, Karen Foong
Translators: Huang Yongqing, Wu Jian

I. Overview

A. General Introduction to the Political, Economic, Social and Legal Environment of the Country Receiving Investment

Brunei Darussalam is an oil-rich sultanate located on the north coast of the island of Borneo. In 1984, Brunei gained independence after having been a British protectorate since 1888.

The official language is Malay, with English as a major second language. Brunei has a population of over 432,000.[①] Nearly two-thirds of the population is officially classified as Malay, with not only ethnic Malays but also certain indigenous peoples included in this category. Approximately one-tenth of the population is Chinese. The rest of the population comprises other indigenous peoples and expatriates.[②]

The official religion in Brunei Darussalam is Islam and its population is predominantly Sunni Muslim.[③]

a. Political

His Majesty The Sultan and Yang Di-Pertuan of Brunei Darussalam is both head of state and head of government. Under the Constitution of Brunei Darussalam 1959 ("1959 Constitution"), His Majesty The Sultan and Yang Di-Pertuan has full executive powers.

Brunei Darussalam is divided into four daerah, or districts, which are each headed by appointed district officers. Each daerah is further subdivided into units called mukim, which are each headed by a headman elected from amongst the various kampungs, or villages, of the mukim.

b. Economic

Brunei's economy is mainly fuelled by its oil and gas industries, with oil and gas consistently accounting for over half of the country's Gross Domestic Product. However in recent years, the Government of Brunei Darussalam has increased efforts to diversify its economy. A large proportion of Brunei's oil and natural gas is produced from offshore fields and is exported to mostly Asian countries. According to Brunei's Department of Economic Planning and Development, exports of oil and liquefied natural gas reached 91.5% of total exports in 2011.[④]

c. Legal

As head of government, His Majesty The Sultan and Yang Di-Pertuan of Brunei Darussalam presides over five councils, namely, the Council of Succession, the Council of Ministers, the Privy Council, the Brunei Islamic Religious Council and the Legislative Council.

The Council of Succession determines who inherits the throne and whether there is a need for a regent in disputes relating to succession.

The Council of Ministers, or Cabinet, is the chief executive body that is the head of government ministries. Members of the Council of Ministers are appointed by the Sultan, who also fulfills the roles of Prime Minister, Minister of Finance and Minister of Defence.

The Privy Council advises the Sultan on issues such as constitutional matters, Malay customs, the conferring of titles and awards and the exercise of official pardons. Members of the Privy Council are appointed by the Sultan and include members of the royal family as well as current and former senior cabinet members.

The Brunei Islamic Religious Council advises the Sultan on matters pertaining to Islam. Members of the Brunei Islamic Religious Council are appointed by the Sultan and include government ministers, the state mufti

---

① World Population Review, Brunei Population 2018.Available at http://worldpopulationreview.com/countries/brunei-population/.
② Encyclopedia Britannica, Brunei.Available at https://www.britannica.com/place/Brunei.
③ Encyclopedia Britannica, Brunei.Available at https://www.britannica.com/place/Brunei.
④ Oxford Business Group, The Report: Brunei Darussalam 2013, page 43.

and sharia law judges.

The Legislative Council was originally established under the 1959 Constitution, with its first election held in 1962. It was subsequently temporarily suspended by the Sultan in 1984 when Brunei gained independence. In 2004, the Sultan revived the Legislative Council by appointing 21 members. It was further expanded in 2005 to include 29 members. It was also announced in 2011 that new members of the Legislative Council would be elected in future.

B. The Status and Direction of the Cooperation with Chinese Enterprises Under the B&R

Chinese investment in Brunei has increased significantly in recent years. In the first half of 2016, China's investments in Brunei increased nine-fold to US$86 million.① It is likely that Brunei's cooperation with Chinese enterprises will continue to flourish given the progress and development of Brunei-China relations.

In 2014, China and Brunei signed an agreement to establish an economic corridor aimed at creating approximately US$500 million of trade and investment in agriculture and food production.②

In July 2016, the Chinese Enterprises Association in Brunei ("CEAB") was established. The establishment of CEAB aimed to promote cooperation between the enterprises from Brunei and China, and further deepen the economic and trade relations between the two countries.③

In February 2017, a China-Brunei joint venture started managing the Muara Container Port, Brunei's largest container terminal. In addition, China's largest private chemical-fibre supplier is constructing a petrochemical plant in Brunei with a total investment of close to US$4 billion, with operations expected to commence in 2019.④

On 13 September 2017, Chinese President Xi Jinping held talks with Brunei's Sultan Haji Hassanal Bolkiah. Both leaders agreed to promote cooperation within the Belt and Road Initiative, in areas such as infrastructure, energy, halal food, agriculture, fishery, and the digital economy, as well as to work towards stronger bilateral ties.⑤

Following China's state visit to Brunei on 13 September 2017, Brunei firms signed five significant economic and bilateral agreements with Chinese companies on 15 September 2017.⑥

II. Investment

A. Market Access

a. Department Supervising Investment

The Brunei government has set up several facilitating agencies in order to promote foreign investment. These include:

(i) the Brunei Economic Development Board ("BEDB"), a statutory body which seeks to promote and facilitate foreign investment into Brunei in the five priority business areas, namely Halal, Technology & Creative Industry, Business Services, Tourism and Downstream Oil & Gas⑦;

(ii) the FDI Action and Support Centre ("FAST") under the Prime Minister's Office which works closely with the BEDB to support incoming investment by facilitating the setting up of investors' business in Brunei. FAST offers a fast-track approval process for high-value investments, from obtaining high level approvals to expediting the set-up of business operations;⑧ and

(iii) the Brunei Industry Development Authority ("BINA") under the Ministry of Industry and Primary Resources, which approves investment projects and oversees the administration of tax incentives.⑨

Notably, the Brunei government also announced in 2016 that it would be setting up the Foreign Direct Investment and Downstream Industry Committee ("FDIDIC") to facilitate the approval process for all FDI projects,

---

① Singh, D., & Cook, M., (2017) Southeast Asian Affairs 2017.ISEAS - Yusof Ishak Institute.
② Belt and Road, Brunei.Available from http://beltandroad.hktdc.com/en/country-profiles/brunei.
③ Embassy of the People's Republic of China in Negara Brunei Darussalam, The Chinese Enterprises Association in Brunei Inaugurated.Available from http://bn.china-embassy.org/eng/sgxws/t1383138.htm.
④ Belt and Road.Brunei.Available from http://beltandroad.hktdc.com/en/country-profiles/brunei.
⑤ Xinhuanet, China, Brunei to boost ties.Available from http://www.xinhuanet.com/english/2017-09/13/c_136607304.htm.
⑥ Borneo Bulletin, Brunei companies ink five key agreements with Chinese firms.Available from https://borneobulletin.com.bn/brunei-companies-ink-five-key-agreements-with-chinese-firms/.
⑦ The Brunei Economic Development Board, Investment Opportunities.Available from http://www.bedb.com.bn/invest-bd.
⑧ BusinessBN, Key Facilitation Agencies.Available at http://business.gov.bn/SitePages/Your%20Partners.aspx.
⑨ http://unctad.org/sections/dite_fdistat/docs/wid_cp_bn_en.pdf.

and provide investors with a single point of contact for project implementation.[1]

b. Laws and Regulations of Investment Industry

The primary piece of legislation on investment in Brunei is the Investment Incentives Order, 2001. Read with the Income Tax Act, the Investment Incentives Order, 2001 offers investment incentives in the form of tax relief to investors.

The Investment Incentives Order, 2001 contains a list of pioneer industries which qualify for tax relief. These pioneer industries largely fall within the non-oil economy and include agri-business, construction, building and heavy equipment, chemicals, petrochemicals and plastics, consumer goods, environmental technologies, food processing, information and communications technology, industrial equipment, marine technology, metal manufacturing, and some services.[2]

Other significant laws which affect business include the Companies Act (Cap.39) (the "Companies Act").

c. Forms of Investment

100% foreign ownership of companies incorporated in Brunei is permitted.

Foreign direct investment in Brunei also often takes the form of joint ventures with local companies.

d. Standards of Market Access and Examination

As mentioned above, there is no restriction on total foreign ownership of companies incorporated in Brunei. The only restriction regarding foreign investment is that when the company has two directors, at least one must be ordinarily resident in Brunei. Where there are more than two directors, at least two of them must be ordinarily resident in Brunei.

B. Foreign Exchange Regulation

a. Department Supervising Foreign Exchange

Not applicable to this region.

b. Brief Introduction of Laws and Regulations of Foreign Exchange

There are no foreign exchange controls in Brunei. Non-resident bank accounts are permitted and there are no foreign exchange restrictions on borrowing by non-residents.[3]

c. Requirements of Foreign Exchange Management for Foreign Enterprises

Not applicable to this region.

C. Financing

a. Main Financial Institutions

The Autoriti Monetari Brunei Darussalam is the central bank of Brunei and was established under the Autoriti Monetari Brunei Darussalam Order, 2010. Its key functions are the formulation and implementation of monetary policies, the regulation and supervision of financial institutions as well as currency management.[4]

There are a number of local, foreign as well as Islamic banks in Brunei. Bank Islam Brunei Darussalam is Brunei's largest bank in both the conventional and Islamic sector.

b. Financing Conditions for Foreign Enterprises

As mentioned above, non-resident bank accounts are permitted and there are no restrictions on borrowing by non-residents.[5] Subject to money-laundering and anti-terrorism regulations, there are no restrictions against financing for foreign enterprises.

---

[1] Energy and Industry Department, Brunei Darussalam, Brunei committed to creating business-friendly environment.Available from http://www.ei.gov.bn/Lists/Industry%20News/NewDispForm.aspx?ID=148.
[2] Section 17 of the Investment Incentives Order, 2001.
[3] International Trade Administration, US Department of Commerce, Brunei-Foreign Exchange Controls.Available from https://www.export.gov/article?id=Brunei-Foreign-Exchange-Controls.
[4] Autoriti Monetari Brunei Darussalam, Establishment of Autoriti Monetari Brunei Darussalam (AMBD).Available from http://www.ambd.gov.bn/about-ambd.
[5] International Trade Administration, US Department of Commerce, Brunei-Foreign Exchange Controls.Available from https://www.export.gov/article?id=Brunei-Foreign-Exchange-Controls.

D. Land Policy

a. Brief Introduction of Land-related Laws and Regulations

The Land Code (Cap.40), Land Code (Strata) Act (Cap.189) and Land Acquisition Act (Cap.41) are the three primary pieces of land-related legislation in Brunei.

b. Rules of Land Acquisition for Foreign Enterprises

Under the Land Code, only Brunei citizens are allowed to own land. However, the Land Code (Strata) Act (Cap.189) which was introduced in 2009 allows foreigners to apply for strata title ownership of property for up to 99 years.[1]

E. The Establishment and Dissolution of Companies

a. The Forms of Enterprises and the Procedure of Establishment

Businesses in Brunei may be established under the following business entities:
(i) sole proprietorship;
(ii) partnership;
(iii) company (private or public); or
(iv) branch of a foreign company.[2]

a) Sole proprietorship

A sole proprietorship is owned and managed by only one person. The sole proprietor has absolute responsibility for all obligations of the sole proprietorship. Upon approval of an application for sole proprietorship, a business name certificate is issued at a fee of B$30. Sole proprietors are not subject to income tax. Generally, registration approval is not granted to foreigners.[3]

b) Partnership

Partnerships are governed by the Contracts Act (Cap.106) (the "Contracts Act"). A partnership may consist of individuals, local companies and / or branches of foreign companies. The maximum permitted number of partners is 20. Applications by foreign individuals are subject to prior clearance by the Immigration Department before they are registered. Upon approval, a business name certificate is issued at a fee of B$30. Partnerships are not subject to corporate or income tax.[4]

Further, pursuant to sections 202 and 206(b) of the Contracts Act, partners will be held jointly and severally liable for the partnership's obligations.

c) Company

Under Section 4 of the Companies Act (Cap.39), four modes of incorporation apply to both private and public companies:
(i) companies limited by shares;
(ii) companies limited by guarantee;
(iii) companies limited by both shares and guarantee; and
(iv) unlimited companies.

Depending on the mode of incorporation, the liability of the individual shareholders will be as such.

A private company must, by its constitution, restrict the right of members to transfer shares. It must have at least two and not more than 50 shareholders. Shareholders need not be citizens or residents of Brunei. A subsidiary company may hold shares in its parent company. No minimum share capital is required. The company must have at least two directors. Where there are two directors, at least one must be ordinarily resident in Brunei. Where there are more than two directors, at least two of them must be ordinarily resident in Brunei.[5]

A public company is one which may issue freely transferable shares to the public. There must be at least seven shareholders. The shareholders need not be citizens or residents of Brunei. A subsidiary company may hold shares in its parent company. No minimum share capital is required for setting up a public company. It may be

---

[1] Lands Department, Ministry of Development, Brunei Darussalam, Information on Strata Ownership.Available from http://www.tanah.gov.bn/SitePages/Information%20on%20Strata%20Ownership.aspx.
[2] Ministry of Foreign Affairs and Trade, Brunei Darussalam, Setting Up Businesses.Available from http://www.mofat.gov.bn/Pages/Setting-Up-Businesses.aspx.
[3] Ministry of Foreign Affairs and Trade, Brunei Darussalam, Setting Up Businesses.Available from http://www.mofat.gov.bn/Pages/Setting-Up-Businesses.aspx.
[4] Ministry of Foreign Affairs and Trade, Brunei Darussalam, Setting Up Businesses.Available from http://www.mofat.gov.bn/Pages/Setting-Up-Businesses.aspx.
[5] Section 138 of the Companies Act (Cap.39).

limited by shares, guarantee or both, or it could be unlimited. There are no restrictions under the Companies Act as to the ownership in the equity of a company. The requirements above relating to directors in private companies apply to public companies as well.

The principal requirements for incorporating a company in Brunei are as follows:

Submit the application to the Registrar of Companies ("ROC") in the prescribed Form A (Application for Approval and Reservation of Name for A Company to be Incorporated under the Companies Act, Cap 39) to determine if the proposed name is available.

The following documents should be submitted to the ROC for the use of an approved name:
(i) Memorandum and Articles of Association;
(ii) Statutory Declaration of Compliance;
(iii) List of Directors;
(iv) Consent to act as director by all the proposed directors;
(v) Notice of Situation of Registered Office; and
(vi) Copies of identity cards or passports of all shareholders and directors.

The registration fees are based on a graduated scale on the authorised share capital of the company. The amount of the authorised share capital and division into shares have to be stated in the company's Memorandum and Articles of Association. Companies incorporated in Brunei are required to pay an amount ranging from B$300 where the capital does not exceed B$25,000 to a maximum of B$35,000 where the capital is in excess of B$150 million. Upon approval, a Registration of Companies certificate will be issued and a fee of B$25 is imposed.[1]

d) Branch of a Foreign Company

Any foreign company wishing to establish a business in Brunei and which does not incorporate as a local company must register as a branch of the foreign company as provided under Part IX of the Companies Act. The branch must have a registered office in Brunei and must appoint local authorised persons. The Companies Act also stipulates the requirements for the registration of a branch of a foreign company in Brunei Darussalam. The proposed name of the branch must first be approved by the ROC prior to the approval for registration.[2]

Under Part IX of the Companies Act, a branch of a foreign company is not a separate legal entity. As such, the foreign company will be held fully liable for losses and debt incurred by the Brunei branch.

The following documents are required for registration:
(i) Form A;
(ii) Certified true copy of the foreign company's Certificate of Incorporation from the Country of Origin; and
(iii) Copies of passports or identity cards for all the directors;
(iv) A certified copy of the Charter, Statutes or other instruments defining the constitution of the foreign company, duly authenticated and when necessary, with English translation;
(v) An original copy of the Board of Directors' Resolution approving the registration of a branch in Brunei Darussalam; and
(vi) A list of directors together with their particulars and the names and addresses of one or more persons residing in Brunei Darussalam authorised to accept notice on the Company's behalf.

Upon approval, a Certificate of Incorporation will be issued and a fee of B$25 is imposed.

The registration fees payable in respect of the registration of a branch depend on the authorised share capital of the holding company but are 50 per cent less than the fees payable for locally-incorporated companies. For example, a company with an authorised capital not exceeding B$25,000 will pay a registration fee of B$150. Where the capital is in excess of B$150 million, the maximum fee imposed is B$17,500.[3]

b. The Application of the Companies Act

The Companies Act applies to all companies incorporated in Brunei as well as to branches of foreign companies, but not to sole proprietorships or partnerships.

As discussed above, the provision in Section 138 regarding the number of directors that must be ordinarily resident in Brunei is of particular importance to foreign investors.

The Ministry of Finance oversees the implementation of the Companies Act.

---

[1] Ministry of Foreign Affairs and Trade, Brunei Darussalam, Setting Up Businesses. Available from http://www.mofat.gov.bn/Pages/Setting-Up-Businesses.aspx.
[2] Ministry of Foreign Affairs and Trade, Brunei Darussalam, Setting Up Businesses. Available from http://www.mofat.gov.bn/Pages/Setting-Up-Businesses.aspx.
[3] Ministry of Foreign Affairs and Trade, Brunei Darussalam, Setting Up Businesses. Available from http://www.mofat.gov.bn/Pages/Setting-Up-Businesses.aspx.

c. Routes and Requirements of Dissolution

In the event of winding up of a company, the liabilities of shareholders or members (as the case may be) to contribute to the payment of the company's debts and liabilities as well as the costs of winding up will depend on the mode of incorporation of the company.[1]

For instance, if a company is limited by shares, a shareholder of such a company will only be liable to contribute to the debt or liability of the company up to the amount unpaid on his shares. In the case of a company limited by guarantee, the member of such a company will only be liable make a contribution up to the amount undertaken to be contributed by him.

In the event of the dissolution of a partnership, the rights and obligations of the partners will continue in all things necessary for winding-up the business of the partnership.[2] The court is also empowered to, in the absence of any contract to the contrary, wind up the business of the partnership, provide for the payment of its debts, and distribute the surplus according to the respective shares of the partners.[3]

a) Dissolution and Liquidation

Pursuant to section 207 of the Contracts Act, partnerships may be dissolved by the court in specified situations. Partnerships may also be dissolved when a member retires from the partnership, or upon the death of any member.[4]

Under the Companies Act, a locally-incorporated company may be wound up voluntarily via special resolution which requires the approval of at least three-fourths of the members. Alternatively, the company may be wound up compulsorily by the court. The company may also be struck off the register.[5]

b) Insolvency

In 2016, Brunei introduced the Insolvency Order, 2016, which consolidates all provisions relating to insolvency under the Companies Act with additional provisions adopted from the United Kingdom and Singapore.[6]

In particular, the Insolvency Order, 2016 includes a new chapter on company voluntary arrangement. Voluntary arrangement under the Insolvency Order, 2016 may include:

(i) a composition in satisfaction of its debts;

(ii) restructuring of debts through restatements of assets and liabilities and agreement with creditors on maintaining payments;

(iii) reorganising the company by restructuring the ownership and management of the company to lead to better decision making and execution; or

(iv) any other acts as may be necessary for the rehabilitation or rescue of the company.

F. Merger and Acquisition

There is no legislation in Brunei governing mergers and acquisitions, neither is there a takeover code.

The Competition Order, 2015 prohibits mergers that have resulted, or may be expected to result in a substantial lessening of competition within any market in Brunei for goods or services.[7] A party to an anticipated merger or involved in a merger who thinks the merger may contravene the aforementioned prohibition may apply to the Competition Commission for a decision. If the Competition Commission decides that the merger contravenes the prohibition, the said party may subsequently apply to the Minister charged with the responsibility for general competition matters (who has not yet been appointed) for the merger to be exempted from the prohibition.[8] It should be noted that these provisions in the Competition Order, 2015 are not yet in force.

Further, the Finance Companies Act (Cap.89) requires finance companies to obtain the approval of the Minister of Finance before merging or consolidating with or acquiring a majority interest in any other finance company.

G. Competition Regulation

a. Department Supervising Competition Regulation

There is currently no department in Brunei that supervises competition regulation. However, the formation of a

---

[1] Section 155(1) of the Companies Act (Cap.39).
[2] Section 216 of the Contracts Act (Cap.106).
[3] Section 218 of the Contracts Act (Cap.106).
[4] Section 206 of the Contracts Act (Cap.106).
[5] Section 276 of the Companies Act (Cap.39).
[6] Ministry of Finance, Brunei Darussalam, Company Insolvency. Available from http://www.mof.gov.bn/divisions/company-insolvency.aspx.
[7] Section 23 of the Competition Order, 2015.
[8] Sections 26 and 27 of the Competition Order, 2015.

Competition Commission is currently underway.[1]

b. Brief Introduction of Competition Law

The Competition Order, 2015 was enacted in January 2015 but has yet to fully come into force. The Order is targeted at prohibiting three key acts, namely:
(i) anti-competitive agreements;
(ii) the abuse of dominant position; and
(iii) anti-competitive mergers.[2]

c. Measures Regulating Competition

The portions of the Competition Order, 2015 which have come into effect are those relating to the constitution, function and powers of the Competition Commission. The provisions targeting anti-competitive practices are not in force yet.

H. Tax

a. Tax Regime and Rules

The Income Tax Act (Cap.35) and Income Tax (Petroleum) Act (Cap.119) govern taxes in Brunei. Under the Brunei tax regime, only companies are subject to tax. There is no personal income tax in Brunei nor is there sales or value added tax.

b. Main Categories and Rates of Tax

The current tax rate for resident and non-resident companies is 18.5%. Companies which engage in the exploration and production of oil and gas will be taxed at a rate of 55%.[3]

c. Tax Declaration and Preference

As discussed above, the Investment Incentives Order, 2001 contains a list of pioneer industries which qualify for tax relief. There are also other categories which qualify for tax relief, including companies engaged in export of qualifying services, companies which engage in production for export, and companies engaged in international trade.

I. Securities

a. Brief Introduction of Securities-related Laws and Regulations

Brunei does not currently have a securities market, although plans have been underway since 2013 to establish one.

In preparation for the launch of its securities market, Brunei has enacted the Securities Market Order 2013 and the Securities Market Regulations 2014.

b. Supervision and Regulation of Securities Market

Under the Securities Market Order, 2013, the Autoriti Monetari Brunei Darussalam will be the regulatory authority in charge of the Brunei stock exchange.

c. Requirements for Engagement in Securities Trading for Foreign Enterprises

In order to engage in securities trading through a public offering, a registration statement and form of prospectus for the public offering must be filed with and declared effective by the Autoriti Monetari Brunei Darussalam.

The requirements for companies to be listed on the Brunei stock exchange have not yet been released.

J. Preference and Protection of Investment

a. The Structure of Preference Policies

There are no official preference policies in Brunei.

b. Support for Specific Industries and Regions

One billion dollars was proposed for the National Development budget for the 2017-2018 financial year. The following is the breakdown of the budget allocation[4]:

---

[1] ASEAN Competition, Brunei Darussalam Department of Economic Planning and Development.Available from https://asean-competition.org/selectcountry=Brunei.
[2] Department of Economic Planning and Development, Brunei Darussalam, Competition Order 2015.Available from http://fwww.depd.gov.bn/SitePages/Competition%20Order%202015.aspx.
[3] Ministry of Finance, Brunei Darussalam, Income Tax.Available from http://www.mof.gov.bn/divisions/income-tax.aspx.
[4] Brudirect, Budget Allocation for National Development.Available from https://www.brudirect.com/news.php?id=24655.

(i) Transport and Communications sector-37.6%;
(ii) Miscellaneous Sector (deals with financing of completed projects that still have liabilities)-24.8%;
(iii) Industrial and Trade Sector-19%;
(iv) Social Services Sector-9.8%;
(v) Public Utilities Sector-6.4%;
(vi) Science and Information Technology, Research and Development and Innovation-1.1%;
(vii) Security Sector-1%;
(viii) Public Buildings Sector-0.3%.

c. Special Economic Areas

There are currently no special economic areas in Brunei. However, a Special Economic Zone is likely to be established in the near future. On 3 May 2017, China Fortune Land Development International (Singapore) Investment Pte Ltd ("CFLD"), the Government of Brunei Darussalam and Darussalam Assets Sdn Bhd signed a Memorandum of Understanding to enter into a public-private partnership for the development of a Special Economic Zone in Brunei using CFLD's industry city model.①

d. Investment Protection

Brunei is a signatory to bilateral investment treaties ("BITs") with eight countries, including China. The BIT with China was signed on 17 November 2000 but is not yet in force.②

III. Trade

A. Department Supervising Trade

The Prime Minister's Office has overall charge over the direction of policies relating to the economy and trade. The Ministry of Foreign Affairs and Trade is in charge of negotiating treaties and agreements in relation to foreign trade, this ministry will also issue certificates of origin. In addition, Brunei Darussalam Economic Development Board (BEDB) and Darussalam Enterprise (DARE) are statutory bodies that have been set up to develop and expand trade and foreign investment into Brunei. Other relevant Ministries and Departments are the Ministry of Finance, under which the Royal Customs and Excise Department operates, the Ministry of Health which is responsible for food, medicines and cosmetics and the Ministry of Religious Affairs, which is responsible for the approval of Halal labelling.

B. Brief Introduction to Trade Laws and Regulations

The main laws which govern import and export are the Customs Order 2006 and the Excise Order 2006.

The importation of foodstuffs is governed by the Public Health (Food) Act (Cap 182) and the Public Health (Food) Regulations. The importation of medicines and cosmetics is governed by the Medicines Order 2007 and the Medicines (Cosmetic Products) Regulations 2007.

The Halal Meat Act applies to the importation of all chicken, beef, lamb and other halal animal meat into Brunei.

The Free Trade Zones Order 2014 provides for the declaration of free trade zones and exemption from the provisions of the customs Act for businesses within such zones. To date, although the Free Trade Zones Order has been published, no free trade zones have been declared.

The Competition Order 2015 establishes a Competition Commission which is tasked to promote and protect competition in markets in Brunei Darussalam.

C. Trade Management

Brunei is a member of the Association of South East Asian Nations (ASEAN), made up of Singapore, Indonesia, Brunei, Malaysia, Thailand, Philippines, Myanmar, Cambodia, Laos and Vietnam.

---

① Yahoo News, CFLD International Inks Landmark MOU with The Government of Brunei Darussalam and Darussalam Assets to Establish Strategic Partnership in Brunei.Available from https://finance.yahoo.com/news/cfld-international-inks-landmark-mou-093200105.html.
② UNCTAD, Agreement Between the Government of the People's Republic of China and the Government of His Majesty the Sultan and Yang Di-Pertuan of Brunei Darussalam Concerning the Encouragement and Reciprocal Protection of Investment (17/11/2000). Available from http://investmentpolicyhub.unctad.org/Download/TreatyFile/514.

Brunei introduced a new Brunei Darussalam Tariff and Trade Classification on 1st April 2017. The new tariff and trade classification incorporates the ASEAN Harmonized Tariff Nomenclature. This was developed by the ASEAN member countries to facilitate trade within ASEAN by having a common commodity classification system or nomenclature.

Brunei Darussalam, is a party to the ASEAN Free trade Agreement, and multilaterally there are Free Trade Agreements between ASEAN and Australia and New Zealand, China, India, Japan and South Korea.

Bilaterally, Brunei Darussalam has concluded an Economic Partnership Agreement with Japan (the Brunei-Japan Economic Partnership Agreement) and a multi-party agreement with Chile, New Zealand and Singapore known as the Trans Pacific Strategic Economic Partnership.

D. The Inspection and Quarantine of Import and Export Commodities

In ensuring food imported and distributed in Brunei is safe and of the quality required, food traders and importers are required to comply with the Public Health (Food) Act 1998 ("Food Act") and the Public Health (Food) Regulations, 2000 ("Food Regulations").

Under Section 2(1) of the Food Act, "food" includes any substance manufactured, processed, sold or represented for use for human consumption, chewing substances, and any ingredient thereof.

Regulation 9 (1) of the Food Regulations states that no person shall import, advertise, manufacture, sell, consign or deliver any prepacked food if the package of any prepacked food does not bear a label containing all the particulars required by these Regulations. The particulars of the labelling requirement shall include name of food, list of ingredients and its sources (including additive), net weight / volume, date marking, storage instruction, name of country of origin and name & address of local importer for imported food.

Regulation 9(4)(f) states that any food containing food additive is required to state the type and the origin whether it is from animal, chemical, plant.

Regulation 20 (1) of the Food Regulations states that no person shall import or manufacture for sale or sell any article of food which contains any food additive which is not permitted by the Regulations.

Regulation 20(4) further state that no person shall import, sell, advertise, manufacture, consign or deliver any permitted food additive unless the purity of that food additive conforms to the specifications as provided in this Part. Where it is not so provided, the purity of the permitted food additive shall conform to the specifications as recommended by the Joint Food and Agriculture Organisation of the United Nations and World Health Organisation (FAO / WHO) Expert Committee on food additives.

Under Regulation 19 of the Food Regulation, no person shall import any food requiring a date marking into Brunei that has not been registered with the Food Safety & Quality Control Division, Department of Health Services. There is no provision for the separate registration of food ingredients / additives but these must comply with the provisions of the Regulations and of they do not then the purity of that food additive must conform to the specifications as provided in FAO / WHO, as the case may be as required under Regulation 20(4).

Under the Medicines Order, all medicines and cosmetics, before they are sold or marketed in Brune,i must be notified to the Department of Pharmaceutical Services of the Ministry of Health.

All chicken, beef, lamb and other halal animal meat which is to be imported into Brunei will need to be approved under the Halal Meat Act, which includes an audit on the slaughterhouse or abattoir to ensure compliance with Halal standards.

E. Customs Management

For import, importers must first register on-line with the Royal Customs and Excise Department. A permit must then be obtained for controlled goods, declarations are made online, after which duty is paid and then goods are subject to inspection and clearance.

For export, exporters must first register with the Royal Customs and Excise Department. A permit for the exportation of controlled goods must be obtained, then declaration, payment and clearance.

IV. Labour

A. Brief Introduction of Labour Laws and Regulations

The Employment Order 2009 regulates certain types of employment contracts only. The Employment Order does not apply to any person employed in a "managerial, executive or confidential position". The employment contracts of such employees are regulated by general contractual principles.

The Employment Order provides that the minimum contractual age for a contract of employment is 16.

The minimum requirements for a contract include names, nature of employment, duration, period of notice for termination, rates of salary, conditions of repatriation.

The Employment Order regulates notice periods, summary dismissals, allowable deductions, remuneration, rest days, holidays, hours of work and overtime and sick leave.

Pursuant to the Workman's Compensation Act (Cap 74) all employees who fall within the definition of "workman" must have workman's compensation insurance obtained for them by their employer for the purpose of making payment of fixed sums under the Act in the event of any industrial accident or illness sustained.

The Workplace Safety and Health Order 2009 ("the WHSO") was introduced to provide for the safety, health and welfare of persons in workplaces and for any related matters.

The WHSO sets out :

(i) Duties of occupiers to ensure the health and safety of premises which they occupy;

(ii) Duties of employers to take reasonable measures to ensure the health and safety of employees and all persons who may be affected by any undertaking carried out by at the workplace;

(iii) A principal's duty to ensure health and safety of their contractors or subcontractors and their employees ;

(iv) The duty to ensure the safety and maintenance of any machinery at the workplace;

(v) The duties to erect modify or install machinery or equipment in a manner that is safe and without risk to health.

The WHSO gives the Authority appointed by the Order the power to remedy the shortfall in the safety, health and welfare of persons at work. In the event of appalling conditions, the commissioner can issue a "stop-work order" which effectively ceases all work operations or processes, with a specified date on which it is to take effect.

Workplaces within the prescribed class or description of workplace must, under Section 28 have a workplace health and safety officer. Section 29 and 30 state that every workplace within the prescribed class or description of workplace must have in place a workplace health and safety committee and have a health and safety auditor.

The WHSO also provides for powers of inspection and investigation and approval for health and safety examiners, officers, auditors and trainers.

B. Requirements of Employing Foreign Employees

a) Work Permit

In order to employ foreign employees in Brunei, an employer must first obtain a foreign workers licence from the Commissioner of Labour. This will allow an employer to employ foreign workers in Brunei. In order to employ a foreign worker, an employer will need to show that they have tried to employ a local Bruneian for the position from Job Centre Brunei.

b) Application Procedure

(i) Register company with Job Centre Brunei.

(ii) Post job vacancy for the position to Job Centre Brunei for 2 weeks. If local jobseekers apply for the position, the application must be considered.

(iii) If position is not filled by a suitable local candidate within 2 weeks, apply for a clearance letter from Job Centre Brunei. This may take up to 3 days.

(iv) Apply for a Foreign Worker License from Department of Labour. A decision should be made in 7 days.

(v) Applications must be submitted via a Registered Employment Agent (Category B).

(vi) Foreign Worker's License Application form must be completed.

(vii) Once approved, security deposit must be paid to Department of Labour.

(viii) Apply for a Foreign Worker Visa for the foreign worker from Immigration. The required documents include:
- Application Letter from Employer;
- Visa Application form;
- Form 23 Work Pass Application;
- 2 passport photo copies;
- Approved Foreign Workers License from Department of Labour;
- Employment Agency Representative's Card;
- Apply for a Medical Examination at the Ministry of Health. (May take 1-2 weeks).

(ix) Worker must go to Department of Labour for the signing of their employment contract.

(x) After the worker signs employment contract, he must go to immigration and apply for a work pass and a green identity card. This may take up to a week). Documents required are.
- Identity Card Application Form;
- Travel Document with photo page and valid Work Pass (original and a photocopy).

(xi) A mandatory inspection will be held within 3-6 months of workers license approval.

c) Social Insurance

Under the Tabung Amanah Pekerja Act (Cap.167 of the Laws of Brunei) ("TAP"), both the employer and employee of Brunei permanent residents and citizens must each contribute 5% of the wage to the TAP.

In 2010, an additional scheme was introduced - the Supplemental Contributory Pension fund ("SCP").Similar to the TAP, it is also compulsory for all employees in the public and private sector. Under the SCP, both the employer and employee must each contribute 3% of the wage, up to a maximum of Brunei Dollars 98.00.

The total contribution for each employee to each fund is therefore 10% for TAP and 6% for SCP. TAP and SCP receive the deduction / contribution on account of each employee, invest the funds and pay them out to the employee at retirement.

C. Exit and Entry

a) Visa Types

The following entry visas are available:

(i) Social Visit Visa;
(ii) Professional Visit Visa;
(iii) Employment Visa;
(iv) Dependents Pass.

b) Restrictions for Exit and Entry

Diplomatic and official passport holders of the Peoples Republic of China may enter Brunei without a visa. For other passport holders, a social visit visa may be obtained as a visa on arrival. Social visit visa are granted on condition that the holder does not enter into employment in Brunei. A professional visit visa may be obtained prior to arrival in Brunei; application is made by a sponsoring employer and a visa may be granted for up to 3 months renewable at the discretion of the Controller of Immigration.

Persons under a professional visit or employment visa may not enter into employment with any other person. Dependents passes may be granted to the dependent of a holder of an employment visa.

D. Trade Union and Labour Organizations

Trade Unions may be registered in Brunei under the Trade Unions Act (Cap.128). Registered Trade Unions are prohibited from having relations with unions outside Brunei. There is very little trade union activity in Brunei, with less than 3 registered unions.

E. Labour Disputes

The Trade Dispute Act (Cap 129) regulates trade disputes. It provides for the creation of certain offences such as intimidation, the offence of a breach of contract in essential services, the offence of a breach of contract that may endanger life or property. This Act makes illegal certain types of strikes or lock outs, allows registered Trade Unions to undertake peaceful pickets, and provides for arbitration of any trade disputes.

V. Intellectual Property

A. Brief Introduction of IP Laws and Regulations

The Brunei Intellectual Property Office ("BruIPO") was set up in 2013 to restructure and govern the national IP administration. It currently oversees the registration for patents, trademarks, industrial designs and plant varieties protection in the country. The objective of the BruIPO is essentially to provide a clear, accessible and widely understood IP system that protects ideas and innovation as well as promoting an 'IP Culture' where creativity and innovation can flourish.

Brunei Darussalam has passed various legislations on trademarks, industrial designs, copyrights and patents since 1999 and has continued to introduce new regulations and legislations over the years to develop the IP legal framework in the country. Relevant laws and regulations relating to the registration and protection of IP in Brunei Darussalam are as follows:

(i) Copyright Order, 1999;
(ii) Industrial Designs Order, 1999;
(iii) Industrial Designs Rules;
(iv) Industrial Designs (International Registration) Rules, 2014;
(v) Patents Order, 2011;

(vi) Patents Rules, 2012;
(vii) Plant Varieties Protection Order, 2015;
(viii) Plant Varieties Protection Rules, 2016;
(ix) Trade Marks Act, Cap.98;
(x) Trade Marks Rules, 2000; and
(xi) Trade Marks (Importation of Infringing Goods) Regulations.

The IP laws and regulations in Brunei Darussalam are in compliance with international standards, complying with international agreements and treaties administered by the World Intellectual Property Organisation ("WIPO"). Brunei Darussalam is a member of multiple international conventions such as the Paris Convention, the Berne Convention, the Patent Cooperation Treaty (PCT), the Hague Agreement Concerning the International Registration of Industrial Designs. Brunei Darussalam is also a signatory of the Agreement on Trade-Related Aspects of Intellectual Property Rights (TRIPS) and more recently, the Protocol Relating to the Madrid Agreement Concerning the International Registration of Marks (Madrid Protocol).

Although Brunei Darussalam has the basic IP legal framework to provide protection levels for basic IP rights such as patent, copyright, trademark and industrial designs, there are currently no legislations protecting other areas relevant to IP such as geographical indications and trade secrets although the same would be protected by the provisions of the common law.

B. Patent Application

Patent protection in Brunei Darussalam is regulated under the Patents Order, 2011 and Patents Rules, 2012. The application system in Brunei Darussalam operates on a "first-to-file" basis, that is, the first person to file an application will have priority over others for the same invention. The key feature of the patent system in Brunei Darussalam is that it is a "self-assessing" system whereby the applicants decide how to proceed and when. The patent system is also "formality-based" and substantive examination work is outsourced to foreign patent offices of Austria, Denmark and Hungary.

All patent applications in Brunei Darussalam must be submitted in English. Supporting documents in a language other than English must be submitted with an English translation.

Application Process

Step	Procedure
1	Lodgment of application (Form PF1) together with: • Prescribed fee (BND160); and • Necessary supporting documents and/or information. This includes the specification and abstract.
2	Preliminary examination is conducted by BruIPO and issuance of letter of acknowledgment.
3	Once application hits 18 months, it will be published in the Patents Journal.
4	Within 21 months from the filing date (Step 1), the applicant may then file for: A. Search-then-Examination request (Form PF11 and PF16); OR B. Combined Search and Examination Request (Form PF12); OR C. Request to rely on the results of a corresponding application linked by priority under the prescribed patent offices or via the PCT; OR D. Request to rely on search results of a corresponding application and request for examination (Form PF16).
5	Applicant files a request for grant within 42 months from the filing date (Step 1), The grant of a patent will take approximately 2-4 years depending on the complexity of the invention

Source: BruIPO website http://www.bruipo.gov.bn/SitePages/patent.aspx

For a patent to qualify for registration in Brunei Darussalam, the invention must meet the following criteria:
(i) It must be new (novel); and
(ii) Involve an inventive step and capable of industrial application.

An invention of a method of treatment on the human and / or animal body involving surgery, therapy, or diagnosis is not patentable as they cannot be applied industrially. An invention that encourages offensive, immoral or anti-social behavior is also not patentable - even if it satisfies the criteria of patentability.

Brunei Darussalam is a signatory to the Patent Cooperation Treaty ("PCT"), which entitles nationals and residents of Brunei Darussalam to file international applications under the PCT and also to seek patent protection for an invention simultaneously in each of a large number of countries by filing an 'international' patent application via the PCT system.

Additionally, Brunei Darussalam is also a participant of the ASEAN Patent Examination Co-operation (ASPEC). ASPEC is a regional work-sharing programme involving nine (9) participating IP Offices in the Member Countries of ASEAN. The purpose of the ASPEC programme is to allow applicants in participating countries to obtain corresponding patents faster and more efficiently so as to reduce duplication on the search and examination work done. ASPEC is free-of-charge and operates in English in all ASEAN IP Offices (except Myanmar).

A patent that has been registered is given a term of twenty (20) years from the date of filing, subject to payment of annual renewal fees.

C. Industrial Designs

The Industrial Designs Order came into force in 2000 and provides for the registration of new industrial designs or the visual appearance of products. BruIPO administers a registration system based on formalities examination only and does not conduct prior art searches.

To be registered, an industrial design must be new at the filing date of the application. An industrial design is new if it has not been registered, published, used or sold in Brunei Darussalam or elsewhere before the date on which the application for registration was lodged. Once accepted for registration, the industrial designs will be published in the Industrial Designs Journal and a certificate of registration will be issued to the applicant. Registration is for an initial period of five (5) years and extendable for two periods of five (5) years each, totaling a maximum of fifteen (15) years subject to the payment of a renewal fee at the end of the 5th year.

The application for registration of an industrial design must be filed with the Registrar of Industrial Designs at the BruIPO. The following has to be submitted:

(i) A completed application form - Designs Form D1;
(ii) One industrial design for articles not forming a set of articles; and
(iii) One industrial design for one set of articles.

It will usually take eight (8) to twelve (12) weeks to register an industrial design in Brunei Darussalam.

As mentioned above, Brunei Darussalam is a member of the Hague Agreement Concerning the International Registration of Industrial Designs, which makes it easier for foreign businesses to obtain industrial designs in Brunei Darussalam.

D. Trademark Registration

Trademarks qualify for protection registration as provided in the Trade Marks Act, Cap.98 and Trade Marks Rules, 2000. A trademark in Brunei Darussalam may be registered if it can be visually perceptible and capable of being represented graphically. In addition, the proposed trademark must satisfy the formalities and substantive requirements set out in the Trade Marks Act, Cap.98 and Trade Marks Rules, 2000. If the proposed trademark is represented in characters other than the English alphabet, for instance Chinese or Japanese characters or Arabic letters, the translation and transliteration must be provided.

As of 2017, Brunei Darussalam can now accept registrations for non-conventional marks, i.e. smell, sound and taste-so long as an applicant can visually represent the product's mark in writing.

Application Process

Step	Procedure
1	Lodgment of Trademark Application: • Covering Letter; • A4-size representation of the proposed trademark; • Form TM1 (and Form TM22 for Foreign Applicants); • Prescribed fee of BND150 per class.
2	A notice will be sent to the applicant with particulars of the trademark and filing date.
3	Application is examined for any deficiencies (formalities examination) and in accordance with the set requirements under the law.
4	Once application is approved, issuance of Form T27 and lodgment of publication fee of BND125 must be made.
5	Publication in Trade Mark Journal for 3 months (Opposition Period).
6	Issuance of Certificate of Registration to applicant.

Source: BruIPO website http://www.bruipo.gov.bn/SitePages/trade-marks.aspx

Protection of a trademark begins on the date on which the application for its registration was filed and it is protected for ten (10) years. This may be renewed indefinitely subject to the payment of a renewal fee.

Protection is only territorial and any registration of trademark with BruIPO is only protected in Brunei Darussalam. However, as mentioned earlier, Brunei Darussalam is now a signatory to the Madrid Protocol and any local applicant wishing to protect their trademark overseas can now do so via the Madrid System, subject to a fee.

E. Plant Variety

Plant Variety is considered an independent type of IP in Brunei Darussalam and this protection system provides an incentive for private research and development into new breeding techniques. All plant genera and species are protectable under the Plant Varieties Protection Order, 2015.

Protection of a plant variety also encourages the development of new and beneficial plant varieties for use by farmers and consumers, as well as enhancing the society's development of agriculture, horticulture and forestry. The protection of a plant variety will also allow plant breeders to gain an exclusive right to produce for sale and sell propagating material of the plant variety and can prevent others from using the variety without their permission.

Application Process

Step	Procedure
1	Lodgment of completed application (Form PVP3) which must also include: • The technical questionnaire (Form PVP-TQ) in English; • The prescribed fee (BND1,600); and • Any necessary supporting documents and information.
2	A preliminary examination will be conducted by BruIPO ("formalities") and a letter of acknowledgment will be issued to the applicant.
3	Information about the application and proposed denomination will be published in the Plant Varieties Protection Journal.
4	Technical examination will then be conducted by one of BruIPO's foreign expert examination partners.
5	The applicant then files a request for grant and a certificate of registration will be issued to the applicant.Details of the registered plant variety will then be published in the Plant Varieties Protection Journal.

Source: BruIPO website http://www.bruipo.gov.bn/SitePages/plant-varieties.aspx

In order to be eligible for protection in Brunei Darussalam, a plant variety has to meet the requirements as provided under the Plant Varieties Protection Order, 2015. As protection is territorial, a plant variety registered with BruIPO is only protected in Brunei Darussalam.

F. Measures for IP Protection

Brunei Darussalam has made efforts in developing a sound IP legal framework to administer and protect IP rights in the country in accordance to international standards. Legislations are amended and updated from time to time to ensure that the IP laws are constantly up to date with current development and practices.

In August 2017, BruIPO hosted a policy dialogue on the best practices for trademark enforcement with support from the International Trade Mark Association (INTA) in efforts to have a comprehensive enforcement system in the country. This was attended by Brunei government representatives.

In August 2017, BruIPO and the Denmark Patent and Trademark Office ("DKPTO") signed a Memorandum of Understanding for a referral arrangement of substantive search and examination of patents. DKPTO has been acting as BruIPO's examiner since the implementation of the patent system in Brunei Darussalam in 2012 and the signing ceremony signified the continuation of collaborative efforts between the two intellectual property offices in the area of patents for a further period of five (5) years.

In September 2017, BruIPO signed a Statement of Intent on Patent Prosecution Highway Plus ("PPH+") with the Japan Patent Office ("JPO") to continue developing measures for IP protection by providing a new patent examination cooperation sharing initiative that aims to accelerate the examination process for corresponding patent applications from Japan and filed in participating intellectual property offices. Under the PPH+ arrangement, each participating patent office will benefit from the work previously done by the other patent office, with the goal of reducing examination workload and improving patent quality. BruIPO has also previously signed a Memorandum of Cooperation with JPO in 2015 to enhance cooperation in the field of industrial property such as trademarks, patents and industrial designs.

VI. Environmental Protection

A. Department Supervising Environmental Protection

The Government of Brunei Darussalam is fully committed to the concept of sustainable development as central to socio-economic development. In the National Development Plan (2012-2017), environment strategy was one of the eight strategies identified to ensure that all aspects of development can be implemented in an organized and effective manner. As part of the country's commitment to promote environment sustainability, Brunei Darussalam signed the Paris Agreement in 2016 and is one of the first countries among the member states of ASEAN to deposit the Instruments of Ratification of the Paris Agreement.

The main government agency responsible for supervising environment protection in the country is the Department of Environment, Parks and Recreation at the Ministry of Development, which issues guidelines and handbook such as the Environmental Acts and Guidelines, Pollution Control Guidelines for the Industrial Development and Recycle 123 Handbook. Reference and tips on recycling for the general public are also published from time to time. Additionally, the Department of Environment, Parks and Recreation is responsible for matters pertaining to Waste Management, Environmental Conservation and Management, Management of Landscape and Recreational Areas, and Environmental Cooperation at national, bilateral and international level.

B. Brief Introduction of Laws and Regulations of Environmental Protection

The Environmental Protection and Management Order, 2016 ("EPMO 2016") came into force on 19th September 2016, the first legislation to be enacted in relation to environment. Prior to the enactment of EPMO 2016, important laws relating to environmental issues were, and still are, covered in the legislations such as below:

(i) Petroleum Mining Act, Cap.44;
(ii) Petroleum (Pipe-lines) Act, Cap.45;
(iii) Mining Act, Cap.42;
(iv) Forest Act, Cap.46;
(v) Water Supply Act, Cap.121;
(vi) Land Code, Cap.40;
(vii) Poison Act, Cap.114;
(viii) Ports Act, Cap.144; and
(ix) Town and Country Planning (Development Control) Act, Cap.143.

EPMO 2016 imposes a duty on every person in Brunei Darussalam to take practical measures to ensure the protection and management of the environment and the prevention, reduction, or control of any potential hazard that may cause pollution or damage to the environment. Every person in Brunei Darussalam shall also comply with the requirements of EPMO 2016 and any subsidiary regulations made after.

The newly enacted legislation also imposes a duty for every person who intends to carry out activities such as agricultural, fishing, forestry and industrial works, to submit a written notification to the authority or any authorised officer at such time that will enable him to take into account any matters relating to the environmental issue prior to undertaking the prescribed activity. Any person carrying out any prescribed activity as set out in EPMO, 2016 without written notification to the authority or any authorised officer is guilty of an offence and liable on conviction to a fine not exceeding BND1,000,000, imprisonment for a term not exceeding 3 years or both.

C. Evaluation of Environmental Protection

The Government of Brunei Darussalam is working together with businesses and non-profit organisations to help accomplish their commitment to conserve and protect the ecosystem in the country by undertaking several initiatives such as recycling services, conducting environmental awareness programmes and activities, and establishing environmental clubs. Apart from making efforts within the country, Brunei Darussalam is also committed on an international level and is a party to several United Nation Conventions such as the Vienna Convention, Montreal Protocol, and Basel Convention on the Control of Transboundary Hazardous Movements of Hazardous Wastes and their Disposal.

Regionally, Brunei Darussalam is a party to the Heart of Borneo, a conservation agreement initiated by the World Wide Fund for Nature in 2005 to protect a 220,000 km2 forested region on Borneo Island and to sustainably manage the area with the other two nations that share the island.

Brunei Darussalam has made credible efforts in the recent years in ensuring its goals of creating an environmentally sustainable environment is achieved amidst the rapid urbanisation and developments. However, the environmental legal framework remains in its early stages and there are gaps to be filled to provide clearer guidance in environmental protection across the country.

New regulations and guidance have been drafted to fill these gaps but have yet to come into force. Such regulations are as follows:

(i) Prevention of Pollution of the Sea Order, 2005;
(ii) Prevention of Pollution of the Sea (Authorised Organisations) Regulations, 2008 (not in force yet);
(iii) Prevention of Pollution of the Sea (Compoundable Offences) Regulations, 2008 (not in force yet);
(iv) Prevention of Pollution of the Sea (Noxious Liquid Substances in Bulk) Regulations, 2008 (not in force yet);
(v) Prevention of Pollution of the Sea (Oil) Regulations, 2008 (not in force yet);
(vi) Prevention of Pollution (Reporting Incidents) Regulation, 2008 (not in force yet);
(vii) Prevention of Pollution (Garbage) Regulation, 2008 (not in force yet);
(viii) Pollution Control Guidelines for Industrial Development.

VII. Dispute Resolution

A. Methods and Bodies of Dispute Resolution

The Supreme Court Act (Cap5) establishes the civil court system in Brunei Darussalam. There are 3 levels of courts of first instance, the Magistrates Courts have jurisdiction for matters or claims of up to Brunei Dollars Fifty Thousand, The Intermediate Court for claims of between Fifty Thousand Brunei Dollars and Three Hundred Thousand, and the High Courts have jurisdiction over claims or matters of over Three Hundred Thousand. Within the Intermediate Court, a specialized Commercial Court hasbeen set up to deal with commercial matters, with the intention that commercial matters may be subject to fast tracking. The High Court has a similar Admiralty Jurisdiction as the English Courts.

Appeals from the Magistrates Courts go to the High Court. From The Intermediate and High Court there is an appeal to the Court of Appeal, which is made up of 3 judges. So long as parties agree before the decision of the Court of Appeal, a further appeal may be made to the Supreme Court in London.

Arbitration is available to parties in Brunei. The Arbitration Order 2009 provides for arbitration between Brunei parties. Brunei is a signatory to the New York Convention and foreign arbitration awards may be enforced in Brunei against Brunei parties as if they were judgements of the courts of Brunei.

The Brunei Arbitration Centre has been established in order to provide a physical venue and to provide support to Brunei based arbitrations.

B. Application of Laws

Brunei courts recognise and give effect to arbitration agreements, and if parties have agreed to resolve disputes by arbitration, if a party seeks redress in court, a Brunei court will stay proceedings so that arbitration may proceed. Brunei courts recognise general choice of law clauses so long as the choice of law is not made in order to avoid the provisions of Brunei Law.

VIII. Others

A. Anti-commercial Bribery

a. Brief Introduction of Anti-commercial Bribery Laws and Regulations

The Prevention of Corruption Act (Cap.131) ("the Act") has 7 Parts, providing for the administration of an Anti-Corruption Bureau ("the Bureau"), corruption offences, powers of search and investigation, evidence and prosecution.

b. Department Supervising Anti-commercial Bribery

His Majesty, the Sultan of Brunei may appoint a Director of the Bureau who shall not be subject to control or direction of any person other than His Majesty.

Section 4A of the Act provides for the duties of the Bureau, they are to:

(i) Receive and consider any report of the commission of an offence under the Act;

(ii) Detect and investigate suspected offences, attempts or conspiracies to commit offences under the Act;

(iii) Examine the practices and procedures of public bodies in order to facilitate the discovery of offence or to revise such practices and procedures;

(iv) Advise public bodies on of any changes in practices and systems to reduce the likelihood of corruption;

(v) Educate the public against corruption; and

(vi) Enlist and foster public support in combating corruption.

The Bureau has substantial powers of arrest and investigation. Section 20 provides that any person must give assistance to an officer of the Bureau in order to discharge his duties.

Section 22 states that any person asked to give information to the Bureau in relation to any offence is legally bound to give such information. The Section makes it an offence to fail to provide information, punishable with a fine of BND 20,000.00 and imprisonment for one year.

Section 23 allows officers of the Bureau to enquire into any bank accounts of any person who is reasonably suspected of having committed an offence. Bankers are bound to provide such information.

Sections 23 A to C provide that officers of the Bureau may seek declarations from third parties as to the assets or office of any person under investigation. There are powers to restrict the disposal of any assets and to freeze bank accounts of any person under investigation. Officers may also impound passports for up to 6 months.

The Act preserves solicitor and client privilege.

Section 24A provides that in any criminal proceeding, any statement made by any accused under any circumstances, whether given to the police or the Bureau or whether under any caution is admissible in any trial of that accused.

c. Punitive Actions

Section 5 of the Act creates an offence by any person to corruptly solicit, receive, agree to receive, give, promise or offer any gratification as an inducement or reward for any person to do or forbear to do anything in respect of a matter or transaction, proposed or actual or likely to take place; or to any member, officer or servant of a public body doing or forbearing to do anything in respect of any matter or transaction whatsoever, in which the public body is concerned.

Section 6 provides for corrupt transactions with agents and provides offences for when:

(i) an agent corruptly accepting or obtaining or agreeing to accept or obtain any gratification to do or not to do any act in relation to his principal's activities;

(ii) any person corruptly giving, agreeing to give any gratification to any agent for that agent to do or forbear to do any act in relation to the agent's principal;

(iii) any person knowingly giving to an agent or an agent using with intent to deceive his principal, any receipt account or other document in respect of the principal's affairs that are false, erroneous or defective in any material particular with the intent to mislead the principal.

The Penalty on conviction for an offence under Sections 5 and 6 is a fine of up to BND30,000 and imprisonment for up to 7 years. If the act is done in relation to a contract or proposal for a contract with a public body, then the penalty is a fine of up to BND30,000 and imprisonment for up to 10 years.

Section 8 states that the acceptor of a gratification under Section 6 may be found guilty even if the purpose of the gratification was not carried out.

Section 9 provides for an offence of corruptly procuring the withdrawal of tenders and Section 10, bribery of a member of the legislature.

Section 11 of the Act provides an offence to offer to or (if a member of any public body) to solicit or accept gratification for the member to:

(i) vote or abstain to vote in relation to any measure resolution or question of a public body;

(ii) to perform or abstain to perform or do any act to expedite, hinder or delay the performance of any official act;

(iii) procure or pass any vote or grant any contract to advantage or favour any person;

(iv) show or forbear or show favour or disfavour to any person in his capacity as member.

Pursuant to Section 12 of the Act, a former or current public officer who maintains a standard of living not commensurate with his present or past income, or who is in control of assets disproportionate to his present or past income commits an offence unless he can give a proper explanation to the court of how he is able to maintain his standard of living or came to be in control of such assets.

The penalty on conviction of any offence pursuant to Sections 9, 10, 11 and 12 is a fine of up to BND30,000 and imprisonment for up to 7 years.

Sections 13, 14 and 15 cover abetments, attempts and conspiracy.

Section 16 provides that it is the duty of any public officer to give information to the Bureau of any corrupt gift, promise or offer to provide any gratification. A failure to do so is an offence punishable with a fine or of up to BND500 and imprisonment for up to 6 months.

Section 25 provides a presumption that any gratification is presumed to be corrupt unless the contrary is proved. Under Section 27 of the Act, evidence of a person's assets may be used as corroborating evidence that a person accepted or obtained or agreed to accept or obtain any gratification, and that it was done so corruptly.

It is also an offence to make frivolous or groundless reports of corruption (Section 33). Section 35 makes it an offence to disclose to any person that he is the subject of an investigation in relation to alleged corruption. Section 37 makes Brunei citizens criminally liable in Brunei for corrupt acts outside Brunei.

The definition of "gratification" is wide and includes:
(i) Money, gift, loan, fee, security, property or interest in movable or immovable property;
(ii) Office, dignity, employment;
(iii) Payment, release, discharge or liquidation of a loan;
(iv) Valuable consideration of any kind;
(v) Forbearance to demand for money;
(vi) Aid, vote, consent or influence;
(vii) Any other service, favour, advantage, including the exercise of any forbearance.

B. Project contracting

Only contractors that are registered with the Ministry of Development may be invited to or bid in tender for Brunei Government public infrastructure projects. Different classes of licences are granted for different types of contracting work. Lower levels of contract will require higher levels of Bruneian ownership and management. More technical or capital intensive classes of contracting will have less requirements for Brunei ownership and management participation.

In the oil and gas sector, principal oil companies which tender our awards of projects and contracts are required to consider the Local Business Development Guidelines issued by the Energy Department of the Prime Ministers Office. The Directive provides, "Oil and gas midstream and down stream operators working in the oil and gas industry in Brunei Darussalam shall adopt the LBD allocation of contract …for their allocation of contracting activities for goods and service". The 4 different quadrants are:

(i) Basic (Low technology, low contract value). Open to local Bruneian companies only, these have a local employment target of 90% and local content target of 70%. Management must be 100% local and managed by local managers or proprietors.

(ii) Development (Low technology higher contract value). These are open to local companies only, have a local employment target of between 50 and 90% and have a 70% local content target. 50% of management must be local and they must maximise the use of local subcontractors.

(iii) Core (High Technology, Higher contract value). Open to all companies. These have a local employment target of between 50 and 90%, and have a 50% local content target. 50% of management must be local and they must maximise the use of local subcontractors.

(iv) Highly specialised (High technology, lower contract value). These are open to all companies and local employment and management is set at best endeavours.

智利

作者：Alberto Cardemil、Ignacio Tornero、Sergio Diez、Daniela Tapia
译者：张毅、张天翼

一、概述

（一）政治、经济、社会和法律环境概述

智利是一个宪政共和国，因此，由宪法确立了一些旨在建立其基本经济体制的原则和规则，这些规则统称为"经济公共秩序"。这些规则是基于对个人自由和个人主动性的尊重，并将其视为促进经济活动的主要驱动力而确立的。除了政治环境之外，智利的外国投资管理主要由两个法律框架实施：2016年智利《外国投资法》（也称"第20848号法"或DFI）和智利中央银行颁布的《外汇兑换规则大全》第十四章（以下简称"第十四章"）。

关于政治环境，智利是一个议会制的共和国，总统拥有广泛的权力。智利近期结束了总统换届选举，于2018年3月组建了新的政府，毫无疑问，新总统上任会非常欢迎国内外投资者，鼓励政府有效地帮助国内外投资者开展项目，这样更容易实现经济增长速度超过3.5%，达到智利中央银行预期的最高目标。除此之外，智利还确立了两院制立法机构，议会和全国代表大会由参议院组成，其成员由民众投票选出，任期8年，众议院及其成员也是由民众投票选出，任期4年。

智利经济环境稳定，发展前景良好。根据福布斯数据统计，智利在全球最佳商业国家中排名第33位，在拉丁美洲的商业国家中处于领先地位。[1]福布斯将智利经济定义为："以高度对外贸易为特征的市场导向型经济，强大的金融机构和稳健的政策使其在南美洲获得了最高主权债券评级。"

世界银行称，智利是以其资产总值而非国内生产总值（GDP）排名拉美第二大富有国家，根据《2018年国民财富变化》报告，2014年智利人均财富为237 713美元，落后于乌拉圭，屈居第二位。智利的财富主要包括人力资本，其次是自然资本，最后是生产性资本。[2]

近年来，虽然社会环境受到了教育制度改革和贫富差距悬殊等问题的影响，但是智利仍然以其财政透明程度而享有盛名（不同于大多数拉丁美洲国家），这直接反映在国家低腐败程度的国际排名中。这一切都得益于国家不断提高行政管理水平。智利积极推进双边、区域和多边贸易协定的发展，不断巩固并增强对外贸易水平和国际竞争力，确立了其积极的国际合作伙伴地位。

由于其政治和经济的稳定性、贸易的开放性、法律安全性和良好的经济增长前景，智利为投资者打造了一个富有吸引力的积极的商业环境。

（二）"一带一路"背景下和中国企业合作的现状和方向

中国是智利在全球的主要商业伙伴，智利出口货物25%以上进入中国，并且与中国达成了多项旨在促进拉丁美洲的交流的合作协议。为贯彻合作精神，中智两国又签署了更多双边条约。[3]2004年智利成为拉美第一个与中国建交的国家，2005年智利成为第一个与中国签订自由贸易条约的国家。截至2016年，两国家间商业往来达到3 147.4万美元，占智利外贸总额的26%。

2018年，来自拉美及加勒比国家共同体的33个国家的代表和中国政府代表在智利圣地亚哥签署了一项协议，为加强深化合作，中国投资2 500亿美元用于该地区的基础设施建设，并邀请拉美及加勒比国家共同体国家加入"一带一路"倡议。

此外，在"一带一路"的倡议下，智利已明确表示愿意促进与亚洲巨头的贸易往来并加强双边关

---

[1] 更多信息参见 https://www.forbes.com/best-countries-for-business/list/#tab:overall。
[2] 参见 https://investchile.gob.cl/world-bank-chile-is-latin-americas-second-wealthiest-country-in-assets/。
[3] 参见 https://chile.gob.cl/china/relacion-bilateral/acuerdos-y-tratados-bilaterales visited 09/03/2018。

系。2017年5月,智利前总统米歇尔·巴切莱特在"一带一路"会议上表示:"智利已做好充分准备,成为亚洲和拉丁美洲之间沟通的桥梁,'一带一路'倡议可以帮助缩短沿线国家间的物理距离和空间距离,加快实现现代化,对推进生产进程,加快经济增长,扩大市场开放,促进贸易投资,繁荣旅游产业发展,加深互信合作有重要意义,从而最终实现平等互信、包容互鉴、合作共赢的和谐社会。"

加入亚洲基础设施投资银行(AIIB)恰恰是智利加入"一带一路"倡议最重要的步骤之一。在领导人会议期间签署的各种协议中,货物服务贸易往来与科学技术合作尤为重要。在"一带一路"倡议下,智利和中国达成了以下协议[①]:
- 《关于南极合作的谅解备忘录》;
- 《关于提升农业合作水平的五年规划》;
- 《关于智利水果途经第三国转运输华的海空联运要求》;
- 《关于智利鲜食鳄梨输往中国植物检疫要求的议定书》;
- 《中国国际贸易促进委员会与智利共和国外国投资促进局合作谅解备忘录》。

正如上文提到的那样,自2018年年初以来,智利政府已经通过智利外国投资促进局推进开展了11个项目,这些项目投资共1.5亿美元,主要涉及以下领域:基础设施、农用工业、葡萄酒业、银行业和能源行业。根据智利中央银行公布的数据,在2009年至2016年期间,中国企业直接投资金额为7.46亿美元,但在2016年5月智利外国投资促进局成立后,仅仅6个项目的投资金额就达到了4亿美元,其中4个项目是在2017年制定的。

二、投资

(一)市场准入

1. 投资监管部门

截至2016年1月1日,智利主要负责投资监管的机构有两个:外国投资促进局和中央银行。

智利《宪法》承认中央银行是一个拥有自主权利的机构,其职能是维护货币稳定和境内外交易的正常运行。此外,《宪法》还赋予中央银行调节控制货币和信贷规模的权利,具体处理信贷和交易所交易,并有权颁布有关货币、信贷、金融和外汇条例的法规。《宪法》同时还规定,中央银行不得担任金融机构担保人,不得获得国家、机构或旗下其他公司发行的文书,也不得直接或间接为公共开支或贷款提供资金。

根据第20848号法的规定,智利外国投资促进局的基本工作任务就是吸引和促进外国投资,但并未对投资金额进行限定。具体来说包括:实施政策推广策略;分析和调查外国投资者的投资能力,颁发资格认证证书,以促进投资者将资金引入国内。

2. 投资行业法律、法规

智利的外国投资监管规定主要体现在两部法律中:一是智利《外国投资法》;二是智利中央银行颁布的《外汇兑换规则大全》第十四章。智利与众多国家签署了贸易互惠投资保护协定(APPIs,也称为"双边投资条约"或"BITs")和自由贸易协定(FTAs),为外国投资者提供双重保护。除此之外,智利还与很多国家达成了避免双重征税协定,这些协定给予来自缔约国的外国投资者更优惠的税收待遇。

2016年1月,智利的外国投资制度主要由两部法律规定,《外国投资法》制定了新的外国投资法规,中央银行《外汇兑换规则大全》第十四章规定投资金额需要超过1万美元,且不设上限。

智利的外国投资制度适用于住所或居住地在世界任何地方的投资者(不论自然人还是法人)。任何非居民且在智利没有住所的外国人或公司,投资金额需要超过500万美元。

(1)《外国投资法》

《外国投资法》规范的是不居住在智利的任何自然人或法人的大于或等于500万美元(或等值外

---

① 参见 https://www.bcn.cl/observatorio/asiapacifico/noticias/hitos-gira-presidencial-asia-pacifico。

汇）的境外投资。

①投资方式
- 可自由兑换的外汇；
- 任何形式和状况的有体物；
- 收益的再投资；
- 信贷资本；
- 任何形式的适于资本化的科技；
- 从关联公司获得的境外投资相关信誉。

②投资的目的和实体化过程

《外国投资法》适用于 2016 年 1 月 1 日后对智利公司进行投资的外国投资者，投资者需要至少直接或者间接持有投资公司 10%的股份，如果不是股份公司，则需要与公司股权同等的资金。

③诉讼和外国投资者证书

为符合外国投资者的资格并获得《外国投资法》赋予的权利，外国投资者需要向外国投资促进局申请资格证书，为证明投资方的身份信息和投资情况，外国投资者需要按照外国投资促进局规定的格式和要求提交相应证明，并详细说明投资的金额、用途和性质。

④《外国投资法》赋予投资人的权利

以下是《外国投资法》赋予的基本权利：
- 海外汇回投资资本及净利润；
- 可进入官方外汇市场；
- 不受法律系统歧视；
- 资本品进口过程中所涉及的营业税和服务税免缴。

⑤税率的稳定性

《外国投资法》规定，至 2019 年 12 月 31 日止 4 年内外资成立的公司或进入智利的外资，在其成立或进入智利后的 10 年期间内，外资所得税税率固定在 44.45%。

⑥采矿项目

自 2016 年起至 2019 年 12 月 31 日止的 4 年期间内，外国投资者如果对采矿行业的项目投资金额超过 5 000 万美元，则可以与智利政府签订为期 15 年的外汇协议，如果选择这种方式，他们有权：首先，适用于采矿行业的税收法律规定保持不变，这些规定体现在《所得税法》（对采矿活动的营业收入或特许经营权收入适用特定的税率）第 64 条之二款和第 64 条之三款，这些规定不受提升税率、扩大税基或任何其他导致税率上涨的影响；其次，受益于稳定的税收政策，在进行具体的采矿活动时，外国投资者可以在投资协议签署之日后确定相应的特许经营权使用费、关税或相关的税收。

⑦制度确立前签署的外国投资协议的效力

根据第 600 号法令，截至 2015 年 12 月 31 日，智利与外国投资者之间签署的投资协议均为有效，因此各外国投资者依然享有根据之前制度签署协议确定的权利和义务。

（2）智利中央银行《外汇兑换规则大全》第十四章

《外汇兑换规则大全》第十四章确立了快捷、基本不受政府干预的外国投资管理体系。根据该法第十四章的规定，外国投资总额必须超过 1 万美元，住所或居住地在世界任何地方的外国投资者（不论自然人还是法人）均可通过第十四章所规定的程序来进行投资。

根据目前外汇兑换规定，所有与境外贷款、存款、投资或出资相关的外汇进入智利均须通过 FEM 并且通知中央银行。然而，不保证外国投资者或出资人和智利借款人分别汇回投资和/或利息、或就外国贷款的本金支付和/或利息（根据 2015 年 12 月 31 日之前签署的外国投资协议为 DL600 项下保留的借款投资）能够进入 FEM。

《外汇兑换规则大全》第十四章仅适用于外国贷款、注资、投资和存款总额超过 1 万美元的投资金额，1 万美元以下的资金可以自由转入智利并汇往国外。

(二)外汇管理条例

1. 外汇监管部门

中央银行(BCCH)是一个拥有自主权利的机构,其职能是维护货币稳定和境内外交易的正常运行。此外,中央银行有权管理和调节货币和信贷规模的权利,具体处理信贷和交易所交易,并有权颁布有关货币、信贷、金融和外汇条例的法规。

欲了解更多信息,请参见"市场准入"部分内容。

2. 外汇相关法律、法规简介

《外汇兑换规则大全》第十四章规定,总额等于或高于1万美元的所有从国外转入智利的贷款、存款、投资或资本。

外汇管理规定,所有从国外向智利转入的贷款、存款、投资或资本都必须通过官方外汇市场进行,并通知中央银行。

欲了解更多信息,请参见"市场准入"部分内容。

3. 外国企业外汇管理要求

(1)国外贷款

① 贷款可能在国内或国外支付;在这两种情况下,贷款都必须通知中央银行。

② 贷款利率、本金和利息的偿还条件及方式可以由债权人和债务人自由商定。

③ 如果债务人违约支付本金和/或利息,保证人需要承担连带责任,该保证也必须按照《外汇兑换规则大全》第十四章的规定通知中央银行。

④ 贷款本金不征税,但如果贷款人是国际金融机构(例如银行),则需要缴纳35%的预扣税。

(2)资本的捐赠、投资和存款

《外汇兑换规则大全》第十四章还对外国资本的捐赠、投资和存款进行了规定,这些规定不适用于实物,仅适用于有关支付义务的行为或在智利居住或有住所的个人向境外转移资金的行为。如上所述,这些从智利转入或转出的资金都必须通过中央银行进行,《外汇兑换规则大全》第十四章允许投资者履行完成赋税义务后,可汇回投资资本及净利润。

不超过1万美元的资金可以自由转入智利和汇往国外。

欲了解更多信息,请参见"市场准入"部分内容。

(三)融资

1. 主要金融机构

智利的融资一般是由银行和其他金融机构通过一套包括贷款协议及一揽子安全措施的合同文件提供的贷款。

融资也可能来自国外,在这些情况下,法律框架将由《外汇兑换规则大全》第十四章(为投资者随时遣返资本和利润提供可能性)或新的《外国投资法》提供,这取决于资金如何进入该国。

2. 外国企业融资条件

由于外国投资对智利经济的重要性,智利已经制定了法律和政策来吸引投资者,确保稳定的法律机制,以保证智利和外国投资者的平等待遇、非自主的和非歧视性的待遇,以及对经济大部分区域的开放。

此外,关于外国投资适用的规定,投资者可以在两种不同的法律制度之间作出选择:新的《外国投资法》和智利中央银行《外汇兑换规则大全》第十四章,第十四章规定了对外国投资的税收优惠和激励措施,如税收制度的不变性、增值税的不变或冻结,以及对投资项目所需要的资本资产的进口的适用关税的冻结等。

对于《外国投资法》,虽然规定外国投资者有权将资本或利润汇往国外,但这些规定只是规定了一项权利,并不能保证进入正式外汇市场,因为他们明确规定,根据《外国投资法》的规定,任何外汇业务均应受该国中央银行(特别是某些限制甚至禁止在外汇市场进行交易的前提是基于国际货币储备货币短缺的假设)的归责。

此外,《外国投资法》规定,自 2016 年 1 月 1 日起的 4 年内(至 2019 年 12 月 31 日),外国投资者可以特别执行一项外国投资协定,并在其中选择一项为期 10 年的稳定为 44.45% 的税率,在将来可能增加适用税率的情况下,可能会比 44.45% 更高。

此外,重要的是,智利的立法也为对智利极端地理区域的投资提供税收优惠。更多信息请参阅下文"投资偏好及投资保护"。

最后,有意开展创新业务或发展高新技术资产和人力资源的公司也有可能申请智利政府提供一些福利("CORFO 补贴"),目的是支持在智利执行这些活动。在这方面,补贴的数额将取决于项目的类型和具体的特点。

(四)土地政策

一般来说,智利法律对非公民的土地所有权没有任何限制。本规则的例外情况包含在第 1939 号法令第 7 条中,其中规定,除非总统授权,否则禁止来自邻国的外国人获取、拥有位于边境地区的不动产。

土地所有权的取得或转让没有具体的税收。取得或转让所涉及的费用,是指在不动产登记簿中起草收购契据、公证和记录财产所有权的相关费用。然而,在购买或租赁带有家具的房地产时,必须支付增值税。

在公共化及都市分区规划中,城市地区的土地利用和土地开发是规划的主题。

这些分区规划是由第 458 号法令(1976 年)中的《城市化与建设总法》,以及第 47 号法令(1992 年)中的《城镇化和建设总条例》所规定的。

住房和城市化部将负责制定有关土地利用和土地开发的法律文书的研究、修订、批准和修改的具体规定。

对于任何设施或建筑物的建设,必须由相应直辖市或自治区的工程总监签发建筑许可证,以证明该建筑项目可根据土地的具体规定进行调整。此授权用于特定的区域和设施。建筑工程施工后,必须由同一单位提供工程验收证明,证明施工符合建筑许可证规定的规范。

(五)公司的设立与解散

1. 公司形式

对于希望在智利建立业务并长期开展业务的外国投资者来说,有两种选择:合并当地子公司、在智利设立分支机构或永久成立一家外国公司。

智利的法律允许通过设立三种类型的企业来开展商业活动,所有类型企业的股东和合伙人均对企业承担有限责任。这三种企业分别为:股份公司、有限责任公司和简化股份公司。

当地子公司的三种公司结构:

① 对于相较于人合更偏向于资合的公司来说,股份公司更合适。这种结构类似于美国的相关机构允许投资者快速筹集资金,让公司获得更好的信贷类型。智利有两种类型的股份公司:公开交易和秘密持有。上市公司受证券市场法律和证券监管制度的制约。

② 另一方面,公司的人合性重于资合性时,当他们想要将责任限制在一定程度或当双方属于同一业务集团时,通常倾向于成立有限责任合伙企业。这种结构给它的合作伙伴提供了很多控制权,因为成员的所有决定都事关它的存在与否,且通常其修整和管理必须得到成员一致同意。

③ 第三种选择是简化股份公司,它可以让单一股东拥有 100% 的股份,与股份公司相比,其程序简单,并且其股东可以自由建立任何管理机制。

除上述之外,智利立法还允许在智利设立分支机构或永久设立外国公司,但这是一个非常简单的结构,通常是建议那些不打算在智利全面开展业务但仍然希望有一个正式的办事处或代表的公司适用。

虽然外国公司的一个分支机构在智利并不被视为自治的法人实体,但它被认为是母公司的代理机构。因此,简要提及相应的规定还是很重要的。

在智利设立外国法律实体的分支机构,必须有"公司章程"以及"外国实体良好信誉证明书",以及授予管理该分支机构的代理人的授权书。

所称原始文件必须经过认证、翻译,再由智利公证处进行公证。

2. 设立程序

有限责任公司、简化股份公司或股份公司的成立,需要一项公共契约,登记在商业登记处的契约摘要及在官方宪报刊登的公告上。在智利成立一家公司大概需要一周时间。

之后,还需要获得纳税人的税号,并在国税局提交一份商业启动通知,如下所述。这是一个简单的过程,包括在税务局提交表格,以及公司的合法注册记录,这就是为什么它可以由任何具有简单的代理权限的人来执行,但它可能会变得很困难(因此,需要一个法律顾问的介入),以防国税局对公司的记录提出法律异议。此外,国税局要求该公司聘请一位在智利定居的律师。

(1)有限责任公司

成立有限责任公司需要至少两名合伙人,最多不能超过 50 名。

(2)股份公司

一般来讲,股份公司的股东不得认购自己公司的股票,并且必须遵从法定的最低分红比例(一般为净收益的 30%)。股东拥有法定赎回权,经过相关批准可要求公司赎回其所持有的股票。

(3)简化股份公司

简化股份公司若想修改章程,不必通过所有股东一致同意。可由一名或多名股东构成(自然人或法人均可),除了必须满足少数几项强制性规则外,可拟定任何种类的公司协议。

3. 公司解散的程序和要求

公司在其存续期间届满时解散、终止,除非该公司是永久不得转让的。另外,如果在专门的股东大会上,经由发行股份的 2/3 以上同意,则公司解散。或者所有的股份由一个人或实体连续持有超过 10 天,或者合并到另一个公司,公司即告解散。公司的章程可以规定其他导致公司解散的情况。

如果公司解散,其清算将由股东自由选出的清算委员会进行清算,除非清算是不必要的(所有股份由一个自然人或实体收购;或是合并)。

对于公司的解散,主要有四个方面的规定需要遵守,才能达到解散的目的:

① 从财务角度看,必须准备好公司的期末资产负债表。

② 从税收的角度看,必须向智利国内税收服务部门提交"停业"表格。

③ 对于公司解散:专门的股东大会必须批准公司财产的清算,并且必须准备批准的文件。这一契约应当被简化为一项公共契约,在商业登记处进行登记,并在官方公报上公布。公共契约的登记和出版必须经过公证。

④ 最后,在清算公司资产的过程中,公司清算委员会必须决定清算资产的程序,之后将由股东大会批准。双方同意的程序和批准必须通过一项公共契约来完成,其摘要必须在商务登记处进行登记。

(六)公司兼并与收购

1. 简介

智利众所周知的经济稳定吸引了新的外国投资进入其新兴市场。由于这一投资,智利成为投资资本的进口商,并实施了几项激励措施来吸引外国投资者。因此,为了提高智利的经济,企业有一个灵活的法律框架,其中一个明显的例子就是不同类型的企业并购的存在。

在智利的法律框架中有很多不同形式的企业并购,例如合并、合资企业、分销协议、特许经营协议等。下面是智利法律中最常见的企业并购的简要描述。

(1)合并

在智利立法中有两种类型的合并:一种合并是两家公司为了某一特殊目的,而将资产转让给一家新公司;另一种合并是一家公司在另一家即将解散的公司解散之前,即取得其全部资产。

(2)接管

简单地说,"接管"就是指一个公司取得另一个公司 100% 的股份或是资产,最终通常伴随着此公司的解散清算。

合并与接管的主要区别是,在合并中,原公司的股东成为最终公司的股东,因此,股票被交易。

相反，由另一家公司接管的，公司的股东可以获得其股份的价格，但不会成为最终公司的股东。

（3）整体收购公司业务

智利的立法也规定了可以整体收购一家公司正在进行的业务，包括为了执行公司的业务，涉及的所有公司资产、债务、劳动力、无形权利、专有技术等。也就是说并不是转让公司股份，而是整体收购公司业务。

（4）增资

当现有股东并未行使其在公司收购中的首次否决权，可以通过发行新股或是由外部投资者（不同于已经存在的股东）进行增资，以此实现对控制股权的收购。

（5）直接收购

在智利收购一家公司的控制权也可以通过直接从控股股东或股东手中获得股份来实现。在这种情况下，有必要区分不同类型的公司。

在封闭性股票公司里，直接获得控制的股份不需要经过任何特殊的程序，也不需要政府的授权和批准。交易完成后，应告知智利国内税务服务公司的新股份组成。

在公开的股份公司或上市公司中，收购控股股份必须按照法律规定的程序通过一份投标书（强制投标，MTO）。根据智利《公司法》第198条的规定（如下所述），应当在同等条件下向所有股东和其他目标公司的持股者（其股票可以转换为公司股份）告知投标书的内容。根据智利法律，在下列情况下需要进行强制投标：

① 在股票市场上交易其股票的公司，收购的目的是成为控股股东。

② 当控股股东倾向于获得至少2/3的已发行股票，并拥有投票权或其他系列股份。

③ 如果买方希望获得另一家公司的控制权，该公司在股票市场上交易其股票，只要被控制公司的资产总额占控制公司资产总额的75%。该强制投标不是针对控股公司的股东，而是针对被控股公司的股东，目的是为了防止通过购买控制公司来避免强制投标的发生。

④ 当个别股东或处于同一协议中的一些人，已获得2/3的已发行股份，并有投票权。在这种情况下，这些股东必须在收购后的30天内将剩余股份置于强制投标的范围之内。在这种情况下，强制投标的价格不能低于智利《公司法》所规定的撤销权的行使价格。

（6）股权协议

最后，两个或更多的股东或股票持有人（如适用）可以通过股东和股东协议行使对企业或有限责任公司的控制权。对于股东和股东协议，智利法律规定的唯一手续是在相应的股东登记簿上进行书面登记。

2. 法律、法规

智利的企业并购主要受下列法律法规的管辖：

① 智利《公司法》（第18046号法律）及其规定（第702号法律）；

②《证券市场法》（第18045号法律）；

③《证券与保险监督管理（智利证监会）行政法理学》，依照第18045号法律；

④《所得税法》（第824号法律）；

⑤《反托拉斯法》（第211号法律）；

⑥《商法典》；

⑦《民法典》。

此外，企业并购所适用的法律是双方在相关合同中约定的。如果未选择具体适用的法律，则适用其中一个协议执行国的法律。

3. 申请及费用

在接管智利一家公司之前必须提交的申请，取决于该公司的目标类型，在本章中简要介绍过。当针对封闭式股份有限公司或有限责任公司时，不需要遵守之前的申请或经过任何政府部门的批准。相反地，一般来说，针对上市公司时，必须在智利证监会及股票交易场所执行一些强制性的程序。

另一方面，无论受影响的公司类型如何，前置申请必须在智利国税局提交报告，例如，公司代表的免职和任命、公司参与的变更、国家身份证号码的获得、业务终止的通知，以及任何其他由公司合并或并购而产生的章程修改申请。

关于反垄断,虽然智利目前还没有强制合并控制系统,但有几个不同的条件(例如,市场集中度、所涉及的公司的市场份额、进入壁垒的存在等),将使得在国家经济检察官办公室(FNE)或智利反托拉斯法院(TDLC)提交一份报告以获得交易的事先批准是可取的。如果上述情况没有发生,则所提及的操作有可能是违反《反托拉斯法》的。如果反托拉斯法院认为该行动妨碍、限制或阻碍了竞争,可以命令修改或终止协议、修改或解除合伙关系、公司和其他私法规定中的法人组织,或是处以相当于20 000 UTA[①](目前相当于约1.87亿美元)金额的罚款。尽管有上述规定,但有必要指出的是,短期内智利将颁布一项法案,对智利《反托拉斯法》进行几项修订,例如:对卡特尔的刑事化和增加罚款等。在合并控制方面,该法案引入了强制合并控制,在其执行之前,必须将超过一定阈值的集中交易通知FNE。下列非同一业务集团的经济代理间的集中交易(超过以下提及的阈值),必须在其执行前通知FNE:
• 并购;
• 当一个或多个代理人要求直接或间接获得可以单独或联合地对另一方的管理产生决定性影响的权利;
• 两个或两个以上独立的经济实体变成一个单一的经济实体——不同于功能永久性的相关实体;
• 当其中一个代理获得了另一个代理资产的控制权。
上述集中交易必须符合下列要求:
• 所涉及的经济代理的销售总额在过去的日历年里一定超过了经济部设立的门槛;
• 在智利,至少有两名经济代理人在上一个日历年中创造了相当于或超过经济部门设定的门槛的销售额。

该法案还将改变现行的计算罚款的方法,从固定的最高罚款制度(目前总计约为1 600万美元的一般违规罚款以及大约2 400万美元的卡特尔违规),改变成最高罚款额相当于违法后所获经济利益的双倍的制度,或是相当于在侵权期间涉嫌违法的特定系列产品或服务销售额的30%。

4. 信息披露

一般而言,根据智利《公司法》的规定,企业并购的批准要求相关股东及股票持有人能够提前查阅各种文件和信息,例如,涉及交易所有情况的并购企划书、交易双方公司最新的资产负债表、专家评估报告,在某些情况下,还包括并购业务资产负债表。

除了需要向相关股东及股票持有人披露信息外,还需向证券监管部门、股票市场和社会大众等履行与上市公司相对应的一般披露义务。

一般而言,公开上市公司应当在有要求披露的事件发生时,如实、充分、及时地披露与自身及其业务有关的所有实质性信息。特别是,公开上市公司应将以下信息永久地披露给证券监管部门、股票市场和公众:
• "FECU 表格",包括个人和合并的季度和年度财务报表、外部审计师的中期或年度财务报表报告;管理层对影响公司及其公开发行证券期间所报告的所有实质性事实的讨论、分析和披露;
• 公司的年度个人和合并财务报表应在每年截止日期前的60天内发送给证券监管机构,并应至少在股东大会召开之日前20天提交股东大会,由股东大会对报表提出意见;这些财务报表也必须刊登在全国性的报纸上;
• 公司的季度个人和合并财务报表应发送给证券监管机构;
• 公司应告知证券监管部门其任何的股权变动,包括其他方面:支付股息、交换股份和减少资本(至少提前20天)和资本化;
• 准备一份年度报告并将相同的副本递交给证券监督机构和公司股东;
• 公司应立即将有关股份公司、其业务及其公开发行的证券的任何材料事实或信息告知证券监管机构。此类信息应在事实发生之日或股票公司知悉之日,如实、及时地披露。

在另一个问题上,如前所述,智利目前没有强制性的合并控制制度。然而,如果一个操作——在

---

① UTA (Unidad Tributaria Anual) 是智利国家内部税收服务部用于计算税收、罚款和其他费用的年度税收单位。

其完成之前或完成之后——由竞争主管部门审核,就必须向国家经济检察官办公室或是反托拉斯法院提交很多文件。国家经济检察官办公室的横向合并分析和反托拉斯法院内部第 12 号规则的指导方针,提供了关于需要披露的信息和文件的指南。尽管有上述规定,但仍不乏对这一信息进行保密的可能。前面提到的是在短期内将实施的《反托拉斯法》。

5. 重大持股的披露

重大持股人(股票比例超过 10%)仅根据公开股票或上市操作(或其他公司,如金融机构等公司)的要求进行披露,主要是指他们有义务通知智利证监会、股票市场和公众,以修正他们的持股比例。

需要指出的是,在具有特殊经营目的的公司中,大股东的持股比例可能会受到限制。

6. 敌意交易

对于公开的股票和上市公司,在证券市场法律中规定了接管,其规定这类交易应通过强制招标的程序进行。然而,应当注意的是,强制招标程序并非是敌意收购。

强制投标是强制性的公开收购要约,相关规定的适用范围应由有意成为控股股东的人扩及至所有股东。这是一种确保透明度和保护少数股东的方式,如果新公司的控制意味着对他们过去所处环境的改变,他们就可以出售自己的股份。作为一项强制性程序,如果不按照法律规定执行,则将宣告该行为无效,并构成犯罪。

因为智利市场上的股权控制集中在少数股东手中,所以敌意接管在智利是不可预见的,这会缩小希望获得控制权的一方与当前控制公司的一方或双方之间的谈判内容范围。

7. 政府监管

在政府监管的行业中,商业公司受相应的监管主体监管。例如,银行或其他金融机构的业务将在银行和金融机构的监督下进行,而保险公司的并购合同则应在智利证监会的监管之下。被提及的这些监督机构可能会施加强制性条件,甚至禁止企业的进一步发展。

对提供公共或基本服务的公司、媒体、教育和保健公司以及其他公司也有限制;这些公司对政府机关有所依赖。更多信息请参阅"投资偏好及投资保护"。

最后,出于国家安全的目的,对于外国人拥有位于智利合法边界的土地是有限制的,这一情况由国家边境管理局监督。这可能会影响并购交易或其他交易中涉及的地产及外国当事方。有关详情,请参阅"土地政策"。

除了上述以外,政府机构不能也不应该影响或限制企业并购的完成。

8. 跨境交易

在智利的立法中,跨境交易并不是特别规定的,但最惠国原则适用于一般规则,而且根据该原则,各国必须避免对其商业伙伴进行区别对待。通过跨境交易间接产生的权利义务的法律框架,与中央银行《外汇兑换规则大全》第十四章和《外国投资法》的规定相对应。

9. 改革和趋势

近年来,智利经济稳步增长,外国投资在其中发挥了关键作用。在这种情况下,并购交易是必不可少的,并且所述情况反映在该国的高级别并购中。

接受这些投资的主要行业是能源、农业、公用事业,当然还有采矿业。智利因其矿藏和矿床而闻名于世,采矿是该国的主要经济活动之一。能源和公用事业富有吸引力,因为它们是政府监管的行业,能为投资提供安全保障。基础设施和零售业市场也需要予以关注。

与企业并购相关的智利法律主要修正案,已经在税收、破产和劳工法规方面进行修订。

尽管如此,这些修正案并不会影响到全国的并购活动,因为该项法案将持续为并购活动提供稳定的框架。即使世界受到重大经济危机的影响,智利的并购交易也没有减少。相反,他们鼓励欧洲和亚洲国家的投资者将本国资本出售给智利。此外,在秘鲁、哥伦比亚等拉美国家,智利企业也正在成为外国投资者市场的新生力量。

(七) 关于竞争的规则

1. 对竞争规则进行监管的部门

① 国家经济检察官办公室（FNE）：是负责调查被指违反竞争规则的政府机构，负责代表国家利益提起权利主张并向竞争法院主张这些权利。此外，根据竞争法的新修正案，国家经济检察官办公室目前负责强制性的合并控制体系。

② 反托拉斯法院（TDLC）：是独立于政府的机构，其功能是防止、纠正并惩处违反竞争法的行为。

③ 最高法院：对竞争法院作出的惩罚决定、撤销 FNE 的决定、批准以满足不同于当事人向 FNE 提出的补救措施为条件的集中管理判决不服的上诉由最高法院管辖。

2. 对竞争法的简要介绍

智利的反垄断立法主要基于以下法律：

《反托拉斯法》（1973 年），规定了对竞争的保护：本法令规范了竞争的不同领域，从而鼓励并保护市场竞争。本法令对任何妨碍、限制、阻碍竞争或者任何企图达成以上目的的行为或者合约予以处罚。《反托拉斯法》最近被第 20945 号法（2016 年）所修改。本法律对智利的竞争法体系进行了重要的修改，也是建立专门法院后对法律进行的全面修改及最相关的改革，内容包括：建立强制性的合并控制体系，将卡特尔问题入罪，大幅提升对可适用的罚金额度，在竞争者中包含"联合"行为本身就违反竞争规则。

《不正当竞争法》法律规范了不正当竞争行为：对构成不正当竞争的行为以及可能违反竞争法的行为进行定义，规定了可以对这些行为提起的诉讼类型以及相应的管辖法院。

国家经济检察官办公室指引：尽管国家经济检察官办公室指引并非具有严格强制力，但是它们仍然代表了国家经济检察官办公室的评价标准，并指导了对国家经济检察官办公室管辖下的各种事项的评价。

3. 规范竞争的措施

（1）违反反垄断的行为

《反托拉斯法》将违反竞争的行为从广义上定义为"所有妨碍、限制或者阻碍竞争或者企图造成以上效果的事实、行为或者协约"。这一广泛的含义或多或少可以提炼为四个（可以说较宽泛）范例，这些范例属于限制性行为，即：

① 竞争者之间约定或者协商一致的行为，既包括竞争者之间通过约定或者协商一致，进行固定销售或者购买价格，限制产量，划分区域或者市场份额或者影响投标结果等行为；也包括那些竞争者之间协议或者协商一致，通过将市场权力赋予竞争者，以便决定市场上的地位状况或者排除现有或者潜在的竞争者的行为。

② 一间公司或者受同一人控制的或者在市场上具有控制权的公司集团，通过固定购买或者销售价格，强制实行货物的捆绑销售，划分市场的区域或报价，或者实施其他滥用的行为；

③ 实施掠夺性行为或者不公平竞争，以期达到、保持或者增加支配地位；

④ 同一个人同时在两个或者更多的竞争公司里具有相关行政职位或者领导职位，假若上述竞争性的公司集团都从销售、服务或者其他经营性活动中获得超过法律规定的总收入，目前总额 100 000 智利发展单位[①]（约合 440 万美元）。

新的法律也对罚金和惩罚体系的规定进行了修改。竞争法院可以对以上行为施加以下惩罚：禁止与政府机构缔约，禁止某些任职，刑罚和罚金。罚金收归国库，金额可能达到涉及违规的产品服务在违规实施期间销售总额的 30%，或者因违法所得经济利益的 2 倍。如果不能确定销售总额或者经济利益，反托拉斯法院可能处以总额为 60 000 年度税单位（约合 5 500 万美元）的罚金。罚金可能施加于单位，它的领导人、经理或者行为实施相关人。如果单位被处罚金，如果单位领导人、经理者或者行为实施相关人均参与该行为，他们可能需要对以上罚金承担连带责任。

---

① 智利发展单位（Unidad de Fomento）是智利政府根据本国每年通货膨胀率的不同而作出相应调整的金融单位。

通过刑罚处罚以整治顽固卡特尔这一制度曾经在2004年的智利《反托拉斯法》中被废止，但是现在又被重新引入。对顽固卡特尔可施刑罚范围从3年1天的监禁到10年监禁。

最后，就卡特尔而言，如果商业代理人在共谋案件中向国家经济检察官办公室提供完整信息，《反托拉斯法》对这些人规定了特惠计划。该计划同样适用于向国家经济检察官办公室提供信息的第一位当事人所可能承担的刑事责任。应当注意的是，检察机关在针对共谋案件中的调查程序中有权为了逮捕嫌疑人进行凌晨突袭，并且对沟通进行干预。

（2）合并控制体系

最近实施的修正案中，最令人关注的内容是引入了强制性的合并控制体系。该体系包括两个阶段，程序始于当事人通知国家经济检察官办公室。

在这个新系统实施后，当事人在其实施对智利有影响且超过国家经济检察官办公室解决方案的销售门槛的集中管理行为前，必须通知FNE。目前有生效中的通知门槛是：

① 在通知前的上一年度已经确定的在智利的销售总额大于1 800 000智利发展单位（约合79 500 000美元）；

② 在智利，其集中管理行为的两家代理人分别在通知的上一年度销售总额大于或者等于290 000智利发展单位（约合12 800 000美元）。如果必要，国家经济检察官办公室有权对此门槛进行调整。

经济部的第33号规定对当事人提起的案件的格式和所披露的最少信息作了规定。国家经济检察官办公室所进行的分析涉及两个阶段。

第一个阶段始于FNE收到通知之时。从此日起，国家经济检察官办公室在10日内判断文档是否完整，如果完整则开启调查阶段。在调查阶段开启后30日内，国家经济检察官办公室应当：

① 如果其确信交易不会实质上减少竞争，应当单纯地且无条件地同意交易；

② 如果披露方所提出的补救措施让国家经济检察官办公室相信，以采取这些措施为限定条件，所涉交易不会在实质上减少竞争的，应当同意交易；或者

③ 如果国家经济检察官办公室认为单纯地且无条件地同意交易，或者以披露方所提出的补救措施为条件，可能对竞争造成实质上的减少的，则将调查时间延长为90天。在这种情况下，程序需要进入第二阶段。

在第二阶段，国家经济检察官办公室需要将其延长调查的决定通知到所有可能直接涉及的代理人和权力机构以及那些对交易可能有兴趣的经济代理人。那些收到这些相关信息以及对交易有兴趣的第三方，包括供货商、竞争者、客户或者消费者，可以在国家经济检察官办公室延长调查的决定公布后20天内向国家经济检察官办公室网站提供信息。在90日的调查延长期限到期后，国家经济检察官办公室同样应当：

① 或者单纯地且无条件地同意交易；

② 或者同意交易，但以披露方所提出的补救措施为限定条件；

③ 或者若其得出结论，交易存在实质上减少竞争的倾向，则应禁止交易的执行。

在救济体系方面，如果国家经济检察官办公室禁止交易的进行，法律仅考量特别的更正救济权。这种救济权必须在国家经济检察官办公室决定提出后10日内向反托拉斯法院作出。反托拉斯法院必须在收到调查文书的60日内安排公开听证。公开听证可以由提出不服的当事人、国家经济检察官办公室以及其他在调查中提交资料的相关方参加。在听证后的60日内，反托拉斯法院需要作出维持或者撤销国家经济检察官办公室的决定。

如果反托拉斯法院的决定在以披露方向国家经济检察官办公室所提出的补救措施为限定条件同意交易的，当事人和国家经济检察官办公室均可以向最高法院提起申诉。

所有该新程序中所规定的时限均应当以工作日计算。

（3）对少数股权的关联及获取

关联：反竞争的行为的假设直接引起竞争者之间的关联将被认定为一种侵权行为，当一个人同时在两个公司担任相关行政职务或者领导职务应当受到处罚，倘若每一个竞争者的经济集团年度销售、服务以及其他经营活动已经超过100 000智利发展单位（合约4 400 000美元）或者在符合上述门槛的上一年度结束后，同时担任以上职务已经超过90日。

对取得少数股份的通知义务：新的规则设立了必须在行为实施 60 日内通知国家经济检察官办公室的义务，"一间公司或者同属同一个公司集团的实体，无论直接或者间接取得属于竞争公司 10% 以上的公司自身持股或者经由第三方代替持股的股权权益"，国家经济检察官办公室都应当考量开启调查程序。这种通知的义务只有在受让公司或者其所在的经济集团以及转让方分别在上一年度的销售、服务或者其他经营性活动中具有超过法律规定的总收入 100 000 智利发展单位（约合 4 400 000 美元）之时，才被触发。《反托拉斯法》规定任何检察机关对受让公司的追诉期为受让公司向国家经济检察官办公室发出通知后 3 年。

（八）税收

1. 税制及主要规定

根据智利《宪法》，税收、关税和各种公共费用必须通过国会通过的法律来实施。

税务问题上的立法主动权属于总统。因此，除非行政部门采取行动，国会批准上述倡议，否则不得改变税收。与财政政策有关的事项由财政部长管辖。

在税务方面，政府的功能由三个不同的公共机构实现：

① 负责税务法律管理的税务局，有权发布规章及进行税务审核；

② 国库，负责税收；

③ 海关机构，负责处理与适用与进口关税有关的所有事项。

如果因为税务审计的结果导致纳税人提出索赔，主管法院将是税务和海关法院。对其裁决可以向相应的上诉法院提出上诉，并且，通过某些特定的程序，案件可以提交给最高法院。

2. 基本所得税体系

一般而言，在智利，任何应计或已收收入、利润或资本增加，不论其来源、性质或面额如何，均须缴纳所得税。

由智利《所得税法》（ITL）征收的税是基于两个主要因素：纳税人住所和收入来源。

（1）纳税人住所

住所或居住地在智利的任何自然人或法人，不论其起源或来源，均应对其所有收入征税。这意味着智利居民将因其全球收入而被征税。

然而，对于在智利安置住所或在智利定居的外国人来说，前三年仅按其智利所得总额缴纳所得税（智利税收机构可根据自由裁量权给符合资格的人士延长税收优惠期），之后将对其全球收入征税。

（2）收入来源

根据智利《所得税法》，非智利居民只需对其来源于智利的收入征税。为此目的，来源于智利的收入是因在智利境内开展活动而取得的收入或在智利境内因拥有资产而获得的收益。

从这个意义上讲，一个智利居民实体的股份是被视为位于智利境内的。因此，根据智利《所得税法》因拥有这些股份的所有权所产生的利润将是来源于智利的收入。进一步讲，因出售智利居民实体股份所得的任何收入将被视为来源于智利的收入。作为例外情形，根据智利《所得税法》第 10 条，若非智利居民因出售权利份额或所有权利益而从非智利居民实体处获得的收益，而且其资产是位于智利的，在满足上述所有条件的情况下，那么该收入也将被视为来源于智利的收入。

3. 两级税收制度与股利分配方案

总体而言，智利公司、有限责任公司、股份公司和外国公司分支机构的收入或应计收入按两级征税。

在这一制度下，各实体将根据其应纳税所得每年按其税收制度征收 25% 或 27% 的企业所得税（CIT）。其合伙人或股东如果是非智利居民将被征收预扣税（WHT），若系居民则被征收个人所得税。合伙人或股东可以使用已支付企业所得税（CIT）金额的 100% 或 65% 来抵扣最终税收，具体如下。

智利税收体系为"归原税制"，即已缴纳的企业所得税可用来抵免最后税款中相应的部分。最后税款指个人所得税，税基为住所或居住地在智利的自然人的所得。个人所得税采取累进税率，税率为 0%～40%。预扣税对住所及居住地均不在智利的纳税主体征收，采用统一税率，为 35%。因此，按照

"归原税制"，智利企业应根据其普通收入缴纳企业所得税，合伙人或股东根据分红情况缴纳最后税款。

智利全面税制改革（以下简称"税改"）已于 2014 年 9 月 29 日生效，并对智利的税收体系作出了重大调整。税改采取渐进实施的方法，于 2017 年 1 月 1 日全面生效。根据这种税制改革，有两种不同的税收制度或税制：归属所得税制度和半一体化制度。

在这种制度下，任何非智利股份公司或隐名合伙企业，若其股东系个人或非智利居民实体，可选择适用下列制度，以确定该个人或非智利居民实体根据各自实体产生股利最终决定缴税时间及税额。

（1）归属所得税制度

股东对在同一年内所得的收入征税，非居民的征收预扣税。

为此目的，归属收入等于应税收入基数，加上非应税收入，再加上其他须符合预扣税的数额。无论是否存在实际分配，一旦取得收入，就会触发预扣税。如果根据公司章程该合伙人或股东没有实际分配该收入，则按每个合伙人或股东的资本参与比例分配。

根据这一制度，各实体将按 25% 的税率征收企业所得税，并且全部可以抵扣预扣税。该体系对智利公司外籍合伙人或股东征收的总税率为 35%。

（2）半一体化制度

股东只对从公司实际提取或分配的利润（现金基础）征收最终税款，对非居民征收预扣税。

对智利企业征收的一类税也可采取"半一体化制度"，即对企业利润征收 27% 的税。

与归属所得税制度不同的是，按此制度用来抵免最终税款的金额不得超过公司缴纳的一类税的 65%，除非智利公司的外籍合伙人或股东的住所位于一个与智利有现行避免双重赋税协定（以下简称"税收协定"）的国家（如中国、英国、巴西、阿根廷、澳大利亚、加拿大、法国、马来西亚、南非、泰国等），则可把公司缴纳一类税的 100% 用来抵免最终税款。对于已签署但尚未生效的条约国（如美国），同样的规则适用至 2021 年。因此，根据外籍业主住所所在国是否与智利签有税收协定，若非协定国家，税收将高达 44.45%。

请注意，为确定收入的归属（归属所得税制度），并为了在这两种制度下进行红利分配，有一些分配规则适用。所述的分配规则确保已经缴纳的企业所得税正确的抵扣相应的收入。

此外，在这两种制度下，必须保存纳税年度记录。所提交的记录因制度不同而不同，其目的是跟踪已经支付企业所得税和预扣税（在归属收入制度下）的利润部分以及与之相关的抵扣额。这些记录的目的，是防止双重缴税或避免双重缴付税款，以及明确 35% 的预扣税是否到期支付。

请注意，如果纳税人选择两种中的一种，必须至少 5 个连续商业年度适用该制度。

4. 附加税或预扣税

一般来讲，预扣税针对居住地和住所均不在智利的自然人或法人从智利取得的收入征收。

对于智利海外纳税人的某些支付也适用该税收。

总体上，居住地或住所均不在智利的自然人或法人其应当缴纳的预扣税税率为 35%。

不过，智利法律规定，特殊种类的支付可以减免预扣税税率：

① 用于为位于智利境内的设备或其他货物投保，向未在智利设立的保险公司支付款项，以及为居住在智利或住所在智利的个人投保人寿保险或医疗保险支付的保费征收 22% 的税款。在这种情况下，再保险按 2% 的税率征税。

② 工程或技术项目，以及专业或技术服务费（税率为 15%）。

③ 因驶往智利或智利港口的海上运输服务而支付给住所不在智利的自然人或法人的工资或佣金，以及来自智利或外国港口的船舶和货运服务的报酬，税率为 5%。如果在船舶注册国或经营者国不存在类似优惠或不对智利船只优惠，则根据互惠原则，本优惠税率不适用。

④ 在规定使用外国船只作为沿海贸易用途的租金、租赁、租船等其他合同中的支付，税率为 20%。相关合同允许或不禁止沿海贸易时，同样适用。

⑤ 一般而言，向未在智利居住的实体支付特许权使用费、专利和费用，须支付 30% 的预扣税，由付款人支付。对于与发明专利、实用新型、工业设计、集成电路或布图设计、新的蔬菜品种和软件有关的专利使用费，只要许可方既不是与被许可人有关，也不是与避税港居民或注册公司有关的，则税率降至 15%。

不过，如果所购买的是"标准软件"，就是免税的。如果涉及技术帮助或者工程师服务，税率也是15%。但如果服务收款人的一方或者一个个人或者实体是位于避税港，则适用20%的税率。

然而，此类利润已缴纳的一类税可以依规定和比例抵免一部分预扣税。

5. 个人所得税

个人所得税针对所有住所或居住地在智利的自然人全部来源的收入征收，累计税率为0%～35%，税基也包括在相应的年份从国外取得的收入，纳税人必须进行年度申报。

6. 二类税

受雇于他人者因获得工资、薪水、分红需要每月缴纳二类税，累进税率为0%～40%。税制改革将最高税率下调为35%，于2017年生效。

需按照此税制纳税的受雇者如无其他收入来源，则无须缴纳任何其他种类的所得税。

7. 矿业税

矿业税又称矿业使用税，对"矿业开发者"（即开采并在任何一个生产加工环节出售矿业资源的自然人或法人）"因矿业活动取得的应纳税营业收入"（在一类税征收所针对的净收入基础上有一定调整）征收矿业税。

矿业税采取累计税率，税基为矿业产品每年的销售额，销量当量以铜精矿吨（MTFC）为单位，单价按伦敦金属交易所的平均铜价作为参考价格计算。年销量超过50 000 MTFC的矿业开发者应根据其营业利润按5%～14%的累计税率纳税；年销量在15 000～50 000 MTFC的矿业开发者应纳税率为0.5%～4.5%；年销量在12 000 MTFC以下的矿业开发者无须缴纳矿业税。

8. 资本利得税

一般来讲，出售持有的智利股份公司股份所获资本收益应缴纳一类税和最后税款；但在满足某些条件的情况下，因变卖某些资产所获的资本收益可享受特殊的税收规定，即仅需缴纳一类税或可以享受免税待遇。如满足特定条件，如纳税主体出售的是在证券交易所频繁交易的上市股份公司的股份，则可能享受免税待遇。税改未对此规则作出修改。

9. 折旧

根据智利税务局的准则，固定资产折旧，除土地外，可以根据其使用年限采用直线法扣税，根据资产价值计算，均衡地分摊到固定资产预定使用寿命内。不过，对于在当地购买的新资产或者有超过3年使用寿命的进口新产品/旧产品，纳税人可以选择加速折旧。为此目的，这些资产的会计使用寿命减去几个月后将被人为计算为正常使用寿命的1/3。纳税人可随时停止使用加速折旧法，但不得重复选择使用。

智利税务局发布了关于不同业务固定资产使用寿命的一般准则，如工业、采矿或渔业。不过，主管区域税务主任可应纳税人的要求，对折旧额进行合理修改。

一般而言，对无形资产，如商誉、专利、商标等，不予折旧。

10. 外国公司分支机构

外国实体的分支机构按来源于全球的收入征税。所得税法赋予税务局在分支机构的会计记录不足以评估应纳税所得时评估其应纳税所得额的权力。在这种情况下，税务局可以根据总收入、资产、资本投资、销售或进出口百分比来评估应税收入。

11. 利息支付与资本弱化税制

在国外取得的贷款的利息通常按35%的标准计算预扣税；然而，向非智利银行或金融机构支付的利息在某些条件下按4%的减征税率征税。

不过，智利的所得税法包含一些资本弱化的规则，限制了向在智利的境外投资提供资金的可能性，因为这些债务的利息都需要缴纳预扣税。因此，如纳税实体在财政年度的年负债总额超过其权益的三倍，则视为过度负债，那么对于借款人来说，由居住或者住所在条约国的出借人或者外国银行、金融机构提供的超过其权益三倍部分的贷款利息征收35%的预扣税。智利借款人必须承担降低利率（例如4%或15%）与35%的利率之间的差额。

12. 转移定价规则

智利通过了经济合作与发展组织《转让定价准则》，因此，如果有关各方之间的国际交易，当地实体收取或支付的价格、价值或回报与交易中收取或支付的价格不同，则税务局可对这些价格、价值或回报提出异议。

13. 增值税

按交易价格计算，税率为19%。当价格明显低于正常水平时，税务局有权对其进行评估。

（1）须缴纳增值税的交易

①转让动产所有权的销售合同和其他合同，但须是经常出售的；

②经常出售的有形不动产；

③与商业、工业、金融、采矿、建筑、保险、广告、数据处理和其他商业活动相对应的服务；

④动产的租金，以及为进行工业或商业活动而提供或配备的不动产的租金；

⑤所述货物的租金；

⑥保险费用（例外情形除外）；

⑦在某些情况下的建筑活动。

一般情况下，货物或服务的销售者负责纳税。然而，增值税的数额通常是增加到货物和服务中的，因此，实际上是买方承担了税收的经济影响。

在例外情况下，当卖方不在智利居住或由于其他原因难以被税务局管控时，买方必须预留并支付增值税。

除进口等特殊情况外，该税按月缴纳。

（2）贷记制

纳税主体购买商品、服务或参与其他需要缴纳增值税的活动而负担的税务视为税款贷项，纳税主体向消费者出售服务或商品时征收的增值税则为税款借项。应付增值税为税款借项减去税款贷项后的剩余部分。如果税款借项金额超过税款贷项，则超过部分可用于无限抵扣。购置有关有形资产，包括建筑物和建筑的税款也可贷记。

增值税贷项从增值税借项中扣除，差额必须付给智利国库。

如果在任何一个月的贷项超过借项，差额可以结转并加到下一个月的贷项中。

若是因购买固定资产产生的税款贷项已经超过借项6个月，可由国库以现金退还。

（3）增值税豁免

智利的增值税法中很少有免税条款。主要有以下几点：

①出口；

②贷款和其他金融业务的利息，但在延期支付销售价格的情况下，收取利息须缴纳增值税；

③国际货运、空运和海运；

④专业服务；

⑤应收预扣税的服务，除非该服务的提供地点在智利或根据智利法律享受特殊税务豁免，或是根据协议约定避免双重征税；

⑥不被视为收入的进项。

（4）不动产

传统的房地产销售是按增值税征收的，这不适用于没有建筑的土地。

法律中已规定允许从应税基础上扣除土地成本。

（5）出口

如前所述，出口免征增值税。不过，出口商可收回因其出口活动所需的购买或服务而收取的增值税，作为对其当地销售中借方的贷项。此外，他们还可以以现金形式收回这笔贷项，作为退款。

14. 税务申报和优惠

一般而言，在智利应纳税的自然人和实体必须通过第22号表格提交年度纳税申报表，且须在收入产生年份的次年4月提交。

此外，须缴纳公司税的纳税人及须缴付增值税的纳税人，必须在规定期间后的首个12个月内，通过第29号表格提交每月报税表。

此外，每月须缴付预扣税、赌博税、燃油税等税款的纳税人，须提交第50号表格。

请注意，根据智利税务局的规定，在某些情况下，纳税人必须向税务当局提交不同类型的宣誓书（例如利润分配、雇员等）。

（九）证券

1. 证券相关法律、法规简介

智利《证券市场法》（第18045号法律）规定，"证券"是指任何可转让票据，包括股票、股票期权、债券、共同基金份额、储蓄计划以及基本上任何信用票据或投资票据。

自然人及企业可以自由投资证券，不区分国民和外国人。机构投资者满足条件的可以投资证券。

根据《证券市场法》的规定，机构投资者指银行、金融企业、保险公司、境内再保险实体，以及法律授权的基金经理。这些投资者投资证券所需要满足的条件在多部法律和多项决议中均有规定，包括但不限于银行普通法、关于养老基金的第3500号法令、养老基金管理人投资外国证券的规定。

这些规定基于以下方面确定投资限制：证券类型；投资额度；证券评级；投资额与基金净值的比例等。

2. 证券市场监督管理

证券交易委员会（SVS）是监管智利证券市场的主管机构。

发行人或发行经纪商唯一可行的，不必根据监管机构采取行动的发售证券的方法是通过私人配售。私募证券不受智利《证券市场法》的约束，因此对私募（非公开发行）以及经纪人/交易商通过私募方式在智利进行的销售既没有限制，也没有特殊要求。

智利法律对私募或证券发行没有定义。尽管如此，《证券市场法》将"公开发行证券"定义为向公众或某些特定人群发出要约。

外国发行人、中介及其他外国人参与涉及违反《证券市场法》的外国证券的注册、配售、存放、交易等行为或协议均应承担法律责任并受到行政处罚，例如罚款、不超过1年的停业（即注册经纪人或代理人的情形），严重情形下，被取消证券交易委员会授予的许可。

此外，任何违反《证券市场法》而提出要约并给第三方造成损害的人将对此类损害承担责任。

3. 外国企业进行证券交易的要求

（1）必须在智利证券市场注册的公司

根据《证券市场法》第5条的规定，下列实体及契据需在证券注册处进行登记：

① 公开发行证券的发行人；

② 公开发行的证券；

③ 公司股份由500名或500名以上股东持有，或者至少10%的认购股本属于至少100名股东，不包括单独或通过其他个人或法人实体持有超过该百分比的股东；

④ 公司自愿注册或法定要求注册发行股份的。

非公众公司是那些不属于公众公司定义的公司。最后，特殊目的公司是《公司法》第十三章中提到的公司。

（2）在智利证券市场发售外国公司股份

外国公司的股份（外资股）必须在智利证券市场和保险监管部门发售，以允许其公开招股和商业交易。

4. 发售顺序

① 发售可以由发行股票的外国公司或保荐人完成。

② 外国公司进行发售须通过智利的法定代表进行，该代表应具有足够的权力申请发售，提供有关公司的信息，遵守发售义务并接收关于认购过程的信息。

③ 在智利发行股份的外国公司必须来自国际证券委员会组织（IOSCO）的国家成员。根据检索，

中国是该组织的成员。

④ 发售申请应附有一封介绍信，声明外国公司有意在智利股票市场发售其股份。此外，公司必须填报并提交第 1 号表格给证券交易委员会，以提供关于该公司股份、潜在的智利投资者、经济和财务信息等基本信息。

（十）投资偏好及投资保护

1. 对特定行业及地区的支持

根据本国立法，在本国特殊地理区域进行的投资将享受税收优惠。此外，诸如《法律评论》《托科皮亚法》《埃斯特拉法》《纳瓦里诺法》等法律规定了适用于智利特定的行政区域（位于智利的北部和南部偏远地区）进行投资和开展经济活动的特殊海关及税收制度。

此外，有意开创创新业务或开发高科技产业和人力资源的公司也有可能申请智利政府提供的一系列资助（CORFO 补贴），该类资助旨在扶持此类业务在本国落地生根。在这方面，补贴金额将取决于项目类型及其具体特点。①

2. 特殊行业

根据智利法律，某些设立时需要特别批准的公司在兼并、增资和请求提前解散之前需要获得主管单位的批准。

此外，还有一些与特定行业相关的法律规定了强制性的合并前申报，包括媒体、银行、港口、供水、赌场、能源输送和海事特许权。

3. 投资保护

由于外国投资对智利经济的重要性，智利制定了一系列法律和政策以吸引投资者，保证稳定的法律机制以确保外国投资者获得和智利投资者同等的待遇，即非随意性和非歧视性待遇，并且（保证外国投资者）能够进入大部分经济领域。

三、贸易

（一）贸易监管部门

总的来说，除了现行立法明文禁止的商品之外（例如二手汽车和摩托车、任何形式的石棉、色情制品、有毒工业废料等），任何类型的商品都可以进口。国家海关总署是负责核实遵守上述事项的机构。

在这方面，海关是财政部下属的公共服务机构，负责监测和检查共和国沿海、边界和机场的货物通过情况；为进出口和其他税收目的而监管国际运输；生成边界运输的流量统计数据；等等。

（二）贸易相关法律、法规

国家海关总署（SNA）是财政部下属的一个公共服务机构，负责监督和控制通过智利的海岸、边界和机场的货物流通，监管国际运输以依法征收进出口和其他税收，生成这些边境运输的统计数据，以及履行其他法律赋予的职责。它由国家局、地区局和海关管理局组成。

国家海关总署受《组织法》（第 329 号法律）（1979 年）和《海关法》（第 30 号法律）（2004 年）的管制。

（三）贸易管理

由于智利是一个开放市场经济体，它对进口或投资的限制很少，允许外国公司享受与当地公司相同的保护和经营条件。但在农业和其他部门存在一些例外。负责监管对外贸易的是海关，这些内容将在"海关管理"部分详细解释。

---

① 更多信息参见 http://www.foreigninvestment.cl/。

（四）进出口商品检验检疫

尽管通常任何类型的货物都可以进口，但第18164号法律规定了两种由特定的公共机构进行认证的产品制度：

（1）目的地证书

酒精、含酒精饮料及醋饮、蔬菜产品，以及对植物、动物、鸟类等产品和副产品有害的产品，动物或植物用料碎屑及下脚料、肥料和杀虫剂，需要农业牲畜部门（SAG）颁发的证书，证书将指定所述货物的核准存放地点，以及将其从海关处所移至指定存放地点的运输路线和运输条件。

任何种类的食品、有毒或危险物质、医药产品、医疗和化妆品用途的食品、麻醉药品和会产生依赖性的精神药物都需要由卫生部门签发的证书，具体说明该货物的授权存放地点，以及将其从海关处所移至指定存放地点的运输路线和运输条件。

（2）使用和目的地授权

一旦上述文件的处理工作已经完成并且货物已经从海关的主要场所移走，它们将被存放在收货人处并受收货人管理，该收货人在没有获得卫生服务部门和／或农业畜牧部门的许可和事先批准的情况下不能使用、消费、出售、转让或以任何方式处置上述货物。

报告可以包含以下内容：

① 授予许可或批准；

② 拒绝许可或批准；

③ 设立一段安全期（检疫期），以便酌情实施卫生、动物和植物检验检疫控制。在此期间，货物不能投放市场。

不使用上述证书中指明的路线、存放地点或运输条件，以及未经相应许可违规使用、消费、出售、转让或处置的行为，将受到 10～1 000 UTM①（1UTM = 80 美元）的罚款处罚。罚款由相应监管机构作出。

此外，农业畜牧部门还负责控制农业和畜牧业投入及受法律和其他规范监管的产品。例如，农业畜牧部门有权：

① 采取措施防止可能影响动植物健康的病虫害进入国家领土；

② 确定有关方面必须采取的措施以预防、控制、打击和根除需人为控制的病虫害；

③ 根据产品的有害生物风险进行分类，以确定其进入智利必须遵守的进口要求。根据产品的分类和农业畜牧部门颁布的具体规定，前述进口要求会有所不同。

（五）海关管理

一般来讲，进口需要支付金额为货物 CIF 价（商品成本加上保险费和运费）6% 的关税。然而，取决于相关货物和相关国家之间的自由贸易协定，这一税率可能有所变化。

1. 总则

根据第20269号法律的规定，进口的资本货物可以免除智利的所有关税，该法律对符合第18634号法律规定的"资本货物"确定了0%的关税。

在这方面，第18634号法律第2条将资本货物定义为："直接或间接用于生产的货物、服务、用于商品或服务的商业化的机器、车辆、设备和工具。该货物不能在第一次使用时丧失其生产更多商品的能力，而是必须具备至少三年的生产能力，在较长时期内缓慢磨损或贬值。"该条文还指出，"旨在进行补充或支持活动，如对生产出的产品进行整修、选择、养护、分析和商业化等，间接地参与生产过程的产品"也属于资本货物。

只有包含在财政部发布的清单中列明的货物才能被认定为"进口的资本货物"。

上述关税制度适用于与资本货物有关的备件和磨损件，只要它们与资本货物在同一份"海关目的地文件"中一起进口。这些备件、磨损部件的价值不得超过资本货物价值的 10%。

---

① UTM (Unidad Tributaria Mensual) 是智利国家内部税收服务部用于计算税收、罚款和其他费用的月度税收单位。

2. 进口增值税

进口也需缴纳增值税。根据《增值税法》第 8 条 a）款的规定，增值税按 CIF 价或海关价值征收进口增值税。但是，《增值税法》第 12 条 b）款第 10 项规定了对进口资本货物免征增值税的情形：

① 货物是按照《外国直接投资法》（DFI）的规定进口的，包括接受这种投资的企业。为了从该豁免中获益，必须满足以下要求：投资项目必须符合上述法律条款的规定；资本货物必须是投资项目的一部分；资本货物必须列入经济部规定的最高法令列表中。

② 符合以下要求时，智利投资者也可以从豁免中受益：智利无法制造满足质量和数量要求的相关资本货物；资本货物必须是与《外国直接投资法》规定的外国投资项目类似的国内投资项目的一部分，旨在为最终消费者生产与《外国直接投资法》规定的外国投资项目类似的商品或服务；投资必须被认定为"有利于国家利益"；资本货物必须列入经济部颁布的最高法令；上述要求的符合性必须由经济部进行检查及发布决议，并由财政部予以确认。

由于智利《所得税法》（ITL）将来源于智利的收入定义为智利境内的货物或在智利开展的活动产生的收入，因此进口商品无须在智利缴纳所得税。在国外设立或住所地在国外的公司仅对其来源于智利的收入在智利缴纳所得税。

（六）产品认证

在智利，没有行业专属的标准协会。相反，唯一负责制定智利标准的组织是国家标准化研究院（INN）。由该院制定的标准发展的长期计划与智利的主要出口行业相一致，包括铜、林业、农产品和葡萄酒。

在大多数行业中，智利的标准不是强制性的，除非法律和/或法规特别规定，但公司可以自愿遵守这些标准，尤其是在某些行业，遵守这些标准构成一种"认证标准"。

但是，某些进口产品，如与工业安全、建筑和建筑材料、汽车安全以及燃气和电力行业有关的产品，必须符合监管机构的具体要求。例如，新建筑必须符合抗震性的具体规定。国家标准化研究院还在当地制造商中推广 ISO 14000 和 ISO 9000 标准。化工行业是一个将 ISO 9000 标准纳入其工业流程的例子。

四、劳动

（一）劳动法律、法规简介

一般而言，劳动相关事宜主要包含在智利《劳动法》中，该法适用于私人雇员，无论是智利人还是外国人。《劳动法》规定了不同的事项，如个人劳动合同、福利、工会和集体谈判协议、分包和人员供给等。

此外，其他一些具体法律还规定了其他与雇佣有关的事宜，如社会保障（养老和健康）、法定保险、劳动保障等。

1. 劳动合同

劳动合同的订立遵从自愿原则。智利法律规定，企业必须在雇员开始工作之日起 15 天内与其签订书面劳动合同。如企业未能在 15 天内出具书面劳动合同，则劳动合同的条款条件默认为雇员所宣称的条款条件。

法律规定了三种劳动合同：

（1）个人劳动合同

个人劳动合同是雇主和雇员之间签订的，对双方具有约束力的书面合同，即雇员基于依赖和雇佣关系向前者提供个人服务，而雇主为雇员提供的服务支付报酬。

智利法规（主要是《劳动法》）规定了上述合同的最基本条款，这些最基本条款对雇主具有强制性。

（2）集体合同

法律规定了两种类型的集体合同：

① 规范性集体合同。根据《劳动法》的规定，集体合同由一个或多个雇主与一个或多个工会，或与没有公会的员工组成的共同协商团体，或与公会和协商团体达成一致，以确立在一段固定时间内共同的工作条件和薪酬。

② 非规范性集体合同。此外，法律允许雇主和雇员（与工会或至少 8 名雇员组成的团体）签订这种特定类型的合同，来约定公会或专门组织起来协商和执行该协议的员工团体在一段固定的时间内共同的工作条件和报酬。

请注意，在法律上，规范性集体合同和非规范性集体合同之间的唯一区别是后者不需要规范的集体谈判程序。因此，非规范性集体合同的谈判既不受规范程序的约束，也不会导致罢工。但是，一旦执行，两种协议均具有相同的效力，并对双方都具有约束力。

（3）特别合同

智利的法律还规定了特殊的劳动合同。这些合同中的每一种都有自己的特点和要求，例如学徒合同仅限于 21 岁以下的个人；农场雇员合同；船舶或海上雇员和临时码头雇员的合同以及家政服务合同。

2. 劳动合同期限

双方当事人可以同意无固定期限合同、限制合同期限至雇员完成特定工作，或者双方同意的固定期限。

固定期限合同的期限需超过一年，对管理人员、专业人员和技术人员需超过两年。在原定期限或其延展期满时，合同自然终止，但如果员工继续为同一雇主提供服务，根据法律规定合同期限变为无固定期限。

3. 员工国籍

法律规定，拥有 25 名以上员工的公司，必须有至少 85% 的员工为智利籍。计算该比例时，无法被智利籍员工取代的技术人员不计算在内。为此，法律规定下述人员为智利籍：

① 配偶或同性伴侣或子女是智利的外国人，包括配偶是智利籍的寡妇或鳏夫；

② 在该国居住超过 5 年的外国人，不考虑偶然不在国内的情形。

4. 工作时间表

至于工作时间表，《劳动法》规定了每周最长小时数。正常的工作周限制在 45 个小时内，且该最长小时数必须是在不少于 5 个且不超过 6 个的连续的工作日内完成。正常工作日不得超过 10 小时。

加班——即员工超过法定或双方同意的工作日工作的时间（如果较短）——应当根据临时情况进行商定。加班必须视情况决定，该种情形不是公司生产活动中长期存在的，是偶然事件或不可避免的因素引起的，且确实在一定时间内（但每天不超过 2 个小时的加班时间）有较大的工作需求。加班协议需满足某些法律规定，且若引起加班的情况持续存在，则加班协议可能需要更新。智利法律规定必须支付 50% 的额外工资。

最后，根据法律规定，在某些特殊情况下，由于其服务性质，员工的工作周期既不限于 45 小时，也无权获得加班费。

5. 员工休息

（1）工作日休息时间

工作日必须分为两个时间段，两个时间段之间至少有半小时的午餐休息时间，这段时间不计算在工作时间内。

（2）每周休息时间

周日和法定休假日为非工作日，法律授权的活动除外。在后一种情形中，法律规定了如何补偿这些休息日。

在智利，假日有：

① 新年（1 月 1 日）；

② 额外新年[①];
③ 复活节（周五，周六和周日）；
④ 劳动节（5月1日）；
⑤ 海军作战纪念日（5月21日）；
⑥ 圣保罗和彼得日（6月29日）[②]；
⑦ 圣女卡门日（7月16日）；
⑧ 国庆节（9月18日和19日）[③]；
⑨ 哥伦布日（10月12日）[④]；
⑩ 福音派教会日（10月31日）[⑤]；
⑪ 万圣节；
⑫ 圣灵感孕日（12月8日）；
⑬ 圣诞节（12月25日）。

请注意，选举日也是假日。同时还有一些地区性的节日（只适用于在这些特定地区工作的雇员）。

（3）年假

① 基本年假为15个工作日；

② 连续或不连续为同一或不同雇主工作10年后雇员有权享有递增的年假，在达到10年工龄后每满三年服务多1天；

③ 特别地区工作的年假为20天（而不是基本年休假的15天），仅适用于在本国第11区和第12区以及其他特定区域工作的雇员。

6. 报酬

在法律上，根据雇佣协议，雇员从雇主处获得的任何现金和实物现金等价收益均被视为报酬。

报酬[⑥]包括基本工资、加班费、佣金、利润分成和奖金。法律进一步明确规定，某些支付或津贴不构成报酬，例如午餐、雇员的家属津贴、交通津贴等。

报酬必须在商定的固定期间支付，不得超过1个月。但是，在可变薪酬的情况下，这种可变的报酬或佣金通常是按月付、每两个月付或者按季付。其他根据公司季度或年度情况而支付的款项，即奖金及利润分成，是在相应的季度或者营业年度结束时支付。

报酬金额可以由雇主和雇员自由约定，但法律规定了一个最低标准，每周工作45个小时的员工的月薪不能低于法定月最低工资（264 000智利比索，约430美元）。

（1）利润分成

从法律上讲，如果一家公司有利润，它必须与其员工分享部分利润。法律规定，公司必须向员工分配30%的净利润，按员工工资的比例进行计算。用于确定利润的基础是公司应纳税所得额（需进行某些调整）减去净资产的10%。代替上述义务的另一种做法是，雇主可以支付等于员工年薪25%的奖金，但无论员工的工资水平如何，该奖金不得超过每月最低工资的4.75倍。但是，雇主和雇员可以就不同的利润分成办法达成一致，只要向雇员支付的报酬不低于上述两种选择。

（2）额外福利

除个人或集体合同中自愿达成的福利外，雇主没有义务提供附加福利。养老金和疾病津贴由后文所述的社会保障制度覆盖。通常来讲，雇主没有法律义务提供餐饮设施和膳食。

7. 劳动合同的终止

智利《劳动法》适用"就业相对稳定"的原则。因此，劳动合同只能因法定事由并依照法律规定终止。

---

① 如果1月1日是星期天，则随后的星期一为假日。
② 如果此假日在周二、周三或周四，假日将移至上个星期一。如果假日在星期五，则假日将转移到下个星期一。
③ 如果国庆节在周六或周日，9月17日将是额外的假日。
④ 如果此假日在周二、周三或周四，假日将移至上个星期一。如果假日在星期五，则假日将转移到下个星期一。
⑤ 如果此假日在周二、周三或周四，假日将移至上个星期一。如果假日在星期五，则假日将转移到下个星期一。
⑥ 没有法律规定要求雇主根据通货膨胀调整雇员的工资。但是，这是一种常见的做法。

《劳动法》规定了劳动合同终止的法定事由有：
① 客观终止理由，例如双方同意、雇员辞职或死亡等；
② 有理由终止；
③ 基于经济原因或无故终止。

根据上文第①、②种所述的终止理由，员工无权获得法定遣散费。但终止雇佣关系必须符合某些法律规定，特别是关于上述第②种理由。

最后，无故终止合同，雇员有权领取法定遣散费，其中包括：
① 代替通知的遣散费：等于员工收到的最后一份工资总额，代替依法应提前30天通知的要求；
② 工龄遣散费：当双方同意或达成任何低于法律规定的条件时，该薪酬的支付等于该员工收到的最后1个月的总工资乘以工作年数，不满1年但超过6个月的按1年计算，但上限不超过11年。① 请注意，员工只有在具有1年服务年限后才有权获得此遣散费。②

两项法定遣散费都必须根据《劳动法》的规定进行计算。

尽管有上述规定，双方可以就终止合同时依据传统遣散费达成一致。双方可以书面形式约定，并且该约定即使在员工根据离职理由不能享有任何法定离职金的情况下也可以适用。但是，约定的遣散费补偿不得低于法定补偿金数额。这种协议适用于行政和管理职位。

此外，雇主有可能支付自愿离职遣散费，通常适用于雇员根据离职理由不享有法定遣散费的情形。需要格外注意的是，对雇主来说这种遣散费在税务上是不能扣除的，并且适用40%的税收惩罚。

此外，无论解雇援引的法定理由是什么，雇员都有权享受其累积未休假的假期的遣散费用。

最后，终止雇佣还必须符合法律要求，例如书面通知，适用于有理由终止雇佣、经济原因或无故终止雇佣，以及执行终止劳动关系协议。

8. 外包

法律允许劳务外包或分包，即使是用人公司的主营业务，或是通过劳务外包公司来雇用临时工。从劳务外包公司雇用临时工有特殊的限定条件和时间限制。劳务外包公司是在主管机关登记的业务单一的特殊法人。法律详细规定了两种制度。

智利法律允许服务采购或外包，智利法规规定了两种外包类型：

（1）分包

在这种类型下，承包商以自己的名义提供服务并承担风险，提供服务的与其建立劳动关系并接受其管理。因此，在服务的执行过程中，客户不得干涉员工的工作方向。

一般来讲，客户对承包商雇员的劳动和社会保障义务（即雇佣终止时的遣散费、社会保障义务的支付、工资等）、卫生和安全的工作地点等承担连带责任。

尽管如此，如果客户能够证明其已经有效地要求了承包商遵守《劳动法》的，则客户不承担连带责任，只承担补充责任。为此，客户应要求承包商提供智利劳工部颁发的特别证明等文件，证明承包商履行了其所有劳动和社会保障义务。

如果承包商没有及时证明其履行了劳动和社会保障义务，客户有权暂扣任何根据双方协议应当支付的款项或预付款，暂扣的款项以履行其支付员工欠款和/或社保欠款的补充责任为限。

客户还可向劳工部报告承包商违反劳动和社会保障义务，并声明其已经进行暂扣。

分包服务的主要风险之一是有可能员工既被视为承包商的雇员，又对客户有服从性和依赖性。为证明存在直接劳动关系，劳动者应当向劳动法院提起针对主公司的诉讼；如果法院裁定有利于雇员，则主公司将承担直接雇主的义务。

（2）人力派遣

法律规定的特定法人允许向公司提供临时的人力派遣。在该种类型下，公司将在授权并在公司管理下接受人力派遣的雇员。然而，智利《劳动法》仅在一些特别情况下（如顶替休假或请病假的雇员、

---

① 这个11年的上限不适用于1981年8月14日之前雇用的员工。
② 关于上述赔偿，有必要说明该笔款项有90个智利发展单位（Unidades de Fomento，简称"UF"）的上限，约为3 900美元。然而，各方可以同意放弃上限，但必须以书面协议的形式达成一致。

应对活动较多的特殊和临时时期等）和有限的期间内（一般不得超过90或180日）允许人力派遣。

9. 背景调查

根据提供的服务的性质，当雇员身体状况是他是否适合该工作的一个因素时，雇主可以要求提供医疗证明。也就是说，只有在特定情况下，雇主才可以申请医疗证明以确认该雇员能够胜任工作（即与不健康和危险的工作有关，例如采矿或高处的劳动）。如果员工的状况不是他是否适合工作的一个要素，这样的要求可能被认为是歧视性的，并且可能被认定为员工的宪法权利受到侵犯。

犯罪背景调查适用同样的标准。

关于信用调查，法律的一般规定是，雇主不可以将没有信用债务或还款义务作为招聘的条件，也不能要求提供无负债的事实声明。然而，根据智利法律，可以要求具有一般行政权力并且能够代表雇主的人，例如经理或代理人，以及负责收集、管理或保管资金的人员提供此类证明或声明。

教育背景调查是允许的，因为教育背景调查被认为是确定他是否适合担任职位的一个要素。

10. 生育保护

关于这一问题，智利劳动法规制定了一系列保护生育产妇的权利和利益的规定，例如：

（1）禁止进行危险或有害的工作 [①]

如果在怀孕期间，一名员工正在从事被认为对怀孕有害的工作，则该员工必须转入其他工作，而不能改变其报酬。

（2）产假

关于产假，法律规定了不同的休假方式：

① 产前假期。女性雇员在产前有6周全额补贴 [②]（由社会保障系统而不是由雇主支付）的休假（产前休假）。法律还规定了在特定情况下的产前补充休假。

② 产后假期。女性雇员有权在其子女出生后获得12周的假期（产后假期，这笔款项由社会保障系统支付）。在某些条件下，假期还可以延长。

③ 育婴假。此外，根据法律规定，可以根据以下两种选择获得额外的育婴假：一种是全日制：这意味着产后假期结束后还可获得12周的额外假期，并由社会保障系统支付全额补贴；另一种是半日制：只能由员工选择，不能强加。在这种情况下，产后假期结束后可以获得18周的育婴假并获得补贴。至于付款方面，由社会保障体系给予的补贴降低到50%，雇主必须支付另外的50%的工资。法律还规定，育婴假的一部分可以转移给父亲。

请注意，法律规定了特定的额外假期。

（3）父亲的育婴假

父亲在儿子/女儿出生后有权享受5天的带薪假。员工可以选择连续使用或在婴儿出生的第一个月内分散使用。

（4）生育保护

女性雇员自怀孕直至产后休假结束后一年，一直享有产妇特权，受到法律保护。在此期间，雇主不得无故解雇女性雇员。对于因故辞退的，雇主必须要求法院的事先批准。

（二）外籍雇员

一般规则是，不论雇主为智利或外国实体，来智利提供服务的雇员均须受到智利《移民法》和《劳动法》的约束。

概括说来，智利《移民法》在办理签证申请过程中不区分申请人的国籍。但申请签证所需费用因申请人国籍不同会有所不同。

智利为打算到智利工作的外籍人员提供以下两种签证：

① 根据工作合同发放的签证（工作签证）；

[①] 下列工作被认为是危险的：(1) 举起、携带和推重物；(2) 进行剧烈的身体活动，包括长时间站立；(3) 夜班工作；(4) 加班加点；(5) 有关当局宣布的在该阶段不方便从事的其他工作。

[②] 需注意员工有权获得的补贴是由法律决定的，并且其法定上限会定期更改。

② 临时签证。

除此之外，临时签证是签发给那些未与智利的公司或分支机构签订劳动合同但作为独立顾问其服务在智利被认为对国家有用或便利的专业人员、技术人员和专家。外国人必须根据不同的情况来申请临时签证。

申请者均有权在以上签证到期之后申请永久居民。同样，同种类型的签证可签发给签证持有人的家庭成员（如妻子、子女或父母），但不得在智利从事有偿服务。

无特殊限制下，所有签证均是允许持有人在智利居住和从事合法活动的居留许可。工作签证期限为2年，临时签证期限为1年并可续签1年。

工作签证申请程序有下列两种：

① 签证申请可向智利领事馆提交后由外交部受理。申请此类签证的材料由接受申请的领事馆确定。

② 签证申请可当雇员到达智利时提交。在此情况下，申请须向移民局（内政部所属部门）提交。

工作签证申请程序耗时约8个月。在此期间外籍雇员可申请临时工作许可证，允许其在等待签证期间在智利工作。

此外，经特别许可，可允许旅游签证持有人在智利工作。故外籍人员可在到达智利后的1周内合法工作。

（三）出入境限制

值得注意的是，任何外籍游客进入智利均须持有旅游签证。根据其国籍，在境外申请旅游签证将成为必要。有些其他国家不要求持有旅游签证，在入境时亦无其他限制。出境时同样适用该规则。

一般情况下，旅游签证期限为90日，而不论以何种方式获得。然而，请注意边境主管机关有权签发期限更短的旅游签证或自行全权决定禁止外籍人员入境。

旅游签证可续签一次，在首次签证到期后起算最长可续签90日。

（四）劳动争议

智利法律规定了雇主与雇员之间的劳动争议解决的几种程序，可以是行政程序也可通过劳动法院提起诉讼。

从法律上讲说，劳动部是核查雇主合法合规并通过调解解决特定劳动争议的政府机关。在此情况下达成的争议和解具有强制力，并对双方当事人具有约束力，后者是依法通过行政程序实现的。

另一方面，劳动法院在其管辖范围内解决任何由雇主或雇员提起的劳动争议。司法裁决具有强制执行力并约束双方当事人，并可向高等级法院提起（如上诉法院或甚至最高法院）上诉。

双方解决劳动争议的程序为：

1. 劳动赔偿

雇员可单独或集体向劳动部提出劳动赔偿。通常情况是，雇员称雇主在劳动关系存续期间或劳动关系终止时违反了法定义务，并提出劳动赔偿请求。

通常情况下，劳动部可对雇主经营场所进行调查，或召集双方尝试达成合意。如无法达成合意，雇员可就争议事项向劳动法院提起诉讼。

2. 劳动诉讼

智利劳动法院有权审查：

① 任何由雇主和/或雇员提起的有关法律适用、与单独或集体劳动合同、契约或仲裁裁决的解释和适用相关的问题；

② 由雇主或雇员提出的社保相关的问题（审查病假问题除外）；

③ 任何就劳动或社会保险部门发布的决议提起的赔偿；

④ 任何就职业事故或疾病提起的赔偿；

⑤ 法律明确规定须受其管辖的任何其他事项。

请注意，根据具体事由和标的额，法律规定了不同的特定程序。因此，地方法规也规定了在劳动法院进行的不同种类的诉讼程序。但所有的程序大多为口头进行，允许观众旁听。

五、知识产权

（一）知识产权法律、法规简介

在智利，保护知识产权的法律主要包括《宪法》和下列几部法律和法规：
- 《关于专利（包括工业设计和实用新型）、商标、地理标识、集成电路外观设计（制图）和商业秘密的工业产权法》（第 19039 号法律）；
- 《著作权（版权）法》（第 17336 号法律）；
- 《植物多样性权法》（第 19342 号法律）；
- 《不正当竞争法》（第 20169 号法律）；
- 《边境措施（第二章）》（第 19912 号法律）。

智利是多个保护知识产权多边条约的成员国，如：
- 《保护工业产权巴黎公约》；
- 《专利合作条约》（PCT）；
- 《保护文学和艺术作品伯尔尼公约》；
- 《保护表演者、音像制品制作者和广播组织罗马公约》；
- 《关于播送人造卫星传输节目信号布鲁塞尔公约》。

同时，智利作为签署方的一些双边自由贸易协定也包含了知识产权部分，包括与美国签署的自由贸易协定和与欧盟签署的联合协定。

国家工业产权协会（INAPI）是负责注册工业产权（专利、工业设计、实用新型、商标、地理标识和集成电路外观设计）的机构。版权或邻接权在知识产权部登记。农业—畜牧业服务中心负责植物新品种登记。

（二）专利申请

专利可授予任何种类的、被认为是发明的产品或方法。在智利，方法被定义为工业活动中任何技术问题的解决方法。专利有效期为自提交申请之日起的 20 年，且不可延展。

发现、科学理论、数学方法、动植物、软件、商业模式、治疗或手术方法、生物的一部分均不能作为申请授予专利权的主题。但智利确实允许第二医药用途专利以及瑞士型权利要求。

专利申请审查由国家工业产权协会进行。智利有授予专利前异议体系，并在专利申请过程中发布多份审查员实质性报告。总体说来，国家工业产权协会进行专利审查的时间为 3 年左右。如有第三方就该专利申请提出异议，则审查时间将再延长一年。国家工业产权协会的最终决定可在工业产权法院进行上诉。上诉救济程序通常需要 1 年。该最终决定还可向最高法院申请撤销。

此外，值得注意的是，智利允许专利保护期调整和专利保护期延展程序。该两项程序均需向工业产权法院提交，由工业产权法院审查和解决。

可针对已注册的专利提起撤销诉讼，提起诉讼的时效期间是自注册之日起 5 年。

智利是《专利合作条约》国际专利体系的成员国。

（三）商标注册

商标可由文字、图案或文字与图案的结合构成。智利允许注册声音商标。3D 商标并不被法律所认可。商标的保护期限为 10 年，并可每 10 年续展一次。使用商标在智利并非是强制的，不因商标不常用而被注销。

尼斯分类项下产品和服务可获得注册，并增加两类：针对零售商名称的"商业设立"和制造商的"工业设立"。

商标申请向国家工业产权协会提交，并在政府公报上公布之后进行首次正式审查。如有绝对或相对的理由,可在商标申请公布后的 30 个工作日内提出异议,包括对智利境外注册的知名和恶名的商标提出异议,即使该商标未在智利使用。国家工业产权协会同样以绝对和相对理由在异议期间届满后对商标申请进行审查。首先,由国家工业产权协会主任对异议和审查意见(如有)作出决定;专门的工业产权法院对上诉作出决定;特定情况下,可提交最高法院裁定。如无异议或审查意见,商标申请审查时间约为 6 个月。

商标注册可自授予之日起的 5 年内以同一异议理由予以撤销。5 年之后,基于恶意情形,商标注册仍有可能被撤销。

商标代理人代为办理商标注册申请,须向国家工业产权协会提交无格式要求的授权书。

(四)保护知识产权的措施

智利法律就知识产权保护规定了几项措施:

《工业产权法》(第 19039 号法律)和《著作权(版权)法》(第 17336 号法律)就知识产权的执行制定了民事和刑事措施,包括禁止令、扣押令、罚款和获得损失赔偿的权利。

智利海关被授权执行边境措施,包括在无法院指令的情形下,就侵犯商标和版权的货物扣留可达 10 日。

六、环境保护

在过去的 10 年里,智利环境保护法备受关注,标准也逐渐提高。从在无污染环境中生活的宪法权利的司法实施到《环境法》(第 19300 号法律)的颁布以及环境部门和代表性区域地标法学的众多决定,环境法规已形成了一个法律体系,即在审批任何一个新投资项目时都需将环境影响纳入考量范围。

在智利,环境法规并非全部包含在一部法律之中,而是分散在数个不同层级的法规中,每项法规针对一项特定的事由。从实际角度来看,以下从实务角度简要总结与环境保护相关的法规。

(一)环境保护监管部门

在智利与环境法规适用相关的政府部门有三家:

① 环境部,负责制定和适用环境政策、规划和项目,保护生物多样性和可再生资源。

② 环境评估服务局(SEA),主要负责管理环境影响评估系统。

③ 环境监管局(SMA),是一个分散的公共服务机构,负责执行、组织和协调环境资质决议(RCA)的后续和监督,预防和消除污染计划,环境质量和排放法规,管理计划和法律规定的其他环境文件。

此外,还有环境法院,主要负责解决环境争议,如寻求环境损害修复的诉讼,对 SMA 决定的索赔,以及对环保认证决议的请求,等等。

(二)环境影响评估系统(SEIA)

该系统由《环境法》(EA)创建。任何包含在 EA 规定的专门清单上的项目或活动须在执行或修改之前须向该系统提交。

须向环境影响评估系统提交的项目和活动包括:高压输电线路和相关变电站,容量在 3 MW 以上的发电厂;机场、公交和汽车站、火车站、铁路、加油站、公路和能够影响受保护区域的公共干道;港口、航道、船厂和海运码头;特定区域的城市发展和旅游项目;宣布为潜在或饱和的工业和房地产项目;包括煤、石油、天然气等包含勘探和挖掘工作、加工设备、污水和废弃石料处置、工业提取石料、煤炭或黏土等内容的采矿项目;石油、天然气、矿物等运输管道,等等。

如必须向环境影响评估系统提交的项目或活动会产生《环境法》中描述的特定的相关环境影响,则须向环境影响评估系统提交环境影响研究报告(EIA)。如项目或活动未发现产生该种环境影响则无须提交环境影响研究报告,提交环境影响报告(DIA)即可。

就环境影响中要求提交环境影响研究报告而非环境影响报告的法律规定包括:因废水、排放物或残留物的数量和质量对人体健康构成威胁;对可再生自然资源(包括土地、水和空气)的数量和质量产生潜在实质不利影响;对人类居住地迁徙或生活方式、习俗或人口发生重大改变;在人类居住区、资源和保护区、优先保护区、受保护的湿地和可能受到影响的冰川或附近区域,以及拟规划区域的环境价值;对任何特定地区的景观或旅游价值在规模或持续时间上的任何重大改变;对人类学、考古学和历史价值的古迹或遗址的任何改变,以及对属于文化遗产部分的改变。

环境影响研究报告和环境影响报告的处理有几个不同点,主要区别在于环境部门发放环境资质决议的时限,对环境影响研究报告政府部门有120日的处理时限,而环境影响报告则缩短至60日。实践中,办理时限因项目所有人申请暂停而延长,主要是为收集数据和信息,回答相关部门的询问。

该程序的必然结果即环境资质决议,要么不允许,即项目或活动不得实施,要么允许。在允许的情况下,环境资质决议通常会要求项目所有人在项目不同实施和运行阶段必须满足的特定条件。

(三)环境保护法律、法规简介

1. 排放和环境质量标准

对几项特定特殊污染源规定了排放上限的标准。

① 有关大气排放,圣地亚哥首都大区实行的大气污染物排放标准比一般施行的标准更加严格。

② 就工业废水的排放而言,污染源排放必须符合相关的标准,申请取决于接受排放的水体种类(河流、湖泊、地下储水层、海洋)。通常为达到排放标准,需要在水务监管部门的监督下安装一个污水处理设施。

③ 环境质量标准规定了可能对人体健康、环境保护或保育产生危害的污染物浓度上限,以及对大气、内陆和海洋水域产生影响的污染物控制标准。

2. 有害固体废物

第148号最高法令(2003年)对有害废物的处理进行了规定,即《有害废物处理卫生条例》,其中介绍了这些废物的管理、存放和销毁的条件。处置重大有害废物的处理机器须向卫生部门提交废物处理计划以获得批准。

第298号最高法令(1994年)则对有害废物的运输进行了规定,即《有害废物运输条例》,规定了所有运输有害材料或废物的交通工具应达到的安全条件。

3. 原始森林法案

智利《原始森林恢复和林业推广法》(第20283号法律)规定,任何采伐原始森林的活动,不论地点,都须在经国家森林公司(CONAF)的事先批准的管理计划的基础上实施。然而,作为原始森林的一部分和被列为"濒临灭绝""易危""稀少""不足以获知"或"脱离危险"种类的原始森林植物种类苗木,不得采伐、销毁、破坏或移除。

4. 原住民法案

第19253号法律介绍了一项对原住民适用的特别法规。其规定了除在同一族群的原住民社区或个人之间,原住民土地不得转让、添附、抵押或通过逆权侵占获得。然而,原住民土地可经国家原住发展公司(CONADI)授权留置。该留置不得包括原住民人家的住宅和其赖以生存的土地。同样,原住民社区拥有的土地不得出租、委托转让或转让给第三方供其使用、享有或管理。原住民个人拥有的土地可进行上述处置,且时间上限为5年。

无论何种情况,这些土地在CONADI的事先同意下,可与同等商业价值并经正式确定的非原住民土地进行置换;后者将被视为原住民土地,而前者便不再属于原住民土地。

此外,智利签署了国际劳工组织《关于原住民和部落民族》(第169号公约)。根据该公约,政府须通过正当程序,就可能影响原住民的立法或行政措施征询原住民意见。

5. 破坏环境的责任

总的说来,破坏环境的责任为主观责任,如要求该个人和组织就环境破坏进行治理修复,或赔偿相当于损害的赔偿金,不仅必须是造成了损害,而且必须是由于故意不当行为或过失造成的结果。特殊情况下,破坏环境责任为严格责任,如《核安全法》(第18302号法律)(1984年)、第2222号法令(1978年)中的《航海法》、第3557号法令(1981年)中的《农业保护法》关于杀虫剂使用的规定。

（四）环境保护的合规监测

正如上述所言，环境监管局是负责协调监测和控制环境资质决议、防治计划或环境净化计划的措施、环境质量标准和排放标准的内容、管理计划以及法律规定的其他所有环境文件。

环境监管局可在违反环境法规时根据第 20417 号法实施处罚。根据违反严重程度的不同，将面临撤回环境资质决议、关闭工厂或处以 1 000 至 10 000 UTA 的罚款。

尽管如此，撤回或暂停环境资质决议的处罚在智利并不常见，因该处罚要求事先征询环保法院的意见。不论上述何种处罚，均须在环境监管局主导的处罚程序下进行。

七、争议解决

（一）争议解决方法和机构

智利的司法系统由一审法院、上诉法院和最高法院构成。一审法院根据地理位置和管辖事项进行划分。然而，智利没有专门解决商事纠纷的法院，因此由民事法庭来解决。

仲裁在智利司法管辖内被作为一项合法的争议解决途径。在仲裁机制下，各方可以自由地就大多数事项达成一致。根据赋予仲裁员的权力大小，仲裁有三种类型：法定仲裁（严格按照智利《民事诉讼法典》和法律规定进行）、公平合理仲裁（双方当事人和仲裁员可自由制定程序规则，该规则须符合公平和合理原则，可不必遵照法律进行）和混合仲裁（双方当事人可以自由制定程序规则，但最终的裁决必须根据法律作出）。

禁止仲裁的案件有有关赡养费、婚姻财产分割的案件和刑事案件等。相反，必须仲裁的案件有涉及公司、合伙企业清算、股东或合伙人之间的分歧等的案件。除这些案件外，任何一方不得违背其意愿进行仲裁。

准据法的选择通常可得到承认和执行，但也有一些例外。位于智利境内的资产始终受智利法管辖。家庭法的承认和执行也有一些例外。

国际合同（需具有国际因素）仲裁地的选择可得到承认和执行。然而，智利法院在认定是否存在国际因素时较为灵活。

（二）法律的适用

《法庭组织法》规定法院的组织和职权、管辖权等相关事项。

尽管特别的诉讼程序规定在单独的法案中，诉讼程序规则大部分规定于《民事诉讼法典》（针对民事案件）和《刑事诉讼法典》（针对刑事案件）。仲裁的程序规则，智利采取二元模式：国内仲裁依据《民事诉讼法典》进行；国际商事仲裁依据第 19971 号法律（2004 年）进行。

八、其他

（一）反商业贿赂

1. 反商业贿赂法律、法规简介

（1）商业贿赂是可由自然人和/或公司构成的刑事重罪

当自然人犯商业贿赂罪时，适用《刑法典》。自然人可以是商业贿赂罪的积极或被动参与者。被动参与者即在政府部门工作并收取了作为利益交换的报酬。相应的，积极参与者即在私营部门工作，为从政府获得利益而支付报酬。智利《刑法典》规定对贪污和贿赂（包括商业贿赂）的处罚。收取贿赂的公职人员以及行贿的人员都将受到刑事处罚。

智利第 20393 号法律（2009 年）规定了公司的刑事责任，公司仅可就下列三种罪行承担责任：

① 贿赂；
② 资助恐怖主义；
③ 洗钱。

法律规定，公司承担该等罪责的前提，实施犯罪的主体须为公司所有者、控制者、董事会成员、代表、主要管理人员，或任何在公司享有管理和监督责任的人员。此外，为归责于公司而非其直接涉及犯罪的人员，公司须直接或间接从实施该犯罪中获得利益。

在商业联合中，如合并，责任可从一家公司转移到另一家，并与个人责任相分离。责任不因公司的解散而结束。

此外，智利是《联合国反腐败公约》的成员国（自2006年起），以及《美洲反腐败公约》的成员国（自1998年起），此类公约使得打击这些犯罪更加严厉。

（2）预防犯罪政策前提

根据第20393号法律的规定，为预防公司犯罪，如贿赂，首先，公司需指定一名"预防犯罪负责人"，该负责人不得在公司任其他从属职位。其次，须授予该负责人足够的权限来履行其职责。再次，公司须设立一套可检测演变成犯罪的活动的"防范系统"、预防犯罪的机制、规则和指南；设置行政程序和审计以防止犯罪，并建立破坏该系统的人员的处罚机制。最后，该"防范系统"须经外聘审计师、风险评估公司或其他在监管部门（SVS）注册公司的认证。但是，该法未规定获得认证的基本条件，通常只需要一个预防系统就够了，但不一定足够需要或起到作用。

毋庸置疑，犯罪预防政策并不能使公司免除处罚，仅能倒置举证责任。在有政策规定的情况下，法院将假设公司遵守了其监督和管理职责，因此将在决定该公司是否有罪时比较宽容。然而，检察官仍可将法院的假设推翻并证明公司有罪。为证明公司有罪，其需要证明政策不足以防止犯罪，和/或证明公司在除该政策之外未积极采取其他手段履行其监督和管理职责。

2. 监管反商业贿赂的部门

监督反商业贿赂的部门为检察院。检察院将负责与其他公职部门如警察局、证券和保险监督管理委员会（SVS）等联合调查此类犯罪。在就犯罪进行一般不超过两年的调查后，如以此标准调查能够向法院提交足以治罪的证据，检察院将提出控告。一旦提出控告，将由3名法官组成刑事法庭负责案件审理并决定行贿者和受贿者是否有罪。

案件的上诉将在上诉法院或最高法院进行。

3. 惩罚措施

根据第20393号法律的规定，如公司被证实实施了上述犯罪，将会面临下列惩罚：

① 罚款；
② 剥夺特定期限内的全部或部分财政收益；
③ 暂时或永久禁止与政府签订协议、合同或其他文件；
④ 最严厉的处罚为解散公司或取消其法人资格；
⑤ 其他轻微惩罚，如在报纸上公布其被法院定罪的信息。[①]

（二）工程承包

规范采购程序的关于供应和提供服务的行政合同的第19886号法律第4条规定，智利人或外籍人员可与国家行政部门签订合同，只要证明其财政状况和技术实用性符合法规要求和普通权利要求。然而，在其任职的两年内，作为适格的公共、私人或直接承包商，其制订的方案或签署的合约，如被认定为反工会的行为或侵犯了工人的基本权利，或触犯了《刑法典》中破产犯罪的规定，其将不得与国家行政部门签订合同。

1. 许可系统

第19886号法律第9条规定，当承包方不满足施工依据规定的要求时，政府承包方将宣布该报价不可接受。当无报价或对其利益不便时，将宣布报价空缺。在此两种情况下，通知必须通过合理的决议作出。

第10条规定，与国家缔结的合同将通过主管当局的决议授予，并通知提议者。中标人将是整体上

---

① 第20393号法律第8条。

提出最有优势报价的人，同时还考虑到条例中所述报价构成和评价标准。参与方和招标单位必须严格遵守行政规定及技术规范，依照招标程序进行。报价构成须事先得到主管当局的批准，然后提交给有关利益相关方。

2. 禁止投资领域

根据智利法律，外国投资者可参与大部分的经济领域和资产、服务的生产型领域。尽管如此，智利也对一些行业进行限制，如沿海贸易、航空运输、传媒和渔业（渔业的限制依据国际互惠原则）。此外，外国投资者不得拥有位于智利边境的房地产。

第 19886 号法律第 3 条规定了下列不得通过公共契约形式进行的情形：

① 受特殊法令管理的国家行政机构人员聘用合同，和与自然人签署的向公共机构提供劳务的报酬合同，不论该合同的法律渊源如何。

② 1975 年《国家财政管理法组织法》(第 1263 号法令) 及其修改第 2 条第 1 款所列公共机构签署的协定。

③ 根据国际组织的具体程序订立的合同，与其授予的信贷或出资相关联。

④ 有关销售和转让有价证券或其他金融票据的合同。

⑤ 有关公共工程的实施和特许权的合同。

同时不适用该法的情形还有：与住房和城市化服务有关的劳务合同，第三方参与执行、运营和维护的市财工程，这些适用批准市政财政系统的第 19865 号法律。

尽管有适用之除外情形，其涉及的招聘将受该法第五章以及附加条款的规定的约束。

⑥ 处理战争物资的合同；根据第 7144 号法律、第 13196 号法律制定和修改的合同；由军队武装部、秩序武装部军团和国家安全部购买的下列资产：军用或警用车辆（除货车、汽车和公共车外）；先进和新兴技术的设备和信息系统，专门用于指挥、控制、通信、计算机情报系统；用于生产、组装、维护、修理、改进军备及其备件、燃料和润滑油的元件或部件。

同样，为防止对国家安全或公共安全造成特殊风险而必须签订的货物和服务合同，由国防部根据相应的主管指挥官，在适当情况下，由智利武警总局局长或调查局局长提议，通过最高法令予以认证。

3. 招标和投标

如果招标是公开的，招标将对所有可能利益相关方开放。当招标为非公开时，须邀请参与投标。非公开招标中的供应商选择必须非常谨慎，因决定着可能接受的报价，故在招标中包含所要求的产品或服务行业中的知名供应商尤为重要。根据法律，非公开招标须有至少 3 名投标人。但建议邀请更多的投标人参与，因为如此增加了过程的透明度，且随着竞争的增加报价也会更有竞争力。招标不论公开或非公开，均须在信息系统智利政府公共采购网站发布，但该公布程序可以通过联系那些欲参与投标的供应商来完成。

Chile

Authors: Alberto Cardemil, Ignacio Tornero, Sergio Diez, Daniela Tapia
Translators: Zhang Yi, Zhang Tianyi

I. Overview

A. General Introduction to the Political, Economic, Social and Legal Environment of the Country Receiving Investment

Chile is a constitutional Republic and, as such, its Constitution envisages certain principles and rules that seek to establish the foundations for its economic system, which are collectively known as "Economic Public Order". Many of such principles and rules are based on the respect for individual liberties and private initiative as the primary driving forces of economic activities. Besides the political constitution, the regulatory framework for foreign investment in Chile is mainly found in two legal bodies: the framework law for Direct Foreign Investment in Chile ("Law No.20848 / (2016)" or "DFI Law"), and; Chapter XIV of the Compendium of Foreign Exchange Regulations of the Central Bank of Chile. Additionally, Chile has executed Agreements on Reciprocal Promotion and Protection of Investments ("APPIs", also known as Bilateral Investment Treaties or "BITs").

With regards to the political environment, Chile is a Republic based on a parliamentary democracy, in which the president is endowed with extensive powers. A new president was recently elected and has started its government this march 2018. It is well known that the president elected is close to both national and foreign investors and it is expected that his government will be effective in convincing investors to carry out their projects. With this, it is likely to ensure growth of more than 3.5% in our country, which is the upper limit of the projections of the Central Bank of Chile. Besides the President, Chile has a bicameral legislature. The Parliament or the National Congress consists of a Senate with its members elected by popular vote to serve eight-year terms, and the Chamber of Deputies with its members elected by popular vote to serve four-year.

Chile offers a stable economic environment, with excellent growth prospects. According to Forbes statistics[1] Chile ranks No. 33 as the best countries for business in the world, leading as the best country in Latin America for business. Forbes defines Chilean economy as a "market-oriented economy characterized by a high level of foreign trade and a reputation for strong financial institutions and sound policy that have given it the strongest sovereign bond rating in South America."

According to the "World Bank", Chile is Latin America's second wealthiest country in assets, rather than Gross domestic Product (GDP). According to the report "The Changing Wealth of Nations 2018", Chile's per capita wealth consisted of US$237,713 in 2014, this last, positioning us in second place, just after Uruguay. Chile's wealth consists mainly in human capital, followed by natural capital and at last produced capital. [2]

In the recent years, the social environment has been influenced by issues such the educational system reform regarding its gratuity and quality, and a strong economic inequality among Chileans. Despite that, Chile is known for its transparency (dislike the majority of Latin American countries), which is reflected in international rankings that highlight the low level of corruption in the country and, particularly, its finances, due to government efforts to raise standards in administration of the State. Chile has promoted an active policy of bilateral, regional and multilateral trade agreements and has driven a growing increase in foreign trade in goods and services and in the country's international competitiveness, consolidating its position as an active international partner.

Thanks to its political and economic stability, openness to trade, legal security and excellent growth prospects, Chile has maintained an attractive and dynamic business climate for investors.

B. The Status and Direction of the Cooperation with Chinese Enterprises Under the B&R

China is Chile's principal commercial partner in the world. Over 25% of Chilean exports go to China. Also, Chile is nowadays the country that has subscribed more agreements with China to facilitate exchange in Latin

---

[1] For more information, please refer to https://www.forbes.com/best-countries-for-business/list/#tab:overall.
[2] https://investchile.gob.cl/world-bank-chile-is-latin-americas-second-wealthiest-country-in-assets/.

America.[1] Currently, several bilateral treaties are in standing between the two countries, reinforcing the spirit of cooperation that has existed since 2004, when Chile became the first country in Latin America to establish diplomatic relations with China, or in 2005, when Chile became the single first country in the world to enter into a Free Trade Treaty with China. It is important to remember that in 2016, the commercial exchange between these two countries reached US 31.474 million, representing 26% of the Chilean foreign trade.

As of this present year, representatives from 33 countries belonging to CELAC (Community of Latin American and Caribbean States) and delegates of the Chinese government signed an agreement in Santiago, Chile, where they arranged to deepen cooperation in the region, with China offering to invest $250 billion in infrastructure in the region, and inviting the countries from CELAC to join the B&R initiative.

Furthermore, under OBOR (Belt and Road) Chile has shown a clear willingness to facilitate trade with the Asian giant and strengthen its relations. In May, 2017 former Chilean president, Michelle Bachelet, at the OBOR conference said that "Chile is ready to be a bridge between Asia and Latin America, we consider the Belt and Road Initiative, a route for the road to achieve distances and build a modern connectivity, which is a contribution to the productive process, national growth, the opening of new markets, the promotion of investment, the increase of tourist flow and the deepening of mutual understanding that leads to a more inclusive, equal, just, prosperous and peaceful society with development for all".

Precisely one of the most important steps for Chile to materialize participation at OBOR is the incorporation to the Asian Infrastructure and Investment Bank (BAII), an institution in which Chile has already been accepted as a partner. Among the agreements signed during the meeting between the leaders, trade exchanges of goods and services stand out, as well as cooperation in scientific and technological matters. Under OBOR initiative, Chile and China have celebrated the following agreements[2]:
• Cooperation Agreement on Antarctic issues;
• Renewal of the Five-Year Work Plan for agricultural cooperation;
• Convention on requirements for the transport of merchandise from Chile to the Chinese market through third countries by sea and air;
• Protocol on the entry of avocados;
• InvestChile Collaboration Agreement and the Chinese Council for the Promotion of International Trade (CCPIT).

As referred in the previous chapter, the Chilean Government has promoted 11 projects since the beginning of 2018 through InvestChile. These projects in total represent USD 1.500 million in investments, in the following fields: infrastructure, agroindustry, wines, banking and energy. According to the Chilean Central Bank, Chinese enterprises reported a direct investment stock of USD 746 million, between 2009 and 2016. Only after InvestChile was created, in May 2016, USD 400 million were materialized through 6 initiatives, 4 of them made in 2017.

II. Investment

A. Market Access

a. Department Supervising Investment

As of January 1st 2016, there are two main institutions supervising investment in Chile: the Agency for the Promotion of Foreign Investment (InvestChile) and the Central Bank.

The Constitution recognizes the Central Bank as an autonomous entity and, as such, its function is to preserve currency stability and the normal functioning of internal and external payments. In addition, this statute indicates that the Central Bank is empowered to regulate the amount of money and credit in circulation, the execution of foreign credit and exchange transactions, and to issue regulations pertaining to monetary, credit, financial and foreign exchange regulations. Furthermore, the Constitution also sets forth that the Central Bank may not act as guarantor for financial institutions, nor acquire instruments issued by the State, its bodies or the companies it owns. Likewise, it also provides that no public expenditure or loan may be financed by direct or indirect loans issued by the Central Bank.

The Agency for the Promotion of Foreign Investment ("Agency") has the task to promote and attract foreign capital and investments into Chile, regardless of the amounts, according to the powers and faculties granted by Law No.20848. Among its attributions, are the following: implement the Promotion Strategy and analyze and

---

[1] https://chile.gob.cl/china/relacion-bilateral/acuerdos-y-tratados-bilaterales visited 09/03/2018, 12:50 GMT -4:00.
[2] https://www.bcn.cl/observatorio/asiapacifico/noticias/hitos-gira-presidencial-asia-pacifico.

investigate the foreign investors and their capacities and then grant the corresponding certificates in order for the investors to bring their capitals intro the country.

Furthermore, the Agency has a proactive role regarding the attraction and promotion of foreign investment, which will include providing information and free assistance to the possible foreign investors about the process and paperwork required to bring their investments; and, in general, supervising that the Government does not apply unnecessary obstacles for the foreign investors.

b. Laws and Regulations of Investment Industry

The regulatory framework for foreign investment in Chile is mainly found in two legal bodies: The Framework Law for Direct Foreign Investment in Chile [Law No.20848(2016)], and Chapter XIV of the Compendium of Foreign Exchange Regulations of the Central Bank of Chile. Additionally, Chile has executed Bilateral Investment Treaties ("BITs") and Free Trade Agreements ("FTAs") with numerous countries, providing additional protection for foreign investors. This also includes the Agreements for the Avoidance of Double Taxation that Chile has entered into with various States, which grant a more favorable tax treatment to foreign investments that come from such states.

As of January 2016, foreign investment regimes in Chile are mainly regulated by two legal bodies, Law No.20848 that established a New Foreign Investment Statute and Chapter XIV of the Foreign Exchange Regulations of the Central Bank of Chile ("Chapter XIV"), for investments of USD 10,000 or more (with no cap).

The foreign investment regimes in Chile are applicable to any foreign person or company, that is not a resident and does not have a domicile in Chile ("Foreign Investor") and that brings to the country foreign capitals for amounts over USD $5,000,000.

a) Law No.20848

Law No.20848 regulates investments made by any natural or legal person incorporated overseas, not residing or domiciled in Chile, whose investment is equal to or greater than USD$5,000,000, or the equivalent to said sum in other foreign currencies.

(i) Methods of Investment:
• Freely exchangeable foreign currency;
• Tangible goods in all forms and conditions;
• Reinvestment of profits;
• Credit capitalization;
• Technology in its various forms suitable for being capitalized;
• Credits associated with foreign investment derived from related companies.

(ii) Materialization and Purpose of the Investment

The application of the rights conferred to the foreign investor by the DFI Law requires for the investment to be made in a Chilean company that receives the investment after January 1, 2016, and this investment must grant the investor the direct or indirect control over, at least, 10% of the company's voting shares, or an equivalent percentage or stake in the corporate equity if it is not a stock-based company, or in the assets of the respective company.

(iii) Proceedings and Foreign Investor Certificate

In order to qualify as a Foreign Investor and access the rights available under the DFI Law, it is necessary to request a certificate issued by the Agency for the Promotion of Foreign Investments demonstrating the interested party's foreign investor status. The request submitted before the Agency must provide evidence that the investment was materialized in the country, including a detailed description thereof, indicating its amount, purpose and nature, all subject to the manner and conditions determined by the abovementioned Agency.

(iv) Rights of the Foreign Investor under the DFI Law

The following are the basic rights granted by the DFI Law:
• Overseas repatriation of the invested capital and net profits;
• Access to the Formal Exchange Market;
• Right to not be arbitrarily discriminated;
• Right to value added tax (VAT) exemption in the import of capital assets.

(v) Transitory Tax Invariability

The DFI Law establishes that during a period of 4 years, expiring on December 31 of 2019, foreign investments shall be entitled to resort to tax invariability with a total income tax rate of 44.45%, during a term of 10 years, as from the start-up date for the corresponding company or as from the date when the investment entered the country.

(vi) Mining Projects

Additionally, during a 4-year period expiring on December 31, 2019, and regarding investments related to mining projects, for a sum equal or greater than US$ 50,000,000, Foreign Investors are also given the possibility of entering into foreign exchange agreements with the State of Chile. If Foreign Investors choose this alternative, for a term of 15 years, they shall be entitled to: resort to the invariability of the legal provisions regarding the specific tax applicable to mining activities, established in articles 64 bis and 64 ter of the Income Tax Law (specific tax to the operational income of mining activities or "royalty" income), without being affected by the increased rate, expansion of the tax base or any other amendment that causes said tax to increase; benefit from the non-application of new taxes, royalties, tariffs, duties or similar levies, referred specifically to mining activities, that could be established after the date on which the respective foreign investment agreement is executed; and benefit from the non-application of prospective amendments to the sum or manner of calculating the exploitation and exploration permits.

(vii) Effectiveness of the Foreign Investment Agreements Executed under the Previous System

Foreign investment agreements executed until December 31, 2015, between the State of Chile and Foreign Investors subject to Law Decree No.600 ("DL 600"), shall remain in full force and effect and, consequently, the respective Foreign Investors shall retain all of the rights and obligations stipulated under the referenced foreign investment agreements.

b) Chapter XIV of the Compendium of Foreign Exchange Regulations of the Central Bank of Chile

Chapter XIV of the Compendium of Foreign Exchange Regulations of the Central Bank regulates all foreign loans, deposits, investments and capital contributions for an aggregate amount equal to or higher than US$10,000, (minimum amount currently in force under Central Bank's policy) transferred into Chile from abroad.

Pursuant to the current foreign exchange regulations, all transfers of funds into Chile from abroad relating to loans, deposits, investments or capital contributions must be made through the FEM and be informed to the Central Bank. However, no access to the FEM is guaranteed to the Foreign Investor or capital contributor and the Chilean borrower, as applicable, for the repatriation of the capital investment and / or profits, or the payment of the principal of and / or interest on the foreign loan, respectively (save for investments on loans made under DL 600, pursuant to foreign investment contracts signed prior to December 31st, 2015).

Chapter XIV applies only to those transfers from and to other countries under foreign loans, capital contributions, investments and deposits of an aggregate amount of US$ 10,000 or more (minimum amount currently in force under Central Bank's policy). Funds under USD 10,000 can be freely transferred into Chile and remitted abroad.

B. Foreign Exchange Regulation

a. Department Supervising Foreign Exchange

The department supervising foreign exchange is the Chilean Central Bank ("BCCH"). As an autonomous entity, its function is to preserve currency stability and the normal functioning of internal and external payments. In addition, the Central Bank is empowered to regulate the amount of money and credit in circulation, the execution of foreign credit and exchange transactions, and to issue regulations pertaining to monetary, credit, financial and foreign exchange regulations.

For further information, please refer to Chapter A "Market Access", letter a.

b. Brief Introduction of Laws and Regulations of Foreign Exchange

Chapter XIV regulates all foreign loans, deposits, investments and capital contributions for an aggregate amount equal to or higher than US$10,000, (minimum amount currently in force under Central Bank's policy) transferred into Chile from abroad.

Pursuant to the current foreign exchange regulations, all transfers of funds into Chile from abroad relating to loans, deposits, investments or capital contributions must be made through the Formal Exchange Market and be informed to the Central Bank.

For further information, please refer to Chapter A "Market Access", letter b, Section II "Chapter XIV".

c. Requirements of Foreign Exchange Management for Foreign Enterprises

a) Foreign Loans

(i) Loans may be disbursed in Chile or abroad; in both cases, these loans must be informed to the BCCH.

(ii) The terms for repayment of principal and interest may be freely agreed between the creditor and debtor, including the interest rate agreed upon by the parties.

(iii) If the debtor defaults on the payment of principal and / or interest, the law entitles the guarantor to pay and carry out the transfer of the funds. Such guarantee must be informed to the BCCH according to Chapter XIV as well.

(iv) The remittance of principal is not subject to taxation. The remittance of interest is subject to a 35% withholding tax, unless the lender is a foreign or international financial institution (e.g., a bank), in which case the payment of interest is subject to a 4% withholding tax.

b) Capital Contributions, Investments and Deposits

Chapter XIV also establishes certain rules applicable to capital contributions, investments and deposits made in Chile from abroad, in foreign currency. These regulations do not apply to contributions in kind and are only applicable to acts involving payment obligations or the subsequent right to transfer foreign currency abroad by individuals or entities with residence or domicile in Chile. In addition, as mentioned above, payments and transfers from and to Chile, arising from the aforementioned acts, must be made through the FEM. Chapter XIV entitles the investors to freely repatriate the capital contributed or invested in Chile and remit the profits obtained from such capital contributions or investments at any time.

Funds under USD 10,000 can be freely transferred into Chile and remitted abroad.

For further information, please refer to Chapter A "Market Access", letter b, Section II "Chapter XIV".

C. Financing

a. Main Financial Institutions

Financing in Chile is, as a general rule, provided by loans from banks and other financial institutions by means of a set of contractual documents that typically include loan agreements and a security package.

Financing might also come from abroad and in these cases the legal framework will be given by Chapter XIV (which provides the possibility for investors to repatriate capital and profits at any moment) or the new Foreign Investment Statute (Law No.20848), depending on how the funds enter the country.

b. Financing Conditions for Foreign Enterprises

As a consequence of the importance that foreign investment represents for Chilean economy, Chile has developed laws and policies in order to attract investors, guaranteeing the existence of stable legal mechanisms that ensure an equal treatment for Chilean and foreign investors, a non-discretionary and non-discriminatory treatment, and the open access to most of the sections of the economy.

Furthermore, regarding foreign investment applicable regulation, the investor is able to choose between two different legal regimes: the new Foreign Investment Statute (or Law No.20848) and Chapter XIV of the Compendium of Foreign Exchange Regulations of the Central Bank of Chile. Chapter XIV grants taxation benefits and incentives for foreign investment, such as the invariability of taxation regimes, the invariability or freezing of the Value Added Tax and freezing of the applicable tariffs in regard to the importation of capital assets required for the investment project, among others.

As for Law No.20848, and although it sets out that the foreign investor shall have the right to remit the capital or profits abroad, those provisions establish only a right but not a guarantee to access the formal foreign exchange market as they explicitly set forth that any foreign exchange operations under Law No.20848 shall be subject to the attributions of the Chilean Central Bank (particularly, certain restrictions and even prohibitions to operate in the foreign exchange market under hypothetical scenarios of shortfalls of international reserves of currencies, etc).

Furthermore, Law No.20848 establishes the possibility, as of 1 January 2016 and for a four-year period (ie, up to 31 December 2019), that foreign investors may exceptionally execute a foreign investment agreement and opt therein for a tax stability of a 44.45 per cent rate for a term of 10 years, which could be relevant in case of possible future increases of the applicable taxation rate to percentages even higher than 44.45 per cent.

Additionally, it is important to mention that our legislation also provides taxation benefits to the investment on extreme geographic regions of our Country. For more information please refer to "Preference and Protection of Investment".

Finally, companies interested in starting innovative business or in the development of high tech assets and human resources, have also the possibility to apply for some benefits provided by the Chilean government ("CORFO Subsidies"), which are intended to support the implementation of such activities in our country. In this regard, the amount of the subsidies will depend of the type of project and its specific characteristics.

D. Land Policy

In general terms, Chilean law has no restrictions for land ownership by non-citizens. An exception to this rule is contained in Art. 7 of Law Decree No. 1939 whereby foreigners from bordering countries are restricted to acquire, possess or have any rights over real estate located in frontier zones unless authorized by the President.

There are no specific taxes associated with the acquisition or transfer of ownership in land. The costs involved in such acquisition or transfer are those related to drafting the acquisition deed, notarization and recording of the property title in the real estate property register. However, when acquiring or leasing a real estate with furniture in it, Value Added Tax must be paid.

Land use and land development is subject in urban areas to communal, inter-communal or metropolitan zoning plans.

Such zoning plans are regulated by the General Law of Urbanization and Construction contained in Decree with Legal Force No. 458/1976, and the General Ordinance of Urbanization and Construction contained in Law Decree No. 47/1992.

The Ministry of Housing and Urbanization will be in charge of establishing specific regulations for the study, revision, approval and modification of the legal instruments that govern land use and land development.

For the construction of any facility or building, a Building Permit must be issued by the Director of Works from the corresponding Municipality or Borough, which certifies that the building project adjusts to the specific regulations for the land. This authorization is given for a specific area and facilities. After the construction works, a Reception of Works must be issued by the same entity, certifying that the construction adjusts to the specifications that were previously authorized in the Building Permit.

E. The Establishment and Dissolution of Companies

a. The Forms of Enterprises

For Foreign Investors who desire to set up a business in Chile, and conduct said business in a mid to long term, there are two options: to incorporate a local subsidiary or to set up a branch or a permanent establishment of a foreign corporation in Chile.

Chile allows for three main types of legal entities to be used as business vehicles, all of which grant limited liability to their shareholders or partners: stock corporations, limited liability partnerships, and simplified corporations.

In Relation to the Local Subsidiary, there are three Corporate Structures:

(i) For businesses in which capital and equity prevail over the consideration of the persons, a Stock Corporation is more adequate ("Sociedad Anónima"). This structure is similar to its U.S. correlative and allows investors to gather capital quickly, granting the Company access to better types of credit. There are two types of Stock Companies in Chile: publicly traded and closely held. Publicly Traded Corporations are subject to the Securities Market Law and the supervision of the Securities and Insurance Superintendence.

(ii) On the other hand, when the entities or persons incorporating the company are more important that its equity, when they want to limit their liability to a certain amount or when the parties belong to the same business group, it is usually preferred to form a Limited Liability Partnership ("Sociedad de Responsabilidad Limitada"). This structure gives a lot of control to its partners, since all decision regarding its existence; modification and administration usually have to be unanimously agreed upon.

(iii) A third option is the Simplified Corporation ("Sociedad por Acciones") which can allow a single shareholder with 100% of the shares, it has to comply with less formalities compared to the Stock Corporation and the shareholders can freely establish any management mechanism.

In addition to the foregoing, the Chilean legislation also contemplates the structure of a branch or permanent establishment of a foreign corporation in Chile, however, this is a very simple structure that is usually advisable to companies which do not intent to fully conduct a business in Chile, but nonetheless wish to have a formal office or representation in our country.

Even though a branch of a foreign corporation is not considered as an autonomous juridical entity by itself in Chile, it is considered as an agency of the parent company. Thus, it is important for us to refer briefly to the corresponding regulation.

To establish a branch of a foreign legal entity in Chile, it is necessary to have the articles of incorporation or by-laws and certificate of good-standing of the foreign entity, as well as a power of Attorney granted to the agent who will manage the branch).

Said original documents must be apostilled, translated and afterwards filed with a Notary Public in Chile for registration.

b. The Procedure of Establishment

The incorporation of a Limited Liability Partnership, a Simplified Corporation or a Stock Corporation requires a public deed, registration of an excerpt of said deed on the Registry of Commerce and its publication in the Official Gazette. Incorporating a corporation in Chile should take about a week.

Afterwards, it will also be necessary to obtain a Tax Payer Number ("RUT") and submit a Business Start Up Notice before the Internal Revenue Service ("IRS" or "Servicio de Impuestos Internos"), as described below. This is a simple process which entails the submission of certain forms before the Internal Revenue Service together with the company's legal records of incorporation, reason why it can be usually performed by any person with a simple power of attorney, but it could become difficult (and thus, require the intervention of a legal advisor) in case the IRS formulates a legal objection to the company's records. Additionally, the Internal Revenue Service requires that the company appoints an attorney who is domiciled in Chile.

a) Limited Liability Partnership

It requires a minimum of two partners and allows a maximum of 50.

b) Stock Corporation

They are generally prohibited from acquiring their own shares and must distribute minimum statutory dividends (30% of net earnings). There are statutory withdrawal rights for shareholders pursuant to which a shareholder can sell its shares back to the corporation upon certain actions being approved.

c) Simplified Corporation

It does not require unanimous consent for amendments of its by-laws, and can be formed by one or more persons (individuals or legal entities), and allows for any type of corporate agreement, save for a few mandatory rules.

c. Routes and Requirements of Dissolution

A corporation is dissolved and terminated when its term of duration expires, unless it has been incorporated to perpetuity. Additionally, corporations are dissolved if it is so agreed by 2/3 of the total issued shares, in an extraordinary shareholders' meeting called for that purpose, or if all the shares are held by one person on entity for a period exceeding 10 consecutive days, or if merged into another company. The by-laws of the company may include other additional events that result in the dissolution of the corporation.

Should the dissolution of the corporation takes place, its liquidation shall be undertaken by a liquidation committee freely elected by the shareholders, except where no liquidation is necessary (acquisition of all the shares by one person or entity, or merger).

Regarding the dissolution of a company, there are 4 main areas that have to be complied in order to achieve the dissolution:

(i) From a financial point of view, a Closing Balance Sheet of the Company has to be prepared.

(ii) From a taxation point of view, the form for "Closing down of the Business" has to be presented before the Chilean Internal Revenue Service.

(iii) Regarding the dissolution, an Extraordinary Shareholders Meeting has to approve the dissolution and liquidation of the assets of the company, and a deed of said approvals has to be prepared. That deed has to be then reduced into a public deed, which's excerpt has to be registered in the Registry of Commerce and then published in the Official Gazette. Finally the registration and publication of the public deed's excerpt has to be notarized.

(iv) Finally, in relation to the liquidation of the assets of the company, a Company's Liquidation Committee has to decide on the procedure to liquidate the assets, which will later on be approved by the Shareholders Meeting. Both the procedure agreed and its approval has to be done by means of a public deed which's excerpt has to be registered in the Registry of Commerce.

F. Merger and Acquisition

a. Introduction

Chile's well-known economic stability has attracted new foreign investment into its emerging market. Because of this investment, the Chilean economy is nowadays an importer of investment capital and has implemented several incentives to attract foreign investors. As a consequence of this, and in order to enhance the Chilean economy, there is a flexible legal framework for businesses, and a clear example of such is the existence of different types of business combinations.

There are many business combinations considered within the Chilean legal framework, such as mergers, joint ventures, distribution agreements, franchise agreements, among others. Below is a brief description of the most frequent business combinations present under Chilean law.

a) Mergers

There are two types of mergers under Chilean legislation: those mergers that are the result of two companies contributing their assets in a new company, incorporated for a specific purpose; and those mergers that are the result of a company acquiring all of the assets of another company, which is to be dissolved, while the acquiring company prevails.

b) Takeovers

Briefly, a takeover takes place when a company acquires 100 per cent of the corporate capital or interest of another company, which usually ends up being dissolved and liquidated.

Considering, the main difference between mergers and a takeover is that, in mergers, the shareholders of the original companies become shareholders of the resulting company and, thus, shares are traded. Conversely, the shareholders of a company taken over by another company receive a price for their shares but do not become shareholders of the resulting company.

c) Acquisition of Business as a Unit

Chilean legislation contemplates the alternative to acquire the target business of a company as an ongoing unit. That is understood as all those company's assets, debts, operations, labour forces, intangible rights, know-how, etc, with which the company carries out its line of business. Instead of a transfer of shares or interest in the company, the business of the company is acquired as a unit.

d) Capital Increases

The acquisition of a controlling set of shares or equity rights (as applicable) may be executed as a result of a corporate capital increase where new shares or equity rights (as applicable) are subscribed and paid by an external investor (as opposed to an existing shareholder), as a result of the existing shareholders not exercising their legal right of first refusal in the acquisition of new corporate interest.

e) Direct Acquisition

The acquisition of the control of a corporation in Chile can also be achieved by the direct acquisition of shares from a controlling shareholder or shareholders. In this case, it is necessary to distinguish between the different types of corporations.

In closed stock corporations, there are no special procedures that need to be complied with for the direct acquisition of a controlling set of shares and no prior consents or approvals are required from any governmental authority. After the transaction, the Chilean Internal Revenue Service shall be informed of the new share composition of the company.

In open stock or listed corporations, the acquisition of a controlling set of shares must be conducted through a tender offer (Mandatory Tender Offer "MTO"), following the procedure established in the law. Pursuant to article 198 of the Chilean Corporations Act (as defined below), an MTO needs to be addressed to all of the shareholders and other stockholders (whose stocks can be converted into company shares) of the target company, for equal conditions. Under Chilean law, in the following cases an MTO needs to be conducted:

(i) in corporations that trade their shares in the stock market, when the acquisition is made with the purpose of becoming a controlling shareholder;

(ii) when a controlling shareholder pretends to acquire, at least, two-thirds of the issued shares with the right to vote or of any series of shares;

(iii) in cases where the buyer wants to obtain control of the controlling company of another company that trades its shares in the stock market, whenever the controlled company represents 75 per cent of the controller's assets. This MTO is not addressed to the shareholders of the controlling company but to the shareholders of the controlled company. The purpose is to prevent the possibility of avoiding the MTO by buying the controller company; or

(iv) when an individual shareholder, or a group of them working on an agreement basis, have acquired two-thirds of the issued shares with the right to vote. In this case, such shareholders must extend an MTO for the remaining shares before the term of 30 days following the acquisition. The price of the MTO in this scenario cannot be lower than the price established for the exercise of the withdrawal right conferred by the Chilean Corporations Act.

f) Shareholders' or Equity Holders' Agreements

Finally, two or more shareholders or equity holders (as applicable) can exercise control of a corporation or limited liability company by means of a shareholders' or equity holders' agreement. For shareholders' and equity holders' agreements the only formalities required under Chilean law are execution in writing and registration in the corresponding shareholders' register.

b. Statutes and Regulations

Business combinations in Chile are mainly ruled by the following legal statutes:

(i) Law No.18046 (the Chilean Corporations Act), and its Regulation (Decree No.702);

(ii) Law No.18045 (the Securities Market Law);

(iii) the Superintendence of Securities and Insurance ("SVS") administrative jurisprudence, pursuant to Law No.18045;

(iv) Decree-Law No. 824 (the Income Tax Law);

(v) Decree-Law No. 211 (the Antitrust Law);

(vi) the Commerce Code; and

(vii) the Civil Code.

Additionally, the governing law of a business combination will be the one agreed upon by the parties in the relevant contract. If no specific law is selected, the governing law will be the one of the country where the agreement shall be executed.

c. Filings and Fees

Filings that must be made prior to taking control of a company in Chile depend on the type of company being targeted, as briefly exposed above in this chapter. When targeting for closed stock corporations or limited liability companies, there is no need to comply with prior filings or request the approval of any governmental authorities. Conversely and in general terms, when targeting for open stock and listed corporations some mandatory procedures need to be conducted before the SVS and stock markets in which such companies trade their shares, as applicable.

On the other hand, regardless of the type of company being affected, ex-post filings must be presented before the Chilean IRS to report on, for example, the removal and appointment of company's representatives, the changes in the company's participation, the obtaining of a national identity card number, the notification of the business termination and, in general, any other amendment as a result of a merger or other business combinations.

Regarding antitrust, even though there is no mandatory merger control system in Chile to this date, there are several different factors (such as, the market concentration, the market share of the companies involved, the existence of entry barriers, among others) which would make it advisable to file a previous presentation before the National Economic Prosecutors Office ("FNE") or the Chilean Antitrust Court ("TDLC") to obtain the prior approval for the transaction. If the above-mentioned presentation does not take place, there is a risk that the referred operation could be considered a breach of Antitrust Law. If the TDLC considers that the operation impedes, restricts or hinders competition, it could order the modification or termination of the agreements, the modification or dissolution of partnerships, corporations and other legal persons of private law that could have intervened in the acts or contracts, or impose fines for fiscal benefit up to an amount equivalent to 20,000 UTA[①] (currently equivalent to approximately US$18.750 million). Notwithstanding the foregoing, it is relevant to note that a bill is to be enacted in the short term introducing several amendments to the Chilean antitrust statute, such as: criminalization of cartels and increasing fines, among other things. In relation to merger control, the bill introduces mandatory merger control, under which concentration transactions that exceed certain thresholds will have to be notified to the FNE prior to their execution. The following concentration transactions between economic agents that are not members of the same business group (which exceed the thresholds mentioned below) will have to be notified to the FNE prior to their execution:

• mergers;

• if one or more of the agents acquires, directly or indirectly, rights that allow it, individually or jointly, to decisively influence the administration of the other;

• the association of two or more independent economic entities to become a single economic entity - different from associated entities - that functions permanently; or

• if one of the agents acquires the control of the other's agent assets.

The above-mentioned concentration transactions must also fulfill the following requirements:

• the sum of the sales of the economic agents involved must have exceeded, during the last calendar year, the threshold to be established by the Ministry of Economy; and

• that in Chile, separately, at least two of the economic agents involved have generated sales, during the last calendar year, for an amount equal or greater than the threshold to be established by the Ministry of Economy.

The bill will also change the current methodology to calculate fines, moving from a system of fixed maximum fines (currently amounting to approximately US$16 million for general violations and approximately US$24 million for cartels) to a system with a maximum threshold of fines equivalent to double the economic benefit obtained as a result of the violation, or 30 percent of the sales of the offender for the specific line of products or services involved in the violation during the period of the infringement.

d. Information to be Disclosed

In general terms, pursuant to the provisions set forth in the Chilean Corporations Act, approval of business combinations require the affecting shareholders and equity holders to have previous access to various documents and information, such as, the business combination project with all the circumstances surrounding the transaction, last audited balance sheet of all the companies that are parties to the operation, expert appraisal reports and, in

---

① UTA (Unidad Tributaria Anual) is an Annual Tax Unit of Measure that indicates a value considered by Chilean national internal revenue service to calculate taxes, fines, and other fees.

some cases, a balance sheet of the merger itself.

Besides information that needs to be disclosed to the affected shareholders or equity holders, as applicable, in all types of companies general disclosure obligations to the SVS, stock markets and general public apply in relation to open stock or listed corporations.

In general terms, open stock or listed corporations shall truthfully, sufficiently and promptly disclose all material information in relation to themselves and their business at such time as it occurs or as soon as it becomes aware of the same. In particular, open stock or listed corporations shall permanently disclose, among others, the following information to the SVS, the stock markets and to the general public, as the case may be:

• the 'FECU Form', which includes individual and consolidated quarterly and annual financial statements, external auditors' interim or annual report of financial statements; management's discussion and analysis and disclosure of all material facts reported during the period affecting the corporation and its publicly issued securities;

• annual individual and consolidated financial statements of the corporation shall be sent to the SVS within 60 days of the closing date of the annual period and in any case at least 20 days prior to the date of the shareholders' meeting that will render an opinion on the same. These financial statements must also be published in a nationwide newspaper;

• quarterly individual and consolidated financial statements of the corporation shall be sent to the SVS;

• the corporation shall inform the SVS any changes in its equity, including among others, payment of dividends, exchange of shares and reductions of capital (at least 20 days in advance) and capitalizations;

• prepare an annual report and deliver copy of the same to the SVS and corporation shareholders; and

• the corporation shall immediately inform the SVS of any material facts or information regarding the stock corporation, its business and its publicly issued securities, if any. Such information shall be disclosed in a truthful, sufficient and timely manner on the date that the fact occurs or once the stock corporation becomes aware of the same.

On another subject and as previously indicated, there is no mandatory merger control system in Chile to this date. Nevertheless, if an operation - before or after its completion-is analyzed by the competition authorities, there are a number of documents that must be presented, whether to the FNE or to the TDLC. The Guidelines for Horizontal Merger Analysis of the FNE and the Internal Regulation No. 12 of the TDLC provides a guide on the information and documents that would be necessary to be disclosed. Notwithstanding the foregoing, it is possible to request the confidentiality of this information. The aforementioned is notwithstanding the antitrust bill that is to be enacted in the short term.

e. Disclosure of Substantial Shareholdings

Owners of large shareholdings (more than 10 per cent) have disclosure requirements only in relation to open stock or listed corporations (or other corporations with special corporate purposes such as financial institutions) and refer mainly to their obligation to inform the SVS, stock markets and general public of their intention to amend their shareholdings.

It is important to point out that in corporations with special corporate purposes, substantial shareholders may be limited on the maximum percentage of shares they can hold.

f. Hostile Transactions

Regarding open stock and listed companies, takeovers are regulated in the Securities Market Law, which provides that this kind of transactions should be conducted through the procedure of Mandatory Tender Offers. However, it is relevant to note that an MTO is not a hostile takeover.

An MTO is a compulsory public offer of acquisition that the person who is interested on becoming a controlling shareholder must extend to all shareholders. It is the way of ensuring transparency and protecting minority shareholders by allowing them to sell their shares if the new company's control implies a modification of the circumstances that they used to have. As a mandatory procedure, if it is not conducted as established by the law, the nullity of the act will be declared and a crime will be constituted.

Hostile takeovers are not contemplated in Chile because the shareholding control in the Chilean market is concentrated in a small group of shareholders, which shortens the spectrum of negotiation between the party that wishes to obtain control and the party or parties that currently control a company.

g. Government Influence

In industries regulated by the government, business combinations are of interest to the corresponding supervisor entity. For example, banks or other financial institutions operations will be under the supervision of the Superintendence of Banks and Financial Institutions whilst insurance companies' combinations shall be under the supervision of the SVS. The referred institutions might impose conditions or even forbid a business combination from going ahead.

There are also limitations to companies that provide public or basic services, the media, educational and health corporations, among others; all of them dependent of administrative organisms. For more information, please refer to Chapter J "Preference and Protection of Investment", letter e).

Finally, for national security purposes, foreigners have restrictions on acquiring estates located at the legal borders of the country, a situation supervised by the National Directorate of Borders of the State. This might have effects on mergers or other operations involving this estates and foreign parties. For more information, please refer to Chapter I "Land Policy".

Other than the above, government agencies cannot and should not influence or restrict the completion of business combinations.

h. Cross-border Transactions

Cross-border transactions are not specially ruled under Chilean legislation, but the most-favored-nation principle applies as a general rule and, pursuant to it, countries must refrain from discriminating between their business partners. Indirectly the legal framework that establishes some rights and obligations arising from cross-border transactions corresponds to Chapter XIV of the Compendium of Foreign Exchange Rules' of the Central Bank and Law No.20848.

i. Updates and Trends

The Chilean economy has been growing steadily in recent years and foreign investment plays a key role in it. Business combinations are essential in this context and said situation is reflected in the high level of M&A's taking place in the country.

The main industries receiving these investments are energy, agroindustry, utilities and, of course, mining. Chile is internationally known for its deposits and mines, and they are one of the principal economical activities of the country. Energy and utilities are attractive because they are government regulated industries, providing security for investments. Other markets to be considered are infrastructure and retail.

Major amendments to the Chilean legal framework affecting business combinations have already taken place in terms of taxation, bankruptcy and labour regulation.

Nonetheless, these proposals should not affect the level of M&A activity in the country as the legislation will keep providing a stable framework for this kind of operations. Even when the world has been affected by major economic crises, M&A transactions in Chile have not declined. On the contrary, they have encouraged investors from European and Asian countries to sell their capital at home and invest them in Chile. Moreover, Chilean companies are also becoming foreign investors in markets such as Peru, Colombia and other Latin American countries.

G. Competition Regulation

a. Department Supervising Competition Regulation

(i) National Economic Prosecutor ("FNE"): which is a government body in charge of investigating alleged violations to competition, filing claims on behalf of the national interests and pursuing the claims before the Competiton Court. Moreover, according to the new amendments to the competition law, the FNE is now responsible of the mandatory merger control system.

(ii) Competition Court ("TDLC"): which is independent from the Government and whose function is to prevent, correct and punish attempts against competition law.

(iii) Supreme Court: which is responsible of hearing the complaint appeal against the decision of the competition Court related with punishments imposed and decisions which repeals the FNE's decision, approving the transaction in a concentration operation subject to the fulfillment of mitigation measures different from the ones offered by the parties to the FNE.

b. Brief Introduction of Competition Law

The Antitrust Chilean legislation is mainly based on the following laws:

Decree Law No.211/1973 ("DL 211"), which sets forth the statute for the defense of competition: This Law regulates different matters regarding Competition, in order to promote and defend Competition of the markets. It penalizes any act or agreement that prevents, restricts or hinders competition, or that tends to produce any of the aforementioned effects. DL 211 has just recently been modified by Law No.20945/2016, which introduced important changes to the Chilean competition system, representing a major overhaul and the most relevant reform since the creation of the specialized court; including: the inclusion of a mandatory merger control system, the criminalization of hard core cartels, a significant increase of the amount of applicable fines and the inclusion of "interlocking" as a per se anticompetitive conduct among competitors.

Law No.20169 which regulates Unfair Competition: This Law defines the conducts that constitute Unfair

Competition and which may constitute an infringement of the competition law. It also established the actions that can be brought against such conducts and defines the competent courts that should decide upon such matters.

FNE's Guidelines: Even though the FNE's Guidelines are no strictly mandatory, they represent the criteria of the FNE and are useful in assessing the different matters which are under its authority.

c. Measures Regulating Competition

a) Antitrust Infringements

The DL 211 broadly defines the conducts contravening competition as "any fact, act or convention that impedes, restricts or impede competition or tends to produce such effects". This broad definition is then somehow refined by four -also rather- broad examples, which are classified as restrictive practices, namely:

(i) Agreements or concerted practices involving competitors with each other and which consist of fixing sales or purchase prices, limiting production, allocate zones or market shares or affect the outcome of tendering processes, as well as agreements or concerted practices which, by conferring market power on them competitors, are to determine the conditions for placing on the market, or exclude current or potential competitors;

(ii) The abusive exploitation by a company or by a conglomerate of companies with a common controller, of a dominant position in the market, by way of fixing purchases or sales prices, imposing tied sales of products, assigning areas or quotas of market or imposing other abusive practices;

(iii) Predatory practices or unfair competition, carried out with the purpose of reaching, maintaining or increasing a dominant position; and

(iv) The simultaneous participation of a person in a relevant executive position or as a director in two or more competing companies, provided that each of the competitor's company group has annual revenues from sales, services and other operational activities in excess of the amounts determined by the law (currently amounting to 100,000 Unidades de Fomento[1] (app. USD 4,400,000).

The new legislation also introduced changes to the system of fines and penalties. The Competition Court can punish the aforementioned conducts with penalties consistent in prohibitions of entering into agreements with Governmental entities, disqualification to hold certain positions, criminal penalties and fines. The fines are for fiscal benefit, and may amount to up to 30% of the sales of the offender corresponding to the product or service line related to the infraction during the period in which the offense was perpetrated, or up to double the economic benefit gained from the infraction. In case it is not possible to determine the amount of the sales or the economic benefit, the TDLC may apply fines up to the amount of 60,000 annual tax units (app. US$ 55,000,000). The fines may be imposed on the corresponding legal entity, on its directors, managers and on any person involved in the conduction of the relevant act. In the case of fines applied to legal entities, their directors, managers and those persons having benefited from the respective act may be jointly liable to the payment thereof, provided they took part in its execution.

Criminal penalties were reintroduced for hardcore cartels, which had been repealed from the Chilean competition statutes in 2004. The penalty for hardcore cartels may range from 3 years and 1 day of imprisonment, up to 10 years of imprisonment.

Finally, regarding cartels, DL 211 contemplates a leniency program benefitting the business agent that provides the FNE with complete information regarding a collusion case, which is also extensible to criminal liability for the first individual to provide information to the FNE. It should be noted that the Prosecutor entity is entitled to make dawn raids and intervene communications during investigation procedures regarding collusion cases.

b) Merger Control System

The most significant amendment recently enacted is the introduction of a mandatory merger control system. The new system consists of two phases, and is initiated by means of a notification of the parties to the FNE.

With the entry into force of this new system, the parties must notify to the FNE, prior to its execution, the concentration operation that have an impact in Chile and surpass the sales thresholds that the FNE set for that purpose in a resolution. The notification thresholds currently in force are:

(i) that the sum of the sales in Chile of the agents that contemplate its concentration have reached, during the previous year to which the notification is verified amounts equal to or greater than 1,800,000 Unidades de Fomento (app. USD 79,500,000); and

(ii) that in Chile, at least two of the agents that contemplate its concentration, separately have generated sales, during the year prior to the year in which the notification is verified, for amounts equal to or greater than 290,000 Unidades de Fomento (app. USD 12,800,000). The FNE is entitled to adjust these thresholds if necessary.

The procedure is initiated by a filing made by the parties which format and minimum information to be submitted was set forth in Regulation No.33 of the Ministry of Economy.

---

[1] The Unidad de Fomento (UF) is a Unit of account that is used in Chile and constantly adjusted for inflation.

The analysis performed by the FNE involves two phases, the first of which begins once the operation is notified. Since that date, the FNE has 10 days to determine whether the filing is complete, in which case it shall initiate an investigation. Within 30 days following the initiation of the investigation, the FNE shall either:

(i) approve the transaction simply and unconditionally, if it comes to the conviction that the transaction will not substantially lessen competition;

(ii) approve the transaction, conditioning said approval to the fulfillment of mitigation measures offered by the notifying parties, if it comes to the conviction that, subject to said measures, the transaction will not substantially lessen competition; or

(iii) extend the investigation for a maximum of 90 additional days, if it considers that should the transaction be simply and unconditionally executed, or conditioned to the measures offered by the notifying parties, as the case may be, could substantially lessen competition. In such event, the proceeding moves to Phase II.

In Phase II, the FNE shall inform its decision to extend the investigation to all agencies and authorities that may be directly concerned and to the economic agents that may have an interest in the transaction. Those who receive said communication, as well as any third party interested in the transaction, including suppliers, competitors, clients or consumers, may submit information to the investigation within 20 days following the publication of the extension decision in the FNE's website. Upon the expiration of the 90 days during which the investigation has been extended, the FNE shall also either:

(i) approve the transaction simply and unconditionally;

(ii) approve the transaction, conditioning said approval to the fulfillment of mitigation measures offered by the notifying parties;

(iii) prohibit the execution of the transaction, should it conclude that it has the aptitude to substantially lessen competition.

Regarding the recourses system, the law only contemplates special revision recourse in case the FNE forbids the execution of the transaction. The recourse must be filed before the TDLC within 10 days following the notice of the FNE's decision. The TDLC shall schedule a public hearing to be held within 60 days following its reception of the investigation's docket. The public hearing may be attended by the challenging parties, the FNE and all those who submitted information during the investigation. Within 60 days following the hearing, the TDLC shall issue its decision confirming or repealing the FNE's decision.

In case the TDLC's decision repeals the FNE's decision, approving the transaction subject to the fulfillment of mitigation measures different from the ones offered by the parties to the FNE, both the parties and the FNE may file a complaint recourse before the Supreme Court.

All of the terms contemplated in this new procedure must be computed in business days only.

c) Interlocking and Acquisition of Minority Stakes

Interlocking: Among the hypotheses of anticompetitive behavior direct interlocking between competitors is considered as an infringement, punishing the simultaneous participation of a person in a relevant executive positions or as a director in two or more competing companies, provided that each of the competitor's economic group has annual revenues for sales, services and other operational activities in excess of 100,000 Unidades de Fomento (app. USD 4,400,000); and the simultaneous participation in the abovementioned positions is held during 90 continuous days since the end of the calendar year in which the relevant companies exceeded the referred threshold.

Obligation to inform the acquisition of minority stakes: a new provision was introduced setting forth the obligation to inform to the FNE, within 60 days from its execution, "the acquisition, by one company or an entity belonging to its company group, of an interest, whether direct or indirect, representing more than 10% of the equity of a competing company, considering both stakes held in its own name and those held by third parties in their benefit", so as to allow the FNE to evaluate the opening of an investigation. The obligation to inform shall only be triggered in case the acquiring company, or its economic group as the case may be, as well as the company which interest is being acquired, separately have annual revenues for sales, services and other operational revenues exceeding 100,000 Unidades de Fomento (app. USD 4,400,000) in the last calendar year. The DL 211 sets forth that any actions to prosecute infractions to this new provision shall expire within 3 years from the date in which the acquiring company informs the FNE.

H. TAX

a. Tax Regime and Rules

Under the Constitution of the Republic of Chile, taxes, customs duties and all kinds of public charges must be implemented through the enactment of a law passed by the Congress.

The initiative to legislate in tax matters rests only with the President of the Republic. Consequently, taxes may not be changed unless the Executive Branch takes action and Congress approves said initiative. Matters related to fiscal policy are under the authority of the Minister of Finance.

In tax matters, government action is carried out by three different public agencies:

(i) The Internal Revenue Service, which is in charge of the administration of tax laws and has the power to issue regulations and conduct tax audits;

(ii) The Treasury, which is in charge of tax collection; and,

(iii) The Customs Agency, which deals with all matters related with custom duties applicable to imports.

If, as a consequence of a tax audit, a claim is submitted by a taxpayer, the competent court will be the Taxes and Customs Courts. Its decision may be appealed before the corresponding Court of Appeals and, through certain procedures, the case may go up to the Supreme Court.

b. General Income Tax System

In general terms, any earning, profit or capital increase, accrued or received, of any origin, nature or denomination, will be subject to income taxes in Chile.

The tax imposed by the Chilean Income Tax Law ("ITL") is based in two main factors: taxpayer residence; and, source of the income.

a) Taxpayer Residence

Any person or legal entity domiciled or resident in Chile shall be subject to tax over all their income, regardless the origin or source. This means that Chilean residents will be taxed over their worldwide income.

However, foreigners who are domiciled or resident in Chile will be subject to taxes only for their Chilean income during the first 3 years. After that period of time they will be subject to taxes in accordance to their worldwide income.

b) Source of the Income

Article 3 of the Chilean ITL provides that non-Chilean residents would only be subject to tax on their Chilean-source income. For this purpose, Chilean-source income is income derived from activities performed in Chile and assets located therein.

In this regard, the shares of a Chilean resident entity are deemed to be located in Chile and, thus, the profits resulting from the ownership of such shares will be Chilean-source income as per the ITL. Therefore and moreover, any income derived from the sale of shares in a Chilean resident entity would be deemed as Chilean-source income. Exceptionally, article 10 of the Chilean ITL provides that income obtained by a non-Chilean resident that derives from the alienation of rights shares or ownership interests, among others, from a non-resident entity, in cases in which there is as underling Chilean asset, and provided all the requirement are met, it will be deemed to be a Chilean income.

c. Two-tier Taxation and Dividend Distribution Regimen

As a general rule, received or accrued income generated by Chilean corporations, limited liability companies, stock companies and branches of foreign companies, are taxed in two tiers.

In this regard, entities will be subject to 25% or 27% rate of Corporate Income Tax ("CIT"), depending on its tax system, determined annually according to its taxable income. Its partners or shareholders will be subject to Withholding Tax in case they are non-residents ("WHT") or to Personal Progressive Tax in case they are residents. Partners or shareholders may use a 100% or 65% of the amount paid for CIT as tax credit against the final taxes, as explained below.

The Chilean tax system is considered an "integrated system" in that corporate tax can be used as a credit against final taxes. Final taxes are the Personal Income Tax, applied to income received by natural persons that are domiciled or reside in Chile, which has a progressive rate ranging from 0% to 40%, and the Withholding Tax, applied to income received from taxpayers that are not domiciled nor reside in Chile, which has a general rate of 35%. Therefore, under this integrated system, ordinary income obtained by local entities is subject to the corporate tax and to final taxes, as a partner or shareholder, depending on its actual distribution.

During 2014 an important tax reform was approved and as from January 1st, 2017 is fully in force. According to such tax reform there are two different tax regimes or tax systems: Attributed Income System and Partially Integrated System.

In this regards, any entity that is not a Chilean stock corporations or a silent partnership by shares, whose shareholders are individuals or non-Chilean resident entities, may opt for applying the following systems in order to determine the timing and final taxation of such individual or non-Chilean resident entity upon the dividends generated by the respective entity.

a) Attributed Income System

Shareholders are taxed with final taxes (WHT for non-residents) for the income attributed to them in the same year said income is generated. For these purposes, the attributed income equals the taxable income base, plus non-taxable income, plus other amounts subject to WHT.

The WHT would be triggered once the income is attributed, regardless of whether an actual distribution exists. If that income is not allocated by the partners or shareholders in the company bylaws, it will be allocated in proportion to the capital participation of each partner or shareholder.

Under this alternative, the respective entity will be taxed with Corporate Income Tax at a 25% rate, which will be credited against WHT (35%).

b) Partially Integrated System

Shareholders are taxed with final taxes (WHT for non-residents) only on profits that are effectively drawn or distributed from the company (cash basis).

Under this alternative, profits will be taxed at the entity level with a 27% CIT.

Only 65% of the CIT effectively paid would be creditable against the WHT due upon a dividend distribution. Notwithstanding, shareholders residing in a treaty country may use the whole CIT credit against the final withholding tax (e.g. China, UK, Brazil, Argentina, Australia, Canada, France, Malaysia, South Africa, Thailand, etc.). In case of treaties that have been signed but are not in force yet (e.g., USA), the same rule applies until 2021. Thus, the overall tax burden for a shareholder residing on a non-treaty country would rise up to 44.45%.

Please note that for purposes of attributing income (under the Attributed Income System) and for purposes of performing a dividend distribution under both regimes, certain allocation rules apply. The referred allocation rules allow the correct assignment of the CIT credit to the respective income.

Further, under both regimes annual records must be kept. The referred records differ from one regime to another and its purpose is to maintain track of the profits that have paid the CIT and WHT (in case of the Attributed Income System) and the CIT credit associated to them. The purpose of the records is to prevent double tax payment or the avoidance of such payment, as well as determining whether the 35% WHT payment is due or not.

Please note that if a taxpayer opts for a regime, it must remain in that regime for at least 5 continuous commercial years.

d. Additional Tax or WHT

The WHT is assessed, as a general rule, on income from Chilean sources earned by individuals or entities neither domiciled nor residing in Chile.

This tax is also assessed on certain payments made by Chilean taxpayers abroad.

As a general rule payments made to an individual or entity not domiciled in Chile, are subject to WHT to be withheld by the payer, generally 35%.

However, the tax may be reduced among others in the following cases:

(i) Payments made to insurance companies not established in Chile for insuring equipment or other goods located in Chile and for life or medical insurance of individuals who are residents of or domiciled in Chile are taxed 22%. In these cases, reinsurance is taxed at a 2% rate.

(ii) Payments for engineering services or technical assistance, 15%.

(iii) Remunerations paid to individuals or entities not domiciled in Chile for maritime transportation to and from Chilean ports and commissions thereon, as well as remunerations originating from services to vessels and freight in Chilean or foreign ports, 5%. This tax is not applied, on the basis of reciprocity, when, in the country where the vessel is registered or in the country of the operator, a similar charge does not exist or is not applied to Chilean vessels.

(iv) Payments for the rental, lease, charter or any other contract which provides for the use of foreign vessels for coastal trade, 20%. The same is applied when the relevant contract allows or does not forbid coastal trade.

(v) In general, the payment of royalties, patents and fees to entities not domiciled in Chile is subject to a 30% WHT to be withheld by the payer. However, the rate of this tax is reduced to 15% for royalties related to invention patents, utility models, industrial designs, designs of integrated circuits or mask work, new vegetable varieties and software, provided that the licensor is neither related to the licensee nor a resident of or incorporated in a tax haven. Although, if what you are paying is a "standard software" it will be tax exempt. In the case of technical assistance or engineering services, the rate is 15%.

However, the tax rate goes up to 20% if these services are rendered by a related party or by a person or entity residing or incorporated in a tax heaven. All these payments are normally deductible as expenses for tax purposes.

e. Personal Progressive Tax

The Personal Income Tax is applied to income of any origin earned by natural persons that are domiciled or have residence in Chile, at a progressive rate of 0% to 40%, including foreign source income earned during the corresponding annual period. As previously mentioned, the Tax Reform reduced the applicable maximum rate to

35%, which goes into effect in 2017.

f. Second Category Tax

This tax is a progressive tax applied on the aggregate amount received by an employee on account of wages, salaries, profit-sharing or others.

The taxation rates range from 0% to 35% of the relevant income per fiscal year. Second category taxpayers are not subject to any other income taxation, unless they have income from sources other than wages or salaries.

g. Mining Royalty

Also known as Mining Royalties, these types of taxes were structured as an income tax on "oper- ating taxable income from mining activities" (namely, net income determined for pur- poses of the First Category Tax, with certain adjustments) earned by a "mining exploiter" (i.e. a natural person or legal entity that extracts mineral resources and sells them during any stage of production).

The rate for this tax is progressive according to the value of annual sales of mining products expressed in metric tons of fine copper (MTFC), determined in accordance with the average cop- per price traded on the London Metal Exchange. Consequently, mining exploiters whose annual sales exceed 50,000 MTFC are subject to progressive taxes that vary between 5% and 14%, depending on their operating margins. Exploiters whose annual sales are valued at between 12,000 and 50,000 MTFC are subject to progressive taxes that vary between 0.5% and 4.5%. Lastly, mining exploiters with annual sales less than 12,000 MTFC are exempt from this tax.

h. Transfer of Shares and Equity Rights

Transfers of shares and are usually subject to First Category Tax and WHT or Personal Progressive Tax, as the case may be. However, under certain conditions, transfers of shares in a stock exchange could be exempt from all taxation.

i. Depreciation

Depreciation on fixed assets, except for land, is tax-deductible using the straight-line method based on their useful lives, in accordance with the guidelines of the Chilean Internal Revenue Service, calculated on the value of the assets, restated by cost of living variation. However, the taxpayer may opt for accelerated depreciation for new assets if acquired locally, or for new or used assets if imported, with useful lives of over three years. For this purpose, the assets will be assigned useful lives equivalent to one-third of the normal span, eliminating fractions of months. Taxpayers may discontinue the use of the accelerated method at any time but may not opt again for the accelerated method.

The IRS has issued general guidelines on the useful lives of fixed assets for different activities, such as industry, mining or fisheries. However, the competent Regional Tax Director may, at the request of the taxpayer, modify the applicable depreciation if deemed advisable.

In general, no allowance is made for amortization of intangible assets, such as goodwill, patents, trademarks, etc.

j. Branch of Foreign Corporation

Branches of foreign entities are taxed with world source income. The Income Tax Law gives the IRS the authority to assess the taxable income of a branch should the accounting records not prove adequate for assessing it. In such a case, the IRS may assess taxable income on the basis of gross receipts, assets, capital invested, sales, or percentage of exports and imports.

k. Interest Payments and Thin Capitalization Rules

Interest on loans obtained abroad is normally subject to a 35% WHT; nevertheless, interest paid to non-Chilean banks or financial institutions are taxed at a reduced 4% rate under certain conditions.

However, Chilean Income Tax Law contains thin capitalization rules that limit the possibility of funding the foreign investment in Chile with debt subject to a reduced withholding tax on interest. Therefore, if the debt of the Chilean borrower exceeds 3 times its equity (3:1 debt to equity ratio), the applicable withholding tax rate on interest related to loans granted by lenders domiciled or resident in a treaty country or by foreign banks or financial institutions will be 35% on the proportion corresponding to the excess indebtedness of the borrower. Chilean borrower must bear the difference between the reduced rate (e.g., 4% or 15%) and the 35% rate.

l. Transfer Pricing Rules

Chile has adopted the OECD guidelines of Transfer Pricing, and thus in case of international transactions between related parties, the IRS may object to the prices, values or returns charged or paid by the local entity if those prices, values or returns differ from prices charged or paid in arm's length transactions.

m. Value Added Tax

The tax rate is 19% assessed on the price of the transaction. When the price is manifestly below the normal level, the IRS is empowered to assess it.

a) In General Terms, the Following Transactions are Subject to VAT:

(i) Sales and other contracts whereby the title to movable goods is transferred provided that they are executed on a recurrent basis;

(ii) Customary sales of real estate;

(iii) Services corresponding to commercial, industrial, financial, mining, construction, insurance, advertising, data processing and other business activities;

(iv) Rental of movable goods, as well as the rental of real estate furnished or equipped to carry out industrial or commercial activities;

(v) Leasing of said goods;

(vi) Insurance premiums, with some exceptions; and

(vii) In certain cases, construction activities.

As a general rule, the seller of goods or services is responsible for the payment of the tax. The amount of VAT, however, is added to the price of the goods or services. Consequently, it is actually the buyer who bears the economic impact of the tax.

Exceptionally, when the seller is not domiciled in Chile or for other reasons is difficult to control by the IRS, the buyer has to withhold and pay VAT.

The tax is payable monthly, except for special situations such as imports.

b) Credit and Debit System

VAT charged by a company on sales of goods or services is called "VAT debit". VAT borne by a company on purchases of goods or services is called "VAT credit". The tax borne on the acquisition of related physical assets, including buildings and constructions, may also be credited.

VAT credits are deducted from VAT debits and the difference has to be paid to the Chilean Treasury.

If in any given month credits exceed debits, the difference may be carried forward and added to the credits of the following month.

VAT credits incurred in the purchase of fixed assets that remain outstanding for more than six months may be refunded in cash by the Treasury.

c) VAT Exemptions

There are few exemptions in the Chilean VAT law. The main ones are the following:

(i) Exports;

(ii) Interest on loans and other financial operations. In the case of deferred payment of a sales price, interest charged is subject to VAT;

(iii) International freight, both by air and sea;

(iv) Professional services;

(v) Services subjected to WHT, unless the services are provided in Chile and also that those enjoy a specific tax exemption given by the Chilean law or by treaties to avoid double taxation in Chile;

(vi) Revenues which are not considered as income.

d) Real Estate

Customary sale of real estate is levied with VAT. This is not applicable to land without constructions.

Provisions have been established in the law allowing for the deduction of the cost of the land from the taxable basis.

e) Exports

As indicated previously, exports are exempt from VAT. However, exporters may recover VAT charged on purchases or services necessary for their exporting activities as a credit against the debit originated in their local sales. Additionally, they may recover this credit in cash as a refund.

n. Tax Declaration and Preferences

As a general rule, individuals and entities subject to taxes in Chile must submit an annual tax return through Form N°22. It must be submitted on April of the year following of the one the income has been generated.

Furthermore, taxpayers subject to corporate tax and taxpayers subject to VAT must submit a monthly tax return through Form N°29 during the first 12 of the month following the relevant period.

In addition, taxpayers subject to monthly payment of Withholding tax, tax on gambling, fuel tax, etc. must submit a Form N°50.

Please note that according to Chilean IRS' rules in certain cases taxpayers must submit different type of affidavits (e.g. profit distributions, employees, etc.) to the tax authority.

I. Securities

a. Brief Introduction of Securities-related Laws and Regulations

The Chilean Securities Law ("Law No.18045" or "Securities Law") provides that "securities" shall mean any negotiable instruments, including shares, stock options, bonds, debentures, mutual fund shares, savings plans, and, in general, any credit or investment instrument.

Natural persons and corporations are freely allowed to invest in securities, with no distinction between nationals or foreigners. Institutional investors are allowed to invest in securities under certain conditions.

According to Law No.18045, institutional investors are banks, finance companies, insurance companies, domestic reinsurance entities, and fund managers authorized by Law. The conditions under which these investors are allowed to invest are regulated in various laws and resolutions, such as, among others, the Banks General Law, Decree Law No.3500 on Pension Funds and the Regulation for the Investment by Pension Fund Administrators in Foreign Securities.

Such regulations establish restrictions on investments based on: type of securities; amount of the investment; rating of the securities; percentage of the investment vis-a vis the networth; etc.

b. Supervision and Regulation of Securities Market

The SVS (local Securities Exchange Commission) is the institution in charge of supervising and regulating the Chilean Securities market.

The only possible way of offering and selling securities in Chile without the issuer or selling broker-dealer having to take any action with respect to local regulators is through a private placement of them. Private placement of securities is not subject to the Chilean Securities Market Law, and therefore no restrictions nor special requirements apply to the private offering (non public offer) nor the selling by the broker / dealer in Chile through a private offering.

There is no definition in Chilean Law of a private placement or offering of securities. Notwithstanding, the Securities Law defines a "public offering of securities" as an offer made to the general public or to certain and specific groups of people.

Foreign issuers, intermediaries and any other foreign persons participating in the registration, placement, deposit, trading or any other acts or agreements with respect to foreign securities that violate the Securities Law shall be liable and subject to administrative sanctions, such as fines, suspension to carry out its activities for up to one year (i.e. in the case of registered brokers or agents) and, in serious cases, the cancellation of their authorization granted by the SVS.

Additionally, any person that makes an offer in breach of the Securities Law and as a consequence of such offering causes damages to a third party, will be liable for such damages.

c. Requirements for Engagement in Securities Trading for Foreign Enterprises

a) Corporations that have to be Registered in the Chilean Securities Market

Pursuant to Article 5 of the Law No.18045, the following corporations shall be recorded in the Securities Registry:

(i) Issuers of publicly offered securities;

(ii) Securities that are the subject of a public offering;

(iii) Shares of corporations that have 500 shareholders or more, or, in which at least 10% of the subscribed capital belongs to at least 100 shareholders, excluding those that individually or through other individuals or legal entities exceed that percentage; and

(iv) Shares issued by corporations that voluntarily or by statutory requirement request registration.

Closely-held corporations are those not falling within the definition of publicly-held corporations. Finally, special-purpose corporations are those referred to in Chapter XIII of the Corporations Act.

b) Subscriptions Of Shares Of Foreign Companies In Chilean Securities Market

The shares of foreign companies ("Foreign Shares") must be subscribed before the Chilean Securities Market and Insurance Superintendence, in order to allow its public offer and commercial transaction.

d. Inscription Process

(i) The inscription can be done by a foreign company that issues shares, or by a sponsor.

(ii) If the subscription is requested by the foreign company, it shall have to be done through a Chilean legal representative with sufficient powers to request the subscription, supply information about the company, comply with the obligations of the subscription and receive the communications regarding the subscription process.

(iii) The foreign company issuing the shares in Chile shall have to come from a country member of the International Organization of the Securities Commissions (IOSCO). According to our research, the Republic of

China is indeed a member of said organization.

(iv) With the subscription request, there must be an introductory letter declaring the intention of the foreign company to subscribe its shares in the Chilean Stock Market. Additionally, Form N°1 will have to completed and presented to the SVS with general information regarding the Company, the shares, the possible Chilean investors, economic and financial information, etc.

J. Preference and Protection of Investment

a. Support for Specific Industries and Regions

Our legislation provides taxation benefits to the investment on extreme geographic regions of our Country. Moreover, several laws, such as "Ley Arica", "Ley Tocopilla", "Ley Austral" and "Ley Navarino", state special custom and tax regimes that govern investment and economic activities held in specific boroughs of Chile (which are located in the northern and southern extreme regions of our country).

Additionally, companies interested in starting innovative business or in the development of high tech assets and human resources, have also the possibility to apply for some benefits provided by the Chilean government ("CORFO Subsidies"), which are intended to support the implementation of such activities in our country. In this regard, the amount of the subsidies will depend of the type of project and its specific characteristics.[①]

b. Special Economic Areas

Under Chilean law, certain companies subject to authorization of existence need their supervisor's authorization for mergers, capital increases and the request for early dissolution.

Moreover, there are laws relating to special sectors that provide mandatory pre-merger filing, including media, banks, ports, water supply, casinos, energy distribution, and maritime concessions.

c. Investment Protection

As a consequence of the importance that foreign investment represents for Chilean economy, our country has developed laws and policies in order to attract investors, guaranteeing the existence of stable legal mechanisms that ensure an equal treatment for Chilean and foreign investors, a non-discretionary and non-discriminatory treatment, and the open access to most of the sections of the economy.

III. Trade

A. Department Supervising Trade

On a general basis, any type of good can be imported, except for those that are expressly prohibited by current legislation, such as used vehicles and motorcycles, asbestos in any of its forms, pornography, toxic industrial waste, among others. The National Service of Customs is the entity in charge of verifying the compliance with the above.

In this regard the Customs Service is a public service under the Treasury, in charge of monitoring and checking the passage of goods along the coasts, borders and airports of the Republic; to intervene in international traffic for the purposes of tax collection to the import, export and others; and to generate the statistics of that traffic through the borders; among other functions.

B. Brief Introduction of Trade Laws and Regulations

The National Customs Service ("SNA" or "Customs") is a public service under the Ministry of Finance, responsible for supervising and controlling the passage of goods through the coasts, borders and airports of Chile, for intervening in international traffic for the purposes of collecting import, export and other taxes determined by law, and for generating statistics on such traffic at the borders, without prejudice to the other functions entrusted to it by law. It consists of the National Directorate, Regional Directorates and Customs Administrations.

It is governed by an organic law, Decree with Force of Law No.329/1979, and by the Ordinance of Customs, Decree with Force of Law No.30/2004.

C. Trade Management

Being Chile an open-market economy, it has very few barriers to imports or investments, allowing foreign

---

① More information can be found at http://www.foreigninvestment.cl/.

D. The Inspection and Quarantine of Import and Export Commodities

Even though in general any type of goods can be imported, Law No.18164 establishes two product regimes were the certification by certain public agencies is required:

a) Certificate of Destination

Alcohols, alcoholic beverages and vinegars, vegetable products and goods which are dangerous for plants, animals, birds, products, by-products and offal of animal or vegetable origin, and fertilisers and pesticides require a certificate issued by the Agricultural and Livestock Service ("SAG") indicating the approved place where the said goods are to be stored, the route and the conditions of transport to be used for their removal from the customs premises to the indicated place of storage.

Food products of any kind, toxic or dangerous substances, pharmaceutical products, food products for medical and cosmetic use, narcotic drugs and psychotropic substances that cause dependence require a certificate issued by the Health Service, specifying the authorized place where the said goods are to be deposited, the route and the conditions of transport to be used for transporting them from the customs premises to the following places.

b) Use and Destination Authorization

Once the processing of the document indicated above has been completed and the goods have been removed from the primary premises of the customs offices, they will be deposited under the responsibility of the consignee who will not be able to use, consume, sell, transfer or dispose of them in any way, without obtaining the authorization and prior approval issued by the Health Service and / or the SAG.

The report may:

(i) grant the authorization or approval;

(ii) deny the authorization or approval; or

(iii) establish a period of security (quarantine) in order to carry out the sanitary, animal and phytosanitary controls, as appropriate. During this period, the goods may not be placed on the market.

The use of a route, a place of deposit or transport conditions other than those indicated in the certificate referred above, as well as the violation of the prohibitions o use, consume, sell, transfer or dispose without the corresponding authorization, may be sanctioned with a fine of 10 to 1,000 UTM[①] (1UTM = 80 USD). The fine shall be applied by the director of the corresponding inspection body.

Additionally, the SAG is responsible for the control of agricultural and livestock inputs and products subject to regulation in laws and other norms. For example, SAG is empowered to:

(i) Adopt measures to prevent the entrance of pests and diseases into the national territory that may affect animal and plant health.

(ii) Determine the measures that the interested parties must adopt to prevent, control, combat and eradicate the diseases or pests that are controlled mandatorily.

(iii) Establish a categorization of products according to their pest risk, in order to determine the import requirements that must be complied to enter Chile. Said requirements will vary, depending on the category of the products and its specific regulation issued by the SAG.

E. Customs Management

As a general rule, imports are subject to a payment of a 6% custom duty on the CIF value of the good (cost of the merchandise, plus insurance premium and freight). However, this treatment can be modified, under certain conditions and depending on the involved goods and the Free Trade Agreement between the relevant countries.

a. General Rule

Imported capital goods can be exempted from any customs duties in Chile according to Law No.20269 which establishes a 0% custom duty upon "capital goods" qualified as such by Law No.18634.

In this regard, Article 2 of Law No.18634 defines capital goods as: "Machines, vehicles, equipment and tools destined, directly or indirectly, to the production of goods or services or to the commercialization of goods or services. The good's capability of producing more goods must not disappear upon its first use, but must have such capability for at least three years, being subject to a slow wear or depreciation process for a longer period". Said article also state that

---

① UTM (Unidad Tributaria Mensual) is a Monthly Tax Unit of Measure that indicates a value considered by Chilean national internal revenue service to calculate taxes, fines, and other fees.

"goods destined to fulfil complementary or support activities, such as conditioning, selection, maintenance, analysis and commercialization of the produced goods, indirectly participate in the production process".

In order for the goods to be considered as "imported capital goods", they must be included in the list issued by the Ministry of Finance.

The above customs regime applies to spare parts, wear and tear parts related to the capital goods, provided they are imported along with the capital goods in the same "Customs Destination Document". The value of such spare parts, wear and tear parts may not exceed 10% of the capital good's value.

b. VAT on Imports

Imports are also subject to VAT. Pursuant to article 8, letter a) of the VAT Law, VAT levies imports on their CIF value or customs value. However, article 12, Letter b) No. 10 of the VAT Law exempts from VAT on import of capital goods exists provided all of the following requirements are met:

(i) That the goods have been imported in accordance with the provisions of DFI, including the enterprises receiving such investments. For purposes of benefitting from the exemption, the following requirements must be met: an investment project must have been agreed to in accordance with the provisions of the aforementioned legal provision; the capital goods must be part of the investment project; the capital goods must be included in a list set in a Supreme Decree dictated by the Ministry of Economy; or

(ii) Chilean investors may also benefit from the exemption when the following requirements are met: the capital goods must not be produced in Chile in enough quality and amount; the capital goods must be part of a national investment project similar to a foreign investment project subject to the provisions of DFI, destined to produce similar goods or services for the final consumer; the investment must be qualified as "of interest for the country"; the capital goods must be included in a Supreme Decree issued by the Ministry of Economy; the compliance of the above requirements must be checked by the Ministry of Economy which would issue a resolution which must be confirmed by the Ministry of Finance.

Imports are not subject to income tax in Chile, as Chilean Income Tax Law ("ITL") defines Chilean-sourced income as those arising from goods located in Chile or activities performed therein. Companies domiciled or resident abroad are subject to income tax in Chile only on their Chilean-sourced income.

F. Product Certification

In Chile, there are no industry-specific standards associations. Rather, the only organization responsible for developing standards in Chile is the National Institute of Standardization ("INN"). Its long-term plan for the development of standards is aligned with Chile's primary export sectors, which include copper, forestry, agricultural products, and wine.

In most sectors, standards are not mandatory in Chile, unless specifically order by a laws and / or regulation, but companies can voluntarily comply with them, especially in industries where such compliance constitutes a kind of "seal of approval".

However, certain imported products, such as those related to industrial safety, building and construction materials, automotive safety, and the gas and electricity industries, must comply with the specific requirements of the supervising entity. For example, there are specific regulations pertaining to the seismic resistance of new construction. The INN is also promoting ISO 14000 and ISO 9000 standards among local manufacturers. The chemical industry is an example of one industry that has incorporated ISO 9000 standards into its industrial processes.

IV. Labour

A. Brief Introduction of Labour Laws and Regulations

In general terms, our Labour related matters are mainly contained in the Chilean Labour Code, which applies to private employees, either Chilean or foreigner, that provides for different matters, such as individual employment agreements, benefits, unions and collective bargaining agreements, subcontracting and personnel supply, among others.

Additionally, the some other specific laws provides rules to other employment related matters, such as social security (pension and health), statutory insurances, labour security, among others.

a. Employment Agreements

The employment contract is consensual. However, Chilean law requires the employment contract to be executed in writing no later than fifteen days after the date when the employee began rendering the services. If the employer fails to put the employment contract into writing, it will be presumed that the terms and conditions of the employment contract are those stated by the employee.

Our legislation recognizes three categories of agreements:

a) Individual Employment Agreements

The employment agreement is provided as a written contract between an employer and an employee whereby they are bound, the employee to render personal services under ties of dependence and subordination ("vínculo de subordinación y dependencia") to the former, whereas the employer to pay compensation for those services.

Local statute (mainly the Labour Code) provides for minimum provisions applicable to said agreements, which are mandatory to any employer.

b) Collective Agreements

Our Law provides two different types:

(i) Contrato Colectivo: According to the Labour Code, a collective contract is agreed upon one or more employers with one or more unions or with nonunionized employees who unite to negotiate collectively, or with both groups, to establish common working conditions and remunerations for a fixed period of time.

(ii) Convenio Colectivo: Additionally, the law allows the employer and the employees (either with a union or with a group of at least eight employees) to enter into this specific kind of agreements, which provides common working conditions and remunerations for a fixed period of time applicable to a union or group of employees specially organized to negotiate and execute it.

Please note that legally, the only difference between a Contrato Colectivo and Convenio Colectivo is that the latter does not require a regulated collective bargaining process. Therefore, the negotiation leading to a Convenio Colectivo is neither subject to a regulated procedure nor can lead to an eventual strike.

However, once executed, both agreements have the same effects and are binding for both parties.

c) Special Contracts

Our law also provides for special labour contracts. Each of these contracts has its own characteristics and specifications, e.g. the apprenticeship contract which is restricted to individuals under 21 years of age; farm employees' contracts; contracts for employees on ships or at sea and temporary dock employees and contracts for domestic help.

b. Labour Contract Term

The parties may agree on either an indefinite contract, limit the duration of the contract to the completion of a particular job to be performed by the employee, or else agree on a fixed period of time.

As for fixed term contract, its term exceeds one year, or two years in the case of managers, professionals and technicians. At the expiry of the original fixed period or of its extension, the contract terminates ipso facto but, if the employee continues rendering services for the same employer, by law the term of the contract becomes indefinite.

c. Employee's Nationality

The law states that at regarding Companies with 25 or more employees, must fulfill a quota of, at least, 85% Chilean citizens. To determine this ratio, the law excludes technicians who cannot be replaced by Chilean nationals. For this purposes the law deem the following persons as Chileans:

(i) foreigners whose spouse or civil partner or whose children are Chilean, including widows or widowers of a Chilean spouse; and

(ii) foreigners who have resided in the country for more than five years, not considering accidental absences.

d. Work Schedule

As for Work Schedule, labour statute considers a maximum number of hours weekly. The normal workweek is limited to a maximum of 45 hours. This maximum must be worked in no less than five and no more than six consecutive days. The normal workday shall not exceed 10 hours.

Overtime -which is the time worked by the employee exceeding the legal or agreed workday, if shorter- shall be agreed only based on temporary situations. Overtime must be determined on circumstances that, while not permanent in the company's productive activity and deriving from occasional events or from unavoidable factors, do imply a greater work demand in a certain amount of time (but not more than 2 overtime hours per day). Overtime work agreements shall fulfill some legal requirements and may be renovated if the circumstances that originated them persists. Local statute provides a mandatory 50% surcharge on the salary.

Lastly, there are some particular cases provided by law in which the employees, due to the nature of their services, who's workweek is neither limited to 45 hours nor are entitled to overtime payment.

e. Employees' Rest

a) Working day rest period

workday must be divided into two periods, leaving between them at least a half-hour break for lunch, which must not be considered for the purposes of determining the workday.

b) Weekly Rest Period

Sundays and days legally established as holidays shall be nonworking days, except for activities authorized by law to be performed on those days. In the latter, the law provides how the rest days are compensated.

In Chile, holidays are:
(i) New year (January 1st);
(ii) Extra New year day[①];
(iii) Easter (Holy Friday, Saturday and Sunday);
(iv) Labour Day (May 1st);
(v) Naval Combat Commemoration (May 21st);
(vi) Saint Paul and Peter (June 29th)[②];
(vii) Virgen del Carmen day (July 16th);
(viii) National Holiday (September 18th and 19th)[③];
(ix) Columbus Day (October 12th)[④];
(x) Evangelic Church Day (October 31st)[⑤];
(xi) All saints Day;
(xii) Immaculate conception (December 8th); and
(xiii) Christmas (December 25th).

Please note that election days are also holidays. Also, there are some

c) Vacations
(i) basic annual vacations equal to 15 working days;
(ii) progressive vacations, to which employees are entitled to after working 10 years, continuously or not, for the same or different employers, and is equal to 1 day for every three years of service, after achieving the 10 years seniority, and
(iii) special regional vacation, equal to 20 days (instead of the 15 days of the basic annual vacations) and only applicable to employees working in the 11th and 12th Regions of the country and other specific zones.

f. Remuneration

Legally, it is deemed as remuneration any cash payments and cash-equivalent benefits in kind that the employee receives from the employer on account of the employment agreement.

The remuneration[⑥] includes base salary, overtime pay, commissions, profit sharing and bonuses. The law further indicates that certain payments or allowances do not constitute remuneration, such as lunch, family allowance for each charge of the employee, transportation allowance, etc.

The remuneration must be paid in the agreed fixed period, which cannot exceed one month. However, in the case of variable remunerations, this variable remuneration or commission is usually paid monthly, bimonthly or quarterly. Other payments which depend on the quarterly or yearly results of the company, i.e. bonuses and profit sharing, are paid at the end of the quarter or business year, respectively.

The amount of compensation can be freely agreed upon between the employer and the employee. However, the law sets a minimum level, which in the case of the monthly base salary for employees working 45-hour weeks cannot be lower than one legal monthly minimum wage (CL$264,000; US$430 approximately).

a) Profit Sharing

Legally if a company has profits, it must share part of them with its personnel. The law stipulates that companies must distribute 30% of net profit to the employees, calculated in proportion to the employee's salary. The basis used to determine profits is the corporate taxable income (subject to certain adjustments) less 10% of net equity. However and in lieu of the above obligation, the employer may pay a bonus of 25% of the yearly salary, but the bonus in this case, regardless of the level of salary of the employee, cannot exceed 4.75 monthly minimum

---

① In case January 1st is on a Sunday, the following Monday is holiday.
② If this holiday is on a Tuesday, Wednesday or Thursday the holiday will be moved to the previous Monday. In case the holiday is on a Friday, the actual day of rest is transferred to the following Monday.
③ In case national holiday is on a Saturday or Sunday, September 17th will be an extra holiday.
④ If this holiday is on a Tuesday, Wednesday or Thursday the holiday will be moved to the previous Monday. In case the holiday is on a Friday, the actual day of rest is transferred to the following Monday.
⑤ In case the holiday is on a Wednesday, the actual day of rest is transferred to the previous Friday. If the holiday is on a Tuesday, the actual day of rest is transferred to the previous Monday.
⑥ There is no legal provision that obliges the employer to update its employee's salary according to inflation. However, this is a common practice.

wages. However, employer and employees may agree on a different profit-sharing system, provided the payment to the employee is not lower than the two alternatives mentioned above.

b) Additional Benefits

Employers have no legal obligation to provide fringe benefits, other than benefits which may be voluntarily agreed upon in individual or collective contracts or agreements. Pension and sickness benefits are covered by the Social Security System described later. There is no legal obligation to provide catering facilities and meals, as a general rule.

g. Termination of the Labour Contract

Chilean Labour law applies the principle of "relative stability in employment". Therefore, labour agreements may only be terminated due to causes and according to the provisions set forth by law.

Labour law provides for:

(i) objective grounds of termination, such as mutual consent, employee's resignation or death, among others;
(ii) termination with cause; and
(iii) termination based on economic reasons or without cause.

Legal ground mentioned on number (i) and (ii) above does not entitle the employee to legal severance. However, some legal requirements must be fulfilled in order to terminate employment, especially regarding those grounds mentioned in number (ii) above.

Finally, termination without cause, the other, entitle the employee to receive legal severance payments, which includes:

(i) Severance in lieu of notice: equal to the amount of last gross salary payment received by the employee instead of giving the 30 days' notice require by law; and

(ii) Severance for years of service: when the parties agree or agreed to anything less than what is required by law, the payment for this compensation is equal to the last monthly gross salary received by the employee multiplied by the years of work or fraction superior to 6 months by the employee, with a 11 years cap.[1] Please note that employees will be entitled to this severance payment only after they have 1-year service seniority.[2]

Both legal severances must be calculated according the provisions set forth in the Labour Code.

Notwithstanding the foregoing, both parties may agree on a conventional severance payment in case of termination. This can be agreed in writing and to be applicable even if the termination ground does not entitle the employee to any legal severance. However, the agreed severance compensation cannot be lower than the statutory compensation regime. Normally, this sort of agreement is common in executive and management positions.

Also, it is possible for the employer to pay a voluntary termination severance, often applicable to grounds of termination that don't entitle the employee to legal severances. It is very important to bear in mind that this sort of severances are not tax deductible for the employer and a 40% tax penalty applies.

Furthermore, and regardless the legal ground invoked for termination, employees are entitled to their accrued vacation severance.

Lastly, termination of employment must also fulfill some legal requirements, such as written notice, only applicable to terminations with cause and those based on economic reasons or without cause, and release settlement execution.

h. Outsourcing

The law recognizes the possibility to outsource or externalize services even in matters related to the main business of the user company and also the hiring of transitory personnel through special entities named EST("Empresas de Servicios Transitorios"). Hiring of transitory personnel from an EST is limited to specific situations and to a limited period of time. ESTs are special entities with a sole line of business previously registered before the competent autority. Both regimes are regulated in detail in the law.

Local statute provides for two outsourcing types:

a) Subcontracting

Under this option, contractor should provide services on its own account and risk, with personnel under its labour dependence and control. Therefore, the client shall not interfere in the labour direction of the employees during the performance of the services.

As a general rule, the client is jointly liable for all the contractor's employees labour and social security

---

[1] This 11-year cap is not applicable to those employees hired before August 14, 1981.
[2] Regarding the above compensations, it is important to state that their payment has a 90 Unidades de Fomento ("UF") cap, which is roughly USD $3,900.- However, the parties may agree upon waiving that cap. Such agreement must be written.

obligations (i.e., severances in case of termination, payments of social security obligations, salaries, etc.), hygienic and secure place of work, among others.

Notwithstanding the above, joint liability becomes subsidiary in case the client can evidence that it has effectible controlled compliance of labour laws by the contractor. For these purposes, the client shall require the contractor a special certificate granted by the Chilean Department of Labour, which evidences that the contractor has fulfilled all its labour and social security obligations, among other documents.

If the contractor does not timely certify the complete fulfillment of its labour and social security obligations, the client has the right to withhold any payment or advance that must be done according the agreement between the parties up to the extent of its subsidiary liability having the obligation to pay, with the withhold amount, the owed amounts to the employees and / or to the social security institutions.

The client can also report to the Department of Labour the breach of contractor's labour and social security obligations, declaring the withholding made.

One of the main risks of subcontracting services is the possibility that it is considered the contractor's employees, and that it has a subordination and dependence entailment with the client. To claim the existence of a direct labour relationship, the employee shall pursue legal action against the main company before the labour courts; if the court rules in favor of the employee, the main company will have the obligations of an immediate employer.

b) Personnel's Supply

Specific legal entities provided by law are allowed to provide personnel to a company on a temporary basis. Under this alternative, the company will be authorized to use the provided employees under its subordination. However, the Chilean labour law allows this alternative only for some exceptional events (i.e. to replace employees either on vacation or on medical leave; to face an exceptional and temporary period of more activities, etc.) and for limited periods of time (in general no more than 90 or 180 days).

i. Background Checks

The employer could request a medical certificate when the latter physical condition is an aspect for his / her suitability according to the nature of the provided services. That is, only in specific cases the employer can request a medical certificate in order to confirm the employee is capable to perform his job (i.e. related with unhealthy and dangerous works, as a mining or height's labours). In case the employee's condition is not an element for his suitability, such request may be considered as discriminatory and the employee's constitutional rights may deem as violated.

As for criminal checks, the same criteria apply.

Regarding credit checks, the law states as a general rule that no employer may condition a hiring process on the absence of credit debts or obligations, nor require any declaration stating the fact that they are not indebted. However, according to local statute, this requirement can be asked regarding those persons that have general administrative powers to represent the employer, such as managers or agents or proxies, as well as those responsible for the collection, administration or custody of funds.

Regarding educational background, this is permitted for it is considered an element to determine whether she / he is suitable for the position.

j. Maternity Protection

Regarding this particular matter, Chilean Labour statute provides for a set of rights and benefits to protect maternity, such as:

a) Prohibition of Performing Dangerous or Hazardous Works[①]

If during a pregnancy, an employee is performing tasks that are considered hazardous to the pregnancy, the employee must be transferred to another task, without any change in her remuneration.

b) Maternity Leave

Regarding this matter the law provides for different leaves:

(i) Prenatal Leave. Female employees are entitled to six weeks leave before the birth of a child ("prenatal leave") on full subsidy[②] pay (which is made by the Social Security System and not by the employer). The law also provides for a supplementary prenatal leave in specific cases.

(ii) Postnatal Leave. On the other hand, female employees are entitled to 12 weeks after the birth of her child (as

---

① For this purposes the following tasks are considered hazardous: (i) Lifting, carry and push heavy objects; (ii) Exert intense physical activity, including standing up for a long period of time; (iii) Working on night shifts; (iv)Working overtime; (v) Anything that the respective authority declares inconvenient during this stage.

② It is important to note that the subsidies that the employee is entitled are determined by law and has legal caps which change periodically.

prenatal leave, this payment is made by the Social Security system). This could be extended if some requirements are fulfilled.

(iii) Parental Permit. Additionally, an extra parental leave is provided by law which can be taken according to 2 options: Full time: this means an extra permit of 12 weeks after the end of the postnatal leave, with full subsidy payment by the Social Security system; or Half time: this can only be chosen by the employee but not imposed. In this case the parental leave and subsidy is extended to 18 weeks after the postnatal leave ends. As for its payment, the subsidy granted by the Social Security System is reduced to 50% so the employer must pay the other 50% of her salary. The law also provides that part of this permit may be transferred to the father.

Please note that the law provides for specific additional leaves.

c) Father's Permit

The father is entitled to 5 paid days' leave for the birth of a son/daughter. This permit can be used continuously or distributed within the first month of baby's life, as the employee's choosing.

d) Maternity Protection

Female employees are legally protected under maternity privilege since the beginning of her pregnancy until one year as from the end of the postnatal leave. During this period, the employer may not dismiss her without cause. For termination with cause, employers must request the court's previous authorization.

B. Foreign Employees

As a general rule, employees coming to the country to render services will be subject to both Chilean migratory and labour law, regardless if the employer is a Chilean or foreign entity.

Chilean Migratory Law, in general terms, disregards the applicant's nationality in the process of requesting a visa. Some differences may be noted due to the applicant's nationality regarding the fee applicable to the process.

Chilean Law provides for two kinds of visas for foreigners who wish to work in Chile, as follows:

(i) visa subject to a work contract (work visa); and

(ii) temporary visa. The latter is granted, inter alia, to professionals, technicians and experts who do not come to Chile under a labour contract with a company or branch office in Chile, but as independent consultants and whose services in Chile are considered useful or convenient for the country. The foreigner must request a temporary visa, under different assumptions based on each particular situation.

Either visa enables the applicant to apply to a permanent residence after its expiration. Also, the same type of visa can be granted to the members of the family of the visa holder (such as wife, children or parents) who will not be allowed to perform remunerated activities in the country.

Any visa is a residence permit that allows the holder to reside in the country and to perform any licit activity, without special limitations. Work visa is granted for 2 years term and a temporary visa can be granted for a 1-year period, renewable once for the same period.

Regarding the application procedure, there are two options:

(i) The application may be filed before the Chilean Consulate and carried out through the Ministry of Foreign Affairs. The documents to apply for this type of visa will depend on the specific Consulate in which it will be submitted.

(ii) The visa application can be submitted once the employee arrives in Chile. In this case the application must be filed before the Immigration Department (which is part of the Ministry of Internal Affairs).

This procedure takes approximately 8 months, during which the foreign employee can apply for a provisional work permit which allows him to work in Chile during the entire procedure to obtain the visa.

Furthermore, tourist visa allows its holder to work in the country if a special permit is granted. Hence the foreigner can be able to legally work within a week after his arrival.

C. Restrictions for Exit and Entry

It is important to note that any foreigner that enters de country must have a tourist visa. Depending on the person's nationality, it will be necessary to apply for a tourist visa abroad. Some other nationals don not require to have the tourism visa and have no further restrictions for entering the country. This is also applicable to exits.

As a general rule, tourist visa's term is 90 days, regardless of how it was obtained. However, please consider that the border control authority (Policía de Investigaciones) is empower to either grant the tourist visa for a shorter period of time, or prohibit the foreigner to entry the country, at its sole discretion.

The tourist visa can be renewed, once, for a maximum period of 90 days, counted since the first visa has expired.

D. Labour Disputes

Chilean law provides several procedures to solve labour disputes between employers and employees. Said proceedings may be held administratively or before Labour Courts.

Legally, the Department of Labour is a government agency which verifies law compliance by employers and resolves certain labour disputes through mediation procedures. Conflict and dispute settlements achieved in this instance are enforceable and binding for the parties. The latter task is fulfilled through administrative proceeding set forth by law.

On the other hand, Labour Courts are those legally obliged to resolving any dispute, applicable to their jurisdiction, provided by the employer or employees. Judiciary rulings are enforceable and binding for both parties and may be subject through recourses by higher courts (such as Appeal Courts or even the Supreme Court).

Procedures by which the parties may solve labour contingencies are:

a. Labour Claims

These can be submitted by an employee or a group of them before the Department of Labour. Often, they are submitted when the employee is seeking the declaration that the employer has breach its legal obligations either while the employment is in force or upon its termination.

Normally, the Department of Labour can set up an investigation in the employer's premises or summon both parties to try and reach an agreement. If an agreement is not reached, the employee can file a lawsuit before the Labour Courts in order to seek a judiciary ruling on the dispute.

b. Labour Lawsuits

Chilean Labour Courts are competent to review:

(i) any issue raised by employers and / or employees related to the application of the law or provided from the interpretation and application of individual or collective agreements, conventions and arbitration decisions;

(ii) social security related issues, raised by employee or employers, except those that consists in reviewing medical leaves;

(iii) Claims against resolutions issued by labor or social security authorities;

(iv) any claim seeking damages compensation because of occupational accidents or diseases; and

(v) any other matter which the law specifically provides must be subject to them.

Please note that the specific procedures set by law will vary depending on the matter and its amount. Therefore, local statute provides for different kinds of proceedings which can be held before a Labor Court. However, all of them are mainly oral and includes audiences before the judge.

V. Intellectual Property

A. Brief Introduction of IP Laws and Regulations

Several laws and regulations, including the Constitution, protect in Chile the various IP rights, of which the most relevant are:

• Law No.19039 of Industrial Property regarding patents (including industrial designs, utility models), trademarks, geographical indications, layout designs (topographies) of integrated circuits and trade secrets.

• Law No.17336 of Author's Rights (Copyright).

• Law No.19342 of Plant Varieties.

• Law No.20169 of Unfair Competition.

• Law No.19912 (Title II) of Border Measures.

Chile is a member of several Multilateral Treaties concerning the protection of IP rights, such as:

• The Paris Convention for the Protection of Industrial Property;

• The Patent Cooperation Treaty ("PCT");

• The Berne Convention for the Protection of Literary and Artistic Works;

• The Rome Convention for the Protection of Performers, Producers of Phonograms and Broadcasting Organizations;

• The Brussels Convention Relating to the Distribution of Program-Carrying Signals Transmitted by Satellite.

Also, some of the bilateral free trade agreements to which is Chile is a party contain IP Chapters, including the Free Trade Agreement with the US and the Association Agreement with the European Union.

The National Institute of Industrial Property ("INAPI") is the agency responsible for the registration of Industrial Property rights (patents, industrial designs, utility models, trademarks, geographical indications and layout designs of integrated circuits). Copyright and neighboring rights are registered at the Department of Intellectual Rights. The Agriculture-Livestock Service ("SAG") is responsible for the registration of Plant Varieties.

B. Patent Application

Patents may be granted for any type of product or process that is to be considered an invention, the latter of which is defined in Chile as any solution to a problem of the technique resulting in an industrial activity. Patents are valid for 20 years from their filing date and cannot be renewed.

Discoveries, scientific theories, mathematic methods, plants and animals, software, business models, therapeutic or surgical methods, parts of living beings are considered non patentable subject matter. Chile does allow for second medical use patents as well as Swiss type claims.

In regards to the prosecution of a patent application, this is done before the INAPI. Chile has a pre-grant opposition system and several examiners substantive reports are issued during the prosecution of an application. In general, the prosecution of a patent takes around 3 years before INAPI. If the application faces a third party opposition, the prosecution will take about an additional year longer. The final decision of INAPI can be the object of appeal recourse before the Industrial Property Court. Appeal recourse procedures usually take around 1 years' time. Said decision, can be the object of an annulment recourse before the Supreme Court.

Additionally, it should be noted that Chile allows for Patent Term Adjustment and Patent Term Extension procedures. Both of them are filed, prosecuted and resolved by the Industrial Property Court.

A cancelation action can be filed against a registered patent and the statute of limitations for the filing of said action is of 5 years from the registration date.

Chile is a member of the PCT Patent System.

C. Trademark Registration

Trademark may consist of words, designs or the combination of both. Sound trademarks are also permitted. 3D trademarks are not recognized by the law. The duration of the trademark is 10 years and registrations may be renewed every 10 years. Use of trademarks is not mandatory in Chile and trademark registrations cannot be cancelled based on lack of use.

Registrations are granted for products and services as classified under the Nice Classification, with the addition of two categories, "establecimiento comercial" for retailer names and "establecimiento industrial" for manufacturing facilities.

Trademark applications are filed at INAPI and are subject first to a formal examination and after to the publication in the Official Gazette. Oppositions which may be filed within 30 working days from the publication, based on absolute or relative grounds, including the right to oppose based on trademarks registered outside Chile that enjoy fame and notoriety, even if the trademark has not been used in Chile. INAPI also examines the application on absolute and relative grounds after the expiration of the opposition term. The opposition and Office Actions, if any, decided in first instance by the Director of INAPI, appeals are decided by a special Industrial Property Court and under certain circumstances, the matter may be brought up to the Supreme Court. The prosecution of a trademark application takes about 6 months if no opposition / Office Action is raised.

Trademark registration may be cancelled within 5 years from the date of granting on the same grounds as for an opposition. After 5 years, a cancellation action may be still possible but based on bad faith grounds.

The agents representing a trademark applicant must submit a Power of Attorney before INAPI that does not require further formalities.

D. Measures for IP Protection

Chilean laws contemplates several measures for the enforcement of IP rights.

Both Law No.19039 of Industrial Property and Law No.17336 of Author's rights (Copyright) provide civil and criminal actions for the enforcement of IP rights, including injunction orders, seizure orders, fines, and the right to obtain compensation for damages.

Chilean Customs is also authorized to carry out border measures consisting in the retention without a Court order for up to 10 days of goods that infringe trademarks and copyrights.

VI. Environmental Protection

In the last decade, Chilean environmental law has become increasingly important and consistent with far higher standards. From the judicial enforcement of the constitutional right to live in a pollution-free environment to the enactment of the Environmental Act, Law No.19300 ("EA"), and numerous decisions by the environmental authorities and landmark jurisprudence, the environmental regulations have formed a legal body that must be taken very much into account when considering any new investment project with environmental consequences.

In Chile, there is no single body of laws that encompasses the entire gamut of environmental regulations. Rather, it is scattered throughout numerous legal statutes of varying hierarchy, each referring to a specific matter. The following paragraphs provide a brief summary of the regulations we consider most relevant - from a practical standpoint in developing any given activity or project.

A. Department Supervising Environmental Protection

There are three Governmental bodies related with the application of environmental regulations in Chile:

(i) The Environmental Ministry, which is in charge of the design and application of environmental policies, plans and programs, and the protection of the biodiversity and renewable resources.

(ii) The Environmental Evaluation Service ("SEA"), whose main function is to administer the Environmental Impact Evaluation System.

(iii) The Environmental Superintendency ("SMA"), which is a decentralized public service that executes, organizes and coordinates the follow-up and supervision of the Environmental Qualification Resolutions ("RCA"), prevention and decontamination plans, environmental quality and emissions regulations, management plans, and other environmental instruments established by law.

In addition, there are Environmental Courts, whose main role is to resolve environmental controversies, such as lawsuits seeking reparation of environmental damage, claims against decisions by the SMA, and claims against environmental certification resolutions, amongst others.

B. Environmental Impact Evaluation System ("SEIA")

This system was created by the EA. Any project or activity included in a specific list contemplated by the EA must be submitted to this system prior to its performance or modification.

The projects and activities that must be submitted to the SEIA include, inter alia, high-voltage power transmission lines and related substations; power generation facilities with capacity above 3 MW; airports, bus and truck terminals and train stations, railroads, gas stations, highways and public thoroughfares capable of affecting protected areas; ports, waterways, shipyards and maritime terminals; urban development and tourism projects in certain areas; industrial or real estate projects in areas declared to be latent or saturated; mining projects, including coal, oil and gas, and comprising prospection and extraction work, processing facilities and disposal of waste and sterile rock, as well as the industrial extraction of aggregates, peat or clay; oil pipelines, gas pipelines, mineral or comparable ducts, etc.

If the project or activity that must be submitted to the SEIA is found to produce certain relevant environmental impacts, described in the EA, then an Environmental Impact Study ("EIA") must be filed with the SEIA. If the project or activity is not found to produce said impact, then no EIA is necessary, only an Environmental Impact Statement ("DIA").

Among the environmental consequences that require filing of an EIA instead of a DIA the law includes: risks to human health, due to the quantity and quality of effluents, emissions or residues; potential material adverse effects on the quantity and quality of renewable natural resources, including soil, water and air; the relocation of human settlements or significant alteration to the lifestyles and customs or the population; their location in or in the vicinity of human settlements, resources and protected areas, priority conservation sites, protected wetlands and glaciers likely to be affected, as well as the environmental value of the territory where its location is planned; and any significant alteration, in terms of magnitude or duration, to the landscape or tourist value of any given area; and any alteration to monuments or sites of anthropological, archeological and historical value, and in general those that are part of our cultural heritage.

There are several differences between how an EIA and a DIA are processed, chiefly the deadlines that the environmental authorities have to work with in issuing an RCA. In the case of an EIA, the authority has 120 days, whereas for a DIA the deadline is shortened to 60 days. In practice, these deadlines are longer because the procedure is usually suspended at the request of the project owner in order to collect data and information needed to answer inquiries made by the authorities.

The corollary of this process is an RCA, which could be either unfavorable, in which case the project or activity cannot be carried out, or favorable. In this last case, the RCA usually establishes certain conditions that the owner must meet during the various project implementation and operation stages.

C. Brief Introduction of Laws and Regulations of Environmental Protection

a. Emission and Environmental Quality Standards

There are several emission standards that establish maximum limits that certain specific sources may emit.

(i) In relation to atmospheric emissions, specific emission standards apply in the Santiago Metropolitan Region that are more stringent than those generally in force.

(ii) As to industrial liquid waste, emission sources must adhere to the relevant emission standard, the application of which depends on the water mass that receives the discharge (rivers, lakes, underground aquifers, sea). Usually, in order to comply with the emissions standard, one needs to implement a waste treatment plant under the operational supervision of the Water Utilities Superintendency.

(iii) Elsewhere, there are environmental quality standards that set out the maximum limits for the concentration of pollutants likely to pose a risk to human health or an environmental protection or conservation hazard. There are quality standards for the control of pollutants that affect the atmosphere and inland and maritime waters.

b. Hazardous Solid Waste

The handling of hazardous waste is regulated by Supreme Decree 148/2003, i.e. Sanitary Regulations for the Management of Hazardous Waste, which introduces conditions for the management, storage and elimination of these wastes. Significant hazardous waste generators must file a waste management plan with the Sanitary Authority for approval.

Hazardous waste transportation is regulated by Supreme Decree 298/1994, i.e. Regulations for the Transportation of Hazardous Waste, which establishes the safety conditions to be met by all vehicles that carry hazardous materials or wastes.

c. Native Forest Act

Law No.20283 on the Native Forest Recovery and Forestry Promotion generally provides that any tree-felling activity on native forests, regardless of the location, must be conducted on the basis of a management plan previously approved by the National Forest Corporation ("CONAF"). Nevertheless, it does forbid the felling, elimination, destruction or removal of planting stock of native plant species that are part of a native forest and classified as "in danger of extinction," "vulnerable," "rare," "insufficiently known" or "out of danger".

d. Indigenous Peoples Act

Law No.19253 introduced a special statute applicable to indigenous peoples. It provides that indigenous lands may not be disposed of, attached, encumbered or acquired through adverse possession, except among indigenous communities or individuals belonging to the same ethnic group. Nevertheless, they may be subject to liens upon authorization by the National Indigenous Development Corporation ("CONADI"). These liens cannot include the home of an indigenous household and the land it needs to survive. Likewise, lands owned by indigenous communities cannot be leased, conveyed under bailment or assigned to third parties for their use, enjoyment or administration. Lands belonging to indigenous individuals may be subject to the above treatment for a maximum of five years.

In any case, these lands, with the prior consent of CONADI, may be exchanged for non-indigenous lands having comparable commercial value, duly ascertained; the latter will then be deemed to be indigenous lands and the former will no longer enjoy this status.

Additionally, Chile has ratified the International Labour Organization N°169 Convention on Indigenous and Tribal Peoples. Pursuant to that Convention the government must consult the indigenous people, through appropriate procedures, about legislative or administrative measures that may affect them.

e. Liability for Environmental Damages

In general, liability for environmental damages is subjective, i.e. for a person or entity to be required to cure environmental damages or pay indemnification equivalent to said damages, not only must it have caused those damages, but they must also have been the result of willful misconduct or negligence. Exceptionally, there are some cases of strict liability, such as the damage regulated by the Nuclear Safety Act 18302/1984, the Navigation Act contained in Decree Law No.2222/1978, and the Agricultural Protection Act contained in Decree Law No.3557/1981, that regulates the use of pesticides.

D. Compliance Monitoring of Environmental Protection

As previously mentioned, the SMA is the entity in charge coordinating the monitoring and control of the RCA, the measures of the Prevention Plans and or Environmental Decontamination Plans, the contents of the Environmental Quality Standards and Emission Standards, the Management Plans, and all other environmental instruments established by law.

The SMA may apply sanctions pursuant to Law No.20417 in case environmental regulations are infringed. Aaccording the severity of the infringement, sanctions including revoke the RAC, close the facilities, or 1,000 to 10,000 fines UTA may be imposed.

Notwithstanding the above, the revocation or suspension of an RCA is an uncommon sanction in Chile, which requires a previous consultation with the Environmental Court of Law. In any event, the sanctions mentioned above may only be applied after a sanctioning proceeding has been led by the SMA.

VII. Dispute Resolution

A. Methods and Bodies of Dispute Resolution

The Chilean judicial system is composed by courts of first instnce, Courts of Appeal and a Supreme Court. Courts of first instance are divided geographically and according to the matters they decide. However, there are no special courts for disputes concerning commercial issues, therefore they are resolved by civil courts.

Arbitration is also recognized as a legal dispute resolution within Chilean jurisdiction. The parties are free to agree upon this mechanism regarding most matters. There are three kinds of arbitration, according to the powers granted to arbitrator: arbitration at law (which strictly follows the rules of the Chilean Civil Procedure Code and rules according to law), arbitration ex-aequo et bono (where the parties and the arbitrator freely establish the rules of procedure, and the ruling must be in accordance with fairness and equity principles, that is to say, it does not necessarily follow the law) and mixed arbitration (where the parties may freely establish the procedures rules, but the final decision must be made according to law).

There are certain matters of prohibited arbitration such as alimony, the separation of assets during matrimony and criminal cases. Conversely, there are certain matters of mandatory arbitration, such as the liquidation of corporations and partnerships as well as the differences between its partners or shareholders. Other than these matters, no party shall be subject to arbitration against its will.

Choice of law clauses are generally recognized and enforced, with some exceptions. Assets located in Chilean territory are always governed by Chilean Law. There are also some exceptions concerning family law.

Choice of venue clauses are recognized and enforced regarding international contracts, which need to have an international element in them. However, Chilean courts are flexible when determining the existence of an international element.

B. Application of Laws

The rules of organization and faculties of the State Courts, along with the jurisdiction related matters, are contained in the Organic Code of Tribunals.

As to the procedural rules, they are mostly contained in the Civil Procedure Code -for civil matters- and Criminal Procedure Code -for criminal matters-, notwithstanding some special proceedings regulated in separated acts. In the case of arbitration, Chile adopts a dualistic model, regulating domestic arbitration within the Civil Procedure Code and International Commercial Arbitration in Act. No. 19971/ 2004.

VIII. Others

A. Anti-commercial Bribery

a. Brief Introduction of Anti-commercial Bribery Laws and Regulations

a) Commercial Bribery is a Felony that can be Perpetrated by People and / or Companies

When the felony is perpetrated by a person, the Criminal Code will apply. A person can be either an active participant or a passive participant of the felony. The passive participant is the person that works on a governmental institution and receives a payment in exchange of a favor. Accordingly, the active participant is the person that works in the private sector and makes a payment in exchange of a favor from the government. The Chilean Criminal Code proscribes and sanctions corruption and bribery (including commercial bribery). Criminal sanctions are established both for the public officer who receives the bribe and for the person who pays it.

According to the Chilean Law that regulates the criminal responsibility of Companies, according to Law No.20393/2009, Companies can only be liable for 3 types of crimes:

(i) Bribery;
(ii) Financing of terrorism; and
(iii) Money laundering.

The Law establishes than in order to make a company liable for said crimes, they have to be performed by the Company's owners, controllers, board members, representatives, principal executives, or whoever has administrative and supervision duties within the company. Furthermore, in order to attribute the liability to the company and not to the person directly involved in the crime, the company must have had, directly or indirectly, a benefit from the execution of said crimes.

In business combinations such as mergers, liability can be transferred from one company to another, independently from the individual's responsibilities. Responsibility does not end with the dissolution of the liable company.

Furthermore, Chile is a member of the United Nations Convention against Corruption (since 2006) and of the Inter-American Convention against Corruption (since 1998), treaties that make the legal framework against these crimes even stricter.

b) Crime Prevention Policy Requisites

Pursuant to Law No.20393, in order for companies to prevent crimes such as bribery, the company must first appoint a "Person in charge of Crime Prevention" who must not have a subordinate position within the company. Second, it must give sufficient and adequate faculties and powers to that person so that it can perform its duties. Third, the company must create a "Prevention System" with the indication of the activities that could tend toward criminal acts; mechanisms, rules and instructions to prevent the latter; install administrative procedures and audits to prevent crimes and finally the establishment of sanctions for the people who breach system regulation. Finally, the "Prevention System" must be certified by external auditors, risk qualificator companies or other companies subscribed to the Superintendence (SVS). However, the Law does not state basic requisites in order to get said certification, and it is usually enough to just have a Prevention System but not necessarily and adequate or sufficient one.

Needless to say that this Crime Prevention Policy does not make the company exempt of criminal liability, but only reverses the proof obligation. In case of having a Policy, the courts assume that the company was in compliance of its supervision and management duties, and will therefore be more benevolent when deciding whether the company is guilty or not. However, the district attorneys can still revert the Courts' assumptions and prove that the company is guilty of the crimes. For the latter, they need to prove that the policy was not sufficient or adequate enough to prevent the crime and or prove that the company was not diligent enough in the compliance of its supervision and management duties through other means besides the existence of a Policy.

b. Department Supervising Anti-commercial Bribery

The department supervising anti-commercial bribery is the Prosecution Office. Said Office will be in charge of investigating such practices with the collaboration of other public entities such as the Police Department and the Superintendence of Securities and Insurance (SVS). After the investigation of a crime, which shall not take longer than 2 years, the Prosecution Office will be able to press charges and present an indictment if the investigation has, at its own criteria, brought enough evidence for the Courts to sanction the anti-commercial bribery practices. Once the charges are pressed, a Criminal Court composed of 3 judges will be in charge of evaluating the case and deciding whether the briber and bribed are guilty of bribery crimes.

Appeals shall then be presented before the Appeals Courts and the Supreme Court.

c. Punitive Actions

Pursuant to Law No.20393 if a Company is found guilty of any of the aforementioned crimes, the sanctions can be the following:

(i) monetary fine;

(ii) total or partial loss of fiscal benefits for a determined period;

(iii) temporal or perpetual prohibition to enter into agreements, contracts and others with the Government;

(iv) dissolution of the company or cancellation of its legal personality as the worst sanction and;

(v) other minor sanctions such as the publication in the newspapers of the Court's decision where the company is found guilty.[1]

B. Project Contracting

Article 4 of Law No.19886 of Bases on Administrative Contracts of Supply and Provision of Services that governs the procurement procedure, provides that Chileans or foreigners may contract with the Administration of the State as long as they prove their financial situation and technical suitability as provided by the regulation, fulfilling the requirements that commands and that demands the common right. However, people who, within two years at the time of the presentation of the offer, the formulation of the proposal or the subscription to the

---

[1] Article 8 of Law 20.393.

convention, as appropriate public, private or direct contracting, have been convicted of anti-union practices or infringement of the fundamental rights of the worker, or for bankruptcy crimes established in the Penal Code, will remain excluded from the possibility of contracting with the Administration of the State.

a. Permission System

Article 9 of Law No.19886 establishes that the contracting body of the State will declare inadmissible the offers when the persons do not fulfill the requirements established in the bases. It will declare a vacant offer when no offers are present, or when the actions are not convenient for its interests. In both cases, the notification must be by reasoned resolution.

Accordingly, article 10 states the contract with the State will be awarded by resolution of the competent authority, communicated to the proponent. The successful bidder will be the one who, as a whole, makes the most advantageous proposal, taking into account the conditions that have been established in the respectful bases and the evaluation criteria indicated in the regulation. The bidding procedures are carried out with obligatory subjection, of the participants and of the bidding entity, to the administrative and technical bases that they regulate. The bases are always approved in advance by the competent authority and then presented to the interested parties.

b. Prohibited Areas

According to Chilean Law, foreign investors may participate in most of the country's economic areas and productive sectors of assets and services. Notwithstanding the foregoing, there are some restrictions regarding cabotage, air transport, communication media and fishing activities (regarding fishing activities, the restrictions are conditioned to the reciprocity international principle). Additionally, foreign investors cannot own real estates located at the borders of the country.

Article 3 of Law No.19886 indicates situations were public contracting is not permitted, such as:

(i) The hiring of personnel of the State Administration regulated by special statutes and the contracts to honoraria that are celebrated with natural persons so that they render services to the public organisms, whatever is the legal source in which they are sustained.

(ii) The agreements signed by the public bodies listed in article 2, first paragraph, of Decree Law No. 1263/1975, the Organic Law of Financial Administration of the State, and its modifications.

(iii) The contracts made in accordance with the specific procedure of an international organization, associated with credits or contributions that it grants.

(iv) Contracts related to the sale and transfer of negotiable securities or other financial instruments.

(v) The contracts related to the execution and concession of public works.

Also, are excluded from the application of this law, work contracts that celebrate the Housing and Urbanization Services for the fulfillment of its purposes, as well as contracts for the execution, operation and maintenance of urban works, with participation of third parties, that they subscribe pursuant to Law No.19865 that approves the Urban Financing System.

Notwithstanding the exclusions reported in this letter, the hiring to which they refer will be subject to the regulations contained in Chapter V of this law, as well as the rest of its provisions in a supplementary manner.

(vi) Contracts that deal with war material; those celebrated by virtue of the Law No.7144, 13196 and their modifications; and, those that are celebrated for the acquisition of the following species by the Armed Forces or by the Forces of Order and Public Security: military or police vehicles, excluding vans, automobiles and buses; equipment and information systems of advanced and emerging technology, used exclusively for command, control, communications, computational and intelligence systems; elements or parts for the manufacture, integration, maintenance, repair, improvement of armaments, their spare parts, fuels and lubricants.

Likewise, contracts for goods and services necessary to prevent exceptional risks to national security or public security, qualified by supreme decree issued through the Ministry of National Defense on the proposal of the corresponding Commander in Chief or, where appropriate, of the General Director of Chilean police or of the Director of Investigations.

c. Invitation to Bid and Bidding

If the bidding is public, the call to bid will be open to all possible interested parties. When the tender is private, we must decide to invite to participate. The selection of suppliers in a private tender must be very careful, since determine the possible offers to receive and, therefore, it is vital to include recognized suppliers and that it belonged to the item of the product or service required. According to the law, for private bidding, there must be at least three guests. However, it is recommended to invite more, because it increases the transparency of the process and the offers improve when the competition increases. The call for bids-public or private must, necessarily be published at the information system, ChileCompra.cl. However, the process can be complement by contacting those suppliers that are desired to show up.

吉布提

作者：Ayman Said
译者：吴凯、江家喜

一、概述

吉布提共和国（以下简称"吉布提"）是不同民族的聚居地，气候干燥，土地贫瘠，自然资源十分有限。吉布提的经济发展主要来自于服务和贸易行业。吉布提位于亚洲、欧洲和非洲的交汇处，充分利用了非洲之角的地缘战略位置。目前，吉布提拥有法国驻非洲最大的军事基地、美国一个同样重要的军事基地以及其他国家的军事基地（如德国、意大利等）。这些军事基地的存在以及吉布提的政治稳定使其为外国投资者在东非地区投资提供了一个安全的金融区，可确保对外国资金100%的所有权。此外，吉布提拥有该地区最重要的港口，是东非各国的物资中心和货物运输枢纽。

吉布提近20%的人口生活在贫困线以下。干燥的气候和干旱使吉布提的土地产量低下，无法实现食物自给自足。吉布提粮食完全依赖进口。但是，凭借优越的地缘战略位置，自2000年以来，吉布提一直保持着约3.1%的稳定的年经济增长率，据世界银行数据显示，吉布提自2014年以来的年经济增长率达到了7%。这在很大程度上受益于港口区的大规模投资。[①]

二、投资

（一）市场准入

据世界贸易组织数据显示，吉布提的贸易对GDP增长贡献率为59.17%。外国公司进入吉布提市场的要求与本地公司相同。吉布提拥有自由贸易制度，对银行和商业部门不设限制。此外，吉布提还制定了投资法典，为公司提供了很多税收相关优惠。吉布提建立了几个免税区，外国公司仅支付有限的成本便可在该区内开展经营活动，并且免交公司税。

1. 投资监管部门

（1）国家投资促进局（NIPA）

法律渊源：2001年1月21日第114号法律。

国家投资促进中心[②]是一个公众有限公司。在国家投资促进局，由总统事务部代表国家负责促进投资。

自2001年成立之后，国家投资促进中心一直是吉布提社会和经济体系的核心，它通过灵活的投资经营政策以及现代化的监管框架和程序鼓励投资者在吉布提进行投资。在吉布提地区投资促进和知识发展过程中，国家投资促进局负责提供吉布提鼓励投资的环境和投资机遇。

国家投资促进局的任务是为新成立或现有的国内外企业发起人提供充分的建议和支持。国家投资促进中心是私营机构在政府层面强有力的伙伴和代表。

国家投资促进局的目的是在这些部门之间建立协调机制，为他们提供一个共同的平台，以向投资者推介吉布提，便利投资经营活动，同时实现监管框架和程序的现代化。

国家投资促进局高级管理人员重申了一站式服务的原因，谈到了相关负责人之间的角色分工。马赫迪·达拉尔·奥尔谢赫（Mahdi Darar Obsieh）先生作的详细解释中包含以下几点：

第一，建立单一窗口是国家投资促进局的特权。作为一个国家授权的机构，国家投资促进局有权

---

① 来源：世界银行数据。
② 来源：Djiboutiinvest.com。

为私营经济在吉布提的发展壮大作出研判分析、提供技术指导,并进行宣传。这些任务在一定程度上说明了将该机关 49% 的资本向私营机构开放的意义。这可以保障良好的治理环境,以及公共及私营机构对决策层方面的信任。

第二,一站式服务的实体框架设计允许国内外投资者(包括法律实体和个人)在同一地点、以较低的成本、在最短的时间内办理所需遵守的手续和申报要求。

为此,国家投资促进局聚集了来自国家投资促进局各个级别及有关合作机构的人员。

此外,工业产权局(ODPIC)的高级官员负责知识产权和商业财产权的登记和保护,以及商业和公司登记。税务机构代表负责批准公司成立的税务登记、契约登记以及发放营业执照。因此,公司的社会登记事宜由全国社会保障基金(CNSS)代理人填报,其在国家劳动和职业培训局(ANEFIP)的对接岗负责根据缺工情况向外籍侨民发放工作许可证,该等工作要求资质备案。同样,国家警察负责管理外籍劳工并发放居住许可证。

此外,国土和土地保护机构、国家印刷局、邮局、吉布提电力公司、国家水务局和吉布提电信公司为一站式服务派驻专业人员,以便于获得及提供有关服务。

重要细节:吉布提商会和经济发展基金会将建立信息和指导中心。

为了更好地实现商事法院(法庭登记处)和单一窗口之间的协调和跟进,将建立电子链接,通过交互界面进行上传对投资者的法律保护至关重要。出于这种考虑,国家投资促进局将牵头在当地的公证员和律师之间建立紧密的合作关系。

如果投资者不想亲自到单一窗口办理审批手续,可以委托国家投资促进局编制、起草并专门跟进其文档。在向企业家了解情况后,国家投资促进局将指导他们根据需要咨询专业人士,并提供与受监管活动、社会地位、税收制度等相关的信息文件。

简言之,国家投资促进局可就所有问题与合作单位委托的代表进行密切沟通,同时与投资者直接对话,单一窗口是改善吉布提商务环境的一项便利设施。

(2)吉布提港口和免税区管理局(DPFZA)

吉布提港口和免税区管理局[①]是一个管理机构,负责制定规则、指令和总体原则,使吉布提目前和未来的港口及免税区能够顺利、有效地运营。吉布提港口和免税区管理局还负责在国内各个免税区执行并实施这些原则和指令。

吉布提港口和免税区管理局是负责管理及控制吉布提所有免税区和港口的唯一管理机构。其作为免税区公司和其他政府机构之间开展交流的唯一纽带,发挥着积极作用,并直接隶属于吉布提总统办公室。

吉布提港口和免税区管理局担负着多项任务,包括促进吉布提港口和免税区作为商业和物流平台,通过商业导向的法律框架建立友好的商务环境,通过其董事会对港口进行管理,以及在吉布提建立新的港口和免税区等。

(3)吉布提免税区(DFZ)

法律渊源:2004 年针对《免税区法》的第 53 号法律;2005 年管理免税区公司的第 103 号法律。

吉布提为投资和贸易创设了一个良好的商务环境。吉布提免税区[②]从 2004 年 10 月开始运营,吉布提定位于成为从东非各国进口、仓储、加工和再出口货物的区域性物流、贸易和营销枢纽。

吉布提免税区位于港口和机场附近,总占地面积超过 40 公顷,包括两个分别为 614 平方米和 1 340 平方米的仓库以及综合办公楼,配备占地 2 000 平方米至 15 000 平方米的公用设施,配备占地 510 平方米的综合办公楼和经营办公区的轻工业区,还有一个占地 9 100 平方米的飞机棚,用于容纳援助物资。

外国投资者享有的财政和非财政激励措施包括:保证 100% 外资所有权,自由收回资本和利润,在免税区经营的所有公司均免交公司税,免交所得税,外国人就业灵活,可以在本地市场进行销售,并且没有货币管制。

---

① 来源:dpfza.gov.dj。
② 来源:dpfza.gov.dj。

2. 投资行业法律、法规

《投资法》[①]：

法律渊源：1994年10月16日第58号法律，修改1984年2月13日关于吉布提《投资法》的第88号法律。

《投资法》于1984年颁布，并于1994年根据新的国内经济需求完成修订。该法就某些特定的投资活动规定了若干项税收优惠，包括免除5～10年的专利税、免收所得税（适用于自然人和法人），以及对实现投资项目所必需的材料和原材料在5年内免收国内消费税（TIC）。

3. 投资形式

《投资法》给予优惠的投资活动如下：

"A类"，要求最低投资额为500万吉布提法郎：与植物或动物来源产品相关的开发、修理或加工活动；远洋渔业；海鲜食品的制备、冷冻、加工或储存；采矿；采矿和金属产品加工或培训业；能源研究、开采或储存；碳氢化合物精炼；机械、电气、电子化学和造船业的现代化或扩展；陆运、海运和空运；港口和机场活动；运输或捕鱼船只建造、维修和维护；产品或消费品制造或现场包装；促进新投资的银行或信贷活动；咨询服务；工程；计算机数据处理；主机远程信息处理数据库。

对于"B类"，要求最低投资额为5 000万吉布提法郎：

本类别将A类的范围扩大至与工业、商业或旅游专用建筑的建设，社会住房建设，教育和培训设施的建设、创办和经营。

为促进出口，吉布提设立了免税区，使投资者能够从税务优惠和灵活的劳动立法中受益。

4. 市场准入和投资限制

吉布提法律在原则上对外国投资没有任何限制。《投资法》第1条规定，任何人（无论国籍）都可以在吉布提自由投资或开展经营活动，也没有法律或监管的规定要求外国投资者必须与本国人设立合资企业。但是，某些受监管的活动，比如银行、保险、采矿、石油、医疗、制药以及自由职业等，必须事先取得有关行政机关颁发的特定的许可或行政授权，这意味着实际上这些活动专为吉布提本国国民而保留。

法律并未要求本地公司的董事或经理必须是吉布提国民或居民。但是，某些董事居住在吉布提会有助于对公司的管理。对吉布提贸易公司的董事没有最低资质要求（学历或专业程度），但从事银行业务活动的公司除外。

在吉布提，没有关于限制控制权变更或股份收购的专门立法。但是，在港口、机场、铁路、采矿和能源等战略部门的PPP协议中会有标准条款，要求在控制权变更前通知吉布提政府或取得吉布提政府的授权。

（二）外汇条例

吉布提的本国货币是吉布提法郎，与美元的固定汇率是1美元=177 721吉布提法郎。金融管理局是吉布提中央银行（BND），于1977年12月3日成立。该国外汇储备货币是美元。吉布提法郎可以自由兑换。

吉布提中央银行既不参与商业银行再融资，也不进行外汇管制。货币发行范围是中央银行的信用货币的两倍。

二级银行需要持有与其本国货币储备相当的可兑换货币对冲。外部资产（主要是存款）通过美元对冲。

吉布提中央银行向吉布提国库支付股息。中央银行不对财政收入课税，无须支付所得税或外汇交易税。

1. 外汇监管部门[②]

吉布提中央银行是一个监管机构，负责管理吉布提的货币、国家外汇头寸和国民经济核算。中央

---

① 参见吉布提商会（www.ccd.dj）。
② 来源：吉布提中央银行网。

银行根据审慎规则进行合规性监管。吉布提没有强制性储备或存款保险。

吉布提没有活跃的资本市场或固定利率金融工具。

吉布提中央银行有权制定关于信贷机构与客户交易利率和条件的各项规定。其可以规定信贷机构对其贷款、预付款和其他信贷交易收取的利率以及最低和最高费用,以及信贷机构对不同类型的承诺支付的最高和最低利率。

吉布提中央银行可以根据信贷机构的用途和来源适用与其体量和性质相关的规则,并可基于各种因素确定最低和最高利率,也可以根据指令决定信贷机构可依授权持股或者处置部分资产、义务或表外承诺的情形。

信贷机构收购或转让任何资产、负债或资产负债表外承诺,如违反了法律规定,则属无效。

如果信贷机构无力遵守审慎标准或出现严重的现金流危机,吉布提中央银行可以要求该机构的法人或自然人、股东或成员提供其所必需的支持。

2. 外汇法律、法规简介

法律渊源: 关于吉布提中央银行的第 19 号法律,管理信贷机构开办、活动和运营的第 92 号法律。

为了设立及从事金融部门的活动,商业银行必须提前获得许可。[①]根据中央银行确定的国家标准和规范,商业银行可以持有信贷机构最多 30% 的股份,或者从事国际银行的货币再融资业务。金融和银行机构的最低资本额或者总部位于海外的分支机构及办事处的最低出资额为 10 亿吉布提法郎。

所有的经济主体(无论是否居住在吉布提)都有权开立账户。得益于监管充分,经济主体可以向世界各地汇款是吉布提的优势之一。

3. 对外国企业的外汇限制[②]

由于严格执行国际监管规定和审慎标准,吉布提的金融部门可提供可靠的银行体系,其可得到主要银行集团的支持,并受益于自由的资本流动。银行部门的重要性还可归因于对国内外公司没有外汇限制,并且本国货币吉布提法郎具有稳定性。实际上,吉布提银行已经为吉布提吸引了大量外国存款。

随着国民经济的增长,2016 年货币供应量持续加速。这主要是由于向公共和私营部门提供的信贷总额增长所致。

除了吉布提中央银行外,国家金融部门还包括 12 个存款和信贷机构。

新银行也出现在中央银行批准的名单中。吉布提通过开放市场建立了稳定的金融体系。但是,吉布提仍然缺乏专业的银行业务服务提供商,无法应对本地人口和企业不断增长的需求。当局鼓励私营部门在以下领域投资:

① 建立更多设施和客户导向型银行;
② 设立 / 建立向工业、农业优先机构提供资金的投资银行;
③ 由私营和本地合伙企业建立小额贷款和小额金融企业;
④ 共同基金机构。

(三)融资和银行业务

1. 金融部门概述[③]

2006 年至 2010 年期间,金融部门发展迅速,出现了一批新银行。2006 年吉布提仅有两家银行,2012 年增长至 11 家。但全行业 85% 的资产仍然集中在两家银行。

2012 年,金融活动占 GDP 的 13%。随着新的也门银行和索马里银行引进伊斯兰金融工具,并为小额存款者、养老金领取者、退休人员和自由职业者开立账户,吸纳了传统银行部门之前流失的存款。

这些新银行在吉布提市场的出现导致竞争加剧,利率下降。但利率水平仍然相对较高,无担保贷款利率平均为 12%,透支额贷款利率为 15%,住房贷款利率为 10%。

授予的信贷主要是短期信贷或消费信贷。尽管现在开始提供 15 年长期贷款,但与中期贷款一样,

---

① 来源:Djiboutinvest.com。
② 来源:Djiboutinvest.com。
③ 来源:Africaeonomicoutlook.com。

长期贷款仍然占比很少。国际货币基金组织（IMF）的分析表明，金融行业虽然健康、流动性强，但仍然存在弱点。

由于新机构的出现以及越来越多的投资进入房地产行业，近些年信贷增长迅速，导致银行资产质量下降。

在这种情况下，中央银行在国际货币基金组织的帮助下不断强化银行业务监督，2012 年，集中颁布了根据上一年实施的银行法制定的监管文件。

新指令和通告涉及申请信贷机构授权、提交银行定期报表及其年度内部控制报告等程序。

信贷机构的监督和管理任务已得到强化。另外，还与外国中央银行签订了合作备忘录，以便更好地监管外国银行在吉布提的子公司。

吉布提最大的小额信贷基金在年内遇到困难，并被交由中央银行管理，中央银行负责监督其改革和能力建设工作。

2. 主要金融机构

吉布提有两类金融机构：零售银行和伊斯兰银行。所有银行均在吉布提中央银行备案。以下是各银行的相关信息。[①]

零售银行包括：吉布提储蓄信贷银行（BDCD）、非洲银行红海分行、吉布提红海工商银行、吉布提商业银行（CBD）、进出口银行、合作和农业信贷国际银行（CAC）、国际商业银行（ICB）和丝绸之路国际银行（SBI）。

伊斯兰银行包括：东非银行（EAB）、萨巴伊斯兰银行和萨拉姆非洲银行（SAB）。

3. 外国企业的融资条件

吉布提对于贷款用途没有限制。但根据 2002 年 12 月 29 日第 196 号法律的规定，贷款不得来自于犯罪所得，也不得用于犯罪目的或者与犯罪相关的其他目的（比如恐怖主义或洗钱）。

所有本地实体可以根据董事会的事先批准和股东大会的批准，与非本地实体签订贷款协议。其中，贷款协议应规定双方身份、贷款额、贷款利率（免息贷款除外）以及还款计划。

吉布提法律规定可以用各种资产作为担保。实物担保适用于对债务人动产和不动产的所有传统的及法律规定的担保。个人担保是债务人未提供其财产作为担保，而由个人提供担保，比如简单的定金或担保书等。

担保可以是传统性质或司法性质的，由吉布提和殖民时期的法国民法共同调整，包括个人担保（比如保函和独立担保）与动产和/或不动产相关的担保权益等。

可以通过无形财产（公司股份、商誉、债务人享有的债权、银行账户和债务人的知识产权）和/或有形财产（专业材料、股票、商业资产）提供担保。

担保权益包括扣留权、质押权、非占有性抵押权和留置权。某些担保权必须在贸易和公司登记处登记。抵押契据（经公证和法院判决的）必须由财产所有人进行登记。

债权人可以向初审法院院长申请，由法院颁发命令，通过采取保护性财产保全措施和/或对违约债务人的不动产和动产权利进行保全的方式获得保障，作为收回债务的担保。

（四）土地政策

吉布提的土地可由自然人或法人购买，无论其是本国人或者外国人，法律上没有任何限制或禁止性规定。吉布提宪法无差别地保障并保护所有人的所有权，包括在境内合法定居的外国人。获得房产是一项基本的无歧视的权利。

土地所有权受到五部立法规范（通常被称为"地产法典"），这五部立法管理与房地产和征用相关的各类交易。这些法律均未禁止外国自然人或法人取得房地产（包括在建和未开发土地）。外国投资者（商业实体）可以自由购买不动产，用于商业、工业和/或居住目的，并且对土地享有与吉布提国民同等的权利。根据土地使用权持有人的身份和/或土地关系的性质，共有三种土地所有权制度。

---

① 来源：吉布提中央银行收集的数据。

1. 公有土地

公有土地指吉布提公有范围内的所有房地产，无论是否指定适用于公共用途。

公有土地可以通过长期租赁和／或特许的形式（一般通过公私合作模式授予，即 PPP）提供给国内外私人实体。长期租赁的期限不得超过 99 年，特许使用期限不得超过 18 年。持有长期租赁的公共或私有土地的外国投资人可以对其债权人提供抵押担保。

2. 私有土地

私有土地包括无主的未占用土地、国家购买的土地，或者通过捐赠、继承或其他合法方式获得的土地。闲置的未托管土地以及所有未注册或未开发的土地在登记至国家名下前，都可以取得临时占用许可证（城市施工用地）或者授权经营（农业用地），登记至国家名下后，可以通过协议或公开招标的方式出售（城市建设用地），可以授权临时使用（工业或农业用地、农村土地），也可以无偿转让给公共机构。

3. 土地所有权

土地所有权由 1991 年 10 月 10 日第 177 号法律规范。该法律确立了所谓的土地保护服务，通过对土地和房产的所有权登记来保障财产所有人的权益。登记是强制且一次性的。任何登记在私人名下的土地均可以进行交易，如转让或捐赠。这些交易必须由公证人在土地登记簿中填写、签字并备案。

4. 土地登记程序①

吉布提《土地法》第 58 条列举了需要在土地登记簿中登记不动产的人员名单，该名单包括所有权人（即便其行为能力仅限于从事管理行为）、负责管理共有建筑或经其他所有人同意的共同所有人、拥有《土地法》第 19 条列举的不动产物权的所有人（详见 1991 年 10 月 10 日第 177 号法律关于吉布提土地组织的规定），但不包括具备前述资质之一的无民事行为能力人的监护人、管理人或监管人。

除非另有约定，登记费用一般应当由申请人承担，但是对于无民事行为能力者而言，应返还给其法定代理人。

如果法院命令在交付前完成该手续，申请以建筑物抵债的债权人可能也需要登记。

只有建成或未开发土地才能在土地登记簿中登记。

对于由一个或多个相邻地块组成的房地产会特别要求其应当属于单一所有人或多个不可分割的共同所有人。

申请登记前，不动产围墙的边界必须由其所有人通过石块、砖墙或混凝土标记等方式在土地所形成的多边形各顶点确定。

登记申请人必须向房产登记员提供一份由本人或特别代理人签字的法语声明，包括以下信息：姓名、性别、居住地、婚姻状况，位于某司法辖区供司法送达的地址，建筑描述、施工和地表植被情况，并标记其位置、容积、边界、出入口以及地名，租金估值或者收入，估计市值，过去 10 年内售价（如果在 10 年前出售，则仅需提供去年的售价）的说明，相关物权以及与建筑相关的 3 年以上租约的情况，包括受益人的姓名和居住地，以及（如适用）未成年人或禁治产者的监护人的信息、为所述建筑进行登记而向房产登记员提交的申请等。房产登记员会向申请人出具收据。

（五）公司成立和解散②

1. 企业形式

吉布提的法律环境对企业非常宽松。无论具有何国籍或居住地在何处，都可以在吉布提成立公司。

在吉布提注册公司可在 3 天内完成。外国投资者无须吉布提当地的合作伙伴可以直接在吉布提开展业务。

投资者可以通过一站式服务或者通过私营的公证人或律师设立公司（法律实体）。开设企业所需的所有手续均通过国家投资促进局的一站式服务完成。

---

① 来源：Loi n° 177/AN/91/2ème L du 10 october 1991。
② 来源：djiboutinvest.com。

在吉布提，最普遍的公司类型包括有限责任公司（LLC）、有限公司（S.A.）、单一成员（股东）有限责任公司（法语简称 EURL）。

2. 成立程序

为了在当地成立公司，必须完成以下几个步骤：

① 新公司必须提交公司章程所需信息（股东的身份证、股东之间的股份分配、公司名称、公司目的、公司地址）。

② 公司需要在公司登记档案中登记，应该提交公司章程、预定商业名称、银行报表等文件。

③ 公司应该在商业登记簿中登记，为此，应该提供登记表、公司章程和银行报表、股东及经理的犯罪记录、商业名称证明、费用、商业登记簿和商业名称。

④ 公司将对公司章程和商业租约进行财务登记。所需文件包括：公司章程（4份），一致性声明，主要银行报表，公司应该支付公司登记费，登记费根据公司资本额确定（不考虑公司形式），印花税约为1000吉布提法郎／规约页，包括附件。

⑤ 完成以上手续后，公司会获得以下文件：付费收据——背面印有其注册形式（登记簿号、页码和登记号），授权签字，契据日期和官方印鉴。

⑥ 公司将进行社会保险登记，需要在国家社会保险基金会（Caisse Nationale de Securité Sociale）登记。该项登记不收取费用。

成立分支机构的步骤有所不同，需提供的文件包括母公司的公司章程、母公司的董事会会议记录、被委派分公司的代表或经理、母公司的商业登记簿、当地分公司的商业登记簿以及商业名称证书。

3. 解散途径和要求[①]

根据下述具体规定，公司清算应当根据公司章程中的规定进行调整。公司自因故解散之时开始清算，但全体股东会议或一人公司股东决定解散的除外。公司名称后面应该注明"公司正在清算"。公司法人资格在清算期间持续存在，直至清算完成。从商业登记簿公布之日起，公司解散为对第三方产生效力。

根据法律规定的条件和截止时间将公布任命的清算人，还将确定作为商业登记簿附件的备案文件。行使总经理、董事、公司经理、管理委员会或监事会成员职能或被剥夺该职能的人不得作为清算人。

公司解散不会自动终止用于社会活动的建筑物租赁合同，包括相关建筑中的宿舍。如果转让租赁合同，则条款中的担保义务将无法存续，其可能根据法院判决由受让人或第三方提供的担保所替代，并视为充分有效。

除非合伙人一致同意，否则将公司全部或部分清算资产转让给合伙企业的合伙人、一般合伙人、经理、董事、总经理、监事会成员、管理委员会成员、审计师或总监时，必须得到初审法院、清算人和法定审计师或者（如果有）财务总监正式听证后批准。

禁止向清算人或其员工、配偶、父母或子女转让公司全部或部分清算资产。向其他公司整体转让公司资产或以公司资产向另一个公司出资（特别是通过合并方式）需要得到合伙人一致同意或修订章程所需的大部分合伙人同意。

清算结束时，需要召集股东（包括无投票权优先股的持有人）确定清算结果，解除清算人管理职责，解除对清算人的授权并记录清算结束。否则，任何合伙人可以请求法院指派代表召集会议。如果清算结束会议无法商议或者拒绝批准清算人的账目，那么可以根据清算人或利害关系人的要求，提请法院裁定。

清算结束的通知将根据法律规定的条款和条件公布。清算人应对公司和第三方就其在履行职责期间的过错造成的损害承担责任。向清算人追责的诉讼时效为3年，自损害事实发生之日起计算，如果损害是隐秘的，则应当自被发现之日起计算。但是，若此类损害构成犯罪，则诉讼时效为10年。

应当在商业登记簿中公布公司解散5年内对非清算合伙人或其未亡配偶、继承人或受让人提起诉讼。如果没有法定条款或双方明确约定，则应当根据法律规定对解散公司进行清算。

此外，法院亦可命令，清算按上述条件进行。

---

① 来源：吉布提《商业法典》。

在法院判决或公司解散之日（以较晚者为准），董事会或经理的权力终止。公司解散不会终止监事会和法定审计师的职能。

如果没有审计师，合伙人可以任命一名或多名审计师，否则，可能由法院应清算人或利益相关人的要求进行指派。

对审计师的任命规定了审计师的权力、职责和报酬以及任职期限。合伙人与审计师共担责任。如公司根据法定条款或合伙人的决议解散，合伙人将任命一名或多名清算人。

如果合伙人无法任命清算人，任意利益相关方提出要求，依法属于应当指定情形的，法院应当指定。

如果公司由法院判决解散，则法院判决会指定一名或多名清算人。

清算人的任职期限不得超过3年，但是，合伙人或初审法院院长可以延长其任期（取决于清算人是由合伙人任命的还是法院指定）。

如果未有效召集股东会议，则法院可以根据清算人的要求通过法院决定延长其任期。

在要求延长任期时，清算人应当说明无法完成清算的原因、计划采取的措施以及完成清算所需的时间。

在获任命后6个月内，清算人将召开股东会议，报告关于公司的积极和消极情况、清算的进展情况以及完成清算所需的时间。清算人报告期间可以根据其申请由法院决定批准延长至12个月。否则，应当根据利益相关人的要求，由监事会（如果有）或者由法院判决所指定的代表召集会议。

清算人代表公司。清算人被授予最广泛的、将资产变现的权力。由法令或任命行为对其权力的限制不得对抗第三方。清算人有权向债权人付款，并清偿欠款余额。

清算人可以继续处理进行中的案件，或者在得到合伙人或法院判决（取决于清算人是由合伙人任命还是法院指定）授权后提起新的诉讼。

清算人应当在每个会计年度结束后3个月内，根据其制备的当时各项资产和债务的清单制作年度报表，以及前一会计年度清算交易的书面报告。

除法院命令许可外，清算人应当根据公司章程规定的程序，每年至少在会计年度结束后6个月内召开一次股东大会，批准年度会计报表，作出必要授权，并根据情况延长审计师或监事会成员的任期。

如果未召开会议，那么上述所述报告应当在初审法院的登记簿中备案，并告知利益相关人。清算期间，合伙人可以在前述相同条件下披露公司文件。

如果未达到法定多数的要求，则可以根据清算人或利益相关人的要求，由法院命令决定。如果审议需要修改章程，则应当依照各类型公司的相关规定办理。

如需继续开展经营活动，则清算人需要根据上述规定召集合伙人会议，否则，利益相关人可以要求通过法定审计师、监事会或监管机构，或者由法院命令任命的代表召集会议。

除非公司章程另有规定，偿还股份票面价值后的剩余股本应当按照持股比例分配给各股东。

在满足债权人权利的前提下，清算人应当决定是否分配清算过程中可获得的资金。

（六）兼并与收购

吉布提《商业法典》第三卷第四部分第六章关于公司法的规定调整公司合并与分立的相关事宜。

《商业法典》第L.326-1条规定，一个或多个公司可以通过合并的方式将资产转移至一个现有公司或其成立的新公司。

一个公司还可以通过分立的方式将其资产转移至多家现有公司或新成立的公司。

这些措施均适用于清算中的公司，条件是合伙人之间的资产分配不是清算开始进行的原因。

在前述所述交易中转移资产的公司股东可以获得股份或受益公司的股份，如果需要，也可以获得现金支付（现金支付的溢价额不得超过股份或所得股份票面价值的10%）。

不同形式的公司之间均可进行前述操作。

由各相关公司自行决定修改章程所需的条件。

如果交易涉及成立新公司，那么各新公司组建需要适用其公司形式的具体规则。

吉布提《商业法典》第L.326-3条规定如下：

合并或分立公司需要不复存在的公司不经清算而解散，并将其全部资产按其在交易最终完成之日的状态转移至受益公司。被解散公司的合伙人可按合并或分立协议规定的条件，通过收购取得受益公司的合伙人的权益和地位。

但是，受益公司的份额或股份不得与被解散公司的份额或股份进行互换，若此类份额或股份被以下各方持有：

① 由受益公司或代表受益公司的个人持有；
② 由被解散公司或代表被解散公司的个人持有。

在以下条件下，公司合并或分立生效：

① 若是成立一个或多个新公司，自新公司或最后一个新公司在商业登记簿登记之日起生效；
② 在其他情况下，则在最后的全体大会批准交易之时生效，除非合同规定交易在其他日期生效，但不得迟于交易交割之日、受益公司当前会计年度，也不得早于转移资产的公司最后一个会计年度结束之日。

若拟议交易将增加一个或多个相关公司的合伙人或股东的出资额，则必须经所涉合伙人或股东的一致决定通过。

参与上述交易的所有公司将构成拟议的合并或分立。

拟议交易文件草案应当在所涉公司总部所在地的初审法院登记簿中登记，并在公布时以相关条例确定的条款为准。

参与以上操作的公司需要在登记簿中备案一份声明，表明其已完成所有履行交易所需的步骤，并确认交易是依据法律、法规进行的，否则无效。书记员应当确保该声明符合法律规定。

公共有限公司之间互相进行的交易应遵守本节所述的法规条例的规定。

合并应由参与交易的各公司的特别股东大会决定。

如适用，合并应由参与交易的各公司获得特别股东大会的批准（若有）。

拟议合并需要召开投资证书持有人特别会议，并根据全体股东大会的规则进行。

（七）竞争法

1. 竞争监管部门

国内贸易、竞争和欺诈监管理事会是负责实施吉布提竞争监管政策的机构。

在东南非共同市场（COMESA）中，吉布提参与实施区域竞争政策。

2. 竞争法简介 [①]

2008年，吉布提通过了一部法律，禁止经济经营者之间各种形式的有可能约束竞争、限制或控制生产及投资，或导致滥用优势地位的行为。

该法律不适用于公共企业和能确保技术进步但不会对主要的相关产品的竞争造成损害的做法。

第28号法律是有关保障、制止欺诈和保护消费者的法律，规定了在贸易活动中自由竞争和保护消费者的实务规范。该法于2008年制定，规定了以下主要原则：

① 产品、商品和服务在国内可自由定价，仅通过竞争约束。但是，由于垄断或长期供应困难的原因，或者依据特殊法律、法规的规定，使价格竞争受到限制的经济部门或国内地区，价格将由内阁会议法令调整。本条规定适用于所有生产、经销和服务活动，包括公法公司的活动。

② 禁止经济经营者之间企图或可能阻碍、限制或破坏市场竞争的各种形式的协同行动、协议、明示或暗示协议或者联合，尤其是企图限制其他公司进入市场或进行自由竞争，通过人为手段阻碍市场自由定价，限制或控制生产、销售、投资、研究或技术进步。同时，禁止一家公司或多家公司滥用在国内市场或大部分国内市场的支配地位。

③ 禁止任何形式的价格控制。如果设定最高或最低价格，则可被视为控制商品、产品或服务的利润或转售价。同时，禁止以低于实际购买价的价格在国内转售任何产品。实际购买价格应为发票价格

[①] 来源：第28号法律。

加上相关转售税款和运费（如适用）的总价。

总体而言，吉布提政府制定的该法律制度与其他自由竞争市场国家具有相同特征。此外，法律列出了违反市场透明规则的行为和限制竞争的做法。吉布提的消费者保护法要求保护消费者的同意权和安全。

在产品或服务名称、供应、展示、使用说明、担保范围及条件以及发票和收据中，必须使用吉布提的官方语言。允许使用其他文字或同等表述。

3. 竞争管理措施[①]

在竞争、防范欺诈和消费者保护方面，商务部及其官员负责控制并监管良好竞争秩序。

贸易部贸易和标准化理事会的宣誓代理人经特别授权，可以根据第28号法律第19条的规定实施必要的检查和调查。就职前，该等代理人将在区法院宣誓，其有义务保守职业秘密。

根据第28号法律第21条关于欺诈声明的规定，调查员负责调查、侦查并起诉违法行为。

上述商业调查员是贸易与行业理事会的审计人员。

商务部、司法警察、税务官、海关以及任何其他调查部门的官员的调查活动应遵守标准化程序。

如果司法警察和税务代理、海关和所有其他管理部门官员在其权限范围内进行检查或调查时有证据证明或确信存在违反商法的行为，其有义务在发现后两个工作日内以书面形式通知竞争局，制止欺诈行为并保护消费者，以便有关部门采取必要措施。

根据第28号法律第21条的规定，调查员要求提供的文件包括但不限于发票以及可能有用的进口或供货文件。

吉布提有三种反竞争犯罪行为：反竞争行为、违反市场透明规则和限制竞争的行为、违反竞争组织规定的行为。

反竞争行为是指，限制其他公司进入市场或开展自由竞争，通过人为手段阻碍市场自由定价，限制或控制生产、销售、投资、研究或技术进步，分割市场或货源，一家公司或几家公司滥用在国内市场或大部分国内市场的支配地位使客户公司或供应商处于无法获得同等解决方案的经济依附状态。

吉布提《商业法典》第L. 2294-3条规定了反竞争的违法行为。根据该条规定，违反市场透明规则和限制竞争的行为包括：控制价格和亏本转售，不遵守计价规定，不沟通价格表和销售条件，拒绝向消费者销售以及强制销售，专业人士之间的歧视做法，胡乱销售或类购买，不遵守与消费者信息有关的规则，尤其是与可能损害身体健康的产品有关的使用说明书，虚假或误导性广告宣传，不遵守与直接销售相关的规则，等等。

此外，违反与银行业务活动相关的法律规定也会被视为违反竞争组织相关规则的行为。

上述违法行为将记录在商务和卫生主管部门起草的备忘录或司法调查记录中。

（八）税收

吉布提税务部门在欧盟资助下于2008—2009年期间编制的《税法通则》重塑了吉布提税收制度。

《税法通则》颁布后，吉布提又颁布了几项重要的不成文税法：包括税收协定、投资和免税区规定、《采矿和石油法典》（Mining and Petroleum Codes）中的税收规定等。此外，吉布提税务署（BODID）的官方公报细化了《税法通则》某些条款的条件，对其作出了补充。

在吉布提开展业务的实体需要支付以下关税及税费：

（1）契约登记费

契约登记费可以在公司存续期间随时产生，可以按固定金额、按比例或累进收取。固定费用1 000～4 000吉布提法郎（5～20美元）不等，取决于登记契约的性质。按比例收取则在2%～10%之间。

（2）印花税

所有民事、司法和法庭管辖以外的行为必须缴纳印花税，每页1 000吉布提法郎。

（3）所得税

经营第二年开始支付所得税，税率为应纳税利润的25%，可以延期支付。位于批准的管理中心和

---

① 来源：第28号法律。

营业额低于 8 000 万吉布提法郎（455 000 美元）（不包括增值税）的公司，可享受 20% 的减税优惠。利润不超过 120 000 吉布提法郎的公司免交所得税。

从 2017 年起，住所在吉布提境外但通过分公司在吉布提经营的外国公司必须对通过提高或降低买卖价格，或者任何其他措施（过多或无正当理由的费用、免息或低息贷款、销账等）产生的间接利润缴纳税款。这些利润必须计入该实体依一般纳税规则应纳税的利润中。

（4）预提税

根据不同业务类型，税率从 2.5% 至 10% 不等。不适用于自治公共机构，比如吉布提港口和机场，以及银行或金融、保险、电信机构和酒店等。

（5）一次性付清的最低税：税率为营业额的 1%，不包括增值税。根据《投资法》批准的所有公司都适用本项税收，但许可费用低于 120 000 吉布提法郎（约合 600 美元）的除外。本税种应当在超过根据专业利润计算的税额时支付，或者在亏损年度支付。

（6）土地税

根据应纳税建筑物以及商业或工业用非耕地的价值，税率分别为 10%、18% 和 25%。需要扣除 20% 的管理费、保险费、折旧费、维护和维修费。未开发土地的税率为 25%。

（7）增值税

增值税适用于所有交易，不包括与出口和国际空运、海运、陆运和客运相关的交易，根据外部融资公共合同获得的款项，或者社区住房、经济适用住房的开发商进口的货物和处置上述住房获得的收入。标准税率为 10%，但是，增值税的计算方法很复杂。税收部门编制的相关说明书，可在经济和财务部的网站获取。

（8）商品和服务税

商品和服务税适用于提供商品或服务，且年营业额不超过 2 000 万吉布提法郎或 1 000 万吉布提法郎的所有自然人或法人，不包括免收增值税的商品和服务，税率为 7%。水果和蔬菜销售、餐饮业、牛羊肉和鱼类销售的商品和服务税可降至 5%。

（9）国内消费税（ICT）

国内消费税适用于在吉布提进口并消费的所有商品（无论其原产地），以及通过陆运再出口至邻国的烟酒。三个主要国内消费税税率为 8%、20% 和 33%。除了这些税率外，某些产品还需要支付附加费，根据产品性质而定。

吉布提没有外汇管制，资本可以自由流通，无须进出口许可。

（九）投资优惠和保护

为了改善商业环境，吉布提政府委托专家委员会重新起草两份旧的法典：《民法典》和《民事诉讼法典》，这两份法典均在国家独立前制定，现已被废除。

政府希望制定现代的《民法典》和《民事诉讼法典》，以更好地适应经济现状，为投资者提供充分的保障。这两份法典的起草已进入最后阶段，据司法部介绍，专家将在 2018 年向政府提交草案报批。一旦通过，政府会将草案发送至国民议会进行审议，并有望在 2018 年年底前通过。

三、贸易

（一）外国公司贸易管制

根据吉布提《贸易法典》的规定，公司可以按照他们的意愿签订合同。公司成立后不需要授权即可开展活动。

原则上，在一般合同法方面，外国公司无须遵守任何特定程序，但必须遵守《合同法》（对所有合同）的基本规定，如合法性、书面同意、没有不公平条款或遵守特定的规则，如公司合同、担保合同或受管制合同的具体条款。

（二）政策和贸易法规

吉布提在外商投资、进出口方面没有歧视性政策，且除通常的海关申报外，对进口货物或原材料没有任何限制。进口货物申报必须由货物所有人、托运人或收货人作出，或者由海关官员作出。

进口禁令通常受吉布提缔结的国际公约约束。唯一明确禁止进口的产品是方向盘在右侧的汽车，以及不可生物降解的塑料包装袋。为健康缘故，某些产品的进口须经卫生部批准。

进口炸药或武器之类的产品须经主管机关事先批准。阿拉伯茶叶（khat）的进口及其市场营销皆受管制。

吉布提没有任何关于反倾销、反补贴或者保障措施的立法。

（三）政府采购

《政府采购法典》调整国家、公共行政机构、公共工商业机构、国有企业和国家占大多数股份的经济实体授予的金额超过500万吉布提法郎的合同。在吉布提，政府采购的管理机构是国家政府采购委员会（CNMP）。

吉布提对政府和社会资本合作（PPP）合同有具体管制，其规范了适用于这些合同的法律框架。这些管制定义和界定了起草、签署、授予与执行政府和社会资本合作合同的条件。

政府和社会资本合作的制度性框架置于共和国总统权威之下，并由国家政府和社会资本合作委员会监督，该委员会负责协助政府制定政策以及政府和社会资本合作战略。

该政策在国家层面上由一个独立的专门机构（PPP单位）实施。采购程序在政府采购管理局的控制下进行。财政部负责审查所提议项目的财政和预算的可持续性。行业监管机构仍然对其行业内的公司的活动负全部责任。

政府采购是一个商业机会，可以成为业务增长的加速器。代表着每年数百亿美元的生意。平均只有1/4的此等市场授予了吉布提公司[①]，这种情况主要是由两个因素造成的：

① 许多本地企业尤其是中小型企业对此等市场代表的机会缺乏了解；
② 缺乏相关的法律、法规环境。

面对这一情况，吉布提商会（CCD）在世界银行的支持下已经成立了一个商业支持项目，以便为吉布提公司进入公共市场提供更好的渠道。

第53号法律第12条包含《公共市场新法典》（CMP），并将政府采购定义如下："国家为执行工程或提供货物、服务而订立的合同。""国家"一词包括政府部门、公共行政机构、工商业性质的公共机构、国有企业和国家直接或间接拥有多数股份的半公共性公司，以及当地政府。所有这些实体都在"签约行政机构"法律条文中予以了列举。

在吉布提，有四项基本原则适用于政府采购：

- 通过公开招标程序所有公司获得的平等政府采购机会；
- 在采购程序、投标评估和合同授予方面平等地对待所有候选人；
- 采购、评估和合同执行程序透明；
- 公共资源利用的经济性和效率性。

《公共市场法典》区分了三种类型的市场：

- 供应与服务：供应与服务的政府采购是指向一家公司（供应商）采购货物、设备、机器和/或材料，或向供应商采购服务。
- 工程：公共工程合同由一个或多个建筑或民用工程承包商执行。
- 知识型服务：知识型服务（咨询服务）的公共合同与主要是知识性质的服务有关，即其主要元素无法量化。

吉布提有一个国家政府采购委员会（CNMP），控制和管制政府采购。2013年，该机构处理了72份公共合同，合同签发及执行总额达10 396 629 501吉布提法郎。

根据市场类型分类，其中：

---

① 来源：吉布提投资—吉布提商会。

- 39 份工程合同，总额达 8 407 696 300 吉布提法郎；
- 21 份供应合同，总额达 1 024 152 209 吉布提法郎；
- 12 份知识型服务合同，总额达 964 780 992 吉布提法郎。

公司需要对政府采购感兴趣，因为它们提供了商业机会，开发市场和使市场来源多样化，可以获得新的基准，建立新的伙伴关系，提高品牌知名度和公司的信誉，增强其能力以更具有竞争力。

在吉布提，政府采购过程参与者主要有：

- 捐助者，如世界银行、非洲开发银行（ADB）、伊斯兰开发银行（IDB）、欧洲联盟（EU）、法国开发署（AFD）、联合国联合署，等等。在吉布提几乎 80% 的政府采购都是通过官方开发援助由外部提供资金。这些捐助者有时使用他们特定的采购程序。
- 签约当局为技术部委：教育、健康、交通、农业、财政；工商业性质的公共机构：吉布提电力局、吉布提国家水务局、吉布提电信、港口管理、吉布提机场等部门；项目执行局：吉布提社会发展局（ADDS）；当地集体企事业单位。
- 企业：在以下活动领域的商品、服务和工程供应商：健康、教育、能源、运输、水、卫生、信息和通信技术、农村开发、环境、食品。

政府采购对所有感兴趣的当事人开放。

作为投标人，公司可以参与公共合同，以响应由缔约当局发出的招标邀请（AAO）。

为此，有两个要求：首先公司必须在《国家》（La Nation）报纸上找发布的与招标邀请相关的信息，然后响应市场的资格要求（行政、财务、经验、技术能力等）。

有几种方式可以参与：

- 联合：如果公司不完全符合市场的资格要求，它可以通过与另一家能互补的公司联合参与公共市场。要使联合小组具备资格，必须遵循某些条件：必须任命项目主要负责人；后者必须满足至少 40% 的资格标准。其他合作伙伴必须符合至少 25% 的资格标准。联合小组内的合作伙伴联合为一体。
- 分包：公司可以作为合同拥有者的分包商参与公共合同。分包条件为：分包不得超过合同的 30%，分包商的使用必须首先获得拥有合同的签约当局的同意。合同持有人对合同的履行继续负有全部责任。
- 协商市场：对于小型合同（少于 500 万美元），签约当局可以采用除公开招标以外的采购方法，如咨询供应商，或直接协商或互相协商。因此，进入这些较小的市场可以成为中小企业参与政府采购的途径。

四、劳动

（一）劳动法律、法规简介

根据吉布提《劳动法典》的规定，任何外国人都可以在吉布提从事受薪活动，而且没有固定的配额来限制公司可以招聘的外国雇员的数量。但是，有关规定要求只在吉布提没有能够胜任的雇员时，公司才可以招聘外国雇员。

希望雇用外国劳工的雇主必须获得国家劳动和职业培训局的工作许可。提交给国家劳动和职业培训局的申请及相关文件将在 60 天内审查。如果在此期间没有答复，视为已授予工作许可证。

《劳动法典》第 28 条赋予行政机关拒绝工作许可的自由裁量权。此等决定可以上诉到吉布提行政法院。

如果获得工作许可，雇主必须支付费用，其金额因所涉及的就业类别和雇员国籍的不同而不同。

《劳动法典》规定了获得临时工作许可证和居留证的条件。任何临时居留证的有效期不能超过 1 年，也不能超过旅行证件的有效期。

（二）工作许可的申请步骤[①]

要在当地工作，需要几种文件。

所需文件有：入境签证（首先，在吉布提国际机场签发的入境签证有效期为 1 个月，所有外国人都要付 10 000 吉布提法郎）；居留证，任何想在吉布提工作的外国人可以经提供以下文件，在境外获得居留证：4 张照片；至少 6 个月有效期的工作许可证复印件；护照复印件；给国家投资促进局的申请信。

对于没有工作许可证的合伙人或经理（非雇员），提供的文件如下：护照复印件、商业登记或执照、给国家投资促进局的申请信。

根据国籍收费：非洲 196 美元、亚洲 225 美元、欧洲 252 美元、美国 280 美元。

任何想在吉布提从事工作的外国劳工，必须先取得工作许可证。

在第一次申请中，提供的文件为：4 张照片，填写申请表，护照复印件，雇用合同，给国家投资促进局的申请信。

在续签的情况下，提供的文件包括：2 张照片，填写申请表，更新申请，工作许可证的原件和复印件，NIPA 申请信。

2011 年 12 月设立的最低工资标准为每月 200 美元。根据私营部门的估计，以下是一些职位标准的参考性工资。

2016 年工资示范

职位	货币	价值
高级总监	美元	1 200～2 000
资深人员	美元	800～1 500
工程师	美元	1 000～1 600
年轻毕业生	美元	500～1 200
行政助理	美元	400～500
合格者	美元	300～500
销售人员	美元	300～500
司机	美元	200～600
保安	美元	200～400
无技术工人	美元	200～250

（三）劳动合同的终止

根据《劳动法典》的规定，雇主必须提前 1 个月通知一般雇员和劳动者终止劳动合同，提前 3 个月通知主管、经理和其他类似岗位的人员终止劳动合同。雇主可以提出以下解除理由：

① 个人原因（例如雇员的健康状态）；

② 经济原因［包括由于技术变化而导致的职位的重大转变（《劳动法典》第 48 条）；在这种情况下，受影响的雇员在被解雇后的第一年内必须得到优先考虑再上岗的机会，并有资格获得补偿］；

③ 行为严重失当，即《劳动法典》第 59 条明确规定的九种情形之一，或公司规章中规定的任一情形；

④ 雇主还可以选择一个更具灵活性的解除理由，即公司可以选择技术性解雇，一次解雇 3 个月，然后可再延长一次（《劳动法典》第 41 条）。在此种情况下，雇主只需支付最小补偿，但因此遭解雇的员工在遭解雇后的第一年应优先得到考虑给予再就业的机会。

根据公司的规模，无正当理由终止合同而产生的损害赔偿和利息可以为 2 个月至 6 个月的工资，特殊情况适用于不经劳动监察机构批准即可解雇的员工代表。在这种情况下，雇主必须支付 12 个月的

---

① 来源：djiboutinvest.com。

工资。然而，如果用来解雇的理由是真实和严重的理由，即使未遵守通常的通知形式，劳动法庭也可以要求雇主仅支付不超过 1 个月工资的赔偿（《劳动法典》第 55 条）。

五、知识产权[①]

吉布提工业和商业产权局（ODPIC）和版权局共同承担保护知识产权的责任，这些机构都是具有法律和财政自主权的公共机构。

前述机构的任务包括打击工业产权侵权，包括假冒和不正当竞争，以及在吉布提，保障和促进工业产权的保护和使用。

法院可以采取的措施包括没收非法获得的侵犯版权的产品、没收假冒商品和支付损害赔偿（对违反版权法的受害者的赔偿）。

实践中，有关部门的执法能力在工业和商业产权领域是非常有效和成熟的，但在版权和相关权利方面有时有局限性，原因在于资源有限、法官和法律从业者缺乏经验以及公众缺乏对知识产权的保护意识。

根据吉布提法律，工业产权的保护涉及专利、集成电路布图设计、工业设计、商标、产品或服务、商号、地理标志和原产地名称以及反不正当竞争。

工业产权从最广泛意义上加以理解，不仅适用于工业、贸易和服务领域，也适用于农业和采矿业的所有生产以及所有产品制造领域。

加入保护工业产权国际联盟的每一个国家的国民，应当享有本法规定的工业产权保护，但必须符合其规定的条件和形式。

加入吉布提参加的工业产权领域的其他条约的缔约国的国民应当享有同等保护，并在条约中规定给予此等国家国民不低于此等国家的国民待遇。

居住在吉布提的任何自然人或法人都可以申请工业产权，以及随后与之有关的任何交易，或为此目的委派一名在吉布提有住所或其注册办事处在吉布提的代理人。

工业产权所有人的代理人可以提出一个或多个备案或注册申请，或者提出委托人现在或未来的所有备案和登记，但委托人授权有例外规定的除外。

不是保护工业产权国际联盟成员的国家的国民，如果他们的住所地在联盟国家的领土范围内，或他们在联盟国家领土范围内有有效和严肃的工业或商业活动，也可以享有该法规定的权益。

申请人或其受益人在保护工业产权国际联盟的其中一个国家提出发明专利（第一次申请）、关于主专利的增补证书、工业设计或商标、产品、贸易或服务有关的申请，在吉布提提出上述申请时（随后的申请），在法律规定的期间内享有优先权。

事实上，对于专利、主专利的增补证书和集成电路布图设计，上述提及的优先权期限为 12 个月，对于工业设计和商标、产品或服务，优先权期限为 6 个月。期间从在保护工业产权国际联盟的其中一个国家第一次提交申请之日开始计算，因为申请之日并不及时。

任何人希望在保护工业产权国际联盟的其中一个国家获得较早的优先申请需要作出书面的优先声明，写明日期、编号（如果在吉布提申请的时候已经知道），以及提出申请的原有国。如果在吉布提提出申请时不知道优先申请编号，则申请人应尽快提供。

优先声明应在向吉布提提交申请的日期提交。在提交申请之日起 3 个月内，申请人必须根据法律规定的条件，提供文件证明先前的申请正当。

一个专利申请可以提出多个优先权，即使它们来自不同的国家。在适当的情况下，可以就同一个权利要求提出多个优先权。

如果提出多个优先权，相关截止日期从最早的优先权日期起算。

任何发明都可以成为吉布提工业和商业产权局授予专利的对象。专利权在法律规定的条件和限度内，属于发明人或者他的继承人。

保护的发明工业产权有：

---

① 来源：第 50 号法律关于工业产权的保护。

① 专利，从专利申请之日起享受 20 年的保护期；

② 增补证书，是发明的附属权利，附属于至少一个主专利要求。此等证书的有效期应自其申请之日起算，到其所附的主专利期限届满为止。

吉布提《工业产权法》第 23 条规定，如果一项发明不在现有技术之列，即被认为是新的发明。

如果对于一个精通技术的人来说，某项发明并不能清晰地从现有技术中推导出来，该项发明即视为具有创造性。

现有技术包括在向吉布提交申请之日或在国外提交具有有效优先权的专利申请之前，世界上任何地方的公众通过书面或口头描述、使用或以其他方式可能获得的一切技术。

在吉布提交专利申请或国际申请的内容，如果此等申请日期在上述提及的日期之前，也应被认为包含在现有技术之内，即使此等内容只在该日期或在该日期之后公布。

根据法律规定，下列事项不属于发明：发现；自然界存在的实体、物质和组织及其组成部分或成分；科学理论和数学方法；处于不同组成与发展阶段的人体和构成人体的物质及其成分，包括基因序列或部分序列；植物或动物生产的基本生物进程；文学艺术作品或任何其他美学创作、计划、原则；在智力活动、游戏或经济活动中使用的方法；计算机程序、信息展示。

同样，以下事项也不能申请专利：

除了微生物以外的动植物，为了治疗人类或动物疾病的诊断、理疗和手术方法，进行商业开发或实施会违背公共秩序或道德的发明，或者危害人类、动物、植物健康或环境的发明。

六、环境保护

（一）环境保护监管部门

法律来源：《关于设立国家可持续发展委员会的法令》。

国家可持续发展委员会（NCSD）是环境保护的监管部门。

（二）环境保护法律、法规简介

法律来源：《关于环境影响评估程序规定的法令》。

从前吉布提没有环境立法。当时，该国环境遭遇到了一些公司导致的各种破坏，且在 1997 年时污染严重。国家委托进行了一项研究，评估石油公司造成污染的损害程度，而该研究结果促使国家采取措施补救这一领域的立法空白，于 2009 年制定了《环境法典》。

吉布提《环境法典》将环境保护视为国家最高利益。《环境法典》规定了国家生物多样性的原则、所有公民皆可以接受环境教育、管理国家环境和保护吉布提动植物的措施。在吉布提境内经营的所有公司必须遵守该法律，否则将面临刑事处罚。

吉布提政府已制定了一项法律，根据管理和保护环境以抵制一切形式的环境退化或恶化、保护环境资源以确保可持续发展这一根本原则，制定了国家环境保护和管理政策的目标。

为可持续发展而管理和保护环境的根本原则如下：

① 参与原则。环境保护是国家的最高利益，涉及所有公民的集体责任，要求所有人参与环境政策的制定。

② 一体化原则。环境保护和良好的环境管理是国家经济、社会和文化发展政策不可或缺的组成部分，当开发和使用土地时，应考虑环境保护和生态平衡。

③ 污染者负担原则。关于实现和管理经济社会项目以及服务，有效实施使用者负担和污染者负担原则；因环境破坏而产生的任何损坏，都涉及必须确保环境修复的责任方的直接或间接责任。

④ 预防原则。为了保护环境，各国必须根据各自的能力采取预防措施。

⑤ 合作原则。在制定发展计划和项目以及环境立法方面遵守国际环境协定。

环境管理和保护领域的行动是在环境部根据国家环境政策事先批准的情况下进行的。

任何希望在吉布提开展业务的组织、公司或投资者必须了解，所有通过改变其物理、化学、生物或细菌学特征可能导致或增加水资源退化的泄漏、排放、直接或间接沉淀，无论是领水范围内的地表水、地下水或海水，都是禁止的。此外，向领海排放压载水也是禁止的。

政府已经制定特别措施保护特殊领域。环境、卫生、水资源、海洋事务和渔业部负责评估观察到的污染水平以及任何可能加剧环境资源恶化的情况。

任何超过标准的液体排放和任何可能引起或增加水污染的沉淀都是禁止的。拒绝的条件、分析的条件及排放的控制由监管措施规定。

任何液体的排放，即使低于标准，在具有环境破坏风险的情况下，也可能引起时间和空间上有限制的禁令。环境、卫生、水资源、海洋事务和渔业部在进行环境审计后，可以解除这一禁令，但需要从该部门获得适当形式的证书。

任何拥有包含危险或有毒物质的船舶、航空器或海洋设施的投资者或公司，都应当立即采取适当的预防措施，严防发生与海洋环境有关的危急情况。投资者必须尽快向环境和海洋部门通报这些物质的性质及预防污染的措施，如其不履行该义务，国家当局可采取必要措施，费用由此等所有者支付。

对于投资者来说，应该注意的是，吉布提《环境法典》主要适用于任何自然人经营或拥有的、公共或私人的工厂、车间、仓库、采石场和一般工业、工艺或商业设施，以及可能对健康、安全、公共卫生、农业、自然环境造成危害或不便，或者给邻里造成不利或不便的所有其他活动。

工业设施分为两类，根据其运行可能造成的危害严重程度确定，它们必须经过批准或申报。

第一类包括运行会带来严重危险和不便的设施。这类设施的运行只有在环境部长批准、已经采取具体措施预防此等危险或不便时，才允许进行。

第二类包括不构成任何严重危险或危害的设施，必须遵守负责环境事务的部长所制定的一般规定。此类设施必须申报。

七、争议解决

吉布提是1958年《承认及执行外国仲裁裁决公约》的缔约国。

外国判决和外国仲裁裁决要在吉布提执行，必须得到吉布提初审法院的执行令。吉布提初审法院院长根据以下条件发放执行令：

① 外国判决或仲裁裁决，是由一个根据吉布提接受的冲突法规则确定的有管辖权的法院作出的；
② 外国判决或仲裁裁决具有既判力，并且在作出裁判的司法管辖范围内可以强制执行；
③ 案件当事人皆已经正当传唤、代表出席或被宣布缺席；而且该判决不违反吉布提法律意义上的公共秩序，也不违反任何具有既判力的吉布提的司法决定。

任何希望获得执行令的当事人必须向吉布提初审法院院长提交经过认证的外国判决的法语翻译件，或在仲裁的情况下，经过认证的仲裁裁决和仲裁协议的法语翻译件。

在吉布提，法院一般支持仲裁。当合同中有仲裁条款时，当地法院会宣布其无权处理该案，并告知当事人去仲裁。尽管存在仲裁条款，吉布提初审法院院长仍可裁定采取临时措施。

实际上，在将案件交给仲裁员之前，而且在特殊情况下，如果需要紧急采取临时措施和保全措施而仲裁员无法及时作出裁决的，当事人可以向有权司法机关要求采取此等措施（包括在请求之日临时查封债务人位于吉布提的财产）。

吉布提法院一般认可国内仲裁裁决，前提是此等裁决是根据应适用的规则作出的。然而，仲裁裁决可能被有管辖权的地方法院撤销，如果：

① 该裁决是在没有仲裁协议或仲裁协议无效或失效的情况下作出的；
② 仲裁庭的组成不符合规则，或独任仲裁员的任命不符合规则；
③ 仲裁庭违反职责作出裁定；
④ 对抗原则没有得到尊重，或抗辩权受到侵害；
⑤ 裁决的救济违背国际公共政策；
⑥ 仲裁裁决不合理。

八、其他

反商业贿赂[①]：

法律来源：2013年7月16日第3号法律——制定预防和反腐败立法。

第3号法律通过补充相关预防和反腐败的立法规定，创设了国家预防和反腐败委员会。

国家预防和反腐败委员会的职责如下：

① 预防、打击和根除一切形式的腐败；
② 强化预防和打击腐败的法律、行政和其他手段；
③ 进行调查、研究和问卷调查，以了解腐败现象产生的原因和程度；
④ 制定和提出有效打击腐败的政策和策略；
⑤ 教育公共机构、私人部门和公民社会警惕腐败的负面影响；
⑥ 定期评估相关法律文件和行政措施；
⑦ 促进和协调其他监督机构、国际组织、民间组织和私人部门参与打击腐败；
⑧ 促进和支持在预防、侦查和起诉腐败（包括资产追回）方面的国际合作；
⑨ 接受资产申报并在官方公告上公布。

---

① 来源：anticorruption.dj。

Djibouti

Authors: Ayman Said
Translators: Raymond Wu, Eric J. Jiang

I. Overview

The Republic of Djibouti, former French colony now independent, is an ethnic brewing ground of different population. Its dry climate and arid land make it a country very limited in natural resources. However the economy of Djibouti has grown around the service and trade industry. Indeed, the country has been able to take advantage of its geostrategic position in the Horn of Africa at the crossroads of the three continents, European, African and Asian. Today, Djibouti is home to the largest French military base in Africa, an equally important US military base and many other military contients (German, Italian, etc.). The presence of these military base and the political stability of Djibouti make it a secure financial place for foreign investors to invest in the East African region by ensuring 100% ownership of foreign funds. Moreover, having one of the most important port sector in the region, Djibouti is a center of goods and logistics hub for all countries of East Africa.

Nearly 20% of the population of the Republic of Djibouti lives below the poverty line. The climate and the aridity of the region make Djibouti a land of little fertility with an impossibility of food self-sufficiency. Indeed, the country is totally dependent on the import of foodstuffs. However, taking advantage of its privileged geostrategic position, the country maintains stable economic growth with about 3. 1% annual growth since the early 2000s and, according to the World Bank, around 7% since 2014. This growth is largely favored by massive investments in the port area. [1]

II. Investment

A. Market Access

According to the World Trade Organization, Djibouti has a trade-to-GDP ratio of 59,17%. Access to Djiboutian market is granted for all foreign companies with same requirements as for local companies. Djibouti has a free trade regime and unrestricted banking and commercial sector. The country has established and investment code that grant many advantages to companies regarding taxes. Djibouti has also established several free zones areas where international companies can settle with limited cost and no corporate taxes.

a. Department Supervising Investment

a) The National Investment Promotion Agency(NIPA)
Legal source: Law No. 114 of 21 January 2001.

The National Agency for the Promotion of Investment[2], is a public limited company. the State is represented in the ANPI by the Ministry of Presidential Affairs, in charge of the Promotion of Investments.

The National Investment Promotion Agency is in the heart of social and economic system of the country since its establishment in 2001. It encourages the promotion of investment in Djibouti through a policy of flexibility in investment operations, a modern regulatory framework and procedures. As part of the investment promotion and development of knowledge of the Djiboutian territory, NIPA is responsible for putting forward the incentive environment of the Republic of Djibouti and investment opportunities.

Its mission is to provide a full advice and support for new or existing local and foreign promoters. The National Investment Promotion Agency is a strong partner and representative of the private sector at governmental level.

Its purpose is to create synergies between all these actors and to provide them with a common platform for the promotion of Djibouti to investors, the facilitation of investment operations and the modernization of the regulatory framework and procedures.

The senior official took the opportunity to reiterate the reasons for the one-stop shop. He also returned to the

---

[1] Source : World Bank data.
[2] Source : Djiboutiinvest. com.

division of roles between the occupants of the premises. Several infos are to retain detailed explanations of Mr. Mahdi Darar Obsieh.

First, the establishment of the single window is the prerogatives of the ANPI. Which is the national authority empowered to make diagnoses, provide technical guidance, and advocate for the development of a private sector, strong and profitable in the Republic of Djibouti. These are just some of the missions that fairly summarize the value of opening up its capital to private operators up to 49%. This is a guarantee of good governance, and trust between the decision-making spheres of the public and private sectors.

Secondly, the physical architecture of the one-stop shop has been designed to allow investors, both national and foreign, legal entities and individuals to perform in one place, at a reduced cost and in a minimum period of time. formalities and declarations to which they are required to comply.

To this end, the building houses women and men from the respective ranks of ANPI and different partner institutions.

In addition, a senior officer of the ODPIC carries out the registration and protection of intellectual and commercial properties and registration in the commercial and companies register. It is up to the representative of the tax hotel to ratify the tax registration of the companies in formation, the registration of deeds, and the subscription to the business license. Thus, the social registration tasks of companies are filled by an agent of the National Social Security Fund (CNSS). His counterpart of the National Employment Agency and Vocational Training (ANEFIP) is called upon to issue work permits for expatriates subject to the proven lack of Djiboutian applicants corresponding to the profiles of the qualifications sought by the outfitters. jobs. Likewise, a national police officer is in charge of regularizing foreign workers and issuing residence permits.

In addition, the DATUH, the domains and the land conservation, the National Printing, the Post office, the EDD, the ONEAD and Djibouti Télécom dispatch to the one-stop shop of the professionals supposed to facilitate the access to the subscriptions and the services which they offer.

Significant detail: the Chamber of Commerce and the Economic Development Fund of Djibouti will have information and guidance centers.

An electronic link will be established for better coordination and follow-up between the Commercial Court (Registry of the Tribunal) and the Single Window. This uploading by interface is essential in order to guarantee the legal protection of the investors. With this in mind, the ANPI took the lead in forging ties of collaboration with local notaries and lawyers.

If investors wish to free themselves from the administrative procedures with the single window, they can entrust to the skills of the ANPI the preparation, the drafting, and the personalized follow-up of their files. Following a diagnosis of the entrepreneurs› situation, ANPI directs them to consulting professionals when needed and provides them with information documents on regulated activities, social status, the tax system, etc.

In short, the ANPI deals with all the issues in close consultation with the delegates mandated by the partner organizations, while remaining the sole interlocutor of the investors. This is to say that the single window is an asset of readability in the improvement of the Djiboutian business environment.

b) The Djibouti Ports & Free Zones Authority (DPFZA)

The DPFZA[1] is the governing authority that sets the rules, directives and overarching principles for the smooth and efficient running of the current, and any future ports and free zones, in Djibouti. It is also responsible for the enforcement and implementation of these principles and directives at every free zone in the country.

DPFZA is the sole authority in charge of the administration and the control of all the free zones and ports in Djibouti. The entity also plays an instrumental role as the sole interface between the free zone companies and any other governmental bodies and comes under the direct authority of the Djibouti Presidential Office.

DPFZA holds several mandates, among them, the Promotion the Djibouti Ports & Free Zones as a commercial and logistic platform, the establishment of a business friendly environment with a business oriented legal framework, the regulation of the ports through its Board of Directors, the creation of new Ports and Free Zones in Djibouti.

c) Djibouti Free Zone (DFZ)

Legal source : Law No. 53 / AN / 04 / 5eme L aiming the Free Zone Code dated 2004; Law No. 103 / AN / 05 / 5eme L regulating Free Zone Companies dated 2005.

Djibouti has created a good business environment for investment and trade, Djibouti Free Zone (DFZ) [2]in operation since October 2004, positions Djibouti as the regional logistics, trade and marketing hub for the import, warehousing, processing and re-export of goods to and from the eastern African countries.

---

[1] Source : dpfza. gov. dj.
[2] Source : dpfza. gov. dj.

DFZ is developed over 40 hectares near the Port and the Airport. It comprises warehouses of 614 meters square and 1340 meters square with integrated office units, land plots serviced with utilities ranging from 2000 meters square to 15000 meters square, light industrial units of 510 meters square with integrated office units, office units for operations and hangar of 9100 meters square designated to accommodate aid cargo.

The Package of fiscal & non fiscal incentives for foreign investors is the guarantee of 100% of foreign ownership, a free repatriation of capital and profits, an exemption of corporate tax for all companies operating in the free zone, an exemption of income tax, a flexibility for the employment of foreigners, a possibility to sell on local market and no currency restriction.

b. Laws and Regulations of Investment Industry

Investment Code[1]:

Legal source : Law N° 58 / 94 / 3e L of 16th october 1994 modifying law N° 88 / AN / 1e of 13th february 1984 on the Investment Code of Djibouti.

Adopted in 1984 first then completed in 1994, the investment code was amended in 1994 to meet the new needs of the national economy. It provides for certain activities several tax benefits, exemption from patent for a period of 5 to 10 years, exemption from income tax (for natural and legal persons), exemption of the Internal Consumption Tax (TIC) on the materials necessary for the realization of their investment programs and on the raw materials during 5 years.

c. Forms of Investment

The activities benefiting from the benefits of the Investment Code are as follows:

For the "Regime A", which require a minimum investment amount of 5 million Djibouti francs : all activities related to exploitation, repair or processing of products of plant or animal origin, offshore and offshore fishing, preparation, freezing, processing or storage of seafood, mining, processing or training industry for mining and metals products, research, exploitation or storage of any energy source and refining of hydrocarbons, the creation, operation, modernization or extension of the mechanical, electrical, electronic, chemical and shipbuilding industries, land, sea and air transport, port and airport activities, construction, repair and maintenance of shipping or fishing vessels, manufacture or on-site packaging of products or consumer goods, banking or credit activities that promote new investments, consultancy services, engineering, computer data processing host telematics databases.

For the "Regime B" which require a minimum investment amount 50 millions Djibouti francs.

This scheme extends the scope of Plan A to the all activities related to the construction of buildings for exclusively industrial, commercial or tourist use, the construction of social housing, the construction, creation and operation of educational and training establishments.

As part of the promotion of exports, Djibouti has created free zones that allow investors to benefit from tax benefits and flexible labor legislation.

d. Limitation of Market Access and Investment

Djibouti law does not, in principle, provide for any limitation on foreign investment. Article 1 of the Investment Code states that anyone, regardless of their nationality, is free to invest in or undertake an economic activity in Djibouti. There is also no legal or regulatory requirement for a joint venture with a national for foreign investment. However, certain regulated activities such as banking, insurance, mining, petroleum, medical and pharmaceutical, and the liberal professions are subject to the prior authorization of a specific license or administrative authorization from a competent administrative authority, which means these activities are, in practice, reserved for Djiboutian nationals.

There is no requirement for a director or manager of a local company to be a national or a resident in Djibouti. However, it is advantageous that some directors reside in Djibouti to facilitate management. There are no minimum qualifications (academic or professional) required to be a director of a Djiboutian trading company except for a company engaged in banking activities.

There is no specific legislation relating to change of control restrictions or the acquisition of shares in Djibouti. However, in strategic sectors such as ports, airports, railways, mining and energy, there is a standard clause in a PPP agreement, that establishes the obligation to notify or obtain prior authorization of the Djiboutian government, before any change of control.

B. Foreign Exchange Regulation

The national currency of Djibouti is the Djibouti franc, which is indexed to the US dollar by a fixed exchange

---

[1] Djibout Chamber of Commerce - www. ccd. dj.

rate of 1 USD = 177,721 DJF. The Monetary authority is the Central Bank of Djibouti (BND) which has been created the 3th of December 1977. The currency of the foreign exchange reserve is the US Dollar. The Djibouti franc is freely convertible.

The Central Bank of Djibouti does not do neither refinancing of commercial banks nor exchange control. The coverage of issue of the currency is beyond 100% of the fiduciary money by the Central Bank.

Second-tier banks are required to hold convertible currency hedges commensurate with their deposits in the national currency. External assets, mainly deposits, are hedged in US Dollar.

The Central Bank Djibouti pays dividends to the National Treasury of Djibouti. The Central Bank does not tax financial income, it does not pay income taxes on profits nor taxes on foreign exchange transactions.

a. Department Supervising Foreign Exchange[1]

The Central Bank of Djibouti is the supervisory authority responsible for managing the currency of Djibouti, the country's foreign exchange position, the national accounting. The Central Bank is monitoring complicance with prudential rules. No Mandatory reservations nor deposit insurance.

Djibouti does not have active capital markets or fixed rate instruments.

The Central Bank of Djibouti is the institution empowered to make all provisions concerning the rates and conditions of transactions carried out by credit institutions with their customers. It may set the interest rates and maximum and minimum fees that credit institutions are allowed to levy on their loans, advances and other credit transactions, as well as the maximum and minimum interest rates that they are allowed to pay on their different categories of commitments.

The Central Bank of Djibouti may adopt rules relating to the volume and nature of the uses and resources of credit institutions and prescribe minimum or maximum ratios between the various elements thereof. It may also, by order, determine the conditions under which credit institutions are authorized to hold shareholdings or to dispose of any part of their assets, liabilities or off-balance sheet commitments.

Any acquisition or transfer of any part of their assets, liabilities or off-balance sheet commitments, which would be carried out by a credit institution in violation of the law is null and void.

When a credit institution is no longer able to comply with prudential standards or is experiencing a serious cash-flow crisis, the Central Bank of Djibouti may require legal or natural persons, shareholders or members of that institution to provide it with the support it needs. it is necessary for him.

b. Brief Introduction of Laws and Regulations of Foreign Exchange

Legal sources : Law 91 / AN / 05 related to the Central Bank of Djibouti and Law 92 / AN / 05 governing the opening, activities, and functioning of credit institutions.

In order to establish and engage in an activity in the financial sector, commercial banks must obtain prior agreement[2]. It is possible to possess up to 30% of the shares of a credit institution or engage in refinancing in currencies from an international bank subject to the national standards and norms established by the Central Bank. The minimum capital amount for financial and banking institutions, or minimum endowment in capital for branch and agency establishments which are headquartered abroad, is fixed at one billion francs.

All economic actors, whether residing in Djibouti or not, are entitled to open an account. The possibility to make transfers everywhere in the world thanks to an adequate regulation constitutes one of the advantages of Djibouti.

c. Foreign Exchange Restrictions for Foreign Enterprises [3]

Owing to a strict application of international regulatory provisions and prudent standards, Djibouti's financial sector provides reliable banking system, backed by major banking groups, and benefitting from free capital flows. The importance of the banking sector can also be attributed to the absence of exchange restrictions to local and foreign companies and to the stability of the Djiboutian Franc, the national currency. In fact, Djiboutian banks have attracted substantial foreign deposits in Djibouti.

In a context marked by the growth of the national economy, the acceleration of money supply has continued in 2016. This development is mainly due to the growth of total credit granted to the public and the private sector.

Besides the Central Bank of Djibouti, the country's financial sector includes 12 deposit and credit institutions.

New banks have also been included in the list approved by the Central Bank. Djibouti disposes of a stable financial sector with a market that goes beyond borders. However, the country still lacks specialised banking service providers that respond to the increasing demand of the local population and businesses. Authorities

---

[1] Source : Central Bank of Djibouti.
[2] Source : Djiboutinvest. com.
[3] Source : Djiboutinvest. com.

encourage the private sector to invest in the following:
- (i) Establishment of more facilities and customer oriented banks;
- (ii) Establishment of investment banks that provide funds to priority sectors namely in agriculture and industry;
- (iii) Private and local partnerships to develop the microcredit and microfinance sector;
- (iv) Mutual fund agencies.

C. Financing and Banking

a. Overview of the Financial Sector[1]

The financial sector grew rapidly between 2006 and 2010 with the arrival of new banks. In 2012, Djibouti now has eleven establishments against two in 2006. However, the sector remains very concentrated with two banks gathering 85% of assets.

The activity accounted for 13% of GDP in 2012. The introduction of Islamic finance instruments by new Yemeni and Somali banks, as well as the opening of accounts for small savers, pensioners, retirees and self-employed persons, enabled to drain savings that previously escaped the traditional banking sector.

The establishment of new establishments in the Djiboutian market has led to a fall in interest rates as a result of increased competition. However, they remain relatively high averaging around 12% for unsecured loans, 15% for overdrafts and 10% for home loans.

The credits granted are mainly short-term or consumer credits. Although long-term loans with 15-year maturities are beginning to be offered, they remain marginal, as are medium-term loans. The analysis conducted by the IMF shows a healthy and very liquid sector, but nevertheless points to vulnerabilities.

The rapid growth of credit in recent years, due to the emergence of new institutions and the increasing exposure of their portfolio to the real estate sector, could lead to a deterioration in the quality of the banks' portfolio.

In this context, the Central Bank is continuing work to strengthen banking supervision initiated under the auspices of the IMF. In 2012, efforts focused on the promulgation of regulatory texts stemming from the banking law adopted the previous year.

The new instructions and circulars dealt with the procedures for applying for authorization of credit institutions, transmissions of the periodic statements of banks and their annual internal control report.

Supervision and supervision missions in credit institutions have been intensified. In addition, memoranda of cooperation with foreign central banks have been signed to ensure better oversight of foreign bank subsidiaries in Djibouti.

Finally, the country's largest micro-finance fund encountered difficulties during the year and was placed under the administration of the Central Bank, which oversees reform and capacity-building work.

b. Main Financial Institutions

Djibouti have two kind of financial institutions : Retail banks and Islamic banks. All banks are recorded within the Centrak Bank of Djibouti. Following are the information collected for each bank.[2]

Operating as retails banks we have : the "Banque de Dépôts et de Crédits" (BDCD), The Bank of Africa Mer Rouge, The Bank pour le Commerce et l'Industrie Mer Rouge, the Commercial Bank of Djibouti (CBD), The Exim Bank, the Cooperative and agricultural Credit international Bank (CAC Bank), the ICB-International Commercial Bank and the SBI - Silk Road International Bank.

Operating as Islamic banks we have : The East Africa Bank (EAB), the Saba Islamic Bank, and the Salaam African Bank (SAB).

c. Financing Conditions for Foreign Enterprises

There are no restrictions on the purposes for which money can be lent. However, money cannot be part of the proceeds of crime and cannot be used for criminal purposes or for purposes related to crime (e. g. terrorism or money laundering), according to Law No. 196 of 29 December 2002.

All local entities are free to enter into loan agreements with non-resident entities subject to the prior approval of the board of directors and the approval of the general meeting of shareholders. Loan agreements should, among other things, specify the identity of the parties, the loan amount, interest rate (unless the loan is free of charge) and the repayment schedule.

Djiboutian legislation provides for collateral on a wide range of assets. Real security applies to all the conventional and legal guarantees taken on the movable and immovable property of a debtor. Personal collateral

---

[1] Source : Africaeconomicoutlook. com.
[2] Source : data collected from Central Bank of Djibouti - banque-centrale. dj.

is when collateral is not taken from a debtor's property, but is provided by individuals, eg for a simple deposit or surety bond.

Securities may be of a conventional nature and / or of a judicial nature, and are governed by a mix of Djiboutian and colonial-era French civil law. These include personal security (such as bonds and autonomous guarantees) security interests relating to movable property and / or real estate.

Security can be taken on intangible property (shares of a company, goodwill, debts held on behalf of a debtor, bank accounts and intellectual property of a debtor) and or on tangible property (professional materials, stocks, commercial assets).

Security interests include rights of retention, pledge, non-possessory pledges and liens. Certain security rights must be entered in the Trade and Companies Register. Mortgage deeds (notarial and judicial) must be registered by the property owner.

A creditor may apply to the President of the Court of First Instance to be authorised by a court order to obtain security in the form of a protective attachment and / or attachment on the property and movable rights of the defaulting debtor, as collateral and security for the recovery of the debts.

D. Land Policy

Land can be acquired by natural or legal persons, whether Djiboutian or foreign. There is no legal restriction or prohibition. Djibouti's constitution guarantees and protects the right of ownership for all persons without distinction, including foreigners legally established in the territory. Access to property is a fundamental and non-discriminatory right.

Land ownership is regulated by five pieces of legislation, commonly known as the "Code Foncier", which govern various transactions relating to property and expropriation. None of these laws prohibit a natural person or legal person of foreign nationality from acquiring property (either on built and undeveloped land). Foreign investors (commercial entities) can freely acquire ownership of real estate for commercial, industrial and / or residential purposes, and they enjoy all of the same rights over the land as a Djiboutian national. Three types of tenure systems are identified according to the standing of the tenure holder and / or the nature of the relationship established over the land.

a. Land Belonging to the Public Domain

All property in Djibouti as part of the public domain, whether or not assigned to public use.

Public domain land can be made available to a national and foreign private entity, either in the form of an emphyteutic lease and / or in the form of a concession, commonly granted in Public Private Partnerships (PPP). An emphyteutic lease cannot exceed 99 years and a concession cannot exceed 18 years. A foreign investor holding an emphyteutic lease on public or private land can grant a mortgage as security in favour of his creditor.

b. Land Constituting the Private Domain of the State

This includes unowned and unoccupied land, and land acquired by the state or from donations, inheritances or other legal means. Vacant and unmanaged land, and in general all unregistered or undeveloped land can, before being registered in the name of the state, be the subject of a temporary occupation permit, in the case of urban land for construction purposes, or an authorisation to operate in the case of agricultural land, or, after registration in the name of the state, be sold by mutual agreement or public tender if it is urban land for construction use; be granted on an interim basis in the case of urban land for industrial or agricultural use or rural land; or be assigned free of charge to public institutions.

c. Land Ownership

Law No. 177 / AN / 91 / 2eL of 10 October 1991 governs land ownership. This establishes a so-called land conservation service, which guarantees the title of property owners by registering the ownership of land and property. Registration is mandatory and final. Any land registered in the name of a private person may be subject to land transactions such as assignment or donation. These transactions must be prepared, signed and recorded in the land register by a notary.

d. Land Registration Procedure[1]

Article 58 of the Djibouti Land Code enonciates a list of persons that may require the registration of immovables on land books. The list comprise the owner, even if his capacity is restricted to administrative acts only, the co-owner responsible for the administration of the undivided building or the consent of the other rights holders, the owner of one of the real rights enumerated in article 19 of the Land Code (for more information on this

---

[1] Source : Loi n°177/AN/91/2ème L du 10 octobre 1991.

subject, refer to the law No. 177 / AN / 91 / 2nd L of October 10, 1991 on the land organization of Djibouti), other than the owner, the tutor, administrator or curator of an incapable person having one of the above qualities.

In all other cases, the costs of proceedings are, unless otherwise agreed, borne by the applicant, subject to repetition with regard to the legal representatives of the incapable.

The creditor pursuing the appropriation of a building may also require registration when the court ordered the completion of this formality prior to the tender.

Only built or undeveloped land is eligible for registration on the land books.

A special request shall be made for each property belonging to a single owner or to several undivided co-owners, and composed of one or more parcels provided that such parcels are contiguous.

Prior to any application for registration, the boundaries of the immovable fenced must be determined by the care of the owner, by means of stone, masonry or concrete markers planted at each of the vertices of the polygon formed by the land.

Any registration applicant must submit to the Registrar of Property landlord, who gives him a receipt, a statement in French signed by him or a special agent and containing the following informations: his surname, first names, quality and domicile, and civil status, an address for service in a locality of the judicial jurisdiction in which the building to be registered, the description of the building, as well as the constructions and plantations found there, with an indication of its location, capacity, limitations, ins and outs, and, where appropriate, the name under which he is known, the estimate of its rental value or of the income of which it is susceptible, the estimate of its market value, with a reminder of the selling prices of which it has been the object in the last ten years, or the last only, if this sale goes back more than ten years, the details of the real rights and leases of more than three years relating to the building, mentioning the surnames, forenames and domicile of the beneficiaries and, where applicable, those of the subrogated guardian of the minors or interdicts of which he may have guardianship, requisition to the Registrar of Landed Property to proceed with the registration of the described building.

E. The Establishment and Dissolution of Companies[①]

a. The Forms of Enterprises

The Djiboutian lawful environment is favorable to the businesses. You can create your company in Djibouti whatever your nationality or your place of residence is.

The registration of your company in Djibouti can be done within three days. Foreign investor does not need a Djiboutian partner to start a business in Djibouti.

You can use our One Stop Shop services or create the status (legal structure) of your company with a notary or lawyer of the private sector. All steps required to start a business are of course undertaken by the One Stop Shop of NIPA.

In the Republic of Djibouti, the most current types of companies that we find is the Limited Liability Company (LLC), the Limited Company (S. A.), the Limited Liability Single Member (shareholder) Company (EURL in french).

b. The Procedure of Establishment

In order to establish in the local territory, a company must follow several steps:

(i) First of all the new company must deliver required information for the article of association (identity cards of associates, repartition of associates'shares, company'name, company'purpose, company'address).

(ii) Then the Company needs to register to the Company registration file. Documents should be submitted such as article of association Project, reservation of comercial name, bank statements.

(iii) The Company should then proceed to the registration at the register of commerce. For this purpose, it should provide : registration form, Article of association and bank statement, criminal record of associates and manager, comercial name certificate, fees, register of commerce and comercial name.

(iv) The company goes then for the fiscal registration of article of association and commercial lease. The documents required are : Article of association (4 copies), and the declaration of conformity, the main Bank statement, the Company should pay fees for the registration, fixed part:depends of the amount of the capital of the company regardless of is its legal from, and stamps' fees for about 1000 Djibouti francs / statute page including enclosures.

(v) Once all these steps done, the Company is provided with the folowing documents. receipt of fees payment, at the back of the document are reproduced the-registration formalities (registry no. ,foliono. ,and registrationno.),authorized signature,date of the deed and official stamps.

(vi) Finally, the Company goes for a Social registration. It requires, registration at the National social security

---

① Source : djiboutinvest. com.

fund (Caisse Nationale de Securité Sociale). This step is free of charges.

The creation of a branch follows as different process. The documents to present are the article of association of the parent Company, the minutes of the board of directors of the parent Company, a nominated representative or manager of the branch, the Commercial register of the parent Company, the commercial register of the local branch and a commercial name certificate.

c. Routes and Requirements of Dissolution[①]

Subject to the specific provision that we will detail below, the liquidation of companies is governed by the provisions contained in the articles of association. The company is in liquidation from the moment of its dissolution for any reason whatsoever except in the case of the meeting of all the shares or shares in one hand. His name is followed by the words "company in liquidation". The legal personality of the company subsists for the purposes of the liquidation, until the closure of the latter. The dissolution of a company only has effect with respect to third parties from the date on which it is published in the commercial register.

The act of appointment of the liquidator is published, in accordance with the conditions and deadlines set as necessary by law, which shall also determine the documents to be filed as an appendix to the commercial register. The persons to whom the exercise of the functions of general manager, director, company manager, member of the management board or supervisory board are prohibited or who are deprived of the right to perform such functions may not be liquidators.

The dissolution of the company does not automatically entail the cancellation of the leases of the buildings used for its social activity, including living quarters dependent on these buildings. If, in the event of assignment of the lease, the obligation of guarantee can no longer be ensured in the terms thereof, it may be substituted, by court decision, any guarantee offered by the assignee or a third party, and deemed sufficient.

Except with the unanimous consent of the partners, the assignment of all or part of the assets of the corporation in liquidation to a person having been a partner in the partnership, general partner, manager, director, general manager member of the supervisory board, member of the executive board, auditor or controller, can only take place with the authorization of the court of first instance, the liquidator and, if there are any, the statutory auditor. accounts or the controller duly heard.

The assignment of all or part of the assets of the company in liquidation to the liquidator or his employees or their spouses, ascendants or descendants is prohibited. The global transfer of the assets of the company or the contribution of the assets to another company, in particular by way of merger, is authorized by the partners unanimously or by the majority required for the amendment of the statutes.

The shareholders, including the holders of non-voting preferred shares, are called at the end of the liquidation to decide on the final account, on the discharge of the liquidator's management and the discharge of his mandate and to record the closing. liquidation. Failing this, any partner may request in court the appointment of a representative to conduct the convocation. If the closing meeting can not deliberate or if it refuses to approve the accounts of the liquidator, it is decided, by court decision, at the request of the latter or any interested person.

The notice of closure of the liquidation is published in accordance with the terms and conditions laid down by law as required. The liquidator is liable, with regard to both the company and the third parties, for the harmful consequences of the faults committed by him in the performance of his duties. The action for liability against the liquidators is prescribed by three years from the fact harmful or, if it was concealed, its revelation. However, if the fact is described as a crime, the action is prescribed by ten years.

All actions against the non-liquidating partners or their surviving spouses, heirs or assigns, shall be barred after five years from the publication of the dissolution of the company in the commercial register. In the absence of statutory clauses or express agreement between the parties, the liquidation of the dissolved company shall be carried out in accordance with the provisions of the law.

In addition, it may be ordered by court order that this liquidation will be carried out under the same conditions as seen above.

The powers of the board of directors or managers end on the date of the court decision or the dissolution of the company if it is later. The dissolution of the company does not terminate the functions of the Supervisory Board and the Statutory Auditors.

In the absence of auditors, and even in companies that are not required to appoint one or more auditors may be appointed by the partners. Failing that, they may be appointed, by court order, at the request of the liquidator or any interested person.

The act of appointment of the auditors sets their powers, duties and remunerations and the duration of their duties. They bear the same responsibility as the auditors. One or more liquidators are appointed by the partners, if

---

① Source : Commercial Code of Djibouti.

the dissolution results from the statutory term or if it is decided by the partners.

If the partners have not been able to appoint a liquidator, the latter shall be appointed by court order at the request of any interested party, under the conditions determined as necessary by law.

If the dissolution of the company is decided by court decision, this decision designates one or more liquidators.

The term of office of the liquidator may not exceed three years. However, this mandate may be renewed by the partners or the president of the court of first instance, depending on whether the liquidator was appointed by the partners or by court order.

If the meeting of shareholders has not been validly convened, the mandate is renewed by court order, at the request of the liquidator.

In asking for the renewal of his mandate, the liquidator shall indicate the reasons for which the liquidation could not be closed, the measures he intends to take and the time required for the completion of the liquidation.

Within six months of his appointment, the liquidator convenes the meeting of shareholders to which he reports on the active and passive situation of the company, on the continuation of the liquidation operations and the time necessary to complete them. The period within which the liquidator reports may be extended to twelve months upon his request by court order.

Failing this, the meeting shall be convened either by the supervisory body, if one exists, or by a designated representative, by a court decision, at the request of any interested person.

The liquidator represents the company. He is invested with the widest powers to realize the assets, even amicably. The restrictions to these powers, resulting statutes or the act of appointment, are not opposable to third parties. He is entitled to pay the creditors and distribute the available balance.

He may continue the cases in progress or initiate new ones for the purposes of the liquidation only if he has been authorized, either by the partners, or by a court decision if he has been appointed by the same means.

The liquidator shall, within three months of the end of each financial year, draw up the annual accounts in the light of the inventory he has drawn up of the various elements of the assets and liabilities existing on that date and a written report by which he reports on the liquidation transactions during the past financial year.

Except where granted by court order, the liquidator shall convene, in accordance with the procedures provided for in the articles of association, at least once a year and within six months of the end of the financial year, the shareholders' meeting, which shall decide on the annual accounts, give the necessary authorizations and possibly renew the mandate of the auditors, auditors or members of the supervisory board.

If the meeting is not held, the report provided for in the first paragraph above shall be filed with the registry of the court of first instance and communicated to any interested person. During the liquidation period, the partners may make the disclosure of the corporate documents, under the same conditions as before.

If the required majority can not be met, it shall be decided by court order at the request of the liquidator or any interested person. When the deliberation entails modification of the statutes, it is taken under the conditions prescribed for this purpose, for each form of company.

In case of continuation of the social exploitation, the liquidator is required to convene the meeting of partners under the conditions provided above. Failing this, any interested person may request the convocation, either by the statutory auditors, the supervisory board or the supervisory body, or by a representative appointed by court order.

Unless otherwise provided by the articles of association, the remaining share capital after repayment of the par value of the shares or shares is made between the shareholders in the same proportion as their shareholding.

Subject to the rights of the creditors, the liquidator shall decide whether to distribute the funds that became available during liquidation.

F. Merger and Acquisition

Chapter 6 of Title 4 of Book 3 of the Djibouti Commercial Code on Company Law deals with the merger and the demerger.

Article L. 326-1 stipulates that one or more companies may, by way of a merger, transfer their assets to an existing company or to a new company they form.

A company may also, by way of a split, transfer its assets to several existing companies or to several new companies.

These options are open to companies in liquidation provided that the distribution of their assets among the partners has not been the subject of a start of execution.

The shareholders of the companies that transmit their assets in the context of the transactions mentioned in the three preceding paragraphs receive shares or shares of the beneficiary company (s) and, if necessary, a cash payment whose amount can not exceed 10% of the nominal value. shares or shares awarded.

All the aforementioned operations can be carried out between companies of different form.

They are decided, by each of the companies concerned, in the conditions required for the modification of its statutes.

If the transaction involves the creation of new companies, each one of them is constituted according to the rules specific to the form of company adopted.

In its article L. 326-3, the Commercial Code of Djibouti specifies the following things:

The merger or the split entails the dissolution without liquidation of the disappearing companies and the universal transfer of their assets to the beneficiary companies, in the state where it is at the date of final completion of the transaction. It entails the acquisition, by the partners of the companies that disappear, of the status of partners of the beneficiary companies, under the conditions determined by the merger or demerger agreement.

However, there is no exchange of units or shares of the beneficiary corporation for units or shares of the companies that disappear when such units or shares are held:

(i) either by the beneficiary company or by a person acting in his own name but on behalf of that company;

(ii) Either by the company that disappears or by a person acting in his own name but on behalf of that company.

The merger or split takes effect:

(i) In the case of the creation of one or more new companies, at the date of registration, in the commercial register, of the new company or of the last of them;

(ii) In other cases, on the date of the last general meeting that approved the transaction, unless the contract provides for the transaction to take effect on another date, which must not be later than the closing date of the transaction. the current financial year (s) of the beneficiary company (s) and not earlier than the closing date of the last financial year of the company or companies that transmit their assets.

When the proposed transaction has the effect of increasing the commitments of partners or shareholders of one or more companies in question, it can only be decided unanimously by said partners or shareholders.

All companies participating in any of the transactions referred refered above establish a proposed merger or split.

This draft shall be lodged at the registry of the court of first instance at the headquarters of the said companies and shall be the subject of an advertisement the terms of which shall be fixed as and when required by regulation.

On pain of nullity, the companies participating in one of the operations mentioned above are required to file with the registry a statement in which they relate all the acts done in order to proceed and by which they affirm that the transaction was carried out in compliance of laws and regulations. The clerk ensures that the declaration complies with the law.

Transactions carried out only between public limited companies are subject to the provisions of this section.

The merger is decided by the extraordinary general meeting of each of the companies participating in the transaction.

The merger is subject, where applicable, to each of the companies participating in the transaction, to the ratification of special meetings of shareholders, if they exist.

The proposed merger is subject to the special meetings of holders of investment certificates, acting in accordance with the rules of the general meeting of shareholders.

G. Competition Regulation

a. Department Supervising Competition Regulation

The Directorate of Internal Trade, Competition and Fraud Control is the agency responsible for implementing the Government's policy on the regulation of competition.

As part of COMESA, Djibouti participates in the implementation of the regional competition policy.

b. Brief Introduction of Competition Law[①]

In 2008, Djibouti adopted a law which prohibits all forms of action between economic operators which tend, amongst other things, to restrict competition, limit or control production and investment; or result in the abuse of a dominant position.

Excluded from the scope of this law are public enterprises and practices having the effect of ensuring technical progress, without, however, compromising competition for a substantial part of the products in question.

Law No. 28 / AN / 08 / 6th L on the protection, the suppression of fraud and the protection of the consumer is the law which lays down the practical modalities of the trade with regard to the free competition and the protection of the consumer. Established since 2008, this law sets the following main principles:

---

① Source : Law No. 28 / AN / 08 / 6th L.

(i) The prices of products, goods and services are fixed freely throughout the national territory and determined solely by competition. However, in sectors of economic activity or in localities of the national territory where price competition is limited by reason of either monopoly situations or difficulties of long-term supply, or of special legislative or regulatory provisions, prices will be regulated by decree in the Council of Ministers. The provisions of this Title apply to all production, distribution and service activities, including those carried out by public-law corporations.

(ii) All forms of concerted action, agreements, express or tacit agreements or coalitions between economic operators whose object is or may have the effect of preventing, restricting or distorting competition in a market, are prohibited, in particular where they tend to restrict market access or the free exercise of competition by other undertakings; to hinder the setting of prices by the free play of the market by artificially favoring their rise or fall; limit or control production, outlets, investments, research or technical progress. Also prohibited is the abuse by a firm or group of companies of a dominant position in the internal market or a substantial part of it.

(iii) Any form of imposed price practice is forbidden. The margin or the resale price of a good, a product or a service is presumed to be imposed when it is given a minimum or maximum character. Also prohibited is the resale of any product in the state at a price lower than its actual purchase price. The actual purchase price is presumed to be the price charged on the invoice plus any taxes relating to such resale and, where applicable, the price of transport.

In general, the legal framework established by the Government of Djibouti has features in common with free competition markets. In addition, the law lists breaches of the rules of market transparency and restrictive practices of competition. Finally, consumer protection in Djibouti requires the protection of its consent and security.

In the designation, the offer, the presentation, the instructions for use or use, the scope and conditions of guarantee of a good or service, as well as in invoices and receipts, the use of one of the official languages of the Republic of Djibouti is obligatory. The use of any other term or equivalent expression is permitted.

c. Measures Regulating Competition[①]

In the area of competition, fraud prevention and consumer protection, the Ministry of Commerce is responsible, with the help of its officials, for the control and supervision of good competition.

The officials specially empowered to carry out the necessary checks and investigations pursuant to the provisions of Article 19 of Law No. 28 / AN / 08 / 6th L are: sworn agents of the Trade and Standardization Directorate of the Ministry of Trade. Before taking office, these agents take an oath before the district court of their district. They are bound to professional secrecy.

The investigators referred to in Article 21 of Law No. 28 / AN / 08 / 6th L on the Representation of Fraud, are responsible for the investigation, detection and prosecution of regulatory offenses.

The investigators are the auditors of the Directorate of Trade and Industry.

Standardization of the Ministry of Commerce, Judicial Police Officers, Tax Officers, Customs and any officer of any other administration to which the activity under investigation is subject.

If the judicial police officers and the agents of the taxes, the customs and all other administration, in the course of verification or investigations under their jurisdiction come to have the evidence or become convinced that infringements of the commercial law have been committed, are obliged to inform, within two working days following the day of the finding, in writing, of the Competition Bureau, the repression of fraud and the protection of the consumer so that the necessary provisions are committed by the competent service.

In accordance with Article 21 of Law No. 28 / AN / 08 / 6th L, the documents requested by the investigators include, but are not limited to, invoices and import or offering documents that may be useful to them.

There are three types of anti-competitive offenses in Djibouti: offenses classified as anti-competitive practices, breaches of the rules of market transparency and practices restrictive of competition, infringements of the provisions annexed to the organization of competition.

An anti-competitive practice is one of the following practices: to limit the access to the market or the free exercise of competition by others companies, to impede price fixing by the free play of the market by favoring artificially their rise or fall, to limit or control the production, the outlets, the investments, the research or technical progress, to allocate the market or sources of supply, the Exploitation by a company or a group of companies of a dominant position in the internal market or a substantial part of this one, the state of economic dependence in which it finds itself, a client company or supplier that does not have an equivalent solution.

Article L. 2294-3 of the Djibouti Commercial Code specifies anti-competitive offenses. According to the article in question, are considered as infringements of the rules of the transparency of the market and as practices restrictive of the competition. The list comprises : the practices of imposed price and resale at a loss, non-

---

① Source : Law No. 28 / AN / 08 / 6th L.

compliance with billing rules, non-communication of price lists and conditions of sale, the refusal of sale and the subordination of sale to the consumer, discriminatory practices between professionals, wild sales and para-shopping, the non-observance of the rules relating to the information of the consumer particular as regards the instructions for use relating to products likely to to damage health, false or misleading advertising, non-compliance with the regulations relating to direct sales to consumers.

Moreover, it is also considered as a violation of the provisions annexed to the organization of competition, the violation of the legal provisions relating to banking activities.

The offenses enumerated above are recorded in the minutes drawn up by the competent administrations of Commerce and Health or by judicial inquiry.

H. Tax

The General Tax Code of Djibouti is the result of work to recast Djiboutian taxation carried out in 2008-2009 by the Tax Department with funding from the European Union.

The Code is followed by the main uncodified tax laws: tax treaties, investment and free zone provisions, tax provisions of the Mining and Petroleum Codes, etc. It is also complemented by the decisions of the Official Bulletin of the Tax Directorate of the Republic of Djibouti (BODID) which specify the conditions for the application of certain articles of the Code.

An entity doing business in Djibouti is subject to payment of the following duties and taxes:

a) Fees for the Registration of Deeds

They can occur at any time of the life of the company and can be fixed, proportional or progressive. Fixed fee amounts range from 1000 to 4000 DJF (USD 5 to USD 20) depending on the nature of the deeds to be registered. Proportional fees range from 2-10%.

b) Stamp Duty

Mandatory for all civil, judicial and extrajudicial acts and set at 1000 DJF per page.

c) Income Tax

25% of the taxable profit payable from the second year of operation, with the possibility of postponement. Adherence to approved management centres and a turnover of less than 80 million DJF (USD 455,000), exclusive of VAT, entitle you to a 20% reduction. Companies whose profits do not exceed 120,000 DJF are exempt from income tax.

Since 2017, foreign companies residing outside Djibouti, but which operate through their branches in Djibouti, must pay tax on any profits indirectly transferred by increasing or decreasing purchase or selling prices, or by any other means (excessive or unwarranted fees, interest-free or low-interest loans, write-offs, etc.). These must be reported in the taxable profit of the entity subject to the ordinary tax.

d) Withholding Tax

Ranges from 2. 5% to 10% depending on the type of business. Autonomous public institutions such as EDD, Port and Airport of Djibouti are excluded, as well as banks or financial, insurance, telecommunication and hotel establishments.

e) Lump-sum Minimum

tax: 1% of turnover excluding VAT. All companies approved under the Investment Code are subject to this tax, unless the cost of their licence was less than 120,000 DJF (approx. USD 600). It is payable when it exceeds the amount of tax calculated on professional profits or in the case of a loss-making year.

f) Land Tax

Rates are 10%, 18% and 25% depending on the value of the taxable base of buildings and non-cultivated land for commercial or industrial use. There is a reduction of 20% for management, insurance, depreciation, maintenance and repair costs. The rate on undeveloped properties is 25%.

g) VAT

applies to all transactions except those related to exports and international air, sea, land and passenger transport, payments received under an externally financed public contract and the imports made by the real estate promoters of social habitats, economic habitats as well as the disposal of these dwellings. The standard rate is 10%. However, its method of calculation is complex. The Tax Department has prepared an explanatory note, available on the website of the Ministry of Economy and Finance.

h) Goods and Services Tax

applies to all natural or legal persons who deliver goods or services whose annual turnover does not exceed 20,000,000 FDJ or 10,000,000 FDJ. Excluded are all goods and services exempt from VAT. The rate is set at 7%. It is reduced to 5% for fruit and vegetable sales, catering and sales of red meat and fish.

i) Domestic Consumption Tax (ICT)

applicable to all goods imported and consumed in Djibouti, regardless of their origin, as well as to tobacco and alcohol re-exported by road to neighbouring countries. The three main ICT rates are 8. 20% and 33%. In addition to these rates, certain products are subject to the payment of a surcharge, the amount of which varies according to their nature.

There are no exchange controls in Djibouti, and capital can flow freely. Import and export licences are not required.

I. Preference and Protection of Investment

As part of its strategy to improve the business climate, the Djiboutian government has entrusted to an expert committee the project of redrafting two old Napoleonic codes: the Civil Code and the Code of Civil Procedure, which date before independence, and are now obsolete.

The government wants to adopt a modern Civil Code and Code of Civil Procedure, better adapted to economic realities and offering adequate security to investors. The drafting of the codes is in its final phase and according to the Ministry of Justice, experts will submit the drafts to the government for validation in 2018. Once validated, the Government will send them to the National Assembly for discussion and adoption, hopefully before the end of 2018.

III. Trade

A. Trade Regulation for Foreign Companies

Under the Djibouti Trade Code, companies are free to contract as they wish. No authorisation is required after the incorporation of a company to enable it to carry on its activities.

In principle, there are no specific procedures for foreign company to follow with regard to general contract law. They must respect the basic provisions as to contract law (as for all contracts) such as lawfulness, consent in writing, absence of unfair terms, or be subject to specific rules, such as company contracts, guarantee contracts, or terms specific to regulated contracts.

B. Policies and Trade Regulations

Djibouti has no discriminatory policy with respect to foreign investment, imports or exports, and there are no restrictions on the importation of goods or raw materials apart from the usual customs declarations. A declaration of goods must be made by their owners, shippers or consignees or by the customs officer.

Import prohibitions are generally governed by the international conventions to which Djibouti is a signatory. The only products whose import is explicitly prohibited are cars with the steering wheel on the right, and non-biodegradable plastic packaging bags. For health reasons, the importation of certain products is subject to approval by the Ministry of Health.

The importation of products, such as explosives or weapons, requires the prior approval of the competent authorities. The importation of khat, as well as its marketing, is regulated.

Djibouti does not have any anti-dumping, countervailing or safeguard legislation.

C. Public Procurement

The Public Procurement Code governs contracts amounting to more than DF 5 million that are awarded by the state, public administrative establishments, public industrial and commercial establishments, state-owned companies and economic entities in which the state is the majority shareholder. The body of control and regulation of public procurement in Djibouti is the National Commission of Public Procurement (CNMP).

Djibouti has specific regulations for public-private partnership contracts which regulate the legal framework applicable to these contracts. These define and delimit the conditions for the drafting, execution, the award and the execution of the PPP contracts.

The institutional framework of PPPs is under the authority of the President of the Republic and overseen by a National PPP Committee, which is charged with assisting the government in defining its policy and PPP strategies.

This policy is implemented at a national level by an autonomous specialised entity (the "PPP Unit"). The procurement procedure is carried out under the control of the Public Procurement Regulatory Authority. The Finance Ministry is responsible for checking the financial and budgetary sustainability of the projects proposed.

The sectoral regulatory authorities remain fully responsible for the activities of companies in their sector.

Public procurement is a business opportunity and can be an accelerator for business growth. They represent tens of billions of dollars every year. On average only 1/4 of these markets are awarded to Djiboutian companies.[①] This state of affairs is mainly due to two elements:

(i) A lack of knowledge of the opportunities these markets represent for many local businesses, especially SMEs;

(ii) Low ownership of the legal and regulatory environment relating to it.

Faced with this, the Chamber of Commerce of Djibouti (CCD) has set up, with the support of the World Bank, a business support program for better access to public markets.

Law No. 53 / AN / 09 / 6ème L bearing the New Code des Marches Publics (CMP) in its Article 12 defines public procurement as follows: "Contracts entered into by the State for the execution of works, or supply of goods or services " The term "State" includes ministries, public administrative establishments, public establishments of an industrial and commercial nature, state-owned companies and semi-public companies whose capital is majority-owned, directly or indirectly by the State. and local authorities. All these entities are named in the legal texts Contracting Administrations.

In the Republic of Djibouti, four basic principles govern public procurement:

• Equal access of companies to public procurement through the open tender procedure;

• Equal treatment of candidates both in the procurement process and in the evaluation of tenders and the awarding of contracts;

• Transparency of procedures in the procurement, evaluation and execution of contracts;

• Economy and efficiency in the use of public resources.

The Code des Marches Publics distinguishes 3 types of markets:

• Supplies and services: public procurement of supplies and services is the acquisition of goods, equipment, machinery and / or materials to a company (supplier) or the provision of a service with a provider.

• Works: public works contracts are for the execution by one or more contractors of building or civil engineering works.

• Intellectual services: public contracts for intellectual services (consultancy services) relate to services of a mainly intellectual nature whose predominant element is not physically quantifiable.

The Republic of Djibouti has a National Commission for Public Procurement (CNMP) which is a control and regulation body of public procurement in Djibouti. In 2013, this body dealt with 72 public contracts issued and executed for a total amount of 10,396,629,501 DJF.

Breakdown according to the type of markets:

• 39 works contracts for a total amount of 8,407,696,300 DJF;

• 21 supply contracts for a total amount of FDF 1,024,152,209;

• 12 contracts for intellectual services for a total amount of 964,780,992 DJF.

Companies need to be interested in public procurement as they provide access to business opportunities, develop and diversify market sources, acquire new benchmarks, form new partnerships, increase brand awareness and the credibility of the company, to strengthen its capabilities to be more competitive.

There are several actors in the Republic of Djibouti participating in the public procurement process. It is mainly:

• Donors such as the World Bank, the African Development Bank (ADB), the Islamic Development Bank (IDB), the European Union (EU), the French Development Agency (AFD), the UN Agencies United, etc. Almost 80% of public procurement in Djibouti is financed externally through official development assistance. These donors sometimes use procurement procedures specific to each of them.

• The contracting authority as the Technical Ministries: Education, Health, Transport, Agriculture, Finance; -the public establishments of commercial industrial character: ONEAD, Djibouti Telecom, Port S. A, Djibouti Airport, etc. ; Project Implementation Agency: Djiboutian Agency for Social Development (ADDS); the local collectives.

• Enterprises: all suppliers of goods, services and works in the following fields of activity: health; education; energy; transportation; the water; sanitation; Information and Communication Technologies; rural development; the environment; food products.

Participation in public procurement is open to all interested parties.

As a bidder a company may participate in a public contract in responding to an invitation to tender (AAO) issued by a Contracting Authority.

For this, two requirements : first of all, the company must find the information by following the publications

---

① Source : Djibouinvest - Chamber of Commerce of Djibouti.

AAO in the newspaper La Nation and then reply the qualification requirements of the market (administrative, financial, experience, technical capabilities, etc ...).

There a several way to participate:

• In group-If the company does not fully meet the criteria of market qualification, it can participate in public markets by forming a group with another company having a complementary activity. For the group to be qualified, certain conditions must be respected: A leader must be appointed; The latter must fulfill at least 40% of the qualification criteria. The other partners must fulfill at least 25% of the qualification criteria. Partners in a grouping are jointly solidary.

• By subcontracting-A company may participate in a public contract as a subcontractor of a contract holder. The conditions of subcontracting: No more than 30% of the contract may be subcontracted; The use of a subcontractor must first obtain the agreement of the Contracting Authority owning the contract. The Contract Holder retains full responsibility for the performance of the contract with the Contracting Authority.

• Negotiated markets-For small acquisitions (less than 5 million USD), the Contracting Authority may use a procurement method other than open tendering such as consulting suppliers, or the direct agreement or the mutual agreement. Participating in these smaller markets could thus be a gateway to public procurement for SMEs.

IV. Labour

A. Brief Introduction of Labour Laws and Regulations

According to the Djiboutian Labour Code, any foreigner may conduct a salaried activity in Djibouti, and no quota is fixed to limit the number of foreign employees that a company can recruit. However it is stipulated that a company can only call on foreign labour if the required competence is unavailable in Djibouti.

An employer wishing to hire a foreign worker must obtain a work permit from the National Agency for Employment and Vocational Training (ANEFIP). An application, enclosing relevant documents to the ANEFIP will be considered within 60 days. If there is no answer within that period, the work permit is deemed granted.

Article 28 of the Labour Code gives the administration the discretion to refuse a work permit. Such decision is subject to appeal to the Djibouti Administrative Court.

If a work permit is granted, the employer must pay a fee, the amount of which varies according to the category of employment involved, and the nationality of the employee.

The terms and conditions for the award of a temporary work permit and residence card are set out in the Labour Code. The duration of the validity of any temporary residence card cannot be greater than one year and cannot exceed the validity of the travel documents.

B. Steps for Work Permit[①]

Several documents are required in order to work in the local territory.

The documents required are: the Entry visa (first of all, an entry visa valid for 1 month is issued at the international airport of Djibouti against 10000 Djibouti francs for all foreigner ; the residence permit, Any foreigner who intends to work in Djibouti may obtain an identity card in foreign parts providing the following documents : four photos, copy of work permit valid for at least 6 months, copy of passport, request letter for NIPA.

In the case of a partner or manager (not employee) without a work permit, the documents to provide are as follows : copy of Passport, register of commerce or license, request letter for NIPA.

Fees according to nationality: $ 196 Africa, $ 225 Asia, $ 252 Europe and $ 280 American.

Any foreigner worker wishing to pursue a profession in Djibouti must first take a work permit.

In cas of first application, the documents to provide are : 4 photos, application form to fill, copy of Passport, employment contract, request letter for NIPA.

In cas of renewal, the documents to provide are comprising: 2 photos, application form to fill: renewal application, original and copy of the work permit, request letter for NIPA.

The minimum wage established in December 2011 is set at $ 200 per month. The following are indicative wages for some positions standard, based on estimates by the private sector.

---

① Source : djiboutinvest. com.

Exemple of wages for the year 2016

Position	Currency	Value
Senior Director	USD	1 200–2 000
Senior	USD	800–1 500
Engineer	USD	1 000–1 600
Young graduate	USD	500–1 200
Administrative assistant	USD	400–500
Qualified	USD	300–500
Seller	USD	300–500
Driver	USD	200–600
Security guard	USD	200–400
Unskilled worker	USD	200–250

C. Termination

Under the Labour Code, the employer must give one month's notice of termination of a contract to general employees and labourers and three months to supervisors, managers and those in similar positions. The employer may invoke:

(i) Personal reasons (e. g. the employee's state of health);

(ii) Economic reasons (including, among other things, the substantial transformation of a position due to technological change (section 48 of the Labour Code), in which case the affected employee must be given priority for reemployment during the first year following his dismissal and is eligible for compensation;

(iii) Serious misconduct as defined by any of the nine cases clearly stated in article 59 of the Labour Code) or as stipulated in the company's regulations;

(iv) An element of greater flexibility is open to employers, where the company can resort to utilising an option for technical unemployment for a period of three months, renewable once (article 41 of the Labour Code), under which minimal compensation is paid, provided any employees so laid off are given priority for re-employment in the first year following dismissal.

The damages and interest payable in respect of a termination of contract without just reason can be between two and six months' salary depending on the size of the company. Special conditions apply to staff representatives who may be dismissed without the authorisation of the labour inspectorate. In such cases, the employer must pay 12 month's salary. However, if the ground of dismissal invoked constitutes a real and serious reason, even without observance of the usual forms of notice, a labour tribunal may require the employer to pay compensation which will not exceed one month's salary (article 55 of the Labour Code).

V. Intellectual Property[1]

The Djibouti Office of Industrial and Commercial Property (ODPIC) and the Copyright Office share responsibility for the protection of intellectual property rights. These are public bodies with legal and financial autonomy.

Their missions include the fight against infringement of industrial property rights, including counterfeiting and unfair competition, and the guarantee and promotion of the protection and use of industrial property in Djibouti.

Measures that can be taken by the courts include, amongst other things, forfeiture of illegally obtained products of copyright infringement, confiscation of counterfeit goods and payment of damages (compensation for the victims of violations of copyright law).

In practice, the enforcement capacity is very effective and developed in the field of industrial and commercial property, but it is sometimes quite limited for copyright and related rights due to resource constraints, lack of experience of judges and legal practitioners, and lack of public awareness of intellectual property rights.

---

[1] Source : Law No. 50 / AN / 09 / 6th L regarding the Protection of Industrial Property.

Under the law of Djibouti, the protection of industrial property relates to patents, layout designs (topography) of integrated circuits, industrial designs, trademarks, products or services, trade name, geographical indications and appellations of origin and the repression of unfair competition.

Industrial property is understood in the widest sense and applies not only to industry, trade and services, but also to all production in the field of agricultural and mining industries and to all manufactured goods.

Nationals of each of the countries forming part of the International Union for the Protection of Industrial Property shall enjoy the protection of the industrial property rights provided for in this Law, subject to the fulfillment of the conditions and formalities laid down therein.

The same protection shall be accorded to nationals of countries party to any other treaty concluded in the field of industrial property to which the Republic of Djibouti is a party, and providing in its provisions treatment no less favorable than that enjoyed by nationals of such countries.

Any natural or legal person residing in Djibouti may make his own applications for industrial property rights, as well as any subsequent transactions relating thereto, or appoint for this purpose an agent, domiciled or having his registered office in Djibouti.

The power of the agent of the industrial property right may apply to one or more deposits or registrations or to all existing or future filings and registrations of the principal, subject to any exceptions mentioned by the principal in the power.

Nationals of countries which are not part of the International Union for the Protection of Industrial Property enjoy the benefit of the provisions of this Act if they are domiciled or have an effective and serious industrial or commercial activity in the territory of the one of the countries of the Union.

The person who has regularly made the filing of an application (first application) for a patent of invention, a certificate of addition relating to a principal patent, industrial design or trademark, product, trade or service, in one of the countries of the International Union for the Protection of Industrial Property, or its beneficiary, will enjoy, for the purpose of filing the said application in Djibouti (subsequent application), a right of priority during the deadlines provided by law.

In fact, the priority period mentioned above is twelve months for patents, certificates of addition to a main patent, and layout-designs (topography) of integrated circuits, and six months for industrial designs and trademarks, products or services. Time limits begin to run from the date of filing of the first application made in one of the countries of the Union, as the day of filing is not timely.

Anyone wishing to avail himself of the priority of an earlier filing made in one of the countries of the Union will be required to make a written priority declaration indicating the date, the number if it is known at the time of filing in Djibouti, and the country of origin of this deposit. If the priority deposit number is not known at the time of deposit in Djibouti, it is provided by the depositor as soon as possible.

The declaration of priority shall be made on the date of submission of the application to Djibouti. Within three months from the date of filing of the application in Djibouti, the depositor must provide the documents justifying the previous deposit under the conditions to be determined by regulation.

Multiple priorities can be claimed for a patent application, even if they come from different countries. Where appropriate, multiple priorities may be claimed for the same claim.

If multiple priorities are claimed, the deadlines starting from the date of priority are calculated from the date of the earliest priority.

Any invention may be the subject of a patent granted by the Djibouti Office of Industrial and Commercial Property. The right to a patent belongs to the inventor or his successors under the conditions and within the limits set by this law.

The industrial property rights protecting the inventions are:

(i) patents, issued for a term of protection of twenty years from the filing date of the patent application;

(ii) certificates of addition, which are ancillary titles for inventions the object of which is attached to at least one claim of a main patent. Such certificates shall be issued for a period beginning on the date of filing of their application and expiring with the term of the main patent to which they are attached.

Article 23 of the Industrial Property Law of Djibouti explains that an invention is considered new if it is not included in the state of the art.

An invention is considered to involve an inventive step if, for a person skilled in the art, it does not follow clearly from the state of the art.

The state of the art consists of everything made available to the public anywhere in the world by a written or oral description, use or any other means, before the date of filing of the patent application in Djibouti or a patent application filed abroad whose priority is validly claimed.

The content of patent applications filed in Djibouti or of international applications, as filed, which have a filing date prior to that mentioned above, shall also be deemed to be included in the state of the art. and which have been published only on that date or at a later date.

According to the a law, are not considered as inventions, discoveries, substances, materials and organisms as they exist in nature, and their parts or components, scientific theories and mathematical methods, the human body and the materials that make up the human body, at the various stages of its constitution and development, and its components, including the sequence or partial sequence of a gene, essentially biological processes for the production of plants or animals, literary and artistic works or any other aesthetic creation, plans, principles and methods in the exercise of intellectual activities, in gaming or in the field of economic activities, computer programs, information presentations.

In the same way, are not patentable:

Plants and animals other than micro-organisms, diagnostic, therapeutic and surgical methods for the treatment of humans or animals, inventions whose commercial exploitation or implementation would be contrary to public order or morality, or endanger the health or life of persons, animals, plants or the environment.

VI. Environmental Protection

A. Department Supervising Environmental Protection

Legal source: Décret n° 2004-0092 / PR / MHUEAT Portant création d'une Commission Nationale pour le Développement Durable (CNDD).

The National Commission for Sustainable Development (NCSD) has been created as department supervising environment protection.

B. Brief Introduction of Laws and Regulations of Environmental

Law source: Décret n° 2001-0011 / PR / MHUEAT portant définition de la procédure d'étude d'impact environnemental–Law n°51 / AN / 09 / 6ème L establishing the Environmental code.

The Republic of Djibouti had no environmental legislation to date. The country was then exposed to various abuses by some companies and significant pollution was discovered in 1997 by the state. A study was commissioned by the authorities to assess the extent of pollution damage caused by the oil companies and the results led the state to take measures to remedy the lack of legislation in this area. In 2009, a code of the environment was set up by the State.

Today the code of the environment is applicable to Djibouti, it places the preservation of the environment in the supreme interest of the nation. The environmental code lays down the principles of national biodiversity, environmental education accessible to all citizens, instruments for managing the state's environment and protecting the fauna and flora of Djibouti. All companies operating in the territory of Djibouti must abide by it or face criminal sanctions.

The Government of the Republic of Djibouti has established a law which sets the objectives of the national environmental protection and management policy on the basis of the fundamental principles for managing and protecting the environment against all forms of degradation or deterioration of the environment. environmental resources to ensure sustainable development.

Management and protection of the environment for sustainable development are based on the following fundamental principles:

(i) Principle of participation: the preservation of the environment is a supreme interest of the nation, involving the collective responsibility of all citizens and requiring the participation of all in the development of environmental policy.

(ii) Principle of integration: the protection and the good management of the environment are integral parts of the national policy of economic, social and cultural development; Consideration of environmental protection and ecological balance when developing and implementing land use plans.

(iii) Polluter pays principle: the effective implementation of the principles of the paying user and the polluter pays with regard to the realization and management of economic and social projects and the provision of services; Any prejudice resulting from an environmental damage engages the direct or indirect responsibility of its author who must ensure its repair.

(iv) Precautionary principle: To protect the environment, precautionary measures must be widely applied by States according to their capabilities.

(v) Principle of cooperation: compliance with international environmental agreements in the development of development plans and programs as well as environmental legislation.

Actions in the field of environmental management and protection are done with the prior approval of the Ministry of the Environment in accordance with the national environmental policy.

Any organization, firm or investor wishing to establish themselves to work in the Republic of Djibouti must be informed that all spills, discharges, discharges, direct or indirect deposits of any nature which may cause or increase the degradation of the waters by modifying their physical, chemical, biological or bacteriological characteristics, whether they be surface, ground or marine waters within territorial waters. In addition, any discharge of ballast water into territorial waters is prohibited.

Special protection areas under special measures have been established by the Government. The Ministry of the Environment, Public Health, Water Resources, Maritime Affairs and Fisheries takes into account the levels of pollution observed and any circumstances that may aggravate the deterioration of environmental resources.

Any liquid discharge exceeding the standards and any deposit that may cause or increase water pollution are prohibited. Regulatory measures determine the conditions of rejection, the conditions for analysis and control of discharges.

Any liquid discharge, even below the standards, may, in the event of risk of environmental damage give rise to a limited ban in time and space. The Ministry of the Environment, Public Health, Water Resources, Maritime Affairs and Fisheries may lift this ban after an environmental audit, which entails obtaining a certificate in due form form of the Ministry.

An investor or company that owns a ship, aircraft or marine facility containing dangerous or toxic substances shall immediately take the appropriate precautionary measures in the event of a critical situation in relation to the marine environment. It must inform the environmental and maritime authorities as soon as possible of the nature of the substances and the measures taken to combat pollution. In the event of default, the national authorities will have the necessary measures carried out at the expense of the owner.

For investors, it should be noted that the Djibouti environment code is mainly intended for factories, workshops, depots, quarries and generally industrial, craft or commercial facilities operated or owned by any natural person or moral, public or private, and all other activities that present either dangers or inconveniences for health, safety, public health, agriculture, the natural environment, or disadvantages for the convenience of the neighborhood.

Industrial installations are divided into two classes, depending on the degree of seriousness of the hazards and nuisances that may result from their operation. They are subject to either authorization or declaration.

The first class includes facilities whose operation presents serious dangers and inconveniences. The operation of these installations may only be authorized if specific measures are taken to prevent these dangers or inconveniences by an authorization from the Minister for the Environment.

The second class includes installations which, not presenting any serious dangers or nuisances, must respect the general prescriptions enacted by the Minister in charge of the Environment. They are subject to declaration.

VII. Dispute Resolution

The Republic of Djibouti is a party to the 1958 New York Convention on the Recognition and Enforcement of Foreign Arbitral Awards.

In order to be enforceable in Djibouti, foreign judgments and foreign arbitral awards must be granted an exequatur order from the Court of First Instance of Djibouti. The exequatur is granted by the President of the Djibouti Court of First Instance on receipt of a petition made in accordance with the following conditions:

(i) the foreign judgment or arbitral award, was rendered by a competent court in accordance with the rules on conflicts of laws, as accepted in Djibouti;

(ii) the foreign judgment or the arbitral award has the force of res judicata and is enforceable in the jurisdiction where it was rendered; and

(iii) the parties have been duly convened, represented or declared in default; and the judgment does not contravene public order within the meaning of Djiboutian law and is not contrary to any decision of Djiboutian justice having res judicata authority.

A party wishing to obtain an exequatur order must submit to the President of the Djibouti Court of First Instance a copy of a certified French translation of the foreign judgment or, in the case of arbitration, a copy of the certified French translation of the arbitral award and the arbitration agreement.

In Djibouti, the courts are generally in favour of arbitration. When there is an arbitration clause in a contract, a local court will declare that it is not competent to deal with the case and will invite the parties to go to arbitration. The President of the Court of First Instance of Djibouti may grant interim measures notwithstanding the existence of an arbitration clause.

Indeed, before the referral of the case to the arbitrator, and in exceptional circumstances, thereafter, in cases where the urgency of the interim and conservatory measures requested would not allow the arbitrator to take a decision in time, the parties may request such measures (including provisional seizures on the property of a debtor located in Djibouti on the date of the request) should be taken by the competent judicial authority.

The courts of Djibouti generally recognise domestic arbitral awards on the condition that they have been rendered in accordance with the applicable rules. However, the arbitral award maybe the subject of an action for annulment before a competent local court if:

(i) the award was made in the absence of an arbitration agreement or on a null or expired agreement;

(ii) the arbitral tribunal has been irregularly constituted or the sole arbitrator irregularly appointed;

(iii) the arbitral tribunal has ruled without complying with the mission entrusted to it;

(iv) the principle of contradiction has not been respected or where the rights of the defence have been infringed;

(v) the relief awarded is contrary to international public policy; or

(vi) the arbitration award is not reasoned.

VIII. Others

Anti-commercial Bribery[1]:

Law source : Law No. 03 / AN. 13 / 7th L of 16 july 2013 - establishing the prevention and fight against corruption.

The National Commission for the Prevention and Combating of Corruption was created by Law No. 03 / AN / 13 / 7th by supplementing the legislative provisions relating to the prevention and fight against corruption.

The missions of the National Commission for the Prevention and Combating of Corruption are as follows:

(i) Prevent, fight and eradicate all forms of corruption;

(ii) Strengthen legal, administrative and other tools to prevent and combat corruption;

(iii) Conduct research, studies and surveys to know the causes and extent of the phenomenon;

(iv) Develop and propose policies and strategies to effectively fight corruption;

(v) Educate and sensitize public authorities, the private sector and civil society on the negative effects of corruption;

(vi) Periodically evaluate relevant legal instruments and administrative measures;

(vii) Promote and coordinate the participation of other supervisory institutions, international organizations, civil society and the private sector in the fight against corruption;

(viii) Facilitate and support international cooperation in the prevention, detection and prosecution of corruption, including asset recovery;

(ix) Receipt of declaration of heritage and publication in the official journal.

---

[1] Source : anticorruption. dj.

埃塞俄比亚

作者：Mehrteab Leul Kokeb、Mesfin Tafesse
译者：闪涛、邵开俊

一、概述

（一）政治、经济、社会和法律环境概况

埃塞俄比亚联邦民主共和国（以下简称"埃塞俄比亚"）位于非洲东部，与厄立特里亚、吉布提、索马里、苏丹、南苏丹和肯尼亚接壤。截至2016年，人口约为1.02亿。[1] 埃塞俄比亚首都亚的斯亚贝巴是非洲联盟总部所在地。现任总统是穆拉图·特肖梅（Dr.Mulatu Teshome）。埃塞俄比亚是一个联邦共和国，使用语言是阿姆哈拉语，流通货币是埃塞俄比亚比尔。

1. 政治

1995年，《埃塞俄比亚联邦民主共和国宪法》（以下简称《宪法》）规定了联邦国家的结构，其由9个会员国组成联邦。埃塞俄比亚是一个多党联邦民主国家，其政府由行政首长、经选举产生的人民代表院（547个成员）和联邦院（110个成员）组成。[2] 埃塞俄比亚有一个两院制议会，由人民代表院和联邦院组成。人民代表院是联邦政府的唯一立法机构和最高权力机构。联邦院拥有宪法解释权。

通过多党民主国家和联邦州选举执政党后，再由执政党选举总理，每5年举行一次。总统由人民代表院的人民代表选举。总理任命内阁，由人民代表院批准。[3]

2. 经济

埃塞俄比亚是东非地区发展速度最快的经济体。埃塞俄比亚政府已经制定并开始实施第二个五年增长和转型计划（GTP），该计划将持续到2019年或2020年。预计GTP将在很大程度上促进工业发展，尤其是能源和基础设施领域。政府的目标是在2025年达到中等收入国家水平。

促进发展的具体领域包括农业和农产品再加工、皮革和皮革制品、园艺和花卉出口、建筑材料和旅游。国家的经济主要以农业为基础。埃塞俄比亚70%以上的人口仍在农业部门工作，但服务业已超过农业，成为GDP的主要来源。[4] 尽管咖啡仍然是最大的外汇收入来源，但埃塞俄比亚正在丰富出口产品，黄金、芝麻、阿拉伯茶、牲畜和园艺产品等商品正变得越来越重要。制造业在2016年出口总额中所占的比重不到8%，由于国际市场的日益增长，未来几年制造业出口应该会有所增加。[5]

2017年10月，政府将其货币比尔贬值15%，以增加出口，缓解该国长期的外汇短缺。

3. 社会

埃塞俄比亚是一个多民族国家。大约有80种不同的语言和方言，并且存在着文化差异。埃塞俄比亚是一个以青年人为主的国家，超过60%的人口年龄在24岁以下。

投资者可以自由聘用外籍员工担任管理职务，但在投资者需要熟练劳工的时候，不得雇用外籍员工。

4. 法律

宪法具有最高法律效力，其他法律和实践惯例，或者政府机构或政府官员作出的决定都必须遵从宪法的规定。埃塞俄比亚批准的国际条约是当地法律的组成部分，并在全国范围内具有约束力。宪法确立

---

[1] 参见 http://www.worldbank.org/en/country/ethiopia/overview。
[2] 参见 http://www.ethiopia.gov.et/government-overview。
[3] 参见 http://www.ethiopia.gov.et/government-overview。
[4] 参见 https://www.cia.gov/library/publications/the-world-factbook/geos/et.html。
[5] 参见 https://www.cia.gov/library/publications/the-world-factbook/geos/et.html。

了议会式政府，共有两个议院，即联邦院和人民代表院。人民代表院拥有立法权。在埃塞俄比亚联邦立法的层级中，宣言由人民代表院发布，法规由部长理事会发布，指令、指示由特定的理事会发布。

宪法分配了联邦州和地区之间的权力。联邦政府以及各地区都有立法、司法和行政机关。州议会是最高级别的地区国家机关，并有权制定在其辖区内的相关法律。

联邦政府被赋予了一项权力，即可以通过立法来制定联邦事务，这些事务包括自然资源、国家安全、外汇、对外关系、交通和通信等。所有未明确提供予联邦政府或联邦政府和各州的权力都保留给各州。

司法权属于联邦法院和地方法院，根据法律规定，法院系统由三个层级的法院组成。因此，在联邦和地方两级都有一审法院、高等法院和最高法院。在联邦一级法院和州一级联邦高等法院管辖下的事项分别委托给地方高等法院和地方最高法院。

宪法承认宗教和习惯法庭以及一些准司法机构，它们只处理诸如税收、劳工、贸易竞争等具体事项。

虽然埃塞俄比亚是法律多元主义的发源地，但它通常被定性为民事法律体系。这个国家在法国的模式上采用了大量的民商事法规。法典和立法是埃塞俄比亚法律的主要渊源。埃塞俄比亚的法律制度也承认联邦最高法院在不少于由5名法官审理的案件中所作出的在先判例和法律解释对联邦和地方法院具有约束力，并且这些决定已经对外公布，并公开出版。

（二）"一带一路"倡议下与中国企业的合作

埃塞俄比亚是对中国"一带一路"倡议充满热情的非洲国家之一。中国和埃塞俄比亚近年来的关系全面快速发展。[①]中国已表示有意在六个优先领域加深中国和埃塞俄比亚的合作关系：国家层面的管理、治安、产能合作、人力资源、航空和在全球及区域性问题上的协调。[②]埃塞俄比亚已经接受了这个计划，并且认为"一带一路"是一个加速该国经济转型的机会。

"一带一路"的项目之一是振兴非洲东部的铁路网络。中国和埃塞俄比亚签署的合同已授予中国企业通过埃塞俄比亚铁路公司建设新的 Addis Ababa-Djibouti 铁路的权利。埃塞俄比亚计划扩大该项目并在2020年建造一条5 000公里的铁路连接到肯尼亚、苏丹和南苏丹。该计划有可能将东非的多个贸易中心与中国的港口连接起来，以促进他们之间的贸易。[③]

此外，埃塞俄比亚文艺复兴大坝预计将成为铁路运行的可靠能源，并有助于东非地区可再生能源的区域一体化。[④]

埃塞俄比亚也希望增加在"一带一路"倡议下与中国企业的合作，加强在服装、农业、机械与零部件和基础设施方面的生产能力。2016年，中国山东省22家企业投资埃塞俄比亚，进出口总额是2.8亿美元。[⑤]

二、投资

（一）市场准入

1. 投资监管部门

埃塞俄比亚的投资行政机关包括投资委员会、埃塞俄比亚投资审查委员会（EIC）和区域投资委员会。埃塞俄比亚投资审查委员会有权促进、协调和监管在埃塞俄比亚的投资活动，发放投资许可证，进行政策开发并为投资者提供咨询和技术服务。区域投资委员会在各自管辖的区域履行与埃塞俄比亚投资审查委员会相同的职责。投资委员会是由总理和总理指定的其他政府官员组成的。投资委员会有权监督投资及决定投资相关的方针和调控事务。

---

① 参见 https://eng.yidaiyilu.gov.cn/qwyw/rdxw/16964.htm。
② 参见 http://www.xinhuanet.com/english/2017-06/22/c_136386698.htm。
③ 参见 http://usa.chinadaily.com.cn/a/201712/20/WS5a3a0c80a31008cf16da26fc.html。
④ 参见 http://usa.chinadaily.com.cn/a/201712/20/WS5a3a0c80a31008cf16da26fc.html。
⑤ 参见 http://www.scio.gov.cn/32618/Document/1552616/1552616.htm。

2. 投资行业法律、法规

埃塞俄比亚与投资相关的法律、法规是《投资公告》(第 769/2012 号)。《投资公告》规定了最低资本要求、投资许可要求和工业开发区。《投资公告》还规定了投资管理机关和投资担保的相关事宜。该《投资公告》根据之后发布的《投资公告》(修正案)(第 849/2014 号)进行了修订。根据《投资公告》的规定，应制定一项规定以规范为国内投资者保留激励及投资领域的细节。按照此规定，国内投资者投资激励及投资领域保留部长理事会颁布了《部长理事会条例》(第 270/2012 号)，该条例规定了为国内投资者保留的投资领域及投资者申请投资激励的条件。

还有其他直接或间接规范埃塞俄比亚投资的法律规定。埃塞俄比亚《商法典》规定了商业组织应该如何组建和运作。根据法律的适用性，埃塞俄比亚《民法典》规定了合同关系。埃塞俄比亚颁布了《就业公告》，规定了投资者与员工之间的劳资关系。《联邦所得税公告》规定了投资者的税收责任。

根据各类投资领域，制定具体的法律管理投资。采矿和能源领域就是这种拥有具体法律的投资领域的例子。埃塞俄比亚通过了《公私伙伴关系公告》，该公告规定了在埃塞俄比亚的公私伙伴关系投资的相关事宜。还有一些针对特定领域或问题的指令，例如，埃塞俄比亚税收和海关局有一项指令，详细规定了投资者的免税进口权。埃塞俄比亚投资委员会指令规定了投资者可以免税进口车辆。此外，各部门也有一些针对具体领域的指令，《建筑部专业人员和顾问注册指令》就是一个很好的例子，该指令规定了对投资建筑和工程咨询行业的投资者的能力要求。

3. 出资方式

就投资者身份而言，投资可以区分为由外国投资者或国内投资者独资、国内投资者和外国投资者合资，以及政府与国内或外国投资者的合资企业。然而，某些领域是保留给政府、国内投资者或政府和私人投资者之间的联合投资。

外国公司可采取以下形式：

（1）建立一个子公司

子公司的实质就是一家以私人有限公司或股份公司形式存在的新公司。虽然母公司对子公司有控股权，但总有股东可能不属于母公司，这些股东的存在通常是为了满足公司法定最少股东数。

（2）建立一个分公司

当一家外国公司在埃塞俄比亚开设一家分公司时，母公司的股东仍然是该分公司的股东。此外，它将采用母公司的名称，并补充说明它是埃塞俄比亚的分公司。埃塞俄比亚分公司将由母公司指定的经理管理。每一项重大决定都将通过母公司经公证的股东会议记录作出。

在章程方面，分支机构不能与母公司有不同的名称，不能转让其资产或在没有母公司允许的情况下成立新公司，不能将其转换为不同形式的企业组织。

子公司与分公司之间的主要区别是，如果公司是分公司，主要决策将由母公司通过经公证的股东会议记录作出。此外，在埃塞俄比亚法律下建立的子公司，是埃塞俄比亚的公司；但外国公司建立的分公司仍是外国的公司。

本地化的机构有其他存在形式，可以是商业代表处和项目部。商业代表处设立的目的是促进投资并在特定国家开展市场调查。在埃塞俄比亚，商业代表处只允许从事促销和市场调查。商业代表不得销售商品和服务或与客户签订合同。项目部是由外国投资者在国际投标过程中设立的。项目部需在商业登记册登记，并获得营业执照。然而，由于项目部是为需要国际投标的特殊项目而设立的，而不是常设机构，因此更容易进行清算。

（3）购买现有公司的大部分股份

埃塞俄比亚法律下的股份转让被认为是广义定义下的"并购"，因此，并购需获得贸易竞争和消费者保护管理局（TCCPA）的批准。如果并购公司的年营业额、资本或资产超过了 3 000 万比尔（即 110 万美元），则必须经贸易竞争和消费者保护管理局批准。贸易竞争和消费者保护管理局在审查过程中，除了对竞争的影响进行审查外，也对外国投资者是否具有该投资领域资格及是否满足最低资本金门槛进行审查。特别指出，贸易竞争和消费者保护管理局将审查外国投资者的最低资本金门槛及与埃塞俄比亚国家的联合投资是否符合"市场准入和审查标准"。一旦检查无误后，贸易竞争和消费者保护管理局就会以信函的形式告知文件认证和登记管理局（DARA）和贸易部（MOT）授予其批准。

4. 市场准入和审查标准

由于市场准入的限制，埃塞俄比亚存在关税壁垒，进口税从 0～35% 不等，消费税从 10%～100% 不等。埃塞俄比亚对烟草产品、汽车和纺织产品等国家不鼓励进口的货物征收消费税，也有其他商品被认为是奢侈品（如汽车和香水），因此对此类商品征收消费税。另外，对埃塞俄比亚的投资也有领域限制，其中一些领域只面向国内投资者，包括银行和保险、批发、零售、物流、广播、大众传媒、广告、促销、物流以及律师和法律服务。①

另一个市场准入限制是最低资本要求。《投资公告》规定，外国投资者必须为单个项目配置至少 20 万美元。外国投资者与国内投资者共同投资的，最低资本金额将减少至 15 万美元。投资建筑工程及相关技术咨询服务、技术测试和分析或出版工程所需的最低资本为 10 万美元，与国内投资者联合投资的情况下，所需资金为 5 万美元。

（二）外汇监管

1. 外汇监督部门

埃塞俄比亚国家银行（NBE）是该国的中央银行，拥有对银行、保险和其他金融行业的监管权力。埃塞俄比亚国家银行监控所有国际交易的外汇情况及贵重物品的交易情况。②埃塞俄比亚国家银行制定、贯彻落实国家的汇率政策，管理国家的国际储备。埃塞俄比亚国家银行对银行和其他金融机构的存款中持有的黄金和外汇资产设置了限额。此外，埃塞俄比亚国家银行还对净外汇头寸和条款以及银行和其他金融机构的外债数额设置了限额。埃塞俄比亚国家银行有权发布与外汇交易有关的指令。③《设立公告和投资公告》（第 679/2012 号）授予埃塞俄比亚国家银行对外汇和对外贷款的核准权力。

2. 外汇相关法律、法规简介

埃塞俄比亚的外汇和供应商信贷法律制度规定了银行、保险公司和其他金融机构国际支付相关的问题。外汇是由相关的外部贷款指令等立法条例规制的，如《外汇分配和管理透明度指令》《保留和利用出口收入和汇入汇款指令》以及《比尔限制和外汇持有指令》等。

每项立法的目的和范围如下：

（1）《保留和利用出口收入和汇入汇款指令》

该法律鼓励合格的货物和服务出口商，并允许他们在授权银行开立存款账户。④因此，符合条件的客户可以开立两个种类的账户，即外国保留账户 A 和外国保留账户 B⑤，其中账户 A 有 30% 的外币是无限期保留的，70% 的外币可保留 28 天，之后将兑换成当地货币。两个账户应使用在与金融相关和经常性付款的业务上，如进口货物（车辆除外）、结算外部贷款、向旅游经营者提供退款、赞助国际会议、退还未使用的外汇或其他经埃塞俄比亚国家银行批准的款项。

经授权的银行有义务按月对账户 A 和账户 B 所持有的外汇总额进行报告。

（2）《外汇分配和管理透明度指令》

在埃塞俄比亚，外汇是一种稀缺资源，需要谨慎地管理和配给。为此，埃塞俄比亚国家银行已经发布了上述指令，并创建了一个透明的外汇分配和管理制度。分配是根据优先级列表及按需进行。在外汇的分配中，银行必须以先到先得的方式优先考虑某些进口商品，如必需品。⑥同时也有按需服务的项目，并且该项目可以豁免登记。⑦禁止外汇按照非上述规定的方法进行分配。⑧

---

① 参见国内投资者投资激励及投资领域保留部长理事会《部长理事会条例》（第 270/2012）第 3 条。
② 参见《国家银行设立公告》（经修正）（第 592/2008 号）。
③ 参见《国家银行设立公告》（作为修正案）（第 592/2008 号）第 21（5）(b) 条。
④ 参见《保留和利用出口收入和汇入汇款指令》第 3 条。
⑤ 参见《保留和利用出口收入和汇入汇款指令》第 5 条。
⑥ 参见《外汇分配和管理透明度指令》第 6.1 条。
⑦ 参见《外汇分配和管理透明度指令》第 6.2 条。
⑧ 参见《外汇分配和管理透明度指令》第 7 条。

（3）《外部贷款和供应商信贷指令》

外部贷款和供应商信贷按照《外部贷款和供应商信贷指令》的规定执行。该法律要求埃塞俄比亚政府担保的任何贷款都必须在埃塞俄比亚国家银行登记。符合条件的借款人（出口商和外国投资者）的任何外国贷款，均须经埃塞俄比亚国家银行登记并批准。同样，外国投资必须在埃塞俄比亚投资审查委员会登记。[1]只有遵守上述程序，才有可能收回贷款、股息和利润。

（4）《比尔限制和外汇持有指令》

该法律对埃塞俄比亚人和外国人持有比尔和外币作出了规定。[2]一个入境埃塞俄比亚和离开埃塞俄比亚的人最多能持有1 000比尔。[3]另外，居住在埃塞俄比亚的任何人不得持有一种外币超过30天。[4]居住在埃塞俄比亚境内、从境外进入该国并携带超过1 000美元的外币的，应当使用外币申报单进行申报。[5]不居住在埃塞俄比亚但入境该国的人，该数额为3 000美元。该法还规定了对出国和入境的人以及外国人的货币限制。

3. 外国企业外汇管理的要求

对从事出口货物和服务的外国企业的外汇管理，是根据《保留和利用出口收入和汇入汇款指令》来规范的。定期接受国外汇兑、汇款和从事出口货物及服务的客户，均可在商业银行开立存款账户。符合条件的客户可以开立两个种类的账户，外汇存款账户A和外汇存款账户B。合格的客户只能在账户A内无限期地保留30%的外汇收入，其他70%的外汇收入只能在账户B中保留28天，28天后账户B中未被使用的外汇将被转换为当地货币。这两个账户都应直接为业务提供资金，用于支付进口货物的费用、外部贷款结算、顾问的服务费用，以及为国际会议支付款项等。

（三）金融融资

1. 主要金融机构

金融机构被定义为包括保险公司、银行、微型金融机构、邮政储蓄、资金转移机构和其他由埃塞俄比亚国家银行确立的类似机构。在埃塞俄比亚有16个私有和3个政府所有的银行，17个私有和一个政府所有的保险公司，35个微型金融机构。[6]银行和金融业是限制外国人参与的行业之一，只允许埃塞俄比亚公民参与。

埃塞俄比亚的主要金融监管机构是埃塞俄比亚国家银行。埃塞俄比亚国家银行监管国家的金融事务。它监管银行、外汇，充当政府的财政代理和金融顾问。埃塞俄比亚国家银行在各种金融问题上作出指示。埃塞俄比亚国家银行设置了比尔的汇率。目前比尔与美元挂钩。

2. 外国企业融资条件

政府所有的和私有银行都向在埃塞俄比亚的外国企业提供贷款。借款人须接受常规的信用评估。埃塞俄比亚开发银行（DBE）是政府所有的银行，为投资者提供资金。埃塞俄比亚开发银行以50∶50的债务股本比率为投资者提供50%的资本。与任何私有商业银行相比，埃塞俄比亚开发银行具有较强的财务能力，贷款利率相对较低。

埃塞俄比亚对外国控股的当地公司的债务有税务上的要求。根据《联邦所得税公告》的规定，在纳税年度，该公司的债务股本比为2∶1。除非是正常性的债务，否则为支付超额债务的利率不能用于税收减免。

外国投资者可以从外部获得贷款和供应商，债务股本比率为60∶40，但也有附加条件，贷款协议草案应在贷方与企业之间签订贷款协议之前，向NBE提交并得到批准。贷款协议的利率取决于平均偿还期。如果平均偿还期为3年，则利率为半年期的伦敦银行同业拆借利率或相应的欧元银行同业拆

---

[1] 参见《投资公告》第36条（270/2012）。
[2] 参见《比尔限制和外汇持有指令》。
[3] 参见《比尔限制和外汇持有指令》第2条。
[4] 参见《比尔限制和外汇持有指令》第3条。
[5] 参见《比尔限制和外汇持有指令》第4条。
[6] 埃塞俄比亚国家银行（www.nbe.gov.et）。

借利率+2%；如果是3年到5年，则利率为半年期利率或相当于欧元银行同业拆借利率+3%；如果超过5年，则利率为半年期利率或相当于欧元银行同业拆借利率+5%。[①]这些规则和条件也适用于供应商的信用。

无论是外国企业还是国内企业，都不能从银行或股东以外的其他来源借款。有利息的贷款是一种银行业务，个人或实体除非有银行执照，否则不能参与。

（四）土地政策

1. 土地相关法律、法规简介

埃塞俄比亚为管理土地权利而制定的关键法律规定如下：

（1）1995年埃塞俄比亚《宪法》；
（2）1960年埃塞俄比亚《民法典》；
（3）《土地管理及使用公告》（第456/2005号）；
（4）《城市土地租赁权公告》（第721/2011号）；
（5）《征用土地进行公共用途并支付补偿公告》（第455/2005号）；
（6）《为公共目的而征用土地上财产的补偿》（第135/2007号）。

根据埃塞俄比亚法律的规定，埃塞俄比亚无私有土地所有权，埃塞俄比亚《宪法》中的规定，"土地所有权和所有自然资源的所有权都只属于埃塞俄比亚的国家和人民"。土地是埃塞俄比亚国家、民族和人民的共同财产，不得出售或以其他方式交换。

埃塞俄比亚《宪法》赋予联邦政府"制定法律以利用和保护土地和其他自然资源、历史遗迹和文物"的权利。因此，联邦政府颁布了《土地管理及使用公告》。

在埃塞俄比亚，主要的土地立法大致分为城市土地法和农村土地法。城市土地是指位于城市中心的行政边界内的土地，另外，被定义为地方市政管理人口达到2 000名居民或更多居民人口的规模中，有一半的劳动者从事非农业劳动。与联邦法律相一致，《土地管理及使用公告》将"制定农村土地管理及使用法律"的权力授权给地方。

2. 外资企业的土地收购规则

（1）城市土地的持有

城市土地征用以两种方式进行。第一种是分配，第二种是招标。初次从有关政府机构获取土地时，任何获准进行城市土地租赁的人必须与有关政府机构签订租赁合同。租赁人订立的租赁合同的内容包括开工时间、使用期限、付款期限、宽限期以及双方各自的权利和义务。租赁持有证书随后由管理局颁发。

（2）农村土地的持有

农村土地的土地权利人可以利用其土地使用权，按照合同约定与投资者共同进行开发活动。该合同需经主管机关核准登记。持证人和投资者之间土地租赁协议所涉的土地面积和租赁期限由地区法律予以规定。

除了投资者和土地所有者之间的合同约定之外，政府也通过土地租赁协议向投资者出租土地。根据《联邦农村土地使用公告》的规定，从事农业活动的私人投资者有权依照联邦和地方法律的投资政策和规定使用农村土地。农民、半牧民和牧民在土地使用方面优先于投资者。向投资者提供农村土地这一概念在各地方州的立法中得到了进一步重申。

（五）公司的成立和解散

1. 组织形式

埃塞俄比亚《商法典》规定了六种形式的合伙关系：
① 普通合伙企业；

[①] 参见《外部贷款和供应商信贷指令》（经修订）第6条。

② 合资企业;
③ 普通合伙;
④ 有限合伙企业;
⑤ 股份公司;
⑥ 私人有限公司。

前四种形式区别于后两种形式之处在于各实体合伙人需要承担无限责任,这是企业更倾向于选择受股份限制的合伙企业或公司的一个关键因素。在后两种形式中,最普遍的是私人有限公司,主要是由于此类公司的成立更加简单,公司运营过程中涉及的监管需求较小。

股份公司由至少 5 名成员组成,股东承担有限责任。股份可自由转让,资本可以被分为实缴和认购两部分。股份公司需要有一个正式的管理结构,这一结构在《商法典》中有详细规定。

私人有限公司(PLC)由 2～50 名成员组成,在公司成立时需要全部缴付全部资本。股份不能自由转让,公司不能从事银行和保险业务。与股份公司不同,私人有限公司可以由对股东负责的经理运作,而不是必须采用正式的管理结构,比如董事会。

2. 设立程序

外国企业的设立程序包括以下步骤:

① 符合所需的文件要求。所有来自国外的文件都必须由埃塞俄比亚驻该国的大使馆提供,并在埃塞俄比亚进行进一步核实。

② 公司名称核准。

③ 纳税。法律规定,在该国经营的所有企业都必须持有由埃塞俄比亚税务和海关管理局(ERCA)签发的纳税人登记证书(TIN)。

④ 投资许可认证。埃塞俄比亚的所有投资者都必须获得埃塞俄比亚投资审查委员会的投资许可,该许可证是对在埃塞俄比亚的计划投资项目和其满足最低资本要求情况的核准和登记。投资许可证每年更新,直至投资者开始销售其产品或服务。

⑤ 商业登记认证。商业登记是在埃塞俄比亚取得营业执照的先决条件。登记机关向在商业登记簿上注册的公司签发商业登记证,以证明该实体注册的合法性。

⑥ 能力认证。一些业务部门需要从相关权威部门获得能力认证,以验证其在获颁营业执照前具有开展业务的能力。

⑦ 营业执照。依法成立的公司为了开始正常营业并盈利,必须拥有营业执照。没有有效营业执照的,不得从事经营活动。

3. 解散的途径和要求

《商法典》第 217—218 条规定的公司解散事由可分为以下三类:

① 法定的解散事由:是指当商业目的已经达到或不能达到,或当商业组织成立的期限届满,除非合伙人同意继续营业,该公司依法解散。

② 约定的解散事由:合伙人同意在该公司成立时设定的期限届满之前解散公司。

③ 司法解散事由:法院依据合伙人的申请,可以解散一个商业组织。在司法解散时,应当有正当理由,例如一方合伙人严重失职,或因严重疾病或其他任何原因导致无法履行其职责,或在合伙人之间存在严重分歧等。

(六)公司的合并和收购

1. 适用于合并和收购的法律、法规

2013 年《贸易竞争和消费者保护公告》(以下简称《竞争法》)是监管埃塞俄比亚公司并购的法律。《竞争法》将并购定义为:

① 先前独立存在的两个或两个以上的商业组织的合并,或者这些商业组织把全部或部分资源集中起来,以进行某种商业活动;

② 通过直接或间接地获取某一商业组织的股份、证券或资产,或通过购买或者其他方式控制他人

的业务管理。

2. 目标公司的类型

并购的目标公司是私营公司。埃塞俄比亚没有股票市场，因此也就没有上市公司。其大多数公司都是由家庭所有，以私人有限公司的形式存在。

3. 私营公司的合并和收购

在埃塞俄比亚，收购私人公司的常见方式是通过股份转让协议收购股份。如前所述，只有经贸易竞争和消费者保护管理局批准并通过文件认证和登记管理局（DARA）对股份转让协议进行登记后，才能完成收购。任何商业人士若提议订立并购协议，应将该提议通知贸易竞争和消费者保护管理局。并购通知的最低门槛设置在为实施并购规定而准备的并购指令中。如果并购实体的年营业额、资产价值或注册资本超过3 000万比尔的，则需要进行并购通知。

（七）竞争规则

1. 竞争监管部门

负责竞争事务的机构是贸易竞争和消费者保护管理局，该机构在贸易部的监督和管理之下。《竞争法》已在联邦和地区两级赋予贸易竞争和消费者保护管理局贸易竞争和消费者保护法庭（以下简称"法庭"）的职能。

2.《竞争法》简介

埃塞俄比亚《竞争法》是一项旨在负责保护工商界免受反竞争和不公平的市场行为的侵害，创造一个有竞争力的自由市场的法律。同时它还以保护消费者不受市场行为的误导和欺骗，为消费者创造一个公平的商品和服务的交易环境为目的。

埃塞俄比亚《竞争法》于2003年第一次获得通过，并于2014年3月进行了最新一次的修订。该法适用于在埃塞俄比亚进行或在埃塞俄比亚生效的任何有关商品或服务的活动或交易。[①]该法律覆盖范围十分广泛，包括反竞争协议、横向或纵向联合行为或决策。如果某一联合行为能显著防止或减少竞争，或者直接或间接地涉及交易价格或任何其他交易条件，涉及串通投标，或者通过分配客户、供应商、领地或特定类型的商品或服务来划分市场，那么由业务人员或商业团体在横向关系中作出的这一联合行为或决定将受到《竞争法》的禁止。[②]除非协议的一方能够证明这些协议、决定或一致的做法能够在技术层面提升效率或有利于竞争。[③]反竞争协议、纵向的联合行为或决定也被禁止，除非该行为的一方能以上述方式证明其并不具有防止或显著减少竞争的效果。[④]埃塞俄比亚法律对滥用支配地位的行为也进行了管制。虽然法律对滥用支配地位的行为没有明确的界定，但列举了一份很长的关于滥用支配地位的行为的名单。[⑤]除非有正当理由，禁止滥用支配地位。法律还提供了一种用以评估支配地位的机制。[⑥]贸易竞争和消费者保护管理局还参照上述内容对并购事宜进行规范。

3. 竞争监管措施

《竞争法》为竞争监管措施得以实施提供了制度和法律保障机制。一旦有违反竞争法的行为发生，贸易竞争和消费者保护管理局将对其进行调查，并有针对性地采取三种不同的补救措施，分别是民事、行政和刑事救济。经过调查，贸易竞争和消费者保护管理局将对违法行为提起行政诉讼。[⑦]关于刑事救济措施，联邦司法部长[⑧]和联邦警察委员会可以对被指控的违法者进行调查和起诉。任何因该实体的反竞争行为而提出赔偿请求的企业或消费者，也可将其案件提交给同一法庭。[⑨]

---

① 参见《贸易竞争和消费者保护公告》（第813/2013号）第4条。
② 同上，第7（1）（a）条。
③ 同上注。
④ 同上，第7（2）（a）条。
⑤ 同上，第5条。
⑥ 同上，第6条。
⑦ 同上，第37条。
⑧ 参见《联邦总检察长公告》（第943/2016号）。
⑨ 参见《贸易竞争和消费者保护公告》（第813/2013号）第37（2）条。

滥用支配地位的行为的行政处罚额度是年营业额的 5%～10%。① 任何商事主体被发现参与反竞争协议、联合行为或决定的，将被处以年营业额 10% 的罚款。② 任何被发现违反并购规定的商人将被处以其年营业额 5%～10% 的罚款。③ 如果除商事主体以外的任何第三人直接或间接地参与任何违反竞争法的活动，其将承担 1 万到 10 万埃塞俄比亚比尔的责任。④ 商事主体及商事主体以外的任何第三人未能遵守法庭的行政制裁、处罚或有关法庭的判决的，将受到刑事处罚，并将被处 1～5 年的监禁。⑤

（八）税收

1. 税收制度和规则

埃塞俄比亚的所得税制度建立在计划基础上，根据不同的收入类别征收不同的税，不同的收入类别适用不同的税率和扣除额。埃塞俄比亚《所得税法》基于两项税收原则：住宅和收入。《所得税法》适用于埃塞俄比亚居民的全球收入和非本地居民的收入。

《所得税公告》（第 979/2016 号）、《联邦部长委员会所得税条例》（第 410/2017 号）、《联邦税务行政公告》（第 983/2016 号）、《增值税公告》（第 285/2002 号，经第 609/2008 号修订）、《部长委员会增值税条例》（第 79/2002 号）、《营业税公告》（第 308/2002 号，经第 611/2008 号修订）、《货物税公告》（第 307/2002 号）及《印花税公告》（第 110/1998 号）适用于埃塞俄比亚的税务制度和税务管理程序。

2. 税务类别和税率

（1）直接税，包括就业所得税、营业税、建筑物租金税、存款利息所得税、股息税、特许权使用所得税和其他税收。

（2）间接税，包括流转税、消费税、增值税和关税。

（3）印花税，是针对法规所规定的特定公司的注册文件而征收的。公司注册文件包括章程大纲、章程、安全契约、法人授权书、产权证明文件。费率是根据文件的类型计算的，要么按统一费率计算，要么按百分比计算。

（4）适用于企业的主要直接税和间接税如下：

编号	税种	税率
1	企业所得税	30%
2	关税	0%～35%
3	股息税	10%
4	消费税	10%～100%
5	出口税	无
6	就业所得税	0%～35%
7	矿区开采使用税	5%
8	营业税	2% 和 10%
9	增值税	15%
10	代扣所得税	2%
11	资本收益税	15%（针对不动产的处置）
		30%（针对股票和债券的转让）
12	从国外获得技术或管理服务的收入	15%

---

① 参见《贸易竞争和消费者保护公告》（第 813/2013 号），第 42（1）条。
② 同上，第 42（2）条。
③ 同上，第 42（4）条。
④ 同上，第 42（5）条。
⑤ 同上，第 43 条。

3. 税务申报和优惠政策

根据埃塞俄比亚《税法》的规定，纳税年度为财政年度，即从7月8日至次年的7月7日为1年，除非法律另有规定。

（1）纳税人的纳税年度分为：纳税人为个人及由个人组成的协会，指财政年度；纳税人为机构，指该机构的会计年度。

（2）纳税人分为：

① A类纳税人：每年总收入超过100万埃塞俄比亚比尔的机构或个人；

② B类纳税人：除机构外，年总收入在50万至100万埃塞俄比亚比尔的纳税人；

③ C类纳税人：除机构外，年总收入低于50万埃塞俄比亚比尔的纳税人。

（3）纳税申报时间：

雇员不需要申报纳税，除非雇员在一个公历月内有超过一个的雇主，或者他有自我扣缴义务。

① A类纳税人在纳税年度结束后的4个月内有纳税申报义务。

② B类纳税人在纳税年度起始2个月内有纳税申报义务。

③ C类纳税人应按照每年7月7日至8月6日的征税标准缴纳税款。

（九）证券交易

1. 证券相关法律、法规简介

1960年颁布的埃塞俄比亚《商法典》最初设想的是，资本金完全缴足的公司可以发行债务证券（债券、股票等）。① 政府也可以发行债券。② 财政部和经济合作部是被授权发行国库券和债券的政府机构。③ 虽然有通过证券市场发行债券的可能性，但埃塞俄比亚从未有过正式的证券市场。其初级债务证券市场并不是根据法律制定的，只要资本充足的公司都可以发行债务证券。公司发行股票的做法也很普遍。政府偶尔会以短期国库券和长期国库券的形式发行债务证券，但这种现象非常罕见。埃塞俄比亚也没有二级债务证券市场。市场上的证券主要都是通过场外交易或交易商的网站进行，而不是依据相关法律进行有组织的证券交易，对证券交易所的全面监管和证券交易的实体结构在埃塞俄比亚并不存在。

2. 证券市场的监督管理

埃塞俄比亚没有证券市场，也没有监管证券市场的法律。

3. 外国企业从事证券交易业务的要求

由于埃塞俄比亚没有证券市场和证券交易的实体结构（无论是初级市场还是二级市场），也没有法律和相关的监管要求来规范证券交易，因此外国人不能在埃塞俄比亚进行证券交易。

（十）对投资的优惠和保护

（1）优惠政策的结构

埃塞俄比亚增长和转型计划（GTP）确定了不同的优惠领域，这是一份旨在通过实现预计的国内生产总值目标来改善该国经济的政策文件。埃塞俄比亚增长和转型计划对一些支柱产业的发展进行了概述，包括：

① 保持过去10年来快速、广泛和公平的经济增长和发展；

② 通过同时提高生产部门（农业和制造业）的产品质量、生产率和竞争力，提高总体的生产能力和效率；

③ 加快和促进国内私营部门的转型，使其成为强劲的发展力量；

④ 提升国内建筑业实力，尤其注重通过加强对建设部门的执行能力的关注确保基础设施服务的质

---

① 参见埃塞俄比亚《商法典》第429条。
② 参见《国家银行设立公告》（修订版）第5（3）条；《政府特别债券公告》（第531/2007号）。
③ 参见《政府特别债券公告》（第53/2007号）第2（1）条。

量，填补关键的基础设施缺口；

⑤ 对正在进行的快速的城市化进行适当管理和规范，以释放其维持经济增长和促进经济结构转型的潜力；

⑥ 通过提高公共部门的执行能力和加强动员公众的参与，建立对社会民主和发展的良好治理机制。

根据埃塞俄比亚目前的政策结构，投资者所从事的任何与上述支柱产业相关的活动都被认为是可取的。关于投资的法律制度规定了利用下列财政和非财政的投资者保护措施来促进和鼓励投资机制：

① 投资激励措施。在埃塞俄比亚，凡是允许外国企业投资的领域，任何形式的商业组织作为投资者均有资格获得某些奖励和豁免。

② 财政激励措施。

免征所得税：根据投资管理的相关规定，根据投资项目的类型和地点，对投资企业给予1~6年免征所得税的豁免。该豁免适用于新企业、扩大或升级企业，并额外适用于产品或服务出口量至少为总量的60%的投资者。

亏损结转：在免税期内遭受损失的投资者，可以在所得税减免期到期后结转一半的损失。

免除关税：根据《投资条例》的规定，投资者有权进口与建立或扩大其无关税的企业有关的资本货物和建筑材料。

出口激励措施：除少数产品（半加工皮革和皮革）外，出口产品不征收出口税。

（2）对特定行业和区域的支持

国内外的合格投资者在制造业、农业、农产品加工业、能源生产、电力运输和供应、信息通信技术（ICT）、旅游、建筑承包、教育和培训、建筑和工程咨询、技术检测和分析、资本货物等领域建立新企业，均有权获得免税额，其免税率取决于投资者所在的部门类型。此外，在亚的斯亚贝巴的投资者的免税情况不同于其他地区，那些决定前往该地区的投资者将获得长期的所得税豁免。

在 Gambella、Benishangul Gumuz、Afar（除去 Awash 河左右两边15公里以内的地方）、Somali、Oromiya 的 Guji 和 Borana 区域、南 Omo 区、Segen（Derashe、Amaro、Konso 和 Burji）人民区、Benchi-Maji 区、Dawaro 区、Sheka 区、Keffa 区、南方民族和人民区的 Sheka 区、Keffa 区或 Konta 和 Basketo 特别行政区等地区建立了新业务的投资者，在所得税免税期届满后3年内，可以享受30%的所得税减免。法律通过这样做来鼓励投资者到工业化程度较低和发展较为落后的某些地区进行投资。

所有资本货物的进口，如工厂车间、机器设备和建筑材料，都有权享受关税和对此种货物征收的其他税款的100%的豁免。

占进口投资资本货物总价值15%的备件，也可以免缴关税。

生产、出口商品的投资者也可获得非财政奖励，这些投资者有资格通过供应商的信贷进口机器和设备。经营者在所得税减免期内遭受损失的，在所得税减免期满后，可以结转损失。

埃塞俄比亚法律极力鼓励投资者从事制造业和农业。已经投资超过20万美元并为超过50名埃塞俄比亚国民创造了永久就业机会的制造业企业，将有权随时享受资本货物的免税特权。在投资者从事其他行业时，这种特权可持续5年。

（3）特别经济区

埃塞俄比亚成立了工业和发展公司[①]，用以开发和管理工业园区，租用土地，制定详细的国家工业园区总体规划，为工业园区提供必要的基础设施，将工业园区的管理外包出去，促进工业园区效益的增长。

在工业园区内从事制造业的投资者享有额外的福利，例如免除所得税的期限高达8~10年。此外，工业园区内提供一站式的政府服务。

工厂和住宅区的土地租赁期限为60~80年。此外，工业园区还通过保税出口工厂计划，将进口的原材料直接从海关邮寄到工厂，提供海关方面的便利。

关于工业园区开发商与工业园区企业之间的转租，埃塞俄比亚投资审查委员会确保：租赁和分租协

---

① 参见《工业园区公告》（第886/2015号）；《部长会议关于设立工业园区发展公司的条例》（第326/2014号）。

议的签订；施工许可按照规定的制度进行；根据计划建设基础设施；为生产提供相关服务；适当地提供所需的材料。如果不遵守这些要求，转租则无法完成。埃塞俄比亚投资审查委员会不干预转租价格。

根据工业园区的位置，对工业园区的开发商免征 10～15 年的所得税，同时给开发商提供必要的基础设施，包括专用的变电站。

（4）工业园区配备有道路、水、电力、电话、固体垃圾和液体污水排放设施等重要基础设施。因此，工业园区的开发商有资格提供安保、废物处理、电信或仓储等服务。

（5）投资保护

《投资法》为外国投资者提供以下保护：

① 征用保护：除因公共利益或法律明确规定以外，不得征收或者国有化个人资产。因公共利益需要被征用时，应支付与现行市场价值相对应的适当补偿。

② 资金输出：外国投资者依法享有将其外国贷款的任何利润、股息、本金和利息、转让股份或转让所有权的收益、企业销售或清算所得的收益等汇回国内的权利。此外，外籍人士还可将其工资和其他从工作中得到的收入汇回国内。这实际上需要通过埃塞俄比亚投资审查委员会和埃塞俄比亚国家银行来处理。

③ 拥有不动产的权利：《投资公告》授权外国投资者拥有自己的住宅和任何其他不动产，包括经营业务所必需的私人商业车辆。外国投资者在离开该国时，可根据此权利买卖不动产。只要有外国企业在里面，如前文所述，他们就会成为奖励政策的受益者。

上述对投资者的保护政策在埃塞俄比亚与其他国家的双边投资协定中得到重申。迄今为止，埃塞俄比亚与 33 个国家签署了相关协定，其中 21 个协定已生效。[①]这些国家是意大利、科威特、瑞士、马来西亚、也门、中国、苏丹、利比亚、法国、突尼斯、伊朗、土耳其、荷兰、丹麦、瑞典、阿尔及利亚、奥地利、以色列、德国、芬兰和埃及。[②]这些双边投资协定对促进和鼓励投资、保护投资、投资待遇、赔偿损害和损失、公平和公正地对待外国投资者以及在征用时给予充分和及时的补偿等内容作出了规定。埃塞俄比亚作为缔约国的双边投资条约也提供了解决争端的机制。这些双边投资条约为投资者提供了一种选择，即向东道国提出索赔。在其选择向东道国的主管法院提请解决投资纠纷的诉求之前，还可以选择国际投资争端解决中心（ICSID）（双方都是其成员）、由特别协议指定的国际仲裁员或特设仲裁庭或者根据贸易法委员会仲裁规则设立的国际商会仲裁法庭。

双边投资条约为投资者提供了类似于国内法的保护，同时具有有效的争端解决机制。在国内法律保护的情况下，投资者只有权在具有管辖权的国内法院提起解决投资纠纷的诉求。双边投资条约的争端解决机制包括国内法院、国际投资争端解决中心法庭、特设仲裁庭和基于贸易法委员会仲裁规则的仲裁。

三、贸易

（一）贸易监管部门

贸易部是负责贸易监管的主要政府机关。在 2010 年政府部门调整后，贸易部作为一个专门负责规范贸易的部门被设立（依据第 691/2010 号声明）。目前，贸易部的职能由第 916/2015 号声明予以规定。在贸易部的职能中，贸易部有权为了推动和发展出口贸易、控制进出口货物质量创造有利条件。贸易部下的贸易关系和谈判总局负责执行贸易部建立贸易关系和协调贸易谈判。

除了贸易部外，不同的政府机关（例如埃塞俄比亚投资审查委员会、埃塞俄比亚税务和海关总署、埃塞俄比亚贸易竞争和消费者保护管理局和埃塞俄比亚国家银行）在规范、促进埃塞俄比亚贸易方面扮演着不同的角色。

根据 1995 年《宪法》所采用的联邦制度，联邦政府和 9 个地区的州政府有权对各自的司法事务进行监管。联邦政府（贸易部）有权监管州与州之间的贸易和对外贸易，并就国际协议进行谈判和批准。

---

① 参见 http://investmentpolicyhub.unctad.org/IIA/CountryBits/67#iiaInnerMenu accessed on 14 March 2018。
② 参见 http://investmentpolicyhub.unctad.org/IIA/CountryBits/67#iiaInnerMenu accessed on 14 March 2018。

各地区管理商业活动的机关有权规范和发展各州的其他贸易事务。

（二）贸易法律、法规和贸易管理简介

《投资促进以及国内投资者投资保护条例》（第270/2012号，以下简称"第270/2012号规定"）管控允许从事对外贸易的人员。根据第270/2012号规定的规定，进口贸易专门为国内投资者保留。但是，外国投资者可以从事出口贸易，出口贸易的范围不包括出口生咖啡豆、柳絮、油籽、干豆、珍贵的矿物质、市场上采购的兽皮、林业产品，非投资者自己饲养的活的绵羊、山羊、骆驼、牛和马类。

目前，没有单一的限制商品进口和出口的法律。但是目前，议会正在讨论声明草案，旨在规范进出口贸易的监管。在不同的法律中，可以找到一些对进出口贸易的限制。《商业登记及许可公告》（第980/2016号）授权贸易部在部长理事会的批准下，有权禁止从埃塞俄比亚进口或出口某些商品和服务，以满足国家利益。

埃塞俄比亚是《非洲增长与机遇法案》的受益方，因此其有资格向美国出口某些不受关税和配额限制的商品。埃塞俄比亚也是东南非洲共同市场的非自由贸易成员，该市场建立了一个由19个成员国组成的自由贸易区。尽管埃塞俄比亚是东南非共同市场的非自由贸易成员，但目前从埃塞俄比亚进口或出口合格商品可获得10%的关税减免。[①]埃塞俄比亚还与33个国家签署了双边投资协定，旨在建立牢固的贸易关系。

在开放给外国投资者的领域，对各种商品实施出口奖励、免税特权以及限制国内产品的参与，可以看作是埃塞俄比亚对政府自由化的承诺。然而目前埃塞俄比亚的进口贸易受到各种限制，一般情况下，只从事进口贸易的贸易商没有资格获得奖励。

（三）进出口商品的检验检疫

埃塞俄比亚对进出口商品的检验检疫主要是为了征收关税及其他税种，以及检查商品的合法性。因为前述原因，所以埃塞俄比亚尚未成为世界贸易组织的成员，而且征收关税仍占该国财政收入的很大一部分。

关于商品的合法性，海关法禁止任何人进口、出口或转运法律或国际公约禁止的货物，并禁止任何人在未经主管当局事先许可的情况下，对被标记为受限制的货物采取同样做法。是否禁止或限制某一商品，应从埃塞俄比亚的国内法或埃塞俄比亚认可的国际公约中予以确认。

商品检验是由一名官员对货物进行实物检查（不论是通过货物扫描机还是手工检查），以确保货物的原产国和出口国、性质、状态、质量、数量、关税类别和价值符合预先提交的登记声明资料。

检验是在风险管理的基础上进行的，将进出口商划分为某些风险类别。海关当局也有权抽取样品进行检验，检验费用由报关人承担。

（四）海关管理

在埃塞俄比亚联邦政府的安排中，联邦政府有权管制外国商业，征收关税、其他税种和其他进出口费用。埃塞俄比亚税务和海关总署于2008年通过第587/2008号声明而设立，作为一个直接向总理负责的联邦机构，其合并了之前互相独立的税务部、埃塞俄比亚海关局和联邦税务局。

埃塞俄比亚税务和海关总署目前负责管理该国总体的海关事务，并在联邦政府管辖下管理国内税收。由于各州未获授权进行海关管理工作，埃塞俄比亚税务和海关总署目前在埃塞俄比亚各地设有30个负责执行具体的海关管理任务的分支机构。此外，埃塞俄比亚税务和海关总署还有权检查通过海关港口、边境站和其他海关站进出埃塞俄比亚的货物和运输工具，以确保其办理了相应的海关手续，并负责收集和分析控制进出口货物所需的信息，发放仓库许可证，监督免税商店。

在埃塞俄比亚进出口货物，需要从贸易部获得进出口许可证。其他许可证，例如投资许可证，也可以作为进出口投资货物的许可证。此外，贸易部有权禁止某些货物的进出口。

由于埃塞俄比亚是一个内陆国家，海运的进出口货物主要通过吉布提港出入其境。埃塞俄比亚航

---

① 亚的斯亚贝巴商会、东南非共同市场，详见 https://addischamber.com/comesa-common-market-for-eastern-and-southern-africa/。

运公司等独立机构提供从海运到多式联运和单一方式运输以及海关和港口清关服务等全面服务。

四、劳动

（一）劳动法律、法规简介

埃塞俄比亚《劳动公告》将雇佣关系划分为管理性和非管理性的。管理人员是由法律规定或由雇主委托，有权力制定和执行管理政策的人员，和/或有权决定雇用、迁转、停业、裁员、委派或对员工采取惩戒性措施的人员，而且包括法律服务负责人（负责考虑雇主的利益来作出独立判断，从而提出有关建议）。[1] 其他工作人员都被划分为非管理雇员。

《劳动公告》及其修正案适用于非管理雇员，而埃塞俄比亚《民法典》适用于管理人员。虽然每一项法律都规定了最低劳动条件，但雇用合同的当事方可以就更好的条件达成协议。

根据埃塞俄比亚法律的规定，当雇员直接或间接同意在雇主的监督下从事定期或无固定限期的工作，以换取工资时，即称为雇佣关系。[2] 因此，当雇主的要约被雇员接受时，即使申请人还未到雇主处报到，雇佣关系就已经开始。要约和承诺都可以直接或间接作出，雇主在此期间解除协议可能构成非法解除劳动合同。

准备书面形式的劳动合同不是强制性要求。如果劳动合同是书面形式的，必须具体说明：雇主和雇员的个人资料、雇用类型（职位）、工作地点、工资的计算标准和方式、付款间隔和合同期限。如果劳动合同不是书面形式的，雇主有义务在合同订立后15天内向雇员提供载有上述信息的经签字的书面声明。[3]

《劳动公告》和《民法典》都规定雇主可酌情试用雇员。在此期间，雇主和雇员都可以终止雇佣关系，而无须通知对方，也不需要向另一方给予赔偿。但这样的试用期必须以书面形式约定，对于非管理雇员，试用期不得超过连续45天。但是，《民法典》没有规定最长的试用期。《劳动公告》还规定了诸如最长工作时间、加班费、病假、工伤、年假、产假、妇女和青年员工的工作条件等事项。[4]

根据《劳动公告》的规定，劳动合同可因下列任何一种理由而终止：雇主及雇员基于合同法原则，依据法律规定，经双方书面同意，终止劳动合同。该公告还包括一份穷尽式列举的清单，列出了可以在没有通知的情况下终止劳动合同的情况。此外，如果公告中所列的理由之一存在，雇主或雇员也可以通过发出通知而终止劳动合同。约定期限或固定限期合同可以在本合同规定的期限结束时终止，或者在合同中约定的具体工作完成后终止。

对于管理人员，无论是在通知还是没有通知的情况下，雇主终止劳动合同，都需要有正当的理由。因此，在没有正当理由的情况下，是不可以解雇此类雇员的。埃塞俄比亚法律承认《民法典》所列的某些理由构成正当理由，如果存在这些理由，雇主可在发出所需通知后终止合同。在要求通知才可以终止合同的情况下，如果没有通知，则需要支付代替通知的款项。

另外，无论是雇主还是雇员，如果有严重程度足以证明可以立即解除合同的理由，都可以在不通知的情况下解除劳动合同。法律并未明文规定哪些情形是严重程度足以证明可以立即解除合同的理由，不过，仅仅不履行劳动合同下的义务是不可以立即解除合同的。

（二）雇用外籍员工的要求

埃塞俄比亚《投资法》允许投资者雇用成功经营其企业所需要的外国人，该企业必须计划在提供必要培训后的有限时间内，由埃塞俄比亚国民接替外籍员工。[5] 然而，投资者可以在没有任何限制的情况下保留外籍人员的高级管理职位。[6]

---

[1] 参见《劳动公告》（第377/2003号），《尼卡里特·加泽塔联邦投资公告》第10年第12号，第3（2）（C）条，《劳动公告》（修正）（第494/2006号），《尼卡里特·加泽塔联邦投资公告》第12年第30号，第2（1）（C）条。
[2] 参见《劳动公告》（第377/2003号），《尼卡里特·加泽塔联邦投资公告》第10年第12号，第4（1）条。
[3] 同上，第7（1）条。
[4] 同上，第61、66、76、85、88、89、92条。
[5] 参见《尼卡里特·加泽塔联邦投资公告》第18年第63号，第3（2）（c）条、第37（1）（2）条，第769/2012号。
[6] 同上，第37（3）条，第769/2012号。

1. 工作许可

一般来说，获得工作许可是外国人在埃塞俄比亚就业的先决条件。但是，法律对外交使团、联合国会员国、世界银行等的外籍人员规定了某些例外情况。[①]一般情况下，外国雇员在开始在埃塞俄比亚工作之前，必须申请并取得工作许可。工作许可通常发放 3 年，但每年可延期。此外，在社会和劳工事务部（MOLSA）确定在该国国内劳动力市场上是具备还是缺乏该外籍人士具备的技能之后，才发放工作许可。[②]雇主还必须提供一份计划，规定在技能转让后由埃塞俄比亚国民替代外籍人员的时间表。

此外，外籍人士须在抵港后 30 天内到移民及国籍事务主管部门登记。[③]在获得工作许可证后，外国人必须申请并获得有效期为 1 年的居留许可。

2. 申请程序

以下材料需要在向社会和劳工事务部申请工作许可时提供：
① 工作许可申请表（已填）；
② 外籍雇员的教育及工作经历证明材料——在埃塞俄比亚驻外使馆进行过合法认证（原件的照片）；
③ 外籍员工旅行证件的复印件（护照）；
④ 有效的商业签证、投资签证或者工作签证；
⑤ 雇主向社会和劳工事务部发出的请求书，并附上劳动合同的复印件；
⑥ 4 张护照大小的照片；
⑦（副本）雇主填写的表格，指定在技能转让后取代外籍人员的当地雇员；
⑧ 如果外籍人员被指派从事需要技术方面的知识或能力的工作，提供可以证明其精通程度的相应证书；
⑨ 1 700 埃塞俄比亚比尔服务费。

此外，如果雇主是一个私营组织或实体，则必须提供以下材料：
① 雇主的有效营业执照或投资证书或者商业登记证；
② 雇主的有效增值税和纳税登记证；
③ 卫生部或教育部的支持函——如果外籍人员要在卫生或教育部门工作；
④ 来自相关机构的支持信，解释在当地市场上缺乏该外籍人士的专业知识的原因。

（三）社会保险

《私营组织雇员养老金公告》（第 781/2011 号）管理私营组织雇员的养老金计划。所有埃塞俄比亚私营组织雇员（管理和非管理人员）都必须缴纳国家设立和管理的强制性养老金基金。雇主必须为养老金缴纳雇员工资的 11%，雇员则必须缴纳其工资的 7%。但是，该法律（雇主必须每月代扣代缴前述金额的养老金）不适用于外国人。[④]埃塞俄比亚私营组织雇员的退休年龄为 60 岁。雇员必须工作至少 10 年才能领取养老金。外籍人员不需要缴纳养老金。

（四）出入境

《移民公告》（第 354/2003 号）和第 114/2004 号规定规范埃塞俄比亚的出入境事宜。外国人必须持有有效的旅行证件、入境签证或永久居留证，或身份证和健康证明才能进入埃塞俄比亚。如果一个人具备旅游签证或过境签证，他/她还必须持有允许他/她进入目的地国的机票和签证。同样，离开埃塞俄比亚的人必须持有有效的旅行证件、目的地国签证和健康证明（视情况而定）。

1. 签证类型

根据来访者的目的，埃塞俄比亚会签发不同种类的签证：外交、特殊、商业、移民、旅游、过境、

---

① 参见《劳工和社会事务部关于向外国人发放工作许可证的指令》（2002 年），第 5（2）条。
② 同上，第 10（3）条。
③ 参见《移民公告》（第 354/2003 号），《尼卡里特·加泽塔联邦投资公告》第 9 年第 75 号，第 13（C）条。
④ 参见《私营组织雇员养老金公告》（第 715/2011 号），《尼卡里特·加泽塔联邦投资公告》第 17 年第 79 号，第 10 条。

学生、出境和再入境签证。① 下面简要介绍一些签证。

外交签证——为"大使、外交代表、随员、领事代表、国际和区域组织官员及其配偶以及持外交护照入境或过境的外国国民"等人员签发的签证。②

公务签证——"外国使馆、常驻代表团和领事机构的雇员,国际或地区组织的国际公务人员",上述人员的家属持公务签证入境。③

商务签证——是为目的是投资、就业、与外国政府或区域组织、非政府组织签订协议的无报酬的人道主义服务提供者,及为参加专题讨论会、展览、讲习班、培训和相关活动的需前往埃塞俄比亚的外国人发放的签证。④ 商务签证允许一次或多次入境。

移民签证——"被埃塞俄比亚人收养的外国人或与埃塞俄比亚人结婚的外国人,在埃塞俄比亚拥有永久居留许可的外国国民"适用移民签证。⑤

旅游签证——是签发给外国人前来旅游的签证。旅游签证可签发一次或多次入境。需要注意的是,持旅游签证的外国人是不允许工作的。⑥

过境签证——过境埃塞俄比亚的外国人可以申请过境签证(单次过境或者二次过境)。⑦

学生签证——前往埃塞俄比亚求学或者培训的外国人可以申请学生签证。申请人必须出示他/她所收到的埃塞俄比亚教育机构或者培训机构的录取通知书以及可以支付学费、生活费的资金。⑧

2. 出入境的限制

根据埃塞俄比亚《移民公告》的规定,如果签发当局有理由相信申请人可能是"公共负担"或被认定为是罪犯、吸毒者,或者患有危险的传染病、提供虚假信息或违反移民法规定的,则可拒绝或取消签证。⑨ 但是,目前没有任何出境的限制,除非有法院指令。

(五)工会以及劳动组织

埃塞俄比亚《劳动公告》允许工人和雇主分别组成工会和雇主协会。在一个组织中,至少需要10名工人组成工会。⑩ 该公告还允许通过工会联盟和联合会联盟组成联合会。这些组织的目的是确保法律所规定的工作条件得到落实,并保护其成员的权利和权益⑪,还可以代表其成员参加集体谈判和处理劳动纠纷。

(六)劳动争议

《劳动公告》在国家一审法院设立了劳动庭,该庭负责裁决个人劳动纠纷,如纪律措施、解雇、工资、休假、工伤等问题。⑫ 第25/96号联邦法院公告赋予联邦一审法院类似的权力。对一审法院的裁决不满意的一方可向上诉法院提出上诉。

关于雇主和雇员之间的集体劳动纠纷,如工资,其他福利,新的工作条件,集体协议或工作规则的签订、修改和取消,法律允许当事方通过调解或仲裁来解决争议。如未能达成协议,他们可向劳动关系委员会或有关法院主张权利。

另一种办法是,当事方可以把案件交由社会和劳工事务部处理,由社会和劳工事务部任命一名调解人。调解人应在争议提交后30天内解决,如果调解不成功,应向社会和劳工事务部及当事人各方提交一份详细说明问题的报告和他/她的评论。根据争议的性质,当事方可以将此事提交劳动关系委员

---

① 参见《移民公告》(第354/2003号),《尼卡里特·加泽塔联邦投资公告》第9年第75号,第12条。
② 《部长理事会条例》(第114/2004号),《尼卡里特·加泽塔联邦投资公告》,第11年,第4号,第14条。
③ 同上,第15条。
④ 同上,第16条。
⑤ 同上,第17条。
⑥ 同上,第18条。
⑦ 同上,第19条。
⑧ 同上,第20条。
⑨ 参见《移民公告》(第354/2003号),《尼卡里特·加泽塔联邦投资公告》第9年第75号,第5条。
⑩ 参见《劳动公告》(第377/2003号),《尼卡里特·加泽塔联邦投资公告》第10年第12号,第113条。
⑪ 同上,第115条。
⑫ 同上,第137、138条。

会。法律规定，劳动关系委员会的事实调查结果是终局的。然而，当事方有权在劳动关系委员会作出决定后 30 天内，向联邦高等法院提出上诉（基于适用法律错误）。

五、知识产权

（一）知识产权法律、法规简介

埃塞俄比亚联邦民主共和国《宪法》（第 1/1995 号）承认了有形和无形私人财产的所有权。

埃塞俄比亚是世界知识产权组织的成员，但不是主要的国际知识产权公约的缔约国。[①] 埃塞俄比亚知识产权局正在努力加入《保护工业产权巴黎公约》。

埃塞俄比亚颁布了承认和保护各种知识产权的国内立法。构成知识产权法律框架的主要法律有：《发明、小发明和工业设计公告》《版权和邻接权保护公告》（经修订）、《商标注册和保护公告》与《植物培育者权利公告》。

埃塞俄比亚知识产权局成立于 2003 年，是负责保护和维护国家知识产权的政府机构。

（二）专利保护和申请

在埃塞俄比亚，管理专利的主要法律是《关于发明、小发明和工业设计公告》（第 123/1995 号）。除了议会颁布的这一公告外，部长会议关于发明、小发明和工业设计的第 12/1997 号条例也对这一领域作出了更加详细的规定。这些法律涵盖了除专利之外的小发明，如实用新型和工业设计。

专利的保护期为 10～15 年，如果可以证明是在本国合理使用的话，可以再延长 5 年。

依据埃塞俄比亚法律的规定，如果一项发明是新的有创造性的，并且在工业上是可行的，则它是可以申请专利权的。

享有专利权的人，可以按照埃塞俄比亚知识产权局规定的格式，说明申请人的姓名、地址、国籍、住所以及发明的名称，向该局提交专利申请。专利申请的标题必须简短、准确。

在埃塞俄比亚提交专利申请需要以下文件：

① 专利申请文件需要列出发明的说明、权利主张、图样以及摘要；

② 如果申请人想根据外国申请主张优先权，应当提供 12 个月内已提交的外国申请的经核证的真实副本，优先文件最晚可在埃塞俄比亚提交申请之日起 90 天内提交；

③ 申请组织已被该发明人授权就该发明申请权利；

④ 在公证人面前签署的委托书，并经埃塞俄比亚驻国外大使馆/领事馆认可其合法性后，将授权书交给在埃塞俄比亚的专利代理人或专利律师。如果有充分的理由说明委托书材料不能连同申请一并提供，那么提交的时间间隔最多为 2 个月。

在填写专利申请后，登记处将进行一次形式审查，如果不符合上述要求，将会正式要求申请人在 2 个月内修改其申请。如果通过了形式审查，将对申请进行实质性审查。

在形式和实质性审查通过后，专利将会被授予。当专利被授予后，该文件将在政府公报上公布，并将颁发专利证书。专利最初给予 15 年保护期，从申请之日起计算。如果证明该专利在埃塞俄比亚得到合理使用，则保护期可以延长 5 年。每年必须预付保护专利的年费，从填写完日期后一年开始计算。但埃塞俄比亚当局为迟缴年费提供了 6 个月的宽限期。不支付年费，专利申请会被视为撤回或放弃。

（三）商标注册

监管商标的主要两部法律是《商标注册和保护公告》（第 501/2006 号）和部长会议通过《商标注册和保护条例》（第 273/2012 号）。商标注册后，保护期为 7 年，而且可以无限续期。

《商标注册和保护公告》（第 501/2006 号）将商标定义为：能够将货物或服务与类似的货物或服务区分开来的任何标志或标志组合。商标可以是字母、单词、数字、象征元素和颜色组合，也可以是其

[①] 埃塞俄比亚于 1982 年 2 月 17 日加入了《保护奥林匹克标志的内罗毕条约》，并于 2013 年 6 月 28 日签署了《马拉喀什条约》，以方便盲人、视力障碍者或其他印刷品阅读障碍者查阅已出版的作品。

中的任何组合。

商标所有权是通过注册取得的，对第三方具有约束力。

在埃塞俄比亚，商标注册需要下列文件：

① 按照规定经填写的申请表，一式两份；

② 经外国公证和授权委托书签署地的埃塞俄比亚外国大使馆/领事馆认证（合法性）的授权委托书；

③ 根据尼斯分类第十版填写的商品和服务清单；

④ 经公证机关核证的本国或外国商标注册证书的副本，当公司打算注册一个商标，没有本国或外国注册证书的，经认证的营业执照副本也可以，营业执照必须载明公司提供与所注册商标有关的服务或商品；

⑤ 商标中除阿姆哈拉语或拉丁文以外的字符，或除阿姆哈拉语、阿拉伯语或拉丁数字以外的数字表达式，直译为阿姆哈拉语或拉丁字符或阿拉伯数字。

此外，申请人可在提交申请之日起6个月内，通过提供经核证无误的外国申请商标注册的副本，主张优先权。在埃塞俄比亚申请之日起90天内，可以延迟填写优先权文件。

埃塞俄比亚知识产权局将对申请实行形式审查和实质性审查，之后会在全国发行的报刊上发布通知。如果通知发布后60天内无人提出异议，将会发放注册证书。相反，如果有人提出异议，知识产权局会让双方提供证据后再进行裁决。一个注册商标保护期为7年，可以无限期续期。

商标所有人可通过向知识产权局备案的方式许可或转让其商标。其他有关登记人身份或所有权的变动，如姓名、地址和合并等，也应在知识产权局备案。

（四）著作权

埃塞俄比亚的著作权制度包括《著作权和相邻权保护公告》（第410/2004号）及第872/2014号修正案。部长会议通过了《著作权及相邻权部长理事会条例》（第305/2014号），该条例有助于前述公告的执行。

（五）知识产权保护措施

在知识产权侵权案件中，埃塞俄比亚法律规定了民事救济和刑事处罚。

民事救济包括禁止令，以停止对相关权利人的侵犯（或）赔偿所造成的损失。

另外，参与侵犯知识产权的人可能面临1~10年的监禁。此外，在适当的情况下，处罚可包括扣押、没收和销毁侵权货物。

除上述措施外，受指控侵权的货物可能会被海关当局扣押和扣留。

六、环境保护

（一）环境保护监管部门

负责埃塞俄比亚所有环境事务和环境保护的联邦政府机构是环境、森林和气候变化部（以下简称"该部"）。根据《环境保护机构设立公告》（第295/2002号）和《埃塞俄比亚联邦民主共和国行政机关关于权利和义务定义》（第916/2016号）的规定，需要建立一种制度，以便在联邦和地区各级环境保护机构之间相互促进协调但所承担的责任又是有区别的。《环境保护机构设立公告》还要求分别设立部门和地区的环境单位和机构。据此，该部将环境保护权力下放给了6个机构：水、灌溉和电力部；交通部；采矿、石油和天然气部；农业和自然资源部；工业部；城市发展和住房部。

根据《环境影响评估公告》（第299/2002号）的规定，环境影响评估是实施重大发展项目、方案和计划的强制性的法定前置条件。环境影响评估的目的是在项目实施前，充分评估重大项目的影响，并确保重大不利影响的缓解措施落实到位。环境影响评估包括程序性的指引，作为批准任何部门新开发活动和项目的先决条件。除该项目为政府所有外，环境影响评估由经认证的私人专家（由该部认证）进行。如果项目由联邦机构许可、执行和监督，或者可能产生跨区域影响，则由该部负责评估和批准任何环境影响研究报告，并监测其执行情况。如果项目不由联邦机构许可、执行和监督，并且不太可能产生跨区域影响，则由各地区的地区环境机构负责评估和批准其辖区内的环境影响研究报告，并监测其执行情况。

(二) 环境保护法律、法规简介

《埃塞俄比亚环境政策》于1997年印发，是埃塞俄比亚有关环境保护的第一批正式文件之一，为保护和可持续利用该国的环境资源提供了全面指导。《宪法》规定了环境政策的法律框架，其中阐述了环境保护、可持续发展和环境相关权利的概念。

之后又颁布了若干与环境相关的法律。除前述《环境保护机构设立公告》（第295/2002号）和《环境影响评估公告》（第299/2002号）外，接下来将讨论以下主要问题：

颁布《环境污染控制公告》（第300/2002号）的目的是消除或减轻污染，管理危险废物、化学物质和放射性物质。《环境污染控制公告》通过制定惩罚性和奖励措施，逐步培养公民遵守这些标准的责任感，还为执行环境标准提供了框架。该公告第四节规定，"禁止在未经管理部门或有关地区环境机构许可的情况下生成、保管、存储、运输、处置或清理任何危险废物"。此外，《固体废物管理公告》（第513/2007号）第4/2条规定，"任何人在进行固体废物的收集、运输、使用或处置之前，应获得城市行政管理局有关机构的许可"。

此外，《环境影响评估公告》的其中一项要求是实施废物管理计划。根据《环境影响评估公告》第5.1(6)(b)(v)条的规定，项目须指明消除、尽量减少或减轻负面影响的方法。此外，《环境污染控制公告》第6(1)(e)节规定的环境标准之一是废物管理标准，其中规定了在生成、处理、储存、处理、运输和处置各类废物时所允许的标准及所使用的方法。

(三) 环境保护的评估

埃塞俄比亚的农村和城市都正在面临着环境挑战，原因包括大规模砍伐森林、高度城市化、人口急速增长以及国家基础设施和工业基础的扩大。正是因为认识到了这一点，埃塞俄比亚政府在其增长和转型计划中将环境确定为可持续发展的重要支柱，并纳入了诸如气候适应型绿色经济等发展战略，致力于减轻气候变化对可持续利用环境的影响。

在法律框架方面，埃塞俄比亚已成为大多数国际环境条约的缔约国[①]，出台了国家政策和法律，并建立了改善环境质量的机构。[②]虽然埃塞俄比亚的环境保护计划起步缓慢，但随着政府的政策、环境友好型发展计划和战略的实施，其前景变得更加光明。

七、争议解决

(一) 争议解决办法和机构

1. 双法院结构

在埃塞俄比亚，联邦政府和地区之间的司法权力在每个机构不同层次上的水平和垂直划分。分配给联邦法院的事项是全国关注的问题，而非全国关注问题的相关事项则由各地区法院处理。根据第25/1996号公告的规定，在联邦法院结构中有三个不同层级的法院：联邦初审法院只有初审管辖权，联邦高等法院拥有初审和上诉管辖权，联邦最高法院拥有初审、上诉管辖权和撤销原判的权力。第25/1996号公告主要根据两项标准将管辖权分配给联邦法院：法律和人员。联邦法院应根据联邦法律、

---

① 《生物多样性公约》《控制危险废物越境转移及其处置巴塞尔公约》《巴塞尔禁令修正案》《禁止向非洲进口危险废物并在非洲内管理和控制危险废物越境转移的巴马科公约》《粮食和农业植物遗传资源国际条约》《濒危野生动植物种国际贸易公约》《联合国气候变化框架公约》《京都议定书》《联合国关于在发生严重干旱和／或荒漠化的国家特别是在非洲防治荒漠化的公约》《生物多样性公约卡塔赫纳生物安全议定书》《野生动物迁徙物种保护公约》《非洲—欧亚大陆迁徙水鸟保护协定》《保护臭氧层维也纳公约》《关于耗损臭氧层物质的蒙特利尔议定书》《关于国际贸易中对某些危险化学品和农药采用事先知情同意程序的鹿特丹公约》《关于持久性有机污染物的斯德哥尔摩公约》。
② 《通过公平服务促进成果运营 促进共享繁荣》，世界银行，2015年3月，参见 documents.worldbank.org/curated/en/.../pdf/ETHIOPIA-EDUC-PAD-11302017.pdf。

国际条约和地区法律的规定，解决在其管辖范围内提交给它的案件或争议（如果这些案件与联邦法律、国际条约和地区法律有关且不符合这些法律的规定）。地区各州均有自己的一级法院。

埃塞俄比亚法系属于大陆法系——由立法机关来颁布法律。然而，一些人认为，埃塞俄比亚现在采用的是混合法律制度，因为联邦最高法院上诉部门正在开创先例。埃塞俄比亚法律制度中一直没有遵循先例原则，直到最近才根据第 54/2005 号公告提出这一原则。根据第 54/2005 号公告第 2（1）条的规定，联邦最高法院的司法解释对联邦和州各级法院具有约束力。

2. 替代性争议解决方式

埃塞俄比亚法律下的替代性争议解决机制，特别是和解、调解和仲裁，由 1960 年《民法典》第二十章调整。

3. 亚的斯亚贝巴商会和部门协会仲裁研究所

亚的斯亚贝巴商会和部门协会仲裁研究所（ACCSA AI）是仅有的得到合法授权和委托的商业争端解决机构。目前，根据第 341/2003 号公告的规定，在争端各方提出请求时，商会和部门协会有权依法对商业纠纷进行仲裁。这项法律明确规定了商会和部门协会的权力，与世界上大多数法律体系常见的长期和广泛的做法相一致。然而，除了根据上述公告进行的机构仲裁外，现行的《民法典》和《民事诉讼法》也允许特别诉讼和个人诉讼。

4. 专家法庭

某些专家法庭被委托根据有关法律解决争端。受第 813/2013 号公告的委托，贸易竞争和消费者保护管理局的行政法庭通过其一审管辖权和上诉管辖权，对与竞争有关的民事和刑事案件作出裁决。第 377/2003 号公告授权劳动关系委员会审理劳动纠纷，而第 983/2016 号公告规定税务上诉委员会有权审查不满意的纳税人的申诉。

（二）法律的适用

原告一旦作出提起诉讼的决定，必须考虑的第一个问题就是向哪个法院提起诉讼。只有在有管辖权的法院才能够提起诉讼。管辖权有三个要素：司法管辖权、标的管辖权和地方管辖权。所有这些要素都必须存在于一个特定的案件中时，法院对此案件才有管辖权。

埃塞俄比亚是少数的没有加入《承认及执行外国仲裁裁决公约》的国家之一。埃塞俄比亚法律对外国仲裁裁决的承认和执行受 1960 年埃塞俄比亚《民事诉讼法》第 461 条的管辖。

根据《民事诉讼法》第 461 条的规定，外国仲裁裁决不得在埃塞俄比亚执行，除非：

① 确保互惠性，即在作出判决的国家允许执行埃塞俄比亚的裁决；
② 裁决是在裁决作出的国家签订仲裁协议或采取其他法律行为之后作出的；
③ 当事各方在任命仲裁员方面享有平等的权利，并已被传唤参加仲裁；
④ 仲裁庭在规定期限内组成；
⑤ 裁决不涉及埃塞俄比亚法律规定不能提交仲裁的事项，或不违反公共秩序或道德的事项；
⑥ 裁决具有在埃塞俄比亚法律规定的条件下可强制执行的性质。

八、其他

（一）反商业贿赂

1. 反商业贿赂法律、法规简介

埃塞俄比亚反腐败法律主要载于经修订的《联邦道德和反腐败委员会机构公告》和经修订的《反腐败法》，其中将腐败定为刑事犯罪，主要形式包括行贿和受贿、贿赂外国官员和洗钱。此前颁布的《反腐败法》不允许联邦道德和反腐败委员会处理私营企业的腐败犯罪，仅适用于发生在政府组织中的腐败，并且仅在涉及国家层面的腐败案件时才适用于私营企业。然而，根据第 881/2015 号公告的规定，有必要将私营部门实施的类似行为，特别是管理从公共部门筹集或为公共目的筹集资金的人实施的类似行为列为腐败罪,有必要将私营部门实施的贿赂、贪污和其他类似行为归类为腐败行为。

埃塞俄比亚通过了有助于防止和控制腐败的公告和法令。其中包括《刑法》(第414/2004号)、1961年《刑事诉讼法》、经修订的《联邦道德和反腐败委员会机构公告》(第433/2005号)、经修订的《反腐败特别程序和证据规则公告》(第434/2005号)、《资产披露和登记公告》(第668/2010号)、《刑事犯罪证人和举报人保护公告》(第699/2011号)、《防止和制止洗钱和资助恐怖主义公告》(第657/2009号)、《区域道德和反腐败委员会机构公告》(9个地区中有8个地区有这类法律)、经修订的《联邦审计长办公室公告》(第669/2010号)、《联邦法院令》(第733/2012号)、《海关公告》(第622/2009号)、《银行业务许可和监督》和《埃塞俄比亚联邦民主共和国行政机关权力和职责的定义公告》(第691/2010号)。埃塞俄比亚也是国际法律文件的签署国,其中包括《非洲联盟预防和打击腐败公约》(第545/2007号)、《联合国反腐败公约》(第544/2007号)、《伊加特刑事事项司法协助公约》(第732/2012号)。

2. 反商业贿赂监管部门

埃塞俄比亚负责反商业贿赂的监管部门是联邦道德和反腐败委员会。根据经修订的《反腐败特别程序和证据规则公告》(第434/2005号)的规定,只要所涉问题与公职人员、公私串通等事项有关,联邦道德和反腐败委员会即有权调查私营企业的腐败问题。联邦道德和反腐败委员会有权调查除议会外的任何政府机构或实体的腐败行为。在与议会有关的调查中,联邦道德和反腐败委员会必须请求议会撤销豁免权,以便对议员进行调查。联邦道德和反腐败委员会可全部或部分授予联邦或区域犯罪调查机构(视属于何种情况而定)对腐败案件(非重大腐败案件)的一般调查权。

3. 惩罚措施

根据《贪污罪公告》的规定,公职人员、公共组织的工作人员或其他任何人犯有腐败罪的,均应受到所规定的刑罚。公共组织的任何公职人员或雇员,为了谋取自身利益,或者为他人谋取不正当利益或损害他人权利,直接或间接地不当履行职责或义务来接受或索取不正当利益;或以任何其他方式滥用赋予他的责任或公众信任,为自己或他人获取不正当利益;或任何人意图为自己或为他人获得不正当利益或损害他人的权利,承诺、提议、给予或同意给予公职人员或公共机构的工作人员不应有的利益;或者任何人给予任何公职人员或公共组织雇员不正当的利益,或者任何公职人员或公共组织雇员接受不正当利益的,无论是已经完成还是即将完成,都将被视为犯了腐败罪,应当受到规定的处罚。

关于贿赂犯罪的惩罚措施包括:

(1)为了采取行动或不作为,如果直接或间接地寻求、接受或强制承诺为自己或他人带来好处,违反其职务本身的职责的,应处以不少于1年的监禁和不少于3 000比尔的罚款,或不超过10年的监禁和不超过40 000比尔的罚款。

(2)根据意图违背职责或义务来索取好处的程度、罪犯的责任程度或权力范围,或者损害个人、公共或国家利益的程度,使得前述第(1)项所述罪行特别严重,则应处以7年至15年有期徒刑,并处不少于10 000比尔但不超过100 000比尔的罚金。

(3)前述第(2)项所述情形中有两种及以上的情形同时存在的,处10年以上25年以下有期徒刑,并处20 000比尔以上200 000比尔以下的罚金。

(4)任何人意图诱使公职人员或公共组织工作人员违反其职责,向该公职人员或公共组织工作人员提供好处或礼物的,应根据情况处以监禁和罚款,或处以不超过7年的监禁并处7 000比尔以上30 000比尔以下的罚金。

(5)凡向外国或国际组织的任何官员或工作人员提供好处或礼物,意图促使他执行或忽视违反其公务的与国际贸易或交易有关的行为,均应受到处罚。

(6)根据违背职责、义务的意图、所提供或承诺的好处的范围、罪犯的权力或责任范围,或对个人、公共或国家利益或公共组织的损害程度,足以构成犯罪的,将受到5年至15年的监禁,并处以5 000比尔以上100 000比尔以下的罚款。

（二）工程承包

1. 许可和限制

《埃塞俄比亚联邦政府采购和财产管理局公告》（第 649/2009 号）规定，联邦政府通过采用、雇用或通过任何其他合同手段获取货物、工程、咨询或其他服务。尽管该公告旨在规范公共机构使用公共基金进行的采购行为，但不同的公共企业也适用该公告规定的采购程序和限制，无论是正式采纳内部采购准则中的程序和限制，还是在没有任何正式准则的情况下以其作为管理指引。

参与任何公共采购，当地投标人必须在公共采购和财产管理机构保存的供应商名单上登记。如果发现外国公司投标对于确保有效竞争至关重要或该采购高于国家招标水平门槛，公共采购也可以通过国际竞争性招标进行。公开招标是公共采购的法定优先程序。

关于国际采购（无论是由私营企业还是国营企业进行的），根据埃塞俄比亚国家银行 FXD/13/2000 号指令的规定，该采购行为需要得到银行各级管理层的批准。FXD/13/2000 号指令取消了以前对价值超过 100 万美元的进口商品进行国际竞标的要求。

2. 招标和投标

在通知投标人之前，采购方（公共机构采购部门）应编写招标文件，其中包括对投标人的指示、技术规格、投标表格、价格表、合同的通用及专用条款以及评标标准。技术规格将明确说明采购方在质量、安全以及必要时在尺寸、符号术语、包装、标记和标签、生产过程和方法方面的要求。一旦招标文件准备完毕，招标邀请将刊登在国家报纸上，并可在国家电台和（或）电视上刊登。招标文件包括标书的提交地点、截止日期、开标时间和地点以及出席开标会议的人员等信息。在截止日期之前，采购方可以采用制定一个附录的形式修改招标文件，这个附录会告知所有购买了竞标文件的投标人。

投标文件提交后，招标人将向投标人签发收据，注明提交投标书的时间和日期。投标人必须提交与投标一致的投标保证金。投标保证金的目的是约束不负责任的投标人，如果投标人撤回其投标，投标保证金将被没收。如果投标人放弃担任承包商或在必要时不提供履约担保，投标保证金也被没收。

投标将分三个连续阶段进行评估：初评、技术评价和财务评价，在三个阶段中脱颖而出的投标人将成为中标人。招标程序结束后，招标人可以与中标人协商招标文件中未尽事宜。

在采购人通知落标方中标人是谁以及他们为什么落标等信息后，最终版本的合同将由采购人和中标人签订。

Ethiopia

Authors: Mehrteab Leul Kokeb, Mesfin Tafesse
Translators: Shan Tao, Shao Kaijun

I. Overview

A. General Introduction to the Political, Economic, Social and Legal Environment of the Country Receiving Investment

The Federal Democratic Republic of Ethiopia (Ethiopia) is located in the East of Africa and is bordered by Eritrea, Djibouti, Somalia, Sudan, South Sudan and Kenya. The Country's population, in 2016, is approximately 102 million.① Ethiopia's capital city Addis Ababa is where th headquarter of the African Union is located. The current president of the country is Dr. Mulatu Teshome. Ethiopia is a Federal Republic. The federal language of the county is Amharic and the currency is ETB.

a. Political

The 1995 Constitution of the Federal Democratic Republic of Ethiopia provides for a federal state structure with nine member states making up the federation. Ethiopia is a multi-party federal democracy with legislative authority resting with the government headed by an executive prime minister and the elected House of Representatives (547 members) and the House of Federation (110 members).② Ethiopia has a Bicameral Parliament which comprises of the House of the Peoples' Representative and the House of the Federation. The House of the Peoples' Representative is the sole legislature and the highest authority of the federal government. The House of Federation is the ultimate interpreter of the Constitution.

The Prime Minister is chosen by the party in power following multi-party democratic national and federal state elections which are held every five years. The President is elected by the members of the House of People's Representatives. The Prime Minister appoints the Council of Ministers, which is then approved by the House of the Peoples' Representative.③

b. Economic

Ethiopia is the fastest growing economy in the East African region. The Ethiopian Government has formulated and started the implementation of the second five year Growth and Transformation Plan (GTP), which will run up to 2019/20. The GTP is expected to increase industrial development on a significant scale, with particular focus on energy and infrastructure. The Government aims to reach lower-middle-income status by 2025.

Specific areas for increased development include agriculture and agro-processing; leather and hides, horticulture and floriculture exports, building materials and tourism. The Country's economy is mainly based on agriculture. More than 70% of Ethiopia's population is still employed in the agricultural sector, but services have surpassed agriculture as the principal source of GDP.④ Though coffee remains the largest foreign exchange earner, Ethiopia is diversifying exports, and commodities such as gold, sesame, khat, livestock and horticulture products are becoming increasingly important. Manufacturing represented less than 8% of total exports in 2016, but manufacturing exports should increase in future years due to a growing international presence.⑤

In October 2017, the government devalued the birr by 15% to increase exports and alleviate a chronic foreign currency shortage in the country.

c. Social

Ethiopia is a multi-ethnic state. There are approximately eighty different languages, dialects and cultural variations. Ethiopia is a predominantly young population. More than 60% of the population is under the age of 24.

---

① http://www.worldbank.org/en/country/ethiopia/overview.
② http://www.ethiopia.gov.et/government-overview.
③ http://www.ethiopia.gov.et/government-overview.
④ https://www.cia.gov/library/publications/the-world-factbook/geos/et.html.
⑤ https://www.cia.gov/library/publications/the-world-factbook/geos/et.html.

Investors have liberty to employ expatriate staff on managerial positions and in cases where the required skilled labour is not available in the country.

d. Legal

The Constitution is the supreme law of the land. Other laws and customary practices or decisions of organs of state or public officials must conform to it. International agreements ratified by Ethiopia are integral part of the law of the land and are binding throughout the country. The FDRE Constitution establishes a parliamentary form of government and there are two houses, The House of Federation and House of Peoples Representatives. The House of Peoples Representatives is vested with the power of law making. In the hierarchy of federal legislation in Ethiopia, proclamations are issued by the House of People's Representatives, regulations are issued by Council of Ministers, and directives are issued by a particular ministry.

The Constitution allocates power between the federal state and the regional states. The federal Government as well as the Regions have legislative, judicial and executive organs. State Councils are the highest organs of Regional States which have the power to enact laws on matters falling under their jurisdictions.

The Federal Government is vested with a power to legislate on what are considered federal matters such as natural resources, national security, foreign exchange, foreign relations and transport and communication. All powers not given expressly to the Federal Government alone, or concurrently to the Federal Government and the States are reserved to the States.

Judicial authority is vested on federal courts and regional courts which are organized in a three-layer tiers based on their competence as provided by law. Accordingly, there are first instance courts, high courts and supreme courts both at federal and regional levels. Matters falling under the jurisdiction of federal first instance courts and federal high court at the state level are delegated to the regional high courts and regional supreme courts respectively.

The Constitution recognizes religious and customary courts as well as some quasi-judicial bodies which only deal with specify matters such as tax, labour, trade competition and the like.

Although Ethiopia is a home of legal pluralism, it is generally characterized as a Civil Law legal system. The country has adopted Civil and Commercial Codes based, substantially, on the French Model. Code law and legislations are the primary sources of law in Ethiopia. Ethiopian legal system also recognizes the doctrine of precedents and interpretation of law by the Federal Supreme Court rendered in its Cassation division with not less than five judges shall be binding on federal and regional courts. These decisions are published in volumes and are available publicly.

B. The Status and Direction of the Cooperation with Chinese Enterprises Under the B&R

Ethiopia is one of the African countries that has welcomed China's B&R with enthusiasm. China-Ethiopia relations have seen comprehensive and rapid development in recent years.[1] China has expressed interest to deepen the China-Ethiopia cooperation in six priority areas: exchanges on governing a state, peace and security, capacity cooperation, human resources, aviation and coordination on global and regional issues.[2] Ethiopia has accepted this and views the Belt and Road Initiative as an opportunity to speed up the transformation of the country's economy.

One of the projects under the B&R is the revitalization of the Eastern African railway network. Accordingly, contracts have been awarded to Chinese companies by the Ethiopian Railway Corporation for the construction of the new Addis Ababa–Djibouti railway. Ethiopia plans to expand on this project and lay down a 5,000 km railway line connecting it to Kenya, Sudan and, South Sudan by 2020. This plan has the potential to link multiple trading hubs in Eastern Africa to Chinese ports, facilitating trade among them.[3]

Furthermore, the Grand Ethiopian Renaissance Dam is expected to be a reliable source of energy for the railways as well as contribute to the regional integration of renewable energy in East Africa.[4]

Ethiopia is also looking to increase cooperation with Chines enterprises and strengthen production capacity in garments, agriculture, machinery and infrastructure, under the framework of the B&R. Accordingly, in 2016 Ethiopia had received investment from 22 enterprises in the Shandong Province of China and the import and export volume was $280 million.[5]

---

[1] https://eng.yidaiyilu.gov.cn/qwyw/rdxw/16964.htm.
[2] http://www.xinhuanet.com/english/2017-06/22/c_136386698.htm.
[3] http://usa.chinadaily.com.cn/a/201712/20/WS5a3a0c80a31008cf16da26fc.html.
[4] http://usa.chinadaily.com.cn/a/201712/20/WS5a3a0c80a31008cf16da26fc.html.
[5] http://www.scio.gov.cn/32618/Document/1552616/1552616.htm.

II. Investment

A. Market Access

a. Department Supervising Investment

Organs of investment administration in Ethiopia comprises the Investment Board, Ethiopian Investment Commission (EIC) and Regional Investment Commissions. The EIC has the authority to promote, coordinate and supervise investment activities in Ethiopia. It issues investment permit, engages in policy initiation and provides advisory and technical services to investors. The regional investment commissions engage in the same activity as the EIC in the respective regions. The investment board is established with the composition of the Prime Minister and other government officials designated by the Prime Minister. The investment board has the power to supervise investment and decide on policy and regulatory matters on investment.

b. Laws and Regulations of Investment Industry

The primary law regulating investment in Ethiopia is the Investment Proclamation No 769/2012. The proclamation provides rules on minimum capital requirement, investment permit requirements and industrial development zones. Investment administration organs and investment guarantees and protections are provided under the proclamation. The proclamation was later amended with proclamation Investment Amendment Proclamation No. 849/2014. Proclamation 769/2012 provides that there shall be a regulation that regulates the details of incentives and investment areas reserved for domestic investors. In accordance with this rule Investment Incentives and Investment Areas Reserved for Domestic Investors Council of Ministers Regulation No. 270/2012 was promulgated by the Council of Ministers. This regulation provides areas reserved for domestic investors and the conditions with which investment incentives shall be provided to investors.

There are other areas of laws that directly or indirectly regulate investment in Ethiopia. The Commercial Code of Ethiopia regulates business organizations on how these organization shall be formed and shall operate. The Civil Code of Ethiopia regulates contractual relationships depending on the applicability of the law. Ethiopia has Employment Proclamation that governs the labour relationship between investors and employees. The Federal Income Tax Proclamation governs tax duties of investors.

Depending on the areas of investment, specific legislations govern investment. Mining and energy are examples of such investment with specific laws. Recently Ethiopia adopted the Public Private Partnership Proclamation which regulates PPP based investments in Ethiopia. There are also directives that govern specific issues. For instance, the Ethiopian Revenues and Customs Authority has a directive that in detail regulates the duty-free import right of investors. Duty free importation of vehicles for investors is regulated by Ethiopian Investment Board directive. On the other hand, the respective authorities have directives which regulate specific sectors. A good example would be the Directive for the Registration of Professionals and Consultants of Ministry of Construction which regulates competence of investors who want to invest in construction and engineering consultancy sector.

c. Forms of Investment

In terms of who the investor is, investment can be wholly owned by a foreign or domestic investor, it can be a partnership between a domestic investor and a foreign investor or a joint venture between the government and a domestic or foreign investor. There are however, some sectors reserved for the government, for domestic investors or for joint investment between the government and private investors.

Foreign companies may take the following forms:

a) Setting up a Subsidiary Company

A subsidiary for all practical purposes is like any new company having the form of either a private limited company or a share company. Though the parent company has a controlling interest in a subsidiary, there is / are always other shareholder/s that may or may not be affiliated to the parent company usually to fulfil the required legal minimum number of members.

b) Setting up a Branch

When a foreign company opens a branch in Ethiopia the shareholders of the parent company will still remain to be the shareholders. Furthermore, it will take the name of its parent company and add indication it is the branch in Ethiopia. The Ethiopia branch will be administered by a manager appointed by the parent company. Every major decision will come from the parent company through notarized minutes of the shareholders.

In terms constitution, a branch cannot have a different name from the parent, cannot transfer its assets or establish a new company without the resolution of the parent company and cannot be converted in to different form of business organization.

The major difference between a subsidiary and a branch is, if the company is a branch the major decisions will come from the parent company through notarized minutes of the shareholders. Furthermore, because a subsidiary is created under Ethiopian law it will have an Ethiopian nationality where as a branch of a foreign company will have a foreign nationality.

Other forms of local presence can be commercial representative office and project office. Commercial representative offices are established with the aim to promote investments and engage in market research in a given country. In line with this, in Ethiopia commercial representative offices are allowed only to engage in promotion and market survey. Commercial representatives are not allowed to engage in selling goods and services or enter into contracts with customers. Another means of local presence is through project office. Project office is established by foreign investors winning international bid. Project office is required to be registered in the commercial register and have a business license. However, because project offices are set up for a specific project through an international bid and not as a permanent establishment it is easier to liquidate.

c) Purchasing majority shares of an existing company

The transfer of shares is considered as acquisition which is captured under the broad definition given to "merger" under Ethiopian law. Accordingly, merger triggers the obligation to obtain an approval from the Trade Competition and Consumer Protection Authority (TCCPA). The TCCPA approval is mandatory if the annual turnover, capital or assets of the company in which the transfer takes place is more than ETB 30,000,000 (USD 1.1 million). The TCCPA checks in practice, in addition to competition impact, the eligibility of the areas of investment for foreign investors as well as the fulfilment of the minimum required threshold. In particular, the TCCPA checks whether the minimum capital thresholds for foreign investors and for a joint investment with an Ethiopian national are met as mentioned under A. (d) below. Once TCCPA clears the transaction, it grants its approval in the form of a letter to DARA and the Ministry of Trade (MOT).

d. Standards of Market Access and Examination

Ethiopia has tariff barriers as market access restrictions. Import duties range from 0-35%. Excise tax ranges from 10% to 100%. Excise tax is imposed on goods whose import is discouraged in the country such as tobacco products, motor vehicles and textile products. . There are also other goods considered as luxuries goods hence, excise tax is levied on such goods. These are motor vehicles and perfumes. On the other hand, there are sectoral restrictions on investment in Ethiopia by which some sectors are reserved for domestic investors only. Some of these sectors are banking and insurance, wholesale, retail, logistics, broadcasting, mass media, advertisement, promotion, logistics and attorney and legal services.[1]

The other market access restriction is minimum capital requirement. The Investment Proclamation provides that foreign investors shall be required to allocate USD 200,000 for a single project. The amount of minimum capital is reduced to USD 150,000 if the foreign investor invests jointly with domestic investors. The minimum capital required for investors investing in architectural and engineering works and related technical consultancy services technical testing and analysis or publishing works is USD 100,000 unless it is a joint investment with domestic investors in which case the capital required will be USD 50,000.

B. Foreign Exchange Regulation

a. Department Supervising Foreign Exchange

The National Bank of Ethiopia (NBE) is the central bank of the country with a regulatory power over banking, insurance and other financial sectors. The NBE monitors all international transaction in foreign exchange and valuable goods.[2] It formulates, implements and follows-up the country's exchange rate policy, and manages and administers the international reserves of the country. The NBE also set limits on gold and foreign exchange assets held in the deposits of banks and other financial institutions. Furthermore, it sets limits on the net foreign exchange positions and terms, and the amount of external indebtedness of banks and other financial institutions. The NBE is empowered to issue directives relating to transactions in foreign exchange.[3] The National Bank of Ethiopia is also vested by its establishment proclamation and Investment Proclamation No. 679/2012 to regulate foreign exchange and criterion for external loan.

b. Brief Introduction of Laws and Regulations of Foreign Exchange

Ethiopian Foreign exchange legal regime governs issues that require international payments by banks,

---

[1] Investment Incentives and Investment Areas Reserved for Domestic Investors Council of Ministers Regulation no. 270/2012, Article 3.
[2] see The National Bank Establishment Proclamation (as Amended) Proclamation No. 592/2008.
[3] Article 21(5)(b) of the National Bank Establishment (as Amendment) Proclamation, 592/2008.

insurance companies and other financial institutions. Foreign exchange is governed by legislations such as External Loan Directive No. FXD/47/2017, Transparency in Foreign Currency Allocation and Foreign Exchange Management Directive No. FXD 46/2017, the Retention and Utilization of Export Earnings and Inward Remittances Directive No. FXD/48/2017, and Limits on Birr and Foreign Currency Holding Directive FXD/49/2017.

The purpose and scope of each legislations is discussed as follows:

a) Retention and Utilization of Export Earnings and Inward Remittances

This law incentivizes eligible exporters of goods and services and allows them to open retention accounts in an authorized bank.[1] Accordingly, eligible customers may open two types of accounts. These are Foreign Retention Account A and B.[2] In Account A 30% of the foreign currency is retained for an indefinite time and 70% of the foreign currency is retained up to 28 days and then converted to local currency. Both accounts shall be used to finance business related and current payments such as for import of goods (except vehicles), for settlement of external loan, to refund tour operators, contribution to international conferences, to refund unused part of foreign currency transferred or other payments as may be approved by NBE.

Authorized banks have a duty to make a report of aggregate amount of foreign exchange held under retention accounts A and B on monthly basis.

b) Transparency in Foreign Exchange Allocation and Management

Foreign exchange is a scarce resource in Ethiopia and there is a need for managing and carefully allocating the same. For this NBE has issued the above directive and created a transparent allocation and management of foreign currency. The allocation is based on priority list and on demand. In the allocation of foreign currency, a bank is required to give priority, on first come first served basis, to certain import items such as essential goods.[3] There are also items that are to be served on demand and are exempted for the requirement of registration.[4] Allocation foreign currency other than stated above is prohibited.[5]

c) External Loan

External loan and Suppliers credit is regulated by External Loan and Supplier's Credit Directive No. 47/2017. This law requires any loan guaranteed by the Ethiopian Government to be registered by NBE. Any foreign loan by eligible borrowers (exporters and foreign investors), shall be registered and approved by the NBE. Likewise, foreign investment has to be registered by the Ethiopian Investment Commission (EIC).[6] Repayment of loan, repatriation of dividends and profits is only possible if the above procedures are followed.

d) Limits on Birr and Foreign Currency Holding

This law governs the holding of birr and foreign currency for Ethiopians and foreigners.[7] A person entering and departing from Ethiopia may hold up to a maximum of Birr 1000.[8] On the other hand no person residing in Ethiopia is allowed to hold a foreign currency for more than 30 days.[9] Any person residing in Ethiopia and entering into the country from abroad and carrying a foreign currency exceeding 1000 USD shall make declaration using foreign currency declaration form.[10] The amount is 3000 for persons not residing in Ethiopian and entering to Ethiopia, in doing so the law sets limits on currency holds for persons going abroad and entering Ethiopia as well as foreigners.

c. Requirements of Foreign Exchange Management for Foreign Enterprises

Foreign exchange management of foreign enterprises engaged in the export of goods and services is regulated by the Retention and Utilization of Export Earnings and Inward Remittances Directive No. FXD/48/2017. Regular recipients of foreign exchange remittance from abroad and exports of goods and services are eligible customers to open retention accounts at commercial banks. There are two types of retention accounts that can be opened for eligible customers. Foreign Exchange Retention Account A and Foreign Exchange Retention Account B. Eligible customers can retain only 30% of their foreign exchange earnings for an indefinite period of time under account A and 70% of their foreign exchange earnings for 28 days under account B. At the end of the 28 days the foreign currency in account B will be converted to local currency if not utilized. Both accounts shall be used

---

[1] Article 3 of Retention and Utilization of Export Earnings and Inward Remittances Directive.
[2] Article 5 of the Retention and Utilization of Export Earnings and Inward Remittances Directive.
[3] Article 6.1 of Transparency in Foreign Currency Allocation and Foreign Exchange Management Directive.
[4] Article 6.2 of Transparency in Foreign Currency Allocation and Foreign Exchange Management Directive.
[5] Article 7 of Transparency in Foreign Currency Allocation and Foreign Exchange Management Directive.
[6] Article 36 of the Investment Proclamation No. 270/2012.
[7] Limits on Birr and Foreign Currency Holding Directive.
[8] Article 2 of the Limits on Birr and Foreign Currency Holding Directive.
[9] Article 3 of the Limits on Birr and Foreign Currency Holding Directive.
[10] Article 4 of the Limits on Birr and Foreign Currency Holding Directive.

to finance direct businesses related and current payments for import of goods, payment for settlement of external loan, service payment for consultants, payment contributions for international conferences, etc.

C. Financing

a. Main Financial Institutions

Financial institutions are defined as insurance company, bank, micro-finance institutions, postal savings, money transfer institution and others similar institutions as determined by the NBE. There are 16 private 3 government owned banks in Ethiopia; 17 private and one government owned insurance companies and 35 micro finance institutions.[1] Banking and finance is one of the sectors that is restricted to foreigners and allowed only for Ethiopian citizens.

The main financial regulatory body in Ethiopia is the NBE. NBE regulates financial matters in the country. It regulates banks, regulates foreign exchanges, acts as fiscal and agent and financial advisor of the government. The NBE issues directives on various financial issues. The NBE sets exchange rate of Birr (official currency in Ethiopia). Currently Birr is pegged against U.S. Dollar.

b. Financing Conditions for Foreign Enterprises

Both government owned and private banks lend money to foreign enterprises in Ethiopia. Borrowers are subject to the usual credit worthiness check. The Development Bank of Ethiopia (DBE) is government owned bank which finances investors. DBE lends investors 50% of their capital based on 50:50 debt equity ratio. DBE has high financial capacity compared to any of the private commercial banks and lends with relatively low interest rate.

There is a tax implication of debt received by foreign controlled resident company. The Income Tax Proclamation provides that the debt to equity ratio of such company shall be 2:1 for a tax year. The interest rate paid on the excess of debt is not deductible for tax purposes unless the debt is arm's length debt.

Foreign investors are allowed to acquire loan and suppliers from external sources. The debt to equity ratio shall be 60:40. However, there are preconditions attached to it. The draft loan agreement shall be presented to NBE and approved by the same prior to singing the loan agreement between the lender and the enterprise. Emphasis is given to the interest rate of the loan agreement. The interest rate depends on the average maturity period. If the average maturity rate is up to three years the interest rate shall be six-month LIBOR or equivalent EURIBOR plus 2%. If it is three years up to five years, six months or equivalent EURIBOR plus 3%. If it is more than five years six month or equivalent EURIBOR plus 5%.[2] These rules and conditions also apply for supplier's credit.

Any enterprise be it foreign or a domestic enterprise, cannot borrow money with interest from sources other than banks or shareholders. Lending money with interest is a banking business in which individuals or entities cannot engage in unless they have banking license.

D. Land Policy

a. Brief Introduction of Land-related Laws and Regulations

The key legislation that are in place in order to govern land rights in Ethiopia are the following:
(i) The 1995 Constitution Of The Federal Democratic Republic Of Ethiopia (FDRE Constitution);
(ii) The 1960 Civil Code of Ethiopia;
(iii) Land Administration and Use Proclamation No. 456/2005;
(iv) Urban Land Lease Holding Proclamation No. 721/2011;
(v) Expropriation of Landholding for Public Purpose and Payment of Compensation Proclamation No. 455/2005; and
(vi) Payment of Compensation for Property Situated on Land holding Expropriated For Public Purposes Council of Ministers Regulations No. 135/2007.

Under the laws of Ethiopia, there is no private ownership of land inasmuch as the Ethiopian Constitution provides that, "…the right to ownership of rural and urban land, as well as of all natural resources, is exclusively vested in the State and in the peoples of Ethiopia. Land is a common property of the Nations, Nationalities and Peoples of Ethiopia and shall not be subject to sale or to other means of exchange".

The Ethiopian Constitution empowers the Federal government to "enact laws for the utilization and conservation of land and other natural resources, historical sites and objects". Accordingly, the Federal Government has enacted Land administration and Use Proclamation No. 456/2005.

---

[1] National Bank of Ethiopia, www.nbe.gov.et.
[2] Directive for External Loan and Supplier's Credit Directive No. REL/05/2002 (as amended), Article 6.

The main legislation regulating land in Ethiopia can be broadly categorized as urban land law and rural land law. An urban land is defined as land located within an administrative boundary of an urban centre which, in turn, is defined as any locality having a municipal administration or a population size of 2000 or more inhabitants of which at least 50% of its labor force is engaged in non-agricultural activity. The Land administration and Use Proclamation No.456/2005 Proclamation has delegated the power to "enact rural land administration and land use law" to regional stats consistent with federal law and effectively implements it at regional level.

b. Rules of Land Acquisition for Foreign Enterprises

a) Urban Land Holding

Urban land acquisition is conducted in two ways. The first is through allotment the second is through tender. When first receiving the land from the appropriate government body, any person permitted urban land lease holding must conclude a contract of lease with the appropriate government body. The lease contract entered into by the lease holder includes construction start up time, completion time for use of its allowed purpose, payment schedule, grace period, and the respective rights and duties of the parties. A lease holding certificate will then subsequently be issued by the authority.

b) Rural Land Holding

The landholder of a rural land may, using his land use right, undertake development activity jointly with an investor in accordance with the contract he concludes. Such contract shall be approved and registered by the competent authority. The size of the land and period for land lease agreement between holder certificate and investor is regulated by regional laws.

Besides contractual arrangement between investors and land holders, the government also leases land to investors through land lease agreements. The Federal Rural Land Use proclamation states that private investors that engage in agricultural activities are given the right to use rural land in accordance with the investment policies and laws at federal and regional laws. Farmers / semi pastoralists and pastoralist have priority over investors. This concept of providing access to rural land to investors is further reaffirmed under the regional state legislations.

E. The Establishment and Dissolution of Companies

a. The Forms of Enterprises

Ethiopian Commercial Code provides for six forms of partnerships.
(i) Ordinary Partnership;
(ii) Joint Venture;
(iii) General partnership;
(iv) Limited Partnership;
(v) Share Company and;
(vi) Private Limited Company.

The first four are different from the latter two in that members' liability of the partners of the entities is not limited. This is a key factor for business to prefer the two forms of partnerships / companies limited by shares. Of the two, the commonly prevalent is the Private Limited Company mainly due to the simplicity of its formation and the lesser regulatory requirements involved in running it.

Share Companies are formed by a minimum of five members and liability of shareholders is limited. Shares are freely transferable, and capital can be structured into paid and subscribed portions. A share company is required to have a formal management structure which is detailed in the Commercial Code.

Private Limited Companies (PLC) are formed by between two and fifty members with capital that is fully paid at the point of formation. Shares are not freely transferable and the PLC cannot engage in banking and insurance activities. Unlike a share company, a PLCs may be operated by a manager responsible to the shareholders, rather than having to adopt a formal management structure, such as a board.

b. The Procedure of Establishment

The establishment procedure of foreign enterprises constitutes of the following steps:

(i) Fulfilling the required documents. All documents which originate from abroad are required to be apostilled in by the Ethiopian Embassy in the country of origin and further authenticated in Ethiopia.

(ii) Company name verification.

(iii) Tax Identification Number (TIN). All businesses operating in the country are required by law to have a taxpayer's registration certificate (TIN) issued by the Ethiopian Revenue and Customs Authority (ERCA).

(iv) Investment permit. All investors in Ethiopia are required to get an investment permit from the EIC which is an approval and a registration of the planned investment project in Ethiopia and the fulfilment of the minimum capital requirement. The investment permit is renew the permit annually until the investor commences marketing of his / her products or services.

(v) Commercial Registration Certificate. The Commercial Register is a pre-requirement to acquiring a business license in Ethiopia. The registration of a company in the Commercial Register results in the issuance of a Commercial Registration Certificate by the registering authority that certifies the legal incorporation of an entity.

(vi) Competence Certificate. Some business sectors are required to get a competence certificate from the relevant authority validating their competency to conduct the business before a business license is issued.

(vii) Business License. After the legal incorporation of the entity in order to commence its business and start earning income the entity is required to have a business license. No person shall engage in a business activity without having a valid business license.

c. Routes and Requirements of Dissolution

The grounds of dissolution which are a set out in Articles 217-218 of the Commercial Code can be grouped into three categories as follows:

(i) Legal Dissolution-This is when the business purpose has been achieved or cannot be achieved or when the term for which the business organization was formed expires, unless the partners agree to continue the business organization.

(ii) Consensual Dissolution: This is when the partners agree to dissolution prior to the expiry of the term for which the business organization was formed.

(iii) Judicial Dissolution: A business organization may be dissolved for good cause by the court on the application of a partner. for judicial dissolution to be applied there shall be good cause in particular where a partner seriously fails in his duties or becomes through infirmity or permanent illness or for any reason incapable of carrying out his duties or where serious disagreement exists between the partners.

F. Merger and Acquisition

a. Laws and Regulations Applicable to Merger and Acquisition

The Trade Competition and Consumer Protection Proclamation No. 2013 (the Competition Law) is the law that regulates merger in Ethiopia.

The Competition Law defines merger as:

(i) two or more business organizations previously having independent existence amalgamate or when such business organizations pool the whole or part of their resources for the purpose of carrying on a certain commercial activity; or

(ii) by directly or indirectly acquiring shares, securities or assets of a business organization or taking control of the management of the business of another person by a person or group of persons through purchase or any other means.

b. Types of Target Companies

The target companies are private companies. Stock market does not exist in Ethiopia. Therefore, there are no listed companies. Most companies are owned by families and existing in the form of a PLC.

c. Merger and Acquisition of Private Companies

The common way of acquisition of private companies in Ethiopia is through acquisition of shares effected through a share transfer agreement. As indicated earlier[①] acquisition can only be completed after the approval of the TCCPA and registration of the share transfer resolution by the Document Authentication and Registration Authority (DARA). Any business person who proposes to enter into an agreement or arrangement of merger shall notify the TCCPA of such proposal. The minimum threshold for the notification of merger is set in the Merger and Acquisitions Directive prepared for the implementation of merger regulation. Merger notification is required if either the annual turnover, values of assets or registered capital of the merging entities is more than 30,000,000 ETB (Thirty Million Birr).

G. Competition Regulation

a. Department Supervising Competition Regulation

The institution that is entrusted with competition matters is the TCCPA. This institution is under the supervision and umbrella of Ministry of Trade. The Competition Law has established the TCCPA as well as a Trade Competition and Consumer Protection Tribunal (hereinafter the Tribunal) both at Federal and Regional levels.

---

①   Section A(c)iii.

b. Brief Introduction of Competition Law

Ethiopian competition law is a law that is in charge of protecting the business community from anti-competitive and unfair market practices and creation of a competitive and free market. It also has as its objective the protection of consumers from misleading and deceptive market conducts and creating an environment by which consumers get goods and services equivalent to the price they pay.

Ethiopia had adopted competition law for the first time in 2003. The recent amendment to the Competition law is enacted in March 2014. This law is applicable on any commercial activity or transaction in goods or services conducted in Ethiopia or having effect in Ethiopia.[1] The law covers a wide range of anti-competitive agreements, concerted practices and decisions both in horizontal and vertical line. The law states that agreements between, or concerted practices by, business persons or decisions by associations of business persons in a horizontal relationship shall be prohibited, if it has the effect of preventing or significantly lessening competition, or it involves, directly or indirectly, fixing a purchase or selling price or any other trading condition, collusive tendering, or dividing markets by allocating customers, suppliers, territories or specific types of goods or services.[2] The only exception available is when a party to the agreement proves that there is technology efficiency or pro-competitive gain resulting from such agreements, decisions or concerted practices.[3] Anti-competitive agreements, concerted practices or decision on the vertical line are also prohibited, if it has the effect of preventing or significantly lessening competition unless justified in the same way discussed above.[4] Abuse of dominant position is also regulated under Ethiopian law. Abusing dominant position is not clearly defined under the law but a long list activity that constitute abuse of dominant position are provided under the law.[5] Abuse of dominant position is prohibited unless justified. The law also provides a mechanism for the assessment of dominance.[6] The TCCPA also regulates merger as stated in the above section.

c. Measures Regulating Competition

The Competition Law provides the institutional and legal mechanisms for its enforcement. Whenever there is an alleged violation of the competition law the TCCPA will conduct investigation and there are three different remedies that are envisaged. These remedies are civil, administrative and criminal remedies. After investigation the TCCPA, will institute action for administrative sanctions before the Tribunal [7] As regards the criminal remedies, the Federal Attorney General[8] and Federal Police Commission may conduct investigation and prosecute the alleged violator before the Tribunal. Any business or consumer claiming compensation because of the anti-competitive acts of the entity may also bring their case before the same Tribunal.[9]

The administrative penalties for abuse of dominant position is 5%-10% of the annual turnover.[10] Any business person found to be engaged in any anticompetitive agreements, concerted practices or decisions will be fined a 10% of annual turnover.[11] Any business person found to be in violation of the provision regulating merger will be fine 5%-10% of the annual turnover.[12] If a person, other than business person, is involved, directly or indirectly, in any the violation of the Competition Law, he / she will be liable from 10,000 to 100,000 Ethiopian Birr.[13] Any business person or a person other than business person that fails to observe the administrative sanctions and penalties imposed by the Tribunal or decision of a relevant court, he / she shall be guilty of criminal offense and shall be punished with rigorous imprisonment from 1 to 5 years.[14]

H. Tax

a. Tax Regime and Rules

The income tax regime of Ethiopia is structured on a scheduler basis where separate taxes are imposed

---

[1] Article 4 of the Trade Competition and Consumer Protection Proclamation No. 813/2013.
[2] Article 7(1) (a) of the Trade Competition and Consumer Protection Proclamation No. 813/2013.
[3] Article 7(1)(a) of the Trade Competition and Consumer Protection Proclamation No. 813/2013.
[4] Article 7(2)(a) of the Trade Competition and Consumer Protection Proclamation No. 813/2013.
[5] Article 5 of the Trade Competition and Consumer Protection Proclamation No. 813/2013.
[6] Article 6 of the Trade Competition and Consumer Protection Proclamation No. 813/2013.
[7] Article 37 of the Trade Competition and Consumer Protection Proclamation No. 813/2013.
[8] Federal Attorney General Establishment Proclamation No. 943/2016.
[9] Article 37(2) of the Trade Competition and Consumer Protection Proclamation No. 813/2013.
[10] Article 42(1) of the Trade Competition and Consumer Protection Proclamation No. 813/2013.
[11] Article 42(2) of the Trade Competition and Consumer Protection Proclamation No. 813/2013.
[12] Article 42(4) of the Trade Competition and Consumer Protection Proclamation No. 813/2013.
[13] Article 42(5) of the Trade Competition and Consumer Protection Proclamation No. 813/2013.
[14] Article 43 of the Trade Competition and Consumer Protection Proclamation No. 813/2013.

on different categories of income. Different rates and deductions are applied to different categories of income. The income tax law of Ethiopia is based on two taxing principles; residence and source. The Income tax law is applicable to residents of Ethiopia with respect to their worldwide income and to non-residents with respect to their Ethiopian sourced income.

The Income Tax Proclamation (Federal Income Tax Proclamation No. 979/2016), Councils of Ministers Federal Income Tax Regulation 410/2017, Federal Tax Administration Proclamation No. 983/2016) and Value Added Tax Proclamation No. 285/2002 (as amended by Proclamation No. 609/2008) and Council of Ministers Value Added Tax Regulation No.79/2002, Turn Over Tax Proclamation No. 308/2002 (as amended by Proclamation No. 611/2008), Excise Tax Proclamation No. 307/2002 and Stamp Duty Proclamation No. 110/1998 govern the tax regime and the tax administration procedures of Ethiopia.

b. Main Categories and Rates of Tax

(i) Direct taxes include tax on income from employment, business profit tax, tax on income from rental of buildings, tax on interest income on deposits, dividend income tax, tax on income from royalties, and other taxes.

(ii) Indirect Taxes include a turnover tax, an excise tax, a value added tax, and a customs duty.

(iii) Stamp duty is charged on instruments of incorporation defined by certain regulations. The instruments of incorporation include memorandum and articles of association of business organizations, contracts, security deeds, powers of attorney, documents of title to property. The rate is computed depending on the type of instrument, either on flat rate basis or according to value on a percentage basis.

(iv) The major direct and indirect taxes applicable to businesses are the following:

No.	Type of tax	Rate
1	Corporate income tax	30%
2	Custom duties	0% up to 35%
3	Dividend tax	10%
4	Excise tax	10% up to 100%
5	Export tax	Nil
6	Income tax from employment	0% up to 35%
7	Royalty tax	5%
8	Turn over tax	2% and 10%
9	Value added tax	15%
10	Withholding tax	2%
11	Capital gains tax	15% on the disposal of immovable assets
		30% for the transfer of shares and bonds
12	Income from receiving of a technical or management service from abroad	15%

c. Tax Declaration and Preference

Under the Ethiopian tax law, the period for tax assessment ("tax year") is the fiscal year, that is, the one-year period from July 8th to 7th July; unless otherwise provided.

(i) The tax year of a person is: in the case of an individual or an association of individuals, the fiscal year; in the case of a body, the accounting year of the body.

(ii) Tax payers are categorized into:
• Category A-a body or other person having an annual gross income over 1,000,000 Ethiopian Birr;
• Category B-a taxpayer, other than a body, having an annual gross income between 500,000 and 1,000,000 Ethiopian Birr;
• Category C-a taxpayer, other than a body, having an annual gross income less than 500,000 Ethiopian Birr.

(iii) Tax Declaration Periods:
An employee is not required to file a tax declaration unless the employee has more than one employer for a calendar month or he has self-withholding obligations.
• Category A taxpayers have tax declaration obligations within 4 months from the end of the tax year.
• Category B taxpayers have tax declaration obligations within 2 months from the taxpayers tax year.

• Category C taxpayers shall pay the tax determined in accordance with standard assessment on the 7th of July to the 6th of August every year.

I. Securities

a. Brief Introduction of Securities-related Laws and Regulations

The Ethiopian Commercial Code, enacted in 1960, envisages that companies whose capital is fully paid-up may issue debt securities (bonds, stocks, etc.).① The government is also allowed to issue debt securities.② The Ministry of Finance and Economic Cooperation is the authorized government body to issue treasury bills and bonds.③ Despite such possibilities of issuing debt securities, the country has never had a formal securities market. The primary debt market is not that developed Under the law it is provided that companies whose capital is fully paid up can issue debentures. The practices where companies issue shares / equities is also prevalent. The government, occasionally, issue's debt securities in the form of treasury bills and bonds but this is also very rare. The secondary debt market is non-existent. All securities in the primary market are traded in Over The Counter (OTC) transactions or dealers networks as opposed to organized Stock exchange in the relevant law, comprehensive regulation of stock exchange and the physical structure for trade in securities does not exist in Ethiopia.

b. Supervision and Regulation of Securities Market

There is no securities market in Ethiopia. There are also no laws regulating securities market.

c. Requirements for Engagement in Securities Trading for Foreign Enterprises

There is no securities market in Ethiopia. The physical structure for trade in securities, both for primary and secondary markets, do not exist. There are no laws and regulatory requirements dealing with securities exchange and foreigners cannot trade in securities in Ethiopia.

J. Preference and Protection of Investment

a) The Structure of Preference Policies

Various areas of preference have been identified by the Ethiopian Growth and Transformation plan (GTP), which is the policy umbrella document concerned with improving the country's economy by achieving a projected gross domestic product target. The GTP has outlined certain pillars to this effect some of which are:

(i) Sustain the rapid, broad based and equitable economic growth and development witnessed during the last decade;

(ii) Increase the productive capacity and efficiency to reach the economy's production possibility frontier through concurrently improving quality, productivity and competitiveness of productive sectors (agriculture and manufacturing industries);

(iii) Speed up and catalyse transformation of the domestic private sector and render them a capable development force;

(iv) Build the capacity of the domestic construction industry, bridge critical infrastructure gaps with particular focus on ensuring the quality of infrastructure services through strengthening the implementation capacity of the construction sector;

(v) Properly manage and administer the on-going rapid urbanization to unlock its potential for sustaining growth and structural transformation of the economy;

(vi) Establish democratic and developmental good governance through enhancing implementation capacity of the public sector and mobilization of public participation.

Any activity taken up by investors that feed into the above pillars is considered to be preferable by the current policy structure of Ethiopia. The legal regime governing investment has provided for mechanisms to facilitate and encourage investment by making use of fiscal and non-fiscal / investor protection incentives discussed below.

(i) Investment Incentives. Irrespective of the structure of business organization used, a foreign entity investing in Ethiopia in the sector allowed for foreign investment, by virtue of being an investor can be eligible for certain incentives and exemptions.

(ii) Fiscal incentives.

Income tax exemption: under the Investment Regulation, income tax exemption ranging from one to six years

---

① Article 429 of the Commercial Code of Ethiopia.
② Article 5(3) of the National Bank Establishment (as Amended) Proclamation No. 591/2008; see also The Special Government Bond Proclamation No. 531/2007.
③ Article 2(1) of the Special Government Bond Proclamation No. 531/2007.

depending on the types of project and the location of investment projects is offered. The exemption can apply for new enterprises, expanding or upgrading enterprises and additional exemption applies for investors exporting at least 60% of its products or services.

Loss carry forward: an investor who has incurred loss within the period of income tax exemption will be allowed to carry forward such loss for half of the income tax exemption period after the expiry of such period.

Exemptions from customs duty: the Investment Regulation provides that investors are entitled to import capital goods and construction materials relevant for the establishment and / or expansion of its enterprise free of customs duty.

Export incentives; with the exception of few products (semi processed hides and skins), no export tax is levied on export products.

b) Support for Specific Industries and Regions

Eligible investors, domestic and foreign, establishing new enterprises in areas of manufacturing, agriculture, agro-industries, energy generation, transmission and supply of electrical energy, Information Communication Technology (ICT), tourism, construction contracting, education and training, architectural and engineering consultancy works, technical testing and analysis, capital goods etc are entitled to obtain a an Income Tax exemption whose rate depends on the type of sector in which the investor is engaged. The exemption also varies between investors engaged in and around Addis Ababa, and other regions. Those investors who decided to go to the regions will obtain an Income Tax exemption for longer period of time.

An investor who established a new business in regions such as Gambella, Benishangul Gumuz, Afar (except in areas 15 Kilo Meters right and left of the Awash River) Somali, Guji and Borana Zones of Oromiya, South Omo Zone, Segen (Derashe, Amaro, Konso and Burji) Area Peoples Zone, Benchi-Maji Zone, Dawaro Zone, Sheka Zone, Keffa Zone or Konta and Basketo Special Woredas of the Southern Nations Nationalities and Peoples are entitled to an Income Tax deduction of 30% for three consecutive years after the expiry of the income tax exemption period. By doing so the law encourages investors to invest in certain regions where there is less industrialization and development.

The importation of all capital goods, such as plant, machinery and equipment and construction materials is entitled to 100% exemption from custom duties and other taxes levied on such imports.

Spare parts worth 15% of the total value of the imported investment capital goods, provided that they are also exempted from the payment of custom duties.

Non-fiscal incentives are also available for investors who produce export items. Such investors are entitled to import machinery and equipment through suppliers' credit. Business person who suffer losses during the income tax exemption period can carry forward the loss, following the expiration of the income Tax period.

Ethiopian law highly encourages investors to engage in manufacturing and agriculture. Manufacturing industries that have invested more than US$ 200,000 and created permanent employment opportunities for more than 50 Ethiopian nationals will be entitled to duty-free privileges for capital goods at any time. Such privilege is five years only if the investor is engaged in other sectors.

c) Special Economic Areas

The Industrial and Development Corporation[1] has been established to develop and administer industrial parks, lease land, prepare detail national industrial parks master plan, to make necessary infrastructures accessible to industrial parks, to outsource the management of industrial parks and promote the benefits of industrial parks.

Investors who manufacture in the industrial parks enjoy added benefits such as exemption from income tax up to 8-10 years. Furthermore, the parks provide one-stop government services within the parks premises.

The land lease term for factories and residential quarters is 60-80 years at nominal rate. Furthermore, the parks also provide customs facilitation by transporting imported raw materials straight from customs post to factory through bonded export factory scheme.

In regards to the sublease between the Industrial Park Developer and the Industrial Park Enterprise, the EIC ensures: lease and sub-lease agreements are concluded, construction permits are granted in accordance with the system in place; ensures that infrastructure is developed per the plans, the required materials are provided properly and utilised for production and provision of associated services; because sublease cannot be concluded before these requirements are complied with. They do not intervene with regards to sublease price.

Developers of industrial parks are exempted from income tax of 10-15 years depending on the location of the park. The developers are also provided with essential infrastructure, including dedicated power substations.

---

[1] Industrial Parks Proclamation no. 886/2015 and the Council of Ministers to establish Industrial Parks Development Corporation regulation no. 326/2014.

d) The industrial park land is furnished with infrastructure like roads, water, power, telephone, dry and liquid sewages discharging facilities and other important infrastructures. Thus it is possible that the Industrial Park Developer is entitled to provide services like park security service, waste treatment service, telecom services or provision of warehouse.

e) Investment Protection

The investment law provides foreign investors the following protections:

(i) Protection from Expropriation: No investment may be expropriated or nationalized except for public interest and then, only in conformity with the requirements of the law. In case expropriation happens for public interest, adequate compensation, corresponding to the prevailing market value, will be paid.

(ii) Remittance of funds: Foreign investors are legally entitled to repatriate any profits, dividends, principal and interest payments on foreign loans, proceeds from transfer of shares or transfer of ownership, proceeds from the sale or liquidation of the enterprise. In addition, expatriates may also repatriate their salaries and other payments accruing from their employment out of the country. In practice, this needs to be processed through the EIC and the NBE.

(iii) Right to Own Immovable Properties: The Investment Proclamation entitles foreign investors to own a dwelling house and any other immovable properties including private commercial vehicles necessary for running their business operations. Foreign investors may use this right to buy and sale immovable properties upon leaving the country. As long as there is an element of foreign ownership in it and will be the beneficiary of the incentives discussed in the foregoing paragraphs.

The above stated protections of investment are reaffirmed in Bilateral Investment Treaties (BITs) between Ethiopia and other states. To date Ethiopia has signed 33 BITs of which 21 are in force.[1] The BITs that are actually in force are with Italy, Kuwait, Switzerland, Malaysia, Yemen, China, Sudan, Libya, France, Tunisia, Iran, Turkey, Netherlands, Denmark, Sweden, Algeria, Austria, Israel, Germany, Finland and Egypt.[2] These BITs have provisions for the promotion and encouragement of investments, protections of investments, treatment of investments, compensations for damages and loss, fair and equitable treatment of foreign investors and adequate and prompt compensation in the case of expropriation. The BITs to which Ethiopia is a party also provide a dispute settlement mechanism. These BITs provide the investor with a choice to bring claims against the host state, at its option, before the competent Court of the contracting party in whose territory investment is made, ICSID rules in case both contracting parties become members to the ICSID Convention, International Arbitrator or Ad hoc Arbitration tribunal to be appointed by special agreement or established under UNCITRAL Arbitration Rules, Court of Arbitration of International Chamber of Commerce.

The BITs, therefore, provide the similar investment protections to that of the domestic law but with an effective dispute settlement mechanisms. In the case of the domestic law protections the investors are only entitled to bring investment disputes before the domestic court that has jurisdiction. The dispute settlement mechanism of the BITs includes domestic court, ICSID tribunal, Ad hoc arbitration tribunals and arbitration based on UNCITRAL Arbitration rules.

III. Trade

A. Department Supervising Trade

Ministry of Trade is the main government organ responsible for supervising trade. Following the restructuring of the government in 2010, the Ministry of Trade was established as a specialized ministry responsible for regulating trade by Proclamation No. 691/2010. The current powers of the Ministry of Trade are provided under Proclamation No. 916/2015. Among its competencies, the Ministry of Trade is empowered to create conducive conditions for promotion and development of Ethiopia's export trade and control qualities of export and import goods. The trade relation and negotiation directorate general at the Ministry of Trade is responsible for implementing the power of the Ministry of Trade to establish foreign trade relations and coordinate trade negotiations.

In addition to the Ministry of Trade, different government organs such as the Ethiopian Investment Commission, Ethiopia Revenue and Customs Authority, Trade Practice and Consumers' Protection Authority and the National Bank of Ethiopia plays different roles in the regulation and promotion of trade in Ethiopia.

As the result of the federal system adopted in the 1995 Constitution, the federal government and the nine

---

[1] See http://investmentpolicyhub.unctad.org/IIA/CountryBits/67#iiaInnerMenu accessed on 14 March 2018.
[2] See http://investmentpolicyhub.unctad.org/IIA/CountryBits/67#iiaInnerMenu accessed on 14 March 2018.

Regional State Governments have authority to regulate trade on their respective jurisdictional matters. The Federal government (Ministry of Trade) has the power to regulate inter-state and foreign commerce as well as negotiating and ratifying of international agreements. The respective Regional organs administering commercial activities have the power to regulate and develop all other trade matters within their respective states.

B. Brief Introduction of Trade Laws and Regulations and Trade Management

Investment Incentives and Investment Areas Reserved for Domestic Investors Council of Ministers Regulation No. 270/2012 (hereinafter Regulation No. 270/2012) regulates persons permitted to engage in foreign trade. According to Regulation No. 270/2012, import trade is exclusively reserved for domestic investors. However, foreign investors can engage in export trade excluding export of raw coffee, chat, oilseeds, pulses, and precious minerals and hides and skins bought from the market, natural forestry products, and live sheep, goat, camel, cattle and equines not raised by the investor.

So far there is no single body of law that provides for restriction on commodities which can be imported and exported. However, the Parliament is currently discussing a draft proclamation which is aimed at standardizing regulation of the import / export trade. Some restriction on import / export trade can be found in different laws. Commercial Registration and Licensing Proclamation No. 980/2016 empowers the Ministry of Trade, with the approval of the Council of Ministers, to ban importation into or exportation from Ethiopia certain goods and services, for the national interest.

Ethiopia is a beneficiary of the African Growth and Opportunity Act (AGOA) and thus, is eligible to export certain commodities free from tariff and quota to the United States of America. Ethiopia is also a member of Common Market for Eastern and Southern Africa (COMESA), which builds a free trade area with 19 member states. Though Ethiopia is a non-free trade member of COMESA, currently eligible goods imported into or exported from Ethiopia attract 10% tariff reduction.① Ethiopia has also signed bilateral investment treaties with 33 countries with the aim of building strong trade relations.

The presence of export incentives on various commodities, duty-free privileges as well as the absence of domestic participation requirement on investment areas open for foreign investors can be an indication of Ethiopia's commitment towards liberalization. However, there are various restriction on import trade and generally, traders engaged solely in import trade are not be eligible for incentives.

C. The Inspection and Quarantine of Import and Export Commodities

Ethiopia's inspection and quarantine of import and export commodities is mainly targeted towards collection of customs duty and taxes and checking for the legality of commodities. Ethiopia has not yet become a member to the World Trade Organization and for that reason, collection of border taxes and duties still forms a large part of the Country's overall revenue.

Regarding legality of commodities, the customs law prohibits anyone from importing, exporting or transiting goods prohibited by law or international agreements and doing the same with goods labelled as restricted without getting prior permission from a competent authority. Whether a certain good is prohibited or restricted is to be confirmed from domestic laws or international agreements ratified by Ethiopia.

Inspection of commodities involves physical examination of goods by an officer whether by a cargo scanning machine or manually to ensure that the country of origin and export, nature, condition, quality, quantity, tariff classification and value of the goods conforms to the information filed in a registered declaration submitted beforehand.

Inspection is made based on a risk management basis by classifying importers and exporters in to certain risk categories. The Customs Authority is also empowered to take samples for examination and the cost of examination is to be covered by the declarant.

D. Customs Management

In Ethiopia's Federal arrangement, it is the power of the Federal Government to regulate foreign commerce and collect custom duties, taxes and other charges on imports and exports. Accordingly, the Ethiopian Revenues and Customs Authority (ERCA) was established as a Federal institution directly accountable to the Prime Minister in 2008 by Proclamation No. 587/2008 by combining the previously independent institutions of the Ministry of Revenue, the Ethiopian Customs Authority and the Federal Inland Revenue Authority.

ERCA is now charged with managing the country's overall Customs operations together with administering

---

① Addis Ababa Chamber of Commerce & Sectoral Associations, COMESA, Available at: https://addischamber.com/comesa-common-market-for-eastern-and-southern-africa/.

domestic taxes under the Federal Government's jurisdiction. Since the Regional States are not authorised to carry out customs management works, ERCA currently has 30 branch offices all over Ethiopia to perform specific customs management tasks. Among others, it is empowered to examine goods and means of transport entering into or departing from Ethiopia through customs ports, frontier posts and other customs stations, ensure that customs formalities are complied with, collect and analyse information necessary for the control of import and export goods, issue warehouse licenses and supervise duty-free shops.

To import or export goods in Ethiopia, a person needs to secure an import or export license from the Ministry of Trade. Other permits such as an investment license can also serve as an import licence to import investment goods. In addition, the Ministry is empowered to ban the importation and exportation of certain goods.

Since Ethiopia is a land-locked country, import and export items transported by sea enter and exit the country through transit mostly via the port of Djibouti. There are independent institutions such as the Ethiopian Shipping Lines that provide overall services ranging from sea transportation to multimodal and unimodal transportation and customs and port clearing services.

IV. Labour

A. Brief Introduction of Labour Laws and Regulations

The Ethiopian labor law classifies employment relationships into managerial and non-managerial employment. A "managerial employee" is an individual 'who is vested with powers to lay down and execute management policies by law or by the employer's delegation, and / or with the power to hire, transfer, suspend, layoff, assign or take disciplinary measures against employees, and includes legal service head who recommends measures to be taken by the employer regarding managerial issues by using his / her independent judgment in the interest of the employer.'[1] All other workers are classified as non-managerial employees.

The Labor Proclamation and its amendments govern non-managerial employees, while the Ethiopian Civil Code applies to managerial employees. While each of these laws provide for the minimum conditions of labor, it is possible for parties to employment contracts to agree on better terms.

Under Ethiopian law, an employment relationship is said to be formed when an employee agrees directly or indirectly to work under the supervision of the employer for a definite or indefinite period of time in return for a wage.[2] Thus, an employment relationship starts even before the applicant has to report for work, when the employer's offer is accepted by the employee. Both the offer and the acceptance can be made directly or indirectly (e.g., through employment agencies). A withdrawal from the agreement by the employer during this period may constitute an unlawful termination of contract of employment.

It is not mandatory to prepare employment contracts in a written form. However, when it is reduced to writing, it must specify: personal information of the employer and the employee; type of employment (position); place of work; rate and manner of calculation of wages; interval of payment and duration of the contract. Where the contract of employment is not reduced to written form, the employer has the obligation to give the worker, within 15 days from the conclusion of the contract, a written and signed statement containing the information specified above.[3]

Both the Labour Proclamation and the Civil Code provides that an employer may, at his / her discretion, engage an employee on a trial basis. During that period, both the employer and the employee may terminate the employment relationship without any notice and the need to compensate the other party. It is, however, mandatory that such a probation period must be agreed in writing, and that it cannot exceed forty five (45) consecutive days in the case of non-managerial employees. The Civil Code, however, does not specify a maximum probation period. The Labour Proclamation also governs matters such as, maximum working hours, overtime pay, sick leave, occupational injuries, annual leave, maternity leave, working conditions of women and young workers and etc.[4]

Pursuant to the Labour Proclamation, a contract of employment may be terminated for any of the following reasons: on the initiative of either the employer or worker based on contract law principles, in accordance with the provisions of the law, by mutual agreement of the two parties, or pursuant to a collective agreement. The

---

[1] Labour Proclamation no. 377/2003, Federal Negarit Gazeta, Year 10, No.12 Article 3(2(c) , Labour Amendment Proclamation no. 494/2006, Federal Negarit Gazeta, Year 12, No.30 Article 2(1) (c).
[2] Labour Proclamation no. 377/2003, Federal Negarit Gazeta, Year 10, No.12, Article 4(1).
[3] Ibid. Article 7(1) Proc 377/2003.
[4] Ibid. Article 61,66,76,85,88,89,92.

Proclamation also includes an exhaustive list of circumstances where contracts of employment may be terminated without notice. Additionally, a contract of employment may also be terminated by the employer or the employee by giving notice if one of the grounds listed in the proclamation exists. Definite Period / fixed term contracts may be terminated when the period fixed in the agreement comes to an end, or upon the completion of the specific work agreed in the contract.

With respect to managerial employees, the employer should have a good cause to terminate an employee both with and without notice. It is, therefore, not possible to terminate an employee without there being good cause. Ethiopian law recognizes certain grounds listed in the civil code as constituting good cause and when such grounds exist, employer can terminate the contract after giving the required notice. In the case of termination requiring notice, the absence of notice may lead to payment in lieu of notice.

On the other hand, both the employer and the employee can terminate the contract of employment without notice if there exists a reason that is sufficiently serious / gross to justify summary dismissal. The law does not define what constitutes serious reason but it says that a mere non-performance of duties under the employment contract does not justify summary dismissal.

B. Requirements of Employing Foreign Employees

The investment law of Ethiopia permits investors to employ foreigners required for the successful operation of their businesses with a plan of replacing them by Ethiopian nationals within a limited period of time upon provision of the necessary trainings.[1] However, investors are allowed to retain the services of expatriates for top managerial positions without any restrictions.[2]

a. Work Permit

As a general rule, acquiring a work permit is a prerequisite for foreigners to be employed in Ethiopia. However, the law provides certain exceptions to expatriates coming for diplomatic missions, members of the United Nations, World Bank, etc.[3] In all other cases, foreign employees must apply for and acquire work permit before they start working in Ethiopia. Work permit is usually issued for three years, but is renewable every year. Additionally, work permit is issued after the Ministry of Social and Labour Affairs (hereinafter MoLSA) determines the availability, or otherwise lack of the expat's skill in the domestic labour market of the country.[4] The employer is also obliged to provide a plan with a timeline to replace the expats with Ethiopian nationals following transfer of skill.

Additionally, expats are required to register at the Main Department for Immigration and Nationality Affairs within 30 days of their arrival.[5] After a work permit is obtained, the expat must apply for and obtain a residence permit, which is valid for a period of one year.

b. Application Procedure

The following documents are required to process a work permit at the Ministry of Labor and Social Affairs:
• Application form for a work permit- (filled out);
• Educational and work experience credentials of the foreign employee –legalized up to an Ethiopian Embassy abroad (photo copy with original documents);
• A copy of the travel documents of the foreigner (passport);
• A valid business visa (BV) or investment visa (IV) or work visa (WV) ;
• Request Letter addressed to the Ministry by the Employer accompanied by copy of the employment contract;
• Four Passport size photos;
• (Counterpart) form filled out by employer designating local employees who would replace the expat after skills-transfer;
• If the expat is to be assigned on jobs that require knowledge / competence on technical matters, proficiency certificate;
• Service fee of 1700.00 Ethiopian Birr (ETB).
In addition, if the employer is a private organization / entity, the following are required:
• Valid business license or investment certificate or commercial registration certificate of the employer;
• Valid VAT and TIN registration certificate of the employer;
• Support letter from the Ministry of Health or education—if the expat is going to work in the health or

---

[1] Investment Proclamation Federal Negarit Gazeta, Year 18, No.63 Article 3(2(c) 769/2012, Article 37(1)(2) of proc 769/2012.
[2] Ibid. Article 37(3) of proc 769/2012.
[3] Directive issued for the issuance of work permit to foreigners, Ministry of Labour and Social Affairs, 2002, Article 5(2).
[4] Ibid. Article 10(3).
[5] Immigration Proclamation no. 354/2003, Federal Negarit Gazeta, Year 9, No.75, Article 13(c).

education sector; and
• Support letter from appropriate organizations explaining the non-availability of the expat's expertise in the local market.

C. Social Insurance

Private Employees' Pension Proclamation 751/2011 governs the pension scheme for employees in private organizations. All Ethiopian employees (managerial and non-managerial) of private organizations are required to be part of the mandatory pension fund established and managed by the state. The employer is required to contribute 11% of the salary of the employee and an employee is required to contribute 7% of his / her salary towards the pension. This law, however, is not applicable to foreigners[1] the employer is required to withhold said payment and transfer to the Pension Fund on a monthly basis. The age of retirement for private organization employees in Ethiopia is 60 years. An employee has to serve for a period of at least 10 year to receive pension. Expatriates are not required to make pension contributions.

D. Exit and Entry

Immigration Proclamation no. 354/2003 and Regulation 114/2004 govern entry into and exit from Ethiopia. A foreign national must have a valid travel document, entry visa or a permanent residence permit, or an identity card and health certificate in order to enter to Ethiopia. If a person is coming with a tourist or a transit visa, he / she must also have a ticket and a visa which allows him / her to enter the country of destination. Similarly, a person exiting Ethiopia must have a valid travel document, visa to the country of destination, and health certificate (as applicable).

a. Visa Types

There are different kinds of visas that could be issued in Ethiopia, in accordance with the purpose of the visitor. Some of which are, diplomatic, special, business, immigrant, tourist, transit, student, exit and re-entry.[2] A brief description of some of the visas is provided hereunder.

• Diplomatic visa- is a type of visa issued for personnel such as "ambassadors, diplomatic agents, attaches, consular representatives, officials of international and regional organizations and their spouses, and foreign nationals coming or transiting with diplomatic passport." [3]

• Service visa- 'employees of foreign embassies, permanent missions and consular posts, international civil servants in international or reginal organizations,' family members of the above mentioned personnel's enter the country on service visa.[4]

• Business visa- is a visa issued to foreign nationals coming to Ethiopia for 'investment activities, employment purposes, for personnel related to an agreement entered with a foreign governments, international or regional organizations or non-governmental organizations, humanitarian service providers without remuneration, for the purpose of taking part in symposia, exhibitions, workshops, giving trainings and related activities.[5] This visa may be issued on a single or multiple entry basis.

• Immigration visa- 'foreigners adopted by Ethiopians or those married to Ethiopians, foreign nationals who have permanent residence permit in Ethiopia' are some of the categories of personnel's qualified to apply for this type of visa.[6]

• Tourist visa- is a visa issued to foreigners visiting Ethiopia. It is possible to issue this visa with single or multiple entry. It is important to note foreigners entering the country with this visa are not allowed to work.[7]

• Transit visa- foreigners passing through Ethiopia may apply for this visa with single or double entry.[8]

• Student visa- foreigners coming to Ethiopia for education or training purposes may apply for this visa. The applicant must show that he / she has received an acceptance by educational or training institutions in Ethiopia and funds to cover tuition and living expenses.[9]

---

[1] Private Organization Employees Pension Proclamation 715/2011, Federal Negarit Gazeta, Year 17, No.79, Article 10.
[2] Immigration Proclamation no. 354/2003, Federal Negarit Gazeta, Year 9, No.75, Article 12.
[3] Council of Ministers regulation No. 114/2004, Federal Negarit Gazeta, Year 11, No.4, Article 14.
[4] Ibid. Article 15.
[5] Ibid. Article 16.
[6] Ibid. Article 17.
[7] Ibid. Article 18.
[8] Ibid. Article 19.
[9] Ibid. Article 20.

b. Restrictions for Exit and Entry

Under the immigration laws of Ethiopia, a visa could be denied or cancelled if the issuing authority has a reason to believe the applicant could be "public burden or is found to be notorious criminal, a drug addict, the person is suffering from a dangerous contagious disease, has furnished fraudulent information or violated the provisions of the immigration law." [1] There are, however, no exit restrictions currently, unless there is a court order to that effect.

E. Trade Union and Labour Organizations

Ethiopian labour law allows for workers and employers to form trade unions and employers associations respectively. A minimum of 10 workers is required to form trade unions in an organization.[2] The law also allows the formation of federation through the union of trade unions and confederation at the union of federations. The purpose of these organizations is to ensure the proper implementation of the working conditions provided under the law and protecting the rights and interests of its members.[3] It also represents its members in collective negotiations and labour disputes.

F. Labour Disputes

The Labour Proclamation has established labour division in state first instance courts, which adjudicate individual labour disputes such as disciplinary measures, termination, wages, leave, employment injury etc.[4] Federal Courts Proclamation No. 25/96 vests similar power to the federal first instance courts (Addis Ababa and Dire Dawa). Parties dissatisfied with the decision of the first instance courts may bring their claims to the appellate courts.

With regard to collective labour disputes between employer and employees, such as, wages and other benefits, new working conditions, the conclusion, amendment and invalidation of collective agreements or work rules, the law allows for parties to attempt to resolve the dispute through conciliation or arbitration. In the event an agreement is not reached, they may bring their claim to the Labour Relation Board or the appropriate court.

Alternatively, parties may also bring their case to MoLSA, which will appoint a conciliator. The conciliator should attempt to resolve the case within 30 days following the submission of the dispute, and in the event where the conciliation is not successful, a report detailing the issue together with his / her comments should be provided to the Ministry and the parties. Depending on the nature of the dispute, parties could then bring the matter to the Labour Relation Board. The law provides that factual findings of the Board is final. However, parties have the right to appeal to the Federal High Court on basis of error of law within 30 days following the decision of the Board.

V. Intellectual Property

A. Brief Introduction of IP Laws and Regulations

The Constitution of the Federal Democratic Republic of Ethiopia (Proclamation No. 1/1995) recognizes the right to the ownership of both tangible and intangible private property.

Ethiopia is a member of the World Intellectual Property Organization. However, the Country is not state party to major international intellectual property conventions.[5] The Ethiopian Intellectual Property Office is working on acceding to the Paris Convention for the Protection of Industrial Property.

Ethiopia has enacted domestic legislations that recognize and protect different kinds of intellectual property rights. The major laws that constitute the IP legal framework include: The Inventions, Minor Inventions and Industrial Design Proclamation, The Copyright and Neighboring Rights Protection Proclamation (as amended), The Trademark Registration and Protection proclamation and the Plant Breeders' Right Proclamation.

Established in 2003, the Ethiopian Intellectual Property Office (EIPO) is the government body that is in charge of the protection and maintenance of intellectual property rights in the Country.

---

[1] Immigration Proclamation no. 354/2003, Federal Negarit Gazeta, Year 9, No.75, Article 5.
[2] Labour Proclamation no. 377/2003, Federal Negarit Gazeta, Year 10, No.12 Article 113.
[3] Ibid. Article 115.
[4] Ibid. Article 137, 138.
[5] Ethiopia, however, acceded to the Nairobi Treaty on the Protection of the Olympic Symbol on June on February 17, 1982 and signed the Marrakesh Treaty to Facilitate Access to Published Works for Persons Who Are Blind, Visually Impaired or Otherwise Print Disabled on June 28, 2013.

B. Patent Protection and Application

In Ethiopia, the major law that regulates patents is Proclamation no. 123/1995 (The proclamation concerning Inventions, Minor Inventions and Industrial Design). In addition to this Proclamation enacted by the Parliament, Council of Ministers Regulation No. 12/1997 on Inventions, Minor Inventions and Industrial Designs regulates the area in a more detailed fashion. The laws cover minor inventions, such as utility Models and Industrial designs besides patents.

Patents are protected for 10 to 15 years, with an additional five years of protection if proof of properly utilization in the Country can be furnished.

Under Ethiopian law, an invention is patentable if it is new, involves an inventive step and is industrially applicable.

A person who has a right to a patent can apply to EIPO using the form prescribed by the Office by stating the applicant's name, address, title of the invention, nationality and residence. The title of a patent application has to be short and precise.

The following documents are required to file a patent application in Ethiopia:
• A patent document which specifies the description, the claims, drawing and the abstract of the invention;
• If the applicant wants to claim priority based on a foreign application, certified true copy of the foreign application filed within 12 months should be provided. Late filling of a priority document is possible within 90 days from the date of filling in Ethiopia;
• A document proving the applicant organization was given the right over the invention by the individual inventor;
• A Power of attorney signed before a notary and legalized up to an Ethiopian Embassy/Consulate abroad given to the patent agent or patent attorney in Ethiopia. If this cannot be furnished together with the application for good reason, its submission can be differed for up to two months.

After the filling of the patent application, the Registry will undertake a formality examination and failure to conform to the requirements listed above triggers an official action up on which the applicant will be requested to amend its application within two months. If the formality examination is passed, the application will be subject to a substantive examination.

The patent shall be granted after formality and substantive examinations. As soon as the patent is granted it will be published in an official gazette and the certificate of patent will be handed out. The patent initially grants protection for a period of fifteen years starting from the filling date and it can be extended for further five years if proof of working of the invention in Ethiopia is furnished. Annual fees must be paid in advance for each year starting one year after the filling date, in order to maintain the patent. But a six months grace period is provided for late payment of annual fees. Non-payment of annual fees results in the patent application deemed withdrawn or abandoned.

C. Trademark Registration

The two main pieces of legislation that govern trademark in Ethiopia are the Trademark Registration and Protection Proclamation no. 501/2006 and Council of Ministers Trademark Registration and Protection Regulation no. 273/2012. Once registered, trademarks are protected for seven years and they can be renewed indefinitely.

The Ethiopian Trademark Registration and Protection Proclamation defines trademark as any sign or combination of signs capable of distinguishing goods or services from similar goods or services. Trademarks can be letters, words, numerals, figurative elements and combination of colors or any combination thereof.

Ownership rights over a trademark are acquired and become binding on third parties through registration.

The following documents are required for trademark registration in Ethiopia:
• Two copies of filled out applications forms prescribed by the office;
• A power of attorney signed before a foreign notary and legalized up to an Ethiopian foreign Embassy / Consulate where the power of attorney is signed after verification of authenticity;
• List of goods and services based on the Nice Classification 10th edition;
• A certified copy of a home / foreign trade mark registration certificate attested by a notary as being a true copy of the Original. When the company intending to register a trademark does not have a home / foreign registration certificate, a certified copy of its Business License can be an alternative for both domestic & foreign applicant. The business license must authorize the company to provide services / goods in relation to which a trade mark registration is sought;
• Where the trademark contains characters other than Amharic or Latin, or numerical expressions other than Amharic, Arabic or Latin numerals their transliteration into Amharic or Latin characters and Arabic numerals.

Moreover, an applicant can claim priority by providing certified true copy of a foreign application filed within six months from the date on which the application is filed in Ethiopia. Late filling of a priority document is possible and it can be filed within 90 days from the date of filling in Ethiopia.

The Ethiopian Intellectual Property Office conducts formality and substantive examinations on applications and notice of opposition will then be published on a Gazzette having nationwide circulation. If no opposition is lodged within 60 days from the date of publication of the notice, certificate of registration will be issued by the Office. On the other hand, if opposition is lodged, the Office will decide on the opposition after inviting both parties to produce evidence. A registered mark gets protection for seven years and the term of protection is renewable indefinitely.

An owner of the trademark can license or assign its trademark by recording same with the office. Other changes affecting identity or ownership of registrants such as changes of name, address and merger, shall also be recorded in the Office.

D. Copyright Protection

The Ethiopian Copyright regime consists of the Copyright and Neighboring Rights Protection Proclamation (Proclamation No. 410/2004) and its amendment proclamation No. 872/2014. The Council of Ministers passed the Copyright and Neighboring Rights Council of Ministers Regulation No. 305/2014 that helps the implementation of the above mentioned Proclamations.

E. Measures for IP Protection

In cases of infringement of IP rights, Ethiopian laws provide for both civil remedies and criminal sanctions.

The civil remedies consist of injunction orders in order to stop infringing the pertinent right holders and / or compensation to indemnify the damage inflicted.

On the other hand, persons involved in infringement of IP rights could face imprisonment from one to ten years. Moreover, where it is appropriate, the penalty could include seizure, forfeiture and destruction of the infringing goods.

In addition to the above measures, goods subject to an alleged infringement could be seized and detained by the customs authority.

VI. Environmental Protection

A. Department Supervising Environmental Protection

The federal government body in charge of all environmental matters and environment protection in Ethiopia is the Ministry of Environment, Forest and Climate Change (hereinafter referred to as "Ministry"). The Environmental Protection Organs Establishment Proclamation (No.295/2002) and Definition of Powers and Duties of the Executive Organs of the Federal Democratic Republic of Ethiopia Proclamation No. 916/2016 has stipulated the need to establish a system that enables to foster coordinated but differentiated responsibilities among environmental protection agencies at federal and regional levels. The Environmental Protection Organs Establishment Proclamation also requires the establishment of Sectoral and Regional Environmental, Units and Agencies, respectively. Based on that, the Ministry has delegated environment protection powers to six (6) organs: Ministry of Water, Irrigation, and Electricity; Ministry of Transportation; Ministry of Mining, Petroleum, and Natural Gas; Ministry of Agriculture and Natural Resources; Ministry of Industry; and Ministry of Urban Development, and Housing.

The Environmental Impact Assessment Proclamation No. 299/2002 has made Environmental Impact Assessment (EIA) a mandatory legal prerequisite for the implementation of major development projects, programs and plans. EIA is designed to adequately assess the impacts of major projects, prior to the implementation of the project, and ensure that mitigation measures for adverse significant impacts are in place The EIA includes procedural guidelines as a prerequisite for the approval of new development activities and projects in any sector. The environment impact assessment is conducted by certified private experts (certified by the Ministry) unless the project is owned by the government. The Ministry is responsible for the evaluation and approval of an environmental impact study report and the monitoring of its implementation when the project is subject to licensing, execution or supervision by a federal agency or when it is likely to produce trans-regional impact. The regional environmental organ in each region is responsible for the evaluation and approval of any environmental impact study report and the monitoring of its implementation if the project is not subject to licensing, execution and Supervision by a federal agency and if it is unlikely to produce trans-regional impact.

B. Brief Introduction of Laws and Regulations of Environmental Protection

The Environmental Policy of Ethiopia, one of the first official documents with respect to environment protection, was issued in 1997, and provided an overall guidance in the conservation and sustainable utilization of the country's environmental resources. The legal framework for the environmental policy is provided for by the Constitution, where the concept of environmental protection, sustainable development and environmental rights emanate.

Since then, several environment laws have been enacted. In addition to the Environmental Protection Organs Proclamation No 295/2002 and Environmental Impact Assessment Proclamation No. 299/2002, which have been addressed above, the major ones are discussed henceforward:

The Environmental Pollution Control Proclamation No 300/2002 was promulgated with a view to eliminate or mitigate pollution, management of hazardous waste, chemical and radio-active substance. It also provides the framework for the enforcement of environmental standards that instills the duty to respect such standards by setting punitive and incentive measures. Particulary, according to the Environemtnal Pollution Control Proclamation No. 300/2002 (section 4) The generation, keeping, storage, transportation, treatment or disposal of any hazardous waste without a permit from the Authority or the relevant regional environmental agency is prohibited. Additionally, the Solid Waste Managment proclamation no. 513/2007 under Article 4/2 provides that "any person shall obtain a permit from the concerned body of an urban administration prior to his engagement in the collection, transport, use or disposal of solid waste."

Moroever, one of the requirements of the EIA is for projects to implement a waste management plan. The EIA, under Section 5.1 (6)(b)(v) requires projects to specify methods to eliminate, minimize, or mitigate negative impacts. In addition, one of the Environmental Standards set forth under Proclamation No.300/2002 (section 6(1)(e)) is Waste Management Standards specifying the levels allowed and the methods to be used in the generation, handling, storage, treatment, transport and disposal of the various types of waste.

C. Evaluation of Environmental Protection

Ethiopia is facing environmental challenges in both rural and urban setting for reasons such as massive deforestation, high rate of urbanization, a fast growing population and expansion of the country's infrastructural and industrial base. Recognizing that, the Ethiopia government identified environment as a vital pillar for sustainable development in its Growth and Transformation Plan (GTP) and has incorporated development strategies like the CRGE (Climate Resilient Green Economy) to work towards reducing the effects of climate change on the environment for sustainable use.

In terms of the legal framework, Ethiopia has become a party to most of the international environmental treaties[1], adopted national policies and laws, and established institutions to enhance the quality of the environment.[2] While Ethiopia's environmental protection scheme had a slow start, with the government's policy direction, environment friendly development plans and strategies, brighter future lies ahead.

VII. Dispute Resolution

A. Methods and Bodies of Dispute Resolution

a. Dual Court Structure

Ethiopia has organized a dual court structure. Consequently, we see the division of judicial power between

---

[1] The Convention on Biological Diversity; The Basel Convention on the Control of Transboundary Movements of; Hazardous Wastes and Their Disposal and Basel Ban Amendment; The Bamako Convention on the Ban of the Import into Africa and the Control of Transboundary Movement and Management of Hazardous Wastes within Africa; The International Treaty on Plant Genetic Resources for Food and Agriculture; The Convention on International Trade in Endangered Species of Wild Fauna and Flora; The United Nations Framework Convention on Climate Change and its Kyoto Protocol; The United Nations Convention to Combat Desertification in those Countries Experiencing Serious Drought and/or Desertification, Particularly in Africa; The Cartagena Protocol on Biosafety to the Convention on Biological Diversity; The Convention on Migratory Species and the African-Eurasian Water Bird Agreement; The Vienna Convention for the Protection of the Ozone Layer and the Montreal Protocol on Substances that Deplete the Ozone Layer; The Rotterdam Convention on the Prior Informed Consent Procedure for Certain Hazardous Chemicals and Pesticides in International Trade; and The Stockholm Convention on Persistent Organic Pollutants.
[2] World Bank, (March 2015) Enhancing Shared Prosperity through Equitable Services Program for Result Operation retrieved from documents.worldbank.org/curated/en/.../pdf/ETHIOPIA-EDUC-PAD-11302017.pdf.

the courts of the Federal government and that of the Regions, horizontally, and again vertically among the different levels within each structure. The matters allocated to the federal courts appear to be of national concern, while matters relating to the units are left to the courts of the regions. Within the federal court structure, there are three levels of courts according to Proclamation No 25/96. Thus put from bottom to apex: the Federal First Instance Court having only original jurisdictions, the Federal High Court possessing both original and appellate jurisdiction and the Federal Supreme Court with its original, appellate and cassation powers. Proc.No. 25/1996 allocates jurisdiction to Federal Courts mainly on two criteria: laws and persons. Federal Courts are to settle cases or disputes submitted to them within their jurisdiction on the basis of Federal laws, international treaties, and regional laws where the cases relate to same and if not inconsistent with federal laws and international treaties. The regional states do have their own tier of courts.

The Ethiopian legal system belongs to the Continental-a system where law is promulgated by the legislature. However, some argue that nowadays Ethiopia follow a mixed legal system because the Federal supreme court cassation division is rendering precedent. The doctrine of stare decisis had been absent from the Ethiopian legal system until it was introduced very recently by virtue of Proclamation 454/2005. Pursuant to Article 2(1) of this Proclamation, judicial decision by the Cassation Division of the Federal Supreme Court on interpretation of a law is binding on Federal and State Courts at all levels.

b. Alternative Dispute Resolution

Alternative dispute resolution mechanisms under Ethiopian law: particularly compromise / conciliation and arbitration are governed by Title XX of the 1960 Civil Code.

c. Addis Ababa Chamber Commerce and Sectoral Associations Arbitration Institute

The Addis Ababa Chamber Commerce and Sectoral Associations Arbitration Institute (AACCSA AI) is the only legally authorized and mandated commercial disputes settlement body. At present, Chambers of Commerce and Sectoral Associations are legally mandated to conduct arbitration on commercial disputes when requested by disputing parties under proclamation no 341/2003. This law clearly provides such powers to the chambers of commerce and sectoral Associations' in conformity with the long and widespread practices common to most legal systems the world over. Apart from institutional arbitration administered in accordance with the aforementioned proclamation however, existing Civil Code and Civil Procedure Code also allow arbitration to be conducted on an ad hoc and individual basis on arbitrable disputes.

d. Specialist Tribunals

Certain specialist tribunals have been entrusted with the settlement of disputes in accordance with relevant laws. The administrative tribunals of the Trade Practices and Consumer Protection Authority, through its first instance and appellate jurisdiction has been entrusted by Proclamation No. 813/2013 to adjudicate civil and criminal matters related to competition. The Labour Relation Board is empowered by Proclamation No. 377/2003 to hear labour disputes while Proclamation No. 983/2016 provides the powers of the Tax Appeal Commission to review the claims of dissatisfied taxpayers.

B. Application of Laws

Once a decision to bring a case is made, the first question that the plaintiff must consider is where suit may be brought. A suit can only be brought in a court that has jurisdiction. There are three elements of jurisdiction; judicial jurisdiction, material jurisdiction and local jurisdiction. All of these elements must be present in a given case in order for the court to have jurisdiction.

Ethiopia is one of the few countries that is not a member to the New York Convention on the Recognition and Enforcement of Foreign Arbitral Awards (1958). The recognition and enforcement of foreign arbitral awards under Ethiopian law is governed by Article 461 of the Civil Procedure Code of Ethiopia of 1960.

According to Article 461 of the Civil Procedure Code, foreign arbitral awards may not be enforced in Ethiopia unless:

(i) Reciprocity is ensured i.e. the execution of Ethiopian judgments is allowed in the country in which the judgment to be executed was give;

(ii) The award has been made following a regular arbitration agreement or other legal act in the country where it was made;

(iii) The parties have had equal rights in appointing the arbitrators and they have been summoned to attend the proceedings;

(iv) The arbitration tribunal was regularly constituted;

(v) The award does not relate to matters which under the provisions of Ethiopian laws could not be submitted to arbitration or is not contrary to public order or morals; and

(vi) The award is of such nature as to be enforceable on the condition laid down in Ethiopian laws.

VIII. Others

A. Anti-commercial Bribery

a. Brief Introduction of Anti-commercial Bribery Laws and Regulations

Ethiopian anti-corruption law is primarily contained in The Revised Federal Ethics and Anti-corruption Commission Establishment Proclamation and the Revised Anti-Corruption Law which criminalize major forms of corruption including active and passive bribery, bribing a foreign official, and money laundering. The corruption law issued previously was not allowed the Federal Ethics and Anti-Corruption Commission (FEACC) to handle private sector's corruption crimes. It was limited to corruption occurring in government organizations, and was concerned with the private sector only when there is involvement on state level corruption cases. However, under the current proclamation no. 881/2015, it has become necessary to include similar acts committed by the private sector particularly by those who administer funds collected from the public or collected for public purposes in the category of corruption offence, it has become necessary to categorize as corruption acts of bribery, embezzlement and other similar acts committed by the private sector.

Ethiopia has passed proclamations and enactments which would help to prevent and control corruption. These include: The Criminal Code Proclamation No. 414/2004; The Criminal Procedure Code of 1961;The Revised Federal Ethics and Anti-corruption Commission Establishment Proclamation No. 433/2005; The Revised Anti-corruption Special Procedure and Rules of Evidence Proclamation No. 434/2005; Assets Disclosure and Registration Proclamation No. 668/2010; Protection of Witnesses and Whistle-blowers of Criminal Offences Proclamation No. 699/2011; Prevention and Suppression of Money Laundering and the Financing of Terrorism Proclamation No. 657/2009; Regional Ethics and Anti-corruption Commission Establishment Proclamations (8 of the nine regions have such laws); Office of the Federal Auditor General Establishment (as amended) Proclamation No. 669/2010; Federal Courts Advocates' Licensing and Registration Proclamation No. 733/2012; Customs Proclamation No. 622/2009; Licensing and Supervision of Banking Business (Ethiopian National Bank Directive No. SBB/46/2010 Customer Due Diligence of Banks) and Definition of Powers and Duties of the Executive Organs of the Federal Democratic Republic of Ethiopia Proclamation No. 691/2010. Ethiopia is also party to international legal instruments which include among others, The African Union Convention on Preventing and Combating Corruption Ratification Proclamation No. 545/2007; The United Nations Convention against Corruption Ratification Proclamation No. 544/2007; IGAD Convention on Mutual Legal Assistance in Criminal Matters Ratification Proclamation No. 732/2012.

b. Department Supervising Anti-commercial Bribery

The department supervising anti commercial bribery in Ethiopia context is the Federal Ethics and Anti-Corruption Commission (herein after FEACC). In accordance with the Revised Anti-Corruption Special Procedure and Rules of Evidence Proclamation No. 434/2005, the Commission has the authority to investigate corruption in the private sector as long as the issue in question concerns public officials and matters such as public-private collusion. The FEACC has full authority to investigate corruption in any government agency or entity except in the Parliament. In the case of investigations related to Parliament, the Commission must request the Parliament to lift immunity in order to investigate Parliament members. The Commission may delegate, in whole or in part, to Federal or Regional crime investigation bodies, as the case may be, a general investigation power of corruption cases, other than grand corruption.

c. Punitive Actions

According to the Corruption Crimes Proclamation, any public servant or employee of a public organization or any other person who commits anyone of the offenses characterized as corruption shall be subject to the punishments prescribed for such offences. Any public servant or employee of public organization who, with intent to obtain for himself or to procure for another an undue advantage or to injure the right of another, directly or indirectly accepts or solicits an undue advantage by performing his responsibility or duty improperly; or who, in any other way, misuses the responsibility or public trust vested in him to procure an undue advantage for himself or another; or any person who, with intent to obtain for himself or to procure for another an undue advantage or to injure the right of another, promises, offers, gives or agrees to give an undue advantage to a public servant or employee of public organization; or any person, who gives, or any public servant or employee of public organization, who accepts, an undue advantage in consideration for an act of public office, public enterprise or public organization properly performed or to be performed, shall be deemed to have committed crimes of corruption and be liable to the punishments prescribed.

Punitive actions regarding bribery offences are as follows:

(i) When directly or indirectly, seeks, receives or exacts a promise of an advantage for himself or another, in order to act or refrain from acting, in violation of the duties proper to his office, it would be Punishable with simple imprisonment for not less than one year and fine not less than Birr three thousand or rigorous imprisonment not exceeding ten years and fine not exceeding Birr forty thousand.

(ii) Where the purpose of the breach of responsibility or duty solicited the extent of the advantage received, the degree of responsibility or powers of the culprit or the, extent of harm to private, public or State interests or advantages renders the crime committed under sub-article (i) of this Article of particular gravity, the punishment shall be rigorous imprisonment from seven years to fifteen years and fine not less than Birr ten thousand and not exceeding Birr hundred thousand.

(iii) Where two or more of the circumstances mentioned in sub-article (ii) of this Article are present concurrently, the punishment shall be rigorous imprisonment from ten years to twenty-five years and fine not less than Birr twenty thousand and not exceeding Birr two hundred thousand.

(iv) Whosoever, with intent to procure a public servant or employee of a public organization to perform or omit an act in violation of the duty proper to his office, gives or offers an advantage or gift to such public servant or employee of a public organization, shall be punishable, according to the circumstances of the case, with simple imprisonment and fine, or with rigorous imprisonment not exceeding seven years and fine not less than Birr seven thousand and not exceeding Birr thirty thousand.

(v) Whosoever, gives or offers an advantage or gift to any official or employee of a foreign State or international organization, with intent to procure him to perform or omit an act related to international trade or transaction in violation of his official duties shall be punishable.

(vi) Where the purpose of the breach of responsibility or duty solicited, the extent of the advantage offered or promised, the degree powers or responsibility of the culprit or the extent of the harm to private, public or State interests or public organizations renders the crime committed the punishment shall be rigorous imprisonment from five years to fifteen years and fine not less than Birr five thousand and not exceeding Birr one hundred thousand.

B. Project Contracting

a. Permission System and Restrictions

The Ethiopian Federal Government Procurement and Property Administration Proclamation No.649/2009 (Proclamation No. 649/2009) regulates procurement made by the Federal Government to obtain goods, works, consultancy or other services through purchasing, hiring or obtaining by any other contractual means. Even though Proclamation No. 649/2009 aims to regulate procurement by public bodies using a public fund, the different public enterprises also apply the procurement procedures and restrictions provided by Proclamation No. 649/2009 either by formally adopting the procedures and restrictions in their internal procurement guidelines or simply taking a management position without any formal guideline.

To participate in any public procurement, local bidders are required to register in the suppliers' list which is kept by the Public Procurement and Property Administration Agency. The public procurement may also be made by international competitive bidding, if invitation of foreign firms is found to be crucial to ensure effective competition or for procurements above a threshold level for national bidding (when the value of the contract exceeds ETB 50,000,000.00 for works, ETB 10,000,000.00 for goods, ETB 2,500,000.00 for consultancy services and ETB 7,000,000.00 for other services). Open bidding is the statutory preferred procedure of public procurement.

For international procurement (either made by private or public enterprises), the National Bank of Ethiopia Directive No. FXD/13/2000 requires an approval to be obtained from the different levels of Bank's management depending on the value of the importation. Directive No. FXD/13/2000 repeal and replaces a previous requirement for international competitive bidding for the importation of value more than 1 million USD.

b. Invitation to Bid and Bidding

Before calling for potential bidders, the procurer (procurement department of the public body) will prepare the bid document, which includes an instruction to bidders, technical specification, bid form, price schedule, general and specific conditions of contract and bid evaluation criteria. The technical specifications will clearly describe the procurer's requirements with respect to quality performance, safety and where necessary dimensions, symbols terminology, packaging, marking and labelling, the process and methods of production. Once the bid document is prepared, the invitation to bid will be advertised in a national newspaper and optionally in a national radio and / or television. The invitation to bid will contain different information such as the place and deadline for the submission of bids, place and time for the opening of the bid as well as persons permitted to attend the opening procedure. Prior to the deadline for submission of bids, the procurer may modify the bidding documents by issuing an addendum, which will be communicated to all candidates that purchased the bidding documents.

Upon submission of the bid, the procurer will issue a receipt to the bidders indicating the time and date on which the tender was submitted. Bidders are required to submit bid security together with the tender. The bid security is aimed at discouraging irresponsible bidders and will be forfeited if a bidder withdraws his bid or in the case of a successful bidder if the bidder renounces the contractor or fails to furnish performance security if so required.

The bid submission will be evaluated on three successive stage process: preliminary, technical and financial evaluation and a bidder that stands out in all the three stages will become the successful bidder. After the conclusion of the bidding process, the procurer may negotiate matters not dealt in the bidding document with the successful bidder.

The final contract will be executed by the procurer and the successful bidder after the procurer notifies the unsuccessful bidders as to who the successful bidder was and why they have lost the bid.

伊拉克

作者：Ali AL Dabbagh、Greg Englefield、Tom Calvert
译者：邹振东、赵新伟

一、概述

（一）政治、经济、社会、法律投资环境概述

1. 伊拉克地理位置

伊拉克位于中东的战略核心地带，西部接壤叙利亚及约旦，南部毗邻沙特阿拉伯和科威特，东靠伊朗，北接土耳其。伊拉克东南部有连接阿拉伯湾的入海口（通过了位于巴士拉和乌姆盖斯尔的主要港口）。

伊拉克对于世界贸易以及"一带一路"项目也有独特且重要的地缘优势。从中国至俄罗斯南部的最短陆路交通线途径伊拉克。此外，驶经阿拉伯湾的海上丝绸之路的分航线（无论是在历史上还是当今）也经过位于中东中心地带的巴士拉和乌姆盖斯尔港。

2. 人口、社会、宗教及语言

2017年，伊拉克总人口约为3 600万人，其中巴格达地区人口数量约占伊拉克全国总人口的21%。库尔德斯坦自治区人口约为500万人。伊拉克人口及社会呈现多元化特点，其中阿拉伯人占总人口的大多数，此外伊拉克人口中还包括库尔德人、土库曼人、亚述人、波斯人和其他种族。

伊斯兰教是被《宪法》确定的国家官方宗教。穆斯林人口占伊拉克总人口的绝大多数，同时伊拉克也是基督徒、雅兹迪人和其他宗教人士的家园。

伊拉克官方语言为阿拉伯语与库尔德语。民众使用的其他语言还包括土库曼语、波斯语和亚拉姆语。英语通常被用作第二语言。

3. 伊拉克政治发展概述

伊拉克在历史上曾受亚述、巴比伦、波斯、伊斯兰帝国哈里发王朝等统治，是多种文明的故乡。20世纪以前，伊拉克受奥斯曼帝国统治。第一次世界大战之后，位于中东的奥斯曼帝国在战胜国的控制和影响下，分裂成为不同区域。

1920年，国际联盟正式确定了美索不达米亚英国托管地，现代伊拉克地区就此诞生。在托管期内，英国在该区域创立了议会与国王共存的君主立宪制。1921年，经全民公投，伊拉克费萨尔一世的国王身份得以合法化。

1932年，英国的托管期结束，伊拉克成为独立国家。1958年7月14日，伊拉克王权被军队推翻，阿拉伯民族主义与社会主义政党（即复兴社会党，也就是萨达姆·侯赛因统治的政党）上台执政，直至2003年英美两国发动入侵行动。

在被美英联盟占领期间，伊拉克受联盟驻伊拉克临时管理当局（CPA）统治。2004年6月28日，伊拉克的全部政府职权被移交给伊拉克临时政府，联盟驻伊拉克临时管理当局自此不复存在。伊拉克临时政府筹备了伊拉克过渡政府的选举工作。2005年1月30日，伊拉克过渡政府成立，并起草了一部永久性《宪法》。2005年10月15日，伊拉克现行《宪法》以全民公投的形式获得批准，并在2005年10月28日的《政府公报》上公布。2005年12月15日，根据新《宪法》的规定，伊拉克为选举永久性政府进行了第一届国家议会选举。

4. 宪法、政治及法律体系

根据伊拉克《宪法》的规定，《宪法》是伊拉克至高无上、位阶最高的法律。该法还对伊拉克联邦

政府（以下简称"联邦政府"）、公民权利及自由有关的基本原则进行规定。宪法将"伊拉克共和国"定义为一个独立和享有完全主权的联邦制国家，共和国的政府是"共和制、代表制、议会制和民主制的政府"。

联邦政府由立法、行政和司法机关构成，以三权分立及分权管理的联邦制度为基础，行使各自职权。联邦政府的主要机关包括：

① 行政机关：由共和国总统、总理及部长理事会（即内阁）构成（每届任期为4年，由代表委员会选举产生）；

② 立法机关：主要由伊拉克议会（即代表委员会）构成，代表委员由人民投票选举产生，任期为4年；

③ 区域及地方政府：联邦体系由分权管理的首都（巴格达）、联邦区域、省级和地方行政区域构成，省级行政区域选举产生省长以及省议会，省议会享有地方立法权，埃尔比勒、杜胡克、苏莱曼尼亚三省的大部分领土组成了库尔德斯坦自治区（KR）。该地区作为目前唯一被《宪法》承认的半自治地区，由库尔德斯坦自治区区政府进行管理。《宪法》允许其他省份合并成立新的联邦区域，但迄今为止尚未有过这类做法。

除《宪法》之外，《1951年民法典》（以下简称《民法典》）是伊拉克又一部核心法律，该法列明了在伊拉克进行民事交易的规范及原则。此外，该法也对合同的订立以及民事责任进行了规定。

《民法典》的实施已经使伊拉克成为并将继续作为一个受民事法律管辖的国家，这意味着伊拉克法官将依照法律条文作出裁判，尽管某些条文可在一定程度上作出灵活性的解释。《民法典》确立了法律规定的首要地位，以及习俗和伊斯兰教法的次要地位，同时还允许对司法判例进行有限的参考。

5. 伊拉克经济

伊拉克国内生产总值约为240万亿第纳尔（约合2 000亿美金，数据来源：世界银行），是中东地区最大的经济体之一。尽管伊拉克经济在多年的制裁与战争中饱受重创，但近年来伊拉克实际国内生产总值有了较为快速的增长。

伊拉克经济以石油业为支柱，该行业贡献了50%以上的国内生产总值以及80%以上的政府财政收入。伊拉克是世界原油的主要生产及出口国之一。伊拉克估算其拥有的常规石油储量达1 430亿桶，仅次于沙特阿拉伯和伊朗，位居世界第三（信息来源：联合国开发计划署）。

伊拉克的私有行业主要由零售、贸易、建筑和运输服务，以及从事轻工业的众多中小型企业组成。尽管如此，在通信与信息技术产业领域，特别是在移动通信及区域油气产业辅助服务领域，已经有越来越多的大型私有企业崭露头角。

伊拉克与伊斯兰国（ISIS）之间的冲突以及国际油价的下跌，使得伊拉克近几年的经济又遭受了重大打击。2014年，伊拉克实际国内生产总值出现萎缩。尽管伊拉克的未来发展存在不确定性，但自2016年开始，其经济迎来显著增长，据一些组织评估，其经济增长率超过10%（信息来自世界货币基金组织2016年10月～2017年10月《世界经济展望》报告）。随着伊拉克近期从恐怖主义和油气行业动荡的影响中逐渐恢复，人们普遍看好伊拉克未来几年的经济发展。

伊拉克拥有大量的石油与天然气储备，是中东地区除沙特阿拉伯、伊朗之外的第三大石油储备国。此外，伊拉克还拥有磷酸盐、硫黄以及丰富的土地和水资源。

（二）"一带一路"背景下与中国企业合作的现状与方向

伊拉克对有意愿参与或发起新项目的外国公司和投资者持日渐开放和鼓励的态度。伊拉克各领域对投资和项目的需求都是巨大的。尽管政府对各种潜在项目提供了大量的支持，但外国承包商的专业知识和融资帮助也是项目开发的必要条件。

作为历史上中东地区最富裕的国家之一，伊拉克有着丰富的资源和巨大的经济发展潜力。正如上文所提到的，伊拉克对于世界贸易以及"一带一路"项目也有着独特而重要的地缘优势。此外，通往阿拉伯湾的海上丝绸之路的分航线途经位于中东中心地带的巴士拉和乌姆卡瑟尔港口。基于此，伊拉克将是"一带一路"项目中的一个重要合作伙伴，中国企业在伊拉克的活跃度也将日益提高。

近几年，伊拉克与中国的正式合作有所增加，例如，自2015年开始，两国为开展经济、科技、军事和外交事务方面的合作签订了多份备忘录。中国企业目前在伊拉克的多个领域都较为活跃，近年来，伊拉克在法律、政策和投资方面的发展对中国企业有利。关于一般性投资、油气法律、工程承包及其他事项的内容，详见本文相关章节。此外，如下对于一些具有特定发展和新兴机会的关键领域的简要介绍，可能会引起中国企业的兴趣：

1. 油气领域

伊拉克拥有 1 430 亿桶原油储备（以及 2 000 亿桶被认定为可开采的潜在原油储备）和 112 万亿立方英尺的天然气储备，这些资源使伊拉克成为全球油气市场上重要的长期供应者。越来越多的中国国企和私企［例如中国石油天然气集团公司（以下简称"中石油"）、上海振华重工（集团）股份有限公司、中国海洋石油总公司以及众多其他公司］参与到伊拉克油气行业中来。

2017 年 7 月，伊拉克宣布了新一轮上游产业招标。该轮招标已被延长至 2018 年。据我们了解，除非有强制性的限制条件，承包商可以对合同及融资条款提交自己的提案。

伊拉克鼓励对于中下游产业投资。中国企业越来越多地参与到这些领域的开发中来。总的来看，近期的发展包括：随着上游产业的发展，加大了对中下游关键性基础设施的投资整合，例如，结合新的炼油厂的建设和运营（据报道，中石油已与其他公司一同参与了此类项目），提议对油田进行综合开发。近期，已有多个炼油厂发展项目（供国内使用及出口）面向中国的石油和天然气承包商进行了招标。在中游天然气行业，可以看到以公私合作的方式开展的投资，而且伊拉克还计划建造用以加工天然气的新工厂，这些计划已经引起了中国电力供应商、承包商和银行的极大兴趣。

对于其他正在计划中以及正在进行的中下游产业项目，中国企业目前已参与或可能参与的项目包括多个计划性管道工程（例如从伊拉克到约旦的管道）、存储设备以及其他运输设施的开发。此外，伊拉克当局也在考虑增加天然气出口项目。

2. 电力行业

发展伊拉克电力行业对于发展伊拉克国民经济是至关重要的，提高发电能力以及完善输电和配电网络是必经之路。众多中国承包商正积极地供应设备，开发伊拉克电力相关项目。

伊拉克电力部将电力行业对私人投资开放。2017 年，伊拉克通过了一部规范电力部工作的新法律。根据该法的规定，外国开发商和投资者可以参与和投资伊拉克电力行业。近期，我们已经注意到了现有国有电站拟订进行部分私有化，如在政府担保或出口信贷机构（ECA）支持下的独立发电厂（IPP）模式。开发商、工程采购和建设（EPC）承包方、设备提供方及出租方有了越来越多的机会。潜在项目主要涉及燃气发电厂（包括从简单的开口循环到组合循环的技术转换）、热电站和可再生能源。

3. 通用基础设施和其他产业部门

国家投资委员会（NIC），作为伊拉克国家投资协调机构，已对需要外国投资的其他投资项目和行业进行了界定。中国企业已经在积极参与及/或可能参与如下所述的领域：

① 住房类项目：据估计，伊拉克住房缺口已经超过 400 多万套，有超过 118 个住房投资项目已经获得国家投资委员会的确认；

② 铁路项目：计划建设 2 000 公里的铁路轨道，伊拉克各地都存在与伊拉克共和国铁路公司合作的投资机会；

③ 公路项目：伊拉克计划重点发展伊拉克公路系统，包括直通土耳其的六车道高速公路以及位于巴格达的 15 座新桥梁；

④ 机场项目：计划中的新机场、在建机场，以及巴格达、巴士拉和摩苏尔机场的重建工作；

⑤ 港口项目：巴士拉周围（包括 Al-Fao 石油码头、货物港口、经济特区以及交通和通信中心）的重建工作；

⑥ 普通工业：国家投资委员会已经确定了超过 126 个投资机会，涉及钢铁及铝厂，以及生产电气产品、轮胎、塑料、电池、水泥、玻璃、纸张和其他产品的工厂等所有普通行业；

⑦ 电信项目：外国包括中国企业在伊拉克的通信和电信行业表现得较为活跃（潜在的投资包括开发通信基础设施和其他服务的项目）；

⑧ 其他行业：国家投资委员会确认了其他行业存在的众多投资机会，包括卫生（在每个省都需建

设拥有 400 个床位的综合性医院、专业性医院，以及制药厂）、教育（中小学校和大学的建设和运营）、旅游（酒店和其他设施的建设和运营），以及其他行业。

二、投资

（一）市场准入

1. 投资监管部门

负责推动投资的政府部门有：

① 国家投资委员会（以下简称"国家投资委"）。该机构根据《投资法》（2016 年第 13 号法律）设立，负责的事项有：制定和实施全国性投资政策，向符合特定标准的项目发放投资许可证。

② 省级投资委员会（以下简称"省级投资委"）。该机构根据《投资法》（2016 年第 13 号法律）设立，负责的事项有：向位于各省的投资项目发放投资许可证。

③ 其他行业主管部门也对具体行业进行监管，但是，这些行业主管部门通常不涉及投资事宜。

2. 投资行业法律、法规

根据已修订的《投资法》（2016 年第 13 号法律）及其法规和指令，投资者可以申请获得投资许可证，而投资许可证可向投资者提供税务/关税豁免、财产（例如住宅项目）所有权等其他权利保护以及各种投资保护（例如利润汇回）。此外，《原油冶炼投资法》（2007 年第 64 号法律）对于原油冶炼这一特定投资类型提供了针对性的法律保护。

3. 投资形式

伊拉克《投资法》并未根据投资类型提供投资保护。但是，所有投资类型都有资格获得投资许可证，并享受《投资法》规定的各项特权。无论是在私人领域还是公共领域，外国投资者通常都能享受国民待遇。

4. 市场准入标准与审核

伊拉克并不存在明确的市场准入标准。外国投资者可对国家投资委或省级投资委公布的任何项目进行投资，并获得投资许可证。

（二）外汇监管

1. 负责外汇监管的部门

伊拉克中央银行负责对外汇进行监管。

2. 外汇法律、法规简介

在伊拉克提供货币兑换服务的公司属于银行业的一部分，受伊拉克中央银行监管。但是，伊拉克没有适用于外汇监管的法律。

（三）财政

1. 主要金融机构

伊拉克中央银行列举了一项关于目前的持照银行和银行分支机构的名单，详见网站 https://www.cbi.iq/page/24。

伊拉克中央银行向其他金融机构发放许可证。但是，这些金融机构仅能提供其许可证允许范围内的、特定类型的服务。

2. 外国企业融资条件

伊拉克中央银行根据《银行法》（2004 年第 94 号法律）发布了一项有关监管融资公司业务的指令（2010 年第 3 号法律）。根据该指令的规定，投资者可以通过成立股份制公司或者有限责任公司，向按照《公司法》（1997 年第 21 号法律）规定成立的中小企业提供融资。设立股份制信贷公司的最低资本要求为20亿第纳尔,设立有限责任公司的最低资本要求为10亿第纳尔。该指令还对注册各类企业的程序以及对其提供融资的方法进行了进一步阐明。

(四)土地政策

1. 土地相关法律、法规简介

①《不动产登记法》:该项法律对不动产以及与不动产相关的权利的登记进行了规定。

② 伊拉克《外国人不动产所有权法》(1961年第38号法律):该项法律对外国人享有土地和不动产所有权进行了规定。

③ 经修订的《投资法》(2006年第13号):2015年,伊拉克对《投资法》进行了修订,允许外国人和外国投资者在伊拉克购置土地并享有所有权。

2. 外国企业购置土地规定

《不动产登记法》(1971年第43号法律)规定,不动产的购置权仅限于伊拉克国民,而不适用于外国人,除非出现以下例外情形:

① 伊拉克与试图购置不动产的外国人的所在国之间存在互惠待遇;

② 该项购置不存在行政或者军事障碍;

③ 该项财产距离伊拉克边境不少于30公里;

④ 对相关购置必须经伊拉克内政部批准。

法人实体(包括外国实体)可依据《不动产登记法》第152条和第153条的规定购置不动产,但应遵守下列规定:

① 该公司的注册情况必须经伊拉克验证;

② 该公司的公司章程必须允许购置不动产;

③ 对该项财产的登记必须经内政部批准;

④ 该项财产必须位于某一城市的边界范围以内。

此外,截至本文撰写之日,伊拉克已经颁布了多项法律,在特定情况下允许外国人在伊拉克购置不动产。

如上文所述,在1994年以前,伊拉克曾经允许非伊拉克公司在伊拉克拥有不动产,但在革命指挥委员会(目前已解散)废止所有允许外国人拥有不动产的法律以后,形势急剧逆转,中止了允许外国国民拥有不动产的所有法律和法令。

此后,2005年,伊拉克制定了永久性《宪法》,而该《宪法》确认伊拉克国民在伊拉克境内享有财产权,于此同时,《宪法》拒绝承认外国人享有不动产所有权,但相关法律另有规定的除外。

经修订的伊拉克《投资法》(2006年第13号)第10条规定,伊拉克或者外国投资者应享有前述法律规定的所有特权、优惠和保障。此外,根据《投资法》的规定,伊拉克或者外国投资者有权购置下列种类的土地:为住宅项目预留的土地,由国家或公共部门拥有的土地,以及仅由私人部门或公私合伙拥有的土地,但该土地的使用不得与土地使用的首要目的存在冲突。值得注意的是,伊拉克允许本国投资者购置农业或工业用途预留地,并且允许为融资和管理而与外国投资者签订合作伙伴关系协议。

为防止投资者对财产进行任意处分,伊拉克或者外国投资者在购置财产时,应在该项财产上设置留置权,直至投资管理局同意撤销留置权,并且伊拉克或外国投资者的义务履行完毕。此外,还要求投资者将该项财产用于拟定用途,不得利用该项财产从事任何投机活动。如果投资者未能在规定时间内履行其义务,不动产登记部门应在投资管理局提出请求以后,撤销对该项财产的登记,并将该项财产退还给其前所有权人,但前提是应向投资者返还先前支付的买受价格减去占用期租金的剩余部分。

在整个许可期限内,外国投资者按照其签署协议列明的条件负责建造住宅,并将其出售或出租给伊拉克国民,但有权对项目的非住宅部分进行处分。尽管投资者可以在项目完成40%后,对投资项目进行部分转让,但在项目全面完成以前,投资者不得转让项目所有权。还应注意的是,《投资法》禁止对投资项目进行征用或者国有化,也禁止取消部分或全部所有权,为了公共利益而采取上述措施的除外,而在此例外情形下,投资者应有权获得公平补偿。《投资法》还规定,该法的任何后续修订不具有追溯力,以便维护该项法律(对外国投资者)提供的保障和优惠。

《投资法》允许外国投资者为了建设投资项目而向政府和私有领域承租、出租和购买物权,有效期不超过 50 年,但可以续期。

3. 库尔德斯坦自治区的情况

根据库尔德斯坦自治区《投资法》(2006 年第 4 号法律)第 3 条的规定,外国投资者应享受国民待遇。该《投资法》还规定,以遵守库尔德斯坦自治区《投资法》的其他规定为前提,外国投资者为了项目的设立、扩建、多元化和开发,有权购买和租赁必要的土地与不动产。为使其投资项目受益,外国投资者有权根据投资项目的情况购买和租用住宅和车辆。此外,外国投资者有权将其部分或全部投资转让给另一家外国投资者或本国投资者,或者其合作伙伴,但前提是该外国投资者应获得投资管理局的批准。如果项目全部转让,那么受让人应代替让与人享有该项目产生的所有权利并履行所有义务。为防止投资者任意处分投资项目有关财产,相关不动产登记部门将对该项资产设置留置权,直至投资管理局同意撤销以及投资者将其所有义务履行完毕。

4. 其他相关法律

伊拉克《公司法》(1997 年第 21 号法律)禁止外国人参股伊拉克公司。但是,2004 年伊拉克颁布了前述法律的修订版本,允许外国人参股伊拉克公司并对公司享有所有权,但商业代理机构(必须由伊拉克人所有)等特定情形除外。依据《公司法》第 23 条的规定,无论公司股东的国籍如何,在伊拉克注册的公司都被视为伊拉克公司,都具有确切的法律人格和财务地位,因此,这类公司可在伊拉克购置财产。2010 年 5 月 5 日,国务院应司法部长的请求,发布《国务委员会决定》(2015 年第 54 号决定),该决定对"由外国股东直接或间接所有的银行和公司可否在伊拉克购置不动产"这一问题给予了肯定答案。该决定明确规定,即使伊拉克的银行存在外国股东,但该银行仍可采取与公司章程中规定目标相符的方式购置不动产。根据《银行法》(2004 年第 94 号法律)第 33 条第 2 款的规定,(外国股东所有的伊拉克公司)为保证公司运营(包括用于职员和工人的住宿)可以购置必要的不动产。《国务委员会决定》依据该条法律,允许外国人所有的伊拉克银行购置不动产。

值得提及的是,尽管《公司法》明确规定公司创始人的国籍情况并不影响一家公司被视为伊拉克公司,于此同时,《国务委员会决定》也作出类似规定,创始人国籍不存在任何法律障碍,但在实践中,对此问题依然存在不同的做法。事实上,除了受库尔德斯坦自治区《投资法》管辖的公司以外,向外国股东所有的伊拉克公司转让不动产仍具有挑战性。尽管如此,基于具体案例具体分析的原则,此类不动产转让并非不可实现。在撰写本文时,这个问题仍然很严峻。相当一部分外国人所有的公司已经成功地将不动产登记到其在伊拉克注册的公司名下,但有些公司的类似请求却遭到拒绝,尽管伊拉克的法律明确规定,这一操作并不存在任何法律障碍。

我们注意到,根据《不动产登记法》及其修订版本的规定,外国公司在伊拉克设立的分支机构及其相关办事处被视为母公司的延伸,因此,分支机构及其相关办事处不得在伊拉克购置不动产。同样的规定也适用于外国银行在伊拉克设立的持有许可证的分支机构。但是,在获得伊拉克中央银行批准的条件下,这些分支机构或许可在其名下进行抵押登记。唯一的例外情形是,根据伊拉克《投资法》(2015 年第 50 号法律)之规定,外国实体在下列情况下可享有不动产所有权:公司从事住宅工程且满足一定条件,或者土地的所有权人为政府且满足一定条件。

综上所述,正如上文重点强调的,外国投资者在特定情形下是可以在伊拉克购置不动产的。(投资者)对待当地法律须小心谨慎,此外,了解伊拉克当地主管部门的实际处理办法尤为重要。

(五)公司的设立和解散

1. 企业的形式

(1)个人独资企业

该类企业由一名自然人设立。作为公司的唯一持股人,所有权人承担个人无限责任。

(2)简易公司

简易公司是由 2~5 名自然人注册成立的公司,且每一位自然人都对该公司的资本有认缴份额,并承担无限责任。

（3）有限责任公司

此类公司可以是公众公司，也可以是私人公司。出资人数量可以是 1～25 名自然人或者法人。创始人以其各自股份面值为限对公司债务承担有限责任。

（4）股份制公司

此类公司可以是公众性公司，也可以是私人公司。股份制公司成立时至少有 5 名自然人或者法人作为股东。此类公司通过公开认购发行股份。股东以其各自的股份面值为限对公司债务承担有限责任。

（5）共同责任公司

该类公司由 2～25 名自然人或者法人设立。所有权人承担无限责任，并按照各自在公司的持股比例承担责任。

2. 公司设立程序

贸易部/公司注册部门是负责管理外国公司分支机构和当地子公司的成立的政府机构。成立有限责任公司，通常需要 1 个月来签发注册证书，另外需要 2 个月来完成注册后的要求。注册分支机构的程序会稍短一些。上述两种情况均不包括特定行业的审批和许可程序，这一审批和许可程序取决于公司的经营类型。

3. 公司解散的程序和要求

公司应当通过专门的股东大会决议，对清算决定进行批准并指定清算人。签发股东大会决议后的 3 日内，公司应向贸易部办公室提供决议副本，并在官方公报和至少两家当地日报上刊登决议。清算人应监督公司的日常经营，保护公司的财产和资产，代表公司处理所有事宜，直至公司完成清算解散。

清算人应按照下列程序行使公司权利、履行公司义务，并对其资产进行清算：

① 清算人应行使法律授予的有关公司清算的各项权力；

② 清算人应制作公司债务人名单，并就追索债务的情况与程序提交报告，该名单应被视为证明公司债务人的主要证据；

③ 清算人应偿还公司债务，并处理公司权利义务相关事宜；

④ 清算人应提交由指定审计机构编制的总公司财务报表。

提交的法定会计师所签署的公司资产报表和应付款报表应包括下列信息：

① 不动产：是指不产生损坏的情况下无法进行移动的资产，例如：建筑物、某些类型的设备以及某些种类的家具；

② 动产：是指在不产生损坏的情况下能够移动的资产，例如：债务、保险、车辆、无形资产和现金。

此外，清算人应当基于公司活动向某些主管部门致函。

最后，注册部门将签发对公司除名的决议，并在官方公报和一家日报上刊登。

（六）兼并和收购

为进行兼并，公司应采取下列措施：

① 股份制公司兼并其他类型公司的，应对兼并的目的、原因、条件和其他方面进行经济和技术分析，分析报告应提交给（参与兼并收购的）各公司股东大会；

② 各公司股东大会应分别作出兼并决议。兼并决议应写明兼并公司的名称、类型、资本金、股东和业务。兼并决议和分析报告应在被采纳后的 10 日内交义注册部门；

③ 在收到上述材料后的 15 日内，如注册部门并未发现兼并决定与法律不符，将即刻签发许可决定并通知有关公司。此后，兼并决议将在公报和一家日报上刊登；

④ 在决议刊登后的 60 日内，公司将收到注册部门签发的兼并许可，此后召集股东大会联席会议，以对存续公司的合同进行修改，或者为兼并公司起草一份新合同（视情况而定）；该合同应在 10 日之内发送至注册部门申请批准，并在公报和一家日报上刊登；

⑤ 截止至合同（修订后的合同或者新合同，视情况而定）刊登的最后一天，兼并应被视为生效；

同时，被兼并的公司的法人地位应被终止；注册部门对合同的背书等同于颁发许可证；

⑥ 被兼并的公司，其所有权利和义务应转移给实施兼并的公司，或者兼并后设立的新公司。

（七）竞争监管

1. 竞争法简介

伊拉克曾颁布过《反垄断和竞争法》（2010年第14号法律，以下简称《竞争法》），但此后并未颁布实施《竞争法》的指令。因此，对于竞争的监管仍然依照各行业的零散法规进行，我们建议（投资者）可就竞争相关问题获得相关行业针对性的意见。法律明确禁止通过以下方式实施破坏竞争或者反垄断效应、阻碍或阻止竞争的行为，或签署相关协议：

① 固定商品或服务的价格；

② 固定商品或服务的数量；

③ 按照地域、销售量、购买量、客户或者任何其他依据对市场进行分割，并且可能对竞争和反垄断产生不利影响；

④ 阻止或排斥（其他）团体进入伊拉克市场，或以低于成本的价格销售的方式使其他团体遭受亏损；

⑤ 投标时进行"串通"，如果招投标并不具有任何反竞争性质的目的，在此条件下进行联合投标（要约），当事方自开始对此即已知晓，那么此类情形并不被视为"串通"；

⑥ 在价格或者其他销售条件上，对同一种商品或服务的客户进行区别对待；

⑦ 迫使客户不得与竞争对手进行交易；

⑧ 在不存在合法事由的情况下，拒绝按照通常商业条款与特定客户进行交易；

⑨ 意图垄断竞争方为从事其业务所必需的某种原料，或者购买某种商品或服务造成其市场价格上涨，或妨碍其价格下降；

⑩ 以如下任何一项作为销售或者购买某种商品或服务的条件：捆绑销售，或者销售或购买须达到特定数量，或者提供另一种服务；

⑪ 通过利用竞争中的优势地位或制造消极影响，迫使当事方接受或者使其获得特别不公正的价格或销售条件。

2. 竞争监管措施

现行的伊拉克法律允许在私有领域适用竞争法规，因为法律允许受影响的当事人针对反竞争行为申请赔偿相关损失。尽管如此，这在伊拉克并不属于通行做法。在某些情形下，伊拉克法律也对反竞争行为处以罚款并要求登记在案。

（八）税务

1. 税务制度和法规

① 《所得税法》（1983年第13号法律）及其修订版本；

② 《不动产税法》（1959年第162号法律）及其修订版本；

③ 《土地税法》（1962年第26号法律）及其修订版本；

④ 《关于个人所得税扣除的指令》（2005年第1号令）；

⑤ 《关于如何对所得税估值提出异议的指令》（1996年第16号令）。

2. 主要税种和税率

① 企业所得税：该税款金额因公司从事的业务类型不同而有所不同；

② 所得税：个人所得税金额是雇员或者工人工资的10%，但根据雇员的情况，可申请一些税务豁免；

③ 不动产税：按照不动产的类型和价值进行征收；

④ 土地税：按照土地的类型和价值进行征收。

3. 税务申报和优惠

在每一财政年度开始时，各公司都有义务依法提交其上一年度的财务报表和税务申报表，而税款金额则依据公司提交的税务申报表和财务报表进行计算。对于私有领域工人（即公司雇员）应缴纳的税款，则根据公司财务报表和税务申报表上列明的工资进行计算。

（九）证券

1. 证券相关法律、法规简介

伊拉克《证券市场临时法》（美英联盟临时管理当局2004年第74号令）是现行有效的法律，对证券交易所的监管和运行进行了规定。有关证券管理和监督的其他法律还包括：《银行法》（2004年第94号法律）、《商法典》（1984年第30号法律），以及伊拉克中央银行和伊拉克证券交易所发布的指令。

2. 证券市场监督和监管

伊拉克证券交易所和伊拉克中央银行对证券市场实施监督和管理。

3. 关于外国企业从事证券交易的要求

总体而言，伊拉克对于外国企业的证券交易并无特殊要求。

（十）投资优惠和保护

为了努力推进伊拉克的重建与开发，根据《投资法》（2006年第13号）的宗旨，伊拉克特别注重对技术和专业知识的进一步引进。与投资相关的法律进一步支持外国投资者在伊拉克设立投资项目，在多种层次上扩大和发展投资项目，并授予投资项目豁免权。为了吸引和鼓励外国投资，伊拉克还制定了多项投资法律，这与预期目标相符，并有可能使外国投资者获得更多的保障。

根据《投资法》（2015年第50号）的规定，符合条件的投资项目将享受下列优惠和保障：

① 自项目开始之日起的30年内，该投资项目在每一阶段都有权享受税费豁免；

② 依据伊拉克投资者的参股情况延长税费豁免期，如果伊拉克投资者的持股比例达到50%以上，则豁免期将延长至35年；

③ 可在雇用本国工人的同时，雇用外国工人；

④ 根据该项法律新修订版本的规定，如果用于投资项目的外国资产在该工程期间进入伊拉克，伊拉克可对其免征税收和关税；

⑤ 对用于商业运营的进口原材料免征税收（包含关税）；

⑥ 保证不对投资项目进行征用或者国有化，除非受到司法终审判的支持；

⑦ 根据与伊拉克签订的双边国际协议或者伊拉克承认的多边国际协议，外国投资者可享有的其他优惠。

1. 对特定行业和地区的扶持

（1）与伊拉克医疗行业进行贸易往来

① 医疗产品贸易

在伊拉克进口药品、化妆品和医疗用品在内的医用产品，（投资者）可基于不同的买方采取不同的商业模式。在伊拉克，买方的身份存在两种可能：国家药品和医疗用品公司（以下简称"国家医药公司"）或伊拉克私有企业。在公共采购领域，国家医药公司是唯一获得授权、代表伊拉克政府进口医疗产品的政府机构；该公司采用伊拉克通用的公开招标规则进口医疗产品。在进行公开招标时，国家医药公司须遵守关于履行政府合同的两项法规（2014年第1号和第2号法规）。前述法规对投标人必须遵守的合同订立要求进行了规定，比如，在国家医药公司批准合同订立以前，投标人应同时提交标书和初步担保金，并从可被接受的当地银行开立履约保函。

根据伊拉克《药品法》1970年第40号法律）以及规范医药产品市场科研办事处的附属指令（1998年第4号指令）之规定，伊拉克的药品进口必须经过在伊拉克注册的第三方科研办事处来进行。唯一的例外情况是，国家医药公司认为有必要对药品实施直接进口。尽管国家医药公司有权与非伊拉克制造商和营销商进行直接交易，但该公司仍然倾向于通过在伊拉克注册的科研办事处进行交易。在与伊拉克的私有企业交易时，进口药品贸易必须通过科研办事处才能完成。

在伊拉克医疗行业存在以下两个监管机构：一是卫生和环境部（以下简称"卫生部"），二是伊拉克药剂师联合会。一般而言，伊拉克进口医疗产品时，应牢记以下几点：

- 通过第三方代理机构（即科研办事处）进行交易的，相关税务部门视其为在伊拉克进行交易，因此需要缴纳所得税；
- 为了进口或者买卖医疗产品，制造商及医疗产品需要在卫生部进行登记，由卫生部保存已登记的医疗产品和制造商名单；
- 为了对制造商进行登记，卫生部要求（登记方）提供许多文件，包括但不仅限于：制造商或供应商的公司章程、授权书、制造许可证，以及质量管理规范证书（GMP）和药品注册证书（CPP）；
- 卫生部针对出口国不同所要求提交的文件也不同，这取决于原产国是由哪些部门对医疗产品的制造和销售行使批准权；
- 所有提交的文件都需要按照伊拉克法律进行妥善认证和盖章；
- 对于源自某些国家的产品或在某些情形下，卫生部将要求申请方支付卫生部检查员到访并检查生产设施的相关费用；
- 需要向卫生部更新注册信息中的变化，以使登记仍然有效；
- 在大多数情况下，每5年需对登记进行一次续期；
- 在实施进口之前，（有关部门）将向科研办事处签发关于特定产品的进口许可证，例外情形是，（投资方）直接与国家医药公司进行交易的，进口许可证将签发给投资方；
- 在某些特定情况下，国家医药公司将协助进口商加快卫生部的登记程序，使已获准的招标项目得以履行；
- 科研办事处可以在卫生部办理登记，并代表委托方进行投标，但应出示经公证的授权书；
- 同一种医疗产品进行交易时，委托的科研办事处不得超过一家；但对于不同的医疗产品，可委托多家科研办事处；
- 科研办事处可以担任委托人的代理人，也可以作为自营的分销商；
- 科研办事处必须由伊拉克人经营，而如果是法人实体的，则必须由伊拉克人全资所有。

② 在伊拉克的医疗行业进行投资

2015年，伊拉克议会通过了《关于设立私人医疗机构法》（2015年第25号法律）（以下简称《私人医疗机构法》），该法于2015年6月29日生效。该法废除了《私人医院法》（1985年第25号法律）和《公共卫生法》（1981年第89号法律）的部分规定。《私人医疗机构法》包含了（该领域的）若干重要进步，并对私人资本投资医疗行业的法律框架进行了完善。卫生部将对如何实施该法律颁布详细法规。以此同时，该法规定的激励措施和进行的相关调整如下所示：

- 废除了《公共卫生法》规定医疗机构许可证持有人必须是伊拉克人的章节，允许非伊拉克人为经营医疗机构而申请执业许可证；
- 允许在卫生部批准的情况下，医疗实体以经营为目的进行的合并；
- 免除（投资者）开始实际经营之日起3年内的所得税，卫生部对此予以支持；
- 允许根据雇员的类型，提高外国雇员的比例；
- 在卫生部批准的情况下，允许以免费方式划拨土地；
- 在卫生部批准的情况下，允许修建医疗机构的费用中含有不超过30%的贷款。

《私人医疗机构法》并非唯一包含激励措施的法律。根据投资的具体结构，该法及其两项修订可以作为《投资法》（2006年第13号法律）以外的第二位阶、更具体的法律规范。根据《投资法》的规定，必须持有国家投资委签发的许可证才能享受优惠，但《私人医疗机构法》并未要求投资人必须获得国家投资委的先行批准。由于伊拉克公司法允许外国人享有伊拉克公司100%的股权，投资者可以选择在没有领取投资许可证的情况下经营医疗机构。无论医疗机构投资者采取何种方式，都要受卫生部的监管。

③关于伊拉克医疗行业的结语

（投资者）与伊拉克医疗行业进行交易的，必须通过获得许可的伊拉克第三方科研办事处进行，国家医药公司进行公开招标是唯一的例外情形。法律要求投资者首先获得进口许可证，然后再对产品、制造商和供应商进行登记。就私人投资而言，新的《私人医疗机构法》标志着私人资本在投资医疗行业取得了积极发展，标志着该行业对外国资本的开放，这也为伊拉克投资项目赚取利润提供了机会。

（2）伊拉克的电信行业

伊拉克通信和媒体委员会（以下简称"传媒委"）根据美英联盟临时管理委员会2004年第65号令设立，负责对伊拉克的电信、广播、信息服务和其他媒体颁发许可证并进行监管。

在撰写本文时，直接向传媒委或者其他政府机构进行查询是寻求现行法律确切解释的唯一途径。这一过程（如有结果）最短也需数月。为了应对该行业快速发展的需求，传媒委近期向公众发布了多项咨询，为今后起草传媒委全面实施监管的相关法规进行调查。

尽管前述咨询结果并不具有法律效力，但是这表明了传媒委在将来可能会实施监管的意向。本报告在此简要总结了3份涉及竞争、合法监听和服务质量的公众咨询文件。

①《竞争法》（草案）和《市场审查咨询文件》（2016年6月公布）

这一拟订的电信特定竞争法规是在《竞争法》的基础上颁布的。但是，传媒委的法规草案与《竞争法》存在很大不同。传媒委法规草案将仅适用于被传媒委签发许可证的人，原因在于，非许可证持有人还将受到其他监管机构的监督。该项法规草案包含了预防性和救济性竞争保护措施。伊拉克电信业的预防性措施或者事前监管措施具有独特性，致力于在行为尚未发生或者重大竞争损害尚未发生前进行提前干预。传媒委竞争法规草案中的救济性措施或者事后监管措施大部分来自于《竞争法》。电信行业竞争的具体事后监管措施包括：禁止许可证持有人与非终端客户签订非零售协议，禁止反竞争的服务搭售或者捆绑，禁止歧视客户以及禁止以其他形式滥用市场支配权利。根据该项《竞争法》（草案）的规定，传媒委可根据《竞争法》第15条之规定，向具有司法管辖权的法院申请对违反事后监管措施的许可证持有人采取强制执行。

传媒委在电信与信息服务业竞争的事前监管中引入了许多新概念，其中之一就是"重要市场地位"。传媒委将利用从许可证持有人处收到的数据以及传媒委市场审查政策的相关定义与检测方式对"重要市场地位"进行认定。传媒委于2015年公布了市场审查公众咨询文件，于2016年6月公布了相关政策草案和《竞争法》（草案）。市场审查咨询文件通过两个方面对各市场进行了界定：供求产品具有可替代性；若干地理区域在竞争状况上具有类似性。需要注意的是，在进行市场审查时，库尔德斯坦自治区可能被视为一个单独市场。

根据传媒委公布的最新市场审查政策草案，判断某一特定市场是否易受事前监管的影响基于三项标准检测。如果三项标准都符合，则认为该市场易受事前监管影响。如果至少有一项标准不符，则认为不易受事前监管影响。这三项标准是：

- 存在较高的、非暂时性的进入（市场）的壁垒；
- 在相关时间范围内，市场并不倾向于有效竞争；
- 仅靠《竞争法》不足以解决市场失灵问题。

如果认定某一市场易受事前监管的影响，那么接下来将对具有"重要市场地位"的许可证持有人进行指定。要指定拥有"重要市场地位"的许可证持有人，市场份额是最重要的参考标准。例如，2016年6月的《市场审查咨询文件》中表明，Asiacell、Korek和Zain三家公司是移动电话市场具有"重要市场地位"的许可证持有人。指定"重要市场地位"意在使市场持续面向新的竞争者，以使市场保持最佳活力。对于上述三家许可证持有人，《市场审查咨询文件》对其规定了以下义务：

- 允许接入和使用特定的网络设施；
- 不得进行不合理的捆绑销售；
- 不得进行歧视；
- 提高透明度；
- 控制价格；
- 核算成本；

- 单独核算。
②《协助合法监听和数据保留法规》(草案)(2016年6月公布)

《协助合法监听和数据保留法规》(草案)依据现行监听法律,就如何遵循法律作出了进一步解释。该草案包括对通信服务提供商提出的一些数据保留要求,还包括与监听有关的操作程序和标准。该项法规草案界定了需要进行信息披露的授权书类型,以及不向非授权人披露信息的义务。此外,该项法规草案还对实施法律的费用分摊以及违背法律的处罚进行了规定。最后,该项法规草案还就加密(技术)的使用,以及何种信息需要在取得妥善授权后才能进行收集、保管及制作等技术事项进行了规定。

③《服务质量咨询文件》(2016年6月公布)

《服务质量咨询文件》包含《服务质量规定》《零售业服务质量法规》和《批发业服务质量法规》。传媒委意在通过服务质量监管改善伊拉克所提供的服务的选择、价格或者质量,提供质量信息以便在仅有的服务中帮助消费者作出选择,并协助服务提供商维持服务质量。这两项法规和《服务质量规定》涉及以下事项:评估标准、报告日期和范围、评估报告的典型示例、管辖和争议解决、制裁和合规措施,以及旨在确保客户知情权的措施。

传媒委公布《服务质量咨询文件》的目的在于,更好地协商和界定现有许可中规定的服务质量承诺。此外,《消费者保护法》(2010年第1号法律)带来了一些新发展,意在使服务质量与服务提供商收取的价格和声称的情况相符。传媒委实施的监管并不妨碍消费者消费与购买的倾向。但是,如果服务提供商太少,消费者的这一倾向不能被实现,则传媒委须通过监管确保服务具有足够的高质量和低价格。

④关于伊拉克电信行业的结语

通过发布公众咨询文件和寻求利益相关方的建议,传媒委似乎决定通过制定带有一定预见性的法规,保持伊拉克电信业的竞争力以及对新服务提供商的开放性。传媒委的目标是,只在有需要时才进行监管,传媒委已为此作出努力,通过发布《程序规则法规》(草案)以确保规则制定权实施的透明度。传媒委机构的独立性和问责性使其朝着更加符合国际监管标准的方向迈出了积极的一步。

2. 经济特区

伊拉克存在诸多自由贸易区,其中最活跃的是位于巴士拉西南部的巴士拉。在自由贸易区进行运营的(实体),可以免缴所得税(包括外国雇员的个人所得税)。国家对伊拉克雇员工资的50%进行征税。自由贸易区也没有对进出口进行限制,货物进入自由贸易区按过境处理,即国家仅对从自由贸易区进入伊拉克当地消费市场的货物进行征税,对向别国出口的货物不征税,对于进入伊拉克自由贸易区的货物不征收关税。

3. 投资保护

众所周知,武装冲突、政府政策变动和政局不稳使得伊拉克并非理想的投资胜地。但是,为解决前述风险,伊拉克也已采取了相应措施。伊拉克已批准了两部法律(2012年第64号法律和2007年第29号法律),成为解决投资争端国际中心和多边投资担保机构的成员,这使得伊拉克的投资氛围有较大改善,增强了潜在投资者的信心。

伊拉克已于2007年批准了《多边投资担保机构公约》并予以实施。加入多边投资担保机构,意味着目前在伊投资项目可以购买政治风险保险。根据世界银行网站数据显示,截至2016年9月,多边投资担保机构在伊拉克未清偿的贷款总额为800万美元。其次,近期令人振奋的进展是,伊拉克于2012年加入了《关于解决国家和其他国家国民之间投资争端公约》(以下简称《华盛顿公约》)。解决投资争端国际中心通过作出当地终局仲裁裁决,为私人投资者有关独特的投资合同/协定提供了执行机制。

伊拉克目前尚不是《承认及执行外国仲裁裁决公约》(以下简称《纽约公约》)的缔约国,因此其加入解决投资争端国际中心是令人惊叹的。《纽约公约》允许(被申请执行仲裁裁决的)法院基于一系列排除性理由(包括公共政策)而拒绝强制执行他国裁决。而与之不同的是,《华盛顿公约》将解决投资争端国际中心作出的裁决视为国家法院的终局判决。此外,向解决投资争端国际中心裁决提出反对的唯一途径是,请求该中心的另一个仲裁庭取消上述裁决,而这在解决投资争端国际中心的历史上是鲜见成功先例的。

解决投资争端国际中心与多边投资担保机构虽然没有为投资者确定投资待遇,或向投资者提供实质性权利,但是它们分别起到了为投资者提供(投资合同/协定)执行机制和(政治风险)保险的作用。因此,研究合同和投资协定对于理解伊拉克的承诺是很有必要的。值得注意的是,合同是在协定的基础上附加了更多权利。

伊拉克已经签署并批准了多项关于促进和保护投资的双边投资协定。与伊朗、日本、科威特、约旦、白俄罗斯和德国签订的此类双边协定已经在《阿拉伯伊拉克公报》上发布。

三、贸易①

(一)贸易监管部门

伊拉克联邦政府若干部委、政府部门或机关参与监管贸易相关事宜。这些监管部门包括贸易部(MoT)、财政部(MoF)、伊拉克商品交易会和商业服务公司(SCIFCS)以及海关总署(GCC)。

贸易部依照2011年第37号法律成立,其职责为:通过消除妨碍贸易与投资的有关规定和取消进口许可相关规则,鼓励私有领域的发展,鼓励相关项目以改善伊拉克贸易环境。贸易部同时也负责签发与一般商业贸易相关的各类指令和规则(例如商业代理相关法规)。隶属于商务部的伊拉克商品交易会和商业服务公司,目前负责进出口许可证的签发以及相关程序的核准。

财政部依照1981年第92号法律成立,负责国家财政规划与管理。在贸易监察方面,财政部还负责管理海关总署,海关总署是负责海关事务的政府机构。它是财政部的一个部门,由财政部长委任的关长进行领导。海关总署通过海关各部门、海关办公室以及入境点来实施《海关法》的规定。

(二)贸易法律、法规概述

《海关法》(1984年第23号法律)对进出口贸易程序在内的贸易制度整体框架作出了规定。此外,《海关法》还对如下几个方面作出规定:货物进口方、出口方的一般性义务;货物在伊拉克的转运;海关总署的成立与授权;报关程序;海关关税的征收与免除。

《海关法》是一项重要的立法,共有271条规定。而实践中,伊拉克报关及进口程序主要依据第二次立法(如《进口规范》和《临时进口指令》,详见下文)以及海关官员的惯例做法。

《关税法》(2010年第22号法律),经历了2011年与2013年两次修订,规定对进口货物征收关税。通常进口货物的关税税率自0.5%至40%不等(烟酒类除外,烟酒类关税最高可征收至100%),关税由海关总署负责征收。部长理事会以法令的形式对适用的关税进行调整。《关税法》同时对免征关税的特定商品(例如包装、没有商业价值的样本、投资许可证下的进口货物,以及其他物品)作出了规定。总体而言,在伊拉克并不存在对特殊产业的关税优惠,但正如上述所提到的,情况可能会随着部长理事会的法令而有所调整。

要将货物进口至伊拉克需要获得进口许可证。《1978年进口方式实施规范》对进口许可证的签发流程作出了详细的规定。《临时进口指令》(1984年第9号令)允许已经与政府签订合同的外国公司申请临时进口许可证,为其所需的设备免除关税。

其他相关法律法规还包括《商业代理法》(2017年第79号法律)。对于希望在伊拉克市场出售其生产的货物,但又不想在伊拉克注册企业的外国公司而言,可以采用多种途径,其中包括与伊拉克商业代理及分销商签订协议的形式。这些伊拉克企业需在伊拉克进行注册,同时需要遵守《商业代理法》的其他要求。

关于伊拉克的电子贸易,许多法律对电子交易与支付作出了规定。这些法律包括:

①《银行法》(2004年联盟临时管理政府第94号法律)。为伊拉克国内银行系统提供了法律框架。根据《银行法》的规定,在伊拉克的所有人,除非获得伊拉克中央银行(CBI)签发的银行许可证,否则不得从事银行业务。此外,银行业务包括清算、结算和转账服务,付款指令与付款工具;付款指令

---

① 注:本文引用及提供的伊拉克法律译文,为非官方信息。为确保信息无误,请参考阿拉伯语相关原件。本文并不构成法律意见,读者应就具体问题寻求相关法律意见。除特别注明,本文提到的法律法规仅指伊拉克联邦的法律法规。

与付款工具又包括支票、信用卡、借记卡和其他支付卡。

②《电子签名与电子交易法》（2012年第78号法律）。对电子签名与支付活动进行了规定。此外，该法还规定使用电子交易的组织必须采取必要措施，为客户提供安全的服务并维护交易的保密性。

③ 2014年伊拉克部长理事会第3号决议涉及电子支付服务。这一决议对涉及结算和清算系统的电子支付和其他程序进行了规定。所有电子支付服务都必须获得伊拉克中央银行批准。

伊拉克参与了许多促进国际贸易发展的国际协定与组织。伊拉克于2007年1月24日成为世界贸易组织观察员，据报道，伊拉克也有意愿成为其正式成员。伊拉克还批准了1981年《促进和发展阿拉伯国家间贸易交流协定》，以及2005年《大阿拉伯自由贸易区协定》。伊拉克是石油输出国组织（OPEC）和阿拉伯国家联盟的重要成员。2013年，伊拉克与欧盟签署了《贸易和投资框架协议》（TIFA）。伊拉克虽不是许多双边投资协议（BITs）的协议方，但近年来批准了与日本（2012年）和科威特（2013年）的双边投资协议。

目前，伊拉克与中国没有签订双边协议。据了解，两国为建立有关石油与天然气的长期合作，已于2015年12月达成了《谅解备忘录》（MoU）。《谅解备忘录》意在建立两国有关原油贸易、油气勘探开发、油田工程服务技术、存储与运输设备建设、化学冶炼工程、能源设备的合作。我们了解到，伊拉克与中国还签订了其他备忘录，就经济、技术、军事、外交等领域开展合作，上述领域的进展有望促进两国双边贸易及其他领域关系的发展。

（三）贸易管理

伊拉克致力于支持自由贸易与投资体制。当前的伊拉克国家发展计划，表明要促进贸易和投资，以支持私有领域和经济增长。总体而言，伊拉克近年来意在将进出口关税保持在较低水平，并建立一个促进投资和贸易的监管体制。《投资法》（2006年第13号法律）允许（向投资者）颁发投资许可证，投资人因此可享受10年内免征税收和其他费用的好处，也允许（投资者）在巴士拉进行自由贸易区的经营。自由贸易区由隶属于财政部的自由贸易区综合委员会（GCFZ）管辖。在自由贸易区从事商业活动的投资者必须从自由贸易区综合委员会处获得投资许可证。

伊拉克近期还采取了其他支持投资和贸易的措施，包括批准了《关于解决国家和其他国家国民之间投资争端公约》（ICSID）。

（四）进出口商品的检验检疫

货物为通关必须附有海关申报单。递交海关申报单后，货物还需通过检验。检验可能包括为特定商品是否符合相关产品规范而进行的验证。根据《海关法》及相关法规的规定，海关官员有权对违反适用规范的货物进行检疫，或者在货物可能对公共卫生产生危害或经伊拉克卫生主管部门要求的情况下，对货物进行检疫。

（五）海关管理

根据《海关法》规定，任何在伊拉克入境、离境或过境的货物，必须向海关总署海关办公室提交货物清单。进口货物必须附有原产地证书、价值声明、经出产国（也就是货物起运国）商会认证的原始发票。海关总署经一般性授权，可以要求（相关方）进一步提交关于进口货物价值与原产地的证明材料。直至货物通过检验，（相关方）缴纳了所有关税，或者提供的关税担保已被接受，货物才可通关。

上述总结是对伊拉克已公布法律体系的反映，而据我们了解，该总结也在目前的实践中得以印证。但是，在伊拉克入境点实施的通关和进口程序，很大程度上取决于相关官员的做法，因此程序操作可能（与理论）存在一定偏差。特别是，为了使货物报关价值的具体方法得以解释，（相关方）与海关官员进行重要的会谈是非常有必要的。《海关法》规定了确定货物价值的方法，例如根据原材料的商业发票价值进行确认，而实践中，海关官员对于确定估价的详细程序有相当大的自由裁量权，这有时会影响到适用的关税比例。

四、劳动

（一）劳动法律、法规概述

《劳动法》（2015 年第 37 号法律）调整了用人单位与劳动者之间的权利、义务与承诺，并在劳动与社会事务部（MoLSA）的监督下实施相关规定。总体而言，《劳动法》适用于任何在伊拉克受雇的人（包括伊拉克人与外国人）。除《劳动法》之外，还存在诸多命令、指示、决议作为调整就业相关问题（包括工会、卫生、健康、安全规则，以及职业安全）的详细规定。还有许多法律适用于伊拉克签证与工作许可证相关事宜，其中包括规定外国人出入伊拉克相关事宜的经修订的《外国人居住法》（1978 年第 118 号法律），这些法律法规随时间不断调整。

根据《劳动法》之规定，伊拉克法院对于判定一段工作关系是否构成劳动关系具有自由裁量权（即受《劳动法》调整，无论当事人之间如何命名他们之间的关系）。总体而言，《劳动法》更倾向于保护劳动者的权益，并对用人单位提出了许多要求及限制。当事人在合同中约定不受《劳动法》的约束是无效的。

《劳动法》包含诸多规定和要求，包括：

① 在所有劳动关系的环节中，包括合同以及其他文件，都必须使用阿拉伯语或库尔德语；对于向劳动者提起的索赔，如果（用人单位）所依据的文件采用阿拉伯语及库尔德语之外的其他语言，即使文件中有劳动者的签名，该索赔依然可能会败诉；

② 应使用伊拉克货币"第纳尔"支付工资，用人单位必须确保劳动者不受歧视和同工同酬；

③ 还对"最低工资标准"进行了规定，（有关部门）将根据生活成本及其他经济状况随时间的变化，对最低工资标准进行周期性审核；

④ 原则上每天的工作时间为 8 小时，在特殊情况下工作时间可以延长；

⑤ 对劳动者的最长试用期为 3 个月；

⑥ 除了固定期限劳动合同到期，劳动者可以提前 30 日通知辞职，以及双方协议解除合同，用人单位仅可以在特定情形下开除劳动者（例如员工被判一年以上监禁、劳动者或雇主死亡、项目清算或遇不可抗力）；

⑦ 劳动者具有广泛的权利，有权参与工会及参加罢工活动；

⑧ 用人单位必须确保采取了充分的健康与安全措施。

（二）雇用海外劳动者的要求

1. 工作许可证

根据《劳动法》第 30 条的规定，非伊拉克人希望来伊拉克工作的，需要获得工作许可证。经修订的《工作许可证规范》（1987 年第 18 号法规）对取得工作许可证的程序进行了规定。

工作许可证仅适用于能够证明自身专业资格或拥有特定专业技能的个人。通常情况下，向劳动者签发工作许可证需要来自企业的担保。如果用人单位能够为劳动者取得签证，并在没有工作许可证的情况下将其带入伊拉克境内，那么用人单位必须在劳动者入境之后的一个月内为其申请工作许可证。另一种做法是，劳动与社会事务部签发的工作许可证背面有签证，由此申请人可以工作为由入境伊拉克。

就我们了解，这一制度并没有被全面施行。实践中，劳动者通常仅取得了签证（而没有工作许可证）。然而，自 2016 年起，劳动与社会事务部开始积极执行该规定，并将未能遵守该规定的一些公司诉至法庭。

2. 申请程序

《外国人居住法》概述了向外国人签发签证的一些关键性要求。此外，伊拉克签证申请人必须持有有效护照或者替代材料，并在入境伊拉克之前申请并获得签证，除非属于紧急签证的情形。实践中，申请签证前，申请人的护照或旅行证件有效期至少为 6 个月。

联邦政府签发签证的机构是隶属于内政部的国籍、护照及居住权总署（以下简称"居住办"）。据了解，所有签证申请均在巴格达处理及批准，但具体程序会经常变动，而且基于申请人的性质以及入境口岸的不同，具体程序也可能会有所不同。

为了商业目的而获取签证的有效渠道，主要有如下四种：

① 在伊拉克的公司或外国公司在伊拉克的分支机构可以作为一个企业保证人，获得居住办的签证批准；

② 利用相关政府的支持，公司可以通过其国家的外交部，向伊拉克外交部及内政部申请签证；

③ 通过国家投资委申请签证，国家投资委可协助持有投资许可证的项目担保人，为劳动者或承包人获得签证；

④ 劳动与社会事务部签发背面有签证的工作许可证。

实践中，伊拉克企业保证人通常会为在伊拉克境外的申请人申请签证。一旦申请获批，企业担保人将从居住办取得申请批准函，之后进行扫描并通过邮件发送给在伊拉克境外等待签证的申请人。

根据我们的理解，申请工作许可证的普遍原则是，工作许可证只适用于那些能够证明自己的专业资质或专门技能，并足以证明其在伊拉克工作具有合法性的人。工作许可的申请过程尤其需要满足如下几点：

① 在公司注册处以及劳动与社会事务部下属的养老金与社会保障办公室完成在伊拉克雇佣公司或分支机构的注册；

② 为相关劳动者提交申请信息，例如简历、教育或专业资质证书以及其他信息材料。

工作许可证申请书将被送至劳动部部长等待审批，此后劳动与社会事务部将签发函件，列明获得批准的申请人。一旦获得工作许可，申请人即可凭此申请签证。根据《工作许可证规范》的规定，被签发的工作许可证有效期为1年，在接下来的6年内每年均可进行有效期的延展，6年之后则需经劳动部部长批准，方能延展有效期。

3. 社会保险

在伊拉克，用人单位必须向养老金及社会保障办公室代扣代缴劳动者应承担的社会保险金和养老金，并缴纳用人单位所承担的特定份额。劳动与社会事务部已采取行动实施这一规范，近期已将众多不缴纳社会保险金与养老金的公司诉至法院。

依照目前的伊拉克法律的规定，（在伊拉克的）用人单位应当为（在伊拉克的）劳动者（无论外国人还是当地人）缴纳如下社会保险与养老金：

第一，每个劳动者自缴部分为其月工资的5%，该部分由用人单位从其工资中扣除并缴纳给劳动与社会事务部；

第二，各用人单位必须向劳动与社会事务部缴纳的份额为劳动者月工资的13%，这13%由如下几部分构成：

① 1% 为医疗保险；

② 3% 为工伤保险；

③ 9% 为养老金。

上述费用应按月支付，并以每年1月份的劳动者工资为基数进行计算。在劳动者受雇的第一年，则以其首月工资为基数进行计算。逾期缴费的，将会被处以一定数额的罚款。

缴纳社会保险金的劳动者有权利获得相应的保障，例如：

① 退休后的养老金。伊拉克法律并未对强制退休年龄作出规定。在完成20年工作期后，参与工作的男性、女性分别有权自满60岁、55岁开始领取养老金。

② 病假工资（也包括受伤的情形）。单位仅须向劳动者支付每年不超过30天的病假工资。超过30天的部分，由国营的劳动者养老金和社会保障协会支付。该协会通常根据劳动者的临床检查结果和治疗情况承担其医疗费用。

（三）出入境

1. 签证的种类

伊拉克法律规定，外国人（也包括在伊拉克工作的外国人）可申请的签证类型主要包括如下六类：

① 紧急签证：通常有效期最多为 10 天，可以签发给已经到达伊拉克但尚未获得其他类型签证的外国人，对于此种申请，移民局官员有权利决定是否批准及判定申请理由是否合理；

② 单次入境签证：即仅允许外国人在被授予签证之日后的 3 个月内入境伊拉克一次，此类签证通常允许签证持有人自达到伊拉克之日起连续在伊停留 3 个月；

③ 过境签证：即允许外国人穿越伊拉克边境（一些过境签证允许停留），根据目前我们所了解到的情况，此类签证在实践中并不常用；

④ 外交签证：由外交部长授权，签发给以外交身份或以类似身份入境伊拉克的人群；

⑤ 公务签证：公务签证被授予政府雇佣人员，用于与工作相关的行程；

⑥ 旅游—宗教类签证：旅游签证可以签发给信仰伊斯兰教的非伊拉克人，用于到伊拉克圣地进行朝拜。

上述签证中，单次入境签证通常签发给潜在的国际投资者。尽管实践中存在签发多次往返签证的情况，但目前对此尚无明确的立法。

2. 出入境限制

到达伊拉克后，那些已经从居住办获得签证批准函，但在到达之前尚获得伊拉克签证标签的人，必须出示签证批准函，填写签证申请表，并支付 2 美金以获得签证标签。

签证标签上附有入境日期，（旅客获得签证标签后）再通过移民入境点入境。劳动者在获得用于工作的签证时，其用人单位的名称也会附在签证上（该签证禁止此劳动者为其他用人单位工作）。

在到达伊拉克后，所有签证持有者，除持有有效期为 10 天或 10 天以下的签证的持有者外，必须在 15 天内向就近的居住办出示护照。此外，（法律）还要求签证持有者向居住办提交血液和艾滋病检测结果（根据我们了解，签证有效期为 10 天及以内的除外）。

伊拉克的签证持有者，在尚未从居住办获得离境签证之前，不得离开伊拉克，但在入境 10 日内离境的除外。根据居住办报道，签证持有者在签证到期前离境的，需要缴纳 1 美金以获得离境签证。获得离境签证后，签证持有者被允许在 10 日之内离境。就我们对目前做法的了解，签发的长期有效签证（有效期 3 个月以上）通常是允许多次往返的签证。否则，旅客需要为每次离境取得离境签证。

（四）工会与劳工组织

《劳动法》认可工会自由以及集体协商的权利。该法同时禁止用人单位以"劳动者不参与工会，不成为工会成员"为由终止劳动合同，或者以此为条件建立劳动合同。法律没有对伊拉克企业设立工会作出要求。

2003 年之前，伊拉克仅有一家工会，其活动受到之前政权的严格限制。目前，数家工会活跃在伊拉克联邦，包括伊拉克工会联合会、伊拉克工人工会联合会、伊拉克工人委员会与工会联合会、石油工会联合会与独立工会联合会。我们从报道中了解到，尽管罢工并不常见，但目前工会越来越密切的向联邦政府汇报劳动者权利问题，并更多地参与到劳动者与公司之间的争议解决当中。

（五）劳动争议

各省都设有专门的劳动法院。劳动法院由独任法官构成，审理与劳动和就业相关的民事、刑事纠纷和索赔。

根据《劳动法》的规定，伊拉克劳动者享有广泛的权利。对于劳动者与用人单位之间的纠纷，法院倾向于作出有利于劳动者的判决。因此，对于用人单位，明智的做法是依照当地的法律意见来准备劳动合同，认真遵守《劳动法》的规定，并保留准确的记录（例如雇员合同、社会保险金及其他支付凭证）作为合规证明。这在一定程度上可以减轻劳动者根据《劳动法》向用人单位提出索赔的风险。

近期，劳动与社会事务部也采取了积极主动的措施，以保障《劳动法》的实施，包括工作许可证制度的实施。此外，许多公司已经因没有为其外籍雇员获取工作许可证，而被劳动与社会事务部诉至法庭。因此，从合规监管的角度，全面遵守《劳动法》的要求才是明智之举。

五、知识产权

(一)知识产权法律、法规概述

伊拉克已颁布了保护各类知识产权的相关法律。包括如下几种:

① 保护专利权的《专利权法》(1970年第65号法律)(经联盟驻伊拉克临时管理当局第81号令修订);

② 保护贸易与服务商标的《商标法》(1957年第21号法律)(经联盟驻伊拉克临时管理当局第80号令修订);

③ 保护著作权的《著作权法》(1971年第3号法律)(经联盟驻伊拉克临时管理当局第3号令修订)。

一些知识产权,例如专利权、商标权,可以通过在伊拉克进行注册而获得保护。一些特定的知识产权,例如著作权,包括文学及艺术作品,是无法注册的。但根据《著作权法》的规定,著作权人为自然人的,著作权人经济权利的保护期为自著作权人死亡后的50年;著作权人为公司或其他组织的,保护期为自第一次出版发行后的50年。

(二)专利申请

《专利权法》保护的专利范围包括工业应用发明、创新发明,以及参与有关于新工业产品、新工业方法或对熟知工业方法之新应用的创新性行动。

《专利权法》为经登记的专利所有人提供法律保障,保障发明在未经授权的情况下不得被使用、开发、生产、销售或进口。专利可在专利与工业设计登记办公室进行注册。法律对注册专利的保护期为自注册之日起的20年。

(三)商标注册

根据伊拉克《商标法》的规定,在商标注册办公室注册的商标与服务标志,未经授权不得使用。

《商标法》对"商标"概括性地定义为,足以区分一个企业商品与其他企业商品的任何符号或任何符号的组合。商标可以是个人姓名、字母、数字符号、图形要素、颜色以及这几类符号的组合。当符号本身不具备区分相关商品或服务的能力时,该符号是否能被注册为商标将取决于它在使用中已获得的特殊性。

服务标志可以包括任何符号或任何符号的组合,它被用以识别一个人的服务具有唯一性,有别于他人的服务。

注册商标及服务标志以10年为一个周期进行续展申请。申请必须要递交使用阿拉伯文填写的申请表,同时支付申请费。对商标或服务标志的使用并不是注册申请的必要条件。

(四)知识产权保护措施

根据伊拉克诸多法律条款的规定,由伊拉克法院实施对知识产权的保护。在一些案件中,侵犯知识产权的行为也构成犯罪。

《专利权法》明确规定,在伊拉克,经注册的专利或工业设计的所有者可以通过向伊拉克法庭申请,以终止侵权人的侵权行为。《商标法》列明了与侵犯注册商标权相关的各项犯罪。许多情况下,商标注册人可对侵权人提起民事诉讼。伊拉克法院可以下令扣押任何侵犯贸易或服务商标的产品,没收相关平行进口商的因侵权获得的所有收入,并处以其他惩罚。因侵犯著作权而构成犯罪的,侵权人将被处以监禁与赔偿。

《商标法》也规定,"驰名"商标即便未在伊拉克进行注册,其所有权人仍有权利享受《商标法》给予的保护。尽管如此,实践中最好对这类商标申请注册,这是因为欲证明商标是"驰名"的,所有权人还需从伊拉克法院获得相应的裁决。

伊拉克是《保护工业产权巴黎公约》的缔约国。该公约列明了在伊拉克享受国民待遇(即承认其他缔约国的知识产权)、优先权的标准及其他影响知识产权的规定。

伊拉克也是《商标法新加坡条约》的缔约国,该条约使其他缔约国商标注册与确立了世界知识产权组织的《世界知识产权组织公约》之间协调一致。

六、环境保护

（一）环境保护监督部门

环境部依据2008年第37号法律成立，负责伊拉克环境事务的总体监督，以及相关环境法律的执行。此外，在伊拉克，对于可能造成环境影响的活动和项目，需要获得环境部的同意或者许可证书。对于部分特定项目，还需要获得其他部委（例如负责管理伊拉克石油的石油部）的同意。

环境部对部分工作进行分配，一些环境事务交由省级环境中心（以下简称"环境委员会"）进行处理。环境委员会监管各级环境部门的工作，负责环境监测和监督，包括监测空气质量、水、固体废物和危险化学品、生物多样性、土地利用、工业活动等以及监督环境影响评估的准备工作。由环境部以及伊拉克其他部委的高级官员组成"环境保护和改进委员会"，负责监督环境委员会的工作。

其他伊拉克政府部门也获得部分授权，根据具体法律负责相关环境事宜（详情如下）。

（二）环境保护法法律、法规概述

《环境保护法》（2009年第27号法律）建立了环境保护法律体系，并对环境污染作出了禁止性规定。此外，《环境保护法》还包含如下内容：

① 规定大型项目所有人须进行环境影响评估；
② 规定禁止营运任何影响环境的大型项目，除非得到环境部批准；
③ 要求勘探或开采油气的相关方采取防止环境污染的一切必要措施；
④ 概括地规定了有关排放气体、液体、其他物质必须遵循"国家环境法律"的规定；
⑤ 禁止直接或间接地影响土地产量、食物链或造成自然风光的污染。

此外，许多其他法律也对环境保护进行了规范。它们包括：

① 《油气资源保护法》（1985年第84号法律），该法由石油部负责施行，意在保护油气资源免受损害和浪费。此外，根据该法律的规定，油气运营人须采取任何避免污染的必要手段与防范措施；
② 2011年环境部第3号法规，列明了在伊拉克设立项目需要遵守的环境规范，并要求环境部对此进行监督。此外，该法规也制订了针对项目（例如项目位置、废物处理及储存）的环境规范；
③ 2001年部长理事会第B2号关于水资源保护的规定，意在保护河流、湿地等公共水域，禁止在未经允许的情况下向公共水域排放废物、垃圾；
④ 有关在伊拉克公司的环境责任须写入相关合同，例如石油行业的服务合同。

（三）环境保护评估

根据《环境保护法》的规定，违反环境相关法律的行为将被处以高额罚金和严厉制裁。环境部同时有权暂停或者停止活动，直至违反环境相关法律的事项消失。违法者可能被判处监禁以及某些重罪，例如未经授权进行危险品处理，向伊拉克境内进口危险废物，违法者将被处以强制性监禁。根据《刑法典》（1969年第111号法律）（经修订）之规定，法人犯罪的，只能被处以罚金、没收财产或被采取法律规定的预防措施。但是，违规雇员或公司职员可能因犯罪而被处以刑事处罚。

据我们了解，近些年，实践中环境保护的执法力度有所加强。法律要求相关方必须履行取得环境许可证及进行环境影响评估等法律义务。如果外国公司在伊拉克造成污染而没有得以恢复，伊拉克相关部门和国家机构将采取相应的监管行动。

七、争议解决

（一）争议解决的方式与主体

在伊拉克，法院诉讼是争议解决的主要途径。依据法律规定，伊拉克法院系统由各级法院构成，包括：联邦最高法院，即伊拉克最高司法机构；上诉法院，有权对除联邦最高法院之外的其他法院进行审查，审理除来自联邦最高法院之外的上诉案件；其他法院。

受理商事案件的法院主要包括：

① 商事法院：大多数民事法律纠纷受伊拉克初审法院管辖（详情如下），但如果纠纷涉及商业合同且合同一方为外国公司，那么此类纠纷可以受商事法院管辖；

② 初审法院：各省设立初审法院，由独任法官构成；初审法院审理与民事行为及索赔相关的案件；

③ 劳动法院：各省设立劳动法院，该法院由独任法官构成，负责审理与劳动及就业相关的民事、刑事纠纷和索赔；

④ 上诉法院：各省设立上诉法院，由审判长与其他法官构成，他们根据案件的复杂程度，对不服初审判决的上诉案件进行裁判；

⑤ 刑事法院：存在多种刑事法院，包括调查法院、轻罪法院、重罪法院，这些法院审理违反《刑法典》的行为以及其他法律规定的违法犯罪行为。

除了上述伊拉克法院体系，伊拉克法律（例如《投资法》第27条）还允许投资者通过仲裁来解决争议。1951年伊拉克《民法典》对仲裁作出相关规定，并且设有伊拉克国家仲裁中心。尽管如此，实践中，涉外相关方通常也可选择在伊拉克之外的区域或国际仲裁中心提起仲裁（例如迪拜国际金融中心—伦敦国际仲裁院分院）。

（二）法律适用

在伊拉克，法院审理程序有时存在不确定性，主要原因是尚未对以往裁判建立起公共数据库。尽管如此，伊拉克法院还是发挥着作用，并且法院的裁判通常也受到尊重。外国当事人曾有在伊拉克法院成功起诉、抗辩及索赔的先例。

尽管如此，由于伊拉克不是1971年2月1日《国际民商事案件中外国判决的承认和执行公约》的缔约国，在伊拉克执行外国法院判决还存在问题。

但是，根据《民法典》第16条的规定，在伊拉克不得执行外国法院递交的判决，除非根据伊拉克相关法律规定，这些判决被视为是可执行的。综上所述，只有发生法律规定的如下情况，对外国法院判决的申请执行才能得以实现：

① 签发外国判决的国家与伊拉克达成了双边协议；

② 伊拉克法规明确提到判决法院所属国家的判决可以被执行；

③ 判决法院所属国家与伊拉克存在互惠关系。

至少在表面上看，与伊拉克签署过执行外国判决条约的国家较为有限，它们包括埃及、土耳其、意大利、印度和约旦。

关于仲裁，由于伊拉克并非1958年《承认及执行外国仲裁裁决公约》的缔约国，因而在伊拉克执行外国仲裁裁决也存在问题。

尽管如此，1983年《利雅得公约》已经获得伊拉克批准，外国裁决可以通过该公约得以执行。该公约对于外国判决与仲裁裁决的执行也进行了规定。

根据《利雅得公约》的规定，缔约国所属法院必须执行其他缔约国的仲裁裁决，除非：

① 被申请执行仲裁裁决的国家法律规定，该纠纷不属于仲裁解决的范畴；

② 该裁决是基于无效仲裁条款或无效仲裁协议作出的；

③ 该裁决并非终极裁决；

④ 根据仲裁协议或者裁决作出地法律，该仲裁员是不称职的；

⑤ 仲裁庭没有及时传唤当事人参与仲裁；

⑥ 裁决与伊斯兰教法、公共秩序、被申请执行裁决的缔约国之宪法、伦理道德相违背。

上述条件都存在较为广泛的解释空间，伊拉克法院据此可以轻易地拒绝执行非伊拉克的仲裁裁决。尽管如此，为了使裁决在伊拉克具有可执行性，当事人最好在《利雅得公约》的缔约国进行仲裁（例如阿联酋或约旦）。此外，还存在一个重要的限制是，《利雅得公约》不适用于针对伊拉克联邦政府的仲裁裁决。(该条可能被扩大解释为针对任何政府机关或国企的仲裁裁决。)

2015年,伊拉克批准了1965年《关于解决国家和其他国家公民之间投资争端公约》。该公约为投资者解决与东道主国之间的争议提供了途径,对裁决的执行进行了规定。该公约对于伊拉克是较新的公约,市场评论员正饶有兴致地关注着有关公约的进展。此外,该公约条款也可能被写入公司与联邦政府的合同中。

八、其他

(一)反商业贿赂

1. 反商业贿赂法律、法规概述

在伊拉克,涉及商务反贿赂、有反腐败的法律主要有:
① 《刑法典》;
② 《公务员行为准则法》(1991年第14号法律)。

《刑法典》包含了涉及"公职人员"以及与之相对的"私人"的贪腐罪行。在《刑法典》中,"公职人员"被定义为"被联邦政府或其机构委以公共任务的任何官员、劳动者或工作人员(包括国有公司的劳动者)"。

此外,《刑法典》对如下情形作出禁止:
① 任何公职人员或代理人为了自己或他人能够谋取或接受礼物、好处、荣誉(或关于此的承诺)而履行、不履行或违背职责;
② 公职人员接受了礼物或好处(对此虽无明确定义,但我们认为可以进行广义解释),继而采取或避免采取一些行为(即使这些行为不属于其职责的范畴,或者该行为尚未被实施);
③ 任何人向公职人员提供或承诺给予礼物或好处,即使公职人员不接受贿赂,上述行贿人员依然会因其行为受到处罚;
④ 任何政府官员或其他人员,作为中间人,分别寻求、收受或提供贿赂。

《公务员行为准则法》禁止政府部门或国有机构的官员组织或参与某些活动,包括利用职务便利为自己或他人谋取私利;接受客户或者承包商(或其他商业人士)提供的好处,或者接受私人因其公职身份而提供的好处;以及公务员参与某些商业活动。

此外,伊拉克也有其他法律包含了反贿赂、反贪污的相关规定,包括:
① 伊拉克革命指挥委员会《革命指挥委员会反贿赂决议》(1983年第160号决议);
② 伊拉克《非法所得法》(1958年第15号法律);
③ 伊拉克2007年第35号法律批准的《联合国反腐败公约》(UNCAC)。

2. 反商业贿赂监督部门

通常来说,伊拉克的检察官有权对贿赂和贪污的罪行提起公诉。我们也注意到联盟驻伊拉克临时管理当局《监察长令》(2004年第57号命令)涉及监察长的职权。根据该命令的规定,联邦政府各部委都要设立监察长办公室。该办公室对包括贪污、滥用职权在内的违法行为享有广泛调查权。此项权利包括强制私人(包括非公职人员)提供与调查有关的信息。

根据《伊拉克廉政委员会法》(2011年第30号法律)的规定,在伊拉克设立了联邦廉政委员会。该机构已经获得特别授权,可在调查法官的监督下,通过调查人员的相关工作,对腐败案件实施调查,以及开展防止和打击腐败的相关工作。根据法律特别规定,联邦廉政委员会将会与联邦最高审计委员会(如下面所讨论的)以及部分监察长办公室合作办案。

根据《联邦最高审计委员会法》(2011年第31号法律)的规定,伊拉克设立联邦最高审计委员会,该委员会作为独立主体审计公共账目、监督公共财政。根据该法律的规定,联邦最高审计委员会监督与公共收入相关的交易,审计公共领域机构(包括国有企业)财务状况。最高审计委员会也有权审阅记录、报告以及其他材料,有权要求公共监察官或联邦廉政委员会实施调查行为。

3. 处罚措施

国内反贿赂法律对贿赂行为的处罚进行了规定,包括:
① 《刑法典》:根据《刑法典》的规定,犯有贪污罪的人将被处以 10 年及以下监禁,并处罚金;
② 《公务员行为准则法》:违反《公务员行为准则法》的公务员,将被处以罚金与监禁;
③ 《革命指挥委员会反贿赂决议》:违反《革命指挥委员会反贿赂决议》的人,将被处以罚金与监禁;
④ 《非法所得法》:惩罚措施包括返还非法所得,撤销公职人员职务,处以 5 年及以下监禁,以及处以罚金。

如下法律对刑罚的减免及抗辩事由进行了规定:
① 《刑法典》:行贿人和中介人,向司法或行政机关告知情况,或者在提起诉讼前承认罪行的,应当被免除处罚;在诉讼开始后以及结束之前告知或承认罪行的,被认定为减刑情形;对于接受贿赂的政府官员,法律并不给予上述类似的保护;
② 《公务员行为准则法》:该法并未规定具体的抗辩事由,但是规定如果犯罪嫌疑人已经得到了官方对其表现的认可,可以被减免相应处罚;
③ 《革命指挥委员会反贿赂决议》:除《刑法典》规定的可能适用的一般性抗辩事由,本法并未对具体抗辩事由进行规定;
④ 《非法所得法》:根据本法规定,相关人向特定机关举报非法所得,或协助依法进行调查的,可以被免于处罚。

(二)项目合同

1. 项目合同

在伊拉克的实务操作中,与外国投资者相关的重要项目,由联邦政府或伊拉克国有企业(SOEs)批准该项目合同。

《公共采购法》(联盟驻伊拉克临时管理当局第 87 号法律)(以及相关的实施规范)是规范联邦政府公共项目合同采购及履约的主要法律。《公共采购法》适用于伊拉克所有可能花费公共资金而进行的物品或服务采购,包括国有企业使用政府拨款,批准订立物品或服务采购合同的行为。

在国际性公司与国有企业组建的合资企业中,如有国家资金的投入,则《公共采购法》也适用于该国际性公司批准订立的采购合同(例如建筑或其他项目合同)。

规划部(MoP)也不时签发与公共采购和招标相关(例如投标文件内容、评标过程等)的实施细则。此外,该部还发布了大量的支持性条例,并已发送至包括石油部在内的所有部委,以鼓励各部委与联邦政府的采购行为保持一致性。

2. 许可制度

"投标资质预审要求"通常适用于希望通过投标订立合同的公司。该要求包括提交法人信息及财务支持(例如对一些投标提供投标保证金或押金)。投标保证金或押金(的金额)通常以合同价值为基础,如果投标不成功,该保证金或押金将被返还给投标者。

法律并未要求投标者在投标前,一定要成立伊拉克当地企业,但投标者通常为了履行公共合同而需要成立当地企业。规划部也为部分服务类工程继续保留了"承包方分类方案",尽管这对参与大型公共合同招标的国际投标者并不适用,但一些伊拉克采购主体可能会根据这一方案对投标者进行分类。

3. 禁止性范围

通常,法律不对外国投资者实施国籍限制。但实践中,如下领域的外商投资会受到这类限制:商业代理与分销安排、某些计算机及通信服务、担保的提供、土地所有权(仅有限的住房开发项目除外)、国防及安全设施。

4. 招标与投标

根据《公共采购法》(以及其实施规范)的规定,公共合同须根据竞争原则批准合同的签订,特定情形除外。例如货物或服务只能从特定供应商处获得，或者出于公共利益而不能进行招标。

对公共合同进行投标，投标者需要提供充足的信息，例如工作状况，预计工作安排，招标评估的条款、条件及标准。招标方同时需要阐明招标的期限，并向投标者答疑。尽管法律规定没有要求公开招标方应仅凭价格作为选择投标人的标准，但通常招标方须确定选标的标准，以此对收到的投标进行评估。

实践中，一些伊拉克部委与国企对于特定合同的招标，适用不同程序规定或标准。比方说，国家石油公司或者其合资公司正在进行的采购项目，实践中并不在《公共采购法》调整的范畴内。

通常而言，联邦政府或者国有企业向私企批准合同订立的行为，须遵守《公共采购法》，否则可能面临其他方对合同的批准订立提出质疑的情况（例如，其他商业实体提出对协议或项目的反对意见）。当《公共采购法》的适用与否并不确定时（比方说，由于特定政府部门或国企提出了特殊要求），合同批准方可采取一些防损措施（例如，通过部长理事会对批准签订的合同进行确认）以降低订立合同所面临的法律挑战。

（三）其他

1.《油气法》

涉及联邦伊拉克油气的相关法律大致可分为两部分：2004年之前的立法，起源于1961—1975年国有化时期；2004年后的立法，包含了关于油气的多部法律，但并没有一部统一的联邦油气法。

与油气相关的主要法律包括：

①《宪法》；

② 部分2004年之前的立法，例如1967年第101号法律，该法起源于1961—1975年的国有化进程；

③ 2010年第19号法律，规定对在伊拉克的外国石油公司以及转包、分包商征收35%的所得税；

④《冶炼投资法》（2007年第64号法律），对私人投资石油冶炼领域规定了若干激励措施；

⑤ 石油部的许多部门规章，例如为进行油田招标而签发的规定。

（1）《宪法》

《宪法》包括对自然资源的有关规定。根据该法第111条的规定，石油和天然气归伊拉克联邦地区以及各省的全体公民所有。此外，根据第112条的规定，联邦政府、资源产出省及地方政府应当对当前油气田开采的油气实施管理，按全国各地人口分布成比例分配油气收入，实现收入的公平分配。

（2）伊拉克石油与天然气许可流程及技术服务合同模板

1967年第97号法律授予伊拉克国家石油公司（目前已并入石油部）对伊拉克境内油气的专属开发权。在此基础上，石油部被视为是有权订立油气资源开发合同的伊拉克政府部门。自2008年起，联邦政府已经启动了多轮许可程序，邀请国际石油公司与其缔结合约，对伊拉克的油气田进行勘探、开发、开采与生产。

参与投标的国际石油公司必须经过石油部的预先资格审查。需要缴纳25 000美金的预先资格审查费，并提交详细的技术、法律和财务信息，以证明其适合参与伊拉克的上游石油和天然气行业。

投标成功的国际石油公司，将（与伊拉克方）签订20年的技术服务合同（TSCs）。技术服务合同的主要条款包括：

① 对每桶石油的固定价格（而非股份）作出约定，根据技术服务合同，国际石油公司将成为伊拉克相关区域国有石油公司（例如南方石油公司、北方石油公司等）的承包商；

② 对"石油作业"进行了较为广泛的定义，包括评估、开发、再开发及生产运作；

③ 对伊拉克国有石油企业及石油部的相关义务进行了约定，包括获取土地、法律、税收稳定及其他事项；

④ 对国际石油公司和石油承包商的义务进行了详细约定，义务涉及"石油作业"的开展，以及对石油勘探、开发及退出计划的准备工作。

在伊拉克石油领域，国际石油公司受诸多法律规范（包括临时性法规）调整。这些规范作出了如下规定：

①"石油作业"的开展必须以石油部批准签订的一定类型的技术服务合同为准；

② 对招投标过程进行了规定，即通过公示公告或向选定的公司（即经预审证实其财务充足、专业知识及在伊拉克石油行业工作经验符合要求的公司）发出邀请函，启动招标程序；

③ 对石油承包商提出了诸多要求，包括勘探活动的评估和计划、开发计划及退出计划。

（3）《冶炼投资法》

为鼓励和利于有意向建设、运行和维护新炼油工业的投资者，伊拉克颁布了《冶炼投资法》。根据该法的规定，联邦政府可以低于市场上巴士拉离岸价的折扣价，向该项目提供原油原料，但需另行支付自就近交货点至炼油厂的运输成本费用。

投资公司负责自交货点到冶炼厂的有关管道建造、运营及维护的相关费用。投资者可以在伊拉克境内销售成品油或将其出口。伊拉克政府保留对任何成品油的优先购买权。

2. 政府在项目及项目结构方面的态度改善

过去，在伊拉克的项目通常是以政府享有所有权为基础而展开的，受国家拨款预算的限制，私营企业仅能在"工程采购与建造"（EPC）类合同下提供服务、设备及专业技能。然而，最近几年，因油价下跌以及在军事及人道主义行动方面的支出，伊拉克财政赤字不断加大，伊拉克对外国投资及融资的态度越来越开放。

此外，我们注意到，联邦政府为了支持融资项目，近些年越来越乐意提供主权担保（尽管主权担保的签发还需取决于联邦政府下一年度预算给予此种担保的财政分配情况）。此外，伊拉克法律（尤其是《民法典》）对"担保的授予"作出了规定，并允许以各类资产提供担保。通常，伊拉克法律适用于以地方资产提供担保的情形。

关于项目结构，我们特别关注到，伊拉克国内有以下两种基础设施投资模式：

① 工程、采购、建筑与融资（EPC+F）合同，由私有企业充当工程、采购与建筑承包方的传统角色，并同时帮助政府安排融资以用于支付其服务费用。近几个月，电力行业达成了几宗此类交易，这种经验可以应用到石油中下游行业。这些成功交易的先例中有一个特别因素，即外国政府（一般是私有承包方所在国政府）通过发展银行贷款及出口信贷机构等方式参与了项目。

② 股权投资，即一个私有企业被授予开发、运营及拥有一项基础设施项目的权利。这似乎与冶炼项目密切相关。《冶炼投资法》对"建设—所有—运营—转让"（BOOT）为基础模式的私人投资法律框架作出了规定。此外，尽管（伊拉克政府）仍然会不情愿准予私有企业对管道等战略性基础设施享有所有权，但据我们了解，按照设想，至少从伊拉克至约旦的部分石油管道将以"建设—所有—运营—转让"的模式进行开发。

3. 库尔德斯坦自治区

我们注意到，伊拉克库尔德斯坦自治区（KR）是被《宪法》承认的现有的联邦地区。库尔德斯坦政府（KRG）已经在其部分领域通过了法律，这些法律仅在库尔德斯坦自治区适用，这一点值得在库尔德斯坦自治区的外国投资者注意。实践中，自1991年库尔德斯坦获得了一定程度的自治权后，该地区通常不再适用在巴格达通过的法律，除非由库尔德斯坦议会批准。但是，如果库尔德斯坦自治区对某些问题没有相关立法，通常仍将适用1991年后的巴格达立法。

Iraq

Authors: Ali AL Dabbagh, Greg Englefield, Tom Calvert
Translators: Zou Zhendong, Zhao Xinwei

I. Overview

A. General Introduction to the Political, Eeconomic, Social and Legal Environment of the Country Receiving Investment

a. Location of Iraq

Iraq lies at the strategic heart of the Middle East — ringed to the west by Syria and Jordan, to the south by Saudi Arabia and Kuwait, to the east by Iran, and to the north by Turkey. At its southeast Iraq has sea access via the Arabian Gulf (in particular via major ports at Basra and Umm Qasr).

Iraq also has a special and important geographic position for world trade and for the Belt and Road project. The shortest land route from China to Europe south of Russia passes through Iraq. Furthermore, the branch of the Maritime Silk Road that proceeds up the Arabian Gulf (historically and in modern times) also meets the Iraqi ports of Basra and Um Qasr in the heart of the Middle East.

b. Population/Society, Religion and Languages

Iraq's population was approximately 36 million people in 2017. Baghdad governorate is home to approximately 21% of the total Iraqi population. The Kurdistan region has a population of around 5 million people. Iraq has a diverse population and society, with Iraqi Arabs making up the majority of the population. Iraq's population also includes Kurds, Turkmen, Assyrians, Persians and others.

Islam is constitutionally recognized as the official religion of the state. Muslims form the overwhelming majority of Iraq's total population and Iraq is also home to Christians, Yazidis, and people of other religions.

Arabic and Kurdish are official languages of Iraq. Other languages spoken in the country include Turkmen, Persian and Aramaic. English is often spoken as a second language.

c. Overview of Political Development of Lraq

Iraq has been home to, or ruled by, various civilizations and empires in its history, including Assyria, Babylon, Persia, Islamic empires / caliphates and others. Prior to the twentieth century Iraq was subject to rule by the Ottoman Empire. After the First World War the Ottoman Empire in the Middle East was divided into regions under the influence or control of the victorious powers.

The British Mandate of Mesopotamia (the "Mandate"), from which modern Iraq emerged, was formally established by the League of Nations in 1920. During the Mandate the British created a constitutional monarchy, with a parliament, as well as a king. In 1921 the monarch Faisal I of Iraq was legitimized as King by a plebiscite.

In 1932 Iraqi independence was achieved when the Mandate officially ended. The Iraqi monarchy was overthrown by the Iraqi army on 14 July 1958 and the country was generally ruled by an Arab nationalist and socialistic party known as the Ba'ath party (also the political party of Saddam Hussein) until the American and British led invasion of 2003.

During the period of occupation by coalition forces Iraq was governed by the Coalition Provisional Authority ("CPA"). On 28 June 2004, all governmental authority in Iraq was transferred to the Iraqi Interim Government, and the CPA ceased to exist. The Iraqi Interim Government prepared for the national election of the Iraqi Transitional Government. Following national elections on 30 January 2005 the Iraqi Transitional Government was formed, which prepared a permanent constitution. Iraq's current Constitution("Constitution") was ratified by a national referendum on 15 October 2005 and published in the Official Gazette on 28 December 2005. The first national parliamentary election under the new Iraqi Constitution was held on 15 December 2005 to elect a permanent Iraqi Government.

d. Constitution, Political and Legal System

The Constitution states that it is the preeminent and supreme law in Iraq and sets out certain fundamental principles in relation to the federal government of Iraq ("Federal Government") and civil rights and liberties. The Constitution also defines the Republic of Iraq as a single federal, independent and fully sovereign state in which the system of government is "republican, representative, parliamentary, and democratic".

The Federal Government is composed of legislative, executive, and judicial branches which exercise their competencies on the basis of the principle of separation of powers and a decentralised federal system. Key institutions include:

• an executive: which consists of the President of Republic, Prime Minister and the Council of Ministers [i. e. the Iraqi cabinet ("CoM")] (each of which usually hold office / are constituted for four years and are confirmed by the CoR, see below);

• a legislature: consisting primarily of the Iraqi parliament, known as the Council of Representatives ("CoR"), which is elected by popular vote for four-year terms; and

• regional and local government: The federal system is made up of a decentralized capital (Baghdad), federal regions, governorates / provinces and local administrations. There are currently 18 Iraqi Governorates. Governorates have their own elected Governors and Governorate councils which enjoy powers to issue local legislation. Most of the territory of three Governorates—Erbil, Dohouk, Sulaymaniya constitute the Kurdistan Region ("KR"). The KR is governed as the only current semi-autonomous region defined in the Constitution by the Kurdistan Regional Government ("KRG"). The Constitution allows other Governorates to group together to create federal regions, but none have done so to date.

In addition to the Constitution, a key law in Iraq is the Civil Code of 1951 (the "Civil Code") which sets out rules and principles for civil transactions in Iraq. Among other matters, the code sets out rules for the formation of contracts and rules of civil liability.

By adopting the Civil Code, Iraq became, and continues to be, a civil law jurisdiction, which means that Iraqi judges rely on the text of statutes to render decisions, although certain rules can be interpreted with a degree of flexibility. The Civil Code establishes the primacy of legislative provisions and the secondary influence of custom and Islamic law, while allowing limited reference to judicial precedent.

e. Economy of Iraq

With a GDP of approximately IQD 240 trillion (US$ 200 billion) (Sources: World Bank), Iraq is one of the largest economies in the Middle East. While the Iraqi economy suffered extensively during the many years of sanctions and war, during the recent past it has experienced high real GDP growth rates.

The Iraqi economy is dominated by its oil sector, which represents more than 50% of GDP and accounts for more than 80% of government revenue. Iraq is one of the leading producers and exporters of crude oil in the world. Iraq estimates that it has 143 billion barrels of conventional oil reserves, placing it third in the world after Saudi Arabia and Iran (Sources: U. N. Development Program).

Iraq's private sector is predominantly comprised of a large number of small and medium sized businesses, which mainly operate in retail, trade, construction and transportation services, and light industry. However, large private businesses have been increasingly emerging in the communication and information technology industry, particularly mobile communications and services supporting the regional oil and gas industry.

As a result of the difficulties related to the conflict with ISIS and a decline in international oil prices, the Iraqi economy has suffered more recently. Real GDP contracted in 2014. While future growth in Iraq remains uncertain, significant economic growth has returned since 2016, measured by some organizations at over 10% (IMF World Economic Outlook October 17th 2016). General expectations are for improvement over the next few years as Iraq recovers from recent set-backs caused by terrorism and hydrocarbon sector volatility.

The country has large reserves of petroleum and natural gas. Iraq has the third largest oil reserves in the Middle East after Saudi Arabia, Iran. Other resources include phosphates, sulfur, rich land and water resources.

B. The Status and Direction of the Cooperation with Chinese Enterprises Under the B&R

Iraq is increasingly open and generally encouraging to foreign companies / investors who wish to participate in, or initiate, new projects. The need for investment and projects in all sectors in Iraq is great. While significant governmental support is available for various potential projects, foreign contractor expertise and finance help may be necessary to develop them.

Iraq is rich in resources and economic potential, being historically one of the richest countries of the Middle East. As also noted above, Iraq also has a special and important geographic position for world trade and for the Belt and Road project. The shortest land route from China to Europe south of Russia passes through Iraq. Furthermore, the branch of the Maritime Silk Road that proceeds up the Arabian Gulf (historically and in modern times) also meets the Iraqi ports of Basra and Um Qasr in the heart of the Middle East. For these reasons Iraq would appear to be an important country to the Belt and Road project and Chinese enterprises are increasingly active in Iraq.

In recent years formal cooperation between Iraq and China has also increased, for instance since 2015 Iraq and China have signed various memoranda to set out cooperation in relation to economic, technological, military and diplomatic matters (see further discussion in trade section). Chinese enterprises are now active in Iraq in many sectors and there have been certain recent legal, policy and investment developments helpful to Chinese enterprises. Please see following sections in relation to general investment, hydrocarbons laws, project contracting and other matters. In addition, a brief description of certain key sectors where there are particular developments and emerging opportunities which may of interest to Chinese enterprises is below.

a. Oil and Gas Sector

Iraq's 143 billion barrels of oil reserves (and a potential further 200 billion recoverable barrels identified), and gas reserves of nearly 112 trillion cubic feet (Tcf), make the country a key long-term supplier to the global oil and gas market. Increasing numbers of Chinese SOEs and private enterprises are involved in the Iraqi oil and gas sector (such as, for instance, CNPC, Zhenhua, CNOOC and many others).

A new upstream bid round was announced in July 2017. The bid-round has been extended into 2018, and we understand that contractors may submit their own proposals for contractual and financial terms, subject to underlying regulatory restrictions.

Iraq is also encouraging investment to develop the midstream and downstream sectors. These developments increasingly involve Chinese enterprises. Recent developments in general include the increased integration of investment in key mid and downstream infrastructure with upstream development, such as the proposed integrated development of oil fields, together with the construction and operation of new refineries (this kindof project has reportedly involved PetroChina among other companies). Several tenders have been issued recently for the development of refineries (for both domestic use and export) to Chinese oil and gas contractors. The midstream gas sector has also seen investment based on public/private partnerships and there also are plans to build new plants to process natural gas which have received interest from Chinese power sector suppliers, contractors and banks.

Other proposed and ongoing downstream projects which have current or potential involvement from Chinese enterprises include the development of several proposed pipelines (such as the Iraq-Jordan pipeline), storage facilities and other related transport infrastructure. Additional gas export projects are also under consideration by Iraqi authorities.

b. Power Sector

Developing the Iraqi power sector is vital to develop the Iraqi national economy and there is great need to increase electricity generating capacity and transmission and distribution networks. A number of Chinese contractors are active supplying equipment and developing power-related projects in Iraq.

The Iraqi Ministry of Electricity is open to investment by the private sector in the electricity sector and a new law regulating the Ministry of Electricity, which contains provisions which allow for the potential involvement and investment by foreign developers and investors in the Iraqi power sector, was passed in 2017. Recently we have seen the proposed partial privatization of existing state-owned plants; and the potential use of the IPP model with government guarantees and, typically, ECA backing. There are increasing opportunities for developers, EPC contractors, equipment suppliers and lenders. Potential projects involve mainly gas fired plants (including conversions from simple open-cycle to combined-cycle technology), but also thermal power stations and renewable energy sources.

c. General Infrastructure and Other Industry Sectors

The National Investment Commission ("NIC"), the national coordinating body for investment in Iraq, has identified numerous other investment projects and sectors where foreign investment is required. Chinese companies are already active and / or can participate in sectors including those described below:

- Housing: the housing deficit in Iraq has been estimated by some sources at more than four million units. Over 118 housing investment projects have been identified by the NIC;
- Railways: plans exist for the construction of 2,000 km of track and various investment opportunities with the Iraqi Republic Railways Company in various locations across Iraq;
- Roads: plans for major development of Iraq's highway system including a six-lane expressway connecting to Turkey and 15 new bridges in Baghdad;
- Airports: new airports planned / under construction, and the rehabilitation of Baghdad, Basra and Mosul airports;
- Ports: rehabilitation around Basra, including Al-Fao oil terminals, cargo port, special economic zone and transport and communications centres;
- General industry: over 126 investment opportunities have been identified by the NIC in relation to all kinds of general industry, including (among others) steel and aluminum plants, factories producing electrical goods, tires, plastics, batteries, cement, glass, paper and other products;
- Telecoms: foreign and Chinese enterprise are active in the communications and telecoms industry (potential

investments include projects to develop communication infrastructure and other services); and

• Other sectors: numerous opportunities identified by the NIC exist in other sectors, including health (in each governorate there is a need to establish 400-bed general hospitals, specialized hospitals and factories to produce pharmaceuticals), education (construction and operation of schools and colleges), tourism (construction and operation of hotels and other facilities) and other sectors.

II. Investment

A. Market Access

a. Department Supervising Investment

The government departments responsible for the promotion of investment are:

(i) The National Investment Commission (NIC). Established under the Investment Law No. 13 for 2016 and it is responsible for the setting and the implementation of national investment policies and granting the investment license to projects that satisfy certain criteria.

(ii) Provinces Investment Commission. Established under the Investment Law No. 13 for 2006, responsible for granting investment licenses for investment projects in provinces.

(iii) Other sectoral authorities are involved in regulation of the specific sector. However, they are not typically investment related.

b. Laws and Regulations of Investment Industry

Under the Investment Law No. 13 for 2006 as amended and its regulations and instructions, investors can apply for investment licenses which grant them tax \ customs exemptions and other rights such as owning property (for housing projects) and a number of investment protections (e. g. repatriation of profits). In addition, there is the private Investment Law in Refinery of Crude Oil No. 64 of 2007, which provides sector specific laws for this particular type of investment.

c. Forms of Investment

The Iraqi Investment Law does not provide for investment protections by the type of investment. However, all types of investment are eligible to obtain an investment licence, and enjoy the privileges of the Investment Law. Whether with the private sector or with the public sector. Foreign investors generally receive the same treatment as national investors.

d. Standards of Market Access and Examination

There is no set standard for market access; foreign investors may invest in any of the projects declared by the NIC or the Province Investment Commission, and obtain an Investment License.

B. Foreign Exchange Regulation

a. Department Supervising Foreign Exchange

The Central Bank of Iraq regulates foreign exchange.

b. Brief Introduction of Laws and Regulations of Foreign Exchange

The Central Bank of Iraq regulates companies providing currency exchange in Iraq as a part of the banking sector. However, there are no applicable foreign currency.

C. Financing

a. Main Financial Institutions

The Iraqi Central Bank maintains a list of currently licensed banks and branches of banks at https://www.cbi.iq/page/24.

The Iraqi Central Bank licenses other financial institutions. However, such institutions are limited to providing the specific types of services allowed by their licenses.

b. Financing Conditions for Foreign Enterprises

According to Banking Law No. 94 of 2004, the Central Bank of Iraq issued Instruction No. 3 of 2010 regulating the work financing companies "The Instructions". According to this instruction, Joint or limited liability companies may be established to finance small and medium enterprises established in accordance with the provisions of the Companies Law No. (21) of 1997. The instructions provided that minimum capital requirement for the establishment of joint stock financing company to be IQD 2 Billion and IQD 1 Billion of capital for the establishment of limited liability company. The instructions further explained the registration procedures and means of financing all kind of enterprises.

D. Land Policy

a. Brief Introduction of Land-related Laws and Regulations

(i) Real Estate Registration Law. This law governs the registration of real estates and the rights pertaining to real estates.

(ii) Law of Foreigner Real Estate Ownership in Iraq No. (38) Of 1961. This law governs foreigners ownership of land and real estates.

(iii) Investment Law No. 13 for 2006 as amended. The investment law was emended in 2015 to allow for the acquisition and ownership of land by foreigners and foreign investors.

b. Rules of Land Acquisition for Foreign Enterprises

The Real Estate Registration Law Number 43 of 1971 as amended (the "Real Estate Registration Law"), provides that the right to acquire real estate is restricted to Iraqi nationals only and does not extend to foreigners save where the following exceptions apply:

(i) there must be reciprocity in treatment between Iraq and the country of the relevant foreigner who is seeking to acquire the real estate;

(ii) there must be no administrative or military impediment in respect of the acquisition;

(iii) the property must not be less than 30 kilometers from Iraq's borders; and

(iv) the Iraqi Ministry of Interior must approve the relevant acquisition.

Corporate entities, including foreign entities, may acquire real estate pursuant to Articles 152 and 153 of the Real Estate Registration Law subject to the following:

(i) the company's registration must be attested in Iraq;

(ii) the articles of association of such company must allow the acquisition of real estate;

(iii) the Minister of Interior must approve the registration of the property; and

(iv) the property must be located within the borders of a city.

Further, at the date of writing, a number of laws have been issued to allow the acquisition by foreigners of real estate in Iraq in particular situations.

Non Iraqi nationals were permitted to own real estate until 1994 (as set out above) when the situation was dramatically reversed with the issuance of a decision by the now dissolved Revolutionary Command Council which suspended all laws and decrees that allowed the ownership of real estate by foreign nationals.

Thereafter, in 2005 the permanent constitution of Iraq was introduced which granted Iraqi nationals the right to own properties anywhere in Iraq and denied foreigners the right to own immoveable properties except as provided under the law. We consider the laws that have been introduced since this date and their effect.

Article 10 of the amended Iraq Investment Law Number 13 of 2006 (the "Iraq Investment Law") provides that an Iraqi or foreign investor shall enjoy all of the privileges, benefits and guarantees set out in the aforementioned law. Furthermore, the Investment Law provides that an Iraqi or foreign investor shall have the right to acquire land reserved for residential projects and owned by the state or public sector, as well as land owned by the private sector solely or in partnership with the public sector provided that the use of the same shall not conflict with the principally intended purpose. It is also worth noting that an Iraqi investor is allowed to acquire land reserved for agriculture or industrial use and to enter into a partnership agreement with a foreign investor for financing and management purposes.

When an Iraqi or foreign investor acquires a property, a lien shall be inscribed for the purpose of preventing any disposal of the property until the Iraqi or foreign investor satisfies its obligations as verified by the Investment Authority and the investor shall be required to use the property as intended and refrain from entering into any speculative activity with respect to such property. In the event that the investor fails in performing its obligations within the relevant period, the real estate registration department shall, upon request from the Investment Authority, cancel the registration of the property and return the property to its previous owner, provided that the investor shall receive back the previously paid purchase price less the equivalent rent in respect of the occupancy period.

The foreign investor is obligated to build residential units and to sell or lease such units to Iraqi nationals but shall have the right to dispose of the non-residential parts of the project during the entire licensing term in accordance with the conditions stated in the agreement executed with such investor. While the investor may transfer part of the investment project after completion of 40% of the project, it shall not be allowed to transfer the ownership of the project unless it is entirely completed. We also note that the Iraq Investment Law has prohibited the expropriation or nationalization of an investment project or the revocation of its ownership, whether in part or in whole, except for public interest, and in which case, the investor shall be entitled to a fair compensation. The Iraq Investment Law further states that any future amendment shall not operate retroactively so as not to affect the guarantees and benefits afforded under such law.

The Iraq Investment Law allows the foreign investor to rent, lease and acquire Musataha rights from the government and the private sector for the purpose of constructing investment projects for a period not exceeding 50 years subject to renewal.

c. The Position in Kurdistan

Article 3 of the Investment Law of Kurdistan Region Number 4 of 2006 (the "Kurdistan Investment Law") states that the foreign investor shall be treated in the same manner as the national investor. The Investment Law further provides that, subject to the other provisions of the Investment Law, the foreign investor is entitled to purchase and lease lands and real estate as required for establishing, expanding, diversifying and developing a project. The foreign investor is entitled to purchase and rent for the benefit its investment project such residential properties and vehicles as required in the context of the investment project. Moreover, the foreign investor is entitled to assign its investment, in part or in whole, to a foreign investor or to a national investor or to assign the project to its partner, provided that the investor obtains the approval of the Investment Authority. In the event of assignment, the new investor shall substitute the previous investor in all of its rights and obligations ensuing from the project. A lien shall be inscribed on the property by the relevant real estate registration authority for the purpose of preventing any disposal affecting a property which is dedicated for an investment project. The lien shall not be lifted unless the Investment Authority approves and provided that the investor satisfied all of its obligations.

d. Other Relevant Laws

The Iraqi Companies Law Number 21 of 1997 (the "Companies Law") prohibited foreigners from participating in Iraqi companies. However, an amendment to the aforementioned law was introduced in 2004 to allow foreigners to participate in and entirely own Iraqi companies, except in specific cases such as commercial agencies which must still be Iraqi owned. Given that companies incorporated in Iraq are considered Iraqi pursuant to Article 23 of the Companies Law and have a distinct legal personality and financial position irrespective of the nationality of its shareholders, these companies may acquire properties in Iraq. This has been confirmed in decision number 54/2010 issued by the State Council on 5 May 2010 (the "State Council Decision") at the request of the Minister of Justice who wished clarity as to whether banks and companies owned directly or indirectly by foreign shareholders are allowed to acquire real estate in Iraq. The decision expressly states that, notwithstanding the existence of foreign shareholders in Iraqi banks, these banks are allowed to acquire real estate in a manner consistent with their objectives as set out in their articles of association. The State Council Decision also provides that Iraqi banks owned by foreigners are allowed to acquire real estate on the basis of Paragraph 2 of Article 33 of the Banks Law Number 94 of 2004 which allows the acquisition of property when required in the context of undertaking their operations, including for staff and workers' accommodation.

It is worth mentioning that, despite the clear provision of the Companies Law which considers a company Iraqi notwithstanding the nationality of its founders, as well as the State Council Decision, and the absence of any legal impediment, the practice remains different on the ground. As a matter of fact, and save for companies that are subject to the Kurdistan Investment Law, it is challenging to transfer properties to Iraqi companies who have foreign shareholders. Although challenging, such transfers are not impossible to achieve on case by case basis. As at the date of this article, the issue remains of critical importance. A number of companies owned by foreigners have succeeded in registering properties under the respective company name in Iraq, while other companies were denied this request despite the clear provisions of the law and the absence of any legal impediment.

In relation to branches of foreign companies and their relevant offices established in Iraq, in accordance with Real Estate Law No. 43 of 1971 and its amendments, we note that they are considered as an extension of the parent company under the applicable laws and therefore are not allowed to acquire real estate in Iraq. The same treatment applies with regard to branches of foreign banks that are licensed in Iraq and which are not allowed to own real estate. However, subject to obtaining the approval of the Central Bank of Iraq, it is possible for these branches to register mortgages under their names. The only exception, is granted according to Iraqi Investment Law No. 50 of 2015, where it allows foreign entities to own real estates, with certain conditions, if the company is working on housing project, or to own real estate if the land is owned by the government, with certain conditions.

In conclusion, the acquisition of property in Iraq is possible for foreign investors in particular situations as highlighted in this article. Care requires to be taken in navigating local laws and it is important to understand the practical approach of the local Iraqi authorities.

E. The Establishment and Dissolution of Companies

a. The Forms of Enterprises

a) Sole Proprietorships

Can be established by one natural person, the owner of the sole holdings in the company the owner assumes personal, unlimited liability.

b) Simple companies

Simple companies are incorporated by number of natural persons ranging from 2-5 each contributes a share in the company's capital and assumes unlimited liability.

c) Limited liability companies—mixed or private

The number of contributors can be one and no more than twenty-five natural or moral persons. Founders are responsible for company debts to the extent of the nominal value of their respective shares.

d) Joint stock companies—mixed or private

At least five natural or legal persons must establish joint stock companies. They offer shares through public subscription. The shareholders are responsible for company debts to the extent of the value of their respective shares

e) Joint liability companies

Established by a number of persons ranging between two and twenty-five natural or legal. The liability of the owners is unlimited and they participate in proportion to their respective shares in the company.

b. The Procedure of Establishment

The Ministry of Trade / Registrar of Companies Department is the governmental entity responsible for the regulation of the establishment of foreign branches as well as incorporating local subsidianes, Incorporating an LLC typically takes one month to issue a registration certificate and two to three months to complete post registration requirements. Branch registration is a shorter process. Neither of the above include sector specific approvals and licenses, which depend on the type of activity to be conducted.

c. Routes and Requirements of Dissolution

The Company should adopt an extraordinary General Assembly Resolution to approve the liquidation decision, and appoint the liquidator. The company shall provide the Companies General Control at the Ministry of Trade ('the Controller') with a copy of the GA resolution with 3 days of its issuance, and publish the same in the Official Gazette and in at least 2 local daily newspapers. The liquidator shall supervise the ordinary operations of the Company, safeguard its properties and assets, and represent the Company on all matter until its dissolution after finalizing the liquidation of the Company;

The liquidator shall settle the Company's rights and obligations, and liquidate its assets in accordance with the following procedures:

(i) The liquidator shall exercise the powers conferred upon him by the applicable law for carrying out the Company's liquidation.

(ii) The liquidator shall organize a list of the names of the Company debtors, and submit a report on the transactions and procedures he carried out to claim the payment of the debts due to the company by its debtors. This list shall be considered as primary evidence of the persons whose names appear in the list as debtors of the Company.

(iii) The liquidator shall pay the Company's debts and shall settle its rights and obligations.

(iv) The liquidator should submit the headquarters' financial statement, as prepared by the appointed auditor.

Submitting the company's assets and the payables' statement signed by the legal accountant, which includes the following:

(i) Immovable assets: Assets that cannot be moved without damage, e.g. buildings, certain types of equipment, and in some cases furniture.

(ii) Movable assets: Assets that can be moved freely without damage, e.g. Debts, insurance, vehicles, intangibles, and cash.

Further letters should be addressed to certain authorities based on the activity of the company to obtain clears letters.

Thereafter, the Registrar shall issue his decision to delete the Company's name from the records and publish the decision in the bulletin and one daily newspaper.

F. Merger and Acquisition

For the purposes of the merger, the following measures shall be taken:

(i) An economic and technical study shall be made of the joint-stock possibly of merging other types of companies to be merged, including the aims, reasons, conditions of the merger, and any other studies. The studies shall be submitted to the general assembly of each company.

(ii) The merge decision shall be made by the general assembly of each company separately. The decision shall specify the name and type of the merger company as well as its capital, members, and activity. The decisions and the studies shall be sent to the Registrar within 10 days from their adoption.

(iii) If, within 15 days of receiving them, the Registrar has not found that the decisions are inconsistent with the law, it will promptly issue its permission and inform the companies concerned of this decision; the companies will then cause it to be published in the Bulletin and one daily paper.

(iv) The companies receiving the Registrar's permission for their merger will call their general assemblies to a joint meeting within 60 days from the date of the publication of the merger decision in order to amend the contracts of the existing companies or draw up a new contract for the merger company, depending on the circumstances. The contract shall be sent to the Registrar within 10 days for endorsement and publication in the bulletin and one daily paper.

(v) The merger shall be considered effective as of the last publication date of the amended or new contract, depending on the circumstances. On this date, the corporate status of the companies merging into the new company shall be terminated. The Registrar's endorsement of the contract is tantamount to a license of establishment.

(vi) All the rights and commitments of the merger shall be transferred to the company with which it was merged, or the company resulting from the merger.

G. Competition Regulation

a. Brief Introduction of Competition Law

Iraq passed the Anti-monopoly and Competition Law no. 14 in 2010. However, no instructions implementing said law were promulgated thereafter. As such, competition regulation remains subject to scattered rules in various sectors and sector specific advice is recommended on competition related questions. The applicable primary legislation specifically prohibits practices or agreements if they disrupt competition or anti-monopoly effects, or otherwise hinder, or prevent competition especially if the object or if the purpose is to:

(i) Fix prices of goods or services and so on;

(ii) Fix quantity of goods or services;

(iii) Dividing markets on geographical basis, sale quantities, purchase quantities, customers, or any other basis that may negatively affect competition and anti-monopoly;

(iv) Conduct inhibiting entry of organizations to Iraqi markets or their exclusion from it or exposing them to large loses including selling lower than cost (with a loss);

(v) Collusion in bids to tenders, and it is not considered a collusion if joint bids (offers) are presented and their parties are aware of this from the beginning on condition that the purpose of such bids and offers is not anti-competitive in any way;

(vi) Discrimination between customers of the same goods or services in prices or other sale conditions;

(vii) Compelling a customer to not deal with a competitor;

(viii) Refusing to deal with a specific customer with the usual commercial terms without a legal excuse;

(ix) Aiming to monopolize a certain material necessary for a competing party to conduct its activity or buying a good or service in a quantity that causes its price to increase or prevent it from decreasing in the market;

(x) Making sale or purchase of a good or service conditional on, sale or purchase of another good or service, or on sale or purchase of a specific quantity, or on providing another service;

(xi) Compelling a party or obtaining such a party a special unjustified price or sale conditions in a manner that gives an advantage in competition or negatively affect it.

b. Measures Regulating Competition

Current Iraqi law allows private enforcement of competition regulation as it allows affected private parties to claim damages from anti-competitive conduct. However, this is not a common practice in Iraq. Iraqi law also imposes fines and requires registration in some cases.

H. Tax

a. Tax Regime and Rules
(i) Income Tax Law No. 13 for 1983 as amended.
(ii) Real Estate Tax law No. 162 for 1959 as amended.
(iii) Land Tax Law No. 26 for 1962 as amended.
(iv) Instruction Regarding the Deduction of Personal Income Tax No. 1 for 2005.
(v) Instruction on how to object on Income Tax Estimation No. 16 for 1996.

b. Main Categories and Rates of Tax
(i) Corporate Tax: the amount of corporate tax differs depending on the type of activity performed by the company.

(ii) Income Tax: the amount of personal income Tax is 10% of the employee's or worker's salary, however, a number of tax exemptions may be applied depending on the employee's states.

(iii) Real estate Tax : subject to the type and value of the real estate.

(iv) Land Tax: subject to the type and value of land.

c. Tax Declaration and Preference
Each company is obligated by law to submit at the beginning of each fascial year its financial statements and the tax declaration for the previous year, the calculation of tax will be based on the tax declaration and financial statements submitted by the company. For workers in the private sector, i. e. company's employees the amount of tax on their salaries will be based on the salaries paid to them, which is stated in the company's financial statements and tax declaration.

I. Securities

a. Brief Introduction of Securities-related Laws and Regulations
The Iraq Securities Market Interim Law (CPA order No. 74 of 2004) is the currently effective law governing the regulation and workings of the stock exchange. Other laws such as the Banking Law No. 94 of 2004, the Code of Commerce No. 30 of 1984, and instructions issued by the Central Bank of Iraq and the Iraqi Stock Exchange govern and regulate securities.

b. Supervision and Regulation of Securities Market
The Iraqi Stock Exchange and the Central Bank of Iraq supervise and regulate securities.

c. Requirements for Engagement in Securities Trading for Foreign Enterprises
Generally speaking there are no special requirements for foreign companies to trade in securities.

J. Preference and Protection of Investment

In light of the efforts to rebuild and develop Iraq and as per the objectives of the Investment Law (No. 13 of the year 2006), there has been a marked focus on further attracting technical and professional expertise to the country. the investment laws further support the process of establishing investment projects in Iraq, expanding and developing the same at various levels and granting exemptions to these projects. Investment laws have been legislated for the purpose of attracting and encouraging foreign investments within Iraq and as appropriate with the desired objectives and it is possible to obtain different guarantees.

According to Investment law No. 50 of 2015, eligible investment project will enjoy the following benefits and guarantees:

(i) Exemption from taxes and fees for 30 years from the date of commencement of the project and for every stage of the project;

(ii) Extending the exemption periods from taxes and fees based on the Iraqi investor participation, and it will extend to the period of 35 years if the rate of the Iraqi investor increased to reach more than 50%;

(iii) Employing foreign workers alongside local workers;

(iv) According to the new amendment to the law, the imported assets for the purpose of investment projects are exempted from tax and customs fees, provided that they were entered to the country during the stages of the project;

(v) Exempting the imported raw materials for the purpose of commercial opertation from taxes and customs duties;

(vi) Guaranteeing that the investment project will not be expropriated or nationalized except through a final judicial decision;

(vii) Foreign investors enjoy additional benefits in accordance with bilateral international agreements with Iraq or multilateral international agreements recognized in Iraq.

a. Support for Specific Industries and Regions

a) Trading with the Iraqi Healthcare Industry

(i) Trade in Medical Products. Importation of medical products, which include medicines, cosmetics, and medical appliances, can follow different business models depending on who the buyer is. There are two broad possibilities in Iraq: the buyer can be the State company for marketing drugs and medical appliances ('KIMADIA') or it can be a buyer from the Iraqi private market. On the public procurement side, KIMADIA is the only governmental body authorised to import medical products on behalf of the Iraqi government, and it does so using the usual regulations for public tendering applicable in Iraq. When KIMADIA solicits bids for public tenders, it follows regulations No. 1 and 2 of 2014 on implementing government contracts. This entails certain contracting requirements that must be followed by the bidder, such as submitting preliminary guarantees with bids and posting performance bonds from an acceptable local bank, prior to KIMADIA awarding a bid.

According to Iraq's Pharmaceutical Law (Federal Law No. 40 of 1970) and accompanying instructions (Instructions No. 4 of 1998) regulating scientific offices in the business of marketing pharmaceutical products, importing medical products to Iraq must be done exclusively through Iraqi registered third parties "scientific offices". The only exception is if KIMADIA deems it necessary to import products directly. While KIMADIA has the authority to deal directly with non-Iraqi manufacturers or marketers, it still prefers to deal through Iraqi registered scientific offices whenever possible. Where dealing with the Iraqi private sector, the only way to trade in medical products is through a scientific office.

There are two relevant regulators in the Iraqi healthcare sector, the Ministry of Health and Environment ("Ministry of Health") and the Syndicate of Iraqi Pharmacists. Generally speaking the following should be kept in mind when importing medical products to Iraq,

• There are income tax obligations when doing business through third party agents, i. e. scientific offices, as this is considered doing business in Iraq by the relevant tax authorities;

• To import or market medical products, both the manufacturer and the medical product need to be registered with the Ministry of Health, who keeps a list of registered products and manufacturers;

• To register a manufacturer, the Ministry of health requires a number of documents including, but not limited to, the manufacturer's / vendor's articles of incorporation, letters of authorisation, manufacturing licence, and Good Manufacturing Practice ("GMP") and Certificate of Pharmaceutical Product ("CCP") certificates;

• The required documents are different from originating country to country, depending on which authorities are responsible for granting approvals for the manufacturing and selling medical products in the country of origin;

• All submitted documents need to be properly legalised and stamped, as per Iraqi law;

• For products originating from certain countries, and in certain cases, the Ministry of Health will require the applying party to pay for Ministry inspectors to visit and inspect production facilities;

• Changes affecting information provided to the Ministry of Health need to be updated for the registration to remain active;

• Registrations need to be renewed after five years, in most cases;

• Import licences are issued to scientific offices to import a specific product prior to import, and, as an exception, to parties dealing directly with KIMADIA;

• There are certain circumstances where KIMADIA will provide assistance to importers to expedite the registration process at the Ministry of Health for performance of awarded bids;

• Scientific offices can carry out registration at the Ministry of Health, and bid on behalf of the parties they represent using properly notarised authorisation letters;

• No more than one scientific office can be used to market the same medical product, but multiple offices can be engaged to market different products;

• Scientific offices can be agents acting on behalf of their principles or distributers acting on their own;

• Scientific offices must be operated by Iraqis and, if they are an incorporated entity, must be fully owned by Iraqis.

(ii) Investing in Lraq's Healthcare Sector

In 2015, the Iraqi parliament passed the Law on Establishing Private Healthcare Institutions (Federal Law No. 25 of 2015) (the 'Private Healthcare Institutions Law'), which came into force on 29 June 2015. The new law repealed the old private hospitals law (Federal Law No. 25 of 1985) and some articles in the public health law (Federal Law No. 89 of 1981). The Private Healthcare Institutions Law included major developments and improved the legal framework for private investment in healthcare. The Ministry of Health will issue regulations detailing how it intends to implement the new law. In the meantime, we can point out the following incentives and changes introduced by the new law:

• Repealing parts of the public health law requiring licence holders to be Iraqis and allowing non-Iraqis to apply for licences to operate healthcare institutions;

• Allowing incorporation of entities with the purpose of operating healthcare institutions, with the approval of the Ministry of Health;

• Exempting health care institutions from income tax for the first three years from actual operation, as supported by the Ministry of Health;

• Allowing further employment of foreign staff up to certain percentages, depending on the type of employed staff;

• Allowing land allocation for free, with approval from the Ministry of Health;

• Allowing loans of up to 30 per cent of the cost of establishing hospitals, with the approval of the Ministry of Health.

The Private Healthcare Institutions Law is not the only piece of applicable legislation with incentives. Depending on how the investment is structured, it can be a second, more specific, layer which operates on top of the Investment Law (Federal Law No. 13 of 2006), with its two amendments. Unlike the Investment Law, which requires holding a licence from the National Investment Commission ('NIC') to enjoy its benefits, the Private Healthcare Institutions Law does not require prior approval from the NIC. Since Iraqi corporate law allows foreign parties to own 100 per cent of Iraqi corporations, investors can choose to operate without an investment licence. Regardless of the path investors choose to follow, the Ministry of Health remains the relevant regulator for healthcare businesses.

(iii) Conclusion on Iraqi Healthcare Sector

Dealing with the Iraqi healthcare industry must be done through licensed Iraqi third parties; the only exception is public tenders from KIMADIA. Prior registration of products as well as manufacturers and vendors is required to grant import licences. As far as private investment is concerned, the new Private Healthcare Institutions Law marks a positive development for private investment in the healthcare industry, opening it to foreign capital and creating lucrative opportunities for investment in Iraq.

b) The Telecommunications Sector in Iraqii

The Iraqi Communications and Media Commission ("Commission") was established by Coalition Provisional Authority Order No. 65 in 2004 to license and regulate telecommunications, broadcasting, information services and other media in Iraq.

As of the date of this article, the only way to interpret the available laws with certainty is by direct inquiry with the Commission or other government bodies. A process that, when fruitful, takes a few months at best. To address the needs of this rapidly developing sector, the Commission has recently published a number of public consultations detailing draft future regulations pertaining to various aspects of the Commission's legal domain.

While these consultations are not in force as law, they give a good indication of the Commission's likely future regulatory requirements. This article provides a brief summary of three key public consultations on competition, lawful interception, and quality of service.

(i) Competition Regulation Draft and the Market Reviews Consultation (Published in June 2016)

This proposed telecommunications specific competition regulation builds on the Competition and Monopoly Prevention Law No. 14 of 2010 ('Competition Law'). That said, the Commission's draft regulation is quite different from the Competition Law. The Commission's anticipated regulation will apply only to holders of licenses issued by the Commission because regulation of non-licensed parties requires involvement of other regulatory bodies. The draft regulation contains both preventative and remedial competition preserving measures. Preventative measures or ex-ante regulations are unique to the telecommunication industry in Iraq and aim to intervene in the market before anti-competitive behaviour can occur or cause significant damage to competition. Remedial measures or ex-post regulations in the Commission's competition regulation draft are largely derived from the Competition Law. The telecommunication specific ex-post competition regulation includes prohibitions on licensees from entering into non-retail agreements with parties who are not end customers, anti-competitive tying or bundling of services, customer discrimination, and other forms of abuse of dominant market power. The draft competition regulation states that the Commission will seek enforcement action against licensees for violations of ex-post regulation in a court with jurisdiction under the Competition Law as provided for under Article 15 of that law.

The Commission introduces a number of new concepts in its ex-ante regulation of competition in telecommunications and information services. One such new concept is "Significant Market Power". The Commission uses data it collects from licensees as well as definitions and tests set out in a market review policy issued by it to determine Significant Market Power. The Commission published a public consultation on market review in 2015 and a draft policy followed in June 2016 along with the draft Competition Regulation. The market review consultation defines each market using two parameters having demand-side or supply-side substitutability of products, and geographic areas where the conditions of competition are similar. It is important to note that the Kurdistan region is likely to be considered a separate market for market review purposes.

According to the most recent draft market-review policy published by the Commission, the decision whether a given market is susceptible to ex-ante regulation is based on a three criteria test. If all three criteria are met, the market is considered susceptible to Ex-ante regulation. If at least one of the criteria is not met, the market is not susceptible to ex-ante regulation. The three criteria are:

- presence of high and non-transitory barriers to entry;
- the market does not tend towards effective competition within the relevant time horizon; and
- insufficiency of competition law alone to adequately address the market failure(s).

When a determination that a market is susceptible to ex-ante regulation, designation of licensees with Significant Market Power will follow. Market share is the most important criterion to designate licensees with significant market power. For example, the June 2016 consultation concluded that Asiacell, Korek and Zain are licensees with Significant Market Power in the mobile market. Designation of Significant Market Power imposes regulations aimed at keeping the market open to new competitors and achieving the best market dynamics possible. For the three licensees mentioned above the market review consultation imposed the following obligations:

- to allow access to and use of specific network facilities;
- not to unreasonably bundle;
- non-discrimination;
- transparency;
- price control;
- cost accounting; and
- separate accounting.

(ii) Assistance for Lawful Interception and Data Retention Regulation Draft (Published in June 2016)

The Assistance for Lawful Interception and Data Retention Regulation Draft builds on existing interception laws and provides more clarity on compliance requirements. The draft includes some data retention requirements for providers of communications services, as well as operating procedures and standards relevant to interception. The draft regulation defines the type of authorization required to disclose information and contains obligations not to disclose information to unauthorised persons. In addition, the draft regulation contains provisions on cost allocation of its implementation and the penalties for failure to comply. Finally, the draft regulation addresses technical matters such as the use of encryption and what information needs to be collected, retained, and made available on properly authorised request.

(iii) Quality of Service Consultation (Published in June 2016)

The Quality of Service Consultation (QOS) contains a Quality of Service Policy, a Retail Quality of Service Regulation and a Wholesale Quality of Service Regulation. The Commission intends QOS regulation to improve the choice, price or quality of services offered in Iraq and to provide information about quality that will help consumers to make choices and service providers to maintain quality when there are too few choices available. The two regulations and the Quality of Service Policy cover measurements standards, reporting periods and areas, representative samples for reporting of measurements, governance and dispute resolution, sanctions and compliance measures, and measures aimed at ensuring customer awareness.

The Commission published the Quality of Service Consultation to better negotiate and define the quality of service commitments under the existing licenses. In addition, some of the new developments were motivated by the Consumer Protection Law (Law No. 1 of 2010) and aim to keep the quality of service consistent with prices charged by service providers and claims made by them. The Commission's regulatory requirements do not prevent consumers from exercising preferences that might actually to be to have low prices with low quality or high prices with high quality. However, when consumers are unable to exercise their preferences because there are too few service providers, the Commission's regulatory requirements aim to ensure sufficiently high quality and sufficiently low prices.

(iv) Conclusion on Iraqi telecommunications Sector

By publishing public consultations and asking for the input of stakeholders, the Commission seems determined to keep the Iraqi telecommunications industry competitive and open to new service providers by offering a level of predictability to future regulations. The Commission aims to regulate only as and when deemed necessary and has made efforts to ensure transparent implementation of its rule making by publishing a draft Rules of Procedure Regulation that will govern its processes. Institutional independence and accountability of the Commission make the new developments a positive step towards better regulation in line with international standards.

b. Special Economic Areas

Iraq has a number of free zones, the most active free zone is in khor AL-Zubair south-west of Basra. Operations in free zones are exempt from income taxes and this includes salaries of foreign employees. Iraqi employees' salaries are taxed at 50%. Free Zones also do not have import \ Export restrictions and materials enter into free zones as transit., i. e., duties are only levied if goods exit the free zone to enter Iraq for local consumption, no duties are levied when exporting outside Iraq and no customs are levied when goods enter the free zone.

c. Investment Protection

It is no secret that armed conflict, turbulent government policy and political unrest paints Iraq as an unlikely place to invest. However, there are ways to deal with such risks and Iraq has taken steps to address those concerns. By passing ratification laws No. 64 of 2012 and No. 29 of 2007, Iraq is now listed as a member of the International Center for the Settlement of Investment Disputes (ICSID) and the Multinational Investment Guarantee Agency (MIGA). Being able to make use of those two World Bank organizations in Iraq can make a significant difference in Iraq's investment climate and give measure of confidence to prospective investors.

Iraq had ratified the Convention Establishing the Multilateral Investment Guarantee Agency back in 2007, and is since providing for its implementation. MIGA membership means that investments in Iraq are now eligible for political risk insurance. According to the World Bank's website MIGA's outstanding gross exposure in Iraq stood at US$8 million as of September 2016. The second, more recent and exciting development, is Iraq's accession to the Washington Convention on the Settlement of Investment Disputes between States and Nationals of Other States in 2012. ICSID provides private investors a unique enforcement mechanism for investment contracts and treaties through arbitration awards that cannot be appealed locally.

Iraq's accession to ICSID may be surprising in light of the fact that Iraq is still not a member of the New York Convention on Recognition and Enforcement of Foreign Arbitral Awards. Unlike the New York Convention which allows courts to refuse enforcement of awards relying on a list of exclusive grounds that includes public policy, the Washington Convention considers ICSID awards to be final judgments from national courts. Further, unlike normal arbitration awards the only recourse against an ICSID award that is sought to be enforced with pressure from the World Bank is a request for annulment before another ICSID tribunal, which has rarely been successful throughout ICSID's history.

Neither ICSID nor MIGA determine investment treatment or provide substantive rights to investors rather, they work as an enforcement mechanism and an insurance provider respectively. As such it is necessary to look to contracts and investment treaties for an understanding of Iraq's commitments. Noting that contracts add another layer of rights on top of the treaties.

Iraq has signed and ratified a number of Bilateral Investment Treaties (BITs), titled investment promotion and protection. Example of such treaties published in the Arabic Iraqi gazette include treaties with Iran, Japan, Kuwait, Jordan, Belarus, and Germany.

III. Trade[①]

A. Department Supervising Trade

Several ministries of the Iraqi federal government ("Federal Government") and governmental departments or authorities may be involved with the supervision of trade-related matters. These include the Ministry of Trade (the "MoT"), the Ministry of Finance (the "MoF"), the State Company for Iraqi Fairs and Commercial Services (the "SCIFCS") and the General Commission for Customs (the "GCC").

The MoT was established by Law No. 37 of 2011 and is responsible for encouraging private sector development by removing regulations blocking trade and investment, eliminating import licensing rules, and projects to promote the trading environment in Iraq. The MoT is also responsible for issuing various instructions and rules in relation to general commerce and trade (such as for instance regulations in relation to commercial agency). A state company affiliated to the MoT, the SCIFCS, is currently responsible for the issuance of export and import licences and related procedures.

---

① Please note: translations of Iraqi legislation cited in, and provided with, this information are unofficial. Reference should be made to the Arabic language originals for reliance purposes. This information is not legal advice and for any reliance purposes readers should obtain legal advice. Other than where specifically stated, we refer to laws and regulations in relation to federal Iraq only.

MoF was established by Law No. 92 of 1981 and is responsible for the state's financial planning and management. In relation to trade supervision, the MoF is particularly responsible for the GCC which is the governmental body responsible for customs matters. The GCC is a division of the MoF and headed by a Director General appointed by the Minister of Finance. The GCC implements the Customs Law (discussed below) through customs departments, customs offices and entry points.

B. Brief Introduction of Trade Laws and Regulations

The Customs Law No. 23 of 1984 (the "Customs Law") provides a general regulatory framework for trade including procedures for the export of goods from and import of goods into Iraq. Among other matters, the Customs Law provides for the general obligations of importers and exporters of goods; transit of goods through Iraq, the establishment and authorities of customs authorities (the GCC); customs clearance procedures; and the imposition of, and exemption from, customs tariffs.

The Customs Law is a substantial piece of legislation, running to 271 Articles. In practice, the actual customs and import procedures followed in Iraq are informed largely by secondary legislation (such as the Import Instructions and the Temporary Import Instructions, see below) and by the practice of customs officials.

Customs Tariff Law No. 22 of 2010, as amended by Law of First Amendment No. 34 of 2011 and Law of Second Amendment No. 27 of 2013, imposes customs duties on imported goods. Customs duties generally range from 0. 5% to 40% (with the exception in particular of alcohol and cigarettes which are subject to duties of up to 100%) and are collected by the GCC. The Council of Ministers changes applicable customs duties from time to time by decree. The Customs Tariff Law also provides that certain items are exempt from customs duties (such as packaging, samples which have no commercial value, imports subject to an investment licence, and other items). Generally, there are no tariff preferences for any particular industries in Iraq but, as noted above, this could be subject to change by decree of the Council of Ministers.

The Instructions of 1978 on Implementing the Import Method (the "Import Instructions") set out detailed procedures for the issuance of import licences which are required in order to import goods into Iraq. The Instructions No. 9 of 1984 on Temporary Imports (the "Temporary Import Instructions") allow a foreign company which has entered into a contract with a governmental entity to apply for a temporary import permit for required equipment to be generally exempt from customs duties.

Other relevant laws and regulations include Law No. 79 of 2017 (the "Commercial Agency Law"). Where a foreign manufacturer wishes to sell goods into the Iraqi market but does not wish to register an entity in Iraq, various structures can be used, including contracting with Iraqi commercial agencies and distributorships. Such Iraqi entities are subject to local registration in Iraq and also other requirements under the Commercial Agencies Law.

In relation to electronic trade in Iraq various laws govern electronic transactions and payments. Among other laws these include:

(i) CPA Order No. 94 of 2004 ("Banking Law"): which provides a legal framework for the domestic Iraqi banking system. Under the terms of the Banking Law no person in Iraq may engage in banking activities without a banking license issued by the Central Bank of Iraq ("CBI"). Banking activities include, among other matters, clearing, settlement and transfer services for money, payment orders and payment instruments—this includes checks, credit, debit and other payment cards;

(ii) Electronic Signature & Electronic Transactions Law No. 78 of 2012 which sets out certain rules in relation to electronic signatures and payment activities. Among other matters this law also sets out a general obligation that entities engaged in electronic transfers of funds must take necessary measures to provide secured services for customers and maintain the confidentiality of transactions; and

(iii) Iraqi Council of Ministers Resolution No. 3 of 2014 regarding the Electronic Payment Services of Money. This resolution sets out regulations for activities relating to electronic payment and other processes in accordance with settlement and clearing systems. All electronic payment services must be licensed by the CBI.

Iraq is party to several international agreements and organisations that promote international trade. Iraq became an observer at the World Trade Organization (WTO) on 24 January 2007 and reportedly still intends to become a full member. Iraq has also ratified the Agreement to Facilitate and Develop Trade among Arab States (1981) and the Greater Arab Free Trade Area Agreement (2005). Iraq is a significant member of the Organization of the Petroleum Exporting Countries (OPEC) and of the League of Arab States. In 2013, Iraq ratified a Trade and Investment Framework Agreement (TIFA) with the European Union. Iraq is not party to a large number of bilateral investment agreements (BITs), but in recent years ratified BITs with Japan (2012) and Kuwait (2013).

There is not yet a BIT between Iraq and China. However, in December 2015 we understand that China and Iraq entered into a memorandum of understanding ("MoU") to establish long term cooperationin relation to oil and gas. According to reports the MoU seeks to develop cooperation in the areas of crude oil trade, oil-gas exploration and development, oilfield engineering service technology, construction of storage and transportation facilities, chemical refining engineering, and energy equipment. We understand that Iraq and China have also signed other memoranda to set out cooperation in relation to general economic, technological, military and diplomatic matters and that it is hoped that these developments will help lead to increased bilateral trade and other ties.

C. Trade Management

Iraq aims to support a liberal trade and investment regime. The current National Development Plan for Iraq sets out to foster trade and investment to support the private sector and economic growth. Generally Iraq has in recent years sought to keep import and export tariffs low and develop a regulatory regime intended to facilitate investment and trade. This includes Investment Law No. 13 of 2006, which allows for the granting of investment licences that allow benefits including exemptions from taxation and other "fees" for a period of 10 years, and the opening of an operational free zone in Basra (Khor Al-Zubair). The zone is governed by the General Commission for Free Zones (the "GCFZ"), which is affiliated to the Ministry of Finance. An investor who carries out business within a free zone must obtain an investment licence from the GCFZ.

Iraq has recently been taking other steps with a view to support investment and trade, including the ratification of the Convention on the Settlement of Investment Disputes between States and Nationals of Other States of 1965 ("ICSID").

D. Inspection and Quarantine of Import and Export Commodities

In order to clear customs, goods must be accompanied by a customs declaration. Following submission of the customs declaration, the goods are subject to an inspection. This may include analysis to determine compliance with any relevant product specifications. The Customs Law and related instructions also set out certain rights for customs officials to quarantine goods which breach applicable specifications or in circumstances where goods may be harmful to public health or where requested by Iraqi health authorities.

E. Customs Management

Under the Customs Law, a manifest for any goods entering to, or departing from, or in transit through Iraq shall be submitted to the relevant GCC customs office. Imported goods must be accompanied by a certificate of origin, a declaration of value, and an original invoice attested by the chamber of commerce in the relevant home country (i. e. the country from which the goods were shipped). The GCC is generally authorised to require submission of further documents to provide satisfactory evidence of the value and origin of imported goods. Goods may not clear customs until after inspection and applicable customs duties have been paid in full, or a deposit has been accepted as security for customs duties.

The summary reflects published legislation which we understand is reflected in current practice. However, the customs and import procedures applied at points of entry in Iraq depend to a large extent on the practice of the relevant officials. There can therefore a degree of deviation in procedures. We note in particular that sometimes significant discussion can be necessary with customs officials to clarify the detailed approach to the valuation of goods for customs purposes. Where the Customs Law may set out the framework for the valuation of goods, such as the commercial invoice value of raw materials, in practice customs officials have considerable discretion to determine the detailed valuation procedure and this can sometimes affect applicable customs duties.

IV. Labour

A. Brief Introduction of Labour Laws and Regulations

Law No. 37 of 2015 ("Labour Law") deals with the rights, duties and commitments of employers and employees and its implementation is overseen by the Ministry of Labour and Social Affairs ("MoLSA"). Generally, the Labour Law applies to any person employed in Iraq (i.e. including Iraqis and foreigners). In addition to the Labour Law there are also numerous Orders, Directives and Resolutions dealing with detailed requirements of a host of employment-related issues such as trade unions, hygiene, health and safety rules and occupational safety. Various laws and regulations also apply in respect of visas and work permits in Iraq which change from time to time, including Law No. 118 of 1978 (as amended) ("Foreigner Residency Law") which provides for certain matters relating to the entry and exit of foreign nationals to / from Iraq.

Under the Labour Law an Iraqi court has the discretion in determining whether a working relationship is an employment relationship (i.e. governed by the Labour Law, irrespective of the label given by the parties). Generally, the Labour Law is employee-friendly and places a number of requirements and restrictions upon employers. It is not possible to contract out of the Labour Law.

The Labour Law contains numerous provisions / requirements, these include:

(i) Arabic or Kurdish must be used in all employment relationships, including contracts and other documents. A claim against a worker may fail if the document upon which it is relied is drawn up in another language, even if it bears the worker's signature;

(ii) wages should be paid in Iraqi Dinars and the employer is required to ensure non-discrimination and equal pay;

(iii) a minimum wage is also provided for, to be periodically reviewed from time to time in line with the living costs and other economic conditions;

(iv) hours of work are generally eight hours per day, although this can be increased in exceptional circumstances;

(v) the maximum probationary period for an employee is three months;

(vi) employers may only dismiss employees in certain circumstances other than by expiry of a fixed-term employment contract, resignation of an employee on 30 days' notice or mutual agreement with an employee (such as the imprisonment of an employee for more than one year, death of employee or employer, liquidation of a project or force majeure);

(vii) employees have extensive rights to belong to trade unions and participate in strike action; and

(viii) it is the responsibility of an employer to ensure sufficient health and safety measures are in place.

B. Requirements of Employing Foreign Employees

a. Work Permit

Article 30 of the Labour Law requires non-Iraqis to obtain a work permit if they wish to work in Iraq. Instructions No. 18 of 1987 (as amended) ("Work Permit Instructions") set out procedures in order to obtain a work permit.

Work permits are only available for individuals who are able to demonstrate a level of professional qualification or have specific expertise. Generally the issuance of a work permit for an employee would require sponsorship from a corporate entity. Where an employer is able to obtain a visa to bring employees without a work permit into Iraq then the employer must apply for a work permit within one month from the date of the entry of the employee into Iraq. Alternatively, visas can be obtained on the back of work permits issued by the MoLSA, in order to allow the applicant enter the country for work purposes.

Traditionally we understand this system was not fully implemented and in practice only a visa (and no work permit) was obtained by an employee. However, since 2016 MoLSA been proactively implementing this requirement and taking certain companies to court for failing to comply.

b. Application Procedure

The Foreigner Residency Law outlines certain key requirements for the issuance of visas to foreign nationals. Among other matters, visa applicants to Iraq must hold a valid passport, or substitute document, andapply for and obtain a visa prior to entering Iraq, other than in the case of an Emergency Visa. As a matter of practice, a passport / travel document should be valid for at least six months in advance of a visa application.

The Federal Government body responsible for issuing visas is the General Directorate for Nationality, Passport and Residency (the "Residency Office"), which is affiliated to the Ministry of Interior. We understand that all applications for visas are processed and approved in Baghdad, however detailed procedures for visa applications are subject to frequent change and may vary according to the nature of the applicant and intended port of entry.

To obtain visas for business purposes in Iraq there are four main routes available:

(i) companies and / or foreign company branch offices in Iraq may be able to act as a sponsor entity and obtain a visa letter of approval from the Residency Office;

(ii) using the support of a relevant governmental counterparty. Companies may be able to obtain visas through the relevant foreign affairs ministry of its country requesting this from the Iraqi Ministry of Foreign Affairs and the Ministry of Interior;

(iii) by way of application through the National Investment Commission, which may assist the sponsor of a project with an investment licence to obtain visas for its employees or contractors; or

(iv) on the back of work permits issued by the MoLSA.

In practice an Iraqi sponsor entity usually applies for a visa for an overseas applicant from within Iraq. Upon approval of the application, the sponsor entity collects a visa letter of approval from the Residency Office, which is then scanned and emailed to the applicant waiting outside of Iraq.

We understand as a general principle that work permits will only be available for individuals who are able to demonstrate a level of professional qualification or have specific expertise to justify their employment in Iraq. The application process for work permits in particular requires:

(i) completion of registration of the relevant employing company or branch office in Iraq at the Companies Registry and the Pensions and Social Security Office of MoLSA ("PSSO"); and

(ii) submission of application information for the relevant employees such as a C. V. and evidence such as educational or professional qualification certificates and other information.

The work permit application will be sent to the Minister of Labour for approval, following which MoLSA will issue a letter listing the individuals whose work permit applications have been approved. Once the issuance of the work permits has been approved, the relevant individuals will be able to use such approval as the basis for obtaining visas. Under the Work Permit Instructions, work permits would be issued for one year, renewable annually for up to six years, following which approval for renewal should be sought from the Minister of Labour.

c. Social Insurance

In Iraq an employer is required to withhold and remit to the PSSO certain social security and pensions contributions on behalf of employees and to also make certain employer contributions. MoLSA has taken steps to enforce these requirements and has recently taken a number of companies to court for the non-payment of social security and pensions contributions.

In accordance with current Iraqi Law, employers are required to remit the following social security and pensions contributions for their employees (foreign and local) in Iraq:

First, each employee should make a contribution of five per cent of his / her monthly salary, which the employer deducts from his / her salary and remits to MoLSA; and

Second, each employer should make a contribution to MoLSA of 13 per cent of each of its employees' monthly salary. The 13 per cent contribution paid by the employer constitutes:

(i) one per cent for health insurance;
(ii) three per cent for work injuries insurance; and
(iii) nine per cent retirement pension.

Contributions are payable monthly and are calculated upon the employee's salary in January of each calendar year or, during the employee's first year of employment, upon the employee's salary in the first month of the employee's employment. In circumstances of late payment certain fines will apply.

The insuredemployee is entitled to receive certain benefits. These for instance include:

(i) a pension salary upon retirement. There is no compulsory retirement age under Iraqi law. A working man or woman is entitled to receive a pension, at 60 and 55 years of age, respectively, upon the completion of 20 years of service.

(ii) sick leave (also in case of injury). An employer is only required to pay sick leave not exceeding 30 days per year. Any days in excess are paid by the state-run Institute of employees Pensions and Social Security. The Institute covers medical costs of employees pertaining to clinical examinations and treatment generally.

C. Exit and Entry

a. Visa Types

Iraqi law provides for six main types of visa for foreigners including those working in Iraq.

(i) Emergency Visa, usually for up to ten days, may be granted to foreigners on arrival in Iraq who have not yet obtained another type of visa. The immigration officer at the time of application has the authority to decide or justify the reasons for granting this visa;

(ii) Single Entry Visa; which permits a foreigner to enter Iraq one time during three months from the date of grant. This usually allows the visa holder to stay in Iraq for three months from the date of their arrival;

(iii) Transit Visa; permits a foreigner to transit through Iraqi borders (some transit visas may allow stopping). As far as we are aware this visa is not often used in practice;

(iv) Diplomatic Visa; issued under the authority of the Minister of Foreign Affairs for those persons wishing to enter Iraq in the capacity of a diplomat or such;

(v) Service Visa; a Service Visa is granted to government employees for work-related travel; and

(vi) Tourist-Religious Visa; tourist visas may be granted to non-Iraqi persons of Islamic faith who obtain such visas to make a pilgrimage to holy sites in Iraq.

Of these, the Single Entry Visa is generally the most relevant for potential international investors. There is no clear legislative basis for multiple-entry visas, although in practice these are granted.

b. Restrictions for Exit and Entry

Upon arrival in Iraq, those persons who have received a visa approval letter from the Residency Office and who do not have an Iraqi visa sticker affixed into their passport prior to arrival (i. e. those who have not received it from an Iraqi Embassy or Consulate), will be required to present a copy of their visa approval letter from the Residency Office, fill in a visa application form and a pay USD 2 fee to obtain a visa sticker.

The visa sticker is stamped with an entry date and then individual passes through the immigration entry point. Upon obtaining a visa for employment purposes, the name of the employer of the employee is also affixed to the visa (an employee is restricted from working for other employers under the visa).

After arrival in Iraq all visa-holders, other than those holding visas valid for ten days or less, must present their passport to the nearest Residency Office within 15 days. There is also a requirement for a blood / HIV test to be submitted to the Residency Office by visa-holders (other than, we understand, holders of visas valid for ten days or less).

A visa holder in Iraq may not leave until he has obtained an Exit Visa from the Residency Office unless the visa-holder exits Iraq within ten days of arrival. The cost for an Exit Visa if the visa-holder is leaving before the expiry date of their visa is reported by the Residency Office as being USD 1. Upon obtaining an Exit Visa this will allow a visa holder ten days to leave Iraq. Based on our understanding of current practice, where a longer-term visa is issued (i. e. more than three months) this is generally in the form of a multiple entry and exit visa. Otherwise, individuals would need to obtain an Exit Visa for each exit.

D. Trade Union and Labour Organizations

The Labour Law recognises the freedom of trade unions and the right to collective negotiation. The Labour Law also prohibits employers from terminating employment, or making employment conditional, upon employees not joining, or being not members of, trade unions. There is no general requirement for the establishment of trade unions within an entity in Iraq.

There was only one trade union in Iraq before 2003 and its activities were heavily circumscribed by the previous regime. At present, there are various trade unions active in federal Iraq, including the General Federation of Trade Unions of Iraq, the Iraqi Federation of Workers Trade Unions, the Federation of Workers Councils and Unions in Iraq, the Federation of Oil Unions and the Federation of Independent Trade Unions. We understand from reports that unions have recently become increasingly involved with representing workers' rights issues to the Federal Government and in relation to disputes between individuals and companies, although strikes are not generally very common.

E. Labour Disputes

Specialised Labour Courts are established in each governorate. Comprised of a single judge, the Labour Courts look into both civil and criminal disputes / claims relating to labour and employment.

Employees in Iraq have strong rights under the Labour Law. Disputes between employees and employers therefore tend to result in favourable judgments for employees. It is therefore advisable for employers to prepare employment agreements based upon local legal advice and carefully comply with the rules set out under theLabour Law and also keep accurate records to prove compliance with the law (such as employee contracts and evidence of payment of social security and other payments). This may somewhat mitigate some of the risks of claims by employees under the Labour Law.

Recently MoLSA has also taken pro-active steps to generally enforce provisions of the Labour Law. This includes the enforcement of the work permit regime. Among other matters, several companies have been taken to court by MoLSA for not obtaining work permits for their foreign employees. Full compliance with Labour Law requirements is therefore also advisable from a regulatory perspective.

V. Intellectual Property

A. Brief Introduction of Intellectual Property Laws and Regulations

Iraq has enacted laws to protect various types of intellectual property rights. These include in respect of:
(i) patents, which are protected in Iraq under Law No. 65 of 1970 (as amended CPA Order No. 81) ("Patent

Law");

(ii) trademarks, Iraqi law provides for the protection of trade and service marks under Law No. 21 of 1957 (as amended by CPA Order No. 80) ("Trade Mark Law"); and

(iii) copyright, the Iraqi law on copyright is contained in Law No. 3 of 1971 (as amended CPA Order No. 83) ("Copyright Law").

Some intellectual property rights, such as patents and trademarks, can be registered in Iraq to allow their protection. Certain other intellectual property rights, such as copyright which extends to a wide range of written and artistic works, is not registrable. The Copyright Law however provides for protection of a person's economic rights for a period of 50 years from death (in the case of an individual) and 50 years from the date of first publication of the works (in the case of a corporate or other entity).

B. Patent Application

The Patent Law allows patents in respect for inventions that are industrially applicable, novel and involves an inventive step, either concerning new industrial products, new industrial methods, or new application of known industrial methods.

The Patent Law grants the registered owner of the patent protection for its invention from unauthorised use, exploitation, production, sale or importation. Registration may be carried out at the Registry of Patents and Industrial Designs. Protection for registered patents lasts for 20 years from the date of registration.

C. Trademark Registration

Iraqi law provides for the protection against unauthorized use of trademarks and service marks under the Trade Mark Law by way of registration at the Trademark Registration Office.

Trade marks are generally defined under the Trade Mark Law as any sign, or any combination of signs, capable of distinguishing the goods of one undertaking from those of other undertakings. This may include particular words including personal names, letters, numerals, figurative elements and colours as well as any combination of such signs. Where signs are not inherently capable of distinguishing the relevant goods or services, the ability of a person to register that sign will depend on the distinctiveness it has acquired through use.

Service marks may include any sign, or any combination of signs, used by a person to identify and distinguish the services of one person, including a unique service, from the services of others.

Registration for such trade and service marks is renewable for a ten year period. Applications must be submitted in Arabic and an application fee paid. Use of trademarks and / or a service mark is not a requirement for the filing of applications for registration.

D. Measures for Intellectual Property Protection

Various provisions of Iraq law allow for enforcement of intellectual property rights through the Iraqi courts. In certain cases criminal offences also apply in relation to infringement of intellectual property rights.

The Patent Law specifically provides that the owner of a patent or industrial design registered in Iraq may apply through an Iraqi court to have any infringer cease the infringement. The Trade Mark Law sets out various criminal offences in relation to infringement of registered trademarks. The owner of a registered trademark could also take civil action against infringers in various circumstances. An Iraqi court may order the seizure of any products which infringe trade / service marks, the confiscation of any revenues obtained by the parallel importer in connection with them and impose other penalties. A copyright infringement gives rise to a criminal offence, with penalties including imprisonment and compensation.

The Trade Mark Law also provides that the owner of a "well-known" trademark has the right to enjoy the protection provided by the Trade Mark Law even if the trade mark is not registered in Iraq. In practice, it is preferable to nevertheless proceed with an application for registration of such trademarks—particularly because in order to prove that a trade mark is "well-known", its owner may need to obtain an order to that effect from an Iraqi court.

Iraq is a signatory to the Paris Convention for the Protection of Industrial Property. This sets certain standards in Iraq for the national treatment (i.e. recognition of intellectual property of other signatory countries), priority and other rules affecting intellectual property.

Iraq is also a signatory to the Singapore Treaty on the Law of Trademarks which provides for certain harmonization of trademark registration with other signatory countries and the WIPO Convention which establishes the World Intellectual Property Organisation.

VI. Environmental Protection

A. Department Supervising Environmental Protection

The Ministry of Environment ("MoE") was established by Law No. 37 of 2008 and is responsible for the general oversight of environmental matters and related enforcement of environmental laws in Iraq. Among other matters, the consent or a licence from the MoE may be a direct requirement for activities and projects in Iraq if these could have an environmental impact. For certain projects this may also be a requirement before another Ministry (such as for instance the Ministry of Oil ("MoO") in the Iraqi petroleum sector) grants its consent.

Some work of the MoE is decentralised, with certain environmental matters handled by provincial environmental centres ("Environmental Directorates"). The Environmental Directorates oversee various local units with responsibilities for environmental monitoring and supervision including units for monitoring air quality, water, solid waste and hazardous chemicals, bio-diversity, land use, industrial activities and for supervising the preparation of environmental impact assessments. The Environment Directorates are overseen by a body of senior officials from the MoE and other Iraqi Ministries known as the Environmental Protection and Improvement Council.

Other Iraqi Ministries also have certain authorities and responsibilities in relation to environmental matters under sector specific laws (see below).

B. Brief Introduction of Laws and Regulations of Environmental Protection

Law No. 27 of 2009 ("Environment Protection Law") establishes a legislative framework for environmental protection and set outs certain prohibitions on causing environmental pollution. Among other matters, the Environment Protection Law:

(i) requires environmental impact assessments to be prepared by owners of large projects;

(ii) requires that any large project that may impact the environment will be prevented from operating unless it has an approval from the MoE;

(iii) requires parties exploring for or extracting hydrocarbons to take all necessary measures to prevent pollution;

(iv) generally provides that the emission of gases, other matter and liquids must be made in accordance with "national environmental legislation"; and

(v) prohibits direct or indirect pollution that damages land affecting its capacity of production, the food chain or natural beauty.

Various other requirements in relation to environmental protection are also included in other laws and certain contracts. These include:

(i) the Conservation of Hydrocarbon Resources Law no. 84 of 1985 which is implemented by the MoO and aims to conserve hydrocarbon wealth resources from damage and waste. Among other matters, the law requires oil and gas operators to take all necessary measures and precautions to prevent pollution;

(ii) MoE Instructions No. 3 of 2011, which set out the environmental specifications for the establishment of projects in Iraq and requirements for their supervision by the MoE. Among other matters, the instructions set out environmental specifications for projects, such as in relation to project location, waste treatment, and storage;

(iii) Council of Ministers' Regulation No. B 2 of 2001 on Preservation of Water Sources, which aims to protect public waters such as rivers and wet lands and prohibits all unpermitted disposal of waste and pollutants into public waters; and

(iv) environmental obligations on companies in Iraq included in the terms of contracts e. g. petroleum sector services contracts.

C. Evaluation of Environmental Protection

The Environment Protection Law makes strong provision for fines and sanctions for violations of environmental law. The MoE also has the right to temporarily stop or shut down activities until the violation of environmental law is removed. A violator may also or alternatively be sentenced to imprisonment and certain felonies, such as the disposal of hazardous materials without proper authorization or the import of hazardous waste into Iraq, carry a mandatory prison sentence. Under Law No. 111 of 1969 (as amended) ("Penal Code"), corporate bodies may only be sentenced to a fine, confiscation or such precautionary measures as are prescribed by law for that offence. However, individual offending employees or company personnel could also be punished by criminal penalties for an offence.

In practice, our understanding is that the level of enforcement activity in respect of environmental protection has increased in recent years. Compliance with legal obligations such as obtaining environmental licences and environmental impact assessments is required. Instances of pollutionby foreign companies in Iraq which are not remediated may result in regulatory action by the relevant Iraqi Ministries and state entities.

VII. Dispute Resolution

A. Methods and Bodies of Dispute Resolution

The primary means of dispute resolution in Iraq is the Iraqi courts. The Iraqi courts are composed of various courts regulated by law, including the Federal Supreme Court, the ultimate judicial organ in Iraq, the Court of Cassation, which has authority to review all courts in Iraq and hear appeals other than from the Federal Supreme Court, and other courts.

The main Iraqi courts of relevance to commercial matters are:

(i) Commercial court: most civil law disputes will be under jurisdiction of the Iraqi court of first instance (see below) but, where a party to a contract is a foreign company and the dispute relates to a commercial contract, the dispute may fall under the jurisdiction of the commercial court;

(ii) Courts of first instance: comprised of a single judge and established in each governorate, the court of first instance decides on actions and matters relatingto civil actions / claims.

(iii) Labour courts: Labour courts are established in each governorate. Comprised of a single judge, the Labour courts look into both civil and criminal disputes / claims relating to labour and employment;

(iv) Courts of appeal: Courts of appeal are established in each governorate and consist of a presiding judge and other judges depending upon the complexity of the case, to decide on appeals against judgments delivered by the courts of first instance;

(v) Criminal Courts: Various criminal courts operate, including Investigation Courts, Misdemeanour Courts and Felony Courts. These courts hear cases relating to alleged offences under the Penal Code and criminal offences established pursuant to other laws.

In addition to the Iraq court system, Iraq law permits the use of arbitration by investors (for instance under Article 27 of Investment Law No. 13 of 2006). Certain provision is made for arbitration under the Iraqi Civil Code and there are Iraqi national arbitration centers. However, in practice international parties are in general free to choose arbitration conducted by regional or international arbitration centers outside of Iraq (such as DIFC-LCIA).

B. Application of Laws

Court procedures in Iraq can sometimes be uncertain, in particular due to a lack of a centralised public database of previous decisions. However, Iraqi courts are functioning and their decisions are usually respected. Foreign parties have been able to successfully bring, and defend, claims in the Iraqi court system.

The enforcement of foreign court judgments in Iraq is however problematic because Iraq is not a party to the Hague Convention on Recognition of Foreign Judgements (The Hague, 1 February 1971).

Also, Article 16 of the Civil Code provides that judgments rendered by foreign courts shall not be executory in Iraq unless they have been deemed to be enforceable in accordance with the rules laid down in the laws enacted in this respect. In summary, the laws enacted in relation to enforcement of judicial awards provide that a foreign award can only be enforced in Iraq in the following cases:

(i) foreign judgments issued in a country that has a bilateral agreement with Iraq; or

(ii) where the country of the awarding court is specifically named by Iraqi regulations; and, in either case

(iii) where there is "reciprocity" with the country of the awarding court.

Treaties which establish at least prima facie enforceability in Iraq of foreign judgments exist with a limited number of other nations including Egypt, Turkey, Lebanon, Italy, India, and Jordan.

In relation to arbitration, the enforcement of foreign arbitral awards has been problematic because Iraq has not been a signatory to the1958 New York Convention on the Recognition and Enforcement of Foreign Arbitral Awards.

Foreign judgments may however be enforced under the 1983 Riyadh Convention on Judicial Cooperation between States ("Riyadh Convention"), which has been ratified by Iraq. The Riyadh Convention deals with the recognition and enforcement of foreign judgments and arbitral awards.

The Riyadh Convention states that the courts of a signatory country must enforce arbitral awards made in another signatory country unless:

(i) the law of the signatory country which is requested to enforce the award does not allow settlement of the subject of the dispute by arbitration;

(ii) the award is issued pursuant to a void term or void arbitration contract;
(iii) the award has not become final;
(iv) the arbitrator was not competent according to the agreement to arbitrate or according to the law under which the award was issued;
(v) the parties were not duly summoned to the arbitration; or
(vi) the award is contradictory to Shari'a law or public order or the constitution or ethics of the signatory country in which the award is to be enforced.

These conditions are open to a wide range of interpretation and could easily allow an Iraqi court to refuse the direct enforcement of non-Iraqi arbitral awards upon the slightest pretext. Nevertheless, for arbitral awards to be enforceable in Iraq, generally an arbitration should best take place in one of the signatory countries of the Riyadh Convention (for example, the United Arab Emirates or Jordan). One significant limitation, however, is that the Riyadh Convention does not apply to awards rendered against the Federal Government (which may be interpreted to extend to any government authority or SOE).

During 2015 Iraq ratified ICSID. Among other matters ICSID can provide investors with access to a form of settlement for disputes they may have with a host State and ICSID contains certain enforcement provisions relating to ICSID awards. ICSID is relatively new to Iraq and market commentators are watching its evolution with interest. Among other matters, it may be possible for ICSID provisions to be incorporated into contracts between companies and Federal Government counterparties.

VIII. Others

A. Anti-commercial Bribery

a. Brief Introduction of Anti-commercial Bribery Laws and Regulations

The principal Iraqi laws in respect of anti-bribery and corruption (which may also relate to commercial matters) are:
(i) the Penal Code; and
(ii) Law No. 14 of 1991, the Civil Servants Disciplinary Law, (the "Disciplinary Code").

The Penal Code includes offences relating to corruption applicable to both "public officials" and private persons who interact with them. A "public official" is defined in the Penal Code as any official, employee or worker who is entrusted with a public task in the service of the Federal Government or its agencies (this include employees of state owned entities).

The Penal Code prohibits, among other matters:
(i) any public official or agent from seeking or accepting for himself or for another a gift, benefit, honour (or a promise of these things) to carry out any duty of his employment or to refrain from doing so or to contravene such duty;
(ii) a public official accepting a gift or benefit (which are not fully defined but in our view should be interpreted broadly) to carry out or to refrain from carrying out acts (even if such acts do not fall within his duties or the act is not carried out);
(iii) any person giving, offering or promising a public official a gift or benefit. Such a person is subject to penalties for bribery even if the public official does not accept the bribe; and
(iv) any intermediary of a public official or other person respectively seeking / receiving or offering / giving a bribe.

The Disciplinary Code prohibits various activities carried out by officials within a government ministry or state entities. The Disciplinary Code prohibits such officials from engaging in various activities. This includes an official exploiting his position for personal benefit or profit for himself or others; accepting benefits from clients or contractors (or other commercial persons) related to his employment or from anyone with whom he has a relationship because of his civil service position; and a civil servant engaging in certain commercial activities

There are a number of provisions of other Iraqi laws which also contain anti-bribery and corruption provisions, among other matters these include:
(i) The Iraqi Revolutionary Command Council (RCC) Resolution No. 160 of 1983 (the "RCC Anti-Bribery Resolution");
(ii) The Iraqi Law of Unlawful Gains No. 15 of 1958 (the "Unlawful Gains Law"); and
(iii) The Iraqi Law Ratifying the United Nations Convention Against Corruption (UNCAC) No. 35 of 2007.

b. Department Supervising Anti-commercial Bribery

As a general matter, public prosecutors in Iraq are empowered in Iraq to prosecute bribery and corruption offenses. We also note the Coalition Provisional Authority (CPA) Order No. 57 of 2004 regarding Iraqi Inspectors General (the "Inspectors General Order"). The Inspectors General Order provides for the establishment of an office of an Inspector General within each ministry of the Federal Government. An Inspector General has wide-ranging powers to investigate violations and abuses, including in respect of corruption. These include powers to compel persons (including private persons) to provide information in connection with investigations.

The Iraqi Commission of Integrity Law No. 30 of 2011 (the "Commission of Integrity Law"); establishes the Federal Commission of Integrity. It has specific authority to investigate corruption cases through the work of investigators under the supervision of an investigation judge and generally to perform work to prevent and combat corruption. The Federal Commission of Integrity is specifically stated to co-operate with the Federal Board of Supreme Audit (as discussed further below) and individual offices of inspector general.

The Iraqi Board of Supreme Audit Law No. 31 of 2011 establishes the Board of Supreme Audit as an independent body to audit public accounts and oversee public finances. It provides for the Board of Supreme Audit to oversee transactions relating to public revenues and generally to audit public sector authorities (including state-owned companies). The Board of Supreme Audit also has the authority to review records, reports and other documentation and request the conduct of investigations by a public inspector or the Federal Commission of Integrity.

c. Punitive Actions

Possible penalties under domestic anti-bribery laws include:

(i) Penal Code: The penalties for persons found guilty of anti-corruption offences under the Penal Code can include imprisonment for up to 10 years and fines;

(ii) Disciplinary Code: Penalties for officials who breach the Disciplinary Code include fines and imprisonment;

(iii) RCC Anti-Bribery Resolution: Penalties for persons who breach the RCC Anti-Bribery Resolution include fines and imprisonment; and

(iv) Unlawful Gains Law: Sanctions include the return of "illegal gains"; removal of persons in public service from their positions; imprisonment for up to five years; and fines.

Certain mitigations and defences to the penalties under these laws exist, including the following:

(i) Penal Code: a person who offers a bribe as well as the intermediary shall be exempt from the penalty if the person undertakes to notify the legal or administrative authorities, or confesses to the offence before legal action is brought. It is considered a mitigating circumstance if the notification or confession occurs after an action is brought but before the end of the proceedings. There is no similar protection for the public official recipient of a bribe.

(ii) The Civil Servants' Disciplinary Law: this law does not provide specific defences, but sanctions may be reduced or avoided where the accused has previously received official commendations in respect of his performance.

(iii) The RCC Anti-Bribery Resolution: this law does not provide specific defences, although general defences under the Penal Code may potentially apply.

(iv) Unlawful Gains Law: a person may be able to avoid sanction under the Unlawful Gains Law by informing "the specialized authority" about cases of illegal gains or by assisting in investigations carried out under the law.

B. Project Contracting

a. Project Contracting

In practice in Iraq most significant project contacts with foreign investors are awarded by the Federal Government or Iraqi state-owned enterprises ("SOEs").

CPA Order No. 87 (and its related implementing regulations) ("Public Procurement Law") is the principal legislation governing the procurement and performance of Federal Government / public project contracts. The Public Procurement Law applies to all procurement of goods or services by the State of Iraq that may commit public funds, including SOEs when awarding public contracts for the procurement of goods or services that are directly financed by government funds.

The Public Procurement Law could apply to international companies awarding contacts (such as a construction or other project contracts) when in a joint venture with a State entity, provided that State funds are committed to that joint venture.

From time to time the Ministry of Planning ("MoP") also issues detailed implementing instructions for public procurement and tendering (such as for the content of tender documents, the process of evaluation of bids etc.). The MoP has also issued numerous supporting regulations which are sent to all Ministries, including the MoO, to encourage consistency in Federal Government procurement.

b. Permission System

Bid prequalification requirements generally apply to companies wishing to tender for a contract. These requirements may include submission of corporate information and financial support such as bid-bonds or deposits for certain bids. Bid-bonds or deposits are usually based upon the value of the contract and returned to unsuccessful tenders.

A local Iraqi entity is not generally required to be established before bidding for a contract, however at law and in practice it would be necessary to establish a local entity to perform a public contract. The MoP also maintains a contractor classification scheme for certain engineering related services and some Iraq procurement entities may require that bidders are classified under this scheme, although this tends not to apply to international bidders bidding for larger public contracts.

c. Prohibited Areas

Generally, nationality restrictions do not apply to investment in Iraq. However, foreign investment in the following sectors may be limited at law and in practice: commercial agency and distribution arrangements, certain IT and communications services, provision of security services, ownership of land (subject to limited exceptions for housing development projects), and investment in national defence or security assets.

d. Invitation to Bid and Bidding

Under the Public Procurement Law (and implementing instructions) public contracts must be awarded on a competitive basis subject to certain exceptions, such as where goods or services are only available from a particular supplier or there is a public interest in avoiding a tender.

A tender for a public contract is required to provide sufficient information, such as a statement of work, anticipated work schedule, terms and conditions and criteria against which bids will be evaluated. A tender should also state the timing for the tender and procedures for clarificatory questions from bidders. While there is no requirement for the public issuer of the tender to choose the successful bidder based on pricing alone, the tender should usually identify the particular criteria upon which the received bids will be evaluated.

In practice, some Iraqi Ministries or SOEs may apply different procurement rules or standards for the tender of certain contracts. For instance, on-going procurement by the State oil companies and their joint ventures generally remains outside of the Public Procurement Law as matter of practice.

Generally, the award of a contract to a private company by the Federal Government or State entity should comply with the Public Procurement Law, otherwise a potential challenge to the award of the contract could be brought by, for instance, another commercial entity which opposes the agreement / project. In circumstances where application of the Public Procurement Law is uncertain (e. g. due to the particular requirements from a particular Ministry or State entity) it may be possible to mitigate the risk of a legal challenge to the award of a contract by taking certain mitigating steps such as ratification of a contract award by the Council of Ministers.

C. Others

a. Hydrocarbon Laws

Hydrocarbon laws in federal Iraq can be broadly separated into pre 2004 legislation, which was largely derived from the nationalisation process occurring between 1961-1975, and post 2004 legislation which includes various laws on the subject but no overarching federal hydrocarbon legislation.

Principal hydrocarbon related legislation includes:

(i) the Constitution;

(ii) certain pre-2004 legislation, such as Law No. 101 of 1967, which was largely derived from the nationalisation process occurring between 1961-1975;

(iii) Law No. 19 of 2010 which imposes income tax on foreign oil companies and their subcontractors in Iraq at a rate of 35%;

(iv) Law No. 64 of 2007 (as amended) ("Refinery Investment Law") which provides certain incentives for the private investment in oil refineries; and

(v) various MoO regulations, such as those issued for the conduct of petroleum field bid rounds.

a) The Constitution

The Constitution contains certain provisions regarding natural resources. This includes Article 111 which states that oil and gas is owned by all the people of Iraq in all the federal regions and governorates. Article 112 states, among other matters, that the Federal Government, with the producing governorates and regional governments, shall undertake the management of oil and gas extracted from present fields, provided that it distributes its revenues in a fair manner in proportion to the population distribution in all parts of the country.

b) Iraq Oil and Gas Licensing Rounds and Model TSC

Law No. 97 of 1967granted to the Iraqi National Oil Company (now subsumed with the MoO) the exclusive right to develop hydrocarbons in Iraqi territory. It is on this basis that the MoO is viewed as having the authority to enter into contracts for the development of hydrocarbon resources in Iraq. The Federal Government has opened several licensing rounds since 2008 inviting international oil companies (IOCs) to contract to explore / develop and produce hydrocarbons from Iraqi oilfields and gas fields.

To participate in bid rounds IOCs are required to pre-qualify with the MoO. This requires the payment of a USD 25,000 pre-qualification fee and the submission of detailed technical, legal and financial information which evidences its suitability to participate in Iraq's upstream oil and gas sector.

The contracts awarded in the bidding rounds to IOCs are 20-year technical service contracts ("TSCs"). Key provisions of TSCs include:

(i) a fixed fee per barrel of oil instead of an equity stake. Under a TSC, the IOC becomes a "Contractor" for the relevant Iraqi regional oil SOE (e. g. such as the South Oil Company, North Oil Company etc.) for the development of the relevant oil fields;

(ii) a broad definition of "petroleum operations" which includes the appraisal, development, redevelopment and production operations;

(iii) obligations of the relevant Iraqi oil SOE and MoO, including access to land, legal and tax stabilisation and other matters;

(iv) detailed requirements for IOCs / petroleum contractors in relation to the carrying out of "petroleum operations" and the preparation of exploration, development and decommissioning plans.

Various regulations (including provisional regulations) apply to IOCs in the Iraqi petroleum sector, among other matters these regulations set out that:

(i) petroleum operations can only be conducted on the basis of certain types of TSCs and that the MoO awards, and enters into, TSCs;

(ii) the rules governing "Bid Round" process which is initiated by in the form of a public announcement or a letter of invitation to selected companies (who are pre-qualified according to requirements including sufficient financial resources, expertise, and petroleum sector experience in Iraq); and

(iii) various requirements for petroleum contractors including as to evaluations and plans for exploration activities, development plans and decommissioning plans.

c) Refining Investment Law

The Refining Investment Law has been enacted to encourage and benefit those investors who wish to construct, work and maintain new refinery capacity. Under the Refining Investment Law, the Federal Government may provide crude feedstock to such a project at a discount to the market price for crude delivered FOB Basra, but with an addition to cover transport costs to the refinery from the nearest delivery point.

The investor company is responsible for the costs of construction, operation and maintenance of the pipeline from the delivery point to the refinery. The investor may market the refined product within Iraq or export it. The Government of Iraq maintains the right of first refusal to any such refined product.

b. Evolving Government Attitudes to Projects and Project Structures

Historically, as a general matter projects in Iraq have tended to be structured on the basis of government ownership, with private sector involvement being limited to the provision of services, equipment or expertise under engineering procurement and construction ("EPC") style contracts financed by the state budget. In recent years, however, as Iraq's budget deficit has increased in the face of lower oil prices and the cost of military and humanitarian operations, there has been an increasing openness to foreign investment participation and financing in Iraq.

Among other matters we note that the Federal Government appears increasingly willing in recent years to provide sovereign guarantees to support financed projects (although the issuance of sovereign guarantees going forwards will depend on the budgetary allocation for such issuance inforthcoming annual Federal Government budgets). Further, Iraqi law (primarily the Civil Code) regulates the granting of security in Iraq and allows for the granting of security over various types of asset. Generally, Iraq law will apply to the granting of security over local assets.

In relation to project structuring, we are aware in particular in Iraq of the following two models for infrastructure investments:

(i) EPC + F (engineering, procurement, construction and financing) contracts, where a private entity fulfils the traditional role of an EPC contractor but also helps to arrange financing for the government in order to pay for its services. In recent months a number of these transactions have been concluded in the power sector and it may be that this experience can be translated to the mid—and downstream petroleum sector. A particular factor in the success of these precedent transactions has been the involvement of foreign governments (typically, the home governments of the relevant private contractors) through development bank loans and export credit agencies; and

(ii) equity investment, whereby a private entity is granted rights to develop, operate and own an infrastructure project. This would appear to be particularly relevant in relation to refinery projects, where the Refining Investment Law provides a legal framework for private investment on a build-own-operate-transfer (BOOT) basis. Further, while there may be continuing reluctance to allow private ownership of strategic infrastructure such as pipelines, we understand that it is envisaged that at least part of the proposed Iraq-Jordan oil pipeline will be developed on a BOOT basis.

c. Kurdistan Region

We note that the Kurdistan Region of Iraq ("KR") is specifically recognised as an existing federal region under the Constitution. The KR Government ("KRG") has passed legislation in certain areas which apply only in the KR and this should be borne in mind by foreign investors in the KR. In practice the KR does not generally apply Iraqi legislation passed in Baghdad since the KR gained a measure of autonomy in 1991 unless approved by the KR parliament. However, in the event that there is no suitable equivalent KR legislation to cover a particular issue, it is common for the KRG to adopt post 1991 Baghdad legislation.

意大利

作者：Sara Marchetta
译者：金笑、姚远

一、概述

(一) 国家概况

作为地中海地区与欧洲的天然桥梁，意大利共和国（以下简称"意大利"）是欧盟中杰出的成员国之一。它在地中海东部和西部新崛起的国家之间、欧洲的中部和东部之间起着商业、贸易联系桥梁的作用。意大利北部位于欧洲中心，与法国、瑞士、奥地利及斯洛文尼亚接壤。意大利的人口近 6 000 万。意大利语是其官方语言，全国各地都说区域性方言。

意大利是欧洲最大的农业生产国，也是在服务业、工业及科学等方面领先的国家之一，拥有悠久的发明传统。创造工作机会、减税、提高竞争、降低预算赤字和债务是意大利政府近年来关注的焦点。

罗马作为意大利首都及最大的城市在制度方面起主要作用，而米兰则在商业方面起到重要作用。除罗马和米兰外，意大利还有都灵、那不勒斯、威尼斯和热那亚等大城市。国家铁路系统由普通铁路系统和高速铁路系统组成，覆盖整个意大利，并延伸至邻国。有数条高速公路和国家级、省级公路贯穿意大利，意大利的公路系统也与其他欧洲国家的公路系统相连接。通过意大利高速公路，可以方便地到达意大利最大的城镇和城市。

由于意大利的地理位置，海运在意大利的对外贸易中起到了至关重要的作用。热那亚、里窝那、的里雅斯特、拉文纳、拉斯佩齐亚和那不勒斯是意大利最重要的港口。拉斯佩齐亚和塔兰托则是两个重要的海军基地。目前，意大利运营着超过 100 个机场，其中包括国际机场和区域性机场。罗马的费米齐诺机场和米兰的马尔彭萨机场是重要的国际航空枢纽。另一些重要的国际机场有米兰的利纳特机场、威尼斯马可波罗机场和博洛尼亚机场。

意大利近十年来以提高竞争力、效率和服务为目标，主要在能源、天然气、交通和电信领域展开了经济自由化进程。政府继续持有银行、能源制造、流通和运输等行业企业的股份。

意大利拥有现代化且高度发达的通信系统，已经有全自动化电话、电报及数据服务，以及高容量光缆系统。意大利的移动电话普及率排名全球第三。意大利和其他欧盟国家一起从 1999 年 1 月开始使用欧元作为新货币，因此，货币政策是由位于德国法兰克福的欧洲中央银行制定。2002 年 1 月，意大利顺利地引入了新的硬币和纸币。

(二) 外交关系

意大利是联合国大多数专门机构及相关组织的成员。意大利与大多数国家都建立了外交关系，并开展了商业活动。意大利在世界范围拥有广泛的领事网络，世界主要国家在意大利的大多数重要城市设有领事馆，很多国家在罗马都有自己的外交代表。

除特别情况可能需要旅行者根据其国籍国要求提供签证外，进入意大利或在意大利国内没有任何旅行限制。

(三) 宪法制度

意大利实行民主共和制。1948 年宪法通过的意大利民主联邦的三个权力机构实行民主制度：①议会，行使最高立法权，包括由众议院（Camera dei Deputat）和参议院（Senato della Repubblica）组成的两院制；②内阁（Consiglio dei ministry），由内阁总理领导（Presidente del Consiglio）；③自由、中立且独立的司法权，由独立的法院系统行使，其中包括在"司法制度"部分进一步讨论的宪法法院

(Corte Costituzionale)。

(四)总统和政府

意大利共和国总统是由议会的联席会议以及共和国地区代表选举产生,任期7年。总统的权力包括:①任命内阁总理,以及根据内阁总理的推荐任命部长;②解散议会;③批准国际条约。政府的日常运行由内阁总理、部长及其共同组成的内阁负责。内阁总理通常由在议会中代表人数最多的党派首领担任,负责协调部长的行动。内阁(通常但非必须由议会成员组成)制定政府总体政治事务并监督事务的实施,须维持议会两院对它的信任。

现任共和国总统是2015年1月31日选举的塞尔焦·马塔雷拉(Sergio Mattarella)。

1. 议会

意大利议会由普选产生的众议院和参议院组成,任期5年。根据2005年生效的法律的规定,选举制度以人口数量为基础。参议会还包括共和国前总统和根据特别宪法条款享有终身特权的其他人员。立法议案可以由议会两院中任意一个提出,且必须经议会两院的大多数成员同意。公民必须年满25周岁才有权选举参议员,年满18周岁即有权参加其他所有选举。

2. 司法制度

意大利司法制度以罗马法为基础,由民法、刑法、宪法、行政法、会计法、军事法及税法构成。

民法、刑法构成意大利法律的常规部分,这些常规职能一般会受两个层级的司法审查:一审法庭和上诉法院。上诉法院关于民法、刑法案件的判决(仅限于法律问题)将由意大利最高法院(Corte di Cassazione)审查。

行政法、会计法、军事法及税法构成意大利法律的专业部分。这些专业化职能一般会受到两个层级的司法审查:一审法庭、上诉法庭或其他机构。地区行政法庭(Tribunali Amministrativi Regionali)和国务院(Consiglio di Stato)分别是一审法庭和对行政法事宜享有管辖权的上诉机构。

有关宪法的事宜由宪法法院管辖。宪法法院还负责立法审查,判定其是否符合宪法,并对政府三大分支机构(立法、行政和司法)间的冲突、共和国和地区间的冲突及不同地区间的冲突作出裁决。

(一审)案件的审理程序一般平均持续9个月到3年,上诉程序会将审理程序延长2年到3年。通常意大利法院的判决可以在境外被执行,相应地,外国法院的判决也可以在意大利得到执行。意大利是一些关于认可和执行外国判决的国际条约的缔约国,例如:

1968年9月27日的《关于民商事案件管辖权及判决执行的公约》,目前已经被2000年12月22日的关于管辖权、认可和执行民商事判决的2001第44号欧盟条例替代;

1958年6月10日的《承认及执行外国仲裁裁决公约》。

此外,意大利司法系统还提供了各种形式的争议解决方式,例如仲裁、调解、调停以及被认可的有关国际条约。

二、投资

(一)市场准入

1. 投资产业法律、法规

在意大利,银行、金融业务受1993年9月1日颁布的《银行法》(第385号法令)规制。这一法令实施了对银行设置管理、监督体系的欧盟银行指令。

只有根据《银行法》获得批准的银行才可以从事银行业务(例如,向公众收取存款、授予信贷)。《银行法》规定,在意大利从事银行业务应当获得意大利中央银行的批准,但是,欧盟银行(例如,已在意大利以外的欧盟成员国注册有办事处或总部的银行)可以在所谓的"互相认可"制度下开展经营活动(例如,在意大利设立分支机构的银行可以在根据所属国授予的许可在意大利从事经营活动,而不需获得意大利中央银行的批准,前提是意大利中央银行已收到同为欧盟成员国的该银行所属国主管机构的通知)。

1998年2月24日颁布的《金融法》（第58号法令）规定了投资服务和活动、资产管理及交易，该法令在意大利实施了欧盟有关投资的指令。《金融法》在意大利实施了欧盟《金融工具市场指令》（MIFID），尤其是关于投资服务的规定。

保险和再保险业务在意大利受2005年9月7日颁布的《保险法》（第209号法令）规制，该法令在意大利实施了对保险、再保险设定的监管体制（包括人身保险和非人身保险）的欧盟保险指令。

2004年5月21日的第170号法令被2011年4月24日的第48号法令修订，该法令实施了欧盟关于金融担保安排的指令（第2002/47/CE号），还规定了一项保障金融担保品安全的特别制度，旨在鼓励金融担保机制的完善和执行。

2. 外商投资

意大利没有针对外商投资的具体规定，所有投资都必须遵循《民法典》和《公司法》的有关规定。外国投资者可以以设立代表处、合资企业、外商独资企业或以兼并收购的形式进行投资。

投资公司、资产管理公司由意大利中央银行与意大利公司和证券交易所监管委员会监管。意大利中央银行监督中介机构的风险控制和财务稳定性，意大利公司和证券交易所监管委员会监督关于披露要求和客户关系稳健性的合规性。

意大利证券交易所和衍生产品市场由意大利证券交易所股份公司进行管理。意大利证券交易所是意大利设立的第一家（证券）市场管理公司。

除意大利法律提供的保护之外，外商投资者还受到国际法保护。意大利已加入了一些保护外国投资的多边、双边协议，例如，1965年的《华盛顿公约》以及大量为外国投资提供保护的双边投资协议（也被称为"BIT"）。

中国与意大利于1985年1月28日签署了一份双边投资协议，协议于1987年8月28日生效。

3. 市场准入和审查标准

根据互惠原则，中国和意大利有双边投资协议，双方为在对方国家投资的个人提供优惠待遇。根据意大利《民法典》的规定，外国投资的市场准入标准与本地投资者相同。如果兼并、收购涉及欧盟内部市场竞争，还应当遵守欧盟市场竞争政策。如果兼并、收购涉及意大利国内市场，则应当遵循意大利竞争法规，并经意大利竞争和市场管理局审查和批准。此外，如果被兼并或收购的是意大利上市公司超过2%的股份，则必须向主管机构意大利证券监督管理委员会报告，并由该机构进行审批。

意大利没有针对外国投资者的国家安全审查机制，但是，当涉及公共利益，以及具有重要战略意义的行业、企业或资产时，意大利政府可以通过"黄金股权"对有关投资进行审查和评估，并享有最终决定权。"黄金股权"通常由财政部或政府的其他行业法定代表持有。

意大利对国防工业、飞机制造业、石油和天然气开采业等行业设有严格的市场准入条件，这些行业有明确的市场准入限制和标准。

意大利的工业园主要集中在东北部传统工业地区，共有45个工业园。西北部地区有37个工业园，中部地区有38个工业园，南部地区有17个工业园。

另外，意大利设有出口加工自由贸易区，在自由贸易区内实施免税政策，自由贸易区内的商品可进行任何形式的加工，而不受任何海关限制。外国投资者可以根据意大利劳工法规、社会安全法规在自由贸易区内雇用其本国的劳动者。

（二）外汇管理规定

1. 外汇监管部门

意大利中央银行负责决定欧元区的单一货币政策，并履行欧元体系国家中央银行授予的职责。意大利中央银行可以根据欧元体系设置的规则实施外汇业务，管理自己的外汇储备，以及代表欧洲中央银行管理其部分外汇储备。

作为国家监管机构，意大利中央银行设法稳健、审慎地管理金融中介机构，确保金融系统整体的稳定和效率，以及受其监管的金融中介机构的合规性。

意大利中央银行是单一监管机制下指定的国家主管机构（NCA）。

2. 外汇法律、法规简介

欧元体系根据《欧盟运行条约》第 127 条和第 129 条的规定进行外汇交易的运营。在欧元体系内，意大利中央银行可能会按要求与其他国家中央银行（NCB）和欧洲中央银行（ECB）共同干预市场。

意大利中央银行还会被要求干预第二汇率机制（ERM II），该机制用于确定欧洲中央银行和还未采用欧元的欧盟成员国国家中央银行间关于汇率政策的主要合作方针。

外汇运营业务还可以被用来改变意大利中央银行的外汇储备组成，从而达到风险和收益的最佳平衡。

意大利中央银行还需要从市场交易方手中购入和出售外汇，从而在不改变外汇储备组成或数量的情况下，解决国家的外币债务，平衡现金的流入和流出。

意大利中央银行还通过主要新闻机构和市场经营者提供的信息，分析主要货币每日的情况。

意大利中央银行还按照意大利法律确定适用于财政目的的平均月利率、年利率，并通知给经济财政部，并在《意大利共和国公报》（Official Journal）进行公开。与此相关的法案有所得税法律汇编（DPR917/86）（第 110 条）和第 167/90 号法令（第 4 条）。

3. 针对外国企业的外汇管理要求

意大利没有外汇限制，实行资本账户自由化。意大利允许资本在国际间自由流动。利润在缴纳所得税后可以汇出意大利。

（三）金融

1. 主要金融机构

（1）银行、金融中介机构，从事保险、再保险活动、投资服务及资产管理活动的金融机构。

（2）市场管理公司——意大利证券交易所，分为线上证券交易市场（用于进行股票交易）、证券化衍生产品市场（用于进行证券化衍生产品交易）、"延时交易"市场（用于在不同于线上证券交易市场、证券化衍生产品市场的交易时间内，对符合意大利证券交易所流动性要求的上市股票交易和按照发行人的要求在证券化衍生品市场进行的证券化衍生产品金融工具的交易）、AMI Italia（专门用于有强劲成长潜能的中小型意大利企业）、开放式电子基金和证券化衍生金融工具市场、债券、政府债券电子市场（Mercato Telematico delle Obbligazioni e dei Titoli di Stato，用于进行债券、国库券、欧元债券、外国企业发行的公司债券及资产抵押证券的交易）、投资工具电子化交易市场（用于进行投资公司、房产投资公司的股权交易）。

（3）衍生金融工具市场（IDEM），用于受《金融法》规制的衍生金融工具的交易。

（4）债券、政府债券批量交易电子市场，用于进行国库券的批发交易，由政府债券市场公司管理。

（5）EuroTLX，一家多边交易公司，用于进行国库券、公司债券、资产担保证券、基金股份的交易，由 EuroTLX 股份有限公司管理。

2. 外国投资者的银行账户和贷款

意大利没有需要在意大利银行机构开立账户才可以从事投资活动的明确法律要求。但是，反洗钱法律已经对现金的使用设置了某些限制。更明确地说，累计价值等于或高于 1 000 欧元的现金（银行存折、股票）转账交易都是被禁止的，因此，不可避免地必须通过银行机构或其他经认可的中介机构进行交易。这一条款实际上暗示着任何在意大利从事商业活动的投资者都必须在意大利开立银行账户，银行账户可由非意大利机构持有。

非本地居民的自然人可以在意大利自行开立银行账户。总的来说，对外国顾客而言，使用银行账户没有任何限制。银行仅需根据其国籍国法律确认非本地居民的身份和行为能力。另外，为了遵循反洗钱规定，银行必须要求客户提供身份信息、可能的交易受益人的身份信息以及交易目的，还应当获取有关商业关系目的及其意图本质的信息。

投资者接受银行贷款没有任何法律限制，可由银行与投资者根据相关法律的规定自由协商。相关法律规定包括反高利贷法，对利率和适用于金融业务的其他收益设置了一些门槛。

（四）房地产

1. 房地产法律、法规简介

根据意大利法律，原则上，非意大利的私人投资者可以自由取得意大利不动产权，但是会受到同样适用于意大利国民的限制。上述原则的唯一限制是（不适用于欧盟投资者），如果意大利公民在某投资者的国籍国不能取得不动产的权利，则来自于该国的投资者不得就意大利不动产取得相同的权利。这一限制不经常适用（而且经常被忽略），但是违反这一要求可能会引发纠纷，其中包括诉讼。如果意大利与投资者的国籍国之间就这一事项存在对等协定，则这一要求不适用。

大多数对意大利不动产的投资都需要取得不动产的全部所有权。理论上，投资者还可以要求从所有人处取得不动产的"部分"对物权，例如，使用权，在不动产之上或之下建造建筑物或构造物的权利，或特定的留置优先权，如特定他物权。除非在极少数特定情形下，商业投资者很少会对这类"部分"物权进行投资。不动产的所有权和其他对物权一般需要在不动产登记处进行登记，以确保具有对抗第三方的强制执行力，同时也进一步确保对不动产的所有权和在不动产上不存在任何对物的财产负担（例如抵押）。有关文件必须公证，方可对不动产权利进行登记。

作为取得对物权的替代选择，投资者可以与不动产所有人签订协议。根据协议，投资人可以在特定时期内使用不动产，将使用权授予第三方，在某些情形下，还有权取得不动产的全部所有权。上述协议通常体现为直接的不动产租约、融资租赁或运营企业的租约。上述权利不能在不动产登记处进行登记，因此相较对物权，上述权利更难以被确认和强制执行。

2. 所有权

所有权是不动产上最普遍的对物权。

所有权人可以按照他的想法使用不动产（有一些限制，大多来自行政法方面），可以出售不动产，向第三方出租不动产，向第三方授予部分对物权，也可以将不动产用于债务担保（通常以抵押的方式）。

取得不动产所有权需要履行特定的手续，这些手续会延长取得过程，或使该过程复杂化，包括如下手续：

① 买卖合同必须是书面形式的，但是实践中强烈推荐进行公证，以便在不动产登记处进行登记；

② 如果不动产为建筑物，出让人应当在买卖合同中记载建筑物许可证，建筑物许可证是建筑物建造的基础，表明建筑物已经登记在不动产登记处不动产清册中，未按照相关建筑物许可证建造或未在不动产登记处进行登记的建筑物无法转让；

③ 如果不动产为建筑物，双方应当在买卖合同中注明建筑物"能源等级"，"能源等级"根据具体"能源等级"证书确定，这一证书记载了建筑物的能源消耗，由双方（通常为出让人）指定的专业机构出具；

④ 如果不动产为地块，双方应当在买卖合同中附上一份由有关政府出具的"许可使用"证书——出具此类证书需1个月；

⑤ 双方应当在买卖合同中表明交易是否有任何经纪人协助，如有经纪人，则还需表明向经纪人支付的费用金额；

⑥ 双方应当在买卖合同中表明对价是以何种方式支付（或即将如何支付）的；

⑦ 如果不动产具有"历史"或"艺术"价值，转让将受到一些限制（包括意大利公共机构的优先购买权）；

⑧ 在一些情形下，建筑物的承租人可能对建筑物享有优先购买权，优先购买权也适用于农业用地。

3. 使用权

使用物权的权利人与所有人享有基本相同的权利。主要的差异在于，使用权有时间限制（最长期限等同于原物权权利人有生之年，如原物权权利人为法人的，最长期限为30年）。使用权通常可向第三人出售或抵押（除非权利文件另有规定），使用权人还可以向第三人出租不动产。

取得使用权的程序和手续与前述"房地产法律、法规简介"部分所述取得完全所有权的程序和手续基本相同。

4. 建造权（diritto di superfice）

建造权人有权在有关不动产之上（或之下）建造建筑物或构筑物，并取得其建造的建筑物或构筑物的完全的永久所有权。

建造权（和根据建造权取得的建筑物完全所有权）可以出售或抵押。

取得建造权的程序和手续与前述"房地产法律、法规简介"部分所述取得完全所有权的程序和手续基本相同。

5. 地役权（diritti di servitù）

地役权通常表现为不动产所有权人可以向其他不动产行使某些权利。最常见的地役权是通行权（diritto di passaggio），根据这一权利，不动产所有权人有权在临近不动产上通行（一般为地块），以进出其不动产。

地役权通常不会被认为是不动产投资本身，但可极大地增加（或减少）"主要"资产的价值。

创设地役权的协议必须是书面形式的，实践中强烈推荐进行公证，以便将地役权在不动产登记处进行登记。

在一些情形下，如果未签署任何协议，地役权也可以（根据主管机关的指令或地面上的具体情形）创设。但是，大部分地役权是通过协议创设的，一般可以向不动产登记处进行查询确定。

6. 不动产租约

不动产的普通租约（与金融租约相对应）大多由企业采用，企业倾向于直接使用租赁的资产从事经营活动。承租人有权根据租赁合同中规定的限制和规则使用承租的资产（租赁合同可能会极大地限制资产的使用）。如果租赁合同允许，承租人可以将资产全部或部分转租，或者转让整个租赁合同。

承租人来源于租约的权利不能作为承租人债务的抵押物（即这些权利不能抵押）。

签署租约的方式比取得不动产物权的方式简单得多，但是，租约通常是书面形式（住宅租约强制规定必须是书面的），长期租约（超过9年租期的）则建议进行公证，在不动产登记处进行登记，以确保可以要求该不动产的未来所有人强制履行承租人的权利。

涉及建筑物租赁的期限和条件很大程度上取决于法律规定，包括以下内容：

① 住宅租约的租赁期限不得少于4年，非住宅租约为6年，酒店租约为9年，需注意，部分条款规定了最低租赁期限；

② 租约一旦到期会自动延续，除非合同一方提前通知——第一次到期时，出租人仅可在特定情形下发出不续期的通知；

③ 承租人在一些情形下可以单方终止租约——承租人可单方终止租约的具体情形由判例法确定，基本原则是，如果在签署租约时不可预见的新情况下租约负担变得过重的，承租人可以终止租约；

④ 租约可以约定授予承租人额外的终止权，但是，出租人仅可在承租人严重违约的情形下终止租约；

⑤ 对于租期不超过6年的商业租约（酒店租约不超过9年的），租金浮动水平不得超过意大利统计局通货膨胀指数的75%，更长租期的商业租约可以规定更高的租金浮动水平；

⑥ 部分商业资产的租约中，如果出租人出售租赁资产的，承租人享有优先购买权，如部分租约到期的情形下，承租人有权向出租人要求相当的补偿。

7. 金融租约

金融租约授予承租人使用有关资产的权利，以及在租约到期时选择购买这一资产的权利。仅有银行和一些其他金融机构可以作为金融租约的出租人。

金融租约交易的基本目的，即授予承租人使用的权利和在租约到期时购买资产而无须预先支付全款的权利。出租人首先是为购买（部分时候为建造）某一资产提供资金，取得该资产的所有权（维持资产的所有权，直至承租人行使购买权），从承租人处收取预先确定的租金。租约到期时，资产的出售价格通常低于其剩余市场价值，因为承租人在租期内支付的租金通常定在可以充分确保出租人收入的水平，以逐步补偿出租人购买（或建造）该资产所支付的部分初始财务支出。有时，交易的形式为售后回租。此时,出租人从承租人处购得资产(因此,出租人向承租人提供大体相当于购买价格的资金),然后再将这一资产出租给承租人。考虑到意大利法律原则上不允许以向债权人转让资产所有权作为担保,售后回租交易必须有正规的出租公司参与,并谨慎地评估和安排。签署金融租约的方式比取得不动产物权的方式要简单得多。基本上,协议应为书面形式,出租人应提供交易成本的有关信息。

适用于不动产普通租约的法律强制规定不适用于金融租约。

8. 运营企业租约

如果不动产是运营企业的组成部分,运营企业租约可以包含不动产。

由于运营企业租约不仅准许出租人给予承租人使用不动产的权利,还允许出租人授予承租人承接运营企业的合同关系(即雇佣合同、供应合同)、有关设备、相关行政许可证和审批的权利,运营企业租约常常被购物中心、酒店的所有人和运营人采用。更进一步而言,意大利的购物中心(和一些酒店)的开发和管理中最常见的构架即为运营企业租约,如下所示:

① 不动产开发商取得建造和运营购物中心的行政审批和许可证;

② 此后,开发商建造建筑物,通过运营企业租约将购物中心的各个商铺出租给商铺的最终运营者,具体包括商铺、水电供应合同及运营商铺的行政许可证;

③ 开发商再将整个购物中心(作为一家运营企业)出售给最终运营者或所有人,成为拥有每一商铺使用权的运营企业租约的出租人。

签署运营企业租约的手续要求租约必须经公证,且必须向公司注册处提交租约协议。如果租约包括行政许可证,可能会要求提供转让这一行政许可证的特定合约。

即便运营企业包括不动产在内,适用于不动产的普通租约的法律强制规定也不适用于运营企业租约。但是,有一些关于运营企业租约的规定应当受到谨慎评估,包括:

① 租约被认为是运营企业的"暂时转让",其后果是,在签署租约后,承租人即成为运营企业所签署合同的一方(包括任何雇佣合同),收取运营企业的应收账款,对该运营企业的特定债务承担责任;同样,租约到期或终止时,出租人将成为运营企业所签署合同的一方(包括任何雇佣合同),收取运营企业的应收账款,对该运营企业的特定债务承担责任。这一后果在某种程度上受制于精心构建的租约以及被出租的运营企业。

② 运营企业租约有时可能涉及反垄断,因而有必要向反垄断主管机关告知运营企业租约。

③ 运营企业出租人不应在租约期限内从事任何可能与被出租运营企业相竞争的活动,出租人和承租人可以在租约中约定降低这一非竞争义务。

④ 运营企业应当谨慎组织管理,企业存续相关文件应当妥善保存,防止承租人主张租约应当受适用于不动产租约的规定制约(适用有关有利于承租人的强制性规定)。

9. 可以取得不动产的投资形式和方式

意大利法律不限制意大利人或外国投资者在意大利直接取得不动产(前提是符合"房地产法律、法规简介"部分描述的"互惠"要求)。

尽管如此,大多数投资者选择不直接在意大利取得不动产,而是通过其他形式和方式取得此类资产。这一方法有多种好处,主要是限制责任,易于组织"有限追索权"融资,便于资金流动,易于设立合资企业、合作投资,有专业资产管理人参与,可能有成本和税费的优惠。

最常见的投资形式有:

① 设立一家特定目的公司(通常为有限责任公司,有时为股份有限公司)获得资产;

② 向不动产基金投资,然后取得不动产。

下面列举了对这些形式的简要描述:

(1)设立特定目的公司

设立特定目的公司是获取不动产资产最传统的形式,在很多方面来说,也是获取不动产资产最简单的形式。

通过设立特定目的公司持有资产主要具有如下好处:

① 投资者对资产享有完全的控制权(限于投资者持有公司主要注册资本和指定大部分董事的

情况）；

② 投资者最大的责任限于公司注册资本金额，以及股东贷款（限于公司是谨慎组织和管理的情况）；

③ 此类公司的设立简化了有限追索权融资的设置；

④ 通过对章程进行充分设计，并在必要时签署股东协议，此类公司可以被用作合资企业或合作投资的工具；

⑤ 资金可以简单地按照每一投资者在此类公司中持有的注册资本比例分配给多个投资者；

⑥ 公司收益一般比不动产资产直接收益更容易转出，可用于为任一融资主体提供担保。

通过设立特定目的公司投资的主要缺点有：

① 投资者需要设立一个管理机构（某些情形下还需要审计机构，以及承担有关开支）；

② 与直接通过投资不动产基金方式相比，税制较为不利。

（2）向不动产基金投资

作为设立不动产公司的替代选择，投资者可以选择向不动产基金投资，然后取得不动产资产。

根据意大利法律，不动产基金是由专业的（受规制的）资产管理公司为多名投资者的利益管理的资产。向不动产公司和向不动产基金投资的差异主要在于投资者的角色：基本上，投资者在不动产公司中扮演的是一个"积极的"角色，可以指挥公司及其资产（通过任命公司董事会）；投资者在不动产基金中扮演的是一个"消极的"角色，几乎所有关于基金的管理、资金的决定都由资产管理公司作出。投资者的角色仅限于某些具体（且非常有限）的范围，例如，前期投入基金的资金数量、初期商业计划、大体投资政策，以及投资公司发生利益冲突时的决定。

需注意，根据意大利法律，不动产基金必须有多个投资者——"多个"的含义必须根据个案确定，如果基金中的投资者属于特定类别（即国家或国家控制的企业、集体投资企业、保险公司），可以很容易满足"多个投资者"的条件。

除具备设立特定目的公司的常见优点外，投资不动产基金还有以下好处：资产管理委托给专业（且受规制的）资产管理公司进行。

通过不动产基金投资的主要缺点有：

① 投资者扮演着"消极的"投资者角色，因此其参与资产管理的程度受到极大的限制（请参见上述详细信息）；

② 资产管理公司的费用和开支由基金支付（最终由投资者承担）；

③ 基金必须有多个投资者。

（五）从事经营活动的业务方式

1. 政府参与

意大利经济属于市场经济。欧洲的政治、经济共同体决定了意大利外商投资在商业、工业中近乎完全自由化。政府还控制着某些行业，例如国防和提供重要公共服务的其他领域。

政府控制公司的典型方式是通过所谓的"黄金股权"的方式，即通过特定控制权实现，此种特定控制权不要求政府必须绝对控股。鉴于黄金股权参与方式在某些情况下违反了现行的欧盟条例，并且考虑到其他政策原因，意大利政府已经将大多数过去由国家控制的公司私有化。尽管如此，仍有许多公司由政府所有，特别是由地方政府所有，大多数存在于供水供电、运输等特殊领域。

2. 合资企业

在意大利设立合资企业的第一步，通常是签署一份合资协议，确定各方间合作的条款和条件。在设立合资企业前，需要进行反垄断评估。

合资企业可以通过设立特定目的公司的方式实现，也可以通过合资企业合资人简单地签署合作协议来规制他们间的商业关系。

在设立新的合资企业的情况下，未来股东在选择设立公司的类型和将要遵守的管理政策时需要考虑以下因素。

合资企业可以设立的企业类型没有限制,包括股份有限公司(Società di Capitali)和合伙企业(Società di Persone)。公司设立程序、开支、费用大多数取决于股东所选择的企业类型。

公司可以由外国人进行管理或代表,而没有任何限制。意大利法律仅要求董事在任职前必须取得社会保险号。这一原则的唯一限制(但不适用于欧盟投资者)是外国股东的国籍国应当使意大利国民享有同等权利。其后果是,如果外国董事的国籍国不允许意大利国民作为董事,则非欧盟的投资者无权担任意大利公司的董事。如果意大利与涉及此事的投资者的国籍国间存在协议,则这一对等要求不适用。

根据目前的欧盟商业实践(已在欧盟委员会2003年5月6日的建议中被认可),企业被分为大型、小型、中型(SMEs)及微型企业:

① 雇员:微型企业最多10名雇员,小型企业最多50名雇员,中型企业最多250名雇员;

② 收益:微型企业的收益最高不超过200万欧元,小型企业最高1 000万欧元,中型企业最高5 000万欧元;

③ 股权:不属于小型企业、中型企业的公司不得持有实益权益公司25%以上的股份。

3. 有限责任公司

在意大利,外国企业扩张时常常使用的公司类型有两种,分别为股份公司(S.p.A.)和有限责任公司(S.r.l.)。

(1)股份公司

股份公司是有大额投资的大中型企业最为常见的商业形式。股份公司的设立通过公证员起草的公共合同的方式生效。在公司设立后的20日内,必须将这一合同提交给商务部设立的公司注册处。股份公司的最低注册资本为12万欧元(注册资本的25%必须在公司设立时缴纳)。另外,在经公司章程允许或批准的情况下,股份公司可以发行股票、债券和其他债务或风险金融工具。

股份公司由股东指定的董事会或独立董事进行管理。股东还可以指定法定审计师委员会,对公司的管理、账目有监管权。监事会的所有成员必须是在特定注册处经登记的会计专家,或者是任命外部审计师。

股份公司章程可以规定股东指定的董事会,可以从审计师委员会成员中选出。必须由外部审计机构监督公司账目。

股份公司章程可以规定监事会由股东指定。监事会负责监督公司的管理。此外,由监事会指定负责管理公司事务的管理委员会(Consiglio di Gestione)。如果股东解散公司,应当指定一名外部审计师监督公司账目。

(2)有限责任公司

有限责任公司是最适合股东数量有限的中小型企业的商业形式。有限责任公司的最低注册资本为1万欧元(注册资本的25%应当在设立时缴纳,或者支付同等金额的保单或银行保函)。

股东可以指定公司董事,由董事会或独立董事按照章程管理公司。除非公司资本超过12万欧元,或者连续两年符合以下三项限制条件中的两项,否则不必设立法定审计师委员会:

① 总资产(根据最近一期财务报表)超过440万欧元;

② 销售利润超过880万欧元;

③ 上一财政年度的平均员工数量高于50名。

公司组织文件必须在签署之日起的20日内由公证员公证,并将这些文件提交给公司注册处。

总体而言,在意大利设立公司的成本(按照标准章程)主要是公证和法律费用。这些费用同样适用于设立分支机构。

设立股份公司和有限责任公司(以简单标准形式)的程序需要1~2周。

2011年,意大利法律简化了35岁以下自然人设立有限责任公司的程序。这种情况下,最低注册资本减少至1欧元。

股份公司和有限责任公司均可由一名或数名股东设立。上述适用于数名股东的公司程序和规定同样适用于一名股东。

如果是一名股东的,需要符合特定的披露要求,否则,这一股东将对公司的全部债务负责。

4. 合伙

在意大利，"公司"一词包括了所有营利性实体，例如，合伙型实体（Società di Persone）和股份公司（Società di Capitali）。

合伙型实体包括简单合伙企业、无限合伙企业和有限合伙企业。这些企业的特点是合伙人承担无限连带责任，但有限合伙企业是例外（参见"其他类型的企业"部分）。下面介绍了简单合伙企业和无限合伙企业两种合伙企业的主要特点。

（1）简单合伙企业

简单合伙企业是常用于非商业性活动的合伙企业（特别是农业活动），以股东承担无限连带责任为特征。

除非公司章程另有规定，简单合伙企业由每一股东分别管理。简单合伙企业的设立没有最低注册资本的要求，合伙人对其个人收益进行纳税。

（2）无限合伙企业

无限合伙企业是最常见的用于商业性活动的合伙型企业。在无限合伙企业中，所有的股东都对企业的对外债务承担连带责任。除非股东以特定资产作为出资（例如不动产或经注册的资产），设立此类企业不受特定形式的限制。设立无限合伙企业没有最低资本要求。

此类企业可以由一个或多个董事进行管理。除非按照特定手续要求向商会设立的公司注册处提交特定文件，他们的权力不受限制。

5. 其他类型的企业

在意大利，还可以设立另外两种类型的企业。这些企业从管理职能和责任制度方面对其合伙人进行划分。在一个有限合伙企业（Società in Accomandita）中，主要有两种类型的合伙人：①有限合伙人，由于不允许此类合伙人代表企业履行经营管理职能，此类合伙人只承担有限责任；②普通合伙人，负责管理企业，并对他们代表企业作出的任何行为承担全部的连带责任。

有限合伙人相当于出资人或财务合伙人，而普通合伙人被认为是管理合伙人。

合伙人在有限合伙企业中的参与形式可能是持有股份（即股份有限合伙企业），也有可能仅是被登记在公司的股东名册上（即有限合伙企业）。

6. 子公司、分支机构和代表处

外国公司在意大利设立的子公司适用关于国内实体的法律规定，也适用关于披露和控股公司责任制的特定要求（以防为了控股公司单独的利益而实施的经营行为）。总体而言，意大利公司法适用于在意大利注册的实体，或者公司总部（sede del amministrazione）或主要营业场所（oggetto principale）在意大利的实体。

按照意大利法律的规定，分支机构（它是建立子公司的替代选择）是没有独立法律地位的实体，是其外国母公司的一部分。因此，（外国公司的分支机构）必须符合适用于母公司的法律所规定的所有要求，还必须同时符合意大利法律对外国分支机构的要求。特别是某些母公司的文件必须在意大利备案（如现行的公司章程和批准设立分支机构的公司决议）。另外，分支机构应当向意大利公司注册处提交其在意大利代表公司的永久性代理人的相关信息，并且明确永久代理人的经营管理权或代表权。

在意大利，设立一个代表处十分容易（不需要任何公司组织或特定的注册程序），并且从会计的角度来看也很方便。但是，这样的代表处在重要的经营方面受到许多限制，比如，代表处可能无法从事产品营销；另外，代表处的常规活动仅限于收集信息、市场调研和推广外国企业的名称和品牌。

7. 信托及其他信托实体

1985年7月1日《关于信托的法律适用及其承认的公约》（以下简称《海牙公约》）于1989年10月16日根据意大利第364号法律被签署，并于1992年1月1日生效。由于没有涉及信托的国内立法，在意大利，只能按照《海牙公约》的规定设立信托，并且适用外国法律。由于缺乏国内立法，关于信托的判例法发展起来。在过去的几年里，意大利有70多个关于信托的判决。意大利议会根据2006年12月27日第296号法律批准了一整套针对信托的税收规定。

根据意大利《民法典》第2645条的规定，可以意大利法律制度认可的目的将个人所有的部分财产进行分割（以不动产和其他经登记的资产为代表），最长期限可达 90 年（或者受益人终身）。要达到此类目的，必须由转让方或第三方来完成，而除出让人指定的目的外，第三人不得就此类资产或此类资产所产生的收入主张权利。

在意大利，信托公司（fiduciary companies）是被认可的，前提是该信托公司根据 1995 年 1 月 16 日部长令的规定获得批准。这一法令规定了信托公司必须履行特定的资本和公司要求，以便在意大利进行经营活动。

（六）企业设立的要求

1. 外商投资

一般来说，外国在意大利的投资是不受限制的，例外是拥有和经营飞机或船舶必须由意大利或者欧盟的公民或公司进行控制和管理。但是，需要注意的是，任何收购特定公司（比如银行和保险公司）的大量股份的行为都必须获得主管部门的批准。

2. 反托拉斯法

基本的反垄断立法由 1990 年 10 月 10 日的《竞争法》（第 279/90 号法律）和 1998 年 4 月 30 日的第 217 号法令规定。《竞争法》规定了对国内市场竞争的保护，第 217 号法令则根据《竞争法》规定了调查程序。

意大利反垄断机构（Authorità Garante della Concorrenza e del Mercato）主要负责规制以下行为：
① 经营者集中；
② 防止、限制或者扭曲竞争的协议；
③ 滥用市场支配地位。

另外，意大利竞争与市场管理局是处理误导性、比较性广告和协调在意大利政府工作的官员间利益冲突的主管机构。

在意大利竞争与市场管理局向申请人通知决定的 60 天内，申请人可以对意大利竞争与市场管理局的决定向拉齐奥地区行政法院 (TAR Lazio) 提出异议。拉齐奥地区行政法院的判决可以被上诉至最高行政法院（Consiglio di Stato）。

如果该交易属于欧盟反垄断规定的范围，那么意大利的反垄断规则就不适用于该交易。

在意大利，违反竞争法的行为不受刑事处罚。

3. 政府批准

在意大利，企业经营活动不需要特定的政府批文，除非这类企业从事受监管的商业活动，比如媒体、电信、能源生产或分配（电力或者天然气），或者是银行、保险、投资和相关金融服务等行业。在这种情况下，政府部门会就从事此类活动颁发特定批文。

4. 执照、许可证

在某些特定活动中，执照和许可证可能是必须的，比如食品或保健产品的经销和生产。

（七）企业的运营

1. 广告

对于误导性和比较性的广告（后者仅在一定程度内被允许）有一般性的规定，对于与特定产品（比如烟草、处方药物和酒精）和专业服务（比如法律服务）有关的推广活动则没有特别的限制。此外，电视和无线电广告禁止侵犯个人尊严、宗教或信仰，引起种族、性别或国籍歧视，以及引导公众以危险的方式行事。大多数媒体都加入了一个广告行业自律监管体制，这个体制被称为广告自律协会，它的目的是确保广告诚实、真实和适当。

2. 商业道德和准则

一般来说，商业活动必须遵守意大利法律。此外，根据投资者所从事的活动，职业行为准则、特定的道德准则或专业组织及行业协会所采用的合同范本均可适用（比如为专业、金融或银行服务的特许经营网络），尽管这些条款通常不具有约束力。在会计方面，投资者必须遵守国家会计准则（或在某种情况下遵守国际会计准则）。某些活动（如银行、保险和金融活动）必须遵守独立监管机构发布的严格规定，且受到此监管机构的监督管理。

需要注意的是，根据 2001 年第 231 号法令的规定，在意大利经营的公司可能会因公司职员为公司利益实施的某些犯罪行为而受到行政裁（包括危害公共管理的犯罪、危害员工健康和安全的犯罪、滥用市场支配地位、单位犯罪等）。在这种情况下，公司可能受到罚金处罚或其他制裁，包括禁止开展经营活动、禁止在公共管理事务上进行投标。公司可以通过采取适当的内部控制模式来限制其在这方面的潜在风险，防止其职员犯罪。

3. 消费者保护法

近年来，为了执行与消费者权利有关的欧盟指令，意大利已经通过了若干规定（其中的某些条款已被纳入《消费者保护法》中）。保护消费者的专门条款主要是关于：①在营业场所以外协商达成的合同；②远程合同；③消费者与非消费者之间不公平的合同条款；④缺陷产品造成的损害。此外，为保障消费者，通常通过向消费者提供：①充分了解即将签署的交易条款的权利；②在合同履行后的特定时期内撤销合同的权利；③举证责任倒置制度。在某些情况下，某些"不公平"条款可以被认定为无效或无法执行。

4. 建筑

根据工程的特点和地点，（工程）需要从区域或地方行政机构获得特定的批准，例如建筑许可和特许。只要通知地方政府，且地方政府在一定期限内不禁止施工，内部工程通常不经任何批准就可以开工。受一般土地使用限制的地区内的建造活动或涉及历史或艺术性建筑的建造活动，可能会受到特定限制。

获得许可、特许和批准所需要的时间因工程的关联性和涉及的行政机关不同而有所不同。

5. 合同

根据到意大利投资的法规和意大利和投资国签署的国际投资双边或多边条约的规定，投资者可以在意大利自由地签订合同。这一原则的唯一限制是（不适用于欧盟投资者），投资者的国籍国应给予意大利国民对等的权利，因此，如果意大利国民不能在投资者国籍国订立合同，非欧盟投资者就无权根据意大利法律订立同样的合同。这样的限制并不经常适用（通常是被忽略），但违反这样的要求可能会引发纠纷。如果意大利和投资者的国籍国之间有管辖该事项的条约，则互惠要求不适用。

如果投资合同根据有关冲突规则适用外国法，则投资合同可能会适用外国法律，或者当事人合意选择的法律。然而，意大利的法律规定了一些强制性规定以增加确定性，这些强制性规定也适用于受外国法律管辖的合同。

6. 价格控制

一般来说，价格不受行政控制。然而，在某些经济领域，如公共服务（如交通、能源和天然气）或烟草零售，其价格由公共部门监管或指定。

7. 产品注册

除特定行业（例如制药和医疗器械），在意大利推广和销售产品不需要事前注册。然而，为了在市场上进行销售，产品必须符合所有国内和欧盟有关产品安全、成分、包装和消费者指示的规定。

8. 减少或返还资本

一般来说，资本流动没有限制，在特定（有限）情况下，需要与主管机构进行初步沟通。

9. 产品销售

为了向客户销售产品，在某些情况下（主要取决于商店的大小），产品销售企业必须从当地政府获得商业许可证。对于与公共安全有关的特定活动和服务、推广和销售必须符合《公共安全综合法案》（Consolidated Act on Public Safety）或其他规则（例如药店需要取得特定的许可证）的规定。此外，作为一般规则，营业场所必须遵守与所出售产品或提供服务有关的卫生和健康规定。

10. 行业协会

意大利有许多行业协会，但是加入此类协会通常不是强制性的。相反，个人提供某些专业服务（如律师、建筑师和医生）则要求必须要成为专业机构的成员。行业协会和专业机构通常都需要支付年费。（行业协会）常常会为成员制定强制性贸易做法，但是，如果这些做法涉及价格操纵或为成员制定商业战略，则可能会违反竞争规则。

（八）终止营业

1. 终止

企业（股份公司、股份有限公司、有限责任公司）可以自动终止其存续，或者在发生载于法律或公司章程中的特定事项时终止。终止程序分三个阶段执行：

① 初步阶段：导致终止的事件发生后，必须在股东（或法官，视情况而定）召开的特别会议上指定一名或多名管理人。公司董事必须向管理人交付公司的资产和账簿及最新的财务报表（记载着最后一次资产负债表批准之日到终止之日之间的财务数据）。

② 清算阶段：为清盘公司的业务，管理人可执行所有普通或特殊交易而向公司债权人清偿债务，并将剩余资产分配给股东。

③ 最终阶段：公司资产清算后，管理人起草最终资产负债表，所有债权人都获清偿后仍有剩余资产的，管理人则应制订分配计划。最后，管理人把资产分配给股东，并要求该公司在公司登记主管机关进行注销。

2. 资不抵债、破产

意大利有关破产的立法目前记载于1942年3月16日的第267号法令，分别于2005年、2006年及2007年进行修改和增补。在意大利，过去法院在破产程序中扮演着核心角色，而在庭外重组中却是很少见的。尽管存在一定的不确定性，但上述改革仍取得了进展，即通过在意大利破产实践中引入与债权人的和解制度及新融资协议，为困境中的债务人提供了解决暂时性财务困难的契机。

一方面，破产程序的主要目的在于清算债务人的资产，并以公平原则（par condicio）向债权人进行清偿。另一方面，这一特别行政程序的目的也在于企业重整以及维持就业，并通过以持续经营为目的的业务转让及确保雇员同所售业务一并转移来平衡前述目的。

根据意大利法律的规定，法院仅根据资不抵债就可以宣告公司破产。资不抵债是指债务人（比如公司）没有能力定期偿还其债务，且当其债务可能存在需长期应付而非临时清偿的情况。根据意大利破产法的规定，以下重组和破产程序是陷入财务困难的公司可用的替代措施。

（1）司法程序外的重整措施。在意大利，重整通常通过正式的司法程序进行，因为相较非司法程序而言，其对债务人更为有利，同时非司法重整中签订的非正式协议在后续的破产程序中容易被法院审查，并且可能被质疑为无效交易。但是，如果公司具备清偿能力，只是遇到财务困难的，则其可以通过与债权人签订庭外协议（concordato stragiudiziale）来保障公司的存续。

（2）法庭监督下的破产前债权人和解（concordato preventivo）。破产宣告前，任何处于危机（stato di crisi）下的公司都可以提议与债权人进行和解（concordato preventio），以避免宣告破产以及启动清算程序。破产前和解的申请应当向有管辖权的法院提出。只有处于危机中的公司（而非其债权人）才能申请破产前和解，并且该申请必须经过董事会批准。申请破产前和解必须基于和解方案。该方案可包括：① 任何手段的债务重组和贷款清偿，包括财产转让、债务继承（accollo）以及其他特别的交易，比如将股票、债券（包括可转债）或者其他融资借款票据发行给债权人、债权人成立或（全部或部分）所有的公司；② 向第三方转让债务人业务，包括债权人、由债权人成立或（全部或部分）所有的公司，或者在该方案实施期间新设的由债权人持股的公司；③ 将债权人根据法律地位及共同经济利益进行分类；④ 区别对待不同类别的债权人。除此之外，申请破产前和解还需附带一份由具有相关资质的专业人员草拟的报告。代表过半数债权且有投票资格的债权人同意，即为通过该和解方案。存在多种类别债权人时，每一表决组中代表过半数债权的债权人同意，即为和解方案通过。担保债权人不得参与和解方案的投票，放弃其担保利益的除外。和解程序未决时，债权人的所有诉讼及请求均被中止。

和解协议的执行阶段由债务人对公司进行管理，但应受到法院指定之人员的监视及法院的监督。和解程序失败的，法院会宣告公司破产，并进入破产程序（fallimento）。

（3）债务重整协议（accordi di ristrutturazione dei debiti）。债务人公司可以与代表至少全部债权60%的债权人达成重整协议，或者根据公司注册处的公告，需向法院报批重整协议。就破产前和解程序而言，申请必须由债务人董事会批准，且债权人无权在破产重整协议公布之日起60天内发起诉讼及请求。重整协议可包括债务的重新安排、债务的部分免除、转让财产给债权人、债转股和以容许重整及债务人企业存续为目的再融资。债权人并非都需要获得同等待遇，因为每一个债权人都有权评估债务人的提案并自主保护自身地位。债务重整协议必须附带一份经过对债务人能力进行特别评估后所作出的关于重整协议可行性的专家报告，其中需要特别注明，在债务人不实施重整计划时债务人定期（或者全部）清偿债权人的能力。依破产协议的约定，不存在剥夺管理权的情况，即债务人仍有权管理该企业。若重整协议没有被执行，参与协议的债权人根据意大利《民法典》有关合同的规定，将有权以不履行为由，终结破产协议。

（4）重整方案（piani di risanamento）。债务人资产上所为的行为、清偿以及担保或保证，如果是在执行重整方案（该方案须具有重整债务实现财务再平衡的可能性）时作出的，同时与意大利《民法典》第四部分第2501条之二精神相吻合的，则免于被追回。重整不受任何形式的司法控制，也不需要获得批准，因此不需要向法院或者其他监督机关提出申请。重整方案需要专家出具合理的证明文件，该专家必须是审计员或者是特殊登记注册过的审计公司，普遍认为，其应由公司指定而非法院指定。债权人并非都需要获得同等待遇，因为每一个债权人都有权评估债务人的提案并自主保护自身地位。重整方案不需要取得全部未受清偿的特定多数债权人的同意。依破产协议的约定，不存在剥夺管理权的情况，债务人仍有权管理该企业。法院或债权人不指定管理人，同时法院对此不进行日常监督。

（5）大型公司适用的特别行政管理程序（amministrazione straordinaria delle imprese in crisi）。在意大利法下，大型工商业企业可适用特殊行政管理程序。该程序的目的在于挽救一个陷于财务危机的公司（考虑其在科技、商业及生产价值方面的重要性）与维持就业。根据1999年7月8日的第270号法令的规定，为适用特别行政管理程序，企业应符合以下要求：① 程序开始前一年内拥有200名及以上的员工；② 债务至少相当于总资产的2/3及上一个财务年度源自销售和服务的总收益的2/3。该程序的效果有：① 以下修复计划，择其一：公司重整计划（最长持续2年）或者资产处置（最长持续1年）；② 中止债权人的诉讼及请求；③ 由1~3名政府指定的破产管理人（commissario straordinario）代替公司进行运营管理。法院必须根据破产管理人递交的报告对该计划的可实现性进行评估，之后也许会作出企业进入该行政程序的裁定，或者裁定司法清算。

新特别行政程序已经颁发（后续修订于2003年12月23日的第347号法令），适用于在程序开始前一年内拥有超过500名员工且有相当于至少3亿欧元（包括来自于未偿担保的债务）无力偿还之债的公司。当前的立法是对旧程序的优化，原因在于新法加快了批准满足上述条件的公司的特别行政程序的进程。但是，该程序的实质效果并没有改变，主要的差异在于"追回"条款也适用于由政府授权的重整计划。

鉴于意大利的股份公司所面临的财务困难，意大利政府在2008年8月28日通过的第134号法令修正案对347号法令作出修改（法令原颁布于2003年12月23日，修正后的法令根据2008年第166号法令上升为法律），该修正案旨在处理意大利的股份公司所面临的特定危机。2008年第134号法令所制定的若干改革，为从事公共基础服务的公司制定了具体的适用规则，并为适用2003年12月23日第347号法令的"巨型公司"提供了适用于以转让持续经营（cessione dei complessi agiendali）而非挽救公司为目的的特别行政程序的可能性。

（6）破产程序（fallimento）。商业实体届期没有能力清偿其到期债务的，被认定为资不抵债（《破产法》第5条）。公司、其债权人或公诉人有权申请宣告公司破产并开始公司清算的破产程序。宣告破产后：① 除个别情况外，债权人的所有诉讼及请求暂停，且只能在指定时期内提起诉讼及请求；② 债务人将公司治理及资产管理的权限转交给破产管理人；③ 宣告破产后公司所做的任何行为对其债权人而言都是无效的。由法院指定的破产管理人、副法官及债权人委员会对破产程序进行实施和监督。由作出破产宣告的法院控制整个程序，并且对所有因破产程序引起的或者有关破产程序的诉讼及请求具有专属管辖权。副法官有权管理程序的规范性,并向法院报告任何属于管辖权的事宜。破产管理人有权在副法官及债权人委员会的控制下管理债务人企业并且负责:① 根据债权人各自的优先权,制作债权人名单;② 评估债务人资产的数量及状况;③ 管理和清算资产;④ 终结和继续履行破产企业签订的合同;⑤ 提起对"暂停期"内所进行的交易撤销或宣告无效的诉讼及请求;⑥ 在被清算的资产允许的范围内,根据债权人各自的优先权对债权人进行清偿;⑦ 对破产公司的前董事及审计人员提起诉讼;⑧ 向公诉人告知其所意识到的任何刑事责任;⑨ 起草债务人财产的清算方案。债权人委员会由副法官在债权人中按照其所代表的不同组群与其债权的实际获偿可能性所指定的三3~5名债权人组成。债权人委员会监督破产管理人开展的事项并授权其履行重大行为。清算中所得的收益根据法定优先权进行分配。意大利破产法对包括雇员及意大利财政部在内的某些优先债权人授予优先获偿权。

像其他司法权一样,在意大利法律中,存在"追回"诉讼,其可能导致破产宣告前的付款或者给予的担保利益被撤销或宣告无效。在破产程序中,意大利法律还规定了长达1年的追回期。破产管理人有权申请对破产宣告前一年内债务人的某些交易无效。在集团的内部交易中,追回期可以被延长至5年。但不论何种情况,都应当注意的是:① 根据第267/1942号法令第64条的规定,在某些情况下,在破产宣告前的两年内公司与债权人之间缔结的无对价交易对债权人不发生效力;② 根据1942年第267号法令第65条的规定,在宣告破产的当天及之后到期的应收账款,如果是在破产宣告前的两年内发生的,被认为对债权人不发生效力。

(7)债权人破产后和解(concordato fallimentare)。公司向破产法院提出与债权人进行破产后和解的申请后,破产程序可以在管理人进行清算前终结。该提案可以规定:① 根据债权人之间类似的司法地位及经济利益,将其分成不同类别;② 区别对待不同类别的债权人,并证明区别对待的理由;③ 采用具体的技术或法律手段进行债务重整及对债权人的清偿,包括债务继承、合并或者公司的任何其他交易如将股份、配额(如"债转股")或债券(可转债或者其他金融票据及债务证券)转让给债权人或者债权人持有利益的公司;④ 担保债权人的部分清偿(条件是该部分还款不低于通过出售该担保资产所收回的金额,以独立专家所估计的价值为基准);⑤ 将债权人资产及由管理人为了实现该程序目的而提起的诉讼(包括"追回"和补偿诉讼)转让给第三方。经代表过半数有表决权的债权人同意,视为提案通过。存在多种类别债权人的,需每个类别中代表过半数有表决权的债权人均同意后,提案视为通过。破产后和解对所有破产程序开始前已存在的债权人(无论是基于财产权、事实还是其他理由)都有效,也包括没有申请参与该程序的债权人。

应当注意的是,2000年5月29日的第1346号欧盟理事会破产程序规则规定了处理欧盟内有关破产程序的法律冲突的规则,该规则特别规定了破产程序适用的法律以及在成员国领土开展的该破产程序的效力,该破产程序在其他所有成员国均被自动承认。

(九)兼并与收购

在过去几年,意大利并购市场稳步发展,主要是因为跨境交易,这表明意大利市场对外国(工业和金融)投资者有着很大的吸引力。公开并购领域也受到了这种发展的影响,每年都会发生几项重大的交易。对公开并购交易的复杂法律、法规的掌握,以及具备专业知识及经验的律师的意见,是此类交易能够更好地策划并且成功实施的基础。

1. 一般公司事项

适用于公开并购交易的主要法律、法规有:① 意大利《民法典》;② 1998年第58号法令;③《意大利公司和证券交易所监督委员会条例》(1999年第11971号);④ 企业治理法规(自愿适用)。

投资者应注意,在规划收购意大利上市公司的股份时,股东单独或与其他一致行动的股东持有的股份或投票权超过25%(如果有其他股东持有25%以上的股份或投票权,则超过30%)时意味着,对于这样的股东来说,有义务对所有剩余股份发起收购要约。这种义务的存在导致了"强制性收购"和"自愿收购"之间的区别。

此外,一方面,如果一方持有意大利上市公司90%以上的股份,则应根据该公司的任何一个持有人的要求购买其剩余股份,除非在90天内恢复足够保证正常交易业绩的交易流通量。另一方面,如果由于全球收购要约,要约人持有意大利上市公司超过95%的股份,则要约人除了有义务根据该公司任一持有人的要求购买剩余的股份外，还有权在要约期之后3个月内（即所谓的"强制排除权"）购买剩余的股份。

上市公司的收购可以通过公开收购要约、合并、场外收购或认购库存股来进行。

应当指出的是，当投资者选择公开收购要约方式时，他们必须制作用以公示的要约通知，并在上述通知发布后20天内向意大利公司和证券交易所监管委员会提交要约文件（意大利法律规定了上述文件的详细内容）。意大利公司和证券交易所监管委员会必须在收到文件后的15天内批准要约文件，而要约期限最少为15个交易日，在强制性收购时最多为25个交易日，自愿收购时最多为40个交易日。在为促进要约收购所需满足的要求中，投标人应当确保履行与要约相关的付款承诺的能力，并向意大利公司和证券交易所监管委员会提供有利于此目的的担保证据。

根据意大利法律的规定，目标上市公司没有义务为潜在投标人提供相关的尽职调查信息。尽管如此，市场惯例是上市公司为潜在的友好投标人提供机密资料，但前提是这些投标人签署保密协议并从全体股东的利益出发对并购的发起进行评估。但需注意，投标人可以获取意大利上市公司的多个数据，因为根据意大利法律的规定，这些实体必须向公众提供有关其本公司及其子公司的一系列信息，包括敏感价格信息。

2. 收购竞投之出价

关于意大利的收购出价，应当指出的是，虽然可以自由设定自愿并购的对价，但强制收购的对价不得低于投标人在通知本次要约前12个月内作出的最高报价。如果在此期间没有作出过对价交易，则要约对价不得低于过去12个月或者更短的可参考期间的平均加权市场价格。

需注意的是，如果投标人以发出要约的意向通知和要约期结束后6个月之间的更高对价收购股份的，那么自愿或者强制收购的出价应当随之增加。

3. 反收购防御

当投资者计划发起收购要约时，他们应适当考虑反收购防御措施，其可能会以不同的方式破坏投资人收购要约的成功实施。意大利公司和证券交易所监管委员会明确了三种不同的防御措施：① 旨在提高收购对价的总价值的行为；② 旨在对目标公司的经济状况造成重大影响的行为；③ 旨在阻碍投标人活动的任何其他行为。

需注意的是，一般而言，作为被收购对象的公司应避免采取防御性措施（所谓的"被动规则"），除非在要约期间得到普通或特别股东大会的批准。意大利上市公司有权通过修改其公司章程的方式放弃全部或部分被动性规则。

针对防御性措施的最佳方法是阐明要约收购的好处，从而防止股东大会批准由董事会提请的反收购防御提案（意大利上市公司的组织形式不鼓励敌意收购，因为控股股东通常持有大部分股份，因此，在意大利，成功的敌意收购仅有少数几例）。如果所采取的防御措施不符合法律规定的要求，则投标人有权向法院或意大利公司和证券交易所监管委员会提出异议。

4. 保护友好交易免受恶意干涉者的侵害

意大利法律没有为投标人提供任何针对敌意收购的保护措施，因为法律的目的是保护股东的利益。然而，为了巩固自己的地位，投标人可以与前控股股东签订协议，约定前控股股东接受反要约时需交违约金，以控制其接受其他收购要约，或者与目标公司股东签订协议来避免竞争性报价的成功，但须遵守公示要求。

5. 反垄断和其他监管问题

根据意大利法律的规定，达到以下累积营业额门槛条件的，需要向意大利竞争管理局（ICA）申报：① 所有相关经营者上个财政年度在意大利的营业额合计超过4.92亿欧元的；② 目标公司上个财政年度在意大利的营业额超过4 900万欧元的。对于银行和金融机构来说，营业额必须等于排除备查账户后的总资产的1/10。对于保险公司而言，营业额必须等于所收取保险费的价值。

相关经营者必须在其就交易的主要方面达成协议后且在经营者集中实施前进行申报。需注意，申报本身不必然导致交易的暂停，但是如果出现竞争隐患，意大利竞争和市场管理局可以发出指令，要求其放弃欲收购的全部或部分企业。

拒绝申报的可能导致产生高达公司营业额1%的罚款；通常情况下，如果经营者集中对当地的竞争没有重大影响，意大利竞争和市场管理局会对其处以低额罚款（例如5 000欧元）。

关于反垄断审查的时间，应注意的是，合并规制程序的第一阶段自申报起需30日（对于同样向大利公司和证券交易所监管委员会提请的公开招标需15天）。对于保险公司，上述30日的审核期间会被暂停，以便有关监管机构提出意见，有关监管机构必须在收到申请后的30天内给出意见。在开展深入调查的情况下，有关监管机构必须在调查开始后的45日内作出决定。

除上述情况外，还应注意的是，收购银行、保险、基金等企业的大量股份时，须经主管部门批准。意大利政府有权对在国防和国家安全、能源、交通和通信领域经营的企业行使"黄金股权"，包括否决股权收购、战略决策和对收购提出具体条件。互惠原则适用于非欧盟国家。

6. 税务问题

在意大利，对于并购交易没有特别的税收规定，适用第917/86号法令规定的关于资本利得税的规定。值得注意的是，并购交易的税务后果会因交易结构的差异而有很大的不同，并且通常取决于几个因素。

无论并购交易所涉及的当事方的居住地或合同执行地在哪里，转移意大利本国公司发行的股份所有权的，均需缴纳金融交易税（FTT）。应税基数是已付对价。标准税率为0.2%，在受监管市场中或在欧盟成员国或白名单所列欧洲经济区国家所建立的多边贸易机构中执行的交易，则税率则下调至0.1%。由受让方支付金融交易税。

支付给非意大利居民股东的股息，原则上须按照等同于普通税率的26%缴纳预扣税。

非意大利本国投资者是否征收资本利得税取决于若干因素，其中包括参股比例。

（十）竞争管制

1. 竞争监管部门

意大利竞争和市场管理局是反不正当竞争和反垄断的监管部门，主要负责监管：
① 经营者集中；
② 排除、限制或扭曲竞争的协议；
③ 滥用支配地位。

在意大利竞争和市场管理局向申请人通知决定的60天内，申请人可以向拉齐奥地区行政法院（TAR Lazio）提出异议。拉齐奥地区行政法院的判决可以被上诉至最高行政法院（Consiglio di Stato）。

2. 竞争法规简介

反竞争的基本立法载于1990年10月10日的《竞争法》（第287/90号法令）和1998年4月30日的第217号法令，《竞争法》规定了对国内市场竞争的保护，第217号法令则根据《竞争法》规定了调查程序。

交易属于欧盟反垄断条款范围的，则不适用意大利反垄断法规。在意大利，违反竞争的行为不受刑事处罚。

3. 竞争的监管措施

（1）经营者集中

合资协议与通过合同等手段购买股份或资产来直接或间接地实现公司并购与控制的行为，可能会受到意大利竞争和市场管理局的前置审查，如果其认定该拟议的交易对竞争进行了非法限制，则可以禁止此类交易的进行。

涉及具体经济部门的经营者集中可能需要提交多份申请给不同部门，其中每个部门都会就交易的不同方面进行分析和评估。这些部门包括银行、金融部门，电信、广播电视部门，保险部门和能源部门。

意大利关于经营者集中的规定大量借鉴了欧洲的并购立法及实践。"一站式"原则（即经营者总营业利润超出一定标准时由欧盟行使排他性审查权）适用于此。根据欧盟2004年第139号条例的规定，意大利竞争和市场管理局原则上遵循欧盟委员会关于经营者集中的通知中所确定的准则。

满足以下标准之一的，经营者需事先向意大利竞争和市场管理局申报：

① 所有相关公司在意大利的营业额合计（比如买方和目标公司在意大利的营业额）超过4.61亿欧元的；

② 目标公司或拟被收购的企业的国内营业额超过4 600万欧元的（意大利反垄断机构每年会更新门槛）。

"营业额"一词是指相关公司与其各自的组织于上一财政年度在意大利的销售额。

相关经营者可能要求意大利竞争和市场管理局主动提供非正式指导。在预先申报阶段，相关经营者可以提交一份有关交易的书面说明，以供与竞争和市场管理局官员讨论用。

签订合并或购买协议后立即填写表格，即可完成申报。申报费按照该交易在意大利境内部分价值的1.2%缴纳，最低金额为3 000欧元，最高金额为60 000欧元。在收到表格后的30天内，如果意大利竞争和市场管理局认为拟议的交易可能在意大利市场建立或加强其支配地位并持续严重地排除或限制竞争的，则可以对其进行深入调查。在这种情况下，主管部门必须在调查开始之日起的45天内作出决定。如果意大利竞争和市场管理局认定交易不会引起竞争问题，则必须在收到表格后的30天内将批准通知给各方。

与欧盟在交易完成前必须获得反垄断批准不同，在意大利，收购或合并可以在反垄断机构作出决定前进行。但是，意大利反垄断机构在启动调查时可以指示双方在其作出最终决定前暂停交易的实施。

意大利反垄断机构对经营者集中可以作出批准与禁止的决定。此外，相关经营者对其造成的竞争扭曲作出结构性承诺或行为承诺的，意大利反垄断机构也可以据此批准经营者集中。

在经营者未申报的情况下，意大利竞争和市场管理局可以对负申报义务的经营者处以其年度全球营业额的1%的罚款；其还可以对构成违反有效竞争的经营者集中的企业，处以其年度全球营业额的1%～10%的罚款，并要求其消除因未遵守程序制度对有效竞争所造成的扭曲影响。

（2）排除、限制或扭曲竞争的协议

与《欧共体条约》第81条相似，《竞争法》第2条禁止企业间签订明显以排除、限制或扭曲在国内市场或其主要部分的竞争为目的或效果的协议。这项禁止规定适用于例如价格操纵或分割市场的企业联合的协议。

意大利竞争和市场管理局可以主动开展调查，或者根据企业、公共政策机构或个人的投诉进行调查。

被调查的公司可以在调查程序开始后的3个月内提交承诺书。如果意大利竞争和市场管理局接受该承诺书，承诺书的内容将具有强制性，同时调查程序将被终结，并不宣告其违法。不履行承诺的，意大利竞争和市场管理局可以对其处以其营业额的10%的行政罚款。

自2007年2月以来，从宽方案已落实。第一个自愿提交有关违法事实存在的信息或证据的公司将不会受到任何罚款。如果所提交的证据，依其详细程度，显著强化了意大利竞争和市场管理局所掌握的证据，则可以减少不超过50%的罚款。

（3）滥用支配地位

禁止在国内市场或其主要部分处于支配地位的一个或多个企业滥用其地位，包括实行不公平的购销价格或其他不公平的交易条件，以及实施限制生产、市场或投资、技术开发等行为。被调查的公司可以在调查程序开始后的3个月内提交承诺书。如果意大利竞争和市场管理局接受该承诺书，承诺书的内容将具有强制性，同时调查程序将被终结，并宣告其不违法。不履行承诺的，意大利竞争和市场管理局可以对其处以其营业额的10%的行政罚款。

（十一）征税

1. 税收机制及规则

税制建立在直接税和间接税的基础上。意大利税收体制适用于境内的每一个个人和企业，这意味着意大利同时对国内收入和国外收入征收所得税，其中应纳税额扣除了在国外已支付的部分。意大利的外国非居民个人只针对其在意大利获得的收入纳税。

2. 税收的主要类别和税率

税收主要有三种：

（1）对企业征税

意大利企业所得税（IRES）从 2004 年 1 月 1 日开始全面改革，随后进一步修改。普通公司税率为 27.5%。从 2011 年纳税年度开始，在上一个财政年度中，收入超过 1 000 万欧元的公司，应纳税所得额高于 100 万欧元的公司，以及在能源生产和供应领域进行某些类型活动的公司，税率为 38%。从 2011 年纳税年度开始，"非经营实体"享受 38% 的企业税率。

公司还需要缴纳关于生产活动的地区税（IRAP），其征收对象是意大利每个行政区的净产值，标准税率为 3.9%。地方当局可以增加或减少该标准税率。提交纳税申报表及支付意大利地区生产税应当遵循适用于企业所得税的规定。意大利地区生产税纳税申报表与企业所得税纳税申报表应分开提交。

注册税是对应主动到公共登记机构进行登记的契据或合同所征收的税。税率根据契据或合同性质的不同而有所不同，为 0.5% 至 8%（出售农地的税率为 15%）。一般来说，如果交易需缴纳增值税（IVA），注册税则为 168 欧元的固定税费。在意大利拥有房地产的公司需要统一市政税（IMU）。目前标准税率为 0.76%，税率可根据不同的市政当局和具体的房地产增加或减少。

增值税适用于意大利境内应纳税人提供的货物和服务以及进口货物。公司一直被视为应纳税人，一般税率自 2011 年 9 月 17 日后为 21%，优惠税率为 4%~10% 不等。

（2）对个人征税

个人需缴纳个人所得税（IRPEF），其为累进税，适用于纳税人的累计应税收入。

以下税率适用于应税收入和资本收益：

应税收入（欧元）	税率（%）
15 000 欧元及以下	23
15 000~28 000 欧元	27
28 000~55 000 欧元	38
55 000~75 000 欧元	41
超过 75 000 欧元	43

2011 年 1 月 1 日至 2013 年 12 月 31 日，收入超过 300 000 欧元的个人需支付 3% 的附加费。上述费率因地区不同而有所不同，范围在 0.9% 至 1.4% 之间。由各省、市确定的省、市级附加税可进一步提高税率，但上述税率合计最高为 0.8%。

（3）对其他法律实体征税

意大利的非商业实体（即不以开展商业活动为唯一或主要目的的公司及公私主体）应缴纳企业所得税，税率为 27.5%。

非商业实体即使专门从事非商业活动，也必须缴纳意大利地区生产税。生产税的税率为 3.9%，生产税的税基基于以下方式计算：①非商业实体向雇员及其他应缴纳所得税的人员所支付的报酬；②非商业实体向非经常性提供服务的自主就业人员支付的报酬（仅部分人员的费用可扣除）。

某种程度上，只有在进行持续性商业活动的情况下，非商业实体才是增值税纳税人。增值税申请、备案、支付和税率的相关规则，适用于公司的规则。

3. 纳税申报与优惠

由于税收的复杂性和税收种类的繁多，企业应向特定的会计师事务所进行咨询。一般来说，增值税应在交易完成后的 3 个月内申报。商业实体进行所得税申报的，应在最后一个应纳税月后的 9 个月内提交税务文件。

（十二）证券

1. 与证券相关的法律、法规简介

关于证券交易，在意大利注册的外国公司享受与本地公司相同的待遇。规范证券的主要法律、法规有《金融法》《金融中介机构监督条例》《从事投资或资产管理服务的金融中介机构的组织结构和议定书》《中介机构管理办法》和《统一银行法》。

2. 证券市场的监督和管理

金融业主要由意大利证券监督委员会和意大利中央银行监督管理。意大利证券监督管理委员会主要负责审查金融业务人员行为的透明度和正确性，维护证券市场的声誉和公平竞争，保护投资者利益，保证证券市场符合有关法律、法规的要求，并制裁非法行为。意大利中央银行负责维持货币和金融的稳定性。

3. 外国企业证券交易参与要求

根据《金融中介机构监督条例》的规定，地方金融机构必须向意大利公司和证券交易所监管委员会提交从事投资服务的申请。意大利1993年9月1日的第385号法令和1999年4月21日的第229号意大利中央银行条例对外资银行进入意大利市场的准入要求有明确规定。

三、贸易

（一）贸易监督部门

在意大利，经济发展部是贸易监管部门，在经济发展部下设部长办公厅、7个业务司和1个局：① 部长办公厅（协调内部关系、新闻发布、国际发展等）；② 合作团体管理司，内务服务司，贸易、保险业和服务业管理司，企业促进司，市场协调和消费者保护司，能源及矿产资源管理司，生产力发展和竞争力司；③ 经济发展政策协调局（国家层面的协调与规划）。

（二）贸易法律、法规简介

除了国内关于进出口产品的技术安全和检测的法规是从欧盟指引转变而来的，作为欧盟成员国，意大利还实施统一的欧盟共同贸易政策。

（三）贸易管理

意大利的贸易管理主要集中在国家间进出口贸易，适用海关管理规定与欧盟共同贸易政策。

（四）出口与进口

出口。一般而言，意大利对出口没有具体限制。然而，欧盟条例和意大利法律也对某些商品的出口作出了具体限制，例如武器和军民两用货物、医药产品、国家珍宝和艺术品。

进口。欧盟成员国有固定的共同体海关税则及常规税率，但根据协会协议、自由贸易协定或一般关税优惠制度，也实行优惠税率。适用于货物的各种措施都载于海关税则在线数据库（也称为"TARIC"），数据库整合了与关税、商业和农业立法有关的所有措施。海关税则在线数据库包括复合关税暂停征收、关税配额、关税优惠和贸易防卫措施（反倾销、反补贴、保障措施）等规定。一般而言，进口壁垒仅限于出于政治和环境卫生的理由。

（五）海关管理

自1950年开始，意大利成为《关税和贸易总协定》（GATT）的签署国，并于世界贸易组织成立起（1995年1月1日）就是其成员国。

意大利也是欧洲联盟的创始国成员。欧盟的基础是关税联盟，这需要：

① 取消欧盟成员国间进出口的所有关税和其他限制（货物可以从一个欧盟成员国转移到另一个国家，而不需要完成海关手续）；
② 对从欧盟以外进口的货物实行共同关税；
③ 共同的商业政策。

1992年10月12日的欧洲经济共同体第（EEC）2913/92号条例及其修订案（《欧洲共同体海关法》）、1993年7月2日的欧洲经济共同体第（EEC）2454/93号条例及其修订案（《欧洲共同体海关法实施条例》）和1987年7月23日的欧洲委员会第（EC）2658/87号条例及其修订案（《欧洲共同体关税税则》）是构成欧盟成员国海关管理立法框架的主要文件，直接适用于所有欧盟成员国，并优先于成员国的国内法。

但是，《欧洲共同体海关法》由成员国的国家机构施行。

《欧洲共同体海关法实施条例》规定了实施《欧洲共同体海关法》所需的详细条款。在国家层面，执行措施载于1973年1月23日的第43号法令批准的有关关税的统一规定中。

根据《欧洲共同体关税税则》的规定，货物按联合命名法（CN）进行分类，该方法是一个以世界海关组织的统一制度（HS）为基础并辅以欧盟进一步细化的货物分类系统。

通过共同商业政策，欧盟拥有与第三国谈判关税和贸易协定的专有权限，授予单边优惠，并采取贸易保护措施，如反倾销措施、反补贴措施和保障措施等。欧盟还可以根据《贸易壁垒规则》发起调查，并启动世界贸易组织争端解决程序。

2001年1月1日，意大利立法机关成立了一个海关机构，以加强对贸易的动态管理。该机构是一个具有司法权力和广泛行政自由裁量权和自主权的政府机构。希望从意大利进口或出口产品的经营商可以向海关机构申请出具关税信息或原产地信息。

欧盟成员国的领土共同组成了欧盟的关税领土。但利维尼奥和坎皮奥内，以及卢加诺湖的国家水域被排除在欧盟关税领土之外（虽然在意大利境内）。

四、劳动

（一）劳动法律、法规简介

依据意大利劳动法的规定，雇佣劳动关系受成文法、国家集体协议、公司补充协议、个人劳动合同及劳动规章等规制。

1. 成文法

意大利《民法典》载有关于雇员职责、忠诚义务、保密义务、纪律制裁、社会保障、终止雇佣关系和赔偿（遣散费）、雇佣关系存续期间和结束之后的竞业禁止条款以及企业转让时雇员的权利等条款。除此之外，其他特别法也有关于解雇、社会保障及雇佣关系等内容的规定。

2. 国家集体协议

国家集体协议是由工会和雇主协会在国家层面上签订的协议，每隔一段时间会进行一次协商（通常每四年进行一次，不过工资条款须每两年更新一次）。每个产业或行业都有特定的国家集体协议，适用于在特定产业或行业中受雇的个人。此外，管理岗位与非管理岗位适用不同的协议。雇主可以自由选择所适用的国家集体协议，但实践中通常都会选择涉及公司所属产业或行业的合同。

国家集体协议的内容包括工资、工作职责、工龄计算、工龄津贴、工作时间、假期、病假、育儿假、申诉程序、调动、借调、终止雇佣关系（通知期限、理由、解雇方式）、养老金计划、社会保障、仲裁、工会代表和其他事项等。

国家集体协议的规定一般比法律规定更有利于雇员，或者说，这些合同规定了适用一般法定规则的具体细则（如纪律处罚和申诉程序）。这些条款不具有法律地位，但在实践中普遍适用，因此认为对所有雇主都具有约束力（此外，在诉讼中，此类协议通常由劳动法院适用）。

因此，当需要确定某种特定的雇佣关系适用哪些规则时，须同时考虑成文法和国家集体协议。

3. 公司层级的集体协议

国家集体协议可以由公司层级的集体协议来进行补充。这些补充协议旨在补充国家集体协议中只进行了部分规定或没有规定之处，例如工作条件和附加利益等。

4. 个人劳动合同

除了国家集体协议和公司层级的集体协议（如有），劳动关系还受个人劳动合同的约束。个人劳动合同规定了雇员的工资，有时可能依据雇员个人的能力和表现而制定高于国家集体合同规定的最低标准的额外补偿。

由于法律、法规和国家集体协议对劳动关系进行了详细的规定，个人劳动合同的自由性会受到限制，往往只需要变更基础的工资条款。

需注意，个人劳动合同不得违反法律和国家集体协议的规定，而且不得不利于雇员。

5. 劳动规章

意大利《宪法》第36条赋予了雇员获得报酬的权利，员工工资应当与其从事的工作的数量和质量相当，无论如何应足够保证他（她）的家人过上有尊严/小康的生活。

工资的充足水平（即最低工资）由适用的国家集体协议决定。个人劳动合同不能将此类工资降低至上述集体协议规定的最低水平以下。

管理岗位雇员不适用于限制工时的规章。

法定年假期限由法律规定。但是，国家集体协议可能会提供更有利的条件，雇员有权享受至少4周的带薪假期，至少12个法定假期/法定假日。个人劳动合同不得减损假期待遇。

生病时，雇员有权在其所适用的国家集体协议规定的期限内保留自己的职位。休假期间，雇员有权获得全部或部分工资。相关花费主要由社会保障体系支付。

管理岗雇员在休病假期间有权保留自己的职位，并得到全部12个月的工资。由其所在的公司支付此薪水和相关的社会保障费用。

意大利公司雇用雇员时不应对国籍有具体限制。国籍限制将被视为歧视，并且是非法的。

（二）雇用外籍雇员的要求

1. 工作签证

将要在意大利工作或者希望在意大利工作的非欧盟成员国的国民，无论是临时工作还是永久工作，都应当在进入意大利之前获得工作签证。通常，要取得意大利每年的移居签证"配额"后，才可以申请工作签证。

意大利《移民法》还规定了一项特殊工作签证，只能向某些类别的雇员发放。与上述工作签证相反，这类签证不受任何配额限制，但仍有一些特殊要求，即雇员必须是就职于总部或分支机构位于意大利境内的企业，处于管理层和或具有高度专业性的岗位，且在国内至少有6个月的相关资历，或者是大学教授或讲师、专业翻译或口译员、艺术家或音乐家、公立或私立医院的专业护士等。

2. 申请程序

非欧盟国家的国民申请工作签证及工作许可须经以下程序：

① 意大利企业必须向当地移民局（即雇用外籍雇员的企业所在地区的办事处）申请工作许可；
② 一旦获得工作许可，雇员将在意大利驻该国的领事馆申请工作签证，以进入意大利；
③ 雇员（及家属）在抵达意大利后的8天内，应向其在意大利境内居住地的移民局申请居留许可。

整个申请程序约在2～3个月内完成。

3. 社会保险

工作场所的健康和安全保障主要由第626/94号法令及其修订案规定。根据该法令的规定，雇员有权享受企业设置的安全保障制度，比如委派一名代表参加企业组织的安全培训课程，其他义务必须由雇主履行（即起草风险评估文件和委任一名合格的医师）。如果违背了工作场所的健康和安全保障义务，雇主须承担民事和刑事责任。

(三) 出入境

1. 签证种类

签证主要分为以下三种：

(1) 统一申根签证 (USV)：适用于所有申根国家，这种签证可能是：

① 机场过境签证 (A类)；

② 过境签证 (B类)；

③ 短期或旅行签证 (C类)，有效期最长为90天，适用于单人或多人入境。

(2) 有限地区签证 (LTV)：此类签证仅适用于签发签证的申根国家（或其他申请签证时特别注明的申根国家），但无法进入或通过任何其他申根国家。

(3) 长期居留或"国家签证" (NV)：此类签证仅适用于访问签发签证的申根国家超过90天 (D类) 时，可以一次或多次进入该国，以及需要从其他申根国家经过不超过5天时。

入境签证类型：2000年7月12日的《部门间法令》规定了21种（20种仍有效）入境签证，以及发放这些签证的要求。20种入境签证为：领养、商务、医疗、外交、随行受养人、体育竞赛、邀请、准许在签证国就业的受养人、不准许在签证国就业的受养人、代表团、宗教理由、再入境、住所选择、家庭团聚、学习、机场过境、过境、交通、旅游、工作假期、求职（已废除）等。

2. 出入境限制

意大利在逐渐适应《关于执行申根协定的协定》规定的一般签证制度后，于1997年10月26日加入了申根体系。在加强共同外部边界管制的同时，内部边界管制被逐步取消，为申根协议签署国提供了充分的人口流动自由。最终申根区得以成立。

外国人只能通过以下途径从申根区外部边界进入意大利领土：

① 由边境口岸入境；

② 持有允许过境的有效护照或同等认可的旅行证件；

③ 持有可证明其入境目的及停留条件的文件，证明其拥有足够的资金以确保在意大利停留期间的花费及回国（或前往第三国）的旅费；

④ 如果需要，持有有效的入境或过境签证；

⑤ 申根信息系统中无禁止入境的警告；

⑥ 不被意大利法律或其他申根国法律认为威胁到意大利或其他申根国的公共政策、国家安全或国际关系。

不满足上述任一项条件，外国人都可能会被拒绝入境，无论其是否持有有效入境或过境签证。

(四) 工会及劳动组织

意大利有许多工会，入会没有门槛或其他强制要求。相反，行业协会要求会员必须是提供某类专业服务的人（例如律师、建筑师和医生）。工会和行业协会一般都会要求交年费。行业协会会为成员规制强制性交易惯例，但如果这些惯例涉及固定价格或共谋经营策略，则可能触犯《竞争法》。

根据意大利《劳动者条例》第14条的规定，雇员有权成立工会委员会，并有权加入工会和在企业内开展工会活动（即集会和组织工会的权利）。

根据《劳动者条例》第15条、第16条的规定，禁止在行使工会权利和参与工会活动方面歧视雇员。此外，根据该法第19条的规定，如果公司雇用的雇员超过15人，则雇员有权要求选举工会代表。

在意大利，工会是合法的，并获得政府的承认。最具代表性的工会有：

1. 雇员组织

① 意大利总工会 (Confederazione Generale Italiana del Lavoro)；

② 意大利工会联合会 (Confederazione Sindacati Lavoratori Italian)；

③ 意大利劳动联盟 (Unione Italiana del Lavoro)；

④ 劳工总会 (Unione Generale del Lavoro)。

2. 雇主组织

① 意大利工业联合会；
② 意大利商业联合会。
还有其他的独立小型工会，代表特殊雇佣关系雇员的利益。

（五）劳动争议

意大利各省都有自己的劳动部门负责协调和处理劳动争议。此外，意大利宪兵队还有一个"劳动保护宪兵队"，负责保护劳工的权利。

（六）2014 年第 183 号法令

2014 年第 183 号法案也被称为《就业法案》，对劳资关系进行了深度改革。随着上述劳动法改革进入生效期，在 2015 年不到 9 个月的时间里，意大利议会批准了八项执行法令，对意大利就业法律框架作出重大调整。

1. 全新的解雇规则

2015 年 2 月的第 23 号法令对《劳动者条例》第 18 条（关于不公平解雇的救济）进行了实质性修改，自 2015 年 3 月 7 日起生效。

2015 年第 23 号法令引入了"按工龄支付补偿合同"，使雇主可灵活地终止与雇员的雇佣关系（适用于 2015 年 3 月 7 日之后新聘用的雇员）。新规定取消了此前公司在不公平解雇其雇员时所负的恢复其职位的义务，但因为歧视而解雇雇员或口头解雇雇员的情况除外。只有出现法律明确规定的情况（如结婚或怀孕）或者没有相关事实表明构成惩戒性解雇理由的情况下，才能适用恢复原职的规定。

因此，新规定取消了此前恢复原职的义务（上述列举的极个别情况除外），取而代之的是根据雇员的在职时间支付辞退补偿金。从公司角度看，在一套更简单的规章制度背景下，公司更容易计算每个雇员的"裁员成本"。

尤其是在不公平解雇的情况下，雇主向雇员支付补偿金的标准为每一年工龄对应两个月的工资（补偿金数额最低为 4 个月工资，最高不得超过 24 个月工资）。雇佣合同应自解雇之日起失效，雇员无须就补偿金缴纳社会保险。如果仅是因为违反形式规定（如违反惩戒性程序）而导致解雇的不公平性，补偿金可相应降低（金额为 2～12 个月的工资）。

此外，还特别引入了有关"小型雇主"（即单个业务部门的雇员数量不超过 15 人、在意大利的全部雇员数量不超过 60 人的公司）的规定。如果是没有任何理由的不公平解雇，法律不再要求小型雇主恢复雇员原职，而是根据工龄支付赔偿金，按照每一年对应 1 个月的工资计算（最少 2 个月，最多 6 个月）。

为了鼓励采取和解方式解决争议，新法案还规定，雇主可以在雇员被解雇后的 60 天内向被解雇的雇员提供一张支票，根据工龄支付补偿金，按照每一年对应 1 个月的工资计算（最少 2 个月，最多 18 个月），该补偿金免缴社会保障金和税款。

需注意，关于不公平解雇补救措施的新规则适用于从 2015 年 3 月 7 日起被雇用的雇员，以及雇主本应在此日期之前招聘，实际上却在此之后才开始聘用的雇员，且在一个公司内聘用超过 15 名雇员或在意大利聘用超过 60 名雇员的情形。

新规则也适用于集体解雇的情况（仅限于 2015 年 3 月 7 日之后雇用的雇员），即在 120 天内解雇 5 人及以上。

在这种情况下，如果解雇没有以书面形式进行，则雇员有权要求复职；不遵守其他程序要求或违背了"选择标准"（法律规定集体解雇时可以家庭负担、工作年限以及组织、技术和生产原因确定被解雇的雇员），将导致雇主就其错误向被解雇的雇员支付赔偿金。

2."社会减震器"

2015 年 5 月的第 22 号法令出台了有关"社会减震器"的新规定（即雇主因经济财务状况比较困难，

造成雇员工作时间或者薪酬下降时，由公共机构向雇员支付报酬）。

这项新的失业福利制度被称为"纳斯皮"，最长可救济 24 个月。因享受该制度的人数比以前有所增加，因而救济额有略微的下调。

2015 年第 22 号法令规定了享受"纳斯皮"福利待遇需要满足的申请条件：
① 非自愿失业（即因辞职而终止雇佣关系的雇员不享有福利制度，除非辞职具有正当理由，在哺乳期辞职，因雇员拒绝转移到距离其居住地超过 50 公里的另一工作地点而导致雇佣关系终止，以及双方决定终止雇佣关系的雇员，除非劳动关系的终止系基于先前劳动法的强制性解雇程序，该程序仅适用于 2015 年 3 月 7 日之前雇用的员工）；② 失业；③ 在失业前的四年内支付过 13 周的社会保障金；④ 在开始领取失业救济金起之前的 12 个月内完成了 30 天的实际工作。

该法令还规定，如果企业被注销，则不再适用这些福利待遇。

3. 全新的降职规则

2015 年 6 月，根据 2015 年第 81 号法令的规定，关于工作内容的规则也进行了修改，尤其是雇主有更大的权力单方决定雇员的职责。

雇主可以在不降低雇员薪酬的前提下，单方面决定同一集体合同、同一级别或同一类别的雇员的职责。

该法令还规定，雇主如果因为公司重组而影响雇员工作职位，则可以将该雇员分配到同一类别的较低职位（无须经雇员同意），但应保持雇员先前的报酬。

此外，该法令规定，各方（雇主和雇员）在有管理职能的公共机构或者工会组织介入之前，可以通过签署协议来协商改变甚至降低就业条件（即职责、水平和薪水），以便于保持雇佣关系，获得拥有不同技能的人才，以及提高雇员的生活水平。

4. 劳动合同新调整

根据 2015 年第 81 号法令的规定，规制不同类型合同的规则被集中到了统一的立法中，特别是兼职合同、固定期限合同、零时合同、人力型劳务合同和学徒制合同（因为合同类型变得更加灵活，公司会有更大的可能性采用这些合同）。

通过取消以前对定期合同的限制，吸引了更多雇主采用固定期限合同。唯一的限制是固定期限合同的最长期限（36 个月，且延期不得超过 5 次），以及无固定期限合同与固定期限合同的比例——无固定期限合同最多不得超过固定期限合同的 20%。雇主提供固定期限合同时可以不说明原因（意大利法律规定的此类"原因"通常是企业出于组织或生产的考虑）。

此外，从 2015 年 12 月 31 日起，项目工作合同已被取消，但已签订的合同在合同期限届满前仍然有效。

该法令还允许签订标准合作合同（不涉及具体项目）和增值税顾问合同（不产生额外费用，并保持合作者的专业性），明确规定在满足以下两个条件的前提下，此类合同应视为劳动合同：① 合作者或顾问的办公室位于该公司；② 合作者或顾问的活动由该公司管理，公司确定其活动的时间和方式，并对其进行指导。

上述情况的例外情形也规定在该法令中（例如该劳动关系受集体合同调整，或者该雇员是专业协会注册的专业人员，比如律师）。

5. 电子监控雇员

2015 年 9 月的第 151 号法令对关于对雇员活动的监控的规定作出了实质性改动。

该法令允许公司通过使用多种电子设备来监控雇员。上述立法旨在"提高工人的生产力"，但是受到了强烈批评，因为可能会侵犯雇员的隐私和个人自由。

雇主不再需要工会的授权，也不需要签署工会协议，就可以为雇员提供工作的设备（如移动电话或个人电脑），即使雇主可能会用该电子设备来监控雇员。因此，公司可以使用这些工具来监管雇员，甚至是出于公司纪律的目的，只要雇员已经充分了解情况，并且该监管行为不侵犯隐私。

雇主还必须与工会代表签署合同或获得行政机关授权，才能安装用来监管雇员行为的设备（例如摄像头）。

6. 工作与生活的平衡

6月，政府出台了各种措施，试图更好地实现劳动者工作与个人生活的平衡，特别是对正在抚育幼儿的父母。

例如，育儿假可以一直延长至孩子12岁（不再是以前法律规定的8岁）。带薪假（支付部分薪酬的假期，支付比例为30%）从3年提高到6年，对于低收入家庭来说，这种福利可能会持续到孩子8岁。收养或寄养的情况也适用同样的规则。此外，双亲中的一位可以要求不休育儿假，而是将全职改为兼职工作。育儿假几乎涵盖所有类型的雇员。父亲和养父母通常也能享受该假期。

五、知识产权

（一）法律及条例

意大利已实施了两项重要的保护知识产权的法律，即2005年2月10日的《工业产权法典》（第30号法令）和1941年4月22日的《著作权法》（第663号法令）及其后续的修订案。

意大利还签署了下列条约和协定：
① 1883年3月20日签署的《保护工业产权巴黎公约》（斯德哥尔摩文本）；
② 1886年9月9日签署的《保护文学和艺术作品伯尔尼公约》（巴黎文本）；
③ 1891年4月14日签署的《商标国际注册马德里协定》（斯德哥尔摩文本）；
④ 1891年4月14日签署的《制止商品来源虚假或欺骗性标记马德里协定》（里斯本文本和斯德哥尔摩附加文本）；
⑤ 1952年9月6日签署的《世界版权公约》（巴黎文本）；
⑥ 1957年6月15日签署的《商标注册用商品和服务国际分类尼斯协定》（日内瓦文本）；
⑦ 1961年10月26日签署的《保护原产地名称及其国际注册里斯本协定》（斯德哥尔摩文本）；
⑧ 1961年10月26日签署的《保护表演者、录音制品制作者和广播组织罗马公约》；
⑨ 1961年12月2日签署的《国际植物新品种保护公约》（日内瓦文本）；
⑩ 1968年10月8日签署的《建立工业品外观设计国际分类洛迦诺协定》；
⑪ 1970年6月19日签署的《专利合作条约》（PCT）；
⑫ 1971年3月24日签署的《国际专利分类斯特拉斯堡协定》；
⑬ 1971年10月29日签署的《保护录音制品制作者禁止未经许可复制其录音制品公约》；
⑭ 1973年10月5日签署的《欧洲专利公约》（EPC）；
⑮ 1974年5月21日签署的《发送卫星传输节目信号布鲁塞尔公约》；
⑯ 1977年4月28日签署的《国际承认用于专利程序的微生物保存布达佩斯条约》；
⑰ 1981年9月28日签署的《保护奥林匹克会徽内罗毕条约》；
⑱ 1989年6月27日签署的《商标国际注册马德里协定有关议定书》；
⑲ 1994年4月15日签署的《与贸易有关的知识产权协定》（TRIPs Agreement）；
⑳ 1996年12月20日签署的《世界知识产权组织版权条约》（未批准）；
㉑ 1996年12月20日签署的《世界知识产权组织表演和录音制品条约》（未批准）；
㉒ 1999年7月2日签署的《工业品外观设计国际注册海牙协定》（日内瓦文本）。

（二）专利、商标、著作权保护

专利和商标申请可以直接通过意大利专利商标局提交，或通过地方专利商标局提交。特别是，专利授权期限为自申请之日起20年，且不得延长。相反，法律对商标的保护为10年，每10年续展一次，可以无限期续展。自2011年7月起，意大利引进了一项行政异议程序，该程序在商标申请公开后向意大利专利商标局提出，类似欧洲共同体商标异议程序。

著作权的保护（期限）通常是作者有生之年及死后70年，如果是集体创作作品，著作权保护期限则持续至最后去世的一名合著者死后70年。商业秘密根据下列规定受保护：
① 意大利《民法典》关于不正当竞争的条款；

②意大利《刑法典》；
③《工业产权法典》。

（三）财产权

关于专利或商标的财产权转让必须在意大利专利商标局进行登记后方可对第三方生效。专利权转让协议的登记必须经出让人和受让人签署的转让声明确认才有效，但无须公证手续。

意大利没有关于许可的监管方针，也没有关于知识产权许可、支付许可费的政府批准制度。转让或许可著作权必须提供书面形式的证明。

意大利知识产权法就某些产品作出了特别要求或是例外规定，例如受严格行政许可程序管制的新植物品种、医药产品。

在意大利，没有关于许可费支付的特别规定。关于关联公司间的许可费应考虑知识产权的转让价格合理确定。

当地的反垄断法及竞争法同样适用于（知识产权）许可。

一般而言，许可协议是外国公司及其全资控股公司间的典型协议。

六、环境保护

公众对关于环境保护的承诺和规定越来越敏感，这一态度转化成了越来越强的环境保护意识和行动力。从政府的角度而言，由于受公众意见和欧盟条例的共同压力，关于环境保护的强制执行变得更加严格。

意大利已批准了多个国际环境协议，其中包括与空气污染、南极海洋生物资源、南极海豹、生物多样化、气候变化、沙漠化、濒临灭绝物种、环境改善、有害废弃物、海洋法、海洋倾废、臭氧层保护、船舶污染、湿地和捕鲸等方面的国际环境协议。地区性条约方面，意大利加入了《欧洲野生鸟类指令》，并且是欧洲委员会的成员国之一，该指令指定了许多生物保护区。

以下介绍意大利两部重要的环境法律：

（1）2006年4月12日的《环境法》（第152号法令）包括了关于主要环境领域的重要规定，例如，污染场地的清理程序、废物处理和处置、空气排放规定、水资源使用和分配，以及环境影响评估。

（2）随着欧盟第96/61/CE号关于预防和减少污染的指令的通过，意大利政府颁布了2005年2月18日的第59号法令，该法令规定了环境综合许可证的批准（一项单独的许可证，代替了目前从事工业活动所必需的主要的环境许可证，上述法令对此进行了详尽的规定）。

在其他几部重要的环境法律中，下列规定值得注意：

① 1995年10月26日的第447号关于声音污染的法令；
② 1992年2月26日的第257号关于停止使用含石棉材料规定的法令；
③ 1997年9月8日的第357号法令——实施欧盟第92/43/CEE号关于保护自然栖息地、野生动植物栖息地指令的规定；
④ 2001年2月22日的第36号关于电力、电磁污染的法令（及2003年7月8日的内阁总理令）。

七、争议解决

（一）争议解决的方法和机构

争议解决的主要方法是诉讼、调解和仲裁。意大利拥有完整的《民法典》和《企业破产法》，以保证财产和合同权利。双边投资协议被视为外国投资的"特殊法"，其效力优先于国内法，如有争议，依照双边投资协议的规定解决。意大利有许多调解中心，包括意大利国家仲裁商会和米兰国际仲裁商会。此外，2004年，中意商会共同成立了中意商事调解中心，为中意企业提供服务。意大利也是国际投资争端解决中心的成员，对于合作投资争议，意大利法院通常会承认外国仲裁机构的裁决。

（二）法律适用

管辖权适用2001年第44号欧盟条例、意大利1995年第218号法令和1986年《布鲁塞尔条约》的规定。

八、其他

（一）反商业贿赂法

1. 反商业贿赂法律、法规简介

近年来，意大利大力集中实施反腐败法规。2012年11月6日发布了第190号法令，即《反腐败法》。关于反商业贿赂问题主要规定在2011年第231号法令中。此外，意大利在2004年通过了第215/04号法令，授权意大利竞争和市场管理局调查和处理政府官员的商业利益冲突，以保护正常的商业行为免受政府官员的影响。

2. 具有反商业贿赂职责的部门

意大利负责反商业贿赂的部门是意大利竞争和市场管理局。

3. 惩罚措施

《反腐败法》采用"综合治理"方式，结合刑事和非刑事责任实施惩处，包括对个人或公司实施经济制裁、对个人实施监禁或其他处罚（包括取消资格、没收违法所得、要求赔偿损失等）。对于企业来说，这些惩处行为还会影响企业的声誉和融资能力，影响力和震慑力更为深远。

（二）国内外公司刑事责任

1. 简介

意大利是大陆法系国家中第一个引入公司刑事责任的国家，该制度通过2001年6月8日颁布的第231号法令确立。即使第231号法令将公司责任描述为"行政责任"，实务中法院还是在判决中将其认定为刑事责任。近年来，通过修订法律、扩大公司犯罪相关上游犯罪的范围以及实务中意大利法院对该条款的广泛运用，该法案令适用范围有所扩大。因此，公司对高级管理人员所犯罪行的起诉日益增加。

第231号法令没有明确说明外国公司（即总部设在境外的公司）是否受其规制。然而，意大利法院认为，在某些情况下，只要在意大利开展业务的公司就应受该法令规制。此外，意大利《统一银行法》也与第231号法令不同，该法明确了外国银行的责任。具体来说，根据《统一银行法》第97条之二第5款的规定，为意大利银行设定的特别责任制度也适用于外国银行在意大利的分支机构，无论该外国银行的主要营业地在欧盟内部还是在欧盟之外。

从法律角度来看，在满足一定主观和客观构成要件时，公司才应承担第231号法令规定的责任。客观构成要件为，法定代表人、经理或受其监督的人员的犯罪行为是为了公司利益或者为了增加公司的利益。罪行种类包括进行公共欺诈、洗钱、侵犯版权、公司犯罪、滥用市场地位、奴役劳动和奴隶贩卖、因违反公共场所健康与安全条例而致人死亡，以及环境犯罪。获利的含义应作广泛解释，例如，依据第231号法令的规定，雇员在工作场合死亡时，可以指控公司过失致人死亡，一些判决强调"获利"应包括公司因没有完善工作场合的健康和安全条件而节省的成本。主观构成要件指公司未能设计并实施预防犯罪的合规制度。这一点对于减轻第231号法令规定的刑罚以及免于承担刑事责任至关重要。

第231号法令对外国公司和银行在意大利的经营和投资有重大影响。公司可能受到严厉处罚，比如罚金、吊销资格以及没收犯罪所得。因此，在意大利境内投资和开展业务时，外国投资者应对这些规则有所了解。所以，以下将简要概述第231号法令中与外国公司相关的部分。

2. 第231号法令的适用法域及其对外国公司的影响

虽然第231号法令没有直接规制外国公司的责任，但在大量判例中，法院判决了外国公司可以受

到起诉并且应为其没能阻止其高级管理人员犯罪而负责（米兰法院第四法庭2013年2月4日第13976号判决）。如果犯罪行为、过失犯罪行为或犯罪结果发生在意大利或者意属地区，就认为犯罪发生在意大利。意大利法学界现在倾向于宽泛解释犯罪地的概念，以扩大第231号法令的司法管辖权。具体来说，意大利法院认为，无论是整个犯罪行为还是部分犯罪行为，甚至只有一小部分犯罪行为发生在意大利境内，意大利法院就有管辖权。意大利最高法院近来认为，即使是仅在意大利境内计划实施犯罪行为，比如贿赂外国官员，意大利法院也有管辖权（最高法院第六刑事法庭2016年2月12日第11442号判决）。因此，外国公司也可能因其基本上在外国实施的罪行而被意大利法院传唤，即使该罪行与意大利仅有微弱的联系。从域外司法管辖的角度来看，即关于完全在国外实施的上游犯罪，第231号法令第4条只明确规定，在意大利设有总部的公司在海外犯下的罪行，将根据意大利《刑法典》（第7条至第10条）中个人犯罪的构成要件对其进行起诉，前提是外国司法机关未就该公司同样的行为提起诉讼。如果外国公司的主要经营地设在境外，且该公司完全在另一个国家领土内实施的犯罪行为不属于本法规制的范围。

3. 跨国犯罪与禁止双重诉讼原则

意大利《刑法典》并未明确承认个人犯罪适用禁止双重诉讼原则。现行有效的1930年《刑法典》第11条允许对于已经在国外被裁定的相同事实提起新的诉讼。如果犯罪事实全部或部分发生在意大利境内，就可以提起一项新的诉讼。另外，如果罪行完全是在国外发生的，司法部长也可以要求提起新的诉讼。

近20年来，该项法律制度已经被完全改变，欧盟扩大了它的适用范围。《欧盟基本权利宪章》（CFREU）第50条规定了跨国犯罪的禁止双重诉讼原则，规定"就欧盟境内已依法宣告无罪或处罚之犯罪，不得重复受刑事审判或刑罚"。这一条款与《关于执行1985年6月14日〈申根协定〉的公约》第54条至第58条主旨相同，后者明确了这一原则的适用条件及例外情况（见欧盟法院Spasic法官作出的2014年5月27日第C-129/14 PPU号判决）。根据学界意见，"禁止双重诉讼"原则也应适用于公司犯罪，所以，如果一家公司在一个欧洲国家已经得到终局判决，就不能在另一个欧洲国家再被判决。

关于意大利的法律规定，应当明确两种情况：一方面，意大利最高法院认为，一家公司在非欧盟成员国被宣告无罪或者有罪，在意大利又重复受到刑事审判或刑罚的情形不适用该原则。在一起已经在尼日利亚和美国得到判决的国际贿赂刑事案件中，一部分犯罪行为发生在意大利，而且犯罪主体包含一家意大利公司，意大利最高法院表示，美国司法机关作出的和解书不能排除意大利法院提起新的诉讼，因为两国之间不存在司法协议，且不能将禁止双重诉讼原则作为国际法原则（意大利最高法院第六刑事法庭2016年2月12日第11442号判决）。另一方面，意大利仍尊重禁止双重诉讼原则，甚至为某些被刑事指控的公司提供了有力保护。第231号法令第4条规定，如果一个总部在意大利的公司受到外国司法机关的指控，并且其全部犯罪事实发生在国外，则该公司在国内不能因完全相同的事实被调查。但该条并未说明这个规定适用于外国公司。此外，第231号法令也没有指出在国外受到最终判决的意大利公司或者外国公司不能被意大利司法机关再次起诉或处罚。

4. 并购交易与外国投资

许多外国投资者对涉及意大利公司的并购交易感兴趣，在这种情况下，建议投资者事先进行尽职调查，以评估参与交易的公司是否有涉第231号法令的诉讼，或者其管理人员是否涉及公司犯罪刑事调查。考虑到第231号法令，这种调查对预判并购交易后的责任转移很有必要。

第231号法令对公司在特殊公司交易（即转型、兼并、分立和收购）中的责任作出了具体规定。对于公司转型，该法令规定受诉公司仍然对转型生效前的犯罪行为负责；对于公司兼并，兼并后的公司仍然对兼并前的公司的犯罪行为负责；公司分立和公司收购适用的法律更加复杂。关于公司合并或分立，第231号法令就如何适用刑罚作出了规定。尽职调查和潜在诉讼的风险提示能使有问题的公司作出更明智的决定并评估其潜在的风险。

5. 外国控股公司及其在意大利的子公司

第231号法令并未明确规定集团公司的责任。尽管如此，意大利法院最近作出的判决明确指出，如果子公司是为了母公司的利益进行了上游犯罪，则法院可以就此犯罪指控母公司。为了避免自己及其外国控股公司受到指控，在意大利境内营业的子公司应当遵循第 231 号法令。

6. 合规之路

根据法律，无论是意大利公司还是外国公司，如果其法人代表或者雇员犯罪，可以通过证明其拥有有效运行的合规制度来豁免第 231 号法令设定的法律责任。但是公司完全豁免法律责任的案例很少，因为意大利法院倾向于拒绝排除公司责任，除了几种例外情况，比如公司责任事故罪。合规制度的存在可以为公司减轻其他责任，比如不吊销其营业资格、减轻罚金刑。第 231 号法令采取了奖励与惩罚并重的方法，鼓励公司加强组织、控制和管理，以预防犯罪。

应当区分法人代表与雇员实施上游犯罪的案件。如果是法人代表实施犯罪，则公司可以通过证明以下内容来豁免责任：①管理部门在犯罪行为发生前已经制定并有效实施适当的防止此类犯罪行为发生的组织性和管理性方案；②犯罪行为人通过欺诈手段规避该组织管理；③犯罪主体以欺诈手段逃避管控而犯下罪行；④管理部门没有监管不力（第 231 号法令第 6 条）。

另外，如果是公司雇员在受到监管的情况下仍然实行了犯罪（虽然这种指控在实践中较为罕见），公司依然要承担责任。但是，在犯罪发生前，公司已经针对该种犯罪采用和有效实施了组织、管理和控制办法。这样的办法应符合以下要件：①针对被发现的犯罪行为，公司应定期进行检查，以及对相关监管制度定期进行修改，或者对公司结构和经营范围进行过调整；②规定了配备有惩处手段的纪律制度（第 231 号法令第 7 条）。因此，如果满足了第 231 号法令规定的合规要求，则可以减轻公司的刑罚或者豁免部分刑事责任。

因此，从预防和补救的角度来说，外国公司应当采纳和实施符合意大利法律的合规制度。

（三）工程承包

1. 许可制度

作为欧盟成员国，意大利是世界贸易组织《政府采购协定》的缔约方，有义务向其他成员国采购方提供某个标的额（6 242 000 欧元）以上的公共建筑项目。由于目前中国不是《政府采购协定》的缔约方，所以在这个标的额下的项目，意大利没有义务对中国企业开放。

2. 禁止投资领域

意大利禁止外国公司从事军事、国防和其他相关行业的项目。此外，意大利对能源和电力等行业也有严格的许可制度，并对这些行业的外国投资者实施一定的限制。

3. 招投标

公共工程项目应严格执行招标制度，不实施公开招标的项目必须说明具体原因。招标方式主要有四种：

①公开招标采购项目，主要针对一般采购协议，价格因素对其决定性较大；

②两阶段招标采购，是指对某个项目的设计和实施部分分别招标，即同一项目的设计和实施可由一个公司完成或两个公司分别完成；

③谈判采购，指直接邀请供应商就采购进行谈判，以略过公告程序；

④快速招标采购，指紧急情况下的非标准招标采购。

Italy

Authors: Sara Marchetta
Translators: Jin Xiao, Yao Yuan

I. Overview

A. Glance of Country

A natural bridge between the Mediterranean and Europe, Italy is one of the most prominent members of European Union. It acts as a base for commercial and trade links with the emerging countries of the eastern and western Mediterranean as well as with the central-eastern parts of Europe. Northern Italy is located in the centre of Europe and is bordered by France, Switzerland, Austria and Slovenia and its population is approximately 60 million. Italian is the official language and regional dialects are spoken throughout the country.

Italy is one of Europe's biggest agricultural producers and is also one of its leaders in services, industry and technology, with a long tradition of innovation. Creating jobs, cutting taxes, enhancing competitiveness and reducing the budget deficit and debt have been the focus of recent Italian governments.

Rome, Italy's capital and largest city, plays a leading role on the institutional side while Milan plays a prominent role in business. In addition to Rome and Milan, there are several large cities, including Turin, Naples, Venice and Genova. The national railway system extends throughout Italy and into neighbouring countries and consists of a regular and high-speed train lines' network Italy is traversed by a number of highways and state and provincial roads and the Italian road network is linked to those of other European countries. Italian highways provide very good access to the country's largest towns and cities.

Due to Italy's geographical position, sea transport plays an essential role in the country's foreign trade. Genova, Livorno, Trieste, Ravenna, La Spezia and Naples are the most important Italian ports. La Spezia and Taranto are two naval bases of significant importance. Currently, there are over 100 airports operating in Italy, including a number of international and regional airports. Rome's Fiumicino and Milan's Malpensa are the major international air hubs. The other major international airports are Milan Linate, Venice Marco Polo and Bologna Borgo Panigale.

Italy has been engaged over the past ten years in a process of economic liberalization mainly in the energy, gas, transportation and telecommunications sectors with a view of enhancing competition, efficiency and quality of service. The government continues to own shares in corporations in a range of sectors including banking, energy production and distribution, and transportation.

Italy's communications system is modern and well developed. The country has fully automated telephone, telex and data services, and high-capacity cable systems; the country has the third-highest mobile phone penetration rate in the world Italy, along with other countries from the European Union (the "EU") adopted the Euro as its new currency in January 1999. As such, monetary policy is set by the European Central Bank in Frankfurt, Germany. The introduction of the new coins and bills in January 2002 has been quite smooth.

B. Diplomatic Relations

Italy is a member of most of the United Nations specialized and related agencies. Italy has established diplomatic relations and conducts business with nearly every country in the world. Italy has a wide consular network in the world. Most major cities in Italy have consulates from the world's leading nations. Almost every country has in Rome its own diplomatic representation.

There are no travel restrictions to or within the country except on a case by case basis where visas may be required depending on a traveller's country of origin.

C. The Constitutional Asset

Italy is a democratic republic. The 1948 Constitution rules the life of its democracy through the three Powers of the democratic Italian State: (i) the Parliament, sovereign of the legislative power, a bicameral organ consisting of the Chamber of Deputies (Camera dei Deputat) and the Senate (Senato della Repubblica); (ii) the Council of Ministers (Consiglio dei ministri), headed by the President of the Council of Ministers (Presidente del Consiglio),

(iii) the free, neutral and independent judicial power headed by an independent Court system including the Constitutional Court (Corte Costituzionale) as further discussed in Section "The Judicial System" below.

D. The President and the Government

The president of the Republic is elected by a joint session of the Parliament, with the addition of the representatives of the republic's regions, and holds a seven-year term The powers of the President include (i) the appointment of the President of the Council of Ministers and, on his / her recommendation, the Ministers, (ii) the dissolution of Parliament and (iii) the ratification of international treaties. The day-to-day functioning of the Government is in the hands of the President of the Council of Ministers and the Ministers, jointly forming the Council of Ministers. The President of the Council, who is normally the leader of the party with the largest representation in the Parliament, co- ordinates the action of the Ministers. The Council of Ministers (usually, but not necessarily composed of members of Parliament) sets and oversees the implementation of the government's general political agenda and must retain the confidence (fiducia) of both houses of Parliament.

The current President of the Republic is Sergio Nattarella who was elected on January 30, 2015.

a. The Parliament

The Italian Parliament consists of the Chamber of Deputies and the Senate of the Republic elected by popular suffrage for five-year terms of office. Pursuant to legislation enacted in 2005, the electoral system is on proportional basis. The Senate also includes former Presidents of the Republic and several other persons appointed for particular life merits according to special constitutional provisions. Legislative bills may originate in either Houses and must be passed by a majority in both. Citizens must be 25 years of age or older to vote for senators; in all other elections, all citizens over age 18 are eligible to vote.

b. The Judicial System

The judicial system is based on Roman Law comprising of the following areas: civil, criminal, constitutional, administrative, accounting, military and tax.

The civil and criminal areas constitute the system's ordinary function. Such ordinary system has generally two levels of judicial review: first instance Tribunals and appellate Courts. Decisions of the appellate Courts related to civil and criminal matters (only as to issues of law) can be submitted to the syndicate of the Supreme Court of Italy (Corte di Cassazione).

The administrative, accounting, military and tax areas constitute the systems specialized functions. Such specialized system has generally two levels of review: first instance Tribunals and appellate Courts or other bodies. Regional Administrative Courts (Tribunali Amministrativi Regionali) and the Council of State (Consiglio di Stato) are examples of first instance Tribunals and an appellate body with jurisdiction over administrative matters.

The constitutional matters are subject to the jurisdiction of the Constitutional Court (Corte Costituzionale) which also examines legislation and decides whether it conforms to the Constitution and adjudicates on conflicts among the three branches of government (legislative, executive and judicial), between the Republic and its Regions or among different Regions.

The average duration of a trial Is between 9 months and 3 years. An appeal can add up to 2-3 years to the litigation process. To the extent recognized by other countries, Italian decisions can generally be enforced outside the country. Reciprocally, foreign decisions can also be enforced in Italy. Italy is a party to several international conventions which govern recognition and enforcement of foreign decisions, such as:

The Brussels Convention on Recognition and Enforcement of Judgments in Civil and Commercial Matters of September 27, 1968 which is now superseded by the European Regulation 44 / 2001 of December 22, 2000, concerning jurisdiction, recognition and the enforcement of judgments in civil and commercial matters.

The New York Convention on the Recognition and Enforcement of Foreign Arbitral Awards of June 10, 1958.

In addition, the Italian legal system provides a variety of forms of alternative dispute resolution such as arbitration, mediation, conciliation and recognition of the related international conventions.

II. Investment

A. Market Access

a. Laws and Regulations of Investment Industry

Banking and financial activities are regulated in Italy by the Legislative Decree No.385 of September 1, 1993 (the "Banking Law"), which implements the EU Banking Directives setting forth the regulatory and supervision regime for banks.

Banking activities (i.e., the collection of savings from the public and the granting of credit) may be conducted only by banks authorized to perform such activities pursuant to the Banking Law. The Banking Law requires the authorization of the Bank of Italy in order to conduct banking activities in Italy, while EU banks (i.e., banks having registered office and head office in an Eu State other than Italy) may operate under the so-called "Mutual Recognition" framework (i.e., they can act in Italy availing themselves the authorization granted to them in their home country, without any obligation to establish a branch in Italy, provided that the Bank of Italy has been duly informed by the competent authority of the home member EU State).

Legislative Decree No.58 of February 24, 1998 (the "Financial Law") which provides for the regulation of investment services and activities, asset management and exchanges, implemented in Italy and relevant investment directive of the EU.The Financial Law has, inter alia, implemented in Italy the EU Directive "MIFID", on the provision of investment services.

Insurance and reinsurance activities are regulated in Italy by Legislative Decree No.209 of September 7, 2005 (the "Insurance Code"), which implements in Italy the EU Insurance Directives setting forth the regulatory and supervision regime for insurances and reinsurances (both for life insurance and for non-life insurances).

Italian Legislative Decree No.170 of May 21, 2004 as amended by the Italian Legislative Decree No.48 of April 24, 2011 (the "Decree 170"), implemented the EU Directive 2002/47/CE on Financial Collateral Arrangements. Decree 170 provides for a special regime for security over financial collaterals, aimed at fostering the perfection and enforcement of financial collateral arrangements.

b.Foreign Investment

Italy does not have specific regulations on foreign investment, all investments have to oblige to the Civil Code, regulations related to Company Law. Foreign investors can invest in the form of setting up representation offices, joint ventures, foreign wholly-owned enterprises, and merger and acquisition.

Both investment firms and asset management companies are subject to supervision exercised by the Bank of Italy and Consob. While the former supervises the risk management and the financial stability of the intermediary, Consob supervises the compliance with disclosure requirements and the soundness of customer relationship.

The markets Borsa Italian and IDEM are managed by Borsa Italiana S.p.A., the first market managing company established in Italy.

In addition to the protection available under the Italian law, foreign investors can rely on the protection available under international law. Italy has indeed entered into several multilateral and bilateral treaties for the protection of foreign investments such as, inter alia, the Washington Convention of 1965 (also known as the ICSID Convention) and a multitude of Bilateral Investment Treaties (also known as BIT) for the protection of foreign investments.

China and Italy signed a BIT on January 28, 1985, it entered into force on August 28, 1987.

c. Standards of Market Access and Examination

According to the principle of reciprocity, China and Italy have bilateral treaties which benefit individuals to invest in the other country. The standard of market access for foreign investments are same as local investors, in accordance with the Italian Civil Code. If the merger and acquisition involves the EU domestic market competition, then it must follow the EU market competition policies. If it involves Italian domestic market, then it shall follow regulations of Italian competition regulations and shall be examined and approved by the Italian Competition and Market Bureau (AGCM). Also, if merged or acquired an Italian listed company for more than 2% of share, then it shall be examined and reported to the competent authority CONSOB.

Italy does not have a national security examination mechanism for foreign investors, but when it comes to matters of public interest and industries, enterprises and assets with significant strategic meanings, the Italian government through its "golden share" can implement examinations and assessments to related investments and have the final decision right. The "golden share" is usually obtained by the Ministry of Finance or other competent industry representatives of the government.

Italy has strict market access on national defence industry, airplane industry, petrol and gas resources excavation industry, and etc. These industries have specific restrictions and standards of market access.

Italy's Industrial Park is mainly focused in northeast traditional industrial region, with an amount of 45 industry parks, 37 in northwest regions, 38 in middle area, and 17 in southern region.

Also, Italy has Export Processing Free Trade Zone, which enjoy free tax inside the zone, and merchandise can process in any forms with no custom restrictions within the zone, and foreign investor can employee employees from their own country in the zone under the Italian Labour Law regulations and Social Security Law regulations.

B. Foreign Exchange Regulation

a. Department Supervising Foreign Exchange

The Bank of Italy contributes to the decisions on the single monetary policy of the euro area and performs the tasks entrusted to as national central bank in the Euro system. It may carry out foreign exchange operations in accordance with the rules laid down by the Euro system. It manages its own foreign currency reserves and a portion of those of the ECB on the latter's behalf.

As the national supervisory authority, the Bank of Italy seeks to ensure the sound and prudent management of intermediaries, the overall stability and efficiency of the financial system and compliance with the rules and regulations of those subject to supervision.

The Bank of Italy is the designated National Competent Authority (NCA) under the Single Supervisory Mechanism.

b. Brief Introduction of Laws and Regulations of Foreign Exchange

The Euro system conducts foreign exchange operations in accordance with Articles 127 and 219 of the Treaty on the Functioning of the European Union. Within the Euro system, the Bank of Italy may be called upon to intervene on the market together with the other national central banks (NCBs) and the European Central Bank (ECB).

The Bank of Italy may also be asked to intervene in connection with the Exchange Rate Mechanism II (ERM II), which sets out the main lines of cooperation in exchange rate policies between the ECB and the NCBs in EU member states that have not adopted the euro.

Foreign exchange operations may also be used to alter the composition of the Bank's foreign currency reserves in order to achieve the best balance between risk and return.

Lastly, the Bank of Italy may be required to buy and sell foreign currency with market counterparties in connection with the servicing of the country's foreign currency debt, in order to balance inflows and outflows without changing the amount or composition of foreign currency reserves.

The Bank analyses the performance of the main currencies daily, using information provided by the main news agencies and market operators.

The Bank of Italy also makes available, in compliance with Italian law, the average monthly and yearly exchange rates valid for fiscal purposes, which it then notifies to the Ministry for the Economy and Finance for publication in the Gazzetta Ufficiale della Repubblica Italiana (Official Journal). The relevant acts are the Consolidated Law on Income Tax DPR 917/86(Article 110) and Decree Law 167/90 (Article 4).

c. Requirements of Foreign Exchange Management for Foreign Enterprises

In Italy there is no foreign exchange restriction and implements Capital Account Liberalization. Italy allows capital to freely exchange through international regions. Profits can be brought out of the country after taxing the income tax.

C. Financing

a. Main Financial Institutions

(i) Banking Institutions; Financial Intermediaries; Insurance and Reinsurance Activities; Investment Services and Asset Management Activities; and

(ii) Market Management Companies, Borsa, which is divided into Mercato Telematico Azionario, MTA, for the trading of shares; SeDeX, for the trading of the securitized derivatives; "Trading After Hours" Market, TAH, for the trading of listed shares that satisfy the liquidity requirements established by Borsa Italiana, securitised derivative financial instruments traded on the SEDEX market at the request of the issuer at different times from those established for the MTA and SEDEX market; AMI Italia, dedicated to small and medium-sized Italian enterprises with strong growth potential; Electronic open-end funds and securitised derivative financial instruments market; Mercato Telematico delle Obbligazioni e dei Titoli di Stato, for the trading of bonds and Treasury Bonds, Eurobonds, bonds issued by foreign companies and asset-backed securities; Electronic investment vehicles market, for the trading of shares of investment companies and real estate investment companies;

(iii) Mercato degli Strumenti Derivati (IDEM), for the trading of derivative financial instruments regulated by the Financial Law;

(iv) Mercato Telematico all'ingrosso dei Titoli di Stato, for the wholesale trading of Treasure bonds; managed by Società per il Mercato dei titoli di Stato - MTS S.p.A.; and

(v) EuroTLX, a Multilateral Trading Facility for the trading of Treasure Bonds, corporate bonds, asset-backed securities, fund shares, sovereign bonds, managed by EuroTLX SIM S.p.A..

b. Bank Accounts and Granting Loans for Foreign Investors

There is no specific legal requirement to open an account with an Italian banking institution in order to conduct investments in Italy. However, anti-money laundering legislation has set certain limitations for the use of cash. More specifically, transferring of cash (or bearer's bankbooks or stocks to bearer) with an aggregate value equal to or exceeding 1,000.00 EURO is prohibited and, therefore, must unavoidably be effected via a banking institution or other authorized intermediary. This provision de facto implies that any investor conducting business in Italy needs to have a bank account, which could be maintained with a non-Italian entity.

A non-resident person is free to open a bank account in Italy. In general terms, there are no restrictions on the use of a bank account by a foreign customer. The bank must only verify the non-resident's identity and capacity according to his / her national law. Further, in order to comply with anti-money laundering provisions, banks must (i) require identification information of their clients and of the possible beneficial owner of the transaction and also the purpose of it and (ii) obtain information on the purpose and intended nature of the business relationship.

There are no legal prohibitions on an investor receiving bank loans, which are freely negotiated between a bank and an investor, subject to applicable provisions of law, which include usury legislation, which sets forth certain thresholds for the interest rates and other forms of remuneration applicable to financing transactions.

D. Real Estate

a. Brief Introduction of Real Estate Related Laws and Regulations

Pursuant to Italian law non-Italian private investors can, in principle, freely acquire rights on Italian real estate subject to the same limits applicable to Italian nationals. The sole limitation (which does not apply to EU investors) to such principle is that the country of nationality of the investor cannot acquire rights on Italian real estate if Italian nationals cannot acquire the same rights on real estate assets in the country of nationality of the investor. Such limitation is not often applied (and is often ignored) but violations of the requirement may cause complications, inter alia in case of litigation. The reciprocity requirement does not apply if there is a treaty between Italy and the country of nationality of the investor governing the matter.

Most investments in Italian real estate assets envisage the (direct or indirect) acquisition of the full ownership of a real estate asset. In theory, investors could also acquire from the owner of the asset "partial" in-rem rights over the asset, such as a right of use, a right to build buildings or structures over or under the asset or specific liens such as specific easement rights. Commercial investors seldom invest in such "partial" in-rem rights, other than in some very specific situations. Ownership and other in-rem rights over real estate assets are usually registered in the real estate registry, which ensures the enforceability of the right against third parties as well as a high level of certainty with respect to title over real estate assets and to the absence of in-rem encumbrances (such as mortgages) over the asset. In order to register rights over real estate rights, the relevant document must be notarized.

As an alternative to the acquisition of in-rem rights, investors may enter into an agreement with the owner of the real estate asset, pursuant to which the investor is entitled to use the asset for a certain period of time, may in turn grant using rights to third parties and, in some cases, may be entitled to acquire the full ownership of the asset. Such agreements are usually structured as "straightforward" leases of real estate, "financial" leases or leases of going concern. Such rights cannot be registered in the real estate register and therefore may be harder to identify and enforce than the in-rem rights mentioned above.

b. Full Ownership

Ownership is the broadest in-rem right over real estate assets.

The owner can use the asset as he sees fit (with some limitations mostly arising from administrative law), can sell the asset, can lease the asset to third parties, can grant partial in-rem rights to third parties and can use the asset as security for its obligations (usually by way of mortgage).

The acquisition of the ownership of a real estate asset requires certain formalities which may complicate or delay the acquisition, including the following:

(i) The purchase agreement must be in writing although in practice notarization is strongly recommended in order to allow the registration of the purchase in the real estate registry;

(ii) If the asset is a building, the transferor must indicate in the purchase agreement the building permits on which basis the building has been built and that the building is duly registered with the cadastral real estate registry; buildings which are not compliant with the relevant building permits or which are not registered in the cadastral real estate registry cannot be easily transferred;

(iii) If the asset is a building, the parties must indicate in the purchase agreement the "energetic class" of the building on the basis of a specific "energetic class" certificate; such certificate describes the energy consumption of the building and is issued by professional appointed by the parties (usually the transferor);

(iv) If the asset is a land parcel, the parties must attach to the purchase agreement a "permitted use" certificate issued by the relevant municipality - the issuance of such a certificate may take up to a month;

(v) The parties must indicate in the agreement whether the transaction has been assisted by any broker and in such a case how much has been paid in fees to such broker;

(vi) The parties must indicate in the agreement how the price has been (or will be) paid;

(vii) If the asset has "historical" or "artistic" value, certain limitations to transfers (including a pre-emption right of Italian public entities) may apply; and

(viii) In certain cases, the tenant of the building may have a pre-emption right for the purchase of the building - pre-emption right may apply also to the sale of agricultural land.

c. Right of Use (Usufrutto)

The holder of an in-rem right of use has basically the same rights as the owner. The main difference is that the right of use is limited in time (its maximum term is equal to the life of the original holder or to thirty years if the original holder is a legal entity). The right of use can usually (unless the title provides otherwise) be sold to third parties or mortgaged, and the holder of the right of use can lease the asset to third parties.

The procedure and formalities for the acquisition of an in-rem right of use are basically the same applicable to the acquisition of the full ownership described under the paragraph a above.

d. Right to Build Building or Structures over or Under the Asset (Diritto di Superfice)

The holder of a diritto di superfice is entitled to build buildings or structures over (or under) the relevant real estate asset and acquires the full ownership of the buildings or structures so built for the full term of the diritto di spuerfice.

The diritto di superfice (and the full ownership of the buildings built pursuant to the diritto di superfice) can be sold or mortgaged.

The procedure and formalities for the acquisition of a diritto di superfice are basically the same applicable to the acquisition of the full ownership described under paragraph a. above.

e. Easement Rights

Easement rights (diritti di servitù) are "minor" in-rem usually finalized to allow the owner of a real estate asset to exercise some rights over another real estate asset. The most typical lien is the right of way (diritto di passaggio), pursuant to which the owner of a real estate asset is entitled to cross a nearby asset (usually a land parcel) to access his property.

Easement rights are not usually considered as real estate investments "per se", but may significantly increase (or decrease) the value of a "main" asset.

The agreements for the creation of an easement right must be in writing; in practice notarization is strongly recommended in order to allow the registration of the easement right in the real estate registry.

In some cases an easement right may be created (by order of the competent authorities or due to a de facto situation on the ground) also if no agreement has been entered into; however most easement rights are created by means of an agreement and their existence can usually be ascertained through a search in the real estate registry.

f. Leases of Real Estate Assets

Straightforward (as opposed to "financial") leases of real estate assets are mostly used by entities which intend to use the leased asset directly to carry out their activity. The lessee is entitled to use the leased asset in compliance with the limits and rules set forth in the lease agreement (which may significantly limit the allowed uses of the asset).If allowed by the lease agreement, the lessee can sublease the asset (in whole or in part) or assign the lease agreement.

The rights of the lessee arising from the lease cannot easily be used as security for the lessee's obligations (i.e. they cannot be mortgaged).

The formalities for the execution of a lease agreement are significantly simpler than those required for the acquisition of in-rem rights over real estate assets; however lease agreements are usually in writing (residential leases shall mandatorily be in writing) and it is advisable that long term lease agreements(those exceeding a nine year term)be notarized and registered in the real estate registry to ensure that the rights of the lessee are enforceable vis à vis any future owner of the leased real estate asset.

The terms and conditions of lease agreements concerning buildings are to a significant extent imposed by mandatory provisions of law, including the following:

(i) the term of the lease cannot be shorter than 4 years (for residential leases), 6 years (for non-residential leases) and 9 years (for leases of hotels); please consider that there are some extreme minimum terms;

(ii) upon expiry the lease is automatically renewed unless one of the parties gives notice in advance-on the first expiry the lessor can give notice only in certain specific cases;

(iii) the lessee can unilaterally terminate the lease in certain cases-the exact scope of the cases where the lessee can terminate the lease has been defined by the case law, the basic principle is that the lessee can terminate the lease if the lease has become excessively burdensome due to new circumstances which were not foreseeable at the time of execution of the lease agreement;

(iv) the lease agreement can grant to the lessee additional termination rights, while the lessor can terminate the lease only in case of serious breach by the tenant;

(v) indexation is limited to 75% of the ISTAT inflation index for those commercial leases whose term does not exceed 6 years (9 years for hotels); commercial leases with a longer term can provide for a higher level of indexation; and

(vi) in certain cases of lease of commercial property, the lessee is entitled to a pre-emption right if the lessor sells the leased asset, and the lessee is entitled to receive a significant indemnity by the lessor in some cases of expiry of the lease.

g. Financial Leases

Financial lease agreements grant to the lessee the right to use the relevant asset and the option to purchase such asset at the end of the lease period. Only banks and certain other financial institutions can act as lessor in a financial lease.

The basic purpose of a financial lease transaction is to grant to the lessee the right to use the asset and to purchase the same at the end of the lease period without paying upfront the entire purchase price. The lessor basically finances the acquisition (and sometimes the construction) of the asset, acquires the ownership of the asset (and retains such ownership until the lessee exercises its call option) and receives from the lessee the payment of a pre-agreed rent. Usually the purchase price of the asset at the end of the lease is lower than the residual market value of the asset, as the amount of the rent paid by the lessee during the term of the lese is usually set at a level sufficient to ensure an adequate remuneration to the leasing company and to gradually reimburse to the leasing company part of the initial financial outlay for the purchase(or construction) of the asset. Sometimes the transaction is structured as a sale and leaseback. whereby the lessor acquires the asset from the lessee (thus basically financing the lessee for an amount equal to the purchase price) and then leases such asset back to the lessee. Sale and leaseback transactions must be carefully evaluated and structured, with the involvement of regulated leasing companies, in view of the fact that Italian law does not allow in principle the transfer of ownership of assets as a mechanism to give security to creditors. The formalities for the execution of a financial lease agreement are significantly simpler than those for the acquisition of in-rem rights over real estate assets; basically the agreement shall be in writing and the lessor shall provide certain information concerning the costs of the transaction.

The mandatory provisions of law which govern "straightforward" leases of real estate assets do not apply to financial leases of such assets.

h. Leases of Going Concerns

Leases of going concerns may include real estate assets if such assets are part of the going concern.

Leases of going concerns are often used by the owners and operators of shopping malls and hotels, as a lease of going concern allows the lessor to grant to the lessee not only the right to use the real estate asset and contractual relationships included in the going concern (i.e., employment contracts and supply agreements), but also the relevant equipment and, most important, the relevant administrative licenses and permits. More in detail, the most common structure for the development and management of shopping malls (and to a certain extent of hotels) in Italy is based on leases of a going concern, as follows:

(i) a real estate developer obtains the administrative permits and licenses for building and operating the shopping mall;

(ii) the developer then builds the structure and leases each shop within the shopping mall to the final operator of the shop by means of leases of a going concern which include, inter alia, the premises, agreements for the supply of utilities and the administrative license for operating the shop;

(iii) the developer then sells the whole shopping mall (as a going concern) to the final operator / owner, who therefore becomes the lessor under the leases of going concern governing the use of each shop.

The formalities for the execution of a lease of going concern require the notarization of lease agreement and the filing of the agreement with the companies' register and, if the lease includes an administrative license, a specific deed of transfer of such licence could be required.

The mandatory provisions of law which govern "straightforward" leases of real estate assets do not apply to leases of going concern, even if such going concerns include real estate assets. There are however certain rules concerning leases of going concern which should be carefully evaluated, including the following:

(i) the lease is considered as a "temporary transfer" of the going concern; as a consequence, upon execution of the lease the lessee becomes a party to the agreements included in the going concern (including any employment agreements), acquires the receivables of the going concern and becomes liable for certain liabilities of the going concern; similarly, upon expiry or termination of the lease the lessor becomes a party to certain agreements included in the going concern (including any employment agreements), acquires the receivables of the going concern and becomes liable for certain liabilities of the going concern. This effect may to a certain extent be limited by carefully structuring the lease agreement and the going concern to be leased;

(ii) the lease of the going concern can sometimes be relevant for antitrust purposes and therefore it may be necessary to notify the lease to the antitrust authorities;

(iii) the lessor of a going concern shall not-for the full term of the lease - carry out any activity which may compete with the leased going concern; such non- compete obligation can however be derogated in the agreement between the lessor and the lessee; and

(iv) the going concern shall be carefully structured and its existence properly documented to avoid any attempts by the lessee to claim that the agreement should be governed by the rules concerning leases of real estate assets (and the application of the relevant mandatory rules, which favour the lessee).

i. Structures and Vehicles Which May Be Set Up to Acquire Real Estate Assets

Italian law does not limit the right for Italian or foreign investors to acquire directly real estate assets in Italy (provided that the "reciprocity" requirement described under Paragraph "D.a. Brief Introduction of Real Estate Ralated Laws and Regulations" above is met).

Nevertheless, most investors elect not to acquire Italian real estate assets directly, but to acquire such assets through other structures and vehicles. This approach can offer multiple benefits, mostly in terms of limitation of liability, ease of structuring "limited recourse" financing, liquidity of the investment, greater ease in setting up joint ventures and co-investments, involvement of specialized asset managers and potential cost and tax efficiencies.

The most commonly used investment structures are the following:

(i) setting up a specific purpose company (usually a limited liability company, sometimes a joint stock company) which acquires the assets; and

(ii) investing in real estate fund, which then acquires the real estate assets.

We set forth below a short description of such structures:

a) Setting Up a Specific Purpose Company

This is the most traditional and in many respects the simplest structure for the acquisition of real estate assets. Holding the assets through a specific purpose company offers the following main benefits:

(i) the investor has full control of the assets (to the extent the investor holds the majority of the corporate capital of the company and appoints the majority of its directors);

(ii) the maximum liability of the investor is limited to the amount of the corporate capital of the company and of any shareholder loans (to the extent the company is carefully structured and managed);

(iii) the incorporation of such company simplifies the setting up of limited recourse financing;

(iv) the company can easily be used as vehicle for joint ventures or co-investments by structuring adequately the by-laws and if necessary by executing shareholders agreements;

(v) the investment can easily be split among multiple investors by allocating to each investor a certain percentage of the corporate capital of the company;

(vi) interests in the company can usually be transferred more easily than a transfer of a direct interest in real estate assets and can be used to grant security to any financing entities.

The main drawbacks of investing through a company are the following:

(i) the investor needs to set up a management (and in some cases an audit structure, with all the relevant costs;

(ii) the tax regime may be less beneficial than in the event of acquisition through a al estate fund.

b) Investing in a Real Estate Fund

As an alternative to setting up a real estate company, the investor may decide to invest in a real estate fund, which then acquires the real estate assets.

Pursuant to Italian law real estate funds are pools of assets managed by a specialized (and regulated) asset management company in the interest of a plurality of investors. The main difference between an investment in a real estate company and an investment in a real estate funds concerns the role of the investor: basically, while the investor in a real estate company has an "active" role and can to a certain extent direct (through the appointment of the board of directors of the company) appointment of the board of directors of the company) the management of the company and of its asset, the investor in an Italian real estate fund is a "passive" investor, and almost all the decisions concerning the management of the fund and of its assets are taken by the fund management company. The investor has a role only with respect to certain specific (and very limited decisions, such as the initial term of the fund, the amount of equity to be contributed to the fund, its initial business plan, its general investment policy and certain decisions where the management company is in conflict of interests).

Please note also that, pursuant to Italian law, real estate funds must have a plurality investors-the concept of "plurality" must be evaluated on a case by case basis and can more easily be met if the investors in the fund fall within certain categories (i.e. states or state-controlled entities, collective investment undertakings, insurance companies).

Besides the common benefits of setting up a special purpose company, investing in a real estate fund may also offer the following benefits: the management of the assets is entrusted to a specialized (and regulated) asset management company.

The main drawbacks of investing through a real estate fund are the following:

(i) the investor shall act as a "passive" investor, and therefore its involvement in the management of the assets shall be extremely limited (see above for more details);

(ii) the fees and costs of the asset management company are paid by the fund (and therefore, ultimately, by the investors); and

(iii) the fund must have a plurality of investors.

E. Structures for Doing Business

a. Governmental Participation

The Italian economy is a market-based economy. The European political and economic common space has determined the almost total liberalization of the commercial and industrial foreign investments. The government is still present in certain industries such as, for example, defence and certain other sectors which provide essential public services.

Typically, governmental control over a company is exercised through a so-called "golden share" participation, i.e. by means of specific control rights which are not necessarily based upon a majority shareholding by the government. In light of the fact that golden share participations in some cases violate existing EU regulations and for other policy reasons, the Italian government has privatized most companies which in the past were state controlled; nevertheless, there are still plenty of companies which are owned by the government and especially by local authorities, mostly in specific fields such as utilities and transports.

b. Joint Ventures

The first step to establish a joint venture in Italy is usually the execution of a joint venture agreement, setting forth the terms and conditions of the alliance between or among the parties. An antitrust assessment may be necessary before setting up the joint venture.

The joint venture may be realized either through the establishment of a special purpose corporate vehicle, or simply by entering into cooperation agreements among the partners of the joint venture regulating their commercial relationship.

In the event that a new company is established for the joint venture, prospective shareholders may consider several factors when selecting the type of company to be incorporated and management policies to be followed.

There are no restrictions as to the type of entities which can be established for a joint venture. Both stock companies (Società di Capitali) and partnerships (Società di Persone) may be used as corporate vehicles by the joint venture parties. Incorporation procedures and related costs and fees mostly depend upon the type of entity selected by the parties.

The corporate vehicle may be managed and / or represented by foreigners without restrictions; Italian law requires only directors to obtain a Italian social security number before accepting their designation as directors of an Italian corporate entity. The sole limitation (which does not apply to EU investors) to such principle is that the country of nationality of the foreign director shall allow reciprocal rights to Italian nationals; as a consequence, non-EU investors are not entitled to act as directors of Italian companies if Italian nationals cannot act as directors in the country of nationality of the foreign director. The reciprocity requirement does not apply if there is a treaty between Italy and the country of nationality of the investor governing the matter.

Under the current EU commercial practice (which has been acknowledged in the Recommendation of the European Commission of May 6, 2003), business is divided into large, small and medium-sized (SMEs) and micro enterprises:

(i) Employees: a maximum of 10 employees for micro enterprises, 50 employees for small companies, and 250 for medium-sized one;

(ii) Turnover: a maximum turnover not exceeding 2 million euro for micro business, 10 million euro for small and 50 million euro for medium-sized companies;

(iii) Shareholding: the beneficial company may not be more than one quarter participated (25%) by companies or groups not failing within the category of small to medium-sized company.

c. Limited Liability Companies

In Italy, there are two types of companies which are customary used for the expansion of foreign businesses. Such companies are the Società per Azioni (S.p.A.) and the Società a Responsabilita' Limitata (S.r.l.).

a) Società per Azioni

The S.p.A. is arguably the most common business form for medium and large companies with significant investments. Incorporation of a S.p.A. is effected by means of a public deed drafted by a notary public; such deed must then be filed with the Companies Register maintained by the competent Chamber of Commerce within 20 days from the date of incorporation. The minimum statutory capital of a S.p.A. is 120,000 EURO (25% of such capital must be paid upon incorporation). Furthermore, a S.p.A. may issue shares, bonds and other financial instruments of debt or risk, if duly authorized and permitted by its by-laws.

The management of the company may be entrusted to a Board of Directors or to a Sole Director, appointed by Shareholders. The shareholders also appoint a Board of Statutory Auditors that has supervisory powers over the company's management and its accounts. All members of the Board of Statutory Auditors must be accounting experts registered in a special register. Alternatively, external auditors may be appointed.

The by-laws may provide for a Board of Directors appointed by the shareholders, which, in turn, elects from within its members an Audit Committee (Comitato di Controllo). An external auditing body must supervise the company's accounts.

The by-laws may provide for a Supervisory Board (Consiglio di Sorveglianza) appointed by shareholders. The Supervisory Board is in charge of supervising the company's management. Moreover, the Supervisory Board appoints a Management Board (Consiglio di Gestione) which manages the affairs of the company. If resolved upon by shareholders, an external auditor is appointed to supervise the company's accounts.

b) Società a Responsabilità Limitata

S.r.l. is the legal form most suitable for small and medium companies with a limited number of shareholders. The minimum statutory capital for a S.r.l. is 10,000 EURO (25% of such capital must be paid in upon incorporation, alternatively is possible to substitute the payment with an insurance policy or a bank guaranty of the same amount.

Shareholders may be appointed as directors of the company and its management can be entrusted to either one director or to a Board of Directors, as prescribed by the by-laws. A Board of Statutory Auditors is not required unless the company's capital exceeds 120,000 EURO or, if two consecutive years, two of the following three threshold limits are exceeded:

(i) Total assets (as per the latest financial statements) exceeding 4,400,000 EURO;

(ii) Revenues from sales in excess of 8,800,000 EURO;

(iii) Average number of employees during the preceding fiscal year higher than 50.

The organizational documents must be drafted by a notary public who, within 20 days from the signature, must file such documents with the Companies' Register.

In general, the main costs associated with the formation of an Italian company (with standard by-laws) are related to Public Notary and legal fees. The same costs are applicable for the establishment of a branch.

The procedures for the establishment of a S.p.A. and a S.r.l. (in their simple standard forms) ordinary may take from one to two weeks.

In 2011, a simplified procedure has been introduced by the law for S.r.l.s incorporated by individuals under 35 years. In this case the minimum initial capital is reduced to 1 EURO.

Both the S.p.A. and the S.r.l. may be incorporated by a sole shareholder or by a number of shareholders. The same procedures and provisions mentioned above with reference to companies with a number of shareholders are applicable to a sole shareholder.

Specific disclose is required in the case of a sole shareholder; otherwise, such shareholder would become fully liable for the company's obligations.

d. Partnerships

In Italy the term Società or company includes all profit-making entities, i.e. partnership-type entities (Società di Persone) and stock companies (Società di Capitali).

Partnership-type companies are Società Semplice, Società in Nome Collettivo, and Società in Accomandita

Semplice. Such companies are characterized by the joint and unlimited liability of the partners, with the exception of Accomandanti in the case of a Società in Accomandita Semplice (see below paragraph "other types of Companies"). In the next paragraphs, a brief description of the main featuresof the two main type of partnership-type entities, the Società Semplice and the Società in Nome Collettivo are given.

a) Società Semplice

The Società Semplice is a partnership-type company which may be used for non-commercial activities (in particular, agricultural activities), characterized by the joint and unlimited liability of its shareholders.

Unless otherwise prescribed by its by-laws, the management of the Società Semplice is severely entrusted to each of its shareholders. No minimum capital is required for its incorporation and its profits are taxed at the partner's level.

b) Società in Nome Collettivo

The Società in Nome Collettivo is the most common partnership-type company which may be used for commercial activities. In a Società in Nome Collettivo, all shareholders are jointly and severally liable for the company's obligations towards third-party. The incorporation of such company is not subject to particular formalities, unless certain assets are contributed by shareholders (i.e. real estate or registered assets). No minimum capital is required for its incorporation.

One or more directors may manage the company. Their powers may be unlimited unless certain formalities are fulfilled by filling specific documentation with the Companies Register held by the Chamber of Commerce.

e. Other Types of Companies

Two other types of companies may be incorporated in Italy. Such companies categorize partners for purpose of management duties and liability. In a Società in Accomandita, there are two main categories of partners: (i) the Accomandanti which are exposed to limited liability since such partners are not allowed to perform any management acts on behalf of the company and (ii) the Accomandatari which manage the company and are held fully and jointly liable for any acts they perform on behalf of the company.

Accomandanti are comparable to contributing / financial partners, while Accomandatari may be considered as managing partners.

The participation in the Società in Accomandita may be in the form of share (Società in Accomandita per Azioni) or may be simply recorded in the stakeholders' register kept by the company (Società in Accomandita Semplice).

f. Subsidiaries / Branches / Representative Offices

Italian subsidiaries of foreign companies are subject to the provisions of law applicable to national entities. Certain requirements related to disclosure and holding company liability (in case of operations executed for the sole benefit of the group) are applicable. In general, Italian corporate law applies to those entities incorporated in Italy or that have in Italy their main office (sede del amministrazione) or their main place of business (oggetto principale).

Pursuant to Italian law, a branch office (which is an alternative to the establishment of a subsidiary) is an entity with no independent legal status, and as such forms part of its foreign parent company. Therefore, all requirements pursuant to parent company legislation must be fulfilled together with applicable requirements provided by Italian law for foreign owned branches. In particular, certain parent company documents must be filed in Italy (i.e, the current by-laws and the corporate resolutions authorizing the establishment of the branch office). In addition, a branch office must file with the Companies Register information related to the agents permanently representing the company in Italy, with specific reference to their management and / or representative powers.

A representative office can be easily established in Italy (no corporate structure or specific procedures for incorporation are required) and may be convenient from a fiscal stand point. However, such office is subject to a number of important operational limits. For example, representative offices may not be active in product marketing. Moreover, customary activities for a representative office are limited to collecting information, conducting market research and promoting the foreign enterprise's name and brand.

g. Trusts and Other Fiduciary Entities

The Hague Convention of 1 July 1985 on the Law Applicable to Trusts and on their Recognition was ratified pursuant to Italian Law No.364 of 16 October 1989 and came into force on 1 January 1992. As there is no domestic legislation relating to trusts, they can only be established in Italy in accordance with The Hague Convention and subject to a foreign law. Due to lack of domestic legislation, case law has developed with respect to trusts. There have been over seventy judgements relating to trusts in Italy in the past few years. The Italian Parliament has approved a complete set of tax provisions on trusts in Italy pursuant to law No.296 of December 27, 2006.

Article No 2645 ter of the Italian Civil Code offers the opportunity to separate part of an individual's own assets (represented by real estate and other "registered assets") for purposes recognized by the Italian legal system and for a maximum period of ninety years (or for the term of the beneficiary's life). The pursuit of such purposes must be made by the transferor or third parties and neither the assets nor the income produced by such assets may be claimed by third parties for purposes other than those assigned by the transferor.

Societa Fiduciarie (fiduciary companies) are recognized in Italy to the extent that they are authorized pursuant to the provisions of the Ministerial Decree of January 16, 1995. Such decree provides for specific capitalization and corporate requirements which must be fulfilled by the fiduciary companies in order to perform their activity in Italy.

F. Requirements for the Establishment of a Business

a. Foreign Investments

In general, foreign investments in Italy are not restricted with the exception of owning and operating aircrafts or ships: these must be under control and management of Italian or EU citizens or companies. However, please note that any acquisition of a considerable shareholding in certain corporations (such as, for example, banks and insurance companies) must be approved by the competent authorities.

b. Antitrust Laws

The basic antitrust legislation is contained in Law No.287/90 of October 10, 1990 (the "Competition Act"), which provides for the protection of competition on the national market and Presidential Decree No.217 of April 30, 1998, which regulates investigation procedures pursuant to the Competition Act.

The Italian antitrust authority (Authorità Garante della Concorrenza e del Mercato) is mainly responsible for controlling:

(i) Concentrations;
(ii) Agreements that prevent, restrict or distort competition; and,
(iii) Abuses of dominant position.

Furthermore, the AGCM is competent for misleading and comparative advertising and conflicts of interest of officials working for the Italian Government.

Decisions issued by the AGCM can be challenged before the Lazio Regional Administrative Court (Tribunale Ammistrativo Regionale per il Lazio - TAR Lazio) within 60 days from their notification to the filing parties. The judgements of TAR Lazio can be appealed before the Administrative Supreme Court (Consiglio di Stato).

The Italian antitrust rules are not applicable if the transaction falls within the scope of EU antitrust provisions.

In Italy, offences against the Competition Act are not subject to criminal penalties.

c. Governmental Approvals

No specific governmental approvals are required to operate businesses in Italy, unless such businesses conduct regulated activities such as media and telecommunication, production or distribution of energy (gas and / or electricity), or banking, insurance, investment services, and related financial services. In such cases, governmental authorities issue specific authorizations for the performance of such activities.

d. Licenses / Permits

Licenses and permits may be required in connection with certain specific activities such as the production of distribution of food products or health care products.

G. Operation of a Business

a. Advertising

There general regulations on misleading and comparative advertising (the latter is allowed only to a certain extent) and specific restrictions on the promotional activities related to specific products (such as tobacco, prescription drugs and alcohol) and professional services (such as legal services). In addition, television and radio advertising must not (i) offend human dignity or religious or idealistic beliefs, (ii) evoke racial, sexual or citizenship discrimination, (ii) lead the public to behave in a dangerous way. Mostly the media adheres to an advertising self-regulatory system referred to as the Istituto dell' Autodisaplina Pubblicitaria which aims to guarantee an honest, truthful and appropriate advertising.

b. Business Ethics / Codes

In general, commercial activities must be conducted in compliance with Italian law. Furthermore, depending on the activity performed by the investor, professional codes of conduct, specific ethics codes or contract models adopted by professional and trade associations may be applicable (i.e. for professional, financial or banking services franchising networks), although such provisions are usually not binding. As for accounting, national accounting principles (or in some cases international accounting principles) must be followed by the investor. Certain activities (i.e. banking, insurance and financial activities) are subject to strict regulation issued by independent regulatory authorities and to the supervision of such authorities.

In addition, please note that, according to Legislative Decree No.231/2001. the companies operating in Italy may be subject to administrative sanctions for certain crimes committed by the company's officers in the interest of the company (including, crimes against the Public Administration, crimes against the health and safety of workers, market abuse, corporate crimes, etc.). In such case, the company may be subject to monetary fines and other sanctions, including the prohibition to carry out the business and the prohibition to negotiate with the Public Administration. The company may seek to limit its potential liability in this respect by adopting appropriate models of internal control aimed to prevent its officers' crimes.

c. Consumer Protection Laws

In recent years, several regulations have been adopted in order to implement EC directives related to consumer rights (certain of these provisions have been incorporated into the Consumer Protection Code). There are specific Provisions which protect consumers mainly in respect of (i) contracts negotiated outside the business premises, (ii) distance contracts, (iii) unfair contractual terms between a consumer and a non-consumer, and (iv) damages caused by defective products. Furthermore, consumer protection is generally assured by providing the consumer with (i) an adequate knowledge of the terms of the transaction to be concluded, (ii) the right to revoke the contract for a specific period subsequent to its execution, and (iii) the inversion of the burden of proof. In some cases, certain "unfair" clauses may be held invalid or unenforceable.

d. Construction

Specific authorizations such as building permits and concessions must be requested from regional or local administrative authorities, depending on the features and the location of the work. Interior works may usually be commenced without any authorization, as long as notification is provided to local authorities and the authorities do not forbid the works within a certain period of time. Specific limitations may apply for construction activities in areas which are protected by general land-use restrictions or for works concerning historical or artistic buildings.

Time necessary to obtain permits, concessions and authorizations varies according to the relevance of the works and to the administrative authorities involved.

e. Contracts

An investor can freely enter into Italian contracts taking into consideration Italian investment regulations and bilateral / multilateral treaties on international investments signed by Italy and the country of the investor. The sole limitation (which does not apply to EU investors) to such principle is that the country of nationality of the investor shall allow reciprocal rights to Italian nationals; as a consequence, non-EU investors are not entitled to enter into contracts under Italian law if Italian nationals cannot enter into the same contracts in the country of nationality of the investor. Such limitation is not often applied (and is often ignored) but violations of the requirement may cause complications in case of litigation. The reciprocity requirement does not apply if there is a treaty between Italy and the country of nationality of the investor governing the matter.

Investment contracts can be governed by a foreign law if such law is applicable according to relevant conflict rules, which include a choice of law by parties to the contract. However, Italian regulations provide certainty for mandatory provisions which are also applicable to contracts governed by foreign laws.

f. Price Controls

In general, there are no administrative controls over prices. However, in certain sectors of the economy such as public services (i.e. transport, energy, and gas) or tobacco retailing, prices are regulated or fixed by public authorities.

g. Product Registration

With the exception of specific industries (such as, for example, pharmaceuticals and medical devices), no prior registration of the product is required for its marketing and sale in Italy. However, in order to be sold in the market, products must be in compliance with all relevant national and EC provisions in terms of product safety, ingredients packaging and consumer instructions.

h. Reductions or Return on Capital

In general, there are no restrictions on the movement of capital; in certain (limited) cases, a preliminary communication to the competent authorities is required.

i. Sale of Goods

In order to sell products to customers, in some cases (mostly depending on the size of the shop) a commercial permit must be obtained from a local authority. For specific activities and services related to public safety, marketing and sale must be in compliance with the provisions of the T.U.L.P.S. (Consolidated Act on Public Safety) or other regulations (i.e. chemist's shops require a specific permit). Furthermore, as a general rule, premises must be in compliance with hygienic and sanitary provisions related to the products which are sold or to the services which are offered.

j. Trade Associations

In Italy there are numerous trade associations although membership in such associations is usually not compulsory. In contrast, membership in professional organizations is required for individuals providing certain professional services (such as lawyers, architects and doctors). Both trade associations and professional organizations usually require the payment of annual fees. Mandatory trade practices for members are often stipulated; however, such practices may be in breach of competition rules if they involve price fixing or the formulation of commercial strategies for members.

H. Cessation of Termination of a Business

a. Termination

The so-called Società di Capitali (S.p.A., S.a.p.a. and S.r.l.) may be terminated voluntarily or upon occurrence of specific events prescribed by the law or set forth in the company's certificate of incorporation. Termination is implemented pursuant to a three-phase procedure:

(i) Preliminary Phase: Upon occurrence of an event of termination, an extraordinary meeting of the shareholder (or a judge, as the case may be) must appoint once or more receivers. The directors of the company must deliver to the receiver(s) the company's assets and books, and updated financial statements from the date of the latest approved balance sheet and the date of termination;

(ii) Liquidation Phase: The receivers(s) may implement all ordinary or extraordinary transactions aimed at winding up the company's business, in order to pay the company's creditors and distribute the remaining assets to the shareholders; and

(iii) Final Phase: Once the company's assets have been liquidated, the receiver(s) will draft a final balance sheet and, if the company still has assets after satisfaction of all of its creditors, a distribution plan. Finally, the receiver(s) will distribute the assets to the shareholders and request the company to be cancelled from the competent Companies Register.

b. Insolvency / Bankruptcy

The Italian insolvency legislation is currently set forth by Royal Decree No.267 of March 16, 1942, as amended and supplemented in 2005, 2006 and 2007. In Italy, the courts play a central role in the insolvency process and out-of-court restructurings have been infrequent in the past. Though some uncertainties remain, the afore mentioned reforms have gone a long way from introducing into Italian insolvency practice the opportunity for distressed debtors to resolve temporary financial difficulties through settlements with creditors and contracting new financing.

The primary aim of the bankruptcy proceedings is to liquidate the debtor's assets for the satisfaction of creditors, with a view to ensuring an equal treatment (par condicio) to all creditors. On the other side, the extraordinary administration procedure is also aimed to restructure the business and maintain employment and these aims often have been balanced by the sale of businesses as going concerns and ensuring that employees are transferred along with the businesses being sold.

Under Italian law, a company may be declared insolvent by a court only, based on insolvency (insolvenza). Insolvency occurs when a debtor (i.e. a company) is no longer able to regularly meet its obligations as and when they become due on a permanent, rather than temporary, basis. The following restructuring and bankruptcy alternatives are available under Italian law for companies facing financial difficulties:

a) Restructuring outside of judicial process. In Italy, restructuring generally takes place through the formal judicial process because of the more favourable conditions for the debtor and the fact that informal arrangements put in place as a result of a non-judicial restructuring are vulnerable to being reviewed by a court in the event of a subsequent insolvency and possibly challenged as voidable transactions. However, in cases where a company is solvent, but financial difficulties, it may be possible for the company to enter into an out-of- court arrangement with its creditors (concordato stragiudiziale), which may safeguard the existence of the company.

b) Court-supervised pre-bankruptcy composition with creditors (concordato preventivo). Prior to the declaration of bankruptcy, any company that is in a distressed condition (stato di crisi) may make a proposal for a composition with its creditors (concordato preventio), in order to avoid a declaration of bankruptcy and the initiation of liquidation proceedings. Application for pre-bankruptcy composition shall be filed with the competent Court. Only the distressed company (and not its creditors) can file for pre-bankruptcy composition and the filing must be approved by its board of directors. Applications for a pre-bankruptcy composition must be based on a composition plan. The plan may include:(i) debt restructuring and payment of credits through any means, including assignment of assets, assumptions of the debt (accollo) and other extraordinary transactions, such as the granting to creditors, and companies formed or owned (in whole or in part) by creditors, of shares, bonds, including convertible bonds, or other financial and debt instruments; (ii) the assignment of the debtor business to third parties including creditors, and companies formed or owned (in whole or in part) by creditors, or to be formed during implementation of the plan, the shares of which are to be attributed to creditors as a result of the plan; (iii) the division of creditors into classes according to like legal position and homogenous economic interest; and (iv) differential treatment of creditors belonging to different classes. The application for pre-bankruptcy composition must be accompanied by, amongst others, a report drafted by an eligible professional. The composition plan is approved with the favourable vote of creditors representing the majority of credits entitled to vote. If there are different classes of creditors, approval of the composition plan requires the favourable vote of creditors representing the majority of credits admitted to each class Secured creditors shall be excluded from voting on the composition plan except to the extent that they renounce their security interest. During the pendency of the concordato preventivo proceedings, all actions by creditors are stayed. During the implementation of the arrangement, the company is managed by the debtor but under the surveillance of an official appointed by the court, and under the supervision of the court. If the concordato preventivo fails, the company could be declared bankrupt by the court and enter bankruptcy (fallimento) proceedings.

 c) Debt restructuring agrements (accordi di ristrutturazione dei debiti). Companies may: (i) reach an agreement with their creditors representing at least 60% of all claims; and (ii) following publication in the companies register, submit the agreement to the Court for approval. Application to the Court to obtain approval for the restructuring agreements shall be filed by the debtor. As for the pre-bankruptcy composition, the filing must be approved by the debtor's board of directors and creditors are not entitled to take the initiative for a 60-day period starting from the date of publication of the restructuring agreement. Restructuring agreements may include a wide range of provisions such as rescheduling of debts, partial debt forgiveness, transfer of assets to creditors, conversion of credits into equity and refinancing of the company with the purpose of permitting a restructuring and the continuation of the debtor's business. All creditors are not required to receive the same treatment as each is free to evaluate the debtor's proposals and to autonomously protect its own position. The restructuring agreement must be accompanied by an expert's report regarding the feasibility of the restructuring agreement with particular reference to the debtor's ability to ensure the regular (i.e. complete) payment of creditors not adhering to the restructuring agreement Following a restructuring agreement, there is no dispossession and the debtor remains entitled to manage its business. If a restructuring agreement is not implemented, the adhering creditors would be able to terminate it for non-performance in accordance with the provisions set out in the Italian civil code on contracts.

 d) Restructuring plans (piani di risanamento). Acts, payments and securities / guarantees granted on the debtor's assets, provided they are made in implementation of a plan that appears to be capable of permitting the restructuring of the debtor's indebtedness and to ensure the rebalancing of its financial condition and the rationality of which is attested in accordance with the provisions of Article 2501-bis, fourth paragraph of the Italian civil code, are exempt from bankruptcy claw back. Restructuring plans are not under any form of judicial control or approval and, therefore, no application is to be made to the Court or other supervising authority. An expert's reasonableness attestation is required in relation to a restructuring plan. The expert must be either an auditor or an auditing company enrolled in a special register and, according to the prevailing opinion, is appointed by the company and not by the Court. Creditors are not required receive the same treatment as they are free to evaluate the debtor's proposals and to autonomously protect their own position. Restructuring plans do not require the consent of a specific majority of all outstanding claims. Following a restructuring agreement, there is no dispossession and the debtor remains entitled to manage its business. No Court or creditors' appointed officer is contemplated nor any Court's supervision.

 e) Extraordinary administration for large companies (amministrazione straordinaria delle imprese in crisi). Under Italian law, large industrial and commercial enterprises may avail themselves of special administration proceedings. The purpose of the administration proceedings is to rehabilitate a company in financial distress in light of the significance of the company's technical, commercial and productive value and to maintain employment. Pursuant to the Legislative Decree No.270 of July 8, 1999, the requirements to be admitted to amministrazione straordinaria are (i) 200 or more employees in the year before the procedure was commenced; (ii) debt equal to at least two-thirds of its total assets and two-thirds of its total income generated by sales and services for the last fiscal year. The effects of the procedure consist of: (i) the adoption of a rehabilitation program which might alternatively be a program of corporate restructuring (lasting a maximum of two years), or a program of asset disposal (lasting a maximum of one year); (ii) stay of actions by creditors; (iii) appointment by the Government of one or three receivers (commissario straordinario) to substitute the existing management in the company's operations. The court must assess the prospects of the plan's success in light of reports submitted by the receiver / s; the court may then either issues a decree to place the enterprise under the administration procedure or orders judicial liquidation.

New extraordinary administration proceedings have been enacted (amministrazione straordinaia delle grandi imprese in crisi ex Law Decree No.347 of December 23, 2003, as subsequently amended) and are available to insolvent companies having more than 500 employees in the year before the procedure was commenced and debt (including those from outstanding guarantees) equal to at least 300 million EURO. This recent legislation represents a refinement of the old proceedings as it expedites the admission to extraordinary administration for the companies which satisfy the aforementioned conditions. The substantial effects of the procedure, however, remain unchanged. the main difference being that the claw-back provisions apply also in case of a restructuring program authorized by the Government.

Finally, in light of the financial difficulties currently faced by Alitalia S.p.A., the Italian government has enacted an amendment to Law Decree No.347 of 23 December 2003 adopting the Law Decree No.134 of August 28, 2008 (converted into law with amendments by Law No.166 of 2008), that addresses the specific distressed state of Alitalia S.p.A.. The reforms enacted by means of Law Decree No.134 of 2008 have introduced some specific provisions applying to companies which carry out public essential services and allow also to "very large companies'", to which the provisions of Law Decree No.347 of 23 December 2003 applies, the possibility to be subject to an amministrazione straordinaria delle grandi imprese in crisi not aimed at the rescue of the company but rather to the assignment of the going concern (cessione dei complessi agiendali).

f) Bankruptcy proceeding (fallimento). A commercial entity may be deemed insolvent when it is unable to pay its debts as they fall due (Article 5 of the Insolvency Act). A request to declare a company bankrupt and to commence a bankruptcy proceeding (fallimento) for the liquidation of a company can be made by the company, the creditor(s) or a public prosecutor. Upon the declaration of bankruptcy: (i) subject to certain exceptions, all actions of creditors are stayed, and creditors must file claims within a defined period; (ii) the administration of the company and the management of its assets pass from the debtor to the receiver; and (iii) any act made by the company after a declaration of bankruptcy is ineffective with respect to the creditors. The bankruptcy proceeding is carried out and supervised by a court-appointed receiver, a deputy judge and a creditors' committee. The Court declaring the bankruptcy has the control over the entire procedure and has the exclusive jurisdiction with respect to all the actions arising from and related to the bankruptcy procedure. The deputy judge is empowered to control the regularity of the procedure and reports to the Court with respect to any matter subject to the jurisdiction of the Court. The receiver is empowered to manage the business of the debtor under the control of the deputy judge and of the creditors committee and is in charge of (i) forming the list of the creditors, on the basis of their respective priority rights, (ii) assessing the number and status of the debtor's assets, (iii) managing and liquidating the assets, (iv) terminating or continuing the contracts to which the bankrupt company is party (v) initiating any action to set aside and revoke the transactions carried out during the so called "suspect period", (vi) satisfying the creditors in accordance with their respective priority rights and to the extent the liquidation of the assets allows it, (vii) initiating any action against the former directors and auditors of the insolvent company, (viii) notifying the public prosecutor of any criminal liability of which he becomes aware of; and (ix) drafting the liquidation plan of the debtor's estate. The creditors' committee, constituted by 3 or 5 members, is appointed by the deputy judge among the creditors in order to represent the various groups of creditors and taking into account the actual possibilities of repayment of the respective claims. The committee controls the activity carried out by the receiver and gives the relevant authorizations with respect to the performance of the receiver's material acts. The proceeds from the liquidation are distributed in accordance with statutory priority. Italian insolvency law grants priority to the payment of certain preferential creditors, including employees and the Italian treasury.

Under Italian law, as in other jurisdictions, there are the so-called "claw-back" actions (azioni revocatorie) that may give rise to the revocation of payments or the setting aside of grants of security interests made by the company prior to the declaration of bankruptcy. In a bankruptcy proceeding (fallimento), Italian law provides for a claw-back period of up to one year. A bankruptcy receiver can request that certain transactions of the debtor during the one year-period preceding the declaration of bankruptcy be declared ineffective. In case of infra-group transactions, the claw-back period can be extended to up to five years. In any case, it should be noted that: (i) under article 64 of Royal Decree No.267/1942, all transactions for no consideration, depending on certain circumstances, are ineffective vis-d-vis creditors if entered into by the bankrupt entity in the two-year period prior to the bankruptcy declaration, and (ii) under article 65 of Royal Decree no 267/1942, payments of receivables becoming due on the day of the insolvency declaration or thereafter are ineffective vis-a-vis creditors, if made by the bankrupt entity in the two-year period prior to the bankruptcy declaration.

g) post-bankruptcy composition with creditors (concordato fallimentare). A bankruptcy (fallimento) can be terminated prior to the receiver's liquidation by a company filing a petition to the insolvency court for a post-bankruptcy composition with creditors (concordato fallimentare). The proposal may provide for (i) the division of the creditors into different classes, in accordance with their similar juridical position and economic interests; (ii) the differential treatment for creditors belonging to different classes, giving evidence of the reasons of the different treatments; (iii) the restructuring of the debt and the satisfaction of the creditors by specific technical or legal means, including the assumption of the debt (accollo), merger or any other corporate transaction, such as the assignment to creditors or to companies in which they hold an interest, of shares or quotas (i.e. "debt to equity swap"), or bonds, including those convertible into shares or other financial instruments and debt securities; (iv) the partial payment of the secured creditors (subject to the condition that said partial payment is not lower than the amount that could be recovered through the sale of the secured asset, on the basis of the value estimated by an independent expert); (v) the transfer to a third party (the "assuntore") of the assets of the debtor and of actions (including the claw-back and indemnity actions) filed by the receiver in the interest of the procedure. The proposal is deemed approved if it receives the favourable vote of the creditors which represent the majority of the claims admitted to mvote. If theproposal provides for different classes of creditors, the proposal is deemed approved if it receives the favourable vote of the creditors which represent the majority of the claims admitted to vote in each class. The concordato fallimentare is effective with respect to all creditors, which were creditors for title, fact, reason or cause prior to the opening of the bankruptcy procedure, including those who have not filed a request of participation to the procedure.

It should also be noted that the EU Council Regulation no.1346/2000 of May 29, 2000, contains rules for addressing conflicts of laws in relation to insolvency proceedings within the European Union. In particular, such Regulation provides (i) that the law applicable to insolvency proceedings and its effects shall be that of the Member State within the territory of which such proceedings are opened (lex fori) and (ii) the automatic recognition of the insolvency proceedings in all the other Member States.

I. Merger and Acquisition

Italy's M&A market is steadily growing in the last years mainly due to cross-border transactions, which demonstrate the strong appeal of Italian market to foreign (industrial and financial) investors. Such a growth has also affected the public M&A sector, which is registering the consummation of several significant transactions every year. The knowledge of the main provisions of the complex regulation applicable to public M&A deals, as well as - of course - the advice of lawyers of proven expertise and experience, is fundamental for a better planning of such transactions, as well as for the successful execution of the same.

a. General Corporate Issues

The main laws and regulations applicable to public M&A transactions are the following: (i) the Italian Civil Code; (ii) the legislative decree no.58/1998; (iii) the Regulation no.11971/1999 of Commissione Nazionale per le Società e la Borsa (Consob-the Italian Securities and Exchange Commission); and (iv) the corporate governance code (applicable on a voluntary basis).

In the planning of acquisitions of interests in Italian listed companies, investors shall be aware that the holding by a shareholder-alone or together with other shareholders acting in concert with him-of a stake or voting rights higher than 25% (or 30%, if another shareholder holds a stake or voting rights higher than the threshold of 25%) implies, for such a shareholder, the obligation to promote a takeover bid on all the remaining shares. The existence of such an obligation leads to the distinction between "mandatory takeovers" and "voluntary takeovers".

In addition, if a party holds more than 90% of the share capital of an Italian listed company, the same must purchase the remaining securities on the request of any holder thereof, unless a float sufficient to ensure regular trading performance is restored within 90 days. On the other side, if - as a result of a global takeover bid - the offeror holds more than 95% of the share capital of an Italian listed company, the offeror, in addition to the obligation to purchase the remaining securities on the request of any holder thereof, has also the right to purchase the remaining securities within three months of the offer period (so-called "squeeze-out").

The acquisition of a listed company may be carried out by public tender offer, merger, acquisition outside the market or subscription of a reserved share capital increase.

It is worth pointing out that when the investors choose the way of the public tender offer, then they must prepare an offer communication for the public and file an offer document with Consob within 20 days from the issuance of the aforesaid communication (the Italian law provides for a detailed content of both the aforesaid documents). Consob must approve the offer document within 15 days from the filing, while the offer period shall last a minimum of 15 trading days up to a maximum 25 trading days for mandatory takeovers, or 40 trading days for voluntary takeovers. Among the requirements which shall be met in order to promote tender offers, bidders are required to ensure their capacity to fulfil the payment commitments related to the offer, providing Consob with evidence of guarantees issued in their favor for this purpose.

Under Italian law, listed target company are not obliged to provide potential bidder with due diligence information on the same. Nevertheless, it is market practice that public companies provide potential friendly bidders with confidential information, provided that such bidders execute confidentiality agreements and are evaluating a launch of a tender offer for the benefit of all the shareholders. Having said that, please note that bidders may acquire several data on Italian listed companies since, pursuant to Italian law, such entities must make available to the public a set of information concerning themselves and their subsidiaries, including those of price sensitive nature.

b. Price of Takeover Bids

With respect to the price of takeover bids in Italy, it should be noted that while consideration of voluntary takeovers can be freely set, consideration of mandatory takeovers must not be lower than the highest consideration paid by the bidder to acquire the securities subject to the offer during the 12 months before communication of the intention to launch the offer. If no purchase for consideration was made in this period, the offer consideration must not be lower than the average weighted market price over the previous 12 months or the shorter available period.

Please note that if the bidder purchases securities subject to the offer in the period between the communication of his intention to launch the offer and the six months following the end of the offer period at a higher consideration, the price offered for the voluntary / mandatory takeover shall be increased.

c. Anti-takeover Defences

When investors are planning to launch a takeover bid, they shall take in due account that anti-takeover defences may jeopardise-in different ways-the success of their offer. In this respect, Consob identifies three different defensive measures: (i) actions aimed at increasing the total value of the tender consideration; (ii) actions aimed at materially affecting the economic conditions of the target; and (iii) any other action aimed at obstructing the activity of the bidder.

However, please note that, generally speaking, issuers whose securities are involved in tender offers shall abstain from adopting defensive measures (so-called "passivity rule"), unless the latter have been approved by the ordinary or extraordinary shareholders' meeting during the tender offer. Italian listed companies are entitled to waive the passivity rule, in whole or in part, by amending their by-laws.

The best way to overcome defensive measures is to make clear the benefits of the tender offer, thus preventing the shareholders' meeting from approving anti-takeover defenses envisaged by the board of directors (the composition of the Italian listed company does not encourage hostile acquisitions, since controlling shareholders typically hold a large stake of the share capital; as a consequence, in Italy there are only few examples of successful hostile acquisitions). Should defensive measures be taken without the requirements set forth by the law are met, then the bidder shall be entitled to challenge such measures before the courts or Consob.

d. Protection of Friendly Deals from Hostile Interlopers

The Italian regulation does not provide the bidders with any protective measures against hostile interlopers, since the only purpose of the law is the protection of the interests of shareholders. However, in order to strengthen its position, a bidder can execute (i) an agreement with the former controlling shareholder to regulate his acceptance of the envisaged tender offer providing a penalty in case the former controlling shareholder accepts a counter-offer; or (ii) an agreement with target shareholders to prevent the success of competing offers, subject to publicity requirements.

e. Antitrust and Other Regulatory Issues

Under Italian law, notification to the Italian Competition Authority (ICA) is required if the following cumulative turnover thresholds are met: (i) the combined aggregate turnover achieved in Italy in the last financial year by the undertakings concerned is higher than Euro 492 million; and (ii) the aggregate turnover achieved in Italy in the last financial year by the target company is above Euro 49 million. For banks and financial institutions, the turnover must be equal to the value of one-tenth of their total assets, with the exclusion of memorandum accounts. For insurance companies, the turnover must be equal to the value of premiums collected.

A concentration must be notified before it is carried out, after the parties have reached an agreement on the main aspects of the transaction. Please note that notification does not entail any obligation to suspend the transaction. However, if competition concerns arise, the ICA may order divestiture of the whole or part of the business acquired.

Failure to notify may result in fines of up to one percent of the companies' turnover; however, for failure concerning concentrations that do not have a significant local competition effects, as a matter of practice, the ICA imposes low fines (for example, Euro 5,000).

As far as the timing of antitrust review is concerned, please note that the first phase of the merger control procedure takes 30 calendar days from notification (15 days in the case of a public bid also filed with Consob). In the case of insurance companies, the 30-day period is suspended to allow the relevant regulatory authority to issue its opinion. This must be issued within 30 days of receiving the request. In the case of opening an in-depth investigation, a decision must be taken within 45 calendar days from opening the investigation.

In addition to the above, please note that acquisition of a significant stake in banks, insurance companies, funds etc., is subject to the approval of the competent authorities and that the Italian government can exercise the so-called "golden powers" over undertakings operating in the defense and national security, energy, transport, and communications sectors. These powers range from vetoing acquisitions of holdings and strategic decisions, to imposing specific conditions on the acquisition. The reciprocity principle applies vis-à-vis non-EU states.

f. Tax Issues

There are no special tax regulations for M&A deals, to which the rules on direct taxation of capital gains set forth by Italian Presidential Decree 917/86 apply. It is worth noting that the tax consequences of M&A deals can vary hugely in relation to the structure of the transaction and generally depend on several factors.

A financial transaction tax (FTT) is levied on transfers of ownership of shares issued by Italian resident companies, regardless of the place of residence of the parties involved or the place where the contract was executed. The taxable basis is the consideration paid. The standard rate is 0.2%, reduced to 0.1% for transactions executed on regulated markets or in multilateral trading facilities established in an EU member state or a European Economic Area country that is included on the whitelist. The FTT is payable by the transferee.

Dividends paid to non-Italian resident shareholders are in principle subject to a withholding tax applied at an ordinary rate equal to 26%.

Whether capital gains tax is levied on the non-resident investor depends on several factors, including the percentage of the participation.

J. Competition Regulation

a. Department Supervising Competition Regulation

The Italian Antitrust Authority (Autorità Garante dela Concorrenza e del Mercato AGCM) is the supervising department of anti-unfair competition and antitrust, and is mainly responsible for controlling:
(i) Concentrations;
(ii) Agreements that prevent, restrict or distort competition; and,
(iii) Abuses of dominant position.

Decisions issued by the AGCM can be challenged before the Lazio Regional Administrative Court (Tribunale Amministrativi Regionale per il Lazio-TAR Lazio) within 60 days from their notification to the filling parties. The judgements of TAR Lazio can be appealed before the Administrative Supreme Court (Consiglio di Stato).

b. Brief Introduction of Competition Law

The basic antitrust legislation is contained in Law No.287/90 of October 10, 1990 (the "Competition Law"), which provides for the protection of competition on the national market and Presidential Decree NO.217 of April 30, 1998, which regulated investigation procedures pursuant to the Competition Act.

The Italian antitrust rules are not applicable if the transaction falls within the scope of EU antitrust provisions. In Italy, offences against the Competition Act are not subject to criminal penalties.

c. Measures Regulating Competition

a) Concentrations

Joint venture agreements, mergers and acquisition of control (whether direct or indirect) of companies or business entities through the purchase of shares or assets, by contract or other means, may be subject to prior scrutiny of the AGCM which may prohibit the implementation of such transactions if it determines that the proposed transaction unlawfully limits competition.

Concentrations in specific economic sectors may require multiple filings to different authorities, each of them analysing and assessing different aspects of the transaction. These sectors are the banking and financial sector, the telecommunications and radio and television broadcasting sector, the insurance sector and the energy sector.

The Italian provisions concerning concentrations are widely modelled on European merger legislation and practice. The "one-stop shop" principle applies. The AGCM follows, in principle, the guidelines set forth in the European Commission's notices relating to concentrations subject to Regulation (EC) 139/2004.

Prior notification to the AGCM is required if either one of the following two criteria is met:

(i) The aggregate total turnover in Italy of all the companies involved (i.e., the Italian turnover of the purchaser and the target) exceeds 461 million EURO in the aggregate; or

(ii) The domestic turnover of the target company or business to be acquired exceeds 46 million EURO (the thresholds are updated by the Italian Antitrust Authority on a yearly basis).

The term "turnover" means sales made in Italy in the previous financial year by the involved companies and their respective groups.

Informal guidance may be requested from the AGCM. During the pre-notification phase, the parties may submit a written description of the transaction to be discussed with the Authority's officials.

Notification must be done through the completion of a form which must be filled immediately upon execution of the merger or purchase agreement. A filing fee must be paid of 1.2% of the transaction value referred to the Italian part of the concentration, ranging between a minimum of 3,000 EURO and a maximum of 60,000 EURO. Within 30 days from receipt of the form, the AGCM can launch an in-depth investigation if it believes that the proposed transaction may create or strengthen a dominant position on the Italian market with the effect of eliminating or restricting competition significantly and on a lasting basis. In such case, the authority is required to issue its decision within 45 days from the date of opening of the investigation. If, on the contrary, the AGCM decides that the transaction does not give rise to competition concerns, it must communicate its approval to the parties within 30 days from its receipt of the form.

Contrary to EU antitrust approval, which must be obtained prior to the closing of a transaction, an acquisition or a merger can be implemented in Italy prior to the decision of the IAA. However, the IAA, upon launching an investigation, may instruct the parties to suspend the implementation of the transaction pending tis final decision.

The IAA can clear or prohibit a concentration. In addition, it can make the approval of a concentration subject to structural or behavioural commitments by the parties to remedy any resulting distortion of competition.

In the case of failure to notify, the AGCM can impose on the parties responsible for the notification a fine up to 1% of their annual worldwide turnover. The AGCM can also impose fines ranging between 1% and 10% of the annual worldwide turnover of the business forming the object of the concentration of effective competition and remove the effects that caused he distortion has not been complied with.

b) Agreements that Prevent, Restrict or Distort Competition

Article 2 of the Competition Act, similar to Article 81 of the EC Treaty, provides that agreements are prohibited between undertakings, which have as their object or effect an appreciable prevention, restriction or distortion of competition within the national market or within a substantial part of it. The prohibition applies for example to price-fixing or market sharing cartels.

An investigation may be started by the AGCM on its own initiative, or following a complaint by an undertaking, a public policy agency or a private individual.

Companies being investigated may submit commitments within 3 months of the opening of a proceeding. If the AGCM accepts such commitments, they will become compulsory and the proceeding will be closed without reporting an infringement. In the event of a failure to comply with commitments the Authority may impose an administrative fine of up to 10% of turnover.

Since February 2007 a leniency programme is in place. A company will not receive any fine if it is the first to submit voluntarily information or evidence as to the existence of infringement. A reduction of no more than 50% of the fine may be applied if the submitted evidence significantly strengthens, by its very nature of its level of detail, the evidence already in the possession of the AGCM.

c) Abuses of Dominant Position

The abuse by one or more undertakings of a dominant position within the domestic market or in a substantial part of it is prohibited. Examples of such abuse include imposing unfair purchase or selling prices or other unfair contractual conditions, and limiting or restricting production, markets or investment, technical development or progress, Companies being investigated may submit commitments within 3 months of the opening of a proceeding into abuses of a dominant position. If the AGCM accepts the commitments, they will become compulsory and the proceeding will be closed without reporting an infringement. In the event of a failure to comply with commitments, the Authority may impose an administrative fine of up to 10% of turnover.

K. Tax

a. Tax Regime and Rules

The tax regime is built on direct and indirect tax. Italy implements tax regime per person to its domestic individuals and enterprises, meaning that Italy taxes income tax on both domestic income and income abroad, in which payable tax does not include tax paid abroad. Foreign non-resident individuals in Italy tax only income received in Italy.

b. Main Categories and Rates of Tax

Taxes are mainly categorized in 3 categories:

a) Taxation on Corporations

The Italian corporate income tax ("IRES") has been substantially reformed starting from January 1, 2004 and subsequently further modified. The ordinary corporate tax rate is 27.5%. From tax year 2011, the rate is 38% for companies that, in the previous financial year, had (i) revenues exceeding 10 million EURO, (ii) a taxable income higher than 1 million EURO, and (iii) carry on certain types of activities in the fields of energy production and supply. Starting from tax year 2011, "non-operating entities" are subject to a 38% corporate tax rate.

Companies are also subject to a regional tax on productive activities ("IRAP") that is levied on the net value of the production derived in each Italian region. The standard rate is 3.9%. Regional authorities may increase or decrease the standard rate. The filing of the tax return and the payment of IRAP follow the rules applicable for corporate income tax. The IRAP tax return is filed separately from the IRES tax return.

Registration tax is due on deeds and contracts which are subject to registration in public registers on which are voluntarily registered in such registers. Rates vary according to the nature of the deed or contract from 0.5% to 8% (15% on sale of farm land). As general rule, if a transaction is subject to Value Added Tax ("IVA") registration tax is applicable at the fixed rate of 168.00 EURO. Companies which have real estate properties situated in Italy are subject to unified municipal tax ("IMU"). Currently, the standard rate is 0.76%. which can be increased or decreased depending on the municipality and depending on the real estate property.

VAT applies to the supply of goods and services within Italy by a taxable person and to the importation of goods by anyone. Companies are always considered taxable persons. With effect from 17 September 2011, the general rate is 21%. Reduced rates range from 10% to 4%.

b) Taxation on Individuals

Individuals are subject to individual income tax ("IRPEF") that is a progressive tax which applies to the aggregate taxable income of the taxpayer.

The following rates apply to taxable income and capital gains:

Taxable income (EURO)	Rate (%)
Up to 15,000	23
15,000 - 28,000	27
28,000 - 55,000	38
55,000 - 75,000	41
Over 75,000	43

From January 1, 2011 until December 31, 2013 a surcharge of 3% applies for individuals earning income which exceeds 300,000 EURO. The above rates are increased by a regional surcharge ranging between 0.9% - 1.4%, depending on the region. The rate may be further increased by the municipal and provincial surtax, determined by each municipally and province at an aggregate rate up to 0.8%.

c) Taxation on Other Legal Entities

Non-commercial entities resident in Italy (i.e. public or private entities other than companies not having as their sole or main purpose the conduct of a business activity) are subject to IRES. The rate is 27.5%.

Non-commercial entities are subject to IRAP even if they exclusively carry on non-commercial activities. In such case, the taxable base for IRAP purposes is the remuneration paid by the entity to (i) employees and other persons treated as employees for income tax purpose and (ii) independent workers who conduct such activity on a non-habitual basis. Only certain costs of personnel are deductible. The standard rate is 3.9%.

Non-commercial entities are taxable persons for VAT purposes only if, and to the extent that, they carry on a commercial activity habitually. As for the application of VAT, filing, payment, and rates, the rules provided for companies apply.

c. Tax Declaration and Preference

Due to the complicity and wide variety of taxes, enterprises shall consult to specific accounting firms. Generally, VAT shall be declared within 3 months after completion of transaction. For the declaration of commercial entities income tax, tax papers shall be submitted within the ninth month after the final taxable month.

L. Securities

a. Brief Introduction of Securities-related Laws and Regulations

Regarding securities transactions, Foreign companies registered in Italy enjoy the same treatments as local companies. The main laws and regulations regulating securities are: "Testo Unico Finanziario", "Disposizioni di Vigilanza per gli intermediary finanziari", "Organization Structure and Protocol of Financial Intermediaries Engaging in Investments or Asset Management Services", "Regolamento Intermediari", "Testo Unico Bancario".

b. Supervision and Regulation of Securities Market

The financial industry is mainly supervised and regulated by the "Italian Security Supervision Committee" and the "Italian Central Bank". The "Italian Security Supervision Committee" is mainly responsible for examining the transparency and correctness of finance operating personnel's behaviours, maintaining the reputation and fair competition of the security market, protecting investors' interests, guarantying the security market is in accordance with related laws and regulations, and penalizing illegal activities. On the other hand, the "Italian Central Bank" is in charge of maintaining the stability of currency and finance.

c. Requirements for Engagement in Securities Trading for Foreign Enterprises

According to the "Financial Intermediates Regulation", local finance institutions have to submit application to "CONSOB" to engage in investment services. The Italian Decree No.385 of September 1st, 1993 and Italian Central Bank's Regulation No.229 of April 21st, 1999 have clear regulations on access requirements for foreign banks entering in the Italian market.

III. Trade

A. Department Supervising Trade

In Italy the department supervising trade is the Economic Development Department (Ministero dello Sviluppo Economico), and under the Economic Development Department, there are Cabinet offices, seven divisions and a bureau, including: (i) Cabinet offices (responsible for coordinating different government departments, news publication and international relationship developent); (ii) Division for the supervision of institutions, the cooperative system and the commission, internal affairs division, division for market, insurance, and so.ice industry, division for company development, division for market reguJa (ion and consumer protection, division for mineral and energy resources and division for business incentives; (iii) Economic development and policy coordination bureau (in charge of national-scale planning and policies coordination).

B. Brief Introduction of Trade Laws and Regulations

As State Member of the EU, Italy implements uniform EU Common Trade Policy although technology safety and examination of products imported and exported are transformed to local regulations from EU indications.

C. Trade Management

Italy's trade management is mainly focused in national import and export, and customs regulations, and under the EU Common Trade Policy.

D. Import and Export

Exports: in general, there are no specific restrictions on exports. However, EU Regulations and Italian law also provide specific restrictions with respect to the export of certain goods such as, for example, arms and dual use goods, pharmaceutical products and national treasures and works of art.

Import: as mentioned above, the EU Member States have a fixed Community Customs Tariff with conventional duty rates, but also apply preferential rates on the basis of association agreements, free trade agreements or general tariff preferences. All the various measures applicable to goods are included in the online customs tariff database (also known as TARIC), in which are integrated all measures relating to tariff, commercial and agricultural legislation. The TARIC includes the provisions of the combined tariff suspensions, tariff quotas, tariff preferences and trade defence measures (anti-dumping, anti-subsidy, safeguards). In general, import barriers are limited to those justified by political and sanitary reasons.

E. Customs Management

Italy is a signatory of the General Agreement of Tariffs and Trade ("GATT") since 1950 and is a member of the World Trade Organization since it came into begin on January 1, 1995.

Italy is also a founding member of the European Union (EU). The EU is based on a customs union, which entails:

(i) The elimination of all customs duties and other restrictions on imports and exports between EU Member States (goods can be transferred from one EU Member State to another without completing customs formalities);

(ii) The application of a common customs tariff to goods imported from outside the EU;

(iii) The common commercial policy.

Regulation (EEC) 2913/92 of October 12, 1992, as amended, (the "Community Customs Code"), Regulation (EEC) 2454/93 of July 2, 1993, as amended, (the "Implementing Regulation") and Regulation (EC) No.2658/87 of July 23, 1987, as amended, (the "Community Customs Tariff") are the main instruments comprising the legislative framework for customs administration in the EU Member States. They are directly applicable in all EU Member States and have primacy over the national law of the Member States.

However, Community customs law is executed by the national authorities of the Member States.

Detailed provisions necessary for the implementation of the Community Customs Code are set out in the Implementing Regulation. At the national level, implementing measures are also contained in the Consolidated version of the provisions relating to customs duties approved by Decree No.43 of the President of the republic of January 23, 1973.

For the purpose of the Community Customs Tariff, goods are classified in the Combined Nomenclature (CN), a system of classification of goods based on the Harmonized System (HS) of the World Customs Organization, with further EU subdivisions.

Through the common commercial policy, the EU has exclusive competence for negotiating tariff and trade agreements with third countries, granting unilateral preferences and adopting measures to protect trade such as anti-dumping measures, countervailing measures and safeguard measures. The EU may also initiate investigations under the "Trade Barriers Regulation" and start WTO Dispute Settlement proceedings.

On January 1, 2001, the Italian legislature formed a customs agency in order to enhance the dynamic administration of trade. Such agency is a public entity with judicial powers and broad administrative discretion and autonomy. Economic operators wishing to import or export a product in or from Italy may request the customs agency to issue a binding tariff information (BTI) or binding origin information (BOI).

The territories of the EU Member States together form the customs territory of the EU. However, the municipalities of Livigno and Campione d'Italia and the national waters of Lake Lugano, although being in Italy, are excluded from the EU customs territory.

IV. Labour

A. Brief Introduction of labour Laws and Regulations

Under Italian employment law, terms of employment are governed by (i) statutory law, (ii) national collective agreements, (iii) supplemental agreements at company level, (iv) individual employment contracts and (v) employment regulations.

a. Statutory Law

The Italian civil code contains several provisions related to the duties of the employee, loyalty obligations, confidentiality, disciplinary sanctions, social security, termination of the employment relationship and indemnities (severance payments), non-competition clauses during and after the employment relationship and rights of employees upon transfer of undertakings. In addition to such provisions, certain laws contain provisions applicable to dismissal, social security and other aspects of the employment relationship.

b. National Collective Agreements

National collective agreements are negotiated on a national level from time to time (usually every 4 years, although the economic terms are negotiated every 2 years) by unions and associations of employers. Each industry or trade has a specific national collective agreement, which applies to individuals employed in that particular industry or trade. Furthermore, executive-level employees are subject to a different agreement than non-executive level employees. The employer may freely choose which national collective agreement should be applicable, but usually the agreement referring to the industry sector or trade to which the company belongs is utilized.

National Collective Agreements contain provisions related to salary, job duties, seniority increases, seniority bonus, working time, vacations, sickness leave, parental leave, grievance procedures, transfers, secondment, termination of the employment relationship (notice periods, justification, form of the dismissal), pension schemes, social security, arbitration, union representations and other matters.

National collective Agreements contain provisions generally provide for more favourable conditions than statutory provisions or, in other cases, such agreements stipulate specific rules for the application of the general statutory rules (as in the case of disciplinary sanctions and grievance procedures). They do not have the status of law but, in practice, are generally applied and are therefore considered binding upon all employers (further, in the event of litigation, such agreements are usually applied by labour courts).

Therefore, in order to determine which rules are applicable to a specific employment relationship, both statutory law and national collective agreements must be considered.

c. Company Level Collective Agreements

National collective agreements may be supplemented by agreements at the company level. The purpose of such supplemental agreements is to regulate areas which are partially covered or not covered by the national collective agreements, such as for example work conditions and additional benefits.

d. Individual Employment Agreements

Collectively with the national collective agreements and supplemental agreements (if any), the employment relationship is governed by the individual employment agreement which contains the salary applicable to the relevant employee, including any additional compensation over and above the minimum levels set forth in the national collective agreement in consideration of the employee's capability and performance.

As a result of the detailed regulation of the employment relationship by statutory law and national collective agreements, often the scope of individual employment agreements is limited and mainly provides for the improvement of the basic economic terms.

Please note that individual employment agreements cannot derogate from the provisions of law and national collective agreements to the detriment of the employee.

e. Employment Regulations

Pursuant to section 36 of the Italian Constitution, an employee is entitled to receive a salary proportional to the quantity and quality of his / her working activities. Such salary must be "sufficient" in order to assure a dignified life to him / her and his / her family.

The sufficiency level of the salary (i.e. minimum wage) is determined by the applicable national collective agreement. An employment contract cannot reduce such salary below the minimum level established by the aforementioned collective agreement.

Executive-level employees are not subject to the regulation on working time.

The duration of the annual holidays is determined by law. However, national collective agreements may provide for a more favourable treatment. Employees are entitled to a minimum 4-week paid vacations. There are at least 12 bank holidays. Individual agreements may not stipulate a detrimental treatment for employees related to holidays.

In case of sickness, employees have the right to retain their position for the period of time which is set forth by the applicable national collective agreement. During such leave, employees are entitled to be paid their whole salary or part of their salary. The relevant costs are mainly covered by the social security system.

Executive-level employees in sickness leave are entitled to retain their position and to be paid their whole salary for a period of 12 months. However, the company will pay such salary and related social security contributions.

There are no specific restrictions related to the citizenship of the employees hired by an Italian company. Recruitment of personnel on the basis of citizenship is considered discriminatory and it is illegal.

B. Requirements of Employing Foreign Employees

a. Work Permit

Non-EU nationals who have a job offer in Italy, or wish to work in Italy, either temporarily or permanently, must obtain a work visa before coming to Italy. As a general rule, a work visa may be applied for only if the individual is able to enter the yearly "quotas" of immigrant visa established every year from the Italian Government.

Notwithstanding the foregoing principle, Italian immigration law provides for a special work visa which can be granted only to certain categories of employees. As opposite to the work visa addressed above, this type of visa is not restricted by any quota. However, to be eligible for this work visa some particular requirements must be met (i.e. the employee must be (i) an executive or a high-skilled employee with a seniority in his own country of at least 6 months and must demonstrate that he / she is employed by a foreign company who is seconding him / her to an Italian branch, a subsidiary or an affiliated legal entity of the foreign company, or (ii) a professor or a lecturer at university, (iii) a professional translator or interpreter, (iv) an artist or musician, (v) a professional nurse hired by public and / or private hospital, etc.).

b. Application Procedure

There are three main stages in the procedure related to visa and work permits for non-Eu citizens:

(i) The Italian legal entity must apply for a work authorisation to the local immigration office (i.e. the local office of the district where the foreign employee will be employed);

(ii) Once the work authorisation is issued, a prospective employee applies for a work visa in the Italian consulate in his / her country of residence in order to enter Italy;

(iii) The employee (and family members), within 8 days of their in arrival in Italy, apply for a Permit of Stay at the Immigration Office where they intend to reside.

The foregoing procedure may take approximately 2 to 3 months to complete.

c. Social Insurance

Health and safety in the workplace are mainly governed by Legislative Decree No.626/94 as subsequently amended. According to such regulation, employees are entitled to participate in the safety and protection system implemented by the company, by, among other things, appointing a representative and attending special safety training courses organized by the employer. Additional obligations must be satisfied by the employer (i.e. drafting the risk assessment document and appointing a competent physician). In the event of breach of workplace health and safety obligations, the employer is subject to civil and criminal liability.

C. Exit and Entry

a. Visa Types

Visas are divided into three main categories:

a) Uniform Schengen Visas (USV): valid for all territories of the Contracting Parties; such visa may be:
(i) an airport transit visa (type A);
(ii) a transit visa (type B); or
(iii) a short-stay or travel visas (type C), valid up to 90 days, for single or multiple entry.

b) Limited Territorial Validity Visas (LTV): such visa is valid for the Schengen State that issued the visa (or for other Schengen States that are named) without any possibility of access to or transit through the territory of any other Schengen State.

c) Long stay or "national Visas" (NV): such visa is valid for only for visits that are longer than 90 days (type D), with one or more entries, in the territory of the Schengen State that issued the visa, and to transit through the territory of other Schengen States for a period not exceeding five days.

Types of Entry Visa: The Interdepartmental Decree of July 12, 2000 introduced 20 types of entry visa, as well as the requirements and the conditions for granting such visas: adoption, business, medical treatment, diplomatic, accompanying dependent, athletic competition, invitation, non-dependent employment, dependent employment, mission, religious grounds, re-entry, choice of residence, family reunion, study, airport transit, transit, transport, tourism, working holidays, job-seeking (abolished).

b. Restrictions for Exit and Entry

On October 26, 1997, Italy joined the Schengen system after a gradual process of adjusting to the common visa regime provided by the Convention Implementing the Schengen Agreement. While strengthening the common external border, there was a parallel and gradual removal of internal border controls, providing total freedom of movement within the signatory states of the Schengen Agreement. This resulted in the establishment of what has become known as the Schengen Area.

Admission to Italian territory through the external borders of the Schengen Area is permitted only to foreigners who:

(i) Seek entry through a border crossing point;

(ii) Are in possession of a valid passport or equivalent recognised travel document permitting them to cross the border;

(iii) Are in possession of documents substantiating the purpose and the conditions of the planned visit and have sufficient means of support, both for the period of the planned visit and to return to their country of origin (or to travel in transit to a Third State);

(iv) Are in possession of a valid entry or transit visa, if required:

(v) Are not prohibited from entering due to an alert in the Schengen Information System; and

(vi) Are not considered to be a threat to public policy, national security or the international relations of any of the Contracting Parties, under Italian or the law of another Schengen State.

If any of aforementioned conditions are not satisfied, a foreigner may be denied entry by border authorities regardless of whether such foreigner is in possession of a valid entry or transit visa.

D. Trade Union and Labour Organizations

In Italy there are numerous trade associations although membership in such associations is usually not compulsory. In contrast, membership in professional organizations is required for individuals providing certain professional services (such as lawyers, architects and doctors). Both trade associations and professional organizations usually require the payment of annual fees. Mandatory trade practices for members are often stipulated; however, such practices may be in breach of competition rules if they involve price fixing or the formulation of commercial strategies for members.

Under Italian law (section 14 of the Worker's Statute), employees are entitled to establish union committees, to join trade unions and to perform union activities within the company (i.e. right to assemble and union permits).

Pursuant to Sections 15 and 16 of the Worker's Statute, discrimination against employees on the basis of their exercise of union rights and activities is prohibited. Furthermore, according to Section 19 of such law, if the company employs more than 15 workers, such employees are entitled to request the election of union representative in the work place.

In Italy, unions are legal and recognized by the government. The most representative unions are the following:

a. Employees

(i) CIGL ("Confederazione Generale Italiana del Lavoro");

(ii) CISL ("Confederazione Sindacati Lavoratori Italian");

(iii) UIL ("Unione Italiana del Lavoro");

(iv) UGL ("Unione Generale del Lavoro").

b. Employers

(i) CONFINDUSTRIA;

(ii) CONFCOMMERCIO.

Other independent and minor Unions represent the interests of employees belonging to specific employment sectors.

E. Labour Disputes

Each province has its own labour department in charge of coordinating and handling labour disputes. Also, the "Italian Carabinieri" has a "Labour Protection Carabinieri" department, protecting labour workers' rights.

F. The Law No.183/2014

The so called "Jobs Act" has determined a deep change in industrial relations. Following the entrance into force of the abovementioned employment law reform, in less than nine months during the course of 2015, eight implementation decrees have been approved by the Italian Parliament, providing for important amendments to the Italian employment law framework.

a. New Dismissal Rules

In February 2015, the first decree (Legislative Decree no.23/2015) provided substantial amendments to Article 18 of the "Workers' Statute" (concerning remedies for unfair dismissal) with effect from March 7th, 2015.

The decree introduced more flexibility for the employers to terminate an employment relationship (for those employees hired later than 7th March 2015) by introducing the "contratto a tutele crescenti". The new provisions removed any form of obligation of reinstatement in the instance of an unfair dismissal of a worker by the company, unless the dismissal is based on discrimination or communicated orally. In addition, the reinstatement is also applicable in limited cases expressly provided for by law (e.g. marriage or pregnancy) and in cases where there are no relevant facts that may constitute grounds for a disciplinary dismissal.

The reinstatement obligation is therefore replaced (with the exclusion of the limited cases mentioned above) with a payoff proportionate to the length of the employee's time of service. Thus, from the companies' point of view, the "redundancy cost" for an employee becomes easier to calculate and this against the background of a simpler set of rules.

In particular, the amount to be paid by the employer to the employee in case of unfair dismissal is now equal to two months' salary per year of service (with a minimum of four and a maximum of 24 months' salary). Employment contracts will end on the date of dismissal and the compensation for damages will not be subject to social security contributions. Compensation may be lower (between two and 12 month's salary) if the unfairness of the dismissal solely derives from a breach of formal requirements (e.g. the instance of a disciplinary procedure).

In addition, special rules have been introduced in relation to "small employers" (i.e. with 15 or fewer employees in the single business unit and 60 in Italy). In the case of an unfair dismissal in the absence of any reason, small employers will not be required to reinstate the employee but instead they shall have the obligation to pay an amount of damages equal to 1 month salary per year of service (with a minimum of 2 and a maximum of 6 months' salary).

With the aim of encouraging settlements, the new rules also provide for the possibility for the employer, within 60 days of the dismissal, to make an offer to the dismissed employee consisting in a check equal to one month's salary for each year of service (with a minimum of 2 months and a maximum of 18) free from social security payments and taxes.

Lastly, please note that new rules on remedies for unfair dismissal apply to employees hired from 7th March 2015 - and to employees hired before should the employer, after such date, start to employ more than 15 employees in a plant or more than 60 in Italy, while the previous provisions continue to apply to employees hired before that date.

The new rules will be applicable also in the case of collective dismissals (limited to employees hired following the 7th March 2015), defined by statute as at least five dismissals over a period of 120 days.

In this case, (i) if the dismissal was not communicated in writing, then the employee will have the right to demand reinstatement, while (ii) non-compliance with other procedural requirements or mistakes in the application of the "selection criteria" (mandatory criteria provided for by law to determine those employees to be made redundant during a collective dismissal - i.e. family burden, seniority and organizational, technical and productive reasons) will trigger liability on the part of the employer to pay to the dismissed employee a compensation for damages in the measure indicated above for individual dismissal.

b. Social Shock-Absorbers

In May 2015, the second decree (Legislative Decree no.22/2015) introduced new rules concerning 'social shock-absorbers' (i.e. financial benefits paid to employees by a public body if their working hours or salary are reduced because of the economic and financial difficulties of the employer).

The new unemployment benefit system, known as "Naspi", has therefore been introduced, providing for a maximum duration of 24 months. More people are eligible than before, but with a slightly reduced amount compared to today.

In particular, the decree set out the following requirements in order to be eligible to benefit from the Naspi treatment:

involuntary loss of employment (i.e., the benefit will not be enjoyed by those employees who have terminated the employment relationship by resignation, unless (i) if the resignation took place for a just cause, or (ii) if resignation occurred during the protected period of maternity, (iii) if the termination of the employment relationship for mutual termination deriving from the employee's refusal to his / her transfer to another location that is more than 50 kilometers far away from his / her residence and (iv) for those employees who have mutually terminated the employment relationship, unless it is a mutual termination deriving from the mandatory procedure for dismissal provided by the previous labour law and applicable to the employees hired prior to 7th March 2015); unemployment; 13 weeks of social security contribution payment in the 4 years preceding the beginning of the unemployment period; having carried out 30 days of actual work in the 12 months preceding the beginning of the period of unemployment benefits payment.

The decree also provides that these financial benefits are no longer available in the cases of closure of a business.

c. New Rules on Demotion

In June 2015, with a new decree (Legislative Decree no.81/2015) the rules governing changes in job description were also modified.

In particular, employers have been granted with greater power to unilaterally alter employees' duties.

Employers may now unilaterally change employees' duties within the same collective bargaining agreement, level and category without reducing the employees' remuneration.

Moreover, the decree also provides the possibility for the employer, in case of a structure reorganization which affects the employee's job position, to assign to the employee (also without the employee's consent) duties referring to a lower level within the same category and with the right of the employee to maintain the same remuneration.

In addition, the decree provides for the possibility for the parties (employer and employee) to agree to alter, and even worsen, employment conditions (i.e. duties, level and salary) by signing an agreement before a competent public body, or trade union association, in order to: (i) preserve the employment relationship; (ii) favor the acquisition of different skills; or (iii) improve the employees' living standards.

d. Reorganization of Employment Contracts

With the same Legislative Decree no.81/2015, new rules concerning different kinds of contracts have been concentrated into a single piece of legislation. The changes particularly affect part-time, fixed-term and zero-hours contracts, manpower workers' contracts and apprenticeships (the relative types of contracts have been made more flexible and therefore companies have more of an incentive to use them).

The use of fixed-term contracts is facilitated by the elimination of previous restrictions on their adoption. The only limitations concern maximum contract duration (36 months, also considering a series of maximum 5 extensions) and the open-ended / fixed term contract ratio, which is a maximum of 20% of the fixed term. The new decree confirmed the possibility for the employer to offer a fixed-term contract without indicating, at the outset, the precise technical reason - known as "causali" in Italian and reflecting organizational or production-related factors.

In addition, from 31 December 2015 onwards, project work contracts have been abolished. Project agreements still in force on such date remain in force until their expiration date.

The decree also confirms the possibility to enter into standard collaboration agreements (not connected to a specific project) and V.AT. consultancy agreements (without incurring in additional costs and maintaining the collaborators the same professionality), specifying that such agreements have to be considered as employment agreements, in case (i) the collaborator / consultant's office is located at the company's premises and (ii) the collaborator / consultant's activity is managed by the company, which sets timing and means of the activity and "heads" the collaborator / consultant.

The decree also provides some exceptions to the above (e.g. in cases governed by collective bargaining agreements and professionals enrolled in a specific professional association, for example lawyers).

e. Electronic Monitoring of Employees

In relation to the monitoring of the employees' activities, substantial changes have been introduced by Legislative Decree no.151/2015 in September 2015.

The decree gives companies the possibility to monitor employees through the use of many kinds of electronic devices. The aforementioned legislation-strongly criticized for the risk of damaging privacy as well as workers' individual freedoms-is aimed at "improving workers productivity".

Employers are no longer required to obtain unions' authorization nor to sign a unions agreement for providing employees with equipment to be used in order to carry out their work (e.g. mobile phones or personal computers), even if the equipment is electronic and if employers could use it to monitor employees' activities. Therefore, companies are now allowed to use these tools to check on employees even for disciplinary purposes, provided that employees have been adequately informed and, in any case, in accordance with rules regarding privacy.

Employers must also either sign an agreement with trade union representatives or obtain authorization from a public authority to install any other equipment (e.g. cameras), through which they could also monitor employees' activities.

f. Work-life Balance

In June, the government introduced various measures to try and balance work and personal life, with particular regard to parents with young children.

For example: parental leave may now be used until a child reaches the age of 12 (and no longer the age of 8, as provided before). The partially paid leave (30%) is raised from 3 years to 6 years; for low-income families the benefit may last up to the child's 8th year of age. The same rule was introduced for the case of adoption or foster care. Further, one of the parents may ask to work part-time instead of using parental leave. Maternity leave has been extended to almost all kinds of workers. Fathers and adoptive parents are also generally granted the same protection as mothers.

V. Intellectual Property

a. Laws and Rules

Italy has enacted two major pieces of legislation for the protection of intellectual property, and namely: Legislative Decree No.30 of February 10, 2005 (the so-called "Industrial Property Code") and Law No.663 of April 22,1941-as subsequently amended-the "Copyright Law".

Italy has also entered into the following conventions and treaties:

(i) Paris Convention for the Protection of Industrial Property (Stockholm text), signed on March 20, 1883;

(ii) Berne Convention for the Protection of Literary and Artistic Works (Paris text), signed on September 9, 1886;

(iii) Madrid Agreement concerning the International Registration of Marks (Stockholm text), signed on April 14, 1891;

(iv) Madrid Agreement for the Repression of False or Deceptive Indications of Source on Goods (Lisbon text and Stockholm Integration), signed on April 14, 1891;

(v) Universal Copyright Convention (Paris text), signed on September 6, 1952;

(vi) Nice Agreement concerning the International Classification of Goods and Services for the Registration of Marks (Geneva text), signed on Jun 15, 1957;

(vii) Lisbon Agreement for the Protection of Appellations of Origin and their International Registration (Stockholm text), signed on October 26, 1961;

(viii) Rome Convention for the Protection of Performers, Producers of Phonograms and Broadcasting Organizations, singed on October 26, 1961;

(ix) International Convention for the Protection of New Varieties of Plants (Geneva text), signed on December 2, 1961;

(x) Locarno Agreement establishing an International Classification for Industrial Designs, signed on October 8, 1968;

(xi) Patent Cooperation Treaty (PCT), signed on June 19, 1970;

(xii) Strasbourg Agreement concerning the International Patent Classification, signed on March 24, 1971;

(xiii) Convention for the Protection of Producers of Phonograms Against Unauthorized Duplication of their Phonograms, signed on October 29, 1971;

(xiv) European Patent Convention (EPC), signed October 5, 1973;

(xv) Brussels Convention relating to the Distribution of Program-Carrying Signals Transmitted by Satellite, signed on May 21, 1974;

(xvi) Budapest Treaty on the International Recognition of the Deposit of microorganisms for the Purposes of Patent Procedure, signed on April 28, 1977;

(xvii) Nairobi Treaty on the Protection of the Olympic Symbol, signed on September 26, 1981;

(xviii) Protocol relating to the Madrid Agreement concerning the International Registration of marks, signed on June 27, 1989;

(xix) Agreement on Trade-Related Aspects of Intellectual Property Rights (TRIPS Agreement), signed on April 15, 1994;

(xx) WIPO Copyright Treaty (WCT), signed on December 20, 1996 (not ratified);

(xxi) WIPO Performances and Phonograms Treaty (WPPT) signed on December 20, 1996 (not ratified); and

(xxii) Geneva Act of the Hague Agreement concerning the International Registration of Industrial Designs, signed on July 2, 1999.

b. Patents, Trademarks, Copyright Protection

Patent and trademark applications are filed with the Italian Patents and Trademarks Office, either directly or through local offices. In particular, patents are granted for a period of twenty years from the filing date and cannot be extended. Conversely, legal protection for trademarks lasts for ten years and may be perpetually renewed for further ten years' terms. Since July 2011, an administrative opposition procedure has been introduced in Italy, similar to the Community Trademark Opposition, to be carried out before the Italian Patents and Trademarks Office after publication of a trademark application.

Copyright protection is generally granted for the lifetime of the author plus seventy years, and in the event of collective works, the copyright protection lasts seventy years after the death of the last co-author. Know-how is protected by several provisions of:

(i) The Italian Civil Code related to unfair competition.
(ii) The Italian Criminal Code, and
(iii) The Industrial Property Code.

c. The Economic Rights

The assignment of economic rights related to a patent or trademark must be registered with the Italian Patents and Trademarks Office in order to be effective vis-à-vis third parties. The registration of a deed of assignment of patent rights must be legalized by a simple declaration of transfer executed by the assignor and the assignee without notarial formalities.

Italy has neither regulatory guidelines for licenses nor a system of governmental approval for intellectual property licensing or payment of royalties. Evidence of the assignment or license of copyrights must be given in writing.

The Italian intellectual property laws provide for particular requirements / exceptions related to certain products, such as, new varieties of plants and pharmaceutical products which are subject to a strict administrative licensing procedure.

In Italy, there are no specific provisions on payment of royalties. Provisions on transfer pricing are to be taken into account when transactions between related companies are to be carried out.

Local antitrust and / or competitions laws do apply to licenses.

In general term, typical agreements between foreign companies and their wholly owned subsidiaries are licensing agreements.

VI. Environmental Protection

The public is increasingly sensitive to environmental protection undertakings and regulations. This attitude translates into greater awareness and activism. From a government standpoint, enforcement actions tend to be more stringent due to the combined pressure of public opinion and EU regulations.

Italy has ratified numerous international environmental agreements including those related to air pollution, Antarctic-marine living resources, Antarctic seals, biodiversity, climate change, desertification, endangered species, environmental modification, hazardous wastes, law of the Sea, marine dumping, ozone layer protection, ship pollution, wetlands and whaling. Regionally, Italy is a party to the European Wild Birds Directive and the council of Europe, under which dozens of biogenetic reserves have been designated.

Among the major pieces of Italian environmental legislation, we can recollect:

(i) the legislative decree No.152 of April 12, 2006-the Environmental Code-which contains major provisions with respect to the main environmental sectors such as the contaminated sites cleaning up procedures, the waste treatment and waste disposal, air emissions regulation, water use and distribution, environmental impact assessment.

(ii) Following the adoption of the EU directive No.96/61/CE on the prevention and reduction of pollution, the Italian government has enacted the legislative decree No.59 of February 18, 2005, which sets forth the procedure for the granting of the Environmental Integrated Permit (a sole permit which substitutes the main existing environmental permits necessary for the carrying out of certain industrial activities duly detailed within the mentioned legislative decree).

Among the other important pieces of environmental legislation, the following are noteworthy:

(i) Italian law No.447 of October 26, 1995 on noise pollution;

(ii) Law No.257 of February 26, 1992 containing rules on the termination of the use of asbestos containing material;

(iii) Presidential Decree September 8,1997, No.357-regulation of implementation of EU directive 92/43/CEE on the protection of natural habitats and of wild flora and fauna; and

(iv) Law No.36 of February 22,2001 (and Decree of the President of the Council of Ministries July 8, 2003) on electric and electromagnetic pollution.

VII. Dispute Resolution

A. Methods and Bodies of Dispute Resolution

The main methods of dispute resolution are litigation, mediation, and arbitration. Italy has a complete Civil Code and Enterprise Bankruptcy Law such guarantees property and contractual rights. Bilateral investments are deemed as "lex specialis" of foreign investments, and its effect prevail domestic law. In case of dispute, bilateral investment agreement a major legislative authority. Italy has many mediation centres, including the Italy National Arbitration Chamber of Commerce and Milan International Arbitration Chamber of Commerce. Also, in 2004, the Sino-Italy Chamber of Commerce co-established a Sino-Italy Arbitration Centre, providing services between Sino-Italian enterprises. Italy is also a member of the ICSID, and for investment cooperation disputes, under demand, Italy's courts usually accept foreign arbitration organizations' arbitration award.

B. Application of Laws

The right of jurisdiction is regulated in accordance with the EU No.44/2001 regulation, Italy No.218/1995 regulation, and Brussels Convention of 1986.

VIII. Others

A. Anti–commercial Bribery

a. Brief Introduction of Anti-commercial Bribery Laws and Regulation

In recent years, Italy has strongly and concentratedly implemented the Anti-corruption regulations. On November 6, 2012 published the Italian Decree No.190, and the "Anti-corruption Law". Italy's anti-commercial bribery is mainly regulated in the Decree No.231/2011. Also, in 2004 Italy has passed the law No.215/04, authorizing Italy's competition and market management bureau to investigate and process government officials commercial interest conflicts to protect normal business behaviour from being affected by government officials.

b. Department Supervising Anti-commercial Bribery

The department supervising anti-commercial bribery is the Italian Competition and Market Supervision Bureau.

c. Punitive Actions

The "Anti-Bribery Law" utilizes "Comprehensive Governance" method, combining with penal and non-penal methods to implement punitive actions, including: economic sanctions to individuals or corporates, imprisonment or other penal to individuals (including disqualification, confiscate ill-gotten gains or compensation for damages and etc.). Moreover, such kind of punitive actions will also affect enterprises' reputation and financing ability, which might cause major influences.

B. Corporate Criminal Liability and Foreign Companies

a. Introduction

Italy was one of the first European countries with civil-law jurisdiction to introduce corporate "criminal" liability through the adoption of Legislative Decree no.231, dated 8 June 2001 ("Decree no.231"). Even if this corporate liability is expressly referred to as formally 'administrative' in Decree no.231 itself, the stance of Italian courts in certain decisions is that this liability is criminal in substance. The ambit of applicability of the Decree has expanded in recent years both through the adoption of legislative amendments, extending the list of predicate crimes giving rise to corporate liability, and in judicial practice, with Italian courts strengthening the application of its provisions. As a result, there has been a progressive increase in prosecutions of companies for crimes committed by their executives.

Foreign companies, namely companies with headquarters abroad, are not expressly covered in Decree no.231. Nevertheless, Italian Courts have held that under certain conditions companies doing business in Italy are subject to this legislative framework. In addition, the Italian Consolidating Bank Act, differently from Decree no.231, contains an express reference to the liability of foreign banks. More specifically, Article 97-bis, paragraph 5 thereof establishes that the special liability regime provided for Italian banks shall apply-insofar as compatible - to Italian subsidiaries of foreign banks having their principal seat within and outside the European Union.

From a legal point of view, corporate liability under Decree no.231 arises from the presence of certain objective and subjective elements. The objective element includes the commission of a predicate crime in the interest or to the advantage of a company on the part of its representatives, managers or personnel subject to their surveillance. The material scope of the Decree is extended to several predicate crimes, among which public frauds, money laundering, copyright laws violations, corporate crimes, market abuse, slavery and slave trade, injuries and death caused by breach of the rules concerning health and safety regulations in the workplace, and environmental crimes. The notions of interest and advantage are interpreted in a broad sense. For instance, in proceedings brought under Decree no.231 against companies charged with having failed to prevent involuntary manslaughter in the case of the death of an employee at the workplace, some decisions stress that a company receives an advantage pursuant to Decree no.231 when the death was a result of cost-savings in health and safety matters. The subjective element on the other hand concerns the failure on the part of the company to adopt and effectively implement a compliance program aimed at preventing the crimes in question. This final element is essential to reduce the gravity of the sanctions that can be imposed under the Decree and, under certain conditions, to avoid corporate criminal liability (see para. 6).

The application of Decree no.231 to foreign companies and banks has a potentially significant impact on their operations and investments in Italy. Companies may be punished with severe sanctions such as financial penalties, disqualification sanctions, and the confiscation of the proceeds of the offence. Therefore, foreign investors have a strong interest in complying with these legislative dispositions when investing and conducting business within the Italian territory. With the above in mind, this article will briefly outline the aspects of Decree no.231 which most concern and affect foreign companies.

b. Territorial Scope of Decree No.231 and Its Impact on Foreign Companies

Although Decree no.231 does not expressly regulate the liability of foreign companies, prevailing case law dictates that such companies may be prosecuted and held liable for having failed to prevent the commission of predicate crimes by their corporate officers in Italy (among others, Court of Milan, section IV, 4 February 2013, no.13976). In this regard, a criminal offence is deemed to be committed in Italy if the act or omission occurs in whole or in part in the territory of the State or if the result of such act or omission takes place therein (criterion of ubiquity). There is a tendency in Italian jurisprudence to employ a broad interpretation of the criterion of ubiquity so as to extend the territorial application of Decree no.231. More specifically, the Italian Courts consider that a crime has been committed in whole or in part within the Italian territory even where only a small part of the conduct has occurred within the territory of the State. Recently the Italian Supreme Court held that the mere planning of the offence, namely bribery of foreign officials, that occurred in Italy has to be considered enough in order to find the Italian jurisdiction (Supreme Court, criminal section VI, 12 February 2016, n. 11442). As a result, there is a significant possibility that foreign companies can be called to respond for acts committed principally abroad but that have tenuous connection with the Italian territory. From an extra-territorial jurisdiction point of view, namely with regards to predicate crimes committed entirely abroad, Article 4 of Decree no.231 only establishes expressly that a company with headquarters in Italy will be prosecuted for offences committed abroad according to the conditions set out for individuals in the Italian Criminal Code (Articles 7-10), provided the authorities of a foreign State have not commenced proceedings against that company for the same acts. Foreign companies, having their principal seat abroad, that commit crimes entirely in the territory of another country do not fall within this legislative provision.

c. Transnational Double Jeopardy

The Italian Criminal Code does not expressly recognize the ne bis in idem principle in criminal law with regard to individuals. Following the drafting of 1930, still in force, Article 11 of the Criminal Code allows for new proceedings to be undertaken for the same facts that have been already adjudicated upon abroad. If the fact is committed in the Italian territory in whole or in part, a new proceeding is instituted. If on the other hand the crime is committed entirely abroad, the Minister of Justice may request for new proceedings to be instituted.

In the last twenty years this legal framework has deeply changed. The European Union law has prompted an evolution in this ambit. Article 50 of the Charter of the Fundamental Rights of the European Union (CFREU) enshrines the transnational ne bis in idem principle according to which "No one shall be tried or punished again in criminal proceedings for an offence for which he or she has already been finally acquitted or convicted within the Union in accordance with the law". This provision is interpreted in accordance with Articles 54-58 of the Convention implementing the Schengen Agreement of 14 June 1985 (CAAS) which expressly outline the conditions and exceptions for the application of this principle (see, among others, EU Court of Justice, 27 May 2014, Case C 129/14 PPU, Spasic). Following the opinion of scholars, the ne bis in idem principle covers also the corporate criminal liability, so that a company cannot be judged in a European State when it has been already judged with a definitive decision in another European State.

Concerning the Italian legal order, two specifications are needed. On the one hand, the Supreme Court of Italy has held that this rule cannot be applied in the event that a company is tried or punished again in Italy for a fact for which it has already been finally acquitted or convicted in a non-Member State of the European Union. In the context of criminal proceedings concerning a case of international corruption committed in part in Italy and involving an Italian company already judged in Nigeria and U.S.A., the Italian Supreme Court stated that the settlement reached with U.S. authorities for the same facts did not exclude a new proceeding in Italy since no international agreement exists between the two countries and the ne bis in idem principle cannot be considered a general principle of transnational law (Italian Supreme Court, criminal section VI, 12 February 2016, no.11442). On the other hand, Italy offers an even stronger guarantee to corporations who are criminally prosecuted by prohibiting the institution of a double proceeding (lis pendens). Article 4 of Decree no.231 provides that an investigation cannot be started against a company with headquarters in Italy that is in parallel being prosecuted by a foreign authority for the same fact committed entirely abroad. This rule does not expressly apply to foreign companies. In addition, Decree no.231 does not expressly state that an Italian or a foreign company that has been finally judged abroad cannot be prosecuted or punished twice by Italian judicial authorities.

d. M&A Transactions and Foreign Investments

Foreign investors are often interested in carrying out M&A transactions that involve Italian companies. In these situations, it is advisable to carry out Due Diligence evaluations aimed at assessing whether the companies involved in the transactions are subject to proceedings under Decree no.231 or if their managers are the subject of criminal investigations for crimes that may trigger corporate liability. Such evaluation becomes necessary on the basis of several provisions within the Decree which foresee the shift of responsibility in M&A transactions.

In particular, Decree no.231 lays down specific provisions governing the liability of a company in case of extraordinary corporate transactions, namely transformation, merger, division, and sale of the company. As for transformation of the company, Decree no.231 establishes that a company involved in a proceeding continues to be liable for offenses committed prior to the date on which the transformation takes effect. In the case of a merger, even by incorporation, the company resulting from the merger shall be liable for the offences committed by the merging entities, while more complex rules shall apply in the case of division and sale of the company. Concerning mergers or divisions, several provisions aimed at regulating the issue of applicable sanctions are set out in Decree no.231. A due diligence evaluation and an advice on any potential proceedings will allow the company in question to make more informed decisions and assess potential risks.

e. Foreign Holding Companies and Their Subsidiaries in Italy

Decree no.231 does not expressly provide for the responsibility of groups of companies. Nevertheless, recent decisions of the Italian courts have established that the parent company can be prosecuted and judged for facts committed within their Italian subsidiaries, provided that a predicate crime has been committed and the crime has been committed by a qualified person belonging to the parent company in the interest of this latter. An Italian subsidiary carrying out business in Italy should comply with Decree no.231 in order to avoid incurring liability itself and on the part of the foreign holding company.

f. The Road of Compliance Programs

Following the legal texts, a company-no matter whether Italian or foreign - investigated for having failed to prevent the commission of a predicate crime committed by a representative or an employee can escape liability under Decree no.231 by proving the adoption and implementation of a compliance program. Such a positive outcome of the adoption of the compliance program is quite rare in practice: Italian judges tend to refuse the exclusion of corporate liability, with a few relevant exceptions, namely in case of corporate manslaughter. That said, the adoption and effective implementation of a compliance program offers other advantages for the company, like the exclusion of disqualifications as precautionary measures and the reduction of financial penalties. Following the 'stick-and-carrot approach', Decree no.231 has hereby introduced strong incentives for companies to adopt and implement an organizational, management and control model, the main aim of Decree no.231 being to strengthen a culture of crime prevention in the context of corporate activities.

A general distinction must be made between cases in which a predicate crime has been committed by a representative or and cases where it has been committed by an employee. On the one hand, if a predicate crime has been committed by a representative, the company avoids liability if it proves that: (i) management has adopted and effectively implemented, prior to the commission of the fact, organizational and management models aimed at preventing offences of the type that occurred; (ii) the task of supervising the functioning of and compliance with such models has been delegated to a body with independent powers of initiative and control; (iii) the corporate officer has committed the offence by fraudulently eluding the organization and management models; and (iv) there has been supervision on the part of the supervisory board (Article 6 of Decree no.231).

On the other hand, if the offence has been committed by the employees that are under the supervision of management–even if this kind of accusations are rarer in practice–the corporation is liable if the commission of the offences is a result of noncompliance with management and supervision obligations. However, a company is deemed compliant with management and supervision obligations when, prior to commission of the offence, it has adopted and effectively implemented an organizational, management and control model aimed at preventing offences of the type that occurred. A model is effectively implemented if: (i) it is regularly monitored and amended in the event that relevant breaches of its rules are discovered, or corporate structure and activities are changed; and (ii) a disciplinary system to punish noncompliance with the measures is laid down in the model (Article 7 of Decree no.231). Sanctions may be reduced or in part avoided according to the Decree if, inter alia, the compliance program is adopted and implemented during a proceeding under Decree no.231.

Foreign companies may thus be well served, in both a preventative and remedial sense, by adopting and implementing a compliance program aligned with applicable Italian legislation.

C. Project Contracting

a. Permission System

As State Member of the EU, Italy is a contracting party of WTO's "Government Procurement Agreement" and has the duty to provide threshold above certain amount (6,242,000 EURO) to other contracting parties regarding public construction projects. Currently, China is not a contracting party of the "Government Procurement Agreement", and projects under this threshold, Italy does not have the duty to open for foreign enterprises.

b. Prohibited Areas

Italy prohibits foreign companies engaging in military, national defence and other related industries' projects. Also, Italy has strict permission in industries such as energy and electricity and implements certain restriction to foreign investors on these industries.

c. Invitation to Bid and Bidding

Public engineering projects strictly implement bidding system although projects which do not implement open tendering must specify. Bidding method is mainly through 4 methods, including:

(i) Open tendering procurement is mainly performed for general procurement agreements mostly depending on price factor;

(ii) Two phase bidding procurement is the separate bidding of certain project's design and implementation, which means the design and implementation can be performed by one or two companies;

(iii) Negotiating procurement means directly inviting suppliers to negotiate about the purchase, avoiding notification processes;

(iv) Fast bidding procurement is a non-standard bidding procurement under emergency circumstances.

日本

作者：森胁章、野村高志、早川一平
译者：朱翊、杨青

一、概述

（一）政治、经济、社会与法律环境概述

在日本经济的繁荣时期，许多日本公司对中国进行了巨额投资。当繁荣过后，一种新的趋势正在形成——来自中国的游客、访客和投资正在不断增加。在"一带一路"框架下，中日政府双方对这种新趋势基本持肯定态度，并正在将这种趋势推向下一个阶段，即"在'一带一路'所覆盖的地区内进行双边合作"。

1. 政治环境

日本的政体为"议会制君主立宪制"。根据1947年生效的日本《宪法》的规定，天皇被定义为"国家和人民团结的象征"，没有实际权力。与之相对，首相由天皇根据议会的提名任命，是内阁的领导。首相从国会议员中选出，这种任命方式代表着人民主权的思想。

日本《宪法》采纳了三权分立体制，将政治权力分为三个部分：属于国会的立法权、属于内阁的行政权、属于最高裁判所和地方裁判所的司法权。采取三权分立的原因是期望这些权力能够相互"监督与平衡"。

2. 经济环境

从1968年至2009年，日本的GDP总值一直保持在世界第二位。但是日本泡沫经济的繁荣结束于1991年。自此，严峻的经济环境持续了近20年。这段时期又被称作"失去的20年"。

现在的日本被认为处于一种温和增长的阶段。尽管GDP增长较慢，土地和股票价格却稳定增长。这种温和增长态势可能由多种因素促成，包括即将于2020年举办的东京奥运会，近期剧增的来自其他国家或地区的游客的数量，以及当前的货币政策（例如量化宽松政策和低利率政策）。

3. 社会环境

日本国土面积狭小，土地面积约378 000平方公里，只有中国的1/25，排在世界第61位；然而，日本的人口数量却排在世界第10位。

近年来，日本面临着两个严峻的问题：不断降低的人口出生率和不断加重的人口老龄化。由于出生率低，日本总人口自2015年开始减少，目前日本总人口大约为1.27亿人，但是日本的外国人口正在增加。另外，日本的老年人口刺激了许多行业的创新，这些创新也可能适用于其他老龄化国家和地区。

4. 法律环境

（1）司法系统

如前文所述，《宪法》将全部司法权赋予了裁判所。日本裁判所独立于其他国家机构，日本的法官也独立行使他们的公权力。此外，下级裁判所可以不接受上级裁判所的指示或监督。

在日本，裁判所系统由最高裁判所、高等裁判所、地方裁判所、简易裁判所和家庭裁判所组成。裁判所处理民事、刑事和行政案件。最高裁判所设于东京，高等裁判所分布于日本国内的8个城市。每个县设1个地区裁判所，北海道作为例外设置了4个地区裁判所。日本司法系统基本为三层结构，每个案件理论上可以上诉两次。一般而言，民事案件的初审依所涉金额的不同由地方裁判所或简易裁判所审理，家庭事务则由家庭裁判所审理。

最高裁判所具有对所有案件的终审权。最高裁判所共有15名法官，其中包括1名首席法官。最高裁判所的案件由所有法官组成的大合议庭或由3名或3名以上法官组成的小合议庭审理。

最高裁判所的首席法官经内阁指定后由天皇任命，其他法官由内阁任命。下级裁判所的法官由内阁从最高裁判所提名的名单中选任。除简易裁判所的法官外，所有法官必须通过被称为"第二次考试"的最终考试。第二次考试要在至少一年的实习训练结束后在最高裁判所下属的司法研究所进行。

（2）法源

① 宪法

日本《宪法》在日本具有最高法律效力。任何下位阶法律、法规（例如议案或决议）如与《宪法》相悖，则将被认定为无效。裁判所有权判定下位阶法律、法规是否合宪，并可以在涉及特定案件的情况下，判定任何与《宪法》相悖的下位阶法律、法规不应实施。裁判所还可以认定违宪的决议无效。但是在实践中，由于缺乏民主基础，最高裁判所对于合宪性的判定相对保守。

《宪法》修正案可以由任意一级议会的全体议员的 2/3 或以上议员发起，并需要在全民投票中经多数国民同意。迄今为止，日本《宪法》自 1947 年生效后从未修改过。

② 法律

日本是大陆法系国家，成文法是其重要的法源。国会一般采用由两议院出席议员过半数决议通过的方式，以成文法的形式制定法规。依照日本《宪法》的规定，某些重要的事项只能由法律规定，如处以刑罚或征收新租税。但是，通常做法则是将一些立法权力委托给其他机构，由其采用命令、条例以处理被委托的事项。

③ 内阁政令和省令

命令包括内阁制定的内阁政令、各省制定的省令，以及内阁制定的内阁府令。命令分为两类：第一，"受法律委托制定的命令"，指基于法律委托而制定的命令；第二，"执行命令"，指并非基于委托，而是为了执行上位法律、法规而制定的命令。

④ 县或市条例和规则

县或市条例是由普通地方公共团体的议会通过的规章制度。与之相对，规则是由县长或市长和地方公共团体的委员会通过的。《地方自治法》[①] 允许县、市条例规定刑事惩罚（此类案例需由地方公共实体正式通过）和非刑事罚款。

⑤ 司法判例

尽管没有关于司法判例约束力的明文规定，但最高裁判所的司法判例对下级裁判所的后续判决具有很大的影响力，在司法实践中也非常重要。根据日本法律、法规的规定，如果判决中含有与最高裁判所的司法判例冲突的内容，则构成刑事案件的上诉理由或受理民事案件上诉申请的理由。最高裁判所的司法判例只能通过大合议庭修正，司法实践中，最高裁判所的司法判例被认为有一定程度的约束力。

（二）"一带一路"倡议下与中国企业合作的现状与趋势

在一段时间内，日本政府没有明确表明其对中国"一带一路"倡议的立场。但在 2017 年年末，日本政府公开对"一带一路"倡议表示了支持。特别是在 2017 年 12 月初，日本政府发布了一份名为《关于中日在第三国的私有经济合作》的指导文件，该指导文件主要涉及节能环保领域、工业园区和基础建设现代化以及亚欧间物流等方面的合作。

另外，在 2016 年 12 月，《综合度假区建设推进法案》（又名《赌场促进法》）公布。该法案的目标是促进日本包括赌场的综合度假区的建立。日本政府由此建立了一个名为综合度假区促进咨询委员会的政府机构。该委员会于 2017 年发布了一份白皮书，白皮书中阐述了招商流程和其他事项的细节，并期待国外企业参与综合度假区的建立。

二、投资

（一）市场准入

1. 投资监管部门

在日本，主要的政府投资监管部门包括：

---

① 1947 年第 67 号法律。

① 对日直接投资推进会议，由日本内阁府设立，目的为促进外国对日本的直接投资；
② 日本贸易振兴机构（JETRO），是为促进其他国家与日本之间的相互贸易投资的政府相关机构。

其他省、厅也大多为外国投资者在日本的投资设立了特别办公室，如经济产业省和金融厅。这些特别办公室为外国投资者提供各种各样的服务，包括但不限于提供与投资机会相关的信息。

另外，一些地方政府（包括东京、横滨和大阪的政府）针对地区内的外国投资设立了各自的特别办公室。以东京为例，日本中央政府和东京市政府联合成立了东京开业一站式中心，旨在帮助任何希望在东京投资的企业。该中心提供在东京成立经济实体和开始营业所需的各种政府手续方面的协助，包括公司章程认证、公司注册、报税以及与年金、社会保险和移民相关的雇用事务。

- 日本贸易振兴机构（http://www.jetro.go.jp/）。
- 内阁府关于外国直接投资的一般信息（http://www.invest-japan.go.jp/en_index.html）。
- 东京开业一站式中心（http://www.seisakukikaku.metro.tokyo.jp/onestop/english/top/）。

2. 投资行业法律、法规

外国投资者在日本投资可能会遇到的许多障碍都已消除，现在只有少数特定行业的主要法律、法规中保留着一些限制，这些限制列于下表中。这些为了促进日本国家、产业和经济安全而设定的限制采取的方法各不相同，其中最常用的方法是限制外国投资者对日本国内企业的持股和投票权，以及限制其取得个人营业许可。

商业领域	对外国投资的限制
电信	拒绝转让注册股份（《日本电信电话株式会社法》[①]第6条第1款、第2款）
电台	限制取得电台许可（《电波法》[②]第5条第1款、第4款） 撤销电台许可（《电波法》第75条第1款）
广播基站	拒绝授予开展广播基站业务的批文（《广播法》[③]第93条第1款第6项） 撤销进行广播基站业务的批文（《广播法》第103条第1款、第2款） 拒绝转让注册股份（《广播法》第116条第1款、第2款） 限制投票权（《广播法》第116条第3款、第4款）
广播基站供应商	拒绝转让注册股份（《广播法》第125条第1款、第2款） 限制投票权（《广播法》第125条第2款）
注册广播股份公司	拒绝授权建立注册广播股份公司（《广播法》第159条第2款第5项） 撤销授权建立注册广播股份公司（《广播法》第166条第1款第1项） 拒绝转让注册股份（《广播法》第161条第1款） 限制投票权（《广播法》第116条第2款）
货物物流等	拒绝注册一级物流服务商（《货物利用运输事业法》[④]第6条第1款第5项） 终止一级货物物流业务并撤销注册（《货物利用运输事业法》第16条第3款） 取消二级货物物流许可（《货物利用运输事业法》第22条） 拒绝批准航空器登记（《航空法》[⑤]第4条第1款） 取消航空运输业务许可（《航空法》第101条第1款第5项） 拒绝航空运输公司转让注册股份（《航空法》第120-2条第1款） 禁止拥有日籍船舶（《船舶法》[⑥]第1条） 拒绝登记船级注册业务（《关于国际航海船舶及国际港湾设施安全法》[⑦]第20条第5款第4项）

---

① 1984年第85号法律。
② 1950年第131号法律。
③ 1950年第132号法律。
④ 1989年第82号法律。
⑤ 1952年第231号法律。
⑥ 1899年第46号法律。
⑦ 2004年第31号法律。

（续表）

商业领域	对外国投资的限制
银行	申请银行业务许可时的审查（《银行法》[①]第4条第3款）
渔业	禁止在日本领海和内部水域捕鱼（《外国人渔业规则法》[②]第3条）
矿业	禁止持有采矿权（《矿业法》[③]第17条）

日本政府一般不对日本国内公司持股和投票权进行限制，但是他们限制了外国股东的比例。在大多数情况下，外国投资者在取得股份方面并不受限制，相反却被限制登记于公司股东名册[④]中。这可能会导致外国股东无法行使股东权利。

除了前述限制以外，根据日本《外汇及外国贸易法》的规定[⑤]，外国投资者对日本进行直接投资时将被要求履行事前通知或事后报告的手续，详细内容将在"外汇监管"部分进行说明。

3. 投资方式

外国企业对日本投资最常用的方法是：①在日本建立商业实体；②与日本公司设立合资公司；③收购日本公司的股份。关于在日本建立商业实体，更多的信息将在"企业设立和解散"部分进行说明。

4. 准入条件及审查

如前文所述，对在日本的外国投资的限制是有限的。不仅如此，日本政府目前正在积极吸引外国对日本的投资。2016年5月，日本政府导入了"以全球管理中心为目标促进对日本直接投资的配套政策"[⑥]。尽管如此，复杂的法规和管理程序、语言障碍和独特的商业习惯仍然是外国企业进入日本市场的障碍。最近，在世界银行《2018全球经商环境报告》中，日本在经商便利程度方面排名第34位。

（二）外汇监管

1. 外汇主管部门

对日本的外国投资主要受《外汇及外国贸易法》规制。尽管经济产业省的管辖权高于FEFTA，多数与外国投资者对日本直接投资的商业交易仍然由日本银行处理。例如，日本银行接受许可申请、通知表格和事前通知或事后报告等手续（《外汇及外国贸易法》第69条）。

日本银行通过电话接受《外汇及外国贸易法》与备案程序相关的一般询问，更多信息可以在日本银行的网站上查询。

- 日本银行（http://www.boj.or.jp/en/index.htm）。
- 关于《外汇法》报告制度的说明 [https://www.boj.or.jp/about/services/tame/t_seido.htm/（仅有日文版）]。

2. 外汇法律、法规概况

（1）《外汇及外国贸易法》概述

根据《外汇及外国贸易法》的规定，外国投资者实施涉及对内直接投资的特定外国交易时，需要通知日本政府。1998年4月修订后的《外汇及外国贸易法》废除了以前采用的"事前通知和批准制度"（特别是资本交易方面），取而代之的是"事后报告制度"。根据新制度的规定，当一笔外国交易完成后，必须向财务大臣和/或其他对交易目标行业具有管辖权的主管大臣提交包含外国交易细节在内的报告。目前，根据《外汇及外国贸易法》的规定，除特殊情况外，包括在日本投资在内的外国交易一般可根据

---

① 1981年第59号法律。
② 1967年第60号法律。
③ 1950年第289号法律。
④ 股东名册是对公司股东的记录，由公司保管并用于授予股东权利。对于上市公司的股东，股东名册也可以是股东对第三方主张权利的依据。
⑤ 1949年第228号法律。
⑥ 关于该政策的更多信息可以在对日直接投资推进会议的网站上找到。

"事后报告制度"自由进行。该除外情况包括：①与日本国家安全或公共秩序有关的产业的投资；②日本向经济合作与发展组织（OECD）提交通知决定根据经济合作与发展组织资本流动自由化和无形资本经营准则的要求保持自由化的产业的投资。将在"事前通知"部分对该除外情况进一步说明。

（2）对内直接投资的定义

根据《外汇及外国贸易法》的规定，对内直接投资被定义为下列几类行为：

① 收购非上市企业的股权或股份（通过外国投资者转让的收购除外）；

② 持有人在成为非日本居民前持有的非上市企业的股权或股份等的转让（限于非日本居民个人向外国投资者的转让）；

③ 收购例如上市公司的股份以至收购者对该公司的持股比例（包括与收购者有特定关系的他人所持有的股份）达到该公司已发行股份的 10% 或以上；

④ 同意对公司经营范围进行实质性的变更（对于商业公司，限于持有商业公司全体股东 1/3 或以上投票权的股东的同意）；

⑤ 设立日本分支机构或实质性改变日本分支机构的种类或经营范围（限于内阁政令明确指明的种类和范围，和在"外国投资者"的定义的第①或第②项中所确定的种类和范围）；

⑥ 向主要办事机构在日本的法人贷款，贷款额超过了内阁政令规定的额度且偿还期限超过 1 年的；

⑦ 对特定外国投资者提出债券收购要约；

⑧ 对依据特别法律设立的法人所发行的投资证券的收购；

⑨ 对内阁政令指定的上市公司的任意投资。

（3）外国投资者的定义

根据《外汇及外国贸易法》的规定，外国投资者是指下列所述对日本直接投资的人员：

① 非日本居民的个人；

② 依照外国法律、法规设立或主要办事机构设在国外的法人或其他组织；

③ 前述①项或②项所列人员直接或通过其他公司间接持有投票权的比例及根据内阁政令指定的投票权的总数超过所有股东或公司成员的投票权 50% 的；

④ 除上述②项和③项所列人员外，前述①项所列的非日本居民的个人作为法人、过半数的高级管理人员（是指董事或其他同级人员）或具有代表权限的高级管理人员由前述①项所列的非日本居民的个人所组成的其他组织。

3. 外资企业外汇管理要求

（1）事后报告

发生"外国投资者"的"对内直接投资"外国交易时，一般而言，"外国投资者"在投资发生后 15 日内，需（通过日本银行）向财务大臣或其他任何对交易目标行业具有管辖权的主管大臣提交一份事后报告。但这些当局没有批准或否决该交易的权力。提交事后报告的要求主要出于统计分析的需要。

与对内直接投资相关的内阁政令中列出了要求提交事后报告的除外情况。因此，有必要在投资前基于相关事实确认是否需要适用除外规定。

（2）事前通知

如外国投资者试图"对内直接投资"下列相关行业，该外国投资者将被要求在进行投资的 30 日前（通过日本银行）向财务大臣或其他任何对交易目标行业具有管辖权的主管大臣提交一份事前通知（而不是事后报告）：

① 国家安全（如武器、航空器、原子能、宇宙开发和爆炸物）；

② 公共秩序维护（如发电、供电和售电，天然气和供暖，通信和广播）；

③ 公共安全（如生物制品和安保产品制造业）；

④ 高科技制造业；

⑤ 日本通过向经济合作与发展组织提交通知允许根据经济合作与发展组织资本流动自由化和无形资本经营准则的要求保持自由化的产业（如农业、林业和渔业，空运和海运，石油业和皮革业）。

因为前述所列行业会不定时更新，因此，有必要关注日本银行网站的相关内容，以确保获得最新的信息。

投资者在日本银行接到事前通知后的 30 日内不能进行投资。但这段"等待时间"经常会依相关条例被缩短为自接到通知起两周。不仅如此,为了促进外国投资者对日本的投资,财务大臣和其他相关大臣对绿地投资(如某些涉及设立投资者的全资日本子公司的投资)、滚动投资(如同一个投资者在过去 6 个月之内进行过同类投资)和被动投资(投资者进行的不主动参与管理或控制公司,且被主管大臣认为适用快速通道选项的某些投资)提供了快速通道选项。如适用快速通道选项,"等待时间"可进一步被缩短为 5 日。

政府可能会根据对外国投资者提交的事前报告的审查,建议投资修改或取消投资。接到这类建议的外国投资者可选择接受或拒绝。但如果外国投资者不接受建议,政府可下令修改或取消投资。该命令对投资者具有法律约束力。

(三)融资

1. 主要金融机构

(1)银行

截至 2017 年年末,日本约有 200 家持有银行牌照的银行。在这 200 家银行中,有 4 家大型银行财团——瑞穗、三井住友、三菱东京 UFJ 和理索纳。但应当注意的是,其中还有 60 家持有银行牌照的海外银行日本分行,其中包括总部设在中国的 5 家银行:交通银行、中国银行、中国工商银行、中国建设银行和中国农业银行。

(2)证券公司

根据《金融商品交易法》(FIEA)的规定[①],证券公司被划分为与金融商品行业相关的四个子类:①第一类金融商品业务;②第二类金融商品业务;③投资咨询/代理业务;④投资管理业务。销售基金相关利益依照其经营的证券的种类被认为构成第一类金融商品业务或第二类金融商品业务。截至 2017 年年末,约有 293 家公司被批准从事第一类金融商品业务,1 171 家公司被批准从事第二类金融商品业务。

日本 5 家大型证券公司为:野村证券、大和证券、日兴证券、瑞穗证券和三菱日联摩根士丹利证券。

2. 外资企业融资条件

外资企业有数种方法可以在日本融资,包括债务融资(银行贷款、向母公司贷款)和证券融资(发行股票或公司债券)。

(1)债务融资

日本没有特别针对向外资企业提供贷款的限制。外资企业与日本企业一样享有获得银行贷款的权利。

日本政策投资银行作为一家政府银行向外国附属公司提供长期低息贷款。该行还有一个专门负责协助外国投资者的团队。不仅如此,一些地方公共团体也提供额外的融资激励措施,且对各国企业开放。这些融资激励措施大多与不动产相关,并大多采用长期低息贷款或土地税补贴的形式。

外资企业如果想要从中国母公司获得贷款,在满足中国法律的程序要求后即可获得贷款。但外资企业支付贷款利息时,在税务方面应注意"资本弱化规则"[②]和"超额利息征税规则"[③],建议其在向中国母公司贷款时可以咨询日本税务会计师的意见。

(2)证券融资

如外国企业以全资股份制子公司的形式在日本设立子公司(株式会社),该股份公司可以和其他日本公司一样,以发行股票或公司债券的形式进行融资。日本没有特别针对外国主体的股票或公司债券的发行进行限制。关于日本证券法规的更多信息请参见"证券"部分。

---

① 1948 年第 25 号法律。
② 当一家国内企业从其外国母公司获得的贷款超过母公司向子公司注资的 3 倍时,超出部分的利息不得包含在该子公司可抵扣费用中。
③ 超额利息征税规则规定,向关联人员支付的"净利息"超过公司"调整后收入"的 50% 时,该支付不能用于抵消企业收入。

(四)土地政策

1. 土地法律、法规概况

日本有许多与不动产交易相关的法律、法规。这是因为人们普遍认为,经营者和消费者在获取信息的能力和谈判技巧方面存在巨大差距。

规范不动产交易的代表性法律列举如下:

(1)购买、销售和出租不动产

《宅地建物取引业法》[1]规范在日本购买、销售不动产和不动产中介等行为。对于建筑用地或建筑物的经营者作为销售者的销售合同,《宅地建物取引业法》为保护消费者就合同内容进行了限制。这些限制与《民法》[2]中的限制有所不同,《宅地建物取引业法》特别对定金、取消费用及违反合同瑕疵担保责任的限额进行了限制,并规定违反这些限制的合同条款一律无效。

相反,《宅地建物取引业法》对于租赁合同的内容没有特别的规定。租赁合同由《借地借家法》[3]、《民法》和《消费者合同法》[4]规制。还有一些关于公寓等共有产权建筑物交易的专门规定(参见《建筑物单元所有权法律》[5]和《关于推进公寓管理规范化的法律》[6])。

(2)不动产登记

为了向第三方主张土地和住宅的所有权和其他权利,不动产必须依照《民法》和《不动产登记法》[7]进行登记。通过登记,将不动产的现状、所有权和权利情况向公众公示,由此向第三方公示明示不动产的权利(包括所有权)所有者和其拥有的具体权利。

(3)土地使用和建筑建设

土地使用法规的目的是实现全面系统化的土地使用以及避免城镇的无序发展(参见《城市规划法》[8]《国土利用规划法》[9]和《农业用地法》[10])。对建筑建设的限制是为了保证建筑的建设符合城市规划以及保证建筑的安全和性能(参见《建筑基准法》[11])。

投资日本的不动产时,投资者应当确保对不动产的使用不违反土地使用限制,且建筑建设符合《建筑基准法》。

2. 外资企业取得土地的规定

外国人在日本购买不动产没有法律限制,在缴税方面也和日本人没有区别。外国个人和公司无论国籍、居住地和居住情况如何,均可在日本购买不动产。但居民和非居民需要提交的文件(主要是确认购买人身份的文件)有所不同。在接收购买不动产款项和购买后缴税方面,银行的要求也有所不同。

需注意的是,在日本购买不动产的外国居民(无论国籍)需要根据《外汇及外国贸易法的规定》,在购买不动产后20日内(通过日本银行)向财务大臣或其他任何对交易目标行业具有管辖权的主管大臣提交报告。

(五)企业的设立和解散

1. 企业的形式

(1)可选形式

外国企业在日本开展业务的方法主要有以下三种:

---

[1] 1952年第176号法律。
[2] 1896年第89号法律。
[3] 1991年第90号法律。
[4] 2000年第61号法律。
[5] 1962年第69号法律。
[6] 2000年第149号法律。
[7] 1899年第24号法律。
[8] 1968年第160号法律。
[9] 1974年第92号法律。
[10] 1952年第229号法律。
[11] 1950年第201号法律。

① 在日本成立营业所（分支机构）；
② 在日本设立新公司；
③ 设立合伙企业，例如有限责任合伙企业。

需要注意的是，外国企业有意进入日本市场的，在采用上述第②种和第③种方法前可以先在日本设立代表处。尽管代表处不能在日本开展业务活动，但可以进行一些准备和辅助性工作，例如进行市场调查和为计划的各类业务活动收集信息。

（2）分支机构

外国公司有意在日本进行持续的业务活动时，应指定一名或多名驻日代表，并作为外国公司进行注册。[①]尽管在日本设立营业所不是必须的，但实际上外国企业一般会设立营业所作为在日本进行业务活动的基地。外国公司的日本营业所（分支机构）必须进行注册。

分支机构的业务活动由外国公司的授权机构（如董事会）决定。分支机构不是独立法人而是被视为外国公司的一部分。相应地，外国公司一般直接对分支机构业务活动中产生的义务负责。另外，外国公司还将负责为其分支机构在日本的收入在日本纳税。

（3）在日本设立新公司

当外国公司选择在日本设立新公司时，有四种类型的公司可供选择：

- 股份公司（株式会社）；
- 有限责任公司（合同会社）；
- 一般合伙公司（合名会社）；
- 有限合伙公司（合资会社）。

其中，股份公司是在日本被采用最多的公司形式。尽管有限责任公司不像股份公司一样普遍，但这种公司形式经常被用于进行结构性融资。一般合伙公司和有限合伙公司这两种公司形式则不常被采用。

这四种公司形式的重要区别在于各自承担责任的范围和日常运营模式不同。股份公司的股东和有限责任公司的出资人只承担有限责任，而一般合伙公司和有限合伙公司的全部或部分出资人需对公司的债务和义务承担个人责任（即无限责任）。需承担无限责任的风险是一般合伙公司和有限合伙公司很少被采用作为公司形式的原因。关于日常运营，股份公司的日常运营由董事或董事会负责，而在有限责任公司、一般合伙公司和有限合伙公司中，除非在公司章程中指定了负责运营的管理人员，否则将由出资人直接负责公司的运营。

如果外国公司在日本成立子公司（即日本公司），子公司将被视为独立于外国公司的独立公司。如果该子公司是一家有限责任公司、一般合伙公司或有限合伙公司，那么外国公司将作为投资者依法对子公司在业务活动中产生的全部责任负责。与之相对，如果子公司是一家股份公司，外国公司只承担子公司股价下跌的风险，对子公司的债务不承担任何法律责任。

（4）设立合伙企业

外国公司也可以通过设立合伙企业进行业务活动而不设立公司。合伙企业的特征是它的内部规定由投资人（即合伙人）协议决定，且合伙企业本身无须纳税。但需注意，向合伙人分配的利润仍需纳税。

2. 设立程序

股份公司是在日本最常见的公司形式，以下集中讨论股份公司的设立和解散程序。

（1）设立股份公司的概述

根据《公司法》的规定，股份公司的设立被称为公司注册。股份公司的公司注册是指股份公司通过获得法人资格而成为法人的过程。这个过程需要一个组织：①准备作为组织基本规则的公司章程；②安排公证机构对公司章程进行公证；③决定公司注册中股份发行相关事宜（即在股份公司注册公司时发行的股份）；④确定对公司发行股份的认购；⑤根据出资选择公司注册时的股东；⑥决定管理机构和/或管理人，包括公司注册时的董事（即在公司成立时被设定的董事）；⑦注册股份公司使其获得

---

① 最少应登记一名代表。该代表必须在日本居住，但不必是日本国籍。

法人资格。

除此之外，《公司法》规定了两种公司注册方法：①不进行招股的公司注册；②进行招股的公司注册。在不进行招股的公司注册中，公司发起人（即在公司章程上签名或盖章的个人）作为公司注册的策划人和执行人认购公司注册中发行的全部股份，并成为原始股东。而在进行招股的公司注册中，公司发起人只认购公司注册中发行的部分股份，并招募他人认购其余股份，公司发起人和认购股份者一同成为原始股东。

在日本，《公司法》的颁布废除了对最低注册资本的要求（股份公司1 000万日元，有限个人公司300万日元）。因此，尽管最低出资至少为1日元，但扣除公司注册费用后公司注册资本的原始金额可以低至0日元。①

（2）股份公司注册后需要提交的通知

除了公司注册文件，公司注册后还需提交下列通知：

一般而言，根据《外汇及外国贸易法》的要求，外国投资者在日本设立分支机构，在日本注册公司或收购现有日本公司的股份或股权后，必须提交事后通知。

如果在日本设立的分支机构和/或在日本注册的外国公司雇用员工的，可能会被要求向税务机构和劳动相关机构提交相关文件。

根据公司所属行业法律的规定，还有可能被要求提交其他授权文件或通知。

向50人以上募集新发行证券认购者的，依情况可能需要依据《金融商品交易法》的规定提交有价证券备案书。

3. 公司解散的途径与要求

（1）解散与清算

在日本，解散与清算过程更为简单和迅速。根据《公司法》的要求，解散股份公司意味着公司法人终止存在。解散后自动启动清算流程。在清算过程中，股份公司结束经营，回收债务并进行其他终止股份公司法人身份的必要步骤。

《公司法》规定了数种导致公司解散的事由，但公司解散的主要原因还是股东大会的决议。根据《公司法》的规定，解散公司的特别决议需要满足以下条件：① 出席股东的投票权在可就该决议投票的全体股东投票权中过半数；② 同意解散提案的股东投票权占出席股东投票权的2/3以上。另外，公司解散须向法务省登记。

解散股份公司的决议将引发清算程序。在清算过程中，公司董事一般作为清算人对公司的清算流程负责。清算人的任命应当向法务省登记。清算程序的关键部分在于向股份公司的债权人发送通知，要求其在特定期间内提出索要债务的主张。该期间必须超过两个月，以便债权人有足够的时间提出他们的主张。

在必要的内部流程完成后，清算人应向法务局申请办理清算完成的登记。清算人还必须申请关于注销登记信息的证明书，该证明书可于申请登记后约两周内取得。此后，公司清算完成的通知还必须寄给税务机构和其他相关机构。

（2）破产/倒闭

在日本，破产和重组程序被分为两大类：①在裁判所监督下的司法破产；②无裁判所介入的基于利益相关各方协议的非司法破产。

司法破产程序进一步分为两类：①债务重整；②债务清算。关于债务重整，分为两种破产程序：①民事重整程序（民事再生）；②公司重整程序（会社更生）。民事重整程序可被用于个人和公司，无论公司大小和类型如何。公司重整程序则一般仅用于股份公司。关于债务清算，分为两种破产程序：①破产清算程序；②特别清算程序。破产清算程序可被用于个人或任意实体，而特别清算程序仅用于陷入财务困境的股份公司。

但应注意的是，处于困境的债务人经常试图和债权人达成协议而不申请司法破产。这种无裁判所

---

① 需注意的是，某些行业可能会有最低资本金的要求，以便从相关部门获得经营许可后开展业务。因此，如果某行业需要从相关部门获得许可，则有必要确认相关要求。

介入的非司法破产越来越受到青睐，原因是这种方式被认为可以保持债务人产业的价值，且更节约费用与时间。

（六）合并收购

1. 合并收购的方法

一般而言，企业并购一家公司（目标公司）的方法包括：①收购公司股份；②业务转让；③依照《公司法》的规定进行企业重组。实践中，收购目标公司的过半数股份可以立即变更目标公司的控制权的归属，这是取得目标公司控制权最简单的方法。与之相对，业务转让是向买方出售目标业务或目标公司。企业重组可以通过多种方式实现，但都必须符合《公司法》规定的程序。

（1）股份收购

当某一方持股达到或超过一定的投票权标准时，该方就可能通过在股东大会上行使该等投票权来控制目标公司。尽管股份收购改变了股东构成，但目标公司的组织结构不会受到影响。

如目标公司为非上市公司，其公司章程通常会包含转让或收购公司股份必须获得目标公司批准的条款（通常是公司董事会的批准）。因此，股份转让方会在转让前请求获得目标公司的批准。

如目标公司为上市公司，买方从现有股东手中购买股份需遵守《金融商品交易法》的相关程序规定。这些程序包括规范要约收购的相关程序和大量持股时需要提交的报告（详情参见"证券市场法规"部分）。

（2）业务转让

业务转让包括一方向另一方转让全部或部分业务。通过该程序，可以转让全部或部分目标公司的业务。与收购股份相比，业务转让的优点是无须承担意外风险，因为所有转让项目都会被明确区分并列出。没有列出的财产或债务由原所有人保留。但如果受让人继续使用转让人的商号而未遵守相关程序，受让人也将为业务转让产生的任何义务的履行负责。

（3）企业重组

企业重组包括合并、股权交换、股权转让和公司分离，也常见于企业收并购交易。

合并一般需要所有参与合并公司的股东大会的特别决议批准。合并使存续公司或新设公司继承被解散公司的所有权利和义务，并自动获得被解散公司的财产、债务、合同和雇员。

在股权交换中，一家现有股份公司将另一家现有股份公司变成自己的全资子公司。这类交易一般要求双方股东大会的特别决议批准。通过股权交换，股份公司可以获得目标公司100%的所有权。

在股权转让中，根据《公司法》的规定，一家新设股份公司可以使另一家现有股份公司成为其全资子公司。股权转让一般需要现有股份公司股东大会的特别决议批准。

《公司法》也对公司分离进行了规定。在公司分离过程中，一家公司将其全部或部分权利和义务转移给另一家公司，该公司继承被分离公司的财产、债务、雇佣合同以及其他权利和义务。

2. 企业并购法规

根据企业并购的对象是目标公司的全部业务还是部分特定业务，该交易可能会适用《公司法》和一般性法律、法规（如《劳动法》和《税法》）和/或行业特定法规的规定。此外，是否需要获得特定政府部门的批准和许可根据情况也有所不同，必须分别确认。

（1）证券市场法规

《金融商品交易法》是日本证券市场的基本规定。因此，《金融商品交易法》经常在上市公司等企业并购交易中发挥重要作用。其中，以大量持股报告制度（即5%规则）和要约收购法规最为常见。

大量持股报告制度原则上要求任何人收购公司已发行股份5%以上股权（包括新股预约权等潜在股份，以下简称"股份"）时必须提交大量持股报告。该报告必须在收购后5个工作日内提交。此报告制度在频繁以大额买卖股份为日常业务的机构投资者（如证券公司、银行和信托公司等）满足特定要求时会减轻其报告义务。减轻报告义务的制度称为"特别报告制度"。特别报告制度仅要求投资者在其选定的基准日每月提交两次持股报告。

关于要约收购法规，《金融商品交易法》要求对主要从金融商品交易所以外的来源收购超过特定数额股份的收购方进行要约收购。

（2）竞争法规

适用企业并购的竞争法规有两类。

第一，实体法禁止可能会对市场造成负面冲击的企业合并。实务中，需要注意企业合并指导方针中规定的避风港条款，如果企业合并达到下列标准，则日本公平贸易委员会（JFTC）不太可能作出该企业合并严重限制竞争的结论：

① 当企业合并满足下列条件之一时：
- 赫芬达尔—赫希曼指数（HHI）[①] 在企业合并后不超过 1 500；
- 企业合并后赫芬达尔—赫希曼指数为 1500 以上但不超过 2500，且赫芬达尔—赫希曼指数的增加值不超过 250；
- 企业合并后赫芬达尔—赫希曼指数超过 2500，但赫芬达尔—赫希曼指数的增加值不超过 150。

② 当企业合并同时满足以下两项条件时：
- 赫芬达尔—赫希曼指数在企业合并后不超过 2 500；
- 企业合并后的公司集团所占市场份额不超过 35%。

第二，相关程序法要求企业合并超过一定规模时需要事前申报。如果企业合并需要提交事前申报，原则上禁止在提交通知后的 30 日内进行目标交易的交割。但在日本公平贸易委员会认为必要时可以缩短该时间。

（七）竞争管制

1. 竞争管制主管机构

日本公平贸易委员会是负责实施《禁止私人垄断和维护公平交易法》（以下简称《反垄断法》）[②] 的主要机构。

2. 竞争法律简介

《反垄断法》是日本反不正当竞争政策中最重要的法律。但是在日本从事业务的公司除关注法律条文之外，还应关注日本公平贸易委员会发布的司法判例和指导方针。这些指导方针可以在日本公平贸易委员会的网站[③] 上查询，其中一些已翻译成英文。

《反垄断法》禁止：①不合理的交易限制；②私人垄断；③不正当交易；④可能严重限制竞争的企业合并。不仅如此，《反垄断法》要求当企业合并达到上述标准后，经营者（事业者）需提交事前申报。日本也有与经营者团体相关的法规。

为了避免不合理的交易限制，《反垄断法》禁止企业与其竞争对手通过如卡特尔或操纵投标等方式对竞争进行实质性限制。近几年日本公平贸易委员会对大量价格垄断案件开出了罚单。

为了避免私人垄断，《反垄断法》禁止任何企业单独或与其他竞争企业联合，通过排他或控制其他企业业务活动的方式对竞争进行实质性限制。

《反垄断法》禁止的不正当交易限制的是纵向竞争。该类限制存在各种实例，包括协同拒绝交易、歧视性价格以及不正当低价销售。

3. 竞争管制措施

对违反《反垄断法》的行为存在多种处罚形式。最常见的处罚为禁止令和罚款（课征金）支付令，两者皆为行政处分。禁止令由日本公平贸易委员会依据《反垄断法》作出，要求企业采取"必要的措施消除违法行为或保证违法行为被消除"。日本公平贸易委员会可以对任何违反《反垄断法》的行为发出禁止令。[④] 罚款支付令中计算罚款的方法因违法行为的类型有所不同。罚款支付令不适用于部分不正

[①] 赫芬达尔-赫希曼指数是公认用于测量市场集中程度的方法。
[②] 1947 年第 54 号法律。
[③] 参见 http://www.jftc.go.jp/en/legislation_gls/imonopoly_guidelines.html。
[④] 实务中，截至 2018 年 2 月，尚未有就私人垄断发出罚款支付令的情形。

当交易行为。个人或企业可能会因不合理的交易限制和私人垄断行为而受到刑事处罚。[1]

为了更好地监控违反《反垄断法》的行为并促进公平与自由竞争，日本从2005年起就不合理的交易限制建立了宽恕制度。根据宽恕制度的规定，在申请宽恕并满足了特定条件的公司中，最多5家公司可以被免除或减轻因限制竞争行为受到的制裁。第一名申请人将被全额免除，第二名申请人可以减少支付罚金的50%，第三、四、五名申请人可以减少支付罚金的30%。该制度在日本被证实十分有效。

（八）税收

1. 税收体系与制度

（1）税收体制

在日本，规定国家和地方征税的法律有很多，包括《法人税法》[2]和《消费税法》[3]。国税厅（NTA）是财务省下设的特别管理机构，主要负责处理国家征税的相关事宜。下级地区税务局及其下级税务署负责协助国税厅。另外，国税厅设立国税不服审判所，该审判所作为国税厅的机构之一，负责审查和批准纳税人提出的税务评估再调查或再审查请求。税务署负责征税和一般税务的调查、修正、评估，因此税务署与纳税人的关系最为紧密。

地方政府及其下级税务所，以及市政府和村镇政府负责处理地方税务事宜。

（2）针对外国企业的法规

外国企业在日本设立常设机构后，该外国企业在日本国内的收入将成为征税对象并被要求自行评估后纳税。因此，一般而言，外国企业不在日本设立常设机构更为有利。按照《法人税法》的规定，常设机构是指分支机构、建设工程和代理人。代表处不视为常设机构，因其只进行信息收集和市场研究等准备性和辅助性工作。尽管如此，代表处和分支机构之间的界限模糊，其性质主要由其所从事的活动决定。

2. 主要税种及税率

（1）适用于业务的主要税种

适用于在日本业务的主要税种包括法人税和消费税。法人税适用于公司收入（包括资本收益），由公司自行评估纳税。日本国内企业不论收入来源如何均有义务就所有收入纳税。与之相反，外国企业只对其在日本国内的收入承担纳税义务。依照日本公认会计准则下的会计处理方法，法人税针对的收入等于总收入减去可抵扣费用。

消费税由国家评估并征收，是对几乎所有国内交易（如商品销售和租赁以及提供服务）和进口交易征收的增值税。任何从事国内或进口交易的商业实体，如果该实体在特定时期（原则上为上一个财年的前一个财年）内的收入超过1 000万日元的应缴纳消费税。

（2）税率

法人税率正在逐渐降低。法人税税率曾高至25.5%，于2015年4月1日以后开始的财年降至23.9%，于2016年4月1日以后开始的财年降至23.4%，并于2018年4月1日以后开始的财年降至23.2%。另外，如果公司资本金少于1亿日元，其第一个800万日元收入的税率则为19%，但此后直至2019年3月31日以前的财年税率降至15%。

消费税从2015年4月起由5%升至8%，原本预计于2015年10月起升至10%（其中7.8%作为国家税，2.8%作为地方税）。但为配合经济复兴和财政稳定，消费税提升至10%的计划被推迟至2017年4月，之后再次被推迟至2019年10月。为了减轻消费税的累退性，减少低收入群体的负担，消费税提高至10%时将同时实施对食品等产品的减税。

3. 纳税申报与优惠

（1）报税

公司必须向相关税务署提交纳税申报单，并在每个财年结束后2个月内缴纳税费。如公司因不可

---

[1] 迄今为止尚未出现对私人垄断作出刑事制裁的情形。
[2] 1965年第34号法律。
[3] 1988年第108号法律。

避免的原因在期限内无法提交纳税申报单，或因公司章程等原因于该期间内持续不能举行年度股东大会进行决算，那么该公司可延期提交纳税申报单，但该公司必须就该等延期提交事前申请。

（2）税收优惠

为了促进在日本投资，针对在日本从事业务活动的外国企业，日本政府提供了各种税务优惠措施。这些优惠措施包括：

- 雇用促进税：对符合特定要求的公司提供税务优惠，例如在适用的财年内雇用 5 名以上的雇员且雇员人数达到雇员总数 10% 的公司。
- 对于将公司总部从东京 23 区迁移至其他地区，或在该地区增强、扩展总部功能的公司提供税收优惠。
- 与经济特区相关的优惠措施（参见"特殊经济区域"部分）。

地方政府也对拟于各地区开设办事机构的外国企业提供了各种优惠措施。①

（九）证券

1. 证券法律、法规概况

日本制定了多部与证券相关的法律、法规，其中主要法律、法规如下：

（1）《金融商品交易法》②

在日本，《金融商品交易法》是适用于证券的最为基本的法律。其规定证券的发行、募集和交易，也对日本证券的一级和二级市场作出规定。

（2）《投资信托和投资法人法》（ITICA）③

《投资信托和投资法人法》对国内和国外的投资信托和投资法人进行规范。

（3）《外汇及外国贸易法》④

《外汇及外国贸易法》对非日本居民向日本居民发行或销售在日本以外国货币为主的证券进行规范。

（4）《日本证券业协会规则》（JSDA 规则）

《日本证券业协会规则》是证券业自行建立的行业内控机制，对证券相关交易具有重大影响。

2. 证券市场的监管

日本金融厅（FSA）是证券市场最重要的监管机关，主要作用是保证稳定和顺畅的金融交易。日本金融厅作为内阁府的外部机关而设立。部分日本金融厅理事的权力被委托给证券交易监督委员会，该委员会同时为日本金融厅和地方金融局的下属委员会（地方金融局是财务省的下属机构）。

另外，各类行业组织如日本证券业协会和其他证券交易所自行规定了各种证券规则。这些自我约束的规则在规范证券市场中发挥了重要作用。

3. 外资企业参与证券交易的要求

外国企业有两种方法在日本从事证券交易。第一种方法是在日本证券交易所通过首次公开发行（IPO）上市。第二种方法是进行公募但不在日本证券交易所上市（POWL）。在第二种方法中，发行方在外国证券交易所上市的同时，也在日本公开发行证券。

当前，大多数外国企业选择第二种方法。由于在日本上市和 POWL 均涉及外国股票的首次发行和二次发售，原则上发行公司必须满足日本对披露的要求。因此，根据《金融商品交易法》的规定，发行人必须提交有价证券报告书并制定和递交招股说明书。除此之外，选择在日本上市的发行公司需遵守相关日本证券交易所的上市程序以及上市之后适用的披露义务。

对于 IPO 来说，东京证券交易所（TSE）是日本最具有代表性的证券交易所，所有在日本上市的外国企业均是在东京证券交易所上市。东京证券交易所运营的市场包括第一板块、第二板块、

---

① 更多关于在日本投资的税收优惠细节可以在查询下网站：https://www.jetro.go.jp/en/invest/incentive_programs.html。
② 1948 年第 25 号法律。
③ 1951 年第 198 号法律。
④ 1949 年第 228 号法律。

JASDAQ 和创业板（为初创公司设立）。每个市场都有特定的上市要求和股票转让要求。东京证券交易所的上市要求包括已有 200 名股东、市值不低于 5 亿日元和上市时估值不低于 10 亿日元等。

（十）投资优惠及保护

1. 优惠政策框架

日本政府没有官方优惠政策。另外，如"市场准入"部分所述，日本政府积极致力于"以全球管理中心为目标促进对日本直接投资的配套政策"以吸引外国对日本的投资。除该政策之外，日本政府设立了工作组以简化和修改与外国对日本投资相关的法规和行政手续。

2. 特定行业与地区鼓励

日本政府在国家和地区层面为鼓励和促进外国对日本投资提供了优惠措施，还在各省和机构向外国投资者提供与在日本从事业务相关的全面咨询和支持的一站式服务。有一些优惠措施专门针对外国投资者，另一些优惠措施则面向所有投资者，不论投资者国籍如何。

日本政府提供的投资优惠之一是《促进日本成为亚洲商业中心法案》。此法案确定了适用于在日本的跨国企业运营新研发中心和公司总部的重要支持措施（如资金筹集协助、加快专利审查和减少专利费用），并得到了对此类业务有管辖权的各省的保证。

日本还通过"国家战略特区"和"综合特区"对个别行业进行支持。政府的支持还体现在暂停规制适用和提供优惠税率等方面，下文对此有详细叙述。地方政府还特别向外国企业提供各类优惠措施，包括东京提供的以下两项优惠措施：

• 海外金融企业业务开展补贴计划（参见 http://www.seisakukikaku.metro.tokyo.jp/bdc_tokyo?english/business-support/subsidy.html）。

• 外企增长计划（参见 http://www.seisakukikaku.metro.tokyo.jp/bdc_tokyo?english/invest-tokyo/fhr.html）。

对在日本投资的优惠计划将会不定时更新，因此，建议关注日本贸易振兴机构官网以获得最新的信息（http://www.jetro.go.jp/en/invest/incentive_programs.html）。

3. 特殊经济区域

（1）国家战略特区

日本政府已选定 10 个地区，在这些地区暂停适用诸多规制并提供优惠的税收政策，以打造最有利的商业环境。这 10 个被称为"国家战略特区"的地区分别是：仙北市、仙台市、新泻市、东京地区（东京都、神奈川县、千叶市、成田市）、爱知县、关西地区（大阪府、兵库县、京都府）、养父市、广岛县/今治市、福冈市/北九州市和冲绳县。"市场准入"部分提到的东京开业一站式中心的建立就是东京地区暂停适用规制的成果。

根据选定地区有所不同，其规制的暂停适用将不定时变更。因此，建议登录内阁府关于"国家战略特区"网站确认最新详情［http://www.kantei.go.jp/jp/singi/tiiki/kokusentoc/index.html（仅有日文版）］。

（2）综合特区

内阁府选定数个城市作为"综合特区"（CSZ）。通过建立综合特区，内阁府旨在为被选定的地区所面临的综合战略挑战提供定制化和整合性支持（其中 11 个选定地区旨在增强国际竞争力，77 个选定地区旨在地区复兴）。对在指定地区内有商业计划的公司提供特别规制措施、优惠的税收政策（针对所得税）和财政/货币支持。

关于综合特区的详细信息可以通过内阁府网站查询［http://www.kantei.go.jp/jp/singi/tiiki/sogotoc/index.html（仅有日文版）］。

（3）复兴特区

对于在受东日本大地震影响的地区（227 座城市）内有商业计划的公司，日本政府会提供例如暂停适用管制以及税收优惠等特殊措施。

关于复兴特区的详细信息可以在日本复兴厅的网站上查询（http://www.reconstruction.go.jp/english/）。

4. 投资保护

（1）投资协定

截至2018年2月，日本与中国签订了下列两份投资协定。中国、日本、韩国三边投资协定明文批准各缔约方将争端提交至国际投资争端解决中心（ICSID）进行仲裁（日本于1965年9月23日签署了《国际投资争端解决中心公约》，于1967年8月17日批准，并自1967年9月16日起在日本生效）。

	签署日期	生效日期
《关于鼓励和相互保护投资协定》（BIT）中国—日本	1988年8月	1989年5月14日
《关于促进、便利和保护投资的协定》（TIP）中国—韩国—日本	2012年5月	2014年5月17日

尽管中国、日本、韩国三边投资协定于2014年5月17日起生效，中日双边投资协定仍继续有效。

（2）投资保护

依据中日之间的投资协议，投资者和投资财产受如下政策保护：
- 国民待遇；
- 最惠国待遇；
- 公平待遇；
- 全面保护和安保；
- 遵守义务条款（保护伞条款）；
- 征用；
- 内部纷争和冲突保护；
- 业绩要求；
- 资本转移保证。

三、贸易

（一）贸易监管部门

在日本，经济产业省（2001年以前称"通商产业省"）是监督贸易的政府机构，其负责确定贸易政策方向，并促进国际经济合作与交流。

就贸易相关的检疫而言，厚生劳动省监管食品检疫，而农林水产省则监管动植物检疫。此外，海关（财务省的地方分局）监管关税。

（二）贸易法律、法规简述

有关进出口的基本法是《外汇及外国贸易法》及内阁和各省根据该法颁布的法令，如《出口贸易管制令》《进口贸易管制令》及《外汇交易令》。这些法律、法规规定了有关货物、服务与技术进出口的管制措施及其进出口程序，《进出口贸易法》也规定了进出口卡特尔，禁止侵犯知识产权、伪造原产地等货物的进出口，旨在禁止不公平的出口交易。

有关通关的基本法是《海关法》《关税法》及《关税暂定措施法》。《海关法》规定了关税的确定与支付规则、禁止进口的商品及海关手续等；《关税法》则规定了长期适用的基本关税税率；《关税暂定措施法》是针对上述两部法律的特别规定，其规定了由于日本国内外经济形势变化而实行的暂定税率。

除上述法律、法规外，根据货物具体情形，将适用国内各种法律项下对进出口的管制，例如《食品卫生法》《家畜传染病防预法》《植物防疫法》及《药事法》。

（三）贸易管理

自 1955 年加入《关税及贸易总协定》（GATT）后，日本从 20 世纪 60 年代初开始实行贸易自由化。在保持并强化多元自由贸易的同时，日本还基于国家安全、人类与动物生命保护及可耗尽的自然资源保护等目的而采取特定的管控措施。

1. 出口

从维护国际和平与安全的角度而言，若出口特定的货物、服务及技术（如武器或大规模杀伤性武器）（清单管制），或向特定区域（美国、英国及法国等发达国家除外）出口特定种类的货物、服务及技术（可能转化为大规模杀伤性武器或类似武器的技术）（全面管制），应获得经济产业省的许可。而且，从维持国际贸易差额的平衡及对外贸易与国民经济健康发展的角度而言，为实现与特定货物、目的地及交易有关的出口，也必须获得经济产业省的批准。

此外，根据《海关法》的规定，以下物品将禁止出口：①麻醉剂、精神药物、大麻、兴奋剂等；②儿童色情制品；③侵犯知识产权（专利权、实用新型专利、外观设计专利、商标权、著作权、邻接权和育种者权）的产品；④同他人的货物或业务标识类似或模仿他人的货物或业务标识的货物等。但就第①类物品而言，若获得政府许可，则允许其出口。

2. 进口

从维持对外贸易与国民经济健康发展的角度而言，特定货物的进口会受到限制。对于《蒙特利尔公约》附件中规定的属于未放开物品的海产品与管制药品（如氯氟烃），由于其属于"进口配额类"货物，因此应当事先从经济产业省处获得进口配额。对于"进口批准类"，须获得经济产业省的事先批准；对于"事先确认类"及"海关确认类"货物，则须分别获得主管省与海关的确认。

此外，根据《海关法》的规定，以下物品的进口将受到限制：①麻醉剂、精神药物、大麻、兴奋剂等，以及鸦片吸食工具；②指定药物；③手枪、机枪等武器以及弹药等；④炸药；⑤火药；⑥极可能用于生产化学武器或其原材料的有毒物质；⑦可能用于生物恐怖主义的病原体等；⑧假币等；⑨有损公共安全或公共道德的书籍等；⑩儿童色情制品；⑪侵犯知识产权（专利权、实用新型专利、外观设计专利、商标权、著作权、邻接权和育种者权）的产品；⑫同他人的货物或业务标识类似或模仿他人的货物或业务标识的货物等。但是，就上述第①至⑦类以及第⑧类中的印花税票仿制品及邮票仿制品而言，若获得政府的许可或类似批准，则允许其进口。

（四）进出口商品的检查和检疫

1. 食品类

根据《食品卫生法》等法律规定，进口食品、食品添加剂等时，应当向厚生劳动省管辖的检疫所提交"食品进口申请书"，并要求对货物进行检查。若通过书面审查确定须进行检查的，应进一步对货物进行有序检查、行政检查、监督检查及其他检查，除非通过该等检查，否则该食品不能进口。对于监督检查，可不等待检查结果作出，即可进口食品，但是，若后来其进口的食品未能通过检查，则将会被采取召回等措施。对于畜产品和农产品，还需要在动物检疫所及植物防疫所进行进一步检查。

2. 畜禽产品

进口畜禽产品时，根据《家畜传染病预防法》等法律规定，除非向农林水产省管辖的动物检疫所提交"进口检验申请书"，且货物需通过书面审查以及各种检查（比如针对动物的临床检查、血液检查等，针对畜禽产品的实际货物检查、详细检查等），否则不允许其进口。需要检验的货物，即所谓的指定检疫类货物，包括偶蹄类动物、鸡、鹌鹑与其他家禽，类属雁形目的鸟类（及鸟蛋）、狗、兔与蜜蜂以及此类物种产品。对于从国内动物传染病发病率高的地区（禁止进口地区）发运或经过该等地区的畜禽产品，则是被禁止进口的。

3. 植物类

在进口植物等货物时，根据《植物防疫法》等法律规定，应当在农林水产省管辖的植物防疫所对其是否存在害虫、是否属于禁止进口类货物等事项进行检查。应接受检查的货物包括幼苗、接穗、鳞茎、种子、切花与切枝、水果、蔬菜、谷物、豆类、香料、木材等。对于从特定地区（禁止进口地区）发运或经过禁止进口地区的特定植物、检疫性有害生物［其蔓延可能对有用植物造成损害的无脊椎动物（如节肢动物）、脊椎动物、真菌、寄生植物和病毒］等货物，则禁止其进口。

（五）海关管理

关税的征收与进出口货物的通关程序等由九大海关部门（函馆、东京、横滨、名古屋、大阪、神户、门司、长崎、冲绳）管理。目前，就通关手续而言，已引入日本货物自动化通关系统（NACCS，用于在线处理进出口货物的通关程序的系统），并且物流的便捷度及相关程序的简化程度已得到了提升（其同样适用于食品及动植物进口申请）。

就关税税率而言，《关税法》中列出了"关税税率表"，各海关编码的基本关税税率、临时关税税率、世界贸易组织关税税率、一般优惠关税税率（以支持发展中国家的各行业）及特别优惠关税税率（针对最不发达国家）可得到确认。在所有类别中，约35%的货物被免除关税。而且，就诸如玉米、乳制品、各种豆类、花生、魔芋根、牛皮、马革及羊皮等共计25项物品已采取关税配额制度。根据该制度，上述物品在满足特定进口总量时，可免除关税或适用较低税率，而超出该总量则适用较高关税税率。其他特别关税包括季节性关税、进口价关税、浮动关税、特殊关税（反倾销关税、反补贴关税等）等。采用海关的预先咨询系统，可确认适用于有待进出口货物的关税税率。

四、劳动

（一）劳动法律、法规简介

1. 日本的劳动法规

在日本，一些立法规范了雇员和雇主之间的关系，比如《劳工标准法》规范了员工的工作条件；《劳动合同法》规定了劳动合同；《工会法》保障了成立工会的权利；《最低工资法》则规定了劳动合同中最低工资标准。这些法案在细节和适用方面并不区分是否是日本国籍的雇员和雇主。

2. 雇员类型

在日本，雇员可以大致分为无固定期限雇员和固定期限雇员。无固定期限雇员是指其工作条件中不会固定其工作期限的雇员，无固定期限雇佣是传统的雇佣制度。但是，近年来，除无固定期限雇佣制度外，固定期限雇佣与劳务派遣的人数一直在增加。需注意，如果固定期限合同的合同期限持续了5年或因续期而持续更长期限，则固定期限雇员可以要求将其劳动合同转换为无固定期限劳动合同，而雇主不得拒绝该要求。

3. 薪酬

雇主应当在规定的日期以法定货币直接向雇员全额支付工资，且每月不少于一次。在日本，最低工资由各县决定。自2017年10月起，主要城市的最低工资如下：①东京：每小时958日元；②爱知：每小时871日元；③大阪：每小时909日元；④福冈：每小时789日元。国家平均工资是每小时848日元。

4. 解雇与退休

在日本，雇主不能任意解雇雇员，雇主只被允许在具有客观合理的理由且解雇被认为符合社会认可的标准的情况下方可解雇员工。

（二）外籍雇员的要求

1. 工作许可证

在日本，没有规定外籍雇员的雇用许可证制度。雇主可以雇用任何有工作签证的外国人。日本主要有13种类型的工作签证：①教授；②研究人员；③艺术家；④宗教活动；⑤记者；⑥业务经理；⑦法律服务；⑧医疗服务；⑨讲师；⑩工程师；⑪公司内部的被调任人员（例如，在境外工作的人被转到日本分公司工作的情况）；⑫艺人；⑬技术劳工。

2. 申请程序

关于工作签证，下面介绍了每种情况所需要的程序：

① 若一名已取得工作签证的外国人被雇用，且其签证类型与上述工作签证类型相同，则其不需要进一步的程序。

② 若一名已取得工作签证的外国人被雇用，其工作签证类型与上述工作签证类型不同，或者是一个没有工作签证，但持有另一种签证（例如学生签证）的外国人被聘用，则雇主须与外籍雇员签订劳动合同，并在日本入境管理局办理工作签证的变更手续。

③ 若雇用一名没有签证的外国人，则须前往驻该外国人所在国家的日本大使馆申请相应的工作签证。

3. 社会保险

雇主有义务参加的社会保险如下：工伤事故赔偿保险、失业保险、健康保险以及员工养老金保险。除由雇员负担的部分外，上述保险的额外保险费须由雇主承担。社会保险的具体情况和适用，不区分是否是日本国籍的雇员与雇主。

（三）出入境

1. 签证的类型

除具有可免签证短期居留的国家国籍的外国人外，外国人进入日本需获得签证［有关工作签证的获得请参阅"外籍雇员的要求"相关部分］。具有中华人民共和国国籍的人在满足特定要求时可以获得多次入境的商务／旅游签证（入境时长：15 天、30 天或 90 天；有效期：1 年、3 年、5 年或 10 年）。

2. 出入境限制

若有居留身份的外国人在日本境外停留 1 年以上，则须在离开日本前取得再次入境许可。此外，需注意，自 2018 年 3 月起，如果有居留身份的外国人离开日本前往朝鲜民主主义人民共和国，那么在某些情况下，该外国人可能被禁止再次进入日本。

（四）工会和劳工组织

以企业为基础而组成的企业工会在日本是很常见的。然而，近年来，一些工会将会员资格扩展到在无工会企业工作的雇员上。按照《工会法》的规定，工会有权与雇主签订"劳动协议"（Rodo kyoyaku），雇主不能将该工会或属于工会成员的雇员或已经针对雇主的不公平待遇向劳动委员会主张权利的雇员置于不利境地，不能拒绝与工会进行集体谈判，也不能控制和干预工会的事务。

（五）劳动纠纷

在日本，劳动纠纷主要通过劳资审裁或民事审判解决。劳资审裁是为迅速解决劳资纠纷而设立的制度，原则上，如果纠纷不能在程序进行的第三天达成和解，劳资审裁委员会将作出裁决，该裁决可强制执行。但是，如果对方提出异议，劳动争议将移交至裁判所进行审判。

五、知识产权

（一）知识产权法律概述

日本的知识产权相关法律包括《专利法》《实用新型法》《意匠法》《商标法》《著作权法》及《防止不正当竞争法》等。

1.《专利法》

《专利法》（1959 年第 121 号法律）是一部旨在保护发明的法律。"发明"被定义为"利用自然法则的高度先进的技术理念"（《专利法》第 2 条第 1 款）。待授予专利的发明包括产品发明与方法发明。

当软件信息处理利用硬件资源来实现时，与该软件有关的发明可通过专利权将其作为利用自然规律进行的技术思想的创作而进行保护。专利权在日本专利厅（JPO）注册后生效。原则上，专利权的存续期限为自申请提交之日起 20 年（《专利法》第 67 条第 1 款）。

2.《实用新型法》

《实用新型法》（1959 年第 123 号法律）是一部旨在保护设计的法律。"设计"被定义为"利用自然法则创造技术理念"（《实用新型法》第 2 条第 1 款），并且与《专利法》一样用于保护技术。然而，与《专利法》不同的是，《实用新型法》并不要求该技术极其先进。此外，仅有与物品或物品组合的形状或结构相关的设计受到《实用新型法》的保护（《实用新型法》第 3 条第 1 款），而方法发明与计算机软件均不受实用新型专利的保护。与专利权一样，实用新型专利自在日本专利厅注册后生效。然而，与《专利法》不同的是，《实用新型法》规定在权利登记时不需要进行任何实质性审查，而且实用新型专利的存续期限为自申请提交之日起 10 年（《实用新型法》第 15 条），其存续期限短于专利权的存续期限。

3.《意匠法》

《意匠法》（1959 年第 125 号法律）是一部旨在保护外观设计的法律。"外观设计"被定义为"通过视觉引起美感的物品（包括物品的一部分）的形状、图案或颜色或其任何组合"（《意匠法》第 2 条第 1 款第 1 项），简而言之，其是物品的外观设计。外观设计专利自在日本专利厅注册后生效。外观设计专利的存续期限为自其注册登记之日起 20 年（《意匠法》第 21 条第 1 款）。若外观设计满足著作权的权利性质，其亦可受《著作权法》的保护。

4.《商标法》

《商标法》（1959 年第 127 号法律）是一部旨在保护商业活动主体的货物或服务上所用标识（商标）的法律，商标将商业主体的货物或服务与其他商业主体的货物或服务区分开来，并代表着货物或服务的来源。除了任何文字、图形、符号、三维形状或其任何组合外，自 2015 年以来，能够注册的商标现在还包括非传统商标，例如运动商标、全息商标、仅由颜色组成的商标、声音商标和位置商标（《商标法》第 2 条第 1 款）。商标权经注册后生效（《商标法》第 18 条第 1 款）。商标权的存续期限为自注册之日起 10 年，且可以更新（《商标法》第 19 条）。未经注册的商标，若其被广泛认可或广为人知，其可受《防止不正当竞争法》和/或《民法》的保护。

5.《著作权法》

《著作权法》（1970 年第 48 号法律）是一部旨在保护作品的法律。"作品"被定义为"创作性地表现思想或感情的属于文艺、学术、美术或者音乐领域的成果"（《著作权法》第 2 条第 1 款第 1 项）。作品种类包括文学作品、音乐作品、美术作品、建筑作品、电影作品、摄影作品及计算机编程作品。根据作品的使用方式，著作权可进一步细分为复制权、舞台表演权、音乐演奏权、银幕放映权、传播权、口述权、展览权、发行权、转让权、租赁权、翻译权、原著改编权。作品创作后，著作权人享有与作品相关的著作权（《著作权法》第 51 条第 1 款），且著作权的获得无须履行诸如注册等手续（《著作权法》第 17 条第 2 款：无正式手续原则）。对于著作权人以真实姓名（包括知名笔名）创作的作品，著作权保护将持续至著作权人死后 50 年（《著作权法》第 51 条第 2 款）；对于以法人等组织创作的作品，原则上，著作权保护将持续至该作品发表后 50 年（《著作权法》第 53 条）。著作权人享有著作人格权（《著作权法》第 17 条）。

（二）专利申请

为了使发明获得专利权并作为《专利法》下的权利而得到保护，必须满足以下要求：

① 实用性（《专利法》第 29 条第 1 款：引言条款）；
② 新颖性（《专利法》第 29 条第 1 款：引言条款）；
③ 创造性（《专利法》第 29 条第 2 款）。

在提交专利申请时，须向日本专利厅提交描述特定事项的申请，必要时附上说明、权利请求范围及图片，并随附摘要（《专利法》第 36 条第 1 款、第 2 款；需注意，专利申请通常通过在线程序作为电子数据提交）。该说明应包括"发明的详细解释"，内容陈述应清楚且详细，以便该发明所属领域的普通技术人员能够使用该发明（《专利法》第36条第3款、第4款第1项）。在权利请求范围部分，须列举被认为详细说明申请人请求授予专利权的发明所需要的所有事项（《专利法》第36条第5款）。关于权利请求范围的描述须满足以下要求：请求授予专利权的发明在发明的详细说明中进行了陈述（《专利法》第36条第6款第1项：支持要求）；请求授予专利权的发明是清楚的（《专利法》第36条第6款第2项：清晰）；各项请求陈述应简明（《专利法》第36条第6款第3项）。

无论其审查进度如何，专利申请的内容将于专利申请提交之日起一年六个月后予以公布（《专利法》第64条：公布专利申请）。包括申请人在内的个人可提请对专利申请进行审查，经申请后审查程序启动。若自专利申请提交之日起3年内对该申请未提出审查请求的，该专利申请将被视为已撤销（《专利法》第48-3条）。

若未发现拒绝专利申请的任何理由，审查官应作出授予专利权的决定（《专利法》第51条）。相反，若审查官发现拒绝授予专利权的理由，其应向申请人出具拒绝申请的理由通知。作为回复，申请人将有机会陈述意见（《专利法》第50条）。若申请人已提交书面意见，或已对申请作出修改，且审查官已确定无任何理由拒绝该申请的，可作出授予专利权的决定。若申请人未陈述任何意见，或未对申请作出任何修改，或申请人确已提交书面意见或对申请作出修改，但审查官仍然认为拒绝理由尚未得到妥善解决的，审查官可再次作出拒绝申请的决定。如果申请人对拒绝决定不满，其可对审查官的拒绝决定提出申诉（《专利法》第121条）。

若作出授予专利权决定的，该专利将于支付专利费后进行注册，注册后专利开始生效（《专利法》第66条第1款、第2款）。专利权生效后，将在日本专利厅发布的专利公报中发布以下事项：专利申请中陈述的事项；说明中陈述的事项；权利请求范围以及其他事项（《专利法》第66条第3款）。自公开该专利的专利公报发行后6个月内，任何人可对授予的专利权提出异议，要求重新审议该专利（《专利法》第103条）。该期限届满后，唯有利益相关人士可提交专利无效审判请求（《专利法》第123条）。

（三）商标注册

为了使商标得以注册，须满足以下要求：该商标是用于与申请人业务有关的货物或服务的商标（《商标法》第3条第1款：引言条款）；该商标能将申请人的货物或服务与任何其他人的货物或服务区分开来（《商标法》第3条第1款各项）；商标从公共利益和私人利益等方面而言，不是一个不可注册的商标。

提交商标申请后，审查官将对是否有任何拒绝申请的理由（例如不符合注册要求）而对申请进行实质性审查（《商标法》第15条）。商标申请的内容在申请提交1个月后在商标公报上予以公布（《商标法》第12-2条）。

若未发现任何拒绝的理由，审查官应作出对商标予以注册的决定（《商标法》第16条）。相反，若审查官发现拒绝理由，其应向申请人出具拒绝其申请的理由的通知。作为回复，申请人将有机会陈述意见（《商标法》第15-2条）。若申请人已提交书面意见，或已对申请作出修改，且审查官已确定无任何理由拒绝该申请的，可作出对商标予以注册的决定。若申请人未陈述任何意见，或未对申请作出任何修改，或如申请人确已提交书面意见或对申请作出修改，但审查官仍然认为拒绝理由尚未得到妥善解决的，审查官将作出拒绝申请的决定。如果申请人对拒绝决定不满，其可对审查官的拒绝决定提出申诉（《商标法》第44条）。若作出对商标予以注册的决定的，该商标将于支付注册费后进行注册（《商标法》第18条第2款），其内容将在商标公报上予以发布。就商标而言，同样允许他人对商标的注册提出异议（《商标法》第43-2条），并允许提出注册商标无效的审判请求（《商标法》第46条）。

（四）知识产权保护

1. 专利权

由于专利权人享有将专利发明作为业务运作的专属权利（《专利法》第68条），专利权人有权对任何未经许可将专利发明作为业务运作的人士采取寻求禁令（《专利法》第100条）等措施，若存在故意或过失侵权的，还可要求对任何损害进行赔偿（《民法》第709条）。鉴于损害金额难以确定，因此存在推定损害金额等规定（《专利法》第102条）。

2. 实用新型专利

由于实用新型专利持有人享有将经注册的实用新型专利作为业务运作的专属权利（《实用新型法》第 16 条），实用新型专利持有人有权对任何未经许可将经注册的实用新型专利作为业务运作的人士采取寻求禁令（《实用新型法》第 27 条）等措施，若存在故意或过失侵权的，还可要求对任何损害进行赔偿（《民法》第 709 条）。然而，实用新型专利的注册无须经过实质审查，比如新颖性与独创性审查。因此，在行使权利时，须首先出示已注册的实用新型专利的实用新型技术意见（《实用新型法》第 12 条），以作为警告（《实用新型法》第 29 条第 2 款）。实用新型和专利权一样，有推定损害金额等规定（《实用新型法》第 29 条）。

3. 外观设计专利

由于外观设计专利持有人享有将经注册的外观设计作为业务运作的专属权利（《意匠法》第 23 条），外观设计专利持有人有权对任何未经许可将经注册的外观设计作为业务运作的人士采取寻求禁令（《意匠法》第 37 条）等措施，若存在故意或过失侵权的，还可要求对任何损害进行赔偿（《民法》第 709 条）。外观设计和专利权一样，有推定损害金额等规定（《意匠法》第 39 条）。

4. 商标权

由于商标权人享有使用与指定商品或服务有关的注册商标的专属权利（《商标法》第 25 条），并有权禁止他人使用任何相似的商标（《商标法》第 37 条第 1 款：禁止权），商标权人有权对侵犯该等权利的人士采取寻求禁令（《商标法》第 36 条）等措施，若存在故意或过失侵权的，还可要求对任何损害进行赔偿（《民法》第 709 条）。《商标法》中含有推定损害赔偿数额等类似规定（《商标法》第 38 条）。

5. 著作权

著作权人有权针对著作权侵权（包括对著作权细分权利的侵权等）行为采取寻求禁令（《著作权法》第 12 条）等措施，若存在故意或过失侵权的，还可要求对任何损害进行赔偿（《民法》第 709 条）。就复制权及原著改编权侵权而言，要求验证其依赖性（即他人在受到著作权人作品的影响后将著作权人作品融入自己的作品中）及相似性（即与著作权人作品中的创意表达的相似性）。《著作权法》中含有推定损害赔偿数额等类似规定（《著作权法》第 104 条）。

六、环境保护

（一）环境保护监督部门

环境省（MOE）是管理环境保护的主要行政部门。除一般环境政策外，环境省还负责并执行其他环境政策，如全球与国际环境合作政策，大气环境措施与汽车排放物措施，水土、地面及海洋环境保护，废弃物及回收利用政策，健康措施与化学物质控制措施，以及自然环境与生物多样性保护。

另外，经济产业省负责管理节能与可再生能源推广领域，而国土交通省负责管理建筑节能标准法规等领域。

而且，各地区的行政机关下级分支机构及有关地方政府负责监督并执行相关地区的具体规定与活动。

（二）环境保护法律、法规概述

《环境基本法》规定了日本的整体环境政策。另外，根据该法制定的《环境基本规划》表明了日本政府环境保护措施的基本方向。

而且，根据《推进全球气候变暖对策法》的规定，日本政府应通过诸如制定《全球气候变暖对策规划》，采取措施控制温室气体排放等对策加强应对全球气候变暖的措施。

除该等与环境政策相关的基本法律、法规外，日本还制定了针对各种环境保护问题的具体法律、法规以及与此类法律、法规相关的规定。

首先，就污染物排放等事宜而言，《大气污染防治法》《水质污染防治法》《土壤污染对策法》《废弃物处理和公共清洁法》以及其他法律、法规规范并限制了污染物的排放，并规范了废弃物的处置方法等事宜。

其次，诸如《森林法》《自然环境保护法》及《自然公园法》等法律、法规规范并限制了在森林区与国家公园区的开发行为。

日本还出台了《环境影响评估法》，根据该法规定，在特定地域开展的开发行为可能需要事先评估开发行为对环境的影响，并且根据评估结果，可能需要对开发方案予以修改，以减少对环境的影响，视具体情形还可能停止开发行为。

就该等环境保护法律、法规而言，各地区出台了相应的市政法令，某些地区采用的标准甚至比法律规定的标准更为严格。

在节能领域，《提高建筑物能耗性能法》及其他法律、法规规定了建筑物节能标准等事宜。因此，在某些情况下，如修建建筑物时，须满足某些节能标准。

最后，一些地区已采用了关于某些建筑物温室气体排放量的规定。因此，为了符合该等规定的要求，有时须采取节能措施，并安装节能设备等。

在可再生能源领域，根据《电力供应商利用可再生能源电力特别措施法》的规定已引入回购电价制度。

（三）环境评估

日本的环境保护政策及法律、法规历经了数个阶段。

从 20 世纪 60 年代至 70 年代，随着经济的发展，日本出现了严重的污染问题。为了应对这些污染问题，日本制定了环境保护法律、法规，其中包括《大气污染防治法》《水质污染防治法》以及其他与防止环境污染的环境保护措施相关的法律、法规。

此后，诸如全球气候变暖和生物多样性减少等环境问题成为国际性问题。为实现可持续发展，从 20 世纪 90 年代起，日本也制定了相应的法律、法规，对气候变暖对策、节能及回收利用等事宜予以规定。

因此，可以说日本现有的环境保护政策及法律、法规涵盖了全面且详尽的环境保护政策，其能够满足不同领域的需求。

另外，各地方政府均已制定了符合本地区具体情况的法规，其中一些法规提出的要求甚至比法律规定的要求更为严格。

此外，自 2011 年东日本大地震后，地震造成的损害及后果导致的环境问题及节能措施再次受到关注与反思。为了实现 2015 年通过的可持续发展目标及 2016 年生效的《巴黎协定》的目标，在国际关系方面，日本政府预计将比之前作出更多努力并出台更多政策。

七、争议解决

（一）纠纷解决的方法及机构

在日本，解决纠纷的方法大致分为审判和替代性纠纷解决方式（ADR）。替代性纠纷解决方式主要包括仲裁和调解。

1. 审判

审判机构包括最高裁判所、高等裁判所、地方裁判所、简易裁判所和家事裁判所（处理家事关系案件的裁判机构）。日本实行三级审判制度，根据该制度，纠纷当事人可以对下一级裁判所作出的判决提起上诉，原则上最多给予纠纷当事人三次审判的机会。各种诉讼程序法，主要是指《民事诉讼法典》和《刑事诉讼法典》，均规定了严格的审判程序。应注意的是，审判过程中只可使用日语。若书面证据是以外文书写的，须随附其日文译本，若审判过程中的宣誓人不会日语，须有口译员在场。

劳资审裁是类似于裁判所审判的一种制度。劳资审裁处理个体劳动者与雇主之间与劳资关系相关的民事纠纷。劳资委员会在必要时在各方当事人之间进行调解，若当事人之间未能达成调解协议，劳资委员会将作出裁决。原则上，劳资审裁的程序是通过召开三次庭审来完成的，因此可以比普通审判程序更快地作出裁判。此外，除一名法官外，两名具有劳资关系专业知识和经验的劳资审判人员担任劳资委员会成员，因此可灵活地解决复杂的劳资问题。

2. 替代性纠纷解决方式（ADR）

与审判相比，替代性纠纷解决方式具有以下特点：

- 该程序不对公众公开，因此，替代性纠纷解决方式可能更适合于纠纷事实含有高度机密事项，或纠纷本身应保密的案件。
- 纠纷当事人可选择仲裁员或调解员。因此，替代性纠纷解决方式可能更适合于需要技术判断以解决纠纷的案件，因为当事人可选择具有适当专业知识的仲裁员或调解员。
- 通常来说，该程序所需时限比普通审判程序更短。

（1）仲裁

若纠纷各方当事人签订仲裁协议，即将某特定法律关系中已出现或未来可能出现的民事纠纷提交仲裁解决并接受仲裁结果的协议，可申请仲裁解决争议。若当事人未签订仲裁协议，则无法申请仲裁。仲裁协议可以防止任何一方当事人向裁判所提起诉讼（即使一方当事人提起诉讼，另一方当事人抗辩称存在仲裁协议的，该诉讼应驳回）。在仲裁程序中，所使用的语言由当事人之间的协议确定，并可将包括日语在内的任何语言设定为仲裁语言。应指出的是，与公司相比通常处于弱势地位的消费者和雇员可能被迫签订对其不利的仲裁协议，因此在某些情况下，从保护消费者和雇员的角度而言，法律允许终止公司与消费者之间的仲裁协议，并可认定公司与雇员之间的仲裁协议无效。在政府或私营部门组织的众多仲裁机构中，日本商事仲裁协会（JCAA）因解决国际商事纠纷而闻名。

（2）调解

调解是由第三方介入当事人之间的纠纷以解决争议。不同于仲裁，调解是根据当事人之间的和解协议解决纠纷的程序。即调解员不作出任何裁决，只是提出和解方案，由当事人自行决定是否接受该和解方案。调解由裁判所、政府或私营部门组织的机构进行，而由裁判所进行的调解也应由当事人决定是否接受和解方案。

（二）法律适用

包括《民事诉讼法典》和《刑事诉讼法典》在内的各种程序法均适用于审判。仲裁根据《仲裁法》及各仲裁机构的仲裁规则进行。对于调解，《民事调解法》适用于由裁判所进行的调解。但是对于其他调解机构进行的调解程序，并没有普遍适用的法律，基本上这种调解按照各调解机构的规则进行。

对于中国和日本之间仲裁机构作出的仲裁裁决的可执行性而言，两国均是《承认及执行外国仲裁裁决公约》的成员国，因此，可在中国执行日本仲裁机构作出的仲裁裁决，也可在日本执行中国仲裁机构作出的仲裁裁决。对于司法判决，日本法律规定了日本裁判所执行外国法院所作司法判决的条件。其中一项条件是在日本与作出该司法判决的法院所属国家之间"存在相互担保"（《民事诉讼法典》第118条第4款）。具体而言，在作出判决的外国法院所属国家，由日本裁判所作出的同该外国法院所作的同类别司法判决必须在某些条件下被认定为有效，且这些条件在重要方面应与日本法律项下的条件实质性相似。从这方面来说，一般认为中国与日本之间无相互担保，因此不可能在日本执行中国法院作出的司法判决，也无法在中国执行日本裁判所作出的司法判决。

八、其他

（一）反商业贿赂

属于日本《刑法》下的公职人员受贿犯罪的案件当事人将根据贿赂类型受到法定处罚。例如，在简单贿赂的情况下，规定受贿者应被判处5年以下有期徒刑，且没收受贿款项，无法没收全部或部分受贿款项的，应追征等额罚金。

若属于日本公职人员的贿赂犯罪案件，行贿者将被判处3年以下有期徒刑，或250万日元以下的罚金。各项特别法均对被视为公职人员的人员和从事公共事务的人员的贿赂犯罪行为作出了规定。

《防止不正当竞争法》规定了对外国公职人员的行贿行为。在属于《防止不正当竞争法》中规定的对外国公职人员行贿的案件中，行贿者应被判处 5 年以下有期徒刑，或处以 500 万日元以下的罚金，或两者并罚，公司应被处以 3 亿日元以下的罚金。法人代表或法人的代理人、雇员或任何其他工作人员对外国公职人员犯有行贿犯罪的，违法者和该法人均应被处以 3 亿日元以下的罚金。

与中国不同的是，在日本并无关于商业贿赂（所谓的非公职人员之间的贿赂）的一般规定。但是，董事等的行贿或受贿行为，或与股东权利行使相关的行贿与受贿行为均属于《公司法》下的特殊贿赂犯罪。

（二）工程外包

根据世界贸易组织《政府采购协定》及其他相关法律的规定，对于合同金额不少于规定金额（例如，合同金额为 6.8 亿日元以上的建筑工程采购合同，或合同金额为 1 500 万日元以上的货物及其他物品采购合同）的中央及地方政府的采购合同均需经过招标程序。招标程序的目的是确立非歧视性待遇，并确保采购过程透明。

招标程序分为一般竞争性招标（公开招标）、指定竞争性招标（选择性招标）和自决合同（限制性招标）。原则上，希望参加一般竞争性招标和指定竞争性招标的企业需通过采购机构的资格筛选。

若采购机构希望进行一般竞争性招标或指定竞争性招标的，采购机构应至少于招标日期前 40 天在官方公报、地方公告上发布公开招标通知（公告），并向公众公布拟议招标。此外，为了广泛提供政府采购有关信息，官方公报中公布的信息将存储于数据库之中，可通过日本贸易振兴机构驻日本办事处、商业支持中心，或通过在线检索服务（http://www.jetro.go.jp/gov_procurement/）访问该等信息。

Japan

Authors: Akira Moriwaki, Takashi Nomura, Ippei Hayakawa
Translators: Zhu Yi, Eagle Yang

I. Overview

A. General Introduction to the Political, Economic, Social and Legal Environment of the Country Receiving Investment

When the Japanese economy prospered, many Japanese companies made huge investments into China. However, after the end of that prosperity, a new trend is being established–the number of tourists, visitors, and investments from China are increasing. Under the "Belt and Road" ("B&R") initiative, the governments of both China and Japan generally welcome this new trend and are moving forward to the next stage, "mutual cooperation in the whole area covered by B&R".

a. Political Environment

The political framework of Japan is known as a "bicameral parliamentary representative democratic constitutional monarchy". Pursuant to the Constitution of Japan, which came into effect in 1947, the Emperor is defined as "the symbol of the State and of the unity of the people", and holds no power. By contrast, the Prime Minister, who is the head of the Cabinet, is appointed by the Emperor in accordance with the nomination of the Diet. The Prime Minister is chosen from the diet members. This method of appointment represents the principle of popular sovereignty.

The Constitution of Japan has adopted the trias politica model which divides governmental power into three– the legislative power, which is vested in the National Diet, the executive power, which is vested in the Cabinet, and the judiciary power, which is vested in the Supreme Court and other local courts. As a result of this tripartite division, there is an expectation that "Checks and Balances" will be exercised among those powers.

b. Economic Environment

From 1968 to 2009, Japan had the second highest GDP in the world. However, the prosperity of Japan's "bubble economy" ended in 1991. Thereafter, severe economic conditions continued for almost twenty years. That period became known as the "lost two decades".

Now, Japan is said to be in a phase of moderate growth. Although Japan's GDP growth has been quite small, land and stock prices have steadily increased. This phase of moderate growth could be caused by several factors, including the fact that the Olympic Games are to be held in Tokyo in 2020, the recent dramatic boost of the number of tourists from foreign countries and regions, and the current monetary policies, i.e., the quantitative easing policy and the low interest rate policy.

c. Social Environment

Japan is a small country in terms of its total land area of approximately 378,000 square kilometers. As a result, Japan is almost one-twenty fifth the size of China, which is ranked 61st in the world for total land area. Nevertheless, in terms of population, Japan is ranked tenth in the world.

Recently, Japan is said to be facing two serious problems–decreasing birthrate and an aging population. Because of its decreasing birthrate, the total population of Japan has been decreasing since 2015. To date, the total population is approximately 127 million. However, the foreign population in Japan is increasing. Additionally, Japan's aging population provides many opportunities for innovation in various industry sectors which may possibly apply to other aging countries and regions.

d. Legal Environment

a) Judicial System

As mentioned above, the Constitution of Japan vests the judicial power entirely in the courts. Courts in Japan are independent from the other state institutions. Likewise, all judges are independent in the exercise of their official duties. Furthermore, lower courts may not be instructed or supervised by superior courts.

In Japan, the court system consists of the Supreme Court, high courts, district courts, summary courts and family courts. The courts handle civil, criminal and administrative cases. The Supreme Court is located in Tokyo, and high courts are located in eight cities throughout Japan. There is one district court in every prefecture, with the exception of Hokkaido which has four district courts. The Japanese judicial system basically has a three-tier structure, and appeals may, in principle, be made twice. Normally, the court of first instance is, depending on the claimed amount (in civil cases), either the district court or the summary court, and in family affairs, the family court.

The Supreme Court is the court of last resort for all cases. It is composed of 15 justices, one of whom is the Chief Justice. Cases in the Supreme Court are heard by either a full bench comprised of all justices, or a petty bench, which is a panel of three or more justices.

The Chief Justice of the Supreme Court is appointed by the Emperor, but he or she is designated by the Cabinet. The other justices of the Supreme Court are appointed by the Cabinet. Judges in the lower courts are appointed by the Cabinet from a list of persons nominated by the Supreme Court. Except for the judges of the summary courts, all judges must have passed the final examination, which is known as "the second exam". The second exam is given at the end of at least one year of legal apprentice training at the Legal Training and Research Institute, which is under the authority of the Supreme Court.

b) Source of Law

(i) Constitution

The Constitution of Japan is the supreme law of Japan. If any subordinate laws and regulations, such as acts and dispositions, are contrary to the Constitution of Japan, they are deemed invalid. The courts have the power to determine constitutionality, and may, in relation to a specific case, determine that any subordinate laws and regulations which contravene the Constitution should not be applied. The courts may also invalidate dispositions that are contrary to the Constitution. However, in practice, the Supreme Court acts relatively conservatively when making constitutionality determinations because of its lack of democratic grounds.

An amendment to the Constitution may be initiated only by a majority of two thirds or more of all the members of each Diet house and with the consent of the majority of the people, which is established through a referendum. To date, the Constitution of Japan has never been amended since it came into effect in 1947.

(ii) Acts

Because Japan is a civil law country, statutes are the essential source of law. An act is a law adopted by the Diet in the form of a statute, which normally has to be approved by a majority of the members present of each National Diet house. Under the Constitution of Japan, certain important matters, such as the adoption of punitive provisions and the imposition of new taxes, can only be regulated through acts. However, it is common for an act to be used to delegate legislative authority to other institutions, which can then adopt orders, ordinances, etc. to address the delegated matters.

(iii) Cabinet Orders and Ordinances of The Ministry

Orders include cabinet orders adopted by the Cabinet, ordinances of the Ministry adopted by the Ministries, and cabinet office ordinances adopted by the Cabinet Office. There are two types of orders: "orders delegated by an act", which are orders adopted based on a delegation in an act, and "enforcement orders", which are orders that are not based on delegation, but are issued to execute superior laws and regulations.

(iv) Prefectural / Municipal Ordinances and Rules

Prefectural / municipal ordinances are rules of law adopted by a council of an ordinary local public entity. By contrast, rules are adopted by governors / mayors and committees of local public entities. The Local Autonomy Act[1] permits prefectural / municipal ordinances to prescribe criminal penalties and the rules (adopted by governors / mayors of local public entities) may govern non-penal fines.

(v) Judicial Precedents

Although there is no provision which expressly defines the legally binding effect of judicial precedents, judicial precedents of the Supreme Court have a strong influence on the subsequent judgments of the lower courts, and their importance in legal practice is exceedingly high. Under the laws and regulations of Japan, conflicting judicial precedents from the Supreme Court may be a reason for a final appeal (in criminal cases) or reason for a petition for acceptance of a final appeal (in civil cases). The judicial precedents of the Supreme Court may be only be amended through a full bench, and, in practice, the judicial precedents of the Supreme Court are considered to have certain legally binding effect.

---

[1] Act No.67 of 1947.

B. The Status and Direction of the Cooperation with Chinese Enterprises Under the B&R

The Japanese government did not express their position on China's B&R initiative for a time. However, in late 2017, the Japanese government expressly stated its support of the B&R initiative. In particular, in early December 2017, the Japanese government issued a guideline entitled "Regarding Japan-China Private Economic Cooperation in the Third-Party Countries". That guideline addressed cooperation mainly with respect to the energy-saving and environmental sectors, the modernization of industrial parks and infrastructure, and logistics between Asia and Europe.

In addition, in December 2016, the Act Promoting Implementation of Specified Integrated Resort Areas, the so called "Casino Promotion Law", was promulgated. Its aim was to promote the establishment of an integrated resort ("IR") with casino in Japan. Subsequently, the Japanese government established a new governmental body called the IR Promotion Advisory Council. This new council issued a whitepaper in 2017, which described the details concerning the selection process and other matters. It is also expected that foreign enterprise will be involved in that area.

II. Investment

A. Market Access

a. The Agencies Supervising Investment

The primary governmental agencies supervising investments are:

(i) the Council for Promotion of Foreign Direct Investment in Japan, which was organized by the Cabinet Office of Japan to promote the foreign direct investment in Japan, and

(ii) the Japan External Trade Organization ("JETRO"), which is a government-related organization that works to promote mutual trade and investment between Japan and the rest of the world.

Most other ministries and government offices, such as the Ministry of Economy, Trade and Industry ("METI") and the Financial Services Agency ("FSA"), also have their own specialized offices for foreign investment in Japan. These specialized offices offer various services to foreign investors, including, but not limited to, providing information about investment opportunities.

Additionally, a few local governments (including Tokyo, Yokohama, and Osaka) have their own specialized offices for foreign investment in their local prefecture. In Tokyo, for example, the Japanese government and the Tokyo metropolitan government joined together to launch the Tokyo One-Stop Business Establishment Center. This center is intended to support any foreign company wishing to invest in Tokyo. It provides assistance in connection with the wide range of administrative procedures which are required when forming a business entity and commencing operations in Tokyo, including the certification of articles of incorporation, corporate registration, tax issues, and employment matters related to pensions, social insurance and immigration.

• JETRO, Official website: http://www.jetro.go.jp/;

• General information from the Cabinet Office regarding foreign direct investment, Official Website: http://www.invest-japan.go.jp/en_index.html;

• Tokyo One-Stop Business Establishment Center, Official Website: http://www.seisakukikaku.metro.tokyo.jp/onestop/english/top/

b. Laws and Regulations Governing Investment Industry

Many of the barriers to foreign investment in Japan have been abolished. Now, only a few restrictions remain in the laws which govern specific business areas, and those are listed in the table below. These restrictions, which are intended to promote the national security policies, national industrial policies, and economic policies of Japan, vary in method. However, as the table demonstrates, restrictions on holding shares and voting rights in Japanese domestic companies and the acquisition of licenses concerning individual businesses are the most common methods of restriction.

Business Area	Outline of Restrictions Targeted at Foreign Investment
Telecommunications	Refusal to Register Share Transfer (Act on Nippon Telegraph and Telephone Corporation, etc.① (the "NTT Act"), Article 6, Paragraphs 1 and 2)
Radio Stations	Restrictions on the Acquisition of Radio Licenses (Radio Act②, Article 5, Paragraphs 1 and 4) Revocation of Radio Licenses (Radio Act, Article 75, Paragraph 1)
Basic Broadcasting	Refusal to Grant Approval to Conduct Basic Broadcast Business (Broadcast Act③, Article 93, Paragraph 1, Item 6) Revocation of Approval to Conduct Basic Broadcast Business (Broadcast Act, Article 103, Paragraphs 1 and 2) Refusal to Register Share Transfer (Broadcast Act, Article 116, Paragraphs 1 and 2) Restrictions on Voting Rights (Broadcast Act, Article 116, Paragraphs 3 and 4)
Basic Broadcast Station Supplier	Refusal to Register Share Transfer (Broadcast Act, Article 125, Paragraphs 1 and 2) Restrictions on Voting Rights (Broadcast Act, Article 125, Paragraph 2)
Certified Broadcast Holding Companies	Refusal to Grant Authorization to Establish a Certified Broadcast Holding Company (Broadcast Act, Article 159, Paragraph 2, Item 5) Revocation of Authorization to Establish a Certified Broadcast Holding Company (Broadcast Act, Article 166, Paragraph 1, Item 1) Refusal to Register Share Transfer (Broadcast Act, Article161, Paragraph 1) Restrictions on Voting Rights (Broadcast Act, Article 116, Paragraph 2)
Cargo Forwarding, etc.	Refusal to Register as Class 1 Cargo Forwarder Servicer (Cargo Forwarder Service Act④, Article 6, Paragraph 1, Item 5) Suspension of Business and Revocation of Registration concerning Class 1 Cargo Forwarding (Cargo Forwarder Service Act, Article 16, Item 3) Disqualification of License of Class 2 Cargo Forwarding (Cargo Forwarder Service Act, Article 22) Refusal to Approve Aircraft Registration (Civil Aeronautics Act⑤, Article 4, Paragraph 1) Disqualification of License for Air Transportation Business (Civil Aeronautics Act, Article 101, Paragraph 1, Item 5) Refusal to Register Share Transfer by Air Transportation Companies (Civil Aeronautics Act, Article 120-2, Paragraph 1) Prohibition of Ownership of Japanese Vessels (Ship Act⑥, Article 1) Refusal to Register Ship Class Register Business (Act on Assurance of Security of International Ships and Port Facility⑦, Article 20, Paragraph 5, Item 4)
Banking	Examination When Appling for Banking Business License (Banking Act⑧, Article 4, Paragraph 3)
Fishing	Prohibition on Fishing in Japanese Territorial Sea and Internal Waters (Act on Regulation of Fishing Operations by Foreign Nationals⑨, Article 3)
Mining	Prohibition on Holding Mining Rights (Mining Act⑩, Article 17)

The restrictions on holding shares and voting rights in Japanese domestic companies generally do not require the involvement of the Japanese government because they stipulate the ratio of permitted foreign shareholders. In most cases, foreign investors are not restricted from acquiring shares, but instead will be prevented from

① Act No.85 of 1984.
② Act No.131 of 1950.
③ Act No.132 of 1950.
④ Act No.82 of 1989.
⑤ Act No.231 of 1952.
⑥ Act No.46 of 1899.
⑦ Act No.31 of 2004.
⑧ Act No.59 of 1981.
⑨ Act No.60 of 1967.
⑩ Act No.289 of 1950.

registering in the company's register of shareholders[①]. This may result in foreign shareholders not being able to exercise their rights as shareholders.

Apart from the foregoing restrictions, under the Foreign Exchange and Foreign Trade Act[②] ("FEFTA") of Japan, foreign investors are required to follow pre-notification or after-the-fact reporting procedures when performing direct investment in Japan as explained in detail in section B. Foreign exchange regulation.

c. Forms of Investment

The most common methods used by foreign entities to invest in Japan are: (i) the establishment of a business presence in Japan, (ii) the establishment of a joint venture with Japanese companies, or (ii) the acquisition of shares from a Japanese company. Additional information about the establishment of a business presence in Japan will be described in section E. The establishment and dissolution of companies.

d. Market Access

As stated above, the restrictions on foreign investment in Japan are limited. Furthermore, the Japanese government is now actively working to attract foreign investment in Japan. In May 2016, the Japanese government introduced the "Policy Package for Promoting Foreign Direct Investment into Japan to Make Japan a Global Hub"[③]. Nonetheless, complex regulations and administrative procedures, language barriers, and unique business customs still act as barriers to the entry of foreign entities into the Japanese market. Recently, Japan was ranked No.34 with respect to the ease of doing business in the "A World Bank Group Flagship Report : Doing Business 2018".

B. Foreign Exchange Regulation

a. The Agencies Supervising Foreign Exchange

Foreign investment in Japan is primarily regulated by the FEFTA. Although the METI have jurisdiction over the FEFTA, the Bank of Japan performs many of the business transactions required when foreign investors directly invest in Japan. For example, the Bank of Japan accepts permit applications, notification forms and reports of pre-notification or after-the-fact report procedures (FEFTA, Article 69).

The Bank of Japan accepts general inquiries in relation to the filing procedures under the FEFTA over the telephone; additional information can also be found on its website as listed below.

• Bank of Japan, Official website: http: //www.boj.or.jp/en/index.htm

• Reports under the Foreign Exchange Act:https://www.boj.or.jp/about/services/tame/t_seido.htm/ (Japanese Version Only)

b. Brief Introduction to the Laws and Regulations Governing Foreign Exchange

a) Outline of The FEFTA

Under the FEFTA, the Japanese government must receive notification when certain foreign transactions involving "inward direct investment" by a "foreign investor" are performed. The revisions to the FEFTA in April 1998, abolished the "prior notification / approval system" which was used previously, particularly in capital transactions. In its place, the "after-the-fact reporting system" was introduced. Under this new system, after a foreign transaction is completed, a report providing the details of the foreign transaction must be submitted to the Minister of Finance and/or any other ministers who have jurisdiction over the business which is the subject of such transaction. Today, under the FEFTA, foreign transactions including investments in Japan may, in general, be freely conducted in accordance with such "after-the-fact reporting system" except in certain cases. Those exceptions include investments in: (i) industries which interfere with Japan's security or the public maintenance of order, or (ii) industries wherein Japan has determined to stay the liberalization required by the OECD Codes of Liberalisation of Capital Movements and of Current Invisible Operations by giving notice to the Organisation for Economic Co-operation and Development ("OECD"). We will explain further on those exceptions in subsection c b) below.

b) Definition of "Inward Direct Investment"

Under the FEFTA, the term "inward direct investment" is defined as an act that falls within any of the following categories:

---

① The register of shareholders is a record of a company's shareholders which is maintained by the company and used to grant shareholder rights. For the shareholders of listed companies, the register of shareholders could also be a requirement to assert claims against third parties.

② Act No.228 of 1949.

③ Additional information on the policy can be found on the website of the Council for Promotion of Foreign Direct Investment in Japan.

(i) an acquisition of the shares or equity of an unlisted corporation (excluding an acquisition through a transfer from foreign investors);

(ii) a transfer of the shares or equity of a corporation other than listed corporations, etc., which have been held by a person prior to his or her becoming a non-resident (limited to transfers from an individual who is a non-resident to foreign investors);

(iii) an acquisition of the shares of, for example, a listed corporation, to the extent that the acquirer's total shareholding in such a company (including the shares held by those who have a certain relationship with the acquirer) reaches 10% or more of the issued and outstanding shares;

(iv) the consent given for a substantial change of the business purpose of a corporation (for a business corporation, limited to a consent given by those holding one-third or more of the voting rights of all shareholders of the business corporation);

(v) the establishment of, for example, branch offices in Japan or a substantial change of the kind or business purpose of a branch office in Japan (limited to those specified by Cabinet Order and conducted by those identified in items c)(i) or c)(ii) of the definition of "foreign investors");

(vi) a loan of money to a juridical person having its principal office in Japan which exceed the amount specified by Cabinet Order and for which the period for repayment exceeds one year;

(vii) an acquisition of bonds which are offered to specified foreign investors;

(viii) an acquisition of investment securities which are issued by juridical persons established under special acts; and

(ix) a discretionary investment in shares in, for example, a listed company as specified by Cabinet Order.

c) Definition of "Foreign Investor"

Under the FEFTA, the term "foreign investor" is defined as any one of the following persons who, for example, directly invest in Japan:

(i) an individual who is a non-resident of Japan;

(ii) a juridical person or other organization either established pursuant to foreign laws and regulations, or having its principal office in a foreign state;

(iii) a corporation of which the ratio of a) the sum of the number of voting rights directly held by those listed in items (i) or (ii) and the number of voting rights specified by Cabinet Order as those indirectly held through other corporations, to b) the number of voting rights of all shareholders or members of the corporation is 50% or higher; and

(iv) in addition to what is listed in items (ii) and (iii), a juridical person or other organization in which the persons identified in item (i) comprise a majority of either the officers (meaning directors or other persons equivalent thereto) or the officers having the power of representation.

c. Foreign Exchange Management Requirements for Foreign Enterprises

a) After-the-fact Reporting

When foreign transactions involving "inward direct investment" by a "foreign investor" occur, generally, the "foreign investor" will be required to submit an after-the-fact report to the Minister of Finance and any other ministers who have jurisdiction over the business which is the subject of such transaction (through the Bank of Japan) within 15 days after the investment is made. The authorities, however, will not have the authority to either approve or reject the transactions. The after-the-fact reports are mostly required for the purpose of statistical analysis.

The exceptions to the after-the-fact reporting requirement are listed in the Cabinet Order on Inward Direct Investment. It is good practice, therefore, to confirm whether an exception applies based on the relevant facts before investing.

b) Pre-notification

If the intended "inward direct investment" by foreign investors is related to any of the industries described below, such foreign investors will be required to file a pre-notification (instead of after-the fact reporting) with the Minister of Finance and the minister who has jurisdiction over the business which is the subject of such transaction (through the Bank of Japan) at least 30 days prior to making the investment:

(i) national security (i.e., weapons, aircraft, nuclear power, space development and explosives);

(ii) the maintenance of public order (i.e., the production, sale and supply of electricity, gas and heat, and communications and broadcasting);

(iii) public security (i.e., the manufacture of biological products and security);

(iv) manufacturing involving advanced technologies; and

(v) industries wherein Japan is allowed to stay the liberalization required under the OECD Codes of Liberalisation of Capital Movements and of Current Invisible Operations by giving notice to the OECD (i.e., agriculture, forestry and fishing, air and marine transportation, petroleum and leather).

Because the foregoing list of industries is updated from time to time, it is good practice to check the current list, which is maintained on the Bank of Japan's website to ensure the latest information.

An investor may not invest for a period of 30 days after the Bank of Japan accepts a pre-notification. However, this "waiting period" will normally be shortened to two weeks from acceptance in accordance with the relevant ordinance. Moreover, in an effort to facilitate foreign investment in Japan, the Ministry of Finance and other relevant ministries have implemented expedited fast-track options for green field investments (i.e., certain investments which involve setting up a wholly owned Japanese subsidiary of the investor), rollover investments (i.e., certain investments which are the same type as those which were made within the preceding six months by the same investor) and passive investments (i.e., certain investments undertaken by the investor so as not to proactively participate in the management or take control of the company and to which the competent minister decided that the fast-track option may be applied). If the fast-track option is applicable, the "waiting period" will be further reduced to five business days.

The government may recommend a change to, or the cancellation of the investment upon its review of the pre-notification filed by the foreign investor(s). A foreign investor who receives such a recommendation may either accept or reject it. However, if the foreign investor does not accept the recommendation(s), the government may then order a change to, or the cancellation of the investment. Such an order is legally binding on the investor.

C. Financing

a. Main Financial Institutions

a) Banks

At the end of 2017, there were approximately 200 banks with banking licenses in Japan. Within those 200 banks, there are currently 4 mega-banking groups in Japan--Mizuho, Sumitomo Mitsui, Mitsubishi UFJ and Resona. However, it should be noted that there are also approximately 60 overseas bank branches with banking licenses in Japan, including the following 5 banks which have head offices registered in China: Bank of Communications, Bank of China, China Business Bank, China Construction Bank, and Agricultural Bank of China.

b) Securities Firms

Under the Financial Instruments and Exchange Act of Japan[①] ("FIEA"), securities firms are classified into the following four subcategories of financial instruments related businesses: (i) Type I Financial Instruments Businesses, (ii) Type II Financial Instruments Businesses, (iii) Investment Advisory / Agency Businesses, and (iv) Investment Management Businesses. The marketing of interests in funds is considered to constitute either a Type I Financial Instruments Business or Type II Financial Instruments Business depending on the type of securities being marketed. At the end of 2017, there were approximately 293 firms approved as Type I Financial Instruments Businesses, and 1,171 firms approved as Type II Financial Instruments Businesses.

The 5 mega-securities firms in Japan are Nomura Securities Co., Ltd., Daiwa Securities Co.Ltd., SMBC Nikko Securities Inc., Mizuho Securities Co., Ltd. and Mitsubishi UFJ Morgan Stanley Securities Co., Ltd.

b. Financing Conditions for Foreign Enterprises

When foreign entities wish to finance a business in Japan, there are numerous ways to do so, including debt financing (bank loans, loan from parent company) and equity financing (issuance of shares or corporate bonds).

a) Debt Financing

There are no restrictions on bank loans in Japan which are specifically targeted at foreign entities. Foreign entities are just as entitled to receive loan financing from banks as Japanese companies.

The Development Bank of Japan, which is a government bank, offers low interest long term loans to foreign affiliated companies. It also has a team dedicated to assisting foreign investors. Moreover, some local government offices have their own financial incentives which are open to businesses regardless of their nationality. These financial incentives are mostly property related and are usually in the form of long-term, low interest loans or land tax subsidies.

If a foreign company wishes to receive a loan from its parent company in China, it is certainly entitled to do so after satisfying any procedures required by Chinese law. However, the foreign company should consider thin

---

① Act No.25 of 1948.

capitalization rules[1] and excess interest taxation rules[2] from a tax perspective when paying interest on such loan. Accordingly, we recommend that you contact a tax accountant in Japan when receiving loans from a parent company in China.

b) Equity Financing

If foreign company has established a subsidiary in Japan in the form of a wholly-owned subsidiary in the form of a stock corporation (Kabushiki Kaisha or "KK"), such KK could issue shares or company bonds to finance its business just like any other Japanese company. There is no restriction in Japan which is specifically targeted at foreign entities in connection with the issuance of shares or company bonds. Please see section I. Securities below for additional information on regulation regarding securities in Japan.

D. Land Policy

a. Brief Introduction to Land-related Laws and Regulations

There are many laws and regulations governing real estate transactions in Japan. This is because it is commonly understood that there is a considerable disparity between business operators and consumers with respect to their respective abilities to obtain information and negotiation skills.

Representative regulations which govern real estate transactions are set forth in more detail below:

a) Buying, Selling and Leasing Real Estate

The Building Lots and Buildings Transaction Business Act[3] is a law which regulates the acts of buying, selling and intermediating real estate in Japan. For sale and purchase contracts in which building lots and buildings transaction business operators are the seller, the Building Lots and Buildings Transaction Business Act includes restrictions on the content of such contracts to ensure consumer protection. These restrictions may be somewhat different from those set forth in the Civil Code[4]. Specifically, the Building Lots and Buildings Transaction Business Act limits the amount of earnest money, cancellation penalties and restrictions on the warranty against defects in such contracts and invalidates any contract provisions which contravene these restrictions.

By contrast, the Building Lots and Buildings Transaction Business Act has no special regulations governing the content of lease contracts. Lease contracts, in principle, are handled pursuant to, among other things, the Act on Land and Building Leases[5], the Civil Code and the Consumer Contract Act[6]. There are also a number of specialized regulations for transactions related to condominiums and other buildings with unit ownership (See the Act on Building Unit Ownership[7] and the Act on Advancement of Proper Condominium Management[8]).

b) Real Estate Registration

In order to assert (perfect) one's ownership and other rights on lands and residences against third parties, the real property must be registered in accordance with the Civil Code and Real Property Registration Act[9]. Through registration, the current status of the real property and the titles and rights thereto are public knowledge, and the holders of rights (including ownership) in such real property and the details of the rights are clearly indicated to third parties.

c) Land Use/Construction of Buildings

Land use regulations are intended to realize comprehensive and systematic land usage and to prevent towns from being developed in a disorderly manner (See the City Planning Act[10], National Land Use Planning Act[11], and Agricultural Land Act[12]). Similarly, restrictions on building construction ensure that buildings are constructed appropriately in accordance with city planning and that the safety and proper performance of the buildings is

---

[1] A domestic corporation that receives a loan from its foreign parent company which is more than three times the amount of capital contributed by such foreign parent to the subsidiary is not allowed to include in its deductible expenses the interest corresponding to such excess.
[2] Under the excess interest taxation rule, "net interest" payments to affiliated persons in excess of 50% of the "adjusted revenue" of a corporation cannot be offset against the corporation's revenues.
[3] Act No.176 of 1952.
[4] Act No.89 of 1896.
[5] Act No.90 of 1991.
[6] Act No.61 of 2000.
[7] Act No.69 of 1962.
[8] Act No.149 of 2000.
[9] Act No.24 of 1899.
[10] Act No.160 of 1968.
[11] Act No.92 of 1974.
[12] Act No.229 of 1952.

assured (See the Building Standards Act[1].).

When investing in any real estate in Japan, investors should confirm that the usage of the property does not violate the restrictions on the land usage and that the building construction complies with the Building Standards Act.

b. Rules Governing Land Acquisitions by Foreign Companies

There are no legal restrictions on foreigners acquiring real estate in Japan, nor are there any differences in the applicable taxes. Foreign individuals and companies may purchase real estate in Japan regardless of their nationality and where they live and have residence status. However, there are differences in the documents required by residents and non-residents (mainly documents for confirming the person's identity), and in the banking requirements with regard to receiving purchase funds and paying taxes on real estate after purchase.

Please note that foreign residents (regardless of nationality) who acquire real estate in Japan are required to submit a report to the Minister of Finance and the minister who has jurisdiction over the business which is the subject of such transaction (through the Bank of Japan) within 20 days after acquiring real estate under the FEFTA.

E. The Establishment and Dissolution of Companies

a. The Forms of Enterprises

a) Options

The three principal methods by which foreign entities may start a business in Japan are:
(i) Setting up a business office ("branch office") in Japan;
(ii) Incorporating a new Japanese company; and
(iii) Forming a partnership such as a limited liability partnership.

It should be noted that foreign entities, which are willing to enter the Japanese market, may establish a representative office in Japan prior to performing the procedures necessary to implement methods (ii) and (iii) above. Although a representative office is not permitted to engage in business activities in Japan, such office could be used as a base for preparatory and ancillary activities such as performing market research and collecting information for the planned full-scale business activities.

b) Branch Office

When a foreign company intends to conduct continuous business activities in Japan, it must identify its representative(s) in Japan[2] and register as a foreign company. Although it is not required to establish a business office in Japan, in practice, foreign entities often do so in order to provide a base for their business activities. A foreign company's business office (branch office) in Japan must be registered.

The business activities of a branch office are determined by the appropriately authorised organs of the foreign company (for example, the board of directors). The branch office has no independent legal personality, and it may be treated as a part of the foreign company. Accordingly, the foreign company will generally be directly liable for the obligations that arise from the business activities of its branch office in Japan. In addition, the foreign company itself will be subject to taxation in Japan on the income of its branch office in Japan.

c) Incorporating a New Japanese Company

When a foreign company chooses to implement method, incorporating a new Japanese company, there are four types of companies which can be formed:
• Stock company (Kabushiki Kaisha);
• Limited liability company (Godo Kaisha);
• General partnership company (Gomei Kaisha);
• Limited partnership company(Goshi Kaisha).

Of these, a stock company is the most widely used corporate form in Japan. Nevertheless, while a limited liability company is not as popular as a stock company, it is often used as a vehicle in structured finance. By contrast, a general partnership company and a limited partnership company are not commonly used corporate forms.

The key differences among these four types of companies can be seen in the extent of their respective liabilities and their methods of daily operation. Shareholders in a stock company and members in a limited liability company are only liable to a limited extent, whereas all or some members in a general partnership company and a

---

[1] Act No.201 of 1950.
[2] At least one representative must be registered. The representative must be a resident in Japan, but not necessarily a Japanese national.

limited partnership company are personally liable for the company's debts and obligations (i.e., unlimited liability). The risks associated with unlimited liability are why general and limited partnership companies are rarely used as corporate forms. With respect to daily operations, directors or a board of directors is responsible for the daily operation of a stock company. By contrast, members of a limited liability company, a general partnership company, and a limited partnership company (collectively "Membership Company") conduct the daily operations of the business on their own unless they appointed managing members in the articles of incorporation.

If a foreign company incorporates a subsidiary company (a Japanese company) in Japan, the subsidiary company is considered to be a separate company from the foreign company. If such subsidiary company (a Japanese company) is a Membership Company, the foreign company will be liable for all of the obligations arising from the business activities of the subsidiary company as an investor as specified by law. By contrast, if the subsidiary company (a Japanese company) is a stock company, the foreign company only bears a risk that the shares of its subsidiary company will decrease in value; it does not assume any legal liability for the debt of the subsidiary company.

d) Forming a Partnership

It is also possible for a foreign company to conduct business by forming a partnership instead of a company, in other words, by implementing method. Partnerships are characterized by the fact that their internal regulations are determined by the mutual agreement of the capital investors (i.e., the partners) and that the partnership itself is not obligated to pay tax. Please note, however, that the distribution of profits to the partners is subject to taxation.

b. The Procedure of Establishment

As a stock company is the most common corporate form in Japan, we will focus our discussion relating to establishment and dissolution procedures on those applicable to a stock company.

a) General Explanation of The Establishment of A Stock Company

Under the Companies Act, the establishment of a stock company is called incorporation. The incorporation of a stock company refers to the process by which a Stock Company becomes a juridical person through the acquisition of legal personality. This process requires an organisation to: (i) prepare articles of incorporation which are the basic rules of the organisation; (ii) arrange for certification of the articles of incorporation by a notary public; (iii) make decisions about matters concerning the Shares Issued at Incorporation (i.e., the shares which are issued at the time of incorporation of the stock company); (iv) determine the subscription for the Shares Issued at Incorporation; (v) select the Shareholders at Incorporation based on the contributions; (vi) determine the governing entities and / or persons, including the Director at Incorporation (i.e., the person who is expected to become a director at the time of incorporation); and (vii) register the stock company so that it acquires legal personality.

Furthermore, the Companies Act prescribes two incorporation methods: (i) Incorporation without Solicitation, and (ii) Incorporation by Solicitation. Incorporation without Solicitation is the method by which the Incorporator (i.e., the person who has signed or affixed his / her name and seal on the articles of incorporation), who is the planner and the executor of the incorporation, subscribes for all of the Shares Issued at Incorporation and becomes the original shareholder. By contrast, Incorporation by Solicitation is the method by which the Incorporator only subscribes for a portion of the Shares Issued at Incorporation and other person(s), who subscribe for the remainder of the Shares Issued at Incorporation, are solicited. Both the Incorporator and the person(s) who subscribe for such shares become the original shareholders.

In Japan, the minimum capital requirement (JPY10 million for a stock company and JPY3 million for a limited private company) was abolished by the enactment of the Companies Act. As a result, while the contribution amount needs to be at least one yen, the original amount of the stated capital at incorporation may be as low as zero yen since such amounts are determined after deduction of incorporation expenses, etc.[1]

b) Notifications to Be filed Upon the Incorporation of A Atock Company

In addition to registration of incorporation, the following notifications must be submitted when the company is incorporated:

Generally, under the FEFTA, after-the-fact notifications must be submitted when a foreign investor establishes a branch office in Japan, incorporates a Japanese company or acquires the shares or equity interests of an existing Japanese company.

A foreign company which establishes a branch office in Japan and / or incorporates a Japanese company may be required to submit certain documents to the competent tax office and labor related office if it hires employment workers.

---

[1] Please note that some businesses are subject to minimum capital requirements in order to receive permission from the relevant authorities to start the business.Therefore, if a business requires permission from the relevant authorities, it is important to check the requirements.

Other authorizations and notifications may be required under the laws which regulate the specific industry to which the company belongs.

In the case of soliciting applications for the acquisition of newly issued securities from 50 or more people, a securities registration statement (yukashoken todokedesho) may be required under the FIEA depending on the situation.

c. Routes and Requirements of Dissolution

a) Dissolution and Liquidation

The dissolution and liquidation process is simple and quick in Japan. Under the Companies Act, the dissolution of a stock company is grounds for termination of its existence as a juridical person. After dissolution, the liquidation process ensues. During the liquidation process, the stock company winds up its business, recovers debts and conducts other procedures necessary to terminate the stock company's juridical personality.

Although the Companies Act identifies several events which cause the dissolution of a stock company, the principal cause of dissolution is a resolution at a shareholders' meeting. Pursuant to the Companies Act, the special resolution needed to dissolve a stock company requires: (i) the attendance of the shareholders having a majority of the total voting rights of those shareholders who are eligible to exercise their voting rights at the shareholders' meeting in question, and (ii) adoption of a dissolution proposal by not less than two-thirds (2/3) of the voting rights of the attending shareholders. The dissolution of the company should be registered with the Ministry of Justice.

A resolution to dissolve the stock company triggers the liquidation process. In the liquidation process, directors of the company generally become liquidators who are responsible for the liquidation process. The appointment of the liquidator(s) should be registered with the Ministry of Justice. The key part of the liquidation process is the notification sent to the creditors of the stock company which advises them to state their claims, if any, during a certain period. This period must be more than two months to allow creditors sufficient time to submit their claims.

After the necessary internal procedures are completed, the liquidator(s) is required to apply for registration of the completion of liquidation with the Legal Affairs Bureau. The liquidator(s) must also apply for a certificate concerning the registered closure information, which can be acquired approximately two weeks after the application for registration. Thereafter, notifications of the completion of the company's liquidation must be sent to tax authorities and other relevant authorities.

b) Insolvency/Bankruptcy

Insolvency and restructuring proceedings in Japan are largely categorized as either (i) judicial insolvency proceedings, which are supervised by the court, or (ii) out-of-court workouts, which are based on agreements among the interested parties without involvement of the court.

Judicial insolvency proceedings are further categorized as either (i) proceedings for rehabilitation and reorganization of a debtor, or (ii) proceedings for liquidation of a debtor. With respect to proceedings for rehabilitation and reorganization of a debtor, there are two types of insolvency proceedings: (i) civil rehabilitation proceedings (minji saisei), and (ii) corporate reorganization proceedings (kaisha kosei). Civil rehabilitation proceedings can be used to rehabilitate individuals and companies of any size and type. Corporate reorganization proceedings, however, are principally only available for stock companies. With respect to proceedings for liquidation of a debtor, there are two types of insolvency proceedings: (i) bankruptcy proceedings (hasan), and (ii) special liquidation (tokubetsu seisan). While bankruptcy proceedings can be used for individuals and any type of entity, special liquidation proceedings are used solely to wind up stock companies (kabushiki kaisha) in financial difficulty.

Please note, however, that a distressed debtor usually seeks to reach an agreement with its creditors without filing a petition for judicial insolvency proceedings. Such out-of-court workouts are increasingly preferred over the judicial insolvency proceedings referenced above. This is because out-of-court workouts are generally considered more likely to preserve the value of the debtor's business and are more cost and time efficient.

F. Merger and Acquisition ("M&A")

a. Methods of M&A

In general, the M&A methods used to acquire a company (the "target company") include: (i) acquisition of the target company's shares; (ii) a business transfer; or (iii) corporate reorganisation as stipulated in the Companies Act. In practice, acquiring the majority of the target company's shares could result in an immediate change in control of the target company. This is the easiest way to gain control over a target company. A business transfer, by contrast, is a transfer of the target business to the buyer or a company which is under the control of the buyer. Corporate reorganisation can be accomplished using various methods, all of which require compliance with the procedures stipulated in the Companies Act.

 a) Acquisition of Shares

 If the shares held by a party reach or exceed a certain threshold of voting rights, it is possible to control the target company by exercising such voting rights at the general shareholders' meeting. Although a share acquisition changes the composition of shareholders, the organisation of the target company remains unaffected.

 If the target company is a non-listed company, its articles of incorporation will often contain provisions stipulating that the acquisition of shares by transfer requires the target company's approval (usually its board of directors). Therefore, the seller usually requests the target company's approval prior to transferring the shares.

 If the target company is a listed company, purchasing shares from the existing shareholders may require the buyer to comply with certain procedures stipulated in the FIEA. Such procedures include those concerning tender offer regulations and the filing of a large shareholding report (Please refer to F.b.a) for more details.).

 b) Business Transfer

 A business transfer involves transferring a business, in whole or in part, from one entity to another. Using this procedure, it is possible to transfer all or a part of a target company's business. A business transfer's advantage over a share acquisition is that there is no risk of taking on unexpected liabilities, since each item to be transferred must be specifically identified and listed. To the extent that an asset or liability is not listed, it will be retained by the original owner. However, if a transferee continues to use the trade name of the transferor without having followed certain procedures, the transferee will also be liable for the performance of any obligation which arose from the business of the transferor.

 c) Corporate Reorganisation

 Corporate reorganisation includes mergers, share exchanges, share transfers and company splits, which are also frequently used for M&A transactions.

 A merger generally requires a special resolution of the shareholders' meeting of each of the companies involved. A merger enables a surviving company as well as a newly-established company to succeed to all of the rights and obligations of the dissolving company and to automatically acquire the assets, liabilities, agreements and employees of the dissolving company.

 In a share exchange, an existing stock company makes another existing stock company its wholly-owned subsidiary. This transaction generally requires special resolutions of the shareholders' meetings of both stock companies. Through a share exchange, a stock company can acquire 100% ownership of the target company.

 As stipulated in the Companies Act, in a share transfer, a newly-established stock company makes another existing stock company its wholly-owned subsidiary. A share transfer generally requires a special resolution of the shareholders' meeting of the existing stock company.

 A company split is also stipulated in the Companies Act. In a company split, a company transfers all or a part of its rights and obligations to another entity. Furthermore, the succeeding company succeeds to the assets, liabilities, employment agreements and other rights and obligations of the company being split.

b. Regulations Governing M&A Transactions

 Depending on whether the subject of the M&A transaction is the whole business or just specific divisions of the target company, the transaction may be subject to the Companies Act, general laws and regulations (such as labor and tax laws) and / or industry-specific regulations. Likewise, whether certain governmental authorizations and approvals are required also varies and must be determined.

 a) Securities Market Regulations

 The FIEA is the principal source of Japanese securities market regulations. As such, it frequently plays a central role in M&A transactions involving listed companies. Regulations relating to the large shareholding reporting system (i.e., the 5% Rule), and tender offer regulations are the most common.

 Under the large shareholding reporting system, a "large shareholding report" must, in principle, be filed by any person who acquires certain equity interests (including potential shares such as share options, hereafter "Shares") of a listed company which are equivalent to more than 5% of the total number of issued shares of the relevant company. Such report must be filed within five business days of the purchase. This filing obligation is reduced for institutional investors (such as securities companies, banks, trust companies, etc.), which frequently buy and sell Shares in large quantities as part of their daily business, when they meet certain requirements. The reduced filing obligation is called the "special reporting system". Under that system, it will suffice for the investors to report on their holdings twice a month on certain record dates selected by the investors.

 With respect to tender offer regulations, the FIEA requires purchasers to conduct tender offers if they intend to purchase more than a certain number of Shares from sources primarily outside of the financial instruments exchange market.

b) Competition Regulations

Regarding the competition regulations, there are two types applicable to M&A. First, there is a substantive regulation which forbids a business combination if the business combination is judged to have a probable negative impact. In practice, it is important to know that there is a safe harbor under the Business Combination Guidelines. If a business combination falls within the thresholds specified below, the JFTC is highly unlikely to conclude that those business combinations substantially restrain competition.

(i) The business combination satisfies one of the following items:
• the Herfindahl-Hirschman Index ("HHI")[①] after the business combination is completed is not more than 1,500;
• the HHI after the business combination is completed is more than 1,500, but not more than 2,500, while the increment of the HHI is not more than 250; or
• the HHI after the business combination is completed is more than 2,500, while the increment of the HHI is not more than 150.

(ii) The business combination satisfies both of the following items:
• the HHI after the business combination is completed is not more than 2,500, and
• the market share of the company groups after the business combination is completed is not more than 35%.

Second, there is procedural regulation which requires prior notification for business combinations of a certain size. If a business combination is subject to the prior notification regulation, it is prohibited, in principle, from closing the subject transactions for a period of 30 days after submitting the notification. The JFTC may, however, shorten this period when it deems necessary.

G. Competition Regulation

a. Department Supervising Competition Regulation

The JFTC is the main agency in charge of implementing the Act on Prohibition of Private Monopolisation and Maintenance of Fair Trade[②] ("Antimonopoly Act").

b. Brief Introduction of Competition Law

The Antimonopoly Act plays a predominant role in Japan's competition policy. However, entities who are conducting business in Japan should refer not only to its provisions, but also, to judicial precedents and the guidelines issued by the JFTC. These guidelines are available on the JFTC's web site[③], many of which are translated into English.

The Antimonopoly Act prohibits: (i) unreasonable restraints of trade; (ii) private monopolisation; (iii) unfair trade practices; and (iv) business combinations which might substantially restrain competition. Furthermore, the Antimonopoly Act requests that entrepreneurs (jigyosha) provide prior notification of any business combination that satisfies certain thresholds as explained above. There are also regulations related to trade associations (jigyosha dantai).

To prevent unreasonable restraints of trade, the Antimonopoly Act prohibits entities from substantially restricting competition by acting in coordination with competing entities through, for example, cartels or bid-rigging. The JFTC has recently been sanctioning an increasing number of price cartels.

To prevent private monopolization, the Antimonopoly Act prohibits entities from substantially restraining competition by excluding or controlling the business activities of other entities, whether individually or by coordinating with competing entities.

The unfair trade practices which are prohibited by the Antimonopoly Act are the restraints on competition arising from vertical relationships. There are various examples of this type of restraint including a concerted refusal to trade, discriminatory pricing, and unjust low price sales.

c. Measures Regulating Competition

The sanctions imposed in response to a violation of the Antimonopoly Act vary widely. The most common sanctions are a cease and desist order and a payment order for surcharge (kachokin); both of which are administrative dispositions. A cease and desist order is issued by the JFTC pursuant to the Antimonopoly Act and requires an entity to take "the measures necessary to eliminate the violation or to ensure that the violation is eliminated". The JFTC can issue a cease and desist order in response to all types of Antimonopoly Act violations.[④]

[①] HHI is a commonly accepted measure of market concentration.
[②] Act No.54 of 1947.
[③] http://www.jftc.go.jp/en/legislation_gls/imonopoly_guidelines.html.
[④] From practical viewpoint, it is important to note that there has been no payment order for surcharge in connection with a finding of private monopolization as of February 2018.

With respect to a payment order for surcharge, the method of calculating the surcharge is different depending on the type of violation. It should be noted that some unfair trade practices are not subject to a payment order for surcharge. Criminal punishment may also be imposed on individuals and entities in response to unreasonable restraints of trade and private monopolization.[1]

To detect more Antimonopoly Act violations and further promote fair and free competition, the Leniency System has been available in Japan since 2005 in connection with unreasonable restraints of trade. Under the Leniency System, a maximum of 5 companies, which have applied for leniency and satisfied certain conditions, will either be exempted from or receive reduced sanctions for their anti-competitive conduct. The first applicant is granted full immunity, while the second applicant is granted a 50% reduction and the third, fourth and fifth applicants are granted 30% reductions in the surcharge payments. This system has proved very successful in Japan.

H. Tax

a. Tax Regime and Rules

a) Tax Regime

In Japan, there are many laws which govern the imposition of both national and local taxes including the Corporate Tax Act[2] and the Consumption Tax Act[3]. The National Tax Agency ("NTA"), which is an extra-ministerial bureau of the Ministry of Finance, is the governmental agency that has primary responsibility for handling national tax related matters. It is assisted by its subordinate Regional Taxation Bureaus and their subordinate Tax Offices. In addition, the National Tax Tribunal has been established as an agency of the NTA to examine and make decisions regarding taxpayer requests for reinvestigation or reconsideration of tax assessments. The Tax Offices are responsible for ordinary tax investigations, corrections, assessments and collections. As a result, the Tax Offices maintain the closest relationship with taxpayers.

Local governments, their subordinate prefectural Tax Offices, city offices and town / village offices handle matters regarding local taxes.

b) Rules for Foreign Entities

When foreign entities have a permanent establishment in Japan, such foreign entities become subject to Japanese taxation on their domestic (i.e., Japan) source income and are required to pay self-assessed taxes. Therefore, it is more beneficial, in general, for foreign entities not to have a permanent establishment in Japan. Under the Corporate Tax Act, a permanent establishment means a branch office, a construction site or an agent. It is worth noting a "representative office" is not considered to be a permanent establishment since it only conducts preparatory or auxiliary operations such as information gathering or market research. Nonetheless, the distinction between a representative office and a branch office is not always clear and is highly dependent on the activities carried out by the office.

b. Main Categories and Rates of Tax

a) Main Taxes Applicable to Businesses

The main taxes which are generally applicable to a business in Japan are corporate taxes and consumption taxes. The corporate tax applies to corporate income (including capital gains) and is paid through self-assessment. Domestic corporations are obliged to pay tax on all income regardless of the source. By contrast, foreign entities have tax liability only for domestic (i.e., Japan) source income. The corporate tax is imposed on income which, in accordance with the accounting treatment under generally accepted accounting principles in Japan ("Japanese GAAP"), is substantially equal to the amount of gross revenue less the amount of deductible expenses.

The consumption tax, which is assessed and collected nationally, is a value-added tax imposed on nearly all domestic transactions (e.g., sale and lease of goods and provision of services) and import transactions. The consumption tax is payable by a business entity conducting any domestic or import transaction if such business entity's amount of revenue for a certain period (in principle, the fiscal year preceding the last fiscal year) was more than JPY10 million.

b) Rates of Tax

The corporate tax rate is gradually being reduced. The corporate tax rate, which was as high as 25.5%, was reduced to 23.9% for the fiscal years commencing on or after April 1, 2015, and 23.4% for the fiscal years commencing on or after April 1, 2016. It will be further reduced to 23.2% for the fiscal years commencing on or

---

[1] To date, there has been no criminal sanction imposed in response to private monopolization.
[2] Act No.34 of 1965.
[3] Act No.108 of 1988.

after April 1, 2018. Additionally, if the corporation's capital account has JPY100 million or less, the tax rate with regard to the first JPY8 million of income is 19%, but it was reduced to 15% until the year commencing on or before March, 31 2019.

The consumption tax rate was raised from 5% to 8% in April 2015, and then was expected to increase to 10% (of that amount, 7.8% is imposed as a national tax and 2.2% is imposed as a local tax) in October 2015. However, in order to achieve compatibility between economic renewal and financial soundness, the increase to 10% was postponed to April 2017, and then to October 2019. As a measure to alleviate the regressive nature of the consumption tax and reduce the burden on low-income brackets, a reduced tax rate on foodstuff, etc. will be introduced at the time the consumption tax increases to 10%.

c. Tax Declaration and Preference

a) Tax Declaration

A corporation must submit its tax return to the relevant Tax Office and pay the applicable taxes within two months from the end of each fiscal year. If a corporation either (i) cannot submit its tax return by the deadline for unavoidable reasons, or (ii) is consistently unable to hold the annual shareholders' meeting for the settlement of accounts within such time period because of the articles of incorporation, etc., the corporation can be granted an extension of time to file its tax return. However, the corporation must have submitted a prior application for such extension.

b) Tax Preference

To facilitate investment in Japan, the Japanese government offers various tax incentives targeting foreign entities doing business in Japan. These incentives include:

• Employment promotion taxation which gives tax incentives to companies who meet certain requirements, such as hiring 5 or more new employees to increase the number of employees by 10%, in the applicable business year.

• Tax incentives for companies that either relocate their headquarters from one of the 23 wards in Tokyo to other regions or enhance and expand the function of their headquarters in those regions.

• Incentives relating to special economic areas which is explained below (please refer to J.c.).

Local governments also offer various incentives to foreign entities which are planning to open offices in their respective regions.[1]

I. Securities

a. Brief Introduction to Securities-related Laws and Regulations

Although there are various laws and regulations relevant to securities, the primary ones which should be noted are as follows:

(i) FIEA[2]

In Japan, the FIEA is the most basic law applicable to securities. It regulates the issuance, placement and trading of securities; it also regulates the primary and secondary markets of securities in Japan.

(ii) the Act on Investment Trusts and Investment Corporations ("ITICA")[3]

The ITICA regulates investment trusts and investment corporations, both domestic and foreign.

(iii) the Foreign Exchange and Foreign Trade Act ("FEA")[4]

The FEA regulates the issuance and sale in Japan of securities denominated in foreign currencies by non-residents to residents.

(iv) the Rules of the Japan Securities Dealers Association ("JSDA Rules")

The JSDA Rules are a control mechanism which is self-imposed by the industry. These rules have a huge impact on security-related transactions.

b. Supervision and Regulation of Securities Market

In the securities market, the most important supervisory authority is the FSA. The primary role of the FSA is to ensure stable and smooth financial transactions. The FSA was established as an external agency of the Cabinet Office. Some of the FSA Commissioner's powers have been delegated to the Securities and Exchange Surveillance Commission (shoken torihiki tou kanshi iinnkai), which was established as a subordinate commission

---

[1] More details on the tax incentives available for investments in Japan can be found at https://www.jetro.go.jp/en/invest/incentive_programs.html.
[2] Act No.25 of 1948.
[3] Act No.198 of 1951.
[4] Act No.228 of 1949.

of both the FSA and the local finance bureau (zaimu kyoku) (The local finance bureau is a subordinate agency of the Ministry of Finance.).

Additionally, there are various securities regulations which were self-imposed by various industry organizations such as the Japan Securities Dealers Association and other securities exchanges. These self-imposed regulations play an important role in regulating the securities market.

c. Requirements for Engagement in Securities Trading for Foreign Enterprises

There are two ways for foreign enterprises to engage in securities trading in Japan. The first is an Initial Public Offering ("IPO") with a listing on a Japanese stock exchange ("Listing in Japan"). The second is a public offering without a listing on a Japanese stock exchange ("POWL"). In this second method, the issuer becomes listed on a foreign stock exchange while simultaneously conducting a public offering in Japan.

Currently, the majority of foreign enterprises have used POWL. As both Listing in Japan and POWL involve a primary offering or secondary distribution of foreign stocks, issuing companies, in principle, must fulfill Japanese disclosure requirements. Issuers, therefore, must file a Securities Registration Statement and prepare and deliver a statutory prospectus in accordance with the FIEA. Moreover, issuing companies opting for Listing in Japan will be subject to the listing procedures of the relevant Japanese stock exchange as well as the disclosure obligations, which become applicable after listing.

For an IPO, the Tokyo Stock Exchange ("TSE") is the representative stock exchange in Japan and all foreign entities listed in Japan are listed on the TSE. The markets operated by the TSE include the First Section, the Second Section, JASDAQ and the "Mothers Section" (which is for start-up companies). There are specific listing and assignment requirements prescribed for each market. The listing requirements for the TSE include, among other things, a prerequisite of 200 shareholders, market capitalization of JPY500 million or more and expected market capitalization at the time of listing of JPY1 billion or more).

J. Investment Preference and Protection

a. Structure of Preference Policies

The Japanese government has no official preference policies. Additionally, as stated above in section A. Market access, the Japanese government is now actively working to attract foreign investment in Japan with the introduction of the "Policy Package for Promoting Foreign Direct Investment into Japan to Make Japan a Global Hub". In furtherance of this policy, the Japanese government had set up a working group to simplify and revise the regulations and administrative procedures related to foreign investment in Japan.

b. Support for Specific Industries and Regions

The Japanese government, at both a national and regional level, offers incentives to encourage and facilitate foreign investment in Japan. It also offers single contact points in various ministries and agencies that can comprehensively handle enquiries and provide support to foreign investors with respect to doing business in Japan. Some incentives are targeted at foreign entities, while others are provided regardless of nationality.

One investment incentive offered by the Japanese government is the "Act for Promotion of Japan as an Asian Business Center". This Act makes certain key support measures (such as assistance for fund raising, acceleration of patent examinations and reduction of patent fees) applicable to new R&D and headquarters operations which are conducted by global companies in Japan and are certified by the minister who has jurisdiction over the business which is the subject of such transaction.

The Japanese government is also supporting individual industries in "National Strategic Special Zones" and "Comprehensive Special Zones". It does so by suspending certain regulations and providing favorable tax treatment as explained in more detail below. There are also many incentives provided by local governments exclusively to foreign affiliated companies, including the two following incentives which are provided by Tokyo Metropolis.

• Overseas Financial Corporation Business Establishment Subsidy Program (http://www.seisakukikaku.metro.tokyo.jp/bdc_tokyo/english/business-support/subsidy.html).

• Program to Increase Foreign Entrepreneurs (http://www.seisakukikaku.metro.tokyo.jp/invest_tokyo/english/invest-tokyo/fhr.html).

The incentive programs for investment in Japan will be updated from time-to-time. Accordingly, we recommend checking the web site of JETRO for the latest information (https://www.jetro.go.jp/en/invest/incentive_programs.html).

c. Special Economic Areas

a) National Strategic Special Zones

The Japanese government has selected 10 areas to establish the most business friendly environment by suspending various restrictions and providing favorable tax treatment. These 10 areas, which are known as the "National Strategic Special Zones", are Senboku-shi, Sendai-shi, Niigata-shi, the Tokyo Area (Tokyo prefecture, Kanagawa prefecture, Chiba-shi, Narita-shi), Aichi prefecture, the Kansai Area (Osaka prefecture, Hyogo prefecture, Kyoto prefecture), Yabu-shi, Hiroshima prefecture / Imabari-shi, Fukuoka-shi / Kitakyushu-shi, and Okinawa prefecture. The establishment of Tokyo One-Stop Business Establishment Center, which was mentioned in section A. Market access, is a result of the suspension of restrictions in the Tokyo Area.

The restrictions which are suspended vary between the selected areas, and the selected cities and they will be updated from time-to-time. Accordingly, we recommend checking the web page of the Cabinet Office concerning the "National Strategic Special Zones" for the latest and most detailed information. The official website: http://www.kantei.go.jp/jp/singi/tiiki/kokusentoc/index.html (Japanese only).

b) Comprehensive Special Zones

The Cabinet Office has selected a number of cities as "Comprehensive Special Zones ('CSZ')". In so doing, it aims to provide tailored and integrated support for comprehensive and strategic challenges in the selected regions (Eleven regions were selected to increase international competitiveness, and 77 regions were selected for local revitalization.). Special regulatory measures, favorable tax treatment (for corporate income tax), and financial / monetary support are available to companies with business plans in the designated zones.

For detailed information about the areas selected for the CSZ, please check the website of the Cabinet office. The official website: http://www.kantei.go.jp/jp/singi/tiiki/sogotoc/index.html (Japanese only).

c) Special Zone for Reconstruction

Special measures, such as the suspension of regulations and tax incentives, are available for companies with business plans in the areas afflicted by disasters due to the East Japan earthquakes (227 cities).

For more information on the Special zone for reconstruction, please check the website of the Reconstruction Agency. The official website: http://www.reconstruction.go.jp/english/.

d. Investment Protection

a) Investment Treaties

As of February 2018, Japan has entered into two investment treaties with China, as listed below. The Japan-China-Korea Trilateral Investment Provision explicitly allows parties to refer disputes to arbitration at the International Centre for Settlement of Investment Disputes ("ICSID") (Japan signed the ICSID Convention on 23 September 1965, and ratified it on 17 August 1967. It came into force in Japan on 16 September 1967.).

	Date of Signature	Date of Entry into Force
Bilateral Investment Treaty(BIT) China-Japan	August 1988	14 May 1989
Trilateral Investment Provision (TIP) China -Republic of Korea- Japan	May 2012	17 May 2014

Although the Japan-China-Korea Trilateral Investment Provision was entered into force on 17 May 2014, it is understood that the Japan-China BIT still continues to operate in parallel.

b) Investment Protections

The following substantive protections are available for investors and investment property pursuant to the investment treaties between China and Japan which are listed above:
- national treatment;
- most-favored-nation treatment;
- fair and equitable treatment;
- full protection and security;
- obligation observance clause (umbrella clause);
- expropriation;
- protection from civil disturbance or strife;
- performance requirements; and
- guarantee of capital transfers.

III. Trade

A. Department Supervising Trade

In Japan, the Ministry of Economy, Trade and Industry (its former name until 2001: the Ministry of International Trade and Industry) is the governmental body supervising trade, and it establishes policy directions concerning trade, and also promotes the enhancement of international economic cooperation and exchange.

With respect to quarantines related to trade, the Ministry of Health, Labour and Welfare supervises the quarantine of foods in general, and the Ministry of Agriculture, Forestry and Fisheries supervises the quarantine of plants and animals. Furthermore, customs, the local branch bureaus and departments of the Ministry of Finance, supervises customs tariffs.

B. Brief Introduction of Trade Laws and Regulations

The basic law concerning export and import is the Foreign Exchange and Foreign Trade Act, and together with its cabinet orders and ministerial orders, such as the Export Trade Control Order, the Import Trade Control Order, and the Foreign Exchange Order, they provide for the control measures concerning export and import of goods, services, and technologies, and the procedures therefor. Furthermore, the Export and Import Transaction Act, which also provides for export and import cartel, prohibits export and import of goods that infringe upon intellectual property rights, goods carrying a false indication of the place of origin, and the like, with the aim of prohibiting unfair export transactions.

The basic laws concerning customs clearance are the Customs Act, the Customs Tariff Act, and the Act on Temporary Measures concerning Customs. The Customs Act provides for the determination and payment of the customs tariffs, the import-prohibited goods, customs procedures, and the like, and the Customs Tariff Act provides for the basic tariff rates that apply on a long-term basis. The Act on Temporary Measures concerning Customs, the special measures of the aforementioned two laws, provides for a provisional tariff rate to be applied owing to changes in the economic situation in Japan and abroad.

In addition to these laws and regulations, depending on the goods, export and import control under various domestic laws, such as the Food Sanitation Act, the Act on Domestic Animal Infectious Diseases Control, the Plant Protection Act, and the Law on Securing Quality, Efficacy and Safety of Products Including Pharmaceuticals and Medical Devices, would be applicable.

C. Trade Management

Japan has, following its entry into the General Agreement on Tariffs and Trade (GATT) in 1955, proceeded with trade liberalization, since the early 1960s. While Japan maintains and enhances multifaceted free trade, Japan also takes certain control measures, based on the purposes such as national security, protection of human and animal life, and conservation of exhaustible natural resources.

a. Export

From the perspective of the maintenance of international peace and security, in the case of exporting specific kinds of goods, services, and technologies (such as weapons or weapons of mass destruction) (list control) or in the case of exporting specific kinds of goods, services, and technologies (those that are likely to be converted into weapons of mass destruction or the like) to specific regions (regions other than developed countries such as the U.S., the U.K., and France) (catch-all control), a permission from the Minister of Economy, Trade and Industry shall be obtained. Furthermore, from the perspective of the maintenance of equilibrium in the international balance of trade, and the sound development of foreign trade and the national economy, for carrying out exports relating to specific kinds of goods, destinations, and transactions, an approval from the Minister of Economy, Trade and Industry would be necessary.

Moreover, under the Customs Act, the exports of (i) narcotics, psychotropic drugs, cannabis, stimulants, and the like, (ii) child pornography, (iii) products that infringe upon intellectual property rights (patent rights, utility model rights, design rights, trademark rights, copyrights, neighboring rights, and breeder's rights), and (iv) goods that are similar to or imitate another person's indication of goods or business, and the like are prohibited (however, with respect to (i), the export thereof will be permitted if the permission from the government is obtained.).

b. Import

From the perspective of the sound development of foreign trade and the national economy, imports of specific goods are restricted. With respect to marine products that are unliberalized items, and controlled substances (such as chlorofluorocarbons) provided for in the Annex of the Montreal Protocol, as they are "import quota items", an import quota is required to be obtain in advance from the Minister of Economy, Trade and Industry. With respect to "import approval items," prior approval from the Minister of Economy, Trade and Industry is necessary, and with respect to "prior confirmation items" and "confirmation items at customs," the confirmation of the competent Minister in charge, and customs, is respectively necessary.

Moreover, under the Customs Act, the imports of (i) narcotics, psychotropic drugs, cannabis, stimulants, and the like, and opium smoking tools, (ii) designated substances, (iii) pistols, machine guns and the like, and ammunition and the like, (iv) explosives, (v) gun powder, (vi) toxic substances that are highly likely to be used for the purpose of the production of chemical weapons or raw materials thereof, (vii) pathogens and the like that are likely to be used in biological terrorism, (viii) counterfeit currencies and the like, (ix) books and the like detrimental to public security or public morals, (x) child pornography, (xi) products that infringe upon intellectual property rights (patent rights, utility model rights, design rights, trademark rights, copyrights, neighboring rights, and breeder's rights), and (xii) goods that are similar to or imitate another person's indications of goods or businesses, and the like, are prohibited (however, with respect to (i) through (vii), as well as imitation revenue stamps and imitation postage stamps among (viii), the import thereof will be permitted if a permission or the like from the government is obtained.).

D. The Inspection and Quarantine of Import and Export Commodities

a. Foods, etc.

Under the Food Sanitation Act and the like, when importing foods, food additives, and the like, a "Notification Form for Importation of Foods, etc." is required to be submitted to the quarantine station (over which the Ministry of Health, Labour and Welfare has jurisdiction,) and it is required for the goods to be examined. As a result of the documentary examination, if it is determined that an inspection is necessary, it is required for the goods to further undergo ordered inspection, administrative inspection, monitoring inspection, and the like, and unless the inspections are passed, the food cannot be imported (with respect to monitoring inspections, the food may be imported without awaiting the results of the inspection; however, in the case where it fails the inspection thereafter, measures, such as recall, will be taken). With respect to livestock products and agricultural products, it is required for the goods to further undergo inspection at the animal quarantine service and the plant protection station, as follows.

b. Animals and Livestock Products

When importing animals and livestock products, under the Act on Domestic Animal Infectious Diseases Control and the like, unless an "Import Inspection Application Form" is submitted to the animal quarantine service (over which the Ministry of Agriculture, Forestry and Fisheries has jurisdiction), and the goods pass the documentary examination, as well as various inspections (such as clinical inspection, blood inspection, and the like for animals; and actual goods inspections, detailed inspection, and the like for livestock products), such import will not be permitted. Those goods that require inspection, the so-called designated quarantine items, are cloven-hoofed animals and cattle; chickens, quails, and the like; birds belonging to the orders Anseriformes (and these eggs); dogs, rabbits, and honeybees; and products and the like of these animals. With respect to these animals and livestock products that are shipped from or via regions in which the incidence of domestic animal infectious diseases is high (prohibited import regions), the import thereof is prohibited.

c. Plants, etc.

When importing plants and the like, under the Plant Protection Act and the like, the goods are required to undergo inspections from the plant protection station (over which the Ministry of Agriculture, Forestry and Fisheries has jurisdiction) for the existence of pests, whether they fall under an import-prohibited goods, and the like. Those subject to the inspections are seedlings, scions, bulbs, seeds, cut flowers and cut branches, fruits, vegetables, grains, beans, spices, woods, and the like. With respect to specific plants that are shipped from specific regions (prohibited import regions) or via prohibited import regions; quarantine pests (invertebrates, such as arthropods, vertebrates, fungi, parasitic plants, and viruses, that could do harm to useful plants in case of their spread); and the like, the import thereof is prohibited.

E. Customs Management

The collection of customs tariffs, customs clearance procedures of exported and imported goods, and the like are managed by nine customs departments (Hakodate, Tokyo, Yokohama, Nagoya, Osaka, Kobe, Moji, Nagasaki, and Okinawa). Presently, with respect to customs clearance procedures and the like, Nippon Automated Cargo and Port Consolidated System (NACCS) (a system by which the customs clearance procedures and the like of exported and imported goods are processed online) has been introduced, and the expediting of logistics and simplification of procedures have been enhanced (which is also available for import notification of foods and animals and plants).

With respect to the tariff rates, the "Customs Tariff Schedule" is provided for in the Customs Tariff Act, and the basic tariff rates, provisional tariff rates, WTO tariff rates, general preferential tariff rates (those with the purpose of support for the industries of developing countries), special preferential tariff rates (targeting least developed countries (LDC)), and the like for each HS code may be confirmed. Among all items, approximately 35% are customs tariff-free. Furthermore, with respect to 25 items in total, such as corns, dairy products, variety-beans, peanuts, konjac roots, cowhides and horse leathers, and sheepskin, a tariff-quota system (a system by which a tariff exemption or low tariff rate is applicable thereto, within a certain import quantity, and a high tariff rate is applicable thereto that exceeds such certain amount) has been adopted. With respect to other special tariffs, there are seasonal tariffs, gate price tariffs, sliding tariffs, special tariffs (anti-dumping tariffs, countervailing duties, and the like), and the like. By using the advance-counseling system of customs, the tariff rate applicable to the goods to be exported or imported may be confirmed.

IV. Labour

A. Brief Introduction of Labour Laws and Regulations

a. Labour Legislations in Japan

In Japan, some legislations regulate the relationship between employees and employers, such as the "Labour Standards Act," which regulates employees' working conditions; the "Labour Contracts Act," which regulates labour contracts; the "Labour Union Act," which guarantees rights to unionize; and the "Minimum Wage Act," which sets forth minimum wages for labour contracts. The details and application of these acts do not distinguish between employees and employers of Japanese nationality and those of other foreign nationalities.

b. Type of Employees

In Japan, employees can be broadly divided into nonfixed-term employees and fixed-term employees. The nonfixed-term employees are employees for whom their working conditions do not fix their employment term, and the non-fixed-term employment is a traditional employment system. However, in recent years, employment systems other than nonfixed-term employment, such as fixedterm employment and dispatching employees, have been increasing. Please note that, if the contract term of the fixed-term contracts continues for five consecutive years or more due to renewal, then the fixed-term employees can request conversion of their labour contracts to nonfixed-term labour contracts, and the employers cannot refuse such requests.

c. Wage Regulations

Employers must pay wages, in legal tender, directly to employees in full amount, not less than once per month, and on a specified date. In Japan, minimum wages are determined by each prefecture, and the minimum wages in major cities as of October 2017 are as follows: (i) Tokyo: JPY 958 per hour; (ii) Aichi: JPY 871 per hour; (iii) Osaka: JPY 909 per hour; and (iv) Fukuoka: JPY 789 per hour, and national average is JPY 848 per hour.

d. Dismissal Regulations and Retirement

In Japan, employers are restricted from dismissing employees at their convenience, and an employer is only allowed to dismiss an employee if there is an objectively reasonable ground and if dismissal is deemed to be appropriate in light of socially-accepted norms.

B. Requirements of Employing Foreign Employees

a. Work Permit

In Japan, there is no permit system regulating employment of foreign employees. Employers can employ any foreigners who have work visas. Mainly, the following 13 types of work visas exist in Japan: (i) Professor; (ii) Researcher; (iii) Artist; (iv) Religious Activities; (v) Journalist; (vi) Business Manager; (vii) Legal Services; (viii) Medical Services; (ix) Instructor; (x) Engineer; (xi) Intracompany Transferee (e.g., in the case where a person working overseas is transferred to a Japanese branch office); (xii) Entertainer; and (xiii) Skilled Labour.

b. Application Procedure

Regarding work visas, procedures required for each situation are introduced below.

(i) If a foreigner who already has a work visa is employed in the same workvisa category as that of the foreigner's work visa, then no further procedures are required.

(ii) If a foreigner who already has a work visa is employed in a different workvisa category from that of the foreigner's work visa, or if a foreigner who does not have a work visa but another visa (i.e., student visa) is employed, then it will be necessary to execute a labour contract with the foreign employee and to perform change procedures for a work visa at the Immigration Bureau of Japan in Japan.

(iii) If a foreigner without a visa is employed, then it will be necessary to apply for a work visa at the Embassy of Japan in the foreigner's country.

c. Social Insurance

Social insurance in which employers are obligated to take part are as follows: "Industrial Accident Compensation Insurance;" "Employment Insurance;" "Health Insurance;" and "Employee's Pension Insurance." Excluding portions to be borne by the employees, insurance premiums for the aforementioned insurance must be borne by employers. The details and application of the social insurance do not distinguish between employees and employers of Japanese nationality and those of other foreign nationalities.

C. Exit and Entry

a. Visa Types

Excluding foreigners of nationalities of foreign countries with visa exemption for shortterm stay, foreigners need to obtain visas to enter Japan (regarding obtaining a work visa, see relevant portions in "B.Requirements of employing foreign employees"). Persons of nationality of People's Republic of China who meet certain requirements can obtain multipleentry visas for commercial business / sightseeing (visit duration: 15 days, 30 days, or 90 days; validity period: 1 year, 3 years, 5 years, or 10 years).

b. Restrictions for Exit and Entry

If a foreigner with resident status stays outside Japan for more than one year, then the foreigner needs to obtain reentry permission before leaving Japan. Further, please note that, as of March 2018, if a foreigner with resident status leaves Japan for Democratic People's Republic of Korea, then the foreigner may be prohibited from re-entering Japan in certain cases.

D. Trade Union and Labour Organizations

Enterprise labour union organized on an enterprise basis is common in Japan. However, in recent years, there have been labour unions that extend membership to employees who work for a company without a labour union. In accordance with the Labour Union Act, a labour union is authorized to execute a "labour agreement" (Rodo kyoyaku) with employers, and employers are prohibited from disadvantaging such labour union or employees who are members of the labour union or who have made claims to the Labour Relations Commission for the unfair labour practices of the employer; refusing collective bargaining with the labour union; and controlling and intervening with the affairs of the labour union.

E. Labour Disputes

In Japan, a few major avenues to resolve labour disputes are through labour tribunals or a trial. Labour tribunals are systems established for the purpose of promptly resolving labour disputes, and, in principle, if the dispute is not reconciled by the third date of the proceedings, then the labour tribunal members will render a decision. The decision is enforceable. However, if the other party files a challenge, then the labour dispute will be transferred to a court for its judgment.

V. Intellectual Property

A. Overview of Intellectual Property Laws

The laws pertaining to intellectual property rights in Japan include the Patent Act, the Utility Model Act, the Design Act, the Trademark Act, the Copyright Act, the Unfair Competition Prevention Act, and the like.

a. The Patent Act

The "Patent Act" (Act No.121 of 1959) is an Act for the protection of inventions. An "invention" is defined to be "the highly advanced creation of technical ideas utilizing the laws of nature" (Article 2, paragraph 1 of the same Act). The inventions to be patented include the invention of a product, and the invention of a process. When information processing by way of software is embodied using hardware resources, that invention pertaining to that software can be protected by a patent right, as a creation of technical ideas utilizing the laws of nature. A patent right takes effect on registration at the Japan Patent Office (JPO). The duration of a patent right is 20 years from the filing date, in principle (Article 67, paragraph 1 of the same Act).

b. The Utility Model Act

The "Utility Model Act" (Act No.123 of 1959) is an Act to protect a device. A "device" is defined to be "the creation of technical ideas utilizing the laws of nature" (Article 2, paragraph 1 of the same Act), and serves to protect a technique, just as the Patent Act does. However, unlike the Patent Act, the Utility Model Act does not require the technique to be highly advanced. The Utility Model Act is also different from the Patent Act, in that only a device that relates to the shape or structure of an article, or a combination of articles, is to be protected by a utility model right (Article 3, paragraph 1 of the same Act), and neither a process nor computer software is to be protected by a utility model right. Just as with a patent right, a utility model right takes effect on registration at the JPO; however, unlike the Patent Act, the Utility Model Act does not require any substantive examination in the registration of the right, and the duration of a utility model right is 10 years from the filing date (Article 15 of the same Act), which is shorter than that for a patent right.

c. The Design Act

The "Design Act" (Act No.125 of 1959) is an Act to protect a design. A "design" is defined to be "the shape, patterns or colors, or any combination thereof, of an article (including a part of an article), which creates an aesthetic impression through the eye" (Article 2, paragraph 1, item (i) of the same Act), which is the design of an article, in short. A design right also takes effect on registration at the JPO. The duration of a design right is 20 years from the date of registration of its establishment (Article 21, paragraph 1 of the same Act). If a design satisfies copyrightability, it can also be protected under the Copyright Act.

d. Trademark Act

The "Trademark Act" (Act No.127 of 1959) is an Act to protect a mark (trademark) used for a person's goods or services in business, so as to distinguish the person's goods or services from others' goods or services, and to represent the identity of the origin of the goods or services. In addition to any character(s), figure(s), sign(s), or three-dimensional shape(s) or any combination thereof, the trademarks that can be registered now include non-traditional trademarks, such as a trademark for motion, a hologram trademark, a trademark solely comprised of color(s), a sound trademark, and a position trademark, since 2015 (Article 2, paragraph 1 of the same Act). A trademark right takes effect upon the registration (Article 18, paragraph 1 of the same Act). The duration of a trademark right is 10 years, from the date of registration of its establishment, and it is renewable (Article 19 of the same Act). An unregistered trademark can be protected under the Unfair Competition Prevention Act and / or the Civil Code if they are widely recognized or well known.

e. The Copyright Act

The "Copyright Act" is an Act to protect a work (Act No.48 of 1970). A "work" is defined to be "a production in which thoughts or sentiments are creatively expressed and which falls within the literary, academic, artistic or musical domain" (Article 2, paragraph 1, item (i) of the same Act). The types of works include literary works, musical works, works of fine art, works of architecture, cinematographic works, photographic works, and works of computer programming. Depending on how the work is used, copyrights are defined as subdivided rights, and specifically include a right of reproduction, a right of stage performance, a right of giving a musical performance, a right of on-screen presentation, a right of transmission to the public, a right of recitation, a right of exhibition, a right of distribution, a right of transfer, a right of rent, a right of translation, and a right of adapting a pre-existing work. An author will enjoy a copyright pertaining to the work, upon the creation of the work (Article 51, paragraph 1 of the same Act), and no formalities such as a registration are required in order to obtain a copyright (the non-formality rule, Article 17, paragraph 2 of the same Act). For a work by an author produced under a true name (including a commonly-known pseudonym), the copyright protection continues 50 years following the death of the author (Article 51, paragraph 2 of the same Act); and for a work by an organization, such as a corporation, the copyright protection continues 50 years after the work is made public, in principle (Article 53 of the same Act). An author enjoys the moral rights of an author (Article 17 of the same Act).

B. Patent Application

The following requirements must be satisfied in order for an invention to be given a patent right, and to be protected as a right under the Patent Act:

(i) Industrial applicability (Article 29, paragraph 1, the introductory clause of the Patent Act);
(ii) Novelty (the same paragraph, each item as in the above);
(iii) Inventive step (the same Article, paragraph 2).

In filing a patent application, an application describing certain matters must be submitted to the JPO, with the description, scope of claims, drawings where necessary, and abstract attached thereto (Article 36, paragraphs 1 and 2 of the same Act; It should be noted here that the patent application is often submitted as electronic data, via an online procedure). The description must include a "detailed explanation of the invention," in which the statement should be clear, and sufficient to enable any person ordinarily skilled in the art to which the invention pertains to work the invention (same Article, paragraph 3, and paragraph 4, item (i)). In the scope of claims, all matters deemed necessary to specify the invention for which the applicant requests the grant of a patent must be recited (same Article, paragraph 5). Concerning the recitation of the scope of claims, the following requirements must be satisfied, among others: the invention for which a patent is sought is stated in the detailed explanation of the invention (the support requirement; Article 36, paragraph 6, item (i) of the same Act); the invention for which a patent is sought is clear (clarity: same paragraph, item (ii)); and the statement for each claim is concise (same paragraph, item (iii)).

The content of a patent application will be published after one year and six months from the date of the filing of the patent application, regardless of the state of progress of its examination (publication of a patent application; Article 64 of the same Act). A person, including the applicant, may file a request for the examination of the patent application, upon which the examination starts. Where a request for the examination of an application is not filed within three years from the filing date thereof, the patent application will be deemed to have been withdrawn (Article 48–3 of the same Act).

Where no reasons for refusal are found for a patent application, the examiner renders a decision to grant a patent (Article 51 of the same Act). On the contrary, where the examiner has found a reason for refusal, the examiner issues a notification of reasons for refusal to the applicant. In response, the applicant will have an opportunity to state an opinion (Article 50 of the same Act). Where the applicant has submitted a written opinion, or made an amendment, and where the examiner has determined that the application is not subject to any reason for refusal, a decision to grant a patent is given. Where the applicant has not stated any opinion, or made any amendment, or where the applicant did submit a written opinion or make an amendment and yet the examiner still deems that the reason for refusal has not been satisfactorily addressed, the examiner will issue a decision of refusal to the application. If an applicant is dissatisfied with that decision of refusal, the applicant may file appeals against the examiner's decision of refusal (Article 121 of the same Act).

Where a decision to grant a patent is made, the patent is registered upon payment of the patent fee, thereby causing the patent right to be effective (Article 66, paragraphs 1 and 2 of the same Act). Thereafter, the following matters will be published in the Patent Gazette issued by the JPO: the matters stated in the application; the matters stated in the description, the scope of claims, and the like (the same Article, paragraph 3). Only within six months from the issuance of the Patent Gazette in which the patent is laid open, any person may file an opposition to a granted patent, to request re-consideration of the patent (Article 103 of the same Act). After this period, only an interested person may file a request for an invalidation trial (Article 123 of the same Act).

C. Trademark Registration

The following requirements must be satisfied for a trademark to be registered, among others: the trademark is a trademark to be used in connection with goods or services pertaining to the business of an applicant (Article 3, paragraph 1, the introductory clause of the Trademark Act); the trademark distinguishes between goods or services of the applicant and goods or services of any other parties (Article 3, paragraph 1, each item of the same Act); the trademark is not an unregistrable trademark from the aspects of public interest and private interest, and the like.

When a trademark application is filed, an examiner will perform a substantive examination as to whether the application is subject to any reason for refusal, such as not satisfying the registration requirements (Article 15 of the same Act). The content of the trademark application will be published after about one month from the filing of the application in the Trademark Gazette (Article 12–2 of the same Act).

Where no reasons for refusal are found, the examiner renders a decision to the effect that a trademark is to be registered (Article 16 of the same Act). On the contrary, where the examiner has found a reason for refusal, the examiner issues a notification of reasons for refusal to the applicant. In response, the applicant will have an opportunity to state an opinion (Article 15–2 of the same Act). Where the applicant has submitted a written opinion, or made an amendment, and where the examiner has determined that the application is not subject to any reason for refusal, a decision to grant a trademark is given. Where the applicant has not stated any opinion, or made any amendment, or where the applicant did submit a written opinion or make an amendment and yet the examiner still deems that the reason for refusal has not been satisfactorily addressed, the examiner will issue a decision of refusal to the application. If an applicant is dissatisfied with that decision of refusal, the applicant may file appeals against the examiner's decision of refusal (Article 44 of the same Act). Where a decision to grant a trademark is made, the trademark is registered upon payment of the registration fee (Article 18, paragraph 2 of the same Act), and the content thereof will be published in the Trademark Gazette. With respect to trademarks, too, an opposition to the registration of a trademark is allowed to be filed (Article 43–2 of the same Act), and a request for an invalidation trial is also allowed to be filed (Article 46 of the same Act).

D. Protection of Intellectual Property

a. Patent Right

Because a patentee has the exclusive right to work the patented invention as a business (Article 68 of the Patent Act), the patentee has a right to seek an injunction (Article 100 of the same Act) and the like against those who work the patented invention as a business without permission, and may request compensation of any damages, in the case of intentional or negligent infringement (Article 709 of the Civil Code). There is a provision for presuming the amount of damage, or the like, as establishing the damage amount is difficult (Article 102 of the Patent Act).

b. Utility Model Right

Because a holder of a utility model right has the exclusive right to work the registered utility model as a business (Article 16 of the Utility Model Act), the holder of a utility model right has a right to seek an injunction (Article 27 of the same Act) and the like against those who work the registered utility model as a business without permission, and may request compensation of any damages, in the case of intentional or negligent infringement (Article 709 of the Civil Code). However, registration of a utility model is made without going through a substantive examination, such as on novelty and inventive steps; and therefore, in exercising a right, a utility model technical opinion for the registered utility model (Article 12 of the Utility Model Act) must first be presented, for warning (Article 29–2 of the same Act). Just as in the case of patent rights, there is a provision for presuming the amount of damage, or the like (Article 29 of the Utility Model Act).

c. Design Right

Because a holder of a design right has the exclusive right to work the registered design, and designs similar thereto, as a business (Article 23 of the Design Act), the holder of a design right has a right to seek an injunction (Article 37 of the same Act) and the like against those who work the registered design as a business without permission, and may request compensation of any damages, in the case of intentional or negligent infringement (Article 709 of the Civil Code). Just as in the case of patent rights, there is a provision for presuming the amount of damage, or the like is also prescribed (Article 39 of the Design Act).

d. Trademark Right

Because a holder of a trademark right has the exclusive right to use the registered trademark in connection with the designated goods or designated services (Article 25 of the Trademark Act), and has a right to prohibit usage of any trademark in a similar range (Right to prohibit: Article 37, paragraph 1 of the same Act), the holder of a trademark right has a right to seek an injunction (Article 36 of the same Act) and the like against those who infringe on these rights, and may request compensation of any damages, in the case of intentional or negligent infringement (Article 709 of the Civil Code). Under the Trademark Act, there is a provision for presuming the amount of damage, or the like (Article 38 of the Trademark Act).

e. Copyright

A copyright owner has a right to seek an injunction (Article 112 of the Copyright Act) and the like against infringement on the copyright (infringement on each subdivided right of the copyright, etc.), and may request compensation of any damages, in the case of intentional or negligent infringement (Article 709 of the Civil Code). Regarding infringement on a right of reproduction and a right of adapting a pre-existing work, it is required to verify the dependence (i.e., after having been exposed to the works of others, incorporating them into its own work), as well as similarity (i.e., similarity to the creative expressions in others' work). Under the Copyright Act, there is a provision for presuming the amount of damage, or the like (Article 104 of the Copyright Act).

VI. Environmental Protection

A. Department Supervising Environmental Protection

The Ministry of the Environment (the "MOE") is the main administrative authority that administers environmental protection. In addition to general environmental policies, the MOE takes charge of, and executes, a broad range of environmental policies, such as policies on cooperation for global and international environment; measures for aerial environment and measures against automobile emissions; preservation of water, soil, ground, and marine environment; policies on waste and recycling; health measures and measures to control chemical substances; and preservation of natural environment and biodiversity.

In addition, the Ministry of Economy, Trade and Industry administers the fields of energy conservation and renewable energy promotion, whereas the Ministry of Land, Infrastructure, Transport and Tourism administers certain fields such as regulations on energy conservation standards for buildings.

Furthermore, both the administrative authority's lower branch organization in each regional area and the relevant local government supervise and execute specific regulations and activities in the relevant regional area.

B. Brief Introduction of Laws and Regulations on Environmental Protection

The Basic Environment Act has been enacted as a law that generally governs the Japanese environmental policies; further, pursuant to this Act, the Basic Environmental Plan has been established that shows the basic direction of the Japanese government's environmental conservation measures.

Further, the Act on Promotion of Global Warming Countermeasures provides that the Japanese government should promote global warming countermeasures by such means as formulating a Global Warming Countermeasure Plan and taking measures to promote, among others, the control of greenhouse gas emissions.

In addition to these basic laws and regulations relating to environmental policies, specific laws and regulations for various types of environmental protection, and many rules relating to these laws and regulations have been established.

First, regarding the emission of pollutants and so on, the Air Pollution Control Act, the Water Pollution Prevention Act, the Soil Contamination Countermeasures Act, the Waste Management and Public Cleansing Act, and other laws and regulations restrict the emission of pollutants and regulate waste disposal methods and so on.

Further, laws and regulations such as the Forest Act, the Nature Conservation Act, and the Natural Parks Act regulate and restrict development in forest zones and national park zones, etc.

The Environmental Impact Assessment Act has also been established, pursuant to which, certain acts of development conducted in certain regional areas would require prior assessment of the impact of the development on the environment; and depending on the assessment results, the development plan needs to be revised in order to decrease the impact on the environment, or, as the case may be, the development might possibly have to be stopped.

Regarding these environmental protection laws and regulations, corresponding municipal ordinances have been established in each regional area; and some regional areas impose even stricter standards than those imposed under laws.

In the energy conservation field, the Act on Improvement of Energy Consumption Performance of Buildings, and other laws and regulations prescribe energy conservation standards for buildings and so on. Accordingly, in cases such as the case of constructing buildings, certain energy conservation standards must be satisfied.

Further, certain regional areas have adopted regulations on the amounts of greenhouse gas emissions from certain buildings; accordingly, there are cases where execution of energy conservation measures and installment of energy conservation devices, etc. will be necessary in order to meet these regulations.

In the renewable energy field, the Feed-in Tariff program has been introduced pursuant to the Act on Special Measures Concerning Procurement of Electricity from Renewable Energy Sources by Electricity Utilities.

C. Evaluation of Environmental Protection

The Japanese environmental protection policies, laws, and regulations have undergone several stages.

From the 1960s to the 1970s, along with economic development, serious pollution problems arose in Japan. In order to respond to these pollution problems, environmental protection laws and regulations were developed, including, among others, the Air Pollution Control Act, the Water Pollution Prevention Act, and other laws and regulations regarding anti-pollution measures.

Thereafter, environmental problems such as global warming and decreasing biodiversity became international issues. For the purpose of sustainable development, laws and regulations were also developed in Japan from the

1990s onward, prescribing matters such as warming countermeasures, energy conservation, and recycling.

As a result, we can say that environmental protection policies, laws, and regulations in Japan now have comprehensive and exhaustive environmental protection policies which can meet the demands of various fields.

In addition, each local government has enacted regulations tailored to fit the region's own circumstances, and some of these regulations impose even stricter requirements than those imposed under laws.

Further, after the Great East Japan Earthquake that occurred in 2011, environmental problems and energy conservation measures have gained renewed attention and reconsideration, triggered by the damage and consequences resulting from the earthquake. Even more efforts and policies than before are expected to be promoted also in terms of international relationships, in order to achieve the SDGs adopted in 2015 and the goals under the Paris Agreement that came into effect in 2016.

VII. Dispute Resolution

A. Method and Bodies of Dispute Resolution

The methods for resolving disputes in Japan are classified broadly into trial and Alternative Dispute Resolution (ADR). ADR mainly includes arbitration and mediation.

a. Trial

The bodies that hold trials consist of the Supreme Court, High Courts, District Courts, Summary Courts, and Family Courts (the body addressing domestic relations cases). A three-tiered judicial system is adopted whereby a party to a dispute may appeal a judgment rendered by a lower court and is, in principle, given an opportunity for trial up to three times in total. Various procedural laws, mainly the Code of Civil Procedure and the Code of Criminal Procedure, stipulate strict procedures in a trial. It should be noted that only the Japanese language can be used in the trial process. If documentary evidence is written in a foreign language, a Japanese translation thereof must be attached; if a deponent in the trial process cannot speak Japanese, an interpreter must be present.

The labour tribunal is a system similar to a trial held by a court. The labour tribunal addresses civil disputes over labour relations which occur between individual workers and employers. The labour tribunal commission mediates between the parties to resolve the dispute as necessary, and if they fail to reach an agreement, the commission renders a labour tribunal decision. In principle, proceedings in the labour tribunal are completed by conducting three hearings, and thus, a conclusion may be reached more rapidly than by trial. Further, in addition to one judge, two labour tribunal members who have expert knowledge and experience in labour relations serve as labour tribunal commissioners; thus, complicated labour issues may be flexibly addressed.

b. Alternative Dispute Resolution (ADR)

ADR has the following features as compared with a trial:

• The process is closed to the public. As such, ADR may be more appropriate for cases where the facts in a dispute include highly confidential matters, or where the existence of the dispute itself should remain confidential.

• Parties to a dispute may choose arbitrators or mediators. Thus, ADR may be more appropriate for cases where a technical judgment is required to resolve the dispute as the parties can choose arbitrators or conciliators with appropriate expertise.

• In general, the process may be completed more quickly than a trial.

a) Arbitration

Arbitration is available in cases where the parties to a dispute enter into an "arbitration agreement"; namely, an agreement to submit a civil dispute which has already arisen or which may arise in the future in respect of a certain legal relationships, to arbitration, and to accept the award made therein. Arbitration is not available without entering into an arbitration agreement. The arbitration agreement may prevent either party from filing litigation in a court (even if one party files litigation, when the other party claims the existence of the arbitration agreement as demurrer, the litigation should be dismissed). In an arbitration, the language used is determined by agreement between the parties, and it is possible to set any language, including those other than Japanese, as the language for arbitration. It should be noted that consumers and workers, who are generally in a weaker position than companies are susceptible to being forced to enter into an arbitration agreement that is disadvantageous to them, and thus, in certain cases, from the viewpoint of consumer / worker protection, the law allows for termination of an arbitration agreement between a company and a consumer and may deem an arbitration agreement between a company and an employee invalid. Among many arbitration bodies organized by the government or private sector, the Japan Commercial Arbitration Association (JCAA) is relatively famous for international commercial disputes.

b) Mediation

In mediation, a third party intervenes in a dispute between the parties to resolve it. Unlike arbitration, it is a procedure to resolve the dispute based on a settlement agreement between the parties. Namely, a mediator does not render any adjudication but just presents a settlement proposal; it is at the parties' discretion to approve such settlement proposal. Mediation is conducted either by a court, or bodies organized by the government or private sector, and mediation conducted by the courts adheres to the above description as well.

B. Application of Laws

Various procedural laws, including the Code of Civil Procedure and the Code of Criminal Procedure, apply to the trial. Arbitration is conducted pursuant to the Arbitration Act and the arbitration rules of each arbitration body. Meanwhile, for mediation, the Civil Conciliation Act applies to mediation conducted by a court; however, there is no law generally and comprehensively regulating the procedure of mediation conducted by other mediation bodies, and basically, that type of mediation is conducted pursuant to the rules of each mediation body.

Regarding the enforceability of judicial decisions by the court and arbitral awards between Japan and China, Japan is a member state of the Convention on the Recognition and Enforcement of Foreign Arbitral Awards (New York Convention), and so is China. Therefore, it is possible to enforce an arbitral award rendered by a Japanese arbitration body in China and to enforce an arbitral award rendered by a Chinese arbitration body in Japan. Meanwhile, for judicial decisions, Japanese law stipulates the conditions for a Japanese court to enforce a judicial decision rendered by a foreign court. One of the conditions is that "A mutual guarantee exists" (Article 118, item (iv) of the Code of Civil Procedure) between the country to which a foreign court rendering such judicial decision belongs and Japan; more specifically, in the county to which the foreign court rendering such decision belongs, a judicial decision by a Japanese court that is of the same kind as that by the foreign court must be held valid on conditions that are substantially similar to those under the Japanese law in material aspects. In this regard, it is generally construed that there is no mutual guarantee between Japan and China, and thus it is impossible to enforce judicial decisions rendered by Chinese courts in Japan and to enforce judicial decisions rendered by Japanese courts in China.

VIII. Others

A. Anti-commercial Bribery

Cases falling under the crime of bribery of public officers under Japanese criminal law are subject to a statutory penalty prescribed according to the type of bribery. For example, in the case of simple bribery, it is provided that (i) a bribe-taker shall be punished by imprisonment for not more than 5 years, (ii) the bribe shall be confiscated, and (iii) when all or part of the bribe cannot be confiscated, an equivalent sum of money shall be collected.

If a case falls under the crime of bribery of public officers in Japan, a briber shall be punished by imprisonment with work for not more than 3 years or a fine of not more than 2,500,000 yen. Bribery of people who are deemed public officers and people engaged in public work is provided by each special law.

The Unfair Competition Prevention Act provides for the bribery of foreign public officers. In cases that fall under the crime of bribery of a foreign public officer provided in the Unfair Competition Prevention Act, a briber shall be punished by imprisonment with work for not more than 5 years or a fine of not more than 5,000,000 yen, or both. Companies shall be punished by a fine of not more than 300 million yen. When a representative of a juridical person, or an agent, employee or any other worker of a juridical person falls under the crime of bribery of a foreign public officer, not only the offender but also the juridical person shall be punished by a fine of not more than 300 million yen.

Unlike China, there is no general regulation concerning commercial bribery (so-called bribery between non-public officers) in Japan; however, the crime of giving or accepting a bribe by a director, etc. and the crime of giving or accepting a bribe in relation to the exercise of a right of a shareholder, etc. are provided as a special bribe crime under the Companies Act.

B. Project Contracting

In accordance with the WTO's "Agreement on Government Procurement" and other relevant laws, both central and local government's procurement contracts for which the contract amount is not less than the specified amount, respectively (e.g., a contract on procurement of construction work for which the contract amount is 680 million yen or more, or a contract on procurement of goods and other items for which the contract amount is 15 million yen or more), require bidding procedures. The purpose of these bidding procedures is to establish nondiscriminatory treatment and to ensure procurement procedural transparency.

Bidding procedures are divided into general competitive bidding (public bidding), designated competitive bidding (selective bidding), and discretionary contract (limited bidding). An enterprise that wishes to participate in general competitive bidding and designated competitive bidding, in principle, needs to undergo qualification screening conducted by a procurement agency.

If a procurement agency wishes to conduct general competitive bidding or designated competitive bidding, then at least 40 days before the bidding date, the procurement agency will give a public notice (public announcement) in the Official Gazette, prefectural bulletin, etc. and make the proposed bidding publicly known. Further, in order to broadly provide information regarding the government procurement, information published in the Official Gazette is stored in databases. Such information is accessible at the Japan External Trade Organization's offices in Japan, Business Support Centers, etc. or accessible through an online retrieval service (http://www.jetro.go.jp/gov_procurement/).

肯尼亚

作者：Adil Khawaja、Sigee Koech、John Ohaga、Franklin Cheluget
译者：蒙启红、贾红卫

一、概述

（一）政治、经济、社会和法律环境介绍

1. 政治

肯尼亚的政体是总统制民主共和国。根据2010年通过的《宪法》的规定，肯尼亚实行多党制度，肯尼亚总统既是国家元首也是政府首脑。全国有47个郡，由各郡郡长领导。

行政权力由政府行政部门行使，行政部门由总统领导，总统主持内阁，内阁成员从外部议会选出。立法权完全归属于议会，议会由两院组成，即国民议会和参议院。参议院由来自各个郡的代表组成，代表的主要职责是对各郡的相关事宜进行立法。司法独立于行政和立法。

2. 经济

肯尼亚采用市场经济，有少量国有基础设施企业，实行自由化的外贸体系。该国通常被视为东非和中非的金融、通信和运输服务枢纽。主要行业包括：农业、林业和渔业，采矿业，工业制造业，能源产业，旅游和金融服务业。据估计，截至2015年，肯尼亚的国内生产总值为69.977亿美元，这使之成为世界第72大经济体。人均国内生产总值约为1 587美元。

3. 社会

肯尼亚的社会以分布于47个郡的44个部落组合为特征。主要居民为班图人和尼罗克人，北部有一些讲库什族语言的少数民族。截至2017年，其总人口大约为4 700万。

4. 法律

2010年的肯尼亚《宪法》是规定肯尼亚法律制度的主要法律文件。它确立了法院系统，各方将争议提至法院以作出裁决。在法院体系中设立了具有不同管辖权的不同类型的法院，即最高法院、上诉法院、高等法院、就业与劳动关系法院（原为工业法院）、环境与土地法院、下属法院、裁判法院，其中包括卡迪法院和军事法院。法律也允许通过调解、谈判、仲裁和其他选择性争议解决机制私下解决争端。

（二）"一带一路"倡议下与中国企业合作的现状及方向

中国和肯尼亚之间存在着长期的经济合作，特别是在与肯尼亚建设道路和铁路方面的合作。2015年12月在约翰内斯堡举行的中非合作论坛第二次峰会期间，中国承诺协助加强非洲工业能力。据此承诺，肯尼亚于2017年12月13日至16日在内罗毕的肯雅塔国际会议中心（KICC）首次举办了中国非洲产能合作展览会。

此外，肯尼亚积极响应中国"一带一路"倡议，与中国的合作将会达到高峰。为实现这一倡议，需要理顺肯尼亚和中国的法律制度。

二、投资

（一）市场准入

国际贸易在肯尼亚经济中发挥着关键作用。货物贸易在国内生产总值中所占的份额平均为43%，

就说明了这一点。服务贸易进一步增强了国际贸易的重要性,这体现在服务贸易在全球经济中的作用。据世界贸易组织(2010年)统计,2015年服务贸易已占全球国内生产总值的2/3,即49.5万亿美元。肯尼亚通过其侨民社区从此市场中获得了收益,2015年汇出了1 454亿克朗(14.3亿美元)。

肯尼亚的国际贸易政策意在通过有助于将肯尼亚转变为有竞争力的出口导向型经济和促进国内市场蓬勃发展的政策措施,挖掘商品贸易和服务贸易的潜力。国际贸易政策是在肯尼亚已经签署的多边、区域和优惠关税协定(PTAs)的框架内制定的,包括世界贸易组织(WTO)、东非共同体(EAC)、东南非共同市场(COMESA)三方自由贸易区《非洲增长与机遇法案》(AGOA)和东非—欧盟经济伙伴关系协议。下文将详述贸易体制中的这些安排。

1. 多边贸易安排

肯尼亚已经认可了世界贸易组织的各项协议所定义的多边贸易安排,这源于肯尼亚对WTO的承诺。在"国家贸易政策设计"中提及的协议包括:《关税及贸易总协定》(GATT)、《实施卫生与植物检疫措施协议》(SPS)、《技术性贸易壁垒协议》(TBT)、《反倾销协议》《补贴和反补贴措施协议》《海关估价协议》《原产地规则协议》《保障措施协议》《与贸易有关的知识产权协定》《国际服务贸易协议》等等。

2. 区域贸易安排

影响肯尼亚国际贸易政策的区域贸易安排包括东非共同体、东南非共同市场、政府间发展组织(IGAD)和环印度洋地区合作联盟(IOR-ARC)。这些安排的意义和影响如下:

(1)东非共同体(EAC)

东非共同体成员包括肯尼亚、坦桑尼亚、乌干达、卢旺达、布隆迪和南苏丹。共同体将六国汇集在一起,讨论经济、社会和政治合作问题。通过《东非共同体关税同盟议定书》和《共同市场议定书》以及其他区域一体化手段、行业战略和政策,东非共同体已经创建了一个广泛的商品和服务贸易市场。

(2)东南非共同市场(COMESA)

东南非共同市场是包括肯尼亚在内的19个国家的区域经济共同体。通过自由贸易区框架,以免税为基础,东南非共同市场为成员国提供了拓宽出口目的地和进口来源地的机会。2015年,东南非共同市场的出口额占肯尼亚出口总额的16%。2011年至2015年期间,贸易增长迟滞,增长率几乎不变。另外,东南非共同市场在同一时期实现了巨大的进口增长,这意味着贸易潜力的存在,可以利用这一潜力来增加这一区域的出口量。

(3)政府间发展组织(IGAD)

政府间发展组织在非洲之角,包括以下国家——吉布提、索马里、南苏丹、苏丹、埃塞俄比亚、乌干达和肯尼亚。政府间发展组织现在是一个区域经济共同体(REC),其任务是从抗干旱和抗荒漠化扩大到经济和贸易等事项。因此,通过它提供的区域一体化框架,七国之间的贸易可以通过其他区域经济共同体(比如东南非共同市场)的共同承诺来扩大贸易一体化。

(4)东非共同体、东南非共同市场、南部非洲发展共同体(SADC)三方自由贸易区(TFTA)

根据2008年10月22日国家元首首脑会议的指令,东非共同体、东南非共同市场、南部非洲发展共同体三方自由贸易区的建立最终于2015年6月10日启动。它涵盖了包括货物贸易在内的第一阶段的整合。根据自由贸易区的协定,肯尼亚从26个国家扩大后的区域市场中获益匪浅。

(5)2000年《非洲增长和机遇法案》

与其他撒哈拉以南的非洲受益国一样,肯尼亚受益于美国通过的《非洲增长与机遇法案》所提供的优惠贸易协定。受益国必须符合该法案规定的资格标准,其中包括建立市场经济和良好的政府治理。该贸易初步预计于2015年到期,但在2015年7月1日,该计划又延长了15年。

(6)经济伙伴关系协议(EPAs)

为了与《欧盟市场准入条例》(1528/2007)相一致,2016年9月20日,肯尼亚议会批准了《经济伙伴关系协议》。根据此《欧盟市场准入条例》,肯尼亚必须签署和批准该协议,以避免失去自1975年以来该国享有的免税市场准入资格。不签署和批准该协议会使肯尼亚自2016年10月1日起丧失在欧盟的免税市场地位。

3. 双边贸易协定

肯尼亚与众多发达国家和发展中国家均订立有双边贸易和投资协定，以达成下列目标：

① 相互参加展览和交易会，以及各国的贸易促进周活动；
② 共享市场情报，调查市场信息；
③ 鼓励机构合作，例如标准化机构、工会商会、海关组织、研究机构等；
④ 对双边会议期间提出的问题进行及时和重点跟进；
⑤ 一般和特定产品贸易交流和投资任务；
⑥ 促进贸易和投资。

4. 影响出口市场准入的制约因素和挑战

肯尼亚产品在区域和国际市场的市场准入仍然受到一系列限制并面临一些挑战。这导致肯尼亚在地方贸易中的份额较低，并在一些情况下出现下滑。区域市场尤其如此，一些产品的出口大幅下降。其中最关键的约束条件如下：

（1）非关税壁垒的盛行（NTBs）

东非共同体和东南非共同市场的区域内贸易受到非关税壁垒的严重阻碍，这些非关税壁垒的形式是大量的海关文件和繁琐的行政程序。此外，拒绝承认原产地证书，适用《实施卫生与植物检疫措施协议》（SPS）要求时采用不同的标准和不同的尺度，另外，延误过境、路障、地磅、警察检查和服务人员费用以及未统一的过境费和程序也阻碍了贸易。

非关税壁垒的应用限制了各国之间的货物流通。该国面临的主要挑战是，确保双边、区域和多边贸易体系的谈判能够减少或消除非关税壁垒。肯尼亚的出口在国际市场上也面临非关税壁垒的威胁，主要与《实施卫生与植物检疫措施协议》和技术标准，以及通过关税配额季节性限制产品相关。

（2）东非共同体贸易推广计划的应用效果不佳

由于东非共同体免税计划执行力差，肯尼亚企业面临进入东非共同体市场的挑战。

（3）原材料、中间产品和生产资料的关税征收

用于生产成品的原材料和中间产品不承担进口关税，出口产品才具有竞争力。在中非共同体的共同外部关税框架下，有些产业部门并非如此。确定原材料或中间产品是否应该缴纳关税的判断标准是是否存在区域供应产品的能力以满足相应区域工业需求。迄今为止东非共同体的关税结构并未依据这一原则，我们可以看到，因需要缴纳进口关税，这类原材料和中间产品正持续从东非共同体以外的国家进口。

总体的影响是，成品在区域和国际市场上都没有竞争力。

（4）较高的和多重的国内税费

在生产、投资和服务方面广泛征收的各种税费扭曲了产品价格，使产品和服务在国内和国际市场上失去竞争力。此外，多重征税对工商界来说是繁重的负担。政府面临的挑战是审查所有税收法律、法规并使之合理化，以提高产品竞争力。

（5）关税高峰和关税升级的挑战

虽然平均关税在经过连续几轮谈判后下降，但发达国家对来自发展中国家的增值产品实行高关税和关税升级继续限制了发展中国家的产品出口。实际上，这种做法保护了进口国家的国内工业，同时也阻碍了产品增值。

（6）优惠侵蚀和竞争力丧失

由于世界贸易组织框架下的持续自由化所带来的优惠侵蚀，肯尼亚面临着由于竞争激烈导致其对欧盟和美国市场出口量下降的问题。

（二）外汇管制

1. 根据《银行法》（第488章）制定的条例和准则

由肯尼亚中央银行颁布的条例和准则要求银行遵守某些要求、限制和准则。这一监管结构旨在使银行机构和与其开展业务的个人和公司之间形成透明的关系。

鉴于银行业与国家（和全球）经济对银行的依赖性之间的相互关联性，监管部门需要保持对这些机构标准化实践的控制。这些规定的目标是：

① 谨慎监管——降低银行债权人所面临的风险水平（如保护存款人）；
② 减少系统性风险——降低不利交易条件导致的多家银行或重要银行倒闭造成的中断风险；
③ 避免滥用银行——降低银行被利用于犯罪的风险，例如洗钱；
④ 保护银行秘密；
⑤ 信用分配——指导信贷投入到受欢迎的行业，以在竞争激烈的时期提供最佳的客户服务。

肯尼亚中央银行对金融体系进行监管，并在外汇业务管理方面发挥监督作用。维持（国际）收支平衡也是该银行的目标之一。

肯尼亚中央银行受以下立法监管：

① 肯尼亚《宪法》（2010年）；
② 肯尼亚《中央银行法》（2015年）；
③《银行法》（2015年）；
④《微型金融法》（2006年）；
⑤《国家支付系统法》（2011年）；
⑥ 肯尼亚《存款保险法》（2012年）。

中央银行的主要担忧之一是外汇交易商是否能准确收集并及时提交统计信息，否则央行将无法实现肯尼亚《中央银行法》规定的目标。

应注意到，在1995年12月27日生效的《外汇管制法》被废止后，管理外汇业务的责任被授予经授权的外汇交易商。中央银行注意到，根据1996年8月19日发布的肯尼亚中央银行第12号通告和1996年11月11日的《外汇局指南》，交易商已经有效地发挥了其自身的作用。

在管理外汇业务时，外汇交易商（被授权银行和外汇局）需要遵守以下原则：

① 必须始终遵守"了解你的客户"原则（KYC）；
② 谨慎行事，确保跨境支付与非法金融交易无关，所有外汇交易商都应采用适当的反洗钱政策；
③ 在市场上推出新产品之前，推出产品的外汇交易商应先与中央银行进行协商；
④ 外汇交易商（的员工）必须是合适的且有能力胜任的，也就是说，他们必须高度诚实、正直，具备高度的声誉、竞争力和能力。

2. 外汇局

外汇局可以买卖外币现金，购买旅行支票、私人支票、银行本票和进行银行汇款。外汇局也可以出售旅行支票，但必须事先获得肯尼亚中央银行的批准。外汇局只允许从事现汇交易，不许从事衍生性外汇交易。

3. 允许办理外汇业务的人员

根据1996年2月28日第23号法律公告的规定，依肯尼亚《中央银行法》第33A条第3款的规定，获得肯尼亚中央银行授权的可以接受外汇收据的任何人不得买卖（买入或卖出）外汇。

第33A条规定如下：

① 依第3款规定，除授权经销商以外，任何人均不得在肯尼亚办理外汇业务；
② 任何人违反第1款的规定，即属犯罪，一经定罪，可处不超过50万先令罚款，或处3年以下有期徒刑，或两者并处；
③ 尽管有第1款的规定，银行可以允许其指定的人或某一类别的人在没有许可证的情况下处理外汇业务，但须遵守银行可能施加的条件。

根据《旅游业许可法》的规定，获得许可的已注册的旅游企业、免税店的所有者或经营者，或者由于其业务的性质需要定期以外币进行交易的经营者，均可以获得上述许可。其收到的外币应按以下方式处理：

① 记入贷方外币账户；
② 卖给授权经销商；

③用于通过授权银行对外部债务进行结算；
④清偿以外币结算的本地债务。

4. 货币买卖

除非交易的其中一方是根据肯尼亚《中央银行法》（第491章）第33B条许可的授权经销商，否则禁止买卖外币。

5. 假币

所有的外汇交易商都应该有检测假币的必要设备。应当扣留客户提供的假币，向客户提供收据，并在向有关当局咨询后交付肯尼亚中央银行调查。

6. 汇率显示板

外汇交易商必须在其场所内显著且方便公众观看的位置展示其柜台汇率。每个外汇交易商必须配备一个汇率显示板，并为每笔外汇交易签发收据。

7. 交易

肯尼亚居民和非居民可以：
①以肯尼亚先令或外币为货物和服务开具发票；
②持有外汇；
③向授权经销商出售外汇或从其处购买外汇；
④根据肯尼亚第118号法律公告（载于1998年9月4日发布的第48号政府补充公告）进出口货币。

8. 市场操纵

所有外汇交易商均应避免参与误导市场上其他参与者的投机交易，也不得滥用任何受保护的信息。鼓励所有外汇交易尽可能具有真实的相关商业活动基础。

9. 外汇交易文件

对10 000美元等值以上的交易，所有外汇交易商必须获得并保留适当的文件。或者，在采用电子银行记账时，授权经销商可以接受经恰当签署的声明表格，以代替存档文件。客户应按要求向银行出示交易文件，且授权经销商应将文件提供给肯尼亚中央银行以供其进行审查。

10. 外向投资

所有外汇交易商应取得并保留以下副本：
①外国政府对投资的批准文件（如果持有）；
②申请人与东道国有关机构之间的合同，如股票交易合同；
③中介（文件）；
④有关投资的条款和条件（文件）。

11. 外交使团的外币账户（FCY）

被授权银行可以自由为外交使团或其认可的任何官员，或依据国际条约在肯尼亚境内或境外设立的任何组织及其认可的任何官员，开设和经营外币账户。

应当指出，这些组织的进口活动不受进口申报单（IDF）或装运前检验程序（PSI）的限制。因此，他们的外汇账户可能在缺少必要的进口文件的情况下被扣款。此类账户的所有其他借项应遵循谨慎的银行业务惯例。每日流入量和每周持有量应按要求在返回肯尼亚中央银行时进行记录。

12. 以外币计值的信贷

被授权银行可以自由地将以外币计价的信贷融资延伸至肯尼亚居民和非居民，但须受审慎贷款惯例之限制。

13. 向肯尼亚居民贷款

向肯尼亚居民提供的贷款，贷款银行应保留相应的信息，包括：
①正式签署的贷款协议（融资函）复印件，详细说明信贷和担保的条款和条件（如果适用的话）；
②借款人的声明，保证其在信贷融资期限内保留居民身份，或其居民身份改变时通知银行；

③ 作为还款替代方式的担保财物。

14. 向非居民贷款

对于向非居民提供的贷款，贷款银行应保存适当的信息，包括以下内容：
① 正式签署的贷款协议，详细说明贷款和担保的条款和条件（如果适用）；
② 证明抵押物可以用外币变现的文件；
③ 偿还资金来自国外的声明。

15. 肯尼亚居民的离岸借款

肯尼亚居民可以从境外借款。然而，被授权经纪人必须适当考虑其客户的利益，就其客户离岸借款的风险给予适当的建议。如果需要的话，应该建议借款人寻求商业律师的帮助。

应保留下列相关信息作为离岸债务的证据：借款人与外国贷方正式签署的融资协议，确认贷款收入的资金转账文件以及贷款偿还日程。

16. 内向投资

允许内向投资。非居民可自由投资于房地产、股票、货币和证券交易或其他合理类型的投资。投资程序的详细信息可以从位于肯尼亚内罗毕哈兰比大道肯尼亚国家银行总部大楼的投资促进中心（IPC）获得。

（三）融资

1. 监管和所有权限制

（1）无外汇管制

肯尼亚没有外汇管制法。然而，根据肯尼亚《中央银行法》的规定，以下每笔付款必须通过被授权银行进行。任何相悖的程序机制都需要中央银行的批准：
① 在肯尼亚境内给肯尼亚境外的人付款或贷款；
② 在肯尼亚境外给肯尼亚境内的人付款或贷款；
③ 在肯尼亚居民与非居民之间的付款（除常规项目交易外）。

根据该法，授权银行是指由肯尼亚中央银行许可的特许经营外汇业务的特定银行。实际上，包括所有持有银行执照的机构。因此，涉及向肯尼亚实体发放贷款或认购股份的交易可能会被认定为违反该条款。

2. 五个主要的金融监管部门

（1）肯尼亚中央银行

中央银行通过制定货币政策来实现和维持稳定，从而规范银行业。它通过执行《银行法》的规定监管商业银行、国家和地区的支付系统。

（2）保险监管机构

保险监管机构为保险和再保险公司、保险经纪人、代理商、评估员、理赔员和健康管理组织（HMOs）颁发执照。根据《保险法》的规定，保险监管机构调节监督和发展肯尼亚的保险业。

（3）资本市场管理局

资本市场管理局批准和监督资本市场中介机构的所有活动，确保所有持牌人和市场机构的行为适当，并规范资本市场产品（债券，股票等）的发行。

（4）退休福利机构

退休福利机构调节和监督养老金计划的建立和管理，保护退休福利计划成员和发起人的利益，促进退休福利部门发展。

（5）合作社管理机构

合作社管理机构根据 SACCO 法案，授权储蓄和信贷合作社（SACCO）开展存款业务，对储蓄和信贷合作社进行管理和监督。

3. 肯尼亚的银行业结构

（1）商业银行
- 42家商业银行；
- 8个代表处；
- 为公司和消费者提供银行服务。

（2）移动支付运营商
- 4个移动支付运营商；
- 为个人和企业的移动支付提供解决方案。

（3）小额信贷银行
- 12家小额信贷银行；
- 专为微型和小型企业提供银行服务。

（4）抵押贷款机构
- 1家抵押贷款公司；
- 重点关注房地产开发的贷款。

（5）外汇局
- 86个外汇局；
- 提供外汇兑换服务。

（6）汇款服务提供商
- 14个汇款服务提供商；
- 为个人和中小企业提供国家间汇款服务。

（7）征信机构
- 4家征信机构；
- 向金融机构、公用事业和个人提供信息共享服务。

（四）税收

1. 公司、企业税

肯尼亚公司税的计算基于应税利润：
- 营业税：营业额的3%（自2007年1月1日起实施，以营业额500万肯尼亚先令为限）；
- 居民企业：30%；
- 非居民企业：37.5%。

2. 资本利得税

资本利得税（CGT）于2015年1月1日起重新推出，税率为财产转让净收益的5%。这是最终的税收，不能抵消其他所得税。

3. 分公司利得税

外国实体的分公司按37.5%的税率缴纳税款。

4. 增值税（VAT）

增值税率为16%和0%。出口税率为零。一些商品和服务，如未加工的农产品和金融服务可免除增值税。

5. 就业福利税

一般来说，就非现金利益应向雇主承担的成本和公平市场价值中的较高者征税。为了税收目的，应税价值应被添加到薪酬中。如果累计总额不超过每年36 000肯尼亚先令，则免除征收。

6. 机动车税

每月按车辆初始成本的2%或规定费率中的较高者缴纳。租赁车辆的税则是按照租赁成本计算。

7. 住房税

对于非执行董事而言，按总收入（全职董事薪酬）的15%，或公平市场中的租金价值，或已付租金中的较高者征税。对于农业雇员来说，按薪酬的10%征税。对于其他员工而言，支付的全部租金或薪酬的15%，取二者中的较高者征税。

8. 员工贷款

给雇员的贷款税按公司税率计算，按税收专员所规定的利率与雇员支付的实际利率之间的差额征税。

9. 其他收益

家具的应税收益是每月成本的1%，电话是每月话费的30%，员工持股计划（ESOP）是股票市价与期权合约当日的报价的差额。

10. 地方税

就业收入税在员工收入的基础上征收，按10%至30%的累进税率预扣。

11. 股息

股息是在预提税基础上征收的最终税。因此，不允许使用费用抵消股息收入或纳税人的任何其他收入。对于持股超过12.5%的居民企业，股息免税。金融机构收到的股息应被视为应纳税所得。

然而，如果分配了非税收入，可能会产生补偿税（公司税）。例如，因资本消耗补偿而产生的资本收益。这是通过年度股息税账户达成的，该账户记录了已收和已付股息的变动情况，并考虑了该实体已缴纳的税款。

12. 利息扣除

完全和纯粹为取得收入而产生的利息是可抵免的。但是，如果一家公司由1名非居民以及4名或4名以下的居民所控制，则该抵免仅限于公司总负债不超过实收股本和收入的3倍，或利息的数额（在资本稀薄时）。

所得税专员有权规定计算利息的形式和方式。

若公司资本稀薄，已发生的外汇损失可递延纳税。

13. 税损

税损可结转以抵消未来应纳税所得额。从2010年1月1日起，抵消以5年为限。

税损仅适用于从特定来源获得的应纳税所得额。这些来源是：

① 租赁或占用不动产所得收入；
② 就业收入；
③ 农业、园艺、林业等收入；
④ 雇主从注册退休金、公积金中提取的收入；
⑤ 业务活动。

但是，损失不能从一个实体转移到另一个实体。

14. 海外收入

非在肯尼亚发生或产生的收入不可征税，除非是：

① 在肯尼亚境外或境内的肯尼亚居民在受雇期间作为雇员而取得的就业收入；
② 跨境进行的商业活动；
③ 外国银行分行利用当地产生的收入进行的投资或海外贸易收入。

15. 税收优惠

根据资产分类，资产减值是可进行税收抵免的。

肯尼亚与下列国家签有双重税收协定：加拿大、丹麦、东非共同体、法国、德国、印度、毛里求斯、挪威、南非、瑞典、英国、赞比亚。

为某些指定企业提供10年免税期，这些企业仅从事出口产品（在出口加工区）的生产。在免税期结束时，可按 25% 的税率纳税。

对新上市的证券交易公司，前 3～5 年适用较低的公司税率，对于至少已发行上市股本 20%、30% 和 40% 的公司，其对应的税率分别为 27%、25% 和 20%。

对从事慈善、医疗、扶贫和宗教活动的组织免征税款。

16. 外国税收减免

外国税收减免仅适用于与肯尼亚订有双重征税协议的国家。

17. 企业集团

一般来说，在肯尼亚，不论属于哪个企业集团，所有注册公司的税率均为 30%。非居民企业的税率为 37.5%。

18. 关联方交易

全部且专门为取得收入而进行的关联方交易可以免缴税款。如果关联方交易作为商业活动在肯尼亚发生，则应当作为收入纳税。

根据自 2006 年 7 月 1 日起生效的肯尼亚《转让定价规则》，需要进行关联方交易的公司须准备和存档转让定价文件。

（五）土地政策

外国人只能根据租赁权持有土地。授予非公民的租赁不得超过 99 年。

肯尼亚通过《土地管理法》管理农业用地的交易。任何涉及销售、转让、租赁、抵押、交换、分割或其他处置或处理任何农业用地的交易，必须获得土地管理局的批准。非肯尼亚公民不能就此类交易获得批准（除非为非肯尼亚贷款人提供抵押或付款）。

然而，非肯尼亚公民可以申请总统豁免令以免于适用该法，尽管实际上这种方法仅在涉及重要公共利益的极特殊的情况下适用。

从广义上讲，农业用地是指不在自治市、乡镇或市场范围内的土地，或者是以公报形式公布的土地（但不包括因有任何特定使用限制而未用于农业用途的土地）。

依照肯尼亚《宪法》，2012 年 5 月 2 日颁布并实施了三项议会法案：
- 2012 年《土地法》；
- 2012 年《土地注册法》；
- 2012 年《国家土地委员会法》。

1. 非肯尼亚公民的土地所有权

在这方面，土地法的突出特点是，永久业权土地不能由非肯尼亚公民所有，99 年以上的租赁权益不能由非肯尼亚公民持有。

因此，非肯尼亚公民拥有的任何永久业权自 2010 年 8 月 27 日起被转换为 99 年的租赁权益；任何超过 99 年的租赁权益自 2010 年 8 月 27 日起被转换为 99 年的租赁权益。

《宪法》规定，一个企业或公司只有 100% 被肯尼亚公民所有才能被视为肯尼亚法人。因此，即使是只有一个股东是非肯尼亚公民的公司也只能享有 99 年或以下的租赁权益。

肯尼亚公民和非肯尼亚公民共同拥有的永久业权或未满期的超过 99 年的租赁权益是否会被转换为 99 年的租赁权益，目前还未规定。

2. 根据肯尼亚法律，谁是外国人或非公民？

肯尼亚《宪法》没有对公民、非公民或外国人提供明确的法律定义。相反，《宪法》规定了公民的权利、利益、特权和义务。

2011 年《公民和移民法》规定了这些权利和特权的规范性内容。例如，在全国任何地区拥有土地和其他财产的权利，并有权获得给予公民的任何注册文件，包括"注册证书"。

《公民和移民法》将外国人定义为"任何非肯尼亚公民的人"。但是，这些法规似乎仅涉及自然人的地位，而不是公司。但公司才是外国直接投资的主要参与者。因此，自然人即使涉及投资，其国籍将根据移民法确定。而公司的法人国籍问题,以及确定一家企业或公司是否为外国法人的具体国籍标准涉及公司机构和投资的概念和相关法律。

尽管如此,自然人的移民身份或公民身份依然与此具有相关性,特别是在适用外国控制原则的情况下,法人团体的国籍可以根据对该团体的决策进行控制的自然人的公民身份来确定。

3. 根据肯尼亚法律确定公司实体的法人国籍

在肯尼亚法律体系中,公司实体的法人国籍可以通过各种法律规定来确定,如下所述:

(1)投资促进和公司立法

就一般投资法而言,《投资促进法》旨在提供"一站式服务",指导外国投资者申请必要的执照和许可证,并评估其是否适合在肯尼亚投资。在确定投资者的"外国国籍"时,该法对合伙企业只适用"外国控制"的概念,即如果企业的权益由非肯尼亚公民控制,则该合伙企业被视为外国企业。然而,有其他法律采用了"正式国籍"的概念,即公司根据其注册地在国外被视为非公民(或外国投资者),因此公司若根据外国法律注册成立,则视为外国投资者。

这是《公司法》所采纳的观点,其中的规定为,外国公司是指"……在肯尼亚境外注册……并在肯尼亚境内设立营业场所的公司"。因此,公司立法同样以公司注册地为首要标准来确定公司的"外国国籍",同时也要求该实体在当地设立营业场所。

(2)与私人或集体土地所有者签订直接合同协议的征地机制

以租赁的方式,外国公司可以通过几种可行的机制对土地进行投资。持有私有土地的人有权处理该土地,包括根据自愿租赁协议向其他人许可租赁,以约定的金额作为对价。根据《土地法》第六章的规定,这些租赁或分租可以是定期的、短期的、未来的租约,也可以是固定期限的协议。

外国公司投资土地时,无权通过签订租赁或分租协议取得任何私人土地的永久产权,这是《宪法》所禁止的。

(六)公司的设立和解散

在肯尼亚,企业合法注册的形式包括:有限责任公司、独资企业、合伙企业、合作企业、担保有限公司(大多数为非营利组织)以及代表处。外国投资者青睐于有限责任公司,因其提供类似于在其他国家的公司所享有的优惠。

1. 设立的程序

设立的程序在很大程度上取决于希望设立的企业类型以及企业所属的行业部门。

投资者需先在司法部长办公室的公司注册处登记拟注册的公司名称。此申请可由申请人直接作出或通过法定代表和政策专家作出。一旦获得批准,公司组织章程将提交给注册员,由他颁布公司注册证书。必须填写的表格包括名义资本声明、董事和股东情况、注册办公室情况以及参与组建公司的律师的资格证。

注册企业的法律要件是必须获得增值税号码、个人识别号码(PIN)、全国社会保障基金(NSSF)号码和国家医院保险基金(NHIF)号码。其他要件依业务类型而定。

"投资证书"授予投资者享有其经营所需的所有许可证的权益,以及3名管理人员或技术人员、3名股东或合伙人各自有效期为两年的工作许可证。

2. 肯尼亚公司的自愿清算

自愿清算适用的是肯尼亚《破产法》(2015年第18号法令)和《公司法》(2015年第17号法令)。

根据上述两项法案,在肯尼亚终止公司有两种选择:《破产法》规定的自愿清算程序和在公司注册处根据《公司法》注销公司。

(1)自愿清算

当公司董事有意通过清算程序终止公司时,应当根据《破产法》的规定作出法定声明。

公司的自愿清算从确认公司偿付能力的第一次决议获得通过时开始,决议中应包括其资产和负债报表的声明。第二次自愿清算决议必在其后5周内由全体或大多数董事通过。但是,在通过自愿清算决议之前,公司应将该决议通知公司财产的任何适格的浮动抵押权人。

公司自愿清算开始之时及其后，公司必须停止经营业务，除非可能是必要的且有益于清算的业务，包括公司股份的转让、变更或尝试变更公司成员的职位。

公司在通过自愿清算决议后的14天后，应在《肯尼亚公报》和两家全国性报纸上发布有关于清算决议的通知，否则该公司可能会被罚款。

然后，公司的成员在为清算目的召开的股东大会上任命一位经授权的破产执行人为清算人。获得任命后，清算人需要就整个清算程序编制一份会计报表，并说明公司的债务（如果有）应如何结算。将这些资料提交给公司成员并获得批准后，清算人将在公司注册处提交一份这些资料的复印件和报税表。所有这些会议必须在日报和《肯尼亚公报》刊登广告30天之后开始。

清算人须出席股东大会并于7天后提交会计报表及报税表。公司注册处将在收到账目后登记上述账户，在公示此账户3个月之后，此公司视为已经解散。

这一过程的支出由被指定的破产执业人自行决定，并受限于被清算公司的规模和类型。

（2）注销登记

《公司法》为清算业务提供了另一种选择。《公司法》规定了公司注销登记的两种方式。

首先，它赋予注册处注销其认为没有实际开展业务或运营的公司的权利。

第二种选择是由公司申请。公司可以选择向注册员提出申请，在公司注册处注销。如果公司申请注销公司注册，则必须确保其在申请日期后7日内向公司的每位成员、债权人、员工和董事提供申请书副本。

该申请应是由其董事代表公司或由多数董事通过决议提出的。注册处将在《肯尼亚公报》发布通知，3个月后将在册公司注销，声明注册员将根据《公司法》第897条对相关公司行使该项权力，并说明任何人均可提出公司不应被注销的原因。

在将公司的名称从登记册上注销后，注册员应尽快在《肯尼亚公报》上发布通知，说明该公司的名称已从登记册中注销，并说明注销日期。在《肯尼亚公报》发布该通知时，该公司被认为已经解散。

请注意，如果公司实施下列行为，则不能向注册处提出注销申请：在申请前的3个月内更改了名称；正在开展业务；处置财产，且该财产是在停止经营之前为了在正常经营过程中获益而持有的；根据与破产有关的法律提出了关于公司的自愿安排的提议；已根据有关破产的法律向法院提出申请，要求就该公司作出破产管理的命令；法院已出具清算公司的申请文件；或者该公司从事过任何其他停止公司事务所必需的活动。

《公司法》明确这不是一个清算程序，但这的确为肯尼亚的公司提供了另一个终止途径来移除其在肯尼亚的任何公司机构。请注意，新《公司法》中的此项规定尚未被适用过。

（七）竞争条例

肯尼亚《竞争法》涵盖的主要领域是限制性交易行为，控制和固定价格，合并、收购以及控制无根据的经营者集中。下面将简要讨论这些专项问题。

1. 限制性交易行为

肯尼亚关于限制性交易行为的法律涵盖非常广泛的领域。它包括旨在减少或排除以下法人和自然人参与经济活动的行为，包括垄断协议、行业协会垄断、拒绝交易和歧视性交易、掠夺性交易行为、串通投标和在拍卖销售中合谋竞价的行为。

受害者可向委员会投诉，或者委员会可自行调查。委员会拥有广泛的权力，包括有权要求行为人停止行为。该要求通过委员会经公告的"承诺协议"来实现。如果没有"承诺协议"，那么将举行听证会，然后由部长作出必要的命令。要求停止行为的命令可能同时要求行为人采取积极措施协助现有或潜在的供应商、竞争对手或客户，以消除过去违规行为的影响。

部长命令发出的相对人有权向限制性交易行为仲裁庭上诉并最终向高等法院提出上诉。通常，大多数被控告的人倾向于与投诉人达成某种协议，此时大多数投诉都会消失，这使得调查过程非常艰难。

关于委员会自行发起的调查，通常，即使行为人否认其错误，其违法行为也会被停止。因此竞争管理局的监督职能对国民经济十分有利。

2. 兼并和收购

除非获得法律授权，两个或两个以上独立企业之间的兼并和收购本身是被禁止的。这种强制性的告知和授权程序必然使委员会在兼并和收购领域非常活跃。

委员会的观点是应引入某种门槛制度。否则，该委员会在这方面将非常有影响力。当并购被批准时，可能会被附加条件来减少合并或收购对竞争造成的负面影响。

3. 控制无根据的经营者集中

《竞争法》要求部长审查肯尼亚的产品和服务的生产和分配结构，以确定经营者集中对经济的不利影响是否超出了生产和销售一体化所带来的效率优势（如果有的话）。

竞争管理部门承担行业研究的任务，并在投标中力求完成这一法定任务。如有必要，部长可以命令任何他认为在任一部门进行无根据的经营者集中的人在生产、分配或服务提供方面处置其部分权益，因为情况紧急时可能有必要解除这种无根据的集中。

4. 控制和固定价格

自1994年10月以来，肯尼亚取消了价格管制。关于控制和固定价格的整个章节有望在适当的时候被废除。

5. 制度框架

肯尼亚的竞争案件由5个主要机构处理。分别为立法机关（议会）、财政部长办公室、垄断和价格专员办公室、限制性交易行为仲裁庭和肯尼亚高等法院。立法中明确规定了每个机构的职能、责任和权力。

（1）立法机关（议会）

议会是肯尼亚公共利益的主要管理者，它为促进和保护公共利益创造了制度和法律框架。在竞争领域，议会颁布了相关法律文件，即《限制性交易行为、垄断和价格管制法》。而且，由于市场是动态的，必须不时地审查管制市场运作的法律，以便使其与市场的动态变化相适应。

（2）财政部长办公室

肯尼亚竞争政策的责任总体归属于财政部长。该法第3（2）条规定，垄断和价格专员受部长指挥，专员通过部长命令，使部长关于市场的专业指示得以遵循。部长在很大程度上依赖垄断和价格专员的专业意见。专员的团队包括经济学家、财务分析师、律师和其他必要的市场分析师，该团队是肯尼亚竞争政策的主要管理者。

专员是根据第3节第1条任命的。他作为监督者，关注整体的商业活动，在有需要的情况下对其进行初步调查或下令进行深入调查。专员对所有可能情形下的反竞争行为，如限制性交易行为、滥用市场支配地位、兼并和收购等的调查活动负有首要责任。实际上，这些调查是由专员团队在垄断和价格委员会的工作人员中实施的。这些调查工作包括回应公司竞争对手或客户的投诉和对那些被认为存在竞争问题的市场进行非正式调查。

（3）垄断和价格专员办公室

根据肯尼亚《竞争法》第3（1）条的规定任命垄断和价格专员，他可根据法律赋予的权力，或依部长认为适合的限制，来直接或间接控制、管理和影响竞争。该法没有规定负责任命垄断和价格专员的权力机构。然而，一旦专员被任命，他即可独立拥有一系列的法定职责。他领导财政部垄断和价格司，负责有效的行政管理和《竞争法》的执行。他还在消费者保护领域负有责任。他寻求长期的消费者福利的最大化，并通过以下方式保护弱势消费者的利益：

① 通过提供信息和补救措施赋予消费者权力；
② 通过禁止权利滥用保护消费者权利；
③ 促进富有竞争力和责任感的供应商的发展。

（4）限制性交易行为仲裁庭（RTPT）

根据《限制性交易行为、垄断和价格管制法》第64（1）条，自1991年2月8日起每隔5年指定一个准司法机构，即限制性交易行为仲裁庭。限制性交易行为仲裁庭由1名主席和4名成员组成，该主席必须在肯尼亚高等法院任职不少于7年。限制性交易行为仲裁庭的成员有5年的固定任期，并可在 5 年期满时延续任期。

这里必须强调的是，一旦财政部长组建了限制性交易行为仲裁庭，限制性交易行为仲裁庭即绝对独立于部长办公室及垄断和价格专员办公室。仲裁庭的主要职能是仲裁因垄断和价格委员会建议的部长令而产生的竞争政策争议。当受损害的一方提起上诉时，限制性交易行为仲裁庭有权推翻、修改、确认或撤回部长令。

不服仲裁庭的命令和决定的只能向肯尼亚高等法院提出上诉，而且这种上诉需在仲裁庭的判决或命令通知有关方后的 30 天内提出。

（5）肯尼亚高等法院

限制性交易行为仲裁庭根据《限制性交易行为、垄断和价格管制法》第 20（1）、251 和 31（1）条的规定，对依据相应的第 18（1）、24（1）和 31（1）条的规定发出的部长命令作出决定。所有不服该限制性交易行为仲裁庭决定的上诉人，可以在该决定的通知送达后 30 天内向肯尼亚高等法院提起上诉，高等法院的判决是终局判决。

（八）证券

1. 内罗毕证券交易所（NSE）的权力

关于内罗毕证券交易所基本权力的具体规定在其基本文件《资本市场管理局（CMA）条例》《会员和交易规则》以及《上市手册》中。《资本市场法》没有直接提及其权力。虽然基本文件赋予证券交易所广泛的权力，但其行使权力要遵循《资本市场法》和根据该法制定的条例的规定，此类条款使得这些权利在很大程度上归于无效。

例如，虽然交易所有权鼓励任一公司收购资产、收购或持有其他公司股份，但资本市场管理局已将其股权限制在中央存管结算有限责任公司（CDSC）。

《管理和成员规则》《交易规则》和《上市手册》中所载的内罗毕证券交易所的使命同样要遵循《资本市场法》及其条例。一些例子充分地阐述了这一点。首先，交易所必须接纳资本市场管理局许可的所有公司为正式或准成员。第二，尽管证券交易所有权批准证券上市，但证监会批准的证券必须被"无条件"地接纳上市。第三，未经管理局事先批准，交易所制定的规则不可被修改、变更或撤销。同时，管理局有权对规则进行补充，并有权酌情废止这些规定。第四，未经管理局批准，交易所的成员资格不得被中止。此外，管理局除名成员的方式是拒绝续展或撤销其许可。第五，内罗毕证券交易所对成员或上市公司采取的任何处罚措施必须在 7 日内通知管理局。管理局有权根据自己的动议或受影响方的申请对决定进行审查，并有权在听取关于此事的证券交易所的意见之后废除该决定。第六，管理局批准交易所的年度预算。最后，交易所只能在资本市场管理局给予处罚的情况下决定成员停牌或退市。

只有一次报道称，2008 年一家上市公司向内罗毕证券交易所申请免除其因迟交财务报告而被处以的财务处罚。除此之外，没有证据表明内罗毕证券交易所对会员资格及其披露义务方面在进行积极执法。

此外，它既没有调查权，也没有追诉权，不能在其领域内执行《资本市场法》的规定。资本市场管理局对肯尼亚证券市场的监管权限延伸至中央存管结算有限责任公司（其附属机构）。

赋予公司的权力可以在资本市场管理局的权力范围内行使或与资本市场管理局协商行使。虽然中央存管结算有限责任公司有权任命中央存管代理人，但它只能与管理局"协商"后才能暂停或撤销其任命。2003 年《中央存管（业务）规则》所设想的协商的作用尚不明确。当中央存管结算有限责任公司暂停颁发公平银行有限责任公司的托管许可证（中央存管代理许可证）时，争议出现了。资本市场管理局命令中央存管结算有限责任公司立即恢复许可证，并承诺对两个实体之间的争议进行仲裁。资本市场管理局认为中央存管结算有限责任公司没有按照 2000 年《中央存管法》的规定批准暂停。令人惊讶的是，《中央存管法》并没有涉及解决暂停或撤销保管许可的问题，并且现在适用的规则仍然要求"协商"。

这些事例表明，虽然内罗毕证券交易所和中央存管结算有限责任公司似乎都享有某些权力，这些权力表面上由其他司法管辖区的自律组织行使，但这些权力受到《资本市场法》及其条例的严格限制。

不言而喻，证券市场的动态性，全球化的影响，技术进步和市场中介机构的不可靠性，使自我管制在许多方面变得不切实际。自律的效用逐渐被市场中介的贪婪破坏，因此需要政府大力干预。

因此，资本市场管理局对内罗毕证券交易所和市场中介机构行使全体立法权和监督权力。它的权力无处不在，在证券市场各个方面的首要地位都是无可争议的。这种包罗性权力在满足保护投资者和增强投资者信心方面的需求上是合理的。重要的是，资本市场管理局承认其全面的监督地位，并认为监管改革应该实现对自律组织的认可并赋予他们重大的权力和责任。在内罗毕证券交易所即将实施的将交易所的商业和监管职能分离的股份化背景下，这一点特别重要。

不言而喻，市场中介机构在证券市场的治理中发挥着至关重要的作用。资本市场管理局的公司事务部门可以通过与技术和经验更丰富的股票经纪人和投资银行联合会合作来提高投资者意识，从而获益匪浅。总之，资本市场管理局负责审慎监督证券交易所和其他市场中介机构的业务操作。

2. 有关外国投资者的证券法规

（1）《资本市场（外国投资者）条例》（2002年）

《资本市场（外国投资者）条例》（2002年）于2002年7月15日生效。根据该条例的规定，外国投资者是指任何非本地投资者。发行人是指根据东非共同体成员国的法律成立的公司或其他法律实体，向所有或一部分公众提供证券，无论这些证券是否为准入申请的对象或已被允许上市。机构投资者是指法人机构，包括金融机构、集体投资计划管理人、基金管理人、交易商或其他日常业务是作为委托人或代表客户管理或投资资金的法人团体；

该条例进一步定义了个人本地投资者，它指的是拥有东非共同体成员国公民身份的自然人。就法人团体而言，它将本地投资者定义为根据《公司法》或东非共同体成员国的任何成文法成立或注册的公司或任何其他法人团体，且东非共同体成员国的公民或政府在其普通股中拥有百分之百（100%）权益。

（2）外国投资者的参与

外国投资者的参与遵循《资本市场（外国投资者）条例》第3条的规定。该条规定，首次公开发行后发行人的任何有表决权的股份可供外国投资者投资，且不受任何持股水平的限制，除非《资本市场（收购与合并）规则》（2002年）另有规定。然而，尽管有此条例，内阁秘书仍然可以通过宪报公告规定发行人或上市公司的最大外资持股量。内阁秘书只能行使第3条第2款下的权力，在私有化交易中，政府或其代理机构将其股份出售给公众，但对国家战略性行业或部门，要维持一定程度的地方所有权以符合国家利益。

（3）肯尼亚境外上市股票的限制

根据《资本市场（外国投资者）条例》第9条的规定，资本市场管理局可能会指定部分股票或其他资本市场工具在肯尼亚境外挂牌，除非经资本市场管理局书面批准并经证券登记，任何人不得在肯尼亚向公众发行拟在境外上市公司的股票或其他资本市场工具。

（九）投资的优先和保护

在肯尼亚，投资的优先和保护受《外国投资保护法》管辖。它是对某些经核准的外国投资和其附带事项给予保护的一项议会立法。根据该法的规定，外国资产包括外国的货币、信贷、权利、利益或财产，通过外币支出获得的任何货币、信贷、权利、利益或财产，外国信贷，外国权利、利益或财产，以及根据第3条的规定就该企业的执照持有人在核准企业内投资所获得的利润。

1. 外国投资者可以申请并获得证书

根据《外国投资保护法》第3条的规定，拟向肯尼亚海外资产投资的外国公民可向财政部部长申请执照，证明其拟投资的企业为符合本法规定的核准企业。财政部部长须考虑根据第3条第1款提出的每一项申请，并且在他认为该企业将促进肯尼亚的经济发展或对肯尼亚有利的情况下，酌情向申请人颁发执照。

每份执照都应载明持证人的姓名、企业的名称和对企业的描述。还应该载明执照持有人在企业中投资或将要投资的海外资产的数额。这些资本代表企业持有者权益且应当符合本法案规定的固定数额，故应在执照中标明，其可以以肯尼亚货币或相关外币计价；就本法案而言，任何贷款均可以采用肯尼亚货币或相关外币计价。

该执照还应载明所投资或将投资的外币以及为实现本法的目的所必要或可能需要的其他事项。如果外国资产尚未投资,则应签发附条件的执照,除记载第3条第3款所规定的细节外,还应说明其出资期限。

在依本法颁发执照时,如果执照所涉及的外国资产或其中的一部分尚未投资于核准的企业,该笔资产应在批准的期限内投资,否则,该执照视为被撤销。

2. 投资促进和保护的特殊安排

法律还授权财政部长可不时通过《肯尼亚公报》公告声明,说明此安排是与其他国家的政府共同达成的,目的是为促进和保护外国投资人在肯尼亚的投资,使投资按其标书生效。

政府通过彻底修改影响商业便利的立法将重点放在吸引外商直接投资(FDI)和快速落实"肯尼亚2030愿景"的经济支柱上。鉴于出口加工区尚未对经济产生预期影响,其中一项重要举措就是推广经济特区。

3. 经济特区

肯尼亚总统于2015年9月11日批准《经济特区法》(2015年)(SEZ法案),该法随后于2015年9月15日发布。《经济特区法》的目的是通过对投资者提供有利的投资环境来促进全球和当地投资者的投资。经济特区必须在指定的地理区域建立,具体地区由工业发展内阁秘书在《肯尼亚公报》公告刊登。

(1)依该法颁发许可证

《经济特区法》规定,依该法可颁发下列许可证:

• 经营者许可——针对从事经济特区管理的公司实体;
• 开发者许可证——针对从事开发和运营经济特区的公司实体;
• 企业许可证——针对在经济特区开展业务的企业实体。

(2)经济特区类型

宣布为特别经济区的区域可以被指定为单一或多部门经济区,可以涵盖以下部门:

• 农业区:促进农业区域及相关活动和服务的经济特区;
• 业务处理外包(BPO):提供外包服务,如人力资源、财务、会计和采购等后台支持服务的经济特区;
• 商业服务园区:用以方便经济特区为地区总部提供服务,包括业务处理外包、呼叫中心、管理顾问、咨询服务和其他相关服务;
• 自由港区:指定的港口区域,进入此地的货物被视为处于关境(东非共同体成员国)之外;
• 自由贸易区:海关控制区,货物在此卸载后进行转运、仓储,可能包括拆除包装、重新包装、分拣、混合、交易或其他形式的处理,但不包括制造和加工;
• 工业园区:基础设施完备的区域,便于促进制造业和加工业的发展;
• 通信技术园区:促进信息通信技术行业及其服务和相关活动的发展;
• 畜牧区:进行牲畜调度、检疫、喂养、育肥、屠宰、冷藏、剔骨、增值以及兽医产品制造和其他相关活动的区域;
• 科学技术园区:发展科技行业的区域;
• 旅游和娱乐中心:发展旅游和娱乐行业的区域。

(3)经济特区管理局

经济特区将由经济特区管理局管理,其职责为:

• 审查申请并向经济特区开发商、运营商和企业授予许可;
• 向潜在的开发商、运营商和其他投资者推广经济特区;
• 实施政府的政策和计划;
• 确定、规划并向开发商和运营商提供指定为经济特区的土地;
• 确定投资标准和门槛;

- 管理一站式中心，通过该中心，经济特区企业可以提交所有有关许可证、审批、执照和设施等的申请，由其转交给受理机构。

（4）经济特区商品和服务贸易

经济特区生产的商品和服务可以出口到国外，或像从境外进口（须遵守海关规定）一样在肯尼亚境内出售，或在经济特区内用于制造其他商品或提供其他服务。

（5）成为经济特区开发者或企业的资格

在注册成为经济特区开发商或企业前，需满足以下要求：
- 在肯尼亚注册成立；
- 具备实施经济特区拟开展业务的财务能力和技术专长；
- 在经济特区内拥有或租有土地或房屋；
- 从事在经济特区有资格从事的任何活动；
- 不应对环境产生负面影响或参与威胁国家安全的活动。

（6）在肯尼亚经济特区经营的优惠

《经济特区法》规定了各种优惠，例如：

① 税收豁免

根据《消费税法》《所得税法》《东非共同体海关管理法》和《增值税法》的规定，对所有经济特区的企业、开发商和运营商应免除所有应缴税款包括（关税）。

② 其他豁免

经济特区企业、开发商和经营者也可享受如下豁免：
- 与经济特区商业活动有关的文书的印花税；
- 《外国投资和保护法》的规定；
- 《统计法》的规定；
- 郡政府征收的广告费和商业服务许可费；
- 2010年《酒精控制法》规定的普通酒类牌照和宾馆酒类牌照；
- 《茶叶法》规定的制造许可证；
- 未经加工的贵重金属贸易许可；
- 制片许可；
- 租赁或租金控制；
- 依据《肯尼亚公报》通知，法律可能授予的任何其他豁免。

③ 工作许可

经济特区允许有最多可占劳动力总人数20%的外籍人士，且可获得工作许可，并可根据要求获得额外的工作许可。

④ 其他优惠
- 保护财产免遭国有化和征用；
- 没有任何外汇障碍的资本和利润回流；
- 保护知识产权。

（7）争议解决

《经济特区法》设立了争议解决机制，以解决经济特区实体与管理局或政府之间可能出现的任何争端。通过谈判和双边协商解决争议的期限是30天。争议未解决的，当事人应当在14日内将争议提交仲裁。

（8）处罚

《经济特区法》规定，对于任何违反该法规定的人员，处以高达2 000万肯尼亚先令的罚款或最长3年的监禁或二者并罚，并没收货物。

三、贸易

（一）贸易监管部门

根据肯尼亚《宪法》的规定，贸易监管由中央政府和 47 个郡政府共同完成。

工业和贸易合作部是国家政府促进贸易、工业化和企业发展以及国际贸易监管的主要机构。该部由三个国家部门组成：国家贸易部、国家投资与产业部和国家合作部。

另一方面，郡政府负责各自郡的贸易发展和规制，包括市场、贸易许可（不包括行业监管）、公平贸易惯例，以及当地旅游业和合作社。

（二）贸易法律、法规简介

肯尼亚没有规范贸易的一般法律。有关贸易的规定散见于以下立法条文中。

肯尼亚《海关法》第 472 章是规定肯尼亚货物进出口的主要法律。该法规定了货物进出肯尼亚应适用的关税。该法还禁止某些货物的进出口，如未经法律授权的火器和弹药、假币或假票据、变性烈酒、淫秽物品和含有香精油或化学产品对健康有害的蒸馏饮料等。肯尼亚税务局局长在内阁财政部长的监督下负责确保《海关法》的实施。

其他进出口货物禁令载于其他国会立法，包括 1998 年的禁止在肯尼亚处理或处置有害物质的《环境管理和协调法》以及肯尼亚的《禁止进口货物贸易法》。

各郡制定本郡管辖范围内的贸易活动法规。

（三）贸易管理

肯尼亚颁布了若干旨在管理贸易的法律，其中包括肯尼亚的《投资促进法》，该法规定肯尼亚的外商独资企业有权申请投资证书。该证书赋予企业获得所有该企业所需的必要许可证和外籍员工的某些工作许可的权利，并要求企业在 1 年内获得这些许可证，在此期间内允许企业可以在没有许可证的情况下运营。

另一方面，《外商投资保护法》旨在保护外国投资者免受歧视，并根据《宪法》规定适用公平公正的征收规则。

《出口加工区法》和《经济特区法》下的经济特区旨在通过给予额外的税收优惠和豁免，以吸引更多的本地和外国投资。

国家政府设立了一个名为 Huduma 中心的一站式服务中心，在此中心可以及时有效地享受到所有政府和公共服务。政府还有一个名为 eCitizen 的在线门户网站，它是一个数字支付平台，使肯尼亚公民、居民和游客能够获得政府服务并为之付款，如签证申请、公司注册和网上许可申请。各郡政府还建立了在线平台，向各郡居民提供网上支付途径。

（四）进出口商品的检验检疫

《标准法》规定了商品标准和业务守则。

肯尼亚根据《标准法》设立了肯尼亚标准局（KEBS），其职能是起草、制定、修订或修改规范和业务守则。该法还设立了国家标准委员会，可以通过《肯尼亚公报》公告宣布由肯尼亚标准局制定的任何规范或准则为肯尼亚的国家标准。

肯尼亚标准局负责管理进口货物符合质量标准（PVoC）的出口前验证。质量标准的总体目标是最大限度地降低不安全和不合格产品进入肯尼亚市场的风险，从而确保肯尼亚人的健康、安全和肯尼亚的环境保护。进口商有责任确保进口货物符合肯尼亚的标准或批准的规格。

如果是由肯尼亚标准局列入的进口货物，应由肯尼亚标准局授权的检验机构以肯尼亚标准或原产国认可的规格进行核查。如需要，可在主管局的入境口岸进行复验。肯尼亚标准局随后应颁发合格证书或不合格报告。不合格货物将不允许进入肯尼亚，并应由进口商承担费用予以重新装运、退回或销毁。任何到达入境口岸的没有合格证书的货物，都会被收取货物成本、保险和货运价值的 15% 的费用以及与上述费用等价的执行保证金。

《标准法》进一步规定，在肯尼亚，任何人都必须按照符合有关方法、程序的规定或行为准则来制造或销售商品。此外，符合标准的商品和产品须贴上标准化商标。

《植物保护法》和《农产品（出口）法》为植物的进出口以及进出口适用的标准提供了立法框架。肯尼亚植物检疫局（KEPHIS）根据该法管理植物的进口和出口。

（五）海关管理

根据《海关税法》的规定，肯尼亚税务局局长按照内阁财政部长的指示负责控制和管理海关和执行部门，以及收缴关税和核算肯尼亚关税收入。

2000年7月成立的东非共同体旨在扩大和深化成员国（即布隆迪、肯尼亚、卢旺达、南苏丹、坦桑尼亚和乌干达）之间在政治、经济和社会领域的合作互利。该条约强调在运输和通信、贸易和工业、安保、移民，以及促进地区投资这些优先领域的合作。

为此，东非共同体合作伙伴国于2005年建立了关税同盟。2004年《东非共同体海关管理法》（EACCMA）是根据《建立东非共同体议定书》制定，是已被采纳且生效的用于管理东非共同体关税同盟的法律。

根据该法的规定，伙伴国之间的货物流动不构成"进口"或"出口"，而是构成共同体内货物的"转移"。货物进口或出口是指货物从伙伴国以外的其他国家的输入或输出。

该法涉及出口加工区（EPZ's）和自由港的规定是，根据东非共同体《海关联盟议定书》，进入这些区域的货物应免税。但该法并没有涉及经济特区的概念。

根据该法案，同盟委员拥有如下权力：

① 允许在出口加工区或自由港内取走货物供家庭消费，但须缴纳应交税款。在没有委员授权的情况下从这些区域取走货物将涉嫌犯罪；

② 指定办理海关手续的出口加工区和自由港。

《东非共同体海关管理法》还要求，出口加工区运营商或自由港运营商授权的任何工业、商业或服务活动必须事先通知同盟委员。

肯尼亚还是东南非共同市场等几个贸易区块的成员。此外，一个涉及东南非共同市场、东非共同体和南部非洲发展共同体的三方自由贸易区（TFTA）正在计划设立中，这将成为非洲最大的自由贸易区。肯尼亚已经签署了声明，表明它有意成为TFTA的成员。自1995年1月1日起，肯尼亚成为世界贸易组织（WTO）的成员，自1964年2月5日起成为关税及贸易总协定（GATT）的缔约方，自2007年11月起成为欧盟经济伙伴协定的一员。这些国际协议都为海关管理提供了规则。

四、劳动

（一）劳动法规简介

在肯尼亚，劳工事宜主要由以下法律规定：

① 2010年肯尼亚《宪法》规定了劳动关系和各类人员的劳动权利；

② 2007年《就业法》确立了雇员的基本权利，为肯尼亚的就业基本条件提供了法定的最低雇用期限和条件；

③ 2011年《就业与劳动关系法院法》设立了就业与劳动关系法院，并规定了其目标、组成、管辖和程序；

④ 2007年《劳资关系法》规定了雇主与工会之间的关系；

⑤ 2007年《劳工机构法》建立了肯尼亚劳工机构；

⑥ 2007年《工作福利和工伤法》规定了雇员在工作中受伤的工伤赔偿；

⑦ 2007年《职业安全与卫生法》规定了保障在工作场所的工作人员和合法在场人员的安全、健康和福利。

（二）雇用外籍雇员的要求

1. 工作许可证

2011年肯尼亚《公民和移民法》（以下简称《移民法》）以及肯尼亚《公民和移民条例》（以下简称《移民条例》）规定，任何外国人必须首先获得工作许可或特别通行证才能在肯尼亚工作。非肯尼亚公民在肯尼亚持有有效的工作许可、居留许可或通行证，即为合法。

根据《移民法》的规定，在雇佣关系成立之前，所有雇主必须为外籍雇员申请并获得授予外国人就业权利的工作许可证或特殊通行证。在实践中，申请并获得工作许可证或特殊通行证的费用由雇主承担。

移民局被授权通过签发和续签入境许可证和其他通行证来控制和规范居住权。

工作许可分为从A级到M级的不同级别。每个级别适用于满足特定要求的特定人员。

例如，D类许可证签发给由肯尼亚政府、联合国组织或其他一些经批准的机构批准的技术援助计划的特定雇主雇用的外籍人员。

为了获得工作许可证，外籍人员必须满足以下条件：

① 个人必须拥有在肯尼亚无法获得的技能或资格，并且他们参与这项工作对肯尼亚有益；

② 外籍人员必须有一名替补的肯尼亚公民，替补人员应该接受培训，以接手该外籍人员申请的职位；

③ 外籍人员必须按照《移民条例》规定的金额存入保证金。这笔款项存放在肯尼亚公民和外国公民管理处，金额大小根据发放许可证的类型有所不同。移民局长有权允许外国人签署保函提供保证以代替押金，可以要求或不要求提供保证人。入境事务处处长亦可准许雇主订立合同，为雇员及其配偶、子女及其他受养人提供保证金。

目前，移民申请需要2～4个月才能获得批准。如果申请人希望在短时间内开始工作，可以申请特别通行证。特别通行证是发给移民局的短期批准文件，有效期为6个月，不可续期。

2. 申请程序

通常，雇主将向移民局的外国国民服务（eFNS）电子系统提交工作许可申请。虽然有关各类工作许可证的申请文件各不相同，但以下文件对于所有申请都是必需的：

① 填妥并签名的申请表格；

② 雇主/本人/组织签署的致移民局局长的求职信；

③ 护照复印件；

④ 两张最近的彩色护照照片；

⑤ 当前的移民身份（如已在国内）。

如果移民局局长认为就该特定类型的要求全部达到，并且申请人在肯尼亚的存在对肯尼亚有利，则签发许可证。

如果雇员因任何原因停止为雇主工作，则工作许可证中规定的雇主必须在15日内以书面形式向入境事务处处长报告，证明许可证持有人已停止许可证所载的雇佣关系，否则此雇主将涉嫌犯罪。

如果没有遵守申请和注册程序，雇主和雇员都会受到严厉的处罚。如果法律没有特别规定，对于此类犯罪的一般刑罚为100万肯尼亚先令以下的罚金或5年以下的监禁。

3. 社会保险

现有的国家养老金制度是2013年《全国社会保障基金法》中规定的全国社会保障基金制度（NSSF）。

全国社会保障基金按照确定缴费基数运营，根据该制度，成员退休时应领取的金额取决于基金投资在一段时间内的情况以及缴费总额。缴费由雇主和雇员共同完成。

全国社保基金涵盖以下几种单位的雇主和雇员：

① 私营部门，包括非正式部门的公司、非政府组织、国际组织和组织团体；

② 政府部委；

③ 半国营机构；
④ 个体经营者或任何其他没被纳入任何保险计划的人；
⑤ 劳动、社会和安全部宣布的任何其他人员。

《全国社会保障基金法》将员工定义为"任何年满18岁且根据服务合同在肯尼亚就业的人"。因其定义范围之广，外籍雇员也必须向该基金缴费。

然而，《全国社会保障基金法》免除了以下人士在基金下注册的义务：
① 根据任何国际公约有权豁免缴纳社会保险的人员；
② 通常不在肯尼亚居住的人；一次性在肯尼亚就业的时间不超过3年的人；内阁秘书以书面形式批准的，有权或应当有权从任何其他国家的社会保险基金或类似机构中受益的人。

除强制性的社会保障基金计划外，雇员可选择加入职业计划或个人退休金计划。职业计划由雇主为其员工的利益而设立。这些计划是在自愿的且相互信任的情况下建立。另一方面，个人养老金计划由机构提供者（主要是金融机构）设立，专门为一些不能明确界定雇主或正式职业的个人采用。

国家健康保险由《国家健康保险基金法》中规定的国家健康保险基金（NHIF）负责。该法规定了有责任向基金缴款的主体：任何定居在肯尼亚且年满18岁的人。定居居民包括被允许在肯尼亚工作或学习的外国游客。

除国家健康保险基金外，外籍员工可以向其雇主提供的私人医疗保险计划缴纳费用。

（三）出入境

1. 签证类型

进入肯尼亚境内的签证类型取决于许多因素，例如访问的目的和预计访问持续的时间。《移民条例》明确规定了侨民免签进入肯尼亚的人员和国家，还规定了可以依申请向其侨民发放签证的国家。

打算通过肯尼亚境内至第三方目的地而在肯尼亚境内停留不超过3天的人可以获得过境签证。此签证允许此人在这段时间内离开机场。

因其国籍需要签证才能进入肯尼亚访问或居留的人将获得单程或普通签证，有效期限应在签证中注明。

需要签证的国家的国民，如果因业务或形势需要经常访问肯尼亚，可能将获得多次往返签证。

执行公务的外交护照持有者可免费获得外交签证。必须指出，对肯尼亚进行私人访问的外交官和政府官员，如果属于需要提供签证的国家的国民，也必须以常规的方式申请签证。

应向持有官方或公务护照的公务人员和持有普通护照且没有外交签证的人员（被认为应该具有国际礼仪的情形）颁发官方或礼遇签证，有效期限亦会在签证中注明。

2. 出入境限制

如果正在离境的外国人被发现其违反《移民法》而在该国逾期居留，移民官员应通知其可选择书面承认违规行为。

在收到上述书面承认后，移民官员可以对其处以不超过5万肯尼亚先令的罚款。移民官员可以起诉任何不立即支付罚金的人。

根据该法被归类为禁止移民的人以及没有有效许可证或通行证的人将被禁止进入肯尼亚。

（四）工会和劳工组织

肯尼亚《宪法》第41条和《劳资关系法》第233章涉及雇主或雇员组建的工会，规定组建工会是雇主和雇员的权利。这意味着雇主或雇员可以选择是否加入或组建工会。

肯尼亚法律没有强制组建工会的要求。

（五）劳动争议

劳动纠纷由劳动关系法院（ELRC）裁定。劳动关系法院的成立的目的是为了受理和判决与就业和劳动关系有关的纠纷。

《就业法》明确规定，当雇主或雇员忽视或拒绝履行服务合同时，当出现与任何一方的权利或义务有关的问题，变更或争议，或在任何服务合同下侵犯任何一方的不当行为、疏忽，或任何一方的虐待，以及关于任何一方的人身或财产受到侵害的纠纷，劳动关系法院是唯一可以受理和解决争议的法院。

希望将争议诉诸劳动关系法院的一方当事人可以依据任何成文法提出申诉、请求或申请司法复审程序。

《就业和劳动关系法院法》规定，任何情况下都不排除 ELRC 自行或应当事方要求采取和执行任何其他适当的争议解决方式，包括内部方法、和解、调解和宪法第 159（2）（c）条规定的传统争端解决机制。

《劳资关系法》还规定了劳资纠纷的争议解决机制。劳资纠纷是指雇主与雇员之间、雇主和工会之间、雇主组织与雇员或工会之间的任何关于雇佣事宜的争议，包括关于解雇、停职或员工冗余、工作分配或工会认可的争议。

根据该法的规定，作为争议一方的工会、雇主、雇主组织或其授权代表须向负责就业事务的内阁秘书报告劳资纠纷。在劳资纠纷报告后 21 日内，内阁秘书应指定一名调解人解决劳资纠纷。除非对争议当事人具有约束力的集体协议中的调解程序尚未用尽，否则法律或对双方有约束力的集体协议禁止就争议问题进行协商。

如果任何一方对此决定不服，可将此争议提交给就业与劳动关系法院。

五、知识产权

（一）知识产权法律、法规简介

知识产权保护是国家政府的职能。因此，肯尼亚的所有关于知识产权的立法和条例都是在国家一级制定的。

肯尼亚还加入了许多知识产权条约和国际组织，为知识产权人提供更多保护，这些条约包括《商标国际注册马德里协定》及其议定书，《专利合作条约》《保护文学和艺术作品伯尔尼公约》《保护工业产权巴黎公约》《与贸易有关的知识产权协定》，以及非洲地区工业产权组织框架内的《专利和工业品外观设计哈拉雷议定书》等。

1. 专利保护

肯尼亚的专利由 2001 年《知识产权法》规制。《知识产权法》的制定旨在为专利、实用新型、技术和工业品外观设计的获取、授予和管理提供立法框架。

依据《知识产权法》设立有肯尼亚工业产权局（KIPI），该机构负责审议和批准各种工业产权申请，筛选并注册技术转让协议和许可证，向公众提供技术和经济发展的工业产权信息以及在肯尼亚推动创新。

依《知识产权法》还设立有工业产权法庭，审理和裁定被肯尼亚工业产权局局长拒绝注册知识产权的人的上诉。

涉及的其他机构包括非洲地区工业产权组织，已经向其提交了区域备案文件以及"国际申请专利合作条约"。

知识产权保护期限为 20 年，须缴纳年费。

2. 商标保护

肯尼亚《商标法》是肯尼亚商标管理的主要立法文件。根据《商标法》制定的《商标规则》规定了更多适用的条款。

商标一经注册，有效期为 10 年。

就标志和图形元素的注册而言，肯尼亚采纳《商标注册用商品和服务国际分类尼斯协定》和《建立商标图形要素国际分类维也纳协定》。

3. 版权保护

肯尼亚的版权保护由肯尼亚《版权法》规定，该法规定了保护文学、音乐和艺术作品、音像作品、录音和广播版权的立法框架。

依《版权法》建立了肯尼亚版权委员会，这是一个受委托管理肯尼亚版权相关事宜的法人团体。版权委员会的主要职能包括：指导、协调和监督与版权有关的法律的实施，提高公众版权意识以及维护作者及其作品的有效数据库。

2004年《版权条例》规定了版权作品的注册。肯尼亚版权局执行主任的任务是开设和维护名为"版权注册"的注册簿，用以记录注册版权作品的详情。

注册的目的是将版权作品记录下来，使版权委员会能够建立和维护有关作者及其作品的有效数据库，并将作品所有者的权利公之于众。作者对版权作品的注册是自愿的，注册不是保护版权的先决条件。

版权作品的注册程序有以下步骤：
① 以肯尼亚版权局的规定格式提交申请，并附交《版权条例》规定的费用；
② 如果作品被认为符合《版权法》规定的相关标准，肯尼亚版权委员会执行主任在收到申请后，在版权登记处记录此类作品；
③ 随后颁发注册证书。

肯尼亚还是《保护文学和艺术作品伯尔尼公约》的缔约国，该公约在其他缔约国内为肯尼亚的版权持有人提供更广泛的保护。

4. 工业设计保护

《知识产权法》管理肯尼亚的工业品外观设计。该法将工业品外观设计定义为线条、颜色或任何三维图形组成的整体，不一定与线条或颜色相关，只要这种组合物或图形在工业品或手工艺产品上形成了特殊的外观，并可作为图案印于工业品或手工艺产品上即可。

肯尼亚的工业品外观设计申请向肯尼亚工业产权局提交。

5. 专利申请

根据《知识产权法》的规定，如果一项发明是新的，具有创造性并可在工业上适用，则该项发明可被授予专利。专利申请须向肯尼亚工业产权局局长提交。

专利注册程序有以下步骤：
① 准备和提交专利申请；
② 审查申请（自申请日起3年内）；
③ 审查员批准申请，要求提交更多资料或拒绝申请；
④ 如果要求提交更多资料，须向审查员作出答复；
⑤ 审查员批准、重新考虑或要求进一步修改申请；
⑥ 如果审查员批准申请，即为同意授予专利（如果拒绝授予专利，申请人可以就下列程序提出上诉）；
⑦ 在《肯尼亚公报》或工业产权杂志上公布专利内容；
⑧ 授予专利。

注册专利的时间约为18个月。

如果专利申请被驳回，申请人可以向工业产权法庭提出上诉。不服工业产权法庭裁决的可向肯尼亚高等法院上诉。不服肯尼亚高等法院裁决的可向肯尼亚上诉法院上诉。

6. 商标注册

若商标符合以下任一条件，即可在肯尼亚注册：
① 以特殊方式表示的个人或公司的名称；
② 申请人或其前任的签名；
③ 一个或多个新创的单词；
④ 没有提及货物的特征和质量并且不包含地理名称或别名的词；
⑤ 任何与众不同的标志。

在肯尼亚申请注册商标的程序有如下步骤：
① 在肯尼亚工业产权局注册处进行搜索以确定拟议商标的可用性；
② 以规定格式填写和提交申请表，详细说明拟议的商标及其所有人；

③ 审查；

④ 经批准后，商标应在肯尼亚工业产权局的月刊上刊登公告，任何人均可在 60 日内提出反对声明；

⑤ 在没有异议的情况下，商标注册处处长应当自公告发布之日起 60 天内注册登记该商标，并向注册申请人出具注册证书。

7. 知识产权保护

肯尼亚制定了一个强大的法律框架来打击与知识产权有关的违法行为。《商标法》禁止涉及商标的各种罪行，对伪造注册商标的处以不超过 20 万肯尼亚先令的罚金和 / 或不超过 5 年的监禁，对伪造登记册的处以 5 年以下有期徒刑和 / 或 1 万肯尼亚先令以下的罚金。

此外，肯尼亚于 2008 年颁布了《反假冒法》，该法建立了一个反假冒机构，负责打击肯尼亚制造假冒商品和买卖假冒商品的行为。

根据《知识产权法》的规定，任何故意侵犯专利或注册实用新型或工业品外观设计的行为均构成犯罪，可处以 3 年以上 5 年以下监禁和 / 或 1 万肯尼亚先令以上 5 万肯尼亚先令以下的罚金。

此外，根据《版权法》的规定，侵犯版权的行为可导致 10 万肯尼亚先令至 40 万肯尼亚先令罚金和 2 至 10 年监禁。版权所有者还有权享受各种补救措施，包括损害赔偿、禁令和代替特许权使用费和物品交付的赔偿金。

六、环境保护

（一）环境保护监督部门

《宪法》将肯尼亚的环境和自然资源保护责任授予中央政府。环境和自然资源部的内阁秘书负责制定政策、指导和国家目标，并决定保护环境的政策和优先事项。

根据法律成立的国家环境管理局（NEMA）负责对所有与环境有关的事务进行全面监督和协调，是政府执行所有与环境有关事务的主要机构。

在肯尼亚履行环境职能的其他机构包括肯尼亚林务局、渔业局和野生动物局。

（二）环境保护法律、法规简介

1999 年的《环境管理和协调法》是肯尼亚环境管理和保护的主要法律，该法对河流、湖泊、海洋、湿地、山区、森林和其他重要环境区域提供了保护。

该法涵盖的其他领域包括：环境审计和监测、环境质量标准、环境规划以及综合环境影响评估、检查、分析和记录。该法还建立了各种执法机构，包括国家环境管理局、国家环境法庭和环境与土地法院来裁定环境纠纷。此外，该法将若干行为定义为刑事犯罪，处罚范围从 100 万肯尼亚先令至 500 万肯尼亚先令的罚款以及 1 年至 4 年的监禁不等。为了落实该法的规定，另外颁布了 13 项条例。

其他法律，如 2016 年《森林保护和管理法》、2013 年《野生动物保护和管理法》以及 2016 年《渔业管理和发展法》等，也在环境保护方面起着补充作用。

（三）评估环境保护

从上面列举的各种立法规定来看，肯尼亚的环境立法框架在很大程度上是非常先进的。肯尼亚也批准了若干与环境有关的国际条约。但是在一些地区，执法仍然存在问题。

七、争议解决

（一）解决争端的方式和机构

1. 解决纠纷的普通法系统

肯尼亚的法律体系从英国普通法体系继承而来。普通法的基本原则之一是遵循先例原则，即下级法院必须遵循上级法院的裁决,而且上诉法院也必须遵循自己先前的裁决。

2. 法院层级

根据肯尼亚《宪法》的规定,法院分为两个级别,高等法院和基层法院。其组成如下:

(1)高等法院

① 最高法院——是肯尼亚最高一级的法院,只能受理和裁定与总统办公室选举有关的争议,以及不服上诉法院和国家立法规定的其他法院或法庭判决的上诉。

来自上诉法院的上诉只能是涉及肯尼亚《宪法》的解释或适用权利的争议,以及最高法院或上诉法院认为与公众重要利益有关的其他案件。

最高法院也可以应国家政府、国家机关或郡政府的请求提供咨询意见。

② 上诉法院——肯尼亚第二高级别的法院,受理高等法院和议会法案规定的其他法院或法庭的上诉。

③ 高等法院——该法院在刑事和民事方面拥有无限的初始管辖权,这意味着它可以受理和裁定任何实际事项。

它还有权受理有关人权法案中的权利或基本自由是否被剥夺、违反、侵犯或威胁的案件,受理就根据《宪法》任命的审判庭的裁决提出的上诉和任何有关宪法解释的问题。

④ 就业和劳动关系法院——是具有高等法院地位的专门法院。它受理和裁定与劳动和就业事务有关的争议。

⑤ 环境与土地法院——是另一个具有高等法院地位的专门法院。该院受理和裁定有关土地和环境问题以及处理土地和环境问题的所有法庭的上诉。

(2)基层法院

① 地方法院——根据涉案金额的大小,这些法庭分别由1名首席裁判官,1名高级主任裁判官,1名主任判官,1名高级地方治安官或1名地方治安官主持。例如,地方治安官可以判决标的物价值不超过500万肯尼亚先令的案件,而首席裁判官可以审理并判决标的物价值不超过2 000万肯尼亚先令的案件。

② 卡迪斯法院——其管辖范围仅限于当所有当事人都信奉伊斯兰教并服从卡迪斯法院管辖时,关于与个人身份、婚姻、离婚或继承有关的穆斯林法问题。

③ 军事法庭——根据《武装部队法》的规定,军事法庭有权审判任何受《武装部队法》规制的人并有权执行刑罚。

3. 专门法庭

在肯尼亚,专门法庭是由《议会法案》建立的行使司法或准司法职能的机构。每个法庭的任命和构成均有所不同。专门法庭对普通法院的司法起补充作用,但它们没有刑事管辖权。

专门法庭和法院一样,必须在其决定中尊重《人权法案》,不得作出不符合正义和道德、违背宪法或本国其他法律的判决。大多数专门法庭都受到高等法院的监督。

在肯尼亚有许多不同类型的专门法庭。肯尼亚精神健康法庭等一些法庭的功能仅限于调控和咨询,而其他诸如租赁法庭和所得税法庭则可以裁决公民之间或公民与公共机构之间的纠纷。

4. 案件审理程序

案件材料须在相关的法院登记处亲自提交,相应的法院登记处会给案件分配一个案件编号。对于民事诉讼,在每一方都提交并送达诉状或答辩之后,各方再填写并提交给法庭一份预审问卷,之后召开案件会议。案件会议可以帮助法院确定争议焦点,并确定其进行诉讼的方式。法院还可以帮助当事方解决全部或部分案件争议。

法院随后举行庭审会议来确认开庭时间和最快的开庭方式。庭审会议结束后,法院再公布开庭日期。

开庭时,原告有权先行陈述案件。原告陈述案件时需提交口头和书面证据。原告陈述完毕后,被告开始陈述案件、传唤证人,以及提供口头和书面证据。最后双方可提交最终意见书,之后法院确定判决日。庭审结束后,法院将在审判结束后60天内作出判决。

宣读判决结果后，书记官起草、盖章并发布法院命令或法令。该命令或法令应反映法院的判决，并应分段落阐明判决结果。

5. 替代性争议解决程序

《宪法》第 159 条规定了解决争议的其他形式，包括和解、调解、仲裁和传统争端解决机制。这些争议解决方法在不违反《人权法案》，不违反司法公正以及《宪法》或其他任何成文法的情况下均应被推广适用。

对于民事诉讼，根据《民事诉讼法》的规定，如果双方同意或法院认为案件适合如此，诉讼可转用任何其他争议解决方法。其他替代性争议解决方法应受双方自己同意的条件或法院酌情决定的命令的规制。

任何由诉讼引起的、由法院或当事人协议采纳的其他争议解决方法得出的结果，均可作为法院判决得以强制执行，且不可上诉。

（1）仲裁

1995 年的《仲裁法》（2010 年修订）是肯尼亚管理仲裁的首要法律。尽管该法并没有明确规定何种争议禁止仲裁，但人们普遍认为刑事纠纷不可仲裁。

肯尼亚是 1958 年《承认及执行外国仲裁裁决公约》（以下简称《纽约公约》）的缔约国。肯尼亚于 1989 年签署了该公约并提出互惠保留。《仲裁法》规定，根据《纽约公约》和肯尼亚签署的有关仲裁裁决的其他公约的规定，肯尼亚承认国际仲裁裁决的约束力和执行力。

根据《仲裁法》的规定，在下列情况下，仲裁裁决不论在哪个国家作出，都可能被拒绝：

① 仲裁协议当事人无行为能力；

② 仲裁协议按照属人原则无效，或按法律的指示无效，或根据仲裁裁决所在国的法律无效；

③ 申请仲裁裁决的当事人没有得到有关仲裁员的指定或仲裁程序的通知，进而未有机会对案件进行陈述；

④ 仲裁裁决涉及不属于仲裁条款所规定或不在仲裁条款范围内的争议，或者裁决了超出仲裁范围的事项；

⑤ 仲裁庭的组成或仲裁程序不符合当事人的协议，或者当事人未能达成任何协议，或者违背仲裁地的法律；

⑥ 仲裁裁决尚未对当事人产生约束力，或者裁决已被裁决制定国的法院或根据该国法律被撤销或中止；

⑦ 仲裁裁决的作出涉及欺诈、贿赂、腐败或可能产生不正当影响。

国内和国际仲裁的主要机构是特许仲裁员协会（肯尼亚分会）、内罗毕国际仲裁中心和国际商会仲裁院以及伦敦国际仲裁院。

（2）和解

《就业法》《劳工机构法》和《劳资关系法》对通过和解程序解决争议有所规定。和解协议必须为书面形式并由当事双方和调解人签名。

（3）调解

调解是自愿的、非正式的、合意的、严格保密的、不具约束力的争议解决程序，主要按照不同的肯尼亚调解机构制定的规则进行。

在肯尼亚，调解争议的机构有特许仲裁员协会肯尼亚分会、内罗毕国际仲裁中心、调解培训协会和斯特拉斯莫尔争议解决中心。依当事人的同意，这些机构用其自行制定的规则来进行调解。

（4）法院调解

2016 年，肯尼亚司法部门推出了法院附带调解程序。这是在法庭程序内进行的调解程序。迄今为止，该项目已在内罗毕 Milimani 高等法院的家庭和商业司内试行。

所有向家庭和商业部门提交的案件都由调解副登记官（MDR）审查，以评估案件是否适合调解。一旦将案件进入调解程序，调解副登记官将通知当事方这一决定，然后提名 3 名司法部门认可的调解员。

一旦当事双方被告知 3 名被提名调解员的信息，当事双方可以按照先后排序选择他们偏好的调解员,并以书面形式通知调解副登记官他们的选择。当事双方也可以从司法部门认可的调解员中自由选择调解员。随后调解副登记官任命选定的调解员来处理案件。

调解程序应在提交调解之日起 60 日内完成。此期间可延长 10 天。当各方达成协议,他们将在 10 天内签署调解协议并将其提交给调解副登记官。如果没有达成协议,调解员会通知调解副登记官,然后由法院以一般程序处理案件。

（5）传统的争端解决机制

传统的争端解决机制（TDRM）受到了肯尼亚 2010 年《宪法》第 159 条的认可和保护。传统的争端解决机制在解决冲突方面尤其是对发生在肯尼亚牧民社区之间的自然资源冲突非常有效。

所使用的一些机制包括协商、和解、非正式调解、长老理事会调解、当地长老和解决问题协调会调解。

实施这些机制的唯一限制是不得违反《人权法案》,不得违背正义和道德,不得违反《宪法》或其他任何成文法的规定。

（二）法律的适用

在法庭提起诉讼之前,当事人必须确保其选择的法院有管辖权。

通常,除非《仲裁法》另有规定,法院不会干预双方同意提交仲裁的事宜。如果法院诉讼案件涉及仲裁协议,法院可在收到申请后中止诉讼程序并将此事提交仲裁。

如果外国法院具有类似的管辖权来受理和裁判肯尼亚法院管辖的案件,肯尼亚法院可酌情决定是否行使其管辖权。由认为外国法院更适合管辖此案的一方承担举证责任。

例如,如果合同双方约定同意接受外国法律的约束,或因合同引起的任何争议在外国法院解决,肯尼亚法院通常会支持此类协议。

如果争议由与肯尼亚签有互惠执行协议的国家的法院受理和裁判,则适用《外国判决（互惠执行）法》。根据该法的规定,与肯尼亚有互惠协议的国家有澳大利亚、马拉维、塞舌尔、坦桑尼亚、乌干达、赞比亚、卢旺达和英国。

如果外国判决来自与肯尼亚签有互惠执行协议的国家,当事人不得在肯尼亚法院重新提起索赔。当事人仅可向高等法院申请判决登记。

如果判决来自尚未与肯尼亚达成互惠执行协议的国家,则要求执行外国判决的当事人必须通过提交一份阐明索赔性质的声明,向肯尼亚高等法院重新提出索赔。外国判决可列入支持索赔的证据之中。

八、其他

（一）反商业贿赂

1. 反商业贿赂法律、法规简介

根据《反贿赂法》的规定,在私营或公共部门行贿或受贿都属于犯罪行为。根据该法的规定,公共和私营实体必须根据其规模大小及其运作性质制定适当的制度并落实到位,以预防贿赂和腐败,若不这样做则相当于犯罪。值得注意的是,该法也规定了向外国公职人员行贿亦属犯罪,使此法在肯尼亚境内外均可适用。

依托于《宪法》的《反腐败和经济犯罪法》《公职人员道德法》和《领导廉洁法》等法律对在公共部门的贿赂和其他腐败行为的处罚有指导性。根据这些法律的规定,在公共场合或正式场合向国家官员赠送或捐赠的礼物,或捐赠给国家的礼物应交付给国家,根据《议会法案》获得豁免的除外。所有国家官员,无论是以公职还是私人身份,都有责任避免个人利益和公职之间的冲突,不能为了个人利益而损害任何公共或官方利益。

《反腐败和经济犯罪法》进一步禁止了行贿和受贿、操纵投标或参与公共服务中的腐败行为。该法案设立有追回因腐败或经济犯罪而损失的金额的机制。此外,公职人员贿赂违反了《公职人员道德法》和《领导廉洁法》中规定的行为准则。

此外，肯尼亚还是《联合国反腐败公约》和《非洲联盟预防和打击腐败公约》的缔约国。根据《宪法》第2（6）条的规定，这两项公约构成肯尼亚法律的一部分。

2. 反商业贿赂监督部门

在肯尼亚，道德与反腐败委员会是负责打击贿赂、经济犯罪和腐败的主要机构。除其他职能外，其还依法负责调查并向检察长揭露任何有关贪污、贿赂或经济犯罪的犯罪行为以供起诉。任何人都可以向道德与反腐败委员会提出申诉以进行调查，该委员会也有权自行调查其请求。

根据《反贿赂法》的规定，公职人员和在私人企业拥有实权的人员在获知任何信息或嫌疑后，在24小时内向道德与反腐败委员会报告其所知悉的或怀疑的贿赂事件的情况。

需要注意的是，尽管有上述规定，该委员会迄今为止处理的大部分事项都只与公共部门有关。

其他机构也参与监督肯尼亚公共部门的反商业贿赂行动。这些机构包括：审计长办公室、行政司法委员会（监察员）和其他部门特定委员会，这些机构负责根据《公职人员道德法》实施行为守则。

3. 惩罚措施

惩罚措施大致可以分为两类：个人犯罪惩罚和单位犯罪惩罚。以下是对个人性质的贿赂罪定罪的最高处：

① 行贿或受贿可处以不超过10年的监禁或不超过500万肯尼亚先令的罚款或二者并罚，并可能承担额外的强制性罚款，其金额为其获得的任何可量化收益或他人所遭受的可量化损失金额的5倍。

② 打压贿赂的告密者或证人，可处不超过10年监禁或不超过500万肯尼亚先令的罚款或二者并罚。

③ 贿赂外国公职人员可处以不超过10年的监禁或不超过500万肯尼亚先令的罚款或二者并罚。

④ 如果被定罪的人是公司的董事，则该人在一段时间内禁止在肯尼亚任何公司任职董事，禁止时间不得超过10年。

⑤ 被判定犯有贿赂罪的人在定罪后一段时间内禁止被选任或任命担任国家机关的公职，禁止时间不得超过10年。

在涉及私营单位的贿赂犯罪中，处罚如下：

① 单位董事在一段时间内禁止在肯尼亚任何公司担任董事，禁止时间不得超过10年。

② 被判贿赂罪的单位定罪后10年内不得与国家和郡政府有业务往来。

（二）项目合同

1. 许可制度

肯尼亚的政府采购遵循2015年第33号《政府采购和资产处置法》。该法和其下设立的法规的目的是为公共实体建立有效的政府采购和资产处置程序。

该法案设立了政府采购监管局，其职责是执行该法的规定，特别是监督、评估和审查政府采购和资产处置系统，以确保他们尊重国家价值观和《宪法》的其他规定。

在郡一级，郡财政部门是负责实施各郡政府采购和资产处置政策的机构。

国家机关和公共实体的所有采购行为都必须遵守《政府采购和资产处置法》的规定和原则。

2. 限制

根据《政府采购和资产处置法》的规定，不符合政府采购条件的采购类型有：

① 在采购个人提供的定期服务中，提供服务的个人涉嫌受他人雇佣的（基于服务合同项下的个人提供服务的除外）；

② 缺乏财政考虑而将资产从一个国家机关或公共实体转移给另一个国家机关或公共实体；

③ 获得由政府或政府部门提供的服务；

④ 购买和出售股票或证券；公共实体的财政机构；合作社、国有企业或其他公共实体购买股票等投资；

⑤ 根据2013年《公私伙伴关系法》采购和处置的资产；

⑥ 根据肯尼亚政府与其他外国政府、机构、实体或多边机构的双边或多边协议采购和处置的资

产,《政府采购和资产处置法》另有规定的除外。

3. 招标和投标邀请

根据《政府采购和资产处置法》的招标程序如下:

(1) 资格预审

资格预审是招标程序的初步阶段,旨在编制一份能够满足工程或项目技术标准的公司名单,在此阶段不考虑价格因素。这一阶段对于大型或复杂的项目来说也许是必要的。

资格预审应考虑是否有类似合同的经验、过去表现如何、建筑和生产设施的水平以及财务状况等因素。招标对象仅限于已经过资格预审的公司。

(2) 招标邀请

采购实体随后应准备招标邀请函,邀请函应包括以下内容:

① 采购实体的名称和地址;
② 采购实体分配给采购程序的招标编号;
③ 对所要采购的货物、工程或服务进行简要说明,包括交付或完成的时限;
④ 如何获得招标文件的说明,包括所有的费用的数额;
⑤ 阐明于何时何地必须提交标书以及招投标会议在何时何地开幕;
⑥ 投标人或其代表可以参加开标的声明。

(3) 提交投标书

投标人必须在截止日期之前提交投标书,在截止日期之后收到的任何投标书均应在未开封的状态下退回。提交报价的时间和地点由招标文件规定。

意向投标人必须在投标文件中提交指定期限内有效的投标。采购实体可以要求投标人缴纳投标保证金,该投标保证金可以是固定金额或占合同估计价值的一定比例的金额。保证金由招标文件规定,可以高达合同价格的2%。

(4) 评标

评审委员会在开标后不久进行初步评估,以确定投标书以正确的格式提交、已被签署以及被提供了正确的份数。有投标保证的,保证具备有效性且提供了要求的样品。任何不符合要求的投标书将被拒绝。

随后对投标进行更严格的技术合格评估,之后进行财务评估,其中包括在开标时宣读的价格、计算错误的更正、货币单位、折扣等。最低价的合格投标书通常会获得缔约机会。

采购实体有权不签订合同,随时拒绝所有收到的投标书并终止采购程序。

(5) 接受投标的通知

采购实体将通知中标者其投标书已被接受,同时通知其他投标者其投标未成功。

但是,在签订书面合同之前,至少需等待14天,以便有时间申请行政审查。如果中标人拒绝签订书面合同,可将该合同授予下一个最佳评估投标人。

Kenya

Authors: Adil Khawaja, Sigee Koech, John Ohaga, Franklin Cheluget
Translators: Meng Qihong, David Jia

I. Overview

A. General Introduction to the Political, Economic, Social and Legal Environment of the Country Receiving Investment

a. Political

The Politics of Kenya take place in a framework of a presidential representative democratic republic, whereby the President of Kenya is both head of state and head of government, and of a multi-party system in accordance with the Constitution passed in 2010. The country also has 47 counties which are all headed by Governors.

Executive power is exercised by the executive branch of government, headed by the President, who chairs the cabinet, that is composed of people chosen from outside parliament. Legislative power is vested exclusively in Parliament which is comprised of two houses, the National Assembly and the Senate. The Senate contains representatives from each county whose primary function is to legislate on law touching on the counties. The judiciary is independent of the executive and the legislature.

b. Economic

Kenya's economy is market-based with a few state-owned infrastructure enterprises and maintains a liberalised external trade system. The country is generally perceived as Eastern and central Africa's hub for Financial, Communication and Transportation services. Major industries include: agriculture, forestry and fishing, mining and minerals, industrial manufacturing, energy, tourism and financial services. As of 2015 estimates, Kenya had a GDP of $69.977 billion making it the 72nd largest economy in the world. Per capita GDP was estimated at $1,587.

c. Social

Kenya's social scene is characterized by a combination of 44 tribes spread across 47 counties. It is inhabited primarily by Bantu and Nilotic populations, with some Cushitic-speaking ethnic minorities in the north. Its total population was estimated at 47 million as of 2017.

d. Legal

The Constitution of Kenya, 2010 is the primary legal document which prescribes the legal system in Kenya. It prescribes a court system where disputes are referred to by parties for determination. The court system creates different categories of courts and with diverse jurisdiction, namely Supreme Court, Court of Appeal, High Court, Employment & Labour Relations Court (formerly the Industrial Court), Environment and Land Court, Subordinate Courts, the Magistrate Court which encompasses under it the Kadhi's Court, and Courts Martial. The law nevertheless still anticipates settling of disputes privately through mediations, negotiations, arbitrations among other alternative dispute resolution mechanisms.

B. The Status and Direction of the Cooperation with Chinese Enterprises Under the B&R

There has long been economic cooperation between China and Kenya, especially arising from the partnerships that Kenya has entered into with China in its major construction of roads and railway. Following the commitment made by China in strengthening Africa's industrial capacity during the second summit of the Forum on China-Africa Cooperation (FOCAC) held in Johannesburg in December 2015, Kenya has hosted the maiden launch of China-Africa Industrial Capacity Cooperation Exhibition that kicked off on December 13-December 16 at the Kenyatta International Convention Centre (KICC) in Nairobi.

Moreover, there has been positive response and reception by Kenya regarding the cooperation that will ultimately culminate in the China Belt and Road initiative. What only remains is streamlining of the legal regime in Kenya and China to accommodate the initiative.

II. Investment

A. Market Access

International trade plays a key role in Kenya's economy. This is illustrated by the share of trade in goods in total GDP, which averages 43 percent. Trade in services increases the significance of international trade even further. This is evidenced by the role that trade in services plays in the global economy, which according to WTO (2010) accounts for two thirds of Global GDP or USD 49.5 trillion by 2015. Kenya is already reaping from this market through its diaspora community, which in 2015 remitted KES 145.4 billion (or USD 1.43 billion).

Kenya's international trade policy, seeks to exploit the potential in both the trade in goods and trade in services through policy measures that contribute towards transforming Kenya into a competitive export led economy and a thriving domestic market. The International trade policy is formulated within the framework of Multilateral, Regional and Preferential Tariff Arrangements (PTAs) that Kenya has entered into. These include the WTO, EAC, COMESA, Tripartite FTA (COMESA, EAC and SADC) AGOA and EAC-EU EPA. Trade regimes under these various arrangements are further detailed herebelow.

a. Multilateral Trade Arrangement

Kenya has subscribed to the multilateral trade arrangements that are defined by various WTO Agreements. This has been because of through her commitment under the WTO. The agreements which are alluded to in the Design of the National Trade Policy include the following: General Agreement on Trade and Tariffs (GATT), Sanitary and Phytosanitary (SPS) Agreement, Technical Barriers to Trade (TBT) Agreement, Anti-dumping Agreement, Subsidies and Countervailing Measures Agreement, Customs Valuation Agreement, Rules of Origin Agreement, Safeguards, Trade Related Intellectual Properties (TRIPs) Agreement, Trade in Services, among others.

b. Regional Trade Arrangements

Regional trade arrangements that shape Kenya's international trade policy include the East African Community (EAC); the Common Market for Eastern and Southern Africa (COMESA); the Intergovernmental Authority on Development (IGAD) and the Indian Ocean Rim-Association of Regional Cooperation (IOR-ARC). The significance and impacts of these arrangements are highlighted below:

a) The East African Community (EAC)

The membership comprises Kenya, Tanzania, Uganda, Rwanda, Burundi and South Sudan. The community brings the five countries together on issues of economic, social and political cooperation. The EAC has created an expanded market for trade in goods and services, through the provisions of the EAC Customs Union Protocol and the Common Market Protocol as well as other regional integration instruments and sectoral strategies and policies.

b) The Common Market for Eastern and Southern Africa (COMESA)

COMESA is a Regional Economic Community of 19 countries, which includes Kenya. Through the Free Trade Area framework, COMESA affords Member States an opportunity for expanding their trade with the region as a destination for exports or a source for imports on duty free basis. In 2015, COMESA accounted for 16 percent of Kenya's total exports. Over the period 2011–2015 trade was characterized by sluggish and near constant growth rate. Over the same period, on the other hand, COMESA recorded tremendous growth in imports, implying existence of trade potential that needs to be exploited in order to increase exports o this regional block.

c) The Intergovernmental Authority on Development (IGAD)

IGAD comprises of the following countries in the horn of Africa-Djibouti, Somalia, South Sudan, Sudan, Ethiopia, Uganda and Kenya. IGAD is now a Regional Economic Community (REC). Its mandate expanded from drought and desertification to include an economic and trade agenda. It therefore provides a regional integration framework through which trade between the seven countries can be expanded using shared commitments in other RECs (such as COMESA) to deepen trade integration.

d) EAC- COMESA / SADC Tripartite Free Trade Area (TFTA)

The EAC / COMESA / SADC Tripartite FTA, whose formation is based on the directive of the Heads of State Summit of 22nd October 2008, was eventually launched on 10th June 2015. It covers the first phase of integration that includes trade in goods. Kenya gains immensely from the expanded regional market of 26 countries, to be accessed under a Free Trade Area arrangement.

e) African Growth and Opportunity Act (AGOA) 2000

Kenya, along with other beneficiary Sub-Saharan African countries, has benefited from a preferential trade arrangement provided by the USA through the African Growth and Opportunity Act (AGOA). The beneficiary countries have to meet the eligibility criteria set out in the Act which includes establishment of a market based economy and issues of good governance. This trading program was initially expected to expire in 2015, but was on 1st July 2015 extended by another 15 years.

f) Economic Partnership Agreements (EPAs)

The EPA was ratified by Kenya Parliament on 20th September 2016 in order to comply with the EU Market Access Regulation 1528/2007. Under these Regulatuions, Kenya was required to sign and ratify the Agreement in order not to lose duty free market access which the country had been enjoying since 1975. Not signing and ratifying the EPA would have triggered the duty free market status in the EU with effect from 1st October 2016.

c. Bilateral Trade Agreements

Kenya has signed various bilateral trade and investment agreements with both developed and developing countries that fulfil the following objectives:

(i) Reciprocal participation in exhibitions and trade fairs as well as respective country week promotional events;

(ii) Exchange of market intelligence, missions / surveys for market information;

(iii) Encouragement of institutional cooperation such as the Standards Institutions; Chambers of Commerce and Industry, Customs Organizations, Research Institutions among others;

(iv) Prompt and focused follow up of issues raised during bilateral meetings;

(v) Exchange of general and product specific trade and investment missions; and,

(vi) Promotion of Trade and Investment.

d. Constraints and Challenges Affecting Market Access for Exports

Market access for Kenyan products in the regional and international markets continues to be limited by a swarm of constraints and challenges. This has led to Kenya's dismal share in local trade and in some cases experiencing decline. This has especially been the case in the regional market, where some products have recorded substantial decline in exports. Among the most critical constraints are the ones discussed herebelow:

a) Prevalence of Non-Tariff Barriers (NTBs)

Intra-regional trade within EAC and COMESA has been greatly hampered by Non-Tariff Barriers. These take the form of cumbersome and numerous customs documentation and administrative procedures. Also, non-recognition of the certificates of origin, varying standards and stringent application of SPS requirements play a critical role. Further, delays at border crossing, road blocks, weighbridges, police check and attendant costs and un-harmonized transit charges and procedures hamper the trade.

Applications of NTBs restrict the flow of goods among nations. The main challenge confronting the country is to ensure that negotiations at bilateral, regional and multilateral trading system lead to a reduction or elimination of all NTBs. Kenya exports also faces NTBs in international markets, associated mainly with SPS and Standards as well as season restriction of products through tariff quotas.

b) Ineffective Application of EAC Trade Promotion Schemes

Kenyan firms have faced challenges accessing the EAC market as a result of weaknesses in the implementation of the EAC Duty Exemption Scheme.

c) Charging of Tariffs on Some Raw Material, Intermediate Products and Capital Goods

Competitive export products require that the raw material and intermediate products that are used in the production of final products be subjected to no import duty. In the case of EAC CET, there are some sectors where this is not the case. The yard stick for determining whether raw material or intermediate product should attract duty is existence of regional capacity to supply the product to meet regional industrial demand for the same. This principle has so far not guided the EAC tariff architecture, as demonstrated by continued importation of such raw material and intermediate products from outside the EAC, with such imports being subjected to import duty.

The overall effect is that the final products are made uncompetitive in the regional as well as international market.

d) High and Multiple Internal Duties and Taxes

A wide range of taxes, levies, cesses, and fees charged on production, inputs, and services, distort prices and make products and services uncompetitive in domestic and world markets. In addition, the multiple taxes are burdensome and cumbersome to the business community. The challenge for the Government is to review and rationalize all taxation laws and regulations to enhance competitiveness in production.

e) Challenges of Tariff Peaks and Escalations

While average customs duties have come down after successive rounds of negotiations, application of high tariffs and tariff escalations by developed countries for value added products originating from developing countries has continued to restrict exports of developing countries. In effect, this practice protects domestic industries of the importing country while discouraging value addition.

f) Preference Erosion and Loss of Competitiveness

As a result of the erosion of preferences arising from the continued liberalization under WTO, Kenya faces the problem of declining exports in EU and US markets caused by stiff competition.

B. Foreign Exchange Regulations

a. Regulations and Guidelines Pursuant to the Banking Act (Cap 488)

Regulations and Guidelines issued by the Central Bank of Kenya subject banks to certain requirements, restrictions and guidelines. This regulatory structure is designed to create transparency between banking institutions and the individuals and corporations with whom they conduct business, among other things.

Given the interconnectedness of the banking industry and the reliance that the national (and global) economy hold on banks, it is important for regulatory agencies to maintain control over the standardised practices of these institutions. The objectives of these regulations are:

(i) Prudential—to reduce the level of risk to which bank creditors are exposed (i.e.to protect depositors);

(ii) Systemic risk reduction—to reduce the risk of disruption resulting from adverse trading conditions for banks causing multiple or major bank failures;

(iii) Avoid misuse of banks—to reduce the risk of banks being used for criminal purposes, e.g.laundering the proceeds of crime;

(iv) To protect banking confidentiality;

(v) Credit allocation—to direct credit to favoured sectors to provide the best customer service in this competitive age.

The Central Bank of Kenya regulates the financial system and plays a supervisory role with regard to the management of the foreign exchange business. The Bank is also responsible for the preparation of the balance of payments among other objectives.

The Central Bank of Kenya is in various ways guided by the following pieces of legislation:

(i) Constitution of Kenya (2010);

(ii) Central Bank of Kenya Act (2015);

(iii) Banking Act (2015);

(iv) Microfinance Act (2006);

(v) The National Payment System Act (2011);

(vi) Kenya Deposit Insurance Act (2012).

One of the major concerns of the Central Bank is the accurate collection and timely submission of statistical information by the foreign exchange dealers without which the Bank cannot fulfil its objectives as laid down in the Central Bank of Kenya Act.

It may be noted that the responsibility of managing foreign exchange business was delegated to the authorised foreign exchange dealers following repeal of the Exchange Control Act effective December 27, 1995. The Central Bank noted that the dealers have performed this role efficiently in accordance with the Central Bank of Kenya Circular No.12 dated August 19, 1996 and Forex Bureau Guidelines of November 11, 1996.

In managing foreign exchange business, foreign exchange dealers (authorised banks and forex bureaus) need to observe the following principles:

(i) The maxim of Know Your Customer (KYC) must be observed at all times.

(ii) Exercising caution to ensure that cross-border payments are not connected with illegal financial transactions and appropriate money laundering policies should be adopted by all the foreign exchange dealers.

(iii) New products should be introduced in the market after consultations between the originating foreign exchange dealer and the Central Bank.

(iv) The foreign exchange dealers (staff) must be fit and proper, that is, they must be officers with a high degree of honesty, integrity and reputation, competence and capability.

b. Foreign Exchange Bureaus

Forex bureaus may engage in buying and selling foreign currency cash; buying travellers cheques; personal cheques; banker's drafts and bank transfers. A Forex bureau may also sell travellers cheques but must seek and obtain prior approval from the Central Bank of Kenya. Forex bureaus are only allowed to engage in spot foreign exchange transactions and should not engage in derivative foreign exchange deals.

c. Persons Permitted to Transact Foreign Exchange Business

According to Legal Notice No.23 of 28-02-1996, any person permitted by the Central Bank of Kenya under Section 33A (3) of the Central Bank of Kenya Act to accept foreign exchange receipts should not deal in (buy and sell) foreign exchange.

The section provides as follows:33A

(i) Subject to sub-section c), no person shall, in Kenya transact foreign exchange business except an authorized dealer.

(ii) A person who contravenes the provisions of subsection a) commits an offence and shall, on conviction be liable to a fine not exceeding five hundred thousand shillings, or to imprisonment for term not exceeding three years, or to both.

(iii) Notwithstanding the provisions of subsection a), the Bank may permit such person or class of persons as it may specify, to transact foreign exchange business without a licence, subject to such conditions as it may impose.

The permission is granted to any person who is licensed under the Tourist Industry Licensing Act to carry on any registered tourist enterprise; or owns or operates a Duty Free Shop; or, by the nature of his / her business requires to transact regularly in foreign currency. The foreign currency received should be dealt with as follows:

(i) Credited to a foreign currency account;
(ii) Sold to an authorised dealer;
(iii) Used to settle external obligations through authorized banks;
(iv) Settle local debts billed in foreign currency.

d. Currency Sales and Purchases

Buying and selling of foreign currency is prohibited unless one of the parties to the transaction is an authorised dealer licensed under section 33(B) of the Central Bank of Kenya Act (Cap.491).

e. Counterfeits/Forged Currency Notes

All foreign exchange dealers should have the necessary equipment to detect counterfeit currencies. The counterfeits presented by customers should be seized, the customer issued with evidencing receipt and counterfeit currencies delivered to the Central Bank of Kenya for investigation in consultation with the relevant authorities.

f. Exchange Rate Display Board

Foreign exchange dealers must display their counter exchange rates prominently and in locations within their premises convenient to the public. Each foreign exchange dealer must have an Exchange Rate Display Board and issue a receipt in respect of each foreign exchange transaction.

g. Transactions

Kenya residents and non residents may:
(i) Invoice for their goods and services in Kenya Shilling or foreign currency.
(ii) Possess foreign currency.
(iii) Sell foreign currency to and buy foreign currency from authorised dealers.
(iv) Export and import currency in accordance with the legal Notice No.118, contained in the Kenya Gazette Supplement No.48 dated 4th September 1998.

h. Market Manipulation

All foreign exchange dealers must avoid engaging in speculative transactions that tend to mislead the other participants in the market and must also avoid misuse of any privileged information. It is encouraged that as much as possible, all foreign exchange transactions should be supported by the underlying commercial activity.

i. Foreign Exchange Documentation

All foreign exchange dealers are required to obtain and retain appropriate documents for all transactions above the equivalent of US$ 10,000. Alternatively, authorized dealers may accept duly executed declaration forms in lieu of documents where e-banking is adopted. The customers would undertake to produce the transaction documents to the bank on demand; and it would be the authorized dealer to avail the documents to the Central Bank of Kenya for examination purposes.

j. Outward Investments

All foreign exchange dealers shall obtain and retain copies of:
(i) Foreign government approvals for the investment, if held;
(ii) The contracts between the applicant and the relevant bodies in the host country, say stock;
(iii) brokers;
(iv) Terms and conditions of the investment.

k. Foreign Currency (FCY) Accounts for Diplomatic Missions

Authorised banks are free to open and operate foreign currency accounts for diplomatic missions or any of their accredited officials or any organisation established in or outside Kenya by international treaty or any of its accredited officials.

It should be noted that imports by these organisations are not subject to the Import Declaration Form (IDF) or pre-shipment inspection (PSI) procedures. Their foreign currency accounts may therefore be debited without the requisite importation documents. All other debits to such accounts should be done in accordance with prudent banking practice. The daily inflows and weekly holdings should, however, be captured in the return to the Central Bank of Kenya as required.

l. Credit Facilities Denominated in Foreign Currency

Authorised banks are free to extend foreign currency denominated credit facilities to Kenya residents and non-residents subject to the prudential lending practice.

m. Advances to Kenya Residents

On advances made to Kenya residents, the lending banks shall maintain appropriate information, including:

(i) A copy of the loan agreement (facility letter) duly executed, specifying terms and conditions of the credit and guarantee, if applicable.

(ii) A declaration to the effect that the borrower shall remain a resident during the term of the credit facility or advise the bank if and when the residential status changes.

(iii) Items lodged as security as an alternative way of repayment.

n. Advances to Non-Residents

On advances made to non-residents, the lending banks shall maintain appropriate information including, the following:

(i) Loan agreements duly executed, specifying terms and conditions of the loans and guarantees, if applicable.

(ii) Documents to show that the collaterals pledged are realisable in foreign currency.

(iii) Declaration to the effect that funds for repayment shall be from abroad.

o. Offshore Borrowing by Kenya Residents

Kenyan residents may borrow offshore. Authorised dealers must however pay due regard to the interests of their customers and give them appropriate advice on risks associated with offshore borrowing. The borrowers, if need be, should be advised to seek the services of commercial lawyers.

Records relating to the following should be maintained as evidence of the offshore debt: financial agreements duly executed between the borrower and the foreign lender, funds transmission instruments confirming receipts of loan proceeds and loans amortization schedule.

p. Inward Investments

Inward investments are permitted. Non-residents are free to invest in real estate, equities, money and stock exchange securities or other types of investments as appropriate. Detailed information on investment procedures can be obtained from the Investment Promotion Centre (IPC) currently located at the National Bank of Kenya Headquarters building on Harambee Avenue, Nairobi.

C. Financing

a. Regulatory and Ownership Restrictions

a) No Exchange Control

There are no exchange control laws in Kenya. The Central Bank of Kenya Act however, provides that for every payment made:

(i) In Kenya to or for the credit of a person outside Kenya; or

(ii) Outside Kenya to or for the credit of a person in Kenya; or

(iii) In Kenya (other than a payment for a current transaction) between a resident and non-resident, such payment must be effected through an authorised bank. Any contrary mechanism would require approval from the Central Bank.

An authorised bank under the Act is a specified bank licensed by the Central Bank of Kenya to transact foreign exchange business. In practical terms, this effectively captures all institutions with banking licenses. Accordingly, transactions that involve the disbursement of loans to or the subscription of shares in a Kenyan entity would arguably fall foul of this provision.

b. Five Main Actors Regulating the Financial Sector Activities

a) Central Bank of Kenya

Regulates the Banking sector by formulation of monetary policy to achieve and maintain stability. It supervises commercial banks through enforcement of the Banking Act regulations and facilitates and provides oversight on national and regional payment systems.

b) Insurance Regulatory Authority

Licenses insurance and reinsurance companies, insurance brokers, agents, assessors, adjustors and health management organizations (HMOs). In accordance with the Insurance Act regulations, it regulates, supervises and develops the insurance industry in Kenya.

c) Capital Markets Authority

It licenses and supervises all the activities of capital market intermediaries, ensures proper conduct of all licensed persons and market institutions and regulates the issuance of the capital market products (bonds, shares etc.).

d) Retirement Benefit Authority

It regulates and supervises the establishment and management of pension schemes, protects the interest of members and sponsors of retirement benefits schemes and develops and promotes the retirement benefits sector.

e) Societies Regulatory Authority

It licenses Savings and Credit Cooperatives (SACCO) societies to carry out deposit-taking business in accordance with the SACCO Act. It also regulates and supervises deposit taking savings and credit cooperative societies.

c. Kenya's Banking Sector Structure

a) Commercial Banks
- 42 Commercial Banks;
- 8 Representative offices;
- Corporate and consumer banking services.

b) Mobile Money Operators
- 4 Mobile Money Operators;
- Mobile payment solutions for individuals and corporates.

c) Microfinance Banks
- 12 Microfinance Banks;
- Banking services focused on Micro and Small enterprises.

d) Mortgage Finance Institutions
- 1 Mortgage Finance company;
- Lending focused on property development.

e) Foreign Exchange Bureaus
- 86 Foreign Exchange Bureaus;
- Foreign currency exchange services.

f) Money Remittance Providers
- 14 Money Remittance Providers;
- Inter country money transfer for individuals and SMEs.

g) Credit Reference Bureaus
- 4 Credit Reference Bureaus;
- Credit information sharing services to financial institutions, utilities and individuals.

D. Tax

a. Company/Corporate Tax

Company tax in Kenya is based on computed tax profits as follows:
- Turnover tax: 3% of turnover (with effect from 1 January 2007 for turnover of up to KES 5,000,000);
- Resident companies: 30%;
- Non-resident companies: 37.5%.

b. Capital Gains Tax

Capital Gains Tax (CGT) was re-introduced effective 1st January 2015. The rate of tax is 5% of the net gain on the transfer of property. It is a final tax and cannot be offset against other income taxes.

c. Branch Profits Tax

Branch of a foreign entity pays tax at the rate of 37.5%.

d. Value Added Tax (Vat)

The VAT rates are 16% and 0%. Exports are zero rated. Some goods and services such as unprocessed agricultural products and financial services are exempt.

e. Fringe and Employment Benefits Tax

Generally, non-cash benefits are taxable on the higher of the cost incurred by the employer or the fair market value.

The taxable value is added to the emoluments for tax purposes. Exempt if aggregate total does not exceed KES 36,000 per annum.

f. Motor Vehicles

The benefit is the higher of 2% per month of the initial cost of the vehicle or the prescribed rates. For leased vehicles the benefit is the cost of leasing.

g. Housing

For non-executive directors the benefit is the higher of 15% of total income (emoluments—for a whole time service director), fair market rental value and rent paid. For agricultural employees it is 10% of emoluments. For other employees it is the higher of rent paid and 15% of emoluments.

h. Loans to Employees

Loans to employees are taxed at a corporate tax rate on the difference between the interest rate prescribed by the Commissioner and the actual interest rate paid by the employee.

i. Other Benefits

The taxable benefit of furniture is 1% of cost per month, telephone is 30% of the cost per month, and employee share ownership plans (ESOPs) is the difference between the market price of shares and the offer price at the date the option is granted.

j. Local Taxes

Employment income is taxed on a withholding tax (WHT) basis known as Pay As You Earn (PAYE) at a graduating scale of 10%-30%.

k. Dividends

Dividends are taxed on a WHT basis which is final tax. Expenses are therefore not allowable on the dividends' income or any other income of the taxable person. Dividends are tax-exempt for resident companies controlling more than 12.5% shareholding. Dividends received by financial institutions shall be deemed to be income chargeable to tax.

However, compensating tax (corporation tax) may arise if non-taxed income is distributed, e.g.capital gain or profits on capital allowances. This is arrived at through an annual Dividends Tax Account which captures the movement of dividends received and paid and takes into consideration taxes paid by the entity.

l. Interest Deductions

Interest incurred wholly and exclusively in the production of income is tax allowable. However, where a company is controlled by a non-resident person together with four or fewer resident persons, the interest deductibility is restricted only to the extent that the total indebtedness of the company does not exceed three times the paid-up share capital and revenue reserves or an amount of deemed interest (thinly capitalised).

The Commissioner of Income Tax is empowered to prescribe the form and manner in which deemed interest is to be computed.

Realised foreign exchange losses are deferred as long as the firm is thinly capitalised.

m. Losses

Tax losses can be carried forward to be offset against future taxable income. However this is subject to a five year limit effective 1 January 2010.

The tax loss is only allowable on taxable income derived from the same specific source. These sources are:
(i) Income from renting or occupation of immovable property;
(ii) Income from employment;
(iii) Income from agriculture, horticulture, forestry, etc;
(iv) Income from withdrawals from a registered pension / provident fund by employer;
(v) Business activities.

Losses are, however, not transferable from one entity to another.

n. Foreign Source Income

Income that is not income accrued or derived from Kenya is not assessable in Kenya except:
(i) Employment income for an employee who at the time of employment was a resident person in respect of

any employment by him outside or inside Kenya;
  (ii) Business activities carried out across borders; and,
  (iii) Foreign bank branches' income on investments or trading abroad using locally generated income.

o. Tax Incentives

Capital deductions are allowable and provided for on assets based on the asset classification.

Kenya has Double Tax Agreements with the following countries: Canada, Denmark, East African Community, France, Germany, India, Mauritius, Norway, South Africa, Sweden, United Kingdom, and, Zambia.

A ten year tax holiday is available to certain designated enterprises that undertake activities consisting of the manufacture of goods for exports only (under the Export Processing Zones). At the end of the tax holiday, a reduced rate of tax of 25% is available.

A lower rate of corporation tax at 27%, 25% and 20%, for the first 3-5 years for companies newly listed on a securities exchange, with at least 20%, 30% and 40% respectively, of the issued share capital listed.

Tax exemptions apply for organisations undertaking charitable, medical, alleviation of poverty, and religious activities.

p. Foreign Tax Relief

Foreign tax relief is limited only to countries which have a Double Taxation Agreement with Kenya.

q. Corporate Groups

Generally for tax purposes, a corporation tax rate of 30% applies to all incorporated companies irrespective of groups in Kenya. The rate is 37.5% for non-resident companies.

r. Related Party Transactions

Related party transactions are allowable expenses if incurred wholly and exclusively in the production of income and taxed as income if earned or accrued in Kenya as business activities.

Companies which have related party transactions are required to prepare and document Transfer Pricing Documentation, as per the Kenyan Transfer Pricing Rules effective 1 July 2006.

E. Land Policy

Foreigners may only hold land on the basis of leasehold tenure. Leases granted to non-citizens may not exceed a period of 99 years.

Dealings in agricultural land are controlled in Kenya by the Land Control Act. Consent must be obtained from the Land Control Board for any transaction involving the sale, transfer, lease, mortgage, exchange, partition or other disposal of or dealing with any agricultural land. Consent will not be given to non-Kenyan citizens for any such transactions (save in the case of a mortgage or charge created in favour of a non-Kenyan lender).

However, a non-Kenyan citizen may apply for a presidential exemption from the application of the Act, although in practice this method is exercised in the most exceptional of circumstances in which there are significant public interest considerations.

Broadly defined, agricultural land is any land that is not within a municipality, township or market or is gazetted as such (but excludes land in such areas which by reason of any specific restriction on its use, the land may not be used for agricultural purposes).

Pursuant to the Constitution of Kenya, three Acts of Parliament have been enacted and came into force on 2nd May, 2012:
  • Land Act, 2012;
  • Land Registration Act, 2012;
  • National Land Commission Act, 2012.

a. Ownership of Land by Non-Kenyan Citizens

Salient features in the Land laws in this respect to this is that freehold land cannot be owned by a non-Kenyan citizen; and a leasehold interest of over 99 years cannot be held by a non-Kenyan citizen.

Therefore any freehold land owned by a non-Kenyan citizen is deemed to have been converted into a 99 year leasehold interest commencing from 27/8/2010 and any leasehold interest with an unexpired term of over 99 years is deemed to be converted into a 99 year leasehold interest commencing from 27/8/2010.

The Constitution states that a body corporate / company is deemed to be a Kenyan citizen only if it is 100% owned by Kenyan citizens. Therefore a company with even one shareholder who is a non-Kenyan citizen would only be entitled to own a leasehold interest of 99 years or less.

It is unclear whether a freehold title or title with an unexpired term of over 99 years that is owned jointly by a Kenyan citizen and a non-Kenyan citizen would be converted to a lease of 99 years or whether the tenure would remain intact.

b. Who Is a Foreigner/non-citizen under Kenyan Law?

The Constitution of Kenya does not offer an explicit legal definition of a citizen, non-citizen or foreigner. The Constitution, instead, sets out the rights, benefits, privileges and duties of a citizen.

The 2011 Citizenship and Immigration Act sets out the normative content of these rights and privileges, for instance, including the right to own land and other property in any part of the country; and entitlement to any document of registration given to citizens, including a "certificate of registration."

This immigration law defines a foreign national to mean "any person who is not a citizen of Kenya." These statutes however appear to concern the status of natural persons, and not corporations, which are the principal players in foreign direct investments. Thus, while the nationality of a natural person, even with respect to investments will be determined on the basis of immigration law, the question of citizenship concerning corporations, and the specific national criteria adopted to determine whether a company or other corporation is a foreign national involves concepts and laws regarding corporate bodies and investments.

Nonetheless, the immigration status or citizenship of natural persons remains relevant, particularly in context of the doctrine of foreign control, whereby the nationality of a body corporate could be determined on the basis of the citizenship of the natural persons that hold decision making control over such body corporate.

c. Determination of Citizenship Status of Corporate Bodies under Kenyan Law

In the Kenyan legal system, the foreign citizenship status of a body corporate, as a legal person, can be determined through the provisions of a variety of laws, as evaluated below:

a) The Investments Promotion, and Companies Legislation

In terms of general investments law the Investment Promotion Act is designed to provide a "one-stop shop" through which foreign investors are guided in application for necessary licences and permits, and assessed for suitability to invest in Kenya. In determining the "foreign status" of an investor, this law only applies the notion of foreign control with regard to partnerships, which are deemed as foreign if the controlling interest is owned by person(s) who are not citizens of Kenya. However, the law employs the concept of formal nationality whereby companies are deemed as non-citizen (or foreign investor) based on their place of incorporation, such that a company is a foreign investor is it was incorporated under the laws of a foreign country.

This is the view taken by the Companies Act, which in reference to foreign companies, refers to "... companies incorporated outside Kenya which ... establish a place of business within Kenya." The companies' legislation thus equally applies the place of incorporation as the primary criterion to determine the "foreign" status of a company, but also requires such entity to establish a local place of business.

b) Direct Contractual Agreements With Private Or Community Landholders As a Mechanisms For Land Acquisitions

There are several possible mechanisms through which a non-citizen corporation could acquire land for investments, on the leasehold terms. Persons who hold land under private tenure are entitled to deal with that land, including granting leases under voluntary lease agreements to other people, for an agreed amount of money as consideration. According to Part VI of the Land Act, these leases or sub-leases could be periodic, short-term, future leases, or could be an agreement for a fixed term.

In context of investment land by a non-citizen corporation, such a foreign entity would not be entitled to enter into lease or sub-lease agreements over any private land on freehold tenure, as this is prohibited by the constitution.

F. Establishment and Dissolution of Companies

Forms of legal incorporation of business enterprises in Kenya include: incorporated limited liability companies, sole proprietorships, partnerships, cooperatives, companies limited by guarantees for most non-profit organizations, and representative offices. Foreign investors favour limited liability companies which offer advantages similar to those offered by corporate bodies in other countries.

a. The Formal Procedures of Establishment

These are to a great extent determined by the type of business one wishes to establish and the sector which the business belongs.

Investors must first log their proposed business names with the Registrar of Companies at the Attorney General's office. This application can be made by the applicants directly or through legal representatives and policy experts. Once approved, Memorandum and Articles of Association are filed with the Registrar who issues a Certificate of Incorporation. Forms that must be completed include Statement of Nominal Capital, Particulars of Directors and Shareholders, Situation of Registered Office and Certificate of a Lawyer involved in the Formation of the Company.

Legal requirements that registered businesses must acquire include VAT number, Personal Identification Number (PIN), National Social Security Fund (NSSF) number, and the National Hospital Insurance Fund (NHIF) number. Other requirements are specific to business type.

An Investment Certificate grants the investor such benefits as entitlement to all licenses required for his or her operations, and work permits for three members of management or technical staff and three shareholders or partners valid for 2 years each.

b. Voluntary Winding up of a Company in Kenya

The applicable Kenyan statutes are the Insolvency Act No.18 of 2015 (Insolvency Act hereinafter) and the Companies Act No.17 of 2015 (Companies Act hereinafter).

Under the two Acts there are two options of winding up a company in Kenya: Voluntary liquidation process under the Insolvency Act; Deregistration of the Company at the Companies Registry under the Companies Act.

a) Voluntary Liquidation

This occurs when the directors of the company being liquidated make a statutory declaration subject to the provisions of the Insolvency Act as to the intention to wind-up a company by the liquidation process.

The voluntary liquidation of a company commences when a first resolution affirming the solvency of the company is passed, which should include a statement of its assets and liabilities. Five weeks thereafter a second resolution for voluntary liquidation must be passed by all or a majority of the directors. However, before passing a resolution for voluntary liquidation, the company shall give notice of the resolution to holders of any qualifying floating charge in respect of the company's property.

On and after the commencement of voluntary liquidation of a company, the company must cease to carry on its business, except in so far as may be necessary for its beneficial liquidation, including the transfer of the company's shares and an alteration in, or an attempt to alter, the status of the company's members.

Fourteen days after the company passes the resolution for its voluntary liquidation, it should publish in the Kenya Gazette and two national newspapers a notice setting out the resolution. Failure to do this may result into a fine penalty.

The members of the company then appoint an authorized insolvency practitioner as the liquidator in a general meeting convened for that purpose. Once this is done, the liquidator is required to prepare a statement of account on the entire liquidation process and specify how the company's debt and liabilities, if any, have been settled. He will table this to the members and once approved, the liquidator will file a copy together with returns at the Companies Registry. All these meetings must be commenced thirty days after the advertisement of the notice in the dailies and Kenya Gazette.

The liquidator is required to lodge the statement of account and the returns seven days after presentation at the general meeting. The registrar of companies will register the said statement of account upon receipt and three months after presentation of the said account, the company shall be deemed to have been dissolved.

Costs for this process are at the discretion of the appointed insolvency practitioner and are subject to the size and type of company being liquidated.

b) Deregistration

The Companies Act provides another option of winding up business. The Companies Act provides for two ways in which a company can be deregistered.

First, it gives power to the Registrar to strike off a company which the Registrar believes is not carrying on business or in operation.

The second option is upon application by the company. A company may opt to deregister itself from the Companies Registry, on application to the registrar to do the same. Where the company applies to be struck of the Register of Companies (the "Register") it must ensure that it provides a copy of the application to every member, creditor, employee and director of the company within seven days of the date of the application.

The application is made on behalf of the company by its directors or by a majority of them passing a resolution to do so. The registrar will strike off the company from the Register three months after publishing a notice in the Kenya Gazette stating that the registrar may exercise the power under section 897 of the Companies Act in relation to the company; and inviting any person to show cause why the name of the company should not be struck off.

As soon as practicable after striking the name of the company off the Register, the registrar shall publish in the Kenya Gazette a notice to the effect that the company's name has been struck off the Register and the date of the striking off. On the publication of this second notice in the Kenya Gazette, the company is considered dissolved.

Note that a company will not be able bring an application to be struck off the Register, if, during the preceding three months the company has changed its name; carried on business; made a disposal for value of property that, immediately before ceasing to carry on business, it held for the purpose of disposal for gain in the normal course of carrying on business; made a proposal for a voluntary arrangement in relation to the company under the laws relating to insolvency; there has been the making of an application to the court for an administration order in respect of the company under the laws relating to insolvency; there has been the presenting of an application to liquidate the company by the court; or the company has engaged in any other activity necessary for closing down the affairs of the company.

The Companies Act states that this is not a liquidation process but does provide the company with another avenue to remove any corporate establishment that exists in Kenya. Note that we are yet to attempt this process under the new Companies Act.

G. Competition Regulations

The main areas covered by the Competition Law in Kenya are Restrictive Trade Practices, Control and Display of Prices, Mergers and Takeovers and Control of unwarranted concentrations of economic power. These topical issues are each discussed briefly below.

a. Restrictive Trade Practices

The Kenya law on restrictive trade practices is intended to cover a very wide area. It covers acts intended to reduce or eliminate the participation of legal and natural persons in economic activities. It embraces trade agreements, trade associations, refusal and discrimination in supply, predatory trade practices, collusive tendering and collusive bidding at auction sales.

Offended persons can complain to the Commission or the Commission may initiate an investigation ex proprio motu. The Commission has wide powers including powers to require the offending persons to cease and desist. This is done through Consent Agreements which the Commissioner is required to Gazette. Where there are no Consent Agreements, a hearing is held after which the Minister makes requisite orders. The orders to desist may require the offender to take positive steps to assist existing or potential suppliers, competitors or customers, in order to compensate for the past effects of the offending practices.

A person against whom a Ministerial Order is made has a right to appeal to the Restrictive Trade Practices Tribunal and eventually to the High Court. The Kenya experience has been that most people against whom complaints are made tend to reach some sort of an agreement with the complainants. At that point most complainants just vanish into thin air. They thus make the investigation process very difficult.

Regarding investigations initiated ex proprio motu by the Commission, the Kenyan experience is that even where the suspected offenders deny wrong-doing, the offensive practices cease. The surveillance function of the Competition Authority is, thus, beneficial to the national economy.

b. Mergers and Takeovers

Mergers and takeovers between two or more independent enterprises are prohibited per se unless they are authorized in accordance with the law. This compulsory notification and authorization procedure has, of necessity, ensured that the Commission is quite active in the Mergers / takeovers area.

The Commission is of the view that some sort of a threshold should be introduced. Otherwise the Commission is quite effective in this area. When the merger or takeover is being approved, a condition may be imposed that certain steps be taken to reduce the negative effects of the merger or takeover on competition.

c. Control of Unwarranted Concentrations of Economic Power

The competition law requires the Minister to keep the structure of production and distribution of goods and services in Kenya under review to determine where concentrations of economic power exist whose detrimental impact on the economy out-weighs the efficiency advantages, if any, of integration in production and distribution.

The Competition Authority undertakes sectoral studies in a bid to consummate this legal mandate. Where necessary the Minister may make an order directing any person whom he deems to hold an unwarranted concentration of economic power in any sector to dispose of such portion of his interests in production or distribution or the supply of services as the exigency of the situation may deem necessary to remove the unwarranted concentration.

d. Control and Display of Prices

Kenya has abolished price controls since October, 1994. It is hoped that the whole part will be repealed in due course.

e. Institutional Framework

Competition cases in Kenya are handled by five principal institutions. These are Legislature (Parliament), Office of the Minister in-charge of Finance, the Office of the Commissioner for Monopolies and Prices, the

Restrictive Trade Practices Tribunal and the High Court of Kenya. Each one of these institutions has its functions, responsibilities and powers clearly spelt out in the legislation.

a) Legislature (Parliament)

Parliament is the principal custodian of public interest in Kenya and it creates both the institutional and legislative frameworks for the promotion and protection of public interest. In the competition area, Parliament enacted the current legal instrument, i.e.the Restrictive Trade Practices, Monopolies and Price Control Act, Cap.504 of the Laws of Kenya. And because the market is dynamic, the Law that regulates the functioning of the market must be reviewed from time to time so as to align it with the dynamic changes in the market place.

b) Office of the Minister for Finance

The overall responsibility for competition Policy in Kenya is in the hands of the Minister for Finance. Section 3(2) of the Act subjects the Commissioner for Monopolies and Prices to the control of the Minister and the Commissioner obtains compliance with his professional prescriptions for the market through Ministerial orders. The Minister relies heavily on the professional advice of the Commissioner for Monopolies and Prices, who, with a team of economists, financial analysis, lawyers and other necessary market analysts is the principal custodian of Kenya's Competition policy.

The Commissioner, whose appointment is mandated under section 3(1) acts as a watchdog, keeping an eye on commerce as a whole, carrying out initial enquiries and ordering in-depth investigations whenever situations demand. The Commissioner has the primary responsibility for conducting investigations into all possible situations of anti-competitive practices such as restrictive trade practices, abuse of dominant market power, mergers and take-overs. In practical terms, such investigations are carried out by the Commissioner's staff in the Monopolies and Prices Commission. The work involves responding to complaints by a company's competitors or customers, and carrying out informal research into markets where competition problems are thought or alleged to be present.

c) The Office of the Commissioner for Monopolies and Prices

The Commissioner for Monopolies and Prices is appointed in pursuant to the provisions of Section 3(1) of Kenya's Competition Law and he, in turn, directly and indirectly controls, manages and influences competition in exercise of the powers conferred upon him by the Law and such limitations as the Minister may think fit. The Law does not provide the authority that is responsible for the appointment of the Commissioner for Monopolies and Prices. However, once the Commissioner is appointed he is independent and has a range of statutory duties and responsibilities. He heads the Monopolies and Prices Department of the Treasury and has responsibilities for efficient administration and enforcement of Competition Law. He has also responsibilities in the consumer protection field. He seeks to maximise consumer welfare in the long term, and to protect the interests of vulnerable consumers by:

(i) Empowering consumers through information and redress.

(ii) Protecting them by preventing abuse.

(iii) Promoting competitive and responsible supply.

d) The Restrictive Trade Practices Tribunal (RTPT)

Pursuant to Section 64(1) of the Restrictive Trade Practices, Monopolies & Price Control Act, a quasi-judicial authority, that is the RTPT, is appointed every other five years since 8th February 1991. The RTPT consists of a Chairman who must be an advocate of the High Court of Kenya of not less than seven years standing and four members. The members of the RTPT have a five years secure term of office and may be appointed for other terms of office at the expiry of the five years.

It must be stressed here that once constituted by the Minister for Finance, the RTPT is absolutely independent of the Office of the Minister and the Office of the Commissioner for Monopolies and Prices. The principal function of the Tribunal is to arbitrate our competition policy disputes resulting from ministerial orders made on the recommendation of the Commissioner for Monopolies and Prices. The RTPT has powers to overturn, modify, confirm and / or refer back to the Minister orders appealed against by aggrieved parties.

Orders and decisions of the Tribunal are only appealable to the High Court of Kenya and such appeals are only feasible within 30 days following the communication of the Tribunal's decisions / orders to the concerned parties.

e) The High Court of Kenya

All appellants to the RTPT in pursuant to the provisions of Sections 20(1), 251 and 31(1) in respect to ministerial orders made in pursuant to the provisions of Sections 18(1), 24(1) and 31(1) respectively who are dissatisfied with the decision of the RTPT may appeal to the High Court of Kenya against that decision within thirty days after the date on which a notice of that decision was served on him and the decision of the High Court should be final.

H. Securities

a. Powers of the Nairobi Securities Exchange (NSE)

The basic powers of the NSE are embodied in its constitutive documents, the Capital Markets Authority (CMA) Regulations, Membership and Trading Rules and the Listing Manual. The Capital Markets Act makes no direct reference to the powers. Although the constitutive documents accord the stock exchange an extensive mandate the objects and powers conferred are exercisable subject to the provisions of the Capital Markets Act and Regulations made under the Act which render them largely ineffectual.

For instance, although the exchange is empowered to promote any other company to facilitate acquisition of property or acquire or hold shares in other companies, the CMA has restricted its shareholding to the Central Depository and Settlement Corporation Ltd (CDSC).

The mandate of the NSE contained in the Management and Membership Rules, Trading Rules and the Listing Manual is equally subordinated to the Capital Markets Act and its Regulations. A few examples sufficiently contextualize this argument. First, the exchange is required to admit all firms licensed by the CMA as full or associate members. Second, although the stock exchange is empowered to approve securities for listing, securities approved by the Authority must be admitted to listing "without any other conditions." Third, rules made by the exchange cannot be amended, varied or rescinded without prior approval of the Authority. Relatedly, the Authority is empowered to make additions to the rules and has discretion to abrogate them. Fourth, a member of the exchange cannot be suspended without approval of the Authority. Moreover, a member can only be expelled by non-renewal or revocation of license by the Authority. Fifth, the Authority must be notified of any disciplinary action taken by the NSE against members or listed companies within seven days. The Authority is empowered to review the decision either on its own motion or on application by the affected party and has jurisdiction to set the decision aside after hearing the securities exchange on the matter. Sixth, the Authority approves the annual budget of the exchange. Finally, the exchange can only suspend or delist securities with sanction of the CMA.

Except in one instance where a listed company was reported as having petitioned the NSE to waive a financial penalty it had imposed for late submission of financial reports in 2008, there is no evidence that NSE has been enforcing its membership and continuing disclosure obligations aggressively.

Additionally, it has neither investigative nor prosecutorial power and cannot enforce the provisions of the Capital Markets Act in its domain. The oversight jurisdiction of the CMA over Kenya's securities markets extends to its relationship with the Central Depository and Settlement Corporation, its affiliate.

Powers conferred on the corporation are exercisable subject to those of or in consultation with the CMA. Although the CDSC is empowered to appoint Central Depository Agents, it can only suspend or revoke their appointment in "consultation" with the Authority. The character of the consultation contemplated by the Rules remains unclear. This was the issue at hand when the CDSC suspended the custodial license (central depository agent license) of Equity Bank Company Ltd. The CMA ordered the CDSC to reinstate the license immediately and undertook to arbitrate the dispute between the two entities. The CMA argued that it had not "approved" the suspension as required by the provisions of the Central Depositories Act, 2000. Surprisingly, the Central Depositories Act does not address the issue of suspension or revocation of custodial licenses and the applicable Rules require "consultation."

These instances demonstrate that although the NSE and the CDSC appear to enjoy certain powers, ostensibly exercised by self-regulatory organizations in other jurisdictions, the powers are deeply circumscribed by the Capital Markets Act and its regulations. Concededly, the dynamism of the securities markets coupled with, globalization, advancement in technology and the unreliability of market intermediaries have rendered self-regulation impracticable in many respects. The utility of self-regulation has progressively been undermined by the insatiable greed of market intermediaries which has necessitated substantial government intervention.

Consequently, the CMA exercises plenary legislative and supervisory powers over the NSE and market intermediaries. Its powers are ubiquitous and its primacy over all aspects of the securities markets is incontestable. The enveloping powers are justified on the need to protect investors and bolster investor confidence. Significantly, the CMA has acknowledged its overarching oversight and has conceded that regulatory reforms should provide for the recognition of self-regulatory organizations and confer significant powers and responsibilities to them. This is exceedingly important particularly in the context of the impending demutualization of the NSE which constitutes the separation of business and regulatory functions of the exchange.

Concededly, market intermediaries play a crucial role in securities markets governance. The corporate affairs department of the CMA could enormously benefit by partnering with the more skilled and experienced NSE and KASIB in promoting investor awareness. In sum, the CMA is responsible for prudential, supervision and conduct of business of the securities exchange and other market intermediaries.

b. Securities Regulations in Respect to Foreign Investors

a) The Capital Markets (Foreign Investors) Regulations, 2002

These Regulations are cited as the Capital Markets (Foreign Investors) Regulations, 2002 and came into force on July 15, 2002. Under the regulations, a foreign investor means any person who is not a local investor. An issuer means a company or other legal entity incorporated or established under the laws of East African Community Partner States that offers securities to the public or a section thereof, whether or not such securities are the subject of an application for admission or have been admitted to listing. An institutional investor refers to a body corporate including a financial institution, collective investment scheme, fund manager, dealer or other body corporate whose ordinary business includes the management or investment of funds whether as principal or on behalf of clients;

The regulations further defines a local investor in relation to an individual, to mean a natural person who is a citizen of an East African Community Partner State. In relation to a body corporate, it defines a local investor as a company or any other body corporate established or incorporated under the Companies Act or under the provisions of any written law of an East African Community Partner State in which the citizens or the government of an East African Community Partner State have beneficial interests in one hundred per centum (100%) of its ordinary shares.

b) Participation by Foreign Investors

The participation of foreign investors is governed by Regulation 3. The section provides that any proportion of the voting shares of an issuer after an initial public offering shall be available for investment by foreign investors without any restrictions in the level of holdings except as provided under the Capital Markets (Takeovers and Mergers) Regulations, 2002. Notwithstanding this regulation, however, the Cabinet Secretary may by notice in the gazette, prescribe a maximum foreign shareholding in an issuer or listed company. The Cabinet Secretary may only exercise the power under paragraph 3(2) where in a privatization transaction, the government or its agency is divesting its shares to the public, some level of local ownership in a strategic industry or sector in the country is to be maintained or it is in national interest.

c) Restrictions of Outside Kenya

Under regulation 9, no person shall, in Kenya, offer or cause to be shares issued offered to the public any shares or other capital market instrument as the Authority may specify which are listed or to be listed outside Kenya except with the prior written approval and registration of such security with the Authority.

I. Preference and Protection of Investments

In Kenya, this is governed by the Foreign Investments Protection Act. It is an Act of Parliament to give protection to certain approved foreign investments and for matters incidental thereto. It understands foreign assets to include foreign currency, credits, rights, benefits or property, any currency, credits, rights, benefits or property obtained by the expenditure of foreign currency, the provision of foreign credit, or the use or exploitation of foreign rights, benefits or property, and any profits from an investment in an approved enterprise by the holder of a certificate issued under section 3 in relation to that enterprise.

a. Foreign Investors May Apply for and Be Granted Certificates

Under section 3, a foreign national who proposes to invest foreign assets in Kenya may apply to the Minister for a certificate that the enterprise in which the assets are proposed to be invested is an approved enterprise for the purposes of this Act. The Minister shall consider every application made under subsection (1) and in any case in which he is satisfied that the enterprise would further the economic development of, or would be of benefit to Kenya, he may in his discretion issue a certificate to the applicant.

Every certificate should state the name of the holder, the name and a description of the enterprise. It should also state the amount of the foreign assets invested or to be invested by the holder of the certificate in the enterprise divided as between capital, being deemed to be a fixed amount representing the equity of the holder in the enterprise for the purposes of this Act and which shall be expressed in the certificate in, and shall for the purposes of this Act be in, either Kenya currency or the relevant foreign currency; and any loan, which may be expressed in, and may for the purposes of this Act be in, either Kenya currency or the relevant foreign currency.

The certificate should also state the foreign currency invested or to be invested and such other matters as may be necessary or desirable for the purposes of the Act. If it so happens that the foreign assets have not yet been invested a conditional certificate shall be issued stating, in addition to the details specified in subsection (3), the period in which they shall be invested.

If, at the time at which a certificate is issued under this Act, any foreign assets or part thereof to which the certificate relates have not been invested in the approved enterprise, they shall be so invested within the approved period, and, if not so invested within that period, the certificate shall be deemed to have been revoked.

b. Special Arrangement for Investment Promotion and Protection

The law also empowers the Minister for Finance may, from time to time, by notice in the Gazette declare that the arrangement specified in the notice, being arrangements made with the Government of any country with a view to promoting and protecting the investments of that country in Kenya, shall have effect according to its tenor.

The Government has put emphasis on attracting Foreign Direct Investment (FDI) and fast tracking implementation of the economic pillar under the Vision 2030 through the overhaul of legislation which impact the ease of doing business. One of the key initiatives is the promotion of Special Economic Zones, a recognition that Export Processing Zones have not had the expected impact on the economy.

c. Special Economic Areas

The President assented to the Special Economic Zone Act, 2015 (SEZ Act) on 11 September 2015 and the Act was subsequently published on 15 September 2015. The purpose of the Act is to promote and facilitate investment by global and local investors by promoting an enabling environment for such investments. An SEZ has to be established in a designated geographical area to be gazetted by the Cabinet Secretary for Industrialization.

a) Licences to Be Issued Under The Act

The SEZ Act provides for the following licences to be issued under the Act:
- Operator Licence—corporate entity engaged in the management of a special economic zone;
- Developer Licence—corporate entity engaged in developing and operating a special economic zone;
- Enterprise Licence—corporate entity carrying out business in a special economic zone.

b) Types of Special Economic Zones

Areas declared as a special economic zones may be designated as a single sector or multiple sector special economic zones and can cover the following sectors:
- Agricultural Zone: SEZ to facilitate agricultural sector and relates activities and services;
- Business Processing Outsourcing (BPO): SEZ to provide outsourcing services such as back office support services in human resources, finance, accounting, and procurement among others;
- Business Service Park: SEZ to facilitate provision of services to regional headquarters, BPOs, call centres, management consulting, advisory services and other associated services;
- Freeport Zone: A designated area at the port where goods introduced there are regarded to be outside the customs territory (EAC Countries);
- Free Trade Zone: A customs controlled area where goods are off-loaded for transshipment, storage and may include bulk breaking, repacking, sorting, mixing, trading or other forms of handling excluding manufacturing and processing;
- Industrial park: A zone with integrated infrastructure to facilitate manufacturing and processing industries;
- Formation Communication Technology park: A zone to facilitate ICT sector, its services and related activities;
- Livestock zone: A zone where livestock marshalling and inspection, livestock feeding or fattening, abattoir and refrigeration, deboning, value addition, manufacture of veterinary products and other related activities are carried out;
- Science and Technology Park: A zone to facilitate the science and technology sector;
- Tourism and recreation Centre: A zone to facilitate tourism and recreation sector.

c) Special Economic Zones Authority

The SEZ will be governed by the Special Economic Zones Authority (Authority) whose roles shall be:
- Reviewing applications and granting licenses to SEZ developers, operators and enterprises;
- Promoting and marketing SEZs to potential developers, operators and other investors;
- Implementing policies and programmes of the Government;
- Identifying, mapping and availing to developers and operators the areas of land to be designated as SEZ;
- Determining investment criteria and threshold;
- Administering a one-stop centre through which SEZ enterprise can channel all their applications for permits, approvals, licences and facilities not handled directly by the authority; among others.

d) Trading in SEZ Goods and Services

Goods and services produced in a SEZ can be exported out of the country, sold within Kenya as though imported from outside (subject to customs requirements) or be used within the SEZ for the manufacture of other goods or provision of other services.

e) Qualification to Be An SEZ Developer / Enterprise

An SEZ developer / enterprise is expected to meet the following requirements before registration:
- Be incorporated in Kenya;
- Have financial capacity and technical expertise to carry-out the SEZ proposed operations;
- Own or lease land or premise within SEZ;

• Engage in any activity eligible to be undertaken by an SEZ;
• Should not have a negative impact on the environment or engage in activities that are a threat to national security.

f) Benefits of Operating in An SEZ in Kenya

The Act provides for various benefits such as:

(i) Tax Exemption

An SEZ enterprise, developer and operator shall be granted exemption from all taxes and duties payable under the Excise Duty Act, Income Tax Act, East Africa Community Customs Management Act and the Value Added Tax Act on all SEZ transactions.

(ii) Other Exemption

SEZ enterprises, developers and operators shall also enjoy exemptions from:
• Stamp Duty on execution of instruments relating to business activities of the SEZ;
• Provisions Foreign Investments and Protection Act;
• The provisions of the Statistics Act;
• Payment of advertisement fees and business service permit fees levied by County Governments;
• General liquor licence and hotel liquor licence under the Alcoholic Drinks Control Act, 2010;
• Manufacturing licence under the Tea Act;
• Licence to trade in unwrought precious metals;
• Filming licence;
• Rent or tenancy controls; and
• Any other exemption as may be granted by the Act through a Gazette notice.

(iii) Work Permits

SEZ shall be allowed to have expatriates and obtain work permits for up to 20% of the total workforce, with additional work permits available on request.

(iv) Other Benefits

• Protection of property against nationalization and expropriation;
• Repatriation of capital and profits without any foreign exchange impediments; and
• Protection of intellectual property.

g) Dispute Resolution

The SEZ Act has set out a dispute resolution mechanisms, for any dispute that may arise between an SEZ entity and the Authority or Government. The timelines for dispute resolution is 30 days for negotiations and mutual agreement. Where the dispute is not resolved, the parties shall submit the issue to arbitration within 14 days.

h) Penalties

The SEZ Act provides for a stiff penalty of KShs 20,000,000 or imprisonment for up to three years or both and forfeiture of goods for any person found violating the provisions of the Act.

III. Trade

A. Department Supervising Trade

Pursuant to the Kenyan Constitution, trade supervision is done by both the National Government and the 47 County Governments.

The Ministry of Industry, Trade and Cooperatives is the main organ through which the National Government promotes trade, industrialization and enterprise development as well as supervision of international trade. The Ministry is made up of three State Departments; the State Department of Trade, the State Department of Investment and Industry and the State Department of Cooperatives.

On the other hand, County Governments are tasked with trade development and regulation including markets, trade licenses (excluding regulation of professions), fair trade practices, local tourism and cooperative societies in theirrespective Counties.

B. Brief Introduction of Trade Laws and Regulations

There is no general law regulating trade in Kenya. Trade is regulated under several difference pieces of legislation as discussed below.

The Customs and Excise Act, Chapter 472 Laws of Kenya is the primary legislation regulating importation and exportation of goods in Kenya. The Act sets out the duties applicable on importation an exportation of goods into and out of Kenya. The Act also prohibits the importation and exportation of prohibited goods such as firearms and ammunition (unless authorized by law), false money or counterfeit currency notes, denatured spirits, obscene materials and distilled beverages containing essential oils or chemical products which are injurious to health amongst others. The Commissioner General of the Kenya Revenue Authority under the supervision of the Cabinet Secretary in charge of Finance, is responsible for ensuring compliance with the stipulations of the Customs and Excise Act.

Further prohibitions with respect to importation and exportation of goods into Kenya are contained in other Acts of Parliament including the Environment Management and Coordination Act of 1998 which prohibits handling and disposal of hazardous substances in Kenya as well as the Trading in Prohibited Goods Act of Kenya.

Various Counties have enacted County legislations regulating trade activities within their respective jurisdictions.

C. Trade Management

Kenya has enacted several pieces of legislation seeking to manage trade including the Investment Promotion Act in Kenya which entitles a foreign owned business in Kenya to apply for an investment certificate. This certificate entitles the business to obtain (as a right) all necessary licenses for that business and certain work permits for expatriate staff and allows the business a period of one year within which to obtain the licenses and permits, the business can operate without the licenses and permits in this period.

The Foreign Investments Protection Act on the other hand aims to protect foreign investors from discrimination and provide for fair and equitable rules on expropriation as set out in the Constitution.

Additional tax benefits and exemptions are issued to Companies set up in Economic Processing Zones under the Export Processing Zones Act and the Special Economic Zones under the Special economic Zones Act which aims to attract more local and foreign investments into the country.

The National Government has set up one stop shops known as Huduma Centres, where one can access all government and public services in a timely efficient manner. The Government also has an online portal known as eCitizen which is a digital payments platform that enables Kenyan citizens, residents and visitors' access and pay for government services such as visa applications, company incorporation, and license application online. Various County Governments have also set up online platforms to provide access to payment services by residents of their counties.

D. The Inspection and Quarantine of Import and Export Commodities

The Standards Act provides for the standardization of commodities and codes of practice.

The Standards Act also establishes the Kenya Bureau of Standards ("the KEBS") whose functions are, inter alia, to prepare, frame, amend or modify specifications and codes of practice. The Act also establishes the National Standards Council which may by gazette notice declare any specification or code prepared by the KEBS to be a Kenya Standard.

The KEBS administers the Pre-Export Verification of Conformity to Standards for the regulation of the quality of imported goods ("PVoC"). The overall objective of PVoC is to minimize the risk of unsafe and substandard goods entering Kenyan market, thus ensuring health, safety and environmental protection for Kenyans. It is incumbent upon an importer of goods into Kenya to ensure that the said goods meet Kenya's standards or approved specifications.

Imported goods if listed by the KEBS shall be subjected to a verification of conformity to Kenya Standards or approved specifications in the country of origin by an inspection body authorized by the KEBS and may be re-inspected at the port of entry by the Bureau if it is deemed necessary. KEBS shall then issue a certificate of conformity or a non-conformity report. Non-conforming goods will not be allowed entry into Kenya and shall be re-shipped, returned or destroyed at the expense of the importer. Any listed goods arriving at the port of entry without a certificate of conformity shall be subjected to a fee of 15% of the cost, insurance and freight value of the good and a duly executed security bond equivalent to the said fee.

The Standards Act further stipulates that no person shall manufacture or sell any commodity, method or procedure to which the relevant specification or code of practice relates in Kenya, unless it complies with the prescribed specification or code of practice. Further, a standardization mark shall be applied to compliant goods and products.

The Plant Protection Act and Agricultural Produce (Export) Act provides the legislative framework for import and exportation of plants and the standards applicable thereto. The Kenya Plant Health Inspectorate Service (KEPHIS) regulates the importation and exportation of plants pursuant to this Act.

E. Customs Management

Pursuant to the Customs and Excise Act, the Commissioner General of the Kenya Revenue Authority, subject to the direction of the Cabinet Secretary in charge of Finance, is responsible for the control and management of customs and excise department and for the collection of, and accounting for, customs and excise revenue in Kenya.

The East African Community which came into force in July 2000 aims at widening and deepening co-operation among the Partner States thereto (i.e.Burundi, Kenya, Rwanda, South Sudan Tanzania, and Uganda) (the "EAC") in, inter alia, political, economic and social fields for their mutual benefit. The treaty emphasises co-operation in the priority areas of transport and communication, trade and industry, security, immigration and the promotion of investment in the region.

To this end the EAC Partner States established a Customs Union in 2005. The East African Community Customs Management Act 2004 is the piece of legislation enacted and adopted by to govern the East African Community Customs Union created under the Protocol on the Establishment of the East African Customs Union.

The Act specifies that the movement of goods between Partner States do not constitute "imports" or "exports" but instead constitute "transfers" of goods within the Community. Goods are only deemed to be exported or imported when they originate from any country other than a Partner State.

The Act deals with Export Processing Zones (EPZ's) and Freeports and provides that goods entering such areas shall be free from duty in accordance with the EAC Customs Union Protocol. It however does not provide for the concept of SEZ's.

Under the Act, the Commissioner has power:

(i) To permit removal of goods in EPZ's or freeports for home consumption subject to the payment of duties due. Removal of goods from these zones without the authority of the Commissioner is an offence.

(ii) To designate areas in EPZ's and freeports in which customs formalities shall be carried out.

The EACCMA also requires the Commissioner to be notified in advance of any industrial, commercial or service activity authorized by the operator of an EPZ or a freeport.

Kenya is also a member of several trade blocks such as the Common Market for Eastern and Southern Africa (COMESA). Further, plans are underway for the establishment of a Tripartite Free Trade Area (TFTA) involving COMESA, EAC and Southern African Development Community (SADC) creating the largest free trade area in Africa. Kenya has signed the Declaration intimating its intention to be TFTA's member. Kenya has also been a World Trade Organization (WTO) member since 1 January 1995 and a party to the General Agreement on Tariffs and Trade (GATT) since 5 February 1964 as well as European Union Economic Partnership Agreement since November 2007. All these international agreements make provision for customs management.

IV. Labour

A. Brief Introduction of Labour Laws and Regulations

In Kenya, labour matters are primarily founded on the following laws:

(i) The Constitution of Kenya 2010 which makes provision for labour relations and various labour rights due to persons;

(ii) The Employment Act, 2007 which defines the fundamental rights of employees, provides the basic conditions of employment in Kenya and provides the statutory minimum terms and conditions of employment;

(iii) The Employment and Labour Relations Court Act, 2011 which establishes the Employment and Labour Relations Court and sets out its objectives, composition, jurisdiction and procedure;

(iv) The Labour Relations Act, 2007 which regulates the relationship between employers and trade unions;

(v) The Labour Institutions Act, 2007 which establishes the labour institutions in Kenya;

(vi) The Work Benefits Injuries Act, 2007 which provides for the compensation to employees for work related injuries and diseases contracted in the course of employment; and

(vii) The Occupational Safety and Health Act, 2007 which provides for the safety, health and welfare of workers and all persons lawfully present at workplaces.

B. Requirements of Employing Foreign Employees

a. Work Permit

The Kenya Citizenship and Immigration Act, 2011 (the "Immigration Act") and the Kenya Citizenship and

Immigration Regulations (the Immigration Regulations) provide that in order for any foreign national to work in Kenya, he / she must first obtain a work permit or special pass. The presence in Kenya of a person who is not a citizen of Kenya shall be unlawful unless that person holds a valid work permit, residence permit or pass.

Pursuant to the Immigration Act, every employer must apply for and obtain a work permit or special pass conferring on the foreign national the right to engage in employment before granting the foreign national employment. In practice, this translates into employers incurring the cost of the work permit or special pass.

The Department of Immigration has been given the mandate to control and regulate residency through the issuance and renewal of entry permits and other passes.

There are different classes of work permits ranging between Class A to M. Each class is intended for a specific person who fulfils specific requirements.

For example, a Class D permit is issued to a foreign person who is offered specific employment by a specific employer, the Government of Kenya or an approved technical aid scheme under the United Nations Organization or some other approved Agency.

In order for a work permit to be issued, a foreigner must satisfy certain conditions as follows:

(i) The individual must be in possession of skills or qualifications that are not available in Kenya and that their engagement in that employment will be of benefit to Kenya.

(ii) The foreigner must have an understudy who is a Kenyan citizen. The understudy shall be trained to take up the position being applied for by the foreigner.

(iii) A foreigner is required to deposit as security an amount of money prescribed by the Regulations. This amount is deposited with the Kenya Citizens and Foreign Nationals Management Service and is dependent on the type of permit being issued. In lieu of a deposit, the Director of Immigration may permit a foreigner to enter into a bond to provide security, with or without sureties. The Director of Immigration may also permit the employer to enter into a covenant to provide general security in respect of the employee and his or her spouse, children and other dependants in lieu of a deposit or security bond.

At present, it takes between 2-4 months for an immigration application to be approved. In case an applicant wishes to start employment within a short time, one can apply for a special pass. A special pass is a short-term approval document issued to the Department of Immigration that is valid for a period of six (6) months and is not renewable.

b. Application Procedure

Ordinarily, the employer will file the work permit application on the Department of Immigration's Electronic Foreign National Service (eFNS) system. Although the application documents in relation to the various classes of work permits vary, the following documents are necessary for all applications:

(i) Duly filled and signed application Form;

(ii) Signed cover letter from the employer / self / organization addressed to the Director of Immigration Services;

(iii) Copies of national passport;

(iv) Two recent coloured passport size photo; and

(v) Current Immigration status if in the country.

If the Director of Immigration is satisfied that the requirements of that particular class have been met and the engagement or the applicant's presence in Kenya will be of benefit to Kenya, the permit will be issued.

In the case of an employee ceasing to work for the employer for any reason, the employer specified in the work permit is required to report in writing to the Director of Immigration within fifteen (15) days that the holder of a permit has ceased to engage in the employment in respect of which the permit was issued and any employer who fails to do so commits an offence.

Serious penalties are prescribed for both employer and employee if the application and registration processes are not adhered to. Where no penalty is prescribed in the Act, a general penalty of a fine not exceeding one million shillings or imprisonment for a term not exceeding five years is applied to any person that is convicted of an offence under the Act.

c. Social Insurance

The state pension system that is in place is the National Social Security Fund ("NSSF") that is set out in the National Social Security Fund Act 2013 (the "NSSF Act").

The NSSF operates on a defined contribution basis in that the amount that a member shall receive upon retirement under this plan depends on the performance of the fund's investments over time and the total amount contributed. Contribution is made by both the employer and employee.

NSSF covers the following categories of employers and employees:

(i) Private Sector, this includes companies, non-governmental organizations, international organizations and organized groups in the informal sector;
(ii) Government Ministries;
(iii) Parastatal organizations ;
(iv) Self-employed or any other person not covered by any other scheme; and
(v) Any other category as declared by the Ministry of Labour, Social and Security Services.

The NSSF Act defines an employee as 'any person who has attained the age of eighteen years and who is employed in Kenya under a contract of service'. As the scope of this definition is broad, foreign employees are required to be registered under the Fund.

The NSSF Act however exempts the following persons from registration under the Fund:
(i) persons entitled to exemption from contribution to social security under any International Convention; and
(ii) persons not ordinarily resident in Kenya who are employed in Kenya for periods not exceeding three years at any one time being persons who are liable to contribute to or are or shall be entitled to benefit from the social security Fund or similar body of any country other than Kenya approved by the Cabinet Secretary in writing.

Apart from the mandatory NSSF scheme an employee may opt to join an occupational scheme or individual pension scheme. Occupational schemes are set up by employers for the benefit of their staff. Such schemes are voluntary and are established under trust. Individual pension schemes on the other hand are set up by institutional providers (mostly financial institutions) to target individual members not necessarily tied to an employer or any formal setting.

The state health insurance system is the National Health Insurance Fund (NHIF) that is set out in the National Health Insurance Fund Act (the "NHIF Act"). The NHIF Act sets out who is liable to contribute to the Fund. It provides that any person who is ordinarily resident in Kenya and who has attained the age of 18 years shall be liable to contribute to the fund. Persons ordinarily resident include foreign visitors permitted to work or study in Kenya.

Apart from NHIF, a foreign employee can be registered under a private health insurance scheme offered by their employer.

C. Exit and Entry

a. Visa Types

The type of visa issued to persons wishing to gain entry into Kenya depends on a number of factors such as the purpose and intended duration of the visit. The Immigration Regulations set out clearly the various persons and countries whose nationals do not require visas to enter Kenya. The Regulations also prescribe the countries whose nationals may be issued with visas on application.

Persons intending to transit through Kenya to a third destination for periods not exceeding three (3) days can obtain a transit visa. This visa allows one to leave the airport for this duration.

Persons whose nationalities require visas to enter Kenya for visits or residence shall be issued with a Single Journey / Ordinary Visa. The validity period is specified in the visa.

Persons who are nationals of countries which require visas for Kenya and who by nature of the business or circumstances require to make frequent visits to Kenya may be issued with a Multiple Journey Visa.

Holders of diplomatic passports who are on official duty shall be issued a Diplomatic Visa free of charge. It is important to note that diplomats and government officials on private visits to Kenya and who are nationals of countries that require referred visas are required to make applications for a visa in the usual manner.

Persons holding official or service passports on official duty and ordinary passport holders who are not entitled to a Diplomatic Visa (where it is considered to be desirable on the grounds of international courtesy) shall be issued an Official / Courtesy Visa. The validity period is specified in the visa.

b. Restrictions for Exit and Entry

If a departing foreign national is found to have overstayed in the country in contravention of the Immigration Act, an immigration officer has the power to bring it to the notice of that person the option to enter a written admission of contravention.

Upon receipt of the said written admission of contravention the immigration officer may impose a fine not exceeding fifty thousand Kenyan shillings. An immigration officer may prosecute any person who fails to immediately pay the penalty.

Persons categorized as prohibited immigrants under the Act and persons without valid permits or passes will be restricted from entering Kenya.

D. Trade Union and Labour Organizations

Article 41 of the Constitution of Kenya and the Labour Relations Act Cap 233 deal with the formation of trade unions by either an employer or an employee and they provide that formation of a trade union is a right of both an employer and an employee. This means that an employer or employee may choose whether to join or form a trade union or not.

There is no mandatory requirement for formation of a labour union under Kenyan law.

E. Labour Disputes

Labour disputes are determined by the Employment and Labour Relations Court (the "ELRC"). The ELRC was set up to hear and determine disputes relating to employment and labour relations.

The Employment Act provides clearly that the ELRC is the only court that can hear and determine disputes where an employer or employee neglects or refuses to fulfil a contract of Service, where any question, difference or dispute arises as to the rights or liabilities of either party or disputes touching any misconduct, neglect or ill-treatment of either party or any injury to the person or property of either party, under any contract of service.

A party who wishes to refer a dispute to the ELRC under any written law may file a statement of claim, a petition or judicial review proceedings.

The Employment and Labour Relations Court Act provides that nothing precludes the ELRC from adopting and implementing, on its own motion or at the request of the parties, any other appropriate means of dispute resolution, including internal methods, conciliation, mediation and traditional dispute resolution mechanisms in accordance with Article 159(2)(c) of the Constitution.

The Labour Relations Act also provides for a dispute resolution mechanism for trade disputes. It defines a trade dispute as a dispute between employers and employees, employers and trade unions, or between an employers' organisation and employees or trade unions, concerning any employment matter, and includes disputes regarding the dismissal, suspension or redundancy of employees, allocation of work or the recognition of a trade union.

It makes provision for a trade union, employer or employers' organization that is a party to the dispute or their authorized representative to report a trade dispute to the Cabinet Secretary in charge of Employment matters. Within twenty-one days of a trade dispute being reported, the Cabinet Secretary shall appoint a conciliator to attempt to resolve the trade dispute unless the conciliation procedures in an applicable collective agreement binding on the parties to the dispute have not been exhausted or a law or collective agreement binding upon the parties prohibits negotiation on the issue in dispute.

If any party is aggrieved with the decision arrived at, the party may refer the matter to the Employment and Labour Relations Court.

V. Intellectual Property

A. Brief Introduction of IP Laws and Regulations

Intellectual Property Rights as a function is a preserve of the National Government. Consequently all legislations and regulations governing intellectual property rights in Kenya are enacted at the national level.

Kenya is also party to numerous treaties and bodies on intellectual property rights, granting proprietors more protection including the Madrid Agreement Concerning the International Registration of Marks as well as its Protocol, Patent Cooperation Treaty, Berne Convention for the Protection of Literary and Artistic Works, Paris Convention for the Protection of Industrial Property, WTO TRIPS Agreement, and the Harare Protocol on Patents and Industrial Designs Within the Framework of the African Regional Industrial Property Organization (ARIPO), amongst others.

a. Patent Protection

Patents in Kenya are governed by the Industrial Property Act of 2001 (the "IP Act"). The IP Act was enacted to provide the legislative framework for the acquisition, granting and regulation of patents, utility models, technovations and industrial designs.

The IP Act establishes the Kenya Industrial Property Institute ("KIPI") a body corporate mandated to consider and approve applications for the various industrial property rights; screen and register technology transfer agreements and licenses; provide industrial property information for technology and economic development to the public; and to generally promote innovation in Kenya.

The IP Act also establishes the Industrial Property Tribunal which hears and determines appeals from persons whose registration of IP rights has been denied by the Managing Director of KIPI.

Other bodies involved include ARIPO where regional filings are done and the Patent Co-operation Treaty for international filings.

The length of protection runs for a period of 20 years subject to remittance of annual fees.

b. Trademark Protection

The Trade Marks Act is the primary legislation regulating trade marks in Kenya. Further applicable provisions are stipulated by the Trademark Rules enacted pursuant to the Trademark Act.

Trademarks once registered are valid for a period of 10 years.

Kenya has also adopted the Nice Agreement on International Classification of Goods and Services and the Vienna Agreement on International Classification of the Figurative Elements of Marks in so far as registration of marks and figurative elements is concerned.

c. Copyright Protection

Copyright protection in Kenya is regulated by the Copyright Act of Kenya which provides for the legislative framework for the protection of copyright in literary, musical and artistic works, audio-visual works, sound recordings and broadcasts.

The Copyright Act establishes the Kenya Copyright Board, a body corporate mandated to administer all matters relating to copyright in Kenya. The primary functions of the Copyright Board include directing, coordinating and overseeing the implementation of laws which relate to copyright; enlightening the public on matters relating to copyright; and maintaining an effective data bank on authors and their works.

The Copyright Regulations of 2004 provide for registration of copyright work. The Executive Director of the Kenya Copyright Board is mandated to open and maintain a register known as the "Copyright Register" wherein the particulars of registered copyright work shall be recorded.

The purpose of registration is to maintain a record of copyright works, enable the Copyright Board to establish and maintain an effective data bank on authors and their works and to publicize the rights of the owners of works. Registration of copyright work by authors is voluntary and is not a prerequisite for protection thereof.

The procedure for registering of copyright works involves the below steps:

(i) Filing an application in the prescribed form obtained from the Kenya Copyright Board accompanied by the fees prescribed in the Copyright Regulations;

(ii) On receipt of the application the Executive Director of the Kenya Copyright Board may enter such work in the copyright register if the work is deemed to meet the relevant standards set out in the Copyright Act; and

(iii) a certificate of registration is then issued.

Kenya is also party to the Berne Convention for the Protection of Literary and Artistic Works granting extended protection to Kenya's copyright holders in other contracting States.

d. Industrial Design Protection

The IP Act governs Industrial designs in Kenya. The Act defines an industrial design as a composition of lines or colours or any three dimensional form, whether or not associated with lines or colours provided that such composition or form gives a special appearance to a product of industry or handicraft and can serve as a pattern for a product of industry or handicraft.

Applications for industrial designs in Kenya are made to the KIPI.

e. Patent Application

Pursuant to the IP Act, an invention is patentable if it is new, involves an inventive step and, is industrially applicable. Applications for patents are filed with the Managing Director of KIPI.

The procedure for registering of a patent involves the below steps:

(i) preparing and filing a patent application;

(ii) request for examination (within 3 years from the filing date);

(iii) approval, request for further information or rejection of application by an examiner;

(iv) if further information requested, a response to examiner is made;

(v) examiner approves, reconsiders or calls for further amendments;

(vi) if the examiner approves the patent then the same is granted (where a patent is rejected, one may appeal which procedure is set out below);

(vii) publication of the contents of the patent in the Kenya Gazette or the industrial property journal; and

(viii) grant of patent issued.

The time frame for registering a patent is approximately eighteen months.

Where an application for patent is rejected, an applicant may appeal to the Industrial Property Tribunal. Appeals from the decisions of the Industrial Property Tribunal lie with the High Court of Kenya. Appeals from the decisions of the High Court of Kenya lie with the Court of Appeal of Kenya.

f. Trademark Registration

A trademark is registrable in Kenya, if it contains any of the following particulars:

(i) Name of a individual or firm, represented in a special or particular manner;

(ii) Signature of the applicant or some predecessor in his business;

(iii) An invented word or invented words.

(iv) Words with no reference to the character / quality of the goods and that do not contain a geographical name / surname;

(v) Any distinctive mark.

The procedure for application of a trademark in Kenya involves the below steps:

(i) Conducting a search at the KIPI registry to determine the availability of the proposed mark;

(ii) Completion and submission of an application in the prescribed form detailing the proposed trade mark and proprietors thereto;

(iii) Examination;

(iv) Upon approval, the trademark shall proceed to advertisement in KIPI's monthly Journal. Any opposing party is at liberty to oppose by filing a statement of opposition within sixty days;

(v) Where there is no opposition, the Registrar of Trademarks shall on expiry of sixty days from date of advertisement, register the trademark and issue the applicant with a certificate of registration.

g. Measures for IP Protection

Kenya has put in place a robust legal framework to combat IP related violations. The Trademarks Act prohibits various offences in relation to trade marks ranging from forgery of registered trademarks which is punishable by a fine not exceeding two hundred thousand shillings or to imprisonment for a term not exceeding five years or both, to falsification of entries in register which is punishable by imprisonment for a term not exceeding five years or to a fine not exceeding ten thousand shillings, or both.

Further, the country enacted the Anti-Counterfeit Act of 2008, which establishes an Anti-Counterfeit Agency, a body tasked with combating counterfeiting, trade and other dealings in counterfeit goods in Kenya.

The IP Act provides that any intentional infringement of a patent or registered utility model or industrial design shall constitute an offence punishable by imprisonment for a term not less than three years and not more than five years or a fine of not less than ten thousand shillings and not exceeding fifty thousand shillings or with both.

Additionally, infringement of copyright under the Copyright Act attracts fines ranging between one hundred thousand shillings to four hundred thousand shillings and imprisonment for terms between two to ten years. The owner is also entitled to various remedies ranging from damages, injunction, damages in lieu of royalty and delivery of article in possession.

VI. Environmental Protection

A. Department Supervising Environmental Protection

The Constitution vests protection of the environment and natural resources in Kenya to the National Government. The Cabinet Secretary in charge of the Ministry of Environment and Natural Resources is responsible for policy formulation, directions, setting of national goals and objectives as well as determination of policies and priorities for the protection of the environment.

The National Environment Management Authority ("NEMA") is the main body established under the law to exercise general supervision and co-ordination over all matters relating to the environment and to be the principal instrument of Government in the implementation of all policies relating to the environment.

Other agencies performing environmental functions in Kenya, include the Kenya Forest Service, Kenya Fisheries Service and the Kenya Wildlife Service.

B. Brief Introduction of Laws and Regulations of Environmental Protection

The Environmental Management and Co-ordination Act of 1999 is the primary law governing environment management and protection in Kenya. It provides for protection of rivers, lakes, seas, wet lands, mountain areas, forests and other environmentally significant areas.

Other areas covered by the Act include: environmental audit and monitoring, environmental quality standards, environmental planning, integrated environmental impact assessment, inspection, analysis and records. The Act also establishes various enforcement bodies, these include; NEMA, National Environment Tribunal and the Environment and Land Court to adjudicate environment disputes. Moreover, several acts have been criminalized by the Act, with penalties ranging from fines of one million shillings to five million shillings as well as imprisonment for terms ranging from one year to four years. To give effect to the stipulations of the Act, thirteen regulations have since been enacted.

Other laws such as Forest Conservation and Management Act of 2016, Wildlife Conservation and Management Act of 2013 and the Fisheries Management and Development Act of 2016, all play complementary role in so far as environmental protection is concerned.

C. Evaluation of Environmental Protection

The Country's legislative framework on environment is to a large extent very progressive as set out in the various legislations discussed above. Kenya has ratified several environment related international treaties as well. Enforcement however remains an issue in some areas.

VII. Dispute Resolution

A. Methods and Bodies of Dispute Resolution

a. Common Law System Governing Disputes in Kenya

The legal system in Kenya descends from the English Common Law system. One of the fundamental doctrines of Common Law is the doctrine of precedent which provides that every court is bound to follow the decisions made by the court above it and, on the whole, appellate courts also have to follow their own decisions.

b. Hierarchy of Courts

Under the Constitution of Kenya, courts operate on two levels, Superior Courts and Subordinate Courts. These consist of the following:

a) Superior Courts

(i) The Supreme Court—this is the highest court in Kenya. It can only hear and determine disputes relating to the elections to the office of the President, appeals from the Court of Appeal and any other court or tribunal prescribed by national legislation.

The Appeals from the Court of Appeal are only those that lie as of right in any case involving the interpretation of or application of the Constitution of Kenya or any other case in which the Supreme Court or Court of Appeal certifies that a matter of general public importance is involved.

The Supreme Court can also give advisory opinions at the request of National Government, any state organ or county government.

(ii) The Court of Appeal—the second highest court in Kenya can hear appeals from the High Court and any other court or tribunal as prescribed by an Act of Parliament.

(iii) The High Court— It has unlimited original jurisdiction in criminal and civil matters which means that it can hear and determine practically any actionable matter.

It also has the jurisdiction to hear to determine the question whether a right or fundamental freedom in the Bill of Rights has been denied, violated, infringed or threatened, to hear an appeal from a decision of a tribunal appointed under the Constitution to consider the removal of a person from office and any question respecting the interpretation of the Constitution.

(iv) The Employment and Labour Relations Court—this is a specialised court with the status of the High Court. It hears and determines disputes relating to labour and employment matters.

(v) The Environment and Land Court—this is another specialised court with the status of the High Court. It hears and determines land and environment matters and appeals from all tribunals dealing in land and environment matters.

b) Subordinate Courts

(i) Magistrate Courts—These courts are presided over by a chief magistrate, a senior principal magistrate, a principal magistrate, a senior resident magistrate or a resident magistrate. Parties are appointed a different magistrate depending on the value of the subject matter of their claim. For example, a resident magistrate can hear and determine claims where the value of the subject matter does not exceed five (5) million Kenyan Shillings whereas the chief magistrate can hear and determine claims where the value of the subject matter does not exceed twenty (20) million shillings.

(ii) Kadhis Court—Their jurisdiction is limited to the determination of questions of Muslim Law relating to personal status, marriage, divorce or inheritance in proceedings in which all the parties profess the Muslim Religion and submit to the jurisdiction of the Kadhis' courts.

(iii) Court Martial—It has the power to try any person subject to the Armed Forces Act for any offence which under the Armed Forces Act is triable by court martial, and to award punishment for such an offence.

c. Specialist Tribunals

In Kenya, tribunals are bodies established by Acts of Parliament to exercise judicial or quasi-judicial functions. Each tribunal is appointed and constituted differently. Tribunals supplement ordinary courts in the administration of justice however, they do not have penal jurisdiction.

Tribunals, like the courts, have to respect the Bill of Rights in their decisions and not be repugnant to justice and morality or be inconsistent with the Constitution or other laws of the land. Most tribunals are subject to the supervision of the High Court.

There are many different types of tribunals in Kenya. Some tribunals like the Kenya Board of Mental Health are purely regulatory and advisory while others such as the Rent Tribunals and the Income Tax Tribunals adjudicate disputes between citizens or between citizens and public bodies.

d. Procedure for Filing and Conduct of Cases

Cases are filed physically at the relevant court registry upon which a case number is allocated. For civil suits, after each party has filed and served its pleadings, each party completes, files and serves a pre-trial questionnaire upon which the Court convenes a Case Conference. The purpose of the Case Conference is to help the Court identify the disputed issues as well as set up the manner in which it will conduct the proceedings. The Court could also help the parties to settle the whole or part of the case.

The Court then conducts a trial conference to plan the trial time, as well as decide on the fastest way to conduct the trial. After Trial Conference is concluded, the court then issues a hearing date.

During the hearing, the Plaintiff has the right to start and thus presents their case first. The Plaintiff is required to state their case and present both oral and written evidence. Once the Plaintiff has finished presenting their case, the Defendant also presents their case, calls witnesses and produces both oral and written evidence. Both parties are then allowed to file their final submissions, after which the court sets a day for judgment. After the trial has been concluded, the court will proceed to give a judgment within Sixty (60) days of concluding the trial.

After the judgment has been read out, the Registrar draws, seals and issues an order or decree of the court. The order or decree should reflect the decision of the Court and should specify clearly in paragraphs the award sought and granted.

e. Alternative Dispute Resolution Procedures

Article 159 of the Constitution recognises alternative forms of dispute resolution including reconciliation, mediation, arbitration and traditional dispute resolution mechanisms. It provides that they shall all be promoted as long as they do not contravene the Bill of Rights and are not repugnant to justice or inconsistent with the Constitution or any written law.

For civil suits, the Civil Procedure Act provides for suits to be referred to any other method of dispute resolution where the parties agree or the Court considers the case suitable for such referral. It sets out that any other method of alternative dispute resolution shall be governed by such procedure as the parties themselves agree to or as the Court may, in its discretion, order.

Any settlement arising from a suit referred to any other alternative dispute resolution method by the Court or agreement of the parties shall be enforceable as a judgment of the Court and no appeal shall lie in respect of any judgment entered under this section.

a) Arbitration

The Arbitration Act, 1995 (as amended in 2010) is the principle piece of legislation governing arbitration in the Republic of Kenya. Although the Act does not specifically prohibit any dispute from being arbitrated, it is generally accepted that arbitration is not the correct medium for resolving criminal disputes.

Kenya is party to the New York Convention of 1958 ("the Convention"). Kenya signed the Convention in 1989 with a reciprocity reservation. The Arbitration Act provides that an international arbitration award shall be recognised as binding and enforced in accordance to the provisions of the New York Convention or any other convention to which Kenya is signatory and relating to arbitral awards.

The Arbitration Act provides that the recognition or enforcement of an arbitral award, irrespective of the state in which it was made, may be refused in the following circumstances:

(i) Where a party to the arbitration agreement was under some incapacity;

(ii) Where the arbitration agreement is not valid under the law to which the parties have subjected it or, failing any indication of that law, under the law of the state where the arbitral award was made;

(iii) Where the party against whom the arbitral award is invoked was not given proper notice of the appointment of an arbitrator or of the arbitral proceedings or was otherwise unable to present his case;

(iv) Where the arbitral award deals with a dispute not contemplated by or not falling within the terms of the reference to arbitration, or it contains decisions on matters beyond the scope of the reference to arbitration;

(v) Where the composition of the arbitral tribunal or the arbitral procedure was not in accordance with the agreement of the parties or, failing any agreement by the parties, was not in accordance with the law of the state where the arbitration took place;

(vi) Where the arbitral award has not yet become binding on the parties or has been set aside or suspended by a court of the state in which, or under the law of which, that arbitral award was made; or

(vii) Where the making of the arbitral award was induced or affected by fraud, bribery, corruption or undue influence.

The main institutions used in Kenya for both domestic and international arbitrations are the Chartered Institute of Arbitrators (Kenya Branch), The Nairobi Centre for International Arbitration and the International Chamber of Commerce and the London Court of International Arbitration.

b) Conciliation

The Employment Act, Labour Institutions Act and Labour Relations Act are among the statutes that make provision for the resolution of disputes through conciliation. The conciliation agreement must be in writing and signed by both parties and the conciliator.

c) Mediation

Mediation is a voluntary, informal, consensual, strictly confidential and nonbinding dispute resolution process and it is mostly governed by rules set by the various bodies that mediate disputes in Kenya.

Some of the bodies used in Kenya for mediating disputes are the Kenyan Chartered Institute of Arbitrators, The Nairobi Centre for International Arbitration, the Mediation Training Institute and the Strathmore Dispute Resolution Centre. These bodies often come up with their own rules governing the mediation process which the parties may agree to use.

d) Court Annexed Mediation

In 2016, the Judiciary of Kenya introduced court annexed mediation. This is a mediation process conducted under the umbrella of the court. So far, it has been implemented within the Family and Commercial Divisions of the Milimani High Court in Nairobi on a pilot basis.

All cases filed at the Family and Commercial Division undergo screening by the Mediation Deputy Registrar ("MDR") who assesses whether or not they are suitable for mediation. Once a case is referred to mediation, the MDR notifies the parties of this decision and then nominates three (3) mediators from the Register of Judiciary accredited mediators.

Once the parties are notified of the 3 nominated mediators, the parties then select their preferred mediator from the three names in the order of priority, and inform the MDR of their preference in writing. Parties are also free to select their own mediator from the Register of Judiciary accredited mediators. The MDR then appoints the selected mediator to handle the case.

The mediation proceedings are to be concluded within sixty (60) days from the date the matter is referred for mediation. However, this period may be extended for a further ten (10) days. Where parties reach an agreement, they sign a mediation agreement and file it with the MDR within ten (10) days. If no agreement is reached, the mediator notifies the MDR after which the case is processed by the court in the usual manner.

e) Traditional Dispute Resolution Mechanisms

Traditional dispute resolution mechanisms ("TDRM's") are now recognized and protected under Article 159 of the Constitution of Kenya, 2010. TDRM's have been very effective in resolving conflicts especially natural resource-based conflicts among the pastoralist communities in Kenya.

Some of the mechanisms used include negotiation, reconciliation, informal mediation, council of elders, local elders and problem solving workshops.

The only limitation to the application of these mechanisms is that they must not contravene the Bill of Rights, they must not be repugnant to justice and morality or inconsistent with the Constitution or any written law.

B. Application of Laws

Before filing suit in court, parties must make sure that their court of choice has the jurisdiction to hear and determine the matter.

Ordinarily, courts do not intervene in matters to which parties have agreed to refer to arbitration unless otherwise provided for in the Arbitration Act. Where court proceedings are brought in a matter which is the subject of an arbitration agreement, the court upon application can stay the proceedings and refer the matter to arbitration.

In cases where a foreign court has similar jurisdiction to hear and determine a matter as a Kenyan court, Kenyan courts have the discretion to determine whether or not to exercise their jurisdiction. The burden falls on a party to convince the court that the foreign court is a more appropriate forum.

For example where parties to a contract have agreed to be bound by the laws of a foreign country or to have any disputes arising from the contract to be settled in a foreign court, courts in Kenya ordinarily uphold such agreements.

If a dispute arises and is heard and determined by a court in a country with which Kenya has a reciprocal enforcement arrangement, the Foreign Judgments (Reciprocal Enforcement) Act (the "Foreign Judgments Act") shall apply. The countries with which Kenya has reciprocal agreements under this Act are Australia, Malawi, Seychelles, Tanzania, Uganda, Zambia, Rwanda and the United Kingdom.

Where the foreign judgment is from a country with which Kenya has a reciprocal enforcement arrangement, a party does not re-institute the claim in a Kenyan court. A party merely applies to the High Court to have the judgement registered.

Where the judgment is from a country which has not entered into a reciprocal enforcement arrangement with Kenya, parties seeking to enforce foreign judgments are required to re-institute the claim at the High Court in Kenya by filing a plaint setting out the nature of the claim. The foreign judgment will be among the documents filed in support of the claim.

VIII. Others

A. Anti-commercial Bribery

a. Brief Introduction of Anti-commercial Bribery Laws and Regulations

The Bribery Act makes it an offence to give or receive a bribe in both the private and public sector. Public and private entities are required under this Act to put in place procedures appropriate to their size and scale and to the nature of its operation, for the prevention of bribery and corruption, failure to which amounts to an offence. It is of importance to note that this Act introduced an aspect of culpability for issuance of bribes to foreign public officials, making it applicable to operations of entities within and outside Kenya.

The Constitution with the backing of the Anti-Corruption and Economic Crimes Act, the Public Officer Ethics Act and the Leadership and Integrity Act, is instructive when it comes to bribery and other corrupt acts in the public sector. These laws stipulate that a gift or donation to a State officer on a public or official occasion is a gift or donation to the Republic and shall be delivered to the State unless exempted under an Act of Parliament. All state officers, whether in public or private capacity, are mandated to avoid conflicts between personal interests and official duties as well as compromising any public or official interest in favour of a personal interest.

Issuance or receiving of bribes, secret inducement, bid rigging or involvement in corrupt conduct in the public service, is further prohibited by the Anti-Corruption and Economic Crimes Act. Under this Act, mechanisms have been set in place for recovery of amounts lost as a result of corruption or economic crimes. Moreover, engaging in bribery by public officers' amounts to violations of the code of conduct set out in the Public Officer Ethics Act and the Leadership and Integrity Act.

Kenya is also party to the UN Convention on Corruption and the African Union Convention on Preventing and Combating Corruption. As such, the two Conventions do form part of Kenyan law pursuant to Article 2(6) of the Constitution.

b. Department Supervising Anti-commercial Bribery

The Ethics and Anti-Corruption Commission is the main body tasked with combating bribery, economic crimes and corruption in Kenya. Amongst other functions, the law tasks it with investigating and recommending to Director of Public Prosecutions any acts of corruption, bribery or economic crimes for prosecution. Whereas any person can lodge a complaint with the Commission for investigation, the Commission does have power to investigate claims on its own motion.

The Bribery Act mandates public officers and persons holding positions' of authority in private entities to report to the Commission any knowledge or suspicion of instances of bribery within a period of twenty four hours after acquiring such knowledge or suspicion.

Nonetheless, it is important to note that despite the above stipulations, most of the matters handled so far by the Commission are public sector related.

Other bodies also do take part in supervision of anti-commercial bribery in Kenya's public sector. These include; the office of the Auditor General, Commission on Administrative Justice (Ombudsman) and other sector specific commissions tasked with enforcing codes of conduct under the Public Officer Ethics Act.

c. Punitive Actions

The punitive measures can broadly be dichotomized into two; personal offences and offences against entities. The following are maximum penalties upon conviction of bribery offences of a personal nature:

(i) Bribing or receiving a bribe is punishable by imprisonment for a term not exceeding 10 years or a fine not exceeding Kshs.5,000,000/- or both and may be liable to an additional mandatory fine of five times the amount of any quantifiable benefit gained by the person or the quantifiable loss suffered by another person.

(ii) Imprisonment for a term not exceeding 10 years or a fine not exceeding Kshs.5,000,000, or both for taking disciplinary action against a whistle blower or a witness of bribery.

(iii) Bribing foreign public officials is punishable by imprisonment for a term not exceeding 10 years or a fine not exceeding Kshs.5,000,000, or both.

(iv) If the convicted person is a director of a company, such person shall be disqualified from holding the position of director in that or any other company in Kenya for a period of not more than 10 years.

(v) A person who is convicted of an offence involving bribery shall be disqualified from being elected or appointed to hold a state office or a public office for a period of not more than 10 years after conviction.

In bribery offences involving private entities, the following penalties accrue;

(i) disqualification of director from holding the position of director in that or any other company in Kenya for a period of not more than 10 years.

(ii) An entity convicted of bribery shall be disqualified from doing business with the National and County Government for a period of 10 years after such conviction.

B. Project Contracting

a. Permission system

Public procurement in Kenya is governed by the Public Procurement and Asset Disposal Act, No 33 of 2015 ("the PPAD Act"). The purpose of the PPad Act and the Regulations created thereunder is to establish procedures for efficient public procurement and for assets disposal by public entities.

The PPAD Act establishes the Public Procurement Regulatory Authority whose role is to enforce the provisions of the Act and in particular to monitor, assess and review the public procurement and asset disposal system to ensure that they respect the national values and other provisions of the Constitution.

At County level, County Treasuries are the organs responsible for the implementation of public procurement and asset disposal policy in the respective County.

All procurement by State organs and public entities are subject to the rules and principles of the PPAD Act.

b. Restrictions

The PPAD Act provides that the following types of procurement that do not qualify as public procurement. These are:

(i) retaining of the services of an individual for a limited term if, in providing those services, the individual works primarily as though he or she were an employee, but this shall not apply to persons who are under a contract of service;

(ii) transfer of assets being disposed of by one state organ or public entity to another state organ or public entity without financial consideration;

(iii) acquiring of services provided by government or government department;

(iv) acquisition and sale of shares or securities, fiscal agency by a public entity, investments such as shares purchased by cooperative societies, state corporations or other public entities;

(v) procurement and disposal of assets under the Public Private Partnership Act, 2013; and

(vi) procurement and disposal of assets under bilateral or multilateral agreements between the Government of Kenya and any other foreign government, agency, entity or multilateral agency unless as otherwise prescribed in the Regulations to the Public Procurement and Asset Disposal Act.

c. Invitation to Bid and Bidding

The tendering process under the PPAD Act is as follows:
a) Prequalification
Prequalification is a preliminary stage of the tendering process that is designed to produce a short-list of

companies that would be capable of meeting the technical standards of the works or project, without regard to price considerations at this stage. It may be necessary for large or complex works or projects.

Prequalification should take into account experience and past performance on similar contracts, capabilities with respect to construction and manufacturing facilities and financial position. Tendering is then confined to companies that have been prequalified.

b) Invitation to Tender

The procuring entity shall then prepare an invitation to tender that sets out the following:

(i) the name and address of the procuring entity;

(ii) the tender number assigned to the procurement proceedings by the procuring entity;

(iii) a brief description of the goods, works or services being procured including the time limit for delivery or completion;

(iv) an explanation of how to obtain the tender documents, including the amount of any fee;

(v) an explanation of where and when tenders must be submitted and where and when the tenders will be opened; and

(vi) a statement that those submitting tenders or their representatives may attend the opening of tenders.

c) Submission of Tenders

Bidders are required to submit the tender before the deadline and any tender received after that deadline shall be returned unopened. The time and place for submission of offers will be specified in the tender documents.

Potential bidders are required to submit bids that are valid for a period specified in the bidding documents. Procuring entities have the option to demand bid security which can be a fixed sum or a percentage of the estimated value of the contract. This is specified in the bidding documents and can be up to 2% of the contract price.

d) Evaluation of Tenders

A preliminary evaluation is undertaken by an evaluation committee soon after opening tenders to ascertain that the tender has been submitted in the correct format, has been signed, and that the correct number of copies, tender security, validity and any required samples have been provided. Any tender that does not meet the requirements is rejected.

Tenders are then evaluated more rigorously for technical conformity, followed by the financial evaluation which considers prices read out at tender opening, corrections for arithmetic errors, currency, discounts etc. The lowest priced conforming tender is usually awarded the contract.

The procuring entity has the right to reject all tenders received and to terminate the procurement proceedings at any time without entering into a contract.

e) Notification of Acceptance of Tender

The procuring entity will notify the successful bidder that his tender has been accepted, while at the same time notifying other bidders that their tenders were not successful.

However, at least 14 days must elapse before a written contract may be entered into, to allow time for an application to be made for administrative review. If the successful bidder refuses to enter into a written contract, the entity may award the contract to the next best evaluated bidder.

韩国

作者：殷炫浩、John Sangho Park
译者：姜金姬、金瑛

一、概述

（一）政治、经济、社会和法律环境概述

大韩民国（以下简称"韩国"）是位于朝鲜半岛南部的富裕的东亚国家。其领土由山地大陆和3 000多个无人居住的相邻岛屿组成。韩国拥有5 100万[1]的同一民族的人口。韩国的首都和人口最多的城市是首尔。

韩国是一个技术先进和发达的国家，在国内生产总值、医疗保健质量、经营便利性和预期寿命等国际业绩指标方面有很好的排名。韩国是经济合作与发展组织（OECD）和G20的成员。

1. 政治

韩国是一个总统民主共和制国家，总统由人民直接投票选出，任期5年。总统是国家元首、政府首脑和军队总司令。政府由三个独立的部门组成：行政机关、立法机关（由300名一院制国民议会成员组成，任期4年，可以连任）和司法机关（由14名最高法院法官组成，除首席大法官以外，任期6年，可以连任），有17个地方政府和226个基层地方政府，地方政府首脑和各地方议会均以可连续的4年任期方式当选。

现任韩国总统是文在寅，于2017年5月10日就职。韩国总统任期5年，不可连任。

2. 经济

按照GDP计算，韩国是世界第十一位经济大国，也是亚洲第四大经济体。[2]在过去50年中，韩国已经展现出并持续保持着较快的经济增长速度和全球一体化，逐渐成为高科技工业化经济体。20世纪60年代，韩国的人均国内生产总值与非洲和亚洲较贫穷国家的水平相当。这一时期之后，韩国GDP年增长率从1961年至2017年[3]平均为7.46%，因此，韩国如今是一个高收入经济体，GDP超过1.4万亿美元，人均收入接近35 000美元（购买力平价调整后）。[4]韩国也是三星、LG和现代等标志性和世界领先品牌的所在地。

3. 社会

韩语是韩国的官方语言，而韩语的书面形式使用的是韩文———一种由韩国王朝世宗（1397—1450年）[5]委托发明的文字体系。尽管韩国不同地区的方言存在差异，但来自不同地区的演讲者和听众可以相互理解。

韩国支持宗教自由。儒教、佛教和基督教是主要宗教。韩国是单一民族国家，但自20世纪末以来，移民工人和外国学生人数迅速增加。到2017年12月，韩国的外国人口达到218万[6]，相当于韩国人口的4.21%。[7]

---

[1] 2018年韩国人口，参见 http://worldpopulationreview.com/countries/south-korea-population。
[2] 2017年世界GDP排名，参见 http://cn.knoema.com/nwnfkne/world-gdp-ranking-2017-gdp-by-country-data-and-charts。
[3] 韩国GDP增长率，参见 https://tradingeconomics.com/south-korea/gdp-growth-annual。
[4] 同上注。
[5] 韩国一摘要，参见 http://www.korea.net/AboutKorea/Society/South-Korea-Summary。
[6] 法务部：《移民政策月报》2017年12月，载 tpp://www.moj.go.kr/HP/COM/bbs_03/ListShowData.do?strNbodCd=noti0097&strWrtNo=241&strAnsNo=A&strNbodCd=noti0703&strFilePath=moj/&strRtnURL=MOJ_40402000&strOrgGbnCd=104000&strThisPage=1&strNbodCdGbn=。
[7] 《韩国时报》称，外国人口增加到218万，参见 https://www.koreatimes.co.kr/www/nation/2018/01/177_243054.html。

4. 法律

韩国是一个大陆法系国家，由多种法律形式组成，包括《宪法》、国民议会制定的立法文件和行政机关颁布的条例。《宪法》是韩国的法律基础，并建立了民主共和国政府体系。司法系统一般被认为是独立的，由最高法院、宪法法院、6个高等法院、13个地区法院和其他专门法院组成。尽管最高法院是韩国的最高级别法院，但宪法法院是所有有关合宪性问题的最后诉讼法院。产权和商业企业的相关法律通常被认为是发达的。

为了促进外商投资，韩国政府将对外商投资的监督和审查保持在最低限度。事实上，韩国积极促进外国直接投资，源于1998年政府利用外国直接投资以克服亚洲金融危机，并为进一步开放经济作出了贡献。通过这些努力，韩国已经放开了外国投资，并建立了保护外国投资者的框架。在政府基于国家利益对外国投资的监督上，相关法规和政策更关注于产业市场细分，而不是投资者的来源或其他因素。原因在于国家在某类业务上对外国所有权或业务总量有限制，例如电信、电力传输、布局和防御等。

从历史上看，韩国的货币——韩元一直受到严格的外汇管制。然而，近年来，韩国在实现货币市场自由化方面取得了重大进展。这始于1990年，当时实施了一系列放松管制的措施以放开外汇管制。在2006年，韩国政府宣布实施"外汇自由化计划"，采取了进一步的措施。在该计划下，政府加速开放外汇市场。

（二）"一带一路"倡议下与中国企业合作的现状与方向

"一带一路"倡议为韩国和整个东北亚地区提供了经济机遇。根据《推动共建丝绸之路经济带和21世纪海上丝绸之路的愿景与行动》，中国东北三省（辽宁、吉林和黑龙江）已被指定为连接俄罗斯、蒙古和远东其他地区的中国"窗口"。在这一点上，与韩国政府的欧亚倡议合作还有很多合作，这样可以推动"一带一路"倡议为建设东北亚经济区作出贡献。

2017年5月14日，由民主党立法委员李秉硕率领的韩国政府代表团出席了在北京举办的"一带一路"国际合作高峰论坛。随后，在2017年12月13日，韩国总统文在寅上任后首次访华。中国国家主席习近平和文在寅总统同意推进双边关系，以确保中国与韩国之间的长期稳定关系。习近平主席表示，中国欢迎韩国参与"一带一路"建设，推动"一带一路"倡议与韩国的发展战略保持一致。文在寅总统还宣布，他和习近平主席已经同意积极寻求中国"一带一路"倡议和韩国自己的外交政策倡议（"新北区"和"新南区"政策）的实际合作方式，以此来寻求与欧亚以及东南亚国家进行更大的经济和外交合作。

二、投资

（一）市场准入

1. 投资监管部门

韩国产业通商资源部对在韩国的外商直接投资进行监管。另外，当外国投资者需要将其投资转入或转出韩国时，企划财政部与韩国银行（中央银行）也会根据外汇规定共同进行监管。

2. 投资产业规制法律、法规

在韩国，规制外商直接投资最重要的法律是《外国人投资促进法》与《外汇交易法》。《外汇交易法》主要规定外汇汇率系统、外汇业务及外汇收支。当韩国政府确定很可能出现某些紧急情况（如利率与汇率的突然波动、稳定国际收支严重困难，或者韩国金融市场与资本市场受到严重干扰），韩国政府可能会实行某些限制来维持正常的市场秩序。这些限制包括要求外商投资者在收购韩国证券、利益返还、获取股息或销售利润前取得韩国企划财政部的批准。但是，如果外国直接投资符合《外国人投资促进法》及根据其制定的某些条件，将不受前述根据《外汇交易法》制定的具体规定的约束。《外国人投资促进法》为外商投资者提供了许多投资保护及激励措施制度，详情参见"投资偏好与保护"部分。

3. 投资方式

外商投资者在正式进入韩国前，必须首先选择一种合适的投资方式。无论外商投资者是自然人或法人，均可在韩国设立公司实体。如果外商投资者是公司法人，其还可以选择在韩国设立联络处或者分支机构。

如果外商投资者选择在韩国设立公司实体，两种最普遍的外商投资形式是设立股份公司或有限公司。另外，其还可选择设立有限责任公司。每种公司形式都分别规定了股东或拥有股权利益的成员在其向公司投资限额的范围内承担有限责任。

如上所述，外国实体可以在韩国设立联络处或分支机构以负责其在韩国的经营。由于分支机构被视为在韩国的常设机构，因此，在韩国的外国公司分支机构对其运营收入将被政府征收所得税，而汇往其海外总部的收入则不需要缴纳韩国的股息税。①然而，设立分支机构不会为其总部提供有限责任保护，因为在韩国，分支机构不被视为独立的法律实体。

4. 市场准入和考核标准

根据韩国法律规定，某些特定种类的韩国公司会因特殊法律的规定而限制外国控股。此外，根据《银行法》等法律的规定，在收购某些公司的股份时会有持股水平的报告或批准的要求。这些要求与投资者的身份无关。

外资所有权的限制适用于：①韩国电力公司等"公益性公司"；②某些政府拥有的公司，如韩国煤气公司；③ KT Corp. 及 SK Telecom 等若干电讯及网络服务业务；④某些海洋产业；⑤某些航空业；⑥广播产业；⑦某些农业产业；⑧某些出版行业。审批要求和阈值根据具体情况而有所不同。

通常情况下，超额持股必须以规定的形式得到相关机关批准后，方可进行相关投资。公益公司的超额持股必须事先经过韩国金融委员会的许可。其他限制外资所有权的企业，通常需要经过相关监管部门或政府部门（例如，产业通商资源部或国土交通部）的批准。韩国证券交易所通过韩国证券电产（KOSCOM）运行的电脑网络/订单系统，对上市的受限实体的外国投资进行监控。除公益公司以外的任何超过外商投资限制的上市公司的订单，都将被系统标记后不予通过。

在韩国证券交易所上市的某些韩国公司，也会根据某些适用于这些公司的法律，受到外资所有权的限制（注意：某些所有权限制适用于国内外投资者）。韩国没有一部限制外商所有权的普遍法律，也没有专门的执行机关。每一部相关法律都有其特定的立法目的，以专业术语及范围，规定了特定的外资所有权限制。此外，某些受外资所有权限制的公司，其公司章程也会规定更多或更严格的所有权限制。

例如，《外国人投资促进法》规定，如果外商投资者想取得一家韩国防务公司的现有股份，外商投资者必须取得韩国产业通商资源部的事先批准，而产业通商资源部在批准前必须得到国防部长的认可。《外国人投资促进法》还规定，如果外商投资者想取得韩国防务公司的新发行股份，外商投资者必须提前通知产业通商资源部。产业通商资源部在接到通知后，如果认为此次收购不违反《防卫事业法》的规定——任何一家韩国防务公司管理层的控制权变更均需要产业通商资源部的事先批准的相关规定，则不会采取进一步行动。但是，如果产业通商资源部认定，外商投资者收购新发行的股份将导致这家韩国防务公司管理层的控制权发生变化，产业通商资源部将根据《防卫事业法》的规定，将此事提交外国人投资委员会进行进一步审核。

（二）外汇监管

1. 外汇监管部门

韩国企划财政部及韩国银行共同监管和监督外汇事宜。

2. 外汇相关法律、法规简介

一般来说，与非居民向居民的贷款延期相关的外汇法规为《外汇交易法施行令》及《外汇交易规定》。某种程度上，《外国人投资促进法》也适用。根据《外汇交易法》及《外汇交易规定》的相关规

---

① 分支机构可以进行创收活动，但是联络处仅可从事非应税活动。

定,外国银行或特定外币不享受优惠待遇。

《外汇交易法》规制非居民对韩国证券的投资行为,以及韩国公司在韩国以外的证券发行行为。根据《外汇交易法》的规定,非居民可根据此法的规定投资韩国证券。韩国金融委员会也会根据《金融投资企业与资本市场法》的授权,引用相关规定来限制外国人投资韩国证券,并监管韩国公司在韩国境外发行证券。

3. 对外国企业的外汇管理要求

根据韩国外汇相关法律规定,外汇交易通常分为"资本交易"或"贸易交易"两种。资本交易指存款、贷款、提供担保、发行或收购证券,而贸易交易指进出口货物或服务。原则上,根据《外汇交易法》[①]的规定,任何人(包括外国人)参与跨境资本交易,必须在达成协议之前,根据交易类型向韩国企划财政部、韩国银行或外汇银行[②]提交报告,但是贸易交易没有这种报告义务。因此,根据韩国法律规定,从事货物或服务进出口的韩国居民(如外国公司在韩国注册的子公司)没有义务就该交易、支付进口货款以及出口收益向相关部门进行汇报,而是根据企划财政部规定的程序,向外汇银行提供支付进口货款、收到出口款项的证明文件即可。[③]但是也有例外,例如,向伊朗支付进口货款或收取伊朗出口货款,必须事先向韩国银行报告,或取得韩国银行的事先批准。[④]

(1)来自外国分支机构公司贷款的报告要求

根据《外汇交易法》第18条第1款及《外汇交易规定》第7条、第14条第1款的规定,韩国居民有意向非居民(如韩国子公司向外国母公司)借入外币资金的,借款交易必须符合报告要求。[⑤]如果贷款金额不超过3 000万美元,则必须向指定的外汇银行提交报告并获得批准。如贷款金额超过3 000万美元,则必须向韩国企划财政部提交报告并获得批准,该报告必须在签订前述相关交易文件前提交。另外,借款人还必须指定一家韩国银行进行贷款及还款的收付。借款必须存入该指定韩国银行的外汇账户,然后由借款人从该账户中支出。

(2)外国人收购韩国股票的程序

根据《外汇管理法》的规定,外国投资者有意收购韩国公司股份的,必须指定一家韩国的外汇银行,并在该银行开设外汇账户和韩元账户,专门用于股票投资。汇款入韩国及在外汇账户中存入外汇资金无须经过批准。外汇资金可以在需要购买股票或结算购买股票价款时,从外汇账户汇入在证券公司开设的韩元账户中。在外汇账户中的外汇资金可不经韩国政府机关批准汇至境外。

股票的股息以韩元支付。外国投资者在韩国支付、接受或保留此类股票的股息或出售韩元所得收益时无须,取得政府部门的批准。非居民的股票收益和出售韩元所得收益,必须存入外国投资者在证券公司开设的韩元账户,或在指定的外汇银行开设的韩元账户。投资者在外汇银行韩元账户中的资金可转至其外汇账户,或根据本地生活需要进行现金取款(有取款上限)。在外汇银行韩元账户中的资金亦可用于未来股票投资,或用以支付通过优先购买权获得新股的认购价款。

(三)金融

1. 主要金融机构

韩国的金融机构可分为银行及可交易类似银行存款的金融产品的非银行金融机构、证券公司、资产管理公司、保险公司及其他金融公司。

在韩国,企划财政部、韩国银行、金融委员会及金融监督院四个部门主要负责对金融机构的监管。

- 企划财政部负责经济政策的制定、国家预算的编制、外汇政策的建立和实施,以及国家财政的管理。

[①] 参见《外汇交易法》第18条。
[②] 外汇银行,指在韩国企划财政部注册的,具有从事外汇交易业务,如买卖外汇或外汇存款业务资质的银行,例如韩国产业银行。
[③] 根据《外汇交易规定》第5(11)条的规定,从韩国汇往他国的汇款必须经外汇银行进行。
[④] 《外汇交易法》第15(2)条;为维护国际和平与安全而制定的支付批准和资金接受的准则。
[⑤] 根据《外汇交易规定》第7(15)条第一段的内容,需要提交报告的类似规定也适用于韩国居民向非韩国居民借入韩元的情形。

- 韩国银行,作为韩国的中央银行,致力于价格的稳定,并通过其建立的金融通货委员会来实施货币政策。
- 金融委员会的主要职责是整合金融政策并进行金融监管。为执行这一职能,金融委员会对金融机构的许可进行监督,并对违反金融规定的机构实施制裁。金融委员会的另一重要职能是准备、制定并修改各种与金融相关的法律、法规,以实施其金融政策并执行其金融监管职能。
- 金融监督院在金融委员会的主持下,对金融机构进行审查和监督。

2. 外国企业的融资条件

在韩国有业务的外商投资者有资格获得市场上各种类型的融资,不会因为其外国投资实体的身份而遭受任何歧视。

最常见的融资形式是公司间贷款(或股东贷款)(例如,外国分支机构向韩国公司发放贷款),在贷款协议的起草中,必须体现适当的条款和条件。虽然没有特定的语言要求,但贷款协议的条款和条件必须充分考虑下面提到的各种因素,谨慎起草。

(1)《外汇交易法》报告

根据《外汇交易法》的规定,任何非居民与居民间的借款交易都必须遵守《外汇交易法》相关规定要求的报告/批准程序。通常情形下,此类借款需事先向韩国借款人指定的外汇银行报告和取得批准,如果贷款金额超过3 000万美元,则必须事先通过外汇银行向韩国企划财政部报告。

(2)公司内部认可

借款公司的董事会必须通过同意贷款的决议,且董事会的会议记录必须以此目的进行起草。

(3)其他相关问题

如果以公司间借款的形式向在韩国的公司提供额外资金的,需要考虑以下几点:

- 股息、利息的预扣所得税:根据《韩国税法》相关规定,外国公司(假设其在韩国没有常设机构)在韩国取得的股息及利息需要缴纳27.5%(包括附加税)的预扣税。如果外国收款人符合税收协定中的优惠资格,则可根据相关税收协定适用低于27.5%的优惠税率。不同的税收协定针对股息及利息规定了不同的税率。如果贷款的形式为债券,且符合相关特殊条件(如以外币计价),则可根据《税收特例限制法》的规定减免预扣税。
- 借款人可扣除利息或股息:按照下文提到的"资本弱化"规则,借款人可在缴纳企业所得税时扣除其支付的利息,但股息的支付则不可抵扣。
- 资本弱化规则:根据《国际税收协调法》的规定,对于韩国借款人向其"外国控股股东"借用的资金,利息的可抵扣程度可能会受到限制。具体来说,如果韩国借款人欠其外国控股股东或由其外国控股股东提供担保而发放贷款的第三方的债务金额超过该韩国借款人的"净外国控股股东股本"(定义见下文)的3倍时,这种过度债务的利息支付将不能在韩国借款人缴纳企业所得税时进行抵扣。另外,如果借款的出借人为外国控股股东,则上述不可抵扣的利息将被视为股息。在这里,"外国控股股东"指的是直接或间接拥有借款人50%以上投票权的实质上控制着借款人的商业策略的股东。表示实质控制的因素包括连锁董事、重大财务支持、业务依赖、无形资产许可等。借款人的"净外国控股股东股本"指控股股东在本公司的净资产(即总资产−总负债)或截至财务年度结束时股东投资额(即实投资本+股本溢价+减资收益−增资折价−减资损失)中所占份额中数额较大者。然而,如果在财务年度中存在增资或减资,新的控股股东股本应按照平均水平计算。因此,通过在财政年度结束前暂停贷款或在财政年度结束前注入额外资本,是无法避免资本弱化问题的。
- 转让定价规则:根据《国际税收协调法》的规定,如果外国出借人与借款公司之间存在某种涉及韩国定价转让规则(通常为公司借贷)的"特殊关系",税务机关可能会详细审查贷款条款是否符合公平交易原则。因此,应仔细审查贷款协议的条款和条件(利率、违约条款等)以反映公平交易。如果利率高于国际交易的公平市场利率,则借款公司支付的超额利息将不能在缴纳企业所得税时进行抵扣。

(四）土地政策

1. 土地相关法律、法规

与英美法的绝对所有权概念类似，韩国法律关于房地产的所有权仅承认土地私有制。韩国法律不承认部分不动产，例如终身地产权（只在某个人存活状态下拥有的所有权）、附条件不动产（只在持续满足某些条件时才拥有的所有权）以及未来利益（只有在未来某种情况发生时才产生的所有权）。韩国法律也承认租赁权、表面权（土地的使用权）和某些地役权。

（1）所有权登记

根据韩国法律，土地所有权和建筑物所有权是区分开的，因此，韩国实行包括土地登记与房产登记的不动产双重登记制度（统称为不动产登记）。

（2）转让

已登记的不动产所有人可不经任何机关批准，自由地转让其名下的不动产所有权。

（3）征用

与土地征用相关的法律制度框架为《为公共事业征收土地和补偿相关法》（以下简称《征收法》）。根据《征收法》的相关规定，中央及地方政府只有在法定的公共需求下，才可命令中央土地征用委员会征用私人所有的不动产。这时，中央土地征用委员会将根据市场价值、政府公布价等全方面因素决定购买价格。

2. 外国公司的土地收购规则

根据《外国人土地法》的规定，如果外国人打算购入韩国的土地，外国购买者必须在签订购买协议的 60 日内，向政府机关报备其土地收购情况。如果是一家由外国人持有 50% 以上已发行股票的韩国公司，即使这家公司是在韩国注册成立的，其在土地收购中也将被视为外国实体，适用《外国人土地法》。如果一家外国公司收购了拥有土地所有权的韩国公司，那么根据上述规则，目标公司将被视为外国实体。如目标公司打算继续持有土地，则必须在韩国公司被收购的 6 个月内报告其土地收购利润。

根据《不动产交易申报法》的规定，土地或房产的买卖双方，必须于签订合同之日起 60 日内，且在登记变更不动产所有权之前，共同向政府机关进行不动产买卖合同的申报。只要外国人在购买不动产时已经根据《不动产交易申报法》进行了不动产交易申报，其就无须再根据《外国人土地法》进行土地收购申报。

如果外国人打算以境外汇入的资金在韩国购买不动产的，则必须事先向外汇银行报备其不动产购买计划。

（五）公司的建立与解散

1. 公司的形式

外商投资者可根据需要建立以下三种形式的子公司或合资公司：股份公司、有限公司及有限责任公司。三种形式的公司的主要区别为：

- 除非公司章程另有规定，股份公司和有限公司的股份（即成员权益）原则上是可以自由转让的；而有限责任公司的股份（即成员权益），除非公司章程另有规定，原则上不可以自由转让；
- 只有股份公司要求必须设立董事会，设立法定监事一人以上，实收注册资本小于 10 亿韩元的小型股份公司则例外；
- 上一会计年度结束时，总资产超过 120 亿韩元的股份公司必须聘请外部会计审计，并向金融委员会提交该财务审计报告；
- 对于有限公司与有限责任公司，如果所有成员均同意的，书面决议可以代替实际会议；但是，对于股份公司，书面决议代替实际会议通常是被禁止的。[①]

外商投资者也可以选择另外一种方式，即在韩国设立联络办公室或分支机构。联络办公室通常指一家外国公司进行非纳税经营活动的辅助机构。由于联络办公室不能被视为一个独立的法人实体，也

---

① 需要注意的是，实收注册资本小于 100 亿韩元的小型股份公司，如果所有成员均书面同意，书面决议可以代替实际会议。

不能被视为一个能够产生收入的营业场所，因此联络办公室不能进行以下活动：①创收活动；②在税务机关登记注册（因此不符合纳税申报条件，解释见下文）；③以其名义持有资产（如设施、设备或不动产）。因此，外国投资者为了在韩国从事创收活动，设立分公司等分支机构是一个可行的选择。

分支机构/分公司是其外国总公司的延伸，分公司的权利和义务也因此而延伸至其总公司。根据韩国法律规定，分支机构/分公司可以在韩国法院进行注册，也可以在税务部门进行注册。由于规模通常较小、法律规定的管理要求较少，设立分支机构/分公司的一个优势在于，分支机构在设立、维护及管理方面不像设立子公司那样繁琐。此外，如下文所述，分支机构的盈利转出至海外总公司时，其可能会享受到一些税收优惠政策。但是设立分支机构的弊端是，其法律责任不能与海外总公司相互独立。

2. 设立程序

在韩国，外国投资者如欲设立公司实体，必须在注入资本前准备和通过公司章程。另外，设立股份公司或有限公司要求首先举行首届股东大会或发起人会议，以指定拟设立公司的董事和/或法定监事。除此之外，还需向相关外汇银行提交收购股权报告，在完成注资后，外国投资者还需向法院注册处和当地税务部门进行注册。新公司需要一份租赁协议来完成税务局注册。

在韩国，股份公司、有限公司和有限责任公司的设立均没有最低注册资本的要求，但是根据《韩国商法典》的规定，外国公司如欲获得符合《外国人投资促进法》规定的"外商直接投资"资格而享受的各项优惠政策，其投资额不得少于1亿韩元。这些优惠政策包括投资回流的保证、对适格的外商直接投资给予的税收优惠等。

3. 解散的步骤和要求

下面将简单概括韩国的股份公司及有限公司的解散/清算程序。①

（1）解散程序

为了清算一家股份公司或有限公司，其股东首先应通过解散公司决议。只有以下程序全部完成时，公司才正式解散：①公司所有资产均被处置完成；②所有义务均已履行完毕；③所有剩余资产均已被股东分配完毕。如果上述任何一项没有完成的，公司将被视为仍在清算过程中。另外，还需注意以下几点：

- 股东大会：自愿解散一家韩国公司需要股东会决议。
- 选举和注册清算人：清算一家公司可能有一个或多个清算人来清算公司资产。在决定解散公司的股东会议中，可同时决定指派清算人。如果指派多个清算人的，在清算人会议上还须指定清算人代表。除非公司章程另有协议或股东会另有决议，公司的董事将自动被指派为清算人。
- 向股东发出解散通知：公司解散的股东会决议通过时，代表董事须向所有股东发出公司解散通知。
- 解散登记：股东自通过解散公司的股东会决议起两周内，必须向公司主要办公室所在地具有管辖权的法院注册登记公司解散的决议、指派的清算人及清算代表。

（2）清算程序

下面简单列出韩国公司的清算程序：

- 向法院报告：清算代表（如仅指派一个清算人，则清算人）须在被指派之日起两周内，向法院报告以下事项：
  - 解散的原因（如解散决议的内容）及日期；
  - 清算人姓名、身份证号码（或外国人护照号码）及地址。

除此之外，清算代表还须经股东大会同意，向法院提交资产汇总表与资产负债表。

- 资产处置：清算代表可根据《韩国商法典》的规定将公司的资产处置变现。
- 处理未决事项：公司解散时未决事项必须得到全部解决。持续履行的第三方合同必须是与公司员工雇佣关系密切相关的。

---

① 除各自适用的股权利益形式不同外，股份公司及有限公司的解散与清算程序基本一致（例如，股份公司适用"股东"，而有限公司适用"成员"）。

- 债权人保护程序：清算人/清算代表必须在其被委派后的两个月内，至少两次向所有债权人发出公司解散的公告（如报纸等出版物），通知债权人在不少于两个月的通知期限内向清算人提出债权申报。除公告外，清算人还须向所有已知债权人发出书面债权申报通知。
- 解雇员工及其他劳动相关事务：公司停业或清算要求与所有员工解除劳动关系，必须分次或一次性地，提前30天书面通知员工，解除劳动关系。员工的工资、强制遣散费、津贴及其他需要支付给员工的款项，需要在解雇之日起14日内完成支付。如果公司与员工之间另有协议的，此期限可以得到延长。
- 分配清算所得：清算所得指在公司清算程序中公司履行了所有义务后仍剩余的资产。公司在清偿全部债务，或预留足够资产以履行存在争议的义务前，公司股东不能分配公司资产。
- 股东会批准清算程序完成：当清算程序全部完成（即所有资产均已分配完毕，且无未结清的债务或应收款项），清算代表应及时准备财务报表并提交股东大会批准。股东大会批准后，可以视为公司解除清算人义务。
- 向法院登记完成清算：清算代表须在公司股东大会批准通过清算程序完成之日起两周内，向公司主要办公室所在地具有管辖权的法院进行清算完成登记。

（六）合并与收购

在韩国，并购类交易通常以股权转让或股权认购、资产转让（包括业务转让）、合资或合并等方式进行。根据韩国法律规定，拆分和合并可以在一次交易中一并完成。值得注意的是，《韩国商法典》（2012年修订）中引入了现金合并与三角合并的概念。修正案针对新发行股票份额不足其公司总股份10%（修订前为5%）的合并后新公司，免除了其股东批准要求，从而对小规模合并放宽了要求。

1. 法律、法规

《韩国商法典》规定了韩国公司的一般业务及公司相关规定，包括涉及股权收购、资产收购、公司合并、分立及其他交易结构的相关法规。如果股票收购涉及在韩国证券交易所主板上市，或韩国证券交易所创业板科斯达克（KOSDAQ）上市的韩国公司，该交易将适用《金融投资业与资本市场法》及其他相关法律。根据《反垄断法》和《公平交易法》等反垄断法的规定，并购交易需要向韩国公平交易委员会提交报告。如果涉及跨境交易的，则须适用《外国人投资促进法》及《外汇交易法》。

2. 法律适用

一般来说，股份认购协议（包括发行和购买新股）、合资或股东协议（涉及公司管理事物）及合并协议均应适用韩国法律。其他交易文件的法律适用，则根据当事人的协议而定。

3. 申请和费用

如果收购的公司是外国公司，根据《外国人投资促进法》的规定，需要事先通过外汇银行向韩国产业通商资源部提交报告。如果一项合并、分立或业务转让交易涉及上市公司的，除一般的披露要求外，《金融投资业与资本市场法》还要求上市公司向韩国证券交易所主板与创业板科斯达克（KOSDAQ）及金融委员会提交报告。

此外，上市公司5%以上实际所有权的收购还要求申请报告。收购要约和代理申请也需要提交申请。某些情况下，对韩国公司或在韩国开展业务的公司投资，可能会涉及向公平交易委员会提交反垄断报告并接受审查。

根据《公平交易法》的规定，当交易涉及以下事项时，需要提交反垄断报告：
- 收购目标公司所有或大部分业务或资产；
- 购买现存公司的股票后，收购方（及其附属公司）持有公司20%以上（如被收购公司为在韩国证券交易所主板或创业板上市的公司，则为15%）的投票权；
- 公司间合并；以及在前述任何一种情况下，并购交易的一方（及其附属公司）的资产或收入等于或超过2 000亿韩元，另一方（其附属公司）的资产或收入等于或超过200亿韩元。

此外，如果交易任意一方资产或收入超过2万亿韩元，还要求提交交割前报告。在公平交易委员会进行审查的30日内（可能被延长90日），交易不可完成。如果交易满足上述要求的反垄断申报条件，那么将被要求提供交割后报告。在这种情况下，报告须于交易完成后 30 日内提交，公平交易委员会也将审查 30 日，可延长 90 日。某些影响韩国市场的海外交易，还须根据其相关方（及其附属机构）在韩国的收入提交相关报告。

在韩国，并购相关业务不需要缴纳特别的印花税及其他行政费用（与根据交易金额收取的印花税不同），但是根据交易结构的不同，可能要缴纳相关不同种类的税费。

4. 信息披露

上市公司必须针对其并购类交易向韩国金融委员会及韩国证券交易所主板或创业板科斯达克提交报告。并购报告中必须披露与并购计划各方及其相关的事项信息，且此报告是公开的。

如果交易类型为业务或资产的转让或分立的，也需要提交类似的报告。收购要约和代理申请也需要根据《金融投资业与资本市场法》的规定披露相关信息。根据《公平交易法》的规定向韩国公平交易委员会提交的报告，可以不被公开。

5. 重大股权的披露

根据《金融投资业与资本市场法》的规定，如果投资者（包括特殊关系者及相关方）持有上市公司 5% 以上的股权，或该公司发行的其他特定债权的，必须在交易完成的 5 个工作日内向金融委员会报告相关收购交易。投资者被视为因签订股权购买协议而持有股票。任何超过 1% 的股权变动，均应在 5 个工作日内（被动投资的情况下，为下个月 10 日前）提交一份附加报告。在这份报告中，投资者必须明确表示，此交易是否为被动投资，或其是否打算影响公司的经营管理。投资目的的变化也将导致报告义务，如果投资者的目的是参与公司的经营管理，在 5% 报告提交后，将面临一个 5 天的冷却期。投资者在此期间内不得行使股东的投票权，也不能购入额外的股份。当投资者持有韩国上市公司 10% 以上的股份时，应当在 5 个工作日内向韩国证券期货委员会另外提交一份报告。此后任何股权变动都应当在 5 个工作日内向证券期货委员会报告。此外，上市公司必须在其向金融委员会提交的定期报告中披露与最大股东（及其关联公司）交易的所有细节。

6. 批准及评估权

对于收购公司产生重大影响的合并、全部或大部分业务转让、全部或部分业务的并购类交易，需要收购公司股东大会的特别决议的批准。根据《金融投资业与资本市场法》的规定，特别决议需要出席股东大会的 2/3 以上股东的赞成方可通过，出席股东大会的股东必须持有公司 1/3 以上的股份。当然，公司章程也可约定比上述规定更加严格的特别决议批准程序。在这种情况下，如果异议股东在股东大会上恰当地做好异议记录的，异议股东将获得评估权，股东的评估权可通过一套固定公式（上市公司的情况）、个人协商或法院来决定。

7. 恶意交易

韩国的法律没有区分善意或恶意的收购，二者均受到韩国收购相关法律的约束。法律并未要求，但允许目标公司的董事会表达其对收购要约的意见。

8. 政府的角色

韩国的政府机构通常无权限制并购类交易的完成。但是，跨境交易受到某些政府报告或批准的限制，包括外汇管理规定等。此外，银行、通信、防务等特定监管行业的并购类交易，可能会根据相关法律、法规，要求审批或存在其他限制。某些特定的跨境交易也可能因国家安全原因（如妨碍当地国防工业产品的制造或泄露国家机密）及核心技术保护因素而受到限制。

（七）竞争规则

1. 监管竞争规则的部门

韩国公平交易委员会是经国务总理授权的部级中央管理机构。作为类似司法机关，公平交易委员会制定和执行竞争政策，处理、审议及决定反垄断案件。

2. 竞争法简介

《公平交易法》是韩国最主要的反垄断和竞争法。《公平交易法》中的许多原则与美国、欧盟及日本的反垄断法非常相似。《公平交易法》包含了许多竞争行为的不同方面的不同规定，例如：①经营者集中、垄断和滥用市场支配地位；②合并及收购等并购类交易；③不公平合作活动；④不公平贸易行为。

（1）滥用市场支配地位

《公平交易法》禁止拥有市场主导地位的公司参与下列活动：①不合理定价、维持或改变价格；②不合理地控制商品销售或提供服务；③不合理地阻碍其他企业的经营活动；④不合理地妨碍新竞争者进入市场；⑤不合理排除竞争者的交易。

（2）并购类交易

《公平交易法》第7条规定了各种并购类交易的类型（如横向、纵向及混合类并购），极大地限制了在特定领域中贸易的竞争。《公平交易法》第12条规定，某些类型的并购类交易需要在交易完成前或完成后，向韩国公平交易委员会提交备案报告。只有全球范围内总资产或总营业额超过2 000亿韩元的企业，在并购类交易另一方总资产或总营业额超过200亿韩元，才需要提交备案报告。如果并购类交易发生在外国企业之间，或另一方为外国企业的，只有当外国公司在韩国的营业额（不仅限于在韩国注册的企业，包括所有相关公司的总营业额）超过200亿韩元时，才要求提交报告。这种并购类交易包括以下几种：

① 收购股份：收购现有公司20%（上市公司15%）以上的股份；已持有该公司20%（上市公司15%）以上股份的股东，进一步收购股份后成为该公司最大股东（除非收购方已经是该公司最大股东）。

② 收购业务或资产：收购或租赁另一公司业务的全部或主要部分；收购另一公司全部或主要部分的固定资产；被委托管理另一公司。主要部分指收购价格在目标公司上一会计年度财务报表中总资产的10%以上，或超过50亿韩元。

③ 并购另一企业。

④ 连锁大型企业的董事会（连锁关联公司的董事会除外）。

⑤ 参与设立新公司并成为该公司最大股东。

原则上，应在收购股份、资产或业务，或设立新公司等交易完成后30日内提交报告。但是，在上述第①、②、③、⑤种情形下，如果收购方或转让方任何一方交易后的总资产或总营业额超过2万亿韩元的，必须在交易完成前提交交易报告。需要注意的是，在提交报告后的30日（可能被延长90日）内，不可以完成交易。根据《公平交易法》的规定，虽然可以在签订股权收购、资产收购或并购协议之日后，或股东大会/董事会作出设立新公司决议之日后提交报告，但是也可以在此之前向公平交易委员会申请提前审查，通过包含合同主要条款的最终协议草案，审查拟进行的交易是否存在不正当竞争的效果。在合同各方实际履行了最终协议时，还需要提交一份正式报告。即使是可以在交易完成后提交报告的交易类型中，也可以自愿申请提前审查。但是，前述提到的公平交易委员会的初步审查，并没有免除相关方向公平交易委员会提交正式商业并购类交易报告的义务。

公平交易委员会对这些交易进行审查后，会下发可以进行交易的批文，或当其认为该交易将在某一特定领域的竞争中起到实质性抑制作用时，会下发禁止交易的命令。为此，韩国公平交易委员会首先对相关市场、产品市场、地域市场等进行界定，而后根据交易的不同类型（如横向、纵向或混合类并购），审查交易各方及竞争者的市场份额，市场份额的历史趋势，单方及共同影响，引入外商的竞争程度，国际竞争形式，引入、阻止或消除潜在竞争者的可能性，排除竞争者等。此外，公平交易委员会也审查该并购类交易可否被定性为"有效率"或"不符合公司原则"。

（3）竞争者之间的不公平合作行为

《公平交易法》第四章禁止企业从事某些合作行为。例如，针对以下行为达成协议：①制定、维持或改变商品价格；②对商品及服务贸易、支付价格或补偿，制定条件与条款；③限制商品或服务的生产、运输和贸易；④限制贸易或消费者的范围；⑤妨碍或限制生产商品或提供服务的设备，或设施的扩大及设备的安装；⑥在生产、经营时，限制货物的种类或规格；⑦设立新企业或类似企业，共同经营或管理企业的主要业务；⑧在投标或拍卖时，确定中标价格或中标人；⑨妨碍或限制其他企业的商业行为或业务性质，从而实质上抑制相关贸易行业的竞争。

上述大多数合作行为通常都被认为是恶性卡特尔，其本身是违法的（第⑦项可能除外）。《公平交易法》对这些行为的审查虽然"很大程度上抑制了竞争"，但是在实践中，公平交易委员会并不一定会评估这种减少或限制竞争的效果。

联合经营某些业务（如营销和分销职能）或联合经营资源的协议（如共同研究和开发），也可被确定为合作行为，但是这些行为将根据"合理原则"进行审查，而不是"自身违法"审查。

当签订上述活动的协议（并不一定是书面协议）时，这些企业将被视为完成了一个卡特尔。无论该协议是否实际上履行，均不会影响卡特尔的合法与否，即使在实践中，如果协议各方在达成协议后退出的，那么针对该卡特尔，退出方受到的制裁可能不会很严重。

值得注意的是，《公平交易法》第19条第5款规定，如两个或两个以上的企业进行上述行为，且"极大可能"地进行了合作行为的——考虑到：①相关交易的属性；②商品或服务；③相关行为的经济原因及连锁反应；④企业联系的方式及频率，它们将被"推定"为进行了不正当的合作行为。无论是否缺乏证据（进行这类行为的明确合同），这种推论都会成立。根据这一规定，即使缺乏证据，韩国公平交易委员会通常也会认定这种两个或两个以上的企业在同时或类似的时间，以同样或类似的比例或数量，提高商品价格，改变供应货物的其他条款的情形为卡特尔，而不会认为是因市场情况和产业结构而出现的巧合。这是为了减轻政府举证证明相关企业是否存在这类协议的负担，因为在实践中举证证明是非常困难的。如上所述的卡特尔一旦被推定，相关企业必须证明它们没有不正当合作的协议，市场上"看似卡特尔"的事件仅仅是一个巧合。

（4）不公平贸易行为

根据"合理原则"审查，以下几种行为将被视为不公平贸易行为：

① 抵制：无理由地拒绝与某些特定的人进行交易，或阻止与特定的人交易；

② 价格或条件的歧视：以显著有利或不利的价格，或其他条件进行交易；

③ 消除竞争对手：掠夺性定价；

④ 错误地吸引客户：向客户提供不合理的过分的经济利益，如溢价或以欺诈方案诱使客户交易；

⑤ 捆绑交易或强迫交易；

⑥ 滥用市场支配地位：例如，以其市场主导地位向另一方强加销售目标，被认为是滥用市场支配地位；

⑦ 限制性条件：限制另一方仅与自己交易，不能与其他竞争者交易，这种做法被认为是不公平和不合理的；限制另一方的交易范围与客户同样会被视为不公平和不合理；

⑧ 干涉其他公司的业务活动：如不合理地使用合作方的技术、不恰当地从其他公司挖人；

⑨ 通过提供预付款、贷款、人力、资产、证券、商品、服务等，或以优惠条件进行交易的方式，不正当地协助有特殊关系的人或其他公司；

⑩ 固定转售价格：与大部分国家一样，韩国禁止固定转售价格，但是《公平交易法》规定，固定某些受版权保护的材料的转售价格是被允许的。原则上，《公平交易法》允许对某些符合特定要求的消费品固定转售价格，如容易识别的质量统一及公平交易委员会批准前存在的市场自由竞争。另外，如果有合理的理由，也可以固定价格上限。

3. 竞争监管措施

根据违规的类型，公平交易委员会有权：①责令更改；②发布违规公告；③实施现金罚款；④对严重违规行为，移交检察长提起刑事诉讼。公平交易委员会可针对合作行为处以高达相关商品或服务销售额10%的罚款（如无法估计销售额，最高可处20亿韩元的罚款）。

（八）纳税

1. 税收制度和规则

韩国的税收包括国税和地税。国税包括企业所得税、增值税、遗产和赠与税及个人所得税等；地税包括地方所得税、收购税、登记税及财产税等。韩国的税法包括《企业所得税法》《增值税法》《个人所得税法》《地方税法》及《国际税收协调法》等。国家税收政策的制定由韩国企划财政部指导，韩国国税厅管理和收缴各项税收。

2. 主要税种及税率

（1）居民企业

居民企业按照其全球范围内的收入进行征税，非居民企业则只针对来源于韩国的收入进行征税。居民企业的判定标准为，企业在韩国是否有总部或有效管理地点。

纳税年度始于 2018 年 1 月 1 日及之后时间的企业，企业所得税率（包括地方所得税）为：应纳税所得额中 2 亿韩元以下的部分为 11%，应纳税所得额 2 亿韩元以上 200 亿韩元以下的部分为 22%，应纳税所得额中 200 亿韩元以上 3 000 亿韩元以下的部分为 24.2%，应纳税所得额超过 3 000 亿韩元的部分为 27.5%。即使企业有资格享受税收优惠政策，也需要缴纳替代最低限度税，企业净亏损可在 10 个纳税年度中进行不超过 70%（2019 年起为 60%）的抵扣。企业所得税税基中包括居民企业的资本收益或亏损。

（2）居民个人

居民按照其全球范围内的收入进行征税，非居民则只针对来源于韩国的收入进行征税。个人是否为居民的判定标准为，其是否在韩国居住或在一个自然年中在韩国累计居住 183 天以上。

纳税年度始于 2018 年 1 月 1 日及之后时间的个人，个人所得税率（包括地方所得税）为：应纳税所得额中 1 200 万韩元以下的部分为 6.6%，应纳税所得额中 1 200 万韩元以上 4 600 万韩元以下的部分为 16.5%，应纳税所得额中 4 600 万韩元以上 8 800 万韩元以下的部分为 26.4%，应纳税所得额中 8 800 万韩元以上 1.5 亿韩元以下的部分为 38.5%，应纳税所得额中 1.5 亿韩元以上 3 亿韩元以下的部分为 41.8%，应纳税所得额中 3 亿韩元以上 5 亿韩元以下的部分为 44%，应纳税所得额超过 5 亿韩元的部分为 46.2%。截至 2018 年，在韩国工作的外国人可适用 20.9% 的统一税率。用人单位及员工在交纳国家养老金和医疗保险的情况下，需要根据职工的总收入交纳社会保险费（国家养老金、医疗保险、工伤保险及失业保险）。

（3）非居民企业和个人

非居民企业或个人提供的服务，一般被划为个人服务收入，适用 22%（包括当地所得税）的预扣税，也可以根据相关税收条约予以免除。对涉及技术转让等特定服务的纳税，可参照特许权使用费。一般来说，不存在分支机构利润税，但根据有关税收条约的规定，可以征收分支机构的企业所得税，对商品和服务的提供按照 10% 的比例征收增值税。在某些情况下（例如出口、服务出口等），可以适用零增值税。

（4）税收协定

为防止双重征税，并降低预扣税税率，截至 2018 年 1 月，韩国已与 93 个国家签订了税收协定。非居民公司或个人的股息、利息、特许权使用费等被动收入应缴纳 22%（包括当地所得税）的所得税，也可根据相关税收协定予以减免。非居民企业的资本收益或亏损应按照销售额的 11%（包括当地所得税）及资本收益的 22%（包括当地所得税）中较小者缴纳所得税。如转让一家韩国公司股票所得的资本收益，在韩国的纳税义务可根据相关税收协定被免除。

3. 纳税申报及优惠政策

企业必须在纳税年度结束后的 3 个月内提交年终企业所得税申报表（在统一企业所得税申报的情况下为 4 个月）。如果公司的纳税年度超过 6 个月，则必须在头 6 个月后的 2 个月内申报并支付临时税。税务评估的时效一般为 5 年。

一般情况下，居民个人需要在次年 5 月 31 日之前申报并支付个人所得税。如果纳税人的收入仅由工资和/或遣散费构成，由于用人单位每月会代扣个人所得税，纳税人就不必另外申报和缴纳个人所得税。在这种情况下，纳税人需要在次年 2 月准备一份年终税务结算表。

申报和缴纳增值税一般是按季度进行的。如果企业提供的货物和服务符合零增值税条件的，则可每月申报提前退税。

经韩国企划财政部批准，位于特定外商投资区或自由贸易区内，或从事特定高科技行业的外商投资企业可享受免税的优惠政策。外商投资企业可享受自产生应纳税收入额起 3～5 年的免税（企业所得税）政策，及之后2年企业所得税减半的优惠。自2018年1月起，因国内企业受到歧视而引发争议，对外商投资企业的税收优惠措施预计将会被修改。

（九）证券

1. 证券相关法律、法规简介

在韩国，规制资本市场及金融投资业务行为最主要的法律为《金融投资业与资本市场法》（总统令），列举了《金融投资业与资本市场法》处理的事项及相关的规章制度。《金融投资业与资本市场法实施规则》（总理令）规定了总统令所赋予的权力和规章制度的实施。金融委员会颁布的规章，包含了解释总统令所产生的职责与上文所述规章制度具体实施的条文。《金融投资业与资本市场法》的规定包括：金融投资业务的监管、证券发行和披露的监管、对短期利润回报的监管、对不公平交易行为的调查和报告、对资本市场调查的监管、对金融机构的检查和制裁的监管等。金融委员会在其监管执行规则中明确，金融委员会授权其主席和根据《金融投资业与资本市场法》设立的金融监督院，颁布法令和执行细则。这些规则与金融委员会规定、其他相关法律法规、具体要求及所需文件，构成了对上文所述法律、法规的具体实施。

其他可能适用于资本市场的法律主要包括：管制流入韩国的货币的《外汇交易法》，以及关于反洗钱、金融交易信息的法律，如《关于特定金融交易信息的报告与使用的法令》《关于惩罚隐匿犯罪收益行为的法令》《关于实名金融交易及隐私保护的法令》《个人信息保护法令》及《信用信息的使用和保护法令》等。

2. 证券市场的监管

在韩国，金融业的主要权威监管机构是金融委员会。其主要职责为：①商议和制定财政政策；② 监管金融机构及金融市场；③ 保护消费者的金融交易；④促进金融业发展。韩国金融委员会经特别授权，参与制定和修改金融机构及金融行业的相关法规，批准金融机构的设立、合并、兑换、转让和收购，并为金融投资企业颁发相关营业执照。

金融监督院是金融委员会的执行机构，与金融委员会密切相关。金融监督院的主要职责是监督、审计和检察金融机构，并调查操控市场及其他不公平交易行为。

此外，还有其他金融监管机构，包括：①韩国企划财政部，负责制定经济和财政政策、国家预算及税收政策，并负责外汇管理；②韩国银行（央行）负责维持金融稳定、货币和信贷政策，包括外汇兑换。虽然韩国证券交易所是一个主要由某些金融投资公司（金融投资产品的经纪人和经销商）所有的机构，但是作为韩国唯一的证券交易所，韩国证券交易所是经营证券和金融衍生品的市场，且在某些情况下可以行使监管权，根据《韩国证券交易所上市规则》的规定暂停特定公司股票的交易，使某一证券下市，或限制股价变动。此外，韩国金融投资协会是一个由金融投资公司根据《金融投资业与资本市场法》成立的自治组织，其主要活动包括：①制定行业规章制度；②审查标准协议和广告；③对会员单位进行检查；④金融专业人员资格考试的登记和管理；⑤争议解决。

3. 外国企业进行证券交易的要求

一般情况下，根据投资的规模和目的，外国人对韩国公司的投资分为两类：①根据《资本市场与金融投资业相关法律》和《外汇交易法》的规定进行的间接投资；②根据《外国人投资促进法》的规定进行的外商直接投资。

（1）《外国人投资促进法》投资

如果外国投资者收购一个韩国公司10%以上的股份，或参与公司的经营管理（通常以有权任命公司一个或以上董事为标准），即使收购比例可能不足10%，根据《外国人投资促进法》的规定，本次投资也将被视为外商直接投资。

在这种情况下，外商投资者必须在投资（交易日或结算日）之前向外汇银行或大韩贸易投资振兴公社（KOTRA）（负责接收《外国人投资促进法》报告的韩国产业通商资源部授权其可以接收报告）提交报告。但是，如果被收购股票是上市公司发行的股票，但是并非新发行的股票（即收购上市公司的现有股票），那么在投资之日起30日内提交报告即可。在外商直接投资的情况下，发行公司必须将自己注册为外商投资企业。

《外国人投资促进法》报告一旦被提交,任何收购或抛售相关公司股份的行为,都需要提交修改报告(该公司的外商投资企业注册也需要相应修改)。

(2)间接投资

不符合《外国人投资促进法》规定的外商直接投资的投资,都是间接证券投资("间接投资")。

一般来说,根据《金融投资业与资本市场法》《外汇交易法》及相关规定,外国公司的间接投资必须:①获得金融监督院的外商投资登记号码;②在外汇银行开设用于间接投资的外币账户及韩元账户;③在韩国的证券经销商或代理人(如证券公司)处开设证券交易账户;④通过韩国证券公司购买证券。除此之外,外商投资者必须指定一个当地托管人(可以指定开设相关账户的外汇银行)。就第①项要求,获得外商投资登记号码通常是一个简单明了的过程,可以在几天内完成,往往是由当地的证券经纪人或托管人代为处理。

间接投资于上市证券的情况,应符合上述所有条件;对于非上市证券的投资,除没有明确要求投资者必须获得外商投资登记号码外,其他所有要求都将被适用。这是因为投资韩国证券交易所上市公司的股票,需要获得外商投资注册号码。

以间接投资的目的,在证券公司开设证券账户,或在银行开设账户时,证券公司或银行会根据《实名法》要求核实投资者的身份,通常做法是要求投资者提供外商投资登记号码来验证身份。因此,虽然对非上市公司的证券投资并没有要求必须获得外商投资登记号码(如上文所述),但在实践中可能还是需要获得外商投资登记号码。

另外一种方式为,以间接投资的目的,在外汇银行开设外币账户及韩元账户之前,将收购韩国公司股份的事项,向韩国银行提交报告并获得批准。如此,外商投资者可免除上述所有程序要求(韩国银行投资)。这种方式的好处在于,无须两种货币的转换。但是,韩国银行并不是很愿意接受这种报告,且可能裁定拒绝接受,因此需要提前与韩国银行讨论该问题。

(3)《外汇交易法》投资

对于非上市公司股份的投资,根据《外汇交易法》的规定,不符合《外国人投资促进法》规定的外商直接投资的外国投资者,可以通过向外汇银行提交报告,投资非韩国证券交易所上市公司的股票。在这种情况下,可以不适用上述要求。

(4)外国公司对韩国公司投资的限制

在很大程度上,外国公司投资韩国公司是没有特别限制的。但是,某些韩国公司根据相关具体法律规定,受到外国所有权的限制。如上文所述,韩国没有一部专门限制外商所有权的普遍法律,也没有专门的执行机关。《通信事业法》《广播法》《互联网多媒体广播事业法》《新闻法》《报纸法和期刊法》《航空法》《电子设施法》《韩国水资源公司法》及《海洋交通法》等法律根据各自的立法目的,使用相关的术语及不同上限,分别规定了相关的外商所有权限制。

(十)投资偏好与保护

1. 偏好政策的结构

除对外商投资进行限制的某些特定行业外,韩国并没有任何偏向于韩国国民及内资企业的法律、法规及政策。

相反,为吸引外商直接投资,韩国政府对某些符合特定条件的外商投资企业提供了许多税收减免政策。具体来说,《特殊税收限制法》《外国人投资促进法》及其他相关法律向适格的外商投资企业给予一定的税收减免,让他们在企业所得税、购置税、登记税、财产税、关税等方面享受减免。在韩国,某些符合特定条件的外商投资企业甚至可以享受来自政府的现金补助。

2. 对特定产业及地区的支援

对于符合标准的高科技产业外商投资企业,会有一些税收减免或其他鼓励措施。外商投资企业在韩国开展业务所引进的高新技术,必须是《税收优惠限制法》总统令中被列为"未来成长动力/原始技术"的高新技术门类之一。

(1) 免税

具有高新技术类别资格的外商投资企业享受以下免税政策：

- 外商投资企业在取得资格后的前 5 年享受企业所得税免税政策，此后 2 年将享受企业所得税减半政策。免税时间始于以下几项中最早的时间：在不考虑税收亏损结转的情况下，外商投资企业具有可纳税收入的第一个纳税年度；取得免税资格起 5 年内的纳税年度。
- 一般而言，自取得资格之日起 5 年内免征与符合条件产业相关的购置税及财产税等地方税，此后 2 年内减半征收。
- 根据《外国人投资促进法》的规定，根据企业报告的外商投资额及股权形式的程度，针对直接用于免税产业的进口资本设备，5 年内予以免征关税、个人消费税及增值税。

(2) 现金补助

当外商投资满足特定条件时，韩国中央政府及地方政府将对其提供现金补助，以资助新工厂及新设施等的建设。在审核过程中，韩国政府将综合考虑外商投资企业是否引入新科技、转让技术的影响、就业机会的规模、外商投资企业是否与国内投资相重叠、外商投资地点的适当性等因素。

3. 特别经济区

韩国向工业区内符合条件的、为工业区的战略发展特别设计出外国投资的工业综合体提供不同种类的支援。另外，韩国的外商投资区、自由贸易区、自由经济区等亦向外国投资者提供了优越的投资环境。

这些吸引外商投资的工业区支援系统包括：①根据《外国人投资促进法》的规定设立的"外商投资区"；②根据自由贸易区的指定及运营相关法律设立的"自由贸易区"；③根据自由经济区的指定及运营相关法律设立的"自由经济区"。外商投资区可进一步分类为子类型、复杂类、个别类及服务类。

为外商直接投资指定的区域可能根据投资目的的不同，在当地职业资格、目标行业和投资奖励（例如租金、税收、关税和现金补助）等方面提供不同的支援措施。因此，即使是在审批手续较为简易的指定区域内，投资者也需要仔细检查及分析投资地点。

4. 投资保护

《外国人投资促进法》保证在韩国外商投资公司可以向韩国境外汇出由外国投资者出售证券而获得的收益，根据贷款协议支付的本金、利息及服务费用，以及根据许可协议支付的特许费用。

(1) 外汇交易保障条款中的例外

根据《外国人投资促进法》的规定，无论是自然灾害、战争、武装冲突、国内外经济条件的严重且突然变化，及其他类似情况，均不会影响适格外商投资企业取得相应资格。

(2) 国民待遇

除非韩国法律另有规定，外商投资者与外商投资企业与韩国国民及内资企业享受同等待遇。

(3) 平等适用税收减免条例及其他

除非韩国法律另有规定，按照《外国人投资促进法》的规定扩大贷款及提供技术的外商投资者及外商投资企业与韩国国民及内资企业同等地适用税法中关于税收减免的条款。

三、贸易

(一) 贸易监管部门

韩国产业通商资源部是韩国重要的政府监管贸易机构。韩国产业通商资源部的主要任务包括，通过谈判和监督执行涉及外贸和投资的条约和协议来鼓励外国在韩投资。此外，它还负责制定贸易、工业和能源部门的经济政策。在韩国产业通商资源部内部，贸易部长特别负责贸易政策、贸易谈判和跨境投资政策。

韩国贸易委员会（KTC）是韩国产业通商资源部下属的重要贸易机构。其负责对反倾销税、反补贴税和保障措施进行贸易救济调查。根据韩国贸易委员会的调查结果和建议，企划财政部负责实施贸易救济措施，而韩国海关负责征收贸易救济案件引起的任何关税。

（二）贸易法规简介

《对外贸易法》是规定贸易活动总体政策方向和原则的基本法规。其下属法规包括了总统令、部委法令和公告等。为了反映现行的国际标准并遵守世界贸易组织（WTO）的义务，《对外贸易法》对进出口活动进行最低限度的监管。但是，在特殊情况下（例如保护国家安全、环境或公共健康），《对外贸易法》可以授权政府限制进出口活动。它还为进口数量突然增加（例如保障措施）提供进口救济的法律依据，并在需要遵守国际法的情况下，在相关贸易活动可能违反韩国或其贸易伙伴的法律时管制交易商。

有关贸易救济的主要内国法载于：①《海关法》；②《关于调查不公平的国际贸易惯例和补救措施以防止工业损害法》及其附属条例。适用于国内的其他贸易补救措施也包括在《1994年关税与贸易总协定》第6条执行协定中。韩国加入的WTO协定和其他《自由贸易协定》（FTA）是充分具有拘束力的，并且与国内法具有相同的效力，构成韩国贸易和监管体系的一部分。

（三）贸易管理

作为世界贸易组织的成员，韩国一直赞成支持自由贸易。在这方面，韩国已与智利、新加坡、欧洲自由贸易联盟、东盟、印度、欧盟、秘鲁、美国、土耳其、澳大利亚、加拿大、中国、哥伦比亚、新西兰和越南15个国家签订贸易协定。为遵守WTO协定，韩国作出了巨大的努力，并作为投诉方、应诉方或第三人参与了WTO的若干贸易争端。

（四）进出口商品检验检疫

如果韩国海关认为有必要评估进出口商的合规水平、货物特性或进出口商的境外对手方的，可以检查进出口商品。如果知识产权的所有者或被许可人向韩国海关报告其知识产权需要保护的，韩国海关也可以检查某些商品是否侵犯知识产权。

动植物检疫机构（APQA）检疫和检查进出口动物、畜产品和植物，以保护社区免受国际贸易和旅游带来的风险。动植物检疫机构对进出口商品的检疫和检验受到规制，以符合WTO的卫生和植物检疫措施要求。所有进入韩国的动物和动物产品必须附有离境国签发的有效检疫或热处理证书。所有进口动物和动物产品必须在抵达时进行申报和检验。否则将导致动物或动物产品分别被送回或销毁。植物、水果、蔬菜、种子、兰花、苗木、切花、土壤和类似性质的物品也必须在抵达时进行申报和检查。

（五）海关管理

韩国海关成立于1970年5月13日，是独立于财政部的独立政府机构。韩国海关被授权进行以下活动：①决定征收或免除关税；②征收关税；③控制进出口货物的清关；④根据《海关法》的规定调查犯罪活动和采取行动。

适用的关税税率规定在韩国的协调制度中。进口到韩国的工业产品的正常关税一般为8%从价税，而农产品的关税通常要高得多。除韩国海关的审核和批准外，还可以设立海关保税区或自由贸易区，将货物运送到这些区域不会引起关税责任（除非货物实际进入韩国境内，在这种情况下，应支付适用的关税和其他与进口相关的税款。）。

如果按照规定某些进口商符合参加月度综合计划（允许进口商按月支付关税）和附带计划（允许进口商推迟支付关税等，最长为期15天）的资格并参与其中的，该韩国进口商也可以免除在清关时应支付所有适用的关税和其他税款这一要求。

此外，根据进口产品的不同，韩国进口商可能需要遵守各种有关进口此类产品的法律和法规（即《海关法》以外）的某些认证、报告和一些特殊产品的批准要求，例如《药品事务法律》《医疗器械法》和《化学品管制法》等。虽然通常没有对进口的事先通知要求，但海关会要求进口某些医药和医疗器械产品的进口商必须在取得通关前向相关行业协会提交进口前报告。同时，相关行业协会接受此类报告是清关的先决条件。鉴于韩国海关的积极执法行为，强烈建议寻求进口任何根据《海关法》以外的法律和规定的产品的进口商，要确保进口完全合规。

"战略物资"和"战略技术"的出口需要有关当局的批准，以保持多国战略物资出口管制措施的完整性。韩国政府还根据《防止韩国工业技术分离和保护法》的规定控制"国家核心技术"的出口。

四、劳动

(一) 劳动法律、法规简介

《劳工标准法》(以及许多执行法令)是适用于所有拥有 5 名或 5 名以上员工的企业和工作场所的主要劳动法规制度。不超过 4 名"一般"雇员的企业或工作场所可能仍受到总统令规定的《劳工标准法》的某些规定的拘束。就业和劳动部负责执行《劳工标准法》。涉及劳资纠纷的诉讼由最高法院、5 所高等法院(中级上诉法院)以及许多地方法院(审判法院)裁决。

《劳工标准法》规定了就业的各个方面,包括就业合同、工资支付、工作和休息时间、女性和未成年人的就业、安全和健康、学徒、工业事故补偿、劳动监察和罚款条款。例如,《劳工标准法》第 23 条规定,在对雇员实施纪律处分之前,雇主必须有"正当理由",直至终止雇用。正当理由在法规中没有定义,但根据法院的先例,以下三种理由通常被视为正当理由的基础:①严重或重复的不当行为;②长时间表现不佳;③"业务的紧急需要"(裁员)。《劳工标准法》第 26 条还要求雇主至少提前 30 天以书面形式通知非自愿离职者(或以 30 天的普通工资代替)。

除了《劳工标准法》《工会和劳动关系调整法》,其他相关劳动法、民事和刑事法律、雇主与雇员之间的协议(包括集体谈判协议、雇用规则和雇佣合同)以及劳动关系惯例都适用于雇佣关系和劳资关系。

发生法律冲突时,根据惯用的法律原则来确定哪些具有优先权。上级法律优先于下级法律(因此,《宪法》优先于《性别平等就业和工作与家庭平衡支持法》等法律),特殊法律优先于一般法律(因此,适用于《海员法》的人优先适用《海员法》而不是《劳工标准法》)。当两个同级法律相互冲突时,优先适用颁布时间最近的法律。

韩国劳动法的一个最重要的原则是为员工提供更好的条件。因此,如果劳动法、雇用规则和个人雇用合同中规定的工作条件彼此不同,则将适用对雇员最有利的条件。一般来说,法律规定的标准不得因私人协议而损害雇员利益。

(二) 雇用外籍雇员的要求

1. 工作许可

只要外国人在韩国拥有允许他们在韩国就业的适当签证,外国公民就可以在韩国工作。外国工人最常见的长期工作签证是 D-7、D-8 和 E-7。如何选择适当的签证类型,取决于分配或就业的性质以及企业在韩国的类型等因素。

(1) D-7 签证

韩国外商投资企业的分支机构或联络处的外籍员工可以获得 D-7 长期签证,他们需要已经在总部、分支机构或其他附属机构工作过,并在到韩国之前至少工作过 1 年。D-7 签证的办理需要移民局(出具)预先批准证书。在收到预先批准证书后,外籍人士可以到韩国领事馆,在护照上加盖签证。

(2) D-8 签证

D-8 长期签证可向韩国子公司或外商投资的合资企业的外籍员工提供。对于大多数国籍的人(有例外情况),在没有签证、持旅游签证或是短期签证进入韩国,都可以申请将签证状态从入境签证转为 D-8 长期工作签证。

(3) E-7 签证

E-7 长期签证适用于外国人直接由韩国公司(包括外商投资公司的分公司)雇用的情况。因此,一般来说,申请 E-7 长期签证的外国人不是从外国子公司借调的受让人(与持有 D-7 或 D-8 长期签证的外籍劳工相反)。作为该流程的一部分,需要来自韩国有关部门或机构的推荐信。

其他类型的工作签证将在"出境和入境"部分讨论。

2. 社保

韩国国家社会保障体系包括社会保险、公共援助和社会福利服务。社会保障福利包括:①国民年金;②国民健康保险;③失业保险;④工伤保险。

（1）国民年金
- 通过支付保险福利来改善公共健康并促进社会福利，以预防、诊断、治疗人们的疾病或伤害，预防死亡，促进健康；
  - 养老金福利：养老金、残疾人养老金、幸存者养老金；
  - 整笔津贴：养老金退款、死亡福利。

（2）国民健康保险
- 通过支付保险福利来预防、诊断、治疗和康复人们的疾病或伤害，并预防死亡、促进健康，从而改善公共卫生和促进社会保障；
  - 服务福利：保健福利、健康检查；
  - 现金福利：治疗费用、共同支付上限制度、超额共同支付的补偿、残疾人辅助器械费用、怀孕和分娩检查费用。

（3）失业保险
- 防止失业并促进就业；
- 提高工人的职业能力发展；
- 加强职业指导和培训；
- 通过提供失业救济来保障工人生活的稳定。

员工健康保险费目前为员工月平均工资的6.12%（由雇主和员工平均分摊）。

（4）工伤保险
- 快速、公平地补偿工人的工伤事故；
- 实施和运营促进工人康复和回归社会所需的保险设施；
- 通过防灾和促进工人福利来帮助保护工人；
- 护理福利、暂时丧失工作能力的福利、残疾福利、护理福利金、幸存者福利、丧葬费用、伤害和疾病补偿养老金。

（三）出境和入境

1. 签证类型

任何计划在韩国停留期间工作的人都必须依法申请签证。此外，如果个人的家庭成员也计划在韩国工作，他们还必须申请工作签证以获得合法的工作权限（外籍劳工就业许可）。

最常见的就业签证包括：
- 短期工作签证（C-4）；
- 公司驻地/公司转让（公司内部转移）（D-7）；
- 外国投资签证（D-8）；
- 贸易管理签证（D-9）；
- 专业工作签证（E-5）；
- 特定工作签证（E-7）。

申请人必须亲自到韩国驻申请人所在国的领事馆或大使馆申请，并由韩国雇主批准。许多签证是由申请人的韩国雇主获得的。一旦申请获得批准，即可获得签证确认书。必须将该确认书连同签证申请一并提交给韩国申请人所在国的大使馆。

2. 出境和入境限制

外国人进入韩国时，必须持有有效的护照和司法部长签发的签证。一般来说，与韩国缔结签证免除协议的国家的外国人，或出于国际友谊、观光或访问性质等有利于韩国利益而进入韩国的外国人，可以在没有签证的情况下入境。

司法部长得禁止以下人进入韩国：①携带传染病；②吸毒成瘾者；③被认为可能对公共健康造成危害和伤害；④被认为极有可能实施任何有损韩国利益或公共安全的行为。

就业保障办公室可限制对欠缺有效就业许可证或特别许可就业证明的外籍工作人员的雇用，以及违反《外国工人就业法》或《移民管理法》的人员的雇用。

(四) 工会和劳工组织

就业和劳动部宣布,截至 2016 年,10.3% 的工人参加了韩国工会。韩国有两个国家工会中心:韩国工会联合会(FKTU)和韩国民主工会联合会(KCTU)。2015 年,韩国工会联合会拥有 84.3 万名会员(占韩国工会会员的 43.5%),韩国民主工会联合会拥有 63.6 万名会员(占韩国工会会员的 32.8%),45.9 万名工作人员属于以上两个联合会以外的独立工会。

(五) 劳动争议

韩国最常见的个人劳动争议形式是发生在不公平待遇(如没有正当理由的解雇或纪律处分)方面。此类个人权利争议的法律依据是禁止《劳工标准法》第 23 条规定的不公平解雇。

2016 年,集体劳动争议数量为 120 起,多于 2015 年的 105 起。在 2016 年,因劳资争议而损失的工作天数为 2 035 天,比 2015 年多(丢失了 447 个工作日)。

五、知识产权

(一) 知识产权法律、法规简介

韩国有许多知识产权(IP)权利。知识产权保护的最重要形式包括专利、实用新型、外观设计权、版权、商标和商业秘密。这些权利基于各种法规,包括《专利法》《实用新型法》《外观设计保护法》《商标法》《版权法》和《不公平竞争预防与商业秘密保护法》(UCPA)。

1. 专利和实用新型

在韩国,可申请专利事项包括装置、方法、工艺和材料发明,而实用新型仅保护物品的形状或结构。因此,方法、工艺和材料发明不能作为实用新型来保护。此外,专利和实用新型都必须具有新颖性和创造性才能获得批准,但《专利法》和《实用新型法》对创造性的规定有不同的标准。实用新型与专利的基本区别在于,实用新型要求较低的技术含量。

有一个相关的事项是,自 1979 年 3 月 1 日起,韩国成为《建立世界知识产权组织公约》的成员国。自 1980 年 5 月 4 日起,韩国也成为《保护工业产权巴黎公约》的成员国,并自 1995 年 1 月 1 日起成为世界贸易组织《与贸易有关的知识产权协定》的成员国。此外,韩国也是《专利合作条约》的成员国,第一章于 1984 年加入,第二章于 1990 年加入。因此,除了直接向韩国知识产权局(KIPO)提交申请外,《专利合作条约》下的国际申请可以在任何受理局提交并指定进入韩国国内。

2. 商标

商标用于识别个人或企业的商品或服务,并将其与他人的商品和服务区分开来。标志、字符、数字、3D 形状、颜色和声音是可保护的商标类型。经过韩国知识产权局的一系列手续和实质性审查后,将在注册后授予商标权。根据《商标国际注册马德里协定有关议定书》(即《马德里议定书》)的规定,商标可以直接与韩国知识产权局或通过世界知识产权组织进行注册。驰名商标即使没有注册,也可以得到《不公平竞争预防与商业秘密保护法》的保护。

3. 外观设计

《外观设计法》将"外观设计"定义为在视觉上产生审美印象的物品(包括物品的一部分)的形状、图案、颜色或这些的组合。因此,外观设计应用应该涉及单个产品或包含特定形状或图案的产品的任何部分。字体也可以根据《设计保护法》进行保护。此外,如果某些要求得到满足,未注册的物品设计可以在《不公平竞争预防与商业秘密保护法》的"复制品"条款下免受仿制品的侵害,其中包括:①仿制产品是在原产品生产之日起 3 年内制造的;②产品外观不是该类商品的常用形式。

4. 版权

要获得版权,作品必须具有原创性、创造性和表现力。获得版权不需要任何程序或手续,版权始于作者完成原作时。版权注册不是强制性的,但它为权利人提供了一定的优势,包括在创建或发布登记日期时的推定利益、登记作者身份和推定侵权人的疏忽。

5. 商业秘密

根据《不公平竞争预防与商业秘密保护法》的规定，可用于商业活动的技术或管理性质的机密信息可作为商业秘密加以保护。具体而言，为了成为《不公平竞争预防与商业秘密保护法》标准下有权被保护的商业秘密，信息必须符合特定要求，包括以下内容：
- 这些信息一般不为公众所知；
- 信息具有独立的经济价值；
- 努力保密这些信息。

应当指出，刑事诉讼是商业秘密保护的重要组成部分。韩国当局（检察官办公室和警察）在这方面表现得相当活跃，往往热衷追查涉及违反商业秘密的案件。另一个趋势是，近年来，侵犯商业秘密和违反不正当竞争条款的争议数量在稳步增加。造成这一趋势的一个重要原因是，员工的工作流动性增加，这可以为海外泄露商业秘密案件的增加作出解释。在犯罪方面尤其如此，因为韩国公司越来越多地与国外对手竞争，并在海外设有分支机构。

6.《不公平竞争预防与商业秘密保护法》下的知识产权保护

《不公平竞争预防与商业秘密保护法》被认为是通过防止不公平竞争手段来保护知识产权的一种有效方式，韩国法院越来越愿意通过《不公平竞争预防与商业秘密保护法》来扩大对知识产权侵权的保护范围。值得注意的是，2014年1月31日，《不公平竞争预防与商业秘密保护法》采用了一般性的"一揽子"规定，"通过使用该权利人付出非常多的努力和投资的产品侵犯他人权利获得利益的行为，和通过违反公平的商业贸易惯例或竞争秩序的方法未经其授权而侵犯个人权益的行为"，以便为各方提供适当手段来应对进行新类型不正当竞争的第三方。

7. 知识产权监管

《垄断监管和公平交易法》（MRFTA）适用于获取、授予、行使和转让知识产权。《垄断监管和公平交易法》第59条规定："本法不适用于任何被视为合理行使《版权法》《专利法》《实用新型法》《外观设计保护法》或《商标法》权利的行为。" 2000年8月颁布的《不正当行使知识产权准则》为确定知识产权行使是否构成企业滥用其市场支配地位或多个企业之间不公平的合作行为提供了指导。值得注意的是，韩国公平交易委员会于2016年12月宣布成立新的"知识产业反垄断部门"。韩国公平交易委员会表示，该部门的主要职责包括监测标准必要专利的滥用情况、监控不正当竞争行为以及损害与药品专利相关的消费者利益，例如原始和非专利药厂之间的"延迟支付协议"。

（二）专利申请

专利和实用新型权利是在向韩国知识产权局申请经过一系列正式和实质性审查后颁发的。在韩国注册时，专利申请和实用新型申请必须向韩国知识产权局提交。在这方面，需要提交专利申请和实用新型申请的人必须向韩国知识产权局专员提交下列文件：
- 发明人和申请人的名称和地址（申请人为法人的，需要法定代表人的姓名），发明名称和优先权数据（如果要求优先权）的申请；
- 规范，包括对发明和至少一项索赔的详细描述；
- 图纸（如有）；
- 摘要；
- 如果由申请人以外的当事人提交申请，需提交授权书。

在提交所需文件后，专利或实用新型申请将受到实质审查。对于专利和实用新型而言，采用延期审查制度，直到正式提出审查申请（可以在申请日后3年）才开始进行实质性审查。在提出审查申请后，申请的审查内容包括：①工业适用性；②新颖性；③创造性；④描述要求。实质审查决定通常在专利和实用新型申请审查日期后10至13个月内发布。

如果审查员不拒绝专利申请，其必须发布授予专利的决定通知。申请人必须在收到决定通知之日起3个月内缴纳前3年的年金作为注册费。此后，申请人可以每年支付年费。专利保护的期限从注册开始，到申请提交日期 20 年后结束；而实用新型的保护期从注册开始，到申请提交日期 10 年后结束。

（三）商标注册

根据《商标法》的规定，商标、证明商标、地理标志和其他商标在韩国受到保护。驰名商标即使没有注册，也受到《不公平竞争预防与商业秘密保护法》的保护。此外，韩国是一些国际公约的签署国，例如《保护工业产权巴黎公约》《与贸易有关的知识产权协定》《商标注册用商品和服务国际分类尼斯协定》《商标法条约》《商标国际注册马德里协定有关议定书》和《建立商标图形要素国际分类维也纳协定》，这些条约具有与国内法相同的法律效力。

韩国《专利法》的许多程序条款已适用于《商标法》。此外，韩国《刑法》的一般规定适用于《商标法》关于商标侵权刑事制裁的规定；《刑事诉讼法》适用于此类案件的侦查、起诉和刑事法院审理；《民事诉讼法》规定了商标侵权的民事救济方法；《海关法》规定了对韩国商标的保护。与其他司法管辖区一样，根据《公平贸易法》和《不公平贸易惯例和补救措施国内产业损害调查法》的规定，特定商标的权利也有其限制。此外，公平贸易委员会准则制定了允许平行进口的标准。

韩国采用了"注册"制度，而不是"使用"制度来保护商标。在这种制度下，商标权通常只有在商标注册时才会被认可。商标的实际使用不是获得商标注册的必要条件，可以基于使用意图提出申请。

（四）知识产权保护措施

在韩国，技术知识产权的拥有者可以采取多种不同的措施来保护其知识产权。具体而言，可采取以下措施：民事主要诉讼（寻求禁令或损害赔偿）、民事初步禁令诉讼（与民事主要诉讼分开的诉讼程序或仅寻求禁令救济）或刑事诉讼［可以寻求侵犯技术知识产权（包括专利、实用新型和外观设计）的刑事诉讼］；韩国贸易委员会的措施（类似于美国国际贸易委员会的行动）；韩国海关办公室的韩国海关措施；在韩国知识产权局（知识产权局内知识产权审判处的行政程序，以确定权利人的产品是否属于知识产权范围）之前的范围确认措施。

在韩国，首尔、大田、大邱、釜山和光州地区法院对知识产权侵权案件拥有专属管辖权。虽然知识产权侵权案件可能在这五个地区法院提出，并满足相关场所要求，但首尔中央法院有权审理任何知识产权侵权案件，无论哪个地区。此外，知识产权侵权案件的上诉仅由专利法院审理。在这方面，专利法院拥有一份上诉审判手册，手册上载明了关于知识产权侵权案件上诉的具体指导方针。

还有一项旨在保护工业技术和国家核心技术的《防止工业技术泄密和保护法》。工业技术指的是由相关部分指定、通知或发布并符合以下任何一项标准：①在韩国发展起来的原创技术，与先进国家相同或超出发达国家先进水平，并可商业化；②可降低成本或改善现有产品的性能或质量的技术；③具有技术和经济潜力，有助于提高国家技术基础和竞争力；④基于应用或利用上述技术的技术。此外，工业技术包括"国家核心技术"此一术语，其被韩国产业通商资源部定义为具有高技术或经济价值，或在国内外市场上具有高增长潜力的工业技术，并且其在韩国以外的披露会严重威胁国家安全或经济。韩国产业通商资源部负责维护一份已公布的国家核心技术列表。

六、环境保护

（一）环境保护监管部门

环境部负责保护环境，涵盖空气、水、土壤、自然、废物、回收利用、化学品、环境健康和气候变化等。此外，环境部还有许多机构支持其任务，其中包括但不限于国立环境研究所、中央环境争议调解委员会、韩国环境公司、韩国环境产业技术研究所、韩国国立公园管理局和首都圈垃圾填埋场管理公司等。

（二）环境保护法律、法规简介

韩国的环境法基于环境保护概念和清洁环境权（这是《宪法》中的一项权利）。根据《环境政策框架法》的原则，许多环境相关法律已经根据各种主题制定。

1. 环境评估

作为预防和警戒措施，《环境影响评估法》要求在执行行政决定或业务计划之前进行环境评估，以确定活动对该地区的环境影响。

2. 自然环境

《自然环境保护法》《野生动物保护和管理法》《生物多样性保护和利用法》以及《湿地保护法》等已经颁布，以保护自然环境和野生动植物群。

3. 空气

《空气环境保护法》在总体上规定了大气污染物的排放，《首尔大都市区空气质量改善特别法》对首尔大都市区的排放设施实施了更严格的标准。此外，还制定了《恶臭预防法》和《内部空气质量管理法》等，以改善韩国空气质量状况。

4. 水

《水环境保护法》规定了水污染物排放。《供水和水厂安装法》《污水处理法》《饮用水管理法》《居民对四大河流流域管理法》等法律进一步规范了水质和废水管理。

5. 土壤

《土壤环境保护法》等法律规定了防止土壤污染，并规定了对被污染土壤的修复要求。

6. 废物和资源循环

《废物管理法》规定了废物的处理方式，列出了适用于废物管理的一般性要求和标准。此外，《控制危险废物越境转移及其处置巴塞尔公约》规定了国家之间如何转移废物。最近颁布的《资源流通基本法》给处置废弃物这一工作设置了更大的负担，其目的是鼓励回收废物。《废弃物回收再利用促进法》《电气、电子设备和车辆资源循环法》和《资源回收利用促进法》等法律进一步促进了废弃物的再利用。

7. 化学制品

《化学品注册、评估法》等法律要求对化学物质、危险性/毒性测试进行登记以及规定了受管制的化学物质。此外，《化学品管理法》规定了处理有害物质的营业执照的颁发，并规定了化学物质如何储存和管理以防止事故发生。

8. 气候变化

《低碳和绿色增长框架法》规定了降低碳排放的目标管理方案。《温室气体排放许可证的分配和贸易法》提供了一个温室气体排放交易系统，企业可以在这个交易系统中交易其温室气体排放许可。

9. 石棉

《石棉安全管理法》禁止使用石棉、制造或进口含有石棉的产品，并要求对建筑物进行石棉检查。《石棉伤害救济法案》还提供了一种方法来弥补石棉造成的损害。

10. 环境纠纷

《环境损害和救济责任法》使环境污染受害者能够通过降低受害人的举证责任来寻求损害赔偿。此外，《环境争议调解法》规定了安排、调解和仲裁的详细程序，从而促使环境争议能够迅速公正地得到解决。

此外，《污染物排放设施综合管理法》对在综合管理系统下可能对环境产生重大影响的主要行业（例如钢铁制造、化学、电气或电子制造等）的排放设施进行了规定，并通过对为该按特定设施提供最佳技术，来确保能够对该设施进行适当的监管。

(三) 环境保护评估

截至2017年，环境部主管约60项环境法律，涵盖了几乎所有与环境保护有关的事项。这些法律不断更新，符合其他国家最近的法律、法规（标准）。由于这个原因，韩国环境法通常被认为是有条理的、最新的。

但是，对这些环境法律、法规的执行仍然存在担忧。例如，虽然环境部的 2016 年预算为 5.7 兆韩元，但大部分预算并没有平均分配给地方政府，因此在全国各地实施的执法和环境质量改善情况有所不同。此外，也有批评指出，当新政府介入时，监管领域和执行强度似乎发生了变化。

七、争议解决

（一）争议解决的方法和机构

在韩国，大部分大型商业争议都由法院解决，尽管近年来替代性争议解决方式越来越受欢迎，特别是作为解决商业争议手段的仲裁在跨境争议中越来越受欢迎。法院往往鼓励通过调解来解决争议。

调解可由主持争议的法官，或与主持争议以外的法官（仅用于调解的目的），或由包括一名法官和两名或多名以上的公民在内的调解委员会进行。韩国之所以增加仲裁的使用，是基于若干因素，其中包括韩国公司参与国际交易的增加以及韩国法院执行仲裁裁决的总体趋势。

原则上，韩国的民事诉讼是对抗性的，虽然也有纠问程序的要素。例如，主审法官可以直接向当事人询问事实或法律事项并敦促当事人提出进一步的证据（韩国《民事诉讼法》第 136 条第 1 款），向当事人寻求关于未决诉讼的澄清。此外，除了程序问题（如诉讼要件）外，法官必须调查和确定一些实质性问题（例如，当事方之间的共同过失程度、赔养费的量定，等等）。在民事诉讼中，证据负担使用的是"证据的优势"原则，而不是刑事案件中使用的"超越合理怀疑"的标准。

除了专利法院（专门为处理知识产权问题而设立的）必须审理的某些争议外，所有大型商业纠纷均由具有管辖权的普通民事法庭审理。

在地方法院审理的民事案件中，法官的人数取决于索赔的金额：
- 索赔金额在 2 亿韩元以下的案件，由 1 名法官审理；
- 索赔金额超过 2 亿韩元或无法确定索赔额的案件，由 3 名法官组成的小组审理；
- 在高级（上诉）法院，所有案件都由 3 名法官组成的小组审理。

地方法院和高级法院内的细分部门负责民事、刑事、家庭、青少年、行政、专利和破产事宜。如果初审法院的裁决被上诉，高等法院会重新进行审理。对于高等法院的裁决，只能在法律问题上向最高法院提起上诉。首尔高等法院对专利法院作为初审法院审理的知识产权争议裁决只能由最高法院二审。同样，如果韩国公平交易委员会作为当事人一方，且该争议由作为初审法院的首尔高等法院审理的，只能由最高法院进行二审。

为了更有效地处理涉及专业问题的复杂争议，一些法院指定某些法官小组负责处理某些争议，以便他们可以更加熟悉专业行业背后的技术和细微差别（例如，建筑行业的规划）。促使这种司法安排的实践领域包括国际交易、证券、建筑、人力资源和环境。

（二）法律的适用

根据《韩国法律冲突法》第 25 条的规定，当事人一般可以自由选择合同的管辖法律。为此，韩国法院尊重合同中主体对外国管辖法律和管辖权的选择。但是，如果合同中的主体涉及韩国任何强制性的法律，那么这些法律将优先适用。

最高法院还宣布，如果满足以下要求，关于承认外国法院专属管辖权协议的条款有效：
- 此案不涉及韩国法院专属管辖的事宜；
- 被指定为具有专属管辖权的外国法院，根据外国有关法律规定，对该事项具有管辖权；
- 被指定为具有专属管辖权的外国法院与争议事项有合理的联系。

最高法院还裁定，如果外国法院的专属管辖权协议明显不合理且/或不公平，那么该协议将因违反公共秩序和公序良俗而无效。

八、其他

（一）反商业贿赂

1. 反商业贿赂法律、法规简介

许多法律和条例都规定了贿赂政府官员的内容，其中包括《刑法》《关于加重处罚特定罪行的法令》《特定经济犯罪的加重处罚等法》《反腐败和民权委员会和防止腐败的创立和运作法》（即《反贪污法》或 ACA）和《禁止不正当征求和提供/收受货币和贵重物品法》（《反贪污法》或 AGA）。

《国际商业交易法》中的"外国贿赂预防"规制贿赂外国公职人员的问题。《公职人员维护诚信行为准则》（即《行为准则》）为各政府机构和国有企业收受付款、餐饮、礼品等活动提供指导。

反腐败和民权委员会发布了《关于不当请求和提供/收受贵重物品的处理投诉指导方针》和《不正当征求和贪污法手册》，详细解释了《反贪污法》。

2. 监督反商业贿赂的部门

地方检察官办公室有权起诉、调查和执行所有刑事案件，包括商业贿赂。警察在地方检察官办公室的监督下有权进行刑事侦查。如果检察官办公室决定起诉罪犯，主管法院有权对犯罪人实施刑事制裁。

反腐败和民权委员会是负责制定国家反腐败战略的主要反腐机构。它有权接受投诉，但无权进行独立的刑事侦查。相反，它必须将问题提交给其他机构或向刑事执法机构（即警察和检察官办公室）寻求帮助。

对于违反《反贪污法》的情况，相关公共机构（即涉案公职人员所在的机构）和韩国审计和检查委员会也有权在内部调查涉嫌违反《反贪污法》的指控，但不是启动刑事侦查。

3. 惩罚措施

（1）《刑法》

向政府官员行贿而违反《刑法》规定的人可能面临最高达 5 年的监禁或高达 2 000 万韩元的罚款。进行商业贿赂的人可能面临最高 2 年的监禁或高达 500 万韩元的罚款。对于《刑法》中任何类型的贿赂，公司不承担责任。

接受、索取或同意贿赂的公职人员可能面临长达 5 年的监禁，或被褫夺公权长达 10 年。

（2）《关于加重处罚特定罪行的法令》/《特定经济犯罪的加重处罚等法》

最高惩罚规定于《关于加重处罚特定罪行的法令》，而《特定经济犯罪的加重处罚等法》的规定高于《刑法》。处罚与贿赂的金额成正比。

（3）《反贪污法》

根据《反贪污法》的规定，单一案件超过 100 万韩元或每年获得超过 300 万韩元收益的公职人员，可处以 3 000 万韩元以下的罚款或 3 年以下的监禁。罚金将适用于给付人和收受人。

对于收益低于上述货币门槛的，但所托事项与收受贿赂的公职人员的公务职责直接相关，给付人和收受人都可能受到行政罚款的 2 至 5 倍的罚款。

根据《反贪污法》的规定，公司得对其员工的行为承担责任。

（二）项目承包

1. 许可制度

原则上，公共采购处代表韩国政府、地方政府和公共机构签订采购合同。集中采购流程的目的是提高效率。

但是，政府机构或公共机构可以在下列情况下直接签订采购合同：①自然灾害；②不可抗力事件；③与国防有关的采购或者必须保密的采购；④自然灾害或重大事故的紧急救援活动。①

---

① 参见《政府采购法》第 5 条（2）。

对于国防采购来说，国防采办计划管理局是有权签订与国防有关的采购合同的主要机构。

2. 禁区

传统上，韩国公民可以获得政府或公共采购工程。但是，自从韩国成为WTO《政府采购协议》的缔约方，外国公司也可能参与超过一定数量的政府或公共采购项目。

政府或公共采购招标分为以下三类：
- 国内投标，只有韩国公民可以参加；
- 国际招标，韩国公民和外国人均可参加；
- 外国招标，只有外国人可以参加（由于缺乏当地资源）。

3. 招标和投标邀请

原则上，政府采购项目通过竞标获得。①但是，如果承包商拥有的专业技术和此技术对项目的成功尤为重要，相关的政府机构或公共机构可能会与被认为最有利于该国的公司签订非竞争性的唯一来源合同。在这种情况下，承包商的业绩记录、技术能力和项目实施计划等非价格因素将被认为具有更高的重要性。此外，这些标准将提前提供给投标人。②

如果难以在制造或购买商品或服务的协议中列出规范或要求，或者根据协议的特点要求，则可能首先要求投标人参与竞标规格或技术。只有那些被视为具备所需能力的投标人才会被邀请参加投标。③

（三）隐私和数据保护

《个人信息保护法》规定了公共或私人部门收集的个人信息的整体流程。《个人信息保护法》与现有的《促进信息和通信网络利用和信息保护法》等同时执行，该法规定了个人信息的收集（通过电信网络，如互联网）。《信用信息使用和保护法》规定了信用信息的收集。在这方面，收集客户信息的公司可能会按照上述法律，并参考收集方法和收集的信息类型。

个人信息被广义地定义为，涉及与自然人相关的信息，其包含识别特定人员的信息（例如，名字、地址或类似形式的图像等，包括其本身不包含的但是与其他信息结合起来可以轻松识别一个人的信息）。个人信息的常见示例包括姓名、地址、电话号码、性别和爱好等。信息必须与自然人相关，因此，关于公司实体的信息不属于个人信息的范围，并且不受《个人信息保护法》的保护。来自个人客户和员工的个人信息，属于《个人信息保护法》定义的个人信息范围。

根据韩国法律，敏感信息被定义为个人信息，其包括意识形态、信仰、工会成员资格、政治观点、政党成员资格、健康信息或医疗、性生活、基因信息和犯罪记录（例如，量刑、豁免、暂缓宣判、保护性关押、缓刑）等。同样，独特的身份信息被定义为一个人的居民身份证号码、护照号码、驾驶证号码或外国人登记号码。

---

① 国家作为缔约方的条款，《合同法》第10条。
② 国家作为缔约方的条款，《合同法执行法令》第43条。
③ 国家作为缔约方的条款，《合同法执行法令》第18条。

Republic of Korea

Authors: Hyun-Ho Eun, John Sangho Park
Translators: Jiang Jinji, Jin Ying

I. Overview

A. General Introduction to the Political, Economic, Social and Legal Environment of the Country Receiving Investment

The Republic of Korea ("Korea") is a wealthy East Asian state that occupies the southern part of the Korean Peninsula. Its territory consists of a mountainous mainland and over 3000 largely uninhabited adjacent islands. Korea has a relatively homogenous population of 51 million.[1] The capital and most-populated city of Korea is Seoul.

Korea is a technologically advanced and developed country that ranks well in international performance indicators such as gross domestic product, healthcare quality, ease of doing business and life expectancy. Korea is a member of the Organization for Economic Cooperation and Development (OECD) and the G-20.

a. Political

Korea is a presidential democratic republic system whereby the president is elected by a direct vote of the people for a five-year term. The president is the chief of the state, head of the government and commander-in-chief of the armed forces. The government is composed of three independent branches: the executive; the legislature (made up of 300 members of the unicameral National Assembly who serve renewable four-year terms); and the judiciary (made up of 14 Supreme Court justices who, with the exception of the Chief Justice, serve renewable six-year terms). There are 17 regional local governments and 226 basic local governments. The heads of the local governments and the members of local councils are each elected for renewable four-year terms.

The current President of Korea is Moon Jae-in, who was inaugurated into office on 10 May 2017. The President of Korea is elected for a non-renewable and single term of 5 years.

b. Economic

Korea is the world's 11th largest economy by GDP and the 4th largest in Asia[2] Over the past five decades, Korea has demonstrated and sustained incredible economic growth and global integration to become a high-tech industrialized economy. In the 1960s, GDP per capita was comparable to levels in the poorer countries of Africa and Asia. Since this period, GDP Annual Growth Rate in Korea averaged 7.46 percent from 1961 until 2017[3] and as a consequence, Korea is today a high-income economy with a GDP in excess of $1.4 trillion and a per capita income nearing $35,000 (PPP adjusted)[4]. Korea is also home to iconic and world-leading brands such as Samsung, LG, and Hyundai.

c. Social

Korean is the official language of Korea while the written form of Korean uses Hangeul, a writing system commissioned by King Sejong (1397–1450)[5] during the Joseon Dynasty. Despite differences in the dialects inherent to different regions within Korea, speakers and listeners from these different regions can understand each other.

Korea supports religious freedom. Confucianism, Buddhism and Christianity are the main religions. Korea has long been a homogeneous society, but the number of migrant workers and foreign students has increased rapidly since the end of the 20th century. By December 2017, the number of foreign people in Korea reached up to 2.18

---

[1] South Korea Population 2018. Available from: http://worldpopulationreview.com/countries/south-korea-population.
[2] World GDP Ranking 2017. Available from: http://cn.knoema.com/nwnfkne/world-gdp-ranking-2017-gdp-by-country-data-and-charts.
[3] South Korea GDP Annual Growth Rate. Available from: https://tradingeconomics.com/south-korea/gdp-growth-annual.
[4] South Korea GDP Annual Growth Rate. Available from: https://tradingeconomics.com/south-korea/gdp-growth-annual.
[5] Republic of Korea-Summary. Available from: http://www.korea.net/AboutKorea/Society/South-Korea-Summary.

million[1], equivalent to roughly 4.21% of the Korean population.[2]

d. Legal

Korea is a civil law system and comprises of many levels of codified forms of law. These include the Constitution, legislation enacted by the National Assembly and regulations promulgated by the Executive. The Constitution forms the legal foundation of Korea and sets out a democratic republic system of government. The judicial system is generally regarded as independent and is composed of the Supreme Court, the Constitutional Court, 6 High Courts, 13 District Courts and other specialized courts. While the Supreme Court is the highest court in Korea, the Constitutional Court is the court of last resort for all matters relating to constitutionality. Property rights and commercial enterprise laws are generally regarded as being well-developed.

To promote foreign investment, the Korean government has kept its involvement in the oversight and review of foreign investment to a minimum. In fact, Korea's active promotion of foreign direct investment (FDI) stemmed from the government's efforts to utilise FDI to help overcome the 1998 Asian financial crisis and to further liberalise the economy. Through such efforts, Korea has liberalised foreign investment and established a framework to protect foreign investors. In terms of the government oversight of foreign investments on grounds of national interest, the relevant regulations and policies are focused more on industry segments rather than origin of the investors or other factors in the sense that a limited number of restrictions for aggregate foreign ownership or business activities by foreign-owned entities exist with respect to certain types of businesses such as telecommunications, electric transmission and distribution and defence.

Historically, the currency of Korea, the Korean won, has been subject to significant exchange controls. In recent years, however, Korea has made significant progress toward liberalising its currency markets. This began in 1990 when a series of deregulatory measures was put in place to liberalise foreign exchange controls. Further measures were introduced in 2006 when the Korean government announced a "Foreign Exchange Liberalisation Plan". Under this plan, the government accelerated liberalising foreign exchange markets.

B. The Status and Direction of the Cooperation with Chinese Enterprises Under the B&R

The Silk Road Economic Belt and the 21st-century Maritime Silk Road (the "Belt and Road Initiative") provides economic opportunities for Korea and the broader Northeast Asia region. According to the "Vision and Actions on Joint Building Silk Road Economic Belt and 21st-Century Maritime Silk Road", three northeastern provinces (Liaoning, Jilin, and Jeilongjiang) have been designated to become sea-land 'windows' linking Russia, Mongolia and other areas in the Far East. In this light, there are many points for cooperation with the Eurasia Initiative of the Korean government and ways in which Belt and Road Initiative can contribute to building a Northeast Asian economic zone.

On 14 May 2017, a Korean government delegation led by Democratic Party lawmaker Byeong-seok Park attended the Belt and Road Forum for International Cooperation in Beijing. This was followed up on 13 December 2017 when Korean President Moon Jae-in made his first trip to China since taking office, whereby Chinese President Xi Jinping and President Moon agreed to advance bilateral relations to ensure the long-term stability of ties between China and Korea. President Xi Jinping said China welcomed Korea's participation in the Belt and Road construction and promoted the alignment of the Belt and Road Initiative with Korea's development strategy. President Moon also announced that he and President Xi Jinping had agreed "to actively look for ways of actual cooperation between China's Belt and Road Initiative" and Korea's own foreign policy initiative—the "New North" and "New South" policies-which seek greater economic and diplomatic cooperation with Eurasian as well as with Southeast Asian nations.

II. Investment

A. Market Access

a. Department Supervising Investment

The Ministry of Trade, Industry and Energy ("MOTIE") oversees foreign direct investments in Korea. As a

---

[1] Ministry of Justice, Monthly Report on Immigration Policy, December 2017.Available from: http://www.moj.go.kr/HP/COM/bbs_03/ListShowData.do?strNbodCd=noti0097&strWrtNo=241&strAnsNo=A&strNbodCd=noti0703&strFilePath=moj/&strRtnURL=MOJ_40402000&strOrgGbnCd=104000&strThisPage=1&strNbodCdGbn=.
[2] Foreign population jumps to 2.18 million, The Korea Times.Available from: https://www.koreatimes.co.kr/www/nation/2018/01/177_243054.html.

related matter, the Ministry of Strategy and Finance ("MOSF") and the Bank of Korea ("BOK") jointly oversee foreign exchange regulation, which may apply when a foreign investor needs to remit its investment to and from Korea.

b. Laws and Regulations of Investment Industry

The principal laws governing foreign direct investments ("FDI") in Korea are the Foreign Investment Promotion Act ("FIPL") and the Foreign Exchange Transaction Act ("FETL"). The FETL generally regulates the exchange rate system, foreign exchange operations, and the payment and receipt of foreign exchange. In the event that the Korean government determines that certain exigent circumstances are likely to occur (e.g., sudden fluctuations in interest rates or exchange rates, extreme difficulty in being able to stabilize the balance of payments, or a substantial disturbance in the Korean financial and capital markets), then the Korean government may implement restrictions to protect the markets. These restrictions may involve requiring foreign investors to obtain approval from the MOSF before acquiring Korean securities or repatriating interest, dividends or sales proceeds arising from Korean securities. If, however, the FDI meets certain conditions and is made pursuant to the FIPL, then the FDI will not be subject to the foregoing restrictions under the FETL. The FIPL provides for investment protection and certain incentives, which the details are set out in Section II, J.

c. Forms of Investment

A foreign investor who intends to establish a presence in Korea must first select an appropriate form of the FDI to be made in Korea. Regardless of whether the foreign investor is a natural person or a legal entity, the foreign investor can establish a corporate entity in Korea. If the foreign investor is an entity, then the foreign entity also has the option to establish a liaison or branch office.

If a foreign investor elects to establish a corporate entity, then the two most popular entity forms used by the foreign investors in Korea have been a joint stock company (or Jusik Hoesa in Korean) or a limited company (or Yuhan Hoesa in Korean). It is also possible for the foreign investor to establish a limited liability company (or Yuhan Chaegim Hoesa in Korean). Each of the entity types provide limited liability to the shareholders or members having an equity interest in the relevant company where their respective liability will be limited to the capital amounts that they have invested in the company.

As mentioned above, a foreign entity can establish a liaison or branch office in Korea for its Korean operations. Since a branch is viewed as a permanent establishment in Korea, a branch in Korea is subject to Korean income tax on income attributable to the branch's operation whereas the earnings remitted to its overseas head office are not subject to Korean dividend tax.[1] However, a branch will not provide limited liability protection for its head office since a branch is not treated as a separate legal entity in Korea.

d. Standards of Market Access and Examination

Under Korean law, certain Korean companies are subject to foreign ownership limitations based on laws specifically applicable to such companies. Also, under certain legislation such as the Banking Law, acquisition of shares in certain companies is subject to reporting / approval requirements depending on the shareholding level. These requirements are irrespective of the identity of the investors.

Foreign ownership restrictions apply to ownership in: (i) "public-interest corporations" such as Korea Electric Power Corporation; (ii) certain government-owned corporations such as Korea Gas Corporation; (iii) certain telecommunications and network services businesses such KT Corp. and SK Telecom; (iv) certain marine industries; (v) certain aviation industries; (vi) the broadcasting industry; (vii) certain agriculture industries; and (viii) certain publishing industries. Approval requirements and thresholds vary on a case-by-case basis.

Generally, prior approval for excess shareholding must be sought from the appropriate authority and through a prescribed form before such investment may be made. In the case of public-interest corporations, prior approval for excess shareholding must be obtained from the Financial Services Commission ("FSC"). For other foreign-ownership restricted corporations, authorization is generally sought from the appropriate regulator or governmental ministry (e.g., MOTIE or the Ministry of Land, Infrastructure, and Transport. Automatic monitoring of foreign investment in restricted entities listed on the Korea Exchange is made through a computer network / order placing system operated by the Korean Securities Computers Corporation. Any order exceeding foreign investment limits in a listed but restricted public-interest corporation is flagged by the system and will not be processed.

Certain Korean companies that are listed on the Korea Exchange are subject to foreign ownership limitations based on laws specifically applicable to such companies (please note that some of the ownership limitations apply to both domestic and foreign investors). There is no single law that sets out a common rule on foreign ownership limitations and nor is there a centralized enforcement authority in this regard. Each of the relevant laws set out

---

[1] While a branch office may engage in revenue generating activities, a liaison office may only undertake non-taxable activities.

specific foreign ownership limitations using its own terminology as well as different ceilings in order to serve the purposes of that specific law. In addition, the articles of incorporation of certain companies subject to ownership restrictions may impose additional or more stringent ownership limitations.

For example, the FIPL stipulates that in order for a foreign investor to acquire existing shares of a Korean defense company, the foreign investor is required to obtain MOTIE's prior approval, which MOTIE may do so only after it has consulted the Minister of National Defense. The FIPL further stipulates that in order for a foreign investor to acquire newly issued shares of a Korean defense company, the foreign investor must provide advance notice to MOTIE. Upon receiving the advance notice, if MOTIE judges that the acquisition will not trigger the relevant provision in the Defense Acquisition Program Act ("DAPA Act"), which stipulates that the change of control in any Korean defense company's management requires MOTIE's prior approval, MOTIE will take no further action. However, if MOTIE determines that the proposed acquisition of newly issued shares by a foreign investor would cause a change of control in a Korean defense company's management, then MOTIE will refer the matter to the Foreign Investment Committee for further determination pursuant to the DAPA Act.

B. Foreign Exchange Regulation

a. Department Supervising Foreign Exchange

The MOSF and the BOK jointly regulate and supervise foreign exchange matters in Korea.

b. Brief Introduction of Laws and Regulations of Foreign Exchange

In general, the foreign exchange regulation relevant to the extension of a loan by a non-resident to a resident is the FET Act and the Foreign Exchange Transaction Regulations ("FETR"). To some extent, the FIPL is also applicable. Under the FETL and FETR, no preferential treatment is given to a particular nationality of a foreign lender or a particular foreign currency.

The FETL regulates investment in Korean securities by non-residents and issuance of securities outside Korea by Korean companies. Under the FETL, non-residents may invest in Korean securities pursuant to the FETL. The FSC has also adopted, pursuant to its authority under the Financial Investment Services and Capital Markets Act ("FSCMA"), regulations that restrict investment by foreigners in Korean securities and regulates the issuance of securities outside of Korea by Korean companies.

c. Requirements of Foreign Exchange Management for Foreign Enterprises

Under the Korean foreign exchange laws and regulations, foreign exchange transactions are generally classified as "capital transactions" or "trade transactions". Capital transactions refer to making deposits, lending, provision of guarantee, or issuance or acquisition of securities, whereas trade transactions refer to import / export of goods or services. In principle, any person (including a foreigner) engaging in a cross-border capital transaction must file a report under the FETL[①] with the MOSF, the BOK or a foreign exchange bank[②] depending on the relevant transaction, prior to entering into an agreement, but there is no such reporting obligation in the case of a trade transaction. As such, a Korean resident (e.g., a Korean subsidiary of a foreign company) importing or exporting goods or services does not have any obligation to file any reports under Korean law with respect to the transaction or with respect to making payments for the imports or receiving export proceeds; it would be sufficient for the Korean resident to submit to a foreign exchange bank[③] documents evidencing the import payments to be made and the export proceeds to be received, in accordance with the procedures prescribed by the MOSF. There are, however, some important exceptions. For example, a report must be filed in advance to the BOK, or approval must be obtained from the BOK, to pay for imports from Iran or to receive payment for exports to Iran.[④]

a) Reporting Requirement for Intercompany Loans from Foreign Affiliates

Under Article 18, Paragraph 1 of the FETL and Article 7-14, Paragraph 1 of the FETR, where a Korean resident intends to borrow foreign currency funds from a non-resident (e.g., the foreign parent company of the Korean subsidiary), the borrowing transaction is subject to reporting requirements.[⑤] If the amount of the loan is not

---

[①] FETL, Article 18.
[②] The term "foreign exchange bank" refers to a bank registered with the MOSF to conduct foreign exchange business such as buying and selling foreign currency and taking foreign currency deposits. For example, the Industrial Bank of Korea is a foreign exchange bank.
[③] Pursuant to Article 5(11) of the FETR, all remittances from Korea to other countries are required to be made through a foreign exchange bank.
[④] FETL, Article 15(2); Guidelines on Approval of Payment and Receipt of Funds to Enable Maintenance of International Peace and Safety.
[⑤] Under Article 7(15), Paragraph 1 of the FETR, there is a similar reporting requirement applicable in case a Korean resident intends to borrow Korean Won funds from a non-resident.

more than USD 30 million, such report must be filed with, and accepted by, a designated foreign exchange bank. If the amount exceeds USD 30 million, the report must be filed with, and accepted by, the MOSF. The report must be filed prior to the signing of the transaction documents. In addition, the borrower is required to designate one Korean bank for the loan and its repayment. The loan must be deposited into the foreign currency account at the designated Korean bank, and then may be withdrawn from the account by the borrower.

b) Procedures Applicable to Acquisition of Shares in Korea by Foreigners

Under the FETL, a foreign investor who intends to acquire shares of a Korean company must designate a foreign exchange bank at which to open a foreign currency account and a Korean Won account exclusively for stock investments. No approval is required for remittance into Korea and deposit of foreign currency funds in the foreign currency account. Foreign currency funds may be transferred from the foreign currency account at the time required to place a deposit for, or settle the purchase price of, a stock purchase transaction to a Korean Won trading account opened at a securities company. Funds in the foreign currency account may be remitted abroad without any governmental approval.

Dividends on shares are paid in Korean Won. No governmental approval is required for foreign investors to receive dividends on, or the Korean Won proceeds of the sale of, any such shares to be paid, received and retained in Korea. Dividends paid on, and the Korean Won Proceeds of the sale of, any such shares held by a non-resident of Korea must be deposited either in a Korean Won account with the investor's securities company or the Korean Won account at the designated foreign exchange bank. Funds in the investor's Korean Won account at a foreign exchange bank may be transferred to the foreign currency account or withdrawn for local living expenses up to certain limitations. Funds in the Korean Won account at a foreign exchange bank may also be used for future investment in shares or for payment of the subscription price of new shares obtained through the exercise of preemptive rights.

C. Financing

a. Main Financial Institutions

Financial institutions in Korea are categorized into banks, non-bank deposit handling institutions that handle financial products similar to bank deposits, securities companies and asset management companies, insurance companies, and other financial institutions.

The four major administrative bodies engaged in the regulation of financial institutions in Korea are the MOSF, the BOK, the FSC and the Financial Supervisory Service ("FSS").

• The MOSF engages in the establishment of economic policy, the preparation of the national budget, the establishment and implementation of foreign exchange policy, and the management of the national treasury.

• The BOK, as Korea's central bank, pursues price stability and implements monetary policies through the Monetary Policy Committee established therein.

• The FSC's main role is to integrate financial policy and provide financial supervision, and to carry out this role, it oversees the licensing of Korean financial institutions and administers sanctions to institutions that are in violation of financial regulations. Another important function of the FSC relates to the preparation and enactment of various finance-related laws and regulations and its amendments for the purpose of carrying out its financial policy implementation and financial supervision roles.

• The FSS operates under the auspices of the FSC, and its primary function is the examination and supervision of financial institutions.

b. Financing Conditions for Foreign Enterprises

Foreign investors with a presence in Korea are eligible to obtain various types of financing available in the market without any discrimination for being a foreign invested entity.

The most common form of financing is an intercompany loan (or shareholder loan) (e.g., where a foreign affiliate extends a loan to the company in Korea) and the loan agreement would have to be drafted reflecting the appropriate terms and conditions. While there is no specific language that must be inserted in the form, the terms and conditions of the loan agreement shall be carefully drafted, with due consideration of various factors mentioned below.

a) Fetl Report

Under the FETL, any loan transaction between a non-resident and a resident is subject to the reporting / approval procedure prescribed in the FETL and the regulations thereunder. In general, such a loan is required to be reported to and accepted by the Korean borrower's designated foreign exchange bank in advance; however, if the principal of the loan exceeds USD 30 million, it must be reported to the Ministry of Strategy and Finance through a foreign exchange bank.

b) Internal Corporate Approval

The Board of Directors of the borrowing entity must adopt a resolution approving the loan. Board minutes must be drafted for this purpose.

c) Other Relevant Issues

When considering intercompany loans as a means of providing additional funds to the company in Korea, the following points are relevant:

• Withholding Tax on Repatriation of Dividends or Interests: Under Korean tax law, a foreign corporate recipient (assuming that it does not have any permanent establishment in Korea) would be subject to withholding tax at 27.5% (including surtax) on both dividends and interest payments. If the foreign recipient is qualified to receive benefits of any tax treaty, the lower withholding tax rates specified in the relevant tax treaty would apply instead of 27.5%. Tax treaties may provide different tax rates for dividends and interest. If the loan is structured instead as bonds and meet certain relevant conditions (e.g., denominated in foreign currency), an exemption or reduction of Korean withholding tax may be obtained in accordance with the Tax Incentives Limitation Law;

• Deduction of Interest or Dividends to the Borrower: Subject to the thin capitalization rule as discussed below, interest payments are generally deductible to the borrower for its corporate income tax purposes. On the other hand, no deduction is provided for dividend payments under Korean tax law;

• Thin Capitalization Rule: Under the International Tax Coordination Law ("ITCL"), the deductibility of interest payments with respect to a loan extended by a "foreign controlling shareholder" ("FCS") of the Korean borrower may be limited. More specifically, if the amount of the Korean borrower's debt, owed to an FCS or to a third party under a guarantee issued by an FCS, exceeds 300% of the "net FCS equity" (as defined below) in the Korean borrower, interest expenses on such excessive debt will not be deductible to the Korean borrower for its corporate income tax purposes. In addition, such non-deductible interest amount would be treated as dividends if the debt is owed to an FCS. An FCS for this purpose means a foreign shareholder who (i) directly or indirectly owns 50% or more of the voting power in the borrower, or (ii) in substance controls the business policies of the borrower. Factors indicating control include interlocking directors, significant financial support, business dependency, licensing of intangible property, etc. The "net FCS equity" in the borrower for this purpose is defined, in principle, as its proportionate share of the larger of (i) the net equity (i.e., total assets minus total liabilities) amount of the Company or (ii) the shareholder's investment amount (i.e., paid-in capital plus share premium plus gain from capital reduction minus discount from capital increase minus loss from capital reduction) as of the end of the fiscal year. If there is any capital increase or capital reduction during the fiscal year, however, the new FCS equity should be calculated under the average basis. Accordingly, a thin capitalization problem cannot be avoided by extinguishing loans just before the end of the fiscal year or by an injection of additional capital immediately before the end of the fiscal year; and

• Transfer Pricing Regulations: If there is any "special relationship" between the foreign lender and the Company within the meaning of the Korean transfer pricing regulations (which usually exists in the case of an inter-company loan) which are stipulated in the ITCL, the terms of the loan may come under scrutiny by the tax authorities to see if they are arm's length terms. Accordingly, the terms and conditions (interest rate, default provision, etc.) of the loan should be carefully fixed to reflect an arms-length dealing. If the interest rate is higher than the fair market interest rate for the international transaction, the excessive interest paid by the Company would be treated as non-deductible expenses for its corporate income tax purpose.

D. Land Policy

a. Brief Introduction of Land-related Laws and Regulations

With respect to ownership of real estate, Korean law only recognizes complete ownership, which is similar to the Anglo-American law concept of a fee simple absolute. Korean law does not recognize partial estates such as life estates (ownership lasting only during a certain person's lifetime), conditional estates (ownership lasting only as long as certain conditions remain satisfied) and future interests (ownership arising only upon the occurrence of a future contingency). Leasehold interests, rights of superficies (the right to use land without ownership) and certain easements are also recognized under Korean law.

a) Registration of Ownership

Land ownership interests and building ownership interests are separate rights under Korean law. As a consequence, Korea has a dual registration system for real property, consisting of a land registry and a building registry (collectively, the "Real Property Registry").

b) Transferability

Title to real estate is freely transferrable by the registered owner(s) of the subject real estate registered on the land registry and the building registry and such title transfer is not subject to any approval of the authorities.

c) Expropriation

The framework for the legal regime relating to expropriation is the Act on Acquisition and Compensation for Land for Public Projects ("Takings Act"). Pursuant to the Takings Act, central or local governments can only order the Central Land Taking Committee to expropriate private real property when there is a statutory public need. In this case, the Central Land Taking Committee determines the purchase price, based on all the circumstances, including the market value and the government-posted value.

b. Rules of Land Acquisition for Foreign Enterprises

Pursuant to the Foreigner's Land Act ("FLA"), if a foreigner wishes to acquire land in Korea, the foreign purchaser must report its acquisition of the land to the government authorities within 60 days of the execution date of the sale and purchase agreement. A company incorporated in Korea will be deemed a foreign company for the purpose of the FLA if foreigners own 50% or more of the outstanding shares in the company. If a foreign entity acquires a Korean company that owns land, and therefore the target company becomes a foreigner according to the above standard and intends to continue to own the land going forward, the acquisition of interests in the land must be reported within six months of the acquisition of that Korean company.

Pursuant to the Act on Real Property Transaction Report, the parties to a land or building sale and purchase agreement must jointly report to the government authorities the execution of such an agreement within 60 days from the date of the execution and prior to the registration of the ownership transfer. A foreigner may be exempt from filing a land acquisition report under the FLA as long as the foreigner has filed the real estate transaction report in accordance with the Act on Real Estate Transaction Report.

Finally, when a foreigner desires to acquire real property in Korea with money remitted from abroad, such foreigner purchasing the real property must report the acquisition to a foreign exchange bank in advance.

E. The Establishment and Dissolution of Companies

a. The Forms of Enterprises

A foreign investor can establish a subsidiary or joint venture company in one of the following three forms: joint stock company (or "Jusik Hoesa" in Korean); limited company ("Yuhan Hoesa" in Korean); and limited liability company ("Yuhan Chaegim Hoesa" in Korean). The major differences between the three forms are as follows:

• While shares of a joint stock company and equity interest in a limited company (i.e., membership units) are in principle freely transferable unless otherwise provided in the relevant articles of incorporation, equity interest in a limited liability company (i.e., membership units) is not in principle freely transferable unless otherwise provided in the relevant articles of incorporation;

• Only a joint stock company is required to have a board of directors and one or more statutory auditors, provided that there is certain exception for small joint stock companies with paid-in capital of less than KRW 1 billion;

• A joint stock company with total assets of at least KRW 12 billion as of the previous year-end must have its financial statements audited by an external accountant and file such audited financial statements with the FSC; and

• While written resolutions in lieu of a meeting are generally prohibited for a joint stock company, such written resolutions are permitted for a limited company and a limited liability company if all members consent to the same.[①]

As an alternative, foreign investors may consider establishing a liaison office or branch office in Korea. The "liaison office" generally refers to an office engaging in non-taxable activities of a preliminary and auxiliary nature for the business of a foreign corporation. As a liaison office is not treated as an independent legal entity nor a place of business that generates revenue, it cannot (i) engage in income-generating activities; (ii) be registered with the tax office (and thus is not eligible to file a tax return, as explained below); and (iii) own any assets (e.g., facilities, equipment or real property) under its name. In order for the foreign investor to engage in revenue generating activities in Korea, establishing a branch office can be a viable option.

A branch office is an extension of its (foreign) head office, and accordingly, the rights and liabilities of a branch extend to the company to which it belongs. Under Korean law, a branch can be registered with the court and also with the tax office as a place of business in Korea. One benefit of establishing a branch office is that a branch office may be less cumbersome to operate than a subsidiary, in terms of maintenance and management, because it is usually smaller in size and the law imposes fewer statutory managerial requirements. Also, a branch may

---

① Please note that shareholders of a corporation with paid-in capital of less than KRW one billion may pass resolutions of a general meeting of shareholders in writing without convening an actual meeting if all shareholders of the corporation consent to the same in writing.

have certain tax advantages with respect to the earnings remitted to its overseas head office, as further described below. On the other hand, the downside of conducting business by a branch office is that the foreign company would not be insulated from the liabilities of the branch.

b. The Procedure of Establishment

In order to incorporate an entity in Korea, a foreign investor must prepare and execute the articles of incorporation of such entity prior to the capital injection, and in the case of a joint stock company or limited company, the inaugural general meeting of shareholders or members must be held in order to appoint the entity's directors and / or statutory auditor. Also, a report of acquisition of equity interest in the newly incorporated entity should be filed with the relevant foreign exchange bank in Korea and, after the completion of the capital injection, the foreign investor must have the new entity registered with the court registry and the local tax office. To register with the local tax office, the new entity must have a lease agreement in place.

Although there is no minimum capital amount required to incorporate a joint stock company, limited company or limited liability company, under the Korean Commercial Code ("KCC"), a foreign investor must, among others, make an investment of at least KRW 100,000,000 in order for its investment to be qualify for various benefits consequent upon "foreign direct investment" within the meaning of the FIPL. Some examples of these benefits include a guarantee of repatriation of the investment, and tax benefits to certain qualifying foreign direct investment.

c. Routes and Requirements of Dissolution

A summary of the requirements and procedures for dissolution / liquidation of a joint stock company ("jusik hoesa" in Korean) / limited company ("yuhan hoesa" in Korean) in Korea is set out below.①

a) Dissolution Process

In order to liquidate a joint stock company or a limited company, the shareholders / members must first adopt a resolution to dissolve the company. Liquidation is complete when: (i) all the assets of the company have been disposed of; (ii) all the obligations have been performed; and (iii) all the remaining assets have been distributed among the shareholders / members. There is no time limit to completing these procedures. If there are any matters unresolved, the company will be deemed to be still in the process of liquidation. Further issues worth being mindful of are considered below:

• Meeting of shareholders / members: Voluntary dissolution of a Korean company requires a shareholders' / members' resolution;

• Election and registration of liquidator(s): A company in liquidation may have one or more liquidators who will be in charge of the liquidation of the company. The appointment can be made at the same shareholders' / members' meeting at which the shareholders / members adopt the resolution for dissolution. If more than one liquidator is appointed, a "representative liquidator" should be appointed from among the liquidators at the meeting of liquidators. Unless the company's articles of incorporation or its shareholders / members approve otherwise, the directors of the company will automatically become the liquidators;

• Notice of dissolution to shareholders / members: Upon adoption of the resolution for the dissolution at a shareholders' / members' meeting, the representative director must give notice thereof to all shareholders / members; and

• Registration of dissolution: After the shareholders / members approve the dissolution of the company at the shareholders' / members' meeting, the dissolution and the appointment of the liquidators and the representative liquidator must be registered with the courts having jurisdictions over the company's principal office within two weeks from the date of the shareholders' / members' resolution.

b) Liquidation Process

The following list generally sets out the liquidation process in Korea:

• Report to the court: The representative liquidator (in case a sole liquidator is appointed, the liquidator) must report the following matters to the appropriate court within two weeks from the date of appointment:

-The cause of dissolution (i.e., the contents of the resolution for dissolution) and the date thereof; and

-The names, resident registration numbers (or passport numbers for foreigners) and addresses of the liquidators.

In addition, the representative liquidator must file the inventory of assets and balance sheet with the court following the shareholders' / members' approval.

---

① The process of dissolution and liquidation for a joint stock company and a limited company are essentially the same, except the different forms of equity interest applicable to a joint stock company and a limited company (i.e., "shareholders" applicable to a joint stock company, while "members" applicable to a limited company).

• Disposal of assets: The representative liquidator may dispose of the company's assets and reduce them to cash. The disposal of the assets must be completed in accordance with the requirements of the KCC.

• Winding up of pending affairs: Any contractual affairs left uncompleted by the company at the time of dissolution must be settled. Continuous contractual relationships with third parties must be wound up as well as the employment relationship with the company's employees.

• Creditor protection procedures: The representative liquidator must give public notice of the dissolution to the creditors of the company (e.g., by newspaper publication) at least twice within the twomonth period following his / her appointment. In the public notice, the representative liquidator should request the creditors to present the company with their claims within the period set out in such notice, which period should not be less than two months. In addition to the public notice, the representative liquidator is required to give personal notice in writing to all known creditors of the company.

• Dismissal of employees and other labor matters: The closure of business and liquidation of the company will require the dismissal of all employees, either in phases or at one time by giving at least 30 days' prior notice in writing. Salaries, mandatory severance payments, allowances or other payments to employees would need to be finally settled within fourteen days of dismissal; however, such period may be extended subject to the mutual agreement between the company and the dismissed employees.

• Distributing liquidation proceeds: Liquidation proceeds are those assets which remain after the company has discharged all of its obligations. The company may not distribute its property to its shareholders / members until after all the obligations of the company have been discharged completely or, in the case of any obligation which is in dispute, until after the company sets aside sufficient property for the discharge of such obligation.

• Approval of completion of liquidation by general meeting of shareholders / members: When the liquidation procedures have been completed (i.e., when all assets have been distributed and there are no unsettled debt or receivables), the representative liquidator should without delay prepare a statement of the financial accounts and submit it to the shareholders' / members' meeting for approval. When the approval has been given, the company shall be deemed to have relieved the liquidators of their responsibility.

• Court registration of completion of liquidation: The representative liquidator must register the completion of the liquidation with the court having jurisdiction over the company's principal office within two weeks after the shareholders' / members' meeting approving the completion of liquidation.

F. Mergers and Acquisitions

In Korea, business combinations typically take the form of a share transfer or subscription, asset transfer (including business transfer), joint venture, merger or consolidation. Under Korean law, a spin-off and merger can be completed in one transaction. Notably, certain amendments to the KCC that became effective in 2012 introduced cash-out mergers and triangular mergers. The amendments also relaxed the requirements for small-scale mergers by allowing the merged company's shareholders approval requirement to be waived in a merger where the surviving company issues new shares that are less than 10% of its total shares (the ceiling was 5% prior to the amendment).

a. Statutes and Regulations

The KCC provides for general business and corporate regulations governing Korean companies, including regulations relating to the acquisition of shares or assets, mergers, spin-offs and other transaction structures. If the acquisition involves shares of a Korean company listed on the Stock Market Division of the Korea Exchange or registered on the KOSDAQ Market Division of the Korea Exchange, the FSCMA and other related rules and regulations will apply. M&A transactions are also subject to the reporting requirements of the Korea Fair Trade Commission ("KFTC") under the Monopoly Regulation and Fair Trade Law ("FTL"), which is the general antitrust statute. If the business combination is a cross-border transaction, the FIPL or the FETL, may apply.

b. Governing Law

Typically, the share subscription agreement (involving issuance and purchase of new shares), a joint venture or shareholders' agreement (involving, among others, corporate governance matters) and the merger agreement are governed by Korean law. The governing law of the other transaction documents varies depending on the agreement of the parties.

c. Filings and Fees

If an acquiring company is a foreign company, it must file a prior report on the acquisition of shares with the MOTIE through a foreign exchange bank pursuant to the FIPL. When a merger, spin-off or business transfer involves a listed company, in addition to the general disclosure requirements, the FSCMA requires the listed company to file a report with the Stock Market Division or KOSDAQ Market Division of the Korea Exchange and the FSC.

In addition, beneficial ownership of 5% or more of the shares of a listed company triggers a filing requirement. A tender offer or proxy solicitation is also subject to a filing requirement. In certain circumstances, investments in a Korean company or a company that has business in Korea may trigger an antitrust filing requirement and a review by the KFTC.

Under the FTL, an antitrust filing should be made when the transaction involves, among others:

• the acquisition of all of (or a major portion of) the business or assets of a target company;

• the purchase of shares of an existing company, and as a result of such transaction, the acquirer (together with its affiliates) becomes a shareholder holding 20% (15% in the case of a company publicly listed (or registered) on the Stock Market Division or Kosdaq Market Division of the KRX) or more of the voting shares of the target company; or

• a merger between companies, and, with respect to each of the foregoing cases, one of the parties to the business combination has (together with its affiliates) assets or revenues equal to or exceeding KRW 200 billion and the other party has (together with its affiliates) assets or revenues equal to or exceeding KRW 20 billion.

Further, if either party to the transaction has assets or revenues equal to or exceeding KRW 2 trillion, in general a pre-closing filing will be required. The transaction may not be closed while the KFTC is undertaking its 30-day review (which can be extended by an additional 90 days). If a transaction that satisfies the aforementioned thresholds for antitrust filing is not subject to pre-closing filing requirements, it will be subject to post-closing filing obligations. In such cases, the filing must be made within 30 days after the close of the transaction. Such post-closing filing will also be subject to a review period of 30 days, which can be extended by an additional 90 days. Certain overseas transactions having an effect on the Korean market may also trigger a Korean filing requirement based on the amount of revenue the relevant parties (together with its affiliates) have in relation to Korea.

There are no stamp taxes or other governmental fees (other than stamp duties which are nominal in amount) relating specifically to business combinations. However, the transaction will be subject to various Korean taxes depending on the structure of the transaction.

d. Information to be Disclosed

A publicly listed company involved in a merger must submit a merger report to the FSC and the Stock Market Division or KOSDAQ Market Division of the Korea Exchange. A merger report is required to disclose certain matters relating to the contemplated merger and the parties to the merger. This report is made publicly available.

In the case of a business or asset transfer or spin-off, a similar filing is required. A tender offer or proxy solicitation also requires certain information to be disclosed in the prescribed forms provided under the FSCMA. In the case of the report filed with the KFTC under the FTL, the contents of such report are submitted to the KFTC and are not made publicly available.

e. Disclosure of Substantial Shareholdings

Under the FSCMA, once an investor (including specially related persons and other parties acting in concert) holds 5% or more of the voting shares or certain other equity securities issued by a listed company, the investor must file within five business days a report regarding such acquisition with the FSC. For the purpose of this report, the investor is deemed to hold the shares upon entering into a share purchase agreement. An addendum report should be filed within five business days of any change of 1% or more in such holdings (in the case of passive portfolio investment, by the 10th day of the following month). When filing this report, the investor must indicate whether the investment is a passive portfolio investment, or whether the investor has any intent to exert any influence over the management of the company. A filing obligation is also triggered if the purpose of the investment changes. In the case of an investment with the purpose of participating in the management of a company, a five-day cooling-off period will be applicable after the 5% report is filed, during which period the investor may not exercise voting rights or purchase additional shares. Where the holdings of the investor reaches 10% or more of the issued and outstanding voting shares of the listed Korean company, a separate report should be filed with the Securities & Futures Commission ("SFC") within five business days, and any change in shareholding must be reported to the SFC within five business days of such change. In addition, a public company must disclose the details of all transactions with the largest shareholder (including affiliates) in its periodic reports filed with the FSC.

f. Approval and Appraisal Rights

Certain transactions such as mergers, the transfer of a whole or a significant part of a business or the acquisition of a whole or a part of a business of another company that significantly affects the acquiring company's business are subject to approval of a special resolution of the shareholders of the company. Under the KCC, a special resolution of shareholders requires the affirmative vote of two-thirds of the shareholders at a shareholders' meeting. This meeting must be attended by shareholders comprising at least one-third of the total issued and outstanding shares, although the articles of incorporation of the company could provide for a higher voting threshold for such special resolutions. In such cases, the shareholders have appraisal rights that are determined by a set formula (in the case of publicly listed companies), by private negotiation, or by the court. Such appraisal rights are available to shareholders who have duly recorded their dissent to the proposed transaction at the relevant shareholders' meeting.

g. Hostile Transactions

Korean law does not distinguish between hostile and friendly takeover bids. They are both subject to the same takeover laws and regulations. The board of the target company is allowed, but not required, to express its opinion on the tender offer.

h. Role of Government

Other than through antitrust regulations, government agencies do not generally have the authority to restrict the completion of a business combination. However, a cross-border transaction will be subject to certain government reporting or approval requirements, including foreign exchange regulations. Further, business combinations in certain regulated industries such as banking, telecommunications and defense may be subject to certain approval requirements or other restrictions under the relevant laws and regulations. Certain cross-border transactions may also be restricted for reasons of national security (e.g., impeding local manufacturing of defense industry items or disclosing state secrets) and the protection of core technology.

G. Competition Regulation

a. Department Supervising Competition Regulation

The KFTC is an independent ministerial-level central administrative organization under the authority of the Prime Minister. Functioning as a quasi-judicial body, the KFTC formulates and administers competition policies and handles, deliberates and decides antitrust cases.

b. Brief Introduction to Competition Law

The FTL is the primary antitrust and competition law in Korea. Many of the principles contained in the FTL are quite similar to the antitrust laws of other countries, including those of the United States, EU and Japan. The FTL contains various sections that regulate particular aspects of competitive behavior. For example, the FTL regulates and covers, among others: (i) monopolies, monopolization and abuse of monopolistic power in general; (ii) business combination, including mergers and acquisitions; (iii) unfair collaborative activity; and (iv) unfair trade practices.

a) Abuse of Monopolistic Power

The FTL prohibits an enterprise in a market-dominant position from engaging in, among others: (i) unreasonable fixing, maintenance, or alteration of price; (ii) unreasonable controlling of the sale of goods or rendering of services; (iii) unreasonable hampering of another enterprise's business activities, (iv) unreasonable hindering of the entry of a new competitor; and (v) unreasonable transaction to exclude competitors.

b) Business Combination

Article 7 of the FTL regulates various types of business combinations (e.g., horizontal, vertical and conglomerate mergers and acquisitions) that may substantially restrain competition in a particular field of trade. Under Article 12 of the FTL, certain types of business combinations are required to be filed with the KFTC Filing may take place either prior to or after closing. Only those companies whose total assets or total sales of not less than KRW 200 billion on a global basis are subject to such filing requirement when total assets or sales amount of the counterpart company exceeds KRW 20 billion. In case a business combination occurs between foreign companies, or the counterpart company is a foreign company, a filing obligation will be triggered only when the foreign company's sales amount in Korea (as determined by total affiliated companies' sales in Korea, not necessarily limited to the company at issue) exceeds KRW 20 billion. Such business combinations include the following:

(i) Acquisition of shares: acquisition of 20% (15% if a listed company) or more of the voting shares of an existing company; or additional acquisition of shares by the acquirer who already holds 20% (15% if a listed company) or more of the company's shares, resulting in the acquirer's becoming the largest shareholder of the company (unless the acquirer is already the largest shareholder at the time of the additional acquisition);

(ii) Acquisition of business or assets: either acquisition or lease of all or an important portion of the business of another company; acquisition of all or important portion of fixed assets for business of another company; or being entrusted with the management of another company. A "important portion" is defined as when the acquisition price is 10% or more of the transferor company's total assets as stated in the financial statement of the most recent fiscal year, or KRW 5 billion won or more;

(iii) Merger with another company;

(iv) Interlocking directorate of a large-scaled corporation (except for cases of interlocking directorate of affiliates); and

(iv) Participating in the establishment of a new company and becoming the largest investor thereof.

The filing should be made, in principle, within 30 days after the closing of the transactions i.e., the acquisition of shares, assets or a business or the incorporation of a new company. However, in scenarios (i), (ii), (iii) and (v) above, if the total consolidated assets or total annual consolidated sales of the business group to which either the transferor or the transferee belongs to are KRW 2 trillion or more, the business combination report will need to be filed before closing. It should be noted that the closing cannot take place within 30 days from the filing date, which might be extended for another 90 days. While the FTL stipulates that filing may take place after the date of signing the share purchase, asset acquisition, or merger agreement or the date of the general meeting / board's resolution on the establishment of the new company, it is possible to submit an application to the KFTC for a preliminary review on whether there is any anti-competitive effect with regard to the contemplated transaction, with a draft of the definitive agreement as long as the draft contains major terms of the transaction and with the understanding that an official filing will be made when the definitive agreement is actually executed by the parties. Even in the case of a post-closing filing obligation, making a voluntary filing for pre-clearance is allowed. The KFTC's preliminary review as mentioned above does not exempt the relevant party from filing a formal business combination report with the KFTC.

The KFTC will review the cases as filed with them and may issue an order to enjoin the transaction or an order to divest if it finds that the business combination has an effect of substantially restraining competition in a specific field. For this purpose, the KFTC will first define the relevant markets, product market, geographic market, etc., and then review, among others, the market shares of the parties and other competitors, the historical trend of the market shares, unilateral effects, coordinated effects, degree of foreign competition introduced and international competition situation, likelihood of entry, foreclosure, elimination of potential competition, exclusion of competitors, etc., based on the type of business combination (i.e., horizontal, vertical or conglomerate mergers). The KFTC also reviews whether the business combination can be justified by "efficiency" or "failing company doctrine".

c) Unfair Collaborative Acts Among Competitors

Chapter 4 of the FTL prohibits businesses from engaging in certain collaborative acts or behaviors. Examples of such collaborative acts include entering into an agreement to: (i) fix, maintain, or alter prices; (ii) determine the terms and conditions for trade in goods or services or for payment of prices or compensation thereof; (iii) restrict the production, shipment, transportation of, or trade in goods or services; (iv) restrict the territory of trade or customers; (v) hinder or restrict the establishment or expansion of facilities or installation of equipment necessary for the manufacturing of products or the rendering of services; (vi) restrict the types or specifications of the goods at the time of production or trade thereof; (vii) establish a corporation or the like aimed to jointly conduct or manage primary areas of businesses; (viii) decide successful bidder or bidding price, etc. in biddings or auctions; or (ix) hinder or restrict the business activities or the nature of the business of other enterprises, thereby substantially restraining competition in a relevant field of trade.

Most of the above mentioned collaborative acts are generally deemed to be hard core cartels and as a consequence, illegal per se (although item (vii) may be an exception to this rule). While the FTL provides for a test of such activities would "substantially restrain competition". In practice, however, the KFTC does not necessarily evaluate the effect of lessening or restraining competition.

An agreement to jointly operate certain parts of business (e.g., marketing and distribution functions) or to pool resources, for example into joint research and development, may also be determined a collaborative act even though they may be reviewed under "rule of reason" test instead of per se illegal test.

A cartel will be deemed completed when an agreement to do the above mentioned activities is entered into. Such an agreement does not have to be in a written form. Whether or not the agreement was actually implemented does not affect the legality of the cartel, even though in practice the sanction on violation would likely be less severe if the parties withdrew from implementation after agreement.

One notable provision, Article 19 (5) of the FTL, provides that when two or more enterprises commit any of the acts listed above, and there is a 'substantial probability' that they committed the act in collaboration—taking into consideration: (i) the characteristics of the relevant transaction; (ii) goods or services; (iii) economic reasons and ripple effects of the relevant activity; and (iv) frequency, mode of contact among enterprisers, the parties shall be "presumed" to have committed an improper collaborative act. This presumption holds irrespective of whether there exists a lack of evidence for an explicit agreement to engage in such an act. Based on this provision, the KFTC often rules-even with only a paucity of supporting evidence-that there was a cartel when two or more competitors increase the price or change other terms of supply of goods at the same or similar rate or amount at the same or similar time, and it is difficult to consider it as a mere coincidence in light of the market situation or industry structure. This is to alleviate the burden of the government to prove the existence of an agreement that in practice is difficult to prove.If the cartel is presumed as above, then the parties must prove that there was in fact no agreement among the parties and the look-alike-cartel incident in the market is a mere result of parallel activities.

d) Unfair Trade Practices

There are several categories of trade practices that fall within the scope of an unfair trade practice when assessed under the "rule of reason" test:

• Boycott: Refusing to transact with a certain party or to stop transacting with a certain party, without justification;

• Discrimination in price and other terms and conditions: Wrongfully transacting at a significantly advantageous or disadvantageous price or other terms and conditions;

• Act to eliminate competitors: Predatory pricing;

• Wrongfully alluring customers: Providing customers with unreasonably excessive economic benefits such as premium or alluring them with fraudulent schemes;

• Tying and other types of coerced transaction;

• Abusing dominant market position when transacting with others: For example, imposing sales target on the other party using its dominant market power is deemed abuse of such dominant market power;

• Restrictive conditions: To restrict the other party of a transaction to deal with him / herself on an exclusive basis and not to transact with competitors can be deemed unfair and unreasonable. To restrict territory and customer of the other party can also be deemed unfair and unreasonable;

• Interfering with other company's business activities, such as using a partner's technology improperly, improperly scouting employees of another company; and

• Wrongfully assisting person with special relationship or other companies by providing advanced payments, loans, manpower, assets, security, goods, services, etc., or by transacting under substantially favorable terms therewith;

• Resale Price Maintenance: As in most other countries, resale price maintenance is strictly prohibited. The FTL does, however, provide that the restriction on resale price maintenance will not apply in the case of certain copyrighted material. In principle, the FTL does allow resale price maintenance in the case of consumer goods that meet certain requirements, i.e., easily identifiable uniform quality and the existence of free competition in the market with prior KFTC approval. In addition, maintaining a price cap is allowed if there are reasonable grounds.

c. Measures Regulating Competition

Depending on the type of violation, the KFTC has the authority to: (i) issue corrective orders; (ii) issue orders for public announcement of violation; (iii) impose monetary fines; and (iv) file a criminal complaint with the Prosecutor General for serious violations. For collaborative acts, the KFTC may impose a monetary fine of up to 10% of the sales volume of the related goods or service of a defendant (in the event that it is difficult to calculate the sales volume or there is no sales volume at all, a monetary fine up to KRW 2 billion won may be imposed).

H. Tax

a. Tax Regime and Rules

In Korea, there are both national and local taxes. National taxes include corporate income tax, value-added tax ("VAT"), inheritance and gift tax, personal income tax, etc. Local taxes include local income tax, acquisition tax, registration tax, property tax, etc. The Korean tax laws include Corporate Income Tax Law, VAT Law, Personal Income Tax Law, Local Tax Law, ITCL, etc. National tax policy is formulated and directed by the MOSF. The National Tax Service administers and collects taxes.

b. Main Categories and Rates of Tax

a) Resident Companies

Resident companies are taxed on their worldwide income, and non-resident companies are only taxed on Korean-source income. A company is a resident if its headquarters or place of effective management is in Korea.

For taxable years beginning on or after January 1, 2018, the corporate income tax rate (including local income tax) is 11% on the first KRW 200 million of taxable income, 22% on taxable income above KRW 200 million up to KRW 20 billion, 24.2% on taxable income above KRW 20 billion up to KRW 300 billion, and 27.5% on taxable income above KRW 300 billion. Corporations are subject to an Alternative Minimum Tax even if the corporation is eligible for tax incentives. Net operating loss may be carried forward up to 10 years. Net operative loss is only deductible up to 70% (60% beginning in 2019) of taxable income. Capital gains or losses of a resident company are included in the corporate income tax base.

b) Resident Individuals

Resident individuals are taxed on their worldwide income, and non-resident individuals are taxed only on Korean-source income. An individual is a resident if he or she has a domicile in Korea or resides in Korea for a period of at least 183 days in the aggregate during a calendar year.

For taxable years beginning on or after January 1, 2018, the personal income tax rate (including local income tax) is 6.6% on the first KRW 12 million of taxable income, 16.5% on taxable income above KRW 12 million up to KRW 46 million, 26.4% on taxable income above KRW 46 million up to KRW 88 million, 38.5% on taxable income above KRW 88 million up to KRW 150 million, 41.8% on taxable income above KRW 150 million up to KRW 300 million, 44% on taxable income above KRW 300 million up to KRW 500 million, and 46.2% on taxable income above KRW 500 million. Until 2018, foreigners working in Korea are eligible for a flat tax rate of 20.9% (including local income tax). Employer and employee are liable to make social security contributions (national pension, medical insurance, worker's compensation, and unemployment insurance) based on the gross income of the employee subject to a ceiling amount in the case of national pension and medical insurance.

c) Non-Resident Companies and Individuals

The payment for services provided by a non-resident company or individual is generally characterized as personal services income and subject to withholding tax at the rate of 22% (including local income tax), which may be exempt under the relevant tax treaty. The payment of consideration for certain services involving conveyance of know-how, etc. may be characterized as a royalty. Generally, there is no branch profits tax, but imposition of branch profits tax may be allowed under the relevant tax treaty and VAT is levied on the supply of goods and services at the rate of 10% of the total value of supply. In certain cases (i.e., exports, services rendered outside of Korea, etc.), zero-rate VAT may apply.

d) Tax Treaties

As of January 2018, Korea has entered into tax treaties with 93 countries in order to prevent double taxation and provide reduced withholding tax rates. Passive income, such as dividends, interest, and royalties, that are paid to a non-resident company or individual are subject to withholding tax at the rate of 22% (including local income tax), which may be reduced under the relevant tax treaty. Capital gains or losses of a non-resident company are subject to tax at the rate of the lesser of 11% (including local income tax) of the sales price or 22% (including local income tax) on capital gains. In case of capital gains from a transfer of shares in a Korean company, the Korean tax may be exempt under the relevant tax treaty.

c. Tax Declaration and Preference

Companies must file a year-end corporate income tax return within three months (four months in the case of a consolidated corporate income tax return) from the end of the tax year. If a company has a tax year longer than 6 months, interim tax must be filed and paid within two months after the first 6 month period. The statute of limitation for tax assessment is generally five years.

Generally, a resident individual is required to file and pay PIT by 31 May of the following year. In the event that a taxpayer's income is comprised of only salary and / or severance, the taxpayer may not be required to file a return since the employer withholds income tax on a monthly basis. In that case, the taxpayer would be required to prepare a year-end tax settlement in February of the following year.

Filing and paying of VAT is generally made on a quarterly basis. Monthly filing is allowed for early VAT refund in the event the goods or services provided by the company are subject to zero-rate VAT.

Subject to the approval of the MOSF, a tax exemption may be granted for foreign investment in a company engaged in certain high-tech activities or companies located in certain foreign investment zones or free economic zones. The foreign invested company will be eligible for a 100% corporate income tax exemption for a 3 or 5 year period from the tax year in which taxable income has first accrued, and 50% corporate income tax exemption for the next 2 years. As of January 2018, the tax incentives for foreign investment are expected to undergo modification due to controversy over discrimination against domestic companies.

I. Securities

a. Brief Introduction of Securities-related Laws and Regulations

The primary law governing the capital market and activities of financial investment business in Korea is the FSCMA. The Enforcement Decree of the FSCMA, which is a Presidential Decree, enumerates matters addressed by the FSCMA and the rules and regulations prescribed to be implemented under the FSCMA. The Enforcement Rules of the FSCMA (Ordinance of the Prime Minister) stipulate the powers ensured by the Decree and the rules and regulations prescribed to be implemented. Regulations promulgated by the FSC contain articles that explain the duties created by the Decree and the rules and regulations prescribed to be implemented. The FSCMA regulations include, among others, the Regulation on Financial Investment Business, Regulation on Issuance and Disclosure of Securities, Regulation on the Return of Short-Swing Profits and the Investigation and Reporting of Unfair Trading Practices, Regulation on Capital Market Investigation, Regulations on Inspection and Sanction on Financial Institutions. In its regulatory enforcement rules, the FSC defines the authority entrusted to its Chairperson and the FSS by the FSCMA, its decrees and enforcement rules, the FSC Regulations and the other relevant laws and regulations, along with detailed requirements and documents needed for the concrete implementation of the above-mentioned laws and regulations.

Other major laws which may be applicable to the capital markets include FETL which governs, among other things, the flow of currency outside of Korea, and laws concerning anti-money laundering and financial transaction information e.g., the Act on Reporting and Use of Information Concerning Certain Financial Transactions, Act on Regulation of Punishment of Criminal Proceeds Concealment, Act on Real Name Financial Transactions and Protection of Confidentiality ("Real Name Act"), Personal Information Protection Act and Use and Protection of Credit Information Act.

b. Supervision and Regulation of Securities Market

The main regulatory body having authority over the financial industry of Korea is the FSC. The FSC is primarily charged with: (i) deliberating and establishing financial policies; (ii) supervising financial institutions and markets; (iii) protecting consumers in financial transactions; and (iv) promoting financial industry. The FSC is particularly authorized to formulate and amend regulations relevant to financial institutions and industry, make an approval on establishment, merger, conversion, business transfer and acquisition of Korean financial institutions and grant relevant business licenses of financial investment businesses.

Working closely with the FSC is the FSS, which is the executive arm of the FSC. The FSS's primary function is to supervise, audit and inspect financial institutions and to investigate market manipulation and other unfair trading activities.

There are other financial authorities relevant to regulated businesses, including: (i) the MOSF, which is responsible for the establishment of economic and fiscal policy, national budget and tax policies and management of foreign exchange; and (ii) the BOK, which is responsible for maintaining the financial stability and currency and credit policy, including foreign exchange. While it is a private institution mostly owned by certain financial investment companies (brokers and dealers of financial investment products), the Korea Exchange, as the sole exchange of Korea, operates the securities and derivatives markets and has the regulatory power in some circumstances to suspend trading in the shares of a given company or to de list a security pursuant to the Regulation on Listing on the Korea Exchange as well as to restrict share price movements. In addition, the Korea Financial Investment Association ("KFIA") is a self-regulating organization formed by financial investment companies pursuant to the FSCMA. The KFIA's main activities involve: (i) establishing rules and regulations; (ii) reviewing standard agreements and advertisements; (iii) conducting inspections of members; (iv) registering and administering qualification exams for financial professionals; and (v) resolving disputes.

c. Requirements for Engagement in Securities Trading for Foreign Enterprises

As a general matter, depending on the size and objective of the investment, a foreigner's investment in a Korean company is categorized as either: (i) a portfolio investment in securities under the FSCMA and the FETL; or (ii) a foreign direct investment under the FIPL.

a) FIPL Investment

If a foreign investor acquires 10% or more of the issued and outstanding voting shares of a Korean company or participates in the management of the company (which is generally evidenced by a contractual right to appoint one or more directors of the company) even though its acquisition ratio may be less than 10%, such investment will be considered as a foreign direct investment under the FIPL.

In such case, the foreign investor is required to file a report with a foreign exchange bank or the Korea Trade-Investment Promotion Agency (MOTIE, which is in charge of accepting FIPL reports, has delegated its authority to grant such acceptance to these entities) prior to the date of the foreign direct investment (i.e., the closing or settlement date). However, if the shares are: (i) issued by a listed company; but (ii) not newly issued (i.e., the acquisition of existing shares in a listed company), this report can be filed within 30 calendar days from the date of the foreign direct investment. The issuer company must register itself as a foreign invested enterprise in the case of a foreign direct investment.

Once subject to the filing of an FIPL report, any additional acquisition (or disposal) of the relevant company's voting shares will trigger the requirement to file an amendment thereto (and the company's foreign invested enterprise registration should also be amended).

b) Portfolio Investment

Investments that do not qualify as foreign direct investment under the FIPL are treated as portfolio securities investments (a "Portfolio Investment").

Generally, under the FSCMA, FETL and their subordinate regulations, a foreign entity making a Portfolio Investment must: (i) obtain a foreign investment registration number from the FSS; (ii) establish foreign currency and Korean Won accounts with a foreign exchange bank for portfolio investment purposes; (iii) open a securities trading account with a investment dealer or a broker (i.e., a securities company) in Korea (including Korean branches of foreign securities companies); and (iv) effect the purchase of the securities through a securities company in Korea. In addition, the foreign investor must appoint a local custodian (which can be the foreign exchange bank at which the relevant accounts are opened). In respect of item (i), normally, the issuance of a foreign investment registration number is a straightforward process and may be completed in a few days. This procedure is typically handled by the local securities broker or custodian on the applicant's behalf.

In case of a portfolio investment in listed securities, all of the requirements described in the foregoing paragraph should be met. As for non-listed securities, the same requirements apply, except that there is no express requirement that the investor obtain a foreign investment registration number. This is because the relevant regulations require the foreign investor to obtain a foreign investment registration number with respect to investment in a company listed on the Korea Exchange.

When opening a securities account with a securities company or opening an account with a bank in Korea for purposes of a portfolio investment, the securities company or the bank is required to verify the identity of the investor pursuant to the Real Name Act and the general practice of securities companies and banks is to request the investor to provide the foreign investment registration number to verify the identity. Therefore, although there is no express requirement under the regulations that the investor obtain a foreign investment registration number when making a portfolio investment in a non-listed company (as noted above), such may be required as a matter of practice.

As an alternative to establishing a foreign currency and Korean Won accounts with a foreign exchange bank for portfolio investment purposes, if the foreign investor files a prior report to, and obtains acceptance from, the BOK with respect to the acquisition of securities in a Korean company, the foreign investor is exempted from satisfying the above mentioned procedures (a "BOK Investment"). The merit of the BOK Investment is that there will not have to be two currency conversions. However, the BOK does not readily accept the report and may refuse to accept such report at its discretion. Accordingly, it would be prudent to discuss this with the BOK in advance.

c) FETL Investment

As for investments in non-listed shares, under the FETL, a foreign investor that is not able to satisfy the requirements for foreign direct investment under the FIPL may invest in the shares of a non-Korea Exchange listed company by filing a report with (and obtaining the acceptance from) a foreign exchange bank (an "FETL Investment"). Under this alternative, none of the foregoing requirements will be applicable.

d) Restrictions in Respect to Investment in Korean Companies by a Foreign Entity

For the most part, there are no particular restrictions in respect to investment in Korean companies by a foreign entity. However, certain Korean companies are subject to foreign ownership limitations based on laws specifically applicable to such companies. As explained earlier, there is no single law that sets out a common rule on foreign ownership limitations and there is no centralized enforcement authority in this regard. Each of the relevant laws set out specific foreign ownership limitations using its own terminology as well as different ceilings in order to serve the purposes of that specific law.

J. Preference and Protection of Investment

a. The Structure of Preference Policies

Other than those limited types of businesses that are subject to foreign investment restrictions, there are no preferential laws, regulations or policies in Korea that are especially favorable to Korean nationals or local companies.

To the contrary, the Korean government offers certain tax exemptions to qualified foreign investors to promote foreign direct investment in Korea. More specifically, the Restriction of Special Taxation Act, the FIPL and other applicable laws offer certain tax holidays to certain qualified foreign-invested enterprises, which allow them to enjoy exemptions from corporation income tax, acquisition tax, registration tax, property tax, customs duty, etc. in Korea. It also possible for foreign-invested enterprises to receive cash grants if the foreign-invested enterprise meets certain qualifications.

b. Support for Specific Industries and Regions

There exist tax exemptions and other incentives for certain qualified high-tech businesses of foreign-invested enterprises. The high-tech introduced by foreign-invested enterprises in performing their business in Korea must fall into one of the eligible high-tech categories for "new growth engines / original" technologies as listed under the Presidential Decree of the Tax Incentive Limitation Law.

a) Tax Exemptions

Foreign investment that accompanies a qualifying high-tech category confers tax exemptions to foreign-invested enterprises as follows:

• 100% exemption for five years from corporate income tax on income from qualified business of the foreign-invested enterprises and 50% exemption for two years thereafter. The exemption period starts from the earlier of (i) the first taxable year in which the foreign-invested enterprise has taxable income from the qualified business without considering any tax loss carryovers and (ii) the taxable year in which five years from the commencement date of the qualified business falls.

• 100% exemption for five years generally from the business commencement date on local taxes such as acquisition tax and property tax on properties purchased in connection with the qualified business and 50% reduction for two years thereafter.

• 100% exemption for five years from customs duties, individual consumption taxes and VAT on imported capital equipment to be used directly for the tax exempt business, to the extent of the foreign investment amount reported and induced in the form of equity under FIPL.

b) Cash Grant

Where foreign investment satisfies certain conditions, the central and local governments provide cash grants to be used for the construction of a new factory, new facility, etc. In the review process, the Korean government takes into account whether the relevant foreign investment accompanies high technology, the effect of technology transfer, the size of job creation, whether the foreign investment overlaps with domestic investment, the propriety of the location in which the foreign investment is made, etc.

c. Special Economic Areas

Korea provides various types of support to certain qualifying foreign-invested enterprises that operate in industrial complexes, which are designated and developed strategically for industrial development. In addition, foreign investment zones, free trade zones and free economic zones in Korea offer investment environments favorable to foreign investors.

Under the industrial site support system to facilitate and induce foreign investment, different zones are operated: (i) "foreign investment zone" designated by the FIPL; (ii) "free trade zone" under the Act on Designation and Management of Free Trade Zones; (iii) and "free economic zones" as prescribed by the Special Act on Designation and Management of Free Economic Zones. Foreign investment zones can be further classified into sub-types: complex-type, individual-type and service-type.

The locations designated for foreign direct investment may vary in terms of eligibility for occupation, targeted industries and investment incentives (e.g., rent, taxation, customs duty and cash grant) depending on their purpose of designation. Therefore, it is advised that one carefully examines and analyzes the investment sites, even for planned sites where the approval procedures for factory establishment are simpler compared to others.

d. Investment Protection

FDI made pursuant to the FIPL guarantees that a foreign-invested enterprise may remit proceeds outside of Korea for the sale of securities by a foreign investor, the principal, interest and service charges paid in accordance with a loan agreement and royalties paid pursuant to a license agreement.

a) Exceptions to the Safeguard Clause on Foreign Exchange Transactions

Irrespective of the outbreak of a natural disaster, war, conflicts of arms, grave and sudden changes in domestic or foreign economic conditions or other situations equivalent thereto as provided in the FETL, such restrictions will not apply to qualified foreign-invested enterprises qualified under the FIPL.

b) National Treatment

Unless otherwise prescribed under applicable Korean laws, foreign investors and foreign-invested enterprises are treated no differently to Korean nationals and local companies.

c) Equal Application of Tax Abatement Regulations, etc.

Unless otherwise prescribed under applicable Korean laws, the same provisions concerning the abatement or exemption of taxes from tax laws will be applied to foreign investors, foreign-invested enterprises, persons who have extended loans as prescribed by the FIPL, and persons who have provided technology thereto, as Korean nationals and local companies.

III. Trade

A. Department Supervising Trade

The MOTIE is the key governmental body supervising trade in Korea. The main tasks of MOTIE include encouraging foreign investment in Korea by negotiating and monitoring the implementation of treaties and agreements covering foreign trade and investment. In addition, it also develops economic policies with regard to the trade, industrial and energy sectors. Within the MOTIE, the Minister for Trade is specifically responsible for trade policy, trade negotiations and cross-border investment policies.

The Korea Trade Commission ("KTC") is another important trade agency that operates under the MOTIE. It is responsible for conducting trade remedy investigations with regard to anti-dumping duties, countervailing duties and safeguard measures. The MOSF is responsible for imposing trade remedy measures pursuant to the Korea Trade Commission's investigation results and recommendations while the Korea Customs Services is responsible for collecting any duties arising from trade remedy cases.

B. Brief Introduction of Trade Laws and Regulations

The Foreign Trade Law is the basic statute that provides general policy directions and principles regarding trade activities. Its subordinate regulations include Presidential Decrees, Ordinances of Ministries and Public Notices, etc. To reflect prevailing international standards and to comply with World Trade Organization ("WTO") obligations, the Foreign Trade Law adopts a minimal approach to the regulation of export and import activities. However, under exceptional circumstances (e.g., the protection of national security, environment or public health), the Foreign Trade Law empowers the government to restrict export / import activities. It also provides legal grounds for imposing import relief against a sudden increase in imports (e.g., safeguard) and regulates traders when it is necessary to secure compliance with international law or when relevant trade activities may violate the laws of Korea or its trading partners.

The primary domestic laws covering trade remedies are contained in the: (i) Customs Act; (ii) Act on the Investigation of Unfair International Trade Practices and Remedy against Injury to Industry and their subordinate regulations. Other trade remedies that apply domestically are also included in the Agreement on Implementation of Article VI of the General Agreement on Tariffs and Trade 1994. The WTO Agreement and other Free Trade Agreements ("FTA"s) to which Korea is a party to are fully binding and have identical effects as domestic laws constituting a part of the trade and regulation regime in Korea.

C. Trade Management

As a member of the World Trade Organization, Korea has been in favor of supporting free trade. In this regard, Korea has entered into 15 FTAs-Chile, Singapore, EFTA, ASEAN, India, the European Union, Peru, the United States, Turkey, Australia, Canada, China, Colombia, New Zealand and Vietnam. Korea has made great efforts to comply with the WTO Agreement and is involved in several WTO trade disputes as a complainant, respondent and / or intervening third party.

D. The Inspection and Quarantine of Import and Export Commodities

Korean Customs can inspect import / export goods if it determines it is necessary to assess the compliance level of importer / exporter, characteristics of goods, or foreign counter parties of importer / exporter. Korean Customs can also inspect whether certain goods are infringing intellectual properties if the owner / licensee of such intellectual properties reports to Korean Customs that its intellectual property rights are in need of protection.

The Animal and Plant Quarantine Agency (the "APQA") quarantines and inspects imported / exported animals / livestock products and plants to protect the community from risks arising out of international trade and travel. APQA's quarantine and inspection of import / export commodities is regulated to meet the WTO's Sanitary and Phytosanitary Measures. All live animals and animal products entering Korea must be accompanied by a valid quarantine or heat treatment certificates issued by the country of departure. All import animals and animal products must be declared and inspected upon arrival. Failure to do so will result in the animal or animal product being sent back or destroyed, respectively. Plants, fruits, vegetables, seeds, orchids, nursery stock, cut flowers, soil and items of a similar nature must also be declared and inspected upon arrival.

E. Customs Management

Korean Customs was established on 13 May 1970 as an independent government agency separate from the Ministry of Finance. Korean Customs is mandated to: (i) levy or waive on customs duties; (ii) collect customs duties; (iii) control clearance of imported / exported goods; and (iv) investigate and enforce criminal activities under the Customs Act.

Applicable custom duty rates are shown in the Harmonized System of Korea. The normal customs duty rate for industrial products imported into Korea is generally 8% ad valorem, while the customs duty rates for agricultural products are generally much higher. Subject to Korean Customs' review and approval, it is possible to set up a customs-bonded area or a free trade zone where the movement of goods into such areas or zones would not attract customs duty liability (unless the goods actually are entered into the territory of Korea, in which case the applicable customs duties and other import-related taxes would be payable).

Certain Korean importers may also be exempt from the general requirement that all applicable customs duties and other taxes should be paid at the time of customs clearance, if provide that such importers are eligible qualify for and participate in for the monthly aggregate program (which would allow the importers to pay the customs duties, etc., on a monthly basis) and collateral program (allowing the importers to delay the payment of the customs duties, etc.for up to a period of 15 days.).

Furthermore, depending on the imported products, Korean importers may be subject to certain certification, reporting and / or approval requirements stipulated under various laws and regulations governing the importation of such products (i.e., other than the Customs Act), such as the Pharmaceutical Affairs Law, Medical Devices Law and Chemicals Control Law, among others. While there are generally no prior notification requirements for imports, Korean importers seeking to import certain pharmaceutical and medical device products are required to submit a pre-importation report to the relevant industry association before obtaining customs clearance, and the relevant industry association's acceptance of such report is a precondition for customs clearance. Importers seeking to import any products that are subject to additional requirements under laws and regulations other than the Customs Act are strongly encouraged to ensure full compliance in view of Korean Customs' aggressive enforcement actions.

Exports of 'strategic items' and 'strategic technology' require approval from the relevant authorities for the purposes of maintaining the integrity of multinational strategic materials export control measures. The Korean government also controls exports of 'national core technologies' under the Act on Prevention of Divulgence and Protection of Industrial Technology Korea.

IV. Labour

A. Brief Introduction of Labour Laws and Regulations

The Labor Standards Act (along with the many enforcement decrees) is the main labor-related statutory regime that applies to all businesses and workplaces with five or more employees. A business or workplace with no more than four 'ordinary' employees may still be subject to some provisions of the Labor Standards Act as prescribed by Presidential Decree. The Ministry of Employment and Labor is responsible for enforcing the Labor Standards Act. Litigation involving labor disputes is adjudicated by the Supreme Court, five High Courts (intermediate appellate courts), and many District Courts (trial courts) in Korea.

The Labor Standards Act governs all aspects of employment, including employment contracts, payment of wages, hours of work and recesses, employment of women and minors, safety and health, apprenticeship, as well as industrial accident compensation, labor inspections, and penalty provisions. For example, Article 23 of the LSA, employers must have a "just cause" before carrying out disciplinary action against an employee, up to and including termination of employment. Just cause is not defined in the statute, but in accordance with court precedents, the following 3 grounds are generally accepted as bases of just cause: (i) serious and / or repeated acts of misconduct; (ii) poor performance over an extended period of time; and (iii) an "urgent business necessity" (for a layoff). Article 26 of the LSA also requires that an employer provide at least 30 days' written notice of involuntary separation of employment (or 30 days' ordinary wage in lieu thereof).

In addition to the LSA, the Trade Union and Labor Relations Adjustment Act, other related labor laws, the civil and criminal codes, agreements between employers and employees (including collective bargaining agreements, rules of employment, and employment contracts), and labor customs also govern the employment relationship and labor relations generally.

Where laws conflict, familiar legal principles are applied to determine which will have priority. Higher-level laws take precedence over lower-level laws (thus, the Constitution takes precedence over, for example, the Gender Equality Employment and Work-Family Balance Support Act. Special laws are preferred over general laws (thus as applied to persons covered by it, the Seamen's Act takes precedence over the LSA). When two laws at the same level conflict with each other, the more recent law will prevail.

One overriding principle of Korean labor law is to promote better conditions for employees. Thus, if the working conditions specified in labor laws, rules of employment, and individual employment contracts are different from each other, the conditions most favorable to employees will apply. As a general rule, the standards provided by law may not be varied to the detriment of employees by private agreements.

B. Requirements of Employing Foreign Employees

a. Work Permit

A foreign citizen can work in Korea so long as the foreigner possesses an appropriate visa permitting employment activities in Korea. The most common long-term work visas for foreign workers are D-7, D-8 and E-7. The appropriate visa type depends on the nature of the assignment / employment and the type of entity located in Korea, among other factors.

a) D-7 Visa

The D-7 long-term visa is available to a foreign employee of a branch or liaison office of a foreign-invested enterprise in Korea who has been assigned from and worked with the head office, branch or other affiliates for at least one year prior to the Korea assignment. D-7 visa processing requires a pre-approval certificate from the immigration office. Upon receipt of the pre-approval certificate, the expatriate may visit a Korean consulate to have the visa stamped in his / her passport.

b) D-8 Visa

D-8 long-term visa is available to a foreign employee of a Korean subsidiary or joint venture of a foreign-invested enterprise who is being assigned from the foreign affiliate to the Korean entity. For most nationalities (exceptions apply), upon entering Korea with either no visa, a tourist visa or a short term visa, a request can be made for a visa status change from the entry visa to a long-term D-8 work visa.

c) E-7 Visa

The E-7 visa applies when a foreigner is directly hired by a Korean company (including a branch of a foreign-invested company). Thus, in general, a foreigner applying for an E-7 visa is not an assignee seconded from a foreign affiliate (as opposed to foreign workers holding D-7 or D-8 visas). As part of the process, a recommendation letter from the appropriate Korean ministry or agency is required.

Other types of working visas are discussed in the "visa" section under C. Exit and Entry.

b. Social Insurance

The Korean National Social Security System consists of social insurance, public assistance and the social welfare service. Social security benefits include: (i) National Pension; (ii) National Health Insurance; (iii) Unemployment Insurance; and (iv) Workers' Compensation Insurance.

a) National Pension

• Contributes to stabilizing people's lives and promotes their welfare by implementing a public pension benefit for geriatric diseases or death.

• Pension Benefit: Old-age Pension, Disability Pension, Survivor's Pension.

• Lump sum allowance: Pension Refund, Death Benefit.

b) National Health Insurance

• Improves public health and promotes social security by paying insurance benefits to prevent, diagnose, treat, and rehabilitate people's diseases or injuries and prevent death, and to promote health.

• Service Benefits: Health care benefits, Health check-up.

• Benefits in cash: Treatment expenses, Co-payment Ceiling System, Compensation for excessive co-payments, Appliance expenses for the disabled, Pregnancy & childbirth examination expenses.

c) Unemployment Insurance

• Prevents unemployment and promotes employment.

• Increases a worker's vocational competency development.

• Strengthens occupational guidance and training.

• Promotes stabilization of a worker's life and his / her job search by providing unemployment benefits.

The employee health insurance premium is currently 6.12% of the worker's monthly average wage (shared evenly by the employer and the employee).

d) Workers' Compensation Insurance

• Compensates workers for industrial accidents rapidly and fairly.

• Implements and operates the insurance facilities required for promoting workers' rehabilitation and return to

society.
 • Helps protect workers with operations addressing disaster prevention and promotion of workers' welfare.
 • Care Benefit, Temporary Incapacity Benefit, Disability Benefit, Nursing Benefit, Survivor Benefit, Funeral Expenses, Injury & Disease Compensation Pension.

C. Exit and Entry

a. Visa Types

Anyone who is planning to work during their stay in Korea is legally required to apply for a visa. In addition, if the individual has family members who also plan to work while in Korea, they must also apply for work visas in order to be legally entitled to work (Employment Permission for Foreign Workers).
 The most common employment visas include:
 • the Short Term Employment Visa (C-4);
 • the Corporate Resident / Company Assignment (Intra-company Transfer) (D-7);
 • the Foreign Investment Visa (D-8);
 • the Trade Management Visa (D-9);
 • the Professional Job Visa (E-5); and
 • the Specific Job Visa (E-7).
 An application must be made in person at a Korean Consulate or Embassy in their home country, with the endorsement of their Korean employer. Many visas are obtained by an applicant's Korean employer. Once this application has been approved, a Certificate of Confirmation of Visa Issuance is granted. The Certificate must then be submitted, along with a Visa Issuance application, to the Korean Embassy in the applicant's home country.

b. Restrictions for Exit and Entry

When a foreigner enters Korea, the foreigner must hold a valid passport and a visa issued by the Minister of Justice. In general, a foreigner of a country that has concluded a Visa Exemption Agreement with Korea, or a foreigner who enters Korea for purposes of international friendship, sightseeing or the nature of the visit is in the interests of Korea, etc.may enter without a visa.
 The Minister of Justice may prohibit a person from entering Korea if that person is: (i) carrying a contagious disease; (ii) a narcotics addict; (iii) deemed likely to cause danger and harm to public health; or (iv) deemed highly likely to commit any act detrimental to the interests of Korea or public safety from entering Korea.
 The Office of Employment Security may place limitations on employment of foreign workers who have no valid employment permit or certificate of exceptionally permissible employment, or who have been punished for a violation of the Act on Foreign Workers' Employment, etc.or the Immigration Control Act.

D. Trade Union and Labour Organizations

The Ministry of Employment and Labor announced that as of 2016, 10.3% of workers were in trade unions in Korea. There are two national trade union centres in Korea: the Federation of Korean Trade Unions ("FKTU") and the Korean Confederation of Trade Unions ("KCTU"). In 2015, the FKTU had 843 thousand members (43.5% of trade union members in Korea), the KCTU had 636 thousand members (32.8%), and 459 thousand workers were members of independent trade unions affiliated to neither national centre.

E. Labor Disputes

The most common form of individual labor dispute in Korea is one that occurs over unfair treatment (e.g.dismissal or disciplinary action without a just cause). The legal basis for such individual rights disputes is the prohibition against unfair dismissal stipulated in Article 23 of the Labor Standards Act.
 The number of collective labor disputes in 2016 was 120, which was more than in 2015 (105). The number of working days lost due to labor disputes in 2016 was 2,035, which was more than 2015 (447 lost working days).

V. Intellectual Property

A. Brief Introduction of IP Laws and Regulations

There are many types of intellectual property ("IP") rights available in Korea. The most significant forms of IP protection include patents, utility models, design rights, copyrights, trademarks and trade secrets. These rights are based on various statutes, including the Patent Act, the Utility Model Act, the Design Protection Act, the Trade Mark

Act, the Copyright Act and the Unfair Competition Prevention & Trade Secret Protection Act ("UCPA"), respectively.

a. Patent and Utility Model

Patentable subject matter in Korea includes devices, methods, processes and material inventions, while utility models protect only the shape or structure of an article. Thus, methods, processes and material inventions cannot be protected as a utility model. Moreover, both patents and utility models must be novel and inventive to be granted, but the Patent Act and the Utility Model Act respectively set out slightly different standards for inventiveness. The basic difference between a utility model and a patent is that a utility model requires a lower level of technical content.

On a related matter, Korea has been a member of the Convention Establishing the World Intellectual Property Organization ("WIPO") since 1 March 1979. Korea has also been a member of the Paris Convention for the Protection of Industrial Property since 4 May 1980, and the World Trade Organization Agreement on Trade-Related Aspects of Intellectual Property Rights since 1 January 1995. In addition, Korea has been a member of the Patent Cooperation Treaty-Chapter I since 1984 and Chapter II since 1990. Therefore, an international application under the Patent Cooperation Treaty can be filed in any of the Receiving Offices and designate Korea for the national entry, in addition to being filed directly with the Korean Intellectual Property Office ("KIPO").

b. Trademark

Trademarks are used to identify the goods or services of a person or business, and distinguish them from the goods and services of others. Signs, characters, figures, 3D shapes, colors and sounds are protectable trademarks. Trademark rights are granted upon registration after going through a series of formalities and substantive examination by KIPO. Filing trademarks can be done directly with KIPO or through WIPO, based on the WIPO Protocol Relating to the Madrid Agreement Concerning the International Registration of Marks 1989 ("Madrid Protocol"). Well-known marks can also be protected under the UCPA, even if they are not registered.

c. Design

The Design Act defines "designs" as the shape, pattern or color, or a combination of these, in an article (including part of an article) which produces an aesthetic impression in the visual sense. Thus, a design application should relate to a single product or to any part of a product containing a specific shape and / or pattern. A typeface can also be protected under the Design Protection Act. Also, unregistered designs of an article can be protected against an imitation product under the "dead copy" provision of the UCPA if certain requirements are met, including: (i) the imitation product is manufactured within three years from the date of creation of an original product; and (ii) the product appearance is not a commonly used form for the subject goods.

d. Copyrights

To be copyrightable, a work must be original, creative and expressive. A copyright does not require any procedures or formalities to come into existence. A copyright arises the moment at which an original work of authorship is completed. The registration of copyrights is not mandatory, but it provides certain advantages for the right-holder, including presumptive benefits for the registered date of creation / publication, the registered authorship and the presumed negligence of an infringer.

e. Trade Secrets

Confidential information of a technical or managerial nature that can be used in business activities can be protected as a trade secret under the UCPA. Specifically, to be entitled to protection as a trade secret under the UCPA, the information must meet certain requirements, including the following:
- the information is generally unknown to the public;
- the information possesses an independent economic value; and
- the information is kept secret through reasonable efforts.

It is to note that criminal actions comprise a substantial part of trade secret protection. The Korean authorities (the public prosecutor's office and the police) are quite active in this area and often eager to pursue cases involving a breach of a trade secret. Another trend is that the number of disputes alleging trade secret breach and a violation of non-competition provisions has been steadily increasing in recent years. One important reason for this trend is increased job movement by employees, which can explain the increase in cases alleging leakage of trade secrets overseas. This is particularly the case on the criminal side but is also relevant on the civil side as Korean companies increasingly compete with rivals abroad and / or have affiliates abroad.

f. IP Protection under UCPA

The UCPA is considered an effective way to protect intellectual property rights by preventing unfair methods of competition, and Korean courts are becoming increasingly willing to expand the scope of protection against intellectual property infringement through the UCPA. Notably, on 31 January 2014, the UCPA adopted a general "catch-all" provision, "an act of infringing a person's right to profit by using that person's product, which was the result of considerable effort and investment, without authorization for one's business through a method that contravenes fair commercial trade practice or competition order", in order to provide parties with appropriate means against third parties that conduct new types of unfair competition.

g. IP Regulation

The Monopoly Regulation and Fair Trade Act ("MRFTA") is applicable to the obtainment, grant, acquisition, exercise and transfer of intellectual property rights. Article 59 of the MRFTA stipulates, "This Act shall not apply to any act which is deemed the justifiable exercise of the right under the Copyright Act, the Patent Act, the Utility Model Act, the Design Protection Act or the Trademark Act." The Guidelines on Unfair Exercise of Intellectual Property Rights, first promulgated in August 2000, provides guidance for determining whether an exercise of intellectual property rights constitutes an abuse by enterprises of their market dominance or unfair collaborative acts between multiple enterprises. Notably, the KFTC announced in December 2016 the creation of a new "Knowledge Industry Anti-Monopoly Division". The KFTC stated that major responsibilities for the Division will include monitoring of any abuse of standard essential patents and monitoring of unfair competition and conduct harming consumer welfare in relation to pharmaceutical patents, such as 'pay for delay' agreements between original and generic pharmaceutical companies.

B. Patent Application

Patent and utility model rights are awarded after an application goes through a series of formal and substantive examinations by KIPO. For registration in Korea, patent applications and / or utility model applications must be filed with KIPO. In this regard, a person who wishes to file a patent application and / or a utility model application must submit to the Commissioner of KIPO the following documents:
- An application stating the name and address of the inventor and the applicant (including the name of a representative, if the applicant is a legal entity), the title of the invention, and priority data (if priority is claimed);
- A specification, comprising a detailed description of the invention and at least one claim;
- Drawing(s) (if any);
- An abstract; and
- A power of attorney, if the application is filed by a party other than the applicant.

After the required documents are filed, patents and / or utility model applications are subject to substantive examination. For patents and utility models, a deferred examination system is used, where substantive examination does not begin until a formal request for examination is filed (which can be up to three years after the filing date). After a request for examination is filed, the application is examined in terms of its: (i) industrial applicability; (ii) novelty;(iii) inventiveness; and (iv) description requirements. The substantive examination decision is typically issued within 10 to 13 months from the date at which the request for examination is filed for both patents and utility models.

If the examiner does not reject a patent application, he or she must issue a notice of decision to grant the patent. The applicant must then pay, as a registration fee, the annuities for the first three years within three months from the date of receiving the notice of allowance. Thereafter, the applicant may pay annual fees on an annual basis. The term of protection for a patent commences upon its registration and ends 20 years after the filing date of the application, while the term of protection for a utility model commences upon registration and ends 10 years after the filing date of the application.

C. Trademark Registration

Trademarks, certification marks, geographical indications and other marks can be protected in Korea under the Trademark Act. Well-known marks can be protected under the UCPA, even if they are not registered. Further, the international conventions to which Korea is a signatory - such as the Paris Convention for the Protection of Industrial Property, the Agreement on Trade-Related Aspects of Intellectual Property Rights, the Nice Agreement Concerning the International Classification of Goods and Services for the Purposes of the Registration of Marks, the Trademark Law Treaty, the Protocol Relating to the Madrid Agreement Concerning the International Registration of Marks, and the Vienna Agreement Establishing an International Classification of the Figurative Elements of Marks—have the same legal effect as domestic laws.

Many procedural provisions of the Korean Patent Act have been applied to the Trademark Act. In addition, the general provisions of the Korean Criminal Act apply to the provisions of Trademark Act regarding the criminal sanction of trademark infringement, and the Criminal Procedure Act applies to the investigation, indictment, and Criminal Court hearing of such cases. The Civil Procedure Act sets out the civil remedies for trademark infringement, while the Customs Act provides for the protection of trademarks within Korea. As in other jurisdictions, the rights to a given trademark have their limits under the Fair Trade Act and the Act on Investigation of Unfair Trade Practices and Remedies against Injury of Domestic Industry. In addition, the Fair Trade Commission Guidelines establish standards for permitting parallel imports.

Korea has adopted a "registration," as opposed to a "use," system for the protection of trademarks. Under this system, a trademark right is normally recognized only when the mark is registered. The actual use of the mark is not a necessary condition for obtaining a trademark registration and an application can be filed on the basis of intent to use.

D. Measures for IP Protection

In Korea, an owner of a technical IP right can bring several different types of actions to protect his / her IP rights. In particular, the following actions are available: a civil main action (seeking an injunction and / or damages), a civil preliminary injunction action (a separate procedure from the civil main action; seeking only an injunctive relief), or a criminal action (criminal proceedings can be sought for infringement of technical IP rights including patents, utility models and designs); a Korean Trade Commission action (similar to United States ITC actions); a Korean Customs Action before the Korean Customs Office; or a scope confirmation action before the Korean Intellectual Property Office (administrative proceedings before the Intellectual Property Tribunal within KIPO to determine whether the products identified by the right-holder fall within the scope of the IP right).

In Korea, the Seoul, Daejeon, Daegu, Busan, and Gwangju district courts have exclusive jurisdiction of IP infringement cases. Although IP infringement cases may be brought before whichever of these five district courts satisfies the relevant venue requirements, the Seoul Central District Court will have additional jurisdiction to hear any IP infringement cases regardless of the venue. Further, intermediate appeals of IP infringement cases are heard exclusively by the patent court. In this regard, the patent court has a manual for appeal trials with specific guidelines on how the appeals of IP Infringement cases are progressed.

There is also the Act on the Prevention of Divulgence and Protection of Industrial Technology, which is purported to protect "Industrial Technology" and "National Core Technology." The term "Industrial Technology" refers to technology that is designated, notified, or published by the relevant ministries and satisfies any one of the following criteria: (i) original technology developed in Korea, which is advanced at the same level or beyond those of advanced countries and can be commercialized; (ii) technology which can reduce costs or improve the performance or quality of existing products; (iii) technology which has technical and economic potential and can contribute to the improvement of the nation's technological base and competitiveness; or (iv) technology based on application or exploitation of the above technologies. Further, Industrial Technology includes the term "National Core Technology", which is defined as industrial technology designated by the MOTIE as having high technical or economic value, or high growth potential in the domestic / foreign market, and whose disclosure outside of Korea poses a serious threat to national security or economy. The MOTIE maintains a published list of National Core Technologies.

VI. Environmental Protection

A. Department Supervising Environmental Protection

The Ministry of Environment is responsible for protecting the environment, which covers air, water, soil, nature, waste, recycling, chemicals, environmental health, climate change, etc. In addition, the MOE has numerous institutions supporting its mission which include, but are not limited to, National Institute of Environmental Research, Central Environmental Dispute Mediation Committee, Korea Environment Corporation, Korea Environmental Industry & Technology Institute, Korea National Park Service, Sudokwon Landfill Site Management Corporation.

B. Brief Introduction of Laws and Regulations of Environmental Protection

Environmental law in Korea is based upon the concept of environmental protection and the right to clean environment, which is a right contained in the Constitution. Under the principle of the "Framework Act on Environmental Policy", many environmental laws have been enacted on various topics.

a. Environmental Assessment

As a preventive and cautionary measure, the Environmental Impact Assessment Act requires that an environmental assessment be made prior to implementing an administrative decision or a business plan to ascertain the environmental impact the activity will have on the area.

b. Natural Environmental

The Natural Environment Conservation Act, the Wildlife Protection & Management Act, the Act on the Conservation and Use of Biological Diversity, and the Wetlands Conservation Act, etc. have been enacted to protect the natural environment, wild flora and fauna.

c. Air

The Air Environment Conservation Act regulates emission of air pollutants in general, and the Special Act on the Improvement of Air Quality in Seoul Metropolitan Area applies stricter standards to the emission facilities in the Seoul metropolitan area. Moreover, the Malodor Prevention Act, the Inside Air Quality Management Act, etc. have been enacted to improve air-quality-related health in Korea.

d. Water

Under the Water Environmental Conservation Act, which regulates discharge of water pollutants, the Water Supply and Waterworks Installation Act, the Sewerage Act, the Drinking Water Management Act, the Acts on the Management of Water and Resident's Support for Four Major River Basins, etc. further regulate the water quality and wastewater management.

e. Soil

The Soil Environment Conversation Act, among others, prevents soil contamination and provides requirements on how contaminated soil must be remediated.

f. Waste & Resource Circulation

The Waste Control Act specifies how wastes must be processed, setting out the general requirements and standards applicable to waste management. In addition, the Act on the International Movement of Wastes and Their Disposal regulates how wastes may be transferred between countries. The recently-enacted Resource Circulation Basic Law has placed a greater burden on those disposing wastes, the purpose of which is to encourage recycling of wastes. The Construction Waste Recycling Promotion Act, the Act on Resource Circulation of Electrical / Electronic Equipment and Vehicles, and the Act on the Promotion of Saving and Recycling of Resources, etc., further promote recycling of wastes.

g.Chemicals

The Act on Registration, Evaluation, etc., of Chemicals requires registration of chemical substances, hazardousness / toxicity tests, and designation of regulated chemical substances. Moreover, the Chemical Control Act regulates the issuance of business licenses to handle hazardous substances, and sets out the requirements on how chemical substances need to be stored and managed to prevent accidents.

h. Climate Change

The Framework Act on Low Carbon and Green Growth sets out the target management scheme to lower carbon emission, and the Act on the Allocation and Trading of Greenhouse-Gas Emission Permits provides a greenhouse-gas emission trading system where businesses may trade their greenhouse-gas emission permits.

i. Asbestos

The Asbestos Safety Management Act prohibits the use of asbestos and the manufacturing / import of products containing asbestos, and requires buildings to be inspected for asbestos. The Asbestos Injury Relief Act also provides a means to redress damages caused by asbestos.

j. Environmental Disputes

The Act on Liability for Environmental Damage and Relief enables victims of environmental contamination to seek damages by lowering the burden of proof on the victim plaintiffs. In addition, the Environmental Dispute Mediation Act set out the detailed processes on arrangement, mediation, and arbitration, thereby facilitating resolution of environmental disputes in a prompt and fair manner.

Moreover, the Act on the Integrated Control of Pollutant-Discharging Facilities regulates emission facilities in the major industries (e.g., steel manufacture, chemical, electrical / electronic manufacture, etc.) which may have a significant impact on the environment under the integrated management system, and ensures that an appropriate regulation be applied to each facility by setting out the best available technology for that particular facility.

C. Evaluation of Environmental Protection

As of 2017, the Ministry of Environment oversees approximately 60 environmental laws, which covers almost all matters relating to environmental protection. These laws are continuously updated in line with recent environmental laws and regulations in other countries. For this reason, Korean environmental laws are generally considered to be well-organized and up-to-date.

There still remains a concern about enforcement of these environmental laws and regulations. For example, although the 2016 budget for the MOE was KRW 5.7 trillion, most of the budget was not evenly allocated to local governments, thereby creating different levels of enforcement and improvement of environmental quality across the country. Moreover, there is also criticism, noting that the emphasized regulated areas and the intensity of enforcement appear to have changed when new governments stepped in.

VII. Dispute Resolution

A. Methods and Bodies of Dispute Resolution

Most large commercial disputes in Korea are resolved by the courts, although alternative dispute resolution has increased in popularity in recent years. In particular, arbitration as a means of settling commercial disputes has steadily become more popular for cross-border disputes. The courts have tended to encourage the resolution of disputes through mediation.

Mediation can be conducted by a judge presiding over the dispute, by a different judge (solely for the purpose of the mediation), or by a mediation committee comprising one judge and two or more private citizens. The increased use of arbitration in Korea is based on several factors, including an increase in Korean companies' involvement in international transactions and the general tendency of the Korean courts to enforce arbitral awards.

In principle, civil litigation in Korea is adversarial, although there are elements of inquisitorial proceedings as well. For example, the presiding judge can seek clarification from the parties regarding the pending litigation by directly questioning the parties about factual or legal matters and by urging the parties to present further evidence (Article 136(1), Korean Civil Procedure Act). In addition, the judge must investigate and determine sua sponte not only procedural matters (such as elements for a cause of action), but also certain substantive matters (for example, the degrees of contributory negligence between the parties, quantification of alimony and so on). In civil litigation, the evidentiary burden is the "preponderance of evidence", rather than the "beyond a reasonable doubt" standard applicable in criminal cases.

All large commercial disputes are brought before regular civil courts with the requisite jurisdiction, except for certain disputes that must be heard by the Patent Court (specifically established to deal with IP issues).

The number of judges sitting on a civil case at the district court level depends on the size of the claim:
• where the claim amount is KRW 200 million or less, the case is heard by a single judge;
• where the claim amount is more than KRW 200 million, or if the claim amount cannot be determined; the case is heard by a panel of three judges; and
• in the high (appellate) courts, all cases are heard by a panel of three judges.

Subdivisions within the district and high courts are responsible for civil, criminal, family, juvenile, administrative, patent and bankruptcy matters. If a decision of the court of first instance is appealed, the high court conducts the proceedings de novo (afresh). The decision of the high courts can be appealed to the Supreme Court only on questions of law. The decision of the Seoul High Court on IP disputes tried by the Patent Court as the court of first instance can only be reviewed by the Supreme Court. Similarly, disputes in which the KFTC is a party are heard at the Seoul High Court as the court of first instance, and can only be reviewed by the Supreme Court.

To more efficiently deal with complex disputes involving specialized issues, some courts have assigned certain panels of judges to oversee certain disputes so that they may become more familiar with the technicalities and nuances behind specialized industries (e.g., programming in the construction industry). Practice areas that have attracted this judicial arrangement include international transactions, securities, construction, HR and the environment.

B. Application of Laws

Under Article 25 of the Korean Conflicts of Law, parties generally have the freedom to choose the governing law for their contract. To this end, Korean courts respect the choice of a foreign governing law and jurisdiction in a contract. However, if the contract includes the subject which involves any mandatory laws of Korea, those laws will prevail.

The Supreme Court has also declared that a provision regarding an agreement to recognize the exclusive jurisdiction of a foreign court is effective if the following requirements are met:
- The case is not about a matter subject to the exclusive jurisdiction of the Korean courts;
- The foreign court designated as the court with exclusive jurisdiction has jurisdiction in the matter under the relevant law of the foreign country; and
- The foreign court designated as the court with exclusive jurisdiction has a reasonable connection to the matter in dispute.

The Supreme Court has also ruled that if the agreement on exclusive jurisdiction of a foreign court is clearly unreasonable and / or unfair, then that agreement will be void for being against the public order and good morals.

VIII. Others

A. Anti-commercial Bribery

a. Brief Introduction of Anti-commercial Bribery Laws and Regulations

A number of laws and regulations govern bribery of domestic government officials, including the Criminal Code; the Act Concerning Aggravated Punishment of Specific Crimes ("SCA"); the Act on the Aggravated Punishment, etc., of Specific Economic Crimes ("SECA"); the Act on the Creation and Operation of the Anti-Corruption and Civil Rights Commission and the Prevention of Corruption (the "Anti-Corruption Act" or "ACA"); and the Act on Prohibition of Improper Solicitation and Provision / Receipt of Money and Valuables (the "Anti-Graft Act" or AGA").

The Foreign Bribery Prevention in International Business Transactions Act governs bribery of foreign public officials. The Public Official's Code of Conduct for Maintenance of Integrity ("Code of Conduct") provides guidelines on the receipt of payment, meals, gifts, etc., in various government agencies and state-owned enterprises.

The Anti-Corruption & Civil Rights Commission ("ACRC") published the "Guidelines on Processing Complaints on Improper Request and Providing / Receiving Valuables" and the "Handbook of Improper Solicitation and Graft Act", which explains the AGA in detail.

b. Department Supervising Anti-commercial Bribery

The district prosecutor's office has the powers to prosecute, investigate and enforce all criminal cases, including commercial bribery. The police, under supervision of the district prosecutor's office, has the authority to conduct criminal investigations. If the prosecutor's office decides to indict the offender, the competent court has the authority to impose criminal sanctions on the offender.

The ACRC is a major anti-corruption agency responsible for formulating national anti-corruption strategies. It has the authority to accept complaints but does not have the authority to conduct an independent criminal investigation. Instead, it must refer matters to other agencies or solicit help from the criminal enforcement bodies (i.e., the police and the prosecutor's office).

For violations of the AGA, the relevant public institution (i.e., the institution where the implicated public official is employed) and the Board of Audit and Inspection of Korea also have the authority to internally investigate alleged violations of the AGA, but not to initiate a criminal investigation.

c. Punitive Actions

a) Criminal Code

A person who gives a bribe to a government official, in violation of the Criminal Code, may face imprisonment of up to five years or a fine of up to KRW20 million. A person found undertaking commercial bribery may face imprisonment of up to two years or a fine of up to KRW5 million. Companies cannot be held liable for either type of bribery under the Criminal Code.

A public official who receives, solicits or agrees to a bribe may face imprisonment of up to five years or be disqualified from serving in a public / official capacity for up to 10 years.

b) SCA / SECA

Maximum penalties are under the SCA and the SECA are higher than those under the Criminal Code. Penalties are proportionate to the amount given as a bribe.

c) AGA

Under the AGA, any benefit to public officials above KRW1 million in a single instance, or above KRW3 million in a yearly aggregate, is subject to either a fine of up to KRW 30 million or imprisonment of up to three years. The penalty would apply to the both the giver and the recipient of the benefit.

For benefits below the monetary thresholds mentioned above, but are directly related to the official duties of the recipient public official, both the giver and the recipient may be subject to an administrative fine of two to five times the amount of the benefit.

A company may be held liable for the acts of its employees under the AGA.

B. Project Contracting

a. Permission System

In principle, the Public Procurement Service ("PPS") enters into procurement contracts on behalf of the Korean government, local governments and public institutions. The purpose of centralizing the procurement process is to increase the efficiency.

However, a government agency or public institution may directly enter into a procurement contract in the following cases: (i) natural disaster; (ii) force majeure event; (iii) procurement which relates to national defense or must otherwise be kept secret; and (iv) emergency relief activities for natural disaster or major accident.①

For defense procurement, the Defense Acquisition Program Administration is the primary agency with the authority to enter into procurement contracts relating to national defense.

b. Prohibited Areas

Traditionally, government or public procurement contracts have been awarded to Korean nationals. However, a foreign company may also participate in government or public procurement projects exceeding a certain amount since Korea became a party to the WTO Agreement on Government Procurement.

The tender for government or public procurement is divided into the following three categories:
- Domestic tender, where only Korean nationals may participate;
- International tender, where both Korean nationals and foreigners may participate; and
- Foreign tender, where only foreigners may participate (due to lack of local sources).

c. Invitation to Bid and Bidding

In principle, a government procurement projects are awarded through a competitive bidding process.② However, if expertise and technology owned by a contractor is more important for the success of a project, a relevant government agency or public institution may enter into a non-competitive sole source contract with a company that is deemed to be most favorable to the country. In such cases, non-price factors such as the contractor's performance record, technological capability and project implementation plan will be considered with a higher degree of importance. Such criteria are made available to the bidders in advance.③

If it is difficult to set out specifications or requirements in agreements for manufacturing or purchase of goods or service agreements, or otherwise required based on the characteristics of an agreement, bidders may firstly be required to participate in a bid for specification or technology. Only those bidders who are subsequently deemed to have the required capability will then be invited to participate in the bidding process.④

C. Privacy and Data Protection

The Personal Information Protection Act ("PIPA") regulates the overall processing of personal information gathered either in the public or private sectors. PIPA is enforced in parallel with the already existing Act on Promotion of Information and Communication Network Utilization and Information Protection, etc., which governs the collection of personal information through telecommunications networks (e.g., the internet) and "Use and Protection of Credit Information Act", which governs the collection of credit information. In this regard, a company collecting customer information may be subject to the above mentioned laws with reference to the methods of collection and the types of information being collected.

"Personal information" is broadly defined to refer to information relating to a living individual that contains information identifying a specific person (e.g., name, address, or similar in a form of an image, etc., including information that does not, by itself, make it possible to identify a specific person, but that enables identification of a person easily when combined with other information). Common examples of personal information include one's name, address, phone number, gender, hobbies, etc. Information must be related to a living individual, and therefore, information about a corporate entity does not fall within the scope of personal information and is not

---

① Government Procurement Act, Article 5(2).
② Act on Contracts to Which the State is a Party, Article 10.
③ Enforcement Decree of the Act on Contracts to Which the State is a Party, Article 43.
④ Enforcement Decree of the Act on Contracts to Which the State is a Party, Article 18.

protected under PIPA. Accordingly, personal information from both individual customers and employees are within the scope of personal information as defined under PIPA.

Under Korean law, sensitive information is defined as personal information that details ideology, faith, labor union membership, political views or membership in a political party, health information or medical treatment, sex life, genetic information, criminal records (e.g., sentencing, exemptions, suspended sentences, protective custody, probation). Similarly, unique identification information is defined as one's resident registration number, passport number, driver's license number or alien registration number.

科威特

作者：Ibrahim Sattout、Akusa Batwala
译者：余盛兴、高俊

一、概述

（一）政治、经济、社会和法律环境概述

科威特是一个君主立宪制国家，将立法权、行政权、司法权的三权分立制度写入了《宪法》。立法权归属于埃米尔（Amir）和国会，埃米尔是王室成员，并由王室选出。科威特《宪法》将埃米尔定位为国家首脑并给予官方称谓"科威特最高领袖酋长"。同时，《宪法》规定埃米尔通过他的大臣行使权力，并且埃米尔有豁免权且不可被侵犯。

国会成员由科威特国民直接选举产生。行政权由内阁行使，总理和政府各部门领导统领内阁。内阁同样也被称为部长会议。部长由总理和埃米尔任命，整个内阁对埃米尔和国民议会负责，虽然事实上内阁是和埃米尔紧紧联系在一起的。司法机构由指定的司法官员组成。虽然1962年的《宪法》保证了独立的司法权，但行政部门仍然保留对其行政和财政预算所控制，并没有实现真正的独立。在经过司法部的推荐之后，埃米尔任命普通法院的法官。对于科威特国民来说，这种任命是终身制的；而对于外国人来说，这种任命的任期是1～3年。

科威特的民事法律体系遵循法国并且深受埃及法律体系的影响。科威特的法律体系在很大程度上是世俗的，尽管伊斯兰教法对穆斯林居民实行家庭法。科威特《宪法》规定伊斯兰教为国教。

科威特虽然国土面积狭小却很富裕，经济相对开放，并自称其原油储量约占世界储量的8%。石油占国内生产总值的近一半，占出口收入的95%和政府收入的95%。[①]

科威特原则上是一个支持外国资本对本国进行投资的国家，并且在最近几年引进了新的法律；科威特对外国资本持一种开放的态度。2013年，科威特通过了2013年第116号法律——科威特《促进直接投资法》（DLL）。该法律旨在使与直接投资相关的法律条文更现代化，并且可以在不断涌现的经济和投资的挑战面前更加灵活和透明。科威特最近还颁布了一部新的《公共投标法》（2016年第49号法律及其执行条例，通过2017年30号法令）管理政府投标的程序。这部新法律被普遍认为是对先前法律的改进，鼓励外国参与和在政府投标中使用现代技术。

（二）在"一带一路"倡议下与中国企业合作的状态和方向

中国和科威特从1955年开始贸易往来，1971年正式确立外交关系。两国建立外交关系以来，双边经济和贸易沟通日渐频繁，贸易数额也逐渐增大。2016年，中国和科威特之间的贸易总额达到了95亿美元，相比刚建交的时候增加了60多倍。科威特是阿拉伯国家对中国优惠贷款的最大供应商之一。从1982年起，科威特阿拉伯经济发展基金为中国提供了超过10亿美元的贷款。[②]

科威特和中国之间有诸多经济和贸易的协定，包括：1980年签订的《贸易协定》；1985年签订的《鼓励和相互保护投资协定》；1986年签订的《关于成立经济、技术和贸易合作混合委员会的协定》；1989年签订的《避免双重征税协定》；1989年签订的《经济技术合作协定》以及2004年7月签订的《贸易协定》。

中国驻科威特大使王镝表示，2014年在首相贾比尔·穆巴拉克·哈马德·萨巴赫（Sheikh Jaber Al-Mubarak Al-Hamad Al-Sabah）参加丝绸之城、丝绸之路活动时，科威特和中国签署了一份合作文

[①] 参见 World Bank – Kuwait Country Report October 2017。
[②] 参见 http://kw.china-embassy.org。

件。① 他同时表明，2013年习近平主席提出的"丝绸之路经济带"和"21世纪海上丝绸之路"与埃米尔·萨巴赫·艾哈迈德·贾比尔·萨巴赫（Amir Sheikh Sabah Al-Ahmad Al-Jaber Al-Sabah）希望将科威特建立称谓一个全球经济和商业中心这一想法不谋而合。同时，王镝也强调科威特是第一个在一带一路下和中国签订合作协定的阿拉伯国家。

科威特和中国未来的关系一定会更加紧密。中国的发展需要石油，而科威特的发展需要中国现有的技术和人才条件。两个国家互相支持对方，从而达到一种积极向上的，可持续并多样化的发展。②

二、投资

（一）市场准入

1. 投资监管部门

根据投资的性质和被投资行业的不同，政府监管部门也会不同。总体来说，主要的监管部门有：科威特中央银行（以下简称"中央银行"，它与其他部门一起，对科威特的银行业和金融业进行规则的制定）、商务和工业部（以下简称"工商部"，是科威特所有企业的总监管者）、资本市场管理局（以下简称"资本管理局"，是一个被工商部监督的独立公共部门，监管所有科威特的证券活动，包括证券活动执照等）以及科威特直接投资促进管理局（以下简称"投资促进局"），根据《促进直接投资法》出具执照，由工商部部长主持，旨在改进科威特整体投资环境，使外国投资者可以更好地根据《促进直接投资法》进行投资。

2. 投资行业法律、法规

在科威特，最重要的规范投资的法律是《商法典》（1980年第68号法律），《公司法》（2016年第1号法律及其实施条例，以下统称《公司法》）、《促进直接投资法》以及《资本管理法》（经修订的2010年第7号法律及其根据2015年第72号法律修订的实施条例，以下简称《资本管理法实施条例》）。

（1）《商法典》

《商法典》为科威特的商业关系提供了最基本的框架和法律原则。除了一些例外（包括一些《促进直接投资法》规定的例外豁免），《民法典》第23条、第24条规定，外国公司必须通过代理人或通过科威特"合作伙伴"在科威特开展业务（通常通过成立一家科威特公司，科威特参与者拥有至少51%该公司的资本）。

（2）《公司法》

《公司法》设立了科威特公司在科威特设立和运营的监管框架。《公司法》还规定不同形式的主体，包括合伙企业、合资企业和公司。根据投资的需要，可以建立不同类型的公司，包括一人公司（只有1个股东）、有限责任公司（拥有2～50个股东）和股份公司（适用于规模比较大的企业，必须至少5个股东）。

（3）《促进直接投资法》

《促进直接投资法》的目的是促进和便利对科威特的外国投资，并为有利于科威特经济多样化的项目提供重要激励措施。重要的是，根据这项法律，外国当事人可以免受科威特公司外国所有权的限制。其他的利好包括税收抵免和海关豁免。

（4）《资本管理法》

《资本管理法》建立了资本管理局，并为科威特证券交易所、清算代理机构和证券行业的其他主体制订了规则。此外，针对证券市场出现的各种问题，修订后的《资本管理法实施条例》连同资本管理局发布的其他通告和决议都规定了关键监管原则。修订后的《资本管理法实施条例》和其他资本管理规定并不是被动启动的。相反，资本管理局有权对受监管实体进行监督和控制。

---

① 参见 http://www.timeskuwait.com/Times_Kuwait-is-China-s-key-trade-partner-envoy。
② 参见 http://en.people.cn/n3/2017/1128/c90000-9297520.html 。

（5）其他法律

还有其他法律可能与希望在科威特开展业务的外国当事人有关，例如《商业代理法》（2016 年第 13 号法律，该法规定了外国负责人与科威特当地的代理、经销商、特许经营人等之间的关系）、经修正的《中央银行法》（1968 年第 32 号法律，其中规定了中央银行、科威特货币调节、货币兑换、科威特银行、融资等）、《工业法》（1996 年第 56 号法律，建立了由工商部监督并负责和发展科威特工业活动的工业公共管理机构），以及 1995 年第 26 号已修订的关于自由贸易区的法律（以下简称《自由贸易区法》），其允许建立自由贸易区，并为那些获准在自由贸易区内经营的人提供某些优惠（例如豁免外国所有权限制、税收及关税，然而目前《自由贸易区法》尚未实施）。

3. 投资形式

根据《自由贸易区法》的规定，外国实体可在自由贸易区内自由运营而无须委任科威特代理人或设立科威特公司，但须遵守某些规定（例如，运营限于自由贸易区内），以此来激励对科威特的投资。考虑到在自由贸易区建立商业运营的困难和成本，外方在过去往往会寻求其他投资形式（例如根据《促进直接投资法》等）。目前在科威特有三个自由贸易区，即舒瓦克（Shuwaikh）港、Al-Abdally 和 Nuwaiseeb。在自由贸易区开展业务时，实体必须取得许可证才能进行《自由贸易区法》第 2 条规定的许可活动（但是，目前尚无根据《自由贸易区法》颁发的许可证）。

为了取得《促进直接投资法》给予的优惠，投资者必须在科威特进行重大投资（例如技术转让、国家产品多样化、积极的环境影响、科威特国民就业等）。这种资格要求旨在确定科威特整体如何从拟议的项目、活动中受益。2015 年第 75 号部长理事会决议列出了某些行业直接投资的负面清单，这些行业不符合《促进直接投资法》规定的许可条件（如石油勘探和生产、安全和国防等），但确实规定了某些行业的股权割让。合格的投资者可获得的优惠包括 100% 的外资所有权、税收抵免、海关豁免、政府土地使用等。

4. 市场准入的标准和审查

根据上文所述，非科威特人可以拥有在科威特境内经营的公司中不超过 49% 的股份。该一般规则的例外情况包括：

① 在自由贸易区内运营——在这种情况下，所有运营必须在自由贸易区内进行；

② 根据《促进直接投资法》成立——这要求其对科威特进行重大投资；

③ 根据 2002 年第 141 号和 2011 年部长会议第 237 号决议——仅适用于海湾阿拉伯国家合作委员会（以下简称海合会）的个人或者由海合会成员国国民全资拥有的海合会公司。另外，根据行业的不同，对外资所有权适用特殊的限制。例如，出版和教育部门在外国投资上还受到其他的规制和限制。

（二）外汇管理规则

根据《中央银行法》的规定，中央银行负责稳定科威特经济及其货币。因此，它控制和管理货币兑换业务，任何从事此类业务的公司必须经过批准并向中央银行注册。

财政部长于 1984 年 3 月颁布的关于将货币兑换公司控制在中央银行（MR 19/3/1984），以及中央银行针对货币兑换公司于 2014 年 12 月 2 日发布的指导意见（以下简称《指导意见》）都是外汇管理的重要规则。

根据指导意见第 6—9 条的规定，创设货币兑换公司需要获得中央银行的批准，中央银行应考虑到这些公司在当地金融市场的需要以及任何提议的外国合作伙伴或投资者的必要性。中央银行还负责货币兑换公司的注册，除非他们在注册簿中注册，否则这些公司不可以从事货币兑换业务。如果货币兑换公司同时执行与银行业务的货币兑换活动（例如接受现金或储蓄存款、提供贷款等）或其他活动（例如交易、房地产、工业活动），而没有为这些活动建立单独的实体，货币兑换公司可能会从注册簿中被移除。值得注意的是，《指导意见》第 13 条和《中央银行法》第 71 条规定，中央银行可以向货币兑换公司发出这样的指示，如果它认为有必要实现中央银行的政策。此外，《指导意见》第 14—17 条允许中央银行对货币兑换公司行使一定的检查权。这些条款还允许中央银行向货币兑换公司提供广泛的自我报告要求。根据《指导意见》第 17 条的规定，如果货币兑换公司违背其创始文件的条款，发布虚假信息，或违反中央银行的指示的，中央银行有权实施《中央银行法》第 85 条规定的警告、罚款和其他处罚。根据《指导意见》第 7 条的规定，中央银行允许货币兑换公司采取各种法律形式，而不像银行必须采取股份公司（KSC）的形式。

外国投资者在进口和资本汇回方面没有外汇管制限制。除 2013 年第 106 号《关于打击洗钱和资助恐怖主义的法律》（以下简称《反洗钱法》）的规定之外，科威特货币兑换为外币也不受限制，反之亦然，也不限制利润汇回本国、交易对手以当地货币进行交易，或交易对手进行外汇交易。

在科威特，洗钱、反恐融资及相关活动主要由《反洗钱法》进行管制。《反洗钱法》的颁布旨在为科威特打击洗钱和反恐怖主义融资，特别是在金融机构和某些受监管机构方面提供更有力的监管制度。《反洗钱法》是根据 2013 年第 37 号部长决议发布的执行条例实施的。反恐融资还受到准许科威特加入《制止向恐怖主义提供资助的国际公约》的第 85 号法律的管辖。

除了《反洗钱法》外，2013 年 7 月 23 日 2/BS，IBS/38/2013 号文件中关于打击洗钱和恐怖融资交易的指示以及最近修订的《资本管理法实施条例》都对洗钱、科威特相关的反恐融资活动作出了补充规定。修订后的《资本管理法实施条例》对"被许可人员"（由《资本管理法实施条例》界定）在打击洗钱和恐怖主义融资方面规定了额外义务。新法规旨在：

① 提高资本市场的完整性和可信度；
② 保护被许可人员及其客户。

已修订的《资本管理法实施条例》适用于所有"被许可人员"，这些人员被定义为持有资本管理局执照且从事以下任何行为的自然人或法人：

① 证券交易所；
② 清算机构；
③ 投资组合管理人；
④ 集体投资计划；
⑤ 投资经理；
⑥ 认购代理人；
⑦ 托管人；
⑧ 在资本管理局注册的经纪人；
⑨ 投资管理人；
⑩ 信用评级机构；
⑪ 评估资产；
⑫ 由资本管理局指定为证券活动的任何其他活动。

《反洗钱法》的实施细则要求法律界定的金融机构或指定的非金融机构企业和专业人员（DNFBP）进行金额超过 3 000 科威特第纳尔或其等值外币的交易时，需通过文件核实客户的身份，或者不居住在科威特的人的护照或旅行证件。

此外，根据《反洗钱法》通过的条例规定，所有从科威特转移的、超过 3 000 科威特第纳尔（或等值其他货币）的货币必须通过当地银行或交易所电汇资金完成。因此，一些银行会寻求中央银行的批准，以便向其他方大量转移资金。银行未遵守《反洗钱法》的规定的，将会被处以罚款、没收资金和/或监禁。但是，《反垄断法》明确规定罚款和没收资金不应损害到善意第三人的权利。

（三）融资

1. 主要金融机构

根据《中央银行法》设立的中央银行监管科威特境内的银行活动，并更具体地监督在科威特从事融资活动的所有当地银行和投资公司。

在科威特的一般原则是，在科威特（即在岸上）进行的"银行活动"需要从中央银行获得适当的许可证。还应该注意的是，除了在中央银行所持有的银行登记册中登记的机构外，没有其他机构可以从事银行业务，或在其营业地点、出版物或广告中使用"银行""银行家""银行所有人"或任何在机构性质上可能误导公众的措辞。为了能够在科威特建立一个新的银行机构，应向中央银行董事会提出申请。

此外，禁止外国银行在科威特当地开设分行开展银行业务，除非它首先获得了中央银行的许可证。没有具体的规定限制在科威特的自然人或法律实体在离岸／跨境基础上从科威特获得金融服务。外国金融机构提供此类金融服务应遵守该外国金融机构所在司法管辖区适用的法律。

科威特有一些当地的银行和几家伊斯兰银行。几家外国银行也在科威特建立了分行。

2. 外国企业融资条件

（1）银行账户

在符合洗钱法规定的前提下，开设和运营银行账户相对容易，只要相关实体在科威特境内合法存在，符合监管要求即可。但是，在科威特境内没有直接实际存在的外国实体（包括正在通过代理人执行政府项目的实体）可能无法在科威特开设银行账户。科威特的银行将允许持有科威特民事身份证的科威特国民和外国居民开设银行账户。

（2）融资

请注意，依据各种各样的通函，中央银行对本地受监管银行向非居民公司／个人贷款的能力施加了限制。更具体地说，中央银行对本地银行向非居民客户提供科威特第纳尔信贷额度进行了一定的限制。

更具体地说，允许当地银行将科威特第纳尔的信贷服务提供给与政府共同执行项目的非居民，无须事先征得中央银行的同意，只要融资合同价值不超过 4 000 万科威特第纳尔，并且信贷额度不超过每个合同总价值的 70%。至于其他合同或超出此限额的信贷额度，必须事先征得中央银行的同意。

对于本地银行向非居民客户提供的所有科威特第纳尔信贷额度，还需满足以下条件：

① 向非居民提供的科威特第纳尔信贷额度应该仅限于为以科威特第纳尔计价的合同提供融资，并且得到科威特政府机构的授权。融资银行必须核实这些融资合同是真合同，并且必须保留副本。

② 具体的融资金额应根据每份具体的合同单独衡量确定，而且不能通过相关客户提供的一般信用额度来概括。

③ 所有融资合同付款的转让函应该以贷款银行为受益人来签署。这些款项应用于根据这些额度条件授予的信贷额度的偿还。

④ 银行可代表其非居民客户进行货币远期交易，条件是此类交易要与合同预期付款的到期日一致。这些交易的金额不得超过预计在每个阶段收取的金额，并且交易的到期日应该与该金额的到期日相匹配或在接近的日期内到期。所提供的科威特第纳尔信贷额度要兑换成外币，限于合同中的外国部分。中央银行应允许覆盖远期外汇合同，以及科威特第纳尔现金额度转换为外汇，但是最多不超过合同价值的 50%，银行应该以自身资源为合同的剩下部分融资承担责任。

⑤ 银行必须立即通知中央银行的外国业务部门向非居民客户授予贷款或补助，并且不需要中央银行事先同意。该通知应包含以下信息：项目业主名称；借款方名字；融资合同的规模及付款时间表；授予的信用限制。上述部门也应被告知这些案子被授予额度的还款进度。对于价值超过 4 000 万科威特第纳尔或超过最高限制的额度，申请获得中央银行的事先同意——每个案子应该分开申请，应包括与申请批准的案件有关的所有信息和数据。所有此类申请应发送至监管部门（部门）。

⑥ 有关银行应继续按非居民客户的要求，在科威特提供信贷，以承保由当地机构发起的投标所需的投标保证金。

⑦ 信贷延期决定是贷款银行的责任，贷款银行将承担由此可能导致的任何风险，包括获得中央银行事先同意的情况。在这种情况下，相关银行必须遵守中央银行发布的监管规则，包括但不限于：资本充足率、信贷集中度和信贷政策等。值得一提的是，中央银行应对每家银行可分别向其非居民客户提供的总信贷额度设定一个内部限额，这需要求银行停止提供任何新的信贷额度直到获得同意。

（四）土地政策

1959 年第 5 号法律和 1979 年第 74 号法律规定科威特公民可以自由拥有房地产。上述法律也规定了外国在科威特房地产的所有权。作为一般前提，非科威特人不能——除非在有限的情况下——拥有科威特的房地产。对房地产的永久产权通常限于科威特国民或其全资拥有的公司实体。然而，此一般性规定的例外情况总结如下：

（1）海合会成员国（GCC states）

2004年关于在科威特建造的土地和房地产的所有权问题上将海合会成员国公民视为科威特人的第1号法律规定，海合会成员国国民及其全资拥有的公司实体可以在科威特拥有土地。实际上，这种权利只扩展到由海合会成员国国民全资拥有的科威特公司以及居住在科威特的海合会成员国/阿拉伯公民，这些公民必须拥有足够的收入来购买该财产，并且不得是科威特另一家房地产的所有者。

（2）外交使团

外国可以对其外交使团和使团团长的住所拥有不动产。但是对于这种所有权，每个国家不得超过4 000平方米。这种例外建立在假定外国也给予科威特互惠待遇的基础上。此外，必须签发一份埃米尔法令，以便在个案基础上允许这种所有权。

（3）《促进直接投资法》

根据促进科威特直接投资的《促进直接投资法》，外国实体可以全部拥有科威特公司或在科威特设立的分支机构。根据《促进直接投资法》的规定，激励外国人在科威特建立一个当地实体的措施包括但不限于为投资目的分配土地（不必然是该土地的所有权）。根据《促进直接投资法》授予许可和特权/奖励（包括土地分配）时，有关当局将根据具体情况评估该外国实体的项目或企业，同时考虑所使用的技术、涉及的专业知识、为科威特人力资源创造就业机会和培训机会、以发展为目标的部门、项目的地点等。

（4）在科威特证券交易所上市的公司

尽管可能有外国非海合会股东，在科威特证券交易所上市的科威特公司可能被允许在科威特拥有房地产。一般来说，外国公司不得在科威特拥有土地。同样，一家拥有外国（非海合会）股东的科威特公司也可能不拥有土地。然而，尽管有这项禁令，适用的法律规定可以获得一份埃米尔法令，以允许一家拥有外国股东的科威特公司拥有其在科威特的营业场所（因此也是其所在的土地）。首先需要获得部长理事会的决定，此后埃米尔必须颁布执行部长理事会决定的法令。

（5）登记

根据1959年关于房地产登记的第5号法律，科威特有一个中央土地登记册，由不动产登记部门（即土地登记处）管理，该部门是司法部的一部分。中央登记册可被社会利益相关方查看，但须象征性支付费用。

房地产抵押和其他权利也根据其优先顺序被记录在登记册中。抵押权的登记权利从出售抵押财产的收益中享有优先于普通债权人的权利。如果抵押权未登记，那么从抵押中产生的权利仅仅属于个人权利，并且可能无法对第三方实施。

永久产权的转让以及其他创造房地产权利的文件必须在土地登记处登记。房地产的所有权只能通过将这种财产的所有权登记到新的所有人名下来转移。

（6）租赁

所有人（即外国公民和实体）均可享受租赁的利益。根据《民法典》（1980年第67号法律）和1978年关于房地产租赁的第35号法律，可以批准土地租赁。

如果私人土地的租赁期超过10年，则应该在土地登记处登记。租赁期限不得超过25年。如果据称已经签订的租约期限较长或无期限，则该期限将减至25年。但是，如果签订的租约时间为"出租人或承租人的终身期限"，则法律允许按照租赁约定的期限运行，即使它可能超过25年。除非协议另有规定，否则承租人不得转让租约。

国有土地的租赁不像私有土地的租赁一样要进行登记。由相关机构（通常是财政部—国家房地产部门）签署并盖章的租赁合同就是这种租赁的证据，并且在科威特市政厅（负责总体规划的实体）和财政部记录同样的内容。

国家为工业发展而授予的房地产租赁由工业主管部门（PAI）管理，这些协议由工业主管部门签署。与国有土地一样，由工业主管部门签署并盖章的合同也是这种租赁的证据，并且在工业主管部门、科威特市政厅和财政部也保留了相同的记录。

（7）征用土地

根据科威特《宪法》（第18条）的规定，政府有权为公共利益收回某些私人权利，但是要以"公正补偿"为交换条件。因此，法律允许强制征用土地。

1964年第33号关于为了公共利益而征用和暂时扣押的法律规定了为公共利益而征用或扣押土地的过程。根据1964年第33号法律，除公共利益外，不得征收和临时扣押不动产。财政部的下属部门公益征用部，对征用负责，该部门负责调查和确定哪些土地可能被征用，并执行征用程序。公益征用部征地委员会由财政部主持，就征收土地的必要性作出决定。此外，在公益征用部设立的评估委员会提供了在征用和没收土地时应支付的赔偿金的预估值。

（五）公司的成立与解散

科威特法律一般规定，外国公司（除《促进直接投资法》规定的特殊情况下）在科威特开展业务时必须通过代理商或者通过科威特合作伙伴（通常通过设立科威特公司并由科威特参与者拥有该公司至少51%的资本）。目前，只有拥有至少51%的资本的科威特个人或实体可以成为非科威特实体的代理。此外，科威特境内各种法律实体的设立和注册受到经修订的《公司法》的管辖，并且作为一般规则要求科威特国民的参与。

《促进直接投资法》于2013年12月生效，其实施条例于一年后发布。寻求在科威特开展业务和投资的外国当事人可以根据《促进直接投资法》的规定，并且这样做可能会从其中规定的各种激励措施和利益中得到好处。例如，根据《促进直接投资法》的规定，外国投资者可以享受的主要好处之一是可以持有科威特公司100%的股份。

1. 公司的形式

下面列出了《公司法》准许的公司类型：
① 普通合伙公司；
② 有限合伙公司；
③ 股份合伙有限公司；
④ 合资企业；
⑤ 股份公司（无论是公开交易还是非公开交易）；
⑥ 有限责任公司；
⑦ 一人公司。

科威特最常见的实体类型是有限责任公司（WLL）和封闭式股份公司（KSCC）。下面是封闭式股份公司和有限责任公司之间的主要区别：

① 股权：封闭式股份公司和有限责任公司的股权持有者既可以是个人，也可以是法人实体。对于封闭式股份公司的股东人数没有上限，但必须至少有5个人。有限责任公司必须有至少2名但不多于50名的股东。

② 股本：封闭式股份公司或有限责任公司所需的最低资本取决于公司的活动。除某些活动外，封闭式股份公司所需的最低资本为10 000科威特第纳尔（约33 000美元），有限责任公司的最低资本为1 000科威特第纳尔（约3 300美元）。

③ 税：科威特目前没有对有限责任公司征税。然而，封闭式股份公司需要：

• 在向强制性储备缴款后、向股东分配股息之前，向科威特科学促进基金会（KFAS）提供其净利润的1%；

• 根据2006年第46号《扎卡特法》（Zakat Law），将年净利润的1%作为扎卡特税。作为伊斯兰教的五大支柱之一，扎卡特是所有符合财富标准的穆斯林的宗教义务。这不是慈善捐款，并且被认为是税收或义务施舍。

其股票在科威特交易所上交易的封闭式股份公司必须从其净利润中支付2.5%的额外捐款，以资助旨在鼓励科威特国民在私营部门就业的科威特国家项目。

目前，有限责任公司和封闭式股份公司中的非科威特或非海合会的公司股东对其从这些公司所得的收入按15%的税率纳税。

通过投资促进局注册成立的公司可能会获得免税，免税年限不超过10年。

④ 管理层和董事会：封闭式股份公司由董事会管理，董事会的组成和任期在公司章程和公司备忘

录有详细说明。有限责任公司通常由一名或多名管理人员管理。

2. 成立过程

与封闭式股份公司过程相比,有限责任公司的建立通常更快并且过程更简单。在某些情况下,有限责任公司以在5—7周内成立(即直至发放交易许可证的时间点)。但是,封闭式股份公司的成立过程通常需要更多时间,并且必须办理特殊的手续。例如,成立封闭式股份公司有一些需要信息公开的要求,每个股东都必须经过各个主管部门的批准,这种批准要考虑到封闭式股份公司的相关活动。

成立过程从提交给工商部的申请开始。在获得有关批准(例如从市政府和科威特消防局获得批准,从内政部获得经理、主席、合伙人/股东的批准等)并完成公司名称的注册后,工商部将此事提交司法部在公证机构签署公司备忘录和/或公司章程。一旦公司备忘录和/或公司章程被签署并经过公证后,该事项会被退到工商部,以便在商业登记处登记公司。注册后,将向公司发放交易许可证,允许其开始运营。

3. 公司的解散

根据《公司法》的规定,公司可因以下任何原因解散:
① 公司章程规定的期限已届满,除非依照公司章程或本法规定另行延期的。
② 实现公司成立的目标或目标不可能实现时。
③ 公司全部或大部分资产在一定程度上贬值以至于以剩余资产投资被认为是不可行的。
④ 合伙人一致同意在公司任期届满前解散公司,除非公司章程有规定需要特定多数同意。
⑤ 公司和其他公司合并。
⑥ 宣告公司破产。
⑦ 因公司不从事业务或未连续3年发布公司财务报表,发布吊销公司执照的决定。
⑧ 判决解散公司。

除上述情况外,如果"一般合伙公司"或"合资公司"的合伙人或"有限合伙公司的普通合伙人"或"合伙制股份有限公司"的合伙人死亡,公司应解散。此外,在公布判决宣告公司合伙人无法律能力或破产的情况下,公司应予解散。但是,在这种情况下,如果公司章程规定该公司剩余合作伙伴之间继续存续,则该公司仍然是一个法律实体。

如果其损失相当于实收资本的3/4,封闭式股份公司也可能被解散。在此情况下,董事会成员应召开临时股东大会,以解决公司是否应继续存续或在公司章程规定的期限之前解散或采取其他适当措施。

就有限责任公司而言,有限责任公司可能会在其损失相当于公司资本3/4的情况下解散。在这种情况下,经理应向合伙人的临时股东大会提出资本不足的建议补救措施,或可提出解散公司或其他适当措施以供合伙人作出决定。

(六)合并和收购

在科威特的兼并和收购主要受《公司法》《资本管理法》和修订后的《资本管理法实施条例》的约束。监管机构主要是科威特工商部、资本管理局、科威特证券交易所、竞争保护委员会(由2007年第10号法律即《竞争法》设立)及其他部门——具体监管机构视情况而定。

合并可能采取的形式:
① 所涉公司被清算,其资产和负债归属于一家新成立的公司的融合。清算公司的股东获得新公司的股份,以换取其在清算公司中的股份。
② 合并,其中一家或多家公司被现有公司吸收。一家公司的所有资产和负债转移到另一家公司,被吸收公司的股东接收现有公司的新股,被吸收公司被清算。
③ 通过将公司的权利和义务分为两个或两个以上部分来分割和吸收以及将每个部分合并为现有公司。

关于收购,目标公司的地位(例如,公司的活动、上市与否等)决定了《资本管理法》和修订后的《资本管理法实施条例》是否适用于收购。与大多数司法管辖区一样,收购私人公司的股份或资产通常通过资产或股份购买协议实施。如上所述,科威特存在外资所有权限制。科威特法律一般规定,除了在特殊情况下，在科威特开展业务的外国公司必须通过当地代理或通过科威特"合作伙伴"（通常通过与科威特参与者建立科威特公司——科威特参与者拥有该公司至少51%的资本）。如上所述，这些限制有一些例外情况，例如属于海合会个人或实体全权控股的个人和实体，这些个人和实体可以设立并全部拥有当地的科威特实体或其可以在科威特开展业务的分支机构（只有少数限制）；在自由贸易区设立；根据2000年第20号法律，获得建立并拥有一家科威特公司49%以上资本的许可证，并且外国投资者在遵守科威特证券交易所的规则和《资本管理法》规定的情形下可以获得最多100%的股份（科威特银行除外，外国所有权仍然限于49%以下）。

如果公司是上市公司，《资本管理法》和修订后的《资本管理法实施条例》（特别是修订后的《资本管理法实施条例》第9条）为科威特的公众并购提供了法定框架。《资本管理法》和修订后的《资本管理法实施条例》适用于：

① 科威特证券交易所的上市公司的股本为100%的自愿收购要约（VTO）；

② 要约人收购超过上市公司30%的股份时必须向其余股东作出的强制收购要约（MTO）。在这方面，上市公司可能是在科威特证券交易所上市的科威特注册公司，也可能是在科威特证券交易所上市的非科威特注册公司。

在科威特，敌对投标并不常见。根据修订后的《资本管理法实施条例》，可以通过自愿收购要约或强制收购要约收购上市公司。应该注意的是，根据修订后的《资本管理法实施条例》，一旦出价人（直接或间接）占目标公司30%以上的有表决权的股份且该公司在科威特证券交易所上市，就要发起强制收购要约。也可以通过大宗交易拍卖程序获得上市公司的股权，其中可以收购在科威特证券交易所上市的目标公司超过5%的有表决权的股份。大宗交易受科威特证券交易所市场主管2014年第28号决议的约束。如果大宗交易拍卖过程完成后，大宗交易拍卖中的中标人持有上市公司30%以上的有表决权的股份，那么这将迫使投标人根据修订后的《资本管理法实施条例》以强制要约收购方式进行大宗交易。

额外的监管考虑将取决于目标所属的部门，如《中央银行法》适用于中央银行；《保险法》（1961年第24号法律）适用于保险公司；与石油部门有关的法律适用于石油公司。此外，如果并购可能导致控制地位（即占股权比例35%或以上），或者如果它已经处于控制地位，投标人应当将并购情况通知竞争保护委员会。

公共和私人收购通常都有适用外国法律的交易文件。但在这两种情况下，股份转让的手续必须按照科威特的法律完成。

（七）竞争监管

1. 竞争监督部门的保护

竞争保护委员会是负责确保科威特市场公平竞争的实体。竞争保护委员会是根据《竞争法》设立的。根据《竞争法》的规定，竞争保护委员会拥有独立的法人资格，隶属于工商部。根据《竞争法》第14条的规定，竞争保护委员会可以制定政策、接受投诉、进行调查、制定有关科威特竞争的法律和法规，并采取必要措施保护公平竞争。

2.《竞争法》简介

《竞争法》从本质上保证以不损害或影响科威特自由竞争的方式从事经济活动的自由，并且不影响在科威特实施的国际条约和协定。

竞争保护委员会的活动不限于《竞争法》规定的非法活动和/或做法，它可以根据其自由裁量权，参照其他科威特的法律和法规，确定可能对科威特自由竞争有害的活动。

《竞争法》通常限制任何有损自由竞争的协议、合同或做法。但是，竞争保护委员会可以根据当事人的要求允许一些可能限制竞争的做法、协议、合同和决议，以便为消费者带来明显和固定的收益，这些收益大于限制自由竞争的影响。

根据《竞争法》第7条的规定，对自由竞争产生影响的知识产权滥用存在普遍限制。《竞争法》进一步规定，它适用于所有在国外实施的影响科威特竞争的行为；但是，这个域外申请将如何实施还有待观察。

(1) 主导市场地位

《竞争法》将占据支配地位或控制地位定义为一个人或一群人占有35%或更多的科威特市场来直接或间接控制市场的地位。

《竞争法》规定，处于主导市场地位或控制地位的人员不得参与某些被认为是反竞争或滥用其控制地位的特定行为。

根据《竞争法执行条例》第1条的规定，处于控制地位的自然人或法人之间明示或默示的投标、合同或协议不得违反法律规定，最大限度地减少或防止《竞争法》第4条规定的任何形式的竞争。在这方面，《竞争法》第4条明确禁止以下列方式滥用控制地位：

① 通过提高、减少或固定价格或者通过虚构交易或通过违背自然市场机制的其他方法来影响市场上产品的价格，以便损害竞争对手。

② 限制产品进入市场的自由，完全或部分撤回产品，禁止买卖流通，错误地储存或以任何其他方式进行储存。

③ 调配丰富的产品，导致以不切实际的价格流通，影响竞争对手。

④ 禁止或阻碍任何人在市场上随时进行任何经济活动。

⑤ 完全或部分扣留来自市场的产品。

⑥ 以低于实际成本的价格销售产品，目的是损害竞争对手。

⑦ 影响出售、采购、提供或供应产品和服务，无论是邀请招标、投标或供应。

⑧ 在投标邀请的条件下提供供应，用于指定拟购买的商品的品牌或类型。

⑨ 完全或部分停止商品和服务的制造、开发、分销或销售流程，或对其可用性施加限制或条件。

⑩ 根据地理区域、配送中心、客户类型、季节或时间来分割或分配产品市场，以期损害竞争对手。

⑪ 在与原始交易或协议目标无关的条件下，暂停签订合同或协议。

⑫ 通过歧视或有利于其中一个竞争者的信息泄露，忽视竞争者之间的机会平等。

一些确定与具体的义务包含在向竞争委员会报告当事人之间的某些特定交易中，这些交易可能会在特定市场上创造或增加某人的控制地位，并使其处于市场支配地位。在这方面，根据《竞争法》第8条和《竞争法执行条例》第3条的规定，如果包括收购资产、合并或合并管理等在内的交易导致某人达到控制地位或增加控制程度，《竞争法》要求竞争保护委员会通告此类交易（包括交易的具体细节和交易的预期经济效果）。此外，交易需要竞争保护委员会的批准，否则无法进行。此类批准申请必须在拟进行交易日期前至少60天提出。

重要的是，如上所述，《竞争法》不区分当地人和外国人。这意味着，如果合并导致外国当事人拥有超过35%的对当地市场的控制权，其有义务向竞争保护委员会申请批准。

(2) 竞争规范措施

《竞争法》规定了适用于特定条款的各种制裁措施。例如，违反《竞争法》第4条的规定将导致罚款或罚款不超过10万第纳尔或相当于非法收益的价值，以较大者为准。在重复的情况下，罚款可能会翻倍。此外，有关法院可以下令没收与违法行为有关的商品。

竞争保护委员会本身也受《竞争法》的规制，竞争保护委员会的雇员/官员违反《竞争法》的规定也要受到特定的处罚。例如，违反第14条（禁止竞争保护委员会的职员/官员披露他们在履行职责期间获得的任何信息）将会被处以2 000～10 000第纳尔的罚款，甚至更严厉的处罚。

根据《竞争法执行条例》的规定，对于行为、合同、决定或协议是否有害于竞争的最终评估，是竞争保护委员会的责任。因此，如果任何人希望明确遵守《竞争法》，此类人员可向竞争保护委员会询问，以确定竞争保护委员会认为此类人员所提出的行为、合同、决定或协议是否违反《竞争法》。

(八) 税

1. 税制和规则

科威特的主要税收立法是经由2008年第2号法律（以下简称《税法》）及其章程修订的1955年第

3号法律。根据《税法》，在科威特开展贸易或业务的公司实体对其从科威特取得的净收入缴纳所得税。

所得税部（DIT）还要向拥有科威特公司股份的外国非海合会成员国的公司实体征税，通过其从科威特公司获得的净利润的百分比利息征税。无论是科威特人还是非科威特人，个人都不需要在科威特缴纳所得税。

所得税部目前的做法是不对科威特实体和其他海合会成员国设立的企业和公司实体征收所得税。然而，这不是根据《税法》明确豁免的，而仅仅是基于所得税部的现行做法。

科威特与白俄罗斯、比利时、中国、克罗地亚、塞浦路斯、埃塞俄比亚、法国、德国、匈牙利、印度尼西亚、意大利、约旦、韩国、黎巴嫩、毛里求斯、蒙古、荷兰、巴基斯坦、波兰、罗马尼亚、瑞士、叙利亚、突尼斯、土耳其和英国签署了双重税收协定。在科威特或与科威特交易方开展业务时，这些条约能为外国实体减少税务风险。

2. 主要类别和税率

如上所述，科威特适用的主要税种是所得税。根据《税法》的规定，所得税按15%的统一税率征收，允许纳税人按照《税法》的规定扣除某些损失和费用。

科威特适用的附加税包括某些科威特实体应缴纳的关税和其他税款。进口到科威特的物品的关税通常等于这些物品价值的5%。但是，应付的关税可能会根据进口商品的性质而有所不同。

如上所述，封闭式股份公司有义务根据《扎卡特法》的规定按净年利润的1%缴纳宗教税。科威特股份公司还必须每年向科威特科学促进基金会贡献其利润的1%。科威特股份公司的股份在科威特证券交易所上交易，每年还需要支付2.5%的净利润作为劳动力贡献，以资助旨在鼓励科威特国民在私营部门就业的计划。

海合会成员国于2016年执行了《海合会增值税框架协议》。框架协议的签署为在海合会成员国引入增值税铺平了道路。科威特正在起草其国内增值税立法以执行框架协议。科威特的增值税实施日期尚未正式公布。最初预计增值税于2018年年初在科威特实施，但有媒体报道说它不大可能在2019年前实施。预计增值税率将为5%。

3. 税务申报和优惠

纳税人有义务以规定的形式提交阿拉伯文版本的纳税申报表，显示相关纳税期的应纳税所得额，并反映应纳税款。税务申报必须在该公司的纳税期结束后的第4个月的第15天或之前提交给所得税部，除非纳税人要求延期并得到所得税部的批准。纳税人每过30天（或其中一部分）未能提交纳税申报，可以处以1%的罚款。如果纳税人未能提交纳税申报或提交不准确的纳税申报，所得税部有权根据纳税人提供的任何信息估算纳税人的纳税额。

如上所述，目前所得税部的做法不是让科威特实体和海合会成员国在科威特缴纳所得税。同样，根据《促进直接投资法》获得投资许可的外国实体，在向科威特直接投资促进委员会提出申请后，根据科威特直接投资促进委员会制定的规则，从开始运营之日起获得不超过10年的收入和其他税收抵免。

根据《自由贸易区法》的规定，在科威特自由贸易区内设立的项目以及从在其中独家进行的活动所获得的利润免征所得税和关税。

根据修订后的《资本管理法实施条例》的规定，科威特交易所的贸易业务所产生的利润，无论是直接进行还是通过投资组合或基金进行，均可在科威特免交所得税。

（九）证券

1. 概述

在科威特发行的证券（包括外国发行的证券）的市场营销、提供和出售，受《资本管理法》（经修订）和修订后的《资本管理法实施条例》（《资本管理法实施条例》和《资本管理法》一同构成资本管理的法律）的管辖。

资本管理局是监管科威特所有资本市场和证券活动的主要监管机构，包括市场营销、提供和出售本地和外国的发行证券。在科威特，任何证券的市场营销、提供和出售都是允许的。但是，如果外国发行人希望在科威特（即科威特在岸市场）营销、提供和出售外国已发行证券，则必须满足这些要求：无论证券的市场营销、提供和出售是基于私募还是公开发行，都需从资本管理局取得许可证。

2. 监督和监管

根据《资本管理法实施条例》的规定，在科威特营销、提供和出售任何外国证券的许可不能直接发给外国发行人或其外国代表。这种许可证只能由资本管理局向代表外国发行人的科威特当地代理人发放，并且该当地代理人必须是符合特定标准的正式持牌的科威特股份公司。此外，根据《资本管理法实施条例》的规定，当地代理人还必须获得资本管理局颁发的"许可人"许可（定义见《资本法管理实施条例》），以便它可以在科威特从事"证券活动"（例如，向科威特的投资者营销、提供和出售外国发行的证券），尤其是必须获得代表第三方（例如，证券的外国发行人）营销、提供和出售境外发行证券的许可。

换句话说，外国发行人将被禁止在科威特直接营销、提供和出售证券，除非它通过当地代理人获得了必要的从事此类活动的许可。只有当地的银行或投资公司可以成为当地代理商，获得从事此类活动的批准。对于在科威特销售的不同的证券，必须获得单独的许可证。该许可证由外国发行人指定的当地代理人获得。

（十）投资的优惠和保护

1. 优惠政策的结构

虽然科威特没有正式的优惠政策，但其通过某些决议和一般性实践，给予科威特国民优惠，并且在类似程度上给予海合会成员国公民优惠（科威特、阿联酋、巴林、阿曼、卡塔尔和沙特阿拉伯）。但是，科威特继续致力于鼓励外国投资，这体现在建立直接投资促进委员会及其与其他国家缔结的众多投资条约。

也就是说，对海合会成员国的公民给予优惠待遇。例如，关于税收问题，虽然科威特《税法》规定，在科威特经营业务的任何法人团体在科威特产生的纯利润按照15%的固定税率征税，但作为惯例，所得税部不向海合会成员国国民全资拥有的海合会成员国公司实体征税。如果公司实体部分归非海合会成员国公民所有，公司实体将按照外资所有权比例征税。所得税部将对外资所有权比例进行审查。

外国公民通常也只能获得科威特商业企业49%的所有权。然而，根据2002年第141号部长决议，海合会成员国公民以及由海合会成员国公民100%控股的海合会成员国公司可以直接设立当地实体，并拥有该实体100%的股份。同样，作为关于在科威特境内运营的外国营业部门的一般规则的例外情况，2011年第237号部长决议允许满足一定条件的全资海合会成员国实体在科威特建立其分支机构。为了获得类似的权利，非海合会成员国国民必须根据这些一般规则的特殊规定获得许可（例如获得在自由贸易区之一的许可或根据《促进直接投资法》的规定）。

2. 支持特定行业和地区

鉴于最近油价下跌，科威特政府正在鼓励公共和私营部门多元化。尽管《促进直接投资法》不支持特定的行业或地区，但位于负面清单上的产业如原油生产、天然气、氮肥、公共管理、房地产活动等无法享受《促进直接投资法》提供的优惠和奖励。任何符合标准的其他项目都是可以接受的。基于合格投资促进局开发的评分系统的结果，合格的申请人将有权获得某些利益（例如，税收和海关关税豁免、土地分配）。

申请人是否符合《促进直接投资法》的要求和标准，将根据特定的评分系统进行衡量。最重要的是，申请人应该说服投资促进局认真考虑其在科威特投资的重要性；特别是，对科威特市场和经济有积极影响的投资（例如，创造就业机会、技术转让、增加科威特出口、利用科威特产品或服务等）。这些事宜将根据申请人向投资促进局提交的商业研究进行评估。

2013年4月，科威特颁布了支持中小企业的法律。虽然这可能不被视为对特定行业的支持，但根据该法律，一个项目（无论是小型企业还是中型企业）可能包括工业、商业、农业、专业、服务或技术企业，这些企业对于国民收入的发展和多元化起到了直接的促进作用，也符合国内市场和国际市场的要求。此外，这些项目应尽可能地为国民提供工作和培训机会，增强国家实力。

3. 特殊经济区

根据《自由贸易区法》，外国实体可在科威特自由贸易区独立运营，无须委任科威特代理人或设立科威特公司。但是，公司的运营仅限于获得许可的自由贸易区，这对计划在科威特整个区域进行贸易的实体来说是不切实际的。目前在科威特有三个自由贸易区，即 Shuwaikh 港、Al-Abdally 和 Nuwaiseeb。

最近部长理事会决定将这些自由贸易区的管理权转交给投资促进局，以发展和鼓励更多的投资。这一决定尚未实施。

4. 投资保护

科威特是各种双边投资条约（与各国签订了 64 个双边投资条约，目前已生效）、有投资条款的条约（该条约主要调整海合会与诸如美国等国家之间的关系）、与投资有关的文书（例如《纽约公约》《服务贸易总协定》《与贸易有关的知识产权协定》等）以及某些双重征税条约的缔约国。

此外，《促进直接投资法》为外国投资提供了另一层保护，其规定任何持有执照的投资实体（即经投资促进局许可）除依据适用法律的公共利益外，不得以没收或征用，并以项目的实际经济价值来进行补偿。

三、贸易

（一）贸易管理部门

科威特工商部是主要负责监督管理科威特境内商业活动的政府部门，同时还负责与科威特其他政府部门，如科威特中央银行、科威特财政部（以下简称"财政部"）等其他监管机构，一起制定和实施科威特的贸易政策。

科威特海关总署（以下简称"海关总署"）是主要负责承担与科威特的港口以及其他主管部门或其他政府部门指定的检查地点（例如机场、陆上过境点等）的与海关事务相关的所有工作和职责的政府部门。海关总署负责执行由科威特政府部门和其他部门就货物进口所作出的决定，也向其他政府部门（如财政部）提交关于海关流程的建议，供其审议及实施。

（二）贸易类法律、法规简介

科威特有若干管理贸易活动的法律法规。其中，具有特别意义的是《进口法》（1964 年第 43 号法律）、《海合会统一海关法》（以下简称《统一海关法》，经 2003 年第 10 号法律在科威特颁布）以及根据《统一海关法》经 2003 年第 200 号法律颁布的科威特法规。

《进口法》授予工商部向科威特的实体/个人颁发进口许可证的权利，以及制定该种许可证的程序。如果没有前述许可证，不得出于商业目的将物品进口到科威特。《统一海关法》适用于所有通过陆路、海路或空运跨越关税线的进口商品或出口商品。目前，《统一海关法》也适用于其他海合会成员国（即科威特、巴林、阿联酋、沙特阿拉伯、卡塔尔和阿曼）。《统一海关法》及其规定适用于整个海合会成员国域内。然而，根据《统一海关法》的规定，各个国家域内的海关法律之间可能存在一些变化（例如，科威特有专门适用于科威特自由贸易区的规定）。

科威特其他与境内贸易相关的法律包括：经修订的 1997 年第 128 号法律（关于货物的标准规格）、《自由贸易区法》（关于设立自由贸易区）和经修订的 1979 年第 10 号法律（关于监管货物贸易和决定某些指定物品的价格和质量）。

（三）贸易管理

无论是在本国，还是在其他由科威特向贸易组织承诺的地区和科威特缔结各种贸易协定的地区，科威特多年来一直致力于贸易自由化。在这方面，科威特是《关税及贸易总协定》《服务贸易总协定》和《与贸易有关的知识产权协定》的签署国，并且自 1995 年以来一直是世贸组织的成员国。科威特是海合会关税联盟成员国之一，是《大阿拉伯自由贸易协定》的缔约国，也是其他以独立国家身份或以海合会成员国身份与外国签订的其他贸易协定的一方。例如，在 2008 年和 2009 年，海合会与新加坡、欧洲自由贸易联盟（EFTA）签署了第一批自由贸易协定，科威特作为海合会成员国也承认了前述自由贸易协定。科威特以独立国家的身份与德国、印度、荷兰、摩洛哥、中国等国家签订了数十个双边投资条约。

科威特通过执行旨在简化外国实体在科威特开展业务的法律，进一步践行了其对自由贸易的承诺。在这方面，虽然工商部通常要求外国实体在特定的监管范围内运营，但外国实体可以通过在科威特的自由贸易区内经营或由科威特直接投资的项目，使得其商业行为被许多监管法律豁免（例如外国所有权限制、关税、税收等）。其他监管例外适用于海合会成员国的实体和公民。

（四）进出口商品的检验、检疫

《统一海关法》第 52 条至第 59 条规定了货物检验。根据这些条款，指定的海关官员应在关税申报登记后检查货物。一般而言，该等申报包括商业发票、原产地证书、装箱单以及所有商业货物附带的提货单或航空货运单。这些文件必须包含足够的信息，以便适用相关法规、税收和关税。关税根据关税申报的内容进行征收。检查、开箱、运输和其他与检查相关的费用由货物所有人承担。

许多商品或者被特殊管制进口到科威特，或者被完全禁止进口到科威特。举例来说，医疗器械、枪支、爆炸物和烟草制品是受到特殊管制的货物，需要额外的检查程序并得到指定机构进一步批准（例如，药品需要经卫生部批准）。被禁止进口到科威特的商品包括猪肉、含酒精饮料、赌博机器、色情物品、来自被联合抵制国家的货物、毒品和其他违反科威特法律的货物。

（五）海关管理

虽然科威特的出口程序对于自然人和公司来说相对简单，但是科威特的进口程序相对复杂。如果要合法地将商品进口到科威特，进口商必须向工商部申请进口许可证，并且必须在科威特商会登记。只有在科威特商会登记的科威特国民和/或实体才可以持有进口许可证。进口许可证的有效期通常为 1 年，并且相关当事方可以向工商部申请延期。在实践中，在科威特开展业务的外国实体（如果未单独获得许可），通常会通过其在科威特的代理人将其货物/产品进口到科威特。在这种情况下，当地代理人必须持有有效的进口许可证，用以进口该外国实体的货物/产品。

除非另有豁免，否则应对所有进口到科威特的货物缴纳关税。该关税直接支付给海关总署。如果进口商已经跨越了某一海合会成员国的关税线，并且已经因此支付了进口货物的关税，那么他们将不需要缴纳额外的关税。

四、劳动

（一）劳动相关法律、法规简介

私营企业的雇用（本地人和外派人员/外国人）主要受经修订的《私营企业劳动法》（2010 年第 6 号法律）的规制，而石油企业的雇用受经修订的《石油企业劳动法》（1969 年第 28 号法律）的规制，公共部门的雇用受《公共服务法》（1979 年第 15 号法律）的规制。

外国人（不包括海合会成员国公民）想要在科威特合法生活和工作，必须持有工作许可证和居留签证（即"居住证"）。未持有有效居留签证的外国人可能被罚款及驱逐出境。所有外籍雇员（即外籍人员）必须在科威特实体（或个人）担保下，获得允许他们在科威特工作的工作许可。基于前述工作许可，外籍人员可以获得居留签证。

《私营企业劳动法》规定了雇用的最低期限和福利，包括最低工资标准（目前为每月 75 科威特第纳尔）、30 个工作日的带薪年假、每周休息 1 天、8 小时工作制、加班费、70 天产假、病假、解约金、强制性的劳工赔偿保险等。缔约双方不得约定任何低于《私营企业劳动法》规定的最低标准的条款。但是，雇主可以在与员工达成的协议中提供更优越的条款，而且这些条款对双方都具有约束力。

（二）聘用外籍员工的要求

在社会事务和劳工部（以下简称"社工部"）拥有有效劳工档案的在科威特设立的法律实体或科威特个人，可以雇佣外籍员工，并作为担保人为他们取得工作许可和居留签证。根据《人力资源法》（2000年第19号法律）的规定，每个私营公司在雇用外籍员工的同时，必需雇用一定数量的科威特国民。但是，海合会成员国国民不需要前述担保。

1. 工作许可

所有在科威特工作的外籍人员都需要获得工作许可和居留签证。《居留法》（1959年第17号法律）对与居留签证相关的工作许可（工作许可的期限决定了居留签证的期限）进行了规定。工作许可包括多种类型，但通常颁发给私营企业雇员的是《居留法》第18条所规定的工作许可。获得工作许可/居留身份的过程可能很漫长。获得工作许可所需的时间各不相同，取决于雇员的国籍、申请人的职业以及担保人/雇主拥有的可作为担保人办理居留签证的配额等。前述过程可能需要4到8周才能完成。工作许可的期限最少为1年。但是，如果持有居留许可的外国人在科威特以外停留超过6个月（未经事先批准），该外国人的工作许可将被取消。另外，科威特不存在临时工作许可或短于1年期限的工作许可。

2. 工作许可申请程序

申请工作许可和居留签证的程序通常由科威特担保人/雇主践行。如果雇主想要为仍停留在其居住国的雇员获得工作许可，雇主需要提交雇员的身份证明（如护照）和资格证明文件（如大学学位证书），以及签订的雇佣合同。前述文件应附在提交给社工部的工作许可申请中。提交文件后，通常需要大约10—15个工作日才能收到相应的回复。如果申请成功，雇主将获得该雇员的工作许可。该雇员在前往科威特之前，必须在其原籍国接受体检。在抵达科威特时，该雇员的生物识别信息（包括指纹）将被收集及记录，且该雇员需接受进一步的体检。雇主必须支付员工的健康保险，并承担因在雇员的护照上加盖居留签证所产生的费用。

3. 社会保险

缴纳社会保险仅适用于科威特国民和其他海合会成员国国民。私营公司必须为其雇佣的科威特籍（和具有海合会成员国国籍）雇员缴纳社会保险相关费用，其法律依据是《社会保险法》（1976年第61号法律）建立的保险/养老基金制度。《社会保险法》（以及其中所规定的福利）仅适用于在政府、私营公司和石油企业工作的科威特籍（和具有海合会成员国国籍）的雇员。

为了保证基金的资金来源，根据《社会保险法》的规定，雇主需要每月从支付给科威特工人的月薪中扣除10.5%，并缴纳相同数额至社会保险公共机构（即"社保机构"）。此外，雇主有义务每月直接向该基金进行捐款，捐款金额应相当于其所雇佣的科威特籍雇员每月薪水的11.5%。

根据与海合会成员国国民不在其母国工作相关的《统一海合会成员国法》（即《统一社会保险法》），在科威特工作的海合会成员国国民也必须根据科威特的社会保险计划缴纳相应费用。

（三）出入境

1. 签证类型

（1）商务访问签证

商务访问签证/商务签证是通过科威特担保人（通常是公司或其他形式的商业机构）进行申请的一种签证类型。其主要目的是为了容许申请人的商业伙伴能够短期访问停留。该签证通常在签发后90天内有效，在科威特的有效停留期为30天。

（2）工作签证

提供工作签证是为了最终取得由公司或机构作为担保人的居留/工作许可。该签证包括第17条（发给由政府部门或政府机构协助雇用的雇员）、第18条（发给私营企业的雇员）、第19条（被称为自雇签证/工作许可）和第20条（发给家政人员和家庭帮佣）所列出的签证种类。

（3）旅游签证

这种签证适用于特定国家和地区，并可以在科威特国际机场获得，其有效期为签发后 3 个月。可以申请此类签证的国家和地区包括：美国、英国、法国、意大利、希腊、荷兰、卢森堡、芬兰、西班牙、梵蒂冈、圣马力诺、加拿大、澳大利亚、瑞士、奥地利、新西兰、日本、比利时、丹麦、瑞典、葡萄牙、爱尔兰、摩纳哥、安道尔、列支敦士登、中国香港特区、韩国、新加坡、马来西亚、文莱、波兰、挪威、德国、不丹、格鲁吉亚、斯洛文尼亚和越南。上述名单可以由移民局自行修改。

（4）医疗签证

这种签证是出于医疗原因而签发的。这种签证的申请过程和有效期将取决于个案中的医疗报告和医生建议。

（5）探亲访问签证

这种签证适用于外国居民为其非居留家庭成员申请。这种签证通常仅限于第一级亲属关系的非居民（即母亲、父亲、姐妹、兄弟、丈夫、妻子、孩子）。该种访问关系需要签署承诺书，保证探亲访问签证不会转为居留和工作许可。根据国籍，该种签证所签发的有效期为 1 个月至 3 个月不等。

2. 出入境限制

一旦外籍人员获得了居留签证，他们就可以自由出入境。但是，如果外籍人员一次性在国外停留超过 6 个月（除非事先获得政府的批准），其居留签证可能会被取消。然而，在办理居留签证期间，外派人员必须停留在科威特（3 周左右）。

（四）工会和劳工组织

《私营企业劳动法》中，有关设立"企业联合组织"的设想，即通过将该等企业联合组织联合起来，组成"工会"，用来组织和保护其成员（即员工）在工作场所的利益。创建一个企业联合组织，需要经过社工部的批准。但是，根据目前的做法，社工部只批准组建只有科威特国民才能成为相关成员的企业联合组织。

（五）劳动纠纷

《私营企业劳动法》规定了个人对雇主索赔的具体程序以及雇主向个人索赔的程序。在向法庭起诉前，劳动争议应当先提交至社工部的劳动部门。社工部应当召集双方并尝试以友好的方式解决争议。如果无法达成和解，那么在雇员提出要求的 1 个月之内，社工部必须将该等争议提交至初审法院，并附上案件摘要、双方的证据以及社工部自己的意见。法院必须在 3 天内确定庭审日期，并通知双方。案件会以简易程序进行审理。

五、知识产权

（一）知识产权法律、法规简介

知识产权（即商标、有版权保护的资料、专利、设计等）的取得、转让和保护受科威特法律的规定和管理，特别是认可了《海合会成员国商标法》的《商标法》（2015 年第 13 号法律）、经 2013 年第 71 号法律修订的《专利法》（1962 年第 4 号法律）以及《著作权法》（2016 年第 22 号法律）。

科威特在努力保护知识产权的方面取得了重大进展。科威特批准了《保护工业产权巴黎公约》和《保护文学和艺术作品伯尔尼公约》，前述条约于 2014 年 12 月 2 日在科威特生效。同日，科威特成为国际保护工业产权联盟（即巴黎联盟）和国际保护文学和艺术作品联盟（即伯尔尼联盟）的成员国之一。通过加入前述公约，科威特成为保护商标和著作权的国际体系中的一部分，并且扩大了受版权保护的商品和服务的国际贸易体系。这是科威特在文化、娱乐、信息和技术交流层面的重要举措。

（二）专利申请

科威特在 2013 年通过了新《专利法》，同时废止了旧《专利法》（1962 年第 4 号法律）中的某些规定。旧《专利法》中的某些规定仍然有效,并且继续对该法律所覆盖的专利所有人的权利义务进行规制(除了某些专门由新《专利法》规范的事项外)。

《专利法》规定了发明、工业设计和集成电路专利的申请和注册。在原法律通过后的很多年里,科威特专利和商标局(以下简称"专利商标局")收到过前述项目的申请,但从未对该等申请进行审查。专利商标局没有采取进一步行动的原因是,除了工业设计外,它没有检查其他专利申请的专业技术。根据上述制度,申请人只会收到一份证书,证明当事方提交过申请,除此之外再无其他作用。

目前,专利商标局继续受理有关工业设计的申请,而其他专利申请则会被转交至位于沙特阿拉伯利雅得的海合会专利局。在利雅得的海合会专利局获得注册的专利,在科威特同样有效。

(三)商标注册

除非涉及某些违禁物品,即酒类、猪肉产品以及与某些受限制活动(例如赌博)相关的商品,商标、服务标志、标识和商品名称可根据《商标法》在科威特按照国际分类标准申请注册。前述注册的有效期从提交注册申请开始最长为10年,并且可以在到期前申请延展相同的期限。

在科威特使用外国商标时,所有人应考虑根据《商标法》对该外国商标进行注册。因为比起未在科威特注册商标,根据《商标法》注册的规定会给该商标的所有人提供更多的保护。

最近颁布的《商标法》及其实施条例包含了新的规定,用以增加对已注册和未注册商标所有人的保护。同时,新法还规定了商标许可协议。新法规定了缔约双方在签订商标许可协议时所应遵守的形式要件和限制,以及登记此类协议的程序。

(四)著作权法

《著作权法》第3条规定,该法所给予的保护适用于任何类型、表达形式、目的等的创作作品。寻求保护其著作权的一方无须为了获得《著作权法》所给予的保护在注册处登记相同的内容。然而,为了提高作者对于著作权保护权利的证明能力,其可以向科威特国家图书馆(以下简称"国家图书馆")申请并要求存放需要保护的作品。

国家图书馆有权接受作者或创作人或其继承者或官方代表存放作品的申请。每项申请只允许申请一个作品分类。如果作品被接受存放,国家图书馆将对该作品进行分类并出具一份能示明序列号、存放日期和国际分类的证书。

(五)知识产权保护措施

1. 专利

专利、图纸、设计或实用新型的所有权人或权利持有人可以根据《专利法》提出控告,以保护其知识产权。在民事或刑事诉讼中,原告可请求法院发出采取预防措施的命令,特别是扣押仿制品以及用于实施该等犯罪的设备和机器。原告可提交一份要求采取前述措施的申请,同时提交一份记载了其发明、实用新型或工业图纸或设计登记的声明文件作为证据。如有需要,可以指定专家和其他法院工作人员协助执行为采取此类措施而发出的命令。

《商标法》和《著作权法》特别授权了权利或所有权的持有人可在提交实质侵权诉讼(和必要的单方依据)前,为防止专利侵权和违法行为,向科威特法院申请执行预防措施的命令,以作为初步措施。然而,《专利法》则不同,仅在专利侵权或违反《专利法》的实质案件被提起后,《专利法》才授予此类权利。

《专利法》规定,如构成下列行为,将受到监禁期限不超过一年且罚款不超过1 000科威特第纳尔的处罚或两者择一的处罚:复制已经获得专利或实用新型的发明;复制已注册的工业图纸或设计;销售、许诺销售或交易、进口、为交易之目的而获取任何仿制产品或材料,显示所复制的仿制产品的工业图纸或设计所包含的知识,与在科威特已注册的是一致的;以及在产品、广告、商标或其他方面非法放置任何信息,导致被认为已经取得工业图纸或设计的专利或注册。

2. 商标

《商法典》中对商标侵权的救济规定已经被《商标法》中的规定所废止。《商标法》将《商法典》

中关于预防措施的规定替换为一套更详细的规定。根据这些规定，如果存在侵害商标所有人或商标权利持有人的行为，或有必要避免即将发生的侵权行为，商标所有人或商标权利持有人可以在向主管法院提交诉状后获得法院命令，以利用一个或多个的预防程序，包括：

① 为描述侵权行为或违法行为而对某一地点进行检查；获取此类被侵权物品或货物的详细信息；已经用于或将用于上述侵权行为或违法行为的材料、工具和设备；采取某些行为以保存侵权行为的证据。

② 附上上述提到的物品以及任何显示侵权行为结果或产品的物品。

③ 防止侵权物品或货物到达商业销售点；停止基于海关放行的分销；以及防止其出口。

④ 停止或防止侵权行为或违反商标法律法规行为的发生。

根据《商标法》的有关规定，在考虑采取预防措施时，简易法庭的法官必须适用的检验标准是：是否有正在进行的针对权利或权利持有人的侵权行为或违法行为，该等侵权行为或违法行为是否具有紧迫性，以及该等拟被采取的预防措施对于防止侵权行为或违法行为的继续进行或预防侵权行为或违法行为的发生，是不是必要的。

除上述检验标准外，法院可自行决定视情况要求申请人提供证据证明侵权行为或者证明违法行为或侵权行为即将发生；提供充分信息，使法院能够执行此类预防措施；确定特定的产品或商品等。

除了由法院决定的特殊案件外，简易法庭须在前述申请提交之日起10日内作出决定。若简易法庭在审查事实后，发现迟延可能对申请人造成不可挽回的损害或妨碍司法或证据的销毁等情况的，简易法庭可以通知该等申请的被告或单方面行使其自由裁量权发布命令。

根据《商标法》的规定，伪造或假冒已经根据《商标法》注册的商标且以使大众混淆或误导大众的方式伪造此类商标者、恶意使用伪造商标或假冒商标者或者恶意将第三方所有的商标用于其产品或商品或服务者，在任何其他法律未规定更严厉处罚的情况下，将被判处1个月至3年的监禁和金额不低于5 000沙特里亚尔或与之相当的海合会成员国等值货币且不高于2 000 000沙特里亚尔的罚款，或两项处罚中的一项。

明知产品或商品带有或使用假冒或伪造的商标，没有法律依据地销售或许诺销售或交易或为销售而持有者及为该等假冒、伪造商标提供服务者；使用未经注册的商标；在其商标、信头纸、纸张或商业文件上非法书写或标注导致大众相信其商标是注册商标；故意不将已经注册的可以对其产品或商品进行区分的商标放置于或用于其产品或商品；以及持有并使用工具或材料对注册商标或驰名商标进行仿冒或伪造，在任何其他法律未规定更严厉处罚的情况下，将被判处1个月至1年的监禁和金额不低于1 000沙特里亚尔或与之相当的海合会成员国等值货币且不高于100 000沙特里亚尔的罚款，或两项处罚中的一项。

在反复进行侵权行为或违法行为的情况下，违法行为人应被处以不超过违法行为所适用的最高处罚双倍的处罚，且违法行为人的店铺或企业应被关闭15日以上6个月以下。根据《商标法》执行细则中规定的程序，前述裁判或命令应当由违法行为人承担。根据《商标法》的规定，违法行为或侵权行为的累犯是指，因构成《商标法》所规定的违法行为或不当行为已经被宣告有罪的人，自其前一项违法行为或不当行为被终审法院宣告有罪之日起的3年内再次进行类似的违法行为。

3. 著作权

根据《著作权法》的规定，当对《著作权法》规定的任何权利有侵害时，被侵害人可向有关法院提出申请，请求法官发出执行一项或多项预防措施的命令。

不同于《商标法》要求原告自预防命令发出后20日内向有关法院提起实质性诉讼，《著作权法》规定的期限较短，即要求原告自预防命令发出后15日内提起实质性诉讼。不同于《商标法》所规定的针对预防命令的发出有20天的申诉期限，《著作权法》为相关当事方规定了30天的申诉期限。

根据《著作权法》的规定，未获得作者或有关权利所有者的书面许可，侵害《著作权法》所规定的属于作者或有关权利所有者的文学权利或财产权利的，包括将任何作品公布于众，将被判处6个月至两年的监禁，以及500纳尔以上1 000第纳尔以下的罚款，或两项处罚中的一项。

六、环境保护

(一)环境保护监督部门

为了控制环境污染以及努力维护其自然资源,科威特颁布了《环境保护法》(2014年第42号法律)。该法第三章通过设立以总理(或副总理)为首、由该总理或副总理选出的部长级成员所组成的最高环境委员会,来进行环境事务的管理。

此外,《环境保护法》还设立了一个有关环境事务的公共机构,被称为公共环境保护局(以下简称"环保局"),负责与保护科威特环境相关的所有工作和职责,包括科威特境内项目建设许可证的颁发。在这方面,《环境保护法》要求所有计划执行将对环境产生影响的项目的公司,向环保局提供环境影响评估报告。该等报告的批准通常由环保局颁发的允许该等项目继续进行的"作业许可单"加以证明。

环保局局长(或他授权的任何人)有权给予违反《环境保护法》及其相关规定[该法第四部分第一章所涵盖的事项(即保护海洋环境不受污染)除外]的违法行为人宽限期,用以快速纠正其违法行为。如果该违法行为人在30天内未纠正其违法行为的,或确定该违法行为的继续将对环境造成严重损害的,环保局有权采取必要的法律措施制止这种违法行为,关闭该企业或取消已颁发的许可证,但不影响《环境保护法》中规定的任何其他处罚的实施和对因此类违法行为造成的损害的赔偿要求。

(二)环境保护法律、法规简介

《环境保护法》及其相关条例(由部长决议定期颁布)是关于科威特环境保护的主要法律。

根据《环境保护法》的规定,污染被广泛地定义为——在一定期间内,在数量上或特征上有益于环境中的任何污染材料或因素存在的所有人类活动和自然活动,该等活动可能直接地或间接地、个别地或与其他材料或因素相关联地,导致公共卫生的损害;或从事可能导致自然生态系统恶化或妨害享受生活和得益于私人和公共财产的工作和活动。

污染源被《环境保护法》定义为一个地方,通过它,材料、污染物或能源被排出、释放或排放到周围的环境中(无论是空气、水还是土壤)。污染源可以是固定的(如烟囱、污水和工业区域管道以及垃圾处理场),也可以是可移动的(如车辆、船只和飞机)。

污染损害被定义为由有害物质导致的环境污染所造成的损失,无论其造成的原因是什么。这一损失包括因采取旨在打击污染和修复的措施所产生的费用,以及这些措施所造成的任何损失或损害。

根据《环境保护法》第52条和第53条的规定,所有实体和设施都必须采取指定的措施,防止排放物或空气污染物高于允许的限值。该等设施的所有者或运营者须采取一切必要的预防措施,以防止可能导致环境污染的污染物泄露或排放。

根据《环境保护法》第54条的规定,所有实体和个人都必须遵守相关规定,且在进行生产活动、提供服务或参与任何其他活动时不得超过允许的噪音水平。

《环境保护法》第八章提出了对造成任何环境损害的民事责任和赔偿。该法的第七章还规定了处罚。这些处罚包括可能的罚款和监禁,包括因违反《环境保护法》第25条(关于核废料的进口/储存)的规定而可能被判处死刑。

《环境保护法》规定在内政部设立一个名为"环境警察"的专门警务单位。该单位的任务是执行最高环境委员会规定的环境法律和条例。该单位还为与环保局合作的司法工作人员的活动提供支持。

(三)环境保护评估

许多实体(政府的和非政府的)都参与了环境保护。然而,环保局在环境保护以及任何(潜在的或实际的)环境污染物的评估中,扮演着主要角色。环保局最近推出了许多项目和培训课程,用以提高科威特个人、居民和实体对环境保护的认识,在科威特居民中构建负责任的环境行为的意识。为此,政府推出了一个名为"Beatona"(意指我们的环境)的网站,提供有关环境保护的信息。

环保局还建立了自己的网站,努力让参与到环境保护的众多组织、参与到科威特项目开发的其他政府机构以及保护科威特环境的个人之间建立合作关系。环保局还旨在提供与环境保护相关的有效电子服务和信息来源。这是通过提供有利于研究人员和非专业人员的信息来完成的。环保局的网站包括有关环境状况的最新信息；提供了一个综合的环境数据库，其中包括：科威特的数字地图、一个完整的用于环保目的的地理信息系统以及适用于所有省的列明了水、土壤和空气数据的环境地图集。

另一个在环境问题上至关重要的组织是1974年3月31日成立的科威特环境保护协会。它是在第一次联合国人类环境会议（瑞典斯德哥尔摩，1972年）上发起的。这是科威特环境保护协会的起点，也是科威特保护环境新时代的开端。科威特环境保护协会多年来一直与各政府机构合作，建议环境保护立法，并采取措施健全环保法律，以加强对环境的保护。

农业事务和渔业资源公共局是根据1983年第94号法律设立的。其设立是为了开展与农业发展和提升相关的工作，包括在植物和畜牧领域。其设立还为了渔业资源的开发和保护，以及对道路、庭院、公共花园、公园、造林区域和动物园的环境美化和植树造林进行设计、监督和追踪。

科威特科学研究院（以下简称"科研院"）是一个独立的国立科学研究机构。它是在1967年因日本的阿拉伯石油有限公司部分履行其与科威特政府签订的石油特许协议项下的义务而设立。科研院的最初作用是致力于开发三个领域：石油、沙漠农业和海洋生物学。自那时起，科研院的作用和责任大大扩展，包括促进国家工业的进步和开展研究以应对主要挑战，如保护环境、可持续管理科威特的自然资源、负责任地管理水和能源，以及农业创新方法的发展。

七、争议解决

（一）争议解决的方法和机构

科威特司法体系是与埃及和几个欧洲国家类似的大陆法系。但是，它具有以下独特的特点：
① 公共政策在司法审查过程中起着重要作用；
② 采用审问式程序而非控告式程序，大量依赖书面的法律备忘录；
③ 大量依赖法院的专家部门，尤其是涉及复杂的商业和技术事项的争议；
④ 程序性和实质性方面主要受成文法和指令的制约，判例法不具有优先权。

1. 科威特司法体系的结构

（1）普通（Al Kulliya）法院及其巡回法庭
① 小额诉讼/简易法庭：该等法庭的管辖范围涉及紧急和相对较小的事项，包括临时保护令、旅行禁令、对固定资产和动产的司法扣押及临时执行程序；此外，小额诉讼/简易法庭的管辖权是有限的，仅审查5 000科威特第纳尔（约15 250美元）以下的民事和商事诉求；
② 一审法庭：审查不属于小额诉讼/简易法庭管辖范围的事项；
③ 行政法庭：审查涉及科威特政府及其下属部门和公共机构的事项；
④ 政府法庭：审查不属于行政法院管辖范围的所有政府事项；
⑤ 民事和商事法庭：审查根据科威特《民法典》和《商法典》提起的诉讼；
⑥ 劳动法庭：审查与私营和石油企业的雇用相关的所有事项；
⑦ 租赁法庭：审查根据1978年35号关于不动产租赁的法律（提起的）所有诉讼，包括出租人和承租人的权利和义务；
⑧ 刑事法庭：审查涉及刑事违法行为和交通违规的事项；
⑨ 个人事务法庭：审查与家庭、个人身份、离婚、监护、信托和遗产有关的事项；
⑩ 未成年人事务法庭：审查与21岁以下公民有关的事项。

除上述法庭外，普通法院还有三个更重要的部门：
① 认证部门：认证部门专门从事以下各项事务：
• 签名和文件的认证；
• 文件的公证；
• 有关文件官方性质的认定。
② 专家部门：专家部门审查法院可能涉及的技术和复杂事项，并经常在影响案件结果方面发挥决

定性的作用。当某一事项被提交给专家部门时,适用以下内容:
- 在专家部门提出报告和建议之前,法院的诉讼程序有效地被搁置;
- 专家部门的主要职能涉及收集和分析证据;
- 专家部门有权要求当事人合作,以及在不合规或出现进一步问题时将争议转回法院;
- 专家部门向法院报告其调查结果和结论;
- 专家部门的报告通常会得到法院的认可,但不具有约束力,也可能被受影响的当事人反驳;
- 不同意专家部门报告的当事人可提交一份书面备忘录,说明其事实和法律异议。

③ 执行部门:执行部门通常负责:
- 法律通知送达,包括传票;
- 使法院的决定和规则生效,包括处罚;
- 执行法院判决。

(2)上诉法院

上诉法院的管辖权通常是对来自普通法院的上诉案件进行审查,但是上诉法院也有权对上诉案件进行重新审理(案件审理由高等法院进行,对所有在下级法院或法庭审理过的事实或法律重新审理,就如同之前没有进行过审理)。上诉法院定期进行重审。除了最高法院接受的上诉外,上诉法院作出的判决是最终判决。

(3)最高法院

最高法院对于与科威特法律适用、解释及执行相关的事项拥有最终审判权,同时最高法院也有权修正下级法院在审理中出现的程序瑕疵和实质瑕疵。

2. 仲裁

科威特是《承认及执行外国仲裁裁决公约》(1958年,以下简称《纽约公约》)的签约国。然而,科威特仅承认其他已经签署了《纽约公约》的成员国所作出的仲裁裁决。

如果当事人各方在所达成的协议中一致同意以仲裁作为解决争议的途径,那么科威特法院对于因该等协议所引发的争议将不享有管辖权。对某一外国仲裁裁决的执行请求与其他的原始请求相同,只是科威特法院不会对案件的实体问题进行审查。

海合会成员国的法院判决在科威特可以得到承认和执行。非海合会成员国的判决和仲裁裁决(当《纽约公约》不适用时),如果满足以下条件,可以得到执行:

① 争议中的外国法律需要有承认和执行科威特判决或仲裁的条约或先例。

② 外国判决、命令或裁决需提交给对应管辖权的司法法庭或仲裁庭根据该外国司法管辖权的实质和程序规则进行判决。

③ 当事方有被传唤和充分表达自身观点的,法院的判决或仲裁裁决对于案件的实体问题有明确的判断。

④ 外国判决、命令或仲裁裁决是终局的,没有进一步上诉且可被立即执行。

申请执行的外国判决、命令或仲裁裁决不得与科威特判决相冲突,也不得有违科威特的公共政策或公序良俗。

科威特与海合会成员国和/或阿拉伯国家有签署关于承认及执行法院命令和判决的区域性条约。

(二)外国法律的适用

当事人通常可以自由选择外国法律来管辖他们的合同。在这方面,《处理涉外关系法》(1961年第5号法律,以下简称《冲突法》)第59条作了相关规定。根据该规定,应当适用合同当事人居住国的法律。如果当事人居住地不同,除非当事人另有协议或有安排显示有适用其他法律的意图,否则应当适用该等合同执行地所在国的法律。

然而,《冲突法》第73条规定,如果外国法律违反科威特公共秩序或公共道德而无法在科威特适用,则应当适用科威特法律。

实践中,政府实体不太可能同意受外国法律的管辖。

八、其他

（一）反商业贿赂

1. 反商业贿赂法律、法规简介

商业贿赂是本部分的主题，是一种腐败形式，其未必涉及政府人员或机构。商业贿赂是贿赂的一种，通常涉及潜在购买者代理人或雇员进行的腐败交易，其目的是为了使供应商获得超出其他商业竞争者的优势。

（1）刑法

科威特关于贿赂犯罪的主要法律是 1970 年第 31 号法律。该法律对于科威特《刑法典》（1960 年第 16 号法律）中的某些条款进行了修订，并且包含了限制支付、接受及促进贿赂的条款。

在科威特，任何公职人员为其自身或其他人，要求或接受任何礼物或馈赠，用以履行或放弃履行任何与该公职人员的公共职责有关的行为，应被视为违反《刑法典》关于贿赂的条款（经 1970 年第 31 号法律修订），构成贿赂。公职人员如被认定为犯有该等犯罪的，将会被处以监禁和 / 或罚款。

任何个人为了让公职人员履行或放弃履行任何与该公职人员的公共职责有关的行为，向公职人员提供礼物或馈赠的，应被视为违反《刑法典》关于贿赂的条款。该人如被认定为构成该等犯罪的，也将会被处以监禁和 / 或罚款。

《刑法典》第 43 条规定：贿赂所指的"公职人员"，不仅指政府官员和雇员，也指在商业交易中，由政府或政府的某一实体担任股东 / 所有者的企业、公司、协会和组织的董事会成员、董事、经理和雇员。因此，《刑法典》中对贿赂条款也可以作为对在政府或政府某一实体担任股东或所有的企业、公司、协会和组织中工作的非政府或私营部门雇员提起贿赂指控的基础和潜在依据。

对于向政府雇员或官员给予贿赂的行为，除了《刑法典》的规定外，建立起科威特反腐败机构的科威特 2016 年第 2 号法律的规定也应当加以参考。

《刑法典》中针对贿赂的禁止性规定不仅仅适用于政府官员履行他们的公共职责方面，该等规定也可以适用于政府作为股东或所有者的非政府企业实体或商业公司中的个人。

（2）竞争法

科威特在 2007 年 4 月 29 日通过了"关于竞争保护"的科威特《竞争法》（2007 年第 10 号法律），用以取代之前科威特关于非法竞争的法律。《竞争法》于 2009 年 8 月 22 日在《科威特政府公报》上公布其实施条例之后开始生效。

《竞争法》的意义在于它列举了被禁止的商业行为，创设了一个负责执行和管理该等法律规定的政府机构，确立了对处于控制位置（指直接或间接控制 35% 的市场）的个人的限制和报告义务，并且要求个人在进行法律规定的可能被视为威胁市场自由竞争的交易前需要获得某些批准。

《竞争法》禁止对科威特的自由竞争有限制或危害的行为。该法律进一步限制处于控制地位的自然人和法人的某些行为。《竞争法》第 4 条规定，对自由竞争有危害的协议、合同和做法是被禁止的。该法律进一步规定了处于控制地位的个人或实体被禁止滥用该等控制地位。

根据《竞争法》的规定，任何意图危害竞争的做法都是必须被禁止的。任何意图处于"控制"地位的当事方都被禁止滥用其控制地位从事任何有害于自由竞争的行为。

我们进一步注意到，违反《竞争法》可能会构成一种"腐败犯罪"，从而触发《反腐败法》（2016 年第 2 号法律）的适用。

（3）资本市场法

经修订的《资本市场法（细则）》的第八章第 1 条至第 6 条规定："被许可人"（指经资本市场管理局许可，从事一项或多项经修订的《资本市场法（细则）》规定的证券活动的自然人或公司法人）在从事证券活动时，不得直接或间接地向其客户支付任何费用或佣金、提供财产性或非财产性的利益或礼物。

此外，被许可人禁止接受任何利益或礼物，除非遇到下列情况：

① 与鼓励被许可人向其客户提供更好的服务无关的费用、佣金或非财产性利益，例如：象征性的

礼物；

② 被许可人因向客户提供服务而产生的费用或消费金额，例如：安全保护费用、交割和结算的佣金以及其他与被许可人忠诚、公平和专业履行其职责以实现客户利益不冲突的费用，该等禁止同样适用于被许可人的雇员。

2. 反商业贿赂监管部门

针对违反《刑法典》中反贿赂规定的行为，检察官办公室将对该等罪犯进行起诉，同时反腐败委员会对腐败和贿赂相关犯罪拥有进行调查、管理、报告、劝阻及监督管理的权力。虽然反腐败委员会与检察官办公室及社会组织紧密协作，但是，它主要侧重于公职人员的违法行为。

对于违反《竞争法》的行为，负责执行反竞争规定的政府机关是反竞争管理局。资本市场管理局是负责执行《资本市场法》的政府机关。

3. 惩罚性行为

根据《刑法典》的规定，收受贿赂的，将被判以最高10年的监禁以及相当于受贿金额2倍的罚款（最低不少于50科威特第纳尔——相当于178美元）。

根据《竞争法》的规定，任何人如果违反了《竞争法》第4条的规定，将被处以不超过100 000科威特第纳尔的罚款或相当于已经获得的非法收入金额的罚款，以较高者为准。法官也可以命令没收货物。如果再犯，罚款将翻倍，同时物品将被没收。

被许可人如果违反《资本市场法》的规定，将会被处于不少于5 000科威特第纳尔且不多于50 000科威特第纳尔的罚款。

（二）工程承包

1. 许可制度

《公开招标法》（2016年第49号法律）是一部规定了科威特公共机构在进行采购货物、签署合同，以及接受服务时与公开招标相关的法律。有权在公开招标中参与投标的当事方包括：

① 根据招标性质登记的且在供应商或承包商中注册过的科威特公司；

② 外国公司。如果外国公司被邀请参与投标，该外国公司不需要为了投标聘请代理人或科威特合伙人，但是，出于实际操作的考虑，在竞标成功后，应该聘请当地代理人或合伙人从事相应的工作。根据招标的技术规格和需求，招标可以仅针对国有企业或外国公司。

公开招标可以分为单个或两个阶段进行。根据要履行的合同的要求，单个阶段招标可以包括两类报价（技术报价和财务报价）或者仅包括财务报价。如果实际上无法向参与投标者完全展示规定采购的技术要求和合同要求以获得有竞争力的报价的，可以分两个阶段进行招标。在此情况下，单个阶段的招标文件需要说明目的、期望的表现、对规格的总体描述、其他特性以及对于履行合同的资质要求。对于投标人的公告应根据该等文件进行制作。在第一阶段结束时，相关政府机构将排除不符合要求的投标者或因某些缺点而导致实质上不符合条件的投标者。然后，相关政府机构会邀请技术报价没有被排除的投标者进行最终投标，包括价格。

2. 禁区

《公开招标法》不适用于：

① 国防、国民警卫队及内政部；

② 科威特中央银行；

③ 科威特石油公司及该公司全资拥有的公司；

④ 公共单位和机构的即时投资交易。

对于前述①到③项，将设立专门委员会负责处理采购交易。

3. 投标邀请和投标

科威特的投标程序包括以下阶段：

（1）邀请投标的公告或邀请出价或资格预审的公告

该等公告应当刊登在政府公报上，同时在中央招标委员会网站上公布。该等公告也可能被刊登在定期的商业刊物或适当的技术杂志或专业杂志上。邀请信息需包括：

① 负责招标的政府部门及其地址；
② 需求项目、承包工程或服务的性质；
③ 投标文件或资质的要求及费用；
④ 申请资格预审或出价要求的方式，包括地点和截止日期。

在下列情况下，投标邀请或资格要求必须同时以阿拉伯语以外的另一语种进行刊登：

① 招标或出价在外国；
② 招标仅限于外国公司。

（2）资格预审

投标人必须满足招标文件中所列的要求或满足被筛选的资格预审的要求。根据要求，可以为一个项目或在特定阶段进行资格预审。如果投标人认为其符合要求，应提交所要求的具体文件。相关机构会列出通过资格预审的投标人。

（3）参与投标

在大多数情况下，技术方案和财务方案在这一阶段是需要被提交的。这两份方案应被分开提交。技术方案包括：

① 投标保证金；
② 所提供的方案的总体条件、具体条件和技术数据；
③ 如果根据招标文件要求，有一部分工作需要转包，需要提供分包商的完整信息、数据；
④ 招标文件需要的其他文件或数据。

财务方案包括：

① 投标人认可的出价公式；
② 价格清单和工程量清单；
③ 根据投标期间其他可能影响方案条款中的财务价值的因素；
④ 招标文件需要的其他文件或数据。

（4）评估及开标

在不需要技术检验的情况下，最终的中标者应是符合招标文件要求的最低出价者。如果招标需要技术方案和财务方案的，且需要复杂的技术、高水平的工程、精密的技术特性和高成本，中标人应是满足招标文件要求的最低出价者——在对技术方案和财务方案评估完成之后。中标者将会得到书面通知，同时中标决定将会被刊登在政府公报及中央招标委员会网站。

（5）履约保证金及签约

中标人应在得知中标后10天内为项目提交履约保证金。中标人将在提交履约保证金后30天内被邀请签约。如果中标人未能签约或提交履约保证金，或因其他原因退出，相关政府部门将会没收其投标保证金。未能签约的，也可能被没收履约保证金。

（三）公私合营模式

根据当地的具体情况，本文对其他与投资相关的法律法规作如下介绍。

在过去的几年中，科威特颁布了若干与公私合营模式（PPP）相关的法律。2007年以前，由私营部门运营的国营部门经济项目基本上是根据大量法律的结合，这些法律包括《公共采购法》（1964年第37号法律——已经被《公共招标法》替代）和管理政府土地出租的法律（经1980年第105号法律修订）。

然而，2007年科威特政府颁布了关于建设——经营——转让运营及类似制度的法律，即2008年第7号法律（以下简称《BOT法》）。该法是首次被载入名册的专门监管公私合作模式的法律。《BOT法》及其执行规定针对科威特不同行业部门规定了设立法律实体（项目公司）以执行项目和建立公私合作项目的采购流程。随着《BOT法》的颁布，合伙技术局（PTB）在众多行业中启动了大量的公私合作项目，包括能源、铁路、医院、劳动城市、学校等。执行规定和与世界银行合作制定的合伙技术局指南,为采购程序提供了进一步的指导。

然而,《BOT法》被与公共部门和私营部门之间合伙相关的《公私合营法》(2014年第116号法律)及其执行规定所废止及替代。《公私合营法》作为《BOT法》的改进版本,是源自于科威特政府在根据《BOT法》购买首个公私项目的过程中,为了应对投资者、贷方和采购实体所遇到的困难和障碍而积累的经验来制定的。这被视为积极和主动的行为。《公私合营法》建立了科威特公私合营项目管理局(KAPP)以取代合伙技术局。《公私合营法》现在是基本法,为在政府拥有的土地上进行跨部门采购、实施公私合作项目提供指导。

在《公私合营法》颁布前,政府部门颁布了关于建立科威特股份公司的2010年第39号法律(以下简称《IWPP法》),该公司将承担电力、海水淡化工厂的建设和执行。《IWPP法》后来被2012年第28号法律和2015年第19号法律修订。《IWPP法》专门规定了与能源和海水淡化相关的公私合营项目。该法律确定了能源项目由于其技术性质和对于国家的经济和社会重大影响,需要由专门的法律予以监管。

《公私合营法》废止了关于在科威特设立股份公司的2008年第40号法律,该公司承担对劳动力城市所在州的建设、运营和转移。虽然能源和海水淡化项目仍然要根据《IWPP法》进行采购,但是劳动力城市项目现在根据《公私合营法》进行采购。换言之,对于那些属于IWPP项目的,但却不能适用《IWPP》的事项,可适用《公私合营法》(《公私合营法》被视为兜底的监管法律)。

至今,成功完成的公私合营项目只有一个[即北祖尔(Az Zour北部)海水淡化项目一期]。换言之,大量的公私合营项目仍在继续进行中,包括乌姆海曼(Um Al Hayman)废水项目和卡布德(KABD)城市固体废弃物项目(该项目在采购程序上大有改进,有望于2018年结束)。虽然从总体进度上看,公私合营项目在采购和完成速度上比较慢,但是政府正积极提升其在这些公私合营项目中的建设经验和采购经验,有望在将来转化为更顺畅和有效的采购程序。

Kuwait

Authors: Ibrahim Sattout, Akusa Batwala
Translators: Steven Yu, Gao Jun

I. Overview

A. General Introduction to the Political, Economic, Social and Legal Environment of the Country Receiving Investment

Kuwait is a constitutional monarchy with separation of powers between the three branches of the government: the legislature, the executive and the judiciary. The powers of the three branches of the Kuwaiti government are outlined in the Constitution. The legislature consists of the Amir and the National Assembly. The Amir iS a member of the royal family of Kuwait, who iS selected by the members of that family. The Constitution of Kuwait defines the Amir as the"Head of the State"with his official title as"His Highness the Amir of the State of Kuwait". It also provides that the Amir will assume his authorities through his ministers, and his person shall be immune and inviolable.

The National Assembly iS made uD of members elected directly by nationals of the State of Kuwait. Executive power is exercised by the Cabinet, which is headed by the Prime Minister and the various Ministers of the Government. The Cabinet is also known as the Council of Ministers. Thc Ministets are appointed by the Prime Minister and the Amir. The entire Cabinet iS answerable to the Amir and the National Assembly, though in practice the Cabinet is closely tied to the Amir. The judiciary is made up of appointed judicial officers. while the 1962 constitution guarantees all independent judiciary, the executive branch retains control over its administration and budget. The Emir, after recommendation ofthe Justice Ministry, appoints judges in the regular courts. Kuwaiti nationals receive lifetime appointments while non-Kuwaiti judges receive renewable terms of one to three years.

Kuwait follows the civil law system after the French legal system and influenced greatly by the Egyptian legal system. Kuwait'S legal system is largely secular though Sharia law governs family law for Muslim residents. The Constitution of Kuwait makes Islam the state religion.

Kuwait is a geographically small but wealthy country with a relatively open economy and self-reported crude oil reserves of approximately 8% of world reserves. Petroleum accounts for nearly halfofthe country'S GDP, 95% ofexport revenues and 95% of government income.[1]

Kuwait has, in principle, been a country open to foreign investment and with the introduction ofnew laws in recent years; the country would appear to be even more open to foreign capital. In 2013 Kuwait passed Law No.116 of 2013 Regarding the Promotion of Direct Investment in the State of Kuwait (the"DIL Law") aimed at promoting and stimulating direct investment in the State of Kuwait. This law is intended to modernize direct investment legislation and to become more accommodating and transparent in the face of emerging economic and investment challenges. Kuwait also recently issued a new Public Tenders Law(Law No.49 of 2016 and its executive regulations through Decree Law No. 30 of 2017)governing the process of the award of government tenders. This new law is generally viewed as an improvement on the previous law that encourages foreign participation and the use of modern technology in government tenders.

B. The Status and Direction of the Cooperation with Chinese Enterprises Under the B&R

China and Kuwait began trading in 1955 and established diplomatic relations in 1971. Following the establishment of diplomatic relations between the two countries, bilateral economic and trade transactions have become more frequent and the trade volume between the two countries has been on the increase. The trade volume between China and Kuwait reached 9.5 billion U.S. dollars in 2016, more than 60 times the volume since the inception of diplomatic ties. Kuwait has been one of the largest suppliers of preferential loans to China among the Arab States and in this regard, the Kuwait Fund for Arab Economic Development has provided China with over US$one billion as loans since 1982.[2]

---

[1] World Bank-Kuwait Country Report October 2017.
[2] http://km.china-embassy.org.

There have been several economic and trade agreements signed between the Chinese and Kuwaiti governments and these include: an Agreement on Trade (signed in 1980), an Agreement on Promotion and Protection ofInvestment (signed in 1985), an Agreement on Establishing Joint Economic and Trade Committee (signed in 1986), an Agreement on Avoiding Double Taxation (signed in 1989), an Agreement (signed in July 2004).

China'S Ambassador to Kuwait Wang Di (in 2016) indicated that a cooperation document was signed between Kuwait and China during the visit of His Highness Prime Minister Sheikh Jaber Al-Mubarak Al-Hamad Al-Sabah in 2014 on participating in establishing the Silk City and Silk Road[①]. He further stated that the Silk Road Economic Belt and the 21st-Century Maritime Silk Road Initiative, first put forward in 2013 bv Chinese President Xi Jinping, concurs with the vision of Amir Sheikh Sabah Al-Abroad Al-Jaber Al-Sabah to transform Kuwait into a global center for finance and commerce. He also noted that Kuwait iS one of the first Arab countries to have signed a cooperation agreement with China under the Belt and Road Initiative.[②]

The future of the relationship between Kuwait and China appears to be set to grow from strength to strength. With China'S growing need for fuel and Kuwait's development plans requiring the expertise already developed and available in China, the two countries appear set to support each other in their goals to achieve positive, sustainable and diversified development in their respective countries.

II. Investment

A. Market Access

a. Departments Supervising Investment

The relevant governmental institutions which would regulate an investment will vary depending on the nature of the investment and the sector where the investment is being made. Having said that, the primary authorities which may be involved include: the Central Bank of Kuwait (the "CBK") (which, with other authorities, is involved in the regulation of banking and financing in Kuwait), the Ministry of Commerce and Industry (the "MOCI") (which is the general regulator of all companies in Kuwait), the Capital Market Authority (the "CMA") (which is an independent public authority supervised by the MOCI and regulates all securities activities in Kuwait, licenses entities that engage in securities activities etc.) and the Kuwait Direct Investment Promotion Authority (the "KDIPA") (an institution which issues licenses under the DIL Law, is chaired by the Minister of Commerce and Industry and aims to improve the overall investment climate in Kuwait with respect to foreign investors and to apply the provisions of the DIL Law).

b. Laws and Regulations of the Investment Industry

The primary laws which regulate investments in Kuwait are the Commercial Code (being Law No.68 of 1980), the Companies Law [being Law No.1 of 2016 and its executive regulations (the "Companies Law")] , the DIL Law and the Capital Markets Authority Law [being Law No.7 of 2010 as amended ("CMA Law") and its amended executive regulations issued by Decree No.72 of 2015 (the "Amended CML Bylaws")] .

a) Commercial Code

The Commercial Code provides for the general framework and principles which regulate business relations in Kuwait. Subject to certain limited exceptions (including the exemption provided under the DIL Law, etc.), Articles 23 and 24 of the Commercial Code provide that foreign companies conducting business in Kuwait must do so either through an agent or through a Kuwaiti "partner" (generally facilitated through the establishment of a Kuwaiti company with Kuwaiti participants owning at least 51% of the capital of such company).

b) Companies Law

The Companies Law sets out the regulatory framework within which a Kuwaiti company is established and operates in Kuwait. The Companies Law also regulates different forms of entities including partnerships, joint ventures and companies. Different types of companies may be established depending on the needs of the investment including a Single Person Company (which only has one shareholder), a With Limited Liability Company (which has between two and fifty shareholders) and Joint Stock Companies (which is used for larger scale ventures and must have at least five shareholders).

c) Investment Law

The DIL Law has as its purpose to promote and facilitate foreign investment into Kuwait and provides

---

① http://www.timeskuwaity.com/Times Kuwait-is-China-a-key-trade-partner-envoy.
② http://en.people.cn/n3/2017/1128/c90000-9297520.html.

significant incentives for projects that help to diversify the Kuwaiti economy. Significantly, foreign parties can be exempted under this law from the restrictions on foreign ownership of Kuwaiti companies. Other benefits include, tax credits and customs exemptions.

d) CMA Law

The CMA Law establishes the CMA and sets out regulations for the Kuwait stock exchanges, clearing agencies and other actors in the securities industry. Additionally, the Amended CML Bylaws together with other circulars and decisions issued by the CMA take into account key regulatory principals for a wide variety of issues which arise in the securities market. The Amended CML Bylaws and the other CMA regulations are not of a passive monitoring variety; rather the CMA is empowered to exert supervision and control of regulated entities.

e) Other Laws

There are other laws which may also be relevant to foreign parties who wish to conduct business in Kuwait such as the Commercial Agency Law (being Law No.13 of 2016) (which regulates relations between foreign principals and their local agents, distributors, franchisees etc.), the CBK Law (being Law No.32 of 1968), as amended (which establishes the CBK, Currency Regulafion in Kuwait, currency exchange, Kuwaiti banks, financing, etc.), the Industrial Law (being Law No.56 of 1996) (which establishes the Public Authority for Industry, an institution that is supervised by the MOCI and is tasked with developing and supervising the industrial activities in Kuwait) and Law No.26 of 1995 as amended regarding Free Trade Zones (the "FTZ Law"), which allows for the establishment of free trade zones ("FTZ") and grants certain benefits (e.g.exemptions from foreign ownership restrictions, taxes and customs duties) for those licensed to operate in such zones; however at present, the FTZ Law is not being implemented.)

c. Forms of Investment

Pursuant to the FTZ Law, but subject to certain regulations (e.g.operations being limited to within the FTZ), a foreign entity may operate independently in the FTZ without having to appoint a Kuwaiti agent or establish a Kuwaiti company in addition to other benefits designed encourage investment in Kuwait. Given the difficulties and cost in establishing commercial operations in the FTZ, foreign parties have in the past tended to pursue other options to establish in Kuwait (such as that under the Direct Investment Law etc.). There are currently three FTZ in Kuwait namely, Shuwaikh Port, Al-Abdally and Nuwaiseeb. To carry on business in the FTZ, an entity must obtain a license to carry on one of the permitted activities outlined in Article 2 of the FTZ Law (however, no licenses are being issued / granted at present under the FTZ Law).

To qualify for advantages under the DIL Law, investors must make a significant investment in Kuwait (e.g.transfer of technology, diversification of national products, positive environmental impact, employment of Kuwaiti nationals, etc.). Such qualification requirements are designed to ascertain how Kuwait as a whole will benefit from the proposed project / activities. Council of Ministers Resolution No.75 of 2015 sets out a negative list of direct investments for certain industries which will not qualify for licensing under the Direct Investment Law (e.g.oil exploration and productions, security and defense, etc.) but does provide for certain carve-outs. The advantages available for qualifying investors include 100% foreign ownership, tax credits, customs exemptions, utilization of government land, etc.

d. Standards of Market Access and Examination

In line with that noted above, non-Kuwaitis may not own more than 49% of a company which operates in Kuwait. Exceptions to this general rule include:

(i) operation in the FTZ–in which case all operations must be conducted within the FTZ;

(ii) establishment under the DIL Law–which requires a significant investment into Kuwait; and

(iii) establishment under Ministerial Resolution no.141 of 2002 and Ministerial Resolution no.237 of 2011—which is only available to Gulf Cooperation Council ("GCC") individuals or GCC companies wholly owned by GCC nationals. Additional restrictions on foreign ownership may apply depending on the industry. For example, the publishing and educational sectors are subject to additional regulations and restrictions on foreign participation.

B. Foreing Exchange Regulations

The CBK, pursuant to the CBK law, Law 32 of 1968, is charged with the responsibility of stabilizing Kuwait's economy and thereby its currency. It therefore controls and regulates the business of money exchange and any company engaging in such business has to be approved and registered with the CBK.

Ministerial Order issued by the Minister of Finance in March 1984 concerning the subjugation of currency exchange companies to the control of the CBK (MR 19/3/1984) together with CBK instructions to exchange companies issued on 2 December 2014 are among the legislations concerned with the regulation of the foreign exchange sector.

Pursuant to Articles 6-9 of MR 19/3/1984, establishing currency exchange companies requires the approval of the CBK which shall take into consideration the need for such companies in the local financial market as well as the necessity of any proposed foreign partners / investors. The CBK also maintains a register of currency exchange companies and such companies may not practice the business of currency exchange unless they are registered in the CBK register. Currency exchange companies may be removed from the register if, among other things, they simultaneously perform currency exchange activities with banking activities (e.g.receiving cash / savings deposits, offering loans, etc.) or other activities (e.g.trading, real estate, industrial activities, etc.) without establishing a separate entity for such activities. Notably, Article 13 of MR 19/3/1984 and Article 71 of the CBK Law state that the CBK may issue such instructions to currency exchange companies when it is necessary for them to realize the policies of the CBK. Furthermore, Articles 14-17 of MR 19/3/1984 empower the CBK with certain inspection rights over currency exchange companies. These articles also allow the CBK to instill broad self-reporting requirements over currency exchange companies. Pursuant to Article 17 of MR 19/3/1984, the CBK is entitled to apply warnings, fines and other penalties listed in Article 85 of the CBK Law should a currency exchange company breach the provisions of its founding documents, release false information, or violate the instructions of the CBK. Pursuant to Article 7 of MR 19/3/1984, the CBK allows currency exchange companies to take various legal forms unlike banks which have to take the form of a joint stock company (KSC).

There are no exchange control restrictions in relation to the importation or repatriation of capital by foreign investors. There are also no restrictions on conversion of the currency of Kuwait into foreign currency or vice versa or the repatriation of profits, restrictions on counterparties conducting transactions in local currency, or restrictions on counterparties entering into transactions involving foreign exchange other than those set out in Law No.106 of 2013 regarding the Combating of Money Laundering and Financing of Terrorism (the "AML Law").

Money laundering, counter-terrorist financing and related activities in Kuwait are regulated primarily by the AML Law. The AML Law was enacted to provide a more robust regulatory regime to counter money laundering and financing of terrorism in Kuwait, especially with regard to financial institutions and certain regulated bodies. The AML Law is implemented by executive regulations that were issued under Ministerial Resolution No.37 of 2013. Counter-terrorism financing is additionally governed by Law No.85 of 103 Approving Kuwait's Accession to the International Convention for the Suppression of the Financing of Terrorism.

The AML Law is supplemented by the CBK instructions to banks in Kuwait no.2/BS, IBS/308/2013 of 23 July 2013 regarding the combating of money laundering and terror financing transactions and subsequent instructions and the recent Amended CML Bylaws. The Amended CML Bylaws impose additional obligations on Licensed Persons (defined by the CML Bylaws) with respect to combating of money laundering and financing of terrorism. The new regulations are intended to:

(i) enhance the integrity and credibility of the capital markets; and
(ii) to protect Licensed Persons and their customers.

The Amended CML Bylaws apply to all "Licensed Persons" who are defined in the Amended CML Bylaws as natural or corporate persons that have a license from the CMA to practice any of the following:

(i) securities exchange;
(ii) clearing agency;
(iii) investment portfolio manager;
(iv) collective investment schemes;
(v) investment manager;
(vi) subscription agent;
(vii) custodian;
(vii) broker registered with the CMA;
(ix) investment controller;
(x) credit rating agency;
(xi) appraising assets; and
(xii) any other activities designated as securities activities by the CMA.

The executive regulations to the AML Law require a financial institution or Designated Non-Financial Businesses and Professions (DNFBP) as defined in the law to verify the identity of customers for any transaction of KD 3,000 (three thousand Kuwaiti Dinar) or its equivalent in foreign currency through documentation such as a civil identity card for citizens and residents; or a passport or travel document for persons not residing in the State of Kuwait.

In addition, regulations passed pursuant to the AML Law require that all transfers of currency in excess of KD 3,000 (or its equivalent in other currency) out of Kuwait must be done via a wire transfer of funds through a local bank or exchange company. Accordingly, some banks will seek the approval of the CBK for what the bank may consider large transfers of funds to other parties. Failure on the part of a bank to comply with the AML Law will result in fines, confiscation of funds and / or imprisonment. However, the AML Law specifically provides that the imposition of fines and confiscation of funds is to be "without prejudice to the rights of good-faith third parties".

C. Financing

a. Main Financial Institutions

The CBK established pursuant to the CBK Law regulates banking activities onshore of Kuwait and more specifically supervises all local banks and investment companies engaged in financing activities in Kuwait.

The general principle in Kuwait is that "banking activities" conducted in Kuwait (i.e., on an onshore basis) require that the appropriate licenses be obtained from the CBK. It should also be noted that no institutions other than those registered in the Register of Banks held at the CBK are permitted to engage in banking business or use in their business addresses, publications or advertise the terms "bank", "banker", "bank owner" or any other wording which has the potential to mislead the public as to the nature of the institution. In order to be able to incorporate a new banking institution in Kuwait, an application should be presented to the board of directors of the CBK.

Also, a foreign bank is prohibited from opening a local branch to conduct banking business in Kuwait unless it has first obtained a license from the CBK. There are no specific regulations which would restrict natural persons or legal entities in Kuwait from obtaining financial services from outside of Kuwait on an offshore / cross-border basis. The rendering of such financial services by a foreign financial institution would be subject to the applicable laws of the jurisdiction where such foreign financial institution is incorporated.

There are a number of local banks and several Islamic banks in Kuwait. Several foreign banks have also established foreign bank branches in Kuwait.

b. Financing Conditions for Foreign Enterprises

a) Bank Accounts

Subject to compliance with money laundering regulations, it is relatively easy to open and operate a bank account provided the relevant entity has a legal presence onshore of Kuwait in compliance with regulatory requirements. However, foreign entities which do not have a direct and physical presence onshore of Kuwait (including those who are undertaking the execution of government projects through agents), will likely be unable to open bank accounts in Kuwait. Banks in Kuwait will allow Kuwaiti nationals and foreign residents holding a Kuwait civil identification card to open bank accounts.

b) Financing

Please note that pursuant to various circulars, the CBK has imposed restrictions on the ability of locally regulated banks to lend to non-resident companies / individuals. More specifically the CBK's Rules & Regulations Concerning Local Banks'Extension of KD Credit Facilities to Non-Resident Customers provide for certain limitations.

More specifically, local banks are allowed to extend credit facilities in KD to nonresidents carrying out projects with the government, without the need of seeking the CBK's prior consent, for financing contracts whose value shall not exceed KD 40 Million, provided such facilities do not exceed 70% of the total value of each contract. As for other contracts or credit facilities exceeding such limits, they shall require the prior consent of the CBK.

The following conditions are also required to be satisfied in respect of all KD credit facilities extended by the local banks to their non-resident customers:

(i) The credit facilities extended in KD to non-residents shall be limited to financing the contracts denominated in KD, and awarded by Government bodies in the State of Kuwait. The financing bank must verify that the contracts to be financed are in fact real contracts, and must retain copies thereof.

(ii) Finance extended for such cases shall be limited for each separate contract, and shall not be concluded through general credit lines extended to the concerned customers.

(iii) A Letter of Assignment over all the financed contract payments shall be signed in favor of the lending bank. Such payments shall be utilized for repayment of the granted credit facilities in compliance with such facilities conditions.

(iv) The bank may perform currency forward transactions on behalf of its nonresident customers, provided that such transactions concur with the maturity dates of the contract expected payments. The amounts of these transactions shall not exceed the amount expected to be collected at each stage, and the maturity date of the transaction shall match the maturity date of this amount or shall fall due on a date close thereto. The conversion of the extended KD credit facilities to foreign currency shall be limited only to the foreign component of the contract. The CBK shall allow the coverage of forward foreign exchange contracts, as well as the conversion of

KD cash facilities into foreign currencies, up to a maximum of 50% of the contract value, where the bank shall be responsible for financing the remaining portion of the contract value from its own resources.

(v) Banks are required to immediately advise the Foreign Operations Department at the CBK of any loan or facility granted to a non-resident customer, and not requiring the CBK's prior consent. Such notice shall include the following information: Name of the project owner; Name of the borrowing party; Size of the financed contract, and schedule of payments and The granted credit limits. The said department shall also be advised of the repayment progress of the facilities granted for all such cases. As regards the facilities whose value exceed KD 40 Million, or exceed the established maximum limits, the application for obtaining the CBK's prior consent—for each case separately—shall include all the information and data related to the case for which the approval is sought. All such applications shall be sent to the Supervision Department (Sector).

(vi) The concerned bank shall continue to extend the credit facilities in KD requested by their non-resident customers for the issuance of bid bonds required by such customers to submit bids for tenders launched by local bodies.

(vii) The credit extension decision is the responsibility of the lending bank, which will bear any risks that may result therefrom, including those cases, for which the CBK's prior consent is obtained. In such cases, the concerned bank is required to comply with the supervisory rules issued by the CBK, including but not limited to: Capital Adequacy, Credit Concentration and Credit Policy, etc. It is worth mentioning that the CBK shall set an internal limit for total KD credit facilities that can be extended by each bank separately to its non-resident customers, and this would entail requiring any bank to stop extending any new credit facilities until the permission is established.

D. Land Policy

Law No.5 of 1959 and Law No.74 of 1979 essentially provide that Kuwaiti citizens may freely own real estate properties. The same laws regulate foreign ownership of real estate property in Kuwait. As a general premise, non-Kuwaitis may not—except in limited circumstances—own real estate in Kuwait. Freehold ownership of real estate is generally limited to nationals of Kuwait or corporate entities wholly owned by them. There are, however, exceptions to this general rule which are summarized as follows:

a) GCC States

Law No.1 of 2004 concerning the treatment of GCC citizens as Kuwaitis in respect to ownership of Lands and Real Estate built in Kuwait, provides that GCC nationals as well as corporate entities wholly owned by them, may own land in Kuwait. In practice, such right is only extended to Kuwaiti companies wholly owned by GCC nationals, and to GCC / Arab citizens resident in Kuwait who must have sufficient income to purchase the property and must not be the owner of another property in Kuwait.

b) Diplomatic Missions

Foreign states may own real estate properties for purposes of their diplomatic missions and head of mission's residence. Any such ownership, however, must not exceed 4,000 m^2 for each state. This exception assumes that the foreign state also grants Kuwait reciprocal treatment. In addition, an Amiri Decree must be issued to allow such ownership on a case by case basis.

c) Direct Investment Law

Under the DIL law promoting direct investment in Kuwait, foreign entities may wholly own a Kuwaiti company or establish branches in Kuwait. There are incentives to foreigners establishing a local presence in Kuwait under the DIL Law which include, but are not limited to, the allocation of land (and not necessarily ownership in such land) for investment purposes. In granting licenses and privileges / incentives under the DIL Law (including land allocation), the relevant authority will assess the project or enterprise of the foreign entity on a case by case basis taking into account the technology which is to be used, expertise involved, creation of jobs and training opportunities for Kuwaiti manpower, sectors which are being targeted for development, the location of the project, etc.

d) Companies Listed On The Kuwait Stock Exchange

Notwithstanding it may have foreign non-GCC shareholders, Kuwait companies listed on the Kuwait Stock Exchange may be permitted to own real estate in Kuwait. As a general rule, a foreign company may not own land in Kuwait. Similarly, a Kuwaiti company with foreign (non-GCC) shareholders may not own land either. However, despite this prohibition, the applicable laws make provision for an Amiri Decree to be obtained that could allow a Kuwaiti company which has foreign shareholders to own its business premises (and therefore the land on which it is built) in Kuwait. A decision of the Council of Ministers to this effect would first need to be obtained, and thereafter the Amiri must issue a Decree implementing the Council of Ministers' decision.

e) Registration

Kuwait has a central register of land for privately owned land that is administered by the Real Estate

Registration Department (the "Land Register") which is part of the Ministry of Justice in accordance with Law No.5 of 1959 in respect to Real Estate Registration. The central register may be inspected by interested members of the public, subject to the payment of a nominal fee.

Mortgages and other rights in real estate are also recorded in the register in accordance with their priority ranking. Mortgagee's rights which are registered enjoy preference over the rights of ordinary creditors from the proceeds of a sale of the mortgaged property. Should the mortgage not be registered, then rights which arise from the mortgage will only be of a personal nature and may not be enforceable against third parties.

Transfer of freehold ownership, as well as all other documents creating rights to real estate, must be registered at the Land Register. Ownership of real estate may only be transferred by the registration of ownership of such property into the new owner's name.

f) Leases

All nationalities (i.e.foreign nationals and entities) may enjoy the benefit of a lease. Leases over land can be granted under the Civil Code Law 67 of 1980 and Law No.35 of 1978 Concerning Leasing of Real Estate Property.

If the lease is for more than 10 years on privately owned land, it should be registered at the Land Register. A lease term can however not exceed 25 years. If a lease has purportedly been concluded for a longer or an indefinite term, the term will be reduced to 25 years. However, if a lease is concluded for a period covering "the life time of either the lessor or lessee", the Law will permit the lease to run for the agreed term, even though it may exceed 25 years. A lease may not be assigned by the tenant unless provided for in the agreement.

Leases on State owned land are not registered in the same manner as leases on privately owned land. With State owned land, the lease contract signed and stamped by the relevant government authority (typically the Ministry of Finance ("MOF")—State Real Estates Department) is evidence of such lease and records of the same are maintained at the Kuwait Municipality (which is the entity in charge of master planning) and the MOF.

Leases granted by the State for industrial development are managed by the Public Authority for Industry (PAI) and these agreements are signed by the PAI. As with State owned land, the lease contract signed and stamped by the PAI, is evidence of such lease and records of the same are maintained at the PAI, the Kuwait Municipality and the MOF.

g) Expropriation of Land

Under the Kuwait Constitution (Article 18), the Government is empowered to confiscate certain private rights for public interest, but only in exchange for "just compensation". Accordingly, the compulsory acquisition of land is permitted by the Law.

Law No.33 of 1964 regarding the Expropriation and Temporary Seizure for Public Interest provides for the process by which land may be expropriated or seized for public interest. Pursuant to Law No.33 of 1964, expropriation of real estate and temporary seizure shall not be carried out except for public interest. A department within the MOF called the Expropriation Department for Public Interest is responsible for expropriation. The department is charged with surveying and determining which lands may be expropriated and implementing the expropriation procedures. The Expropriation Committee of the Expropriation Department for Public Interest, chaired by the MOF, issues decisions regarding the necessity to expropriate land. Furthermore, an evaluation committee established within the Expropriation Department for Public Interest provides the estimate of the indemnity to be paid when land is expropriated or seized.

E. The Estabilishment and Dissolution of Companies

Kuwaiti law generally provides that foreign companies (except in limited circumstances e.g.under the DIL Law), conducting business in Kuwait must do so either through an agent or through a Kuwaiti partner (generally facilitated through the establishment of a Kuwaiti company with the Kuwaiti participants owning at least 51% of the capital of such company). Currently, only a Kuwaiti individual or Kuwait entity that is 51% owned by Kuwaitis can act as an agent to a non-Kuwaiti entity. Additionally, establishment and registration of various legal entities in Kuwait is governed by the Companies Law as amended and as a general rule requires participation of Kuwaiti nationals.

The DIL Law came into force in December 2013 and its executive regulations were issued a year later. A foreign party seeking to do business and to invest in Kuwait may be able to do so under the DIL Law and in doing so, may be able to benefit from the various incentives and benefits provided for therein. For example, one of the key benefits which a foreign investor may enjoy under the DIL Law is that it may be able to own up to 100% of a Kuwaiti company.

a. The Forms of Companies

We set out below the types of companies permitted under the Companies Law;

(i) General Partnership Company;
(ii) Limited Partnership Company;
(iii) Partnership Limited by Shares;
(iv) Joint Venture Company;
(v) Shareholding Company (whether publicly traded or closed);
(vi) With Limited Liability Company; and
(vii) Single Person Company.

The most common types of entities in Kuwait are the With Limited Liability Companies ("WLL") and Closed Shareholding Companies ("KSCC"). We set out below the primary differences between KSCCs and WLLs:

(i) Shareholding: The shareholders of a KSCC and a WLL may either be individuals or legal entities. There is no limit on the number of shareholders for a KSCC but it must have a minimum of five shareholders. However, a WLL must have at least two shareholders but not more than 50.

(ii) Share capital: The minimum capital required for a KSCC or WLL is subject to the activities of the company. With the exception of certain activities, the minimum capital required for a KSCC is KD 10,000 (approximately USD 33,000) and for a WLL is KD 1,000 (approximately USD 3,300).

(iii) Tax: A WLL is not, at present, subject to any tax in Kuwait. A KSCC, however, is required to:

• Contribute one percent of its net profits to the Kuwaiti Foundation for the Advancement of Science (KFAS) after contributions have been made to the compulsory reserve and before any dividends are distributed to the shareholders; and

• Pay one percent of its net annual profit as Zakat tax under the Zakat Law No.46 of 2006 ("Zakat Law"). As one of the five pillars of Islam, Zakat is a religious obligation for all Muslims who meet the necessary criteria of wealth. It is not a charitable contribution, and is considered to be a tax, or obligatory alms.

KSCC whose shares are traded on the Boursa Kuwait must pay an additional 2.5% contribution from its net profits to help fund a program in the State of Kuwait designed to encourage the employment of Kuwaiti nationals in the private sector.

Non-Kuwaiti / non-GCC corporate shareholders in a WLL and KSCC are at present taxed on their income derived from their percentage ownership in such companies at the rate of 15%.

Companies incorporated through KDIPA may obtain exemptions in respect of their tax liabilities for certain number of years that should not exceed 10 years.

(iv) Management and Board of Directors: A KSCC is managed by a Board of Directors whose composition and term of office are described in the company's Memorandum and Articles of Association. WLLs are generally managed by one or more managers.

b. Establishment Process

The establishment of a WLL is generally quicker and the process is simpler compared to the KSCC process. Subject to certain considerations, a WLL may be incorporated (i.e.up to the point of the issuance of the trading license) within 5-7 weeks. However, the incorporation process for a KSCC typically takes more time and additional formalities will have to be complied with. For example, there are publication requirements regarding the incorporation of a KSCC and each of its shareholders must be approved by various authorities taking into account the relevant activities of the KSCC.

The incorporation process starts with an application submitted to the MOCI. After obtaining the relevant approvals regarding the incorporation (e.g.approvals for the premises from the Municipality and Kuwait Fire Service Directorate, approvals regarding the manager, chairman and partners / shareholder from the Ministry of Interior, etc.) and completing the registration of the name of the company, the MOCI will refer the matter to the Ministry of Justice for the signing of the memorandum and / or articles of the company before the Notary Public. Once the memorandum and / or articles of the company are signed and then notarized, the matter is referred back to the MOCI for registration of the company in the Commercial Registry. Following registration, a trading license will be issued to the company allowing for it to begin its operations.

c. Dissolution of a Company

Pursuant to the Companies Law, a company may be dissolved for any of the following reasons:

(i) Expiry of the term of the company as set out in the company's articles, unless otherwise extended in accordance with the provisions of the company's articles or this law.

(ii) Fulfillment of the objective for which the company was established or when such objective has become impossible to fulfill.

(iii) Depreciation of all or most of the company's assets to the extent that the investment of the remaining assets is deemed unfeasible.

(iv) Unanimous approval by the partners to dissolve the company before the expiry of its term, unless the company's Articles provides for specific majority.

(v) Merger of the company into another company.

(vi) Declaration of the company's bankruptcy.

(vii) Issuing of a decision terminating the company's license for not undertaking its activities or failing to issue financial statements of the company for a period of three consecutive years.

(viii) Issuance of a judgment on the dissolution of the company.

In addition to the above, a company shall be dissolved in the event of the death of a partner in the "General Partnership Company" or the "Joint Venture Company" or of a "general partner in the Limited Partnership Company" or the "Partnership Limited by Shares". Further, a company shall be dissolved in the case of issuance of a judgment declaring one of company's partners legally incompetent or bankrupt. However, a company shall remain a legal entity where a company shall survive among the remaining partners is included in the articles.

A KSCC may also be dissolved where its losses amount to three quarters of the paid-up capital. In such case, the members of board of directors shall call an extraordinary general meeting to resolve whether the company shall continue or be dissolved before the term specified in the Company Contract or to take other appropriate measures.

With respect to WLLs, a WLL may be dissolved where its losses amount to three-quarters of the company's capital. In such case, the managers shall present to the extraordinary general meeting of the partners proposed remedies of the undercapitalization or may propose the dissolution of the company or other appropriate measures for a decision by the partners.

F. Merger and Acquisition

Mergers and acquisitions in Kuwait are primarily governed by the Companies Law, the CMA Law and the Amended CML Bylaws. The regulatory bodies are primarily the MOCI, the CMA, Boursa Kuwait (formerly known as the Kuwait Stock Exchange), the Competition Protection Board (established by the Competition Law No.10 of 2007 (the "Competition Law")) and other sector—specific regulators as the case may be.

Mergers may take the form of:

(i) a fusion where companies involved are liquidated and their assets and liabilities are contributed to a newly incorporated company. The shareholders of the liquidated companies receive shares in the new company in exchange for their shares in the liquidated companies;

(ii) amalgamation, where one or more companies is absorbed by an existing company. All the assets and liabilities of one company are transferred to another company, and the shareholders of the absorbed company receive new shares in the remaining company, and the absorbed company is liquidated;

(iii) by division and absorption through the division of the rights and obligations of a company into two or more parts and the merger of each part into an existing company.

With respect to acquisitions, the status (e.g., activities of the company, listed or not etc.) of the target company determines whether or not the CMA Law and the Amended CML Bylaws would apply to the acquisition. As with most jurisdictions, acquisitions of shares or assets of a private company are ordinarily implemented throughy an asset or share purchase agreements. As noted above, there are foreign ownership restrictions in Kuwait. Kuwaiti law generally provides that foreign companies conducting business in Kuwait must—except in limited circumstances—do so either through a local agent or through a Kuwaiti "partner" (generally facilitated through the establishment of a Kuwaiti company with Kuwaiti participants—with the Kuwaiti participants owning at least 51% of the capital of such company). As discussed above, there are certain exceptions to the restrictions, such as individuals and entities wholly owned by GCC individuals or entities which are permitted to establish and wholly own a local Kuwaiti entity or a branch through which they may carry on business (with a few limitations) in Kuwait; establishment in the FTZ; Obtaining a license to establish and own more than 49% of a Kuwaiti company pursuant to Law No.20 of 2000 and according to which foreign investors may be able to acquire up to 100% of the shares (except for Kuwaiti banks where foreign ownership is still limited to 49%) subject to complying with Boursa Kuwait's rules and those of the CMA.

If the company is a listed company, the CMA Law and the Amended CML Bylaws (particularly Book 9 of the Amended CML Bylaws), provide a statutory framework for public M&A in Kuwait. The CMA Law and the Amended CML Bylaws apply where there is:

(i) a voluntary takeover offer ("VTO") for 100% of the share capital of a company listed on Boursa Kuwait; and

(ii) a mandatory takeover offer ("MTO") which must be made to the remaining shareholders when the offeror acquires more than 30% of a listed company. In this regard, the public company may be a Kuwait incorporated company listed on Boursa Kuwait or a non-Kuwait incorporated company with a primary listing on Boursa Kuwait.

Hostile bids are uncommon in Kuwait. A takeover of a listed company may be by way of a VTO or a MTO under the Amended CML Bylaws. It should be noted that pursuant to the Amended CML Bylaws that an MTO is required to be launched by a bidder once the same has (whether directly or indirectly) come into possession of more than 30 per cent of the voting shares of a target company which is listed on Boursa Kuwait. It is also possible to acquire a stake in a listed company by way of a block trade auction process where more than 5% of the voting shares of a target company which is listed on Boursa Kuwait may be acquired. The block trade is governed by the Kuwait Stock Exchange Market Directors Resolution No.28 of 2014. If post completion of the block trade auction process, the successful bidder at the block trade auction holds more than 30% of the voting shares of a listed company, then this will oblige the bidder to follow up the block trade with an MTO under the Amended CML Bylaws.

Additional regulatory considerations will depend on the sector to which the target belongs; such as the CBK Law for banks under the jurisdiction of the CBK; and the Insurance Law (Law No.24 of 1961) for insurance companies; and laws relating to the oil sector for oil companies (to mention a few). In addition, with regard to merger control, the bidder is required to inform the Competition Protection Board in the event of an offer which may lead to a control position (i.e.35% or more) or if it already is in a control position, an offer that may increase the existing control position in the concerned market.

It is quite usual to have foreign law governed transaction documents for both public and private acquisitions. In both instances, the formalities of the share transfer would however have to be concluded in accordance with the laws of Kuwait.

G. Competition Regulation

a. Department Supervision Competition Protection

The Competition Protection Board is the entity responsible for ensuring fair competition in the Kuwaiti market place. The Competition Protection Board was established by the Competition Law. Under the Competition Law, the Competition Protection Board has a separate legal personality and it is affiliated with of the Minister of Commerce and Industry. Pursuant to Article 14 of the Competition Law, the Competition Protection Board may, among other things, make policies, receive complaints, undertake investigations, propose laws and regulations concerning competition in Kuwait and generally do what is necessary to protect fair competition.

b. Brief Introduction to the Competition Law

The Competition Law essentially guarantees the freedom to exercise economic activity in a manner that does not harm or affect free competition in Kuwait and without prejudicing international treaties and agreements that are enforced in Kuwait.

The activities of the Competition Protection Board are not limited to illegal activities and / or practices under the Competition Law but in its discretion, it is authorized to determine and identify activities which may be detrimental to free competition in Kuwait by reference to other Kuwaiti laws and regulations.

The Competition Law generally restricts any agreements, contracts or practices, which are harmful to free competition. However, the Competition Protection Board may, upon the concerned parties' request, permit some practices, agreements, contracts and resolutions which may limit the competition, in order to achieve clear and fixed benefits to the consumers that are greater than the impact of limiting the freedom of competition.

Pursued to Article 7 of the Competition Law, there is a general restriction on the misuse of intellectual property in so far as it affects free competition. The Competition Law further provides that it shall apply to all acts perpetrated abroad that affect competition in Kuwait; however, it remains to be seen how this extrajudicial application will be implemented.

a) Dominant Market Position

The Competition Law defines a dominant market position or a control position as a position in which a person or group of persons directly or indirectly control a market by possessing 35% or more of the Kuwaiti market.

The Competition Law provides that persons in such dominant market position or control position are restricted from engaging in certain specified acts which are considered anti-competitive or an abuse to their control position.

Pursuant to Article 1 of the executive regulations of the Competition Law, tenders, contracts or agreements, either explicit or implicit, between controlling natural or legal persons may not be concluded on the basis of being illegal and constituting violation to, minimization or prevention of competition pursuant to the forms stipulated in Article 4 of the Competition Law. In this regard, Article 4 of the Competition Law specifically prohibits the misuse of a control position in the following ways:

(i) Affect the prices of the products which are in the market, by raising, reducing, or fixing them or by fictitious transactions or by any other method which is contrary to the natural market mechanism with the aim of doing harm to competitors.

(ii) Limiting the freedom of the flow of products into the market or withdrawing them totally or partially, abstaining from dealing in them, wrongfully storing them or in any other manner.

(iii) Concocting abundance of the products that leads to circulating them at unrealistic prices that affects the competitors.

(iv) Prohibit or hinder the exercise of the economic activities of any person in the market at any time.

(v) Withhold products totally or partially from the market.

(vi) Sell the products at a price less than the actual cost with the aim of doing harm to competitors.

(vii) Affect the bids of selling, purchasing, providing or supplying products and services whether in the invitation for tenders, bidding or supply offers.

(viii) Provide provisions, in the conditions of the invitations for tenders, in which the brand or the type of the commodity, which is intended to be purchased, is named.

(ix) The complete or partial ceasing of the processes of manufacturing, development, distribution or marketing of commodities and services or applying restrictions or conditions on its availability.

(x) Divide or assign the product markets on the basis of geographical territories, distribution centers, types of customers, seasons or times with the aim of doing harm to the competition.

(xi) Suspend the conclusion of a contract or an agreement on conditions which are not connected to the object of the original dealing or the agreement.

(xii) Disregard the equality of opportunities among the competitors through discrimination or through information leaking in favor of one of the competitors.

Certain specific obligations are also included with regards to reporting to the Competition Protection Board certain transactions between parties which may create or increase a person(s) control position over a particular market and place them in a dominant market position. In this regard, pursuant to Article 8 of the Competition Law and Article 3 of the executive regulations, if a transaction including the acquisition of assets, merger or combining management, etc. results in a person achieving a control position or increasing the extent of control, the Competition Law requires notification of the Competition Protection Board of such transaction (including specified details of the transaction and the intended economic effect of the transaction). Additionally, the transaction will require the approval of the Competition Protection Board without which it cannot proceed. The application for such approval has to be made at least sixty days prior to the date the transaction is intended to take place.

Importantly, as stated above, the Competition Law does not distinguish between local and foreign persons. This means that, if a merger results in a foreign party(ies) obtaining more than 35% control over the relevant local market, there would be an obligation to apply for approval from the Competition Protection Board.

b) Measures Regulating Competition

There are various sanctions provided for in the Competition Law which apply to specified Articles. For example, violations of Article 4 of the Competition Law will result in a penalty or a fine not exceeding one hundred thousand Dinars or to the equivalent of the illegal gains' value, whichever is greater. This fine may be doubled in case of repetition. Additionally, the relevant court may order the confiscation of commodities which relate to the violation.

The Competition Protection Board itself is also regulated by the Competition Law and the employees / officers of the Competition Protection Board face specific penalties for violating the Competition Law. For example, violations of Article 14 (which prohibits the employees / officers of the Competition Protection Board from disclosing any information that they have gained during the course of their duties) will result in a penalty of a fine not less than two thousand Dinars and not exceeding ten thousand Dinars without prejudice to more severe penalties.

According to the Executive Regulations, the ultimate evaluation of whether actions, contracts, decisions, or agreements are harmful to competition is the responsibility of the Competition Protection Board. Therefore, if anyone desire clarity regarding compliance with the Competition Law, such person(s) may inquire with the Competition Protection Board to determine whether, in the Competition Protection Board's opinion, such person(s) proposed actions, contracts, decisions or agreements violate the Competition Law.

H. Tax

a. Tax Regime and Rules

The primary tax legislation in Kuwait is Decree No.3 of 1955 which was amended by Law No.2 of 2008 (the "Tax Law") and its Bylaws. Under the Tax Law, corporate entities carrying on trade or business in Kuwait are subject to income tax on the net income derived by them from Kuwait.

The Department of Income Tax (the "DIT") also seeks to tax foreign non-GCC corporate entities that own shares in Kuwaiti companies by taxing their percentage interest of net profits obtained from Kuwaiti companies.

Individuals, whether Kuwaiti or non-Kuwaiti, are not subject to income tax in Kuwait.

The current practice of the DIT is not to apply income tax on Kuwaiti entities and entities established in the other Gulf Cooperation Council countries. However, this is not an express exemption under the Tax Law but is simply based on the current practice of the DIT.

Kuwait is a signatory to double tax treaties with a number of countries including Belarus, Belgium, China, Croatia, Cyprus, Ethiopia, France, Germany, Hungary, Indonesia, Italy, Jordan, Korea, Lebanon, Mauritius, Mongolia, the Netherlands, Pakistan, Poland, Romania, Switzerland, Syria, Tunisia, Turkey and the United Kingdom. These treaties may provide foreign entities with reduced tax exposure when doing business in Kuwait or with Kuwaiti counterparties.

b. Main Categories and Rates of Tax

As noted above, the primary tax applicable in Kuwait is income tax. Under the Tax Law, income tax is charged at a flat rate of fifteen percent (15%). A taxpayer is allowed to deduct certain losses and expenses in accordance with the rules established under the Tax Law.

Additional taxes applicable in Kuwait include customs duty and other taxes that are payable by certain Kuwaiti entities. The customs duty on items imported into Kuwait is generally an amount equal to five percent (5%) of the value of such items. However, the customs duty payable may vary depending on the nature of the imported items.

As noted above, KSCCs are obliged to pay Zakat tax from their net annual profits under the Zakat Law at the rate of one percent (1%). Kuwaiti joint stock companies are also required to contribute one percent (1%) of their net profits to the Kuwaiti Foundation for the Advancement of Science on an annual basis. Kuwaiti joint stock companies whose shares are traded on Boursa Kuwait are also on an annual basis required to pay an additional 2.5 percent as a labor contribution from their net profits to help fund a program designed to encourage the employment of Kuwaiti nationals in the private sector.

The GCC countries executed the Gulf Cooperation Council Value Added Tax (VAT) Framework Agreement in 2016. The signing of the Framework Agreement paved the way for the introduction of VAT in the GCC countries. Kuwait is in the process of drafting its domestic VAT legislation to implement the Framework Agreement. The date of implementation of VAT in Kuwait has not yet been formally announced. It was initially anticipated that VAT would be implemented in Kuwait in early 2018 but there have been press reports that it is unlikely that it will be implemented before 2019. It is expected that the VAT rate will be five percent (5%).

c. Tax Declaration and Preference

A taxpayer is obliged to submit a tax declaration in Arabic in the prescribed format to the DIT showing the taxable income for the relevant taxable period and reflecting the value of tax due thereon. The tax declaration must be submitted to the DIT on or before the fifteenth day of the fourth month following the end of the taxable period of such company unless an extension is sought by the taxpayer and granted by the DIT. A penalty of one percent (1%) may be applied for each 30 day period (or part thereof) of failure by the tax payer to file a tax declaration. If a taxpayer fails to submit a tax declaration or submits an inaccurate tax declaration, the DIT has the right to estimate the tax payable by the taxpayer based on any information available to it.

As noted above, the current practice of the DIT is not to subject Kuwaiti entities and entities established in the GCC countries to income tax in Kuwait. Similarly, foreign entities that obtain an investment license under the DIL Law may, upon application to KDIPA, be granted tax credits for income and other taxes for a period not exceeding 10 years from the date of commencement of operations based on rules established by KDIPA.

Pursuant to the FTZ Law, projects that are established within the Kuwait FTZ as well as profits realized from activities that are exclusively conducted therein are exempt from income tax and customs duties.

Under the Amended CML Bylaws, profits generated from trading operations in Boursa Kuwait whether performed directly or through investment portfolios or funds are also exempt from income tax in Kuwait.

I. Securities

a. Brief Introduction

The marketing, offering and sale of securities (including foreign issued securities) in Kuwait is governed by The CMA Law (as amended) and the Amended CML Bylaws (together with the CMA Law, the "CML Rules").

The CMA is the primary regulator which regulates all capital markets and securities activity in Kuwait, including, the marketing, offering and sale of both local and foreign issued securities. The marketing, offering and sale of any securities in Kuwait is permissible. However, there are requirements which would have to be met by a foreign issuer in the event that it wishes to market, offer and sell its foreign issued securities in Kuwait (that is, "onshore" of Kuwait). Such requirements would entail the procurement of a license from the CMA regardless of whether the marketing, offering or sale of the Securities occurs on the basis of a private placement or a public offering.

b. Supervision and Regulation

According to the CML Rules, a license to market, offer and sell any foreign securities in Kuwait cannot be issued directly to a foreign issuer or its foreign representative. Such a license will only be issued by the CMA to a local agent in Kuwait on behalf of the foreign issuer and such local agent must be a duly licensed Kuwait joint stock company that meets specific criteria. In addition, and pursuant to the CML Rules, the local agent must also be licensed as a "Licensed Person" (as defined in the CML Rules) by the CMA so that it may engage in "Securities Activities" in Kuwait (e.g., to market, offer and sell foreign issued securities to investors in Kuwait), and in particular, must be licensed to market, offer and sell foreign issued securities on behalf of third parties (e.g., a foreign issuer of securities).

In other words, a foreign issuer would be prohibited from directly marketing, offering and selling securities in Kuwait unless the requisite license to engage in such activity has been obtained via a local agent. Only a local bank or an investment company can be retained as a local agent to obtain any such required approval. A separate license must be obtained with respect to each different security being marketed in Kuwait. This license would be obtained by the local agent appointed by the foreign issuer.

J. Preference and Protection of Investment

a. The Structure of Preference Policies

While there are no official preference policies in the State of Kuwait, through certain resolutions and generally in practice, preference is given to Kuwaitis and, to a similar degree, to citizens of the GCC countries (Kuwait, the U.A.E., Bahrain, Oman, Qatar and Saudi Arabia). However, Kuwait continues to remain committed to the encouragement of foreign investment as evidenced by the establishment of KDIPA and its numerous investment treaties with other countries.

That said, preferential treatment is given to citizens of GCC countries. For example, in regards to taxes, while the Kuwaiti Tax Law provides that tax will be levied at a flat rate of 15% on the net profits generated in Kuwait by any corporate body carrying on business in Kuwait, as a matter of practice, the DIT does not tax GCC corporate entities wholly owned by GCC nationals. Where corporate entities are partially owned by non GCC citizens, the corporate entity will be taxed in proportion to the foreign ownership percentage. Such foreign ownership percentage will be scrutinized by the DIT.

Foreign nationals are also typically limited to either a 49% ownership stake in commercial enterprises in Kuwait. However, pursuant to Ministerial Resolution No.141 of 2002, GCC citizens and GCC companies owned 100% by GCC citizens may directly establish local entities and own up to 100% of the shares of such entity. Similarly, as an exception to the general rule regarding foreign business branches operating in Kuwait, Ministerial Resolution No.237 of 2011 permits wholly owned GCC entities that satisfy certain conditions to establish branches of their businesses in Kuwait. To obtain similar rights, non-GCC nationals must be licensed under one of the limited exceptions to these general rules (e.g.obtain a license to operate in one of the FTZ or under the DIL Law).

b. Support for Specific Industries and Regions

Given the recent drop in oil prices, the Kuwait government is encouraging diversification both in the public and private sectors. While the DIL Law does not support or favor a specific industry or region, there is a negative list of activities (e.g., production of crude oil, natural gas, azote fertilizers, public management, real estate activities, etc.) that would not qualify for the benefits and incentives provided by the DIL Law. Any other projects that meet the criteria would however be acceptable. A successful applicant would be entitled to certain benefits (e.g., tax and custom tariff exemptions, allocation of land) depending on the results of the scoring system developed by KDIPA.

Whether an applicant meets the requirements and criteria of the DIL Law or not will be measured on the basis of a particular scoring system. Most importantly the applicant should convince KDIPA of the seriousness of its intention to invest significantly in Kuwait; specifically, the positive impact of such investment on the Kuwaiti market and economy (e.g., creating jobs, technology transfer, increase Kuwaiti exports, utilization of Kuwaiti products / services, etc.). These matters will be assessed based on a business study submitted by the applicant to KDIPA.

In April 2013, Kuwait enacted a law to support Small and Medium Enterprises. While this may not be considered as support for a specific industry, under this law, a project (either a small or medium enterprises) may include industrial, commercial, agricultural, professional, service or technological enterprises that directly support the development and diversification of the national income and also meet the requirements of the national market and international markets. Additionally, such projects should, where possible, provide job and training opportunities for nationals and build capacity.

c. Special Economic Areas

Pursuant to the FTZ Law, a foreign entity may operate independently in the Kuwait FTZ without having to appoint a Kuwaiti agent or establish a Kuwaiti company. However, the operations of the company are limited to the FTZ where it is licensed, which typically makes operations in such FTZ for entities intending to trade in Kuwait impractical. There are currently three (3) FTZ in Kuwait namely, Shuwaikh Port, Al-Abdally and Nuwaiseeb.

The Council of Ministers recently decided to transfer the management of these FTZ to KDIPA in order to develop and encourage more investment. This decision is yet to be implemented.

d. Investment Protection

Kuwait is a signatory to various bilateral investment treaties (64 bilateral investment treaties with various countries are currently in force), treaties with investment provisions (which generally regard GCC relationships with certain foreign countries like the United States), investment related instruments (e.g., the New York Convention, GATS, TRIPS, etc.), and certain double taxation treaties.

In addition, the DIL Law provides another layer of protection to foreign investment by stipulating that any licensed investment entity (i.e., licensed by KDIPA) may not be subject to forfeiture or expropriation except for public interest pursuant to the applicable laws, and in consideration of a fair compensation equivalent to real economic value of the project.

III. Trade

A. Department Supervising Trade

The MOCI is the government entity which primarily supervises commercial practices within Kuwait. The MOCI is also responsible for formulation and implementation of Kuwait's trade policies, in conjunction with other government entities such as the MOF the CBK and other regulatory authorities.

The General Administration of Customs ("GAC") is the government entity that is primarily responsible for undertaking all tasks and duties which are related to the customs affairs of Kuwait's ports and other inspection locations (e.g.airports, overland border crossings, etc.) which have been designated by competent ministers and other authorities. The GAC is responsible for implementing the decisions which have been issued by the government ministries and other departments in the State of Kuwait with respect to the import of goods. The GAC also makes submissions and submits proposals regarding customs processes to other government entities like the MOF for their consideration and implementation.

B. Brief Introduction of Trade Laws and Regulations

Several laws and regulations govern trading activities in Kuwait. Of particular significance are the Import Law (Law No.43 of 1964), the GCC Unified Customs Law (enacted in Kuwait by Law No.10 of 2003) and the Kuwaiti regulations which were issued under the Unified Customs Law by Decree No.200 of 2003.

The Import Law grants the MOCI the right to issue import licenses to Kuwaiti entities / individuals and determine the procedures to obtain such licenses. Without such license a party cannot import items into Kuwait for commercial purposes. The Unified Customs Law applies to all commodities, whether imported or exported, crossing the customs line by land, sea or air. The Unified Customs Law is currently also implemented in other GCC member states (i.e.Kuwait, Bahrain, the UAE, Saudi Arabia, Qatar and Oman). The Unified Customs Law and its regulations were designed to be applied across the whole of the GCC. However, certain variations may be found amongst these customs laws with each jurisdiction as provided for in the Unified Customs Law (e.g., Kuwait has certain regulations which apply to the Kuwaiti FTZ).

Other Kuwaiti laws which are relevant to trade in Kuwait include Law No.128 of 1997 as amended (regarding the standard specifications for goods), the FTZ Law (regarding the establishment of Free Trade Zones) and Decree Law No.10 of 1979 as amended (regarding the supervision of trade in goods and the determination of the prices and quality for certain prescribed items).

C. Trade Management

Kuwait has evidenced its commitment over the years to liberalizing trade, both in Kuwait and in the region by committing itself to trade organizations and concluding various trade agreements. In this regard, Kuwait is a signatory to the GATT, GATS and TRIPS treaties and has been a WTO member since 1995. Kuwait is a member of the GCC customs union, is party to the Great Arab Free Trade Agreement and also other trade agreements with foreign countries in both its capacity as an individual country and as a member of the GCC. For example, in 2008 and 2009, the GCC concluded its first free trade agreements with Singapore and the European Free Trade Association and Kuwait accepted these free trade agreements in its capacity as a GCC member state. In its capacity as an individual country, Kuwait is a party to dozens of bilateral investment treaties with countries like Germany, India, the Netherlands, Morocco, China, etc.

Kuwait has further evidenced its commitment to free trade through the implementation of laws that are designed to simplify doing business in Kuwait for foreign entities. In this regard, although the MOCI typically requires entities to operate within certain regulatory confines, businesses may be exempt from many of these regulations (e.g.foreign ownership restrictions, customs duties, taxes, etc.) by operating in one of Kuwait's free trade zones or through Kuwait's direct investment program. Additional regulatory exceptions apply to GCC entities and nationals.

D. Inspection and Quarantine of Import and Export Commodities

Articles 52 through 59 of the Unified Customs Law govern the inspection of goods. These provisions state that designated customs officers shall examine the goods following the registration of the customs declarations. In general, such declarations include a commercial invoice, certificate of origin, packing list, and a bill of lading or airway bill to accompany all commercial shipments. These documents must include sufficient information to enable the application of the appropriate regulations, taxes and duties. Customs duties are levied based on the contents of the customs declaration. The examination, unpacking, transportation and other expenses required for examination are borne by the owner of the goods.

Numerous items are specially regulated or are prohibited outright from being imported into Kuwait. For instance, medical devices, firearms, explosives and tobacco products are specially regulated goods that are subject to additional inspection procedures and further approvals from designated authorities (e.g.pharmaceuticals require the approval of the Ministry of Health). Items which cannot be legally imported into Kuwait include pork, alcoholic beverages, gambling machines, pornographic materials, goods from boycotted countries, narcotics and other goods which violate Kuwaiti laws.

E. Customs Management

Although export procedures in Kuwait are relatively simple for both natural persons and companies, Kuwaiti importation procedures are comparatively complex. To legally import commercial goods into Kuwait, importers must apply for an import license from the MOCI, and must be registered with the Kuwait Chamber of Commerce. Only Kuwaiti nationals and / or entities registered in Kuwait are allowed to hold an importing license. Importing licenses are typically valid for one year and are renewable upon the relevant parties request to the MOCI. In practice, foreign entities that are doing business in Kuwait (and who are not separately licensed), typically import their goods / products into Kuwait through their Kuwaiti agents. In such cases, the local agent must be in a possession of a valid importing license that enables it to import the foreign entity's goods / products.

Unless otherwise exempted, customs duties are payable in relation to all goods imported into Kuwait. Such customs duties are paid directly to the GAC. If the importer has already crossed a customs line in one of the GCC states and has therefore paid customs duties on the goods being imported, they would not be subject to additional customs duties.

IV. Labour

A. Brief Introduction of Labour Laws and Regulations

Employment in the private sector (for locals and expatriates / foreigners) is regulated primarily by Law No.6 of 2010 as amended (the "Private Sector Labour Law"), while employment in the oil sector is regulated by the Oil Sector Labour Law (Law No.28 of 1969 as amended) and employment in the public sector is regulated by the Public Service Law (Law No.15 of 1979).

To live and work legally in Kuwait, foreigners (other than GCC citizens) must have a work permit and a residence visa (i.e.an "iqama"). A person without a valid residency visa may be fined and deported. All foreign employees (i.e.expatriates) must be sponsored by a Kuwaiti entity (or individual) in order be granted a work permit allowing them to work in Kuwait. It is on the basis of such work permit that an expatriate will be granted a residence visa.

The Private Sector Labour Law provides for the minimum terms and benefits of employment. These include, a minimum wage (currently KD 75 per month), 30 working days paid annual leave, one day off each week, eight hour working days, overtime pay, 70 days of maternity leave, sick leave, an end of service payment, compulsory workmen's compensation insurance, etc. Parties cannot contract for anything less than the minimum provided for in the Labour Law. However, employers may provide for better terms in their agreements with their employees and such terms would be binding on the parties.

B. Requirements of Employing Foreign Employees

An established legal entity in Kuwait that has an active labor file at the Ministry of Social Affairs and Labour ("MOSAL") or a Kuwaiti individual may employ expatriates and sponsor their work permits and residence visas. Pursuant to the Manpower Law (Law No.19 of 2000), there is a requirement for each private sector company to also employ a certain number of Kuwaiti nationals alongside the expatriate employees as well. GCC nationals however do not require sponsorship.

a. Work Permits

All expatriates working in Kuwait require a work permit and a residence visa. Work permits, which are linked to residence visas (i.e.the duration of a person's work permits determines the duration of his / her residency visa), are provided for under the Residency Law (Law No.17 of 1959). There are various types of work permits that can be issued but typically Article 18 work permits are issued to private sector employees. The process of obtaining a work permit / residency status can be lengthy. The duration of time to obtain a work permit varies and depends on, among other things, the nationality of the employee, the applicant's profession and the quota of sponsored residency visas which the sponsor / employer is entitled to maintain. This process may take anywhere from four to eight weeks to complete. A work permit is granted for a minimum of one year. It will however be cancelled if the individual with residence status stays outside of the country for more than six months (without prior approval). There are no temporary work permits or work permits granted for shorter periods of time.

b. Work Permit Application Procedure

The process for applying for both the work permit and residence visa is typically undertaken by the Kuwaiti sponsor / employer. If the employer intends to obtain a work permit for the employee while the employee is still in their country of residence, then the employee's identification (e.g.passport) and qualification documents (e.g.university degree certificates) will be required including the employment contract entered into. These documents will be attached to the work permit application submitted to MOSAL. It typically take about 10—15 working days from submission of the documentation to receive a response to the same. If the application is successful, the employer will be issued with a work permit for the employee. The employee will have to undergo medical tests in his / her country of origin before travelling to Kuwait. Upon arrival in Kuwait, the employee will have their biometric information collected and recorded (including finger prints) and will also undergo further medical examinations. The employer is required to pay for the employee's health insurance and the stamping of the employee's residence visa in the employee's passport.

c. Social Insurance

Social Security contributions only apply to Kuwaiti nationals and other GCC nationals. Private sector companies are required to contribute towards the social security payments for their Kuwaiti (and GCC) employees. This is pursuant to Law No.61 of 1976 (the "Social Security Law") which created an insurance / pension fund. The Social Security Law (and the benefits prescribed therein) only applies to Kuwaiti (and GCC) employees in the government, private and oil sectors.

To finance the fund, employers are required under the Social Security Law to deduct 10.5% from the monthly salaries paid to Kuwaiti workers and remit same to the Public Institution for Social Security ("PIFSS"). Additionally, employers are obligated to directly contribute to the fund (on a monthly basis) an amount equal to 11.5% of the monthly salary payable to such Kuwaiti employee.

Pursuant to the Unified GCC Law concerning GCC employees who are not working in their home countries (the "Unified Social Securities Law"), GCC nationals working in Kuwait are also required to contribute to the social security scheme in Kuwait.

C. Exit and Entry

a. Visa Types

a) Commercial visit visas

A commercial visit visa / business visa is a type of visa applied for by a Kuwaiti sponsor who is typically either a company or other form of business establishment. It is essentially provided to facilitate a short term visit of business associates of the applicant. It is typically valid for use for 90 days upon issuance and valid for 30 days stay upon entry into Kuwait.

b) Work Visas

This type of visa is provided to facilitate eventual residency / work permit sponsored by a company or establishment. These include Article 17 (issued to government sponsored employees employed by Ministries and governmental bodies), Article 18 (issued to private sector employees), Article 19 (referred to as self sponsorship visas / work permit) and Article 20 (issued to housekeepers and domestic helpers) visas.

c) Tourism Visas

This type of visa is available to certain nationalities and regions and is obtained at Kuwait International Airports. It is valid for 3 months upon issuance. The nationalities and regions that can apply for such visa are: USA, Britain, France, Italy, Greece, Holland, Luxemburg, Finland, Spain, Vatican, San Marino, Canada, Australia, Switzerland, Austria, New Zealand, Japan, Belgium, Denmark, Sweden, Portugal, Ireland, Monaco, Andorra, Lichtenstein, Hong Kong (China), South Korea, Singapore, Malaysia, Brunei, Poland, Norway, Germany, Bhutan, Georgia, Slovenia and Vietnam. This list may be amended at the discretion of the immigration authorities.

d) Medical Visas

This type of visa is issued for medical reasons. The processing and validity of such a visa will depend on medical reports and doctors recommendations in each case.

e) Family visit visas

This type of visa is applied for by a foreign resident for a non-resident family member. These are usually restricted to the 1st degree relations of such resident (i.e.mother, father, sister, brother, husband, wife, children). The visiting relation is required to sign an undertaking that the family visit visa will not be transferred into a residency and work permit. This visa may be issued for a month or up to three months depending on nationality.

b. Restrictions for Exit and Entry

Once an expatriate has been issued with his / her residence visa, they may enter and exit the country freely. The residence visa may however be cancelled if the expatriate remains outside of the country for more than six months at a time (except with prior approval of the authorities). However, during the processing of the residence visa, the expatriate will not be able to leave the country (for a period of about three weeks).

D. Trade Unions and Labour Organizations

The Private Sector Labour Law contemplates the creation of "syndicates" and syndicates may join to form a "union" of syndicates to organize and protect its members' (i.e.employees) interests in the workplace. The creation of a syndicate is subject to the approval of the MOSAL. However, under its current practice, MOSAL only approves the forming of syndicates where only Kuwaiti nationals may become members of the relevant syndicate.

E. Labour Disputes

The Private Sector Labour Law provides for specific procedures which must be followed by an individual pursing a claim against their employers and vice versa. The dispute must be submitted to the Labour Department at the MOSAL before a law suit is initiated in the courts. The MOSAL must call the two parties together and try to settle the matter amicably. If no settlement is reached then, within one month of being asked by the employee, the MOSAL must refer the dispute to the First Instance Court, along with a summary of the matter, the evidence of the parties, and the MOSAL's own comment's. Within three days the court must fix a date for a hearing, and notify both parties. The case is heard in an expedited manner.

V. Intellectual Property

A. Brief Introduction of IP Laws and Regulations

The acquisition, transfer and protection of intellectual property ("IP") rights, i.e.trademarks, copyrighted materials, patents, designs, etc., are provided for and regulated under Kuwaiti legislation, in particular, Law No.13 of 2015, Approving the Trademarks Law of GCC States (the "TM Law"); Law No.4 of 1962, Kuwait Patent Law as amended by Law No.71 of 2013 (the "Patent Law") and the new Copyright Law, Law No.22 of 2016 ("Copyright Law").

The State of Kuwait has made important strides in joining the global effort to protect IP rights. It ratified the Paris Convention for the Protection of Industrial Property and the Berne Convention for the Protection of Literary and Artistic Works; these treaties entered into force with respect to Kuwait on December 2, 2014. On said date, Kuwait became a member of the International Union for the Protection of Industrial Property (Paris Union) and the International Union for the Protection of Literary and Artistic Works (Berne Union). By joining these conventions, Kuwait became part of the international system for protection of trademarks and authors' rights and by extension, the international trading system for goods and services protected by copyright; an important step in the exchange of culture, entertainment, information and technology.

B. Patent Application

The new Patent Law was passed in Kuwait in 2013, which repealed certain provisions of the old patent law, Law No.4 of 1962. Portions of the earlier patent law remain valid and (except on matters solely within the scope of the Patent Law) continue to regulate the rights and obligations of patent owners covered by said law.

The Patent Law provides for the application and registration of patents for invention, industrial design and integrated circuits. For a number of years after the passage of the original law, applications were received by the Kuwait Patent &Trademark Office ("PTO") but not examined. No further action was taken by PTO since it did not have the technical expertise to examine patents except in respect of industrial designs. Under said regime, the applicant would only receive a certificate to the effect that an application was submitted by the specified parties and nothing else.

Presently, the PTO continues to process applications for industrial designs while other patent applications are being directed to the GCC Patent Office in Riyadh, Saudi Arabia. An application for registration in the GCC Patent Office in Riyadh, when approved, may be enforced in Kuwait.

C. Trademark Registration

Except in relation to certain prohibited items, i.e.alcohol, pork products, and in relation to certain restricted activities (e.g.gaming), trademarks, service marks, logos and trade names may be registered in Kuwait under the TM Law in accordance with international classification standards. These registrations are valid for up to 10 years from submission of the application for registration and may be renewed for similar periods prior to its expiration.

When foreign marks are to be used in Kuwait, the owner should consider registering them in accordance with the TM Law as the latter affords the marks' owners more protection than when the marks have not been registered in Kuwait.

The recently issued TM Law and its implementing regulations contain new provisions that increase protection for both registered and unregistered owners of marks. It also regulates trademark licensing agreements. These new legislations sets forth the formal requirements and restrictions which parties should observe when entering into trademark licensing agreements as well as the procedure for registering such agreements.

D. Copyright Law

Article 3 of the Copyright Law provides that the protection granted by said law applies to creative works of whatever type, way of expression, purpose, etc. A party seeking to protect its copyright need not register same in a registry in order for it to be granted protection under the Copyright Law; however, it may wish to apply and file a request with the Kuwait National Library ("KNL") to deposit the works sought to be protected in order to enhance their ability to evidence the author's entitlement to copyright protection.

The KNL is authorized to accept applications for deposit of works from authors or creators or their descendants or official representatives. Only one classification of work will be allowed for each application. If the material is accepted for deposit, KNL will classify the material and issue a certificate indicating the serial number, the date of deposit and an international classification.

E. Measures for IP Protection

a. Patent

An owner or rights holder of a patent, a drawing, a design or a utility model may file a complaint under the Patent Law to protect their IP. During a civil or criminal lawsuit, the complainant may request the court to issue an order to take precautionary measures, in particular the seizure of imitated products or merchandise and the equipment and machines used for committing the offense. The complainant may submit an application for taking such measures supported by a statement documenting the registration of its invention, utility model, or industrial drawing or design. Where necessary, the order issued for taking such measures, may require the appointment of an expert and other court officers to assist in its implementation.

Unlike under the TM Law and the Copyright Law, which specifically grants a rights or title holder to seek an order from a Kuwait court for the enforcement of precautionary measures as a preliminary measure prior to the filing of a substantive infringement action (and on an ex parte basis when necessary) to prevent patent infringements and violations, the Patent Law grants such right only after the substantive case for patent infringement or violation of the Patent Law has been filed.

The Patent Law provides for the imprisonment for a period of not more than a year and a fine of not more than KD 1,000 or by either punishment for committing the following: copying an invention for which a patent or the utility model has been previously awarded; copying an industrial drawing or design already registered; selling, offering for sale or trade, importing, or obtaining for trading purposes of any imitated products or materials showing the copied industrial drawing or design with the imitated products with the knowledge thereof if same is registered in Kuwait; and placing, unjustly, on products, advertisements, trademarks, packing machines or others any information leading to the belief that a patent or registration of an industrial drawing or design has been obtained.

b. Trademarks

The remedies for TM infringement under the Commercial Code were repealed by provisions in the TM Law. The TM Law replaced the provisions of the Commercial Code with a more detailed set of provisions on precautionary measures. Under these provisions, when there is an infringement or violation of the rights of a TM owner of rights holder, or where it is necessary to avert an imminent infringement, the latter may obtain a court order after filing a petition with the competent court to avail of one or more precautionary procedures, including the following:

(i) Carry out an inspection of a location in order to describe the infringement or violation; obtain details of the items or goods subject of such infringement; materials, tools and equipment used or which are to be used in or for any of the above; and do such acts as to preserve the evidence of infringement.

(ii) Attach the items mentioned above and any item showing the results or products of the infringement.

(iii) Prevent items and goods subject of the infringement from reaching commercial outlets; stop distribution upon customs release; and prevent their export.

(iv) Stop or prevent the occurrence of infringements or violation of the TM laws and regulations.

Under relevant provisions of the TM Law, when considering an application for precautionary measures, the test that the summary court judge is required to apply is: whether there is an on-going infringement, or violation of the rights or title holder or such infringement or violation is imminent and the measures applied for are necessary to prevent the continued infringement or violation or imminent occurrence of the same.

Aside from the above test, the court may in its discretion, require the petitioner to provide such evidence of infringement as circumstances may require or to show proof that a violation or infringement is imminent; present adequate information to enable the court to execute such precautionary measures; identify specific products or commodities, etc.

The summary court is required to decide on said petition no later than 10 days from the date of its filing except in special cases to be decided by the court. The summary court may notify the respondent of the petition or exercise its discretion to issue the order/s on ex parte basis if the court, upon reviewing the facts, finds that a delay may cause irreparable damage to the petitioner, obstruction of justice, destruction of evidence, etc.

Under the TM Law, without prejudice to any tougher penalty provided for in any other laws, a penalty of a minimum of one month up to three years in prison and a fine no less than Saudi Riyal five thousand or its equivalent in a GCC state currency but no more than Saudi Riyal two million, or either one of the two penalties shall apply to and be imposed on anyone who forged or faked a trademark which has been registered in accordance with the provisions of the TM Law and imitated such trademark in a manner which may be confusing or misleading to the public as well as anyone who used a false or counterfeit trademark in bad faith or anyone who in bad faith put or used a trademark owned by a third party on a product or commodity or used such third party owned trademark in connection with its services.

Without prejudice to any tougher penalty provided for in any other law, a penalty of a minimum of one month up to one year in prison and a fine no less than Saudi Riyal one thousand or its equivalent in a GCC state currency but no more than Saudi Riyal one hundred thousand, or either one of the two penalties shall apply to and be imposed on anyone who sold or offered for sale or trading or possessed for sale a product or commodity knowingly and deliberately carrying or using a counterfeit or false trademark for no legal basis as well as anyone who offered his services under such trademark; anyone who used a trademark which is not registered; anyone who illegally wrote or noted on his mark, letterheads, papers, or commercial documents anything which may lead to the belief or impression that it is a registered trademark; and anyone who knowingly and deliberately in bad faith failed to put or use the registered trademark on the products or commodities which are distinguished by such trademark; and anyone who possessed tools or materials with the intention to use the same towards the imitation or forgery of registered or reputable trademarks.

In the event of repeated infringement or violation, the violator shall be penalized by no more than double the maximum applicable penalty for the violation and the violator's shop or enterprise shall be closed for a minimum of 15 days and up to a maximum of 6 months. Such verdict or order shall be published at the cost of violator in accordance with the procedures set forth in the executive by-laws of the TM Law. For purposes of the TM Law, a frequent violator or repeater of the violation or infringement is anyone who has been convicted of one of the violations or wrongdoings stipulated in the TM Law who then repeats a similar violation within three years from the date on which he / she was convicted by a final court verdict on the previous violation or wrongdoing.

c. Copyright

Under the Copyright Law, a complainant may, by application to the relevant court, petition the judge to issue an order to enforce one or more precautionary measures when there is a violation of any rights stipulated under the Copyright Law.

Unlike the TM Law, which requires the complainant to file a substantive action with the relevant court within 20 days from issuance of the precautionary order, the Copyright Law provides for a shorter period, i.e. requires the complainant to file the substantive action within 15 days from issuance of the precautionary order. Unlike the TM Law, which provides for a term of 20 days to file a grievance in relation to the issuance of the precautionary order, under the Copyright Law, the concerned party has a period of 30 days to appeal the same.

The Copyright Law provides for imprisonment for a period of not less than six months and not more than two years, in addition to a fine of not less than five hundred dinars and not more than one thousand Dinars, or either of the two penalties, for whoever commits one of the following acts without obtaining written permission from author or owner of related rights: violates a literary or financial right pertaining to the author or owner of the related rights stipulated under the Copyright Law including making any work available to the public.

VI. Environmental Protection

A. Department Supervising Environmental Protection

In order to control environmental pollution and in an effort to maintain its natural resources, the Kuwaiti legislators enacted Law No.42 of 2014 (the "Environment Protection Law"). The third chapter of this law deals with the management of environmental affairs through the establishment of the Supreme Environment Council headed by the Prime Minister (or any of his deputies) and with a membership of the ministers selected by the head of the Supreme Environment Council.

Additionally, a public authority concerned with environmental affairs called the Environment Public Authority ("EPA") was also established by the Environment Protection Law to undertake all works and duties to protect the environment in Kuwait, including the issuance of project and construction licenses for developments in Kuwait. In this regard, the Environment Protection Law requires all companies who intend to execute projects which will have an impact on the environment to provide the EPA with an environmental impact assessment report. The approval of said report is typically evidenced by the issuance of a "Clearance Certificate" by the EPA allowing for the project to proceed.

The Director General of the EPA (or whoever he authorizes) has the right to grant violators of the Environment Protection Law and its related regulations (other than with respect to matters covered by the First Chapter of the Fourth Section of the law (i.e.protecting the marine environment from pollution)), a grace period for the prompt rectification of their violation. If the violator has not rectified the violation within thirty days or it is established that the continuation of the violation would cause gross damage to the environment, then the EPA will have the right to take the necessary legal measures to stop such violating activity, close the establishment or cancel the license issued without prejudice to any other penalties provided for in the Environment Protection Law and the compensations for the damages resulting from such violations.

B. Brief Introduction of Laws and Regulations of Environmental Protection

The Environment Protection Law and its related regulations (issued regularly by Ministerial Resolution) are the primarily legislation concerning the protection of Kuwait's environment.

Pursuant to the Environment Protection Law, pollution is defined broadly as—all human and natural activities that contribute to the existence of any of the pollutant materials or factors in the environment in quantities or characteristics for a time period that may lead, directly or indirectly, individually or in connection with other materials or factors, to damaging public hygiene; or doing works and activities that may lead to deterioration of the natural ecological system or hinder enjoying life and benefiting from private and public properties.

A source of pollution is defined by the law as a place, through which materials, pollutants or energy is drained, released or emitted into the surrounding environment (whether air, water and / or soil). A source of pollution can be a fixed structure (such as chimneys, sewage and industrial area drains, and waste disposal landfills) or it could be movable (e.g.vehicles, ships and aircrafts).

Pollution damage is defined as any loss that results from environmental pollution by a harmful material, whatever its cause may be. This loss includes the cost of measures aimed at combating pollution and rehabilitation as well as any loss or damage that results from such measures.

Pursuant to Articles 52 and 53 of the Environment Protection Law, all entities and facilities are required to abide by the designated measures preventing emissions or air pollutants higher than the allowable limits. The owner or the operator of such facilities is required to take all necessary precautionary measures to prevent any leakages or emissions of pollutants that may lead to the pollution of the environment.

Pursuant to Article 54 of the Environment Protection Law all entities and individuals are required to abide by the designated regulations and not exceed the permitted levels of noise while conducting production activities, providing services or when involved in any other activities.

Civil liability and compensation for any environmental damage caused is addressed in Chapter 8 in the Environment Protection Law. Penalties are also prescribed in Chapter 7 of the same Law. These penalties include potential fines and imprisonment (including a potential death penalty for the violation of Article 25 of the Environment Protection Law (concerning the import / storage of nuclear waste).

The Environment Protection Law provides for the establishment of a specialized policing unit within the Ministry of Interior called the "Environment Police". This unit has been entrusted with the task of implementing the environment laws and regulations as specified by the Supreme Environment Council. This unit also supports the activities of the judicial officers working with the EPA.

C. Evaluation of Environmental Protection

A number of entities (both governmental and non-governmental) are involved in environment protection. The EPA however plays the primary role in the protection of the environment and therefore in the evaluation of any (potential or actual) environmental pollution. The EPA has recently launched a number of programs and training courses to raise the awareness of Kuwaiti individuals, residents and entities with respect to the protection of the environment and to create consciousness about responsible environmental behavior among the residents of Kuwait. For these purposes, the government launched a website called "Beatona" (which means our environment) which provides information on the protection of the environment.

The EPA also launched its own website in an effort to build cooperation between various organizations involved in environment protection, other governmental bodies involved in the development of projects in Kuwait, as well as between individuals to protect Kuwait's environment. The EPA also aims to provide effective e-services and information sources that are relevant to environment protection. This is done through the provision of information that benefits both researchers and non-professional. The EPA's website includes updates concerning the environmental situation; it provides a comprehensive environmental database that includes digital maps of Kuwait, a complete Geographic Information System for environmental purposes and an environmental Atlas for all governorates with lists of water, soil and air data.

Another organization that has been vital in environmental issues is the Kuwait Environment Protection Society that was founded in March 31, 1974. It was initiated at the First UN Conference on the Human Environment (Stockholm, Sweden 1972). This was the starting point of the Kuwait Environment Protection Society and the beginning of a new era in Kuwait's protection of its environment. The Kuwait Environment Protection Society has over the years been working with various governmental bodies in lobbying for environment protection legislation and the adoption of means to develop the environmental laws to enhance the protection of the environment.

The Public Authority for Agriculture Affairs and Fish Resources was established by Law No.94 of 1983. It was established to carry out the work related to agricultural development and advancement; both in the plant and the livestock sectors. It was also established for the development and protection of fish resources, as well as designing, supervising and following up on landscaping and afforestation of roads, yards, public gardens, parks, afforestation areas, and zoos.

Kuwait Institute of Scientific Research (KISR) is an independent, national institute of scientific research. It was established in 1967 by Japan's Arabian Oil Company Limited, in partial fulfillment of its obligations under an oil concession agreement with the government of the State of Kuwait. KISR's initial role was dedicated to developing three fields: petroleum, desert agriculture and marine biology. Since then, KISR's role and responsibilities have expanded greatly to include the advancement of national industry and the undertaking of studies to address key challenges, such as the preservation of the environment, sustainable management of Kuwait's natural resources, responsible management of water and energy, and development of innovative methods of agriculture.

VII. Dispute Resolution

A. Methods and Bodies of Dispute Resolution

The Kuwaiti judicial system is a civil law system similar to that of Egypt and several European countries. However, it has the following distinctive features:

(i) Public policy plays a substantial role in the judicial review process.

(ii) Substantial reliance on written legal memoranda, in an inquisitorial rather than accusatorial process.

(iii) Substantial reliance on the Experts Department of the Court, particularly in disputes involving complicated commercial and technical matters.

(iv) The procedural and substantive aspects are primarily governed by written laws and directives; case law does not control precedence.

a. The Structure of the Kuwaiti Judicial System

a) The General (Al Kulliya) Court and Its Circuits

(i) Small Claims / Summary Court: The jurisdiction of this Court extends to urgent and relatively minor matters including provisional protective orders, travel bans, judicial custody over fixed and movable assets and provisional execution proceedings. Additionally, the Small Claims / Summary Court has limited jurisdiction and reviews only civil and commercial claims of up to KD 5,000 (about US$ 15,250).

(ii) Court of First Instance: Reviews matters that do not fall under the jurisdiction of the Small Claims / Summary Court.

(iii) Administrative Court: Reviews matters involving the Kuwaiti government and its subdivisions and public authorities.

(iv) Government Court: Reviews all government matters not falling under the jurisdiction of the Administrative Court.

(v) Civil and Commercial Court: Reviews matters arising under the Civil and Commercial Codes of Kuwait.

(vi) Labour Court: Reviews all matters relating to employment in the private and oil sectors.

(vii) Court of Rents: Reviews all matters falling under Law No.35 of 1978 Concerning the Rental of Real Property including the rights and obligations of lessors and lessees.

(viii) Criminal Court: Reviews matters involving criminal violations and traffic infractions.

(ix) Court of Personal matters: Reviews matters relating to family, personal status, divorce, custody, trust and estate.

(x) Court of Minors' Affairs: Reviews matters relating to citizens under the age of 21.

In addition to the above courts, the General Court also has three more important divisions:

(i) The Authentication Department: The Authentication Department specializes in various matters including;
• Authentication of signatures and documents.
• Notarization of documents.
• Determination of the official nature of relevant documents.

(ii) The Experts Department: The Experts Department reviews those technical and complicated matters that the court may refer to it, and frequently plays a decisive role in influencing the outcome of cases. When a matter is referred to the Experts Department, the following applies:

• The court proceedings are effectively stayed, pending the Experts Department's report and recommendations.

• The primary functions of the Experts Department relates to gathering and analysing evidence.

• The Experts Department is empowered to demand the litigants' co-operation and to refer the dispute back to the court in the event of non-compliance or if further questions arise.

• The Experts Department reports to the court on its findings and conclusions.

• The Experts Department's report usually receives the court's favorable consideration, but is not binding. It may also be rebutted by affected litigants.

• A litigant disagreeing with the Experts Department's report may submit a written memorandum setting forth its factual and legal objections.

(iii) The Execution Department: Execution Department is generally responsible for:
• Serving legal notices including summons.
• Giving effect to the court decisions and rules including penalties.

- Executing court judgements.

b) The Court of Appeals

The jurisdiction of the Court of Appeals is generally limited to the review of the issue being appealed from the Al Kulliya Court, but the Court of Appeals is also empowered to make a de novo review of appealed cases (trial in a higher court in which all the issues of fact or law tried in a lower court or tribunal are reconsidered as if no previous trial had taken place). The Court of Appeal regularly conducts trial de novo. Except for those appeals taken to and accepted by the Court of Cassation, judgements rendered in the Court of Appeals are final.

c) The Court of Cassation

The Court of Cassation has final jurisdiction covering matters relating to the proper application, interpretation and enforcement of Kuwaiti law and rectifies procedural and substantive defects committed by the lower courts.

b. Arbitration

Kuwait is a signatory to the New York Convention on the Recognition and Enforcement of Foreign Arbitral Awards (1958). Kuwait's ratification however only applies to awards made in countries which are also signatories to the said convention.

Where the parties to an agreement have agreed to arbitration as the dispute resolution mechanism, a Kuwaiti court should decline jurisdiction over a dispute arising from the same. The enforcement of a foreign arbitral awards is typically commenced like other original claims but without the Kuwaiti court examining the merits of the matter.

Judgements from GCC states courts may be recognized and enforced in Kuwait. Non-GCC judgments and arbitral awards (where the New York Convention does not apply) may be enforced in accordance with the following criteria:

(i) There must be a treaty or precedent to the effect that the foreign law in question is reciprocal in the recognition and enforcement of Kuwaiti judgements or awards.

(ii) The foreign judgement, order or award was rendered by a competent judicial forum or arbitration tribunal having jurisdiction to decide the matter in accordance with the substantive and procedural rules of that foreign jurisdiction.

(iii) The parties were duly summoned and represented, and the court judgement or arbitration award was on the merits.

(iv) The foreign judgement, order or arbitration award is final, subject to no further appeal, and immediately executable.

A foreign judgement, order or arbitration award must neither contradict a Kuwaiti judgement nor offend Kuwaiti public policy or morals.

Kuwait is party to regional (with GCC states and / or with Arab states) treaties concerning the recognition and enforcement of courts orders and judgments.

B. Application of Foreign Laws

Parties are generally free to choose a foreign law to govern their contracts. In this regard, Article 59 of the Law No.5 of 1961 Governing Legal Relations Involving a Foreign Element (the "Conflicts Law") provides in pertinent part that the law of the country where the contractual parties reside should apply. In case those parties reside in different places, then the law of the country where the contract has been executed should apply unless the parties agree otherwise or it appears from the arrangement that another law was intended to apply.

That said however, Article 73 of the Conflicts Law provides that the rules of a foreign law may not apply in Kuwait should they violate the public order or morality of Kuwait and in such event, Kuwaiti law shall apply.

In practice, government entities are unlikely to agree to be subject to foreign law.

VIII. Others

A. Anti-commercial Bribery

a. Brief lintroduction of Anti-commercial Bribery Laws and Regulations

Commercial bribery, which is the subject matter of this section, is a form of corruption that does not necessarily involve government personnel or facilities. It is a form of bribery which often involves corrupt dealings by agents or employees of potential buyers to enable suppliers to secure an advantage over business competitors.

a) The Criminal Law

The primary legislation with respect to the offence of bribery is Kuwait Law No.31 of 1970 ("Law 31 of 1970") which amends certain provisions of Kuwait's Criminal Code, Law No.16 of 1960 ("Criminal Code") and contains provisions prohibiting the payment, receipt and facilitation of bribes.

In Kuwait, any public officer who requests or accepts for himself or for another person any gift or favor to perform, or abstain from performing, any act related to the public duties of such public officer, i.e.a bribe, is considered to have violated the provisions of the Criminal Code on bribery (as amended by Law No.31 of 1970). The public officer, if found guilty of such offences, may be punished with imprisonment and / or a fine.

Any individual who provides such gift or favor to a public officer to perform, or abstain from performing, any act related to the public duties of such officer would also be considered to have violated the provisions of the Criminal Code on bribery. Such individual, if found guilty of such offence, would receive a similar punishment.

Article 43 of the Criminal Code defines a "public official" for the purposes of bribery, to include not just government officials and employees but also board members, directors, managers and employees of corporations, companies, associations and organizations where the government or one of its entities, is a shareholder / owner involving commercial transactions. Hence, the provisions in the Criminal Code on bribery also stand as basis and potential grounds to file a complaint for bribery against non-government or private sector employees working in corporations, companies, associations and organizations where the government or one of its entities is a shareholder or owner.

Where bribery involves the giving of a bribe to a government employee or official, aside from the Criminal Code, the provisions of Kuwait's Law No.2 of 2016, which set-up Kuwait's Anti-Corruption Authority should also be considered.

The prohibition against bribery in the Criminal Code is not limited to government officials in respect of their public duties. They may also apply to both individuals in non-government corporate entities or commercial companies where the government is a shareholder or owner.

b) Competition Law

Kuwait passed Kuwait Law No.10 of 2007, "Regarding the Protection of Competition" ("Competition Law") on 29 April 2007; same replaced Kuwait's prior laws on unlawful competition. The Competition Law came into effect on August 22, 2009 after its implementing regulations were published in the Kuwaiti Official Gazette.

The significance of the Competition Law that it sets out certain business conduct that is prohibited; it created an authority tasked with enforcing and administering the provisions of said law; and established restrictions and reporting obligations in respect of persons who are in positions of control (defined as having direct or indirect control of 35% of the market) and requires persons to obtain certain approvals to conclude prescribed transactions that may be deemed to threaten free competition in the market.

The Competition Law prohibits conduct which restricts or harms free competition in Kuwait. The law goes on to restrict certain conduct by both natural and juristic persons who are in positions of control. Article 4 of the Competition Law provides in pertinent part that agreements, contracts and practices that are harmful to free competition are prohibited. It goes on to provide that people or entities who are in control positions are prohibited from abusing the same.

Pursuant to the provisions of the Competition Law, any practice determined harmful to competition is essentially prohibited. Any party who is determined to be in a "control" position is prohibited from abusing their position by engaging in acts to harm free competition.

We further note that violation of the Competition Law is considered a "corruption crime" and therefore subject to the application of the Anti-Corruption Law (Law No.2 of 2016).

c) Capital Markets Law

Articles 1 to 6 of Book 8 of the Amended CML Bylaws provide in part that a "Licensed Person" (defined as a natural or corporate person licensed by the CMA to practice one or more of the Securities Activities as defined in the Amended CML Bylaws) while practicing an activity involving Securities, is prohibited from paying any fees or commissions, and from providing monetary or non-monetary benefits or gifts, whether directly or indirectly, to his clients.

In addition, the Licensed Person is not permitted to receive any such benefits or gifts except in the following cases:

(i) Fees, commissions or non-monetary benefits that are not intended to encourage the Licensed Person to provide better service for its clients, such as symbolic gifts; and

(ii) any charges or monetary amounts incurred by the Licensed Person for providing services to its client such as, costs of safekeeping , commissions of settlement and clearing and fees that do not contradict in its nature with the duty to act honestly, fairly and professionally, in a manner that fulfills the interests of the clients. This prohibition applies also to employees of the Licensed Person.

b. Department Supervising Anti-commercial Bribery

For the violation of anti-bribery provisions of the Criminal Code, the Office of the Public Prosecutor ("OPP") is tasked with prosecuting offenders while the Anti-Corruption Commission has investigative, administrative, reportorial, recommendatory and regulatory powers in respect of corruption and bribery-related offenses. The Anti-Corruption Commission works closely with the OPP and civic organizations. It is however, primarily focused on violations by public officials.

For violations of the Competition Law, the government agency tasked with enforcing anti-competition regulations is the Anti-Competition Authority. For enforcement of CML Rules, the agency enforcing said rules is the CMA.

c. Punitive Actions

Under the Criminal Code, the receipt of a bribe is punishable by imprisonment of up to 10 years and a fine equal to an amount that is double the value of the bribe in question (with a minimum fine of KD 50—approximately USD $178).

Under the Competition Law anyone who violates Article 4 of the Competition Law shall be penalized by a fine that shall not exceed KD 100,000 or the equivalent of the illegal gains that were realized, whichever is greater. The judge may also order the confiscation of the commodities. In case of repetition, the fine shall be doubled and the goods shall be confiscated.

A Licensed Person in violation of the CML Rules may be penalized with a fine of not less than KD 5,000 and not more than KD 50,000.

B. Project Contracting

a. Permission System

Law No.49 of 2016 relating to Public Tenders (the "Public Tenders Law") organizes the purchase of commodities, contracting and services made for public bodies in Kuwait. The party submitting a bid in public tenders shall be either:

(i) a Kuwaiti company registered in the suppliers or contractors registers according to the nature of the tender; or

(ii) a foreign company. In circumstances where a foreign company is invited to bid, the foreign company does not need to engage an agent or Kuwaiti partner for the purposes of bidding but should, as a matter of practice, engage a local agent or partner to perform the works if awarded the contract. Tenders may be exclusive to national companies or to foreign companies depending on the technical specifications and requirements of the tender.

Public tenders may be conducted in one or two phases. A one phase tender could involve two offers (a technical and financial offer) or a financial offer only, as required by the contract to be performed. A two phase tender may be conducted when it is not practically possible to specify the technical and contractual aspects of the procurement thoroughly to attain competitive offers. In such case, the tender documents at the first phase would specify the purpose, expected performance, general description of specification and such other characteristics required - together with the qualifications required to perform the contract. The announcement to the bidders would be made according to such documents. At the end of the first phase the relevant governmental body would decline the offers that do not satisfy the requirements or where there are weaknesses which make the offer substantially non-compliant with the tender conditions. The relevant governmental body would then invite the bidders whose technical offers were not declined to submit their final tenders, including the price.

b. Prohibited Areas

The Public Tenders Law does not apply to (i) Defense, National Guard and Interior Affairs, (ii) the CBK, (iii) Kuwait Petroleum Corporation and the companies wholly owned by it and (iv) instant investment transactions of public institutions and bodies. Specialized committees have been established to handle procurement transactions for categories (i) through (iii) above.

c. Invitation to Bid and Bidding

The phases of the tendering process within Kuwait are as follows:

a) Announcement of Invitation to the Tender or for Submitting Bids or Pre-Qualification Requests

The announcement for invitation for the tender or to submit bids or pre-qualification requests shall be published in the Official Gazette, as well as on the Central Tender Committee's website. The announcement may also be published in a periodic commercial print, or appropriate technical or professional magazine. The invitation must include:

(i) the competent authority and its address;

(ii) the nature of the required items, contracting works or services;

(iii) the places of tender documents or qualification and its cost; and

(iv) the method of applying pre-qualification or bid requests, including place and deadline date. Tender invitations or qualification requests must also be published in a language other than Arabic in circumstances where:

(i) the tender or bid shall be external; or

(ii) if the offering is limited to foreign companies.

b) Pre-qualification

A bidder must satisfy the conditions provided for in the tender documents or within the pre-qualification requirements to be selected. Pre-qualification can be done for one project or for a specified period, according to the requirements. Prospective bidders who believe that they meet the requirements will submit the required details. The relevant authority will list those who pass the qualification in the activities applied for.

c) Submitting Bids

In most cases, a technical and financial proposal will be required at this stage. The two proposals should be submitted separately. The technical bid should include:

(i) a bid bond;

(ii) general and special conditions and technical data of the provided proposal;

(iii) complete data for subcontractors that may be assigned a part of the implementation if required by the tender documents; and

(iv) any other documents or data that may be required by the tender documents.

The financial proposal should include the following:

(i) the approved bidding formula by the bidder;

(ii) the price list and bill of quantities;

(iii) any other elements that may affect the financial value of the proposal as required by the terms of the offering; and

(iv) any other documents or data required by the tender documents.

d) Evaluation and Award

In cases that do not require technical inspection, the award shall be made to the bidder who meets the requirements of the tender documents with the lowest price. In the case of tenders with technical and financial proposals, and which require complicated technology, high levels of engineering, precise technical characteristics and high cost, the award shall be made to the bidder who fulfills the tender requirements and offers the lowest cost—after a technical and financial evaluation of the bids has been completed. The winning bidder shall be notified in writing and the decision shall also be published in the Official Gazette and on the Central Tenders Committee website.

e) Performance Bond and Contract Signing

The winning bidder should submit the performance bond for the project within 10 days of being awarded the tender. The bidder will also be invited to sign the contract within 30 days of submitting the performance bond. If the winning bidder fails to sign the contract or provide the performance bond, or withdraws for any other reason, the bid bond may be called by the relevant authority. Failure to sign the contract may also be cause for the performance bond to be called.

C. Public Private Partnerships (PPPs)

Writers can make an introduction to other investment-related laws and regulations according to the needs of local situation.

Kuwait has over the past few years promulgated a number of laws concerning public private partnerships (PPP). Prior to 2007, public sector projects carried out by the private sector were essentially procured based on a combination of number of laws including Public Procurement Law (Law No.37 of 1964—which has since been repealed and replaced with Public Tenders Law) and laws regulating the leasing of government owned land (in particular Law No.105 of 1980 as amended).

However, in 2007, the Kuwaiti government enacted Law No.7 of 2008 regarding Regulation of BOT Operations and Similar Systems (the "BOT Law") which was essentially the first specialized law on the books regulating PPPs. The BOT Law and its Executive Regulations provided for the incorporation of a legal vehicle (the Project Company) to implement the projects and established the procurement process of PPP projects across various industry sectors in Kuwait. Following the enactment of the BOT Law, the Partnership Technical Bureau ("PTB"), launched a number of PPP projects in various sectors including power, railroad, hospitals, labor cities, schools, etc. The procurement process was further guided by the Executive Regulations and the PTB Guide Book that had been developed in partnership with the World Bank.

The BOT Law was however repealed and replaced by Law No.116 of 2014 Concerning Partnerships between the Public and Private sectors (the "PPP Law") and its Executive Regulations. The PPP Law was developed as an improvement to the BOT Law as the Kuwaiti government at this point had been engaged in the procurement of its first PPP projects and had to respond to the difficulties and hurdles experienced by the investors, lenders and the procuring entities as a result of the implementation of the BOT Law. This was generally viewed as a positive and proactive step by the government. The PPP Law provides for the establishment of the Kuwait Authority of Public-Private Partnership Projects ("KAPP") which replaced the PTB. The PPP Law is now the general law which sets the guidelines for the procurement and implementation of public private partnership projects on government owned land across the sectors.

Prior to enacting the PPP Law, the government had enacted Law No.39 of 2010 regarding the establishment of Kuwaiti Joint Stock Companies which would undertake the construction and implementation of electrical power and water desalination plants (the "IWPP Law"). The IWPP law was subsequently amended by Law No.28 of 2012 and Law No.19 of 2015. The IWPP Law specifically regulates power and water desalination PPP projects, it having been identified that power projects would require their own special law given their specific technical nature and economic and social importance to the country.

The PPP Law repealed Law No.40 of 2008 regarding the establishment of Kuwaiti Joint Stock Companies that would undertake the building, operation and transfer to the State of workers cities. These projects (i.e.workers cities) are now procured under the PPP Law, while power and water desalination projects would still be implemented under the IWPP Law. That said, the provisions of the PPP Law would apply to IWPP projects to the extent a particular matter is not specifically regulated by the IWPP Law (the PPP Law acts as a catchall in effect).

To date, only one PPP project has been successfully closed (i.e.the Az Zour North IWPP Phase 1). That said, a number of PPP projects continue to progress through the pipeline including the Um Al Hayman Waste Water Project and the KABD Municipal Solid Waste Project which are quite advanced in the procurement process and it is hoped will close in 2018. Though progress is generally viewed as being slow with the procurement and closing on PPP projects; the Government is positively developing its experience in the structuring and procuring of these PPP projects and this should hopefully translate into smoother and more efficient procurement processes.

附录
APPENDIX

阿富汗——撰稿人介绍 / Afghanistan—Introduction to Authors

律所介绍 / Introduction to Law Firms

云南建广律师事务所

云南建广律师事务所创建于 2000 年，是一家综合性律师事务所。

得益于海纳百川的精神，经过十多年的发展，建广律师事务所在东南亚、南亚的金融、房地产建设、知识产权等专业领域作出了突出成绩，得到了社会的广泛认同，积累了不可多得的人脉资源和丰富的客户资源。2005 年，建广律师事务所获得云南省地产风云榜"最佳房地产法律服务机构奖"。2008 年，建广律师事务所作为云南省内三家律师事务所之一，被评为"全国优秀律师事务所"。

云南建广律师事务所现有执业律师、律师助理及行政管理人员 60 人，律师均毕业于优秀大学。

Established in 2000, Yunnan Jianguang Law Firm is a leading comprehensive law firm.

Harboring the spirit embracing diversities, through over a decade of development. Jianguang Law Firm has accumulated rich experiences in various legal fields such as Southeast Asia & South Asian, financing, construction, real estate, intellectual property, and set up diversified connections with clients and precious harmonious relationships with different governmental branches of each level. Jianguang Law Firm has been widely acknowledged for its prominent achievement in legal services. In 2005, Jianguang Law Firm was awarded as "the best legal service award for real estate industry of Yunnan", and in 2008, elected as top three in Yunnan Province "National Excellent Law Firms in China".

Yunnan Jianguang Law Firm has 60 staff so far, including practicing lawyers, lawyer assistants and administration personnel. All of the staff graduated from prestigious Chinese Universities.

律师介绍 / Introduction to Lawyers

刘晓炜

刘晓炜，合伙人，执业 10 年，处理了大量诉讼事务，主要涉及房地产、土地、知识产权纠纷、投资纠纷，经办过诸如企业风险管理、并购、知识产权战略的许多非诉事务，为矿业、装饰、旅游、物流、建筑、医药、银行等企业提供常年法律顾问服务。于 2007 年开始为企业对越南、缅甸、老挝等东南亚、南亚国家直接投资服务。

Xiaowei Liu, a partner of Yunnan Jianguang Law firm, has been practicing as a lawyer for ten years, when he dealt with a lot of litigation cases about real estate, land dispute, IP tort and permission, investment dispute, contract dispute, labor and employment, criminal, and administrative lawsuit, as well as many non-litigation affairs such as enterprise risk control, M&A, IP strategy, provided long-term legal counselor services for mining, building decoration, travel, logistics, construction, pharmacy, bank, and other enterprises. He has been providing legal services for FDI in Vietnam, Myanmar, Laos, and other Southeast & South countries. since 2007.

律所介绍 / Introduction to Law Firms

广东众翔律师事务所

广东众翔律师事务所是中国首家在深圳市前海深港现代服务业合作区设立的个人律师事务所。该所律师不仅办理中外知识产权诉讼和仲裁案件，代理美国337调查业务，还为政府提供专项法律服务，担任过在香港联合交易所上市的公司以及多家大型公司的常年法律顾问。该所律师能够熟练运用中英文和西班牙语工作，与美国和欧洲著名知识产权专业律师事务所保持着密切的业务交流和合作，在中外知识产权法领域拥有专业的执业空间和良好的执业信誉。该所的宗旨是："做专业的国际知识产权律师事务所，联合各国律师，共同为已经和即将走出国门的中国公司和个人的智慧财产提供优质高效的法律服务。"

AF Law Firm, Guangdong was the first individual lawyer established in Qianhai Shenzhen-Hong Kong Modern Service Industry Cooperation Zone of shenzhen. Our lawyers not only handle IP litigation and arbitration cases in China and other countries, Response to the 337-survey business; but also provide special legal services to the government. We have served as legal counsel for many large companies including Hong Kong Stock Exchange listed companies. Proficient in English, Chinese and Spanish, and has close business communication and cooperation with well - known European IP law firms and US. It has professional practice space and good practice reputation in Chinese and foreign intellectual property law field. The purpose of the Firm is: "To do professional international intellectual property law firms, joint national lawyers, and has been about to go out of the country's Chinese companies and individuals to provide high - quality intellectual property and efficient legal services."

律师介绍 / Introduction to Lawyers

江知芸

江知芸，一级律师，广东众翔律师事务所负责人。业务专长领域为中外知识产权法。西北政法大学法学学士，美国伊利诺伊理工学院芝加哥肯特法学院国际比较法硕士。欧美同学会会员，中华全国律师协会涉外律师领军人才，中华全国律师协会"一带一路"跨境律师人才库律师，广东省律师协会知识产权专业委员会副主任，广东律师专家库知识产权法律事务专家，广东省知识产权法律专家库专家，深圳市知识产权局知识产权专家委员会专家，深圳市WTO法律服务专家库专业律师。

Ms. Dennia Jiang, Licensed in China, One-grade lawyer, Director and Attorney at Law of AF Law Firm, Guangdong. Western Returned Scholars Association, Member. The Foreign Affair's talent lawyer in All China Lawyers Association. Lawyer of the Cross-border Lawyer of the "Belt and Road" of the All China Lawyers Association. Guangdong Province Lawyers Association, deputy director of the professional committee of the intellectual property. The experts in Guangdong lawyers expert database. The experts in Guangdong intellectual property office of the expert committee. The experts in Shenzhen intellectual property office of the expert committee. Shenzhen WTO law service expert professional lawyers.

阿尔巴尼亚——撰稿人介绍 / Albania—Introduction to Authors

律所介绍 / Introduction to Law Firms

Boga & Associates 律师事务所

Boga & Associates 律师事务所成立于1994年，为阿尔巴尼亚领先的律师事务所之一。该所以为客户提供最高质量的法律服务、税务服务和会计服务而享有盛誉。该所还在科索沃（普里什蒂纳）开展业务，并提供全方位的服务。2007年5月，该所成为毕马威的国际成员所。高级合伙人／管理合伙人 Genc Boga 先生同时担任毕马威阿尔巴尼亚的高级合伙人／执行合伙人。

该所擅长为客户提供多领域的服务，并始终追求卓越。除了广泛扎实的法律实践之外，该所对阿尔巴尼亚和科索沃快速变化的商业环境具有敏锐的洞察力，在税务和会计服务方面能够提供最高标准的专业知识。

该所服务的主要客户所涉行业包括大型实业、银行业、金融机构，并为从事保险、建筑、能源和公用事业、娱乐传媒、采矿、石油和天然气、专业服务、房地产、技术、电信、旅游、运输、基础设施和消费品行业的公司提供服务。

该所连续被 The Legal 500、钱伯斯法律评级机构的商事、争议解决、项目、知识产权领域以及《国际金融法律评论》在金融法、公司法领域评为"顶级律师事务所"。该所被客户和同行称赞为"具有高水平专业知识的律师事务所""市场领先的业务实践""阿尔巴尼亚精英"，并以"亲近、负责和明智"而著称。

Boga & Associates, established in 1994, has emerged as one of the premier law firms in Albania, earning a reputation for providing the highest quality of legal, tax and accounting services to its clients. The firm also operates in Kosovo (Pristina) offering full range of services. Until May 2007, the firm was a member firm of KPMG International and the Senior Partner/Managing Partner, Mr. Genc Boga was also Senior Partner/Managing Partner of KPMG Albania.

The firm's particularity is linked to the multidisciplinary services it provides to its clients, through an uncompromising commitment to excellence. Apart from the widely consolidated legal practice, the firm also offers the highest standards of expertise in tax and accounting services, with keen sensitivity to the rapid changes in the Albanian and Kosovo business environment.

The firm delivers services to leading clients in major industries, banks and financial institutions, as well as to companies engaged in insurance, construction, energy and utilities, entertainment and media, mining, oil and gas, professional services, real estate, technology, telecommunications, tourism, transport, infrastructure and consumer goods.

The firm is continuously ranked as a "top tier firm" by The Legal 500, by Chambers and Partners for Corporate/Commercial, Dispute Resolution, Projects, Intellectual Property, Real Estate, as well as by IFLR in Financial and Corporate Law. The firm is praised by clients and peers as a "law firm with high-calibre expertise", "the market-leading practice", "a unique legal know-how", distinguished "among the elite in Albania" and described as "accessible, responsive and wise".

律师介绍 / Introduction to Lawyers

Genc Boga

Genc Boga 是 Boga & Associates 律师事务所的创始合伙人和管理合伙人。Boga 先生的专业领域包括商业和公司法、特许权法、能源法、公司法、银行和金融、税务、诉讼、竞争法、房地产、环境保护法等。

Boga 先生担任多家银行、金融机构，以及经营能源、基础设施和房地产等重大项目的国际投资者的顾问，拥有扎实的专业知识。凭借他的执业经历，Boga & Associates 一直被最重要的金融机构和外国投资者定期聘为法律顾问。

Boga 先生经常为欧洲复兴开发银行、国际金融公司和世界银行在阿尔巴尼亚和科索沃的各种投资项目提供咨询。

Boga 先生连续被钱伯斯法律评级机构和 IFLR1 000 评为阿尔巴尼亚领先律师。

Boga 先生精通英语、法语和意大利语。

Genc Boga is the founder and Managing Partner of Boga & Associates which operates in both jurisdictions of Albania and Kosovo. Mr. Boga's fields of expertise include business and company law, concession law, energy law, corporate law, banking and finance, taxation, litigation, competition law, real estate, environment protection law etc.

Mr. Boga has solid expertise as advisor to banks, financial institutions and international investors operating in major projects in energy, infrastructure and real estate. Thanks to his experience, Boga & Associates is retained as legal advisor on regular basis by the most important financial institutions and foreign investors.

He regularly advises EBRD, IFC and World Bank in various investment projects in Albania and Kosovo.

Mr. Boga is continuously ranked as leading lawyer in Albania by Chambers and Partners and IFLR 1000.

He is fluent in English, French and Italian.

Jonida Skendaj

Jonida 女士于 2004 年加入 Boga & Associates 律师事务所，现为合伙人。

Jonida 女士是一名专业的商业律师，协助客户处理涉及商事法律方面的问题，包括公司、雇用、公司税务、竞争法、兼并和收购以及知识产权。

Jonida 女士还为银行和金融机构在阿尔巴尼亚的日常经营活动提供协助，包括合规需求。

除与客户有关的工作之外，Jonida 女士还发表了大量有关税务和反垄断方面的文章。

Jonida 女士是国际商会仲裁和替代性争议解决委员会和国际商会竞争法委员会委员，CSR 网络阿尔巴尼亚公司董事会成员。

Jonida 女士于 2002 年毕业于法国巴黎第十大学，并于 2003 年获得法国巴黎第十大学商业法硕士学位。

Jonida 女士精通法语、英语和意大利语。

Jonida is a Partner at Boga & Associates, which she joined in 2004.

She is a specialised business lawyer and assists clients on any business law aspects, including corporate, employment, taxation of corporations, competition law implications, mergers and acquisitions and intellectual property.

Jonida also assists banks and financial institutions in their day-to-day activity in Albania including regulatory compliance requirements.

In addition to her client related work, Jonida has published extensively on tax and antitrust issues.

She is a member of ICC Commission on Arbitration and ADR and ICC Commission on Competition. Jonida is a member of the Board of Directors of CSR Network Albania.

She graduated in Business Law ("Maîtrise en Droit des Affaires") at the University of Paris X Nanterre, Paris, France in 2002 and obtained a Master Degree in Business Law ("Diplôme d'Etudes Approfondies en Droit des Affaires"), in 2003 at the University of Paris X Nanterre, Paris, France.

Jonida is fluent in French, English and Italian.

律所介绍 / Introduction to Law Firms

Hoxha, Memi & Hoxha 律师事务所

Hoxha, Memi & Hoxha 律师事务所是一家独立的商业律师事务所，在商业法律的核心领域为客户提供法律服务，并协助一些本地公司和国际公司在阿尔巴尼亚开展业务。

该所在商业法核心领域拥有丰富的专业知识，并且能够在相关领域提供优质的服务。该所在协助和处理复杂而敏感的事务方面有出色的表现且经验丰富。

该所协助客户开展业务活动，如从公司组建到企业融资、税务规划、就业问题、获取许可证、收购或进行复杂交易。

Hoxha, Memi & Hoxha is an independent Albanian business law firm. The firm provides legal services in all core areas of business law to assist clients in the development of their venture, and assist some of the largest local companies and international corporations operating in Albania.

HM&H has a first class expertise in all core areas of business law and are able to offer unrivalled expertise in the relevant fields, with in depth knowledge of the business sector. The Firm have an excellent and proven track- record in assisting and handling complicated and sensitive tasks.

We assist clients in all aspects related to the conduct of a business activity, starting from company formation to financing the business, tax planning, employment issues, obtaining licenses and permits, acquiring assets and property or entering into complex transactions.

律师介绍 / Introduction to Lawyers

Elion Shkodrani

Elion Shkodrani 是 Hoxha, Memi & Hoxha 律师事务所的执业律师，他的执业领域侧重于行政法、特许经营权和环境问题，曾协助私人客户和公共部门组织和实施 PPP 和公共服务特许经营项目。

此外，Elion 还协助投资者开展了一系列房地产开发和能源项目，从而在项目运营方面积累了丰富的经验。Elion 一直是起草阿尔巴尼亚公共当局现行特许权手册和其他相关法律、法规的法律团队中的一员。Elion 获得了博洛尼亚大学法学院的法学博士和硕士学位。

Elion Shkodrani is an associate at Hoxha, Memi & Hoxha. Elion's practice focuses in administrative law, concessions and environment matters. He has assisted both private clients and the public sector in the structuring and implementation of PPP and public service concession projects.

Additionally, Elion has assisted investors in a number of real estate development and energy projects, thus gaining substantial experience in running project procedures. Elion has been part of the legal team that drafted the current concessions manual of the Albanian public authorities and other related key legal acts. Elion received a J.D. equivalent and a master degree from the Bologna University Law School. He is a qualified Albanian lawyer.

Dorant Ekmekçiu

Dorant Ekmekçiu 是 Hoxha, Memi & Hoxha 律师事务所的执业律师，专业领域主要是合同法、房地产和就业，此外，Dorant 的执业领域还包括破产法、争议解决和诉讼。

Dorant 在合同起草和谈判以及与雇用有关的事务方面拥有非常丰富的经验，其在争议解决方面也拥有非常丰富的经验，曾协助客户进行大量的高价值的诉讼以及破产程序。

Dorant 获得了地拉那大学法学院的法学博士学位，他在阿尔巴尼亚的各级司法部门具有代理资格。

Dorant Ekmekçiu is an associate at Hoxha, Memi & Hoxha. Dorant's practice on contracts law, real estate and employment matters. His practice additionally includes bankruptcy Law, disputes and litigation.

He has moreover a significant experience in contract drafting and negotiations, as well as in employment related matters. Dorant has a very strong experience in contentious matters and has assisted clients in a large number of sensitive and high value litigation and bankruptcy proceedings.

Dorant received a J.D. equivalent from the Tirana University Law School. He is qualified for representation in front of all levels of the Albanian judiciary.

阿尔巴尼亚——翻译及协调人介绍 / Albania—Introduction to Translators and Cooperators

律所介绍 / Introduction to Law Firms

国浩律师事务所

国浩律师事务所是中国大型的法律服务机构，是中国投融资领域尤其是资本市场非常专业的法律服务提供者，在跨境投资、海外并购等涉及中国企业"走出去"和"一带一路"相关法律服务方面优势明显，并积累了丰富的项目经验。迄今已为包括俄罗斯、蒙古、哈萨克斯坦、伊朗、印度、印度尼西亚、柬埔寨、越南、孟加拉国、马来西亚、巴基斯坦、阿尔巴尼亚、新加坡在内的许多"一带一路"沿线国家提供过法律服务，而由"国浩'一带一路'法律研究与服务中心"推出的"一带一路"沿线国家相关法律问题研究系列成果更是引起了业界的广泛关注。

Grandall Law Firm is one of the largest trans-regional partnership law firm in China. Grandall is the most professional legal service provider in the field of investment and financing in China, especially the capital market. Grandall has obvious advantages in relevant legal services to Chinese companies "going out" and "Belt and Road", such as cross-border investment, overseas mergers and acquisitions, and has accumulated rich project experiences. So far, Grandall has provided legal services to many countries along "Belt and Road", including Russia, Mongolia, Kazakhstan, Iran, India, Indonesia, Cambodia, Vietnam, Bangladesh, Malaysia, Pakistan, Albania and Singapore. The series of research results on related legal issues in the countries along the "Belt and Road" published by the "Grandall Belt and Road Legal Research and Service Centre" have attracted widespread concern.

律师介绍 / Introduction to Lawyers

胡静

胡静，中华全国律师协会国际业务专业委员会委员。胡静律师主要从事的业务领域有贸易救济及国际贸易、涉外并购、公司业务以及涉外诉讼和仲裁等。

胡静律师获得了中国政法大学硕士学位。

Dora Hu is the Member of All China Lawyers Association. Her fields of expertise include trade remedy and international trade, cross-border investment, corporate business and foreign related litigation and arbitration.

She obtained a LLM from China University of Political Science and Law.

律所介绍 / Introduction to Law Firms

广信君达律师事务所

广信君达律师事务所是广东省较早设立的合伙制律师事务所之一。2012年11月29日，原广东广信律师事务所、信利盛达律师事务所、安道永华律师事务所三家"广州十佳"律师事务所及其他所的优秀律师团队，合并为广东广信君达律师事务所。合并后，该所成为广东省内首家采用特殊普通合伙形式，实行公司化运营和专业化分工的广东最大的律师事务所。2017年6月，广信君达律师事务所总部入驻广州第一高楼——广州周大福金融中心，办公面积超过7000平方米；在东京、南宁、深圳、中山、东莞、清远、武汉设有分所，并在泰国曼谷设有联络办公室。

广信君达律师事务所拥有一支由400多名资深律师、专家学者领衔组成的专业法律服务团队，20年来，全所累计受理了近60万宗各类民商事、刑事、行政案件或项目。广信君达律师事务所也一直致力于为广大客户提供金融与保险、公司及证券、投资与并购、城市基础设施建设、建筑与房地产、知识产权、国际贸易等诉讼与非诉讼的优质法律服务。

ETR Law Firm is one of the earliest established partnership law firms in Guangdong Province. On November 29th, 2012, the then three top ten "Guangzhou Top Ten" lawyers' offices of Guangdong Guangxin, Xinli Shengda, and Ando Yonghua, and other outstanding lawyers successfully achieved a "strong strong alliance" and merged into Guangdong ETR Law Firm. After the merger, the Firm became the largest law firm in Guangdong Province which adopts a special general partnership form and implement corporate operations and specialization. In June 2017, ETR's headquarter office moved into the highest building in Guangzhou - Guangzhou Chow Tai Fook Financial Center, with an office area of more than 7000m². It has set up branches in Tokyo, Nanning, Shenzhen, Zhongshan, Dongguan, Qingyuan, and Wuhan, and a liaison office is set up in Bangkok, Thailand.

ETR has more than 400 professional legal service teams led by senior lawyers, experts and scholars, and maintains good cooperation with various professional service agencies. Over the past 20 years, ETR has handled nearly 600,000 various civil and commercial, criminal and administrative cases or projects. On the way forward, ETR is striving to provide its clients with high quality legal services in financial and insurance, corporate and securities, investment and mergers and acquisitions of urban infrastructure, construction and real estate, intellectual property, international trade, litigation and non-litigation areas.

律师介绍 / Introduction to Lawyers

陈赞

陈赞是广东广信君达律师事务所的执业律师,在跨境投资及融资、国际贸易、并购、知识产权、争议解决及其他与涉外相关的业务领域等方面拥有非常丰富的经验。陈赞律师在英国获得国际商法学硕士学位并通过英国律师资格考试,入选司法部、中华全国律师协会"中国涉外律师领军人才",也是广东省律师协会港澳台和外事工作委员会副主任。

Ms. Zan Chen is a practicing lawyer of Guangdong ETR Law Firm and has extensive experience in cross-border investment and financing, international trade, mergers and acquisitions, intellectual property, dispute resolution and other foreign-related business areas. Ms. Chen received a master's degree in International Commercial Law from the United Kingdom and passed the UK Bar Examination. She is the "Leading PRC Lawyer of International Practice" selected by the Ministry of Justice and the All Chinese Lawyers Association. She is also Deputy Director of the Hong Kong, Macao, Taiwan and Foreign Affairs Committee of the Guangdong Provincial Lawyers' Association.

阿根廷——撰稿人介绍 / Argentina—Introduction to Authors

律所介绍 / Introduction to Law Firms

Allende & Brea 律师事务所

Allende & Brea 律师事务所是阿根廷最大、最负盛名的综合性律师事务所之一。该事务所成立于 1957 年,致力于用专业的水平、严谨的态度、丰富的经验,为客户提供优质的法律服务。

该所的律师拥有哥伦比亚大学、纽约大学、杜克大学、芝加哥大学、弗吉尼亚州大学、密歇根州大学、西北大学、宾夕法尼亚大学、杜克大学等知名学府的法学硕士学位,并在纽约、芝加哥、迈阿密、华盛顿、旧金山和伦敦等地的律师事务所担任过外国律师。

为更好地满足客户需求,该所组成了各领域的专业化团队,包括反垄断、仲裁、银行、资本市场、消费者、公司、合规、海关、能源和自然资源、许可和特许经营、保险和再保险、知识产权、劳动和社会保障、诉讼、并购、重组和破产、税务、技术、电信和广播。

Allende & Brea is one of the largest and most prestigious full-service law firms in Argentina. Established in 1957, it provides legal advice to cover the needs of its clients, helping them to achieve their goals. In an ever-changing environment, the ability to adapt is crucially important. Allende & Brea's lawyers provide the highest level of commitment, intellectual rigor and experience, which has been the key of our success for 60 years.

The firm's lawyers have obtained over the years Master of Law degrees at universities such as Columbia, New York University, Duke, Chicago, Virginia, Michigan, Northwestern, Penn and Duke, and have held foreign lawyer's positions at major New York, Chicago, Miami, Washington, San Francisco and London law firms.

To better serve the clients' business needs, the firm is organized into dedicated, specialized, focused groups in all areas of business law and industry sectors, such as: antitrust, arbitration, banking, capital markets, consumer, corporate, compliance, customs, energy and natural resources, licensing and franchising, insurance and reinsurance, intellectual property, labor and social security, litigation, mergers and acquisitions, restructuring and bankruptcy, tax, technology, telecommunications and broadcasting.

律师介绍 / Introduction to Lawyers

Valeriano Guevara Lynch

Valeriano Guevara Lynch 是 Allende & Brea 律师事务所的管理合伙人,1995 年从阿根廷天主教大学毕业,1996 年加入该所,1999 年获得杜克大学法学硕士学位,2003 年成为该所合伙人。他在杜克大学法学院攻读了公司法,并在富卡商学院学习金融。1991 年至 1996 年期间,他曾在布宜诺斯艾利斯担任法官助理,并于 2000 年至 2002 年期间在纽约的 Cravath, Swaine & Moore 律师事务所工作。

Mr. Guevara Lynch is currently the Managing Partner of Allende & Brea. He joined the firm in 1996 after graduating from the "Universidad Católica Argentina" in 1995 and became partner in 2003 after obtaining a Masters in Laws in 1999 from Duke University where he studied general corporate law in the Law School, and finance at the Fuqua School of Business. Between 1991 and 1996 he served as law clerk to Judge Liliana Filgueira de Casares in the City of Buenos Aires and between 2000 and 2002 he worked at the law firm of Cravath, Swaine & Moore in New York.

Raúl Fratantoni

Raúl Fratantoni 于 1998 年毕业于阿根廷天主教大学，2001 年获得伊利诺伊大学厄本纳—香槟分校法律硕士学位。他是布宜诺斯艾利斯律师协会、纽约州律师协会、纽约市律师协会的会员。作为公司和并购业务的合伙人，他主要为客户提供并购、海外投资、公司法、合同、房地产和税务筹划等方面的法律服务。

Mr. Fratantoni graduated as a lawyer from the Facultad de Derecho y Ciencias Políticas of Universidad Católica Argentina in 1998. In 2001, he obtained a Master of Laws degree (LL.M.) at University of Illinois at Urbana-Champaign. He is a member of the Bar of the City of Buenos Aires, the New York State Bar, and the New York City Bar. He is a partner of the Corporate and M&A practice, and has advised our clients in merger and acquisitions, foreign investments, corporate law, contracts, and estate and tax planning.

律所介绍 / Introduction to Law Firms

Beccar Varela 律师事务所

Beccar Varela 律师事务所成立于 1897 年，是阿根廷领先的全方位服务律师事务所，为公司法领域的当地和国际公司提供咨询服务。凭借超过 120 年的服务，该所结合对现代法律的理解，总结出一套独特的创新实践经验。

该所总部位于布宜诺斯艾利斯市。该所在布宜诺斯艾利斯市北部的 Tigre 有一个分所。该所的团队协助客户在全国范围内开展活动，并得到大型网络及其他律师事务所的支持。Beccar Varela 律师事务所与国际网络结成联盟，将全球高度可靠的律师事务所聚集在一起。

该所有 150 多名律师，专门从事不同领域的法律服务，其中许多律师曾在世界商业中心学习或工作过。该所律师可以用西班牙语、英语、法语、德语、意大利语、普通话和葡萄牙语为客户提供服务。

2017 年，在 Chambers and Partners Latin America，Beccar Varela 被评为阿根廷的年度律师事务所。

Founded in 1897, Beccar Varela is a leading full-service law firm in Argentina, which advises local and international companies in all areas of corporate law across all industries. With over 120 years of service, it has built a unique and innovative practice, combining experience and understanding of modern law.

Beccar Varela's head office is in the city of Buenos Aires. It also has a branch in Tigre, in northern Buenos Aires. The firm's team assist clients with activities across the country, supported by a large network of correspondent firms. Throughout its history, Beccar Varela has forged alliances with international networks that bring together highly reliable law firms worldwide.

The firm's team consists of over 150 lawyers specializing in different areas of law, many of whom have studied or worked in the world's business capitals. They are supported by motivated paralegals and interns, and by talented and creative administrative staff. Beccar Varela's lawyers can serve clients in Spanish, English, French, German, Italian, Mandarin and Portuguese.

In 2017, Beccar Varela was named "Argentina Law Firm of the Year" by Chambers and Partners Latin America.

律师介绍 / Introduction to Lawyers

Roberto A. Fortunati

Roberto A. Fortunati 是 Beccar Varela 律师事务所的合伙人，也是该所执行委员会的成员。他主管律师事务所的资源部门，并主管银行、金融机构以及并购部门。

他的主要业务领域是银行和金融机构、兼并与收购以及项目融资，特别关注自然资源。他是采矿、能源和石油、天然气行业公认的专家。他还担任世界银行破产事务的顾问。

1979 年，Roberto 从布宜诺斯艾利斯大学获得法律学位。他是布宜诺斯艾利斯律师协会、国际律师协会和美国律师协会的成员，同时还是几家公司的董事会成员。

他会讲西班牙语、英语、法语、葡萄牙语和意大利语。

Roberto A. Fortunati is a partner at Beccar Varela and a member of the firm's Executive Committee. He heads the firm's Natural Resources Department and co-heads the Banking and Financial Institutions and M&A departments.

His main practice areas are banking and financial institutions, mergers & acquisitions and project finance, with particular focus on natural resources. He is a recognized expert in the mining, energy and oil & gas industries. He has also acted as consultant to The World Bank on insolvency matters.

Roberto obtained his Law degree from Universidad de Buenos Aires (1979). He is a member of the Buenos Aires Bar Association, the International Bar Association and the American Bar Association. He is on the Board of Directors of several companies, and is a member of various professional associations, both national and international.

He speaks Spanish, English, French, Portuguese and Italian.

Nicolás Rukavina Mikusic

Nicolás Rukavina Mikusic 于 2011 年加入 Beccar Varela 律师事务所,是该所的资深律师。他的业务领域包括公司法,重点关注并购,商业实体的形成和结构,公司治理问题,与商业公司有关的一般公司事务,为国内和国际客户提供咨询服务。

Nicolás Rukavina Mikusic is a senior lawyer of Beccar Varela. He joined the firm in 2011. His practice area includes corporate law with a focus on M&A, the formation and structuring of business entities, corporate governance issues, corporate disputes and general corporate matters related to commercial companies, advising domestic and international clients.

阿根廷——翻译及协调人介绍 / Argentina—Introduction to Translators and Cooperators

律所介绍 / Introduction to Law Firms

广东恒福律师事务所

广东恒福律师事务所是一家处理海事、海商、保险、贸易、房地产、知识产权、金融、刑事、行政、劳资、海外仲裁等法律事务的综合性律师事务所。

广东恒福律师事务所在处理海事、海商和保险业务方面是有较强实力的律师事务所之一。多年来,广东恒福律师事务所处理了大量疑难、复杂的案件,获得当事人的高度评价。2013 年,广东恒福律师事务所被世界著名法律评级机构钱伯斯评为中国华南地区"最佳海事海商律师事务所",2016 年被中华全国律师协会评为"2011—2014 年度全国优秀律师事务所"。

Yang & Lin Co. Law Firm is a comprehensive law firm dealing with maritime, admiralty, insurance, trade, real estate, intellectual property rights, finance, criminals, administrative affairs, labor relations, and overseas arbitration disputes and affairs.

Yang & Lin is recognized as one of the top law firms dealing with maritime, admiralty, trade and insurance cases in China. Over the years, Yang & Lin has handled numerous complicated cases and won high praises. In 2013, Yang & Lin was highly recommended by Chambers and Partners - a world-renowned legal rating agency as the Leading Law Firm in Shipping in Southern China. In 2016, Yang & Lin was elected as National Elite Law Firm from 2011 to 2014 by the All China Lawyers Association.

律师介绍 / Introduction to Lawyers

林翠珠

林翠珠,广东恒福律师事务所创始合伙人,双博士学位、双法学硕士学位,有丰富的工作经验。

林翠珠律师是中华全国律师协会首批"全国涉外律师领军人才",兼任多家大学教授,广东省律师协会"一带一路"法律服务研究中心四大项目小组组长之一,广州市律师协会"一带一路"法律业务专业委员会主任,广州仲裁委员会仲裁员,并被聘请为华南理工大学、华南师范大学校外硕士生导师。

Judy Lin, founding partner of Yang & Lin Co. Law Firm, has a rich experience of studying and working aboard with two doctoral degrees and two LLM degrees.

As one of the first Leading Talent Lawyer awarded by All China Lawyers Association, Judy serves as part-time professor in several universities, and she is also appointed as team leader of "the Belt and Road" Legal Research Center of Guangdong Lawyers Association and director of "the Belt and Road" Committee of Guangzhou Lawyers Association. She's an arbitrator of Guangzhou Arbitration Commission. She is also appointed as extramural academic advisor for postgraduate students by both South China Normal University and South China University of Technology.

律所介绍 / Introduction to Law Firms

天册律师事务所

天册律师事务所(以下简称"天册所")始创于 1986 年,总部位于杭州,在北京、上海、宁波设有分所,是合伙制律师事务所。天册所同时获有中国律师事务所两项最高荣誉——司法部授予的"部级文明律师事务所"称号和中华全国律师协会授予的"全国优秀律师事务所"称号,并且多次荣获《亚洲法律杂志》(Asia Legal Business)中国中东部年度最佳律师事务所大奖、《中国法律与实践》(China Law & Practice)年度地区最佳律师事务所奖,并入选《钱伯斯亚太领先商事律师客户指南》。

天册所核心服务领域为公司业务、金融证券、外商投资、国际贸易、房地产、知识产权及民商事诉讼和仲裁。该所与国际律师事务所以及国内各中心城市的优秀律师事务所组建了业务协作和联营组织[即中世律所联盟(SGLA)],可以为客户开展境内外商务活动提供宽领域、高质素和跨地域的法律服务。

Formed in 1986, T&C is one of the earliest partnership law firms in China, being headquartered in Hangzhou with branch offices in Beijing, Shanghai and Ningbo. T&C has been awarded the two top honors in the legal service sector in China—National Civilized Law Firm by Ministry of Justice of P. R. China and National Outstanding Law Firm by All China Lawyers Association. Moreover, T&C has been awarded the "East and Central China Law Firm of the Year" of ALB(Asia Legal Business) and the "Regional Firm of the Year" of CLP(China Law & Practice) for several times, and has been selected to "A Client's Guide: Asia-Pacific's Leading Lawyers for Business" of Chambers.

T&C's core practices focus on the areas of corporate business, finance& securities, foreign investment, international trade, real estate, intellectual property, civil and commercial litigation and arbitration. T&C, together with a number of excellent law firms from all over the major cities in China and international law firms, formed the Sino-Global Legal Alliance ("SGLA"), which aims to provide the clients of the members of SGLA with wide-range, professional and cross-regional legal service.

律师介绍 / Introduction to Lawyers

郭芳

郭芳律师，浙江天册律师事务所合伙人。浙江省律师协会涉外与海事海商业务委员会副主任，中国国际贸易促进委员会、中国国际商会调解员，中国（杭州）跨境电子商务就业创业导师团导师，浙江大学法学院实务导师。2013 年入选司法部、中华全国律师协会"涉外律师领军人才库"，2016 年入选中华全国律师协会"'一带一路'跨境律师人才库"。主要执业领域为国际投资与并购、外商投资及相关争议解决等。

Ms. Guo Fang, Partner & Attorney of Zhejiang T&C Law Firm, Vice Chief Director of International Business Affairs Business Committee of Zhejiang Lawyers Association, Mediator of the Mediation Center of China Council for the Promotion of International Trade(CCPIT)/China Chamber of International Commerce(CCOIC), Mentor of China (Hangzhou) Cross-border E-commerce Employment & Entrepreneurship Mentor Group, Mentor of Law School of Zhejiang University. Ms. Guo has been selected into the China National Talent Pool of International Lawyers in 2013 and the Cross-border Lawyer Talent Pool of "the Belt and Road" Strategic Construction Project in 2013 by All China Lawyers Association. Ms. Guo specializes in international mergers and acquisitions, foreign direct investment, and relevant dispute resolution.

亚美尼亚——撰稿人介绍 / Armenia—Introduction to Authors

律所介绍 / Introduction to Law Firms

Concern-Dialog 律师事务所

Concern-Dialog 律师事务所设立于 1998 年，其业务涉及广泛，致力于在公司法、竞争法、合同法、劳动法、物权法以及税法等方面提供高质量的专业服务。同时，该所业务涉及电子通信、传媒、矿业、能源、博彩、银行法规、公共法律咨询、立法政策的发展以及政府关系等方面。

该所及其律师多次登上钱伯斯排名，以及 Legal 500、《国际金融法律评论》等著名机构排行榜。

该所在业界拥有广泛的合作，包括与大成律师事务所在 TAGLaw 与 NextLaw 平台上的广泛合作。该所还积极参与亚美尼亚美国商会、亚美尼亚德国商会（DWV）、亚美尼亚法国商业与工业协会和亚美尼亚英国商会等商业组织。

该所加入了伊斯兰新兴金融咨询平台。

Concern-Dialog Law Firm is a full–service law firm founded in 1998. The company's specialization includes the legal aspects in various spheres providing high-level services in corporate, competition, contract, labor, property and tax laws; on electronic communications, media, mining, energy, gambling, banking regulatory issues, legal consulting to public entities and legislation and policy development and governmental relations.

The firm and its lawyers have been ranked by several reputable organizations, including Chambers and Partners, Legal 500, IFLR 1000.

Concern-Dialog is a member of several legal networks, such as TAGLaw and NextLaw by Dentons, and is an active member of several business associations, including the American Chamber of Commerce in Armenia, the German Business Association in Armenia (DWV), Chamber of Commerce and Industry France Armenia and Armenian British Business Chamber.

Recently, Concern Dialog has become a member of the ISFIN platform (Islamic Finance advisory for emerging markets).

律师介绍 / Introduction to Lawyers

Sedrak Asatryan

Sedrak Asatryan 自 2003 年成为 Concern Dialog 律师事务所管理合伙人，执业领域涉及劳动法、行政法及房地产法等，在代理诉讼和行政申诉方面拥有丰富的经验。

除律师工作外，Asatryan 先生也在倡导者学校授课，并于 2017 年当选为亚美尼亚倡导者协会理事会理事。

Asatryan 先生撰写了多篇文章和多部著作［包括手册，如亚美尼亚《新劳动法：雇佣合同》《新劳动法：雇主的内部和个人法律行为》《律所管理》和涉及"雇佣和劳动法"的著作，ICLG 第 6 版（2016）、ICLG 第 7 版（2017），《理事会和合伙中的雇佣关系》等］。

Sedrak Asatryan has been the Managing Partner of Concern Dialog law firm since 2003. He practices in the areas of Labor Law, General Administrative Law and issues regarding Real Estate. Mr. Asatryan has wide experience in representing clients in courts and various administrative bodies.

In addition to his attorney practice, Mr. Asatryan lectures at the School of Advocates. In 2017, Mr. Asatryan was elected to the Board of the Chamber of Advocates of the Republic of Armenia.

Mr. Asatryan has authored several articles and publications (including handbooks: "The New Labor Code of the RA: Employment Contracts"; "The New Labor Code of the RA: Employer's Internal and Individual Legal Acts"; "Law Firm Management" and publications referring "Employment and Labor Law", ICLG, 6th Edition, 2016 and 7th Edition, 2017; "Employment" in Chambers and Partners 2018) and etc..

Roustam Badasyan

Roustam Badasyan 是 Concern Dialog 律师事务所的合伙人，业务领域为税法，自 2015 年成为亚美尼亚倡导者协会会员。

Badasyan 先生参与了与收购亚美尼亚一家大型矿业公司有关的税务优化事宜的咨询，并为某大型金融机构就发行欧洲债券的税务事宜提供法律意见。

Badasyan 先生在代理涉税的行政和司法程序案件方面具有丰富的经验，其中包括代表一家矿业公司解释关于支付自然资源使用费的法律，以及代表跨国组织分支机构在亚美尼亚的母公司就增值税应税交易提供法律服务。

Roustam Badasyan is Partner at Concern Dialog Law Firm who is responsible for Tax Law practice. He is a member of the Chamber of Advocates of the RA since 2015.

Roustam Badasyan was involved in consultancy on tax optimization matters related to the acquisition of a major mining company in Armenia and on tax consequences related to the issuance of Eurobonds by one of the major financial organization.

Roustam Badasyan has significant experience in representing his clients in tax related cases in the scope of administrative and judicial proceedings. Significant cases include representation of a mining company in connection with the interpretation of the legislation concerning the payment of royalties for the use of natural recourses and representation of a branch of a transnational organization concerning VAT taxable transactions implemented by the parent company in Armenia and attributed to the branch by Tax Authorities.

律所介绍 / Introduction to Law Firms

Grant Thornton 法律及税务事务所

Grant Thornton 法律及税务事务所（GTLT）是一个多专业的律师、税务和会计顾问团队。该所是由 Grant Thornton（GT）CJSC 的法律和税务部门拆分并组成的一个独立的业务实体。GT 亚美尼亚办公室成立于 20 世纪 90 年代初，以专业的视角致力于为客户提供高质量的服务。经过二十多年的奉献和承诺，客户享受了高度专业、诚信和精准的服务。通过在"GT 国际"的会员资格，该所保持着与全球成员公司和"GT 国际"IBC 的交流与合作。除了高度的专业精神之外，该所的专家以其专业的外语能力闻名，并帮助各地区客户进行对外经济活动及与海外公司合作。

Grant Thornton Legal & Tax LLC (GTLT) is a multi-professional group of lawyers, tax and accounting advisors. The firm was founded by spinning off the legal and tax departments of Grant Thornton (GT) CJSC into a separate business entity. GT Armenia was founded in the early 1990s, organized by a common professional vision and especially focused on providing high-quality services to clients. For more than 20 years of dedication and commitment, its clients have enjoyed high professionalism, integrity and deep understanding of the requirements of their businesses. Through its membership in GT International, the firm has access to a network of member firms and GT International IBCs worldwide. In addition to high professionalism, the firm's specialists are renowned for their profound foreign languages proficiency which helps local clientele in foreign economic activity and co-operation with overseas companies.

律师介绍 / Introduction to Lawyers

Hakob Tadevosyan

Hakob 先生在 2001 年加入 Grant Thornton 法律及税务事务所，并负责该所的战略方向、运营执行和整体领导。

Hakob joined Grant Thornton in 2001. He is responsible for the strategic direction, operational execution and overall leadership of GTLT.

Tatevik Harutyunyan

Tatevik Harutyunyan 在 2009 年加入 Grant Thornton 法律及税务事务所，对公司法律法规、中小企业部门法律和行政法律有深入的研究。

Legal Department, GTLT Tatevik Harutyunyan joined Grant Thornton network in 2009. She has strong knowledge on corporate laws and regulations, SME sector legislation and administrative law.

亚美尼亚——翻译及协调人介绍 / Armenia—Introduction to Translators and Cooperators

律所介绍 / Introduction to Law Firms

锦天城律师事务所

锦天城律师事务所是一家提供全方位法律服务的中国律师事务所。该所在中国 22 个城市及伦敦设有分所，为境内外客户制订法律解决方案并提供法律服务。

该所多次被司法部、中华全国律师协会及国际知名的法律媒体和权威机构列为中国顶尖的法律服务提供者之一。

该所有执业律师 2 000 多人，可以使用多种语言工作，许多律师拥有美国多个州、英国、法国和日本等地的执业资格。

该所为其客户在涉及公司、商业与并购、证券与资本市场、银行与金融、房地产与建筑、争议解决（诉讼与仲裁）、国际贸易及"一带一路"法律服务、海商海事、知识产权保护领域的商业交易和争议中，提供有效的解决方案和服务。该所的客户遍及全球，涉及大中型国有企业、事业单位、跨国集团、外商投资企业、民营企业、各类金融机构等。

AllBright Law Offices is a leading full-service Chinese law firm in China. As a national law firm headquartered in Shanghai, it provides a comprehensive range of high-quality legal services to both domestic and international clients from its twenty-two domestic offices and branch in London.

Widely acknowledged as one of the top legal service providers by Ministry of Justice P.R.C., ACLA and numerous international legal media and institutions, AllBright Law Offices has been in the front rank of the country.

AllBright has approximately 2,000 lawyers, who can provide legal service in multiple languages. Many of the lawyers are admitted in the United States, the U.K., France, Japan and other foreign jurisdictions.

AllBright Law Offices provides cost-efficient and world-class legal solutions and services to clients in corporations, mergers and acquisitions, securities and capital markets, banking and financing, real estate and construction, dispute resolution (litigations and arbitrations), international trade and "Belt and Road" service, maritime and shipping, intellectual property and other practice areas. Our clients come from all over the country and the world, which include state-owned powerhouses, institutions, international groups, foreign invested enterprises, private enterprises, banks and financial institutions.

律师介绍 / Introduction to Lawyers

李玛林

李玛林律师现为锦天城律师事务所高级合伙人，专注海商海事和涉外领域法律服务，在跨境船舶建造、跨境贸易和投资争议方面有丰富的经验，曾先后代理船舶建造出口和融资项目数十起，自 2000 年以来，在国内海事法院及新加坡国际仲裁中心、中国香港国际仲裁中心、伦敦国际仲裁院等代理仲裁机构案件逾 500 件。

李玛林律师现为中华全国律师协会国际业务委员会和海商海事业务委员会委员，并任江苏省律师协会海商海事业务委员会副主任等。

As a senior partner of Allbright Law Offices and experienced in maritime and foreign-related issues, Li Malin has handled more than 500 litigation proceedings, items or projects for state departments, shipping companies, insurance companies and foreign-invested enterprises since 2000 before domestic maritime court, CIETAC, SIAC, HKIAC, LCIA and LMAA.

Malin has been certified as member of All-China Lawyers Association international business committee and maritime affairs committee, and has been chosen director of Maritime Professional Committee of Jiangsu Bar Association.

律所介绍 / Introduction to Law Firms

安徽天禾律师事务所

安徽天禾律师事务所成立于1987年，自成立以来，秉承"专业、诚信、勤勉、规范"的执业理念，为社会各界提供了优质高效的法律服务，赢得了社会各界的普遍认可和赞誉。该所先后获得了"全国优秀律师事务所""全国优秀青少年维权岗""安徽省司法行政系统先进集体""安徽省优秀律师事务所""安徽省律师事务所综合实力十强""安徽省综合实力五十强律师事务所"等光荣称号。该所现有执业律师及行辅人员140余名，拥有2000多平方米现代办公写字楼，业绩名列安徽省前茅，勇于承担社会责任，已发展为安徽省内具有较大影响力的综合性律师事务所。

安徽天禾律师事务所在金融证券、投资融资、大型建设项目、涉外等法律业务领域，在业内享有较高声誉。

Since its foundation in 1987, Anhui Tian He Law Firm has been upholding four guiding principles: professionalism, integrity, diligence, and compliance. It receives wide recognition and good reputation on account of its qualified and efficient legal service. It has been awarded National Outstanding Law Firm, National Excellent Protecting Base of Children's Rights, Leading Group in the Judicial and Administrative System of Anhui Province, Outstanding Law Firm in Anhui Province, the Top 10 Law Firms in Anhui Province, and the Top 50 Law Firms in Anhui Province. At present, we have 140-odd practicing attorneys and administrators and a modern office of more than 2000 square meters. Our performance is one of the best in Anhui province and we are passionate to undertake social responsibilities. All of these have enabled us to develop into an influential and full-service law firm in Anhui province.

Tian He Law Firm enjoys prestige in financing, securities, investment, large-scale construction projects and foreign-related legal affairs.

律师介绍 / Introduction to Lawyers

李结华

李结华律师，安徽天禾律师事务所合伙人，毕业于安徽大学，先后获英语学士学位和法律硕士学位。现任安徽省律师协会外事工作委员会主任委员、涉外法律专业委员会副主任委员，入选首批"全国涉外律师领军人才"（全国总计348人）、首批安徽省律师协会"青年律师人才库"金融证券类（全省总计34人），入选司法部"全国千名涉外律师人才"。

2015年10月至11月，被中华全国律师协会、司法部公派到美国费城天普大学和Pepper Hamilton LLP律师事务所进行交流学习。

李结华在跨境投资与并购法律事务、资本市场业务、企业改制、私募股权投资基金等领域具有丰富经验，熟悉财务会计及税收等专业知识。

Li Jiehua is a partner in Tian He Law Firm. As a graduate of Anhui University, he has received bachelor's degree in English and then Juris Master Degree. He is currently the chairman of the Foreign Affairs Committee, and the vice-chairman of the Foreign-related Law Committee of Anhui Lawyers Association. He is included in The First National Talent Pool of Lawyers for Foreign-related Affairs (altogether 348 lawyers across the country), The First Talent Pool of Young Lawyers for Finance and Securities of Anhui Lawyers Association (34 lawyers in total across the province), The National Talent Pool of Thousands of foreign-related lawyers.

From October 2015 to November 2015, he was sponsored by All China Lawyers Association and Ministry of Justice to be a visiting scholar in Temple University and Law Firm of Pepper Hamilton LLP.

He is quite experienced in such sectors as cross-border investment and M&A, operations in capital market, restructuring of enterprises, private equity and etc. In addition, he has profound knowledge of accounting and taxation.

澳大利亚——撰稿人介绍 / Australia—Introduction to Authors

律所介绍 / Introduction to Law Firms

金杜律师事务所澳大利亚办公室

金杜律师事务所澳大利亚办公室（以下简称"金杜澳大利亚"）是全球领先的律师事务所，有着深厚的澳大利亚文化和传统，在澳洲拥有超过1350名成员，分别负责法律专业工作或业务支持工作，其中包括超过165名合伙人及600多名律师。

该所在墨尔本、珀斯、布里斯班、堪培拉和悉尼都设有办公室,其中悉尼办公室为金杜澳大利亚的总部。在超过 185 年的发展历程中,金杜澳大利亚从一家澳洲本土律师事务所,发展为一个联结全世界成长型市场和金融资本的综合性全球网络。

在 2018 年钱伯斯亚太评选中,金杜澳大利亚有 19 项业务名列第一梯队(数量为澳洲律师事务所之最),包括公司/并购等业务,也是个人排名方面领先的律师事务所。

KWM AU is a leading global law firm with a deeply Australian heart and heritage. Nationally, KWM AU has a staff of over 1,350 across all legal and support functions including over 165 partners and 600 lawyers. KWM AU has centres in Melbourne, Perth, Brisbane, Canberra, and Sydney (which serves as the Australian headquarters). For over 185 years, KWM AU has grown from a collection of Australian city-based firms to become an integrated global network spanning the world's growth markets and financial capitals.

KWM AU in Australia has 19 tier-one rankings (most by any firm), including for Corporate/M&A, and most ranked individuals of any firm in Chambers Asia Pacific 2018.

律师介绍 / Introduction to Lawyers

Will Heath

Will Heath 是金杜律师事务所墨尔本办公室的合伙人。Will 曾为众多跨国企业及澳大利亚公司的并购交易、股权资本市场业务、合资经营及公司法律事务等项目提供法律服务。

2010 年至 2013 年,Will 曾在亚洲工作,期间他代理了一系列有影响力的跨境交易。Will 曾为众多中国企业在澳大利亚的投资项目提供法律服务,包括能源、基础设施建设、科技行业、健康产业及消费者业务等。

Will 是墨尔本大学法学院的高级研究员,为法学硕士讲授公司法课程。同时,他也在莫纳什大学讲授公司治理等法律课程。他曾在牛津大学以优异成绩取得了两个法学硕士学位,同时还获得了牛津大学 Menzies 纪念学者(法律)的荣誉。

Will Heath is a partner at King & Wood Mallesons' Melbourne office. Will advises multinational and Australian companies on public and private M&A, ECM, joint ventures and corporate advisory work.

Will acted on a number of significant cross-border transactions in Asia, where he worked and lived from 2010 to 2013. He has worked on a number of PRC corporate investments in Australia, including in the energy, infrastructure, technology, health and consumer sectors.

Will is a Senior Fellow at the Melbourne Law School where he teaches an LLM course in corporate law. He also teaches an undergraduate law course at Monash University focusing on corporate governance. He is a graduate of the University of Oxford, where he completed two masters' degrees in law, as a Menzies Memorial Scholar.

律所介绍 / Introduction to Law Firms

Gilbert + Tobin 律师事务所

Gilbert + Tobin 律师事务所是一家出色的律师事务所,也是澳大利亚法律市场的关键参与者。从悉尼、墨尔本到珀斯,该所为澳大利亚乃至全球,特别是在亚太地区的最重要的公司及政府客户提供新颖、中肯且富有商业眼光的法律对策。

该所关注不断进化的各市场部门,并参与定义和指导市场的交易项目和案件。Gilbert + Tobin 律师事务所一直是重视企业文化且拥有成功决心的行业领导者们首选的法律服务提供者。

Gilbert + Tobin 律师事务所以在许多领域提供的法律意见而享有盛名,包括银行和金融、公司顾问(基金、企业并购、私募股权投资、资本市场、税收及印花税)、竞争和监管、能源、知识产权、媒体、诉讼和争议解决、不动产和项目工程、技术和数字化。

Gilbert + Tobin 律师事务所成立于 1988 年,雇员超过 600 人。该所也被认为是提供公益服务的先行者。

Gilbert + Tobin is a leading corporate law firm and a key player in the Australian legal market. From our Sydney, Melbourne and Perth offices, the firm provides innovative, relevant and commercial legal solutions to major corporate and government clients across Australia and internationally, particularly in the Asia-Pacific region.

With a focus on dynamic and evolving market sectors, the firm works on transactions and cases that define and direct the market. Gilbert + Tobin has become the legal adviser of choice for industry leaders who value our entrepreneurial culture and determination to succeed.

Gilbert + Tobin's reputation for expert advice extends across a broad range of areas including: banking and finance; corporate advisory – funds, mergers and acquisitions, private equity, capital markets, tax and stamp duty; competition and regulation; energy and resources; intellectual property; media; litigation and dispute resolution; real estate and projects and technology and digital.

Established in 1988, Gilbert + Tobin employs more than 600 people. The firm is acknowledged as a pioneer in providing pro bono services.

律师介绍 / Introduction to Lawyers

Charles Coorey

Charles 是 Gilbert + Tobin 律师事务所竞争和监管部门的合伙人。

Charles 精通竞争法,包括并购通关、滥用市场支配地位及卡特尔;澳大利亚消费者法,包括混淆或欺诈行为、消费者保障及产品责任问题;基础设施市场准入,包括申报及准入承诺。

Charles 擅长数字经济、零售、航空、能源等领域的事务。特别是在数字经济领域,他参与了包括《全球竞争评论》主办的"GCR Live 新加坡——亚太法律领导人年度论坛"、《澳大利亚财经评论》主办的"国家创新峰会"、澳大利亚竞争政策峰会、新南威尔士州法律协会"未来法律及创新调研委员会"在内的许多重要会议。

Charles 被 Who's Who Legal 评为竞争法领域"未来领导者",同时被列入"最佳律师"及"Legal 500",并被评价为具有"非凡的客户服务精神"和"能迅速了解商机并清楚地运用在法律中"。

Charles is a partner in Gilbert + Tobin's Competition + Regulation group.

Charles' expertise includes competition law matters, including merger clearances, misuse of market power matters and cartel matters; the Australian Consumer Law including misleading or deceptive conduct, the consumer guarantees and product liability issues; and access to infrastructure including declaration applications and access undertakings.

Charles has experience in a broad range of industries, but specialises in digital economy, retail, aviation and energy and resources matters. His expertise in the digital economy has seen him present at a number of major conferences including the Global Competition Review's "GCR Live Singapore - Annual Asia Pacific Law Leaders Forum"; the Australian Financial Review's National Innovation Summit, the Australian Competition Policy Summit, "The Sunrise" as part of the Vivid Festival, the General Counsel Summit and the Law Society of New South Wales' "Commission of Inquiry into the Future of Law and Innovation".

Charles is recognised as a "Future Leader" by Who's Who Legal Competition, as well as being listed in Best Lawyers and The Legal 500, which describes Charles as having "phenomenal client service ethics" and "the ability to see the commercial drivers very quickly and clearly apply them to the law".

Michael Williams

Michael 是 Gilbert + Tobin 律师事务所知识产权团队负责人。

Michael 以其策略、学识、快速地解决复杂争议的能力和提供知识产权建议而闻名。他为来自电子、软件、娱乐、快速消费品、矿产、金融服务等广泛领域的澳大利亚及全球客户服务。

Michael 在技术和知识产权领域有很强的实务经验,包括:虚假宣传、品牌争议和反仿冒;版权和数据保护;商业秘密、内部威胁和网络安全建议及调查;技术争议和专利诉讼。

Michael 被认为是澳大利亚 IP 领先从业者。他入选钱伯斯亚太知识产权领域第一等律师,并被评价为"令人敬畏、非常专业且聪明"。

Michael is the head of Gilbert + Tobin's Intellectual Property team.

Michael is well known for his strategic skills, subject matter knowledge and robust approach to complex disputes and IP advice. He acts for a wide range of Australian and international clients in fields such as electronics, software, content, entertainment, FMCG, mining and financial services.

Michael has a keen interest in technology and IP and has built a strong digital practice. Michael's practice covers, amongst other things: false advertising, brand disputes and anti-counterfeiting; copyright and data protection; trade secrets, insider threat and cybersecurity advice and investigations; and technology disputes and patent litigation.

Michael is recognised as a leading IP practitioner in Australia. With a Tier 1 ranking in IP in Chambers Asia Pacific, he has been described as "formidable, extremely professional and incredibly bright".

澳大利亚——翻译及协调人介绍 / Australia—Introduction to Translators and Cooperators

律所介绍 / Introduction to Law Firms

金杜律师事务所

金杜律师事务所(以下简称"金杜")被广泛认为是全球最具创新力的律师事务所之一,能够提供与众不同的商业化思维和客户体验。金杜拥有 2000 多名律师,分布于全球 27 个城市,在中国、澳大利亚、新加坡、日本、美国、英国、德国、西班牙、意大利等国家的主要城市和中东均设有办公室,是一家能同时提供中国法、澳大利亚法、英国法、美国法、德国法、意大利法等法律服务的全球性律师事务所。

2018年2月，金杜荣获钱伯斯亚太评选的"亚太地区年度最佳律师事务所"大奖。2017年6月，金杜获《金融时报》亚太创新律师大奖的两个奖项。金杜中国在2018年钱伯斯亚太评选中有20项业务名列第一梯队，在中国律师事务所中处于领先地位。

Recognised as one of the world's most innovative law firms, King & Wood Mallesons ("KWM") offers a different perspective to commercial thinking and the client experience. Around the world, KWM has over 2,000 lawyers with an extensive global network of 27 international offices spanning PRC, Australia, Singapore, Japan, the US, the UK, Germany, Spain, Italy, as well as presences in the Middle East. KWM is a global law firm which provides a one-stop legal service covering laws in PRC, Australia, the UK, the US, Germany, Italy, etc.

In February 2018, KWM received the award Asia-Pacific Law Firm of the Year at the Chambers Asia-Pacific Awards. In June 2017, KWM was recognised with two awards at the 2017 Financial Times Asia-Pacific Innovative Lawyers Awards. KWM PRC has 20 tier-one rankings (leading in all Chinese firms) in Chambers Asia Pacific 2018.

律师介绍 / Introduction to Lawyers

莫海波

莫海波律师是金杜律师事务所广州办公室合伙人，拥有中国律师和澳大利亚注册会计师资格，主要执业领域为公司重组与并购、证券（境内外上市）、银行金融。

莫海波律师曾为众多境外大型跨国企业和境内知名企业的跨境投资项目提供法律服务，涵盖股权收购、项目投资、公司治理、公司日常性法律事务及合规咨询等。莫海波律师曾作为牵头律师参与了众多金融机构设立、改制、重组并购、发债、资产证券化和上市等项目，也曾为多家知名上市企业就教育机构、互联网创新业务和基础设施建设方面提供法律服务。

莫海波律师入选中华全国律师协会评选的"全国涉外律师领军人才"，于2014年以及2017年分别完成由司法部专项资金支持的欧洲专项培训。莫海波律师入选了广东省律师协会"广东省涉外律师领军人才"。

Mr. Mo Haibo is a partner at King & Wood Mallesons' Guangzhou office and has been admitted to the All China Lawyer Association and CPA Australia. He specializes in corporate restructuring and M&A, securities (IPO), and banking and finance.

Mr. Mo has extensive experience in multinational enterprises' foreign direct investment projects and well-known domestic enterprises' outbound investments. He has participated in and headed many establishment, reorganization, restructuring and merger, bonds issuance, assets securitization and IPO projects involving financial institutions, and provided legal services to many well-known listed companies regarding education institutions, Internet Finance and infrastructure construction projects.

Mr. Mo has been selected for the Legal Talents Scheme in Foreign-related Business launched by All China Lawyers Association, and has completed his training course in Europe in 2014 and 2017 funded by the Ministry of Finance. He is also been selected for the Legal Talents Scheme in Foreign-related Business launched by Guangdong Lawyers Association.

律所介绍 / Introduction to Law Firms

国浩律师事务所

国浩律师事务所是中国大型的法律服务机构，是中国投融资领域尤其是资本市场非常专业的法律服务提供者，在跨境投资、海外并购等涉及中国企业"走出去"和"一带一路"相关法律服务方面优势明显，并积累了丰富的项目经验。迄今已为包括俄罗斯、蒙古、哈萨克斯坦、伊朗、印度、印度尼西亚、柬埔寨、越南、孟加拉、马来西亚、巴基斯坦、阿尔巴尼亚、新加坡在内的许多"一带一路"沿线国家提供过法律服务，而由"国浩'一带一路'法律研究与服务中心"推出的"一带一路"沿线国家相关法律问题研究系列成果更是引起了业界的广泛关注。

Grandall Law Firm is a large law firm in China, and a professional legal service provider in China investment and financing area, and capital markets, in particular. It has remarkable advantages in providing legal service in cross-border investment, overseas M&A and other legal services relating to the Go Global of Chinese enterprises and the Belt and Road（"B&R"）Initiative and has accumulated abundant experience in project service and dispute resolution. Grandall has rendered services to a number of properties in the related B&R countries, Russia, Mongolia, Kazakhstan, Iran, India, Indonesia, Cambodia, Vietnam, Bangladesh, Malaysia, Pakistan, Albania and Singapore to name a few. Moreover, Grandall B&R Legal Research and Service Centre has made great achievements of research on the legal issues of the countries along the B&R and has drawn extensive attention in the industry.

律师介绍 / Introduction to Lawyers

陶海英

陶海英律师是国浩律师事务所的合伙人,现任中华全国律师协会国际业务专业委员会秘书长、委员,杭州仲裁委员会仲裁员。陶海英律师在金融、国际投融资领域拥有丰富的执业经验,担任或曾担任多家银行、保险公司、资产管理公司、期货公司、进出口公司、外商投资企业的顾问律师,经办了多个重大境内外投融资项目,包括企业并购重组、私募股权投资、结构性融资、融资租赁、境外基金的设立和运作。

Mrs. Tao is a Partner of Grandall Law Firm, and she is currently the secretary-general and committee member of International Business Committee of All China Lawyers Association (ACLA), the arbitrator of Hangzhou Arbitration Commission. Mrs. Tao is mainly specialised in the field of international investment and financing. She has been a legal counsel for numbers of banks, insurance companies, AMCs, futures companies, import and export corporations, foreign-invested enterprises and participated in several significant domestic and foreign investment and financing projects, including M&A, PE, structure financing, finance lease, establishment and operation of funds.

阿塞拜疆——撰稿人介绍 / Azerbaijan—Introduction to Authors

律所介绍 / Introduction to Law Firms

Ekvita 律师事务所

Ekvita 律师事务所是一家提供全方位服务的法律和税务咨询事务所。2011 年年初,该所与一家成立于 1999 年的当地税务咨询事务所合并,从而大大扩展了其业务领域,税务咨询是该所主要领域之一。该所已有超过 15 年的历史。

该所的主要业务是石油和天然气行业。客户一致认为 Ekvita 律师事务所是所有石油和天然气工业部门的"首选"事务所,特别是海洋业务。

管理合伙人 Ilgar Mehti 和合伙人 Anar Karimov manage 管理着 25 名全职专业人士。2000 年,两名合伙人在阿塞拜疆获得了律师资格,并拥有美国著名法学院(西北大学和华盛顿法学院)的 LLM 学位。

一些大的石油项目、建筑项目和电信项目选择了 Ekvita 律师事务所,让该所在涉及法律和税务问题的各种交易中代表他们的利益。

Ekvita is a full-service legal and tax consulting firm. In early 2011, the firm merged with a local tax consulting firm established in 1999, thereby significantly expanding its practice areas, and claiming tax consulting as one of its main areas. EKVITA now brings together 15 years of local expertise and knowledge.

The main focus for the firm remains the oil and gas industry. Ekvita is perceived by the clients as a 'go-to' firm for all oil and gas industry sub-sectors, including, specifically, marine operations.

Managing partner Ilgar Mehti and partner Anar Karimov manage 25 full-time professionals. Both partners qualified in Azerbaijan in 2000 and hold LLM degrees from leading US law schools (Northwestern University and Washington College of Law).

The firm's work speaks for itself: some of the largest oil projects, the largest construction projects and the largest telecommunications projects in Azerbaijan have selected Ekvita to represent their interests in various transactions covering both legal and tax matters.

律师介绍 / Introduction to Lawyers

Ilgar Mehti

Ilgar Mehti 是 Ekvita 律师事务所的创始人和管理合伙人。2000 年以来,他有资格在阿塞拜疆从事法律工作。

在 Ekvita 律师事务所成立之前,Ilgar Mehti 在 Baker McKenzie 的巴库办公室工作,担任劳动法实践的负责人和能源法律实践的成员。在此之前,他曾在英国石油公司工作了 9 年。目前主要专注于阿塞拜疆的沙阿德尼兹天然气项目的上游部分。

Ilgar 除了在巴库国立大学获得阿塞拜疆法律资格外,还获得了美国西北大学 LLM 学位。

Ilgar 在商业管理方面也有资格证书,即西班牙商业管理证书。

Ilgar 的从业领域主要包括能源、企业和税收。

Ilgar Mehti is a founder and managing partner of the law firm Ekvita based in Baku, Azerbaijan. He is qualified to practice law in Azerbaijan since 2000.

Prior to establishing Ekvita, Ilgar Mehti worked at Baker McKenzie Baku office as the head of the Employment Law Practice and member of the Energy Law Practice; before that he had spent 9 years in BP, lately as Legal Adviser focusing on the upstream segment of the giant Shah Deniz gas project in Azerbaijan.

In addition to his Azerbaijani legal qualification from the Baku State University, Ilgar also holds an LLM degree from Northwestern University, a top tier U.S. law school based in Chicago.

Ilgar also has qualification in business management - Certificate in Business Administration from IE Business School (Spain).

Ilgar's practice areas include mostly Energy, Corporate and Taxation.

阿塞拜疆——翻译及协调人介绍 / Azerbaijan—Introduction to Translators and Cooperators

律所介绍 / Introduction to Law Firms

北京德和衡律师事务所

北京德和衡律师事务所是中国规模较大、发展较快的综合商务型律师事务所，在国内外各主要城市均设有分所或办事机构，作为中国商务部指定的首批"国际投资法律服务供应商"、The lawyer 2017 年"亚太地区 100 强律所"第七名等荣誉获得者，该所吸纳了多位复合型法律人才，所内律师可以英、法、德、日、韩等多国语言，在证券与资本市场、公司商事、国际贸易、境内外投资并购、知识产权、刑事、政府法律服务、反垄断及跨国争议解决等领域为全球客户提供高品质的法律服务。

Beijing DHH Law Firm is one of the largest and fastest-growing comprehensive commercial law firms in China, it has branches or offices in major cities at home and abroad. As the first batch of international investment legal service providers designated by the Ministry of commerce of China, the owner of the lawyer ranked seventh among the top 100 law firms in Asia and the Pacific in 2017 and other honorary owners, Beijing DHH has absorbed a number of complex legal talents, the lawyers in the firm can practice in English, French, German, Japanese, Korean and other languages, and can provide the highest quality legal service in the fields of securities and capital markets, corporate commerce, international trade, domestic and foreign investment and mergers and acquisitions, intellectual property rights, criminal, government legal services, antitrust, etc.

律师介绍 / Introduction to Lawyers

刘克江

刘克江律师，德衡律师集团常务副总裁，北京德和衡律师事务所主任、高级合伙人，中华全国律师协会"中国涉外律师领军人才"，中国商务部"国际投资法律事务"首期入库律师、伦敦国际仲裁院仲裁员、北京联合大学兼职教授。

刘克江律师于 1996 年获得中国政法大学法学学士学位，2007 年获得格拉斯哥大学管理学硕士学位。执业 18 年来，在并购项目管理、企业合规、商务谈判、法律风险管理、反垄断法律事务等领域积累了丰富的经验，客户多为国有大中型企业、上市公司及大型中外跨国公司。

Kejiang(Michael) LIU, executive VP of Deheng Law Group, Managing Partner of Beijing DHH Law Firm, Senior Partner, the Member of China Leading International Attorney selected by All China Layers Association and Ministry of Justice, Member of MOFCOM Attorney Bank for International Investment and Dispute Resolution, Arbitrator of The London Court of International Arbitration(LCIA), Visiting Professor of Beijing Union University.

Mr. Liu has been awarded a Bachelor Degree of Law by China University of Political Science and Law in 1996 as well as a MBA degree by University of Glasgow(UK) in 2007. During his 18 years legal career, he dedicated in project management of M&A, enterprise compliance management, investment &financing, business negotiation, legal risk management, anti-trust legal affairs and international dispute resolution. His clients are mainly state-owned large and medium-sized enterprises, listed companies and large multinational companies.

律所介绍 / Introduction to Law Firms

北京从真律师事务所

北京从真律师事务所由具有 10 多年从业经验的律师、专利代理人、商标代理人和仲裁员组成。根据公司化管理的理念，按照专业化分工，该所分设知识产权部、公司事务部、争议解决部等法律业务部门。目前，凭借深厚的专业知识、丰富的实践经验以及出色的团队精神,该所已成为一家能够运用多种语言服务国内外大中型企业及初创企业的精品律师事务所。

Conzen is a general law firm founded by the experienced lawyers, patent attorneys, trademark attorneys and arbitrators. Especially, Conzen is skilled in intellectual property legal services in all aspects, including patent prosecution, invalidation, infringement litigation, trademark prosecution and litigation as well as IP transactions and strategic counseling, copyright, domain name, trade secret, crackdown on counterfeit, custom protection, etc. Conzen approaches client service by first understanding our clients' priorities, objectives, and challenges. We work hard to understand our clients' issues and forge long-term relationships with them to help achieve successful outcomes and solve their legal issues through practical business advice and cutting-edge legal insight. Our clients view us as trusted business advisors because we understand that great legal service is only valuable if it is relevant, practical and beneficial to their businesses.

律师介绍 / Introduction to Lawyers

程义贵

程义贵律师是北京从真律师事务所的管理合伙人,具有律师、专利代理人资格和司法鉴定人资格。程义贵律师的主要专业领域为知识产权事务和仲裁业务,包括知识产权商业化和许可、知识产权保护、知识产权管理和争议解决,国内外专利侵权之诉,专利无效、许可与转让,以及商事仲裁。程义贵律师担任多家仲裁机构的仲裁员,入选国家知识产权局"国家知识产权人才工程百名高层次人才"库、国家知识产权专家库专家,司法部涉外律师人才库,京津冀司法行政机构服务北京冬奥会、雄安新区法律服务团成员。

Michael Cheng is the managing partner of ConZen law firm. He is the qualified Chinese lawyer, Chinese Patent Agent, Arbitrator and Judicial Appraiser. He worked for SINOPEC as engineer, for Vivien Chan & Co, Lehman, Lee & Xu, Zhonglun Law Firm in turn as legal counsel, patent attorney and partner. Michael's main professional field includes intellectual property affairs and arbitration, including the commercialization of intellectual property and licensing, the protection of intellectual property rights, intellectual property management and dispute resolution, domestic and foreign patent infringement lawsuit, patent invalid, licensing and transfer; and commercial arbitration.

巴林——撰稿人介绍 / Bahrain—Introduction to Authors

律所介绍 / Introduction to Law Firms

Haya Rashed Al Khalifa 律师事务所

Haya Rashed Al Khalifa 律师事务所是巴林颇具盛名和活力的提供综合法律服务的律师事务所之一。该所为重大而具有开创性的国内外交易及诉讼提供法律服务。

该所拥有超过20年的诉讼和咨询经验,是巴林重要的法律服务提供者。特别是在重大国际项目方面,其已成为巴林发展的促进者。

该所广受巴林政府、国际和本地银行、投资顾问、国际会计师事务所、跨国公司和全球高净值人士的青睐。

该所的工作语言包括英语、阿拉伯语、法语和波斯语。

Haya Rashed Al Khalifa is a full service legal practice based in the Kingdom of Bahrain and is regarded as one of the most prestigious and dynamic law firms in the Kingdom. The firm advise on high-profile and groundbreaking domestic and international transactions and litigation matters.

With over 20 years of exceptional litigation and advisory experience, the Firm has proven to be pivotal to the provision of legal counsel to the Bahraini community, especially in regards to major international projects, and has focused extensively on serving as a catalyst to national development.

The Firm is widely retained by the Bahraini Government departments & institutions, international and local banks, investment advisers, international accountancy firms, multinational companies and high net worth individuals from around the world.

The diversity of languages spoken in the Firm has come to include English, Arabic, French and Farsi.

律师介绍 / Introduction to Lawyers

Abdulrahman Zainal

Abdulrahman Zainal 是 Haya Roshed Al Khalifa 律师事务所备受尊敬的团队的最新成员。他毕业于雷丁大学，尔后在吉尔福德法学院完成法律实践课程并获得一等荣誉，被授予法律、商业和管理硕士学位，2017 年加入 Haya Rashed Al Khalifa 律师事务所。

在加入该所之前，Abdulrahman 拥有多家分属不同行业的当地公司的工作经验，这些经历使他明确了未来继续钻研的法律领域。他还曾任职于普华永道国际会计师事务所位于巴林的税务部门，因此能够深入了解 GCC 地区的税收情况并提供法律建议。

Abdulrahman Zainal is the newest addition to the firm's esteemed team. Having recently graduated from the University of Reading and subsequently awarded a Master of Science in Law, Business and Management upon completing the Legal Practice Course with First Class Honors at the University of Law in Guildford, he then came to join Haya Rashed Al Khalifa Law Firm in 2017.

Prior to joining the firm, Abdulrahman gathered experience from multiple local firms that specialize in different areas of law which he aims to pursue further. He was also a member of PricewaterhouseCoopers' tax department in Bahrain, and thus is capable of providing insight into taxation in the GCC region as well as legal advice.

律所介绍 / Introduction to Law Firms

Zu'bi & Partners 律师事务所

Zu'bi & Partners 律师事务所由 Hatim S. Zu'bi & Partners（是巴林成立较早的综合性律师事务所之一）和 Qays H. Zu'bi 合并创建。

该所为所有主导行业提供法律服务，包括银行和金融、企业、商业、建筑、能源、信息技术、通信、房地产、保险、知识产权等，还为企业和高端客户提供诉讼、仲裁、财产法、劳动法、贸易法和家事法等。

该所的业务能力和成就得到了法律评级机构和各大刊物的广泛认可，深受客户好评，客户包括私营机构、公共机构、政府和准政府机构以及高端客户群体。

ZU'BI & PARTNERS (the "Firm") is the merged firm between two long-established Bahrain law firms: Hatim S. Zu'bi & Partners, the oldest established local law firm in Bahrain, and Qays H. Zu'bi Attorneys & Legal Consultants.

The Firm provides legal services across all leading sectors, including banking and finance, corporate, commercial, construction, energy, IT, communications, real estate, insurance, IP, to name just a few. The Firm also acts for both corporate and high net worth individuals in many diverse areas, including litigation, arbitration, property, labour, trade and family law.

The breadth of expertise and success of the Firm has been widely recognized by independent legal commentators and publications and is reflected in its client base of leaders in their fields, including both private and public institutions, government and quasi-government bodies, as well as high net worth individuals.

律师介绍 / Introduction to Lawyers

Qays H. Zu'bi

Qays H. Zu'bi 持有英国剑桥大学文学学士（BA）和文学硕士（MA）学位，并在美国杜克大学获得经济学、公共政策及政治科学的文学学士学位。1981 年开始法律职业生涯。

目前担任巴林（最高法院）执业律师、GCC 商事仲裁中心仲裁员、阿联酋迪拜法律顾问、加拿大驻巴林荣誉领事、美国巴林商会主席、国际律师协会会员、英格兰与威尔士法学会会员，以及巴林牛津剑桥校友会创始人兼主席等职务。

Qays read law at the University of Cambridge in the United Kingdom achieving a BA and an MA in Legal Studies. Prior to that he achieved a Bachelor of Arts degree in Economics, Public Policy and Political Science from Duke University in the United States. He commenced his legal career in Bahrain in 1981 and is a licensed litigator and arbitrator. He is qualified to appear before the Court of Cassation in Bahrain and holds a legal consultancy licence in Dubai, UAE.

Qays' positions include: Licensed Lawyer (Cassation Court) Bahrain; Certified Arbitrator, GCC Commercial Arbitration Centre; Legal Consultant, Dubai UAE; Honorary Consul for Canada in Bahrain; President, American Chamber of Commerce in Bahrain (AmCham); Member, International Bar Association; Member, Law Society of England & Wales (International Division); Oxford & Cambridge Alumni of Bahrain.

Noor Al Taraif

Noor Al Taraif 持有伦敦大学东方与非洲研究学院荣誉学士学位，2014 年加入 Zu'bi and Partners 律师事务所。她具备破产清算、协议起草、合同咨询、民航法、商业公司法、知识产权法、巴林中央银行法、劳动法及电信法方面的经验，曾为 LexisNexis 等数据库、世界银行《营商环境报告》项目、高伟绅律师事务所中东及北非妇女工作项目、The Oath 等杂志作出了贡献。

Noor Al Taraif 近期执业经历：主办两家巴林中央银行授权客户的清算业务。代理一家巴林企业进行股权收购，完成股权收购的尽职调查。

Noor joined Zu'bi and Partners in 2014 and holds a Bachelor of Laws (Hons) degree from SOAS, University of London. She has experience in liquidation procedures, drafting legal agreements, advising on contracts, civil aviation law, commercial companies' law, copyright law, Central Bank of Bahrain law, labor law and telecommunications law. Noor has been contributing to legal databases such as LexisNexis, projects such as The World Bank's Doing Business series and Clifford Chance's MENA Women and magazines such as The Oath.

Recent Assignments, Major role in liquidation of two Central Bank of Bahrain licensees. Acted for a purchaser of shares in a Bahraini company, along with completing due diligence for the share purchase transaction.

巴林——翻译及协调人介绍 / Bahrain—Introduction to Translators and Cooperators

律所介绍 / Introduction to Law Firms

锦天城律师事务所

锦天城律师事务所是一家提供全方位法律服务的中国律师事务所。该所在中国 22 个城市及伦敦设有分所，为境内外客户制订法律解决方案并提供法律服务。

该所多次被司法部、中华全国律师协会及国际知名的法律媒体和权威机构列为中国顶尖的法律服务提供者之一。

该所有执业律师 2 000 多人，可以使用多种语言工作，许多律师拥有美国多个州、英国、法国和日本等地的执业资格。

该所为其客户在涉及公司、商业与并购、证券与资本市场、银行与金融、房地产与建筑、争议解决（诉讼与仲裁）、国际贸易及"一带一路"法律服务、海商海事、知识产权保护领域的商业交易和争议中，提供有效的解决方案和服务。该所的客户遍及全球，涉及大中型国有企业、事业单位、跨国集团、外商投资企业、民营企业、各类金融机构等。

AllBright Law Offices is a leading full-service Chinese law firm in China. As a national law firm headquartered in Shanghai, it provides a comprehensive range of high-quality legal services to both domestic and international clients from its twenty-two domestic offices and branch in London.

Widely acknowledged as one of the top legal service providers by Ministry of Justice P.R.C., ACLA and numerous international legal media and institutions, AllBright Law Offices has been in the front rank of the country.

AllBright has approximately 2,000 lawyers, who can provide legal service in multiple languages. Many of the lawyers are admitted in the United States, the U.K., France, Japan and other foreign jurisdictions.

AllBright Law Offices provides cost-efficient and world-class legal solutions and services to clients in corporations, mergers and acquisitions, securities and capital markets, banking and financing, real estate and construction, dispute resolution (litigations and arbitrations), international trade and "Belt and Road" service, maritime and shipping, intellectual property and other practice areas. Our clients come from all over the country and the world, which include state-owned powerhouses, institutions, international groups, foreign invested enterprises, private enterprises, banks and financial institutions.

律师介绍 / Introduction to Lawyers

刘炯

刘炯律师是锦天城律师事务所高级合伙人，现任多家国内外仲裁机构仲裁员，英国皇家特许仲裁员协会（FCIArb）研究员，业务专长为争议解决。

自 2000 年以来，刘炯律师曾代表诸多国内外客户处理过近百件诉讼与仲裁案件，在上海市、江苏省、广东省高级人民法院、中国国际经济贸易仲裁委员会、上海国际经济贸易仲裁委员会，有优异的出庭表现，并取得令人满意的结果。

刘炯律师被评为"ALB 2017 年度中国十五佳诉讼律师""ALB 2016 年度中国十五佳律师新星"，入选"全国涉外律师领军人才"等。

John Liu is a Senior Partner of AllBright based in Shanghai, specialized in dispute resolution. Being a member of FCIArb, he is also arbitrator and/or mediator of several domestic and international arbitral institutions.

Since 2000, Mr. Liu has represented many international and domestic clients and handled nearly one hundred lawsuits and arbitration cases. His excellent performance before Shanghai High Court, Jiangsu High Court, Guangdong High Court, CIETAC, and SHIAC has achieved satisfactory results. Invited by China Legal Association, Mr. Liu delivered a lecture on dispute resolution and liquidation for foreign-invested enterprises together with judges from the Supreme Court.

Mr. Liu was honored as ALB Top 15 China Litigators 2017, ALB Top 15 China Rising Star Lawyers 2016, Leading Pioneer of Foreign-related Lawyers in China, and Best Ten Young Lawyers in Pudong New Area of Shanghai..

律所介绍 / Introduction to Law Firms

北京金诚同达律师事务所

北京金诚同达律师事务所创立于 1992 年，现已发展成为中国规模最大、最富活力的律师事务所之一，在诸多业务领域处于行业领先，为客户提供法律服务。此外，该所还拥有国际化的业务网络，力求在全球范围内实现资源共享。

JINCHENG TONGDA & NEAL (JT&N) is widely recognized as one of the leading full-service law firms in China and Asia as a whole, with deep expertise across a broad spectrum of practice areas. Founded in 1992, JT&N has grown to become one of the largest and most respected law firms in China. We are a full-service law firm and advise clients on a wide variety of matters. The broad extent of our legal services enables JT&N to promptly deliver needed legal support to our clients. JT&N has a broad domestic and international business network. JT&N's extensive international business and legal network help us optimize resource sharing and business interaction for the benefit of our clients.

律师介绍 / Introduction to Lawyers

杨晨

杨晨律师是金诚同达律师事务所高级合伙人。杨晨律师多次代表中国政府应诉国际贸易救济案件，还为大量国内外进出口企业提供法律服务，并精通风险投资和并购业务。

Chen YANG is a Senior Partner with JT&N and specializes in M&A, international trade and antitrust. He is also a managing partner in charge of public relationship and publicity of the firm. Mr. Yang is a market-leading lawyer in the fields of M&A and antitrust law, as well as private equity and venture capital (PE/VC). Mr. Yang is also acknowledged by his peers to be an expert in the field of international trade dispute matters.

波斯尼亚和黑塞哥维那——撰稿人介绍 / Bosnia and Herzegovina—Introduction to Authors

律所介绍 / Introduction to Law Firms

Tkalcic-Dulic, Prebanic & Jusufbasic-Goloman 律师事务所

Tkalcic-Dulic, Prebanic & Jusufbasic-Goloman 律师事务所由 BojanaTkalcic-Dulic 女士创始于 1994 年，此前其曾在波黑法院及司法部任职。

作为规模较大的律师事务所之一，该所致力于民商事领域法律服务。该所因向其国内外客户提供优质的法律服务而在业内享有极高声誉。同时，该所被一些外国大使馆和多家国际组织机构聘为法律顾问，并为金融、工业及服务领域的大量跨国公司提供法律服务。

该所密切关注国际法理论和实践的最新发展，经常参加各种研讨会、讲座和律师国际交流项目。

Lawyers' Office Tkalcic-Dulic, Prebanic & Jusufbasic-Goloman was founded in 1994 by Bojana Tkalcic-Dulic, after she spent a part of her career in courts and the Ministry of Justice of Bosnia and Herzegovina.

This makes it one of the larger lawyers' offices in the Bosnia and Herzegovina legal environment, which is specialized in legal services in the area of commercial and civil law. The Office has acquired an indisputable reputation for outstanding quality of services rendered to its foreign and local clients. The Office acts in capacity of an advisory body to a number of foreign embassies and international organizations and agencies in Bosnia and Herzegovina and it represents a significant number of large international corporations in the areas of finances, industrial and service-related sectors.

The Office closely monitors the developments in theory and practice of the international law on a daily basis, while its lawyers frequently participate in different workshops and seminars, as well as in international exchange programs for lawyers.

律师介绍 / Introduction to Lawyers

Olodar Prebanic

Olodar Prebanic，高级合伙人，毕业于萨拉热窝大学法学院，在该所从业18年以上，自2004年2月起成为联邦律师协会的注册律师。其为国内外多领域客户提供法律顾问服务，尤其擅长公司法、国内及国际公司重组、改制、跨境并购等领域业务，其为跨国公司在波黑的业务提供服务长达20年，被钱伯斯法律评级机构评为行业领军人物。Olodar Prebanic的工作语言为英语、波斯尼亚语、克罗地亚语及塞尔维亚语等。

Mr. Olodar Prebanic is a Senior Partner at Lawyers' Office Tkalcic-Djulic, Prebanic and Jusufbasic-Goloman. He has more than 18 years of experience, as a trainee, associate, lawyer and senior partner at Lawyers' Office Tkalcic-Djulic, Prebanic and Jusufbasic-Goloman. He graduated from the Law Faculty at the University in Sarajevo, Bosnia and Herzegovina and is registered in the FB&H Bar Chamber since February 2004. Olodar frequently advises national and international clients in a variety of sectors, particularly in corporate matters, domestic and international reorganizations and restructurings and cross-border M&A transactions in different industries. He has been supporting multinational companies in their operations in Bosnia and Herzegovina for more than 20 years. He has been recognized as a leading individual in Bosnia and Herzegovina by the Chambers & Partners publication for the past several years. He speaks English and Bosnian/Croatian/Serbian language.

Tijana Blesic

Tijana Blesic，律师助理，毕业于萨拉热窝大学法学院。自2016年7月起在该所工作至今，为国内不同行业客户日常经营活动中产生的法律问题提供咨询服务，其主要专注于公司法、劳动法以及外国公民就业等领域的相关业务。Tijana Blesic的工作语言为英语、波斯尼亚语、克罗地亚语及塞尔维亚语等。

Ms. Tijana Blesic is an Associate in the Lawyers' Office Tkalcic-Djulic, Prebanic & Jusufbasic-Goloman. She graduated from the Law Faculty at the University of Sarajevo, Bosnia and Herzegovina and has worked in the Office since July 2016. Tijana is advising clients from different industries on their day-to-day operations on the territory of Bosnia and Herzegovina on various issues arising from the Office's regular activities, particularly focusing on corporate, labor and issues related to employment of foreign citizens in Bosnia and Herzegovina. She speaks English and Bosnian/Croatian/Serbian language.

波斯尼亚和黑塞哥维那——翻译及协调人介绍 / Bosnia and Herzegovina—Introduction to Translators and Cooperators

律所介绍 / Introduction to Law Firms

天津华盛理律师事务所

天津华盛理律师事务所是一家经天津市司法局批准正式挂牌营业的市司法局直属合伙制律师事务所。该所于2001年正式成立，过往业绩良好。

2006年，该所被评为"天津市政法系统优秀律师事务所"，2009年被授予"人民满意律师事务所"，2011年被授予"2010—2011年度优秀律师事务所"，2016年2月被中华全国律师协会评为"全国优秀律师事务所"。

Tianjin Wisely Law Office was approved into operation by Tianjin Bureau of Justice in 2001. Over the past years, the office has enjoyed a high reputation for its credible legal services.

Tianjin Wisely Law Office was awarded "The Outstanding Law Frim of Tianjin Political and Legal System" in 2006; "The Most Satisfied Law Firm" in 2009; "The Outstanding Firm of The Year of 2010-2011" in 2011; "The National Outstanding Law Firm" by All China's Lawyers' Association in February 2016.

律师介绍 / Introduction to Lawyers

刘尔婵

刘尔婵律师，天津华盛理律师事务所高级合伙人、中国及美国纽约州执业律师、英国皇家御准仲裁员协会中级会员；2016年入选中华全国律师协会"中国涉外律师领军人才"。刘尔婵律师擅长的业务领域包括但不限于商事争议解决、涉外法律服务等。

Ms. Erchan Liu is a senior partner of Tianjin Wisely Law Office, who is licensed to practice law in both China and

State of New York. She is invited to be a member of Chartered Institute of Arbitrators (CIArb). In 2016 she is awarded as "The China Leading International Lawyer" by All China's Lawyers Association. Her experiences mainly focus on commercial dispute resolution, foreign legal services.

律所介绍 / Introduction to Law Firms

陕西海普睿诚律师事务所

陕西海普睿诚律师事务所（以下简称"海普睿诚"）总部位于中国西安，北京设有分所，具有 26 年的发展历史，是以特殊的普通合伙制为组织形式，公司制管理为主导运营模式的专业化、规范化、规模化、国际化发展的大型综合性律师事务所。

该所秉持"价值思维、规则导向"与"诚信、笃行、责任、共赢"的发展理念，追求"以奋斗者为本，打造百年强所"的目标，致力于提供优质、高效、专业的法律服务。

该所获得 ISO9001：2008 国际质量管理体系认证、军工涉密业务安全保密资质，先后两次荣膺"全国优秀律师事务所"以及"全省优秀律师事务所""省级文明所""全省规范建设先进律师事务所"等多项殊荣。

Shaanxi Helpreaching Law Firm（"Helpreaching"）is a large comprehensive law firm with its headquarter in Xi'an and branch office in Beijing, China. It has a history of over 26 years. It takes the organizational form of special general partnership, adopts the corporate management as the main operation mode, is engaged in the development of professionalization, standardization, scale and internationalization.

Helpreaching adheres to the development concepts of valuable thinking, rule-oriented, good faith, earnest behavior, responsibility, win-win, and pursues the goal of taking the striver as the foremost, and building Helpreaching into a powerful law firm with a hundred-year-old history. It has been committing itself to providing excellent, efficient, and professional legal service.

Helpreaching has passed standard attestation of ISO9001：2008 International Quality System, and got the Service Qualification Certificate for the Military Confidential Business. It has been awarded the prizes of National Excellent Law Firm twice, Provincial Excellent Law Firm, Provincial Civilized Law Firm, and the Provincial Excellent Law Firm in Standardization Building, etc.

律师介绍 / Introduction to Lawyers

张玉明

张玉明律师，法学硕士学位。1981 年，张玉明律师在北京大学攻读国际政治关系，于 1985 年获法学学士学位，同年在中国政法大学研究生院攻读法律，于 1988 年获法学硕士学位。自 1988 年起在中国国际贸易促进委员会陕西省分会（中国国际商会陕西商会）法律事务部工作，后在中国国际贸易促进委员会陕西调解中心和中国国际经济贸易仲裁委员会陕西办事处工作。

现执业于陕西海普睿诚律师事务所，为中国法学会会员和陕西省律师协会涉外法律事务专业委员会主任，为"中国涉外律师领军人才"和"一带一路"跨境律师，被中国国际贸易促进委员会 / 中国国际商会调解中心选聘为调解员。

Mr. Zhang, a professional lawyer, studied the International Politics in Peking University and obtained Bachelor of Law Degree in 1985, and studied the Science of Law in Graduate School of China University of Political Science and Law and obtained Master of Law Degree in 1988. Mr. Zhang was enrolled to serve in Legal Affairs Department, China Council for the Promotion of International Trade Shaanxi Sub-Council (China International Chamber of Commerce Shaanxi Chamber of Commerce), and China International Economic and Trade Arbitration Commission Shaanxi Office.

Mr. Zhang is now serving for Shaanxi Helpreaching Law Firm. He is a member of China Law Society, the director of Professional Committee for Foreign Legal Affairs of Shaanxi Lawyers Association, China Leading International Lawyer, Cross-Border Lawyer in the Belt and Road Initiative by All China Lawyers Association, and a mediator of CCPIT/CCOIC Mediation Center.

巴西——撰稿人介绍 / Brazil—Introduction to Authors

律所介绍 / Introduction to Law Firms

Machado, Meyer, Sendacz e Opice Advogados 律师事务所

Machado, Meyer, Sendacz e Opice Advogados（以下简称"Machado Meyer 律师事务所"）建所 45 年来，以专业人员的卓越执业标准、优质执业技能以及与客户间的密切关系而著称。作为巴西优秀的律师事务所之一，该所拥有超过 700 名执业律师。

基于当今投资流动频繁，该所拥有为外国客户提供高效优质服务的专业团队。该所还与各国当地团队共同组建跨专业服务团队，特别是亚洲、德国和西班牙。除了对当地语言的娴熟运用，该所还积累了丰富的消除跨文化交流障碍、促进新兴产业、提高竞争优势以及增强项目价值方面的经验。我们的网站为：www.machadomeyer.com.br.

Machado, Meyer, Sendacz e Opice Advogados（"Machado Meyer"）has been building its history for more than 45 years, inspired by sound ethical principles, technical skills of its professionals, and a close relation with its clients. The firm is ranked as one of the leading top law firms in Brazil, with over 700 professionals.

Because of the significant flow of today's existing investment, Machado Meyer has organized professionals specialized in advising clients abroad. The firm has also created multidisciplinary groups, especially in Asia, Germany and Spain with its special desks. In addition to fluency in the respective foreign languages, professionals of the special desks have accumulated experience to eliminate any specific cultural barriers, facilitating the conduct of new business, generating competitive advantage and adding value to the project of clients coming from those regions. Our website is: www.machadomeyer.com.br.

律师介绍 / Introduction to Lawyers

Celso Costa

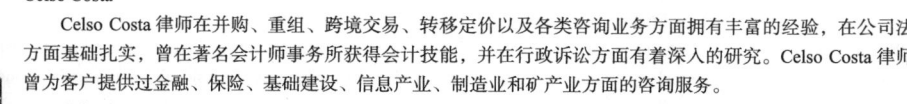

Celso Costa律师在并购、重组、跨境交易、转移定价以及各类咨询业务方面拥有丰富的经验，在公司法方面基础扎实，曾在著名会计师事务所获得会计技能，并在行政诉讼方面有着深入的研究。Celso Costa律师曾为客户提供过金融、保险、基础建设、信息产业、制造业和矿产业方面的咨询服务。

Celso has extensive experience in M&A, reorganizations, cross-border transactions, transfer pricing and general advisory. Solid background in corporate law. Accounting skills acquired in a leading accounting firm. In depth knowledge of administrative litigation. His practice includes advisory on financial and insurance services, infrastructure, information technology, manufacturing and mining advisory.

Thales Saito

Thales Saito律师是当地和国际金融交易、并购、银行监管、应收账款证券化、设立投资基金、金融衍生品和证券监管方面的专家。Saito律师为当地和外国客户提供设立不同结构公司及金融交易的谈判与执行，包括与设立投资基金和受监管行为相关的业务。Saito律师是Machado Meyer律师事务所亚洲团队的核心成员，对于为亚洲客户特别是日本和中国客户提供法律服务有着丰富的经验。

Thales Saito is specialist in local and international financial transactions, M&A, banking regulations, securitization of receivables, incorporation of investment funds, derivatives and exchange regulations. His practice encompasses the rendering of legal assistance to local and international clients in the negotiation and implementation of corporate and financial transactions of different structures. He is one of the members and organizers of our Asian Desk, having extensive experience in the rendering of legal assistance to Asian clients, specially from Japan and China.

巴西——翻译及协调人介绍 / Brazil—Introduction to Translators and Cooperators

律所介绍 / Introduction to Law Firms

天元律师事务所

天元律师事务所创立于1992年，是中国成立时间较早和规模较大的综合性合伙制律师事务所，目前分别在北京、上海、深圳、成都、香港设有办公室，约有120多名合伙人，500多名执业律师及其他专业人士，涉及各个法律领域。其中大多数律师都有国内外知名院校的博士和硕士学位。

成立二十多年来，天元律师事务所在中国律师业发展历程中创造了多项第一，深得客户的认可和信赖。1998年，该所成为司法部授予的全国首届20家部级"文明律师事务所"。2005年至今，该所连续四次获得中华全国律师协会授予的"全国优秀律师事务所"荣誉称号。

Founded in 1992, Tian Yuan Law Firm ("Tian Yuan") is one of leading law firms in China. As one of the earliest partnership law firms, it has five offices around China, respectively in Beijing, Shanghai, Shenzhen, Chengdu and Hong Kong. Tian Yuan has a team of over 120 partners and more than 500 practitioners who have extensive experience in all legal fields. Most of our lawyers have received master's or doctoral degrees from well-known domestic and/or overseas law schools.

Tian Yuan has provided over two decades of high quality legal services to its clients, gaining recognition and trust. In 1998, Tian Yuan was acknowledged as one of the first twenty ministry-level "Civilized Law Firms" by China's Ministry of Justice. From 2005 until the present, Tian Yuan was awarded the "National Outstanding Law Firm" prize four times in a row by China's National Bar Association.

律师介绍 / Introduction to Lawyers

高文杰

高文杰律师，天元律师事务所高级合伙人，擅长处理国际争议解决业务，并对此业务有浓厚的兴趣。曾在多个跨境诉讼案件和仲裁案件中担任牵头律师和合作律师。在仲裁领域，高文杰律师处理过适用香港国际仲裁中心 (HKIAC)、国际商会国际仲裁院 (ICC)、伦敦海事仲裁协会 (LMAA)、斯德哥尔摩商会仲裁院 (SCC)、美国仲裁协会国际争议解决中心 (AAA-ICDR) 以及中国国际经济贸易仲裁委员会 (CIETAC)、深圳国际仲裁中心 (SCIA)、北京仲裁委员会 (BAC) 等仲裁机构仲裁规则的机构仲裁，以及适用联合国国际贸易法委员会《贸易法委员会仲裁规则》(UNCITRAL) 的临时仲裁。在诉讼领域，处理过包括我国最高人民法院、美国法院、伦敦上诉法院、阿联酋沙迦法院等法院审理的民商事诉讼案件。

高文杰律师在国际贸易、跨境并购和收购业务等方面有丰富的经验。

高文杰律师现为深圳市律师协会理事，国际律师协会会员，中国工作组成员。曾获得商法"年度杰出大奖—国际仲裁"及 The Legal 500"争议解决—特别推荐律师"等荣誉。工作语言为中文、英文。

Mr. Gao Wenjie is a national partner of Tian Yuan law firm. He owns passionate interest and expertise in international commercial dispute resolutions. He has acted as lead counsel or co-counsel in many cross-border litigations and arbitrations. He has dealt with the arbitrations both in the types of institutional arbitration and ad hoc arbitration by adopting the arbitration rules of ICC, HKIAC, LMAA, LCIA, SCC, AAA (ICDR), SCIA, BAC, SZAC and UNCITRAL respectively. He often appears in all level of courts within China and outside China, including the Supreme Court of China and the courts in UK, US, UAE etc.

Mr. Gao also have much experience on various transactions, international trading and cross boarder merger and acquisition etc.

Mr. Gao is the Council Member of Shenzhen Lawyers Association, the member of International Bar Association, also as the member of China Working Group. He was awarded the "Deal of the year – International arbitration" by The China Business Law Journal and the "Recommended Lawyer - Dispute Resolution" by The Legal 500 Asia Pacific in 2017. His working languages are Chinese and English.

律所介绍 / Introduction to Law Firms

安杰律师事务所

安杰律师事务所是一家跨地区的综合性律师事务所，在多个领域有着丰富的法律服务经验和卓越的业绩。该所律师既有丰富的实务经验，又有深厚的理论基础。该所多名合伙人均为中国某一特定领域法律及相关专业之著名专家学者，被钱伯斯、Who's Who legal、Legal 500、ALB、Legalband、《商法》等相关国际法律评级机构与专业刊物评定为专业领域的优秀中国律师和重点推荐律师。该所大多数合伙人具有在国外知名律师事务所工作或在海外长期学习的经历，并能用中文、英文、韩文、日文等语言为客户提供服务。

AnJie Law Firm is a full-service law firm with offices in Beijing, Shanghai and Shenzhen. The firm serve our clients in a wide variety practice areas. As successful practitioners in their fields, our lawyers demonstrate remarkable experience and legal excellence. Many of our partners have received considerable accolade in particular practice areas. Some have been honored as excellent Chinese lawyers or are highly recommended by a number of international ranking institutions and legal journals, including Chambers & Partners, Who's Who Legal, Legal 500, Asian Legal Business, and the China Business Law Journal. Most of our partners have practiced within leading international law firms, having accrued many years of experience before joining AnJie. Our lawyers and professionals are capable of providing legal services directly in Chinese, English, Korean and Japanese.

律师介绍 / Introduction to Lawyers

冯婧

冯婧律师是安杰律师事务所的合伙人，长期从事跨境、涉外业务，擅长金融、贸易、投融领域的境内外商事诉讼、仲裁，尤其对境内外客户"平行诉讼、诉仲结合"等系列跨境争议案件的穿插配合应对有着丰富的积累和经验。冯婧律师长期代理贸易融资领域的重大复杂案件，同时为境内外客户提供跨境贸易合规、金融合规、银行法律服务。冯婧律师还多次代理境外客户在国内进行仲裁或外国裁决的承认与执行案件，以及中国客户在境外的商事仲裁和境外法院诉讼。冯婧律师中英文娴熟。

Ms Feng Jing is a partner of AnJie Law Firm. She specializes in cross-border legal services in finance, trade and investment etc. Her practice focuses on the international dispute resolution in such areas and has gained extensive experiences as to parallel proceedings in different countries. Ms Feng Jing represents clients in significant and complex cases in trade finance and provides legal services in regulatory compliance in trade, trade finance, and banking etc. She frequently represents foreign clients in arbitration and seeking enforcement of foreign awards in China, and also represents Chinese clients in international arbitration and in foreign court proceedings. She is proficient in English and Chinese.

文莱——撰稿人介绍 / Brunei—Introduction to Authors

律所介绍 / Introduction to Law Firms

Eversheds Harry Elias 律师事务所

  Eversheds Harry Elias 律师事务所由新加坡 Harry Elias 合伙制律师事务所与 Eversheds Sutherland 全球化律师事务所合并设立，吸纳了兼具国际标准、当地知识和关系的全方位法律人才。Eversheds Sutherland 律师事务所在参与"一带一路"倡议的许多国家都设有办公室，特别是在东南亚，其业绩呈增长趋势。

  该所有能力为北京、新加坡和伦敦等地参与"一带一路"倡议的客户提供中国业务法律咨询服务。该所为客户提供便利的独立联络点，为其提供多领域法律服务及重要的管理信息，并随时准备为其提供法律意见，以及时应对环境变化。

  该所期待在"一带一路"倡议中发挥作用，并坚信有能力为各国法律环境的发展作出巨大贡献。

  Eversheds Harry Elias is a merger between Harry Elias Partnership in Singapore and Eversheds Sutherland, a global firm. Eversheds Harry Elias represents a combination of full-spectrum legal expertise of international standards and local knowledge and connections. Much of the Belt and Road Initiative ("BRI") involves countries in which Eversheds Sutherland has offices, and in particular South-East Asia, where Eversheds Harry Elias has a growing presence.

  Eversheds Harry Elias has Chinese transactional advisory capabilities for those involved in BRI, including Beijing Singapore and London. The firm's clients will have the convenience of a single point of contact for multi-jurisdictional matters, crucial management information at one's fingertips and on-call legal advice to enable timely adaptions to changing circumstances.

  Eversheds Harry Elias looks forward to the materialisation of the BRI and strongly believes it makes a strong contribution to the developing legal landscape in the region and beyond.

律师介绍 / Introduction to Lawyers

Philip Fong

  Philip 是 Eversheds Harry Elias 律师事务所的执行合伙人，也是新加坡诉讼实务团队的负责人。

  Philip 在民事诉讼、国际仲裁和调解领域经验丰富，承办的争议案件涉及合同、公司、不动产、业务过失、信托和财产。

  Philip 承办了大量合规性监管业务，包括证券法、公司治理、投资和医疗实践。

  Philip 被多家独立媒体评为杰出律师，包括亚太法律 500 强榜单、《法律界名人录》《亚洲法律杂志》《海峡时报》《亚太杰出律师事务所指南》《今日报》《商业时报》和亚洲新闻频道。

  Philip is the Managing Partner of Eversheds Harry Elias and heads the Litigation Practice Group in Singapore.

  Philip has extensive experience in civil litigation, international arbitration and mediation. His dispute resolution cases involve contracts, companies, property, professional negligence, trusts and estates.

  Philip also advises extensively in regulatory compliance matters, including securities laws, corporate governance, investments and medical practice.

  Philip has been highly recommended as a star name and leading lawyer by independent publications such as The Asia Pacific Legal 500, Who's Who Legal, Asian Business Legal, The Straits Times, The Guide to Asia-Pacific's Leading Law Firms, TODAY Paper, The Business Times and Channel News Asia.

Kennedy Chen

  Kennedy 是公司与公司金融领域的执业律师，尤其致力于并购与收购、战略合资企业、债务/破产重组、公私合伙企业以及公司法律咨询业务。

  Kennedy 精通英语及普通话，粤语与闽南语流利，是文莱、缅甸、印度尼西亚、越南及其他东南亚和亚太地区在并购与收购、合资企业领域的专家。Kennedy 拥有较高的法律、社会、文化、商业意识，观察力敏锐，思路开放，在工业、司法、商业地理领域都有影响力。

Kennedy is a corporate and corporate finance practitioner. He particularly works on mergers and acquisitions, strategic joint ventures, solvent/insolvent restructuring, private-public partnerships, and corporate law advisory matters.

Fully proficient in spoken and written English, Mandarin, and fluent in Cantonese and Min-Chinese, Kennedy is a specialist in M&A and joint ventures into Brunei, Myanmar, Indonesia, Vietnam and other parts of Southeast Asia and the Asia-Pacific. Armed with requisite legal, social, cultural and commercial awareness, a keen eye for detail and an open mind, he is effective regardless of the industry, jurisdiction, and the business geographical forum.

律所介绍 / Introduction to Law Firms

Pengiran Izad & Lee 律师事务所

Pengiran Izad & Lee 律师事务所最初由马来西亚三大律师事务所之一的 Skrine & Co., Kuala Lumpur 律师事务所的数名合伙人以及本所现任两名合伙人共同创立。马来西亚合伙人退休后，该所在 1999 年改名为 Pengiran Izad & Lee。

该所的定位是一家"精品所"，专注于公司、商事和银行法领域，包括符合伊斯兰教法的融资。

自 1999 年起至今，该所始终是文莱银行协会的法律顾问，也是跨国公司，如法国道达尔、法国石油和三菱公司等的法律顾问。同时，该所也获批为所有在文莱设立的银行提供法律服务，如渣打银行、大华银行、马来亚银行、兴业银行、伊斯兰文莱达鲁萨兰国银行有限公司、Baiduri 银行、Perbadanan TAIB 和汇丰银行。

该所还为各种离岸金融机构服务，同时也接收大量来自如新加坡、马来西亚等地大型律师事务所的推介。

Pengiran Izad & Lee established its office in Brunei late 1996, initially under the name Skrine & Co., Brunei. Skrine & Co., Brunei was a joint venture between some of the partners of Skrine & Co., Kuala Lumpur, which is one of the three major law firms in Malaysia, and the two current Brunei partners of Pengiran Izad & Lee. After the retirement of the Malaysian partners, the firm changed its name to Pengiran Izad & Lee on the 1st day of June 1999.

Pengiran Izad & Lee considers itself a "boutique law practice" specializing in corporate, commercial and banking law, which encompasses Sharia compliant financing.

The firm is the first-ever appointed retained legal advisers to the prestigious The Brunei Association of Banks, since 1999 to to date. It is also the retained legal counsel to a number of MNCs such as Total, the French oil and gas producer and Mitsubishi Corporation. It is also an approved law firm to the panels of all licensed banks in Brunei, notably Standard Chartered Bank, United Overseas Bank Limited, Malayan Banking Berhad, RHB Bank Berhad, Bank Islam Brunei Darussalam Berhad, Baiduri Bank Berhad, Perbadanan TAIB and HSBC.

The firm also acts for various offshore financial institutions. It also receives significant amount of referral works from major law firms in the region, such as from Singapore, Malaysia.

律师介绍 / Introduction to Lawyers

Pengiran Izad

Pengiran Izad 曾在新加坡和英格兰萨默塞特郡上过中学，于 1993 年在基尔大学获得政治与法律学士学位，于 1994 年在林肯律师学院加入英国律师协会，之后在伦敦大学学院完成了商事和公司法的法学硕士学位。他还在文莱达鲁萨兰大学完成了符合伊斯兰教法的财务研究生学位。Pengiran Izad 在伦敦大律师行工作后，在文莱达鲁萨兰国司法部服务了 1 年。其业务涵盖民事诉讼、商业和企业咨询、交易和知识产权。他是文莱法律协会前副主席。2015 年，Pengiran Izad 被任命为瑞士联邦文莱达鲁萨兰国联盟的名誉领事。

Pengiran Izad attended secondary school in Singapore and Somerset, England. Pengiran Izad obtained a BA in Politics and Law from the University of Keele in 1993 and was called to the English Bar at Lincolns Inn in 1994, before completing his LLM specialising in Commercial and Corporate Law at University College London. Pengiran Izad has also completed a post graduate diploma at University Brunei Darussalam on Sharia compliant finance. After chambering with barristers chambers in London, Pengiran Izad served for one year in the Judiciary of Brunei Darussalam. Pg Izad's practice encompasses civil litigation, commercial and corporate advisory and transactions and intellectual property. Pengiran Izad is a Past-President of and is currently the Vice-Present of the Law Society of Brunei Darussalam. In 2015 Pengiran Izad was appointed as Honorary Consul for the Confederation of Switzerland to Brunei Darussalam.

Karen Foong

Karen Foong 在 2013 年获得肯特大学学士（荣誉）学位。在她完成律师职业培训课程后，于 2015 年 10 月在林肯律师学院加入英格兰及威尔士律师协会。此后她开始在 Pengiran Izad & Lee 律师事务所实习，并于 2016 年 11 月 19 日开始作为文莱达鲁萨兰国最高法院辩护律师执业。

Karen Foong 的业务领域包含公司和诉讼事务。

Karen Foong graduated from University of Kent with a LLB (Hons) degree in 2013. Following her completion of the Bar Professional Training Course, she was admitted to the Bar of England and Wales by the Honourable Society of Lincoln's Inn in October 2015. She then commenced her pupillage with Pengiran Izad & Lee and was admitted to practice as an Advocate and Solicitor of the Supreme Court of Brunei Darussalam on 19th November, 2016.

Her area of work covers corporate and litigation matters.

文莱——翻译及协调人介绍 / Brunei—Introduction to Translators and Cooperators

律所介绍 / Introduction to Law Firms

隆安律师事务所

隆安律师事务所成立于 1992 年，总所设于北京，是中国较早的合伙制律师事务所之一，并于 2017 年成功改制为特殊普通合伙律师事务所。经过 25 年的发展，该所已有执业律师 800 余人、合伙人 200 余人，在上海、深圳、广州等二十多个城市设有分所，在美国和欧洲拥有战略合作伙伴。

该所曾为世界 500 强等大中型企业提供了知识产权、资本市场及金融、公司项目、诉讼和仲裁等领域的法律服务。该所多次被全国律师管理机构评为全国优秀律师事务所，成功入围《亚洲法律杂志》多项年度法律大奖，入选"中国十佳成长律所"，在"亚洲最大 50 家律所"及"中国律所 30 强"榜单中均位列前十，亦在英国《律师》杂志"亚太地区百强律所"榜单及中国经营律所 30 强榜单中位居前列。

Established in 1992 and headquartered in Beijing, Longan Law Firm is one of the earliest privately owned law firms in China, and has been restructured into a firm in limited liability partnership in 2017. Longan has been looking to provide extraordinary, effective legal services to our clients, with diligence and integrity. After 25 years' development, Longan has grown into a large law firm with over 800 practicing lawyers and over 200 partners, with offices covering over 20 cities including Shanghai, Shenzhen and Guangzhou, and has established strategic cooperation with large and renowned law firms throughout America and Europe. Longan, in the wave of globalisation, is going from strength to strength.

In the past 25 years, Longan provided professional and premium legal services for numerous medium and large enterprises including those listed in the Fortune Global 500 in multiple fields including but not limited to intellectual property rights, capital market and finance, corporation projects, litigation and arbitration. Longan's overall strength won and evidenced by various awards and credentials. For many times, Longan has been rated as one of the most outstanding law firms by national lawyers administrative organisations, shortlisted in several annual legal awards of Asian Legal Business (ALB), ranked in ALB China Fast 10, and ranked top 10 in both the ALB Top 50 largest Asian Law Firms and ALB China Top 30 Law Firms. In addition, Longan has also ranked among the best in Top 100 Law Firms in Asian-Pacific Area and Top 30 Elite Law Firms in China by the Lawyer Magazine of Britain.

律师介绍 / Introduction to Lawyers

黄永庆

黄永庆律师，北京市隆安律师事务所高级合伙人、管委会成员，北京隆安（成都）律师事务所主任，中国政法大学"一带一路"法律研究中心执行主任。

黄永庆律师在民商法，特别是公司法、期货法、证券法方面有较高的理论造诣和实务经验，代理了大量外商投资、涉外贸易、股份制改造、知识产权、证券纠纷、期货纠纷案件或项目。

Yongqing Huang is the Senior Partner and member of Managing Committee of Beijing Longan Law Firm, the Director of Longan Chengdu Office and the Executive Director of the Research Center for "the Belt and Road" Law of China University of Political Science and Law.

Mr. Huang has particular expertise and substantial experience in civil and commercial laws, especially contract law, company law, investment law, futures law and securities law. Mr. Huang maintains strong prevailing records in terms of dispute resolution, and has advised large quantities of complex civil and commercial cases/projects covering a large range of fields, such as foreign investment, international trade, shareholding restructure, intellectual property, securities disputes and futures disputes.

律所介绍 / Introduction to Law Firms

段和段律师事务所

段和段律师事务所成立于1993年，是中国改革开放后由中国留学生回国投资创办的第一家与国际接轨的律师事务所，是中国法律界能够提供高端的国际和涉外法律服务的律师事务所。

该所在涉外领域历经了二十多年的发展，拥有专业化和国际化的资深律师团队，提供全方位的、高端法律服务。该所已成为众多国际、国内500强企业选择法律服务的首选，并为多家国内知名的大型国企、民企处理国内业务和踏入国际市场提供专业法律服务。

该所在中国上海、北京、南京、深圳、昆明、合肥、大连、成都、重庆、厦门、郑州、长沙、青岛、济南、德阳、乌鲁木齐、香港特别行政区，美国西雅图，日本名古屋，柬埔寨均设有办公室，分别拥有专业的执业律师队伍，工作语言中有中文、英文和日文等。

Founded in 1993, Duan & Duan was the first law firm established in China with international standards after the Reform and Opening-up. Its founders were Chinese students, who returned from overseas study and work. Duan & Duan has become one of the most prestigious international PRC law firms with a commitment to providing legal services professionally and with integrity.

Duan & Duan is devoted to providing first class legal advice for domestic and foreign matters and clients since its establishment. In more than two decades, Duan & Duan has built a team of professionals with extensive local and international experience on complex and sophisticated legal matters. Duan& Duan has been engaged by numerous Chinese well-known state-owned or private enterprises both for their domestic legal needs and for expanding their business into international market. Duan & Duan is also the first choice of many Fortune 500 domestic or international businesses.

Duan & Duan has offices in Shanghai, Beijing, Nanjing, Shenzhen, Kunming, Hefei, Dalian, Chengdu, Chongqing, Xiamen, Zhengzhou, Changsha, Qingdao, Ji'nan, Deyang, Urumqi, Hong kong(China), Seattle(USA), Nagoya(Japan), Cambodia, each of which has a professional legal team with fluency in Chinese, English, Japanese and other languages.

律师介绍 / Introduction to Lawyers

吴坚

上海段和段律师事务所主任，具有20多年的律师执业经验。吴坚律师擅长世界贸易组织及协议、知识产权保护、国际投资、反垄断及反倾销，对国际贸易、公司购并、反垄断、知识产权、反倾销及金融领域有长期研究和实务经验，在能源领域法律服务具有高知名度。他还担任上海市人大代表、上海市国有资产监督管理委员会外部董事、中华全国律师协会理事等。

William Wu is the Chief Director of Shanghai Duan&Duan Law Firm. He has expertise in World Trade Organization and Agreement, Intellectual Property protection, international investment, international anti-monopoly, international anti-dumping. He has long term researching and practicing experience in international trade, M&A, Intellectual Property, anti-dumping and financial area, and has high reputation in legal service relating to resource area. He has several thesis and publications in his specialized area. Meanwhile, William Wu is Member of Shanghai Municipal People's Congress, Shanghai SASAC outside director, Member of Environment and Development Project of UN executive, and director of All China Lawyers Association.

智利——撰稿人介绍 / Chile—Introduction to Authors

律所介绍 / Introduction to Law Firms

佳理律师事务所

佳理律师事务所是智利较大的律师事务所，也是智利成立时间较长、服务范围全面的律师事务所之一，有多达250余名专业法律人士。其团队覆盖了各专业领域，有众多高水准律师。佳理律师事务所的客户包括一些较大的跨国及国际组织，及当地一些重要的公司和机构。该所经常被有影响力的法律杂志认可为智利及拉丁美洲领军的律师事务所之一。

Carey is the largest, and one of the oldest, full-service law firms in Chile, with more than 250 legal professionals. Its various corporate, litigation and regulatory groups include highly-specialized attorneys and practice areas covering all areas of law. Carey's clients include some of the world's largest multinationals, international organizations, and some of the most important local companies and institutions. It is regularly recognized as one of the leading law practitioners in Chile and Latin America by the most influential publications.

律师介绍 / Introduction to Lawyers

Alberto Cardemil

Alberto Cardemil 是智利佳理律师事务所的合伙人，也是该所自然资源及环境团队的主任。其专业领域集中在水法、自然资源交易及立法、农商业、公司法及商法。另外，他还是佳理律师事务所中国区的负责人。他被钱伯斯、最佳律师及拉美律师等国际知名法律杂志认可为领军律师。近年来，他担任环太平洋律师协会环境委员会的副主席，同时也是中智钱伯斯协会的会员及智利律师协会的会员。

Alberto Cardemil is a partner at Carey and co-head of the firm's Natural Resources and Environment Group. His professional practice is focused on water law, natural resources transactions and litigation, agribusiness, corporate law and commercial law. Additionally, he leads Carey's China Desk. He has been recognized as a leading lawyer by several international publications such as Chambers & Partners, Best Lawyers and Latin Lawyer. Currently, he is Vice-Chair of the Environmental Committee of the Inter-Pacific Bar Association and a member of the board of the Chinese-Chilean Chamber of Commerce. Also, he is member of the Chilean Bar Association. Mr. Cardemil graduated from Universidad Católica de Chile and has an LL.M. from the University of Sydney. During 2005 and 2006, he worked as Foreign Associate in the Projects and Corporate Groups at Herbert Smith Freehills, in Melbourne and Perth.

Ignacio Tornero（罗焱）

罗焱是佳理律师事务所中国代表处的高级合伙人及上海地区协调人。他的专业领域主要是为在智利的亚洲公司和在中国的拉美律师事务所提供一般的法律援助。罗焱先生从智利天主教大学获得法律学士学位，并于近期申请了哥伦比亚大学尚德商学院的工商管理硕士。他于2013年、2014年分别在国浩律师事务所北京分所及大成律师事务所上海分所工作。他也是《中国在拉美的对外投资：智利篇》的创作者，得到了智利银行及金融组织的表彰（2011）。另外，他在2011年还赢得了"中国桥"普通话比赛智利赛区的奖项。

Ignacio Tornero is a senior associate and coordinator in Shanghai of Carey's China Practice. His professional practice focuses on general legal assistance to Asian companies in Chile, and to Latin American companies in their endeavors in China. Mr. Tornero obtained his law degree from Universidad Católica de Chile, and is currently MBA candidate at Sauder School of Business, University of British Columbia. In 2013 and 2014 he worked at Grandall Law Firm and Dacheng Dentons in their Beijing and Shanghai offices respectively. Mr. Tornero has written several publications regarding trade and Chinese Outward Direct Investment (ODI) in Chile and Latin America, and is a regular speaker in international conferences regarding the matter. He is also the author of the thesis 'Chinese ODI in Latin America: the Chilean Case', awarded by the Chilean Banks Association and Financial Institutions (2011). In addition, also in 2011, he won the Chilean stage of the Chinese language competition 'Chinese Bridge'.

律所介绍 / Introduction to Law Firms

Cariola Diez Pérez Cotapos 律师事务所

Cariola Diez Pérez Cotapos 律师事务所是智利领先的律师事务所之一，是一家向客户提供全方面、高质量法律服务，充分满足客户需求的律师事务所。该所的服务覆盖银行、金融和资本市场、商法和公司法、并购、合规、家庭、能源、酒店、度假区、赌场、工程和建造、房地产和城市开发、破产、境外投资、劳动法、雇用和移民、竞争和反垄断、诉讼、调解和仲裁、环境、矿业和自然资源、渔业和农业、保险、科技、隐私和媒体、运输和基建、税务和知识产权。

Cariola Díez Pérez-Cotapos is one of Chile's major business law firms. We are a full-service firm that delivers high-quality legal advice to our clients and provides a comprehensive range of legal services to meet today's business needs. Those services include: banking, finance and capital markets; commercial and corporate law; mergers and acquisitions; regulatory law; family businesses; energy; hotels, resorts and casinos; engineering and construction; real estate and urban development; insolvency; foreign investment; labor, employment and immigration; competition and antitrust; litigation, mediation and arbitration; environmental; mining and natural resources; fisheries and aquaculture; insurance; technology, privacy and media; transportation and infrastructure; taxation; and intellectual property (IP).

律师介绍 / Introduction to Lawyers

Sergio Diez

Sergio Diez，Cariola Diez Pérez Cotapos 律师事务所合伙人，擅长公司、条例与合同事务，为多个领域的国内外客户提供长期咨询服务，所涉行业包括石油、工业、农工、酒店、渔业和水产，以及实验室、赌场等。塞尔希奥曾经参与众多项目，在相关项目的交易和融资过程中为国外客户提供咨询，设计在智利的合法投资工具，为实现在智利投资或将资金汇出国外制订替代方案以及相关的税务事项。同时，塞尔希奥律师还参与了尽职调查、起草股权交易、公司持股合同和股东协议等方面的工作。

Sergio, Partner, his areas of practice are Corporate Law, contracts and agreements and serves as legal counsel for local and foreign clients of the most diverse areas, such as oil, energy, industrial, agro industrial, laboratories, gaming casinos, hotel industry, fishing and aquaculture industry, among others. He has participated in several transactions for the purchase, sale and financing of various companies, assisting foreign clients through the whole purchase process, including the incorporation in Chile of a suitable investment vehicle; advising in the evaluation of different alternatives to carry out foreign investment in Chile or the remittance of capital abroad and its tax implications; due diligence processes; share purchase agreements, equity capital assignment and shareholder's agreements.

Daniela Tapia

Daniela Tapia，助理律师，2016 年加入该所。2015 年毕业于智利天主教大学法学院。专注于公司法和合同法。Daniela Tapia 曾参与数家企业的出售、购买及融资交易项目，在整个交易过程中予以协助，还曾参与矿业、渔业、不动产和建设工程等项目。

Daniela Tapia is an associate of Cariola Díez Pérez-Cotapos since 2016. She graduated from Pontificia Universidad Católica de Chile, School of Law in 2015. Her areas of practice are Corporate Law and contracts and agreements. She has participated in several transactions for the purchase, sale and financing of various companies, assisting through the whole purchase process. She has been involved in mining, fishing, real estate and construction projects among others.

智利——翻译及协调人介绍 / Chile—Introduction to Translators and Cooperators

律所介绍 / Introduction to Law Firms

锦天城（青岛）律师事务所

锦天城律师事务所是一家提供全方位法律服务的全国领先的律师事务所，是一家总部设在上海的全国性律师事务所。上海锦天城（青岛）律师事务所成立于 2014 年，该所现有执业律师、律师助理及行政人员共计 130 人。锦天城（青岛）律师事务所目前建立了房地产及建筑工程、金融、证券、知识产权、税务等十余个优质、高效的服务团队。该所多次被律师协会、国际知名法律媒体和权威评级机构列为中国顶尖的法律服务提供者之一。

AllBright Law Firm is one of the leading full-service Chinese law firms in the People's Republic of China（"PRC"）. As the only national law firm headquarter in Shanghai, we provide a comprehensive range of legal solutions and services to both domestic and international clients. AllBright (Qingdao) Law Firm was founded in 2014. We have currently more than 130 registered lawyers, legal assistants and administrative officers. AllBright (Qingdao) Law Firm has more than 10 practice areas, including Real Estate and Construction, Finance, Securities, Intellectual Property, Tax and so on. We are consistently recognized by various institutions and in major rankings as one of the top PRC law firms.

律师介绍 / Introduction to Lawyers

张毅

张毅律师系上海锦天城（青岛）律师事务所高级合伙人，主要执业领域为国际投资、国际贸易、保险等，担任多家著名跨国公司及众多欧美外商投资企业的常年法律顾问。张毅律师在外商投资和中国企业海外投资业务，特别是"一带一路"领域具有丰富的执业经验，曾代表多家境内外投资者设立外商投资企业，进行投资、重组、并购、融资等业务。作为中国涉外律师领军人才，张毅律师参加了中华全国律师协会组织的在美国以及欧盟的跨境投资并购和反倾销的培训。

David Zhang is the Senior Partner in Shanghai AllBright(Qingdao) Law Firm. Mr. Zhang specializes in International investment, international trade and insurance. He has acted as corporate counsel to a large number of well-known multinationals and foreign investment companies, providing high quality, comprehensive legal services. Mr. Zhang has extensive practical experience in inbound and outbound investment, especially "Belt and Road" area, having represented a number of Chinese and multinational investors in the incorporation of foreign-owned enterprises, mergers and acquisitions, corporate restructuring, and financing. Mr. Zhang took part in the cross-border investment and anti-dumping training in USA and Europe, as one of the "China International Legal Professionals". In 2017, Mr. Zhang was one of the 15 lawyers that selected to participate in the international lawyer institution activities by the All China Lawyer Association (ACLA).

律所介绍 / Introduction to Law Firms

云南八谦律师事务所

云南八谦律师事务所是云南省第一家执业律师数量超过110人的律师事务所、特殊普通合伙律师事务所，现有合伙人36名、执业律师120名。连续多年被钱伯斯评为"公司与商事"业务西部第一等律师事务所，获得全国优秀律师事务所、云南省优秀律师事务所称号。多年来为众多客户提供包括政府法律事务、国有资产管理、金融、涉外法律、房地产、纠纷解决、知识产权方面的服务。

云南八谦律师事务所还在老挝万象设立了八谦老挝律师事务所，在缅甸仰光设立了中国澜湄律师事务所，业务范围覆盖东南亚和南亚主要国家。

Yunnan Baqian Law Firm is the first Yunnan law firm with more than a hundred lawyers and limited liability partnership LLP. It is with 36 partners and 120 licensed attorneys. It has been ranked as the Grade One of Cooperate/Commerce Western Law Firm by Chambers for years, awarded with National Excellent Law Firm and Yunnan Excellent Law Firm. Yunnan Baqian has been provided clients with various legal services in the practice field, including government administration, State-owned assets management, finance, foreign-related practice, real estate, dispute resolution, and intellectual property.

Yunnan Baqian set up Baoqian Law and Consultancy (Lao) in Vientiane, Lao PDR, and jointly incorporated China Panmekong Law Firm in Yangon, Myanmar, rendering cross-border legal services covering South and Southeast Asia.

律师介绍 / Introduction to Lawyers

张天翼

张天翼律师2008年开始执业，云南八谦律师事务所合伙人，八谦老挝律师事务所主任，中国澜湄律师事务所高级顾问，中华全国律师协会"涉外律师领军人才库"律师，中国国际贸易促进委员会/中国国际商会调解中心调解员。

张天翼律师的业务领域为境外投资、外商对华投资、并购、重大基础设施建设、国际商事仲裁等。

Mr. Zhang Tianyi, Partner of Yunnan Baqian Law Firm, Director of Baoqian Law&Counsltancy (Lao), Senior Advisor of China Panmekong Law Firm, member of the "Leading Chinese Lawyers in Foreign-related Legal Practice" of All China Lawyers Association, mediator of China Council for the promotion of International Trade/China Chamber of International Commerce Resolution Center.

His main areas of practice are overseas investments, foreign investments in China, M&A, major infrastructure constructions, and international commercial arbitrations.

吉布提——撰稿人介绍 / Djibouti—Introduction to Authors

律所介绍 / Introduction to Law Firms

ASM律师事务所

ASM律师事务所已成立多年，一直致力于提高本地的法律专业水平。该所可提供建立在对吉布提现状广泛而透彻的了解基础上的经验和知识。该所可对私营企业及政府部门提供服务。

ASM律师事务所一直积极响应吉布提全球化的需求，积极参与非洲、欧洲及中东地区的各种研讨会和智库。

ASM律师事务所的团队清楚非洲面临的各种挑战和需要，据此提供兼顾各种法律体系（大陆法、普通法、伊斯兰法）特点的务实、有效的解决方案。

Established in Djibouti for many years, ASM Law firm contributes to strengthening the local legal expertise. The law firm offers an experience and a knowledge of ground which give it wide knowledge to know the ins and outs of the current problems of the country. The firm delivers counsel to the private sector and the public sector.

ASM Law firm has been proactive in responding to the globalization of Djibouti by actively participating in numerous conferences and think tanks throughout Africa, Europe and the Middle East.

ASM Law firm team understands the challenges of the African context and the need to provide practical and effective solutions that take into account the specificities of each legislation (Civil Law, Common Law, Islamic Law etc.).

律师介绍 / Introduction to Lawyers

Ayman Said

Ayman Said 专长于商法和刑法。

Ayman Said 毕业于法国克莱蒙费朗（Clermont-Ferrand）大学法学系，拥有商法和税法的硕士学位及高等教育文凭。

Ayman Said 基于其从业经历对于银行专业法律颇有研究，此外他还获得了银行及保险公司等金融专业机构认可的由银行技术学院（巴黎银行培训中心）颁发的国际专业证书。

2012 年，Ayman Said 在吉布提法院宣誓，并开始作为吉布提律师协会的注册律师执业。

Ayman Said 是非洲商业及法律专家（又称"ABLE"）网络的成员。ABLE 的成员为资深律师，其在非洲大陆的法律、经济等领域发展及推广新思想和有效的解决方案方面扮演着重要的角色。

Ayman Said 是 ABLE 网络东部和南部非洲共同市场地区商法协调专家组的成员。通过他的网络可获得非洲大陆重要的法律信息资源。

Mr. Ayman Said is specialized in Business Law and Criminal Law.

Ayman has completed a degree in Private Law and Business Law of which he graduated with a Master's degree in Law and a Diploma of Specialized Higher Education in Business Law and Taxation of the Faculty of Law of Clermont-Ferrand, France.

Ayman completed his legal studies by developing a banking expertise thanks, on the one hand, to his professional experience and, on the other hand, by obtaining the international professional diploma of the Technical Institute of Bank (Center of Banking Training of Paris), recognized by the financial professions of banks and insurance companies.

In 2012, Ayman was sworn in at the Judicial Court of Djibouti and since then has been successfully practicing as a lawyer registered with the Bar Association of Djibouti.

Ayman is a member of the AFRICA BUSINESS AND LEGAL EXPERTISE (ABLE) network. ABLE members are experienced lawyers who play an important role in the African continent to develop and promote new ideas and effective solutions all, legal and economics area.

Ayman is a member of the experts of the ABLE network on the harmonization of business law in the COMESA region. His network allows him to access important resources in terms of legal information throughout the continent.

吉布提——翻译及协调人介绍 / Djibouti—Introduction to Translators and Cooperators

律所介绍 / Introduction to Law Firms

广东恒益律师事务所

广东恒益律师事务所原名为"广州市对外经济律师事务所"，成立于 1984 年 8 月，是中国改革开放后首批成立的涉外专业律师事务所之一。

经过三十多年的发展，本所现已成为华南地区规模较大的综合性律师事务所之一，业务范围涵盖公司、金融、证券、知识产权、房地产、外商投资、国际贸易、反垄断、诉讼、仲裁等各个重要的法律服务领域，可为国内外客户提供全方位的法律服务。

该所多次受到政府主管部门和行业协会的表彰与肯定。1998 年，该所荣获司法部授予的"部级文明律师事务所"称号。2005 年，该所被中华全国律师协会评为"全国优秀律师事务所"。此外，该所连续六年被广州市律师协会授予"规范管理奖"。国际著名的法律媒体 Legal 500 亦对该所予以肯定及推介。

GFE Law Office (the "Firm") used to known as Guangzhou Foreign Economic Law Office, which was founded on 28th August, 1984. In those days, the Firm was designated by the Ministry of Justice of China as one of the principal law firms in China practicing foreign-related legal affairs.

Over the years, the Firm has grown into one of the leading law firms in the South of China, which can provide full services for its domestic and foreign clients, including corporate, banking, securities, intellectual property, real property, FDI, international trade, antitrust and competition, litigation and arbitration.

The Firm is highly acknowledged and recommended by the authorities and bar associations in China. In 1998, the Firm was ranked by the Ministry of Justice as one of the 20 "Model Law Firms" in China. In 2005, the Firm was recognized as "Excellent Law Firm" in China by the All China Lawyers Association. Moreover, the Firm was granted Outstanding Management Award by Guangzhou Lawyers Association for consecutive 6 years. The Firm was also recommended by Legal 500 as one of the leading law firms in Guangzhou.

律师介绍 / Introduction to Lawyers

吴凯

吴凯律师是广东恒益律师事务所高级合伙人，现任广东省律师协会竞争与反垄断法律专业委员会副主任、广州市律师协会公平贸易法律业务专业委员会副主任。

吴凯律师为中山大学国际法硕士、英国格拉斯哥大学反垄断法硕士。

吴凯律师长期从事外商投资、企业并购、境外上市、公司法、反垄断法、商业诉讼、仲裁等领域的法律事务，执业经验丰富。

2013年，吴凯律师被评为中华全国律师协会"中国涉外律师领军人才"；2017年吴凯律师入选中华全国律师协会"一带一路"跨境律师人才库。

Mr. Raymond Wu is a senior partner of GFE Law Office in Guangzhou, China. Moreover, he is the Vice Director of Competition and Anti-trust Laws Committee under Guangdong Lawyers Association, Vice Director of Fair Trade Laws Committee under Guangzhou Lawyers Association in these days.

Mr. Wu obtained his LLM degree of International Competition Laws and Policies from Glasgow University in UK and Master Degree of International Laws from Zhong Shan University in China.

Mr. Wu mainly practices corporate and commercial laws. His specializations include FDI, M&A, overseas listing, antimonopoly legal affairs, general corporate legal affairs, commercial litigation and arbitration. He has extensive experience in advising domestic and foreign clients on their investments and transactions.

In 2013, Mr. Wu was elected as one of the leading Chinese lawyer talents practicing foreign related legal affairs by All China Lawyers Association ("ACLA"); in 2017, he was enrolled to the "Belt and Road Cross-border Transaction Lawyers Pool" by ACLA.

律所介绍 / Introduction to Law Firms

北京市时代九和律师事务所

北京市时代九和律师事务所是我国创立较早、服务全面深入的大型律师事务所之一，前身为1994年成立的北京市时代律师事务所，以及稍后成立的北京市华地律师事务所和北京市九和律师事务所。2001年，北京市时代律师事务所与北京市华地律师事务所为适应规模化、专业化需要，合并成立了提供全面商业法律服务的北京市时代华地律师事务所。2007年年初，为了进一步扩大规模和提升专业层次，北京市时代华地律师事务所与北京市九和律师事务所合并成立了北京市时代九和律师事务所。经过两次合并后，该所的律师人数已达一百多名，业务收入已经昂然全国前列，业务规模不断扩大，成为中国知名律师事务所之一。该所在公司、证券、金融、融资、资本市场、房地产、诉讼仲裁、国际投资、国际贸易、海商海事、知识产权等领域拥有一流的专家级律师。

Jurisino Law Group is a large law firm offering comprehensive and thorough legal services to clients from within and outside China. Founded in 2001 by a merger between the Times Law Firm and the Highland Law Firm, both among the oldest private law firms in mainland China, and a further merger in 2007 between the Times Highland Law Firm and the Jusers Law Firm, With over 100 lawyers, Jurisino is distinguished by its expertise and reputation in capital markets, banking and financing, crossborder investment, international trade, marine and maritime law, land development, sports and entertainment, information technology, intellectual property, dispute settlement and many other areas of practice. For their unparalleled expertise and uncompromisable commitment to excellence, Jurisino lawyers have been known for many activities. One of Jurisino lawyers acted as the lead counsel for the Beijing Bidding Committee for the 2008 Olympics, another became an expert consultant to the Ministry of Commerce of the P.R. China in the WTO Doha Round rules negotiation, and yet another led the Chinese legal profession for six years as the President of the All China Lawyers Association.

律师介绍 / Introduction to Lawyers

江家喜

江家喜律师为北京市时代九和律师事务所高级合伙人,具有中国、美国和加拿大律师执业许可,北京大学法学学士和法学硕士、女王大学法律硕士、约克大学法律博士。主要从事公司治理、资本市场、国际投资、国际贸易、国际诉讼仲裁等业务。国家律师学院客座教授,在国际律师协会、中华全国律师协会、美国律师协会多个专业委员会担任职务。在公司治理、跨境投资、反倾销法、反垄断法等领域发表了多部(篇)中英文法律专著和专文。

Eric J. Jiang is a Senior Partner at Jurisino Law Group, based in Beijing. He is licensed to practise law in China, USA and Canada. He obtained an LL.B. and M. Jur. from Peking University, an LL.M. from Queen's University and a J.D. from York University. Currently he focuses on corporate governance, capital markets, mergers & acquisitions, cross-border investments, international trade and international arbitration. He serves in multiple positions at several specialized commitees of the International Bar Association, the All China Lawyers Association, and the American Bar Association, and is a Visiting Professor to the China National Lawyers College. He has many publications including A Practical Guide on Corporate Governance in China, "Towards A Truly Globalized Competition Initiative", "From TPP to 'Belt and Road': Some Thoughts on Establishing Institutional Supports", and "Ten Years After Accession to the WTO: Recent Developments in the Non-market Economy Issue".

埃塞俄比亚——撰稿人介绍 / Ethiopia—Introduction to Authors

律所介绍 / Introduction to Law Firms

Mehrteab Leul and Associates 律师事务所

Mehrteab Leul and Associates 律师事务所由 Mehrteab Leul Kokeb 于 1997 年创立,是埃塞俄比亚领先的全方位服务型的律师事务所,在该国商业和投资方面的法律问题上有超过 20 年的为客户提供咨询和代理服务的经验。该所提供公司组建、投资、知识产权、就业、税务、能源、采矿、石油和天然气、慈善和社会服务、酒店和休闲服务、房地产、银行和金融、航空、项目融资、私募股权等方面的法律咨询服务。其客户范围从创业公司到政府部门以及可口可乐和通用电气(GE)等跨国公司。该所约 99% 的客户是外国公司。

该所是英国欧华律师事务所非洲集团的特别成员,DLA Piper 非洲集团是一家独立律师事务所联盟,与国际和非洲的 DLA Piper 共同合作。

该所还是国际律师协会、埃塞俄比亚律师协会和国际商标协会的成员。此外,该所也是非洲商业法律公司协会的创始成员之一。

Founded in 1997 by Mehrteab Leul Kokeb, Mehrteab Leul and Associates ("MLA") is a leading full service law office in Ethiopia with over twenty years experience advising and representing clients on wide range of legal issues concerning business and investment in the country. MLA offers a broad range of legal advisory services on company formation, Investment, Intellectual Property, Employment, Taxation, Energy, Mining, Oil and Gas, Charities and Societies, Hospitality and Leisure, Real Estate, Banking and Finance, Aviation, Project Finance, Private Equity, and other related matters. MLA's clients range from start-up companies, to government entities and multinational corporations, such as, Coca Cola and General Electric (GE). About 99% of our clientele is foreign companies.

MLA is a proud member of DLA Piper Africa Group, an allianceofleadingindependent law firms, working together in association with DLA Piper, both internationally and across Africa.

MLA is also a member of the International Bar Association, the Ethiopian Lawyers' Association, and the International Trademark Association. Moreover, MLA is a founding member of the African Business Law Firms Association.

律师介绍 / Introduction to Lawyers

Mehrteab Leul Kokeb

Mehrteab Leul Kokeb 是一位资深法律专家,在公司和资产交易方面拥有 25 年的经验。Mehrteab 在法庭诉讼案件、处理合同纠纷、仲裁、非法竞争案件、清算和劳动案件方面也有着十分丰富的经验。目前在律所从事项目融资和公司业务。擅长为个人和公司提供多方面的法律服务,并且精通资产交易、企业相关问题、审判、听证会、调解、取证和相关文件准备以及在演讲技巧方面有着卓越的成果。

Mehrteab Leul Kokeb is a senior law professional with 25 years of experience in corporate and transactional matters. Mehrteab have also experience in managing court cases, dealing with contractual disputes, arbitration, unlawful competition cases, liquidations, and employment matters. Currently in MLA Mehrteab Leul is practicing on project finance and corporate matters. He is skilled in providing multidimensional legal services to individual and corporate clients, and proficient in achieving excellent results in transaction, corporate issues, trials, hearings, mediations, dispositions pleading and document preparation with excellent oratory skills.

律所介绍 / Introduction to Law Firms

Mesfin Tafesse & Associates 律师事务所

  Mesfin Tafesse & Associates 律师事务所在埃塞俄比亚是一家领先的律师事务所，为商业和投资、并购、银行和金融、税务、采矿和能源、建筑和制造业、知识产权、IT 和电信、环境和民间社会法以及酒店业提供高质量的法律咨询服务。

  该所由一批在埃塞俄比亚多个领域具有丰富经验的律师组成，提供一系列服务，包括为各种交易准备前的法律尽职调查报告，代表客户进行商业谈判，起草投资报告协议，促进各种法律形式的本地存在。

  2018 年，钱伯斯法律评级机构将该所评为埃塞俄比亚第一品牌法律顾问。IFLRS 1000 将该所评为金融和企业业务领域的二级法律顾问。该所也被 The Legal 500 评为埃塞俄比亚一级法律律所。

  Mesfin Tafesse & Associates Law Office (MTA) is a leading law office providing high quality legal advisory services in the areas of commercial and investment law, M&A, banking and finance, taxation, mining and energy, construction and manufacturing industry, intellectual property, hospitality, IT and Telecom, Environment, and civil society law.

  The law office is made up of a team of attorneys with substantial experience in diversified areas of Ethiopian law, offering a range of services, including preparation of legal due diligence opinion relating to various transactions, conducting business negotiations on behalf of clients, drafting of investment agreements, facilitating the local presence of various legal forms.

  In 2018, Chambers and Partners ranked MTA as a Brand 1 legal adviser in Ethiopia. The IFLRS 1000 ranked MTA as a Tier 2 legal adviser in financial and corporate practice area. MTA is also ranked by Legal 500 as a Tier 1 law firm in Ethiopia.

律师介绍 / Introduction to Lawyers

Mesfin Tafesse

  Mesfin Tafesse 是 Mesfin Tafesse & Associates 律师事务所的首席律师。他在埃塞俄比亚的私营、公共和公民社会领域拥有超过 25 年的法律实践经验。Mesfin Tafesse 在电力和能源、银行与金融、并购、石油与天然气以及基础设施等行业中代表跨国投资者有着丰富的经验，是一位评价很高的律师。他被钱伯斯法律评级机构评为埃塞俄比亚"普遍商业法"领域的 I 类法律服务提供者。

  Mesfin Tafesse is the Principal Attorney who founded MTA. He has over 25 years of legal experience in the private, public, and civil society sectors in Ethiopia. Mr. Mesfin is a top-rated attorney with substantial experience representing multinational investors in sectors including power and energy, banking and finance, M&A, oil and gas, and infrastructure. He is recognized by Chambers & Partners as Band I legal service provider in Ethiopia in the area of General Business Law.

埃塞俄比亚——翻译及协调人介绍 / Ethiopia—Introduction to Translators and Cooperators

律所介绍 / Introduction to Law Firms

北京市盈科律师事务所

  北京市盈科律师事务所是一家源自中国的全球化法律服务机构，致力于在全球范围内为客户提供"一站式"商务法律服务，其总部设于中国北京，在中国大陆拥有 47 家分所，同时该所全球法律服务联盟已覆盖海外 53 个国家的 113 个国际城市。

  该所的业务范围覆盖国际贸易、海外投资、公司、资本证券、两岸事务、私募、投融资与并购、知识产权、房地产、环境保护、海商海事等专业领域。

  该所的专业服务水平得到了国际评级机构的认可。2014 年、2016 年均被《亚洲法律杂志》评为"亚洲规模最大律所"之一、2017 年"中国国内律所" 30 强；2016 年、2017 年被英国《律师》杂志评为"亚太地区 100 强律所"。

  Beijing Yingke Law Firm is a global legal service organization from China. It is committed to providing "one-stop" business legal services to customers worldwide. Its headquarters is located in Beijing, China and has 47 points in China. At the same time, Yingke Global Legal Services Alliance has covered 113 international cities in 53 countries.

  The firm's business scope covers international trade, overseas investment, companies, capital securities, cross-strait affairs, private equity, investment and financing and mergers and acquisitions, intellectual property, real estate, environmental protection, maritime affairs and other specialized fields.

YingKe's professional service level has been recognized by international rating agencies. In 2014 and 2016, he was named "The Largest Law Firm in Asia" by the *Asia Legal Business* and the top 30 law firms in China in 2017; In 2016 and 2017,The top 100 law firms list in the Asia Pacific region by the *The Lawyer*.

律师介绍 / Introduction to Lawyers

闪涛

闪涛，盈科国际合作委员会副主任；盈科（广州）律师事务所高级合伙人，国际法律事务部主任；法学博士。作为中华全国律师协会"中国涉外律师领军人才"赴美国天普大学培训以及英国伦敦 BPP Law School 培训。

专注于涉外法律服务、公司法务、解散、破产、清算、金融、证券、私募等领域。

闪涛律师迄今代理过各类具有涉外因素的民商事诉讼案件上百件，其中包含股权转让纠纷、资产转让纠纷、土地使用权转让纠纷、董事竞业禁止纠纷、国际贸易买卖合同纠纷、海上货物运输合同纠纷、借贷合同纠纷以及传统民商法领域的债权债务纠纷，具有丰富的诉讼经验。

Shan Tao, Vice Director of Yingke International Cooperation Committee; Senior Partner, Director of International Legal Affairs Department; Doctor of Law. As a leader in foreign legal affairs of the National Bar Association, he trained at Temple University in the United States and trained at BPP Law School in London, England.

Focus on foreign-related legal services, corporate legal affairs, dissolution, bankruptcy, liquidation, finance, securities, private equity and other fields.

Shan Tao has so far represented hundreds of civil and commercial litigation cases involving foreign factors, including equity transfer disputes, asset transfer disputes, land use rights transfer disputes, directors' non-competition disputes, international trade contract disputes, and marine cargo Disputes over transport contract disputes, loan contract disputes and creditor's rights and debts in the field of traditional civil and commercial law have extensive litigation experience.

律所介绍 / Introduction to Law Firms

北京尚公（上海）律师事务所

北京尚公（上海）律师事务所是全国优秀律师事务所——尚公律师事务所旗下规模最大的分所。曾荣获"闸北区优秀律师事务所""闸北区文明单位""静安区文明单位"等称号。

本着"合作、敬业、高效、发展"的宗旨，该所自成立伊始就以涉外法律业务作为核心业务之一，为境内外客户提供股权结构设计、内部治理规范、兼并收购策划、商事争议解决等法律事务。担任多家政府机构、大型国有企业、外资企业的常年法律顾问；参与跨国公司间并购方案的策划、谈判及实施等法律事务。与新加坡、韩国、泰国、迪拜、印度等地的服务机构有稳定的业务合作关系，以满足客户境外投资所需的相关法律服务

Beijing Shanggong (Shanghai) Law Firm is the largest branch of the Shanggong Law Firm, an excellent national law firm. Won the title of "Zhabei District Excellent Law Firm", "Zhubei District Civilization Unit", "Jingan District Civilized Unit" and so on.

With the tenet of "cooperation, dedication, efficiency, and development", since its establishment, Shanggong Shanghai has been involving foreign-related legal operations as one of its core businesses, providing domestic and foreign clients with equity structure design, internal governance regulations, mergers and acquisitions planning, and commercial disputes. Solve such legal affairs. Acted as a perennial legal advisor for various government agencies, large state-owned enterprises, and foreign-funded enterprises; participated in the planning, negotiation, and implementation of legal affairs among MNCs. With local service agencies such as Singapore, South Korea, Thailand, Dubai, India, etc., they have a stable business cooperation relationship to meet the relevant legal services required by customers for overseas investment.

律师介绍 / Introduction to Lawyers

邵开俊

邵开俊，北京尚公（上海）律师事务所创始合伙人、执行主任。上海市律师协会国际投资业务研究委员会副主任，上海仲裁委员会仲裁员。荣获"上海市静安区优秀政协委员""上海市优秀青年律师"等称号。

留学于英国，并在新加坡工作多年，拥有丰富的海外工作经验。擅长政府法律事务、股权结构设计、内部治理规范、兼并收购策划、私募股权投资、资本市场运作、商事争议解决等法律事务。

Mr. Shao Kaijun is the Founding Partner and Executive Director of Beijing S&P (Shanghai) Law Firm. Vice Director of the International Investment Research Committee of Shanghai Bar Association, The Arbitrator of Shanghai Arbitration Commission. He was awarded the title of "Excellent CPPCC Member of Jing'an District of Shanghai" and "Outstanding Young Lawyer of Shanghai".

He graduated from the University of Exeter, UK and major in International Business Law. He worked in Singapore for many years and has extensive overseas working experiences. He specializes in Equity Structure Design, Company Internal Governance, Mergers and Acquisitions Planning, Private Equity Investment, Capital Market Operations and Commercial Dispute Resolution.

伊拉克——撰稿人介绍 / Iraq—Introduction to Authors

律所介绍 / Introduction to Law Firms

Al Tamimi 律师事务所

Al Tamimi 律师事务所成立于 1989 年,是中东地区最大的律师事务所,共有 17 个办事处,遍布世界 9 个国家。是一家集知识、经验和专业知识为一体的提供综合服务的商业律所,致力于为客户提供符合商业目标、成本效益最佳的法律解决方案。

多年来,该所为众多类型的客户提供服务,包括政府机构、政府或半政府实体、本地、区域和国际公司、银行和金融机构,与国际和地区律师事务所进行合作。

该所能够在 9 个国家的法院代理案件,这一独特优势使该所与竞争对手拉开距离,这也是该所骄傲之处。

Al Tamimi & Company is the largest law firm in the Middle East with 17 offices across nine countries. Established in 1989, we are a full service commercial firm combining knowledge, experience and expertise to ensure our clients have access to the best legal solutions that are commercially sound and cost effective.

Over the years, we have acted for a wide variety of clients, including: government bodies; government or semi-government owned entities; local, regional and international companies; banks and financial institutions; along with both international and regional law firms.

As a firm, we have the ability to practice local law in each of the nine jurisdictions where we have a presence. This means that each of our licensed litigators have rights of audience before local courts. We are proud of this unique strength, which truly sets us apart from the competition.

律师介绍 / Introduction to Lawyers

Ali AL Dabbagh

诉讼律师助理,2016 年在匹兹堡大学获得法学硕士学位,2014 年在巴格达大学获得法学学士学位。

阿里擅长商业诉讼及国际商事仲裁。此外,阿里具有医疗、投资和电信方面的交易经验。在加入 Al Tamimi 律师事务所之前,他致力于分析和寻找伊拉克投资法律框架(尤其是国际承诺)的空白。

使用语言:阿拉伯语、英文。

Ali specialises in commercial litigation and arbitration. In addition, Ali has transactional experience in healthcare, investment, and telecommunications. Prior to joining Al Tamimi Ali worked on analysing and finding gaps in the Iraqi investment legal framework, particularly Iraq's international commitments.

Languages: Arabic, English.

Education: 2016–LLM, University of Pittsburgh; 2014 – Bachelor of Law, University of Baghdad.

律所介绍 / Introduction to Law Firms

Confluent 律师事务所

Confluent 律师事务所是伊拉克领先的法律咨询服务机构,也是唯一能提供汉语法律服务的伊拉克法律服务供应商。

Confluent Law Group is the leading legal consultancy advising on Iraq. It is the only such advisor with a Chinese-language capability.

律师介绍 / Introduction to Lawyers

Greg Englefield

Greg Englefield, Confluent 律师事务所合伙人,负责该所的管理事宜。他曾在高伟绅律师事务所位于英国、多哈及迪拜的办公室供职 18 年。他在多个司法管辖区从事过油气以及基础设施项目融资的相关工作。近些年,Greg 投身于伊拉克(包括库尔德斯坦地区)的电力项目以及一个重要的石油项目。他从事的领域包括对位于伊拉克以及中东地区的、有国际融资人以及出口信贷机构参与的公司(包括电信公司)进行融资,包含了伊斯兰以及传统意义的融资。

Partner–Greg manages the Confluent practice. He previously worked with Clifford Chance in the UK, Doha and Dubai for 18 years. Greg has worked on oil and gas and infrastructure project financings in numerous jurisdictions. Greg has recently worked on power projects and a major petroleum project in Iraq including the Kurdistan Region. He has also worked on major financings for corporates including telecoms companies in Iraq and the Middle East involving international financiers and ECAs. This has included Islamic and conventional financings.

Tom Calvert

Confluent 律师事务所合伙人,曾经在美国领先的以及欧亚顶级的律师事务所工作。他具备多个领域的商业经验,并专注于能源以及自然资源领域,为不同类型客户提供服务。Tom 的专业领域包括国际并购、合资、相关能源项目的开发以及一般性公司事务。他讲中文,中英文法律文件读写流利。

Partner–Tom previously worked for leading U.S. and major circle law firms in Europe and Asia. His extensive commercial experience spans a number of sectors but he has a particular focus on energy and natural resources acting for a diverse range of clients. Tom's areas of expertise include international mergers and acquisitions, joint ventures, energy related project development and general corporate matters. He speaks Chinese and is fully familiar with the review of legal documents in English and Chinese.

伊拉克——翻译及协调人介绍 / Iraq–Introduction to Translators and Cooperators

律所介绍 / Introduction to Law Firms

北京市中鹏律师事务所

北京市中鹏律师事务所成立于 2001 年,拥有合伙人、律师及职员三十余人,是一家专注于融资并购和上市业务的高度专业化律师事务所,有着丰富的资本市场相关法律经验,包括首次公开募股、企业并购、债务融资等。该所在反倾销和解决其他跨国投资纠纷方面也有突出表现。该所大部分律师具有美国、英国及其他国家的法律学位或者执业经历。

该所专为众多国际知名公司及本土企业提供高效的法律服务,这些公司的跨境业务已经有了实质性的拓展。该所的律师相信,高端专业的服务能力将满足客户日益增长的国际业务需求。

Sinowing Law LLP was established in 2001 in Beijing, the firm has 4 partners, and more than 30 other lawyers and support staff. Sinowing Law LLP positions itself as a highly-specialized firm focusing on foreign related cases. It is experienced in capital market related legal services, including IPO, M&A, foreign direct investment, etc. Its experience in cross border dispute resolutions is also well recognized. Majority of its attorneys have hand-on practicing experiences or own law degrees from USA, UK and other countries.

Sinowing has proudly worked with some of the well-known international companies. These companies have substantial business growth in China, benefiting from the legal services provided by Sinowing. The attorneys in Sinowing believe that their cutting edge expertise and fine professional ethics will contribute to the prosperity of their clients.

律师介绍 / Introduction to Lawyers

邹振东

北京市中鹏律师事务所主任,中国人民大学国际政治及国际经济双学士。曾参选英国政府与中国司法部联合主办的赴英工作培训项目,曾在伦敦 Bird & Bird 律师事务所及 Brick Court Chambers 大律师楼工作,并参加伦敦大学法律集训,获英国司法大臣培训证书。邹振东律师目前是国际保护知识产权理事会中国委员和国际许可贸易工作者协会(LES)中国执行委员,中国电信业投融资国际论坛副秘书长,中华全国律师协会信息网络与高新技术专业委员会执行委员,中华全国律师协会国际业务专业委员会委员。

Zou Zhendong, Senior Partner of Sinowing Law LLP, graduated from Renmin University of China with a bachelor's degree in international politics and international economics. He has been elected jointly by The Lord Chancellor's Office of UK and the Ministry of Justice of PRC to work at Bird & Bird and Brick Court Chambers in London for a year. He is the Deputy Secretary General of TeleChina Investment Forum, executive member of High-Tech and Ecommerce Committee of ACLA, member of Cross-Border Investment Committee of Beijing Lawyer Association, PRC executive member of LES and AIPPI.

律所介绍 / Introduction to Law Firms

山东海允律师事务所

山东海允律师事务所是一家专业从事海事海商、保险、国际贸易及投资等涉外业务的律师事务所，长期为国际船东保赔协会、保险、航运、贸易等领域的中外客户提供切实有效的法律服务。

该所多名合伙人及律师具有国外留学、培训及工作经历，具有国际视野，能够很好地理解客户需求。

该所奉行客户利益至上的服务理念，以卓越服务实现法律服务价值最大化，协助客户实现商业目标，赢得了客户的广泛信任与好评。

Hihonor Law Firm is specializing in providing legal services in dry shipping and admiralty, in insurance, international trade and cross boarder investment. We have been retained as service provider by leading P&I Clubs, insurance, shipping and trade companies both home and abroad.

HiHonor lawyers have sound educational background, some lawyers have overseas studying, training and working experiences, which enabled our better communication and understanding the needs of clients.

Upholding the honor of our clients, Hihonor are dedicated to provide clients with best available legal services and commercial-minded practical solution on cost-effective basis.

律师介绍 / Introduction to Lawyers

赵新伟

山东海允律师事务所主任，一级律师。华东政法学院法学学士、英国南安普敦大学海商法硕士。中华全国律师协会海事海商专业委员会委员，伦敦海事仲裁员协会（LMAA）支持会员，韩国商事仲裁院（KCAB）仲裁员。入选中华全国律师协会"涉外律师领军人才"库，于2014年、2016年被选派西班牙、欧盟总部及美国参加海外投资并购等培训项目。

Zhao Xinwei, Managing Partner of HiHonor Law Firm. LL.B from ECUPL Shanghai, LL.M from University of Southampton UK. Committee Member of the Maritime Law Committee of All China Lawyers' Association (ACLA); Supporting Member of London Maritime Arbitrators' Association (LMAA), Arbitrator of Korea Commercial Arbitration Board (KCAB). In 2014 being selected by ACLA, attended Elite PRC Lawyers' Overseas Training Course in Spain and Brussels on cross-border investment and European law; In 2016 being selected by ACLA, attended the Elite PRC Lawyers' Training Course in USA on foreign investment etc. US law.

意大利——撰稿人介绍 / Italy—Introduction to Authors

律所介绍 / Introduction to Law Firms

凯明迪律师事务所

深厚的法律知识功底和国际视野是凯明迪律师事务所一直以来的突出特色。该所由帕斯卡尔·齐奥门蒂律师事务所（Pasquale Chiomenti）于1948年创建，一直以其在服务企业、机构方面的独立性和法律专长闻名。

凯明迪律师事务所拥有一支由多专业背景人士组成的律师团队，致力于确保企业、机构在遵循法律的前提下实现其最复杂的目标。该所300名专业人士的共同目标是：勤奋工作、追求卓越，这也是凯明迪律师事务所设立以来的特色。这些原则和创新、建设性的途径使得凯明迪律师事务所可以向客户提供综合、多专业的意见，协助客户全面理解影响其商业决定的法律建议，抓住商机。

该所的专业特长、敬业程度体现在其所服务的多种交易中，特别是在曾服务过的企业、机构的成长和市场定位方面。

该所的客户包括意大利和国外工业、银行、保险和金融行业的领军企业。该所是意大利主要公共机构、外国政府、公共机构、国际组织的长期顾问。

Deep knowledge of the law and an international outlook have always been Chiomenti Studio Legale's ("Chiomenti") distinctive characteristics. From 1948, the year in which Pasquale Chiomenti founded the Firm, Chiomenti has always known how deploy its independence and legal expertise in the service of businesses and institutions.

Chiomenti has always worked to ensure that businesses and institutions achieve their most complex objectives in compliance with the applicable law thanks to a team of professionals organized to make the most of a multiplicity of skills. 300 professionals with one common objective: hard work and dedication to achieving excellence, which have characterised our Firm since its outset. These principles, together with our innovative and constructive approach, allow us to provide our clients with integrated and multidisciplinary advice, helping them seize opportunities through a complete understanding of the myriad legal complexities that affect their business decisions.

Our professionals' excellence and level of commitment is demonstrated in the types of transactions on which we have worked and in the contribution that we have made to the growth and market positioning of the businesses and institutions we have assisted.

Chiomenti's clients include leading Italian and foreign industrial, banking, insurance and financial groups. Chiomenti has always been an adviser to the key Italian public institutions, to foreign governments and public authorities, and to international organisations.

律师介绍 / Introduction to Lawyers

Sara Marchetta

Sara Marchetta 1998 年毕业于北京大学商法专业，2002 年毕业于意大利帕尔玛大学法律专业。她的主要职业领域包括公司、跨境并购、技术转让及外商直接投资。她拥有近 20 年的法律实务经验，特别是在以下方面：协助意大利客户在中国进行投资（涉及能源、机械、零售及餐饮等），以及协助中国国有企业和私营企业在并购及合同相关问题上与意大利公司进行交涉（涉及能源分布、餐饮、机械、零部件及健康医疗等）。她的工作语言包括意大利语（母语）、英语（流利）和中文（流利）。

Sara Marchetta 还是中国欧盟商会的董事会及监事会成员。

Sara Marchetta, Chief Representative of Chiomenti Studio Legale Beijing Representative Office. Ms. Marchetta graduated from Peking University with the diploma in Business Law in 1998 and University of Parma with the degree in Italian Law in 2002. Her main areas of expertise include Corporate, Cross Border Acquisitions, Technology Transfers and Foreign Direct Investment. She has almost 20 years of experiences in law, especially in assisting Italian clients in their investments into the PRC (energy, machinery, retail, food and beverage) and Chinese SOEs and private companies in acquisitions and contracts with Italian Companies (energy distribution, food and beverage, machinery, components and healthcare). Ms. Marchetta's working languages include Italian (mother tongue), English(fluent) and Mandarin Chinese(fluent).

Ms. Marchetta also serve as Member of ExCo in the EU- China Chamber of Commerce.

意大利——翻译及协调人介绍 / Italy—Introduction to Translators and Cooperators

律所介绍 / Introduction to Law Firms

湖南人和律师事务所

湖南人和律师事务所成立于 1989 年，是一家兼具本土智慧和国际视野的综合性专业法律服务机构。历经近 30 载，该所因其高水准的服务和较强的社会责任感，已经发展成为湖南省规模领先的律师事务所之一。该所的法律服务领域涵盖房地产、金融、公司、知识产权、国际投资等众多业务领域。该所总部设在长沙，在北京、上海、深圳、珠海、中国香港特别行政区、吉隆坡等设有分所、联营所或办事处。

该所律师经验丰富，具有出色的能力和较高效率，具备法律、金融、建筑工程和税务方面的专业经验，从而能为国内外客户提供专业、全方位的法律支持。该所目前具有执业律师及其他专业人员约 300 名。作为一家有声望的律所，该所为全球客户提供多语言的法律服务。

Hunan Renhe Law Firm, founded in 1989, and provides comprehensive professional legal service with both local experiences and international perspective. After nearly 30 years, Renhe has become one of the largest and leading law firms in Hunan Province because of its top-level service and extraordinary social responsibility. Renhe offers a diverse range of sophisticated legal services including but not limited real estate, finance, corporate, Intellectual Property, international investment. Renhe sets its head office in Changsha and has branch offices in Beijing, Shanghai, Shenzhen, Zhuhai, Hong Kong, Kuala Lumpur and other cities.

Renhe is comprised of well-experienced, highly competent and efficient professionals with experiences in law, finance, construction and tax, and provides professional and comprehensive legal support for clients from domestic and overseas. Renhe currently has about 300 licensed lawyers and other professional staff in total. Most of Renhe Lawyers graduated from famous law schools in China and abroad. As a reputable law firm, Renhe provides its clients with multi language legal services throughout the world.

律师介绍 / Introduction to Lawyers

金笑

湖南人和律师事务所合伙人。

金笑律师2003年毕业于瑞典斯德哥尔摩大学，获法律与信息技术专业法学硕士。她的执业领域主要专注于知识产权，包括商标、知识产权的尽职调查、授权、技术转让和与知识产权有关的交易和跨境投资。她在版权、商标、不正当竞争的侵权诉讼方面有着丰富的经验，并曾代理过一些在中国有影响力的案件，例如中国第一例电视节目模仿案件。金笑律师还协助客户制定知识产权战略。金笑律师在与互联网有关的知识产权和境外知识产权保护方面是一个活跃的研究者。金笑律师是中华全国律师协会"中国涉外律师领军人才"和"青年律师领军人才"。

金笑律师在涉外知识产权、境外直接投资、国际贸易领域也有着丰富的经验，曾在跨境投资和技术引进项目中为一些中国大型企业提供服务。金笑律师是国内为数不多的具有国际仲裁出庭经验的律师。她还担任着几家仲裁机构及中国国际贸易促进委员会的仲裁员和调解员。

Jin Xiao, senior partner of Hunan Renhe Law Firm.

Ms. Jin holds a Master degree (Stockholm University, Sweden 2003) in Law & IT. Her main areas of expertise include Intellectual Property, involving trade mark prosecution, IP due diligence, licensing, technology transfer, IP-related business transactions and cross border investments. She has extensive experiences in copyright, trade mark, unfair competition infringement litigation, and she has handled some influential IP cases in China, such as the first television program imitation case in China. Ms. Jin advises clients on IP strategies. Ms. Jin has been an active speaker on intellectual property law related to Internet and cross-border IP protection for Chinese Companies. Ms. Jin has received numerous important honors, including "Leading Talents in Foreign-Related Lawyers" and "Leading Talents in Young Lawyers" honored by All China Lawyers Association.

Ms. Jin has extensive experience in cross-border IP, international trade, and international arbitration. She also helps quite a few large Chinese enterprises in cross border investments and technological acquisition projects. Ms. Jin is one of the few Chinese lawyers who have represented clients before international arbitration tribunal as co-counsel. Ms. Jin also serve as arbitrator and mediator in several arbitration commissions and China Council for the Promotion of International Trade.

律所介绍 / Introduction to Law Firms

北京德和衡律师事务所

北京德和衡律师事务所是1993年创立的中国早期合伙制律师事务所德衡律师集团在北京创建的总部机构。自成立以来，该所秉持"专业、专心、专才、专注"的服务理念，以客户需求为核心，坚持专业分工和团队协作，依托先进的管理经验，已发展成为中国具有规模性的综合商务型律师事务所。

该所在中国多省以及多个国家的数十家机构拥有千余名执业律师。该所律师均拥有国内外知名院校专业教育背景及执业培训经历；此外，多名律师同时具有外国律师执业资格以及注册会计师、税务师、经济师、专利代理人等专业资格，助力客户应对日益复杂的商业挑战。

该所致力于作为品牌律师事务所，用精英律师，以国际化视野，发挥本地优势，为国内外客户提供专业、优质、高效的全方位商事法律服务。

Beijing DHH Law Firm is the Headquarter of Deheng Law Group founded in 1993 as one of China's first partnership law firms. Since its founding, DHH has been adhering to the service concepts of Professionalism, Concentration, Specialization and Dedication, serving the clients' business needs with expertise and teamwork. Relying on its advanced management experience, DHH has now become one of the leading full-service business law firms in China.

DHH has over 1,000 lawyers working from over 50 offices covering every major province and region in China as well as major countries around the world. DHH's strong team of elite lawyers have received education and professional training from reputable domestic and overseas law schools, and some are also certificated public accountants, tax agents, public economists and patent agents, which enables the firm to assist clients in coping with the increasingly complicated business challenges.

As a leading law firm with professional lawyers with international perspectives and local advantages, DHH is committed to providing high-quality, efficient and effective business legal services for its clients both at home and abroad.

律师介绍 / Introduction to Lawyers

姚远

姚远律师，北京德和衡律师事务所高级合伙人。

作为国际业务团队的负责人之一，姚远律师在外商投资、公司收购及兼并、股权私募投资、企业境外上市等方面拥有超过10年的工作经验，为众多领先的外国公司在中国的经营业务和投资项目提供法律服务，涉及汽车、医药医疗生产、机械制造、天然气、石油、化工、酒店管理、互联网、咨询和媒体等多个行业。

姚远律师曾代理外企在中国进行并购、外商直接投资，协助客户进行战略规划和谈判；代表中国公司在海外建立实体、建设设施，并协助他们进行金融和并购业务。此外，姚远律师还曾代表外国公司解决国际贸易和投资争端，特别是参与中国多家仲裁机构管辖的涉外仲裁。姚远律师在处理复杂商事纠纷方面具有丰富的经验，尤其擅长处理因股权、资产收购合同、合资合同、国际贸易合同等引起的跨境争议。

Yao Yuan, senior partner of Beijing DHH Law Firm.

As one of leaders of DHH International Practice, Mr. Yao has ten years of experience in foreign investment, M&A transactions, private equity investment and overseas listing. He advised many leading companies in a number of industries and sectors, including Automobile, Medicine and Medical Equipment Production, Machinery Manufacture, Gas and Oil, Chemical, Hotel Management, IT and Consulting and Media.

Mr. Yao has represented foreign companies for M&A and FDI in PRC and participated in strategic planning and negotiations of the projects. He has also represented Chinese leading companies to form offshore entities, build facilities and engage in their finance and M&A projects. Additionally, he has represented his foreign clients in cross-bounder disputes resolution with a particular focus on foreign-related arbitration seated in numerous arbitration organizations in PRC. He has extensive experience in dealing with complex commercial disputes, with an expertise on disputes arising out of joint venture agreement, international trade contracts, M&A and equity transfer.

日本——撰稿人介绍 / Japan—Introduction to Authors

律所介绍 / Introduction to Law Firms

安德森·毛利·友常律师事务所

安德森·毛利·友常律师事务所是由自1950年代初期即作为日本的国际性律师事务所开拓者的安德森·毛利律师事务所与在国际金融交易及跨境投资案件领域拥有众多实绩的友常木村律师事务所合并而设立，2015年，在国际破产、业务重组领域等方面具有丰富经验的Bingham·坂井·三村·相泽律师事务所的主要律师也加入本所，形成目前规模的综合律所。该所拥有众多在企业并购、融资、资本市场、业务重组、破产、诉讼和仲裁等专业领域经验丰富的高水准律师。除东京总部外，还在大阪、名古屋、北京、上海、新加坡、胡志明、曼谷、雅加达等地设立了分所及办公地。

Anderson Mori & Tomotsune is a full-service law firm formed by the merger and consolidation of the practices of three leading Japanese law firms: Anderson Mori, which established its reputation as one of the largest and most established international law firms in Japan since its inception in the early 1950s; Tomotsune & Kimura, which is particularly known for its expertise in international finance transactions; and Bingham Sakai Mimura Aizawa, a premier international insolvency/restructuring and crisis-management firm. Their combined expertise enables us to deliver advice on virtually all legal issues that may arise from a corporate transaction, including M&A, finance, capital markets, restructuring/insolvency, and litigation/arbitration. The majority of Their lawyers are multi-lingual and experienced with communicating, drafting and negotiating across borders around the globe. Their main office is in Tokyo. The firm also maintain offices in Osaka, Nagoya, Beijing, Shanghai, Singapore, Ho Chi Minh City, and Bangkok, and operate a Jakarta Desk.

律师介绍 / Introduction to Lawyers

森胁章

安德森·毛利·友常律师事务所合伙人（东京总部）、上海代表处首席代表。同时担任中国人民大学法学院客座教授、庆应义塾大学法学院客座教授、上海国际经济贸易仲裁委员会仲裁员等。

森胁章律师于1995年取得日本律师执业许可，1998年到中国开始处理日本企业对中国投资及中国企业对日本投资的各种法律问题，其专业领域为M&A、反垄断法、通商法、一般企业法务等。

Partner (Tokyo) and Chief Representative of Shanghai Office. In addition to his work at AMT, Akira Moriwaki is a visiting professor at Renmin University of China Law School, an arbitrator at the Shanghai International Economic and Trade

Arbitration Commission (Shanghai International Arbitration Center) and a visiting professor at the Law School of Keio University.

Akira Moriwaki qualified as a Japanese lawyer in 1995. Shortly thereafter in 1998, he skillfully handled a diverse array of complex legal issues encountered by Japanese companies when entering the Chinese market and then by Chinese companies when entering the Japanese market. His practice has focused on M&A, merger control, competition compliance, international competition practice, and corporate governance.

律所介绍 / Introduction to Law Firms

西村朝日律师事务所

西村朝日律师事务所通过与数家一流律师事务所强强联手，逐步成为综合性律师事务所。该所拥有近600名日本律师和外国律师，使得本所成为日本规模最大的律师事务所。作为国际法领域的专家，伴随日本企业采取新的进军海外市场战略，自2010年起该所在亚洲各地开设了办公网点（包括相关事务所），例如北京、上海、香港特别行政区、胡志明、河内、新加坡、仰光、曼谷、雅加达与迪拜。同时，该所与当地实力雄厚的律师事务所建立密切的合作关系，使得该所可以根据当地法律及国情，为客户提供完善的法律服务。

Nishimura & Asahi has evolved into a firm capable of providing a full range of legal services through the integration of several top law firms. Our firm comprises close to 600 Japanese and foreign lawyers, making it the largest firm in Japan. As experts in international law, since 2010 we have opened offices (including affiliate offices) in various cities across Asia, as follows: Beijing, Shanghai, Hong Kong, HCMC, Hanoi, Singapore, Yangon, Bangkok, Jakarta and Dubai, as Japanese corporations have adopted new overseas expansion strategies. At the same time, we have established close affiliations with major law firms overseas, enabling us to provide legal services tailored to the laws and circumstances of those countries.

律师介绍 / Introduction to Lawyers

野村高志

西村朝日律师事务所上海代表处代表（合伙人）。早稻田大学法学部毕业，对外经济贸易大学留学。

1998年，东京辩护士会注册；2001—2014年西村朝日律师事务所、富而德律师事务所；2012—2014年期间为东京理科大学客座教授，研究方向为中国知识产权战略；2014年至今任西村朝日律师事务所上海代表处代表。

专业领域为中国境内外并购、知识产权、合规、诉讼/纠纷等。

Nishimura & Asahi Shanghai Office, Representative/Partner.

1988 Waseda University (LL.B.); 1998 Registered as Japanese Lawyer; 2004 University of International Business and Economics, Beijing; 2001-2014 Nishimura & Asahi, Freshfields Bruckhaus Deringer LLP; 2012-2014 Visiting Professor, Tokyo University of Science Graduate School of Innovation Studies; 2014-Now Representative of Nishimura & Asahi Shanghai Office.

Practice Areas: Cross-border M&A, IP, Compliance, Litigation and ADR, etc.

早川一平

西村朝日律师事务所律师。2008年毕业于庆应义塾大学法学部；2010年毕业于庆应义塾大学法科大学院；2011年，在第二东京辩护士会注册；2013年，北京语言大学（汉语进修课程）毕业；2012年至今，西村朝日律师事务所执业。

专业领域为日本境内一般公司法务、劳动法等，以及中国境内外并购、中国当地法人的公司法务等。

Nishimura & Asahi, Associate; 2008 Keio University (LL.B.); 2010 Keio University Law School (J.D.); 2013 Beijing Language and Culture University (Chinese Course); 2012-Now Nishimura & Asahi.

Practice Areas: General Corporate, Labor Law, M&A involving China.

日本——翻译及协调人介绍 / Japan—Introduction to Translators and Cooperators

律所介绍 / Introduction to Law Firms

北京高文律师事务所

北京高文律师事务所成立于2001年，在中国境内和境外设立有3家分所（上海、大连、合肥），17个办事处，总计拥有200余名律师、专家顾问和律师辅助人员。

该所致力于将专业分工与团队合作密切结合。该所分设知识产权、公司、诉讼仲裁、刑事辩护、海事海商、银行与国际金融、房地产与建设工程、劳动与人力资源等专业部门,保证了高文律师在相关领域的专业化水平。同时,高文还秉承团队化工作模式,根据项目涉及的专业领域整合专家律师团队共同承办,并为客户提供极具专业性和建设性的解决方案。

该所代理了大量的有广泛社会影响的案例,其中多起案件被评为"最高法院十大案例""最高人民法院中国知识产权50典型案例""北京市十大外商知识产权保护案""北京市知识产权十大案例""国家知识产权局专利复审委十大案件"。

Beijing Globe-Law Law Firm was established in 2001. Headquartered in Beijing, Globe-Law now has branches in Shanghai, Dalian, and Hefei, along with its 17 offices worldwide. Globe-Law is now home to nearly 200 experienced lawyers and paralegals.

In providing services to clients, Globe-Law are firmly committed to the principle and spirit of specialization and teamwork. Globe-Law divide our team into several departments, including intellectual property, corporate, litigation and arbitration, criminal defense, maritime, banking and international finance, real estate and construction, labor and human resources, etc. Globe-Law will assign the case to a working team of professionals from various departments, optimizing personnel resources in order to provide the most professional, efficient, and quality legal service to meet our clients' needs.

Globe-Laws lawyers have resoundingly handled a number of cases with enormous social impact, including cases that marked as Top Ten Cases of The Supreme Court of China, 50 Typical Cases of IPR Infringement From The Supreme People's Court of China, Top Ten Cases of IPR Infringement In Beijing, Top Ten Cases of Patent Re-examination Board of SIPO, Top Ten Cases of IPR Infringement for Foreign Investors In Beijing, etc.

律师介绍 / Introduction to Lawyers

朱翊

北京高文律师事务所法学博士,纽约法学院法学博士。进入法律行业前在IT领域有多年工作经验,对电子商务、移动互联网和大数据有较深的研究。

执业领域包括专利、知识产权和公司法业务。

工作语言为中文、英语、日语。

Mr. Zhu Yi, is a Juris Doctor of Globe-Law law firm. He obtained his J.D. degree from New York Law School in the United States. Before entering into his legal career, he used to work in IT industry for many years, and he has great understanding of E-commerce, Mobile Internet and Big-data.

Mr. Zhu Yi mainly practices in patent, intellectual property and corporation laws.

Chinese, English and Japanese are his working languages.

律所介绍 / Introduction to Law Firms

中豪律师事务所

中豪律师事务所系中国领先的综合性一流公司化律师事务所。该所在北京、重庆、上海、成都、贵阳、香港、纽约的CBD中心设有办公室,拥有由50多名合伙人、逾250名执业律师和专业人员组成的精英团队。该所在诸多领域表现卓越,多次荣获"司法部部级文明律师事务所"、中华全国律师协会"全国优秀律师事务所"、ALB"亚洲最具发展潜力的30家律所"、The Lawyer"亚太100强律师事务所""中国精英律所30强"、钱伯斯"全球顶尖律师",以及《商法》杂志评选的"年度卓越律所"等称号。

Zhonghao Law Firm is an international law firm with fully integrated partnership in China. Zhonghao has offices in such metropolis as Beijing, Chongqing, Shanghai, Chengdu, Guiyang, Hong Kong and New York. Zhonghao has an elite team with more than 50 partners and 250 professionals. Zhonghao has been recognized as Civilized Law Firm at Ministerial Level by the Ministry of Justice, World's Top Lawyers by Chambers Global, Outstanding Law Firm of China by ACLA, Top 30 Potential Law Firms in Asia by ALB,Top 100 Law Firm in Asia-Pacific and China Elite Top 30 by The Lawyer,China Business Law Awards by China Business Law Journal.

律师介绍 / Introduction to Lawyers

杨青

杨青,中豪律师事务所合伙人,西南政法大学和英国格拉斯哥大学双法学硕士,香港注册内地律师,英国志奋领学者、中华全国律师协会"中国涉外律师领军人才""全国千名涉外律师人才""青年律师领军人才",执业领域包括海外投融资与并购、外商投资与并购、私募基金等。多年来,杨青代理过诸多重大跨境投资融资与并购项目，如为金科控股集团、博赛集团、华宇地产集团、安徽新华传媒、上海乾立基金等在海外的投资与收购，以及麦当劳、住友、巴斯夫、霍尼韦尔、拉法基、沃尔玛等在中国的投资与收购提供全程法律服务。

Eagle Yang, is a partner of Zhonghao law firm, graduated from SWUPL and University of Glasgow has been granted double LLMs. Eagle Yang is Hong Kong Registered Mainland Chinese Lawyer a Chevening Scholar sponsored by the British Foreign and Commonwealth Office, the Leading Chinese Lawyer Dealing with Cross-border Legal Affairs, the Leading One Thousand Chinese Lawyer Dealiing with Foreign Related Affairs and Leading Chinese Young Lawyer. He has been practicing in such sectors as Foreign Direct Investment, Cross-border Investment and Financing, M&A and PE. Over years, Eagle Yang has dealt with many cross-board transactions, for example, overseas investment and M&A by Jinke Holding Group, Bosai Mining Group, Huayu Real Estate Group, as well as foreign direct investment and M&A by MacDonald, Sumitomo, Honeywell, BASF, Lafarge, Wal-Mart, etc.

肯尼亚——撰稿人介绍 / Kenya—Introduction to Authors

律所介绍 / Introduction to Law Firms

Hamilton Harrison & Mathews 律师事务所

Hamilton Harrison & Mathews 律师事务所是肯尼亚法律行业的市场领导者。该所有116年源远流长的历史。该所由10名合伙人、33名执业律师以及80多名辅助人员组成，其中辅助人员包括法律助理、实习生、法律秘书和行政人员。

该所通过其积累的在各个国家、区域管辖范围内被公认为是顶尖律师的人脉资源，为在东非地区的跨境交易提供咨询服务。该所还与在英国、欧洲、美洲和亚洲的一些国际律师事务所建立了稳定的合作关系。

该所有一个专门的公司商事和房地产部门以及一个诉讼部门，这些部门在处理各种领域的复杂问题方面有丰富的经验。其中，商事部门由金融、公司商事、私有化、项目、房地产和规划、知识产权和公私合作领域的顶尖专家组成；诉讼部门在处理各法院和各个特殊法庭的事务上均有丰富的专业知识。

凭借其丰富的历史，该所拥有对肯尼亚商业环境深入而独到的认识，能够为客户提供有关各种法律事务的全面解决方案。

该所有着来自各行各业的丰富的客户群体。他们包括：跨国公司、肯尼亚政府、本地和外国银行和金融机构、外国投资者及其肯尼亚子公司和分支机构、石油、天然气和能源公司、运输和物流公司、通信和ICT（信息、通信和技术）公司、保险公司、外国使馆和特派团以及非政府组织和国际援助组织。

Hamilton Harrison & Mathews (HH&M) is a market leader in the legal industry in Kenya. The firm has a long history of excellence in the legal market spanning 116 years. The firm comprises of 10 partners and 33 qualified lawyers and over 80 support staff including legal assistants, pupils, para-legal, legal secretaries and administration staff.

The firm provides advice in cross border transactions in the East African region through our network of firms who are also recognised leaders in their respective jurisdictions. We also have strong relationships with international law firms in the U.K, Europe, Americas and Asia.

The firm has a dedicated Corporate Commercial and Real Estate department and a Litigation department with significant experience in handling complex matters across an array of areas. The Commercial department comprises of leading experts in all areas of finance, corporate commercial, privatisation, projects, real estate and planning, intellectual property and public private partnerships. The Litigation department has built a wealth of expertise having handled matters in all our courts and various specialised tribunals.

Drawing from its rich history, HH&M has the unique quality of an in-depth understanding of the Kenyan business environment and is able to provide holistic solutions to clients on a broad spectrum of legal matters.

The firms' client base is equally rich and diverse cutting across all sectors. They include: Multinational companies, the Government of Kenya, local and foreign banks and financial institutions, foreign investors and their Kenyan subsidiaries and branches, oil, gas and energy companies, transport and logistic companies, communication and ICT companies, insurance companies, foreign embassies and missions and non-governmental and international aid organisations.

律师介绍 / Introduction to Lawyers

Adil Khawaja

Adil Khawaja 是 Hamilton Harrison & Mathews 律师事务所执行合伙人，他在房地产、环境和规划法、商业诉讼和仲裁方面有着23年的经验和深入的认识。他是肯尼亚在房地产、项目开发、规划和环境法方面知名的律师之一。他在肯尼亚处理过许多复杂的土地问题，并为银行提供了许多复杂的公司重整、变现和债务整理方案。他被 IFLR 1000、Legal 500 和《钱伯斯全球法律指南》评为顶尖律师。

Adil Khawaja the Managing Partner of the Firm has 23 years' experience and in-depth knowledge in real estate, environmental and planning law, commercial litigation and arbitration. He is one of the most renowned lawyers in Kenya with respect to real estate, project development, planning and environmental law. He has dealt with complicated land issues in Kenya and undertaken many complex company restructurings, realizations and schemes of arrangement for banks. He is recognised as a leading lawyer by IFLR 1000, Legal 500, and Chambers Global (all internationally recognized legal directories).

Sigee Koech

Sigee Koech 是 Hamilton Harrison & Mathews 律师事务所合伙人，她在公司法和商法领域拥有丰富的经验。她擅长银行金融、房地产和一般的公司商事法律事务。她处理过大量的银行和金融领域方面的境内和跨境交易。她目前专注于多个肯尼亚的基础设施项目，并担任相关项目融资交易的首席法律顾问。

Sigee Koech, a partner in the Firm has significant experience in corporate and commercial law. She specialises in banking and finance, real estate and general corporate commercial law. She has dealt with a number of local and cross-border transactions in the area of banking and finance. She is currently lead advisor on several project finance transactions focusing on infrastructure projects in Kenya.

律所介绍 / Introduction to Law Firms

TripleOKLaw 律师事务所

TripleOKLaw 律师事务所是一家在肯尼亚注册的有限合伙律所，提供顶尖且全方位的法律服务。该所拥有六十多名员工，其中有 8 名合伙人、超过 20 名的专职律师，以及一些法律助理和辅助人员。

该所是 Meritas Worldwide 的成员，Meritas Worldwide 是由众多的有着全方位经营业务的独立的律所组成的全球性的联盟，该联盟的律师事务所成员遍布七十多个国家，该联盟遍布全球 7 个地区，这使该所能够自信地处理各种跨国法律事务，因为该所是这个联盟的成员，而这个联盟具有积极的商业磋商方法和为优秀成员提供服务的普遍性承诺。法律、法规在全球司法管辖下可能是复杂而多样的，但作为 Meritas 的成员，该所能够有效地为客户提供具有连贯性的和世界一流水平的服务。

TripleOKLaw Advocates LLP is registered as a Limited Liability Partnership and a leading full service Kenyan law firm. The firm has a staff of over 60 personnel comprised of 8 partners and over 20 Associates who are assisted by a pool of legal assistants and support staff.

The firm are members of Meritas Worldwide, an established global alliance of independent full-service law firms with a geographical presence across over 70 countries. The alliance is found in seven global regions namely Africa, Asia, Australia, New Zealand, Canada, Europe, Latin America and the Caribbean and the United States of America. This enables us to navigate transnational legal issues with confidence as the firm are part of an alliance that has a positive, consultative approach to business and a common commitment to excellent client service. The rule of law may be complex and diverse across global jurisdictions but as a member firm of Meritas the firm are able to ofer consistency and world class quality that our clients need to conduct business eficiently.

律师介绍 / Introduction to Lawyers

John Ohaga

John Ohaga 擅长争议解决，特别是在商业领域方面。John 在民事诉讼的其他方面也有相当丰富的经验，包括劳动纠纷、租赁纠纷、公共采购和保健法。因为在争议解决方面高质量的工作和专业的知识，John 获得 Legal 500、Chambers Global 和 Best Lawyers 的认可。John 被 International Law Office（ILO）授予 2010 年、2016 年和 2017 年肯尼亚在诉讼类别的客户选择奖。

John 是肯尼亚替代性争议解决委员会法律协会的发起人。John 是英国特许仲裁委员会的资深会员，也是特许仲裁委员会（肯尼亚分会）理事，是一位有着丰富经验的仲裁员，被 Chambers Global 评为肯尼亚顶尖仲裁员之一。John 是 2013 年第 26 号文件公布的内罗毕国际仲裁法中心的董事会成员。他还是一名调解员，是依据《民事诉讼法》第 59A 章设立的调解委员会的成员。他还是 2013 年依据《体育法》成立的体育纠纷法庭的主席，并担任广告标准委员会上诉委员会的主席。

John Ohaga has a passion for dispute resolution, particularly in the commercial sphere. He also has considerable experience in other aspects of civil litigation including employment and labour disputes, landlord and tenant, public procurement and constitutional law. He has been recognized for his high-quality work and expertise in dispute resolution by Legal 500, Chambers Global and Best Lawyers. John was declared the 2010, 2016 and 2017 winner for Kenya in the category of litigation by the International Law Office (ILO) Client Choice Awards.

John is the Convener of the Law Society of Kenya's Committee on Alternative Dispute Resolution. He is a Fellow of the

Chartered Institute of Arbitrators as well as a Trustee of the Chartered Institute of Arbitrators (Kenya Branch). He is an experienced arbitrator and is recognized by Chambers Global as one of the leading arbitrators in Kenya. He sits on the board of the Nairobi Centre for International Arbitration established under the Nairobi Centre for International Arbitration Act, No. 26 of 2013. He is also a Certified Mediator and is a member of the Mediation Accreditation Committee established under the Section 59A of the Civil Procedure Act. He is also the Chairman of the Sports Disputes Tribunal which is established under the Sports Act, 2013 and also chairs the Appeals Committee of the Advertising Standards Board.

Franklin Cheluget

Franklin Cheluget 是 TripleOKLaw 律师事务所的公司争端解决部门的合伙人。他以这种身份参与了多种争议解决的庭审。他具有处理商事、环境与土地、民事、劳动关系等方面诉讼案件的经验。他也处理过房地产管理与继承、体育法、退休福利法以及采购法等方面的诉讼事务。他还参与过庭外和解的谈判。

Franklin 是肯尼亚司法部门认可的调解员。他以法院授权的调解员身份加入了法院的劳动关系、民事、商事和家庭部门调解员名录，还与私人企业和个人进行调解。

他在人权、体育法、经济法、商法、肯尼亚调解法律和实践、投资法、刑法以及新兴法律领域撰写和出版了大量的文章。Franklin 是一位后起之秀。

Franklin Cheluget is an Associate in the Dispute Resolution Department of the Firm of TripleOKlaw LLP. In this capacity he is involved in diverse dispute resolution fora. Specifically, he litigates matters in the Commercial, Environment & Land, Civil, Employment & Labor relations courts and tribunals. He also litigates matters in the fields of Commercial Law, Estate Administration and Succession, Sports Law, law relating to retirement benefits as well as procurement law. He also negotiates out of court settlements.

Franklin is a Certified and Accredited Mediator by the Judiciary in Kenya. He is enrolled on the panel of mediators of the Employment and Labor Relations, Civil, Commercial and Family divisions of the court as a Court Mandated Mediator. He also conducts mediations for private corporates as well as individual parties.

He has written and published extensively in the areas of Human Rights, Sports Law, Economic law, Commercial Law, Mediation law and practice in Kenya, Investment Law, Criminal Law as well as emerging areas of law. Franklin is a rising star.

肯尼亚——翻译及协调人介绍 / Kenya—Introduction to Translators and Cooperators

律所介绍 / Introduction to Law Firms

大成（哈尔滨）律师事务所

大成律师事务所成立于 1992 年，在中国 42 个城市设有分所，是中国规模最大的综合性律师事务所。2015 年，大成律师事务所和 Dentons 律师事务所正式合并。合并后，该所拥有逾 8 000 名律师，服务于五十多个国家，业务遍及美洲、欧洲、非洲及整个亚太地区；已建立了覆盖全国、遍布世界重要城市的全球法律服务网络，其境内外机构及各地客户均可共享该所全球化法律服务网络内的项目信息、专业知识、业务经验、专业人才、社会关系等资源。该所现已建立了先进的管理体制，依赖专业化团队为国内外客户及时提供专业、全面、务实的法律及商务解决方案。大成（哈尔滨）律师事务所在东北亚、俄罗斯业务中享有优势。它与大成律师事务所其他分支机构共同致力于使大成律师事务所成为品牌化、国际化的律师事务所。

Founded in 1992, Dacheng Law Offices is the largest partnership law firms in China, with branch offices in 42 cities. In 2015, Dacheng Law Offices and Dentons Law Offices officially merged. Now Dacheng has over 8000 lawyers and have presence in over 50 countries, covering Canada, the USA, Europe, Central East, Africa and Asia-Pacific Areas. Dacheng Dentons has established a global legal service network across the nation and worldwide. Dacheng Dentons' offices and clients from all over the world can share project information, professional knowledge, business experience, professional talents and other resources through its global legal service network. Dacheng Dentons has established advanced management system and relies on teamwork and cooperation to provide professional, all-round and pragmatic legal and commercial solutions. Dacheng Dentons Harbin Office enjoys advantages in providing legal service in North-eastern Asia and Russia. Its legal professionals are committed to building Dacheng Dentons into one of the world's most sought-after law firms.

律师介绍 / Introduction to Lawyers

蒙启红

蒙启红律师在中国政法大学取得法学学士学位，在芬兰赫尔辛基大学法学院取得法律硕士学位（商法和合同法方向）。她目前是哈尔滨商业大学法学院副教授，大成（哈尔滨）律师事务所执业律师。蒙启红律师在商事领域为客户提供广泛的法律服务，担任多家外资企业的法律顾问。

2013至2014年间，她在美国哥伦比亚大学法学院做访问学者、公益法研究所研究员。在此期间，她在纽约法律援助中心工作3个月。

蒙启红律师入选中华全国律师协会"涉外律师领军人才库"，并参加了中华全国律师协会主办的西班牙和美国的培训项目，是中国法学会世界贸易组织法研究会理事、黑龙江省法学会经济法研究会副会长、哈尔滨市仲裁委员会仲裁员。

Qihong Meng graduated from China University of Political Science and Law with an LL.B and the Faculty of Law of the University of Helsinki with an LL.M (contract and commercial law). She is now an associate professor at the Law School of Harbin University of Commerce, and a practicing attorney at Dacheng Dentons Harbin Office. Qihong is experienced in advising clients in a wide variety of commercial law matters. She has also counseled joint-ventures.

Qihong was a visiting scholar to Columbia Law School and a PILnet (Global Network for Public Interest Law) fellow from 2013 to 2014. She also has worked as an intern at New York Legal Aid Society for three months during her stay in NY.

Qihong participated China International Legal Professionals Association's training program (Spain and U.S.). She is a director of WTO Studies of China Law Society, the vice chair of Heilongjiang Economic Law Research Society. She serves as an arbitrator at Harbin Arbitration Tribunal.

律所介绍 / Introduction to Law Firms

隆安律师事务所

隆安律师事务所成立于1992年，总所位于北京，是中国较早的合伙制律师事务所之一，并于2017年成功改制为特殊普通合伙律师事务所。经过25年的发展，该所已有执业律师八百余名、合伙人二百余名，在上海、深圳、广州等20个城市设有分所，在美国和欧洲拥有战略合作伙伴。

隆安律师事务所曾为世界500强等大中型企业提供知识产权、资本市场及金融、公司项目、诉讼和仲裁等领域的法律服务。该所多次被全国律师管理机构评为中国优秀的律师事务所之一，成功入围《亚洲法律杂志》多项年度法律大奖，入选"中国十佳成长律所"，在"亚洲最大50家律所"及"中国律所30强"榜单中均位列前十，亦在英国《律师》杂志"亚太地区100强律师事务所"榜单及"中国国内律所30强"榜单中位居前列。

Established in 1992 and headquartered in Beijing, Longan Law Firm is one of the earliest privately owned law firms in China, and has been restructured into a firm in limited liability partnership in 2017. Longan has been looking to provide extraordinary, effective legal services to our clients, with diligence and integrity. After 25 years' development, Longan has grown into a large law firm with over 800 practicing lawyers and over 200 partners, with offices covering 20 cities including Shanghai, Shenzhen and Guangzhou, and has established strategic cooperation with large and renowned law firms throughout America and Europe. Longan, in the wave of globalisation, is going from strength to strength. Many lawyers in Longan have graduated from prestigious domestic and foreign law schools with progressives and extensiveexperience. Some of them hold multiple certifies qualifying them to practice in China and other countries after years of legal practices in America, United Kingdom, and Japan.

In the past 25 years, Longan provided professional and premium legal services for numerous medium and large enterprises including those listed in the Fortune Global 500 in multiple fields including but not limited to intellectual property rights, capital market and finance, corporation projects, litigation and arbitration. Longan's overall strength won and evidenced by various awards and credentials. For many times, Longan has been rated as one of the most outstanding law firms by national lawyers administrative organisations, shortlisted in several annual legal awards of Asian Legal Business (ALB), ranked in ALB China Fast 10, and ranked top 10 in both the ALB Top 50 largest Asian Law Firms and ALB China Top 30 Law Firms. In addition, Longan has also ranked among the best in Top 100 Law Firms in Asian-Pacific Area and Top 30 Elite Law Firms in China by the Lawyer Magazine of Britain.

律师介绍 / Introduction to Lawyers

贾红卫

北京市隆安（深圳）律师事务所主任、创始合伙人，北京大学法学学士、北京大学国际经济学硕士、美利坚大学华盛顿法学院国际商法硕士，"中国涉外律师领军人才"三、四期（英国班）班长。现为广东省律师协会常任理事、港澳台和外事工作委员会主任、深圳市人大常委会法律助理、深圳国际仲裁院等机构的仲裁员。

执业领域为:跨境争议解决、兼并收购、合同法、公司法、企业清算。

Managing Partner of Longan Law Firm Shenzhen Office, obtained his LLB from Peking University Law School, Master Degree of Economics from Peking University Business School and LLM from American University Washington College of Law. He is the monitors of Class III and Class IV (UK) Training Programs for China Leading International Lawyers. He is the standing director of Guangdong Lawyers Association, in charge of the Committee of Foreign Affairs, as well as the arbitrator of Shenzhen Court of International Arbitration and Nanjing Arbitration Commission.

Practice area: cross border dispute resolutions, M&A, contract, company and liquidation.

韩国——撰稿人介绍 / Republic of Korea—Introduction to Authors

律所介绍 / Introduction to Law Firms

金·张律师事务所

金·张律师事务所是韩国规模最大、专业化程度最高的国际性律师事务所。自1973年起,该所向世界一流企业和金融机构提供服务。该所是位于首尔的提供全领域服务的律师事务所,专业人员有1 400多名,包括韩国、中国、美国和欧洲律师、税务师、专利与商标代理人、会计师及其他行业的专家。

该所对客户的坚定承诺在独特的团队合作和"一站式"服务中体现。该所通过合理组建专家团队,充分发挥律所人才多方面的知识技能和丰富的经验为客户服务。该所也利用较强的专业经验、在各行业中的丰富知识和前沿性洞察力,来帮助客户成功应对当今急速变化和发展的环境并解决他们所面临的复杂商业挑战。

金·张律师事务所在出色的客户服务方面一直受到认可。该所最近获得过的一些奖项包括:《亚洲法律杂志》(2017)评选的"年度亚太律所"和 IFLR Asia(2017)评选的"韩国年度律师事务所";该所同时也在 Chambers Asia-Pacific(2018)、Legal 500(2018)和 IFLR 1000(2018)的所有领域中获得一等排名。

Kim & Chang is Korea's largest and most specialized law firm with a premier global practice. Since 1973, we have advised the world's leading companies and financial institutions. Based in Seoul, the firm are a full service law firm with over 1,400 dedicated professionals, including Korean, Chinese, US, and European-licensed lawyers, tax lawyers, patent and trademark attorneys, accountants, and other subject matter and industry experts.

The firm's steadfast commitment to our clients is reflected in Kim & Chang's unique team-oriented and "one-stop" legal service approach. The firm leverage the multifaceted expertise and broad experience of our talent, bringing together the right mix of professionals for each client. The firm leverage The firm's strong specialized practice area experience, The firm's deep industry group expertise and forward industry insight to help our clients successfully navigate through today's dynamic and fast-changing environment to solve their most complex business challenges.

Kim & Chang has been consistently recognized for our outstanding client work. Some recent awards and recognitions for our commitment to excellence include, "Asia-Pacific Firm of the Year" from Asialaw (2017) and "National Law Firm of the Year for Korea" from IFLR Asia (2017). Kim & Chang also received top rankings in all practices by Chambers Asia-Pacific (2018), Legal 500 (2018), and IFLR 1000 (2018).

律师介绍 / Introduction to Lawyers

殷炫浩

殷炫浩律师是金·张律师事务所合伙人,执业领域涉及公司法的各个方面,主要提供和企业并购、私募股权、风险投资和合资、娱乐、体育和休闲、公司治理、外商直接投资、破产和重组相关的法律服务。

殷炫浩律师1991年毕业于首尔大学法学院并获得法学学士学位,2003年于纽约大学法学院取得法学硕士学位。1994年至1995年在韩国大法院司法研修院进行研修。殷律师具有韩国律师资格。

Hyun-Ho Eun is a partner at Kim & Chang practicing in a wide range of corporate areas, with a focus on mergers and acquisitions, private equity, venture capital and joint venture, entertainment, sports and leisure, corporate governance, foreign direct investment, and insolvency and restructuring.

Mr. Eun received an LL.M. from the New York University, School of Law in 2003, and his LL.B. from the Seoul National University College of Law in 1991. He attended the Judicial Research and Training Institute of the Supreme Court of Korea in 1994 and 1995. He is admitted to the Korea bar.

John Sangho Park

John Sangho Park 是金·张律师事务所的资深外国律师，主要业务领域为项目投资与能源，在跨境并购、合资公司、项目融资、能源（油气）和资源项目开发及相关争议解决方面具有十分丰富的经验。

John 于 2002 年从悉尼大学取得法学学士学位，后于 2003 年取得法学硕士学位。他同时也是新南威尔士大法院和澳洲高等法院的法务官 / 出庭律师。

John Sangho Park is a senior foreign attorney at Kim & Chang specializing in projects and energy with extensive experience in cross-border mergers and acquisitions, joint ventures, project financing, development of various energy (oil & gas) and resources projects, and related disputes.

John received an LL.B. from the University of Sydney in 2002 and Graduate Diploma in Law from the College of Law in 2003. He is admitted as a solicitor/barrister of the Supreme Court of New South Wales and the High Court of Australia.

韩国——翻译及协调人介绍 / Republic of Korea—Introduction to Translators and Cooperators

律所介绍 / Introduction to Law Firms

北京高文律师事务所

北京高文律师事务所成立于 2001 年，在中国境内和境外设立有 3 家分所（上海、大连、合肥）、17 个办事处，总计拥有 200 余名律师、专家顾问和律师辅助人员。

该所致力于将专业分工与团队合作紧密结合。该所分设知识产权、公司、诉讼仲裁、刑事辩护、海事海商、银行与国际金融、房地产与建设工程、劳动与人力资源等专业部门，保证了高文律师在相关领域的专业化水平。同时，高文还秉承团队化工作模式，根据项目涉及的专业领域整合专家律师团队共同承办，并为客户提供极具专业性和建设性的解决方案。

该所代理了大量的有广泛社会影响的案例，其中多起案件被评为"最高法院十大案例""最高人民法院中国知识产权 50 典型案例""北京市十大外商知识产权保护案""北京市知识产权十大案例""国家知识产权局专利复审委十大案件"。

Beijing Globe-Law Law Firm was established in 2001. Headquartered in Beijing, Globe-Law now has branches in Shanghai, Dalian, and Hefei, along with its 17 offices worldwide. Globe-Law is now home to nearly 200 experienced lawyers and paralegals.

In providing services to clients, Globe-Law are firmly committed to the principle and spirit of specialization and teamwork. Globe-Law divide our team into several departments, including intellectual property, corporate, litigation and arbitration, criminal defense, maritime, banking and international finance, real estate and construction, labor and human resources, etc. Globe-Law will assign the case to a working team of professionals from various departments, optimizing personnel resources in order to provide the most professional, efficient, and quality legal service to meet our clients' needs.

Globe-Laws lawyers have resoundingly handled a number of cases with enormous social impact, including cases that marked as Top Ten Cases of The Supreme Court of China, 50 Typical Cases of IPR Infringement From The Supreme People's Court of China, Top Ten Cases of IPR Infringement In Beijing, Top Ten Cases of Patent Re-examination Board of SIPO, Top Ten Cases of IPR Infringement for Foreign Investors In Beijing, etc.

律师介绍 / Introduction to Lawyers

姜金姬

姜金姬律师是北京高文律师事务所合伙人、管委会成员、北京市律师协会第 10 届外事委员会委员、朝阳区律师协会"一带一路"法律服务工作小组秘书长。

姜金姬律师专注于商业秘密、知识产权商用化、特许经营等知识产权业务领域，擅长于企业知识产权整体战略、品牌战略的策划。姜金姬律师精通韩语，对韩国法律制度和法律环境有较深的了解，在涉韩法律服务方面有非常丰富的经验。姜金姬律师还致力于知识产权课题研究，先后承接了国家知识产权局、中国知识产权研究会、北京市知识产权局、重庆市知识产权局等部门的多项课题。

Jiang Jinji is a partner of Beijing Globe-Law Law Firm, and a member of management committee as well. She is a member of the tenth Foreign Affairs Committee of Beijing Lawyers Association, also the Secretary-General of the Belt and Road Legal Service Group of Beijing Chaoyang Lawyers Association.

Lawyer Jiang focuses on trade secrets, commercialization of intellectual property, commercial franchising and other intellectual property business, specialized in intellectual property strategy of enterprises, brand strategy planning. Lawyer Jiang is proficient in Korean and has complete understanding of Korean legal system and legal environment. She has rich experience in Korean legal services. Lawyer Jiang is also committed to research on intellectual property rights and has successfully undertaken many subjects, such as the projects from State Intellectual Property Office, China Intellectual Property Society, Beijing Intellectual Property Office, Chongqing Intellectual Property Office and so on.

律所介绍 / Introduction to Law Firms

北京市盈科律师事务所

北京市盈科律师事务所是一家源自中国的全球化法律服务机构，致力于在全球范围内为客户提供"一站式"商务法律服务，其总部设于中国北京，在中国大陆拥有47家分所，同时该所全球法律服务联盟已覆盖海外53个国家的113个国际城市。

该所的业务范围覆盖国际贸易、海外投资、公司、资本证券、两岸事务、私募、投融资与并购、知识产权、房地产、环境保护、海商海事等专业领域。

该所的专业服务水平得到了国际评级机构的认可。2014年、2016年均被《亚洲法律杂志》评为"亚洲规模最大律所"之一，2017年"中国30强国内律师"；2016年、2017年被英国《律师》杂志评为"亚太地区100强律所"。

Beijing Yingke Law Firm is a global legal service organization from China. It is committed to providing "one-stop" business legal services to customers worldwide. Its headquarters is located in Beijing, China and has 47 points in China. At the same time, Yingke Global Legal Services Alliance has covered 113 international cities in 53 countries.

The firm's business scope covers international trade, overseas investment, companies, capital securities, cross-strait affairs, private equity, investment and financing and mergers and acquisitions, intellectual property, real estate, environmental protection, maritime affairs and other specialized fields.

YingKe's professional service level has been recognized by international rating agencies. In 2014 and 2016, he was named "The Largest Law Firm in Asia" by the *Asia Legal Business* and the top 30 law firms in China in 2017; In 2016 and 2017,The top 100 law firms list in the Asia Pacific region by the *The Lawyer*.

律师介绍 / Introduction to Lawyers

金瑛

北京盈科（沈阳）律师事务所合伙人，毕业于中山大学，曾于英国华威大学、美国哈佛大学、韩国高丽大学深造学习及交流。专注于涉外领域法律服务，专业方向为对外投资、跨境并购及国际贸易等。工作语言有中文（普通话及粤语）、英文、韩文。现为司法部、中华全国律师协会"中国涉外律师领军人才"，并任辽宁省律师协会涉外法律专业委员会委员。

Ms JIN Ying, a partner of Yingke Law Firm Shenyang office, graduated from Sun Yat-sen University in China, and further educated in the University of Warwick in UK, Harvard University in USA, and Korea University in South Korea. Ms JIN focuses her practice area in International legal affairs especially in cross-boarder Investment, M&A, International Trade and etc. Her working languages are Chinese (Mandarin & Cantonese), English and Korean. She is awarded the title of "Chinese Foreign-related Lawyers Leading Talent" by the Ministry of Justice and All China Lawyers Association, and is also a member of Foreign-related Law Committee of Liaoning Lawyers Association.

科威特——撰稿人介绍 / Kuwait—Introduction to Authors

律所介绍 / Introduction to Law Firms

ASAR-Al Ruwayeh & Partners（ASAR）律师事务所

ASAR-Al Ruwayeh & Partners（ASAR）是科威特最大的提供全方位服务的商业律师事务所，也是中东地区较大的律师事务所之一，其在整个海湾地区拥有强大的连接网络。

该所在科威特和巴林的办公室共有30多名专业律师，该所拥有卓越的企业和商业实践经验，并专注于商业交易、兼并和收购、私有化、首次公开募股、银行和金融、特许经营、建筑、政府项目、公私合作、证券、税务、商业诉讼和仲裁。该所可以提供多语种法律服务，包括英语、阿拉伯语和法语。

该所的律师团队横跨海湾阿拉伯国家合作委员会的两个新兴的、富有竞争力的市场，该所的专业业务涉及的领域十分广泛，包括本地和外国跨国公司、银行和投资公司、工业集团、政府和国家以及私人客户业务。

该所参与了科威特和巴林的一些最具有创新性和复杂性的项目以及被视为先例的交易，因此有能力为涉及科威特和巴林市场的事务提供关键的法律和实践见解。

该所一直被权威的法律服务评估机构，例如国际金融法律评论（IFLR）、钱伯斯全球指南以及 Legal 500 和汤森路透公司评为科威特领先的商业律师事务所。2017年，该所荣获 IFLR 国内律师事务所年度大奖，这也是该所连续第九年获得该奖项。

ASAR-Al Ruwayeh & Partners (ASAR) is the largest full service corporate and commercial law firm in Kuwait and one of the largest in the Middle East, with strong connections throughout the Gulf region.

With more than a 30 member team of professional lawyers based across the Kuwait and Bahrain offices of ASAR, the firm has a leading corporate and commercial practice with a focus on corporate and commercial transactions, mergers and acquisitions, privatizations, IPOs, banking and finance, franchising, construction, government projects, PPPs, securities, taxation, commercial litigation and arbitration. The firm has multilingual capabilities, including being able to provide services in English, Arabic and French.

With our team of lawyers spanning two emerging, and highly competitive markets in the GCC, our expertise extends over a wide range of areas that cover local and foreign multinational corporations, banks and investment companies, industrial conglomerates, governments and state authorities, and private clients.

ASAR has been involved in some of the most innovative and complex projects and precedent setting transactions in Kuwait and Bahrain and is therefore well placed to provide key legal and practical insight into Kuwait and Bahrain markets.

The firm has been consistently rated as the leading corporate and commercial law firm in Kuwait by reputable legal guides such as the International Financial Law Review (IFLR), Chambers Global Guide, and the Legal 500 and the Practical Law Company. In 2017, ASAR was awarded with the IFLR National Law Firm of the Year Award; an award which ASAR has been delighted to receive for a record setting 9th consecutive year.

律师介绍 / Introduction to Lawyers

Ibrahim Sattout

Ibrahim Sattout 是 ASAR 律师事务所的合伙人之一，他拥有超过25年的法律执业经验，其中有17年在科威特执业。

Ibrahim 具有包括银行和金融、公私合伙、政府项目、商法和公司法、并购、资本市场和仲裁的经验。除了并购、股权债权配置以及融资交易之外，他还在科威特的重要公私合伙项目中，作为首席和协理律师顾问，为科威特政府、当地和外国投资者以及贷款人提供法律服务。

Ibrahim 精通英语、阿拉伯语和法语。

Ibrahim Sattout is a Partner at ASAR – Al Ruwayeh & Partners with over 25 years of experience, 17 years of which have been spent in Kuwait.

Ibrahim's experience includes banking and finance, public private partnerships, government projects, commercial and corporate law, acquisition transactions, capital markets and arbitration. He has been extensively involved as lead and co-counsel for the Kuwaiti government, local and foreign investors and lenders on the major PPP projects in Kuwait, in addition to acquisition transactions, debt and equity arrangements and financing transactions.

Ibrahim is fluent in English, Arabic and French.

Akusa Batwala

Akusa 是 ASAR 律师事务所的合伙人之一，具有超过16年的法律执业经验。Akusa 在英格兰利兹大学获得法律学位，并在苏格兰斯特拉斯克莱德大学获得信息技术和电信法硕士学位。在 ASAR 律师事务所，Akusa 在商业和公司法、政府合同、公私合伙、保险、电信和就业等领域开展业务。

Akusa is a Partner at ASAR – Al Ruwayeh & Partners with over sixteen years of legal experience. She received her law degree from the University of Leeds in England and her Masters degree in IT and Telecommunications Law from the University of Strathclyde in Scotland. At ASAR, she practices in the areas of commercial and corporate law, government contracts, public private partnerships, insurance, telecommunications and employment.

科威特——翻译及协调人介绍 / Kuwait—Introduction to Translators and Cooperators

律所介绍 / Introduction to Law Firms

上海市海华永泰律师事务所

上海市海华永泰律师事务所总部位于上海，是中国首批获准成为"特殊的普通合伙"的律师事务所之一。该所设有八大业务部门：金融部、证券部、房地产与建设工程部、公司与商事部、国际业务部、刑事业务部、知识产权部和争端解决部。

该所不仅在上海有着规模庞大的专业律师队伍，还在北京、长沙、成都、济南、哈尔滨、南京等地设有分支机构。经过二十余年的发展，该所已经迅速成长为在国内外有重大影响力的综合法律服务机构。

Hiways Law Firm is one of the first approved liability limited partnership law firms in China, with its headquarter in Shanghai. We have eight major practice groups: Finance, Securities, Real Estate & Infrastructure, Corporate & Commercial, International, Criminal Defense, Intellectual Property and Dispute Resolution.

Hiways not only has a large-scale professional lawyer team in Shanghai, but also has branches in Beijing, Changsha, Chengdu, Jinan, Harbin, and Nanjing etc. Since the establishment in 1995, Hiways has rapidly flourished into a comprehensive legal service provider with great reputation both at home and aboard.

律师介绍 / Introduction to Lawyers

余盛兴

余律师曾在上海 WTO 事务咨询中心任职，现主要帮助中国企业处理在美国、欧盟及其他国家和地区的贸易和投资领域的法律事务。

2008 年 12 月—2011 年 6 月，余律师在美国华盛顿某知名律师事务所工作，同时担任美国乔治城大学法学院的访问学者。

2013 年，余盛兴律师入选"中国涉外律师领军人才"；2015 年、2016 年连续两年被《亚洲法律评论》评为中国最受客户推荐的律师（20 强）；2016 年，余盛兴律师荣获《商法》杂志"法律精英 100 强"称号。

Dr. Yu once worked at the Shanghai WTO Affairs Consultation Center and now mainly helps Chinese companies handle their legal affairs in trade and investment in the United States, the European Union and other countries and regions.

From December 2008 to June 2011, he worked for a well-known law firm in Washington, DC, and served as a visiting scholar at the Georgetown University School of Law in the United States.

In 2013, Dr. Yu was named one of the "Chinese Foreign Leading Lawyers" by All China Bar; in 2015 and 2016, he was consecutively awarded "Client Choice Top 20" by Asia Law Business. He also sits in the "A List" for top 100 lawyers in mainland China and Hong Kong, a survey by China Business Law Journal.

律所介绍 / Introduction to Law Firms

中伦律师事务所

中伦律师事务所创立于 1993 年，是中国司法部较早批准设立的合伙制律师事务所之一，拥有 290 多名合伙人和 1 500 多名专业人员，在北京、上海、深圳、广州、武汉、成都、重庆、青岛、杭州、南京、香港、东京、伦敦、纽约、洛杉矶和旧金山 16 个城市设有办公室。该所是世界律师联盟（WLG）的成员，也是国际上有重大影响力的律师联盟 Terralex 的成员。

该所及其律师经常得到钱伯斯、《亚洲法律与实务》《亚洲法律杂志》《国际金融法律评论》等著名法律媒体推荐。

该所拥有强大的海外投资法律服务团队，由具有中国、美国、英国、法国、加拿大、澳大利亚及日本等国家或地区执业资格的律师组成，海外投资项目涉及石油、天然气、矿产、能源、电力、交通、电信、制造业、零售业及高科技等行业。

Founded in 1993, Zhong Lun is one of the first Private Law partnership to receive approval from the Ministry of Justice of PRC, with over 290 partners and more than 1500 professionals working in sixteen offices strategically located in Beijing, Shanghai, Shenzhen, Guangzhou, Wuhan, Chengdu, Chongqing, Qingdao, Hangzhou, Nanjing, Tokyo, Hong Kong, London, New York, Los Angeles and San Francisco. Zhong Lun is the member of World Law Group (WLG), and also the member of Terralex, an influential network worldwide.

Zhong Lun's outstanding work has achieved broad recognition and its practice groups and lawyers are frequently cited and recommended in their respective markets by distinguished legal media groups such as Chambers & Partners, Asia Law & Practice, Asian Legal Business, International Financial Law Review and others.

Zhong Lun's outbound investment team consists of attorneys with qualifications in China, USA, UK, France, Canada, Australia and Japan. Zhong Lun has undertaken projects in a broad range of industry sectors such as oil, gas, mining, energy, power, transport, telecommunication, manufacturing, retail industry and high technology.

律师介绍 / Introduction to Lawyers

高俊

高俊律师是中伦律师事务所争议解决部合伙人，也是该所合规部门的负责人。高俊律师至今已执业长达 23 年，具有丰富的法律服务经验。高俊律师先后荣获《中国法律商务》"2017 年度合规律师"大奖，被评选为《亚洲法律杂志》"2016 年客户首选 20 强律师"、钱伯斯"2013 年度争议解决推荐律师"。此外，在高俊律师及合规团队的共同努力下,中伦律师事务所被评选为《商法》"2017—2018 年度合规领域卓越律所""2016—2017 年度合规领域卓越律所"及《中国法律商务》"2016 年度公司合规中国律师事务所"。

Mr. Gao Jun is the Partner and the Head of Compliance Team of Beijing Zhong Lun Law Firm. So far, Mr. Gao has practiced in legal for about 23 years, which makes Mr. Gao as an experienced lawyer. Mr. Gao has been awarded as the 2017 "Regulatory & Compliance Lawyer of the Year" by China Law & Practice, the 2016 "Client Choice Top 20 Lawyer" by ALB and the 2013 "Annual Recommended Litigator" by Chambers & Partners. Under the joint efforts of Mr. Gao Jun and the Compliance Team, Zhong Lun Law Firm was awarded as 2016-2017 and 2017-2018 "Outstanding Firm in Compliance" by China Business Law Journal and "China Firm of the Year 2016 (Compliance)" by China Law & Practice.